HALSBURY'S
Laws of England

FIFTH EDITION
2018

Volume 70

This is volume 70 of the Fifth Edition of Halsbury's Laws of England, containing the title LOCAL GOVERNMENT FINANCE.

The title LOCAL GOVERNMENT FINANCE replaces the title of the same name contained in volume 70 (2012). Upon receipt of volume 70 (2018), the old volume 70 (2012) may be archived.

For a full list of volumes comprised in a current set of Halsbury's Laws of England please see overleaf.

Fifth Edition volumes:

1 (2017), 1A (2017), 2 (2017), 3 (2011), 4 (2011), 5 (2013), 6 (2011), 7 (2015), 8 (2015), 9 (2017), 10 (2017), 11 (2015), 12 (2015), 12A (2015), 13 (2017), 14 (2016), 15 (2016), 15A (2016), 16 (2017), 17 (2017), 18 (2009), 19 (2011), 20 (2014), 21 (2016), 22 (2012), 23 (2016), 24 (2010), 25 (2016), 26 (2016), 27 (2015), 28 (2015), 29 (2014), 30 (2012), 31 (2012), 32 (2012), 33 (2017), 34 (2011), 35 (2015), 36 (2015), 37 (2013), 38 (2013), 38A (2013), 39 (2014), 40 (2014), 41 (2014), 41A (2014), 42 (2011), 43 (2011), 44 (2011), 45 (2010), 46 (2010), 47 (2014), 47A (2014), 48 (2015), 49 (2015), 50 (2016), 50A (2016), 51 (2013), 52 (2014), 53 (2014), 54 (2017), 54A (2017), 55 (2012), 56 (2017), 57 (2018), 58 (2014), 58A (2014), 59 (2014), 59A (2014), 60 (2011), 61 (2010), 62 (2016), 63 (2016), 64 (2016), 65 (2015), 66 (2015), 67 (2016), 68 (2016), 69 (2018), 70 (2018), 71 (2013), 72 (2015), 73 (2015), 74 (2011), 75 (2013), 76 (2013), 77 (2016), 78 (2018), 79 (2014), 80 (2013), 81 (2018), 82 (2018), 83 (2018), 84 (2013), 84A (2013), 85 (2012), 86 (2017), 87 (2017), 88 (2012), 88A (2018), 89 (2011), 90 (2011), 91 (2012), 92 (2015), 93 (2017), 94 (2017), 95 (2017), 96 (2012), 97 (2015), 97A (2014), 98 (2013), 99 (2012), 100 (2018), 101 (2018), 102 (2016), 103 (2016), 104 (2014)

Consolidated Index and Tables:

2018 Consolidated Index (A–E), 2018 Consolidated Index (F–O), 2018 Consolidated Index (P–Z), 2018 Consolidated Table of Statutes, 2018 Consolidated Table of Statutory Instruments, 2018 Consolidated Table of Cases (A–G), 2018 Consolidated Table of Cases (H–Q), 2018 Consolidated Table of Cases (R–Z, ECJ Cases)

Updating and ancillary materials:

2018 annual Cumulative Supplement; monthly Noter-up; annual Abridgments 1974–2017

May 2018

HALSBURY'S
Laws of England

Volume 70

2018

Members of the LexisNexis Group worldwide

United Kingdom	RELX (UK) Ltd, trading as LexisNexis, 1–3 Strand, London WC2N 5JR and 9–10 St Andrew Square, Edinburgh EH2 2AF
Australia	Reed International Books Australia Pty Ltd trading as LexisNexis, Chatswood, New South Wales
Austria	LexisNexis Verlag ARD Orac GmbH & Co KG, Vienna
Benelux	LexisNexis Benelux, Amsterdam
Canada	LexisNexis Canada, Markham, Ontario
China	LexisNexis China, Beijing and Shanghai
France	LexisNexis SA, Paris
Germany	LexisNexis GmbH, Dusseldorf
Hong Kong	LexisNexis Hong Kong, Hong Kong
India	LexisNexis India, New Delhi
Italy	Giuffrè Editore, Milan
Japan	LexisNexis Japan, Tokyo
Malaysia	Malayan Law Journal Sdn Bhd, Kuala Lumpur
New Zealand	LexisNexis New Zealand Ltd, Wellington
Singapore	LexisNexis Singapore, Singapore
South Africa	LexisNexis, Durban
USA	LexisNexis, Dayton, Ohio

FIRST EDITION	*Published in 31 volumes between 1907 and 1917*
SECOND EDITION	*Published in 37 volumes between 1931 and 1942*
THIRD EDITION	*Published in 43 volumes between 1952 and 1964*
FOURTH EDITION	*Published in 56 volumes between 1973 and 1987, with reissues between 1988 and 2008*
FIFTH EDITION	*Published between 2008 and 2014, with reissues from 2014*

A CIP Catalogue record for this book is available from the British Library.

ISBN 978-1-4743-0954-7

9 781474 309547

ISBN for the set: 9781405734394

ISBN for this volume: 9781474309547

Typeset by LexisNexis
Printed and bound by CPI Group (UK) Ltd, Croydon, CR0 4YY

Visit LexisNexis at www.lexisnexis.co.uk

HALSBURY ADVISORY BOARD

Editors of this Volume

DAVID HAY, MA, LLM

of the Inner Temple, Barrister

MOHINI TULLOCH, LLM

AMANDA WILLIS, LLM

LOCAL GOVERNMENT FINANCE

Consultant Editor

Colin Crawford, LLM,
of Middle Temple, Barrister;
Formerly of Kings Chambers, Manchester, Leeds and Birmingham

The law stated in this volume is in general that in force on 25 March 2018, although subsequent changes have been included wherever possible.

Any future updating material will be found in the Noter-up and annual Cumulative Supplement to Halsbury's Laws of England.

TABLE OF CONTENTS

HOW TO USE HALSBURY'S LAWS OF ENGLAND

Volumes

Each text volume of Halsbury's Laws of England contains the law on the titles contained in it as at a date stated at the front of the volume (the operative date).

Information contained in Halsbury's Laws of England may be accessed in several ways.

First, by using the tables of contents.

Each volume contains both a general Table of Contents, and a specific Table of Contents for each title contained in it. From these tables you will be directed to the relevant part of the work.

Readers should note that the current arrangement of titles can be found in the Noter-up.

Secondly, by using tables of statutes, statutory instruments, cases or other materials.

If you know the name of the Act, statutory instrument or case with which your research is concerned, you should consult the Consolidated Tables of statutes, cases and so on (published as separate volumes) which will direct you to the relevant volume and paragraph.

(Each individual text volume also includes tables of those materials used as authority in that volume.)

Thirdly, by using the indexes.

If you are uncertain of the general subject area of your research, you should go to the Consolidated Index (published as separate volumes) for reference to the relevant volume(s) and paragraph(s).

(Each individual text volume also includes an index to the material contained therein.)

Updating publications

The text volumes of Halsbury's Laws should be used in conjunction with the annual Cumulative Supplement and the monthly Noter-up.

The annual Cumulative Supplement

The Supplement gives details of all changes between the operative date of the text volume and the operative date of the Supplement. It is arranged in the same volume, title and paragraph order as the text volumes. Developments affecting particular points of law are noted to the relevant paragraph(s) of the text volumes.

For narrative treatment of material noted in the Cumulative Supplement, go to the annual Abridgment volume for the relevant year.

Destination Tables

In certain titles in the annual *Cumulative Supplement*, reference is made to Destination Tables showing the destination of consolidated legislation. Those Destination Tables are to be found either at the end of the titles within the annual *Cumulative Supplement*, or in a separate *Destination Tables* booklet provided from time to time with the *Cumulative Supplement*.

The Noter-up

The Noter-up is issued monthly and notes changes since the publication of the annual Cumulative Supplement. Also arranged in the same volume, title and paragraph order as the text volumes, the Noter-up follows the style of the Cumulative Supplement.

For narrative treatment of material noted in the Noter-up, go to the annual Abridgment volume for the relevant year.

REFERENCES AND ABBREVIATIONS

ACT	Australian Capital Territory
A-G	Attorney General
Admin	Administrative Court
Admlty	Admiralty Court
Adv-Gen	Advocate General
affd	affirmed
affg	affirming
Alta	Alberta
App	Appendix
art	article
Aust	Australia
B	Baron
BC	British Columbia
C	Command Paper (of a series published before 1900)
c	chapter number of an Act
CA	Court of Appeal
CAC	Central Arbitration Committee
CA in Ch	Court of Appeal in Chancery
CB	Chief Baron
CCA	Court of Criminal Appeal
CCR	County Court Rules 1981 (as subsequently amended)
CCR	Court for Crown Cases Reserved
CJEU	Court of Justice of the European Union
C-MAC	Courts-Martial Appeal Court
CO	Crown Office
COD	Crown Office Digest
CPR	Civil Procedure Rules
Can	Canada
Cd	Command Paper (of the series published 1900–18)
Cf	compare
Ch	Chancery Division
ch	chapter
cl	clause
Cm	Command Paper (of the series published 1986 to date)
Cmd	Command Paper (of the series published 1919–56)
Cmnd	Command Paper (of the series published 1956–86)
Comm	Commercial Court

Comr .... Commissioner
Court Forms (2nd Edn) .... Atkin's Encyclopaedia of Court Forms in Civil Proceedings, 2nd Edn. See note 2 post.
CrimPR .... Criminal Procedure Rules
DC............................. Divisional Court
DPP........................... Director of Public Prosecutions
EAT........................... Employment Appeal Tribunal
EC .... European Community
ECJ .... Court of Justice of the European Community (before the Treaty of Lisbon (OJ C306, 17.12.2007, p 1) came into force on 1 December 2009); European Court of Justice (after the Treaty of Lisbon (OJ C306, 17.12.2007, p 1) came into force on 1 December 2009)
EComHR .... European Commission of Human Rights
ECSC......................... European Coal and Steel Community
ECtHR Rules of Court ..... Rules of Court of the European Court of Human Rights
EEC........................... European Economic Community
EFTA .... European Free Trade Association
EGC .... European General Court
EWCA Civ .... Official neutral citation for judgments of the Court of Appeal (Civil Division)
EWCA Crim .... Official neutral citation for judgments of the Court of Appeal (Criminal Division)
EWHC .... Official neutral citation for judgments of the High Court
Edn .... Edition
Euratom...................... European Atomic Energy Community
EU .... European Union
Ex Ch .... Court of Exchequer Chamber
ex p........................... ex parte
Fam........................... Family Division
Fed............................ Federal
Forms & Precedents (5th Edn) .... Encyclopaedia of Forms and Precedents other than Court Forms, 5th Edn. See note 2 post
GLC .... Greater London Council
HC............................ High Court
HC............................ House of Commons
HK............................ Hong Kong
HL .... House of Lords
HMRC .... Her Majesty's Revenue and Customs
IAT .... Immigration Appeal Tribunal
ILM........................... International Legal Materials

INLR .... Immigration and Nationality Law Reports
IRC .... Inland Revenue Commissioners
Ind .... India
Int Rels .... International Relations
Ir .... Ireland
J .... Justice
JA .... Judge of Appeal
Kan .... Kansas
LA .... Lord Advocate
LC .... Lord Chancellor
LCC .... London County Council
LCJ .... Lord Chief Justice
LJ .... Lord Justice of Appeal
MR .... Master of the Rolls
Man .... Manitoba
n .... note
NB .... New Brunswick
NI .... Northern Ireland
NS .... Nova Scotia
NSW .... New South Wales
NY .... New York
NZ .... New Zealand
OHIM .... Office for Harmonisation in the Internal Market
OJ .... The Official Journal of the European Union published by the Publications Office of the European Union
Ont .... Ontario
P .... President
PC .... Judicial Committee of the Privy Council
PEI .... Prince Edward Island
Pat .... Patents Court
q .... question
QB .... Queen's Bench Division
QBD .... Queen's Bench Division of the High Court
Qld .... Queensland
Que .... Quebec
r .... rule
RDC .... Rural District Council
RPC .... Restrictive Practices Court
RSC .... Rules of the Supreme Court 1965 (as subsequently amended)
reg .... regulation
Res .... Resolution
revsd .... reversed

Rly	Railway
s	section
SA	South Africa
S Aust	South Australia
SC	Supreme Court
SI	Statutory Instruments published by authority
SR & O	Statutory Rules and Orders published by authority
SR & O Rev 1904	Revised Edition comprising all Public and General Statutory Rules and Orders in force on 31 December 1903
SR & O Rev 1948	Revised Edition comprising all Public and General Statutory Rules and Orders and Statutory Instruments in force on 31 December 1948
STI	Simon's Tax Intelligence (1973–1995); Simon's Weekly Tax Intelligence (1996-current)
Sask	Saskatchewan
Sch	Schedule
Sess	Session
Sing	Singapore
TCC	Technology and Construction Court
TS	Treaty Series
Tanz	Tanzania
Tas	Tasmania
UDC	Urban District Council
UKHL	Official neutral citation for judgments of the House of Lords
UKPC	Official neutral citation for judgments of the Privy Council
UN	United Nations
V-C	Vice-Chancellor
Vict	Victoria
W Aust	Western Australia
Zimb	Zimbabwe

NOTE 1. A general list of the abbreviations of law reports and other sources used in this work can be found at the beginning of the Consolidated Table of Cases.

NOTE 2. Where references are made to other publications, the volume number precedes and the page number follows the name of the publication; eg the reference '12 Forms & Precedents (5th Edn) 44' refers to volume 12 of the Encyclopaedia of Forms and Precedents, page 44.

NOTE 3. An English statute is cited by short title or, where there is no short title, by regnal year and chapter number together with the name by which it is commonly known or a description of its subject matter and date. In the case of a foreign statute, the mode of citation generally follows the style of citation in use in the country concerned with the addition, where necessary, of the name of the country in parentheses.

NOTE 4. A statutory instrument is cited by short title, if any, followed by the year and number, or, if unnumbered, the date.

TABLE OF STATUTES

TABLE OF STATUTORY INSTRUMENTS

P

R

TABLE OF CASES

B

PARA

Bootle-cum-Linacre Corpn v Lancashire County Council (1890) 60 LJQB 323, 7 TLR 179, CA 301

Bowes Museum and Park Trustees v Cutts (Valuation Officer) (1950) 43 R & IT 881, LT 95

Boyd v South Staffordshire District Council Community Charges Registration Officer and Staffordshire and Shropshire Valuation and Community Charge Tribunal [1992] RA 235, DC 271

Bradford Metropolitan City Council v Anderton (1991) 89 LGR 681, [1991] RA 45, 135 Sol Jo 251, [1991] COD 313, (1991) Times, 15 February 354

Bradford-on-Avon Assessment Committee v White [1898] 2 QB 630, sub nom White v Bradford-on-Avon Assessment Committee 62 JP 533, 67 LJQB 643, 46 WR 603, 42 Sol Jo 540, 78 LT 758, 14 TLR 447 180

Bradgate v Buncombe (Valuation Officer) (1967) 13 RRC 347, LT 162

Bradshaw v Davey [1952] 1 All ER 350, 50 LGR 175, [1952] 1 Lloyd's Rep 65, 45 R & IT 86, 116 JP 119, 96 Sol Jo 132, [1952] 1 TLR 368, 159 Estates Gazette 138 .... 99, 101

Brecon Markets Co v St Mary's, Brecon (1877) 41 JP 325, 36 LT 109 184

Brewis v Hornsey Local Board (1890) 55 JP 389, 64 LT 288, sub nom Hornsey Local Board v Brewis 60 LJMC 48, 7 TLR 27, MagsCt 114

Briant Colour Printing Co Ltd (in liquidation), Re [1977] 3 All ER 968, [1977] 1 WLR 942, 75 LGR 768, 20 RRC 133, 142 JP 1, 121 Sol Jo 592, [1977] 2 EGLR 105, sub nom Southwark London Borough Council v Briant Colour Printing Co Ltd [1977] RA 101, 244 Estates Gazette 379, 463 .... 85, 91, 93

Brickwoods Ltd v Cousins (Valuation Officer) [1968] RA 243, 14 RRC 186, 206 Estates Gazette 1031, [1968] JPL 408 .... 180–181, 184

Bright (Valuation Officer) v British Oil Storage Co Ltd (1962) 9 RRC 203, [1962] RVR 99, [1962] JPL 418 172–173

Brighton Marine Palace and Pier Co v Rees (Valuation Officer) (1961) 9 RRC 77, [1961] RVR 614, 179 Estates Gazette 533, [1961] JPL 689, LT 184–185, 253

Bristol and Bath River Navigation Co v Willis (1840) 4 JP 152, 113 ER 491, sub nom Bruce v Willis 11 Ad & El 463, 9 LJMC 43, 3 Per & Dav 220, sub nom Bath River Navigation Co v Willis 2 Ry & Can Cas 7 .... 88, 101

Bristol Guardians v Bristol Corpn (1887) 18 QBD 549, 51 JP 676, 56 LJQB 320, 35 WR 619, 56 LT 641, 3 TLR 446, CA 94

British Advent Missions Ltd v Cane (Valuation Officer) and Westminster City Council (1954) 48 R & IT 60, 165 Estates Gazette 24, LT 97, 114

British Aluminium Co Ltd v Inverness-shire Assessor 1937 SC 566, 1937 SLT 375, CtSess 186

British American Typewriters v Hill (Valuation Officer) [1962] RA 298, 9 RRC 353, [1962] RVR 374, 182 EG 761, LT 202

British Bakeries Ltd v Gudgion (Valuation Officer) and Croydon London Borough Council [1969] RA 465, 16 RRC 56, 211 EG 1412, LT 172

British Coal Corpn v Aspinall (Valuation Officer) [1988] RA 78, LT 95

British Home Stores Ltd v Brighton Corpn and Burton (Valuation Officer) (1958) 51 R & IT 665, 3 RRC 344, 172 Estates Gazette 223, LT 253

British Portland Cement Manufacturers Ltd v Thurrock UDC (1950) 49 LGR 235, 43 R & IT 841, 114 JP 580, 94 Sol Jo 759, 66 (pt 2) TLR 1003, CA 173

British Railways Board v Hopkins (Valuation Officer) and Birmingham District Council [1981] RA 328, LT 106

PARA

H

PARA

I

PARA

M

PARA

R v Attwood (1827) 6 B & C 277, 5 LJOSMC 47, 4 Dow & Ry MC 348, 9 Dow & Ry KB 328, Pratt 18, 108 ER 455 174

R v Barking and Dagenham London Borough Council, ex p Magon [2004] RA 269, CA 301

R v Barnes Inhabitants (1830) 1 B & Ad 113, 8 LJMC 115, 35 RR 235, 109 ER 729 102

R (on the application of Daniels) v Barnet London Borough Council [2007] EWHC 1885 (Admin), [2007] RVR 300, sub nom Daniels v Barnet London Borough Council [2007] All ER (D) 236 (May) 467

R v Bath Corpn (1811) 14 East 609, 104 ER 736 100

R v Bedminster Union (1876) 1 QBD 503, 40 JP 743, 45 LJMC 117, sub nom Williams v Bedminster Union Assessment Committee 34 LT 795 ..... 102, 271

R v Bedworth Inhabitants (1807) 8 East 387, 103 ER 391 174

R v Bell (1798) 1 Bott 189, 7 Term Rep 598, 101 ER 1152 ..... 88, 100

R v Berwick Assessment Committee (1885) 16 QBD 493, 50 JP 71, 55 LJMC 84, 2 TLR 219, sub nom Berwick Harbour Comrs v Tweedmouth (Churchwardens and Overseers) 5 Asp MLC 532, 54 LT 159 102

R v Bexley Justices, ex p Henry [1971] RA 145, 17 RRC 15 296

R v Birmingham Gas-Light and Coke Co (1823) 1 B & C 506, 1 Dow & Ry MC 385, 2 Dow & Ry KB 735, 107 ER 187 100

R v Birmingham Justices, ex p Turner [1971] RA 65, 17 RRC 12, 219 Estates Gazette 585, DC 296

R v Birmingham Magistrates' Court, ex p Mansell (1988) 87 LGR 82, 152 JP 570, [1988] RVR 112, (1988) Times, 7 May 296

R v Blackfriars Bridge Co (1839) 3 JP 114, 9 Ad & El 828, 8 LJMC 29, 1 Per & Dav 603, 112 ER 1428 102

R (on the application of Curzon Berkeley Ltd) v Bliss (Valuation Officer, London Westminster) [2001] EWHC Admin 1130, [2001] All ER (D) 314 (Dec) 190

R (on the application of Lee) v Bournemouth Magistrates' Court [2002] All ER (D) 378 (Mar) 296

R v Bradford [1908] 1 KB 365, 6 LGR 333, 72 JP 61, 77 LJKB 475, 98 LT 620, 24 TLR 195, [1904–7] All ER Rep Ext 1079, DC 117

R v Bradford (1815) 4 M & S 317, 105 ER 852 179

R (on the application of Risk Management Partners Ltd) v Brent London Borough Council [2008] EWHC 692 (Admin), [2008] LGR 331, [2008] All ER (D) 302 (Apr); affd sub nom Risk Management Partners Ltd v Brent London Borough Council [2008] EWHC 1094 (Admin), [2008] LGR 429, [2008] All ER (D) 226 (May); affd [2009] EWCA Civ 490, [2010] LGR 99, [2010] PTSR 349, [2009] All ER (D) 109 (Jun); revsd [2011] UKSC 7, [2011] 2 AC 34, [2011] 2 All ER 209, [2011] 2 WLR 166, [2011] 2 CMLR 627, [2011] LGR 169, [2011] PTSR 481, [2011] NLJR 256, (2011) Times, 10 February, 155 Sol Jo (no 6) 31, [2011] All ER (D) 103 (Feb), SC 6

R (on the application of Woolcock) v Bridgend Magistrates' Court [2017] EWHC 34 (Admin), [2017] All ER (D) 139 (Jan) 499

R (on the application of Woolcock) v Bridgend Magistrates' Court [2018] EWHC 17 (Admin), [2018] All ER (D) 120 (Jan) 499

R (on the application of Brighton and Hove City Council) v Brighton and Hove Justices [2004] EWHC 1800 (Admin), [2004] All ER (D) 546 (Jul) 294

PARA

R (on the application of Clark-Darby) v Highbury Corner Magistrates' Court [2001] EWHC Admin 959, [2001] All ER (D) 229 (Nov) 478

R v Hodgson. See Hodgson v Carlisle Local Board of Health

R v Hodgetts (Valuation Officer), ex p Nationwide Building Society [2001] RA 30, [2000] 1 EGLR 97, [2000] 05 EG 141, [1999] EGCS 131, [1999] Lexis Citation 3235, [1999] All ER (D) 1195, CA 153

R (on the application of Lampkin) v Horseferry Road Magistrates' Court [2005] EWHC 312 (Admin), [2005] RA 233 294

R (on the application of Pilot Foods Ltd) v Horseferry Road Magistrates' Court [2003] EWHC 1447 (Admin), [2003] RVR 268, [2003] All ER (D) 286 (Jun) 293–294

R (on the application of Williams) v Horsham District Council [2004] EWCA Civ 39, [2004] 1 WLR 1137, [2004] RA 49, [2004] 08 LS Gaz R 30, [2004] 05 EGCS 147, (2004) Times, 29 January, [2004] All ER (D) 167 (Jan), sub nom Williams v Horsham District Council [2004] 3 All ER 30 354

R v Huelin (Valuation Officer), ex p Murphy Ltd [2001] RA 30, [2000] 1 EGLR 97, [2000] 05 EG 141, [1999] EGCS 131, [1999] Lexis Citation 3235, [1999] All ER (D) 1195, CA 153

R v Hull Dock Co (1845) 7 QB 2, 9 JP 405, 1 New Sess Cas 621, 115 ER 388, 5 LTOS 126, sub nom R v Kingston-upon-Hull Dock Co 41 LJMC 114, 9 Jur 444, 1 New Mag Cas 296 102

R v Institution of Civil Engineers (1879) 5 QBD 48, 44 JP 265, 49 LJMC 34, 28 WR 253, 42 LT 145, DC 149

R v Joliffe (1787) 1 Bott 162, 1 RR 437, 2 Term Rep 90 ..... 89, 100

R v Kingston Justices and Philips (1858) 23 JP 5, EB & E 256, 27 LJMC 199, 6 WR 551, 120 ER 503, 31 LTOS 162, sub nom R v Mason and Phillips 4 Jur NS 758 294

R v Lands Tribunal, ex p City of London Corpn [1981] 1 All ER 753, [1981] 1 WLR 985, [1981] RA 106, 125 Sol Jo 81; revsd [1982] 1 All ER 892, [1982] 1 WLR 258, 80 LGR 564, 125 Sol Jo 792 271

R v Leicester City Justices, ex p Barrow [1991] 2 QB 260, [1991] 3 All ER 935, [1991] 3 WLR 368, [1991] RA 205, 155 JP 901, (1991) Times, 5 August 293

R v Leith (1852) 16 JP 310, 1 E & B 121, 21 LJMC 119, 16 Jur 522, 118 ER 382, 18 LTOS 221 ..... 88, 101

R v Lewis. See Lewis v Swansea Overseers

R v Liverpool City Justices, ex p Greaves (1979) 77 LGR 440, [1979] RA 119, 21 RRC 315 296

R v Liverpool City Justices, ex p Lanckriet (1976) 75 LGR 605, [1977] RA 85, [1977] Crim LR 299, [1977] 1 EGLR 70, 241 Estates Gazette 685, DC 296

R v London and North Western Rly Co (1874) LR 9 QB 134, 38 JP 245, 43 LJMC 81, [1874–80] All ER Rep 549, 29 LT 910 ..... 162, 184

R v London and South Western Rly Co (1842) 1 QB 558, 6 JP 393, 11 LJMC 93, 2 Gal & Dav 49, 6 Jur 686, 113 ER 1246 184

R v London, Brighton and South Coast Rly Co (1851) 15 QB 313, 15 JP 240, 6 Ry & Can Cas 440, 20 LJMC 124, 15 Jur 372, 4 New Sess Cas 511, 117 ER 477, 16 LTOS 533 185

R v London City Assessment Committee [1907] 2 KB 764, 5 LGR 819, 71 JP 377, 76 LJKB 1087, 2 Konst Rat App (1904–8) 596, 97 LT 346, 23 TLR 502, CA 188

R v London Corpn (1790) 4 Term Rep 21, 100 ER 872 101

R v London Justices [1899] 1 QB 532, 63 JP 388, 68 LJQB 383, 47 WR 316, 43 Sol Jo 398, 80 LT 286, 15 TLR 196, DC 89

PARA

R (on the application of Veolia ES Nottinghamshire Ltd) v Nottinghamshire County Council [2010] EWCA Civ 1214, [2011] LGR 95, [2012] PTSR 185, [2010] 44 LS Gaz R 18, (2010) Times, 9 November, [2010] All ER (D) 01 (Nov) 599

R (on the application of Makro Properties Ltd) v Nuneaton & Bedworth Borough Council [2012] EWHC 2250 (Admin), [2012] RA 285, [2012] All ER (D) 136 (Aug) 98

R v Oundle and Thrapston Justices and Delaney, ex p East Northamptonshire District Council [1980] RA 232, DC 296

R (on the application of Secerno Ltd) v Oxford Magistrates' Court [2011] EWHC 1009 (Admin), [2011] RA 247, [2011] 17 EG 71 (CS), [2011] All ER (D) 198 (Apr) 294

R v Oxfordshire Local Valuation Panel, ex p Oxford City Council (1981) 79 LGR 432, [1981] RA 239, [1981] 2 EGLR 138, 259 Estates Gazette 46 271

R v Paddington Valuation Officer, ex p Peachey Property Corpn Ltd [1964] 3 All ER 200, [1964] 1 WLR 1186, 62 LGR 549, [1964] RA 165, 10 RRC 330, 10 RRC 317, 128 JP 550, 108 Sol Jo 692, [1964] CLY 3112, [1964] RVR 500; affd [1966] 1 QB 380, [1965] 2 All ER 836, [1965] 3 WLR 426, 63 LGR 353, [1965] RA 177, 11 RRC 141, 129 JP 447, 109 Sol Jo 475, [1965] RVR 384, 194 EG 993, CA 54, 157, 162–163, 183, 188, 231

R v Page (1792) 4 Term Rep 543, 100 ER 1166, Nolan 35 102

R v Parker (1857) 21 JP 549, 7 E & B 155, 26 LJMC 199, 3 Jur 771, 5 WR 681, 119 ER 1205, 29 LTOS 197 294

R v Parrot (1794) 1 Bott 182, 5 Term Rep 593, 101 ER 332 95

R v Paynter (1845) 7 QB 255, 9 JP 31, 14 LJMC 179, 115 ER 485; affd sub nom Paynter v R (1847) 10 QB 908, 13 JP 457, 16 LJMC 136, 11 Jur 973, 116 ER 344, Exch 89

R v Philip Reid [1973] 3 All ER 1020, [1973] 1 WLR 1283, 57 Cr App Rep 807, 138 JP 51, 117 Sol Jo 681, 137 JP Jo 697 226

R v Ponsonby (1842) 3 QB 14, 6 JP 266, 4 State Tr NS App 1369, 11 LJMC 65, 1 Gal & Dav 713, 6 Jur 642, 114 ER 412 88

R (on the application of Williams) v Pontefract Magistrates' Court [2002] All ER (D) 465 (May) 478

R v Poole Justices, ex p Fleet [1983] 2 All ER 897, [1983] 1 WLR 974, 81 LGR 802, 147 JP 330, 127 Sol Jo 536, [1983] LS Gaz R 2215, [1983] RVR 106 296

R (on the application of Watts) v Preston City Council [2009] EWHC 2179 (Admin), [2009] RA 334, [2009] All ER (D) 264 (Oct) 356

R v Reading Assessment Committee, ex p McCarthy E Fitt Ltd [1948] 1 All ER 194, 46 LGR 190, 112 JP 127, 92 Sol Jo 142, 64 TLR 191, 151 EG 64, DC 202

R v Rebowe (1771) cited in Cald Mag Cas 102

R (on the application of Hodkin) v Registrar General of Births, Deaths and Marriages [2013] UKSC 77, [2014] AC 610, [2014] 1 All ER 737, [2014] 2 WLR 23, [2014] 4 LRC 49, [2014] PTSR 1, [2014] 1 FCR 577, [2014] 1 P & CR D36, [2013] All ER (D) 100 (Dec), SC 114

R v Registrar General, ex p Segerdal [1970] 2 QB 697, [1970] 3 All ER 886, [1970] 3 WLR 479, [1970] RA 439, 114 Sol Jo 703 114

R v Rhymney Rly Co (1869) LR 4 QB 276, 33 JP 549, 10 B & S 198, 38 LJMC 75, 17 WR 530 184

R v Richmond Justices, ex p Atkins [1983] RVR 148 296

R v Richmond upon Thames London Borough Council, ex p Stubbs (1988) 87 LGR 637, [1989] RA 1, (1989) Times, 3 January, CA 301

PARA

PARA

T

PARA

Y

Z

LOCAL GOVERNMENT FINANCE

PARA.

1. POWERS OF LOCAL AUTHORITIES TO INCUR EXPENDITURE

1. Legal status of local authorities in financial matters.

Local authorities[1] have independent status as distinct corporate bodies[2], subject to the direction, control and supervision of central government[3] to the extent authorised by Parliament[4]. This status is reflected in relation to finance in that each individual local authority is responsible for making arrangements for the proper administration of its own finances[5]. The rule of law by which the powers of a statutory corporation are limited to those functions expressly or impliedly conferred by Parliament[6] is of paramount importance in confining expenditure to authorised purposes[7].

Central government control is particularly significant in relation to non-domestic rating with the Secretary of State and the Welsh Ministers having a substantial role in relation to the collection and distribution of funds as well as other extensive powers[8]. Central government also has extensive powers in relation to the amount and collection of council tax[9]; and more general powers in relation to such matters as the keeping of accounts[10], audit[11] and returns of financial information[12].

1 As to local government areas and authorities in England and Wales see LOCAL GOVERNMENT vol 69 (2018) PARA 36 et seq.

2 As to the independent status of local authorities see LOCAL GOVERNMENT vol 69 (2018) PARA 1.

3 Ie the Secretary of State or, in relation to Wales and to the extent that functions have been delegated, the Welsh Ministers.

4 As to supervision of local authorities by central government generally see LOCAL GOVERNMENT vol 69 (2018) PARA 27 et seq.

5 See the Local Government Act 1972 s 151; and PARA 665.

6 See LOCAL GOVERNMENT vol 69 (2018) PARA 504.

7 If the expenditure is for an unauthorised purpose, the authority may be restrained by injunction: see *A-G v Aspinall* (1837) 2 My & Cr 613; *A-G v Norwich Corpn* (1837) 2 My & Cr 406; *A-G v Newcastle-upon-Tyne Corpn and North Eastern Rly Co* (1889) 23 QBD 492, CA (affd [1892] AC 568, HL); *A-G v Manchester Corpn* [1906] 1 Ch 643; *A-G v De Winton* [1906] 2 Ch 106; *A-G v West Ham Corpn* [1910] 2 Ch 560. However, the doing of things calculated to facilitate, or conducive or incidental to the discharge of functions is specifically authorised by the Local Government Act 1972 s 111(1): see LOCAL GOVERNMENT vol 69 (2018) PARA 506. See also *A-G v Smethwick Corpn* [1932] 1 Ch 562, CA.

8 See PARAS 49, 51.

9 As to council tax see PARA 344 et seq.

10 As to accounts see PARA 588 et seq.

11 As to audit see PARA 591 et seq.

12 As to returns of financial arrangements see PARA 662.

2. Expenditure, receipts, investment and lending.

The expenditure of a local authority[1] comprises the cost of functional work[2] and the cost of staff, land, buildings and other establishment activities authorised by the Local Government Act 1972 or by other enactments[3]. Some of these costs are charged to revenue and some to capital[4]. To meet the total of such expenditure the local authority has available receipts in the form of precepts[5], council tax and non-domestic rates[6], grants[7], rents, charges and fees[8], profits from undertakings[9], contributions from general and collection funds[10], and money borrowed[11]. There may also be contributions received from other local authorities[12]. The income of a local authority is exempt from corporation tax[13] and capital gains tax[14].

Local authorities have a general power of investment[15]. Without prejudice to powers conferred by or under any other enactment, an authority[16] may invest property held by the authority in accordance with a scheme submitted to the Treasury[17] by any association of local authorities and approved by the Treasury as enabling investments to be made collectively without in substance extending the scope of powers of investment[18].

Among the purposes for which local authorities[19] are empowered to lend money are the erection of buildings on land sold or leased by a local authority[20]. There are further specific powers for certain principal authorities which have serious inner urban area problems to make loans for a wide range of purposes within a designated area[21].

1 As to local government areas and authorities in England and Wales see LOCAL GOVERNMENT vol 69 (2018) PARA 36 et seq.
2 Ie under the specific legislation relating to eg education, housing, highways, planning, police, fire service, public health and social services.
3 In this sense a local authority is empowered or required to arrange for meetings, to appoint staff, to build halls and offices, to purchase, appropriate and dispose of land, to carry out research, to provide information, to safeguard archives, to calculate and collect non-domestic rates and council tax, to establish a range of funds and to do other things as part of a comprehensive set of functions.
4 As to the power to incur expenditure see PARA 3. As to capital finance see PARA 563 et seq.
5 Ie under the Local Government Finance Act 1992 Pt I Ch IV (ss 39–52): see PARA 11 et seq.
6 As to non-domestic rating see PARA 49 et seq. As to council tax see PARA 344 et seq.
7 As to grants see PARA 29 et seq.
8 See PARA 577.
9 See PARA 578.
10 As to funds see PARA 579 et seq.
11 As to borrowing see PARA 567 et seq.
12 Ie under the Local Government Act 1958 s 56 or the Local Government Act 1972 s 136: see PARA 9.
13 See the Corporation Tax Act 2010 s 984(1).
14 See the Taxation of Chargeable Gains Act 1992 s 271(3); and CAPITAL GAINS TAXATION vol 6 (2011) PARA 884.
15 See the Local Government Act 2003 s 12; and PARA 574.
16 For the purposes of the Trustee Investments Act 1961 s 11, the authorities are:
(1) in England and Wales, the Greater London Authority, the council of a county, a county borough, a borough a district or a parish, the Common Council of the City of London, a functional body (within the meaning of the Greater London Authority Act 1999), the Broads Authority, a National Park authority, a police and crime commissioner (see POLICE AND INVESTIGATORY POWERS vol 84 (2013) PARA 56 et seq), a joint authority established by the Local Government Act 1985 Pt IV (ss 23–42) (see LOCAL GOVERNMENT vol 69 (2018) PARA 71), an economic prosperity board established under the Local Democracy, Economic Development and Construction Act 2009 s 88 (see TRADE AND INDUSTRY vol 97 (2015) PARA 1086 et seq), a combined authority established under the Local Democracy, Economic Development and Construction Act 2009 s 103 (see TRADE AND INDUSTRY vol 97 (2015) PARA 1092 et seq) and the Council of the Isles of Scilly (Trustee Investments Act 1961 s 11(4)(a) (amended by the London Government Act 1963 s 93(1), Sch 18 Pt II; the Local Government Act 1972 s 272(1), Sch 30; the Local Government Act 1985 ss 84, 102, Sch 14 para 38, Sch 17; the Norfolk and Suffolk Broads Act 1988 s 21, Sch 6; the Education Reform Act 1988 s 237, Sch 13 Pt I; the Water Act 1989 s 190, Sch 25 para 29; the Local Government (Wales) Act 1994 s 66(6), Sch 16 para 19(1); the Police and Magistrates' Courts Act 1994 s 43, Sch 1 Pt II para 46; Environment Act 1995 s 78, Sch 10 para 5; Police Act 1996 s 103, Sch 7 para 1(2)(a); the Police Act 1997 s 134(1), Sch 9 para 4(a); Greater London Authority Act 1999 s 387(1), (2); Serious Organised Crime and Police Act 2005 ss 59, 174(2), Sch 4 paras 7, 8(a), Sch 17 Pt 2; Local Government and Public Involvement in Health Act 2007 s 209(2), Sch 13 Pt 2 para 26; Local Democracy, Economic Development and Construction Act 2009 s 119, Sch 6 para 2; the Police Reform and Social Responsibility Act 2011 s 99, Sch 16 paras 76, 77; and the Deregulation Act 2015 s 59, Sch 13 para 6(1), (3)));

(2) in Scotland, a local authority within the meaning of the Local Government (Scotland) Act 1947 (Trustee Investments Act 1961 s 11(4)(b));

(3) in any part of Great Britain, a joint board or joint committee constituted to discharge or advise on the discharge of the functions of any two or more authorities mentioned in heads (1) and (2) above (including a joint committee established by those authorities acting in combination in accordance with regulations made under the Superannuation Act 1972 s 7 (see PERSONAL AND OCCUPATIONAL PENSIONS vol 80 (2013) PARA 321) (Trustee Investments Act 1961 s 11(4)(c) (amended by the Superannuation Act 1972 s 29(1), Sch 6 para 40)).

As to the Greater London Authority see LONDON GOVERNMENT vol 71 (2013) PARA 67 et seq. As to the Common Council of the City of London see LONDON GOVERNMENT vol 71 (2013) PARAS 34–38. As to the Broads Authority see WATER AND WATERWAYS vol 101 (2009) PARA 734. As to National Park authorities see OPEN SPACES AND COUNTRYSIDE vol 78 (2010) PARA 526. As to the meaning of 'Great Britain' see PARA 4 note 10.

'England' means, subject to any alteration of boundaries of local government areas, the area consisting of the counties established by the Local Government Act 1972 s 1 (see LOCAL GOVERNMENT vol 69 (2018) PARAS 5, 36), Greater London and the Isles of Scilly: Interpretation Act 1978 s 5, Sch 1. 'Wales' means the combined area of the counties which were created by the Local Government Act 1972 s 20 (as originally enacted) (see LOCAL GOVERNMENT vol 69 (2018) PARAS 5, 51), but subject to any alteration made under s 73 (consequential alteration of boundary following alteration of watercourse) (see LOCAL GOVERNMENT vol 69 (2018) PARA 116): Interpretation Act 1978 Sch 1 (definition substituted by the Local Government (Wales) Act 1994 s 1(3), Sch 2 para 9). As to local government areas see LOCAL GOVERNMENT vol 69 (2018) PARA 36 et seq; and as to boundary changes see LOCAL GOVERNMENT vol 69 (2018) PARA 99 et seq. As to Greater London see LONDON GOVERNMENT vol 71 (2013) PARA 14. Note that references to 'England' in Acts passed before 1967 include references to Wales (see the Interpretation Act 1978 Sch 2 para 5(a)).

17 As to the meaning of 'the Treasury' see PARA 30 note 15.

18 Trustee Investments Act 1961 s 11(1) (amended by the London Government Act 1963 s 93(1), Sch 8 Pt II; and the Local Government Act 1985 s 102, Sch 17). A scheme may apply to a specified authority or to a specified class of authorities, may make different provisions as respects different authorities or different classes of authorities or as respects different descriptions of property or property held for different purposes, and may impose restrictions on the extent to which the power controlled by the Trustee Investments Act 1961 s 11(1) is to be exercisable: s 11(2).

In approving a scheme, the Treasury may direct that the Financial Services and Markets Act 2000 is not to apply to dealings undertaken or documents issued for the purposes of the scheme, or to such dealings or documents of such descriptions as may be specified in the direction: Trustee Investments Act 1961 s 11(3) (amended by the Financial Services Act 1986 s 212(2), Sch 16 para 2; and by SI 2001/3649).

19 Local authorities' powers to lend money are in nearly all cases contained in specific housing, planning or land development legislation, which it is necessary to examine in order to determine which authorities may lend.

20 See the Local Authorities (Land) Act 1963 ss 3, 4: see LOCAL GOVERNMENT vol 69 (2018) PARA 579.

21 See the Inner Urban Areas Act 1978 ss 2, 3, 5–9: see PLANNING vol 83 (2018) PARAS 1488 et seq. The authorities which may lend are district and county councils in the district or county of which are included the districts designated as having special social need: see ss 1(2), 17(1).

3. Powers to incur expenditure.

The power of local authorities[1] to incur expenditure stems from three main classes of legislation:

(1) the enactments which confer powers or impose duties to execute specific statutory functions[2];

(2) the enactments which provide a wide spectrum of administrative, financial or other management powers[3]; and

(3) certain specific enactments which are intended as reserve powers to enable reasonable expenditure to be incurred on matters not the subject of other statutory authorisation for local government action[4].

As statutory corporations, local authorities are subject to the ultra vires rule which prohibits them from spending money or from executing matters for which they have no statutory power[5]. However, a local authority is empowered to do anything (whether or not involving the expenditure, borrowing or lending of money or the acquisition or disposal of any property or rights) calculated to facilitate, or which is conducive or incidental to, the discharge of its functions[6]. However, a local authority may not, by virtue of this provision, raise money, whether by means of rates, precepts or borrowing, or lend money, except in accordance with the enactments relating to those matters respectively[7]. This general subsidiary power must be borne in mind when interpreting specific statutory powers or duties.

1 As to local government areas and authorities in England and Wales see LOCAL GOVERNMENT vol 69 (2018) PARA 36 et seq.
2 As to the specific functions of local authorities see LOCAL GOVERNMENT vol 69 (2018) PARA 504 et seq.
3 The Local Government Act 1972 contains many provisions which make specific reference to expenditure: see eg s 103 (expenses of joint committees: see LOCAL GOVERNMENT vol 69 (2018) PARA 410); s 112(2) (terms of remuneration for officers: see LOCAL GOVERNMENT vol 69 (2018) PARA 466).
4 As to powers for expenditure on matters not otherwise authorised see the Local Government Act 1972 s 137; and PARA 4. As to powers in relation to emergencies or disasters see s 138; and PARA 7.
5 As to the ultra vires rule see LOCAL GOVERNMENT vol 69 (2018) PARA 505.
6 See the Local Government Act 1972 s 111(1); and LOCAL GOVERNMENT vol 69 (2018) PARA 506.
7 See the Local Government Act 1972 s 111(3); and LOCAL GOVERNMENT vol 69 (2018) PARA 506. As to non-domestic rating see PARA 49 et seq. As to council tax PARA 344 et seq. As to precepts see PARA 11 et seq. As to borrowing see PARA 567 et seq. As to lending see PARA 2.

4. Expenditure for the benefit of a local authority's area.

A local authority[1] may, subject to the following provisions, incur expenditure which in its opinion is in the interests of, and will bring direct benefit to, its area or any part of it or all or some of its inhabitants[2]; but it may not, by virtue of this power, incur any expenditure:

(1) for a purpose for which it is, either unconditionally or subject to any limitation or to the satisfaction of any condition, authorised or required to make any payment by or by virtue of any other enactment[3]; nor

(2) unless the direct benefit accruing to its area or any part of it or to all or some of the inhabitants of its area will be commensurate with the expenditure to be incurred[4].

A local authority may incur expenditure under heads (1) and (2) above on publicity[5] only by way of assistance to a public body or voluntary organisation[6] where the publicity is incidental to the main purpose for which the assistance is given[7].

A local authority[8] may incur expenditure on contributions to any of the following funds, that is to say[9]:

(a) the funds of any charitable body in furtherance of its work in the United Kingdom[10];

(b) the funds of any body which provides any public service (whether to the public at large or to any section of it) in the United Kingdom otherwise than for the purposes of gain[11]; or

(c) any fund which is raised in connection with a particular event directly affecting persons resident in the United Kingdom on behalf of whom a public appeal for contributions has been made by the Lord Mayor of London[12] or the chairman of a principal council[13] or by a committee of which the Lord Mayor of London or the chairman of a principal council is a member or by such a person or body as is referred to in the Local Government (Scotland) Act 1973[14].

The expenditure of a local authority under these powers[15] in any financial year[16] may not exceed the amount produced by multiplying such sum as is for the time being appropriate to the authority[17] by the relevant population[18] of the authority's area[19]. For the purpose of determining whether a local authority has exceeded this limit, its expenditure in any financial year under these provisions[20] must be taken to be the difference between its gross expenditure under these provisions for that year and the aggregate of the amounts specified in heads (i) to (vi) below[21]. The amounts are:

(i) the amount of any expenditure which forms part of the authority's gross expenditure under these provisions and in respect of which any grant has been or is to be paid under any enactment by a Minister of the Crown[22] (whether or not the grant covers the whole of the expenditure)[23];

(ii) the amount of any repayment in that year of the principal of a loan for the purpose of financing expenditure under these provisions in any year[24];

(iii) so much of any amount raised by public subscription as is spent in that year for a purpose for which the authority is authorised by these provisions to incur expenditure[25];

(iv) any grant received by the authority for that year out of the European Regional Development Fund or the Social Fund of the European Union, in so far as the grant is in respect of an activity in relation to which the authority incurred expenditure under these provisions[26];

(v) the amount of any repayment in that year of a loan under these provisions made by the authority in any year[27]; and

(vi) the amount of any expenditure which is incurred by the authority in that year in circumstances specified in an order made by the appropriate national authority[28], which is incurred by the authority in that year and is of a description so specified, or which is defrayed by any grant or other payment to the authority which is made in or in respect of that year and is of a description so specified[29].

The accounts of a local authority by whom expenditure is incurred under these provisions must include a separate account of that expenditure[30].

1 In the Local Government Act 1972 s 137 (except s 137(3): see note 8),'local authority' means a parish council which is not an eligible parish council for the purposes of the Localism Act 2011 Pt 1 Ch 1 (ss 1–8) (general power of competence: see LOCAL GOVERNMENT vol 69 (2018) PARA 507 et seq), or a community council: Local Government Act 1972 s 137(9) (substituted by the Local Government Act 2000 s 8; and amended by the Local Government and Public Involvement in Health Act 2007 s 101, Sch 5 paras 1, 7; and the Localism Act 2011 s 1(7), Sch 1 para 1). As to parish councils generally see LOCAL GOVERNMENT vol 69 (2018) PARA 41 et seq. As to community councils see LOCAL GOVERNMENT vol 69 (2018) PARA 63 et seq.

2 Local Government Act 1972 s 137(1) (amended by the Local Government and Housing Act 1989 s 36). The power of a local authority to incur expenditure under the Local Government Act 1972 s 137(1) includes power to do so by contributing towards the defraying of expenditure by another local authority in or in connection with the exercise of that other authority's functions: s 137(2). As to contributions between authorities to expenditure see further PARA 9.

In *Manchester City Council v Greater Manchester Metropolitan County Council* (1980) 78 LGR 560, HL, it was held that a scheme by the county council (although that council was not a local education authority) to pay money in order to advance the education of children living in the county was within the powers of the county council under the Local Government Act 1972 s 137(1), and that the county council had power to set up a trust for that purpose as being incidental to its power to expend such money.

3 Local Government Act 1972 s 137(1)(a) (as amended: see note 2). In any case where by virtue of s 137(1)(a) a local authority is prohibited from incurring expenditure for a particular purpose, and the power or duty of the authority to incur expenditure for that purpose is in any respect limited or conditional (whether by being restricted to a particular group of persons or in any other way), the prohibition must extend to all expenditure to which that power or duty would apply if it were not subject to any limitation or condition: s 137(1A) (added by the Local Government and Housing Act 1989 s 36).

4 Local Government Act 1972 s 137(1)(b) (as amended: see note 2).

5 'Publicity' means any communication, in whatever form, addressed to the public at large or to a section of the public: Local Government Act 1972 s 137(2D) (added by the Local Government Act 1986 s 3(3)).

6 'Voluntary organisation' means a body which is not a public body but whose activities are carried on otherwise than for profit: Local Government Act 1972 s 137(2D) (as added: see note 5).

7 Local Government Act 1972 s 137(2C) (added by the Local Government Act 1986 s 3(3); and amended by the Local Government and Housing Act 1989 ss 36, 194(2), Sch 12 Pt III).

8 In the Local Government Act 1972 s 137(3), 'local authority' means:

(1) in relation to England, a county council, a district council, a London borough council, the Common Council of the City of London or a parish council (Local Government Act 1972 s 137(10)(a) (s 137(10) added by the Local Government Act 2000 s 8));

(2) in relation to Wales, a county council, a county borough council or a community council (Local Government Act 1972 s 137(10)(b) (as so added).

As to the meanings of 'England' and 'Wales' see PARA 2 note 16. As to local government areas and authorities in England and Wales see LOCAL GOVERNMENT vol 69 (2018) PARA 36 et seq. As to the London boroughs and their councils see LONDON GOVERNMENT vol 71 (2013) PARAS 15, 20–22, 55 et seq. As to the Common Council of the City of London see LONDON GOVERNMENT vol 71 (2013) PARAS 34–38.

9 Local Government Act 1972 s 137(3). This provision is expressed to be subject, in the case of a parish or community council, to s 137(4)–(10) (see the text to notes 15–30): see s 137(3) (amended by the Local Government and Housing Act 1989 s 36; and the Local Government Act 2003 s 127(1), Sch 7 para 4).

10 Local Government Act 1972 s 137(3)(a). 'United Kingdom' means Great Britain and Northern Ireland: Interpretation Act 1978 s 5, Sch 1. 'Great Britain' means England, Scotland and Wales: Union with Scotland Act 1706, preamble art I; Interpretation Act 1978 s 22(1), Sch 2 para 5(a). Neither the Channel Islands nor the Isle of Man are within the United Kingdom. See further CONSTITUTIONAL AND ADMINISTRATIVE LAW vol 20 (2014) PARA 3. As to charities and charitable purposes see CHARITIES vol 8 (2015) PARA 1 et seq.

11 Local Government Act 1972 s 137(3)(b) (amended by the Local Government and Housing Act 1989 s 36).

12 As to the Lord Mayor of the City of London see LONDON GOVERNMENT vol 71 (2013) PARA 27 et seq.

13 'Principal council' means a council elected for a principal area; and 'principal area' means a non-metropolitan county, a district or a London borough but, in relation to Wales, means a county or county borough: Local Government Act 1972 s 270(1) (definition of 'principal area' amended by the Local Government (Wales) Act 1994 s 1(8)).

14 Local Government Act 1972 s 137(3)(c) (amended by the Local Government and Housing Act 1989 s 36). The relevant provision of the Local Government (Scotland) Act 1973 for these purposes is s 83(3)(c): see the Local Government Act 1972 s 137(3)(c) (as so amended).

15 Ie under the Local Government Act 1972 s 137. The relevant proportion of pay and expenses of a local authority's officers attributable to time spent on functions authorised under s 137, is to be taken into account when calculating the expenditure of a local authority under those powers: *Leicester City Council v District Auditor for Leicester* [1989] RVR 162, CA.

16 'Financial year' means the period of 12 months ending with 31 March in any year: Local Government Act 1972 s 270(1). As to the meaning of 'month' see PARA 11 note 1.

17 Ie under the Local Government Act 1972 Sch 12B: see s 137(4)(a), Sch 12B (s 137(4) amended by the Local Government and Housing Act 1989 s 36; the Local Government Act 1972 s 137(4)(a) further amended by the Local Government Act 2003 s 118(1); the Local Government Act 1972

Sch 12B added by the Local Government Act 2003 s 118(2); amended by the Statistics and Registration Service Act 2007 s 60(1), Sch 3 para 1). See also the Local Authorities (Discretionary Expenditure Limits) (England) Order 2005, SI 2005/419.

18 The relevant population of a local authority's area must be determined in accordance with regulations made by the Secretary of State or, in relation to Wales, the Welsh Ministers; and a statutory instrument containing such regulations made by the Secretary of State is subject to annulment in pursuance of a resolution of the House of Commons: see the Local Government Act 1972 s 137(4AB) (added by the Local Government and Housing Act 1989 s 36). As to the equivalent procedure in relation to subordinate legislation made by the Welsh Ministers see the Government of Wales Act 2006 Sch 11 paras 33–35; and STATUTES AND LEGISLATIVE PROCESS vol 96 (2012) PARA 1035. As to the regulations made see the Local Authorities (Discretionary Expenditure) (Relevant Population) Regulations 1993, SI 1993/40.

The functions of the Secretary of State under the Local Government Act 1972 s 137, so far as exercisable in relation to Wales, were transferred to the National Assembly for Wales (see the National Assembly for Wales (Transfer of Functions) Order 1999, SI 1999/672, art 2, Sch 1) and are now vested in the Welsh Ministers (see the Government of Wales Act 2006 s 162(1), Sch 11 para 30). As from 1 April 2018, the Welsh Assembly has general legislative competence except in relation to reserved matters: see the Government of Wales Act 2006 s 108A, Sch 7A, Sch 7B (added by the Wales Act 2017 s 3, Sch 1, Sch 2); and the Wales Act 2017 (Commencement No 4) Regulations 2017, SI 2017/1179, reg 2.

In any enactment, 'Secretary of State' means one of Her Majesty's principal secretaries of state: see the Interpretation Act 1978 s 5, Sch 1. As to the office of Secretary of State see CONSTITUTIONAL AND ADMINISTRATIVE LAW vol 20 (2014) PARA 153. 'The Welsh Ministers' means the First Minister and the Welsh Ministers appointed under the Government of Wales Act 2006 s 48: see s 45(2). As to the First Minister and the Welsh Ministers see the Government of Wales Act 2006 ss 46–48; and CONSTITUTIONAL AND ADMINISTRATIVE LAW vol 20 (2014) PARAS 374, 475. As to devolved government in Wales generally see CONSTITUTIONAL AND ADMINISTRATIVE LAW vol 20 (2014) PARA 82.

19 Local Government Act 1972 s 137(4)(b) (amended by the Local Government and Housing Act 1989 s 36).

20 Ie under the Local Government Act 1972 s 137.

21 Local Government Act 1972 s 137(4A) (added by the Local Government (Miscellaneous Provisions) Act 1982 s 44).

22 Ie within the meaning of the Ministers of the Crown Act 1975: see PARA 41 note 1.

23 Local Government Act 1972 s 137(4B)(a) (s 137(4B) added by the Local Government (Miscellaneous Provisions) Act 1982 s 44; the Local Government Act 1972 s 137(4B)(a) substituted by the Local Government and Housing Act 1989 s 36).

24 Local Government Act 1972 s 137(4B)(b) (as added: see note 23).

25 Local Government Act 1972 s 137(4B)(c) (as added: see note 23).

26 Local Government Act 1972 s 137(4B)(d) (as added: see note 23; and amended by virtue of the European Union (Amendment) Act 2008 s 3(6)).

27 Local Government Act 1972 s 137(4B)(e) (as added: see note 23).

28 Ie the Secretary of State or, in relation to Wales, the Welsh Ministers: see note 18.

29 Local Government Act 1972 s 137(4B)(f) (as added: see note 23). A statutory instrument containing an order under s 137 may apply to all local authorities or may make different provision in relation to local authorities of different descriptions: s 137(5) (amended by the Local Government (Miscellaneous Provisions) Act 1982 s 44). Any such instrument made by the Secretary of State is subject to annulment in pursuance of a resolution of either House of Parliament: see the Local Government Act 1972 s 137(6). As to the equivalent procedure in relation to subordinate legislation made by the Welsh Ministers see the Government of Wales Act 2006 Sch 11 paras 33–35; and STATUTES AND LEGISLATIVE PROCESS vol 96 (2012) PARA 1035. As to the orders made see the Local Authorities (Expenditure Powers) Order 1984, SI 1984/197; and the Local Authorities (Expenditure Powers) Order 1995, SI 1995/3304.

30 Local Government Act 1972 s 137(7) (amended by the Public Audit (Wales) Act 2004 ss 66, 72, Sch 2 para 1(1), (2), Sch 4). In relation to England, the Local Audit and Accountability Act 2014 s 25 (inspection of statements of accounts etc: see PARA 599) applies in relation to a separate account included in a local authority's accounts by virtue of the Local Government Act 1972 s 137(7) as it applies in relation to a statement of accounts prepared by the authority pursuant to the Local Audit and Accountability Act 2014 s 3(3) (see 588): Local Government Act 1972 s 137(7A) (s 137(7A), (7B) added by the Public Audit (Wales) Act 2004 s 66, Sch 2 para 1(1), (3); the Local Government Act 1972 s 137(7A) amended by the Local Audit and Accountability Act 2014 s 45, Sch 12 paras 4, 7). In relation to Wales, the Public Audit (Wales) Act 2004 s 29 (rights of

inspection: see PARA 627) applies in relation to a separate account included in a local authority's accounts by virtue of the Local Government Act 1972 s 137(7) as it applies in relation to a statement of accounts prepared by the authority pursuant to regulations under the Public Audit (Wales) Act 2004 s 39: Local Government Act 1972 s 137(7B) (as so added). As to accounts generally see PARA 588 et seq.

5. General power of competence: England.

A local authority in England[1] has power to do anything that individuals generally may do[2], which power includes:

(1) power to do it anywhere in the United Kingdom[3] or elsewhere;
(2) power to do it for a commercial purpose or otherwise for a charge, or without charge; and
(3) power to do it for, or otherwise than for, the benefit of the authority, its area or persons resident or present in its area[4].

The generality of the power conferred by these provisions ('the general power') is not limited by the existence of any other power of the authority which (to any extent) overlaps the general power, but it is subject to the important limitations imposed by statute[5]. Any such other power is not limited by the existence of the general power[6].

1 In the Localism Act 2011 Pt 1 Ch 1 (ss 1–8), 'local authority' means a county council in England, a district council, a London borough council, the Common Council of the City of London in its capacity as a local authority, the Council of the Isles of Scilly, or an eligible parish council: s 8(1). A parish council is 'eligible' for the purposes of Pt 1 Ch 1 if the council meets the conditions prescribed by the Secretary of State by order for the purposes of s 8: s 8(2). See the Parish Councils (General Power of Competence) (Prescribed Conditions) Order 2012, SI 2012/965. As to the meaning of 'England' see PARA 2 note 16.

2 Localism Act 2011 s 1(1). This applies to things that an individual may do even though they are in nature, extent or otherwise unlike anything the authority may do apart from s 1(1) or unlike anything that other public bodies may do: s 1(2). In s 1, 'individual' means an individual with full capacity: s 1(3).

3 As to the meaning of 'United Kingdom' see PARA 4 note 10.

4 Localism Act 2011 s 1(4).

5 Localism Act 2011 s 1(5). As to the limitations see ss 2–7; and LOCAL GOVERNMENT vol 69 (2018) PARAS 509–511.

6 Localism Act 2011 s 1(6). However, if the Secretary of State thinks that the general power is overlapped (to any extent) by another power then, for the purpose of removing or reducing that overlap, the Secretary of State may by order amend, repeal, revoke or disapply any statutory provision (whenever passed or made): see s 5(2);and LOCAL GOVERNMENT vol 69 (2018) PARA 511.

6. Promotion of well-being by local authorities in Wales.

Every local authority in Wales has power to do anything which it considers is likely to achieve any one or more of the following objects:

(1) the promotion or improvement of the economic well-being of its area;
(2) the promotion or improvement of the social well-being of its area;
(3) the promotion or improvement of the environmental well-being of its area;

and this power includes power for a local authority to incur expenditure or give financial assistance to any person[1].

1 See the Local Government Act 2000 s 2(1), (4) (s 2(1) amended by the Localism Act 2011 s 1(7), Sch 1 paras 2, 3). The power is subject to the limitations imposed by the Local Government Act 2000 s 3. See *R (on the application of Risk Management Partners Ltd) v Brent London Borough Council; Risk Management Partners Ltd v Brent London Borough Council* [2008] EWHC 692 (Admin), [2008] LGR 331, which adopted a very restrictive interpretation of the power; and LOCAL GOVERNMENT vol 69 (2018) PARA 506.

7. Expenditure in the case of emergencies or disasters.

Where an emergency or disaster involving destruction of or a danger to life or property occurs or is imminent or there is reasonable ground for apprehending such an emergency or disaster, and a principal council[1] is of the opinion that it is likely to affect the whole or part of its area or all or some of its inhabitants, the council may[2]:

(1) incur such expenditure as it considers necessary in taking action itself[3] which is calculated to avert, alleviate or eradicate in its area or among those inhabitants the effects or potential effects of the event[4]; or

(2) make grants or loans to other persons or bodies on conditions determined by the council in respect of any such action taken by those persons or bodies[5].

Subject to certain exceptions in relation to land drainage work[6], the above powers are in addition to, and not in derogation of, any power conferred[7] on a local authority[8].

1 For these purposes, 'principal council' includes the Common Council of the City of London: see the Local Government Act 1972 ss 138(4), 270(1). As to the meaning of 'principal council' generally see PARA 4 note 13. As to the Common Council of the City of London see LONDON GOVERNMENT vol 71 (2013) PARAS 34–38.

2 Local Government Act 1972 s 138(1). With the consent of the Secretary of State, a metropolitan county fire and rescue authority and the London Fire and Emergency Planning Authority may incur expenditure in co-ordinating planning by principal councils in connection with their functions under s 138(1): s 138(5) (added by the Local Government and Housing Act 1989 s 156(3); and amended by the Greater London Authority Act 1999 s 328, Sch 29 Pt I para 16; and the Civil Contingencies Act 2004 s 32(1), Sch 2 Pt 1 para 10(1), (2)). Prospectively, the reference to the London Fire and Emergency Planning Authority is replaced by a reference to the London Fire Commissioner: see the Local Government Act 1972 s 138(5) (as so added; amended, as from a day to be appointed, by the Policing and Crime Act 2017 s 9(3)(c), Sch 2 paras 35, 40; at the date at which this volume states the law, no such day had been appointed). As to the Secretary of State see PARA 4 note 18. As to metropolitan county fire and rescue authorities see FIRE AND RESCUE SERVICES vol 51 (2013) PARA 17. As to the London Fire and Emergency Planning Authority see LONDON GOVERNMENT vol 71 (2013) PARA 315.

3 Ie either alone or jointly with any other person or body and either in its area or elsewhere in or outside the United Kingdom: see the Local Government Act 1972 s 138(1)(a). As to the meaning of 'person' see PARA 11 note 13. As to the meaning of 'United Kingdom' see PARA 4 note 10.

4 Local Government Act 1972 s 138(1)(a). As to emergency financial assistance to local authorities see PARA 48.

5 Local Government Act 1972 s 138(1)(b).

6 Nothing in the Local Government Act 1972 s 138 authorises a local authority to execute any drainage or other works in any part of a main river within the meaning of the Water Resources Act 1991 Pt IV (ss 105–113) (see WATER AND WATERWAYS vol 101 (2009) PARA 574), or of any other watercourse which is treated for the purposes of any of the provisions of that Act as part of a main river, or any works which local authorities have power to execute under the Land Drainage Act 1991 ss 14–17 (see WATER AND WATERWAYS vol 101 (2009) PARA 587 et seq), s 62(2), (3) (see WATER AND WATERWAYS vol 101 (2009) PARA 609), s 66 (see WATER AND WATERWAYS vol 101 (2009) PARAS 605–607): Local Government Act 1972 s 138(3) (amended by the Local Government and Housing Act 1989 s 156(2)(a); and the Water Consolidation (Consequential Provisions) Act 1991 s 2(1), Sch 1 para 22(2)).

7 Ie by or under any other enactment, including any enactment contained in the Local Government Act 1972.

8 See the Local Government Act 1972 s 138(3) (amended by the Local Government and Housing Act 1989 s 156(2)(b); and the Civil Contingencies Act 2004 s 32(1), Sch 2 para 7(b)). As to local arrangements for civil protection see the Civil Contingencies Act 2004 Pt 1 (ss 1–18); and ARMED CONFLICT AND EMERGENCY vol 3 (2011) PARA 155 et seq.

8. Expenses of parish and community councils.

In a parish having a separate parish council[1] or in a community having a council, whether separate or common[2], the expenses of the parish meeting[3] or any community meeting[4] must be paid by the parish or community council[5]. In a community not having a community council, whether separate or common, the expenses of any community meeting must be paid by the council of the principal area[6] in which the community is situated[7].

1 As to parish councils see LOCAL GOVERNMENT vol 69 (2018) PARA 41 et seq.
2 As to community councils see LOCAL GOVERNMENT vol 69 (2018) PARA 63 et seq.
3 References in the Local Government Act 1972 s 150 to the expenses of a parish or community meeting include references to the expenses of any poll consequent on a parish or community meeting: s 150(7). As to parish meetings see LOCAL GOVERNMENT vol 69 (2018) PARA 48.
4 See also note 3. As to community meetings see LOCAL GOVERNMENT vol 69 (2018) PARA 70.
5 See the Local Government Act 1972 s 150(2).
6 As to the meaning of 'principal area' see PARA 4 note 13.
7 Local Government Act 1972 s 150(3) (amended by the Local Government (Wales) Act 1994 s 66(5), Sch 15 para 34).

9. Inter-authority contributions to expenditure.

Two or more local authorities[1] may make arrangements for defraying any expenditure incurred by one of them in exercising any functions exercisable by both or all of them[2].

A county council may make any contribution it thinks fit to the expenditure[3] of a council of a district in the county[4]. A county council may also make any contribution it thinks fit towards expenditure by a parish council or a parish meeting in connection with the exercise of the functions[5] of the council or meeting relating to public open spaces[6].

A parish or community council has a general power to contribute towards the defraying of expenditure by another such authority if the contributing authority considers that the contribution is in the interests of and will bring direct benefit to its area or any part of it or all or some of its inhabitants, and the purpose of the expenditure is not otherwise authorised[7].

1 'Local authority' means a county council, a district council, a London borough council or a parish council but, in relation to Wales, means a county council, county borough council or community council: Local Government Act 1972 s 270(1) (definition amended by the Local Government Act 1985 s 102, Sch 16 para 8, Sch 17; and the Local Government (Wales) Act 1994 s 1(5)). As to local government areas and authorities in England and Wales see LOCAL GOVERNMENT vol 69 (2018) PARA 36 et seq.
2 Local Government Act 1972 s 136. Such arrangements may arise informally and are terminable on reasonable notice: *R v Rossendale Borough Council, ex p Whitworth Town Council* (1997) 96 LGR 507.
3 'Expenditure' includes sums paid by virtue of a precept or other instrument or by way of contribution: Local Government Act 1958 s 66(1).
4 Local Government Act 1958 s 56(1) (amended by the Statute Law (Repeals) Act 1974; and the Statute Law (Repeals) Act 1978).
5 'Functions' means powers or duties: Local Government Act 1958 s 66(1).
6 Local Government Act 1958 s 56(2) (amended by the Local Government Act 1972 s 272(1), Sch 30). As to the regulation and management of public open spaces see OPEN SPACES AND COUNTRYSIDE vol 78 (2010) PARA 508.
7 See the Local Government Act 1972 s 137(1), (2); and PARA 4.

10. Constraint on local authority procurement.

Whenever a local authority seeks offers in relation to a proposed public supply contract, a public works contract or certain other contracts it must comply with regulations implementing EU legislation[1] on the coordination of procedures for the award of such contracts[2].

1 Ie European Parliament and Council Regulation (EU) 2014/24 (OJ L94, 28.3.2014, p 65) on public procurement.

2 See the Public Contracts Regulations 2015, SI 2015/102; and CONSTITUTIONAL AND ADMINISTRATIVE LAW.

2. DETERMINATION OF BUDGET REQUIREMENTS

11. Issue of precepts by major precepting authorities in England and Wales.

For each financial year[1] a major precepting authority[2] must issue a precept or precepts[3]. A precept must be issued before 1 March in the financial year preceding that for which it is issued, but is not invalid merely because it is issued on or after that date[4]. A precept may only be challenged by way of judicial review[5].

A precept may only be issued to an appropriate billing authority[6]. A precept must state:

(1) the amount which, in relation to the year and each category of dwellings[7] in the billing authority's area, has been calculated (or last calculated)[8] by the precepting authority[9]; and

(2) the amount which has been calculated (or last calculated)[10] by the precepting authority as the amount payable by the billing authority for the year[11].

A major precepting authority must assume for these purposes that each of the valuation bands is shown in the billing authority's valuation list as applicable to one or more dwellings situated in its area or (as the case may be) each part of its area as respects which different calculations have been so made[12].

Before issuing the first precept to be issued by it for the financial year, a major precepting authority is under a duty to consult persons[13] or bodies appearing to the authority to be representative of persons subject to non-domestic rates[14] in the authority's area concerning its proposals for expenditure in that financial year[15].

1 'Financial year' means any period of 12 months beginning with 1 April: Local Government Finance Act 1992 s 116(1). In Pt I (ss 1–69), 'financial year', except in references to earlier or preceding financial years, does not include the financial year beginning in 1992 or earlier financial years: s 69(1). 'Month' means calendar month: Interpretation Act 1978 s 5, Sch 1.

2 Each of the following is a 'major precepting authority' for the purposes of the Local Government Finance Act 1992 Pt I, namely:

(1) a county council in England (s 39(1)(a) (amended by the Local Government (Wales) Act 1994 s 35(6)));

(2) the Greater London Authority (Local Government Finance Act 1992 s 39(1)(aa) (added by the Greater London Authority Act 1999 s 82(1), (2)));

(3) a mayoral combined authority, as defined by the Local Democracy, Economic Development and Construction Act 2009 s 107A(8) (see TRADE AND INDUSTRY) (Local Government Finance Act 1992 s 39(1)(ab) (added by the Cities and Local Government Devolution Act 2016 s 5(1)));

(4) a police and crime commissioner (see POLICE AND INVESTIGATORY POWERS vol 84 (2013) PARA 56 et seq) (Local Government Finance Act 1992 s 39(1)(b) (substituted by the Police Reform and Social Responsibility Act 2011 s 26(1), (2)));

(5) a metropolitan county fire and rescue authority (Local Government Finance Act 1992 s 39(1)(d) (amended by the Civil Contingencies Act 2004 s 32(1), Sch 2 Pt 1 paras 10(1), (2)));

(6) a fire and rescue authority in England constituted by a scheme under the Fire and Rescue Services Act 2004 s 2 or a scheme to which s 4 of that Act applies (see FIRE AND RESCUE SERVICES vol 51 (2013) PARAS 18–20) (Local Government Finance Act 1992 s 39(1)(da) (added by the Local Government Act 2003 s 83(1); and substituted by the Fire and Rescue Services Act 2004 s 53(1), Sch 1 para 81));

(7) a fire and rescue authority created by an order under the Fire and Rescue Services Act 2004 s 4A (see FIRE AND RESCUE SERVICES) (Local Government Finance Act 1992 s 39(1)(db) (added by the Policing and Crime Act 2017 s 6, Sch 1 para 71(1), (2)).

Where an order under the Local Government and Public Involvement in Health Act 2007 Pt 1 Ch 1 (ss 1–23) (structural and boundary change in England: see LOCAL GOVERNMENT vol 69 (2018) PARA 95 et seq) transfers the functions of district councils in relation to any area to a council for a county consisting of that area, the county council is not, for any such year, a major precepting authority for the purposes of the Local Government Finance Act 1992 Pt I (ss 1–69): see the Local

Government and Public Involvement in Health Act 2007 s 19(1)(b); and the Local Government (Structural Changes) (Finance) Regulations 2008, SI 2008/3022, reg 7(1), (2)(b). The Local Government and Public Involvement in Health Act 2007 s 19 does not limit any power to make provision by order under Pt 1 Ch 1 or any power to make incidental, consequential, transitional or supplementary provision in connection with the provisions of any such order: s 19(2). For these purposes 'financial year' means 12 months beginning with 1 April: s 19(3).

In respect of the financial year beginning on 1 April 2000, and subsequent financial years, for the purposes of the Local Government Finance Act 1992 Pt I Ch IV (ss 39–52), the receiver for the metropolitan police district's area is to be the area of the inner London boroughs; and the receiver may only issue precepts to the councils of the inner London boroughs: s 39(5) (added by SI 1999/3435). As to the meaning of 'England' see PARA 2 note 16.

As to the scrutiny of precepts issued by the relevant police and crime commissioner under the Local Government Finance Act 1992 s 40 by police and crime panels, see the Police Reform and Social Responsibility Act 2011 Sch 5 paras 1–6. The Secretary of State may make regulations concerning the scrutiny of precepts by police and crime panels: see Sch 5 paras 7, 8. See the Police and Crime Panels (Precepts and Chief Constable Appointments) Regulations 2012, SI 2012/2271.

As to local government areas and authorities in England see LOCAL GOVERNMENT vol 69 (2018) PARA 36 et seq. As to the Greater London Authority see LONDON GOVERNMENT vol 71 (2013) PARA 67 et seq. As to metropolitan county fire and rescue authorities see FIRE AND RESCUE SERVICES vol 51 (2013) PARA 17. As to the metropolitan police see POLICE AND INVESTIGATORY POWERS vol 84 (2013) PARA 53. As to the inner London boroughs see LONDON GOVERNMENT vol 71 (2013) PARA 15.

3 See the Local Government Finance Act 1992 s 40(1). It is the authority itself and not a committee which must discharge the function of issuing a precept: see s 67(1), (2)(d) (s 67(1) amended by the Local Government Act 2003 s 84(1), (2)). As to constitutional and operational arrangements of local authorities see LOCAL GOVERNMENT vol 69 (2018) PARA 294 et seq.

4 Local Government Finance Act 1992 s 40(5). No such precept may be issued by a precepting authority in England to a billing authority (see note 6) before the earlier of the following:

(1) the earliest date on which, for the financial year for which the precept is issued, each of the periods prescribed for the purposes of item 'T' in the Local Government Finance Act 1992 s 31B(1) (see PARA 383), item 'T' in s 42B(1) (see PARA 13) and item 'TP' in s 45(3) (see PARA 14) has expired (s 40(5A)(a) (s 40(5A) added by the Localism Act 2011 s 79, Sch 7 paras 7, 17(1), (4)));

(2) the earliest date on which, for that year, each billing authority has notified its calculations for the purposes of those items to the precepting authority (Local Government Finance Act 1992 s 40(5A)(b) (as so added)).

No such precept may be issued to a billing authority in Wales before the earlier of the following:

(a) the earliest date on which, for the financial year for which the precept is issued, each of the periods prescribed for the purposes of item T in s 33(1) (see PARA 385), item T in s 44(1) (see PARA 14) and item TP in s 45(3) (see PARA 14) has expired (s 40(6)(a) (s 40(6) amended by the Localism Act 2011 Sch 7 paras 7, 17(1), (5)));

(b) the earliest date on which, for that year, each billing authority has notified its calculations for the purposes of those items to the precepting authority (Local Government Finance Act 1992 s 40(6)(b) (as so amended)).

As to the meaning of 'Wales' see PARA 2 note 16.

No such precept may be issued unless the precepting authority has made in relation to the year the calculations required by Pt 1 Ch IV (ss 39–52): s 40(7). A purported issue of such a precept, if done in contravention of s 40(5A), (6) or (7) must be treated as not having occurred: s 40(8) (amended by the Localism Act 2011 Sch 7 paras 7, 17(1), (6)).

5 See the Local Government Finance Act 1992 s 66(1), (2)(e). If on an application for judicial review the court decides to grant relief, it must quash the precept: see s 66(3) (amended by the Local Government Finance Act 2012 s 10(2), (3)(b), Sch 4 paras 3, 5(1), (3)). As to judicial review generally see JUDICIAL REVIEW vol 61 (2010) PARA 601 et seq.

6 Local Government Finance Act 1992 s 39(3). If the whole or part of a billing authority's area falls within a precepting authority's area, it is an appropriate billing authority in relation to the precepting authority to the extent of the area which so falls: s 39(4). As to the meaning of 'billing authority' see PARA 346.

Where an order under the Local Government and Public Involvement in Health Act 2007 Pt 1 Ch 1 (ss 1–23) (see LOCAL GOVERNMENT vol 69 (2018) PARA 95 et seq) transfers the functions of district councils in relation to any area to a council for a county consisting of that area, the county council is, for any financial year beginning at the same time as or after that transfer, a billing authority for the purposes of the Local Government Finance Act 1992 Pt I (ss 1–69) in relation to the area, and is not, for any such year, a major precepting authority for those purposes: Local Government and Public Involvement in Health Act 2007 s 19(1). Section 19 does not limit any power to make provision by order under Pt 1 Ch 1 or any power to make incidental, consequential, transitional or supplementary provision in connection with the provisions of any such order: s 19(2). For these purposes, 'financial year' means 12 months beginning with 1 April: s 19(3).

If the Secretary of State or, in relation to Wales, the Welsh Ministers so requires by regulations, a billing authority must supply prescribed information within a prescribed period to any precepting authority which has power to issue a precept to the billing authority: see the Local Government Finance Act 1992 s 52. The functions of the Secretary of State under ss 52, 65 (see note 15), so far as exercisable in relation to Wales, were transferred to the National Assembly for Wales (see the National Assembly for Wales (Transfer of Functions) Order 1999, SI 1999/672, art 2, Sch 1) and are now vested in the Welsh Ministers (see the Government of Wales Act 2006 s 162(1), Sch 11 para 30). 'Prescribed' means prescribed by regulations made by the Secretary of State or, as the case may be, the Welsh Ministers: see the Local Government Finance Act 1992 s 116(1). As to the regulations made see the Local Authorities (Calculation of Council Tax Base) (Supply of Information) Regulations 1992, SI 1992/2904 (amended by SI 1995/3150; and, in relation to England, by SI 2012/2914). As to the Secretary of State and the Welsh Ministers see PARA 4 note 18.

7 Dwellings fall within different categories for the purposes of the Local Government Finance Act 1992 s 40(2) according as different calculations have been made in relation to them in accordance with:
   (1) in the case of a precepting authority in England, ss 42A, 42B and ss 45–47 (see PARAS 12–13) (s 40(3)(a) (s 40(3) amended by the Localism Act 2011 Sch 7 paras 7, 17(1), (3))); or
   (2) in the case of a precepting authority in Wales, the Local Government Finance Act 1992 ss 43–47 (see PARA 14) (s 40(3)(b) (as so amended)).

   As to the meaning of 'dwelling' see PARA 349.

8 Ie in accordance with:
   (1) in the case of a precepting authority in England, the Local Government Finance Act 1992 ss 42A, 42B (see PARAS 12–13) and ss 45–47; or
   (2) in the case of a precepting authority in Wales, ss 43–47 (see PARA 14).

9 Local Government Finance Act 1992 s 40(2)(a) (amended by the Localism Act 2011 Sch 7 paras 7, 17(1), (2)). As to the amount to be stated under the Local Government Finance Act 1992 s 40(2)(a) for any financial year in respect of any category of dwellings listed in a particular valuation band see s 47 (amended by the Greater London Authority Act 1999 s 92; and the Localism Act 2011 Sch 7 paras 7, 24).

10 Ie in accordance with the Local Government Finance Act 1992 s 48. Section 48 makes provision for calculating the amount required by s 40(2)(b) to be stated in a precept as the amount payable by a billing authority for any financial year: see s 48 (amended by the Greater London Authority Act 1999 s 93; and the Localism Act 2011 Sch 7 paras 7, 25). See also the Local Authorities (Calculation of Council Tax Base) (England) Regulations 2012, SI 2012/2914; and the Local Authorities (Calculation of Council Tax Base) (Wales) Regulations 1995, SI 1995/2561 (amended by SI 1999/2935, SI 2004/3094 and SI 2016/969).

11 Local Government Finance Act 1992 s 40(2)(b).

12 Local Government Finance Act 1992 s 40(4). As to the modifications to s 40 where the precepting authority is the Greater London Authority see s 40(9), (10) (added by the Greater London Authority Act 1999 s 83; the Local Government Finance Act 1992 s 40(9) amended by the Localism Act 2011 Sch 7 paras 7, 17(1), (7)).

   Where the precepting authority is a mayoral combined authority a precept may be issued only in relation to expenditure incurred by the mayor for the authority's area in, or in connection with, the exercise of mayoral functions and the issuing and calculation of a precept is subject to any provision made in an order under the Local Democracy, Economic Development and Construction Act 2009 s 107G (see TRADE AND INDUSTRY): Local Government Finance Act 1992 s 40(11) (added by the Cities and Local Government Devolution Act 2016 s 5(2)).

13 'Person' includes a body of persons corporate or unincorporate: Interpretation Act 1978 s 5, Sch 1. As to bodies corporate see COMPANIES vol 14 (2016) PARA 2; CORPORATIONS vol 24 (2010) PARA 301 et seq.

14 Ie under the Local Government Finance Act 1988 ss 43, 45: see PARAS 133, 135.

15 See the Local Government Finance Act 1992 s 65(1), (3), (4)(b) (s 65(3) amended by the Greater London Authority Act 1999 s 423, Sch 34 Pt I; the Police Reform and Social Responsibility Act 2011 s 26(1), (3); and the Policing and Crime Act 2017 s 6, Sch 1 para 71(1), (3)). Consultations must be made as to each financial year, and must be about the authority's proposals for expenditure (including capital expenditure) in that financial year; and the Secretary of State or, in relation to Wales, the Welsh Ministers may by regulations prescribe matters which are to be treated as expenditure for this purpose: Local Government Finance Act 1992 s 65(2). In performing the duty to consult, an authority must have regard to any guidance issued by the Secretary of State or, in relation to Wales, the Welsh Ministers concerning:

(1) persons or bodies to be regarded for these purposes as representative of persons subject to non-domestic rates as regards hereditaments situated in the authority's area (s 65(5)(a)); and

(2) the timing and manner of the consultations (see s 65(5)(b)).

An authority must make available to persons or bodies it proposes to consult such information as may be prescribed and is in its possession or control; and it must do so in such form and manner, and at such time, as may be prescribed: s 65(6). As to the regulations made see the Non-Domestic Ratepayers (Consultation) Regulations 1992, SI 1992/3171.

12. Calculation of council tax requirement by major precepting authorities in England.

In relation to each financial year[1] a major precepting authority in England[2] must make the following calculations[3].

The authority must calculate the aggregate of[4]:

(1) the expenditure the authority estimates it will incur in the year in performing its functions and will charge to a revenue account for the year in accordance with proper practices[5];

(2) such allowance as the authority estimates will be appropriate for contingencies in relation to amounts to be charged or credited to a revenue account for the year in accordance with proper practices[6];

(3) the financial reserves which the authority estimates it will be appropriate to raise in the year for meeting its estimated future expenditure[7]; and

(4) such financial reserves as are sufficient to meet so much of the amount estimated by the authority to be a revenue account deficit for any earlier financial year as has not already been provided for[8].

The authority must also calculate the aggregate of[9]:

(a) the income which it estimates will accrue to it in the year and which it will credit to a revenue account for the year in accordance with proper practices, other than income which it estimates will accrue to it in respect of any precept issued by it[10]; and

(b) the amount of the financial reserves which the authority estimates that it will use in order to provide for the items mentioned in heads (1) and (2) above[11].

If the aggregate calculated under heads (1) to (4) above exceeds that calculated under heads (a) and (b) above, the authority must calculate the amount equal to the difference; and the amount so calculated is to be its council tax requirement for the year[12].

The Secretary of State may by regulations[13] do one or both of the following:

(i) alter the constituents of any calculation to be made under heads (1) to (4) or heads (a) and (b) above (whether by adding, deleting or amending items)[14];

(ii) alter[15] the rules governing the making of any such calculation[16].

1 As to the meaning of 'financial year' see PARA 11 note 1.

2 As to the meaning of 'major precepting authority' see PARA 11 note 2. As to the meaning of 'England' see PARA 2 note 16.

3 See the Local Government Finance Act 1992 s 42A(1) (s 42A added by the Localism Act 2011 s 75). The Local Government Finance Act 1992 s 42A is subject to s 52ZT (which requires a direction to a major precepting authority that the referendum provisions in Pt 1 Ch 4ZA (ss 52ZA–52ZY) are not to apply to the authority for a financial year to state the amount of the authority's council tax requirement for the year) (see PARA 406): s 42A(12) (as so added).

The function of making a calculation under s 42A must be discharged only by the authority: see s 67(1), (2)(b) (s 67(1) amended by the Local Government Act 2003 s 84(1), (2); the Local Government Finance Act 1992 s 67(2)(b) amended by the Localism Act 2011 s 79, Sch 7 paras 7, 30). Where an authority to which the Local Government Finance Act 1992 s 42A applies is making calculations in accordance with that section, the chief finance officer of the authority must report to it on matters such as the robustness of the estimates made for the purposes of the calculations, and the adequacy of the proposed financial reserves, and must review those calculations throughout the year: see the Local Government Act 2003 s 25; and PARA 16.

A calculation made in accordance with the Local Government Finance Act 1992 s 42A may not be questioned except by an application for judicial review: see s 66(1), (2)(c) (amended by the Localism Act 2011 Sch 7 paras 7, 29). If, on an application for judicial review, the court decides to grant relief in respect of any matter, it must quash the calculation: see the Local Government Finance Act 1992 s 66(3) (amended by the Local Government Finance Act 2012 s 10(2), (3)(b), Sch 4 paras 3, 5(1), (3)). As to judicial review see JUDICIAL REVIEW vol 61 (2010) PARA 601 et seq.

4 In making the calculation under the Local Government Finance Act 1992 s 42A(2) the authority must ignore payments which must be met from a trust fund: s 42A(5) (as added: see note 3).

5 Local Government Finance Act 1992 s 42A(2)(a) (as added: see note 3). As to the meaning of 'proper practices' see PARA 590 note 4. As to accounts generally see PARA 588 et seq. In estimating under s 42A(2)(a) an authority must take into account:

(1) the amount of any expenditure which it estimates it will incur in the year in making any repayments of grants or other sums paid to it by the Secretary of State (s 42A(6)(a) (as so added)); and

(2) in the case of an authority which is a county council, the amount of any levy issued to it for the year (s 42A(6)(b) (as so added)).

But (except as provided by regulations under the Local Government Finance Act 1988 s 74: see PARA 24) the authority must not anticipate a levy not issued: Local Government Finance Act 1992 s 42A(7) (as so added). In estimating under s 42A(2)(a) an authority must take into account the amount of expenditure which it estimates it will incur in the year in accordance with regulations under the Local Government Finance Act 1988 s 99(3) (see PARA 583): Local Government Finance Act 1992 s 42A(7A) (added by SI 2014/389).

As to the Secretary of State see PARA 4 note 18. As to grants see PARA 29 et seq. 'Levy' means a levy under regulations made under the Local Government Finance Act 1988 s 74 (see PARA 24): Local Government Finance Act 1992 s 69(1).

6 Local Government Finance Act 1992 s 42A(2)(b) (as added: see note 3).

7 Local Government Finance Act 1992 s 42A(2)(c) (as added: see note 3). For these purposes an authority's estimated future expenditure is:

(1) that which the authority estimates it will incur in the financial year following the year in question, will charge to a revenue account for the year in accordance with proper practices and will have to defray in the year before the following sums are sufficiently available (s 42A(8)(a) (as so added)):

(a) sums which will be payable to it for the year (s 42A(8)(a)(i) (as so added)); and

(b) sums in respect of which amounts will be credited to a revenue account for the year in accordance with proper practices (s 42A(8)(a)(ii) (as so added)); and

(2) that which the authority estimates it will incur in the financial year referred to in head (1) above or any subsequent financial year in performing its functions and which will be charged to a revenue account for that or any other year in accordance with proper practices (s 42A(8)(b) (as so added)).

In relation to the estimation of financial reserves for the purpose of calculations in accordance with s 42A, in the case of a controlled reserve, it is not to be regarded as appropriate for the balance of the reserve at the end of the financial year under consideration to be less than the minimum amount determined in accordance with regulations made by the appropriate person: see the Local Government Act 2003 s 26(1)(b), (2) (s 26(1)(b) amended by the Localism Act 2011 Sch 7 paras 42, 44). As to the meanings of 'controlled reserve' and 'appropriate person' see PARA 16 note 8. At the date at which this volume states the law, no such regulations had been made. The provisions relating to the making of a report by the chief finance officer on the inadequacy of controlled reserves and budget monitoring also apply: see the Local Government Act 2003 ss 27, 28; and

PARAS 16–17.

8 Local Government Finance Act 1992 s 42A(2)(d) (as added: see note 3).

9 In making the calculation under the Local Government Finance Act 1992 s 42A(3) the authority must ignore payments which must be made into a trust fund: s 42A(9) (as added: see note 3).

10 Local Government Finance Act 1992 s 42A(3)(a) (as added: see note 3). In estimating under s 42A(3)(a) the authority must take into account the sums which the authority estimates will be paid to it in the year by billing authorities in accordance with regulations under the Local Government Finance Act 1988 s 99(3) (see PARA 583): Local Government Finance Act 1992 s 42A(10) (as so added). As to the meaning of 'billing authority' see PARA 346.

11 Local Government Finance Act 1992 s 42A(3)(b) (as added: see note 3).

12 Local Government Finance Act 1992 s 42A(4) (as added: see note 3).

13 At the date at which this volume states the law, no such regulations had been made.

14 Local Government Finance Act 1992 s 42A(11)(a) (as added: see note 3).

15 Ie whether by deleting or amending the Local Government Finance Act 1992 s 42A(5)–(10) (see notes 4, 5, 7, 9, 10), or any of those provisions, or by adding other provisions, or by a combination of those methods.

16 Local Government Finance Act 1992 s 42A(11)(b) (as added: see note 3).

13. Calculation of basic amount of tax by major precepting authorities in England.

In relation to each financial year[1] a major precepting authority in England[2] must calculate the basic amount of its council tax[3] by applying a specified formula[4].

The Secretary of State may by regulations[5] do either or both of the following:

(1) alter the constituents of any such calculation to be made (whether by adding, deleting or amending items)[6];

(2) provide[7] for rules governing the making of any such calculation[8].

Additional calculations must be made where special items relate to part only of a major precepting authority's area[9]. A major precepting authority which has made calculations in relation to a financial year[10] (originally or by way of substitute), may[11] make calculations in substitution in relation to the year[12].

1 As to the meaning of 'financial year' see PARA 11 note 1.

2 As to the meaning of 'major precepting authority' see PARA 11 note 2. As to the meaning of 'England' see PARA 2 note 16.

3 The function of setting an amount of council tax for a financial year under the Local Government Finance Act 1992 Pt I Ch III (ss 30–38), whether originally or by way of substitute, must be discharged only by the authority (see s 67(1), (2)(c)) but this does not apply to the determination of an amount for item 'T' in s 42B(1) (see the text to notes 6–8) (s 67(2A)(ba) (s 67(2A) added by the Local Government Act 2003 s 84(1), (3); the Local Government Finance Act 1992 s 67(2A)(ba) added by the Localism Act 2011 s 79, Sch 7 paras 7, 30(1), (3))). However, that function may, if the authority so directs, be exercised by a committee of the authority appointed by it for that purpose; and as respects a committee so appointed the number of members and their term of office must be fixed by the authority, and each member must be a member of the authority: see the Local Government Finance Act 1992 s 67(3) (amended by the Localism Act 2011 Sch 7 paras 7, 30(1), (4)).

4 See the Local Government Finance Act 1992 s 42B (s 42B added by the Localism Act 2011 s 75). Regulations prescribing certain periods for the purposes determining the calculation must be determined in the prescribed manner by such authority or authorities as may be prescribed: Local Government Finance Act 1992 s 42B(4) (as so added). 'Prescribed' means prescribed by regulations: see s 116(1). At the date at which this volume states the law, no such regulations had been made.

The Secretary of State must make regulations containing rules for making for any year certain calculations required by the formula: see s 42B(3) (as so added). As to the Secretary of State see PARA 4 note 18. As to the regulations made see the Local Authorities (Calculation of Council Tax Base) (England) Regulations 2012, SI 2012/2914.

5 See the Local Authorities (Calculation of Council Tax Base) (England) Regulations 2012, SI 2012/2914.

6 Local Government Finance Act 1992 s 42B(5)(a) (as added: see note 5).

7 Ie whether by adding provisions to, or deleting or amending provisions of, the Local Government Finance Act 1992 s 42B, or by a combination of those methods.
8 Local Government Finance Act 1992 s 42B(5)(b) (as added: see note 5).
9 See the Local Government Finance Act 1992 ss 45–46 (s 45 amended by the Localism Act 2011 Sch 7 paras 7, 22; and the Local Government Finance Act 2012 s 15(2); the Local Government Finance Act 1992 s 46 amended by the Police and Magistrates' Courts Act 1994 s 93, Sch 9 Pt I; the Greater London Authority Act 1999 ss 91(1), (2), 423, Sch 34 Pt I; the Localism Act 2011 Sch 7 paras 7, 23; and SI 1996/3071).
10 Ie in accordance with the Local Government Finance Act 1992 ss 42A, 42B and ss 45–48, (originally or by way of substitute): see s 49(1)(za) (s 49(1) substituted by the Greater London Authority Act 1999 s 94(1), (2); the Local Government Finance Act 1992 s 49(1)(za) added by the Localism Act 2011 Sch 7 paras 7, 26).
11 See note 10.
12 See the Local Government Finance Act 1992 s 49 (amended by the Greater London Authority Act 1999 s 94; and the Localism Act 2011 Sch 7 paras 7, 26).

14. Calculations by major precepting authorities in Wales.

A major precepting authority in Wales[1] is required to make certain calculations in order to determine its annual budget requirements[2]. The authority must calculate:

(1) the aggregate of:
  (a) the expenditure the authority estimates it will incur in the year in performing its functions and will charge to a revenue account for the year[3];
  (b) the expenditure that the authority estimates it will incur in the year in making repayments of grant paid to it by the Secretary of State or the Welsh Ministers or amounts paid to it by the Welsh Ministers in respect of redistributed non-domestic rates[4];
  (c) such allowance as the authority estimates will be appropriate for contingencies in relation to expenditure to be charged to a revenue account for the year[5];
  (d) the financial reserves which the authority estimates it will be appropriate to raise in the year for meeting its estimated future expenditure[6]; and
  (e) such financial reserves as are sufficient to meet so much of the amount estimated by the authority to be a revenue account deficit for any earlier financial year as has not already been provided for[7]; and

(2) the aggregate of
  (a) the sums which it estimates will be payable to it for the year[8] and in respect of which amounts will be credited to a revenue account for the year[9];
  (b) the sums that it estimates will be payable to it for an earlier financial year in respect of redistributed non-domestic rates, revenue support grant, additional grant, floor funding or police grant[10]; and
  (c) the amount of the financial reserves which the authority estimates that it will use in order to provide for the items mentioned in heads (1)(a), (b) above[11].

If the aggregate calculated under head (1) above exceeds that calculated under head (2) above, the authority must calculate the amount equal to the difference; and the amount so calculated is its budget requirement for the year[12].

The Welsh Ministers[13] may by regulations do one or both of the following:

(i) alter the constituents of any calculation to be made under head (1) or head (2) above;

(ii) alter the rules governing the making of any calculation under head (1) or head (2) above[14].

A major precepting authority in Wales must also calculate the basic amount of its council tax in relation to each financial year[15]. A major precepting authority which has made calculations in relation to a financial year[16] (originally or by way of substitute), may[17] make calculations in substitution in relation to the year[18].

1 As to the meaning of 'major precepting authority' see PARA 11 note 2. As to the meaning of 'Wales' see PARA 2 note 16.

2 See the Local Government Finance Act 1992 s 43(1) (amended by the Localism Act 2011 s 79, Sch 7 paras 7, 20(1), (3)). As to the robustness of estimates made for the purposes of budget calculations and other related matters see PARA 16. As to budget monitoring generally see PARA 17.

3 Local Government Finance Act 1992 s 43(2)(a) (amended by the Localism Act 2011 ss 79, 237, Sch 7 paras 7, 20(1), (4), Sch 25 Pt 13). As to revenue accounts see PARA 590.

4 Local Government Finance Act 1992 s 43(2)(aa) (added in relation to Wales by SI 2013/216).

5 Local Government Finance Act 1992 s 43(2)(b).

6 Local Government Finance Act 1992 s 43(2)(c). For the purposes of s 43(2)(c) an authority's estimated future expenditure is:

(1) that which the authority estimates it will incur in the financial year following the year in question, will charge to a revenue account for the year and will have to defray in the year before the following sums are sufficiently available, namely, sums which will be payable to it for the year and in respect of which amounts will be credited to a revenue account for the year (s 43(6)(a)); and

(2) that which the authority estimates it will incur in the financial year referred to in head (1) above or any subsequent financial year in performing its functions and which will be charged to a revenue account for that or any other year (s 43(6)(b)).

As to the meaning of 'financial year' see PARA 11 note 1.

7 Local Government Finance Act 1992 s 43(2)(d).

8 Ie other than those which it estimates will be so payable:

(1) in respect of redistributed non-domestic rates, revenue support grant, additional grant, special grant, floor funding or police grant (Local Government Finance Act 1992 s 43(3)(a)(i) (amended by the Localism Act 2011 Sch 7 paras 7, 20(1), (5)(a); and by SI 1995/234, SI 2011/313, SI 2012/521 and SI 2013/216)); or

(2) in respect of any precept issued by it (Local Government Finance Act 1992 s 43(3)(a)(ii) (amended by the Localism Act 2011 Sch 7 paras 7, 20(1), (5)(b), Sch 25 Pt 13)).

In the Local Government Finance Act 1992 ss 43, 44 'police grant', in relation to a major precepting authority and a financial year, means the total amount of grant payable to the authority in accordance with the police grant report for that year; and 'police grant report' means a police grant report approved by a resolution of the House of Commons pursuant to the Police Act 1996 s 46: see the Local Government Finance Act 1992 s 43(6A), (6B) (substituted by the Localism Act 2011 Sch 7 paras 7, 20(1), (7)).

In the Local Government Finance Act 1992 ss 43, 44:

(a) references to sums payable for a financial year in respect of floor funding are to sums that are payable by the Secretary of State in the year to a major precepting authority in addition to the police grant referred to in s 43(6A) (s 43(6C)(a) (s 43(6C) added in relation to Wales by SI 2013/216)); and

(b) references to sums payable for a financial year in respect of:

(i) redistributed non-domestic rates,

(ii) revenue support grant,

(iii) additional grant, or

(iv) special grant,

are to be construed in accordance with the Local Government Finance Act 1992 s 32(12) (see PARA 384) (s 43(6C)(b) (as so added)).

As to non-domestic rates see PARA 49 et seq. As to grants see PARA 29 et seq. As to the Secretary of State see PARA 4 note 18.

9 Local Government Finance Act 1992 s 43(3)(a).

10 Local Government Finance Act 1992 s 43(3)(aa) (added in relation to Wales by SI 2013/216).

11 Local Government Finance Act 1992 s 43(3)(b).

12 Local Government Finance Act 1992 s 43(4). As to the limitation of precepts where the amount calculated is excessive see PARA 21.
13 As to the Welsh Ministers see PARA 4 note 18.
14 See the Local Government Finance Act 1992 s 43(7) (amended by the Localism Act 2011 Sch 7 paras 7, 20(1), (8)). The following regulations have been made under the Local Government Finance Act 1992 s 43(7) and continue to have effect: the Local Authorities (Alteration of Requisite Calculations and Funds) Regulations 1994, SI 1994/246 (amended by the Localism Act Sch 25 Pt 13); the Local Authorities (Alteration of Requisite Calculations and Funds) Regulations 1995, SI 1995/234 (amended by the Localism Act 2011 Sch 25 Pt 13); the Local Authorities (Alteration of Requisite Calculations) (Wales) Regulations 1999, SI 1999/296 (amended by the Localism Act 2011 Sch 25 Pt 13); the Local Authorities (Alteration of Requisite Calculations) (Wales) Regulations 2000, SI 2000/717 (amended by the Localism Act 2011 Sch 25 Pt 13); the Local Authorities (Alteration of Requisite Calculations) (Wales) Regulations 2004, SI 2004/451; the Local Authorities (Alteration of Requisite Calculations) (Wales) Regulations 2006, SI 2006/344; the Local Authorities (Alteration of Requisite Calculations) (Wales) Regulations 2007, SI 2007/571; the Local Authorities (Alteration of Requisite Calculations) (Wales) Regulations 2008, SI 2008/476; the Local Authorities (Alteration of Requisite Calculations) (Wales) Regulations 2009, SI 2009/267; the Local Authorities (Alteration of Requisite Calculations) (Wales) Regulations 2010, SI 2010/317; the Local Authorities (Alteration of Requisite Calculations) (Wales) Regulations 2011, SI 2011/446; the Local Authorities (Alteration of Requisite Calculations) (Wales) Regulations 2012, SI 2012/521; and the Local Authorities (Alteration of Requisite Calculations) (Wales) Regulations 2013, SI 2013/216.
15 See the Local Government Finance Act 1992 ss 44–46 (s 44 amended by the Localism Act 2011 Sch 7 paras 7, 21; and by SI 1994/246, SI 1995/234, SI 2011/313, SI 2012/521 and SI 2013/216; the Local Government Finance Act 1992 s 45 amended by the Localism Act 2011 Sch 7 paras 7, 22; and the Local Government Finance Act 2012 s 15(2); the Local Government Finance Act 1992 s 46 amended by the Police and Magistrates' Courts Act 1994 s 93, Sch 9 Pt I; the Greater London Authority Act 1999 ss 91(1), (2), 423, Sch 34 Pt I; the Localism Act 2011 Sch 7 paras 7, 23; and SI 1996/3071).
16 Ie in accordance with the Local Government Finance Act 1992 ss 43–48 (see the text to notes 1–15) (originally or by way of substitute): see s 49(1)(a) (s 49(1) substituted by the Greater London Authority Act 1999 s 94(1), (2)).
17 See note 16.
18 See the Local Government Finance Act 1992 s 49 (amended by the Greater London Authority Act 1999 s 94; and the Localism Act 2011 Sch 7 paras 7, 26).

15. Setting of council tax and calculation of budget requirement: England and Wales.

For each financial year and each category of dwellings in its area, a billing authority must set an amount of council tax[1]. For this purpose a billing authority must make the requisite calculations as to its budget requirement[2], which then forms the basis on which it calculates the amount of tax[3].

1 See the Local Government Finance Act 1992 s 30; and PARA 380.
2 See the Local Government Finance Act 1992 s 32; and PARA 384.
3 See the Local Government Finance Act 1992 s 33; and PARA 385. As to special items see s 34; and PARA 386.

16. Budget calculations: robustness of estimates etc: England and Wales.

Where a major precepting authority[1] is making calculations of budget requirements[2], the chief finance officer[3] of the authority must report to it on the following matters:

(1) the robustness of the estimates made for the purposes of the calculations[4]; and

(2) the adequacy of the proposed financial reserves[5].

An authority to which such a report is made must have regard to the report when making decisions about the calculations in connection with which it is made[6].

In relation to the estimation of financial reserves for the purpose of calculations of budget requirements[7], in the case of a controlled reserve[8], it is not to be regarded as appropriate for the balance of the reserve at the end of the financial year[9] under consideration to be less than the minimum amount determined in accordance with regulations made by the appropriate person[10].

Where a major precepting authority[11] is making calculations of budget requirements[12], if in relation to the previous financial year it appears to the chief finance officer that a controlled reserve[13] is or is likely to be inadequate[14], he must report to the authority on the reasons for that situation[15], and the action, if any, which he considers it would be appropriate to take to prevent such a situation arising in relation to the corresponding reserve for the financial year under consideration[16]. An authority to which such a report is made must have regard to the report when making decisions about the calculations in connection with which it is made[17].

1 Ie an authority to which the Local Government Finance Act 1992 s 42A (see PARA 12) or s 43 (see PARA 14) applies: see the Local Government Act 2003 s 25(1) (amended by the Localism Act 2011 s 79, Sch 7 paras 42, 43). The Local Government Act 2003 s 25 also applies to an authority to which the Local Government Finance Act 1992 s 31A or s 32 applies: see the Local Government Act 2003 s 25(1); and PARAS 382, 384. The Local Government Act 2003 ss 25–27 apply to the Isles of Scilly subject to such exceptions, adaptations and modifications as the Secretary of State may by order provide: see s 125. As to the Secretary of State see PARA 4 note 18. As to the Council of the Isles of Scilly see LOCAL GOVERNMENT vol 69 (2018) PARA 50. At the date at which this volume states the law no such order had been made.

2 Ie in accordance with the Local Government Finance Act 1992 s 42A (see PARA 12) or s 43 (see PARA 14).

3 'Chief finance officer', in relation to an authority, means the officer having responsibility for the administration of the authority's financial affairs for the purposes of the Local Government Act 1972 s 151, the Local Government Act 1985 s 73, the Local Government Finance Act 1988 s 112, the Local Government and Housing Act 1989 s 6 (as to all of which see PARA 665), the Greater London Authority Act 1999 s 127(2) (see LONDON GOVERNMENT vol 71 (2013) PARA 154) or the Police Reform and Social Responsibility Act 2011 Sch 1, 2 or 4 (see POLICE AND INVESTIGATORY POWERS vol 84 (2013) PARA 56 et seq, 112 et seq, 117 et seq): Local Government Act 2003 s 25(3) (amended by the Police Reform and Social Responsibility Act 2011 s 99, Sch 16 paras 316, 318).

4 Local Government Act 2003 s 25(1)(a).

5 Local Government Act 2003 s 25(1)(b).

6 Local Government Act 2003 s 25(2).

7 Ie calculations in accordance with the Local Government Finance Act 1992 s 42A (see PARA 12) or s 43 (see PARA 14): see the Local Government Act 2003 s 26(1)(b) (amended by the Localism Act 2011 Sch 7 paras 42, 44). See also *R (on the application of Buck) v Doncaster Metropolitan Borough Council* [2013] EWCA Civ 1190, [2013] LGR 847. The Local Government Act 2003 s 26 applies also to calculations in accordance with the Local Government Finance Act 1992 s 31A and s 32: see the Local Government Act 2003 s 26(1)(a); and PARAS 382, 384.

8 'Controlled reserve' means a financial reserve of a description specified for these purposes by regulations made by the appropriate person: Local Government Act 2003 s 26(3). 'Appropriate person' means, in relation to England, the Secretary of State, and, in relation to Wales, the Welsh Ministers: s 124. The functions under the Local Government Act 2003 were formerly vested in the National Assembly for Wales and are now exercisable by the Welsh Ministers by virtue of the Government of Wales Act 2006 s 162(1), Sch 11 paras 30, 32. As to the Secretary of State and the Welsh Ministers see PARA 4 note 18. As to the meanings of 'England' and 'Wales' see PARA 2 note 16. At the date at which this volume states the law no regulations had been made under the Local Government Act 2003 s 26(3).

9 'Financial year' means a period of 12 months beginning with 1 April: Local Government Act 2003 s 124. As to the meaning of 'month' see PARA 11 note 1.

10 Local Government Act 2003 s 26(2). Different provision may be made under s 26(2) for different descriptions of financial reserve: s 26(4). At the date at which this volume states the law no regulations had been made under s 26(2).

11 Ie an authority to which the Local Government Finance Act 1992 s 42A (see PARA 12) or s 43 (see

PARA 14) applies: see the Local Government Act 2003 s 27(1) (amended by the Localism Act 2011 Sch 7 paras 42, 45). The Local Government Act 2003 s 27 applies also to an authority to which the Local Government Finance Act 1992 s 31A or s 32 applies: see the Local Government Act 2003 s 27(1); and PARAS 382, 384. See also note 1.

12 See the Local Government Act 2003 s 27(1). The calculations referred to are those made in accordance with the Local Government Finance Act 1992 s 43 (see PARA 14): see the Local Government Act 2003 s 27(1).

13 For these purposes, a 'controlled reserve' is a financial reserve of a description specified by regulations under the Local Government Act 2003 s 26(3) (see note 8): s 27(3)(a).

14 A controlled reserve is 'inadequate' if the balance of the reserve at the end of the financial year concerned is less than the minimum amount determined in accordance with regulations under the Local Government Act 2003 s 26(2) (see the text to notes 8–10): s 27(3)(b).

15 Local Government Act 2003 s 27(2)(a).

16 Local Government Act 2003 s 27(2)(b).

17 Local Government Act 2003 s 27(4).

17. Budget monitoring: England and Wales.

Where in relation to a financial year[1] a major precepting authority[2] has made its calculations of budget requirement[3], it must review them from time to time during the year[4]. In carrying out such a review, an authority must use the same figures for financial reserves as those used in the calculations under review, except in the case of financial reserves to meet a revenue account[5] deficit from an earlier financial year[6]. If as a result of carrying out a review it appears to the authority that carried out the review that there has been a deterioration in its financial position[7], it must take such action, if any, as it considers necessary to deal with the situation[8].

1 As to the meaning of 'financial year' see PARA 16 note 9.

2 Ie an authority to which the Local Government Finance Act 1992 s 42A (see PARA 12) or s 43 (see PARA 14) applies: see the Local Government Act 2003 s 28(1) (amended by the Localism Act 2011 s 79, Sch 7 paras 42, 46). The Local Government Act 2003 s 28 also applies to an authority to which the Local Government Finance Act 1992 s 31A (see PARA 382) or s 32 (see PARA 384) applies: see the Local Government Act 2003 s 28(1) (as so amended). Section 28 applies to the Isles of Scilly subject to such exceptions, adaptations and modifications as the Secretary of State may by order provide: see s 125. As to the Secretary of State see PARA 4 note 18. As to the Council of the Isles of Scilly see LOCAL GOVERNMENT vol 69 (2018) PARA 50. At the date at which this volume states the law no such order had been made.

3 Ie the calculations required by the Local Government Finance Act 1992 s 42A (see PARA 12) or s 43 (see PARA 14).

4 See the Local Government Act 2003 s 28(1). Where substitute calculations have effect, it is those calculations to which the duty under s 28(1) applies: s 28(5). As to substitute calculations see the Local Government Finance Act 1992 s 49; and PARAS 13, 14.

5 As to the meaning of 'revenue account' see PARA 590 note 4.

6 Local Government Act 2003 s 28(2).

7 There is a deterioration in an authority's financial position if on the review an amount falls to be calculated under the Local Government Finance Act 1992 s 42A(4) (see PARA 12) or s 43(4) (see PARA 14) and:

(1) none fell to be calculated under that provision at the time of the calculations under review (Local Government Act 2003 s 28(4)(a) (s 28(4) amended by the Localism Act 2011 Sch 7 paras 42, 46)); or

(2) an amount did then fall to be calculated under that provision and the amount then calculated is less than the amount calculated on the review (Local Government Act 2003 s 28(4)(b) (as so amended)).

8 Local Government Act 2003 s 28(3).

18. Issue of precepts by local precepting authorities: England and Wales.

For each financial year[1] a local precepting authority[2] may issue a precept[3]. Such a precept must be issued before 1 March in the financial year preceding that for which it is issued, but is not invalid merely because it is issued on or after that date[4]. A precept may only be challenged by way of judicial review[5].

A precept issued to a billing authority[6] must state, as the amount payable by that authority for the year, the amount which has been calculated (or last calculated) by the precepting authority[7] as its budget requirement for the year[8].

If so required by regulations[9], a billing authority must supply prescribed information within a prescribed period to any precepting authority which has power to issue a precept to the billing authority[10].

1 As to the meaning of 'financial year' see PARA 11 note 1.

2 Each of the following is a 'local precepting authority' for the purposes of the Local Government Finance Act 1992 Pt I (ss 1–69), namely:
 (1) the sub-treasurer of the Inner Temple (s 39(2)(a));
 (2) the under-treasurer of the Middle Temple (s 39(2)(b));
 (3) a parish or community council (s 39(2)(c));
 (4) the chairman of a parish meeting (s 39(2)(d)); and
 (5) charter trustees (s 39(2)(e)).

As to the Temples see LONDON GOVERNMENT vol 71 (2013) PARA 17. As to parish councils see LOCAL GOVERNMENT vol 69 (2018) PARA 41 et seq. As to parish meetings see LOCAL GOVERNMENT vol 69 (2018) PARA 48. As to community councils see LOCAL GOVERNMENT vol 69 (2018) PARA 63 et seq. As to charter trustees see LOCAL GOVERNMENT vol 69 (2018) PARA 144.

3 Local Government Finance Act 1992 s 41(1).

4 Local Government Finance Act 1992 s 41(4).

5 See the Local Government Finance Act 1992 s 66(1), (2)(e). If on an application for judicial review the court decides to grant relief, it must quash the precept: see s 66(3) (amended by the Local Government Finance Act 2012 s 10(2), (3)(b), Sch 4 paras 3, 5(1), (3)). As to judicial review generally see JUDICIAL REVIEW vol 61 (2010) PARA 601 et seq.

6 As to the meaning of 'billing authority' see PARA 346.

7 Ie, in the case of a precepting authority in England, under the Local Government Finance Act 1992 s 49A (see PARA 19) and, in the case of a precepting authority in Wales, under s 50 (see PARA 20). As to the meanings of 'England' and 'Wales' see PARA 2 note 16.

8 Local Government Finance Act 1992 s 41(2) (amended by the Localism Act 2011 s 79. Sch 7 paras 7, 18(1), (2)). The Secretary of State may by regulations make provision that a billing authority in England making calculations in accordance with the Local Government Finance Act 1992 s 31A (see PARA 382) (originally or by way of substitute) may anticipate a precept under s 41; and the regulations may include provision as to the amounts which may be anticipated by billing authorities in pursuance of the regulations, the sums (if any) to be paid by such authorities in respect of amounts anticipated by them and the sums (if any) to be paid by such authorities in respect of amounts not anticipated by them: s 41(2A) (added by the Localism Act 2011 Sch 7 paras 7, 18(1), (3)). As to the Secretary of State see PARA 4 note 18.

The Welsh Ministers may by regulations make provision that a billing authority in Wales making calculations in accordance with the Local Government Finance Act 1992 s 32 (see PARA 384) (originally or by way of substitute) may anticipate a precept under s 41; and the regulations may include provision as to the amounts which may be anticipated by billing authorities in pursuance of the regulations, the sums (if any) to be paid by such authorities in respect of amounts anticipated by them and the sums (if any) to be paid by such authorities in respect of amounts not anticipated by them: s 41(3) (amended by the Localism Act 2011 Sch 7 paras 7, 18(1), (4)). As to the Welsh Ministers see PARA 4 note 18.

As to the regulations made see the Billing Authorities (Anticipation of Precepts) Regulations 1992, SI 1992/3239 (amended by SI 1995/235, SI 2006/3395 and SI 2014/35).

9 Ie regulations made by the Secretary of State or, in relation to Wales, the Welsh Ministers: see the Local Government Finance Act 1992 s 52. At the date at which this volume states the law no such regulations had been made.

The functions of the Secretary of State under the Local Government Finance Act 1992 s 52 so far as exercisable in relation to Wales, were transferred to the National Assembly for Wales (see the National Assembly for Wales (Transfer of Functions) Order 1999, SI 1999/672, art 2, Sch 1) and are now vested in the Welsh Ministers (see the Government of Wales Act 2006 s 162(1), Sch 11 para 30).

10 See the Local Government Finance Act 1992 s 52.

19. Calculation of council tax requirement by local precepting authorities in England.

In relation to each financial year[1] a local precepting authority in England[2] must make the following calculations[3].

The authority must calculate the aggregate of:

(1) the expenditure the authority estimates it will incur in the year in performing its functions and will charge to a revenue account for the year in accordance with proper practices[4];

(2) such allowance as the authority estimates will be appropriate for contingencies in relation to amounts to be charged or credited to a revenue account for the year in accordance with proper practices[5];

(3) the financial reserves which the authority estimates it will be appropriate to raise in the year for meeting its estimated future expenditure[6]; and

(4) such financial reserves as are sufficient to meet so much of the amount estimated by the authority to be a revenue account deficit for any earlier financial year as has not already been provided for[7].

The authority must also calculate the aggregate of:

(a) the income which it estimates will accrue to it in the year and which it will credit to a revenue account for the year in accordance with proper practices, other than income which it estimates will accrue to it in respect of any precept issued by it[8]; and

(b) the amount of the financial reserves which the authority estimates that it will use in order to provide for the items mentioned in heads (1) and (2) above[9].

If the aggregate calculated under heads (1) to (4) above exceeds that calculated under heads (a) and (b) above, the authority must calculate the amount equal to the difference; and the amount so calculated is to be its council tax requirement for the year[10].

A local precepting authority which has made such calculations[11] in relation to a financial year (originally or by way of substitute) may[12] make calculations in substitution in relation to the year[13]. None of the substitute calculations are to have any effect if the amount calculated as its council tax requirement for the year[14] would exceed that so calculated in the previous calculations[15]; but this does not apply if the previous calculation has been quashed because of a failure to comply with the statutory provisions[16] in making the calculation[17].

1 As to the meaning of 'financial year' see PARA 11 note 1.

2 As to the meaning of 'local precepting authority' see PARA 18 note 2. As to the meaning of 'England' see PARA 2 note 16.

3 See the Local Government Finance Act 1992 s 49A(1) (ss 49A, 49B added by the Localism Act 2011 s 78). The Local Government Finance Act 1992 s 49A is subject to s 52ZV (which requires a direction to a local precepting authority that the referendum provisions in Pt 1 Ch 4ZA (ss 52ZA–52ZY) are not to apply to the authority for a financial year to state the amount of the authority's council tax requirement for the year) (see PARA 406): s 49A(6) (as so added).

4 Local Government Finance Act 1992 s 49A(2)(a) (as added: see note 3). As to the meaning of 'proper practices' see PARA 590 note 4. As to accounts generally see PARA 588 et seq.

5 Local Government Finance Act 1992 s 49A(2)(b) (as added: see note 3).

6 Local Government Finance Act 1992 s 49A(2)(c) (as added: see note 3). For these purposes, an authority's estimated future expenditure is:

(1) that which the authority estimates it will incur in the financial year following the year in question, will charge to a revenue account for the year in accordance with proper practices and will have to defray in the year before the following sums are sufficiently available, namely, sums:

(a) which will be payable to it for the year (s 49A(5)(a)(i) (as so added)); and

(b) in respect of which amounts will be credited to a revenue account for the year in accordance with proper practices (s 49A(5)(a)(ii) (as so added)); and

(2) that which the authority estimates it will incur in the financial year referred to in head (1) above or any subsequent financial year in performing its functions and which will be charged to a revenue account for that or any other year in accordance with proper practices (s 49A(5)(b) (as so added)).

7 Local Government Finance Act 1992 s 49A(2)(d) (as added: see note 3).

8 Local Government Finance Act 1992 s 49A(3)(a) (as added: see note 3). As to the issue of precepts see PARA 18.

9 Local Government Finance Act 1992 s 49A(3)(b) (as added: see note 3).

10 Local Government Finance Act 1992 s 49A(4) (as added: see note 3).

11 Ie calculations in accordance with the Local Government Finance Act 1992 s 49A: see the text to notes 1–10.

12 Ie in accordance with the Local Government Finance Act 1992 s 49A: see the text to notes 1–10.

13 Local Government Finance Act 1992 s 49B(1) (as added: see note 3).

14 Ie the amount calculated under the Local Government Finance Act 1992 s 49A(4): see the text to note 10.

15 Local Government Finance Act 1992 s 49B(2) (as added: see note 3).

16 Ie the Local Government Finance Act 1992 s 49A: see the text to notes 1–10.

17 Local Government Finance Act 1992 s 49B(3) (as added: see note 3).

20. Calculation of budget requirements by local precepting authorities in Wales.

A local precepting authority in Wales[1] is required to make certain calculations in order to determine its annual budget requirements[2]. The authority must calculate:

(1) the aggregate of:

(a) the expenditure the authority estimates it will incur in the year in performing its functions and will charge to a revenue account for the year[3];

(b) such allowance as the authority estimates will be appropriate for contingencies in relation to expenditure to be charged to a revenue account for the year[4];

(c) the financial reserves which the authority estimates it will be appropriate to raise in the year for meeting its estimated future expenditure[5]; and

(d) such financial reserves as are sufficient to meet so much of the amount estimated by the authority to be a revenue account deficit for any earlier financial year as has not already been provided for[6]; and

(2) the aggregate of the sums which it estimates will be payable to it for the year and in respect of which amounts will be credited to a revenue account for the year, other than sums which it estimates will be so payable in respect of any precept issued by it[7], and the amount of the financial reserves which the authority estimates that it will use in order to provide for the items mentioned in heads (1)(a) and (b) above[8].

If the aggregate calculated under head (1) above exceeds that calculated under head (2) above, the authority must calculate the amount equal to the difference; and the amount so calculated is to be its budget requirement for the year[9].

A local precepting authority which has made calculations[10] in relation to a financial year (originally or by way of substitution) may[11] make calculations in substitution in relation to the year[12].

1 As to the meaning of 'local precepting authority' see PARA 18 note 2. As to the meaning of 'Wales' see PARA 2 note 16.

2 See the Local Government Finance Act 1992 s 50(1) (amended by the Localism Act 2011 s 79, Sch 7 paras 7, 27). A calculation made in accordance with the Local Government Finance Act 1992 s 50, whether originally or by way of substitute, may not be questioned except by an application for judicial review: see s 66(1), (2)(c). If on an application for judicial review the court decides to grant relief, it must quash the calculation: s 66(3) (amended by the Local Government Finance Act 2012 s 10(2), (3)(b), Sch 4 paras 3, 5(1), (3)). As to judicial review generally see JUDICIAL REVIEW vol 61 (2010) PARA 601 et seq.
3 Local Government Finance Act 1992 s 50(2)(a). As to revenue accounts see PARA 590.
4 Local Government Finance Act 1992 s 50(2)(b).
5 Local Government Finance Act 1992 s 50(2)(c). For these purposes an authority's estimated future expenditure is:
(1) that which the authority estimates it will incur in the financial year following the year in question, will charge to a revenue account for the year and will have to defray in the year before the following sums are sufficiently available, namely, sums which will be payable to it for the year and in respect of which amounts will be credited to a revenue account for the year (s 50(5)(a)); and
(2) that which the authority estimates it will incur in the financial year referred to in head (1) above or any subsequent financial year in performing its functions and which will be charged to a revenue account for that or any other year (s 50(5)(b)).
As to the meaning of 'financial year' see PARA 11 note 1.
6 Local Government Finance Act 1992 s 50(2)(d).
7 Local Government Finance Act 1992 s 50(3)(a).
8 Local Government Finance Act 1992 s 50(3)(b).
9 Local Government Finance Act 1992 s 50(4).
10 Ie in accordance with the Local Government Finance Act 1992 s 50: see the text to notes 1–9.
11 Ie in accordance with the Local Government Finance Act 1992 s 50: see the text to notes 1–9.
12 Local Government Finance Act 1992 s 51(1). None of the substitute calculations is to have any effect if the amount calculated under s 50(4) (see the text to note 9) would exceed that so calculated in the previous calculations: s 51(2). However, s 51(2) does not apply if the previous calculation under s 50(4) has been quashed because of a failure to comply with that provision in making the calculation: s 51(3).

21. Limitation of precepts in Wales.

An authority in Wales[1] must notify the Welsh Ministers[2] in writing[3] of any amount calculated by it as its budget requirement[4] for a financial year, whether originally or by way of substitute[5].

If in the Welsh Ministers opinion the amount calculated by an authority as its budget requirement for a financial year (the 'year under consideration') is excessive, the Welsh Ministers may exercise their power[6] to designate or nominate the authority[7]. The Welsh Ministers may make a report specifying in relation to any year under consideration, and any authority, an amount which in the Welsh Ministers opinion should be used as the basis of any comparison in place of the amount calculated by the authority as its budget requirement for a financial year falling before the year under consideration (the 'alternative notional amount')[8].

If in the Welsh Ministers' opinion[9] the amount calculated by an authority as its budget requirement for the year under consideration is excessive[10], the Welsh Ministers may designate the authority as regards the year under consideration[11], or nominate the authority[12]. If the Welsh Ministers designate an authority as regards the year under consideration[13] they must notify the authority in writing of the designation[14]. A designation is invalid unless this requirement as to notification is complied with[15]. A designation is treated as made at the beginning of the day on which the authority receives the notification[16]. Before the end of the period of 21 days beginning with the day it receives a notification, an authority may inform the Welsh Ministers by notice in writing that:

(1) for reasons stated in the notice, it believes the maximum amount stated in the notice[17] should be such as the authority states in its notice[18]; or
(2) it accepts the maximum amount stated[19] in the notice[20].

The Local Government Finance Act 1992 sets out the procedures to be followed depending on whether head (1) above applies and the designated authority challenges the amount[21], or head (2) above applies and the authority accepts the maximum amount[22]. Where there is neither a challenge nor an acceptance following the 21 day period, the Welsh Ministers must make an order stating the amount which the amount calculated by the authority as its budget requirement for the year is not to exceed[23].

If the Welsh Ministers nominate an authority[24], they must notify the authority in writing of the nomination[25]. A nomination is invalid unless this requirement as to notification is complied with[26]. A nomination is treated as made at the beginning of the day on which the authority receives the notification[27].

After nominating an authority, the Welsh Ministers must decide whether to proceed by designating the authority[28] or by not designating the authority[29]. If the former, the Welsh Ministers must designate the authority as regards the financial year immediately following the year under consideration[30], determine an amount which they propose should be the maximum for the amount calculated by the authority as its budget requirement for the year as regards which the designation is made[31], and determine the target amount for the year as regards which the designation is made, that is, the maximum amount which they propose the authority could calculate as its budget requirement for the year without the amount calculated being excessive[32]. The Welsh Ministers must notify the authority in writing of the designation[33]. A designation is invalid unless this requirement as to notification is complied with[34]. A designation is treated as made at the beginning of the day on which the authority receives the notification[35]. Before the end of the period notified to it[36] an authority may inform the Welsh Ministers by notice in writing that:

(a) for reasons stated in the notice, it believes the maximum amount stated in the notice[37] should be such as the authority states in its notice[38]; or

(b) it accepts the maximum amount stated in the notice[39].

Failing either a challenge or acceptance, the Welsh Ministers must make an order stating the amount which the amount calculated by the authority as its budget for the year is not to exceed[40].

If the Welsh Ministers nominate the authority[41] and decide to proceed by not designating the authority[42], they must determine an amount which they propose should be the notional amount calculated by the authority as its budget requirement for the year under consideration[43]. The Welsh Ministers must notify in writing the authority of the amount so determined[44]. Before the end of the period of 21 days beginning with the day it receives the notification an authority may inform the Welsh Ministers by notice in writing that, for reasons stated in the notice, it believes the notional amount stated in the notification should be such as the authority states in its notice[45]. After the end of that period the Welsh Ministers must, if they receive such a notice, reconsider their determination (taking the notice into account)[46], and must notify the authority in writing of the amount which is to be the notional amount calculated by the authority as its budget requirement for the year under consideration[47].

1 In the Local Government Finance Act 1992 Pt I Ch IVA (ss 52A–52Y), reference to an 'authority' is to a billing authority in Wales or a major precepting authority in Wales: s 52A(1) (ss 52A–52Z added by the Local Government Act 1999 s 30, Sch 1 Pt I para 1; the Local Government Finance Act 1992 s 52A(1) amended by the Localism Act 2011 s 72(2), Sch 6 paras 1, 4). As to the meaning of 'billing authority' see PARA 346. As to the meaning of 'major precepting authority' see PARA 11 note 2. As to the meaning of 'Wales' see PARA 2 note 16.

2 As to the Welsh Ministers see PARA 4 note 18.

3 'Writing' includes typing, printing, lithography, photography and other modes of representing or reproducing words in a visible form, and expressions referring to writing are construed accordingly: Interpretation Act 1978 s 5, Sch 5.

4 Any reference in the Local Government Finance Act 1992 Pt I Ch IVA (ss 52A–52Y) to the amount calculated (or already calculated) by a major precepting authority as its budget for a financial year is a reference to the amount calculated by it in relation to the year under s 43(4) (see PARA 14): s 52W(1) (as added (see note 1); amended by the Localism Act 2011 ss 72(2), 237, Sch 6 paras 1, 25, Sch 25 Pt 12).

Any reference in the Local Government Finance Act 1992 Pt I Ch IVA to the amount calculated (or already calculated) by a billing authority as its budget requirement for a financial year is a reference to the amount calculated by it in relation to the year under s 32(4) (see PARA 384); but this is subject to s 52X: see ss 52W(3), 52X (both as so added; s 52X amended by the Localism Act 2011 Sch 6 paras 1, 26).

5 Local Government Finance Act 1992 s 52Y(1) (s 52Y as added (see note 1); amended by the Localism Act 2011 Sch 6 paras 1, 27). A billing authority must also notify the Welsh Ministers in writing of the aggregate amount for any financial year of any precepts which were taken into account by it in making a calculation in relation to the year under the Local Government Finance Act 1992 s 32(2) (see PARA 384) and which were:

(1) issued to it by local precepting authorities (s 52Y(2)(a) (as so added and amended)); or
(2) anticipated by it in pursuance of regulations under s 41 (see PARA 18) (s 52Y(2)(b) (as so added and amended)).

A notification under s 52Y(1) or (2) must be given before the end of the period of seven days beginning with the day on which the calculation was made: s 52Y(3) (as so added). As to the meaning of 'local precepting authority' see PARA 18 note 2.

The Welsh Ministers may serve on an authority a notice requiring it to supply to them such other information as is specified in the notice and required by them for the purpose of deciding whether to exercise their powers, and how to perform their functions, under Pt I Ch IVA (ss 52A–52Y): s 52Y(4) (as so added and amended). The authority must supply the information required if it is in its possession or control, and must do so in such form and manner and at such time as the Welsh Ministers specify in the notice: s 52Y(5) (as so added and amended). An authority may be required under s 52Y(4) to supply information at the same time as it gives a notification under s 52Y(1) or (2) or at some other time: s 52Y(6) (as so added).

If an authority fails to comply with s 52Y(1), (2) or (5), the Welsh Ministers may decide whether to exercise their powers, and how to perform their functions, under Pt I Ch IVA on the basis of such assumptions and estimates as they think fit: s 52Y(7) (as so added and amended). In deciding whether to exercise their powers, and how to perform their functions, under Pt I Ch IVA the Welsh Ministers may also take into account any other information available to them, whatever its source and whether or not obtained under a provision contained in or made under the Local Government Finance Act 1992 or any other Act: s 52Y(8) (as so added and amended).

6 Ie under the Local Government Finance Act 1992 s 52D: see the text to notes 9–12.

7 Local Government Finance Act 1992 s 52B(1) (s 52B as added (see note 1); amended by the Localism Act 2011 Sch 6 paras 1, 5). The question whether the amount so calculated is excessive must be decided in accordance with a set of principles determined by the Welsh Ministers: Local Government Finance Act 1992 s 52B(2) (as so added and amended). As to the set of principles see s 52B(3)–(7) (as so added and amended). In applying s 52B the Welsh Ministers must ignore any calculation for which another has been substituted at the time designation or nomination is proposed: s 52B(8) (as so added and amended). As to the exercise of the power under s 52B see *R (on the application of South Cambridgeshire District Council) v First Secretary of State* [2005] EWHC 1746 (Admin), [2006] LGR 529, [2005] RVR 369, [2005] All ER (D) 04 (Oct).

8 Local Government Finance Act 1992 s 52C(1), (2) (s 52C as added (see note 1); amended by the Localism Act 2011 Sch 6 paras 1, 6). A report:

(1) may relate to two or more authorities (Local Government Finance Act 1992 s 52C(3)(a) (as so added));
(2) may be amended by a subsequent report (s 52C(3)(b) (as so added));
(3) must contain such explanation as the Welsh Ministers think desirable of the calculation by them of the alternative notional amount (s 52C(3)(c) (as so added and amended));
(4) must be laid before the National Assembly for Wales (s 52C(3)(d) (as so added and amended)).

If a report is approved by resolution of the National Assembly for Wales, s 52B has effect, as regards the year under consideration and any authority to which the report relates, as if the reference in s 52B(4) (see note 7) to the amount calculated by the authority as its budget requirement for a financial year falling before the year under consideration were to the alternative notional amount for the year so falling: s 52C(4) (as so added and amended). As to the National Assembly for Wales see CONSTITUTIONAL AND ADMINISTRATIVE LAW vol 20 (2014) PARA 351 et seq.

9 Ie reached after applying the Local Government Finance Act 1992 s 52B: see the text to notes 6–7.

10 Local Government Finance Act 1992 s 52D(1) (as added (see note 1); amended by the Localism Act 2011 Sch 6 paras 1, 7).

11 Local Government Finance Act 1992 s 52D(2)(a) (s 52D(2), (3) as added (see note 1); amended by the Localism Act 2011 Sch 6 paras 1, 7). The Welsh Ministers may proceed under different paragraphs of the Local Government Finance Act 1992 s 52D(2) in relation to different authorities: s 52D(3) (as so added and amended).

12 Local Government Finance Act 1992 s 52D(2)(b) (as added: see note 1). See also note 11.

13 Local Government Finance Act 1992 s 52E(1) (as added (see note 1); amended by the Localism Act 2011 Sch 6 paras 1, 8).

14 Local Government Finance Act 1992 s 52E(2)(a) (s 52E(2) as added (see note 1); amended by the Localism Act 2011 Sch 6 paras 1, 8). The notification must also set out:

(1) the set of principles determined for the authority under the Local Government Finance Act 1992 s 52B (see the text to notes 6–7) (s 52E(2)(b) (as so added));

(2) the category in which the authority falls (if the Welsh Ministers determine categories under s 52B) (s 52E(2)(c) (as so added and amended));

(3) the amount which the Welsh Ministers propose should be the maximum for the amount calculated by the authority as its budget requirement for the year (s 52E(2)(d) (as so added and amended));

(4) the target amount for the year, that is, the maximum amount which the Welsh Ministers propose the authority could calculate as its budget requirement for the year without the amount calculated being excessive (s 52E(2)(e) (as so added and amended)); and

(5) the financial year as regards which the Welsh Ministers expect the amount calculated by the authority as its budget requirement for that year to be equal to or less than the target amount for that year (assuming one to be determined for that year) (s 52E(2)(f) (as so added and amended)).

15 See the Local Government Finance Act 1992 s 52E(3)(a) (as added: see note 1).

16 Local Government Finance Act 1992 s 52E(3)(b) (as added: see note 1).

17 Ie under the Local Government Finance Act 1992 s 52E(2)(d): see note 14.

18 Local Government Finance Act 1992 s 52E(5)(a) (s 52E(5) as added (see note 1); amended by the Localism Act 2011 Sch 6 paras 1, 8).

19 Ie under the Local Government Finance Act 1992 s 52E(2)(d): see note 14.

20 See the Local Government Finance Act 1992 s 52E(5)(b) (as added: see note 1). If an authority has been designated under s 52D(2)(a) (see the text to note 11), and after the designation is made the authority makes substitute calculations in relation to the year, the substitute calculations are invalid unless they are made in accordance with s 52I or s 52J (see PARA 22) (as the case may be): s 52E(4) (as so added).

21 See the Local Government Finance Act 1992 s 52F (as added (see note 1); amended by the Localism Act 2011 Sch 6 paras 1, 9).

22 See the Local Government Finance Act 1992 s 52G (as added (see note 1); amended by the Localism Act 2011 Sch 6 paras 1, 10).

23 See the Local Government Finance Act 1992 s 52H(1), (2) (s 52H as added (see note 1); amended by the Localism Act 2011 Sch 6 paras 1, 11). The amount stated must be that stated in the notice under the Local Government Finance Act 1992 s 52E(2)(d) (see the text to note 14): s 52H(2) (as so added). An order must not be made unless a draft of it has been laid before and approved by resolution of the National Assembly for Wales (s 52H(3)(a) (as so added and amended)), and may relate to two or more authorities (s 52H(3)(b) (as so added)). As soon as is reasonably practicable after an order is made the Welsh Ministers must serve on the authority (or each authority) a notice stating the amount stated in the case of the authority concerned in the order: s 52H(4) (as so added and amended). When the Welsh Ministers serve a notice under s 52H(4) on a precepting authority the Welsh Ministers must also serve a copy of it on each billing authority to which the precepting authority has power to issue a precept: s 52H(5) (as so added and amended). Orders made under s 52H, being of local effect, are not recorded in this work.

24 Ie under the Local Government Finance Act 1992 s 52D(2)(b) (see the text to note 12): see s 52L(1) (as added (see note 1); amended by the Localism Act 2011 Sch 6 paras 1, 15).

25 Local Government Finance Act 1992 s 52L(2)(a) (s 52L(2) as added (see note 1); amended by the Localism Act 2011 Sch 6 paras 1, 15). The notification must also set out:
   (1) the set of principles determined for the authority under the Local Government Finance Act 1992 s 52B (see the text to notes 6–7) (s 52L(2)(b) (as so added));
   (2) the category in which the authority falls (if the Welsh Ministers determine categories under s 52B) (s 52L(2)(c) (as so added and amended)); and
   (3) the amount which the Welsh Ministers would have proposed as the target amount for the year under consideration if they had designated the authority as regards that year under s 52D(2)(a) (see the text to note 11) (s 52L(2)(d) (as so added and amended)).
26 Local Government Finance Act 1992 s 52L(3)(a) (as added: see note 1).
27 Local Government Finance Act 1992 s 52L(3)(b) (as added: see note 1).
28 Ie under the Local Government Finance Act 1992 s 52M (see the text to notes 30–39): see s 52L(4)(a) (s 52L(4) as added (see note 1); amended by the Localism Act 2011 Sch 6 paras 1, 15).
29 Ie under the Local Government Finance Act 1992 s 52N (see the text to notes 41–47): see s 52L(4)(a) (as added and amended: see note 28). The Welsh Ministers may decide to proceed under different sections in relation to different authorities: s 52L(4)(b) (as so added and amended).
30 Local Government Finance Act 1992 s 52M(1), (2)(a) (s 52M as added (see note 1); amended by the Localism Act 2011 Sch 6 paras 1, 16).
31 Local Government Finance Act 1992 s 52M(1), (2)(b) (as added and amended: see note 30). In making the determinations under s 52M(2) the Welsh Ministers must take into account:
   (1) the amount which they would have proposed as the target amount for the year under consideration if they had designated the authority as regards that year under s 52D(2)(a) (see the text to note 11) (s 52M(3)(a) (as so added and amended)); and
   (2) any information they think is relevant (s 52M(3)(b) (as so added and amended)).
32 Local Government Finance Act 1992 s 52M(1), (2)(c) (as added and amended: see note 30). See also note 31.
33 Local Government Finance Act 1992 s 52M(1), (4)(a) (as added and amended: see note 30). The notification must also set out:
   (1) the amount determined under s 52M(2)(b) (see the text to note 31) (s 52M(1), (4)(b) (as so added and amended));
   (2) the target amount determined under s 52M(2)(c) (see the text to note 32) (s 52M(1), (4)(c) (as so added and amended));
   (3) any information taken into account under s 52M(3)(b) (see note 31) (s 52M(1), (4)(d) (as so added and amended));
   (4) the financial year as regards which the Welsh Ministers expect the amount calculated by the authority as its budget requirement for that year to be equal to or less than the target amount for that year (assuming one to be determined for that year) (s 52M(1), (4)(e) (as so added and amended));
   (5) the period within which the authority may inform the Welsh Ministers that it challenges or accepts the amount stated under head (1) above (s 52M(1), (4)(f) (as so added and amended)).

   The period notified under s 52M(4)(f) must be a period of at least 21 days beginning with the day the authority receives the notification: s 52M(9) (as so added).
34 Local Government Finance Act 1992 s 52M(5)(a) (as added: see note 1).
35 Local Government Finance Act 1992 s 52M(5)(b) (as added: see note 1). If an authority has been designated under s 52M as regards a financial year the Welsh Ministers may not designate it under s 52D(2)(a) (see the text to note 11) as regards that year: s 52M(6) (as so added; and as amended (see note 30)). If an authority has been designated under s 52M as regards a financial year, and after the designation is made the authority makes calculations or substitute calculations in relation to the year, the calculations (or substitute calculations) are invalid unless they are made in accordance with s 52T or s 52U (see note 38) (as the case may be): s 52M(7) (as so added).
36 Ie under the Local Government Finance Act 1992 s 52M(4)(f): see note 33.
37 Ie stated under the Local Government Finance Act 1992 s 52M(4)(b): see note 33.
38 Local Government Finance Act 1992 s 52M(8)(a) (as added and amended: see note 30). As to the procedure with regard to such challenges see ss 52Q, 52T, 52U (all as so added; s 52Q amended by the Localism Act 2011 Sch 6 paras 1, 19, Sch 25 Pt 12; the Local Government Finance Act 1992 s 52T amended by the Localism Act 2011 Sch 6 paras 1, 22; the Local Government Finance Act 1992 s 52U amended by the Localism Act 2011 Sch 6 paras 1, 23, Sch 25 Pt 12).
39 See the Local Government Finance Act 1992 s 52M(8)(b) (as added and amended: see note 30). As to the procedure with regard to such acceptances see ss 52P, 52R (both as so added; s 52P amended by the Localism Act 2011 Sch 6 paras 1, 18; the Local Government Finance Act 1992 amended by the Localism Act 2011 Sch 6 paras 1, 20).

40 See the Local Government Finance Act 1992 s 52S(1)(a), (2) (s 52S as added (see note 1); amended by the Localism Act 2011 Sch 6 paras 1, 21). The amount stated must be that stated in the notice under the Local Government Finance Act 1992 s 52M(4)(b) (see note 33): s 52S(2) (as so added). An order:
(1) must not be made unless a draft of it has been laid before and approved by resolution of the National Assembly for Wales (s 52S(3)(a) (as so added and amended));
(2) may relate to two or more authorities (s 52S(3)(b) (as so added)).
As soon as is reasonably practicable after an order is made the Welsh Ministers must serve on the authority (or each authority) a notice stating the amount stated in the case of the authority concerned in the order: s 52S(4) (as so added and amended). When the Welsh Ministers serve a notice under s 52S(4) on a precepting authority the Welsh Ministers must also serve a copy of it on each billing authority to which the precepting authority has power to issue a precept: s 52S(5) (as so added and amended). Orders made under s 52S, being of local effect, are not recorded in this work.
41 Ie under the Local Government Finance Act 1992 s 52D(2)(a) (see the text to note 11): see s 52N(1)(a) (s 52N as added (see note 1); amended by the Localism Act 2011 Sch 6 paras 1, 17).
42 See the Local Government Finance Act 1992 s 52N(1)(b) (as added and amended: see note 41).
43 Local Government Finance Act 1992 s 52N(2) (as added and amended: see note 41). In making the determination the Welsh Ministers must take into account:
(1) the amount which they would have proposed as the maximum for the amount calculated by the authority as its budget requirement for the year under consideration if they had designated it as regards that year under s 52D(2)(a) (see the text to note 11) (s 52N(3)(a) (as so added and amended)); and
(2) any information they think is relevant (s 52N(3)(b) (as so added and amended)).
44 Local Government Finance Act 1992 s 52N(4)(a) (as added and amended: see note 41). The notification must also set out the amount mentioned in s 52N(3)(a) and any information taken into account under s 52N(3)(b) (see note 43): s 52N(4)(b), (c) (as so added).
45 See the Local Government Finance Act 1992 s 52N(5) (as added and amended: see note 41).
46 Local Government Finance Act 1992 s 52N(6)(a) (as added and amended: see note 41).
47 Local Government Finance Act 1992 s 52N(6)(b) (as added and amended: see note 41). Such a notification must be treated as made at the beginning of the day on which the authority receives it: s 52N(7) (as so added). In applying Pt I Ch IVA (ss 52A–52Y) at any time after such a notification is made of the amount which is to be the notional amount calculated by the authority as its budget requirement for a financial year, the amount calculated by the authority as its budget requirement for that year must be taken to be the notional amount notified: s 52N(8) (as so added).

22. Substitute calculations by an authority in Wales following designation.

If an authority in Wales[1] has been designated as regards excessive budget requirement calculations[2], and after the designation is made the authority makes substitute calculations in relation to the year[3], the substitute calculations will be invalid unless they are made in accordance with specified statutory provisions[4].

If an authority has been designated[5] as regards a financial year following nomination in respect of excessive budget requirement calculations[6], and after the designation is made the authority makes calculations or substitute calculations in relation to the year[7], the calculations (or substitute calculations) will be invalid unless they are made in accordance with specified statutory provisions[8].

1 As to the meaning of 'authority' see PARA 21 note 1. As to the meaning of 'Wales' see PARA 2 note 16.
2 Ie under the Local Government Finance Act 1992 s 52D(2)(a) (see PARA 21): see s 52E(4)(a) (s 52E added by the Local Government Act 1999 Sch 1 Pt I para 1).
3 Local Government Finance Act 1992 s 52E(4)(b) (as added: see note 2).
4 Local Government Finance Act 1992 s 52E(4) (as added: see note 2). As regards a designated billing authority the statutory provision is s 52I (ss 52I–52K added by the Local Government Act 1999 Sch 1 Pt I para 1; and amended by the Localism Act 2011 Sch 6 paras 1, 12); and as regards a designated precepting authority the statutory provision is the Local Government Finance Act 1992 s 52J (as so added; and amended by the Localism Act 2011 Sch 6 paras 1, 13, Sch 25 Pt 12): see the Local Government Finance Act 1992 s 52E(4) (as so added). As to the consequences of failure to comply with the substitute calculation provisions in s 52I or s 52J see s 52K (as so added; amended by the Localism Act 2011 Sch 6 paras 1, 14, Sch 25 Pt 12).
5 Ie under the Local Government Finance Act 1992 s 52M: see PARA 21.

6 Local Government Finance Act 1992 s 52M(7)(a) (ss 52M, 52T, 52U added by the Local Government Act 1999 Sch 1 Pt I para 1).
7 Local Government Finance Act 1992 s 52M(7)(b) (as added: see note 6).
8 See the Local Government Finance Act 1992 s 52M(7) (as added: see note 6). As regards a designated billing authority the statutory provision is s 52T (as so added; amended by the Localism Act 2011 Sch 6 paras 1, 22); and as regards a designated precepting authority the statutory provision is the Local Government Finance Act 1992 s 52U (as so added; amended by the Localism Act 2011 Sch 6 paras 1, 23, Sch 25 Pt 12): see the Local Government Finance Act 1992 s 52M(7) (as so added). As to the consequences of failure to comply with the substitute calculation provisions in s 52T or s 52U, see s 52V (added by the Local Government Act 1999 Sch 1 Pt I para 1; and amended by the Localism Act 2011 Sch 6 paras 1, 24, Sch 25 Pt 12).

23. Substituted precepts: England and Wales.

Where a precepting authority[1] has issued a precept or precepts for a financial year[2] (originally or by way of substitute)[3] and at any time it makes substitute calculations[4], it must as soon as reasonably practicable after that time issue a precept or precepts in substitution so as to give effect to those calculations[5]. Where a precepting authority issues a precept in substitution (a 'new precept') anything paid to it by reference to the precept for which it is substituted (the 'old precept') must be treated as paid by reference to the new precept[6]. If the amount stated[7] in the old precept exceeds that of the new precept, the following applies as regards anything paid if it would not have been paid had the amount of the old precept been the same as that of the new precept:

(1) it must be repaid if the billing authority[8] by whom it was paid so requires[9];

(2) in any other case it must (as the precepting authority determines) either be repaid or be credited against any subsequent liability of the billing authority in respect of any precept of the precepting authority[10].

1 'Precepting authority' means a major precepting authority or a local precepting authority: Local Government Finance Act 1992 s 69(1). As to the meaning of 'major precepting authority' see PARA 11 note 2. As to the meaning of 'local precepting authority' see PARA 18 note 2.
2 As to the meaning of 'financial year' see PARA 11 note 1. As to the issue of precepts see PARAS 11, 18.
3 Local Government Finance Act 1992 s 42(1)(a).
4 Ie under the Local Government Finance Act 1992 s 49 (see PARAS 13, 14), s 49A (see PARA 19), s 52ZU (see PARA 406), s 52J or s 52U (see PARA 22) or (as the case may be) s 51 (see PARA 20) or the Greater London Authority Act 1999 s 95 (see LONDON GOVERNMENT vol 71 (2013) PARA 150): see the Local Government Finance Act 1992 s 42(1)(b) (amended by the Local Government Act 1999 s 30, Sch 1 Pt II paras 2, 4; the Greater London Authority Act 1999 s 84; and the Localism Act 2011 ss 72(3), 79, Sch 6 paras 1, 3, Sch 7 paras 7, 19).
5 Local Government Finance Act 1992 s 42(1). Any precept issued in substitution under s 42(1) must be issued in accordance with s 40 (see PARA 11) or (as the case may be) s 41 (see PARA 18), but s 40(5) and s 41(4) must be ignored for this purpose: s 42(2).
6 Local Government Finance Act 1992 s 42(3).
7 Any reference in the Local Government Finance Act 1992 s 42(4) to the amount stated in a precept is to be construed, in relation to a precept issued by a major precepting authority, as a reference to the amount stated in the precept in accordance with s 40(2)(b) (see PARA 11): s 42(5).
8 As to the meaning of 'billing authority' see PARA 346.
9 Local Government Finance Act 1992 s 42(4)(a).
10 Local Government Finance Act 1992 s 42(4)(b).

24. Levies: England and Wales.

In respect of any chargeable financial year[1] no levying body[2] has power under the Local Government Finance Act 1988 concerned to issue a precept to, make a levy on or have its expenses paid by the council concerned[3]. Whereas a levying body[4] has[5] no such power under the Act concerned in respect of a chargeable financial year, the appropriate national authority[6] may make regulations conferring on each levying body power to issue to the council concerned[7] and in accordance with the regulations a levy in respect of any chargeable financial year[8].

In relation to any body which has no power to levy a rate by virtue of regulations[9] or whose power to levy a rate is modified by regulations[10], the appropriate national authority[11] may make regulations conferring on any such body power to issue in respect of prescribed chargeable financial years and in accordance with the regulations:

(1) a special levy to such billing authority as is prescribed as regards the body concerned[12]; or

(2) special levies to such billing authorities as are prescribed as regards the body concerned[13].

A levy or special levy so issued[14] may only be challenged by way of judicial review[15].

1 'Chargeable financial years' are financial years beginning in 1990 and subsequent years: Local Government Finance Act 1988 s 145(1). A 'financial year' is a period of 12 months beginning with 1 April: s 145(3). As to the meaning of 'month' see PARA 11 note 1.

2 For the purposes of the Local Government Finance Act 1988 s 117(6), 'levying body' means any body which:

(1) is established by or under an Act (s 117(5)(a));

(2) apart from s 117(6) would have in respect of the financial year beginning in 1990 power (conferred by or under an Act passed before, or in the same session as, the Local Government Finance Act 1988, ie the 1987–1988 session) to issue a precept to, make a levy on or have its expenses paid by a county council or charging authority (s 117(5)(b)); and

(3) is not a precepting authority or combined fire and rescue authority in Wales (s 117(5)(c) (amended by the Courts Act 2003 s 109(1), Sch 8 para 305(b); the Fire and Rescue Services Act 2004 s 53(1), Sch 1 para 68(1), (4); and the Police Reform and Social Responsibility Act 2011 s 99, Sch 16 paras 180, 191)).

In the Local Government Finance Act 1988 s 117(5), (6), 'Act' includes a private or local Act: s 117(7). As to private Acts see STATUTES AND LEGISLATIVE PROCESS vol 96 (2012) PARA 624; and as to local Acts see STATUTES AND LEGISLATIVE PROCESS vol 96 (2012) PARA 626. Each of the following is a 'charging authority': a district council; a London borough council; the Common Council of the City of London; and the Council of the Isles of Scilly: ss 144(1), 146(4). As to local government areas and authorities see LOCAL GOVERNMENT vol 69 (2018) PARA 36 et seq. As to the London boroughs and their councils see LONDON GOVERNMENT vol 71 (2013) PARAS 15, 20–22, 55 et seq. As to the Common Council of the City of London see LONDON GOVERNMENT vol 71 (2013) PARAS 34–38. As to the Council of the Isles of Scilly see LOCAL GOVERNMENT vol 69 (2018) PARA 50.

As to the meaning of 'precepting authority' see PARA 23 note 1 (definition applied by s 144(2) (substituted by the Local Government Finance Act 1992 ss 117(1), 118(1), Sch 13 para 81(1); and amended by the Local Government Finance Act 2012 s 5(1), (2)(b), Sch 3 paras 23, 29)). A 'combined fire and rescue authority' is a fire and rescue authority constituted by a scheme under the Fire and Rescue Services Act 2004 s 2 or a scheme to which s 4 of that Act applies (see FIRE AND RESCUE SERVICES vol 51 (2013) PARAS 18–20): Local Government Finance Act 1988 s 144(5) (substituted by the Fire and Rescue Services Act 2004 s 53(1), Sch 1 para 68(1), (5)). As to police authorities see POLICE AND INVESTIGATORY POWERS vol 84 (2013) PARA 55 et seq. As to the meaning of 'Wales' see PARA 2 note 16.

3 Local Government Finance Act 1988 s 117(6).

4 For the purposes of the Local Government Finance Act 1988 s 74, 'levying body' means any body which:

(1) is established by or under an Act (s 74(1)(a));

(2) apart from s 117 (see the text to notes 1–3) would have in respect of the financial year beginning in 1990 power (conferred by or under an Act passed before, or in the same session as, the Local Government Finance Act 1988) to issue a precept to, make a levy on or have its expenses paid by a county council or charging authority (s 74(1)(b)); and

(3) is not a precepting authority or a combined fire and rescue authority in Wales (s 74(1)(c) (amended by the Courts Act 2003 Sch 8 para 305(a); the Fire and Rescue Services Act 2004 Sch 1 para 68(1), (2); and the Police Reform and Social Responsibility Act 2011 Sch 16 paras 180, 182(a))).

In the Local Government Finance Act 1988 s 74, 'Act' includes a private or local Act: s 74(6).

Additionally with respect to regulations which may be made under s 74(2):

(a) a Welsh joint planning board constituted under the Town and Country Planning Act 1990 s 2(1B) (see PLANNING vol 81 (2018) PARA 188) is to be treated as a levying body (see s 74(7) (added by the Local Government (Wales) Act 1994 s 20(4), Sch 6 para 21; and amended by the Environment Act 1995 s 120, Sch 24)); and

(b) a combined authority established under the Local Democracy, Economic Development and Construction Act 2009 s 103 (see LOCAL GOVERNMENT vol 69 (2018) PARA 83) is to be treated as a levying body, and the reference in the Local Government Finance Act 1988 s 74(2) to the council concerned must be treated as a reference to the combined authority's constituent councils (see s 74(8) (s 74(8)–(10) added by the Local Democracy, Economic Development and Construction Act 2009 s 119, Sch 6 paras 74, 75)).

Regulations under the Local Government Finance Act 1988 s 74 by virtue of s 74(8) may only make provision in relation to the expenses of a combined authority that are reasonably attributable to the exercise of its functions relating to transport or, subject to s 74(11), to the exercise of any other functions: s 74(10) (as so added; amended by the Cities and Local Government Devolution Act 2016 s 9(1)).

Regulations under the Local Government Finance Act 1988 s 74 by virtue of s 74(8) that include provision within s 74(10)(b) may be made only with the consent of the constituent councils and, in the case of regulations in relation to an existing combined authority, with the consent of the combined authority: s 74(11) (s 74(11)–(14) added by the Cities and Local Government Devolution Act 2016 s 9(2)). The Local Government Finance Act 1988 s 74(11) is subject to the Local Democracy, Economic Development and Construction Act 2009 s 106A (which enables regulations to be made without the consent of all the constituent councils in certain circumstances: see TRADE AND INDUSTRY vol 97 (2015) PARA 1094): Local Government Finance Act 1988 s 74(12) (as so added).

Regulations under s 74 by virtue of s 74(8) may not make provision in relation to expenses of a combined authority that are attributable to the exercise of mayoral functions: s 74(13) (as so added).

In s 74(8)–(13), 'constituent council' means a county council the whole or any part of whose area is within the area of the combined authority, or a district council whose area is within the area of the combined authority; and 'mayoral functions' has the meaning given by the Local Democracy, Economic Development and Construction Act 2009 s 107G: Local Government Finance Act 1988 s 74(14) (as so added).

The power to make regulations under s 74, so far as they are made in relation to a combined authority by virtue of s 74(8), is exercisable by statutory instrument, and no such regulations can be made unless a draft of them has been laid before and approved by a resolution of each House of Parliament: Local Government Finance Act 1988 s 143(4B) (added by the Cities and Local Government Devolution Act 2016 s 23(1), Sch 5 paras 9, 11).

5 Ie by virtue of the Local Government Finance Act 1988 s 117: see the text to notes 1–3.

6 Ie the Secretary of State or, in relation to Wales, the Welsh Ministers. As to the Secretary of State and the Welsh Ministers see PARA 4 note 18. The functions of the Secretary of State under the Local Government Finance Act 1988 ss 74, 75 (but see note 11) so far as exercisable in relation to Wales, were transferred to the National Assembly for Wales (see the National Assembly for Wales (Transfer of Functions) Order 1999, SI 1999/672, art 2, Sch 1) and are now vested in the Welsh Ministers (see the Government of Wales Act 2006 s 162(1), Sch 11 para 30).

7 The reference in the Local Government Finance Act 1988 s 74(2) to 'the council concerned' includes a reference to a council to which the functions of the council concerned in relation to the whole or any part of its area have been transferred by or in consequence of an order under the Local Government Act 1992 s 17 (repealed) or the Local Government and Public Involvement in Health Act 2007 Pt 1 (ss 1–30) (see LOCAL GOVERNMENT vol 69 (2018) PARA 95 et seq): Local Government Finance Act 1988 s 74(2A) (added by SI 1994/2825; and amended by the Local Government and Public Involvement in Health Act 2007 s 22, Sch 1 para 16(1), (2); and the Local Democracy, Economic Development and Construction Act 2009 s 146(1), Sch 7 Pt 4). See also note 4.

8 Local Government Finance Act 1988 s 74(2). The regulations may include provision:

(1) as to when levies are to be issued (s 74(3)(a));

(2) imposing a maximum limit on levies (s 74(3)(b));
(3) as to apportionment where a body issues levies to more than one council (s 74(3)(c));
(4) conferring a power to issue levies by way of substitute for others (s 74(3)(d));
(5) as to the payment (in instalments or otherwise) of amounts in respect of which levies are issued (s 74(3)(e)); and
(6) conferring a right to interest on anything unpaid (s 74(3)(f)).

The regulations may also contain additional provisions: see s 74(4), (5) (s 74(4) amended by the Local Government Finance Act 1992 s 117(1), Sch 13 para 72(1); the Greater London Authority Act 1999 s 105; the Localism Act 2011 s 79, Sch 7 paras 1, 2; and the Police Reform and Social Responsibility Act 2011 Sch 16 paras 180, 182(b); the Local Government Finance Act 1988 s 74(5) substituted by the Local Government Finance Act 1992 Sch 13 para 72(2)).

As to the regulations made see the Transport Levying Bodies Regulations 1992, SI 1992/2789 (amended by SI 2012/213, SI 2012/2914 (England), SI 2015/27 and SI 2017/603); the Levying Bodies (General) Regulations 1992, SI 1992/2903 (amended by SI 1992/697, SI 2001/3649 and, in relation to England, SI 2012/460 and SI 2012/2914); the National Park Authorities (Levies) (Wales) Regulations 1995, SI 1995/3019 (amended by SI 1996/2913, SI 1998/1129, SI 2001/429 and SI 2001/3649); the National Park Authorities (Levies) (England) Regulations 1996, SI 1996/2794 (amended by SI 1996/2976, SI 1997/2971, SI 1998/1129, SI 2001/3649 and SI 2012/460); the Joint Waste Disposal Authorities (Levies) (England) Regulations 2006, SI 2006/248; and the Environment Agency (Levies) (England and Wales) Regulations 2011, SI 2011/696 (amended by SI 2012/2914 (England) and SI 2013/755).

9 Ie regulations under the Local Government Finance Act 1988 s 118: see s 75(1)(a). Section 118 applies as regards any body:
(1) which is established by or under an Act (s 118(1)(a));
(2) which as regards the financial year beginning in 1989 has power (conferred by or under an Act) to levy a rate by reference to the value or yearly value of property (s 118(1)(b)); and
(3) which is not a billing authority (s 118(1)(c) (amended by the Local Government Finance Act 1992 Sch 13 para 74)),

and, in the case of an internal drainage board, there must be disregarded for the purposes of head (2) above any agreement under the Land Drainage Act 1976 s 81 (repealed) under which the board has agreed that no drainage rate will be levied on occupiers or owners of certain rateable hereditaments (Local Government Finance Act 1988 s 118(1) (amended by the Local Government and Housing Act 1989 s 139, Sch 5 paras 67(1), (3), 79(3))). As to the meaning of 'billing authority' see PARA 346 (definition applied by the Local Government Finance Act 1988 s 144(2) (as substituted and amended: see note 2)). As to internal drainage boards see WATER AND WATERWAYS vol 101 (2009) PARA 569 et seq. In s 118, 'Act' includes a private or local Act: s 118(5).

Regulations under s 118(2) may provide as regards any such body:
(a) that the body is to have no power to levy the rate as regards any time specified in the regulations and falling after 31 March 1990 (s 118(2)(a)); or
(b) that the body's power to levy the rate as regards any time specified in the regulations and falling after 31 March 1990 is to be modified in a manner specified in the regulations (s 118(2)(b)).

Before making regulations under s 118 or s 75, other than regulations relating to an internal drainage board, the appropriate national authority must by means of a notice in a newspaper take such steps as it thinks reasonably practicable to bring the contents of the proposed regulations to the notice of persons likely to be affected: see s 143(10) (amended by the Local Government and Housing Act 1989 Sch 5 paras 1, 72, 79(3)). As to the meaning of 'person' see PARA 11 note 13. At the date at which this volume states the law no regulations had been made under the Local Government Finance Act 1988 s 118.

10 Ie under the Local Government Finance Act 1988 s 118 (see note 9): see s 75(1)(b).

11 As respects any internal drainage board whose district is partly in England and partly in Wales, that Secretary of State and the Welsh Ministers must act jointly: see the Local Government Finance Act 1988 ss 75(8), 118(5) (s 75(8) added by the Local Government and Housing Act 1989 Sch 5 paras 55(4), 79(3); definition in the Local Government Finance Act 1988 s 118(5) added by the Local Government and Housing Act 1989 Sch 5 paras 67(1), (3), 79(3)). As to the meaning of 'England' see PARA 2 note 16.

12 Local Government Finance Act 1988 s 75(2)(a) (amended by the Local Government and Housing Act 1989 Sch 5 paras 55(2), 79(3); and the Local Government Finance Act 1992 s 117(1), Sch 13 para 73(1)).

13 Local Government Finance Act 1988 s 75(2)(b) (amended by the Local Government and Housing Act 1989 Sch 5 paras 55(2), 79(3); and the Local Government Finance Act 1992 Sch 13 para 73(1)).

The regulations may include provision as to the body's expenditure, or the proportion of its expenditure, which may be met from the proceeds of a special levy or special levies: Local Government Finance Act 1988 s 75(3). They may also include provision:

(1) as to when special levies are to be issued (s 75(4)(a));
(2) imposing a maximum limit on special levies (s 75(4)(b));
(3) as to apportionment where a body issues special levies to more than one billing authority (s 75(4)(c) (amended by the Local Government Finance Act 1992 Sch 13 para 73(2), (3));
(4) conferring a power to issue special levies by way of substitute for others (Local Government Finance Act 1988 s 75(4)(d));
(5) as to the payment (in instalments or otherwise) of amounts in respect of which special levies are issued (s 75(4)(e)); and
(6) conferring a right to interest on anything unpaid (s 75(4)(f)).

The regulations may also include certain additional provision: see s 75(5)–(7) (s 75(5), (6) amended, s 75(7) substituted, by the Local Government Finance Act 1992 Sch 13 para 73(2)–(4); the Local Government Finance Act 1988 s 75(6) amended by the Localism Act 2011 Sch 7 paras 1, 3). Regulations made by the Welsh Ministers may include provision for appeals to be made to the Welsh Ministers from special levies issued to meet expenses incurred in the exercise of functions relating to land drainage: Local Government Finance Act 1988 s 75(7A) (added by the Environment (Wales) Act 2016 s 84(1), (2)). As to the regulations made see the Internal Drainage Boards (Finance) Regulations 1992, SI 1992/3079.

14 Ie a levy issued under regulations under the Local Government Finance Act 1988 s 74 or a special levy issued under regulations under s 75, subject to s 138(4): see the text to notes 4–13. Section 138(1) does not affect appeals made by virtue of provision made in regulations under s 75(7A) (see note 13): s 138(4) (added by the Environment (Wales) Act 2016 s 84(1), (3)(b)).

15 See the Local Government Finance Act 1988 s 138(1), (2)(e), (f) (s 138(2)(f) amended by the Environment (Wales) Act 2016 s 84(1), (3)(a)). If on an application for judicial review the court decides to grant relief, it must quash the levy or special levy (as the case may be): see the Local Government Finance Act 1988 s 138(3) (substituted by the Local Government Finance Act 1992 Sch 13 para 76(2)). As to judicial review see JUDICIAL REVIEW vol 61 (2010) PARA 601 et seq.

3. CENTRAL GOVERNMENT GRANTS

(1) Separate Administration in England and Wales

25. Commutation of, and interest on, periodic payments of grants, etc.

Where the appropriate national authority[1] has a power or duty to make any annual or other periodic payment by way of contribution, grant or subsidy towards expenditure incurred or to be incurred by a local authority[2], the appropriate national authority may commute such payments[3] which would otherwise fall due on or after 1 April 1990 either into a single payment or into a lesser number of payments than would otherwise be payable[4]. The appropriate national authority may also, if it thinks it appropriate, pay to the Public Works Loans Commissioners, in whole or in part, any single or other payment so as to reduce or extinguish a local authority's debt to the commissioners[5].

If, after a commuted payment has been made to a local authority or to the Public Works Loans Commissioners, it appears to the appropriate national authority that the payment was smaller or greater than it should have been (whether by miscalculation or otherwise), the appropriate national authority may make a further payment to the local authority or the commissioners[6], or may require the local authority to repay such sum as the appropriate national authority may direct[7].

1 Ie the Secretary of State or, in relation to Wales, the Welsh Ministers. The functions of the Secretary of State under the Local Government and Housing Act 1989 s 157, so far as exercisable in relation to Wales, were transferred to the National Assembly for Wales (see the National Assembly for Wales (Transfer of Functions) Order 1999, SI 1999/672, art 2, Sch 1) and are now vested in the Welsh Ministers (see the Government of Wales Act 2006 s 162(1), Sch 11 para 30). As to the Secretary of State and the Welsh Ministers see PARA 4 note 18. As to the meaning of 'Wales' see PARA 2 note 16.

2 'Local authority' means any of the following:

(1) a county council (Local Government and Housing Act 1989 s 157(6)(a));
(2) a county borough council (s 157(6)(aa) (added by SI 1996/3071));
(3) a district council (Local Government and Housing Act 1989 s 157(6)(b));
(4) a London borough council (s 157(6)(c));
(5) the Common Council of the City of London (s 157(6)(d));
(6) the Council of the Isles of Scilly (s 157(6)(e));
(7) the Metropolitan Police Authority (now the Mayor's Office for Policing and Crime) (see POLICE AND INVESTIGATORY POWERS vol 84 (2013) PARA 78 et seq) (s 157(6)(f) (substituted by the Greater London Authority Act 1999 ss 325, 423, Sch 27 para 64, Sch 34 Pt I));
(8) a police authority established under the Police Act 1996 s 3 (see POLICE AND INVESTIGATORY POWERS vol 84 (2013) PARA 55) (Local Government and Housing Act 1989 s 157(6)(g) (amended by the Police and Magistrates' Courts Act 1994 s 43, Sch 4 para 43; and the Police Act 1996 s 103(1), Sch 7 para 1(1), (2)(zd)));
(9) a joint authority established by the Local Government Act 1985 Pt IV (ss 23–42) (see LOCAL GOVERNMENT vol 69 (2018) PARA 71) (Local Government and Housing Act 1989 s 157(6)(h));
(10) a residuary body established under the Local Government Act 1985 Pt VII (ss 57–67) (see LOCAL GOVERNMENT vol 69 (2018) PARA 17) (Local Government and Housing Act 1989 s 157(6)(i));
(11) an economic prosperity board established under the Local Democracy, Economic Development and Construction Act 2009 s 88 (see TRADE AND INDUSTRY vol 97 (2015) PARA 1086 et seq) (Local Government and Housing Act 1989 s 157(6)(j) (s 157(6)(j), (k) added by the Local Democracy, Economic Development and Construction Act 2009 s 119, Sch 6 paras 81(1), (7))); and
(12) a combined authority established under the Local Democracy, Economic Development

and Construction Act 2009 s 103 (see TRADE AND INDUSTRY vol 97 (2015) PARA 1092 et seq) (Local Government and Housing Act 1989 s 157(6)(k) (as so added)).

As to local government areas and authorities in England and Wales see LOCAL GOVERNMENT vol 69 (2018) PARA 36 et seq. As to the London boroughs and their councils see LONDON GOVERNMENT vol 71 (2013) PARAS 15, 20–22, 55 et seq. As to the Common Council of the City of London see LONDON GOVERNMENT vol 71 (2013) PARAS 34–38. As to the Council of the Isles of Scilly see LOCAL GOVERNMENT vol 69 (2018) PARA 50. As to the Mayor's Office for Policing and Crime see POLICE AND INVESTIGATORY POWERS vol 84 (2013) PARA 78 et seq.

3 A single or other payment falling to be made by virtue of the Local Government and Housing Act 1989 s 157(1) is for these purposes referred to as a 'commuted payment' and the calculation of the amount of any commuted payment must be such as appears to the appropriate national authority to be appropriate: s 157(4). A local authority must furnish the appropriate national authority with such information as the appropriate national authority may by notice in writing reasonably require for the purposes of s 157 and, if the notice so specifies, any information must be certified and audited in such manner and supplied not later than such date and in such form as may be so specified: s 157(9). As to the meaning of 'writing' see PARA 21 note 3.

4 Local Government and Housing Act 1989 s 157(1)(a). Where the amount of any annual or other periodic payment as is mentioned in s 157(1) is, at 16 November 1989, calculated by reference to a variable rate of interest, the appropriate national authority may substitute a fixed rate of interest: s 157(5). See also note 5.

5 See the Local Government and Housing Act 1989 s 157(1)(b). It is for the Public Works Loans Commissioners to determine the amount owing to them and, if only part of a commuted payment is paid to them, the balance must be paid to the local authority concerned: s 157(2). As to borrowing by a local authority see PARA 567 et seq. As to the Public Works Loan Commissioners see FINANCIAL INSTRUMENTS AND TRANSACTIONS vol 49 (2015) PARA 160 et seq.

Section 157(1) applies whether the annual or other periodic payments began before, on or after 16 November 1989 and applies notwithstanding anything in any enactment requiring the payments to be made over a period of 20 years or any other specified period: s 157(3).

6 Local Government and Housing Act 1989 s 157(7)(a).

7 Local Government and Housing Act 1989 s 157(7)(b).

26. Separate administration in England and Wales.

The provisions of the Local Government Finance Act 1988 relating to grants[1] apply separately, and must be administered separately, in England and Wales[2]. Those provisions must be construed accordingly so that (for instance) references to authorities must be read as references to those in England or Wales, as the case may be[3].

1 Ie the Local Government Finance Act 1988 Pt V (ss 76–88C).

2 Local Government Finance Act 1988 s 140(1) (amended by the Local Government Finance Act 1992 s 117(1), Sch 13 para 78(1), (3)). In practice, specific provision is made as to the application of the Local Government Finance Act 1988 Pt V, with Pt V Ch 2 (ss 77A–84C) applying in relation to England only (see s 77A; and PARA 30 et seq), Pt V Ch 3 (ss 84D–84P) applying in relation to Wales only (see s 84D; and PARA 33 et seq), and Pt V Ch 4 (ss 84Q–88C) applying in relation to either England or Wales or both (see s 84Q; and PARA 36 et seq). As to the meanings of 'England' and 'Wales' see PARA 2 note 16.

3 Local Government Finance Act 1988 s 140(3) (amended by the Local Government Finance Act 1992 Sch 13 para 78(1), (3)).

27. Power to make regulations relating to set off.

The appropriate national authority[1] may make regulations[2] in relation to any case where:

(1) the appropriate national authority is liable to pay[3] to a receiving authority[4] at any time an amount or amounts[5]; and

(2) the receiving authority is liable to pay[6] an amount or amounts to the appropriate national authority at the same time[7].

The regulations may provide that if the total of the amount or amounts mentioned in head (1) above exceeds the total of the amount or amounts mentioned in head

(2) above, the appropriate national authority may set off the latter in paying the former[8]; and that if the total of the amount or amounts mentioned in head (2) above exceeds the total of the amount or amounts mentioned in head (1) above, the receiving authority is to set off the latter in paying the former[9]. The regulations may also provide that if the total of the amount or amounts mentioned in head (1) above is the same as the total of the amount or amounts mentioned in head (2) above, no payment need be made[10]. The regulations may include provision:

(a) treating any liability as discharged accordingly[11];

(b) requiring prescribed[12] provisions of the Local Government Finance Act 1988 to be read subject to the regulations[13];

(c) requiring prescribed provisions of the Local Government Finance Act 1988 to be read as if references to sums received or payments made were to sums or payments which would have been received or made apart from the regulations[14].

1 Ie the Secretary of State or, in relation to Wales, the Welsh Ministers. The functions of the Secretary of State under the Local Government Finance Act 1988 s 141, so far as exercisable in relation to Wales, were transferred to the National Assembly for Wales (see the National Assembly for Wales (Transfer of Functions) Order 1999, SI 1999/672, art 2, Sch 1) and are now vested in the Welsh Ministers (see the Government of Wales Act 2006 s 162(1), Sch 11 para 30). As to the Secretary of State and the Welsh Ministers see PARA 4 note 18. As to the meaning of 'Wales' see PARA 2 note 16.

2 As to the regulations made see the Local Government Finance (Payments) (English Authorities) Regulations 1992, SI 1992/2996; the Local Government Finance (Payments) (Welsh Authorities) Regulations 1993, SI 1993/613; and PARA 28.

3 Ie under the Local Government Finance Act 1988 s 83 (see PARA 31), s 84C (see PARA 32), s 84K (see PARA 35), s 84N (see PARA 35) and s 86B (see PARA 36), regulations under s 99(3) (see PARA 583), regulations made under Sch 7B para 7 (see PARA 60), Sch 7B paras 14(2), (9) and (10), 17(7), (8) and 27(1) (see PARAS 62, 63, 66), regulations made under Sch 7B para 28 (see PARA 67), Sch 7B para 30(6) (see PARA 67), regulations made under Sch 7B para 33 (see PARA 68), regulations made under Sch 7B para 42 (see PARA 72), Sch 8 para 5(10), (14) (see PARA 75), regulations made for the purpose mentioned in Sch 8 para 4(7) (see PARA 75), regulations made under Sch 8 para 5(15) (PARA 75) or Sch 8 para 6(5) (see PARA 76) and Sch 8 paras 12, 15 (see PARAS 78, 79): see s 141(1)(a), (7) (s 141(7) substituted by the Local Government Finance Act 1992 s 117(1), Sch 13 para 79(1); and amended by the Local Government Act 2003 s 127(1), Sch 7 paras 9(1), 23; and the Local Government Finance Act 2012 ss 5(1), (2), 7(1), (3), Sch 3 paras 23, 28(1), (3)).

4 Each of the following is a 'receiving authority': a billing authority; and a major precepting authority: Local Government Finance Act 1988 s 141(6) (substituted by the Local Government Finance Act 1992 Sch 13 para 79(1)). As to the meaning of 'billing authority' see PARA 53; and as to the meaning of 'major precepting authority' see PARA 11 note 2 (definitions applied by the Local Government Finance Act 1988 s 144(2) (substituted by the Local Government Finance Act 1992 Sch 13 para 81(1); and amended by the Local Government Finance Act 2012 s 5(1), (2)(b), Sch 3 paras 23, 29)).

5 See the Local Government Finance Act 1988 s 141(1)(a).

6 Ie under the Local Government Finance Act 1988 s 83 (see PARA 31), s 84C (see PARA 32), s 84K (see PARA 35) and s 84N (see PARA 35), regulations under s 99(3) (see PARA 583), Sch 7B para 6 (see PARA 60), regulations made under Sch 7B para 7 (see PARA 60), Sch 7B paras 14(1), (6), (7), 17(4), (5) and 24(1) (see PARAS 62, 63, 65), regulations made under Sch 7B para 28 (see PARA 67), regulations made under Sch 7B para 33 (see PARA 68), regulations made under Sch 7B para 42 (see PARA 72), Sch 8 para 5 (see PARA 75), regulations made under Sch 8 para 5(15) (see PARA 75) and Sch 8 paras 12, 15 (see PARAS 78, 79), and, as from a day to be appointed, the Local Government and Housing Act 1989 s 80ZA (negative amounts of Housing Revenue Account subsidy and interest and costs where payment made late): see the Local Government Finance Act 1988 s 141(1)(b), (8) (s 141(8) substituted by the Local Government Finance Act 1992 Sch 13 para 79(1); and amended by the Local Government Finance Act 2012 ss 5(1), (2), 7(1), (4), Sch 3 paras 23, 28(1), (4); and, as from a day to be appointed, the Local Government Act 2003 s 90(4); at the date at which this volume states the law, no such day had been appointed).

7 See the Local Government Finance Act 1988 s 141(1)(b).
8 Local Government Finance Act 1988 s 141(2).
9 See the Local Government Finance Act 1988 s 141(3).
10 See the Local Government Finance Act 1988 s 141(4).
11 Local Government Finance Act 1988 s 141(5)(a).
12 'Prescribed' means prescribed by the regulations: see the Local Government Finance Act 1988 s 146(6).
13 Local Government Finance Act 1988 s 141(5)(b) (amended by the Local Government Finance Act 2012 s 3(1), (4)(a)).
14 Local Government Finance Act 1988 s 141(5)(c) (amended by the Local Government Finance Act 2012 Sch 3 paras 23, 28(1), (2)).

28. Power to set off.

Regulations[1] have been made providing for the set off of payments where:

(1) the appropriate national authority[2] is liable to pay[3] to a receiving authority[4] at any time an amount or amounts[5]; and

(2) the receiving authority is liable to pay[6] an amount or amounts to the appropriate national authority at the same time[7].

If the total of the amount or amounts mentioned in head (1) above exceeds the total of the amount or amounts mentioned in head (2) above, the appropriate national authority may set off the latter in paying the former[8]; and if the total of the amount or amounts mentioned in head (2) above exceeds the total of the amount or amounts mentioned in head (1) above, the receiving authority is to set off the latter in paying the former[9]. If the total of the amount or amounts mentioned in head (1) above is the same as the total of the amount or amounts mentioned in head (2) above, no payment need be made[10].

1 Ie the Local Government Finance (Payments) (English Authorities) Regulations 1992, SI 1992/2996, and the Local Government Finance (Payments) (Welsh Authorities) Regulations 1993, SI 1993/613. These regulations are made under the Local Government Finance Act 1988 s 141: see PARA 27.
2 Ie the Secretary of State or, in relation to Wales, the Welsh Ministers. The functions of the Secretary of State under the Local Government Finance (Payments) (Welsh Authorities) Regulations 1993, SI 1993/613, were transferred to the National Assembly for Wales (see the National Assembly for Wales (Transfer of Functions) Order 1999, SI 1999/672, arts 2, 3, Sch 1) and are now vested in the Welsh Ministers (see the Government of Wales Act 2006 s 162(1), Sch 11 para 30). As to the Secretary of State and the Welsh Ministers see PARA 4 note 18. As to the meaning of 'Wales' see PARA 2 note 16.
3 Ie under the Local Government Finance Act 1988 s 79(2), (3) (see PARA 30), s 83 (see PARA 31) or s 84C(1)–(3) (see PARA 32), or Sch 8 para 5 (see PARA 75), Sch 8 para 12 (see PARA 78) or Sch 8 para 15 (PARA 79): see the Local Government Finance (Payments) (English Authorities) Regulations 1992, SI 1992/2996, reg 2(1)(a); and the Local Government Finance (Payments) (Welsh Authorities) Regulations 1993, SI 1993/613, regs 2, 3(1)(a).
4 As to the meaning of 'receiving authority' see PARA 27 note 4.
5 See the Local Government Finance (Payments) (English Authorities) Regulations 1992, SI 1992/2996, reg 2(1)(a); and the Local Government Finance (Payments) (Welsh Authorities) Regulations 1993, SI 1993/613, reg 3(1)(a).
6 Ie under the Local Government Finance Act 1988 s 83(5) (see PARA 31) or s 84C(4) (see PARA 32), or Sch 8 para 5 (see PARA 75), Sch 8 para 12 (see PARA 78) or Sch 8 para 15 (PARA 79): see the Local Government Finance (Payments) (English Authorities) Regulations 1992, SI 1992/2996, reg 2(1)(b); and the Local Government Finance (Payments) (Welsh Authorities) Regulations 1993, SI 1993/613, regs 2, 3(1)(b).
7 See the Local Government Finance (Payments) (English Authorities) Regulations 1992, SI 1992/2996, reg 2(1)(b); and the Local Government Finance (Payments) (Welsh Authorities) Regulations 1993, SI 1993/613, reg 3(1)(b).
8 Local Government Finance (Payments) (English Authorities) Regulations 1992, SI 1992/2996, reg 2(2); Local Government Finance (Payments) (Welsh Authorities) Regulations 1993, SI 1993/613, reg 3(2). Where the appropriate national authority exercises these powers, any liability of the receiving authority which has been set off in accordance with these provisions, and the part of the

liability of the appropriate national authority against which that liability has been set off, are to be treated as discharged: Local Government Finance (Payments) (English Authorities) Regulations 1992, SI 1992/2996, reg 3(1); Local Government Finance (Payments) (Welsh Authorities) Regulations 1993, SI 1993/613, reg 4(1).

9 Local Government Finance (Payments) (English Authorities) Regulations 1992, SI 1992/2996, reg 2(3); Local Government Finance (Payments) (Welsh Authorities) Regulations 1993, SI 1993/613, reg 3(3). Where a receiving authority sets off any amount in accordance with these provisions, any liability of the appropriate national authority which is so set off, and the part of the liability of the receiving authority against which that liability has been set off, are to be treated as discharged: Local Government Finance (Payments) (English Authorities) Regulations 1992, SI 1992/2996, reg 3(2); Local Government Finance (Payments) (Welsh Authorities) Regulations 1993, SI 1993/613, reg 4(2).

10 Local Government Finance (Payments) (English Authorities) Regulations 1992, SI 1992/2996, reg 2(4); Local Government Finance (Payments) (Welsh Authorities) Regulations 1993, SI 1993/613, reg 3(4). Where, in accordance with the Local Government Finance (Payments) (English Authorities) Regulations 1992, SI 1992/2996, reg 2(4), no payment is made by the Secretary of State or an English receiving authority, their respective liabilities which are taken into account are to be treated as discharged: reg 3(3).

(2) Revenue Support Grants

(i) Introduction

29. Abolition and replacement of rate support grants.

The system of rate support grants introduced by the Local Government, Planning and Land Act 1980[1] was replaced by a new system of revenue support grants introduced by the Local Government Finance Act 1988[2]. Under the Local Government Finance Act 1988, no payments by way of rate support grants may be made for a financial year beginning in or after 1990[3].

The appropriate national authority[4] may by order repeal any enactment relating to rate support grants[5]. If a sum paid to an authority under any provision so repealed is less than the amount which should have been paid to it under that provision, the appropriate national authority must calculate the amount equal to the difference and pay a sum equal to that amount to the authority[6].

If a sum in excess of an amount payable to an authority has been paid under any provision so repealed, the appropriate national authority must calculate the amount equal to the excess and a sum equal to the amount is due from the authority to the appropriate national authority[7]. If the appropriate national authority decides that a sum so due is to be recoverable by deduction, it may deduct a sum equalling (or sums together equalling) that sum from anything the authority is entitled to receive from the appropriate national authority (whether by way of revenue support grant or otherwise)[8]. If the appropriate national authority decides that a sum so due is to be recoverable by payment, it is payable on such day as the appropriate national authority may specify; and if it is not paid on or before that day it is recoverable in a court of competent jurisdiction[9].

1 See the Local Government, Planning and Land Act 1980 ss 53–68 (repealed).

2 See the Local Government Finance Act 1988 Pt V (ss 76–88C); and PARA 30 et seq.

3 See the Local Government Finance Act 1988 s 124(1). As to the meaning of 'financial year' see PARA 24 note 1.

4 Ie the Secretary of State or, in relation to Wales, the Welsh Ministers. The functions of the Secretary of State under the Local Government Finance Act 1988 s 124, so far as exercisable in relation to Wales, were transferred to the National Assembly for Wales (see the National Assembly for Wales (Transfer of Functions) Order 1999, SI 1999/672, art 2, Sch 1) and are now vested in the Welsh Ministers (see the Government of Wales Act 2006 s 162(1), Sch 11 para 30). As to the

Secretary of State and the Welsh Ministers see PARA 4 note 18. As to the meaning of 'Wales' see PARA 2 note 16.

5 Local Government Finance Act 1988 s 124(2). At the date at which this volume states the law no such order had been made.

6 Local Government Finance Act 1988 s 124(3).

7 Local Government Finance Act 1988 s 124(4).

8 Local Government Finance Act 1988 s 124(5). The appropriate national authority may decide that a sum due under s 124(4) is to be recoverable partly by deduction and partly by payment, and in such a case the provisions of s 124(5) and s 124(6) (see the text to note 9) have effect with appropriate modifications: s 124(7). The appropriate national authority may decide differently under s 124(5)–(7) as regards sums due from different authorities or as regards sums due from the same authority in respect of different financial years: s 124(8).

9 Local Government Finance Act 1988 s 124(6). See also note 8.

(ii) England

30. Revenue support grants and the reporting process.

The following provisions apply in relation to England only[1].

For each chargeable financial year[2] the Secretary of State[3] must pay[4] a grant (a 'revenue support grant') to receiving authorities[5], specified bodies[6] or both[7]. For each chargeable financial year for which revenue support grant is to be paid the Secretary of State must make a determination[8], stating:

(1) the amount of the grant for the year[9];

(2) whether the Secretary of State proposes to pay grant to receiving authorities[10];

(3) if so, what amount of the grant he proposes to pay to receiving authorities[11];

(4) whether the Secretary of State proposes to pay grant to specified bodies[12]; and

(5) if so, what amount of the grant he proposes to pay to each specified body[13].

Before making a determination, the Secretary of State must consult such representatives of local government as appear to him to be appropriate[14], and obtain the Treasury's consent[15].

Such a determination must be specified in the local government finance report for the year[16]. If the determination provides for grant to be paid to receiving authorities, the report must also specify the basis (the 'basis of distribution') on which the Secretary of State proposes to distribute among receiving authorities the amount of revenue support grant which[17] falls to be paid to such authorities for the financial year to which the report relates (the 'financial year concerned')[18]. Before making such a report the Secretary of State must notify to such representatives of local government as appear to him to be appropriate the general nature of the basis of distribution[19].

Where a determination as regards revenue support grant has been made for a financial year and specified in a report which has been laid before the House of Commons the following provisions apply[20]. If the report is approved by resolution of the House of Commons, the Secretary of State must pay the amount stated in the determination as the amount of the revenue support grant for the year[21]. If the determination provides for grant to be paid to receiving authorities, the Secretary of State must pay to receiving authorities the amount stated in the determination under head (3) above and, if the determination provides for grant to be paid to specified bodies, the Secretary of State must pay to specified bodies the aggregate of the amounts stated in the determination under head (5) above[22]. Where a sum falls to be paid to a specified body by way of revenue support grant it must be paid at such time, or in instalments of such amounts and at such times, as the Secretary of State determines with the Treasury's consent; and any such time may fall within or after the financial year concerned[23].

It is likely to be difficult to obtain judicial review of decisions in relation to revenue support grants as they involve questions of political judgment[24].

1 See the Local Government Finance Act 1988 s 77A (added by the Local Government Act 2003 s 127(1), Sch 7 paras 9, 14). As to the meaning of 'England' see PARA 2 note 16.

2 As to the meaning of 'chargeable financial year' see PARA 24 note 1.

3 As to the Secretary of State see PARA 4 note 18.

4 Ie in accordance with the provisions of the Local Government Finance Act 1988 Pt V Ch 2 (ss 77A–84C): see the text to notes 5–23 and PARAS 31–32.

5 In the Local Government Finance Act 1988 Pt V (ss 76–88C), 'receiving authority' means any billing authority or major precepting authority: Local Government Finance Act 1988 s 76(1), (2) (s 76(2) substituted by the Local Government Finance Act 1992 s 104, Sch 10 para 8). As to the meaning of 'billing authority' see PARA 53; and as to the meaning of 'major precepting authority' see PARA 11 note 2 (definitions applied by the Local Government Finance Act 1988 s 144(2) (substituted by the Local Government Finance Act 1992 s 117(1), Sch 13 para 81(1); and amended by the Local Government Finance Act 2012 s 5(1), (2)(b), Sch 3 paras 23, 29)).

6 In the Local Government Finance Act 1988 Pt V (ss 76–88C), 'specified body' means any body which provides services for local authorities and is specified in regulations made by the Secretary of State under the Local Government Finance Act 1988 s 76(4); but a body is not a specified body as regards a financial year unless the regulations specifying it are in force before the year begins: s 76(1), (4). Before exercising the power to make regulations under s 76(4), the Secretary of State must consult such representatives of local government as appear to him to be appropriate: s 76(5). In relation to any financial year beginning on or after 1 April 2011, the Improvement and Development Agency for Local Government (company registration number 3675577) is specified for the purposes of s 76(4): Revenue Support Grant (Specified Body) (England) Regulations 2010, SI 2010/2568, reg 3.

7 Local Government Finance Act 1988 s 78(1) (substituted by the Local Government Finance Act 2012 s 2(1), Sch 2 paras 1, 2(1), (2)).

8 Local Government Finance Act 1988 s 78(2) (amended by the Local Government Finance Act 2012 Sch 2 paras 1, 2(1), (3)).

9 Local Government Finance Act 1988 s 78(3)(a).

10 Local Government Finance Act 1988 s 78(3)(aa) (added by the Local Government Finance Act 2012 Sch 2 paras 1, 2(1), (4)(a)).

11 Local Government Finance Act 1988 s 78(3)(b) (amended by the Local Government Finance Act 2012 Sch 2 paras 1, 2(1), (4)(b)).

12 Local Government Finance Act 1988 s 78(3)(ba) (added by the Local Government Finance Act 2012 Sch 2 paras 1, 2(1), (4)(c)).

13 Local Government Finance Act 1988 s 78(3)(c) (amended by the Local Government Finance Act 2012 Sch 2 paras 1, 2(1), (4)(d)). Different amounts may be stated under the Local Government Finance Act 1988 s 78(3)(c) in relation to different specified bodies: s 78(4).

14 Local Government Finance Act 1988 s 78(5)(a).

15 Local Government Finance Act 1988 s 78(5)(b). 'The Treasury' means the Commissioners of Her Majesty's Treasury: Interpretation Act 1978 s 5, Sch 1. As to the Treasury see CONSTITUTIONAL AND ADMINISTRATIVE LAW vol 20 (2014) PARA 262 et seq.

16 Local Government Finance Act 1988 s 78A(1) (s 78A added by the Local Government Finance Act 1992 s 104, Sch 10 para 10; the Local Government Finance Act 1988 s 78A(1) amended by the Local Government Finance Act 2012 Sch 2 paras 1, 3(1), (3)). As to the local government finance report see the Local Government Finance Act 1988 Sch 7B para 5; and PARA 59.

17 Ie under the Local Government Finance Act 1988 Pt V Ch 2 (ss 77A–84C).

18 Local Government Finance Act 1988 s 78A(2) (as added (see note 16); amended by the Local Government Act 2003 s 127(1), Sch 7 paras 9, 15; and the Local Government Finance Act 2012 Sch 2 paras 1, 3(1), (4)).

19 Local Government Finance Act 1988 s 78A(3) (as added (see note 16); amended by the Local Government Finance Act 2012 Sch 2 paras 1, 3(1), (5)).

20 Local Government Finance Act 1988 s 79(1) (amended by the Local Government Finance Act 1992 s 104, Sch 10 para 11).

21 Local Government Finance Act 1988 s 79(2). The provisions of s 79(2), (3) must be read subject to the Local Government Finance (Payments) (English Authorities) Regulations 1992, SI 1992/2996 (see PARA 28): see the Local Government Finance (Payments) (English Authorities) Regulations 1992, SI 1992/2996, reg 4(1).

22 Local Government Finance Act 1988 s 79(3) (amended by the Local Government Finance Act 2012 Sch 2 paras 1, 4(1), (2)). See also note 21. Any amount falling to be paid to receiving authorities must be distributed among and paid to them in accordance with the Local Government Finance Act 1988 ss 82, 83 (see PARA 31): s 79(4) (amended by the Local Government Finance Act 1992 Sch 10 para 11; and the Local Government Finance Act 2012 Sch 2 paras 1, 4(1), (3)). Any amount to be paid to a particular specified body must be the amount stated in relation to it under the Local Government Finance Act 1988 s 78(3)(c) (see head (5) in the text; and note 13): s 79(5) (amended by the Local Government Finance Act 2012 Sch 2 paras 1, 4(1), (4)).

23 Local Government Finance Act 1988 s 79(6).

24 See *R v Secretary of State for the Environment, ex p Avon County Council* (1990) 89 LGR 498; *R v Secretary of State for the Environment, ex p Hammersmith and Fulham London Borough Council* [1991] 1 AC 521, sub nom *Hammersmith and Fulham London Borough Council v Secretary of State for the Environment* [1990] 3 All ER 589, HL. As to judicial review generally see JUDICIAL REVIEW vol 61 (2010) PARA 601 et seq.

31. Calculation and payment of revenue support grants.

The following provisions apply in relation to England only[1], if:

(1) a determination as regards revenue support grant has been made[2] for a financial year[3] and specified in a local government finance report which has been laid before the House of Commons[4];

(2) the determination provides for grant to be paid to receiving authorities[5]; and

(3) the report is approved by resolution of the House of Commons[6].

As soon as is reasonably practicable after the report has been approved, the Secretary of State[7] must calculate what sum, if any, falls to be paid to each receiving authority by way of revenue support grant for the year in accordance with the basis of distribution[8] specified in the report[9]. Where such a calculation is made, the Secretary of State must pay to each receiving authority any sum calculated as falling to be paid to it[10].

After making a calculation[11], the Secretary of State may, at any time before the end of the financial year following the financial year concerned, make one further calculation of what sum, if any, falls to be paid to each receiving authority by way of revenue support grant for the year in accordance with the specified basis of distribution[12]. Where such a further calculation is made and the sum it shows as falling to be paid to a receiving authority exceeds that shown as falling to be paid to it by the calculation for the financial year concerned[13], the Secretary of State must pay to the authority a sum equal to the difference[14]; and where the sum it shows as falling to be paid to a receiving authority is less than that shown as falling to be paid to it by the calculation for the financial year concerned[15], a sum equal to the difference must be paid by the authority to the Secretary of State on such day after the end of the financial year concerned as he may specify[16].

If the Secretary of State decides that he will leave out of account information[17] received by him after a particular date in making a calculation under the above provisions[18], the calculation must be made accordingly; and he may decide different dates for different kinds of information[19]. However, this applies only if the Secretary of State informs each receiving authority in writing[20] of his decision and of the date (or the dates and kinds of information) concerned; but he may do this at any time before the calculation is made, whether before or after a determination is made[21] for the year[22].

As soon as is reasonably practicable after making a calculation under these provisions[23], the Secretary of State must inform each receiving authority of the sum he calculates as falling to be paid to it by way of revenue support grant for the year[24]. If the Secretary of State calculates in the case of a particular receiving authority that no such sum falls to be paid to it, he must inform the receiving authority of that fact[25].

The calculation used to distribute revenue support grant to local authorities is, in practice, often referred to as the 'standard spending assessment' or 'SSA'[26].

1 See the Local Government Finance Act 1988 s 77A (added by the Local Government Act 2003 s 127(1), Sch 7 paras 9, 14). As to the meaning of 'England' see PARA 2 note 16.

2 Ie in accordance with the Local Government Finance Act 1988 ss 78, 78A: see PARA 30.

3 As to the meaning of 'financial year' see PARA 24 note 1.

4 Local Government Finance Act 1988 s 82(A1)(a) (s 82 substituted by the Local Government Finance Act 1992 s 104, Sch 10 Pt II para 13; the Local Government Finance Act 1988 s 82(A1) added by the Local Government Finance Act 2012 s 2(1), Sch 2 paras 1, 5(1), (2)). As to local government finance reports see PARA 59.

5 Local Government Finance Act 1988 s 82(A1)(b) (as added: see note 4). As to the meaning of 'receiving authority' see PARA 30 note 5.

6 Local Government Finance Act 1988 s 82(A1)(c) (as added: see note 4).

7 As to the Secretary of State see PARA 4 note 18.

8 As to the meaning of 'basis of distribution' see PARA 30.

9 Local Government Finance Act 1988 s 82(1) (as substituted (see note 4); amended by the Local Government Finance Act 2012 Sch 2 paras 1, 5(1), (3)).

10 Local Government Finance Act 1988 s 83(1). The sum must be paid in instalments of such amounts, and at such times in the financial year concerned, as the Secretary of State determines with the Treasury's consent: s 83(2). As to the meaning of 'financial year concerned' see PARA 30. As to the meaning of 'Treasury' see PARA 30 note 15. The provisions of s 83 must be read subject to the Local Government Finance (Payments) (English Authorities) Regulations 1992, SI 1992/2996 (see PARA 28): see reg 4(1).

11 Ie under the Local Government Finance Act 1988 s 82(1): see the text to notes 7–9.

12 Local Government Finance Act 1988 s 82(2) (as substituted: see note 4). The power to make a calculation under s 82(2) is not exercisable after the approval by resolution of the House of Commons of any amending report made under s 84A (see PARA 32) in relation to the local government finance report: s 82(3) (as so substituted).

13 Ie under the Local Government Finance Act 1988 s 82(1): see the text to notes 7–9.

14 Local Government Finance Act 1988 s 83(3). The sum must be paid at such time, or in instalments of such amounts and at such times, as the Secretary of State determines with the Treasury's consent; but any such time must fall after the end of the financial year concerned: s 83(4). See also note 10.

15 Ie under the Local Government Finance Act 1988 s 82(1): see the text to notes 7–9.

16 Local Government Finance Act 1988 s 83(5). If the sum is not paid on or before the specified day, it is recoverable in a court of competent jurisdiction: see s 83(5). See also note 9.

17 Unless the context otherwise requires, 'information' includes accounts, estimates and returns: Local Government Finance Act 1988 s 146(5A) (added by the Local Government and Housing Act 1989 s 139, Sch 5 paras 75, 79(3)).

18 Ie under the Local Government Finance Act 1988 s 82(1) (see the text to notes 7–9) or s 82(2) (see the text to notes 11–12).

19 Local Government Finance Act 1988 s 82(4) (as substituted: see note 4).

20 As to the meaning of 'writing' see PARA 21 note 3.

21 Ie under the Local Government Finance Act 1988 s 78: see PARA 30.

22 Local Government Finance Act 1988 s 82(5) (as substituted: see note 4).

23 Ie under the Local Government Finance Act 1988 s 82(1) (see the text to notes 7–9) or s 82(2) (see the text to notes 11–12).

24 See the Local Government Finance Act 1988 s 82(6) (as substituted: see note 4).

25 Local Government Finance Act 1988 s 82(7) (as substituted: see note 4).

26 A total SSA for a local authority is made up of component SSAs for each service (eg education) that the authority provides.

32. Amending reports.

The following provisions apply in relation to England only[1].

After a local government finance report containing a determination as to revenue support grant[2] has been made the Secretary of State[3] may, at any time before the end of the financial year[4] following the financial year concerned[5], make in relation to the report one or more amending reports[6]. Such an amending report must contain amendments to the basis of distribution[7] specified in the local government finance report[8]. Before making the report the Secretary of State must notify to such representatives of local government as appear to him to be appropriate the general nature of the amendments which he proposes to make[9]. The report must be laid before the House of Commons[10]; and, as soon as is reasonably practicable after the report is so laid, the Secretary of State must send a copy of it to each receiving authority[11].

As soon as is reasonably practicable after an amending report has been approved by resolution of the House of Commons, the Secretary of State must calculate what sum, if any, falls to be paid to each receiving authority by way of revenue support grant[12] for the financial year concerned in accordance with the basis of distribution specified in the local government finance report as amended by the amending report[13]. After making such a calculation, the Secretary of State may make one further calculation of what sum, if any, falls to be paid to each receiving authority by way of revenue support grant for the year in accordance with that basis of distribution[14].

Where a calculation (the 'relevant calculation') is made[15] in relation to an amending report[16] and the sum shown by the relevant calculation as falling to be paid to a receiving authority for the financial year concerned exceeds that shown as falling to be paid to it by the relevant previous calculation[17], the Secretary of State must pay to the authority a sum equal to the difference[18]; and where the sum shown by the relevant calculation as falling to be paid to a receiving authority for the financial year concerned is less than that shown as falling to be paid to it by the relevant previous calculation, a sum equal to the difference must be paid by the authority to the Secretary of State[19].

1 See the Local Government Finance Act 1988 s 77A (added by the Local Government Act 2003 s 127(1), Sch 7 paras 9, 14). As to the meaning of 'England' see PARA 2 note 16.

2 Ie a under the Local Government Finance Act 1988 s 78: see PARA 30. As to local government finance reports see PARA 59.

3 As to the Secretary of State see PARA 4 note 18.

4 As to the meaning of 'financial year' see PARA 24 note 1.

5 As to the meaning of 'financial year concerned' see PARA 30.

6 Local Government Finance Act 1988 s 84A(1) (ss 84A–84C added by the Local Government Finance Act 1992 s 104, Sch 10 para 15; the Local Government Finance Act 1988 s 84A(1) amended by the Local Government Finance Act 2012 s 2(1), Sch 2 paras 1, 6). Where an amending report has been approved by resolution of the House of Commons, the Secretary of State may not make a subsequent amending report in relation to the same local government finance report: Local Government Finance Act 1988 s 84A(6) (as so added).

7 As to the meaning of 'basis of distribution' see PARA 30.

8 Local Government Finance Act 1988 s 84A(2) (as added: see note 6).

9 Local Government Finance Act 1988 s 84A(3) (as added: see note 6).

10 Local Government Finance Act 1988 s 84A(4) (as added: see note 6). As to the laying of documents before Parliament see STATUTES AND LEGISLATIVE PROCESS vol 96 (2012) PARA 1052.

11 Local Government Finance Act 1988 s 84A(5) (as added: see note 6). As to the meaning of 'receiving authority' see PARA 30 note 5.

12 As to the meaning of 'revenue support grant' see PARA 30.

13 Local Government Finance Act 1988 s 84B(1) (as added: see note 6). The provisions of s 82(4)–(7)

(see PARA 31) apply in relation to calculations made under s 84B(1), (2) (see the text to note 14) as they apply in relation to calculations made under s 82(1), (2): s 84B(4) (as so added).

14 Local Government Finance Act 1988 s 84B(2) (as added: see note 6). A calculation may not be made under s 84B(2) after whichever is the later of:
(1) the end of the financial year following the financial year concerned (s 84B(3)(a) (as so added)); and
(2) the end of the period of three months beginning with the day on which the amending report is approved by resolution of the House of Commons (s 84B(3)(b) (as so added)).
See also note 13. As to the meaning of 'month' see PARA 11 note 1.

15 Ie under the Local Government Finance Act 1988 s 84B(1) or s 84B(2): see the text to notes 12–14.

16 Local Government Finance Act 1988 s 84C(1) (as added by: see note 6). The provisions of s 84C must be read subject to the Local Government Finance (Payments) (English Authorities) Regulations 1992, SI 1992/2996 (see PARA 28): see reg 4(1).

17 'Relevant previous calculation' means:
(1) in relation to a calculation made under the Local Government Finance Act 1988 s 84B(1) (see the text to notes 12–13), the calculation under s 82(1) (see PARA 31) or, where a further calculation has been made under s 82(2) (see PARA 31), that further calculation (see s 84C(6)(a) (as added: see note 6));
(2) in relation to a calculation made under s 84B(2) (see the text to note 14), the calculation made under s 84B(1) (see s 84C(6)(b) (as so added)).

18 Local Government Finance Act 1988 s 84C(2) (as added: see note 6). The sum must be paid at such times, or in instalments of such amounts and at such times, as the Secretary of State determines with the Treasury's consent; but any such time must fall after the end of the financial year in which the amending report was made: s 84C(3) (as so added). As to the meaning of 'Treasury' see PARA 30 note 15. See also note 16.

19 Local Government Finance Act 1988 s 84C(4) (as added: see note 6). The sum must be paid on such day after the end of the financial year in which the amending report was made as the Secretary of State may specify; and if it is not paid on or before that day it is recoverable in a court of competent jurisdiction: s 84C(5) (as so added). See also note 16.

(iii) Wales

33. Revenue support grants.

The following provisions apply in relation to Wales only[1].

The Welsh Ministers[2] must pay[3] a grant (known as 'revenue support grant') for each financial year[4] to receiving authorities[5], and specified bodies[6].

The Welsh Ministers must for each financial year make[7]:

(1) a determination stating:
  (a) the total amount of revenue support grant for the year[8];
  (b) the amount of the grant the Welsh Ministers propose to pay to receiving authorities[9]; and
  (c) the amount of the grant the Welsh Ministers propose to pay to each specified body[10]; or
(2) a determination stating:
  (a) the total amount of revenue support grant for the year for receiving authorities (other than police and crime commissioners)[11] and specified bodies[12];
  (b) the amount of the grant the Welsh Ministers propose to pay to receiving authorities that are not police and crime commissioners[13]; and
  (c) the amount of the grant the Welsh Ministers propose to pay to each specified body[14]; and
(3) a determination stating the total amount of revenue support grant for the year for police and crime commissioners[15].

Before making any such determination, the Welsh Ministers must consult such representatives of local government as appear to the Welsh Ministers to be appropriate[16].

1 Local Government Finance Act 1988 s 84D (ss 84D–84F added by the Local Government Act 2003 s 40(1), Sch 2 para 1). As to the meaning of 'Wales' see PARA 2 note 16.
2 As to the Welsh Ministers see PARA 4 note 18.
3 Revenue support grant is payable in accordance with the Local Government Finance Act 1988 Pt V Ch 3 (ss 84D–84P) (see the text to notes 4–16 and PARAS 34–35): s 84E(3) (as added: see note 1).
4 See the Local Government Finance Act 1988 s 84E(1), (2) (s 84E as added (see note 1); s 84E(1) amended by SI 2007/1388). As to the meaning of 'financial year' see PARA 24 note 1.
5 Local Government Finance Act 1988 s 84E(1)(a) (as added: see note 1). As to the meaning of 'receiving authority' see PARA 30 note 5.
6 Local Government Finance Act 1988 s 84E(1)(b) (as added: see note 1). As to the meaning of 'specified body' see PARA 30 note 6.
7 See the Local Government Finance Act 1988 s 84F(1) (as added (see note 1); amended by SI 2007/1388).
8 Local Government Finance Act 1988 s 84F(1)(a), (2)(a) (as added: see note 1).
9 Local Government Finance Act 1988 s 84F(1)(a), (2)(b) (as added (see note 1); s 84F(2)(b) amended by SI 2007/1388).
10 Local Government Finance Act 1988 s 84F(1)(a), (2)(c) (as added (see note 1); s 84F(2)(c) amended by SI 2007/1388). Different amounts may be stated under the Local Government Finance Act 1988 s 84F(2)(c) in relation to different specified bodies: see s 84F(6) (as so added).
11 Local Government Finance Act 1988 s 84F(1)(b), (3)(a)(i) (as added (see note 1); s 84F(3)(a)(i) amended by the Police Reform and Social Responsibility Act 2011 s 99, Sch 16 paras 180, 183(a)). As to police and crime commissioners see POLICE AND INVESTIGATORY POWERS vol 84 (2013) PARA 56 et seq.
12 Local Government Finance Act 1988 s 84F(1)(b), (3)(a)(ii) (as added: see note 1).
13 Local Government Finance Act 1988 s 84F(1)(b), (3)(b) (as added (see note 1); s 84F(3)(b) amended by the Police Reform and Social Responsibility Act 2011 Sch 16 paras 180, 183(a); and SI 2007/1388).
14 Local Government Finance Act 1988 s 84F(1)(b), (3)(c) (as added (see note 1); s 84F(3)(c) amended by SI 2007/1388). Different amounts may be stated under the Local Government Finance Act 1988 s 84F(3)(c) in relation to different specified bodies: see s 84F(6) (as so added).
15 Local Government Finance Act 1988 s 84F(1)(b), (4) (as added (see note 1); s 84F(4) amended by the Police Reform and Social Responsibility Act 2011 Sch 16 paras 180, 183(a)).
16 Local Government Finance Act 1988 s 84F(5) (as added (see note 1); amended by SI 2007/1388).

34. Local government finance reports.

The following provisions apply in relation to Wales only[1].

The Welsh Ministers[2] must specify a determination of revenue support grant[3] in a report, to be called a 'local government finance report'[4]. A local government finance report must also specify the basis on which the Welsh Ministers propose to distribute among the receiving authorities[5] to which the report relates the amount[6] stated in the determination[7].

Before making a report, the Welsh Ministers must notify the general nature of the basis of distribution proposed to be specified in the report to such representatives of local government as appear to the Welsh Ministers to be appropriate[8]. A report must be laid before the National Assembly for Wales[9]; and as soon as is reasonably practicable after a report is laid before the Assembly, the Welsh Ministers must send a copy of the report to each of the receiving authorities to which the report relates[10].

Where[11] a determination as regards revenue support grant has been made for a financial year[12] and specified in a report which has been laid before the Assembly[13], if the report is approved by resolution of the Assembly the Welsh

Ministers must pay the amount stated in the determination as the amount of revenue support grant for the year[14].

Where the Welsh Ministers have made a local government finance report for a particular financial year, they may, at any time before the end of the financial year following the financial year concerned, make a report (an 'amending report') containing amendments to the basis of distribution specified[15] in the local government finance report[16]. Where the Welsh Ministers have made two local government finance reports relating to the same financial year, this power may (in particular) be exercised by making a single amending report relating to both of the local government finance reports[17]. Before making an amending report, the Welsh Ministers must notify to such representatives of local government as appear to the Welsh Ministers to be appropriate the general nature of the amendments they propose to make[18].

An amending report must be laid before the National Assembly for Wales[19]. As soon as is reasonably practicable after an amending report is laid before the Assembly, the Welsh Ministers must send a copy of the amending report to each receiving authority to which the local government finance report relates[20]. Where an amending report has been approved by resolution of the Assembly, the Welsh Ministers may not make a subsequent amending report[21] in relation to the same local government finance report[22].

1 Local Government Finance Act 1988 s 84D (ss 84D, 84G added by the Local Government Act 2003 s 40(1), Sch 2 para 1). As to the meaning of 'Wales' see PARA 2 note 16.
2 As to the Welsh Ministers see PARA 4 note 18.
3 Ie a determination under the Local Government Finance Act 1988 s 84F: see PARA 33.
4 Local Government Finance Act 1988 s 84G(1) (as added (see note 1); amended by SI 2007/1388).
5 As to the meaning of 'receiving authority' see PARA 30 note 5.
6 Ie the amount under the Local Government Finance Act 1988 s 84F(2)(b) or, as the case may be, s 84F(3)(b) or (4): see PARA 33.
7 See the Local Government Finance Act 1988 s 84G(2) (as added (see note 1); and amended by SI 2007/1388).
8 Local Government Finance Act 1988 s 84G(3) (as added (see note 1); amended by SI 2007/1388).
9 See the Local Government Finance Act 1988 ss 76(7), 84G(4) (s 76(7) added by SI 2007/1388; the Local Government Finance Act 1988 s 84G(4) as added (see note 1); amended by SI 2007/1388). As to the National Assembly for Wales see CONSTITUTIONAL AND ADMINISTRATIVE LAW vol 20 (2014) PARA 351 et seq.
10 Local Government Finance Act 1988 s 84G(5) (as added (see note 1); substituted by SI 2007/1388).
11 Ie in accordance with the Local Government Finance Act 1988 s 84F (see PARA 33) and s 84G (see the text to notes 2–10).
12 As to the meaning of 'financial year' see PARA 24 note 1.
13 Local Government Finance Act 1988 s 84H(1) (ss 84H, 84L added by the Local Government Act 2003 Sch 2 para 1; and substituted by SI 2007/1388).
14 Local Government Finance Act 1988 s 84H(2) (as added and substituted: see note 13). The amount of revenue support grant to be paid to receiving authorities in accordance with s 84H(2) must be distributed among, and paid to, them in accordance with ss 84J and 84K (see PARA 35): s 84H(3) (as so added and substituted). The amount of revenue support grant to be paid to a specified body in accordance with s 84H(2) must be paid at such time, or in instalments of such amounts and at such times, as the Welsh Ministers may determine: s 84H(4) (as so added and substituted). The time of payment under s 84H(2) may be during or after the financial year for which the grant is payable: s 84H(5) (as so added and substituted). As to the meaning of 'specified body' see PARA 30 note 6.
15 Ie under the Local Government Finance Act 1988 s 84G(2): see the text to notes 5–7.
16 Local Government Finance Act 1988 s 84L(1) (as added and substituted: see note 13).
17 Local Government Finance Act 1988 s 84L(2) (as added and substituted: see note 13).
18 Local Government Finance Act 1988 s 84L(3) (as added and substituted: see note 13).
19 See the Local Government Finance Act 1988 ss 76(7), 84L(4) (s 76(7) as added (see note 9); s 84L(4) as added and substituted: see note 13).

20 Local Government Finance Act 1988 s 84L(5) (as added and substituted: see note 13).
21 Ie under the Local Government Finance Act 1988 s 84L.
22 Local Government Finance Act 1988 s 84L(6) (as added and substituted: see note 13).

35. Calculation and payment of grant.

The following provisions apply in relation to Wales only[1].

As soon as is reasonably practicable after a local government finance report[2] for a financial year[3] has been approved by resolution of the National Assembly for Wales[4], the Welsh Ministers[5] must calculate what sum, if any, falls to be paid to each receiving authority[6] by way of revenue support grant[7] for the year in accordance with the basis of distribution specified in the report as so approved[8]. The Welsh Ministers may carry out such a calculation again at any time before the end of the financial year immediately following the one to which the report relates[9]; and where they do so must pay any sum so calculated as falling to be paid by way of revenue support grant to a receiving authority in instalments of such amounts, and at such times in the financial year for which the grant is payable, as the Welsh Ministers may determine[10]. As soon as is reasonably practicable after making a calculation[11], the Welsh Ministers must inform each receiving authority to which the report relates of the outcome, so far as relating to it[12].

Where the Welsh Ministers make a calculation[13] that shows an increase in the sum that falls to be paid to a receiving authority, the Welsh Ministers must pay the authority a sum equal to the difference[14]. Where the Welsh Ministers make such a calculation that shows a decrease in the sum that falls to be paid to a receiving authority, the authority must pay to the Welsh Ministers a sum equal to the difference[15].

Where the National Assembly for Wales, by resolution, approves a report[16] (the 'amending report') relating to a local government finance report ('the original report')[17], as soon as is reasonably practicable after the Assembly has approved the amending report, the Welsh Ministers must calculate[18] in relation to each receiving authority to which the original report relates what sum, if any, falls to be paid to the authority by way of revenue support grant for the financial year to which the original report relates[19]. The Welsh Ministers may carry out the calculation again at any time before[20]:

(1) the end of the financial year immediately following the one to which the original report relates[21]; or
(2) if later, the end of the period of three months[22] beginning with the day on which the Assembly approves the amending report[23].

As soon as is reasonably practicable after making a calculation[24], the Welsh Ministers must inform each receiving authority to which the original report relates of the outcome, so far as relating to it[25].

Where the Welsh Ministers make a calculation[26] that shows an increase in the sum that falls to be paid to a receiving authority, the Welsh Ministers must pay the authority a sum equal to the difference[27]. Where the Welsh Ministers make such a calculation that shows a decrease in the sum that falls to be paid to a receiving authority, the authority must pay a sum equal to the difference to the Welsh Ministers[28].

1 Local Government Finance Act 1988 s 84D (ss 84D, 84J, 84K, 84M, 84N, 84P added by the Local Government Act 2003 s 40(1), Sch 2 para 1). As to the meaning of 'Wales' see PARA 2 note 16.
2 As to local government finance reports see PARA 34.
3 As to the meaning of 'financial year' see PARA 24 note 1.
4 As to the National Assembly for Wales see CONSTITUTIONAL AND ADMINISTRATIVE LAW vol 20 (2014) PARA 351 et seq.

5 As to the Welsh Ministers see PARA 4 note 18.
6 As to the meaning of 'receiving authority' see PARA 30 note 5.
7 As to revenue support grants see PARA 29 et seq.
8 See the Local Government Finance Act 1988 ss 76(7), 84J(1) (s 76(7) added by SI 2007/1388; the Local Government Finance Act 1988 s 84J added by the Local Government Act 2003 Sch 2 para 1; and substituted by SI 2007/1388).
9 Local Government Finance Act 1988 s 84J(2) (as added and substituted: see note 8). The power under s 84J(2) may only be exercised once and is not exercisable after the approval by resolution of the Assembly of any amending report made under s 84L (see PARA 34) in relation to the local government finance report: s 84J(3) (as so added and substituted).

The Welsh Ministers may set a deadline for the receipt of information to be taken into account by them when making a calculation under s 84J(2), or s 84J(4) (see the text to notes 11–12), s 84M(2) or (4) (see the text to notes 19–23): s 84P(1) (s 84P as added (see note 1); s 84P(1), (3), (5) amended by SI 2007/1388). Different deadlines may be set in relation to different kinds of information: Local Government Finance Act 1988 s 84P(2) (as so added). A deadline has effect only if the Welsh Ministers notify each receiving authority concerned of the deadline and of the information to which it relates: s 84P(3) (as so added and amended). Such notification may be given at any time before the making of the calculation to which the deadline relates, including a time before the making of a determination under s 84F (see PARA 33) for the year concerned: s 84P(4) (as so added). When making a calculation in relation to which a deadline has effect, the Welsh Ministers must leave information to which the deadline applies out of account if it is received after the passing of the deadline: s 84P(5) (as so added and amended).
10 See the Local Government Finance Act 1988 s 84K(1) (as added (see note 1); amended by SI 2007/1388).
11 Ie under the Local Government Finance Act 1988 s 84J(1) or (2): see the text to notes 2–9.
12 Local Government Finance Act 1988 s 84J(4) (as added and substituted: see note 8). The Welsh Ministers may set a deadline for the receipt of information to be taken into account by them when making a calculation under s 84J(4): see s 84P; and note 9.
13 Ie under the Local Government Finance Act 1988 s 84J(4): see the text to notes 11–12.
14 Local Government Finance Act 1988 s 84K(2) (s 84K as added (see note 1); s 84K(2), (3), amended by SI 2007/1388). Such payment must be at such time, or in instalments of such amounts and at such times, as the Welsh Ministers may determine: Local Government Finance Act 1988 s 84K(3) (as so added and amended). The time for payment must be after the end of the financial year for which the grant is payable: s 84K(4) (as so added).
15 Local Government Finance Act 1988 s 84K(5) (s 84K as added (see note 1); s 84K(5), (6), amended by SI 2007/1388). The time for payment is such day after the end of the financial year for which the grant is payable as the Welsh Ministers may specify: Local Government Finance Act 1988 s 84K(6) (as so added and amended).
16 Ie a report made under the Local Government Finance Act 1988 s 84L: see PARA 34.
17 See the Local Government Finance Act 1988 ss 76(7), 84M(1) (s 76(7) as added (see note 8); s 84M(1) as added (see note 1); and substituted by SI 2007/1388).
18 The calculation must be in accordance with the amended basis of distribution: Local Government Finance Act 1988 s 84M(3) (as added: see note 1).
19 Local Government Finance Act 1988 s 84M(2) (as added (see note 1); substituted by SI 2007/1388). The Welsh Ministers may set a deadline for the receipt of information to be taken into account by them when making a calculation under the Local Government Finance Act 1988 s 84M(2): see s 84P; and note 9.
20 Local Government Finance Act 1988 s 84M(4) (as added (see note 1); amended by SI 2007/1388). The power under the Local Government Finance Act 1988 s 84M(4) may only be exercised once: s 84M(5) (as so added). The Welsh Ministers may set a deadline for the receipt of information to be taken into account by them when making a calculation under s 84M(4): see s 84P; and note 9.
21 Local Government Finance Act 1988 s 84M(4)(a) (as added: see note 1).
22 As to the meaning of 'month' see PARA 11 note 1.
23 Local Government Finance Act 1988 s 84M(4)(b) (as added (see note 1); amended by SI 2007/1388).
24 Ie under the Local Government Finance Act 1988 s 84M(2) or (4): see the text to notes 19–23.
25 Local Government Finance Act 1988 s 84M(6) (as added (see note 1); amended by SI 2007/1388).
26 Ie under the Local Government Finance Act 1988 s 84M(2) or (4): see the text to notes 19–23.
27 Local Government Finance Act 1988 s 84N(1) (s 84N as added (see note 1); s 84N(1), (2) amended by SI 2007/1388). Payment must be at such time, or in instalments of such amounts and at such times, as the Welsh Ministers may determine: Local Government Finance Act 1988 s 84N(2) (as so added and amended). The time for payment must be after the end of the financial year in which

the report under s 84L (see PARA 34) was made: s 84N(3) (as so added).
28 Local Government Finance Act 1988 s 84N(4) (s 84N as added (see note 1); s 84N(4), (5) amended by SI 2007/1388). The time for payment is such day after the end of the financial year in which the report under the Local Government Finance Act 1988 s 84L (see PARA 34) was made as the Welsh Ministers may specify: s 84N(5) (as so added and amended).

(3) Additional Grants

36. Additional revenue support grants in Wales.

In relation to Wales[1], where a local government finance report[2] for a chargeable financial year[3] has been approved by the National Assembly for Wales[4] and, before the year ends, the Welsh Ministers[5] form the view that fresh circumstances affecting the finances of local authorities have arisen since the approval[6], for the year concerned the Welsh Ministers may pay[7] a grant ('additional grant') to receiving authorities[8].

Where the Welsh Ministers propose to pay additional grant for a financial year they must make a determination[9] stating the amount of grant for the year[10], and the basis on which the Welsh Ministers propose to distribute it among receiving authorities[11]. A determination must be specified in a report and the report must be laid before the Assembly[12]; and as soon as is reasonably practicable after the report is laid before the Assembly the Welsh Ministers must send a copy of it to each receiving authority[13].

Where a determination as regards additional grant has been made for a financial year and specified in a report which has been laid before the Assembly[14], if the report is approved by resolution of the Assembly the Welsh Ministers must pay the amount stated in the determination as the amount of the additional grant for the year[15], and the amount must be distributed on the basis stated in the determination[16]. Where a sum falls to be paid to a receiving authority by way of additional grant it must be paid at such time, or in instalments of such amounts and at such times, as the Welsh Ministers determine; and any such time may fall within or after the financial year concerned[17].

1 The Local Government Finance Act 1988 ss 86A, 86B apply in relation to Wales only: s 84Q(1)(b) (s 84Q added by SI 2007/1388). As to the meaning of 'Wales' see PARA 2 note 16.
2 As to local government reports see PARA 34.
3 As to the meaning of 'chargeable financial year' see PARA 24 note 1.
4 As to the National Assembly for Wales see CONSTITUTIONAL AND ADMINISTRATIVE LAW vol 20 (2014) PARA 351 et seq.
5 As to the Welsh Ministers see PARA 4 note 18.
6 See the Local Government Finance Act 1988 ss 76(7), 86A(1) (ss 76(7), 86A, 86B added by SI 2007/1388).
7 Ie in accordance with the Local Government Finance Act 1988 ss 86A, 86B: see the text to notes 8–17.
8 Local Government Finance Act 1988 s 86A(2) (as added: see note 6). As to the meaning of 'receiving authority' see PARA 30 note 5.
9 Local Government Finance Act 1988 s 86A(3) (as added: see note 6).
10 Local Government Finance Act 1988 s 86A(4)(a) (as added: see note 6).
11 Local Government Finance Act 1988 s 86A(4)(b) (as added: see note 6).
12 Local Government Finance Act 1988 s 86A(5) (as added: see note 6).
13 Local Government Finance Act 1988 s 86A(6) (as added: see note 6).
14 Local Government Finance Act 1988 s 86B(1) (as added: see note 6).
15 Local Government Finance Act 1988 s 86B(2)(a) (as added: see note 6).
16 Local Government Finance Act 1988 s 86B(2)(b) (as added: see note 6).
17 Local Government Finance Act 1988 s 86B(3) (as added: see note 6).

37. Transport grants: England and Wales.

The appropriate national authority[1] must pay to a defined council[2] a grant for a chargeable financial year[3] if the appropriate national authority accepts that at least some of the council's estimated relevant transport expenditure[4] for the year is appropriate to be taken into account for these purposes[5]. The amount of the grant is a proportion of so much of the council's estimated relevant transport expenditure for the year as the appropriate national authority so accepts[6]. The proportion is such as is determined for the year by the appropriate national authority and must be the same as regards each council to which a grant is paid for the year under these provisions[7]. A grant must be paid at such time, or in instalments of such amounts and at such times, as the appropriate national authority thinks fit; and any such time need not fall within the financial year concerned[8].

In deciding whether to accept any of a council's estimated relevant transport expenditure for a financial year, and how much of it to accept, the appropriate national authority may have regard to the following matters (in addition to any other matters the appropriate national authority thinks fit):

(1) whether the council's relevant transport expenditure[9] for any preceding financial year or years is greater or smaller than its estimated relevant transport expenditure for that year or those years[10];

(2) the extent (if any) to which it is greater or smaller[11].

In relation to England[12], the total accepted as regards all defined councils for a particular financial year must not exceed such amount as is approved by the Treasury for the year[13].

1 Ie the Secretary of State or, in relation to Wales, the Welsh Ministers. The Local Government Finance Act 1988 ss 87, 88 apply in relation to England and Wales: see s 84Q(1)(c) (s 84Q added by SI 2007/1388). In the application of the Local Government Finance Act 1988 s 87 in relation to Wales, references to the Secretary of State are references to the Welsh Ministers: s 87(7) (added by SI 2007/1388). As to the Secretary of State and the Welsh Ministers see PARA 4 note 18. As to the meanings of 'England' and 'Wales' see PARA 2 note 16.

2 Each of the following is a defined council: a county council; a county borough council; and a metropolitan district council: Local Government Finance Act 1988 s 88(1), (2) (s 88(2) amended by the Local Government Wales Act 1994 s 66(6), Sch 16 para 85; and the Greater London Authority Act 1999 ss 159(8), 423, Sch 34 Pt II). As to local government areas and authorities in England and Wales see LOCAL GOVERNMENT vol 69 (2018) PARA 36 et seq.

3 As to the meanings of 'chargeable financial year' and 'financial year' see PARA 24 note 1.

4 A council's 'estimated relevant transport expenditure' for a financial year is the expenditure it estimates it will incur in the year in connection with:

(1) highways or the regulation of traffic, where the council is English (Local Government Finance Act 1988 s 88(1), (5)(a)); or

(2) highways, the regulation of traffic or public transport, where the council is Welsh (s 88(1), (5)(b)).

In making the estimate expenditure must be left out of account unless, at the time the estimate is made, it is capital expenditure for the purposes of the Local Government Act 2003 Pt 1 Ch 1 (ss 1–20) (capital finance: see PARA 563 et seq): Local Government Finance Act 1988 s 88(1), (6) (s 88(6) amended by the Local Government Act 2003 s 127(1), Sch 7 paras 9(1), 18).

5 Local Government Finance Act 1988 s 87(1).

6 Local Government Finance Act 1988 s 87(2).

7 Local Government Finance Act 1988 s 87(3).

8 Local Government Finance Act 1988 s 87(4).

9 A council's 'relevant transport expenditure' for a financial year is the expenditure it calculates it incurred in the year in connection with:

(1) highways or the regulation of traffic, where the council is English (Local Government Finance Act 1988 s 88(1), (3)(a)); or

(2) highways, the regulation of traffic or public transport, where the council is Welsh (s 88(1), (3)(b)).

In making the calculation expenditure must be left out of account unless, at the time the calculation is made, it is capital expenditure for the purposes of the Local Government Act 2003 Pt 1 Ch 1 (ss 1–20) (capital finance: see PARA 563 et seq): Local Government Finance Act 1988 s 88(1), (4) (s 88(4) amended by the Local Government Act 2003 Sch 7 paras 9(1), 18).

10 Local Government Finance Act 1988 s 87(5)(a).

11 Local Government Finance Act 1988 s 87(5)(b).

12 The functions of the Treasury under the Local Government Finance Act 1988 s 87, so far as exercisable in relation to Wales, were transferred to the National Assembly for Wales (see the National Assembly for Wales (Transfer of Functions) Order 1999, SI 1999/672, art 2, Sch 1) and are now vested in the Welsh Ministers (see the Government of Wales Act 2006 s 162(1), Sch 11 para 30).

13 Local Government Finance Act 1988 s 87(6). As to the meaning of 'Treasury' see PARA 30 note 15.

38. Council tax grants: England and Wales.

Regulations may make provision for reduced amounts of council tax for certain cases[1].

If such regulations relating to reduced amounts of council tax have effect as regards a financial year[2], the appropriate national authority[3] may pay[4] a grant to a billing authority[5] as regards that financial year[6]. The amount of the grant is such as the appropriate national authority may determine[7]. A grant must be paid at such time, or in instalments of such amounts and at such times, as the appropriate national authority may determine[8]. In making any payment of a grant the appropriate national authority may impose such conditions as it may determine[9]; and the conditions may relate to the repayment in specified circumstances of all or part of the amount paid, or otherwise[10].

In deciding whether to pay a grant under these provisions, and in determining the amount of any such grant, the appropriate national authority must have regard to its estimate of any amount which, in consequence of the regulations, the billing authority might reasonably be expected to lose, or to have lost, by way of payments in respect of the council tax set by it for the financial year concerned[11].

1 See the Local Government Finance Act 1992 s 13; and PARA 377.

2 As to the meaning of 'financial year' see PARA 24 note 1.

3 Ie the Secretary of State or, in relation to Wales, the Welsh Ministers. The Local Government Finance Act 1988 s 88A applies in relation to England and Wales: see s 84Q(1)(c) (s 84Q added by SI 2007/1388). In the application of the Local Government Finance Act 1988 s 88A in relation to Wales, references to the Secretary of State are references to the Welsh Ministers: s 88A(6) (s 88A added by the Local Government and Housing Act 1989 s 139, Sch 5 paras 1, 61, 79(3); substituted by the Local Government Finance Act 1992 s 104, Sch 10 para 18; the Local Government Finance Act 1988 s 88A(6) added by SI 2007/1388). As to the Secretary of State and the Welsh Ministers see PARA 4 note 18. As to the meanings of 'England' and 'Wales' see PARA 2 note 16.

4 In relation to England, payment made by the Secretary of State requires the consent of the Treasury: see the Local Government Finance Act 1988 s 88A(1) (as added and substituted: see note 3). The functions of the Treasury under the Local Government Finance Act 1988 s 88A, so far as exercisable in relation to Wales, were transferred to the National Assembly for Wales (see the National Assembly for Wales (Transfer of Functions) Order 1999, SI 1999/672, art 2, Sch 1) and are now vested in the Welsh Ministers (see the Government of Wales Act 2006 s 162(1), Sch 11 para 30). As to the meaning of 'Treasury' see PARA 30 note 15.

5 As to the meaning of 'billing authority' see PARA 53 (definition applied by the Local Government Finance Act 1988 s 144(2) (substituted by the Local Government Finance Act 1992 s 117(1), Sch 13 para 81(1); and amended by the Local Government Finance Act 2012 s 5(1), (2)(b), Sch 3 paras 23, 29)).

6 Local Government Finance Act 1988 s 88A(1) (as added and substituted: see note 3).

7 Local Government Finance Act 1988 s 88A(2) (as added and substituted: see note 3). In relation to England, the determination of the Secretary of State requires the consent of the Treasury: see s 88A(2) (as so added and substituted). See also note 4.

8 Local Government Finance Act 1988 s 88A(3) (as added and substituted: see note 3). In relation to England, the determination of the Secretary of State requires the consent of the Treasury: see s 88A(3) (as so added and substituted). See also note 4.
9 In relation to England, the determination of the Secretary of State requires the consent of the Treasury: see the Local Government Finance Act 1988 s 88A(4) (as added and substituted: see note 3). See also note 4.
10 Local Government Finance Act 1988 s 88A(4) (as added and substituted: see note 3).
11 Local Government Finance Act 1988 s 88A(5) (as added and substituted: see note 3).

39. Special grants: England and Wales.

The appropriate national authority[1] may pay[2] a grant (a 'special grant') to a relevant authority[3]. Where the appropriate national authority proposes to make one special grant it must, before making the grant, make a determination[4] stating with respect to the grant:

(1) to which relevant authority it is to be paid[5];
(2) the purpose for which it is to be paid[6]; and
(3) the amount of the grant or the manner in which the amount is to be calculated[7].

Where the appropriate national authority proposes to make two or more special grants to different relevant authorities it must, before making the grants, make a determination[8] stating with respect to the grants:

(a) to which relevant authorities they are to be paid[9];
(b) the purpose for which they are to be paid[10]; and
(c) either:
   (i) the amount of the grant which the appropriate national authority proposes to pay to each relevant authority or the manner in which the amount is to be calculated[11]; or
   (ii) the total amount which the appropriate national authority proposes to distribute among the relevant authorities by way of special grants and the basis on which the appropriate national authority proposes to distribute that amount[12].

A determination[13] must be specified in a report (a 'special grant report'), which must contain such explanation as the appropriate national authority considers desirable of the main features of the determination[14]. A special grant report must be laid before the House of Commons or as the case may be, the National Assembly for Wales[15] and, as soon as is reasonably practicable after the report has been so laid, the appropriate national authority must send a copy of it to any relevant authority to whom a special grant is proposed to be paid in accordance with the determination in the report[16]. No special grant may be paid unless the special grant report containing the determination relating to the grant has been approved by a resolution of the House of Commons or, as appropriate, the National Assembly for Wales[17].

A special grant report may specify conditions which the appropriate national authority intends to impose[18] on the payment of (or of any instalment of) any special grant to which the report relates[19]. The conditions may:

(A) require the provision of returns or other information[20] before a payment is made to the relevant authority concerned[21]; or
(B) relate to the use of the amount paid, or to the repayment in specified circumstances of all or part of the amount paid, or otherwise[22].

Without prejudice to compliance with any such conditions, a special grant must be paid at such time or in instalments of such amounts and at such times as the appropriate national authority may determine[23].

1 Ie the Secretary of State or, in relation to Wales, the Welsh Ministers. The Local Government Finance Act 1988 s 88B applies in relation to England and Wales: see s 84Q(1)(c) (s 84Q added by SI 2007/1388). As to the Secretary of State and the Welsh Ministers see PARA 4 note 18. As to the meanings of 'England' and 'Wales' see PARA 2 note 16.

The functions of the Secretary of State under the Local Government Finance Act 1988 s 88B, so far as exercisable in relation to Wales, were transferred to the National Assembly for Wales (see the National Assembly for Wales (Transfer of Functions) Order 1999, SI 1999/672, art 2, Sch 1) and are now vested in the Welsh Ministers (see the Government of Wales Act 2006 s 162(1), Sch 11 para 30). The functions of the Secretary of State under the Local Government Finance Act 1988 s 88B and the functions of the Welsh Ministers under s 88C (see PARA 40) are exercisable concurrently so far as they relate to police and crime commissioners in Wales: s 84Q(2) (as so added; amended by the Police Reform and Social Responsibility Act 2011 s 99, Sch 16 paras 180, 184(a)). As to police and crime commissioners see POLICE AND INVESTIGATORY POWERS vol 84 (2013) PARA 56 et seq. See further note 3. The functions under the Local Government Finance Act 1988 s 88B so far as exercisable by the Welsh Ministers are exercisable free from the requirements for Treasury consent: see the National Assembly for Wales (Transfer of Functions) Order 1999, SI 1999/672, Sch 1.

2 In relation to England, payment by the Secretary of State requires the consent of the Treasury: see the Local Government Finance Act 1988 s 88B(1) (s 88B added by the Local Government Finance Act 1992 s 104, Sch 10 para 18). See also note 1. As to the meaning of 'Treasury' see PARA 30 note 15.

3 Local Government Finance Act 1988 s 88B(1) (as added: see note 2). For these purposes each of the following is a 'relevant authority': a receiving authority; an integrated transport authority for an integrated transport area in England (see LOCAL GOVERNMENT vol 69 (2018) PARA 73); and a combined authority established under the Local Democracy, Economic Development and Construction Act 2009 s 103 (see LOCAL GOVERNMENT vol 69 (2018) PARA 83): Local Government Finance Act 1988 s 88B(9) (as so added; amended by the Local Transport Act 2008 s 77(5), Sch 4 para 56(1), (2); and the Local Democracy, Economic Development and Construction Act 2009 s 119, Sch 6 paras 74, 76). In the application of the Local Government Finance Act 1988 s 88B in relation to Wales, 'relevant authority' means only a police and crime commissioner (see POLICE AND INVESTIGATORY POWERS vol 84 (2013) PARA 56 et seq): Local Government Finance Act 1988 s 88B(10) (s 88B as so added; s 88B(10) added by SI 2007/1388; and amended by the Police Reform and Social Responsibility Act 2011 s 99, Sch 16 paras 180, 185). As to special grants to receiving authorities in Wales see PARA 40.

4 In relation to England, such a determination made by the Secretary of State requires the consent of the Treasury: see the Local Government Finance Act 1988 s 88B(4) (as added: see note 2). See also note 1.

5 Local Government Finance Act 1988 s 88B(2)(a) (as added: see note 2).

6 Local Government Finance Act 1988 s 88B(2)(b) (as added: see note 2).

7 Local Government Finance Act 1988 s 88B(2)(c) (as added: see note 2).

8 In relation to England, such a determination made by the Secretary of State requires the consent of the Treasury: see the Local Government Finance Act 1988 s 88B(4) (as added: see note 2). See also note 1.

9 Local Government Finance Act 1988 s 88B(3)(a) (as added: see note 2).

10 Local Government Finance Act 1988 s 88B(3)(b) (as added: see note 2).

11 Local Government Finance Act 1988 s 88B(3)(c)(i) (as added: see note 2).

12 Local Government Finance Act 1988 s 88B(3)(c)(ii) (as added: see note 2).

13 Ie under the Local Government Finance Act 1988 s 88B(2) or s 88B(3): see the text to notes 4–12.

14 Local Government Finance Act 1988 s 88B(4) (as added: see note 2).

15 As to the laying of documents before the National Assembly for Wales see the Government of Wales Act 2006 s 86. As to the National Assembly for Wales see CONSTITUTIONAL AND ADMINISTRATIVE LAW vol 20 (2014) PARA 351 et seq.

16 Local Government Finance Act 1988 s 88B(5) (as added: see note 2).

17 See the Local Government Finance Act 1988 s 88B(6) (as added: see note 2); and the National Assembly for Wales (Transfer of Functions) Order 1999, SI 1999/672, art 2, Sch 1.

18 In relation to England, the imposition of such conditions by the Secretary of State requires the consent of the Treasury: see the Local Government Finance Act 1988 s 88B(7) (as added: see note 2). See also note 1.
19 Local Government Finance Act 1988 s 88B(7) (as added: see note 2).
20 As to the meaning of 'information' see PARA 31 note 17.
21 Local Government Finance Act 1988 s 88B(7)(a) (as added: see note 2).
22 Local Government Finance Act 1988 s 88B(7)(b) (as added: see note 2).
23 Local Government Finance Act 1988 s 88B(8) (as added: see note 2). In relation to England, such a determination made by the Secretary of State requires the consent of the Treasury: see s 88B(8) (as so added). See also note 1.

40. Special grants: additional provision in relation to Wales.

The Welsh Ministers[1] may pay a grant (a 'special grant') to a receiving authority[2] in Wales[3]. Where the Welsh Ministers propose to make one special grant they must, before making the grant, make a determination stating with respect to the grant:

(1) to which authority it is to be paid[4];
(2) the purpose for which it is to be paid[5]; and
(3) the amount of the grant or the manner in which the amount is to be calculated[6].

Where the Welsh Ministers propose to make two or more special grants to different authorities they must, before making the grants, make a determination stating with respect to the grants:

(a) to which authorities they are to be paid[7];
(b) the purpose for which they are to be paid[8]; and
(c) either:
 (i) the amount of the grant which they propose to pay to each authority or the manner in which the amount is to be calculated[9]; or
 (ii) the total amount which they propose to distribute among the authorities by way of special grants and the basis on which they propose to distribute that amount[10].

A determination[11] must be specified in a report (a 'special grant report') which must contain such explanation as the Welsh Ministers consider desirable of the main features of the determination[12]. A special grant report must be laid before the National Assembly for Wales[13] and, as soon as is reasonably practicable after the report has been so laid, the Welsh Ministers must send a copy of it to any receiving authority to whom a special grant is proposed to be paid in accordance with the determination in the report[14]. No special grant must be paid unless the special grant report containing the determination relating to the grant has been approved by a resolution of the Assembly[15].

A special grant report may specify conditions which the Welsh Ministers intend to impose on the payment of (or of any instalment of) special grant to which the report relates; and the conditions may:

(A) require the provision of returns or other information before a payment is made to the receiving authority concerned[16]; or
(B) relate to the use of the amount paid, or to the repayment in specified circumstances of all or part of the amount paid, or otherwise[17].

Without prejudice to compliance with any such conditions, a special grant must be paid at such time or in instalments of such amounts and at such times as the Welsh Ministers may determine[18].

1 As to the Welsh Ministers see PARA 4 note 18.
2 As to the meaning of 'receiving authority' see PARA 30 note 5.

3 Local Government Finance Act 1988 s 88C(1) (ss 76(7), 84Q, 88C added by SI 2007/1388). The Local Government Finance Act 1988 s 88C applies only in relation to Wales: s 84Q(1)(d) (as so added). The functions of the Secretary of State under s 88B (see PARA 39) and the functions of the Welsh Ministers under s 88C are exercisable concurrently so far as they relate to police and crime commissioners in Wales: s 84Q(2) (as so added; amended by the Police Reform and Social Responsibility Act 2011 s 99, Sch 16 paras 180, 184(a)). As to police and crime commissioners see POLICE AND INVESTIGATORY POWERS vol 84 (2013) PARA 56 et seq. As to the meaning of 'Wales' see PARA 2 note 16.
4 Local Government Finance Act 1988 s 88C(2)(a) (as added: see note 3).
5 Local Government Finance Act 1988 s 88C(2)(b) (as added: see note 3).
6 Local Government Finance Act 1988 s 88C(2)(c) (as added: see note 3).
7 Local Government Finance Act 1988 s 88C(3)(a) (as added: see note 3).
8 Local Government Finance Act 1988 s 88C(3)(b) (as added: see note 3).
9 Local Government Finance Act 1988 s 88C(3)(c)(i) (as added: see note 3).
10 Local Government Finance Act 1988 s 88C(3)(c)(ii) (as added: see note 3).
11 Ie under the Local Government Finance Act 1988 s 88C(2) or (3): see the text to notes 4–10.
12 Local Government Finance Act 1988 s 88C(4) (as added: see note 3).
13 As to the National Assembly for Wales see CONSTITUTIONAL AND ADMINISTRATIVE LAW vol 20 (2014) PARA 351 et seq.
14 See the Local Government Finance Act 1988 ss 76(7), 88C(5) (both as added: see note 3).
15 Local Government Finance Act 1988 s 88C(6) (as added: see note 3).
16 Local Government Finance Act 1988 s 88C(7)(a) (as added: see note 3).
17 Local Government Finance Act 1988 s 88C(7)(b) (as added: see note 3).
18 Local Government Finance Act 1988 s 88C(8) (as added: see note 3).

41. Expenditure grants: England and Wales.

A Minister of the Crown[1] may pay[2] a grant to a local authority in England towards expenditure incurred or to be incurred by it[3]; and a Minister of the Crown, or the Welsh Ministers[4], may pay a grant to a local authority in Wales[5] towards expenditure incurred or to be incurred by it[6].

The amount of a grant and the manner of its payment are to be such as the person[7] paying it may determine[8]. A grant may be paid on such conditions as the person paying it may determine[9]; and such conditions may, in particular, include:

(1) provision as to the use of the grant[10];
(2) provision as to circumstances in which the whole or part of the grant must be repaid[11].

The Welsh Ministers may pay a grant to a community council[12] towards expenditure incurred or to be incurred by it[13]. The amount of such a grant and the manner of its payment are to be such as the Welsh Ministers may determine[14]. A grant may be paid on such conditions as the person paying it may determine[15]; and such conditions may include (but are not limited to):

(a) provision as to the use of the grant[16];
(b) provision as to circumstances in which the whole or part of the grant must be repaid[17].

1 'Minister of the Crown' means the holder of an office in Her Majesty's Government in the United Kingdom, and includes the Treasury, the Board of Trade and the Defence Council: Ministers of the Crown Act 1975 s 8(1) (definition applied by the Local Government Act 2003 s 33(2)). As to Ministers of the Crown see CONSTITUTIONAL AND ADMINISTRATIVE LAW vol 20 (2014) PARA 151. As to the meaning of 'United Kingdom' see PARA 4 note 10.
2 In the case of a grant to a local authority in England, the powers under the Local Government Act 2003 s 31 are exercisable with the consent of the Treasury: s 31(6). As to the meaning of 'England' see PARA 2 note 16. As to the meaning of 'Treasury' see PARA 30 note 15.
The following are local authorities for these purposes:
(1) a county council (s 33(1)(a));
(2) a county borough council (s 33(1)(b));
(3) a district council (s 33(1)(c));
(4) the Greater London Authority (s 33(1)(d));

(5) a London borough council (s 33(1)(e));
(6) the Common Council of the City of London, in its capacity as a local authority, police authority or port health authority (s 33(1)(f));
(7) the Council of the Isles of Scilly (s 33(1)(g));
(8) an authority established under the Local Government Act 1985 s 10 (waste disposal authorities: see LOCAL GOVERNMENT vol 69 (2018) PARA 17) (Local Government Act 2003 s 33(1)(i));
(9) a joint authority established by the Local Government Act 1985 Pt IV (ss 23–42) (fire and rescue services and transport: see LOCAL GOVERNMENT vol 69 (2018) PARAS 71, 72) (Local Government Act 2003 s 33(1)(j) (amended by the Civil Contingencies Act 2004 s 32(1), Sch 2 para 10(3)(e)));
(10) an economic prosperity board established under the Local Democracy, Economic Development and Construction Act 2009 s 88 (see TRADE AND INDUSTRY vol 97 (2015) PARA 1086 et seq) (Local Government Act 2003 s 33(1)(jb) (added by the Local Democracy, Economic Development and Construction Act 2009 s 119, Sch 6 para 117(1), (3)));
(11) a combined authority established under Local Democracy, Economic Development and Construction Act 2009 s 103 (see TRADE AND INDUSTRY vol 97 (2015) PARA 1092 et seq) (Local Government Act 2003 s 33(1)(jc) (added by the Local Democracy, Economic Development and Construction Act 2009 Sch 6 para 117(1), (3)));
(12) a joint planning board constituted for an area in Wales outside a National Park by an order under the Town and Country Planning Act 1990 s 2(1B) (see PLANNING vol 81 (2018) PARA 188) (Local Government Act 2003 s 33(1)(k));
(13) a fire and rescue authority constituted by a scheme under the Fire and Rescue Services Act 2004 s 2 or a scheme to which s 4 applies (see FIRE AND RESCUE SERVICES vol 51 (2013) PARAS 18–20) (Local Government Act 2003 s 33(1)(l) (substituted by the Fire and Rescue Services Act 2004 s 53(1), Sch 1 paras 99, 101));
(14) a fire and rescue authority created by an order under the Fire and Rescue Services Act 2004 s 4A (see FIRE AND RESCUE SERVICES) (Local Government Act 2003 s 33(1)(la) (added by the Policing and Crime Act 2017 s 6, Sch 1 para 83(1), (3)));
(15) a police and crime commissioner (see POLICE AND INVESTIGATORY POWERS vol 84 (2013) PARA 56 et seq) (Local Government Act 2003 s 33(1)(m) (substituted by the Police Reform and Social Responsibility Act 2011 ss 27(4), 99, Sch 16 paras 316, 319)).

As to local government areas and authorities in England and Wales see LOCAL GOVERNMENT vol 69 (2018) PARA 36 et seq. As to the Greater London Authority see LONDON GOVERNMENT vol 71 (2013) PARA 67 et seq. As to the London boroughs and their councils see LONDON GOVERNMENT vol 71 (2013) PARAS 15, 20–22, 55 et seq. As to the Common Council of the City of London see LONDON GOVERNMENT vol 71 (2013) PARAS 34–38. As to the Council of the Isles of Scilly see LOCAL GOVERNMENT vol 69 (2018) PARA 50.

3 Local Government Act 2003 s 31(1). As to the application of s 31 to the Greater London Authority see further s 32.
4 As to the Welsh Ministers see PARA 4 note 18. The functions under the Local Government Act 2003 s 31 were formerly vested in the National Assembly for Wales and are now exercisable by the Welsh Ministers by virtue of the Government of Wales Act 2006 s 162(1), Sch 11 paras 30, 32.
5 As to the meaning of 'Wales' see PARA 2 note 16.
6 Local Government Act 2003 s 31(2).
7 As to the meaning of 'person' see PARA 11 note 13.
8 Local Government Act 2003 s 31(3).
9 Local Government Act 2003 s 31(4).
10 Local Government Act 2003 s 31(5)(a).
11 Local Government Act 2003 s 31(5)(b).
12 As to community councils in Wales see LOCAL GOVERNMENT vol 69 (2018) PARA 63 et seq.
13 Local Government (Wales) Measure 2011 s 129(1).
14 Local Government (Wales) Measure 2011 s 129(2).
15 Local Government (Wales) Measure 2011 s 129(3).
16 Local Government (Wales) Measure 2011 s 129(4)(a).
17 Local Government (Wales) Measure 2011 s 129(4)(b).

42. Grants in connection with designation for service excellence: England and Wales.

The appropriate person[1] may pay any of the following to a best value authority[2] which, in relation to any of its functions, is subject to best value duty[3], or to a Welsh improvement authority[4]:

(1) a grant towards expenditure incurred by the authority in applying for the award of a designation based on excellence in the provision of services[5]; and

(2) where the authority is awarded such a designation:

  (a) a grant as a reward for being awarded such a designation[6]; and

  (b) a grant towards expenditure incurred or to be incurred by the authority in disseminating information about best practices[7].

The amount of a grant and the manner of its payment are to be such as the appropriate person may determine[8]. A grant may be paid on such conditions as the appropriate person may determine as to the circumstances in which the whole or any part of the grant must be repaid[9].

1 As to the meaning of 'appropriate person' see PARA 16 note 8.
2 'Best value authority' means an authority or body which is a best value authority for the purposes of the Local Government Act 1999 Pt I (ss 1–29) (see LOCAL GOVERNMENT vol 69 (2018) PARA 779): Local Government Act 2003 s 124.
3 Ie the duty in the Local Government Act 1999 s 3(1): see LOCAL GOVERNMENT vol 69 (2018) PARA 780.
4 Local Government Act 2003 s 36(1) (amended by the Local Government and Public Involvement in Health Act 2007 s 144(2), Sch 8 Pt 2 para 25(1), (2); and the Local Government (Wales) Measure 2009 s 51(1), Sch 1 paras 23, 24). A 'Welsh improvement authority' is one within the meaning of the Local Government (Wales) Measure 2009 s 1 (see LOCAL GOVERNMENT vol 69 (2018) PARA 789): see the Local Government Act 2003 s 36(1) (as so amended).
5 Local Government Act 2003 s 36(1)(a).
6 Local Government Act 2003 s 36(1)(b)(i).
7 Local Government Act 2003 s 36(1)(b)(ii).
8 Local Government Act 2003 s 36(2).
9 Local Government Act 2003 s 36(3).

43. Grants in respect of best value and improvement authorities: England and Wales.

A Minister of the Crown[1] may pay a grant to a person[2] for use in, or in connection with, promoting or facilitating the economic, efficient and effective exercise of functions by a best value authority[3] or best value authorities or a Welsh improvement authority[4] or Welsh improvement authorities[5]. The power to make such a grant is exercisable only with the consent of the Treasury[6] and, in the case of a grant in respect of the exercise of functions by a Welsh improvement authority, the Welsh Ministers[7].

The amount of a grant, and the method of payment, are to be such as the Minister of the Crown may determine[8]; but the power to pay a grant does not include power to pay a grant to a best value authority or a Welsh improvement authority[9]. A grant may be paid on such conditions as the Minister of the Crown may determine[10]. Such conditions may, in particular, include:

(1) provision as to the use of the grant[11];

(2) provision as to circumstances in which the whole or part of the grant must be repaid[12].

The Welsh Ministers may pay a grant to a person for use in, or in connection with, promoting or facilitating compliance by a Welsh improvement authority or Welsh improvement authorities with the statutory requirements[13] relating to local government improvement[14]. The amount of a grant, and the method of payment, are to be such as the Welsh Ministers may determine[15]; but the power to pay a grant does not include power to pay a grant to a best value authority[16] or Welsh improvement authority[17]. A grant may be paid on such conditions as the Welsh Ministers may determine[18]. Such conditions may, in particular, include:

(a) provision as to the use of the grant[19];

(b) provision as to circumstances in which the whole or part of the grant must be repaid[20].

1 As to the meaning of 'Minister of the Crown' see PARA 41 note 1 (definition applied by the Local Government Act 2003 s 36A(7) (ss 36A, 36B added by the Local Government and Public Involvement in Health Act 2007 s 143(1))).

2 As to the meaning of 'person' see PARA 11 note 13.

3 As to the meaning of 'best value authority' see PARA 42 note 2. For the purposes of the Local Government Act 2003 ss 36A, 36B, 'best value authority' includes the Greater London Authority, whether exercising its functions through the Mayor or otherwise: see ss 36A(7), 36B(6) (both as added: see note 1). As to the Greater London Authority see LONDON GOVERNMENT vol 71 (2013) PARA 67 et seq.

4 For the purposes of the Local Government Act 2003 ss 36A, 36B, 'Welsh improvement authority' means an authority which is a Welsh improvement authority within the meaning of the Local Government (Wales) Measure 2009 s 1 (see LOCAL GOVERNMENT vol 69 (2018) PARA 789): Local Government Act 2003 ss 36A(7), 36B(6) (ss 36A, 36B as added (see note 1); definitions added by the Local Government (Wales) Measure 2009 s 51(1), Sch 1 paras 23, 25(d), 26(c)).

5 Local Government Act 2003 s 36A(1) (as added (see note 1); amended by the Local Government (Wales) Measure 2009 Sch 1 paras 23, 25(a)).

6 Local Government Act 2003 s 36A(2)(a) (as added: see note 1). As to the meaning of 'Treasury' see PARA 30 note 15.

7 Local Government Act 2003 s 36A(2)(b) (as added (see note 1); amended by the Local Government (Wales) Measure 2009 Sch 1 paras 23, 25(b)). As to the Welsh Ministers see PARA 4 note 18.

8 Local Government Act 2003 s 36A(4) (as added: see note 1).

9 Local Government Act 2003 s 36A(3) (as added (see note 1); amended by the Local Government (Wales) Measure 2009 Sch 1 paras 23, 25(c)).

10 Local Government Act 2003 s 36A(5) (as added: see note 1).

11 Local Government Act 2003 s 36A(6)(a) (as added: see note 1).

12 Local Government Act 2003 s 36A(6)(b) (as added: see note 1).

13 Ie the requirements of the Local Government (Wales) Measure 2009 Pt 1 (ss 1–36): see LOCAL GOVERNMENT vol 69 (2018) PARA 789 et seq.

14 Local Government Act 2003 s 36B(1) (as added (see note 1); amended by the Local Government (Wales) Measure 2009 Sch 1 paras 23, 26(a)).

15 Local Government Act 2003 s 36B(3) (as added: see note 1).

16 See note 3.

17 Local Government Act 2003 s 36B(2) (as added (see note 1); amended by the Local Government (Wales) Measure 2009 Sch 1 paras 23, 26(b)).

18 Local Government Act 2003 s 36B(4) (as added: see note 1).

19 Local Government Act 2003 s 36B(5)(a) (as added: see note 1).

20 Local Government Act 2003 s 36B(5)(b) (as added: see note 1).

44. Loans by Public Works Loan Commissioners.

The Secretary of State[1] may, if he thinks it appropriate, make payments to the Public Works Loan Commissioners[2] so as to reduce or extinguish such debt (whether then due or not) of a local authority in England[3] to those Commissioners as he thinks fit[4]; and the Welsh Ministers[5] may, if they think it appropriate, make payments to the Public Works Loan Commissioners so as to reduce or extinguish such debt (whether then due or not) of a local authority in Wales[6] to those Commissioners as the Welsh Ministers think fit[7].

The amount required to extinguish a debt[8], or by which a payment reduces a debt[9], is such as may be determined by the Commissioners[10]. The Commissioners may refuse to accept a payment which the Secretary of State or the Welsh Ministers propose to make to them under these provisions[11].

1 As to the Secretary of State see PARA 4 note 18.
2 As to the Public Works Loan Commissioners see FINANCIAL INSTRUMENTS AND TRANSACTIONS vol 49 (2015) PARA 160 et seq.
3 'Local authority', in relation to England, means:
 (1) a district council (Local Government Act 2003 s 38(5)(a)(i));
 (2) a county council that is the council for a county in which there are no district councils (s 38(5)(a)(ii));
 (3) a London borough council (s 38(5)(a)(iii));
 (4) the Common Council of the City of London (s 38(5)(a)(iv)); or
 (5) the Council of the Isles of Scilly (s 38(5)(a)(v)).
 As to the meaning of 'England' see PARA 2 note 16. As to local government areas and authorities in England see LOCAL GOVERNMENT vol 69 (2018) PARA 36 et seq. As to the London boroughs and their councils see LONDON GOVERNMENT vol 71 (2013) PARAS 15, 20–22, 55 et seq. As to the Common Council of the City of London see LONDON GOVERNMENT vol 71 (2013) PARAS 34–38. As to the Council of the Isles of Scilly see LOCAL GOVERNMENT vol 69 (2018) PARA 50.
4 Local Government Act 2003 s 38(1).
5 As to the Welsh Ministers see PARA 4 note 18. The functions under the Local Government Act 2003 s 38 were formerly vested in the National Assembly for Wales and are now exercisable by the Welsh Ministers by virtue of the Government of Wales Act 2006 s 162(1), Sch 11 paras 30, 32.
6 'Local authority', in relation to Wales, means a county council or a county borough council: Local Government Act 2003 s 38(5)(b). As to the meaning of 'Wales' see PARA 2 note 16. As to local government areas and authorities in Wales see LOCAL GOVERNMENT vol 69 (2018) PARA 51 et seq.
7 Local Government Act 2003 s 38(2).
8 Local Government Act 2003 s 38(3)(a).
9 Local Government Act 2003 s 38(3)(b).
10 Local Government Act 2003 s 38(3).
11 Local Government Act 2003 s 38(4).

45. Payments towards local authority indebtedness.

The Secretary of State[1] may, if he thinks it appropriate, make payments to a local authority in England[2] for application by the authority in reducing or extinguishing such debt (whether then due or not) of the authority as he thinks fit[3]; and the Welsh Ministers[4] may, if they think it appropriate, make payments to a local authority in Wales[5] for application by the authority in reducing or extinguishing such debt (whether then due or not) of the authority as the Welsh Ministers think fit[6].

The person[7] making such payments to a local authority may specify how the payments are to be applied by the authority and may in particular specify:
 (1) the debt or debts to be extinguished[8], or
 (2) the debt or debts to be reduced[9].

A payment may be made subject to conditions imposed by the person making the payment[10], including (in particular) conditions relating to the repayment in specified circumstances of all or part of the payment[11].

Payments made to a local authority under these provisions may not be applied in reducing or extinguishing any debt of the authority to the Public Works Loan Commissioners[12].

1 As to the Secretary of State see PARA 4 note 18.
2 'Local authority', in relation to England, means:
 (1) a district council (Local Government Act 2003 s 39(7)(a)(i));
 (2) a county council that is the council for a county in which there are no district councils (s 39(7)(a)(ii));
 (3) a London borough council (s 39(7)(a)(iii));

(4) the Common Council of the City of London (s 39(7)(a)(iv)); or
(5) the Council of the Isles of Scilly (s 39(7)(a)(v)).

As to the meaning of 'England' see PARA 2 note 16. As to local government areas and authorities in England see LOCAL GOVERNMENT vol 69 (2018) PARA 36 et seq. As to the London boroughs and their councils see LONDON GOVERNMENT vol 71 (2013) PARAS 15, 20–22, 55 et seq. As to the Common Council of the City of London see LONDON GOVERNMENT vol 71 (2013) PARAS 34–38. As to the Council of the Isles of Scilly see LOCAL GOVERNMENT vol 69 (2018) PARA 50.

3 Local Government Act 2003 s 39(1).
4 As to the Welsh Ministers see PARA 4 note 18. The functions under the Local Government Act 2003 s 39 were formerly vested in the National Assembly for Wales and are now exercisable by the Welsh Ministers by virtue of the Government of Wales Act 2006 s 162(1), Sch 11 paras 30, 32.
5 'Local authority', in relation to Wales, means a county council or a county borough council: Local Government Act 2003 s 39(7)(b). As to the meaning of 'Wales' see PARA 2 note 16. As to local government areas and authorities in Wales see LOCAL GOVERNMENT vol 69 (2018) PARA 51 et seq.
6 Local Government Act 2003 s 39(2).
7 As to the meaning of 'person' see PARA 11 note 13.
8 Local Government Act 2003 s 39(3)(a).
9 Local Government Act 2003 s 39(3)(b).
10 Local Government Act 2003 s 39(4).
11 See the Local Government Act 2003 s 39(5).
12 Local Government Act 2003 s 39(6). As to the making of payments to reduce or extinguish local authority debts to the Public Works Loan Commissioners see s 38; and PARA 44. As to the Public Works Loan Commissioners see FINANCIAL INSTRUMENTS AND TRANSACTIONS vol 49 (2015) PARA 160 et seq.

46. Grants for specific services.

Certain enactments provide for specific grants in aid of revenue expenditure of local authorities. These grants are paid to the particular local authority responsible for a function or service and in accordance with any conditions and limits in the appropriate enactment.

Specific grants are payable, for instance, in respect of police[1], derelict land[2], ethnic minorities[3], special social need in urban areas[4], and provision of employment for disabled persons[5].

The appropriate national authority[6] may from time to time by order made by statutory instrument[7] provide that, with effect from such year as may be specified in the order, no grant may be paid under any such local authority grant provision[8] as may be so specified or that no such grant may be paid except in respect of expenditure of a description so specified[9]. No such order has effect unless it is approved by a resolution of each House of Parliament or, as the case may be, the National Assembly for Wales[10].

1 See the Police Act 1996 ss 46, 47, 48; and POLICE AND INVESTIGATORY POWERS vol 84 (2013) PARAS 155–156. As to grants financing new police and crime commissioners see s 94; and POLICE AND INVESTIGATORY POWERS vol 84 (2013) PARA 159. As to grants by local authorities to police and crime commissioners see s 92; and POLICE AND INVESTIGATORY POWERS vol 84 (2013) PARA 158.
2 See the Derelict Land Act 1982 s 1; and TRADE AND INDUSTRY vol 97 (2015) PARAS 1067–1069.
3 See the Local Government Act 1966 s 11; and PARA 47.
4 See the Local Government Grants (Social Need) Act 1969; and PARA 47.
5 See the Disabled Persons (Employment) Act 1944 s 15(5)(c); and EMPLOYMENT vol 40 (2014) PARA 610.

6 Ie the Secretary of State or, in relation to Wales, the Welsh Ministers. The functions of the Secretary of State under the Local Government Act 1974 Sch I Pt III, so far as exercisable in relation to Wales, were transferred to the National Assembly for Wales (see the National Assembly for Wales (Transfer of Functions) Order 1999, SI 1999/672, art 2, Sch 1) and are now vested in the Welsh Ministers (see the Government of Wales Act 2006 s 162(1), Sch 11 para 30). As to the Secretary of State and the Welsh Ministers see PARA 4 note 18. As to the meaning of 'Wales' see PARA 2 note 16.

7 The following order has been made: the Education Act 1944 (Termination of Grants) Order 1980, SI 1980/660 (amended by SI 2010/1172).

8 'Local authority grant provision' means an enactment providing for the payment of grants to local authorities (within the meaning of the enactment concerned) in respect of expenditure incurred in connection with a specific function: Local Government Act 1974 Sch 1 Pt III para 11(2).

9 Local Government Act 1974 Sch 1 Pt III para 11(1). An order under Sch 1 Pt III para 11 may contain such provisions as appear to the appropriate national authority to be necessary or proper in consequence of the termination of the grants, including provision amending, repealing or revoking, with or without savings, any enactment or instrument made under an enactment: Sch 1 Pt III para 11(3).

10 See the Local Government Act 1974 Sch 1 Pt III para 11(4); and the Government of Wales Act 2006 Sch 11 para 33. As to the National Assembly for Wales see CONSTITUTIONAL AND ADMINISTRATIVE LAW vol 20 (2014) PARA 351 et seq.

47. Grants for special social needs.

The appropriate national authority[1] may pay, to local authorities[2] which in its opinion are required to make special provision in the exercise of any of their functions in consequence of the presence within their areas of persons belonging to ethnic minorities whose language or customs differ from those of the rest of the community, grants of such amounts as the appropriate national authority may determine[3] on account of expenditure in respect of the employment of staff[4].

Out of money provided by Parliament, the appropriate national authority[5] may also pay grants, of such amounts as it may determine[6], to local authorities[7] which in its opinion are required in the exercise of any of their functions to incur expenditure by reason of the existence in any urban area of special social need[8].

1 Ie the Secretary of State or, in relation to Wales, the Welsh Ministers. The functions of the Secretary of State under the Local Government Act 1966, so far as exercisable in relation to Wales, were transferred to the National Assembly for Wales (see the National Assembly for Wales (Transfer of Functions) Order 1999, SI 1999/672, art 2, Sch 1) and are now vested in the Welsh Ministers (see the Government of Wales Act 2006 s 162(1), Sch 11 para 30). As to the Secretary of State and the Welsh Ministers see PARA 4 note 18. As to the meaning of 'Wales' see PARA 2 note 16.

2 'Local authority' means the council of a county, district, London borough or county borough, the Common Council of the City of London, and the Council of the Isles of Scilly: Local Government Act 1966 s 41(1) (definition amended by the Statute Law (Repeals) Act 1978; the Local Government Act 1985 s 102, Sch 17; the Local Government (Wales) Act 1994 s 66(6), Sch 16 para 27; and by virtue of the Local Government Act 1972 s 179(1), (3)). As to local government areas and authorities see LOCAL GOVERNMENT vol 69 (2018) PARA 36 et seq. As to the London boroughs and their councils see LONDON GOVERNMENT vol 71 (2013) PARAS 15, 20–22, 55 et seq. As to the Common Council of the City of London see LONDON GOVERNMENT vol 71 (2013) PARAS 34–38. As to the Council of the Isles of Scilly see LOCAL GOVERNMENT vol 69 (2018) PARA 50.

The Local Government Act 1966 s 11 also applies to a fire and rescue authority created by an order under the Fire and Rescue Services Act 2004 s 4A (see FIRE AND RESCUE SERVICES), the London Fire and Emergency Planning Authority (see FIRE AND RESCUE SERVICES vol 51 (2013) PARA 17), a police and crime commissioner (see POLICE AND INVESTIGATORY POWERS vol 84 (2013) PARA 56 et seq), the Mayor's Office for Policing and Crime (see POLICE AND INVESTIGATORY POWERS vol 84 (2013) PARA 78 et seq), a joint authority established by the Local Government Act 1985 Pt IV (ss 23–42) (see LOCAL GOVERNMENT vol 69 (2018) PARA 71), an economic prosperity board established under the Local Democracy, Economic Development and Construction Act 2009 s 88 (see TRADE AND INDUSTRY vol 97 (2015) PARA 1086 et seq) and a combined authority established under the Local Democracy, Economic Development and Construction Act 2009 s 103 (see TRADE AND INDUSTRY vol 97 (2015) PARA 1092 et seq) as it applies to a local authority: Local Government Act 1966 s 11(2) (s 11 substituted by the London Government (Amendment) Act 1993 s 1; the Local Government Act 1966 s 11(2) amended by the Greater London Authority Act 1999 ss 325, 328, Sch 27 para 19, Sch 29 para 7; the Local Democracy, Economic Development and Construction Act 2009 s 119, Sch 6 para 4; the Police Reform and Social Responsibility Act 2011 s 99, Sch 16 para 84; and the Policing and Crime Act 2017 s 6, Sch 1 para 16). Prospectively, the reference to the London Fire and Emergency Planning Authority is replaced with a reference to the London Fire Commissioner: see the Local Government Act 1966 s 11(2) (as so substituted; amended, as from a day to be appointed, by the Policing and Crime Act 2017 s 9(3)(c), Sch 2 para 26). At the date at which this volume states the law, no such day had been appointed.

3 A determination of the Secretary of State requires the consent of the Treasury: see the Local Government Act 1966 s 11(1) (as substituted: see note 2). As to the meaning of 'Treasury' see PARA 30 note 15.

4 See the Local Government Act 1966 s 11(1) (as substituted: see note 2).

5 The functions of the Secretary of State under the Local Government Grants (Social Need) Act 1969, so far as exercisable in relation to Wales, were transferred to the National Assembly for Wales (see the National Assembly for Wales (Transfer of Functions) Order 1999, SI 1999/672, art 2, Sch 1) and are now vested in the Welsh Ministers (see the Government of Wales Act 2006 s 162(1), Sch 11 para 30). Those functions are exercisable by the Welsh Ministers concurrently with the Secretary of State and are exercisable by the Welsh Ministers free from the requirement for Treasury consent: see the National Assembly for Wales (Transfer of Functions) Order 1999, SI 1999/672, Sch 1; and the Government of Wales Act 2006 Sch 11 para 30.

6 A determination of the Secretary of State requires the consent of the Treasury: see the Local Government Grants (Social Need) Act 1969 s 1(1).

7 'Local authority' has the same meaning as in the Local Government Act 1966 s 41 (see note 2) and also includes a fire and rescue authority created by an order under the Fire and Rescue Services Act 2004 s 4A, the London Fire and Emergency Planning Authority, a police and crime commissioner, the Mayor's Office for Policing and Crime, a joint authority established by the Local Government Act 1985 Pt IV (ss 23–42), an economic prosperity board established under the Local Democracy, Economic Development and Construction Act 2009 s 88 and a combined authority established under s 103 of that Act: see the Local Government Grants (Social Need) Act 1969 s 1(3) (amended by the Local Government Act 1985 s 84, Sch 14 para 44; the Greater London Authority Act 1999 Sch 27 para 23, Sch 29 Pt I para 10; the Local Democracy, Economic Development and Construction Act 2009 Sch 6 para 7; the Police Reform and Social Responsibility Act 2011 Sch 16 para 93; and the Policing and Crime Act 2017 Sch 1 para 20). Prospectively, the reference to the London Fire and Emergency Planning Authority is replaced with a reference to the London Fire Commissioner: see the Local Government Grants (Social Need) Act 1969 s 1(3) (amended, as from a day to be appointed, by the Policing and Crime Act 2017 Sch 2 para 30). At the date at which this volume states the law, no such day had been appointed.

8 Local Government Grants (Social Need) Act 1969 s 1(1). The grants may be paid at such times, subject to such conditions and on account of such expenditure as the appropriate national authority may determine: s 1(2). As to urban development see PLANNING vol 83 (2018) PARA 1488 et seq; and as to urban regeneration see PLANNING vol 83 (2018) PARA 1504 et seq.

48. Emergency financial assistance.

In any case where an emergency or disaster occurs involving destruction of or danger to life or property[1] and, as a result, one or more local authorities[2] incur expenditure[3] on, or in connection with, the taking of immediate action (whether by the carrying out of works or otherwise) to safeguard life or property, or to prevent suffering or severe inconvenience, in the area or among the inhabitants[4], the appropriate national authority[5] may establish a scheme for the giving of financial assistance to those authorities in respect of that expenditure[6]. Financial assistance given pursuant to a scheme takes the form of grants paid by the appropriate national authority[7], the terms and conditions of a scheme being such as the appropriate national authority considers appropriate to the circumstances of the particular emergency or disaster concerned[8]. A scheme may:

(1) make the payments of grants conditional upon the making of claims of a description specified in the scheme[9];
(2) make provision with respect to the expenditure qualifying for grant and the rates and amounts of grants[10];
(3) make provision in certain specified circumstances for the repayment of any grant, in whole or in part[11]; and
(4) make different provision for different local authorities or descriptions of authorities and for different areas[12].

1 Local Government and Housing Act 1989 s 155(1)(a).
2 'Local authority' means:
  (1) a county council (Local Government and Housing Act 1989 s 155(4)(a));
  (2) a county borough council (s 155(4)(aa) (added by SI 1996/3071));
  (3) a district council (Local Government and Housing Act 1989 s 155(4)(b));
  (4) the Greater London Authority (Local Government and Housing Act 1989 s 155(4)(bb) (added by the Greater London Authority Act 1999 s 104(1), (3)(a)));
  (5) a London borough council (Local Government and Housing Act 1989 s 155(4)(c));
  (6) the Common Council of the City of London (s 155(4)(d));
  (7) the Council of the Isles of Scilly (s 155(4)(e));
  (8) a police and crime commissioner (see POLICE AND INVESTIGATORY POWERS vol 84 (2013) PARA 56 et seq) (s 155(4)(ea) (added by the Police and Magistrates' Courts Act 1994 s 43, Sch 4 para 42; substituted by the Police Reform and Social Responsibility Act 2011 ss 27(1), (3), 99, Sch 16 paras 199, 206(1), (3)));
  (9) a joint authority established by the Local Government Act 1985 Pt IV (ss 23–42) (see LOCAL GOVERNMENT vol 69 (2018) PARA 71) other than an integrated transport authority (Local Government and Housing Act 1989 s 155(4)(g) (amended by the Local Transport Act 2008 s 77(5), Sch 4 para 57));
  (10) a fire and rescue authority constituted by a scheme under the Fire and Rescue Services Act 2004 s 2 or a scheme to which s 4 applies (see FIRE AND RESCUE SERVICES vol 51 (2013) PARAS 18–20) (Local Government and Housing Act 1989 s 155(4)(h) (added by the Local Government Act 2003 s 37; substituted by the Fire and Rescue Services Act 2004 s 53(1), Sch 1 para 71(1), (5)));
  (11) a fire and rescue authority created by an order under the Fire and Rescue Services Act 2004 s 4A (see FIRE AND RESCUE SERVICES) (Local Government and Housing Act 1989 s 155(4)(ha) (added by the Policing and Crime Act 2017 s 6, Sch 1 paras 60, 66));
  (12) a National Park authority (Local Government and Housing Act 1989 s 155(4)(i) (added by the Natural Environment and Rural Communities Act 2006 s 65(1), (2))); or
  (13) the Broads Authority (Local Government and Housing Act 1989 s 155(4)(j) (added by the Natural Environment and Rural Communities Act 2006 s 65(1), (2))).

As to local government areas and authorities in England and Wales see LOCAL GOVERNMENT vol 69 (2018) PARA 36 et seq. As to the Greater London Authority see LONDON GOVERNMENT vol 71 (2013) PARA 67 et seq. As to the London boroughs and their councils see LONDON GOVERNMENT vol 71 (2013) PARAS 15, 20–22, 55 et seq. As to the Common Council of the City of London see LONDON GOVERNMENT vol 71 (2013) PARAS 34–38. As to the Council of the Isles of Scilly see LOCAL GOVERNMENT vol 69 (2018) PARA 50. As to National Park authorities see OPEN SPACES AND COUNTRYSIDE vol 78 (2010) PARA 526. As to the Broads Authority see WATER AND WATERWAYS vol 101 (2009) PARA 734.

Expenditure incurred as mentioned in the Local Government and Housing Act 1989 s 155(1) by the London Fire and Emergency Planning Authority, the Mayor's Office for Policing and Crime or Transport for London in respect of places or areas within Greater London is to be treated for these purposes as expenditure so incurred by the Greater London Authority (and, accordingly, as so incurred by a local authority): s 155(1A) (s 155(1A), (1B) added by the Greater London Authority Act 1999 s 104(1), (2); the Local Government and Housing Act 1989 s 155(1A) amended by the Police Reform and Social Responsibility Act 2011 s 27(1), (2)). Prospectively, the reference to the London Fire and Emergency Planning Authority is replaced with a reference to the London Fire Commissioner: see the Local Government and Housing Act 1989 s 155(1A)(a) (substituted, as from a day to be appointed, by the Policing and Crime Act 2017 s 9(3)(c), Sch 2 paras 85, 91). At the date at which this volume states the law, no such day had been appointed.

To the extent that any financial assistance given to the Greater London Authority under the Local Government and Housing Act 1989 s 155 is referable to expenditure incurred by a body mentioned in s 155(1A), the financial assistance is to be treated for the purposes of the Greater London Authority Act 1999 s 103 (see LONDON GOVERNMENT vol 71 (2013) PARA 150) as a payment made to the Greater London Authority for the purposes of that body: Local Government and Housing Act 1989 s 155(1B) (as so added). As to the London Fire and Emergency Planning Authority see FIRE AND RESCUE SERVICES vol 51 (2013) PARA 17. As to the Mayor's Office for Policing and Crime see POLICE AND INVESTIGATORY POWERS vol 84 (2013) PARA 78 et seq. As to Transport for London see LONDON GOVERNMENT vol 71 (2013) PARA 163 et seq. As to Greater London see LONDON GOVERNMENT vol 71 (2013) PARA 14.

3 The reference in the Local Government and Housing Act 1989 s 155(1)(b) to expenditure incurred by a local authority includes expenditure incurred in defraying, or contributing towards defraying, expenditure incurred by a parish or community council: s 155(6). As to expenditure in the case of emergencies or disasters see PARA 7. As to parish councils see LOCAL GOVERNMENT vol 69 (2018) PARA 41 et seq. As to community councils see LOCAL GOVERNMENT vol 69 (2018) PARA 63 et seq.

4 Local Government and Housing Act 1989 s 155(1)(b).

5 Ie the Secretary of State or, in relation to Wales, the Welsh Ministers. The functions of the Secretary of State under the Local Government and Housing Act 1989 s 155, so far as exercisable in relation to Wales, were transferred to the National Assembly for Wales (see the National Assembly for Wales (Transfer of Functions) Order 1999, SI 1999/672, art 2, Sch 1) and are now vested in the Welsh Ministers (see the Government of Wales Act 2006 s 162(1), Sch 11 para 30). As to the Secretary of State and the Welsh Ministers see PARA 4 note 18. As to the meaning of 'Wales' see PARA 2 note 16.

6 Local Government and Housing Act 1989 s 155(1).

7 Grants paid by the Secretary of State require the consent of the Treasury: see the Local Government and Housing Act 1989 s 155(2). As to the meaning of 'Treasury' see PARA 30 note 15.

8 Local Government and Housing Act 1989 s 155(2).

9 Local Government and Housing Act 1989 s 155(3)(a).

10 Local Government and Housing Act 1989 s 155(3)(b).

11 Local Government and Housing Act 1989 s 155(3)(c).

12 Local Government and Housing Act 1989 s 155(3)(d).

4. NON-DOMESTIC RATING

(1) Introduction

49. Non-domestic rating and council tax and the funding of local authorities.

For each financial year, major precepting authorities and local precepting authorities issue to billing authorities precepts, which state the amount payable to them by the billing authority on the basis of calculations made by the precepting authority as its budget requirement for the year[1].

The non-domestic rating of hereditaments[2] and council tax[3] are the principal means whereby a billing authority obtains monies from occupiers and owners of properties in its area[4]. Sums collected by a billing authority for council tax and non-domestic rating of hereditaments in the local non-domestic rating list[5] must be paid, in England, into the collection fund of that authority[6] and, in Wales, into the council fund of that authority[7]. Non-domestic rates payable on hereditaments in the central non-domestic rating list[8] are collected by the Secretary of State or, in Wales, by the Welsh Ministers[9]. Non-domestic rates collected by billing authorities are pooled and placed in a non-domestic rating account held by the Secretary of State or the Welsh Ministers, who determine the collection and distribution of such funds in accordance with statutory provisions[10].

1 As to the issuing of precepts see PARA 11 et seq.

2 As to non-domestic rating see PARA 52 et seq.

3 As to council tax see PARA 344 et seq.

4 As to local government finance generally see PARA 1 et seq. The other principal source of income for local authorities (ie apart from non-domestic rating and council tax) is central government grants: see PARA 29 et seq. As to the special financial provisions applicable to the Greater London Authority see LONDON GOVERNMENT vol 71 (2013) PARA 150 et seq.

5 As to the local non-domestic rating lists see PARA 191 et seq.

6 Collection funds are established and maintained by billing authorities in England under the Local Government Finance Act 1988 s 89: see PARA 581.

7 Council funds are established and maintained by billing authorities in Wales under the Local Government (Wales) Act 1994 s 38: see the Local Government Finance Act 1988 s 89A; and PARA 585.

8 As to the central non-domestic rating lists see PARA 196 et seq.

9 As to the Secretary of State and the Welsh Ministers see PARA 51.

10 See PARA 58 et seq.

50. Historical background.

The modern law of rating and council tax is statutory[1] but, with some aspects of rating law having been carried through into the new legislation, much of the case law decided under earlier rating legislation continues to be relevant to its interpretation and to the understanding of underlying principles[2].

Prior to 1990, the principal Act was the General Rate Act 1967, which consolidated earlier legislation from the Poor Relief Act 1601 to the Local Government Act 1966[3]. The 1967 Act imposed liability to rates on occupiers of rateable property and empowered rating authorities to levy rates on unoccupied hereditaments. There was a division of responsibility between rating authorities which set and levied rates, and the valuation officers appointed by the Commissioners for Inland Revenue whose duty it was to prepare and maintain valuation lists for each area.

The General Rate Act 1967 was repealed by the Local Government Finance Act 1988 with effect for financial years beginning on or after 1 April 1990, subject to certain savings[4]. The 1988 Act created a new non-domestic rating system, abolished rating in relation to domestic property[5] and introduced the community charge[6]. The community charge was later abolished and replaced by the council tax with effect from 1 April 1993[7]. The local authorities' role in setting the rate applicable to non-domestic property was abolished and replaced by a uniform business rate set by the Secretary of State or, in relation to Wales, the Welsh Ministers and applicable at the same level throughout the country[8].

1 As to council tax see PARA 344 et seq.

2 See eg *Williams v Scottish & Newcastle Retail Ltd* [2001] EWCA Civ 185 at [16], [2001] RA 41 at [16], sub nom *Scottish & Newcastle Retail Ltd v Williams (Valuation Officer)* [2001] 1 EGLR 157 at [16] per Robert Walker LJ: 'The law of rating is statutory and ancient [. . .] Apart from comparatively recent upheavals (in the form of community charge and council tax) in relation to residential property, the body of statute law has shown extraordinary stability. [. . .] This slow and steady process of evolution means that there is a large volume of case law, some of it quite old, which is still relevant to the understanding of the principles underlying the modern law'.

3 The General Rate Act 1967 assimilated the rating of Greater London to that of the rest of England and Wales, although the rating in the City of London continued as before under the City of London (Union of Parishes) Act 1907. Rating in the City of London has now been generally assimilated to that of the rest of England and Wales by virtue of the inclusion of the Common Council of the City of London as a billing authority (see PARA 53) although the Common Council maintains a separate City fund under the Local Government Finance Act 1988 ss 93, 94 (see PARA 586). The Inner Temple and the Middle Temple are to be taken as falling within the area of the Common Council: see s 146(4), (5). As to the Common Council of the City of London see LONDON GOVERNMENT vol 71 (2013) PARA 34 et seq; and as to the Inner and Middle Temple see LONDON GOVERNMENT vol 71 (2013) PARA 17.

4 As to the repeal of the General Rate Act 1967, which ceased to have general effect any time after 31 March 1990, see the Local Government Finance Act 1988 ss 67(11), 117(1), 149, Sch 13 Pt 1. Notwithstanding this, many of the provisions of the General Rate Act 1967 continued to have effect, subject to amendments, for a number of purposes including those relating to the following (see the Local Government Finance (Repeals, Savings and Consequential Amendments) Order 1990, SI 1990/776; and the General Rate Act and Related Provisions (Savings and Consequential Provision) Regulations 1990, SI 1990/777):

(1) any rate made under the 1967 Act in respect of any period ending before 1 April 1990;
(2) any liability for rates in respect of such a period; and
(3) the alteration of any valuation list in force prior to 1 April 1990 pursuant to a proposal made before that date but to which effect had not been given immediately before that date.

The most notable survival of the General Rate Act 1967 is the definition of 'hereditament' in s 115(1) (repealed), which is invoked for the purposes of the Local Government Finance Act 1988 s 64(1): see PARA 106.

5 As to the meaning of 'domestic property' see PARA 190.

6 As to the community charge see PARA 344. The Local Government Finance Act 1988 long title states (in part) that it is '[a]n Act to create community charges in favour of certain authorities, to create new rating systems, [. . .] to abolish existing rates [. . .] and to provide for the establishment of valuation and community charge tribunals, and for connected purposes'.

7 See the Local Government Finance Act 1992 s 100; and PARA 344.

8 As to the Secretary of State and the transfer of statutory powers to the Welsh Ministers see PARA 51. As to the calculation of the non-domestic rate see PARA 84.

(2) Administration and Disclosure of Information

(i) Administration

51. The Secretary of State and Welsh Ministers.

Despite the fact that older statutes refer to ministers, to specific ministers or to government departments, in law the office of Secretary of State is one and accordingly many modern statutes refer simply to the 'Secretary of State' without reference to a particular department or ministry[1]. The rating legislation confers the functions of central government in relation to the administration of the non-domestic rating system upon the 'Secretary of State' without reference to a particular department or ministry, but in practice the Secretary of State for Housing, Communities and Local Government has responsibility for rating[2]. Many statutory functions vested in a Secretary of State or a Minister of the Crown are transferred so as to be exercisable in relation to Wales[3] by the Welsh Ministers[4].

Central government control is far greater under the current provisions than under previous rating legislation[5] and the Secretary of State and the Welsh Ministers have wide powers (which have been extensively exercised) to make orders and regulations under the rating legislation, as a consequence of which the current state of the law has to be ascertained by reference to numerous statutory instruments, as well as to the Acts of Parliament themselves[6]. The power to make an order or regulations under the Local Government Finance Act 1988[7] may be exercised differently in relation to different areas or in relation to different cases or descriptions of case[8]. The appropriate national authority[9] may at any time by order make such supplementary, incidental, consequential or transitional provision as appears to it to be necessary or expedient for the general purposes or any particular purpose of the Local Government Finance Act 1988, or in consequence of any of its provisions or for giving full effect to it[10]. The appropriate national authority may also make regulations saving powers for issuing precepts and making levies under earlier legislation which has now been repealed[11], may provide for the abolition or modification of powers to levy rates[12], and may make regulations in relation to payments to and from authorities[13].

In circumstances where:

(1) the appropriate national authority serves a notice on a relevant authority[14] or relevant officer[15] requiring it or him to supply to the appropriate national authority information specified in the notice[16];

(2) the information is required by the appropriate national authority for the purpose of deciding whether to exercise its powers (and how to perform its functions) under the Local Government Finance Act 1988[17]; and

(3) the information is not personal information[18],

the authority or officer must supply the information required, and must do so in such form and manner and at such time as the appropriate national authority specifies in the notice[19]. In deciding whether to exercise its powers, and how to perform its functions, under the Local Government Finance Act 1988 the appropriate national authority may also take into account any other information available to it, whatever its source and whether or not obtained under a provision contained in or made under that Act or any other Act[20].

1 As to the Secretary of State see PARA 4 note 18.

2 As to the Secretary of State in relation to council tax see PARA 345.

3 As to the meaning of 'Wales' see PARA 2 note 16.

4 As to the Welsh Ministers and the general legislative competence of the Welsh Assembly see PARA 4 note 18. Where functions are transferred this is referred to in the paragraphs concerned.

5 Ie under the General Rate Act 1967 (repealed) and earlier enactments.

6 Where subordinate legislation has been made under the main primary legislation, a reference will be given but the detail of current rating law residing in secondary legislation, much of which is technical, is set out in this title only where it furthers the exposition of a principle of law.

7 As to orders, rules and regulations under the Local Government Finance Act 1992 see PARA 345.

8 Local Government Finance Act 1988 s 143(1). An order or regulations under the Local Government Finance Act 1988 may include such supplementary, incidental, consequential or transitional provisions as appear to the Secretary of State, the Minister of Agriculture, Fisheries and Food the Treasury or the Welsh Ministers (as the case may be) to be necessary or expedient: see s 143(2) (amended by the Local Government and Housing Act 1989 s 139, Sch 5 paras 72, 79(3)). The functions of the former Minister of Agriculture, Fisheries and Food are now exercised by the Secretary of State for Environment, Food and Rural Affairs: see the Ministry of Agriculture, Fisheries and Food (Dissolution) Order 2002, SI 2002/794.

9 Ie the Secretary of State or, in relation to Wales, the Welsh Ministers. The functions of the Secretary of State under the Local Government Finance Act 1988 s 117 (see the text to note 11), s 118 (see the text to note 12), s 139A (see the text to notes 14–20), s 141 (see the text to note 13) and s 147, so far as exercisable in relation to Wales, were transferred to the National Assembly for Wales (see the National Assembly for Wales (Transfer of Functions) Order 1999, SI 1999/672, art 2, Sch 1) and are now vested in the Welsh Ministers (see the Government of Wales Act 2006 s 162(1), Sch 11 para 30).

10 Local Government Finance Act 1988 s 147(1). Such orders may in particular make provision for amending, repealing or revoking (with or without savings) any provision of an Act passed before or in the same session as the Local Government Finance Act 1988, or of an instrument made under an Act before the passing of the 1988 Act, and for making savings or additional savings from the effect of any amendment or repeal made by the 1988 Act: s 147(2). Any provision that may be made under this power is to be in addition and without prejudice to any other provision of the Local Government Finance Act 1988: s 147(3). No other provision of the Local Government Finance Act 1988 is to be construed as prejudicing the generality of the powers conferred by s 147: s 147(4). For these purposes, 'Act' includes a private or local Act: see s 147(5). As to the orders so made see the Local Government Finance Act 1988 (Miscellaneous Amendments and Repeals) Order 1990, SI 1990/10; the Local Government Finance (Garden Squares) (Consequential Amendments) Order 1990, SI 1990/525 (amended by SI 1993/616); the Local Government Finance (Repeals, Savings and Consequential Amendments) Order 1990, SI 1990/776; the Local Government Finance (Consequential Amendments) (Debt Administration) Order 1990, SI 1990/1114; the Local Government Finance (Miscellaneous Amendments and Repeal) Order 1990, SI 1990/1285; the Rates and Precepts (Final Adjustments) Order 1991, SI 1991/185 (amended in relation to England by SI 1999/2629; and in relation to Wales by SI 2000/975); the Local Government Finance (Miscellaneous Provisions) (England) Order 1991, SI 1991/241; the Local Government Finance (Repeals and Consequential Amendments) Order 1991, SI 1991/1730; the Rates and Precepts (Final Adjustments) (Amendment) (England) Order 1999, SI 1999/2629; the Rates and Precepts (Final Adjustments) (Amendment) (Wales) Order 2000, SI 2000/975; and the Control of Fuel and Electricity, Local Government and Transport (Revocations and Savings) Order 2013, SI 2013/2986. As to local Acts see STATUTES AND LEGISLATIVE PROCESS vol 96 (2012) PARA 626. As to private Acts see STATUTES AND LEGISLATIVE PROCESS vol 96 (2012) PARA 624.

11 See the Local Government Finance Act 1988 s 117(8).

12 See the Local Government Finance Act 1988 s 118; and PARA 24.

13 See the Local Government Finance Act 1988 s 141; and PARA 27.

14 For these purposes, each of the following is a relevant authority, namely: a billing authority, a precepting authority, or a functional body within the meaning of the Greater London Authority Act 1999 (see LONDON GOVERNMENT vol 71 (2013) PARA 148): Local Government Finance Act 1988 s 139A(5) (s 139A added by the Local Government and Housing Act 1989 s 139, Sch 5 para 68; the Local Government Finance Act 1988 s 139A(5) amended by the Local Government Finance Act 1992 s 117(1), Sch 13 para 77(1); and the Greater London Authority Act 1999 s 109(2)). As to the meaning of 'billing authority' see PARA 53; and as to the meaning of 'precepting authority' see PARA 23 note 1 (definitions applied by the Local Government Finance Act 1988 s 144(2) (substituted by the Local Government Finance Act 1992 s 117(1), Sch 13 para 81(1); and amended by the Local Government Finance Act 2012 s 5(1), (2)(b), Sch 3 paras 23, 29)).

15 Ie a proper officer within the meaning of the Local Government Act 1972 (see LOCAL GOVERNMENT vol 69 (2018) PARA 477) of a relevant authority: see the Local Government Finance Act 1988 s 139A(6) (s 139A as added (see note 14); s 139A(6) substituted by the Local Government Finance Act 1992 Sch 13 para 77(2)).
16 Local Government Finance Act 1988 s 139A(1)(a) (as added: see note 14).
17 Local Government Finance Act 1988 s 139A(1)(b) (as added: see note 14).
18 Local Government Finance Act 1988 s 139A(1)(c) (as added: see note 14). 'Personal information' is information which relates to an individual (living or dead) who can be identified from that information or from that and other information supplied to any person by the authority or officer concerned; and personal information includes any expression of opinion about the individual and any indication of the intentions of any person in respect of the individual: see s 139A(7) (as so added). As to the meaning of 'person' see PARA 11 note 13.
19 Local Government Finance Act 1988 s 139A(2) (as added: see note 14). If an authority or officer fails to comply with s 139A(2), the appropriate national authority may assume the information required to be such as it sees fit; and in such a case the appropriate national authority may decide in accordance with the assumption whether to exercise its powers, and how to perform its functions, under the Local Government Finance Act 1988: s 139A(3) (as so added).
20 Local Government Finance Act 1988 s 139A(4) (as added: see note 14).

52. Separate administration in England and Wales.

The rating legislation extends to England and Wales[1].

The provisions of the Local Government Finance Act 1988 relating to non-domestic rating[2] must be read as applying separately, and must be administered separately, in England and Wales[3]. In particular, separate central non-domestic rating lists must be compiled and maintained separately for England and Wales[4] and separate estimates must be made[5] for the purpose of determining non-domestic rating multipliers[6].

1 See the Local Government Finance Act 1988 s 151; and the Local Government and Housing Act 1989 s 195(4)–(6). The Local Government and Housing Act 1989 applies to the Isles of Scilly subject to such exceptions, adaptations and modifications as the Secretary of State may direct: s 193(1). At the date at which this volume states the law no such order had been made. As to the Secretary of State see PARA 4 note 18. As to the meanings of 'England' and 'Wales' see PARA 2 note 16. As to the Council of the Isles of Scilly see LOCAL GOVERNMENT vol 69 (2018) PARA 50.
2 Ie the Local Government Finance Act 1988 Pt III (ss 41–67) and Schs 4A–9.
3 See the Local Government Finance Act 1988 s 140(1) (s 140(1), (3) amended by the Local Government Finance Act 1992 s 117(1), Sch 13 para 78). The Local Government Finance Act 1988 Pt III must be construed so that references to authorities are read as references to those in England or Wales, as the case may be: s 140(3) (as so amended).
4 Local Government Finance Act 1988 s 140(2)(a). As to local non-domestic rating lists see PARA 191 et seq.
5 Ie under the Local Government Finance Act 1988 Sch 7 para 5(6), (7): see PARA 156.
6 Local Government Finance Act 1988 s 140(2)(b).

53. Billing authorities.

In relation to England[1], a district council[2] or London borough council[3], the Common Council of the City of London[4] or the Council of the Isles of Scilly[5] and, in relation to Wales[6], a county council or county borough council[7] are 'billing authorities'[8] charged with the collection and recovery[9] of non-domestic rates[10] for each chargeable financial year[11].

Where there is a reorganisation of local government areas provision is made as to the exercise of functions in relation to the non-domestic rating[12].

1 As to the meaning of 'England' see PARA 2 note 16.
2 As to local government areas and authorities in England see LOCAL GOVERNMENT vol 69 (2018) PARA 36 et seq.
3 As to the London boroughs and their councils see LONDON GOVERNMENT vol 71 (2013) PARAS 15, 20–22, 55 et seq.

4 The Inner Temple and the Middle Temple are to be taken to fall within the area of the Common Council: Local Government Finance Act 1992 s 69(3) (applied by the Local Government Finance Act 1988 s 144(2) (substituted by the Local Government Finance Act 1992 s 117(1), Sch 13 para 81(1); and amended by the Local Government Finance Act 2012 s 5(1), (2)(b), Sch 3 paras 23, 29)). As to the Common Council of the City of London see LONDON GOVERNMENT vol 71 (2013) PARAS 34–38. As to the Temples see LONDON GOVERNMENT vol 71 (2013) PARA 17.

5 Local Government Finance Act 1992 s 1(2)(a) (s 1(2) substituted by the Local Government (Wales) Act 1994 s 35(5); and applied by the Local Government Finance Act 1988 s 144(2) (as substituted and amended: see note 4)). As to the Council of the Isles of Scilly see LOCAL GOVERNMENT vol 69 (2018) PARA 50.

6 As to the meaning of 'Wales' see PARA 2 note 16.

7 Local Government Finance Act 1992 s 1(2)(b) (as substituted and applied: see note 5). As to local government areas and authorities in Wales see LOCAL GOVERNMENT vol 69 (2018) PARA 51 et seq.

8 Local Government Finance Act 1992 s 1(2) (as substituted and applied: see note 5). The functions of a billing authority in relation to the administration and enforcement of non-domestic rates may, to the prescribed extent, be exercised by, or by the employees of, such person as may be authorised to exercise them by the authority whose functions they are: see the Local Authorities (Contracting Out of Tax Billing, Collection and Enforcement Functions) Order 1996, SI 1996/1880, art 49. As to the meaning of 'person' see PARA 11 note 13.

9 As to the recovery of rates and demand notices see PARA 272 et seq.

10 As to non-domestic rating see PARA 80 et seq.

11 As to the meaning of 'chargeable financial year' see PARA 24 note 1.

12 See the Local Government (Structural Changes) (Finance) Regulations 2008, SI 2008/3022, regs 8–11. These regulations are made under the Local Government and Public Involvement in Health Act 2007 s 14: see LOCAL GOVERNMENT vol 69 (2018) PARA 102. As to local government structural and boundary change see LOCAL GOVERNMENT vol 69 (2018) PARA 95 et seq.

54. Appointment and functions of valuation officers.

The Commissioners for Her Majesty's Revenue and Customs[1] must appoint a valuation officer for each billing authority[2] and a central valuation officer[3]. A valuation officer for a billing authority must compile and maintain local non-domestic rating lists[4], and the central valuation officer must compile and maintain the central non-domestic rating lists[5].

Valuation officers may disclose information to each other to assist in the performance of their statutory functions. Hence, where a rating official[6] requests another rating official to disclose any information to him in order to assist him in the performance of his statutory functions[7], the other official must not be prevented from so disclosing the information merely because it is held by him in connection with his statutory functions[8].

Valuation officers may request information from owners or occupiers of hereditaments if the officers believe it will assist them in carrying out their functions[9]. They may also enter on, survey and value a hereditament on giving at least 24 hours' notice of the proposed entry[10]. A person may require a valuation officer to provide access to specified information upon request[11].

1 Local Government Finance Act 1988 s 61(1) (amended by virtue of the Commissioners for Revenue and Customs Act 2005 s 50). As to the Commissioners for Her Majesty's Revenue and Customs see INCOME TAXATION vol 58 (2014) PARAS 33–34.

2 Local Government Finance Act 1988 s 61(1)(a) (amended by the Local Government Finance Act 1992 s 117(1), Sch 13 para 69). As to the meaning of 'billing authority' see PARA 53.

3 Local Government Finance Act 1988 s 61(1)(b). Unless the context otherwise requires, references to 'valuation officers' in the Local Government Finance Act 1988 Pt III (ss 41–67) are to valuation officers for billing authorities and the central valuation officer: s 67(2), (13) (s 67(2) amended by the Local Government Finance Act 1992 Sch 13 para 71). The remuneration of, and any expenses incurred by, valuation officers in carrying out their functions under the Local Government Finance

Act 1988 Pt III, including the remuneration and expenses of persons, whether or not in the service of the Crown, employed to assist them, are to be paid out of money provided by Parliament: s 61(2).

The position of the valuation officer in rating is that 'he is a neutral official charged with the statutory and recurring duty of bringing into existence a valuation list and maintaining its contents in correct and legal form': *Society of Medical Officers of Health v Hope (Valuation Officer)* [1960] AC 551 at 565, [1960] 1 All ER 317 at 322, HL, per Lord Radcliffe. See also *R v Paddington Valuation Officer, ex p Peachey Property Corpn Ltd* [1964] 3 All ER 200, [1964] 1 WLR 1186, DC; affd [1966] 1 QB 380, [1965] 2 All ER 836, CA.

4 See the Local Government Finance Act 1988 s 41; and PARA 191 et seq.

5 See the Local Government Finance Act 1988 s 52; and PARA 196 et seq.

6 'Rating official' means a valuation officer; and 'valuation officer' means a person appointed under the Local Government Finance Act 1988 s 61(1)(a) or s 61(1)(b) (see the text to notes 1–3): Non-Domestic Rating (Information) Act 1996 s 1(2).

7 'Statutory functions' means, in relation to a valuation officer, functions under the Local Government Finance Act 1988 Pt III (ss 41–67) or the function under the Business Rate Supplements Act 2009 s 12(4) (see PARA 332): Non-Domestic Rating (Information) Act 1996 s 1(2) (definition amended by the Business Rate Supplements Act 2009 s 12(10)).

8 Non-Domestic Rating (Information) Act 1996 s 1(1).

9 See the Local Government Finance Act 1988 Sch 9 paras 5, 5A–5H, 6, 6A; and PARAS 226–227.

10 See the Local Government Finance Act 1988 Sch 9 para 7; and PARA 228.

11 See the Local Government Finance Act 1988 Sch 9 paras 8, 9; and PARAS 229–230.

(ii) Disclosure of Revenue and Customs Information

55. Disclosure of HMRC information in connection with non-domestic rating.

An officer of the Valuation Office of Her Majesty's Revenue and Customs[1] may disclose Revenue and Customs information[2] to a qualifying person[3] for a qualifying purpose[4]. Information disclosed to a qualifying person may be retained and used for any qualifying purpose[5].

1 As to the Commissioners for Her Majesty's Revenue and Customs see INCOME TAXATION vol 58 (2014) PARAS 33–34.

2 'Revenue and Customs information' means information held as mentioned in the Commissioners for Revenue and Customs Act 2005 s 18(1) (see INCOME TAXATION vol 59 (2014) PARA 2325): Local Government Finance Act 1988 s 63A(5) (s 63A added by the Enterprise Act 2016 s 31(1), (2)).

3 Each of the following is a 'qualifying person' (Local Government Finance Act 1988 s 63A(3) (as added: see note 2).

(1) a billing authority (s 63A(3)(a) (as so added));
(2) a major precepting authority (s 63A(3)(b) (as so added));
(3) a person authorised to exercise any function of an authority within head (1) or (2) relating to non-domestic rating (s 63A(3)(c) (as so added));
(4) a person providing services to an authority within head (1) or (2) relating to non-domestic rating (s 63A(3)(d) (as so added));
(5) the Secretary of State (s 63A(3)(e) (as so added));
(6) the Welsh Ministers (s 63A(3)(f) (as so added));
(7) a prescribed person (s 63A(3)(g) (as so added)).

'Prescribed' means, in relation to England, prescribed by regulations made by the Secretary of State; and, in relation to Wales, prescribed by regulations made by the Welsh Ministers: s 63A(5) (as so added). Regulations under s 63A may only be made with the consent of the Commissioners for Her Majesty's Revenue and Customs: s 63A(6) (as so added).

As to the meaning of 'billing authority' see PARA 53. As to the meaning of 'major precepting authority' see PARA 11 note 2 (definition applied by s 144(2) (substituted by the Local Government Finance Act 1992 s 117(1), Sch 13 para 81(1); and amended by the Local Government Finance Act 2012 s 5(1), (2)(b), Sch 3 paras 23, 29)). As to the Secretary of State and the Welsh Ministers see PARA 51.

4 Local Government Finance Act 1988 s 63A(1) (as added: see note 2). Each of the following is a 'qualifying purpose' (s 63A(4) (as so added):
(1) enabling or assisting the qualifying person to whom the disclosure is made, or any other qualifying person, to carry out any functions conferred by or under Pt III (ss 41–67) which are not functions of the Secretary of State or the Welsh Ministers (s 63A(4)(a) (as so added));
(2) enabling or assisting the Secretary of State or the Welsh Ministers to carry out functions conferred by or under s 53, s 54 or s 54ZA (central non-domestic rating: see PARAS 142, 197), or by or under Sch 9 (see PARA 226 et seq) so far as relating to central non-domestic rating lists (s 63A(4)(b) (as so added; amended by the Telecommunications Infrastructure (Relief from Non-Domestic Rates) Act 2018 Schedule para 5);
(3) any other prescribed purpose relating to non-domestic rating (s 63A(4)(c) (as so added)).
As to restrictions on onward disclosure see PARA 56.
5 Local Government Finance Act 1988 s 63A(2) (as added: see note 2).

56. Restrictions on onward disclosure of HMRC information.

Information disclosed by an officer of the Valuation Office of Her Majesty's Revenue and Customs in connection with non-domestic rating[1] may not be further disclosed unless that further disclosure is:
(1) to a qualifying person[2] for a qualifying purpose[3];
(2) for the purposes of the initiation or conduct of any proceedings relating to the enforcement of any obligation imposed by or under Part III[4] of the Local Government Finance Act 1988[5];
(3) in pursuance of a court order[6];
(4) with the consent of each person to whom the information relates[7]; or
(5) required or permitted under any other enactment[8].

Information disclosed to a qualifying person under these provisions may be retained and used for any qualifying purpose[9].

A person commits an offence if the person contravenes the prohibition on further disclosure[10] by disclosing information relating to a person whose identity:
(a) is specified in the disclosure; or
(b) can be deduced from it[11].

It is a defence for a person charged with such an offence of disclosing information to prove that the person reasonably believed:
(i) that the disclosure was lawful; or
(ii) that the information had already lawfully been made available to the public[12].

A prosecution for an offence under these provisions may be instituted only by or with the consent of the Director of Public Prosecutions[13].

These provisions are without prejudice to the pursuit of any remedy or the taking of any action in relation to a contravention of the prohibition[14] on further disclosure of information[15].

1 Ie under the Local Government Finance Act 1988 s 63A (see PARA 55) or s 63B. As to the Commissioners for Her Majesty's Revenue and Customs see INCOME TAXATION vol 58 (2014) PARAS 33–34.
2 As to the meaning of 'qualifying person' see PARA 55 note 3; definition applied by the Local Government Finance Act 1988 s 63B(10) (s 63B added by the Enterprise Act 2016 s 31(1), (2)).
3 Local Government Finance Act 1988 s 63B(1)(a) (as added: see note 2). As to the meaning of 'qualifying purpose' see PARA 55 note 4; definition applied by s 63B(10) (as so added). Information may not be disclosed under s 63B(1)(a) to a qualifying person within s 63A(3)(c), (d), (e), (f) or (g) (see PARA 55 note 3 heads (3)–(7)) except with the consent of the Commissioners for Her Majesty's Revenue and Customs (which may be general or specific): 63B(2) (as so added).
4 Ie the Local Government Finance Act 1988 Pt III (ss 41–67).
5 Local Government Finance Act 1988 s 63B(1)(b) (as added: see note 2).

6 Local Government Finance Act 1988 s 63B(1)(c) (as added: see note 2).
7 Local Government Finance Act 1988 s 63B(1)(d) (as added: see note 2). As to the meaning of 'person' see PARA 11 note 13.
8 Local Government Finance Act 1988 s 63B(1)(e) (as added: see note 2).
9 Local Government Finance Act 1988 s 63B(3) (as added: see note 2).
10 Ie the Local Government Finance Act 1988 s 63B(1) or (2).
11 Local Government Finance Act 1988 s 63B(4) (as added: see note 2). A person guilty of an offence under s 63B is liable, on summary conviction, to imprisonment for a term not exceeding 12 months or to a fine, or to both; or, on conviction on indictment, to imprisonment for a term not exceeding two years or to a fine, or to both: s 63B(6) (as so added). In relation to an offence under s 63B committed before the commencement of the Criminal Justice Act 2003 s 154(1) (increase in maximum term that may be imposed on summary conviction of offence triable either way) the reference in the Local Government Finance Act 1988 s 63B(6)(a) to 12 months is to be taken as a reference to six months: s 63B(8) (as so added). As to the powers of magistrates' courts to issue fines on summary conviction see SENTENCING vol 92 (2015) PARA 176.
12 Local Government Finance Act 1988 s 63B(5) (as added: see note 2).
13 Local Government Finance Act 1988 s 63B(7) (as added: see note 2).
14 Ie under the Local Government Finance Act 1988 s 63B(1) or (2) (whether or not s 63B(4) (see the text to notes 10–11) applies to the contravention).
15 Local Government Finance Act 1988 s 63B(9) (as added: see note 2).

57. Freedom of information.

Revenue and Customs information relating to a person[1] which has been disclosed[2] in connection with non-domestic rating is exempt information[3] for the purposes of the Freedom of Information Act 2000 if its further disclosure:

(1) would specify the identity of the person to whom the information relates[4]; or
(2) would enable the identity of such a person to be deduced[5].

1 In the Local Government Finance Act 1988 s 63C, 'revenue and customs information relating to a person' has the same meaning as in the Commissioners for Revenue and Customs Act 2005 s 19(2) (see INCOME TAXATION vol 59 (2014) PARA 2325): Local Government Finance Act 1988 s 63C(2) (s 63C added by the Enterprise Act 2016 s 31(1), (2)). As to the meaning of 'person' see PARA 11 note 13.
2 Ie under the Local Government Finance Act 1988 s 63A (see PARA 55) or s 63B (see PARA 56).
3 Ie by virtue of the Freedom of Information Act 2000 s 44(1)(a) (prohibition on disclosure: see CONSTITUTIONAL AND ADMINISTRATIVE LAW vol 20 (2014) PARA 457).
4 Local Government Finance Act 1988 s 63C(1)(a) (as added: see note 1).
5 Local Government Finance Act 1988 s 63C(1)(b) (as added: see note 1).

(3) Local Retention of Non-domestic Rates

(i) In England

58. Non-domestic rating accounts.

In relation to England, the Secretary of State[1] must, for each year, keep an account, to be called a 'main non-domestic rating account'[2], and each such account must be kept in accordance with the statutory provisions[3] that apply to a main non-domestic rating account[4]. The Secretary of State must keep each such account in such form as the Treasury may direct and must, at such time as the Treasury may direct, send copies of each such account to the Comptroller and Auditor General[5]. The Comptroller and Auditor General must examine, certify and report on any account of which copies are so sent to the Comptroller and Auditor General and must arrange for copies of the account and of the

Comptroller and Auditor General's report on it to be laid before each House of Parliament[6].

For each year the following are to be credited (as items of account) to the main non-domestic rating account kept for the year[7]:

(1) amounts received by the Secretary of State in the year[8] in respect of central non-domestic rating liability[9];

(2) amounts received by the Secretary of State in the year[10] in respect of contributions in aid relating to property occupied for the purposes of visiting forces or headquarters[11];

(3) amounts received by the Secretary of State in the year under regulations relating to the treatment of a surplus or deficit in a collection fund[12] that make provision in relation to non-domestic rates[13];

(4) amounts received by the Secretary of State in the year in respect of payments of the central share[14] and amounts received by the Secretary of State in the year under regulations[15] relating to administrative arrangements for such payments[16];

(5) amounts received by the Secretary of State in the year[17] in respect of payments following a local government finance report[18];

(6) amounts received by the Secretary of State in the year[19] in respect of payments following an amending report[20];

(7) amounts received by the Secretary of State in the year under regulations[21] relating to transitional protection payments[22]; and

(8) amounts received by the Secretary of State in the year under regulations[23] relating to payments following estimates of amounts to be disregarded[24].

For each year the following are to be debited (as items of account) to the main non-domestic rating account kept for the year[25]:

(a) payments made by the Secretary of State in the year under regulations[26] that make provision in relation to non-domestic rates[27];

(b) payments made by the Secretary of State in the year under regulations[28] relating to administrative arrangements for payments of the central share[29];

(c) payments made by the Secretary of State in the year[30] in respect of payments following a local government finance report[31];

(d) payments made by the Secretary of State in the year[32] in respect of payments following an amending report[33];

(e) payments made by the Secretary of State in the year under regulations[34] relating to transitional protection payments[35]; and

(f) payments made by the Secretary of State in the year under regulations[36] relating to payments following estimates of amounts to be disregarded[37].

If a local government finance report for a year has been approved by resolution of the House of Commons, an amount may be debited (as an item of account) to the main non-domestic rating account kept for the year, for use for the purposes of local government in England[38].

As soon as is reasonably practicable after the end of each year, the Secretary of State must calculate:

(i) the aggregate of the items of account credited to the main non-domestic rating account kept for the year and;

(ii) the aggregate of the items of account debited to the main non-domestic rating account kept for the year[39].

If the aggregate mentioned in head (i) above exceeds that mentioned in head (ii), an amount equal to the excess must be debited (as an item of account) to the main non-domestic rating account kept for the year and credited (as an item of account) to the main non-domestic rating account kept for the next year[40].

If the aggregate mentioned in head (ii) exceeds that mentioned in head (i), an amount equal to the excess must be credited (as an item of account) to the main non-domestic rating account kept for the year and debited (as an item of account) to the main non-domestic rating account kept for the next year[41].

1 As to the Secretary of State see PARA 51.
2 Local Government Finance Act 1988 Sch 7B paras 1(1), 45 (Sch 7B added by the Local Government Finance Act 2012 s 1(1), (4), Sch 1). 'Year' means a chargeable financial year: Local Government Finance Act 1988 Sch 7B para 45 (as so added). As to the meaning of 'chargeable financial year' see PARA 24 note 1.
3 Ie the provisions of the Local Government Finance Act 1988 Sch 7B.
4 Local Government Finance Act 1988 Sch 7B para 1(2) (as added: see note 2).
5 Local Government Finance Act 1988 Sch 7B para 1(3) (as added: see note 2). As to the Treasury see CONSTITUTIONAL AND ADMINISTRATIVE LAW vol 20 (2014) PARA 262 et seq. As to the Comptroller and Auditor General see CONSTITUTIONAL AND ADMINISTRATIVE LAW vol 20 (2014) PARA 494 et seq.
6 Local Government Finance Act 1988 Sch 7B para 1(4) (as added: see note 2).
7 Local Government Finance Act 1988 Sch 7B para 2(1) (as added: see note 2).
8 Ie under the Local Government Finance Act 1988 s 54: see PARA 142.
9 Local Government Finance Act 1988 Sch 7B para 2(1)(a) (as added: see note 2).
10 Ie under the Local Government Finance Act 1988 s 59: see PARA 113.
11 Local Government Finance Act 1988 Sch 7B para 2(1)(b) (as added: see note 2).
12 Ie under regulations made under the Local Government Finance Act 1988 s 99(3): see PARA 583.
13 Local Government Finance Act 1988 Sch 7B para 2(1)(c) (as added: see note 2).
14 Ie under the Local Government Finance Act 1988 Sch 7B para 6: see PARA 60. In Sch 7B, 'the central share' has the meaning given by Sch 7B para 4 (see PARA 59): Sch 7B para 45 (as so added).
15 Ie under the Local Government Finance Act 1988 Sch 7B para 7: see PARA 60.
16 Local Government Finance Act 1988 Sch 7B para 2(1)(d) (as added: see note 2).
17 Ie under the Local Government Finance Act 1988 Sch 7B para 14: see PARA 62.
18 Local Government Finance Act 1988 Sch 7B para 2(1)(e) (as added: see note 2). As to the meaning of 'local government finance report' see PARA 59.
19 Ie under the Local Government Finance Act 1988 Sch 7B para 17: see PARA 63.
20 Local Government Finance Act 1988 Sch 7B para 2(1)(f) (as added: see note 2).
21 Ie under the Local Government Finance Act 1988 Sch 7B para 33: see PARA 68.
22 Local Government Finance Act 1988 Sch 7B para 2(1)(g) (as added: see note 2).
23 Ie under the Local Government Finance Act 1988 Sch 7B para 42: see PARA 72.
24 Local Government Finance Act 1988 Sch 7B para 2(1)(h) (as added: see note 2).
25 Local Government Finance Act 1988 Sch 7B para 2(2) (as added: see note 2).
26 Ie under regulations made under the Local Government Finance Act 1988 s 99(3): see PARA 583.
27 Local Government Finance Act 1988 Sch 7B para 2(2)(a) (as added: see note 2).
28 Ie under the Local Government Finance Act 1988 Sch 7B para 7: see PARA 60.
29 Local Government Finance Act 1988 Sch 7B para 2(2)(b) (as added: see note 2).
30 Ie under the Local Government Finance Act 1988 Sch 7B para 14: see PARA 62.
31 Local Government Finance Act 1988 Sch 7B para 2(2)(c) (as added: see note 2).
32 Ie under the Local Government Finance Act 1988 Sch 7B para 17: see PARA 63.
33 Local Government Finance Act 1988 Sch 7B para 2(2)(d) (as added: see note 2).
34 Ie under the Local Government Finance Act 1988 Sch 7B para 33: see PARA 68.
35 Local Government Finance Act 1988 Sch 7B para 2(2)(e) (as added: see note 2).
36 Ie under the Local Government Finance Act 1988 Sch 7B para 42: see PARA 72.
37 Local Government Finance Act 1988 Sch 7B para 2(2)(f) (as added: see note 2).
38 Local Government Finance Act 1988 Sch 7B para 2(3) (as added: see note 2). The amount that may be debited under Sch 7B para 2(3) for a year may not exceed the total amount credited for the year under heads (1), (2), (3), (4) and (8) in the text, minus the total amount debited for the year under heads (a), (b) and (f) in the text: Sch 7B para 2(4) (as so added).

The reference in the text to use for the purposes of local government in England includes the making of payments under an Act or an instrument made under an Act (whenever passed or made) to billing authorities in England, precepting authorities in England,levying bodies in England (and for this purpose 'levying body' has the meaning given by s 74(1)) or bodies to which s 75(1) applies: Sch 7B para 2(5) (as so added). As to the meaning of 'billing authority' see PARA 346.

39 Local Government Finance Act 1988 Sch 7B para 3(1) (as added: see note 2).

40 Local Government Finance Act 1988 Sch 7B para 3(2) (as added: see note 2).

41 Local Government Finance Act 1988 Sch 7B para 3(3) (as added: see note 2).

59. Determination of the central and local share.

The Secretary of State[1] must, for each year and in relation to each billing authority[2] in England, determine:

(1) the percentage ('the central share') that is to be the billing authority's central share for the year for the purposes of Part III[3] of the Local Government Finance Act 1988[4]; and

(2) the percentage ('the local share') that is to be the billing authority's local share for the year for the purposes of Part IV[5] of that Act[6].

Such a determination must be specified in a report, to be called a 'local government finance report'[7]. The Secretary of State must lay, or make arrangements for laying, the local government finance report before the House of Commons[8]. As soon as is reasonably practicable after a local government finance report is laid before the House of Commons, the Secretary of State must send a copy of the report to each relevant authority[9].

1 As to the Secretary of State see PARA 51.

2 As to the meaning of 'year' see PARA 58 note 2. As to the meaning of 'billing authority' see PARA 346.

3 Ie the Local Government Finance Act 1988 Pt III (ss 41–67) (payments to the Secretary of State in respect of the central share): see PARA 191 et seq.

4 Local Government Finance Act 1988 Sch 7B para 4(a) (Sch 7B added by the Local Government Finance Act 2012 s 1(1), (4), Sch 1).

5 Ie the Local Government Finance Act 1988 Pt IV (ss 74–75A) (payments by billing authorities to major precepting authorities): see PARA 24.

6 Local Government Finance Act 1988 Sch 7B para 4(b) (as added: see note 4).

7 Local Government Finance Act 1988 Sch 7B para 5(1) (as added: see note 4). In Sch 7B, 'local government finance report' has the meaning given by Sch 7B para 5(1): Sch 7B para 45 (as so added).

8 Local Government Finance Act 1988 Sch 7B para 5(2) (as added: see note 4).

9 Local Government Finance Act 1988 Sch 7B para 5(3) (as added: see note 4). 'Relevant authority' means a billing authority in England or a major precepting authority in England: Sch 7B para 45 (as so added). As to the meaning of 'major precepting authority' see PARA 11 note 2 (definition applied by s 144(2) (substituted by the Local Government Finance Act 1992 s 117(1), Sch 13 para 81(1); and amended by the Local Government Finance Act 2012 s 5(1), (2)(b), Sch 3 paras 23, 29)).

60. Payments in respect of the central share.

The following provisions apply if a local government finance report for a year[1] is approved by resolution of the House of Commons[2]. Each billing authority[3] in England must make a payment for the year to the Secretary of State[4] of an amount equal to the central share of the billing authority's non-domestic rating income[5] for the year[6]. This is subject to regulations[7] about deductions from central share payments[8].

The Secretary of State may by regulations make provision about the administration of such payments[9]. The regulations may, in particular, make provision:

(1) about the time and manner in which a payment under the provisions above or under such regulations is to be made (including for payment by instalments), and as to the consequences of non-payment[10];

(2) about the making of a payment by a billing authority to the Secretary of State or vice versa where:

  (a) a payment under the provisions above is made in the course of the year to which it relates; and

  (b) it is subsequently determined that the amount of the payment required to be made is more or less than that actually made[11];

(3) about the making of a payment by a billing authority to the Secretary of State or vice versa where:

  (a) a calculation of a payment under the provisions above is made by reference to an estimate of an amount; and

  (b) it is subsequently determined that the actual amount is more or less than the estimate[12].

The Secretary of State may by regulations make provision for the deduction from a payment to be made under the provisions above by a billing authority to the Secretary of State of an amount to be determined in accordance with the regulations[13]. The regulations may, in particular, make provision for the determination of an amount to be deducted to be made by reference to the operation in relation to the billing authority of the statutory provision[14] as to discretionary relief[15]. The consent of the Treasury is required to such regulations[16].

1 As to the meaning of 'local government finance report' see PARA 59. As to the meaning of 'year' see PARA 58 note 2.

2 Local Government Finance Act 1988 Sch 7B para 6(1) (Sch 7B added by the Local Government Finance Act 2012 s 1(1), (4), Sch 1).

3 As to the meaning of 'billing authority' see PARA 346.

4 As to the Secretary of State see PARA 51.

5 For these purposes, an authority's 'non-domestic rating income' has the meaning given by regulations made by the Secretary of State: Local Government Finance Act 1988 Sch 7B para 6(3) (as added: see note 2). The regulations may, in particular, define that term by reference to the total which, if the authority acted diligently, would be payable to it in respect of the year under ss 43, 45 (see PARAS 133, 135), subject to such adjustments as may be specified in the regulations: Sch 7B para 6(4) (as so added). The regulations may, in particular, make provision for adjustments by reference to changes to the calculation of the amount of a billing authority's non-domestic rating income for an earlier year but not taken into account in that calculation: Sch 7B para 6(5) (as so added). See the Non-Domestic Rating (Rates Retention) Regulations 2013, SI 2013/452 (amended by SI 2014/96, SI 2015/628, SI 2016/317, SI 2016/1268, SI 2017/318, SI 2017/496 and SI 2017/1321); and the Non-Domestic Rating (Shale Oil and Gas and Miscellaneous Amendments) Regulations 2015, SI 2015/628.

6 Local Government Finance Act 1988 Sch 7B para 6(2) (as added: see note 2). As to the central share see PARA 59.

7 Ie regulations under the Local Government Finance Act 1988 Sch 7B para 8 (see the text to notes 13–16).

8 Local Government Finance Act 1988 Sch 7B para 6(6) (as added: see note 2).

9 Local Government Finance Act 1988 Sch 7B para 7(1) (as added: see note 2). See the Non-Domestic Rating (Rates Retention) Regulations 2013, SI 2013/452 (as amended: see note 5).

10 Local Government Finance Act 1988 Sch 7B para 7(2)(a) (as added: see note 2).

11 Local Government Finance Act 1988 Sch 7B para 7(2)(b) (as added: see note 2).

12 Local Government Finance Act 1988 Sch 7B para 7(2)(c) (as added: see note 2).

13 Local Government Finance Act 1988 Sch 7B para 8(1) (as added: see note 2). See the Non-Domestic Rating (Rates Retention) Regulations 2013, SI 2013/452 (as amended: see note 5); the Non-Domestic Rating (Designated Areas etc) Regulations 2016, SI 2016/317 (amended by SI 2017/318); and the Non-Domestic Rating (Designated Areas etc) Regulations 2017, SI 2017/318.

14 Ie the Local Government Finance Act 1988 s 47: see PARA 149.

15 Local Government Finance Act 1988 Sch 7B para 8(2) (as added: see note 2).

16 Local Government Finance Act 1988 Sch 7B para 8(3) (as added: see note 2). As to the Treasury see CONSTITUTIONAL AND ADMINISTRATIVE LAW vol 20 (2014) PARA 262 et seq.

61. Payments by billing authorities to major precepting authorities.

The Secretary of State[1] may by regulations make provision requiring billing authorities[2] in England to make payments for a year to major precepting authorities[3] in England[4]. The regulations must provide that a billing authority is not required to make a payment for a year unless the local government finance report[5] for the year has been approved by resolution of the House of Commons[6]. The regulations may, in particular, make provision as to:

(1) the billing authorities that are required to make payments under the regulations[7];
(2) the major precepting authorities that are entitled to receive payments under the regulations[8];
(3) the amounts of the payments that are required to be made[9].

The regulations may, in particular, make provision for the amount of a payment to be made by a billing authority for a year to be such proportion of its non-domestic rating income[10] for the year as is specified in or determined in accordance with the regulations[11]. The regulations may not have the effect that the total amount payable by a billing authority under the regulations for a year exceeds the billing authority's local share of its non-domestic rating income for a year[12].

The Secretary of State may by regulations make provision about the administration of payments under regulations under the provisions above[13]. The regulations may, in particular, make provision:

(a) about the making of calculations, and the supply of information to a major precepting authority, by a billing authority in connection with the determination of a payment to be made under regulations about payments or administrative arrangements[14] or under Part VI (funds) of the Local Government Finance Act 1988[15] so far as applying to non-domestic rates[16];
(b) about the assumptions and adjustments to be made, and the information to be taken into account, in making such calculations[17];
(c) about the consequences of non-compliance with provision under head (a) or (b)[18];
(d) about the time and manner in which a payment under regulations about payments or administrative arrangements[19] is to be made (including for payment by instalments), and as to the consequences of non-payment[20];
(e) about the making of a payment by a billing authority to a major precepting authority or vice versa where:
    (i) a payment under regulations about payments[21] is made in the course of the year to which it relates; and
    (ii) it is subsequently determined that the amount of the payment required to be made under the regulations is more or less than that actually made[22];
(f) about the making of a payment by a billing authority to a major precepting authority or vice versa where:
    (i) a calculation of a payment under regulations about payments is made by reference to an estimate of an amount, and
    (ii) it is subsequently determined that the actual amount is more or less than the estimate[23];

(g) for the certification of calculations made, or information supplied to a major precepting authority, by a billing authority in connection with the determination of a payment under regulations about payments or administrative arrangements or under Part VI (funds) of the Local Government Finance Act 1988 so far as applying to non-domestic rates[24];

(h) about the consequences where a certified calculation or certified information does not match that made or supplied by the billing authority, including (in particular) about the use of the certified calculation or certified information[25].

The regulations may confer power on the Secretary of State to give directions about the certification of calculations or information[26].

The Secretary of State may by regulations make provision for a billing authority to make a payment for a year to one or more major precepting authorities of an amount equal to a proportion of the amount that is to be deducted in accordance with regulations[27] from the billing authority's payment in respect of the central share[28] to the Secretary of State for the year[29]. The regulations may make provision about the administration of payments to major precepting authorities under the regulations[30]. The regulations may, in particular, make provision in relation to payments to major precepting authorities of the same kind as the provision that may be made under heads (a) to (h) above in relation to payments to major precepting authorities to which those heads apply[31].

1 As to the Secretary of State see PARA 51.

2 As to the meaning of 'billing authority' see PARA 346.

3 As to the meaning of 'major precepting authority' see PARA 11 note 2 (definition applied by the Local Government Finance Act 1988 s 144(2) (substituted by the Local Government Finance Act 1992 s 117(1), Sch 13 para 81(1); and amended by the Local Government Finance Act 2012 s 5(1), (2)(b), Sch 3 paras 23, 29)). As to the meaning of 'year' see PARA 58 note 2.

4 Local Government Finance Act 1988 Sch 7B para 9(1) (Sch 7B added by the Local Government Finance Act 2012 s 1(1), (4), Sch 1). See the Non-Domestic Rating (Rates Retention) Regulations 2013, SI 2013/452 (amended by SI 2014/96, SI 2015/628, SI 2016/317, SI 2016/1268, SI 2017/318, SI 2017/496 and SI 2017/1321).

5 As to the meaning of 'local government finance report' see PARA 59.

6 Local Government Finance Act 1988 Sch 7B para 9(2) (as added: see note 4).

7 Local Government Finance Act 1988 Sch 7B para 9(3)(a) (as added: see note 4).

8 Local Government Finance Act 1988 Sch 7B para 9(3)(b) (as added: see note 4).

9 Local Government Finance Act 1988 Sch 7B para 9(3)(c) (as added: see note 4).

10 For these purposes, an authority's 'non-domestic rating income' has the meaning given by the regulations: Local Government Finance Act 1988 Sch 7B para 9(5) (as added: see note 4). The regulations may, in particular, define that term by reference to the total which, if the authority acted diligently, would be payable to it in respect of the year under ss 43, 45 (see PARAS 133, 135), subject to such adjustments as may be specified in the regulations: Sch 7B para 9(6) (as so added). The regulations may, in particular, make provision for adjustments by reference to changes to the calculation of the amount of a billing authority's non-domestic rating income for an earlier year but not taken into account in that calculation: Sch 7B para 9(7) (as so added). See the Non-Domestic Rating (Shale Oil and Gas and Miscellaneous Amendments) Regulations 2015, SI 2015/628.

11 Local Government Finance Act 1988 Sch 7B para 9(4) (as added: see note 4).

12 Local Government Finance Act 1988 Sch 7B para 9(8) (as added: see note 4). In Sch 7B, 'the local share' has the meaning given by Sch 7B para 4 (see PARA 59): Sch 7B para 45 (as so added).

13 Local Government Finance Act 1988 Sch 7B para 10(1) (as added: see note 4). See the Non-Domestic Rating (Rates Retention) Regulations 2013, SI 2013/452 (as amended: see note 4); and the Non-Domestic Rating (Shale Oil and Gas and Miscellaneous Amendments) Regulations 2015, SI 2015/628.

14 Ie regulations under the Local Government Finance Act 1988 Sch 7B para 9 or Sch 7B para 10.

15 Ie the Local Government Finance Act 1988 Pt VI (ss 89–99): see PARA 579 et seq.

16 Local Government Finance Act 1988 Sch 7B para 10(2)(a) (as added: see note 4).
17 Local Government Finance Act 1988 Sch 7B para 10(2)(b) (as added: see note 4).
18 Local Government Finance Act 1988 Sch 7B para 10(2)(c) (as added: see note 4).
19 See note 14.
20 Local Government Finance Act 1988 Sch 7B para 10(2)(d) (as added: see note 4).
21 Ie under the Local Government Finance Act 1988 Sch 7B para 9.
22 Local Government Finance Act 1988 Sch 7B para 10(2)(e) (as added: see note 4).
23 Local Government Finance Act 1988 Sch 7B para 10(2)(f) (as added: see note 4).
24 Local Government Finance Act 1988 Sch 7B para 10(2)(g) (as added: see note 4).
25 Local Government Finance Act 1988 Sch 7B para 10(2)(h) (as added: see note 4).
26 Local Government Finance Act 1988 Sch 7B para 10(3) (as added: see note 4).
27 Ie under the Local Government Finance Act 1988 Sch 7B para 8: see PARA 60.
28 Ie under the Local Government Finance Act 1988 Sch 7B para 6: see PARA 60. As to the meaning of 'the central share' see PARA 58 note 14.
29 Local Government Finance Act 1988 Sch 7B para 11(1) (as added: see note 4). See the Non-Domestic Rating (Rates Retention) Regulations 2013, SI 2013/452 (as amended: see note 4); and the Non-Domestic Rating (Shale Oil and Gas and Miscellaneous Amendments) Regulations 2015, SI 2015/628.
30 Local Government Finance Act 1988 Sch 7B para 11(2) (as added: see note 4).
31 Local Government Finance Act 1988 Sch 7B para 11(3) (as added: see note 4).

62. Principal payments in connection with local retention of non-domestic rates.

The local government finance report for a year[1] must specify the basis ('the basis of calculation') on which the Secretary of State[2] intends to:

(1) calculate which relevant authorities are to make payments in connection with the local retention of non-domestic rates[3] to the Secretary of State for the year[4];

(2) calculate which relevant authorities are to receive payments in connection with the local retention of non-domestic rates from the Secretary of State for the year[5]; and

(3) calculate the amount of each payment within head (1) or (2)[6].

Before making the local government finance report for a year, the Secretary of State must notify such representatives of local government as the Secretary of State thinks fit of the general nature of the basis of calculation[7].

The following provisions apply if a local government finance report for a year is approved by resolution of the House of Commons[8]. As soon as is reasonably practicable after the report has been approved, the Secretary of State must:

(a) calculate which relevant authorities are to make payments in connection with the local retention of non-domestic rates to the Secretary of State for the year[9];

(b) calculate which relevant authorities are to receive payments in connection with the local retention of non-domestic rates from the Secretary of State for the year[10]; and

(c) calculate the amount of each payment within head (a) or (b)[11].

Subject as follows, the Secretary of State may, at any time before the end of the year following the year to which the report relates, make one further set of calculations of the kind described in heads (a) to (c) above[12]. The power to make a further set of calculations is not exercisable after the approval by the House of Commons of any amending report[13] made in relation to the local government finance report[14]. Calculations under these provisions must be made in accordance with the basis of calculation specified in the report[15]. As soon as is reasonably practicable after making such calculations[16] under sub-paragraph (2) or (3), the Secretary of State must notify each relevant authority of:

(i) whether any payments are to be made by the authority to the Secretary of State in accordance with the calculations[17];

(ii) whether any payments are to be made to the authority by the Secretary of State in accordance with the calculations[18]; and

(iii) if any payments are to be made by or to the authority, the amount of each payment[19].

Where calculations under heads (a) to (c) above show that a relevant authority is to make a payment to the Secretary of State, the authority must make that payment to the Secretary of State[20]. Where calculations under heads (a) to (c) above show that the Secretary of State is to make a payment to a relevant authority, the Secretary of State must make that payment to the authority[21].

The following provisions apply if further calculations ('the revised calculations') are made under for a year[22]. Where a payment the revised calculations show as falling to be made by a relevant authority to the Secretary of State exceeds that shown as falling to be made by the original calculations, or a payment the revised calculations show as falling to be made by the Secretary of State to a relevant authority is less than that shown as falling to be made by the original calculations[23], the authority must make a payment to the Secretary of State of an amount equal to the difference[24].

Where the original calculations did not show that a relevant authority was to make a payment to the Secretary of State, but the revised calculations show that the authority is to make a payment to the Secretary of State, the authority must make that payment to the Secretary of State and the authority must make a payment to the Secretary of State of an amount equal to the amount of the payment shown by the original calculations as falling to be made by the Secretary of State to the authority[25].

Where a payment the revised calculations show as falling to be made by a relevant authority to the Secretary of State is less than that shown as falling to be made by the original calculations, or a payment the revised calculations show as falling to be made by the Secretary of State to a relevant authority exceeds that shown as falling to be made by the original calculations, the Secretary of State must make a payment to the authority of an amount equal to the difference[26].

Where the original calculations did not show that the Secretary of State was to make a payment to a relevant authority, but the revised calculations show that the Secretary of State is to make a payment to the authority, the Secretary of State must make that payment to the authority and the Secretary of State must make a payment to the authority of an amount equal to the amount of the payment shown by the original calculations as falling to be made by the authority to the Secretary of State[27].

1 As to the meaning of 'local government finance report' see PARA 59. As to the meaning of 'year' see PARA 58 note 2.

2 As to the Secretary of State see PARA 51.

3 Ie under the Local Government Finance Act 1988 Sch 7B Pt 5 (paras 12–18). Schedule 7B Pt 5 is subject to Sch 7B Pt 9 (paras 34–38) (pooling of authorities: see PARAS 69–70) and Pt 10 (paras 39–42) (designation of areas and classes of hereditament: see PARAS 71–73): Sch 7B para 18 (Sch 7B added by the Local Government Finance Act 2012 s 1(1), (4), Sch 1). As to the meaning of 'relevant authority' see PARA 59 note 9.

4 Local Government Finance Act 1988 Sch 7B para 12(1)(a) (as added: see note 3).

5 Local Government Finance Act 1988 Sch 7B para 12(1)(b) (as added: see note 3).

6 Local Government Finance Act 1988 Sch 7B para 12(1)(c) (as added: see note 3).

7 Local Government Finance Act 1988 Sch 7B para 12(2) (as added: see note 3).

8 Local Government Finance Act 1988 Sch 7B para 13(1) (as added: see note 3).

9 Local Government Finance Act 1988 Sch 7B para 13(2)(a) (as added: see note 3).

10 Local Government Finance Act 1988 Sch 7B para 13(2)(b) (as added: see note 3).
11 Local Government Finance Act 1988 Sch 7B para 13(2)(c) (as added: see note 3).
12 Local Government Finance Act 1988 Sch 7B para 13(3) (as added: see note 3).
13 Ie made under the Local Government Finance Act 1988 Sch 7B para 15: see PARA 63.
14 Local Government Finance Act 1988 Sch 7B para 13(4) (as added: see note 3).
15 Ie made under the Local Government Finance Act 1988 Sch 7B para 13(2) or (3).
16 Local Government Finance Act 1988 Sch 7B para 13(5) (as added: see note 3).
17 Local Government Finance Act 1988 Sch 7B para 13(6)(a) (as added: see note 3).
18 Local Government Finance Act 1988 Sch 7B para 13(6)(b) (as added: see note 3).
19 Local Government Finance Act 1988 Sch 7B para 13(6)(c) (as added: see note 3).
20 Local Government Finance Act 1988 Sch 7B para 14(1) (as added: see note 3). A payment by a relevant authority to the Secretary of State under Sch 7B para 14(1):
(1) must be made on or before such day in the year to which the local government finance report relates, and in such manner, as the Secretary of State may specify (Sch 7B para 14(11)(a) (as so added)); and
(2) if not made on or before that day, is recoverable in a court of competent jurisdiction (Sch 7B para 14(11)(b) (as so added)).
21 Local Government Finance Act 1988 Sch 7B para 14(2) (as added: see note 3). A payment by the Secretary of State to a relevant authority under Sch 7B para 14(2) must be made:
(1) in instalments of such amounts; and
(2) at such times in the year to which the local government finance report relates,
as the Secretary of State determines with the Treasury's consent: Sch 7B para 14(12) (as so added.
22 Local Government Finance Act 1988 Sch 7B para 14(3) (as added: see note 3).
23 In the Local Government Finance Act 1988 Sch 7B para 14, 'the original calculations' means the calculations for the year under Sch 7B para 13(2): Sch 7B para 14(4) (as added: see note 3).
24 Local Government Finance Act 1988 Sch 7B para 14(5), (6) (as added: see note 3). A payment by a relevant authority to the Secretary of State under Sch 7B para 14(6) or (7):
(1) must be made on or before such day after the end of the year to which the local government finance report relates, and in such manner, as the Secretary of State may specify (Sch 7B para 14(13)(a) (as so added)); and
(2) if not made on or before that day, is recoverable in a court of competent jurisdiction (Sch 7B para 14(13)(b) (as so added)).
25 Local Government Finance Act 1988 Sch 7B para 14(7), (8) (as added: see note 3). See note 24.
26 Local Government Finance Act 1988 Sch 7B para 14(8), (9) (as added: see note 3). A payment by the Secretary of State to a relevant authority under Sch 7B para 14(9) or (10) must be made:
(1) at such time; or
(2) in instalments of such amounts and at such times,
as the Secretary of State determines with the Treasury's consent; but any such time must fall after the end of the year to which the local government finance report relates: Sch 7B para 14(14) (as so added).
27 Local Government Finance Act 1988 Sch 7B para 14(10) (as added: see note 3). See note 26.

63. Amending reports.

After a local government finance report[1] has been made, the Secretary of State[2] may, at any time before the end of the year following the year to which the report relates, make in relation to the report one or more amending reports under the following provisions[3].

An amending report must contain amendments to the basis of calculation specified in the local government finance report[4]. Before making the report, the Secretary of State must notify such representatives of local government as the Secretary of State thinks fit of the general nature of the amendments the Secretary of State proposes to make[5]. The Secretary of State must lay, or make arrangements for laying, the report before the House of Commons[6]. As soon as is reasonably practicable after the report is laid before the House of Commons, the Secretary of State must send a copy of the report to each relevant authority[7]. Where an amending report has been approved by resolution of the House of Commons, the Secretary of State may not make a subsequent amending report in relation to the same local government finance report[8].

The following provisions apply if an amending report for a year is approved by resolution of the House of Commons[9]. As soon as is reasonably practicable after the amending report has been approved, the Secretary of State must:

(1) calculate which relevant authorities are to make payments[10] to the Secretary of State for the year[11];

(2) calculate which relevant authorities are to receive payments from the Secretary of State for the year[12]; and

(3) calculate the amount of each payment within head (1) or (2)[13].

Subject as follows, the Secretary of State may make one further set of calculations of the kind described in heads (1) to (3) above[14]. The power to make a further set of calculations is not exercisable after whichever is the later of:

(a) the end of the year following the year to which the amending report relates[15]; and

(b) the end of the period of three months beginning with the day on which the amending report is approved by resolution of the House of Commons[16].

Calculations in respect of amending reports must be made in accordance with the basis of calculation specified in the local government finance report as amended by the amending report[17].

As soon as is reasonably practicable after making calculations or further calculations, the Secretary of State must notify each relevant authority of:

(i) whether any payments are to be made by the authority to the Secretary of State in accordance with the calculations[18];

(ii) whether any payments are to be made to the authority by the Secretary of State in accordance with the calculations[19]; and

(iii) if any payments are to be made by or to the authority, the amount of each payment[20].

The following provisions apply if calculations ('the revised calculations') are made in consequence of an amending report for a year[21].

Where a payment shown by the revised calculations as falling to be made by a relevant authority to the Secretary of State exceeds that shown as falling to be made by the relevant previous calculations[22] or a payment shown by the revised calculations as falling to be made by the Secretary of State to a relevant authority is less than that shown as falling to be made by the relevant previous calculations, the authority must make a payment to the Secretary of State of an amount equal to the difference[23].

Where the relevant previous calculations did not show that a relevant authority was to make a payment to the Secretary of State, but the revised calculations show that the authority is to make a payment to the Secretary of State, the authority must make that payment to the Secretary of State and the authority must make a payment to the Secretary of State of an amount equal to the amount of the payment shown by the relevant previous calculations as falling to be made by the Secretary of State to the authority[24].

Where a payment shown by the revised calculations as falling to be made by a relevant authority to the Secretary of State is less than that shown as falling to be made by the relevant previous calculations or a payment shown by the revised calculations as falling to be made by the Secretary of State to a relevant authority exceeds that shown as falling to be made by the relevant previous calculations, the Secretary of State must make a payment to the authority of an amount equal to the difference[25].

Where the relevant previous calculations did not show that the Secretary of State was to make a payment to a relevant authority, but the revised calculations show that the Secretary of State is to make a payment to the authority, the Secretary of State must make that payment to the authority and the Secretary of State must make a payment to the authority of an amount equal to the amount of the payment shown by the relevant previous calculations as falling to be made by the authority to the Secretary of State[26].

A payment by a relevant authority to the Secretary of State under these provisions:

(A) must be made on or before such day after the end of the year in which the amending report was made, and in such manner, as the Secretary of State may specify[27]; and

(B) if not made on or before that day, is recoverable in a court of competent jurisdiction[28].

A payment by the Secretary of State to a relevant authority under these provisions must be made:

(I) at such time; or

(II) in instalments of such amounts and at such times,

as the Secretary of State determines with the Treasury's consent; but any such time must fall after the end of the year in which the amending report was made[29].

1 As to the meaning of 'local government finance report' see PARA 59.
2 As to the Secretary of State see PARA 51.
3 Local Government Finance Act 1988 Sch 7B para 15(1) (Sch 7B added by the Local Government Finance Act 2012 s 1(1), (4), Sch 1). As to the meaning of 'year' see PARA 58 note 2. The Local Government Finance Act 1988 Sch 7B Pt 5 (paras 12–18) is subject to Sch 7B Pt 9 (paras 34–38) (pooling of authorities: see PARAS 69–70) and Pt 10 (paras 39–42) (designation of areas and classes of hereditament: see PARAS 71–73): Sch 7B para 18 (as so added).
4 Local Government Finance Act 1988 Sch 7B para 15(2) (as added: see note 4). As to the meaning of 'basis of calculation' see PARA 62; definition applied by Sch 7B para 45 (as so added).
5 Local Government Finance Act 1988 Sch 7B para 15(3) (as added: see note 4).
6 Local Government Finance Act 1988 Sch 7B para 15(4) (as added: see note 4).
7 Local Government Finance Act 1988 Sch 7B para 15(5) (as added: see note 4). As to the meaning of 'relevant authority' see PARA 59 note 9.
8 Local Government Finance Act 1988 Sch 7B para 15(6) (as added: see note 4).
9 Local Government Finance Act 1988 Sch 7B para 16(1) (as added: see note 4).
10 Ie under the Local Government Finance Act 1988 Sch 7B Pt 5.
11 Local Government Finance Act 1988 Sch 7B para 16(2)(a) (as added: see note 4).
12 Local Government Finance Act 1988 Sch 7B para 16(2)(b) (as added: see note 4).
13 Local Government Finance Act 1988 Sch 7B para 16(2)(c) (as added: see note 4).
14 Local Government Finance Act 1988 Sch 7B para 16(3) (as added: see note 4).
15 Local Government Finance Act 1988 Sch 7B para 16(4)(a) (as added: see note 4).
16 Local Government Finance Act 1988 Sch 7B para 16(4)(b) (as added: see note 4).
17 Local Government Finance Act 1988 Sch 7B para 16(5) (as added: see note 4).
18 Local Government Finance Act 1988 Sch 7B para 16(6)(a) (as added: see note 4).
19 Local Government Finance Act 1988 Sch 7B para 16(6)(b) (as added: see note 4).
20 Local Government Finance Act 1988 Sch 7B para 16(6)(c) (as added: see note 4).
21 Local Government Finance Act 1988 Sch 7B para 17(1) (as added: see note 4).
22 In the Local Government Finance Act 1988 Sch 7B para 17, 'the relevant previous calculations' means the last calculations of the kind referred to in Sch 7B para 13(2) or (3) (see PARA 62) or Sch 7B para 16(2) (see the text to notes 11–13) made for the year: Sch 7B para 17(2) (as added: see note 4).
23 Local Government Finance Act 1988 Sch 7B para 17(3), (4) (as added: see note 4).
24 Local Government Finance Act 1988 Sch 7B para 17(5) (as added: see note 4).
25 Local Government Finance Act 1988 Sch 7B para 17(6), (7) (as added: see note 4).
26 Local Government Finance Act 1988 Sch 7B para 17(8) (as added: see note 4).
27 Local Government Finance Act 1988 Sch 7B para 17(9)(a) (as added: see note 4).

28 Local Government Finance Act 1988 Sch 7B para 17(9)(b) (as added: see note 4).
29 Local Government Finance Act 1988 Sch 7B para 17(10) (as added: see note 4).

64. Levy accounts.

The Secretary of State[1] must, for each year, keep an account, to be called a 'levy account'[2]. Each such account must be kept in accordance with the relevant statutory provisions[3] that apply to a levy account[4]. The Secretary of State must keep each such account in such form as the Treasury may direct and must, at such time as the Treasury may direct, send copies of each such account to the Comptroller and Auditor General[5]. The Comptroller and Auditor General must examine, certify and report on any account of which copies are so sent to the Comptroller and Auditor General, and must arrange for copies of the account and of the Comptroller and Auditor General's report on it to be laid before each House of Parliament[6].

For each year the following are to be credited (as items of account) to the levy account kept for the year[7]:

(1) amounts received by the Secretary of State in the year[8] in respect of levy payments[9]; and
(2) amounts received by the Secretary of State in the year under regulations[10] in respect of payments on account[11].

If a local government finance report[12] for a year has been approved by resolution of the House of Commons, and that report provides for an amount to be credited to the levy account kept for the year, that amount may be credited (as an item of account) to that account[13].

For each year the following are to be debited (as items of account) to the levy account kept for the year[14]:

(a) payments made by the Secretary of State in the year[15] in relation to safety net payments[16];
(b) payments made by the Secretary of State in the year under regulations in respect of payments on account[17]; and
(c) payments made by the Secretary of State in the year[18] in respect of the distribution of the remaining balance[19].

As soon as is reasonably practicable after the end of each year, the Secretary of State must calculate:

(i) the aggregate of the items of account credited to the levy account kept for the year[20]; and
(ii) the aggregate of the items of account debited to the levy account kept for the year[21].

If the aggregate mentioned in head (i) above exceeds that mentioned in head (ii), an amount equal to the excess must be debited (as an item of account) to the levy account kept for the year and credited (as an item of account) to the levy account kept for the next year[22].

If the aggregate mentioned in head (ii) above exceeds that mentioned in head (i), an amount equal to the excess must be credited (as an item of account) to the levy account kept for the year and debited (as an item of account) to the levy account kept for the next year[23].

1 As to the Secretary of State see PARA 51.
2 Local Government Finance Act 1988 Sch 7B para 19(1) (Sch 7B added by the Local Government Finance Act 2012 s 1(1), (4), Sch 1). As to the meaning of 'year' see PARA 58 note 2.
3 Ie the relevant provisions of the Local Government Finance Act 1988 Sch 7B.
4 Local Government Finance Act 1988 Sch 7B para 19(2) (as added: see note 2).
5 Local Government Finance Act 1988 Sch 7B para 19(3) (as added: see note 2). As to the Treasury

see CONSTITUTIONAL AND ADMINISTRATIVE LAW vol 20 (2014) PARA 262 et seq. As to the Comptroller and Auditor General see CONSTITUTIONAL AND ADMINISTRATIVE LAW vol 20 (2014) PARA 494 et seq.

6 Local Government Finance Act 1988 Sch 7B para 19(4) (as added: see note 2).

7 Local Government Finance Act 1988 Sch 7B para 20(1) (as added: see note 2).

8 Ie under the Local Government Finance Act 1988 Sch 7B para 24: see PARA 65.

9 Local Government Finance Act 1988 Sch 7B para 20(1)(a) (as added: see note 2). In Sch 7B, 'levy payment' has the meaning given by Sch 7B para 22(1) (see PARA 65): Sch 7B para 45 (as so added).

10 Ie under the Local Government Finance Act 1988 Sch 7B para 28: see PARA 67.

11 Local Government Finance Act 1988 Sch 7B para 20(1)(b) (as added: see note 2).

12 As to the meaning of 'local government finance report' see PARA 59.

13 Local Government Finance Act 1988 Sch 7B para 20(2) (as added: see note 2).

14 Local Government Finance Act 1988 Sch 7B para 20(3) (as added: see note 2).

15 Ie under the Local Government Finance Act 1988 Sch 7B para 27: see PARA 66.

16 Local Government Finance Act 1988 Sch 7B para 20(3)(a) (as added: see note 2). In Sch 7B, 'safety net payment' has the meaning given by Sch 7B para 25(1) (see PARA 66): Sch 7B para 45 (as so added).

17 Local Government Finance Act 1988 Sch 7B para 20(3)(b) (as added: see note 2).

18 Ie under the Local Government Finance Act 1988 Sch 7B para 30: see PARA 67.

19 Local Government Finance Act 1988 Sch 7B para 20(3)(c) (as added: see note 2).

20 Local Government Finance Act 1988 Sch 7B para 21(1)(a) (as added: see note 2).

21 Local Government Finance Act 1988 Sch 7B para 21(1)(b) (as added: see note 2).

22 Local Government Finance Act 1988 Sch 7B para 21(2) (as added: see note 2).

23 Local Government Finance Act 1988 Sch 7B para 21(3) (as added: see note 2).

65. Levy payments.

The Secretary of State[1] may by regulations make provision for calculating whether a relevant authority is required to make a payment under the relevant statutory provisions[2] (a 'levy payment') to the Secretary of State for a year and, if so, the amount of the levy payment[3]. The regulations must make provision for calculations for a year to be made after the end of that year[4].

The regulations may, in particular, make provision for calculations in relation to a relevant authority to be made:

(1) if the relevant authority is a billing authority[5], by reference to the total payable to it in respect of the year[6], subject to such adjustments as may be specified in the regulations[7];

(2) if the relevant authority is a major precepting authority[8], by reference to the total of the amounts payable in respect of the year[9] to the billing authorities that are required to make payments to it for the year[10], subject to such adjustments as may be specified in the regulations[11];

(3) by reference to payments of a kind specified in the regulations made to the authority by the Secretary of State[12];

(4) by reference to such other factors as may be specified in the regulations[13].

The regulations may, in particular, make provision for adjustments to an amount calculated under provision made under heads (1) to (4) by reference to changes affecting the calculation of such an amount for an earlier year but not taken into account in that calculation[14].

The Secretary of State must calculate in relation to each relevant authority whether it is required to make a levy payment for a year and, if so, the amount of that payment[15]. The calculation must be made:

(a) as soon as is reasonably practicable after the end of the year[16]; or

(b) if the authority is subject to a requirement imposed by a direction[17] to make calculations or supply information or by or under regulations[18] about calculations and supply of information for the purposes of these provisions, as soon as is reasonably practicable after the time for compliance with that requirement[19],

whichever is the later[20].

The calculation must be made in accordance with regulations[21] about calculating levy payments[22]. As soon as is reasonably practicable after making a calculation in relation to a relevant authority, the Secretary of State must notify that authority of:

(i) whether, in accordance with the calculation, it is required to make a levy payment for the year[23]; and

(ii) if so, the amount of that payment in accordance with the calculation[24].

If a calculation[25] shows that a levy payment is to be made to the Secretary of State by a relevant authority, the authority must make that payment to the Secretary of State[26].

The levy payment:

(A) must be made on or before such day and in such manner as the Secretary of State may specify[27]; and

(B) if not made on or before that day, is recoverable in a court of competent jurisdiction[28].

1 As to the Secretary of State see PARA 51.
2 Ie under the Local Government Finance Act 1988 Sch 7B Pt 7 (paras 22–31). As to the meaning of 'relevant authority' see PARA 59 note 9. Schedule 7B Pt 7 is subject to Sch 7B Pt 9 (paras 34–38) (pooling of authorities: see PARAS 69–70) and Pt 10 (paras 39–42) (designation of areas and classes of hereditament: see PARAS 71–73): Sch 7B para 31 (Sch 7B added by the Local Government Finance Act 2012 s 1(1), (4), Sch 1).
3 Local Government Finance Act 1988 Sch 7B para 22(1) (as added: see note 2). As to the meaning of 'year' see PARA 58 note 2. See the Non-Domestic Rating (Levy and Safety Net) Regulations 2013, SI 2013/737 (amended by SI 2014/822, SI 2015/617, SI 2015/2039 and SI 2017/496).
4 Local Government Finance Act 1988 Sch 7B para 22(2) (as added: see note 2).
5 As to the meaning of 'billing authority' see PARA 346.
6 Ie under the Local Government Finance Act 1988 ss 43, 45: see PARAS 133, 135.
7 Local Government Finance Act 1988 Sch 7B para 22(3)(a) (as added: see note 2).
8 As to the meaning of 'major precepting authority' see PARA 11 note 2 (definition applied by the Local Government Finance Act 1988 s 144(2) (substituted by the Local Government Finance Act 1992 s 117(1), Sch 13 para 81(1); and amended by the Local Government Finance Act 2012 s 5(1), (2)(b), Sch 3 paras 23, 29)).
9 Ie under the Local Government Finance Act 1988 ss 43, 45.
10 Ie under regulations under the Local Government Finance Act 1988 Sch 7B para 9: see PARA 61.
11 Local Government Finance Act 1988 Sch 7B para 22(3)(b) (as added: see note 2).
12 Local Government Finance Act 1988 Sch 7B para 22(3)(c) (as added: see note 2).
13 Local Government Finance Act 1988 Sch 7B para 22(3)(d) (as added: see note 2).
14 Local Government Finance Act 1988 Sch 7B para 22(4) (as added: see note 2).
15 Local Government Finance Act 1988 Sch 7B para 23(1) (as added: see note 2).
16 Local Government Finance Act 1988 Sch 7B para 23(2)(a) (as added: see note 2).
17 Ie under the Local Government Finance Act 1988 Sch 7B para 43: see PARA 73.
18 Ie under the Local Government Finance Act 1988 Sch 7B para 44: see PARA 73.
19 Local Government Finance Act 1988 Sch 7B para 23(2)(b) (as added: see note 2).
20 Local Government Finance Act 1988 Sch 7B para 23(2) (as added: see note 2).
21 Ie under the Local Government Finance Act 1988 Sch 7B para 22: see the text to notes 1–14.
22 Local Government Finance Act 1988 Sch 7B para 23(3) (as added: see note 2).
23 Local Government Finance Act 1988 Sch 7B para 23(4)(a) (as added: see note 2).
24 Local Government Finance Act 1988 Sch 7B para 23(4)(b) (as added: see note 2).
25 Ie under the Local Government Finance Act 1988 Sch 7B para 23: see the text to notes 15–24.
26 Local Government Finance Act 1988 Sch 7B para 24(1) (as added: see note 2).

27 Local Government Finance Act 1988 Sch 7B para 24(2)(a) (as added: see note 2).
28 Local Government Finance Act 1988 Sch 7B para 24(2)(b) (as added: see note 2).

66. Safety net payments.

The Secretary of State[1] may by regulations make provision for calculating whether the Secretary of State is required to make a payment under the relevant statutory provisions[2] (a 'safety net payment') to a relevant authority for a year and, if so, the amount of the payment[3]. The regulations must make provision for calculations for a year to be made after the end of that year[4].

The regulations may, in particular, make provision for calculations in relation to a relevant authority to be made:

(1) if the relevant authority is a billing authority[5], by reference to the total payable to it in respect of the year[6], subject to such adjustments as may be specified in the regulations[7];
(2) if the relevant authority is a major precepting authority[8], by reference to the total of the amounts payable in respect of the year[9] to the billing authorities that are required to make payments to it for the year[10], subject to such adjustments as may be specified in the regulations[11];
(3) by reference to payments of a kind specified in the regulations made to the authority by the Secretary of State[12];
(4) by reference to such other factors as may be specified in the regulations[13].

The regulations may, in particular, make provision for adjustments to an amount calculated under provision made under heads (1) to (4) by reference to changes affecting the calculation of such an amount for an earlier year but not taken into account in that calculation[14].

The Secretary of State must calculate in relation to each relevant authority whether the Secretary of State is required to make a safety net payment to the authority for the year and, if so, the amount of that payment[15]. The calculation must be made:

(a) as soon as is reasonably practicable after the end of the year[16]; or
(b) if the authority is subject to a requirement imposed by a direction[17] to make calculations or supply information or by or under regulations[18] about calculations and supply of information for the purposes of these provisions, as soon as is reasonably practicable after the time for compliance with that requirement[19],

whichever is the later[20].

The calculation must be made in accordance with regulations[21] about the calculation of safety net payments[22]. As soon as is reasonably practicable after making a calculation in relation to a relevant authority, the Secretary of State must notify that authority of:

(i) whether, in accordance with the calculation, the Secretary of State is required to make a safety net payment to the authority for the year[23]; and
(ii) if so, the amount of that payment in accordance with the calculation[24].

If a calculation[25] shows that a safety net payment is to be made by the Secretary of State to a relevant authority, the Secretary of State must make that payment to the authority[26]. The safety net payment must be made in instalments of such amounts, and at such times, as the Secretary of State determines with the Treasury's consent[27].

The provisions about calculation are subject to regulations[28] about payments on account[29].

1 As to the Secretary of State see PARA 51.
2 Ie under the Local Government Finance Act 1988 Sch 7B Pt 7 (paras 22–31). Schedule 7B Pt 7 is subject to Sch 7B Pt 9 (paras 34–38) (pooling of authorities: see PARAS 69–70) and Sch 7B Pt 10 (paras 39–42) (designation of areas and classes of hereditament: see PARAS 71–73): Sch 7B para 31 (Sch 7B added by the Local Government Finance Act 2012 s 1(1), (4), Sch 1).
3 Local Government Finance Act 1988 Sch 7B para 25(1) (as added: see note 2). As to the meaning of 'relevant authority' see PARA 59 note 9. As to the meaning of 'year' see PARA 58 note 2. See the Non-Domestic Rating (Levy and Safety Net) Regulations 2013, SI 2013/737 (amended by SI 2014/822, SI 2015/617, SI 2015/2039 and SI 2017/496).
4 Local Government Finance Act 1988 Sch 7B para 25(2) (as added: see note 2).
5 As to the meaning of 'billing authority' see PARA 346.
6 Ie under the Local Government Finance Act 1988 ss 43, 45: see PARAS 133, 135.
7 Local Government Finance Act 1988 Sch 7B para 25(3)(a) (as added: see note 2).
8 As to the meaning of 'major precepting authority' see PARA 11 note 2 (definition applied by the Local Government Finance Act 1988 s 144(2) (substituted by the Local Government Finance Act 1992 s 117(1), Sch 13 para 81(1); and amended by the Local Government Finance Act 2012 s 5(1), (2)(b), Sch 3 paras 23, 29)).
9 Ie under the Local Government Finance Act 1988 ss 43, 45.
10 Ie under regulations under the Local Government Finance Act 1988 Sch 7B para 9: see PARA 61.
11 Local Government Finance Act 1988 Sch 7B para 25(3)(b) (as added: see note 2).
12 Local Government Finance Act 1988 Sch 7B para 25(3)(c) (as added: see note 2).
13 Local Government Finance Act 1988 Sch 7B para 25(3)(d) (as added: see note 2).
14 Local Government Finance Act 1988 Sch 7B para 25(4) (as added: see note 2).
15 Local Government Finance Act 1988 Sch 7B para 26(1) (as added: see note 2).
16 Local Government Finance Act 1988 Sch 7B para 26(2)(a) (as added: see note 2).
17 Ie under the Local Government Finance Act 1988 Sch 7B para 43: see PARA 73.
18 Ie under the Local Government Finance Act 1988 Sch 7B para 44: see PARA 73.
19 Local Government Finance Act 1988 Sch 7B para 26(2)(b) (as added: see note 2).
20 Local Government Finance Act 1988 Sch 7B para 26(2) (as added: see note 2).
21 Ie under the Local Government Finance Act 1988 Sch 7B para 25: see the text to notes 1–14.
22 Local Government Finance Act 1988 Sch 7B para 26(3) (as added: see note 2).
23 Local Government Finance Act 1988 Sch 7B para 26(4)(a) (as added: see note 2).
24 Local Government Finance Act 1988 Sch 7B para 26(4)(b) (as added: see note 2).
25 Ie under the Local Government Finance Act 1988 Sch 7B para 26: see the text to notes 15–24.
26 Local Government Finance Act 1988 Sch 7B para 27(1) (as added: see note 2).
27 Local Government Finance Act 1988 Sch 7B para 27(2) (as added: see note 2). As to the Treasury see CONSTITUTIONAL AND ADMINISTRATIVE LAW vol 20 (2014) PARA 262 et seq.
28 Ie under the Local Government Finance Act 1988 Sch 7B para 28: see PARA 67.
29 Local Government Finance Act 1988 Sch 7B paras 26(5), 27(3) (as added: see note 2).

67. Payments on account.

The Secretary of State[1] may by regulations make provision:

(1) for a relevant authority[2] to request the Secretary of State to make a calculation before the end of a year of:
  (a) whether the Secretary of State is likely to be required to make a safety net payment[3] to the authority for the year[4]; and
  (b) if so, the amount of the payment[5];

(2) about the time at which and the manner in which a request must be made, and the information that must be provided in connection with the request[6];

(3) about the circumstances in which the Secretary of State may or must make a calculation in response to a request[7];

(4) about the making of the calculation, including for the Secretary of State to make the calculation by reference to estimates of any of specified[8] amounts[9].

The regulations may make provision:

(i) about the timing of a calculation in response to a request[10];

(ii) about the notification of the results of the calculation to the relevant authority to whom it relates[11];

(iii) for the making, as a result of the calculation, of a payment (a 'payment on account') to the authority before the end of the year to which the calculation relates[12].

The regulations may, in particular:

(A) make provision in relation to a calculation that is similar to that made in relation to the calculation of safety net payments[13], or apply the relevant provisions with modifications in relation to such a calculation[14];

(B) make provision in relation to a payment on account that is similar to that made in relation to the calculation of safety net payments following calculations[15] or apply the relevant provisions with modifications in relation to such a payment[16].

The regulations may make provision:

(I) about the calculation of safety net payments[17] to be made in relation to a relevant authority for a year where a payment on account has been made to the authority for the year[18];

(II) for the making of a further payment by the Secretary of State to the authority, or of a payment by the authority to the Secretary of State, as a result of that calculation[19].

The Secretary of State must, in each year other than the first year for which the levy account is kept, calculate in accordance with the statutory formula[20] whether there is a remaining balance on the levy account for the year[21]. The calculation must be made as soon as is reasonably practicable after all of the required calculations of levy payments[22] have been made for the previous year[23], all of the required calculations of safety net payments[24] have been made for the previous year[25], and all of the required calculations of safety net payments on account[26] have been made for the year[27].

The Secretary of State may determine that an amount equal to the whole or part of the remaining balance on a levy account for a year is to be distributed among one or more relevant authorities (rather than being debited or credited[28] to the levy account)[29]. The Secretary of State may by regulations make provision about the basis ('the basis of distribution') on which such an amount is to be distributed[30].

If the Secretary of State makes such a determination, the Secretary of State must calculate what amount (if any) falls to be paid to each relevant authority as its share of the amount to be distributed[31]. The calculations must be made as soon as is reasonably practicable after the determination is made and in accordance with the basis of distribution specified in the regulations[32].

As soon as is reasonably practicable after making the calculations, the Secretary of State must notify each relevant authority of whether a payment is to be made by the Secretary of State to the authority out of the amount to be distributed and, if such a payment is to be made, the amount of the payment[33].

If the calculations show that a payment is to be made by the Secretary of State to a relevant authority, the Secretary of State must make that payment to the authority[34]. A payment from the Secretary of State to a relevant authority under these provisions must be made at such time or in instalments of such amounts and at such times, as the Secretary of State determines with the Treasury's consent; but any such time must fall within the year to which the remaining balance relates[35].

1 As to the Secretary of State see PARA 51.
2 As to the meaning of 'relevant authority' see PARA 59 note 9.
3 Ie under the Local Government Finance Act 1988 Sch 7B para 27: see PARA 66.
4 Local Government Finance Act 1988 Sch 7B para 28(1)(a)(i) (Sch 7B added by the Local Government Finance Act 2012 s 1(1), (4), Sch 1). As to the meaning of 'year' see PARA 58 note 2.
5 Local Government Finance Act 1988 Sch 7B para 28(1)(a)(ii) (as added: see note 4).
6 Local Government Finance Act 1988 Sch 7B para 28(1)(b) (as added: see note 4).
7 Local Government Finance Act 1988 Sch 7B para 28(1)(c) (as added: see note 4).
8 Ie any amounts mentioned in the Local Government Finance Act 1988 Sch 7B para 25(3): see PARA 66.
9 Local Government Finance Act 1988 Sch 7B para 28(1)(d) (as added: see note 4). For regulations made under Sch 7B para 28 see the Non-Domestic Rating (Levy and Safety Net) Regulations 2013, SI 2013/737 (amended by SI 2014/822, SI 2015/617, SI 2015/2039 and SI 2017/496).
10 Local Government Finance Act 1988 Sch 7B para 28(2)(a) (as added: see note 4).
11 Local Government Finance Act 1988 Sch 7B para 28(2)(b) (as added: see note 4).
12 Local Government Finance Act 1988 Sch 7B para 28(2)(c) (as added: see note 4).
13 Ie by the Local Government Finance Act 1988 Sch 7B para 26: see PARA 66.
14 Local Government Finance Act 1988 Sch 7B para 28(3)(a) (as added: see note 4).
15 Ie by the Local Government Finance Act 1988 Sch 7B para 27: see PARA 66.
16 Local Government Finance Act 1988 Sch 7B para 28(3)(b) (as added: see note 4).
17 Ie under the Local Government Finance Act 1988 Sch 7B para 26: see PARA 66.
18 Local Government Finance Act 1988 Sch 7B para 28(4)(a) (as added: see note 4).
19 Local Government Finance Act 1988 Sch 7B para 28(4)(b) (as added: see note 4).
20 Ie in accordance with the Local Government Finance Act 1988 Sch 7B para 29(2)–(4).
21 Local Government Finance Act 1988 Sch 7B para 29(1) (as added: see note 4). In Sch 7B, 'levy account' has the meaning given by Sch 7B para 19(1) (see PARA 64): Sch 7B para 45 (as so added).
22 Ie required by the Local Government Finance Act 1988 Sch 7B para 23(1): see PARA 65. As to the meaning of 'levy payment' see PARA 65.
23 Local Government Finance Act 1988 Sch 7B para 29(2)(a) (as added: see note 4).
24 Ie required by the Local Government Finance Act 1988 Sch 7B para 26(1): see PARA 66.
25 Local Government Finance Act 1988 Sch 7B para 29(2)(b) (as added: see note 4).
26 Ie required by regulations under the Local Government Finance Act 1988 Sch 7B para 28: see the text to notes 1–19.
27 Local Government Finance Act 1988 Sch 7B para 29(2)(c) (as added: see note 4). The calculation must be made as follows (Sch 7B para 29(3) (as so added)):

Step 1: Calculate the aggregate of the amounts of all of the levy payments calculated for the previous year under Sch 7B para 23(1).

Step 2: Add any amount credited to the levy account for the year in accordance with Sch 7B para 21(2) (credit from previous year) to the amount found under step 1, or subtract any amount debited to that account in accordance with Sch 7B para 21(3) (debit from previous year) from the amount found under step 1.

Step 3: Add to the amount found under steps 1 and 2 any amount credited to the levy account for the year in accordance with Sch 7B para 20(2) (credit in accordance with local government finance report).

Step 4: Subtract from the amount found under steps 1–3 the aggregate of the amounts of all the safety net payments calculated for the previous year under Sch 7B para 26(1).

Step 5: Subtract from the amount found under steps 1–4 the aggregate of all the payments to be made by the Secretary of State under regulations under Sch 7B para 28(4)(b) (adjustments following safety net payment on account).

Step 6: Add to the amount found under steps 1–5 the aggregate of all the payments to be made to the Secretary of State under regulations under Sch 7B para 28(4)(b).

Step 7: Subtract from the amount found under steps 1–6 the aggregate of all the payments on account to be made in the year under regulations under Sch 7B para 28.

If the amount found under step 7 is a positive amount, that is the remaining balance on the levy account for the year: Sch 7B para 29(4) (as so added).

If, in the first year for which the levy account is kept:

(1) an amount is credited to the levy account for the year in accordance with Sch 7B para 20(2); and

(2) that amount exceeds the aggregate of all the payments on account to be made in the year under regulations under Sch 7B para 28,

the amount of the excess is to be treated as the remaining balance on the levy account for the year (Sch 7B para 29(5), (6) (as so added)).

28 Ie rather than being treated in accordance the Local Government Finance Act 1988 Sch 7B para 21(2): see PARA 64.
29 Local Government Finance Act 1988 Sch 7B para 30(1) (as added: see note 4).
30 Local Government Finance Act 1988 Sch 7B para 30(2) (as added: see note 4).
31 Local Government Finance Act 1988 Sch 7B para 30(3) (as added: see note 4).
32 Local Government Finance Act 1988 Sch 7B para 30(4) (as added: see note 4).
33 Local Government Finance Act 1988 Sch 7B para 30(5) (as added: see note 4).
34 Local Government Finance Act 1988 Sch 7B para 30(6) (as added: see note 4).
35 Local Government Finance Act 1988 Sch 7B para 30(7) (as added: see note 4). As to the Treasury see CONSTITUTIONAL AND ADMINISTRATIVE LAW vol 20 (2014) PARA 262 et seq.

68. Transitional protection payments.

The Secretary of State[1] may by regulations make provision for calculating in accordance with the regulations:

(1) the total amount which would be payable to a billing authority in England in respect of a year[2] if:
  (a) regulations[3] as to transitional relief following the compilation of the local rating list were not in force for the year[4]; and
  (b) the authority acted diligently[5]; and
(2) the total amount which would be payable to a billing authority in England in respect of a year if the authority acted diligently[6].

The regulations may include provision for adjustments to be made to an amount calculated under provision under heads (1) and (2)[7]. The regulations may, in particular, make provision for adjustments to that amount by reference to changes affecting the calculation of such an amount for an earlier year but not taken into account in that calculation[8].

The Secretary of State may by regulations make provision for the making of a payment (a 'transitional protection payment') for a year by the Secretary of State to a billing authority in England or by a billing authority in England to the Secretary of State[9]. The regulations must provide for the amount (if any) of a transitional protection payment in relation to an authority for a year to be calculated by reference to its deemed and actual rating income[10] for the year[11], so that:

(i) if its deemed rating income for a year exceeds its actual rating income for the year, the Secretary of State is to be liable to make a transitional protection payment to the authority for the year of an amount equal to the excess[12];
(ii) if its actual rating income for a year exceeds its deemed rating income for the year, the authority is to be liable to make a transitional protection payment to the Secretary of State for the year of an amount equal to the excess[13];
(iii) if its deemed rating income for a year is equal to its actual rating income for the year, no transitional protection payment is to be made to or by the authority for the year[14].

The regulations may, in particular, make provision:

(A) about the making of calculations, and the supply of information to the Secretary of State, by a billing authority in connection with the determination of the transitional protection payment (if any) to be made to or by the authority[15];

(B) about the assumptions and adjustments to be made, and the information to be taken into account, in making such calculations[16];

(C) about the consequences of non-compliance with provision under head (A) or (B), including (in particular):

(I) for the making by the Secretary of State of calculations, or of assumptions as to the information that would otherwise have been supplied by the authority[17];

(II) for the suspension of payments to the authority[18].

The regulations may, in particular, make provision:

(AA) for the making by a billing authority or the Secretary of State of a payment on account of a transitional protection payment[19];

(BB) for the calculation, where a payment on account has been made, of the amount of the final transitional protection payment (if any) to be made to or by the authority[20];

(CC) for the certification of calculations made, or information supplied to the Secretary of State, by a billing authority in connection with the determination of the final transitional protection payment (if any) to be made to or by the authority[21];

(DD) about the consequences where a certified calculation or certified information does not match that made or supplied by the authority, including (in particular) about the use of the certified calculation or certified information[22];

(EE) about the making of financial adjustments where the final transitional protection payment to be made to or by the authority for the year is different from a payment on account made to or by the authority for the year[23].

The regulations may confer power on the Secretary of State to give directions about the certification of calculations or information[24]. The regulations may, in particular, make provision about the time and manner in which a payment under the regulations is to be made (including for payment by instalments), and as to the consequences of non-payment[25].

1 As to the Secretary of State see PARA 51.

2 Ie under the Local Government Finance Act 1988 ss 43, 45: see PARAS 133, 135. As to the meaning of 'year' see PARA 58 note 2.

3 Ie under the Local Government Finance Act 1988 s 57A: see PARA 154.

4 Local Government Finance Act 1988 Sch 7B para 32(1)(a)(i) (Sch 7B added by the Local Government Finance Act 2012 s 1(1), (4), Sch 1).

5 Local Government Finance Act 1988 Sch 7B para 32(1)(a)(ii) (as added: see note 4).

6 Local Government Finance Act 1988 Sch 7B para 32(1)(b) (as added: see note 4).

7 Local Government Finance Act 1988 Sch 7B para 32(2) (as added: see note 4).

8 Local Government Finance Act 1988 Sch 7B para 32(3) (as added: see note 4). For regulations made under Sch 7B para 32(1)–(3) see the Non-Domestic Rating (Transitional Protection Payments) Regulations 2013, SI 2013/106.

9 Local Government Finance Act 1988 Sch 7B para 33(1) (as added: see note 4). For regulations made under Sch 7B para 33 see the Non-Domestic Rating (Transitional Protection Payments) Regulations 2013, SI 2013/106; and the Non-Domestic Rating (Shale Oil and Gas and Miscellaneous Amendments) Regulations 2015, SI 2015/628.

10 In the Local Government Finance Act 1988 Sch 7B Pt 8 (paras 32–33), a billing authority's 'deemed rating income' for a year means the amount calculated for the authority and the year under provision under Sch 7B para 32(1)(a), (2) (see the text to notes 2–5, 7), and a billing authority's 'actual rating income' for a year means the amount calculated for the authority and the year under provision under Sch 7B para 32(1)(b), (2) (see the text to notes 6, 7): Sch 7B paras 32(4), 45 (as added: see note 4).

11 Local Government Finance Act 1988 Sch 7B para 33(2) (as added: see note 4).

12 Local Government Finance Act 1988 Sch 7B para 33(2)(a) (as added: see note 4).

13 Local Government Finance Act 1988 Sch 7B para 33(2)(b) (as added: see note 4).
14 Local Government Finance Act 1988 Sch 7B para 33(2)(c) (as added: see note 4).
15 Local Government Finance Act 1988 Sch 7B para 33(3)(a) (as added: see note 4).
16 Local Government Finance Act 1988 Sch 7B para 33(3)(b) (as added: see note 4).
17 Local Government Finance Act 1988 Sch 7B para 33(3)(c)(i) (as added: see note 4).
18 Local Government Finance Act 1988 Sch 7B para 33(3)(c)(ii) (as added: see note 4).
19 Local Government Finance Act 1988 Sch 7B para 33(4)(a) (as added: see note 4).
20 Local Government Finance Act 1988 Sch 7B para 33(4)(b) (as added: see note 4).
21 Local Government Finance Act 1988 Sch 7B para 33(4)(c) (as added: see note 4).
22 Local Government Finance Act 1988 Sch 7B para 33(4)(d) (as added: see note 4).
23 Local Government Finance Act 1988 Sch 7B para 33(4)(e) (as added: see note 4).
24 Local Government Finance Act 1988 Sch 7B para 33(5) (as added: see note 4).
25 Local Government Finance Act 1988 Sch 7B para 33(6) (as added: see note 4).

69. Pooling of authorities.

The Secretary of State[1] may, in accordance with the following provisions, designate two or more relevant authorities as a pool of authorities for the purposes of the statutory provisions[2] applying to such pools[3]. The Secretary of State may make a designation only if each authority covered by the designation has agreed to it[4].

The Secretary of State:

(1) may revoke a designation (in particular if any condition of the designation is breached)[5]; and

(2) must do so if any authority covered by the designation asks the Secretary of State to do so[6].

Subject to the following, a designation has effect for the year beginning after it is made and for each subsequent year, unless previously revoked[7]. However, a designation or revocation has effect for a year only if it is made before the Secretary of State gives the required notification[8] of the general basis of calculation for the year, unless the following provision applies[9]. A revocation made after the Secretary of State has given that notification has effect for the year for which the notification was given if:

(a) it is made in response to a request[10] for revocation by an authority made within the period of 28 days beginning with the date on which the notification was given[11]; and

(b) it is made before the local government finance report[12] for that year is laid before the House of Commons[13].

After making or revoking a designation, the Secretary of State must notify the authorities covered by the designation[14]. Such a notification must be given before or at the same time as the Secretary of State gives the notification of the general basis of calculation for the year to which the designation or revocation relates, unless the following provision applies[15]. A notification of a revocation made in the circumstances described in heads (a) and (b) above must be given as soon as is reasonably practicable after it is made[16].

A designation must be made subject to conditions:

(i) requiring the authorities to which it relates to appoint a lead authority to exercise the functions specified in the conditions[17]; and

(ii) requiring the authorities, if the designation is revoked, to take the steps specified in the conditions before the revocation takes effect[18].

A designation may be made subject to such other conditions as the Secretary of State thinks fit[19].

The Secretary of State may vary a designation by:

(A) adding a condition[20];

(B) modifying a condition[21]; or

(C) removing a condition (other than one mentioned in heads (i) and (ii))[22].

Before varying a designation, the Secretary of State must consult the authorities covered by the designation[23]. After varying a designation, the Secretary of State must notify those authorities[24].

1 As to the Secretary of State see PARA 51.
2 Ie the relevant provisions of the Local Government Finance Act 1988 Sch 7B (see Sch 7B paras 36, 37; and PARA 70).
3 Local Government Finance Act 1988 Sch 7B para 34(1) (Sch 7B added by the Local Government Finance Act 2012 s 1(1), (4), Sch 1). In the Local Government Finance Act 1988 Sch 7B, a 'pool of authorities' means two or more relevant authorities designated as a pool of authorities under Sch 7B para 34: Sch 7B para 45 (as so added). As to the meaning of 'relevant authority' see PARA 59 note 9.
4 Local Government Finance Act 1988 Sch 7B para 34(2) (as added: see note 3).
5 Local Government Finance Act 1988 Sch 7B para 34(3)(a) (as added: see note 3).
6 Local Government Finance Act 1988 Sch 7B para 34(3)(b) (as added: see note 3).
7 Local Government Finance Act 1988 Sch 7B para 34(4) (as added: see note 3). As to the meaning of 'year' see PARA 58 note 2.
8 Ie the notification required by the Local Government Finance Act 1988 Sch 7B para 12(2): see PARA 62.
9 Local Government Finance Act 1988 Sch 7B para 34(5) (as added: see note 3).
10 Ie under the Local Government Finance Act 1988 Sch 7B para 34(3)(b).
11 Local Government Finance Act 1988 Sch 7B para 34(6)(a) (as added: see note 3).
12 As to the meaning of 'local government finance report' see PARA 59.
13 Local Government Finance Act 1988 Sch 7B para 34(6)(b) (as added: see note 3).
14 Local Government Finance Act 1988 Sch 7B para 34(7) (as added: see note 3).
15 Local Government Finance Act 1988 Sch 7B para 34(8) (as added: see note 3).
16 Local Government Finance Act 1988 Sch 7B para 34(9) (as added: see note 3).
17 Local Government Finance Act 1988 Sch 7B para 35(1)(a) (as added: see note 3).
18 Local Government Finance Act 1988 Sch 7B para 35(1)(b) (as added: see note 3).
19 Local Government Finance Act 1988 Sch 7B para 35(2) (as added: see note 3).
20 Local Government Finance Act 1988 Sch 7B para 35(3)(a) (as added: see note 3).
21 Local Government Finance Act 1988 Sch 7B para 35(3)(b) (as added: see note 3).
22 Local Government Finance Act 1988 Sch 7B para 35(3)(c) (as added: see note 3).
23 Local Government Finance Act 1988 Sch 7B para 35(4) (as added: see note 3).
24 Local Government Finance Act 1988 Sch 7B para 35(5) (as added: see note 3).

70. Effect of pooling of authorities.

Where a designation of a pool of authorities has effect for a year[1], the statutory provisions relating to principal payments in connection with local retention of non-domestic rates[2] apply in relation to the pool as if:

(1) the authorities in the pool were not relevant authorities[3]; but
(2) the pool were itself a relevant authority[4].

This does not prevent:

(a) the local government finance report[5] for the year, or an amending report[6] in relation to that report, from also making provision in relation to the individual authorities in the pool[7];
(b) the Secretary of State[8] from making calculations based on the local government finance report, or any such amending report, in relation to each of those authorities[9]; or
(c) the Secretary of State from notifying the results of the calculations to each of those authorities[10].

However, the provisions as to payments following reports[11] do not apply in relation to such calculations[12].

Regulations under specified provisions[13] as to payments may provide for a pool of authorities to be treated as a relevant authority for the purposes of the regulations[14]. Such regulations may, in particular, make provision:

(i) that is similar to provision which may be made under the provision in question apart from the application to pooling[15]; or

(ii) that applies such provision with modifications[16].

Where regulations as to levy payments[17] apply to a pool of authorities for a year, the provisions as to the calculation and making of levy payments[18] apply in relation to the authorities and the year as if references in them to a relevant authority were to the pool[19].

Where regulations as to safety net payments[20] apply to a pool of authorities for a year, the provisions as to the calculation and making of safety net payments[21] apply in relation to the authorities and the year as if references in them to a relevant authority were to the pool[22].

Where a designation of a pool of authorities has effect for a year, the provisions as to the distribution of the remaining balance[23] apply in relation to the pool as if:

(A) the authorities in the pool were not relevant authorities[24]; but

(B) the pool were itself a relevant authority[25].

Regulations as to the distribution of the remaining balance[26] may provide for a pool of authorities to be treated as a relevant authority for the purposes of the regulations[27].

These provisions do not prevent:

(I) regulations as to payments or the distribution of the remaining balance[28] from also making provision in relation to the individual authorities in a pool[29];

(II) the Secretary of State from making calculations[30] based on such regulations in relation to each of those authorities[31]; or

(III) the Secretary of State from notifying the results of the calculations to each of those authorities[32].

However, the provisions as to payments following calculations[33] do not apply in relation to such calculations[34].

A requirement[35] to notify a pool of authorities of any matter is a requirement to notify each authority in the pool of that matter[36].

Where, by virtue of the provisions above[37], a pool of authorities is required to make a payment to the Secretary of State, each authority in the pool is jointly and severally liable to make that payment[38]. Where, by virtue those provisions, the Secretary of State is required to make a payment to a pool of authorities, the payment is to be made to the lead authority appointed in accordance with the conditions[39] of the designation[40].

1 Ie under the Local Government Finance Act 1988 Sch 7B para 4: see PARA 69. As to the meaning of 'pool of authorities' see PARA 69 note 3. As to the meaning of 'year' see PARA 58 note 2.

2 Ie the Local Government Finance Act 1988 Sch 7B Pt 5 (paras 12–18): see PARAS 58–63. However, Schedule 7B para 36(1) does not apply in relation to Sch 7B para 15(5) (duty to send copy of amending report to each relevant authority: see PARA 63): Sch 7B para 36(2) (Sch 7B added by the Local Government Finance Act 2012 s 1(1), (4), Sch 1).

3 Local Government Finance Act 1988 Sch 7B para 36(1)(a) (as added: see note 2). As to the meaning of 'relevant authority' see PARA 59 note 9.

4 Local Government Finance Act 1988 Sch 7B para 36(1)(b) (as added: see note 2).

5 As to the meaning of 'local government finance report' see PARA 59.

6 Ie under the Local Government Finance Act 1988 Sch 7B para 15.

7 Local Government Finance Act 1988 Sch 7B para 36(3)(a) (as added: see note 2).

8 As to the Secretary of State see PARA 51.

9 Local Government Finance Act 1988 Sch 7B para 36(3)(b) (as added: see note 2).

10 Local Government Finance Act 1988 Sch 7B para 36(3)(c) (as added: see note 2).

11 Ie the Local Government Finance Act 1988 Sch 7B paras 14, 17: see PARAS 62, 63.

12 Local Government Finance Act 1988 Sch 7B para 36(4) (as added: see note 2).

13 Ie under the Local Government Finance Act 1988 Sch 7B para 22, 25 or 28 (levy payments, safety net payments and safety net payments on account): see PARAS 65–67.
14 Local Government Finance Act 1988 Sch 7B para 37(1) (as added: see note 2). See the Non-Domestic Rating (Levy and Safety Net) Regulations 2013, SI 2013/737 (amended by SI 2014/822, SI 2015/2039 and SI 2017/496).
15 Local Government Finance Act 1988 Sch 7B para 37(2)(a) (as added: see note 2).
16 Local Government Finance Act 1988 Sch 7B para 37(2)(b) (as added: see note 2).
17 Ie under the Local Government Finance Act 1988 Sch 7B para 22.
18 Ie under the Local Government Finance Act 1988 Sch 7B paras 23, 24: see PARA 65.
19 Local Government Finance Act 1988 Sch 7B para 37(3) (as added: see note 2).
20 Ie under the Local Government Finance Act 1988 Sch 7B para 25.
21 Ie under the Local Government Finance Act 1988 Sch 7B paras 26, 27: see PARA 66.
22 Local Government Finance Act 1988 Sch 7B para 37(4) (as added: see note 2).
23 Ie the Local Government Finance Act 1988 Sch 7B para 30: see PARA 67.
24 Local Government Finance Act 1988 Sch 7B para 37(5)(a) (as added: see note 2).
25 Local Government Finance Act 1988 Sch 7B para 37(5)(b) (as added: see note 2).
26 Ie under the Local Government Finance Act 1988 Sch 7B para 30.
27 Local Government Finance Act 1988 Sch 7B para 37(6) (as added: see note 2).
28 Ie under the Local Government Finance Act 1988 Sch 7B para 22, 25, 28 or 30.
29 Local Government Finance Act 1988 Sch 7B para 37(7)(a) (as added: see note 2).
30 Ie under the Local Government Finance Act 1988 Sch 7B para 23, 26 or 30(3).
31 Local Government Finance Act 1988 Sch 7B para 37(7)(b) (as added: see note 2).
32 Local Government Finance Act 1988 Sch 7B para 37(7)(c) (as added: see note 2).
33 Ie the Local Government Finance Act 1988 Sch 7B paras 24, 27 and 30(6).
34 Local Government Finance Act 1988 Sch 7B para 37(8) (as added: see note 2).
35 Ie under the Local Government Finance Act 1988 Sch 7B Pt 5 (paras 12–18) or Pt 7 (paras 22–31) in its application by virtue of Sch 7B para 36 or 37.
36 Local Government Finance Act 1988 Sch 7B para 38(1) (as added: see note 2).
37 Ie by virtue of the Local Government Finance Act 1988 Sch 7B para 36 or 37.
38 Local Government Finance Act 1988 Sch 7B para 38(2) (as added: see note 2).
39 Ie under the Local Government Finance Act 1988 Sch 7B para 35(1): see PARA 69.
40 Local Government Finance Act 1988 Sch 7B para 38(3) (as added: see note 2).

71. Designation of areas and classes of hereditament.

The Secretary of State[1] may by regulations:

(1) designate one or more areas in England (a 'designated area')[2];
(2) provide for the calculation in accordance with the regulations, for each year for which the designation has effect and in relation to each billing authority[3] all or part of whose area falls within a designated area, of the amount mentioned below[4];
(3) provide for the calculation of a proportion of that amount in accordance with the regulations[5];
(4) provide for that amount or that proportion to be disregarded for the purposes of calculations under any of certain specified provisions[6] in its application to the authority for that year[7].

Subject as follows, the amount referred to in head (2) above is the total amount which, if the authority acted diligently, would be payable to it for the year[8] in respect of the hereditaments within the designated area[9].

The regulations may provide for that amount, or any proportion calculated under head (3) above, to be adjusted in accordance with the regulations (and references in these provisions to that amount or proportion include the amount or proportion as adjusted in accordance with such provision)[10]. The regulations may, in particular, provide for adjustments to that amount or that proportion by reference to changes affecting a calculation under regulations under these provisions for an earlier year but not taken into account in that calculation[11]. The regulations must:

(a) specify the date on which the designation takes effect, which must be the first day of a year[12]; or

(b) provide that the designation is to take effect on the first day of the first year after specified[13] conditions have been met[14].

The regulations may specify the years for which the designation has effect[15].

Regulations under these provisions must specify each area designated by the regulations by means of a plan or map (whether or not each area is specified by any other means)[16]. An area may be designated by regulations by reference to such factors as the Secretary of State thinks fit[17]. The consent of the Treasury is required to regulations under these provisions[18].

The Secretary of State may by regulations:

(i) designate one or more classes of hereditaments in England (a 'designated class')[19];

(ii) provide for the calculation in accordance with the regulations, for each year for which the designation has effect and in relation to each billing authority whose area includes hereditaments within the designated class, of the amount mentioned below[20];

(iii) provide for the calculation of a proportion of that amount in accordance with the regulations[21];

(iv) provide for that amount or that proportion to be disregarded for the purposes of calculations under any of certain specified provisions[22] in its application to the authority for that year[23].

Subject as follows, the amount referred to in head (ii) above is the total amount which, if the authority acted diligently, would be payable to it for the year[24] in respect of the hereditaments within the designated class[25].

The regulations may provide for that amount, or any proportion calculated under head (iii) above, to be adjusted in accordance with the regulations (and references in these provisions to that amount or proportion include the amount or proportion as adjusted in accordance with such provision)[26]. The regulations may, in particular, provide for adjustments to that amount or that proportion by reference to changes affecting a calculation under regulations under these provisions for an earlier year but not taken into account in that calculation[27]. The regulations may include provision imposing duties or conferring powers on valuation officers (whether as regards determinations, certificates or otherwise) for the purpose of the calculation referred to in head (iii)[28]. The regulations:

(A) must specify the date on which the designation takes effect (which must be at the beginning of a year)[29]; and

(B) may specify the years for which the designation has effect[30].

A class may be designated by regulations under these provisions by reference to such factors as the Secretary of State thinks fit[31]. Before making regulations the Secretary of State must consult such persons as the Secretary of State thinks fit[32].

The consent of the Treasury is required to regulations under these provisions[33].

1 As to the Secretary of State see PARA 51.

2 Local Government Finance Act 1988 Sch 7B para 39(1)(a) (Sch 7B added by the Local Government Finance Act 2012 s 1(1), (4), Sch 1).

3 As to the meaning of 'billing authority' see PARA 346. As to the meaning of 'year' see PARA 58 note 2.

4 Local Government Finance Act 1988 Sch 7B para 39(1)(b) (as added: see note 2).

5 Local Government Finance Act 1988 Sch 7B para 39(1)(c) (as added: see note 2).

6 Ie:

(1) the Local Government Finance Act 1988 Sch 7B para 6 (payments in respect of the central share: see PARA 60);

(2) regulations under Sch 7B para 7 (administrative arrangements for payments in respect of

the central share: see PARA 60);
(3) regulations under Sch 7B para 9 (payments by billing authorities to major precepting authorities);
(4) regulations under Sch 7B para 10 (administrative arrangements for payments by billing authorities to major precepting authorities: see PARA 61);
(5) Sch 7B para 13 (calculations following local government finance report: see PARA 62);
(6) Sch 7B para 16 (calculations following amending report: see PARA 63);
(7) Sch 7B para 23 (calculations of levy payments: see PARA 65);
(8) Sch 7B para 26 (calculations of safety net payments: see PARA 66);
(9) regulations under Sch 7B para 28 (calculations of payments on account: see PARA 67);
(10) Sch 7B para 30 (calculations relating to distribution of remaining balance: see PARA 67).

7 Local Government Finance Act 1988 Sch 7B para 39(1)(d) (as added: see note 2). See the Non-Domestic Rating (Designated Areas) Regulations 2013, SI 2013/107; the Non-Domestic Rating (Designated Areas) Regulations 2014, SI 2014/98; the Non-Domestic Rating (Designated Area) Regulations 2015, SI 2015/353; the Non-Domestic Rating (Northern Line Extension) Regulations 2015, SI 2015/354; the Non-Domestic Rating (Designated Areas etc) Regulations 2016, SI 2016/317; the Non-Domestic Rating (Designated Areas etc) Regulations 2017, SI 2017/318 (amended by SI 2017/471); and the Non-Domestic Rating (Designated Areas) Regulations 2018, SI 2018/213. See also the Non-Domestic Rating (Rates Retention) Regulations 2013, SI 2013/452 (amended by SI 2014/96, SI 2015/628, SI 2016/317, SI 2016/1268, SI 2017/318, SI 2017/496 and SI 2017/1321).

8 Ie under the Local Government Finance Act 1988 ss 43, 45: see PARAS 133, 135.

9 Local Government Finance Act 1988 Sch 7B para 39(2) (as added: see note 2). As to hereditaments see PARA 106 et seq.

10 Local Government Finance Act 1988 Sch 7B para 39(3) (as added: see note 2).

11 Local Government Finance Act 1988 Sch 7B para 39(4) (as added: see note 2).

12 Local Government Finance Act 1988 Sch 7B para 39(5)(a) (as added: see note 2).

13 In the Local Government Finance Act 1988 Sch 7B para 39, 'specified' means specified in the regulations: Sch 7B para 39(14) (as added: see note 2).

14 Local Government Finance Act 1988 Sch 7B para 39(5)(b) (as added: see note 2). Conditions under Sch 7B para 39(5)(b) may require compliance with specifications or requirements contained in a document of a specified kind: Sch 7B para 39(6) (as so added). If the regulations make provision under Sch 7B para 39(5)(b), they must provide that they will cease to have effect at the end of a specified period unless the conditions are met by the end of that period: Sch 7B para 39(7) (as so added).

15 Local Government Finance Act 1988 Sch 7B para 39(8) (as added: see note 2). If the regulations contain provision under Sch 7B para 39(8):
(1) amendments within Sch 7B para 39(10) may not be made to the regulations unless (in the case of amendments within Sch 7B para 39(10)(a), (b) or (c)) the amendments are expressed to come into force after the end of that period (Sch 7B para 39(9)(a) (as so added)); and
(2) the regulations may not be revoked unless the revocation is expressed to come into force after the end of that period (Sch 7B para 39(9)(b) (as so added)).

The amendments mentioned in Sch 7B para 39(9)(a) are those which have the effect of:
(a) altering the boundaries of a designated area (Sch 7B para 39(10)(a) (as so added));
(b) where provision made under Sch 7B para 39(1)(d) (see head (4) in the text) has the effect that the amount referred to in that paragraph is to be disregarded, providing for a proportion of that amount to be disregarded (Sch 7B para 39(10)(b) (as so added));
(c) where provision made under Sch 7B para 39(1)(d) has the effect that a proportion is to be disregarded, reducing that proportion (Sch 7B para 39(10)(c) (as so added)); or
(d) reducing the period for which the designation has effect (Sch 7B para 39(10)(d) (as so added)).

16 Local Government Finance Act 1988 Sch 7B para 39(11) (as added: see note 2).

17 Local Government Finance Act 1988 Sch 7B para 39(12) (as added: see note 2).

18 Local Government Finance Act 1988 Sch 7B para 39(13) (as added: see note 2). As to the Treasury see CONSTITUTIONAL AND ADMINISTRATIVE LAW vol 20 (2014) PARA 262 et seq.

19 Local Government Finance Act 1988 Sch 7B para 40(1)(a) (as added: see note 2).

20 Local Government Finance Act 1988 Sch 7B para 40(1)(b) (as added: see note 2).

21 Local Government Finance Act 1988 Sch 7B para 40(1)(c) (as added: see note 2).

22 Ie:
(1) the Local Government Finance Act 1988 Sch 7B para 6 (payments in respect of the

central share: see PARA 60);
(2) regulations under Sch 7B para 7 (administrative arrangements for payments in respect of the central share: see PARA 60);
(3) regulations under Sch 7B para 9 (payments by billing authorities to major precepting authorities);
(4) regulations under Sch 7B para 10 (administrative arrangements for payments by billing authorities to major precepting authorities: see PARA 61);
(5) Sch 7B para 13 (calculations following local government finance report: see PARA 62);
(6) Sch 7B para 16 (calculations following amending report: see PARA 63);
(7) Sch 7B para 23 (calculations of levy payments: see PARA 65);
(8) Sch 7B para 26 (calculations of safety net payments: see PARA 66);
(9) regulations under Sch 7B para 28 (calculations of payments on account: see PARA 67);
(10) Sch 7B para 30 (calculations relating to distribution of remaining balance: see PARA 67).

23 Local Government Finance Act 1988 Sch 7B para 40(1)(d) (as added: see note 2). See the Non-Domestic Rating (Renewable Energy Projects) Regulations 2013, SI 2013/108 (amended by SI 2017/1132); and the Non-Domestic Rating (Shale Oil and Gas and Miscellaneous Amendments) Regulations 2015, SI 2015/628.
24 Ie under the Local Government Finance Act 1988 ss 43, 45: see PARAS 133, 135.
25 Local Government Finance Act 1988 Sch 7B para 40(2) (as added: see note 2).
26 Local Government Finance Act 1988 Sch 7B para 40(3) (as added: see note 2).
27 Local Government Finance Act 1988 Sch 7B para 40(4) (as added: see note 2).
28 Local Government Finance Act 1988 Sch 7B para 40(5) (as added: see note 2).
29 Local Government Finance Act 1988 Sch 7B para 40(6)(a) (as added: see note 2).
30 Local Government Finance Act 1988 Sch 7B para 40(6)(b) (as added: see note 2).
31 Local Government Finance Act 1988 Sch 7B para 40(7) (as added: see note 2).
32 Local Government Finance Act 1988 Sch 7B para 40(8) (as added: see note 2). The fact that Sch 7B para 40 was not in force when consultation in relation to proposed regulations under it took place is to be disregarded in determining whether there has been compliance with Sch 7B para 40(8): Sch 7B para 40(9) (as so added).
33 Local Government Finance Act 1988 Sch 7B para 40(10) (as added: see note 2).

72. Payments where areas or classes of hereditament have been designated.

Where areas or classes of hereditament have been designated[1], regulations[2] may make provision for a billing authority[3] to make a payment for a year to a relevant authority of an amount equal to the whole or part of the amount or proportion that, in relation to the billing authority and the year, is to be disregarded for the purposes of the relevant calculations[4].

Where the regulations include provision for payments to be made to two or more relevant authorities, the regulations may include provision for imposing duties or conferring powers on valuation officers (whether as regards determinations, certificates or otherwise) for the purpose of arriving at the amounts of those payments[5].

The regulations may make provision about the administration of payments to relevant authorities under the regulations[6]. The regulations may, in particular, make provision in relation to payments to relevant authorities of the same kind as the provision that may be made[7] in relation to payments to major precepting authorities[8] to which the relevant provisions apply[9].

The Secretary of State[10] may by regulations make provision for:

(1) calculations of deductions[11] to be made on the basis of an estimate of an amount or proportion that is to be disregarded under regulations under the relevant statutory provision[12];
(2) for the making of a payment by the Secretary of State to a billing authority or vice versa where it is subsequently determined that the amount or proportion to be disregarded is more or less than the amount of the estimate[13].

Such regulations may make provision about the administration of payments under the regulations, including as to:

(a) the time and manner in which a payment is to be made[14]; and
(b) the consequences of non-payment[15].

1 Ie under the Local Government Finance Act 1988 Sch 7B para 39 or 40: see PARA 71. As to hereditaments see PARA 106 et seq.
2 Ie under the Local Government Finance Act 1988 Sch 7B para 39 or 40: see PARA 71.
3 As to the meaning of 'billing authority' see PARA 346.
4 Local Government Finance Act 1988 Sch 7B para 41(1) (Sch 7B added by the Local Government Finance Act 2012 s 1(1), (4), Sch 1). The calculations referred to in the text are those mentioned in the Local Government Finance Act 1988 Sch 7B para 39(1)(d) or 40(1)(d) (as the case may be): see PARA 71 heads (4), (iv). As to the meaning of 'year' see PARA 58 note 2.
5 Local Government Finance Act 1988 Sch 7B para 41(2), (3) (as added: see note 4). As to the meaning of 'relevant authority' see PARA 59 note 9.
6 Local Government Finance Act 1988 Sch 7B para 41(4) (as added: see note 4).
7 Ie under the Local Government Finance Act 1988 Sch 7B para 10(2): see PARA 61.
8 As to the meaning of 'major precepting authority' see PARA 11 note 2 (definition applied by s 144(2) (substituted by the Local Government Finance Act 1992 s 117(1), Sch 13 para 81(1); and amended by the Local Government Finance Act 2012 s 5(1), (2)(b), Sch 3 paras 23, 29)).
9 Local Government Finance Act 1988 Sch 7B para 41(5) (as added: see note 4).
10 As to the Secretary of State see PARA 51.
11 Ie calculations of a kind mentioned in the Local Government Finance Act 1988 Sch 7B para 39(1)(d) or 40(1)(d) (as the case may be): see PARA 71 heads (4), (iv).
12 Local Government Finance Act 1988 Sch 7B para 42(1)(a) (as added: see note 4).
13 Local Government Finance Act 1988 Sch 7B para 42(1)(b) (as added: see note 4).
14 Local Government Finance Act 1988 Sch 7B para 42(2)(a) (as added: see note 4).
15 Local Government Finance Act 1988 Sch 7B para 42(2)(b) (as added: see note 4).

73. Calculations and supply of information.

The Secretary of State[1] may, for the purposes of any provision of or made under the relevant legislation[2] so far as applying to non-domestic rates, direct a relevant authority[3] to make calculations, or to supply information to the Secretary of State, in accordance with the direction[4]. The direction may require the calculations to be made, or the information to be supplied, before such time as is specified in the direction[5]. The direction may require the calculations or information to be certified in accordance with the direction[6].

If a relevant authority does not comply with a direction, the Secretary of State may make the calculations that the Secretary of State thinks would have been made, or make assumptions as to the information that would have been supplied, by the authority if it had complied with the direction[7]. If the Secretary of State proceeds under this provision, the Secretary of State must notify the authority of that fact and of the calculations or assumptions that the Secretary of State has made[8].

If any calculation or information certified in accordance with a direction does not match that made or supplied by the authority in question, the Secretary of State may use the certified calculation or information[9]. If the Secretary of State proceeds under this provision, the Secretary of State must notify the authority of that fact[10].

For the purposes of any provision made by or under the legislation relating to principal payments, levy payments or safety net payments[11] that applies to pools of authorities[12], the provisions above have effect as if references to a relevant authority included a reference to such a pool[13]. Where the Secretary of State is required to notify a pool of authorities[14], the Secretary of State must notify each relevant authority in the pool of the matters in question[15].

The Secretary of State may by regulations:

(1) make any provision that could be made by a direction under the provisions above[16];

(2) make provision for the Secretary of State to give a direction that could be given under those provisions[17];

(3) make any provision made by those provisions in relation to a direction under them:

 (a) in relation to provision made by regulations under this provision[18]; or

 (b) in relation to a direction given by the Secretary of State under regulations under this provision[19].

1 As to the Secretary of State see PARA 51.
2 Ie the Local Government Finance Act 1988 Sch 7B or Pt VI (ss 89–99).
3 As to the meaning of 'relevant authority' see PARA 59 note 9.
4 Local Government Finance Act 1988 Sch 7B para 43(1) (Sch 7B added by the Local Government Finance Act 2012 s 1(1), (4), Sch 1).
5 Local Government Finance Act 1988 Sch 7B para 43(2) (as added: see note 4).
6 Local Government Finance Act 1988 Sch 7B para 43(3) (as added: see note 4).
7 Local Government Finance Act 1988 Sch 7B para 43(4) (as added: see note 4).
8 Local Government Finance Act 1988 Sch 7B para 43(5) (as added: see note 4).
9 Local Government Finance Act 1988 Sch 7B para 43(6) (as added: see note 4).
10 Local Government Finance Act 1988 Sch 7B para 43(7) (as added: see note 4).
11 Ie the Local Government Finance Act 1988 Sch 7B Pt 5 (paras 12–18) or Pt 7 (paras 22–31): see PARAS 62–63, 65–67.
12 As to pooling see PARAS 69–70. As to the meaning of 'pool of authorities' see PARA 69 note 3.
13 Local Government Finance Act 1988 Sch 7B para 43(8) (as added: see note 4).
14 Ie where the Local Government Finance Act 1988 Sch 7B para 43(5) or (7) applies by virtue of Sch 7B para 43(8).
15 Local Government Finance Act 1988 Sch 7B para 43(9) (as added: see note 4).
16 Local Government Finance Act 1988 Sch 7B para 44(a) (as added: see note 4).
17 Local Government Finance Act 1988 Sch 7B para 44(b) (as added: see note 4).
18 Local Government Finance Act 1988 Sch 7B para 44(c)(i) (as added: see note 4).
19 Local Government Finance Act 1988 Sch 7B para 44(c)(ii) (as added: see note 4). For regulations made under Sch 7B para 44 see the Non-Domestic Rating (Rates Retention) Regulations 2013, SI 2013/452 (amended by SI 2014/96, SI 2015/628, SI 2016/317, SI 2016/1268, SI 2017/318, SI 2017/496 and SI 2017/1321).

(ii) In Wales

74. Non-domestic rating accounts: Wales.

In relation to Wales, the Welsh Ministers[1] must, in accordance with the statutory provisions[2], keep for each chargeable financial year[3] an account (to be called a non-domestic rating account)[4]. The Welsh Ministers must keep each account in such form as the Treasury may direct and must at such time as the Treasury may direct send copies of each account to the Auditor General for Wales[5]. The Auditor General for Wales must examine, certify and report on any account of which copies are so sent to him and must lay copies of the account and of his report before the National Assembly for Wales[6].

For each chargeable financial year the following must be credited (as items of account) to the account kept for the year[7]:

(1) sums received by the Welsh Ministers in the year[8] in respect of central non-domestic rating liability[9];

(2) sums received by them in the year[10] in respect of contributions in aid[11]; and

(3) sums received by them in the year[12] in respect of non-domestic rating contribution or under regulations[13] relating to financial adjustment[14].

For each chargeable financial year the following must be debited (as items of account) to the account kept for the year[15]:

(a) specified payments made by the Welsh Ministers in the year[16] in respect of non-domestic rating contributions[17]; and

(b) distribution payments made by them in the year[18] to receiving authorities[19].

As soon as is reasonably practicable after the end of each chargeable financial year the Welsh Ministers must calculate the following[20]:

(i) the aggregate of the items of account credited to the account kept for the year[21]; and

(ii) the aggregate of the items of account debited to the account kept for the year[22].

If the aggregate mentioned in head (i) above exceeds that mentioned in head (ii), a sum equal to the excess must be debited (as an item of account) to the account kept for the year and credited (as an item of account) to the account kept for the next financial year[23].

If the aggregate mentioned in head (ii) exceeds that mentioned in head (i), a sum equal to the excess must be credited (as an item of account) to the account kept for the year and debited (as an item of account) to the account kept for the next financial year[24].

1 As to the Welsh Ministers see PARA 51.
2 Ie in accordance with the Local Government Finance Act 1988 Sch 8.
3 As to the meaning of 'chargeable financial year' see PARA 24 note 1.
4 Local Government Finance Act 1988 Sch 8 para 1(1) (amended by the Local Government Finance Act 2012 s 5(1), (2)(a), Sch 3 paras 2, 3(1), (2)).
5 Local Government Finance Act 1988 Sch 8 para 1(2) (amended by the Local Government Finance Act 2012 Sch 3 paras 2, 3(1), (3)). As to the Auditor General for Wales see PARA 615; and CONSTITUTIONAL AND ADMINISTRATIVE LAW vol 20 (2014) PARA 400 et seq.
6 Local Government Finance Act 1988 Sch 8 para 1(4) (added by SI 2007/1388; amended by the Local Government Finance Act 2012 Sch 3 paras 2, 3(1), (5)). As to the Treasury see CONSTITUTIONAL AND ADMINISTRATIVE LAW vol 20 (2014) PARA 262 et seq.
7 Local Government Finance Act 1988 Sch 8 para 2(1).
8 Ie under the Local Government Finance Act 1988 s 54: see PARA 142.
9 Local Government Finance Act 1988 Sch 8 para 2(1)(a) (amended by the Local Government Finance Act 2012 Sch 3 paras 2, 4(1), (2)(a)).
10 Ie under the Local Government Finance Act 1988 s 59: see PARA 113.
11 Local Government Finance Act 1988 Sch 8 para 2(1)(b) (amended by the Local Government and Housing Act 1989 s 139, Sch 5 paras 41, 79(3); and the Local Government Finance Act 2012 Sch 3 paras 2, 4(1), (2)(b)).
12 Ie under the Local Government Finance Act 1988 Sch 8 para 5: see PARA 75.
13 Ie under the Local Government Finance Act 1988 Sch 8 para 5(15): see PARA 75.
14 Local Government Finance Act 1988 Sch 8 para 2(1)(c) (amended by the Local Government Finance Act 1992 s 117(1), Sch 13 para 86; and the Local Government Finance Act 2012 Sch 3 paras 2, 4(1), (2)(b)).
15 Local Government Finance Act 1988 Sch 8 para 2(2).
16 Ie under the Local Government Finance Act 1988 Sch 8 para 5(10) or (14), under regulations made for the purpose mentioned in Sch 8 para 4(7) or under regulations made under Sch 8 para 5(15) or 6(5): see PARAS 75, 76.
17 Local Government Finance Act 1988 Sch 8 para 2(2)(a) (amended by the Local Government Finance Act 1992 Sch 13 para 86; the Local Government Act 2003 s 127(1), Sch 7 paras 9(1), 26(1), (2); and the Local Government Finance Act 2012 Sch 3 paras 2, 4(1), (3)(a)).
18 Ie under the Local Government Finance Act 1988 Sch 8 para 12 or 15: see PARAS 78, 79.

19 Local Government Finance Act 1988 Sch 8 para 2(2)(b) (amended by the Local Government Finance Act 1992 Sch 13 para 86; and the Local Government Finance Act 2012 Sch 3 paras 2, 4(1), (3)(b)).
20 Local Government Finance Act 1988 Sch 8 para 3(1) (amended by the Local Government Finance Act 2012 Sch 3 paras 2, 5).
21 Local Government Finance Act 1988 Sch 8 para 3(1)(a).
22 Local Government Finance Act 1988 Sch 8 para 3(1)(b).
23 Local Government Finance Act 1988 Sch 8 para 3(2).
24 Local Government Finance Act 1988 Sch 8 para 3(3).

75. Non-domestic rating contributions.

The Welsh Ministers[1] may make regulations containing rules for the calculation of an amount for a chargeable financial year[2] in relation to each billing authority[3] (to be called its non-domestic rating contribution for the year)[4]. The rules must be so framed that the amount calculated under them in relation to an authority is broadly the same as the total which, if the authority acted diligently, would be payable to it[5] in respect of the year[6]. The rules may include provision for such deductions as the maker of the rules thinks fit for the purpose of enabling an authority to retain part, or all, of so much of the total payable to it in respect of the year[7] as exceeds an amount determined for the authority by or under the rules[8].

The Welsh Ministers may incorporate in the rules provision for deductions (of such extent as they think fit) as regards:

(1) the operation of the statutory provisions[9] as to discretionary relief and reduction or remission in the case of hardship[10];
(2) costs of collection and recovery[11];
(3) such other matters (if any) as they think fit[12];

and the requirement as to the framing of the rules[13] has effect subject to this[14].

Regulations under these provisions in their application to a particular financial year (including regulations amending or revoking others) are not effective unless they come into force before 1 January in the preceding financial year[15]. This does not apply to regulations made only for the purpose of amending the rules to increase deductions as regards the operation of the statutory provision for reduction or remission of liability[16] for the whole or part of the financial year[17].

The following provisions apply where regulations[18] are in force for a chargeable financial year and have effect subject to any provision made[19] for adjustments to the calculation of the amount of an authority's non-domestic rating contribution[20]. By such time before the year begins as the Welsh Ministers may direct, a billing authority must calculate the amount of its non-domestic rating contribution for the year and must notify the amount to the Secretary of State[21]. If the authority fails to comply with this requirement or if the Welsh Ministers believe the amount notified is not likely to have been calculated in accordance with the regulations they may make their own calculation of the amount; and where they make such a calculation they must inform the authority why they have done so and inform it of the amount calculated[22].

The authority is liable to pay to the Welsh Ministers an amount (the provisional amount) equal to either that calculated and notified by it or that calculated by the Welsh Ministers[23]. The authority must pay the provisional amount during the course of the year, in such instalments and at such times as the Welsh Ministers may direct[24]. After the year ends the authority must:

(a) calculate the amount of its non-domestic rating contribution for the year[25];
(b) notify the amount so calculated to the Welsh Ministers[26];

(c) notify to the Welsh Ministers, the amount of any deduction that[27] is made in calculating the amount mentioned in head (a)[28]; and

(d) arrange for the calculation and the amount[29] to be certified under arrangements made by the Auditor General for Wales[30].

The Auditor General for Wales must send a copy of the certification of the calculation and the amount or amounts to the Welsh Ministers[31].

If the authority fails to comply with the requirements of heads (a) to (d) above by such time as the Welsh Ministers direct, they may suspend payments which would otherwise fall to be made to the authority under the relevant provisions[32]; but if the authority then complies with the requirements they must resume payments falling to be made to the authority under the relevant provisions and make payments to it equal to those suspended[33].

If, at any time after the year ends, the Welsh Ministers receive notification from an authority under head (b) above they must calculate the amount of the difference (if any) between the amount notified and the provisional amount and, if there is a difference, inform the authority of the amount of the difference[34]. If the amount notified under head (b) above exceeds the provisional amount the authority must pay an amount equal to the difference to the Welsh Ministers at such time as they may direct[35]. If the amount notified under head (b) above is less than the provisional amount, the Welsh Ministers must:

(i) if they believe that the amount so notified is not likely to have been calculated in accordance with the regulations[36], inform the authority of their reasons for that belief[37];

(ii) if they are not of that belief, pay to the authority, at such time as they decide, an amount equal to the difference between the amount so notified and the provisional amount[38].

The following provisions apply where:

(A) at any time after the year ends the Welsh Ministers have received both a notification from an authority under head (b) above and a copy of a certification sent to them[39] by the Auditor General for Wales in relation to the authority[40]; and

(B) the amount which is certified by the certification to be the authority's non-domestic rating contribution for the year (the certified amount) is different from the amount notified to the Welsh Ministers under head (b) above[41].

In such event, the Welsh Ministers must calculate the amount of the difference (if any) between the certified amount and the provisional amount and, if there is a difference, inform the authority of the amount of the difference[42].

If at the time the Welsh Ministers make the required calculation no payment has been made[43] in relation to the amount notified under head (b) above, the following provisions apply instead[44] in relation to that amount[45]. In such a case, if the certified amount exceeds the provisional amount the authority must pay an amount equal to the difference to the Welsh Ministers at such time as they may direct and, if the certified amount is less than the provisional amount the Welsh Ministers must pay an amount equal to the difference to the authority, and the amount is to be paid at such time as they decide[46].

Where an amount has become payable under any of these provisions[47], and it has not been paid, it is recoverable in a court of competent jurisdiction[48].

1 As to the Welsh Ministers and the Secretary of State see PARA 51.

2 As to the meaning of 'chargeable financial year' see PARA 24 note 1.

3 Any reference in the Local Government Finance Act 1988 Sch 8 Pt II (paras 3A–7) to a billing authority is a reference to a billing authority in Wales: Sch 8 para 3A (added by the Local Government Finance Act 2012 s 5(1), (2)(a), Sch 3 paras 2, 6). As to the meaning of 'billing authority' see PARA 346.
4 Local Government Finance Act 1988 Sch 8 para 4(1) (amended by the Local Government Finance Act 1992 ss 104, 117(2), Sch 10 para 6(2)–(5), Sch 14; and the Local Government Finance Act 2012 Sch 3 paras 2, 7(1), (2)). As to the rules for the calculation of non-domestic rating contributions see the Non-Domestic Rating Contributions (Wales) Regulations 1992, SI 1992/3238 (amended by SI 1993/1505, SI 1993/3077, SI 1994/547, SI 1994/1742, SI 1994/3125, SI 1996/619, SI 2000/3382, SI 2007/3343, SI 2014/3193, SI 2016/1169 and SI 2017/1159). See also the Non-Domestic Rating Contributions (England) Regulations 1992, SI 1992/3082 (amended by SI 1992/3259, SI 1993/1496, SI 1993/3082, SI 1994/421, SI 1994/1431, SI 1994/3139, SI 1995/3181, SI 1996/561, SI 1996/3245, SI 1999/3275, SI 2002/3021, SI 2003/3130, SI 2004/3234, SI 2008/3078, SI 2009/1307, SI 2010/2952, SI 2011/1665, SI 2011/2993 and SI 2012/664).
5 Ie under the Local Government Finance Act 1988 ss 43, 45: see PARAS 133, 135.
6 Local Government Finance Act 1988 Sch 8 para 4(2). This has effect subject to Sch 8 para 4(4A) (see the text to notes 7–8): Sch 8 para 4(4C) (Sch 8 para 4(4A), (4C) added by the Local Government Act 2003 s 70(1)).
7 Ie under the Local Government Finance Act 1988 ss 43, 45.
8 Local Government Finance Act 1988 Sch 8 para 4(4A) (as added: see note 6).
9 Ie the Local Government Finance Act 1988 ss 47, 49: see PARAS 149, 151.
10 Local Government Finance Act 1988 Sch 8 para 4(5)(a) (Sch 8 para 4(5) amended by the Local Government Finance Act 2012 Sch 3 paras 2, 7(1), (4)(a), (b)).
11 Local Government Finance Act 1988 Sch 8 para 4(5)(b).
12 Local Government Finance Act 1988 Sch 8 para 4(5)(c) (as amended: see note 10).
13 Ie the Local Government Finance Act 1988 Sch 8 para 4(2).
14 Local Government Finance Act 1988 Sch 8 para 4(5) (amended by the Local Government Finance Act 2012 Sch 3 paras 2, 7(1), (4)(c)).
15 Local Government Finance Act 1988 Sch 8 para 4(6).
16 Ie the Local Government Finance Act 1988 s 49: see PARA 151.
17 Local Government Finance Act 1988 Sch 8 para 4(7) (added by the Local Government Act 2003 s 71(1), (2)). Regulations made for this purpose may include provision:
  (1) for or in connection with the recalculation of the provisional amount for the financial year concerned, including provision for the procedure to be adopted for recalculation (Local Government Finance Act 1988 Sch 8 para 6(6A)(a) (Sch 8 para 6(6A) added by the Local Government Act 2003 s 71(1), (3)); and
  (2) as to financial adjustments to be made, including provision for the making of reduced payments under the Local Government Finance Act 1988 Sch 8 para 5 or of repayments (Sch 8 para 6(6A)(b) (as so added)).
18 Ie under the Local Government Finance Act 1988 Sch 8 para 4: see the text to notes 1–14.
19 Ie by virtue of the Local Government Finance Act 1988 Sch 8 para 6(2A): see PARA 76.
20 Local Government Finance Act 1988 Sch 8 para 5(1) (amended by the Local Government and Housing Act 1989 s 139, Sch 5 paras 42, 79(3)).
21 Local Government Finance Act 1988 Sch 8 para 5(2) (amended by the Local Government Finance Act 1992 s 104, Sch 10 para 6(6)–(10); and the Local Government Finance Act 2012 Sch 3 paras 2, 8(1), (2)). The power to give a direction under the Local Government Finance Act 1988 Sch 8 para 5 includes power to revoke or amend a direction given under the power and may be exercised differently for different authorities: Sch 8 para 6(3).
22 Local Government Finance Act 1988 Sch 8 para 5(3) (amended by the Local Government Finance Act 2012 Sch 3 paras 2, 8(1), (3)).
23 Local Government Finance Act 1988 Sch 8 para 5(4) (amended by the Local Government Finance Act 2012 Sch 3 paras 2, 8(1), (4)).
24 Local Government Finance Act 1988 Sch 8 para 5(5) (amended by the Local Government Finance Act 2012 Sch 3 paras 2, 8(1), (5)).
25 Local Government Finance Act 1988 Sch 8 para 5(6)(a).
26 Local Government Finance Act 1988 Sch 8 para 5(6)(b) (substituted by the Local Government Finance Act 1992 Sch 10 para 6(6)–(10); amended by the Local Government Finance Act 2012 Sch 3 paras 2, 8(1), (6)(a)).
27 Ie in accordance with provision under the Local Government Finance Act 1988 Sch 8 para 4(4A): see the text to notes 7–8.

28 Local Government Finance Act 1988 Sch 8 para 5(6)(ba) (added by the Local Government Act 2003 s 70(2)(a); amended by the Local Government Finance Act 2012 Sch 3 paras 2, 8(1), (6)(b); and by SI 2007/1388).

29 Prospectively, for the words 'the amount' there is substituted a reference to the amount or amounts notifiable under the Local Government Finance Act 1988 Sch 8 para 6(b) and (ba): see Sch 8 para 5(6)(c) (amended, as from a day to be appointed, by the Local Government Act 2003 s 70(2)(b); at the date at which this volume states the law, no such day had been appointed).

30 Local Government Finance Act 1988 Sch 8 para 5(6)(c) (amended by the Public Audit (Wales) Act 2004 s 66, Sch 2 para 8(a); and the Local Government Finance Act 2012 Sch 3 paras 2, 8(1), (6)(c)). As to the Auditor General for Wales see PARA 615; and CONSTITUTIONAL AND ADMINISTRATIVE LAW vol 20 (2014) PARA 400 et seq.

31 Local Government Finance Act 1988 Sch 8 para 5(6A) (added by the Local Government Finance Act 1992 Sch 10 para 6(6)–(10); amended by the Local Government Act 2003 s 70(3); the Public Audit (Wales) Act 2004 Sch 2 para 8(b); and the Local Government Finance Act 2012 Sch 3 paras 2, 8(1), (7)).

32 Ie within the meaning given by the Local Government Finance Act 1988 para 6(7). For the purposes of Sch 8 para 5(7) the relevant provisions are:

(1) Sch 8 para 5(10) (Sch 8 para 6(7)(a));

(2) regulations made for the purpose mentioned in Sch 8 para 4(7) (see the text to notes 16–17) (Sch 8 para 6(7)(aa) (added by the Local Government Act 2003 s 71(1), (4)));

(3) regulations made under the Local Government Finance Act 1988 Sch 8 para 6(5) (Sch 8 para 6(7)(b)); and

(4) Sch 8 paras 12, 15 (Sch 8 para 6(7)(c) (amended by the Local Government Finance Act 1992 s 117(1), Sch 13 para 86(3))).

33 Local Government Finance Act 1988 Sch 8 para 5(7) (amended by the Local Government Finance Act 2012 Sch 3 paras 2, 8(1), (8)).

34 Local Government Finance Act 1988 Sch 8 para 5(8) (amended by the Local Government Finance Act 1992 Sch 10 para 6(6)–(10); and the Local Government Finance Act 2012 Sch 3 paras 2, 8(1), (9)).

35 Local Government Finance Act 1988 Sch 8 para 5(9) (amended by the Local Government Finance Act 1992 Sch 10 para 6(6)–(10); and the Local Government Finance Act 2012 Sch 3 paras 2, 8(1), (10)).

36 Ie the regulations under the Local Government Finance Act 1988 Sch 8 para 4.

37 Local Government Finance Act 1988 Sch 8 para 5(10)(a) (Sch 8 para 5(10) substituted by the Local Government Finance Act 1992 Sch 10 para 6(6)–(10); and amended by the Local Government Finance Act 2012 Sch 3 paras 2, 8(1), (11)).

38 Local Government Finance Act 1988 Sch 8 para 5(10)(b) (as substituted and amended: see note 37).

39 Ie under the Local Government Finance Act 1988 Sch 8 para 5(6A).

40 Local Government Finance Act 1988 Sch 8 para 5(11)(a) (Sch 8 para 5(11)–(15) added by the Local Government Finance Act 1992 Sch 10 para 6(6)–(10); and amended by the Local Government Finance Act 2012 Sch 3 paras 2, 8(1), (12)).

41 Local Government Finance Act 1988 Sch 8 para 5(11)(b) (as added and amended: see note 40).

42 Local Government Finance Act 1988 Sch 8 para 5(12) (as added (see note 40); amended by the Local Government Finance Act 2012 Sch 3 paras 2, 8(1), (13)). Regulations under the Local Government Finance Act 1988 Sch 8 para 5(15) may make provision for financial adjustments to be made where at the time the Welsh Ministers make the calculation required by Sch 8 para 5(12) a payment has already been made under Sch 8 para 5(9) or (10) in relation to the amount notified under Sch 8 para 5(6)(b); and the regulations may include provision for the making of payments by the Welsh Ministers or the authority, and as to the time at which any such payment must be made: Sch 8 para 5(15) (as so added; amended by the Local Government Finance Act 2012 Sch 3 paras 2, 8(1), (16)).

43 Ie under the Local Government Finance Act 1988 Sch 8 para 5(9) or (10).

44 Ie the Local Government Finance Act 1988 Sch 8 para 5(9), (10) does not apply in relation to that amount.

45 Local Government Finance Act 1988 Sch 8 para 5(13) (as added (see note 40); amended by the Local Government Finance Act 2012 Sch 3 paras 2, 8(1), (14)).

46 Local Government Finance Act 1988 Sch 8 para 5(14) (as added (see note 40); amended by the Local Government Finance Act 2012 Sch 3 paras 2, 8(1), (15)).

47 Ie provision of or made under the Local Government Finance Act 1988 Sch 8 Pt II (paras 3A–7).

48 Local Government Finance Act 1988 Sch 8 para 7.

76. Calculation of non-domestic rating contributions.

Any calculation[1] of the amount of a billing authority's non-domestic rating contribution[2] for a chargeable financial year[3] must be made in accordance with the regulations[4] made by the Welsh Ministers[5]. Such a calculation must be made on the basis of the information before the person making the calculation at the time he makes it; but the Welsh Ministers may make regulations:

(1) requiring a calculation of the amount of an authority's non-domestic rating contribution by the authority or the Welsh Ministers[6] to be made on the basis of that information read subject to prescribed assumptions[7];

(2) enabling a calculation by an authority after the year ends[8] to be made without taking into account any information as regards which the following conditions are satisfied[9]:

 (a) it is not reasonably practicable for the person making the calculation to take it into account[10]; and

 (b) it was received by the authority after a prescribed date (which may be before or after the end of the year in question)[11].

Regulations[12] may incorporate in the rules provision for adjustments to be made in the calculation of the amount of an authority's non-domestic rating contribution[13], being adjustments to take account of relevant changes affecting the amount of the authority's non-domestic rating contribution for an earlier year[14].

The Welsh Ministers may make regulations providing that, once the provisional amount has been arrived at[15] as regards an authority for a financial year and if prescribed conditions are fulfilled, the provisional amount is to be treated as being an amount smaller than it would otherwise be[16].

1 Ie under the Local Government Finance Act 1988 Sch 8 para 5: see PARA 75.

2 As to the meaning of 'non-domestic rating contribution' see PARA 75. As to the meaning of 'billing authority' see PARA 75 note 3.

3 As to the meaning of 'chargeable financial year' see PARA 24 note 1.

4 Ie under the Local Government Finance Act 1988 Sch 8 para 4: see PARA 75.

5 Local Government Finance Act 1988 Sch 8 para 6(1). As to the Welsh Ministers and the Secretary of State see PARA 51.

6 Ie under the Local Government Finance Act 1988 Sch 8 para 5(2) or (3): see PARA 75.

7 Local Government Finance Act 1988 Sch 8 para 6(2)(a) (Sch 8 para 6(2) substituted by the Local Government Finance Act 1992 s 104, Sch 10 para 6(11); and amended by the Local Government Finance Act 2012 s 5(1), (2)(a), Sch 3 paras 2, 9(1), (2)).

8 Ie under the Local Government Finance Act 1988 Sch 8 para 5(6): see PARA 75.

9 Local Government Finance Act 1988 Sch 8 para 6(2)(b) (as substituted: see note 7).

10 Local Government Finance Act 1988 Sch 8 para 6(2)(b)(i) (as substituted: see note 7).

11 Local Government Finance Act 1988 Sch 8 para 6(2)(b)(ii) (as substituted: see note 7).

12 Ie under the Local Government Finance Act 1988 Sch 8 para 4.

13 Ie under the Local Government Finance Act 1988 Sch 8 para 5(2) or (6).

14 Local Government Finance Act 1988 Sch 8 para 6(2A) (Sch 8 para 6(2A), (2B) added by the Local Government and Housing Act 1989 s 139, Sch 5 paras 42, 79(3)). For the purposes of the Local Government Finance Act 1988 Sch 8 para 6(2A), a change is a relevant change if it results from a decision, determination or other matter which (whether by reason of the time at which it was taken, made or occurred or otherwise) was not taken into account by the authority in the calculation under Sch 8 para 5(6) of the amount of its non-domestic rating contribution for the earlier year in question: Sch 8 para 6(2B) (as so added).

15 Ie under the Local Government Finance Act 1988 Sch 8 para 5.

16 Local Government Finance Act 1988 Sch 8 para 6(5) (amended by the Local Government Finance Act 2012 Sch 3 paras 2, 9(1), (4)). Regulations under the Local Government Finance Act 1988 Sch 8 para 6(5) may include:

 (1) provision as to the re-calculation of the provisional amount (see PARA 75), including provision for the procedure to be adopted for re-calculation if the prescribed conditions are fulfilled (Sch 8 para 6(6)(a));

(2) provision as to financial adjustments to be made as a result of any re-calculation, including provision for the making of reduced payments under Sch 8 para 5 or of repayments (Sch 8 para 6(6)(b)).

77. Distribution.

Before a financial year begins the Welsh Ministers[1] must estimate:

(1) the aggregate of the items of account which will be credited to the non-domestic rating account[2] kept for the year[3]; and

(2) the aggregate of the items of account which will be debited to the account[4] kept for the year[5].

In making any estimate under heads (1) and (2) the Welsh Ministers may make such assumptions as they see fit[6]. If the aggregate estimated under head (1) exceeds the aggregate estimated under head (2) the Welsh Ministers must calculate the amount equal to the difference[7]. In the local government finance report[8] for the year the Welsh Ministers must specify the amount arrived at under these provisions (the distributable amount for the year)[9]. However, where the Welsh Ministers make two local government finance reports for a particular financial year, the requirement to specify the distributable amount for the year[10] does not apply as respects that year[11] and the Welsh Ministers must decide whether:

(a) distribution among all receiving authorities of the amount arrived at[12] for the year is to be dealt with in just one of those reports (the chosen report)[13]; or

(b) each of those reports is to deal with the distribution of so much of that amount as is for the receiving authorities[14] to which that report relates[15].

If the Welsh Ministers decide as mentioned in head (a) above, the Welsh Ministers must specify that amount (the distributable amount for the year) in the chosen report and the chosen report is the local government finance report for that year to which the requirement to specify the basis of distribution[16] applies[17]. If the Welsh Ministers decide as mentioned in head (b) above;

(i) the provisions as to local government finance reports[18] do not apply as respects the year[19];

(ii) the power to make an amending report[20] may (in particular) be exercised by making a single amending report relating to both of the local government finance reports for the year[21]; and

(iii) the requirement to calculate the shares of the distributable amount[22] does not apply in relation to any report amending either of those reports[23].

1 As to the Welsh Ministers and the Secretary of State see PARA 51.

2 Ie under the Local Government Finance Act 1988 Sch 8 para 2(2)(a): see PARA 74.

3 Local Government Finance Act 1988 Sch 8 para 9(1)(a) (Sch 8 paras 8–15 substituted by the Local Government Finance Act 1992 s 104, Sch 10 para 7; the Local Government Finance Act 1988 Sch 8 para 9(1) amended by the Local Government Finance Act 2012 s 5(1), (2)(a), Sch 3 paras 2, 11(1), (2)).

4 Ie under the Local Government Finance Act 1988 Sch 8 para 3(3)(b): see PARA 74.

5 Local Government Finance Act 1988 Sch 8 para 9(1)(b) (as substituted: see note 3).

6 Local Government Finance Act 1988 Sch 8 para 9(2) (as substituted (see note 3); amended by the Local Government Finance Act 2012 Sch 3 paras 2, 11(1), (3)).

7 Local Government Finance Act 1988 Sch 8 para 9(3) (as substituted (see note 3); amended by the Local Government Finance Act 2012 Sch 3 paras 2, 11(1), (4)).

8 Any reference in the Local Government Finance Act 1988 Sch 8 Pt III (paras 8–16) to a local government finance report is a reference to a report made under s 84G (see PARA 34): Sch 8 para 8(2) (as substituted (see note 3); amended by the Local Government Act 2003 s 40(1), Sch 2 para 2(1), (2); and the Local Government Finance Act 2012 Sch 3 paras 2, 10(1), (3)).

9 Local Government Finance Act 1988 Sch 8 para 9(4) (as substituted (see note 3); amended by the Local Government Finance Act 2012 Sch 3 paras 2, 11(1), (4)). This is subject to the Local Government Finance Act 1988 Sch 8 para 9A: Sch 8 para 9(4) (as so substituted; amended by the Local Government Act 2003 s 40(1), Sch 2 para 2(1), (3)).
10 Ie the Local Government Finance Act 1988 Sch 8 para 9(4).
11 Local Government Finance Act 1988 Sch 8 para 9A(1)(a) (Sch 8 para 9A added by the Local Government Act 2003 Sch 2 para 2(1), (4); the Local Government Finance Act 1988 Sch 8 para 9A(1) amended by the Local Government Finance Act 2012 Sch 3 paras 2, 12; and by SI 2007/1388).
12 Ie under the Local Government Finance Act 1988 para 9.
13 Local Government Finance Act 1988 Sch 8 para 9A(1)(b)(i) (as added and amended: see note 11).
14 For the purposes of the Local Government Finance Act 1988 Sch 8 Pt III a receiving authority is any billing authority in Wales or any major precepting authority in Wales: Sch 8 para 8(1) (as substituted (see note 3); amended by the Local Government Finance Act 2012 Sch 3 paras 2, 10(1), (2)). As to the meaning of 'billing authority' see PARA 346. As to the meaning of 'major precepting authority' see PARA 11 note 2 (definition applied by the Local Government Finance Act 1988 s 144(2) (substituted by the Local Government Finance Act 1992 s 117(1), Sch 13 para 81(1); and amended by the Local Government Finance Act 2012 s 5(1), (2)(b), Sch 3 paras 23, 29)).
15 Local Government Finance Act 1988 Sch 8 para 9A(1)(b)(ii) (as added and amended: see note 11).
16 Ie the requirement under the Local Government Finance Act 1988 Sch 8 para 10(1): see PARA 78.
17 Local Government Finance Act 1988 Sch 8 para 9A(2) (as added (see note 11); amended by SI 2007/1388).
18 Ie the Local Government Finance Act 1988 Sch 8 paras 10, 11. See, however, Sch 8 paras 11A–11C; and PARA 78.
19 Local Government Finance Act 1988 Sch 8 para 9A(3)(a) (as added (see note 11); Sch 8 para 9A(3) amended by the Local Government Finance Act 2012 Sch 3 paras 2, 12; and by SI 2007/1388).
20 Ie under the Local Government Finance Act 1988 Sch 8 para 13.
21 Local Government Finance Act 1988 Sch 8 para 9A(3)(b) (as added: see note 11).
22 Ie the Local Government Finance Act 1988 Sch 8 para 14.
23 Local Government Finance Act 1988 Sch 8 para 9A(3)(c) (as added: see note 11). See, however, Sch 8 para 14A; and PARA 79.

78. Local government finance reports and calculations.

A local government finance report[1] for a financial year must specify the basis (the basis of distribution) on which the Welsh Ministers[2] propose to distribute among receiving authorities[3] the distributable amount for the year[4]. Before making the report the Welsh Ministers must notify to such representatives of local government as appear to them to be appropriate the general nature of the basis of distribution[5].

The following provisions apply where, in relation to a financial year, the distributable amount for the year has been calculated and specified in a report[6] and the report has been laid before the Assembly[7].

If the report is approved by resolution of the Assembly, the distributable amount for the year must be distributed among and paid to receiving authorities in accordance with the relevant statutory provisions[8].

As soon as is reasonably practicable after the report has been so approved, the Welsh Ministers must calculate what sum falls to be paid to each receiving authority as its share of the distributable amount for the year in accordance with the basis of distribution specified in the report as so approved[9]. After making such a calculation, the Welsh Ministers may, at any time before the end of the financial year following the financial year to which the report relates, make one further calculation of what sum falls to be paid to each receiving authority as its share of the distributable amount for the year in accordance with the basis of distribution so specified[10]. The power to make a further calculation is not exercisable, however, after the approval by resolution of the Assembly of any amending report[11] in relation to the local government finance report[12].

If the Welsh Ministers decide that they will leave out of account information received by them after a particular date in making a calculation under these provisions, the calculation must be made accordingly, and they may decide different dates for different kinds of information[13]. This applies only if the Welsh Ministers inform each receiving authority in writing of their decision and of the date (or the dates and kinds of information) concerned; but they may do this at any time before the calculation is made (whether before or after the distributable amount for the year is calculated)[14].

As soon as is reasonably practicable after making a calculation under these provisions, the Welsh Ministers must inform each receiving authority of the sum they calculate falls to be paid to it as its share of the distributable amount for the year[15].

Where the Welsh Ministers propose to make two local government finance reports for a particular financial year and as respects that year decide that each of those reports is to deal with the distribution of so much of that amount as is for the receiving authorities to which that report relates[16], the Welsh Ministers must in each of those reports:

(1) specify the distributable amount[17] for the year[18];
(2) specify how much of that amount is for the receiving authorities to which the report relates[19]; and
(3) specify the basis on which the Welsh Ministers propose to distribute among those authorities the amount specified under head (2)[20].

Before making such a report, the Welsh Ministers must notify the general nature of the basis of distribution proposed to be specified in the report to such representatives of local government as appear to the Welsh Ministers to be appropriate[21].

Where:

(a) the Assembly approves by resolution a local government finance report that is one of two being made by the Welsh Ministers for a particular financial year[22]; and
(b) as respects that year the Welsh Ministers decide that each of those reports is to deal with the distribution of so much of that amount as is for the receiving authorities to which that report relates[23],

the amount specified under head (2) above in the report must be distributed among and paid to the receiving authorities to which the report relates in accordance with the relevant statutory provisions[24].

As soon as is reasonably practicable after the report is approved by the Assembly, the Welsh Ministers must calculate in relation to each of those authorities what sum falls to be paid to the authority as its share of the amount specified under head (2) above[25]. The calculation must be in accordance with the basis of distribution specified in the report[26]. The Welsh Ministers may carry out this calculation again at any time before the end of the financial year immediately following the one to which the report relates[27]. This power may only be exercised once and ceases to be exercisable if the Assembly approves by resolution an amending report made by the Welsh Ministers[28]. As soon as is reasonably practicable after making a calculation under these provisions, the Welsh Ministers must inform each receiving authority to which the report relates of the outcome, so far as relating to it[29].

The Welsh Ministers may set a deadline for the receipt of information to be taken into account by them when making a calculation under the provisions above[30]. Different deadlines may be set in relation to different kinds of information[31]. A deadline only has effect if the Welsh Ministers inform each receiving authority concerned of the deadline and of the information to which it relates[32]. Notification may be given at any time before the making of the calculation to which the deadline relates, including a time before the distributable amount for the year is calculated[33]. When making a calculation in relation to which a deadline has effect, the Welsh Ministers must leave information to which the deadline applies out of account if it is received after the passing of the deadline[34].

Where a calculation is made of the sum to be paid to each receiving authority as its share of the distributable amount for the year[35], the Welsh Ministers must pay to each receiving authority any sum calculated as falling to be paid to it[36]. The sum must be paid in instalments of such amounts, and at such times in the financial year to which the report relates (the financial year concerned), as the Welsh Ministers determine[37].

Where a revised calculation is made[38] and the sum it shows as falling to be paid to a receiving authority exceeds that shown as falling to be paid to it by the original calculation for the financial year concerned[39], the Welsh Ministers must pay to the authority a sum equal to the difference[40]. The sum must be paid at such time, or in instalments of such amounts and at such times, as the Welsh Ministers determine; but any such time must fall after the end of the financial year concerned[41].

Where a revised calculation is made and the sum it shows as falling to be paid to a receiving authority is less than that shown as falling to be paid to it by the original calculation for the financial year concerned, a sum equal to the difference must be paid by the authority to the Welsh Ministers[42]. The sum must be paid on such day after the end of the financial year concerned as the Welsh Ministers may specify; and if it is not paid on or before that day it is recoverable in a court of competent jurisdiction[43].

1 As to the meaning of 'local government finance report' see PARA 77 note 8.
2 As to the Welsh Ministers and the Secretary of State see PARA 51.
3 As to the meaning of 'receiving authority' see PARA 77 note 14.
4 Local Government Finance Act 1988 Sch 8 para 10(1) (Sch 8 paras 8–15 substituted by the Local Government Finance Act 1992 s 104, Sch 10 para 7; the Local Government Finance Act 1988 Sch 8 para 10(1) amended by the Local Government Finance Act 2012 s 5(1), (2)(a), Sch 3 paras 2, 13(1), (2)).
5 Local Government Finance Act 1988 Sch 8 para 10(2) (as substituted (see note 4); amended by the Local Government Finance Act 2012 Sch 3 paras 2, 13(1), (3)).
6 Ie in accordance with the Local Government Finance Act 1988 Sch 8 paras 9, 9A: see PARA 77.
7 Local Government Finance Act 1988 Sch 8 para 11(1) (as substituted (see note 4); amended by the Local Government Act 2003 s 40(1), Sch 2 para 2(1), (5); and the Local Government Finance Act 2012 Sch 3 paras 2, 14(1), (2)). In the Local Government Finance Act 1988 Sch 8 Pt III (paras 8–16), 'the Assembly' means the National Assembly for Wales: Sch 8 para 8(3) (added by SI 2007/1388).
8 Local Government Finance Act 1988 Sch 8 para 11(2) (as substituted (see note 4); amended by the Local Government Finance Act 2012 Sch 3 paras 2, 14(1), (3)). The relevant statutory provisions are the Local Government Finance Act 1988 Sch 8 paras 11, 12. Sums required for the making of payments by the Welsh Ministers under Sch 8 Pt III are to be charged on the Welsh Consolidated Fund: Sch 8 para 16 (added by the Government of Wales Act 2006 s 160(1), Sch 10 para 21).
9 Local Government Finance Act 1988 Sch 8 para 11(3) (as substituted (see note 4); amended by the Local Government Finance Act 2012 Sch 3 paras 2, 14(1), (4)).
10 Local Government Finance Act 1988 Sch 8 para 11(4) (as substituted (see note 4); amended by the Local Government Finance Act 2012 Sch 3 paras 2, 14(1), (4)).
11 Ie under the Local Government Finance Act 1988 Sch 8 para 13: see PARA 79.
12 Local Government Finance Act 1988 Sch 8 para 11(5) (as substituted (see note 4); amended by the Local Government Finance Act 2012 Sch 3 paras 2, 14(1), (5)).

13 Local Government Finance Act 1988 Sch 8 para 11(6) (as substituted (see note 4); amended by the Local Government Finance Act 2012 Sch 3 paras 2, 14(1), (6)).
14 Local Government Finance Act 1988 Sch 8 para 11(7) (as substituted (see note 4); amended by the Local Government Finance Act 2012 Sch 3 paras 2, 14(1), (7)).
15 Local Government Finance Act 1988 Sch 8 para 11(8) (as substituted (see note 4); amended by the Local Government Finance Act 2012 Sch 3 paras 2, 14(1), (8)).
16 Ie decided as mentioned in the Local Government Finance Act 1988 Sch 8 para 9A(1)(b)(ii): see PARA 77 head (b).
17 Ie the amount arrived at under the Local Government Finance Act 1988 Sch 8 para 9: see PARA 77.
18 Local Government Finance Act 1988 Sch 8 para 11A(1)(a) (Sch 8 paras 11A–11C added by the Local Government Act 2003 Sch 2 para 2(1), (6); and amended by SI 2007/1388).
19 Local Government Finance Act 1988 Sch 8 para 11A(1)(b) (as added: see note 18).
20 Local Government Finance Act 1988 Sch 8 para 11A(1)(c) (as added and amended: see note 18).
21 Local Government Finance Act 1988 Sch 8 para 11A(2) (as added and amended: see note 18).
22 Local Government Finance Act 1988 Sch 8 para 11B(1)(a) (Sch 8 para 11B(1) as added (see note 18); substituted by SI 2007/1388).
23 Local Government Finance Act 1988 Sch 8 para 11B(1)(b) (Sch 8 para 11B as added (see note 18); and substituted (see note 22).
24 Local Government Finance Act 1988 Sch 8 para 11B(2) (as added: see note 18). The relevant statutory provisions are the Local Government Finance Act 1988 Sch 8 paras 11, 12.
25 Local Government Finance Act 1988 Sch 8 para 11B(3) (as added and amended: see note 18).
26 Local Government Finance Act 1988 Sch 8 para 11B(4) (as added: see note 18).
27 Local Government Finance Act 1988 Sch 8 para 11B(5) (as added and amended: see note 18).
28 Local Government Finance Act 1988 Sch 8 para 11B(6) (as added and amended: see note 18).
29 Local Government Finance Act 1988 Sch 8 para 11B(7) (as added and amended: see note 18).
30 Local Government Finance Act 1988 Sch 8 para 11C(1) (as added and amended: see note 18).
31 Local Government Finance Act 1988 Sch 8 para 11C(2) (as added: see note 18).
32 Local Government Finance Act 1988 Sch 8 para 11C(3) (as added and amended: see note 18).
33 Local Government Finance Act 1988 Sch 8 para 11C(4) (as added: see note 18).
34 Local Government Finance Act 1988 Sch 8 para 11C(5) (as added and amended: see note 18).
35 Ie under the Local Government Finance Act 1988 Sch 8 para 11(3) or 11B(3).
36 Local Government Finance Act 1988 Sch 8 para 12(1) (as substituted (see note 4); amended by the Local Government Act 2003 Sch 2 para 2(1), (7); and the Local Government Finance Act 2012 Sch 3 paras 2, 12(1), (2)).
37 Local Government Finance Act 1988 Sch 8 para 12(2) (as substituted (see note 4); amended by the Local Government Finance Act 2012 Sch 3 paras 2, 12(1), (3)).
38 Ie under the Local Government Finance Act 1988 Sch 8 para 11(4) or 11B(5).
39 Ie under the Local Government Finance Act 1988 Sch 8 para 11(3) or 11B(3).
40 Local Government Finance Act 1988 Sch 8 para 12(3) (as substituted (see note 4); amended by the Local Government Act 2003 Sch 2 para 2(1), (8); and the Local Government Finance Act 2012 Sch 3 paras 2, 12(1), (4)).
41 Local Government Finance Act 1988 Sch 8 para 12(4) (as substituted (see note 4); amended by the Local Government Finance Act 2012 Sch 3 paras 2, 12(1), (5)).
42 Local Government Finance Act 1988 Sch 8 para 12(5) (as substituted (see note 4); amended by the Local Government Act 2003 Sch 2 para 2(1), (8); and the Local Government Finance Act 2012 Sch 3 paras 2, 12(1), (6)).
43 Local Government Finance Act 1988 Sch 8 para 12(6) (as substituted (see note 4); amended by the Local Government Finance Act 2012 Sch 3 paras 2, 12(1), (6)).

79. Amending reports.

After a local government finance report has been made[1] the Welsh Ministers[2] may, at any time before the end of the financial year following the financial year concerned, make in relation to the report one or more amending reports[3]. An amending report must contain amendments to the basis of distribution specified in the local government finance report[4]. Before making the report the Welsh Ministers must notify to such representatives of local government as appear to them to be appropriate the general nature of the amendments which they propose to make[5].

The report must be laid before the Assembly[6]. As soon as is reasonably practicable after the report is laid before the Assembly, the Welsh Ministers must send a copy of it to each receiving authority[7].

Where an amending report has been approved by resolution of the Assembly, the Welsh Ministers may not make a subsequent amending report in relation to the same local government finance report[8].

As soon as is reasonably practicable after an amending report has been approved by resolution of the Assembly, the Welsh Ministers must calculate what sum falls to be paid to each receiving authority as its share of the distributable amount for the year in accordance with the basis of distribution specified in the local government finance report as amended by the amending report[9]. After making such a calculation the Welsh Ministers may make one further calculation of what sum falls to be paid to each receiving authority as its share of the distributable amount for the year in accordance with that basis of distribution[10]. A further calculation may not be made after whichever is the later of:

(1) the end of the financial year following the financial year concerned[11]; and

(2) the end of the period of three months beginning with the day on which the amending report is approved by resolution of the Assembly[12].

The power for the Welsh Ministers to leave out of account information received by them after a certain date in making a calculation and the requirement to inform each receiving authority of the sum which they calculate falls to be paid to it as its share of the distributable amount for the year[13] apply in relation to calculations made under these provisions[14].

The following provisions apply where:

(a) a report is made amending a report ('the original report') that is one of two local government finance reports that the Welsh Ministers make for a particular financial year[15]; and

(b) as respects that year the Welsh Ministers decide[16] that each of those reports is to deal with the distribution of so much of that amount as is for the receiving authorities to which that report relates[17].

As soon as is reasonably practicable after the amending report is approved by resolution of the Assembly, the Welsh Ministers must calculate in relation to each of the authorities to which the original report relates what sum falls to be paid to the authority as its share of the amount specified[18] in the original report[19]. The calculation must be in accordance with the amended basis of distribution[20]. The Welsh Ministers may carry out the revision of the calculation again at any time before:

(i) the end of the financial year immediately following the one to which the original report relates[21]; or

(ii) if later, the end of the period of three months beginning with the day on which the Assembly approves by resolution the amending report[22].

The power to make a revised calculation may only be exercised once[23]. The requirement to give notice to each receiving authority to which the report relates and the power to set a deadline for the receipt of information[24] apply in relation to calculations made under these provisions[25].

The following provisions apply where a calculation (the relevant calculation) is made[26] in relation to an amending report[27].

Where the sum shown by the relevant calculation as falling to be paid to a receiving authority for the financial year concerned exceeds that shown as falling to be paid to it by the relevant previous calculation[28], the Welsh Ministers must pay to the authority a sum equal to the difference[29]. The sum must be paid at such times, or in instalments of such amounts and at such times, as the Welsh Ministers determine; but any such time must fall after the end of the financial year in which the amending report was made[30].

Where the sum shown by the relevant calculation as falling to be paid to a receiving authority for the financial year concerned is less than that shown as falling to be paid to it by the relevant previous calculation, a sum equal to the difference must be paid by the authority to the Welsh Ministers[31]. The sum must be paid on such day after the end of the financial year in which the amending report was made as the Welsh Ministers may specify; and if it is not paid on or before that day it is recoverable in a court of competent jurisdiction[32].

1 As to the meaning of 'local government finance report' see PARA 77 note 8. As to the making of local government finance reports see PARA 78.
2 As to the Welsh Ministers and the Secretary of State see PARA 51.
3 Local Government Finance Act 1988 Sch 8 para 13(1) (Sch 8 paras 8–15 substituted by the Local Government Finance Act 1992 s 104, Sch 10 para 7; the Local Government Finance Act 1988 Sch 8 para 13(1) amended by the Local Government Finance Act 2012 s 5(1), (2)(a), Sch 3 paras 2, 16(1), (2)). This is subject to the Local Government Finance Act 1988 Sch 8 para 13(6) (see the text to note 8): Sch 8 para 13(1) (as so substituted).
4 Local Government Finance Act 1988 Sch 8 para 13(2) (as substituted: see note 3).
5 Local Government Finance Act 1988 Sch 8 para 13(3) (as substituted (see note 3); amended by the Local Government Finance Act 2012 Sch 3 paras 2, 16(1), (3)).
6 Local Government Finance Act 1988 Sch 8 para 13(4) (as substituted (see note 3); amended by the Local Government Finance Act 2012 Sch 3 paras 2, 16(1), (4)). As to the meaning of 'the Assembly' see PARA 78 note 7.
7 Local Government Finance Act 1988 Sch 8 para 13(5) (as substituted (see note 3); amended by the Local Government Finance Act 2012 Sch 3 paras 2, 16(1), (5)). As to the meaning of 'receiving authority' see PARA 77 note 14.
8 Local Government Finance Act 1988 Sch 8 para 13(6) (as substituted (see note 3); amended by the Local Government Finance Act 2012 Sch 3 paras 2, 16(1), (5)).
9 Local Government Finance Act 1988 Sch 8 para 14(1) (as substituted (see note 3); amended by the Local Government Finance Act 2012 Sch 3 paras 2, 17(1), (2)).
10 Local Government Finance Act 1988 Sch 8 para 14(2) (as substituted (see note 3); amended by the Local Government Finance Act 2012 Sch 3 paras 2, 17(1), (3)). This is subject to the Local Government Finance Act 1988 Sch 8 para 14(3) (see the text to notes 11–12): Sch 8 para 14(2) (as so substituted).
11 Local Government Finance Act 1988 Sch 8 para 14(3)(a) (as substituted: see note 3).
12 Local Government Finance Act 1988 Sch 8 para 14(3)(b) (as substituted (see note 3); amended by the Local Government Finance Act 2012 Sch 3 paras 2, 17(1), (4)).
13 Ie under the Local Government Finance Act 1988 Sch 8 para 11(6)–(8): see PARA 78.
14 See the Local Government Finance Act 1988 Sch 8 para 14(4) (as substituted: see note 3).
15 Local Government Finance Act 1988 Sch 8 para 14A(1)(a) (Sch 8 para 14A added by the Local Government Act 2003 s 40(1), Sch 2 para 2(1), (9); and amended by SI 2007/1388).
16 Ie as mentioned in the Local Government Finance Act 1988 Sch 8 para 9A(1)(b)(ii): see PARA 77 head (b).
17 Local Government Finance Act 1988 Sch 8 para 14A(1)(b) (as added and amended: see note 15).
18 Ie under the Local Government Finance Act 1988 Sch 8 para 11A(1)(b): see PARA 77 head (2).
19 Local Government Finance Act 1988 Sch 8 para 14A(2) (as added and amended: see note 15).
20 Local Government Finance Act 1988 Sch 8 para 14A(3) (as added: see note 15).
21 Local Government Finance Act 1988 Sch 8 para 14A(4)(a) (as added and amended: see note 15).
22 Local Government Finance Act 1988 Sch 8 para 14A(4)(b) (as added and amended: see note 15).
23 Local Government Finance Act 1988 Sch 8 para 14A(5) (as added: see note 15).
24 Ie the Local Government Finance Act 1988 Sch 8 paras 11B(7) and 11C: see PARA 78.
25 See the Local Government Finance Act 1988 Sch 8 para 14A(6) (as added: see note 15).
26 Ie under the Local Government Finance Act 1988 Sch 8 para 14(1) or (2) or 14A(2) or (4).
27 Local Government Finance Act 1988 Sch 8 para 15(1) (as substituted (see note 3); amended by the Local Government Act 2003 Sch 2 para 2(1), (10)).
28 For these purposes, 'the relevant previous calculation' means:

(1) in relation to a calculation made under the Local Government Finance Act 1988 Sch 8 para 14(1) or 14A(2), the calculation under Sch 8 para 11(3) or 11B(3) or, where a further calculation has been made under Sch 8 para 11(4) or 11B(5), that further calculation (Sch 8 para 15(6)(a) (as substituted (see note 3); Sch 8 para 15(6) amended by the Local Government Act 2003 Sch 2 para 2(1), (11)));
(2) in relation to a calculation made under the Local Government Finance Act 1988 Sch 8 para 14(2) or 14A(4), the calculation made under Sch 8 para 14(1) or 14A(2) (Sch 8 para 15(6)(b) (as so substituted and amended)).

29 Local Government Finance Act 1988 Sch 8 para 15(2) (as substituted (see note 3); amended by the Local Government Finance Act 2012 Sch 3 paras 2, 18(1), (2)).
30 Local Government Finance Act 1988 Sch 8 para 15(3) (as substituted (see note 3); amended by the Local Government Finance Act 2012 Sch 3 paras 2, 18(1), (3)).
31 Local Government Finance Act 1988 Sch 8 para 15(4) (as substituted (see note 3); amended by the Local Government Finance Act 2012 Sch 3 paras 2, 18(1), (4)).
32 Local Government Finance Act 1988 Sch 8 para 15(5) (as substituted (see note 3); amended by the Local Government Finance Act 2012 Sch 3 paras 2, 18(1), (4)).

(4) Outline of Non-domestic Rating System

80. Rateable property.

Rateable property consists of relevant non-domestic[1] and composite hereditaments[2] entered in the local rating lists[3], and property of certain bodies which the appropriate national authority[4] has designated by regulation[5] to be entered in a central non-domestic rating list[6]. Rates are chargeable on:

(1) lands[7];
(2) coal mines[8];
(3) mines of any other description, other than a mine of which the royalty or dues are for the time being wholly reserved in kind[9]; and
(4) rights to use land for the purpose of exhibiting advertisements[10] or for the purpose of operating meters which measure a supply of gas or electricity (or some other specified service) and which are not operated by consumers[11]. Moorings let out for non-domestic purposes may be rateable[12].

Hereditaments in a number of classes are exempt from non-domestic rates[13], and in other cases hereditaments have been relieved of the full burden of rates by various means[14]. Exemptions from or privileges in respect of rating are in some instances conferred by local Acts and those exemptions and privileges may be continued by regulations made by the appropriate national authority[15]. The power to continue such privileges is subject to limitations[16].

Unoccupied property is also liable to be rated[17], and a mechanism exists whereby newly completed or altered buildings are deemed to be liable to be rated[18].

1 Ie a non-domestic hereditament falling within the Local Government Finance Act 1988 s 64(4): see PARA 106. As to hereditaments see PARA 106 et seq.
2 As to the meaning of 'composite hereditament' see PARA 106 note 6.
3 As to local non-domestic rating lists see PARA 191 et seq.
4 Ie the Secretary of State or, in relation to Wales, the Welsh Ministers. As to the Secretary of State and the Welsh Ministers see PARA 4 note 18. As to the meaning of 'Wales' see PARA 2 note 16. As to the separate administration of the non-domestic rating provisions (Local Government Finance Act 1988 Pt III (ss 41–67)) in England and Wales see PARA 52.
5 See the Local Government Finance Act 1988 s 53(1); and PARAS 197–198.
6 As central non-domestic rating lists see PARA 196 et seq.
7 See the Local Government Finance Act 1988 s 64(4)(a); and PARA 106.
8 See the Local Government Finance Act 1988 s 64(4)(b); and see PARA 106.

9 See the Local Government Finance Act 1988 s 64(4)(c); and see PARA 106.
10 See the Local Government Finance Act 1988 s 64(2), (4)(e); and PARAS 104–106.
11 See the Local Government Finance Act 1988 s 64(2A), (4)(e); and PARA 104.
12 See the Local Government Finance Act 1988 s 64(3A); and PARA 107.
13 As to the exemptions from non-domestic rating see PARA 110 et seq.
14 See PARA 143 et seq.
15 See the Local Government Finance Act 1988 Sch 5 para 20; and PARA 110. In *Wiltshire County Valuation Committee v Boyce* [1948] 2 KB 125, [1948] 1 All ER 694, CA, a special exemption, expressed to be perpetual and granted by a local and personal Act to the owner of a particular piece of land in respect of all parochial taxes and duties whatsoever, was held to exempt the land from the general rate by virtue of the Rating and Valuation Act 1925 s 64(1)(b) (repealed), on the principle *generalia specialibus non derogant* ('general things do not derogate from special things'), and the making of a scheme under s 64(2) (repealed) was not a condition for the continuance of the exemption. Although this case was decided prior to the coming into force of the Local Government Finance Act 1988 it may continue to be of relevance: see PARA 50.
16 See PARA 110 et seq.
17 See the Local Government Finance Act 1988 ss 45–46; and PARA 135 et seq.
18 See the Local Government Finance Act 1988 Sch 4A; and PARA 138 et seq.

81. Valuation for rating.

Rates are assessed on the rateable value of the hereditament[1]. The amount depends whether the hereditament is:

(1) a non-domestic hereditament (none of which consists of domestic property and none of which is exempt from local non-domestic rating)[2];
(2) a composite hereditament (none of which is exempt from local non-domestic rating)[3]; or
(3) a non-domestic hereditament which is partially exempt from local non-domestic rating[4].

1 The Local Government Finance Act 1988 Sch 6 has effect to determine the rateable value of non-domestic hereditaments: see Sch 6 para 1; and PARA 157 et seq. As to hereditaments see PARA 106 et seq.
2 See the Local Government Finance Act 1988 Sch 6 para 2(1); and PARA 157.
3 See the Local Government Finance Act 1988 Sch 6 para 2(1A); and PARA 157.
4 See the Local Government Finance Act 1988 Sch 6 para 2(1B); and PARA 157.

82. Rating lists.

The Local Government Finance Act 1988 makes provision for three types of rating lists[1]:

(1) non-domestic rating lists[2];
(2) central non-domestic rating lists[3]; and
(3) rural settlement lists[4].

For the purpose of deciding what is shown in a list for a particular day the state of the list as it has effect[5] immediately before the day ends is to be treated as having been its state throughout the day[6].

When ascertained, values for rating purposes are embodied in local non-domestic rating lists prepared by valuation officers for billing authorities[7]. A local rating list must contain such particulars as may be prescribed by regulations with respect to every relevant non-domestic hereditament in the billing authority's area[8].

The central valuation officer must compile and maintain central non-domestic rating lists[9]. The contents of a central non-domestic rating list are prescribed by regulations with a view to securing the central rating en bloc of certain hereditaments[10].

Each billing authority in England must compile and maintain a rural settlement list[11]. This enables certain hereditaments to be entitled to a reduction of the non-domestic rate[12].

1 Unless the context otherwise requires, references in the Local Government Finance Act 1988 to 'lists' are to local and central non-domestic rating lists: s 67(1), (13).
2 As to local non-domestic rating lists see PARA 191 et seq.
3 As to central non-domestic rating lists see PARA 196 et seq.
4 As to rural settlement lists see PARA 195.
5 'Effect' here includes any effect which is retrospective by virtue of an alteration of the list: Local Government Finance Act 1988 s 67(8). As to the alteration of rating lists see PARA 199 et seq.
6 Local Government Finance Act 1988 s 67(8).
7 See the Local Government Finance Act 1988 ss 41, 41A; and PARAS 191, 192.
8 See the Local Government Finance Act 1988 s 42; and PARA 194. As to hereditaments see PARA 106 et seq.
9 See the Local Government Finance Act 1988 s 52; and PARA 196.
10 See the Local Government Finance Act 1988 s 53; and PARA 197.
11 See the Local Government Finance Act 1988 s 42A; and PARA 195.
12 See PARA 145.

83. Valuation list procedure; appeals.

Valuation officers[1] have a duty to maintain non-domestic rating lists[2], which must, by inference, allow them to alter a list[3]. In addition regulations may be made with regard to the alteration of a list by a valuation officer[4], and with regard to proposed alterations by a valuation officer to a list with a view to its being accurately maintained[5]. Detailed provision has been made in this respect[6].

1 As to valuation officers see PARA 54.
2 See the Local Government Finance Act 1988 s 41(1) (local non-domestic rating lists) (see PARA 191), s 52(1) (central non-domestic rating lists) (see PARA 196).
3 See *BMC Properties and Management Ltd v Jackson (Valuation Officer)* [2015] EWCA Civ 1306, [2016] RA 1, [2016] All ER (D) 67 (Jan).
4 See the Local Government Finance Act 1988 s 55(1); and PARA 199.
5 See the Local Government Finance Act 1988 s 55(3): and PARA 199.
6 See PARA 200 et seq.

84. Calculating the chargeable amount.

Subject to transitional provisions, exemptions and reliefs, the chargeable amount for an occupied hereditament for each day that it is both occupied and shown in a local non-domestic rating list is calculated by multiplying the rateable value shown for the hereditament in the appropriate list by the multiplier and then dividing the product by the number of days in the financial year[1].

Unoccupied hereditaments in a local non-domestic rating list fall to be rated for each day in a financial year on which certain conditions are met[2]. Liability for unoccupied hereditaments is equal to the basic level of liability as for occupied hereditaments but with provision made for that liability to be reduced by order and for zero-rating to apply in specified cases[3]. There are specific provisions relating to when new buildings are deemed to be completed for these purposes[4].

Where part of a hereditament in a local non-domestic rating list is unoccupied but will remain so for a short time only, the billing authority may require the valuation officer to apportion the rateable value of the hereditament between the occupied and unoccupied parts of the hereditament[5].

The ratepayer becomes liable to the non-domestic rate in respect of any day of the chargeable financial year if his name is shown as a designated person in a central rating list[6].

1 See the Local Government Finance Act 1988 ss 43–44; and PARA 133. As to hereditaments see PARA 106 et seq.
2 See the Local Government Finance Act 1988 s 45; and PARAS 135–136.
3 See the Local Government Finance Act 1988 ss 45–46; and PARA 135 et seq. Regulations may be made to prevent changes in the state of an unoccupied hereditament affecting liability: see s 66A; and PARA 137.
4 See the Local Government Finance Act 1988 s 46A(1), Sch 4A; and PARAS 138–141.
5 See the Local Government Finance Act 1988 s 44A; and PARA 134.
6 See the Local Government Finance Act 1988 s 54; and PARA 142.

(5) Rateable Occupation

(i) Introduction

85. Necessary ingredients of rateable occupation.

Rateable occupation in relation to non-domestic property[1] is determined in accordance with rules explained and developed by extensive case law[2]. These rules, which applied under the General Rate Act 1967 (now repealed), have been preserved under the Local Government Finance Act 1988, but any express statutory rules contained in the 1967 Act must be ignored[3].

The courts have accepted that there are four necessary ingredients in rateable occupation[4]:

(1) there must be actual occupation[5];
(2) the occupation must be exclusive for the particular purposes of the possessor[6];
(3) the possession must be of some value or benefit to the possessor[7]; and
(4) the possession must not be for too transient a period[8].

Provision is made for the rating of certain non-domestic unoccupied property[9].

1 As to rateable property generally see PARA 80.
2 Cases decided under previous statutes continue to be of relevance to the current statutory regime of rating: see PARA 50.
3 See the Local Government Finance Act 1988 s 65(2); and PARA 86.
4 *John Laing & Son Ltd v Assessment Committee for Kingswood Assessment Area* [1949] 1 KB 344 at 350, [1949] 1 All ER 224 at 228, CA, per Tucker LJ, and at 357 and 232 per Jenkins J; *LCC v Wilkins (Valuation Officer)* [1957] AC 362, [1956] 3 All ER 38, HL; *Hall (Valuation Officer) v Darwen Corpn* (1957) 2 RRC 329 at 337, Lands Tribunal; *Holly Lodge Estate Committee v Hope (Valuation Officer)* (1958) 3 RRC 176 at 180, Lands Tribunal. See also *Re Briant Colour Printing Co Ltd (in liquidation)* [1977] 3 All ER 968, [1977] 1 WLR 942, CA (liquidator of a company was held not to be in rateable occupation of the company's premises as he had been totally excluded by the workers); *Walker (Valuation Officer) v Ideal Homes Central Ltd* [1995] RA 347, Lands Tribunal (show houses were held to be occupied as non-domestic rateable hereditaments).

For the leading discussions of rateable occupation see *R v St Pancras Assessment Committee* (1877) 2 QBD 581; *Liverpool Corpn v Chorley Union Assessment Committee and Withnell Overseers* [1913] AC 197, HL; *Westminster City Council and Kent Valuation Committee v Southern Rly Co, Rly Assessment Authority and Pullman Car Co Ltd* [1936] AC 511, [1936] 2 All ER 322, HL.

5 See note 4; and as to actual occupation see PARA 87 et seq.
6 See note 4; and as to exclusive occupation see PARA 89 et seq.
7 See note 4; and as to beneficial occupation see PARA 94 et seq.

8 See note 4; and as to permanence of occupation see PARA 99.
9 See the Local Government Finance Act 1988 s 45; and PARAS 135–136, 148.

86. Owners and occupiers.

For the purposes of the non-domestic rating provisions[1], the 'owner' of a hereditament[2] or land is the person[3] entitled to possession of it[4]. Whether a hereditament or land is occupied, and who is the occupier, must be determined by reference to the rules which would have applied for the purposes of the General Rate Act 1967 (now repealed) had the Local Government Finance Act 1988 not been passed, ignoring any express statutory rules contained in the General Rate Act 1967[5].

A hereditament which is not in use is to be treated as unoccupied if it would otherwise be treated as occupied by reason only of there being kept in or on the hereditament plant, machinery or equipment which was used in or on the hereditament when it was last in use[6], or which is intended for use in or on the hereditament[7]. A hereditament is to be treated as unoccupied if it would otherwise be treated as occupied by reason only of the use of it for the holding of public meetings in furtherance of a person's candidature at a parliamentary or local government election[8], or if it is a house, the use of a room in it by a returning officer[9] for the purpose of taking the poll in a parliamentary or local government election[10].

The appropriate national authority[11] may make such regulations as it sees fit to deal with any case where (apart from the regulations) there would be more than one owner or occupier of a hereditament or part or of land at a particular time[12].

1 Ie for the purposes of the Local Government Finance Act 1988 Pt III (ss 41–67): see s 67(13).
2 As to the meaning of 'hereditament' see PARA 106 et seq.
3 As to the meaning of 'person' see PARA 11 note 13.
4 Local Government Finance Act 1988 s 65(1). A person is the owner, or in occupation of all or part, of a hereditament on a particular day if (and only if) he is its owner or in such occupation (as the case may be) immediately before the day ends: s 67(6). The Local Government Finance Act 1988 s 65(1), (2) (see the text to note 5) has effect subject to s 65(4) (see PARA 106), s 65(5)–(7) (see the text to notes 6–10), s 65(8)–(8A) (see PARA 104 note 3): s 65(3) (amended by the Local Government and Rating Act 1997 s 2(3)(a)). As to Crown property see PARA 111.
5 Local Government Finance Act 1988 s 65(2). See also note 4. As to occupation see PARA 87 et seq.
6 Local Government Finance Act 1988 s 65(5)(a).
7 Local Government Finance Act 1988 s 65(5)(b).
8 Local Government Finance Act 1988 s 65(6)(a).
9 'Returning officer' is to be construed in accordance with the Representation of the People Act 1983 s 24 (returning officers for parliamentary elections) (see ELECTIONS AND REFERENDUMS vol 38 (2013) PARA 350) or s 35 (returning officers for local government elections) (see ELECTIONS AND REFERENDUMS vol 38 (2013) PARA 354) as the case may be: Local Government Finance Act 1988 s 65(7).
10 Local Government Finance Act 1988 s 65(6)(b).
11 Ie the Secretary of State or, in relation to Wales, the Welsh Ministers. The functions of the Secretary of State under the Local Government Finance Act 1988 s 50, so far as exercisable in relation to Wales, were transferred to the National Assembly for Wales (see the National Assembly for Wales (Transfer of Functions) Order 1999, SI 1999/672, art 2, Sch 1) and are now vested in the Welsh Ministers (see the Government of Wales Act 2006 s 162(1), Sch 11 para 30). As to the Secretary of State and the Welsh Ministers see PARA 4 note 18. As to the meaning of 'Wales' see PARA 2 note 16. As to the separate administration of the non-domestic rating provisions (Local Government Finance Act 1988 Pt III (ss 41–67)) in England and Wales see PARA 52.
12 Local Government Finance Act 1988 s 50(1). The regulations may provide for the owner or occupier at the time concerned to be taken to be such one of the owners or occupiers as is identified in accordance with prescribed rules: s 50(3). The regulations may provide that:
(1) as regards any time when there is only one owner or occupier, s 43 (occupied hereditaments: see PARAS 133, 143 et seq) or s 45 (unoccupied hereditaments: see

PARAS 135–136, 148), as the case may be, is to apply (s 50(4)(a));

(2) as regards any time when there is more than one owner or occupier, the owners or occupiers are to be jointly and severally liable to pay a prescribed amount by way of non-domestic rate (s 50(4)(b)).

The regulations may include that prescribed provisions are to apply instead of prescribed provisions of Pt III (ss 41–67), or that prescribed provisions of Pt III are not to apply or are to apply subject to prescribed amendments or adaptations: s 50(5). Nothing in s 50(3)–(5) prejudices the generality of s 50(1): s 50(2). 'Prescribed' means prescribed by the regulations: see s 146(6). As to the regulations made see the Non-Domestic Rating (Collection and Enforcement) (Miscellaneous Provisions) Regulations 1990, SI 1990/145; and PARA 272.

(ii) Actual Occupation

87. Meaning of 'actual occupation'.

Actual occupation involves physical possession of the hereditament in the sense that some degree of use of it is made, however slight[1]. Legal possession is not synonymous with actual occupation[2].

In certain circumstances, unoccupied property is rateable and so the concept of occupation does not apply[3].

1 See eg *Vtesse Networks Ltd v Bradford* [2006] EWCA Civ 1339, [2006] RA 427, [2006] All ER (D) 242 (Oct) (a network provider was in actual occupation of the whole of a fibre optic telecommunications network, which was a unit of property so as to form a hereditament, despite its being contained in cables partly owned by the network provider and partly owned by third parties). See also *Clydesdale Bank plc v Lanarkshire Valuation Joint Board Assessor* [2005] RA 1, sub nom *Lanarkshire Valuation Joint Board Assessor v Clydesdale Bank plc* 2005 SLT 167 (where ATMs owned by banks were placed in shops, the areas of floor space on which the machines were placed could not be entered in the roll as separate rateable occupation by the banks because the agreements to supply, use and control the ATMs did not confer a right of occupation of the floor space upon the banks).

2 *R v St Pancras Assessment Committee* (1877) 2 QBD 581. A trespasser may be rateable: see PARA 88.

3 As to the rating of unoccupied property see PARA 135 et seq.

88. Title not always material.

Occupation does not depend on title[1], although evidence of title may be material, for instance where it is doubtful which of two persons is the rateable occupier[2], or whether there is any person who can be so described[3].

A mere trespasser may be rateable[4], as may licensees or tenants at will[5] or companies allowed certain use of land for commercial purposes[6].

1 *Lord Bute v Grindall* (1786) 1 Term Rep 338; *R v Leith* (1852) 1 E & B 121 at 131; *Mersey Docks and Harbour Board Trustees v Cameron, Jones v Mersey Docks and Harbour Board Trustees* (1865) 11 HL Cas 443; *Kittow v Liskeard Union* (1874) LR 10 QB 7; *Cory v Bristow* (1877) 2 App Cas 262 at 273, HL, per Lord Cairns LC; *Holywell Union and Halkyn Parish v Halkyn District Mines Drainage Co* [1895] AC 117 at 121, HL, per Lord Herschell LC, and at 127 per Lord Macnaghten.

2 See eg *Holywell Union and Halkyn Parish v Halkyn District Mines Drainage Co* [1895] AC 117 at 134, HL, per Lord Davey; *Hall (Valuation Officer) v Darwen Corpn* (1957) 2 RRC 329, Lands Tribunal. See also the cases cited in PARA 90.

3 See eg *New Shoreham Harbour Comrs v Lancing* (1870) LR 5 QB 489; *Swansea Union Assessment Committee v Swansea Harbour Trustees* (1907) 71 JP 497, sub nom *Swansea Harbour Trustees v Swansea Union Assessment Committee* (1907) 1 Konst Rat App 250, HL; *Doncaster Union Assessment Committee v Manchester Sheffield and Lincolnshire Rly Co* (1894) 71 LT 585, HL; *Margate Corpn v Pettman* (1912) 106 LT 104, DC. As to the liability of a trustee as a rateable occupier see *R v Brighton Justices, ex p Howard* [1980] RA 222, DC; *Marshall v Camden London Borough Council* [1981] RVR 94, DC; *Verrall v Hackney London Borough Council* [1983] QB

445, [1983] 1 All ER 277, CA (person who authorised or ratified occupation on behalf of an unincorporated body was held not liable for the rates as occupation by such a body is impossible in law).

4 *Forrest v Greenwich Overseers* (1858) 8 E & B 890 at 897 per Lord Campbell CJ; *Bruce v Willis* (1840) 11 Ad & El 463 at 479; *R v Bell* (1798) 7 Term Rep 598 at 601. Cf *Kittow v Liskeard Union* (1874) LR 10 QB 7 at 15 per Lush J; *Coomber v Berkshire Justices* (1882) 10 QBD 267 at 282, CA, per Brett LJ. In Scotland, squatters were held to have been correctly included in the valuation list in *Langlands v Midlothian Assessor* [1962] RA 504, 1962 SLT 326, Land Val App Ct. See also *Westminster City Council v Tomlin* [1990] 1 All ER 920, [1989] 1 WLR 1287, CA.

5 *R v Munday* (1801) 1 East 584; *R v Green* (1829) 9 B & C 203 (occupants of almshouses); *R v Lady Ponsonby* (1842) 3 QB 14 (occupant of rooms in palace). An inmate of a lunatic asylum was not a rateable occupant: *R v St Luke's Hospital* (1760) 2 Burr 1053 at 1065.

6 Eg a company which provides bookstalls on a railway station (*Westminster City Council and Kent Valuation Committee v Southern Rly Co, Rly Assessment Authority and Pullman Car Co Ltd* [1936] AC 511, [1936] 2 All ER 322, HL); a water company (*R v Chelsea Water Works Co* (1833) 5 B & Ad 156; *R v East London Waterworks Co* (1852) 18 QB 705); or, prior to the nationalisation of the gas undertaking, a gas company (*R v Stevens and Anderson* (1865) 12 LT 491); or a telegraph company (*Electric Telegraph Co v Salford Overseers* (1855) 11 Exch 181). Cf *Clydesdale Bank plc v Lanarkshire Valuation Joint Board Assessor* [2005] RA 1, sub nom *Lanarkshire Valuation Joint Board Assessor v Clydesdale Bank plc* 2005 SLT 167 (ATMs owned by banks were placed in shops to attract retail custom and the agreements to supply, use and control the ATMs did not confer a right of occupation of the floor space upon the banks).

(iii) Exclusive Occupation

89. Occupation must be exclusive.

In order to be rateable, occupation must be exclusive[1]. Exclusive occupation means that the person using the land may prevent any other person from using it in the same way[2]. Occupation therefore does not cease to be exclusive because other persons have simultaneous, although different, rights of user over the same land, for all may be rateable in respect of their different occupations[3]. A person is not divested of occupation because he lets the land or parts of it to transient users[4]. Several persons, as in the case of partners, may be in joint occupation of a single hereditament, in which case each is liable for the rates on the whole[5].

1 *Cory v Bristow* (1877) 2 App Cas 262, HL; *Holywell Union and Halkyn Parish v Halkyn District Mines Drainage Co* [1895] AC 117, HL; *Peak (Valuation Officer) v Burley Golf Club* [1960] 2 All ER 199, [1960] 1 WLR 568, CA; *John Laing & Son Ltd v Assessment Committee for Kingswood Assessment Area* [1949] 1 KB 344, [1949] 1 All ER 224, CA. See also *R v Trent and Mersey Navigation Co* (1825) 4 B & C 57; *Kittow v Liskeard Union* (1874) LR 10 QB 7; *R v Jolliffe* (1787) 2 Term Rep 90; *Greenall (Valuation Officer) v Castleford Brick Co Ltd* (1959) 5 RRC 253, Lands Tribunal; *Mildmay v Churchwardens and Overseers of Wimbledon* (1872) 41 LJMC 133; *Renore Ltd v Hounslow London Borough Council* (1970) 15 RRC 378, DC, where exclusive occupation of car parking spaces rendered the occupiers liable to rates. See also *Vtesse Networks Ltd v Bradford* [2006] EWCA Civ 1339, [2006] RA 427, [2006] All ER (D) 242 (Oct) (where a fibre optic telecommunications network was contained in cables partly owned by the network provider and partly owned by third parties, the occupation of the network by the network provider was exclusive, not being shared with and therefore not subordinate to that of the third party).

2 *Cory v Bristow* (1877) 2 App Cas 262 at 276, HL, per Lord Hatherley. Exclusive right to remove all but certain materials from a colliery tip amounts to rateable occupation: *Ryan Industrial Fuels Ltd v Morgan (Valuation Officer)* [1965] 3 All ER 465, [1965] 1 WLR 1347, CA. The inability of a golf club to exclude the public and commoners from the course meant that the club's occupation was not exclusive and therefore not rateable: *Peak (Valuation Officer) v Burley Golf Club* [1960] 2 All ER 199, [1960] 1 WLR 568, CA; distinguished in *Pennard Golf Club v Richards (Valuation Officer)* (1976) 20 RRC 225, Lands Tribunal, where the occupation of land by a golf club was held to be exclusive despite the rights of commoners and rights of way; and in *Greater Manchester Passenger Transport Executive v Carter (Valuation Officer)* [1981] RA 271, Lands Tribunal, where the owner in possession of bus turning circles was held rateable despite trespass by the public and unauthorised use by another bus operator. See also *Eden (Valuation Officer) v Grass Ski Promotions Ltd* [1981] RA 7, Lands Tribunal (where occupation of a grass ski course was held

to be not exclusive and not rateable); and *Pratt (Valuation Officer) v United Automobile Services Ltd* [1987] RA 257, Lands Tribunal (a bus company was not in rateable occupation of parts of a bus station shared with public and other bus companies).

3 Eg *Young & Co v Liverpool Assessment Committee* [1911] 2 KB 195, DC (warehouse and hydraulic mains in separate occupation); *Lancashire Telephone Co v Manchester Overseers* (1884) 14 QBD 267, CA (telephone wires attached to roof). As to instances where there may be a rival occupancy in some person who, to some extent, may have occupancy rights over the premises in question see PARA 90.

4 *Roberts v Aylesbury Overseers* (1853) 1 E & B 423 (lettings to stall-holders in a market); cf *Williams v Wednesbury and West Bromwich Churchwardens and Overseers Union Assessment Committee* (1890) Ryde Rat App (1886–90) 327, DC. See also *Magon v Barking and Dagenham London Borough Council* [2000] RA 459 (premises used as a business for the purpose of allowing third parties to store their goods, subject to very limited rights, did not divest the owner of the premises of actual occupation).

5 *Griffiths v Gower RDC* (1972) 17 RRC 69 (holiday flat jointly owned); *Pamplin v Preston Borough Council* [1980] RA 246; *R v Paynter* (1845) 7 QB 255 (affd sub nom *Paynter v R* (1847) 10 QB 908, Ex Ch). Where, however, premises are incorrectly rated as a single hereditament, the occupier of a part only cannot be compelled to pay the rates on the whole: *R v London Justices* [1899] 1 QB 532 at 539, DC. A person in occupation of part of a hereditament for only part of the year is liable to pay only a proportion of the rates: see *Croydon London Borough Council v Maxon Systems Inc (London) Ltd* [1999] RA 286, [1999] EGCS 68; and PARA 133.

90. Paramount occupier is rateable.

In certain cases, there may be a rival occupancy in some person who, to some extent, may have occupancy rights over the premises. The question in every such case is one of fact, namely whose position in relation to occupation is paramount, and whose position in relation to occupation is subordinate, but that question must be considered and answered in regard to the position and rights of the parties in respect of the premises in question, and in regard to the purpose of the occupation of those premises[1]. Neither the control of access to, nor the existence of restrictive covenants on, the user of the portion is decisive[2]. A person allowed the use of offices[3] is not, if he is subject to the landlord's control, the rateable occupier of the offices[4]. Similar considerations apply to parts of commercial or industrial undertakings appropriated to the use of persons conducting subsidiary enterprises[5]. The agreement which allows the separate user may contain words of demise, but it does not necessarily follow that the grantor has transferred to the grantee the rateable occupation[6]; and the grantee may be the rateable occupier even though no words of demise appear in the agreement[7].

1 *Westminster City Council and Kent Valuation Committee v Southern Rly Co, Rly Assessment Authority and Pullman Car Co Ltd* [1936] AC 511, [1936] 2 All ER 322, HL; and see *Holywell Union and Halkyn Parish v Halkyn District Mines Drainage Co* [1895] AC 117, HL (occupation is not exclusive where it is subject to control and regulation by others).

Control over the occupation of the land is to be distinguished from control over the occupier such as the control which a building owner has over the performance of a building contract: see *John Laing & Son Ltd v Assessment Committee for Kingswood Assessment Area* [1949] 1 KB 344, [1949] 1 All ER 224, CA; followed in *Wimborne District Council v Brayne Construction Co Ltd* [1985] RA 234, [1985] 2 EGLR 175, CA. See also *Andrews v Hereford RDC* [1963] RA 75, DC (where the owner of a gravel pit permitted a company to extract gravel under licence, but also permitted others to take gravel, and the owner was held rateable); *Ryan Industrial Fuels Ltd v Morgan (Valuation Officer)* [1965] 3 All ER 465, [1965] 1 WLR 1347, CA (where a company had exclusive right to extract all materials in a colliery tip, other than red ash, for a period of 15 years, and was held to be in rateable occupation of the tip); *Bartlett (Valuation Officer) v Reservoir Aggregates Ltd* [1985] RA 191, [1985] 2 EGLR 171, CA (a company deepening a reservoir and extracting minerals was held to be in rateable occupation of the gravel stratum); *Croydon London Borough Council v Maxon Systems Inc (London) Ltd* [1999] RA 286, [1999] EGCS 68 (a person was permitted to occupy the second floor and part of the third floor of a building on payment of a licence fee which included an apportionment in respect of non-domestic rates, but the owner of the building retained general control of all parts of the building and was held to be in paramount occupation).

2 *Westminster City Council and Kent Valuation Committee v Southern Rly Co, Rly Assessment Authority and Pullman Car Co Ltd* [1936] AC 511, [1936] 2 All ER 322, HL (shops on railway station and builders' depots in goods yard). The purpose of the occupation must also be considered: *Westminster City Council and Kent Valuation Committee v Southern Rly Co, Rly Assessment Authority and Pullman Car Co Ltd* [1936] AC 511, [1936] 2 All ER 322, HL at 529–530 and at 326–327 per Lord Russell of Killowen; and see *Field Place Caravan Park Ltd v Harding* [1966] 2 QB 484, [1966] 3 All ER 247, CA, where the occupier of a caravan was rateable despite a certain amount of control by the site owner. As to the discretionary treatment for caravan pitches provided under certain legislation that has been overtaken to all practical effect but which has not yet been repealed see PARA 109. See also *Hampton Wick v Hatchetts' White Horse Cellars Ltd* (1931) 14 R & IT 8, DC (occupation of tea gardens by refreshment caterers subordinate to owner's occupation and so not rateable); *Dover Harbour Board v Dover Borough Rating Authority* (1931) 13 R & IT 199 (occupation of a landing place by the board subordinate to that of the owners who had certain rights of access); *Orkney Assessor v Highland Airways Ltd* (1935) 23 R & IT 100 (occupation as a landing place for aeroplanes paramount to that of the farmer); *Greenwoods Building Industries Ltd v Sainsbury (Valuation Officer)* (1955) 48 R & IT 155, Lands Tribunal (occupation of a site by subcontractors); *Hall (Valuation Officer) v Darwen Corpn* (1957) 2 RRC 329, Lands Tribunal (occupation of vacant land for holding fairs periodically).

3 *R v Smith* (1860) 30 LJMC 74.

4 See *Westminster City Council and Kent Valuation Committee v Southern Rly Co, Rly Assessment Authority and Pullman Car Co Ltd* [1936] AC 511, [1936] 2 All ER 322, HL at 530 and 327 per Lord Russell of Killowen, and at 556 and 345 per Lord Wright.

5 Eg banks, shops and bookstalls on a railway station and builders' depots in a goods yard (*Westminster City Council and Kent Valuation Committee v Southern Rly Co, Rly Assessment Authority and Pullman Car Co Ltd* [1936] AC 511, [1936] 2 All ER 322, HL); building contractors' offices, canteens and other structures on a building site (*John Laing & Son Ltd v Assessment Committee for Kingswood Assessment Area* [1949] 1 KB 344, [1949] 1 All ER 224, CA); three properties within the curtilage of a single factory but separately occupied by three companies, one being the parent company and the other two being separate subsidiary companies, and each company being a separate legal entity carrying on separate businesses (*Barr (Valuation Officer) v Manley and Regulus Ltd* (1960) 53 R & IT 213, Lands Tribunal); portions of dock undertakings appropriated to shippers (*Allan v Liverpool Overseers* (1874) LR 9 QB 180, DC), or to a canal company (*Rochdale Canal Co v Brewster* [1894] 2 QB 852, CA). In the last two cases the dock board retained the control, and the persons using were held not rateable; but where the board appropriated a portion to a firm of wine merchants, for use as bonded stores, the firm was held to have such control as to be rateable: *Young & Co v Liverpool Assessment Committee* [1911] 2 KB 195, DC. See also *Watson (Valuation Officer) v Thornbury RDC and Miller* (1959) 53 R & IT 107, Lands Tribunal (chalets on camping site in separate occupation). In cases concerning the following properties the persons allowing the use retained control of the whole and were the rateable occupiers: a portion of an exhibition appropriated to a caterer (*R v Morrish* (1863) 32 LJMC 245); part of a set of telegraph wires appropriated by the Postmaster General to the use of a private company (*Paris and New York Telegraph Co v Penzance Union* (1884) 12 QBD 552, DC); portions of electric cables and equipment appropriated to the use of a tramways company (*New St Helens and District Tramways Co Ltd v Prescot Union* (1904) 1 Konst Rat App 150, DC); portions of a cemetery in which the cemetery company had sold exclusive rights of burial (*R v St Mary Abbot's, Kensington* (1840) 12 Ad & El 824), or which it had sold for graves (*R v Abney Park Cemetery Co* (1873) LR 8 QB 515). See also *Porter (Valuation Officer) v Gray, Son and Cook and Cambridge Corpn* (1952) 46 R & IT 28, Lands Tribunal, where a municipal car park was held to be in the occupation of the corporation notwithstanding the letting out of parking spaces. Cf *Renfrewshire Assessor v Old Consort Car Co Ltd* 1960 SC 226, where bars and shops at an airport were run by contractors, and the contractors, not the airport authority, were held to be in rateable occupation; and *Clydesdale Bank plc v Lanarkshire Valuation Joint Board Assessor* [2005] RA 1, sub nom *Lanarkshire Valuation Joint Board Assessor v Clydesdale Bank plc* 2005 SLT 167, where a right of occupation was not conferred on banks whose ATMs were placed in shops as the agreements controlling their supply did not give the banks a right to occupy floor space.

6 *Allan v Liverpool Overseers* (1874) LR 9 QB 180, DC; *Rochdale Canal Co v Brewster* [1894] 2 QB 852, CA. See the comments on these cases in *Westminster City Council and Kent Valuation Committee v Southern Rly Co, Rly Assessment Authority and Pullman Car Co Ltd* [1936] AC 511

at 557–559, [1936] 2 All ER 322 at 346–347, HL, per Lord Wright; and see also *Dunham Bridge Co v Retford Assessment Committee* [1949] WN 419, CA (owner in occupation where purported lease of toll bridge ultra vires).

7 *R v Stevens and Anderson* (1865) 12 LT 491; *Westminster City Council and Kent Valuation Committee v Southern Rly Co, Rly Assessment Authority and Pullman Car Co Ltd* [1936] AC 511, [1936] 2 All ER 322, HL.

91. Occupation by employee or agent.

An employee or agent occupying a separately rateable hereditament, even if he does so by virtue of his employment, may be the rateable occupier if the occupation is for his own purposes rather than those of his employer or principal[1]. Where an employee or agent[2] is required to occupy a hereditament in order to carry out the purposes of his employer's business, or to secure the better performance of his duties, the occupation for rating purposes is that of the employer[3]. A member of an unincorporated association cannot be in occupation since occupation by such an organisation is impossible in law[4].

1 *R v Catt* (1795) 6 Term Rep 332; *R v Lynn* (1838) 8 Ad & El 379; *Smith v Seghill Overseers* (1875) LR 10 QB 422, DC; and see *Morrell (Valuation Officer) v Glamorgan County Council* (1958) 4 RRC 20 at 23, Lands Tribunal. If a factory is taken over by the owner's former employees, and they have exclusive occupation, the owner will not be in rateable occupation: *Re Briant Colour Printing Co Ltd (in liquidation)* [1977] 3 All ER 968, [1977] 1 WLR 942, CA. As to the distinction between occupancy and a tenancy see LANDLORD AND TENANT vol 62 (2016) PARA 15.

2 *Solihull Corpn v Gas Council* [1961] 1 All ER 542, [1961] WLR 619, CA (affd [1962] 1 All ER 898n, [1962] 1 WLR 583, HL) (gas board not occupying research station as agents of Gas Council); *Greenwoods Building Industries Ltd v Sainsbury (Valuation Officer)* (1955) 48 R & IT 155, Lands Tribunal (one company not the employee or agent of another).

3 *Glasgow Corpn v Johnstone* [1965] AC 609, [1965] 1 All ER 730, HL (church house occupied by church officer in order to perform duties); *Northern Ireland Comr of Valuation v Fermanagh Protestant Board of Education* [1969] 3 All ER 352, [1969] 1 WLR 1708, HL (house owned by school and used as schoolmasters' residences); *Hirst v Sargent* [1966] RA 605, DC (house owned by school and occupied by school groundsman who was able to prevent trespass and damage to playing fields from the hereditament). See also *Yates v Chorlton-upon-Medlock Union* (1883) 47 JP 630, DC (dwelling house occupied by means of a caretaker); *R v Field* (1794) 5 Term Rep 587 (school occupied by means of a matron); *R v Tynemouth Inhabitants* (1810) 12 East 46 (lighthouse occupied by means of a lightkeeper); *LCC v Hackney Borough Council* [1928] 2 KB 588 (caretaker on premises); *Reed v Cattermole* [1937] 1 KB 613, [1937] 1 All ER 541, CA (manse occupied by means of minister, who was required by the church to reside there for the more effectual performance of his duty).

4 *Verrall v Hackney London Borough Council* [1983] QB 445, [1983] 1 All ER 277, CA.

92. Occupation by a caretaker or guest.

A mere caretaker cannot himself be a rateable occupier[1]. Whether the caretaker's employer is rateable depends upon whether the occupation is beneficial[2]. Where the hereditament consists of parts capable of separate rateable occupation, the fact that a caretaker is residing in one such part does not make his employer the rateable occupier of the whole[3]. The current law makes provision for rating partly occupied hereditaments[4].

1 *Yates v Chorlton-upon-Medlock Union* (1883) 47 JP 630, DC; *R v Simmonds* (1893) Ryde Rat App (1891–93) 316; and see PARA 91.

2 See *Bertie v Walthamstow Overseers* (1904) 68 JP 545, DC, where a caretaker was looking after other property belonging to the same owner and supervising workmen, and the owner was held to be the rateable occupier of the caretaker's house because the occupation was beneficial to him.

3 *Langford v Cole* (1910) 74 JP 229, DC.

4 See the Local Government Finance Act 1988 s 44A; and PARA 134.

93. Occupation by bankrupt, liquidators or receiver.

A bankrupt may be in rateable occupation even though he holds indirectly through the trustee in bankruptcy[1]. In winding up, liquidators who carry on the company's business continue the rateable occupation of its premises[2]; and they are in rateable occupation even if they occupy merely for the purpose of fulfilling outstanding contracts[3], or of preventing damage to the company's property[4].

Where a receiver and manager of a company's business is appointed by order of the court, by which the company is not directed to deliver up possession of land to him, he has no rateable occupation of the company's land[5]; but a receiver appointed out of court under the terms of a deed by which the company is to give up possession at a certain date is in rateable occupation as from the date when possession is given up[6].

Specific exemptions to the unoccupied rate now exist in relation to the above categories[7].

1 Cf *Re Thomas, ex p Ystradyfodwg Local Board* (1887) 57 LJQB 39.

2 *Re Wearmouth Crown Glass Co* (1882) 19 ChD 640; *Taggs Island Casino Hotel Ltd v Richmond-upon-Thames London Borough Council* (1966) 14 RRC 119; *Banister v Islington London Borough Council* (1972) 17 RRC 191, DC, where the receiver was also liable for unoccupied rate after vacating the premises. See also COMPANY AND PARTNERSHIP INSOLVENCY vol 17 (2017) PARA 785.

3 *Re National Arms and Ammunition Co* (1885) 28 ChD 474, CA. Cf *Re International Marine Hydropathic Co* (1884) 28 ChD 470, CA.

4 *Re Blazer Fire Lighter Ltd* [1895] 1 Ch 402.

5 The occupation remains in the company (*Re Marriage, Neave & Co, North of England Trustee, Debenture and Assets Corpn v Marriage, Neave & Co* [1896] 2 Ch 663, CA; followed in *National Provincial Bank of England Ltd v United Electric Theatres Ltd* [1916] 1 Ch 132 at 135; and *Gyton v Palmour* [1945] KB 426, [1944] 2 All ER 540, DC), but rates due by the company must be paid by the receiver, in priority to the claim of a debenture holder, out of assets coming into the receiver's hands (*Westminster City Council v Treby* [1936] 2 All ER 21; *Westminster Corpn v Haste* [1950] Ch 442, [1950] 2 All ER 65). See also COMPANIES vol 15A (2016) PARA 1557. The company will not be in occupation when it and the liquidator are totally excluded from its premises by ex-employees: *Re Briant Colour Printing Co Ltd (in liquidation)* [1977] 3 All ER 968, [1977] 1 WLR 942, CA.

6 *Richards v Kidderminster Overseers* [1896] 2 Ch 212. See also *Re Marriage, Neave & Co, North of England Trustee, Debenture and Assets Corpn v Marriage, Neave & Co* [1896] 2 Ch 663 at 678, CA, per Rigby LJ. As to a receiver's duty to pay rates see RECEIVERS vol 88 (2012) PARA 106.

7 As to exemptions generally see PARA 110 et seq.

(iv) Beneficial Occupation

94. Occupation for the use of the public.

The public cannot be a rateable occupier, and land occupied by a body as custodians or guardians for the public is exempt from rates[1]. The exemption arises where land is held under an irrevocable obligation to keep it for the use of the public[2] pursuant to statute. An obligation created by non-statutory means, such as a voluntary trust, may be sufficient[3], but the trust must confer such rights upon the public as to exhaust the possibility of the hereditament being of value to a local authority[4]. The public must in fact have free and unrestricted use of the land[5]. Thus highways[6], bridges[7] and public parks[8] may be occupied by the public and exempt from rates. In relation to public places such as parks, the local authority is the occupier but its occupation is not beneficial as the unrestricted use by the public exhausts all possible value of the hereditament to the local authority[9]. Certain parks which for the time being are available for free and unrestricted use by members of the public are exempt from rates[10]. Cases decided under previous legislation held that the exemption extended to uses ancillary to the main public user[11] even if the ancillary part is let out at a rent[12].

1 *Lambeth Overseers v LCC* [1897] AC 625, HL (the 'Brockwell Park' case); *Manchester Corpn v Chorlton Union Assessment Committee* (1899) 15 TLR 327, DC; *Liverpool Corpn v West Derby Assessment Committee* [1908] 2 KB 647, CA; *Burnell (Valuation Officer) v Downham Market UDC* [1952] 2 QB 55, [1952] 1 All ER 601, CA; *Blake (Valuation Officer) v Hendon Corpn* [1962] 1 QB 283, [1961] 3 All ER 601, CA. The claim for exemption failed in *Liverpool Corpn v West Derby Union* (1905) 69 JP 277, DC; *London Playing Fields Society v South West Essex Assessment Committee* (1930) 144 LT 233, DC; *Sir John Soane's Museum Trustees v St Giles-in-the-Fields and St George's, Bloomsbury, Joint Vestry* (1900) 83 LT 248, DC; *North Riding of Yorkshire County Valuation Committee v Redcar Corpn* [1943] 1 KB 114, [1942] 2 All ER 589, DC; *Kingston-upon-Hull Corpn v Clayton (Valuation Officer)* [1963] AC 28, [1961] 3 All ER 118, HL. Public parks are now exempt by statute: see the text to note 10.

2 The dedication must be to the public; dedication to a more limited class is not enough: *Holly Lodge Estate Committee v Hope (Valuation Officer)* (1958) 3 RRC 176, Lands Tribunal; *Hyde Borough Council v Wilkes (Valuation Officer) and Ashton Trustees* (1958) 4 RRC 151, Lands Tribunal.

3 *Burnell (Valuation Officer) v Downham Market UDC* [1952] 2 QB 55, [1952] 1 All ER 601, CA; *Burnell (Valuation Officer) v Terrington St Clement Parish Council* (1954) 47 R & IT 172, Lands Tribunal. Cf *Hyde Borough Council v Wilkes (Valuation Officer) and Ashton Trustees* (1958) 4 RRC 151, Lands Tribunal; *New Windsor Borough Council v Cleaver (Valuation Officer)* (1959) 53 R & IT 123, Lands Tribunal.

4 *Kingston-upon-Hull Corpn v Clayton (Valuation Officer)* [1963] AC 28, [1961] 3 All ER 118, HL, where premises were left in trust for the public as an art gallery but the public was excluded from certain parts and did not have free and unrestricted access, and as therefore its value to the corporation was not exhausted the gallery was rateable.

5 *Lambeth Overseers v LCC* [1897] AC 625, HL (the 'Brockwell Park' case). Reasonable restrictions on user may not be inconsistent with the public's free and unrestricted use of the land: *Liverpool Corpn v West Derby Assessment Committee* [1908] 2 KB 647, CA; *Burnell (Valuation Officer) v Downham Market UDC* [1952] 2 QB 55, [1952] 1 All ER 601, CA; cf *Kingston-upon-Hull Corpn v Clayton (Valuation Officer)* [1963] AC 28, [1961] 3 All ER 118, HL; *South Yorkshire County Council v Jones (Valuation Officer)* [1984] RA 204, [1985] JPL 124, Lands Tribunal; *Max Pullan Management Committee v Simpson (Valuation Officer)* [1989] RVR 128, Lands Tribunal.

6 *Lambeth Overseers v LCC* [1897] AC 625 at 630, HL. See also *Wheeler v Metropolitan Board of Works* (1869) LR 4 Exch 303 at 307; *Stratton v Metropolitan Board of Works* (1874) LR 10 CP 76 at 85; *Bristol Guardians v Bristol Corpn* (1887) 18 QBD 549, CA.

7 *Hare v Putney Overseers* (1881) 7 QBD 223, CA.

8 See the cases cited in note 1; and the text to notes 9–12.

9 See *Kingston-upon-Hull Corpn v Clayton (Valuation Officer)* [1963] AC 28, [1961] 3 All ER 118, HL, in which the House of Lords took the view that the exemption of public parks from rating depended upon the absence of beneficial occupation.

10 See PARA 126.

11 See eg *Liverpool Corpn v West Derby Assessment Committee* [1908] 2 KB 647, CA (bandstand, bowling green, park keepers' houses, refreshment kiosk); *Bexley Borough Council v Draper (Valuation Officer)* (1954) 47 R & IT 431, Lands Tribunal (changing rooms, staff mess-room, nursery garden, stables and garage, groundsman's house); *Redbridge London Borough Council v Wand (Valuation Officer)* (1970) 16 RRC 280 (swimming pool in local authority park). Cf *LCC v Fulham Metropolitan Borough Council* (1951) 44 R & IT 327, Lands Tribunal (civic restaurant in park rateable); *Denman (Valuation Officer) v Brandon Town Bowling Club* (1950) 44 R & IT 54, Lands Tribunal (bowling green rateable); *LCC v Robinson (Valuation Officer) and Lambeth Metropolitan Borough Council* (1955) 48 R & IT 455, Lands Tribunal (restaurant in park rateable); *Crosby Borough Council v Lyster (Valuation Officer)* (1955) 49 R & IT 23, Lands Tribunal (park officials' houses rateable); *Weston-super-Mare Borough Council v Escott (Valuation Officer)* (1953) 47 R & IT 23, Lands Tribunal (putting green and kiosk rateable); *New Windsor Borough Council v Cleaver (Valuation Officer)* (1959) 53 R & IT 123, Lands Tribunal (tea gardens rateable); *Smith (Valuation Officer) v St Albans City and District Council* [1978] RA 147, Lands Tribunal (swimming baths not part of a park nor ancillary to it; rateable); *Cumbria County Council v Sture (Valuation Officer)* [1975] JPL 226, Lands Tribunal (nature reserve rateable). See also *Hampshire County Council v Broadway (Valuation Officer)* [1982] RA 309 (charges made for car parking and other services did not render a country park provided by the county council liable to rates).

12 *Sheffield Corpn v Tranter (Valuation Officer)* [1957] 2 All ER 583, [1957] 1 WLR 843, CA (refreshment pavilion in park let to a caterer not rateable); *Southern Miniature Railways Ltd v Hake (Valuation Officer)* (1959) 5 RRC 179, Lands Tribunal (privately owned miniature railway in public park not rateable).

95. Occupation must be of value or benefit.

To be rateable, occupation must be of value or benefit[1]. The value or benefit need not take the form of pecuniary profit[2], and a hereditament may be rateable even though the occupation of it involves a pecuniary loss[3]. Beneficial occupation can arise if the occupation of the hereditament affords to the occupier the facility for the exercise of a statutory duty[4] or a statutory power[5], or for discharging the duties of a trust[6].

1 Potential beneficial occupation may be enough: *Hare v Putney Overseers* (1881) 7 QBD 223 at 233–234, CA, per Lord Esher; *Winstanley v North Manchester Overseers* [1910] AC 7 at 15, HL, per Lord Atkinson; *R v Heaton* (1856) 20 JP Jo 37; *City of London Real Property Co Ltd v Stewart (Valuation Officer)* [1962] RVR 246, Lands Tribunal. However, there must be actual occupation (ie acts of user) first: *R v Fayle* (1856) 4 WR 460; *Liverpool Corpn v Chorley Union Assessment Committee and Withnell Overseers* [1913] AC 197 at 207–209, HL, per Lord Atkinson; *Re London and North Eastern Rly Co's Appeal* [1946] KB 27 at 34–36 per Wrottesley J. See also *Tyne Coal Co v Wallsend Parish Overseers* (1877) 46 LJMC 185 (drowned-out mine not rateable); *Consett Iron Co Ltd v Assessment Committee for No 5 or North-Western Area of County of Durham* [1931] AC 396, HL (mine running at a loss rateable); *Cumbria County Council v Sture (Valuation Officer)* [1975] JPL 226 (occupation of nature reserve beneficial); *Appleton v Westminster Corpn* [1963] RVR 374, DC (whether or not premises are beneficially occupied is a matter of fact and degree); *British Coal Corpn v Aspinall (Valuation Officer)* [1988] RA 78, Lands Tribunal (surface structures used during the construction of a coal mine were not rateable until the mine was operational).

2 *Mersey Docks and Harbour Board Trustees v Cameron, Jones v Mersey Docks and Harbour Board Trustees* (1865) 11 HL Cas 443; *R v London School Board* (1886) 17 QBD 738, CA; *Burton-upon-Trent Corpn v Burton-upon-Trent Union Assessment Committee and Stretton Overseers* (1889) 24 QBD 197, CA; *LCC v Churchwardens etc of Erith Parish and Dartford Union Assessment Committee* [1893] AC 562, HL; *West Kent Main Sewerage Board v Dartford Union Assessment Committee etc* [1911] AC 171, HL; *Greig v Edinburgh University* (1868) LR 1 Sc & Div 348, HL; *Clyde Navigation Trustees v Adamson* (1865) 4 Macq 931, HL.

3 Eg *R v Parrot* (1794) 5 Term Rep 593; *Consett Iron Co Ltd v Assessment Committee for No 5 or North-Western Area of County of Durham* [1931] AC 396, HL; *O'Malley v Congested Districts Board* [1919] 2 IR 28.

4 *R v London School Board* (1886) 17 QBD 738, CA; *Robinson Bros (Brewers) Ltd v Houghton and Chester-le-Street Assessment Committee* [1937] 2 KB 445 at 480, 487, [1937] 2 All ER 298 at 314–315, 319, CA, per Scott LJ.

5 See eg *Swindon Borough Council v Tavener (Valuation Officer)* (1952) 45 R & IT 410, Lands Tribunal; *Erith Borough Council v Draper (Valuation Officer)* (1952) 45 R & IT 315, Lands Tribunal; *Working UDC v Baker (Valuation Officer)* (1959) 4 RRC 330, Lands Tribunal.

6 See eg *Bowes Museum and Park Trustees v Cutts (Valuation Officer)* (1950) 43 R & IT 881, 900, Lands Tribunal; *Holly Lodge Estate Committee v Hope (Valuation Officer)* (1958) 3 RRC 176, Lands Tribunal.

96. Occupation for public purposes.

The occupation of property for public purposes, other than those of general national administration[1], is rateable[2]. Thus an education authority is rateable for its schools[3]; a water authority is rateable for its sewage disposal works[4]; and a local authority is rateable for its public conveniences[5], town hall[6], fire station[7], swimming pool[8] or seaside entertainments undertaking[9]. The exemption of property which is dedicated to the use of the public, such as highways, arises[10] because the public, which is not rateable, is held to be in occupation[11].

1 However, county buildings, so far as they are used for other than judicial business, are rateable: *Middlesex County Council v St George's Union Assessment Committee* [1897] 1 QB 64, CA; *Worcestershire County Council v Worcester Union* [1897] 1 QB 480, CA. County buildings used

for judges' lodgings are not rateably occupied (*Hodgson v Carlisle Local Board of Health* (1857) 8 E & B 116), but buildings provided for the former assizes in which quarter sessions were also accommodated on payment by the corporation were rateable to the extent of the payment (*Lancashire Justices v Cheetham* (1867) LR 3 QB 14).

2 *Mersey Docks and Harbour Board Trustees v Cameron, Jones v Mersey Docks and Harbour Board Trustees* (1865) 11 HL Cas 443; cf *Leith Harbour and Docks Comrs v Inspector of the Poor* (1866) LR 1 Sc & Div 17, HL; *Williams v Neath Assessment Committee* (1935) 154 LT 261, DC (sub-post office).

3 *West Bromwich School Board v West Bromwich Overseers* (1884) 13 QBD 929, CA; *R v London School Board* (1886) 17 QBD 738, CA; *Laughlin v Saffron-Hill Overseers* (1865) 12 LT 542; *London School Board v Wandsworth and Clapham Unions Assessment Committee* (1900) 16 TLR 137, DC. As to the rating of educational premises see EDUCATION vol 36 (2015) PARA 1369 et seq; and see *Kent County Council v Ashford Borough Council* [1999] RA 367, [1999] All ER (D) 893, CA.

4 *Burton-upon-Trent Corpn v Burton-upon-Trent Union Assessment Committee and Stretton Overseers* (1889) 24 QBD 197, CA; *Leicester Corpn v Beaumont Leys and Barrow-on-Soar Union Assessment Committee* (1894) Ryde & K Rat App 140. See also *Re Burnell (Valuation Officer)* (1959) 53 R & IT 198, Lands Tribunal. Sewers are exempt from rates: see PARA 123.

5 *Erith Borough Council v Draper (Valuation Officer)* (1952) 45 R & IT 315, Lands Tribunal; *Bell (Valuation Officer) v Colne Borough Council* (1958) 6 RRC 36, Lands Tribunal.

6 *Chandler (Valuation Officer) v East Suffolk County Council* (1958) 3 RRC 328, Lands Tribunal.

7 *North Riding of Yorkshire County Council v Bell (Valuation Officer)* (1958) 3 RRC 133, Lands Tribunal.

8 *Working UDC v Baker (Valuation Officer)* (1959) 4 RRC 330, Lands Tribunal; *Smith (Valuation Officer) v St Albans City and District Council* [1978] RA 147, Lands Tribunal. Open air swimming pools in public parks may not be rateable: see *Redbridge London Borough Council v Wand (Valuation Officer)* (1970) 16 RRC 280; and see also PARA 126.

9 *Morecambe and Heysham Corpn v Robinson (Valuation Officer)* [1961] 1 All ER 721, [1961] 1 WLR 373, CA; *Lowestoft Borough Council v Scaife (Valuation Officer)* (1960) 7 RRC 296.

10 See PARA 94.

11 *Hare v Putney Overseers* (1881) 7 QBD 223, CA; *Lambeth Overseers v LCC* [1897] AC 625, HL; *Newham London Borough Council v Hampsher (Valuation Officer)* (1970) 16 RRC 292, Lands Tribunal.

97. Buildings in course of construction or unused.

Buildings in course of construction or alteration are not in the beneficial occupation of the building owner[1], although it may be otherwise while repairs or adaptations of a building already in use are in progress[2]. However, parts of a building site may be in the rateable occupation of the building contractor[3]. Statutory provisions now determine the date when newly constructed or altered buildings become liable to be rated[4]; and statutory provision is also made for unoccupied non-domestic hereditaments to be rateable[5]. In cases where they do not fall to be so rated, the following situations may still be of some relevance. Mere preservation of a building otherwise unused does not create beneficial occupation[6]. An owner may keep a caretaker in a building without becoming rateable for it[7]; nor is the caretaker rateable[8]. However, the presence of a caretaker may result in beneficial occupation if the caretaker does more than merely look after the building[9].

1 *Arbuckle Smith & Co Ltd v Greenock Corpn* [1960] AC 813, [1960] 1 All ER 568, HL. There is also no actual occupation (as to which see PARA 87). See also *Liverpool Corpn v Chorley Union Assessment Committee and Withnell Overseers* [1913] AC 197 at 211, HL, per Lord Atkinson; *John Laing & Son Ltd v Assessment Committee for Kingswood Assessment Area* [1948] 2 KB 116, [1948] 1 All ER 943 (affd on other grounds [1949] 1 KB 344, [1949] 1 All ER 224, CA); *Mid-Northamptonshire Water Board v Lee (Valuation Officer)* [1958] AC 68, [1957] 2 All ER 143, HL; *East London Waterworks Co v Edmonton Union* (1904) Ryde & K Rat App 120.

2 *Hackney Borough Council v Metropolitan Asylums Board* (1924) 131 LT 136, DC; *British Advent Missions Ltd v Cane (Valuation Officer) and Westminster City Council* (1954) 48 R & IT 60, Lands Tribunal. The former case may not have been correctly decided on its facts: see *Arbuckle Smith & Co Ltd v Greenock Corpn* [1960] AC 813, [1960] 1 All ER 568, HL.

3 *Mitchell Bros v Workshop Union Assessment Committee* (1904) 69 JP 53; *John Laing & Son Ltd v Assessment Committee for Kingswood Assessment Area* [1948] 2 KB 116, [1948] 1 All ER 943 (affd [1949] 1 KB 344, [1949] 1 All ER 224, CA); *LCC v Wilkins (Valuation Officer)* [1957] AC 362, [1956] 3 All ER 38, HL; *Croydon Corpn v Hardiman (Valuation Officer) and Wates Ltd* [1962] RA 565, where a show house was held to be in the developer's beneficial occupation. See, however, *Cobley (Valuation Officer) v Horlock (Dredging) Co Ltd* [1972] JPL 713, Lands Tribunal, where gravel winning in order to dredge a channel in a harbour was held not to be rateable occupation of the river bed.

4 See PARA 138 et seq.

5 See PARA 135 et seq.

6 *LCC v Hackney Borough Council* [1928] 2 KB 588; *Arbuckle Smith & Co Ltd v Greenock Corpn* [1960] AC 813, [1960] 1 All ER 568, HL. Cf *Henderson v Liverpool Metropolitan District Council* [1980] RA 238, DC.

7 *R v Morgan* (1834) 2 Ad & El 618n; *North Dublin Union Guardians v Scott* (1850) 1 ICLR 76; *Limerick Union v White* (1852) 2 ICLR 630; *LCC v Hackney Borough Council* [1928] 2 KB 588; *Arbuckle Smith & Co Ltd v Greenock Corpn* [1960] AC 813, [1960] 1 All ER 568, HL.

8 *Yates v Chorlton-upon-Medlock Union* (1883) 48 LT 872, DC; and see PARA 92.

9 *Bursledon Overseers v Clarke* (1897) 61 JP 261, DC; *Bertie v Walthamstow Overseers* (1904) 68 JP 545, DC; *Hicks v Dunstable Overseers* (1883) 48 JP 326, DC; *LCC v Hackney Borough Council* [1928] 2 KB 588 at 597–598 per Wright J.

98. Buildings used for storing goods or abandoned property.

The storage of goods or furniture in a building may amount to beneficial occupation; whether it does or not is a matter of fact and degree[1]. However, if goods are left behind when premises are vacated because they are not worth the cost of their removal, there may be no beneficial occupation[2]. Unoccupied property may now be rateable[3], in which case these earlier cases will be of limited application.

1 *Wirral Borough Council v Lane* [1979] RA 261; *Camden London Borough Council v Peureula Investments Ltd* [1976] RA 169, DC, where there was no beneficial occupation of a theatre where the ceiling had collapsed but the seats and carpets remained. See also *Staley v Castleton Overseers* (1864) 5 B & S 505; *Townley Mill Co (1919) Ltd v Oldham Assessment Committee* [1937] AC 419, [1937] 1 All ER 11, HL; *Gage v Wren* (1902) 67 JP 32, DC; *R (on the application of Makro Properties Ltd) v Nuneaton and Bedworth Borough Council* [2012] EWHC 2250 (Admin), [2012] All ER (D) 136 (Aug); *Sunderland City Council v Stirling Investment Properties LLP* [2013] EWHC 1413 (Admin), [2013] All ER (D) 325 (May).

2 *LCC v Hackney Borough Council* [1928] 2 KB 588; *Offaly County Council and Riordan v Williams* [1930] IR 39; *Holyoak (Valuation Officer) v Sheppard* [1969] RA 524, Lands Tribunal.

3 See PARA 135 et seq.

(v) Permanence of Occupation

99. Test of permanency.

A degree of permanence is an essential element in rateable occupation[1]. Permanence does not depend on the length of the term for which the land is held, and a weekly tenant, for example, is rateable[2], as may also be licensees and tenants at will[3]; but intermittent or casual occupation, such as that of a site for a travelling show[4], a floating dock shifted from place to place[5], stalls in a market[6] or yacht moorings only put down for part of a year[7], may not be rateable. Contractors' huts placed on a building site for 18 months have been held to be rateable[8]. Under the Local Government Finance Act 1988, liability to the non-domestic rate arises on a daily basis[9], but this does not affect the requirement that occupation must satisfy the test under the cases cited in this paragraph since the old rules relating to occupation still apply[10].

1 *R v St Pancras Assessment Committee* (1877) 2 QBD 581; *Westminster City Council and Kent Valuation Committee v Southern Rly Co, Rly Assessment Authority and Pullman Car Co Ltd* [1936] AC 511 at 529, [1936] 2 All ER 322 at 326, HL, per Lord Russell of Killowen; *LCC v Wilkins (Valuation Officer)* [1957] AC 362, [1956] 3 All ER 38, HL; *Field Place Caravan Park Ltd v Harding* [1966] 2 QB 484, [1966] 3 All ER 247, CA; *Renore Ltd v Hounslow London Borough Council* (1970) 15 RRC 378, DC; *Cinderella Rockerfellas Ltd v Rudd* [2003] EWCA Civ 529, [2003] 3 All ER 219, [2003] 1 WLR 2423.

2 *Cory v Bristow* (1877) 2 App Cas 262 at 275, HL, per Lord Cairns LC; *Dick Hampton (Earth Moving) Ltd v Lewis (Valuation Officer)* [1976] QB 254, [1975] 3 All ER 946, CA (short-term quarrying operations of six and nine months held rateable). As to the nature and determination of a weekly tenancy see LANDLORD AND TENANT vol 62 (2016) PARAS 227–228.

3 See PARA 88.

4 *R v St Pancras Assessment Committee* (1877) 2 QBD 581 at 588–589 per Lush J; cf *Hall (Valuation Officer) v Darwen Corpn* (1957) 2 RRC 329, Lands Tribunal.

5 *R v Morrison* (1852) 1 E & B 150.

6 *Roberts v Aylesbury Overseers* (1853) 1 E & B 423 at 433; cf *Williams v Wednesbury and West Bromwich Churchwardens and Overseers Union Assessment Committee* (1890) Ryde Rat App (1886–90) 327, DC (exclusive occupation of market on two days a week held rateable); and see MARKETS vol 71 (2013) PARAS 833, 838.

7 *Bradshaw v Davey* [1952] 1 All ER 350, DC (in so far as the decision was based on the mooring being a chattel the case must be regarded as doubtful since *LCC v Wilkins (Valuation Officer)* [1957] AC 362, [1956] 3 All ER 38, HL). See also PARA 100.

8 *LCC v Wilkins (Valuation Officer)* [1957] AC 362, [1956] 3 All ER 38, HL. See also *Mitchell Bros v Worksop Union Assessment Committee* (1904) 21 TLR 156, DC (more than a year); *John Laing & Son Ltd v Assessment Committee for Kingswood Assessment Area* [1949] 1 KB 344, [1949] 1 All ER 224, CA. See also *Watson (Valuation Officer) v Thornbury RDC and Miller* (1959) 53 R & IT 107, Lands Tribunal (chalets on site for at least a year held rateable); *Dick Hampton (Earth Moving) Ltd v Lewis (Valuation Officer)* [1976] QB 254, [1975] 3 All ER 946, CA (six months' and nine months' quarrying operations).

9 See the Local Government Finance Act 1988 s 43(1); and PARA 133. Liability to the rate is incurred in respect of any day in a year, but only if all the ingredients of occupation exist.

10 See the Local Government Finance Act 1988 s 65(2); and PARA 86.

(vi) Incorporeal Rights and Chattels

100. Easements and exclusive licences.

The mere enjoyment of an easement over land does not itself constitute rateable occupation[1], but a person may be the rateable occupier of land even though the rights granted to him are only in the nature of an easement if the exercise of those rights requires, and brings with it, the exclusive occupation[2]. Under similar conditions, the enjoyment of a licence may be such as to confer rateable occupation[3].

A person may be in rateable occupation of land for the purpose of enjoying an easement, even if others, including the grantor and persons deriving title from him, also have rights of user of another kind[4]. A user of land in a certain way may amount to rateable occupation if the person so using it can prevent any other person from using it in the same way[5], but not if the grantor reserves a right to a similar user[6].

1 *R v Trent and Mersey Navigation Co* (1825) 4 B & C 57; *Doncaster Union Assessment Committee v Manchester, Sheffield and Lincolnshire Rly Co* (1894) 71 LT 585, HL; *R v Mersey and Irwell Navigation Co of Proprietors* (1829) 9 B & C 95; *Liverpool Corpn v Chorley Union Assessment Committee and Withnell Overseers* [1913] AC 197 at 206, HL, per Lord Atkinson. As to easements see REAL PROPERTY AND REGISTRATION vol 87 (2017) PARA 731 et seq.

2 *Doe d R v Archbishop of York* (1849) 14 QB 81; *Talargoch Mining Co v St Asaph Union* (1868) LR 3 QB 478; *Southport Corpn v Ormskirk Union Assessment Committee* [1894] 1 QB 196, CA; *Holywell Union and Halkyn Parish v Halkyn District Mines Drainage Co* [1895] AC 117, HL; *Margate Corpn v Pettman* (1912) 106 LT 104, DC. It is on this principle that public utility companies are rateable for their pipes: *R v Bath Corpn* (1811) 14 East 609; *R v Rochdale Waterworks Co* (1813) 1 M & S 634; *R v Birmingham Gas-Light and Coke Co* (1823) 1 B & C 506; *R v Brighton Gas Light Co* (1826) 5 B & C 466; *R v Chelsea Water Works Co* (1833) 5 B & Ad 156; *R v West Middlesex Waterworks* (1859) 1 E & E 716; *London and North Western Rly Co v Giles* (1869) 33 JP 776; *Liverpool Corpn v Birkenhead Union* (1905) 70 JP 146. The rating of public utility undertakings is now covered by special statutory provisions: see PARAS 169–171. Sewers are now exempt from rating: see PARA 123.

3 *Westminster City Council and Kent Valuation Committee v Southern Rly Co, Rly Assessment Authority and Pullman Car Co Ltd* [1936] AC 511 at 533, [1936] 2 All ER 322 at 329, HL, per Lord Russell of Killowen (bookstalls on a railway station); *R v Stevens and Anderson* (1865) 12 LT 491; *Kittow v Liskeard Union* (1874) LR 10 QB 7; *Roads v Trumpington Overseers* (1870) LR 6 QB 56; *R v Whaddon* (1875) LR 10 QB 230. The three cases last cited refer to licences to dig for various minerals, as to which see MINES, MINERALS AND QUARRIES vol 76 (2013) PARAS 349–354. Such a licence does not, however, constitute rateable occupation if it is not in fact exercised: *R v Fayle* (1856) 4 WR 460. See also *Re Nott and Cardiff Corpn* [1918] 2 KB, 146, CA (revsd on other points sub nom *Brodie v Cardiff Corpn* [1919] AC 337, HL) (railway taken over for construction of reservoir); *Ryan Industrial Fuels Ltd v Morgan (Valuation Officer)* [1965] 3 All ER 465, [1965] 1 WLR 1347, CA.

4 *Holywell Union and Halkyn Parish v Halkyn District Mines Drainage Co* [1895] AC 117, HL, where the company was held rateable for a tunnel constructed by it for the purpose of mine drainage, even though the owner and his lessees had the right to use the tunnel for tramways; *Westminster City Council and Kent Valuation Committee v Southern Rly Co, Rly Assessment Authority and Pullman Car Co Ltd* [1936] AC 511, [1936] 2 All ER 322, HL (storage depots in railway yard).

5 Thus user by a wagon-way (*R v Bell* (1798) 7 Term Rep 598), by a tramway (*Pimlico Tramway Co v Greenwich Union* (1873) LR 9 QB 9), or by telegraph and telephone apparatus (*Electric Telegraph Co v Salford Overseers* (1855) 11 Exch 181; *Lancashire Telephone Co v Manchester Overseers* (1884) 14 QBD 267, CA) creates rateability. The tenant of a sewage farm was rateable for the whole, including the sewage carriers and works, even though the lessors retained the right to inspect, alter, and repair them (*Stourbridge Main Drainage Board v Seisdon Union* (1902) 66 JP 372); and the tenant of the tolls was rateable for a swing-bridge, even though the grantors had the right to open it (*Percy v Hall* (1903) 67 JP 293, DC). Swing-bridges are now statutorily exempt from non-domestic rating: see PARA 130.

6 *R v Jolliffe* (1787) 2 Term Rep 90. See also *Mogg v Yatton Overseers* (1880) 6 QBD 10, DC, where, however, the rights reserved were very narrow.

101. Moorings, artificial watercourses, towing-paths and harbours.

Land may be rateably occupied by means of moorings, if these are fixed in one place and the person rated has the exclusive right of using them[1], but not if they are in fact constantly removed[2], or are mere accessories to a floating vessel[3], or if the right to use them is not exclusive[4].

A canal or navigation company is in rateable occupation of a canal or an artificial cut[5] (with the towing-path[6]), but not of a natural river or the towing-path alongside, unless the soil is vested in the company[7]. A towing-path which is so vested is capable of rateable occupation, although the natural river which it adjoins is not[8]. There may also be a rateable occupation of a sluice in a natural river[9].

A harbour authority is in rateable occupation of any portion of the harbour of which the soil is vested in it[10].

1 *R v Leith* (1852) 1 E & B 121; *Forrest v Greenwich Overseers* (1858) 8 E & B 890; *Cory v Bristow* (1877) 2 App Cas 262, HL. Cf *Grant v Oxford Local Board* (1868) LR 4 QB 9, which is in conflict with these decisions; but it would seem that, in view of *Cory v Bristow* (above), this case cannot be relied on. The licensee of moorings on a river bank was held rateable in *Gooding v Benfleet UDC* (1933) 49 TLR 298.

Regulations may be made for the way in which two or more non-domestic moorings owned by the same person but separately occupied are to be rated: see the Local Government Finance Act 1988 s 64(3A), (3B); and PARA 107. As to the rating of ferry landing places in relation to which tolls are taken see PARA 102.

2 *R v Morrison* (1852) 1 E & B 150; *Manchester, Sheffield and Lincolnshire Rly Co v Governor and Guardians of the Kingston-upon-Hull Poor* (1896) 60 JP 789, CA; *Bradshaw v Davey* [1952] 1 All ER 350, DC (yacht mooring).

3 *Cory v Churchwardens of Greenwich* (1872) LR 7 CP 499. See also *Cinderella Rockerfellas Ltd v Rudd* [2003] EWCA Civ 529, [2003] 3 All ER 219, [2003] 1 WLR 2423 (vessel moored and berthed on river and used as a night-club was rateable). Swinging moorings are now exempt provided they fall within the provisions of the Local Government Finance Act 1988 Sch 5 para 18: see PARA 129.

4 *Watkins v Milton-next-Gravesend Overseers* (1868) LR 3 QB 350.

5 As to inland waterways generally see WATER AND WATERWAYS vol 101 (2009) PARA 713 et seq.

6 *R v Mersey and Irwell Navigation Co of Proprietors* (1829) 9 B & C 95; *R v Thomas* (1829) 9 B & C 114; *Bruce v Willis* (1840) 11 Ad & El 463. Land structures and appliances occupied or maintained by a drainage authority are exempt from rates: see the Local Government Finance Act 1988 Sch 5 para 14; and PARA 124.

7 *R v Mersey and Irwell Navigation Co of Proprietors* (1829) 9 B & C 95; *R v Thomas* (1829) 9 B & C 114; *R v Aire and Calder Navigation Co* (1829) 9 B & C 820; *Doncaster Union Assessment Committee v Manchester Sheffield and Lincolnshire Rly Co* (1894) 71 LT 585, HL. As to the right of navigation in inland waters generally see WATER AND WATERWAYS vol 101 (2009) PARA 688 et seq.

8 *R v London Corpn* (1790) 4 Term Rep 21.

9 *R v Cardington Inhabitants* (1777) 2 Cowp 581; but see, to the contrary, *R v Aire and Calder Navigation Co* (1832) 3 B & Ad 139. It is submitted that the latter decision is unsound.

10 *New Shoreham Harbour Comrs v Lancing* (1870) LR 5 QB 489; *Swansea Union Assessment Committee v Swansea Harbour Trustees* (1907) 71 JP 497, sub nom *Swansea Harbour Trustees v Swansea Union Assessment Committee* (1907) 1 Konst Rat App 250, HL, where the decision of the King's Bench Division on this point was not questioned on appeal. As to harbour authorities generally see PORTS AND HARBOURS vol 85 (2012) PARA 20 et seq.

102. Tolls.

Tolls are not rateable as such, that is if they are not a payment for the use of the soil[1]. If, however, a person, as a necessary consequence of his ownership or occupation of land, possesses the right to take tolls and in fact takes them, he is in rateable occupation of the land[2]. Where these conditions are fulfilled, the occupiers or occupying owners of canals, locks and sluices[3], harbours and docks[4], the landing places of a ferry[5] and toll bridges[6] are in rateable occupation of those hereditaments, the value of which should be taken, not as the value of the land merely, but as the value of the land as enhanced by its availability for the purpose of earning the tolls[7].

Lighthouses belonging to or occupied by Trinity House are exempt from rates by statute[8].

A person having the right to take market tolls has no rateable occupation of land[9] unless the tolls are paid for such privileges as of erecting stalls or of standing carts[10].

1 *R v Nicholson* (1810) 12 East 330; *Williams v Jones* (1810) 12 East 346; *R v Eyre* (1810) 12 East 416; *R v North and South Shields Ferry Co* (1852) 1 E & B 140; *Lewis v Swansea Overseers* (1855) 5 E & B 508. Tolls (so called) levied, without statutory authority, for the privilege of passing through a gate are paid for the right of using the land, and the occupiers are rateable for the land: *R v St George The Martyr, Southwark Inhabitants* (1855) 3 WR 515. A toll thorough is not rateable: *R v Snowdon* (1833) 4 B & Ad 713. As to tolls on highways see HIGHWAYS, STREETS AND BRIDGES vol 55 (2012) PARA 213 et seq.

2 The cases which support this positive proposition are cited in notes 3–6. Where the tolls, although received by the occupier, are not received as a necessary consequence of his occupation, they are not an element in rateable occupation: *R v Aire and Calder Navigation Co, Hunslet Mills Case* (1832) 3 B & Ad 533.

3 *R v Cardington Inhabitants* (1777) 2 Cowp 581; *R v Aire and Calder Navigation Co* (1788) 2 Term Rep 660; *R v Page* (1792) 4 Term Rep 543; *R v Staffordshire and Worcestershire Canal Navigation Co* (1799) 8 Term Rep 340; *R v Macdonald* (1810) 12 East 324; *R v Lower Mitton Inhabitants* (1829) 9 B & C 810.

4 *R v Earl of Durham* (1859) 5 Jur NS 1306; *R v Hull Dock Co* (1845) 7 QB 2; *Faversham Navigation Comrs v Faversham Union Assessment Committee* (1867) 31 JP 822; *New Shoreham Harbour Comrs v Lancing* (1870) LR 5 QB 489; *R v Berwick Assessment Committee* (1885) 16 QBD 493; *Swansea Union Assessment Committee v Swansea Harbour Trustees* (1907) 71 JP 497, sub nom *Swansea Harbour Trustees v Swansea Union Assessment Committee* (1907) 1 Konst Rat App 250, HL.

5 *R v North and South Shields Ferry Co* (1852) 1 E & B 140.

6 *R v Barnes Inhabitants* (1830) 1 B & Ad 113; *R v Marquis of Salisbury* (1838) 8 Ad & El 716; *R v Blackfriars Bridge Co* (1839) 9 Ad & El 828; *R v Hammersmith Bridge Co* (1849) 15 QB 369; *R v Bedminster Union* (1876) 1 QBD 503; *Percy v Hall* (1903) 67 JP 293, DC; *Dunham Bridge Co v Retford Assessment Committee* [1949] WN 419, CA.

7 *Faversham Navigation Comrs v Faversham Union Assessment Committee* (1867) 31 JP 822; *Ipswich Dock Comrs v St Peter, Ipswich, Overseers* (1866) 7 B & S 310; *New Shoreham Harbour Comrs v Lancing* (1870) LR 5 QB 489; *Blyth Harbour Comrs v Churchwardens etc of Newsham and South Blyth and Tynemouth Union Assessment Committee* [1894] 2 QB 675, CA: *R v Berwick Assessment Committee* (1885) 16 QBD 493; *Swansea Union Assessment Committee v Swansea Harbour Trustees* (1907) 71 JP 497, sub nom *Swansea Harbour Trustees v Swansea Union Assessment Committee* (1907) 1 Konst Rat App 250, HL; *R v North and South Shields Ferry Co* (1852) 1 E & B 140; cf *Dover Harbour Board v Dover Borough Rating Authority* (1931) 13 R & IT 199, where one board was held not to be in rateable occupation of a landing place, the owners' occupation being paramount, and the passenger dues payable were held to be tolls in gross and not part of the value of the landing place.

8 See the Local Government Finance Act 1988 Sch 5 para 12; and PARA 128. It follows that lighthouses in the hands of bodies other than Trinity House which levy tolls may still be rateable, although it must be exceptional in practice for lighthouse tolls to be levied today. Historically, rulings on the subject contributed to the development of the principles on which the present law relating to tolls is founded: see *R v Rebowe* (1771) cited in Cald Mag Cas at 351; *R v Tynemouth Inhabitants* (1810) 12 East 46; *R v Coke* (1826) 5 B & C 797; *R v Fowke* (1826) 5 B & C 814n.

9 *Oswestry Corpn v Hudd (Valuation Officer)* [1966] 1 All ER 490, [1966] 1 WLR 363, CA; and see MARKETS vol 71 (2013) PARA 833.

10 *Oswestry Corpn v Hudd (Valuation Officer)* [1966] 1 All ER 490, [1966] 1 WLR 363, CA; and see MARKETS vol 71 (2013) PARA 838.

103. Rights of common.

A right of common is not itself a rateable subject matter[1], but the exercise of such a right over land may bring with it such an exclusive enjoyment of the land as to constitute rateable occupation[2]. If the persons who feed cattle on the land in the exercise of the right are tenants in common for the whole year, they are rateable[3]; if the rights of common are vested in trustees to manage and to receive money paid for the grazing during part of the year, the trustees are rateable[4]. However, a municipal corporation which manages a common on behalf of the freemen is not rateable for the common[5].

1 *Kempe v Spence* (1779) 2 Wm Bl 1244; *R v Churchill* (1825) 4 B & C 750; *R v Alnwick Corpn* (1839) 9 Ad & El 444. As to the different kinds of common see COMMONS vol 13 (2017) PARA 308 et seq. As to exclusive rights of pasture and of foldage see COMMONS vol 13 (2017) PARA 351 et seq.

2 *R v Aberavon Inhabitants* (1804) 5 East 453.

3 *R v Watson* (1804) 5 East 480; cf *R v Sudbury Corpn* (1823) 1 B & C 389.

4 *R v Tewkesbury (Trustees for Burgesses)* (1810) 13 East 155. Similar decisions were given where the trustees were a municipal corporation (*R v Sudbury Corpn* (1823) 1 B & C 389; *R v York Corpn* (1837) 6 Ad & El 419); but the status of a corporation having been changed by the Municipal Corporations Act 1835 (repealed), these two cases apparently no longer apply to municipal corporations (*Lincoln Corpn v Holmes Common Overseers* (1867) LR 2 QB 482). See also *Trenfield v Lowe* (1869) LR 4 CP 454. See also see note 5.

5 This was held on the ground that the profit à prendre belonging to the freemen exhausted the whole value of the land: *Lincoln Corpn v Holmes Common Overseers* (1867) LR 2 QB 482. If the principle of this decision is good law, it appears to overrule not only *R v Sudbury Corpn* (1823) 1 B & C 389 and *R v York Corpn* (1837) 6 Ad & El 419, but also *R v Tewkesbury (Trustees for Burgesses)* (1810) 13 East 155. It is doubtful, however, how far this principle can be reconciled with those laid down in *Mersey Docks and Harbour Board Trustees v Cameron, Jones v Mersey Docks and Harbour Board Trustees* (1865) 11 HL Cas 443 and *LCC v Churchwardens etc of Erith Parish and Dartford Union Assessment Committee* [1893] AC 562, HL (cited in PARAS 95–96).

104. Hereditaments arising from rights to use land for certain purposes.

For the purposes of the non-domestic rating provisions[1], the right to use land[2] for the purpose of exhibiting advertisements, which is let out or reserved to someone other than the occupier[3] of the land (or, where the land is not occupied for any other purpose, which is let out or reserved to any person other than the owner of the land) is a hereditament[4]. In addition, a right is a hereditament if:

(1) it is a right to use any land[5] for the purpose of operating a meter[6] to measure a supply of gas or electricity or such other service as the appropriate national authority[7] may by order specify[8]; and

(2) the meter is owned by a person other than the consumer of the service[9].

1 Ie for the purposes of the Local Government Finance Act 1988 Pt III (ss 41–67): see s 67(13).
2 For these purposes, 'land' includes a wall or other part of a building and a sign, hoarding, frame, or other structure erected or to be erected on land: see the Local Government Finance Act 1988 s 64(11).
3 A right which is a hereditament by virtue of the Local Government Finance Act 1988 s 64(2) must be treated as occupied by the person for the time being entitled to the right: s 65(8). Where land consisting of a hereditament is used, permanently or temporarily, for the exhibition of advertisements or for the erection of a structure used for advertisements, but it is not a hereditament to which s 64(2) applies, and the hereditament is not occupied, it must be treated as occupied by the person permitting it to be used or, if that person cannot be ascertained, its owner: see s 65(8A) (added by the Local Government and Housing Act 1989 s 139, Sch 5 paras 1, 34, 79(3)). As to the meaning of 'hereditament' see PARA 106 et seq. As to the meaning of 'owner', and as to the occupier and occupation of land, see PARA 86 et seq. As to the meaning of 'person' see PARA 11 note 13.
4 Local Government Finance Act 1988 s 64(2). See *O'Brien v Secker (Valuation Officer)* [1996] RA 409, 95 LGR 560, CA (advertising hoarding fixed by a ratepayer to a wall of a building under licence from the occupier).
5 For this purpose, 'land' includes a wall or other part of a building: Local Government Finance Act 1988 s 64(11B) (s 64(11A), (11B) added by the Local Government Act 2003 s 66(3)).
6 The Secretary of State in relation to England, and the Welsh Ministers in relation to Wales, may by regulations make provision as to what is to be regarded as being a meter for these purposes: see the Local Government Finance Act 1988 s 64(11A) (as added: see note 5). At the date at which this volume states the law, no such regulations had been made. The functions under the Local Government Finance Act 1988 s 64(2A), (11A) were formerly vested in the National Assembly for Wales and are now exercisable by the Welsh Ministers by virtue of the Government of Wales Act 2006 s 162(1), Sch 11 paras 30, 32. As to the Secretary of State and the Welsh Ministers see PARA 4 note 18. As to the meanings of 'England' and 'Wales' see PARA 2 note 16. As to the separate administration of the non-domestic rating provisions (Local Government Finance Act 1988 Pt III (ss 41–67)) in England and Wales see PARA 52.
7 Ie the Secretary of State (in relation to England) or the Welsh Ministers (in relation to Wales): see the Local Government Finance Act 1988 s 64(2A)(a) (s 64(2A) added by the Local Government Act 2003 s 66(1)).
8 Local Government Finance Act 1988 s 64(2A)(a) (as added: see note 7). At the date at which this volume states the law no such order had been made.
9 Local Government Finance Act 1988 s 64(2A)(b) (as added: see note 7).

105. Chattels.

In general, stock-in-trade and personal property are not rateable[1]. However, chattels, although not a part of the land, may be rated together with land as one unit of occupation if they are enjoyed with it[2] and enhance its value[3]. On this principle, contractors' huts[4], a caravan[5], kiosks and showcases[6], moorings[7], material in a colliery tip[8], a lean-to shelter[9], a car port[10], and a floating clubhouse[11] have been held to be rateable.

1 As to rateable property see PARA 80.
2 The chattel does not have to be enjoyed on the land it is occupied with, but must be sufficiently connected with it: *Ryan Industrial Fuels Ltd v Morgan (Valuation Officer)* [1965] 3 All ER 465, [1965] 1 WLR 1347, CA.
3 *LCC v Wilkins (Valuation Officer)* [1957] AC 362, [1956] 3 All ER 38, HL.
4 *LCC v Wilkins (Valuation Officer)* [1957] AC 362, [1956] 3 All ER 38, HL; *Mitchell Bros Ltd v Worksop Union Assessment Committee* (1904) 1 Konst Rat App 181, DC; *John Laing & Son Ltd v Assessment Committee for Kingswood Assessment Area* [1948] 2 KB 116, [1948] 1 All ER 943 (affd [1949] 1 KB 344, [1949] 1 All ER 224, CA); *Woodward (Valuation Officer) v Brading and Blundell Ltd* (1951) 44 R & IT 758. See also *Farrans Ltd v Valuation Comr* [1970] RA 147, Lands Tribunal; *Cartwright v Shaw* (1954) 44 R & IT 678, Lands Tribunal.
5 *Field Place Caravan Park Ltd v Harding* [1966] 2 QB 484, [1966] 3 All ER 247, CA; *Baker v Horwell and Halton Borough Council* [1975] RA 317, Lands Tribunal.
6 *Westminster City Council and Kent Valuation Committee v Southern Rly Co, Rly Assessment Authority and Pullman Car Co Ltd* [1936] AC 511, [1936] 2 All ER 322, HL.
7 *Cory v Bristow* (1877) 2 App Cas 262, HL (moorings in the bed of the river Thames).
8 *Ryan Industrial Fuels Ltd v Morgan (Valuation Officer)* [1965] 3 All ER 465, [1965] 1 WLR 1347, CA; *Brook v National Coal Board and Burnwell Coal Co Ltd* [1975] RA 367 (spoil heaps worked for shale rateable); but see *National Coal Board v Brook (Valuation Officer)* (1970) 16 RRC 357, where small coal in a spoil heap constituted stock-in-trade and was not rateable.
9 *Knight v Etteridge* [1971] RA 129, Lands Tribunal.
10 *Barton v Paul (Valuation Officer)* (1969) 15 RRC 186.
11 *Thomas v Witney Aquatic Co Ltd* [1972] RA 493, Lands Tribunal (floating clubhouse on a lake held to be rateable as part of a hereditament comprising the lake itself and a strip of land along one shore). In *Westminster City Council v Woodbury (Valuation Officer) and the Yard Arm Club Ltd* [1992] RA 1, [1991] 2 EGLR 173, CA, a floating vessel used as a restaurant, together with the river bed over which it was moored, and the anchors and attachments which secured the vessel by connection to the river bed, were held to be a hereditament in the occupation of the club company, but were held exempt from rates under a local Act, the Port of London Act 1968, which applied to the bed of the river beneath the vessel (see further PARA 110 note 23). In *Felgate (Valuation Officer) v Lotus Leisure Enterprises Ltd* [2000] RA 89, Lands Tribunal, a floating restaurant and the moorings securing it to the dock side formed a rateable hereditament together with the dock bed; and in *Cinderella Rockerfellas Ltd v Rudd* [2003] EWCA Civ 529, [2003] 3 All ER 219, [2003] 1 WLR 2423, a vessel housing a nightclub, permanently moored by means of horizontal connection to an adjacent quay, was held to be rateable, together with the riverbed which formed part of the same hereditament.

(vii) The Hereditament

106. Unit to be assessed.

For the purposes of the non-domestic rating provisions[1], the unit of assessment is the 'hereditament', which for the purposes of non-domestic rating is anything which, by virtue of the definition of hereditament in the General Rate Act 1967 (now repealed)[2], would have been a hereditament for the purposes of that Act if the Local Government Finance Act 1988 had not been passed[3]. The General Rate Act 1967 defined hereditament as 'property which is or may become liable to a rate, being a unit of such property which is, or would fall to be, shown as a separate item in the valuation list'[4].

A hereditament is 'non-domestic' if either it consists entirely of property which is not domestic[5], or it is a composite hereditament[6]. A hereditament is a 'relevant hereditament' if it consists of property of any of the following descriptions:

(1) lands[7];
(2) coal mines[8];

(3) mines of any other description, other than a mine of which the royalty or dues are for the time being wholly reserved in kind[9]; and

(4) any right to use land[10] for the purpose of exhibiting advertisements or for the purpose of operating meters which measure a supply of gas or electricity (or some other specified service) and which are not operated by consumers[11].

All relevant hereditaments must be entered in the local non-domestic rating list[12].

A single property is not necessarily rateable as a whole[13]; where parts of a building are separately occupied, the parts form separate hereditaments. Structural severance of the parts is not essential[14]. However, property in one occupation[15] may in some circumstances form more than one hereditament. It has been held that where parts of the property are not within the same curtilage, or are not contiguous[16] to one another[17], or are capable of separate letting[18], or are used for entirely different purposes[19], the parts may form separate hereditaments[20]. Where premises in one occupation are divided by a highway they will form separate hereditaments unless they are so essential in use to one another that they should be regarded as a single hereditament[21]. The approach to deciding this issue has recently been clarified as follows[22]. There are three broad principles relevant to cases where the question is whether distinct spaces under common occupation form a single hereditament[23].

(a) The first and primary test is geographical, based on visual or cartographic unity, so that contiguous spaces would normally be a single hereditament, but unity is not simply a question of contiguity. Thus, if adjoining houses do not intercommunicate and can be accessed only via other property of which the common occupier is not in exclusive possession, this will be a strong indication that they are separate hereditaments, and if direct communication were to be established, by piercing a door or a staircase, that would usually create a new, larger single hereditament.

(b) Secondly, where in accordance with this principle two spaces are geographically distinct, a functional test[24] may nevertheless enable them to be treated as a single hereditament, but only where the use of the one is necessary to the effectual enjoyment of the other (thus situations where the two spaces can reasonably be let separately are excluded).

(c) Thirdly, whether the use of one section is necessary to the enjoyment of the other depends not on the business needs of the ratepayer but on the objectively ascertainable character of the hereditaments.

The application of the principles in heads (a) to (c) cannot be a mere mechanical exercise. They will commonly call for a factual judgment on the part of the valuer and the exercise of a large measure of professional common sense[25].

The appropriate national authority[26] may make regulations providing that in prescribed cases[27]:

(i) anything which would (apart from the regulations) be one hereditament must be treated for rating purposes as more than one hereditament[28]; and

(ii) anything which would (apart from the regulations) be more than one hereditament must be treated as one hereditament[29].

1 Ie for the purposes of the Local Government Finance Act 1988 Pt III (ss 41–67): see s 67(13).

2 Ie by virtue of the General Rating Act 1967 s 115(1): see the text to note 4.

3 Local Government Finance Act 1988 s 64(1). Provision is also made for hereditaments to arise out of certain rights associated with land rather than from properties or structures on the land: see PARA 104.

4 See the General Rate Act 1967 s 115(1) (repealed). See also *Vtesse Networks Ltd v Bradford* [2006] EWCA Civ 1339, [2006] RA 427, [2006] All ER (D) 242 (Oct) at [40] per Sedley LJ: 'The key to the apparently circular definition given by the General Rate Act 1967 s 115(1), which defines a hereditament by its liability to rating, is that it assumes and relies on an existing fund of knowledge of what is and is not capable of being shown as a separate item in the valuation list'. As to valuation lists see PARA 188 et seq.
5 Local Government Finance Act 1988 s 64(8)(a). As to the meaning of 'domestic property' in relation to non-domestic rating see PARA 190.
6 Local Government Finance Act 1988 s 64(8)(b). A hereditament is composite if part only of it consists of domestic property: s 64(9).
7 Local Government Finance Act 1988 s 64(4)(a).
8 Local Government Finance Act 1988 s 64(4)(b).
9 Local Government Finance Act 1988 s 64(4)(c). As to rights to work mines generally see MINES, MINERALS AND QUARRIES vol 76 (2013) PARA 363 et seq.
10 Ie a right which is a hereditament by virtue of the Local Government Finance Act 1988 s 64(2): see PARA 104.
11 Local Government Finance Act 1988 s 64(4)(e) (amended by the Local Government Act 2003 s 66(2)).
12 See PARA 194.
13 *Langford v Cole* (1910) 74 JP 229, DC; *Curzon v Westminster Corpn* (1916) 86 LJKB 198, DC; *Holyoak (Valuation Officer) v Sheppard* [1969] RA 524, Lands Tribunal (unused upper floors a separate hereditament); *Moffatt (Valuation Officer) v Venus Packaging Ltd* (1977) 20 RRC 335, Lands Tribunal (occupied part of factory premises treated as separate hereditament from unoccupied part); *British Railways Board v Hopkins (Valuation Officer) and Birmingham District Council* [1981] RA 328, [1982] JPL 187, Lands Tribunal (unoccupied part of multi-storey office building constituted separate hereditament); *Eagle Construction Ltd v Casey (Valuation Officer) and Croydon London Borough Council* [1981] RA 347, [1982] JPL 114, Lands Tribunal (old and new office building a single hereditament); *Post Office v Orkney and Shetland Assessor* [1987] RA 169, Lands Valuation Appeal Court (post office, regional administrative office and sorting office in one premises treated as a single hereditament); *Baker (Valuation Officer) v Citibank NA* [2007] RA 93, Lands Tribunal (each successive increase in floor space constituted in parts of two multi-storey office buildings occupied by a ratepayer created a new hereditament consisting of the enlarged occupation).
14 *Allchurch v Hendon Union Assessment Committee* [1891] 2 QB 436, CA; *Barr (Valuation Officer) v Manley and Regulus Ltd* (1960) 53 R & IT 213, Lands Tribunal.
15 As to occupation see PARA 85 et seq.
16 Premises are not contiguous unless all connect with one another: see *Ind Coope Ltd v Burton-upon-Trent County Borough Council and Thomas (Valuation Officer)* [1961] RVR 341, Lands Tribunal.
17 *Gilbert (Valuation Officer) v S Hickinbottom & Sons Ltd* [1956] 2 QB 40, [1956] 2 All ER 101, CA; *Spillers Ltd v Cardiff Assessment Committee and Pritchard (Cardiff Revenue Officer)* [1931] 2 KB 21. See also *Rawlence v Hursley Union* (1877) 3 Ex D 44, DC; *Whiteley v Fulham Union* (1895) Ryde & K Rat App 5; *Consett Overseers v Durham County Council* (1922) 87 JP 1, DC; *Hudson's Bay Co v Thompson (Valuation Officer)* (1957) 2 RRC 211, Lands Tribunal (this point, decided by the Lands Tribunal, was not raised on appeal: see [1960] AC 926, [1959] 3 All ER 150, HL); *English, Scottish and Australian Bank Ltd v Dyer (Valuation Officer)* (1958) 4 RRC 27, Lands Tribunal; *Wylie and Lockhead Ltd v Glasgow Assessor* (1933) 18 R & IT 93; *Watkins v Herefordshire Assessment Committee* (1935) 154 LT 262, DC.

Gilbert (Valuation Officer) v S Hickinbottom & Sons Ltd [1956] 2 QB 40, [1956] 2 All ER 101, CA, was doubted in *Woolway v Mazars LLP* [2015] UKSC 53, [2015] AC 1862, [2016] 1 All ER 299 (two floors occupied by same firm in office block amounted to separate hereditaments); discussed in Under Occupation, Joseph Ollech and James Tipler: 165 NLJ 7675, p 13 (the geography should be paramount in all but exceptional cases). See the text to notes 22—25.
18 *Standen (Valuation Officer) v Glaxo Laboratories Ltd* (1957) 1 RRC 338, Lands Tribunal; *Spencer (Valuation Officer) and Thurrock UDC v Thames Board Mills Ltd* (1954) 47 R & IT 809, Lands Tribunal. The fact that several parts are capable of separate occupation does not necessarily involve a separation of the assessment when all are occupied together: see *Burton v Marshall (Valuation Officer)* (1966) 12 RRC 128, Lands Tribunal (on appeal (1966) 15 RRC 1, CA); *May v Rotherham Metropolitan Borough Council* [1990] RVR 98, 154 JP 683; *Coventry and Solihull Waste Disposal Co Ltd v Russell (Valuation Officer)* [2000] 1 All ER 97, [1999] 1 WLR 2093, [2000] RA 1, HL.

19 *North Eastern Rly Co v York Union* [1900] 1 QB 733; *English, Scottish and Australian Bank Ltd v Dyer (Valuation Officer)* (1958) 4 RRC 27, Lands Tribunal. See also *Watkins v Herefordshire Assessment Committee* (1935) 154 LT 262, DC; *Morley (Valuation Officer) v Society for Promoting Christian Knowledge* (1960) 53 R & IT 326, Lands Tribunal; *Murdoch (Valuation Officer) v Lanes (Costumiers) Ltd* (1959) 52 R & IT 456, Lands Tribunal.

20 *Gilbert (Valuation Officer) v S Hickinbottom & Sons Ltd* [1956] 2 QB 40, [1956] 2 All ER 101, CA (see note 17). See also *Glasgow University v Glasgow Assessor* 1952 SC 504; *Re Bellamy (Valuation Officer) and Hinckley UDC Appeal* (1952) 45 R & IT 691; *Spencer (Valuation Officer) and Thurrock UDC v Thames Board Mills Ltd* (1954) 47 R & IT 809, Lands Tribunal; *Sussex Caravan Parks Ltd v Richardson (Valuation Officer)* [1961] 1 All ER 731, [1961] 1 WLR 561, CA; *Scaife (Valuation Officer) v Birds Eye Foods Ltd* [1962] RVR 298, Lands Tribunal; *Leeds University v Leeds City Council and Burge (Valuation Officer)* [1962] RVR 311, Lands Tribunal; and see *Trafford Metropolitan Borough Council v Pollard (Valuation Officer)* [2007] RA 49, Lands Tribunal (a sports centre, built within school grounds but not under the management of the school, was held to be a single hereditament together with the school for the purposes of the Non-Domestic Rating (Miscellaneous Provisions) (No 2) Regulations 1989, SI 1989/2303 (see note 23)).

21 *Gilbert (Valuation Officer) v S Hickinbottom & Sons Ltd* [1956] 2 QB 40, [1956] 2 All ER 101, CA (see note 17); *Spillers Ltd v Cardiff Assessment Committee and Pritchard (Cardiff Revenue Officer)* [1931] 2 KB 21. In the following cases the premises divided by the highway were held to form one hereditament: *Gilbert (Valuation Officer) v S Hickinbottom & Sons Ltd* (bakery and repair shop); *Catton & Co Ltd v Burge (Valuation Officer)* (1957) 1 RRC 343, Lands Tribunal (foundry and pattern store); *Leicester City Council v Burkitt (Valuation Officer) and Chilprufe Ltd* (1958) 3 RRC 45, Lands Tribunal (factory and special packing department); *Burkitt (Valuation Officer) v Fielding and Johnson Ltd* (1958) 4 RRC 128, Lands Tribunal (mill and garage, wool store, machinery store, canteen and cycle shed); *Hughes (Valuation Officer) v Imperial Chemical Industries Ltd* (1958) 4 RRC 190, Lands Tribunal (paint factory and stores, fire appliance house and fitter's shop); *Pritchard (Valuation Officer) v William Crawford & Sons Ltd* (1959) 4 RRC 351, Lands Tribunal (factory and vehicle depot, joiner's shop and store); *Newbold (Valuation Officer) v Bibby and Baron Ltd* (1959) 4 RRC 345, Lands Tribunal (factory and garage, and stores); *Wilkins (Valuation Officer) v Martineaus Ltd* (1959) 5 RRC 1, Lands Tribunal (sugar refinery and drum store); *Burton Latimer UDC v Weetabix Ltd and Lee (Valuation Officer)* (1958) 3 RRC 270, Lands Tribunal (factory and land used for warehouse and sports ground).

In the following cases the premises were held to form more than one hereditament: *Rennick (Valuation Officer) v Weathershields Ltd* (1957) 1 RRC 185, Lands Tribunal (factory storage premises and packing and dispatch department); *Standen (Valuation Officer) v Glaxo Laboratories Ltd* (1957) 1 RRC 338, Lands Tribunal (factory and car park); *Carborundum Co Ltd v Duckworth (Valuation Officer)* (1957) 2 RRC 245, Lands Tribunal (factory and laboratory); *John Dickinson & Co Ltd v Presland (Valuation Officer)* (1958) 4 RRC 159, Lands Tribunal (mill and canteen and cycle shed). See also *JW Barker Ltd v Westbury (Valuation Officer)* (1951) 44 R & IT 458, Lands Tribunal; *Re Bellamy (Valuation Officer) and Hinckley UDC Appeal* (1952) 45 R & IT 691, Lands Tribunal; *Spencer (Valuation Officer) and Thurrock UDC v Thames Board Mills Ltd* (1954) 47 R & IT 809, Lands Tribunal; *Raven v Enfield Cables Ltd* (1960) 53 R & IT 422; *Butterley Co Ltd v Tasker (Valuation Officer)* [1961] 1 All ER 574, [1961] 1 WLR 300, CA; *Edwards (Valuation Officer) v BP Refinery (Llandarcy) Ltd* [1974] RA 1, Lands Tribunal (pipelines separately rateable from refinery); *Rank Xerox (UK) Ltd v Johnson (Valuation Officer)* [1987] RA 139, [1986] 2 EGLR 226, Lands Tribunal; *Trunkfield (Valuation Officer) v Camden London Borough Council* [2010] UKUT 391 (LC), [2011] RA 1.

22 *Woolway v Mazars LLP* [2015] UKSC 53, [2015] AC 1862, [2016] 1 All ER 299.

23 *Woolway v Mazars LLP* [2015] UKSC 53 at [12], [2015] AC 1862, [2016] 1 All ER 299 per Lord Sumption, who (at [17]) held that the decision in *Gilbert (Valuation Officer) v S Hickinbottom & Sons Ltd* [1956] 2 QB 40, [1956] 2 All ER 101, CA, could not be supported.

24 The reference to functionality in heads (b) and (c) in the text is not a reference to the use that the ratepayer chooses to make of the premises. It is a reference to a necessary interdependence of the separate parts that is objectively ascertainable. See *Woolway v Mazars LLP* [2015] UKSC 53 at [39], [2015] AC 1862, [2016] 1 All ER 299 per Lord Gill.

25 *Woolway v Mazars LLP* [2015] UKSC 53 at [12], [2015] AC 1862, [2016] 1 All ER 299 per Lord Sumption. Note the criticism (at [20]–[21]) of the approach of the Upper Tribunal (Lands Chamber) below, which had not applied either the geographical or the functional test, but considered itself bound by the dominant interpretation of *Gilbert (Valuation Officer) v S Hickinbottom & Sons Ltd* [1956] 2 QB 40, [1956] 2 All ER 101, CA, and introduced an arbitrary distinction between horizontal and vertical separation.

26 Ie the Secretary of State or, in relation to Wales, the Welsh Ministers. The functions of the Secretary of State under the Local Government Finance Act 1988 s 64, so far as exercisable in relation to Wales, were transferred to the National Assembly for Wales (see the National Assembly for Wales (Transfer of Functions) Order 1999, SI 1999/672, art 2, Sch 1) and are now vested in the Welsh Ministers (see the Government of Wales Act 2006 s 162(1), Sch 11 para 30). As to the Secretary of State and the Welsh Ministers see PARA 4 note 18. As to the meaning of 'Wales' see PARA 2 note 16. As to the separate administration of the non-domestic rating provisions (Local Government Finance Act 1988 Pt III (ss 41–67)) in England and Wales see PARA 52.

27 Local Government Finance Act 1988 s 64(3). 'Prescribed' means prescribed by the regulations: see s 146(6). Regulations under s 64(3) may include rules for ascertaining:
(1) whether the different hereditaments or the one hereditament (as the case may be) must be treated as occupied or unoccupied (s 65(4)(a));
(2) who is to be treated as the owner or occupier of the different hereditaments or the one hereditament (as the case may be) (s 65(4)(b)).

As to the meaning of 'owner', and as to the occupier and occupation of land, see PARA 86 et seq.

As to the regulations so made see the Non-Domestic Rating (Miscellaneous Provisions) Regulations 1989, SI 1989/1060 (amended by SI 1989/2303, SI 1993/616, SI 2009/1307 and SI 2017/327); the Non-Domestic Rating (Miscellaneous Provisions) (No 2) Regulations 1989, SI 1989/2303 (amended by SI 1991/2906; SI 1993/544; SI 1993/616; SI 1994/3122, SI 2000/532, SI 2000/908, SI 2004/1000, SI 2004/1494, SI 2008/2997, SI 2010/1172, SI 2015/1759 and SI 2016/777); the Non-Domestic Rating (Caravan Sites) Regulations 1990, SI 1990/673 (amended by SI 1991/471); the Non-Domestic Rating (Ports of London and Tilbury) Regulations 1991, SI 1991/2906; the Non-Domestic Rating (Telecommunications Apparatus) (England) Regulations 2000, SI 2000/2421; the Non-Domestic Rating (Telecommunications Apparatus) (Wales) Regulations 2000, SI 2000/3383; the Central Rating List (Wales) Regulations 2005, SI 2005/422 (amended by SI 2005/3050, SI 2008/2672, SI 2016/645 and SI 2017/327); the Non-Domestic Rating (Communications and Light Railways) (England) Regulations 2005, SI 2005/549; the Central Rating List (England) Regulations 2005, SI 2005/551 (amended by SI 2005/3050, SI 2006/495, SI 2008/429, SI 2010/456, SI 2010/2692, SI 2011/2743, SI 2012/1292, SI 2013/408, SI 2013/2887, SI 2016/146, SI 2016/645, SI 2016/714 and SI 2016/882); the Non-Domestic Rating (Waterways) (England) Regulations 2012, SI 2012/1291; the Non-Domestic Rating (Waterways) (Wales) Regulations 2015, SI 2015/539; and the Non-Domestic Rating (Miscellaneous Provisions) (Wales) Regulations 2017, SI 2017/327.

28 Local Government Finance Act 1988 s 64(3)(a). In relation to any hereditament which consists of or includes a dock or harbour undertaking carried on under authority conferred by or under any enactment, and in relation to which on the relevant day certain conditions are satisfied, see the Non-Domestic Rating (Miscellaneous Provisions) (No 2) Regulations 1989, SI 1989/2303, reg 5 (amended by SI 1991/2906, SI 1993/616 and SI 1994/3122); and see *Barratclough (Valuation Officer) v Tees and Hartlepool Port Authority* [2004] RA 1, Lands Tribunal (hereditament occupied by harbour undertaking comparable with land in general rather than with statutory undertaking land).

29 Local Government Finance Act 1988 s 64(3)(b). In relation to cross-boundary property in England see the Non-Domestic Rating (Miscellaneous Provisions) Regulations 1989, SI 1989/1060, reg 6 (amended by SI 1993/616 and SI 2017/327); and in relation to certain hereditaments which consist of or include a dock or harbour see the Non-Domestic Rating (Miscellaneous Provisions) (No 2) Regulations 1989, SI 1989/2303, reg 5 (as amended: see note 24). In relation to cross-boundary property in Wales see the Non-Domestic Rating (Miscellaneous Provisions) (Wales) Regulations 2017, SI 2017/327, reg 4.

107. Multiple moorings may be treated as one hereditament.

For the purposes of the non-domestic rating provisions[1], the appropriate national authority[2] may make regulations[3] providing that where on any land there are two or more moorings which:
(1) are owned by the same person[4];
(2) are not domestic property[5]; and
(3) are separately occupied[6] (or available for separate occupation) by persons other than that person[7],

a valuation officer[8] may determine that, for the purposes of the compilation or alteration of a local non-domestic rating list[9], all or any of the moorings or all or any of them together with any adjacent moorings or land owned and occupied by that person are to be treated as one hereditament[10]. Such regulations may provide that where a valuation officer makes such a determination, he must, if prescribed[11] conditions are fulfilled, supply prescribed persons with prescribed information[12].

While such a determination is in force:

(a) the person who on any day is the owner[13] of the moorings (or the moorings and land) which constitute the hereditament is to be treated for the purposes of determining liability under the provisions relating to occupied, partly occupied or unoccupied hereditaments[14] as being in occupation of all of the hereditament on that day[15]; and

(b) no other person is to be treated for those purposes as being in occupation of all or any part of the hereditament on that day[16].

1 Ie for the purposes of the Local Government Finance Act 1988 Pt III (ss 41–67): see s 67(13).

2 Ie the Secretary of State or, in relation to Wales, the Welsh Ministers. The functions of the Secretary of State under the Local Government Finance Act 1988 s 64, so far as exercisable in relation to Wales, were transferred to the National Assembly for Wales (see the National Assembly for Wales (Transfer of Functions) Order 1999, SI 1999/672, art 2, Sch 1) and are now vested in the Welsh Ministers (see the Government of Wales Act 2006 s 162(1), Sch 11 para 30). As to the Secretary of State and the Welsh Ministers see PARA 4 note 18. As to the meaning of 'Wales' see PARA 2 note 16. As to the separate administration of the non-domestic rating provisions (Local Government Finance Act 1988 Pt III (ss 41–67)) in England and Wales see PARA 52.

3 As to the regulations made see the Non-Domestic Rating (Multiple Moorings) Regulations 1992, SI 1992/557.

4 Local Government Finance Act 1988 s 64(3A)(a) (s 64(3A), (3B) added by the Local Government Finance Act 1992 s 104, Sch 10 para 2). As to the meaning of 'person' see PARA 11 note 13.

5 Local Government Finance Act 1988 s 64(3A)(b) (as added: see note 4). As to the meaning of 'domestic property' in relation to non-domestic rating see PARA 190. As to whether a hereditament is non-domestic see the Local Government Finance Act 1988 s 64(8), (9); and PARA 106. If the boat is the sole or main residence of an individual, the mooring and the boat, together with any garden, yard, outhouse or other appurtenance belonging to or enjoyed with them, are domestic property: s 66(4) (s 66(4) substituted, (4A) added, by the Rating (Caravans and Boats) Act 1996 s 1(3)). The Local Government Finance Act 1988 s 66(4) does not have effect in the case of a pitch occupied by a caravan, or a mooring occupied by a boat, which is an appurtenance enjoyed with other property to which s 66(1)(a) (see PARA 190) applies: s 66(4A) (as so added). As to the relevant retrospective effects upon non-domestic rating lists see also s 1(5), (6). As to the council tax for domestic property see PARA 344 et seq.

6 As to occupation see PARA 85 et seq.

7 Local Government Finance Act 1988 s 64(3A)(c) (as added: see note 4).

8 As to the meaning of 'valuation officer' see PARA 54 note 3.

9 As to local non-domestic rating lists see PARA 191 et seq.

10 Local Government Finance Act 1988 s 64(3A) (as added: see note 4).

11 'Prescribed' means prescribed by the regulations: see the Local Government Finance Act 1988 s 146(6).

12 Local Government Finance Act 1988 s 64(3B)(a) (as added: see note 4). As to the meaning of 'information' see PARA 31 note 17.

13 For these purposes, 'owner' in relation to a mooring, means the person who (if the mooring is let) is entitled to receive rent, whether on his own account or as agent or trustee for any other person, or (if the mooring is not let) would be so entitled if the mooring were let; and 'owned' is to be construed accordingly: see the Local Government Finance Act 1988 s 64(12) (added by the Local Government Finance Act 1992 Sch 10 para 2).

14 Ie for the purposes of the Local Government Finance Act 1988 s 43 (occupied hereditaments: see PARAS 133, 143 et seq), s 44A (partly occupied hereditaments: see PARA 134) or s 45 (unoccupied hereditaments: see PARAS 135–136, 148).

15 Local Government Finance Act 1988 s 64(3B)(b)(i) (as added: see note 4).

16 Local Government Finance Act 1988 s 64(3B)(b)(ii) (as added: see note 4).

108. Rating of caravan sites.

The rating of caravan sites was formerly governed by the Rating (Caravan Sites) Act 1976[1]. The 1976 Act has not yet been repealed but is of little relevance today[2], and the rating of caravan sites is now governed by the Non-Domestic Rating (Caravan Sites) Regulations 1990[3].

Where pitches for caravans[4] on a relevant site[5] would constitute separate hereditaments[6] because they are occupied[7] by persons[8] other than the site operator[9], those pitches[10] must, together with so much of the site as constitutes a hereditament in the occupation of the site operator, be treated as one hereditament occupied by the site operator[11]. Where a local rating list[12] is being compiled or altered and it includes a hereditament consisting of a caravan site[13], the valuation officer[14] must inform the site operator in writing[15] of that fact within one month[16] of the compilation or alteration[17]. The information must also state in writing:

(1) how many caravans stationed on pitches which do not consist of domestic property are included in the hereditament[18]; and

(2) how much (if any) of the rateable value of the hereditament is attributable to those caravans, together with their pitches[19].

Any person occupying a pitch for a caravan on a relevant site may, after giving reasonable notice to the valuation officer at any reasonable time and without payment, inspect a copy of any statement[20] supplied to the operator of the site[21].

1 The Rating (Caravan Sites) Act 1976 made provision for the rating of caravan sites under the system of rating governed by the General Rate Act 1967 (now repealed). For most purposes, the General Rate Act 1967 has had no effect as regards any time after 31 March 1990 and, consequently, the Rating (Caravan Sites) Act 1976 would appear to be of little relevance after 1 April 1990: see further PARA 109.

2 See note 1; and PARA 109.

3 Ie the Non-Domestic Rating (Caravan Sites) Regulations 1990, SI 1990/673 (see the text to notes 4–21) made under the Local Government Finance Act 1988 s 55(2), (6) (see PARA 199), ss 64(3), 65(4) (see PARA 106).

4 For these purposes, a 'caravan pitch', and any area comprising it, is to be taken as including the caravan for the time being on the pitch if, apart from the Non-Domestic Rating (Caravan Sites) Regulations 1990, SI 1990/673, reg 3, the caravan would be included as part of the rateable hereditament: reg 3(3). 'Caravan' has the same meaning as it has for the purposes of the Caravan Sites and Control of Development Act 1960 Pt I (ss 1–32) (see PLANNING vol 83 (2018) PARA 1137): Non-Domestic Rating (Caravan Sites) Regulations 1990, SI 1990/673, reg 2(a).

5 'Relevant site' means a caravan site which includes some property which is not domestic and which has an area of 400 square yards or more: Non-Domestic Rating (Caravan Sites) Regulations 1990, SI 1990/673, reg 2(d). 'Caravan site' means any land in respect of which a site licence is required under the Caravan Sites and Control of Development Act 1960 Pt I (ss 1–32) (see PLANNING vol 83 (2018) PARA 1136), or would be so required but for s 2, Sch 1 paras 4, 11, 11A (exemption of certain land: see PLANNING vol 83 (2018) PARA 1140): Non-Domestic Rating (Caravan Sites) Regulations 1990, SI 1990/673, reg 2(b).

Where a pitch is occupied by a caravan which is the sole or main residence of an individual, the pitch and the caravan, together with any garden, yard, outhouse or other appurtenance belonging to or enjoyed with them, are domestic property: see the Local Government Finance Act 1988 s 66(3); and PARA 190.

6 As to the meaning of 'hereditament' see PARA 106.

7 As to occupation see PARA 85 et seq.

8 As to the meaning of 'person' see PARA 11 note 13.

9 'Site operator' means the person who is, for the purposes of the Caravan Sites and Control of Development Act 1960 Pt I (ss 1–32), the occupier of the caravan site (see PLANNING vol 83 (2018) PARA 1136): Non-Domestic Rating (Caravan Sites) Regulations 1990, SI 1990/673, reg 2(e).

10 A pitch which is occupied by a charity or trustees for a charity, and which is wholly or mainly used for charitable purposes (whether of that charity or of that and other charities) is not subject to the regulations for rating of caravans: Non-Domestic Rating (Caravan Sites) Regulations 1990, SI 1990/673, reg 3(2). As to exemptions from rating for charities generally see CHARITIES vol 8 (2015) PARA 431 et seq. As to charitable purposes see CHARITIES vol 8 (2015) PARA 2 et seq.

11 Non-Domestic Rating (Caravan Sites) Regulations 1990, SI 1990/673, reg 3(1) (amended by

SI 1991/471). As to the liability of caravans for council tax see PARA 355.
12 As to local non-domestic rating lists see PARA 191 et seq.
13 Ie a relevant caravan site to which the Non-Domestic Rating (Caravan Sites) Regulations 1990, SI 1990/673, reg 3 applies: see the text to notes 4–11.
14 As to the meaning of 'valuation officer' see PARA 54 note 3.
15 As to the meaning of 'writing' see PARA 21 note 3.
16 As to the meaning of 'month' see PARA 11 note 1.
17 Non-Domestic Rating (Caravan Sites) Regulations 1990, SI 1990/673, reg 4(1).
18 Non-Domestic Rating (Caravan Sites) Regulations 1990, SI 1990/673, reg 4(1)(a) (amended by SI 1991/471). Where it appears to a valuation officer that the information supplied is no longer accurate, but no alteration of the local rating list is required, he must inform the site operator of that fact and supply him with a further statement of the matters in the Non-Domestic Rating (Caravan Sites) Regulations 1990, SI 1990/673, reg 4(1)(a), (b) (see head (2) in the text): reg 4(2).
19 Non-Domestic Rating (Caravan Sites) Regulations 1990, SI 1990/673, reg 4(1)(b). See also note 18.
20 Ie any statement supplied under the Non-Domestic Rating (Caravan Sites) Regulations 1990, SI 1990/673, reg 4: see the text to notes 12–19.
21 Non-Domestic Rating (Caravan Sites) Regulations 1990, SI 1990/673, reg 4(3) (amended by SI 1991/471).

109. Rating of caravan sites under the Rating (Caravan Sites) Act 1976.

Provision for the rating of caravan sites under the system of rating governed by the Local Government Finance Act 1988 is made by the Non-Domestic Rating (Caravan Sites) Regulations 1990[1]. However, the Rating (Caravan Sites) Act 1976, which made provision for the rating of caravan sites under the system of rating governed by the General Rate Act 1967 (now repealed), remains unrepealed[2] and, although it would now appear to be of little relevance, its provisions are set out here for the sake of completeness.

Where, in a caravan site[3] having an area of not less than 400 square yards, pitches for leisure caravans[4] are separately occupied by persons other than the site operator[5] so that the pitches so occupied are separate hereditaments for the purposes of rating[6], the valuation officer may, if he thinks fit[7], in the valuation list treat all or any of those pitches as forming a single hereditament together with so much, if any, of the site as is in the occupation of the site operator[8]. For these purposes, a caravan pitch (and any area comprising it) is to be taken as including the caravan for the time being on the pitch if, but only if, apart from these provisions, the caravan would be included as part of a rateable hereditament[9]. Where any area of a caravan site is treated as a single hereditament, it must be deemed, for the purposes of rating[10], to be a single hereditament in the occupation of the site operator[11].

1 Ie the Non-Domestic Rating (Caravan Sites) Regulations 1990, SI 1990/673: see PARA 108.
2 For most purposes, the General Rate Act 1967 has had no effect as regards any time after 31 March 1990 and, consequently, the Rating (Caravan Sites) Act 1976 would appear to be of little relevance after 1 April 1990.
3 'Caravan site' means any land in respect of which a site licence is required under the Caravan Sites and Control of Development Act 1960 Pt I (ss 1–32) (see PLANNING vol 83 (2018) PARA 1136) or the Mobile Homes (Wales) Act 2013 Pt 2 (ss 4–39), or would be so required if the Caravan Sites and Control of Development Act 1960 Sch 1 paras 4, 11 (exemption of certain land: see PLANNING vol 83 (2018) PARA 1140) or the Mobile Homes (Wales) Act 2013 Sch 1 paras 4, 11 were omitted: see the Rating (Caravan Sites) Act 1976 s 6(b) (amended by the Mobile Homes (Wales) Act 2013 s 58(1), Sch 4 para 3(a)).
4 A 'caravan pitch' is a 'pitch for a leisure caravan' if in accordance with any licence or planning permission regulating the use of the caravan site a caravan stationed on the pitch is not allowed to be used for human habitation throughout the year: see the Rating (Caravan Sites) Act 1976 s 6(c). 'Caravan' has the same meaning as it has for the purposes of the Caravan Sites and Control of Development Act 1960 Pt I (see PLANNING vol 83 (2018) PARA 1137): see the Rating (Caravan Sites) Act 1976 s 6(a).

5 'Site operator' means the person who is, for the purposes of the Caravan Sites and Control of Development Act 1960 Pt I, the occupier of the caravan site (see PLANNING vol 83 (2018) PARA 1136) or is for purposes of the Mobile Homes (Wales) Act 2013 the owner of the caravan site: see the Rating (Caravan Sites) Act 1976 s 6(d) (amended by the Mobile Homes (Wales) Act 2013 Sch 4 para 3(b)). As to the meaning of 'person' see PARA 11 note 13.

6 Ie the system of rating under the General Rate Act 1967 (repealed): see the Rating (Caravan Sites) Act 1976 s 1(1).

7 Note the element of discretion which is present in the Rating (Caravan Sites) Act 1976 but not in the Non-Domestic Rating (Caravan Sites) Regulations 1990, SI 1990/673 (see PARA 108).

8 Rating (Caravan Sites) Act 1976 s 1(1).

9 Rating (Caravan Sites) Act 1976 s 1(2).

10 Ie for the purposes of rating within the meaning of the General Rate Act 1967 (repealed): see the Rating (Caravan Sites) Act 1976 s 1(3).

11 Rating (Caravan Sites) Act 1976 s 1(3). As to mixed hereditaments see s 1(4) (amended by the Local Government, Planning and Land Act 1980 ss 47, 194, Sch 34 Pt IX). Provision is made in relation to the alteration of valuation lists: see the Rating (Caravan Sites) Act 1976 s 1(5)–(7), (9). As to the information to be provided for caravanners about the rating of sites mentioned in s 1, and the provision that is made for a penalty in cases where the requirements so imposed are contravened, see s 2 (amended by the Criminal Justice Act 1982 ss 37, 38, 46).

(6) Exemptions from Non-domestic Rating

(i) In General

110. Items exempt from local non-domestic rating.

Provision is made to determine the extent (if any) to which a hereditament[1] is exempt from local non-domestic rating for the purposes of the Local Government Finance Act 1988[2], in relation to:

(1) agricultural land and buildings[3];
(2) fish farms[4];
(3) places of religious worship[5];
(4) certain property of Trinity House[6];
(5) sewers[7];
(6) property of drainage authorities[8];
(7) certain parks[9];
(8) property used for the disabled[10];
(9) air-raid protection works[11];
(10) swinging moorings[12];
(11) road crossings over watercourses[13];
(12) property used for road user charging schemes[14];
(13) property in enterprise zones[15]; and
(14) visiting forces[16].

The appropriate national authority[17] may make regulations[18] providing that prescribed[19] hereditaments[20] or hereditaments falling within any prescribed description are exempt[21] to such extent (whether as to the whole or some lesser extent) as may be prescribed[22]. However, this power may not be exercised so as to confer exemption which in the opinion of the appropriate national authority goes beyond certain existing exemptions or privileges[23].

For the purposes of these exemptions from local non-domestic rating[24]:

(a) any land, building or property not in use is to be treated as used in a particular way if it appears that when next in use it will be used in that way[25];

(b) any land or building which is not occupied is to be treated as occupied in a particular way if it appears that when next occupied it will be occupied in that way[26]; and

(c) a person is to be treated as an occupier of any land or building which is not occupied if it appears that when it is next occupied he will be an occupier of it[27].

1 As to the meaning of 'hereditament' see PARA 106.
2 Ie the Local Government Finance Act 1988 Pt III (ss 41–67): see s 51.
3 See the Local Government Finance Act 1988 Sch 5 paras 1–8; and PARAS 116–121.
4 See the Local Government Finance Act 1988 Sch 5 para 9; and PARA 122.
5 See the Local Government Finance Act 1988 Sch 5 para 11; and PARAS 114–115.
6 See the Local Government Finance Act 1988 Sch 5 para 12; and PARA 128.
7 See the Local Government Finance Act 1988 Sch 5 para 13; and PARA 123.
8 See the Local Government Finance Act 1988 Sch 5 para 14; and PARA 124.
9 See the Local Government Finance Act 1988 Sch 5 para 15; and PARA 126.
10 See the Local Government Finance Act 1988 Sch 5 para 16; and PARA 125.
11 See the Local Government Finance Act 1988 Sch 5 para 17; and PARA 127.
12 See the Local Government Finance Act 1988 Sch 5 para 18; and PARA 129.
13 See the Local Government Finance Act 1988 Sch 5 para 18A; and PARA 130.
14 See the Local Government Finance Act 1988 Sch 5 para 18B; and PARA 131.
15 See the Local Government Finance Act 1988 Sch 5 para 19; and PARA 132.
16 See the Local Government Finance Act 1988 Sch 5 para 19A; and PARA 113.
17 Ie the Secretary of State or, in relation to Wales, the Welsh Ministers. The functions of the Secretary of State under the Local Government Finance Act 1988 Sch 5, so far as exercisable in relation to Wales, were transferred to the National Assembly for Wales (see the National Assembly for Wales (Transfer of Functions) Order 1999, SI 1999/672, art 2, Sch 1) and are now vested in the Welsh Ministers (see the Government of Wales Act 2006 s 162(1), Sch 11 para 30). As to the Secretary of State and the Welsh Ministers see PARA 4 note 18. As to the meaning of 'Wales' see PARA 2 note 16. As to the separate administration of the non-domestic rating provisions (Local Government Finance Act 1988 Pt III (ss 41–67)) in England and Wales see PARA 52.
18 Such regulations in their application to a particular financial year (including regulations amending or revoking others) are not effective unless they come into force before 1 January in the preceding financial year: Local Government Finance Act 1988 s 51, Sch 5 para 20(5). As to the meaning of 'financial year' see PARA 24 note 1. At the date at which this volume states the law no such regulations had been made.
19 'Prescribed' means prescribed by the regulations: see the Local Government Finance Act 1988 s 146(6).
20 As to the meaning of 'hereditament' see PARA 106.
21 For the purposes of the Local Government Finance Act 1988 Sch 5, 'exempt' means exempt from non-domestic rating: Sch 5 para 21(1), (2).
22 Local Government Finance Act 1988 Sch 5 para 20(1).
23 See the Local Government Finance Act 1988 Sch 5 para 20(2). The exemptions or privileges concerned are those which fulfil the following conditions (see Sch 5 para 20(2)):
   (1) that the exemption or privilege operated or was enjoyed in practice, immediately before the passing of the Local Government Finance Act 1988 (ie 29 July 1988), in respect of a general rate in its application to the hereditaments prescribed or falling within the prescribed description (see Sch 5 para 20(3)); and
   (2) that the exemption or privilege was conferred by a local Act or order passed or made on or after 22 December 1925 or was conferred by a local Act or order passed or made before 22 December 1925 and was saved by the General Rate Act 1967 s 117(5)(b) (repealed) (Local Government Finance Act 1988 Sch 5 para 20(4)).

   Nothing in a private or local Act passed before the Local Government Finance Act 1988 is to have the effect that a hereditament is exempt from non-domestic rating, or prevent a person being subject to a non-domestic rate, or prevent a person being designated or a description of a hereditament being prescribed under s 53 (see PARA 197): s 67(12). As to the meaning of 'person' see PARA 11 note 13. This provision operates to remove earlier exemptions in private and local Acts, as the purpose of the Local Government Finance Act 1988 was to provide a comprehensive code for non-domestic rating: see eg *Woodbury (Valuation Officer) v Toby Restaurants Ltd* [1998]

RA 315 (floating restaurant complex moored on the River Thames and permanently connected to all main utilities was a hereditament which was removed by the Local Government Finance Act 1988 s 67(12) from exemption by virtue of the Port of London Act 1968, which operated so long as the conditions specified in the 1968 Act were satisfied).

24 Ie for the purposes of the Local Government Finance Act 1988 Sch 5: see Sch 5 para 21(1).

25 Local Government Finance Act 1988 Sch 5 para 21(3).

26 Local Government Finance Act 1988 Sch 5 para 21(4). As to rateable occupation see PARA 85 et seq.

27 Local Government Finance Act 1988 Sch 5 para 21(5). As to the meaning of 'occupier' in relation to a hereditament see PARA 86.

111. Crown property.

The non-domestic rating provisions[1] apply to the Crown as they apply to other persons[2]. Accordingly, liability to a non-domestic rate in respect of a hereditament[3] is not affected by the fact that:

(1) the hereditament is occupied by the Crown or by a person acting on behalf of the Crown or is used for Crown purposes[4]; or

(2) the Crown or a person acting on behalf of the Crown is the owner of the hereditament[5].

If any property would consist of two or more Crown hereditaments[6], the property is to be treated[7] as if it were a single hereditament occupied by such one of the occupiers[8] as appears to the billing authority[9] to occupy the largest part of the property[10]. For the purpose of deciding the extent (if any) to which a hereditament is a Crown hereditament[11] on a particular day, the state of affairs existing immediately before the day ends is to be treated as having existed throughout the day[12].

1 Ie the Local Government Finance Act 1988 Pt III (ss 41–67): see ss 65A(1), 67(13) (s 65A added by the Local Government and Rating Act 1997 s 3). References in the Local Government Finance Act 1988 s 65A to Pt III include any subordinate legislation within the meaning of the Interpretation Act 1978 made under it: see the Local Government Finance Act 1988 s 65A(5)(a) (as so added). 'Subordinate legislation' means Orders in Council, orders, rules, regulations, schemes, warrants, byelaws and other instruments made or to be made under any Act: see the Interpretation Act 1978 s 21(1); and STATUTES AND LEGISLATIVE PROCESS vol 96 (2012) PARA 1030 et seq.

2 Local Government Finance Act 1988 s 65A(1) (as added: see note 1). As to the meaning of 'person' see PARA 11 note 13.

3 As to the meaning of 'hereditament' see PARA 106.

4 Local Government Finance Act 1988 s 65A(2)(a) (as added: see note 1).

5 Local Government Finance Act 1988 s 65A(2)(b) (as added: see note 1). As to the meaning of 'owner' see PARA 86.

6 'Crown hereditament' means a hereditament:

(1) which is occupied by a Minister of the Crown or government department or by any officer or body exercising functions on behalf of the Crown (Local Government Finance Act 1988 s 65A(4)(a) (as added: see note 1)); but

(2) which is not provided or maintained by a local authority or by a police and crime commissioner (see POLICE AND INVESTIGATORY POWERS vol 84 (2013) PARA 56 et seq) (Local Government Finance Act 1988 s 65A(4)(b) (as so added; amended by the Criminal Justice and Police Act 2001 s 128(1), Sch 6 para 73; and the Police Reform and Social Responsibility Act 2011 s 99, Sch 16 paras 180, 181)).

The Secretary of State or, in relation to Wales, the Welsh Ministers may by order amend the Local Government Finance Act 1988 s 65A(4)(b) so as to alter the persons for the time being referred to there: s 65A(6) (as so added). At the date at which this volume states the law no such order had been made. 'Local authority' has the same meaning as in the Local Government Act 1972 (see LOCAL GOVERNMENT vol 69 (2018) PARA 37) and includes the Common Council of the City of London: Local Government Finance Act 1988 s 65A(5)(b) (as so added). As to the Common Council of the City of London see LONDON GOVERNMENT vol 71 (2013) PARA 34 et seq. As to Ministers of the Crown see CONSTITUTIONAL AND ADMINISTRATIVE LAW vol 20 (2014) PARA 151.

The functions of the Secretary of State under s 65A, so far as exercisable in relation to Wales, were transferred to the National Assembly for Wales (see the National Assembly for Wales (Transfer of Functions) Order 1999, SI 1999/672, art 2, Sch 1) and are now vested in the Welsh Ministers (see the Government of Wales Act 2006 s 162(1), Sch 11 para 30). As to the Secretary of State and the Welsh Ministers see PARA 4 note 18. As to the meaning of 'Wales' see PARA 2 note 16. As to the separate administration of the non-domestic rating provisions (Local Government Finance Act 1988 Pt III (ss 41–67)) in England and Wales see PARA 52.

7 Ie for the purposes of the Local Government Finance Act 1988 Part III (ss 41–67). See also note 1.

8 As to the meaning of 'occupier' in relation to a hereditament see PARA 86.

9 As to the meaning of 'billing authority' see PARA 53.

10 Local Government Finance Act 1988 s 65A(3) (as added: see note 1). This provision does not affect the power conferred by s 64(3) (see PARA 106): s 65A(7) (as so added).

11 For these purposes, 'Crown hereditament' has the same meaning as in the Local Government Finance Act 1988 s 65A (see note 6): s 67(5A) (added by the Local Government and Rating Act 1997 s 33(1), Sch 3 para 26).

12 Local Government Finance Act 1988 s 67(5) (amended by the Local Government and Housing Act 1989 s 139, Sch 5 paras 35(2), 79(3)).

(ii) Diplomatic Immunity and Visiting Forces

112. Persons entitled to immunity.

Immunity from rates is enjoyed by foreign states and monarchs. In respect of a diplomatic mission, the sending state and the head of the mission are immune from rates[1]. Diplomatic agents (within certain limitations) and members of the family of a diplomatic agent forming part of his household can also benefit from the immunity[2]; however, the extent to which the immunity from rates will benefit an individual diplomat or his family now that rates are no longer charged in respect of domestic property is likely to be small[3]. Commonwealth organisations and certain international organisations and their members are immune from rates[4]. The immunity may, however, be waived. Consular premises are exempt from rates, and exemption from all dues and taxes (other than certain indirect taxes) operates as regards consular officers and employees and members of their families forming part of their households, but this does not exempt them from rates on private property. A similar immunity and exemption extends to representatives of members of the Commonwealth and the Republic of Ireland[5].

1 See generally INTERNATIONAL RELATIONS LAW vol 61 (2010) PARA 269 et seq.

2 See generally INTERNATIONAL RELATIONS LAW vol 61 (2010) PARA 275 et seq.

3 As to council tax in respect of dwellings generally see PARA 348 et seq.

4 See generally COMMONWEALTH vol 13 (2017) PARA 623; and INTERNATIONAL RELATIONS LAW vol 61 (2010) PARAS 302, 304 et seq. That diplomatic privilege extends to immunity from rates was recognised in *Novello v Toogood* (1823) 1 B & C 554; *Parkinson v Potter* (1885) 16 QBD 152; *Macartney v Garbutt* (1890) 24 QBD 368; *Re City of Ottawa Corpn and Rockcliffe Park Village Corpn* [1943] SCR 208.

5 See COMMONWEALTH; and INTERNATIONAL RELATIONS LAW vol 61 (2010) PARA 298 et seq.

113. Visiting forces.

A hereditament[1] is exempt from local non-domestic rating[2] to the extent that it consists of property which is occupied[3] for the purposes of a visiting force[4], or a headquarters[5], in pursuance of arrangements made in that behalf with any government department[6].

Where a contribution in aid of non-domestic rating is made in respect of a hereditament which is exempt from local non-domestic rating by virtue of this exemption, the contribution is to be paid to the appropriate national authority[7].

1 As to the meaning of 'hereditament' see PARA 106.
2 Ie for the purposes of the Local Government Finance Act 1988 Pt III (ss 41–67): see s 51. As to the meaning of 'exempt' see PARA 110 note 21.
3 As to the occupier and occupation of land see PARA 86 et seq. As to the treatment for the purposes of exemptions under the Local Government Finance Act 1988 Sch 5 of any land or building which is not occupied see PARA 110.
4 'Visiting force' means any such body, contingent or detachment of the forces of any country as is a visiting force for the purposes of any provision of the Visiting Forces Act 1952 (see ARMED FORCES vol 3 (2011) PARA 322): Local Government Finance Act 1988 Sch 5 para 19A(2) (Sch 5 para 19A added by the Local Government and Rating Act 1997 s 4). As to the occupier and occupation of land see PARA 86 et seq.
5 'Headquarters' means an international headquarters or defence organisation designated by an Order in Council under the International Headquarters and Defence Organisations Act 1964 s 1 (see ARMED FORCES vol 3 (2011) PARA 420): Local Government Finance Act 1988 Sch 5 para 19A(2) (as added: see note 4).
6 Local Government Finance Act 1988 Sch 5 para 19A(1) (as added: see note 4). It would seem that effect may be given to an exemption which affects part only of a hereditament; a hereditament that is completely exempt under Sch 5 para 19A is not to be entered into a rating list: see s 42(1); and PARA 194.
7 Local Government Finance Act 1988 s 59 (substituted by the Local Government and Housing Act 1989 s 139, Sch 5 paras 32, 79(3); and amended by the Local Government and Rating Act 1997 s 33(1), Sch 3 para 24). 'Appropriate national authority' means the Secretary of State or, in relation to Wales, the Welsh Ministers. The functions of the Secretary of State under the Local Government Finance Act 1988 s 59, so far as exercisable in relation to Wales, were transferred to the National Assembly for Wales (see the National Assembly for Wales (Transfer of Functions) Order 1999, SI 1999/672, art 2, Sch 1) and are now vested in the Welsh Ministers (see the Government of Wales Act 2006 s 162(1), Sch 11 para 30). As to the Secretary of State and the Welsh Ministers see PARA 4 note 18. As to the meaning of 'Wales' see PARA 2 note 16. As to the separate administration of the non-domestic rating provisions (Local Government Finance Act 1988 Pt III (ss 41–67)) in England and Wales see PARA 52.

(iii) Places of Worship

114. Churches, chapels, church halls etc.

A hereditament[1] is exempt from local non-domestic rating[2] to the extent that it consists of any of the following:

(1) a place of public religious worship which belongs to the Church of England[3] or the Church in Wales[4] or is for the time being certified as required by law[5] as a place of religious worship[6];
(2) a church hall[7], chapel hall or similar building[8] used[9] in connection with a place of public religious worship falling within head (1)[10] for the purposes of the organisation responsible for the conduct of public religious worship in that place[11].

'Public religious worship' has been held to mean the gathering together of people in a church for the purpose of taking part in an act of public worship[12]. The showing of religious films to an audience as part of a service can constitute public religious worship[13]. However, places of religious worship are not exempt if, even though they are public as opposed to domestic from the worshippers' point of view, they are not in the ordinary sense public because they are not open to all properly disposed persons who wish to be present; in other words, because the public are excluded[14].

1 As to the meaning of 'hereditament' see PARA 106.

2 Ie for the purposes of the Local Government Finance Act 1988 Pt III (ss 41–67): see s 51. As to the meaning of 'exempt' see PARA 110 note 21.

3 As to the Church of England see ECCLESIASTICAL LAW vol 34 (2011) PARA 50 et seq.

4 Ie within the meaning of the Welsh Church Act 1914: see ECCLESIASTICAL LAW vol 34 (2011) PARA 26 et seq.

5 Ie certified under the Places of Worship Registration Act 1855: see ECCLESIASTICAL LAW vol 34 (2011) PARA 47.

6 Local Government Finance Act 1988 Sch 5 para 11(1)(a). A hereditament that is completely exempt under this head is not to be entered in a rating list: see s 42(1); and PARA 194. See Application 7552/09 *Church of Jesus Christ of Latter-Day Saints v United Kingdom* [2014] RA 322, (2014) Times, 19 March, ECtHR (tax on Mormon temple did not amount to religious discrimination).

As from a day to be appointed, head (1) in the text is substituted so as to refer simply to 'a place of public religious worship': see the Local Government Finance Act 1988 Sch 5 para 11(1)(a) (prospectively substituted by the Local Government Act 2003 s 68). At the date at which this volume states the law no such day had been appointed.

7 A former church building registered for public worship which was owned by the church and used in connection with it and used by a social club was a church hall for the purposes of obtaining exemption under the General Rate Act 1967 (repealed): *Swansea City Council v Edwards (Valuation Officer) and Trustees of Our Lady of Lourdes Roman Catholic Church* [1977] RA 209, Lands Tribunal.

8 'Similar building' has been held to include a building used for purposes such as a youth club, religious meetings, sales of work, church socials, a luncheon club, mission offices, living accommodation for staff, a Sunday school, crèche and roof playground (*West London Methodist Mission Trustees v Holborn Borough Council* (1958) 3 RRC 86), and a Christian Science reading room, committee room and librarian's room (*Board of Directors of Ninth Church of Christ Scientist v Westminster City Council and Cane (Valuation Officer)* (1958) 3 RRC 35, Lands Tribunal), but not a building used as diocesan offices (*Church House Trustees v Dimmick (Valuation Officer)* (1959) 5 RRC 185, Lands Tribunal). Cf *Morley (Valuation Officer) v Society for Promoting Christian Knowledge* (1960) 53 R & IT 326, Lands Tribunal. Premises used partly as a hostel have been held to be within the exemption: *Westminster Roman Catholic Diocese Trustee v Hampsher (Valuation Officer)* [1975] RA 1, Lands Tribunal; and see *Stamp (Valuation Officer) v Birmingham Catholic Archdiocesan Trustees* [1975] JPL 34, Lands Tribunal, where a car park was held exempt although physically separated from the church hall by a road. See also *Mageean v Valuation Comr* [1960] NI 141, NI CA, where a building used by university students of a particular religious denomination for recreation or social purposes was entitled to exemption. Exemption has also been held to extend to a social centre attached to a Roman Catholic church (*Liverpool Roman Catholic Archdiocesan Trustees Inc v Mackay (Valuation Officer)* [1988] RA 90, Lands Tribunal) and to a school in the grounds of a mosque (*Ludkin (Valuation Officer) v Trustees of Anjuman-E-Isthahul Muslimen of UK* [1988] RA 209, Lands Tribunal).

9 As to the treatment for the purposes of exemptions under the Local Government Finance Act 1988 Sch 5 of any land or building which is not in use see PARA 110.

10 Premises used by the diocese of Worcester were held not exempt on the grounds, inter alia, that the hereditament was not connected with a place of religious worship but with all the churches in the diocese: *Church House Trustees v Dimmick (Valuation Officer)* (1959) 5 RRC 185.

11 Local Government Finance Act 1988 Sch 5 para 11(1)(b). A hereditament that is completely exempt under this head is not to be entered in a rating list: see s 42(1); and PARA 194.

12 *First Church of Christ Scientist, Seaford v Thompson (Valuation Officer)* (1953) 46 R & IT 783, Lands Tribunal. It had been said that worship must have some, at least, of the following characteristics: submission to the object worshipped, veneration of that object, praise, thanksgiving, prayer or intercession: see *R v Registrar General, ex p Segerdal* [1970] 2 QB 697 at 709, [1970] 3 All ER 886 at 892, CA, per Buckley LJ, where a 'chapel' of the Church of Scientology was held not to be a place of religious worship for the purposes of the Places of Worship Registration Act 1855. This case, however, was overruled by *R (on the application of Hodkin) v Registrar General of Births, Deaths and Marriages* [2013] UKSC 77, [2014] AC 610, [2014] 1 All ER 737 (see at [62] per Lord Toulson SCJ: 'I interpret the expression "religious worship" as wide enough to include religious services, whether or not the form of service falls

within the narrower definition adopted in *Ex p Segerdal*'). See ECCLESIASTICAL LAW vol 34 (2011) PARA 47).

The following cases, decided under the provisions of the Poor Rate Exemption Act 1833 (repealed), may still be relevant on the meaning of 'public religious worship': *Booth v St Martin, Worcester, and Worcester Union Assessment Committee* (1884) 48 JP 441 (selling church newspaper; holding tea meetings); *College Street United Free Church v Edinburgh Parish Council* (1901) 3 F 414, Ct of Sess (mission schools; temperance meetings; church socials); *Walton-le-Dale UDC v Greenwood* (1911) 105 LT 547 (performance of trial scene from the Merchant of Venice); *Hornsey Local Board v Brewis* (1890) 60 LJMC 48, DC (chapel lecture hall); *North Manchester Overseers v Winstanley* [1908] 1 KB 835 at 849, 857, CA (affd on other points sub nom *Winstanley v North Manchester Overseers* [1910] AC 7, HL) (burial ground).

13 *British Advent Missions Ltd v Cane (Valuation Officer) and Westminster City Council* (1954) 48 R & IT 60, Lands Tribunal.

14 *Church of Jesus Christ of Latter-Day Saints v Henning (Valuation Officer)* [1964] AC 420, [1963] 2 All ER 733, HL; *Broxtowe Borough Council v Birch* [1981] RA 215, Lands Tribunal; *Gallagher (Valuation Officer) v Church of Jesus Christ of Latter-Day Saints* [2008] UKHL 56, [2008] 4 All ER 640, [2008] 1 WLR 1852.

115. Administrative and other buildings.

A hereditament[1] is exempt from local non-domestic rating[2] to the extent that it is occupied[3] by an organisation responsible for the conduct of public religious worship[4] in a place of public religious worship[5], and:

(1) is used for carrying out administrative or other activities relating to the organisation of the conduct of public religious worship in such a place[6]; or

(2) is used as an office or for office purposes, or for purposes ancillary to its use as an office or for office purposes[7].

1 As to the meaning of 'hereditament' see PARA 106.

2 Ie for the purposes of the Local Government Finance Act 1988 Pt III (ss 41–67): see s 51. As to the meaning of 'exempt' see PARA 110 note 21. A hereditament that is completely exempt under Sch 5 para 11 is not to be entered into a rating list: see s 42(1); and PARA 194.

3 As to the occupier and occupation of land see PARA 86 et seq. As to the treatment for the purposes of exemptions under the Local Government Finance Act 1988 Sch 5 of any land or building which is not occupied see PARA 110.

4 As to the meaning of 'public religious worship' see PARA 114.

5 Ie a place falling within the Local Government Finance Act 1988 Sch 5 para 11(1)(a) (see PARA 114): see Sch 5 para 11(2) (Sch 5 para 11(2) substituted by the Local Government Finance Act 1992 s 104, Sch 10 para 3). The meaning and extent of the exemption under Sch 5 para 11 was considered in *Gallagher (Valuation Officer) v Church of Jesus Christ of Latter-Day Saints* [2008] UKHL 56, [2008] 4 All ER 640, [2008] 1 WLR 1852.

6 Local Government Finance Act 1988 Sch 5 para 11(2)(a) (as substituted: see note 5).

7 Local Government Finance Act 1988 Sch 5 para 11(2)(b) (as substituted: see note 5). 'Office purposes' includes administration, clerical work and handling money; and 'clerical work' includes writing, book-keeping, sorting papers or information, filing, typing, duplicating, calculating (by whatever means), drawing and the editorial preparation of matter for publication: Sch 5 para 11(3) (added by the Local Government Finance Act 1992 Sch 10 para 3). See *Gallagher (Valuation Officer) v Church of Jesus Christ of Latter-Day Saints* [2008] UKHL 56, [2008] 4 All ER 640, [2008] 1 WLR 1852.

(iv) Agricultural Land and Buildings

116. Exemption for agricultural land and buildings.

A hereditament[1] is exempt from local non-domestic rating[2] to the extent[3] that it consists of:

(1) agricultural land[4];

(2) agricultural buildings[5].

Fish farms are also exempt[6].

1 As to the meaning of 'hereditament' see PARA 106.
2 Ie for the purposes of the Local Government Finance Act 1988 Pt III (ss 41–67): see s 51. As to the meaning of 'exempt' see PARA 110 note 21. A hereditament that is completely exempt under Sch 5 para 1 is not to be entered into a rating list: see s 42(1); and PARA 194.
3 In *Withers v Dalling (Valuation Officer)* [2004] RA 182, Lands Tribunal, the contention was rejected that, so long as the greater part of the hereditament consisted of agricultural land or agricultural buildings for the purposes of the Local Government Finance Act 1988 Sch 5 para 1, the entirety was exempt.
4 Local Government Finance Act 1988 Sch 5 para 1(a). In Sch 5 para 1, 'agricultural land' is to be construed in accordance with Sch 5 para 2 (see PARA 117): see Sch 5 para 8(1).
5 Local Government Finance Act 1988 Sch 5 para 1(b). In Sch 5 paras 1, 5(5)(b) (see PARA 119), 'agricultural building' is to be construed in accordance with Sch 5 paras 3–7 (see PARAS 118–121): Sch 5 para 8(2).
6 See the Local Government Finance Act 1988 Sch 5 para 9; and PARA 122.

117. Agricultural land.

For the purposes of the exemption of agricultural land from local non-domestic rating[1], 'agricultural land' is:

(1) land[2] used[3] as arable, meadow or pasture ground[4] only[5];
(2) land used for a plantation or a wood or for the growth of saleable underwood[6];
(3) land exceeding 0.10 hectare used for the purpose of poultry farming[7];
(4) anything which consists of a market garden[8], nursery ground[9], orchard[10] or allotment[11];
(5) land occupied with, and used solely in connection with the use of, a building[12] which (or buildings each of which) is[13] an agricultural building[14].

However, agricultural land does not include:

(a) land occupied together with a house as a park[15];
(b) gardens (other than market gardens)[16];
(c) pleasure grounds[17];
(d) land used mainly or exclusively for purposes of sport or recreation[18]; or
(e) land used as a race course[19].

1 As to such exemption see PARA 116.
2 'Land' has been held not to include buildings: *Smith v Richmond* [1899] AC 448, HL; *Hall-Mark Hatcheries Ltd v Spencer (Valuation Officer) and Basildon UDC* (1956) 1 RRC 20, Lands Tribunal; *Gilmore (Valuation Officer) v Baker-Carr* [1962] 3 All ER 230, [1962] 1 WLR 1165, CA; *National Pig Progeny Testing Board v Greenall (Valuation Officer)* [1960] 3 All ER 556, [1960] 1 WLR 1265, CA; *W & JB Eastwood Ltd v Herrod (Valuation Officer)* [1971] AC 160, [1970] 1 All ER 774, HL.

Some of the cases cited in this paragraph were decided prior to the coming into force of the Local Government Finance Act 1988 but continue to be of relevance: see PARA 50.

3 It is the present use and not, for example, the fact that the land has been purchased with a view to building on it that is relevant: see *Abercorn Estates Co v Edinburgh Assessor* 1935 SC 868. As to the treatment for the purposes of exemptions under the Local Government Finance Act 1988 Sch 5 of any land, building or property which is not in use see PARA 110.
4 Meadow or pasture ground used for exercising race horses or riding stable horses may be agricultural land: *Tattersalls Ltd v Marlborough Area Assessment Committee* (1930) 11 R & IT 149; *Kirk v Newmarket Assessment Committee* (1937) 26 R & IT 374; *Jarvis v Cambridgeshire Rural Assessment Area Assessment Committee* [1938] 4 All ER 186, DC; *Young (Valuation Officer) v West Dorset District Council* [1977] RA 234, Lands Tribunal.
5 Local Government Finance Act 1988 s 51, Sch 5 para 2(1)(a). Minimal user may be ignored: *Honiton and District Agricultural Association v Wonnacott (Valuation Officer)* (1955) 48 R & IT 589, Lands Tribunal (agricultural show on one day a year). However, if it goes beyond the minimal, a non-agricultural user will defeat the exemption: see eg *Butser Turf and Timber Co Ltd*

v Petersfield Rating Authority [1950] 1 All ER 288, DC (turf cutting); *Meriden and Solihull Rating Authority v Tyacke* [1950] 1 All ER 939 (turf cutting); *Lewis v Rubery (Valuation Officer)* (1951) 44 R & IT 566, Lands Tribunal (turf cutting); *Fowler v Tavener (Valuation Officer)* (1953) 47 R & IT 39, Lands Tribunal (spoil tip); *Young (Valuation Officer) v Morris, Barker and Poole* [1961] RVR 784, Lands Tribunal (sheep sales); *Moore v Williamson (Valuation Officer)* [1973] RA 172 (site used for caravan); *United Counties Agricultural Society v Knight (Valuation Officer)* [1973] RA 13, Lands Tribunal (agricultural show involving use of land for 12 days or more); *Hadley & Sons v Dickman (Valuation Officer)* (1978) 21 RRC 324, Lands Tribunal (tipping of land for a drainage scheme); *Re Forrest (Valuation Officer)* [1981] RVR 66, Lands Tribunal (aircraft runway); *Forster v Simpson (Valuation Officer)* [1984] RA 85, Lands Tribunal (racehorse gallops); *Hayes (Valuation Officer) v Loyd* [1985] 2 All ER 313, [1985] 1 WLR 714, HL (point-to-point once a year). Nevertheless, it is impossible to give the word 'only' its full meaning when the arable, meadow or pasture land is used for sport or recreation within the latter part of the definition of 'agricultural land' (see head (d) in the text), and in such cases the test adopted in practice is that of the primary use: see the cases cited in note 18.

6 Local Government Finance Act 1988 Sch 5 para 2(1)(b). Whether woods are saleable underwoods depends on the mode and object of their cultivation: *Lord Fitzhardinge v Pritchett* (1867) LR 2 QB 135.

7 Local Government Finance Act 1988 Sch 5 para 2(1)(c).

8 As to the meaning of 'market garden' see *Hood Barrs v Howard (Valuation Officer)* (1967) 13 RRC 164, CA. The Lands Tribunal has held that the production of mushroom spawn is not market gardening: *Darlington & Sons (Holdings) Ltd v Langridge (Valuation Officer)* [1973] RA 207. See also *Andsome Garden Products Ltd v King (Valuation Officer)* [1990] RVR 31, [1990] 1 EGLR 235; and *Tunnel Tech Ltd v Reeves (Valuation Officer)* [2015] EWCA Civ 718, [2015] RA 399, [2015] All ER (D) 141 (Jul) (which examined the meaning of market garden and nursery).

9 As to the meaning of 'nursery ground' see *James and Daniel Provan Ltd v Croydon Corpn* (1938) 29 R & IT 277 (cultivation of turf a nursery ground); *Butser Turf and Timber Co Ltd v Petersfield Rating Authority* [1950] 1 All ER 288, DC (turf cutting not a nursery ground). See also *Meriden and Solihull Rating Authority v Tyacke* [1950] 1 All ER 939; *Lewis v Rubery (Valuation Officer)* (1951) 44 R & IT 566, Lands Tribunal; *Thornton (Valuation Officer) v Maxwell M Hart (Glasgow) Ltd* (1957) 2 RRC 156, Lands Tribunal; *Lanarkshire Assessor v Findlay Bros* 1930 SLT 278; *Bomford v Osborne* [1942] AC 14, [1941] 2 All ER 426, HL; *Henshaw (Valuation Officer) v Hatton Borough Council and Watmore* [1984] RVR 237, Lands Tribunal; *Tunnel Tech Ltd v Reeves (Valuation Officer)* [2015] EWCA Civ 718, [2015] RA 399, [2015] All ER (D) 141 (Jul).

10 An orchard occupied together with a house and not used commercially was held to be exempt on its particular facts: *Drury-Heath v Wallace (Valuation Officer)* (1960) 7 RRC 104, CA; but see also *Hood-Barrs v Howard (Valuation Officer)* [1966] RA 212, 12 RRC 118, Lands Tribunal (on appeal on a different point [1967] RA 50, 13 RRC 164, CA).

11 Local Government Finance Act 1988 Sch 5 para 2(1)(d). The reference to allotments includes allotment gardens within the meaning of the Allotments Act 1922 (ie an allotment not exceeding a quarter of an acre in extent which is wholly or mainly cultivated by the occupier for the production of vegetable or fruit crops for his own or his family's consumption: see the Allotments Act 1922 s 22(1); and AGRICULTURAL LAND AND ALLOTMENTS vol 1 (2017) PARA 649): see the Local Government Finance Act 1988 Sch 5 para 2(1)(d).

12 For these purposes, 'building' includes a separate part of a building: see the Local Government Finance Act 1988 Sch 5 para 8(4).

13 Ie by virtue of the Local Government Finance Act 1988 Sch 5 paras 4–7: see PARAS 118–121.

14 Local Government Finance Act 1988 Sch 5 para 2(1)(e).

15 Local Government Finance Act 1988 Sch 5 para 2(2)(a). 'Park' is not limited to an ancient legal park: *Earl of Devon v Rees (Valuation Officer)* (1951) 44 R & IT 74, Lands Tribunal. See also the following decisions under other statutory provisions: *Huish Overseers v Surveyor of Taxes* (1897) 61 JP 487 (home farm worked by landowner's bailiff not a park); *Pease v Courtney* [1904] 2 Ch 503 (in relation to what is now the Settled Land Act 1925 s 65); *Re Ripon (Highfield) Housing Confirmation Order 1938, White and Collins v Minister of Health* [1939] 2 KB 838, [1939] 3 All ER 548, CA (in relation to the Housing Act 1936 s 75 (repealed)); *R v Bradford* [1908] 1 KB 365, DC (in relation to what is now the Highways Act 1980 s 45). See also PARA 126.

16 Local Government Finance Act 1988 Sch 5 para 2(2)(b).

17 Local Government Finance Act 1988 Sch 5 para 2(2)(c). However, certain pleasure grounds dedicated to the public are exempt: see PARA 126.

18 Local Government Finance Act 1988 Sch 5 para 2(2)(d). In the case of arable, meadow or pasture ground (see head (1) in the text) which is also used for sport or recreation, it is difficult to reconcile that part of the definition of 'agricultural land' with this part of the definition. The Lands Tribunal

has in a number of cases considered whether the agricultural or sporting use was predominant: see *Watkins v Herefordshire Assessment Committee* (1935) 154 LT 262, DC (river with uses for agriculture and fishing held agricultural); *Fenwick v Capstick (Valuation Officer) and Weardale RDC* (1956) 49 R & IT 38, Lands Tribunal (moorland used for grazing and shooting not agricultural); *Waller v Builth RDC* (1954) 47 R & IT 727, Lands Tribunal (land adjoining fishing river held agricultural); *Abernant Hotel and Estate Co Ltd v Davies (Valuation Officer)* (1954) 47 R & IT 694, Lands Tribunal (golf course mown for hay and grazed by animals not agricultural; for a similar decision in Scotland see *Inland Revenue Officer v Assessor for Ross and Cromarty* 1930 SC 404, Ct of Sess); *Clay and Clay v Newbigging (Valuation Officer)* (1956) 1 RRC 13, Lands Tribunal (river with uses for agriculture and fishing held not agricultural); *Cutts (Valuation Officer) v Viscount Ingleby* (1957) 1 RRC 254, Lands Tribunal (moorland used for grazing and shooting held agricultural); *Bloodworth (Valuation Officer) v Marquis of Exeter* (1958) 4 RRC 135, Lands Tribunal (land used for grazing and for golf held agricultural); *Govett's Executors v Wand (Valuation Officer)* (1959) 5 RRC 232, Lands Tribunal (land used for agriculture and for fishing held rateable); *Garnett v Wand (Valuation Officer)* (1960) 7 RRC 99, CA (pasture land kept mainly for the purposes of fishing held not agricultural); *Young (Valuation Officer) v West Dorset District Council* [1977] RA 234, Lands Tribunal (land used for grazing horses in connection with riding stables held agricultural); *Eden (Valuation Officer) v Grass Ski Promotions Ltd* [1981] RA 7 (pasture land used as grass ski slope on 25 occasions a year held agricultural).

19 Local Government Finance Act 1988 Sch 5 para 2(2)(e). 'Race course' has been held to include a course for motor-cycle racing: *Wimborne and Cranborne RDC v East Dorset Assessment Committee* [1940] 2 KB 420, [1940] 3 All ER 201, CA.

118. Buildings occupied together with agricultural land.

For the purposes of the exemption of agricultural buildings from local non-domestic rating[1], a building[2] is an 'agricultural building' if it is not a dwelling[3], and if:

(1) it is occupied together with[4] agricultural land[5] and is used solely[6] in connection with agricultural operations[7] on that or other agricultural land[8]; or

(2) it is or forms part of a market garden[9] and is used solely in connection with[10] agricultural operations[11] at the market garden[12].

A building is also an 'agricultural building' if it is used solely in connection with agricultural operations carried on agricultural land[13] and is occupied either:

(a) by the occupiers[14] of all the land concerned[15]; or

(b) by individuals each of whom is appointed by the occupiers of the land concerned to manage the use of the building[16], and is:

  (i) an occupier of some of the land concerned[17], or

  (ii) a member of the board of directors or other governing body of a person who is both a body corporate[18] and an occupier of the land concerned[19].

1 As to such exemption see PARA 116.

2 For these purposes, 'building' includes a separate part of a building: Local Government Finance Act 1988 Sch 5 para 8(4). 'Building' in this context has been held not to be restricted to enclosures of brick and stonework, and may include structures which would not be considered as buildings under other statutes: see *Shaw v Borrett (Valuation Officer)* [1967] RA 90, Lands Tribunal, where a timber framed poultry house clad with timber and asbestos was held to be an agricultural building.

Some of the cases cited in this paragraph were decided prior to the coming into force of the Local Government Finance Act 1988 but continue to be of relevance: see PARA 50.

3 'Dwelling' has a broader meaning than dwelling house: see *Winterton (Valuation Officer) v Friday Bridge Agricultural Camp Ltd* [1974] RA 309, where seasonal accommodation for fruit pickers was held to be a dwelling, not an agricultural building.

4 As to the occupier and occupation of land see PARA 86 et seq. As to the treatment for the purposes of exemptions under the Local Government Finance Act 1988 Sch 5 of any land or building which is not occupied see PARA 110.

For one building to be 'occupied together with' agricultural land or another building the two must be in the same occupation and the activities must be jointly controlled or managed; there is no conclusive geographical test, but as it is necessary to show that the two are occupied together 'so as to form in a real sense a single agricultural unit' propinquity and distance may give a good indication: *Farmer (Valuation Officer) and Hambleton District Council v Buxted Poultry Ltd* [1993] AC 369, [1993] RA 1, HL. In earlier cases, including one in the House of Lords (*W & JB Eastwood Ltd v Herrod (Valuation Officer)* (1967) 13 RRC 108, [1967] RA 82, Lands Tribunal; on appeal [1971] AC 160, [1970] 1 All ER 774, HL) separation by a distance of a number of miles was not considered fatal to exemption: see eg *Plumpton (Valuation Officer) v Treasures Farms (Ludlow) Ltd* [1965] RA 313, 11 RRC 247; *GC Taylor (Farms) Ltd v Perth and Kinross Assessor* 1962 SC 444; *Hilleshog Sugar Beet Breeding Co Ltd v Wilkes (Valuation Officer)* (1971) 17 RRC 275; *Maurice E Taylor (Merchants) Ltd v Commissioner of Valuation* [1981] NI 236; *Handley (Valuation Officer) v Bernard Matthews plc* [1988] RA 222. These cases must now be read in the light of *Farmer (Valuation Officer) and Hambleton District Council v Buxted Poultry Ltd* above.

The building and land must be in the same occupation: *Perrins v Draper* [1953] 2 All ER 863, [1953] 1 WLR 1178, CA, where dairy buildings were not exempt as the milk was produced on an adjoining farm in separate occupation. See also *Ellerby v March (Valuation Officer)* (1953) 46 R & IT 718, Lands Tribunal (on appeal [1954] 2 QB 357, [1954] 2 All ER 375, CA); *Evans v Day (Valuation Officer)* [1967] RA 266, Lands Tribunal, where a building used for the maintenance of agricultural machinery was not exempt as the machines were used on land in other occupation; *Hall-Mark Hatcheries Ltd v Spencer (Valuation Officer) and Basildon UDC* (1956) 1 RRC 20, where hatchery buildings were not exempt as the eggs were produced on another farm.

5 As to the meaning of 'agricultural land' see PARA 117.

6 In determining for the purposes of the Local Government Finance Act 1988 Sch 5 paras 3–7 whether a building used in any way is solely so used, no account is to be taken of any time during which it is used in any other way, if that time does not amount to a substantial part of the time during which the building is used: Sch 5 para 8(3). As to the treatment for the purposes of exemptions under Sch 5 of any land, building or property which is not in use see PARA 110. The Court of Appeal has held that there is no room to import the *de minimis* concept in deciding whether a use is the sole use: *Hambleton District Council v Buxted Poultry Ltd* [1992] 2 All ER 70, [1991] RA 267, CA (affirmed on a different point sub nom *Farmer (Valuation Officer) and Hambleton District Council v Buxted Poultry Ltd* [1993] AC 369, [1993] RA 1, HL).

See also *Parry v Anglesey Assessment Committee* [1949] 1 KB 246, [1948] 2 All ER 1060, DC (shed housing farmer's car which was used for both farm and domestic purposes held not an agricultural building); *Winterton (Valuation Officer) v Friday Bridge Agricultural Camp Ltd* [1974] RA 309, Lands Tribunal (10% of labour staying in a camp worked in a canning factory; held not to be an agricultural operation or ancillary operation); *Glasgow Assessor v Berridale Allotments and Gardens Association* [1973] RA 236 (use of hut for storing furniture occupied a substantial part of the year; building not exempt); *Home Grown Fruits Ltd v Paul (Valuation Officer)* [1974] RA 329, Lands Tribunal (offices of fruit growers' marketing organisation held not an agricultural building as they were used by other non-members and for imported fruit); *Corser (Valuation Officer) v Gloucester Marketing Society Ltd* [1981] RA 83, CA (auction hall of marketing society used a substantial part of the time by non-members held not exempt).

7 As to which see note 11.

8 Local Government Finance Act 1988 Sch 5 para 3(a) (substituted by the Local Government Act 2003 s 67(1), (2)). The Local Government Finance Act 1988 Sch 5 para 3(a) is worded so as to apply to 'operations on that or other agricultural land' in order to reflect modern farming practices whereby farmers work on other agricultural land, perhaps on a share or contract basis, or through the pooling of resources or machinery.

9 Glasshouses and cucumber frames may be buildings being or forming part of a market garden: *Purser v Worthing Local Board of Health* (1887) 18 QBD 818, CA; *Godber v Bedford Assessment Committee* (1929) 10 R & IT 177; *Jagger v Hayter (Valuation Officer)* (1966) 12 RRC 351, Lands Tribunal. Rooms used for the production of mushroom spawn do not constitute a market garden (*Darlington & Sons (Holdings) Ltd v Langridge (Valuation Officer)* [1973] RA 207), although the growing of mushrooms is an agricultural operation (*J Beveridge & Co Ltd v Perth and Kinross Assessor* [1967] RA 482). As to the meaning of 'market garden' see the relevant cases cited in PARA 117 note 8.

10 In *W & JB Eastwood Ltd v Herrod (Valuation Officer)* (1967) 13 RRC 108, [1967] RA 82, Lands Tribunal (on appeal [1971] AC 160, [1970] 1 All ER 774, HL), intensive poultry farming buildings were held not to be occupied together with agricultural land on which 4% of the poultry's feed was grown because the use of the building was not ancillary to the operations on the land.

11 'Agricultural operations' has been held to mean operations by way of cultivating the soil or rearing livestock: *Gilmore (Valuation Officer) v Baker-Carr* [1962] 3 All ER 230 at 232, [1962] 1 WLR 1165 at 1172, CA, per Lord Denning MR. Pig raising to collect statistical material to assist farmers is an agricultural operation: *National Pig Progeny Testing Board v Greenall (Valuation Officer)* [1960] 3 All ER 556, [1960] 1 WLR 1265, CA; *National Pig Progeny Testing Board v Stirlingshire Assessor* 1959 SC 343. See also *Hallam v James (Valuation Officer)* (1958) 4 RRC 142, Lands Tribunal (mink farming an agricultural operation); *J Beveridge & Co Ltd v Perth and Kinross Assessor* [1967] RA 482 (growing of mushrooms an agricultural operation); cf *Darlington & Sons (Holdings) Ltd v Langridge (Valuation Officer)* [1973] RA 207; *Perth and Kinross Assessor v Scottish Milk Marketing Board* 1963 SLT 109, CA (extraction of semen for artificial insemination not an agricultural operation); *Priestner v Avery (Valuation Officer)* [1964] RA 143, Lands Tribunal. The grazing of thoroughbred racehorses is not an agricultural operation: *Whitsbury Farm and Stud Ltd v Hemens (Valuation Officer)* [1988] AC 601 sub nom *Hemens (Valuation Officer) v Whitsbury Farm and Stud Ltd* [1988] 1 All ER 72, HL. Agricultural operations may also include operations reasonably necessary to make the product marketable or disposable for profit: *W & JB Eastwood v Herrod (Valuation Officer)* [1971] AC 160, [1970] 1 All ER 774, HL; *Midlothian Assessor v Buccleuch Estates Ltd* 1962 SC 453; *Home Grown Fruits Ltd v Paul (Valuation Officer)* [1974] RA 329, Lands Tribunal (marketing operations of a fruit farm syndicate held an agricultural operation); *Hinks & Sons v Ackland (Valuation Officer)* (1951) 44 R & IT 517, Lands Tribunal (buildings and sale ring for auctioning animals fattened on occupier's land held used for agricultural operations); *Thomas (Valuation Officer) v Kenneth Beeston Farms Ltd* (1958) 4 RRC 1 (use of building as loose boxes for stabling hunters held not an activity connected with agricultural operations); *Covell (Valuation Officer) v Streatfield Hood & Co Ltd* [1984] RA 193, [1985] JPL 123, Lands Tribunal (building used for cheese making); *Lowland Cereals Ltd v Lothian Assessor* [1980] RA 85 (use of silos as grain store prior to sale held more of a commercial nature and not part of agricultural operation); *Fletcher v Bartle (Valuation Officer)* [1988] RA 284, Lands Tribunal (shop selling produce of the agricultural land not exempt); *Cartwright (Valuation Officer) v Cherry Valley Farms Ltd* [2003] RA 21, Lands Tribunal (a feather plant that merely prepared duck feathers for marketing and transport was held to be exempt on the basis that its use was ancillary to or consequential on operations in the exempt duck-rearing buildings).

12 Local Government Finance Act 1988 Sch 5 para 3(b).

13 Local Government Finance Act 1988 Sch 5 para 4(1).

14 Local Government Finance Act 1988 Sch 5 para 4 does not apply unless the number of occupiers of the land concerned is less than 25: Sch 5 para 4(4).

15 Local Government Finance Act 1988 Sch 5 para 4(2).

16 Local Government Finance Act 1988 Sch 5 para 4(3).

17 Local Government Finance Act 1988 Sch 5 para 4(3)(a).

18 As to the meaning of 'person' see PARA 11 note 13. As to buildings occupied by bodies corporate see PARA 120.

19 Local Government Finance Act 1988 Sch 5 para 4(3)(b).

119. Livestock buildings.

For the purposes of the exemption of agricultural buildings from local non-domestic rating[1], a building[2] is an 'agricultural building' if:

(1) it is used[3] for the keeping or breeding of livestock[4];

(2) it is not a dwelling[5] and it is occupied[6] together with one or more buildings falling within head (1) and it is used in connection with the operations carried on in that building or those buildings[7].

However:

(a) head (1) does not apply unless either the building is solely used[8] as mentioned in head (1)[9]; or it is occupied together with agricultural land[10] and used also in connection with agricultural operations[11] on that land, and that other use together with the use mentioned in head (1) is its sole use[12];

(b) head (2) does not apply unless either the building is solely used as mentioned in head (2)[13]; or it is occupied also together with agricultural land and used also in connection with agricultural operations on that land, and that other use together with the use mentioned in head (2) is its sole use[14];

(c) a building is not an agricultural building unless it is surrounded by or contiguous to an area of agricultural land which amounts to not less than two hectares[15]; and in determining for this purpose whether an area is agricultural land and what is its size, there must be disregarded:
   (i) any road, watercourse or railway[16];
   (ii) any agricultural building[17] other than the building in question[18]; and
   (iii) any building occupied together with the building in question[19].

1 As to such exemption see PARA 116.

2 For these purposes, 'building' includes a separate part of a building: Local Government Finance Act 1988 Sch 5 para 8(4).

3 As to the treatment for the purposes of exemptions under the Local Government Finance Act 1988 Sch 5 of any land, building or property which is not in use see PARA 110.

4 Local Government Finance Act 1988 Sch 5 para 5(1)(a). 'Livestock' includes any mammal or bird kept for the production of food or wool or for the purpose of its use in the farming of land: see Sch 5 para 8(5). Pigs used in experiments, not kept for the production of food and so not livestock, are not within this meaning: *Meat and Livestock Commission v Stirlingshire Assessor* [1975] RA 234. Pig raising may, however, be an agricultural operation: see PARA 118. Horses at a stud farm do not come within the definition: *Whitsbury Farm and Stud Ltd v Hemens (Valuation Officer)* [1988] AC 601, sub nom *Hemens (Valuation Officer) v Whitsbury Farm and Stud Ltd* [1988] 1 All ER 72, HL. See also, as to the meaning of livestock, *Cresswell (Valuation Officer) v British Oxygen Co Ltd* [1980] 3 All ER 443, [1980] 1 WLR 1556, CA (fish not livestock; but as to the exemption of fish farms see PARA 122); *Gunter (Valuation Officer) v Newton Oyster Fishery Co Ltd* (1977) 20 RRC 313, Lands Tribunal (oysters not livestock; but as to the exemption of fish farms see PARA 122); *Jones (Valuation Officer) v Davies* (1977) 21 RRC 40, Lands Tribunal (mink not livestock); *Cook (Valuation Officer) v Ross Poultry Ltd* [1982] RA 187, Lands Tribunal (pheasant and partridge not livestock).

Some of the cases cited in this paragraph were decided prior to the coming into force of the Local Government Finance Act 1988 but continue to be of relevance: see PARA 50.

5 As to the meaning of 'dwelling' see PARA 118 note 3.

6 As to the occupier and occupation of land see PARA 86 et seq. As to the treatment for the purposes of exemptions under the Local Government Finance Act 1988 Sch 5 of any land or building which is not occupied see PARA 110.

7 Local Government Finance Act 1988 Sch 5 para 5(1)(b). See *Ayrshire Assessor v Macster Poultry Ltd* [1977] RA 189 (where an egg packing station used solely in connection with the activities of laying houses was held exempt); *Womersley (Valuation Officer) v Jisco Ltd* [1990] RA 211, Lands Tribunal (where an abattoir was held exempt). See also the cases cited in PARA 94 note 4.

8 As to sole use see PARA 118 note 6.

9 Local Government Finance Act 1988 Sch 5 para 5(2)(a).

10 As to the meaning of 'agricultural land' see PARA 117.

11 As to the meaning of 'agricultural operations' see PARA 118 note 11.

12 Local Government Finance Act 1988 Sch 5 para 5(2)(b).

13 Local Government Finance Act 1988 Sch 5 para 5(3)(a).

14 Local Government Finance Act 1988 Sch 5 para 5(3)(b).

15 Local Government Finance Act 1988 Sch 5 para 5(4). See eg *Lothian Regional Assessor v Hood* 1988 SLT 161, [1987] RVR 132, Lands Tribunal; *Sovereign Chicken Ltd v Stebbing (Valuation Officer)* [1988] RVR 223, Lands Tribunal. However, a building which is ancillary to a livestock building exempt under the Local Government Finance Act 1988 Sch 5 para 5(1)(a) may itself be exempt under Sch 5 para 7(2), (4), (8) without itself meeting the two hectare requirement: see PARA 120.

16 Local Government Finance Act 1988 Sch 5 para 5(5)(a). The reference to railway includes the former site of a railway from which railway lines have been removed: see Sch 5 para 5(5)(a).

17 As to the meaning of 'agricultural building' see PARA 116 note 5.

18 Local Government Finance Act 1988 Sch 5 para 5(5)(b).
19 Local Government Finance Act 1988 Sch 5 para 5(5)(c).

120. Buildings occupied by bodies corporate.

For the purposes of the exemption of agricultural buildings from local non-domestic rating[1], a building[2] is an 'agricultural building' if it is not a dwelling[3], and if:

(1) it is used[4] in connection with agricultural operations[5] carried on agricultural land[6];
(2) it is occupied[7] by a body corporate[8] any of whose members are (or are together with the body) the occupiers of the land[9]; and
(3) the members who are occupiers of the land together have control of the body[10].

A building is also an 'agricultural building' for these purposes if it is not a dwelling, and:

(a) it is used in connection with the operations carried on in a building which (or buildings each of which) is used for the keeping or breeding of livestock[11], and is[12] an agricultural building[13]; and
(b) the building in question[14]:
  (i) is occupied by a body corporate any of whose members are (or are together with the body) the occupiers of the building or buildings mentioned in head (a)[15], and the members who are occupiers of the land together have control of the body[16]; or
  (ii) is occupied by the same persons[17] as the building or buildings mentioned in head (a)[18]; or
  (iii) is occupied by individuals each of whom is appointed by the occupiers of the building or buildings mentioned in head (a) to manage the use of the building in question[19], and each of whom is either an occupier of part of the building (or of part of one of the buildings) mentioned in head (a)[20], or is a member of the board of directors or other governing body of a person who is both a body corporate and an occupier of the building or buildings mentioned in head (a)[21].

A building does not qualify for either set of exemption conditions set out above[22] unless the use mentioned in either of those conditions (or that use together with the use mentioned in the other of those conditions) is its sole use[23].

1 As to such exemption see PARA 116.
2 In the Local Government Finance Act 1988 Sch 5 para 7, 'building' includes a separate part of a building: see s 51, Sch 5 para 8(4).
3 As to the meaning of 'dwelling' see PARA 118 note 3.
4 As to the treatment for the purposes of exemptions under the Local Government Finance Act 1988 Sch 5 of any land, building or property which is not in use see PARA 110.
5 As to the meaning of 'agricultural operations' see PARA 118 note 11. See also *Courtman (Valuation Officer) v West Devon and North Cornwall Farmers Ltd* [1990] RA 17, [1990] 2 EGLR 213, Lands Tribunal.
Some of the cases cited in this paragraph were decided prior to the coming into force of the Local Government Finance Act 1988 but continue to be of relevance: see PARA 50.
6 Local Government Finance Act 1988 Sch 5 para 7(1)(a). As to the meaning of 'agricultural land' see PARA 117.
7 As to the occupier and occupation of land see PARA 86 et seq. As to the treatment for the purposes of exemptions under the Local Government Finance Act 1988 Sch 5 of any land or building which is not occupied see PARA 110.
8 As to bodies corporate see COMPANIES vol 14 (2016) PARA 2; CORPORATIONS vol 24 (2010) PARA 301 et seq.

9 Local Government Finance Act 1988 Sch 5 para 7(1)(b) (amended by the Local Government and Housing Act 1989 s 139, Sch 5 paras 37(2), 79(3)). See *Re Pyrke (Valuation Officer)* [2003] RA 318, Lands Tribunal (warehouse was occupied by a body corporate but none of the member co-operatives of that body corporate occupied any of the agricultural land; it was the members of the co-operatives that did).

10 Local Government Finance Act 1988 Sch 5 para 7(1)(c) (added by the Local Government Act 2003 s 67(1), (3)). In the Local Government Finance Act 1988 Sch 5 para 7, 'control' must be construed in accordance with the Corporation Tax Act 2010 ss 450, 451 (see INCOME TAXATION vol 59 (2014) PARA 1813): Local Government Finance Act 1988 Sch 5 para 7(9) (added by the Local Government Act 2003 s 67(1), (5); and amended by the Corporation Tax Act 2010 s 1177, Sch 1 Pt 2 paras 206, 210). The amendments made to the Local Government Finance Act 1988 Sch 5 para 7(1)(c) by the Local Government Act 2003 s 67 accommodate premises used for ancillary activities such as food processing and packaging and ensure that the exemption will only apply to such premises where the company is controlled by occupiers of related agricultural land. Previously, the exemption applied provided that the occupier of the premises was a company and any of the members of that company was an occupier of related agricultural land.

11 As to the meaning of 'livestock' see PARA 119 note 4.

12 Ie by virtue of the Local Government Finance Act 1988 Sch 5 para 5: see PARA 119.

13 Local Government Finance Act 1988 Sch 5 para 7(2)(a).

14 See the Local Government Finance Act 1988 Sch 5 para 7(2)(b). As to the nature of occupancy arrangements in relation to such a building that qualified for the exemption as it was set out in earlier legislation see *Prior (Valuation Officer) v Sovereign Chicken Ltd* [1984] 2 All ER 289, [1984] 1 WLR 921, CA; and *Farmer (Valuation Officer) v Hambleton District Council* [1999] RA 61, [1999] EGCS 5, CA (both cases considering the Rating Act 1971 s 4(2)(b)).

15 Local Government Finance Act 1988 Sch 5 para 7(3)(a) (Sch 5 para 7(3) substituted by the Local Government Act 2003 s 67(1), (4)).

16 Local Government Finance Act 1988 Sch 5 para 7(3)(b) (as substituted: see note 15).

17 As to the meaning of 'person' see PARA 11 note 13.

18 Local Government Finance Act 1988 Sch 5 para 7(4). This head does not apply unless the number of occupiers of the building or buildings mentioned in Sch 5 para 7(2)(a) (see head (a) in the text) is less than 25: see Sch 5 para 7(8).

19 Local Government Finance Act 1988 Sch 5 para 7(5). This head does not apply unless the number of occupiers of the building or buildings mentioned in Sch 5 para 7(2)(a) (see head (a) in the text) is less than 25: see Sch 5 para 7(8).

20 Local Government Finance Act 1988 Sch 5 para 7(5)(a).

21 Local Government Finance Act 1988 Sch 5 para 7(5)(b).

22 Ie the conditions set out either in the Local Government Finance Act 1988 Sch 5 para 7(1) (see the text to notes 1–10) or in Sch 5 para 7(2) (see the text to notes 11–14).

23 See the Local Government Finance Act 1988 Sch 5 para 7(6), (7). As to sole use see PARA 118 note 6.

121. Buildings occupied in connection with bee-keeping.

For the purposes of the exemption of agricultural buildings from local non-domestic rating[1], a building[2] is an 'agricultural building' if it is not a dwelling[3], if it is occupied[4] by a person[5] keeping bees, if it is used solely[6] in connection with the keeping of those bees[7], and if it is surrounded by or contiguous to an area of agricultural land[8] which amounts to not less than two hectares[9]. In deciding for these purposes whether an area is agricultural land and what is its size, the following are to be disregarded, namely:

(1) any road, watercourse or railway[10];
(2) any agricultural building[11] other than the building in question[12];
(3) any building occupied together with the building in question[13].

1 As to such exemption see PARA 116.

2 In the Local Government Finance Act 1988 Sch 5 para 6, 'building' includes a separate part of a building: see s 51, Sch 5 para 8(4).

3 As to the meaning of 'dwelling' see PARA 118 note 3.

4 As to the occupier and occupation of land see PARA 86 et seq. As to the treatment for the purposes of exemptions under the Local Government Finance Act 1988 Sch 5 of any land or building which is not occupied see PARA 110.

5 As to the meaning of 'person' see PARA 11 note 13.
6 As to sole use see PARA 118 note 6. As to the treatment for the purposes of exemptions under the Local Government Finance Act 1988 Sch 5 of any land, building or property which is not in use see PARA 110.
7 Local Government Finance Act 1988 Sch 5 para 6(1).
8 As to the meaning of 'agricultural land' see PARA 117.
9 See the Local Government Finance Act 1988 Sch 5 para 5(4) (applied by Sch 5 para 6(2)).
10 See the Local Government Finance Act 1988 Sch 5 para 5(5)(a) (applied by Sch 5 para 6(2)). The reference to railway includes the former site of a railway from which railway lines have been removed: see Sch 5 para 5(5)(a) (as so applied).
11 As to the meaning of 'agricultural building' see PARA 116 note 5.
12 See the Local Government Finance Act 1988 Sch 5 para 5(5)(b) (applied by Sch 5 para 6(2)).
13 See the Local Government Finance Act 1988 Sch 5 para 5(5)(c) (applied by Sch 5 para 6(2)).

122. Fish farms.

A hereditament[1] is exempt from local non-domestic rating[2] to the extent that it consists of land or buildings[3] (other than dwellings[4]) used[5] solely for or in connection with fish farming[6].

In determining whether land or a building used for or in connection with fish farming is solely so used, no account is to be taken of any time during which it is used in any other way, if that time does not amount to a substantial part of the time during which the land or building is used[7].

1 As to the meaning of 'hereditament' see PARA 106.
2 Ie for the purposes of the Local Government Finance Act 1988 Pt III (ss 41–67): see s 51, Sch 5 para 21(2). A hereditament that is completely exempt under Sch 5 para 9 is not to be entered into a rating list: see s 42(1); and PARA 194.
3 'Building' includes a separate part of a building: Local Government Finance Act 1988 Sch 5 para 9(3).
4 As to the meaning of 'dwelling' see PARA 118 note 3.
5 As to the treatment for the purposes of exemptions under the Local Government Finance Act 1988 Sch 5 of any land, building or property which is not in use see PARA 110.
6 Local Government Finance Act 1988 Sch 5 para 9(1). 'Fish farming' means the breeding or rearing of fish or the cultivation of shellfish (including crustaceans and molluscs of any description) for the purpose of (or for purposes which include) transferring them to other waters or producing food for human consumption: see Sch 5 para 9(4), (5). However, an activity does not constitute fish farming if the fish or shellfish are or include fish or shellfish which are purely ornamental, or which are bred, reared or cultivated for exhibition: Sch 5 para 9(4A) (added by the Local Government and Housing Act 1989 s 139, Sch 5 paras 37(3), 79(3)).
7 Local Government Finance Act 1988 Sch 5 para 9(2). In this connection see also the cases cited in PARA 118 note 6.

(v) Sewers and Watercourses

123. Sewers.

A hereditament[1] is exempt from local non-domestic rating[2] to the extent that it consists of a sewer[3] or an accessory[4] belonging to a sewer[5].

Sewage disposal works are, however, rateable[6].

1 As to the meaning of 'hereditament' see PARA 106.
2 Ie for the purposes of the Local Government Finance Act 1988 Pt III (ss 41–67): see s 51, Sch 5 para 21(2). A hereditament that is completely exempt under Sch 5 para 13 is not to be entered into a rating list: see s 42(1); and PARA 194.
3 Local Government Finance Act 1988 Sch 5 para 13(1)(a). 'Sewer' has the meaning given by the Public Health Act 1936 s 343 (see ENVIRONMENTAL QUALITY AND PUBLIC HEALTH vol 46 (2010) PARA 998): Local Government Finance Act 1988 Sch 5 para 13(2).

4 'Accessory' means a manhole, ventilating shaft, pumping station, pump or other accessory: Local Government Finance Act 1988 Sch 5 para 13(3). It has been held that 'accessory' should be given its ordinary meaning and not one *eiusdem generis* with the preceding words: *Jones (Valuation Officer) v Eastern Valleys (Monmouthshire) Joint Sewerage Board (No 2)* (1960) 6 RRC 387, Lands Tribunal (storm water tanks for sewer exempt); *Gudgion (Valuation Officer) v Erith Borough Council and LCC* (1961) 8 RRC 324, [1961] RVR 492, CA (screen and pumps to assist flow through sewer exempt); cf *Hoggett (Valuation Officer) v Cheltenham Corpn* [1964] RA 1, Lands Tribunal (screens, a detritor and storm water tanks held to be preparatory to sewage treatment and not accessories). See also *Northumberland Water Authority v Little (Valuation Officer)* [1986] RA 61, [1986] JPL 612, Lands Tribunal.

The cases cited in this paragraph were decided prior to the coming into force of the Local Government Finance Act 1988 but continue to be of relevance: see PARA 50.

5 Local Government Finance Act 1988 Sch 5 para 13(1). The Secretary of State or, in relation to Wales, the Welsh Ministers may by order repeal Sch 5 para 13(1)–(3): Sch 5 para 13(4). At the date at which this volume states the law no such order had been made. The functions of the Secretary of State under Sch 5, so far as exercisable in relation to Wales, were transferred to the National Assembly for Wales (see the National Assembly for Wales (Transfer of Functions) Order 1999, SI 1999/672, art 2, Sch 1) and are now vested in the Welsh Ministers (see the Government of Wales Act 2006 s 162(1), Sch 11 para 30). As to the Secretary of State and the Welsh Ministers see PARA 4 note 18. As to the meaning of 'Wales' see PARA 2 note 16. As to the separate administration of the non-domestic rating provisions (Local Government Finance Act 1988 Pt III (ss 41–67)) in England and Wales see PARA 52.

6 See PARA 186. A sewer, on the other hand, may continue to be exempt even within the curtilage of a sewage disposal works: *Gudgion (Valuation Officer) v Erith Borough Council and LCC* (1961) 8 RRC 324, [1961] RVR 492, CA. Cf *Leicester Corpn v Churchwardens of Beaumont Leys and Barrow-on-Soar Union Assessment Committee* (1894) 63 LJMC 176; *Hoggett (Valuation Officer) v Cheltenham Corpn* [1964] RA 1, Lands Tribunal. As to the plant and machinery rateable at a sewage disposal works see *Jones (Valuation Officer) v Eastern Valleys (Monmouthshire) Joint Sewerage Board* (1960) 6 RRC 379, Lands Tribunal (see also PARA 173 note 23).

124. Property of drainage authorities.

A hereditament[1] is exempt from local non-domestic rating[2] to the extent that it consists of any of the following, namely:

(1) land which is occupied[3] by a drainage authority[4] and forms part of a main river[5] or of a watercourse[6] maintained[7] by the authority[8];

(2) a structure[9] maintained by a drainage authority, for the purpose of controlling or regulating the flow of water in, into or out of a watercourse which forms part of a main river or is maintained by the authority[10];

(3) an appliance so maintained for the purpose mentioned in head (2)[11].

1 As to the meaning of 'hereditament' see PARA 106.

2 Ie for the purposes of the Local Government Finance Act 1988 Pt III (ss 41–67): see s 51, Sch 5 para 21(2). A hereditament that is completely exempt under Sch 5 para 14 is not to be entered into a rating list: see s 42(1); and PARA 194.

3 As to the occupier and occupation of land see PARA 86 et seq. As to the treatment for the purposes of exemptions under the Local Government Finance Act 1988 Sch 5 of any land or building which is not occupied see PARA 110.

4 'Drainage authority' means the Environment Agency, the Natural Resources Body for Wales or any internal drainage board: Local Government Finance Act 1988 Sch 5 para 14(2) (substituted by the Water Consolidation (Consequential Provisions) Act 1991 s 2, Sch 1 para 49(b); and amended by SI 2013/755). As to the Environment Agency see ENVIRONMENTAL QUALITY AND PUBLIC HEALTH vol 45 (2010) PARA 68 et seq. As to the Natural Resources Body for Wales see ENVIRONMENTAL QUALITY AND PUBLIC HEALTH vol 45 (2010) PARA 1 et seq. As to internal drainage boards see WATER AND WATERWAYS vol 101 (2009) PARA 569 et seq.

5 'Main river' has the same meaning as in the Water Resources Act 1991 (see WATER AND WATERWAYS vol 101 (2009) PARA 574): Local Government Finance Act 1988 Sch 5 para 14(2) (as substituted: see note 4).

6 'Watercourse' has the same meaning as in the Land Drainage Act 1991 (see WATER AND WATERWAYS vol 101 (2009) PARA 573): Local Government Finance Act 1988 Sch 5 para 14(2) (as substituted: see note 4).
7 As to powers of maintenance of watercourses see WATER AND WATERWAYS vol 101 (2009) PARA 589 et seq.
8 Local Government Finance Act 1988 Sch 5 para 14(1)(a).
9 The meaning of 'structure' was considered in *Jewish Blind Society Trustees v Henning (Valuation Officer)* [1961] 1 All ER 47, [1961] 1 WLR 24, CA. See also *Hobday v Nicol* [1944] 1 All ER 302, DC; *Mills and Rockleys Ltd v Leicester Corpn* [1946] KB 315 at 319, [1946] 1 All ER 424 at 427, DC, per Lord Goddard LCJ; and *Cardiff Rating Authority and Cardiff Assessment Committee v Guest Keen Baldwin's Iron and Steel Co Ltd* [1949] 1 KB 385 at 396, [1949] 1 All ER 27 at 31, CA, per Denning LJ.
These cases were decided prior to the coming into force of the Local Government Finance Act 1988 but continue to be of relevance: see PARA 50.
10 Local Government Finance Act 1988 Sch 5 para 14(1)(b). As to the treatment for the purposes of exemptions under Sch 5 of any land, building or property which is not in use see PARA 110.
11 Local Government Finance Act 1988 Sch 5 para 14(1)(c).

(vi) Miscellaneous Exemptions

125. Property used for the disabled.

A hereditament[1] is exempt from local non-domestic rating[2] to the extent that it consists of property used[3] wholly for any of the following purposes:

(1) the provision of facilities for training, or keeping suitably occupied[4], persons who are disabled[5] or who are or have been suffering from illness[6];
(2) the provision of welfare services for disabled persons[7];
(3) the provision of certain facilities for disabled persons[8];
(4) the provision of a workshop or of certain other facilities[9].

1 As to the meaning of 'hereditament' see PARA 106.
2 Ie for the purposes of the Local Government Finance Act 1988 Pt III (ss 41–67): see s 51, Sch 5 para 21(2). A hereditament that is completely exempt under Sch 5 para 16 is not to be entered into a rating list: see s 42(1); and PARA 194.
3 As to the treatment for the purposes of exemptions under the Local Government Finance Act 1988 Sch 5 of any land, building or property which is not in use see PARA 110.
4 As to the occupier and occupation of land see PARA 86 et seq. As to the treatment for the purposes of exemptions under the Local Government Finance Act 1988 Sch 5 of any land or building which is not occupied see PARA 110.
The phrase 'suitably occupied' is to be understood from the context of its juxtaposition to 'training': *Chilcott (Valuation Officer) v Day* [1995] RA 285, Lands Tribunal; *O'Kelly v Davey (Valuation Officer)* [1996] RA 238, Lands Tribunal. See also *Halliday (Valuation Officer) v Priory Hospital Group of the Nottingham Clinic* [2001] RA 355, Lands Tribunal ('training' refers to the instruction of a person for some particular occupation or practice that is suitable to his condition and does not extend to group therapy, counselling and other procedures that are aimed at helping that person to address and cope with his illness). Occupation, however suitable, which is for the purpose of reward is not contemplated by the Local Government Finance Act 1988 Sch 5 para 16: see *O'Kelly v Davey (Valuation Officer)*. See also *Evans (Valuation Officer) v Suffolk County Council* [1997] RA 120, Lands Tribunal.
5 For the purposes of the Local Government Finance Act 1988 Sch 5 para 16 in its application to hereditaments in England, a person is disabled if he has a disability within the meaning given by the Equality Act 2010 s 6 (see DISCRIMINATION vol 33 (2017) PARA 47): Local Government Finance Act 1988 Sch 5 para 16(1A) (added by SI 2015/914). For the purposes of the Local Government Finance Act 1988 Sch 5 para 16 in its application to hereditaments in Wales, a person is disabled if he is disabled within the meaning of the Social Services and Well-being (Wales) Act 2014 s 3: Local Government Finance Act 1988 Sch 5 para 16(2) (substituted by SI 2016/413).

'Illness' has the meaning given by the National Health Service Act 2006 s 275 (see HEALTH SERVICES vol 54 (2017) PARA): Local Government Finance Act 1988 Sch 5 para 16(3) (amended by the National Health Service (Consequential Provisions) Act 2006 s 2, Sch 1 paras 109, 110).

6 Local Government Finance Act 1988 Sch 5 para 16(1)(a).

7 Local Government Finance Act 1988 Sch 5 para 16(1)(b). 'Welfare services for disabled persons' means services or facilities (by whomsoever provided):

(1) of a kind which a local authority in England had power to provide under the National Assistance Act 1948 s 29 (see SOCIAL SERVICES vol 95 (2017) PARA 329) before it ceased to apply to local authorities in England (Local Government Finance Act 1988 Sch 5 para 16(4)(a) (Sch 5 para 16(4) substituted by SI 2016/413));

(2) of a kind which a local authority in Wales has power to provide, or arrange to provide, to an adult in the exercise of its functions under the Social Services and Well-being (Wales) Act 2014 s 35 or s 36 (Local Government Finance Act 1988 Sch 5 para 16(4)(b) (as so substituted)).

The National Assistance Act 1948 s 29 did not empower authorities to provide residential accommodation: see *Jewish Blind Society Trustees v Henning (Valuation Officer)* [1961] 1 All ER 47, [1961] 1 WLR 24, CA; and *Vandyk v Oliver (Valuation Officer)* [1976] AC 659, [1976] 1 All ER 466, HL. See also *Evans (Valuation Officer) v Suffolk County Council* [1997] RA 120, Lands Tribunal. It has been held that part of a hereditament used by a community drugs advisory service and run by the health care trust was not exempt under head (2) in the text on grounds that the assessment process (because it was a form of diagnosis) and the counselling programme (because it constituted treatment of illness) went beyond the welfare services that were envisaged by the relevant statutory definition used for these purposes: see *Reid (Valuation Officer) v Barking, Havering and Brentwood Community Health Care Trust* [1997] RA 385, Lands Tribunal.

8 Local Government Finance Act 1988 Sch 5 para 16(1)(c). The facilities referred to are those provided under the Disabled Persons (Employment) Act 1944 s 15 (see EMPLOYMENT vol 40 (2014) PARA 610): see the Local Government Finance Act 1988 Sch 5 para 16(1)(c). Facilities for disabled persons provided under any other enactment are outside this exemption: see *Davey (Valuation Officer) v O'Kelly* [1999] RA 245, Lands Tribunal. Where a hereditament is adapted for wheelchair use so that the hereditament can be used by a disabled person as his business workshop, it cannot be said that the hereditament is used wholly for the provision of that wheelchair: see *Davey (Valuation Officer) v O'Kelly* above.

9 Local Government Finance Act 1988 Sch 5 para 16(1)(d). The facilities referred to are those provided under the Disabled Persons (Employment) Act 1958 s 3(1) (see EMPLOYMENT vol 40 (2014) PARA 611): see the Local Government Finance Act 1988 Sch 5 para 16(1)(d).

126. Parks.

A hereditament[1] is exempt from local non-domestic rating[2] to the extent that it consists of a park[3] which:

(1) has been provided by, or is under the management of, a relevant authority[4] (or two or more relevant authorities in combination)[5]; and

(2) is available for free and unrestricted use by members of the public[6].

1 As to the meaning of 'hereditament' see PARA 106.

2 Ie for the purposes of the Local Government Finance Act 1988 Pt III (ss 41–67): see s 51, Sch 5 para 21(2). A hereditament that is completely exempt under Sch 5 para 15 is not to be entered into a rating list: see s 42(1); and PARA 194.

3 Reference to a 'park' includes a reference to a recreation or pleasure ground, a public walk, an open space within the meaning of the Open Spaces Act 1906 (see OPEN SPACES AND COUNTRYSIDE vol 78 (2010) PARA 560 et seq), and a playing field provided under the Physical Training and Recreation Act 1937 (see EDUCATION vol 35 (2015) PARA 502): Local Government Finance Act 1988 Sch 5 para 15(2). See also PARA 94 and the cases cited there which are relevant to the question as to what constitutes a 'park'.

A swimming pool provided by a local authority has been held not to be a park: *Smith (Valuation Officer) v St Albans City and District Council* [1978] RA 147, 21 RRC 22. See also *Oxford City Council v Broadway (Valuation Officer)* [1999] RA 169, Lands Tribunal (open-air swimming pools within a park exempt from rating because they were used simply to enhance the park as a park and had not acquired a distinct and separate status). For examples of cases discussing whether land or buildings are part of a park see *Lancashire County Council v Lord (Valuation Officer)* [1987] RA 153, Lands Tribunal (information centre and ranger's house serving country park 570 yards away); *Whitby (Valuation Officer) v Cole* [1987] RA 161, Lands Tribunal (miniature railway rateable).

Some of the cases cited in this paragraph were decided prior to the coming into force of the Local Government Finance Act 1988 but continue to be of relevance: see PARA 50.

4 Each of the following is a 'relevant authority' for these purposes:
(1) a Minister of the Crown or government department or any officer or body exercising functions on behalf of the Crown (Local Government Finance Act 1988 Sch 5 para 15(3)(aa) (added by the Local Government and Rating Act 1997 s 33(1), Sch 3 para 27));
(2) a county council (Local Government Finance Act 1988 Sch 5 para 15(3)(a));
(3) a county borough council (Sch 5 para 15(3)(aa) (added by SI 1996/3071));
(4) a district council (Local Government Finance Act 1988 Sch 5 para 15(3)(b));
(5) a London borough council (Sch 5 para 15(3)(c));
(6) the Common Council of the City of London (Sch 5 para 15(3)(d));
(7) the Council of the Isles of Scilly (Sch 5 para 15(3)(e));
(8) a parish or community council (Sch 5 para 15(3)(f)); and
(9) the chairman of a parish meeting (Sch 5 para 15(3)(g)).

As to Ministers of the Crown see CONSTITUTIONAL AND ADMINISTRATIVE LAW vol 20 (2014) PARA 151. As to local government areas and authorities in England and Wales see LOCAL GOVERNMENT vol 69 (2018) PARA 36 et seq. As to London boroughs and their councils see LONDON GOVERNMENT vol 71 (2013) PARAS 15, 20–22, 55 et seq. As to the Common Council of the City of London see LONDON GOVERNMENT vol 71 (2013) PARA 34 et seq. As to the Council of the Isles of Scilly see LOCAL GOVERNMENT vol 69 (2018) PARA 50. As to parish councils see LOCAL GOVERNMENT vol 69 (2018) PARA 41 et seq. As to community councils see LOCAL GOVERNMENT vol 69 (2018) PARA 63 et seq. As to parish meetings see LOCAL GOVERNMENT vol 69 (2018) PARA 48. As to the separate administration of the non-domestic rating provisions (Local Government Finance Act 1988 Pt III (ss 41–67)) in England and Wales see PARA 52.

5 Local Government Finance Act 1988 Sch 5 para 15(1)(a).

6 Local Government Finance Act 1988 Sch 5 para 15(1)(b). In construing this provision any temporary closure (at night or otherwise) is to be ignored: Sch 5 para 15(4). As to the tests to be applied for the purposes of head (2) in the text see *Manchester City Council v Fogg (Valuation Officer)* [1990] RA 181 at 191, [1991] 2 EGLR 221 at 224, Lands Tribunal; and *Galgate Cricket Club v Doyle (Valuation Officer)* [2001] RA 21, Lands Tribunal (cricket clubhouse situated on recreation ground not exempt). See also *North Riding of Yorkshire County Valuation Committee v Redcar Corpn* [1943] 1 KB 114, [1942] 2 All ER 589, DC; *Sheffield Corpn v Tranter (Valuation Officer)* [1957] 2 All ER 583, [1957] 1 WLR 843; *Burnell v Downham Market UDC* [1952] 2 QB 55, [1952] 1 All ER 601, CA (clubs paying to use field for organised matches and to charge admission for about 40 hours a year not an infringement of free and unrestricted use by the public); *Hampshire County Council v Broadway (Valuation Officer)* [1982] RA 309, [1983] JPL 122 (charges for car park did not restrict free use of a country park); *South Yorkshire County Council v Jones (Valuation Officer)* [1984] RA 204, [1985] JPL 124, Lands Tribunal; *Max Pullan Management Committee v Simpson (Valuation Officer)* [1989] RVR 128, Lands Tribunal.

127. Air-raid protection works.

A hereditament[1] is exempt from local non-domestic rating[2] to the extent that it consists of property which:
(1) is intended to be occupied[3] or used[4] solely for the purpose of affording protection in the event of hostile attack from the air[5]; and
(2) is not occupied or used for any other purpose[6].

1 As to the meaning of 'hereditament' see PARA 106.

2 Ie for the purposes of the Local Government Finance Act 1988 Pt III (ss 41–67): see s 51, Sch 5 para 21(2). A hereditament that is completely exempt under Sch 5 para 17 is not to be entered into a rating list: see s 42(1); and PARA 194.

3 As to the occupier and occupation of land see PARA 86 et seq. As to the treatment for the purposes of exemptions under the Local Government Finance Act 1988 Sch 5 of any land or building which is not occupied see PARA 110.

4 As to the treatment for the purposes of exemptions under the Local Government Finance Act 1988 Sch 5 of any land, building or property which is not in use see PARA 110.
5 Local Government Finance Act 1988 Sch 5 para 17(a).
6 Local Government Finance Act 1988 Sch 5 para 17(b).

128. Certain property of Trinity House.

A hereditament[1] is exempt from local non-domestic rating[2] to the extent that it belongs to or is occupied[3] by Trinity House[4] and consists of any of the following, namely:

(1) a lighthouse[5];
(2) a buoy[6];
(3) a beacon[7];
(4) a property within the same curtilage as, and occupied for the purposes of, a lighthouse[8].

No other hereditament (or part of a hereditament) belonging to or occupied by Trinity House is exempt, notwithstanding any exemptions provided for under the Merchant Shipping Act 1995[9].

1 As to the meaning of 'hereditament' see PARA 106.
2 Ie for the purposes of the Local Government Finance Act 1988 Pt III (ss 41–67): see s 51, Sch 5 para 21(2). A hereditament that is completely exempt under Sch 5 para 12 is not to be entered into a rating list: see s 42(1); and PARA 194.
3 As to the occupier and occupation of land see PARA 86 et seq. As to the treatment for the purposes of exemptions under the Local Government Finance Act 1988 Sch 5 of any land or building which is not occupied see PARA 110.
4 As to the Corporation of Trinity House of Deptford Strond see SHIPPING AND MARITIME LAW vol 94 (2017) PARA 1018.
5 Local Government Finance Act 1988 Sch 5 para 12(1)(a). See also PARA 102, where lighthouse tolls are discussed, although their relevance is now largely historical.
6 Local Government Finance Act 1988 Sch 5 para 12(1)(b).
7 Local Government Finance Act 1988 Sch 5 para 12(1)(c).
8 Local Government Finance Act 1988 Sch 5 para 12(1)(d).
9 Local Government Finance Act 1988 Sch 5 para 12(2) (amended by the Merchant Shipping Act 1995 s 314(2), Sch 13 para 83). For these purposes, the relevant provision of the Merchant Shipping Act 1995 is s 221(1) (exemption from public or local taxes, duties or rates: see SHIPPING AND MARITIME LAW vol 94 (2017) PARA 1046): see the Local Government Finance Act 1988 Sch 5 para 12(2) (as so amended).

129. Swinging moorings.

A hereditament[1] is exempt from local non-domestic rating[2] to the extent that it consists of a mooring which is used[3] or intended to be used by a boat or ship and which is equipped only with a buoy attached to an anchor, weight or other device, which:

(1) rests on the bed of the sea or any river or other waters when in use[4]; and
(2) is designed to be raised from that bed from time to time[5].

1 As to the meaning of 'hereditament' see PARA 106.
2 Ie for the purposes of the Local Government Finance Act 1988 Pt III (ss 41–67): see s 51, Sch 5 para 21(2). A hereditament that is completely exempt under Sch 5 para 18 is not to be entered into a rating list: see s 42(1); and PARA 194. As to the rateability of moorings and of floating vessels secured to moorings see also PARA 101.
3 As to the treatment for the purposes of exemptions under the Local Government Finance Act 1988 Sch 5 of any land, building or property which is not in use see PARA 110.
4 Local Government Finance Act 1988 Sch 5 para 18(a).
5 Local Government Finance Act 1988 Sch 5 para 18(b).

130. Roads crossing watercourses.

A hereditament[1] which is occupied[2] is exempt from local non-domestic rating[3] to the extent that it consists of (or any of the appurtenances of) a fixed road crossing over an estuary, river or other watercourse[4].

For these purposes, a 'fixed road crossing' means a bridge[5], viaduct, tunnel or other construction providing a means for road vehicles or pedestrians or both to cross the estuary, river or other watercourse concerned[6]; and the reference to the 'appurtenances' of a fixed road crossing is a reference to:

(1) the carriageway and any footway of a fixed road crossing[7];
(2) any building, other than office buildings, used[8] in connection with the crossing[9]; and
(3) any machinery, apparatus or works used in connection with the crossing or with any of the items mentioned in heads (1) and (2)[10].

1 As to the meaning of 'hereditament' see PARA 106.
2 Ie as mentioned in the Local Government Finance Act 1988 s 65: see PARA 86. As to the treatment for the purposes of exemptions under Sch 5 of any land or building which is not occupied see PARA 110.
3 Ie for the purposes of the Local Government Finance Act 1988 Pt III (ss 41–67): see s 51, Sch 5 para 21(2). A hereditament that is completely exempt under Sch 5 para 18A is not to be entered into a rating list: see s 42(1); and PARA 194.
4 Local Government Finance Act 1988 Sch 5 para 18A(1) (Sch 5 para 18A added by the Local Government and Housing Act 1989 s 139, Sch 5 paras 37(4), 79(3)).
5 For these purposes, a bridge may be a fixed road crossing notwithstanding that it is designed so that part of it can be swung, raised or otherwise moved in order to facilitate passage across, above or below it: Local Government Finance Act 1988 Sch 5 para 18A(3)(a) (as added: see note 4). However, the expression 'bridge' does not include a floating bridge, ie a ferry operating between fixed chains: Sch 5 para 18A(3)(b) (as so added).
6 Local Government Finance Act 1988 Sch 5 para 18A(2) (as added: see note 4). An aerial ropeway has been held to qualify for this exemption: *Griffin v Sansom (Valuation Officer)* [1996] RA 454, Lands Tribunal.
7 Local Government Finance Act 1988 Sch 5 para 18A(4)(a) (as added: see note 4).
8 As to the treatment for the purposes of exemptions under the Local Government Finance Act 1988 Sch 5 of any land, building or property which is not in use see PARA 110.
9 Local Government Finance Act 1988 Sch 5 para 18A(4)(b) (as added: see note 4).
10 Local Government Finance Act 1988 Sch 5 para 18A(4)(c) (as added: see note 4).

131. Property used for road user charging schemes.

A hereditament[1] which is occupied[2] is exempt from local non-domestic rating[3] to the extent that:

(1) it consists of a road in respect of which charges are imposed by a charging scheme[4]; or
(2) it is used[5] solely for or in connection with the operation of such a scheme[6].

1 As to the meaning of 'hereditament' see PARA 106.
2 Ie as mentioned in the Local Government Finance Act 1988 s 65: see PARA 86. As to the treatment for the purposes of exemptions under Sch 5 of any land or building which is not occupied see PARA 110.
3 Ie for the purposes of the Local Government Finance Act 1988 Pt III (ss 41–67): see s 51, Sch 5 para 21(2). A hereditament that is completely exempt under Sch 5 para 18B is not to be entered into a rating list: see s 42(1); and PARA 194.
4 Local Government Finance Act 1988 Sch 5 para 18B(1)(a) (Sch 5 para 18B added by the Transport Act 2000 s 200). A 'charging scheme' is one under the Greater London Authority Act 1999 Sch 23 (see LONDON GOVERNMENT vol 71 (2013) PARAS 218–219) or under the Transport Act 2000 Pt III (ss 163–200) (see ROAD TRAFFIC vol 89 (2011) PARA 659 et seq): see the Local Government Finance Act 1988 Sch 5 para 18B(1)(a) (as so added).
5 As to the treatment for the purposes of exemptions under the Local Government Finance Act 1988

Sch 5 of any land, building or property which is not in use see PARA 110.

6 Local Government Finance Act 1988 Sch 5 para 18B(1)(b) (as added: see note 4). Office buildings are not exempt under this provision: Sch 5 para 18B(2) (as so added).

132. Property in enterprise zones.

A hereditament[1] is exempt from local non-domestic rating[2] to the extent that it is situated in an enterprise zone[3].

1 As to the meaning of 'hereditament' see PARA 106.

2 Ie for the purposes of the Local Government Finance Act 1988 Pt III (ss 41–67): see s 51, Sch 5 para 21(2). A hereditament that is completely exempt under Sch 5 para 19 is not to be entered into a rating list: see s 42(1); and PARA 194.

3 Local Government Finance Act 1988 Sch 5 para 19(1). An 'enterprise zone' is an area for the time being designated as an enterprise zone under the Local Government, Planning and Land Act 1980 Sch 32 (see PLANNING vol 83 (2018) PARA 1563 et seq): Local Government Finance Act 1988 Sch 5 para 19(2).

(7) Chargeable Amount

(i) Local Non-domestic Rating Lists

A. OCCUPIED HEREDITAMENTS

133. Calculating the amount payable for occupied hereditaments in the local rating list.

A person[1] (the 'ratepayer') is, as regards a hereditament[2], subject to a non-domestic rate in respect of a chargeable financial year[3] if the following conditions are fulfilled in respect of any day in the year, namely if:

(1) on that day he is in occupation[4] of all or part of the hereditament[5]; and

(2) the hereditament is shown for that day in a local non-domestic rating list[6] in force for the year[7].

The amount payable is calculated by:

(a) finding the chargeable amount for each chargeable day[8]; and

(b) aggregating the amounts found under head (a) above[9].

For most cases, the chargeable amount for a chargeable day is calculated by multiplying the rateable value[10] by the non-domestic rating multiplier for the financial year[11], and using the number of days in the financial year[12] to divide the product[13]. However, where the relevant conditions are met, rate relief schemes may apply variations to this formula in cases where the hereditament relates to a small business[14], to a charity or registered club[15], to a qualifying general store, food store or office on the rural settlement list[16], or to certain former agricultural land or buildings[17].

The amount the ratepayer is liable to pay in any case must be paid to the billing authority in whose local non-domestic rating list the hereditament is shown[18].

1 As to the meaning of 'person' see PARA 11 note 13.

2 As to the meaning of 'hereditament' see PARA 106.

3 As to the meaning of 'chargeable financial year' see PARA 24 note 1.

4 As to the occupier and occupation of land see PARA 85 et seq.

5 Local Government Finance Act 1988 s 43(1)(a). The reference to a part of a hereditament in this provision ensures that an occupier who was in occupation (but not in occupation of the whole building) for a temporary period is liable for an apportioned rate in respect of that period, by virtue of the combined effect of s 43(1) and s 44A(1) (see PARA 134): see *Croydon London Borough Council v Maxon Systems Inc (London) Ltd* [1999] RA 286, [1999] EGCS 68.

6 As to local non-domestic rating lists see PARA 191 et seq.
7 Local Government Finance Act 1988 s 43(1)(b).
8 Local Government Finance Act 1988 s 43(2)(a). A 'chargeable day' is one which falls within the financial year and in respect of which the conditions in s 43(1) (see heads (1) and (2) in the text) are fulfilled: s 43(3).
9 Local Government Finance Act 1988 s 43(2)(b).
10 Ie the rateable value shown for the day in the local non-domestic rating list under the Local Government Finance Act 1988 s 42(4) (see PARA 194) as regards the hereditament: see s 44(1), (2) (s 44(2) amended by the Local Government and Housing Act 1989 s 194(4), Sch 5 paras 1, 21, 79(3), Sch 12 Pt II).
11 See the Local Government Finance Act 1988 s 44(1), (4). The 'non-domestic rating multiplier' is a uniform amount applying to every billing authority area and is fixed annually by the Secretary of State or, in relation to Wales, the Welsh Ministers using the method set out in s 56(2), Sch 7: see PARA 156. As to the Secretary of State and the Welsh Ministers see PARA 4 note 18. As to the meaning of 'billing authority' see PARA 53. As to the separate administration of the non-domestic rating provisions (Local Government Finance Act 1988 Pt III (ss 41–67)) in England and Wales see PARA 52.

Where the billing authority is a special authority, the figure used for the non-domestic rating multiplier is the authority's non-domestic rating multiplier for the financial year: see s 44(1), (5) (s 44(5) amended by the Local Government Finance Act 1992 s 117(1), Sch 13 para 61). A billing authority is a 'special authority' if its population on 1 April 1986 was less than 10,000 and its gross rateable value on that date divided by its population on that date was more than £10,000: Local Government Finance Act 1988 s 144(6) (amended by the Local Government Finance Act 1992 Sch 13 para 81(2)). An authority's population on 1 April 1986 was the Registrar General's estimate of its population on that date as certified by him to the Secretary of State for the purposes of the enactments relating to rate support grant; and an authority's gross rateable value on that date was the aggregate of the rateable values on that date of the hereditaments in its area: Local Government Finance Act 1988 s 144(7).

12 See the Local Government Finance Act 1988 s 44(1), (6).
13 See the Local Government Finance Act 1988 s 43(4) (amended by the Local Government and Rating Act 1997 s 1, Sch 1 para 2(a); and the Local Government Act 2003 s 61(1), (2)). The calculation of the chargeable amount for a chargeable day using the formula set out in the Local Government Finance Act 1988 s 43(4) is subject to s 43(4A), (5), (6A) (see the text to notes 14–16): see s 43(4) (as so amended).
14 See the Local Government Finance Act 1988 s 43(4A); and PARA 143.
15 See the Local Government Finance Act 1988 s 43(5); and CHARITIES vol 8 (2015) PARA 433.
16 See the Local Government Finance Act 1988 s 43(6A); and PARA 145.
17 See the Local Government Finance Act 1988 s 43(6F)–(6L); and PARA 146.
18 Local Government Finance Act 1988 s 43(7) (amended by the Local Government Finance Act 1992 Sch 13 para 60). The liability to pay any such amount is discharged by making a payment or payments in accordance with regulations made under the Local Government Finance Act 1988 Sch 9 (see PARA 272 et seq): s 43(8).

B. PARTLY OCCUPIED HEREDITAMENTS

134. Calculating the amount payable for partly occupied hereditaments in the local rating list.

Where a hereditament[1] is shown in a billing authority's[2] local non-domestic rating list[3] and it appears to the authority that part of the hereditament is unoccupied[4] but will remain so for a short time only, the authority may require the valuation officer for the authority[5] to apportion the rateable value of the hereditament[6] between the occupied and unoccupied parts of the hereditament and to certify the apportionment to the authority[7]. For these purposes, an apportionment is to be treated as applicable for any day which:

(1) falls within the operative period[8] in relation to the apportionment[9]; and
(2) is a day for which the rateable value shown[10] as regards the hereditament to which the apportionment relates is the same as that so shown for the day on which the authority requires the apportionment[11].

In circumstances where:

(a) a billing authority requires such an apportionment[12]; and

(b) the hereditament to which the apportionment relates either does not fall within a class prescribed by regulations[13] or would (if unoccupied) be[14] zero-rated[15],

then, in relation to any day for which the apportionment is applicable, the provisions relating to the liability for occupied hereditaments[16] have effect with modifications as regards the hereditament[17]. Similarly, where:

(i) a billing authority requires such an apportionment[18];

(ii) the hereditament to which the apportionment relates both falls within a class prescribed by regulations[19] and would (if unoccupied) not be[20] zero-rated[21]; and

(iii) an order[22] is in force and has effect in relation to the hereditament[23],

then, in relation to any day for which the apportionment is applicable, the provisions relating to the liability for occupied hereditaments[24] have effect with modifications as regards the hereditament[25].

However, in relation to any day where neither set of circumstances[26] applies to the hereditament, an apportionment does not have any effect in relation to the chargeable amount[27].

1 As to the meaning of 'hereditament' see PARA 106. References in the Local Government Finance Act 1988 s 44A(1)–(5) (see the text to notes 2–11) to the hereditament, in relation to a hereditament which is partly domestic property or partly exempt from local non-domestic rating, are to be construed, except where the reference is to the rateable value of the hereditament, as references to such part of the hereditament as is neither domestic property nor exempt from local non-domestic rating: s 44A(10) (s 44A added by the Local Government and Housing Act 1989 s 139, Sch 5 paras 22, 79(3)). As to the meaning of 'domestic property' in relation to non-domestic rating see PARA 190. As to the exemptions from non-domestic rating see PARA 110 et seq.

2 As to the meaning of 'billing authority' see PARA 53.

3 As to local non-domestic rating lists see PARA 191.

4 As to the occupier and occupation of land see PARA 85 et seq.

5 As to valuation officers see PARA 54.

6 This reference to the rateable value of the hereditament is a reference to the rateable value shown under the Local Government Finance Act 1988 s 42(4) (see PARA 194) as regards the hereditament for the day on which the authority makes its requirement: s 44A(2) (as added: see note 1).

7 Local Government Finance Act 1988 s 44A(1) (as added (see note 1); and amended by the Local Government Finance Act 1992 s 117(1), Sch 13 para 62). See *Croydon London Borough Council v Maxon Systems Inc (London) Ltd* [1999] RA 286, [1999] EGCS 68; and PARA 133 note 5.

8 References to the 'operative period' in relation to an apportionment are references to the period beginning:

(1) where requiring the apportionment does not have the effect of bringing to an end the operative period in relation to a previous apportionment under the Local Government Finance Act 1988 s 44A(1) (see the text to notes 1–7), with the day on which the hereditament to which the apportionment relates became partly unoccupied (s 44A(4)(a) (as added: see note 1)); and

(2) where requiring the apportionment does have the effect of bringing to an end the operative period in relation to a previous apportionment under s 44A(1), with the day immediately following the end of that period (s 44A(4)(b) (as so added)),

and ending with the first day on which one or more of the following events occurs (s 44A(4) (as so added)), namely:

(a) the occupation of any of the unoccupied part of the hereditament to which the apportionment relates (s 44A(5)(a) (as so added));

(b) the ending of the rate period in which the authority requires the apportionment (s 44A(5)(b) (as so added));

(c) the requiring of a further apportionment under s 44A(1) in relation to the hereditament to which the apportionment relates (s 44A(5)(c) (as so added));

(d) the hereditament to which the apportionment relates becoming completely unoccupied (s 44A(5)(d) (as so added)).

9 Local Government Finance Act 1988 s 44A(3)(a) (as added: see note 1).
10 Ie under the Local Government Finance Act 1988 s 42(4): see PARA 194.
11 Local Government Finance Act 1988 s 44A(3)(b) (as added: see note 1).
12 Local Government Finance Act 1988 s 44A(6)(a) (as added (see note 1); amended by the Local Government Finance Act 1992 Sch 13 para 62).
13 Ie within a class prescribed by regulations under the Local Government Finance Act 1988 s 45(1)(d) (see PARAS 135–136): see s 44A(6)(b)(i) (s 44A as added (see note 1); s 44A(6)(b) substituted by the Rating (Empty Properties) Act 2007 s 2(1), Sch 1 para 1(1), (2)).
14 Ie under the Local Government Finance Act 1988 s 45A: see PARA 147.
15 Local Government Finance Act 1988 s 44A(6)(b)(ii) (as added (see note 1) and substituted (see note 13)).
16 Ie the Local Government Finance Act 1988 s 43: see note 17.
17 See the Local Government Finance Act 1988 s 44A(7) (as added: see note 1). Generally the chargeable amount for a chargeable day is calculated by multiplying the rateable value by the non-domestic rating multiplier for the financial year, and dividing the product by the number of days in the financial year in the same way as for occupied hereditaments: see the Local Government Finance Act 1988 s 43; and PARA 133. However, the rateable value in this case is only such part of the rateable value shown for the day as regards the hereditament as is assigned by the relevant apportionments to the occupied part of the hereditament: s 44(2) (substituted by s 44A(7) (as so added)). For these purposes, 'relevant apportionment' means the apportionment under s 44A(1) (see the text to notes 1–7) which relates to the hereditament and is treated for the purposes of s 44A as applicable for the day: s 44(2A) (substituted by s 44A(7) (as so added)).
18 Local Government Finance Act 1988 s 44A(8)(a) (as added (see note 1); amended by the Local Government Finance Act 1992 Sch 13 para 62).
19 Ie within a class prescribed by regulations under the Local Government Finance Act 1988 s 45(1)(d) (see PARAS 135–136): see s 44A(8)(b)(i) (s 44A as added (see note 1); s 44A(8)(b) substituted by the Rating (Empty Properties) Act 2007 Sch 1 para 1(1), (3)).
20 Ie under the Local Government Finance Act 1988 s 45A: see PARA 147.
21 Local Government Finance Act 1988 s 44A(8)(b)(ii) (as added (see note 1) and substituted (see note 19)).
22 Ie under the Local Government Finance Act 1988 s 45(4A): see PARA 148.
23 Local Government Finance Act 1988 s 44A(8)(c) (s 44A as added (see note 1); s 44A(8)(c) added by the Rating (Empty Properties) Act 2007 Sch 1 para 1(1), (3)).
24 Ie the Local Government Finance Act 1988 s 43: see note 25.
25 See the Local Government Finance Act 1988 s 44A(9) (as added (see note 1); amended by the Rating (Empty Properties) Act 2007 Sch 1 para 1(1), (4)). Generally the chargeable amount for a chargeable day is calculated by multiplying the rateable value by the non-domestic rating multiplier for the financial year, and dividing the product by the number of days in the financial year in the same way as for occupied hereditaments: see the Local Government Finance Act 1988 s 43; and PARA 133. However, the rateable value in this case is the sum of:
(1) such part of the rateable value shown for the day under s 42(4) (see PARA 194) as regards the hereditament as is assigned by the relevant apportionment to the occupied part of the hereditament (s 44(2)(a) (substituted by s 44A(9) (as so added and amended))); and
(2) such part of that rateable value as is assigned by the relevant apportionment to the unoccupied part of the hereditament, divided by the number prescribed by the order under s 45(4A) (see PARA 148) as it has effect in relation to the hereditament (s 44(2)(b) (substituted by s 44A(9) (as so added and amended))).

For these purposes, 'relevant apportionment' means the apportionment under s 44A(1) (see the text to notes 1–7) which relates to the hereditament and is treated for the purposes of s 44A as applicable for the day: s 44(2A) (substituted by s 44A(9) (as so added and amended)).
26 Ie neither the Local Government Finance Act 1988 s 44A(7) nor s 44A(9): see the text to notes 12–25.
27 Local Government Finance Act 1988 s 44A(9A) (s 44A as added (see note 1); s 44A(9A) added by the Rating (Empty Properties) Act 2007 Sch 1 para 1(1), (5)).

C. UNOCCUPIED HEREDITAMENTS

135. Liability for unoccupied hereditaments.

A person[1] (the 'ratepayer') is, as regards a hereditament[2], subject to a non-domestic rate in respect of a chargeable financial year[3] if the following conditions are fulfilled in respect of any day in the year, namely if:

(1) on the day none of the hereditament is occupied[4];
(2) on the day the ratepayer is the owner[5] of the whole of the hereditament[6];
(3) the hereditament is shown for the day in a local non-domestic rating list[7] in force for the year[8]; and
(4) on the day the hereditament falls within a class prescribed by the appropriate national authority[9] by regulations[10].

In such a case, the ratepayer is liable to pay an amount calculated by:

(a) finding the chargeable amount for each chargeable day[11]; and
(b) aggregating the amounts found under head (a)[12].

The chargeable amount for a chargeable day is calculated by multiplying the rateable value[13] by the non-domestic rating multiplier for the financial year[14], and using the number of days in the financial year[15] to divide the product[16]. However, liability for unoccupied properties may be reduced by order[17], and unoccupied hereditaments used by charities or by registered community amateur sports clubs may be zero-rated[18].

The amount the ratepayer is liable to pay must be paid to the billing authority in whose local non-domestic rating list the hereditament is shown[19].

1 As to the meaning of 'person' see PARA 11 note 13.
2 As to the meaning of 'hereditament' see PARA 106.
3 As to the meaning of 'chargeable financial year' see PARA 24 note 1.
4 Local Government Finance Act 1988 s 45(1)(a). As to the occupier and occupation of land see PARA 85 et seq. The actions of a receiver and manager in managing a company's business do not, without more, amount to rateable occupation of the company's premises by the receiver and manager: see *Ratford v Northavon District Council* [1987] QB 357, [1986] RA 137, CA (for rating purposes, any occupation enjoyed by a receiver and manager in running the company's business as agents of the company was occupation by the company), applied in *Rees v Boston Borough Council* [2001] EWCA Civ 1934, [2002] 1 WLR 1304, [2002] RA 23. See also the cases cited in note 5.

Where a day is determined under the Local Government Finance Act 1988 Sch 4A as the completion day in relation to a new building (see PARA 138), and the building is not occupied on that day, it is deemed for the purposes of s 45 to become unoccupied on that day: s 46A(4) (s 46A added by the Local Government and Housing Act 1989 s 139, Sch 5 paras 25, 79(3)). Where a day is determined under the Local Government Finance Act 1988 Sch 4A as the completion day in relation to a new building, and the building is one produced by the structural alteration of an existing building, the hereditament which comprised the existing building is deemed for the purposes of s 45 to have ceased to exist (and to have been omitted from the list) on that day: s 46A(5) (as so added).

5 As to the meaning of 'owner' see PARA 86. A person is entitled to possession of a hereditament only if he is immediately entitled to possession of it, so a receiver under a debenture is not entitled to possession of a hereditament if he remains just the agent of the company: *Brown v City of London Corpn* [1996] 1 WLR 1070, sub nom *Re Sobam BV and Satelscoop BV* [1996] RA 93. However, he may become the owner if he has exercised a right to take possession: see *Banister v Islington London Borough Council* (1973) 17 RRC 191, DC. See also *Ratford v Northavon District Council* [1987] QB 357, [1986] 3 All ER 193, CA. As to the position on the forfeiture of a lease see *Kingston-upon-Thames London Borough Council v Marlow* [1996] RA 87, [1996] 1 EGLR 101. As to whether non-domestic rates are chargeable as an expense in an administration see *Exeter City Council v Bairstow* [2007] EWHC 400 (Ch), [2007] 4 All ER 437, [2007] RA 109 (non-domestic rates accrued on occupied business premises during a company's administration were payable as expenses of the administration); and COMPANY AND PARTNERSHIP INSOLVENCY vol 16 (2017) PARA 293.
6 Local Government Finance Act 1988 s 45(1)(b).

7 As to local non-domestic rating lists see PARA 191 et seq.
8 Local Government Finance Act 1988 s 45(1)(c).
9 Ie the Secretary of State or, in relation to Wales, the Welsh Ministers. The functions of the Secretary of State under the Local Government Finance Act 1988 s 45, so far as exercisable in relation to Wales, were transferred to the National Assembly for Wales (see the National Assembly for Wales (Transfer of Functions) Order 1999, SI 1999/672, art 2, Sch 1) and are now vested in the Welsh Ministers (see the Government of Wales Act 2006 s 162(1), Sch 11 para 30). As to the Secretary of State and the Welsh Ministers see PARA 4 note 18. As to the meaning of 'Wales' see PARA 2 note 16. As to the separate administration of the non-domestic rating provisions (Local Government Finance Act 1988 Pt III (ss 41–67)) in England and Wales see PARA 52.
10 Local Government Finance Act 1988 s 45(1)(d) (amended by the Local Government and Housing Act 1989 Sch 5 paras 23(2), 79(3)). A class may be prescribed by reference to such factors as the appropriate national authority sees fit: see the Local Government Finance Act 1988 s 45(9) (added by the Local Government and Housing Act 1989 Sch 5 paras 23(3), 79(3)). As to the classes prescribed see PARA 136.
11 Local Government Finance Act 1988 s 45(2)(a). A 'chargeable day' is one which falls within the financial year and in respect of which the conditions mentioned in s 45(1) (see heads (1)–(4) in the text) are fulfilled: s 45(3).
12 Local Government Finance Act 1988 s 45(2)(b).
13 Ie the rateable value shown for the day in the local non-domestic rating list under the Local Government Finance Act 1988 s 42(4) (see PARA 194) as regards the hereditament: see s 46(1), (2) (s 46(2) amended by the Local Government and Housing Act 1989 s 194(4), Sch 5 paras 1, 21, 79(3), Sch 12 Pt II).
14 See the Local Government Finance Act 1988 s 46(1), (3). Where the billing authority is a special authority, the figure used for the non-domestic rating multiplier is the authority's non-domestic rating multiplier for the financial year: see s 46(1), (4) (s 46(4) amended by the Local Government Finance Act 1992 s 117(1), Sch 13 para 64). As to the meaning of 'billing authority' see PARA 53. As to the meaning of 'special authority' and as to the non-domestic rating multiplier see PARA 133 note 11.
15 See the Local Government Finance Act 1988 s 46(1), (5).
16 See the Local Government Finance Act 1988 s 45(4) (substituted by the Rating (Empty Properties) Act 2007 s 1(1)). The calculation of the chargeable amount for a chargeable day using the formula set out in the Local Government Finance Act 1988 s 45(4) is subject to s 45(4A) and s 45A: see s 45(4) (as so substituted); and the text to notes 17–18.
17 See the Local Government Finance Act 1988 s 45(4A); and PARA 148.
18 See the Local Government Finance Act 1988 s 45A; and PARA 147.
19 Local Government Finance Act 1988 s 45(7) (amended by the Local Government Finance Act 1992 Sch 13 para 63). The liability to pay any such amount is discharged by making a payment or payments in accordance with regulations under the Local Government Finance Act 1988 Sch 9 (see PARA 272 et seq): s 45(8).

136. Prescribed class of unoccupied hereditament.

A person[1] (the ratepayer) is subject to a non-domestic rate in respect of a hereditament[2] if it falls within a class prescribed by regulations[3]. A class may be prescribed by reference to such factors as the appropriate national authority[4] sees fit[5]. In particular a class may be prescribed by reference to one or more of the following factors:

(1) the physical characteristics of the hereditaments[6];
(2) the fact that hereditaments have been unoccupied[7] at any time preceding the day[8] in question[9];
(3) the fact that the owners[10] of hereditaments fall within prescribed descriptions[11].

The class of non-domestic hereditaments prescribed for these purposes consists of all relevant non-domestic hereditaments[12] other than those of the following descriptions[13], namely any hereditament:

(a) which has been unoccupied[14] for a continuous period not exceeding three months[15];

(b) which is a qualifying industrial hereditament[16] that has been unoccupied[17] for a continuous period not exceeding six months[18];
(c) whose owner is prohibited by law from occupying it or allowing it to be occupied[19];
(d) which is kept vacant by reason of action taken by or on behalf of the Crown or any local or public authority with a view to prohibiting the occupation of the hereditament or to acquiring it[20];
(e) which is the subject of a building preservation notice[21] or is included in a list[22] of buildings of special architectural or historic interest[23];
(f) which is included in the schedule of monuments compiled[24] under the Ancient Monuments and Archaeological Areas Act 1979[25];
(g) in the case of a hereditament in England, whose rateable value in relation to financial years beginning on or after 1 April 2017 is less than £2,900[26] or, in the case of a hereditament in Wales, whose rateable value is less than £2,600[27];
(h) whose owner is entitled to possession only in his capacity as the personal representative of a deceased person[28];
(i) where, in respect of the owner's estate, there subsists a bankruptcy order[29];
(j) whose owner is a company which is subject to a winding-up order made under the Insolvency Act 1986 or which is being wound up voluntarily under that Act[30];
(k) whose owner is a company in administration[31] or is subject to an administration order made under the former administration provisions[32];
(l) whose owner is entitled[33] to possession of the hereditament in his capacity as liquidator[34].

1 As to the meaning of 'person' see PARA 11 note 13.
2 As to the meaning of 'hereditament' see PARA 106.
3 See the Local Government Finance Act 1988 s 45(1)(d); and PARA 135.
4 Ie the Secretary of State or, in relation to Wales, the Welsh Ministers. The functions of the Secretary of State under the Local Government Finance Act 1988 s 45, so far as exercisable in relation to Wales, were transferred to the National Assembly for Wales (see the National Assembly for Wales (Transfer of Functions) Order 1999, SI 1999/672, art 2, Sch 1) and are now vested in the Welsh Ministers (see the Government of Wales Act 2006 s 162(1), Sch 11 para 30). As to the Secretary of State and the Welsh Ministers see PARA 4 note 18. As to the meaning of 'Wales' see PARA 2 note 16. As to the separate administration of the non-domestic rating provisions (Local Government Finance Act 1988 Pt III (ss 41–67)) in England and Wales see PARA 52.
5 Local Government Finance Act 1988 s 45(9) (s 45(9), (10) added by the Local Government and Housing Act 1989 s 139, Sch 5 paras 23(3), 79(3)).
6 Local Government Finance Act 1988 s 45(10)(a) (as added: see note 5).
7 As to the occupier and occupation of land see PARA 85 et seq.
8 Ie the day mentioned in the Local Government Finance Act 1988 s 45(1): see PARA 135.
9 Local Government Finance Act 1988 s 45(10)(b) (as added: see note 5).
10 As to the meaning of 'owner' see PARA 86.
11 Local Government Finance Act 1988 s 45(10)(c) (as added: see note 5).
12 'Relevant non-domestic hereditament' means any non-domestic hereditament consisting of, or of part of, any building, together with any land ordinarily used or intended for use for the purposes of the building or part: Non-Domestic Rating (Unoccupied Property) (England) Regulations 2008, SI 2008/386, reg 2; Non-Domestic Rating (Unoccupied Property) (Wales) Regulations 2008, SI 2008/2499, reg 2. As to the meaning of 'non-domestic hereditament' see PARA 106. It is submitted that a hereditament consisting primarily of land as opposed to buildings would not qualify for these purposes.
13 Non-Domestic Rating (Unoccupied Property) (England) Regulations 2008, SI 2008/386, reg 3; Non-Domestic Rating (Unoccupied Property) (Wales) Regulations 2008, SI 2008/2499, reg 3.

14 A hereditament which has been unoccupied and becomes occupied on any day must be treated as having been continuously unoccupied for the purposes of the Non-Domestic Rating (Unoccupied Property) (England) Regulations 2008, SI 2008/386, reg 4(a), (b) and the Non-Domestic Rating (Unoccupied Property) (Wales) Regulations 2008, SI 2008/2499, reg 4(a), (b) (see the text to notes 15–18) if it becomes unoccupied again on the expiration of a period of less than six weeks beginning with that day: Non-Domestic Rating (Unoccupied Property) (England) Regulations 2008, SI 2008/386, reg 5; Non-Domestic Rating (Unoccupied Property) (Wales) Regulations 2008, SI 2008/2499, reg 5.

15 Non-Domestic Rating (Unoccupied Property) (England) Regulations 2008, SI 2008/386, reg 4(a); Non-Domestic Rating (Unoccupied Property) (Wales) Regulations 2008, SI 2008/2499, reg 4(a). As to the meaning of 'month' see PARA 11 note 1.

16 'Qualifying industrial hereditament' means any hereditament other than a retail hereditament in relation to which all buildings comprised in the hereditament are:

(1) constructed or adapted for use in the course of a trade or business; and

(2) constructed or adapted for use for one or more of the following purposes, or one or more such purposes and one or more purposes ancillary thereto:

(a) the manufacture, repair or adaptation of goods or materials, or the subjection of goods or materials to any process;

(b) storage (including the storage or handling of goods in the course of their distribution);

(c) the working or processing of minerals; and

(d) the generation of electricity;

and 'retail hereditament' means any hereditament where any building or part of a building comprised in the hereditament is constructed or adapted for the purpose of the retail provision of either goods or services, other than storage for distribution services, where the services are to be provided on or from the hereditament: Non-Domestic Rating (Unoccupied Property) (England) Regulations 2008, SI 2008/386, reg 2; Non-Domestic Rating (Unoccupied Property) (Wales) Regulations 2008, SI 2008/2499, reg 2.

The following cases and the others cited in this paragraph were decided prior to the coming into force of the Non-Domestic Rating (Unoccupied Property) (England) Regulations 2008, SI 2008/386, and the Non-Domestic Rating (Unoccupied Property) (Wales) Regulations 2008, SI 2008/2499, but continue to be of relevance relating as they do to similar provisions in the previous regulations.

'Goods' provides for a broad ambit of operation: see *Southwark London Borough Council v Bellway Homes Ltd* [2000] RA 437, [2000] EGCS 90 (postal sorting office was a qualifying industrial hereditament because mail was considered to be 'goods' and the office's activities at that sorting office in franking, sorting and packaging the mail for distribution, amounted to subjecting goods to a process and to handling them in the course of distribution). However, the exemption relates to tangible objects subject to a physical process, and computer data does not fall within the term 'goods or materials' for these purposes: *Leda Properties Ltd v Kennet District Council* [2002] EWHC 2040 (Admin), [2003] RA 69, [2002] All ER (D) 18 (Jul) (operation of computer programmes far removed from the type of industrial processes envisaged in the industrial exemption).

In *Barnet London Borough Council v London Transport Property* [1995] RA 235, [1995] EGCS 78, it was held that 'storage' will cover a wide range of goods and might conceivably apply to activities which would not normally be described in that way but that in the instant case 'storage' did not include the overnight parking of buses in a bus garage. For these purposes, it does not necessarily follow from the fact that something is stored at a location that the location is used for storage: *Leda Properties Ltd v Kennet District Council* above (unoccupied accommodation providing storage and data handling services on computers housed within it could not act as a store for the data, which could only be stored on suitably programmed computers).

17 See note 14.

18 Non-Domestic Rating (Unoccupied Property) (England) Regulations 2008, SI 2008/386, reg 4(b); Non-Domestic Rating (Unoccupied Property) (Wales) Regulations 2008, SI 2008/2499, reg 4(b).

19 Non-Domestic Rating (Unoccupied Property) (England) Regulations 2008, SI 2008/386, reg 4(c); Non-Domestic Rating (Unoccupied Property) (Wales) Regulations 2008, SI 2008/2499, reg 4(c). The owner is not prohibited by law from occupying the hereditament if he is required to demolish it by a condition of a planning permission: *Henderson v Liverpool Metropolitan District Council* [1980] RA 238, DC. In *Hailbury Investments Ltd v Westminster City Council* [1986] 3 All ER 440, [1986] 1 WLR 1232, HL, the owner was not prohibited by law from occupying a hereditament described in the list as 'offices' but subject to a planning condition prohibiting office use. In *Regent Lion Properties Ltd v Westminster City Council* [1990] RA 121, [1990] 2 EGLR 175, CA, the owner was not prohibited by law from occupying a hereditament for which there was

no permitted use for the purposes of the planning legislation; however in the same case the Court of Appeal held that, where a notice was served under the Health and Safety at Work etc Act 1974 prohibiting certain activities because of the presence of asbestos, the owner was prohibited from occupying the hereditament or allowing it to be occupied until the steps which the notice required to be taken were taken. In *Tower Hamlets London Borough Council v St Katharine-by-the-Tower Ltd* (1982) 80 LGR 843, [1982] RA 261, DC, the owner of a building which had inadequate means of escape in case of fire and no certificate as required by the London Building Acts (Amendment) Act 1939 s 34 was prohibited from occupying the hereditament or allowing it to be occupied. See also *Pall Mall Investments (London) Ltd v Gloucester City Council* [2014] EWHC 2247 (Admin), [2014] PTSR 1184, [2014] All ER (D) 78 (Jul) (which held that exemption did not result from the owner establishing that he would be liable for prosecution under health and safety legislation if the premises were to be occupied in their current state, but only if there was a legal prohibition on him entering the premises to rectify the defects).

20 Non-Domestic Rating (Unoccupied Property) (England) Regulations 2008, SI 2008/386, reg 4(d); Non-Domestic Rating (Unoccupied Property) (Wales) Regulations 2008, SI 2008/2499, reg 4(d). See *Regent Lion Properties Ltd v Westminster City Council* [1990] RA 121, CA (reversing on this point [1989] RA 190).

21 Ie within the meaning of the Planning (Listed Buildings and Conservation Areas) Act 1990: see s 3; and PLANNING vol 83 (2018) PARA 1188 et seq.

22 Ie a list compiled under the Planning (Listed Buildings and Conservation Areas) Act 1990 s 1: see PLANNING vol 83 (2018) PARA 1181 et seq.

23 Non-Domestic Rating (Unoccupied Property) (England) Regulations 2008, SI 2008/386, reg 4(e); Non-Domestic Rating (Unoccupied Property) (Wales) Regulations 2008, SI 2008/2499, reg 4(e). See *Providence Properties Ltd v Liverpool City Council* [1980] RA 189; *Debenhams plc v Westminster City Council* [1987] AC 396, [1987] 1 All ER 51, HL. Where two hereditaments (one occupied, the other not) have been wholly included in a listed building, the two may not be treated for these purposes as separate units and, accordingly, exemption from paying rates has to follow for both: *Ge Bowra Group Ltd v Thanet District Council* [2007] EWHC 1077 (Admin), [2007] RVR 120, [2007] All ER (D) 184 (Apr).

24 Ie under the Ancient Monuments and Archaeological Areas Act 1979 s 1: see NATIONAL CULTURAL HERITAGE vol 77 (2016) PARA 1014.

25 Non-Domestic Rating (Unoccupied Property) (England) Regulations 2008, SI 2008/386, reg 4(f); Non-Domestic Rating (Unoccupied Property) (Wales) Regulations 2008, SI 2008/2499, reg 4(f).

26 Non-Domestic Rating (Unoccupied Property) (England) Regulations 2008, SI 2008/386, reg 4(g)(v) (substituted by SI 2017/102). In relation to earlier financial years the exemption applies where the rateable value is less than the following :

(1) in relation to the financial year beginning on 1st April 2008, £2,200 (Non-Domestic Rating (Unoccupied Property) (England) Regulations 2008, SI 2008/386, reg 4(g)(i) (as so substituted));

(2) in relation to the financial year beginning on 1 April 2009, £15,000 (reg 4(g)(ii) (as so substituted));

(3) in relation to the financial year beginning on 1 April 2010, £18,000 (reg 4(g)(iii) (as so substituted));

(4) in relation to the financial years beginning on 1 April 2011, 1 April 2012, 1 April 2013, 1 April 2014, 1 April 2015 and 1 April 2016, £2,600 (reg 4(g)(iv) (as so substituted)).

27 Non-Domestic Rating (Unoccupied Property) (Wales) Regulations 2008, SI 2008/2499, reg 4(g) (amended by SI 2011/197).

28 Non-Domestic Rating (Unoccupied Property) (England) Regulations 2008, SI 2008/386, reg 4(h); Non-Domestic Rating (Unoccupied Property) (Wales) Regulations 2008, SI 2008/2499, reg 4(h). As to personal representatives see WILLS AND INTESTACY vol 103 (2016) PARA 605.

29 Non-Domestic Rating (Unoccupied Property) (England) Regulations 2008, SI 2008/386, reg 4(i); Non-Domestic Rating (Unoccupied Property) (Wales) Regulations 2008, SI 2008/2499, reg 4(i). A bankruptcy order is one within the meaning of the Insolvency Act 1986 s 381(2) (see BANKRUPTCY AND INDIVIDUAL INSOLVENCY vol 5 (2013) PARA 198 et seq): see the Non-Domestic Rating (Unoccupied Property) (England) Regulations 2008, SI 2008/386, reg 4(i); Non-Domestic Rating (Unoccupied Property) (Wales) Regulations 2008, SI 2008/2499, reg 4(i).

30 Non-Domestic Rating (Unoccupied Property) (England) Regulations 2008, SI 2008/386, reg 4(k); Non-Domestic Rating (Unoccupied Property) (Wales) Regulations 2008, SI 2008/2499, reg 4(k). As to winding-up orders see COMPANY AND PARTNERSHIP INSOLVENCY vol 16 (2017) PARA 342 et seq.

31 Ie within the meaning of the Insolvency Act 1986 Sch B1 para 1: see COMPANY AND PARTNERSHIP INSOLVENCY vol 16 (2017) PARA 141.

32 Non-Domestic Rating (Unoccupied Property) (England) Regulations 2008, SI 2008/386, reg 4(l); Non-Domestic Rating (Unoccupied Property) (Wales) Regulations 2008, SI 2008/2499, reg 4(l). The 'former administration provisions' means those within the meaning of the Enterprise Act 2002 (Commencement No 4 and Transitional Provisions and Savings) Order 2003, SI 2003/2093, art 3 (see COMPANY AND PARTNERSHIP INSOLVENCY vol 16 (2017) PARA 137): see the Non-Domestic Rating (Unoccupied Property) (England) Regulations 2008, SI 2008/386, reg 4(l); Non-Domestic Rating (Unoccupied Property) (Wales) Regulations 2008, SI 2008/2499, reg 4(l).

33 Ie by virtue of an order made under the Insolvency Act 1986 s 112 (see COMPANY AND PARTNERSHIP INSOLVENCY vol 17 (2017) PARA 913) or s 145 (see COMPANY AND PARTNERSHIP INSOLVENCY vol 16 (2017) PARA 485).

34 Non-Domestic Rating (Unoccupied Property) (England) Regulations 2008, SI 2008/386, reg 4(m); Non-Domestic Rating (Unoccupied Property) (Wales) Regulations 2008, SI 2008/2499, reg 4(m).

137. Power to prevent changes in state of unoccupied hereditament affecting liability.

Regulations[1] may provide that, for the purposes of the non-domestic rating provisions[2] as they apply in relation to an unoccupied hereditament[3], the state of any property comprising or included in the hereditament is deemed not to have changed[4] either since before any event of a prescribed description[5], or by reason of any act done by or on behalf of a prescribed person[6]. The regulations may make provision as to the circumstances in which, and period for which, that is deemed to be the case[7].

The regulations may:

(1) provide for the making of such assumptions or apportionments as may be prescribed in determining whether, or to what extent, the state of any property has changed in comparison with an earlier point in time[8];

(2) provide that an act is to be treated as done on behalf of a prescribed person if it is done by any person connected with that person[9], and define in what circumstances persons are to be treated for that purpose as connected[10]; and

(3) provide that they have effect (with any necessary adaptations) in relation to omissions as well as to acts[11].

1 Regulations under the Local Government Finance Act 1988 s 66A may be made, in relation to England, by the Secretary of State and, in relation to Wales, by the Welsh Ministers: s 66A(6) (s 66A added by the Rating (Empty Properties) Act 2007 s 2(1), Sch 1 para 4(1)). At the date at which this volume states the law no such regulations had been made. As to the Secretary of State and the Welsh Ministers see PARA 4 note 18. As to the meanings of 'England' and 'Wales' see PARA 2 note 16. As to the separate administration of the non-domestic rating provisions (Local Government Finance Act 1988 Pt III (ss 41–67)) in England and Wales see PARA 52.

2 Ie the Local Government Finance Act 1988 Pt III (ss 41–67).

3 As to the meaning of 'hereditament' see PARA 106. As to the occupier and occupation of land see PARA 85 et seq. As to liability for unoccupied hereditaments see PARA 135.

4 Local Government Finance Act 1988 s 66A(1) (as added: see note 1).

5 Local Government Finance Act 1988 s 66A(1)(a) (as added: see note 1). 'Prescribed' means prescribed by the regulations: see s 146(6).

6 Local Government Finance Act 1988 s 66A(1)(b) (as added: see note 1). As to the meaning of 'person' see PARA 11 note 13.

7 Local Government Finance Act 1988 s 66A(2) (as added: see note 1).

8 Local Government Finance Act 1988 s 66A(3) (as added: see note 1).

9 Local Government Finance Act 1988 s 66A(4)(a) (as added: see note 1).

10 Local Government Finance Act 1988 s 66A(4)(b) (as added: see note 1).

11 Local Government Finance Act 1988 s 66A(5) (as added: see note 1).

138. New buildings; completion notices.

Under the General Rate Act 1967 (now repealed), an unoccupied new building could only be entered in the rating list if a completion notice had been served in respect of it[1]. The Local Government Finance Act 1988 also contains provision with respect to the determination of a day as the completion day in relation to a new building[2]; but such provision does not explicitly prevent the valuation officer entering a new hereditament in the list in the absence of a completion notice[3].

Where a completion notice is served under the Local Government Finance Act 1988[4], and the building[5] to which the notice relates is not completed on or before the relevant day[6], then for the purposes of the content of local lists[7] and the determination of rateable value[8] the building is deemed to be completed on that day[9].

If it comes to the notice of a billing authority[10] that the work remaining to be done on a new building in its area is such that the building can reasonably be expected to be completed within three months[11], the authority must serve a completion notice on the owner[12] of the building as soon as is reasonably practicable unless the valuation officer[13] otherwise directs in writing[14]. Similarly, if it comes to the notice of a billing authority that a new building in its area has been completed, the authority may serve a completion notice on the owner of the building unless the valuation officer otherwise directs in writing[15]. A billing authority may withdraw a completion notice by serving on the owner of the building to which the notice relates a subsequent notice[16].

A completion notice must specify the building to which it relates and state the day which the authority proposes as the completion day in relation to the building[17]. Where at the time a completion notice is served it appears to the authority that the building to which the notice relates is not completed, the authority must propose as the completion day such day, not later than three months from and including the day on which the notice is served, as the authority considers is a day by which the building can reasonably be expected to be completed[18]. Where at the time a completion notice is served it appears to the authority that the building to which the notice relates is completed, the authority must propose as the completion day the day on which the notice is served[19].

The billing authority must supply to the valuation officer a copy of any completion notice served by it[20], and if the billing authority withdraws a completion notice, it must inform the valuation officer of that fact[21].

1 See *Watford Borough Council v Parcourt Investment Co Ltd* (1971) 17 RRC 19, [1971] RA 97.

2 See the Local Government Finance Act 1988 s 46A(1), Sch 4A (both added by the Local Government and Housing Act 1989 s 139, Sch 5 paras 1, 25, 36, 79(3)); and the text to notes 4–21, and PARAS 139–141.

3 See the text to notes 4–21, and PARAS 139–141. As to local non-domestic rating lists see PARA 191 et seq.

4 Ie under the Local Government Finance Act 1988 Sch 4A (see the text to notes 10–21): see s 46A(2)(a) (as added: see note 2). As to the mode of service of completion notices see PARA 139.

5 'Building' includes part of a building: Local Government Finance Act 1988 s 46A(6)(a), Sch 4A para 10(1) (both as added: see note 2). References to a new building include references to a building produced by the structural alteration of an existing building where the existing building is comprised in a hereditament which, by virtue of the alteration, becomes, or becomes part of, a different hereditament or different hereditaments: s 46A(6)(b), Sch 4A para 10(1) (both as so added). As to the meaning of 'hereditament' see PARA 106. The alterations must be such as to make the building a 'new building' either within the statutory definition or in accordance with the natural use of English: *Tull Properties Ltd v South Gloucestershire Council* [2014] RA 180.

6 Local Government Finance Act 1988 s 46A(2)(b) (as added: see note 2). The 'relevant day' in relation to a completion notice is:

(1) where an appeal against the notice is brought under Sch 4A para 4 (see PARA 141), the day stated in the notice (s 46A(3)(a) (as so added)); and

(2) where no appeal against the notice is brought under Sch 4A para 4, the day determined under Sch 4A as the completion day in relation to the building to which the notice relates (s 46A(3)(b) (as so added)).

7 Ie for the purposes of the Local Government Finance Act 1988 s 42: see PARA 194.
8 Ie for the purposes of the Local Government Finance Act 1988 Sch 6: see PARA 157 et seq.
9 Local Government Finance Act 1988 s 46A(2) (as added: see note 2).
10 As to the meaning of 'billing authority' see PARA 53.
11 As to the meaning of 'month' see PARA 11 note 1.
12 'Owner', in relation to a building, means the person entitled to possession of the building: Local Government Finance Act 1988 Sch 4A para 10(2) (as added: see note 2).
13 References to the valuation officer, in relation to a billing authority, are references to the valuation officer for the authority: Local Government Finance Act 1988 Sch 4A para 10(2) (as added (see note 2); amended by the Local Government Finance Act 1992 ss 117(1), 118(1), Sch 13 para 83(5)). As to the meaning of 'valuation officer' see PARA 54 note 3.
14 Local Government Finance Act 1988 Sch 4A para 1(1) (as added (see note 2); Sch 4A para 1(1)–(3) amended by the Local Government Finance Act 1992 Sch 13 para 83(1)). As to the meaning of 'writing' see PARA 21 note 3.
15 Local Government Finance Act 1988 Sch 4A para 1(2) (as added and amended: see note 14).
16 Local Government Finance Act 1988 Sch 4A para 1(3) (as added and amended: see note 14). The power to withdraw a completion notice ceases to be exercisable in relation to a completion notice once a day has been determined under Sch 4A as the completion day in relation to the building to which the notice relates: Sch 4A para 1(5) (as added: see note 2).
17 Local Government Finance Act 1988 Sch 4A para 2(1) (as added: see note 2). As to the interpretation of a completion notice, the test is whether it fairly conveys to the recipient what is the subject matter of the notice: *Henderson v Liverpool Metropolitan District Council* [1980] RA 238, DC. This case was decided prior to the coming into force of the Local Government Finance Act 1988 but continues to be of relevance: see PARA 50.
18 Local Government Finance Act 1988 Sch 4A para 2(2) (as added: see note 2).
19 Local Government Finance Act 1988 Sch 4A para 2(3) (as added: see note 2).
20 Local Government Finance Act 1988 Sch 4A para 7(1) (Sch 4A para 7 as added (see note 2); amended by the Local Government Finance Act 1992 Sch 13 para 83(4)).
21 Local Government Finance Act 1988 Sch 4A para 7(2) (as added and amended: see note 20).

139. Mode of service of completion notices.

Without prejudice to any other mode of service, a completion notice[1] may be served on a person[2]:

(1) by sending it in a prepaid registered letter, or by the recorded delivery service, addressed to that person at his usual or last-known place of abode or, in a case where an address for service has been given by that person, at that address[3];

(2) in the case of an incorporated company or body, by delivering it to the secretary or clerk of the company or body at its registered or principal office[4] or sending it in a prepaid registered letter or by the recorded delivery service addressed to the secretary or clerk of the company or body at that office[5]; or

(3) where the name or address of that person cannot be ascertained after reasonable inquiry, by addressing it to him by the description of 'owner' of the building[6] (describing it) to which the notice relates and by affixing it to some conspicuous part of the building[7].

1 As to completion notices see PARA 138. In the Local Government Finance Act 1988 Sch 4A, 'completion notice' means a notice under Sch 4A para 1: Sch 4A paras 1(6), 10(2) (Sch 4A added by the Local Government and Housing Act 1989 s 139, Sch 5 paras 36, 79(3)).
2 As to the meaning of 'person' see PARA 11 note 13.
3 Local Government Finance Act 1988 Sch 4A para 8(a) (as added: see note 1). Where an Act authorises or requires any document to be served by post (whether the expression 'serve' or the expression 'give' or 'send' or any other expression is used) then, unless the contrary intention appears, the service is deemed to be effected by properly addressing, pre-paying and posting a letter containing the document and, unless the contrary is proved, to have been effected at the time at which the letter would be delivered in the ordinary course of post: see the Interpretation Act 1978 s 7; and STATUTES AND LEGISLATIVE PROCESS vol 96 (2012) PARA 1219. A requirement to send a document by post is not confined to sending it by the Post Office postal system: see the Postal

Services Act 2000 s 127(4), Sch 8 Pt 1. As to proof of posting and proof of delivery see CIVIL PROCEDURE vol 12 (2015) PARAS 1003, 1004.

4 As to the registered office of a company see COMPANIES vol 14 (2016) PARA 124. As to bodies corporate see COMPANIES vol 14 (2016) PARA 2; CORPORATIONS vol 24 (2010) PARA 301 et seq.

5 Local Government Finance Act 1988 Sch 4A para 8(b) (as added: see note 1).

6 As to the meaning of 'building' see PARA 138 note 5.

7 Local Government Finance Act 1988 Sch 4A para 8(c) (as added: see note 1). See also *UKI (Kingsway) Ltd v Westminster City Council* [2017] EWCA Civ 430, [2017] All ER (D) 93 (Jun) (no authorised receipt).

140. Completion date of substantially completed building.

In the case of a building[1] to which work remains to be done which is customarily done to a building of the type in question after the building has been substantially completed[2], it is to be assumed that the building has been or can reasonably be expected to be completed at the end of such period beginning with the date of its completion apart from the work as is reasonably required for carrying out the work[3].

1 As to the meaning of 'building' see PARA 138 note 5.

2 Local Government Finance Act 1988 Sch 4A para 9(1) (Sch 4A added by the Local Government and Housing Act 1989 s 139, Sch 5 paras 36, 79(3)). The test to be applied in determining whether a building is 'completed' has been held to be whether the building as a building is ready for occupation or capable of occupation for the purpose for which it was intended: *Ravenseft Properties Ltd v Newham London Borough Council* [1976] QB 464, [1976] 1 All ER 580, CA; *Post Office v Nottingham City Council* [1976] 2 All ER 831, [1976] 1 WLR 624, CA; and see *Spears Bros v Rushmoor Borough Council* [2006] RA 86, Lands Tribunal (a building without electric lighting is incapable of occupation as a workshop and the building in question could not be occupied without a fire alarm system in any case). See also *Porter (Valuation Officer) v Trustees of Gladman Sipps* [2011] UKUT 204 (LC), [2011] RA 337 (newly erected office units not rateable).

Some of the cases cited in this paragraph were decided prior to the coming into force of the Local Government Finance Act 1988 but continue to be of relevance: see PARA 50.

3 Local Government Finance Act 1988 Sch 4A para 9(2) (as added: see note 2). The time runs from the date of substantial completion whenever that occurred: *Graylaw Investments Ltd v Ipswich Borough Council* [1979] RA 111, CA. In deciding the time, it is not correct to take into account the time necessary to find a tenant, even though the work cannot be carried out until he has specified his requirements (*JLG Investments Ltd v Sandwell District Council* [1977] RA 78, CA); nor can the time required for planning the work be taken into account (*London Merchant Securities plc and Trendworthy Two v Islington London Borough Council* [1988] AC 303, [1987] 2 All ER 961, HL). See also *Provident Mutual Life Assurance Association v Derby City Council* [1981] 1 WLR 173, [1981] RA 117, HL.

141. Determination of completion day.

If the person[1] on whom a completion notice[2] is served[3] agrees in writing[4] with the billing authority[5] by whom the notice is served that a day specified by the agreement is to be the completion day in relation to the building[6], that day must be the completion day in relation to it[7]. Where such an agreement is made, the completion notice relating to the building is deemed to have been withdrawn[8]. The billing authority must supply the valuation officer[9] with details of any agreement to which it is a party and by virtue of which a completion day is determined in relation to a building[10].

A person on whom a completion notice is served may appeal to a valuation tribunal[11] against the notice on the ground that the building to which the notice relates has not been (or, as the case may be, cannot reasonably be expected to be) completed by the day stated in the notice[12].

Provision is made in relation to the completion day pending such an appeal[13].

Where a person appeals against a completion notice and the appeal is not withdrawn or dismissed, the completion day is such day as the tribunal determines[14]. Where an appeal has been brought against a completion notice, the power of the billing authority to withdraw a notice[15] is only exercisable with the consent in writing of the owner[16] of the building to which the notice relates[17].

Where a completion notice is not withdrawn and no appeal is brought against the notice, or where any appeal is dismissed or withdrawn, the day stated in the notice is the completion day in relation to the building[18].

1 As to the meaning of 'person' see PARA 11 note 13.

2 As to completion notices see PARA 138.

3 As to the service of notices see PARA 139.

4 As to the meaning of 'writing' see PARA 21 note 3.

5 As to the meaning of 'billing authority' see PARA 53.

6 As to the meaning of 'building' see PARA 138 note 5.

7 Local Government Finance Act 1988 Sch 4A para 3(1) (Sch 4A added by the Local Government and Housing Act 1989 s 139, Sch 5 paras 36, 79(3)).

8 Local Government Finance Act 1988 Sch 4A para 3(2) (as added: see note 7).

9 As to the meaning of 'valuation officer' see PARA 54 note 3.

10 Local Government Finance Act 1988 Sch 4A para 7(3) (as added (see note 7); amended by the Local Government Finance Act 1992 ss 117(1), 118(1), Sch 13 para 83(4)).

11 'Valuation tribunal' means, in relation to England, the Valuation Tribunal for England; and, in relation to Wales, a valuation tribunal established under the Local Government Finance Act 1988 Sch 11 para 1 (see PARA 236): Sch 4A para 4(3) (Sch 4A as added (see note 7); Sch 4A para 4(3) added by the Local Government and Public Involvement in Health Act 2007 s 220(1), Sch 16 paras 2, 4). As to the meanings of 'England' and 'Wales' see PARA 2 note 16. As to the Valuation Tribunal for England see PARA 232.

12 Local Government Finance Act 1988 Sch 4A para 4(1) (as added (see note 7); amended by the Local Government Finance Act 1992 Sch 13 para 83(2)). As to the procedure for the initiation of such appeals see, in relation to England, the Non-Domestic Rating (Alteration of Lists and Appeals) (England) Regulations 2009, SI 2009/2268, reg 19; and, in relation to Wales, the Non-Domestic Rating (Alteration of Lists and Appeals) (Wales) Regulations 2005, SI 2005/758, reg 19. As to appeals to a valuation tribunal generally see PARA 232 et seq.

13 See the Local Government Finance Act 1988 Sch 4A para 6 (as added: see note 7). Accordingly, where an appeal under Sch 4A para 4 is brought against a completion notice, then in relation to any day on which the appeal is pending s 45 (see PARA 135) applies by virtue of s 46A(4) (see PARA 135 note 4) as if the day stated in the notice had been determined under Sch 4A as the completion day in relation to the building to which the notice relates: Sch 4A para 6(1) (as so added). The Secretary of State or, in relation to Wales, the Welsh Ministers may make regulations providing for the making of financial adjustments where Sch 4A para 6(1) applies but the day stated in the completion notice is not actually determined as the completion day in relation to the building to which the notice relates: Sch 4A para 6(2) (as so added). Such regulations may include provision requiring payments or repayments to be made (with or without interest) and provision as to the recovery (by deduction or otherwise) of sums due: Sch 4A para 6(3) (as so added; amended by the Local Government Finance Act 1992 Sch 13 para 83(3)). For the purpose of deciding, for the purposes of the Local Government Finance Act 1988 Sch 4A para 6, whether an appeal is pending on a particular day, the state of affairs existing immediately before the day ends is to be treated as having existed throughout the day: Sch 4A para 6(4) (as so added). At the date at which this volume states the law no regulations had been made under Sch 4A para 6.

The functions of the Secretary of State under Sch 4A, so far as exercisable in relation to Wales, were transferred to the National Assembly for Wales (see the National Assembly for Wales (Transfer of Functions) Order 1999, SI 1999/672, art 2, Sch 1) and are now vested in the Welsh Ministers (see the Government of Wales Act 2006 s 162(1), Sch 11 para 30). As to the Secretary of State and the Welsh Ministers see PARA 4 note 18. As to the separate administration of the non-domestic rating provisions (Local Government Finance Act 1988 Pt III (ss 41–67)) in England and Wales see PARA 52.

14 Local Government Finance Act 1988 Sch 4A para 4(2) (as added: see note 7).

15 Ie under the Local Government Finance Act 1988 Sch 4A para 1(3): see PARA 138.

16 As to the meaning of 'owner' see PARA 138 note 12.

17 Local Government Finance Act 1988 Sch 4A para 1(4) (as added: see note 7).
18 Local Government Finance Act 1988 Sch 4A para 5 (as added: see note 7).

(ii) Central Non-domestic Rating Lists

142. Hereditaments entered in central rating lists.

A person[1] (the 'ratepayer') is subject to a non-domestic rate in respect of a chargeable financial year[2] if for any day in the year his name is shown in a central non-domestic rating list in force for the year[3]. In such a case, the ratepayer is liable to pay an amount calculated by:

(1) finding the chargeable amount for each chargeable day[4]; and
(2) aggregating the amounts found under head (1)[5].

The chargeable amount for a chargeable day is calculated by multiplying the rateable value[6] by the non-domestic rating multiplier for the financial year[7], and by using the number of days in the financial year[8] to divide the product[9].

The amount the ratepayer is liable to pay must be paid to the appropriate national authority[10].

A specific formula applies where:

(a) for any day in a chargeable financial year a person's name is shown in a central non-domestic rating list in force for the year[11];
(b) on that day ('the chargeable day'), the specified condition[12] is met in relation to any description of hereditament shown against the person's name in the list[13];
(c) the chargeable day falls before 1 April 2022[14]; and
(d) any conditions prescribed by the appropriate national authority by regulations are satisfied on the chargeable day[15].

1 As to the meaning of 'person' see PARA 11 note 13.
2 As to the meaning of 'chargeable financial year' see PARA 24 note 1.
3 Local Government Finance Act 1988 s 54(1). As to central non-domestic rating lists see PARA 196.
4 Local Government Finance Act 1988 s 54(2)(a). A 'chargeable day' is one which falls within the financial year and for which the ratepayer's name is shown in the list: s 54(3).
5 Local Government Finance Act 1988 s 54(2)(b).
6 Ie the rateable value shown for the day in the list against the ratepayer's name: see the Local Government Finance Act 1988 s 54(5).
7 See the Local Government Finance Act 1988 s 54(6).
8 See the Local Government Finance Act 1988 s 54(7).
9 Local Government Finance Act 1988 s 54(4). This is subject to s 54ZA: see s 54(4) (amended by the Telecommunications Infrastructure (Relief from Non-Domestic Rates) Act 2018 s 3(2)).
10 Local Government Finance Act 1988 s 54(8). The liability to pay any such amount is discharged by making a payment or payments in accordance with regulations made under Sch 9 (see PARA 226 et seq): s 54(9). 'Appropriate national authority' means the Secretary of State or, in relation to Wales, the Welsh Ministers. The functions of the Secretary of State under s 54, so far as exercisable in relation to Wales, were transferred to the National Assembly for Wales (see the National Assembly for Wales (Transfer of Functions) Order 1999, SI 1999/672, art 2, Sch 1) and are now vested in the Welsh Ministers (see the Government of Wales Act 2006 s 162(1), Sch 11 para 30). As to the separate administration of the non-domestic rating provisions (Local Government Finance Act 1988 Pt III (ss 41–67)) in England and Wales see PARA 52.
11 Local Government Finance Act 1988 s 54ZA(1)(a) (added by the Telecommunications Infrastructure (Relief from Non-Domestic Rates) Act 2018 s 3(3)). As to the formula to be applied see the Local Government Finance Act 1988 s 54ZA(3) (as so added). Regulations may be made in relation to this formula (see s 54ZA(3) (as so added) which may in particular:
(1) impose duties or confer powers on the central valuation officer (whether as regards determinations, certificates or otherwise) in relation to the ascertainment of rateable values;
(2) make provision as to appeals relating to things done or not done by the central valuation officer: s 54ZA(4) (as so added).

At the date at which this volume states the law no such regulations had been made.

12 The specified condition is met in relation to a description of hereditament if:

(1) in a case where there is only one hereditament falling within the description, the hereditament is wholly or mainly used for the purposes of facilitating the transmission of communications by any means involving the use of electrical or electromagnetic energy; or

(2) in a case where there is more than one hereditament falling within the description, those hereditaments are, taken together, wholly or mainly so used: Local Government Finance Act 1988 s 54ZA(2) (as added: see note 11).

13 Local Government Finance Act 1988 s 54ZA(1)(b) (as added: see note 11).

14 Local Government Finance Act 1988 s 54ZA(1)(c) (as added: see note 11). The Secretary of State or the Welsh Ministers, as appropriate, may by regulations amend s 54ZA(1)(c) so as to substitute a later date for the date for the time being specified in that provision: s 54ZA(5), (6) (as so added).

15 Local Government Finance Act 1988 s 54ZA(1)(d) (as added: see note 11).

(iii) Relief Schemes

A. MANDATORY RELIEF FOR OCCUPIED HEREDITAMENTS

(A) Small Businesses

143. Small business rate relief.

The formula used to calculate the amount payable for occupied hereditaments[1] in the local non-domestic rating list may be modified in certain circumstances in order to reduce the burden for small businesses[2].

Accordingly, in relation to England[3], where, on the day concerned any conditions prescribed[4] by the Secretary of State[5] by order are satisfied[6], the chargeable amount for a chargeable day[7] is calculated by:

(1) multiplying the rateable value[8] by the small business non-domestic rating multiplier for the financial year[9];

(2) multiplying the number of days in the financial year[10] by such amount as may be prescribed for the purpose by the Secretary of State by order[11]; and

(3) dividing the product found under head (1) by the product found under head (2)[12].

In relation to Wales[13], where:

(a) the rateable value of the hereditament shown in the local non-domestic rating list for the first day of the chargeable financial year[14] is not more than any amount prescribed by the Welsh Ministers[15] by order[16]; and

(b) on the day concerned any conditions prescribed by the Welsh Ministers by order are satisfied[17],

the chargeable amount for a chargeable day is calculated by:

(i) multiplying the rateable value[18] by the non-domestic rating multiplier for the financial year[19];

(ii) multiplying the number of days in the financial year[20] by such amount as may be prescribed for the purpose by the Welsh Ministers by order[21]; and

(iii) dividing the product found under head (i) by the product found under head (ii)[22].

The amount the ratepayer is liable to pay must be paid to the billing authority in whose local non-domestic rating list the hereditament is shown[23].

1 As to the meaning of 'hereditament' see PARA 106.

2 As to local non-domestic rating lists see PARA 191 et seq. As to liability to the non-domestic rate for occupied hereditaments in the local non-domestic rating lists see the Local Government Finance

Act 1988 s 43(4); and PARA 133. As to discretionary relief which may be available see PARA 149. Where, before 1 April 2022, the hereditament is wholly or mainly used for the purposes of facilitating the transmission of communications by any means involving the use of electrical or electromagnetic energy and any conditions prescribed by the appropriate national authority by regulations are satisfied on the day concerned, a different calculation applies: see s 43(4E)–(4H) (added by the Telecommunications Infrastructure (Relief from Non-Domestic Rates) Act 2018 s 1(1)–(3)).

3 As to the meaning of 'England' see PARA 2 note 16. As to the separate administration of the non-domestic rating provisions (Local Government Finance Act 1988 Pt III (ss 41–67)) in England and Wales see PARA 52.

4 'Prescribed' means prescribed by regulations: see the Local Government Finance Act 1988 s 146(6).

5 As to the Secretary of State see PARA 4 note 18.

6 Local Government Finance Act 1988 s 43(4B)(a)(ii) (s 43(4A)–(4D) added by the Local Government Act 2003 s 61(1), (3); the Local Government Finance Act 1988 s 43(4B)(a) amended by the Localism Act 2011 ss 70(1), (2), 237, Sch 25 Pt 11). For the purpose of the Local Government Finance Act 1988 s 43(4B)(a)(ii), the condition to be satisfied in respect of chargeable days (see note 7) falling on or after 1 April 2017 is that the rateable value of the hereditament as shown in the local non-domestic rating list for the chargeable day is not more than £50,999: see the Non-Domestic Rating (Reliefs, Thresholds and Amendment) (England) Order 2017, SI 2017/102, arts 1(2), 2.

If the ratepayer makes an application in order to satisfy a condition prescribed under the Local Government Finance Act 1988 s 43(4B)(a)(ii) and makes a statement in the application which he knows to be false in a material particular, or recklessly makes a statement in the application which is false in a material particular, he is liable on summary conviction to imprisonment for a term not exceeding three months or to a fine not exceeding level 3 on the standard scale or to both: s 43(4D) (as so added; amended by the Localism Act 2011 s 70(1), (4)). As to the powers of magistrates' courts to issue fines on summary conviction see SENTENCING vol 92 (2015) PARA 176.

7 A 'chargeable day' is one which falls within the financial year and in respect of which the conditions in the Local Government Finance Act 1988 s 43(1) (see PARA 133) are fulfilled: s 43(3). As to the meaning of 'financial year' see PARA 24 note 1.

8 Ie the rateable value shown for the day in the local non-domestic rating list under the Local Government Finance Act 1988 s 42(4) (see PARA 194 et seq) as regards the hereditament: see s 44(1), (2) (s 44(2) amended by the Local Government and Housing Act 1989 s 194(4), Sch 5 paras 1, 21, 79(3), Sch 12 Pt II).

9 See the Local Government Finance Act 1988 s 44(1), (7) (s 44(7)–(9) added by the Local Government Act 2003 s 61(5)). The small business non-domestic rating multiplier is fixed annually by the Secretary of State using the method set out in the Local Government Finance Act 1988 Sch 7: see PARA 156. Where the billing authority is a special authority, the figure used for the small business non-domestic rating multiplier is the authority's small business non-domestic rating multiplier for the financial year: see s 44(1), (8) (as so added). As to the meaning of 'billing authority' see PARA 53. As to the meaning of 'special authority' see PARA 133 note 11.

10 See the Local Government Finance Act 1988 s 44(1), (6).

11 See the Local Government Finance Act 1988 s 44(1), (9)(a) (as added: see note 9). As to the prescribed amount in respect of chargeable days falling on or after 1 April 2017 see the Non-Domestic Rating (Reliefs, Thresholds and Amendment) (England) Order 2017, SI 2017/102, arts 1(2), 3.

12 See the Local Government Finance Act 1988 s 43(4A)(a) (as added: see note 6). In relation to any hereditament in respect of which both s 43(4A) and s 43(6A) (rural settlements: see PARA 145), but not s 43(5) (charities etc: see CHARITIES vol 8 (2015) PARA 433), have effect on the day concerned, the chargeable amount, in relation to England, is to be calculated in accordance with s 43(6A): s 43(8A)(a) (s 43(8A) added by the Rating (Former Agricultural Premises and Rural Shops) Act 2001 s 1(1), (4); and substituted by the Local Government Act 2003 s 61(1), (4)). In relation to any hereditament in respect of which the Local Government Finance Act 1988 s 43(4A), s 43(5) and s 43(6A) each have effect on the day concerned, or in respect of which s 43(4A) and s 43(5) both have effect on that day, the chargeable amount is to be calculated in accordance with s 43(5): s 43(8B) (added by the Local Government Act 2003 s 61(1), (4)).

13 As to the meaning of 'Wales' see PARA 2 note 16.

14 As to the meaning of 'chargeable financial year' see PARA 24 note 1.

15 As to the Welsh Ministers see PARA 4 note 18. The functions under the Local Government Finance Act 1988 s 43 were formerly vested in the National Assembly for Wales and are now exercisable by the Welsh Ministers by virtue of the Government of Wales Act 2006 s 162(1), Sch 11 paras 30, 32.

16 Local Government Finance Act 1988 s 43(4B)(b)(i) (as added: see note 6). For the purposes of s 43(4B)(b)(i), the amount prescribed for a hereditament is £12,000: Non-Domestic Rating (Small Business Relief) (Wales) Order 2015, SI 2015/229, art 4.

17 See the Local Government Finance Act 1988 s 43(4B)(b)(ii) (as added: see note 6). As to the conditions to be satisfied see the Non-Domestic Rating (Small Business Relief) (Wales) Order 2015, SI 2015/229, arts 5–9.

18 Ie the rateable value shown for the day in the local non-domestic rating list under the Local Government Finance Act 1988 s 42(4) (see PARA 194) as regards the hereditament: see s 44(1), (2) (s 44(2) as amended: see note 8).

19 See the Local Government Finance Act 1988 s 44(1), (4). The non-domestic rating multiplier is a uniform amount applying to every billing authority area and is fixed annually by the Welsh Ministers using the method set out in Sch 7: see PARA 156. Where the billing authority is a special authority, the figure used for the non-domestic rating multiplier is the authority's non-domestic rating multiplier for the financial year: see s 44(1), (5) (amended by the Local Government Finance Act 1992 s 117(1), Sch 13 para 61).

20 See the Local Government Finance Act 1988 s 44(1), (6).

21 See the Local Government Finance Act 1988 s 44(1), (9)(b) (as added: see note 9). As to the prescribed amount see the Non-Domestic Rating (Small Business Relief) (Wales) Order 2015, SI 2015/229, art 10.

22 See the Local Government Finance Act 1988 s 43(4A)(b) (as added: see note 6). In relation to any hereditament in respect of which both s 43(4A) and s 43(6A) (rural settlements: see PARA 145 et seq), but not s 43(5) (charities etc: see CHARITIES vol 8 (2015) PARA 433) have effect on the day concerned, the chargeable amount, in relation to Wales, is to be calculated in accordance with whichever of s 43(4A) and s 43(6A) produces the smaller amount: s 43(8A)(b) (as added and substituted: see note 12). In relation to any hereditament in respect of which s 43(4A), s 43(5) and s 43(6A) each have effect on the day concerned, or in respect of which s 43(4A) and s 43(5) both have effect on that day, the chargeable amount is to be calculated in accordance with s 43(5): s 43(8B) (as added: see note 12).

23 Local Government Finance Act 1988 s 43(7) (amended by the Local Government Finance Act 1992 Sch 13 para 60). The liability to pay any such amount is discharged by making a payment or payments in accordance with regulations made under the Local Government Finance Act 1988 Sch 9 (see PARA 226 et seq): s 43(8).

(B) Charities and Community Amateur Sports Clubs

144. Charitable relief from rating.

Under the Local Government Finance Act 1988, in respect of three categories of hereditament[1], namely where the ratepayers are:

(1) charities;
(2) trustees for a charity; or
(3) qualifying community amateur sports clubs,

the chargeable amount for which the ratepayer is liable is reduced, in relation to any occupied[2] hereditament where the qualifying ratepayer uses the hereditament wholly or mainly for charitable purposes[3] (whether of that charity or of that and other charities) or for the purposes of the registered club (whichever applies)[4]. Hereditaments which are to be used for such purposes but which are temporarily unoccupied may qualify for zero-rating[5].

1 As to the hereditament see PARA 106.

2 As to occupation by a charity see CHARITIES vol 8 (2015) PARA 434

3 As to use wholly or mainly for charitable purposes see CHARITIES vol 8 (2015) PARA 435. See also *South Kesteven District Council v Digital Pipeline Ltd* [2016] EWHC 101 (Admin), [2016] 1 WLR 2971, [2016] RA 113.

4 As to relief for charities and community amateur sports clubs see CHARITIES vol 8 (2015) PARAS 432–433 As to discretionary relief which may be available see PARA 149.

5 See the Local Government Finance Act 1988 s 45A; CHARITIES vol 8 (2015) PARA 436; and PARA 147.

(C) Rural Settlements in England

145. Rural rate relief in England.

The formula used to calculate the amount payable for occupied hereditaments in the local rating list may be modified in certain circumstances in order to reduce the burden for occupied hereditaments in England in the rural settlement list[1].

The circumstances which must be satisfied are that:

(1) the hereditament[2] is situated in England[3];

(2) on the day concerned the hereditament is within a settlement identified in the billing authority's[4] rural settlement list for the chargeable financial year[5];

(3) the rateable value of the hereditament shown in the local non-domestic rating list[6] at the beginning of that year is not more than any amount prescribed by the Secretary of State[7] by order[8]; and

(4) on the day concerned:

(a) the whole or part of the hereditament is used as a qualifying general store[9], a qualifying food store[10] or qualifying office[11]; or

(b) any conditions prescribed by the Secretary of State by order are satisfied[12].

In such a case, the chargeable amount for a chargeable day[13] is calculated by:

(i) multiplying the rateable value[14] by the non-domestic rating multiplier for the financial year[15];

(ii) multiplying by two the number of days in the financial year[16]; and

(iii) dividing the product found under head (i) by the product found under head (ii)[17].

The amount the ratepayer is liable to pay must be paid to the billing authority in whose local non-domestic rating list the hereditament is shown[18].

1 As to rural settlement lists see PARA 195. As to discretionary relief which may be available see PARA 149.

2 As to the meaning of 'hereditament' see PARA 106.

3 Local Government Finance Act 1988 s 43(6B)(aa) (s 43(6A)–(6C), (6D), (6E) added by the Local Government and Rating Act 1997 s 1, Sch 1 para 2(b); the Local Government Finance Act 1988 s 43(6B)(aa) added by the Local Government Act 2003 s 63(2)). As to the meaning of 'England' see PARA 2 note 16.

4 As to the meaning of 'billing authority' see PARA 53.

5 Local Government Finance Act 1988 s 43(6B)(a) (as added: see note 3). As to the meaning of 'chargeable financial year' see PARA 24 note 1.

6 As to local non-domestic rating lists see PARA 191 et seq.

7 As to the Secretary of State see PARA 4 note 18.

8 Local Government Finance Act 1988 s 43(6B)(b) (as added: see note 3). The amount prescribed as the maximum amount of the rateable value for the purposes of s 43(6B)(b) is, in the case of a hereditament shown in local non-domestic rating lists for billing authorities in England a part or the whole of which is used as a public house or petrol filling station, £12,500 and, in the case of any other such hereditament, £8,500: see the Non-Domestic Rating (Rural Settlements) (England) Order 1997, SI 1997/2792, art 3(1), (3) (art 3(1) substituted by SI 2001/1346; and amended by SI 2009/3176).

9 A hereditament, or part of a hereditament, is used as a 'qualifying general store' on any day in a chargeable financial year if:

(1) a trade or business consisting wholly or mainly of the sale by retail of both food for human consumption (excluding confectionery) and general household goods is carried on there (Local Government Finance Act 1988 s 43(6C)(a) (as added: see note 3)); and

(2) such a trade or business is not carried on in any other hereditament, or part of a hereditament, in the settlement concerned (s 43(6C)(b) (as so added)).

Where a hereditament or part is used as a qualifying general store on any day in a chargeable financial year, it is not to be treated as ceasing to be so used on any subsequent day in that year merely because the condition in head (2) above ceases to be satisfied: s 43(6E) (as so added).

10 A hereditament, or part of a hereditament, is used as a 'qualifying food store' on any day in a chargeable financial year if a trade or business consisting wholly or mainly of the sale by retail of food for human consumption (excluding confectionery and excluding the supply of food in the course of catering) is carried on there: Local Government Finance Act 1988 s 43(6CA) (s 43(6CA), (6CB) added by the Rating (Former Agricultural Premises and Rural Shops) Act 2001 s 3(1), (3)). For these purposes, the supply of food in the course of catering includes any supply of food for consumption on the premises on which it is supplied as well as any supply of hot food for consumption off those premises; and for these purposes 'hot food' means food which, or any part of which has been heated for the purposes of enabling it to be consumed at a temperature above the ambient air temperature and is at the time of supply above that temperature: Local Government Finance Act 1988 s 43(6CB) (as so added).

11 Local Government Finance Act 1988 s 43(6B)(c)(i) (as added (see note 3); amended by the Rating (Former Agricultural Premises and Rural Shops) Act 2001 s 3(1), (2)). A hereditament, or part of a hereditament, is used as a 'qualifying office' on any day in a chargeable financial year if:

(1) it is used for the purposes of a universal service provider within the meaning of the Postal Services Act 2011 Pt 3 (ss 27–67) and in connection with the provision of a universal postal service within the meaning of that Part (see POSTAL SERVICES vol 85 (2012) PARA 252) (Local Government Finance Act 1988 s 43(6D)(a) (as so added; amended by the Postal Services Act 2000 s 127(4), Sch 8 para 21; and the Postal Services Act 2011 s 91(1), (3), Sch 12 para 131)); and

(2) no other hereditament, or part of a hereditament, in the settlement concerned is so used (Local Government Finance Act 1988 s 43(6D)(b) (as so added)).

Where a hereditament or part is used as a qualifying office on any day in a chargeable financial year, it is not to be treated as ceasing to be so used on any subsequent day in that year merely because the condition in head (2) above ceases to be satisfied: s 43(6E) (as so added).

12 Local Government Finance Act 1988 s 43(6B)(c)(ii) (as added: see note 3). The conditions prescribed for these purposes are that the whole or part of the hereditament is used as a public house or a petrol filling station, and in either case no other hereditament or part of a hereditament in the settlement concerned is so used: see the Non-Domestic Rating (Public Houses and Petrol Filling Stations) (England) Order 2001, SI 2001/1345, art 2.

13 For these purposes, a 'chargeable day' is one which falls within the financial year and in respect of which the conditions in the Local Government Finance Act 1988 s 43(1) (see PARA 133) are fulfilled: s 43(3).

14 Ie the rateable value shown for the day in the local non-domestic rating list under the Local Government Finance Act 1988 s 42(4) (see PARA 194) as regards the hereditament: see s 44(1), (2) (s 44(2) amended by the Local Government and Housing Act 1989 s 194(4), Sch 5 paras 1, 21, 79(3), Sch 12 Pt II).

15 See the Local Government Finance Act 1988 s 44(1), (4). The non-domestic rating multiplier is a uniform amount applying to every billing authority area and is fixed annually by the Secretary of State using the method set out in Sch 7: see PARA 156. Where the billing authority is a special authority, the figure used for the non-domestic rating multiplier is the authority's non-domestic rating multiplier for the financial year: see s 44(1), (5) (amended by the Local Government Finance Act 1992 s 117(1), Sch 13 para 61). As to the meaning of 'special authority' see PARA 133 note 11.

16 See the Local Government Finance Act 1988 s 44(1), (6).

17 Local Government Finance Act 1988 s 43(6A) (as added (see note 3); amended by the Rating (Former Agricultural Premises and Rural Shops) Act 2001 s 1(1), (2)). This modification has the effect of reducing by 50% the chargeable amount which applies generally to the non-domestic rate for occupied hereditaments in the local non-domestic rating lists (as to which see PARA 133).

In relation to any hereditament in respect of which both the Local Government Finance Act 1988 s 43(4A) (mandatory small business rate relief: see PARA 143) and s 43(6A), but not s 43(5) (charities etc: see CHARITIES vol 8 (2015) PARA 433), have effect on the day concerned, the chargeable amount, in relation to England, is to be calculated in accordance with s 43(6A): s 43(8A)(a) (s 43(8A) added by the Rating (Former Agricultural Premises and Rural Shops) Act 2001 s 1(1), (4); and substituted by the Local Government Act 2003 s 61(1), (4)). In relation to any hereditament in respect of which the Local Government Finance Act 1988 s 43(4A), s 43(5) and s 43(6A) each have effect on the day concerned, or in respect of which s 43(5) and s 43(6A) both have effect on that day, the chargeable amount is to be calculated in accordance with s 43(5): s

43(8B) (added by the Local Government Act 2003 s 61(1), (4)). In relation to any hereditament having effect on the day concerned in respect of which:

(1) s 43(4A), (4E) have effect, s 43(4A) is to be used;
(2) s 43(4E), (5) have effect, s 43(5) is to be used;
(3) s 43(4E), (6A) have effect, s 43(6A) is to be used;
(4) s 43(4A), (4E), (5) have effect, s 43(5) is to be used;
(5) s 43(4A), (4E), (6A) have effect s 43(6A) is to be used;
(6) s 43(4E), (5), (6A) have effect s 43(5) is to be used;
(7) s 43(4A), (4E), (5), (6A) have effect, s 43(5) is to be used: s 43(8C) added by the Telecommunications Infrastructure (Relief from Non-Domestic Rates Act 2018 s 1(4)).

18 Local Government Finance Act 1988 s 43(7) (amended by the Local Government Finance Act 1992 Sch 13 para 60). The liability to pay any such amount is discharged by making a payment or payments in accordance with regulations made under the Local Government Finance Act 1988 Sch 9 (see PARA 226 et seq): s 43(8).

(D) Former Agricultural Premises

146. Mandatory relief for former agricultural land or buildings.

The following provisions are to have effect in relation to Wales as from a day to be appointed[1].

The formula used to calculate the amount payable for occupied hereditaments in the local rating list[2] may be modified in certain circumstances where land and buildings which had previously been (for a qualifying period) agricultural land and buildings are subsequently used for non-agricultural purposes[3].

The circumstances that must be satisfied are that:

(1) on the day concerned, the following condition is fulfilled in respect of the hereditament[4], namely that the hereditament:
  (a) consists wholly or mainly of land or buildings which were, on at least 183 days during the qualifying period[5], agricultural land or agricultural buildings for the purposes[6] of the non-domestic rating agricultural exemption[7]; and
  (b) includes land or a building which is not agricultural for the purposes of that exemption but was agricultural for those purposes on at least 183 days during the period mentioned in head (a)[8]; and
(2) the rateable value of the hereditament shown in the local non-domestic rating list at the beginning of the chargeable financial year[9] is not more than any amount prescribed by the Welsh Ministers by order[10].

In such a case, the chargeable amount for a chargeable day[11] is calculated by:

(i) multiplying the rateable value[12] by the non-domestic rating multiplier for the financial year[13];
(ii) multiplying by two the number of days in the financial year[14]; and
(iii) dividing the product found under head (i) by the product found under head (ii)[15].

The amount the ratepayer is liable to pay must be paid to the billing authority in whose local non-domestic rating list the hereditament is shown[16].

1 The Local Government Finance Act 1988 s 43(6F)–(6L) is added by the Rating (Former Agricultural Premises and Rural Shops) Act 2001 s 1(1), (3) as from a day to be appointed under s 6(2). In relation to England, 17 July 2001 was appointed for the purposes of making an order under the Local Government Finance Act 1988 s 43(6F) and 15 August 2001 was appointed as the day for all other purposes: see the Rating (Former Agricultural Premises and Rural Shops) Act 2001 (Commencement No 1) Order 2001, SI 2001/2580, art 2. However, at the date at which this volume states the law, no such day had been appointed in relation to Wales. As to the meanings of 'England' and 'Wales' see PARA 2 note 16.

The Local Government Finance Act 1988 s 43(6F)–(6L) ceases to have effect at the end of the period of five years beginning with the day on which those provisions come into effect: s 43(6J) (as so added). However, the Secretary of State or, in relation to Wales, the Welsh Ministers may by order extend or further extend that period: s 43(6K) (as so added). If the period is so extended or further extended, s 43(6F) (see heads (1) and (2) in the text) cannot apply to a hereditament after the end of the period of five years beginning with the day on which it first applies and, where a hereditament to which s 43(6F) applies (the 'original hereditament') includes land or a building which is subsequently included in a different hereditament, that provision cannot apply to the different hereditament after the end of the period of five years beginning with the day on which it first applies to the original hereditament: s 43(6L) (as so added). At the date at which this volume states the law, no such order had been made by the Secretary of State and accordingly, s 43(6F)–(6L) no longer has effect in relation to England.

As to the meaning of 'hereditament' see PARA 106. The functions of the Secretary of State under s 43, so far as exercisable in relation to Wales, were transferred to the National Assembly for Wales (see the National Assembly for Wales (Transfer of Functions) Order 1999, SI 1999/672, art 2, Sch 1) and are now vested in the Welsh Ministers (see the Government of Wales Act 2006 s 162(1), Sch 11 para 30). As to the Secretary of State and the Welsh Ministers see PARA 4 note 18.

2 As to local non-domestic rating lists see PARA 191 et seq. As to the separate administration of the non-domestic rating provisions (Local Government Finance Act 1988 Pt III (ss 41–67)) in England and Wales see PARA 52.

3 As to discretionary relief which may be available see PARA 149.

4 Local Government Finance Act 1988 s 43(6F)(a) (as added: see note 1).

5 Ie on at least 183 days during the period of one year ending immediately before the Local Government Finance Act 1988 s 43(6G)(a) comes into effect: see s 43(6G)(a) (as added: see note 1).

6 Ie for the purposes of the Local Government Finance Act 1988 Sch 5 para 1: see PARA 116 et seq.

7 Local Government Finance Act 1988 s 43(6G)(a) (as added: see note 1). In relation to any hereditament which includes property which is 'domestic' within the meaning of s 66 (see PARA 190), s 43(6G)(a) has effect as if that part of the hereditament which does not consist of such property were the entire hereditament (s 43(6H)(a) (as so added)), and a building which has replaced a building which was an agricultural building for the purposes of the exemption mentioned in s 43(6G) (the 'original building') is treated as if it were the original building (s 43(6H)(b) (as so added)).

8 Local Government Finance Act 1988 s 43(6G)(b) (as added: see note 1). See also note 7.

9 As to the meaning of 'chargeable financial year' see PARA 24 note 1.

10 Local Government Finance Act 1988 s 43(6F)(b) (as added: see note 1). At the date at which this volume states the law no such order had been made.

11 A 'chargeable day' is one which falls within the financial year and in respect of which the conditions in the Local Government Finance Act 1988 s 43(1) (see PARA 133) are fulfilled: s 43(3).

12 Ie the rateable value shown for the day in the local non-domestic rating list under the Local Government Finance Act 1988 s 42(4) (see PARA 194) as regards the hereditament: see s 44(1), (2) (s 44(2) amended by the Local Government and Housing Act 1989 s 194(4), Sch 5 paras 1, 21, 79(3), Sch 12 Pt II).

13 See the Local Government Finance Act 1988 s 44(1), (4). The non-domestic rating multiplier is a uniform amount applying to every billing authority area and is fixed annually by the Welsh Ministers using the method set out in Sch 7: see PARA 156. Where the billing authority is a special authority, the figure used for the non-domestic rating multiplier is the authority's non-domestic rating multiplier for the financial year: see s 44(1), (5) (amended by the Local Government Finance Act 1992 s 117(1), Sch 13 para 61). As to the meaning of 'billing authority' see PARA 53. As to the meaning of 'special authority' see PARA 133 note 11.

14 See the Local Government Finance Act 1988 s 44(1), (6).

15 See the Local Government Finance Act 1988 s 43(6A) (added by the Local Government and Rating Act 1997 s 1, Sch 1 para 2(b); and amended by the Rating (Former Agricultural Premises and Rural Shops) Act 2001 s 1(1), (2)). However, the Local Government Finance Act 1988 s 43(6A) does not have effect in relation to a hereditament to which s 43(6F) applies (see heads (1) and (2) in the text) on a chargeable day on which Sch 6 para 2A (see PARA 168) applies in relation to the hereditament: s 43(6I) (as so added). The modification made by s 43(6A) has the effect of reducing by 50% the chargeable amount which applies generally to the non-domestic rate for occupied hereditaments in the local non-domestic rating lists (as to which see PARA 133).

In relation to any hereditament in respect of which both s 43(4A) (mandatory small business rate relief: see PARA 143) and s 43(6A), but not s 43(5) (charities etc: see CHARITIES vol 8 (2015) PARA 433), have effect on the day concerned, the chargeable amount, in relation to Wales, is to be calculated in accordance with whichever of s 43(4A) and s 43(6A) produces the smaller amount: s 43(8A)(b) (added by the Rating (Former Agricultural Premises and Rural Shops) Act 2001 s 1(1), (4); and substituted by the Local Government Act 2003 s 61(1), (4)). In relation to any hereditament in respect of which the Local Government Finance Act 1988 s 43(4A), s 43(5) and s 43(6A) each have effect on the day concerned, or in respect of which s 43(5) and s 43(6A) both have effect on that day, the chargeable amount is to be calculated in accordance with s 43(5): see s 43(8B) (added by the Local Government Act 2003 s 61(1), (4)).

16 Local Government Finance Act 1988 s 43(7) (amended by the Local Government Finance Act 1992 Sch 13 para 60). The liability to pay any such amount is discharged by making a payment or payments in accordance with regulations made under the Local Government Finance Act 1988 Sch 9 (see PARA 226 et seq): s 43(8).

B. MANDATORY RELIEF FOR UNOCCUPIED HEREDITAMENTS

147. Zero-rating for charities and community amateur sports clubs.

Where a person[1] (the 'ratepayer') is liable to pay a non-domestic rate as regards an unoccupied hereditament[2], the chargeable amount[3] for a chargeable day[4] is zero[5] where:

(1) the ratepayer is a charity[6] or trustees for a charity[7], and it appears that when next in use the hereditament will be wholly or mainly used for charitable purposes[8] (whether of that charity or of that and other charities)[9]; or

(2) the ratepayer is a registered community amateur sports club[10], and it appears that when the hereditament is next in use:

(a) it will be wholly or mainly used for the purposes of that club and that club will be such a registered club[11]; or

(b) it will be wholly or mainly used for the purposes of two or more clubs including that club, and each of those clubs will be such a registered club[12].

1 As to the meaning of 'person' see PARA 11 note 13.

2 Ie where the Local Government Finance Act 1988 s 45 (see PARAS 135–136) applies in relation to a hereditament: see s 45A(1) (s 45A added by the Rating (Empty Properties) Act 2007 s 1(2)). As to the meaning of 'hereditament' see PARA 106.

3 For the usual purposes of the Local Government Finance Act 1988 s 45, the chargeable amount is calculated using the formula set out in s 45(4): see PARA 135.

4 A chargeable day is one which falls within the financial year and in respect of which the conditions mentioned in the Local Government Finance Act 1988 s 45(1) are fulfilled: see s 45(3); and PARA 135. Section 45A(2), (3) (see heads (1) and (2) in the text) applies on a particular day if (and only if) it applies immediately before the day ends: see s 67(7) (amended by Rating (Empty Properties) Act 2007 s 2(1), Sch 1 para 5).

5 Local Government Finance Act 1988 s 45A(1) (as added: see note 2).

6 As to the meaning of 'charity' see CHARITIES vol 8 (2015) PARA 1.

7 Local Government Finance Act 1988 s 45A(2)(a) (as added: see note 2).

8 As to the meaning of 'wholly or mainly used for charitable purposes' see PARA 144.

9 Local Government Finance Act 1988 s 45A(2)(b) (as added: see note 2).

10 See the Local Government Finance Act 1988 s 45A(3)(a) (as added (see note 2); amended by SI 2013/463). This provision refers to a registered club for the purposes of the Corporation Tax Act 2010 Pt 13 Ch 9 (ss 658–671) (community amateur sports clubs): see CAPITAL GAINS TAXATION vol 6 (2011) PARA 892.

11 Local Government Finance Act 1988 s 45A(3)(b)(i) (as added: see note 2).

12 Local Government Finance Act 1988 s 45A(3)(b)(ii) (as added: see note 2).

148. Chargeable amount for unoccupied properties may be reduced by order.

An order may be made, in relation to England, by the Secretary of State and, in relation to Wales, by the Welsh Ministers[1] and may provide that the chargeable amount for each chargeable day[2] that a ratepayer[3] is liable to pay as regards an unoccupied hereditament is to be calculated by:

(1) multiplying the rateable value[4] by the non-domestic rating multiplier for the financial year[5];

(2) multiplying the number of days in the financial year[6] by such number (greater than one but not greater than two) as may be prescribed[7]; and

(3) dividing the product found under head (1) by the product found under head (2)[8].

1 See the Local Government Finance Act 1988 s 45(4B) (s 45(4A), (4B) added by the Rating (Empty Properties) Act 2007 s 1(1)). At the date at which this volume states the law no such order had been made. As to the Secretary of State and the Welsh Ministers see PARA 4 note 18. As to the meanings of 'England' and 'Wales' see PARA 2 note 16. As to the separate administration of the non-domestic rating provisions (Local Government Finance Act 1988 Pt III (ss 41–67)) in England and Wales see PARA 52. A different chargeable rate applies where the hereditament is wholly or mainly used for the purposes of facilitating the transmission of communications by any means involving the use of electrical or electromagnetic energy, the chargeable day falls before 1 April 2022 (or a different date prescribed by regulations) and any conditions prescribed by the Secretary of State or the Welsh Ministers (as appropriate) by regulations are satisfied on the chargeable day: see s 45(4C)–(4G) (added by the Telecommunications Infrastructure (Relief from Non-Domestic Rates) Act 2018 s 2).

2 A chargeable day is one which falls within the financial year and in respect of which the conditions mentioned in the Local Government Finance Act 1988 s 45(1) are fulfilled: see s 45(3); and PARA 135.

3 Ie a person who is subject to a non-domestic rate as regards an unoccupied hereditament in a local rating list: see the Local Government Finance Act 1988 s 45(1); and PARA 135.

4 Ie the rateable value shown for the day in the local non-domestic rating list under the Local Government Finance Act 1988 s 42(4) (see PARA 194) as regards the hereditament: see s 46(1), (2) (s 46(2) amended by the Local Government and Housing Act 1989 s 194(4), Sch 5 paras 1, 21, 79(3), Sch 12 Pt II).

5 See the Local Government Finance Act 1988 s 46(1), (3). The non-domestic rating multiplier is a uniform amount applying to every billing authority area and is fixed annually by the Secretary of State or, in relation to Wales, the Welsh Ministers using the method set out in Sch 7: see PARA 156. Where the billing authority is a special authority, the figure used for the non-domestic rating multiplier is the authority's non-domestic rating multiplier for the financial year: see s 46(1), (4) (amended by the Local Government Finance Act 1992 s 117(1), Sch 13 para 64). As to the meaning of 'special authority' see PARA 133 note 11. As to the meaning of 'billing authority' see PARA 53.

6 See the Local Government Finance Act 1988 s 46(1), (5).

7 Local Government Finance Act 1988 s 45(4A) (as added: see note 1). 'Prescribed' means prescribed by the order: see s 146(6). The number so prescribed will control the amount of the reduction (not greater than 50%) that is to be applied by order.

8 See the Local Government Finance Act 1988 s 45(4A) (as added: see note 1). The formula set out in s 45(4A) supplants that used in s 45(4) (see PARA 135) where an order under s 45(4A) has been made: see s 45(4A) (as so added).

C. DISCRETIONARY RELIEF

149. Scope of discretionary relief.

Except where an unoccupied hereditament[1] is zero-rated[2] or where the hereditament is an excepted hereditament[3], where the eligibility condition[4] is fulfilled for a day which is a chargeable day[5] the chargeable amount for the day is such as is determined by (or found in accordance with rules determined by) the billing authority concerned[6]. Consequently, certain provisions[7] do not apply as regards the day[8].

When making a decision under the eligibility condition[9], a billing authority in England must have regard to any relevant guidance issued by the Secretary of State[10] and a billing authority in Wales must have regard to any relevant guidance issued by the Welsh Ministers[11]. In certain circumstances[12] the billing authority may make the decision only if it is satisfied that it would be reasonable for it to do so, having regard to the interests of persons liable to pay council tax set by it[13].

1 As to the meaning of 'hereditament' see PARA 106. If a hereditament is wholly unoccupied but it appears that it or any part of it when next occupied will be occupied for particular purposes, the hereditament or part concerned (as the case may be) is to be treated as occupied for these purposes: Local Government Finance Act 1988 s 48(1), (5) (s 48(1) amended by the Local Government and Rating Act 1997 s 1, Sch 1 para 4; and the Localism Act 2011 s 237, Sch 25 Pt 10)). As to the occupier and occupation of land see PARA 85 et seq.

2 See the Local Government Finance Act 1988 s 47(10) (added by the Rating (Empty Properties) Act 2007 s 2(1), Sch 1 para 2(1), (3)).

3 Local Government Finance Act 1988 s 47(8A) (added by the Localism Act 2011 s 69(1), (7)). A hereditament is an 'excepted hereditament' if all or part of it is occupied (otherwise than as trustee) by: a billing authority; a precepting authority, other than the Receiver for the Metropolitan Police District or charter trustees; or a functional body, within the meaning of the Greater London Authority Act 1999 (see LONDON GOVERNMENT vol 71 (2013) PARA 148): Local Government Finance Act 1988 s 47(9) (amended by the Local Government Finance Act 1992 Sch 13 para 65; and the Greater London Authority Act 1999 s 138). As from a day to be appointed under the Greater London Authority Act 1999 s 425(2), the words 'the Receiver for the Metropolitan Police District or' above are repealed by s 423, Sch 34 Pt I. At the date at which this volume states the law no such day had been appointed. As to the meaning of 'precepting authority' see PARA 23 note 1 (definition applied by the Local Government Finance Act 1988 s 144(2) (substituted by the Local Government Finance Act 1992 s 117(1), Sch 13 para 81(1); and amended by the Local Government Finance Act 2012 s 5(1), (2)(b), Sch 3 paras 23, 29)). As to charter trustees see LOCAL GOVERNMENT vol 69 (2018) PARA 144.

A hereditament which is wholly unoccupied is to be treated as an excepted hereditament if it appears that when any of it is next occupied the hereditament will be an excepted hereditament: Local Government Finance Act 1988 s 48(1), (4) (s 48(1) as amended: see note 1).

4 Ie the condition mentioned in the Local Government Finance Act 1988 s 47(3). The condition is that, during a period which consists of or includes the chargeable day, a decision of the billing authority concerned operates to the effect that s 47 applies as regards the hereditament concerned: s 47(3) (amended by the Local Government Finance Act 1992 Sch 13 para 65; and the Localism Act 2011 ss 69(1), (4), 237, Sch 25 Pt 10).

5 See the Local Government Finance Act 1988 s 47(1) (amended by the Localism Act 2011 s 69(1), (2)). A 'chargeable day' is a chargeable day within the meaning of the Local Government Finance Act 1988 s 43 (occupied hereditaments) (see PARAS 133, 143 et seq) or s 45 (unoccupied hereditaments) (see PARAS 135–136, 148), as the case may be: see s 47(1).

6 Local Government Finance Act 1988 s 47(1)(a) (amended by the Local Government Finance Act 1992 Sch 13 para 65(1)). As to the meaning of 'billing authority' see PARA 53.

7 Ie the Local Government Finance Act 1988 s 43(4)–(6B) (see PARAS 133, 145; and CHARITIES vol 8 (2015) PARA 433), s 44 (see PARA 133), s 45(4) (see PARA 135), s 45(4A)–(4D) (see PARA 148), s 46 (see PARA 135), regulations under s 57A (see PARA 154) or s 58 (see PARA 155), or any provision of or made under Sch 7A (see PARA 153), as the case may be.

8 Local Government Finance Act 1988 s 47(1)(b) (amended by the Local Government and Housing Act 1989 s 139, Sch 5 paras 26, 79(3); the Local Government and Rating Act 1997 s 1, Sch 1 para 3(a); the Local Government Act 2003 s 127(1), Sch 7 paras 9(1), 10; the Rating (Empty Properties) Act 2007 s 2(1), Sch 1 para 2(1), (2); and the Telecommunications Infrastructure (Relief from Non-Domestic Rates) Act 2018 Schedule para 2).

9 Ie a decision under the Local Government Finance Act 1988 s 47(3): see note 4.

10 Local Government Finance Act 1988 s 47(5C) (s 47(5A)–(5D) added by the Localism Act 2011 s 69(1)–(7)). As to the Secretary of State see PARA 4 note 18.

11 Local Government Finance Act 1988 s 47(5D) (as added: see note 39). As to the Welsh Ministers see PARA 4 note 18.

12 Ie so far as a decision under the Local Government Finance Act 1988 s 47(3) (see note 4) would have effect where none of s 43(6), s 43(6B) (see PARA 145) and s 47(5B) applies: see s 47(5A) (as added: see note 39). Section 47(5B) applies on the chargeable day if:

(1) all or part of the hereditament is occupied for the purposes of one or more institutions or other organisations none of which is established or conducted for profit, and each of whose main objects are charitable or are otherwise philanthropic or religious or concerned with education, social welfare, science, literature or the fine arts (s 47(5B)(a) (as so added)); or

(2) the hereditament is wholly or mainly used for purposes of recreation, and all or part of it is occupied for the purposes of a club, society or other organisation not established or conducted for profit (s 47(5B)(b) (as so added)).

The phrase 'occupied for the purposes of' is not to be read as 'occupied exclusively for the purposes of': *Royal London Mutual Insurance Society Ltd v Hendon Corpn* (1958) 3 RRC 76.

Some of the cases cited in this note were decided prior to the coming into force of the Local Government Finance Act 1988 but continue to be of relevance: see PARA 50.

On similar wording in the Rating and Valuation (Miscellaneous Provisions) Act 1955 s 8 (repealed), it was held to be not always right to take the occupier and treat him as the organisation: *Skegness UDC v Derbyshire Miners' Welfare Committee* [1959] AC 807 at 827, [1959] 2 All ER 258 at 265, HL, per Lord Denning; *Isaacs v Market Bosworth RDC* [1960] 1 All ER 433, [1960] 1 WLR 277 (trustees of trade union memorial home; organisation for whose purposes hereditament occupied was the trade union; hereditament not entitled to relief); cf *National Children's Home and Orphanage Registered Trustees v Penarth UDC* (1960) 53 R & IT 166 (trustees of approved school not occupying for purposes of Home Secretary; school entitled to relief); *Benevolent and Orphan Fund Trustees, National and Local Government Officers' Association v Bournemouth Corpn* (1957) 1 RRC 363 (quarter sessions).

The words 'established or conducted for profit' in the Rating and Valuation (Miscellaneous Provisions) Act 1955 s 8 (repealed) were held to mean not established or conducted for the purpose of making profit; accordingly a direction to the trustees of a charity to make investments in order to produce revenue and increase capital does not make the organisation one which is established or conducted for profit: *Guinness Trust (London Fund) Founded 1890, Registered 1902 v West Ham Corpn* [1959] 1 All ER 482, [1959] 1 WLR 233, CA. The financial gains made by a friendly society from investments do not make the society one which is established or conducted for profit: *National Deposit Friendly Society Trustees v Skegness UDC* [1959] AC 293, [1958] 2 All ER 601, HL. A zoo held to be an educational charity is not conducted for profit merely because it makes a financial surplus on its operations: *North of England Zoological Society v Chester RDC* [1959] 3 All ER 116, [1959] 1 WLR 773, CA. See also *Working Men's Club and Institute Union Ltd v Swansea Corpn* [1959] 3 All ER 769, [1959] 1 WLR 1197, CA, where a society registered under what is now the Industrial and Provident Societies Act 1965 was held not to be established or conducted for profit. See also *Ladbroke Park Golf Club Ltd v Stratford-on-Avon RDC* (1957) 1 RRC 202; *Reinshaw Park Golf Club v Chesterfield RDC* (1957) 1 RRC 281; *Mid-Kent Golf Club Ltd v Gravesend Borough Council* (1957) 50 R & IT 613, where golf clubs were held, at quarter sessions, not to be established or conducted for profit merely because of incidental financial gains.

On the same words in the Rating and Valuation (Miscellaneous Provisions) Act 1955 (repealed), it was held that the 'main objects' must be sought in the written constitution, if there is one: *Berry v St Marylebone Borough Council* [1958] Ch 406, [1957] 3 All ER 677, CA; *General Nursing Council for England and Wales v St Marylebone Borough Council* [1959] AC 540 at 559, [1959] 1 All ER 325 at 332, HL, per Lord Keith of Avonholm; *Victory (Ex-Services) Association Ltd v Paddington Borough Council* [1960] 1 All ER 498, [1960] 1 WLR 106, DC; *Royal College of Nursing v St Marylebone Corpn* [1959] 3 All ER 663, [1959] 1 WLR 1077, CA. The activities of the organisation may be relevant in determining which of the objects are the main objects (*Berry v St Marylebone Borough Council*; *Working Men's Club and Institute Union Ltd v Swansea Corpn* [1959] 3 All ER 769, [1959] 1 WLR 1197, CA; *Trustees of National Deposit Friendly Society v Skegness UDC* [1959] AC 293 at 320, [1958] 2 All ER 601 at 612, HL, per Lord Denning); or where there is ambiguity in the objects (*North of England Zoological Society v Chester RDC* [1959] 3 All ER 116, [1959] 1 WLR 773, CA; *Nottingham Mechanics Institution v City of Nottingham* (1958) 3 RRC 359; *English-Speaking Union v Westminster City Council* (1959) 4 RRC 97, DC).

The objects of theosophy were held not to be 'concerned with the advancement of religion' within the meaning of the Rating and Valuation (Miscellaneous Provisions) Act 1955 s 8 (repealed) (*Berry v St Marylebone Borough Council* [1958] Ch 406, [1957] 3 All ER 677, CA); and so were the objects of freemasonry (*United Grand Lodge of Ancient Free and Accepted Masons of England v Holborn Borough Council* [1957] 3 All ER 281, [1957] 1 WLR 1080, CA). See also *Trustees of National Deposit Friendly Society v Skegness UDC* [1959] AC 293 at 322, [1958] 2 All ER 601 at 614, HL, per Lord Denning. As to charitable purposes see CHARITIES vol 8 (2015) PARA 2 et seq.

On the words in the Rating and Valuation (Miscellaneous Provisions) Act 1955 s 8 (repealed) 'concerned with the advancement of religion, education or social welfare', it was held that the organisation must be substantially altruistic or benevolent in its purposes, although not necessarily in the limited sense applied to charities: *Trustees of National Deposit Friendly Society v Skegness UDC* [1959] AC 293, [1958] 2 All ER 601, HL; *Independent Order of Odd Fellows, Manchester*

Unity Friendly Society v Manchester Corpn [1958] 3 All ER 378, [1958] 1 WLR 1171, CA; *Working Men's Club and Institute Union Ltd v Swansea Corpn* [1959] 3 All ER 769, [1959] 1 WLR 1197, CA. The crucial test was the purpose to which the money was devoted, not the motives of its donors: *Skegness UDC v Derbyshire Miners' Welfare Committee* [1959] AC 807 at 824, [1959] 2 All ER 258 at 263, HL, per Viscount Simonds; explained in *Waterson v Hendon Borough Council* [1959] 2 All ER 760, [1959] 1 WLR 985. The size of the class of persons to be benefited was irrelevant: *Skegness UDC v Derbyshire Miners' Welfare Committee*.

The main objects of the Chartered Insurance Institute are not the advancement of education but the benefit of the profession of insurance generally: *Chartered Insurance Institute v London Corpn* [1957] 2 All ER 638, [1957] 1 WLR 867, DC. The main objects of the English-Speaking Union are not concerned with the advancement of education (*English-Speaking Union v Westminster City Council* (1959) 4 RRC 97); nor are those of the Theosophical Society (*Berry v St Marylebone Borough Council* [1958] Ch 406, [1957] 3 All ER 677, CA). See *Trustees of National Deposit Friendly Society v Skegness UDC* [1959] AC 293 at 322, [1958] 2 All ER 601 at 613, HL, per Lord Denning. At quarter sessions, the Oxford Union Society (*Oxford Union Society v City of Oxford* (1957) 2 RRC 54) and two dramatic societies (*Newport Playgoers' Society v Newport County Borough Council* (1957) 1 RRC 279; *Stoke-on-Trent Repertory Players Trustees v Stoke-on-Trent Corpn* (1957) 1 RRC 353) have been held to be concerned with the advancement of education.

It has been said that 'social welfare' is not the same as 'social well-being', but savours more of those needs of the community which, as a matter of social ethics, ought to be met in the attainment of some acceptable standard: *National Deposit Friendly Society v Skegness UDC* [1959] AC 293 at 314, [1958] 2 All ER 601 at 609, HL, per Lord MacDermott. The needs which are met need not be financial: *Victory (Ex-Services) Association Ltd v Paddington Borough Council* [1960] 1 All ER 498, [1960] 1 WLR 106, DC, where it was held that to promote comradeship between and improve the conditions and welfare of all ranks past and present advanced social welfare. Public benefit alone is not the test of social welfare (*General Nursing Council for England and Wales v St Marylebone Borough Council* [1959] AC 540, [1959] 1 All ER 325, HL); and 'social welfare' is a narrower phrase than 'social improvement' (*Nottingham Mechanics Institution v City of Nottingham* (1958) 3 RRC 359). An organisation which provides benefits only for its members is not concerned with the advancement of social welfare: *Working Men's Club and Institute Union Ltd v Swansea Corpn* [1959] 3 All ER 769, [1959] 1 WLR 1197, CA; *Waterson v Hendon Borough Council* [1959] 2 All ER 760, [1959] 1 WLR 985. A holiday camp run by a miners' welfare committee has been held to be concerned with the advancement of 'social welfare': *Skegness UDC v Derbyshire Miners' Welfare Committee* [1959] AC 807, [1959] 2 All ER 258, HL. See also *Independent Order of Odd Fellows, Manchester Unity Friendly Society v Manchester Corpn* [1958] 3 All ER 378, [1958] 1 WLR 1171, CA; *Berry v St Marylebone Borough Council* [1958] Ch 406, [1957] 3 All ER 677, CA; and, at quarter sessions, *Trustees of West Ham Boys' and Amateur Boxing Club v West Ham County Borough Council* (1957) 2 RRC 44; *Fegg Hayes Welfare Club and Institute Trustees v Stoke-on-Trent Corpn* (1957) 1 RRC 353; *Wearmouth Colliery Welfare Fund Trustees v Sunderland County Borough Council* (1956) 1 RRC 272; *Wearmouth Colliery Cricket Club v Sunderland County Borough Council* (1956) 1 RRC 277.

Societies which were instituted for the purpose of science, literature or the fine arts exclusively were at one stage exempted from rates, provided that certain other conditions were fulfilled, by the Scientific Societies Act 1843 s 1 (repealed). Many decisions were made as to societies which were to be treated as exempt, and as to others which were so instituted but were not exempt because a condition of exemption was not satisfied; some societies were held not to be exclusively instituted for the requisite purposes but might now qualify for discretionary relief on the ground that their main objects are concerned with science, literature or the fine arts. 'Science' has been held to include applied science: *R v Royal Medical and Chirurgical Society of London* (1857) 21 JP 789 at 791. The fine arts must be distinguished from the arts: *R v Institution of Civil Engineers* (1879) 5 QBD 48 at 52, DC. Music is one of the fine arts (*Royal College of Music v Westminster Vestry* [1898] 1 QB 809, CA), and drama and acting may be (*Nonentities Society v Linley (Valuation Officer) and Kidderminster Borough Council* (1954) 47 R & IT 426, CA), but folk dancing is not (*O'Sullivan (Valuation Officer) v English Folk Dance and Song Society* [1955] 2 All ER 845, [1955] 1 WLR 907, CA).

13 Local Government Finance Act 1988 s 47(5A) (as added: see note 39).

150. Grant of the relief.

Discretionary relief for the amount payable as regards hereditaments in the local rating list is not available on any day unless a decision of the billing authority[1] concerned operates to the effect that the provisions for discretionary relief[2] apply as regards the hereditament concerned[3]. Such a decision is invalid if made more than six months[4] after the end of the financial year[5] in which the day falls[6]; and such a decision may be revoked by a further decision of the authority[7].

The amount of the relief given may either be determined by the billing authority or be determined in accordance with rules set by it[8]. The determination must be such that the chargeable amount for the day is less than would otherwise[9] be chargeable[10] and may be nil[11]. It may be varied by a further determination of the authority[12].

The appropriate national authority[13] may make regulations[14] containing provision:

(1) requiring notice to be given of any determination or decision[15];
(2) limiting the power to revoke a decision or vary a determination[16];
(3) as to other incidental matters[17].

Accordingly, the billing authority making a decision or making or varying a determination must give notice in writing[18] to the ratepayer or ratepayers concerned stating[19]:

(a) in the case of the making of a decision, the first day with respect to which the decision operates and (if the decision is expressed to operate by reference to a particular period) the last day with respect to which it operates[20];
(b) in the case of the making or variation of a determination, the chargeable amount or the rules in accordance with which that amount is to be found (as the case may be) as so made or varied[21].

The billing authority revoking a decision must give notice in writing to the ratepayer or ratepayers concerned stating the day on which the revocation has effect[22].

1 As to the meaning of 'billing authority' see PARA 53.
2 Ie the Local Government Finance Act 1988 s 47.
3 See the Local Government Finance Act 1988 s 47(3); and PARA 149.
4 As to the meaning of 'month' see PARA 11 note 1.
5 As to the meanings of 'financial year' and 'chargeable financial year' see PARA 24 note 1.
6 Local Government Finance Act 1988 s 47(7) (amended by the Local Government and Rating Act 1997 s 33(1), Sch 3 para 23).
7 Local Government Finance Act 1988 s 47(6).
8 See the Local Government Finance Act 1988 s 47(1)(a); and PARA 149.
9 Ie apart from the Local Government Finance Act 1988 s 47.
10 Local Government Finance Act 1988 s 47(4)(a). In deciding what the chargeable amount for the day would be apart from s 47, the effect of any regulations under s 57A (see PARA 154) or s 58 (see PARA 155) and the effect of any provision of (or made under) Sch 7A (see PARA 153) must be taken into account but anything which has been done or could be done under s 49 (see PARA 151) must be ignored: s 47(5) (amended by the Local Government and Housing Act 1989 s 139, Sch 5 paras 26, 79(3); and the Local Government Act 2003 s 127(1), Sch 7 paras 9(1), 10).
11 See the Local Government Finance Act 1988 s 47(4)(b).
12 See the Local Government Finance Act 1988 s 47(4)(c).
13 Ie the Secretary of State or, in relation to Wales, the Welsh Ministers. The functions of the Secretary of State under the Local Government Finance Act 1988 s 47, so far as exercisable in relation to Wales, were transferred to the National Assembly for Wales (see the National Assembly for Wales (Transfer of Functions) Order 1999, SI 1999/672, art 2, Sch 1) and are now vested in the Welsh Ministers (see the Government of Wales Act 2006 s 162(1), Sch 11 para 30). As to the Secretary of State and the Welsh Ministers see PARA 4 note 18. As to the meaning of 'Wales' see PARA 2 note 16. As to the separate administration of the non-domestic rating provisions (Local Government Finance Act 1988 Pt III (ss 41–67)) in England and Wales see PARA 52.
14 As to the regulations made see the Non-Domestic Rating (Discretionary Relief) Regulations 1989, SI 1989/1059; and the text to notes 16, 18–22.
15 Local Government Finance Act 1988 s 47(8)(a).

16 Local Government Finance Act 1988 s 47(8)(b). A decision under s 47(3) (see PARA 149) may be revoked and a relevant variation of a determination under s 47(1)(a) (see PARA 149) can only be made so that it takes effect at the expiry of a financial year and so that at least one year's notice of the revocation or variation is given under the Non-Domestic Rating (Discretionary Relief) Regulations 1989, SI 1989/1059, reg 2(1) (see the text to notes 18–21) or reg 2(2) (see the text to note 22), as the case may be: see regs 1(2), 2(3). However, reg 2(3) does not apply in relation to Wales where the billing authority revokes a decision or makes a relevant variation of a determination as a consequence only of the commencement of the Local Government Act 2003 s 63 (which amended the Local Government Finance Act 1988 s 42A (see PARA 195), s 43 (see PARAS 133, 143 et seq) and s 47 (see PARA 149)): see the Non-Domestic Rating (Discretionary Relief) Regulations 1989, SI 1989/1059, reg 2(6) (added by SI 2006/3392). A variation of a determination is a 'relevant variation' for the purposes of the Non-Domestic Rating (Discretionary Relief) Regulations 1989, SI 1989/1059, reg 2(3), (4) (see note 19) if it increases the chargeable amount for any day: reg 2(5).

17 Local Government Finance Act 1988 s 47(8)(c).

18 As to the meaning of 'writing' see PARA 21 note 3.

19 Non-Domestic Rating (Discretionary Relief) Regulations 1989, SI 1989/1059, reg 2(1) (reg 2(1), (2) amended by SI 1993/616). Notice under the Non-Domestic Rating (Discretionary Relief) Regulations 1989, SI 1989/1059, reg 2(1) of the making of a decision or determination, or of the variation of a determination which is not a relevant variation, is to be given as soon as practicable after the decision or determination is made or varied: reg 2(4).

20 Non-Domestic Rating (Discretionary Relief) Regulations 1989, SI 1989/1059, reg 2(1)(a). See also note 16.

21 Non-Domestic Rating (Discretionary Relief) Regulations 1989, SI 1989/1059, reg 2(1)(b). See also note 16.

22 Non-Domestic Rating (Discretionary Relief) Regulations 1989, SI 1989/1059, reg 2(2) (as amended: see note 19). See also note 16.

(iv) Reduction for Hardship

151. Reduction or remission in the case of hardship.

A billing authority[1] may[2]:

(1) reduce any amount which a person[3] is otherwise liable to pay to it[4] as regards hereditaments in the local non-domestic rating list[5]; or

(2) remit payment of the whole of any amount a person would otherwise be liable[6] to pay[7].

However, a billing authority may not so act unless it is satisfied that:

(a) the ratepayer would sustain hardship[8] if the authority did not do so[9]; and

(b) it is reasonable for the authority to do so having regard to the interests of persons liable to pay council tax set by it[10].

1 As to the meaning of 'billing authority' see PARA 53.

2 See the Local Government Finance Act 1988 s 49(1) (s 49(1), (2)(b) amended by the Local Government Finance Act 1992 s 117(1), Sch 13 para 66). Where an authority acts under the Local Government Finance Act 1988 s 49, then s 43 (occupied hereditaments) (see PARAS 133, 143 et seq) or s 45 (unoccupied hereditaments) (see PARAS 135–136, 148) are to be construed accordingly as regards the case concerned: s 49(4).

3 As to the meaning of 'person' see PARA 11 note 13.

4 Ie under the Local Government Finance Act 1988 s 43 (occupied hereditaments) (see PARAS 133, 143 et seq) or s 45 (unoccupied hereditaments) (see PARAS 135–136, 148).

5 See the Local Government Finance Act 1988 s 49(1)(a). The amount as regards which a reduction or remittance may be made under s 49(1) is the amount the person would be liable to pay, apart from s 49, taking account of anything done under s 47 (see PARAS 149–150), the effect of any regulations under s 57A (see PARA 154) or s 58 (see PARA 155) and the effect of any provision of (or made under) Sch 7A (see PARA 153): s 49(3) (amended by the Local Government and Housing Act 1989 s 139, Sch 5 paras 27, 79(3); and the Local Government Act 2003 s 127(1), Sch 7 paras 9(1), 11).

6 Ie under the Local Government Finance Act 1988 s 43 (occupied hereditaments) (see PARAS 133, 143 et seq) or s 45 (unoccupied hereditaments) (see PARAS 135–136, 148).
7 Local Government Finance Act 1988 s 49(1)(b). See also note 5.
8 The meaning of 'hardship' for these purposes was discussed by the Court of Appeal in *Windsor Securities Ltd v Liverpool City Council* (1978) 77 LGR 502, [1979] RA 159, CA ('hardship' is a matter of degree and the question whether payment would cause hardship to the applicant has to be resolved in the light of commonsense having regard to all the circumstances). This case was decided prior to the coming into force of the Local Government Finance Act 1988 but continue to be of relevance: see PARA 50.
9 Local Government Finance Act 1988 s 49(2)(a).
10 Local Government Finance Act 1988 s 49(2)(b) (as amended: see note 2). As to council tax see PARA 344 et seq.

152. Cancellation of backdated liabilities for days in years 2005 to 2010.

The Secretary of State[1] may by regulations[2] provide that, in a prescribed[3] case, the chargeable amount[4] for a hereditament[5] in England[6] for a chargeable day is zero[7].

The regulations may give that relief in relation to a hereditament and a chargeable day only if the hereditament is shown for the day in a local non-domestic rating list[8] compiled on 1 April 2005[9], and it is shown for that day as it is shown as the result of an alteration of the list[10] made after the list was compiled[11].

The regulations may give that relief in relation to a hereditament and a chargeable day subject to the fulfilment of prescribed conditions[12]. A prescribed condition may be:

(1) a condition to be fulfilled in relation to the hereditament[13];
(2) a condition to be fulfilled in relation to some other hereditament[14]; or
(3) some other condition[15].

The conditions that may be prescribed include, in particular:

(a) conditions relating to the circumstances in which an alteration of a local non-domestic rating list was made[16];
(b) conditions relating to the consequences of the alteration[17];
(c) conditions relating to the length of the period beginning with the first day from which an alteration had effect and ending with the day on which the alteration was made[18];
(d) conditions relating to a person's[19] liability or otherwise to non-domestic rates at any time[20].

1 As to the Secretary of State see PARA 4 note 18.
2 See the Non-Domestic Rating (Cancellation of Backdated Liabilities) Regulations 2012, SI 2012/537.
3 'Prescribed' means prescribed by the regulations: see the Local Government Finance Act 1988 s 146(6), (7).
4 Ie under the Local Government Finance Act 1988 s 43 (see PARA 143) or s 45 (see PARA 135).
5 As to the meaning of 'hereditament' see PARA 106.
6 As to the meaning of 'England' see PARA 2 note 16.
7 Local Government Finance Act 1988 s 49A(1) (s 49A added by the Localism Act 2011 s 71).
8 As to local non-domestic rating lists see PARA 191 et seq.
9 Local Government Finance Act 1988 s 49A(2)(a) (as added: see note 7).
10 As to the alteration of rating lists see PARA 199 et seq.
11 Local Government Finance Act 1988 s 49A(2)(b) (as added: see note 7).
12 Local Government Finance Act 1988 s 49A(3) (as added: see note 7).
13 Local Government Finance Act 1988 s 49A(4)(a) (as added: see note 7).
14 Local Government Finance Act 1988 s 49A(4)(b) (as added: see note 7).
15 Local Government Finance Act 1988 s 49A(4)(c) (as added: see note 7).
16 Local Government Finance Act 1988 s 49A(5)(a) (as added: see note 7).
17 Local Government Finance Act 1988 s 49A(5)(b) (as added: see note 7).

18 Local Government Finance Act 1988 s 49A(5)(c) (as added: see note 7).
19 As to the meaning of 'person' see PARA 11 note 13.
20 Local Government Finance Act 1988 s 49A(5)(d) (as added: see note 7).

(v) Transitional Relief Schemes

153. Transitional provisions for the 1990 and 1995 lists.

A large number of hereditaments[1] experienced considerable change in their rates burden on revaluation in 1990[2]. The impact of that change, whether increase or (until 1 April 1993) reduction[3], was limited in most cases by transitional arrangements[4] for the period (the 'transitional period') consisting of the financial years beginning in 1990, 1991, 1992, 1993 and 1994[5].

On revaluations for the 1995 list, a transitional relief scheme was again used to protect ratepayers from large changes in their rates liability (both increases and reductions) and this scheme applied for the financial years beginning in 1995, 1996, 1997, 1998 and 1999[6].

Provision for such relief is now made separately in relation to England and Wales respectively[7].

1 As to hereditaments see PARA 106.
2 As to valuation for rating generally see PARA 156 et seq.
3 The effect of the Non-Domestic Rating Act 1992 s 3(3) was to terminate the transitional provisions concerning hereditaments in respect of which the revaluation had brought a reduction in rates liability with effect from 1 April 1993, so that thereafter the ratepayer received the full benefit of the reduction.
4 As to the transitional arrangements see the Local Government Finance Act 1988 s 57, Sch 7A (s 57 substituted, Sch 7A added, by the Local Government and Housing Act 1989 s 139, Sch 5 paras 31, 40, 79(3); the Local Government Finance Act 1988 Sch 7A para 5 amended by the Non-Domestic Rating Act 1992 ss 2(1), 3(3), 8; and the Non-Domestic Rating Act 1994 s 1(2)); the Non-Domestic Rating (Transitional Period) (Appropriate Fraction) Order 1989, SI 1989/2476 (amended by the Non-Domestic Rating Act 1992 s 3(1); and SI 1991/2924); the Non-Domestic Rating (Transitional Period) Regulations 1990, SI 1990/608 (amended by SI 1990/2329, SI 1992/1514 and SI 1993/616; and in relation to England only by SI 2003/2000); the Non-Domestic Rating (Transitional Period) (Amendment and Further Provision) Regulations 1990, SI 1990/2329 (amended by the Non-Domestic Rating Act 1992 s 2(2); and the Non-Domestic Rating Act 1994 s 1(3)); the Non-Domestic Rating (Transitional Period) (Further Provision) Regulations 1992, SI 1992/559; the Non-Domestic Rating (Transitional Period) (Amendment) Regulations 1992, SI 1992/1514; and the Local Government Finance (Repeals, Savings and Consequential Amendments) Order 1993, SI 1993/616. For a case concerning the operation of this scheme see *R v Huelin (Valuation Officer), ex p Murphy Ltd, R v Hodgetts (Valuation Officer) ex p Nationwide Building Society* [2001] RA 30, [2000] 1 EGLR 97, CA.
5 See the Local Government Finance Act 1988 Sch 7A para 1(1) (as added: see note 4). For these purposes, a transitional day was a day falling in the transitional period: see Sch 7A para 1(2) (as so added).
6 See the Non-Domestic Rating (Chargeable Amounts) Regulations 1994, SI 1994/3279 (now spent).
7 As to transitional provision made in relation to England from the year 2000 onwards see PARA 154; and in relation to Wales see PARA 155. As to the separate administration of the non-domestic rating provisions (Local Government Finance Act 1988 Pt III (ss 41–67)) in England and Wales see PARA 52.

154. Power to make special provision for England: lists for 2000 and 2005 and for later years.

In relation to any relevant period[1], the Secretary of State[2] must make regulations in relation to the chargeable amounts[3] which apply in relation to England[4]. In relation to any case where:

(1) as regards a hereditament[5] or hereditaments, the chargeable amount for a chargeable day falls to be determined under the provisions of the Local Government Finance Act 1988[6]; and

(2) the day falls within a prescribed relevant financial year[7],

the regulations may contain provisions that the chargeable amount will be such as is found in accordance with prescribed rules instead[8]. Consequently, certain provisions of the Local Government Finance Act 1988[9] do not apply as regards the day[10].

The regulations may:

(a) contain different provision in relation to locally listed hereditaments[11] whose rateable value exceeds (and those whose rateable value does not exceed) a prescribed figure[12];

(b) include provision imposing duties and conferring powers on valuation officers[13] (whether as regards determinations, certificates or otherwise)[14] in relation to the ascertainment of rateable values[15]; and

(c) include provision as to appeals relating to things done or not done by such officers[16].

In making such regulations, the Secretary of State must have regard to the object of securing (so far as practicable) that the aggregate amount payable to him and all billing authorities[17] by way of non-domestic rates as regards a particular relevant period is, after disregarding any adjustments made to take account of amounts being payable at times other than those at which they would have been payable apart from the regulations, the same as the aggregate amount which would be so payable apart from the regulations[18]. Once the actual aggregate amounts and adjustments for a particular relevant period are ascertained, the Secretary of State may amend the regulations in their application to a financial year which begins after the coming into force of the amending regulations and falls within the same or a later relevant period to reflect the extent to which the actual aggregate amounts and adjustments differ from his estimate of those amounts and adjustments[19].

Regulations have been made in respect of the period beginning 1 April 2005 and ending on 31 March 2009[20], in respect of the period beginning on 1 April 2010 and ending on 31 March 2015[21], and in respect of the period beginning on 1 April 2017 and ending on 31 March 2022[22].

1 For the purposes of the Local Government Finance Act 1988 s 57A, a 'relevant period' is a period of five years beginning on 1 April 2005 or on any 1 April after that date on which lists must be compiled: s 57A(13)(a) (s 57A added by the Local Government Act 2003 s 65(1)). As to rating lists see PARA 188 et seq.

As to transitional provisions made in relation to the 1990–1994 and 1995–1999 rating lists see PARA 153. For the provisions applicable, in relation to England, in respect of the period of five years beginning on 1 April 2000 and ending on 31 March 2005, see the Non-Domestic Rating (Chargeable Amounts) (England) Regulations 1999, SI 1999/3379 (amended by SI 2000/936, SI 2004/1297 and SI 2009/3343), made under the Local Government Finance Act 1988 s 58, which is now applicable only in relation to Wales (see PARA 155). As to the meanings of 'England' and 'Wales' see PARA 2 note 16. As to the separate administration of the non-domestic rating provisions (Local Government Finance Act 1988 Pt III (ss 41–67)) in England and Wales see PARA 52.

2 As to the Secretary of State see PARA 4 note 18.

3 Ie regulations under the Local Government Finance Act 1988 s 57A. As to the chargeable amounts generally see PARA 133 et seq.

4 Local Government Finance Act 1988 s 57A(1) (as added: see note 1). As to the regulations made see the text to notes 20–21.

5 As to the meaning of 'hereditament' see PARA 106.

6 Local Government Finance Act 1988 s 57A(2)(a) (as added (see note 1); amended by the Rating (Empty Properties) Act 2007 s 2(1), Sch 1 para 3(1); and the Telecommunications Infrastructure (Relief from Non-Domestic Rates) Act 2018 Schedule para 3(2)). The relevant provisions of the Local Government Finance Act 1988 in this respect are s 43 (see PARAS 133, 143 et seq), s 45 (see PARAS 135–136, 148), s 45A (see PARA 147) or s 54 or 54ZA (see PARA 142): see s 57A(2)(a) (as so added and amended).

7 Local Government Finance Act 1988 s 57A(2)(b) (as added: see note 1). 'Prescribed' means prescribed by the regulations: see s 146(6). For the purposes of s 57A, a 'relevant financial year', as regards regulations relating to a relevant period, is a financial year falling within the period: s 57A(13)(b) (as so added). Without prejudice to s 143(1) (see PARA 51), regulations under s 57A relating to a relevant period may contain different provisions for different relevant financial years: s 57A(6) (as so added). Regulations under s 57A, in their application to a particular relevant financial year, are not effective unless they come into force before 1 January immediately preceding the year; but this is without prejudice to the power to amend or revoke: s 57A(9) (as so added). As to the meaning of 'financial year' see PARA 24 note 1.

8 See the Local Government Finance Act 1988 s 57A(2), (3)(a) (as added: see note 1). Rules prescribed under s 57A may be framed by reference to such factors as the Secretary of State thinks fit: s 57A(5) (as so added). A chargeable amount found in accordance with rules prescribed under s 57A, and any calculation (or component of a calculation) used to find that amount, may be the same as or different from what it would be apart from the regulations: s 57A(4) (as so added).

9 Ie the Local Government Finance Act 1988 s 43(4)–(6E) (see PARAS 133, 145; and CHARITIES vol 8 (2015) PARA 433), s 44 (see PARA 133), s 45(4) (see PARA 135), s 45(4A)–(4D) (see PARA 148), s 45A (see PARA 147), s 46 (see PARA 135), s 54(4)–(7) or s 54ZA (see PARA 142): see s 57A(2), (3)(b) (s 57A as added (see note 1); s 57A(3)(b) amended by the Rating (Empty Properties) Act 2007 Sch 1 para 3(2); and the Telecommunications Infrastructure (Relief from Non-Domestic Rates) Act 2018 Schedule para 3(3)).

10 Local Government Finance Act 1988 s 57A(2), (3)(b) (as added and amended: see note 9).

11 A 'locally listed hereditament' is a hereditament for the time being shown in a local non-domestic rating list: see the Local Government Finance Act 1988 s 57A(7) (as added: see note 1). As to local non-domestic rating lists see PARA 191 et seq.

12 Local Government Finance Act 1988 s 57A(7) (as added: see note 1). This provision is expressed to be without prejudice to s 143(1) (see PARA 51): see s 57A(7) (as so added).

13 As to the meaning of 'valuation officer' see PARA 54 note 3.

14 As to valuation determinations, certificates, etc see PARA 157 et seq.

15 Local Government Finance Act 1988 s 57A(8)(a) (as added: see note 1). This provision is expressed to be without prejudice to s 143(1), (2) (see PARA 51): see s 57A(8) (as so added).

16 Local Government Finance Act 1988 s 57A(8)(b) (as added: see note 1). This provision is expressed to be without prejudice to s 143(1), (2) (see PARA 51): see s 57A(8) (as so added). As to valuation list appeals see PARA 167 et seq.

17 As to the meaning of 'billing authority' see PARA 53.

18 Local Government Finance Act 1988 s 57A(10) (as added: see note 1). For these purposes, the Secretary of State may rely on his estimate of the aggregate amounts and adjustments mentioned in s 57A(10): s 57A(11) (as so added).

19 Local Government Finance Act 1988 s 57A(12) (as added: see note 1).

20 See the Non-Domestic Rating (Chargeable Amounts) (England) Regulations 2004, SI 2004/3387 (amended by SI 2005/991, SI 2006/3394, SI 2008/428 and SI 2016/1265) which apply in respect of the period beginning 1 April 2005 and ending on 31 March 2009 (see the Non-Domestic Rating (Chargeable Amounts) (England) Regulations 2004, SI 2004/3387, reg 2(1)). For a case concerning these regulations see *R (on the application of the British Waterways Board) v First Secretary of State* [2006] EWHC 1019 (Admin), [2006] RA 241, [2006] All ER (D) 262 (May).

21 See the Non-Domestic Rating (Chargeable Amounts) (England) Regulations 2009, SI 2009/3343, which apply in respect of the period beginning on 1 April 2010 and ending on 31 March 2015 (see reg 2(1)).

22 See the Non-Domestic Rating (Chargeable Amounts) (England) Regulations 2016, SI 2016/1265, which apply in respect of the period beginning on 1 April 2017 and ending on 31 March 2022 (see reg 4(1)).

155. Power to make special provision for Wales.

In relation to any relevant period[1], the Welsh Ministers[2] may make regulations in relation to the chargeable amounts[3] which apply in relation to Wales[4]. As regards any case which falls within a prescribed description[5] and where:

(1) as regards a hereditament[6] or hereditaments, the chargeable amount for a chargeable day falls to be determined under the provisions of the Local Government Finance Act 1988[7]; and

(2) the day falls within the relevant period concerned[8],

the regulations may contain provisions that the chargeable amount will be such as is found in accordance with prescribed rules instead[9]. Consequently, certain provisions of the Local Government Finance Act 1988[10] do not apply as regards the day[11].

The regulations may:

(a) contain different provision in relation to locally listed hereditaments[12] whose rateable value exceeds (and those whose rateable value does not exceed) a prescribed figure[13];

(b) include provision imposing duties and conferring powers on valuation officers[14] (whether as regards determinations, certificates or otherwise)[15] in relation to the ascertainment of rateable values[16]; and

(c) include provision as to appeals relating to things done or not done by such officers[17].

In making such regulations, the Welsh Ministers must have regard to the object of securing (so far as practicable) that the aggregate amount payable to them and all billing authorities[18] by way of non-domestic rates as regards a particular financial year does not exceed that which it would in their opinion be likely to be apart from the regulations[19].

Regulations have been made in respect of the period beginning on 1 April 2017 and ending on 31 March 2022[20].

1 A 'relevant period' is a period of five years beginning on any 1 April (other than 1 April 1990) on which lists must be compiled: Local Government Finance Act 1988 s 58(10)(a). As to rating lists see PARA 188 et seq. As to transitional provisions made in relation to the 1990–1994 and 1995–1999 rating lists see PARA 153.

2 The functions of the Secretary of State under the Local Government Finance Act 1988 s 58, so far as exercisable in relation to Wales, were transferred to the National Assembly for Wales (see the National Assembly for Wales (Transfer of Functions) Order 1999, SI 1999/672, art 2, Sch 1) and are now vested in the Welsh Ministers (see the Government of Wales Act 2006 s 162(1), Sch 11 para 30). As to the Welsh Ministers see PARA 4 note 18. As to the meaning of 'Wales' see PARA 2 note 16. As to the separate administration of the non-domestic rating provisions (Local Government Finance Act 1988 Pt III (ss 41–67)) in England and Wales see PARA 52.

3 Ie regulations under the Local Government Finance Act 1988 s 58: see s 58(1). As to the chargeable amounts generally see PARA 133 et seq.

4 Local Government Finance Act 1988 s 58(1) (amended by the Local Government Act 2003 s 65(2)). Without prejudice to the Local Government Finance Act 1988 s 143(1) (see PARA 51), regulations under s 58 relating to a relevant period may contain different provision for different relevant financial years: s 58(6). As to the meaning of 'financial year' see PARA 24 note 1. Regulations under s 58, in their application to a particular relevant financial year, are not effective unless they come into force before 1 January immediately preceding the year; but this is without prejudice to the power to amend or revoke: s 58(8) (amended by the Non-Domestic Rating Act 1994 s 2(2)). As to the regulations made see the text to note 20.

5 'Prescribed' means prescribed by the regulations: see the Local Government Finance Act 1988 s 146(6).

6 As to the meaning of 'hereditament' see PARA 106.

7 Local Government Finance Act 1988 s 58(2)(a) (amended by the Rating (Empty Properties) Act 2007 s 2(1), Sch 1 para 3(1); and the Telecommunications Infrastructure (Relief from Non-Domestic Rates) Act 2018 Schedule para 4(2)). The relevant provisions of the Local

Government Finance Act 1988 for these purposes are s 43 (see PARAS 133, 143 et seq), s 45 (see PARAS 135–136, 148), s 45A (see PARA 147), s 54 or s 54ZA (see PARA 142): see s 58(2)(a) (as so amended).

8 Local Government Finance Act 1988 s 58(2)(b).

9 See the Local Government Finance Act 1988 s 58(2), (3)(a). Rules prescribed under s 58 may be framed by reference to such factors as the Welsh Ministers think fit: s 58(5). A chargeable amount found in accordance with rules prescribed under s 58 may be the same as or different from what it would be apart from the regulations: s 58(4).

10 Ie the Local Government Finance Act 1988 s 43(4)–(6E) (see PARAS 133, 145; and CHARITIES vol 8 (2015) PARA 433), s 44 (see PARA 133), s 45(4) (see PARA 135), s 45(4A)–(4D) (see PARA 148), s 45A (see PARA 147), s 46 (see PARA 135), s 54(4)–(7) or s 54ZA (see PARA 142): see s 58(2), (3)(b) (amended by the Local Government and Rating Act 1997 s 1, Sch 1 para 5; Rating (Empty Properties) Act 2007 Sch 1 para 3(2); and the Telecommunications Infrastructure (Relief from Non-Domestic Rates) Act 2018 Schedule para 4(3)).

11 See the Local Government Finance Act 1988 s 58(2), (3)(b) (s 58(3)(b) as amended: see note 10).

12 A 'locally listed hereditament' is a hereditament for the time being shown in a local non-domestic rating list: see the Local Government Finance Act 1988 s 58(7). As to local non-domestic rating lists see PARA 191 et seq.

13 Local Government Finance Act 1988 s 58(7). This provision is expressed to be without prejudice to s 143(1) (see PARA 51): see s 58(7).

14 As to the meaning of 'valuation officer' see PARA 54 note 3.

15 As to valuation determinations, certificates, etc see PARA 157 et seq.

16 Local Government Finance Act 1988 s 58(7A)(a) (s 58(7A) added by the Non-Domestic Rating Act 1994 s 2(1)). This provision is expressed to be without prejudice to the Local Government Finance Act 1988 s 143(1), (2) (see PARA 51): see s 58(7A) (as so added).

17 Local Government Finance Act 1988 s 58(7A)(b) (as added: see note 16). This provision is expressed to be without prejudice to s 143(1), (2) (see PARA 51): see s 58(7A) (as so added). As to valuation list appeals see PARA 232 et seq.

18 As to the meaning of 'billing authority' see PARA 53.

19 Local Government Finance Act 1988 s 58(9) (amended by the Local Government Finance Act 1992 s 117(1), Sch 13 para 68; and the Non-Domestic Rating Act 1994 s 2(3)).

20 See the Non-Domestic Rating (Chargeable Amounts) (Wales) Regulations 2016, SI 2016/1247, which apply for the period consisting of the financial years beginning on 1 April 2017, 1 April 2018, 1 April 2019, 1 April 2020 and 1 April 2021 (see regs 14–17).

(8) Valuation for Rating

(i) Basis for Assessment

156. Non-domestic rating multipliers.

Subject to the transitional provisions[1] and to the exemptions and reliefs which may apply to particular hereditaments[2], the amount payable by way of non-domestic rates is calculated for each chargeable year[3] by reference to the rateable value[4] shown in the appropriate list[5] for the hereditament, and the non-domestic rating multiplier[6] (or, in relation to England only, the small business non-domestic rating multiplier[7], where that applies)[8].

The non-domestic rating multiplier for the financial year beginning 1 April 1990 was specified by the Secretary of State[9] in the Revenue Support Grant Report[10]. For subsequent years (other than those for which a new list must be compiled[11]) the non-domestic rating multiplier and the small business non-domestic rating multiplier are calculated on the basis of a formula which reflects any change in the retail prices index (unless, in relation to England, the Treasury specifies a lesser figure)[12]. For the years in which new lists are compiled, a further factor is introduced into the formula to reflect the change in the total amount of rateable values from the old to the new lists[13].

1 As to the transitional provisions see PARA 153 et seq.

2 As to exemptions from non-domestic rating see PARA 110 et seq; and as to relief schemes see PARA 143 et seq.

3 As to the meaning of 'chargeable financial year' see PARA 24 note 1.

4 As to assessment of the rateable value see PARA 157.

5 As to rating lists see PARA 188 et seq.

6 As to the non-domestic rating multiplier generally see the Local Government Finance Act 1988 s 56(2), Sch 7 paras 1, 2 (Sch 7 para 1 amended by the Local Government Act 2003 s 62(1), (2); and by SI 2007/1388). As to the non-domestic rating multipliers which relate to England only see the Local Government Finance Act 1988 Sch 7 para 3A (added by the Local Government Act 2003 s 62(1), (3)) and the Local Government Finance Act 1988 Sch 7 para 4A (added by the Local Government Act 2003 s 62(1), (4)). As to the non-domestic rating multipliers which relate to Wales only see the Local Government Finance Act 1988 Sch 7 para 3B (added by the Local Government Act 2003 s 62(1), (3); and amended by SI 2007/1388) and the Local Government Finance Act 1988 Sch 7 para 4B (added by the Local Government Act 2003 s 62(1), (4)).

As to the calculation of the multipliers see the Local Government Finance Act 1988 Sch 7 para 5 (amended by the Local Government Finance Act 1992 s 117(1), Sch 13 para 84; the Local Government Act 2003 s 62(1), (5)–(7), s 127(1), Sch 7 paras 9(1), 25(1), (2); the Statistics and Registration Service Act 2007 s 60(1), Sch 3 para 5; and by SI 1996/273 and SI 2007/1388), and the Local Government Finance Act 1988 Sch 7 para 6 (amended by the Local Government Finance Act 1992 Sch 13 para 84; the Local Government Act 2003 s 62(1), (8)–(10), Sch 7 paras 9(1), 25(1), (3); and SI 2007/1388). Separate estimates must be made under the Local Government Finance Act 1988 Sch 7 para 5(6), (7) for the purpose of determining non-domestic rating multipliers for England and Wales respectively: see s 140(2)(b); and PARA 52. Special provision was made in relation to the transitional period 1990–95: see the Local Government Finance Act 1988 Sch 7 paras 7, 8 (both amended by the Local Government and Housing Act 1989 s 139, Sch 5 paras 39, 79(3)). As to the meanings of 'England' and 'Wales' see PARA 2 note 16.

As to the non-domestic rating multiplier to be used by a special authority see the Local Government Finance Act 1992 Sch 7 para 9 (amended by the Local Government Finance Act 1992 s 104, Sch 10 para 5; the Local Government Act 2003 Sch 7 paras 9(1), 25(1), (4); and the Localism Act 2011 s 79, Sch 7 paras 1, 6), the Local Government Finance Act 1988 Sch 7 para 10 (amended by the Local Government Act 2003 Sch 7 paras 9(1), 25(1), (5), (6)) and the Local Government Finance Act 1988 Sch 7 para 11 (amended by the Local Government Act 2003 Sch 7 paras 9(1), 25(1), (6)). The setting by a special authority of a non-domestic rating multiplier under the Local Government Finance Act 1988 Sch 7 must be discharged only by the authority: see s 139(1), (2)(d). As to the meaning of 'special authority' see PARA 133 note 11.

For the purposes of Sch 7 paras 3, 3B, see the Local Government Finance Act 1988 (Non-Domestic Rating Multipliers) (England) Order 2014, SI 2014/2 (2014–15 financial year); the Local Government Finance Act 1988 (Non-Domestic Rating Multipliers) (England) Order 2015, SI 2015/135 (2015–16 financial year); the Non-Domestic Rating (Multiplier) (Wales) Order 2014, SI 2014/124 (2014–15 financial year); and the Non-Domestic Rating (Multiplier) (Wales) (No 2) Order 2014, SI 2014/3492 (2015–16 financial year).

The specification of a non-domestic rating multiplier under the Local Government Finance Act 1988 Sch 7 paras 2, 7 and the setting by a special authority of a non-domestic rating multiplier under Sch 7 may not be questioned except by an application for judicial review: see s 138(1), (2)(h)–(j). If, on such an application for judicial review, the court decides to grant relief, it must quash the specification or setting: see s 138(3) (substituted by the Local Government Finance Act 1992 Sch 13 para 76(2)). As to judicial review see JUDICIAL REVIEW vol 61 (2010) PARA 601 et seq.

7 As to the small business non-domestic rating multipliers generally see the Local Government Finance Act 1988 Sch 7 para 1 (as amended: see note 6). As to the calculation of the small business non-domestic rating multiplier see Sch 7 para 3 (substituted by the Local Government Act 2003 s 62(1), (3)) and the Local Government Finance Act 1988 Sch 7 para 4 (substituted by the Local Government Act 2003 s 62(1), (4)). As to the calculation of the multipliers see the Local Government Finance Act 1988 Sch 7 paras 5, 6 (Sch 7 paras 5, 6 as amended: see note 6). See also the Local Government Finance Act 1988 (Non-Domestic Rating Multipliers) (England) Order 2017, SI 2017/1335 which specifies the non-domestic rating multiplier for the purposes of the Local Government Finance Act 1988 Sch 7 para 3.

As to the small business non-domestic rating multipliers to be used by a special authority see Sch 7 para 9A (added by the Local Government Act 2003 s 62(1), (11)) and the Local Government Finance Act 1988 Sch 7 paras 10, 11 (as amended: see note 6). The setting by a special authority of a small business non-domestic rating multiplier under Sch 7 must be discharged only by the authority: see s 139(1), (2)(d) (amended by the Local Government Act 2003 Sch 7 paras 9(1), 21)). The setting by a special authority of a small business non-domestic rating multiplier under the Local Government Finance Act 1988 Sch 7 may not be questioned except by an application for judicial review: see s 138(1), (2)(j) (amended by the Local Government Act 2003 Sch 7 paras 9(1), 20). If, on such an application for judicial review, the court decides to grant relief, it must quash the setting: see the Local Government Finance Act 1988 s 138(3) (as substituted: see note 6).

As to the application of the small business non-domestic rating multiplier see PARA 143.

8 See the Local Government Finance Act 1988 s 43 (see PARAS 133, 143 et seq), s 45 (see PARAS 135–136, 148).

9 As to the Secretary of State see PARA 4 note 18.

10 See the Local Government Finance Act 1988 Sch 7 paras 1, 2; and note 6.

11 As to the compilation of rating lists see PARAS 191, 196.

12 See the Local Government Finance Act 1988 Sch 7 paras 3, 3A, 3B, 5; and note 6. It was proposed in the 2017 Budget that from 2018 the formula would reflect any change in the consumer prices index instead of the (higher) retail prices index: see Budget Statement, 22 November 2017. At the date at which this volume states the law, this change, which would require an amendment to the Local Government Finance Act 1988 Sch 7 para 5(4), has not been implemented. The Treasury function under the Local Government Finance Act 1988 Sch 7, so far as exercisable in relation to Wales, was transferred to the National Assembly for Wales (see the National Assembly for Wales (Transfer of Functions) Order 1999, SI 1999/672, art 2, Sch 1) and is now vested in the Welsh Ministers (see the Government of Wales Act 2006 s 162(1), Sch 11 para 30). As to the meaning of 'Treasury' see PARA 30 note 15. As to the Welsh Ministers see PARA 4 note 18.

13 See the Local Government Finance Act 1988 Sch 7 paras 4, 4A, 4B, 5; and note 6.

(ii) Determination of Rateable Value

A. THE BASIS FOR DETERMINATION

157. Assessment of rateable value.

Rates are assessed on the rateable value of the non-domestic hereditament[1]. The rateable value of a non-domestic hereditament (none of which consists of domestic property[2] and none of which is exempt from local non-domestic rating[3]) is the amount equal to the rent at which it is estimated the hereditament might reasonably be expected to let from year to year on these three assumptions[4], namely:

(1) that the tenancy begins on the day by reference to which the determination is to be made[5];

(2) that, immediately before the tenancy begins, the hereditament is in a state of reasonable repair, but excluding from this assumption any repairs which a reasonable landlord would consider uneconomic[6];

(3) that the tenant undertakes to pay all usual tenant's rates and taxes and to bear the cost of the repairs and insurance and the other expenses (if any) necessary to maintain the hereditament in a state to command the rent mentioned above[7].

The rateable value of a composite hereditament[8] (none of which is exempt from local non-domestic rating) is the amount equal to the rent which, assuming it is let under the statutory terms above, would reasonably be attributed to the non-domestic use of the property[9]. The rateable value of a non-domestic hereditament which is partially exempt from local non-domestic rating is the amount equal to the rent which, assuming it is let under the statutory terms, is reasonably attributable to the non-domestic use of that part of the hereditament which is not exempt[10].

Various methods of valuation are applied in order to arrive at the hypothetical rent, including: by reference to the actual rent paid for the hereditament, or for others comparable to it, or, where there are no rents, by reference to the assessment of comparable hereditaments, or to the profits earned at the hereditament, or to the cost of construction of it[11].

1 The Local Government Finance Act 1988 Sch 6 has effect to determine the rateable value of non-domestic hereditaments for the purposes of Pt III (ss 41–67): s 56(1), Sch 6 para 1 (Sch 6 para 1 amended by the Local Government and Housing Act 1989 ss 139, 194, Sch 5 paras 38, 79(3), Sch 12 Pt II). As to the meaning of 'non-domestic hereditament' see PARA 106. Special provision as to the method of valuation for non-domestic property in relation to the years 1990–95 is made by the Local Government Finance Act 1988 Sch 7A: see PARA 153.

2 As to the meaning of 'domestic property' see PARA 190.

3 As to the exemptions from non-domestic rating see PARA 110 et seq.

4 Local Government Finance Act 1988 Sch 6 para 2(1) (amended by the Local Government and Housing Act 1989 Sch 5 paras 38, 79(3); and the Rating (Valuation) Act 1999 s 1(1), (2)). Where the rateable value would include a fraction of a pound, the fraction must be made up to one pound if it would exceed 50 pence, and the fraction must be ignored if it would be 50 pence or less: Local Government Finance Act 1988 Sch 6 para 2(2).

The definition in Sch 6 para 2(1) (which relies upon a notional annual rent based upon certain assumptions) derives from earlier legislation starting with the Parochial Assessment Act 1836 (repealed), whose purpose was to establish one uniform mode of rating for the relief of the poor; and cases decided under earlier legislation continue to be of relevance to the current statutory definition: see eg *R v Paddington Valuation Officer, ex p Peachey Property Corpn* [1966] 1 QB 380 at 412, [1965] 2 All ER 836 at 848, CA, per Lord Denning MR ('[The] hypothetical rent [. . .] is the rent which an imaginary tenant might be reasonably expected to pay to an imaginary landlord for a tenancy of this dwelling in this locality, on the hypothesis that both are reasonable people, the landlord not being extortionate, the tenant not being under pressure, the dwelling being vacant and to let, not subject to any control, the landlord agreeing to do the repairs and pay the insurance, the tenant agreeing to pay the rates, the period not too short nor yet too long, simply from year to year'). The Court of Appeal has emphasised that the statutory hypothesis is only a mechanism for enabling one to arrive at a value for a particular hereditament for rating purposes and that a rating valuation should not depart from the real world further than the rating hypothesis compels (the 'reality principle'): see *Hoare (Valuation Officer) v National Trust, National Trust v Spratling (Valuation Officer)* [1999] 1 EGLR 155 at 160, [1998] RA 391 at 408, CA, per Schiemann LJ, and at 162 and 415 per Peter Gibson LJ.

The standard by which rating seeks to establish the value of any particular hereditament, being the annual letting value in comparison with the respective values of the rest, must be universal even though in many cases it demands various hypotheses (this being the principle of 'universality' or of 'uniformity'): see *Dawkins (Valuation Officer) v Ash Bros and Heaton Ltd* [1969] 2 AC 366 at 381–382, [1969] 2 All ER 246 at 252, HL, per Lord Pearce. It is a vital principle of the law of rating that each hereditament should be independently assessed: see *Ladies' Hosiery and Underwear Ltd v West Middlesex Assessment Committee* [1932] 2 KB 679 at 686, CA, per Scrutton LJ. Besides the principle of independent valuation, there is another vital principle: that as between different classes of hereditaments, and as between different hereditaments in the same class, the valuation should be fair and equal, but with a third important qualification, that the assessing authority should not sacrifice correctness to ensure uniformity (but, if possible, obtain uniformity by correcting inaccuracies rather than by making an inaccurate assessment in order to secure uniform error): see *Ladies' Hosiery and Underwear Ltd v West Middlesex Assessment Committee* above at 688 per Scrutton LJ.

As to the duration of the hypothetical tenancy and other matters relating thereto see further PARAS 158–163.

5 Local Government Finance Act 1988 Sch 6 para 2(1)(a) (Sch 6 para 2(1)(a)–(c) added by the Rating (Valuation) Act 1999 s 1(1), (2)).

6 Local Government Finance Act 1988 Sch 6 para 2(1)(b) (as added: see note 5). See eg *Henriques v Stephens (Valuation Officer)* [2001] RA 366, Lands Tribunal (statutory assumptions applied to property in exceptionally poor repair where there was no evidence to suggest that repairs would

be uneconomic). The statutory assumption that a hereditament is in a state of reasonable repair does not displace the reality principle that it is to be valued as it in fact existed on the material day: *Newbigin (Valuation Officer) v SJ & J Monk (a firm)* [2017] UKSC 14, [2017] 2 All ER 971, [2017] 1 WLR 851.

For the purposes of the Local Government Finance Act 1988 Sch 6 para 2, the state of repair of a hereditament at any time relevant for the purposes of a list is assumed to be the state of repair in which, under Sch 6 para 2(1), it is assumed to be immediately before the assumed tenancy begins: Sch 6 para 2(8A) (added by the Rating (Valuation) Act 1999 s 1(1), (3)). See eg *Archer Ltd v Robinson (Valuation Officer)* [2003] RA 1, Lands Tribunal (property valued on the assumption that, immediately before the tenancy begins, it has been repaired by way of over-roofing).

7 Local Government Finance Act 1988 Sch 6 para 2(1)(c) (as added: see note 5).

8 As to the meaning of 'composite hereditament' see PARA 106 note 6.

9 Local Government Finance Act 1988 Sch 6 para 2(1A) (Sch 6 para 2(1A), (1B), (13) added by the Local Government and Housing Act 1989 Sch 5 paras 38, 79(3)). In the Local Government Finance Act 1988 Sch 6 para 2, references to the non-domestic use of property are references to use otherwise than in such manner as to constitute the property domestic property: Sch 6 para 2(13) (as so added).

10 Local Government Finance Act 1988 Sch 6 para 2(1B) (as added: see note 9).

11 As to the methods of valuation see PARA 182 et seq.

158. The duration of the hypothetical tenancy.

As the rent to be estimated is such a rent as might reasonably be expected for the hereditament if let from year to year[1], it is not such a rent as might be obtained for it if let for a term of years; equally, it is not to be assumed in valuing that the tenancy will last only for one year because it must be assumed that there is a reasonable prospect of continuance[2].

1 See the Local Government Finance Act 1988 Sch 6 para 2(1); and PARA 157.

2 See *Staley v Castleton Overseers* (1864) 33 LJMC 178 at 181–182 per Blackburn J; *Great Eastern Rly Co v Haughley* (1866) LR 1 QB 666; *Clive v Foy Overseers* (1875) 39 JP Jo 774, DC; *R v South Staffordshire Waterworks Co* (1885) 16 QBD 359, CA (approved in *Railway Assessment Authority v Southern Rly Co* [1936] AC 266, [1936] 1 All ER 26, HL, per Lord Hailsham LC); *Humber Ltd v Jones (Valuation Officer) and Rugby RDC* (1960) 6 RRC 161, CA; *L & A Black Ltd v Burton (Valuation Officer)* (1958) 3 RRC 172, Lands Tribunal; cf *Lloyd (Valuation Officer) v Rossleigh Ltd* [1962] RVR 249, CA. Where a colliery was at the time working at a loss, the rental value was not necessarily nil; the possibility of improvement in future years had to be taken into account: *Consett Iron Co Ltd v Assessment Committee for No 5 or North-Western Area of County of Durham* [1931] AC 396, HL.

The cases cited in this paragraph were decided prior to the coming into force of the Local Government Finance Act 1988 but continue to be of relevance: see PARA 50.

159. Usual tenant's rates and taxes.

The hypothetical rent is to be estimated in the case of all hereditaments on the assumption that the tenant pays all usual tenant's rates and taxes[1]. In the past, a variety of taxes, duties and charges, subsequently repealed, have been considered in this context[2]. The non-domestic rate will normally now be the only rate or tax falling within this phrase. If an actual rent is used as a basis for calculating the hypothetical rent of a hereditament and that rent includes such a rate, a deduction must be made from it. Any rating reliefs enjoyed by the occupier must be taken into account[3].

1 See the Local Government Finance Act 1988 Sch 6 para 2(1)(c); and PARA 157.

2 The poor rate (now the non-domestic rate) was a usual tenant's rate: *Hackney and Lamberhurst Tithe Commutation Rent Charges Case* (1858) EB & E 1 at 47. A water rate was not a 'rate' at all, but a charge for the supply of a commodity: *Re Baker, ex p Eastbourne Waterworks Co v Official Receiver* [1954] 2 All ER 790, [1954] 1 WLR 1144. As to the treatment of the old sewers rate see *R v Adames* (1832) 4 B & Ad 61; *R v Hall Dare* (1864) 5 B & S 785; *R v Gainsborough Union* (1871) LR 7 QB 64; *Green v Newport Union* [1909] AC 35, HL. Landlord's property tax (under legislation now repealed) was not a usual tenant's tax (*R v Southampton Dock Co* (1851) 14 QB 587); the former land tax was not a usual tenant's tax (*Hackney and Lamberhurst Tithe*

Commutation Rent Charges Case above); payments on account of the monopoly value (now abolished) of licensed premises were not a usual tenant's tax (*Appenrodt v Central Middlesex Assessment Committee* [1937] 2 KB 48 at 59, 69, [1937] 2 All ER 325 at 331, 338, CA); and compensation charges, being deductible from rent, would not appear to be a tenant's tax. As to the meaning of 'rates and taxes' in relation to covenants for payment under tenancy agreements see LANDLORD AND TENANT vol 62 (2016) PARA 423.

The cases cited in this paragraph were decided prior to the coming into force of the Local Government Finance Act 1988 but continue to be of relevance: see PARA 50.

3 *Margate Pier and Harbour Co v Yorke (Valuation Officer)* (1955) 48 R & IT 107, Lands Tribunal.

160. Repairs, insurance and other expenses.

The burden of the cost of the repairs and insurance, and of the other expenses, if any, necessary to maintain the hereditament[1] in a state to command the hypothetical rent[2], falls on the tenant[3]. In addition to the cost of repairs, a sinking fund for renewals when the premises are ultimately worn out may be allowed[4].

1 The phrase 'other expenses necessary to maintain the hereditament' is not to be construed *eiusdem generis* with 'repairs' and 'insurance': *Appenrodt v Central Middlesex Assessment Committee* [1937] 2 KB 48, [1937] 2 All ER 325, CA (monopoly value payments (now abolished) held to fall within the phrase); *Waddle v Sunderland Union* [1908] 1 KB 642, CA (compensation charge not such an expense). As to the rules of statutory interpretation see STATUTES AND LEGISLATIVE PROCESS vol 96 (2012) PARA 1078 et seq. The phrase is not limited to expenditure on the hereditament itself but may include expenditure on other land if it is necessary to preserve the physical state of the hereditament. A renewal fund for the hereditament may be such an expense: *R v Wells* (1867) LR 2 QB 542; *Humber Ltd v Jones (Valuation Officer) and Rugby RDC* (1959) 5 RRC 23, Lands Tribunal (on appeal on another point (1960) 6 RRC 161, CA). The former drainage rates, sea defence rates, fishing rates and similar charges were such expenses: see *Green v Newport Union* [1909] AC 35, HL; *R v Hall Dare* (1864) 34 LJMC 17; *R v Gainsborough Union* (1871) LR 7 QB 64; *R v Smith* (1885) 55 LJMC 49. The cost of dredging a channel which does not form part of the hereditament is not such an expense: *White Bros v South Stoneham Union Assessment Committee* [1915] 1 KB 103, DC.

Most of the cases cited in this paragraph were decided prior to the coming into force of the Local Government Finance Act 1988 but continue to be of relevance: see PARA 50.

2 In *Wexler v Playle (Valuation Officer)* [1960] 1 QB 217, [1960] 1 All ER 338, CA, the court inclined to the view that the words 'necessary to maintain the hereditament in a state to command the rent' qualify only 'the other expenses' and not 'the repairs and insurance', but the point was not decided. In *Hoare (Valuation Officer) v National Trust* [1999] 1 EGLR 155, [1998] RA 391, CA, it was held that the unique nature of the heritage properties in question meant that any landlord would have had difficulty in persuading the ratepayer to bear the unusually high costs of any repairs, as was required by the Local Government Finance Act 1988 Sch 6 para 2(1) (see PARA 157), but there would have been no other bidders for the hypothetical tenancy. Accordingly, it was considered to be crucial that, where a hypothetical tenant was also the actual occupier, its policies and reasons for wanting the property were taken into account when determining the hypothetical rent: *Hoare (Valuation Officer) v National Trust* above (ratepayer would not pay a rent for a loss-making property given its self-financing policy in the real world; the factors in this case indicated a nominal hypothetical rent). See also *Harrods Ltd v Baker (Valuation Officer)* [2007] RA 247, Lands Tribunal (appropriate rateable value for Harrods department store).

3 See the Local Government Finance Act 1988 Sch 6 para 2(1)(c); and PARA 157.

4 *R v Wells* (1867) LR 2 QB 542; *Humber Ltd v Jones (Valuation Officer) and Rugby RDC* (1959) 5 RRC 23, Lands Tribunal (on appeal on another point (1960) 6 RRC 161, CA). As to sinking funds when valuing on the profits basis see PARA 185.

161. Actual conditions affecting property when valuation made.

In relation to the assessment of the rateable value of a non-domestic hereditament[1], the rent which a tenant could afford to give is determined *rebus sic stantibus*[2], that is to say with reference to the hereditament in its physical condition[3] on the material day[4], and to the mode in which it is actually used again at the material day[5]. A continuance of the existing conditions affecting the hereditament is *prima facie* assumed[6]. The issue as to whether lack of repair in a hereditament is to be ignored (as it was in cases valued under the previous law[7]) has been decided by statute[8]. The hereditament must be valued subject to any statutory restrictions in respect of it[9], other than those limiting the rent obtainable for it[10]. However, restrictive covenants and other private arrangements affecting the hereditament are irrelevant[11].

1 As to such assessment see the Local Government Finance Act 1988 Sch 6 paras 1, 2; and PARA 157.

2 Ie, literally, 'as things stand'. For an early, possibly the first, use of the term '*rebus sic stantibus*' see *R v Fletton Overseers* (1861) 3 E & E 450 at 465.

Some of the cases cited in this paragraph were decided prior to the coming into force of the Local Government Finance Act 1988 but continue to be of relevance: see PARA 50.

3 *R v Grand Junction Rly Co* (1844) 4 QB 18; *Sculcoates Union v Kingston-upon-Hull Dock Co* [1895] AC 136, HL; *Poplar Metropolitan Borough Assessment Committee v Roberts* [1922] 2 AC 93 at 120, HL; *Townley Mill Co (1919) Ltd v Oldham Assessment Committee* [1937] AC 419 at 436–437, [1937] 1 All ER 11 at 19–20, HL; *Robinson Bros (Brewers) Ltd v Houghton and Chester-le-Street Assessment Committee* [1937] 2 KB 445 at 468, [1937] 2 All ER 298 at 307, CA (affd sub nom *Robinson Bros (Brewers) Ltd v Durham County Assessment Committee (Area No 7)* [1938] AC 321, [1938] 2 All ER 79, HL).

If the land has buildings upon it and is occupied, it must be valued with them (see eg *R v Aberystwith Inhabitants* (1808) 10 East 354), but land must not be valued at the rent at which it would be let if more, or more valuable, buildings were erected on it (*R v Gardner* (1774) 1 Cowp 79; *Kempe v Spence* (1779) 2 Wm Bl 1244; *R v Mast* (1795) 6 Term Rep 154; *R v St Luke's Hospital* (1760) 2 Burr 1053 at 1064 (considered in *Liverpool Corpn v Chorley Union Assessment Committee and Withnell Overseers* [1913] AC 197 at 209, HL, per Lord Atkinson); *East London Rly Co v Whitechurch* (1874) LR 7 HL 81 at 86).

Temporary partitioning put up by the occupier may be ignored without breach of the *rebus sic stantibus* rule: *City of Sheffield v Meadow Dairy Ltd* (1958) 2 RRC 395, CA. No structural alteration may be envisaged such as the making of a fresh entrance or widening an existing one: *Manchester Tennis and Racquet Club v Castle (Valuation Officer)* (1960) 6 RRC 269, Lands Tribunal. But the making of a minor non-structural alteration may be envisaged, such as the removal of battens securing a garage door (*Appeal of Sheppard (Valuation Officer)* (1967) 13 RRC 139, Lands Tribunal), provided that the alteration is not so substantial as to change the mode or category of use (*Fir Mill Ltd v Royton UDC and Jones (Valuation Officer)* (1960) 7 RRC 171, Lands Tribunal). See *Williams v Scottish & Newcastle Retail Ltd* [2001] EWCA Civ 185 at [74], [76], [2001] RA 41 at [74], [76] per Robert Walker LJ; and also *Re Appeal of Clark (Valuation Officer)* [1987] RA 127, Lands Tribunal. As to whether works are repairs or structural improvements see *Civil Aviation Authority v Langford (Valuation Officer) and Camden London Borough Council* [1979] RA 1, (1978) 247 EG 957, Lands Tribunal (on appeal sub nom *Camden London Borough Council v Civil Aviation Authority and Langford (Valuation Officer)* [1980] RA 369, 257 Estates Gazette 273, CA); and *Murphy (Valuation Officer) v Courtney plc (formerly IAF Financial Services plc)* [1999] RA 1, Lands Tribunal.

4 As to the material day see PARA 165.

5 Pursuant to what Parliament has provided for in the Local Government Finance Act 1988 Sch 6 para 2(3)–(7) (see PARA 164), the 'mode or category of occupation of the hereditament' is recognised as being a material factor in valuation for rating purposes, so confirming that the *rebus sic stantibus* principle has a second limb (user) in addition to its first limb (physical condition): *Williams v Scottish & Newcastle Retail Ltd* [2001] EWCA Civ 185, [2001] RA 41, (2001) Times, 6 March. *Williams v Scottish & Newcastle Retail Ltd* above at [69] per Robert Walker LJ disapproves the dictum stated in *Midland Bank Ltd v Lanham (Valuation Officer)* [1978] RA 1 at 26, [1978] 1 EGLR 189 at 195, Lands Tribunal, per Emlyn Jones ('Finally, all alternative uses to which the hereditament in its existing state could be put in the real world, and which would be in the minds of competing bidders in the market, are to be taken as being within the same mode or category, where the existence of such competition can be established by evidence') as being a formulation which either contradicts the rest of the Tribunal's stated conclusion, which referred to the use being limited to the same mode or category as the existing use, or at best reduces the second limb of the rule recognised in the Local Government Finance Act 1988 Sch 6 para 2(7)(b) (see PARA 164) to a pale reflection of the first limb recognised in Sch 6 para 2(7)(a) (see PARA 164). Parliament's adoption of the expression 'mode or category of occupation' as it was used in *Fir Mill Ltd v Royton UDC and Jones (Valuation Officer)* (1960) 7 RRC 171, Lands Tribunal, must be taken as recognising that the formulation in *Fir Mill Ltd v Royton UDC and Jones (Valuation*

Officer) is on the right lines, even if its precise scope has to be worked out on a case by case basis: *Williams v Scottish & Newcastle Retail Ltd* [2001] EWCA Civ 185 at [70], [2001] RA 41, (2001) Times, 6 March.

As to the line taken in *Fir Mill Ltd v Royton UDC and Jones (Valuation Officer)* see also *R v Everist* (1847) 10 QB 178 at 182 per Lord Denman CJ; *Staley v Castleton Overseers* (1864) 33 LJMC 178 at 182 per Blackburn J; *R v Manchester and South Junction etc Rly Co* (1851) 17 LTOS 71; *Port of London Authority v Orsett Union Assessment Committee* [1920] AC 273 at 305, HL, per Lord Buckmaster; *Poplar Metropolitan Borough Assessment Committee v Roberts* [1922] 2 AC 93 at 103, HL, per Lord Buckmaster; *Townley Mill Co (1919) Ltd v Oldham Assessment Committee* [1937] AC 419 at 437, [1937] 1 All ER 11 at 19, HL, per Lord Maugham.

As to the line taken in the dictum in *Midland Bank Ltd v Lanham (Valuation Officer)* above which has been disapproved see also *Henriques v Garland (Valuation Officer)* (1978) 20 RRC 341, Lands Tribunal; *S & P Jackson (Manchester) Ltd v Hill (Valuation Officer)* [1980] RA 195, [1980] JPL 688, Lands Tribunal; *Westminster City Council v British Telecommunications plc and Woolway (Valuation Officer)* [1985] RA 87, [1985] JPL 648, Lands Tribunal.

As to the effect of planning control on possible alternative uses see *London Transport Executive v Croydon London Borough Council and Phillips (Valuation Officer)* [1974] RA 225, Lands Tribunal; *Midland Bank Ltd v Lanham (Valuation Officer)*; *Henriques v Garland (Valuation Officer)* above (all cases to be read in the light of *Williams v Scottish & Newcastle Retail Ltd* [2001] EWCA Civ 185, [2001] RA 41, (2001) Times, 6 March).

6 *Great Eastern Rly Co v Haughley* (1866) LR 1 QB 666 (applied in *Consett Iron Co Ltd v Assessment Committee for No 5 or North-Western Area of County of Durham* [1931] AC 396, HL); *R v Fletton Overseers* (1861) 30 LJMC 89. While premises are undergoing structural alterations, they must be valued in the state in which they are: *Hounslow London Borough Council v Rank Audio Visual Ltd and Browning (Valuation Officer)* (1970) 17 RRC 82, Lands Tribunal; *Paul Rocky & Co v Morley (Valuation Officer)* [1981] RA 208, [1981] JPL 689, Lands Tribunal.

Under the law as it stood before the passing of the Local Government Finance Act 1988, the prospect of demolition of the hereditament by an external authority during the currency of the hypothetical tenancy could be taken into account: *Dawkins (Valuation Officer) v Ash Bros and Heaton Ltd* [1969] 2 AC 366, [1969] 2 All ER 246, HL. Now, however, these cases have to be read in the light of the requirement in the Local Government Finance Act 1988 that some factors are taken as at the antecedent valuation date and others at the material day: see PARA 164 et seq. It seems that future events which would not have affected value as at the antecedent valuation date (for example, a compulsory purchase order promoted well after the antecedent valuation date) are not to be taken into account: *Prodorite Ltd v Clark (Valuation Officer)* [1993] RA 197, Lands Tribunal. However, in *Berrill (t/a Cobweb Antiques) v Hill (Valuation Officer)* [2000] RA 194, Lands Tribunal, it was accepted that regard could be had to possible future changes in the scale of public works which were in progress at the date at which the ratepayer proposed a reduction but that the reduction made by the valuation officer for the effect of those works was held to be justified largely on the evidentiary basis of other agreements made between the valuation officer and the ratepayer or his agents in relation to nearby comparables.

7 See *Wexler v Playle (Valuation Officer)* [1960] 1 QB 217, [1960] 1 All ER 338, CA; *Saunders v Maltby (Valuation Officer)* [1976] RA 109, CA; *Civil Aviation Authority v Langford (Valuation Officer) and Camden London Borough Council* [1979] RA 1, Lands Tribunal (on appeal sub nom *Camden London Borough Council v Civil Aviation Authority and Langford (Valuation Officer)* [1980] RA 369, CA); *Benjamin v Anston Properties Ltd* [1998] RA 53, [1998] 2 EGLR 147; *Murphy (Valuation Officer) v Courtney plc (formerly IAF Financial Services plc)* [1999] RA 1, Lands Tribunal.

8 See now the Local Government Finance Act 1988 Sch 6 para 2(1)(b), (8A); and PARA 157.

9 *Port of London Authority v Orsett Union Assessment Committee* [1920] AC 273 at 305, HL, per Lord Buckmaster; *Marr's Trustees v Ayrshire Assessor* (1934) 20 R & IT 355; *Liverpool Exchange Newsroom Co Ltd v Pritchard (Valuation Officer)* (1959) 4 RRC 374, Lands Tribunal; *Morley (Valuation Officer) v Society for Promoting Christian Knowledge* (1960) 53 R & IT 326, Lands Tribunal; *Black v Oliver* [1978] QB 870, [1978] 3 All ER 408, CA.

10 *Poplar Metropolitan Borough Assessment Committee v Roberts* [1922] 2 AC 93, HL (rent restrictions to be ignored); *McNamara v Dyer (Valuation Officer)* (1952) 45 R & IT 294, Lands Tribunal; *Jones v Tudge (Valuation Officer)* (1952) 45 R & IT 523, Lands Tribunal; *Oster v Gladwin (Valuation Officer)* (1957) 2 RRC 135, Lands Tribunal; *Whitter v Thornber (Valuation Officer)* [1965] RVR 807, 11 RRC 377, CA; *O'Mere v Burley (Valuation Officer)* (1968) 14 RRC

401, Lands Tribunal; *Orange PCS Ltd v Bradford (Valuation Officer)* [2004] EWCA Civ 155, [2004] 2 All ER 651, [2004] RA 61 (beneficial occupation of the hereditament had a value, and the statutory right of the ratepayer to occupy the land without payment was not to be brought into account in determining that value).

11 *Robinson Bros (Brewers) Ltd v Durham County Assessment Committee (Area No 7)* [1938] AC 321 at 336–337, [1938] 2 All ER 79 at 85–86, HL, per Lord Macmillan; *Sunderland near the Sea Overseers v Sunderland Union Guardians* (1865) 18 CBNS 531; *Burley (Valuation Officer) v A & W Birch Ltd* (1959) 5 RRC 147, Lands Tribunal; *Hemingway's Executors v Pulsford (Valuation Officer)* (1959) 53 R & IT 106, Lands Tribunal; *Evans (Valuation Officer) v Farley* (1972) 17 RRC 356, Lands Tribunal; *Eyston v Mundy (Valuation Officer)* [1978] RA 200, Lands Tribunal; *Byrne v Parker (Valuation Officer)* [1980] RA 45, CA; *S & P Jackson (Manchester) Ltd v Hill (Valuation Officer)* [1980] RA 195, Lands Tribunal.

162. Rent that a hypothetical tenant will pay.

In relation to the assessment of the rateable value of a non-domestic hereditament[1], the hypothetical tenant[2] includes all persons who might possibly take the hereditament[3], including the person actually in occupation, even though he happens to be the owner of the hereditament[4]. The rent is that which he[5] will pay in the competitive market[6], taking into account every intrinsic quality of the hereditament[7] and all relevant circumstances[8]. If the occupier is the only possible tenant of a hereditament, his ability to pay is a relevant consideration[9].

1 As to such assessment see the Local Government Finance Act 1988 Sch 6 paras 1, 2; and PARA 157.

2 For an early, possibly the first, use of the term 'hypothetical tenant' see *R v West Middlesex Waterworks* (1859) 28 LJMC 135 at 137.

Most of the cases cited in this paragraph were decided prior to the coming into force of the Local Government Finance Act 1988 but continue to be of relevance: see PARA 50.

3 *Robinson Bros (Brewers) Ltd v Houghton and Chester-le-Street Assessment Committee* [1937] 2 KB 445, [1937] 2 All ER 298, CA (affd sub nom *Robinson Bros (Brewers) Ltd v Durham County Assessment Committee (Area No 7)* [1938] AC 321, [1938] 2 All ER 79, HL). A person who wants it as an adjunct to another hereditament is included: *R v London and North Western Rly Co* (1874) LR 9 QB 134; *Robinson Bros (Brewers) Ltd v Durham County Assessment Committee (Area No 7)* [1938] AC 321 at 338, [1938] 2 All ER 79 at 86, HL, per Lord Macmillan.

4 *R v London School Board* (1886) 17 QBD 738, CA; *LCC v Churchwardens etc of Erith and Dartford Union Assessment Committee* [1893] AC 562, HL; *Davies v Seisdon Union* [1908] AC 315, HL.

5 The test is what the tenant might be expected to pay, not what the landlord might be able to exact: *Poplar Metropolitan Borough Assessment Committee v Roberts* [1922] 2 AC 93 at 116, HL, per Lord Sumner. See also *Sandown Park Ltd v Esher UDC and Castle (Valuation Officer)* (1954) 47 R & IT 351, 367, CA.

6 *Talargoch Mining Co v St Asaph Union* (1868) LR 3 QB 478 at 486; *Mersey Docks and Harbour Board v Liverpool Overseers* (1873) LR 9 QB 84 at 96; *Robinson Bros (Brewers) Ltd v Houghton and Chester-le-Street Assessment Committee* [1937] 2 KB 445 at 470, [1937] 2 All ER 298 at 308, CA (affd sub nom *Robinson Bros (Brewers) Ltd v Durham County Assessment Committee (Area No 7)* [1938] AC 321, [1938] 2 All ER 79, HL).

7 *Robinson Bros (Brewers) Ltd v Houghton and Chester-le-Street Assessment Committee* [1937] 2 KB 445, [1937] 2 All ER 298, CA (affd sub nom *Robinson Bros (Brewers) Ltd v Durham County Assessment Committee (Area No 7)* [1938] AC 321, [1938] 2 All ER 79, HL). As to the application of the principle *rebus sic stantibus* see PARA 161. If the hereditament affords the opportunity for the carrying on of a gainful trade, that fact may be taken into account: *Robinson Bros (Brewers) Ltd v Houghton and Chester-le-Street Assessment Committee* above; *R v Grand Junction Rly Co* (1844) 4 QB 18 at 38; *Watney Mann Ltd v Langley (Valuation Officer)* [1966] 1 QB 457 at 476, [1963] 3 All ER 967 at 979. In *F Cross & Sons v Spencer (Valuation Officer)* [2000] RA 71, Lands Tribunal, it was held to be appropriate to make allowances for the poor location of the property and the fact that the ratepayer was the only likely tenant rather than relying, as the valuation officer had, on list assessments agreed for other car showrooms etc in the same area as demonstrating the established 'tone' for such establishments.

8 Ie affecting value: *Robinson Bros (Brewers) Ltd v Houghton and Chester-le-Street Assessment Committee* [1937] 2 KB 445 at 469, [1937] 2 All ER 298 at 307, CA (affd sub nom *Robinson Bros (Brewers) Ltd v Durham County Assessment Committee (Area No 7)* [1938] AC 321, [1938] 2 All

ER 79, HL). See also *Staley v Castleton Overseers* (1864) 33 LJMC 178; *Harter v Salford Overseers* (1865) 34 LJMC 206; *Townley Mill Co (1919) Ltd v Oldham Assessment Committee* [1937] AC 419, [1937] 1 All ER 11, HL; cf *Hoyle and Jackson v Oldham Poor Law Union Assessment Committee and Churchwardens etc of Oldham* [1894] 2 QB 372, CA (effect of strike); *Consett Iron Co Ltd v Assessment Committee for No 5 or North-Western Area of County of Durham* [1931] AC 396, HL. For a recent case applying these principles see *Harrods Ltd v Baker (Valuation Officer)* [2007] RA 247, Lands Tribunal (appropriate rateable value for Harrods department store).

In valuing a hereditament it is legitimate to take into account its importance as an adjunct of another hereditament: *R v London and North-Western Rly Co* (1874) LR 9 QB 134; *Robinson Bros (Brewers) Ltd v Durham County Assessment Committee (Area No 7)* [1938] AC 321 at 338, [1938] 2 All ER 79 at 86, HL, per Lord Macmillan; *Stafford v Sture (Valuation Officer)* (1959) 6 RRC 109, Lands Tribunal; *Coppin (Valuation Officer) v East Midlands Airport Joint Committee* (1970) 16 RRC 386, Lands Tribunal. The existence of rating reliefs may affect the annual value of a hereditament: *Port of London Authority v Woolwich Corpn* [1924] 1 KB 30 at 49, CA, per Scrutton LJ.

The effect of temporary circumstances and nuisances which can be shown to affect value may be taken into account and examples of Lands Tribunal decisions include the following: *Baird v Wand (Valuation Officer)* (1960) 7 RRC 350 (effect of petrol rationing); *Lewis v Holman (Valuation Officer)* (1961) 9 RRC 116 (use of land adjoining hereditament for contractor's works for a year); *Heath v Holman (Valuation Officer) and Chorleywood UDC* (1961) 9 RRC 8, Lands Tribunal (laying of main sewer for six months did not affect value); *Price v Harrison* [1963] RA 412, Lands Tribunal (delay in completing estate road did not affect value). See also *Lillywhite v Baker (Valuation Officer)* (1967) 13 RRC 50; *Bradgate v Buncombe (Valuation Officer)* (1967) 13 RRC 347, Lands Tribunal; *Beath v Poole (Valuation Officer)* [1973] RA 411 (effect of motorway construction); *Fairhurst v Grice (Valuation Officer)* [1977] RA 246, Lands Tribunal. However, these cases now need to be read in the light of the requirement in the Local Government Finance Act 1988 that some factors are taken as at the antecedent valuation date and others at the material day: see PARA 164 et seq. Cases which also need to be read in that light are those concerning anticipated circumstances: see eg *Railway Assessment Authority v Southern Rly Co* [1936] AC 266 at 285–286, [1936] 1 All ER 26 at 37–38, HL; *Joseph Jones & Co v West Derby Union* (1911) 75 JP 375; *Dawkins (Valuation Officer) v Ash Bros and Heaton Ltd* [1969] 2 AC 366, [1969] 2 All ER 246, HL, in which it was held that the prospect of the demolition of the hereditament for the purposes of a road scheme within a year could be taken into account, and a distinction was drawn between circumstances which are 'essential to' and 'accidental to' the hereditament. See also *King v Johnston (Valuation Officer)* (1957) 2 RRC 20, Lands Tribunal (redevelopment proposals ignored); *Ritchie v Brewin (Valuation Officer)* (1957) 2 RRC 342, Lands Tribunal (future road improvement ignored); *Burley (Valuation Officer) v A & W Birch Ltd* (1959) 5 RRC 147, Lands Tribunal (redevelopment scheme of landlord ignored); *Lloyd (Valuation Officer) v Rossleigh Ltd* [1962] RVR 249, CA (valuation not affected by planning proposals); *R v Paddington Valuation Officer, ex p Peachey Property Corpn Ltd* [1964] 3 All ER 200, [1964] 1 WLR 1186 (affd [1966] 1 QB 380, [1965] 2 All ER 836, CA). See also *Prodorite Ltd v Clark (Valuation Officer)* [1993] RA 197, Lands Tribunal; and *Berrill (t/a Cobweb Antiques) v Hill (Valuation Officer)* [2000] RA 194, Lands Tribunal (both cases cited in PARA 161).

9 *Tomlinson (Valuation Officer) v Plymouth Argyle Football Co Ltd* (1960) 6 RRC 173, CA. Ability to pay was considered in a number of Lands Tribunal decisions including the following: *Blackman (Valuation Officer) v Lowe and Tavistock RDC* (1957) 3 RRC 1, Lands Tribunal; *Hitchin Town Football Club v Wallace (Valuation Officer)* [1961] RVR 462, Lands Tribunal; *Sussex Motor Yacht Club Ltd v Gilmore (Valuation Officer)* [1966] RA 43, Lands Tribunal; *Heaton Cricket Club v Westwood (Valuation Officer)* (1959) 5 RRC 98, Lands Tribunal; *Magdalen, Jesus and Keble Colleges, Oxford v Howard (Valuation Officer) and City of Oxford* (1959) 5 RRC 122, Lands Tribunal (on appeal [1961] RVR 22, CA); *Marylebone Cricket Club v Morley (Valuation Officer)* (1959) 6 RRC 258, Lands Tribunal; *Shrewsbury Schools v Shrewsbury Borough Council and Plumpton (Valuation Officer)* (1960) 7 RRC 313, Lands Tribunal; *Leeds University v Leeds City Council and Burge (Valuation Officer)* [1962] RA 177, Lands Tribunal; *Addington Community Association v Croydon Corpn and Gudgion (Valuation Officer)* (1967) 13 RRC 126, Lands Tribunal; *Co-operative Retail Services Ltd v Oates (Valuation Officer)* [1995] RA 151, Lands Tribunal. See also *Cardiff Corpn v Williams (Valuation Officer)* [1973] RA 46, 18 RRC 1, CA; and *Eastbourne Borough Council v Allen (Valuation Officer)* [2001] RA 273, Lands Tribunal.

163. Assumption that hereditament is vacant and to let.

In estimating the hypothetical rent in relation to the assessment of the rateable value of a non-domestic hereditament[1], the hereditament is assumed to be vacant and to let[2].

1 As to such assessment see the Local Government Finance Act 1988 Sch 6 paras 1, 2; and PARA 157.

2 *LCC v Churchwardens etc of Erith Parish and Dartford Union Assessment Committee* [1893] AC 562 at 588, HL, per Lord Herschell LC; *Humber Ltd v Jones (Valuation Officer)* (1960) 6 RRC 161, CA; *R v Paddington Valuation Officer, ex p Peachey Property Corpn* [1966] 1 QB 380 at 412, [1965] 2 All ER 836 at 848, CA, per Lord Denning MR; *Wyre Forest District Council v Stokes (Valuation Officer)* [1974] RA 361, Lands Tribunal. It is to be assumed, in the case of business premises, that the previous business has closed and any process machinery been removed: *Fir Mill Ltd v Royton UDC and Jones (Valuation Officer)* (1960) 7 RRC 171, Lands Tribunal.

The cases cited in this paragraph were decided prior to the coming into force of the Local Government Finance Act 1988 but continue to be of relevance: see PARA 50.

B. THE DATE OF VALUATION

164. Date of valuation for purpose of compiling or altering rating lists.

Each successive rating list has a single valuation date[1]. That date is either:

(1) the day on which the list must be compiled[2] (or, in the case of an alteration to a list, the day on which the list came into force[3]); or

(2) such day preceding that day as may be specified by the appropriate national authority[4] by order in relation to the list[5].

In determining the rateable value of non-domestic hereditaments, the following factors[6] must be taken into account:

(a) matters affecting the physical state or physical enjoyment of the hereditament[7];

(b) the mode or category of occupation of the hereditament[8];

(c) the quantity of minerals or other substances in or extracted from the hereditament[9];

(d) the quantity of refuse or waste material which is brought onto and permanently deposited on the hereditament[10];

(e) matters affecting the physical state of the locality in which the hereditament is situated or which, though not affecting the physical state of the locality, are nonetheless physically manifest there[11]; and

(f) the use or occupation of other premises situated in the locality of the hereditament[12].

Where the rateable value is determined for the purposes of compiling a list by reference to a day specified by order[13], the matters mentioned in heads (a) to (f) above must be taken to be as they are assumed to be on the day on which the list must be compiled[14]. Where the rateable value is determined with a view to making an alteration to a list which has been compiled (whether or not it is still in force) the matters mentioned in heads (a) to (f) above must be taken to be as they are assumed to be on the material day[15].

1 As to the principles which underlie the concept of a common valuation date see *K Shoe Shops Ltd v Hardy (Valuation Officer)* [1983] 3 All ER 609, sub nom *Saxone Shoe Co Ltd v Hardy (Valuation Officer) and Westminster City Council* [1983] 1 WLR 1273, HL. As to the compilation of local non-domestic rating lists see PARA 191; and as to the compilation of central non-domestic rating lists see PARA 196.

2 Local Government Finance Act 1988 s 56(1), Sch 6 para 2(3)(a). Schedule 6 has effect to determine the rateable value of non-domestic hereditaments for the purposes of Pt III (ss 41–67): Sch 6 para 1 (amended by the Local Government and Housing Act 1989 ss 139, 194, Sch 5 paras 38, 79(3), Sch 12 Pt II). As to the meaning of 'non-domestic hereditament' see PARA 106.

3 See the Local Government Finance Act 1988 Sch 6 para 2(4)(a).

4 Ie the Secretary of State or, in relation to Wales, the Welsh Ministers. The functions of the Secretary of State under the Local Government Finance Act 1988 Sch 6, so far as exercisable in relation to Wales, were transferred to the National Assembly for Wales (see the National Assembly for Wales (Transfer of Functions) Order 1999, SI 1999/672, art 2, Sch 1) and are now vested in the Welsh Ministers (see the Government of Wales Act 2006 s 162(1), Sch 11 para 30). As to the Secretary of State and the Welsh Ministers see PARA 4 note 18. As to the meaning of 'Wales' see PARA 2 note 16. As to the separate administration of the non-domestic rating provisions (Local Government Finance Act 1988 Pt III (ss 41–67)) in England and Wales see PARA 52.

5 See the Local Government Finance Act 1988 Sch 6 para 2(3)(b), (4)(b). If a day is specified under Sch 6 para 2(3)(b) (ie for the purposes of compiling the list), the same specification must be made in relation to all lists to be compiled on the same day: Sch 6 para 2(10).

As to the orders made under Sch 6 para 2(3)(b) see the Rating Lists (Valuation Date) (England) Order 2014, SI 2014/2841, and the Rating Lists (Valuation Date) (Wales) Order 2014, SI 2014/2917. In relation both to England and to Wales, 1 April 2015 is specified as the day by reference to which the rateable values of non-domestic hereditaments are to be determined for the purposes of the local and central non-domestic rating lists which are to be compiled for England and Wales on 1 April 2017: see the Rating Lists (Valuation Date) (England) Order 2014, SI 2014/2841, art 2, and the Rating Lists (Valuation Date) (Wales) Order 2014, SI 2014/2917, art 2. As to the meaning of 'England' see PARA 2 note 16.

6 The line between physical and other factors is not always easily drawn: see eg *Shearson Lehman Bros Ltd v Humphrys (Valuation Officer)* [1991] RA 125, [1991] 2 EGLR 224, Lands Tribunal; *Jafton Properties Ltd v Prisk (Valuation Officer)* [1997] RA 137, Lands Tribunal. In *Walker (Valuation Officer) v Railex Systems Ltd* [1993] RA 55, Lands Tribunal, the parties agreed, and the tribunal accepted, that no account was to be taken of the Town and Country Planning (Use Classes) Order 1987, SI 1987/764 (see PLANNING vol 81 (2018) PARA 340 et seq), in order to anticipate a future change of use because that Order had not been in force on 1 April 1973 (the date by reference to which the valuation was carried out).

7 Local Government Finance Act 1988 Sch 6 para 2(7)(a). The wording of heads (a) and (b) in the text has been cited to confirm the two limbs of the *rebus sic stantibus* principle (which is used to assess the hypothetical rent on the hereditament from which its rateable value is determined): see *Williams v Scottish & Newcastle Retail Ltd* [2001] EWCA Civ 185, [2001] RA 41, (2001) Times, 6 March; and PARA 161.

The wording of heads (a) and (e) in the text is similar to the wording of the Local Government Finance Act 1988 s 121(1)(a), (b), which:

(1) was enacted to amend the old law (contained in the General Rate Act 1967 s 20 (repealed)) in order to restrict the effect of the decision in *Clement (Valuation Officer) v Addis Ltd* [1988] 1 All ER 593, [1988] 1 WLR 301, HL; and

(2) reflects and is consistent with the reasoning of the Court of Appeal in *Addis Ltd v Clement (Valuation Officer)* (1987) 85 LGR 489, [1987] RA 1, CA.

The Local Government Finance Act 1988 s 121(1) applied where for the purposes of the General Rate Act 1967 s 20 (repealed) a hereditament was valued on the basis of the assumptions specified in s 20(1) (basis of valuation for the purposes of a proposal to alter a valuation list to be consistent with the tone of the list), and had effect in relation to any proposal made on or after 10 March 1988 which was outstanding on the passing of the Local Government Finance Act 1988 (ie 29 July 1988) but had no effect in relation to any proposal made before 10 March 1988: see s 121(1), (3).

8 Local Government Finance Act 1988 Sch 6 para 2(7)(b). See also note 7.

9 Local Government Finance Act 1988 Sch 6 para 2(7)(c).

10 Local Government Finance Act 1988 Sch 6 para 2(7)(cc) (added by the Local Government and Housing Act 1989 Sch 5 paras 38, 79(3)).

11 Local Government Finance Act 1988 Sch 6 para 2(7)(d). Cf the wording used to similar effect in the Local Government Finance Act 1992 s 24 (see PARA 417) for the purposes of council tax. For cases as to 'locality' under the Local Government Finance Act 1988 Sch 6 para 2(7)(d) see *K Shoe Shops Ltd v Hardy (Valuation Officer)* [1983] 3 All ER 609, sub nom *Saxone Shoe Co Ltd v Hardy (Valuation Officer) and Westminster City Council* [1983] 1 WLR 1273, HL; and *Jafton Properties Ltd v Prisk (Valuation Officer)* [1997] RA 137, Lands Tribunal.

12 Local Government Finance Act 1988 Sch 6 para 2(7)(e). See also note 7.

13 Ie under the Local Government Finance Act 1988 Sch 6 para 2(3)(b): see note 5.

14 Local Government Finance Act 1988 Sch 6 para 2(5).

15 Local Government Finance Act 1988 Sch 6 para 2(6) (amended by the Local Government and Housing Act 1989 Sch 5 paras 38, 79(3)). The 'material day' is such day as is determined in accordance with rules prescribed by regulations made by the appropriate national authority: see

the Local Government Finance Act 1988 Sch 6 para 2(6A) (added by the Local Government and Housing Act 1989 Sch 5 paras 38, 79(3), Sch 12; substituted by the Local Government Finance Act 1992 s 104, Sch 10 para 4). As to the material day for these purposes see the Non-Domestic Rating (Material Day for List Alterations) Regulations 1992, SI 1992/556; and PARA 165.

165. The material day for list alterations.

Where the rateable value of non-domestic hereditaments is to be determined[1] with a view to making an alteration to a rating list which has been compiled[2] (whether or not it is still in force), the factors to be considered[3] must be taken to be as they are assumed to be on the material day[4], being such day as is determined in accordance with rules prescribed by regulations[5].

The material day is to be determined in accordance with the following provisions[6]. Where the determination is with a view to making an alteration to correct an inaccuracy in the list on the day on which it was compiled, the material day is the day on which the list was compiled[7]. Where the determination is with a view to making an alteration to correct an inaccuracy in the list which arose in the course of making a previous alteration, or is occasioned by a proposal disputing the accuracy of a previous alteration, the material day is the day by reference to which the factors to be considered[8] fell to be assessed when determining the rateable value with a view to making the alteration which gave rise to the inaccuracy or the accuracy of which is disputed[9].

Where the determination is with a view to making an alteration so as to show in (or delete from) the list any hereditament[10] which:

(1) has come into existence or ceased to exist[11];

(2) has ceased to be (or become) domestic property[12] or property exempt[13] from non-domestic rating[14];

(3) has ceased to be (or become) required to be shown in the central non-domestic rating list[15]; or

(4) has ceased to be (or come to form) part of the relevant authority's[16] area by virtue of a change in that area[17],

the material day is[18] the day on which the circumstances giving rise to the alteration occurred[19]. However, where a completion notice[20] has been served in relation to a building which constitutes or includes the hereditament in question, and the notice has not been withdrawn[21], the material day is:

(a) the day proposed in the notice as the completion day in relation to the building[22]; or

(b) where a completion day has been agreed or determined[23], the day so agreed or determined[24].

Where the determination is with a view to making an alteration to the list to reflect part of a hereditament becoming, or ceasing to be, domestic property or exempt, the material day is the day on which the circumstances giving rise to the alteration occurred[25].

In any other case, and where the determination is with a view to making an alteration to a list compiled before 1 April 2005, the material day is the day on which the proposal for the alteration in respect of which a determination falls to be made is served on the valuation officer[26] or, where there is no such proposal, the day on which the valuation officer alters the list[27]. Where the determination is with a view to making an alteration to a list compiled on or after 1 April 2005, the material day is:

(i) where the alteration is made in pursuance of a proposal, the date on which the valuation officer received a confirmation[28];

(ii) where the alteration is not made in pursuance of a proposal, the day on which the circumstances giving rise to the alteration occurred (if the day on which the circumstances giving rise to the alteration is reasonably ascertainable)[29] or the day on which the valuation officer alters the list (if that day is not reasonably ascertainable)[30].

1 Ie in accordance with the Local Government Finance Act 1988 Sch 6: see PARA 157 et seq.
2 As to the compilation of local non-domestic rating lists see PARA 191. As to the compilation of central non-domestic rating lists see PARA 196. As to the alteration of rating lists see PARA 199 et seq.
3 Ie under the Local Government Finance Act 1988 Sch 6 para 2(7): see PARA 164.
4 See the Local Government Finance Act 1988 Sch 6 para 2(6); and PARA 164.
5 See the Local Government Finance Act 1988 Sch 6 para 2(6A); and PARA 164. As to the regulations made see the Non-Domestic Rating (Material Day for List Alterations) Regulations 1992, SI 1992/556 (amended by SI 2005/658 and SI 2017/155), and the text to notes 6–30.
6 See the Non-Domestic Rating (Material Day for List Alterations) Regulations 1992, SI 1992/556, reg 3(1).
7 Non-Domestic Rating (Material Day for List Alterations) Regulations 1992, SI 1992/556, reg 3(2).
8 Ie under the Local Government Finance Act 1988 Sch 6 para 2(7): see PARA 164.
9 Non-Domestic Rating (Material Day for List Alterations) Regulations 1992, SI 1992/556, reg 3(3).
10 As to the meaning of 'hereditament' see PARA 106.
11 Non-Domestic Rating (Material Day for List Alterations) Regulations 1992, SI 1992/556, reg 3(4)(a). The reference in reg 3(4) to a hereditament coming into existence or ceasing to exist includes a reference to a hereditament which comes into existence or ceases to exist by virtue of:
   (1) property previously rated as a single hereditament becoming liable to be rated in parts (reg 3(8)(a)); or
   (2) property previously liable to be rated in parts becoming liable to be rated as a single hereditament (reg 3(8)(b)); or
   (3) any part of a hereditament becoming part of a different hereditament (reg 3(8)(c)).
12 As to the meaning of 'domestic property' see PARA 190.
13 As to exemptions from non-domestic rating see PARA 110 et seq.
14 Non-Domestic Rating (Material Day for List Alterations) Regulations 1992, SI 1992/556, reg 3(4)(b).
15 Non-Domestic Rating (Material Day for List Alterations) Regulations 1992, SI 1992/556, reg 3(4)(c).
16 The 'relevant authority' in relation to a hereditament means, in respect of a day falling before 1 April 1993, the charging authority; or, in respect of any other day, the billing authority in whose area the hereditament is situated: Non-Domestic Rating (Material Day for List Alterations) Regulations 1992, SI 1992/556, reg 2. As to the meaning of 'charging authority' PARA 24 note 2. As to the meaning of 'billing authority' see PARA 53.
17 Non-Domestic Rating (Material Day for List Alterations) Regulations 1992, SI 1992/556, reg 3(4)(d).
18 Ie subject to the Non-Domestic Rating (Material Day for List Alterations) Regulations 1992, SI 1992/556, reg 3(5): see the text to notes 20–24.
19 Non-Domestic Rating (Material Day for List Alterations) Regulations 1992, SI 1992/556, reg 3(4). For an alteration which has effect under the Non-Domestic Rating (Alteration of Lists and Appeals) Regulations 1993, SI 1993/291 (revoked), the material day is 31 March 2000: Non-Domestic Rating (Material Day for List Alterations) Regulations 1992, SI 1992/556, reg 3(4A) (added in relation to England only by SI 2005/658). As to the meaning of 'England' see PARA 2 note 16.
20 Ie under the Local Government Finance Act 1988 Sch 4A para 1: see PARA 138.
21 Non-Domestic Rating (Material Day for List Alterations) Regulations 1992, SI 1992/556, reg 3(5).
22 Non-Domestic Rating (Material Day for List Alterations) Regulations 1992, SI 1992/556, reg 3(5)(a).
23 Ie in accordance with the Local Government Finance Act 1988 Sch 4A para 3 or Sch 4A para 4: see PARA 141.
24 Non-Domestic Rating (Material Day for List Alterations) Regulations 1992, SI 1992/556, reg 3(5)(b).
25 Non-Domestic Rating (Material Day for List Alterations) Regulations 1992, SI 1992/556, reg 3(6).
26 As to the meaning of 'valuation officer' see PARA 54 note 3.

27 Non-Domestic Rating (Material Day for List Alterations) Regulations 1992, SI 1992/556, reg 3(7)(a) (reg 3(7) substituted in relation to England by SI 2005/658, and amended by SI 2017/155; and substituted in relation to Wales by SI 2005/758).

28 Ie a confirmation under the Non-Domestic Rating (Alteration of Lists and Appeals) (England) Regulations 2009, SI 2009/2268, reg 4C (see PARA 201): Non-Domestic Rating (Material Day for List Alterations) Regulations 1992, SI 1992/556, reg 3(7)(b)(i) (as substituted and amended: see note 27). In relation to Wales, the material day is the day on which the proposal was served on the valuation officer: Non-Domestic Rating (Material Day for List Alterations) Regulations 1992, SI 1992/556, reg 3(7)(b)(i) (as substituted in relation to Wales: see note 27).

29 Non-Domestic Rating (Material Day for List Alterations) Regulations 1992, SI 1992/556, reg 3(7)(b)(ii)(aa) (as substituted: see note 27).

30 Non-Domestic Rating (Material Day for List Alterations) Regulations 1992, SI 1992/556, reg 3(7)(b)(ii)(bb) (as substituted: see note 27).

C. DETERMINING RATEABLE VALUES FOR SPECIFIED HEREDITAMENTS

(A) Regulation-making Powers

166. Power to prescribe assumptions or principles in determining the rateable value.

The appropriate national authority[1] may make regulations providing that, in applying the provisions of the Local Government Finance Act 1988 in respect of the determination of the rateable value of non-domestic hereditaments[2] in relation to a hereditament of a prescribed[3] class, prescribed assumptions (as to the hereditament or otherwise) are to be made[4]. A class may be prescribed by reference to such factors as the appropriate national authority sees fit[5], and without prejudice to this, a class may be prescribed by reference to one or more of the following factors, namely:

(1) the physical characteristics of hereditaments[6];

(2) the fact that hereditaments are unoccupied or are occupied for prescribed purposes or by persons[7] of prescribed descriptions[8].

The appropriate national authority may also make regulations providing that in arriving at an amount for the rateable value of a non-domestic hereditament[9] prescribed principles are to be applied[10]; and the regulations may include provision for the preservation of such principles, privileges, and provisions for the making of valuations on exceptional principles, as apply or applied for the purposes of the General Rate Act 1967 (now repealed)[11].

1 Ie the Secretary of State or, in relation to Wales, the Welsh Ministers. The functions of the Secretary of State under the Local Government Finance Act 1988 Sch 6, so far as exercisable in relation to Wales, were transferred to the National Assembly for Wales (see the National Assembly for Wales (Transfer of Functions) Order 1999, SI 1999/672, art 2, Sch 1) and are now vested in the Welsh Ministers (see the Government of Wales Act 2006 s 162(1), Sch 11 para 30). As to the Secretary of State and the Welsh Ministers see PARA 4 note 18. As to the meaning of 'Wales' see PARA 2 note 16. As to the separate administration of the non-domestic rating provisions (Local Government Finance Act 1988 Pt III (ss 41–67)) in England and Wales see PARA 52.

2 Ie the Local Government Finance Act 1988 Sch 6 para 2(1)–(7): see PARA 157. The Local Government Finance Act 1988 Sch 6 has effect to determine the rateable value of non-domestic hereditaments for the purposes of Pt III (ss 41–67): s 56(1), Sch 6 para 1 (Sch 6 para 1 amended by the Local Government and Housing Act 1989 ss 139, 194, Sch 5 paras 38, 79(3), Sch 12 Pt II). As to the meaning of 'non-domestic hereditament' see PARA 106.

3 'Prescribed' means prescribed by the regulations: see the Local Government Finance Act 1988 s 146(6).

4 Local Government Finance Act 1988 Sch 6 para 2(8) (amended by the Local Government and Housing Act 1989 Sch 5 paras 38, 79(3)). As to the regulations made see the Non-Domestic Rating (Miscellaneous Provisions) Regulations 1989, SI 1989/1060 (see PARA 174 et seq); the Non-Domestic Rating (Miscellaneous Provisions) (No 2) Regulations 1989, SI 1989/2303 (see PARAS 171, 178, 186, 199); the Valuation for Rating (Former Enterprise Zones) Regulations

1995, SI 1995/213 (see PARA 177); the Valuation for Rating (Plant and Machinery) (England) Regulations 2000, SI 2000/540 (see PARA 173); and the Valuation for Rating (Plant and Machinery) (Wales) Regulations 2000, SI 2000/1097 (see PARA 173).

5 Local Government Finance Act 1988 Sch 6 para 2(11) (Sch 6 para 2(11), (12) added by the Local Government and Housing Act 1989 Sch 5 paras 38, 79(3)).

6 Local Government Finance Act 1988 Sch 6 para 2(12)(a) (as added: see note 5).

7 As to the meaning of 'person' see PARA 11 note 13.

8 Local Government Finance Act 1988 Sch 6 para 2(12)(b) (as added: see note 5).

9 Ie under the Local Government Finance Act 1988 Sch 6 para 2(1), 2(1A) or 2(1B): see PARA 157.

10 Local Government Finance Act 1988 Sch 6 para 2(9) (amended by the Local Government and Housing Act 1989 Sch 5 paras 38, 79(3)). As to the regulations made see the Non-Domestic Rating (Miscellaneous Provisions) Regulations 1989, SI 1989/1060 (see PARA 174); and the Non-Domestic Rating (Miscellaneous Provisions) (No 2) Regulations 1989, SI 1989/2303 (see PARAS 171, 178, 186, 199).

11 Local Government Finance Act 1988 Sch 6 para 2(9) (as amended: see note 10).

167. Power to make special provision as to rateable value for prescribed classes of hereditament.

Until a day to be appointed, the following provisions have effect[1].

The appropriate national authority[2] may by order provide that, in the case of a non-domestic hereditament[3] of such class as may be prescribed[4], the usual statutory provisions governing the determination of rateable value[5] do not apply, and that its rateable value is to be determined in accordance with prescribed rules instead ('valuation by formula')[6]. For these purposes, a class may be prescribed by reference to such factors as the appropriate national authority sees fit[7] and, without prejudice to this, a class may be prescribed by reference to one or more of the following factors[8]:

(1) the physical characteristics of hereditaments[9];

(2) the fact that hereditaments are unoccupied or are occupied for prescribed purposes or by persons[10] of prescribed descriptions[11].

In the case of non-domestic hereditaments to be shown in a central non-domestic rating list[12], the appropriate national authority may also by order provide that the usual statutory provisions[13] do not apply, and that their rateable value is to be specified in the order or determined in accordance with prescribed rules instead[14]. There are no restrictions on the methods which the appropriate national authority might employ in arriving at a figure so specified[15].

1 The Local Government Finance Act 1988 Sch 6 para 3 is repealed by the Local Government Act 2003 ss 69, 127(2), Sch 8 Pt 1 as from a day to be appointed under s 128(6). At the date at which this volume states the law no such day had been appointed.

2 Ie the Secretary of State or, in relation to Wales, the Welsh Ministers. The functions of the Secretary of State under the Local Government Finance Act 1988 Sch 6, so far as exercisable in relation to Wales, were transferred to the National Assembly for Wales (see the National Assembly for Wales (Transfer of Functions) Order 1999, SI 1999/672, art 2, Sch 1) and are now vested in the Welsh Ministers (see the Government of Wales Act 2006 s 162(1), Sch 11 para 30). As to the Secretary of State and the Welsh Ministers see PARA 4 note 18. As to the meaning of 'Wales' see PARA 2 note 16. As to the separate administration of the non-domestic rating provisions (Local Government Finance Act 1988 Pt III (ss 41–67)) in England and Wales see PARA 52.

3 As to the meaning of 'non-domestic hereditament' see PARA 106.

4 'Prescribed' means prescribed by the order: see the Local Government Finance Act 1988 s 146(6).

5 Ie the Local Government Finance Act 1988 Sch 6 para 2 (see PARAS 157–166), Sch 6 paras 2A–2C (see PARA 168). The Local Government Finance Act 1988 Sch 6 has effect to determine the rateable value of non-domestic hereditaments for the purposes of Pt III (ss 41–67): s 56(1), Sch 6 para 1 (Sch 6 para 1 amended by the Local Government and Housing Act 1989 ss 139, 194, Sch 5 paras 38, 79(3), Sch 12 Pt II).

6 Local Government Finance Act 1988 Sch 6 para 3(1) (Sch 6 para 3(1), (2) amended by the Local Government and Housing Act 1989 s 139, Sch 5 paras 38(12), (13), 79(3); and the Local Government and Rating Act 1997 s 2(6)). As to the orders made under the Local Government Finance Act 1988 Sch 6 para 3(1) see the Electricity Supply Industry (Rateable Values) (England) Order 2000, SI 2000/947; the Docks and Harbours (Rateable Values) (Wales) Order 2000, SI 2000/948; the Docks and Harbours (Rateable Values) (England) Order 2000, SI 2000/951; the Energy from Waste Plants (Rateable Values) (England) Order 2000, SI 2000/952; and the Electricity Supply Industry (Rateable Values) (Wales) Order 2000, SI 2000/1163; and see PARA 170.

Where the Secretary of State prescribed the use of a formula for determining the rateable value of a non-domestic hereditament, it was to be assumed that he intended to provide a simple and convenient method of arriving at a fair valuation, in that context, of the entire hereditament: see *Coventry and Solihull Waste Disposal Co Ltd v Russell (Valuation Officer)* [2000] 1 All ER 97, [1999] 1 WLR 2093, [2000] RA 1, HL (considering the Electricity Generators (Rateable Values) Order 1989, SI 1989/2474 (now revoked with savings)).

7 Local Government Finance Act 1988 Sch 6 para 3(3) (Sch 6 para 3(3), (4) added by the Local Government and Housing Act 1989 Sch 5 paras 38(14), 79(3)).

8 Local Government Finance Act 1988 Sch 6 para 3(4) (as added: see note 7).

9 Local Government Finance Act 1988 Sch 6 para 3(4)(a) (as added: see note 7).

10 As to the meaning of 'person' see PARA 11 note 13.

11 Local Government Finance Act 1988 Sch 6 para 3(4)(b) (as added: see note 7).

12 Ie by virtue of regulations under the Local Government Finance Act 1988 s 53(2) (see PARA 197): see the Local Government Finance Act 1988 Sch 6 para 3(2) (as amended: see note 6). Some large properties which are national in character appear on a central rating list: see PARA 196 et seq.

13 Ie the Local Government Finance Act 1988 Sch 6 para 2 (see PARAS 157–166), Sch 6 paras 2A–2C (see PARA 168).

14 Local Government Finance Act 1988 Sch 6 para 3(2) (as amended: see note 6). As to the orders made under Sch 6 para 3(2) see the Non-Domestic Rating (Appropriate Fraction and Rateable Values) Order 1991, SI 1991/2924 (amended by SI 1994/3281 and SI 1994/3285); the British Waterways Board and Telecommunications Industry (Rateable Values) Revocation Order 1994, SI 1994/3281; the Water Undertakers (Rateable Values) (Wales) Order 2000, SI 2000/299 (amended by SI 2003/944); the BG plc (Rateable Value) (Wales) Order 2000, SI 2000/352 (amended by SI 2003/944); the Railtrack plc (Rateable Value) (Wales) Order 2000, SI 2000/555 (amended by SI 2003/944); the Gas Industry (Rateable Values) (England) Order 2000, SI 2000/946; the Electricity Supply Industry (Rateable Values) (England) Order 2000, SI 2000/947; the Railways (Rateable Values) (England) Order 2000, SI 2000/949; the Water Undertakers (Rateable Values) (England) Order 2000, SI 2000/950; and the Electricity Supply Industry (Rateable Values) (Wales) Order 2000, SI 2000/1163; and see PARA 169.

15 See *R (on the application of Edison First Power Ltd) v Central Valuation Officer* [2003] UKHL 20, [2003] 4 All ER 209, [2003] 2 EGLR 133 (Lord Bingham of Cornhill and Lord Steyn dissenting) (the purpose of the Local Government Finance Act 1988 Sch 6 para 3(2) is to allow the system which Parliament had thought appropriate for the electricity generating industry (inter alia) for the previous 30 years to be retained, with whatever formulae the government thought appropriate and as long as it thought it expedient to do so). The ratepayer in this case was the purchaser of a hereditament which was chargeable to one set of rates, being its liability under the local listing (see the text to notes 2–11) arising from its own rateable occupation, but it had also entered into a voluntary assumption of liability to reimburse the vendor for central rates payable under the statutory scheme in respect of the residual period in the chargeable year (ie the year of purchase): see *R (on the application of Edison First Power Ltd) v Central Valuation Officer* [2003] UKHL 20, [2003] 4 All ER 209, [2003] 2 EGLR 133 (sum paid to vendor was part of the price that it had agreed to pay for the hereditament and was not a double payment of rates to the Secretary of State).

168. Power to make special provision as to rateable value for particular hereditaments.

The rateable value of any hereditament[1], the whole or any part of which consists in buildings which are both used for the breeding and rearing of horses or ponies (or for either of those purposes)[2], and are occupied together with any agricultural land[3] or agricultural building[4], is taken to be the amount determined under the usual statutory provisions governing the determination of rateable value[5] less whichever is the smaller of the following two amounts[6], namely:

(1) such amount as the appropriate national authority[7] may by order specify for these purposes[8]; and

(2) the amount which would be determined[9] in respect of so much of the hereditament as consists of buildings so used and occupied[10].

In circumstances where:

(a) the rateable value of a hereditament consisting of an area of a caravan site[11] is determined with a view to making an alteration to a list[12] which has been compiled (whether or not it is still in force)[13];

(b) the area is treated[14] as one hereditament[15];

(c) immediately before the day the alteration is entered in the list (or, if the alteration is made in pursuance of a proposal, the day the proposal is made), the list includes a hereditament consisting of an area of the caravan site treated[16] as one hereditament[17]; and

(d) the area mentioned in head (b) and the area mentioned in head (c) are wholly or partly the same[18],

then, in relation to a caravan pitch which is included both in the area mentioned in head (b) above and in the area mentioned in head (c) above, the nature of the caravan on the pitch and the physical state of that caravan[19] must be taken to be as they were assumed to be for the purposes of determining the rateable value of the hereditament mentioned in head (c) above when that rateable value was last determined[20]. Accordingly, the usual factors to be considered under statute[21] do not apply for these purposes as respects the nature of the caravan on the pitch and the physical state of that caravan[22].

Where a hereditament consists wholly or in part of land on which a right of sporting[23] is exercisable[24], and the right is not severed from the occupation of the land[25], then, for the purposes of determining the rateable value of the hereditament[26], the rent at which the hereditament might reasonably be expected to let is to be estimated as if the right of sporting did not exist[27].

1 The Local Government Finance Act 1988 Sch 6 has effect to determine the rateable value of non-domestic hereditaments for the purposes of Pt III (ss 41–67): s 56(1), Sch 6 para 1 (Sch 6 para 1 amended by the Local Government and Housing Act 1989 ss 139, 194, Sch 5 paras 38, 79(3), Sch 12 Pt II). As to the meaning of 'non-domestic hereditament' see PARA 106.

2 See the Local Government Finance Act 1988 Sch 6 para 2A(1)(a) (Sch 6 paras 2A, 2B added by the Local Government and Housing Act 1989 s 139, Sch 5 paras 38(11), 79(3)).

3 'Agricultural land' means any land of more than two hectares which is agricultural land within the meaning of the Local Government Finance Act 1988 Sch 5 para 2 (see PARA 117) and is not land used exclusively for the pasturing of horses or ponies: Sch 6 para 2A(3) (as added: see note 2).

4 See the Local Government Finance Act 1988 Sch 6 para 2A(1)(b) (as added: see note 2). As to the meaning of 'agricultural building' see Sch 5 paras 3–7 (see PARA 118 et seq) (definition applied by Sch 6 para 2A(3) (as so added)).

5 Ie under the Local Government Finance Act 1988 Sch 6 para 2: see PARAS 157–166.

6 See the Local Government Finance Act 1988 Sch 6 para 2A(2) (as added: see note 2).

7 Ie the Secretary of State or, in relation to Wales, the Welsh Ministers. The functions of the Secretary of State under the Local Government Finance Act 1988 Sch 6, so far as exercisable in relation to Wales, were transferred to the National Assembly for Wales (see the National Assembly for Wales (Transfer of Functions) Order 1999, SI 1999/672, art 2, Sch 1) and are now vested in the Welsh Ministers (see the Government of Wales Act 2006 s 162(1), Sch 11 para 30). As to the Secretary of State and the Welsh Ministers see PARA 4 note 18. As to the meaning of 'Wales' see PARA 2 note 16. As to the separate administration of the non-domestic rating provisions (Local Government Finance Act 1988 Pt III (ss 41–67)) in England and Wales see PARA 52.

8 Local Government Finance Act 1988 Sch 6 para 2A(2)(a) (as added: see note 2). In relation to Wales, £2,500 is specified for the purposes of Sch 6 para 2A (see the Non-Domestic Rating (Stud Farms) Order 1989, SI 1989/2331, art 2 (revoked in relation to England by SI 2001/2586)). In

relation to England, in respect of the rateable value of any hereditament shown in a non-domestic rating list compiled on or after 1 April 2010, £4,200 is the amount so specified; and in respect of the rateable value of any hereditament shown in a non-domestic rating list compiled on or after 1 April 2017, £4,700 is the amount so specified (see the Non-Domestic Rating (Stud Farms) (England) Order 2009, SI 2009/3177, art 2 (substituted by SI 2017/102)). As to the meaning of 'England' see PARA 2 note 16. As to the compilation of local non-domestic rating lists see PARA 191. As to the compilation of central non-domestic rating lists see PARA 196.

9 Ie under the Local Government Finance Act 1988 Sch 6 para 2: see PARAS 157–166.

10 Local Government Finance Act 1988 Sch 6 para 2A(2)(b) (as added: see note 2).

11 'Caravan site' means any land in respect of which a site licence is required under the Caravan Sites and Control of Development Act 1960 Pt I (ss 1–32) (see PLANNING vol 83 (2018) PARA 1137) or the Mobile Homes (Wales) Act 2013 Pt 2 (ss 4–39), or would be so required if the Caravan Sites and Control of Development Act 1960 Sch 1 paras 4, 11 (exemption of certain land: see PLANNING vol 83 (2018) PARA 1140) or the Mobile Homes (Wales) Act 2013 Sch 1 paras 4, 11 were omitted: Local Government Finance Act 1988 Sch 6 para 2B(5) (as added (see note 2); amended by the Mobile Homes (Wales) Act 2013 s 58(1), Sch 4 para 5). 'Caravan' has the same meaning as it has for the purposes of the Caravan Sites and Control of Development Act 1960 Pt I (see PLANNING vol 83 (2018) PARA 1137): Local Government Finance Act 1988 Sch 6 para 2B(5) (as so added). As to the rating of caravan sites generally see PARAS 108–109.

12 Ie a local list (see PARA 191) or a central non-domestic rating lists (see PARA 196): see the Local Government Finance Act 1988 s 67(1), (13). As to the alteration of rating lists see PARA 199 et seq.

13 Local Government Finance Act 1988 Sch 6 para 2B(1)(a) (as added: see note 2).

14 Ie by virtue of regulations under the Local Government Finance Act 1988 s 64(3)(b): see PARA 106.

15 Local Government Finance Act 1988 Sch 6 para 2B(1)(b) (as added: see note 2).

16 Ie by virtue of regulations under the Local Government Finance Act 1988 s 64(3)(b): see PARA 106.

17 Local Government Finance Act 1988 Sch 6 para 2B(1)(c) (as added: see note 2).

18 Local Government Finance Act 1988 Sch 6 para 2B(1)(d) (as added: see note 2).

19 See the Local Government Finance Act 1988 Sch 6 para 2B(2), (4) (as added: see note 2).

20 See the Local Government Finance Act 1988 Sch 6 para 2B(2), (3) (as added: see note 2).

21 Ie under the Local Government Finance Act 1988 Sch 6 para 2(7), by virtue of Sch 6 para 2(6): see PARA 164.

22 See the Local Government Finance Act 1988 Sch 6 para 2B(2) (as added: see note 2).

23 'Right of sporting' means a right of fowling, shooting, taking or killing game or rabbits, or fishing: Local Government Finance Act 1988 Sch 6 para 2C(3) (Sch 6 para 2C added by the Local Government and Rating Act 1997 s 2(5)).

24 Local Government Finance Act 1988 Sch 6 para 2C(1)(a) (as added: see note 23).

25 Local Government Finance Act 1988 Sch 6 para 2C(1)(b) (as added: see note 23). As to the occupier and occupation of land see PARA 85 et seq.

26 Ie under the Local Government Finance Act 1988 Sch 6 para 2: see PARAS 157–166.

27 Local Government Finance Act 1988 Sch 6 para 2C(2) (as added: see note 23).

(B) Regulations and Orders Made in Relation to Public Utility Undertakings

169. Hereditaments in the central lists associated with public utility undertakings.

In exercise of the power to make provision in relation to non-domestic hereditaments[1] to be shown in a central non-domestic rating list[2], orders have been made so that the usual statutory provisions used to determine rateable value[3] do not apply, and their rateable value is either as specified in the orders so made or determined in accordance with rules by the order[4].

1 As to the meaning of 'non-domestic hereditament' see PARA 106.

2 Ie shown by virtue of regulations under the Local Government Finance Act 1988 s 53(2) (see PARA 197): see the Local Government Finance Act 1988 Sch 6 para 3(2); and PARA 167. As to the central non-domestic rating lists see PARA 196 et seq.

Originally, hereditaments occupied by public utility undertakings were valued on the profits basis (as to which see PARA 184). However, over time they came to be valued by the application of a statutory formula: see the General Rate Act 1967 ss 31–34, Schs 4–7 (repealed); and as to the historical development of rating law and the continuing relevance of the old case law to the current statutory regime see PARA 50. With the coming into force of the Local Government Finance Act 1988, hereditaments occupied by public utility undertakings and a number of other properties which, in the opinion of the Secretary of State or, in relation to Wales, the Welsh Ministers, were more appropriately rated en bloc, were entered in the central non-domestic rating lists and, with a view to securing the central rating en bloc of certain hereditaments, the list identifies persons designated for central list purposes and identifies the hereditament or class of hereditaments in respect of which they are to be rated via the central list: see the Local Government Finance Act 1988 s 53; and PARA 197.

3 Ie the Local Government Finance Act 1988 Sch 6 para 2 (see PARAS 157–166), Sch 6 paras 2A–2C (see PARA 168).

4 See the Local Government Finance Act 1988 Sch 6 para 3(2); and PARA 167. As to the orders made see the Non-Domestic Rating (Appropriate Fraction and Rateable Values) Order 1991, SI 1991/2924 (amended by SI 1994/3281; SI 1994/3285); the British Waterways Board and Telecommunications Industry (Rateable Values) Revocation Order 1994, SI 1994/3281; the Water Undertakers (Rateable Values) (Wales) Order 2000, SI 2000/299 (amended by SI 2003/944); the BG plc (Rateable Value) (Wales) Order 2000, SI 2000/352 (amended by SI 2003/944); the Railtrack plc (Rateable Value) (Wales) Order 2000, SI 2000/555 (amended by SI 2003/944); the Gas Industry (Rateable Values) (England) Order 2000, SI 2000/946; the Electricity Supply Industry (Rateable Values) (England) Order 2000, SI 2000/947; the Railways (Rateable Values) (England) Order 2000, SI 2000/949; the Water Undertakers (Rateable Values) (England) Order 2000, SI 2000/950; and the Electricity Supply Industry (Rateable Values) (Wales) Order 2000, SI 2000/1163.

170. Hereditaments in local rating lists associated with prescribed classes.

In exercise of the power to make provision in relation to non-domestic hereditaments[1] to be shown in a local non-domestic rating list[2], orders have been made to provide that, in the case of a non-domestic hereditament of such class as has been prescribed by the order, the usual statutory provisions governing the determination of rateable value[3] do not apply, and that its rateable value is to be determined in accordance with prescribed rules instead ('valuation by formula')[4].

1 As to the meaning of 'non-domestic hereditament' see PARA 106.

2 As to local non-domestic rating lists see PARA 191 et seq.

3 Ie the Local Government Finance Act 1988 Sch 6 para 2 (see PARAS 157–166), Sch 6 paras 2A–2C (see PARA 168).

4 See the Local Government Finance Act 1988 Sch 6 para 3(1); and PARA 167. As to the orders made see the Electricity Supply Industry (Rateable Values) (England) Order 2000, SI 2000/947; the Docks and Harbours (Rateable Values) (Wales) Order 2000, SI 2000/948; the Docks and Harbours (Rateable Values) (England) Order 2000, SI 2000/951; the Energy from Waste Plants (Rateable Values) (England) Order 2000, SI 2000/952; and the Electricity Supply Industry (Rateable Values) (Wales) Order 2000, SI 2000/1163.

171. Valuation of public utilities.

Notwithstanding any rule of law requiring the rateable value of a hereditament[1] occupied by a public utility undertaking[2] to be estimated solely by reference to the accounts, receipts or profits of the undertaking[3], in arriving at an amount for the rateable value[4] in relation to such a hereditament, any evidence relevant to estimating the amount of rent in accordance with that provision is to be taken into account[5].

1 As to the meaning of 'hereditament' see PARA 106.

2 As to the occupier and occupation of land see PARA 85 et seq.

3 As to which see PARA 184.

4 Ie under the Local Government Finance Act 1988 Sch 6 para 2(1), 2(1A) or 2(1B): see PARA 157 et seq.

5 Non-Domestic Rating (Miscellaneous Provisions) (No 2) Regulations 1989, SI 1989/2303, reg 3. See also the Local Government Finance Act 1988 Sch 6 para 2(9); and PARA 166.

(C) Rateable Values of Plant and Machinery

172. Plant and machinery deemed to be part of the hereditament.

For the purpose of valuing hereditaments[1], certain classes of plant[2] and machinery in or on the hereditament are to be deemed to be a part of the hereditament to be valued and no account is to be taken of the value[3] of any other plant or machinery in or on the hereditament. The rental value of such a hereditament is to be ascertained by estimating the rent which the hypothetical tenant would pay for the land, buildings and plant and machinery comprising the hereditament, on the assumption that the hypothetical landlord provides at his own expense the plant and machinery as well as the land and buildings, and that the hypothetical tenant pays a rent for all that the hypothetical landlord provides[4].

1 As to the determination of rateable value see PARA 157 et seq. As to the hereditament see PARA 106.

2 'Plant' does not include things which are merely part of the setting in which a business is carried on: *J Lyons & Co Ltd v A-G* [1944] Ch 281, [1944] 1 All ER 477. In *Yarmouth v France* (1887) 19 QBD 647, an employer's liability case, it was said that 'plant' includes all the apparatus and instruments employed in a business. In determining whether an item is plant for rating purposes, it is not permissible to have regard to its function as part of a larger whole: *Manchester Marine Ltd v Duckworth (Valuation Officer)* [1973] 3 All ER 838, [1973] 1 WLR 1431, CA; *Union Cold Storage Co Ltd v Phillips (Valuation Officer)* [1975] RA 306, CA (on appeal [1976] RA 173, HL).

'Plant' has been held to include small safes at a safe deposit (*Chancery Lane Safe Deposit and Offices Co Ltd v Steedens (Valuation Officer)* [1961] RVR 261, Lands Tribunal); cloakroom fittings, chalk boards and display panels at a school (*Dawkins (Valuation Officer) v Royal Leamington Spa Borough Council and Warwickshire County Council* [1961] RVR 291, Lands Tribunal); pipelines (*Shell-Mex and BP Ltd v Childs (Valuation Officer)* [1961] RVR 371, Lands Tribunal (on appeal on a different point [1962] RVR 267, CA); *Bright (Valuation Officer) v British Oil Storage Co Ltd* [1962] RVR 99, Lands Tribunal; *Lever Bros, Port Sunlight Ltd v Bright (Valuation Officer) and Bebington Borough Council* [1962] RVR 70, Lands Tribunal); removable partitioning in an office (*Jarrold (Inspector of Taxes) v John Good & Sons Ltd* [1963] 1 All ER 141, [1963] 1 WLR 214, CA; *British Bakeries Ltd v Gudgion (Valuation Officer) and Croydon London Borough Council* [1969] RA 465, Lands Tribunal); and an automatic vending machine (*NH Platts & Sons Ltd v Hanstock (Valuation Officer)* [1963] RVR 344, Lands Tribunal). 'Plant' has also been said to include heating equipment, lifts, sprinklers and incinerators (*Macsaga Investment Co Ltd v Lupton (Inspector of Taxes)* [1967] Ch 167 at 175, [1966] 3 All ER 375 at 379 per Pennycuick J); and a broadcasting mast used to support aerials (*Independent Broadcasting Authority v Strathclyde Assessor* [1987] RA 268, Lands Tribunal).

'Plant' has been held not to include electric lights (*J Lyons & Co Ltd v A-G*); builders' huts (*Woodward (Valuation Officer) v Brading and Blundell Ltd* (1951) 44 R & IT 758, 774 at 793, Lands Tribunal; *LCC v Wilkins (Valuation Officer)* (1954) 47 R & IT 7, Lands Tribunal (on appeal on a different point [1957] AC 362, [1956] 3 All ER 38, HL)); stadium floodlighting (*Hardiman (Valuation Officer) v Crystal Palace Football and Athletic Club Ltd* (1955) 48 R & IT 91, Lands Tribunal); doors of a safe deposit (*Chancery Lane Safe Deposit and Offices Co Ltd v Steedens (Valuation Officer)* above); the shelving, kitchen equipment and serving counters at a school (*Dawkins (Valuation Officer) v Royal Leamington Spa Borough Council and Warwickshire County Council* above); a wallpaper merchant's pattern books (*Rose & Co (Wallpaper and Paints) Ltd v Campbell (Inspector of Taxes)* [1968] 1 All ER 405, [1968] 1 WLR 346); and a prefabricated laboratory and gymnasium at a school (*St John's School v Ward (Inspector of Taxes)* [1974] RA 49, [1974] STC 69; on appeal [1975] RA 481, [1975] STC 7n, CA).

All of the cases cited in this paragraph were decided prior to the coming into force of the Local Government Finance Act 1988 but continue to be of relevance: see PARA 50.

3 The value to be ignored includes the cost of installing the plant or machinery: *English Clays Lovering Pochin & Co Ltd v Bowles (Valuation Officer)* [1974] RA 129, Lands Tribunal. As to classes of plant and machinery deemed to be part of the hereditament by virtue of statutory regulations see PARA 173.

4 *Kirby v Hunslet Assessment Committee* [1906] AC 43, HL; *S Smith & Sons (Motor Accessories) Ltd v Willesden Union Assessment Committee* (1920) 89 LJKB 137. As to the valuation of plant and machinery see *Cardiff Rating Authority and Cardiff Assessment Committee v Guest Keen Baldwin's Iron and Steel Co Ltd* [1949] 1 KB 385, [1949] 1 All ER 27, CA; *Birchenwood Gas and*

Coke Co Ltd v Hampshire (Valuation Officer) (1959) 4 RRC 303, Lands Tribunal; *Thomas (Valuation Officer) v Manor Vinegar Brewery Co Ltd* (1960) 6 RRC 353, Lands Tribunal; *Shell-Mex and BP Ltd v James (Valuation Officer)* [1961] RVR 106, Lands Tribunal; *Ind Coope Ltd v Burton-upon-Trent County Borough Council and Thomas (Valuation Officer)* [1961] RVR 341, Lands Tribunal; *Vickers-Armstrong (Shipbuilders) Ltd v Thornton (Valuation Officer)* (1965) 11 RRC 66, Lands Tribunal; *Staffordshire Potteries (Holdings) Ltd v Garner (Valuation Officer)* [1967] RA 31, Lands Tribunal.

173. Prescribed classes of plant and machinery deemed to be part of the hereditament.

The appropriate national authority[1] may make regulations providing that, in applying the main provisions of the Local Government Finance Act 1988 which determine the rateable value of non-domestic hereditaments[2] in relation to a hereditament of a prescribed[3] class, prescribed assumptions (as to the hereditament or otherwise) are to be made[4].

Accordingly, for the purpose of the rating lists that came into force on 1 April 1990, regulations prescribed six classes of plant and machinery[5], which, if present on the hereditament, were deemed to be part of it[6].

For the purpose of determining the rateable value of a hereditament for any day on or after 1 April 2000, in applying the statutory provisions[7] in relation to a hereditament in or on which there is plant or machinery which belongs to any of the prescribed classes[8], the prescribed assumptions are that any such plant or machinery is part of the hereditament, and that the value of any other plant and machinery has no effect on the rent to be estimated as required by the relevant statutory provision[9]. In relation to any other hereditament, the prescribed assumption is that the value of any plant or machinery has no effect on the rent to be so estimated[10].

For the purpose of determining the rateable value of a hereditament for any day on or after 1 October 2008, in relation to England, or 1 April 2010, in relation to Wales, in applying the statutory provisions[11] in relation to a hereditament in or on which there is plant or machinery which belongs to any of the prescribed classes, the prescribed assumptions are that any such plant or machinery is part of the hereditament except to the extent that it has microgeneration capacity[12], and the value of any other plant and machinery has no effect on the rent to be estimated as required by relevant statutory provision[13]; and in relation to any other hereditament, the prescribed assumption is that the value of any plant or machinery has no effect on the rent to be so estimated[14].

The four prescribed classes of plant and machinery are as follows:

(1) plant and machinery, listed in a table within the class, which is used or intended to be used mainly or exclusively in connection with the generation[15], storage, primary transformation or main transmission of power[16] in or on the hereditament[17] (together with any of the accessories specified for this purpose in the List of Accessories)[18];

(2) plant and machinery, listed in a table within the class, which is used or intended to be used mainly or exclusively in connection with services[19] to the land or buildings of which the hereditament consists, other than any such plant or machinery which is in or on the hereditament and is used or intended to be used in connection with services mainly or exclusively as part of manufacturing operations or trade processes[20] (together with any of the accessories specified for this purpose in the List of Accessories)[21];

(3) items including railway and tramway lines, lifts and elevators, cables, wires and conductors, posts, poles, towers and pylons (including cables, etc used for communications systems) and pipelines[22];

(4) certain miscellaneous items of plant and machinery listed in tables within the class[23] with four specific exceptions[24].

1 Ie the Secretary of State or, in relation to Wales, the Welsh Ministers. As to the Secretary of State and the Welsh Ministers see PARA 4 note 18. As to the meaning of 'Wales' see PARA 2 note 16. As to the separate administration of the non-domestic rating provisions (Local Government Finance Act 1988 Pt III (ss 41–67)) in England and Wales see PARA 52.

2 Ie the Local Government Finance Act 1988 Sch 6 para 2(1)–(7): see PARA 157 et seq. As to the meaning of 'non-domestic hereditament' see PARA 106.

3 'Prescribed' means prescribed by the regulations: see the Local Government Finance Act 1988 s 146(6).

4 See the Local Government Finance Act 1988 Sch 6 para 2(8); and PARA 166.

5 As to the case law relating to the definition of 'plant' and 'machinery' see PARA 172.

6 See the Valuation for Rating (Plant and Machinery) Regulations 1989, SI 1989/441 (revoked with savings), which did not apply to valuations on the profits basis. These regulations were revoked and replaced by the Valuation for Rating (Plant and Machinery) Regulations 1994, SI 1994/2680, which did apply to valuations on the profits basis. These regulations continue to have effect only for the purpose of determining the rateable value of a hereditament for any day before 1 April 2000 and have been re-enacted, without major changes, in relation to England, by the Valuation for Rating (Plant and Machinery) (England) Regulations 2000, SI 2000/540, and, in relation to Wales, by the Valuation for Rating (Plant and Machinery) (Wales) Regulations 2000, SI 2000/1097: see the text to notes 7–24. As to the profits basis see PARA 184.

7 Ie in applying the provisions of the Local Government Finance Act 1988 Sch 6 para 2(1)–(7) (see PARA 157 et seq): see the Valuation for Rating (Plant and Machinery) (England) Regulations 2000, SI 2000/540, reg 2; and the Valuation for Rating (Plant and Machinery) (Wales) Regulations 2000, SI 2000/1097, reg 2.

8 Ie the classes set out, in relation to England, in the Valuation for Rating (Plant and Machinery) (England) Regulations 2000, SI 2000/540, Schedule (amended by SI 2001/846) and, in relation to Wales, in the Valuation for Rating (Plant and Machinery) (Wales) Regulations 2000, SI 2000/1097, Schedule: see the text to notes 15–24. As to the meaning of 'England' see PARA 2 note 16.

9 See the Valuation for Rating (Plant and Machinery) (England) Regulations 2000, SI 2000/540, reg 2(a); and the Valuation for Rating (Plant and Machinery) (Wales) Regulations 2000, SI 2000/1097, reg 2(a). The relevant statutory provision is the Local Government Finance Act 1988 Sch 6 para 2(1) (see PARA 157 et seq): see the Valuation for Rating (Plant and Machinery) (England) Regulations 2000, SI 2000/540, reg 2(a); and the Valuation for Rating (Plant and Machinery) (Wales) Regulations 2000, SI 2000/1097, reg 2(a). The valuation officer must, on being so required in writing by the occupier of any hereditament, supply to him particulars in writing showing what plant and machinery (or whether any particular plant or machinery) has been assumed in this way to form part of the hereditament: see the Valuation for Rating (Plant and Machinery) (England) Regulations 2000, SI 2000/540, reg 3; Valuation for Rating (Plant and Machinery) (Wales) Regulations 2000, SI 2000/1097, reg 3. As to valuation officers see PARA 54. As to the meaning of 'writing' see PARA 21 note 3. As to the meaning of 'occupier' see PARA 86.

10 See the Valuation for Rating (Plant and Machinery) (England) Regulations 2000, SI 2000/540, reg 2(b); and the Valuation for Rating (Plant and Machinery) (Wales) Regulations 2000, SI 2000/1097, reg 2(b).

11 Ie in applying the provisions of the Local Government Finance Act 1988 Sch 6 para 2(1)–(7) (see PARA 157 et seq): see the Valuation for Rating (Plant and Machinery) (England) Regulations 2000, SI 2000/540, reg 2A(1) (reg 2A added by SI 2008/2332); Valuation for Rating (Plant and Machinery) (Wales) Regulations 2000, SI 2000/1097, reg 2A(1) (reg 2A added by SI 2010/146).

12 See the Valuation for Rating (Plant and Machinery) (England) Regulations 2000, SI 2000/540, reg 2A(1)(a)(i); and the Valuation for Rating (Plant and Machinery) (Wales) Regulations 2000, SI 2000/1097, reg 2A(1)(a)(i) (both as added: see note 11). The exception in the Valuation for Rating (Plant and Machinery) (England) Regulations 2000, SI 2000/540, reg 2A(1)(a)(i) and the Valuation for Rating (Plant and Machinery) (Wales) Regulations 2000, SI 2000/1097, reg 2A(1)(a)(i) applies only:

(1) in relation to any item of plant or machinery that is installed on or after 1 October 2008 (in relation to England) or 1 April 2010 (in relation to Wales) and on the day of

installation has microgeneration capacity (Valuation for Rating (Plant and Machinery) (England) Regulations 2000, SI 2000/540, reg 2A(2)(a); Valuation for Rating (Plant and Machinery) (Wales) Regulations 2000, SI 2000/1097, reg 2A(2)(a) (both as so added)); and

(2) in the period starting on the day that the item of plant or machinery is installed (Valuation for Rating (Plant and Machinery) (England) Regulations 2000, SI 2000/540, reg 2A(2)(b)(i); Valuation for Rating (Plant and Machinery) (Wales) Regulations 2000, SI 2000/1097, reg 2A(2)(b)(i) (both as so added)), and ending on the earlier of:

(a) the first day after the day that the item of plant or machinery is installed on which rating lists fall to be compiled for the purposes of the Local Government Finance Act 1988 s 41(2) (see PARA 191) and s 52(2) (see PARA 196) (Valuation for Rating (Plant and Machinery) (England) Regulations 2000, SI 2000/540, reg 2A(2)(b)(ii)(aa); Valuation for Rating (Plant and Machinery) (Wales) Regulations 2000, SI 2000/1097, reg 2A(2)(b)(ii)(aa) (both as so added)); and

(b) the day the item of plant or machinery ceases to have microgeneration capacity (Valuation for Rating (Plant and Machinery) (England) Regulations 2000, SI 2000/540, reg 2A(2)(b)(ii)(bb); Valuation for Rating (Plant and Machinery) (Wales) Regulations 2000, SI 2000/1097, reg 2A(2)(b)(ii)(bb) (both as so added)).

'Microgeneration capacity' is defined by the Valuation for Rating (Plant and Machinery) (England) Regulations 2000, SI 2000/540, reg 2A(3); and the Valuation for Rating (Plant and Machinery) (Wales) Regulations 2000, SI 2000/1097, reg 2A(3) (both as so added) as the capacity of plant or machinery to be used for the generation of electricity or the production of heat:

(i) which, in generating electricity or (as the case may be) producing heat, relies wholly or mainly on a source of energy or a technology mentioned in the Climate Change and Sustainable Energy Act 2006 s 26(2) (interpretation); and

(ii) the capacity of which to generate electricity or (as the case may be) to produce heat does not exceed the capacity mentioned in s 26(3) of that Act (see ENERGY AND CLIMATE CHANGE vol 42 (2011) PARA 114).

13 See the Valuation for Rating (Plant and Machinery) (England) Regulations 2000, SI 2000/540, reg 2A(1)(a)(ii); and the Valuation for Rating (Plant and Machinery) (Wales) Regulations 2000, SI 2000/1097, reg 2A(1)(a)(ii) (both as added: see note 11). The relevant statutory provision is the Local Government Finance Act 1988 Sch 6 para 2(1) (see PARA 157 et seq): see the Valuation for Rating (Plant and Machinery) (England) Regulations 2000, SI 2000/540, reg 2A(1)(a)(ii); Valuation for Rating (Plant and Machinery) (Wales) Regulations 2000, SI 2000/1097, reg 2A(1)(a)(ii) (both as so added).

14 See the Valuation for Rating (Plant and Machinery) (England) Regulations 2000, SI 2000/540, reg 2A(1)(b); and the Valuation for Rating (Plant and Machinery) (Wales) Regulations 2000, SI 2000/1097, reg 2A(1)(b) (both as added: see note 11).

15 As to the phrase 'generation of power' see *Chesterfield Tube Co Ltd v Thomas (Valuation Officer)* [1970] 3 All ER 733, [1970] 1 WLR 1483, CA. See also *W Collier Ltd v Fielding (Valuation Officer)* (1957) 1 RRC 246, Lands Tribunal; affd [1958] 1 All ER 694, [1958] 1 WLR 323, CA. The cases cited in this paragraph were decided prior to the coming into force of the Local Government Finance Act 1988 but continue to be of relevance: see PARA 50.

16 'Power' means any form of energy or force applicable to work, and includes electrical energy used in chemical electrolysis: *Imperial Chemical Industries Ltd v Owen (Valuation Officer) and Runcorn UDC* (1954) 48 R & IT 43, Lands Tribunal. As to the meaning of 'primary transformation of power' and 'main transmission of power' see the Valuation for Rating (Plant and Machinery) (England) Regulations 2000, SI 2000/540, Schedule Class 1 paras (b), (c); and the Valuation for Rating (Plant and Machinery) (Wales) Regulations 2000, SI 2000/1097, Schedule Class 1 paras (b), (c). For the application of the terms in an earlier (slightly different) statutory order to electrical equipment see *South Wales Aluminium Co Ltd v Neath Assessment Area Assessment Committee* [1943] 2 All ER 587, DC; *Richard Thomas & Co Ltd v Monmouth County Valuation Committee and West Monmouth Assessment Committee* [1943] 2 All ER 707, DC.

17 See the Valuation for Rating (Plant and Machinery) (England) Regulations 2000, SI 2000/540, Schedule Class 1, Table 1 (Schedule Class 1 amended by SI 2001/846); and the Valuation for Rating (Plant and Machinery) (Wales) Regulations 2000, SI 2000/1097, Schedule Class 1, Table 1.

18 See the Valuation for Rating (Plant and Machinery) (England) Regulations 2000, SI 2000/540, Schedule Class 2, List of Accessories paras 1, 2; and the Valuation for Rating (Plant and Machinery) (Wales) Regulations 2000, SI 2000/1097, Schedule Class 2, List of Accessories paras 1, 2.

19 For these purposes, 'services' means the heating, cooling, ventilating, lighting, draining or supplying of water and protection from trespass, criminal damage, theft, fire or other hazard: see the Valuation for Rating (Plant and Machinery) (England) Regulations 2000, SI 2000/540, Schedule Class 2; and the Valuation for Rating (Plant and Machinery) (Wales) Regulations 2000, SI 2000/1097, Schedule Class 2.

20 See the Valuation for Rating (Plant and Machinery) (England) Regulations 2000, SI 2000/540, Schedule Class 2, Table 2; and the Valuation for Rating (Plant and Machinery) (Wales) Regulations 2000, SI 2000/1097, Schedule Class 2, Table 2. Refrigeration equipment for trade processes was held not to fall within a predecessor of this class: *Union Cold Storage Co Ltd v Southwark Assessment Committee* (1932) 16 R & IT 160. Similarly, boilers used in trade processes were held not to fall within it: *Burton-upon-Trent Borough Council v Bass, Ratcliff and Gretton Ltd and Thomas (Valuation Officer)* [1961] RVR 310, Lands Tribunal. In *Hays Business Services v Raley (Valuation Officer)* [1986] 1 EGLR 226, Lands Tribunal, fire-fighting equipment was held not rateable as it had been installed to protect sensitive goods stored in the warehouse and not the warehouse itself. See *Iceland Foods Ltd v Berry (Valuation Officer)* [2018] UKSC 15, [2018] All ER (D) 33 (Mar) (specialised air handling system, were 'manufacturing operations or trade processes' for rating purposes and accordingly, non-rateable).

21 See the Valuation for Rating (Plant and Machinery) (England) Regulations 2000, SI 2000/540, Schedule Class 2, List of Accessories para 2; and the Valuation for Rating (Plant and Machinery) (Wales) Regulations 2000, SI 2000/1097, Schedule Class 2, List of Accessories para 2.

22 See the Valuation for Rating (Plant and Machinery) (England) Regulations 2000, SI 2000/540, Schedule Class 3; and the Valuation for Rating (Plant and Machinery) (Wales) Regulations 2000, SI 2000/1097, Schedule Class 3. For these purposes, 'pipeline' means a pipe or system of pipes and associated fixed accessories and equipment for the conveyance of any thing, not being either a drain or sewer or a pipeline which forms part of the equipment of (and is wholly situated within) a factory or petroleum storage depot, a mine, quarry or mineral field or a natural gas storage or processing facility or gas holder site: see the Valuation for Rating (Plant and Machinery) (England) Regulations 2000, SI 2000/540, Schedule Class 3 para (g); and the Valuation for Rating (Plant and Machinery) (Wales) Regulations 2000, SI 2000/1097, Schedule Class 3 para (g).

The onus is on the ratepayer to prove that a particular pipeline is within one of the exceptions: *Edwards (Valuation Officer) v BP Refinery (Llandarcy) Ltd* [1974] RA 1 at 20, Lands Tribunal. As to pipelines conveying slurry over several miles from a china clay quarry to the 'dries' where it was prepared for sale see *English Clays Lovering Pochin & Co Ltd v Davis (Valuation Officer)* [1966] RA 475, Lands Tribunal; *English Clays Lovering Pochin & Co Ltd v Plymouth Corpn* [1974] 2 All ER 239, [1974] 1 WLR 742, CA. Cf *Rugby Portland Cement Co Ltd v Hunt (Valuation Officer)* (1969) 16 RRC 42, Lands Tribunal. As to pipes forming part of the equipment of a factory see *Edwards (Valuation Officer) v BP Refinery (Llandarcy) Ltd*; *Petrofina (Great Britain) Ltd v Harrington (Valuation Officer)* [1973] RA 65, Lands Tribunal; *Russell (Valuation Officer) v Shell-Mex and BP Ltd* (1970) 17 RRC 323, Lands Tribunal. As to pipelines within a mineral field see *Ottewell (Valuation Officer) v BP Exploration Operating Co Ltd* [1995] RA 22, Lands Tribunal.

23 The number and variety of items makes a summary or general description impracticable. For the full list see the Valuation for Rating (Plant and Machinery) (England) Regulations 2000, SI 2000/540, Schedule Class 4, Tables 3 and 4; and the Valuation for Rating (Plant and Machinery) (Wales) Regulations 2000, SI 2000/1097, Schedule Class 4, Tables 3 and 4. With regard to a number of items, including 'economisers', 'condensers', 'towers and columns', 'conduits', 'foundations', 'settings', 'fixed gantries', 'supports', 'platforms' and 'stages', 'tanks', 'blast furnaces', 'superheaters', and a 'still' see *Kent Oil Refinery Ltd v Walker* (1954) 47 R & IT 771, Lands Tribunal (on appeal sub nom *BP Refinery (Kent) Ltd v Walker (Valuation Officer)* [1957] 2 QB 305, [1957] 1 All ER 700, CA). As to 'bins' see *Chancery Lane Safe Deposit and Offices Co Ltd v Steedens (Valuation Officer)* [1961] RVR 261, Lands Tribunal. As to 'chambers and vessels' see *Scaife (Valuation Officer) v British Fermentation Products Ltd* [1971] RA 352, Lands Tribunal; *W Collier Ltd v Fielding (Valuation Officer)* (1957) 1 RRC 246, Lands Tribunal (affd [1958] 1 All ER 694, [1958] 1 WLR 323, CA). As to 'floating pontoons' see *Vickers-Armstrong (Shipbuilders) Ltd v Thornton (Valuation Officer)* (1965) 11 RRC 66, Lands Tribunal. As to 'conduits' see *Shell-Mex and BP Ltd v Childs (Valuation Officer)* [1961] RVR 371, Lands Tribunal (on appeal on another point [1962] RVR 267, CA); *Bright (Valuation Officer) v British Oil Storage Co Ltd* [1962] RVR 99, Lands Tribunal; *Lever Bros, Port Sunlight Ltd v Bright (Valuation Officer) and Bebington Borough Council* [1962] RVR 70, Lands Tribunal. As to

'foundations, settings etc' see *Shell-Mex and BP Ltd v James (Valuation Officer)* [1961] RVR 106, Lands Tribunal; *Lever Bros, Port Sunlight Ltd v Bright (Valuation Officer) and Bebington Borough Council*; *Post Office v Escott (Valuation Officer) and Kerrier RDC* [1974] RA 97, Lands Tribunal. As to 'furnaces' see *Gudgion (Valuation Officer) v Croydon Borough Council* (1970) 16 RRC 305, Lands Tribunal. As to 'silos' see *JW Thompson (Chesterfield) Ltd v Thomas (Valuation Officer)* (1970) 16 RRC 256, Lands Tribunal. As to 'radio telescopes' see *Post Office v Escott (Valuation Officer) and Kerrier RDC*. As to 'tanks' see *Shell-Mex and BP Ltd v Holyoak (Valuation Officer)* [1959] 1 All ER 391, [1959] 1 WLR 188, HL; *Regent Oil Co Ltd v Trevail (Valuation Officer)* (1959) 4 RRC 202, Lands Tribunal; *Shell-Mex and BP Ltd v James (Valuation Officer)*; *Slack v Harrison (Valuation Officer)* (1960) 8 RRC 143, Lands Tribunal; *Ind Coope Ltd v Burton-upon-Trent County Borough Council and Thomas (Valuation Officer)* [1961] RVR 341, Lands Tribunal. As to 'vats' see *Thomas (Valuation Officer) v Manor Vinegar Brewery Co Ltd* (1960) 6 RRC 353, Lands Tribunal. As to 'masts' see *Whitfield (Valuation Officer) v National Transcommunications Ltd* [1995] RA 214, Lands Tribunal.

As to plant at a sewage works see *Jones (Valuation Officer) v Eastern Valleys (Monmouthshire) Joint Sewerage Board* (1960) 6 RRC 379, Lands Tribunal. As to baker's ovens and provers see *Cumber (Valuation Officer) v Associated Family Bakers (South West) Ltd* [1979] RA 328, Lands Tribunal.

24 The exceptions are:

(1) any such item which is not, and is not in the nature of, a building or structure (see the Valuation for Rating (Plant and Machinery) (England) Regulations 2000, SI 2000/540, Schedule Class 4 para (a); and the Valuation for Rating (Plant and Machinery) (Wales) Regulations 2000, SI 2000/1097, Schedule Class 4 para (a));

(2) any part of any such item which does not form an integral part of such item as a building or structure or as being in the nature of a building or structure (see the Valuation for Rating (Plant and Machinery) (England) Regulations 2000, SI 2000/540, Schedule Class 4 para (b); and the Valuation for Rating (Plant and Machinery) (Wales) Regulations 2000, SI 2000/1097, Schedule Class 4 para (b));

(3) so much of any refractory or other lining forming part of any plant or machinery as is customarily renewed by reason of normal use at intervals of less than 50 weeks (see the Valuation for Rating (Plant and Machinery) (England) Regulations 2000, SI 2000/540, Schedule Class 4 para (c); and the Valuation for Rating (Plant and Machinery) (Wales) Regulations 2000, SI 2000/1097, Schedule Class 4 para (c));

(4) any item in the Valuation for Rating (Plant and Machinery) (England) Regulations 2000, SI 2000/540, Schedule Table 4 only or in the Valuation for Rating (Plant and Machinery) (Wales) Regulations 2000, SI 2000/1097, Schedule Table 4 only, as the case may be, the total cubic capacity of which (measured externally and excluding foundations, settings, supports and anything which is not an integral part of the item) does not exceed 400 cubic metres, and which is readily capable of being moved from one site and re-erected in its original state on another without the substantial demolition of the item or of any surrounding structure (see the Valuation for Rating (Plant and Machinery) (England) Regulations 2000, SI 2000/540, Schedule Class 4 para (d); and the Valuation for Rating (Plant and Machinery) (Wales) Regulations 2000, SI 2000/1097, Schedule Class 4 para (d)).

As to what is meant by 'substantial demolition' see *Cumber (Valuation Officer) v Associated Family Bakers (South West) Ltd* [1979] RA 328, Lands Tribunal. An item can be, or be in the nature of, a building or structure notwithstanding that it, or part of it, moves: *Cardiff Rating Authority and Cardiff Assessment Committee v Guest Keen Baldwin's Iron and Steel Co Ltd* [1949] 1 KB 385, [1949] 1 All ER 27, CA (tilting furnaces and gas and blast mains rateable); *British Portland Cement Manufacturers Ltd v Thurrock UDC* (1950) 114 JP 580, CA (rotary cement kilns rateable); *Tunnel Portland Cement Co Ltd v Thurrock UDC and Spencer (Valuation Officer)* (1951) 44 R & IT 632, Lands Tribunal (rotary cement kilns rateable); *Jones (Valuation Officer) v Rugby Portland Cement Co Ltd* (1952) 45 R & IT 807, Lands Tribunal (rotary cement kilns rateable); *Burton (Valuation Officer) v Ogdens (Brighton) Ltd* (1952) 45 R & IT 470, CA (baking ovens rateable). Cf *Engineering Industry Training Board v Foster Wheeler John Brown Boilers Ltd* [1970] 2 All ER 616, [1970] 1 WLR 881, CA. A floating dock was held not to be a structure in *Vickers-Armstrong (Shipbuilders) Ltd v Thornton (Valuation Officer)* (1965) 11 RRC 66, Lands Tribunal. A Lancashire boiler has been held to be a structure, or in the nature of a structure: *Wand (Valuation Officer) v Strong & Co of Romsey Ltd* [1967] RA 45, Lands Tribunal. Refractory brickwork and linings in steel furnaces may be part of the structure (*British Steel Corpn v Pittock (Valuation Officer)* (1970) 16 RRC 374, Lands Tribunal); but these may now be excluded by the exception in head (3). As to refrigeration plant see *Union Cold Storage Co Ltd v Southwark Assessment Committee* (1932) 16 R & IT 160; *Union Cold Storage Co Ltd v Phillips (Valuation Officer)* [1973] RA 148, Lands Tribunal (on appeal [1975] RA 306, CA; affd [1976] RA 173, HL).

(D) *Valuation of Wasting Property*

174. Valuation of mines and quarries.

The prevailing modern method of valuing mines and quarries[1] is by reference to a royalty per ton of output, to which is added a rent for the surface of the land and the buildings and other works occupied as part of the mine[2].

However, the value of mines and quarries may be ascertained alternatively on the same principle as that of an undertaking valued on the profits basis[3], that is, by making deductions from the yearly receipts for working expenses, for the tenant's share of the profits and for expenses of repair[4]. This last deduction includes the cost of maintaining the permanent roads and airways[5], but not the cost of sinking shafts[6]. No deduction is allowed to provide for the ultimate renewal of exhausted mines[7].

An exhausted mine is not rateable, even though a rent continues to be paid for it[8]; nor is a mine which has become unworkable[9].

The appropriate national authority[10] may make regulations under the Local Government Finance Act 1988 providing that, in arriving at an amount for the rateable value of a non-domestic hereditament[11], prescribed[12] principles are to be applied[13]. Accordingly, in arriving[14] at an amount of estimated rent in relation to such part of any mine or quarry[15] as consists of land[16] occupied for the purpose of the winning and working, grading, washing, grinding and crushing of minerals, no account is to be taken of sums payable in respect of the extraction of minerals from such land in so far as such sums are attributable to the capital value of minerals extracted[17]; and it is to be assumed[18] that the proportion of such sums attributable to the capital value of such minerals is 50 per cent[19].

1 There is no definition of 'mine' or 'quarry' in the Local Government Finance Act 1988. As to the meaning of these terms generally see MINES, MINERALS AND QUARRIES vol 76 (2013) PARAS 3, 4. The meaning of 'mine' was considered for the purposes of determining the rateable value of a mine in *Snailbeach Mine Co Ltd v Forden Guardians* (1876) 35 LT 514.

Most of the cases cited in this paragraph were decided prior to the coming into force of the Local Government Finance Act 1988 but continue to be of relevance: see PARA 50.

2 For examples of the use of this method see eg *Queensgate Whiting Co Ltd v Clayton (Valuation Officer)* (1959) 6 RRC 230, Lands Tribunal; *Leicester Lime Co Ltd v Winterton (Valuation Officer)* [1967] RA 5, Lands Tribunal; *The Tivydale Coal Co Ltd v Hanstock (Valuation Officer)* [1966] RA 225, Lands Tribunal; *Tarmac Roadstone Ltd v Longbotham (Valuation Officer)* [1968] RA 291, Lands Tribunal; *Mann (Valuation Officer) v Smiles & Co Ltd* (1968) 15 RRC 72, Lands Tribunal; *Brook (Valuation Officer) v National Coal Board and Burnwell Coal Co Ltd* [1971] RA 148, Lands Tribunal (on appeal on another point [1975] RA 367, CA); *HJ Banks & Co Ltd v Speight (Valuation Officer)* [2005] RA 61, Lands Tribunal; and *HJ Banks & Co Ltd v Speight and Walsh (Valuation Officers)* [2007] RA 187, Lands Tribunal. In valuing a coal mine, the prospect of better trade in years subsequent to the year of assessment is a factor which may be taken into account by a tenant from year to year in estimating the rent he would give; and a tenant is entitled to take into account the possibility of a continuance of his tenancy beyond the year: *Consett Iron Co Ltd v Assessment Committee for No 5 or North-Western Area of County of Durham* [1931] AC 396, HL.

3 As to the profits basis generally see PARA 184.

4 See eg *Brown & Co Ltd v Rotherham Union Assessment Committee and Churchwardens and Overseers of Dalton* (1900) 64 JP 580, DC.

5 *Brown & Co Ltd v Rotherham Union Assessment Committee and Churchwardens and Overseers of Dalton* (1900) 64 JP 580, DC.

6 *R v Attwood* (1827) 6 B & C 277.

7 Cf *R v Westbrook, R v Everist* (1847) 10 QB 178; *Coltness Iron Co v Black* (1881) 6 App Cas 315,

HL (a decision on income tax); and see INCOME TAXATION vol 58 (2014) PARA 194.

8 *R v Bedworth Inhabitants* (1807) 8 East 387.

9 *Tyne Coal Co v Wallsend Parish Overseers* (1877) 46 LJMC 185.

10 Ie the Secretary of State or, in relation to Wales, the Welsh Ministers. As to the Secretary of State and the Welsh Ministers see PARA 4 note 18. As to the meaning of 'Wales' see PARA 2 note 16. As to the separate administration of the non-domestic rating provisions (Local Government Finance Act 1988 Pt III (ss 41–67)) in England and Wales see PARA 52.

11 As to the meaning of 'non-domestic hereditament' see PARA 106.

12 'Prescribed' means prescribed by the regulations: see the Local Government Finance Act 1988 s 146(6).

13 See the Local Government Finance Act 1988 Sch 6 para 2(9); and PARA 166.

14 Ie under the Local Government Finance Act 1988 Sch 6 para 2(1): see PARA 157 et seq.

15 Ie any hereditament which consists of (or includes) a mine or quarry or any hereditament the whole or part of which is occupied together with a mine or quarry in connection with the storage or removal of its minerals or its refuse: Non-Domestic Rating (Miscellaneous Provisions) Regulations 1989, SI 1989/1060, reg 5(1). Any reference to a mine or quarry includes a reference to a well or bore-hole, or to a well and bore-hole combined: see reg 5(3) (substituted by SI 1989/2303). As to the meanings of 'mine' and 'minerals' see the Mines and Quarries Act 1954 ss 180, 182 (definitions applied by the Non-Domestic Rating (Miscellaneous Provisions) Regulations 1989, SI 1989/1060, reg 5(3) (as so substituted)); and MINES, MINERALS AND QUARRIES vol 76 (2013) PARAS 3, 10.

16 'Land' does not include buildings, structures, roads, shafts, adits or other works: Non-Domestic Rating (Miscellaneous Provisions) Regulations 1989, SI 1989/1060, reg 5(3) (as substituted: see note 15). 'Road' does not include an unwalkable outlet; 'unwalkable outlet' means an outlet which, owing to the gradient thereof or of any part thereof (whether alone or in combination with other circumstances), persons cannot walk up with reasonable convenience; and 'shaft' means a shaft the top of which is, or is intended to be, at the surface: see the Mines and Quarries Act 1954 s 182 (definitions applied by the Non-Domestic Rating (Miscellaneous Provisions) Regulations 1989, SI 1989/1060, reg 5(3) (as so substituted)).

17 See the Non-Domestic Rating (Miscellaneous Provisions) Regulations 1989, SI 1989/1060, reg 5(2).

18 Ie in applying the Local Government Finance Act 1988 Sch 6 para 2(1)–(7): see PARA 157 et seq).

19 See the Non-Domestic Rating (Miscellaneous Provisions) Regulations 1989, SI 1989/1060, reg 5(2).

175. Rapidly exhausting hereditaments.

The net annual value of a rapidly exhausting hereditament, such as a brickfield[1], chalk pit[2] or gravel pit[3], is the rent which a tenant might at the date of the valuation be expected to give for a year's tenancy of it; and this may well be something less than a figure arrived at by a calculation based on the rent and the royalties payable upon the maximum quantity of bricks that might be made or of material that might be got[4]. In most cases in which the hereditament becomes exhausted in the course of the year, the value is to be ascertained with regard to the estimated output over a whole year without deduction on account of exhaustion of the mineral in the course of the year[5].

1 *R v Westbrook, R v Everist* (1847) 10 QB 178; *Yorkshire Brick Co Ltd v Hanstock (Valuation Officer)* (1959) 6 RRC 13, Lands Tribunal.

All of the cases cited in this paragraph were decided prior to the coming into force of the Local Government Finance Act 1988 but continue to be of relevance: see PARA 50.

2 *R v North Aylesford Union* (1872) 37 JP 148; *Queensgate Whiting Co Ltd v Clayton (Valuation Officer)* (1959) 6 RRC 230, Lands Tribunal. The profits which the occupiers made by being occupiers also of an adjoining cement works were not to be taken into account: *R v North Aylesford Union*. See also *Leicester Lime Co Ltd v Winterton (Valuation Officer)* [1967] RA 5, Lands Tribunal.

3 *Farnham Flint, Gravel and Sand Co Ltd v Farnham Union* [1901] 1 KB 272, CA; distinguished in *Gilbard (Valuation Officer) v Amey Roadstone Corpn Ltd* [1974] RA 498, CA.

4 See the cases cited in note 1.

5 *Gilbard (Valuation Officer) v Amey Roadstone Corpn Ltd* [1974] RA 498, CA; distinguishing *Farnham Flint, Gravel and Sand Co Ltd v Farnham Union* [1901] 1 KB 272, CA, where it had been held that regard should be had to the amount of mineral remaining unexhausted at the date of the rate.

176. Spoil heaps.

The extraction of minerals from spoil heaps may give rise to rateable occupation, whether the heaps are classed as land or as chattels[1].

1 See *Greenall (Valuation Officer) v Castleford Brick Co Ltd* (1959) 5 RRC 253, Lands Tribunal; *Andrews v Hereford RDC* [1963] RA 75, DC; *Ryan Industrial Fuels Ltd v Morgan (Valuation Officer)* [1965] 3 All ER 465, [1965] 1 WLR 1347, CA; *Tarmac Roadstone Ltd v Longbotham (Valuation Officer)* [1968] RA 291, Lands Tribunal; *Mann (Valuation Officer) v Smiles & Co Ltd* (1968) 15 RRC 72, Lands Tribunal; *National Coal Board v Brook (Valuation Officer)* (1970) 16 RRC 357, Lands Tribunal; *Brook (Valuation Officer) v National Coal Board and Burnwell Coal Co Ltd* [1971] RA 148, Lands Tribunal (on appeal on another point [1975] RA 367, CA).

All of these were decided prior to the coming into force of the Local Government Finance Act 1988 but continue to be of relevance: see PARA 50.

(E) Regulations Made in Relation to Former Enterprise Zones

177. Former enterprise zones.

The appropriate national authority[1] may make regulations providing that, in applying the main provisions of the Local Government Finance Act 1988 to determine the rateable value of non-domestic hereditaments[2] in relation to a hereditament of a prescribed[3] class, prescribed assumptions (as to the hereditament or otherwise) are to be made[4].

Where the rateable value of a hereditament situated wholly or partly in a former enterprise zone[5] is to be entered in a list[6] (or the rateable value shown in a list for such a hereditament is to be altered)[7], it is to be assumed[8] in relation to so much of the hereditament as is situated in the former enterprise zone that on the relevant day no area had been designated as an enterprise zone[9].

1 Ie the Secretary of State or, in relation to Wales, the Welsh Ministers. As to the Secretary of State and the Welsh Ministers see PARA 4 note 18. As to the meaning of 'Wales' see PARA 2 note 16. As to the separate administration of the non-domestic rating provisions (Local Government Finance Act 1988 Pt III (ss 41–67)) in England and Wales see PARA 52.

2 Ie the Local Government Finance Act 1988 Sch 6 para 2(1)–(7): see PARA 157 et seq. As to the meaning of 'non-domestic hereditament' see PARA 106.

3 'Prescribed' means prescribed by the regulations: see the Local Government Finance Act 1988 s 146(6).

4 See the Local Government Finance Act 1988 Sch 6 para 2(8); and PARA 166.

5 'Enterprise zone' means an area so designated under the Local Government, Planning and Land Act 1980 Sch 32 para 5(1) (see PLANNING vol 83 (2018) PARA 1567); and 'former enterprise zone' means an area which has ceased to be so designated since a date on or after the relevant day, being the day by reference to which a rateable value is to be determined in accordance with the Local Government Finance Act 1988 Sch 6 para 2(3) (see PARA 164): Valuation for Rating (Former Enterprise Zones) Regulations 1995, SI 1995/213, reg 1(2).

6 Ie a central non-domestic rating list or a local non-domestic rating list: see the Valuation for Rating (Former Enterprise Zones) Regulations 1995, SI 1995/213, reg 1(2). As to the compilation of local non-domestic rating lists see PARA 191. As to the compilation of central non-domestic rating lists see PARA 196.

7 As to the alteration of rating lists see PARA 199 et seq.

8 Ie in applying the Local Government Finance Act 1988 Sch 6 para 2(1)–(7): see PARA 157 et seq.

9 See the Valuation for Rating (Former Enterprise Zones) Regulations 1995, SI 1995/213, reg 2.

(F) Regulations Made in Relation to Advertising Hereditaments

178. Advertising hereditaments.

The appropriate national authority[1] may make regulations providing that, in applying the main provisions of the Local Government Finance Act 1988 to determine the rateable value of non-domestic hereditaments[2] in relation to a hereditament of a prescribed[3] class, prescribed assumptions (as to the hereditament or otherwise) are to be made[4], or that, in arriving at an amount for the rateable value of a non-domestic hereditament[5], prescribed principles are to be applied[6].

In relation to an advertising hereditament[7], it is to be assumed[8] that the grant or reservation of the right of which the hereditament consists included the grant or reservation of a right to use any structure[9] or sign for the time being available for use for the purpose of exhibiting advertisements by the occupier[10] of that hereditament, notwithstanding that the structure or sign was provided by that occupier or was provided after the making of the grant or reservation concerned[11].

In arriving at an amount of the hypothetical rent for the purposes of determining rateable value[12] in respect of any land[13] over which such an advertising right is exercisable, no account is to be taken of any value (or, as the case may be, increased value) arising from the use of the land for the purpose of exhibiting advertisements in accordance with that right[14]. However, where any hereditament rateable in respect of its occupation for other purposes is used temporarily or permanently for (or for the erection thereon or attachment thereto of any structure used for) the exhibition of advertisements other than in pursuance of an advertising right, in arriving at an amount[15] in respect of that hereditament the increased value from that use of the hereditament is to be taken into account[16].

1 Ie the Secretary of State or, in relation to Wales, the Welsh Ministers. As to the Secretary of State and the Welsh Ministers see PARA 4 note 18. As to the meaning of 'Wales' see PARA 2 note 16. As to the separate administration of the non-domestic rating provisions (Local Government Finance Act 1988 Pt III (ss 41–67)) in England and Wales see PARA 52.

2 Ie the Local Government Finance Act 1988 Sch 6 para 2(1)–(7). As to the meaning of 'non-domestic hereditament' see PARA 106.

3 'Prescribed' means prescribed by the regulations: see the Local Government Finance Act 1988 s 146(6).

4 See the Local Government Finance Act 1988 Sch 6 para 2(8); and PARA 166.

5 Ie under the Local Government Finance Act 1988 Sch 6 para 2(1), 2(1A) or 2(1B).

6 See the Local Government Finance Act 1988 Sch 6 para 2(9); and PARA 166.

7 'Advertising hereditament' means a hereditament consisting of a right to which the Local Government Finance Act 1988 s 64(2) (see PARA 104) applies; and 'advertising right' means a right which is such a hereditament: Non-Domestic Rating (Miscellaneous Provisions) (No 2) Regulations 1989, SI 1989/2303, reg 4(4).

8 Ie in applying the Local Government Finance Act 1988 Sch 6 para 2(1)–(7): see PARA 157 et seq.

9 'Structure' includes a hoarding, frame, or wall: Non-Domestic Rating (Miscellaneous Provisions) (No 2) Regulations 1989, SI 1989/2303, reg 4(4).

10 As to the meaning of 'occupier' see PARA 86.

11 Non-Domestic Rating (Miscellaneous Provisions) (No 2) Regulations 1989, SI 1989/2303, reg 4(1).

12 Ie under the Local Government Finance Act 1988 Sch 6 para 2(1), 2(1A) or 2(1B): see PARA 157.

13 Ie within the meaning of the Local Government Finance Act 1988 s 64(2): see PARA 104.

14 Non-Domestic Rating (Miscellaneous Provisions) (No 2) Regulations 1989, SI 1989/2303, reg 4(2).

15 Ie under the Local Government Finance Act 1988 Sch 6 para 2(1), 2(1A) or 2(1B): see PARA 157.

16 Non-Domestic Rating (Miscellaneous Provisions) (No 2) Regulations 1989, SI 1989/2303, reg 4(3).

(G) Valuation of Licensed Premises

179. Consideration of existence of licence.

In valuing licensed premises, it is necessary to take into account the value due to the existence of the licence, because the trade which the occupier is thereby permitted to carry on may only be carried on upon the premises rated[1]. Consequently, unless there are countervailing circumstances, an increase in the amount of licence duty which a tenant of the house must bear will have the effect of decreasing the rental value of the house[2].

Where the occupier is bound by a 'tying' covenant to take his liquor, or some part of it, from the landlord, the 'tied' house is to be valued as if it were not affected by any such covenant[3].

1 *R v Bradford* (1815) 4 M & S 317; *West Middlesex Waterworks Co v Coleman* (1885) 14 QBD 529, DC; *Cartwright v Sculcoates Union* [1900] AC 150, HL; *R v Shoreditch Assessment Committee, ex p Morgan* [1910] 2 KB 859, CA; *Robinson Bros (Brewers) Ltd v Houghton and Chester-le-Street Assessment Committee* [1937] 2 KB 445 at 471, 474, [1937] 2 All ER 298 at 309, 311, CA, per Scott LJ (affd sub nom *Robinson Bros (Brewers) Ltd v Durham County Assessment Committee (Area No 7)* [1938] AC 321, [1938] 2 All ER 79, HL); *Appenrodt v Central Middlesex Assessment Committee* [1937] 2 KB 48 at 55–56, [1937] 2 All ER 325 at 329, CA, per Lord Wright MR. Cf *Earl Fitzwilliam v IRC* [1914] AC 753, HL, where the value of premises due to the licence was included in the assessment of reversion duty.

All of the cases cited in this paragraph were decided prior to the coming into force of the Local Government Finance Act 1988 but continue to be of relevance: see PARA 50.

2 *R v Shoreditch Assessment Committee, ex p Morgan* [1910] 2 KB 859, CA.

3 Ie as if it were a 'free' house: *Sunderland Overseers v Sunderland Union* (1865) 18 CBNS 531; *Robinson Bros (Brewers) Ltd v Durham County Assessment Committee (Area No 7)* [1938] AC 321 at 337, [1938] 2 All ER 79 at 85–86, HL, per Lord Macmillan. In practice, a tied house is sometimes valued by taking the rent reserved and adding to it a sum estimated to represent the burden of the tying covenant.

180. Evidence of trade done and of outgoings.

The simplest method of valuing a public house would be by ascertaining the rents which are prevalent in the neighbourhood for 'free' houses; but where this evidence is not available, it is not possible to apply this test. Evidence of the trade actually done and of the profits made by the actual occupier is admissible in order to ascertain the rental value[1]. The rent which a brewer would give for a licensed property in order to put in a tied tenant or a manager must be taken into account in estimating the gross value of the house[2]. If evidence of the gross receipts is given, an occupier must be allowed to give evidence of the outgoings which have been found necessary to earn those receipts[3].

1 *Cartwright v Sculcoates Union* [1900] AC 150, HL; *Robinson Bros (Brewers) Ltd v Houghton and Chester-le-Street Assessment Committee* [1937] 2 KB 445, [1937] 2 All ER 298, CA (affd sub nom *Robinson Bros (Brewers) Ltd v Durham County Assessment Committee (Area No 7)* [1938] AC 321, [1938] 2 All ER 79, HL); *Appenrodt v Central Middlesex Assessment Committee* [1937] 2 KB 48 at 65, [1937] 2 All ER 325 at 335, CA, per Scott LJ. As to the calculation of value on the profits basis generally see PARA 185.

The principle was lucidly explained for the purpose of assessing the capital amount payable by way of compensation for the refusal of an old licence in *Ashby's Cobham Brewery Co, Petitioners, Re The Crown, Cobham* [1906] 2 KB 754 at 761–764 per Kennedy J. See also *Brickwoods Ltd v Cousins (Valuation Officer)* [1968] RA 243, Lands Tribunal; *Bass Charrington (North) Ltd v Padgett (Valuation Officer)* [1969] RA 167, Lands Tribunal. It is clear from *Cartwright v Sculcoates Union* that the accounts of the actual occupier, while not necessarily according with those of the hypothetical tenant, form a useful starting point for the valuer when he prepares the accounts of the hypothetical tenant: *Sharp v Griffiths (Valuation Officer)* [1999] RA 265, [1999] 3 EGLR 113, Lands Tribunal (accounts were showing losses and the evidence did not suggest a real likelihood that future trade would improve to such an extent as to persuade a hypothetical tenant to pay a significant annual rent).

Most of the cases cited in this paragraph were decided prior to the coming into force of the Local Government Finance Act 1988 but continue to be of relevance: see PARA 50.

2 *Robinson Bros (Brewers) Ltd v Houghton and Chester-le-Street Assessment Committee* [1937] 2 KB 445, [1937] 2 All ER 298, CA (affd sub nom *Robinson Bros (Brewers) Ltd v Durham County Assessment Committee (Area No 7)* [1938] AC 321, [1938] 2 All ER 79, HL); overruling *Bradford-on-Avon Assessment Committee v White* [1898] 2 QB 630, DC.

3 *Parr v Leigh Union* (1905) 1 Konst Rat App 211.

181. Methods of valuation of licensed premises.

The usual method of valuation of licensed premises when based on trade is to take the profits (actual or estimated) of the last year or over an average of years, together with the tied rent, and to subtract from them the remuneration which the hypothetical tenant would expect for himself, and to apportion the remainder between rent and rates[1]. Valuation by reference to capital values has been rejected in the past[2].

1 This method was described in *Watney Mann Ltd v Langley (Valuation Officer)* [1966] 1 QB 457 at 463, [1963] 3 All ER 967 at 970 per Thompson J. For examples of the application of this method see *Kirk and Lambert Ltd v West Sussex Assessment Committee* (1938) 29 R & IT 272, 308; *Friary, Holroyd and Healy's Ltd v Surrey County* (1939) 30 R & IT 156; *Westall v Reading Rating Authority* (1939) 30 R & IT 192, 208, 272; *Hall and Woodhouse v South Dorset Assessment Committee* (1939) 30 R & IT 256; *Bryan v East Sussex Assessment Committee* (1939) 31 R & IT 26; *Offilers' Brewery v Derby Borough Assessment Committee* (1940) 32 R & IT 344; *Thomas v Herefordshire Assessment Committee* (1940) 32 R & IT 407 (a free house); *Fountain & Co Ltd v County Borough of Derby Assessment Committee* (1941) 34 R & IT 267; *Edlins Ltd v Horsham and Worthing Assessment Committee* (1946) 39 R & IT 392 (a free house); *Smith v East Devon Assessment Committee* (1946) 40 R & IT 15. See also *Steward & Patteson Ltd v County Borough of Great Yarmouth and Vaughan (Valuation Officer)* (1959) 5 RRC 204, Lands Tribunal; *Hutton v Davies (Valuation Officer)* (1959) 6 RRC 124, Lands Tribunal; *Burkitt (Valuation Officer) v Tennant Bros Ltd* (1960) 7 RRC 243, Lands Tribunal; *Warwicks and Richardsons Ltd v Padgett (Valuation Officer)* (1959) 6 RRC 52, Lands Tribunal; *Bloodworth (Valuation Officer) v Home Brewery Co Ltd* (1959) 6 RRC 128, Lands Tribunal; *Billing (Valuation Officer) v Ansells Brewery Ltd* (1960) 7 RRC 395, Lands Tribunal; *Brickwoods Ltd v Cousins (Valuation Officer)* [1968] RA 243, Lands Tribunal; *Bass Charrington (North) Ltd v Padgett (Valuation Officer)* [1969] RA 167, Lands Tribunal; *Brunning & Price Ltd v Cowell (Valuation Officer)* [2008] RA 1, Lands Tribunal; *Assessor for Lothian v Belhaven Brewery Co Ltd* [2008] CSIH 60, [2008] RA 464, 2009 SC 120, 2008 SLT 1126 (over- and under-performance). As to more general methods that are applied to valuation for rating purposes see PARA 182 et seq.

Most of the cases cited in this paragraph were decided prior to the coming into force of the Local Government Finance Act 1988 but continue to be of relevance: see PARA 50.

2 *Sheffield Corpn v John Smith's Tadcaster Brewery Co Ltd and Tranter (Valuation Officer)* (1958) 3 RRC 191, Lands Tribunal; *Steward & Patteson Ltd v County Borough of Great Yarmouth and Vaughan (Valuation Officer)* (1959) 5 RRC 204, Lands Tribunal.

(iii) Methods of Valuation

182. No uniform method of valuation.

There is no longer any rule of law that any class of hereditament must be valued by a particular method[1]. The main methods of rating in general use can be summarised as being: by reference to actual rents; the 'profits' or 'receipts and expenditure' basis; the 'contractor's basis'; and by using evidence of assessments of comparable hereditaments[2]. There are no hard and fast rules as to which method should be used in any particular case.

All relevant evidence is to be admitted, but given weight according to its quality[3]. Nevertheless, it is to be expected that actual rents, where they are available and cannot be impeached, are likely to be the best guide as to value, although not conclusive[4].

1 As to valuation for rating see PARA 156 et seq. As to the hereditament see PARA 106.

2 As to the various methods in use see PARA 183 et seq.

3 *Garton v Hunter (Valuation Officer)* [1969] 2 QB 37, [1969] 1 All ER 451, CA; and see *Baker Britt & Co Ltd v Hampsher (Valuation Officer)* [1975] RA 293, CA; *Lotus & Delta Ltd v Culverwell (Valuation Officer) and Leicester City Council* [1976] RA 141, 21 RRC 1, Lands Tribunal; *United Services and Services Rendered Club (Tooting And Balham) Ltd v Thorneley (Valuation Officer)* [2001] RA 145, Lands Tribunal.

Most of the cases cited in this paragraph were decided prior to the coming into force of the Local Government Finance Act 1988 but continue to be of relevance: see PARA 50.

4 See eg *O'Brien v Harwood (Valuation Officer)* [2003] RA 244, Lands Tribunal, where direct rental evidence of value existed and the ratepayer's evidence of receipts was given little weight. As to actual rent being evidence of rental value see PARA 183.

183. Actual rent as evidence of value.

The actual rent paid for the hereditament[1] is not conclusive evidence of value[2]. However, where the hereditament is let at what is plainly a rack rent[3], that rent is good evidence of value always provided that it was recently fixed by the 'higgling of the market'[4]. If the actual rent is paid on terms which differ from those of the hypothetical tenancy, it must be adjusted, if possible, to the terms of the hypothetical tenancy before it affords evidence of value. Such adjustments may be necessary to allow, for example, for the burden of rates and taxes, the length of the lease[5] or the provision of landlord's services[6]. Rents paid for comparable hereditaments are relevant evidence, subject to similar considerations[7]. The classes of hereditaments which in practice are most commonly valued by reference to rents are shops, offices, warehouses and other commercial premises[8].

1 As to the hereditament see PARA 106. As to valuation for rating see PARA 156 et seq.

2 *R v London School Board* (1986) 17 QBD 738, CA; *Poplar Metropolitan Borough Assessment Committee v Roberts* [1922] 2 AC 93 at 103, HL, per Lord Buckmaster, and at 107–108 per Lord Atkinson. See also *R v Skingle* (1798) 7 Term Rep 549; *Hayward v Brinkworth Overseers* (1864) 10 LT 608; *R v Paddington Valuation Officer, ex p Peachey Property Corpn* [1964] 3 All ER 200 at 218, [1964] 1 WLR 1186 at 1209, DC (affd [1966] 1 QB 380 at 412–413, [1965] 2 All ER 836 at 848, CA); *Garton v Hunter (Valuation Officer)* [1969] 2 QB 37, [1969] 1 All ER 451, CA; *Baker Britt & Co Ltd v Hampsher (Valuation Officer)* [1976] RA 69, HL; *Orange PCS Ltd v Bradford (Valuation Officer)* [2004] EWCA Civ 155, [2004] 2 All ER 651, [2004] RA 61 (statutory right that the ratepayer had to occupy the land without payment was not determinative of the value of its beneficial occupation, in the same way that an actual rent was not determinative).

Most of the cases cited in this paragraph were decided prior to the coming into force of the Local Government Finance Act 1988 but continue to be of relevance: see PARA 50.

3 Ie a rent equal to the full annual value of the land. Rents paid under the statutory restrictions are not good evidence: *Poplar Metropolitan Borough Assessment Committee v Roberts* [1922] 2 AC 93, HL; *R v Paddington Valuation Officer, ex p Peachey Property Corpn Ltd* [1966] 1 QB 380, [1965] 2 All ER 836, CA; *O'Mere v Burley (Valuation Officer)* (1968) 14 RRC 401, Lands Tribunal; *David v Wyeth (Valuation Officer)* [1974] RA 484, Lands Tribunal; *Hilder v Haysom (Valuation Officer)* [1974] RA 517, Lands Tribunal. As to rents fixed by development corporations for industrial premises see *Homerton Rubber Works Ltd v Morrell (Valuation Officer)* (1958) 3 RRC 306, Lands Tribunal. Cf *Lee (Valuation Officer) v Southwark Manufacturing Co Ltd* [1961] RVR 230, Lands Tribunal. It is always open to either party to show that a rent agreed was a misconception, and that, if the agreement had to be made again, a different rent would be agreed: *East London Rly Joint Committee v Greenwich Union* (1890) Ryde's Rat App (1886–1890) 210 at 219; *Glasspool v Buttery (Valuation Officer)* (1957) 2 RRC 28, Lands Tribunal; *Bell (Valuation Officer) v Perry* [1965] RA 9, Lands Tribunal; *Cash and Carry Cleaners (Merseyside) Ltd v Finch (Valuation Officer)* [1966] RA 454, Lands Tribunal; *Mann (Valuation Officer) v Smiles & Co Ltd* (1968) 15 RRC 72, Lands Tribunal. In *Hodges Ltd v Howells (Valuation Officer)* [1993] RA 236, the Lands Tribunal rejected the actual rent for the subject hereditament on the ground that it was out of line with the general pattern of rents.

4 Rents fixed by tender were rejected as evidence in *WA Rawlinson & Co Ltd v Pritchard (Valuation Officer)* (1958) 4 RRC 178, Lands Tribunal; *Leisure UK Ltd v Moore (Valuation Officer)* [1974] RA 237, Lands Tribunal. Rents fixed as part of a 'sale and lease back' transaction were rejected as evidence in *Binns Ltd v Anderson (Valuation Officer)* (1959) 4 RRC 209, Lands Tribunal; *Trocadero (Swanage) Ltd v Perrins (Valuation Officer)* (1957) 51 R & IT 140, Lands Tribunal; *Lewis Separates v Chapman (Valuation Officer)* (1967) 12 RRC 400, Lands Tribunal; *FW Woolworth & Co Ltd v Christopher (Valuation Officer) and Lincoln City Council* (1972) 17 RRC 341, Lands Tribunal; *John Lewis & Son Ltd v Goodwin (Valuation Officer)* [1980] RA 1, Lands Tribunal; and in *Fusetron Ltd v Whitehouse* [1999] RA 295, Lands Tribunal, rents agreed as part of 'sale and lease back' transactions were regarded as suspect evidence of open market rental values unless supported by other evidence. See also *Hudson & Son Ltd v Rennick (Valuation Officer)* (1959) 5 RRC 221, Lands Tribunal; *Wood v Garvie (Valuation Officer)* [1975] RA 257, Lands Tribunal.

5 See *L & A Black Ltd v Burton (Valuation Officer)* (1958) 3 RRC 172, Lands Tribunal; *Humber Ltd v Jones (Valuation Officer) and Rugby RDC* (1960) 6 RRC 161, CA. As to the conversion of a weekly rent to an annual rent see *LCC v Wand (Valuation Officer)* (1957) 2 RRC 220, Lands Tribunal.

6 See *Bell Property Trust Ltd v Hampstead Borough Assessment Committee* [1940] 2 KB 543, [1940] 3 All ER 640, CA.

7 The Lands Tribunal has in the past adopted the rule that rents fixed after the date of the proposal are inadmissible (*Leicester City Council v Burkitt (Valuation Officer) and Perfecto Engineering Co Ltd* [1965] RA 101, Lands Tribunal; *Gilmore (Valuation Officer) v Baker-Carr (No 2)* [1963] RA 458, Lands Tribunal; *Smith v Moore (Valuation Officer)* [1972] RA 269; *Dunbar v Le Grys (Valuation Officer)* (1978) 21 RRC 88, Lands Tribunal), except to prove or disprove a trend or anticipation at the date of the proposal (*Thomas Ware & Sons Ltd v Toovey (Valuation Officer)* (1959) 6 RRC 216, Lands Tribunal; *British Transport Commission v Hingley and Robinson (Valuation Officers) and Grimsby RDC* (1960) 7 RRC 225, Lands Tribunal; *Frank Mason & Co Ltd v Thomas (Valuation Officer)* [1962] RVR 147, Lands Tribunal; *Robinson v Le Grys (Valuation Officer)* [1969] RA 63, Lands Tribunal), or to show the relative values of hereditaments at the relevant date (*Myers v Glynn (Valuation Officer)* [1973] RA 89; *John Lewis & Co Ltd v Goodwin (Valuation Officer)* [1980] RA 1, Lands Tribunal). However, this rule and these cases require to be read in the light of *Garton v Hunter (Valuation Officer)* [1969] 2 QB 37, [1969] 1 All ER 451, CA, where it was held that all relevant evidence is admissible, and that the goodness or badness of it goes to weight, not to admissibility. Rents fixed by tender are viewed with reserve: see *Thomas Cook Group Ltd v Prince (Valuation Officer)* [1981] RA 17, Lands Tribunal.

8 The larger shops present special problems as there is usually a paucity of rental evidence of similar hereditaments, but rental evidence of small shops is usually available. In order to relate the rents of small shops to large shops, the 'zoning method' is sometimes used: see *Footman, Pretty & Co v Chandler (Valuation Officer)* (1960) 7 RRC 18, Lands Tribunal; *FW Woolworth & Co Ltd v Moore (Valuation Officer)* [1978] RA 186, Lands Tribunal. It may be appropriate to make a 'quantum' or 'quantity' allowance: *FW Woolworth & Co Ltd v Christopher (Valuation Officer) and Lincoln City Council* (1972) 17 RRC 341, Lands Tribunal; *John Lewis & Co Ltd v Goodwin (Valuation Officer)* [1980] RA 1, Lands Tribunal. However, recent valuation practice for large shops suggests a movement away from the 'zoning method' to the 'overall method' in which rents for small shops are not of great assistance; it is now established valuation practice to value large stores on an 'overall' basis: see eg *Harrods Ltd v Baker (Valuation Officer)* [2007] RA 247, Lands Tribunal (appropriate rateable value for Harrods department store), in which the Lands Tribunal provides a helpful analysis of the principles which support that approach as well as the issue of 'quantum' or 'quantity' allowance.

184. Valuation on the 'profits' or 'receipts and expenditure' basis.

In the absence of rental evidence of value, the accounts, receipts or profits of the occupier of the hereditament[1] may be relevant[2]. The profits themselves are not rateable[3] but they may serve to indicate the rent at which the hereditament might reasonably be expected to let, especially where the profits can only be earned upon that hereditament and can be earned there by any ordinary tenant. Whether the profits will affect, and how far they will affect, the rent will depend upon the 'higgling of the market'[4]. Profits have been taken into consideration in the valuation for rating of, for instance, public utility undertakings[5], including waterworks[6], docks and harbours[7], light railways[8] and district heating undertakings[9], and also licensed premises[10], railway refreshment rooms[11], hotels[12], a toll bridge[13], race courses[14], football grounds[15], markets[16], mines, quarries and brickfields[17], a zoo[18], a radio relay system[19], piers[20], caravan sites[21], cemeteries[22], crematoria[23] and cinemas[24].

The rent to be ascertained is that which the hypothetical tenant would pay[25]. The inquiry must therefore embrace the whole of the profits made at the hereditament, even though a part of them does not inure to the actual occupier[26], and failure on the part of the occupier to take profits which it is open to him to take must be disregarded[27].

The occupier of a hereditament may be compelled to disclose his trading figures if they are reasonably required to enable the valuation officer accurately to compile the valuation list or to make or object to a proposal[28].

1 As to valuation for rating see PARA 156 et seq. As to the hereditament see PARA 106.

2 *R v London and South Western Rly Co* (1842) 1 QB 558; *R v Grand Junction Rly Co* (1844) 4 QB 18; *Mersey Docks and Harbour Board v Birkenhead Assessment Committee* [1901] AC 175, HL; *Cartwright v Sculcoates Union* [1900] AC 150, HL. Cf *Mersey Docks and Harbour Board v Liverpool Overseers* (1873) LR 9 QB 84 at 97; *R v London and North Western Rly Co* (1874) LR 9 QB 134 at 144; *R v North Aylesford Union* (1872) 37 JP 148. See also *O'Brien v Harwood (Valuation Officer)* [2003] RA 244, where little weight was given to the ratepayer's evidence of receipts on the basis that this indirect method of assessing annual value is of limited assistance where direct rental evidence of value exists.

Most of the cases cited in this paragraph were decided prior to the coming into force of the Local Government Finance Act 1988 but continue to be of relevance: see PARA 50.

3 *R v Grand Junction Rly Co* (1844) 4 QB 18 at 38 per Lord Denman; *Mersey Docks and Harbour Board v Birkenhead Assessment Committee* [1901] AC 175 at 180–181, HL.

4 See *Talargoch Mining Co v St Asaph's Union* (1868) LR 3 QB 478 at 486 per Blackburn J; *Mersey Docks and Harbour Board v Liverpool Overseers* (1873) LR 9 QB 84 at 96 per Blackburn J; *Aberaman Ex-Servicemen's Club and Institute v Aberdare UDC* [1948] 1 KB 332 at 336–337, sub nom *Aberdare UDC v Pontypridd Area Assessment Committee* [1947] 2 All ER 877 at 878–879, per Atkinson J.

5 Notwithstanding any rule of law requiring the rateable value of a hereditament occupied by a public utility undertaking to be estimated solely by reference to the accounts, receipts or profits of the undertaking, in arriving at an amount under the Local Government Finance Act 1988 Sch 6 para 2(1), 2(1A) or 2(1B) in relation to such a hereditament, any evidence relevant to estimating the amount of rent in accordance with that provision is to be taken into account: see the Non-Domestic Rating (Miscellaneous Provisions) (No 2) Regulations 1989, SI 1989/2303, reg 3; and PARA 171. As to the valuation of public utility undertakings generally see PARA 169 et seq.

6 See eg *R v Churchwardens and Overseers of Mile End Old Town* (1847) 10 QB 208; *R v West Middlesex Waterworks* (1859) 1 E & E 716; *Kingston Union Assessment Committee v Metropolitan Water Board* [1926] AC 331, HL.

7 See eg *Port of London Authority v Orsett Union Assessment Committee* [1920] AC 273, HL; *R v Southampton Dock Co* (1851) 14 QB 587; *Clayton (Valuation Officer) v British Transport Commission* [1955] 2 All ER 274, [1954] 1 WLR 504, CA; *Bluebell Railway Ltd v Ball (Valuation Officer)* [1984] RA 113, [1984] JPL 887, Lands Tribunal.

8 *Ebbutt (Valuation Officer) v Nottingham Colwick Estates Light Rly Co* (1960) 7 RRC 346, Lands Tribunal; *Winchester and Alton Rly Ltd v Whyment (Valuation Officer)* [1981] RA 258, Lands Tribunal; *Bluebell Railway Ltd v Ball (Valuation Officer)* [1984] RA 113, [1984] JPL 887, Lands Tribunal.

9 *Swindon Borough Council v Tavener (Valuation Officer)* (1952) 45 R & IT 410, Lands Tribunal.

10 See eg *Cartwright v Sculcoates Union* [1900] AC 150, HL; *Robinson Bros (Brewers) Ltd v Houghton and Chester-le-Street Assessment Committee* [1937] 2 KB 445, [1937] 2 All ER 298, CA (affd sub nom *Robinson Bros (Brewers) Ltd v Durham County Assessment Committee (Area No 7)* [1938] AC 321, [1938] 2 All ER 79, HL); *Sheffield Corpn v John Smith's Tadcaster Brewery Co Ltd and Tranter (Valuation Officer)* (1958) 3 RRC 191, Lands Tribunal. As to the valuation of licensed premises generally see PARA 179 et seq.

11 See *Clark v Alderbury Union Assessment Committee and Fisherton-Angar Overseers* (1880) 6 QBD 139, DC; *British Transport Commission v Glasgow Assessor* (1957) 51 R & IT 29.

12 See *Burden v Bognor Regis UDC* (1957) 2 RRC 256, Lands Tribunal; *AL Mather Ltd v Cockcroft (Valuation Officer)* (1958) 51 R & IT 819, Lands Tribunal.

13 See *R v Hammersmith Bridge Co* (1849) 15 QB 369.

14 See *R v Verrall* (1875) 1 QBD 9; *Racecourse Betting Control Board v Brighton Corpn* [1941] 2 KB 287, [1941] 2 All ER 595 (affd [1942] 2 KB 90, [1942] 1 All ER 611, CA) (totalisator); *Sandown Park Ltd v Esher UDC and Castle (Valuation Officer)* (1954) 47 R & IT 351, CA.

15 *Hardiman (Valuation Officer) v Crystal Palace Football and Athletic Club Ltd* (1955) 48 R & IT 91, Lands Tribunal. Cf *West Ham United Football Club v Smith (Valuation Officer)* (1957) 1 RRC 263, Lands Tribunal; *March (Valuation Officer) v Gravesend and Northfleet Football Club Ltd* (1959) 4 RRC 299, Lands Tribunal. In *Tomlinson (Valuation Officer) v City of Plymouth and Plymouth Argyle Football Co Ltd* (1958) 4 RRC 272, Lands Tribunal (revsd on other grounds (1960) 53 R & IT 297, CA), a valuation by reference to gate receipts was rejected.

16 *Brecon Markets Co v St Mary's, Brecon* (1877) 36 LT 109; *Taunton Borough Council v Sture (Valuation Officer)* (1958) 4 RRC 32, Lands Tribunal; *Oswestry Corpn v Plumpton (Valuation Officer)* [1962] RVR 44, Lands Tribunal; *Thrapston Market v Newton (Valuation Officer)* [1968] RA 415, Lands Tribunal; *Re The Appeal of Ash (Valuation Officer)* [2009] RA 12, Lands Tribunal.

17 See eg *Denaby and Cadeby Colliery Co v Doncaster Union Assessment Committee* (1898) 78 LT 388; *R v Westbrook, R v Everist* (1847) 10 QB 178. Cf *R v North Aylesford Union* (1872) 37 JP 148. As to the valuation of mines, quarries etc generally see PARA 174 et seq.

18 *Surrey County Valuation Committee v Chessington Zoo Ltd* [1950] 1 KB 640, [1950] 1 All ER 154, DC.

19 *Amalgamated Relays Ltd v Burnley Rating Authority* [1950] 2 KB 183, [1950] 1 All ER 253, DC.

20 *Margate Pier and Harbour Co v Yorke (Valuation Officer)* (1955) 48 R & IT 107, Lands Tribunal; *Underdown (Valuation Officer) v Clacton UDC and Clacton Pier Co Ltd* (1958) 3 RRC 274, Lands Tribunal; *Brighton Marine Palace and Pier Co v Rees (Valuation Officer)* [1961] RVR 614, Lands Tribunal.

21 *Bailey v Parsons (Valuations Officer)* (1956) 1 RRC 35, Lands Tribunal; *Bailey v Bognor Regis UDC* (1957) 1 RRC 288, CA; *Hake and Wright v Chandler (Valuation Officer)* (1957) 2 RRC 23, Lands Tribunal (on appeal (1958) 3 RRC 219, CA); *Welford v Cutts (Valuation Officer)* (1958) 3 RRC 323, Lands Tribunal; *Davies v Tavener (Valuation Officer)* (1959) 5 RRC 6. See also *Silvester v Payne (Valuation Officer)* (1959) 4 RRC 315, Lands Tribunal; *Fairlight & Co Ltd v Payne (Valuation Officer)* (1959) 4 RRC 318, Lands Tribunal (camps of holiday chalets); *Isle of Wight RDC v Woodward (Valuation Officer) and Dabell* (1958) 3 RRC 297, Lands Tribunal (natural gorge and model village); *Hodgkinson v Hallett (Valuation Officer)* (1960) 53 R & IT 245, Lands Tribunal (public house and caravan site); *Sussex Caravan Parks Ltd v Richardson (Valuation Officer) and Hastings Borough Council* (1960) 7 RRC 247, Lands Tribunal (revsd [1961] 1 All ER 731, [1961] 1 WLR 561, CA). As to the rating of caravan sites see also the Local Government Finance Act 1988 Sch 6 para 2B; and PARA 168.

22 *R v St Mary Abbot's, Kensington* (1840) 12 Ad & El 824; *R v Abney Park Cemetery Co* (1873) LR 8 QB 515; *R v St Giles, Camberwell Inhabitants* (1850) 14 QB 571. Cf *Bingley UDC v Melville (Valuation Officer)* (1969) 16 RRC 173, Lands Tribunal; *Gudgion (Valuation Officer) v Croydon Borough Council* (1970) 16 RRC 305, Lands Tribunal, where the profits basis was considered inappropriate in respect of cemeteries run at a loss by local authorities.

23 *Melville and Rees (Valuation Officers) v Airedale and Wharfdale Joint Crematorium Committee* [1963] RVR 201, Lands Tribunal.

24 *Rank Organisation Ltd v Billett (Valuation Officer)* (1958) 4 RRC 15, Lands Tribunal.

25 See PARA 157 et seq.

26 *R v Sherford Inhabitants* (1867) LR 2 QB 503; *R v Rhymney Rly Co* (1869) LR 4 QB 276; and see *Davies v Seisdon Union* [1908] AC 315, HL.

27 *Tranter (Valuation Officer) v National Association of Local Government Officers* (1951) 44 R & IT 662, Lands Tribunal; *Welford v Cutts (Valuation Officer)* (1958) 3 RRC 323, Lands Tribunal; *Amble Club Ltd v Robertson (Valuation Officer)* (1958) 4 RRC 9, Lands Tribunal; *Brickwoods Ltd v Cousins (Valuation Officer)* [1968] RA 243, Lands Tribunal; *Sculcoates Union v Kingston-upon-Hull Dock Co* [1895] AC 136 at 147, 148, HL.

28 *Watney Mann Ltd v Langley (Valuation Officer)* [1966] 1 QB 457, [1963] 3 All ER 967. As to valuation officers see PARA 54. As to rating lists see PARA 188 et seq. As to the alteration of lists see PARA 199 et seq.

185. Calculation of value on the 'profits' basis.

The method of valuation on the 'profits' basis is first to ascertain the annual value of the undertaking as a whole[1]. If the undertaking is situated in the area of more than one billing authority[2], it may be necessary to apportion the value so ascertained amongst the various areas concerned[3].

The valuation of the hereditament is based upon the profits which are made or which (subject to any statutory limitations[4]) are capable of being made there[5]. The gross receipts, which form the starting point of the calculation, are those shown in the occupier's accounts for the last account year concluded before the antecedent valuation date[6]; and, if relevant, accounts available at the date of the hearing of an appeal may be admissible in evidence[7].

The gross receipts include any payments (such as the proceeds of water charges) received by the occupier, and proceeds of precepts on other authorities[8]; but contributions made by the government towards the expenses incurred by a water authority in connection with rural water supplies are to be left out of account[9].

When the gross receipts have been ascertained, the next step is to deduct from them the expenses of earning those receipts[10], and the cost of economic repairs, insurance and other expenses necessary to maintain the undertaking in a state to command the hypothetical rent[11]. Provision may be made for a sinking fund for the renewal of any wasting parts of the undertaking[12]. The remaining balance is divisible between the tenant (the 'tenant's share'[13]), the landlord (the hypothetical rent or net annual value) and rates. The tenant's share is often estimated by applying a percentage to the tenant's capital[14], but in other cases it may be taken directly as a proportion of the divisible balance[15] or by applying a percentage to the gross receipts[16].

1 This is commonly known as the 'cumulo'. As to valuation on the profits basis generally see PARA 184. As to valuation for rating see PARA 156 et seq. As to the hereditament see PARA 106.

2 As to billing authorities see PARA 53.

3 Given the provisions which govern hereditaments divided by a boundary between billing authorities (see the Non-Domestic Rating (Miscellaneous Provisions) Regulations 1989, SI 1989/1060, reg 6; and PARA 106) and the fact that many properties of this sort are rated under the central rating list, the occasions on which such apportionment will be necessary are expected to be rare. As to rating lists see PARA 188 et seq.

4 *Worcester Corpn v Droitwich Union Assessment Committee* (1876) 2 Ex D 49, CA; *Sculcoates Union v Kingston-upon-Hull Dock Co* [1895] AC 136, HL.

The cases cited in this paragraph were decided prior to the coming into force of the Local Government Finance Act 1988 but continue to be of relevance: see PARA 50.

5 *Sculcoates Union v Kingston-upon-Hull Dock Co* [1895] AC 136 at 147–148, HL, per Lord Herschell LC. The principle that the premises are to be valued vacant and to let (see PARA 163) requires that the profits to be considered are those of the hypothetical tenant: *Watney Mann Ltd v Langley (Valuation Officer)* [1966] 1 QB 457 at 476, [1963] 3 All ER 967 at 979; and see the cases cited in PARA 184 notes 27–27.

6 In *Barking Rating Authority v Central Electricity Board* [1940] 2 KB 51, [1940] 2 All ER 341 (affd [1940] 2 KB 493, [1940] 3 All ER 477, CA), the concern was with accounts and estimates for periods after the date of the proposal, which at that time was the date of valuation. It would seem that applying the same principles in the context of the Local Government Finance Act 1988, the appropriate accounts are those for the year before the antecedent valuation date.

7 *Bwllfa and Merthyr Dare Steam Collieries (1891) Ltd v Pontypridd Waterworks Co* [1903] AC 426, HL; *LCC v Tobin* [1959] 1 All ER 649, [1959] 1 WLR 354, CA; *Lincolnshire Sugar Co Ltd v Smart (Inspector of Taxes)* [1937] 1 All ER 413 at 419, HL, per Lord Macmillan; *British Transport Commission v Hingley and Robinson (Valuation Officers) and Grimsby RDC* (1960) 7 RRC 225, Lands Tribunal; *Garton v Hunter (Valuation Officer)* [1969] 2 QB 37, [1969] 1 All ER 451, CA.

8 *Dewsbury and Heckmondwike Waterworks Board v Penistone Union Assessment Committee* (1886) 17 QBD 384, CA; *Merthyr Tydfil Local Board of Health v Merthyr Tydfil Assessment Committee* [1891] 1 QB 186. Proceeds from precepts are part of the gross receipts notwithstanding that the precepts are levied in respect of works under construction and not yet in beneficial occupation: *Mid-Northamptonshire Water Board v Lee (Valuation Officer)* [1958] AC 68, [1957] 2 All ER 143, HL. The proceeds of a rate levied to pay off an old accumulated debt of a gas

undertaking were excluded from the gross receipts in *Lanarkshire Assessor v Lanarkshire County Council* 1933 SC 355, Ct of Sess. In *Denny and Dunipace Magistrates v Stirlingshire Assessor* 1933 SC 388, the proportion of an exchequer grant applicable to a deficiency in the accounts of a municipal water undertaking was included in the gross receipts of the undertaking, but an unemployment grant was excluded from the gross receipts as being exceptional in character.

9 See the Water Industry Act 1991 s 151(3) (repealed subject to savings).

10 Directors' fees may be allowed as an expense: *R v Southampton Dock Co* (1851) 14 QB 587; *Welwyn Garden City Electricity Co Ltd v Barnet Assessment Committee* (1938) 29 R & IT 88; *St Albans City Council v St Albans Waterworks Co and Clare (Valuation Officer)* (1954) 47 R & IT 191, Lands Tribunal; *Margate Pier and Harbour Co v Yorke (Valuation Officer)* (1955) 48 R & IT 107, Lands Tribunal; *Brighton Marine Palace and Pier Co v Rees (Valuation Officer)* [1961] RVR 614, Lands Tribunal. However, no deduction falls to be made for income tax (*R v Southampton Dock Co* above) or any additional tax (*Yeovil RDC v South Somerset and District Electricity Co Ltd* [1948] 1 KB 130, [1947] 1 All ER 669, CA), although liability to additional tax may be taken into account in fixing the tenant's share of profits (*Yeovil RDC v South Somerset and District Electricity Co Ltd* above).

11 Ie expenses which fall on the hypothetical tenant under the statutory hypothesis which is used for assessing rateable value: see PARA 157 et seq.

12 *R v London, Brighton and South Coast Rly Co* (1851) 15 QB 313 at 364–366; *Birmingham City Council v Bromsgrove RDC and Linley (Valuation Officer)* (1955) 48 R & IT 511, 530, Lands Tribunal. A reservoir is not an appropriate subject for a sinking fund: *Birmingham City Council v Bromsgrove RDC and Linley (Valuation Officer)* above. Cf *Humber Ltd v Jones (Valuation Officer) and Rugby RDC* (1959) 5 RRC 23, Lands Tribunal (on appeal on other points (1960) 53 R & IT 293, CA). A pier with a structural life of 100 years may be the subject of a sinking fund: *Underdown (Valuation Officer) v Clacton UDC and Clacton Pier Co Ltd* (1958) 3 RRC 274, Lands Tribunal; *Brighton Marine Palace and Pier Co v Rees (Valuation Officer)* [1961] RVR 614, Lands Tribunal.

13 The tenant's share must cover interest on tenant's capital, remuneration for his industry and compensation for risk: *St James' and Pall Mall Electric Light Co Ltd v Westminster Assessment Committee* [1934] AC 33 at 42, HL, per Lord Atkin; *Railway Assessment Authority v Southern Rly Co* [1936] AC 266, [1936] 1 All ER 26, HL. Cf *London Midland and Scottish Rly Co v Assessor of Railways and Canals Scotland* 1933 SC 590.

14 See eg *R v Southampton Dock Co* (1851) 14 QB 587; *Underdown (Valuation Officer) v Clacton UDC and Clacton Pier Co Ltd* (1958) 3 RRC 274, Lands Tribunal.

15 See eg *AL Mather Ltd v Cockcroft (Valuation Officer)* (1958) 51 R & IT 819, Lands Tribunal; *Silvester v Payne (Valuation Officer)* (1959) 4 RRC 315, Lands Tribunal; *Fairlight & Co Ltd v Payne (Valuation Officer)* (1959) 4 RRC 318, Lands Tribunal; *Isle of Wight RDC v Woodward (Valuation Officer) and Dabell* (1958) 3 RRC 297, Lands Tribunal; *City of Sheffield v John Smith's Tadcaster Brewery Co Ltd and Tranter (Valuation Officer)* (1958) 3 RRC 191, Lands Tribunal; *Williamson (Valuation Officer) v Hayes and Hauber's Executors and Trustees of Roman Catholic Diocese of Southwark* (1959) 5 RRC 119, Lands Tribunal.

16 In practice, this was commonly done in the case of water undertakings because so little tenant's capital was needed that a calculation of tenant's share on that basis would give a fallacious result.

186. Valuation with reference to cost of construction: the 'contractor's basis'. Where actual rents do not afford sufficient evidence of annual rental value, a percentage of the cost of construction or structural value of the hereditament, or of a substitute hereditament, is sometimes taken as evidence[1]. The 'contractor's basis' (as this method is called) is applied in five stages[2]:

(1) estimation of the cost of construction of a replacement hereditament[3];

(2) adjustment to reflect differences between the actual hereditament and the alternative, thus arriving at the effective capital value[4];

(3) addition of the value of the land on which the hereditament stands[5];

(4) decapitalisation of the effective capital value by application of the appropriate percentage[6]; and

(5) final adjustment by the valuer to ensure that his valuation has taken into account all factors affecting value and that the result reflects what the prospective tenant would be willing and able to pay[7].

This method of valuation has been applied, for instance, to the indirectly productive parts of public utility undertakings (such as waterworks[8]), to a chemical works[9], to municipal property (such as schools[10], sewage treatment works[11], former sewage systems[12], a town hall[13], a fire station[14], a swimming pool[15], a local authority leisure centre[16] and public conveniences[17]), to a magistrates' court[18], to colleges and university buildings[19], public schools[20], a geological museum[21], a lighthouse[22], an old people's home[23], a nursing home[24], a community centre[25], a football stadium[26], a cricket ground[27], an indoor bowling stadium[28], a tennis centre[29], an airport[30], coke ovens[31], a factory[32], a broiler house[33], a car park[34], and to plant and machinery[35]. However, the selling price of houses[36] and the capital value of licensed premises[37] have been discounted as evidence.

1 As to valuation for rating see PARA 156 et seq. As to the hereditament see PARA 106. Although the statutory measure of rateable value is the rent which might reasonably be expected (see PARA 157 et seq), interest on cost or capital value may be evidence of what a tenant might reasonably be expected to pay. The explanation for the use of this method of valuation (often referred to as the 'contractor's basis') is that the hypothetical tenant will be unwilling to pay more as an annual rent than it would cost him in annual interest on the capital sum necessary to build a similar hereditament (the 'effective capital value'): see *Dawkins (Valuation Officer) v Royal Leamington Spa Borough Council and Warwickshire County Council* [1961] RVR 291 at 295, Lands Tribunal, per Sir William FitzGerald, citing the argument of Sir Jocelyn Simon QC; approved in *Cardiff Corpn v Williams (Valuation Officer)* [1973] RA 46 at 51–52, 18 RRC 1 at 22–23, CA, per Lord Denning. However, this method may do no more than indicate an upper limit (*Crofton Investment Trust Ltd v Greater London Rent Assessment Committee* [1967] 2 QB 955, [1967] 2 All ER 1103, DC) and the annual rent resulting ought to be much below the interest charge in order to allow for any appreciation in capital value that accrues to an owner-occupier (*vice* yearly tenant) over time (see *Cardiff Corpn v Williams (Valuation Officer)* [1973] RA 46 at 51–52, 18 RRC 1 at 22–23, CA, per Lord Denning). See also *Monsanto plc v Farris (Valuation Officer)* [1999] 1 EGLR 199, [1998] RA 107, Lands Tribunal.

The use of this method of valuation in appropriate cases is amply supported by authority: see eg *R v London School Board* (1855) 55 LJMC 33 at 38 (on appeal (1886) 17 QBD 738, CA); *Liverpool Corpn v Llanfyllin Assessment Committee* [1899] 2 QB 14 at 20–22, CA; *Robinson Bros (Brewers) Ltd v Houghton and Chester-le-Street Assessment Committee* [1937] 2 KB 445 at 481, [1937] 2 All ER 298 at 315, CA; *Imperial College of Science and Technology v Ebdon (Valuation Officer)* [1986] RA 233, [1987] 1 EGLR 164, CA; but cf *Great Central Rly Co v Banbury Union* [1909] AC 78 at 86–87, HL. Even where rental evidence is available, a valuation on the contractor's basis is admissible: *Garton v Hunter (Valuation Officer)* [1969] 2 QB 37, [1969] 1 All ER 451, CA.

Many of the cases cited in this paragraph were decided prior to the coming into force of the Local Government Finance Act 1988 but continue to be of relevance: see PARA 50.

2 See *Gilmore (Valuation Officer) v Baker-Carr (No 2)* [1964] RVR 7, where the five stages were referred to. See also *Imperial College of Science and Technology v Ebdon (Valuation Officer)* [1984] RA 213, [1985] 1 EGLR 209, Lands Tribunal; affd [1986] RA 233, [1987] 1 EGLR 164, CA, where a possible sixth stage was suggested. In *Monsanto plc v Farris (Valuation Officer)* [1999] 1 EGLR 199, [1998] RA 107, Lands Tribunal, it was stated that an economic framework for valuation should be maintained to afford credibility to the contractor's basis of valuation but that such a framework can be preserved without a literal interpretation of the principles cited in *Dawkins (Valuation Officer) v Royal Leamington Spa Borough Council and Warwickshire County Council* [1961] RVR 291, Lands Tribunal (see note 1) by the device of regarding the hypothetical tenant as a prospective purchaser of the hereditament for stages 1, 2 and 3 of the valuation (see heads (1)–(3) in the text) (the 'capital sum stages') and then as the hypothetical tenant of rating for stages 4 and 5 (see heads (4) and (5) in the text) (the 'annual value stages').

3 It is disputed whether one should assess the cost of replacing the actual building or the cost of constructing an alternative building. Where the building on the hereditament is old-fashioned, has excessive ornamentation or much excess capacity, it is sometimes convenient to cost not a replica of the actual building but a modern equivalent. The replacement of the actual building method was preferred in *Magdalen, Jesus and Keble Colleges, Oxford v Howard (Valuation Officer) and City of Oxford* (1959) 5 RRC 122, Lands Tribunal (on appeal [1961] RVR 22, CA); *Downing, Newnham, Churchill and King's Colleges, Cambridge v City of Cambridge and Allsop (Valuation*

Officer) [1968] RA 603, Lands Tribunal; *St Catherine's, St Hilda's and Magdalen Colleges, Oxford v Howard (Valuation Officer) and City of Oxford* [1968] RA 627, Lands Tribunal. See also *Shrewsbury Schools v Shrewsbury Borough Council and Plumpton (Valuation Officer)* (1960) 7 RRC 313, Lands Tribunal. The substitute building method was preferred in *Dawkins (Valuation Officer) v Royal Leamington Spa Borough Council and Warwickshire County Council* [1961] RVR 291, Lands Tribunal.

4 This includes taking into account the building's excess capacity and technical obsolescence: see note 3. In *Eastbourne Borough Council v Allen (Valuation Officer)* [2001] RA 273, Lands Tribunal, the application of the contractor's basis to the existing elderly facilities presented a number of problems and valuing a 'modern simple substitute' was agreed in that case to be the best way to take account of such problems.

5 The land must be valued as if it is limited to its existing use with its existing buildings: see eg *Oxford University v Oxford Corpn* (1902) Ryde & K Rat App 87; *Dawkins (Valuation Officer) v Royal Leamington Spa Borough Council and Warwickshire County Council* [1961] RVR 291, Lands Tribunal; *Oswestry Corpn v Plumpton (Valuation Officer)* (1961) 9 RRC 153, Lands Tribunal; *Downing, Newnham, Churchill and King's Colleges, Cambridge v City of Cambridge and Allsop (Valuation Officer)* [1968] RA 603, Lands Tribunal.

6 The Local Government Finance Act 1988 Sch 6 para 2(8) (see PARA 166) empowers the Secretary of State or, in relation to Wales, the Welsh Ministers to prescribe the decapitalisation rate. This power has been exercised in relation to all rating lists compiled since 1 April 1990: see the Non-Domestic Rating (Miscellaneous Provisions) (No 2) Regulations 1989, SI 1989/2303, reg 2 (amended by SI 1993/544, SI 1994/3122, SI 2000/532, SI 2000/908, SI 2004/1000, SI 2004/1494, SI 2008/2997, SI 2010/1172, SI 2015/1759 and SI 2016/777). The purpose of the prescribed decapitalisation rate is discussed in *Eastbourne Borough Council v Allen (Valuation Officer)* [2001] RA 273, Lands Tribunal; and *Lavery (Valuation Officer) v Leeds City Council* [2002] RA 165, Lands Tribunal.

7 As to some of the factors which may be applied in assessing what a hypothetical tenant would pay see *Cardiff Corpn v Williams (Valuation Officer)* [1973] RA 46 at 51–52, 18 RRC 1 at 22–23, CA, per Lord Denning (teachers' training college). Where specifically targeted capital grants have been paid, an apportioned and discounted sum (relative to instalments) is properly deducted before the finalisation of the effective capital value: *Monsanto plc v Farris (Valuation Officer)* [1999] 1 EGLR 199, [1998] RA 107, Lands Tribunal (impact of the grant regime upon rental values of industrial or kindred hereditaments in the local market at the material date should be used to judge the effect, if any, upon rental value of the subject hereditament). As to this final stage of the method see also *Eastbourne Borough Council v Allen (Valuation Officer)* [2001] RA 273, Lands Tribunal; *Lavery (Valuation Officer) v Leeds City Council* [2002] RA 165, Lands Tribunal; and *Winchester City Council v Handcock (Valuation Officer)* [2006] RA 265, Lands Tribunal.

8 See eg *R v West Middlesex Waterworks* (1859) 28 LJMC 135; *Kingston Union Assessment Committee v Metropolitan Water Board* [1926] AC 331, HL; *Liverpool Corpn v Llanfyllin Assessment Committee* [1899] 2 QB 14, CA; *Liverpool Corpn v Chorley Union Assessment Committee and Withnell Overseers* [1912] 1 KB 270, CA (affd [1913] AC 197, HL). However, in *City of Birmingham Water Department v Hughes (Valuation Officer) and Knighton RDC* (1957) 2 RRC 248, Lands Tribunal, no allowance for age and obsolescence was made.

9 *Monsanto plc v Farris (Valuation Officer)* [1999] 1 EGLR 199, [1998] RA 107, Lands Tribunal.

10 *R v London School Board* (1886) 17 QBD 738, CA; *London School Board v Wandsworth and Clapham Unions Assessment Committee* (1900) Ryde & K Rat App 24, DC; *Dawkins (Valuation Officer) v Royal Leamington Spa Corpn Borough Council and Warwickshire County Council* [1961] RVR 291, Lands Tribunal.

11 *Winchester City Council v Handcock (Valuation Officer)* [2006] RA 265, Lands Tribunal.

12 *Hall v Seisdon Union Assessment Committee* (1912) 77 JP 17, DC; *Davies v Seisdon Union* [1907] 1 KB 630, CA (affd [1908] AC 315, HL); cf *LCC v Churchwardens etc of Erith Parish and Dartford Union Assessment Committee* [1893] AC 562, HL.

13 *Chandler (Valuation Officer) v East Suffolk County Council* (1958) 3 RRC 328, Lands Tribunal.

14 *North Riding of Yorkshire County Council v Bell (Valuation Officer)* (1958) 3 RRC 133, Lands Tribunal.

15 *Woking UDC v Baker (Valuation Officer)* (1959) 4 RRC 330, Lands Tribunal.

16 *Eastbourne Borough Council v Allen (Valuation Officer)* [2001] RA 273, Lands Tribunal.

17 *Bell (Valuation Officer) v Colne Borough Council* (1959) 6 RRC 36, Lands Tribunal.

18 *Lavery (Valuation Officer) v Leeds City Council* [2002] RA 165, Lands Tribunal.

19 *Oxford University v Oxford Corpn* (1902) Ryde & K Rat App 87 (quarter sessions); *Magdalen, Jesus and Keble Colleges, Oxford v Howard (Valuation Officer) and City of Oxford* (1959) 5 RRC 122, Lands Tribunal (on appeal [1961] RVR 22, CA); *Leeds University v Leeds City Council and Burge (Valuation Officer)* [1962] RVR 311, Lands Tribunal; *Downing, Newnham, Churchill and*

King's Colleges, Cambridge v City of Cambridge and Allsop (Valuation Officer) [1968] RA 603, Lands Tribunal; *St Catherine's, St Hilda's and Magdalen Colleges, Oxford v Howard (Valuation Officer) and City of Oxford* [1968] RA 627, Lands Tribunal; *Imperial College of Science and Technology v Ebdon (Valuation Officer)* [1986] RA 233, [1987] 1 EGLR 164, CA.

20 *Shrewsbury Schools v Shrewsbury Borough Council and Plumpton (Valuation Officer)* (1960) 7 RRC 313, Lands Tribunal; *Shrewsbury Schools Governors v Hudd (Valuation Officer)* [1966] RA 439, Land Tribunal; *Eton College (Provost and Fellows) v Lane (Valuation Officer) and Eton RDC* (1971) 17 RRC 152, Lands Tribunal.

21 *Cambridge University v Cambridge Union* (1905) 1 Konst Rat App 105.

22 *Lancaster Port Comrs v Barrow-in-Furness Overseers* [1897] 1 QB 166, DC.

23 *Davey (Valuation Officer) v God's Port Housing Society Ltd* (1958) 4 RRC 18, Lands Tribunal.

24 *Leicester City Council v Nuffield Nursing Homes Trust* [1979] RA 299.

25 *West Linton and District Community Centre Trustees v Assessor for East Lothian, Berwick and Peebles* [1963] RVR 12, Lands Tribunal for Scotland.

26 *Tomlinson (Valuation Officer) v City of Plymouth and Plymouth Argyle Football Co Ltd* (1958) 4 RRC 272, Lands Tribunal; on appeal (1960) 6 RRC 173, CA.

27 *Warwickshire County Cricket Club v Rennick (Valuation Officer)* (1959) 5 RRC 322, Lands Tribunal. Cf *Marylebone Cricket Club v Morley* (1959) 6 RRC 258, Lands Tribunal.

28 *Lanarkshire Assessor v Lanarkshire Indoor Bowling Club* [1965] RA 497.

29 *Willacre Ltd (t/a David Lloyd Slazenger Racquet Club) v Bond (Valuation Officer)* [1987] RA 199, [1986] 1 EGLR 224, Lands Tribunal.

30 *Coppin v East Midlands Airport Joint Committee* (1970) 16 RRC 386, Lands Tribunal; on appeal [1971] RA 449, 17 RRC 31, CA.

31 *Birchenwood Gas and Coke Co Ltd v Hampshire (Valuation Officer)* (1959) 4 RRC 303, Lands Tribunal. Cf *Thomas (Valuation Officer) v Manor Vinegar Brewery Co Ltd* (1960) 6 RRC 353, Lands Tribunal (vinegar vats).

32 *British Aluminium Co Ltd v Inverness-shire Assessor* 1937 SC 566, Ct of Sess.

33 *Gilmore (Valuation Officer) v Baker-Carr (No 2)* [1963] RA 458, Lands Tribunal.

34 *Stoke on Trent City Council v McMillan (Valuation Officer)* [1979] RA 359, Lands Tribunal; cf *National Car Parks Ltd v Gudgion (Valuation Officer)* [1979] RA 85, Lands Tribunal.

35 See eg *Birchenwood Gas and Coke Co Ltd v Hampshire (Valuation Officer)* (1959) 4 RRC 303, Lands Tribunal; *Thomas (Valuation Officer) v Manor Vinegar Brewery Co Ltd* (1960) 6 RRC 353, Lands Tribunal; *Shell-Mex and BP Ltd v James (Valuation Officer)* [1961] RVR 106, Lands Tribunal; *Staffordshire Potteries (Holdings) Ltd v Garner (Valuation Officer)* [1967] RA 31, Lands Tribunal. As to the valuation of plant and machinery see also PARA 172 et seq.

36 *Peche v Wilkins (Valuation Officer)* (1959) 4 RRC 49, CA; *Sole v Henning (Valuation Officer)* [1959] 3 All ER 398, [1959] 1 WLR 769, CA; *Munday v Mason (Valuation Officer)* (1960) 7 RRC 109, CA; *Daniels v Peak (Valuation Officer)* [1964] RA 113, CA; see also *Nicholls v Blyth (Valuation Officer)* (1957) 2 RRC 6 at 9, Lands Tribunal; *Eastaway v Rees (Valuation Officer)* (1957) 2 RRC 147 at 150, Lands Tribunal. However, capital values may not be wholly irrelevant: see *Barnard and Barnard v Walker (Valuation Officer)* [1975] RA 383, Lands Tribunal; *Barb v Hayes (Valuation Officer)* (1978) 21 RRC 128, Lands Tribunal.

37 *Sheffield Corpn v John Smith's Tadcaster Brewery Co Ltd and Tranter (Valuation Officer)* (1958) 3 RRC 191, Lands Tribunal. As to the valuation of licensed premises see also PARA 179 et seq.

187. Evidence of assessments of comparable hereditaments.

Evidence may be given of the assessments of comparable hereditaments[1]. To be of use the comparable hereditaments should normally[2] be drawn from the same area as the hereditament under review[3], although this limitation does not apply if the purpose of referring to the comparable hereditaments is to establish valuation practice and method[4]. Comparable assessments may be of little evidential value early in the life of a list when the 'tone of the list' has yet to be established[5]. An assessment under appeal is normally excluded from consideration[6]. A valuation officer will not be allowed to impugn his own list[7]. The admissibility of assessments does not render admissible statements as to the basis of assessment made by a valuation officer who is not party to the proceedings[8].

1 *Pointer v Norwich Assessment Committee* [1922] 2 KB 471, CA; *Stockbridge Mill Co Ltd v Central Land Board* [1954] 2 All ER 360, [1954] 1 WLR 886, CA; *Howarth v Price (Valuation Officer)* (1965) 11 RRC 196, Lands Tribunal; *F Cross & Sons v Spencer (Valuation Officer)* [2000] RA 71, Lands Tribunal (valuation based on comparable assessment with allowances for

poor location and fact that ratepayer was only potential tenant); *HJ Banks & Co Ltd v Speight (Valuation Officer)* [2005] RA 61, Lands Tribunal (comparison of rental values the correct comparative measure). Cf *Lamb v Minards (Valuation Officer)* [1974] RA 153, Lands Tribunal. As to valuation for rating generally see PARA 156 et seq. As to the hereditament see PARA 106.

Most of the cases cited in this paragraph were decided prior to the coming into force of the Local Government Finance Act 1988 but continue to be of relevance: see PARA 50.

2 Assessments from a wide area have been admitted in relation to a golf club (*Stourbridge Golf Club Ltd v Clark (Valuation Officer)* (1959) 5 RRC 38, Lands Tribunal; cf *Prince's Golf Club (Sandwich) Ltd v Millwood (Valuation Officer)* [1961] RVR 246, Lands Tribunal); an advertising station (*Frank Mason & Co Ltd v Thomas (Valuation Officer)* [1962] RVR 147, Lands Tribunal); a petrol filling station (*Petrofina (GB) Ltd v Dalby (Valuation Officer)* [1967] RA 143, Lands Tribunal); a hotel (*Strand Hotels Ltd v Hampsher (Valuation Officer)* [1977] RA 265, Lands Tribunal); a public school (*Shrewsbury Schools v Shrewsbury Borough Council and Plumpton (Valuation Officer)* (1960) 7 RRC 313, Lands Tribunal); universities (*Imperial College of Science and Technology v Ebdon (Valuation Officer)* [1986] RA 233, [1987] 1 EGLR 164, CA); and private opencast coal sites (*HJ Banks & Co Ltd v Speight (Valuation Officer)* [2005] RA 61, Lands Tribunal).

3 *Eastaway v Rees (Valuation Officer)* (1957) 2 RRC 147, Lands Tribunal; *William Hill (Hove) Ltd v Burton (Valuation Officer)* (1958) 3 RRC 355, Lands Tribunal. However, this does not necessarily mean the same billing authority area: *Sleet v Holman (Valuation Officer)* [1966] RA 589, Lands Tribunal; *Royal Naval Association (Runcorn Branch) v Owen (Valuation Officer) and Runcorn UDC* (1967) 13 RRC 58, Lands Tribunal. As to billing authorities see PARA 53.

4 *William Hill (Hove) Ltd v Burton (Valuation Officer)* (1958) 3 RRC 355, Lands Tribunal; *Footman, Pretty & Co v Chandler (Valuation Officer)* (1960) 7 RRC 18, Lands Tribunal; cf *Harrow Corpn v Betts (Valuation Officer)* (1960) 7 RRC 328, Lands Tribunal.

5 *Marks v Eastaugh (Valuation Officer)* [1993] RA 11, Lands Tribunal. See also *K Shoe Shops Ltd v Hardy (Valuation Officer)* [1983] 3 All ER 609, sub nom *Saxone Shoe Co Ltd v Hardy (Valuation Officer) and Westminster City Council* [1983] 1 WLR 1273, HL; and *Jafton Properties Ltd v Prisk (Valuation Officer)* [1997] RA 137, Lands Tribunal. In the latter case, three stages were identified leading to the establishment of 'tone of the list', the final stage being reached when enough assessments of comparable hereditaments have been settled or are unchallenged to establish a pattern of established values: see *Jafton Properties Ltd v Prisk (Valuation Officer)* above at 166–167. For more recent cases in which, by reference to the earlier authorities, the Lands Tribunal has examined the principles upon which evidence of assessments of comparable hereditaments is relied upon for the purposes of determining rateable value, and the stages against which the question whether a 'tone of the list' has been established falls to be considered, see *HJ Banks & Co Ltd v Speight (Valuation Officer)* [2005] RA 61, Lands Tribunal; and *O'Brien v Harwood (Valuation Officer)* [2003] RA 244, Lands Tribunal.

6 *Thomas Scott & Sons (Bakers) Ltd v Davis (Valuation Officer)* [1969] RA 444, Lands Tribunal.

7 *Borroughs Machines Ltd v Mooney (Valuation Officer)* (1976) 20 RRC 324, Lands Tribunal; *Mitchelhill v Slingsby (Valuation Officer)* (1978) 21 RRC 261, Lands Tribunal; *HJ Banks & Co Ltd v Speight (Valuation Officer)* [2005] RA 61, Lands Tribunal. As to valuation officers see PARA 54.

8 *Austin Motor Co Ltd v Woodward (Valuation Officer)* [1968] RA 133, Lands Tribunal.

(9) Rating Lists

(i) Introduction

188. Historical background.

Prior to the Local Government Finance Act 1988, valuation officers prepared and maintained valuation lists for each rating area under the General Rate Act 1967 (now repealed)[1]. Valuation lists contained a description of every hereditament in a rating area, including all domestic or non-domestic property and its value. No distinction was made as between residential and other types of hereditament in the way in which they were treated for rating purposes. Entries in the valuation lists could be subject to objections by persons aggrieved[2], and objections could result in appeals provided for by statutory procedure. As originally enacted, the General Rate Act 1967 provided for new valuation lists to be prepared every five years, but later this was altered by new lists being prepared so as to come into force on 1 April in such year as the Secretary of State specified by order[3]. Every hereditament had to be entered in the list, whether occupied or not[4]. Amendments could be made to the list by proposals from either the valuation officer or persons aggrieved[5]. Generally, alterations had effect from the date the list was made, except where the list was altered to include newly erected or altered hereditaments[6]. Appeals against an entry in the valuation list were heard by local valuation courts[7], with a further right of appeal to the Lands Tribunal[8] and thence to the Court of Appeal on a point of law by way of case stated[9].

1 A rating area was an area covered by a rating authority. Outside the London area, the rating authorities were the district councils; in London, the rating authorities were the London borough councils and the Common Council for the City of London: see the General Rate Act 1967 s 1 (repealed). As to rating lists see Pt V (ss 67–95) (repealed). As to the position under the Local Government Finance Act 1988 see PARA 189. As to the historical development of rating law see PARA 50.

2 For rating purposes, a person aggrieved was usually the ratepayer, but it could be the rating authority, a ratepayer in the same area, or a managing agent of premises who received the rents: see generally *Arsenal Football Club Ltd v Smith (Valuation Officer)* [1979] AC 1, [1977] 2 All ER 267, HL; *R v Paddington Valuation Officer, ex p Peachey Property Corpn Ltd* [1966] 1 QB 380, [1965] 2 All ER 836, CA.

3 See the General Rate Act 1967 ss 67, 68 (both repealed).

4 See *R v Malden Overseers* (1869) LR 4 QB 326, DC; and see *R v The Assessment Committee of the City of London Union* [1907] 2 KB 764 at 789–790, CA, per Fletcher Moulton LJ.

5 As to proposals to alter lists under the General Rate Act 1967 see s 69 (repealed); and as to transitional provisions in relation to non-water hereditaments of a statutory water undertaking see the Local Government Finance Act 1988 s 123.

6 See the General Rate Act 1967 s 79 (repealed).

7 See the General Rate Act 1967 ss 73–76, 88–95 (repealed).

8 See the General Rate Act 1967 s 77 (repealed).

9 See the Lands Tribunal Act 1949 s 3 (repealed in relation to England and Wales).

189. Position under the Local Government Finance Act 1988.

Under the Local Government Finance Act 1988, rating was abolished in relation to domestic property[1]. Valuation officers[2] now have to compile local non-domestic rating lists[3] and central non-domestic rating lists[4], which contain details of all non-domestic hereditaments[5]. Hereditaments in the central valuation list are those designated by regulations[6].

The lists are to be prepared every five years and maintained throughout each five yearly period by the valuation officer, subject to any decision to postpone a revaluation[7]. The valuation officer may cause an alteration to be made to the list[8]. Proposals may be made by a ratepayer to alter the entry in the valuation list[9]. Where the alteration is disputed by the valuation officer, an appeal may be heard by a valuation tribunal[10] to determine the correct entry in the list. An appeal lies from the decision of that tribunal to the Upper Tribunal[11].

1 The Local Government Finance Act 1988 Pt I (ss 1–31), Pt II (ss 32–40) (all repealed) introduced the community charge, which was itself abolished and replaced with the council tax, by virtue of the Local Government Finance Act 1992 ss 100, 117, Schs 13, 14: see PARA 344.

2 As to valuation officers see PARA 54.

3 As to local non-domestic rating lists see PARA 191 et seq.

4 As to central non-domestic rating lists see PARA 196 et seq.

5 As to rating lists generally see PARA 82. As to the meaning of 'hereditament' see PARA 106.

6 See PARA 197.

7 As to the compilation of local non-domestic rating lists, and the postponements of the five year revaluations, see PARA 191. As to the compilation of central non-domestic rating lists see PARA 196.

8 As to alterations to lists by the valuation officer see PARAS 202–212 (local non-domestic rating lists), PARA 224 (central non-domestic rating lists).

9 As to the making of proposals see PARA 202 et seq (local non-domestic rating lists), PARA 224 (central non-domestic rating lists).

10 As to appeals to a valuation tribunal see PARA 242 et seq. There is also provision for arbitration: see PARA 268.

11 As to appeals to the Upper Tribunal see PARA 269.

190. Definition of 'domestic property' for non-domestic rating purposes.

For the purposes of the non-domestic rating provisions[1], property is domestic if[2]:

(1) it is used wholly for the purposes of living accommodation[3];

(2) it is a yard, garden[4], outhouse[5] or other appurtenance[6] belonging to or enjoyed with property falling within head (1)[7];

(3) it is a private garage which either has a floor area of 25 square metres or less or is used wholly or mainly for the accommodation of a private motor vehicle[8]; or

(4) it is private storage premises used wholly or mainly for the storage of articles of domestic use[9].

Property in England is also domestic if it is used wholly or mainly for small scale energy generation using technologies such as solar and wind (microgeneration)[10] and it is situated in or on property which is either used wholly for the purposes of living accommodation, or is a yard, garden, outhouse or other appurtenance belonging to or enjoyed with property used wholly for the purposes of living accommodation[11].

Property is not domestic if it is wholly or mainly used in the course of a business[12] providing short-stay accommodation[13]. However, this definition does not apply if:

(a) it is intended that in the year being considered[14], short-stay accommodation will not be provided within the hereditament[15] for more than six persons simultaneously[16]; and

(b) the person intending to provide such accommodation intends to have his sole or main residence within that hereditament at the same time, and that any use of living accommodation within the hereditament which would otherwise cause it to be treated as non-domestic will be subsidiary to the use of the hereditament for, or in connection with, his sole or main residence[17].

In relation to England[18], a building or self-contained part of a building is not domestic property if:

(i) the relevant person[19] intends that in the year being considered[20], the whole of the building or self-contained part will be available for letting commercially, as self-contained accommodation for short periods totalling 140 days or more[21]; and

(ii) on that day his interest in the building or part is such as to enable him to let it for such periods[22].

In relation to Wales[23], a building or self-contained part of a building is not domestic property if each of the following heads apply in relation to it:

(A) the relevant person intends that, in the year beginning with the end of the day in relation to which the question is being considered, the whole of the building or self-contained part will be available for letting commercially, as self-catering accommodation, for short periods totalling 140 days or more[24];

(B) on that day the relevant person's interest in the building or part is such as to enable the person to let it for such periods[25];

(C) the whole of the building or self-contained part of the building was available for letting commercially, as self-catering accommodation, for short periods totalling 140 days or more in the year prior to the year beginning with end of the day in relation to which the question referred to in head (A) is being considered[26];

(D) the short periods for which it was so let:

(I) amounted in total to at least 70 days[27]; or

(II) taken together with the short periods for which one or more other buildings or self-contained parts of a building so let, amounted to an average of at least 70 days for each building or self-contained part of a building included within the calculation; where each building or self-contained part of the building included in the calculation[28]:

(III) is not included in another calculation under this head for the year in relation to which the question is being considered[29];

(IV) is situated at the same location or in very close proximity to all of the other buildings or self-contained parts of a building included in the calculation[30]; and

(V) is so let as part of the same business or connected businesses[31].

However, neither of these exceptions[32] applies where the building or self-contained part is used as the sole or main residence of any person[33].

Property is not domestic if it is overnight accommodation which is the subject of a timeshare contract[34]; but caravan pitches[35] and moorings[36] are domestic property if certain circumstances are present.

Property not in use is domestic if it appears that when next in use it will be domestic[37].

The appropriate national authority[38] may by order amend, or substitute another definition for, any definition of domestic property for the time being effective for the purposes of the non-domestic rating provisions[39].

1 Ie for the purposes of the Local Government Finance Act 1988 Pt III (ss 41–67): see s 67(13).

2 See the Local Government Finance Act 1988 s 66(1) (amended by SI 1990/162 and SI 2010/682). The Local Government Finance Act 1988 s 66(1) is subject to s 66(2) (see the text to notes 12–13), s 66(2B) (see the text to notes 18–22), s 66(2BB) (see the text to notes 23–31) and s 66(2E) (see the text to note 34): see s 66(1) (as so amended).

3 Local Government Finance Act 1988 s 66(1)(a). As to whether a person's use of a property to work from home allows that property to continue within the scope of this definition see *Tully v Jorgensen (Valuation Officer)* [2003] RA 233, Lands Tribunal (rates liability did not arise in this case where a room was used to carry out employment-related office work because the use remained for the purposes of ordinary domestic living accommodation). See also *Fotheringham v Wood (Valuation Officer)* [1995] RA 315, Lands Tribunal (rates liability arose because persons were employed at the premises in question and some clients visited there); *Bell v Rycroft (Valuation Officer)* [2000] RA 103, Lands Tribunal (rates liability arose because part of the premises had been altered, fitted and staffed for use as a child-care nursery); *Zhou v Osborne (Valuation Officer)* [2008] RA 451, Lands Tribunal (no rates liability: any business use de minimis).

Most of the cases cited in this paragraph were decided prior to the coming into force of the Local Government Finance Act 1988 but continue to be of relevance: see PARA 50.

4 In *Drury-Heath v Wallace (Valuation Officer)* (1960) 7 RRC 104, CA, a separate plot adjoining the occupier's house was held to be an orchard and not a garden, but the court made it clear that an orchard might be part of a garden. In *Bomford v Osborne* [1942] AC 14 at 40 per Lord Wright, the House of Lords cited dictionary definitions of 'garden' which included the idea of its being an enclosed space, and cited the Oxford English Dictionary especially thus: 'a garden is a substantially homogenous area, substantially devoted to the growth of fruits, flowers and vegetables'.

5 An outhouse is a building which belongs to and is part of a dwelling-house: see *Elsmore v St Briavells Inhabitants* (1828) 8 B & C 461; *R v Haughton* (1833) 5 C & P 555; *R v Hammond* (1844) 3 LTOS 342. In *Martin v Hewitt (Valuation Officer)* [2003] RA 275, Lands Tribunal, boathouses on Lake Windermere, whose occupiers lived in houses some distance away, were held not to be outhouses for these purposes.

6 'Appurtenance' in the Local Government Finance Act 1988 s 66(1)(b) was not intended to encompass land or buildings lying outside the curtilage of the property referred to in s 66(1)(a) (see head (1) in the text): *Martin v Hewitt (Valuation Officer)* [2003] RA 275, Lands Tribunal. In *Head (Valuation Officer) v Tower Hamlets London Borough Council* [2005] RA 177, Lands Tribunal, district heating systems, owned and operated by the council to supply heating and hot water to its tenants on council housing estates, were held to be not rateable on the basis of the Local Government Finance Act 1988 s 66(1)(b). However, in *Winchester City Council v Handcock (Valuation Officer)* [2006] RA 265, Lands Tribunal, sewage treatment works were found not to fall within the curtilage of any of the dwellings that they served, and so were rateable. See also *Allen (valuation officer) v Mansfield District Council* [2008] RA 338, Lands Tribunal.

The word 'appurtenance' must be given its normal construction (see *Clymo (Valuation Officer) v Shell-Mex and BP Ltd* [1963] RA 191, [1963] RVR 471, CA) and comprises something appertaining to the principal subject-matter which would normally be included in it without special mention (see *Evans v Angell* (1858) 26 Beav 202).

7 Local Government Finance Act 1988 s 66(1)(b). Only the property mentioned in s 66(1)(b), unlike the garage mentioned in s 66(1)(c) (see head (3) in the text) or the store mentioned in s 66(1)(d) (see head (4) in the text), is required to belong to or be enjoyed with or have any particular physical relationship to a s 66(1)(a) property (see head (1) in the text): see *Andrews (Valuation Officer) v Lumb* [1993] RA 124 at 130, Lands Tribunal.

8 Local Government Finance Act 1988 s 66(1)(c) (amended by SI 1990/162). See also note 7. As to the meaning of the phrase 'wholly or mainly', considered in relation to the rating of charitable property, see: *Fawcett Properties Ltd v Buckingham County Council* [1961] AC 636 at 669, HL, per Lord Morton of Henryton. 'Mainly' probably means more than half: see *Glasgow Corpn v Johnstone* [1965] AC 609, [1965] 1 All ER 730, HL.

9 Local Government Finance Act 1988 s 66(1)(d). See also note 7. Storage in premises quite separate from the house of things to be used for recreation away from the house cannot constitute the storage of articles of domestic use: *Martin v Hewitt (Valuation Officer)* [2003] RA 275, Lands Tribunal (boats in boathouses, stored for use on a lake and not in or about the dwellinghouses, not articles of domestic use). See also *Reeves (Valuation Officer) v Tobias* [2010] UKUT 411 (LC), [2011] RA 149, [2011] 16 EG 80 (car park spaces).

10 Ie the generation of electricity or the production of heat by a source of energy or a technology mentioned in the Climate Change and Sustainable Energy Act 2006 s 26(2), where either the majority of the electricity or heat is generated or produced for use by such persons as may be in the living accommodation, or the plant or equipment used to generate the electricity or produce the heat has a capacity not exceeding 10 kilowatts or 45 kilowatts thermal, as the case may be: Local Government Finance Act 1988 s 66(1B) (s 66(1A), (1B) added by SI 2013/468).

11 Local Government Finance Act 1988 s 66(1A) (as added: see note 10).

12 'Business' includes any activity carried on by a body of persons, whether corporate or unincorporate, and any activity carried on by a charity: Local Government Finance Act 1988 s 66(8A) (added by SI 1990/162). As to the meaning of 'person' see PARA 11 note 13. As to bodies corporate see COMPANIES vol 14 (2016) PARA 2; CORPORATIONS vol 24 (2010) PARA 301 et seq.

13 Local Government Finance Act 1988 s 66(2) (s 66(2) substituted by SI 1990/162). 'Short-stay accommodation' is accommodation:

(1) which is provided for short periods to individuals whose sole or main residence is elsewhere (Local Government Finance Act 1988 s 66(2)(a) (as so substituted)); and

(2) which is not self-contained self-catering accommodation provided commercially (s 66(2)(b) (as so substituted)).

'Commercially' means on a commercial basis, and with a view to the realisation of profits: s 66(8A) (as added: see note 12).

14 Ie the year beginning with the end of the day in relation to which the question is being considered: see the Local Government Finance Act 1988 s 66(2A)(a) (s 66(2A) added by SI 1990/162; and substituted by SI 1991/474).
15 As to the meaning of 'hereditament' see PARA 106.
16 Local Government Finance Act 1988 s 66(2A)(a) (as added and substituted: see note 14).
17 Local Government Finance Act 1988 s 66(2A)(b) (as added and substituted: see note 14).
18 The Local Government Finance Act 1988 s 66(2B) applies only in so far as Pt III (ss 41–67) applies in relation to England: s 66(2AA) (added by SI 2010/682). As to the meaning of 'England' see PARA 2 note 16.
19 For the purposes of the Local Government Finance Act 1988 s 66(2B), (2BB), the 'relevant person' is:
(1) where the building or self-contained part is not subject as a whole to a relevant leasehold interest, the person having the freehold interest in the whole of the building or self-contained part (s 66(2BC)(a) (s 66(2BC) added by the Local Government Finance Act 2012 s 6(1), (2); and amended in relation to Wales by virtue of SI 2016/31)); and
(2) in any other case, any person having a relevant leasehold interest in the building or self-contained part which is not subject (as a whole) to a single relevant leasehold interest inferior to that interest (Local Government Finance Act 1988 s 66(2BC)(b) (as so added and amended)).
'Relevant leasehold interest' means an interest under a lease or underlease which was granted for a term of six months or more and conferred the right to exclusive possession throughout the term: s 66(8A) (as added: see note 12). As to the meaning of 'month' see PARA 11 note 1. There is a clear case of drafting error in s 66(2C)(a), where the word '*building*' ought to be followed by the phrase '*or self contained part*', as in s 66(2C)(b), but the solution to the problem is a matter for Parliament: see *R (on the application of Curzon Berkeley Ltd) v Bliss (Valuation Officer, London Westminster)* [2001] EWHC Admin 1130, [2001] All ER (D) 314 (Dec).
20 Ie the year beginning with the end of the day in relation to which the question is being considered: see the Local Government Finance Act 1988 s 66(2B)(a) (s 66(2B) added by SI 1990/162).
21 Local Government Finance Act 1988 s 66(2B)(a) (as added: see note 20).
22 Local Government Finance Act 1988 s 66(2B)(b) (as added: see note 20).
23 The Local Government Finance Act 1988 s 66(2BB) applies only in so far as Pt III (ss 41–67) applies in relation to Wales: s 66(2BA) (s 66(2BA), (2BB) added by SI 2010/682). As to the meaning of 'Wales' see PARA 2 note 16.
24 Local Government Finance Act 1988 s 66(2BB)(a) (as added: see note 23).
25 Local Government Finance Act 1988 s 66(2BB)(b) (as added: see note 23).
26 Local Government Finance Act 1988 s 66(2BB)(c) (as added: see note 23).
27 Local Government Finance Act 1988 s 66(2BB)(d)(i) (as added (see note 23); s 66(2BB)(d) substituted by SI 2016/31).
28 Local Government Finance Act 1988 s 66(2BB)(d)(ii) (as added (see note 23); and substituted (see note 27)).
29 Local Government Finance Act 1988 s 66(2BB)(d)(ii)(aa) (as added (see note 23); and substituted (see note 27)).
30 Local Government Finance Act 1988 s 66(2BB)(d)(ii)(bb) (as added (see note 23); and substituted (see note 27)).
31 Local Government Finance Act 1988 s 66(2BB)(d)(ii)(cc) (as added (see note 23); and substituted (see note 27)).
32 Ie neither of the Local Government Finance Act 1988 s 66(2B) or s 66(2BB): see the text to notes 18–31.
33 See the Local Government Finance Act 1988 s 66(2D) (added by SI 1990/162; and amended by the Local Government Finance Act 1992 s 117(1), (2), Sch 13 para 70(1), Sch 14; and SI 2010/682).
34 See the Local Government Finance Act 1988 s 66(2E) (added by SI 1993/542; and amended by SI 2010/2960). A 'timeshare contract' is one within the meaning of the Timeshare, Holiday Products, Resale and Exchange Contracts Regulations 2010, SI 2010/2960: see the Local Government Finance Act 1988 s 66(2E) (as so added and amended).
35 The definition of domestic property in the Local Government Finance Act 1988 s 66(1) (see the text to notes 1–9) does not apply in the case of a pitch occupied by a caravan, but if in such a case the caravan is the sole or main residence of an individual, the pitch and the caravan, together with any garden, yard, outhouse or other appurtenance belonging to or enjoyed with them, are domestic property: s 66(3) (substituted by the Rating (Caravans and Boats) Act 1996 s 1). However, this does not have effect in the case of a pitch occupied by a caravan which is an appurtenance enjoyed

with other property to which the Local Government Finance Act 1988 s 66(1)(a) (see head (1) in the text) applies: see s 66(4A) (added by the Rating (Caravans and Boats) Act 1996 s 1). Whether anything is a caravan is to be construed in accordance with the Caravan Sites and Control of Development Act 1960 Pt I (ss 1–32) (see PLANNING vol 83 (2018) PARA 1137): Local Government Finance Act 1988 s 66(7).

36 The definition of domestic property in the Local Government Finance Act 1988 s 66(1) (see the text to notes 1–9) does not apply in the case of a mooring occupied by a boat, but if in such a case the boat is the sole or main residence of an individual, the mooring and the boat, together with any garden, yard, outhouse or other appurtenance belonging to or enjoyed with them, are domestic property: s 66(4) (substituted by the Rating (Caravans and Boats) Act 1996 s 1). However, this does not have effect in the case of a mooring occupied by a boat which is an appurtenance enjoyed with other property to which the Local Government Finance Act 1988 s 66(1)(a) (see head (1) in the text) applies: see s 66(4A) (as added: see note 35).

37 Local Government Finance Act 1988 s 66(5).

38 Ie the Secretary of State or, in relation to Wales, the Welsh Ministers. The functions of the Secretary of State under the Local Government Finance Act 1988 s 66, so far as exercisable in relation to Wales, were transferred to the National Assembly for Wales (see the National Assembly for Wales (Transfer of Functions) Order 1999, SI 1999/672, art 2, Sch 1) and are now vested in the Welsh Ministers (see the Government of Wales Act 2006 s 162(1), Sch 11 para 30). As to the Secretary of State and the Welsh Ministers see PARA 4 note 18. As to the separate administration of the non-domestic rating provisions (Local Government Finance Act 1988 Pt III (ss 41–67)) in England and Wales see PARA 52.

39 Local Government Finance Act 1988 s 66(9). The non-domestic rating provisions are those of Pt III (ss 41–67): see s 66(9). As to the orders made under s 66(9) see the Standard Community Charge and Non-Domestic Rating (Definition of Domestic Property) Order 1990, SI 1990/162; the Standard Community Charge and Non-Domestic Rating (Definition of Domestic Property) (Amendment) Order 1991, SI 1991/474; the Non-Domestic Rating (Definition of Domestic Property) Order 1993, SI 1993/542; and the Non-Domestic Rating (Definition of Domestic Property) (Wales) Order 2010, SI 2010/682, all of which amend the Local Government Finance Act 1988 s 66: see the text to notes 1–35.

(ii) Local Non-domestic Rating Lists

191. Compilation and maintenance of local non-domestic rating lists.

The valuation officer[1] for a billing authority[2] must, in accordance with the non-domestic rating provisions[3], compile, and then maintain, lists for the authority (to be called its 'local non-domestic rating lists')[4].

A list had to be compiled on 1 April 1990 initially, and must be compiled on 1 April falling every fifth year thereafter[5]. In the case of a billing authority in England[6], this does not require a list to be compiled on 1 April 2015 and on 1 April in every fifth year afterwards, and a list must instead be compiled on 1 April 2017 and on 1 April in every fifth year afterwards[7].

Before a list is compiled, the valuation officer must take such steps as are reasonably practicable to ensure that the list is accurately compiled on 1 April concerned[8]. A list comes into force on the day on which it is compiled and remains in force until the next list is compiled[9].

Not later than 30 September preceding the day on which the list is to be compiled, the valuation officer must send the billing authority a copy of the list he proposes (on the information then before him) to compile[10]. As soon as is reasonably practicable after receiving the copy, the authority must deposit it at its principal office and take such steps as it thinks most suitable for giving notice of it[11]. Similarly, as soon as is reasonably practicable after compiling a list, the valuation officer must send a copy of it to the authority[12] which must, as soon as is reasonably practicable after receiving the copy, deposit it at its principal office[13].

A list must be maintained for so long as is necessary for the purposes of the non-domestic rating provisions[14], so that expiry of the period for which it is in force does not detract from the duty to maintain it[15].

These provisions in their application to Wales are subject to the power of the Welsh Ministers[16] to postpone the compilation of Welsh lists for 2015 onwards[17].

1 As to valuation officers see PARA 54.
2 As to the meaning of 'billing authority' see PARA 53.
3 Ie in accordance with the Local Government Finance Act 1988 Pt III (ss 41–67).
4 Local Government Finance Act 1988 s 41(1) (amended by the Local Government Finance Act 1992 s 117(1), Sch 13 para 59). The general duty prescribed by the Local Government Finance Act 1988 s 41(1) does not imply a specific obligation for alterations to the list to be made within a certain time: *National Car Parks Ltd v Baird (Valuation Officer)* [2004] EWCA Civ 967, [2005] 1 All ER 53, [2004] RA 245. As to alterations to local non-domestic rating lists see PARA 202 et seq.
5 See the Local Government Finance Act 1988 s 41(2). This is subject to s 41(2A) (see the text to notes 6–6): s 41(2) (amended by the Growth and Infrastructure Act 2013 s 29(1), (2)). In compiling and maintaining the list for 1 April 1990, the valuation officer was entitled to take into account information obtained under the General Rate Act 1967 s 82 or s 86 (repealed) (information from returns requiring information and from surveys of property by the valuation officer): Local Government Finance Act 1988 s 41(8).
6 As to the meaning of 'England' see PARA 2 note 16.
7 Local Government Finance Act 1988 s 41(2A) (added by the Growth and Infrastructure Act 2013 s 29(1), (3)).
8 Local Government Finance Act 1988 s 41(4).
9 Local Government Finance Act 1988 s 41(3) (amended by the Growth and Infrastructure Act 2013 s 29(1), (4)).
10 Local Government Finance Act 1988 s 41(5) (amended by the Local Government Act 2003 s 60(1)).
11 Local Government Finance Act 1988 s 41(6).
12 Local Government Finance Act 1988 s 41(6A) (s 41(6A), (6B) added by the Local Government and Housing Act 1989 s 139, Sch 5 paras 1, 19, 79(3)).
13 Local Government Finance Act 1988 s 41(6B) (as added: see note 12).
14 Ie the Local Government Finance Act 1988 Pt III (ss 41–67).
15 Local Government Finance Act 1988 s 41(7) (amended by the Growth and Infrastructure Act 2013 s 29(1), (5)).
16 Ie under the Local Government Finance Act 1988 s 54A (see PARA 193).
17 Local Government Finance Act 1988 s 41(9) (added by the Growth and Infrastructure Act 2013 s 30(2)).

192. Amalgamated lists for Welsh billing authorities.

Every new valuation officer[1] had to compile a list (the 'amalgamated list') on 1 April 1996 for the new billing authority for which he was appointed[2]. The amalgamated list had to contain the information which was included in the local non-domestic rating lists compiled on 1 April 1995 for the old billing authorities[3] (referred to then as the 'current lists') so far as that information was relevant[4]. The amalgamated list was also to include the information which was included in any current list by way of an alteration, so far as that information was relevant[5].

A new valuation officer's amalgamated list was to be treated[6] as the local non-domestic rating list for his new billing authority and was deemed to have come into force on 1 April 1995[7]. Where an amalgamated list contained information which was derived from any alteration made to any list or lists from which it was derived, the amalgamated list was to be treated as having been varied on the date on which the alteration was made[8].

Every valuation officer[9] had to provide, on or before 15 October 1995, the appropriate new valuation officer[10] with the information recorded in his local non-domestic rating list[11] as at 30 September 1995, so far as it was relevant[12]. On 31 March 1996, every valuation officer had to provide the appropriate new valuation officer with the information recorded in his local non-domestic rating list as at that date, so far as it was relevant[13].

As soon as was reasonably practicable after compiling an amalgamated list, a new valuation officer was required to send a copy of it to his new billing authority[14].

1 'New valuation officer' meant a valuation officer for a new billing authority; and 'new billing authority' meant a billing authority which was a new principal council: see the Local Government Finance Act 1988 s 41A(11) (s 41A added by the Local Government (Wales) Act 1994 s 37). 'New principal council' had the same meaning as in the Local Government (Wales) Act 1994 (see LOCAL GOVERNMENT vol 69 (2018) PARA 51): see the Local Government Finance Act 1988 s 41A(11) (as so added). As to billing authorities generally see PARA 53. As to valuation officers generally see PARA 54. As to the separate administration of the non-domestic rating provisions (Local Government Finance Act 1988 Pt III (ss 41–67)) in England and Wales see PARA 52.

2 See the Local Government Finance Act 1988 s 41A(1) (as added: see note 1). The local rating list provisions contained in s 41(2)–(6B) (see PARA 191) did not apply in relation to an amalgamated list: see s 41A(6) (as so added).

3 'Old billing authority' meant a billing authority which was an old authority; and 'old authority' had the same meaning as in the Local Government (Wales) Act 1994 (see LOCAL GOVERNMENT vol 69 (2018) PARA 51): see the Local Government Finance Act 1988 s 41A(11) (as added: see note 1).

4 See the Local Government Finance Act 1988 s 41A(2) (as added: see note 1). Information was relevant in relation to a new valuation officer, or his area, if it related to a hereditament which was in his area: see s 41A(12)(d) (as so added). A new valuation officer's area was the area of the new billing authority for which he was appointed: see s 41A(12)(b) (as so added).

5 See the Local Government Finance Act 1988 s 41A(3) (as added: see note 1).

6 Ie for the purposes of the Local Government Finance Act 1988.

7 See the Local Government Finance Act 1988 s 41A(4) (as added: see note 1).

8 See the Local Government Finance Act 1988 s 41A(5) (as added: see note 1).

9 For these purposes, 'valuation officer' meant a valuation officer for an old billing authority: see the Local Government Finance Act 1988 s 41A(11) (as added: see note 1).

10 The appropriate new valuation officer, in relation to any information which related to any hereditament, was the new valuation officer for the new billing authority in whose area the hereditament was situated: see the Local Government Finance Act 1988 s 41A(12)(c) (as added: see note 1). As to the meaning of 'hereditament' see PARA 106.

11 Ie the local non-domestic rating list maintained by him under the Local Government Finance Act 1988: see s 41A(12)(a) (as added: see note 1).

12 See the Local Government Finance Act 1988 s 41A(7)(a) (as added: see note 1). A new valuation officer receiving any information under s 41A(7)(a) had to send a copy of it to his new billing authority as soon as reasonably practicable: see s 41A(8) (as so added).

13 See the Local Government Finance Act 1988 s 41A(7)(b) (as added: see note 1).

14 See the Local Government Finance Act 1988 s 41A(9) (as added: see note 1). A new billing authority receiving a copy of an amalgamated list under this provision had, as soon as reasonably practicable, to deposit it at its principal office: see s 41A(10) (as so added).

193. Power to postpone compilation of Welsh rating lists.

The Welsh Ministers[1] may by order provide that the following lists must be compiled on a date specified in the order ('the specified date') rather than on 1 April 2015[2]. The lists to which these provisions apply are:

(1) each local non-domestic rating list[3] that would otherwise have to be compiled on 1 April 2015 for a billing authority[4] in Wales[5]; and

(2) the central non-domestic rating list[6] that would otherwise have to be compiled for Wales on that date[7].

The specified date must be 1 April in 2016, 2017, 2018, 2019 or 2020; and the same date must be specified for each list to which these provisions apply[8].

If such an order has effect, the statutory requirement to compile local rating lists[9] applies in relation to billing authorities in Wales as if it did not require a list to be compiled on 1 April 2015 and on 1 April in every fifth year afterwards, but instead required a list to be compiled on the specified date and on 1 April in every fifth year afterwards[10].

If such an order has effect, the statutory requirement to compile central rating lists[11] applies in relation to Wales as if it did not require a list to be compiled on 1 April 2015 and on 1 April in every fifth year afterwards, but instead required a list to be compiled on the specified date and on 1 April in every fifth year afterwards[12].

The specified date for these purposes is 1 April 2017[13].

1 As to the Welsh Ministers see PARA 4 note 18.
2 Local Government Finance Act 1988 s 54A(1) (s 54A added by the Growth and Infrastructure Act 2013 s 30(1)). See the Rating Lists (Postponement of Compilation) (Wales) Order 2014, SI 2014/1370.
3 As to the meaning of 'local non-domestic rating list' see PARA 191.
4 As to the meaning of 'billing authority' see PARA 53.
5 Local Government Finance Act 1988 s 54A(2)(a) (as added: see note 2). As to the meaning of 'Wales' see PARA 2 note 16.
6 As to central non-domestic rating lists see PARA 196.
7 Local Government Finance Act 1988 s 54A(2)(b) (as added: see note 2).
8 Local Government Finance Act 1988 s 54A(3) (as added: see note 2).
9 Ie the Local Government Finance Act 1988 s 41: see PARA 191.
10 Local Government Finance Act 1988 s 54A(4) (as added: see note 2).
11 Ie the Local Government Finance Act 1988 s 52: see PARA 196.
12 Local Government Finance Act 1988 s 54A(5) (as added: see note 2).
13 See the Rating Lists (Postponement of Compilation) (Wales) Order 2014, SI 2014/1370, art 2.

194. Contents of local non-domestic rating lists.

A local non-domestic rating list[1] must show, for each day in each chargeable financial year[2] for which it is in force, each hereditament[3], on the day concerned[4], which:

(1) is situated in the billing authority's area[5];
(2) is a relevant non-domestic hereditament[6];
(3) is not (nor any part of it) either domestic property[7] or exempt from local non-domestic rating[8]; and
(4) is not a hereditament which must be shown for the day in a central non-domestic rating list[9].

For each day on which a hereditament is shown in the local list[10], it must also show whether it consists entirely of property which is not domestic[11], or is a composite hereditament[12], and whether any part of the hereditament is exempt from local non-domestic rating[13]. The list must show the rateable value of the hereditament[14]. The list must also contain such information about hereditaments shown in it as may be prescribed by the appropriate national authority[15] by regulations[16]; and this may include information about the total of the rateable values shown in the list[17].

In respect of each hereditament shown in a list[18], the list must contain:

(a) a description of the hereditament[19];
(b) its address[20]; and
(c) any reference number ascribed to it by the valuation officer[21].

A list must show on any day in which it is in force the total of rateable values shown[22] in the list[23]. In respect of any alteration directed to be made by a tribunal, the list must also show whether the direction was given by a valuation tribunal[24] or the Upper Tribunal[25].

1 As to the meaning of 'local non-domestic rating list' see PARA 191.

2 As to the meaning of 'chargeable financial year' see PARA 24 note 1.
3 As to the meaning of 'hereditament' see PARA 106.
4 A right or other property is a hereditament on a particular day if (and only if) it is a hereditament immediately before the day ends: Local Government Finance Act 1988 s 67(3).
5 See the Local Government Finance Act 1988 s 42(1)(a). As to the meaning of 'billing authority' see PARA 53.
6 Local Government Finance Act 1988 s 42(1)(b). A hereditament is relevant, non-domestic, composite, unoccupied or wholly or partly occupied on a particular day if (and only if) it is relevant, non-domestic, composite, unoccupied or wholly or partly occupied (as the case may be) immediately before the day ends: s 67(4). As to the occupier and occupation of land see PARA 85 et seq.
7 As to the meaning of 'domestic property' see PARA 190.
8 Local Government Finance Act 1988 s 42(1)(c). For the purpose of deciding the extent (if any) to which a hereditament consists of domestic property on a particular day, or is exempt from local non-domestic rating on a particular day, the state of affairs existing immediately before the day ends must be treated as having existed throughout the day: see s 67(5). As to exemptions from local non-domestic rating see PARA 110 et seq.
9 Local Government Finance Act 1988 s 42(1)(d). As to when a hereditament is treated as shown in a central non-domestic rating list see PARA 198. As to central non-domestic rating lists generally see PARA 196 et seq.
10 For the purpose of deciding what is shown in a list for a particular day, the state of the list as it has effect immediately before the day ends must be treated as having been its state throughout the day; and 'effect' here includes any effect which is retrospective by virtue of an alteration of the list: Local Government Finance Act 1988 s 67(8). As to the alteration of lists see PARA 202 et seq.
11 Local Government Finance Act 1988 s 42(2)(a). See also note 6.
12 Local Government Finance Act 1988 s 42(2)(b). See also note 6.
13 Local Government Finance Act 1988 s 42(3). See also note 6.
14 Local Government Finance Act 1988 s 42(4) (amended by the Local Government and Housing Act 1989 Sch 5 paras 20, 79(3)).
15 Ie the Secretary of State or, in relation to Wales, the Welsh Ministers. The functions of the Secretary of State under the Local Government Finance Act 1988 s 42, so far as exercisable in relation to Wales, were transferred to the National Assembly for Wales (see the National Assembly for Wales (Transfer of Functions) Order 1999, SI 1999/672, art 2, Sch 1) and are now vested in the Welsh Ministers (see the Government of Wales Act 2006 s 162(1), Sch 11 para 30). As to the Secretary of State and the Welsh Ministers see PARA 4 note 18. As to the meaning of 'Wales' see PARA 2 note 16. As to the separate administration of the non-domestic rating provisions (Local Government Finance Act 1988 Pt III (ss 41–67)) in England and Wales see PARA 52.
16 Local Government Finance Act 1988 s 42(5). As to the regulations made see the Non-Domestic Rating (Miscellaneous Provisions) Regulations 1989, SI 1989/1060 (see the text to notes 18–25); and the Non-Domestic Rating (Alteration of Lists and Appeals) (England) Regulations 2009, SI 2009/2268, and the Non-Domestic Rating (Alteration of Lists and Appeals) (Wales) Regulations 2005, SI 2005/758 (see PARA 199 et seq).
17 Local Government Finance Act 1988 s 42(5).
18 For these purposes, 'list' means a local rating list compiled under the Local Government Finance Act 1988 s 41 (see PARA 191) or s 41A (see PARA 192).
19 Non-Domestic Rating (Miscellaneous Provisions) Regulations 1989, SI 1989/1060, reg 2(a).
20 Non-Domestic Rating (Miscellaneous Provisions) Regulations 1989, SI 1989/1060, reg 2(b).
21 Non-Domestic Rating (Miscellaneous Provisions) Regulations 1989, SI 1989/1060, reg 2(c). As to valuation officers see PARA 54.
22 Ie in accordance with the Local Government Finance Act 1988 s 42(4): see the text to note 14.
23 Non-Domestic Rating (Miscellaneous Provisions) Regulations 1989, SI 1989/1060, reg 4.
24 As to appeals to valuation tribunals see PARA 232 et seq.
25 See the Non-Domestic Rating (Miscellaneous Provisions) Regulations 1989, SI 1989/1060, reg 3 (amended by SI 2009/1307). As to appeals to the Upper Tribunal see PARA 269.

(iii) Rural Settlement Lists

195. Duty of English billing authorities to compile and maintain rural settlement list.

Each billing authority in England[1] must compile and maintain[2] a list (called its 'rural settlement list')[3]. This list has effect for each chargeable financial year[4] and identifies for each such year any settlements[5] which:

(1) are wholly or partly within the authority's area[6];

(2) appear to the authority to have had a population of not more than 3,000 on the last 31 December before the beginning of the chargeable financial year in question[7]; and

(3) in that financial year are wholly or partly within an area designated by the Secretary of State[8] by order[9] as a rural area for these purposes[10].

A rural settlement list must identify the boundaries of each settlement[11], but if a settlement is not wholly within the area of a billing authority the list need not identify the boundaries outside the authority's area[12]. The requirement to compile and maintain such a list does not apply to a billing authority in respect of any chargeable financial year for which there are no such settlements and, accordingly, if the authority has compiled a rural settlement list, it must cease to maintain that list[13].

The billing authority must, throughout the period of three months[14] preceding the beginning of the first chargeable financial year for which a rural settlement list is to have effect, make available for inspection a draft of the list in the form in which the authority proposes that it should have effect for that year[15].

In each chargeable financial year for which a rural settlement list has effect, the billing authority must, if it appears to the authority that the requirement to compile and maintain a list[16] will apply to the authority in respect of the next chargeable financial year, review the list and consider whether or not, for the next chargeable financial year, any alterations are required[17] to the list[18]. If, following the review, the authority considers that any such alterations are required for that year, it must, throughout the three months preceding the beginning of that year, make available for inspection a draft of the list in the form in which the authority proposes that it should have effect for that year[19].

A billing authority which has compiled a rural settlement list must make it available for inspection in the form in which the list has effect for each chargeable financial year to which it relates[20].

1 As to the meaning of 'billing authority' see PARA 53. As to the meaning of 'England' see PARA 2 note 16.

2 Ie in accordance with the Local Government Finance Act 1988 s 42B: see the text to notes 14–20.

3 Local Government Finance Act 1988 s 42A(1) (ss 42A, 42B added by the Local Government Finance Act 1997 s 1, Sch 1 para 1; the Local Government Finance Act 1988 s 42A(1) amended by the Local Government Act 2003 s 63(1)).

4 As to the meaning of 'chargeable financial year' see PARA 24 note 1.

5 See the Local Government Finance Act 1988 s 42A(2) (as added: see note 3).

6 Local Government Finance Act 1988 s 42A(3)(a) (as added: see note 3).

7 Local Government Finance Act 1988 s 42A(3)(b) (as added: see note 3).

8 As to the Secretary of State see PARA 4 note 18.

9 An order under the Local Government Finance Act 1988 s 42A(3)(c) may provide for designating as a rural area any area for the time being identified by any person, in any manner, specified in the order: s 42A(5) (as added: see note 3). As to the meaning of 'person' see PARA 11 note 13. As to the orders made see the Non-Domestic Rating (Rural Settlements) (England) Order 1997, SI 1997/2792 (amended by SI 2001/1346 and SI 2009/3176); the Non-Domestic Rating (Rural Settlements) (England) Order 1998, SI 1998/393; the Non-Domestic Rating (Rural Settlements)

(England) (No 2) Order 1998, SI 1998/2836; the Non-Domestic Rating (Rural Settlements) (England) Order 1999, SI 1999/3158; and the Non-Domestic Rating (Designation of Rural Areas) (England) Order 2001, SI 2001/3916.

10 Local Government Finance Act 1988 s 42A(3)(c) (as added: see note 3).

11 Ie whether by defining the boundaries or referring to boundaries defined in a map or other document: see the Local Government Finance Act 1988 s 42A(4) (as added: see note 3).

12 Local Government Finance Act 1988 s 42A(4) (as added: see note 3).

13 Local Government Finance Act 1988 s 42A(6) (as added: see note 3).

14 As to the meaning of 'month' see PARA 11 note 1.

15 Local Government Finance Act 1988 s 42B(1) (as added: see note 3). Where a billing authority is required to make any list or draft available for inspection, it must make the list or draft available at any reasonable hour (and free of charge) at its principal office: s 42B(5) (as so added).

16 Ie the Local Government Finance Act 1988 s 42A(1): see the text to notes 1–3.

17 Ie in order to give effect to the Local Government Finance Act 1988 s 42A(2): see the text to notes 4–5.

18 Local Government Finance Act 1988 s 42B(2) (as added: see note 3).

19 Local Government Finance Act 1988 s 42B(3) (as added: see note 3). See also note 15.

20 Local Government Finance Act 1988 s 42B(4) (as added: see note 3). See also note 15.

(iv) Central Non-domestic Rating Lists

196. Compilation and maintenance of central non-domestic rating lists.

The central valuation officer[1] must, in accordance with the non-domestic rating provisions[2], compile, and then maintain, lists (known as 'central non-domestic rating lists')[3]. The first such list had to be compiled on 1 April 1990, and a list must be compiled on 1 April falling every fifth year thereafter[4]. In relation to England[5], however, this does not require a list to be compiled on 1 April 2015 and on 1 April in every fifth year afterwards, and a list must instead be compiled on 1 April 2017 and on 1 April in every fifth year afterwards[6].

A list comes into force on the day on which it is compiled and remains in force until the next one is compiled[7].

Before a list is compiled, the central valuation officer must take such steps as are reasonably practicable to ensure that it is accurately compiled on the 1 April concerned[8]. No later than 30 September preceding the day on which a list is to be compiled, the central valuation officer must send to the appropriate national authority[9] a copy of the list he proposes, on the information then before him, to compile[10]. As soon as is reasonably practicable after receiving the copy the appropriate national authority must deposit it at its principal office[11].

As soon as is reasonably practicable after compiling a list, the central valuation officer must send a copy of it to the appropriate national authority[12] who must, as soon as is reasonably practicable after receiving the copy, deposit it at its principal office[13].

A list must be maintained for so long as is necessary for the purposes of the non-domestic rating provisions[14], so that the expiry of the period for which it is in force does not detract from the duty to maintain it[15].

These provisions in their application to Wales are subject to the power of the Welsh Ministers[16] to postpone the compilation of Welsh lists for 2015 onwards[17].

1 As to valuation officers see PARA 54.

2 Ie in accordance with the Local Government Finance Act 1988 Pt III (ss 41–67).

3 Local Government Finance Act 1988 s 52(1). Separate central non-domestic rating lists must be compiled and maintained for England and Wales respectively: see s 104(2)(a); and PARA 52.

4 See the Local Government Finance Act 1988 s 52(2). This is subject to s 52(2A) (see the text to notes 5–6): s 52(2) (amended by the Growth and Infrastructure Act 2013 s 29(6), (7)).

5 As to the meaning of 'England' see PARA 2 note 16.

6 Local Government Finance Act 1988 s 52(2A) (added by the Growth and Infrastructure Act 2013 s 29(6), (8)).
7 Local Government Finance Act 1988 s 52(3) (amended by the Growth and Infrastructure Act 2013 s 29(6), (9)).
8 Local Government Finance Act 1988 s 52(4).
9 Ie the Secretary of State or, in relation to Wales, the Welsh Ministers. The functions of the Secretary of State under the Local Government Finance Act 1988 s 52, so far as exercisable in relation to Wales, were transferred to the National Assembly for Wales (see the National Assembly for Wales (Transfer of Functions) Order 1999, SI 1999/672, art 2, Sch 1) and are now vested in the Welsh Ministers (see the Government of Wales Act 2006 s 162(1), Sch 11 para 30). As to the Secretary of State and the Welsh Ministers see PARA 4 note 18. As to the meaning of 'Wales' see PARA 2 note 16.
10 Local Government Finance Act 1988 s 52(5) (amended by the Local Government Act 2003 s 60(2)).
11 Local Government Finance Act 1988 s 52(6).
12 Local Government Finance Act 1988 s 52(6A) (s 52(6A), (6B) added by the Local Government and Housing Act 1989 s 139, Sch 5 paras 28, 79(3)).
13 Local Government Finance Act 1988 s 52(6B) (as added: see note 10).
14 Ie for the purposes of the Local Government Finance Act 1988 Pt III (ss 41–57).
15 Local Government Finance Act 1988 s 52(7) (amended by the Growth and Infrastructure Act 2013 s 29(6), (10)).
16 Ie under the Local Government Finance Act 1988 s 54A (see PARA 193).
17 Local Government Finance Act 1988 s 52(8) (added by the Growth and Infrastructure Act 2013 s 30(3)).

197. Power to prescribe the contents of central non-domestic rating lists.

With a view to securing the central rating[1] en bloc of certain hereditaments[2], the appropriate national authority[3] may by regulations[4] designate a person[5] and prescribe in relation to him one or more descriptions of relevant non-domestic hereditament[6].

Where the regulations so require, a central non-domestic rating list must show, for each day in each chargeable financial year[7] for which it is in force, the name of the designated person and, against it, each hereditament (wherever situated) which on the day concerned is occupied or (if unoccupied) owned by him[8] and falls within any description prescribed in relation to him[9]. For each such day, the list must also show against the name of the designated person the rateable value (as a whole) of the hereditaments so shown[10].

Where regulations are for the time being in force so prescribing a description of non-domestic hereditament in relation to the previously designated person[11], amending regulations altering the designated person in relation to whom that description of hereditament is prescribed may have effect from a date earlier than that on which the amending regulations are made[12].

A central non-domestic rating list must also contain such information about hereditaments shown in it as may be prescribed by the appropriate national authority by regulations[13].

1 As to central non-domestic rating lists see PARA 196.
2 As to the meaning of 'hereditament' see PARA 106.
3 Ie the Secretary of State or, in relation to Wales, the Welsh Ministers. The functions of the Secretary of State under the Local Government Finance Act 1988 s 53, so far as exercisable in relation to Wales, were transferred to the National Assembly for Wales (see the National Assembly for Wales (Transfer of Functions) Order 1999, SI 1999/672, art 2, Sch 1) and are now vested in the Welsh Ministers (see the Government of Wales Act 2006 s 162(1), Sch 11 para 30). As to the Secretary of State and the Welsh Ministers see PARA 4 note 18. As to the meaning of 'Wales' see PARA 2 note 16. As to the separate administration of the non-domestic rating provisions (Local Government Finance Act 1988 Pt III (ss 41–67)) in England and Wales see PARA 52.

4 As to the regulations made see the Central Rating List (Wales) Regulations, SI 2005/422 (amended by SI 2005/645, SI 2005/3050, SI 2008/2672 and SI 2017/327); the Central Rating List (England) Regulations 2005, SI 2005/551 (amended by SI 2008/429, SI 2010/456, SI 2010/2692, SI 2011/2743, SI 2012/1292, SI 2013/408, SI 2013/2887, SI 2016/146, SI 2016/714 and SI 2016/882); and PARA 198.

5 As to the meaning of 'person' see PARA 11 note 13.

6 Local Government Finance Act 1988 s 53(1) (amended by the Local Government and Housing Act 1989 s 139, Sch 5 paras 29(2), (3), 79(3)). Nothing in a private or local Act passed before the Local Government Finance Act 1988 (ie 29 July 1988) prevents a person being designated or a description of hereditament being prescribed under s 53: see s 67(12). As to local Acts see STATUTES AND LEGISLATIVE PROCESS vol 96 (2012) PARA 626. As to private Acts see STATUTES AND LEGISLATIVE PROCESS vol 96 (2012) PARA 624.

7 As to the meaning of 'chargeable financial year' see PARA 24 note 1.

8 As to the meanings of 'owner' and 'occupier' see PARA 86.

9 Local Government Finance Act 1988 s 53(2) (amended by the Local Government and Housing Act 1989 Sch 5 paras 29(2), (3), 79(3)).

10 Local Government Finance Act 1988 s 53(3). As to the valuation for rating see PARA 156 et seq.

11 Ie a person designated in the regulations: see the Local Government Finance Act 1988 s 53(4) (as substituted: see note 12).

12 Local Government Finance Act 1988 s 53(4) (s 53(4) substituted, s 53(4A) added, by the Local Government and Housing Act 1989 Sch 5 paras 29(4), 79(3)). Where, by virtue of the Local Government Finance Act 1988 s 53(4), the designated person in relation to any description of non-domestic hereditament is changed from a date earlier than the making of the regulations:

(1) any necessary alteration is to be made with effect from that date to a central non-domestic rating list on which any hereditament concerned is shown (s 53(4A)(a) (as so added)); and

(2) an order making the provision referred to in Sch 6 para 3(2) (see PARA 167) and specifying a description of hereditament by reference to the previously designated person is to be treated, with effect from that date, as referring to the person designated by the amending regulations (s 53(4A)(b) (as so added; repealed, as from a day to be appointed, by the Local Government Act 2003 ss 69, 127(2), Sch 8 Pt 1; at the date at which this volume states the law, no such day had been appointed)).

13 Local Government Finance Act 1988 s 53(5). In addition to the regulations cited in note 4, the following regulations have been made: the Non-Domestic Rating (Alteration of Lists and Appeals) (England) Regulations 2009, SI 2009/2268 (amended by SI 2011/434, SI 2015/424 and SI 2017/155); and the Non-Domestic Rating (Alteration of Lists and Appeals) (Wales) Regulations 2005, SI 2005/758 (amended by SI 2006/1035, SI 2010/713 and SI 2017/941): see PARA 199 et seq.

198. Contents of central non-domestic rating lists.

With a view to securing the central rating en bloc of certain hereditaments[1], regulations have been made designating various corporate bodies and prescribing, in relation to them, a group of relevant non-domestic hereditaments[2]. The relevant non-domestic hereditaments[3] so prescribed[4] are:

(1) railway hereditaments[5] (including, in relation to England only, light railway hereditaments)[6];
(2) communication hereditaments[7];
(3) national, regional and local gas transportation hereditaments[8];
(4) gas meter hereditaments[9];
(5) electricity transmission and distribution hereditaments[10];
(6) electricity meter hereditaments[11];
(7) water supply hereditaments[12];
(8) canal hereditaments[13]; and
(9) long-distance pipeline hereditaments[14].

The regulations also designate persons in relation to each relevant hereditament[15].

The central non-domestic rating list must show, for each day in each year for which it is in force, the name of each designated person[16] and, against each name, each hereditament situated in England or Wales (as the case may be) which on the day concerned is occupied (or, if unoccupied, owned[17]) by that person, and which falls within the description prescribed in relation to that person[18]. The list must also show, against the name of each designated person, that person's business details[19], the rateable value (as a whole) of the hereditaments so shown[20] and, if after 1 April 2005, the first day for which the rateable value shown in the list against the name of the designated person has effect[21]. Where the list has been altered in pursuance of a direction by a tribunal[22], the name of the tribunal must also been shown in the list[23].

A hereditament is to be treated as shown in a central non-domestic rating list for a day if on the day it falls within a class of hereditament shown for the day in the list; and for this purpose a hereditament falls within a class on a particular day if (and only if) it falls within the class immediately before the day ends[24].

1 As to central non-domestic rating lists see PARA 196. As to the meaning of 'hereditament' see PARA 106.

2 The regulations have effect in relation to a central list compiled on or after 1 April 2005: see the Central Rating List (Wales) Regulations 2005, SI 2005/422, reg 3; and the Central Rating List (England) Regulations 2005, SI 2005/551, reg 2. As to the power to make such regulations see the Local Government Finance Act 1988 s 53; and PARA 197.

3 See the Central Rating List (Wales) Regulations 2005, SI 2005/422, reg 2(2)(b); and the Central Rating List (England) Regulations 2005, SI 2005/551, reg 1(3)(b).

4 Ie for the purposes of the Local Government Finance Act 1988 s 53(1) (see PARA 197): Central Rating List (Wales) Regulations 2005, SI 2005/422, reg 4(1); Central Rating List (England) Regulations 2005, SI 2005/551, reg 3(1).

5 Central Rating List (Wales) Regulations 2005, SI 2005/422, reg 4(1)(b), Schedule Pt 1; Central Rating List (England) Regulations 2005, SI 2005/551, reg 3(1)(b), Schedule Pt 1. Additional provision is made by the Central Rating List (Wales) Regulations 2005, SI 2005/422, reg 7 (amended by SI 2005/3050 and SI 2016/645); and the Central Rating List (England) Regulations 2005, SI 2005/551, reg 6 (amended by SI 2005/3050 and SI 2016/645). The Non-Domestic Rating (Miscellaneous Provisions) (Wales) Regulations 2017, SI 2017/327, reg 4 (cross-boundary property in Wales: see PARA 106) will not apply to any hereditament falling within any description in the Central Rating List (Wales) Regulations 2005, SI 2005/422, Schedule: reg 4(2) (amended by SI 2017/327).

6 Central Rating List (England) Regulations 2005, SI 2005/551, reg 3(1)(b), Schedule Pt 2. Additional provision is made by reg 7. As to the meaning of 'England' see PARA 2 note 16.

7 Central Rating List (Wales) Regulations 2005, SI 2005/422, reg 4(1)(b), Schedule Pt 2; Central Rating List (England) Regulations 2005, SI 2005/551, reg 3(1)(b), Schedule Pt 3 (amended by SI 2010/2692 and SI 2011/2743). Additional provision is made by the Central Rating List (Wales) Regulations 2005, SI 2005/422, reg 8 (substituted by SI 2008/2672); and the Central Rating List (England) Regulations 2005, SI 2005/551, reg 8 (amended by SI 2008/429).

8 Central Rating List (Wales) Regulations 2005, SI 2005/422, reg 4(1)(b), Schedule Pts 3–4; Central Rating List (England) Regulations 2005, SI 2005/551, reg 3(1)(b), Schedule Pts 4–5 (Schedule Pt 4 amended by SI 2016/714). Additional provision is made by the Central Rating List (Wales) Regulations 2005, SI 2005/422, regs 9–10; and the Central Rating List (England) Regulations 2005, SI 2005/551, regs 9–10.

9 Central Rating List (Wales) Regulations 2005, SI 2005/422, reg 4(1)(b), Schedule Pt 5; Central Rating List (England) Regulations 2005, SI 2005/551, reg 3(1)(b), Schedule Pt 6 (amended by SI 2016/882). Additional provision is made by the Central Rating List (Wales) Regulations 2005, SI 2005/422, reg 11; and the Central Rating List (England) Regulations 2005, SI 2005/551, reg 11.

10 Central Rating List (Wales) Regulations 2005, SI 2005/422, reg 4(1)(b), Schedule Pts 6–7; Central Rating List (England) Regulations 2005, SI 2005/551, reg 3(1)(b), Schedule Pts 7–8 (Schedule Pt 8 amended by SI 2013/408). Additional provision is made by the Central Rating List (Wales) Regulations 2005, SI 2005/422, regs 12–13; and the Central Rating List (England) Regulations 2005, SI 2005/551, regs 12–13 (reg 12 amended by SI 2016/145).

11 Central Rating List (Wales) Regulations 2005, SI 2005/422, reg 4(1)(b), Schedule Pt 8; Central Rating List (England) Regulations 2005, SI 2005/551, reg 3(1)(b), Schedule Pt 9 (amended by SI 2013/408). Additional provision is made by the Central Rating List (Wales) Regulations 2005, SI 2005/422, reg 14; and the Central Rating List (England) Regulations 2005, SI 2005/551, reg 14.

12 Central Rating List (Wales) Regulations 2005, SI 2005/422, reg 4(1)(b), Schedule Pt 9; Central Rating List (England) Regulations 2005, SI 2005/551, reg 3(1)(b), Schedule Pt 10. Additional provision is made by the Central Rating List (Wales) Regulations 2005, SI 2005/422, reg 15; and the Central Rating List (England) Regulations 2005, SI 2005/551, reg 15.
13 Central Rating List (Wales) Regulations 2005, SI 2005/422, reg 4(1)(b), Schedule Pt 10; Central Rating List (England) Regulations 2005, SI 2005/551, reg 3(1)(b), Schedule Pt 11. Additional provision is made by the Central Rating List (Wales) Regulations 2005, SI 2005/422, reg 16; and the Central Rating List (England) Regulations 2005, SI 2005/551, reg 16.
14 Central Rating List (Wales) Regulations 2005, SI 2005/422, reg 4(1)(b), Schedule Pt 11; Central Rating List (England) Regulations 2005, SI 2005/551, reg 3(1)(b), Schedule Pt 12 (amended by SI 2008/429, SI 2010/456, SI 2010/2692, SI 2011/2743, SI 2012/1292, SI 2013/2887 and SI 2016/146).
15 See the Central Rating List (Wales) Regulations 2005, SI 2005/422, reg 4(1)(a), Schedule Pts 1–11; and the Central Rating List (England) Regulations 2005, SI 2005/551, reg 3(1)(a), Schedule Pts 1–12 (as amended: see notes 7, 14).
16 See the Central Rating List (Wales) Regulations 2005, SI 2005/422, reg 5(a); and the Central Rating List (England) Regulations 2005, SI 2005/551, reg 4(a).
17 As to the meanings of 'owner' and 'occupier' see PARA 86.
18 Central Rating List (Wales) Regulations 2005, SI 2005/422, reg 5(b); and the Central Rating List (England) Regulations 2005, SI 2005/551, reg 4. As to the meaning of 'Wales' see PARA 2 note 16.
19 Where the person is a company registered in England and Wales, the list must show its registered office and, in any other case, the person's principal place of business within the United Kingdom: Central Rating List (Wales) Regulations 2005, SI 2005/422, reg 6(1)(a); Central Rating List (England) Regulations 2005, SI 2005/551, reg 5(1)(a). Where the person is a registered company, the list must show its registered number: Central Rating List (Wales) Regulations 2005, SI 2005/422, reg 6(1)(b); Central Rating List (England) Regulations 2005, SI 2005/551, reg 5(1)(b). As to registration under the Companies Act 1985 see COMPANIES vol 14 (2016) PARA 21 et seq. As to the registered office of a company see COMPANIES vol 14 (2016) PARA 124. As to the meaning of 'United Kingdom' see PARA 4 note 10.
20 See the Local Government Finance Act 1988 s 53(3); and PARA 197.
21 Central Rating List (Wales) Regulations 2005, SI 2005/422, reg 6(1)(c); Central Rating List (England) Regulations 2005, SI 2005/551, reg 5(1)(c).
22 As to appeals to tribunals in respect of the contents of valuation lists see PARA 232 et seq.
23 Central Rating List (Wales) Regulations 2005, SI 2005/422, reg 6(2); Central Rating List (England) Regulations 2005, SI 2005/551, reg 5(2).
24 Local Government Finance Act 1988 s 67(9). For these purposes, 'class' means a class expressed by reference to whether hereditaments are occupied or owned by a person designated under s 53(1) and fall within any description prescribed in relation to him under s 53(1) (see PARA 197): s 67(9A) (added by the Local Government Housing Act 1989 s 139, Sch 5 paras 35(3), 79(3)).

(v) Alteration of Rating Lists

A. IN GENERAL

199. Power to make regulations for the alteration of rating lists.

The appropriate national authority[1] may make regulations[2] providing that, where a copy of a proposed local or central non-domestic rating list has been sent to a billing authority[3] and the valuation officer[4] alters the list before it comes into force[5], the officer must inform the billing authority or the appropriate national authority as the case may be[6], who must then alter the deposited copy accordingly[7].

The appropriate national authority may also make regulations[8] governing the alteration by valuation officers of lists which have been compiled, whether or not they are still in force[9]; and such regulations may include provision:

(1) that where a valuation officer intends to alter a list to ensure that it is accurately maintained, he must not alter it unless prescribed[10] conditions (as to notice or otherwise) are fulfilled[11];

(2) as to who (other than a valuation officer) may make a proposal to alter a list with a view to its being accurately maintained[12];
(3) as to the manner and circumstances in which a proposal may be made and the information to be included in it[13];
(4) as to the period within which a proposal must be made[14];
(5) as to the procedure for and subsequent making of a proposal[15];
(6) as to the circumstances within which and the conditions upon which a proposal may be withdrawn[16];
(7) requiring the valuation officer to inform other prescribed persons[17] of the proposal in the prescribed manner[18];
(8) that, where there is disagreement between a valuation officer and another person making a proposal for the alteration of a list, about the validity of the proposal[19] or about the accuracy of the list[20], an appeal may be made to a valuation tribunal[21];
(9) as to the period for which or day from which an alteration of a list is to have effect[22];
(10) requiring the list to be altered so as to indicate the effect (retrospective or otherwise) of the alteration[23];
(11) requiring the valuation officer to inform prescribed persons of an alteration within a prescribed period[24];
(12) requiring the valuation officer to keep for a prescribed period a record of the state of the list before the alteration was made[25];
(13) as to financial adjustments to be made as a result of alterations, including provision requiring payments or repayments to be made, with or without interest[26], and provision as to the recovery (by deduction or otherwise) of sums due[27].

The regulations also may include provision that:

(a) where a valuation officer for a billing authority has informed the authority of an alteration of a list a copy of which has been deposited by the authority[28], the authority must alter the copy accordingly[29];
(b) where the central valuation officer has informed the appropriate national authority of an alteration of a list a copy of which has been deposited[30], the appropriate national authority must alter the copy accordingly[31].

1 Ie the Secretary of State or, in relation to Wales, the Welsh Ministers. The functions of the Secretary of State under the Local Government Finance Act 1988 s 55, so far as exercisable in relation to Wales, were transferred to the National Assembly for Wales (see the National Assembly for Wales (Transfer of Functions) Order 1999, SI 1999/672, art 2, Sch 1) and are now vested in the Welsh Ministers (see the Government of Wales Act 2006 s 162(1), Sch 11 para 30). As to the Secretary of State and the Welsh Ministers see PARA 4 note 18. As to the meaning of 'Wales' see PARA 2 note 16.

2 As to the regulations made see the Non-Domestic Rating (Miscellaneous Provisions) (No 2) Regulations 1989, SI 1989/2303, reg 6 (amended by SI 1993/616).

3 Ie under the Local Government Finance Act 1988 s 41(5) (see PARA 191) or s 52(5) (see PARA 196). As to the meaning of 'billing authority' see PARA 53. As to local rating lists see PARA 191. As to central rating lists see PARA 196.

4 As to the meaning of 'valuation officer' see PARA 54 note 3.

5 Local Government Finance Act 1988 s 55(1).

6 Local Government Finance Act 1988 s 55(1)(a) (amended by the Local Government Finance Act 1992 s 117(1), Sch 13 para 67(1)).

7 Local Government Finance Act 1988 s 55(1)(b).

8 As to the regulations made under the Local Government Finance Act 1988 s 55(2)–(7A) see the Non-Domestic Rating (Payment of Interest) Regulations 1990, SI 1990/1904 (amended by SI 1991/2111, SI 1992/1515, SI 1993/616, SI 1993/1495, SI 2001/3649, SI 2005/659, SI 2005/758, SI 2009/1307 and SI 2011/255); the Non-Domestic Rating (Caravan Sites) Regulations 1990, SI 1990/673 (amended by SI 1991/471) (see PARA 108); the Non-Domestic Rating (Alteration of Lists and Appeals) (Wales) Regulations 2005, SI 2005/758 (amended by SI 2006/1035, SI 2010/713 and SI 2017/941); and the Non-Domestic Rating (Alteration of Lists and Appeals) (England) Regulations 2009, SI 2009/2268 (amended by SI 2011/434, SI 2015/424 and SI 2017/155) (see PARA 200 et seq); the Valuation Tribunal for England (Council Tax and Rating Appeals) (Procedure) Regulations 2009, SI 2009/2269 (amended by SI 2011/434, SI 2013/465 and SI 2017/156) (see PARA 242 et seq); the Non-Domestic Rating (Communications Hereditaments) (Valuation, Alteration of Lists and Appeals and Material Day) (England) Regulations 2008, SI 2008/2333; and the Non-Domestic Rating (Communications Hereditaments) (Valuation, Alteration of Lists and Appeals and Material Day) (Wales) Regulations 2008, SI 2008/2671.

9 Local Government Finance Act 1988 s 55(2). The provisions of s 55(3)–(7) (see heads (1)–(13) in the text) apply for the purposes of s 55(2): see s 55(2). In *BMC Properties and Management Ltd v Jackson (Valuation Officer)* [2015] EWCA Civ 1306, [2016] RA 1, [2016] All ER (D) 67 (Jan), the Court of Appeal accepted that the valuation officer had power to make an alteration during the currency of a rating list, since although the Local Government Finance Act 1988 did not explicitly empower the valuation officer to make alterations to the list of his own volition, and the Non-Domestic Rating (Alteration of Lists and Appeals) (England) Regulations 2009, SI 2009/2268, reg 17 (see PARA 200) seemed to assume that the power of alteration already existed, rather than explicitly conferring it, the scheme of the legislation, and its historical development, required the valuation officer to 'maintain' the list in an accurate state, and not merely to preserve it as an historic snapshot of the position on the date the list came into effect.

10 'Prescribed' means prescribed by the regulations: see the Local Government Finance Act 1988 s 146(6).

11 Local Government Finance Act 1988 s 55(3). As to the duty to maintain lists see PARAS 191, 196.

12 Local Government Finance Act 1988 s 55(4)(a).

13 Local Government Finance Act 1988 s 55(4)(b) (amended by the Local Government and Housing Act 1989 s 139, Sch 5 paras 30(2), 79(3)).

14 Local Government Finance Act 1988 s 55(4)(c).

15 Local Government Finance Act 1988 s 55(4)(d) (amended by the Local Government and Housing Act 1989 Sch 5 paras 30(2), 79(3)).

16 Local Government Finance Act 1988 s 55(4)(dd) (added by the Local Government and Housing Act 1989 Sch 5 paras 30(2), 79(3)).

17 As to the meaning of 'person' see PARA 11 note 13.

18 Local Government Finance Act 1988 s 55(4)(e). In relation to an English list or a Welsh list, the provision that may be included in the regulations by virtue of s 55(4) includes:

(1) provision about the steps that must be taken before a person may make a proposal for an alteration of the list (which may include steps designed to ensure the person checks the accuracy and completeness of any information on which any decision by the valuation officer has been based and gives the valuation officer an opportunity to consider the results of those checks and alter the list) (s 55(4A)(a) (s 55(4A), (4B), (7B) added, s 55(8) substituted, by the Enterprise Act 2016 s 32(1), (2), (4)));

(2) provision restricting the circumstances in which any of those steps may be taken and provision about the timing of any step (Local Government Finance Act 1988 s 55(4A)(b) (as so added));

(3) provision for valuation officers to impose financial penalties on persons who, in, or in connection with, proposals for the alteration of the list, knowingly, recklessly or carelessly provide information which is false in a material particular (s 55(4A)(c) (as so added)).

If provision is made by virtue of s 55(4A)(c):

(a) the maximum amount of any penalty that may be specified in, or determined in accordance with, the regulations is £500 (s 55(4B)(a) (as so added));

(b) the regulations must require any sum received by a valuation officer by way of penalty to be paid into the appropriate fund (s 55(4B)(b) (as so added));

(c) the regulations may include provision for any penalty to be recovered by the valuation officer concerned as a civil debt due to the officer (s 55(4B)(c) (as so added));

(d) the regulations must include provision enabling a person on whom a financial penalty is imposed to appeal against the imposition of the penalty or its amount to the valuation tribunal (see note 21) (s 55(4B)(d) (as so added)).

For the purposes of s 55(4B)(b) (see head (b) above) and s 55(5A)(d) (see note 21 head (4)) 'the appropriate fund' means:

(i) where the provision made by virtue of s 55(4A)(c) or (5) is in relation to a proposal to alter an English list, the Consolidated Fund (s 55(7B)(a) (as so added)); and

(ii) where the provision made by virtue of s 55(4A)(c) or (5) is in relation to a proposal to alter a Welsh list, the Welsh Consolidated Fund (s 55(7B)(b) (as so added)).

'English list' means either a local non-domestic rating list that has to be compiled for a billing authority in England, or the central non-domestic rating list that has to be compiled for England; and 'Welsh list' means either a local non-domestic rating list that has to be compiled for a billing authority in Wales, or the central non-domestic rating list that has to be compiled for Wales: s 55(8) (added by the Local Government and Public Involvement in Health Act 2007 s 220(1), Sch 16 paras 2, 3(1), (3); and substituted by the Enterprise Act 2016 s 32(1), (5)).

19 Local Government Finance Act 1988 s 55(5)(a).

20 Local Government Finance Act 1988 s 55(5)(b).

21 Local Government Finance Act 1988 s 55(5) (amended by the Local Government and Housing Act 1989 Sch 5 paras 30(3), 79(3); the Local Government Finance Act 1992 Sch 13 para 67(2); and the Local Government and Public Involvement in Health Act 2007 ss 220(1), 241, Sch 16 paras 2, 3(1), (2), Sch 18 Pt 17). 'Valuation tribunal' means, in relation to England, the Valuation Tribunal for England and, in relation to Wales, a valuation tribunal established under the Local Government Finance Act 1988 Sch 11 para 1 (see PARA 237)): s 55(8) (as added and substituted: see note 18). As to the Valuation Tribunal for England see PARA 232 et seq and as to valuation tribunals in Wales see PARA 236 et seq. As to the meaning of 'England' see PARA 2 note 16.

In relation to a proposal made by a person to alter an English list or a Welsh list, the provision that may be included in regulations by virtue of s 55(5) includes provision:

(1) about the grounds on which an appeal may be made (s 55(5A)(a) (s 55(5A) added by the Enterprise Act 2016 s 32(1), (3)));

(2) about the matters which are not to be taken into account by the valuation tribunal as part of an appeal (s 55(5A)(b) (as so added));

(3) about the circumstances in which new evidence may be admitted on an appeal, and about the conduct of an appeal in relation to such evidence (s 55(5A)(c) (as so added));

(4) about the payment of fees by ratepayers in relation to appeals, the payment of those fees into the appropriate fund and the circumstances in which those fees are to be refunded (s 55(5A)(d) (as so added)).

Section 55(5A) is without prejudice to the powers to make regulations conferred by Sch 11 Pt 3 (paras 8–12A) (tribunals: procedure, orders, etc: see PARA 240): s 55(5A) (as so added).

22 Local Government Finance Act 1988 s 55(6)(a). This may include provision that it is to have retrospective effect: see s 55(6)(a); and see *R (on the application of Corus UK Ltd) v Valuation Office Agency* [2001] EWHC Admin 1108, [2002] RA 1 (retrospective alteration not conspicuously unfair in the circumstances).

23 Local Government Finance Act 1988 s 55(6)(b).

24 Local Government Finance Act 1988 s 55(6)(c).

25 Local Government Finance Act 1988 s 55(6)(d).

26 Local Government Finance Act 1988 s 55(7)(a) (substituted by the Local Government Finance Act 1992 s 104, Sch 10 para 1).

27 Local Government Finance Act 1988 s 55(7)(c).

28 Ie under the Local Government Finance Act 1988 s 41(6B) (see PARA 191) or s 41A(10) (see PARA 192).

29 Local Government Finance Act 1988 s 55(7A)(a) (s 55(7A) added by the Local Government and Housing Act 1989 Sch 5 paras 30(5), 79(3); the Local Government Finance Act 1988 s 55(7A)(a) amended by the Local Government Finance Act 1992 Sch 13 para 67(3); and the Local Government (Wales) Act 1994 s 66(6), Sch 16 para 84).

30 Ie under the Local Government Finance Act 1988 s 52(6B): see PARA 196.

31 Local Government Finance Act 1988 s 55(7A)(b) (as added: see note 29).

B. ALTERATION OF LOCAL NON-DOMESTIC RATING LISTS

(a) In England

200. Notification of alteration.

Within four weeks of altering a list[1] a valuation officer[2] must notify[3] the relevant authority[4] of the effect of the alteration; and the relevant authority must as soon as reasonably practicable alter the copy of the list deposited at its principal office[5]. The valuation officer must notify the ratepayer[6] and any proposer[7] of the effect of the alteration[8]. However, this does not apply in relation to alterations made solely to correct a clerical error[9], or to reflect a change in the address of the hereditament concerned[10] or a change in the area of the relevant authority[11].

1 In the Non-Domestic Rating (Alteration of Lists and Appeals) (England) Regulations 2009, SI 2009/2268, Pt 2 (regs 3–17): 'alteration' means alteration of a list in relation to a particular hereditament, and 'alter' must be construed accordingly; and 'list' means a local non-domestic rating list compiled on or after 1 April 2017: reg 3(1) (numbered as such and definition amended by SI 2017/155). As to local non-domestic rating lists see PARA 191 et seq. As to the meaning of 'hereditament' see PARA 106. As to the application of Pt 2 to central non-domestic rating lists see PARA 224.

The Non-Domestic Rating (Alteration of Lists and Appeals) (England) Regulations 2009, SI 2009/2268, apply in relation to England only: see reg 1. As to the equivalent provision to reg 17 in relation to Wales see the Non-Domestic Rating (Alteration of Lists and Appeals) (Wales) Regulations 2005, SI 2005/758, reg 17; and PARA 213. As to the meanings of 'England' and 'Wales' see PARA 2 note 16.

2 In the Non-Domestic Rating (Alteration of Lists and Appeals) (England) Regulations 2009, SI 2009/2268, Pt 2 (regs 3–17), 'valuation officer', in relation to a local non-domestic rating list, means the valuation officer for the billing authority for which the list is compiled and maintained: see regs 2(1), 3(1) (reg 3(1) as renumbered: see note 1). As to the meaning of 'billing authority' see PARA 53. As to valuation officers see PARA 54.

3 Without prejudice to the Local Government Act 1972 s 233 (service of notice by local authorities: LOCAL GOVERNMENT vol 69 (2018) PARA 648) and the Non-Domestic Rating (Alteration of Lists and Appeals) (England) Regulations 2009, SI 2009/2268, reg 22(2), and subject to reg 22(1A), (3) and (4) (see below), any notice required by any provision of the regulations to be provided, sent, given or served may be provided, sent, given or served:

(1) by delivering it to the person ('X') to whom it is to be provided, sent, given or on whom it is to be served, or to any other person authorised by X to act as X's agent for the purpose (reg 22(1)(a) (amended by SI 2017/155));

(2) by sending it to X or X's agent by electronic communication, and any notice sent by such means must be regarded as sent when it is received in a legible form (Non-Domestic Rating (Alteration of Lists and Appeals) (England) Regulations 2009, SI 2009/2268, reg 22(1)(b), (5)(d));

(3) by leaving it at or forwarding it by post to:
  (a) X's usual or last-known place of business (reg 22(1)(c)(i)); or
  (b) in the case of a company, its registered office (reg 22(1)(c)(ii)); or
  (c) the usual or last-known place of business or registered office of any other person authorised by X to act as X's agent for the purpose (reg 22(1)(c)(iii));

(4) by delivering it to some person on the premises to which it relates or, if there is no person on the premises to whom it can so be delivered, by fixing it to some conspicuous part of the premises (reg 22(1)(d));

(5) without prejudice to the foregoing provisions, where a hereditament to which the notice relates is a place of business of the person on whom it is to be served, by leaving it at, or forwarding it by post addressed to that person at, that place of business (reg 22(1)(e)).

At the same time as a copy of a notice under reg 4D(1), reg 4F(1), reg 7, reg 8(2), reg 10(2)(b) or reg 13(2) is sent to or served on X's agent, the notice must also be provided to X: reg 22(1A) (added by SI 2017/155).

Where any notice which is to be provided, sent, given to or served on a person is to be provided, sent, given or served by or on behalf of the Common Council of the City of London or by an officer of the Common Council, it may be provided, sent given or served in any manner in which it might be provided, sent, given or served under the Local Government Act 1972 s 233 if the Common Council were a local authority within the meaning of that section: Non-Domestic Rating (Alteration of Lists and Appeals) (England) Regulations 2009, SI 2009/2268, reg 22(2) (amended by SI 2017/155).

Any notice to be served by a valuation officer on a person who made a request under the Non-Domestic Rating (Alteration of Lists and Appeals) (England) Regulations 2009, SI 2009/2268, reg 4B(2) or a proposal using the valuation officer's electronic portal may be served by notifying the person by electronic communication that a notice addressed to the person is posted on that electronic portal: reg 22(2A) (reg 22(2A), (2B) added by SI 2017/155). 'VO's electronic portal' means the online facility provided by the valuation officer ('VO') for use in connection with proposals for the alteration of a local list compiled on or after 1 April 2017: Non-Domestic Rating (Alteration of Lists and Appeals) (England) Regulations 2009, SI 2009/2268, reg 3(1) (as renumbered (see note 1); definition added by SI 2017/155). Any notice to be served by the Valuation Tribunal for England on a person who made an appeal using the Tribunal's electronic portal may be served by notifying the person by electronic communication that a notice addressed to the person is posted on that electronic portal: Non-Domestic Rating (Alteration of Lists and Appeals) (England) Regulations 2009, SI 2009/2268, reg 22(2B) (as so added).

Any notice to be served on the owner or occupier of any premises may be addressed by the description 'owner' or 'occupier' of the premises, without further name or description: reg 22(3).

Except where the Non-Domestic Rating (Alteration of Lists and Appeals) (England) Regulations 2009, SI 2009/2268, require a notice to be provided or served using the VO's electronic portal or in another manner agreed with the VO, any notice to be provided, sent or given to or served on a VO may be provided, sent, given or served by addressing the notice to the VO, and by delivering it or sending it to the VO's office by post or electronic communication: reg 22(4) (substituted by SI 2017/155).

In the Non-Domestic Rating (Alteration of Lists and Appeals) (England) Regulations 2009, SI 2009/2268, reg 22:

(i) 'electronic communication' has the meaning given by the Electronic Communications Act 2000 s 15(1) (see CIVIL PROCEDURE vol 11 (2015) PARA 61) (Non-Domestic Rating (Alteration of Lists and Appeals) (England) Regulations 2009, SI 2009/2268, reg 22(5)(a) (amended by SI 2017/155));

(ii) any reference to the VO's electronic portal includes a reference to the online facility provided by the central valuation officer for use in connection with proposals for the alteration of a central list compiled on or after 1 April 2017 (Non-Domestic Rating (Alteration of Lists and Appeals) (England) Regulations 2009, SI 2009/2268, reg 22(5)(aa) (added by SI 2017/155));

(iii) any reference to a notice includes a reference to a proposal and any other document required or authorised to be provided, sent, given or served (Non-Domestic Rating (Alteration of Lists and Appeals) (England) Regulations 2009, SI 2009/2268, reg 22(5)(b) (amended by SI 2017/155));

(iv) any reference to such requirement or authorisation is to a requirement or authorisation under the Non-Domestic Rating (Alteration of Lists and Appeals) (England) Regulations 2009 (reg 22(5)(c)).

As to the meaning of 'person' see PARA 11 note 13. As to the service of documents by post generally see PARA 139 note 3. As to the registered office of a company see COMPANIES vol 14 (2016) PARA 124. As to the Common Council of the City of London see LONDON GOVERNMENT vol 71 (2013) PARAS 34–38.

4 'Relevant authority', in relation to a hereditament, means the billing authority in whose area the hereditament is situated: Non-Domestic Rating (Alteration of Lists and Appeals) (England) Regulations 2009, SI 2009/2268, reg 2(1).

5 Non-Domestic Rating (Alteration of Lists and Appeals) (England) Regulations 2009, SI 2009/2268, reg 17(1).

6 'Ratepayer', in relation to a hereditament, means the occupier or, if the hereditament is not occupied, the owner: Non-Domestic Rating (Alteration of Lists and Appeals) (England) Regulations 2009, SI 2009/2268, reg 2(1). As to the meanings of 'owner' and 'occupier' see PARA 86.

7 'Proposer' means any proposer for whom an appeal in relation to the hereditament has been made under the Non-Domestic Rating (Alteration of Lists and Appeals) (England) Regulations 2009, SI 2009/2268, reg 13A(1) (see PARA 211) and whose appeal has either not been determined by the tribunal, or has been so determined and either an appeal has been made to the Lands Tribunal or

the Upper Tribunal and has not been determined, or the time for making an appeal to the Upper Tribunal has not yet expired: reg 17(5) (amended by SI 2017/155). As to the Valuation Tribunal for England see PARA 232. As to appeals see PARA 232 et seq.

8 Non-Domestic Rating (Alteration of Lists and Appeals) (England) Regulations 2009, SI 2009/2268, reg 17(2)(a). The notification must also state the effect of the application of Pt 2 (regs 3–17), and of Pt 5 (regs 22–25), in relation to the alteration: reg 17(2)(b). However, reg 17(2)(b) does not apply in relation to an alteration made to reflect:
(1) a decision of the valuation officer that a proposal is well-founded (reg 17(4)(a));
(2) a decision, in relation to the hereditament which is the subject of the proposal, of a valuation tribunal, the Valuation Tribunal for England, the Lands Tribunal, the Upper Tribunal or a court (reg 17(4)(b)); or
(3) an agreement under reg 12 (see PARA 209) (reg 17(4)(c)).
'Valuation tribunal' means a valuation tribunal established in England before 1 October 2009 under the Local Government Finance Act 1988 Sch 11 para 1 (now applicable in relation to Wales only): Non-Domestic Rating (Alteration of Lists and Appeals) (England) Regulations 2009, SI 2009/2268, reg 2(1).

9 Non-Domestic Rating (Alteration of Lists and Appeals) (England) Regulations 2009, SI 2009/2268 reg 17(3).

10 Non-Domestic Rating (Alteration of Lists and Appeals) (England) Regulations 2009, SI 2009/2268 reg 17(3)(a).

11 Non-Domestic Rating (Alteration of Lists and Appeals) (England) Regulations 2009, SI 2009/2268 reg 17(3)(b).

201. Check of information about a hereditament in England.

A person may not make a proposal[1] in relation to a hereditament[2] in England[3] unless a check of information about the hereditament has been completed[4]. Before making a proposal in relation to a hereditament, the person[5] must request from the valuation officer[6] information which the valuation officer holds about the hereditament[7], which the valuation officer must provide if the information reasonably relates to any of the grounds for making a proposal[8] and the valuation officer considers it reasonable to provide the person with that information[9]. On receiving information about the hereditament so provided by the valuation officer, the person must:

(1) if any of that information is inaccurate, provide the valuation officer with the accurate information[10];
(2) if the valuation officer has asked the person to provide the valuation officer with any missing factual information, provide the valuation officer with the missing information[11]; and
(3) confirm to the valuation officer which of the information provided by the valuation officer is accurate and that any information provided to the valuation officer under heads (1) and (2) is accurate[12].

On receiving a confirmation, the valuation officer must serve on the person who made the confirmation a written acknowledgment of receipt which must state the date on which the valuation officer received the confirmation and the date of the acknowledgment[13].

On receiving any information provided under head (1), the valuation officer must:

(a) decide if that information is accurate or inaccurate[14];
(b) alter the list to correct any inaccuracy in relation to the rateable value of the hereditament or any other information shown in the list about the hereditament[15]; and
(c) update any other information held by the valuation officer about the hereditament to correct any inaccuracy[16].

As soon as reasonably practicable after the steps above have been taken in relation to a hereditament, the valuation officer must serve on the person who made the request a notice stating that a check has been completed in relation to the hereditament[17]. A check is taken to be completed:

(i) if the valuation officer has not served a notice stating that a check has been completed before the end of the period of 12 months beginning with the date on which the valuation officer received a confirmation, at the end of that period[18]; or

(ii) if the valuation officer has not served such a notice before the end of any longer period agreed in writing by the valuation officer and the person, at the end of that period[19].

1 See PARA 202.

2 As to the meaning of 'hereditament' see PARA 106.

3 The Non-Domestic Rating (Alteration of Lists and Appeals) (England) Regulations 2009, SI 2009/2268, apply in relation to England only: see reg 1. There are no equivalent provisions to regs 4A–4F in relation to Wales. As to the meanings of 'England' and 'Wales' see PARA 2 note 16.

4 Non-Domestic Rating (Alteration of Lists and Appeals) (England) Regulations 2009, SI 2009/2268, reg 4A(1) (regs 4A–4F added by SI 2017/155). A check consists of the steps in the Non-Domestic Rating (Alteration of Lists and Appeals) (England) Regulations 2009, SI 2009/2268, regs 4B–4F: reg 4A(2) (as so added). For the purpose of the Regulations, a check is completed in relation to a hereditament on:

(1) the date on which the valuation officer serves a notice under reg 4F(1) (see the text to note 17) (reg 4A(3)(a) (as so added)); or

(2) the date on which the check is taken to be completed under reg 4F(3) (see the text to notes 18–19) (reg 4A(3)(b) (as so added)).

5 Ie a person mentioned in the Non-Domestic Rating (Alteration of Lists and Appeals) (England) Regulations 2009, SI 2009/2268, reg 4(2) (see PARA 202): reg 4B(1) (as added: see note 4).

6 As to the meaning of 'valuation officer' see PARA 200 note 2.

7 Non-Domestic Rating (Alteration of Lists and Appeals) (England) Regulations 2009, SI 2009/2268, reg 4B(2) (as added: see note 4). The person must request or provide information under reg 4B either using the valuation officer's electronic portal or in another manner agreed with the valuation officer: reg 4B(5) (as so added).

8 Ie the grounds set out in the Non-Domestic Rating (Alteration of Lists and Appeals) (England) Regulations 2009, SI 2009/2268, reg 4 (see PARA 202).

9 Non-Domestic Rating (Alteration of Lists and Appeals) (England) Regulations 2009, SI 2009/2268, reg 4B(3) (as added: see note 4). When providing the person with information under reg 4B(3), if the valuation officer is missing any factual information about the hereditament the valuation officer may ask the person to provide the valuation officer with the missing information: reg 4B(4) (as so added).

10 Non-Domestic Rating (Alteration of Lists and Appeals) (England) Regulations 2009, SI 2009/2268, reg 4C(1)(a) (as added: see note 4).

11 Non-Domestic Rating (Alteration of Lists and Appeals) (England) Regulations 2009, SI 2009/2268, reg 4C(1)(b) (as added: see note 4).

12 Non-Domestic Rating (Alteration of Lists and Appeals) (England) Regulations 2009, SI 2009/2268, reg 4C(1)(c) (as added: see note 4). A confirmation and any information provided by a person under reg 4C(1) must be provided either using the valuation officer's electronic portal or in another manner agreed with the valuation officer: reg 4C(2) (as so added). A confirmation must include a statement as to whether or not, on the day the person provides the confirmation, the proposer qualifies as a smaller proposer: reg 4C(3) (as so added). 'Smaller proposer' means a person who qualifies as a smaller proposer under reg 3A (see PARA 203) on the day the person provides a confirmation under reg 4C(1)(c): reg 3(1) (renumbered as such and definitions added by SI 2017/155).

13 Non-Domestic Rating (Alteration of Lists and Appeals) (England) Regulations 2009, SI 2009/2268, reg 4D(1) (as added: see note 4). For the purpose of the Regulations, the date on which the valuation officer received a confirmation is the date stated in the acknowledgment in accordance with reg 4D(1)(a): reg 4D(2) (as so added).

14 Non-Domestic Rating (Alteration of Lists and Appeals) (England) Regulations 2009, SI 2009/2268, reg 4E(a) (as added: see note 4).

15 Non-Domestic Rating (Alteration of Lists and Appeals) (England) Regulations 2009, SI 2009/2268, reg 4E(b) (as added: see note 4).

16 Non-Domestic Rating (Alteration of Lists and Appeals) (England) Regulations 2009, SI 2009/2268, reg 4E(c) (as added: see note 4).

17 Non-Domestic Rating (Alteration of Lists and Appeals) (England) Regulations 2009, SI 2009/2268, reg 4F(1) (as added: see note 4). As to the service of notices see PARA 200 note 3. The notice must include the following (reg 4F(2) (as so added)):

(1) the date on which the notice is served (reg 4F(2)(a) (as so added));
(2) the name of the person (reg 4F(2)(b) (as so added));
(3) the identity of the hereditament (reg 4F(2)(c) (as so added));
(4) details of any alteration the valuation officer made to the list as a result of the check (reg 4F(2)(d) (as so added));
(5) a summary of any changes the valuation officer made as a result of the check of information the valuation officer holds about the hereditament (reg 4F(2)(e) (as so added));
(6) a statement of the person's right to make a proposal (reg 4F(2)(f) (as so added)).

18 Non-Domestic Rating (Alteration of Lists and Appeals) (England) Regulations 2009, SI 2009/2268, reg 4F(3)(a) (as added: see note 4).

19 Non-Domestic Rating (Alteration of Lists and Appeals) (England) Regulations 2009, SI 2009/2268, reg 4F(3)(b) (as added: see note 4).

202. Proposals to alter local non-domestic rating lists.

A proposal for the alteration[1] of a local non-domestic rating list[2] may be made by an interested person[3] who has reason to believe that one of the following grounds exists[4]:

(1) the rateable value[5] shown in the list for a hereditament was inaccurate on the day the list was compiled[6];
(2) the rateable value shown in the list for a hereditament is inaccurate by reason of a material change of circumstances which occurred on or after the day on which the list was compiled[7];
(3) the rateable value shown in the list for a hereditament is inaccurate by reason of an amendment to the classes of plant and machinery[8] which comes into force on or after the day on which the list was compiled[9];
(4) the rateable value shown in the list for a hereditament by reason of an alteration made by a valuation officer is or has been inaccurate[10];
(5) the rateable value or any other information shown in the list for a hereditament is shown to be or to have been inaccurate by reason of a decision in relation to another hereditament of the Valuation Tribunal for England, a valuation tribunal, or the Lands Tribunal, the Upper Tribunal or a court determining an appeal or application for review from the Valuation Tribunal for England, a valuation tribunal, the Lands Tribunal or the Upper Tribunal[11];
(6) the day from which an alteration is shown in the list as having effect is wrong[12];
(7) a hereditament not shown in the list ought to be shown in that list[13];
(8) a hereditament shown in the list ought not to be shown in that list[14];
(9) the list should show that some part of a hereditament which is shown in the list is domestic property[15] or is exempt from non-domestic rating[16] but does not do so[17];
(10) the list should not show that some part of a hereditament which is shown in the list is domestic property or is exempt from non-domestic rating but does so[18];
(11) property which is shown in the list as more than one hereditament ought to be shown as one or more different hereditaments[19];
(12) property which is shown in the list as one hereditament ought to be shown as more than one hereditament[20];
(13) the address shown in the list for a hereditament is wrong[21];

(14) the description shown in the list for a hereditament is wrong[22]; and
(15) any statement required to be made about the hereditament[23] has been omitted from the list[24].

A proposal may also be made by a person, other than an interested person, who has reason to believe that a ground set out in head (3), (4) or (6) above exists[25] and was an interested person at any time during which the alteration or amendment in question had effect[26].

However, no proposal may be made by reference to more than one ground unless, for each ground relied on, the material day[27] and the effective date[28] are the same[29].

1 As to the meaning of 'alteration' see PARA 200 note 1. Information about the hereditament must be checked before a person makes a proposal: see PARA 201.

2 As to local non-domestic rating lists see PARA 191 et seq. As to the application of the Non-Domestic Rating (Alteration of Lists and Appeals) (England) Regulations 2009, SI 2009/2268, Pt 2 (regs 3–17) to central non-domestic rating lists see PARA 224.

3 The Non-Domestic Rating (Alteration of Lists and Appeals) (England) Regulations 2009, SI 2009/2268, reg 2(1) provides that 'interested person':

(1) in relation to a hereditament which forms part of the Crown Estate and is held by the Crown Estate Commissioners under their management within the meaning of the Crown Estate Act 1961 s 1 (see CROWN AND CROWN PROCEEDINGS vol 29 (2014) PARA 197), means the Crown Estate Commissioners;
(2) in relation to any other hereditament, means:
  (a) the occupier;
  (b) any other person (other than a mortgagee not in possession) having in any part of the hereditament either a legal estate or an equitable interest such as would entitle him (after the cessation of any prior interest) to possession of the hereditament or any part of it; and
  (c) any person having a qualifying connection with the occupier or a person described in head (b).

A person must be treated as having a 'qualifying connection' with another:

(i) where both persons are companies, and one is a subsidiary of the other, or both are subsidiaries of the same company (Non-Domestic Rating (Alteration of Lists and Appeals) (England) Regulations 2009, SI 2009/2268, reg 2(1), (2)(a)); or
(ii) where only one person is a company, the other person (the 'second person') has such an interest in that company as would, if the second person were a company, result in its being the holding company of the other (reg 2(2)(b)).

As to the meaning of 'hereditament' see PARA 106. As to the Crown Estate Commissioners see CROWN AND CROWN PROCEEDINGS vol 29 (2014) PARA 194 et seq. As to the meaning of 'occupier' see PARA 86. As to the meaning of 'person' see PARA 11 note 13. As to holding and subsidiary companies see COMPANIES vol 14 (2016) PARA 22.

The Non-Domestic Rating (Alteration of Lists and Appeals) (England) Regulations 2009, SI 2009/2268, apply in relation to England only: see reg 1. As to the equivalent provision to reg 4 in relation to Wales see the Non-Domestic Rating (Alteration of Lists and Appeals) (Wales) Regulations 2005, SI 2005/758, reg 4; and PARA 214. As to the meanings of 'England' and 'Wales' see PARA 2 note 16.

4 See the Non-Domestic Rating (Alteration of Lists and Appeals) (England) Regulations 2009, SI 2009/2268, reg 4(2)(a). No proposal may be made by an interested person, where that person (or a person having a qualifying connection with that person), acting in the same capacity, has made a proposal to alter the same list in relation to the same hereditament on the same ground and arising from the same event: reg 4(3)(b)(i). 'Event' means the compilation of the list, a material change of circumstances or an alteration of the list by the valuation officer: reg 4(4). 'Material change of circumstances', in relation to a hereditament, means a change in any of the matters mentioned in the Local Government Finance Act 1988 Sch 6 para 2(7) (see PARA 164): Non-Domestic Rating (Alteration of Lists and Appeals) (England) Regulations 2009, SI 2009/2268, reg 3(1) (numbered as such by SI 2017/155).

Also no proposal may be made by an interested person where a proposal to alter the list in relation to the same hereditament and arising from the same facts has been made by another person (excluding a person having a qualifying connection with the interested person) and has been considered and determined by a valuation tribunal, the Valuation Tribunal for England, the Lands Tribunal or the Upper Tribunal (Non-Domestic Rating (Alteration of Lists and Appeals) (England) Regulations 2009, SI 2009/2268, reg 4(3)(b)(ii)). As to the meaning of 'valuation tribunal' see PARA 200 note 8. As to the Valuation Tribunal for England see PARA 232. As to appeals see PARA 232 et seq. It may be that such a decision only prevents a further proposal being made during the life of that list (ie one five year period): see *Society of Medical Officers of Health v Hope (Valuation Officer)* [1960] AC 551, [1960] 1 All ER 317, HL; *Central Council for Health Education v Hope* (1958) 3 RRC 314; *Gudgeon (Valuation Officer) v Erith Borough Council and LCC* (1960) 7 RRC 9 (affd (1961) 8 RRC 324); *English Clays Lovering Pochin & Co Ltd v Davis (Valuation Officer)* (1966) 12 RRC 307 at 312, 319, Lands Tribunal. All of the cases cited in this paragraph were decided under previous legislation but may continue to be of relevance.

Cases decided under earlier legislation relating to the need to specify particulars of the proposal may still be of some relevance as there may be some issue as to the degree of precision required: see eg *British American Typewriters v Hill (Valuation Officer)* [1962] RA 298, 9 RRC 353, Lands Tribunal; *Firkins v Dyer (Valuation Officer)* (1972) 17 RRC 363, Lands Tribunal. Cf *Evans v Lands (Valuation Officer)* [1973] RA 377, Lands Tribunal; *R v Assessment Committee for Thanet and District Assessment Area and County Valuation Committee for Kent, ex p Isle of Thanet Gas Light and Coke Co* [1939] 2 KB 640, [1939] 2 All ER 489 (a claim that the existing assessment was 'incorrect and unfair' did not amount to a proposal); *R v Heston and Isleworth Rating Authority, ex p Conti* [1941] 2 KB 146, [1941] 2 All ER 116; *Robinson Bros (Brewers) Ltd v Durham Assessment Committee (Area No 7)* [1938] AC 321, [1938] 2 All ER 79, HL; *Motion, ex p St Albans Rubber Co* (1942) 36 R & IT 16; *R v Reading Assessment Committee, ex p McCarthy E Fitt Ltd* [1948] 1 All ER 194; *R v Surrey (Mid Eastern Area) Assessment Committee, ex p Merton and Morden UDC* [1948] 1 All ER 856; *R v Winchester Area Assessment Committee, ex p Wright* [1948] 2 KB 455, [1948] 2 All ER 552, CA; cf *Mayes v Millwood (Valuation Officer)* (1966) 12 RRC 244, Lands Tribunal; *Behrman v Seymour (Valuation Officer)* (1972) 17 RRC 333, Lands Tribunal; *Guest (Valuation Officer) v Boughton* [1981] RA 97; *Melland & Coward Ltd v Hare (Valuation Officer)* [1991] RA 283.

5 As to the valuation for rating see PARA 156 et seq.

6 Non-Domestic Rating (Alteration of Lists and Appeals) (England) Regulations 2009, SI 2009/2268, reg 4(1)(a).

7 Non-Domestic Rating (Alteration of Lists and Appeals) (England) Regulations 2009, SI 2009/2268, reg 4(1)(b).

8 Ie as set out in the Valuation for Rating (Plant and Machinery) (England) Regulations 2000, SI 2000/540, Schedule: see PARA 173.

9 Non-Domestic Rating (Alteration of Lists and Appeals) (England) Regulations 2009, SI 2009/2268, reg 4(1)(c).

10 Non-Domestic Rating (Alteration of Lists and Appeals) (England) Regulations 2009, SI 2009/2268, reg 4(1)(d). No proposal may be made on this ground, to the extent that the alteration was made as a result of a previous proposal relating to that hereditament or gives effect to the decision of a valuation tribunal, the Valuation Tribunal for England, the Lands Tribunal, the Upper Tribunal or a court determining an appeal or an application for a review in relation to the hereditament concerned: reg 4(3)(c) (amended by SI 2017/155).

11 Non-Domestic Rating (Alteration of Lists and Appeals) (England) Regulations 2009, SI 2009/2268, reg 4(1)(e). There must be some causal link between the decision of the tribunal and the opinion of the ratepayer that the existing entry is incorrect. Where reference was made to a decision solely because in that case the valuation was found to be excessive and incorrect, the ratepayer had not based the opinion on any causal link between the proposal and the preceding decision: *Canning (Valuation Officer) v Corby Power Ltd* [1997] RA 60, Lands Tribunal.

12 Non-Domestic Rating (Alteration of Lists and Appeals) (England) Regulations 2009, SI 2009/2268, reg 4(1)(f).

13 Non-Domestic Rating (Alteration of Lists and Appeals) (England) Regulations 2009, SI 2009/2268, reg 4(1)(g).

14 Non-Domestic Rating (Alteration of Lists and Appeals) (England) Regulations 2009, SI 2009/2268, reg 4(1)(h).

15 As to the meaning of 'domestic property' see PARA 190.

16 As to exemptions from non-domestic rating see PARA 110 et seq.

17 Non-Domestic Rating (Alteration of Lists and Appeals) (England) Regulations 2009, SI 2009/2268, reg 4(1)(i).

18 Non-Domestic Rating (Alteration of Lists and Appeals) (England) Regulations 2009, SI 2009/2268, reg 4(1)(j).

19 Non-Domestic Rating (Alteration of Lists and Appeals) (England) Regulations 2009, SI 2009/2268, reg 4(1)(k).
20 Non-Domestic Rating (Alteration of Lists and Appeals) (England) Regulations 2009, SI 2009/2268, reg 4(1)(l).
21 Non-Domestic Rating (Alteration of Lists and Appeals) (England) Regulations 2009, SI 2009/2268, reg 4(1)(m).
22 Non-Domestic Rating (Alteration of Lists and Appeals) (England) Regulations 2009, SI 2009/2268, reg 4(1)(n).
23 Ie under the Local Government Finance Act 1988 s 42: see PARA 194.
24 Non-Domestic Rating (Alteration of Lists and Appeals) (England) Regulations 2009, SI 2009/2268, reg 4(1)(o).
25 Non-Domestic Rating (Alteration of Lists and Appeals) (England) Regulations 2009, SI 2009/2268, reg 4(2)(c)(i).
26 Non-Domestic Rating (Alteration of Lists and Appeals) (England) Regulations 2009, SI 2009/2268, reg 4(2)(c)(ii).
27 'Material day', in relation to a hereditament, means the day determined as regards that hereditament in accordance with rules prescribed by regulations under the Local Government Finance Act 1988 Sch 6 para 2(6A) (see PARA 164): Non-Domestic Rating (Alteration of Lists and Appeals) (England) Regulations 2009, SI 2009/2268, reg 4(4).
28 'Effective date' means the day from which the alteration, if made, would have effect in pursuance of the Non-Domestic Rating (Alteration of Lists and Appeals) (England) Regulations 2009, SI 2009/2268, Pt 2 (regs 3–17) (see PARA 212): reg 4(4).
29 Non-Domestic Rating (Alteration of Lists and Appeals) (England) Regulations 2009, SI 2009/2268, reg 4(3)(a).

203. Smaller proposers.

A person other than an interested person[1] who may make a proposal for the alteration of a local non-domestic rating list[2] qualifies as a smaller proposer on a day if on that day the person meets specified conditions[3]. Those conditions are that the individual;

(1) falls within the definition of 'micro business' in the Small Business, Enterprise and Employment Act 2015[4], subject to specified[5] modifications[6]; or
(2) is an individual who does not fall within the definition of 'undertaking' in the Small Business, Enterprise and Employment Act 2015[7], subject to specified[8] modifications[9].

1 As to the meaning of 'interested person' see PARA 202 note 3.
2 As to proposals see PARA 202. As to local non-domestic rating lists see PARA 191 et seq.
3 Non-Domestic Rating (Alteration of Lists and Appeals) (England) Regulations 2009, SI 2009/2268, reg 3A(1) (reg 3A added by SI 2017/155). The Non-Domestic Rating (Alteration of Lists and Appeals) (England) Regulations 2009, SI 2009/2268, apply in relation to England only: see reg 1. There is no equivalent provision to reg 3A in relation to Wales. As to the meanings of 'England' and 'Wales' see PARA 2 note 16.
4 Ie in the Small Business, Enterprise and Employment Act 2015 s 33(3). Section 33 applies where any subordinate legislation made by a Minister of the Crown (the 'underlying provision') uses the term 'small business or 'micro business', and defines that term by reference to s 33: s 33(1). In the underlying provision 'small business' means an undertaking other than a micro business (see s 33(3)) which meets the following conditions ('the small business size conditions') (s 33(2)):
(1) it has a headcount of staff of less than 50 (s 33(2)(a)); and
(2) it has a turnover or a balance sheet total of an amount less than or equal to the small business threshold (s 33(2)(b)).

In the underlying provision 'micro business' means an undertaking which meets the following conditions ('the micro business size conditions') (s 33(3)):
(a) it has a headcount of staff of less than 10 (s 33(3)(a)); and
(b) it has a turnover or a balance sheet total of an amount less than or equal to the micro business threshold (s 33(3)(b)).

The Secretary of State may by regulations (referred to as 'the small and micro business regulations') make further provision about the meanings of 'small business' and 'micro business': s 33(4). Section 33 and the small and micro business regulations are to be read subject to any modifications made by the underlying provision in any particular case: s 33(5).

In s 33, 'balance sheet total', 'headcount of staff', 'micro business threshold', 'small business threshold' and 'turnover' have such meanings as may be prescribed by the small and micro business regulations; 'Minister of the Crown' has the same meaning as in the Ministers of the Crown Act 1975 (see PARA 41 note 1); 'subordinate legislation' has the same meaning as in the Interpretation Act 1978 (see s 21; and PARA 111 note 1); and 'undertaking' means a person carrying on one or more businesses, a voluntary or community body within the meaning given by s 27 or a body which is formed or recognised under the law of a country or territory outside the United Kingdom and which is equivalent in nature to a body falling within the definition of voluntary or community body: Small Business, Enterprise and Employment Act 2015 s 33(6).

The small and micro business regulations are subject to negative resolution procedure (ie the statutory instrument containing the regulations is subject to annulment in pursuance of a resolution of either House of Parliament): s 33(7).

5 Ie the modifications contained in the Non-Domestic Rating (Alteration of Lists and Appeals) (England) Regulations 2009, SI 2009/2268, reg 3A. In determining whether an undertaking meets the 'micro business size conditions' defined in the Small Business, Enterprise and Employment Act 2015 s 33(3) (see note 4), all business activities within the meaning of s 27 ('business activities') carried on by the undertaking must be taken into account: Non-Domestic Rating (Alteration of Lists and Appeals) (England) Regulations 2009, SI 2009/2268, reg 3A(3) (as added: see note 3). Regulations made under the Small Business, Enterprise and Employment Act 2015 s 33(4) do not apply to the meaning of 'micro business' in s 33: Non-Domestic Rating (Alteration of Lists and Appeals) (England) Regulations 2009, SI 2009/2268, reg 3A(4) (as so added).

The definition of 'micro business' in the Small Business, Enterprise and Employment Act 2015 s 33(3) is to be read as if:

(1) 'balance sheet total' means the aggregate of the amounts shown as assets in a balance sheet of the undertaking's assets and liabilities prepared by the undertaking during the last 12 month period (Non-Domestic Rating (Alteration of Lists and Appeals) (England) Regulations 2009, SI 2009/2268, reg 3A(5)(a) (as so added));

(2) 'head count of staff' means the average number of persons employed by the undertaking, as determined under reg 3A(6) (see below) (reg 3A(5)(b) (as so added));

(3) 'micro business threshold' means:

 (a) in relation to balance sheet total, £2 million (reg 3A(5)(c)(i) (as so added));

 (b) in relation to turnover, for an undertaking that has carried on business activities for at least 12 months, £2 million (reg 3A(5)(c)(ii) (as so added));

 (c) in relation to turnover, for an undertaking that has carried on business activities for less than 12 months, an amount proportionally adjusted (reg 3A(5)(c)(iii) (as so added)); and

(4) 'turnover' has the same meaning as in the Companies Act 2006 s 474(1) (see COMPANIES vol 15 (2016) PARA 766) (Non-Domestic Rating (Alteration of Lists and Appeals) (England) Regulations 2009, SI 2009/2268, reg 3A(5)(d) (as so added)).

The average number of persons employed by the undertaking is determined as follows (reg 3A(6) (as so added)):

(i) for an undertaking that has carried on business activities for at least 12 months, for each month in the last 12 month period, find the number of persons employed under contracts of employment by the undertaking at any time in that month, add together the monthly totals and divide by 12 (reg 3A(6)(a) (as so added));

(ii) for an undertaking that has carried on business activities for less than 12 months, for each of those months, find the number of persons employed under contracts of employment by the undertaking at any time in that month, add together the monthly totals and divide by the number of monthly totals (reg 3A(6)(b) (as so added)).

In reg 3A, 'last 12 month period' means the period of 12 months ending on the day mentioned in reg 3A(1) (see the text to note 3): reg 3A(7) (as so added).

6 Non-Domestic Rating (Alteration of Lists and Appeals) (England) Regulations 2009, SI 2009/2268, reg 3A(1)(a) (as added: see note 3).

7 Ie in the Small Business, Enterprise and Employment Act 2015 s 33(6).

8 Ie the modifications contained in the Non-Domestic Rating (Alteration of Lists and Appeals) (England) Regulations 2009, SI 2009/2268, reg 3A. In para (a) of the definition of 'undertaking' in the Small Business, Enterprise and Employment Act 2015 s 33(6), the reference to 'businesses' is to be read as if s 27 applies to that reference: Non-Domestic Rating (Alteration of Lists and Appeals) (England) Regulations 2009, SI 2009/2268, reg 3A(2) (as added: see note 3).

9 Non-Domestic Rating (Alteration of Lists and Appeals) (England) Regulations 2009, SI 2009/2268, reg 3A(1)(b) (as added: see note 3).

204. Form and contents of proposals.

Subject to specific provision where a proposal to alter a local non-domestic rating list[1] is made on the ground of a material change of circumstances[2], a proposal in relation to a hereditament[3] may only be made within the period of four months beginning with the date on which a check was completed in relation to the hereditament[4]. A proposal must be made by serving it on the valuation officer using the valuation officer's electronic portal or in another manner agreed with the valuation officer[5]. The date a proposal is made is the date on which it is served on the valuation officer[6].

A proposal must include:

(1) the name, address and contact details of the proposer[7];
(2) the grounds of the proposal including the particulars on which each of the grounds is based ('particulars of the grounds of the proposal')[8];
(3) details of the proposed alteration of the list[9];
(4) the date from which the proposer asserts the proposed alteration should have effect[10];
(5) the date on which the proposal is served on the valuation officer[11];
(6) evidence to support the grounds of the proposal[12]; and
(7) a statement as to how the evidence supports the grounds of the proposal[13].

A proposal in relation to a hereditament ('the hereditament') made on the ground that its rateable value or other information shown in the list for it is shown to be or to have been inaccurate by reason of a decision in relation to another hereditament[14] must also include:

(a) the date of the decision made in relation to another hereditament ('the decision')[15];
(b) the name of the tribunal or court which made the decision[16];
(c) information to identify the other hereditament[17];
(d) the reasons the proposer believes that the decision is relevant to the rateable value or other information shown in the list for the hereditament[18]; and
(e) the reasons the proposer believes that, by reason of the decision, the rateable value or other information shown in the list for the hereditament is inaccurate[19].

If a proposal in relation to a hereditament is made on one or more of certain specified grounds[20] and the hereditament is occupied under a lease, easement or licence to occupy, the proposal must also include:

(i) where the proposer is the occupier[21], the amount payable each year by the proposer, as at the date the proposal is made, in respect of the lease, easement or licence to occupy, the date at which that amount first became payable and details of any rent-free periods[22]; or
(ii) where the proposer is not the occupier, the amount payable each year to the proposer, as at the date the proposal is made, in respect of the lease, easement or licence to occupy, the date at which that amount first became payable and details of any rent-free periods[23].

A proposal may deal with more than one hereditament only in prescribed circumstances[24]. A proposal made on the ground that the rateable value shown in the list by reason of an alteration is or has been inaccurate[25] or that the day from which an alteration is shown in the list as having effect is wrong[26] may include a request for either or both of the following:

(A) the restoration of the list to its state before the alteration was made[27]; and

(B) a further alteration of the list in respect of the hereditament[28].

A proposal in relation to a hereditament made on the ground of a material change of circumstances[29] may be made, if the ground relates to a specified material change of circumstances[30], by the later of[31]:

(I) the last day in the period of four months beginning with the date on which a check was completed in relation to the hereditament[32]; and

(II) the last day in the period of 16 months beginning with the date on which the valuation officer received a confirmation[33].

In general, a person may make only one proposal on the ground of material change of circumstances in relation to each material change of circumstances[34]. However, a person may make one proposal on that ground in relation to more than one material change of circumstances[35] if:

(AA) the material day[36] is the same for each material change of circumstances[37]; and

(BB) the effective date[38] is the same for each material change of circumstances[39].

If a person has provided information to the valuation officer[40] in relation to a material change of circumstances but does not make a proposal within the specified period[41], the person may not make a proposal in relation to that material change of circumstances[42].

1 As to proposals see PARA 202. As to the meaning of 'alter' see PARA 200 note 1. As to local non-domestic rating lists see PARA 191 et seq. As to the application of the Non-Domestic Rating (Alteration of Lists and Appeals) (England) Regulations 2009, SI 2009/2268, Pt 2 (regs 3–17) to central non-domestic rating lists see PARA 224. The Non-Domestic Rating (Alteration of Lists and Appeals) (England) Regulations 2009, SI 2009/2268, apply in relation to England only: see reg 1. As to the equivalent provision to regs 6, 6A in relation to Wales see the Non-Domestic Rating (Alteration of Lists and Appeals) (Wales) Regulations 2005, SI 2005/758, reg 6; and PARA 216. As to the meanings of 'England' and 'Wales' see PARA 2 note 16.

2 Ie under the Non-Domestic Rating (Alteration of Lists and Appeals) (England) Regulations 2009, SI 2009/2268, reg 4(1)(b) (see PARA 202): see reg 6A; and the text to notes 29–42.

3 As to the meaning of 'hereditament' see PARA 106.

4 Non-Domestic Rating (Alteration of Lists and Appeals) (England) Regulations 2009, SI 2009/2268, reg 6(1) (reg 6 substituted by SI 2017/155). As to checks in relation to hereditaments see PARA 201.

5 Non-Domestic Rating (Alteration of Lists and Appeals) (England) Regulations 2009, SI 2009/2268, reg 6(2) (as substituted: see note 4). As to the service of notices see PARA 200 note 3. As to valuation officers see PARA 54.

6 Non-Domestic Rating (Alteration of Lists and Appeals) (England) Regulations 2009, SI 2009/2268, reg 6(3) (as substituted: see note 4).

7 Non-Domestic Rating (Alteration of Lists and Appeals) (England) Regulations 2009, SI 2009/2268, reg 6(4)(a) (as substituted: see note 4). 'Proposer' means the person making a proposal: reg 2(1). As to the meaning of 'person' see PARA 11 note 13.

8 Non-Domestic Rating (Alteration of Lists and Appeals) (England) Regulations 2009, SI 2009/2268, reg 6(4)(b) (as substituted: see note 4).

9 Non-Domestic Rating (Alteration of Lists and Appeals) (England) Regulations 2009, SI 2009/2268, reg 6(4)(c) (as substituted: see note 4).

10 Non-Domestic Rating (Alteration of Lists and Appeals) (England) Regulations 2009, SI 2009/2268, reg 6(4)(d) (as substituted: see note 4).

11 Non-Domestic Rating (Alteration of Lists and Appeals) (England) Regulations 2009, SI 2009/2268, reg 6(4)(e) (as substituted: see note 4).
12 Non-Domestic Rating (Alteration of Lists and Appeals) (England) Regulations 2009, SI 2009/2268, reg 6(4)(f) (as substituted: see note 4).
13 Non-Domestic Rating (Alteration of Lists and Appeals) (England) Regulations 2009, SI 2009/2268, reg 6(4)(g) (as substituted: see note 4).
14 Ie on the ground set out in the Non-Domestic Rating (Alteration of Lists and Appeals) (England) Regulations 2009, SI 2009/2268, reg 4(1)(e): see PARA 202.
15 Non-Domestic Rating (Alteration of Lists and Appeals) (England) Regulations 2009, SI 2009/2268, reg 6(5)(a) (as substituted: see note 4).
16 Non-Domestic Rating (Alteration of Lists and Appeals) (England) Regulations 2009, SI 2009/2268, reg 6(5)(b) (as substituted: see note 4).
17 Non-Domestic Rating (Alteration of Lists and Appeals) (England) Regulations 2009, SI 2009/2268, reg 6(5)(c) (as substituted: see note 4).
18 Non-Domestic Rating (Alteration of Lists and Appeals) (England) Regulations 2009, SI 2009/2268, reg 6(5)(d) (as substituted: see note 4).
19 Non-Domestic Rating (Alteration of Lists and Appeals) (England) Regulations 2009, SI 2009/2268, reg 6(5)(e) (as substituted: see note 4).
20 Ie the grounds set out in the Non-Domestic Rating (Alteration of Lists and Appeals) (England) Regulations 2009, SI 2009/2268, reg 4(1)(a)–(g), (i)–(l): see PARA 202.
21 As to the meaning of 'occupier' see PARA 86.
22 Non-Domestic Rating (Alteration of Lists and Appeals) (England) Regulations 2009, SI 2009/2268, reg 6(6)(a) (as substituted: see note 4).
23 Non-Domestic Rating (Alteration of Lists and Appeals) (England) Regulations 2009, SI 2009/2268, reg 6(6)(b) (as substituted: see note 4).
24 A proposal may deal with more than one hereditament only:
(1) if it is made on the grounds set out in the Non-Domestic Rating (Alteration of Lists and Appeals) (England) Regulations 2009, SI 2009/2268, reg 4(1)(k) or (l) (see PARA 202) (reg 6(7)(a) (as substituted: see note 4)); or
(2) where the person making the proposal does so in the same capacity as respects each hereditament and each hereditament is within the same building or the same curtilage (reg 6(7)(b) (as so substituted)).

It is important to specify clearly both hereditaments within one curtilage if it is intended to alter both by proposal: *R v Cardiff Justices, ex p Cardiff Corpn* [1962] 2 QB 436, sub nom *R v City of Cardiff Justices, ex p Cardiff City Council* [1962] 1 All ER 751.
25 Ie the ground set out in the Non-Domestic Rating (Alteration of Lists and Appeals) (England) Regulations 2009, SI 2009/2268, reg 4(1)(d): see PARA 202.
26 Ie the ground set out in the Non-Domestic Rating (Alteration of Lists and Appeals) (England) Regulations 2009, SI 2009/2268, reg 4(1)(f): see PARA 202.
27 Non-Domestic Rating (Alteration of Lists and Appeals) (England) Regulations 2009, SI 2009/2268, reg 6(8)(a) (as substituted: see note 4).
28 Non-Domestic Rating (Alteration of Lists and Appeals) (England) Regulations 2009, SI 2009/2268, reg 6(8)(b) (as substituted: see note 4).
29 Ie under the Non-Domestic Rating (Alteration of Lists and Appeals) (England) Regulations 2009, SI 2009/2268, reg 4(1)(b): see PARA 202.
30 Ie a material change of circumstances mentioned in the Local Government Finance Act 1988 Sch 6 para 2(7)(d) or (e): see PARA 164.
31 Non-Domestic Rating (Alteration of Lists and Appeals) (England) Regulations 2009, SI 2009/2268, reg 6A(1), (2) (reg 6A added by SI 2017/155).
32 Non-Domestic Rating (Alteration of Lists and Appeals) (England) Regulations 2009, SI 2009/2268, reg 6A(2)(a) (as added: see note 31).
33 Non-Domestic Rating (Alteration of Lists and Appeals) (England) Regulations 2009, SI 2009/2268, reg 6A(2)(b) (as added: see note 31). As to confirmation see PARA 201.
34 Non-Domestic Rating (Alteration of Lists and Appeals) (England) Regulations 2009, SI 2009/2268, reg 6A(3) (as added: see note 31).
35 Non-Domestic Rating (Alteration of Lists and Appeals) (England) Regulations 2009, SI 2009/2268, reg 6A(4) (as added: see note 31).
36 As to the meaning of 'material day' see PARA 202 note 27.
37 Non-Domestic Rating (Alteration of Lists and Appeals) (England) Regulations 2009, SI 2009/2268, reg 6A(4)(a) (as added: see note 31).
38 As to the meaning of 'effective date' see PARA 202 note 28.

39 Non-Domestic Rating (Alteration of Lists and Appeals) (England) Regulations 2009, SI 2009/2268, reg 6A(4)(b) (as added: see note 31).
40 Ie under the Non-Domestic Rating (Alteration of Lists and Appeals) (England) Regulations 2009, SI 2009/2268, reg 4C(1): see PARA 201.
41 Ie the period in the Non-Domestic Rating (Alteration of Lists and Appeals) (England) Regulations 2009, SI 2009/2268, reg 6(1) (see the text to notes 1–4) or if applicable the period in reg 6A(2) (see the text to notes 31–33).
42 Non-Domestic Rating (Alteration of Lists and Appeals) (England) Regulations 2009, SI 2009/2268, reg 6A(5) (as added: see note 31).

205. Acknowledgment of proposal.

In relation to England, except where the proposal is incomplete[1], within four weeks of receiving a proposal for the alteration of a local non-domestic rating list[2], the valuation officer for the billing authority[3] for which the list is compiled and maintained must send an acknowledgment of its receipt to the proposer[4]. An acknowledgment must specify the date of receipt of the proposal and must be accompanied by a statement containing prescribed information[5].

1 Non-Domestic Rating (Alteration of Lists and Appeals) (England) Regulations 2009, SI 2009/2268, reg 7(2) (substituted by SI 2017/155). As to incomplete proposals see PARA 206.
2 As to proposals see PARA 202. As to the meaning of 'alteration' see PARA 200 note 1. As to local non-domestic rating lists see PARA 191 et seq. As to the application of the Non-Domestic Rating (Alteration of Lists and Appeals) (England) Regulations 2009, SI 2009/2268, Pt 2 (regs 3–17) to central non-domestic rating lists see PARA 224.
3 As to the meaning of 'billing authority' see PARA 53. As to valuation officers see PARA 54.
4 See the Non-Domestic Rating (Alteration of Lists and Appeals) (England) Regulations 2009, SI 2009/2268, reg 7(1). The Non-Domestic Rating (Alteration of Lists and Appeals) (England) Regulations 2009, SI 2009/2268, apply in relation to England only: see reg 1. As to the equivalent provision to reg 7 in relation to Wales see the Non-Domestic Rating (Alteration of Lists and Appeals) (Wales) Regulations 2005, SI 2005/758, reg 7; and PARA 217. As to the meanings of 'England' and 'Wales' see PARA 2 note 16. As to the meaning of 'proposer' see PARA 204 note 7.
5 See the Non-Domestic Rating (Alteration of Lists and Appeals) (England) Regulations 2009, SI 2009/2268, reg 7(3). The statement must set out the effect of regs 9–13E (see PARA 207 et seq): see reg 7(3) (amended by SI 2017/155).

206. Incomplete proposals.

In England, the valuation officer for the billing authority[1] for which the list is compiled and maintained must refuse a proposal for the alteration of a local non-domestic rating list[2] ('an incomplete proposal') which does not include specified[3] matters[4].

If the valuation officer refuses an incomplete proposal, the valuation officer must serve on the proposer[5] a notice of refusal specifying the information which is missing and the date the notice is served[6]. If an incomplete proposal in relation to a hereditament[7] is refused, the proposer may make a further proposal within the period of four months beginning with the date on which a check was completed[8] in relation to the hereditament[9].

1 As to the meaning of 'billing authority' see PARA 53. As to valuation officers see PARA 54.
2 As to proposals see PARA 202. As to the meaning of 'alteration' see PARA 200 note 1. As to local non-domestic rating lists see PARA 191 et seq. As to the application of the Non-Domestic Rating (Alteration of Lists and Appeals) (England) Regulations 2009, SI 2009/2268, Pt 2 (regs 3–17) to central non-domestic rating lists see PARA 224.
3 Ie the matters specified in the Non-Domestic Rating (Alteration of Lists and Appeals) (England) Regulations 2009, SI 2009/2268, reg 6(5) and, if applicable, reg 6(5), (6): see PARA 204.

4 Non-Domestic Rating (Alteration of Lists and Appeals) (England) Regulations 2009, SI 2009/2268, reg 8(1) (reg 8 substituted by SI 2017/155). The Non-Domestic Rating (Alteration of Lists and Appeals) (England) Regulations 2009, SI 2009/2268, apply in relation to England only: see reg 1. As to the equivalent provision to reg 8 in relation to Wales see the Non-Domestic Rating (Alteration of Lists and Appeals) (Wales) Regulations 2005, SI 2005/758, reg 8; and PARA 218. As to the meanings of 'England' and 'Wales' see PARA 2 note 16.

5 As to the meaning of 'proposer' see PARA 204 note 7.

6 Non-Domestic Rating (Alteration of Lists and Appeals) (England) Regulations 2009, SI 2009/2268, reg 8(2) (as substituted: see note 4). As to the service of notices see PARA 200 note 3.

7 As to the meaning of 'hereditament' see PARA 106.

8 See PARA 201.

9 Non-Domestic Rating (Alteration of Lists and Appeals) (England) Regulations 2009, SI 2009/2268, reg 8(3) (as substituted: see note 4). In calculating the period in reg 8(3), the days beginning with the date on which the incomplete proposal was made and ending with the date on which the notice of refusal was served are to be ignored (reg 8(4)), but this does not apply where a second or subsequent notice of refusal is served in relation to the further proposal (reg 8(5)).

207. Procedure after a proposal is made.

In England, the valuation officer[1] for the billing authority[2] for which the list is compiled and maintained must, within the period of six weeks beginning with the date on which the valuation officer receives a proposal (not being an incomplete proposal[3]) for the alteration of a local non-domestic rating list[4] in relation to a hereditament[5], serve a copy of the proposal on the ratepayer for that hereditament, unless the ratepayer is the proposer[6].

The valuation officer must provide the relevant authority[7] with the information specified below within the period of six weeks beginning with the date on which the valuation officer receives the proposal and the proposal is determined[8]. The information is:

(1) the identity of the hereditament[9];
(2) the date the proposal was made in relation to the hereditament[10];
(3) the rateable value of the hereditament shown in the list on the date the information is given to the relevant authority[11];
(4) the proposed rateable value[12];
(5) the date from which the proposer asserts that the proposed rateable value should have effect[13]; and
(6) whether or not the proposal has been determined[14].

The relevant authority may provide the valuation officer with evidence relating to the proposal[15], and if it does so:

(a) the valuation officer must provide a copy of that evidence to the proposer[16]; and
(b) the proposer may provide the valuation officer with further evidence in response to that evidence[17].

On receipt of the proposal, the valuation officer must if the valuation officer considers it reasonable to do so provide the proposer with any information the valuation officer holds that relates to the particulars of the grounds of the proposal[18]. Before the proposal is determined, the proposer in response to the information so provided may provide the valuation officer with further evidence to support the grounds of the proposal[19]. Before the valuation officer determines the proposal, if the valuation officer receives any further information that relates to the particulars of the grounds of the proposal:

(i) the valuation officer must if the valuation officer considers it reasonable to do so provide the proposer with that information[20]; and

(ii) the proposer may provide the valuation officer with further evidence in response to that information[21].

Before the proposal is determined, the proposer may provide the valuation officer with further evidence relating to the grounds of the proposal if that evidence was not known to the proposer and could not reasonably have been acquired by the proposer before the proposal was made[22].

The proposer and the valuation officer may agree in writing that the proposer may provide further evidence in circumstances not mentioned above[23].

Any evidence provided by the proposer under these provisions forms part of the proposal and must be provided to the valuation officer:

(A) using the valuation officer's electronic portal[24]; or

(B) in another manner agreed with the valuation officer[25].

If the valuation officer decides that a proposal is well-founded, the valuation officer must as soon as reasonably practicable after making such a decision[26], alter the list accordingly and serve a notice of the decision[27] on the proposer and, if the proposer is not the ratepayer, the ratepayer[28].

1 As to valuation officers see PARA 54.
2 As to the meaning of 'billing authority' see PARA 53.
3 As to incomplete proposals see PARA 206.
4 As to proposals see PARA 202. As to the meaning of 'alteration' see PARA 200 note 1. As to local non-domestic rating lists see PARA 191 et seq. As to the application of the Non-Domestic Rating (Alteration of Lists and Appeals) (England) Regulations 2009, SI 2009/2268, Pt 2 (regs 3–17) to central non-domestic rating lists see PARA 224.
5 As to the meaning of 'hereditament' see PARA 106.
6 Non-Domestic Rating (Alteration of Lists and Appeals) (England) Regulations 2009, SI 2009/2268, reg 9(1), (2) (regs 9, 10 substituted by SI 2017/155). A copy of a proposal served on a ratepayer must be accompanied by a statement of the effect of the Non-Domestic Rating (Alteration of Lists and Appeals) (England) Regulations 2009, SI 2009/2268, regs 10–13E (see the text to notes 26–28; and PARAS 208–211): reg 9(3) (as so substituted). As to the meaning of 'proposer' see PARA 204 note 7.

The Non-Domestic Rating (Alteration of Lists and Appeals) (England) Regulations 2009, SI 2009/2268, apply in relation to England only: see reg 1. As to the equivalent provision to reg 9 in relation to Wales see the Non-Domestic Rating (Alteration of Lists and Appeals) (Wales) Regulations 2005, SI 2005/758, reg 9; and PARA 219. As to the meanings of 'England' and 'Wales' see PARA 2 note 16.
7 As to the meaning of 'relevant authority' see PARA 200 note 4.
8 Non-Domestic Rating (Alteration of Lists and Appeals) (England) Regulations 2009, SI 2009/2268, reg 9(4) (as substituted: see note 6).
9 Non-Domestic Rating (Alteration of Lists and Appeals) (England) Regulations 2009, SI 2009/2268, reg 9(5)(a) (as substituted: see note 6).
10 Non-Domestic Rating (Alteration of Lists and Appeals) (England) Regulations 2009, SI 2009/2268, reg 9(5)(b) (as substituted: see note 6).
11 Non-Domestic Rating (Alteration of Lists and Appeals) (England) Regulations 2009, SI 2009/2268, reg 9(5)(c) (as substituted: see note 6).
12 Non-Domestic Rating (Alteration of Lists and Appeals) (England) Regulations 2009, SI 2009/2268, reg 9(5)(d) (as substituted: see note 6).
13 Non-Domestic Rating (Alteration of Lists and Appeals) (England) Regulations 2009, SI 2009/2268, reg 9(5)(e) (as substituted: see note 6).
14 Non-Domestic Rating (Alteration of Lists and Appeals) (England) Regulations 2009, SI 2009/2268, reg 9(5)(f) (as substituted: see note 6).
15 Non-Domestic Rating (Alteration of Lists and Appeals) (England) Regulations 2009, SI 2009/2268, reg 9(6) (as substituted: see note 6).
16 Non-Domestic Rating (Alteration of Lists and Appeals) (England) Regulations 2009, SI 2009/2268, reg 9(6)(a) (as substituted: see note 6).
17 Non-Domestic Rating (Alteration of Lists and Appeals) (England) Regulations 2009, SI 2009/2268, reg 9(6)(b) (as substituted: see note 6).

18 Non-Domestic Rating (Alteration of Lists and Appeals) (England) Regulations 2009, SI 2009/2268, reg 9(7) (as substituted: see note 6).
19 Non-Domestic Rating (Alteration of Lists and Appeals) (England) Regulations 2009, SI 2009/2268, reg 9(8) (as substituted: see note 6).
20 Non-Domestic Rating (Alteration of Lists and Appeals) (England) Regulations 2009, SI 2009/2268, reg 9(9)(a) (as substituted: see note 6).
21 Non-Domestic Rating (Alteration of Lists and Appeals) (England) Regulations 2009, SI 2009/2268, reg 9(9)(b) (as substituted: see note 6).
22 Non-Domestic Rating (Alteration of Lists and Appeals) (England) Regulations 2009, SI 2009/2268, reg 9(10) (as substituted: see note 6).
23 Non-Domestic Rating (Alteration of Lists and Appeals) (England) Regulations 2009, SI 2009/2268, reg 9(11) (as substituted: see note 6). The text refers to circumstances not mentioned in reg 9(6)–(10).
24 Non-Domestic Rating (Alteration of Lists and Appeals) (England) Regulations 2009, SI 2009/2268, reg 9(12)(a) (as substituted: see note 6).
25 Non-Domestic Rating (Alteration of Lists and Appeals) (England) Regulations 2009, SI 2009/2268, reg 9(12)(b) (as substituted: see note 6).
26 Ie under the Non-Domestic Rating (Alteration of Lists and Appeals) (England) Regulations 2009, SI 2009/2268, reg 10(1).
27 As to the service of notices see PARA 200 note 3.
28 Non-Domestic Rating (Alteration of Lists and Appeals) (England) Regulations 2009, SI 2009/2268, reg 10(2), (2) (as substituted: see note 6).

208. Withdrawal of proposals.

The proposer[1] may withdraw the proposal for the alteration of a local non-domestic rating list[2] by notice[3] sent to the valuation officer for the billing authority[4] for which the list is compiled and maintained[5]. However, where the proposer was a ratepayer[6] in respect of the hereditament[7] at the date of the proposal but is no longer, the proposal may not be withdrawn unless the person[8] who is currently the ratepayer agrees in writing[9].

Where, within two months[10] from the day on which the valuation officer receives a proposal, an interested person[11] notifies the valuation officer in writing that he wishes to be a party to the proceedings in respect of that proposal (an 'interested person's notice')[12] and, after receiving an interested person's notice, the proposal is withdrawn[13], the valuation officer must give notice of the withdrawal to the interested person[14]. Where, within six weeks from the day on which the interested person receives the valuation officer's notice, the interested person notifies the valuation officer in writing that he is aggrieved by the withdrawal of the proposal:

(1) the notification must, if the interested person would at the date of the proposal have been competent to make that proposal, be treated[15] as if it had been a proposal in the same terms made on the day on which the valuation officer received the notification[16]; and
(2) any resulting alteration[17] has effect from the day which would have been applicable had there been no withdrawal[18].

1 As to the meaning of 'proposer' see PARA 204 note 7.
2 As to proposals see PARA 202. As to the meaning of 'alteration' see PARA 200 note 1. As to local non-domestic rating lists see PARA 191 et seq. As to the application of the Non-Domestic Rating (Alteration of Lists and Appeals) (England) Regulations 2009, SI 2009/2268, Pt 2 (regs 3–17) to central non-domestic rating lists see PARA 224.
3 As to the service of notices see PARA 200 note 3.
4 As to the meaning of 'billing authority' see PARA 53. As to valuation officers see PARA 54.
5 Non-Domestic Rating (Alteration of Lists and Appeals) (England) Regulations 2009, SI 2009/2268, reg 11(1). The Non-Domestic Rating (Alteration of Lists and Appeals) (England) Regulations 2009, SI 2009/2268, apply in relation to England only: see reg 1. As to the equivalent provision to reg 11 in relation to Wales see the Non-Domestic Rating (Alteration of Lists and

Appeals) (Wales) Regulations 2005, SI 2005/758, reg 11; and PARA 220. As to the meanings of 'England' and 'Wales' see PARA 2 note 16.

6 As to the meaning of 'ratepayer' see PARA 200 note 6.

7 As to the meaning of 'hereditament' see PARA 106.

8 As to the meaning of 'person' see PARA 11 note 13.

9 Non-Domestic Rating (Alteration of Lists and Appeals) (England) Regulations 2009, SI 2009/2268, reg 11(2). As to the meaning of 'writing' see PARA 21 note 3.

10 As to the meaning of 'month' see PARA 11 note 1.

11 As to the meaning of 'interested person' see PARA 202 note 3.

12 Non-Domestic Rating (Alteration of Lists and Appeals) (England) Regulations 2009, SI 2009/2268, reg 11(3)(a).

13 Non-Domestic Rating (Alteration of Lists and Appeals) (England) Regulations 2009, SI 2009/2268, reg 11(3)(b).

14 Non-Domestic Rating (Alteration of Lists and Appeals) (England) Regulations 2009, SI 2009/2268, reg 11(3).

15 Ie for the purposes of the Non-Domestic Rating (Alteration of Lists and Appeals) (England) Regulations 2009, SI 2009/2268, regs 12–25.

16 Non-Domestic Rating (Alteration of Lists and Appeals) (England) Regulations 2009, SI 2009/2268, reg 11(4)(a).

17 As to the meaning of 'alteration' see PARA 200 note 1.

18 Non-Domestic Rating (Alteration of Lists and Appeals) (England) Regulations 2009, SI 2009/2268, reg 11(4)(b).

209. Agreed alterations.

Where, following the making of a proposal for the alteration of a local non-domestic rating list[1], all the specified persons[2] agree on an alteration[3] of the list in terms that comply with the statutory requirements[4] but differ from those contained in the proposal, and that agreement is signified in writing, the valuation officer must, not later than two weeks after the day on which the agreement was made, alter the list to give effect to the agreement[5], and the proposal must be treated as having been withdrawn[6].

1 As to proposals see PARA 202. As to the meaning of 'alteration' see PARA 200 note 1. As to local non-domestic rating lists see PARA 191 et seq. As to the application of the Non-Domestic Rating (Alteration of Lists and Appeals) (England) Regulations 2009, SI 2009/2268, Pt 2 (regs 3–17) to central non-domestic rating lists see PARA 224.

2 The specified persons are:

(1) the valuation officer (Non-Domestic Rating (Alteration of Lists and Appeals) (England) Regulations 2009, SI 2009/2268, reg 12(2)(a));

(2) the proposer (reg 12(2)(b));

(3) subject to reg 12(3), the occupier (at the date of the proposal) of any hereditament to which it relates (reg 12(2)(c));

(4) the ratepayer (at the date of the agreement) in relation to any hereditament to which it relates (reg 12(2)(d));

(5) subject to reg 12(3), any interested person who would at the date of the proposal have been competent to make the proposal in question, and not later than two months after the day on which the proposal was received by the valuation officer, informs the valuation officer in writing that the interested person wishes to be a party to the proceedings in respect of the proposal (reg 12(2)(e) (amended by SI 2017/155)).

The specified persons do not include:

(a) the occupier of the hereditament at the date of the proposal who is no longer in occupation of any part of it at the date on which all the other persons mentioned in heads (1) to (5) above have agreed as mentioned in the Non-Domestic Rating (Alteration of Lists and Appeals) (England) Regulations 2009, SI 2009/2268, reg 12(1), provided that the valuation officer has taken all reasonable steps to ascertain that former occupier's whereabouts, and they have not been ascertained (reg 12(3)(a)); or

(b) any interested person referred to in head (5) above who cannot be contacted at the address supplied to the valuation officer (reg 12(3)(b)).

As to the meaning of 'person' see PARA 11 note 13. As to valuation officers see PARA 54. As to the meaning of 'occupier' see PARA 86. As to the meaning of 'hereditament' see PARA 106. As to the meaning of 'ratepayer' see PARA 200 note 6. As to the meaning of 'interested person' see PARA 202 note 3. As to the meaning of 'month' see PARA 11 note 1. As to the meaning of 'writing' see PARA 21 note 3.

The Non-Domestic Rating (Alteration of Lists and Appeals) (England) Regulations 2009, SI 2009/2268, apply in relation to England only: see reg 1. As to the equivalent provision to reg 12 in relation to Wales see the Non-Domestic Rating (Alteration of Lists and Appeals) (Wales) Regulations 2005, SI 2005/758, reg 12; and PARA 221. As to the meanings of 'England' and 'Wales' see PARA 2 note 16.

3 As to the meaning of 'alteration' see PARA 200 note 1.

4 Ie the requirements of the Non-Domestic Rating (Alteration of Lists and Appeals) (England) Regulations 2009, SI 2009/2268, Pt 2 (regs 3–17): see PARA 200 et seq.

5 Non-Domestic Rating (Alteration of Lists and Appeals) (England) Regulations 2009, SI 2009/2268, reg 12(1)(a). Where the period of two weeks mentioned in reg 12(1)(a) would expire before the period of two months mentioned in reg 12(2)(e) (see head (5) in note 2) (reg 12(4)(a)), and the valuation officer has not received a request under reg 12(2)(e) within that two-month period (reg 12(4)(b)), the valuation officer must make the alteration required by reg 12(1)(a) as soon as practicable after that period ends (reg 12(4)).

6 Non-Domestic Rating (Alteration of Lists and Appeals) (England) Regulations 2009, SI 2009/2268, reg 12(1)(b).

210. Disagreement as to proposed alteration.

The following provisions apply if the valuation officer[1] decides that a proposal for the alteration of a local non-domestic rating list[2] is not well-founded, and the proposal has not been withdrawn[3] and there has been no agreement[4] to the alteration[5].

The valuation officer must, as soon as reasonably practicable after making such a decision in relation to a proposal, serve a notice of the decision ('decision notice') on the following[6]:

(1) the proposer[7];

(2) if the proposer is not the ratepayer, the ratepayer[8];

(3) any interested person[9];

(4) the relevant authority[10] if the authority has served a notice on the valuation officer that it wishes to receive a copy of a decision notice[11] in relation to:

  (a) the proposal[12];

  (b) any proposal relating to the hereditament[13] to which the proposal relates[14]; or

  (c) a specified class of proposal or a specified class of hereditament, and the proposal or hereditament to which the proposal relates falls within that class[15].

A decision notice served on a person mentioned in heads (1) to (3) above must contain the following[16]:

(i) a statement that the valuation officer is of the opinion that the proposal is not well-founded, that the valuation officer disagrees with the proposed alteration of the list and that the valuation officer has decided either not to alter the list according to the proposal, or to alter the list otherwise than in accordance with the proposal[17];

(ii) the reasons for that decision, including a statement of the evidence and information used to make the decision[18];

(iii) a statement in relation to each of the grounds of the proposal setting out why in the opinion of the valuation officer the ground is not made out, including a summary of any particulars of the grounds of the proposal with which the valuation officer did not agree[19]; and

(iv) details of the proposer's right to appeal against the decision[20].

A decision notice served on a relevant authority under head (4) above must contain the following[21]:

(A) a statement that the valuation officer is of the opinion that the proposal is not well-founded, that the valuation officer disagrees with the proposed alteration of the list and that the valuation officer has decided either not to alter the list according to the proposal, or to alter the list otherwise than in accordance with the proposal[22];

(B) where the valuation officer considers it reasonable to do so:

(I) the reasons for that decision, including a statement of the evidence used to make the decision[23]; and

(II) a statement in relation to each of the grounds of the proposal setting out why in the opinion of the valuation officer the ground is not made out, including a summary of any particulars of the grounds of the proposal with which the valuation officer did not agree[24].

If the valuation officer decides to alter the list otherwise than in accordance with the proposal the valuation officer must do so as soon as reasonably practicable after making the decision[25].

1 As to valuation officers see PARA 54.

2 As to proposals see PARA 202. As to the meaning of 'alteration' see PARA 200 note 1. As to local non-domestic rating lists see PARA 191 et seq. As to the application of the Non-Domestic Rating (Alteration of Lists and Appeals) (England) Regulations 2009, SI 2009/2268, Pt 2 (regs 3–17) to central non-domestic rating lists see PARA 224.

3 Ie under the Non-Domestic Rating (Alteration of Lists and Appeals) (England) Regulations 2009, SI 2009/2268, reg 11: see PARA 208.

4 Ie under the Non-Domestic Rating (Alteration of Lists and Appeals) (England) Regulations 2009, SI 2009/2268, reg 12: see PARA 209.

5 Non-Domestic Rating (Alteration of Lists and Appeals) (England) Regulations 2009, SI 2009/2268, reg 13(1) (reg 13 substituted by SI 2017/155). For appeals to the Valuation Tribunal for England see PARA 211.

The Non-Domestic Rating (Alteration of Lists and Appeals) (England) Regulations 2009, SI 2009/2268, apply in relation to England only: see reg 1. As to the equivalent provision to reg 13 in relation to Wales see the Non-Domestic Rating (Alteration of Lists and Appeals) (Wales) Regulations 2005, SI 2005/758, reg 13; and PARA 222. As to the meanings of 'England' and 'Wales' see PARA 2 note 16.

6 Non-Domestic Rating (Alteration of Lists and Appeals) (England) Regulations 2009, SI 2009/2268, reg 13(2) (as substituted: see note 5). As to the service of notices see PARA 200 note 3.

7 Non-Domestic Rating (Alteration of Lists and Appeals) (England) Regulations 2009, SI 2009/2268, reg 13(2)(a) (as substituted: see note 5). As to the meaning of 'proposer' see PARA 204 note 7.

8 Non-Domestic Rating (Alteration of Lists and Appeals) (England) Regulations 2009, SI 2009/2268, reg 13(2)(b) (as substituted: see note 5).

9 Non-Domestic Rating (Alteration of Lists and Appeals) (England) Regulations 2009, SI 2009/2268, reg 13(2)(c) (as substituted: see note 5). The text refers to an interested person mentioned in regulation 12(2)(e) (see PARA 209 note 3 head (5)). As to the meaning of 'interested person' see PARA 202 note 3.

10 As to the meaning of 'relevant authority' see PARA 200 note 4.

11 Non-Domestic Rating (Alteration of Lists and Appeals) (England) Regulations 2009, SI 2009/2268, reg 13(2)(d) (as substituted: see note 5).

12 Non-Domestic Rating (Alteration of Lists and Appeals) (England) Regulations 2009, SI 2009/2268, reg 13(2)(d)(i) (as substituted: see note 5).

13 As to the meaning of 'hereditament' see PARA 106.

14 Non-Domestic Rating (Alteration of Lists and Appeals) (England) Regulations 2009, SI 2009/2268, reg 13(2)(d)(ii) (as substituted: see note 5).

15 Non-Domestic Rating (Alteration of Lists and Appeals) (England) Regulations 2009, SI 2009/2268, reg 13(2)(d)(iii) (as substituted: see note 5).

16 Non-Domestic Rating (Alteration of Lists and Appeals) (England) Regulations 2009, SI 2009/2268, reg 13(3) (as substituted: see note 5).
17 Non-Domestic Rating (Alteration of Lists and Appeals) (England) Regulations 2009, SI 2009/2268, reg 13(3)(a) (as substituted: see note 5).
18 Non-Domestic Rating (Alteration of Lists and Appeals) (England) Regulations 2009, SI 2009/2268, reg 13(3)(b) (as substituted: see note 5).
19 Non-Domestic Rating (Alteration of Lists and Appeals) (England) Regulations 2009, SI 2009/2268, reg 13(3)(c) (as substituted: see note 5).
20 Non-Domestic Rating (Alteration of Lists and Appeals) (England) Regulations 2009, SI 2009/2268, reg 13(3)(d) (as substituted: see note 5).
21 Non-Domestic Rating (Alteration of Lists and Appeals) (England) Regulations 2009, SI 2009/2268, reg 13(4) (as substituted: see note 5).
22 Non-Domestic Rating (Alteration of Lists and Appeals) (England) Regulations 2009, SI 2009/2268, reg 13(4)(a) (as substituted: see note 5).
23 Non-Domestic Rating (Alteration of Lists and Appeals) (England) Regulations 2009, SI 2009/2268, reg 13(4)(b)(i) (as substituted: see note 5).
24 Non-Domestic Rating (Alteration of Lists and Appeals) (England) Regulations 2009, SI 2009/2268, reg 13(4)(b)(ii) (as substituted: see note 5).
25 Non-Domestic Rating (Alteration of Lists and Appeals) (England) Regulations 2009, SI 2009/2268, reg 13(5) (as substituted: see note 5).

211. Appeals to the Valuation Tribunal for England.

A proposer[1] may appeal to the Valuation Tribunal for England ('the Tribunal')[2] on either or both of the grounds set out below if the valuation officer[3]:

(1) has decided[4] not to alter[5] the local non-domestic rating list[6];
(2) has decided[7] to alter the list otherwise than in accordance with the proposal[8]; or
(3) has not made a decision that a proposal is well-founded[9] and the proposal is not withdrawn[10], there is no agreement as to the alteration[11] and the period of 18 months beginning with the date on which the proposal was made (or any longer period agreed in writing by the valuation officer and the proposer) has elapsed[12].

The grounds are:

(a) the valuation[13] for the hereditament[14] is not reasonable[15];
(b) the list is inaccurate in relation to the hereditament (other than in relation to the valuation)[16].

A proposer may only make an appeal following a decision of the valuation officer[17] within the period of four months[18] beginning with the date of the decision notice[19]. A proposer may only make an appeal in the circumstances set out in head (3) above within the period of four months beginning with the date on which the period of 18 months beginning with the date on which the proposal was made has elapsed or any longer period agreed has elapsed[20].

An appeal must be made by serving[21] a notice of appeal on the Tribunal, using the Tribunal's electronic portal or in another manner agreed with the Tribunal[22]. A notice of appeal must:

(i) set out the grounds of the appeal[23]; and
(ii) identify which particulars of the grounds of the proposal have not been agreed with the valuation officer[24].

A notice of appeal must be accompanied by:

(A) if a decision has been given[25] by the valuation officer, a copy of that decision[26];
(B) a copy of the proposal including any further evidence provided[27] by the proposer under regulation 9[28];
(C) any evidence or information provided to the proposer[29] by the valuation officer[30]; and

(D) the fee (if any) payable[31].

If a proposer serves the notice of appeal on the Tribunal later than the time specified for making the appeal[32] or allowed by an extension of time[33], the notice of appeal must be accompanied by a request for an extension of time and the reason the notice of appeal was not served in time[34].

As soon as reasonably practicable after receiving a notice of appeal, the Tribunal must send a copy of the notice of appeal to the valuation officer and any parties to the appeal[35].

1 As to the meaning of 'proposer' see PARA 204 note 7.
2 As to the Tribunal see PARA 232.
3 As to valuation officers see PARA 54.
4 Ie under the Non-Domestic Rating (Alteration of Lists and Appeals) (England) Regulations 2009, SI 2009/2268, reg 13: see PARA 210.
5 As to the meaning of 'alter' see PARA 200 note 1.
6 Non-Domestic Rating (Alteration of Lists and Appeals) (England) Regulations 2009, SI 2009/2268, reg 13A(1)(a) (regs 13A–13E added by SI 2017/155). The Non-Domestic Rating (Alteration of Lists and Appeals) (England) Regulations 2009, SI 2009/2268, apply in relation to England only: see reg 1. There are no equivalent provisions to regs 13A–13E in relation to Wales. As to the meanings of 'England' and 'Wales' see PARA 2 note 16.
7 Ie under the Non-Domestic Rating (Alteration of Lists and Appeals) (England) Regulations 2009, SI 2009/2268, reg 13: see PARA 210.
8 Non-Domestic Rating (Alteration of Lists and Appeals) (England) Regulations 2009, SI 2009/2268, reg 13A(1)(b) (as added: see note 6). As to proposals see PARA 202.
9 Ie under the Non-Domestic Rating (Alteration of Lists and Appeals) (England) Regulations 2009, SI 2009/2268, reg 10 (see PARA 207) or reg 13 (see PARA 210).
10 Ie under the Non-Domestic Rating (Alteration of Lists and Appeals) (England) Regulations 2009, SI 2009/2268, reg 11: see PARA 208.
11 Ie under the Non-Domestic Rating (Alteration of Lists and Appeals) (England) Regulations 2009, SI 2009/2268, reg 12: see PARA 209.
12 Non-Domestic Rating (Alteration of Lists and Appeals) (England) Regulations 2009, SI 2009/2268, reg 13A(1)(c) (as added: see note 6).
13 'Valuation' means the rateable value as determined under the Local Government Finance Act 1988 Sch 6 (see PARA 157 et seq): Non-Domestic Rating (Alteration of Lists and Appeals) (England) Regulations 2009, SI 2009/2268, reg 13A(3) (as added: see note 6).
14 As to the meaning of 'hereditament' see PARA 106.
15 Non-Domestic Rating (Alteration of Lists and Appeals) (England) Regulations 2009, SI 2009/2268, reg 13A(2)(a) (as added: see note 6).
16 Non-Domestic Rating (Alteration of Lists and Appeals) (England) Regulations 2009, SI 2009/2268, reg 13A(2)(b) (as added: see note 6).
17 Ie under the Non-Domestic Rating (Alteration of Lists and Appeals) (England) Regulations 2009, SI 2009/2268, reg 13: see PARA 210.
18 As to the meaning of 'month' see PARA 11 note 1.
19 Non-Domestic Rating (Alteration of Lists and Appeals) (England) Regulations 2009, SI 2009/2268, reg 13B(1) (as added: see note 6).
20 Non-Domestic Rating (Alteration of Lists and Appeals) (England) Regulations 2009, SI 2009/2268, reg 13B(2) (as added: see note 6).
21 As to the service of notices see PARA 200 note 3.
22 Non-Domestic Rating (Alteration of Lists and Appeals) (England) Regulations 2009, SI 2009/2268, reg 13C(1) (as added: see note 6). The Tribunal's 'electronic portal' means the online facility provided by the Tribunal for use in connection with appeals made in relation to a local list compiled on or after 1 April 2017 or a central list compiled on or after 1 April 2017: reg 2(1) (definition added by SI 2017/155).
23 Non-Domestic Rating (Alteration of Lists and Appeals) (England) Regulations 2009, SI 2009/2268, reg 13C(2)(a) (as added: see note 6). 'Grounds of the appeal' means the ground or grounds in reg 13A(2) on which an appeal is made: reg 3(1) (numbered as such, and definition added, by SI 2017/155).
24 Non-Domestic Rating (Alteration of Lists and Appeals) (England) Regulations 2009, SI 2009/2268, reg 13C(2)(b) (as added: see note 6).
25 Ie under the Non-Domestic Rating (Alteration of Lists and Appeals) (England) Regulations 2009,

SI 2009/2268, reg 13: see PARA 210.

26 Non-Domestic Rating (Alteration of Lists and Appeals) (England) Regulations 2009, SI 2009/2268, reg 13C(3)(a) (as added: see note 6).

27 Ie under the Non-Domestic Rating (Alteration of Lists and Appeals) (England) Regulations 2009, SI 2009/2268, reg 9: see PARA 207.

28 Non-Domestic Rating (Alteration of Lists and Appeals) (England) Regulations 2009, SI 2009/2268, reg 13C(3)(b) (as added: see note 6).

29 Ie under the Non-Domestic Rating (Alteration of Lists and Appeals) (England) Regulations 2009, SI 2009/2268, reg 9: see PARA 207.

30 Non-Domestic Rating (Alteration of Lists and Appeals) (England) Regulations 2009, SI 2009/2268, reg 13C(3)(c) (as added: see note 6).

31 Non-Domestic Rating (Alteration of Lists and Appeals) (England) Regulations 2009, SI 2009/2268, reg 13C(3)(d) (as added: see note 6). Subject to reg 13D(2), the fee payable on making an appeal following a decision of the valuation officer under reg 13 is, for a smaller proposer (see PARA 203), £150; and, for any other proposer, £300: reg 13D(1) (as so added). A fee is not payable for an appeal in the circumstances set out in reg 13A(1)(c) (see head (3) in the text): reg 13D(2) (as so added). Any fees paid under reg 13D must be paid into the Consolidated Fund: reg 13D(3) (as so added). As to the Consolidated Fund see CONSTITUTIONAL AND ADMINISTRATIVE LAW vol 20 (2014) PARA 480 et seq; PARLIAMENT vol 78 (2010) PARA 1028.

A fee paid under reg 13D must be refunded in full if:

(1) the Tribunal decides that one or more grounds of the appeal are made out (reg 13E(1)(a) (as so added));

(2) the Tribunal makes a consent order under the Valuation Tribunal for England (Council Tax and Rating Appeals) (Procedure) Regulations 2009, SI 2009/2269, reg 35 (see PARA 254) (Non-Domestic Rating (Alteration of Lists and Appeals) (England) Regulations 2009, SI 2009/2268, reg 13E(1)(b) (as so added)); or

(3) an appeal is treated as withdrawn under the Valuation Tribunal for England (Council Tax and Rating Appeals) (Procedure) Regulations 2009, SI 2009/2269, reg 19A(7) (see PARA 250) (Non-Domestic Rating (Alteration of Lists and Appeals) (England) Regulations 2009, SI 2009/2268, reg 13E(1)(c) (as so added)).

A fee paid under reg 13D must be refunded in part in accordance with reg 13E(3) if the appeal is decided under the Valuation Tribunal for England (Council Tax and Rating Appeals) (Procedure) Regulations 2009, SI 2009/2269, without a hearing and the Non-Domestic Rating (Alteration of Lists and Appeals) (England) Regulations 2009, SI 2009/2268, reg 13E(1) does not apply: reg 13E(2) (as so added).

The amount of the refund is:

(a) for a smaller proposer, £50 (reg 13E(3)(a) (as so added));

(b) for any other proposer, £100 (reg 13E(3)(b) (as so added)).

32 Ie in the Non-Domestic Rating (Alteration of Lists and Appeals) (England) Regulations 2009, SI 2009/2268, reg 13B: see the text to notes 18–20.

33 Ie under the Valuation Tribunal for England (Council Tax and Rating Appeals) (Procedure) Regulations 2009, SI 2009/2269, reg 6(3)(a): see PARA 244.

34 Non-Domestic Rating (Alteration of Lists and Appeals) (England) Regulations 2009, SI 2009/2268, reg 13C(4) (as added: see note 6).

35 Non-Domestic Rating (Alteration of Lists and Appeals) (England) Regulations 2009, SI 2009/2268, reg 13C(5) (as added: see note 6).

212. Time from which alteration is to have effect.

The following provisions have effect in relation to alterations[1] made on or after 1 October 2009 to a local non-domestic rating list compiled[2] on or after 1 April 2005[3].

Where an alteration is made to correct any inaccuracy in the list on or after the day it is compiled, the alteration has effect as follows[4]:

(1) from the day on which the circumstances giving rise to the alteration first occurred, if the alteration is made:

(a) before 1 April 2016 otherwise than to give effect to a proposal[5];

(b) in order to give effect to a proposal served on the valuation officer[6] before 1 April 2015[7];

(c) on or after 1 April 2016 where the circumstances giving rise to the alteration first occurred on or after 1 April 2015 and the alteration is made otherwise than to give effect to a proposal[8];

(d) in order to give effect to a proposal served on the valuation officer on or after 1 April 2015 where the circumstances giving rise to the alteration first occurred on or after that date[9];

(2) from 1 April 2015 if the circumstances giving rise to the alteration first occurred before that date and the alteration is made on or after 1 April 2016 otherwise than to give effect to a proposal[10];

(3) from 1 April 2015 if the alteration is made in order to give effect to a proposal served on the valuation officer on or after that date and the circumstances giving rise to the alteration first occurred before that date[11].

Where an alteration (alteration A) is made on or after1 April 2015 in order to give effect to a proposal made on the ground that the rateable value shown in the list by reason of an alteration is or has been inaccurate[12] or that the day from which an alteration is shown in the list as having effect is wrong[13] and the proposal was served on the valuation officer within six months of the alteration which gave rise to the proposal (alteration B), alteration A has effect from the day on which alteration B had effect[14].

Where an alteration is made in order to give effect to a proposal served on the valuation officer on or after 1 April 2015 which was made on the ground that the rateable value or other information shown in the list for a hereditament is shown to be or to have been inaccurate by reason of a decision in relation to another hereditament[15], the decision which gave rise to the proposal was made before 1 April 2015 and the proposal was served on the valuation officer within six months of the decision which gave rise to the proposal, the alteration has effect from the day on which the circumstances giving rise to it first occurred[16].

Where the day on which the relevant circumstances arose is not reasonably ascertainable:

(i) where the alteration is made to give effect to a proposal for the alteration of a list, the alteration has effect from the day on which the proposal was served on the valuation officer for the billing authority for which the list is compiled and maintained[17]; and

(ii) in any other case, the alteration has effect from the day on which it is made[18].

An alteration made to correct an inaccuracy (other than one which has arisen by reason of an error or default on the part of a ratepayer[19]) in the list on the day it was compiled[20], or which arose in the course of making a previous alteration[21], which increases the rateable value[22] shown in the list for the hereditament to which the inaccuracy relates, has effect from the day on which the alteration is made[23].

Where an alteration is made to give effect to a completion notice[24], the alteration has effect from the day specified in the notice[25].

Where an alteration needs to be made after the first anniversary of the day on which the next list is compiled, it has retrospective effect only if it is made to give effect to a proposal[26].

Specific provision is made in relation to advertising rights[27].

Where an alteration is made, the list must show the day from which the alteration is to have effect[28]. Before altering an entry in a list the valuation officer must ensure that a record (which need not be in documentary form) is made of the entry[29].

1 As to the meaning of 'alteration' see PARA 200 note 1.

2 As to the compilation of local non-domestic rating lists see PARA 191. As to the application of the Non-Domestic Rating (Alteration of Lists and Appeals) (England) Regulations 2009, SI 2009/2268, Pt 2 (regs 3–17) to central non-domestic rating lists see PARA 224.

3 Non-Domestic Rating (Alteration of Lists and Appeals) (England) Regulations 2009, SI 2009/2268, reg 14(1). However, the provisions of reg 14(2), (2A), (2B), (6) (see the text to notes 4–16, and note 7) do not apply in relation to a list compiled on or after 1 April 2017: reg 14(1A) (reg 14(1A), (1B) added by SI 2017/155). Subject to the Non-Domestic Rating (Alteration of Lists and Appeals) (England) Regulations 2009, SI 2009/2268, reg 14(3)–(7) (see the text to notes 17–25), for a list compiled on or after 1 April 2017, where an alteration is made to correct any inaccuracy in the list on or after the day on which it is compiled, the alteration has effect from the day on which the circumstances giving rise to the alteration first occurred: reg 14(1B) (as so added).

The Non-Domestic Rating (Alteration of Lists and Appeals) (England) Regulations 2009, SI 2009/2268, apply in relation to England only: see reg 1. As to the equivalent provision to regs 14–16, 23 in relation to Wales see the Non-Domestic Rating (Alteration of Lists and Appeals) (Wales) Regulations 2005, SI 2005/758, regs 14–16, 41; and PARA 223. As to the meanings of 'England' and 'Wales' see PARA 2 note 16.

4 Non-Domestic Rating (Alteration of Lists and Appeals) (England) Regulations 2009, SI 2009/2268, reg 14(2) (substituted by SI 2015/424). This provision is expressed to be subject to the Non-Domestic Rating (Alteration of Lists and Appeals) (England) Regulations 2009, SI 2009/2268, reg 14(2A)–(7) (see the text to notes 13–25)): see reg 14(2) (as so substituted). Under previous legislation, it was held that a provision specifying that certain alterations to the list were to take effect from the date of the event giving rise to the alteration only applied when that was the sole reason for the alteration, and no other reason: *Cox & Co (Watford) Ltd v Bushey UDC* (1961) 9 RRC 119, [1962] RVR 126. All the cases cited in this paragraph were decided under previous legislation but may continue to be of relevance.

5 Non-Domestic Rating (Alteration of Lists and Appeals) (England) Regulations 2009, SI 2009/2268, reg 14(2)(a)(i) (as substituted: see note 4). As to proposals see PARA 202.

6 As to valuation officers see PARA 54.

7 Non-Domestic Rating (Alteration of Lists and Appeals) (England) Regulations 2009, SI 2009/2268, reg 14(2)(a)(ii) (as substituted: see note 4). For these purposes, and the purposes of reg 14(2A), (2B), (5)(a) (see the text to notes 12–17), a proposal which is made under reg 8(6)(a) (see PARA 206) is deemed to have been served on the valuation officer on the day on which the proposal to which the invalidity notice relates was served: reg 14(6) (amended by SI 2015/424). As to the meaning of 'billing authority' see PARA 53.

8 Non-Domestic Rating (Alteration of Lists and Appeals) (England) Regulations 2009, SI 2009/2268, reg 14(2)(a)(iii) (as substituted: see note 4).

9 Non-Domestic Rating (Alteration of Lists and Appeals) (England) Regulations 2009, SI 2009/2268, reg 14(2)(a)(iv) (as substituted: see note 4).

10 Non-Domestic Rating (Alteration of Lists and Appeals) (England) Regulations 2009, SI 2009/2268, reg 14(2)(b) (as substituted: see note 4).

11 Non-Domestic Rating (Alteration of Lists and Appeals) (England) Regulations 2009, SI 2009/2268, reg 14(2)(c) (as substituted: see note 4).

12 Ie on the ground set out in the Non-Domestic Rating (Alteration of Lists and Appeals) (England) Regulations 2009, SI 2009/2268, reg 4(1)(d): see PARA 202.

13 Ie on the ground set out in the Non-Domestic Rating (Alteration of Lists and Appeals) (England) Regulations 2009, SI 2009/2268, reg 4(1)(f): see PARA 202.

14 Non-Domestic Rating (Alteration of Lists and Appeals) (England) Regulations 2009, SI 2009/2268, reg 14(2A) (reg 14(2A), (2B) added by SI 2015/424).

15 Ie on the ground set out in the Non-Domestic Rating (Alteration of Lists and Appeals) (England) Regulations 2009, SI 2009/2268, reg 4(1)(e): see PARA 202. As to the meaning of 'hereditament' see PARA 106.

16 Non-Domestic Rating (Alteration of Lists and Appeals) (England) Regulations 2009, SI 2009/2268, reg 14(2B) (as added: see note 14).

17 Non-Domestic Rating (Alteration of Lists and Appeals) (England) Regulations 2009, SI 2009/2268, reg 14(5)(a).

18 Non-Domestic Rating (Alteration of Lists and Appeals) (England) Regulations 2009, SI 2009/2268, reg 14(5)(b).

19 As to the meaning of 'ratepayer' see PARA 200 note 6.
20 Non-Domestic Rating (Alteration of Lists and Appeals) (England) Regulations 2009, SI 2009/2268, reg 14(7)(a). As to alterations made to correct an inaccuracy in the list on the day it was compiled see *Thomas's London Day School v Jorgensen (Valuation Officer)* [2005] RA 222, Lands Tribunal.
21 Ie a previous alteration in connection with a matter mentioned in any of the Non-Domestic Rating (Alteration of Lists and Appeals) (England) Regulations 2009, SI 2009/2268, reg 14(2)–(5) (see the text to notes 4–6, 13–18, 25): reg 14(7)(b).
22 As to the valuation for rating see PARA 156 et seq.
23 Non-Domestic Rating (Alteration of Lists and Appeals) (England) Regulations 2009, SI 2009/2268, reg 14(7). As to whether an alteration to correct an inaccuracy in a list increases the rateable value shown in the list for the hereditament to which the inaccuracy relates see *Lamb & Shirley Ltd v Bliss* [2001] EWCA Civ 562, [2001] RA 99, [2001] All ER (D) 44 (Apr).
24 'Completion notice' means a notice under the Local Government Finance Act 1988 Sch 4A para 1 (see PARA 138) as it applies for the purposes of Pt III (ss 41–67) of the Act, which states the completion day as 1 October 2009 or later: Non-Domestic Rating (Alteration of Lists and Appeals) (England) Regulations 2009, SI 2009/2268, reg 2(1).
25 Non-Domestic Rating (Alteration of Lists and Appeals) (England) Regulations 2009, SI 2009/2268, reg 14(3). Where under the Local Government Finance Act 1988 Sch 4A a different day is substituted by a different notice under Sch 4A para 1(3) (see PARA 138), is agreed under Sch 4A para 3 (see PARA 141) or is determined in pursuance of an appeal under Sch 4A para 4 (see PARA 141), the alteration has effect from the day so substituted, agreed or determined: Non-Domestic Rating (Alteration of Lists and Appeals) (England) Regulations 2009, SI 2009/2268, reg 14(4).
26 Non-Domestic Rating (Alteration of Lists and Appeals) (England) Regulations 2009, SI 2009/2268, reg 14(8).
27 The Non-Domestic Rating (Alteration of Lists and Appeals) (England) Regulations 2009, SI 2009/2268, reg 14 (see the text to notes 1–27) has effect, where the circumstances giving rise to the alteration are the coming into existence of an advertising hereditament, as if those circumstances occurred when:
(1) any structure or sign is erected, after the right constituting the hereditament has been let out or reserved, to enable the right to be exercised (reg 15(1)(a)); or
(2) any advertisement is exhibited in exercise of the right (reg 15(1)(b)),
whichever is earlier; and such a hereditament must be treated for the purposes of the Local Government Finance Act 1988 Pt III (ss 41–67) as coming into occupation at that time (Non-Domestic Rating (Alteration of Lists and Appeals) (England) Regulations 2009, SI 2009/2268, reg 15(1)).
The erection, dismantling or alteration of any structure or sign for enabling the advertising right to be exercised, after the time mentioned in reg 15(1), must be treated as a material change of circumstances for the purposes of a proposal made on the ground specified in reg 4(1)(b) (rateable value inaccurate by reason of material change of circumstances occurring on or after the day on which the list was compiled: see PARA 202): reg 15(2). 'Advertising hereditament' means a hereditament consisting of a right to which the Local Government Finance Act 1988 s 64(2) (see PARA 104) applies; 'advertising right' means a right which is such a hereditament; and 'structure' includes a hoarding, frame, post or wall: Non-Domestic Rating (Alteration of Lists and Appeals) (England) Regulations 2009, SI 2009/2268, regs 2(1), 15(3).
28 Non-Domestic Rating (Alteration of Lists and Appeals) (England) Regulations 2009, SI 2009/2268, reg 16. As to the notification of alterations see PARA 200. There is no requirement that alterations to the list must be made within a certain time: *National Car Parks Ltd v Baird (Valuation Officer)* [2004] EWCA Civ 967, [2005] 1 All ER 53, [2004] RA 245; and see PARA 191.
29 See the Non-Domestic Rating (Alteration of Lists and Appeals) (England) Regulations 2009, SI 2009/2268, reg 23(1). A record made must be retained until the expiry of six years beginning on the day on which the next list is compiled (see reg 23(2)), save that a record in relation to a list compiled on 1 April 1995 must be retained until 31 March 2016 (reg 23(3)).

(b) *In Wales*

213. Notification of alteration.

Within four weeks of altering a list[1] a valuation officer[2] must serve a notice in writing[3] on the relevant authority[4] stating the effect of the alteration; and the relevant authority must as soon as reasonably practicable alter the copy of the list deposited by it at its principal office[5]. The valuation officer must serve a notice in writing on the ratepayer[6] and on any proposer[7] no later than the day on which the notice is served on the relevant authority[8]. However, this does not apply in relation to alterations effected solely for the purpose of correcting a clerical error[9], or for reflecting a change in the address of the hereditament concerned[10] or a change in the area of the relevant authority[11].

1 In the Non-Domestic Rating (Alteration of Lists and Appeals) (Wales) Regulations 2005, SI 2005/758, Pt 2 (regs 3–17): 'alteration' means alteration of a list in relation to a particular hereditament, and 'alter' must be construed accordingly; and 'list' means a local non-domestic rating list compiled on or after 1 April 2005: reg 3(1). As to local non-domestic rating lists see PARA 191 et seq. As to the meaning of 'hereditament' see PARA 106. As to the application of Pt 2 to central non-domestic rating lists see PARA 225.

The Non-Domestic Rating (Alteration of Lists and Appeals) (Wales) Regulations 2005, SI 2005/758, apply in relation to Wales only: see reg 1. As to the equivalent provision to reg 17 in relation to England see the Non-Domestic Rating (Alteration of Lists and Appeals) (England) Regulations 2009, SI 2009/2268, reg 17; and PARA 200. As to the meanings of 'England' and 'Wales' see PARA 2 note 16.

2 In the Non-Domestic Rating (Alteration of Lists and Appeals) (Wales) Regulations 2005, SI 2005/758, Pt 2 (regs 3–17), 'valuation officer', in relation to a local non-domestic rating list, means the valuation officer for the billing authority for which the list is compiled and maintained: see regs 2(1), 3(1). As to the meaning of 'billing authority' see PARA 53. As to valuation officers see PARA 54.

3 Without prejudice to the Local Government Act 1972 s 233 (service of notice by local authorities: LOCAL GOVERNMENT vol 69 (2018) PARA 648) and the Non-Domestic Rating (Alteration of Lists and Appeals) (Wales) Regulations 2005, SI 2005/758, reg 40(2), and subject to reg 40(3), (4) (see below), any notice to be served may be served:

(1) by delivering it to the person on whom it is to be served, or to any other person authorised by that person to act as that person's agent for the purpose (reg 40(1)(a));
(2) by sending it to that person or that agent by electronic communication, and any notice sent by such means must be regarded as sent when it is received in a legible form (reg 40(1)(b), (5)(d));
(3) by leaving it at or forwarding it by post to:
    (a) the usual or last-known place of business of that person (reg 40(1)(c)(i)); or
    (b) in the case of a company, its registered office (reg 40(1)(c)(ii)); or
    (c) the usual or last-known place of business or registered office of any other person authorised as mentioned in head (1) (reg 40(1)(c)(iii));
(4) by delivering it to some person on the premises to which it relates or, if there is no person on the premises to whom it can so be delivered, by fixing it to some conspicuous part of the premises (reg 40(1)(d));
(5) without prejudice to the foregoing provisions, where a hereditament to which the notice relates is a place of business of the person on whom it is to be served, by leaving it at, or forwarding it by post addressed to that person at, that place of business (reg 40(1)(e)).

Where any notice which is to be served on a person is to be served by or on behalf of the Common Council of the City of London or by an officer of the Common Council, it may be given or served in any manner in which it might be given or served under the Local Government Act 1972 s 233 if the Common Council were a local authority within the meaning of that section: Non-Domestic Rating (Alteration of Lists and Appeals) (Wales) Regulations 2005, SI 2005/758, reg 40(2).

Any notice to be served on the owner or occupier of any premises may be addressed by the description 'owner' or 'occupier' of the premises, without further name or description: reg 40(3).

Any notice to be served on a valuation officer may be served by addressing the notice to the valuation officer for the area in question, without further description, and by delivering it or sending it to the valuation officer's office by post or electronic communication: reg 40(4).

In reg 40:

(i) 'electronic communication' has the meaning given by the Electronic Communications Act 2000 s 15(1) (see CIVIL PROCEDURE vol 11 (2015) PARA 61) (Non-Domestic Rating (Alteration of Lists and Appeals) (Wales) Regulations 2005, SI 2005/758, reg 40(5)(a) (amended by SI 2017/155));
(ii) any reference to a notice includes a reference to a proposal and any other document required or authorised to be served (reg 40(5)(b));

(iii) any reference to such requirement or authorisation is to a requirement or authorisation under the Non-Domestic Rating (Alteration of Lists and Appeals) (Wales) Regulations 2005, SI 2005/758 (reg 40(5)(c)).

'Proposal' means a proposal for the alteration of a local non-domestic rating list or the central non-domestic rating list: reg 2(1). As to the meaning of 'person' see PARA 11 note 13. As to the service of documents by post generally see PARA 139 note 3. As to the registered office of a company see COMPANIES vol 14 (2016) PARA 124. As to the Common Council of the City of London see LONDON GOVERNMENT vol 71 (2013) PARAS 34–38.

4 'Relevant authority', in relation to a hereditament, means the billing authority in whose area the hereditament is situated: Non-Domestic Rating (Alteration of Lists and Appeals) (Wales) Regulations 2005, SI 2005/758, reg 2(1).

5 Non-Domestic Rating (Alteration of Lists and Appeals) (Wales) Regulations 2005, SI 2005/758, reg 17(1).

6 'Ratepayer', in relation to a hereditament, means the occupier or, if the hereditament is not occupied, the owner: Non-Domestic Rating (Alteration of Lists and Appeals) (Wales) Regulations 2005, SI 2005/758, reg 2(1). As to the meanings of 'owner' and 'occupier' see PARA 86.

7 'Proposer' means any proposer for whom an appeal in relation to the hereditament has been referred to the relevant valuation tribunal under the Non-Domestic Rating (Alteration of Lists and Appeals) (Wales) Regulations 2005, SI 2005/758, reg 13(1) (see PARA 222) and whose appeal has either not been determined by the tribunal, or has been so determined and either an appeal has been made to the Lands Tribunal (now the Upper Tribunal (Lands Chamber) (see PARA 270) and has not been determined, or the time for making an appeal to the Lands Tribunal has not yet expired: reg 17(5). 'Relevant valuation tribunal' means the Valuation Tribunal for Wales: reg 2(1) (definition substituted by SI 2010/713): see PARA 236 et seq. As to appeals see PARA 242 et seq.

8 Non-Domestic Rating (Alteration of Lists and Appeals) (Wales) Regulations 2005, SI 2005/758, reg 17(2)(a). The notification must also state the effect of the application of Pt 2 (regs 3–17), and of Pt 5 (regs 21–39), in relation to the alteration: reg 17(2)(b). However, reg 17(2)(b) does not apply in relation to an alteration made to reflect:

(1) a decision of the valuation officer that a proposal is well-founded (reg 17(4)(a));

(2) a decision, in relation to the hereditament which is the subject of the proposal, of a valuation tribunal or the Lands Tribunal, or of a court determining an appeal or an application for review from a valuation tribunal or the Lands Tribunal (reg 17(4)(b)); or

(3) an agreement under reg 12 (see PARA 221) (reg 17(4)(c)).

'Valuation tribunal' means the members of the Valuation Tribunal for Wales convened in accordance with Pt 5 for the purpose of disposing of an appeal under the Non-Domestic Rating (Alteration of Lists and Appeals) (Wales) Regulations 2005, SI 2005/758: reg 2(1) (definition substituted by SI 2010/713).

9 Non-Domestic Rating (Alteration of Lists and Appeals) (Wales) Regulations 2005, SI 2005/758, reg 17(3).

10 Non-Domestic Rating (Alteration of Lists and Appeals) (Wales) Regulations 2005, SI 2005/758, reg 17(3)(a).

11 Non-Domestic Rating (Alteration of Lists and Appeals) (Wales) Regulations 2005, SI 2005/758, reg 17(3)(b).

214. Proposals to alter local non-domestic rating lists.

A proposal for the alteration[1] of a local non-domestic rating list[2] may be made by an interested person[3] who has reason to believe that one of the following grounds exists[4]:

(1) the rateable value[5] shown in the list for a hereditament was inaccurate on the day the list was compiled[6];

(2) the rateable value shown in the list for a hereditament is inaccurate by reason of a material change of circumstances which occurred on or after the day on which the list was compiled[7];

(3) the rateable value shown in the list for a hereditament is inaccurate by reason of an amendment to the classes of plant and machinery[8] which comes into force on or after the day on which the list was compiled[9];

(4) the rateable value shown in the list for a hereditament by reason of an alteration made by a valuation officer is or has been inaccurate[10];

(5) the rateable value or any other information shown in the list for a hereditament is shown, by reason of a decision in relation to another hereditament of a valuation tribunal, the Lands Tribunal or a court determining an appeal or application for review from a valuation tribunal or the Lands Tribunal, to be or to have been inaccurate[11];

(6) the day from which an alteration is shown in the list as having effect is wrong[12];

(7) a hereditament not shown in the list ought to be shown in that list[13];

(8) a hereditament shown in the list ought not to be shown in that list[14];

(9) the list should show that some part of a hereditament which is shown in the list is domestic property[15] or is exempt from non-domestic rating[16] but does not do so[17];

(10) the list should not show that some part of a hereditament which is shown in the list is domestic property or is exempt from non-domestic rating but does so[18];

(11) property which is shown in the list as more than one hereditament ought to be shown as one or more different hereditaments[19];

(12) property which is shown in the list as one hereditament ought to be shown as more than one hereditament[20];

(13) the address shown in the list for a hereditament is wrong[21];

(14) the description shown in the list for a hereditament is wrong[22]; and

(15) any statement required to be made about the hereditament[23] has been omitted from the list[24].

A proposal may also be made by a relevant authority[25] where it has reason to believe that one of the grounds set out in heads (2), (5) and (7) to (9) exists[26], and by a person, other than an interested person, who has reason to believe that a ground set out in head (3), (4) or (6) above exists if that person was an interested person at any time during which the alteration or amendment in question had effect[27].

However, no proposal may be made by reference to more than one ground unless, for each of the grounds relied on, the material day[28] and the effective date[29] are the same[30].

1 As to the meaning of 'proposal' see PARA 213 note 3 and as to the meaning of 'alteration' see PARA 213 note 1.

2 As to local non-domestic rating lists see PARA 191 et seq. As to the application of the Non-Domestic Rating (Alteration of Lists and Appeals) (Wales) Regulations 2005, SI 2005/758, Pt 2 (regs 3–17) to central non-domestic rating lists see PARA 225.

3 The Non-Domestic Rating (Alteration of Lists and Appeals) (Wales) Regulations 2005, SI 2005/758, reg 2(1) provides that 'interested person' means:

(1) in relation to a hereditament which forms part of the Crown Estate and is held by the Crown Estate Commissioners under their management within the meaning of the Crown Estate Act 1961 s 1 (see CROWN AND CROWN PROCEEDINGS vol 29 (2014) PARA 197), the Crown Estate Commissioners;

(2) in relation to any other hereditament:

(a) the occupier;

(b) any other person (other than a mortgagee not in possession) having in any part of the hereditament either a legal estate or an equitable interest such as would entitle him (after the cessation of any prior interest) to possession of the hereditament or any part of it; and

(c) any person having a qualifying connection with the occupier or a person described in head (b).

A person must be treated as having a 'qualifying connection' with another:

(i) where both persons are companies, and one is a subsidiary of the other, or both are subsidiaries of the same company (Non-Domestic Rating (Alteration of Lists and Appeals) (Wales) Regulations 2005, SI 2005/758, reg 2(1), (2)(a)); or

(ii) where only one person is a company, the other person (the 'second person') has such an interest in that company as would, if the second person were a company, result in its being the holding company of the other (reg 2(2)(b)).

As to the meaning of 'hereditament' see PARA 106. As to the Crown Estate Commissioners see CROWN AND CROWN PROCEEDINGS vol 29 (2014) PARA 194 et seq. As to the meaning of 'occupier' see PARA 86. As to the meaning of 'person' see PARA 11 note 13. As to holding and subsidiary companies see COMPANIES vol 14 (2016) PARA 22.

The Non-Domestic Rating (Alteration of Lists and Appeals) (Wales) Regulations 2005, SI 2005/758, apply in relation to Wales only: see reg 1. As to the equivalent provision to reg 4 in relation to England see the Non-Domestic Rating (Alteration of Lists and Appeals) (England) Regulations 2009, SI 2009/2268, reg 4; and PARA 202. As to the meanings of 'England' and 'Wales' see PARA 2 note 16.

4 See the Non-Domestic Rating (Alteration of Lists and Appeals) (Wales) Regulations 2005, SI 2005/758, reg 4(2)(a). No proposal may be made by an interested person, where that person (or a person having a qualifying connection with that person), acting in the same capacity, has made a proposal to alter the same list in relation to the same hereditament on the same ground and arising from the same event: reg 4(3)(b)(i). 'Event' means the compilation of the list, a material change of circumstances or an alteration of the list by the valuation officer: reg 4(4)(b). 'Material change of circumstances', in relation to a hereditament, means a change in any of the matters mentioned in the Local Government Finance Act 1988 Sch 6 para 2(7) (see PARA 164): Non-Domestic Rating (Alteration of Lists and Appeals) (Wales) Regulations 2005, SI 2005/758, reg 3(1).

Also no proposal may be made by an interested person where a proposal to alter the list in relation to the same hereditament and arising from the same facts has been made by another person (excluding a person having a qualifying connection with the interested person) and has been considered and determined by a valuation tribunal (otherwise than as mentioned in reg 30(4) (see PARA 263)), or, on appeal under reg 27, by the Lands Tribunal (reg 4(3)(b)(ii)). As to the meaning of 'valuation tribunal' see PARA 213 note 8. As to the Valuation Tribunal for Wales see PARA 237. As to appeals see PARA 232 et seq. For cases on the equivalent provisions in England see PARA 202 note 4. Note that appeals to the Lands Tribunal are now to the Upper Tribunal (Lands Chamber): see PARA 270.

5 As to the valuation for rating see PARA 156 et seq.

6 Non-Domestic Rating (Alteration of Lists and Appeals) (Wales) Regulations 2005, SI 2005/758, reg 4(1)(a).

7 Non-Domestic Rating (Alteration of Lists and Appeals) (Wales) Regulations 2005, SI 2005/758, reg 4(1)(b).

8 Ie as set out in the Valuation for Rating (Plant and Machinery) (Wales) Regulations 2000, SI 2000/1097, Schedule: see PARA 173.

9 Non-Domestic Rating (Alteration of Lists and Appeals) (Wales) Regulations 2005, SI 2005/758, reg 4(1)(c).

10 Non-Domestic Rating (Alteration of Lists and Appeals) (Wales) Regulations 2005, SI 2005/758, reg 4(1)(d). No proposal may be made on this ground, to the extent that the alteration in question gives effect to the decision of a valuation tribunal, the Lands Tribunal or a court determining an appeal or an application for a review from a valuation tribunal or Lands Tribunal in relation to the hereditament concerned: reg 4(3)(c).

11 Non-Domestic Rating (Alteration of Lists and Appeals) (Wales) Regulations 2005, SI 2005/758, reg 4(1)(e). There must be some causal link between the decision of the tribunal and the opinion of the ratepayer that the existing entry is incorrect. Where reference was made to a decision solely because in that case the valuation was found to be excessive and incorrect, the ratepayer had not based the opinion on any causal link between the proposal and the preceding decision: *Canning (Valuation Officer) v Corby Power Ltd* [1997] RA 60, Lands Tribunal.

12 Non-Domestic Rating (Alteration of Lists and Appeals) (Wales) Regulations 2005, SI 2005/758, reg 4(1)(f).

13 Non-Domestic Rating (Alteration of Lists and Appeals) (Wales) Regulations 2005, SI 2005/758, reg 4(1)(g).

14 Non-Domestic Rating (Alteration of Lists and Appeals) (Wales) Regulations 2005, SI 2005/758, reg 4(1)(h).

15 As to the meaning of 'domestic property' see PARA 190.

16 As to exemptions from non-domestic rating see PARA 110 et seq.

17 Non-Domestic Rating (Alteration of Lists and Appeals) (Wales) Regulations 2005, SI 2005/758, reg 4(1)(i).

18 Non-Domestic Rating (Alteration of Lists and Appeals) (Wales) Regulations 2005, SI 2005/758, reg 4(1)(j).
19 Non-Domestic Rating (Alteration of Lists and Appeals) (Wales) Regulations 2005, SI 2005/758, reg 4(1)(k).
20 Non-Domestic Rating (Alteration of Lists and Appeals) (Wales) Regulations 2005, SI 2005/758, reg 4(1)(l).
21 Non-Domestic Rating (Alteration of Lists and Appeals) (Wales) Regulations 2005, SI 2005/758, reg 4(1)(m).
22 Non-Domestic Rating (Alteration of Lists and Appeals) (Wales) Regulations 2005, SI 2005/758, reg 4(1)(n).
23 Ie under the Local Government Finance Act 1988 s 42: see PARA 194.
24 Non-Domestic Rating (Alteration of Lists and Appeals) (Wales) Regulations 2005, SI 2005/758, reg 4(1)(o).
25 As to the meaning of 'relevant authority' see PARA 213 note 4.
26 Non-Domestic Rating (Alteration of Lists and Appeals) (Wales) Regulations 2005, SI 2005/758, reg 4(2)(b).
27 Non-Domestic Rating (Alteration of Lists and Appeals) (Wales) Regulations 2005, SI 2005/758, reg 4(2)(c).
28 'Material day', in relation to a hereditament, means the day determined as regards that hereditament in accordance with rules prescribed by regulations under the Local Government Finance Act 1988 Sch 6 para 2(6A) (see PARA 164): Non-Domestic Rating (Alteration of Lists and Appeals) (Wales) Regulations 2005, SI 2005/758, reg 4(4).
29 'Effective date' means the day from which the alteration, if made, would have effect in pursuance of the Non-Domestic Rating (Alteration of Lists and Appeals) (Wales) Regulations 2005, SI 2005/758, Pt 2 (regs 3–17) (see PARA 223): reg 4(4).
30 Non-Domestic Rating (Alteration of Lists and Appeals) (Wales) Regulations 2005, SI 2005/758, reg 4(3)(a).

215. Time for making proposals.

A proposal to alter a local non-domestic rating list[1] in relation to Wales compiled on or after 1 April 2005 may generally be made at any time before the day on which the next list is compiled[2]. However, a proposal on the ground that the rateable value shown in the list is inaccurate[3] or that the day from which the alteration shown in the list is to have effect is wrong[4] may only be made before the day on which the next list is compiled or within six months[5] of the date of the alteration, whichever is the later[6]; and a proposal on the ground that the rateable value or any other information shown in the list for a hereditament is inaccurate by reason of a tribunal decision[7] may be made no later than six months after the day on which the next list is compiled[8].

1 As to proposals see PARA 214. As to the meaning of 'proposal' see PARA 213 note 3; and as to the meaning of 'alteration' see PARA 213 note 1. As to local non-domestic rating lists see PARA 191 et seq. As to the application of the Non-Domestic Rating (Alteration of Lists and Appeals) (Wales) Regulations 2005, SI 2005/758, Pt 2 (regs 3–17) to central non-domestic rating lists see PARA 225.
2 Non-Domestic Rating (Alteration of Lists and Appeals) (Wales) Regulations 2005, SI 2005/758, reg 5. The equivalent provision which applied in relation to England has been revoked. As to the meanings of 'Wales' and 'England' see PARA 2 note 16.
3 Ie the ground set out in the Non-Domestic Rating (Alteration of Lists and Appeals) (Wales) Regulations 2005, SI 2005/758, reg 4(1)(d): see PARA 214.
4 Ie the ground set out in the Non-Domestic Rating (Alteration of Lists and Appeals) (Wales) Regulations 2005, SI 2005/758, reg 4(1)(f): see PARA 214.
5 As to the meaning of 'month' see PARA 11 note 1.
6 See the Non-Domestic Rating (Alteration of Lists and Appeals) (Wales) Regulations 2005, SI 2005/758, reg 5(2)(a).
7 Ie the ground set out in the Non-Domestic Rating (Alteration of Lists and Appeals) (Wales) Regulations 2005, SI 2005/758, reg 4(1)(e): see PARA 214.
8 See the Non-Domestic Rating (Alteration of Lists and Appeals) (Wales) Regulations 2005, SI 2005/758, reg 5(2)(b).

216. Form and contents of proposals.

A proposal to alter a local non-domestic rating list[1] must be made by notice[2] sent to the valuation officer for the billing authority[3] for which the list is compiled and maintained which must[4]:

(1) state the name and address of the proposer[5];

(2) state whether the proposer is, in respect of the property:

 (a) the interested person[6] and, if so, the capacity in which the interested person makes the proposal[7];

 (b) the relevant authority[8]; or

 (c) some other person[9];

(3) identify the property to which the proposal relates[10];

(4) identify the respects in which it is proposed that the list be altered[11]; and

(5) include a statement of the grounds for making the proposal[12].

A proposal may deal with more than one hereditament[13] only in prescribed circumstances[14]. A proposal made on the ground that the rateable value shown in the list by reason of an alteration is or has been inaccurate[15] or that the day from which an alteration is shown in the list as having effect is wrong[16] may include a request for either or both of the following:

(i) the restoration of the list to its state before the alteration was made[17]; and

(ii) a further alteration of the list in respect of the hereditament[18].

1 As to proposals see PARA 214. As to the meaning of 'proposal' see PARA 213 note 3; and as to local non-domestic rating lists see PARA 191 et seq. As to the application of the Non-Domestic Rating (Alteration of Lists and Appeals) (Wales) Regulations 2005, SI 2005/758, Pt 2 (regs 3–17) to central non-domestic rating lists see PARA 225.

2 As to the service of notices see PARA 200 note 3.

3 As to the meaning of 'billing authority' see PARA 53. As to valuation officers see PARA 54.

4 See the Non-Domestic Rating (Alteration of Lists and Appeals) (Wales) Regulations 2005, SI 2005/758, reg 6(1). The Non-Domestic Rating (Alteration of Lists and Appeals) (Wales) Regulations 2005, SI 2005/758, apply in relation to Wales only: see reg 1. As to the equivalent provision in relation to England see the Non-Domestic Rating (Alteration of Lists and Appeals) (England) Regulations 2009, SI 2009/2268, reg 6; and PARA 204. As to the meanings of 'England' and 'Wales' see PARA 2 note 16.

5 Non-Domestic Rating (Alteration of Lists and Appeals) (Wales) Regulations 2005, SI 2005/758, reg 6(1)(a). 'Proposer' means the person making a proposal: reg 2(1). As to the meaning of 'person' see PARA 11 note 13.

6 As to the meaning of 'interested person' see PARA 214 note 3.

7 Non-Domestic Rating (Alteration of Lists and Appeals) (Wales) Regulations 2005, SI 2005/758, reg 6(1)(b)(i).

8 Non-Domestic Rating (Alteration of Lists and Appeals) (Wales) Regulations 2005, SI 2005/758, reg 6(1)(b)(ii). As to the meaning of 'relevant authority' see PARA 213 note 4.

9 Ie a person described in the Non-Domestic Rating (Alteration of Lists and Appeals) (Wales) Regulations 2005, SI 2005/758, reg 4(2)(c) (see PARA 214): reg 6(1)(b)(iii).

10 Non-Domestic Rating (Alteration of Lists and Appeals) (Wales) Regulations 2005, SI 2005/758, reg 6(1)(c). An adequate identification may be sufficient: see *Exel Logistics Ltd v Oliver (Valuation Officer)* [1995] RA 336 (proposal was construed using common sense and assuming knowledge of the locality and the valuation list); *Mersey Master Mariners' Club v West Derby Assessment Committee* (1951) 44 R & IT 358. Identification of a hereditament which no longer exists will be invalid: *R v Northamptonshire Local Valuation Court, ex p Anglian Water Authority* [1990] RA 93, [1991] 1 EGLR 171, CA. See also *Westminster City Council v Woodbury (Valuation Officer) and the Yard Arm Club Ltd* [1992] RA 1, [1991] 2 EGLR 173, CA; *Floatels (UK) Ltd v Perrin (Valuation Officer)* [1995] RA 326, where it was held that a proposal to alter a list was invalid as it related not to land but to chattels which are unrateable.

The cases cited in this paragraph were decided under previous legislation but may continue to be of relevance.

11 Non-Domestic Rating (Alteration of Lists and Appeals) (Wales) Regulations 2005, SI 2005/758, reg 6(1)(d).

12 Non-Domestic Rating (Alteration of Lists and Appeals) (Wales) Regulations 2005, SI 2005/758, reg 6(1)(e)(i). There must also be included:

(1) in the case of a proposal made on any of the grounds set out in reg 4(1)(a), (c) or (g)–(o) (see PARA 214), a statement of the reasons for believing that those grounds exist (see reg 6(1)(e)(i));

(2) in the case of a proposal made on the ground set out in reg 4(1)(b) (see PARA 214), a statement of the nature of the change in question and of the date on which the proposer believes the change occurred (reg 6(1)(e)(ii));

(3) in the case of a proposal made on the ground set out in reg 4(1)(d) or (f) (see PARA 214), a statement identifying the alteration in question, whether by reference to the day on which the alteration was made or otherwise (reg 6(1)(e)(iii));

(4) in the case of a proposal made on the ground set out in reg 4(1)(e) (see PARA 214), the specified information (reg 6(1)(e)(iv));

(5) in the case of a proposal made on the ground set out in reg 4(1)(f), a statement of the day proposed in place of the day shown in the list (reg 6(1)(e)(v)); and

(6) in the case of proposal made on one of the grounds set out in reg 4(1)(a)–(g), and 4(1)(i) and 4(1)(l), in respect of a hereditament occupied under a lease, easement or licence to occupy, the specified information (reg 6(1)(e)(vi)).

The information required by reg 6(1)(e)(iv) (see head (4) above) is:

(a) the identity of the hereditament to which the decision in question relates (reg 6(2)(a));

(b) the name of the tribunal or court which made the decision (reg 6(2)(b));

(c) the date of the decision (reg 6(2)(c));

(d) the reasons for believing that the decision is relevant to the rateable value or other information to which the proposal relates (reg 6(2)(d)); and

(e) the reasons for believing, in the light of the decision, that the rateable value or other information to which the proposal relates is inaccurate (reg 6(2)(e)).

The information required by reg 6(1)(e)(vi) (see head (6) above) is the amount payable each year, as at the date of the proposal, in respect of the lease, easement or licence to occupy: reg 6(3).

13 As to the meaning of 'hereditament' see PARA 106.

14 A proposal may deal with more than one hereditament only:

(1) if it is made on the grounds set out in the Non-Domestic Rating (Alteration of Lists and Appeals) (Wales) Regulations 2005, SI 2005/758, reg 4(1)(k) or (l) (see PARA 214) (reg 6(4)(a)); or

(2) where the person making the proposal does so in the same capacity as respects each hereditament and each hereditament is within the same building or the same curtilage (reg 6(4)(b)).

It is important to specify clearly both hereditaments within one curtilage if it is intended to alter both by proposal: *R v Cardiff Justices, ex p Cardiff Corpn* [1962] 2 QB 436, sub nom *R v City of Cardiff Justices, ex p Cardiff City Council* [1962] 1 All ER 751.

15 Ie the ground set out in the Non-Domestic Rating (Alteration of Lists and Appeals) (Wales) Regulations 2005, SI 2005/758, reg 4(1)(d): see PARA 214.

16 Ie the ground set out in the Non-Domestic Rating (Alteration of Lists and Appeals) (Wales) Regulations 2005, SI 2005/758, reg 4(1)(f): see PARA 214.

17 Non-Domestic Rating (Alteration of Lists and Appeals) (Wales) Regulations 2005, SI 2005/758, reg 6(5)(a).

18 Non-Domestic Rating (Alteration of Lists and Appeals) (Wales) Regulations 2005, SI 2005/758, reg 6(5)(b).

217. Acknowledgment of proposal.

Except where a proposal[1] is invalid[2], within the period of four weeks beginning with the day on which he receives a proposal for the alteration of a local non-domestic rating list, the valuation officer[3] must by notice in writing served on the proposer[4] acknowledge its receipt[5]. A notice of acknowledgment must specify the date of receipt of the proposal and be accompanied by a statement containing prescribed information[6].

1 As to the meaning of 'proposal' see PARA 213 note 3. As to proposals see PARA 214.

2 Ie where a valuation officer serves a notice under the Non-Domestic Rating (Alteration of Lists and Appeals) (Wales) Regulations 2005, SI 2005/758, reg 8 in respect of the proposal: PARA 218.

3 As to valuation officers see PARA 54.

4 As to the service of notices see PARA 213 note 3. As to the meaning of 'proposer' see PARA 216 note 5.

5 Non-Domestic Rating (Alteration of Lists and Appeals) (Wales) Regulations 2005, SI 2005/758, reg 7(1), (2). As to the application of the Non-Domestic Rating (Alteration of Lists and Appeals) (Wales) Regulations 2005, SI 2005/758, Pt 2 (regs 3–17) to central non-domestic rating lists see PARA 225. The Non-Domestic Rating (Alteration of Lists and Appeals) (Wales) Regulations 2005, SI 2005/758, apply in relation to Wales only: see reg 1. As to the equivalent provision to reg 7 in relation to England see the Non-Domestic Rating (Alteration of Lists and Appeals) (England) Regulations 2009, SI 2009/2268, reg 7; and PARA 206. As to the meanings of 'England' and 'Wales' see PARA 2 note 16.

6 Non-Domestic Rating (Alteration of Lists and Appeals) (Wales) Regulations 2005, SI 2005/758, reg 7(3). The statement must set out the effect of regs 9–13 (see PARA 219 et seq): see reg 7(3).

218. Invalid proposals.

Where the valuation officer for the billing authority[1] for which the list is compiled and maintained is of the opinion that a proposal for the alteration of a local non-domestic rating list[2] has not been validly made[3], the valuation officer may, within four weeks of its service on the valuation officer, serve notice[4] (an 'invalidity notice') on the proposer[5] that the valuation officer is of that opinion, and stating the reasons for that opinion[6] and the effect of service of the notice[7].

The valuation officer may at any time withdraw an invalidity notice by serving notice in writing on the proposer; and any appeal against the invalidity notice must then be treated as having been withdrawn[8].

Unless an invalidity notice has been withdrawn, the proposer may, within four weeks of its service on him or her make a further proposal in relation to the same property[9] or appeal against the notice to the relevant valuation tribunal[10]. Where a further proposal is so made, the proposal in respect of which the invalidity notice was served must be treated as withdrawn[11].

An appeal against an invalidity notice is initiated by serving notice of disagreement on the valuation officer[12]. Unless the valuation officer withdraws the invalidity notice within four weeks of service of the notice of disagreement, on the expiry of that period the valuation officer must inform the clerk of the relevant valuation tribunal of the entry in the list (if any) which it is proposed to alter[13], the grounds on which the proposal was made[14], and the reasons for the valuation officer's opinion that the proposal had not been validly made[15]. Where such information relating to an invalidity notice has been supplied and the notice is withdrawn, the valuation officer must, as soon as practicable, inform the clerk of the relevant valuation tribunal of the withdrawal[16].

Until it is finally decided that the proposal to which an invalidity notice relates was validly made, the procedural provisions relating to proposals[17] do not apply in relation to the proposal[18]. Where it is finally decided that the proposal was validly made, those provisions have effect as if the proposal had been served on the valuation officer on the date of that final decision[19].

Nothing done under the above provisions prevents any party to an appeal[20] from contending that the proposal to which that appeal relates was not validly made[21].

1 As to the meaning of 'billing authority' see PARA 53. As to valuation officers see PARA 54.

2 As to the meaning of 'proposal' see PARA 213 note 3. As to proposals see PARA 214. As to local non-domestic rating lists see PARA 191 et seq. As to the application of the Non-Domestic Rating (Alteration of Lists and Appeals) (Wales) Regulations 2005, SI 2005/758, Pt 2 (regs 3–17) to central non-domestic rating lists see PARA 225.

3 For examples of invalidity see: *Canning (Valuation Officer) v Corby Power Ltd* [1997] RA 60 (no causal link between valuation decision and opinion of the ratepayer); *Green (Valuation Officer) v Barnet London Borough Council* [1994] RA 235, Lands Tribunal (a proposal is not invalid because it proposes to enter in the list as a separate hereditament property which is not contiguous with a larger hereditament owned by the same ratepayer). See also *Edwards (Valuation Officer) v BP Refining* [1974] RA 1. Cf the conflicting decisions in *Eagle Construction Ltd v Casey (Valuation Officer) and Croydon Borough Council* [1981] RA 347; *Aluwihare (Valuation Officer) v MFI Properties Ltd* [1988] 1 EGLR 219, [1987] RA 189. For earlier examples see *Steel Barrel Co Ltd v Priest (Valuation Officer)* (1951) 44 R & IT 492, Lands Tribunal (additional words in the proposal served on the ratepayer did not render it invalid provided the ratepayer not thereby prejudiced); *Rochdale Canal Co v Walton (Valuation Officer)* (1954) 47 R & IT 473, Lands Tribunal (two proposals made simultaneously in respect of the same hereditament could be treated as one, and could supply each other's defects).

These cases were decided under previous legislation but may continue to be of relevance.

4 As to the service of notices see PARA 213 note 3.

5 As to the meaning of 'proposer' see PARA 216 note 5.

6 Non-Domestic Rating (Alteration of Lists and Appeals) (Wales) Regulations 2005, SI 2005/758, reg 8(1)(a). The Non-Domestic Rating (Alteration of Lists and Appeals) (Wales) Regulations 2005, SI 2005/758, apply in relation to Wales only: see reg 1. As to the equivalent provision to reg 8 in relation to England see the Non-Domestic Rating (Alteration of Lists and Appeals) (England) Regulations 2009, SI 2009/2268, reg 8; and PARA 206. As to the meanings of 'England' and 'Wales' see PARA 2 note 16.

7 Ie the effect of the Non-Domestic Rating (Alteration of Lists and Appeals) (Wales) Regulations 2005, SI 2005/758, reg 8(3)–(6) (see the text to notes 8–12): see reg 8(1)(b).

8 Non-Domestic Rating (Alteration of Lists and Appeals) (Wales) Regulations 2005, SI 2005/758, reg 8(2). As to the meaning of 'writing' see PARA 21 note 3.

9 Non-Domestic Rating (Alteration of Lists and Appeals) (Wales) Regulations 2005, SI 2005/758, reg 8(3)(a) (reg 8(3) amended by SI 2006/1035). For the purposes of the Non-Domestic Rating (Alteration of Lists and Appeals) (Wales) Regulations 2005, SI 2005/758, reg 8(3)(a) the time limit applicable under reg 5 (see PARA 215) may be ignored (reg 8(3)(a)); but a further proposal may not be made where the proposal to which the invalidity notice relates was itself made under reg 8(3)(a) or after the expiry of the time limit applicable under reg 5 (reg 8(4)).

10 Non-Domestic Rating (Alteration of Lists and Appeals) (Wales) Regulations 2005, SI 2005/758, reg 8(3)(b). As to the meaning of 'relevant valuation tribunal' see PARA 213 note 7.

11 Non-Domestic Rating (Alteration of Lists and Appeals) (Wales) Regulations 2005, SI 2005/758, reg 8(5).

12 Non-Domestic Rating (Alteration of Lists and Appeals) (Wales) Regulations 2005, SI 2005/758, reg 8(6).

13 Non-Domestic Rating (Alteration of Lists and Appeals) (Wales) Regulations 2005, SI 2005/758, reg 8(7)(a).

14 Non-Domestic Rating (Alteration of Lists and Appeals) (Wales) Regulations 2005, SI 2005/758, reg 8(7)(b).

15 Non-Domestic Rating (Alteration of Lists and Appeals) (Wales) Regulations 2005, SI 2005/758, reg 8(7)(c).

16 Non-Domestic Rating (Alteration of Lists and Appeals) (Wales) Regulations 2005, SI 2005/758, reg 8(8).

17 Ie the Non-Domestic Rating (Alteration of Lists and Appeals) (Wales) Regulations 2005, SI 2005/758, regs 9–13: see PARA 207 et seq.

18 Non-Domestic Rating (Alteration of Lists and Appeals) (Wales) Regulations 2005, SI 2005/758, reg 8(9). For the purposes of reg 8(9), a final decision is made:

(1) where the invalidity notice is withdrawn, on the day of the withdrawal (reg 8(10)(a));

(2) in any other case, on the day on which:

(a) the valuation tribunal having determined the appeal, the period within which an appeal may be made to the Lands Tribunal (now the Upper Tribunal (Lands Chamber) under reg 37 (see PARA 270) expires without such an appeal being made (reg 8(10)(b)(i)); or

(b) the Lands Tribunal gives a decision on appeal under reg 37 (reg 8(10)(b)(ii)).

19 Non-Domestic Rating (Alteration of Lists and Appeals) (Wales) Regulations 2005, SI 2005/758, reg 8(9).

20 Ie under the Non-Domestic Rating (Alteration of Lists and Appeals) (Wales) Regulations 2005, SI 2005/758, reg 13: see PARA 222.

21 Non-Domestic Rating (Alteration of Lists and Appeals) (Wales) Regulations 2005, SI 2005/758, reg 8(11).

219. Procedure after a proposal is made.

Within the period of six weeks beginning on the day on which a proposal for the alteration of a local non-domestic rating list[1] is served on the valuation officer[2] for the billing authority[3] for which the list is compiled and maintained, the valuation officer must serve a copy of the proposal on each of the following provided that person[4] is not the proposer[5]:

(1) any ratepayer[6] in relation to any hereditament[7] to which the proposal relates[8]; and

(2) the relevant authority[9] where that authority is a special authority[10], or has served notice[11] on the valuation officer that it wishes to receive a copy of a class or classes of proposal and the proposal falls within any such class[12].

Where the valuation officer is of the opinion that a proposal is well founded, the valuation officer must as soon as reasonably practicable alter[13] the list accordingly[14].

1 As to the meaning of 'proposal' see PARA 213 note 3. As to proposals see PARA 214. As to local non-domestic rating lists see PARA 191 et seq. As to the application of the Non-Domestic Rating (Alteration of Lists and Appeals) (Wales) Regulations 2005, SI 2005/758, Pt 2 (regs 3–17) to central non-domestic rating lists see PARA 225.
2 As to valuation officers see PARA 54.
3 As to the meaning of 'billing authority' see PARA 53.
4 As to the meaning of 'person' see PARA 11 note 13.
5 Non-Domestic Rating (Alteration of Lists and Appeals) (Wales) Regulations 2005, SI 2005/758, reg 9(1). As to the meaning of 'proposer' see PARA 216 note 5. The Non-Domestic Rating (Alteration of Lists and Appeals) (Wales) Regulations 2005, SI 2005/758, apply in relation to Wales only: see reg 1. As to the equivalent provision to regs 9, 10 in relation to England see the Non-Domestic Rating (Alteration of Lists and Appeals) (England) Regulations 2009, SI 2009/2268, regs 9, 10; and PARA 207. As to the meanings of 'England' and 'Wales' see PARA 2 note 16.
6 As to the meaning of 'ratepayer' see PARA 213 note 6.
7 As to the meaning of 'hereditament' see PARA 106.
8 Non-Domestic Rating (Alteration of Lists and Appeals) (Wales) Regulations 2005, SI 2005/758, reg 9(1)(a). Each copy of a proposal served on a ratepayer must be accompanied by a statement of the effect of regs 10–13 (see the text to notes 12–13; and PARAS 220–222): reg 9(2).
9 As to the meaning of 'relevant authority' see PARA 200 note 4.
10 Non-Domestic Rating (Alteration of Lists and Appeals) (Wales) Regulations 2005, SI 2005/758, reg 9(1)(b)(i). As to the meaning of 'special authority' see PARA 133 note 11.
11 As to the service of notices see PARA 213 note 3.
12 Non-Domestic Rating (Alteration of Lists and Appeals) (Wales) Regulations 2005, SI 2005/758, reg 9(1)(b)(ii).
13 As to the meaning of 'alter' see PARA 213 note 1.
14 Non-Domestic Rating (Alteration of Lists and Appeals) (Wales) Regulations 2005, SI 2005/758, reg 10.

220. Withdrawal of proposals.

The proposer[1] may withdraw the proposal for the alteration of a local non-domestic rating list[2] by notice in writing served on[3] the valuation officer for the billing authority[4] for which the list is compiled and maintained[5]. However, a proposal may not be withdrawn where the proposer was a ratepayer[6] in respect of the hereditament[7] at the date of the proposal but is no longer, unless the person[8] who currently is the ratepayer agrees in writing[9].

Where, within the period of two months[10] beginning on the day on which a proposal is served on the valuation officer, an interested person[11] serves notice in writing on the valuation officer that that person wishes to be a party to the proceedings in respect of that proposal[12] and, after service of such a notice, the proposal is withdrawn[13], the valuation officer must serve notice of that withdrawal on that interested person[14]. Where, within the period of six weeks beginning with the day on which such a notice is served on an interested person, that person serves notice in writing on the valuation officer that he or she is aggrieved by the withdrawal of the proposal:

(1) the notice must, if that person would at the date of the proposal have been competent to make that proposal, be treated[15] as if it had been a proposal in the same terms made on the day on which the notice was served[16]; and

(2) any resulting alteration[17] has effect from the day which would have been applicable had there been no withdrawal[18].

1 As to the meaning of 'proposer' see PARA 204 note 7.

2 As to the meaning of 'proposal' see PARA 213 note 3. As to proposals see PARA 214. As to local non-domestic rating lists see PARA 191 et seq. As to the application of the Non-Domestic Rating (Alteration of Lists and Appeals) (Wales) Regulations 2005, SI 2005/758, Pt 2 (regs 3–17) to central non-domestic rating lists see PARA 225.

3 As to the service of notices see PARA 213 note 3.

4 As to the meaning of 'billing authority' see PARA 53. As to valuation officers see PARA 54.

5 Non-Domestic Rating (Alteration of Lists and Appeals) (Wales) Regulations 2005, SI 2005/758, reg 11(1). The Non-Domestic Rating (Alteration of Lists and Appeals) (Wales) Regulations 2005, SI 2005/758, apply in relation to Wales only: see reg 1. As to the equivalent provision to reg 11 in relation to England see the Non-Domestic Rating (Alteration of Lists and Appeals) (England) Regulations 2009, SI 2009/2268, reg 11; and PARA 208. As to the meanings of 'England' and 'Wales' see PARA 2 note 16.

6 As to the meaning of 'ratepayer' see PARA 213 note 6.

7 As to the meaning of 'hereditament' see PARA 106.

8 As to the meaning of 'person' see PARA 11 note 13.

9 Non-Domestic Rating (Alteration of Lists and Appeals) (Wales) Regulations 2005, SI 2005/758, reg 11(2). As to the meaning of 'writing' see PARA 21 note 3.

10 As to the meaning of 'month' see PARA 11 note 1.

11 As to the meaning of 'interested person' see PARA 214 note 3.

12 Non-Domestic Rating (Alteration of Lists and Appeals) (Wales) Regulations 2005, SI 2005/758, reg 11(3)(a).

13 Non-Domestic Rating (Alteration of Lists and Appeals) (Wales) Regulations 2005, SI 2005/758, reg 11(3)(b).

14 Non-Domestic Rating (Alteration of Lists and Appeals) (Wales) Regulations 2005, SI 2005/758, reg 11(3).

15 Ie for the purposes of the Non-Domestic Rating (Alteration of Lists and Appeals) (Wales) Regulations 2005, SI 2005/758, regs 12–44.

16 Non-Domestic Rating (Alteration of Lists and Appeals) (Wales) Regulations 2005, SI 2005/758, reg 11(4)(a).

17 As to the meaning of 'alteration' see PARA 213 note 1.

18 Non-Domestic Rating (Alteration of Lists and Appeals) (Wales) Regulations 2005, SI 2005/758, reg 11(4)(b).

221. Agreed alterations.

Where, following the making of a proposal for the alteration of a local non-domestic rating list[1], all the specified persons[2] agree on an alteration[3] of the list in accordance with the statutory requirements[4] in terms other than those contained in the proposal, and that agreement is signified in writing, the valuation officer must, not later than the expiry of the period of two weeks beginning on the day on which the agreement was made, alter the list to give effect to the agreement[5], and the proposal must be treated as having been withdrawn[6].

1 As to the meaning of 'proposal' see PARA 213 note 3. As to proposals see PARA 214. As to local non-domestic rating lists see PARA 191 et seq. As to the application of the Non-Domestic Rating (Alteration of Lists and Appeals) (Wales) Regulations 2005, SI 2005/758, Pt 2 (regs 3–17) to central non-domestic rating lists see PARA 225.

2 The specified persons are:

(1) the valuation officer (Non-Domestic Rating (Alteration of Lists and Appeals) (Wales) Regulations 2005, SI 2005/758, reg 12(2)(a));

(2) the proposer (reg 12(2)(b));

(3) subject to reg 12(3), the occupier (at the date of the proposal) of any hereditament to which it relates (reg 12(2)(c));

(4) the ratepayer (at the date of the agreement) in relation to any hereditament to which it relates (reg 12(2)(d));

(5) subject to reg 12(3), any interested person or relevant authority who would at the date of the proposal have been competent to make the proposal in question, and who has within the period of two months beginning on the day on which the proposal was served on the valuation officer served notice on them in writing indicating a wish to be party to proceedings in respect of the proposal (reg 12(2)(e)).

Where:

(a) the occupier of the hereditament at the date of the proposal is no longer in occupation of any part of it at the date on which all the other persons mentioned in heads (1)–(5) above have agreed as mentioned in reg 12(1), and the valuation officer has taken all reasonable steps to ascertain their whereabouts, but they have not been ascertained; or

(b) any interested person who has given notice as mentioned in head (5) above cannot be contacted at the address supplied to the valuation officer (whether in the notice or otherwise),

the agreement of that person under reg 12(1), (2) is not required: reg 12(3).

As to the meaning of 'person' see PARA 11 note 13. As to valuation officers see PARA 54. As to the meaning of 'occupier' see PARA 86. As to the meaning of 'hereditament' see PARA 106. As to the meaning of 'ratepayer' see PARA 213 note 6. As to the meaning of 'interested person' see PARA 214 note 3. As to the meaning of 'relevant authority' see PARA 213 note 4. As to the meaning of 'month' see PARA 11 note 1. As to the meaning of 'writing' see PARA 21 note 3.

The Non-Domestic Rating (Alteration of Lists and Appeals) (Wales) Regulations 2005, SI 2005/758, apply in relation to Wales only: see reg 1. As to the equivalent provision to reg 12 in relation to England see the Non-Domestic Rating (Alteration of Lists and Appeals) (England) Regulations 2009, SI 2009/2268, reg 12; and PARA 209. As to the meanings of 'England' and 'Wales' see PARA 2 note 16.

3 As to the meaning of 'alteration' see PARA 213 note 1.

4 Ie the requirements of the Non-Domestic Rating (Alteration of Lists and Appeals) (Wales) Regulations 2005, SI 2005/758, Pt 2 (regs 3–17): see PARA 213 et seq.

5 Non-Domestic Rating (Alteration of Lists and Appeals) (Wales) Regulations 2005, SI 2005/758, reg 12(1)(a). Where the period of two weeks mentioned in reg 12(1)(a) would expire before the period of two months mentioned in reg 12(2)(e) (see head (5) in note 2), the alteration required by reg 12(1)(a) must, where no notice is served as mentioned in reg 12(2)(e), be made as soon as practicable after the expiry of that period of two months: reg 12(4).

6 Non-Domestic Rating (Alteration of Lists and Appeals) (Wales) Regulations 2005, SI 2005/758, reg 12(1)(b).

222. Disagreement as to proposed alteration.

Where the valuation officer[1] is not of the opinion that a proposal for the alteration of a local non-domestic rating list[2] is well-founded[3], and the proposal is not withdrawn[4], and there is no agreement[5] as to an alteration[6], the disagreement, no later than the expiry of the period of three months[7] beginning on the day on which the proposal was served on the valuation officer, must be referred by the valuation officer, as an appeal by the proposer[8] against the valuation officer's refusal to alter the list, to the relevant valuation tribunal[9]. A referral must take place by means of the transmission to the clerk of the tribunal of a statement of the following matters[10]:

(1) the entry in the list (if any) which is proposed to be altered[11];
(2) the date of service of the proposal[12];
(3) the names and addresses (where known to the valuation officer) of all persons whose agreement is required[13]; and
(4) the grounds on which the proposal was made[14].

The valuation officer must transmit[15] to the clerk of the tribunal the name and address supplied to him or her by any other person who has given notice[16] that they wish to be a party to the appeal[17].

1 As to valuation officers see PARA 54.

2 As to the meaning of 'proposal' see PARA 213 note 3. As to proposals see PARA 214. As to local non-domestic rating lists see PARA 191 et seq. As to the application of the Non-Domestic Rating (Alteration of Lists and Appeals) (Wales) Regulations 2005, SI 2005/758, Pt 2 (regs 3–17) to central non-domestic rating lists see PARA 225.

3 Non-Domestic Rating (Alteration of Lists and Appeals) (Wales) Regulations 2005, SI 2005/758, reg 13(1). The Non-Domestic Rating (Alteration of Lists and Appeals) (Wales) Regulations 2005, SI 2005/758, apply in relation to Wales only: see reg 1. As to the equivalent provision to reg 13 in relation to England see the Non-Domestic Rating (Alteration of Lists and Appeals) (England) Regulations 2009, SI 2009/2268, reg 13; and PARA 210. As to the meanings of 'England' and 'Wales' see PARA 2 note 16.

4 Non-Domestic Rating (Alteration of Lists and Appeals) (Wales) Regulations 2005, SI 2005/758, reg 13(1)(a). As to the withdrawal of proposals see PARA 220.

5 Ie under the Non-Domestic Rating (Alteration of Lists and Appeals) (Wales) Regulations 2005, SI 2005/758, reg 12: see PARA 221.

6 Non-Domestic Rating (Alteration of Lists and Appeals) (Wales) Regulations 2005, SI 2005/758, reg 13(1)(b).

7 As to the meaning of 'month' see PARA 11 note 1.

8 As to the meaning of 'proposer' see PARA 216 note 5.

9 Non-Domestic Rating (Alteration of Lists and Appeals) (Wales) Regulations 2005, SI 2005/758, reg 13(1). As to the meaning of 'relevant valuation tribunal' see PARA 213 note 7.

10 Non-Domestic Rating (Alteration of Lists and Appeals) (Wales) Regulations 2005, SI 2005/758, reg 13(2).

11 Non-Domestic Rating (Alteration of Lists and Appeals) (Wales) Regulations 2005, SI 2005/758, reg 13(2)(a).

12 Non-Domestic Rating (Alteration of Lists and Appeals) (Wales) Regulations 2005, SI 2005/758, reg 13(2)(b).

13 Non-Domestic Rating (Alteration of Lists and Appeals) (Wales) Regulations 2005, SI 2005/758, reg 13(2)(c). The persons referred to are those whose agreement is required by reg 12 (see PARA 221): see reg 13(2)(c). As to the meaning of 'person' see PARA 11 note 13.

14 Non-Domestic Rating (Alteration of Lists and Appeals) (Wales) Regulations 2005, SI 2005/758, reg 13(2)(d).

15 As to the valuation officer's duty in this respect see *R v West Norfolk Local Valuation Panel, ex p H Prins Ltd* [1975] RA 101, 73 LGR 206, DC; *Knight v Morton Valuation Officer* [1988] RVR 5, Lands Tribunal. These cases cited were decided under previous legislation but may continue to be of relevance.

16 Ie under the Non-Domestic Rating (Alteration of Lists and Appeals) (Wales) Regulations 2005, SI 2005/758, reg 2(3)(b)(ii): see PARA 257 note 2.

17 Non-Domestic Rating (Alteration of Lists and Appeals) (Wales) Regulations 2005, SI 2005/758, reg 13(3) (amended by SI 2006/1035).

223. Time from which alteration is to have effect.

The following provisions have effect in relation to alterations[1] made to a local non-domestic rating list compiled[2] on or after 1 April 2005[3].

Where an alteration is made to correct any inaccuracy in the list on or after the day it is compiled, the alteration has effect from the day on which the circumstances giving rise to the alteration first occurred[4]. Where the day on which the relevant circumstances arose is not reasonably ascertainable:

(1) where the alteration is made in pursuance of a proposal for the alteration of a list, the alteration has effect from the day on which the proposal was served on the valuation officer for the billing authority for which the list is compiled and maintained[5]; and

(2) in any other case, the alteration has effect from the day on which it is made[6].

An alteration made to correct an inaccuracy (other than one which has arisen by reason of an error or default on the part of a ratepayer[7]) in the list on the day it was compiled[8], or which arose in the course of making a previous alteration[9], which increases the rateable value[10] shown in the list for the hereditament[11] to which the inaccuracy relates, has effect from the day on which the alteration is made[12].

Where an alteration is made to give effect to a completion notice[13], the alteration has effect from the day specified in the notice[14].

Where an alteration needs to be made after the first anniversary of the day on which the next list is compiled, it has retrospective effect only if it is made in pursuance of a proposal[15].

Specific provision is made in relation to advertising rights[16].

Where an alteration is made, the list must show the day from which the alteration is to have effect[17]. Before altering an entry in a list the valuation officer must ensure that a record (which need not be in documentary form) is made of the entry[18].

1 As to the meaning of 'alteration' see PARA 200 note 1.

2 As to the compilation of local non-domestic rating lists see PARA 191. As to the application of the Non-Domestic Rating (Alteration of Lists and Appeals) (Wales) Regulations 2005, SI 2005/758, Pt 2 (regs 3–17) to central non-domestic rating lists see PARA 225.

3 Non-Domestic Rating (Alteration of Lists and Appeals) (Wales) Regulations 2005, SI 2005/758, reg 14(1). The Non-Domestic Rating (Alteration of Lists and Appeals) (Wales) Regulations 2005, SI 2005/758, apply in relation to Wales only: see reg 1. As to the equivalent provision to regs 14–16, 41 in relation to England see the Non-Domestic Rating (Alteration of Lists and Appeals) (England) Regulations 2009, SI 2009/2268, regs 14–16, 23; and PARA 212. As to the meanings of 'England' and 'Wales' see PARA 2 note 16.

4 Non-Domestic Rating (Alteration of Lists and Appeals) (Wales) Regulations 2005, SI 2005/758, reg 14(2). This provision is expressed to be subject to reg 14(3)–(7) (see the text to notes 5–14): see reg 14(2). Under previous legislation, it was held that a provision specifying that certain alterations to the list were to take effect from the date of the event giving rise to the alteration only applied when that was the sole reason for the alteration, and no other reason: *Cox & Co (Watford) Ltd v Bushey UDC* (1961) 9 RRC 119, [1962] RVR 126. All the cases cited in this paragraph were decided under previous legislation but may continue to be of relevance.

5 Non-Domestic Rating (Alteration of Lists and Appeals) (Wales) Regulations 2005, SI 2005/758, reg 14(5)(a). As to valuation officers see PARA 54. As to the meaning of 'billing authority' see PARA 53.

6 Non-Domestic Rating (Alteration of Lists and Appeals) (Wales) Regulations 2005, SI 2005/758, reg 14(5)(b).

7 As to the meaning of 'ratepayer' see PARA 213 note 6.

8 Non-Domestic Rating (Alteration of Lists and Appeals) (Wales) Regulations 2005, SI 2005/758, reg 14(6)(a). As to alterations made to correct an inaccuracy in the list on the day it was compiled see *Thomas's London Day School v Jorgensen (Valuation Officer)* [2005] RA 222, Lands Tribunal.

9 Ie a previous alteration in connection with a matter mentioned in any of the Non-Domestic Rating (Alteration of Lists and Appeals) (Wales) Regulations 2005, SI 2005/758, reg 14(2)–(5) (see the text to notes 4–6, 13–14): reg 14(6)(b).

10 As to the valuation for rating see PARA 156 et seq.

11 As to the meaning of 'hereditament' see PARA 106.

12 Non-Domestic Rating (Alteration of Lists and Appeals) (Wales) Regulations 2005, SI 2005/758, reg 14(6). As to whether an alteration to correct an inaccuracy in a list increases the rateable value shown in the list for the hereditament to which the inaccuracy relates see *Lamb & Shirley Ltd v Bliss* [2001] EWCA Civ 562, [2001] RA 99, [2001] All ER (D) 44 (Apr).

13 'Completion notice' means a notice under the Local Government Finance Act 1988 Sch 4A para 1 (see PARA 138) as it applies for the purposes of Pt III (ss 41–67) of the Act, which states the completion day as 1 April 2005 or later: Non-Domestic Rating (Alteration of Lists and Appeals) (Wales) Regulations 2005, SI 2005/758, reg 2(1).

14 Non-Domestic Rating (Alteration of Lists and Appeals) (Wales) Regulations 2005, SI 2005/758, reg 14(3). Where under the Local Government Finance Act 1988 Sch 4A a different day is substituted by a different notice under Sch 4A para 1(3) (see PARA 138), is agreed under Sch 4A para 3 (see PARA 141) or is determined in pursuance of an appeal under Sch 4A para 4 (see PARA 141), the alteration has effect from the day so substituted, agreed or determined: Non-Domestic Rating (Alteration of Lists and Appeals) (Wales) Regulations 2005, SI 2005/758, reg 14(4).

15 Non-Domestic Rating (Alteration of Lists and Appeals) (Wales) Regulations 2005, SI 2005/758, reg 14(7).

16 For the purposes of the Non-Domestic Rating (Alteration of Lists and Appeals) (Wales) Regulations 2005, SI 2005/758, reg 14 (see the text to notes 1–15), where the circumstances giving rise to the alteration are the coming into existence of an advertising hereditament, those circumstances are to be treated as occurring when:

(1) any structure or sign is erected, after the right constituting the hereditament has been let out or reserved, to enable the right to be exercised (reg 15(1)(a)); or

(2) any advertisement is exhibited in exercise of the right (reg 15(1)(b)),

whichever is earlier; and such a hereditament must be treated for the purposes of the Local Government Finance Act 1988 Pt III (ss 41–67) as coming into occupation at that time (Non-Domestic Rating (Alteration of Lists and Appeals) (Wales) Regulations 2005, SI 2005/758, reg 15(1)).

The erection, dismantling or alteration of any structure or sign for enabling the advertising right to be exercised, after the time mentioned in reg 15(1), must be treated as a material change of circumstances for the purposes of a proposal made on the ground specified in reg 4(1)(b) (rateable value inaccurate by reason of material change of circumstances occurring on or after the day on which the list was compiled: see PARA 214): reg 15(2). 'Advertising hereditament' means a hereditament consisting of a right to which the Local Government Finance Act 1988 s 64(2) (see PARA 104) applies; 'advertising right' means a right which is such a hereditament; and 'structure' includes a hoarding, frame, post or wall: Non-Domestic Rating (Alteration of Lists and Appeals) (Wales) Regulations 2005, SI 2005/758, regs 2(1), 15(3).

17 Non-Domestic Rating (Alteration of Lists and Appeals) (Wales) Regulations 2005, SI 2005/758, reg 16. As to the notification of alterations see PARA 213. There is no requirement that alterations to the list must be made within a certain time: *National Car Parks Ltd v Baird (Valuation Officer)* [2004] EWCA Civ 967, [2005] 1 All ER 53, [2004] RA 245; and see PARA 191.

18 See the Non-Domestic Rating (Alteration of Lists and Appeals) (Wales) Regulations 2005, SI 2005/758, reg 41(1). A record made must be retained until the expiry of six years beginning on the day on which the next list is compiled: see reg 41(2).

C ALTERATION OF CENTRAL NON-DOMESTIC RATING LISTS

224. Relevant hereditaments capable of alteration in the central rating list: England.

In relation to a hereditament[1] (a 'relevant hereditament') which is required[2] to be shown in a central non-domestic rating list compiled[3] on or after 1 October 2009, the regulations relating to the alteration of local non-domestic rating lists listed below apply, with modifications, as if any reference to a local list were a reference to the central list[4]; any reference to the valuation officer's electronic portal were a reference to the online facility provided by the central valuation officer for use in connection with proposals for the alteration of a central list compiled on or after 1 April 2017[5]; any reference to a valuation officer were a reference to the central valuation officer[6]; and any reference to an alteration[7] of a list were a reference to its alteration in relation to a description of hereditaments[8].

The regulations are:

(1) that relating to the circumstances in which proposals may be made[9];
(2) those relating to the making of proposals[10];
(3) that relating to the procedure after the making of proposals[11];
(4) those relating to the determination of proposals[12];
(5) that relating to disagreement as to a proposed alteration[13];
(6) those relating to making an appeal to the Valuation Tribunal for England[14].
(7) that relating to the time from which an alteration is to have effect[15];
(8) that relating to the effective date to be shown in the list[16]; and
(9) that relating to notification of an alteration[17].

Before altering an entry in the central list, the central valuation officer must ensure that a record (which need not be in documentary form) is made of the entry[18]. Such a record must be retained until the expiry of six years beginning on the day on which the next list is compiled[19].

1 As to the meaning of 'hereditament' see PARA 106.

2 Ie by regulations under the Local Government Finance Act 1988 s 53: see PARA 197.

3 As to the compilation and maintenance of central non-domestic rating lists see PARA 196.

4 Non-Domestic Rating (Alteration of Lists and Appeals) (England) Regulations 2009, SI 2009/2268, reg 18(1)(a). The Non-Domestic Rating (Alteration of Lists and Appeals) (England) Regulations 2009, SI 2009/2268, apply in relation to England only: see reg 1. As to the equivalent provision to regs 18, 23 in relation to Wales see the Non-Domestic Rating (Alteration of Lists and Appeals) (Wales) Regulations 2005, SI 2005/758, regs 18, 41; and PARA 225. As to the meanings of 'England' and 'Wales' see PARA 2 note 16.

5 Non-Domestic Rating (Alteration of Lists and Appeals) (England) Regulations 2009, SI 2009/2268, reg 18(1)(aa) (added by SI 2017/155).

6 Non-Domestic Rating (Alteration of Lists and Appeals) (England) Regulations 2009, SI 2009/2268, reg 18(1)(b). As to valuation officers see PARA 54.

7 As to the meaning of 'alteration' see PARA 200 note 1.

8 Non-Domestic Rating (Alteration of Lists and Appeals) (England) Regulations 2009, SI 2009/2268, reg 18(1)(c).

9 Ie the Non-Domestic Rating (Alteration of Lists and Appeals) (England) Regulations 2009, SI 2009/2268, reg 4 (see PARA 202), except reg 4(1)(k), (l) and reg 4(3): reg 18(2)(a). Regulation 4(1)(o) applies as if the reference to the Local Government Finance Act 1988 s 42 were a reference to s 53 (see PARA 197): Non-Domestic Rating (Alteration of Lists and Appeals) (England) Regulations 2009, SI 2009/2268, reg 18(3).

10 Ie the Non-Domestic Rating (Alteration of Lists and Appeals) (England) Regulations 2009, SI 2009/2268, regs 4A–8 (see PARAS215–206): reg 18(2)(b) (substituted by SI 2017/155).

11 Ie the Non-Domestic Rating (Alteration of Lists and Appeals) (England) Regulations 2009, SI 2009/2268, reg 9 (see PARA 207), except reg 9(4), (5): reg 18(2)(c) (amended by SI 2017/155). At the same time as the central valuation officer serves a copy of a proposal on the ratepayer under the Non-Domestic Rating (Alteration of Lists and Appeals) (England) Regulations 2009, SI 2009/2268, reg 9(1) in relation to a relevant hereditament the central valuation officer must serve such a copy on the Secretary of State: reg 18(5). As to the Secretary of State see PARA 4 note 18.

12 Ie the Non-Domestic Rating (Alteration of Lists and Appeals) (England) Regulations 2009, SI 2009/2268, regs 10–12 (see PARAS 207–209): reg 18(2)(d) (substituted by SI 2017/155).

13 Ie the Non-Domestic Rating (Alteration of Lists and Appeals) (England) Regulations 2009, SI 2009/2268, reg 13 (see PARA 210), except reg 13(2)(d), (4): reg 18(2)(da) (added by SI 2017/155).

14 Ie the Non-Domestic Rating (Alteration of Lists and Appeals) (England) Regulations 2009, SI 2009/2268, regs 13A–13E (see PARA 211): reg 18(2)(db) (added by SI 2017/155).

15 Ie the Non-Domestic Rating (Alteration of Lists and Appeals) (England) Regulations 2009, SI 2009/2268, reg 14 (see PARA 212), except reg 14(3), (4) and (to the extent to which those paragraphs relate to reg 14(3), (4)) reg 14(2), (7): reg 18(2)(e) (substituted by SI 2011/434).

16 Ie the Non-Domestic Rating (Alteration of Lists and Appeals) (England) Regulations 2009, SI 2009/2268, reg 16 (see PARA 212): reg 18(2)(f).

17 Ie the Non-Domestic Rating (Alteration of Lists and Appeals) (England) Regulations 2009,

SI 2009/2268, reg 17 (see PARA 200), except reg 17(3)(b): reg 18(2)(g). Regulation 17(1) applies as if the reference to the relevant authority and its principal office were a reference to the Secretary of State and the Secretary of State's principal office: reg 18(4).

18 See the Non-Domestic Rating (Alteration of Lists and Appeals) (England) Regulations 2009, SI 2009/2268, reg 23(1).

19 See the Non-Domestic Rating (Alteration of Lists and Appeals) (England) Regulations 2009, SI 2009/2268, reg 23(2).

225. Relevant hereditaments capable of alteration in the central rating list: Wales.

In relation to a hereditament[1] (a 'relevant hereditament') which is required[2] to be shown in a central non-domestic rating list compiled[3] on or after 1 April 2005, the regulations relating to the alteration of local non-domestic rating lists listed below apply, with modifications, as if any reference to a local non-domestic rating list were a reference to the central non-domestic rating list[4]; any reference to a valuation officer were a reference to the central valuation officer[5]; and any reference to an alteration[6] of a list were a reference to its alteration in relation to a description of hereditaments[7].

The regulations are:

(1) that relating to the circumstances in which proposals may be made[8];

(2) those relating to the making of proposals, the procedure subsequent to the making of proposals and the determination of proposals[9];

(3) that relating to the time from which an alteration is to have effect[10];

(4) those relating to the effective date to be shown in the list and to notification of an alteration[11].

Before altering an entry in the central non-domestic rating list, the central valuation officer must ensure that a record (which need not be in documentary form) is made of the entry[12]. Such a record must be retained until the expiry of six years beginning on the day on which the next list is compiled[13].

1 As to the meaning of 'hereditament' see PARA 106.

2 Ie by regulations under the Local Government Finance Act 1988 s 53: see PARA 197.

3 As to the compilation and maintenance of central non-domestic rating lists see PARA 196.

4 Non-Domestic Rating (Alteration of Lists and Appeals) (Wales) Regulations 2005, SI 2005/758, reg 18(1)(a). The Non-Domestic Rating (Alteration of Lists and Appeals) (Wales) Regulations 2005, SI 2005/758, apply in relation to Wales only: see reg 1. As to the equivalent provision to regs 18, 41 in relation to England see the Non-Domestic Rating (Alteration of Lists and Appeals) (England) Regulations 2009, SI 2009/2268, regs 18, 41; and PARA 224. As to the meanings of 'England' and 'Wales' see PARA 2 note 16.

5 Non-Domestic Rating (Alteration of Lists and Appeals) (Wales) Regulations 2005, SI 2005/758, reg 18(1)(b). As to valuation officers see PARA 54.

6 As to the meaning of 'alteration' see PARA 213 note 1.

7 Non-Domestic Rating (Alteration of Lists and Appeals) (Wales) Regulations 2005, SI 2005/758, reg 18(1)(c).

8 Ie the Non-Domestic Rating (Alteration of Lists and Appeals) (Wales) Regulations 2005, SI 2005/758, reg 4 (see PARA 214), except reg 4(1)(k), (l) and reg 4(3): reg 18(2)(a). Regulation 4(1)(o) applies as if the reference to the Local Government Finance Act 1988 s 42 were a reference to s 53 (see PARA 197): Non-Domestic Rating (Alteration of Lists and Appeals) (Wales) Regulations 2005, SI 2005/7588, reg 18(3).

9 Ie the Non-Domestic Rating (Alteration of Lists and Appeals) (Wales) Regulations 2005, SI 2005/758, regs 5–8, 9(1)(a), (2), 10–13 (see PARAS 215–222): reg 18(2)(b). Regulations 8, 13 apply as if references to a relevant valuation tribunal were to the valuation tribunal established by regulations under the Local Government Finance Act 1988 Sch 11 (see PARA 236) for the area in which the designated person has its principal place of business within England and Wales: Non-Domestic Rating (Alteration of Lists and Appeals) (Wales) Regulations 2005, SI 2005/7588, reg 18(5). In reg 18 'the designated person' means the person designated by regulations under the

Local Government Finance Act 1988 s 53 (see PARA 197) in relation to the description of hereditaments which includes the relevant hereditament to which the alteration or proposed alteration relates: Non-Domestic Rating (Alteration of Lists and Appeals) (Wales) Regulations 2005, SI 2005/7588, reg 18(7).

At the same time as the central valuation officer serves a copy of a proposal on the ratepayer under reg 9(1) in relation to a relevant hereditament the central valuation officer must serve such a copy on the Welsh Ministers: reg 18(5). As to the Welsh Ministers see PARA 4 note 18.

10 Ie the Non-Domestic Rating (Alteration of Lists and Appeals) (Wales) Regulations 2005, SI 2005/7588, reg 14 (see PARA 223), except reg 14(3), (4) and the reference to reg 14(3), (4) in reg 14(2): reg 18(2)(c).

11 Ie the Non-Domestic Rating (Alteration of Lists and Appeals) (Wales) Regulations 2005, SI 2005/7588, reg 16 (see PARA 223) and reg 17 (see PARA 213), except reg 17(3)(b): reg 18(2)(d). Regulation 17(1) applies as if the reference to the relevant authority and its principal office were a reference to the Welsh Ministers: reg 18(4).

12 See the Non-Domestic Rating (Alteration of Lists and Appeals) (Wales) Regulations 2005, SI 2005/75888, reg 41(1).

13 See the Non-Domestic Rating (Alteration of Lists and Appeals) (Wales) Regulations 2005, SI 2005/7588, reg 41(2).

(vi) Information, Etc Powers Relating to Lists

226. Request for information.

A valuation officer[1] may serve a notice[2] on a person who is an owner or occupier of a hereditament requesting him to supply to the officer information[3] specified in the notice[4] and which the officer reasonably believes will assist him in carrying out functions conferred or imposed on him by or under the non-domestic rating provisions[5]. The notice must state that the officer believes the information requested will assist him in carrying out those functions[6]. A person on whom such a notice is served must supply the information requested in such form and manner as is specified in the notice[7]. A person commits an offence if he makes a false statement in response to the notice[8].

If a person on whom a notice is so served fails to comply with the request for information[9] within the period of 56 days beginning with the day on which the notice is served, he is liable to a penalty of £100[10], and the valuation officer must serve on him a notice (a 'penalty notice') stating (amongst other things) that he is so liable[11]. If the person on whom a penalty notice is served then fails to comply with the request for information within the period of 21 days beginning with the day on which the penalty notice is served, he is liable to a further penalty of £100[12], and to a further penalty of £20 for each day in respect of which the failure continues after the end of that period[13]. A valuation officer may mitigate or remit any penalty so imposed[14].

A person may appeal to a valuation tribunal[15] if he is aggrieved by the imposition on him of any penalty[16] for a failure to comply with a request for information[17]. An appeal must be made before the end of the period of 28 days beginning with the day on which the penalty notice is served[18]. On an appeal, the valuation tribunal may mitigate or remit any penalty imposed if it is satisfied on either or both of the following grounds[19]:

(1) that the appellant had a reasonable excuse for not complying with the request for information[20]; or

(2) that the information requested is not in the possession or control of the appellant[21].

Any penalty imposed for a failure to comply with a request for information may be recovered by the valuation officer concerned as a civil debt due to him[22].

1 As to the meaning of 'valuation officer' see PARA 54 note 3.

2 Where a valuation officer requires the name or address of a person on whom a notice under the Local Government Finance Act 1988 Sch 9 para 5 or Sch 9 para 5A (see the text to notes 9–14) is to be served, he may serve a notice on a billing authority which he reasonably believes may have that information requesting the authority to supply him with that information: s 62, Sch 9 para 5H (Sch 9 paras 5A–5H added by the Local Government Act 2003 s 72(1), (4)). As to the meaning of 'person' see PARA 11 note 13. As to the meaning of 'billing authority' see PARA 53. As to the meaning of 'information' see PARA 31 note 17.

The Secretary of State, in relation to England, and the Welsh Ministers, in relation to Wales, may by regulations make provision in relation to notices served under the Local Government Finance Act 1988 Sch 9 para 5 or Sch 9 para 5A: Sch 9 para 5F(1) (as so added). The provision that may be made by such regulations includes provision enabling a valuation officer to request or obtain information for the purpose of identifying the owner or occupier of a hereditament, and provision enabling a notice to be served on a person either by name or by such description as may be prescribed: Sch 9 para 5F(2) (as so added). 'Prescribed' means prescribed by the regulations: see s 146(6). At the date at which this volume states the law no such regulations had been made. As to the meanings of 'owner' and 'occupier' see PARA 86. As to the meaning of 'hereditament' see PARA 106. As to the Secretary of State and the Welsh Ministers see PARA 4 note 18. As to the meanings of 'England' and 'Wales' see PARA 2 note 16.

The functions under Schedule 9 paras 5F, 5G (see the text to note 10) were formerly vested in the National Assembly for Wales and are now exercisable by the Welsh Ministers by virtue of the Government of Wales Act 2006 s 162(1), Sch 11 paras 30, 32.

3 Local Government Finance Act 1988 Sch 9 para 5(1) (amended by the Local Government and Housing Act 1989 s 139, Sch 5 paras 1, 46, 79(3)).

4 Local Government Finance Act 1988 Sch 9 para 5(1)(a).

5 Local Government Finance Act 1988 Sch 9 para 5(1)(b). The non-domestic rating provisions are those contained in Pt III (ss 41–67): see Sch 9 para 5(1)(b).

6 See the Local Government Finance Act 1988 Sch 9 para 5(1A) (added by the Local Government and Housing Act 1989 Sch 5 paras 1, 46, 79(3)).

7 Local Government Finance Act 1988 Sch 9 para 5(2) (amended by the Local Government and Housing Act 1989 Sch 5 paras 1, 46, 79(3); and the Local Government Act 2003 ss 72(1), (2), 127(2), Sch 8 Pt 1).

8 If a notice has been served on a person, and in supplying information in purported compliance with the Local Government Finance Act 1988 Sch 9 para 5(2) (see the text to note 7) he makes a statement which he knows to be false in a material particular or recklessly makes a statement which is false in a material particular, he is liable on summary conviction to imprisonment for a term not exceeding three months or to a fine not exceeding level 3 on the standard scale or to both: Sch 9 para 5(4). As to the powers of magistrates' courts to issue fines on summary conviction see SENTENCING vol 92 (2015) PARA 176. As to recklessness in criminal law see CRIMINAL LAW vol 25 (2016) PARA 11.

9 Ie fails to comply with the Local Government Finance Act 1988 Sch 9 para 5(2): see the text to note 7.

10 Local Government Finance Act 1988 Sch 9 para 5A(1) (as added: see note 2). The Secretary of State, in relation to England, and the Welsh Ministers, in relation to Wales, may by order amend Sch 9 para 5A to increase or decrease the amount of any penalty thereunder: Sch 9 para 5G (as so added). At the date at which this volume states the law no such order had been made. Any sums received by a valuation officer by way of penalty under Sch 9 para 5A must be paid into the Consolidated Fund: Sch 9 para 5E (as so added). As to the Consolidated Fund see CONSTITUTIONAL AND ADMINISTRATIVE LAW vol 20 (2014) PARA 480 et seq; PARLIAMENT vol 78 (2010) PARA 1028.

11 See the Local Government Finance Act 1988 Sch 9 para 5A(2) (as added: see note 2). A penalty notice must state:

(1) that the person on whom it is served has failed to comply with Sch 9 para 5(2) (see the text to note 7) within the period mentioned in Sch 9 para 5A(1) (see the text to note 10) (Sch 9 para 5A(2)(a) (as so added));

(2) that he is liable to a penalty of £100 (Sch 9 para 5A(2)(b) (as so added));

(3) the effect of a failure to comply with a penalty notice (ie the effect of Sch 9 para 5A(3), (4) (see the text to notes 12–14) (Sch 9 para 5A(2)(c) (as so added)); and

(4) that he has a right of appeal under Sch 9 para 5C (see the text to notes 15–19) (Sch 9 para 5A(2)(d) (as so added)).

12 Local Government Finance Act 1988 Sch 9 para 5A(3)(a) (as added: see note 2).

13 Local Government Finance Act 1988 Sch 9 para 5A(3)(b) (as added: see note 2). The amount to which a person is liable under Sch 9 para 5A in respect of a failure to comply with a notice served under Sch 9 para 5 (see the text to notes 1–5) must not exceed whichever is the greater of the rateable value of the hereditament concerned for the day on which the penalty notice is served and £500: Sch 9 para 5A(4) (as so added). For these purposes, the hereditament concerned is the hereditament in respect of which the notice under Sch 9 para 5 was served, and a list compiled under Pt III (ss 41–67) must be used to find the rateable value of the hereditament for the day concerned: Sch 9 para 5A(5) (as so added). As to the valuation for rating see PARA 156 et seq. 'List' means a local or central non-domestic rating list: see s 67(1). As to local non-domestic rating lists see PARA 191 et seq. As to central non-domestic rating lists see PARA 196 et seq.

14 Local Government Finance Act 1988 Sch 9 para 5B (as added: see note 2).

15 'Valuation tribunal' means, in relation to England, the Valuation Tribunal for England; and, in relation to Wales, a valuation tribunal established under the Local Government Finance Act 1988 Sch 11 para 1 (see PARA 236): Sch 9 para 5C(7) (Sch 9 para 5C as added (see note 2); Sch 9 para 5C(7) added by the Local Government and Public Involvement in Health Act 2007 s 220(1), Sch 16 paras 2, 5). As to the Valuation Tribunal for England see PARA 232.

16 Ie a penalty imposed under the Local Government Finance Act 1988 Sch 9 para 5A: see the text to notes 9–11.

17 Local Government Finance Act 1988 Sch 9 para 5C(1) (as added: see note 2). An appeal under Sch 9 para 5C is to be treated as an appeal against the penalty imposed under Sch 9 para 5A(1) (see the text to notes 9–10) and any further penalty which may be imposed under Sch 9 para 5A(3) (see the text to notes 12–13): Sch 9 para 5C(4) (as so added). However, an appeal under Sch 9 para 5C does not prevent liability to any further penalty or penalties arising under Sch 9 para 5A(3): Sch 9 para 5C(3) (as so added). As to appeals to a valuation tribunal generally see PARA 232 et seq.

18 Local Government Finance Act 1988 Sch 9 para 5C(2) (as added: see note 2). A person who wishes to appeal against the imposition of a penalty must send or deliver a notice of appeal to the Valuation Tribunal for England so that it is received within 28 days after the date on which the appellant received the notice that the penalty had been imposed: see the Non-Domestic Rating (Alteration of Lists and Appeals) (England) Regulations 2009, SI 2009/2268, reg 19(1). The notice of appeal must be accompanied by:

(1) a copy of the penalty notice (reg 19(2)(a));

(2) a statement of the grounds on which the appeal is made (reg 19(2)(b)); and

(3) the date on which the person received notice of the imposition of the penalty (reg 19(2)(c)).

If the person provides the notice of appeal to the tribunal later than the time required by reg 19(1) or by an extension of time allowed under the Valuation Tribunal for England (Council Tax and Rating Appeals) (Procedure) Regulations 2009, SI 2009/2269, reg 6(3)(a) (see PARA 244), the notice of appeal must include a request for an extension of time and the reason why the notice of appeal was not provided in time: Non-Domestic Rating (Alteration of Lists and Appeals) (England) Regulations 2009, SI 2009/2268, reg 19(3).

The Non-Domestic Rating (Alteration of Lists and Appeals) (England) Regulations 2009, SI 2009/2268, apply in relation to England only: see reg 1. As to the equivalent provision to reg 19 in relation to Wales see the Non-Domestic Rating (Alteration of Lists and Appeals) (Wales) Regulations 2005, SI 2005/758, reg 20.

In Wales, an appeal against imposition of a penalty must be initiated by serving on the clerk of the relevant valuation tribunal a notice in writing (a 'notice of appeal') (reg 20(1)) accompanied by:

(a) a copy of the penalty notice (reg 20(1)(a));

(b) a statement of the grounds on which the appeal is made (reg 20(1)(b)); and

(c) the date of service of the notice of the imposition of a penalty (reg 20(1)(c)).

The clerk must, within two weeks of service of the notice of appeal, notify the appellant that the clerk has received it, and must serve a copy of it on the valuation officer whose notice is the subject of the appeal: reg 20(2). As to the meaning of 'relevant valuation tribunal' see PARA 213 note 7.

19 See the Local Government Finance Act 1988 Sch 9 para 5C(5) (as added: see note 2).

20 Local Government Finance Act 1988 Sch 9 para 5C(6)(a) (as added: see note 2). What is a reasonable excuse is largely a question of fact: *Leck v Epsom RDC* [1922] 1 KB 383. Ignorance of the statutory provisions provides no reasonable excuse (*Aldridge v Warwickshire Coal Co Ltd*

(1925) 133 LT 439), nor does a mistaken view of the provisions (*R v Philip Reid* [1973] 3 All ER 1020, [1973] 1 WLR 1283, CA). As to whether reliance upon the advice of an expert can be a reasonable excuse see *Saddleworth UDC v Aggregate and Sand Ltd* (1970) 69 LGR 103.

These cases were decided prior to the coming into force of the Local Government Finance Act 1988 but continue to be of relevance: see PARA 50.

21 Local Government Finance Act 1988 Sch 9 para 5C(6)(b) (as added: see note 2).

22 Local Government Finance Act 1988 Sch 9 para 5D(1) (as added: see note 2). However, no claim to recover any such penalty may be made either before the end of the period mentioned in Sch 9 para 5C(2) (see the text to note 18) or, if an appeal is made under Sch 9 para 5C (see the text to notes 15–21), before the appeal is finally disposed of: Sch 9 para 5D(2) (as so added).

227. Information from billing authorities.

If, in the course of the exercise of its functions, any information[1] comes to the notice of a billing authority[2] which leads it to suppose that a list[3] requires alteration, it is the billing authority's duty to inform the valuation officer[4] responsible for maintaining the list[5]. The appropriate national authority[6] may make regulations containing provision as to what times and in what manner billing authorities must supply the valuation officer with such information as may be prescribed[7].

Information of the following description is prescribed for these purposes[8]. In relation to any property, in relation to a relevant authority[9]:

(1) which is any non-domestic property[10] in the authority's area[11];
(2) which, in the authority's opinion, is property which is or may become liable to a rate[12]; and
(3) in relation to which there is no entry in the local list[13], or in the authority's opinion any entry in such a list requires to be altered[14],

the information is:

(a) the address of the property[15];
(b) the nature of the event by reason of which, in the opinion of the relevant authority, the local list is required to be altered[16];
(c) the day from which, in the opinion of the relevant authority, such alteration should have effect[17]; and
(d) if the property is shown in a local list, any reference number ascribed to it in that list[18].

The information must be supplied as soon as is reasonably practicable after it comes to the attention of the relevant authority[19].

Where regulations[20] impose a duty on a billing authority to supply information to any person[21], they may also require the appropriate national authority[22], any appropriate precepting authority[23], or any appropriate levying body[24] to supply the billing authority with prescribed information if the appropriate national authority considers it to be information the billing authority needs in order to fulfil its duty[25]. Where any person other than the appropriate national authority fails to supply information to a billing authority in accordance with regulations so made[26], he is liable to indemnify the authority against any loss or damage which the authority sustains in consequence of the failure[27].

1 As to the meaning of 'information' see PARA 31 note 17.

2 As to the meaning of 'billing authority' see PARA 53.

3 'List' means a local or central non-domestic rating list: see the Local Government Finance Act 1988 s 67(1). As to local non-domestic rating lists see PARA 191 et seq. As to central non-domestic rating lists see PARA 196 et seq.

4 As to the meaning of 'valuation officer' see PARA 54 note 3.

5 Local Government Finance Act 1988 s 62, Sch 9 para 6(1) (Sch 9 para 6(1) amended by the Local Government Finance Act 1992 s 117(1), Sch 13 para 87(4)). As to the alteration of lists see PARA 202 et seq.

6 Ie the Secretary of State or, in relation to Wales, the Welsh Ministers. The functions of the Secretary of State under the Local Government Finance Act 1988 Sch 9, so far as exercisable in relation to Wales, were transferred to the National Assembly for Wales (see the National Assembly for Wales (Transfer of Functions) Order 1999, SI 1999/672, art 2, Sch 1) and are now vested in the Welsh Ministers (see the Government of Wales Act 2006 s 162(1), Sch 11 para 30). As to the Secretary of State and the Welsh Ministers see PARA 4 note 18. As to the meaning of 'Wales' see PARA 2 note 16.

7 Local Government Finance Act 1988 Sch 9 para 6(1A) (added by the Local Government and Housing Act 1989 ss 139, 194(4), Sch 5 paras 1, 47, 79(3), Sch 12 Pt II; and amended by the Local Government Finance Act 1992 Sch 13 para 87(4)). 'Prescribed' means prescribed by the regulations: see the Local Government Finance Act 1988 s 146(6). As to the regulations made see the text to notes 8–19.

8 See the Non-Domestic Rating (Alteration of Lists and Appeals) (England) Regulations 2009, SI 2009/2268, reg 24(1). The Non-Domestic Rating (Alteration of Lists and Appeals) (England) Regulations 2009, SI 2009/2268, apply in relation to England only: see reg 1. As to the equivalent provision to reg 24 in relation to Wales see the Non-Domestic Rating (Alteration of Lists and Appeals) (Wales) Regulations 2005, SI 2005/758, reg 42, which is in almost identical terms. As to the meanings of 'England' and 'Wales' see PARA 2 note 16.

9 As to the meaning of 'relevant authority' see PARA 200 note 4.

10 As to the meaning of 'domestic property' see PARA 190.

11 See the Non-Domestic Rating (Alteration of Lists and Appeals) (England) Regulations 2009, SI 2009/2268, reg 24(3).

12 Non-Domestic Rating (Alteration of Lists and Appeals) (England) Regulations 2009, SI 2009/2268, reg 24(3)(a).

13 Non-Domestic Rating (Alteration of Lists and Appeals) (England) Regulations 2009, SI 2009/2268, reg 24(3)(b)(i).

14 Non-Domestic Rating (Alteration of Lists and Appeals) (England) Regulations 2009, SI 2009/2268, reg 24(3)(b)(ii).

15 Non-Domestic Rating (Alteration of Lists and Appeals) (England) Regulations 2009, SI 2009/2268, reg 24(2)(a).

16 Non-Domestic Rating (Alteration of Lists and Appeals) (England) Regulations 2009, SI 2009/2268, reg 24(2)(b).

17 Non-Domestic Rating (Alteration of Lists and Appeals) (England) Regulations 2009, SI 2009/2268, reg 24(2)(c).

18 Non-Domestic Rating (Alteration of Lists and Appeals) (England) Regulations 2009, SI 2009/2268, reg 24(2)(d).

19 Non-Domestic Rating (Alteration of Lists and Appeals) (England) Regulations 2009, SI 2009/2268, reg 24(4).

20 Ie regulations under the Local Government Finance Act 1988 Sch 9.

21 As to the meaning of 'person' see PARA 11 note 13.

22 Local Government Finance Act 1988 Sch 9 para 6A(1)(a) (Sch 9 para 6A added by the Local Government Finance Act 1992 Sch 13 para 87(5)).

23 Local Government Finance Act 1988 Sch 9 para 6A(1)(b) (as added: see note 22). An authority is an 'appropriate precepting authority' in relation to a billing authority if it has power to issue a precept to the billing authority under the Local Government Finance Act 1992 Pt I (ss 1–69): Local Government Finance Act 1988 Sch 9 para 6A(4) (as so added). As to precepts see PARA 11 et seq.

24 Local Government Finance Act 1988 Sch 9 para 6A(1)(c) (as added: see note 22). A body is an 'appropriate levying body' in relation to a billing authority if it has power to issue a levy or special levy to the billing authority or if it has power to issue a levy to a county council which has power to issue a precept to the billing authority under the Local Government Finance Act 1992 Pt I (ss 1–69): Local Government Finance Act 1988 Sch 9 para 6A(5) (as so added). A 'levy' (unless the context otherwise requires) is a levy under regulations made under s 74 (see PARA 24) and a 'levying body' is a body with power to issue a levy under those regulations: s 146(2). A 'special levy' is a special levy under regulations made under s 75 (see PARA 24): s 146(3).

25 Local Government Finance Act 1988 Sch 9 para 6A(1) (as added: see note 22). Similarly, where regulations under Sch 9 contain provision about the contents or form of a notice to be served by a billing authority, they may also require the appropriate national authority or any appropriate precepting authority to supply the billing authority with prescribed information if the appropriate national authority considers it to be information the billing authority needs to ensure that the provision is met: Sch 9 para 6A(2) (as so added).

As to the regulations made under Sch 9 para 6A see the Council Tax and Non-Domestic Rating (Demand Notices) (England) Regulations 2003, SI 2003/2613; the Non-Domestic Rating (Demand

Notices) (Wales) Regulations 2017, SI 2017/113; and PARA 272 et seq.

26 Ie regulation made under the Local Government Finance Act 1988 Sch 9 para 6A(1) or 6A(2): see the text to notes 20–25.

27 Local Government Finance Act 1988 Sch 9 para 6A(3) (as added: see note 22).

228. Power of entry.

If a valuation officer[1] needs to value a hereditament in England[2] for the purpose of carrying out functions conferred or imposed on the officer by or under the non-domestic rating provisions[3], the officer and any person[4] authorised by the officer in writing[5] may enter on, survey and value the hereditament if the statutory requirements[6] are fulfilled[7]. Those requirements are that:

(1) the valuation officer must obtain the approval of the tribunal[8] before the officer or a person authorised by the officer exercises the power to enter on, survey and value[9];

(2) after the tribunal has given its approval, at least three days' notice in writing must be given of the proposed exercise of the power[10]; and

(3) in a case where a person authorised by the valuation officer proposes to exercise the power, the person must if required produce the authorisation[11].

A person who wilfully delays or obstructs[12] a person in the exercise of a power under these provisions is liable on summary conviction to a fine[13].

The tribunal may:

(a) determine any application brought under these provisions and any question arising from that application[14];

(b) specify the arrangements by which any entry approved by it must be conducted, including whether the entry may occur on more than one day[15].

If a valuation officer needs to value a hereditament in Wales[16] for the purpose of carrying out functions conferred or imposed on him by or under the non-domestic rating provisions, he (and any person authorised by him in writing) may enter on, survey and value the hereditament, provided that[17]:

(i) at least 24 hours' notice in writing of the proposed exercise of the power is given[18]; and

(ii) in a case where anyone authorised by the valuation officer proposes to exercise the power, that person produces his authority where required[19].

It is an offence for a person to wilfully delay or obstruct a person in the exercise of the power of entry[20].

1 As to the meaning of 'valuation officer' see PARA 54 note 3.

2 As to the meaning of 'hereditament' see PARA 106. As to the meaning of 'England' see PARA 2 note 16.

3 Ie by or under the Local Government Finance Act 1988 Pt III (ss 41–67).

4 As to the meaning of 'person' see PARA 11 note 13.

5 As to the meaning of 'writing' see PARA 21 note 3.

6 Ie the Local Government Finance Act 1988 Sch 9 para 6B(2), (4) (see the text to notes 8–10) and (where it applies) Sch 9 para 6B(5) (see the text to note 11).

7 Local Government Finance Act 1988 s 62, Sch 9 para 6B(1) (Sch 9 para 6B added by SI 2015/982).

8 For these purposes, 'the tribunal' means the First-tier Tribunal: Local Government Finance Act 1988 Sch 9 para 6B(9) (as added: see note 7). As to the First-tier Tribunal see COURTS AND TRIBUNALS vol 24 (2010) PARA 874 et seq.

9 Local Government Finance Act 1988 Sch 9 para 6B(2) (as added: see note 7). The tribunal must not give its approval unless it is satisfied that the valuation officer needs to value the hereditament: Sch 9 para 6B(3) (as so added).

10 Local Government Finance Act 1988 Sch 9 para 6B(4) (as added: see note 7). For the purpose of the requirement under Sch 9 para 6B(4), the following days are to be disregarded: a Saturday, a Sunday, Christmas Day or Good Friday; and a day which is a bank holiday under the Banking and Financial Dealings Act 1971 in England and Wales (see TIME vol 97 (2015) PARAS 313, 321): Local Government Finance Act 1988 Sch 9 para 6B(7) (as so added).
11 Local Government Finance Act 1988 Sch 9 para 6B(5) (as added: see note 7).
12 An act is done wilfully if it is deliberate and intentional, so that the mind of the person who does the act goes with it: *R v Senior* [1899] 1 QB 283. Anything which makes it more difficult for a person to carry out his duty might amount to obstruction: *Hinchcliffe v Sheldon* [1955] 3 All ER 406, [1955] 1 WLR 1207.
13 Local Government Finance Act 1988 Sch 9 para 6B(6) (as added: see note 7). The fine is not to exceed level 1 on the standard scale: Sch 9 para 6B(6) (as so added). As to the powers of magistrates' courts to issue fines on summary conviction see SENTENCING vol 92 (2015) PARA 176.
14 Local Government Finance Act 1988 Sch 9 para 6B(8)(a) (as added: see note 7).
15 Local Government Finance Act 1988 Sch 9 para 6B(8)(b) (as added: see note 7).
16 As to the meaning of 'Wales' see PARA 2 note 16.
17 See the Local Government Finance Act 1988 Sch 9 para 7(1) (amended by SI 2015/982).
18 Local Government Finance Act 1988 Sch 9 para 7(2).
19 Local Government Finance Act 1988 Sch 9 para 7(3).
20 See the Local Government Finance Act 1988 Sch 9 para 7(4). The penalty for such an offence is, on summary conviction, a fine not exceeding level 1 on the standard scale: Sch 9 para 7(4).

229. Inspection of documents regarding state of lists.

Where a valuation officer[1] is maintaining a list[2], and the list is in force or has been in force at any time in the preceding five years[3], a person[4] may require that officer to give him access to such information[5] as will enable him to establish the current or previous state of the list[6]. Similarly, a person may require:

(1) a billing authority[7] to give him access to such information as will enable him to establish what is the state of a copy of a list, or has been its state at any time since it was deposited[8], if the authority has deposited the copy[9], and the list is in force or has been in force at any time in the preceding five years[10];
(2) a billing authority to give him access to such information as will enable him to establish what is the state of a copy of a proposed list if the authority has deposited the copy[11], and the list itself is not yet in force[12];
(3) the appropriate national authority[13] to give him access to such information as will enable him to establish what is the state of a copy of a list, or has been its state at any time since it was deposited, if the appropriate national authority has deposited the copy[14], and the list is in force or has been in force at any time in the preceding five years[15];
(4) the appropriate national authority to give him access to such information as will enable him to establish what is the state of a copy of a proposed list if the appropriate national authority has deposited the copy[16], and the list itself is not yet in force[17].

These requirements[18] must be complied with at a reasonable time and place and without payment being sought; but the information may be in documentary or such other form as the person or authority giving the information thinks fit[19].

A person having custody of a document containing (or having control of access to) information to which access is sought under these provisions commits an offence[20] if, without reasonable excuse[21], he:

(a) intentionally obstructs a person exercising a right[22] to inspection[23]; or
(b) refuses to comply with a requirement[24] to permit copying of information[25].

1 As to the meaning of 'valuation officer' see PARA 54 note 3.

2 Local Government Finance Act 1988 Sch 9 para 8(1)(a) (Sch 9 para 8 substituted by the Local Government and Housing Act 1989 s 139, Sch 5 paras 48, 79(3)). 'List' means a local or central non-domestic rating list: see the Local Government Finance Act 1988 s 67(1). As to local non-domestic rating lists see PARA 191 et seq. As to central non-domestic rating lists see PARA 196 et seq.
3 Local Government Finance Act 1988 Sch 9 para 8(1)(b) (as substituted: see note 2).
4 As to the meaning of 'person' see PARA 11 note 13.
5 As to the meaning of 'information' see PARA 31 note 17.
6 Local Government Finance Act 1988 Sch 9 para 8(1) (as substituted: see note 2).
7 As to the meaning of 'billing authority' see PARA 53.
8 Local Government Finance Act 1988 Sch 9 para 8(2) (as substituted (see note 2); amended by the Local Government Finance Act 1992 s 117(1), Sch 13 para 87(6)).
9 Ie under the Local Government Finance Act 1988 s 41(6B) (see PARA 191) or s 41A(10) (see PARA 192): Sch 9 para 8(2)(a) (as substituted (see note 2); amended by the Local Government (Wales) Act 1994 s 66(6), Sch 16 para 86).
10 Local Government Finance Act 1988 Sch 9 para 8(2)(b) (as substituted: see note 2).
11 Ie under the Local Government Finance Act 1988 s 41(6) (see PARA 191): Sch 9 para 8(4)(a) (as substituted: see note 2).
12 Local Government Finance Act 1988 Sch 9 para 8(4)(b).
13 Ie the Secretary of State or, in relation to Wales, the Welsh Ministers. The functions of the Secretary of State under the Local Government Finance Act 1988 Sch 9, so far as exercisable in relation to Wales, were transferred to the National Assembly for Wales (see the National Assembly for Wales (Transfer of Functions) Order 1999, SI 1999/672, art 2, Sch 1) and are now vested in the Welsh Ministers (see the Government of Wales Act 2006 s 162(1), Sch 11 para 30). As to the Secretary of State and the Welsh Ministers see PARA 4 note 18. As to the meaning of 'Wales' see PARA 2 note 16.
14 Ie under the Local Government Finance Act 1988 s 52(6B) (see PARA 196): Sch 9 para 8(3)(a) (as substituted: see note 2).
15 Local Government Finance Act 1988 Sch 9 para 8(3)(b) (as substituted: see note 2).
16 Ie under the Local Government Finance Act 1988 s 52(6) (see PARA 196): Sch 9 para 8(5)(a) (as substituted: see note 2).
17 Local Government Finance Act 1988 Sch 9 para 8(5)(b) (as substituted: see note 2).
18 Ie a requirement under any of the Local Government Finance Act 1988 Sch 9 para 8(1)–(5): see the text to notes 1–17.
19 Local Government Finance Act 1988 Sch 9 para 8(6) (as substituted: see note 2). Where access is given to information in documentary form the person to whom access is given may make copies of (or of extracts from) the document (Sch 9 para 8(7)(a) (as so substituted)); and require a person having custody of the document to supply to him a photographic copy of (or of extracts from) the document (Sch 9 para 8(7)(b) (as so substituted)). Where access is given to information in a form which is not documentary the person to whom access is given may make transcripts of (or of extracts from) the information (Sch 9 para 8(8)(a) (as so substituted)); and require a person having control of access to the information to supply to him a copy in documentary form of (or of extracts from) the information (Sch 9 para 8(8)(b) (as so substituted)). If a reasonable charge is required for a facility under Sch 9 para 8(7) or (8) above, the provision concerned does not apply unless the person seeking to avail himself of the facility pays the charge: Sch 9 para 8(9) (as so substituted).
20 The penalty for such an offence is, on summary conviction, a fine not exceeding level 1 on the standard scale: see the Local Government Finance Act 1988 Sch 9 para 8(10) (as substituted: see note 2). As to the powers of magistrates' courts to issue fines on summary conviction see SENTENCING vol 92 (2015) PARA 176.
21 As to what may be regarded as reasonable excuse see PARA 226 note 20.
22 Ie a right under the Local Government Finance Act 1988 Sch 9 para 8(1)–(5) (see the text to notes 1–17) or Sch 9 para 8(7)(a), (8)(a) (see note 19).
23 See the Local Government Finance Act 1988 Sch 9 para 8(10)(a) (as substituted: see note 2).
24 Ie under the Local Government Finance Act 1988 Sch 9 para 8(7)(b) or 8(8)(b): see note 19.
25 See the Local Government Finance Act 1988 Sch 9 para 8(10)(b) (as substituted: see note 2).

230. Inspection of documents relating to list alterations.

A person[1] may, at a reasonable time and without making payment, inspect any proposal made or notice of appeal given under regulations made in relation to the alteration of lists[2], if made or given as regards a list[3] which is in force when inspection is sought or has been in force at any time in the preceding five years[4]. A person may make copies of (or of extracts from) any such document[5], or may require a person having custody of such a document to supply to him a photographic copy of (or of extracts from) the document[6].

A person having custody of any such proposal or notice of appeal[7] commits an offence[8] if, without reasonable excuse[9], he either:

(1) intentionally obstructs a person in exercising a right to inspect without charge[10] or to copy[11] such a document[12]; or

(2) refuses to supply a copy to a person who is entitled to it[13].

1 As to the meaning of 'person' see PARA 11 note 13.

2 Ie regulations made under the Local Government Finance Act 1988 s 55: see PARA 199.

3 'List' means a local or central non-domestic rating list: see the Local Government Finance Act 1988 s 67(1). As to local non-domestic rating lists see PARA 191 et seq. As to central non-domestic rating lists see PARA 196 et seq.

4 Local Government Finance Act 1988 Sch 9 para 9(1) (Sch 9 para 9 added by the Local Government and Housing Act 1989 s 139, Sch 5 paras 48, 79(3)).

5 Local Government Finance Act 1988 Sch 9 para 9(2)(a) (as added: see note 4). If a reasonable charge is required for a facility under Sch 9 para 9(2), then Sch 9 para 9(2) does not apply unless the person seeking to avail himself of the facility pays the charge: Sch 9 para 9(3) (as so added).

6 Local Government Finance Act 1988 Sch 9 para 9(2)(b) (as added: see note 4). See also note 5.

7 Ie a document mentioned in the Local Government Finance Act 1988 Sch 9 para 9(1): see the text to notes 1–4.

8 The penalty for such an offence is, on summary conviction, a fine not exceeding level 1 on the standard scale: Local Government Finance Act 1988 Sch 9 para 9(4) (as added: see note 4). As to the powers of magistrates' courts to issue fines on summary conviction see SENTENCING vol 92 (2015) PARA 176.

9 As to what may be regarded as reasonable excuse see PARA 226 note 20.

10 Ie a right under the Local Government Finance Act 1988 Sch 9 para 9(1): see the text to notes 1–4.

11 Ie a right under the Local Government Finance Act 1988 Sch 9 para 9(2)(a): see the text to note 5.

12 See the Local Government Finance Act 1988 Sch 9 para 9(4)(a) (as added: see note 4).

13 Ie under the Local Government Finance Act 1988 Sch 9 para 9(2)(b) (see the text to note 6): see Sch 9 para 9(4)(b) (as added: see note 4).

(vii) Validity of Lists

231. Challenges to the validity of valuation lists.

Under previous legislation[1], the validity of valuation lists[2] was open to challenge by an application for judicial review[3]. The whole list can be challenged in this way, provided the applicant for review has sufficient interest in the matter[4]. Individual entries may also be challenged in this way where there is no other remedy available[5]. There is nothing in the current legislation which acts as a bar to an application for judicial review.

1 Ie under the General Rate Act 1967 (repealed). As to the historical development of rating law and the continuing relevance of the old case law to the current statutory regime see PARA 50.

2 As to local non-domestic rating lists see PARA 191 et seq. As to central non-domestic rating lists see PARA 196 et seq.

3 *R v Paddington Valuation Officer, ex p Peachey Property Corpn Ltd* [1966] 1 QB 380, [1965] 2 All ER 836, CA.

4 As to judicial review see JUDICIAL REVIEW vol 61 (2010) PARA 601 et seq.

5 *R v Valuation Officer, ex p High Park Investments Ltd* [1987] RVR 84.

(viii) Valuation List Appeals

A. VALUATION TRIBUNALS

(A) The Valuation Tribunal for England

232. Establishment and jurisdiction.

There is a Valuation Tribunal for England[1].

The jurisdiction of the existing English tribunals[2], including their jurisdiction under current legislation[3], was transferred to the tribunal[4]. As regards any matter which falls within the jurisdiction of the tribunal[5], the Secretary of State[6] may by regulations provide that, where persons[7] who, if the matter were to be the subject of an appeal to the tribunal, would be the parties to the appeal[8] agree in writing[9] that the matter is to be referred to arbitration, the matter must be so referred[10].

A valuation tribunal is not a court to which the law of contempt of court applies[11].

1 Local Government Finance Act 1988 Sch 11 para A1 (Sch 11 Pt 1 (paras A1–A20) added by the Local Government and Public Involvement in Health Act 2007 s 219(1), Sch 15 paras 1, 2). As to the meaning of 'England' see PARA 2 note 16. As to membership of the tribunal see PARA 233. As to the procedure of the tribunal see PARA 234. As to the provision of services to the tribunal by the Valuation Tribunal Service see PARA 241. As to appeals to the tribunal see PARA 242 et seq. As to the Valuation Tribunal for Wales see PARA 237.

2 The 'existing English tribunals' are the valuation tribunals established in relation to England by regulations under the Local Government Finance Act 1988 Sch 11 (prior to its amendment by the Local Government and Public Involvement in Health Act 2007) which were in existence immediately before 1 October 2009 (ie the date on which Sch 11 para A2 came into force): Sch 11 para A2(4) (as added: see note 1).

3 The jurisdiction of the existing English tribunals under current legislation was their jurisdiction under any of the following (see the Local Government Finance Act 1988 Sch 11 para A2(2) (as added: see note 1)):

(1) regulations under the Local Government Finance Act 1988 s 55 (see PARA 199); the Local Government Finance Act 1988 Sch 4A para 4 (see PARA 141) and Sch 9 para 5C (see PARA 226);

(2) the Land Drainage Act 1991 s 45 (see WATER AND WATERWAYS vol 101 (2009) PARA 634);

(3) the Local Government Finance Act 1992 s 16 (see PARA 513), regulations under s 24 (see PARA 417), and Sch 3 para 3 (see PARA 471).

4 Local Government Finance Act 1988 Sch 11 para A2(1) (as added: see note 1). The jurisdiction so transferred is to be exercised as regards all appeals under that jurisdiction, whether made before or after the transfer: Sch 11 para A2(3) (as so added).

5 Local Government Finance Act 1988 Sch 11 para A3(1) (as added: see note 1).

6 As to the Secretary of State see PARA 4 note 18.

7 As to the meaning of 'person' see PARA 11 note 13.

8 See the Local Government Finance Act 1988 Sch 11 para A3(3) (as added: see note 1).

9 As to the meaning of 'writing' see PARA 21 note 3.

10 Local Government Finance Act 1988 Sch 11 para A3(2) (as added: see note 1). Regulations under Sch 11 para A3 may include: provision applying enactments relating to arbitration; provision that an award in an arbitration may include any order the Valuation Tribunal for England could have made in the matter concerned; provision requiring the carrying out of an order so included: see Sch 11 para 15 (amended by the Local Government Finance Act 1992 s 117(1), Sch 13 para 88(1), (3), (13); and the Local Government and Public Involvement in Health Act 2007 s 219(1), Sch 15 paras 1, 19). As to the regulations made see the Valuation Tribunal for England (Council Tax and Rating Appeals) (Procedure) Regulations 2009, SI 2009/2269; and PARAS 268, 559.

11 See *A-G v British Broadcasting Corpn* [1981] AC 303, [1980] 3 All ER 161, HL (local valuation court was not an inferior court for the purposes of RSC Ord 52 r 1 (revoked: see now CPR Pt 81) (committal for contempt of court) (see CONTEMPT OF COURT vol 22 (2012) PARAS 65, 95–103)); *Jeremy Pickering (t/a City Agents) v Sogex Services (UK) Ltd* [1982] RVR 225 (local valuation court not a court of law).

These cases were decided prior to the coming into force of the Local Government Finance Act 1988 but may continue to be of relevance: see PARA 50.

233. Membership.

The Valuation Tribunal for England[1] is to consist of the following members:

(1) the president of the Valuation Tribunal for England[2];
(2) one or more vice-presidents of the Valuation Tribunal for England[3];
(3) the members of a panel of persons to act as chairmen of the tribunal[4];
(4) other persons appointed as members of the tribunal[5].

It is for the Lord Chancellor[6] to appoint the members of the tribunal[7]; and it is for the Secretary of State[8] to determine the terms and conditions on which members of the tribunal are to be appointed[9]. It is also for the Secretary of State to determine[10] how many vice-presidents the tribunal is to have[11]; how many members the panel of chairmen is to have[12]; and how many other members the tribunal is to have[13].

A vice-president has the functions assigned to him by the president[14]. If the office of president is vacant[15], or the president is absent or otherwise unable to act[16], the president's functions may be exercised by any vice-president[17].

A member of the tribunal holds office in accordance with the terms and conditions of his appointment[18]. The Lord Chancellor may remove a member of the tribunal from office if the Lord Chancellor is satisfied that the member is unable[19], unwilling[20], or unfit (whether because of misbehaviour or otherwise)[21], to perform his functions as a member of the tribunal[22].

A member of the First-tier Tribunal (an 'FTT member') may act as a member of the Valuation Tribunal for England[23]. An FTT member may only act as a member of the tribunal:

(a) at the request of the president and with the approval of the Senior President of Tribunals[24];
(b) in relation to an appeal[25] that relates, in whole or in part, to a council tax reduction scheme[26] made or having effect as if made by a billing authority[27] in England[28]; and
(c) if the FTT member is not disqualified from being, or acting as, a member of the Tribunal[29].

The President may withdraw a request at any time; and an FTT member acting as a tribunal member in response to a request must cease to do so if it is withdrawn[30].

The Valuation Tribunal Service may make payments to the Lord Chancellor in respect of the expenditure incurred by the Lord Chancellor in paying remuneration, allowances or expenses to an FTT member whilst acting as a member of the tribunal[31].

1 As to the Valuation Tribunal for England see PARA 232. As to the Valuation Tribunal for Wales see PARA 237.

2 Local Government Finance Act 1988 Sch 11 para A4(a) (Sch 11 Pt 1 (paras A1–A20) added by the Local Government and Public Involvement in Health Act 2007 s 219(1), Sch 15 paras 1, 2). All members of the Valuation Tribunal for England are disqualified for membership of the House of Commons: see the House of Commons Disqualification Act 1975 s 1(1)(f), Sch 1 Pt II; and PARLIAMENT vol 78 (2010) PARA 908.

3 Local Government Finance Act 1988 Sch 11 para A4(b) (as added: see note 2).

4 Local Government Finance Act 1988 Sch 11 para A4(c) (as added: see note 2).

5 Local Government Finance Act 1988 Sch 11 para A4(d) (as added: see note 2).

6 As to the Lord Chancellor see CONSTITUTIONAL AND ADMINISTRATIVE LAW vol 20 (2014) PARA 256 et seq. Any function of the Lord Chancellor under the Local Government Finance Act 1988 Sch 11 para A7 is a 'protected function' and, as such, may not be transferred, modified, abolished etc under the Constitutional Reform Act 2005 s 19(1): see s 19(5), Sch 7 para 4 Head A (amended by the Local Government and Public Involvement in Health Act 2007 s 220(1), Sch 16

paras 14, 15); and CONSTITUTIONAL AND ADMINISTRATIVE LAW vol 20 (2014) PARA 261.
7 Local Government Finance Act 1988 Sch 11 para A7(1) (as added: see note 2).
8 As to the Secretary of State see PARA 4 note 18.
9 Local Government Finance Act 1988 Sch 11 para A7(2) (as added: see note 2). As to remuneration, allowances and pension see further Sch 11 paras A7(3), A11–A14 (as so added).
10 A determination may specify, in relation to a class of member:
(1) a particular number (Local Government Finance Act 1988 Sch 11 para A8(2)(a) (as added: see note 2)); or
(2) a minimum number or a maximum number, or both (Sch 11 para A8(2)(b) (as so added)).
Before making a determination the Secretary of State must consult both the president (Sch 11 para A8(3)(a) (as so added)) and the Valuation Tribunal Service (Sch 11 para A8(3)(b) (as so added)). As to the Valuation Tribunal Service see PARA 241.
11 Local Government Finance Act 1988 Sch 11 para A8(1)(a) (as added: see note 2).
12 Local Government Finance Act 1988 Sch 11 para A8(1)(b) (as added: see note 2).
13 Local Government Finance Act 1988 Sch 11 para A8(1)(c) (as added: see note 2).
14 Local Government Finance Act 1988 Sch 11 para A5 (as added: see note 2).
15 Local Government Finance Act 1988 Sch 11 para A6(1)(a) (as added: see note 2).
16 Local Government Finance Act 1988 Sch 11 para A6(1)(b) (as added: see note 2).
17 Local Government Finance Act 1988 Sch 11 para A6(2) (as added: see note 2).
18 Local Government Finance Act 1988 Sch 11 para A9(1) (as added: see note 2). That is subject to the other provisions of Sch 11: Sch 11 para A9(2) (as so added).
19 Local Government Finance Act 1988 Sch 11 para A10(a) (as added: see note 2).
20 Local Government Finance Act 1988 Sch 11 para A10(b) (as added: see note 2).
21 Local Government Finance Act 1988 Sch 11 para A10(c) (as added: see note 2).
22 Local Government Finance Act 1988 Sch 11 para A10 (as added: see note 2).
23 Local Government Finance Act 1988 Sch 11 para A18A(1) (Sch 11 Pt 1 as added (see note 2); Sch 11 para A18A added by the Local Government Finance Act 2012 s 10(2), (3)(b), Sch 4 para 2). As to the First-tier Tribunal see COURTS AND TRIBUNALS vol 24 (2010) PARA 874 et seq.
References in the Local Government Finance Act 1988 Sch 11 and in regulations made under Sch 11 para A19 (see PARA 235) to a member of the tribunal include an FTT member acting as a member of the tribunal: Sch 11 para A18A(6) (as so added). But Sch 11 para A18A(6) does not apply to:
(1) Sch 11 para A7, A8, A9, A10 or A12 (which make provision about the appointment and removal of, numbers of, and payments to, members of the tribunal) (Sch 11 para A18A(7)(a) (as so added)); or
(2) regulations under Sch 11 para A19, if and to extent that the regulations provide that it does not apply (Sch 11 para A18A(7)(a) (as so added)).
24 Local Government Finance Act 1988 Sch 11 para A18A(2)(a) (as added: see note 23). A request under Sch 11 para 18A(2)(a) may relate to a particular appeal or to appeals of a particular kind, and may be made only if the president thinks that FTT members are likely to have particular expertise that is relevant to the determination of the appeal, or to appeals of the kind, to which it relates: Sch 11 para A18A(3) (as so added). An approval under Sch 11 para 18A(2)(a) may relate to a particular appeal or to appeals of a particular kind Sch 11 para A18A(4) (as so added).
25 In the Local Government Finance Act 1988 Sch 11 para A18A, references to an appeal include a review by the tribunal of a decision made by it on an appeal: Sch 11 para A18A(9)(a) (as added: see note 23).
26 'Council tax reduction scheme' has the same meaning as in the Local Government Finance Act 1992 Pt I (ss 1–69) (see s 13A(9); and PARA 378 note 20): Local Government Finance Act 1988 Sch 11 para A18A(9)(b) (as added: see note 23).
27 As to the meaning of 'billing authority' see PARA 53.
28 Local Government Finance Act 1988 Sch 11 para A18A(2)(b) (as added: see note 23).
29 Local Government Finance Act 1988 Sch 11 para A18A(2)(c) (as added: see note 23).
30 Local Government Finance Act 1988 Sch 11 para A18A(5) (as added: see note 23).
31 Local Government Finance Act 1988 Sch 11 para A18A(8) (as added: see note 23).

234. Procedure.

The president of the Valuation Tribunal for England[1] may make arrangements for the organisation of the tribunal (whether in divisions or otherwise)[2].

The president or a vice-president may delegate[3] any of his functions to any other member of the tribunal[4]; and a member of the tribunal to whom a function is so delegated may delegate the function to any other member of the tribunal (unless the delegation to him does not allow such sub-delegation)[5]. However, where the president or a vice-president has been selected to deal with an appeal[6], that person may not delegate any function of deciding that appeal[7].

The president must make tribunal business arrangements[8]. 'Tribunal business arrangements' are arrangements which provide for the selection of the member or members of the tribunal to deal with any appeal made to the tribunal[9]; and such arrangements must provide for at least one senior member of the tribunal to deal with an appeal[10].

If a member of the tribunal dealing with an appeal becomes unable to act[11] the other members dealing with the appeal may continue to deal with the appeal[12]; but if the member who becomes unable to act is the only member dealing with the appeal then a further selection must be made in accordance with tribunal business arrangements[13].

1 As to the Valuation Tribunal for England see PARA 232. As to the president of the Valuation Tribunal for England, and membership of the tribunal generally, see PARA 233.
2 Local Government Finance Act 1988 Sch 11 para A15 (Sch 11 Pt 1 (paras A1–A20) added by the Local Government and Public Involvement in Health Act 2007 s 219(1), Sch 15 paras 1, 2).
3 Any delegation under the Local Government Finance Act 1988 Sch 11 para A16 (1) or (3) (see the text to note 5) must be made in writing: Sch 11 para A16(4) (as added: see note 2). As to the meaning of 'writing' see PARA 21 note 3.
4 Local Government Finance Act 1988 Sch 11 para A16(1) (as added: see note 2).
5 See the Local Government Finance Act 1988 Sch 11 para A16(3) (as added: see note 2). See also note 3.
6 As to non-domestic rating appeals see PARA 242 et seq; and as to council tax appeals see PARA 513 et seq.
7 Local Government Finance Act 1988 Sch 11 para A16(2) (as added: see note 2).
8 Local Government Finance Act 1988 Sch 11 para A17(1) (as added: see note 2). Tribunal business arrangements must comply with, and are subject to, regulations under Sch 11 para A19 (see PARA 235): Sch 11 para A17(5) (as so added).
9 Local Government Finance Act 1988 Sch 11 para A17(2) (as added: see note 2).
10 Local Government Finance Act 1988 Sch 11 para A17(3) (as added: see note 2). The senior members of the tribunal are the president, the vice-presidents and the members of the panel of chairmen: Sch 11 para A17(4) (as so added).
11 Local Government Finance Act 1988 Sch 11 para A18(1) (as added: see note 2).
12 Local Government Finance Act 1988 Sch 11 para A18(2) (as added: see note 2).
13 See the Local Government Finance Act 1988 Sch 11 para A18(3) (as added: see note 2).

235. Regulations.

The Secretary of State[1] may, by regulations[2], make provision in relation to procedure or any other matter relating to the Valuation Tribunal for England[3]. Such regulations may include provision about any of these matters:

(1) the circumstances in which persons are disqualified from becoming or continuing to be members of the tribunal[4];
(2) the circumstances in which members of the tribunal are to be disqualified from acting[5];
(3) the factors which are not to disqualify persons from becoming or continuing to be members of the tribunal[6];
(4) the factors which are not to disqualify members of the tribunal from acting[7];
(5) the functions of the tribunal relating to an appeal[8] which may be discharged on its behalf by the clerk of the tribunal or by any other member of the tribunal's staff[9].

The regulations may not make provision in relation to staff, accommodation and equipment[10].

1 As to the Secretary of State see PARA 4 note 18.
2 Without prejudice to the Local Government Finance Act 1988 s 143(1) (general provision relating to regulations), regulations under Sch 11 make different provision for cases where valuation tribunals exercise jurisdiction conferred on them by or under different provisions of the Local Government Finance Act 1988 or the Local Government Finance Act 1992: see Sch 11 para 16(1) (amended by the Local Government Finance Act 1992 s 117(1), Sch 13 para 88(14)). Without prejudice to the Local Government Finance Act 1988 s 143(2), regulations under Sch 11 may include provision amending, adapting, repealing or revoking any provision of or made under the General Rate 1967 (repealed) or any other Act: Local Government Finance Act 1988 Sch 11 para 16(2). As to the regulations made under Sch 11 para A19 see the Valuation Tribunal for England (Council Tax and Rating Appeals) (Procedure) Regulations 2009, SI 2009/2269; and PARA 242 et seq.
3 Local Government Finance Act 1988 Sch 11 para A19(1) (Sch 11 Pt 1 (paras A1–A20) added by the Local Government and Public Involvement in Health Act 2007 s 219(1), Sch 15 paras 1, 2). As to the Valuation Tribunal for England see PARA 232. The Local Government Finance Act 1988 Sch 11 Pt III (paras 8–12A) (see PARA 240) makes further provision about the kind of regulations that may be made under Sch 11 para A19: Sch 11 para A19(4) (as so added).
4 Local Government Finance Act 1988 Sch 11 para A19(2)(a) (as added: see note 3). As to membership of the tribunal see PARA 233.
5 Local Government Finance Act 1988 Sch 11 para A19(2)(b) (as added: see note 3).
6 Local Government Finance Act 1988 Sch 11 para A19(2)(c) (as added: see note 3).
7 Local Government Finance Act 1988 Sch 11 para A19(2)(d) (as added: see note 3).
8 As to non-domestic rating appeals see PARA 242 et seq; and as to council tax appeals see PARA 513 et seq.
9 Local Government Finance Act 1988 Sch 11 para A19(2)(e) (as added: see note 3).
10 Local Government Finance Act 1988 Sch 11 para A19(3) (as added: see note 3).

(B) The Valuation Tribunal for Wales

236. Regulations as to valuation tribunals in Wales.

The Welsh Ministers[1] must make regulations providing for the establishment, in relation to Wales, of one or more tribunals, to be known as 'valuation tribunals'[2]. The regulations may include such provision as the Welsh Ministers see fit in relation to membership[3], staff[4], accommodation, equipment[5], procedure[6] and other matters relating to tribunals[7]. The Welsh Ministers must make such payments as are necessary to meet any expenditure incurred in or in connection with the performance by the tribunals of their functions (whether as regards remuneration, allowances, accommodation, equipment or otherwise)[8].

1 The functions of the Secretary of State and the Treasury under the Local Government Finance Act 1988 Sch 11, so far as exercisable in relation to Wales, were transferred to the National Assembly for Wales (see the National Assembly for Wales (Transfer of Functions) Order 1999, SI 1999/672, art 2, Sch 1) and are now vested in the Welsh Ministers (see the Government of Wales Act 2006 s 162(1), Sch 11 para 30). As to the Secretary of State and the Welsh Ministers see PARA 4 note 18. As to the meaning of 'Wales' see PARA 2 note 16. As to the Treasury see CONSTITUTIONAL AND ADMINISTRATIVE LAW vol 20 (2014) PARA 262 et seq.
2 Local Government Finance Act 1988 s 136, Sch 11 para 1(1) (Sch 11 para 1(1) amended by the Local Government Finance Act 1992 s 117(1), Sch 13 para 88(1), (3), (13); and the Local Government and Public Involvement in Health Act 2007 s 219(1), Sch 15 paras 1, 4(a)). As to the regulations made see the Valuation Tribunal for Wales Regulations 2010, SI 2010/713; and PARA 237 et seq.
3 As regards membership, the regulations may include provision:
   (1) that the number of members of a tribunal is to be such as is determined by the Welsh Ministers (Local Government Finance Act 1988 Sch 11 para 5(1)(a));
   (2) for the appointment by a prescribed person or persons of the members of each tribunal (Sch 11 para 5(1)(b));
   (3) that one of the members is to be president of the tribunal (Sch 11 para 5(1)(c));

(4) that the president is to be appointed by the members by a prescribed method, and that if one is not so appointed within a prescribed period the president is to be appointed by the Welsh Ministers after consulting such prescribed persons as they see fit (Sch 11 para 5(1)(d));
(5) that some of the members (who may include the president) are to be appointed to the position of chairman, that the number to be appointed is to be stated by a prescribed person or persons, and that the appointments are to be made by the members themselves by a prescribed method or (if they default) by a prescribed person or persons (Sch 11 para 5(1)(e));
(6) that persons are to be disqualified from becoming or continuing to be members in prescribed circumstances (Sch 11 para 5(1)(f));
(7) that members are to be disqualified from acting in cases falling within prescribed descriptions (Sch 11 para 5(1)(g));
(8) that prescribed factors are not to disqualify persons from becoming or continuing to be members (Sch 11 para 5(1)(h));
(9) that prescribed factors are not to disqualify members from acting (Sch 11 para 5(1)(i));
(10) as to the duration (subject to disqualification, termination or resignation) of any appointment as president or member or chairman (Sch 11 para 5(1)(j));
(11) allowing the Welsh Ministers to terminate an appointment as president (Sch 11 para 5(1)(k));
(12) requiring the person or persons who appointed a member to terminate the appointment if the Welsh Ministers so direct after consulting the person or persons who made the appointment (Sch 11 para 5(1)(l));
(13) allowing a president to terminate a person's appointment as chairman, and requiring a president to do so if the Welsh Ministers direct him to do so (Sch 11 para 5(1)(m));
(14) allowing a person appointed as president or member or chairman to resign if such notice as may be prescribed is given (Sch 11 para 5(1)(n));
(15) that a person who ceases to be president or member or chairman is to be eligible for re-appointment in prescribed circumstances (Sch 11 para 5(1)(o));
(16) that a member is to be entitled to such remuneration and travelling, subsistence and other allowances as the Welsh Ministers may from time to time determine (Sch 11 para 5(1)(p) (amended by the Local Government Finance Act 1992 Sch 13 para 88(1), (3), (13); and the Local Government and Public Involvement in Health Act 2007 Sch 15 paras 1, 7));
(17) for the administration of members' allowances to be the responsibility of the clerk of the tribunal (Local Government Finance Act 1988 Sch 11 para 5(2)).

'Prescribed' means prescribed by the regulations: see s 146(6). As to the meaning of 'person' see PARA 11 note 13.

4 As regards staff, the regulations may include provision (Local Government Finance Act 1988 Sch 11 para 6(1) (amended by the Local Government Act 2003 s 127(1), Sch 7 paras 9(1), 27(b); and the Local Government and Public Involvement in Health Act 2007 ss 219(1), 241, Sch 15 paras 1, 8, Sch 18 Pt 17)):
(1) that a tribunal must appoint a clerk of the tribunal and may appoint other employees (Local Government Finance Act 1988 Sch 11 para 6(1)(a));
(2) that a tribunal must pay to its employees such remuneration and allowances as the tribunal determines (Sch 11 para 6(1)(b));
(3) that (subject to disqualification) employees must be appointed on such other terms and conditions as the tribunal may determine (Sch 11 para 6(1)(c));
(4) that an appointment is invalid unless made with the approval of the Welsh Ministers (Sch 11 para 6(1)(d));
(5) that a determination as to remuneration or allowances is invalid unless made with the approval of the Welsh Ministers (Sch 11 para 6(1)(e));
(6) that persons are to be disqualified from becoming or continuing to be employees in prescribed circumstances (Sch 11 para 6(1)(f));
(7) that employees are to be disqualified from acting in cases falling within prescribed descriptions (Sch 11 para 6(1)(g));
(8) that prescribed factors are not to disqualify persons from becoming or continuing to be employees (Sch 11 para 6(1)(h));
(9) that prescribed factors are not to disqualify employees from acting (Sch 11 para 6(1)(i));
(10) that any function of making an appointment, or determining remuneration or allowances or other terms or conditions, may be performed on behalf of a tribunal by two or more of its members (Sch 11 para 6(2)(a));
(11) that one of those members must be the president (Sch 11 para 6(2)(b));

(12) for the administration of employees' remuneration and allowances to be the responsibility of the clerk of the tribunal (Sch 11 para 6(3));

(13) that where a person ceases to be employed by a local valuation panel and immediately becomes employed by a valuation tribunal, for the purposes of the Employment Rights Act 1996 his period of employment by the panel must count as a period of employment by the tribunal and the change of employment does not break the continuity of the period of employment (Local Government Finance Act 1988 Sch 11 para 6(4) (amended by the Local Government Finance Act 1992 s 117(1), Sch 13 para 88(4); and the Employment Rights Act 1996 s 240, Sch 1 para 38)).

For the purposes of head (13) above a 'local valuation panel' is a local valuation panel constituted under a scheme under the General Rate 1967 s 88 (repealed): Local Government Finance Act 1988 Sch 11 para 6(5).

5 As regards accommodation and equipment, the regulations may also include provision:

(1) requiring a tribunal to

(a) maintain a permanent office (Local Government Finance Act 1988 Sch 11 para 7(1)(a) (Sch 11 para 7(1) amended by the Local Government Act 2003 Sch 7 para 27(c); and the Local Government and Public Involvement in Health Act 2007 Sch 15 paras 1, 9, Sch 18 Pt 17)); and

(b) make arrangements to secure that the tribunal has such other accommodation, and such secretarial and other equipment, as is sufficient for the performance of its functions (Local Government Finance Act 1988 Sch 11 para 7(1)(b));

(2) that any function as to accommodation or equipment may be performed on behalf of a tribunal by its clerk (Sch 11 para 7(2)).

6 As regards procedure, the regulations above may include provision:

(1) for determining which tribunal is to deal with an appeal (Local Government Finance Act 1988 Sch 11 para 7A(a) (Sch 11 para 7A added by the Local Government and Public Involvement in Health Act 2007 Sch 15 paras 1, 10(2));

(2) that prescribed functions of a tribunal relating to an appeal may be discharged on its behalf by its clerk or other prescribed employee (Local Government Finance Act 1988 Sch 11 para 7A(b) (as so added));

(3) that prescribed functions of a tribunal relating to an appeal may be discharged on its behalf by one of its members (Sch 11 para 7A(c) (as so added));

(4) that prescribed functions of a tribunal relating to an appeal may be discharged on its behalf by some of its members (Sch 11 para 7A(d) (as so added));

(5) as to the selection of a member who is to discharge functions relating to an appeal on behalf of a tribunal (which may include provision that he must be the president or a chairman) (Sch 11 para 7A(e) (as so added));

(6) as to the number and selection of members who are to discharge functions relating to an appeal on behalf of a tribunal (which may include provision that one of them must be the president or a chairman) (Sch 11 para 7A(f) (as so added)).

7 Local Government Finance Act 1988 Sch 11 para 1(2) (amended by the Local Government Act 2003 s 127(1), Sch 7 paras 9(1), 27(a); and the Local Government and Public Involvement in Health Act 2007 Sch 15 paras 1, 4(b), Sch 18 Pt 17).

8 Local Government Finance Act 1988 Sch 11 para 13 (amended by the Local Government and Public Involvement in Health Act 2007 Sch 15 paras 1, 18(1)).

237. Establishment and jurisdiction of Valuation tribunal for Wales.

There was established on 1 April 2010 the Valuation Tribunal for Wales[1] and a Governing Council for the tribunal[2].

The administrative functions of the valuation tribunal[3] are to be performed on its behalf by the governing council[4].

The tribunal exercises the jurisdiction conferred on it by the Local Government Finance Act 1988 and the Local Government Finance Act 1992[5]. As regards any matter which falls within the jurisdiction conferred on the tribunals[6], the Welsh Ministers[7] may by regulations provide that, where the persons[8] who, if the matter were to be the subject of an appeal to a tribunal, would be the parties to the appeal agree in writing[9] that the matter is to be referred to arbitration, the matter must be so referred[10].

The tribunal must maintain a permanent office; and the chief executive[11] has the function on behalf of the tribunal of making such arrangements as will secure that it has such other accommodation and such equipment as is sufficient for the performance of its functions[12].

A valuation tribunal is not a court to which the law of contempt of court applies[13].

1 See the Valuation Tribunal for Wales Regulations 2010, SI 2010/713, reg 4. Those regulations apply in Wales only: see reg 2. As to membership of the tribunal see PARA 238. The constitution and workings of the Valuation Tribunal for Wales are subject to review and consideration by the Administrative Justice and Tribunals Council: see the Tribunals, Courts and Enforcement Act 2007 s 44, Sch 7; the Administrative Justice and Tribunals Council (Listed Tribunals) (Wales) Order 2007, SI 2007/2876, art 2, Schedule; and COURTS AND TRIBUNALS vol 24 (2010) PARA 986 et seq.

2 See the Valuation Tribunal for Wales Regulations 2010, SI 2010/713, reg 5. The membership of the governing council consists of:

(1) the president of the tribunal (reg 6(1)(a));
(2) the national representatives (reg 6(1)(b) (substituted by SI 2017/941)); and
(3) any persons appointed by the Welsh Ministers (Valuation Tribunal for Wales Regulations 2010, SI 2010/713, reg 6(1)(c) (amended by SI 2017/941)).

As to the president of the tribunal see PARA 238. As to the appointment of regional representatives see the Valuation Tribunal for Wales Regulations 2010, SI 2010/713, reg 13 (substituted by SI 2017/941); and as to the appointment of persons by the Welsh Ministers see the Valuation Tribunal for Wales Regulations 2010, SI 2010/713, reg 7 (amended by SI 2017/941). A meeting of the Governing Council is not quorate unless four or more members of the Governing Council are present: Valuation Tribunal for Wales Regulations 2010, SI 2010/713, reg 5A (added by SI 2017/941).

3 Ie the functions under the Valuation Tribunal for Wales Regulations 2010, SI 2010/713, Pt 2 (regs 4–14) (Establishment of the Valuation Tribunal for Wales), Pt 3 (regs 15–20) (Administration) except reg 18(1) (establishment of committees: see PARA 239), and Pt 4 (regs 21–26) (Transitional Provisions).

4 See the Valuation Tribunal for Wales Regulations 2010, SI 2010/713, reg 8(1). The governing council may determine that the functions of the Valuation Tribunal under Pts 2–4 (except reg 18(1)) may be performed on its behalf by two or more members of the governing council one of whom must be the president (reg 8(2)), but this does not apply to the appointment of the chief executive (reg 8(3)); and these provisions are subject to the provisions in regs 16(6), 17, Sch 2 conferring functions on the chief executive (reg 8(4)). On 1 December 2017 there was established an appointments panel of the governing council: see reg 8A(1) (reg 8A added by SI 2017/941). The appointments panel must consist of three members of the governing council: Valuation Tribunal for Wales Regulations 2010, SI 2010/713, reg 8A(2) (as so added). Where the appointments panel appoints chairpersons, the appointments panel must not consist of any persons appointed by the Welsh Ministers under reg 7: reg 8A(3) (as so added). As to the chief executive see PARA 238.

5 The tribunal exercises the jurisdiction conferred on it under the Local Government Finance Act 1988 Sch 4A para 4 (see PARA 141), Sch 9 para 5C (see PARA 226), and by regulations under s 55 (see PARA 199); and the Local Government Finance Act 1992 s 16 (see PARA 513), Sch 3 para 3 (see PARA 471), and regulations under s 24 (see PARA 417): see the Local Government Finance Act 1988 Sch 11 para 2 (amended by the Local Government and Housing Act 1989 s 139, Sch 5 paras 76, 79(3); the Local Government Finance Act 1992 s 117(1), Sch 13 para 88(2); and the Local Government Act 2003 s 72(5)). Without prejudice to the Local Government Finance Act 1988 s 143(1) (general provision relating to regulations), regulations under Sch 11 may make different provision for cases where valuation tribunals exercise jurisdiction conferred on them by or under different provisions of the Local Government Finance Act 1988 or the Local Government Finance Act 1992: see Sch 11 para 16(1) (amended by the Local Government Finance Act 1992 Sch 13 para 88(14)). Without prejudice to the Local Government Finance Act 1988 s 143(2), regulations under Sch 11 may include provision amending, adapting, repealing or revoking any provision of or made under the General Rate 1967 (repealed) or any other Act: Local Government Finance Act 1988 Sch 11 para 16(2).

6 See the Local Government Finance Act 1988 Sch 11 para 4(1).

7 The functions of the Secretary of State under the Local Government Finance Act 1988 Sch 11, so far as exercisable in relation to Wales, were transferred to the National Assembly for Wales (see the National Assembly for Wales (Transfer of Functions) Order 1999, SI 1999/672, art 2, Sch 1) and are now vested in the Welsh Ministers (see the Government of Wales Act 2006 s 162(1), Sch 11 para 30). As to the Secretary of State and the Welsh Ministers see PARA 4 note 18. As to the meaning of 'Wales' see PARA 2 note 16.

8 As to the meaning of 'person' see PARA 11 note 13.

9 As to the meaning of 'writing' see PARA 21 note 3.

10 See the Local Government Finance Act 1988 Sch 11 para 4(2), (3). Regulations under Sch 11 para 4 may include provision applying enactments relating to arbitration; provision that an award in an arbitration may include any order a valuation tribunal could have made in the matter concerned; provision requiring the carrying out of an order so included: see Sch 11 para 15 (amended by the Local Government Finance Act 1992 Sch 13 para 88(1), (3), (13); and the Local Government and Public Involvement in Health Act 2007 s 219(1), Sch 15 paras 1, 19). As to the regulations made see the Non-Domestic Rating (Alterations of Lists and Appeals) (Wales) Regulations 2005, SI 2005/758 (see PARA 268); and the Valuation Tribunal for Wales Regulations 2010, SI 2010/713 (see above, PARA 238 et seq and PARA 559).

11 As to the chief executive see PARA 238.

12 Valuation Tribunal for Wales Regulations 2010, SI 2010/713, reg 20.

13 See *A-G v British Broadcasting Corpn* [1981] AC 303, [1980] 3 All ER 161, HL (local valuation court was not an inferior court for the purposes of RSC Ord 52 r 1 (revoked: see now CPR Pt 81) (committal for contempt of court) (see CONTEMPT OF COURT vol 22 (2012) PARAS 61, 95–103)); *Jeremy Pickering (t/a City Agents) v Sogex Services (UK) Ltd* [1982] 1 EGLR 42, [1982] RVR 225 (local valuation court not a court of law).

These cases were decided prior to the coming into force of the Local Government Finance Act 1988 but may continue to be of relevance: see PARA 50.

238. Membership and staff.

The first appointment to the office of president of the Valuation Tribunal for Wales[1] is to be made in accordance with relevant statutory provisions[2]; and, in the case of a subsequent vacancy occurring in the office of the president, the members of the tribunal must[3] appoint a person to be president[4]. Where no such appointment has taken place[5], the Welsh Ministers[6] must, after consultation with such of the members of the tribunal as they see fit, appoint one of the tribunal's members to be president[7].

The members of the Valuation Tribunal for Wales, consist of persons appointed by the appointments panel[8] when a vacancy arises[9]. Certain persons are disqualified for membership of the tribunal[10].

The tribunal is to determine the number of its members who are to be appointed to the position of chairperson[11]. The president constitutes one of the chairpersons and the appointments panel must appoint the remaining number of chairpersons[12].

If the president is unable, through illness or absence or any other cause, to carry out the president's functions[13], then those functions must be carried out by such member of the governing council[14] as that council from time to time determines[15].

The tribunal is to have a chief executive[16], and may appoint other employees as it so determines[17].

1 As to the Valuation Tribunal for Wales see PARA 237.

2 Ie in accordance with the Valuation Tribunal for Wales Regulations 2010, SI 2010/713, Sch 2 Pt 1 (amended by SI 2017/941) but subject to the Valuation Tribunal for Wales Regulations 2010, SI 2010/713, Sch 2 Pt 2: see reg 11(1). As to the tenure of office of the president see reg 11(4)–(6) (reg 11(4) amended by SI 2017/941).

3 Ie in accordance with the Valuation Tribunal for Wales Regulations 2010, SI 2010/713, Sch 2 Pt 1.

4 See the Valuation Tribunal for Wales Regulations 2010, SI 2010/713, reg 11(2).

5 Ie in accordance with the Valuation Tribunal for Wales Regulations 2010, SI 2010/713, Sch 2.

6 As to the Welsh Ministers see PARA 4 note 18.

7 Valuation Tribunal for Wales Regulations 2010, SI 2010/713, reg 11(3).
8 As to the appointments panel see PARA 237 note 4.
9 See the Valuation Tribunal for Wales Regulations 2010, SI 2010/713, reg 9(1), (3) (reg 9 substituted by SI 2017/941). The tribunal consists of between 16 members and a maximum number of members specified in the Valuation Tribunal for Wales Regulations 2010, SI 2010/713, reg 9(1)(a)–(d) (as so substituted). As to further provision relating to the appointment of members see the regs 9(2), (4)–(6), 21 (reg 9 as so substituted). As to the tenure of office of members of the tribunal see reg 10 (amended by SI 2017/941). As to the payment of allowances to members of the tribunal see the Valuation Tribunal for Wales Regulations 2010, SI 2010/713, reg 17.

All members of the Valuation Tribunal for Wales are disqualified for membership of the National Assembly for Wales: see the Government of Wales Act 2006 s 16(1)(b); the National Assembly for Wales (Disqualification) Order 2015, SI 2015/1536, art 2, Schedule; and CONSTITUTIONAL AND ADMINISTRATIVE LAW vol 20 (2014) PARA 360.
10 See the Valuation Tribunal for Wales Regulations 2010, SI 2010/713, reg 14 (amended by SI 2016/481).
11 See the Valuation Tribunal for Wales Regulations 2010, SI 2010/713, reg 12(1).
12 See the Valuation Tribunal for Wales Regulations 2010, SI 2010/713, reg 12(2) (substituted by SI 2017/941). As to the appointment of chairpersons and their tenure of office see the Valuation Tribunal for Wales Regulations 2010, SI 2010/713, reg 12(3)–(7) (reg 12(3) amended by SI 2017/941).
13 Ie under the Valuation Tribunal for Wales Regulations 2010, SI 2010/713.
14 As to the governing council see PARA 237.
15 Valuation Tribunal for Wales Regulations 2010, SI 2010/713, reg 11(7).
16 See the Valuation Tribunal for Wales Regulations 2010, SI 2010/713, reg 15. As to the chief executive's function of making arrangements as to accommodation and equipment see reg 20; and PARA 237.
17 See the Valuation Tribunal for Wales Regulations 2010, SI 2010/713, reg 16.

239. Procedure.

The Valuation Tribunal for Wales[1] may establish committees[2]. The governing council[3] may establish sub-committees[4]. A person who is not a member of the tribunal[5] may be appointed to such a committee or a sub-committee[6]. Such a committee or sub-committee may only act in an advisory capacity[7].

Minutes must be kept of proceedings of the tribunal, the governing council, the appointments panel[8] and the other committees and sub-committees of the tribunal and the governing council[9]. Minutes of any such proceedings are evidence of those proceedings if they are signed by the person purporting to have acted as chairperson of the proceedings to which the minutes relate or of any subsequent proceedings in the course of which the minutes were approved as a correct record[10].

1 As to the Valuation Tribunal for Wales see PARA 237.
2 Valuation Tribunal for Wales Regulations 2010, SI 2010/713, reg 18(1).
3 As to the governing council see PARA 237.
4 Valuation Tribunal for Wales Regulations 2010, SI 2010/713, reg 18(2).
5 As to membership of the tribunal see PARA 238.
6 Valuation Tribunal for Wales Regulations 2010, SI 2010/713, reg 18(3).
7 Valuation Tribunal for Wales Regulations 2010, SI 2010/713, reg 18(4).
8 As to the appointments panel see PARA 237 note 4.
9 Valuation Tribunal for Wales Regulations 2010, SI 2010/713, reg 19(1) (amended by SI 2017/941). The Valuation Tribunal for Wales Regulations 2010, SI 2010/713, reg 19 applies to meetings or determinations of members of the governing council when acting under reg 8(2) (see PARA 237) as it applies to proceedings mentioned in reg 19(1): reg 19(4).
10 Valuation Tribunal for Wales Regulations 2010, SI 2010/713, reg 19(2). Where minutes of any such proceedings have been signed as mentioned in reg 19(2), those proceedings must, unless the contrary is shown, be deemed to have been validly convened and constituted: reg 19(3).

(C) Tribunal Procedure

240. Regulations.

Regulations[1] may include provision:

(1) prescribing the procedure to be followed for initiating an appeal[2], and authorising or requiring it to be dismissed if it is not initiated within a prescribed time[3];

(2) authorising an appeal to be disposed of on the basis of written representations in prescribed circumstances[4];

(3) prescribing the procedure to be followed before the hearing of an appeal[5];

(4) authorising an appeal to be withdrawn before the hearing in prescribed circumstances[6];

(5) prescribing the procedure to be followed at the hearing of an appeal[7];

(6) in relation to the making by a tribunal[8] of decisions and orders[9];

(7) as to the recording, correction and communication of decisions and orders of a tribunal[10];

(8) that, subject to any other provision of the regulations, a tribunal may regulate its own procedure[11];

(9) as to appeals from decision or orders of a tribunal[12];

(10) as to inspection of records relating to decisions and orders of a tribunal[13].

1 Ie regulations under the Local Government Finance Act 1988 Sch 11 para A19 (see PARA 235) or Sch 11 para 1 (see PARA 236): see s 136, Sch 11 paras 8(1), 11(1) (Sch 11 para 8(1) substituted by virtue of the Local Government and Public Involvement in Health Act 2007 s 219(1), Sch 15 paras 1, 10(2), 11; the Local Government Finance Act 1988 Sch 11 para 11(1) amended by the Local Government and Public Involvement in Health Act 2007 s 219(1), Sch 15 paras 1, 15).

2 As to non-domestic rating appeals see PARA 242 et seq; and as to council tax appeals see PARA 513 et seq.

3 Local Government Finance Act 1988 Sch 11 para 8(2)(a). 'Prescribed' means prescribed by the regulations: see s 146(6).

4 Local Government Finance Act 1988 Sch 11 para 8(2)(b).

5 Local Government Finance Act 1988 Sch 11 para 8(2)(c).

6 Local Government Finance Act 1988 Sch 11 para 8(2)(d).

7 Local Government Finance Act 1988 Sch 11 para 8(3). Such provision may include provision:

(1) requiring the hearing to take place in public except in prescribed circumstances (Sch 11 para 8(3)(a));

(2) as to the persons entitled to appear and to be heard on behalf of parties to the appeal (Sch 11 para 8(3)(b));

(3) authorising the hearing to proceed in the absence of a party or parties to the appeal in prescribed circumstances (Sch 11 para 8(3)(c));

(4) requiring persons to attend to give evidence and produce documents (Sch 11 para 8(3)(d));

(5) that no rule of confidentiality applicable to the Commissioners for Her Majesty's Revenue and Customs is to prevent the disclosure for the purposes of the appeal of particulars delivered documents (within the meaning of the Local Government Finance Act 1992 Pt I (ss 1–69): see PARA 408 note 8) (Local Government Finance Act 1988 Sch 11 para 8(3)(e) (substituted by the Local Government Finance Act 1992 s 117(1), Sch 13 para 86(6); and amended by virtue of the Commissioners for Revenue and Customs Act 2005 s 50));

(6) as to evidence generally (whether written evidence or oral evidence given under oath or affirmation) and, in particular, as to the use as evidence of particulars delivered documents, of information supplied under the Local Government Finance Act 1988 Sch 9 (see PARAS 226, 227, 272–276) or regulations under Sch 2 (repealed), the General Rate 1967 s 82 (repealed), regulations under the Local Government Finance Act 1992 Sch 2 para 15A or 15B (see PARAS 437, 442), or of information disclosed by virtue of the Non-Domestic Rating (Information) Act 1996 s 1(1) (see PARA 54) or of information

supplied under the Welfare Reform Act 2012 s 131 (see WELFARE BENEFITS AND STATE PENSIONS vol 104 (2014) PARA 555) for purposes relating to council tax (Local Government Finance Act 1988 Sch 11 para 8(3)(ea) (added by the Local Government Finance Act 1992 Sch 13 para 86(6); and amended by the Non-Domestic Rating (Information) Act 1996 s 1(3); and the Local Government Finance Act 2012 s 17(1), (6)(b)));

(7) as to the adjournment of the hearing (Local Government Finance Act 1988 Sch 11 para 8(3)(f));

(8) that a person who without reasonable excuse fails to comply with any requirement imposed by the regulations under Sch 11 para 8(3)(d) (see head (4) above) is liable on summary conviction to a fine not exceeding level 1 on the standard scale (Sch 11 para 8(7)).

As to the meaning of 'person' see PARA 11 note 13. As to the Commissioners for Her Majesty's Revenue and Customs see INCOME TAXATION vol 58 (2014) PARAS 33–34. As to the powers of magistrates' courts to issue fines on summary conviction see SENTENCING vol 92 (2015) PARA 176.

8 In the Local Government Finance Act 1988 Sch 11 Pt 3 (paras 8–12A), references to a 'tribunal' are, in relation to England, references to the Valuation Tribunal for England; and, in relation to Wales, references to a tribunal established under Sch 11 para 1 (see PARA 237): Sch 11 para 12A (added by the Local Government and Public Involvement in Health Act 2007 s 219(1), Sch 15 paras 1, 17). As to the Valuation Tribunal for England see PARA 232. As to the meanings of 'England' and 'Wales' see PARA 2 note 16.

9 The regulations may include provision:

(1) that where two or more members of a tribunal are acting the decision of the majority is to prevail or, if the votes are equal, the appeal is to be reheard (Local Government Finance Act 1988 Sch 11 para 8(4)(a));

(2) requiring reasons for a decision to be given (Sch 11 para 8(4)(b));

(3) authorising a decision to be given orally or in writing (Sch 11 para 8(4)(c));

(4) authorising a decision to be reserved (Sch 11 para 8(4)(d));

(5) authorising or requiring an order to be made in consequence of a decision (Sch 11 para 8(4)(e));

(6) that an order may require a register or list to be altered (prospectively or retrospectively) (Sch 11 para 8(4)(f) (Sch 11 para 8(4)(f) substituted, 8(4)(fa)–(fe) added, by the Local Government Finance Act 1992 s 117(1), Sch 13 para 86(7)));

(7) that an order may require the designation of an individual as a responsible individual or as a certification officer, or a designation under the Local Government Finance Act 1988 s 5 (repealed), to be revoked (Sch 11 para 8(4)(fa) (as so added));

(8) that an order may require an estimate to be quashed or altered (Sch 11 para 8(4)(fb) (as so added));

(9) that an order may require a penalty to be quashed (Sch 11 para 8(4)(fc) (as so added));

(10) that an order may require a decision of a billing authority to be reversed (Sch 11 para 8(4)(fd) (as so added));

(11) that an order may require a calculation (other than an estimate) of an amount to be quashed and may require the amount to be recalculated (Sch 11 para 8(4)(fe) (as so added));

(12) that an order may require any ancillary matter to be attended to (Sch 11 para 8(4)(g));

(13) authorising or requiring a tribunal to review or set aside a decision, or to vary or revoke an order, of the tribunal in prescribed circumstances (Sch 11 para 8(4)(h)).

10 The regulations may include provision:

(1) requiring decisions and orders to be recorded (Local Government Finance Act 1988 Sch 11 para 8(5)(a));

(2) as to the proof of decisions and orders (Sch 11 para 8(5)(b));

(3) authorising the correction of clerical errors in records of decisions and orders (Sch 11 para 8(5)(c));

(4) requiring decisions, orders and corrections to be communicated to the parties to appeals (Sch 11 para 8(5)(d)).

11 Local Government Finance Act 1988 Sch 11 para 8(6).

12 The regulations may include provision:

(1) that an appeal lies to the High Court on a question of law arising out of a decision or order which is given or made by a tribunal on an appeal under the Local Government Finance Act 1988 s 23 (repealed), the Local Government Finance Act 1992 s 16 (see

PARA 513), Sch 3 para 3 (see PARA 471) or regulations under s 24 (see PARA 417) (Local Government Finance Act 1988 Sch 11 para 11(1)(a) (amended by the Local Government Finance Act 1992 Sch 13 para 88(10), (11)));

(2) that an appeal lies to the Upper Tribunal in respect of a decision or order which is given or made by a tribunal on an appeal under the Local Government Finance Act 1988 Sch 4A para 4 (see PARA 141) or regulations under s 55 (see PARA 199) (Sch 11 para 11(1)(b) (amended by the Local Government Finance Act 1992 Sch 13 para 88(10), (11); and by SI 2009/1307));

(3) as to the persons who may appeal to the High Court or the Upper Tribunal (Local Government Finance Act 1988 Sch 11 para 11(2)(a) (Sch 11(2)(a)–(c) amended by SI 2009/1307));

(4) authorising or requiring an appeal to the High Court or the Upper Tribunal to be dismissed if it is not initiated within a prescribed time (Local Government Finance Act 1988 Sch 11 para 11(2)(b) (as so amended));

(5) as to the powers of the High Court or the Upper Tribunal on an appeal to it (which may include provision allowing the tribunal's decision or order to be confirmed, varied, set aside, revoked or remitted, and provision allowing the making of any order the tribunal could have made) (Sch 11 para 11(2)(c) (as so amended));

(6) requiring a charging authority, the community charges registration officer for a charging authority, a billing authority, the valuation officer or listing officer for a billing authority, or the central valuation officer, to act in accordance with any order made by the High Court or the Upper Tribunal, and provision that Sch 11 para 9, 10 or 10A (see PARAS 254 note 21, 533 note 6) is to have effect subject to such a requirement (Sch 11 para 11(2)(d) (substituted by the Local Government Finance Act 1992 ss 117(1), 118(1), Sch 13 para 88(1); and amended by SI 2009/1307)).

13 In respect of records which relate to decisions and orders of a tribunal and which are required to be made under any provision included in the regulations, the regulations may include provision (see Sch 11 para 12(1) (amended by the Local Government and Public Involvement in Health Act 2007 Sch 15 paras 1, 16)):

(1) that a person may, at a reasonable time stated by or on behalf of the tribunal concerned and without making payment, inspect such records at the tribunal's permanent office (Local Government Finance Act 1988 Sch 11 para 12(2));

(2) that if without reasonable excuse a person having custody of such records intentionally obstructs a person in exercising a right under any provision included under head (1) above, he is liable on summary conviction to a fine not exceeding level 1 on the standard scale (Sch 11 para 12(3)).

B. THE VALUATION TRIBUNAL SERVICE

241. The Valuation Tribunal Service.

The Valuation Tribunal Service (the 'Service') is a body corporate[1] which has the following functions in relation to the Valuation Tribunal for England[2]:

(1) providing, or arranging for the provision of, the services required for the operation of the tribunal[3], in particular accommodation[4], staff (including the clerk of the tribunal)[5], information technology[6], equipment[7] and training for members and staff of the tribunal (including the clerk of the tribunal)[8];

(2) making payments in respect of remuneration, allowances and pensions for members of the tribunal[9];

(3) giving general advice about procedure in relation to proceedings before the tribunal[10].

The Service must also provide the Secretary of State with such information, advice and assistance as he may require[11].

The Service may do anything which it considers is calculated to facilitate (or is conducive or incidental to) the carrying out of its functions[12], and must carry out its functions with respect to the tribunal in the manner which it considers best calculated to secure its efficient and independent operation[13]. The Service must, in relation to its functions with respect to the tribunal, consult the president of the tribunal about the carrying out of its functions[14].

The Secretary of State may:

(a) after consultation with the Service, give directions to it for the purpose of securing the effective carrying out of its functions[15]; and
(b) issue guidance to the Service about the carrying-out of its functions[16].

The Service must, in carrying out its functions, comply with any such directions[17] and have regard to any such guidance[18].

Further provision is made in relation to:

(i) membership of the Service and the appointment of its chairman and deputy chairman[19];
(ii) disqualification for membership[20];
(iii) tenure of office[21];
(iv) remuneration, pensions, etc of members[22];
(v) staff[23];
(vi) committees of the Service[24];
(vii) proceedings[25];
(viii) delegation of the Service's functions[26];
(ix) members' interests[27];
(x) vacancies and defective appointments[28];
(xi) minutes of proceedings[29];
(xii) execution and proof of instruments[30]; and
(xiii) finance[31].

1 See the Local Government Act 2003 s 105(1). The Secretary of State may make one or more schemes for the transfer to the Service of such of his property, rights and liabilities, or such of the property, rights and liabilities of a valuation tribunal in England, as appear to him to be appropriate to be transferred for the performance of the Service's functions: see s 106, Sch 5. As to the Secretary of State see PARA 4 note 18. As to bodies corporate see COMPANIES vol 14 (2016) PARA 2; CORPORATIONS vol 24 (2010) PARA 301 et seq.

The Valuation Tribunal Service is subject to investigation by the Parliamentary Commissioner for Administration: see the Parliamentary Commissioner Act 1967 s 4(1), Sch 2; and CONSTITUTIONAL AND ADMINISTRATIVE LAW vol 20 (2014) PARA 634. The administrative records of the Valuation Tribunal Service are public records: see the Public Records Act 1958 s 10(1), Sch 1 para 3 Table Pt II; and CONSTITUTIONAL AND ADMINISTRATIVE LAW vol 20 (2014) PARA 343. The Valuation Tribunal Service is a public authority for the purposes of the Freedom of Information Act 2000: see s 3, Sch 1 Pt VI; and CONSTITUTIONAL AND ADMINISTRATIVE LAW vol 20 (2014) PARA 425.

As from 14 February 2012, a minister may by order abolish the Valuation Tribunal Service: see the Public Bodies Act 2011 ss 1(1), 38(1), Sch 1. Such an order may include provision transferring functions from that body to an eligible person: see s 1(2). 'Eligible person' means:

(1) a minister, the Scottish Ministers, a Northern Ireland department or the Welsh Ministers (s 1(3)(a));
(2) any other person exercising public functions (s 1(3)(b));
(3) a company limited by guarantee (s 1(3)(c));
(4) a community interest company (s 1(3)(d));
(5) a co-operative society (s 1(3)(e));
(6) a community benefit society (s 1(3)(f));
(7) a charitable incorporated organisation (s 1(3)(g)); or
(8) a body of trustees or other unincorporated body of persons (s 1(3)(h)).

'Minister' means a Minister of the Crown (as defined by the Ministers of the Crown Act 1975 s 8: see PARA 41 note 1), or the Commissioners for Her Majesty's Revenue and Customs: Public Bodies Act 2011 s 36(1). As to the Commissioners for Her Majesty's Revenue and Customs see INCOME TAXATION vol 58 (2014) PARAS 33–34.

2 See the Local Government Act 2003 s 105(2) (amended by the Local Government and Public Involvement in Health Act 2007 s 220(1), Sch 16 paras 10, 11(1), (2)(a)). As to the Valuation Tribunal for England see PARA 232.

3 Local Government Act 2003 s 105(2)(a) (amended by the Local Government and Public Involvement in Health Act 2007 Sch 16 paras 10, 11(1), (2)(b)).
4 Local Government Act 2003 s 105(2)(a)(i).
5 Local Government Act 2003 s 105(2)(a)(ii) (amended by the Local Government and Public Involvement in Health Act 2007 Sch 16 paras 10, 11(1), (2)(c)).
6 Local Government Act 2003 s 105(2)(a)(iii).
7 Local Government Act 2003 s 105(2)(a)(iv).
8 Local Government Act 2003 s 105(2)(a)(v) (amended by the Local Government and Public Involvement in Health Act 2007 Sch 16 paras 10, 11(1), (2)(d)).
9 Ie payments in accordance with the Local Government Finance Act 1988 Sch 11 para A14 (see PARA 233) or Sch 11 para A18A(8) (see PARA 233): Local Government Act 2003 s 105(2)(aa) (added by the Local Government and Public Involvement in Health Act 2007 Sch 16 paras 10, 11(1), (2)(e); and amended by the Local Government Finance Act 2012 s 10(2), (3)(b), Sch 4 paras 8, 10).
10 Local Government Act 2003 s 105(2)(b) (amended by the Local Government and Public Involvement in Health Act 2007 Sch 16 paras 10, 11(1), (2)(f)).
11 Local Government Finance Act 1988 s 105(3).
12 Local Government Finance Act 1988 s 105(4).
13 Local Government Finance Act 1988 s 105(5) (amended by the Local Government and Public Involvement in Health Act 2007 Sch 16 paras 10, 11(1), (3)).
14 Local Government Finance Act 1988 s 105(6) (amended by the Local Government and Public Involvement in Health Act 2007 Sch 16 paras 10, 11(1), (4)). As to the president of the tribunal see PARA 233.
15 Local Government Act 2003 s 105(7)(a).
16 Local Government Act 2003 s 105(7)(b).
17 See the Local Government Act 2003 s 105(8)(a).
18 See the Local Government Act 2003 s 105(8)(b).
19 See the Local Government Act 2003 s 105(9), Sch 4 para 1 (Sch 4 para 1 amended by the Local Government and Public Involvement in Health Act 2007 Sch 16 paras 10, 13(1), (2)). All members of the Valuation Tribunal Service are disqualified for membership of the House of Commons: see the House of Commons Disqualification Act 1975 s 1(1)(f), Sch 1 Pt II; and PARLIAMENT vol 78 (2010) PARA 908.
20 See the Local Government Act 2003 Sch 4 para 2 (amended by the Civil Partnership Act 2004 s 261(1), Sch 27 para 171; and SI 2012/2404).
21 See the Local Government Act 2003 Sch 4 paras 3–5 (Sch 4 paras 3, 4 amended by the Local Government and Public Involvement in Health Act 2007 Sch 16 paras 10, 13(1), (3), (4)).
22 See the Local Government Act 2003 Sch 4 para 6.
23 See the Local Government Act 2003 Sch 4 paras 7–9 (Sch 4 para 9 substituted by the Local Government and Public Involvement in Health Act 2007 Sch 16 paras 10, 13(1), (5)). As to pensions payable under the Local Government Pension Scheme in respect of service as an employee of the Valuation Tribunal Service see the Pensions Increase (Valuation Tribunal Service) Regulations 2004, SI 2004/558.
24 See the Local Government Act 2003 Sch 4 para 10.
25 See the Local Government Act 2003 Sch 4 para 11.
26 See the Local Government Act 2003 Sch 4 para 12.
27 See the Local Government Act 2003 Sch 4 paras 13–14.
28 See the Local Government Act 2003 Sch 4 para 15.
29 See the Local Government Act 2003 Sch 4 para 16.
30 See the Local Government Act 2003 Sch 4 para 17.
31 See the Local Government Act 2003 Sch 4 paras 18–20.

C. APPEALS TO VALUATION TRIBUNALS

(A) In General

242. Appeals to valuation tribunals.

Appeals to valuation tribunals[1] arise in relation to non-domestic rating in the following circumstances[2]: where:

(1) there is a disagreement between a valuation officer and a proposer as to the validity of a proposal to alter a local non-domestic rating list[3];

(2) there is a disagreement as to whether the proposal to alter a local non-domestic rating list is well founded[4];
(3) there are disagreements as mentioned in heads (1) and (2) above between a proposer and the central valuation officer in relation to an alteration to a central non-domestic rating list[5];
(4) there is an appeal against a completion notice[6];
(5) there is an appeal against imposition of a penalty for failure to comply with a valuation officer's request for information[7].

1 Ie the Valuation Tribunal for England (see PARA 232) and valuation tribunals in Wales (see PARA 236).
2 See the Valuation Tribunal for England (Council Tax and Rating Appeals) (Procedure) Regulations 2009, SI 2009/2269, reg 2(1) (amended by SI 2017/156); and the Non-Domestic Rating (Alteration of Lists and Appeals) (Wales) Regulations 2005, SI 2005/758, reg 2(1) (amended by SI 2010/713). As to the conduct of such appeals see further PARAS 243 et seq, 257 et seq.
3 Ie an appeal under the Non-Domestic Rating (Alteration of Lists and Appeals) (England) Regulations 2009, SI 2009/2268, reg 8, or the Non-Domestic Rating (Alteration of Lists and Appeals) (Wales) Regulations 2005, SI 2005/758, reg 8: see PARAS 206, 218.
4 Ie an appeal under the Non-Domestic Rating (Alteration of Lists and Appeals) (England) Regulations 2009, SI 2009/2268, reg 13A, or the Non-Domestic Rating (Alteration of Lists and Appeals) (Wales) Regulations 2005, SI 2005/758, reg 13: see PARAS 211, 222.
5 Ie an appeal by virtue of the provisions referred to in heads (1) and (2) in the text as they are applied by the Non-Domestic Rating (Alteration of Lists and Appeals) (England) Regulations 2009, SI 2009/2268, reg 18, or the Non-Domestic Rating (Alteration of Lists and Appeals) (Wales) Regulations 2005, SI 2005/758, reg 18: see PARAS 224, 225.
6 Ie an appeal under the Local Government Finance Act 1988 Sch 4A para 4 as it applies for the purposes of the non-domestic rating provisions in Pt III (ss 41–67): see PARA 141.
7 Ie a penalty under the Local Government Finance Act 1988 Sch 9 para 5C: see PARA 226.

(B) England

243. Conduct of appeals.

In giving effect to the Valuation Tribunal for England (Council Tax and Rating Appeals) (Procedure) Regulations[1] and in exercising any of its functions under the regulations, the Valuation Tribunal for England[2] must have regard to:

(1) dealing with appeals[3] in ways which are proportionate to the importance of the appeal, the complexity of the issues, the anticipated costs and the resources of the parties[4];
(2) avoiding unnecessary formality and seeking flexibility in the proceedings[5];
(3) ensuring, so far as practicable, that the parties are able to participate fully in the proceedings[6];
(4) using any special expertise of the tribunal effectively[7]; and
(5) avoiding delay, so far as compatible with proper consideration of the issues[8].

The tribunal must acknowledge receipt of every notice of appeal within two weeks of its receipt and must send a copy of the notice of appeal and any accompanying documents to every party (other than the appellant) as soon as reasonably practicable after receiving the notice of appeal[9].

An irregularity resulting from failure to comply with any requirement in the regulations or a direction[10] does not of itself render void the proceedings or any step taken in the proceedings[11]. If a party has failed to comply with a requirement in the regulations or a direction, the tribunal may take such action as it considers just, which may include:

(a) waiving the requirement[12];
(b) requiring the failure to be remedied[13]; or
(c) exercising the power[14] to give a direction[15].

The tribunal may not make any order in respect of costs[16].

Provision is made as to the sending and delivery of documents[17]. An act required by the regulations or a direction to be done on or by a particular day must be done by 5 pm on that day[18].

1 Ie the Valuation Tribunal for England (Council Tax and Rating Appeals) (Procedure) Regulations 2009, SI 2009/2269. These regulations apply in England only: see reg 1. As to the equivalent regulations in relation to Wales see the Non-Domestic Rating (Alterations of Lists and Appeals) (Wales) Regulations 2005, SI 2005/758, Pt 5 (regs 21–39); and PARA 257 et seq. As to the meanings of 'England' and 'Wales' see PARA 2 note 16.

2 As to the Valuation Tribunal for England see PARA 232.

3 As to appeals in relation to non-domestic rating see PARA 242.

4 Valuation Tribunal for England (Council Tax and Rating Appeals) (Procedure) Regulations 2009, SI 2009/2269, reg 3(a). Regulation 2(3)(d), (e) (amended by SI 2017/156) provides that any reference to a 'party':
   (1) in relation to an appeal under the Non-Domestic Rating (Alteration of Lists and Appeals) (England) Regulations 2009, SI 2009/2268, reg 8 (see PARA 206) or reg 13 (see PARA 210) or an appeal against imposition of a penalty under the Local Government Finance Act 1988 Sch 9 para 5C (see PARA 226), means the appellant and the valuation officer and includes:
      (a) where the appeal is under the Non-Domestic Rating (Alteration of Lists and Appeals) (England) Regulations 2009, SI 2009/2268, reg 8, reg 13A or reg 19 (see PARAS 141, 211):
         (i) a person whose agreement is required under reg 12 (agreed alterations following proposals: see PARA 209); and
         (ii) any other person who has been a ratepayer in relation to the hereditament since the proposal was made and who has notified the valuation officer in writing before the hearing, or before determination on the basis of written representations, that the person wishes to be a party to the appeal;
      (b) where the appeal is against a completion notice, the relevant authority;
   (2) if the proceedings on an appeal have been concluded, means a person who was a party when the tribunal finally disposed of all issues in the proceedings.

   As to valuation officers see PARA 54. 'Appellant' means the person who makes the appeal or, where a person has been substituted under reg 11(1) (see PARA 245), that person: see reg 2(1). As to the meaning of 'person' see PARA 11 note 13. 'Ratepayer', in relation to a hereditament, means the occupier or, if the hereditament is not occupied, the owner: reg 2(1). As to the meaning of 'hereditament' see PARA 106. As to the meanings of 'owner' and 'occupier' see PARA 86. 'Proposal' means a proposal for the alteration of the central non-domestic rating list or the local non-domestic rating list: see reg 2(1). As to local non-domestic rating lists see PARA 191 et seq. As to central non-domestic rating lists see PARA 196 et seq. As to the alteration of lists see PARA 202 et seq. As to the meaning of 'writing' see PARA 21 note 3.

   'Completion notice' means a notice under the Local Government Finance Act 1988 Sch 4A para 1 (see PARA 138) as it applies for the purposes of Pt III (ss 41–67) of that Act: see the Valuation Tribunal for England (Council Tax and Rating Appeals) (Procedure) Regulations 2009, SI 2009/2269, reg 2(1).

   'Relevant authority', in relation to a hereditament, means the billing authority in whose area the hereditament is situated: see reg 2(1). As to the meaning of 'billing authority' see PARA 53.

5 Valuation Tribunal for England (Council Tax and Rating Appeals) (Procedure) Regulations 2009, SI 2009/2269, reg 3(b).

6 Valuation Tribunal for England (Council Tax and Rating Appeals) (Procedure) Regulations 2009, SI 2009/2269, reg 3(c).

7 Valuation Tribunal for England (Council Tax and Rating Appeals) (Procedure) Regulations 2009, SI 2009/2269, reg 3(d).

8 Valuation Tribunal for England (Council Tax and Rating Appeals) (Procedure) Regulations 2009, SI 2009/2269, reg 3(e).

9 Valuation Tribunal for England (Council Tax and Rating Appeals) (Procedure) Regulations 2009, SI 2009/2269, reg 28(2). If an appellant provides notice of appeal against a completion notice or the imposition of a penalty to the tribunal later than the time required by the Non-Domestic Rating (Alteration of Lists and Appeals) (England) Regulations 2009, SI 2009/2268, or by an extension of time allowed under the Valuation Tribunal for England (Council Tax and Rating Appeals) (Procedure) Regulations 2009, SI 2009/2269, reg 6(3)(a) (appeal management powers: see PARA 244), the tribunal must not admit the notice of appeal unless the tribunal extends time for the notice of appeal under that provision: see reg 28(1). As to the power of the tribunal to correct errors in documents produced by it see PARA 245.

10 As to the power of the tribunal to give directions in relation to the conduct or disposal of proceedings see PARA 244. As to directions generally see PARA 245. As to directions relating to evidence and information see PARA 248.

11 Valuation Tribunal for England (Council Tax and Rating Appeals) (Procedure) Regulations 2009, SI 2009/2269, reg 9(1).

12 Valuation Tribunal for England (Council Tax and Rating Appeals) (Procedure) Regulations 2009, SI 2009/2269, reg 9(2)(a).

13 Valuation Tribunal for England (Council Tax and Rating Appeals) (Procedure) Regulations 2009, SI 2009/2269, reg 9(2)(b).

14 Ie under the Valuation Tribunal for England (Council Tax and Rating Appeals) (Procedure) Regulations 2009, SI 2009/2269, reg 8: see PARA 245.

15 Valuation Tribunal for England (Council Tax and Rating Appeals) (Procedure) Regulations 2009, SI 2009/2269, reg 9(2)(c).

16 Valuation Tribunal for England (Council Tax and Rating Appeals) (Procedure) Regulations 2009, SI 2009/2269, reg 12.

17 Any document to be provided to the tribunal under the regulations or a direction must be:

(1) sent by pre-paid post or delivered by hand to the address specified for the proceedings (Valuation Tribunal for England (Council Tax and Rating Appeals) (Procedure) Regulations 2009, SI 2009/2269, reg 15(1)(a));

(2) sent by fax to the number specified for the proceedings (reg 15(1)(b)); or

(3) sent or delivered by such other method and to such address as may be agreed by the tribunal and the person by whom the documents are to be sent or delivered (reg 15(1)(c)).

If a party provides a fax number, email address or other details for the electronic transmission of documents to it, that party must accept delivery of documents by that method: reg 15(2). However, if a party informs the tribunal and all other parties that a particular form of communication (other than pre-paid post or delivery by hand) should not be used to provide documents to that party, that form of communication must not be used: reg 15(3). If the tribunal or a party sends a document to a party or the tribunal by email or any other electronic means of communication, the recipient may request that the sender provide a hard copy of the document to the recipient (reg 15(4)); and such a request must be made as soon as reasonably practicable after the recipient receives the document electronically (reg 15(5)). The tribunal and each party may assume that the address provided by a party or its representative is and remains the address to which documents should be sent or delivered until receiving written notification to the contrary: reg 15(6). As to service by post generally see PARA 139 note 3.

18 Valuation Tribunal for England (Council Tax and Rating Appeals) (Procedure) Regulations 2009, SI 2009/2269, reg 14(1). If the time specified by the regulations or a direction for doing any act ends on a day other than a working day, the act is done in time if it is done on the next working day: reg 14(2). 'Working day' means any day except a Saturday or Sunday, Christmas Day, Good Friday or a bank holiday under the Bank and Financial Dealings Act 1971 s 1 (see TIME vol 97 (2015) PARA 321): Valuation Tribunal for England (Council Tax and Rating Appeals) (Procedure) Regulations 2009, SI 2009/2269, reg 14(3).

244. Appeal management.

It is the duty of the president of the Valuation Tribunal for England[1] to ensure that arrangements are made for the determination of appeals[2].

Subject as otherwise provided[3], the tribunal may regulate its own procedure[4]. The tribunal may give a direction in relation to the conduct or disposal of proceedings at any time, including a direction amending, suspending or setting aside an earlier direction[5]. In particular, and without restricting these general powers[6], the tribunal may:

(1) extend or shorten the time for complying with any regulation or direction[7];
(2) consolidate or hear together two or more sets of proceedings or parts of proceedings raising common issues, or treat[8] an appeal as a lead appeal[9];
(3) permit or require a party[10] to amend a document[11];
(4) permit or require a party or another person[12] to provide documents, evidence, information, or submissions to the tribunal or a party[13];
(5) deal with an issue in proceedings as a preliminary issue[14];
(6) hold a hearing to consider any matter, including a case management issue[15];
(7) decide the form of any hearing[16];
(8) adjourn or postpone a hearing[17];
(9) require a party to produce a bundle for a hearing[18];
(10) stay proceedings[19]; or
(11) suspend the effect of its own decision pending the determination by the Upper Tribunal[20] or a court of an application for permission to appeal against, and any appeal against or review of, that decision[21].

If two or more related appeals have been made[22] to the tribunal[23], and as regards each of the related appeals the tribunal has not made a decision disposing of the proceedings[24] and the related appeals give rise to common or related issues of fact or law[25], then the tribunal may give a direction specifying one or more of the related appeals as a lead appeal or lead appeals[26] and staying the other related appeals[27]. When the tribunal makes a decision in respect of the common or related issues, it must send a copy of that decision to each party in each of the related appeals[28]; and that decision is binding on each of those parties[29] unless, within one month[30] after the date on which the tribunal sends a copy of the decision to a party, that party applies in writing[31] for a direction that the decision does not apply to, and is not binding on the parties to, a particular related appeal[32].

If before the tribunal makes a decision in respect of the common or related issues the lead appeal is withdrawn[33] or, where there is more than one lead appeal, all of the lead appeals are withdrawn[34], the tribunal must give directions as to whether another appeal or other appeals are to be specified as a lead appeal or appeals[35].

1 As to the Valuation Tribunal for England see PARA 232. As to the president of the tribunal, and membership of the tribunal generally, see PARA 233. The Valuation Tribunal for England (Council Tax and Rating Appeals) (Procedure) Regulations 2009, SI 2009/2269, apply in relation to England only: see reg 1. As to the equivalent regulations in relation to Wales see the Non-Domestic Rating (Alterations of Lists and Appeals) (Wales) Regulations 2005, SI 2005/758, Pt 5 (regs 21–39); and PARA 257 et seq. As to the meanings of 'England' and 'Wales' see PARA 2 note 16.

2 See the Valuation Tribunal for England (Council Tax and Rating Appeals) (Procedure) Regulations 2009, SI 2009/2269, reg 5(1). As to appeals in relation to non-domestic rating see PARA 242. The arrangements must provide for appeals to be determined in accordance with the provisions of regs 6–18, 19A, 28–44 (see the text to notes 3–35; and PARAS 243, 245 et seq): see reg 5(1). The tribunal must not deal with an appeal under the Non-Domestic Rating (Alteration of Lists and Appeals) (England) Regulations 2009, SI 2009/2268, reg 13A (see PARA 211) until any appeal under the Council Tax (Alteration of Lists and Appeals) (England) Regulations 2009, SI 2009/2270, reg 7 (see PARA 422) in respect of the same proposal has been decided: see the Valuation Tribunal for England (Council Tax and Rating Appeals) (Procedure) Regulations 2009, SI 2009/2269, reg 5(2) (substituted by SI 2017/156). As to the meaning of 'proposal' see PARA 243 note 4. Where two or more appeals relating to the same hereditament or hereditaments are made under the Non-Domestic Rating (Alteration of Lists and Appeals) (England) Regulations 2009, SI 2009/2268, reg 13A (see PARA 211), the order in which the appeals are dealt with must be the order in which the alterations in question would, but for the disagreements which occasion the

appeals, have taken effect: Valuation Tribunal for England (Council Tax and Rating Appeals) (Procedure) Regulations 2009, SI 2009/2269, reg 5(3) (amended by SI 2017/156). As to the meaning of 'hereditament' see PARA 106. As to the alteration of non-domestic rating lists see PARA 202 et seq.

3 Ie subject to the provisions of the Local Government Finance Act 1988 Sch 11 Pt I (see PARA 232) and the Valuation Tribunal for England (Council Tax and Rating Appeals) (Procedure) Regulations 2009, SI 2009/2269: see reg 6(1).

4 Valuation Tribunal for England (Council Tax and Rating Appeals) (Procedure) Regulations 2009, SI 2009/2269, reg 6(1).

5 Valuation Tribunal for England (Council Tax and Rating Appeals) (Procedure) Regulations 2009, SI 2009/2269, reg 6(2). As to directions see also PARAS 244, 248. As to the striking out of proceedings see PARA 246.

6 Ie the powers in the Valuation Tribunal for England (Council Tax and Rating Appeals) (Procedure) Regulations 2009, SI 2009/2269, reg 6(1), (2): see the text to notes 3–5.

7 Valuation Tribunal for England (Council Tax and Rating Appeals) (Procedure) Regulations 2009, SI 2009/2269, reg 6(3)(a). As to the calculation of time generally see reg 14; and PARA 243.

8 Ie whether in accordance with the Valuation Tribunal for England (Council Tax and Rating Appeals) (Procedure) Regulations 2009, SI 2009/2269, reg 7 (see the text to notes 22–35) or otherwise.

9 Valuation Tribunal for England (Council Tax and Rating Appeals) (Procedure) Regulations 2009, SI 2009/2269, reg 6(3)(b).

10 As to the meaning of 'party' see PARA 243 note 4.

11 Valuation Tribunal for England (Council Tax and Rating Appeals) (Procedure) Regulations 2009, SI 2009/2269, reg 6(3)(c) (amended by SI 2017/156). The tribunal may permit or require a party to an appeal under the Non-Domestic Rating (Alteration of Lists and Appeals) (England) Regulations 2009, SI 2009/2268, reg 13A to amend a such document only if the amendment is in order to correct an inaccuracy in the document: Valuation Tribunal for England (Council Tax and Rating Appeals) (Procedure) Regulations 2009, SI 2009/2269, reg 6(4) (added by SI 2017/156).

12 As to the meaning of 'person' see PARA 11 note 13.

13 Valuation Tribunal for England (Council Tax and Rating Appeals) (Procedure) Regulations 2009, SI 2009/2269, reg 6(3)(d). Head (4) in the text is subject to regs 17, 17A and 18A (see PARAS 248, 249): reg 6(3)(d) (amended by SI 2017/156). As to the service and delivery of documents see reg 15; and PARA 243.

14 Valuation Tribunal for England (Council Tax and Rating Appeals) (Procedure) Regulations 2009, SI 2009/2269, reg 6(3)(e).

15 Valuation Tribunal for England (Council Tax and Rating Appeals) (Procedure) Regulations 2009, SI 2009/2269, reg 6(3)(f).

16 Valuation Tribunal for England (Council Tax and Rating Appeals) (Procedure) Regulations 2009, SI 2009/2269, reg 6(3)(g).

17 Valuation Tribunal for England (Council Tax and Rating Appeals) (Procedure) Regulations 2009, SI 2009/2269, reg 6(3)(h).

18 Valuation Tribunal for England (Council Tax and Rating Appeals) (Procedure) Regulations 2009, SI 2009/2269, reg 6(3)(i).

19 Valuation Tribunal for England (Council Tax and Rating Appeals) (Procedure) Regulations 2009, SI 2009/2269, reg 6(3)(j).

20 As to the Upper Tribunal see COURTS AND TRIBUNALS vol 24 (2010) PARA 874 et seq.

21 Valuation Tribunal for England (Council Tax and Rating Appeals) (Procedure) Regulations 2009, SI 2009/2269, reg 6(3)(k). As to appeals from decisions of the Valuation Tribunal for England see PARA 269.

22 Ie under the Non-Domestic Rating (Alteration of Lists and Appeals) (England) Regulations 2009, SI 2009/2268, reg 13A: see PARA 211.

23 See the Valuation Tribunal for England (Council Tax and Rating Appeals) (Procedure) Regulations 2009, SI 2009/2269, reg 7(1)(a)(ii) (amended by SI 2017/156).

24 Valuation Tribunal for England (Council Tax and Rating Appeals) (Procedure) Regulations 2009, SI 2009/2269, reg 7(1)(b).

25 Valuation Tribunal for England (Council Tax and Rating Appeals) (Procedure) Regulations 2009, SI 2009/2269, reg 7(1)(c).

26 Valuation Tribunal for England (Council Tax and Rating Appeals) (Procedure) Regulations 2009, SI 2009/2269, reg 7(2)(a).

27 Valuation Tribunal for England (Council Tax and Rating Appeals) (Procedure) Regulations 2009, SI 2009/2269, reg 7(2)(b). The tribunal must give directions in respect of appeals which are so stayed, providing for the disposal of, or further directions in, those appeals: reg 7(5).
28 Valuation Tribunal for England (Council Tax and Rating Appeals) (Procedure) Regulations 2009, SI 2009/2269, reg 7(3)(a).
29 Valuation Tribunal for England (Council Tax and Rating Appeals) (Procedure) Regulations 2009, SI 2009/2269, reg 7(3)(b).
30 As to the meaning of 'month' see PARA 11 note 1.
31 As to the meaning of 'writing' see PARA 21 note 3.
32 See the Valuation Tribunal for England (Council Tax and Rating Appeals) (Procedure) Regulations 2009, SI 2009/2269, reg 7(4).
33 Valuation Tribunal for England (Council Tax and Rating Appeals) (Procedure) Regulations 2009, SI 2009/2269, reg 7(6)(a). As to the withdrawal of appeals see PARA 250.
34 Valuation Tribunal for England (Council Tax and Rating Appeals) (Procedure) Regulations 2009, SI 2009/2269, reg 7(6)(b).
35 Valuation Tribunal for England (Council Tax and Rating Appeals) (Procedure) Regulations 2009, SI 2009/2269, reg 7(6)(i). Any direction affecting the related appeals should be set aside or amended: reg 7(6)(ii).

245. Directions.

The Valuation Tribunal for England[1] may give a direction on the application of one or more of the parties[2] or on its own initiative[3]. An application for a direction must state the reason for making that application[4], and may be made by sending or delivering a written[5] application to the tribunal[6] or orally during the course of a hearing[7]. Unless the tribunal considers that there is good reason not to do so, it must send written notice of any direction to every party and to any other person[8] affected by the direction[9]; and if a party or any other person sent such notice wishes to challenge the direction, he may do so by applying for another direction which amends, suspends or sets aside the first direction[10].

The tribunal may give a direction[11]:

(1) substituting a party if:
 (a) the wrong person has been named as a party[12]; or
 (b) the substitution has become necessary because of a change of circumstances since the start of proceedings[13];
(2) adding a person to the proceedings as a party[14].

The tribunal may at any time correct any clerical mistake or other accidental slip or omission in a direction or any document produced by it by sending notification of the amended direction, or a copy of the amended document, to all parties[15], and making any necessary amendment to any information published in relation to the direction or document[16].

1 As to the Valuation Tribunal for England see PARA 232. The Valuation Tribunal for England (Council Tax and Rating Appeals) (Procedure) Regulations 2009, SI 2009/2269, apply in relation to England only: see reg 1. As to the equivalent regulations in relation to Wales see the Non-Domestic Rating (Alterations of Lists and Appeals) (Wales) Regulations 2005, SI 2005/758, Pt 5 (regs 21–39); and PARA 257 et seq. As to the meanings of 'England' and 'Wales' see PARA 2 note 16.
2 As to the meaning of 'party' see PARA 243 note 4.
3 Valuation Tribunal for England (Council Tax and Rating Appeals) (Procedure) Regulations 2009, SI 2009/2269, reg 8(1). As to the power of the tribunal to give directions in relation to the conduct or disposal of proceedings see PARA 244.
4 Valuation Tribunal for England (Council Tax and Rating Appeals) (Procedure) Regulations 2009, SI 2009/2269, reg 8(3).
5 As to the meaning of 'written' see PARA 21 note 3.
6 Valuation Tribunal for England (Council Tax and Rating Appeals) (Procedure) Regulations 2009, SI 2009/2269, reg 8(2)(a). As to the service and delivery of documents see reg 15; and PARA 243.
7 Valuation Tribunal for England (Council Tax and Rating Appeals) (Procedure) Regulations 2009, SI 2009/2269, reg 8(2)(b).

8 As to the meaning of 'person' see PARA 11 note 13.
9 Valuation Tribunal for England (Council Tax and Rating Appeals) (Procedure) Regulations 2009, SI 2009/2269, reg 8(4).
10 See the Valuation Tribunal for England (Council Tax and Rating Appeals) (Procedure) Regulations 2009, SI 2009/2269, reg 8(5).
11 If the tribunal gives a direction under the Valuation Tribunal for England (Council Tax and Rating Appeals) (Procedure) Regulations 2009, SI 2009/2269, reg 11(1) or (2), it may give such consequential directions as it considers appropriate: reg 11(3).
12 Valuation Tribunal for England (Council Tax and Rating Appeals) (Procedure) Regulations 2009, SI 2009/2269, reg 11(1)(a).
13 Valuation Tribunal for England (Council Tax and Rating Appeals) (Procedure) Regulations 2009, SI 2009/2269, reg 11(1)(b).
14 Valuation Tribunal for England (Council Tax and Rating Appeals) (Procedure) Regulations 2009, SI 2009/2269, reg 11(2).
15 Valuation Tribunal for England (Council Tax and Rating Appeals) (Procedure) Regulations 2009, SI 2009/2269, reg 39(a). The tribunal must make arrangements for the effect of each correction under reg 39 to be recorded: see reg 41; and PARA 256.
16 Valuation Tribunal for England (Council Tax and Rating Appeals) (Procedure) Regulations 2009, SI 2009/2269, reg 39(b).

246. Striking out proceedings.

The proceedings, or the appropriate part of them, will automatically be struck out if the appellant[1] has failed to comply with a direction[2] that stated that failure by a party[3] to comply with the direction would lead to the striking out of the proceedings or that part of them[4].

The Valuation Tribunal for England[5] must strike out the whole or part of the proceedings if it does not have jurisdiction in relation to the proceedings or that part of them[6]. The tribunal may strike out the whole or a part of the proceedings if:

(1) the appellant has failed to comply with a direction that stated that failure by the appellant to comply with the direction could lead to the striking out of the proceedings or that part of them[7];
(2) the appellant has failed to co-operate with the tribunal to such an extent that it cannot deal with the proceedings fairly and justly[8]; or
(3) the tribunal considers there is no reasonable prospect of the appellant's appeal, or part of it, succeeding[9].

However, the tribunal may not strike out the whole or part of the proceedings under the above powers[10] without first giving the appellant an opportunity to make representations in relation to the proposed striking out[11].

If the proceedings, or part of them, have been struck out in certain of the above circumstances[12], the appellant may apply for the proceedings, or part of them, to be reinstated[13].

The above provisions apply to a party to the proceedings other than the appellant as they apply to an appellant with certain exceptions[14].

1 As to the meaning of 'appellant' see PARA 243 note 4. As to appeals in relation to non-domestic rating see PARA 242.
2 As to the power of the tribunal to give directions in relation to the conduct or disposal of proceedings see PARA 244. As to directions generally see PARA 245. As to directions relating to evidence and information see PARA 248.
3 As to the meaning of 'party' see PARA 243 note 4.
4 Valuation Tribunal for England (Council Tax and Rating Appeals) (Procedure) Regulations 2009, SI 2009/2269, reg 10(1). The Valuation Tribunal for England (Council Tax and Rating Appeals) (Procedure) Regulations 2009, SI 2009/2269, apply in relation to England only: see reg 1. As to the equivalent regulations in relation to Wales see the Non-Domestic Rating (Alterations of Lists and Appeals) (Wales) Regulations 2005, SI 2005/758, Pt 5 (regs 21–39); and PARA 257 et seq. As to the meanings of 'England' and 'Wales' see PARA 2 note 16.

5 As to the Valuation Tribunal for England see PARA 232.
6 Valuation Tribunal for England (Council Tax and Rating Appeals) (Procedure) Regulations 2009, SI 2009/2269, reg 10(2). As to the jurisdiction of the tribunal see PARA 232.
7 Valuation Tribunal for England (Council Tax and Rating Appeals) (Procedure) Regulations 2009, SI 2009/2269, reg 10(3)(a).
8 Valuation Tribunal for England (Council Tax and Rating Appeals) (Procedure) Regulations 2009, SI 2009/2269, reg 10(3)(b).
9 Valuation Tribunal for England (Council Tax and Rating Appeals) (Procedure) Regulations 2009, SI 2009/2269, reg 10(3)(c).
10 Ie under the Valuation Tribunal for England (Council Tax and Rating Appeals) (Procedure) Regulations 2009, SI 2009/2269, reg 10(2) or reg 10(3)(b) or (c): see the text to notes 5–6, 8–9.
11 Valuation Tribunal for England (Council Tax and Rating Appeals) (Procedure) Regulations 2009, SI 2009/2269, reg 10(4).
12 Ie under the Valuation Tribunal for England (Council Tax and Rating Appeals) (Procedure) Regulations 2009, SI 2009/2269, reg 10(1) or (3)(a): see the text to notes 1–4, 7.
13 Valuation Tribunal for England (Council Tax and Rating Appeals) (Procedure) Regulations 2009, SI 2009/2269, reg 10(5). An application must be made in writing and received by the tribunal within one month after the date on which it sent notification of the striking out to the appellant: reg 10(6). As to the meaning of 'month' see PARA 11 note 1. As to the meaning of 'writing' see PARA 21 note 3. As to the service and delivery of documents see reg 15; and PARA 243.
14 The Valuation Tribunal for England (Council Tax and Rating Appeals) (Procedure) Regulations 2009, SI 2009/2269, reg 10 applies to a party to the proceedings other than the appellant as it applies to an appellant except that:
   (1) a reference to the striking out of the proceedings is to be read as a reference to the barring of that other party from taking further part in the proceedings (reg 10(7)(a)); and
   (2) a reference to an application for the reinstatement of proceedings which have been struck out is to be read as a reference to an application for the lifting of the bar on that other party from taking further part in the proceedings (reg 10(7)(b)).

   If a party other than the appellant has been barred from taking further part in the proceedings under reg 10 and that bar has not been lifted, the tribunal need not consider any response or other submission made by that party: reg 10(8).

247. Representatives.

A party[1] may appoint a representative (whether a legal representative or not) to represent that party in the proceedings[2], but the representative must not be a member of the Valuation Tribunal for England[3] or the Valuation Tribunal Service[4] or an employee of the Valuation Tribunal Service[5]. If a party appoints a representative, that party (or the representative if the representative is a legal representative) must send or deliver to the tribunal written notice[6] of the representative's name and address unless the representative's name and address have already been given to the valuation officer[7]. If the tribunal receives such notice that a party has appointed a representative, it must send a copy of that notice to each other party[8]. A person[9] who receives due notice of the appointment of a representative must provide to the representative any document which is required to be provided to the represented party, and need not provide that document to the represented party[10]; and may assume that the representative is and remains authorised as such until he receives written notification that this is not so from the representative or the represented party[11].

Anything permitted or required to be done by a party[12] or a direction[13] may be done by the representative of that party, except signing a witness statement[14]. At a hearing a party may be accompanied by another person, other than a member of the tribunal or the Valuation Tribunal Service or an employee of that service, whose name and address has not been notified[15] to the tribunal; and that person may act as a representative or otherwise assist in presenting the party's case at the hearing[16].

1 As to the meaning of 'party' see PARA 243 note 4.

2 As to appeals in relation to non-domestic rating see PARA 242.
3 As to membership of the Valuation Tribunal for England see PARA 233.
4 As to the Valuation Tribunal Service see PARA 241.
5 Valuation Tribunal for England (Council Tax and Rating Appeals) (Procedure) Regulations 2009, SI 2009/2269, reg 13(1). The Valuation Tribunal for England (Council Tax and Rating Appeals) (Procedure) Regulations 2009, SI 2009/2269, apply in relation to England only: see reg 1. As to the equivalent regulations in relation to Wales see the Non-Domestic Rating (Alterations of Lists and Appeals) (Wales) Regulations 2005, SI 2005/758, Pt 5 (regs 21–39); and PARA 257 et seq. As to the meanings of 'England' and 'Wales' see PARA 2 note 16.
6 As to the meaning of 'written' see PARA 21 note 3. As to the service and delivery of documents see PARA 243.
7 Valuation Tribunal for England (Council Tax and Rating Appeals) (Procedure) Regulations 2009, SI 2009/2269, reg 13(2). As to valuation officers see PARA 54.
8 Valuation Tribunal for England (Council Tax and Rating Appeals) (Procedure) Regulations 2009, SI 2009/2269, reg 13(3).
9 As to the meaning of 'person' see PARA 11 note 13.
10 Valuation Tribunal for England (Council Tax and Rating Appeals) (Procedure) Regulations 2009, SI 2009/2269, reg 13(5)(a).
11 Valuation Tribunal for England (Council Tax and Rating Appeals) (Procedure) Regulations 2009, SI 2009/2269, reg 13(5)(b).
12 Ie under the Valuation Tribunal for England (Council Tax and Rating Appeals) (Procedure) Regulations 2009, SI 2009/2269.
13 As to the power of the tribunal to give directions in relation to the conduct or disposal of proceedings see PARA 244. As to directions generally see PARA 245. As to directions relating to evidence and information see PARA 248.
14 Valuation Tribunal for England (Council Tax and Rating Appeals) (Procedure) Regulations 2009, SI 2009/2269, reg 13(4). As to witness statements see PARA 248.
15 Ie under the Valuation Tribunal for England (Council Tax and Rating Appeals) (Procedure) Regulations 2009, SI 2009/2269, reg 13(2): see the text to notes 6–7.
16 Valuation Tribunal for England (Council Tax and Rating Appeals) (Procedure) Regulations 2009, SI 2009/2269, reg 13(6). Regulation 13(2)–(5) (see the text to notes 6–14) does not apply in relation to a person who accompanies a party under reg 13(6): reg 13(7).

248. Evidence and submissions.

The Valuation Tribunal for England[1] may make an order[2] prohibiting the disclosure or publication of:

(1) specified documents or information relating to the proceedings[3]; or
(2) any matter likely to lead members of the public to identify any person[4] whom the tribunal considers should not be identified[5].

The tribunal may give a direction prohibiting the disclosure of information to a person if it is satisfied that such disclosure would be likely to cause that person or some other person serious harm[6], and it is satisfied, having regard to the interests of justice, that it is proportionate to give such a direction[7]. The tribunal must conduct proceedings as appropriate in order to give effect to such a direction[8].

The tribunal may[9] give directions as to:

(a) issues on which it requires evidence or submissions[10];
(b) the nature of the evidence or submissions it requires[11];
(c) whether any parties are permitted or required to provide expert evidence[12];
(d) any limit on the number of witnesses whose evidence a party may put forward, whether in relation to a particular issue or generally[13];
(e) the manner in which any evidence or submissions are to be provided, which may include a direction for them to be given orally at a hearing[14] or by written[15] submissions or witness statement[16]; and
(f) the time at which any evidence or submissions are to be provided[17].

The tribunal may[18]:

(i) admit evidence whether or not the evidence would be admissible in a civil trial in England[19]; or
(ii) exclude evidence that would otherwise be admissible where the evidence was not provided within the time allowed by a direction[20], or the evidence was otherwise provided in a manner that did not comply with a direction[21], or it would otherwise be unfair to admit the evidence[22].

Certain information[23] must not be used in any relevant proceedings[24] by a billing authority[25] or a valuation officer[26] unless:
(A) not less than two weeks' notice[27], specifying in relation to any information to be so used the documents or other media in or on which that information is held and the hereditament[28] to which it relates, has previously been given to every other party to the proceedings[29];
(B) any person who has given not less than 24 hours' notice of his intention to do so has been permitted, at any reasonable time to inspect the documents or other media in or on which such information is held[30] and to make a copy (other than a photographic copy) of, or of any extract from, any document containing such information[31]; and
(C) for an appeal relating to the alteration of a valuation list[32], the information relates to a matter included in the notice of appeal or any document accompanying the notice of appeal, or in new or further evidence admitted[33].

The contents of a central non-domestic rating list or a local non-domestic rating list[34] may be proved by the production of a copy of it, or of the relevant part, purporting to be certified to be a true copy by the valuation officer[35]. The contents of a completion notice[36] may be proved by the production of a copy of it purporting to be certified to be a true copy by the proper officer of the relevant authority[37].

1 As to the Valuation Tribunal for England see PARA 232. The Valuation Tribunal for England (Council Tax and Rating Appeals) (Procedure) Regulations 2009, SI 2009/2269, apply in relation to England only: see reg 1. As to the equivalent regulations in relation to Wales see the Non-Domestic Rating (Alterations of Lists and Appeals) (Wales) Regulations 2005, SI 2005/758, Pt 5 (regs 21–39); and PARA 257 et seq. As to the meanings of 'England' and 'Wales' see PARA 2 note 16.
2 As to the correction of errors in an order see PARA 254.
3 Valuation Tribunal for England (Council Tax and Rating Appeals) (Procedure) Regulations 2009, SI 2009/2269, reg 16(1)(a). As to appeals in relation to non-domestic rating see PARA 242.
4 As to the meaning of 'person' see PARA 11 note 13.
5 Valuation Tribunal for England (Council Tax and Rating Appeals) (Procedure) Regulations 2009, SI 2009/2269, reg 16(1)(b).
6 Valuation Tribunal for England (Council Tax and Rating Appeals) (Procedure) Regulations 2009, SI 2009/2269, reg 16(2)(a).
7 Valuation Tribunal for England (Council Tax and Rating Appeals) (Procedure) Regulations 2009, SI 2009/2269, reg 16(2)(b). If a party ('the first party') considers that the tribunal should give such a direction prohibiting the disclosure of information to another party ('the second party'), the first party must:
(1) exclude the relevant document or information from any documents that will be provided to the second party (reg 16(3)(a)); and
(2) provide to the tribunal the excluded document or information, and the reason for its exclusion, so that the tribunal may decide whether the document or information should be disclosed to the second party or should be the subject of a direction under reg 16(2) (reg 16(3)(b)).

As to the meaning of 'party' see PARA 243 note 4.

If the tribunal gives a direction under reg 16(2) which prevents disclosure to a party who has appointed a representative, the tribunal may give a direction that the documents or information be disclosed to that representative if it is satisfied that:
(a) disclosure to the representative would be in the interests of the party (reg 16(5)(a)); and

(b) the representative will act in accordance with reg 16(6) (reg 16(5)(b)).

Documents or information disclosed to a representative in accordance with a direction under reg 16(5) must not be disclosed either directly or indirectly to any other person without the tribunal's consent: reg 16(6). As to representatives see PARA 247. As to the correction of errors in directions see PARA 245.

8 Valuation Tribunal for England (Council Tax and Rating Appeals) (Procedure) Regulations 2009, SI 2009/2269, reg 16(4).

9 The tribunal's power under the Valuation Tribunal for England (Council Tax and Rating Appeals) (Procedure) Regulations 2009, SI 2009/2269, reg 17(1) is subject to reg 17(1A): reg 17(1) (reg 17(1) amended, reg 17(1A) added, by SI 2017/156). The tribunal may only direct a party to an appeal under the Non-Domestic Rating (Alteration of Lists and Appeals) (England) Regulations 2009, SI 2009/2268, reg 13A (see PARA 211) to provide evidence or submissions that relate to a matter included in:

(1) the notice of appeal or any document accompanying the notice of appeal (Valuation Tribunal for England (Council Tax and Rating Appeals) (Procedure) Regulations 2009, SI 2009/2269, reg 17(1A)(a) (as so added)); or

(2) new or further evidence admitted under reg 17A (reg 17(1A)(b) (as so added)).

On an appeal under the Non-Domestic Rating (Alteration of Lists and Appeals) (England) Regulations 2009, SI 2009/2268, reg 13A, the tribunal may only admit evidence that was not included in the notice of appeal or any document accompanying the notice of appeal ('new evidence') if:

(a) that evidence is provided by a party to the appeal, relates to the ground on which the proposal was made; and was not known to the party and could not reasonably have been acquired by the party before the proposal was determined under Pt 2 (regs 3–17) (Valuation Tribunal for England (Council Tax and Rating Appeals) (Procedure) Regulations 2009, SI 2009/2269, reg 17A(1)(a) (reg 17A added by SI 2017/156)); or

(b) all the parties to the appeal agree in writing to the party providing the new evidence (reg 17A(1)(b) (as so added)).

If the tribunal admits so new evidence, it may admit further evidence provided by another party to the appeal if the further evidence specifically relates to the new evidence and the ground on which the proposal was made: reg 17A(2) (as so added). A party which provides evidence under reg 17A(1) or (2) must also provide that evidence to all the other parties to the appeal: reg 17A(3) (as so added).

10 Valuation Tribunal for England (Council Tax and Rating Appeals) (Procedure) Regulations 2009, SI 2009/2269, reg 17(1)(a).

11 Valuation Tribunal for England (Council Tax and Rating Appeals) (Procedure) Regulations 2009, SI 2009/2269, reg 17(1)(b).

12 Valuation Tribunal for England (Council Tax and Rating Appeals) (Procedure) Regulations 2009, SI 2009/2269, reg 17(1)(c).

13 Valuation Tribunal for England (Council Tax and Rating Appeals) (Procedure) Regulations 2009, SI 2009/2269, reg 17(1)(d).

14 Valuation Tribunal for England (Council Tax and Rating Appeals) (Procedure) Regulations 2009, SI 2009/2269, reg 17(1)(e)(i).

15 As to the meaning of 'written' see PARA 21 note 3.

16 Valuation Tribunal for England (Council Tax and Rating Appeals) (Procedure) Regulations 2009, SI 2009/2269, reg 17(1)(e)(ii).

17 Valuation Tribunal for England (Council Tax and Rating Appeals) (Procedure) Regulations 2009, SI 2009/2269, reg 17(1)(f). As to the calculation of time generally see reg 14; and PARA 243.

18 The tribunal's power under the Valuation Tribunal for England (Council Tax and Rating Appeals) (Procedure) Regulations 2009, SI 2009/2269, reg 17(2) is subject to reg 17A (see note 9): reg 17(2) (amended by SI 2017/156).

19 Valuation Tribunal for England (Council Tax and Rating Appeals) (Procedure) Regulations 2009, SI 2009/2269, reg 17(2)(a). As to evidence in civil proceedings see CIVIL PROCEDURE vol 12 (2015) PARA 685 et seq.

20 Valuation Tribunal for England (Council Tax and Rating Appeals) (Procedure) Regulations 2009, SI 2009/2269, reg 17(2)(b)(i).

21 Valuation Tribunal for England (Council Tax and Rating Appeals) (Procedure) Regulations 2009, SI 2009/2269, reg 17(2)(b)(ii).

22 Valuation Tribunal for England (Council Tax and Rating Appeals) (Procedure) Regulations 2009, SI 2009/2269, reg 17(2)(b)(iii).

23 The Valuation Tribunal for England (Council Tax and Rating Appeals) (Procedure) Regulations 2009, SI 2009/2269, reg 17(4) applies to:

(1) information supplied in pursuance of the Local Government Finance Act 1988 Sch 9 para 5 (see PARA 226) or the Non-Domestic Rating (Alteration of Lists and Appeals) (England) Regulations 2009, SI 2009/2268, reg 24 (see PARA 227) (Valuation Tribunal for England (Council Tax and Rating Appeals) (Procedure) Regulations 2009, SI 2009/2269, reg 17(3)(a)(i), (iv) (reg 17(3)(a) substituted by SI 2011/434; and amended by SI 2013/465)); and

(2) information contained in:

(a) any document which, having been produced to the Commissioners for Her Majesty's Revenue and Customs in pursuance of the Finance Act 1931 s 28 or furnished to them in pursuance of Sch 2 to that Act, is for the time being in their possession or under their control (Valuation Tribunal for England (Council Tax and Rating Appeals) (Procedure) Regulations 2009, SI 2009/2269, reg 17(3)(b)(i)); or

(b) any land transaction return within the meaning of the Finance Act 2003 Pt 4 (ss 42–124) (stamp duty land tax) (Valuation Tribunal for England (Council Tax and Rating Appeals) (Procedure) Regulations 2009, SI 2009/2269, reg 17(3)(b)(ii)).

24 In the Valuation Tribunal for England (Council Tax and Rating Appeals) (Procedure) Regulations 2009, SI 2009/2269, reg 17(4) and (8) (see note 29), 'relevant proceedings' means any proceedings on or in consequence of an appeal under the Non-Domestic Rating (Alteration of Lists and Appeals) (England) Regulations 2009, SI 2009/2268 (see PARA 242) and any proceedings on or in consequence of a reference to arbitration under the Valuation Tribunal for England (Council Tax and Rating Appeals) (Procedure) Regulations 2009, SI 2009/2269, reg 4 (see PARA 268): reg 17(11).

25 As to the meaning of 'billing authority' see PARA 53.

26 As to valuation officers see PARA 54.

27 As to the service and delivery of documents see PARA 243.

28 As to the meaning of 'hereditament' see PARA 106.

29 See the Valuation Tribunal for England (Council Tax and Rating Appeals) (Procedure) Regulations 2009, SI 2009/2269, reg 17(4)(a). Subject to reg 17(7), any person to whom notice relating to any hereditament has been given under reg 17(4)(a) ('P') may before the hearing serve notice on the valuation officer specifying other hereditaments as being hereditaments which are comparable in character or otherwise relevant to P's case, and requiring the valuation officer:

(1) to permit P at any reasonable time specified in the notice to inspect and (if P so desires) to make a copy (other than a photographic copy) of, or of any extract from, any document containing information to which reg 17(4) applies (see note 23) which relates to those other hereditaments and is in the possession of the valuation officer (see reg 17(6)(a)); and

(2) to produce at the hearing or to submit to the tribunal such documents as before the hearing P has informed the valuation officer that P requires (reg 17(6)(b)).

On an appeal under the Non-Domestic Rating (Alteration of Lists and Appeals) (England) Regulations 2009, SI 2009/2268, reg 13A (see PARA 211), the tribunal may only admit as evidence documents produced or submitted under head (2) that relate to a matter included in:

(a) the notice of appeal or any document accompanying the notice of appeal (Valuation Tribunal for England (Council Tax and Rating Appeals) (Procedure) Regulations 2009, SI 2009/2269, reg 17(6A)(a) (reg 17(6A) added by SI 2017/156)); or

(b) new or further evidence admitted under the Valuation Tribunal for England (Council Tax and Rating Appeals) (Procedure) Regulations 2009, SI 2009/2269, reg 17A (see note 9) (reg 17(6A)(b) (as so added)).

The number of hereditaments specified in a notice under reg 17(6) must not exceed four or, if greater, the number specified in the notice under reg 17(4)(a): reg 17(7). Nothing in reg 17(6) is to be construed as requiring the making available for inspection or copying, or the production of, any document in so far as it contains information other than information which is reasonably required for the purposes of the relevant proceedings: reg 17(8).

Where P has given notice to the valuation officer under reg 17(6), and the valuation officer refuses or fails to comply with the notice, P may apply to the tribunal or, as the case may be, the arbitrator appointed to determine the appeal; and the tribunal or the arbitrator may, if satisfied that it is reasonable to do so, direct the valuation officer to comply with the notice as respects all the hereditaments or such of them as the tribunal or the arbitrator may determine: reg 17(9). If any document required to be made available for inspection in accordance with reg 17(6) is not maintained in documentary form, the duty to make it so available is satisfied if a print-out, photographic image or other reproduction of the document which has been obtained from the storage medium adopted in relation to the document is made available for inspection: reg 17(10).

30 Valuation Tribunal for England (Council Tax and Rating Appeals) (Procedure) Regulations 2009, SI 2009/2269, reg 17(4)(b)(i).

31 Valuation Tribunal for England (Council Tax and Rating Appeals) (Procedure) Regulations 2009, SI 2009/2269, reg 17(4)(b)(ii).

32 Ie an appeal under the Non-Domestic Rating (Alteration of Lists and Appeals) (England) Regulations 2009, SI 2009/2268, reg 13A: see PARA 211.

33 Valuation Tribunal for England (Council Tax and Rating Appeals) (Procedure) Regulations 2009, SI 2009/2269, reg 17(4)(c) (added by SI 2017/156). The text refers to new or further evidence admitted under the Valuation Tribunal for England (Council Tax and Rating Appeals) (Procedure) Regulations 2009, SI 2009/2269, r 17A (see note 9).

34 As to central non-domestic rating lists see PARA 196 et seq. As to local non-domestic rating lists see PARA 191 et seq.

35 See the Valuation Tribunal for England (Council Tax and Rating Appeals) (Procedure) Regulations 2009, SI 2009/2269, reg 17(12).

36 As to the meaning of 'completion notice' see PARA 243 note 4.

37 Valuation Tribunal for England (Council Tax and Rating Appeals) (Procedure) Regulations 2009, SI 2009/2269, reg 17(13). As to the meaning of 'relevant authority' see PARA 243 note 4.

249. Summoning of witnesses and orders to answer questions or produce documents.

On the application of a party[1] or on its own initiative, the Valuation Tribunal for England[2] may:

(1) by summons require any person[3] to attend as a witness at a hearing at the time and place specified in the summons[4];

(2) order any person to answer any questions or produce any documents in that person's possession or control which relate to any issue in the proceedings[5].

Any such summons or order must:

(a) state that the person on whom the requirement is imposed may apply to the tribunal to vary or set aside the summons or order if he has not had an opportunity to object to it[6]; and

(b) state the consequences of failure to comply with the summons or order[7].

A summons under head (1) above must give the person required to attend 14 days' notice of the hearing or such shorter period as the tribunal may direct[8], and, where the person is not a party, make provision for the person's necessary expenses of attendance to be paid, and state who is to pay them[9].

No person may be compelled to give any evidence or produce any document that the person could not be compelled to give or produce on a trial of an action in a court of law in England[10].

These provisions are modified in relation to a non-domestic rating appeal[11]. In such an appeal:

(i) the tribunal may only issue a summons under head (1) requiring a person to attend a hearing as a witness in relation to[12];

(ii) the tribunal may only order a person under head (2) above to answer questions in relation to[13]; and

(iii) the tribunal may only order a person under head (2) above to produce documents that relate to[14],

matters included in:

(A) the notice of appeal or any document accompanying the notice of appeal[15];

(B) evidence or submissions provided in accordance with a direction[16] by the tribunal[17];

(C) specified information[18] which is used in the proceedings by the valuation officer[19];

(D) evidence admitted[20] as relating to comparable hereditaments[21]; or

(E) new or further evidence admitted[22] in prescribed circumstances[23].

1 As to the meaning of 'party' see PARA 243 note 4.

2 As to the Valuation Tribunal for England see PARA 232. The Valuation Tribunal for England (Council Tax and Rating Appeals) (Procedure) Regulations 2009, SI 2009/2269, apply in relation to England only: see reg 1. As to the equivalent regulations in relation to Wales see the Non-Domestic Rating (Alterations of Lists and Appeals) (Wales) Regulations 2005, SI 2005/758, Pt 5 (regs 21–39); and PARA 257 et seq. As to the meanings of 'England' and 'Wales' see PARA 2 note 16.

3 As to the meaning of 'person' see PARA 11 note 13.

4 Valuation Tribunal for England (Council Tax and Rating Appeals) (Procedure) Regulations 2009, SI 2009/2269, reg 18(1)(a). As to the service and delivery of documents see reg 15; and PARA 243. As to appeals in relation to non-domestic rating see PARA 242.

5 Valuation Tribunal for England (Council Tax and Rating Appeals) (Procedure) Regulations 2009, SI 2009/2269, reg 18(1)(b).

6 Valuation Tribunal for England (Council Tax and Rating Appeals) (Procedure) Regulations 2009, SI 2009/2269, reg 18(4)(a).

7 Valuation Tribunal for England (Council Tax and Rating Appeals) (Procedure) Regulations 2009, SI 2009/2269, reg 18(4)(b).

8 Valuation Tribunal for England (Council Tax and Rating Appeals) (Procedure) Regulations 2009, SI 2009/2269, reg 18(2)(a). As to the calculation of time see reg 14; and PARA 243.

9 Valuation Tribunal for England (Council Tax and Rating Appeals) (Procedure) Regulations 2009, SI 2009/2269, reg 18(2)(b).

10 Valuation Tribunal for England (Council Tax and Rating Appeals) (Procedure) Regulations 2009, SI 2009/2269, reg 18(3). As to evidence in civil proceedings see CIVIL PROCEDURE vol 12 (2015) PARA 685 et seq. As to the production of documents in civil proceedings see CIVIL PROCEDURE vol 12 (2015) PARA 621 et seq.

11 Ie an appeal under the Non-Domestic Rating (Alteration of Lists and Appeals) (England) Regulations 2009, SI 2009/2268, reg 13A (see PARA 211): Valuation Tribunal for England (Council Tax and Rating Appeals) (Procedure) Regulations 2009, SI 2009/2269, regs 18(A1), 18A(1) (regs 18(A1), 18A added by SI 2017/156).

12 Valuation Tribunal for England (Council Tax and Rating Appeals) (Procedure) Regulations 2009, SI 2009/2269, reg 18A(2) (as added: see note 11).

13 Valuation Tribunal for England (Council Tax and Rating Appeals) (Procedure) Regulations 2009, SI 2009/2269, reg 18A(3) (as added: see note 11).

14 Valuation Tribunal for England (Council Tax and Rating Appeals) (Procedure) Regulations 2009, SI 2009/2269, reg 18A(4) (as added: see note 11).

15 Valuation Tribunal for England (Council Tax and Rating Appeals) (Procedure) Regulations 2009, SI 2009/2269, reg 18A(2)(a), (3)(a), (4)(a) (as added: see note 11).

16 Ie under the Valuation Tribunal for England (Council Tax and Rating Appeals) (Procedure) Regulations 2009, SI 2009/2269, reg 17(1): see PARA 248.

17 Valuation Tribunal for England (Council Tax and Rating Appeals) (Procedure) Regulations 2009, SI 2009/2269, reg 18A(2)(b), (3)(b), (4)(b) (as added: see note 11).

18 Ie to which the Valuation Tribunal for England (Council Tax and Rating Appeals) (Procedure) Regulations 2009, SI 2009/2269, reg 17(4) applies: see PARA 248.

19 Valuation Tribunal for England (Council Tax and Rating Appeals) (Procedure) Regulations 2009, SI 2009/2269, reg 18A(2)(c), (3)(c), (4)(c) (as added: see note 11).

20 Ie under the Valuation Tribunal for England (Council Tax and Rating Appeals) (Procedure) Regulations 2009, SI 2009/2269, reg 17(6A): see PARA 248. As to valuation officers see PARA 54.

21 Valuation Tribunal for England (Council Tax and Rating Appeals) (Procedure) Regulations 2009, SI 2009/2269, reg 18A(2)(d), (3)(d), (4)(d) (as added: see note 11).

22 Ie under the Valuation Tribunal for England (Council Tax and Rating Appeals) (Procedure) Regulations 2009, SI 2009/2269, reg 17A: see PARA 248.

23 Valuation Tribunal for England (Council Tax and Rating Appeals) (Procedure) Regulations 2009, SI 2009/2269, reg 18A(2)(e), (3)(e), (4)(e) (as added: see note 11).

250. Withdrawals and deemed withdrawals of appeals.

An appeal[1] may be withdrawn[2]:

(1) at any time before a hearing[3] to consider the disposal of the proceedings (or, if the Valuation Tribunal for England[4] disposes of the proceedings without a hearing, before that disposal) where notice to that effect is given[5] to the tribunal by:

 (a) in the case of an appeal against a completion notice[6] or an appeal[7] against a penalty, the appellant[8] in writing[9]; or

 (b) in any other case the appellant[10]; or

(2) orally at a hearing by the appellant[11].

Where a party has withdrawn its appeal any other party to the appeal may apply to the tribunal for the appeal to be reinstated[12].

Where, after an appeal has been made[13] to the tribunal in relation to a disagreement as to a proposed alteration of a list, the valuation officer alters the list in accordance with the proposal to which the appeal relates, the valuation officer must notify the tribunal of that fact; and the appeal must be treated as withdrawn on the date on which the notice is served on the tribunal[14]. Where, following the initiation of an appeal against imposition of a penalty[15], the valuation officer decides to remit the penalty, he must notify the tribunal of that fact; and the appeal must be treated as withdrawn on the date on which the notice is served on the tribunal[16].

1 As to appeals in relation to non-domestic rating see PARA 242.

2 As to the striking out of proceedings see PARA 246.

3 As to hearings see PARA 251.

4 As to the Valuation Tribunal for England see PARA 232. The Valuation Tribunal for England (Council Tax and Rating Appeals) (Procedure) Regulations 2009, SI 2009/2269, apply in relation to England only: see reg 1. As to the equivalent regulations in relation to Wales see the Non-Domestic Rating (Alterations of Lists and Appeals) (Wales) Regulations 2005, SI 2005/758, Pt 5 (regs 21–39); and PARA 257 et seq. As to the meanings of 'England' and 'Wales' see PARA 2 note 16.

5 As to the service and delivery of documents see PARA 243.

6 As to the meaning of 'completion notice' see PARA 243 note 4.

7 Ie under the Local Government Finance Act 1988 Sch 9 para 5C: see PARA 226.

8 As to the meaning of 'appellant' see PARA 243 note 4.

9 Valuation Tribunal for England (Council Tax and Rating Appeals) (Procedure) Regulations 2009, SI 2009/2269, reg 19A(1), (2)(a)(i) (reg 19A added by SI 2011/434). The tribunal must notify each party in writing of a withdrawal under the Valuation Tribunal for England (Council Tax and Rating Appeals) (Procedure) Regulations 2009, SI 2009/2269, reg 19A(2): reg 19A(3) (as so added; substituted by SI 2017/156). As to the meaning of 'writing' see PARA 21 note 3. Under previous legislation it was decided that once an appeal is validly withdrawn, the tribunal has no jurisdiction to determine it: *R v East Norfolk Local Valuation Court, ex p Martin* [1951] 1 All ER 743, 49 LGR 627.

10 Tribunal for England (Council Tax and Rating Appeals) (Procedure) Regulations 2009, SI 2009/2269, reg 19A(1), (2)(a)(ii) (as added (see note 9); reg 19A(2)(a)(ii) amended by SI 2017/156). The tribunal must notify each party in writing of a withdrawal under reg 19A(2): reg 19A(3) (as substituted (see note 9)).

11 Valuation Tribunal for England (Council Tax and Rating Appeals) (Procedure) Regulations 2009, SI 2009/2269, reg 19A(1), (2)(b) (as added: see note 9). The tribunal must notify each party in writing of a withdrawal under reg 19A(2): reg 19A(3) (as substituted (see note 9)).

Where a party gives notice of withdrawal at a hearing, the notice of withdrawal does not take effect unless the tribunal panel consents to the withdrawal: reg 19A(4) (as so added). 'Tribunal panel', in relation to an appeal, means the members of the Valuation Tribunal for England selected to deal with the appeal in accordance with tribunal business arrangements: see reg 2(1). As to tribunal business arrangements see PARA 234.

12 Valuation Tribunal for England (Council Tax and Rating Appeals) (Procedure) Regulations 2009, SI 2009/2269, reg 19A(5) (as added (see note 9); amended by SI 2017/156). An application under the Tribunal for England (Council Tax and Rating Appeals) (Procedure) Regulations 2009, SI 2009/2269, reg 19A(5) must be made in writing and be received by the tribunal within one month after:

(1) the date on which the tribunal notifies each party under reg 19A(3) (see notes 9–11) of the withdrawal of the appeal (reg 19A(6)(a) (as so added; substituted by SI 2017/156)); or

(2) the date of the hearing at which the appeal was withdrawn orally under the Tribunal for England (Council Tax and Rating Appeals) (Procedure) Regulations 2009, SI 2009/2269, reg 19A(2)(b) (see the text to note 11) (reg 19A(6)(b) (as so added)).

As to the meaning of 'month' see PARA 11 note 1.

13 Ie under the Non-Domestic Rating (Alteration of Lists and Appeals) (England) Regulations 2009, SI 2009/2268, reg 13A: see PARA 211.

14 Valuation Tribunal for England (Council Tax and Rating Appeals) (Procedure) Regulations 2009, SI 2009/2269, reg 19A(7) (as added (see note 9); amended by SI 2017/156). As to valuation officers see PARA 54.

15 Ie an appeal under the Local Government Finance Act 1988 Sch 9 para 5C: see PARA 226.

16 Valuation Tribunal for England (Council Tax and Rating Appeals) (Procedure) Regulations 2009, SI 2009/2269, reg 19A(8) (as added: see note 9).

251. Hearings.

The Valuation Tribunal for England[1] must hold a hearing before making a decision which disposes of proceedings[2] unless each party has consented to, or has not objected to, the matter being decided without a hearing[3] and the tribunal considers that it is able to decide the matter without a hearing[4]. However, the tribunal may in any event dispose of proceedings without a hearing by striking out[5] the proceedings[6].

The tribunal must give each party entitled to attend a hearing reasonable notice[7] of the time and place of the hearing (including any adjourned or postponed hearing) and any changes to the time and place of the hearing[8]. All hearings must be held in public[9]; but the tribunal or tribunal panel may give a direction[10] that a hearing, or part of it, is to be held in private[11].

Where the tribunal or tribunal panel considers:

(1) that the conduct of any person is likely to disrupt the hearing[12];

(2) that the presence of any person is likely to prevent another person from giving evidence or making submissions freely[13]; or

(3) that the presence of any person is likely to defeat the purpose of the hearing[14],

the tribunal or tribunal panel (as the case may be) may give a direction excluding the person from any hearing, or part of it[15]. The tribunal panel may give a direction excluding from any hearing, or part of it any person whose conduct the panel considers is disrupting the hearing[16]. The tribunal or the tribunal panel may give a direction excluding a witness from a hearing until that witness gives evidence[17].

If a party fails to attend a hearing the tribunal panel may proceed with the hearing if:

(a) it is satisfied that the party has been notified of the hearing or that reasonable steps have been taken to notify the party of the hearing[18]; and

(b) it considers that it is in the interests of justice to proceed with the hearing[19].

1 As to the Valuation Tribunal for England see PARA 232. The Valuation Tribunal for England (Council Tax and Rating Appeals) (Procedure) Regulations 2009, SI 2009/2269, apply in relation

to England only: see reg 1. As to the equivalent regulations in relation to Wales see the Non-Domestic Rating (Alterations of Lists and Appeals) (Wales) Regulations 2005, SI 2005/758, Pt 5 (regs 21–39); and PARA 257 et seq. As to the meanings of 'England' and 'Wales' see PARA 2 note 16.

2 Valuation Tribunal for England (Council Tax and Rating Appeals) (Procedure) Regulations 2009, SI 2009/2269, reg 29(1).

3 Valuation Tribunal for England (Council Tax and Rating Appeals) (Procedure) Regulations 2009, SI 2009/2269, reg 29(1)(a). As to the meaning of 'party' see PARA 243 note 4.

4 Valuation Tribunal for England (Council Tax and Rating Appeals) (Procedure) Regulations 2009, SI 2009/2269, reg 29(1)(b).

5 Ie under the Valuation Tribunal for England (Council Tax and Rating Appeals) (Procedure) Regulations 2009, SI 2009/2269, reg 10: see PARA 246.

6 See the Valuation Tribunal for England (Council Tax and Rating Appeals) (Procedure) Regulations 2009, SI 2009/2269, reg 29(2).

7 As to the service and delivery of documents see PARA 243.

8 Valuation Tribunal for England (Council Tax and Rating Appeals) (Procedure) Regulations 2009, SI 2009/2269, reg 30(1). The period of notice must be at least 14 days except that the tribunal may give shorter notice with the parties' consent (reg 30(2)(a)), or in urgent or exceptional circumstances (reg 30(2)(b)).

9 Valuation Tribunal for England (Council Tax and Rating Appeals) (Procedure) Regulations 2009, SI 2009/2269, reg 31(1).

10 As to the correction of errors in directions see PARA 245.

11 Valuation Tribunal for England (Council Tax and Rating Appeals) (Procedure) Regulations 2009, SI 2009/2269, reg 31(2). Where a hearing, or part of it, is to be held in private, the tribunal or tribunal panel may determine who is permitted to attend the hearing or part of it: reg 31(3). As to the meaning of 'tribunal panel' see PARA 250 note 11.

12 Valuation Tribunal for England (Council Tax and Rating Appeals) (Procedure) Regulations 2009, SI 2009/2269, reg 31(4)(a).

13 Valuation Tribunal for England (Council Tax and Rating Appeals) (Procedure) Regulations 2009, SI 2009/2269, reg 31(4)(b).

14 Valuation Tribunal for England (Council Tax and Rating Appeals) (Procedure) Regulations 2009, SI 2009/2269, reg 31(4)(c).

15 Valuation Tribunal for England (Council Tax and Rating Appeals) (Procedure) Regulations 2009, SI 2009/2269, reg 31(4).

16 Valuation Tribunal for England (Council Tax and Rating Appeals) (Procedure) Regulations 2009, SI 2009/2269, reg 31(5).

17 Valuation Tribunal for England (Council Tax and Rating Appeals) (Procedure) Regulations 2009, SI 2009/2269, reg 31(6). As to evidence and witnesses see PARAS 248, 249.

18 Valuation Tribunal for England (Council Tax and Rating Appeals) (Procedure) Regulations 2009, SI 2009/2269, reg 32(a).

19 Valuation Tribunal for England (Council Tax and Rating Appeals) (Procedure) Regulations 2009, SI 2009/2269, reg 32(b).

252. Entry and inspection of premises.

The tribunal panel[1] may enter and inspect the hereditament[2] which is the subject of the appeal[3] and, so as far as is practicable, any comparable land or property to which the attention of the panel is drawn[4].

When the panel so intends to enter any premises it must give notice[5] to the parties[6], who are entitled to be represented at the inspection[7]. Where the panel considers it appropriate, representation at an inspection may be limited to one person to represent those parties having the same interest in the appeal[8].

1 As to the meaning of 'tribunal panel' see PARA 250 note 11.

2 As to the meaning of 'hereditament' see PARA 106.

3 Valuation Tribunal for England (Council Tax and Rating Appeals) (Procedure) Regulations 2009, SI 2009/2269, reg 34(1)(a). As to appeals in relation to non-domestic rating see PARA 242. The Valuation Tribunal for England (Council Tax and Rating Appeals) (Procedure) Regulations 2009, SI 2009/2269, apply in relation to England only: see reg 1. As to the equivalent regulations in relation to Wales see the Non-Domestic Rating (Alterations of Lists and Appeals) (Wales) Regulations 2005, SI 2005/758, Pt 5 (regs 21–39); and PARA 257 et seq. As to the meanings of

'England' and 'Wales' see PARA 2 note 16.
4 Valuation Tribunal for England (Council Tax and Rating Appeals) (Procedure) Regulations 2009, SI 2009/2269, reg 34(1)(b).
5 As to the service and delivery of documents see PARA 243.
6 As to the meaning of 'party' see PARA 243 note 4.
7 Valuation Tribunal for England (Council Tax and Rating Appeals) (Procedure) Regulations 2009, SI 2009/2269, reg 34(2).
8 Valuation Tribunal for England (Council Tax and Rating Appeals) (Procedure) Regulations 2009, SI 2009/2269, reg 34(3).

253. Decisions.

The tribunal panel[1] may give a decision orally at a hearing[2]. As soon as reasonably practicable after the panel makes a decision which finally disposes of all issues in the proceedings, the Valuation Tribunal for England[3] must provide[4] to each party[5]:

(1) a decision notice stating the panel's decision[6];
(2) notification of any right of appeal against the decision and of any right to make an application for the review of the decision[7]; and
(3) notification of the time within which, and the manner in which, any right referred to in head (2) may be exercised[8].

As soon as reasonably practicable after the panel makes a decision which finally disposes of all issues in the proceedings on an appeal, the tribunal must send to each party a written[9] statement of the panel's reasons for the decision[10]. In the case of an appeal against a completion notice[11], the tribunal must send notice of the decision to the valuation officer[12] for the relevant authority[13].

The aim of the tribunal is to determine the correct rateable value of the hereditament, if that is the issue, and the tribunal may rely on its own expert judgment and is not bound to accept the value of one or other party to the appeal[14].

Under the General Rate Act 1967 (now repealed), the valuation court was limited to 'giving effect to the contention of the parties'[15]. Although no such restriction is contained in the current legislation, it is accepted that the jurisdiction of the tribunal continues to be defined by the issues which are raised in the proposal (and the objection thereto) and that such jurisdiction cannot be extended[16]. This being so, earlier cases on restricting a tribunal's decision to the 'contention of the parties' are still of some relevance[17].

The tribunal may at any time correct any clerical mistake or other accidental slip or omission in a decision by sending notification of the amended decision to all parties[18] and making any necessary amendment to any information published in relation to the decision[19].

1 As to the meaning of 'tribunal panel' see PARA 250 note 11.
2 Valuation Tribunal for England (Council Tax and Rating Appeals) (Procedure) Regulations 2009, SI 2009/2269, reg 36(1). As to hearings see PARA 251. As to consent orders see PARA 254. As to the striking out of proceedings see PARA 246.

The Valuation Tribunal for England (Council Tax and Rating Appeals) (Procedure) Regulations 2009, SI 2009/2269, apply in relation to England only: see reg 1. As to the equivalent regulations in relation to Wales see the Non-Domestic Rating (Alterations of Lists and Appeals) (Wales) Regulations 2005, SI 2005/758, Pt 5 (regs 21–39); and PARA 257 et seq. As to the meanings of 'England' and 'Wales' see PARA 2 note 16.
3 As to the Valuation Tribunal for England see PARA 232.
4 As to the service and delivery of documents see PARA 243.
5 As to the meaning of 'party' see PARA 243 note 4.
6 Valuation Tribunal for England (Council Tax and Rating Appeals) (Procedure) Regulations 2009, SI 2009/2269, reg 36(2)(a). For an appeal under the Non-Domestic Rating (Alteration of Lists and

Appeals) (England) Regulations 2009, SI 2009/2268, reg 13A (see PARA 211):

(1) a decision notice provided under the Valuation Tribunal for England (Council Tax and Rating Appeals) (Procedure) Regulations 2009, SI 2009/2269, reg 36(2)(a) must be accompanied by a written statement of the tribunal panel's reasons for the decision (reg 36(3)(a) (reg 36(3), (4) added by SI 2017/156));

(2) the statement of reasons for the decision must specify which, if any, grounds of the appeal were made out (Valuation Tribunal for England (Council Tax and Rating Appeals) (Procedure) Regulations 2009, SI 2009/2269, reg 36(3)(b) (as so added)); and

(3) the tribunal must send a copy of the decision notice and the statement of reasons for the decision to:

(a) if the appellant is not the ratepayer, the ratepayer (reg 36(3)(c)(i) (as so added)); and

(b) any interested person mentioned in the Non-Domestic Rating (Alteration of Lists and Appeals) (England) Regulations 2009, SI 2009/2268, reg 12(2)(e) (see PARA 209) who was served a notice of the valuation officer's decision under reg 13(2) (see PARA 210) (Council Tax and Rating Appeals) (Procedure) Regulations 2009, SI 2009/2269, reg 36(3)(c)(ii) (as so added)).

In head (2) above, 'grounds of the appeal' has the meaning given in the Non-Domestic Rating (Alteration of Lists and Appeals) (England) Regulations 2009, SI 2009/2268, reg 2 (sic: this should be a reference to reg 3(1)) (see PARA 211 note 23): Council Tax and Rating Appeals) (Procedure) Regulations 2009, SI 2009/2269, reg 36(4) (as so added). As to the meaning of 'ratepayer' see PARA 243 note 4.

In determining an appeal under the Non-Domestic Rating (Alteration of Lists and Appeals) (England) Regulations 2009, SI 2009/2268, reg 13A, the tribunal must not take into account any matter (Council Tax and Rating Appeals) (Procedure) Regulations 2009, SI 2009/2269, reg 37A(1), (2) (reg 37A added by SI 2017/156)) unless it was included in:

(i) the notice of appeal or any document accompanying the notice of appeal (Council Tax and Rating Appeals) (Procedure) Regulations 2009, SI 2009/2269, reg 37A(2)(a) (as so added));

(ii) evidence or submissions provided in accordance with a direction under reg 17(1) (see PARA 248) (reg 37A(2)(b) (as so added));

(iii) information to which reg 17(4) applies (see PARA 248 note 23) which is used in the proceedings by the valuation officer (reg 37A(2)(c) (as so added));

(iv) evidence admitted under reg 17(6A) (see PARA 248 note 29) (reg 37A(2)(d) (as so added)); or

(v) new or further evidence admitted under reg 17A (see PARA 248 note 9) (reg 37A(2)(e) (as so added)).

7 Valuation Tribunal for England (Council Tax and Rating Appeals) (Procedure) Regulations 2009, SI 2009/2269, reg 36(2)(b). As to appeals against decisions see PARA 269. As to the review of decisions see PARA 255.

8 Valuation Tribunal for England (Council Tax and Rating Appeals) (Procedure) Regulations 2009, SI 2009/2269, reg 36(2)(c) (amended by SI 2013/465). As to the calculation of time see PARA 243.

9 As to the meaning of 'written' see PARA 21 note 3.

10 Valuation Tribunal for England (Council Tax and Rating Appeals) (Procedure) Regulations 2009, SI 2009/2269, reg 37(1). This is subject to reg 37(3) in the case of council tax appeals (see PARA 513): reg 37(1) (amended by SI 2013/465).

11 As to the meaning of 'completion notice' see PARA 243 note 4.

12 As to valuation officers see PARA 54.

13 See the Valuation Tribunal for England (Council Tax and Rating Appeals) (Procedure) Regulations 2009, SI 2009/2269, reg 37(2)(b). As to the meaning of 'relevant authority' see PARA 243 note 4.

14 *R v Westminster Assessment Committee, ex p Grosvenor House (Park Lane) Ltd* [1941] 1 KB 53 at 70, CA, per du Parcq LJ; *Morecombe and Heysham Borough Council v Robinson (Valuation Officer)* [1961] 1 All ER 721 at 725, [1961] 1 WLR 373 at 378–379, CA, per Holroyd Pearce LJ; *Hardiman (Valuation Officer) v Crystal Palace Football and Athletic Club Ltd* (1955) 48 R & IT 91, Lands Tribunal. These cases were decided prior to the coming into force of the Local Government Finance Act 1988 but may continue to be of relevance: see PARA 50. As to the rateable value see PARA 156 et seq.

15 See the General Rate Act 1967 s 76(5) (repealed).

16 See *Courtney plc v Murphy (Valuation Officer)* [1998] RA 77 at 85–86, Lands Tribunal, per P H Clarke FRICS, citing *Shaw v Hughes (Valuation Officer)* [1991] RVR 96 at 98, Lands Tribunal, per Marder J (citing in turn *Brighton Marine Palace and Pier Co v Rees (Valuation Officer)* [1961] RVR 614, 9 RRC 77, Lands Tribunal; *R v Winchester Area Assessment Committee, ex p Wright* [1948] 2 KB 455, [1948] 2 All ER 552, CA; and *R v Northamptonshire Local Valuation Court, ex p Anglian Water Authority* [1990] RA 93, [1991] 1 EGLR 171, CA).

17 See *Ellerby v March* [1954] 2 QB 357, [1954] 2 All ER 375, CA (tribunal cannot increase or decrease an assessment beyond the increase or decrease claimed in the proposal); *Rees* (Valuation Officer) *v Johnson* (1957) 50 R & IT 641, Lands Tribunal; *Jones (Valuation Officer) v Eastern Valleys (Monmouthshire) Joint Sewerage Board* (1960) 53 R & IT 280, 6 RRC 379, Lands Tribunal; *JT Dove Ltd v Lloyd (Valuation Officer)* (1960) 53 R & IT 563, 9 RRC 51, Lands Tribunal; *Croydon Corpn v LCC and Hardiman (Valuation Officer)* [1962] RA 197, 9 RRC 302, Lands Tribunal (assessments on parts exceeding assessment on whole); *William Gunstone & Sons Ltd v Sheffield City Council* (1957) 51 R & IT 25, 2 RRC 325, Lands Tribunal (claim for derating only in notice of objection); *British Home Stores Ltd v Brighton County Borough Council and Burton (Valuation Officer)* (1958) 51 R & IT 665, (1958) 3 RRC 344, Lands Tribunal (merger of assessments); *Brighton Marine Palace and Pier Co v Rees (Valuation Officer)* [1961] RVR 614, 9 RRC 77, Lands Tribunal (contention that part of hereditament be separately assessed); and see *Ellesmere Port and Neston Borough Council v Shell UK Ltd* [1980] 1 All ER 383, [1980] 1 WLR 205, CA. Where the proposal is to increase an assessment on grounds of structural additions, the court is not limited to considering the value of the additions; the assessment of the whole hereditament may be reviewed: *S Thomas & Co (Nottingham) Ltd v Emett (Valuation Officer)* (1955) 48 R & IT 761, Lands Tribunal. The court has power neither to direct the insertion of figures which do not represent the true values as at the relevant date nor to direct the date upon which an alteration is to take effect: *City of Sheffield v TB and W Cockayne Ltd and Donmall (Valuation Officer)* (1958) 4 RRC 258, 51 R & IT 810, Lands Tribunal. A court must not be influenced by sympathy: *Inchgreen Amateur Rowing Club v Greenock Assessor* (1956) 49 R & IT 264.

18 See the Valuation Tribunal for England (Council Tax and Rating Appeals) (Procedure) Regulations 2009, SI 2009/2269, reg 39(a). The tribunal must make arrangements for the effect of each correction under reg 39 to be recorded: see reg 41; and PARA 256.

19 See the Valuation Tribunal for England (Council Tax and Rating Appeals) (Procedure) Regulations 2009, SI 2009/2269, reg 39(b).

254. Orders.

The Valuation Tribunal for England[1] may, at the request of the parties[2] but only if the tribunal considers it appropriate, make a consent order disposing of the proceedings and making such other appropriate provision as the parties have agreed[3]. A consent order may provide for the alteration of a central non-domestic rating list or a local non-domestic rating list[4] and, where it does, must specify the day from which the alteration is to have effect[5].

After dealing with an appeal relating to a disagreement relating to alteration of a list[6], the tribunal may by order require a valuation officer[7] to alter a list in accordance with any provision made by or under the Local Government Finance Act 1988[8]. Where it is decided that a disputed rateable value[9] should be an amount greater than the amount shown in the list at the date of the proposal[10] and the amount proposed by the appellant[11], the tribunal must order the valuation officer to alter the list with effect from the day on which the tribunal panel[12] made the decision[13]. Where it appears that circumstances giving rise to an alteration ordered by the tribunal have ceased to exist, the order may require the alteration to be made in respect of such period as appears to the tribunal to reflect the duration of those circumstances[14].

After dealing with an appeal against the imposition of a penalty[15], the tribunal may order the valuation officer whose notice is the subject of the appeal to reduce or remit the penalty[16].

The billing authority[17] or the valuation officer (as the case may be) must comply with an order[18] within two weeks of the day of its making[19]. An order[20] may require any matter ancillary to its subject matter to be attended to[21].

The tribunal may at any time correct any clerical mistake or other accidental slip or omission in an order by sending notification of the amended order to all parties[22] and making any necessary amendment to any information published in relation to the order[23].

1 As to the Valuation Tribunal for England see PARA 232. The Valuation Tribunal for England (Council Tax and Rating Appeals) (Procedure) Regulations 2009, SI 2009/2269, apply in relation to England only: see reg 1. As to the equivalent regulations in relation to Wales see the Non-Domestic Rating (Alterations of Lists and Appeals) (Wales) Regulations 2005, SI 2005/758, Pt 5 (regs 21–39); and PARA 257 et seq. As to the meanings of 'England' and 'Wales' see PARA 2 note 16.

2 As to the meaning of 'party' see PARA 243 note 4.

3 Valuation Tribunal for England (Council Tax and Rating Appeals) (Procedure) Regulations 2009, SI 2009/2269, reg 35(1). Notwithstanding any other provision of the Valuation Tribunal for England (Council Tax and Rating Appeals) (Procedure) Regulations 2009, the tribunal need not hold a hearing before making such an order, or provide reasons for the order: reg 35(3). As to the striking out of proceedings see PARA 246. As to hearings see PARA 251. The tribunal must make arrangements for each order under reg 35 to be recorded: see reg 41; and PARA 256.

4 As to central non-domestic rating lists see PARA 196 et seq. As to local non-domestic rating lists see PARA 191 et seq. As to the alteration of lists see PARA 202 et seq.

5 Valuation Tribunal for England (Council Tax and Rating Appeals) (Procedure) Regulations 2009, SI 2009/2269, reg 35(2).

6 Ie an appeal under the Non-Domestic Rating (Alteration of Lists and Appeals) (England) Regulations 2009, SI 2009/2268, reg 13A: see PARA 211.

7 As to valuation officers see PARA 54.

8 Valuation Tribunal for England (Council Tax and Rating Appeals) (Procedure) Regulations 2009, SI 2009/2269, reg 38(4) (amended by SI 2017/156). The tribunal must make arrangements for each order under the Valuation Tribunal for England (Council Tax and Rating Appeals) (Procedure) Regulations 2009, SI 2009/2269, reg 38 to be recorded: see reg 41; and PARA 256.

9 As to the rateable value see PARA 156 et seq.

10 Valuation Tribunal for England (Council Tax and Rating Appeals) (Procedure) Regulations 2009, SI 2009/2269, reg 38(5)(a).

11 Valuation Tribunal for England (Council Tax and Rating Appeals) (Procedure) Regulations 2009, SI 2009/2269, reg 38(5)(b). As to the meaning of 'appellant' see PARA 243 note 4.

12 As to the meaning of 'tribunal panel' see PARA 250 note 11.

13 Valuation Tribunal for England (Council Tax and Rating Appeals) (Procedure) Regulations 2009, SI 2009/2269, reg 38(5) (reg 38(5), (6) amended by SI 2011/434). See also note 8. The Valuation Tribunal for England (Council Tax and Rating Appeals) (Procedure) Regulations 2009, SI 2009/2269, reg 38(5) does not apply where the order requires the valuation officer to alter the list to show:

(1) property previously rated as a single hereditament becoming liable to be rated in parts (reg 38(6)(a) (as so amended)); or

(2) property previously liable to be rated in parts becoming liable to be rated as a single hereditament (reg 38(6)(b) (as so amended)); or

(3) any part of a hereditament becoming part of a different hereditament (reg 38(6)(c) (as so amended)).

As to the meaning of 'hereditament' see PARA 106.

14 Valuation Tribunal for England (Council Tax and Rating Appeals) (Procedure) Regulations 2009, SI 2009/2269, reg 38(7).

15 Ie an appeal under the Local Government Finance Act 1988 Sch 9 para 5C: see PARA 226.

16 Valuation Tribunal for England (Council Tax and Rating Appeals) (Procedure) Regulations 2009, SI 2009/2269, reg 38(8). See also note 8.

17 As to the meaning of 'billing authority' see PARA 53.

18 Ie an order under the Valuation Tribunal for England (Council Tax and Rating Appeals) (Procedure) Regulations 2009, SI 2009/2269, reg 38: see the text to notes 6–16.

19 Valuation Tribunal for England (Council Tax and Rating Appeals) (Procedure) Regulations 2009, SI 2009/2269, reg 38(9). As to the calculation of time see reg 14; and PARA 243.

20 Ie an order under the Valuation Tribunal for England (Council Tax and Rating Appeals) (Procedure) Regulations 2009, SI 2009/2269, reg 38: see the text to notes 6–16.

21 Valuation Tribunal for England (Council Tax and Rating Appeals) (Procedure) Regulations 2009, SI 2009/2269, reg 38(10). The possible effect of a similar provision in earlier regulations was considered in *Re Appeal of Ebury (Valuation Officer)* [2003] RA 261, Lands Tribunal (regarding the scope of an order where a later proposal, accepted by the valuation officer, was followed by an appeal decision made on an earlier proposal).

Where a tribunal orders the valuation officer for a billing authority to alter a local non-domestic rating list of the authority, or the central valuation officer to alter a central non-domestic rating list, if the order is recorded in accordance with any provision included in regulations under the Local Government Finance Act 1988 Sch 11 para A19 (see PARA 235) or Sch 11 para 1 (see PARA 236), the officer or authority ordered must alter the list concerned accordingly, and attend to any ancillary matter provided for in the order (such as the repayment of an amount, or the allowance of an amount by way of deduction against a sum due): see Sch 11 para 9 (amended by the Local Government Finance Act 1992 s 117(1), Sch 13 para 88(8); and the Local Government and Public Involvement in Health Act 2007 s 219(1), Sch 15 paras 1, 12). As to records of decisions etc see PARA 256.

22 See the Valuation Tribunal for England (Council Tax and Rating Appeals) (Procedure) Regulations 2009, SI 2009/2269, reg 39(a). The tribunal must make arrangements for the effect of each correction under reg 39 to be recorded: see reg 41; and PARA 256.

23 See the Valuation Tribunal for England (Council Tax and Rating Appeals) (Procedure) Regulations 2009, SI 2009/2269, reg 39(b).

255. Review of decisions.

The president of the Valuation Tribunal for England[1] may direct that a review be undertaken of the whole or part of a decision which disposes of proceedings[2] on an appeal[3].

A party[4] may apply to the tribunal in writing[5] for the review of the whole or part of a decision which disposes of proceedings on an appeal[6]. The application must be made within 28 days[7] of the date on which notice of the decision was sent[8] and must be considered by the president of the tribunal[9]. The president of the tribunal must not grant the application unless at least one of the following conditions is satisfied[10]. The conditions are:

(1) a document relating to the proceedings was not sent to, or was not received at an appropriate time by, a party or a party's representative[11];

(2) a document relating to the proceedings was not sent to the tribunal at an appropriate time[12];

(3) a party or its representative was not present at a hearing relating to the proceedings and the party shows reasonable cause for its or its representative's absence[13];

(4) there has been some other procedural irregularity in the proceedings[14];

(5) the decision is affected by a decision of, or on appeal from, the Upper Tribunal or the High Court[15];

(6) where the decision relates to an appeal against a completion notice[16], new evidence, whose existence could not have been discovered by reasonable inquiry or could not have been foreseen, has become available since the conclusion of the proceedings[17].

Where an application is granted or a direction that a review be undertaken is given[18], the tribunal must review the decision or part that is the subject of the review[19]; and if it considers that any of the conditions specified in heads (1) to (6) above is satisfied[20] and that it is in the interests of justice to do so[21], the tribunal must set aside the decision or part[22]. If the tribunal sets aside a decision it must revoke any order made in consequence of the decision and notify the parties in writing of the revocation[23].

1 As to the Valuation Tribunal for England see PARA 232. As to the president of the tribunal see

PARA 233.

The Valuation Tribunal for England (Council Tax and Rating Appeals) (Procedure) Regulations 2009, SI 2009/2269, apply in relation to England only: see reg 1. As to the equivalent regulations in relation to Wales see the Non-Domestic Rating (Alterations of Lists and Appeals) (Wales) Regulations 2005, SI 2005/758, Pt 5 (regs 21–39); and PARA 257 et seq. As to the meanings of 'England' and 'Wales' see PARA 2 note 16.

2 As to decisions and orders disposing of proceedings see PARAS 253, 254.

3 Valuation Tribunal for England (Council Tax and Rating Appeals) (Procedure) Regulations 2009, SI 2009/2269, reg 40(2). As to appeals in relation to non-domestic rating see PARA 242.

4 As to the meaning of 'party' see PARA 243 note 4. Where a valuation officer applies to the tribunal under the Valuation Tribunal for England (Council Tax and Rating Appeals) (Procedure) Regulations 2009, SI 2009/2269, reg 40 for the review of a decision in consequence of which an order requiring the alteration of a list was made, the valuation officer must, at the same time or as soon as reasonably practicable afterwards, notify the authority concerned of the application: see reg 44(1)(a). 'The authority concerned' means:

(1) where the application (or appeal under reg 43) relates to the alteration of a local non-domestic rating list, the relevant authority for whose area the list was compiled (reg 44(2)(b)); and

(2) where head (1) does not apply and the application or appeal relates to a provision of the Non-Domestic Rating (Alteration of Lists and Appeals) (England) Regulations 2009, SI 2009/2268, or an appeal against a completion notice under the Local Government Finance Act 1988 Sch 4A para 1 (see PARA 138) as it applies for the purposes of Pt III of that Act, the Secretary of State (Valuation Tribunal for England (Council Tax and Rating Appeals) (Procedure) Regulations 2009, SI 2009/2269, reg 44(2)(c)).

See also the Non-Domestic Rating (Alteration of Lists and Appeals) (England) Regulations 2009, SI 2009/2268, reg 21 which makes similar provision. As to valuation officers see PARA 54. As to the alteration of lists see PARA 202 et seq. As to the service and delivery of documents see reg 15; and PARA 243. As to the meaning of 'relevant authority' see PARA 243 note 4. As to the Secretary of State see PARA 4 note 18.

5 As to the meaning of 'writing' see PARA 21 note 3.

6 Valuation Tribunal for England (Council Tax and Rating Appeals) (Procedure) Regulations 2009, SI 2009/2269, reg 40(1). The tribunal must notify the parties in writing of the result of an application under reg 40(1): reg 40(9)(a). Where, on the day on which an application under reg 40(1) is made, an appeal to the Upper Tribunal or the High Court in relation to the same issue as is the subject of the application remains undetermined, the tribunal must notify the Upper Tribunal or the High Court as soon as reasonably practicable (reg 40(10)):

(1) after the application is made (reg 40(10)(a)); and

(2) after notice is given under any provision of reg 40(9) (see above and notes 22, 23) (reg 40(10)(b)).

As to the judicial review of decisions of the tribunal see PARA 271. As to the High Court of Justice in England and Wales see COURTS AND TRIBUNALS vol 24 (2010) PARA 695 et seq. As to appeals to the Upper Tribunal see PARA 269. As to the Upper Tribunal see COURTS AND TRIBUNALS vol 24 (2010) PARA 874 et seq.

7 As to the calculation of time see PARA 243.

8 Valuation Tribunal for England (Council Tax and Rating Appeals) (Procedure) Regulations 2009, SI 2009/2269, reg 40(3)(a).

9 Valuation Tribunal for England (Council Tax and Rating Appeals) (Procedure) Regulations 2009, SI 2009/2269, reg 40(3)(b).

10 Valuation Tribunal for England (Council Tax and Rating Appeals) (Procedure) Regulations 2009, SI 2009/2269, reg 40(4).

11 Valuation Tribunal for England (Council Tax and Rating Appeals) (Procedure) Regulations 2009, SI 2009/2269, reg 40(5)(a). As to representatives see PARA 247.

12 Valuation Tribunal for England (Council Tax and Rating Appeals) (Procedure) Regulations 2009, SI 2009/2269, reg 40(5)(b).

13 Valuation Tribunal for England (Council Tax and Rating Appeals) (Procedure) Regulations 2009, SI 2009/2269, reg 40(5)(c). As to hearings see PARA 251. In a case decided under previous legislation it was held that the rating authority had appeared before a local valuation court when a representative had notified the clerk of his presence and sat through the hearing: see *Electricity Supply Nominees Ltd v Sharma (Valuation Officer)* [1985] RVR 188, [1985] 2 EGLR 173, CA.

14 Valuation Tribunal for England (Council Tax and Rating Appeals) (Procedure) Regulations 2009, SI 2009/2269, reg 40(5)(d).

15 Valuation Tribunal for England (Council Tax and Rating Appeals) (Procedure) Regulations 2009, SI 2009/2269, reg 40(5)(e).
16 As to the meaning of 'completion notice' see PARA 243 note 4.
17 Valuation Tribunal for England (Council Tax and Rating Appeals) (Procedure) Regulations 2009, SI 2009/2269, reg 40(5)(f).
18 Ie a direction under the Valuation Tribunal for England (Council Tax and Rating Appeals) (Procedure) Regulations 2009, SI 2009/2269, reg 40(2): see the text to notes 1–3.
19 Tribunal business arrangements apply in relation to the selection of members of the tribunal to review a decision or part of a decision as if the review were an appeal: Valuation Tribunal for England (Council Tax and Rating Appeals) (Procedure) Regulations 2009, SI 2009/2269, reg 40(7). As to tribunal business arrangements see PARA 234.
20 Valuation Tribunal for England (Council Tax and Rating Appeals) (Procedure) Regulations 2009, SI 2009/2269, reg 40(6)(a).
21 Valuation Tribunal for England (Council Tax and Rating Appeals) (Procedure) Regulations 2009, SI 2009/2269, reg 40(6)(b).
22 Valuation Tribunal for England (Council Tax and Rating Appeals) (Procedure) Regulations 2009, SI 2009/2269, reg 40(6). The tribunal must notify the parties in writing of the result of a review under reg 40(6): reg 40(9)(b). See also note 6.
23 Valuation Tribunal for England (Council Tax and Rating Appeals) (Procedure) Regulations 2009, SI 2009/2269, reg 40(8). The tribunal must notify the parties in writing if, under reg 40(8), it revokes an order: reg 40(9)(c). See also note 6. The tribunal must make arrangements for each revocation under reg 40(8) to be recorded: see reg 41; and PARA 256.

256. Records of decisions and orders.

The Valuation Tribunal for England[1] must make arrangements for each decision[2], each order[3], the effect of each correction of a decision, direction, order or document[4], and each revocation of an order[5] to be recorded[6]. Records may be kept in any form, whether documentary or otherwise[7]; and each record must be retained for the period of six years beginning on the day on which an entry was last made in it[8].

Any person[9] may, at a reasonable time stated by or on behalf of the tribunal and without making payment, inspect such records[10]. If without reasonable excuse a person having custody of records ('the custodian') intentionally obstructs a person in exercising this right, the custodian commits an offence[11].

The production in any proceedings in any court of law of a document purporting to be certified by the president of the tribunal[12] or the clerk of the tribunal to be a true copy of a record of the tribunal is, unless the contrary is proved, sufficient evidence of the document and of the facts it records[13].

1 As to the Valuation Tribunal for England see PARA 232. The Valuation Tribunal for England (Council Tax and Rating Appeals) (Procedure) Regulations 2009, SI 2009/2269, apply in relation to England only: see reg 1. As to the equivalent regulations in relation to Wales see the Non-Domestic Rating (Alterations of Lists and Appeals) (Wales) Regulations 2005, SI 2005/758, Pt 5 (regs 21–39); and PARA 257 et seq. As to the meanings of 'England' and 'Wales' see PARA 2 note 16.
2 As to decisions see PARA 253.
3 Ie under the Valuation Tribunal for England (Council Tax and Rating Appeals) (Procedure) Regulations 2009, SI 2009/2269, regs 35 or 38: see PARA 254.
4 Ie under the Valuation Tribunal for England (Council Tax and Rating Appeals) (Procedure) Regulations 2009, SI 2009/2269, reg 39: see PARAS 245, 253, 254.
5 Ie under the Valuation Tribunal for England (Council Tax and Rating Appeals) (Procedure) Regulations 2009, SI 2009/2269, reg 40(8): see PARA 255.
6 Valuation Tribunal for England (Council Tax and Rating Appeals) (Procedure) Regulations 2009, SI 2009/2269, reg 41(1).
7 Valuation Tribunal for England (Council Tax and Rating Appeals) (Procedure) Regulations 2009, SI 2009/2269, reg 41(2) (amended by SI 2011/434).
8 Valuation Tribunal for England (Council Tax and Rating Appeals) (Procedure) Regulations 2009, SI 2009/2269, reg 41(3).
9 As to the meaning of 'person' see PARA 11 note 13.

10 Valuation Tribunal for England (Council Tax and Rating Appeals) (Procedure) Regulations 2009, SI 2009/2269, reg 41(4).
11 See the Valuation Tribunal for England (Council Tax and Rating Appeals) (Procedure) Regulations 2009, SI 2009/2269, reg 41(5). The penalty for such an offence is, on summary conviction, a fine not exceeding level 1 on the standard scale: reg 41(5). As to the powers of magistrates' courts to issue fines on summary conviction see SENTENCING vol 92 (2015) PARA 176.
12 As to the president of the Valuation Tribunal for England see PARA 233.
13 Valuation Tribunal for England (Council Tax and Rating Appeals) (Procedure) Regulations 2009, SI 2009/2269, reg 41(6).

(C) Wales

257. Arrangements for appeals.

It is the duty of the president of the Valuation Tribunal for Wales[1] to ensure that arrangements are made for the determination of appeals[2].

Where the appellant is:

(1) a former member of a valuation tribunal which existed before 1 July 2010[3];
(2) a former employee of a valuation tribunal which existed before 1 July 2010, of the Valuation Service for Wales[4] or of the Valuation Tribunal for Wales[5]; or
(3) an employee or member of the Valuation Tribunal for Wales[6],

the appeal must be dealt with by such members of the tribunal as may be appointed for that purpose by the President of the Valuation Tribunal for Wales[7].

Where it appears to the president that by reason of a conflict of interests, or the appearance of such a conflict, it would be inappropriate for an appeal to be dealt with by particular members of the tribunal, the president must appoint another tribunal to deal with that appeal[8].

1 As to the Valuation Tribunal for Wales see PARA 237. As to the president of the tribunal, and membership of the tribunal generally, see PARA 238. The Non-Domestic Rating (Alterations of Lists and Appeals) (Wales) Regulations 2005, SI 2005/758, apply only in relation to Wales: see reg 1. As to the equivalent regulations in relation to England see the Valuation Tribunal for England (Council Tax and Rating Appeals) (Procedure) Regulations 2009, SI 2009/2269; and PARA 243 et seq. As to the meanings of 'England' and 'Wales' see PARA 2 note 16.
2 See the Non-Domestic Rating (Alterations of Lists and Appeals) (Wales) Regulations 2005, SI 2005/758, reg 23(1) (amended by SI 2010/713). As to appeals in relation to non-domestic rating see PARA 242. The arrangements must provide for appeals to be determined in accordance with the provisions of the Non-Domestic Rating (Alterations of Lists and Appeals) (Wales) Regulations 2005, SI 2005/758, regs 23(2)–(5), 24–39 (see the text to notes 3–8; and PARAS 243, 245 et seq): see reg 23(1). The tribunal must not hear an appeal under reg 13 (see PARA 222) until any appeal under reg 8 (see PARA 422) in respect of the same proposal has been decided: see reg 23(2). As to the meaning of 'proposal' see PARA 213 note 3.

Where two or more appeals relating to the same hereditament or hereditaments are referred under reg 13 (see PARA 222), the order in which the appeals are dealt with must be the order in which the alterations in question would, but for the disagreements which occasion the appeals, have taken effect: reg 23(3).

Where an appeal under reg 13 and an appeal under the Council Tax (Alteration of Lists and Appeals) Regulations 1993, SI 1993/290, reg 13 (see PARA 434) relate to the same property:

(1) the president of the valuation tribunal must secure that appeals are dealt with in such order as appears to the president best designed to secure the interests of justice (Non-Domestic Rating (Alterations of Lists and Appeals) (Wales) Regulations 2005, SI 2005/758, reg 23(4)(a));
(2) the listing officer must be joined as a party to the appeal under reg 13 (reg 23(4)(b)); and
(3) the valuation officer must be joined as a party to the appeal under the Council Tax (Alteration of Lists and Appeals) Regulations 1993, SI 1993/290, reg 13 (Non-Domestic

Rating (Alterations of Lists and Appeals) (Wales) Regulations 2005, SI 2005/758, reg 23(4)(c)).

The clerk must, as soon as is reasonably practicable, give written notice to any person who is made a party to an appeal under reg 23(4): reg 23(5). 'Clerk', in relation to an appeal, means the clerk of the Valuation Tribunal for Wales: reg 2(1) (definition substituted by SI 2010/713).

Any reference in the Non-Domestic Rating (Alterations of Lists and Appeals) (Wales) Regulations 2005, SI 2005/758, to a party to an appeal includes the person making the appeal ('the appellant') (reg 2(3)) and:

(a) in relation to an appeal under reg 8 or an appeal against imposition of a penalty, the valuation officer or, as the case may be, the central valuation officer (reg 2(3)(a));

(b) in relation to an appeal under reg 13:

(i) every person whose agreement is required under reg 12 (see PARA 221) (reg 2(3)(b)(i)); and

(ii) any other person who has been a ratepayer in relation to the hereditament since the proposal was made and who has notified the valuation officer in writing before the hearing, or before determination on the basis of written representations under reg 25, that they wish to be a party to the appeal (reg 2(3)(b)(ii));

(c) in relation to an appeal against a completion notice, the relevant authority (reg 2(3)(c)).

As to the meaning of 'hereditament' see PARA 106. As to the meaning of 'ratepayer' see PARA 213 note 6. As to valuation officers see PARA 54. As to the alteration of non-domestic rating lists see PARA 202 et seq.

3 Non-Domestic Rating (Alterations of Lists and Appeals) (Wales) Regulations 2005, SI 2005/758, reg 22(1)(a) (reg 21 substituted by SI 2010/713).

4 Ie the service established by the Valuation Tribunals (Wales) Regulations 2005, SI 2005/3364 (revoked).

5 Non-Domestic Rating (Alterations of Lists and Appeals) (Wales) Regulations 2005, SI 2005/758, reg 22(1)(b) (as substituted: see note 3).

6 Non-Domestic Rating (Alterations of Lists and Appeals) (Wales) Regulations 2005, SI 2005/758, reg 22(1)(c) (as substituted: see note 3).

7 Non-Domestic Rating (Alterations of Lists and Appeals) (Wales) Regulations 2005, SI 2005/758, reg 22(1) (as substituted: see note 3).

8 Non-Domestic Rating (Alterations of Lists and Appeals) (Wales) Regulations 2005, SI 2005/758, reg 22(2) (as substituted: see note 3).

258. Written representations.

An appeal[1] may be disposed of on the basis of written representations if all the parties[2] have given their agreement in writing[3]. Where all the parties have given their agreement, the clerk of the Valuation Tribunal for Wales[4] must serve notice on the parties accordingly[5]; and within four weeks of service of such a notice on them each party may serve on the clerk a notice stating:

(1) that party's reasons or further reasons for the disagreement giving rise to the appeal[6]; or

(2) that that party does not intend to make further representations[7].

A copy of any notice served on a party must be served by the clerk on the other party or parties to the appeal, and must be accompanied by a statement of the effect of the provisions set out below[8]. Any party on whom a notice is so served may within four weeks of that service serve on the clerk a further notice stating their reply to the other party's statement, or that they do not intend to make further representations, as the case may be; and the clerk must serve a copy of any such further notice on the other party or parties[9]. After the expiry of four weeks beginning with the expiry of that period of four weeks the clerk must submit copies of any information transmitted to the clerk[10] and any notice under these provisions[11] to a valuation tribunal constituted[12] for a hearing[13].

The valuation tribunal to which an appeal is so referred may if it thinks fit:

(a) require any party to furnish in writing further particulars of the grounds relied on and of any relevant facts or contentions[14]; or

(b) order that the appeal be disposed of on the basis of a hearing[15].

Where any party has furnished any particulars in response to a request by a valuation tribunal under head (a) above, the clerk must serve a copy of the particulars on every other party, and each of those other parties may, within four weeks of such service, serve on the clerk any further statement they wish to make in response[16].

1 As to appeals in relation to non-domestic rating see PARA 242.
2 As to the meaning of 'party' see PARA 243 note 4.
3 Non-Domestic Rating (Alterations of Lists and Appeals) (Wales) Regulations 2005, SI 2005/758, reg 25(1). As to the meaning of 'writing' see PARA 21 note 3. As to disposal without a hearing where the parties have come to an agreement see PARA 259.
The Non-Domestic Rating (Alterations of Lists and Appeals) (Wales) Regulations 2005, SI 2005/758, apply only in relation to Wales: see reg 1. As to the equivalent regulations in relation to England see the Valuation Tribunal for England (Council Tax and Rating Appeals) (Procedure) Regulations 2009, SI 2009/2269; and PARA 243 et seq. As to the meanings of 'England' and 'Wales' see PARA 2 note 16.
4 As to the Valuation Tribunal for Wales see PARA 237. As to the meaning of 'clerk' see PARA 257 note 2.
5 Non-Domestic Rating (Alterations of Lists and Appeals) (Wales) Regulations 2005, SI 2005/758, reg 25(2). As to the service of notices see PARA 213 note 3.
6 Non-Domestic Rating (Alterations of Lists and Appeals) (Wales) Regulations 2005, SI 2005/758, reg 25(2)(a).
7 Non-Domestic Rating (Alterations of Lists and Appeals) (Wales) Regulations 2005, SI 2005/758, reg 25(2)(b).
8 Non-Domestic Rating (Alterations of Lists and Appeals) (Wales) Regulations 2005, SI 2005/758, reg 25(3).
9 Non-Domestic Rating (Alterations of Lists and Appeals) (Wales) Regulations 2005, SI 2005/758, reg 25(4).
10 Ie under the Non-Domestic Rating (Alterations of Lists and Appeals) (Wales) Regulations 2005, SI 2005/758.
11 Ie under the Non-Domestic Rating (Alterations of Lists and Appeals) (Wales) Regulations 2005, SI 2005/758, reg 25(2) or (4).
12 Ie as provided in the Non-Domestic Rating (Alterations of Lists and Appeals) (Wales) Regulations 2005, SI 2005/758, reg 30: see PARA 263.
13 Non-Domestic Rating (Alterations of Lists and Appeals) (Wales) Regulations 2005, SI 2005/758, reg 25(5).
14 Non-Domestic Rating (Alterations of Lists and Appeals) (Wales) Regulations 2005, SI 2005/758, reg 25(6)(a).
15 Non-Domestic Rating (Alterations of Lists and Appeals) (Wales) Regulations 2005, SI 2005/758, reg 25(6)(b).
16 Non-Domestic Rating (Alterations of Lists and Appeals) (Wales) Regulations 2005, SI 2005/758, reg 25(7) (amended by SI 2006/1035).

259. Disposal by written representations where parties have come to an agreement.

The Valuation Tribunal for Wales[1] may dispose of an appeal[2] without a hearing if[3]:

(1) a party[4] informs the valuation tribunal in writing[5]:
  (a) that parties have come to an agreement[6];
  (b) what that agreement is and the decision the valuation tribunal is asked to make[7]; and
  (c) that parties agree for the appeal to be disposed of without a hearing[8]; and
(2) the clerk[9] sends a notice to all parties to the proceedings stating[10]:
  (a) that the valuation tribunal is minded to dispose of the appeal without a hearing[11];
  (b) the decision the valuation tribunal is minded to take[12]; and

(c) that any party can object to the appeal being disposed of without a hearing[13].

If a notice is sent under head (2) above, a party may request to the clerk that the appeal be disposed of with a hearing[14]. Such a request must be made in writing[15] and received by the clerk within four weeks of the date on which the clerk sent a notice under head (2)[16].

The valuation tribunal must not dispose of an appeal without a hearing if[17]:

(i) in the opinion of the clerk, the appeal raises issues of public importance such as to require that hearing be held[18];

(ii) a period of four weeks from which the notice under head (2) was sent has not elapsed[19]; or

(iii) a party to the appeal has requested a hearing[20].

The functions of the valuation tribunal under these provisions may be performed on its behalf by the clerk[21].

1 As to the Valuation Tribunal for Wales see PARA 237.
2 As to appeals in relation to non-domestic rating see PARA 242.
3 Non-Domestic Rating (Alterations of Lists and Appeals) (Wales) Regulations 2005, SI 2005/758, reg 25A(1) (reg 25A added by SI 2017/941).
The Non-Domestic Rating (Alterations of Lists and Appeals) (Wales) Regulations 2005, SI 2005/758, apply only in relation to Wales: see reg 1. As to the equivalent regulations in relation to England see the Valuation Tribunal for England (Council Tax and Rating Appeals) (Procedure) Regulations 2009, SI 2009/2269; and PARA 243 et seq. As to the meanings of 'England' and 'Wales' see PARA 2 note 16.
4 As to the meaning of 'party' see PARA 243 note 4.
5 Non-Domestic Rating (Alterations of Lists and Appeals) (Wales) Regulations 2005, SI 2005/758, reg 25A(1)(a) (as added: see note 3).
6 Non-Domestic Rating (Alterations of Lists and Appeals) (Wales) Regulations 2005, SI 2005/758, reg 25A(1)(a)(i) (as added: see note 3).
7 Non-Domestic Rating (Alterations of Lists and Appeals) (Wales) Regulations 2005, SI 2005/758, reg 25A(1)(a)(ii) (as added: see note 3).
8 Non-Domestic Rating (Alterations of Lists and Appeals) (Wales) Regulations 2005, SI 2005/758, reg 25A(1)(a)(iii) (as added: see note 3).
9 As to the meaning of 'clerk' see PARA 257 note 2.
10 Non-Domestic Rating (Alterations of Lists and Appeals) (Wales) Regulations 2005, SI 2005/758, reg 25A(1)(b) (as added: see note 3).
11 Non-Domestic Rating (Alterations of Lists and Appeals) (Wales) Regulations 2005, SI 2005/758, reg 25A(1)(b)(i) (as added: see note 3).
12 Non-Domestic Rating (Alterations of Lists and Appeals) (Wales) Regulations 2005, SI 2005/758, reg 25A(1)(b)(ii) (as added: see note 3).
13 Non-Domestic Rating (Alterations of Lists and Appeals) (Wales) Regulations 2005, SI 2005/758, reg 25A(1)(b)(iii) (as added: see note 3).
14 Non-Domestic Rating (Alterations of Lists and Appeals) (Wales) Regulations 2005, SI 2005/758, reg 25A(2) (as added: see note 3).
15 As to the meaning of 'writing' see PARA 21 note 3.
16 Non-Domestic Rating (Alterations of Lists and Appeals) (Wales) Regulations 2005, SI 2005/758, reg 25A(3) (as added: see note 3).
17 Non-Domestic Rating (Alterations of Lists and Appeals) (Wales) Regulations 2005, SI 2005/758, reg 25A(4) (as added: see note 3).
18 Non-Domestic Rating (Alterations of Lists and Appeals) (Wales) Regulations 2005, SI 2005/758, reg 25A(4)(a) (as added: see note 3).
19 Non-Domestic Rating (Alterations of Lists and Appeals) (Wales) Regulations 2005, SI 2005/758, reg 25A(4)(b) (as added: see note 3).
20 Non-Domestic Rating (Alterations of Lists and Appeals) (Wales) Regulations 2005, SI 2005/758, reg 25A(4)(c) (as added: see note 3).
21 Non-Domestic Rating (Alterations of Lists and Appeals) (Wales) Regulations 2005, SI 2005/758, reg 25A(5) (as added: see note 3).

260. Evidence.

The following provisions apply to information[1] supplied to a valuation officer following a request[2]. Subject to the following provisions, such information is in any relevant proceedings admissible as evidence of any fact stated in it[3]; and any record purporting to contain such information is, unless the contrary is shown, presumed:

(1) to have been supplied by the person by whom it purports to have been supplied[4];

(2) to have been supplied by that person in any capacity in which it purports to have been supplied[5].

Such information must not be used in any relevant proceedings[6] by a valuation officer unless:

(a) not less than three weeks' notice has previously been given to every other party[7] to the proceedings[8];

(b) the notice specifies in relation to any information to be so used:

  (i) the documents or other media in or on which that information is held[9];

  (ii) the hereditament[10] or hereditaments to which it relates, and the rateable value or rateable values in the list current at the date of the notice[11];

  (iii) the name and address of the person providing the information[12]; and

  (iv) a summary of the terms of any lease (including the rent, dates of rental reviews and description of the repairing obligations)[13]; and

(c) any person who has given not less than 24 hours' notice of his intention to do so, has been permitted by that officer at any reasonable time:

  (i) to inspect the documents or other media in or on which such information is held[14]; and

  (ii) to make a copy of, or of any extract from, any document containing such information[15].

Any person to whom notice relating to any hereditament has been given under head (a) above may before the hearing serve notice on the valuation officer specifying other hereditaments as being hereditaments which are comparable in character or otherwise relevant to that person's case, and requiring the valuation officer:

(A) to permit him or her at any reasonable time specified in the notice to inspect and (if they so desire) to make a copy of any document containing information to which these provisions apply which relates to those other hereditaments and is in the possession of the valuation officer[16]; and

(B) to produce at the hearing or to submit to the valuation tribunal such documents as before the hearing they have informed the valuation officer that they require[17].

The number of hereditaments specified in such a notice must not exceed four, or if greater, the number specified in the notice under head (a) above[18].

Nothing in the foregoing provisions is to be construed as requiring the making available for inspection or copying, or the production of, any document in so far as it contains information other than information constituting direct evidence of the rent payable in respect of the specified hereditaments, or which is otherwise reasonably required for the purposes of the relevant proceedings[19].

Where a notice has been given to the valuation officer in respect of comparable hereditaments, and the valuation officer refuses or fails to comply with the notice, the person who gave the notice may apply to the valuation tribunal or, as the case may be, the arbitrator appointed to determine the appeal; and that tribunal or arbitrator may, if satisfied that it is reasonable to do so, direct the valuation officer to comply with the notice as respects all the hereditaments or such of them as the tribunal or arbitrator may determine[20].

If any information required to be made available for inspection in accordance with these provisions is not maintained in documentary form, the duty to make it so available is satisfied if a print-out, photographic image or other reproduction of the document which has been obtained from the storage medium adopted in relation to the document is made available for inspection[21].

The contents of a list may be proved by the production of a copy of it, or of the relevant part, purporting to be certified to be a true copy by the valuation officer; and the contents of a completion notice[22] may be proved by the production of a copy of it purporting to be certified to be a true copy by the proper officer of the relevant authority[23].

1 Ie information supplied in pursuance of the Non-Domestic Rating (Alterations of Lists and Appeals) (Wales) Regulations 2005, SI 2005/758, reg 42 (see PARA 227), the Local Government Finance Act 1988 Sch 9 para 5 (see PARA 226) or the General Rate Act 1967 s 82 (repealed).

2 Non-Domestic Rating (Alterations of Lists and Appeals) (Wales) Regulations 2005, SI 2005/758, reg 31(1). As to valuation officers see PARA 54.

The Non-Domestic Rating (Alterations of Lists and Appeals) (Wales) Regulations 2005, SI 2005/758, apply only in relation to Wales: see reg 1. As to the equivalent regulations in relation to England see the Valuation Tribunal for England (Council Tax and Rating Appeals) (Procedure) Regulations 2009, SI 2009/2269; and PARA 243 et seq. As to the meanings of 'England' and 'Wales' see PARA 2 note 16.

3 Non-Domestic Rating (Alterations of Lists and Appeals) (Wales) Regulations 2005, SI 2005/758, reg 31(2).

4 Non-Domestic Rating (Alterations of Lists and Appeals) (Wales) Regulations 2005, SI 2005/758, reg 31(2)(a).

5 Non-Domestic Rating (Alterations of Lists and Appeals) (Wales) Regulations 2005, SI 2005/758, reg 31(2)(b).

6 'Relevant proceedings' means any proceedings on or in consequence of an appeal, and any proceedings on or in consequence of a reference to arbitration under the Non-Domestic Rating (Alterations of Lists and Appeals) (Wales) Regulations 2005, SI 2005/758, reg 38 (see PARA 268): reg 31(8).

7 As to the meaning of 'party' see PARA 243 note 4.

8 Non-Domestic Rating (Alterations of Lists and Appeals) (Wales) Regulations 2005, SI 2005/758, reg 31(3)(a).

9 Non-Domestic Rating (Alterations of Lists and Appeals) (Wales) Regulations 2005, SI 2005/758, reg 31(3)(b)(i).

10 As to the meaning of 'hereditament' see PARA 106.

11 Non-Domestic Rating (Alterations of Lists and Appeals) (Wales) Regulations 2005, SI 2005/758, reg 31(3)(b)(ii).

12 Non-Domestic Rating (Alterations of Lists and Appeals) (Wales) Regulations 2005, SI 2005/758, reg 31(3)(b)(iii).

13 Non-Domestic Rating (Alterations of Lists and Appeals) (Wales) Regulations 2005, SI 2005/758, reg 31(3)(b)(iv).

14 Non-Domestic Rating (Alterations of Lists and Appeals) (Wales) Regulations 2005, SI 2005/758, reg 31(3)(c)(i).

15 Non-Domestic Rating (Alterations of Lists and Appeals) (Wales) Regulations 2005, SI 2005/758, reg 31(3)(c)(ii).

16 Non-Domestic Rating (Alterations of Lists and Appeals) (Wales) Regulations 2005, SI 2005/758, reg 31(4)(a).

17 Non-Domestic Rating (Alterations of Lists and Appeals) (Wales) Regulations 2005, SI 2005/758, reg 31(4)(b).

18 Non-Domestic Rating (Alterations of Lists and Appeals) (Wales) Regulations 2005, SI 2005/758, reg 31(5).
19 Non-Domestic Rating (Alterations of Lists and Appeals) (Wales) Regulations 2005, SI 2005/758, reg 31(6).
20 Non-Domestic Rating (Alterations of Lists and Appeals) (Wales) Regulations 2005, SI 2005/758, reg 31(7).
21 Non-Domestic Rating (Alterations of Lists and Appeals) (Wales) Regulations 2005, SI 2005/758, reg 31(9).
22 As to the meaning of 'completion notice' see PARA 223 note 13.
23 Non-Domestic Rating (Alterations of Lists and Appeals) (Wales) Regulations 2005, SI 2005/758, reg 32.

261. Withdrawals and deemed withdrawals of appeals.

An appeal[1] may be withdrawn[2] before the commencement of a hearing[3] or of consideration of written representations[4], where notice to that effect is given to the clerk[5]:

(1) in the case of an appeal against a completion notice[6] or an appeal[7] against a penalty, by the appellant[8] in writing[9]; or

(2) in any other case by the valuation officer[10].

Where, after the referral of an appeal[11] to the tribunal in relation to a disagreement as to a proposed alteration of a list, the valuation officer alters the list in accordance with the proposal, or there is an agreement as to the proposal[12], the valuation officer must notify the clerk of the tribunal accordingly; and the appeal must be deemed to have been withdrawn[13]. Where, following the initiation of an appeal against imposition of a penalty[14], the valuation officer decides to remit the penalty, he must notify the clerk accordingly; and the appeal must be deemed to have been withdrawn[15].

1 As to appeals in relation to non-domestic rating see PARA 242.
2 This is without prejudice to the Non-Domestic Rating (Alterations of Lists and Appeals) (Wales) Regulations 2005, SI 2005/758, reg 8(2) (see PARA 218): reg 24(1). As to the striking out of proceedings see PARA 246.
3 As to hearings see PARA 263.
4 As to written representations see PARA 258.
5 Non-Domestic Rating (Alterations of Lists and Appeals) (Wales) Regulations 2005, SI 2005/758, reg 24(1). As to the meaning of 'clerk' see PARA 257 note 2. The Non-Domestic Rating (Alterations of Lists and Appeals) (Wales) Regulations 2005, SI 2005/758, apply only in relation to Wales: see reg 1. As to the equivalent regulations in relation to England see the Valuation Tribunal for England (Council Tax and Rating Appeals) (Procedure) Regulations 2009, SI 2009/2269; and PARA 243 et seq. As to the meanings of 'England' and 'Wales' see PARA 2 note 16.
6 As to the meaning of 'completion notice' see PARA 223 note 13.
7 Ie under the Local Government Finance Act 1988 Sch 9 para 5C: see PARA 226.
8 As to the meaning of 'appellant' see PARA 243 note 4.
9 Non-Domestic Rating (Alterations of Lists and Appeals) (Wales) Regulations 2005, SI 2005/758, reg 24(1)(a). The clerk must notify the appellant when the clerk has received the notice of withdrawal under reg 24(1)(a), and must serve a copy of the notice of receipt on all the other parties to the appeal: reg 24(3). As to the meaning of 'party' see PARA 243 note 4.
10 Non-Domestic Rating (Alterations of Lists and Appeals) (Wales) Regulations 2005, SI 2005/758, reg 24(1)(b). Subject to reg 24(4) (see the text to notes 11–13), notice may not be given by a valuation officer under reg 24(1) unless every other party to the appeal has given written consent to the valuation officer for the withdrawal of the appeal: reg 24(2). As to valuation officers see PARA 54.
11 Ie under the Non-Domestic Rating (Alteration of Lists and Appeals) (England) Regulations 2009, SI 2009/2268, reg 13: see PARA 211.
12 Ie under the Non-Domestic Rating (Alterations of Lists and Appeals) (Wales) Regulations 2005, SI 2005/758, reg 12: see PARA 221.

13 Non-Domestic Rating (Alterations of Lists and Appeals) (Wales) Regulations 2005, SI 2005/758, reg 24(4).
14 Ie an appeal under the Local Government Finance Act 1988 Sch 9 para 5C: see PARA 226.
15 Non-Domestic Rating (Alterations of Lists and Appeals) (Wales) Regulations 2005, SI 2005/758, reg 24(5).

262. Pre-hearing review.

With a view to clarifying the issues to be dealt with at a hearing[1], a chairperson of the Valuation Tribunal for Wales[2]:

(1) may on the application of a party[3] or of the chairperson's own motion, not less than four weeks after giving notice[4] to the parties to that effect, order a pre-hearing review to be held[5]; and

(2) must endeavour at the pre-hearing review to secure that all the parties make such admissions and agreements as ought reasonably to be made by them in relation to the proceedings[6].

1 As to hearings see PARA 263.
2 As to the Valuation Tribunal for Wales see PARA 237.
3 As to the meaning of 'party' see PARA 243 note 4.
4 As to the service of notices see PARA 213 note 3.
5 Non-Domestic Rating (Alterations of Lists and Appeals) (Wales) Regulations 2005, SI 2005/758, reg 26(a). The Non-Domestic Rating (Alterations of Lists and Appeals) (Wales) Regulations 2005, SI 2005/758, apply only in relation to Wales: see reg 1. As to the equivalent regulations in relation to England see the Valuation Tribunal for England (Council Tax and Rating Appeals) (Procedure) Regulations 2009, SI 2009/2269; and PARA 243 et seq. As to the meanings of 'England' and 'Wales' see PARA 2 note 16.
6 Non-Domestic Rating (Alterations of Lists and Appeals) (Wales) Regulations 2005, SI 2005/758, reg 26(b).

263. Hearings.

Where an appeal[1] is to be disposed of on the basis of a hearing, the clerk of the Valuation Tribunal for Wales[2] must give the parties[3] not less than four weeks' notice of the date, time and place appointed for the hearing[4]. The clerk must advertise the date, time and place appointed for any hearing by causing a notice giving such information to be conspicuously displayed[5]:

(1) at the valuation tribunal's office[6];
(2) outside an office of the relevant authority[7] appointed by the authority for that purpose[8]; or
(3) in another place within that authority's area[9].

The notice must name a place where a list of the appeals to be heard may be inspected[10].

Where the hearing of an appeal has been postponed, the clerk must take such steps as are practicable in the time available:

(a) to notify the parties to the appeal of the postponement[11]; and
(b) to advertise the postponement[12].

Where a hearing is requested[13] when parties are notified that the tribunal is minded to dispose of the appeal without a hearing and the hearing is postponed, the clerk must inform parties to the proceedings if the valuation tribunal is of the view that parties to the proceedings can come to an agreement[14].

A person[15] is disqualified from participating as a member in the hearing or determination of, or acting as clerk or officer of a valuation tribunal in relation to:

(i) an appeal against a completion notice[16] if they are a member of the relevant authority concerned[17]; or
(ii) an appeal as to a proposal to alter a local non-domestic rating list[18] if they are a member of the special authority concerned[19].

Any party to an appeal which is to be decided at a hearing may appear in person (with assistance from any person they wish), by counsel or solicitor, or any other representative (other than a person who is a member, clerk or other employee of the Valuation Tribunal for Wales)[20].

The Valuation Tribunal for Wales' functions of hearing or determining an appeal are to be discharged by three members of the tribunal, who must include at least one chairperson[21]; and a chairperson must preside[22]. The hearing must take place in public, unless the valuation tribunal orders otherwise on the application of a party, and on being satisfied that the interests of that party would be prejudicially affected[23].

If at a hearing of an appeal to which a valuation officer[24] is a party every other party fails to appear, the valuation tribunal may dismiss the appeal[25]. If, at a hearing of an appeal against a completion notice, the appellant does not appear, the valuation tribunal may dismiss the appeal[26]. If, at the hearing of an appeal, any party does not appear, the valuation tribunal may hear and determine the appeal in his absence[27].

The valuation tribunal may require any witness to give evidence by oath or affirmation, and has power for that purpose to administer an oath or affirmation in due form[28].

Unless the valuation tribunal determines otherwise, at the hearing of an appeal[29], or arising from an alteration of a list by the valuation officer, the valuation officer must begin the hearing[30], and at the hearing of an appeal against a completion notice, the relevant authority must begin the hearing[31]. In any other case parties at the hearing may be heard in such order as the tribunal may determine[32].

Parties at the hearing may examine any witness before the valuation tribunal and call witnesses[33].

A hearing may be adjourned to such time and place and on such terms (if any) as the valuation tribunal thinks fit; and reasonable notice of the time and place to which the hearing has been adjourned must be given to every party[34].

A valuation tribunal may enter and inspect the hereditament which is the subject of the appeal and, as far as is practicable, any comparable land or property to which the attention of the tribunal is drawn[35]. When a valuation tribunal intends to enter any premises in accordance with this provision it must give notice to the parties, who are entitled to be represented at the inspection; and where the tribunal deems it appropriate, such representation is to be limited to one person to represent those parties having the same interest in the appeal[36].

Where at the hearing of an appeal as to a proposal to alter a local non-domestic rating list[37]:

(A) the valuation officer contends that the proposal was not validly made; and

(B) the valuation tribunal does not uphold his contention,

the tribunal must not immediately proceed to determine the appeal unless every party so agrees[38].

Subject to any provision of the regulations regulating appeals[39], the valuation tribunal:

(I) must conduct the hearing in such manner as it considers most suitable to the clarification of the issues before it, and generally to the just handling of the proceedings[40];

(II) must, so far as appears to it appropriate, seek to avoid formality in its proceedings[41]; and

(III) is not bound by any enactment or rule of law relating to the admissibility of evidence before courts of law[42].

1 As to appeals in relation to non-domestic rating see PARA 242.
2 As to the Valuation Tribunal for Wales see PARA 237. As to the meaning of 'clerk' see PARA 257 note 2.
3 As to the meaning of 'party' see PARA 243 note 4.
4 Non-Domestic Rating (Alterations of Lists and Appeals) (Wales) Regulations 2005, SI 2005/758, reg 27(1). The Non-Domestic Rating (Alterations of Lists and Appeals) (Wales) Regulations 2005, SI 2005/758, apply only in relation to Wales: see reg 1. As to the equivalent regulations in relation to England see the Valuation Tribunal for England (Council Tax and Rating Appeals) (Procedure) Regulations 2009, SI 2009/2269; and PARA 243 et seq. As to the meanings of 'England' and 'Wales' see PARA 2 note 16.
5 Non-Domestic Rating (Alterations of Lists and Appeals) (Wales) Regulations 2005, SI 2005/758, reg 27(2).
6 Non-Domestic Rating (Alterations of Lists and Appeals) (Wales) Regulations 2005, SI 2005/758, reg 27(2)(a).
7 As to the meaning of 'relevant authority' see PARA 213 note 4.
8 Non-Domestic Rating (Alterations of Lists and Appeals) (Wales) Regulations 2005, SI 2005/758, reg 27(2)(b).
9 Non-Domestic Rating (Alterations of Lists and Appeals) (Wales) Regulations 2005, SI 2005/758, reg 27(2)(c).
10 Non-Domestic Rating (Alterations of Lists and Appeals) (Wales) Regulations 2005, SI 2005/758, reg 27(3).
11 Non-Domestic Rating (Alterations of Lists and Appeals) (Wales) Regulations 2005, SI 2005/758, reg 27(4)(a).
12 Non-Domestic Rating (Alterations of Lists and Appeals) (Wales) Regulations 2005, SI 2005/758, reg 27(4)(b).
13 Ie under the Non-Domestic Rating (Alterations of Lists and Appeals) (Wales) Regulations 2005, SI 2005/758, reg 25A(2): see PARA 259.
14 Non-Domestic Rating (Alterations of Lists and Appeals) (Wales) Regulations 2005, SI 2005/758, reg 27(5) (added by SI 2017/941).
15 As to the meaning of 'person' see PARA 11 note 13.
16 As to the meaning of 'completion notice' see PARA 223 note 13.
17 Non-Domestic Rating (Alterations of Lists and Appeals) (Wales) Regulations 2005, SI 2005/758, reg 28(1)(a). References in reg 28 to the relevant authority concerned and to the special authority concerned are references to the relevant authority and the special authority in whose area is situated the hereditament which is the subject of the appeal: reg 28(2). As to the meaning of 'special authority' see PARA 133 note 11. As to the meaning of 'hereditament' see PARA 106.
18 Ie under the Non-Domestic Rating (Alterations of Lists and Appeals) (Wales) Regulations 2005, SI 2005/758, reg 13: see PARA 222.
19 Non-Domestic Rating (Alterations of Lists and Appeals) (Wales) Regulations 2005, SI 2005/758, reg 28(1)(b). See note 17.
20 Non-Domestic Rating (Alterations of Lists and Appeals) (Wales) Regulations 2005, SI 2005/758, reg 29 (amended by SI 2010/713).
21 This is subject to the Non-Domestic Rating (Alterations of Lists and Appeals) (Wales) Regulations 2005, SI 2005/758, reg 30(2): reg 30(1). Where all parties to an appeal who appear so agree, the appeal may be decided by two members of a valuation tribunal, and notwithstanding the absence of a chairman: reg 30(2).
22 Non-Domestic Rating (Alterations of Lists and Appeals) (Wales) Regulations 2005, SI 2005/758, reg 30(1) (amended by SI 2006/1035 and SI 2010/713).
23 Non-Domestic Rating (Alterations of Lists and Appeals) (Wales) Regulations 2005, SI 2005/758, reg 30(3).
24 As to valuation officers see PARA 54.
25 Non-Domestic Rating (Alterations of Lists and Appeals) (Wales) Regulations 2005, SI 2005/758, reg 30(4).
26 Non-Domestic Rating (Alterations of Lists and Appeals) (Wales) Regulations 2005, SI 2005/758, reg 30(5).
27 Non-Domestic Rating (Alterations of Lists and Appeals) (Wales) Regulations 2005, SI 2005/758, reg 30(6).
28 Non-Domestic Rating (Alterations of Lists and Appeals) (Wales) Regulations 2005, SI 2005/758,

reg 30(7). As to oaths and affirmations see CIVIL PROCEDURE vol 12 (2015) PARA 824 et seq.
29 Ie under the Non-Domestic Rating (Alterations of Lists and Appeals) (Wales) Regulations 2005, SI 2005/758, reg 8: see PARA 218.
30 Non-Domestic Rating (Alterations of Lists and Appeals) (Wales) Regulations 2005, SI 2005/758, reg 30(8)(a).
31 Non-Domestic Rating (Alterations of Lists and Appeals) (Wales) Regulations 2005, SI 2005/758, reg 30(8)(b).
32 Non-Domestic Rating (Alterations of Lists and Appeals) (Wales) Regulations 2005, SI 2005/758, reg 30(8).
33 Non-Domestic Rating (Alterations of Lists and Appeals) (Wales) Regulations 2005, SI 2005/758, reg 30(9).
34 Non-Domestic Rating (Alterations of Lists and Appeals) (Wales) Regulations 2005, SI 2005/758, reg 30(10).
35 Non-Domestic Rating (Alterations of Lists and Appeals) (Wales) Regulations 2005, SI 2005/758, reg 30(11). This is subject to reg 30(12) (see the text to note 36): reg 30(11).
36 Non-Domestic Rating (Alterations of Lists and Appeals) (Wales) Regulations 2005, SI 2005/758, reg 30(12).
37 Ie under the Non-Domestic Rating (Alterations of Lists and Appeals) (Wales) Regulations 2005, SI 2005/758, reg 13: see PARA 222.
38 Non-Domestic Rating (Alterations of Lists and Appeals) (Wales) Regulations 2005, SI 2005/758, reg 30(13).
39 Ie the Non-Domestic Rating (Alterations of Lists and Appeals) (Wales) Regulations 2005, SI 2005/758, Pt 5 (regs 21–39).
40 Non-Domestic Rating (Alterations of Lists and Appeals) (Wales) Regulations 2005, SI 2005/758, reg 30(14)(a).
41 Non-Domestic Rating (Alterations of Lists and Appeals) (Wales) Regulations 2005, SI 2005/758, reg 30(14)(b).
42 Non-Domestic Rating (Alterations of Lists and Appeals) (Wales) Regulations 2005, SI 2005/758, reg 30(14)(c).

264. Decisions.

An appeal[1] may be decided by a majority of the members of the tribunal participating; and where[2] it falls to be disposed of by two members and they are unable to agree, it must be remitted by the clerk[3] to be decided by a valuation tribunal consisting of three different members[4].

Where an appeal is disposed of on the basis of a hearing[5], the decision may be reserved or given orally at the end of the hearing[6]. As soon as reasonably practicable after a decision has been made, it must:

(1) in the case of a decision given orally, be confirmed[7];
(2) in any other case, be communicated[8],

by notice in writing to the parties[9]; and the notice must be accompanied by a statement of the reasons for the decision[10]. However, nothing in this provision requires notice to be given to a party if it would be repetitive of any copy record sent[11] to that party[12].

In the case of an appeal against a completion notice[13], the clerk must send notice of the decision to the valuation officer for the relevant authority[14].

1 As to appeals in relation to non-domestic rating see PARA 242.
2 Ie pursuant to the Non-Domestic Rating (Alterations of Lists and Appeals) (Wales) Regulations 2005, SI 2005/758, reg 30(2): see PARA 263.
3 As to the meaning of 'clerk' see PARA 257 note 2.
4 Non-Domestic Rating (Alterations of Lists and Appeals) (Wales) Regulations 2005, SI 2005/758, reg 33(1). The Non-Domestic Rating (Alterations of Lists and Appeals) (Wales) Regulations 2005, SI 2005/758, apply only in relation to Wales: see reg 1. As to the equivalent regulations in relation to England see the Valuation Tribunal for England (Council Tax and Rating Appeals) (Procedure) Regulations 2009, SI 2009/2269; and PARA 243 et seq. As to the meanings of 'England' and 'Wales' see PARA 2 note 16.
5 As to hearings see PARA 263.

6 Non-Domestic Rating (Alterations of Lists and Appeals) (Wales) Regulations 2005, SI 2005/758, reg 33(2).
7 Non-Domestic Rating (Alterations of Lists and Appeals) (Wales) Regulations 2005, SI 2005/758, reg 33(3)(a).
8 Non-Domestic Rating (Alterations of Lists and Appeals) (Wales) Regulations 2005, SI 2005/758, reg 33(3)(b).
9 Non-Domestic Rating (Alterations of Lists and Appeals) (Wales) Regulations 2005, SI 2005/758, reg 33(3). As to the meaning of 'party' see PARA 243 note 4.
10 Non-Domestic Rating (Alterations of Lists and Appeals) (Wales) Regulations 2005, SI 2005/758, reg 33(3). The tribunal must make arrangements for each decision under reg 33 to be recorded: see reg 36; and PARA 267.
11 Ie under the Non-Domestic Rating (Alterations of Lists and Appeals) (Wales) Regulations 2005, SI 2005/758, reg 36: see PARA 267.
12 Non-Domestic Rating (Alterations of Lists and Appeals) (Wales) Regulations 2005, SI 2005/758, reg 33(4).
13 As to the meaning of 'completion notice' see PARA 223 note 13.
14 Non-Domestic Rating (Alterations of Lists and Appeals) (Wales) Regulations 2005, SI 2005/758, reg 33(5). As to valuation officers see PARA 54. As to the meaning of 'relevant authority' see PARA 213 note 4.

265. Orders.

On or after deciding an appeal relating to a disagreement relating to alteration of a list[1], the Valuation Tribunal for Wales[2] may[3] require a valuation officer[4], in consequence of the decision, by order to alter a list in accordance with any provision made by or under the Local Government Finance Act 1988[5]. On or after deciding an appeal against imposition of a penalty[6] the valuation tribunal may order the valuation officer whose notice is the subject of the appeal to mitigate or remit the penalty[7]. The valuation officer must comply with such an order within the period of two weeks beginning on the day of its making[8].

However, where the decision is that a disputed rateable value[9] should be an amount greater than the amount shown in the list at the date of the proposal[10] and the amount contended for in the proposal, the order must require the list to be altered with effect from the day on which the decision is given[11]. This does not apply where the order requires the list to be altered to show:

(1) property previously rated as a single hereditament[12] becoming liable to be rated in parts[13]; or
(2) property previously liable to be rated in parts becoming liable to be rated as a single hereditament[14]; or
(3) any part of a hereditament becoming part of a different hereditament[15].

Where it appears that circumstances giving rise to an alteration ordered by a valuation tribunal have at the date of the decision ceased to exist, the order may require the alteration to be made in respect of such period as appears to the tribunal to be commensurate with the duration of those circumstances[16].

An order under these provisions may require any matter ancillary to its subject-matter to be attended to[17].

1 Ie under the Non-Domestic Rating (Alterations of Lists and Appeals) (Wales) Regulations 2005, SI 2005/758, reg 13: see PARA 222.
2 As to the Valuation Tribunal for Wales see PARA 237.
3 This is subject to the Non-Domestic Rating (Alterations of Lists and Appeals) (Wales) Regulations 2005, SI 2005/758, reg 34(4) (see the text to notes 9–11).
4 As to valuation officers see PARA 54.
5 Non-Domestic Rating (Alterations of Lists and Appeals) (Wales) Regulations 2005, SI 2005/758, reg 34(1). The tribunal must make arrangements for each order under reg 34 to be recorded: see reg 36; and PARA 267.

The Non-Domestic Rating (Alterations of Lists and Appeals) (Wales) Regulations 2005, SI 2005/758, apply only in relation to Wales: see reg 1. As to the equivalent regulations in relation to England see the Valuation Tribunal for England (Council Tax and Rating Appeals) (Procedure) Regulations 2009, SI 2009/2269; and PARA 243 et seq. As to the meanings of 'England' and 'Wales' see PARA 2 note 16.

6 Ie an appeal under the Local Government Finance Act 1988 Sch 9 para 5C: see PARA 226.
7 Non-Domestic Rating (Alterations of Lists and Appeals) (Wales) Regulations 2005, SI 2005/758, reg 34(2).
8 Non-Domestic Rating (Alterations of Lists and Appeals) (Wales) Regulations 2005, SI 2005/758, reg 34(3).
9 As to the rateable value see PARA 156 et seq.
10 As to the meaning of 'proposal' see PARA 213 note 3.
11 Non-Domestic Rating (Alterations of Lists and Appeals) (Wales) Regulations 2005, SI 2005/758, reg 34(4).
12 As to the meaning of 'hereditament' see PARA 106.
13 Non-Domestic Rating (Alterations of Lists and Appeals) (Wales) Regulations 2005, SI 2005/758, reg 34(5)(a).
14 Non-Domestic Rating (Alterations of Lists and Appeals) (Wales) Regulations 2005, SI 2005/758, reg 34(5)(b).
15 Non-Domestic Rating (Alterations of Lists and Appeals) (Wales) Regulations 2005, SI 2005/758, reg 34(5)(c).
16 Non-Domestic Rating (Alterations of Lists and Appeals) (Wales) Regulations 2005, SI 2005/758, reg 34(6).
17 Non-Domestic Rating (Alterations of Lists and Appeals) (Wales) Regulations 2005, SI 2005/758, reg 34(7).

266. Review of decisions.

A valuation tribunal[1] consisting, so far as is reasonably practicable, of the same members as constituted the tribunal which took the decision[2] has power, on written application by a party[3], to review or set aside by certificate under the hand of the presiding member, any decision on any of the grounds mentioned in heads (1) to (3) below, and the decision on an appeal against a completion notice[4] on the specified[5] additional grounds[6]. However, this does not apply where an appeal against the decision in question has been determined by the Lands Tribunal[7].

An application may be dismissed if it is not made within the period of four weeks beginning on the day on which notice is given[8] of the decision in question[9].

The grounds referred to in above are[10]:

(1) that the decision was wrongly made as a result of clerical error[11];
(2) that a party did not appear and can show reasonable cause why he did not do so[12]; and
(3) that the decision is affected by a decision of, or on appeal from, the High Court or the Lands Tribunal in relation to an appeal in respect of the hereditament which was the subject of the valuation tribunal's decision[13].

The additional grounds in respect of an appeal against a decision on a completion notice are that new evidence, the existence of which could not have been ascertained by reasonably diligent inquiry or could not have been foreseen, has become available since the conclusion of the proceedings to which the decision relates[14].

If a valuation tribunal sets aside a decision in pursuance of these provisions, it must revoke any order made in consequence of that decision and must order a re-hearing or redetermination before either the same or a different tribunal[15].

The clerk must as soon as reasonably practicable notify the parties to the appeal in writing of[16]:

(a) a determination that the valuation tribunal will not undertake a review[17];
(b) the determination of the valuation tribunal, having undertaken a review[18], that it will not set aside the decision concerned[19];
(c) the issue of any certificate[20] by the presiding member[21]; and
(d) the revocation[22] of any order made in consequence of the original decision[23].

Where in relation to a decision in respect of which an application for review is made[24], an appeal to the Lands Chamber of the Upper Tribunal[25] remains undetermined on the relevant day[26], the clerk must notify the Lands Chamber of the Upper Tribunal as soon as reasonably practicable after the occurrence of the relevant event[27].

1 As to the Valuation Tribunal for Wales see PARA 237.
2 Non-Domestic Rating (Alterations of Lists and Appeals) (Wales) Regulations 2005, SI 2005/758, reg 35(4). As to the decision see PARA 264.
The Non-Domestic Rating (Alterations of Lists and Appeals) (Wales) Regulations 2005, SI 2005/758, apply only in relation to Wales: see reg 1. As to the equivalent regulations in relation to England see the Valuation Tribunal for England (Council Tax and Rating Appeals) (Procedure) Regulations 2009, SI 2009/2269; and PARA 243 et seq. As to the meanings of 'England' and 'Wales' see PARA 2 note 16.
3 As to the meaning of 'party' see PARA 243 note 4. Where a valuation officer applies to the tribunal under the Non-Domestic Rating (Alterations of Lists and Appeals) (Wales) Regulations 2005, SI 2005/758, reg 35 for the review of a decision in consequence of which an order requiring the alteration of a list was made, the valuation officer must, at the same time or as soon as reasonably practicable afterwards, notify the authority concerned of the application: see reg 39(1)(a). 'The authority concerned' means:
(1) where the application (or appeal under reg 37) relates to the alteration of a local non-domestic rating list, the relevant authority for whose area the list was compiled (reg 39(2)(b)); and
(2) in any other case, the Welsh Ministers (reg 39(2)(b)).
As to valuation officers see PARA 54. As to the alteration of lists see PARA 214 et seq. As to the service and delivery of documents see reg 40; and PARA 213 note 3. As to the meaning of 'relevant authority' see PARA 243 note 4. As to the Welsh Ministers see PARA 4 note 18.
4 As to the meaning of 'completion notice' see PARA 223 note 13.
5 Ie the grounds mentioned in the Non-Domestic Rating (Alterations of Lists and Appeals) (Wales) Regulations 2005, SI 2005/758, reg 35(6). See the text to note 14.
6 Non-Domestic Rating (Alterations of Lists and Appeals) (Wales) Regulations 2005, SI 2005/758, reg 35(1). The tribunal must make arrangements for effect of each certificate and revocation under reg 35 to be recorded: see reg 36; and PARA 267.
7 Non-Domestic Rating (Alterations of Lists and Appeals) (Wales) Regulations 2005, SI 2005/758, reg 35(2). Note that appeals to the Lands Tribunal are now to the Upper Tribunal (Lands Chamber): see PARA 270.
8 Ie whether in accordance with the Non-Domestic Rating (Alterations of Lists and Appeals) (Wales) Regulations 2005, SI 2005/758, reg 33(3) (see PARA 264) or reg 36(3) (see PARA 267).
9 Non-Domestic Rating (Alterations of Lists and Appeals) (Wales) Regulations 2005, SI 2005/758, reg 35(3).
10 Non-Domestic Rating (Alterations of Lists and Appeals) (Wales) Regulations 2005, SI 2005/758, reg 35(5).
11 Non-Domestic Rating (Alterations of Lists and Appeals) (Wales) Regulations 2005, SI 2005/758, reg 35(5)(a).
12 Non-Domestic Rating (Alterations of Lists and Appeals) (Wales) Regulations 2005, SI 2005/758, reg 35(5)(b).
13 Non-Domestic Rating (Alterations of Lists and Appeals) (Wales) Regulations 2005, SI 2005/758, reg 35(5)(c).
14 Non-Domestic Rating (Alterations of Lists and Appeals) (Wales) Regulations 2005, SI 2005/758, reg 35(6).
15 Non-Domestic Rating (Alterations of Lists and Appeals) (Wales) Regulations 2005, SI 2005/758, reg 35(7).

16 Non-Domestic Rating (Alterations of Lists and Appeals) (Wales) Regulations 2005, SI 2005/758, reg 35(8). As to the meaning of 'clerk' see PARA 257 note 2.
17 Non-Domestic Rating (Alterations of Lists and Appeals) (Wales) Regulations 2005, SI 2005/758, reg 35(8)(a).
18 Ie under the Non-Domestic Rating (Alterations of Lists and Appeals) (Wales) Regulations 2005, SI 2005/758, reg 35(1).
19 Non-Domestic Rating (Alterations of Lists and Appeals) (Wales) Regulations 2005, SI 2005/758, reg 35(8)(b).
20 Ie under the Non-Domestic Rating (Alterations of Lists and Appeals) (Wales) Regulations 2005, SI 2005/758, reg 35(1).
21 Non-Domestic Rating (Alterations of Lists and Appeals) (Wales) Regulations 2005, SI 2005/758, reg 35(8)(c).
22 Ie under the Non-Domestic Rating (Alterations of Lists and Appeals) (Wales) Regulations 2005, SI 2005/758, reg 35(7).
23 Non-Domestic Rating (Alterations of Lists and Appeals) (Wales) Regulations 2005, SI 2005/758, reg 35(8)(d).
24 Ie under the Non-Domestic Rating (Alterations of Lists and Appeals) (Wales) Regulations 2005, SI 2005/758, reg 35(1).
25 As to the Lands Chamber of the Upper Tribunal (formerly the Lands Tribunal) see COURTS AND TRIBUNALS vol 24 (2010) PARA 886.
26 'The relevant day' means the day on which, as the case may be, the application under the Non-Domestic Rating (Alterations of Lists and Appeals) (Wales) Regulations 2005, SI 2005/758, reg 35(1) is made or an event referred to in any of reg 35(8)(a)–(d) (see heads (a)–(d) in the text) occurs: reg 35(10).
27 Non-Domestic Rating (Alterations of Lists and Appeals) (Wales) Regulations 2005, SI 2005/758, reg 35(9). 'The relevant event', in relation to a relevant day, means the event occurring on that day: reg 35(10).

267. Records of decisions and orders.

It is the duty of the clerk of the Valuation Tribunal for Wales[1] to make arrangements for each decision[2], each order[3] and the effect of each certificate and revocation[4] to be recorded[5]. Records may be kept in any form, whether documentary or otherwise, and must contain the specified[6] particulars[7].

A copy, in documentary form, of the relevant entry in the record must, as soon as reasonably practicable after the entry has been made, be sent (by post, fax or electronic communication) to each party[8] to the appeal to which the entry relates[9].

Each record must be retained for the period of six years beginning on the day on which an entry was last made in it[10].

Any person[11] may, at a reasonable time stated by or on behalf of the valuation tribunal concerned and without making payment, inspect records which are required to be made by these provisions[12]. If without reasonable excuse a person having custody of records intentionally obstructs a person in exercising the right to inspect them that person commits an offence[13].

The member who presided at the hearing or determination of an appeal may authorise the correction of any clerical error in the record, and a copy of the corrected entry must be sent to the persons to whom a copy of the original entry was sent[14].

The production in any proceedings in any court of law of a document purporting to be certified by the clerk to be a true copy of a record of that valuation tribunal is, unless the contrary is proved, sufficient evidence of the document and of the facts it records[15].

1 As to the Valuation Tribunal for Wales see PARA 237. As to the meaning of 'clerk' see PARA 257 note 2.
2 As to decisions see PARA 264.
3 Ie each order under the Non-Domestic Rating (Alterations of Lists and Appeals) (Wales) Regulations 2005, SI 2005/758, reg 34: see PARA 265.

4 Ie each order under the Non-Domestic Rating (Alterations of Lists and Appeals) (Wales) Regulations 2005, SI 2005/758, reg 35: see PARA 266.
5 Non-Domestic Rating (Alterations of Lists and Appeals) (Wales) Regulations 2005, SI 2005/758, reg 36(1). The Non-Domestic Rating (Alterations of Lists and Appeals) (Wales) Regulations 2005, SI 2005/758, apply only in relation to Wales: see reg 1. As to the equivalent regulations in relation to England see the Valuation Tribunal for England (Council Tax and Rating Appeals) (Procedure) Regulations 2009, SI 2009/2269; and PARA 243 et seq. As to the meanings of 'England' and 'Wales' see PARA 2 note 16.
6 Ie the particulars specified in the Non-Domestic Rating (Alterations of Lists and Appeals) (Wales) Regulations 2005, SI 2005/758, Schedule.
7 Non-Domestic Rating (Alterations of Lists and Appeals) (Wales) Regulations 2005, SI 2005/758, reg 36(2).
8 As to the meaning of 'party' see PARA 243 note 4.
9 Non-Domestic Rating (Alterations of Lists and Appeals) (Wales) Regulations 2005, SI 2005/758, reg 36(3).
10 Non-Domestic Rating (Alterations of Lists and Appeals) (Wales) Regulations 2005, SI 2005/758, reg 36(4).
11 As to the meaning of 'person' see PARA 11 note 13.
12 Non-Domestic Rating (Alterations of Lists and Appeals) (Wales) Regulations 2005, SI 2005/758, reg 36(5).
13 Non-Domestic Rating (Alterations of Lists and Appeals) (Wales) Regulations 2005, SI 2005/758, reg 36(6). The penalty for such an offence is, on summary conviction, a fine not exceeding level 1 on the standard scale: reg 36(6). As to the powers of magistrates' courts to issue fines on summary conviction see SENTENCING vol 92 (2015) PARA 176.
14 Non-Domestic Rating (Alterations of Lists and Appeals) (Wales) Regulations 2005, SI 2005/758, reg 36(7).
15 Non-Domestic Rating (Alterations of Lists and Appeals) (Wales) Regulations 2005, SI 2005/758, reg 36(8).

D. ARBITRATION

268. Reference to arbitration.

In relation to England, where the persons[1] who, if a matter were to be the subject of an appeal[2] to the Valuation Tribunal for England[3], would be the parties[4] to the appeal[5] agree in writing[6] that a matter falling within the tribunal's jurisdiction is to be referred to arbitration, the matter must be so referred[7].

Unless the tribunal considers that there is good reason not to do so, where at any time before the determination of an appeal by the tribunal, the parties to the proceedings on an appeal agree in writing that any matter arising in the proceedings is to be referred to arbitration, the matter must be so referred[8].

In any arbitration under these provisions the award may include any order[9] which could have been made by the tribunal in relation to the matter[10].

In relation to Wales, where at any time before the beginning of a hearing[11] or the consideration by the Valuation Tribunal for Wales[12] of written representations[13] it is so agreed in writing between the persons who, if a dispute were to be the subject of an appeal to the tribunal, would be the parties[14] to the appeal, the question must be referred to arbitration[15].

In any arbitration in pursuance of these provisions the award may include any order which could have been made by a valuation tribunal in relation to the question[16].

1 As to the meaning of 'person' see PARA 11 note 13.
2 As to appeals in relation to non-domestic rating see PARA 242.
3 As to the Valuation Tribunal for England see PARA 232. The Valuation Tribunal for England (Council Tax and Rating Appeals) (Procedure) Regulations 2009, SI 2009/2269, apply in relation to England only: see reg 1. As to the equivalent provision in relation to Wales see the text to notes 11–16. As to the meanings of 'England' and 'Wales' see PARA 2 note 16.
4 As to the meaning of 'party' see PARA 243 note 4.

5 See the Valuation Tribunal for England (Council Tax and Rating Appeals) (Procedure) Regulations 2009, SI 2009/2269, reg 4(2).
6 As to the meaning of 'writing' see PARA 21 note 3.
7 See the Valuation Tribunal for England (Council Tax and Rating Appeals) (Procedure) Regulations 2009, SI 2009/2269, reg 4(1). The provisions of the Arbitration Act 1996 Pt I (ss 1–84) apply to any arbitration under the Valuation Tribunal for England (Council Tax and Rating Appeals) (Procedure) Regulations 2009, SI 2009/2269, reg 4: see the Arbitration Act 1996 s 94; and ARBITRATION vol 2 (2017) PARA 509.
8 Valuation Tribunal for England (Council Tax and Rating Appeals) (Procedure) Regulations 2009, SI 2009/2269, reg 4(3). See also note 7.
9 As to orders see PARA 254.
10 Valuation Tribunal for England (Council Tax and Rating Appeals) (Procedure) Regulations 2009, SI 2009/2269, reg 4(4). The Local Government Finance Act 1988 Sch 11 para 9 (see PARA 254 note 21) applies to such an order as it applies to an order recorded under the Valuation Tribunal for England (Council Tax and Rating Appeals) (Procedure) Regulations 2009, SI 2009/2269: reg 4(4).
11 As to hearings see PARA 263.
12 As to the Valuation Tribunal for Wales see PARA 237.
13 As to written representations see PARA 258.
14 As to the meaning of 'party' see PARA 243 note 4.
15 Non-Domestic Rating (Alterations of Lists and Appeals) (Wales) Regulations 2005, SI 2005/758, reg 38(1). The Non-Domestic Rating (Alterations of Lists and Appeals) (Wales) Regulations 2005, SI 2005/758, apply only in relation to Wales: see reg 1.
16 Non-Domestic Rating (Alterations of Lists and Appeals) (Wales) Regulations 2005, SI 2005/758, reg 38(2). The Local Government Finance Act 1988 Sch 11 para 9 (see PARA 254 note 21) applies to such an order as it applies to an order recorded in pursuance of the Non-Domestic Rating (Alterations of Lists and Appeals) (Wales) Regulations 2005, SI 2005/758: reg 38(2).

E. CHALLENGING TRIBUNAL DECISIONS

269. Appeal to the Upper Tribunal: England.

An appeal lies to the Upper Tribunal[1] in respect of a decision[2] or order[3] given or made by the Valuation Tribunal for England[4] on an appeal under the non-domestic rating appeals regulations[5] or an appeal[6] against a completion notice[7]. Any such appeal lies at the instance of[8]:

(1) any party who appeared at the hearing[9] or, if the appeal was disposed of by written representations, who made such representations[10]; or
(2) any person[11] whose application[12] for the review of the decision relied (whether in whole or part) on satisfaction of the condition[13] relating to non-attendance at a hearing[14].

An appeal may be dismissed if it is not made within four weeks[15] of the date on which notice is given of the decision or order against which the appeal is made[16].

The Upper Tribunal may confirm, vary, set aside, revoke or remit the decision or order, and may make any order the tribunal could have made[17]. Valuation officers must act in accordance with any order made by the Upper Tribunal[18].

Any party to an appeal has a right of appeal to the Court of Appeal on any point of law arising from a decision made by the Upper Tribunal[19].

1 As to the Upper Tribunal see COURTS AND TRIBUNALS vol 24 (2010) PARA 874 et seq.
2 As to decisions see PARA 253.
3 As to orders see PARA 254.
4 As to the Valuation Tribunal for England see PARA 232. The Valuation Tribunal for England (Council Tax and Rating Appeals) (Procedure) Regulations 2009, SI 2009/2269, apply in relation to England only: see reg 1. As to the equivalent provision in relation to Wales see the Non-Domestic Rating (Alterations of Lists and Appeals) (Wales) Regulations 2005, SI 2005/758, reg 37; and PARA 270. As to the meanings of 'England' and 'Wales' see PARA 2 note 16.
5 Ie the Non-Domestic Rating (Alteration of Lists and Appeals) (England) Regulations 2009, SI 2009/2268.

6 Ie under the Local Government Finance Act 1988 Sch 4A para 1 as it applies for the purposes of Part III of that Act: see PARA 138.

7 Valuation Tribunal for England (Council Tax and Rating Appeals) (Procedure) Regulations 2009, SI 2009/2269, reg 42(1).

8 Where a valuation officer appeals to the Upper Tribunal under the Valuation Tribunal for England (Council Tax and Rating Appeals) (Procedure) Regulations 2009, SI 2009/2269, reg 42 against a decision in consequence of which an order requiring the alteration of a list was made, or against such an order, the valuation officer must, at the same time or as soon as reasonably practicable afterwards, notify the authority concerned of the application or appeal: see reg 44(1)(b). See also the Non-Domestic Rating (Alteration of Lists and Appeals) (England) Regulations 2009, SI 2009/2268, reg 21 which makes similar provision. As to valuation officers see PARA 54. As to the alteration of lists see PARA 202 et seq. As to the service and delivery of documents see reg 15; and PARA 243. As to the meaning of 'the authority concerned' see PARA 255 note 4.

Where a valuation officer appeals to the Upper Tribunal under the Valuation Tribunal for England (Council Tax and Rating Appeals) (Procedure) Regulations 2009, SI 2009/2269, reg 42 against a decision in consequence of which an order requiring the alteration of a list was made, or against such an order, or receives notice of such an appeal instituted by another party, he must, as soon as reasonably practicable afterwards, notify the Valuation Tribunal for England of the appeal: reg 44(3). As to the meaning of 'party' see PARA 243 note 4.

Where, in relation to a decision or order made on an appeal against a completion notice, an authority appeals to the Upper Tribunal under reg 42, or receives notice of such an appeal instituted by another party, it must, as soon as reasonably practicable afterwards, notify the Valuation Tribunal for England of the appeal: reg 44(4).

9 As to hearings see PARA 251.

10 Valuation Tribunal for England (Council Tax and Rating Appeals) (Procedure) Regulations 2009, SI 2009/2269, reg 42(2)(a). See *Taissa Wassiljew-Jones v Done Bros (Cash Betting) Ltd (t/a Betfred)* [2015] UKUT 499 (LC); [2016] RVR 60. As to written representations and evidence generally see PARA 248.

11 As to the meaning of 'person' see PARA 11 note 13.

12 Ie under the Valuation Tribunal for England (Council Tax and Rating Appeals) (Procedure) Regulations 2009, SI 2009/2269, reg 40(1): see PARA 255.

13 Ie the condition mentioned in the Valuation Tribunal for England (Council Tax and Rating Appeals) (Procedure) Regulations 2009, SI 2009/2269, reg 40(5)(c): see PARA 255.

14 Valuation Tribunal for England (Council Tax and Rating Appeals) (Procedure) Regulations 2009, SI 2009/2269, reg 42(2)(b).

15 As to the calculation of time see PARA 243.

16 Valuation Tribunal for England (Council Tax and Rating Appeals) (Procedure) Regulations 2009, SI 2009/2269, reg 42(3). However, where the appeal is made by a person of the description specified in reg 42(2)(b) (see the text to notes 11–14) (reg 42(4)(a)) and the tribunal gave notice in relation to the person's application that it would not undertake a review (reg 42(4)(b)(i)) or having reviewed the decision or part, that it would not set aside the decision or part (reg 42(4)(b)(ii)), the appeal may be dismissed if it is not made within four weeks of the date of the tribunal's notice (reg 42(4)).

17 Valuation Tribunal for England (Council Tax and Rating Appeals) (Procedure) Regulations 2009, SI 2009/2269, reg 42(5).

18 See the Valuation Tribunal for England (Council Tax and Rating Appeals) (Procedure) Regulations 2009, SI 2009/2269, reg 42(6). The Local Government Finance Act 1988 Sch 11 para 9 (see PARA 254 note 21) has effect as if the reference to a tribunal included a reference to the Upper Tribunal: Valuation Tribunal for England (Council Tax and Rating Appeals) (Procedure) Regulations 2009, SI 2009/2269, reg 42(6).

19 See the Tribunals, Courts and Enforcement Act 2007 s 13; and COURTS AND TRIBUNALS vol 24 (2010) PARA 929.

270. Appeal to the Upper Tribunal: Wales.

An appeal lies to the Lands Chamber of the Upper Tribunal[1] in respect of a decision[2] or order[3] which is given or made by a valuation tribunal on an appeal relating to an invalid proposal[4] or to a decision about a proposed alteration to a valuation list[5] or an appeal against a completion notice[6].

An appeal against a decision or order lies at the instance of any party[7]:

(1) who appeared at the hearing[8] or, if the appeal was disposed of by written representations[9], who made such representations[10]; or

(2) whose application for the review of the decision on the ground that a party did not appear and can show reasonable cause why he did not do so[11] the tribunal has determined[12] not to set aside[13].

An appeal may be dismissed if it is not made within four weeks of the date on which notice is given of the decision or order that is the subject matter of the appeal[14]. However, where:

(a) in relation to an application for review of a decision[15] made within four weeks of the date on which notice was given of the decision which is the subject matter of the appeal, notice is given of a determination that the valuation tribunal will not undertake a review[16]; or

(b) notice is given of a determination that the tribunal, having undertaken a review, will not set aside the decision concerned[17],

the appeal may be dismissed if it is not made within four weeks of the service of the notice under head (a) or (b) above[18].

The Upper Tribunal may confirm, vary, set aside, revoke or remit the decision or order of the valuation tribunal, and may make any order the tribunal could have made[19].

Valuation officers must act in accordance with any order made by the Upper Tribunal[20].

1 As to the Lands Chamber of the Upper Tribunal (formerly the Lands Tribunal) see COURTS AND TRIBUNALS vol 24 (2010) PARA 886.

2 As to decisions see PARA 264.

3 As to orders see PARA 265.

4 Ie under the Non-Domestic Rating (Alterations of Lists and Appeals) (Wales) Regulations 2005, SI 2005/758, reg 8 (see PARA 218).

5 Ie under the Non-Domestic Rating (Alterations of Lists and Appeals) (Wales) Regulations 2005, SI 2005/758, reg 13 (see PARA 222).

6 Non-Domestic Rating (Alterations of Lists and Appeals) (Wales) Regulations 2005, SI 2005/758, reg 37(1). As to the meaning of 'completion notice' see PARA 223 note 13.

The Non-Domestic Rating (Alterations of Lists and Appeals) (Wales) Regulations 2005, SI 2005/758, apply only in relation to Wales: see reg 1. As to the equivalent provisions in relation to England see the Valuation Tribunal for England (Council Tax and Rating Appeals) (Procedure) Regulations 2009, SI 2009/2269, reg 42; and PARA 269. As to the meanings of 'England' and 'Wales' see PARA 2 note 16.

7 As to the meaning of 'party' see PARA 243 note 4. Where a valuation officer appeals to the Upper Tribunal under the Non-Domestic Rating (Alterations of Lists and Appeals) (Wales) Regulations 2005, SI 2005/758, reg 37 against a decision in consequence of which an order requiring the alteration of a list was made, or against such an order, the valuation officer must, at the same time or as soon as reasonably practicable afterwards, notify the authority concerned of the application or appeal: see reg 39(1)(b). As to the meaning of 'the authority concerned' see PARA 266 note 3. As to valuation officers see PARA 54.

Where a valuation officer appeals to the Upper Tribunal as mentioned in reg 39(1)(b), or receives notice of such an appeal instituted by another party, the valuation officer must, at the same time or as soon as reasonably practicable thereafter, notify the clerk to the relevant valuation tribunal of the appeal: reg 39(3).

Where, in relation to a decision or order made on an appeal against a completion notice , an authority appeals to the Upper Tribunal under reg 37, or receives notice of such an appeal instituted by another party it must, at the same time, or as soon as reasonably practicable thereafter, notify the clerk to the relevant valuation tribunal of the appeal: reg 39(4). As to the meaning of 'relevant valuation tribunal' see PARA 213 note 7.

8 As to hearings see PARA 263.

9 As to written representations see PARA 258.

10 Non-Domestic Rating (Alterations of Lists and Appeals) (Wales) Regulations 2005, SI 2005/758, reg 37(2)(a).

11 Ie on the ground set out in the Non-Domestic Rating (Alterations of Lists and Appeals) (Wales) Regulations 2005, SI 2005/758, reg 35(5)(b): see PARA 266 head (2).
12 Ie as mentioned in the Non-Domestic Rating (Alterations of Lists and Appeals) (Wales) Regulations 2005, SI 2005/758, reg 35(8)(b): see PARA 266 head (b).
13 Non-Domestic Rating (Alterations of Lists and Appeals) (Wales) Regulations 2005, SI 2005/758, reg 37(2)(b).
14 Non-Domestic Rating (Alterations of Lists and Appeals) (Wales) Regulations 2005, SI 2005/758, reg 37(3).
15 Ie under the Non-Domestic Rating (Alterations of Lists and Appeals) (Wales) Regulations 2005, SI 2005/758, reg 35(1): see PARA 266.
16 Ie as mentioned in the Non-Domestic Rating (Alterations of Lists and Appeals) (Wales) Regulations 2005, SI 2005/758, reg 35(8)(a): see PARA 266 head (a).
17 Ie as mentioned in the Non-Domestic Rating (Alterations of Lists and Appeals) (Wales) Regulations 2005, SI 2005/758, reg 35(8)(b): see PARA 266 head (b).
18 Non-Domestic Rating (Alterations of Lists and Appeals) (Wales) Regulations 2005, SI 2005/758, reg 37(4).
19 Non-Domestic Rating (Alterations of Lists and Appeals) (Wales) Regulations 2005, SI 2005/758, reg 37(5).
20 Non-Domestic Rating (Alterations of Lists and Appeals) (Wales) Regulations 2005, SI 2005/758, reg 37(6). The Local Government Finance Act 1988 Sch 11 para 9 (see PARA 254 note 21) has effect subject to this requirement: Non-Domestic Rating (Alterations of Lists and Appeals) (Wales) Regulations 2005, SI 2005/758, reg 37(6).

271. Judicial review of decisions made by valuation tribunals: England and Wales.

Decisions of valuation tribunals[1] may be judicially reviewed by the High Court[2], where there is no other suitable avenue of appeal[3]. By way of remedy, a quashing order may be granted if the tribunal acts without jurisdiction[4]; and where a tribunal refuses to hear or review a matter, it may be possible to have that refusal reviewed and a mandatory order granted[5].

1 As to the Valuation Tribunal for England see PARA 232. As to the Valuation Tribunal for Wales see PARA 237.
2 As to judicial review see JUDICIAL REVIEW vol 61 (2010) PARA 601 et seq.
3 See *R v Oxfordshire Local Valuation Panel, ex p Oxford City Council* (1981) 79 LGR 432, [1981] RA 239 (in which it was held that an appeal to the Lands Tribunal from the local valuation court was more convenient where a breach of natural justice was alleged); *Boyd v South Staffordshire District Council Community Charges Registration Officer and Staffordshire and Shropshire Valuation and Community Charge Tribunal* [1992] RA 235.
The cases cited in this paragraph were decided prior to the coming into force of the Local Government Finance Act 1988 but may continue to be of relevance: see PARA 50.
4 *R v Cardiff Justices, ex p Cardiff Corpn* [1962] 2 QB 436, sub nom *R v City of Cardiff Justices, ex p Cardiff City Council* [1962] 1 All ER 751; *R v Cheshire East Local Valuation Court, ex p Peasnall* [1961] RVR 199; and see *Allchin v Williamson (Valuation Officer)* [1966] RA 297, [1966] RVR 366, Lands Tribunal; *Wolverhampton Association of Ratepayers v Stamp (Valuation Officer)* (1977) 21 RRC 62, 246 Estates Gazette 751, Lands Tribunal; *R v Lands Tribunal, ex p City of London Corpn* [1981] 1 All ER 753, [1981] 1 WLR 985. As to quashing orders see JUDICIAL REVIEW vol 61 (2010) PARA 693 et seq.
5 *R v Bedminster Union* (1876) 1 QBD 503 (refusal by an assessment committee to determine an objection). As to delay see *R v South West Durham Assessment Committee* (1928) 8 R & IT 39. As to mandatory orders see JUDICIAL REVIEW vol 61 (2010) PARA 703 et seq.

(10) Recovery of Rates

(i) In General

272. Power to make regulations for the recovery of rates.

The appropriate national authority[1] may make regulations containing such provision as it sees fit in relation to the collection and the recovery otherwise than by the procedure for taking control of goods[2] of amounts persons[3] are liable to pay[4] in relation to non-domestic rating[5].

Similar provision is made for the collection and enforcement of non-domestic rates for hereditaments in the local non-domestic rating lists[6] as for hereditaments in the central non-domestic rating lists[7].

1 Ie the Secretary of State or, in relation to Wales, the Welsh Ministers. The functions of the Secretary of State under the Local Government Finance Act 1988 Sch 9, so far as exercisable in relation to Wales, were transferred to the National Assembly for Wales (see the National Assembly for Wales (Transfer of Functions) Order 1999, SI 1999/672, art 2, Sch 1) and are now vested in the Welsh Ministers (see the Government of Wales Act 2006 s 162(1), Sch 11 para 30). As to the Secretary of State and the Welsh Ministers see PARA 4 note 18. As to the meaning of 'Wales' see PARA 2 note 16.

2 Ie under the Tribunals, Courts and Enforcement Act 2007 Sch 12: see PARA 295; and CIVIL PROCEDURE vol 12A (2015) PARA 1334 et seq.

3 As to the meaning of 'person' see PARA 11 note 13.

4 Ie under the Local Government Finance Act 1988 s 43 (see PARAS 133, 143 et seq), s 45 (see PARAS 135–136, 148), and s 54 (see PARA 142): see the Local Government Finance Act 1988 s 62, Sch 9 para 1. As to the consolidation of proceedings for the recovery of rates see the Poor Rates Recovery Act 1862 s 1.

5 Local Government Finance Act 1988 Sch 9 para 1 (amended by the Tribunals, Courts and Enforcement Act 2007 s 62(3), Sch 13 paras 87, 89(1), (2)).

The following regulations have been made under the Local Government Finance Act 1988 Sch 9 para 1: the Non-Domestic Rating (Collection and Enforcement) (Local Lists) Regulations 1989, SI 1989/1058 (see PARA 278 et seq); the Non-Domestic Rating (Collection and Enforcement) (Central Lists) Regulations 1989, SI 1989/2260 (see PARA 306 et seq); the Non-Domestic Rating (Collection and Enforcement) (Miscellaneous Provisions) Regulations 1990, SI 1990/145 (amended by SI 1993/616, SI 2014/600; and in relation to England by SI 2008/428); the Non-Domestic Rating (Transitional Period) Regulations 1990, SI 1990/608 (amended by SI 1990/2329, SI 1992/1514, SI 1993/616; and in relation to England by SI 2003/2000); the Non-Domestic Rating (Collection and Enforcement) (Local Lists) (Amendment and Miscellaneous Provision) Regulations 1991, SI 1991/141 (amended by SI 1991/228 and SI 1993/616); the Non-Domestic Rating (Collection and Enforcement) (Amendment and Miscellaneous Provision) (No 2) Regulations 1993, SI 1993/894; the Council Tax and Non-Domestic Rating (Demand Notices) (England) Regulations 2003, SI 2003/2613 (amended by SI 2003/3081, SI 2004/3389, SI 2006/217, SI 2006/492, SI 2006/3395, SI 2007/501, SI 2008/387, SI 2008/3264, SI 2009/355, SI 2009/1597, SI 2010/140, SI 2010/187, SI 2012/538, SI 2012/2914, SI 2013/694, SI 2015/427, SI 2016/316 and SI 2017/39); the Non-Domestic Rating (Deferred Payments) (England) Regulations 2009, SI 2009/1597; the Non-Domestic Rating (Deferred Payments) (Wales) Regulations 2009, SI 2009/2154 (amended by SI 2012/466); the Non-Domestic Rating (Deferred Payments) (Wales) Regulations 2012, SI 2012/466 (amended by SI 2017/113); and the Non-Domestic Rating (Demand Notices) (Wales) Regulations 2017, SI 2017/113.

6 As to the collection and enforcement provisions under the local non-domestic rating lists see PARAS 278–305.

7 As to the collection and enforcement provisions under the central non-domestic rating lists see PARAS 306–318.

273. Provision that may be made for collection and recovery generally.

Regulations made in relation to the collection and recovery of amounts which persons are liable to pay in relation to non-domestic rating[1] may include provision[2]:

(1) that the ratepayer[3] is to make payments on account of the amount payable[4], which may include payments during the course of the financial year[5];

(2) that payments on account must be made in accordance with an agreement between the ratepayer and the payee[6] or in accordance with a prescribed[7] scheme for payment by instalments[8];

(3) that in prescribed circumstances payments on account must be calculated by reference to an estimate of the amount payable[9];

(4) that an estimate must be made on prescribed assumptions (whether as to the ratepayer's interest in property or otherwise)[10];

(5) that the payee must serve a notice or notices on the ratepayer stating the amount payable or its estimated amount and what payment or payments he is required to make (by way of instalment or otherwise)[11];

(6) that no payment on account of the amount payable need be made unless a notice requires it[12];

(7) that a notice must be in a prescribed form[13];

(8) that a notice must contain prescribed matters[14];

(9) that a notice must not contain other prescribed matters[15];

(10) that where a notice is invalid because it does not comply with regulations under head (7) or (8) above, and the circumstances are such as may be prescribed, a requirement contained in the notice by virtue of regulations under head (5) or (6) above is nevertheless to have effect as if the notice were valid[16];

(11) that where a notice is invalid because it does not comply with regulations under head (7) above, and a requirement has effect by virtue of regulations under head (10) above, the payee must take prescribed steps to issue to the ratepayer a document in the form which the notice would have taken had it complied with regulations under head (7) above[17];

(12) that where a notice is invalid because it does not comply with regulations under head (8) above, and a requirement has effect by virtue of regulations under head (10) above, the payee must take prescribed steps to inform the ratepayer of such of the matters prescribed under head (8) above as were not contained in the notice[18];

(13) that the payee must publish prescribed information in the prescribed manner[19];

(14) that the payee must supply prescribed information to the ratepayer when the payee serves a notice or on the request of the ratepayer[20];

(15) that if the ratepayer fails to pay an instalment in accordance with the regulations, the unpaid balance of the amount payable or its estimated amount is payable on the day after the end of a prescribed period which begins with the day of the failure[21]; and

(16) that any amount paid by the ratepayer in excess of his liability (whether the excess arises because an estimate turns out to be wrong or otherwise) must be repaid or credited against any subsequent liability[22].

1 Ie regulations made under the Local Government Finance Act 1988 Sch 9: see PARA 272.

2 Local Government Finance Act 1988 s 62, Sch 9 para 2(2).

3 In the Local Government Finance Act 1988 Sch 9 para 2, references to the 'ratepayer' are to a person liable to pay an amount under s 43 (see PARAS 133, 143 et seq), s 45 (see PARAS 135–136, 148), or s 54 (see PARA 142): Sch 9 para 2(1)(a). As to the meaning of 'person' see PARA 11 note 13.

4 In the Local Government Finance Act 1988 Sch 9 para 2, references to the 'amount payable' are to the amount the ratepayer is liable to pay: Sch 9 para 2(1)(b).
5 Local Government Finance Act 1988 Sch 9 para 2(2)(a). In Sch 9 para 2, references to the 'financial year' are to the financial year concerned: Sch 9 para 2(1)(d). As to the meaning of 'financial year' see PARA 24 note 1.
6 In the Local Government Finance Act 1988 Sch 9 para 2, references to the 'payee' are to the billing authority to which the ratepayer is liable to pay or (where s 54 applies: see PARA 142) the Secretary of State or, in relation to Wales, the Welsh Ministers: see Sch 9 para 2(1)(c) (amended by the Local Government Finance Act 1992 s 117(1), Sch 13 para 87(1)). As to the meaning of 'billing authority' see PARA 53.

The functions of the Secretary of State under the Local Government Finance Act 1988 Sch 9, so far as exercisable in relation to Wales, were transferred to the National Assembly for Wales (see the National Assembly for Wales (Transfer of Functions) Order 1999, SI 1999/672, art 2, Sch 1) and are now vested in the Welsh Ministers (see the Government of Wales Act 2006 s 162(1), Sch 11 para 30). As to the Secretary of State and the Welsh Ministers see PARA 4 note 18. As to the meaning of 'Wales' see PARA 2 note 16.
7 'Prescribed' means prescribed by the regulations: see the Local Government Finance Act 1988 s 146(6).
8 Local Government Finance Act 1988 Sch 9 para 2(2)(b).
9 Local Government Finance Act 1988 Sch 9 para 2(2)(c).
10 Local Government Finance Act 1988 Sch 9 para 2(2)(d).
11 Local Government Finance Act 1988 Sch 9 para 2(2)(e).
12 Local Government Finance Act 1988 Sch 9 para 2(2)(f). Any reference in Sch 9 para 2 to a payment on account of an amount is to any payment (whether interim, final or sole) in respect of the amount: Sch 9 para 2(3).
13 Local Government Finance Act 1988 Sch 9 para 2(2)(g) (Sch 9 para 2(2)(g) substituted, para 2(2)(ga)–(ge) added, by the Local Government and Housing Act 1989 ss 139, 194(4), Sch 5 paras 1, 44, 79(3), Sch 12 Pt II).
14 Local Government Finance Act 1988 Sch 9 para 2(2)(ga) (as added: see note 13).
15 Local Government Finance Act 1988 Sch 9 para 2(2)(gb) (as added: see note 13).
16 Local Government Finance Act 1988 Sch 9 para 2(2)(gc) (as added: see note 13).
17 Local Government Finance Act 1988 Sch 9 para 2(2)(gd) (as added: see note 13).
18 Local Government Finance Act 1988 Sch 9 para 2(2)(ge) (as added: see note 13).
19 Local Government Finance Act 1988 Sch 9 para 2(2)(gf) (added by the Local Government Finance Act 2012 s 8(1), (2)).
20 Local Government Finance Act 1988 Sch 9 para 2(2)(h) (amended by the Local Government and Housing Act 1989 Sch 5 paras 1, 44, 79(3), Sch 12 Pt II; and the Local Government Finance Act 2012 s 8(1), (3)).
21 Local Government Finance Act 1988 Sch 9 para 2(2)(i).
22 Local Government Finance Act 1988 Sch 9 para 2(2)(j). Where an amount paid by the ratepayer in excess of his liability falls to be repaid or credited, and where the circumstances are such as may be prescribed, regulations under Sch 9 may include provision that an additional amount by way of interest is to be paid or credited: Sch 9 para 2(2A) (added by the Local Government and Housing Act 1989 Sch 5 paras 1, 44, 79(3), Sch 12 Pt II).

274. Provision that may be made for recovery of payments due to a billing authority.

In respect of any sum which has become payable to a billing authority[1] and has not been paid[2], regulations[3] may include, as regards the recovery of such a sum, provision[4]:

(1) allowing a liability order to be made[5];
(2) allowing commitment to prison[6];
(3) allowing a bankruptcy petition to be presented[7];
(4) allowing winding-up[8].

The regulations may include provision that such a sum is recoverable in a court of competent jurisdiction[9], and such method of recovery is available as an alternative to recovery by taking control of goods[10] or any method included under heads (1) to (4) above[11].

1 Ie under any provision included under the Local Government Finance Act 1988 Sch 9 para 2: see

PARA 273. As to the meaning of 'billing authority' see PARA 53.

2 Local Government Finance Act 1988 s 62, Sch 9 para 3(1) (Sch 9 para 3(1) amended by the Local Government Finance Act 1992 s 117(1), Sch 13 para 87).

3 Ie regulations under the Local Government Finance Act 1988 Sch 9.

4 Local Government Finance Act 1988 Sch 9 para 3(2). The regulations may include provision equivalent to any provision included in regulations made under the Local Government Finance Act 1992 Sch 4 para 1(1) (council tax) (see PARA 473) subject to any modifications the Secretary of State or, in relation to Wales, the Welsh Ministers thinks fit: Local Government Finance Act 1988 Sch 9 para 3(3) (amended by the Local Government Finance Act 1992 Sch 13 para 87).

The functions of the Secretary of State under the Local Government Finance Act 1988 Sch 9, so far as exercisable in relation to Wales, were transferred to the National Assembly for Wales (see the National Assembly for Wales (Transfer of Functions) Order 1999, SI 1999/672, art 2, Sch 1) and are now vested in the Welsh Ministers (see the Government of Wales Act 2006 s 162(1), Sch 11 para 30). As to the Secretary of State and the Welsh Ministers see PARA 4 note 18. As to the meaning of 'Wales' see PARA 2 note 16.

5 Local Government Finance Act 1988 Sch 9 para 3(2)(a). As to liability orders see PARA 293 et seq.

6 Local Government Finance Act 1988 Sch 9 para 3(2)(c). As to commitment to prison see PARA 296 et seq.

7 Local Government Finance Act 1988 Sch 9 para 3(2)(d). As to such provision see PARA 297.

8 Local Government Finance Act 1988 Sch 9 para 3(2)(e). As to such provision see PARA 297.

9 Local Government Finance Act 1988 Sch 9 para 3(4)(a).

10 Ie any method provided for in the Local Government Finance Act 1988 s 62A: see PARA 295.

11 Local Government Finance Act 1988 Sch 9 para 3(4)(b) (amended by the Tribunals, Courts and Enforcement Act 2007 Sch 13 paras 87, 89(1), (3)).

275. Provision that may be made for recovery of payments due to persons other than a billing authority.

In respect of any sum:

(1) which has become payable[1] to the appropriate national authority[2] and has not been paid[3]; or

(2) which has become payable[4] (by way of repayment) to a person[5] other than a billing authority[6] or the appropriate national authority and has not been paid[7],

regulations[8] may include provision that such a sum is recoverable in a court of competent jurisdiction[9].

1 Ie under any provision included under the Local Government Finance Act 1988 Sch 9 para 2: see PARA 273.

2 The functions of the Secretary of State under the Local Government Finance Act 1988 Sch 9, so far as exercisable in relation to Wales, were transferred to the National Assembly for Wales (see the National Assembly for Wales (Transfer of Functions) Order 1999, SI 1999/672, art 2, Sch 1) and are now vested in the Welsh Ministers (see the Government of Wales Act 2006 s 162(1), Sch 11 para 30). As to the Secretary of State and the Welsh Ministers see PARA 4 note 18. As to the meaning of 'Wales' see PARA 2 note 16.

3 See the Local Government Finance Act 1988 s 62, Sch 9 para 4(1)(a).

4 Ie under any provision included under the Local Government Finance Act 1988 Sch 9 para 2: see PARA 273.

5 As to the meaning of 'person' see PARA 11 note 13.

6 As to the meaning of 'billing authority' see PARA 53.

7 Local Government Finance Act 1988 Sch 9 para 4(1)(b) (amended by the Local Government Finance Act 1992 s 117(1), Sch 13 para 87).

8 Ie regulations under the Local Government Finance Act 1988 Sch 9: see PARA 272.

9 Local Government Finance Act 1988 Sch 9 para 4(2).

276. Provision that may be made for payments by agreement.

Regulations[1] may include provision that a billing authority[2] and a person[3] liable to pay it an amount[4] may enter into an agreement[5]:

(1) that any interest of his in the hereditament[6] as regards which the liability arises must be charged to secure payment of the amount[7]; and

(2) that, in consideration of the charge, the authority will take no steps for a period specified in the agreement to recover any payment in respect of the amount[8].

The regulations may include:

(a) provision that the agreement may also extend to any further amount the person may become liable to pay to the authority[9] as regards the hereditament[10];

(b) provision that the agreement may provide for the payment of interest on sums outstanding and for interest payable to be secured by the charge[11];

(c) provision restricting the period which may be specified as mentioned in head (2) above[12].

1 Ie regulations under the Local Government Finance Act 1988 Sch 9: see PARA 272.

2 As to the meaning of 'billing authority' see PARA 53.

3 As to the meaning of 'person' see PARA 11 note 13.

4 Ie under the Local Government Finance Act 1988 s 43 (see PARAS 133, 143 et seq) or s 45 (see PARAS 135–136, 148).

5 Local Government Finance Act 1988 s 62, Sch 9 para 4A(1) (Sch 9 para 4A added by the Local Government and Housing Act 1989 ss 139, 194(4), Sch 5 paras 1, 44, 79(3), Sch 12 Pt II; the Local Government Finance Act 1988 Sch 9 para 4A(1) amended by the Local Government Finance Act 1992 s 117(1), Sch 13 para 87).

6 As to the meaning of 'hereditament' see PARA 106.

7 Local Government Finance Act 1988 Sch 9 para 4A(1)(a) (as added: see note 5).

8 Local Government Finance Act 1988 Sch 9 para 4A(1)(b) (as added: see note 5).

9 Ie under the Local Government Finance Act 1988 s 43 (see PARAS 133, 143 et seq) or s 45 (see PARAS 135–136, 148).

10 Local Government Finance Act 1988 Sch 9 para 4A(2)(a) (as added: see note 5).

11 Local Government Finance Act 1988 Sch 9 para 4A(2)(b) (as added: see note 5).

12 Local Government Finance Act 1988 Sch 9 para 4A(2)(c) (as added: see note 5).

277. Provision that may be made for recovery or adjustment where ratepayer dies.

The appropriate national authority[1] may make such regulations as it sees fit to deal with any case where a person dies and at any time before his death he was (or is alleged to have been) subject to a non-domestic rate[2]. The regulations may provide:

(1) that where, before his death, a sum has become payable by the deceased but has not been paid, his executor or administrator is liable to pay the sum and may deduct out of the assets and effects of the deceased any payments made (or to be made)[3];

(2) that where, before his death, a sum in excess of his liability has been paid (whether the excess arises because of his death or otherwise) and has not been repaid or credited his executor or administrator is entitled to the sum[4];

(3) for the recovery of any sum which is payable under the regulations and is not paid[5];

(4) that proceedings[6] may be instituted, continued or withdrawn by the deceased's executor or administrator[7].

1 Ie the Secretary of State or, in relation to Wales, the Welsh Ministers. The functions of the Secretary of State under the Local Government Finance Act 1988 s 63, so far as exercisable in relation to Wales, were transferred to the National Assembly for Wales (see the National Assembly for Wales (Transfer of Functions) Order 1999, SI 1999/672, art 2, Sch 1) and are now vested in the Welsh Ministers (see the Government of Wales Act 2006 s 162(1), Sch 11 para 30). As to the

Secretary of State and the Welsh Ministers see PARA 4 note 18. As to the meaning of 'Wales' see PARA 2 note 16.

2 Local Government Finance Act 1988 s 63(1). Nothing in s 63(3)–(6) (see heads (1)–(4) in the text) prejudices the generality of s 63(1): s 63(2). As to liability for a non-domestic rate see PARA 80 et seq.

As to the regulations made see the Non-Domestic Rating (Collection and Enforcement) (Local Lists) Regulations 1989, SI 1989/1058 (see PARA 305); the Non-Domestic Rating (Collection and Enforcement) (Central Lists) Regulations 1989, SI 1989/2260 (see PARA 318); the Non-Domestic Rating (Collection and Enforcement) (Miscellaneous Provisions) Regulations 1990, SI 1990/145 (amended by SI 1993/616, SI 2014/600, SI 2014/600; and in relation to England by SI 2008/428); and the Non-Domestic Rating (Transitional Period) Regulations 1990, SI 1990/608 (amended by SI 1990/2329; SI 1992/1514; SI 1993/616; and in relation to England by SI 2003/2000).

3 Local Government Finance Act 1988 s 63(3).

4 Local Government Finance Act 1988 s 63(4).

5 Local Government Finance Act 1988 s 63(5).

6 Ie whether by way of appeal under regulations under the Local Government Finance Act 1988 s 55 (see PARA 199) or otherwise.

7 Local Government Finance Act 1988 s 63(6).

(ii) Local Non-domestic Rating Lists

A. DEMAND

(A) Demand Notices

278. Demand notices and their service.

For each chargeable financial year[1], a billing authority[2] must[3] serve a written[4] notice (a 'demand notice')[5] on every person who is a ratepayer[6] of the authority in relation to the year[7].

Where any notice which is required or authorised[8] to be given to (or served on) a person relates to a hereditament[9] which is (or, where such a notice relates to more than one hereditament, one or more of which is) a place of business of that person, it may be given or served by leaving it at (or by sending it by to him at) the place of business (or, as the case may be, one of those places of business)[10].

In relation to England, any notice required or authorised to be given to (or served by) a billing authority on any person[11], or any information required by the demand notice regulations[12] to be supplied to any person when a demand notice is served[13]:

(1) may be so given, served or supplied by sending the notice or information to that person by electronic communication[14] to such address[15] as may be notified by that person for that purpose[16]; or

(2) is to be treated as given, served or supplied to that person where:

(a) the billing authority and that person have agreed for that purpose that any documents containing the notice or information may be accessed by that person on a website[17];

(b) the document is a document to which that agreement applies[18];

(c) the billing authority has published the document on a website[19]; and

(d) that person is notified, in a manner for the time being agreed for those purposes between him and the billing authority, of the publication of the document on a website[20], of the address of that website[21] and of the place on the website where the document may be accessed[22].

In relation to Wales, any notice required or authorised to be given to (or served by) a billing authority on any person[23]:

(i) may be so given or served by sending the notice to that person by electronic communication to such address as may be notified by that person for that purpose[24]; or

(ii) is to be treated as given or served to that person where:

(A) the billing authority and that person have agreed for that purpose that any documents containing the notice may be accessed by that person on a website[25];

(B) the document is a document to which that agreement applies[26];

(C) the billing authority has published the document on a website[27]; and

(D) that person is notified, in a manner for the time being agreed for those purposes between him and the billing authority, of the publication of the document on a website[28], of the address of that website[29] and of the place on the website where the document may be accessed[30].

In relation to Wales, any information required by the demand notice regulations to be supplied to any person when a demand notice is served[31]:

(I) may be so supplied by sending the information to that person by electronic communication to such address as may be notified by that person for that purpose[32]; or

(II) (subject to the requirement to supply a hard copy on request)[33] is treated as supplied to that person where the billing authority has published the information on a website and has notified that person by way of the demand notice of the publication of the information on a website, the address of that website and the place on the website where the information may be accessed[34].

Where a person requests a hard copy of the information, the authority must supply the information in hard copy as soon as practicable following the request[35].

For the purpose of any legal proceedings, a notice given by a means described in heads (1) and (2), (i) and (ii) above must, unless the contrary is proved, be treated as served on the second business day after it was sent in accordance with head (1) or (i) above[36] or on the second business day after notification of its publication was given in accordance with head (2)(d) or (ii)(D) above[37].

1 As to the meaning of 'chargeable financial year' see PARA 24 note 1.

2 As to the meaning of 'billing authority' see PARA 53.

3 Ie in accordance with the Non-Domestic Rating (Collection and Enforcement) (Local Lists) Regulations 1989, SI 1989/1058, regs 5–7: see PARAS 280, 281, 285.

4 As to the meaning of 'written' see PARA 21 note 3.

5 'Demand notice' means the notice required to be served by the Non-Domestic Rating (Collection and Enforcement) (Local Lists) Regulations 1989, SI 1989/1058, reg 4(1): reg 3(1).

6 'Ratepayer' in relation to a chargeable financial year and a billing authority means a person liable to pay an amount under the Local Government Finance Act 1988 s 43 (see PARAS 133, 143 et seq) or s 45 (see PARAS 135–136, 148) to the authority in respect of the year: Non-Domestic Rating (Collection and Enforcement) (Local Lists) Regulations 1989, SI 1989/1058, reg 3(1) (definition amended by SI 1993/616). As to the meaning of 'person' see PARA 11 note 13.

7 Non-Domestic Rating (Collection and Enforcement) (Local Lists) Regulations 1989, SI 1989/1058, reg 4(1) (amended by SI 1993/616). As to the requirement for demand notices see further PARA 279.

8 Ie by the Non-Domestic Rating (Collection and Enforcement) (Local Lists) Regulations 1989, SI 1989/1058.

9 As to the meaning of 'hereditament' see PARA 106.

10 Non-Domestic Rating (Collection and Enforcement) (Local Lists) Regulations 1989, SI 1989/1058, reg 2(2). This provision is expressed to be without prejudice to the Local Government Act 1972 s 233 (service of notices to local authorities) (see LOCAL GOVERNMENT vol 69 (2018) PARA 648) and the Non-Domestic Rating (Collection and Enforcement) (Local Lists) Regulations 1989, SI 1989/1058, reg 2(1): see reg 2(2). Where any notice which is required or authorised under the Non-Domestic Rating (Collection and Enforcement) (Local Lists) Regulations 1989, SI 1989/1058, to be given to (or served on) a person falls to be given or served by or on behalf of the Common Council of the City of London or by an officer of the Common Council of the City of London, it may be given or served in any manner in which it might be given or served under the Local Government Act 1972 s 233 if the Common Council of the City of London were a local authority within the meaning of that provision: Non-Domestic Rating (Collection and Enforcement) (Local Lists) Regulations 1989, SI 1989/1058, reg 2(1). As to the Common Council of the City of London see LONDON GOVERNMENT vol 71 (2013) PARA 34 et seq.

11 Ie by a provision of the Non-Domestic Rating (Collection and Enforcement) (Local Lists) Regulations 1989, SI 1989/1058 Pt II (regs 3–9).

12 'Demand notice regulations' means, in relation to England, the Council Tax and Non-Domestic Rating (Demand Notices) (England) Regulations 2003, SI 2003/2613; and, in relation to Wales, the Non-Domestic Rating (Demand Notices) (Wales) Regulations 2017, SI 2017/113) (see PARAS 282–283): see the Non-Domestic Rating (Collection and Enforcement) (Local Lists) Regulations 1989, SI 1989/1058, reg 1(2) (definition added, in relation to England, by SI 2003/2604, and, in relation to Wales, by SI 2009/2706; and amended in relation to England by SI 2003/3052; and in relation to Wales by SI 2017/113). As to the meanings of 'England' and 'Wales' see PARA 2 note 16.

13 Non-Domestic Rating (Collection and Enforcement) (Local Lists) Regulations 1989, SI 1989/1058, reg 2(3) (reg 2(3)–(7) added, in relation to England, by SI 2003/2604; and, in relation to Wales, by SI 2009/2706; the Non-Domestic Rating (Collection and Enforcement) (Local Lists) Regulations 1989, SI 1989/1058, reg 2(3), (5), (6) amended, in relation to Wales, by SI 2014/379). This provision is expressed to be without prejudice to the Local Government Act 1972 s 233 (service of notices to local authorities: see LOCAL GOVERNMENT vol 69 (2018) PARA 648) and the Non-Domestic Rating (Collection and Enforcement) (Local Lists) Regulations 1989, SI 1989/1058, reg 2(1), (2) (see the text to notes 8–10) and subject to reg 2(4)–(7) (see notes 16, 17 and the text to notes 23–24): see reg 2(3) (as so added).

As from 15 February 2012 the following provisions have effect in relation to England only: Notwithstanding the provisions of reg 2(3), subject to reg 2(9), information mentioned in the England, the Council Tax and Non-Domestic Rating (Demand Notices) (England) Regulations 2003, SI 2003/2613, Sch 3 Pt 2 (see PARA 282) which the billing authority is required, by reg 3(4) (see PARA 282), to supply to a person when it serves a rate demand notice on that person, must be treated as supplied by a billing authority to a person where the billing authority has published the information on a website and notified the person in writing of the publication of that information on a website, the address of that website, the place on the website where the information may be accessed and a postal address, email address and telephone number which may be used to request a hard copy of the information: see the Non-Domestic Rating (Collection and Enforcement) (Local Lists) Regulations 1989, SI 1989/1058, reg 2(8), (10) (reg 2(8)–(10) added, in relation to England, by SI 2012/25); Non-Domestic Rating (Electronic Communications) (England) Order 2012, SI 2012/25, art 1. Where the person referred to in the Non-Domestic Rating (Collection and Enforcement) (Local Lists) Regulations 1989, SI 1989/1058, reg 2(8) requests a hard copy of the information to which reg 2(8) applies, the billing authority must comply with that request as soon as practicable following the request: reg 2(9) (as so added). As to the meaning of 'writing' see PARA 21 note 3.

14 'Electronic communication' means a communication transmitted (whether from one person to another, from one device to another or from a person to a device or vice versa) by means of an electronic communications network within the meaning of the Communications Act 2003 s 32(1) (see TELECOMMUNICATIONS vol 97 (2015) PARA 53), or by other means but while in electronic form: Non-Domestic Rating (Collection and Enforcement) (Local Lists) Regulations 1989, SI 1989/1058, reg 1(2) (definition added, in relation to England, by SI 2003/2604, and substituted by SI 2006/237; definition added, in relation to Wales, by SI 2009/2706).

15 'Address', in relation to electronic communications, includes any number or address used for the purposes of such communications: Non-Domestic Rating (Collection and Enforcement) (Local Lists) Regulations 1989, SI 1989/1058, reg 1(2) (definition added, in relation to England, by SI 2003/2604; and, in relation to Wales, by SI 2009/2706).

16 Non-Domestic Rating (Collection and Enforcement) (Local Lists) Regulations 1989, SI 1989/1058, reg 2(3)(a) (as added: see note 13). A person who has notified an address for the purpose of reg 2(3)(a) must, by notice in writing to the billing authority, advise the billing authority of any change in that address; and the change takes effect on the third business day after the date on which the notice is received by the billing authority: reg 2(5) (as so added). A person who has notified an address for the purpose of reg 2(3)(a) may, by notice in writing to the billing authority, withdraw that notification; and the withdrawal takes effect on the third business day after the date on which the notice is received by the billing authority: reg 2(6) (as so added). 'Business day' means any day except a Saturday or Sunday, Christmas Day, Good Friday or a day which is a bank holiday under the Banking and Financial Dealings Act 1971 in England and Wales (see TIME vol 97 (2015) PARAS 313, 321): Non-Domestic Rating (Collection and Enforcement) (Local Lists) Regulations 1989, SI 1989/1058, reg 1(2) (definition added, in relation to England, by SI 2003/2604, and, in relation to Wales, by SI 2009/2706).

17 Non-Domestic Rating (Collection and Enforcement) (Local Lists) Regulations 1989, SI 1989/1058, reg 2(3)(b)(i) (as added: see note 13). A person who has entered into an agreement with the billing authority under reg 2(3)(b)(i) may, by notice in writing to the billing authority, inform the authority that he no longer wishes to be a party to the agreement; and where such notice is given, the agreement is to be treated as revoked on the third business day after the date on which the notice is received by the billing authority: reg 2(7) (as so added).

18 Non-Domestic Rating (Collection and Enforcement) (Local Lists) Regulations 1989, SI 1989/1058, reg 2(3)(b)(ii) (as added: see note 13).

19 Non-Domestic Rating (Collection and Enforcement) (Local Lists) Regulations 1989, SI 1989/1058, reg 2(3)(b)(iii) (as added: see note 13).

20 Non-Domestic Rating (Collection and Enforcement) (Local Lists) Regulations 1989, SI 1989/1058, reg 2(3)(b)(iv)(aa) (as added: see note 13).

21 Non-Domestic Rating (Collection and Enforcement) (Local Lists) Regulations 1989, SI 1989/1058, reg 2(3)(b)(iv)(bb) (as added: see note 13).

22 Non-Domestic Rating (Collection and Enforcement) (Local Lists) Regulations 1989, SI 1989/1058, reg 2(3)(b)(iv)(cc) (as added: see note 13).

23 Ie by a provision of the Non-Domestic Rating (Collection and Enforcement) (Local Lists) Regulations 1989, SI 1989/1058 Pt II (regs 3–9).

24 Non-Domestic Rating (Collection and Enforcement) (Local Lists) Regulations 1989, SI 1989/1058, reg 2(3)(a) (as added and amended: see note 13). A person who has notified an address for the purposes of reg 2(3)(a) or (3A) (see the text to notes 31–34) must, by notice in writing to the billing authority, advise the billing authority of any change in that address; and the change takes effect on the third business day after the date on which the notice is received by the billing authority: reg 2(5) (as so added and amended). A person who has notified an address for the purposes of reg 2(3)(a) or (3A) may, by notice in writing to the billing authority, withdraw that notification; and the withdrawal takes effect on the third business day after the date on which the notice is received by the billing authority: reg 2(6) (as so added and amended).

25 Non-Domestic Rating (Collection and Enforcement) (Local Lists) Regulations 1989, SI 1989/1058, reg 2(3)(b)(i) (as added and amended: see note 13).

26 Non-Domestic Rating (Collection and Enforcement) (Local Lists) Regulations 1989, SI 1989/1058, reg 2(3)(b)(ii) (as added: see note 13).

27 Non-Domestic Rating (Collection and Enforcement) (Local Lists) Regulations 1989, SI 1989/1058, reg 2(3)(b)(iii) (as added: see note 13).

28 Non-Domestic Rating (Collection and Enforcement) (Local Lists) Regulations 1989, SI 1989/1058, reg 2(3)(b)(iv)(aa) (as added: see note 13).

29 Non-Domestic Rating (Collection and Enforcement) (Local Lists) Regulations 1989, SI 1989/1058, reg 2(3)(b)(iv)(bb) (as added: see note 13).

30 Non-Domestic Rating (Collection and Enforcement) (Local Lists) Regulations 1989, SI 1989/1058, reg 2(3)(b)(iv)(cc) (as added: see note 13).

31 Non-Domestic Rating (Collection and Enforcement) (Local Lists) Regulations 1989, SI 1989/1058, reg 2(3A) (reg 2(3A), (3B) added, in relation to Wales, by SI 2014/379). This provision is expressed to be without prejudice to the Local Government Act 1972 s 233 (service of notices to local authorities: see LOCAL GOVERNMENT vol 69 (2018) PARA 648) and subject to the Non-Domestic Rating (Collection and Enforcement) (Local Lists) Regulations 1989, SI 1989/1058, reg 2(5), (6) (see note 24): see reg 2(3A) (as so added).

32 Non-Domestic Rating (Collection and Enforcement) (Local Lists) Regulations 1989, SI 1989/1058, reg 2(3A)(a) (as added: see note 31).

33 Ie subject to the Non-Domestic Rating (Collection and Enforcement) (Local Lists) Regulations 1989, SI 1989/1058, reg 3(3B): see the text to note 35.

34 Non-Domestic Rating (Collection and Enforcement) (Local Lists) Regulations 1989, SI 1989/1058, reg 2(3A)(b) (as added: see note 31).
35 Non-Domestic Rating (Collection and Enforcement) (Local Lists) Regulations 1989, SI 1989/1058, reg 2(3B) (as added: see note 31).
36 Non-Domestic Rating (Collection and Enforcement) (Local Lists) Regulations 1989, SI 1989/1058, reg 2(4)(a) (as added: see note 13).
37 Non-Domestic Rating (Collection and Enforcement) (Local Lists) Regulations 1989, SI 1989/1058, reg 2(4)(b) (as added: see note 13).

279. The requirement for demand notices.

Different demand notices[1] are to be served for different chargeable financial years[2]. A demand notice must be served with respect to the amount payable[3] for every hereditament as regards which a person is a ratepayer of the authority, though a single notice may relate to the amount payable with respect to more than one such hereditament[4].

If a single demand notice relates to the amount payable with respect to more than one hereditament, then[5] the amounts due under it, and the times at which they fall due, are to be determined as if separate notices were issued in respect of each hereditament[6].

1 As to the meaning of 'demand notice' see PARA 278 note 5.
2 Non-Domestic Rating (Collection and Enforcement) (Local Lists) Regulations 1989, SI 1989/1058, reg 4(2) (amended, in relation to England, by SI 2017/39). As to the meaning of 'chargeable financial year' see PARA 24 note 1. As to the service of notices see PARA 278.
3 'The amount payable' for a chargeable financial year or part of a chargeable financial year in relation to a ratepayer, a billing authority and a hereditament means:
   (1) in relation to England, the amount the ratepayer is liable to pay to the authority as regards the hereditament in respect of the year or part under:
      (a) the Local Government Finance Act 1988 s 43 (see PARAS 133, 143 et seq) or s 45 (see PARAS 135–136, 148), whether calculated by reference to s 43(4)–(6) or s 45(4) or (4A) (as those provisions are amended or substituted in any case by or under Sch 7A: see PARA 153) or by reference to an amount or rules determined or prescribed under s 47(1)(a) (see PARA 149), s 57A(3)(a) (see PARA 154) or s 58(3)(a) (see PARA 155); and
      (b) the Business Rate Supplements Act 2009 s 11 (see PARA 332), whether calculated by reference to s 13 (chargeable amount: see PARA 332) or determined in accordance with rules set by the levying authority under s 15 (BRS relief: see PARA 333) (Non-Domestic Rating (Collection and Enforcement) (Local Lists) Regulations 1989, SI 1989/1058, reg 3(1)(a) (definition substituted by SI 1991/141; head (1) further substituted, in relation to England, by SI 2010/187)); or
   (2) in relation to Wales, the amount the ratepayer is liable to pay to the authority as regards the hereditament in respect of the year or part under the Local Government Finance Act 1988 s 43 or s 45, whether calculated by reference to s 43(4)–(6) or s 45(4)–(6) (as those provisions are amended or substituted in any case by or under Sch 7A) or by reference to an amount or rules determined or prescribed under s 47(1)(a) or s 58(3)(a) (Non-Domestic Rating (Collection and Enforcement) (Local Lists) Regulations 1989, SI 1989/1058, reg 3(1)(a) (substituted by SI 1991/141)); or
   (3) in relation to England and Wales, where an amount falls to be credited by the billing authority against the ratepayer's liability in respect of the year or part, the amount (if any) by which the amount referred to in head (1) exceeds the amount falling to be so credited (Non-Domestic Rating (Collection and Enforcement) (Local Lists) Regulations 1989, SI 1989/1058, reg 3(1)(b) (substituted by SI 1991/141; amended by SI 1993/616)).

As to the meaning of 'hereditament' see PARA 106. As to the meaning of 'Wales' see PARA 2 note 16. 'Prescribed' means prescribed by the regulations: see the Local Government Finance Act 1988 s 146(6).

'Amount payable' in the Non-Domestic Rating (Collection and Enforcement) (Local Lists) Regulations 1989, SI 1989/1058, can only have the meaning set out in reg 3(1) and cannot be made to refer to a refund: *AEM (Avon) Ltd v Bristol City Council* [1999] LGR 93, [1998] RA 89.

4 Non-Domestic Rating (Collection and Enforcement) (Local Lists) Regulations 1989, SI 1989/1058, reg 4(3).
5 Ie subject to the Non-Domestic Rating (Collection and Enforcement) (Local Lists) Regulations 1989, SI 1989/1058, Sch 1 para 5 (see PARA 286) and Sch 1 para 8 (see PARA 290).
6 Non-Domestic Rating (Collection and Enforcement) (Local Lists) Regulations 1989, SI 1989/1058, reg 4(4).

280. Time of service of demand notices.

A demand notice[1] must be served[2] on or as soon as practicable after[3]:

(1) except in a case falling within head (2) below, 1 April in the relevant year[4]; or

(2) if the prescribed conditions as to liability[5] are not fulfilled in respect of that day[6] as regards the ratepayer[7] and the hereditament concerned, the first day after that day in respect of which such conditions are fulfilled as regards them[8].

A demand notice may[9], if the non-domestic multiplier for the relevant year has been determined or set[10], be served before the beginning of the relevant year on a person with respect to whom on the day it is issued it appears to the billing authority[11] that the prescribed conditions[12] are fulfilled[13] as regards the hereditament to which it relates[14].

A demand notice must not be served before the authority has set amounts of council tax[15] for the relevant year[16].

1 As to the meaning of 'demand notice' see PARA 278 note 5.
2 Ie subject to the Non-Domestic Rating (Collection and Enforcement) (Local Lists) Regulations 1989, SI 1989/1058, reg 5(2): see the text to notes 9–14. As to the service of notices see PARA 278.
3 Non-Domestic Rating (Collection and Enforcement) (Local Lists) Regulations 1989, SI 1989/1058, reg 5(1). Regulation 5(1) contains a balance between the interests of the ratepayers and the practicalities of administration; Parliament must have intended that if the billing authority has not complied with the requirements of that provision it would be wrong in principle for the ratepayer to have an obligation thereafter to pay: *Encon Insulation Ltd v Nottingham City Council* [1999] RA 382, [1999] 24 LS Gaz R 40, [1999] All ER (D) 588 (council should have taken practicable steps at an earlier stage than November to locate the relevant premises and their failure to do so precluded recovery of the tax). The expression 'as soon as practicable' in the Non-Domestic Rating (Collection and Enforcement) (Local Lists) Regulations 1989, SI 1989/1058, reg 5(1) shows that legislative intent will be satisfied by substantial compliance with the regulation and that any prejudice to the ratepayer should be capable of being a relevant consideration in deciding whether there has been such compliance: *R (on the application of Waltham Forest London Borough Council) v Waltham Forest Magistrates' Court* [2008] EWHC 3579 (Admin), [2009] RA 181,[2008] All ER (D) 22 (Nov). 'A failure to serve a regulation 5 notice as soon as practicable does not result in automatic invalidity. Rather, the court determining any issue resulting from such a failure will have regard to the length of delay and the impact of that delay upon the ratepayer, in the context of the public interest in collecting outstanding rates. The greater the prejudice to the ratepayer flowing from the delay, the more likely will be the conclusion that Parliament intended invalidity to follow': *North Somerset District Council v Honda Motor Europe Ltd* [2010] EWHC 1505 (QB), [2010] RA 285, [2010] All ER (D) 13 (Jul) at [60] per Burnett J.
4 Non-Domestic Rating (Collection and Enforcement) (Local Lists) Regulations 1989, SI 1989/1058, reg 5(1)(a). 'Relevant year' in relation to a notice means the chargeable financial year to which the notice relates: reg 3(1). As to the meaning of 'chargeable financial year' see PARA 24 note 1.
5 Ie the conditions mentioned in the Local Government Finance Act 1988 s 43(1) (see PARA 133) or s 45(1) (see PARA 135): see the Non-Domestic Rating (Collection and Enforcement) (Local Lists) Regulations 1989, SI 1989/1058, reg 5(1)(b). For these purposes, the conditions mentioned in the Local Government Finance Act 1988 s 43(1) or s 45(1) are not to be treated as fulfilled as regards a hereditament on any day on which the chargeable amount for the day in respect of it is nil by virtue of a determination to that effect under s 47(1)(a) (see PARA 149) or, in relation to England only, under s 45A (see PARA 147): Non-Domestic Rating (Collection and Enforcement) (Local Lists) Regulations 1989, SI 1989/1058, reg 3(2) (amended, in relation to England, by SI 2008/428).

As to the meaning of 'hereditament' see PARA 106. As to the meaning of 'England' see PARA 2 note 16.

6 Where references are made in the Non-Domestic Rating (Collection and Enforcement) (Local Lists) Regulations 1989, SI 1989/1058, Pt II (regs 3–9) to the day on which a notice is issued, they must be taken to be references:
   (1) if the notice is served in the manner described in reg 2(2) (see PARA 278) or the Local Government Act 1972 s 233(2) (see LOCAL GOVERNMENT vol 69 (2018) PARA 648), by being left at (or sent by post to) a person's place of business or proper address, to the day on which it is so left or posted (Non-Domestic Rating (Collection and Enforcement) (Local Lists) Regulations 1989, SI 1989/1058, reg 3(3)(a)); or
   (2) in any other case, to the day on which it is served (reg 3(3)(b)).

7 As to the meaning of 'ratepayer' see PARA 278 note 6.

8 Non-Domestic Rating (Collection and Enforcement) (Local Lists) Regulations 1989, SI 1989/1058, reg 5(1)(b).

9 Ie subject to the Non-Domestic Rating (Collection and Enforcement) (Local Lists) Regulations 1989, SI 1989/1058, reg 5(3): see the text to notes 15–16.

10 Ie under the Local Government Finance Act 1988 Sch 7: see PARA 156.

11 As to the meaning of 'billing authority' see PARA 53.

12 Ie the conditions mentioned in the Local Government Finance Act 1988 s 43(1) (see PARA 133) or s 45(1) (see PARA 135).

13 Ie or would be fulfilled if a list sent under the Local Government Finance Act 1988 s 41(5) were in force: see PARA 191.

14 Non-Domestic Rating (Collection and Enforcement) (Local Lists) Regulations 1989, SI 1989/1058, reg 5(2) (amended by SI 1993/616 and SI 1993/774). If a demand notice is so served, references in the Non-Domestic Rating (Collection and Enforcement) (Local Lists) Regulations 1989, SI 1989/1058, Pt II (regs 3–9) to a ratepayer are, in relation to that notice and so far as the context permits, to be construed as references to that person: reg 5(2) (as so amended).

15 Ie under the Local Government Finance Act 1992 s 30: see PARA 380.

16 Non-Domestic Rating (Collection and Enforcement) (Local Lists) Regulations 1989, SI 1989/1058, reg 5(3) (added by SI 1993/774).

281. Payments under demand notices.

If a demand notice[1] is issued before or during the relevant year[2] and it appears to the billing authority[3] that the prescribed conditions as to liability[4] are fulfilled[5] in respect of the day on which the notice is issued[6] as regards the ratepayer[7] and the hereditament[8] to which it relates, the notice must require payment of an amount equal to the billing authority's estimate of the amount payable[9] for the year, made as respects periods after the issue of the notice on the assumption that the conditions concerned will continue to be fulfilled on every day after that day[10].

If a demand notice is issued after the end of the relevant year, it must require payment of the amount payable for the year[11].

1 As to the meaning of 'demand notice' see PARA 278 note 5.

2 As to the meaning of 'relevant year' see PARA 280 note 4.

3 As to the meaning of 'billing authority' see PARA 53.

4 Ie the conditions mentioned in the Local Government Finance Act 1988 s 43(1) (see PARA 133) or s 45(1) (see PARA 135). As to these conditions see further PARA 280 note 5.

5 Ie or would be fulfilled if a list sent under the Local Government Finance Act 1988 s 41(5) were in force: see PARA 191.

6 As to the day on which a notice is issued see PARA 280 note 6.

7 As to the meaning of 'ratepayer' see PARA 278 note 6.

8 As to the meaning of 'hereditament' see PARA 106.

9 Where, as a result of the application of the Non-Domestic Rating (Small Business Rate Relief) (England) Order 2004, SI 2004/3315, art 7 (see PARA 143) or the Non-Domestic Rating (Small Business Relief) (Wales) Order 2008, SI 2008/2770, art 11A (see PARA 143) and in accordance with the Order in question, there is any change to the amount which the ratepayer is liable to pay to the billing authority as regards the hereditament, the authority's estimate of the amount payable must take account of such change: see the Non-Domestic Rating (Collection and Enforcement) (Local Lists) Regulations 1989, SI 1989/1058, reg 6(1A), (1B) (reg 6(1A) added by SI 2010/1656;

the Non-Domestic Rating (Collection and Enforcement) (Local Lists) Regulations 1989, SI 1989/1058, reg 6(1B) added by SI 2010/2222). As to the meaning of 'the amount payable' see PARA 279 note 3.

10 Non-Domestic Rating (Collection and Enforcement) (Local Lists) Regulations 1989, SI 1989/1058, reg 6(1) (amended by SI 1993/616). If a demand notice is issued during the relevant year but the Non-Domestic Rating (Collection and Enforcement) (Local Lists) Regulations 1989, SI 1989/1058, reg 6(1) does not apply, the notice must require payment of an amount equal to the amount payable for the period in the year up to the day on which the conditions mentioned in the Local Government Finance Act 1988 s 43(1) (see PARA 133) or s 45(1) (see PARA 135) were last fulfilled as regards the ratepayer and hereditament concerned: Non-Domestic Rating (Collection and Enforcement) (Local Lists) Regulations 1989, SI 1989/1058, reg 6(2). If, after a notice is served to which reg 6(2) applies, the conditions mentioned in the Local Government Finance Act 1988 s 43(1) or s 45(1) are fulfilled again in the relevant year as regards the ratepayer and the hereditament concerned, a further notice must be served on him requiring payments with respect to the amount payable in relation to the hereditament for the period in the relevant year beginning with the day in respect of which the conditions are so fulfilled again; and the Non-Domestic Rating (Collection and Enforcement) (Local Lists) Regulations 1989, SI 1989/1058, regs 5–8 (see PARAS 280, 285, 291) (and, so far as applicable Sch 1 (see PARAS 286–290)) are to apply to the further notice with respect to that period as if it were a demand notice and the conditions had not previously been fulfilled: reg 6(3).

11 Non-Domestic Rating (Collection and Enforcement) (Local Lists) Regulations 1989, SI 1989/1058, reg 6(4).

282. Content of demand notices.

A rate demand notice[1] issued in England[2] for any financial year[3] beginning on or after 1 April 2004[4] or in Wales[5] for any financial year beginning on or after 1 April 2017[6] must contain certain matters prescribed by regulation[7].

If the rate demand notice is served by the Common Council of the City of London (or an authorised person on behalf of the Common Council of the City of London) it must contain the following[8]:

(1) a statement of the address and description of each hereditament[9] to which the notice relates ('relevant hereditament')[10];

(2) a statement of the rateable value shown for each relevant hereditament in the authority's local non-domestic rating list[11];

(3) where an order under the Local Government Finance Act 1988[12] is or will be in force on any day in the relevant year, a statement of the days (if any) on which, for the purposes of calculating the payments required to be made under the notice, it was understood or assumed that the prescribed conditions[13] were or would be fulfilled in relation to any relevant hereditament, and a statement that as regards those days the chargeable amount is reduced by the proportion provided for in the order as compared with the amount it would be if the ratepayer were in occupation of the hereditament[14];

(4) where the provisions relating to zero rating[15] apply to any relevant hereditament on any day in the relevant year, a statement that as regards those days the chargeable amount is zero under those provisions and a statement of the amount by which the aggregate amount demanded under the notice is reduced as compared with the amount which would have been demanded[16] for those days[17];

(5) a statement that explanatory notes are published on the authority's website, a statement of the website address of the authority where the explanatory notes are published and a statement that hard copies of explanatory notes are available on request from the authority[18];

(6) a statement of the days (if any) on which, for the purposes of calculating the payments required to be made under the notice, certain understandings or assumptions were made[19] together with a statement of the manner in which the chargeable amount for those days was calculated and of the amount by which the aggregate amount demanded under the notice is reduced as compared with the amount which would[20] have been demanded[21];

(7) a statement of the non-domestic rating multipliers set by the Common Council[22] for the relevant year[23].

The Common Council must also publish on its website explanatory notes in the prescribed terms[24], or in substantially similar terms, and supply a hard copy of such explanatory notes to a ratepayer on request[25].

If the rate demand notice is served by or on behalf of a billing authority in England, other than the Common Council of the City of London or a rural settlement authority[26], it must contain the matters as set out in heads (1) to (6) above[27], and the billing authority must publish on its website explanatory notes in the prescribed terms[28], or in substantially similar terms, and supply a hard copy of such explanatory notes to a ratepayer on request[29].

A rate demand notice served by or on behalf of a rural settlement authority must contain the same matters, subject to minor modification[30], as must a notice served by an authority under the Business Rate Supplements Act 2009[31], and the billing authority must similarly publish explanatory notes on its website[32].

Similar provision is made where a rate demand notice is served by or on behalf of a Welsh billing authority[33].

If a rate demand notice is served before the end of the relevant year, a billing authority must also supply other information, relating mainly to local government finance estimates, when it serves the rate demand notice[34].

In relation to England only, so that a billing authority may fulfil these obligations with regard to the specified content of rate demand notices[35], information must be supplied to billing authorities by precepting authorities[36] and by levying bodies[37], while in Wales information must be supplied to billing authorities by police and crime commissioners[38].

1 'Rate demand notice' means a demand notice within the meaning of the Non-Domestic Rating (Collection and Enforcement) (Local Lists) Regulations 1989, SI 1989/1058, Pt II (regs 3–9) (see PARA 278 note 5) which is served by a billing authority or any person authorised by a billing authority to exercise any functions relating to the collection of non-domestic rates (including such a notice served pursuant to the Non-Domestic Rating (Collection and Enforcement) (Miscellaneous Provisions) Regulations 1990, SI 1990/145, Pt II (regs 2–5) (joint owners and occupiers)): Council Tax and Non-Domestic Rating (Demand Notices) (England) Regulations 2003, SI 2003/2613, reg 1(2); Non-Domestic Rating (Demand Notices) (Wales) Regulations 2017, SI 2017/113, reg 2(1). As to the meaning of 'billing authority' see PARA 53. As to the meaning of 'person' see PARA 11 note 13.

2 As to the meaning of 'England' see PARA 2 note 16.

3 As to the meaning of 'financial year' see PARA 24 note 1.

4 See the Council Tax and Non-Domestic Rating (Demand Notices) (England) Regulations 2003, SI 2003/2613, reg 2.

Nothing requires a notice to be given on a single sheet of paper, but if more than one sheet is used, the sheets are to be issued together, whether or not attached, so as to comprise one notice: Council Tax and Non-Domestic Rating (Demand Notices) (England) Regulations 2003, SI 2003/2613, reg 3(6); Non-Domestic Rating (Demand Notices) (Wales) Regulations 2017, SI 2017/113, reg 3(2).

5 As to the meaning of 'Wales' see PARA 2 note 16.

6 See the Non-Domestic Rating (Demand Notices) (Wales) Regulations 2017, SI 2017/113, reg 1(3).

7 Council Tax and Non-Domestic Rating (Demand Notices) (England) Regulations 2003, SI 2003/2613, reg 3(1) (amended by SI 2008/3624); Non-Domestic Rating (Demand Notices) (Wales) Regulations 2017, SI 2017/113, reg 3(1).

8 See the Council Tax and Non-Domestic Rating (Demand Notices) (England) Regulations 2003, SI 2003/2613, reg 3(3)(c) (amended by SI 2017/39). 'Authorised person' means a person to whom an authorisation is given by a billing authority to exercise any functions relating to the collection of non-domestic rates by the Local Authorities (Contracting Out of Tax Billing, Collection and Enforcement Functions) Order 1996, SI 1996/1880 (see PARA 53): Council Tax and Non-Domestic Rating (Demand Notices) (England) Regulations 2003, SI 2003/2613, reg 1(2). As to the Common Council of the City of London see LONDON GOVERNMENT vol 71 (2013) PARA 34 et seq.

9 As to the meaning of 'hereditament' see PARA 106.

10 Council Tax and Non-Domestic Rating (Demand Notices) (England) Regulations 2003, SI 2003/2613, Sch 2 Pt 1 para 1; applied by Sch 2 Pt 3 para 1 (Sch 2 Pts 1–3 substituted by SI 2008/387).

11 Council Tax and Non-Domestic Rating (Demand Notices) (England) Regulations 2003, SI 2003/2613, Sch 2 Pt 1 para 2; applied by Sch 2 Pt 3 para 1 (as substituted: see note 10). As to the compilation and maintenance of local non-domestic rating lists see PARA 191 et seq.

12 Ie under the Local Government Finance Act 1988 s 45(4A): see PARA 148.

13 Ie the conditions mentioned in the Local Government Finance Act 1988 s 45(1): see PARA 135.

14 Council Tax and Non-Domestic Rating (Demand Notices) (England) Regulations 2003, SI 2003/2613, Sch 2 Pt 1 para 4; applied by Sch 2 Pt 3 para 1 (as substituted: see note 10).

15 Ie the Local Government Finance Act 1988 s 45A: see PARA 147.

16 Ie if the Local Government Finance Act 1988 s 45(4) applied to the calculation of the chargeable amount: see PARA 135.

17 Council Tax and Non-Domestic Rating (Demand Notices) (England) Regulations 2003, SI 2003/2613, Sch 2 Pt 1 para 5; applied by Sch 2 Pt 3 para 1 (as substituted: see note 10).

18 Council Tax and Non-Domestic Rating (Demand Notices) (England) Regulations 2003, SI 2003/2613, Sch 2 Pt 1 para 5A (added by SI 2017/39); applied by the Council Tax and Non-Domestic Rating (Demand Notices) (England) Regulations 2003, SI 2003/2613, Sch 2 Pt 3 para 1 (as substituted (see note 10); amended by SI 2017/39).

19 Ie it was understood or assumed that:

(1) the chargeable amount would fall to be calculated under the Local Government Finance Act 1988 s 43(4A) (see PARA 143) or s 43(5) (Council Tax and Non-Domestic Rating (Demand Notices) (England) Regulations 2003, SI 2003/2613, Sch 2 Pt 1 para 6(a) (as substituted and applied: see note 10)); or

(2) the chargeable amount would fall to be calculated by reference to the Local Government Finance Act 1988 s 44(2) and (2A) as substituted by s 44A(7) or (9) (see PARA 134) (Council Tax and Non-Domestic Rating (Demand Notices) (England) Regulations 2003, SI 2003/2613, Sch 2 Pt 1 para 6(b) (as so substituted and applied)); or

(3) rules under the Local Government Finance Act 1988 s 47(1)(a) (see PARA 149) or s 57A(3)(a) (see PARA 154) would apply (Council Tax and Non-Domestic Rating (Demand Notices) (England) Regulations 2003, SI 2003/2613, Sch 2 Pt 1 para 6(c) (as so substituted and applied)).

20 Ie if the Local Government Finance Act 1988 s 43(4) (see PARA 133), without modification, and (so far as is relevant) s 44(2) (see PARA 133) without substitution, applied to the calculation of the chargeable amount for those days.

21 Council Tax and Non-Domestic Rating (Demand Notices) (England) Regulations 2003, SI 2003/2613, Sch 2 Pt 1 para 6; applied by Sch 2 Pt 3 para 1 (as substituted: see note 10).

22 Ie in accordance with the Local Government Finance Act 1988 Sch 7 Pt 2: see PARA 156.

23 Council Tax and Non-Domestic Rating (Demand Notices) (England) Regulations 2003, SI 2003/2613, Sch 2 Pt 3 para 2 (as substituted: see note 10).

24 Ie the explanatory notes contained in the Council Tax and Non-Domestic Rating (Demand Notices) (England) Regulations 2003, SI 2003/2613, Sch 2 Pt 3 para 3 (substituted by SI 2015/427; and amended by SI 2016/316, SI 2017/39 and SI 2018/92).

25 See the Council Tax and Non-Domestic Rating (Demand Notices) (England) Regulations 2003, SI 2003/2613, reg 3(3)(c) (as amended: see note 8).

26 'Rural settlement authority' means a billing authority which has, in respect of the relevant year, identified one or more rural settlements for that year in a list compiled under the Local Government Finance Act 1988 s 42A(2) (see PARA 195): Council Tax and Non-Domestic Rating (Demand Notices) (England) Regulations 2003, SI 2003/2613, reg 1(2). As to rural settlement

authorities see PARAS 145, 195.

27 See the Council Tax and Non-Domestic Rating (Demand Notices) (England) Regulations 2003, SI 2003/2613, reg 3(3)(a) (amended by SI 2017/39).

28 Ie the explanatory notes contained in the Council Tax and Non-Domestic Rating (Demand Notices) (England) Regulations 2003, SI 2003/2613, Sch 2 Pt 1 para 7 (substituted by SI 2015/427; and amended by SI 2016/316, SI 2017/39 and SI 2018/92).

29 See the Council Tax and Non-Domestic Rating (Demand Notices) (England) Regulations 2003, SI 2003/2613, reg 3(3)(a) (as amended: see note 27).

30 See the Council Tax and Non-Domestic Rating (Demand Notices) (England) Regulations 2003, SI 2003/2613, reg 3(3)(b), Sch 2 Pt 1 paras 1–6, Pt 2 (reg 3(3)(b) amended by SI 2017/39; the Council Tax and Non-Domestic Rating (Demand Notices) (England) Regulations 2003, SI 2003/2613, Sch 2 as substituted (see note 10); and amended by SI 2017/39).

31 See the Council Tax and Non-Domestic Rating (Demand Notices) (England) Regulations 2003, SI 2003/2613, reg 3(3)(d), Sch 2 Pt 1 paras 1–6, Pt 2A (reg 3(3)(d), Sch 2 Pts 2A, 3A added by SI 2010/187; the Council Tax and Non-Domestic Rating (Demand Notices) (England) Regulations 2003, SI 2003/2613, Sch 2 Pt 1 as substituted (see note 10) and amended (see note 30)). Where the authority concerned is the Common Council of the City of London, the relevant matters are those mentioned in heads (1)–(6) in the text as modified by Sch 2 Pt 3A: see reg 3(3)(d), Sch 2 Pt 3 paras 1, 2, Pt 3A (as so added, substituted and amended). As to the Business Rate Supplements Act 2009 see PARA 326 et seq.

32 See the Council Tax and Non-Domestic Rating (Demand Notices) (England) Regulations 2003, SI 2003/2613, reg 3(3)(b), (d), Sch 2 Pt 1 para 7 (as substituted: see note 10).

33 See the Non-Domestic Rating (Demand Notices) (Wales) Regulations 2017, SI 2017/113, regs 3(1), Sch 1. As to the explanatory notes to be sent see reg 5, Sch 2.

34 See the Council Tax and Non-Domestic Rating (Demand Notices) (England) Regulations 2003, SI 2003/2613, reg 3(4), (5), Sch 3 (amended by SI 2008/3264 and SI 2012/538); and the Non-Domestic Rating (Demand Notices) (Wales) Regulations 2017, SI 2017/113, reg 5, Sch 3 (Sch 3 amended by SI 2018/122).

35 Ie, in relation to England, under the Council Tax and Non-Domestic Rating (Demand Notices) (England) Regulations 2003, SI 2003/2613, reg 3 (see the text to notes 8–32, 34); or, in relation to Wales, under the Non-Domestic Rating (Demand Notices) (Wales) Regulations 2017, SI 2017/113, regs 3, 5 (see the text to notes 33, 36).

36 See the Council Tax and Non-Domestic Rating (Demand Notices) (England) Regulations 2003, SI 2003/2613, reg 5. As to the issuing of precepts see PARA 11 et seq.

37 See the Council Tax and Non-Domestic Rating (Demand Notices) (England) Regulations 2003, SI 2003/2613, reg 6. As to levying bodies see PARA 24.

38 See the Non-Domestic Rating (Demand Notices) (Wales) Regulations 2017, SI 2017/113, reg 6. As to police and crime commissioners see POLICE AND INVESTIGATORY POWERS vol 84 (2013) PARA 56 et seq.

283. Consequence of omissions.

A rate demand notice[1] in England and Wales[2] is invalid if it does not contain the matters prescribed by regulation[3]. However, where the failure so to comply was due to a mistake[4], and the amounts required to be paid under the notice were demanded in accordance with prescribed provisions[5], the requirement to pay those amounts applies as if the notice were valid[6]. In such circumstances, the billing authority[7] must, as soon as practicable after the mistake is discovered, issue to the liable ratepayer concerned a statement of the matters which were not contained in the notice and which should have been so contained[8].

1 As to the meaning of 'rate demand notice' see PARA 282 note 1.

2 As to the meanings of 'England' and 'Wales' see PARA 2 note 16.

3 Council Tax and Non-Domestic Rating (Demand Notices) (England) Regulations 2003, SI 2003/2613, reg 4(2)(a); Non-Domestic Rating (Demand Notices) (Wales) Regulations 2017, SI 2017/113, reg 4(1). The matters are those prescribed by the Council Tax and Non-Domestic Rating (Demand Notices) (England) Regulations 2003, SI 2003/2613, reg 3(3)(a)–(d) (see PARA 282) (see reg 4(2)(a) (amended by SI 2017/39)); and the Non-Domestic Rating (Demand Notices) (Wales) Regulations 2017, SI 2017/113, reg 3(1) (see reg 4(1)).

4 Council Tax and Non-Domestic Rating (Demand Notices) (England) Regulations 2003, SI 2003/2613, reg 4(2)(b); Non-Domestic Rating (Demand Notices) (Wales) Regulations 2017, SI 2017/113, reg 4(2)(a).

5 Council Tax and Non-Domestic Rating (Demand Notices) (England) Regulations 2003, SI 2003/2613, reg 4(2)(c); Non-Domestic Rating (Demand Notices) (Wales) Regulations 2017, SI 2017/113, reg 4(2)(b). The prescribed provisions are the Non-Domestic Rating (Collection and Enforcement) (Local Lists) Regulations 1989, SI 1989/1058, Pt II (regs 3–9) (see PARAS 278–282, 284 et seq): see the Council Tax and Non-Domestic Rating (Demand Notices) (England) Regulations 2003, SI 2003/2613, reg 4(2)(c); and the Non-Domestic Rating (Demand Notices) (Wales) Regulations 2017, SI 2017/113, reg 4(2)(b).

6 Council Tax and Non-Domestic Rating (Demand Notices) (England) Regulations 2003, SI 2003/2613, reg 4(2); Council Tax and Non-Domestic Rating (Demand Notices) (England) Regulations 2003, SI 2003/2613, reg 4(2).

7 As to the meaning of 'billing authority' see PARA 53.

8 Council Tax and Non-Domestic Rating (Demand Notices) (England) Regulations 2003, SI 2003/2613, reg 4(3); Council Tax and Non-Domestic Rating (Demand Notices) (England) Regulations 2003, SI 2003/2613, reg 4(3).

284. Demand notices: final adjustment.

Where:

(1) a notice has been issued by a billing authority[1] requiring a payment or payments to be made by a ratepayer[2] in respect of the amount payable[3] in relation to a hereditament[4] for a chargeable financial year[5] or part of a chargeable financial year[6];

(2) the payment or payments required to be paid are found to be in excess of or less than the amount payable in relation to the hereditament for the year or the part[7]; and

(3) provision for adjusting the amounts required under the notice and (as appropriate) for the making of additional payments or the repaying or crediting of any amount overpaid is not made by any other provision[8],

the billing authority must, as soon as practicable after the expiry of the year or the part of a year, serve a further notice[9] on the ratepayer stating the amount payable for the year or part in relation to the hereditament, and adjusting (by reference to that amount) the amounts required to be paid under the notice referred to in head (1) above[10].

1 Ie under the Non-Domestic Rating (Collection and Enforcement) (Local Lists) Regulations 1989, SI 1989/1058, Pt II (regs 3–9): see reg 9(1)(a) (amended by SI 1993/616). As to the issue of notices see PARA 278. As to the meaning of 'billing authority' see PARA 53.

2 As to the meaning of 'ratepayer' see PARA 278 note 6.

3 As to the meaning of 'amount payable' see PARA 279 note 3.

4 As to the meaning of 'hereditament' see PARA 106.

5 As to the meaning of 'chargeable financial year' see PARA 24 note 1.

6 Non-Domestic Rating (Collection and Enforcement) (Local Lists) Regulations 1989, SI 1989/1058, reg 9(1)(a) (as amended: see note 1).

7 Non-Domestic Rating (Collection and Enforcement) (Local Lists) Regulations 1989, SI 1989/1058, reg 9(1)(b).

8 Non-Domestic Rating (Collection and Enforcement) (Local Lists) Regulations 1989, SI 1989/1058, reg 9(1)(c). The other provision referred to is any provision of Pt II (regs 3–9), the Local Government Finance Act 1988 or any agreement entered into under the Non-Domestic Rating (Collection and Enforcement) (Local Lists) Regulations 1989, SI 1989/1058, reg 7(3) (see PARA 285): see reg 9(1)(c).

9 As to the service of notices see PARA 278.

10 Non-Domestic Rating (Collection and Enforcement) (Local Lists) Regulations 1989, SI 1989/1058, reg 9(2) (amended by SI 1993/616). No notice can be given under the Non-Domestic Rating (Collection and Enforcement) (Local Lists) Regulations 1989, SI 1989/1058, reg 9(2) requiring the payment of sums refunded in error: *AEM (Avon) Ltd v Bristol City Council* [1999] LGR 93, [1998] RA 89 (where the procedure in the Non-Domestic Rating

(Collection and Enforcement) (Local Lists) Regulations 1989, SI 1989/1058, Pt II (regs 3–9) had been complied with and exhausted by payment of the amount due, the liability order provisions in the regulations had no application and the local authority's proper remedy was in restitution).

If the amount stated in the further notice is greater than the amount required to be paid under the notice referred to in the Non-Domestic Rating (Collection and Enforcement) (Local Lists) Regulations 1989, SI 1989/1058, reg 9(1)(a) (see head (1) in the text), the amount of the difference for which such other provision as is mentioned in reg 9(1)(c) (see head (3) in the text) is not made is due from the ratepayer to the billing authority on the expiry of such period (being not less than 14 days) after the day of issue of the notice as is specified in it: reg 9(3) (amended by SI 1993/616).

If there has been an overpayment in respect of any liability of the ratepayer under the Non-Domestic Rating (Collection and Enforcement) (Local Lists) Regulations 1989, SI 1989/1058, Pt II, the amount overpaid for which such other provision as is mentioned in reg 9(1)(c) is not made:

(1) is to be repaid if the ratepayer so requires (reg 9(4)(a)); or
(2) in any other case is (as the billing authority determines) either to be repaid or be credited against any subsequent liability of the ratepayer to pay anything to the billing authority by way of non-domestic rate (reg 9(4)(b) (amended by SI 1993/616)).

As to the repayment, crediting or adjustment of payments see also the Non-Domestic Rating (Collection and Enforcement) (Local Lists) Regulations 1989, SI 1989/1058, reg 3(4); and PARA 285 note 5.

(B) Payment by Instalments

285. Payment by instalments.

A billing authority[1] and a ratepayer[2] may agree that the estimate of the amount payable[3] which is required to be paid[4] should be paid in such manner as is provided by the agreement, rather than in accordance with the non-domestic rate instalment scheme[5].

If such an agreement[6] in relation to the relevant year[7] has been reached between the billing authority and the ratepayer before the demand notice[8] is issued, a notice[9] must require the estimate of the amount payable to be paid in accordance with that agreement[10].

Unless such an agreement[11] in relation to the relevant year has been reached between the ratepayer and the billing authority before the demand notice is issued or the relevant provisions apply[12], a notice[13] must require the estimate of the amount payable to be paid by instalments[14].

A notice issued retrospectively in relation to a period of liability[15] must require payment of the amount payable on the expiry of such period (being not less than 14 days) after the day of issue of the notice[16] as is specified in it[17].

No payment in respect of the amount payable by a ratepayer in relation to a hereditament for any chargeable financial year[18] (whether interim, final or sole) need be made unless a statutory notice[19] requires it[20].

In relation to England, the following provisions apply where a ratepayer gives notice in writing to the billing authority that the ratepayer wishes to pay the estimate of the amount payable for each chargeable financial year by 12 monthly instalments until further notice[21]. An instalment notice[22] may be given either before or after a demand notice is issued and may specify that it is to take effect starting in relation to the relevant year or the year following the relevant year[23].

Where an instalment notice relates to the relevant year, a demand notice[24] must be issued as soon as reasonably practicable after the date on which the instalment notice is received by the billing authority and must require the estimate of the amount payable to be paid in instalments in accordance with the relevant provision[25].

Where an instalment notice relates to the year following the relevant year, as soon as reasonably practicable after the date on which the instalment notice is received by the billing authority, the billing authority must write to confirm that the estimate of the amount payable for that year is to be paid in instalments in accordance with the relevant statutory provision[26].

For each subsequent chargeable financial year for which the billing authority issues a demand notice to the ratepayer[27] after an instalment notice has been given, the demand notice must require payment of the estimate of the amount payable for the year in accordance with the relevant statutory provision[28].

A ratepayer may give notice in writing to the billing authority that the statutory provision as to payment by instalments[29] is no longer to apply[30]. A notice so given takes effect at the expiry of the chargeable financial year in which it was received[31].

1 As to the meaning of 'billing authority' see PARA 53.
2 As to the meaning of 'ratepayer' see PARA 278 note 6.
3 As to the meaning of 'amount payable' see PARA 279 note 3.
4 Ie under a notice to which the Non-Domestic Rating (Collection and Enforcement) (Local Lists) Regulations 1989, SI 1989/1058, reg 6(1) applies: see PARA 281.
5 Non-Domestic Rating (Collection and Enforcement) (Local Lists) Regulations 1989, SI 1989/1058, reg 7(3) (amended by SI 1993/616, SI 2010/1656, SI 2010/2222, SI 2011/1665 and SI 2012/24). The non-domestic rate instalment scheme referred to is that set out in the Non-Domestic Rating (Collection and Enforcement) (Local Lists) Regulations 1989, SI 1989/1058, Sch 1 (see PARAS 286–290), or Schs 1E, 1F (see note 14) or, until 15 February 2012 in relation to England only, Sch 1G (see note 14): see reg 7(3) (as so amended); Non-Domestic Rating (Collection and Enforcement) (Amendment) (England) Regulations 2012, SI 2012/24, reg 1. As to the meaning of 'England' see PARA 2 note 16.

Notwithstanding anything in the Non-Domestic Rating (Collection and Enforcement) (Local Lists) Regulations 1989, SI 1989/1058, reg 7(1)–(3) (see also the text to notes 6–14), such an agreement may be entered into either before or after the demand notice concerned is issued, and may make provision for the cessation or adjustment of payments, and for the making of fresh estimates, in the event of the estimate mentioned in reg 6(1) (see PARA 281) turning out to be wrong; and if it is entered into after the demand notice has been issued, it may make provision dealing with the treatment for the purposes of the agreement of any sums paid in accordance with Schs 1, 1E or 1F, or, until 15 February 2012 in relation to England only, Sch 1G before it was entered into: see reg 7(4) (amended by SI 2010/1656, SI 2010/2222, SI 2011/1665; and, in relation to England only, by SI 2012/24); Non-Domestic Rating (Collection and Enforcement) (Amendment) (England) Regulations 2012, SI 2012/24, reg 1.

Special provision is made in relation to the collection of certain backdated liability to rates: see the Non-Domestic Rating (Collection and Enforcement) (Local Lists) Regulations 1989, SI 1989/1058, reg 7A, Sch 1A (both added, in relation to England, by SI 2009/204, and in relation to Wales, by SI 2009/461; the Non-Domestic Rating (Collection and Enforcement) (Local Lists) Regulations 1989, SI 1989/1058, Sch 1A amended, in relation to England, by SI 2010/1507 and SI 2011/113; and, in relation to Wales, by SI 2011/966). In relation to England, a ratepayer subject to non-domestic rates in respect of the financial year 2009–10 who satisfies certain conditions may defer payment, to the financial years beginning on 1 April 2010 and 1 April 2011, of a specified proportion of his liability: see the Non-Domestic Rating (Collection and Enforcement) (Local Lists) Regulations 1989, SI 1989/1058, reg 7B, Schs 1B, 1C (all added by SI 2009/1597). Corresponding provision is made in relation to Wales in respect of the financial years beginning on 1 April 2009 and 1 April 2012: see the Non-Domestic Rating (Collection and Enforcement) (Local Lists) Regulations 1989, SI 1989/1058, reg 7C, Sch 1D (both added by SI 2009/2154; the Non-Domestic Rating (Collection and Enforcement) (Local Lists) Regulations 1989, SI 1989/1058, reg 7C substituted, Sch 1D amended, by SI 2012/466). As to the meaning of 'Wales' see PARA 2 note 16.

The provisions of the Non-Domestic Rating (Collection and Enforcement) (Local Lists) Regulations 1989, SI 1989/1058, Pt II (regs 3–9) which provide for the repayment or crediting of any amount or the adjustment of payments due under a notice, including in particular Sch 1 para 7 (see PARA 288), have effect subject to the Local Government Finance Act 1988 Sch 7 para 10(4) (multiplier set in substitution by special authority: see PARA 156): Non-Domestic Rating (Collection and Enforcement) (Local Lists) Regulations 1989, SI 1989/1058, reg 3(4).
6 Ie under the Non-Domestic Rating (Collection and Enforcement) (Local Lists) Regulations 1989, SI 1989/1058, reg 7(3): see the text to notes 1–5.

7 As to the meaning of 'relevant year' see PARA 280 note 4.
8 As to the meaning of 'demand notice' see PARA 278 note 5.
9 Ie a notice to which the Non-Domestic Rating (Collection and Enforcement) (Local Lists) Regulations 1989, SI 1989/1058, reg 6(1) applies: see PARA 281.
10 Non-Domestic Rating (Collection and Enforcement) (Local Lists) Regulations 1989, SI 1989/1058, reg 7(2) (amended by SI 1993/616).
11 Ie under the Non-Domestic Rating (Collection and Enforcement) (Local Lists) Regulations 1989, SI 1989/1058, reg 7(3): see the text to notes 1–5.
12 Ie the Non-Domestic Rating (Collection and Enforcement) (Local Lists) Regulations 1989, SI 1989/1058, reg 7(1A), (1B) or, in relation to Wales only, reg 7(1C): see note 14.
13 Ie a notice to which the Non-Domestic Rating (Collection and Enforcement) (Local Lists) Regulations 1989, SI 1989/1058, reg 6(1) applies: see PARA 281.
14 Non-Domestic Rating (Collection and Enforcement) (Local Lists) Regulations 1989, SI 1989/1058, reg 7(1) (amended by SI 1993/616; in relation to England, by SI 2010/1656, SI 2011/1665 and SI 2012/24; and, in relation to Wales, by SI 2010/2222).

The instalments are to be paid in accordance with the Non-Domestic Rating (Collection and Enforcement) (Local Lists) Regulations 1989, SI 1989/1058, Sch 1 Pt I (paras 1–5) (see PARA 286); and where such instalments are required, Sch 1 Pt II (paras 6–9) (see PARAS 287–290) applies for their cessation or adjustment in the circumstances described in Sch 1 Pt II: reg 7(1) (as so amended). However, where reg 7(1A), (1B) or (1C) applies alternative provisions have effect as follows: see reg 7(1) (as so amended).

In relation to England, unless an agreement under reg 7(3) (see the text to notes 1–5) in relation to the relevant year has been reached between the ratepayer and the billing authority before the demand notice is issued, where:

(1) the chargeable financial year begins on 1 April 2011;
(2) it appears to the billing authority that the estimate of the amount payable for that year would fall to be calculated by reference to the Local Government Finance Act 1988 s 43(4A) (see PARA 143) or by reference to the rules prescribed in the Non-Domestic Rating (Chargeable Amounts) (England) Regulations 2009, SI 2009/3343, reg 10(6) (see PARA 154); and
(3) the rateable value of the hereditament concerned is not more than £12,000,

a notice to which the Non-Domestic Rating (Collection and Enforcement) (Local Lists) Regulations 1989, SI 1989/1058, reg 6(1) (see PARA 281) applies must require the estimate of the amount payable to be paid in instalments in accordance with Sch 1E: see reg 7(1A), Sch 1E (both added by SI 2010/1656; the Non-Domestic Rating (Collection and Enforcement) (Local Lists) Regulations 1989, SI 1989/1058, Sch 1E amended by SI 2011/1665). As to the meaning of 'hereditament' see PARA 106.

In relation to Wales, unless an agreement under the Non-Domestic Rating (Collection and Enforcement) (Local Lists) Regulations 1989, SI 1989/1058, reg 7(3) in relation to the relevant year has been reached between the ratepayer and the billing authority before the demand notice is issued, where:

(a) the chargeable financial year begins on 1 April 2011;
(b) it appears to the billing authority that the estimate of the amount payable for that year would fall to be calculated by reference to the Local Government Finance Act 1988 s 43(4A); and
(c) the rateable value of the hereditament concerned is not more than £12,000,

a notice to which the Non-Domestic Rating (Collection and Enforcement) (Local Lists) Regulations 1989, SI 1989/1058, reg 6(1) applies must require the estimate of the amount payable to be paid in instalments in accordance with Sch 1F: see reg 7(1B), Sch 1F (both added by SI 2010/2222).

Until 15 February 2012, in relation to England, unless an agreement under the Non-Domestic Rating (Collection and Enforcement) (Local Lists) Regulations 1989, SI 1989/1058, reg 7(3) in relation to the relevant year has been reached between the ratepayer and the billing authority before the demand notice is issued, where:

(i) the chargeable financial year begins on 1 April 2012;
(ii) it appears to the billing authority that the estimate of the amount payable for that year would fall to be calculated by reference to the Local Government Finance Act 1988 s 43(4A) or by reference to the rules prescribed in the Non-Domestic Rating (Chargeable Amounts) (England) Regulations 2009 SI 2009/3343, reg 10(6); and
(iii) the rateable value of the hereditament concerned is not more than £12,000,

a notice to which the Non-Domestic Rating (Collection and Enforcement) (Local Lists) Regulations 1989, SI 1989/1058, reg 6(1) applies must require the estimate of the amount payable to be paid in instalments in accordance with Sch 1G: see reg 7(1C), Sch 1G (both added by SI 2011/1665; repealed, as from 15 February 2012, by SI 2012/24); Non-Domestic Rating (Collection and Enforcement) (Amendment) (England) Regulations 2012, SI 2012/24, reg 1.

15 Ie a notice to which the Non-Domestic Rating (Collection and Enforcement) (Local Lists) Regulations 1989, SI 1989/1058, reg 6(2), (4) applies: see PARA 281.

16 As to the day on which a notice is issued see PARA 280 note 6.

17 Non-Domestic Rating (Collection and Enforcement) (Local Lists) Regulations 1989, SI 1989/1058, reg 7(5).

18 As to the meaning of 'chargeable financial year' see PARA 24 note 1.

19 Ie a notice served under the Non-Domestic Rating (Collection and Enforcement) (Local Lists) Regulations 1989, SI 1989/1058, Pt II (regs 3–9).

20 Non-Domestic Rating (Collection and Enforcement) (Local Lists) Regulations 1989, SI 1989/1058, reg 7(6).

21 Non-Domestic Rating (Collection and Enforcement) (Local Lists) Regulations 1989, SI 1989/1058, reg 7(1E) (reg 7(1D)–(1K) added, in relation to England, by SI 2014/479).

22 In the Non-Domestic Rating (Collection and Enforcement) (Local Lists) Regulations 1989, SI 1989/1058, reg 7 and in Sch 1 para 1, 'instalment notice' means a notice given by a ratepayer to a billing authority under reg 7(1E): reg 7(1D) (as added: see note 21).

23 Non-Domestic Rating (Collection and Enforcement) (Local Lists) Regulations 1989, SI 1989/1058, reg 7(1F) (as added: see note 21).

24 Ie a notice to which the Non-Domestic Rating (Collection and Enforcement) (Local Lists) Regulations 1989, SI 1989/1058, reg 6(1) (see PARA 281) applies.

25 Non-Domestic Rating (Collection and Enforcement) (Local Lists) Regulations 1989, SI 1989/1058, reg 7(1G) (as added: see note 21). The relevant provision is Sch 1 para 1(2C): reg 7(1G) (as so added).

26 Non-Domestic Rating (Collection and Enforcement) (Local Lists) Regulations 1989, SI 1989/1058, reg 7(1H) (as added: see note 21). The relevant provision is Sch 1 para 1(2C): reg 7(1H) (as so added).

27 Ie in accordance with the Non-Domestic Rating (Collection and Enforcement) (Local Lists) Regulations 1989, SI 1989/1058, reg 6(1): see PARA 281.

28 Non-Domestic Rating (Collection and Enforcement) (Local Lists) Regulations 1989, SI 1989/1058, reg 7(1I) (as added: see note 21). The relevant provision is Sch 1 para 1(2C): reg 7(1I) (as so added).

29 Ie the Non-Domestic Rating (Collection and Enforcement) (Local Lists) Regulations 1989, SI 1989/1058, Sch 1 para 1(2C): see PARA 286 note 6.

30 Non-Domestic Rating (Collection and Enforcement) (Local Lists) Regulations 1989, SI 1989/1058, reg 7(1J) (as added: see note 21).

31 Non-Domestic Rating (Collection and Enforcement) (Local Lists) Regulations 1989, SI 1989/1058, reg 7(1K) (as added: see note 21). This is subject to reg 7(3) (see the text to notes 1–5): reg 7(1K) (as so added).

286. Payment of the aggregate amount under the non-domestic rate instalment scheme.

Where the demand notice[1] is issued on or before 31 December in the relevant year[2], the aggregate amount[3] is payable in monthly instalments, the number of such instalments being[4] ten or, if less, the number of whole months[5] remaining in the relevant year after the issue of the notice less one[6]. The months in which the instalments are payable must be uninterrupted, but subject to that[7] are to be such months in the relevant year as are specified in the notice; and the instalments are to be payable on such day in each month as is so specified[8].

Detailed provisions apply in respect of calculating the instalments due[9].

The demand notice must be issued at least 14 days before the day on which the first instalment is due under it[10].

1 As to the meaning of 'demand notice' see PARA 278 note 5.

2 Non-Domestic Rating (Collection and Enforcement) (Local Lists) Regulations 1989, SI 1989/1058, Sch 1 para 1(1). This provision is expressed to be subject to Sch 1 para 3 (see note 9): see Sch 1 para 1(1). As to the meaning of 'relevant year' see PARA 280 note 4.

3 For the purposes of the Non-Domestic Rating (Collection and Enforcement) (Local Lists) Regulations 1989, SI 1989/1058, Sch 1 Pt I (paras 1–5), 'aggregate amount' means the amount of the estimate referred to in reg 6(1) (see PARA 281), or if pursuant to reg 4(3) (see PARA 279) the demand notice relates to more than one hereditament for which such an estimate is made, the aggregate of the amount of those estimates: Sch 1 para 5. As to the meaning of 'hereditament' see PARA 106.

4 Ie subject to the Non-Domestic Rating (Collection and Enforcement) (Local Lists) Regulations 1989, SI 1989/1058, Sch 1 para 1(2A), (2B), (2C): see note 6.

5 As to the meaning of 'month' see PARA 11 note 1.

6 Non-Domestic Rating (Collection and Enforcement) (Local Lists) Regulations 1989, SI 1989/1058, Sch 1 para 1(2) (amended by SI 1991/1127; and, in relation to England, by SI 2014/479). Where the demand notice is issued in May, the number of instalments may be ten or the number ascertained in accordance with the Non-Domestic Rating (Collection and Enforcement) (Local Lists) Regulations 1989, SI 1989/1058, Sch 1 para 1(2), as the billing authority determines: Sch 1 para 1(2A) (added by SI 1991/1127; amended by SI 1993/616). As to the meaning of 'billing authority' see PARA 53.

In relation to England, the Non-Domestic Rating (Collection and Enforcement) (Local Lists) Regulations 1989, SI 1989/1058, Sch 1 para 1(2C) applies where a demand notice is issued to a ratepayer that has served an instalment notice on the billing authority: Sch 1 para 1(2B) (Sch 1 para 1(2B), (2C) added, in relation to England, by SI 2014/479). The aggregate amount is to be payable in monthly instalments, the number of such instalments being:

(1) where the demand notice is issued on or before 15 April in the relevant year (including where it is issued before the beginning of the relevant year), 12 (Non-Domestic Rating (Collection and Enforcement) (Local Lists) Regulations 1989, SI 1989/1058, Sch 1 para 1(2C)(a) (as so added));

(2) where the demand notice is issued on or after 16 April in the relevant year, the number of whole months remaining in the relevant year after the issue of the demand notice (Sch 1 para 1(2C)(b) (as so added)).

Where the demand notice is issued between 1 January and 31 March in the relevant year, the aggregate amount is payable in a single instalment on such day as is specified in the notice: Non-Domestic Rating (Collection and Enforcement) (Local Lists) Regulations 1989, SI 1989/1058, Sch 1 para 2.

7 Ie and subject also to the Non-Domestic Rating (Collection and Enforcement) (Local Lists) Regulations 1989, SI 1989/1058, Sch 1 para 4: see the text to note 10.

8 Non-Domestic Rating (Collection and Enforcement) (Local Lists) Regulations 1989, SI 1989/1058, Sch 1 para 1(3).

9 See the Non-Domestic Rating (Collection and Enforcement) (Local Lists) Regulations 1989, SI 1989/1058, Sch 1 para 1(4), (5). Special provisions apply to cases where instalments payable in accordance with Sch 1 para 1 would produce an amount for an instalment of less than £50: see Sch 1 para 3.

10 Non-Domestic Rating (Collection and Enforcement) (Local Lists) Regulations 1989, SI 1989/1058, Sch 1 para 4.

287. Cessation and adjustment of instalments where conditions as to liability not fulfilled.

Where the demand notice[1] has been served on a ratepayer[2] by a billing authority[3], and in respect of a day in the relevant year[4] (the 'relevant day') after its issue[5] the prescribed conditions as to liability[6] are not fulfilled as regards the ratepayer and the hereditament[7] to which the notice relates[8], no payments of instalments falling due after the relevant day are payable under the notice in relation to the hereditament[9]. The billing authority must, on the relevant day or as soon as practicable after that day, serve a notice[10] on the ratepayer stating the amount payable[11] in relation to the hereditament for the period in the relevant year up to the relevant day[12].

If these provisions[13] apply in relation to a demand notice, and after the relevant day the conditions as to liability[14] are fulfilled again in the relevant year as regards the ratepayer and the hereditament concerned, a further notice must be served on him requiring payments with respect to the amount payable in relation to the hereditament for the period in the relevant year beginning with the day in respect of which the conditions are so fulfilled again[15].

1 As to the meaning of 'demand notice' see PARA 278 note 5.
2 As to the meaning of 'ratepayer' see PARA 278 note 6.
3 As to the meaning of 'billing authority' see PARA 53.
4 As to the meaning of 'relevant year' see PARA 280 note 4.
5 As to the day on which a notice is issued see PARA 280 note 6.
6 Ie the conditions mentioned in the Local Government Finance Act 1988 s 43(1) (see PARA 133) or s 45(1) (see PARA 135) (or, as the case may be, conditions as would be fulfilled if a list sent under s 41(5) (see PARA 191) were in force): see the Non-Domestic Rating (Collection and Enforcement) (Local Lists) Regulations 1989, SI 1989/1058, Sch 1 para 6(1). As to these conditions see also PARA 280 note 5.
7 As to the meaning of 'hereditament' see PARA 106.
8 Non-Domestic Rating (Collection and Enforcement) (Local Lists) Regulations 1989, SI 1989/1058, Sch 1 para 6(1) (amended by SI 1990/145 and SI 1993/616).
9 Non-Domestic Rating (Collection and Enforcement) (Local Lists) Regulations 1989, SI 1989/1058, Sch 1 para 6(2). This provision is expressed to be subject to Sch 1 para 6(5), (6) (see note 12 and the text to notes 13–15): see Sch 1 para 6(2). As to payment by instalments see PARA 285.
10 As to the service of notices see PARA 278.
11 As to the meaning of 'amount payable' see PARA 279 note 3.
12 Non-Domestic Rating (Collection and Enforcement) (Local Lists) Regulations 1989, SI 1989/1058, Sch 1 para 6(3) (amended by SI 1993/616). If the amount stated in the Non-Domestic Rating (Collection and Enforcement) (Local Lists) Regulations 1989, SI 1989/1058, Sch 1 para 6(3) is less than the aggregate amount of any instalments which have fallen due on or before the relevant day in relation to the hereditament, the difference is to go in the first instance to discharge any liability to pay the instalments (to the extent that they remain unpaid); and any residual overpayment in respect of any liability of the ratepayer under Pt II (regs 3–9) (see PARAS 278 et seq):
    (1) must be repaid if the ratepayer so requires (Sch 1 para 6(4)(a)); or
    (2) in any other case must (as the billing authority determines) either be repaid or credited against any subsequent liability of the ratepayer to pay anything to the billing authority by way of non-domestic rate (Sch 1 para 6(4)(b) (amended by SI 1993/616)).

    If the amount stated in the Non-Domestic Rating (Collection and Enforcement) (Local Lists) Regulations 1989, SI 1989/1058, Sch 1 para 6(3) is greater than the aggregate amount of any instalments which have fallen due in relation to the hereditament on or before the relevant day, the difference between the two is due from the ratepayer to the billing authority on the expiry of such period (being not less than 14 days) after the day of issue of the notice served under Sch 1 para 6(3) as is specified in it: Sch 1 para 6(5) (amended by SI 1993/616).
13 Ie the Non-Domestic Rating (Collection and Enforcement) (Local Lists) Regulations 1989, SI 1989/1058, Sch 1 para 6.
14 Ie those mentioned in the Local Government Finance Act 1988 s 43(1) (see PARA 133) or s 45(1) (see PARA 135).
15 Non-Domestic Rating (Collection and Enforcement) (Local Lists) Regulations 1989, SI 1989/1058, Sch 1 para 6(6). Regulations 5–8 (see PARAS 280, 285, 291) (and, so far as applicable, Sch 1) apply to the further notice with respect to that period as if it were a demand notice and the conditions had not previously been fulfilled: Sch 1 para 6(6).

288. Cessation and adjustment of instalments where estimate based on false factor or assumption.

Where the demand notice[1] has been served on a ratepayer[2] by a billing authority[3], any factor or assumption by reference to which the estimate made for the purpose of the notice[4] was calculated is shown to be false in respect of a day (the 'relevant day'), and where the circumstances affecting liability have not changed[5] as regards the hereditament[6] to which the notice relates[7], the billing authority must, on or as soon as practicable after the relevant day[8]:

(1) adjust the instalments (if any) payable on or after the adjustment day[9] (the 'remaining instalments') so that they accord with the amounts prescribed[10]; and

(2) serve a notice[11] on the ratepayer stating the amount of the revised estimate[12] and the amount of any remaining instalment[13].

If the revised estimate[14] exceeds the aggregate amount of the instalments payable under the demand notice before the adjustment day, but no instalments are payable under it on or after that day, the amount of the excess is due from the ratepayer to the billing authority in a single instalment on the expiry of such period (being not less than 14 days) after the day of issue[15] of the notice[16] as is specified in it[17].

If in any case the revised estimate is less than the aggregate amount of the instalments payable before the adjustment day, any overpayment in respect of any liability of the ratepayer[18]:

(a) must be repaid if the ratepayer so requires[19]; or

(b) in any other case is (as the billing authority determines) either to be repaid or credited against any subsequent liability of the ratepayer to pay anything to it by way of non-domestic rate[20].

1 As to the meaning of 'demand notice' see PARA 278 note 5.

2 As to the meaning of 'ratepayer' see PARA 278 note 6.

3 As to the meaning of 'billing authority' see PARA 53.

4 Ie the estimate made under the Non-Domestic Rating (Collection and Enforcement) (Local Lists) Regulations 1989, SI 1989/1058, reg 6(1): see PARA 281.

5 Ie where the event mentioned in the Non-Domestic Rating (Collection and Enforcement) (Local Lists) Regulations 1989, SI 1989/1058, Sch 1 para 6(1) has not occurred: see PARA 287.

6 As to the meaning of 'hereditament' see PARA 106.

7 Non-Domestic Rating (Collection and Enforcement) (Local Lists) Regulations 1989, SI 1989/1058, Sch 1 para 7(1) (amended by SI 1992/1512, SI 1993/616, SI 2010/1656 and SI 2010/2222). This provision is expressed to be subject to the Non-Domestic Rating (Collection and Enforcement) (Local Lists) Regulations 1989, SI 1989/1058, Sch 1 para 7(1A), (1B) and (1C): see Sch 1 para 7(1) (as so amended).

Schedule 1 para 7 does not apply in a case to which Sch 1 para 7A or Sch 1 para 7B applies, except as provided in Sch 1 para 9(2): Sch 1 para 7(1A) (added by SI 1992/1512). It should be noted that the Non-Domestic Rating (Collection and Enforcement) (Local Lists) Regulations 1989, SI 1989/1058, Sch 1 paras 7A, 7B contain transitional provisions the effect of which was limited to non-domestic rating lists for the period 1990 to 1995 and those provisions are no longer of any practical significance.

The Non-Domestic Rating (Collection and Enforcement) (Local Lists) Regulations 1989, SI 1989/1058, Sch 1 para 7 does not apply in a case to which Sch 1 para 7D or Sch 1 para 7E applies (see PARA 289): see Sch 1 para 7(1B), (1C) (added by SI 2010/1656; and SI 2010/2222 respectively).

8 Non-Domestic Rating (Collection and Enforcement) (Local Lists) Regulations 1989, SI 1989/1058, Sch 1 para 7(2) (substituted by SI 1991/141; and amended by SI 1993/616).

9 'Adjustment day' means the day 14 days after the day the notice served under the Non-Domestic Rating (Collection and Enforcement) (Local Lists) Regulations 1989, SI 1989/1058, Sch 1 para 7(2) is issued: Sch 1 para 7(7).

10 See the Non-Domestic Rating (Collection and Enforcement) (Local Lists) Regulations 1989, SI 1989/1058, Sch 1 para 7(2)(a) (as substituted: see note 8). The aggregate amount of the remaining instalments payable is equal to the amount by which the revised estimate mentioned in Sch 1 para 7(3) (see note 12) exceeds the aggregate amount of the instalments payable under the demand notice before the adjustment day; and the amount of each remaining instalment (if there are more than one) must be calculated in accordance with Sch 1 para 1(4) and (5) (see PARA 286) as if references to the aggregate amount and to instalments were references to the aggregate amount of the remaining instalments and to the remaining instalments respectively: Sch 1 para 7(4).

11 As to the service of notices see PARA 278.

12 See the Non-Domestic Rating (Collection and Enforcement) (Local Lists) Regulations 1989, SI 1989/1058, Sch 1 para 7(2)(b)(i) (as substituted: see note 8). The amount of the revised estimate is the revised estimate of the billing authority of the amount payable for the relevant year in relation to the hereditament: Sch 1 para 7(3) (amended by SI 1993/616). As to the meaning of 'amount payable' see PARA 279 note 3. As to the meaning of 'relevant year' see PARA 280 note 4.

13 Non-Domestic Rating (Collection and Enforcement) (Local Lists) Regulations 1989, SI 1989/1058, Sch 1 para 7(2)(b)(ii) (as substituted: see note 8).

14 Ie as mentioned in the Non-Domestic Rating (Collection and Enforcement) (Local Lists) Regulations 1989, SI 1989/1058, Sch 1 para 7(3): see note 12.

15 As to the day on which a notice is issued see PARA 280 note 6.

16 Ie the notice served under the Non-Domestic Rating (Collection and Enforcement) (Local Lists) Regulations 1989, SI 1989/1058, Sch 1 para 7(2): see the text to notes 11–13.

17 Non-Domestic Rating (Collection and Enforcement) (Local Lists) Regulations 1989, SI 1989/1058, Sch 1 para 7(5) (amended by SI 1990/145 and SI 1993/616). Where a notice has been given under the Non-Domestic Rating (Collection and Enforcement) (Local Lists) Regulations 1989, SI 1989/1058, Sch 1 para 7(2) (see the text to notes 11–13), in the operation of Sch 1 para 7 as respects any further notice that may fall to be given under it, references in Sch 1 para 7 to the demand notice and to amounts in respect of instalments payable under it are to be construed (so far as the context permits) as references to the demand notice, and amounts in respect of instalments payable under the notice, as from time to time previously adjusted under Sch 1 para 7; and in calculating the aggregate amount of instalments payable under a demand notice before the adjustment day for the purposes of Sch 1 para 7(4) (see note 10) and Sch 1 para 7(5) in consequence of the calculation of the revised estimate mentioned in Sch 1 para 7(3) (see note 12), there is not to count as so payable any amount in respect of such instalments which has fallen to be repaid (or credited) under the Local Government Finance Act 1988 Sch 7 para 10(4) (multiplier set in substitution by special authority: see PARA 156) or (on the occasion of the giving of a previous notice under the Non-Domestic Rating (Collection and Enforcement) (Local Lists) Regulations 1989, SI 1989/1058, Sch 1 para 7(2)) under Sch 1 para 7(5), or has been paid (or credited) by way of interest under the Non-Domestic Rating (Payment of Interest) Regulations 1990, SI 1990/1904 (see PARA 199): Non-Domestic Rating (Collection and Enforcement) (Local Lists) Regulations 1989, SI 1989/1058, Sch 1 para 7(6) (amended by SI 1991/141).

18 Ie under the Non-Domestic Rating (Collection and Enforcement) (Local Lists) Regulations 1989, SI 1989/1058, Pt II (regs 3–9): see PARA 278 et seq.

19 Non-Domestic Rating (Collection and Enforcement) (Local Lists) Regulations 1989, SI 1989/1058, Sch 1 para 7(5)(a).

20 Non-Domestic Rating (Collection and Enforcement) (Local Lists) Regulations 1989, SI 1989/1058, Sch 1 para 7(5)(b) (amended by SI 1993/616). See also note 17.

289. Small Business Rate Relief adjustment notices.

Where:

(1) the demand notice[1] has been served on a ratepayer[2] by a billing authority[3];

(2) the year to which the demand notice relates is the chargeable financial year[4] which began on 1 April 2010[5];

(3) the authority's estimate[6] for the purposes of the demand notice ('the original estimate') was made before 1 October 2010[7];

(4) the original estimate is, as a result of the small business rate relief order changes[8], shown to be false[9]; and

(5) the circumstances affecting liability have not changed[10] as regards the hereditament[11] to which the demand notice relates[12],

the billing authority must as soon as practicable adjust the instalments (if any) payable on or after 1 October 2010[13] ('the remaining instalments') so that they accord with the prescribed amounts[14], and serve a notice[15] ('an adjustment notice') on the ratepayer[16].

In so far as the aggregate of any amounts paid (by reference to the original estimate) before 1 October 2010 exceeds the amount of the new estimate, the amount of the excess:

(a) must be repaid if the ratepayer so requires[17];

(b) in any other case, must (as the billing authority determines) either be repaid or credited against any subsequent liability of the ratepayer to pay anything to the billing authority by way of non-domestic rate[18].

1 As to the meaning of 'demand notice' see PARA 278 note 5.
2 As to the meaning of 'ratepayer' see PARA 278 note 6.
3 Non-Domestic Rating (Collection and Enforcement) (Local Lists) Regulations 1989, SI 1989/1058, Sch 1 para 7D(1)(a) (Sch 1 para 7D added, in relation to England, by SI 2010/1656). As to the meaning of 'billing authority' see PARA 53. As to equivalent provision to the Non-Domestic Rating (Collection and Enforcement) (Local Lists) Regulations 1989, SI 1989/1058, Sch 1 para 7D, in relation to Wales, see Sch 1 para 7E (added by SI 2010/2222). As to the meanings of 'England' and 'Wales' see PARA 2 note 16.
4 As to the meaning of 'chargeable financial year' see PARA 24 note 1.
5 Non-Domestic Rating (Collection and Enforcement) (Local Lists) Regulations 1989, SI 1989/1058, Sch 1 para 7D(1)(b) (as added: see note 3).
6 Ie under the Non-Domestic Rating (Collection and Enforcement) (Local Lists) Regulations 1989, SI 1989/1058, reg 6(1): see PARA 281.
7 Non-Domestic Rating (Collection and Enforcement) (Local Lists) Regulations 1989, SI 1989/1058, Sch 1 para 7D(1)(c) (as added: see note 3).
8 Ie as a result of amendments made to the Non-Domestic Rating (Small Business Rate Relief) (England) Order 2004, SI 2004/3315 (see PARA 143) which have effect on 1 October 2010.
9 Non-Domestic Rating (Collection and Enforcement) (Local Lists) Regulations 1989, SI 1989/1058, Sch 1 para 7D(1)(d) (as added: see note 3).
10 Ie the event mentioned in the Non-Domestic Rating (Collection and Enforcement) (Local Lists) Regulations 1989, SI 1989/1058, para 6(1) has not occurred: see PARA 281.
11 As to the meaning of 'hereditament' see PARA 106.
12 Non-Domestic Rating (Collection and Enforcement) (Local Lists) Regulations 1989, SI 1989/1058, Sch 1 para 7D(1)(e) (as added: see note 3).
13 Ie the 'SBRR adjustment day': see the Non-Domestic Rating (Collection and Enforcement) (Local Lists) Regulations 1989, SI 1989/1058, Sch 1 para 7D(7) (as added: see note 3).
14 Non-Domestic Rating (Collection and Enforcement) (Local Lists) Regulations 1989, SI 1989/1058, Sch 1 para 7D(2)(a) (as added: see note 3). The aggregate amount of the remaining instalments payable after the SBRR adjustment day must be equal to the amount by which the new estimate exceeds the aggregate amount of the instalments payable under the demand notice before the SBRR adjustment day; and the amount of each remaining instalment must be calculated in accordance with Sch 1 paras 1(4), (5) (see PARA 286) as if references in those provisions to the aggregate amount and to instalments were references to the aggregate amount of the remaining instalments and to the remaining instalments respectively: Sch 1 para 7D(5) (as so added).
15 An adjustment notice must be served at least 14 clear days before the day on which an instalment falls to be paid under the demand notice: Non-Domestic Rating (Collection and Enforcement) (Local Lists) Regulations 1989, SI 1989/1058, Sch 1 para 7D(3) (as added: see note 3). An adjustment notice need not be given on a single sheet of paper but if more than one sheet is used, the sheets must be issued together, whether or not attached, so as to comprise one notice: Sch 1 para 7D(8) (as so added). As to the service of notices see PARA 278.
16 See the Non-Domestic Rating (Collection and Enforcement) (Local Lists) Regulations 1989, SI 1989/1058, Sch 1 para 7D(2)(b) (as added: see note 3). The adjustment notice must state the amount of the estimate mentioned in Sch 1 para 7D(4) ('the new estimate') (Sch 1 para 7D(2)(b)(i) (as so added)) and the amount of each remaining instalment (Sch 1 para 7D(2)(b)(ii) (as so added)). The new estimate is the estimate of the billing authority of the revised amount payable for the financial year beginning on 1 April 2010 having regard to the small business rate relief order changes: Sch 1 para 7D(4) (as so added).
17 Non-Domestic Rating (Collection and Enforcement) (Local Lists) Regulations 1989, SI 1989/1058, Sch 1 para 7D(6)(a) (as added: see note 3).
18 Non-Domestic Rating (Collection and Enforcement) (Local Lists) Regulations 1989, SI 1989/1058, Sch 1 para 7D(6)(b) (as added: see note 3).

290. Multiple hereditaments and adjustments.

Adjustments may be made if[1] the demand notice[2] relates to more than one hereditament[3] for which an estimate[4] is made[5]. More than one adjustment of amounts paid or payable[6] under a demand notice may be made as the circumstances require[7].

1 Ie pursuant to the Non-Domestic Rating (Collection and Enforcement) (Local Lists) Regulations 1989, SI 1989/1058, reg 4(3): see PARA 279.
2 As to the meaning of 'demand notice' see PARA 278 note 5.
3 As to the meaning of 'hereditament' see PARA 106.
4 Ie such an estimate as is referred to in the Non-Domestic Rating (Collection and Enforcement) (Local Lists) Regulations 1989, SI 1989/1058, reg 6(1): see PARA 281.
5 See the Non-Domestic Rating (Collection and Enforcement) (Local Lists) Regulations 1989, SI 1989/1058, Sch 1 para 8. The adjustments are as follows:
    (1) references in Sch 1 paras 6(1)–(5), 7(1), (3), 7A(1)(d), (5), 7B(1)(b) (see PARAS 287–288) to 'the hereditament' are to be construed as references to all the hereditaments, so that Sch 1 para 6 (see PARA 287) applies only if the event mentioned in Sch 1 para 6(1) has occurred in relation to all of them (Sch 1 para 8(a) (amended by SI 1992/1512));
    (2) the relevant day is to be determined for the purposes of the Non-Domestic Rating (Collection and Enforcement) (Local Lists) Regulations 1989, SI 1989/1058, Sch 1 para 6 by reference to the hereditament with respect to which the conditions referred to in Sch 1 para 6(1) were (or, as the case may be, would be) last fulfilled (Sch 1 para 8(b));
    (3) the reference to 'the hereditament concerned' in Sch 1 para 6(6) is to be construed as a reference to any of the hereditaments concerned (Sch 1 para 8(c)); and
    (4) where neither the conditions mentioned in the Local Government Finance Act 1988 s 43(1) (see PARA 133) nor those mentioned in s 45(1) (see PARA 135) are fulfilled with respect to a hereditament to which the notice relates but the Non-Domestic Rating (Collection and Enforcement) (Local Lists) Regulations 1989, SI 1989/1058, Sch 1 para 6 does not apply by virtue of head (1) above, references in Sch 1 para 7 (see PARA 288) to the revised estimate mentioned in Sch 1 para 7(3) are to be construed in so far as concerns that hereditament as references to the amount payable in relation to the hereditament for the period in the relevant year up to the day on which the conditions were last fulfilled (Sch 1 para 8(d)).
6 As to the meaning of 'amount payable' see PARA 279 note 3.
7 Non-Domestic Rating (Collection and Enforcement) (Local Lists) Regulations 1989, SI 1989/1058, Sch 1 para 9(1) (Sch 1 para 9 substituted by SI 1992/1512). The adjustment of amounts is to be made under the Non-Domestic Rating (Collection and Enforcement) (Local Lists) Regulations 1989, SI 1989/1058, Sch 1 Pt II (paras 6–9): see Sch 1 para 9(1) (as so substituted).

291. Failure to pay instalments.

Where:

(1) a demand notice[1] has been served by a billing authority[2] on a ratepayer[3];
(2) instalments are payable under the notice[4] in accordance with the non-domestic rate instalment scheme[5]; and
(3) any such instalment is not paid[6] in accordance with the scheme[7],

the billing authority must (unless all the instalments have fallen due) serve a further notice[8] on the ratepayer stating the instalments required to be paid[9]. If, after the service of such a further notice, the ratepayer:

(a) fails to pay, before the expiry of the period of seven days beginning with the day of service of the further notice, any instalments which fall due before the expiry of that period under the demand notice concerned[10]; or
(b) fails to pay any instalment which falls due after the expiry of that period under the demand notice concerned on or before the day on which it so falls due[11],

the unpaid balance of the estimated amount[12] becomes payable by him at the expiry of a further period of seven days beginning with the day of the failure[13].

If any factor or assumption by reference to which the estimated amount was calculated in relation to a hereditament is shown to be false before the amount payable is capable of final determination[14], the billing authority may (and if so required by the ratepayer must) make a calculation of the appropriate amount[15] with a view to adjusting the ratepayer's liability in respect of the estimated amount and (as appropriate) to[16]:

(i) requiring an interim payment from the ratepayer if the appropriate amount is greater than the estimated amount[17]; or

(ii) making an interim repayment to the ratepayer if the appropriate amount is less than the amount of the estimated amount paid[18].

On calculating the appropriate amount, the billing authority must notify the ratepayer in writing of it[19].

1 As to the meaning of 'demand notice' see PARA 278 note 5.

2 As to the meaning of 'billing authority' see PARA 53.

3 Non-Domestic Rating (Collection and Enforcement) (Local Lists) Regulations 1989, SI 1989/1058, reg 8(1)(a) (amended by SI 1993/616). As to the meaning of 'ratepayer' see PARA 278 note 6.

4 Ie in accordance with the Non-Domestic Rating (Collection and Enforcement) (Local Lists) Regulations 1989, SI 1989/1058, Sch 1 (see PARAS 286–290), Sch 1E, 1F or, until 15 February 2012 in relation to England only, Sch 1G (see PARA 285): see reg 8(1)(b) (amended by SI 2010/1656, SI 2010/2222, SI 2011/1665 and SI 2012/24); Non-Domestic Rating (Collection and Enforcement) (Amendment) (England) Regulations 2012, SI 2012/24, reg 1. As to the meaning of 'England' see PARA 2 note 16.

5 See the Non-Domestic Rating (Collection and Enforcement) (Local Lists) Regulations 1989, SI 1989/1058, reg 8(1)(b) (as amended: see note 4).

6 Ie in accordance with the Non-Domestic Rating (Collection and Enforcement) (Local Lists) Regulations 1989, SI 1989/1058, Sch 1 (see PARAS 286–290), Sch 1E, Sch 1F or, until 15 February 2012 in relation to England, Sch 1G (see PARA 285): see reg 8(1)(c) (amended by SI 2010/1656, SI 2010/2222, SI 2011/1665 and SI 2012/24); Non-Domestic Rating (Collection and Enforcement) (Amendment) (England) Regulations 2012, SI 2012/24, reg 1.

7 See the Non-Domestic Rating (Collection and Enforcement) (Local Lists) Regulations 1989, SI 1989/1058, reg 8(1)(c) (as amended: see note 6).

8 As to the service of notices see PARA 278.

9 Non-Domestic Rating (Collection and Enforcement) (Local Lists) Regulations 1989, SI 1989/1058, reg 8(1) (amended by SI 1993/616).

10 Non-Domestic Rating (Collection and Enforcement) (Local Lists) Regulations 1989, SI 1989/1058, reg 8(2)(a).

11 Non-Domestic Rating (Collection and Enforcement) (Local Lists) Regulations 1989, SI 1989/1058, reg 8(2)(b).

12 'The estimated amount' means the amount last estimated under the Non-Domestic Rating (Collection and Enforcement) (Local Lists) Regulations 1989, SI 1989/1058, reg 6(1) (see PARA 281) for the purposes of the demand notice mentioned in reg 8(1)(a) (see head (1) in the text) or any subsequent notice given under Sch 1 para 7(2) or, as the case may be, Sch 1 para 7A, 7B, 7C, 7D or 7E (see PARAS 288, 289), or under Sch 1 para 7 as modified by Sch 1E para 5(3) or Sch 1F para 5(3) (see PARA 288), prior to the failure mentioned in reg 8(2), save that if in any case an interim adjustment has been required or made under reg 8(5) (see the text to notes 14–18) in relation to a hereditament, it means as regards the next payment, repayment or interim adjustment in relation to the hereditament under reg 8 (if any), the appropriate amount by reference to which the previous interim adjustment was so made: reg 8(8) (definition amended by SI 1992/1512, SI 2010/1656 and SI 2010/2222). As to the meaning of 'hereditament' see PARA 106.

13 Non-Domestic Rating (Collection and Enforcement) (Local Lists) Regulations 1989, SI 1989/1058, reg 8(2). If the unpaid balance of the estimated amount has become payable under reg 8(2), and on calculating the amount payable for the relevant year in relation to a hereditament to which the demand notice concerned relates that amount proves to be greater than the estimated amount in relation to the hereditament, an additional sum equal to the difference between the two is, on the service by the billing authority on the ratepayer of a notice stating the amount payable, to be due from the person to the authority on the expiry of such period (being not less than 14 days) after the day of issue of the notice as is specified in it: reg 8(3) (amended by SI 1993/616). As to the meaning of 'relevant year' see PARA 280 note 4. As to the meaning of 'person' see PARA 11 note 13.

However, if the unpaid balance of the estimated amount has become payable under the Non-Domestic Rating (Collection and Enforcement) (Local Lists) Regulations 1989, SI 1989/1058, reg 8(2), and on calculating the amount payable for the relevant year in relation to a hereditament to which the demand notice concerned relates that amount proves to be less than the estimated amount in relation to the hereditament, the billing authority must notify the ratepayer in writing of the amount payable (reg 8(4) (amended by SI 1993/616)); and any overpayment in respect of any liability of the ratepayer under the Non-Domestic Rating (Collection and Enforcement) (Local Lists) Regulations 1989, SI 1989/1058, Pt II (regs 3–9) is to be repaid if the ratepayer so requires (reg 8(4)(a)), or in any other case is (as the billing authority determines) either to be repaid or to be credited against any subsequent liability of the ratepayer to pay anything to the billing authority by way of non-domestic rate (reg 8(4)(b) (amended by SI 1993/616)). As to the meaning of 'writing' see PARA 21 note 3. As to the meaning of 'amount payable' see PARA 279 note 3.

14 Ie for the purposes of the Non-Domestic Rating (Collection and Enforcement) (Local Lists) Regulations 1989, SI 1989/1058, reg 8(3), (4): see note 13.

15 The 'appropriate amount' is the amount which would be required to be paid under a demand notice if such a notice were issued with respect to the relevant year, the ratepayer and the hereditament on the day that the notice under the Non-Domestic Rating (Collection and Enforcement) (Local Lists) Regulations 1989, SI 1989/1058, reg 8(7) (see the text to note 19) is issued or the repayment under reg 8(5)(b) (see head (ii) in the text) is made (as the case may be); and more than one calculation of the appropriate amount and interim payment or repayment may be required or made under reg 8(5) according to the circumstances: reg 8(6).

16 Non-Domestic Rating (Collection and Enforcement) (Local Lists) Regulations 1989, SI 1989/1058, reg 8(5) (amended by SI 1993/616).

17 Non-Domestic Rating (Collection and Enforcement) (Local Lists) Regulations 1989, SI 1989/1058, reg 8(5)(a).

18 Non-Domestic Rating (Collection and Enforcement) (Local Lists) Regulations 1989, SI 1989/1058, reg 8(5)(b).

19 Non-Domestic Rating (Collection and Enforcement) (Local Lists) Regulations 1989, SI 1989/1058, reg 8(7) (amended by SI 1993/616). A payment required under the Non-Domestic Rating (Collection and Enforcement) (Local Lists) Regulations 1989, SI 1989/1058, reg 8(5)(a) (see head (i) in the text) is due from the ratepayer to the billing authority on the expiry of such period (being not less than 14 days) after the day of issue of the notice as is specified in it: reg 8(7) (as so amended).

(C) Security for Unpaid Rates

292. Security for unpaid rates.

A billing authority[1] and a person[2] liable to pay to it an amount[3] may enter into an agreement that[4]:

(1) any interest of his in the hereditament[5] as regards which the liability arises is to be charged to secure payment of the amount[6]; and

(2) in consideration of the charge, the authority will take no steps, for a period specified in the agreement[7], to recover any payment in respect of the amount[8].

Such an agreement:

(a) may also extend to any further amount the person may become liable to pay to the authority[9] as regards the hereditament[10];

(b) may provide for the payment of interest on sums outstanding[11];

(c) may provide for interest payable to be secured by the charge[12].

1 As to the meaning of 'billing authority' see PARA 53.

2 As to the meaning of 'person' see PARA 11 note 13.

3 Ie under the Local Government Finance Act 1988 s 43 (see PARAS 133, 143 et seq) or s 45 (see PARAS 135–136, 148).

4 Non-Domestic Rating (Collection and Enforcement) (Local Lists) (Amendment and Miscellaneous Provision) Regulations 1991, SI 1991/141, reg 5(1) (amended by SI 1993/616).

5 As to the meaning of 'hereditament' see PARA 106.

6 Non-Domestic Rating (Collection and Enforcement) (Local Lists) (Amendment and Miscellaneous Provision) Regulations 1991, SI 1991/141, reg 5(1)(a).

7 The period specified for these purposes may not exceed three years: Non-Domestic Rating (Collection and Enforcement) (Local Lists) (Amendment and Miscellaneous Provision) Regulations 1991, SI 1991/141, reg 5(2).
8 Non-Domestic Rating (Collection and Enforcement) (Local Lists) (Amendment and Miscellaneous Provision) Regulations 1991, SI 1991/141, reg 5(1)(b).
9 Ie under the Local Government Finance Act 1988 s 43 (see PARAS 133, 143 et seq) or s 45 (see PARAS 135–136, 148).
10 Non-Domestic Rating (Collection and Enforcement) (Local Lists) (Amendment and Miscellaneous Provision) Regulations 1991, SI 1991/141, reg 5(3)(a).
11 Non-Domestic Rating (Collection and Enforcement) (Local Lists) (Amendment and Miscellaneous Provision) Regulations 1991, SI 1991/141, reg 5(3)(b).
12 Non-Domestic Rating (Collection and Enforcement) (Local Lists) (Amendment and Miscellaneous Provision) Regulations 1991, SI 1991/141, reg 5(3)(c).

B. ENFORCEMENT

293. Applications for liability orders.

A sum which has become payable to a billing authority[1] and which has not been paid[2] is recoverable[3] under a liability order[4], or in a court of competent jurisdiction[5].

Before a billing authority applies for a liability order, it must serve on the person[6] against whom the application is to be made a notice (a 'reminder notice')[7] stating every amount in respect of which the authority is to make the application[8]. A reminder notice may be served in respect of an amount at any time after it has become due[9]; but a reminder notice need not be served on a person who has been served with a notice relating to a failure to make payment by instalments[10] in respect of the amount concerned where there has been a subsequent failure to pay[11] in relation to that notice[12].

If an amount which has fallen due owing to a failure to pay by instalments[13] is wholly or partly unpaid, or if the amount stated in a reminder notice is wholly or partly unpaid at the expiry of the period of seven days beginning with the day on which the notice was served, the billing authority may apply to a magistrates' court for an order against the person by whom it is payable[14]. Such an application is to be instituted by making complaint to a justice of the peace[15], and requesting the issue of a summons[16] directed to that person to appear before the court to show why he has not paid the sum which is outstanding[17]. No liability order may be made in pursuance of a summons issued in this way unless 14 days have elapsed since the day on which the summons was served[18].

A warrant for the arrest of a defendant who does not appear is not to be issued[19] in any proceedings on application for a liability order[20]. However, the court may proceed to hear the complaint in the absence of the defendant upon proof that the summons was served on him in a reasonable time before the hearing[21].

1 Ie under the Non-Domestic Rating (Collection and Enforcement) (Local Lists) Regulations 1989, SI 1989/1058, Pt II (regs 3–9): see PARA 278 et seq. As to the meaning of 'billing authority' see PARA 53.
2 References in the Non-Domestic Rating (Collection and Enforcement) (Local Lists) Regulations 1989, SI 1989/1058, Pt III (regs 10–23) to a sum which has become payable and which has not been paid include references to a sum forming part of a larger sum which has become payable and the other part of which has been paid: reg 10(3).
3 Ie in accordance with the Non-Domestic Rating (Collection and Enforcement) (Local Lists) Regulations 1989, SI 1989/1058, regs 11–21: see the text to notes 6–21; and PARA 294 et seq.
4 As to liability orders see PARA 294. In relation to enforcement and recovery of a sum with respect to joint owners and occupiers, the Non-Domestic Rating (Collection and Enforcement) (Local Lists) Regulations 1989, SI 1989/1058, Pt III (regs 10–23) applies with certain modifications: see

the Non-Domestic Rating (Collection and Enforcement) (Miscellaneous Provisions) Regulations 1990, SI 1990/145, reg 4(1). As to enforcement in relation to partnerships see reg 5 (amended by SI 2014/600). As to the circumstances in which the Non-Domestic Rating (Collection and Enforcement) (Miscellaneous Provisions) Regulations 1990, SI 1990/145, regs 4, 5 apply, see reg 3 (amended by SI 1993/616 and SI 2008/428).

5 Non-Domestic Rating (Collection and Enforcement) (Local Lists) Regulations 1989, SI 1989/1058, reg 10(2) (amended by SI 1993/616). Nothing in the Non-Domestic Rating (Collection and Enforcement) (Local Lists) Regulations 1989, SI 1989/1058, reg 10(2) indicates that proceedings in a court of competent jurisdiction have to be confined to liability in respect of a single chargeable year: *Tower Hamlets London Borough Council v Merrick* [2001] EWHC Admin 799, [2001] RVR 305, [2001] All ER (D) 225 (Oct).

6 As to the meaning of 'person' see PARA 11 note 13.

7 The reminder notice is in addition to any notice required to be served under the Non-Domestic Rating (Collection and Enforcement) (Local Lists) Regulations 1989, SI 1989/1058, Pt II (regs 3–9) (see PARA 278 et seq): see reg 11(1). As to the service of notices see PARA 278.

8 Non-Domestic Rating (Collection and Enforcement) (Local Lists) Regulations 1989, SI 1989/1058, reg 11(1) (amended by SI 1993/616). This provision is expressed to be subject to the Non-Domestic Rating (Collection and Enforcement) (Local Lists) Regulations 1989, SI 1989/1058, reg 11(3) (see the text to notes 10–12): see reg 11(1) (as so amended).

9 Non-Domestic Rating (Collection and Enforcement) (Local Lists) Regulations 1989, SI 1989/1058, reg 11(2).

10 Ie a notice under the Non-Domestic Rating (Collection and Enforcement) (Local Lists) Regulations 1989, SI 1989/1058, reg 8(1): see PARA 291.

11 Ie such a subsequent failure to pay as is mentioned in the Non-Domestic Rating (Collection and Enforcement) (Local Lists) Regulations 1989, SI 1989/1058, reg 8(2)(a): see PARA 291.

12 Non-Domestic Rating (Collection and Enforcement) (Local Lists) Regulations 1989, SI 1989/1058, reg 11(3).

13 Ie an amount which has fallen due under the Non-Domestic Rating (Collection and Enforcement) (Local Lists) Regulations 1989, SI 1989/1058, reg 8(2) in consequence of such a failure as is mentioned in reg 8(2)(a): see PARA 291.

14 Non-Domestic Rating (Collection and Enforcement) (Local Lists) Regulations 1989, SI 1989/1058, reg 12(1) (amended by SI 1993/616). The Magistrates' Courts Act 1980 s 127(1) (limitation of time: see MAGISTRATES vol 71 (2013) PARA 526) does not apply to such an application; but no application may be instituted in respect of a sum after the period of six years beginning with the day on which it became due under the Non-Domestic Rating (Collection and Enforcement) (Local Lists) Regulations 1989, SI 1989/1058, Pt II (regs 3–9) (see PARA 278 et seq): reg 12(3).

15 As to justices of the peace see PARA 300.

16 A summons issued under the Non-Domestic Rating (Collection and Enforcement) (Local Lists) Regulations 1989, SI 1989/1058, reg 12(2) may be served on a person:

(1) by delivering it to him (reg 13(2)(a));
(2) by leaving it at his usual or last-known place of abode, or in the case of a company, at its registered office (reg 13(2)(b));
(3) by sending it by to him at his usual or last-known place of abode, or in the case of a company, to its registered office (reg 13(2)(c));
(4) where all or part of the sum to which it relates is payable with respect to a hereditament which is a place of business of the person, by leaving it at, or by sending it by to him at, the place of business (reg 13(2)(d)); or
(5) by leaving it at, or by sending it by to him at, an address given by the person as an address at which service of the summons will be accepted (reg 13(2)(e)).

As to service by post generally see PARA 139 note 3. As to the registered office of a company see COMPANIES vol 14 (2016) PARA 124. As to the meaning of 'hereditament' see PARA 106.

In *R (on the application of Pilot Foods Ltd) v Horseferry Road Magistrates' Court* [2003] EWHC 1447 (Admin), [2003] RVR 268, [2003] All ER (D) 286 (Jun), liability orders were quashed in circumstances where the summonses had been served at premises which the claimant had licensed to others (rather than at the claimant's registered office) thereby denying him the opportunity of appearing and opposing the making of the orders, in particular by putting evidence before the justices that he had not been in occupation at the relevant time.

17 Non-Domestic Rating (Collection and Enforcement) (Local Lists) Regulations 1989, SI 1989/1058, reg 12(2). It has been held unfair to refuse a defendant in analogous (community charge) proceedings the assistance of a friend at the hearing: *R v Leicester City Justices, ex p Barrow* [1991] 2 QB 260, [1991] RA 205, CA. Any member or officer so authorised by a local authority may prosecute or defend on its behalf, or appear on its behalf in, proceedings before a magistrates' court: see the Local Government Act 1972 s 223; and LOCAL GOVERNMENT vol 69 (2018) PARA 645.

18 Non-Domestic Rating (Collection and Enforcement) (Local Lists) Regulations 1989, SI 1989/1058, reg 13(2A) (added by SI 1998/3089).

19 Ie under the Magistrates' Courts Act 1980 s 55(2): see MAGISTRATES vol 71 (2013) PARA 533.

20 See the Non-Domestic Rating (Collection and Enforcement) (Local Lists) Regulations 1989, SI 1989/1058, reg 12(4). As to warrants that may be issued in certain circumstances following the making of a liability order see PARA 296.

21 See the Magistrates' Courts Act 1980 s 55(1), (3); and MAGISTRATES vol 71 (2013) PARAS 533, 539.

294. Liability orders.

A magistrates' court must make a liability order[1] if it is satisfied that the sum claimed has become payable by the defendant and has not been paid[2]. Such an order must be made in respect of an amount equal to the aggregate of the sum payable[3] and a sum of an amount equal to the costs reasonably incurred by the applicant in obtaining the order[4]. Where the sum payable is paid after a liability order has been applied for[5] but before it is made, the court is nonetheless (if so requested by the billing authority)[6] to make the order in respect of a sum of an amount equal to the costs reasonably incurred by the authority in making the application[7].

A single liability order may deal with one person[8] and one amount (or aggregate amount)[9], or, if the court thinks fit, may deal with more than one person and more than one such amount (or aggregate amount)[10].

The amount in respect of which a liability order is made is enforceable only in accordance with the appropriate statutory provisions[11].

When considering whether to make the liability order, the court can decide whether the conditions of liability[12] have been fulfilled in respect of the defendant and the relevant hereditament[13]; it can also decide whether a hereditament falls within a category exempted wholly or partly from rateability[14]. They cannot, however, consider within their jurisdiction whether an amendment to the local list was validly made[15], or whether or not to issue a warrant in the light of poverty or hardship of the defendant[16].

1 'Liability order' means an order under the Non-Domestic Rating (Collection and Enforcement) (Local Lists) Regulations 1989, SI 1989/1058, reg 12: reg 10(1). As to applications for liability orders see PARA 293. A liability order may not be made in respect of any amount in relation to which proceedings have been instituted under reg 20(1): see reg 20(2); and PARA 299.

2 Non-Domestic Rating (Collection and Enforcement) (Local Lists) Regulations 1989, SI 1989/1058, reg 12(5). As to the meaning of references to sums payable and not paid see PARA 293 note 2.

The burden of proof (in proceedings for distress and now for enforcement by taking control of goods, as to which see PARA 295) as to whether the rates have been paid has been held to lie with the billing authority: see *Tower Hamlets London Borough Council v Fallows and Fallows* [1990] RA 255, CA. There is authority (in relation to previous legislation) for magistrates to refuse to enforce the collection of rates where the rate has been satisfied without actual payment of the rate in question: see *R v Parker* (1857) 7 E & B 155; distinguished in *R v Kingston Justices and Phillips* (1858) EB & E 256. See also *Shillito v Hinchcliffe* [1922] 2 KB 236 at 248 per Shearman J. These were cases where the defendant had overpaid money in respect of a previous rate reduced on appeal, or where the authority had acted 'in flagrant violation of good faith' in taking the action. See also *London and North Western Rly Co v Bedford* (1852) 17 QB 978.

As to examples where a person subject to a liability order sought judicial review of the order see *R (on the application of Lampkin) v Horseferry Road Magistrates' Court* [2005] EWHC 312 (Admin), [2005] RA 233 (in the event, the application was too late after the grounds had been established and the case lacked sufficient merit to extend the limit); and *R (on the application of Pilot Foods Ltd) v Horseferry Road Magistrates' Court* [2003] EWHC 1447 (Admin), [2003] RVR 268, [2003] All ER (D) 286 (Jun) (see PARA 293 note 16). In *Liverpool City Council v Pleroma Distribution Ltd* [2002] EWHC 2467 (Admin), [2003] RA 34, (2002) Times, 2 December, justices were found not to have exceeded their jurisdiction or to have acted unlawfully when they reopened a case so as to set aside a liability order made in ignorance of a request for an adjournment. See also *R (on the application of Brighton and Hove City Council) v Brighton and Hove Justices* [2004] EWHC 1800 (Admin), [2004] RA 277, [2004] All ER (D) 546 (Jul) where the billing authority sought judicial review of a decision by the magistrates court to set aside liability orders.

3 Non-Domestic Rating (Collection and Enforcement) (Local Lists) Regulations 1989, SI 1989/1058, reg 12(6)(a) (reg 12(6) amended by SI 1990/145).

4 Non-Domestic Rating (Collection and Enforcement) (Local Lists) Regulations 1989, SI 1989/1058, reg 12(6)(b) (as amended: see note 3). In Wales, such costs, including those of instituting the application under the Non-Domestic Rating (Collection and Enforcement) (Local Lists) Regulations 1989, SI 1989/1058, reg 12(2), are not to exceed the prescribed amount of £70: reg 12(6)(b) (amended, in relation to Wales, by SI 2011/528).

5 Ie under the Non-Domestic Rating (Collection and Enforcement) (Local Lists) Regulations 1989, SI 1989/1058, reg 12(2): see PARA 293.

6 As to the meaning of 'billing authority' see PARA 53.

7 Non-Domestic Rating (Collection and Enforcement) (Local Lists) Regulations 1989, SI 1989/1058, reg 12(7) (added by SI 1990/145; amended by SI 1993/616). In Wales, such costs, including those of instituting the application under the Non-Domestic Rating (Collection and Enforcement) (Local Lists) Regulations 1989, SI 1989/1058, reg 12(2), are not to exceed the prescribed amount of £70: reg 12(7) (amended, in relation to Wales, by SI 2011/528).

8 As to the meaning of 'person' see PARA 11 note 13.

9 Ie such amount as is mentioned in the Non-Domestic Rating (Collection and Enforcement) (Local Lists) Regulations 1989, SI 1989/1058, reg 12(6) or reg 12(7): see the text to notes 3–7.

10 Non-Domestic Rating (Collection and Enforcement) (Local Lists) Regulations 1989, SI 1989/1058, reg 13(1) (amended by SI 1990/145, SI 2003/1714 and SI 2003/2210). As to the enforcement and recovery of a claim with respect to joint owners and occupiers and partnerships see the Non-Domestic Rating (Collection and Enforcement) (Miscellaneous Provisions) Regulations 1990, SI 1990/145; and PARA 293 note 4.

11 See the Non-Domestic Rating (Collection and Enforcement) (Local Lists) Regulations 1989, SI 1989/1058, reg 13(3). The appropriate statutory provisions are those of the Pt III (regs 10–23) (see PARA 296 et seq): see reg 13(3). Accordingly for the purposes of any of the provisions of the Magistrates' Courts Act 1980 Pt III (ss 75–96A) (satisfaction and enforcement: see MAGISTRATES vol 71 (2013) PARA 648 et seq), the amount in respect of which a liability order is made is not to be treated as a sum adjudged to be paid by order of the court: see the Non-Domestic Rating (Collection and Enforcement) (Local Lists) Regulations 1989, SI 1989/1058, reg 13(3).

12 Ie the conditions under the Local Government Finance Act 1988 s 43 (see PARAS 133, 143 et seq) or s 45 (see PARAS 135–136, 148).

13 As to the meaning of 'hereditament' see PARA 106.

14 See *Evans v Brook* [1959] 2 All ER 399, 4 RRC 392. As to exemptions from non-domestic rating see PARA 110 et seq.

15 See *County and Nimbus Estates Ltd v Ealing London Borough Council* (1978) 76 LGR 624, [1979] RA 63; *R v Thames Magistrates Court, ex p Christie* [1979] RA 231; *Pebmarsh Grain Ltd v Braintree District Council* [1980] RA 136; *Hackney London Borough Council v Mott and Fairman* [1994] RA 381. See also *R (on the application of Secerno Ltd) v Oxford Magistrates' Court* [2011] EWHC 1009 (Admin), [2011] RA 247, [2011] All ER (D) 198 (Apr).

16 See *R v Handsley* (1881) 7 QBD 398; *Hackney London Borough Council v Izdebski* [1988] RVR 144.

295. Enforcement by taking control of goods.

Where a liability order[1] has been made, payment may be enforced by using the statutory procedure for taking control of goods[2].

1 As to the meaning of 'liability order' see PARA 294 note 1. As to liability orders see PARAS 293–294.

2 Non-Domestic Rating (Collection and Enforcement) (Local Lists) Regulations 1989, SI 1989/1058, reg 14 (substituted by SI 2014/600). The procedure referred to in the text is 'the Schedule 12 procedure', ie the procedure in the Tribunals, Courts and Enforcement Act 2007 Sch 12 (taking control of goods and selling them to recover a sum of money: see CIVIL PROCEDURE vol 12A (2015) PARA 1334 et seq): see the Non-Domestic Rating (Collection and Enforcement) (Local Lists) Regulations 1989, SI 1989/1058, reg 10(1) (definition added by SI 2014/600).

Where a liability order has been made against a person under regulations made under the Local Government Finance Act 1988 Sch 9 (see PARA 272), the billing authority may use the procedure in the Tribunals, Courts and Enforcement Act 2007 Sch 12 to recover the amount in respect of which the order was made, to the extent that it remains unpaid: see the Local Government Finance Act 1988 s 62A (added by the Tribunals, Courts and Enforcement Act 2007 s 62(3), Sch 13 paras 87, 88).

296. Commitment to prison.

Where a billing authority[1] has sought to enforce payment by the procedure for taking control of goods[2], the debtor[3] is an individual, and the enforcement agent[4] reports to the authority that he was unable (for whatever reason) to find any or sufficient goods of the debtor to enforce payment, the authority may apply to a magistrates' court for the issue of a warrant committing the debtor to prison[5].

On such application being made, the court must (in the debtor's presence) inquire as to his means and inquire whether the failure to pay which led to the liability order concerned being made against him was due to his wilful refusal or culpable neglect[6]. If (and only if) the court is of the opinion that his failure was due to his wilful refusal or culpable neglect it may if it thinks fit[7]:

(1) issue a warrant of commitment against the debtor[8]; or
(2) fix a term of imprisonment and postpone the issue of the warrant until such time and on such conditions (if any) as the court thinks just[9].

The warrant must be made in respect of the relevant amount[10]. The warrant:

(a) must state the relevant amount[11];
(b) may be directed to the authority making the application and to such other persons (if any) as the court issuing it thinks fit[12]; and
(c) may be executed anywhere in England and Wales by any person to whom it is directed[13].

If:

(i) before a warrant has been issued, or a term of imprisonment fixed and the issue of a warrant postponed, an amount[14] is paid or tendered to the authority[15]; or
(ii) after a term of imprisonment has been fixed and the issue of a warrant postponed, any amount the court has ordered the debtor to pay is paid or tendered to the authority[16]; or
(iii) after a warrant has been issued, the amount stated in it is paid or tendered to the authority[17],

the authority must accept the amount concerned, no further steps may be taken as regards its recovery, and the debtor, if committed to prison, must be released[18].

The order in the warrant is that the debtor be imprisoned for a time specified in the warrant which is not to exceed three months[19], unless the amount stated in the warrant is sooner paid[20].

Where an application for the issue of such a warrant has been made[21], and after the making of the requisite inquiries[22] no warrant is issued or term of imprisonment fixed, the court may remit all or part of the appropriate amount to which the application relates[23]. Where an application for the issue of such a warrant has been made[24], but no warrant is issued or term of imprisonment fixed, the application may be renewed[25].

In any proceedings for commitment[26], a statement in writing[27] to the effect that wages of any amount have been paid to the debtor during any period, purporting to be signed by or on behalf of his employer, is evidence of the facts there stated[28].

1 As to the meaning of 'billing authority' see PARA 53.

2 Ie by the use of the Schedule 12 procedure pursuant to the Non-Domestic Rating (Collection and Enforcement) (Local Lists) Regulations 1989, SI 1989/1058, reg 14: see PARA 294. As to the meaning of 'the Schedule 12 procedure' see PARA 295 note 2.

3 'Debtor' means a person against whom a liability order has been made: Non-Domestic Rating (Collection and Enforcement) (Local Lists) Regulations 1989, SI 1989/1058, reg 10(1) (amended by SI 2014/600). As to the meaning of 'liability order' see PARA 294 note 1. As to liability orders see PARAS 293–294.

4 'Enforcement agent' has the meaning given in the Tribunals, Courts and Enforcement Act 2007 Sch 12 (see CIVIL PROCEDURE vol 12A (2015) PARA 1334): Rating (Collection and Enforcement) (Local Lists) Regulations 1989, SI 1989/1058, reg 10(1) (definition added by SI 2014/600).

5 Non-Domestic Rating (Collection and Enforcement) (Local Lists) Regulations 1989, SI 1989/1058, reg 16(1) (amended by SI 1992/474, SI 1993/616 and SI 2014/600). A single warrant may not be issued under the Non-Domestic Rating (Collection and Enforcement) (Local Lists) Regulations 1989, SI 1989/1058, reg 16 against more than one person: reg 17(1) (amended by SI 2003/1714 and SI 2003/2210). As to the meaning of 'person' see PARA 11 note 13.

The Non-Domestic Rating (Collection and Enforcement) (Local Lists) Regulations 1989, SI 1989/1058, regs 16–17 have effect subject to the Criminal Justice Act 1982 Pt I (ss 1–11) (largely repealed) (treatment of young offenders) (see now the Powers of Criminal Courts (Sentencing) Act 2000; and see SENTENCING vol 92 (2015) PARA 551): Non-Domestic Rating (Collection and Enforcement) (Local Lists) Regulations 1989, SI 1989/1058, reg 17(7). See also *R v Newcastle Justices, ex p Ashley* [1993] RA 264.

As to the relationship between remedies under a liability order see PARA 298.

6 Non-Domestic Rating (Collection and Enforcement) (Local Lists) Regulations 1989, SI 1989/1058, reg 16(2). For the purpose of enabling such inquiry to be made as to the debtor's conduct and means, a justice of the peace (see PARA 300) may:

(1) issue a summons to him to appear before a magistrates' court and (if he does not obey the summons) issue a warrant for his arrest (reg 17(5)(a)); or

(2) issue a warrant for the debtor's arrest without issuing a summons (reg 17(5)(b)).

A warrant issued under reg 17(5) may be executed anywhere in England and Wales by any person to whom it is directed or by any constable acting within his police area; and the Magistrates' Courts Act 1980 s 125(3) (repealed) (execution of warrants) (see now s 125A et seq; and MAGISTRATES vol 71 (2013) PARA 670) applies to such a warrant: Non-Domestic Rating (Collection and Enforcement) (Local Lists) Regulations 1989, SI 1989/1058, reg 17(6). As to the meanings of 'England' and 'Wales' see PARA 2 note 16. As to the office of constable see POLICE AND INVESTIGATORY POWERS vol 84 (2013) PARA 1 et seq. As to police areas see POLICE AND INVESTIGATORY POWERS vol 84 (2013) PARA 52 et seq.

In *R v Birmingham Justices, ex p Turner* (1971) 17 RRC 12, 219 Estates Gazette 585, DC, commitment was quashed due to insufficiency of inquiry. This was followed in *R v Liverpool City Justices, ex p Lanckriet* (1977) 75 LGR 605, [1977] RA 85. See also *R v Poole Justices, ex p Fleet* [1983] 2 All ER 897, [1983] 1 WLR 974; *R v Richmond Justices, ex p Atkins* [1983] RVR 148 (magistrates wrongly assuming that defendant could borrow further from bank); *R v Birmingham Magistrates' Court, ex p Mansell* [1988] RVR 112, (1988) 152 JP 570 (no account taken of ratepayer's offer to meet debt from capital assets); *R v Liverpool Justices, ex p Greaves* [1979] RA 119 (no proper inquiry as to means); *R v Felixstowe, Ipswich and Woodbridge Magistrates' Court, ex p Herridge* [1993] RA 83, 158 JP 307 (not necessary for magistrates to inquire in every case whether there is an alternative procedure to enforce the debt). See also *R (on the application of Lee) v Bournemouth Magistrates' Court* [2002] All ER (D) 378 (Mar) (claimant's committal quashed because authority had failed to discharge the burden of proof on it to establish that claimant had culpably neglected to pay and the justices had failed to state why they had rejected the claimant's evidence that he did not have the means to pay and that any offers to pay that he had made were conditional on funds becoming available).

Committal proceedings are a 'legal process' within the meaning of the Insolvency Act 1986 s

285(1) (restriction on proceedings and remedies: see BANKRUPTCY AND INDIVIDUAL INSOLVENCY vol 5 (2013) PARA 214); therefore the magistrates have the power to stay such proceedings against a bankrupt: see *Smith (a bankrupt) v Braintree District Council* [1990] 2 AC 215, [1990] RA 1, HL (followed in *Lewis v Ogwr Borough Council* [1996] RA 124). Unlawful commitment to prison may result in damages being awarded to the debtor: see *R v Manchester City Magistrates' Court, ex p Davies* [1989] QB 631, [1989] 1 All ER 90; see also *R v Wolverhampton Magistrates' Court, ex p Mould* [1992] RA 309, 157 JP 1017; *R v Middleton Justices, ex p Tilley* [1995] RVR 101. As to cases where magistrates who jailed unrepresented defaulters for failure to pay local rates or court-imposed fines were found to have acted beyond their powers and in breach of provisions of the Convention for the Protection of Human Rights and Fundamental Freedoms (1950) arts 5, 6 (see RIGHTS AND FREEDOMS vol 88A (2018) PARA 274 et seq) see *Lloyd v United Kingdom* [2006] RA 329, [2006] RA 384, (2005) Times, 10 March, ECtHR.

7 Non-Domestic Rating (Collection and Enforcement) (Local Lists) Regulations 1989, SI 1989/1058, reg 16(3). As to the exercise of discretion in such a case see *R v Oundle and Thrapston Justices and Delaney, ex p East Northamptonshire District Council* [1980] RA 232; *R v Thanet District Council, ex p Haddow* [1992] RA 245, sub nom *R v Ramsgate Magistrates' Court and Thanet District Council* (1993) 157 JP 545, CA; *R v Northampton Magistrates' Court, ex p Newell* [1992] RA 283, CA; *R v Felixstowe, Ipswich and Woodbridge Magistrates' Court, ex p Herridge* [1993] RA 83, 158 JP 307 (effect of change in debtor's circumstances); *Stevenson v Southwark London Borough Council* [1993] RA 113 (failure by magistrate to recognise existence of discretion); *R v Cannock Justices, ex p Ireland* [1996] RA 463, CA; *R v Stoke-on-Trent Justices, ex p Booth* [1997] RA 263, (1996) Independent, 9 February (costs against magistrate). It was held in *R v Ealing Magistrates' Court, ex p Coatsworth* [1980] RA 97, 78 LGR 439, that the magistrates could hear evidence in committal proceedings as to who was the rateable occupier of the relevant hereditament.

As to admissibility of evidence in commitment to prison proceedings see PARA 300.

8 Non-Domestic Rating (Collection and Enforcement) (Local Lists) Regulations 1989, SI 1989/1058, reg 16(3)(a).

9 Non-Domestic Rating (Collection and Enforcement) (Local Lists) Regulations 1989, SI 1989/1058, reg 16(3)(b).

10 Non-Domestic Rating (Collection and Enforcement) (Local Lists) Regulations 1989, SI 1989/1058, reg 16(4). The 'relevant amount' for this purpose is the aggregate of:

(1) the amount outstanding (within the meaning of the Tribunals, Courts and Enforcement Act 2007 Sch 12: see CIVIL PROCEDURE vol 12A (2015) PARA 1356) (Non-Domestic Rating (Collection and Enforcement) (Local Lists) Regulations 1989, SI 1989/1058, reg 16(4)(a) (substituted by SI 2014/600)); and

(2) a sum of an amount equal to the costs reasonably incurred by the applicant in respect of the application (Non-Domestic Rating (Collection and Enforcement) (Local Lists) Regulations 1989, SI 1989/1058, reg 16(4)(b)).

11 Non-Domestic Rating (Collection and Enforcement) (Local Lists) Regulations 1989, SI 1989/1058, reg 16(5)(a).

12 Non-Domestic Rating (Collection and Enforcement) (Local Lists) Regulations 1989, SI 1989/1058, reg 16(5)(b).

13 Non-Domestic Rating (Collection and Enforcement) (Local Lists) Regulations 1989, SI 1989/1058, reg 16(5)(c).

14 Ie determined in accordance with the Non-Domestic Rating (Collection and Enforcement) (Local Lists) Regulations 1989, SI 1989/1058, reg 16(6A): see reg 16(6) (substituted by SI 1998/3089). The amount referred to is the aggregate of the amount outstanding (within the meaning of the Tribunals, Courts and Enforcement Act 2007 Sch 12) and the authority's reasonable costs incurred up to the time of payment or tender in making one or more of the applications referred to in the Non-Domestic Rating (Collection and Enforcement) (Local Lists) Regulations 1989, SI 1989/1058, Sch 4: see reg 16(6A), Sch 4 (reg 16(6A), (6B), Sch 4 added by SI 1998/3089; the Non-Domestic Rating (Collection and Enforcement) (Local Lists) Regulations 1989, SI 1989/1058, reg 16(6A) amended by SI 2014/600; the Non-Domestic Rating (Collection and Enforcement) (Local Lists) Regulations 1989, SI 1989/1058, Sch 4 substituted, in relation to England, by SI 2010/752; and, in relation to Wales by SI 2011/528). For these purposes, the authority's reasonable costs in respect of any application must not exceed the amount specified in the Non-Domestic Rating (Collection and Enforcement) (Local Lists) Regulations 1989, SI 1989/1058, Sch 4: reg 16(6B) (as so added).

15 Non-Domestic Rating (Collection and Enforcement) (Local Lists) Regulations 1989, SI 1989/1058, reg 16(6)(a) (as substituted: see note 14).

16 Non-Domestic Rating (Collection and Enforcement) (Local Lists) Regulations 1989, SI 1989/1058, reg 16(6)(b) (as substituted: see note 14).
17 Non-Domestic Rating (Collection and Enforcement) (Local Lists) Regulations 1989, SI 1989/1058, reg 16(6)(c) (as substituted: see note 14).
18 Non-Domestic Rating (Collection and Enforcement) (Local Lists) Regulations 1989, SI 1989/1058, reg 16(6) (as substituted: see note 14).
19 As to the meaning of 'month' see PARA 11 note 1.
20 Non-Domestic Rating (Collection and Enforcement) (Local Lists) Regulations 1989, SI 1989/1058, reg 16(7). However:

(1) where a warrant is issued after a postponement under reg 16(3)(b) (see head (2) in the text) and, since the term of imprisonment was fixed but before the issue of the warrant, the amount mentioned in reg 16(4)(a) (see note 10) with respect to which the warrant would (but for the postponement) have been made has been reduced by a part payment, the period of imprisonment ordered under the warrant must be the term fixed under reg 16(3) (see the text to notes 7–9) reduced by such number of days as bears to the total number of days in that term less one day the same proportion as the part paid bears to that amount (reg 16(7)(a)); and

(2) where, after the issue of a warrant, a part payment of the amount stated in it is made, the period of imprisonment is to be reduced by such number of days as bears to the total number of days in the term of imprisonment specified in the warrant less one day the same proportion as the part paid bears to the amount so stated (reg 16(7)(b)).

In calculating a reduction required under reg 16(7), any fraction of a day is to be left out of account; and the Magistrates' Courts Rules 1981, SI 1981/552, r 55(1)–(3) (payment after imprisonment imposed: see MAGISTRATES vol 71 (2013) PARA 648 et seq) applies (so far as is relevant) to a part payment as if the imprisonment concerned were imposed for insufficient recovery by way of the Schedule 12 procedure to satisfy a sum adjudged to be paid by a magistrates' court: Non-Domestic Rating (Collection and Enforcement) (Local Lists) Regulations 1989, SI 1989/1058, reg 16(8) (amended by SI 2014/600). The court cannot impose two consecutive periods of three months' imprisonment in one warrant of commitment, despite it relating to two separate sums: see *R v Bexley Justices, ex p Henry* (1971) 17 RRC 15. The principle of proportionality is relevant to fixing a term of imprisonment under the Non-Domestic Rating (Collection and Enforcement) (Local Lists) Regulations 1989, SI 1989/1058, reg 16: see *R v Highbury Corner Magistrates' Court, ex p Uchendu* [1994] RA 51, 158 LGR 481.

21 Ie under the Non-Domestic Rating (Collection and Enforcement) (Local Lists) Regulations 1989, SI 1989/1058, reg 16: see the text to notes 1–5.
22 Ie those mentioned in the Non-Domestic Rating (Collection and Enforcement) (Local Lists) Regulations 1989, SI 1989/1058, reg 16(2): see the text to note 6.
23 Non-Domestic Rating (Collection and Enforcement) (Local Lists) Regulations 1989, SI 1989/1058, reg 17(2). The appropriate amount referred to is now the relevant amount: see note 10.
24 Ie under the Non-Domestic Rating (Collection and Enforcement) (Local Lists) Regulations 1989, SI 1989/1058, reg 16: see the text to notes 1–5.
25 Non-Domestic Rating (Collection and Enforcement) (Local Lists) Regulations 1989, SI 1989/1058, reg 17(3). This provision applies except so far as regards any sum remitted under reg 17(2) (see the text to notes 21–23) on the ground that the circumstances of the debtor have changed: see reg 17(3).
26 Ie any proceedings under the Non-Domestic Rating (Collection and Enforcement) (Local Lists) Regulations 1989, SI 1989/1058, reg 16.
27 As to the meaning of 'writing' see PARA 21 note 3.
28 Non-Domestic Rating (Collection and Enforcement) (Local Lists) Regulations 1989, SI 1989/1058, reg 17(4).

297. Amount due under liability order deemed to be a debt for certain proceedings.

Where a liability order[1] has been made and the debtor[2] against whom it was made is an individual, the amount due is deemed[3] to be a debt for the purposes of a creditor's petition[4]. Where a liability order has been made and the debtor against whom it was made is a company, the amount due is deemed[5] to be a debt for the purposes of winding up proceedings[6].

For the purposes of these provisions, the 'amount due' is an amount equal to any outstanding sum which is or forms part of the amount in respect of which the liability order was made[7].

1 As to the meaning of 'liability order' see PARA 294 note 1. As to liability orders see PARAS 293–294.
2 As to the meaning of 'debtor' see PARA 296 note 3.
3 Ie for the purposes of the Insolvency Act 1986 s 267 (grounds of creditor's petition): see BANKRUPTCY AND INDIVIDUAL INSOLVENCY vol 5 (2013) PARA 132.
4 See the Non-Domestic Rating (Collection and Enforcement) (Local Lists) Regulations 1989, SI 1989/1058, reg 18(1). As to the relationship between remedies under a liability order see PARA 298.
5 Ie for the purposes of the Insolvency Act 1986 s 122(1)(f) (winding up of companies by the court: see COMPANY AND PARTNERSHIP INSOLVENCY vol 16 (2017) PARA 354) or, as the case may be, s 221(5)(b) (winding up of unregistered companies: see COMPANY AND PARTNERSHIP INSOLVENCY vol 17 (2017) PARA 1032).
6 See the Non-Domestic Rating (Collection and Enforcement) (Local Lists) Regulations 1989, SI 1989/1058, reg 18(2) (amended by SI 1990/145).
7 Non-Domestic Rating (Collection and Enforcement) (Local Lists) Regulations 1989, SI 1989/1058, reg 18(3).

298. Relationship between remedies.

Where[1] a warrant of commitment is issued against (or a term of imprisonment is fixed in the case of) a person, no steps (or no further steps) may be taken pursuant to the enforcement provisions[2] by way of the procedure for enforcement by taking control of goods[3] or bankruptcy in relation to the relevant amount[4].

Steps[5] by way of enforcement by taking control of goods, commitment[6], bankruptcy or winding up[7] may not be taken against a person under a liability order[8] while steps by way of another of those methods are being taken against him under it[9].

Where a step is taken by way of the procedure for enforcement by taking control of goods for the recovery of an outstanding sum which is or forms part of an amount in respect of which a liability order has been made, any sum recovered thereby which is less than the aggregate of the amount outstanding and any charges connected with the enforcement procedure are to be treated as discharging first the charges, the balance (if any) being applied towards the discharge of the outstanding sum[10].

1 Ie under the Non-Domestic Rating (Collection and Enforcement) (Local Lists) Regulations 1989, SI 1989/1058, reg 16(3): see PARA 296.
2 Ie under the Non-Domestic Rating (Collection and Enforcement) (Local Lists) Regulations 1989, SI 1989/1058, Pt III (regs 10–23).
3 Ie the Schedule 12 procedure see PARA 295 note 2.
4 Non-Domestic Rating (Collection and Enforcement) (Local Lists) Regulations 1989, SI 1989/1058, reg 19(1) (reg 19 amended by SI 2014/600). The 'relevant amount' is that mentioned in the Non-Domestic Rating (Collection and Enforcement) (Local Lists) Regulations 1989, SI 1989/1058, reg 16(4) (see PARA 296): see reg 19(1). As to the Schedule 12 procedure see PARA 295. As to bankruptcy in relation to the relevant amount see PARA 297.
5 Ie under the Non-Domestic Rating (Collection and Enforcement) (Local Lists) Regulations 1989, SI 1989/1058, Pt III (regs 10–23).
6 As to commitment see PARA 296.
7 As to winding up see PARA 297.
8 As to the meaning of 'liability order' see PARA 294 note 1. As to liability orders see PARAS 293–294.
9 Non-Domestic Rating (Collection and Enforcement) (Local Lists) Regulations 1989, SI 1989/1058, reg 19(2) (as amended: see note 4). Subject to reg 19(1) (see the text to notes 1–3) and reg 19(2), the Schedule 12 procedure may be resorted to more than once: reg 19(3) (as so amended).

10 Non-Domestic Rating (Collection and Enforcement) (Local Lists) Regulations 1989, SI 1989/1058, reg 19(4) (as so amended).

299. Recovery in court of competent jurisdiction.

A sum which has become payable to a billing authority[1], which has not been paid, and in respect of which a liability order[2] has not been made may (as an alternative to recovery under a liability order) be recovered in a court of competent jurisdiction[3].

A sum which has become payable (by way of repayment)[4] to a person[5] other than a billing authority but which has not been paid is recoverable in a court of competent jurisdiction[6].

Recovery of sums due in respect of non-domestic rates by this method is subject to a limitation period of six years[7].

1 Ie under the Non-Domestic Rating (Collection and Enforcement) (Local Lists) Regulations 1989, SI 1989/1058, Pt II (regs 3–9): see PARA 278 et seq. As to the meaning of 'billing authority' see PARA 53.

2 As to the meaning of 'liability order' see PARA 294 note 1. As to liability orders see PARAS 293–294.

3 Non-Domestic Rating (Collection and Enforcement) (Local Lists) Regulations 1989, SI 1989/1058, reg 20(1) (amended by SI 1993/616). A liability order may not be made in respect of any amount in relation to which proceedings have been instituted under the Non-Domestic Rating (Collection and Enforcement) (Local Lists) Regulations 1989, SI 1989/1058, reg 20(1): reg 20(2).

4 Ie under the Non-Domestic Rating (Collection and Enforcement) (Local Lists) Regulations 1989, SI 1989/1058, Pt II (regs 3–9): see PARA 278 et seq.

5 As to the meaning of 'person' see PARA 11 note 13.

6 Non-Domestic Rating (Collection and Enforcement) (Local Lists) Regulations 1989, SI 1989/1058, reg 22 (amended by SI 1993/616).

7 See the Limitation Act 1980 s 9(1) (sums recoverable by statute); and LIMITATION PERIODS vol 68 (2016) PARA 1005.

300. Proceedings in magistrates' courts.

Subject to any other enactment authorising a District Judge (magistrates' courts)[1] or other person to act by himself, a magistrates' court may not[2] hear a summons, entertain an application for a warrant or hold an inquiry as to means on such an application except when composed of at least two justices[3].

In any proceedings relating to an application for a liability order[4] or commitment to prison[5], a statement[6] contained in a document constituting or forming part of a record compiled by the applicant authority or an authorised person[7] is admissible as evidence of any fact stated in it of which direct oral evidence would be admissible[8].

1 As to District Judges (magistrates' courts) see MAGISTRATES vol 71 (2013) PARA 420 et seq.

2 Ie under the Non-Domestic Rating (Collection and Enforcement) (Local Lists) Regulations 1989, SI 1989/1058, Pt III (regs 10–23): see PARA 293.

3 Non-Domestic Rating (Collection and Enforcement) (Local Lists) Regulations 1989, SI 1989/1058, reg 21(2) (amended SI 2000/2026 and SI 2001/1076). References to a 'justice of the peace' in the Non-Domestic Rating (Collection and Enforcement) (Local Lists) Regulations 1989, SI 1989/1058, reg 12(2) (see PARA 293) and reg 15(2) are to be construed subject to the Justices' Clerks Rules 2005, SI 2005/545, r 3 (which authorises certain matters authorised to be done by a justice of the peace to be done by a justices' clerk: see MAGISTRATES vol 71 (2013) PARA 503): Non-Domestic Rating (Collection and Enforcement) (Local Lists) Regulations 1989, SI 1989/1058, reg 21(3).

4 Ie any proceedings under the Non-Domestic Rating (Collection and Enforcement) (Local Lists) Regulations 1989, SI 1989/1058, reg 12: see PARA 293. As to the meaning of 'liability order' see PARA 294 note 1.

5 Ie any proceedings under the Non-Domestic Rating (Collection and Enforcement) (Local Lists)

Regulations 1989, SI 1989/1058, reg 16: see PARA 296. This reference to an application under reg 16 includes a reference to an application made in the circumstances mentioned in reg 17(3) (see PARA 296): see reg 21(6) (added by SI 1992/474).

6 'Statement' includes any representation of fact, whether made in words or otherwise: see the Non-Domestic Rating (Collection and Enforcement) (Local Lists) Regulations 1989, SI 1989/1058, reg 21(6) (as added: see note 6).

7 'Authorised person' means any person authorised by a billing authority to exercise any functions relating to the collection and enforcement of non-domestic rates: Non-Domestic Rating (Collection and Enforcement) (Local Lists) Regulations 1989, SI 1989/1058, reg 21(7) (added by SI 1996/1880). As to the meaning of 'billing authority' see PARA 53.

8 Non-Domestic Rating (Collection and Enforcement) (Local Lists) Regulations 1989, SI 1989/1058, reg 21(4) (added by SI 1992/474; and amended by SI 1996/1880 and SI 2014/600). In proceedings where the applicant authority or an authorised person desires to give a statement in evidence in accordance with the Non-Domestic Rating (Collection and Enforcement) (Local Lists) Regulations 1989, SI 1989/1058, reg 21(4), and the document containing that statement is produced by a computer, a certificate:

(1) identifying the document containing the statement and the computer by which it was produced (reg 21(5)(a) (reg 21(5) added by SI 1992/474));

(2) containing a statement that at all material times the computer was operating properly, or if not, that any respect in which it was not operating properly or was out of operation was not such as to affect the production of the document or the accuracy of its contents (Non-Domestic Rating (Collection and Enforcement) (Local Lists) Regulations 1989, SI 1989/1058, reg 21(5)(b) (as so added));

(3) giving such explanation as may be appropriate of the content of the document (reg 21(5)(c) (as so added)); and

(4) purporting to be signed by a person occupying a responsible position in relation to the operation of the computer (reg 21(5)(d) (as so added)),

is admissible as evidence of anything which is stated in it to the best of the signatory's information and belief (reg 21(5) (as so added; amended by SI 1996/1880)).

301. Payment under a mistake.

A payment of rates under a mistake of fact may be recovered at common law[1].

Historically, money paid for rates under a mistake of law was not recoverable at common law[2] but it now seems that money paid by a subject to a public authority in the form of taxes or other levies paid pursuant to an ultra vires demand by the authority is prima facie recoverable by the subject as of right[3] and it has been established as a principle in the law of restitution that money paid under mistake of law is normally recoverable in restitution[4].

1 See *Meadows v Grand Junction Waterworks Co* (1905) 69 JP 255; *Burland v Hull Local Board of Health* (1862) 3 B & S 271; *North Western Gas Board v Manchester Corpn* (1963) 61 LGR 241, [1963] RA 35 (revsd [1963] 3 All ER 442, [1963] RVR 552, CA); and MISTAKE vol 77 (2016) PARA 35.

2 See *Spiers and Pond Limited v Finsbury Metropolitan Borough Council* (1956) 1 RRC 219, 55 LGR 361; cf *Larner v LCC* [1949] 2 KB 683, [1949] 1 All ER 964. See also *Slater v Burnley Corpn* (1888) 53 JP 70; *Slater v Burnley Corpn (No 2)* (1889) 53 JP 535; *Bootle-cum-Linancre Corpn v Lancashire County Council* (1890) 60 LJQB 323, 7 TLR 179, CA; *Selmes v Judge* (1871) LR 6 QB 724; *Stubbs v Richmond upon Thames London Borough Council* [1989] RA 1, CA. As to the former general rule that money paid under mistake of law was irrecoverable at common law see MISTAKE vol 77 (2016) PARA 64.

Under previous rating legislation, it had been held that Parliament must have intended rating authorities not to retain rates paid under a mistake of law or upon an erroneous valuation unless there were special circumstances justifying retention of the amount paid: see *R v Tower Hamlets London Borough Council, ex p Chetnik Developments Ltd* [1988] AC 858, sub nom *Tower Hamlets London Borough Council v Chetnik Developments Ltd* [1988] 1 All ER 961. However that case was considering the General Rate Act 1967 s 9 (repealed) and the discretionary power so conferred on charging authorities does not appear in current legislation.

3 See *Woolwich Equitable Building Society v IRC* [1993] AC 70, sub nom *Woolwich Building Society v IRC (No 2)* [1992] 3 All ER 737, HL; and MISTAKE vol 77 (2016) PARA 64.

4 See *Kleinwort Benson Ltd v Lincoln City Council* [1999] 2 AC 349, [1998] 4 All ER 513, HL; and

RESTITUTION vol 88 (2012) PARA 436 et seq. See also *R v Barking and Dagenham London Borough Council, ex p Magon* [2004] RA 269, CA (restitution was appropriate where overpayment occurred as the consequence of retrospective alterations to a rating list).

302. Limitation on matters to be raised in enforcement proceedings.

Any matter which could be the subject of an appeal as regards matters connected with the alteration of rating lists[1] may not be raised in proceedings[2] under the enforcement provisions[3].

1 Ie an appeal made under regulations which have been made under the Local Government Finance Act 1988 s 55: see PARA 199. As to the alteration of lists see PARA 202 et seq. As to appeals in respect of the alteration to lists see PARA 242 et seq.
2 Ie under the Non-Domestic Rating (Collection and Enforcement) (Local Lists) Regulations 1989, SI 1989/1058, Pt III (regs 10–23): see PARA 293 et seq.
3 Non-Domestic Rating (Collection and Enforcement) (Local Lists) Regulations 1989, SI 1989/1058, reg 23(1). See *R (on the application of Vtesse Networks Ltd) v North West Wiltshire Magistrates' Court* [2009] EWHC 3283 (Admin), [2010] RA 1, [2009] All ER (D) 101 (Dec).

303. Proof of content of local non-domestic rating lists.

The contents of a local non-domestic rating list[1] (or an extract from such a list) may be proved in proceedings under the enforcement provisions[2] by production of a copy of the list (or relevant part of the list) purporting to be certified by the proper officer of the billing authority[3] to which the list (or extract) relates to be a true copy[4].

1 As to local non-domestic rating lists see PARA 191 et seq.
2 Ie under the Non-Domestic Rating (Collection and Enforcement) (Local Lists) Regulations 1989, SI 1989/1058, Pt III (regs 10–23): see PARA 293.
3 As to the meaning of 'billing authority' see PARA 53.
4 Non-Domestic Rating (Collection and Enforcement) (Local Lists) Regulations 1989, SI 1989/1058, reg 23(2) (amended by SI 1993/616).

304. Notifications.

If a liability order[1] has been made and by virtue of the giving of a notification[2] or the setting of a multiplier in substitution[3] any part of the amount[4] in respect of which the order was made would (if paid) fall to be repaid or credited against any subsequent liability, that part is to be treated[5] as paid on the day the notification is given (or on the day that the multiplier in substitution is set[6], as the case may be) and accordingly as no longer outstanding[7].

If, after a warrant is issued or term of imprisonment is fixed[8], and before the term of imprisonment has begun or been fully served, a billing authority gives such a notification as is prescribed[9], or sets a multiplier in substitution[10], it must forthwith notify accordingly the designated officer for the court which issued the warrant and (if the debtor[11] is detained) the governor or keeper of the prison or place where he is detained or such other person as has lawful custody of him[12].

1 As to the meaning of 'liability order' see PARA 294 note 1. As to liability orders see PARAS 293–294.
2 Ie a notification which is given by the billing authority or an authorised person under the Non-Domestic Rating (Collection and Enforcement) (Local Lists) Regulations 1989, SI 1989/1058, reg 8(4) or reg 8(7) (see PARA 291), reg 9(2) (see PARA 284), Sch 1 para 6(3) (see PARA 287), Sch 1 para 7(2)(a) (see PARA 288) or Sch 1 para 7A(2) (see PARA 288) (including a notification given under Sch 1 para 7A(2) pursuant to Sch 1 para 7B(2) (see PARA 288)): reg 23(3)(a) (amended by SI 1992/1512, SI 1993/616 and SI 1996/1880). For these purposes, 'authorised person' means any person authorised by a billing authority to exercise any functions relating to the collection and enforcement of non-domestic rates: reg 21(7) (added by SI 1996/1880). As to the meaning of 'billing authority' see PARA 53. As to the meaning of 'person'

see PARA 11 note 13.

3 Ie the Local Government Finance Act 1988 Sch 7 para 10(4) (multiplier set in substitution by special authority: see PARA 156) applying in any case: Non-Domestic Rating (Collection and Enforcement) (Local Lists) Regulations 1989, SI 1989/1058, reg 23(3)(b).

4 Ie the amount mentioned in the Non-Domestic Rating (Collection and Enforcement) (Local Lists) Regulations 1989, SI 1989/1058, reg 12(6)(a): see PARA 294.

5 Ie for the purposes of the Non-Domestic Rating (Collection and Enforcement) (Local Lists) Regulations 1989, SI 1989/1058, Pt III (regs 10–23): see PARA 293 et seq.

6 Ie under the Local Government Finance Act 1988 Sch 7 para 10: see PARA 156.

7 Non-Domestic Rating (Collection and Enforcement) (Local Lists) Regulations 1989, SI 1989/1058, reg 23(3).

8 Ie under the Non-Domestic Rating (Collection and Enforcement) (Local Lists) Regulations 1989, SI 1989/1058, reg 16(3): see PARA 296.

9 Ie such a notification as is mentioned in the Non-Domestic Rating (Collection and Enforcement) (Local Lists) Regulations 1989, SI 1989/1058, reg 23(3)(a) in the case in question: see note 2.

10 Ie so that the Local Government Finance Act 1988 Sch 7 para 10(4) applies in the case in question: see PARA 156.

11 As to the meaning of 'debtor' see PARA 296 note 3.

12 Non-Domestic Rating (Collection and Enforcement) (Local Lists) Regulations 1989, SI 1989/1058, reg 23(4) (amended by SI 1993/616, SI 2005/617, SI 2001/362, SI 2001/1076 and SI 2005/617).

305. Outstanding liabilities on death.

Where a person dies and at any time before his death he was (or is alleged to have been) subject to a non-domestic rate[1], and:

(1) before the deceased's death, a sum has become payable by him under the non-domestic rating billing provisions[2] or by way of relevant costs[3] in respect of a non-domestic rate but has not been paid[4]; or

(2) after the deceased's death, a sum would, but for his death (and whether or not on the service of a notice) become payable by him[5] in respect of a non-domestic rate[6],

his executor or administrator is[7] liable to pay the sum and may deduct out of the assets and effects of the deceased any payments made (or to be made)[8].

Where, before the deceased's death, a sum in excess of his liability[9] (including relevant costs[10] payable by him) in respect of a non-domestic rate has been paid (whether the excess arises because of his death or otherwise) and has not been repaid or credited under the non-domestic rating billing provisions[11], his executor or administrator is entitled to the sum[12].

In so far as is relevant to such liability[13] in the administration of the deceased's estate, the executor or administrator may institute, continue or withdraw proceedings (whether by way of appeal[14] or otherwise)[15]. However, any matter which could be the subject of an appeal as regards matters connected with the alteration of rating lists[16] may not be raised in proceedings to enforce a liability arising upon a ratepayer's death[17]. The contents of a local non-domestic rating list[18] (or an extract from such a list) may be proved in such proceedings by production of a copy of the list (or relevant part of the list) purporting to be certified by the proper officer of the billing authority[19] to which the list (or extract) relates to be a true copy[20].

1 Non-Domestic Rating (Collection and Enforcement) (Local Lists) Regulations 1989, SI 1989/1058, reg 24(1). 'Non-domestic rate' includes a business rate supplement within the meaning of the Business Rate Supplements Act 2009 s 1(1) (see PARA 326): Non-Domestic Rating (Collection and Enforcement) (Local Lists) Regulations 1989, SI 1989/1058, reg 1(2) (definition added by SI 2010/187).

2 Ie under the Non-Domestic Rating (Collection and Enforcement) (Local Lists) Regulations 1989, SI 1989/1058, Pt II (regs 3–9): see PARA 278 et seq.

3 Costs are 'relevant costs' for the purposes of the Non-Domestic Rating (Collection and Enforcement) (Local Lists) Regulations 1989, SI 1989/1058, reg 24(2) and reg 24(4) (see the text to notes 9–12) if:

(1) an order or warrant (as the case may be) was made by the court in respect of them under reg 12(6)(b), (7) (see PARA 294) or reg 16(4)(b) (see PARA 296) or in proceedings under reg 20 (see PARA 299) (reg 24(5)(a) (amended by SI 1990/145)); or

(2) they are charges connected with the use of the Schedule 12 procedure which may be recovered pursuant to regulations under the Tribunals, Courts and Enforcement Act 2007 Sch 12 para 62 (reg 24(5)(b) (amended by SI 2014/600)).

As to the meaning of 'Schedule 12 procedure' see PARA 295 note 2.

4 Non-Domestic Rating (Collection and Enforcement) (Local Lists) Regulations 1989, SI 1989/1058, reg 24(2)(a) (amended by SI 1990/145).

5 Ie under the Non-Domestic Rating (Collection and Enforcement) (Local Lists) Regulations 1989, SI 1989/1058, Pt II (regs 3–9): see PARA 278 et seq.

6 Non-Domestic Rating (Collection and Enforcement) (Local Lists) Regulations 1989, SI 1989/1058, reg 24(2)(b). Where this provision applies, the liability of the executor or administrator does not arise until the service on him of a notice requiring payment of the sum: reg 24(3). As to the service of notices see PARA 278.

7 Ie subject to the Non-Domestic Rating (Collection and Enforcement) (Local Lists) Regulations 1989, SI 1989/1058, reg 24(3) (see note 6) and to the extent that it is not in excess of the deceased's liability under the Local Government Finance Act 1988 or the Business Rate Supplements Act 2009 (including relevant costs payable by him) in respect of the rate: see the Non-Domestic Rating (Collection and Enforcement) (Local Lists) Regulations 1989, SI 1989/1058, reg 24(2).

8 Non-Domestic Rating (Collection and Enforcement) (Local Lists) Regulations 1989, SI 1989/1058, reg 24(2) (amended by SI 2010/187). A sum payable under the Non-Domestic Rating (Collection and Enforcement) (Local Lists) Regulations 1989, SI 1989/1058, reg 24(2) is enforceable in the administration of the deceased's estate as a debt of the deceased and accordingly:

(1) no liability order need be applied for in respect of it, after the deceased's death, under reg 12 (see PARA 293) (reg 24(6)(a)); and

(2) the liability of the executor or administrator is a liability in his capacity as such (reg 24(6)(b)).

As to the meaning of 'liability order' see PARA 294 note 1. As to executors and administrators see WILLS AND INTESTACY vol 103 (2016) PARA 605 et seq.

9 Ie his liability under the Local Government Finance Act 1988 or, in relation to England, the Business Rate Supplements Act 2009.

10 As to relevant costs for these purposes see note 3.

11 Ie under the Non-Domestic Rating (Collection and Enforcement) (Local Lists) Regulations 1989, SI 1989/1058, Pt II (regs 3–9): see PARA 278 et seq.

12 Non-Domestic Rating (Collection and Enforcement) (Local Lists) Regulations 1989, SI 1989/1058, reg 24(4) (amended, in relation to England, by SI 2010/187). Interest is usually due on such payments: see the Non-Domestic Rating (Payment of Interest) Regulations 1990, SI 1990/1904; and PARA 199.

13 Ie his liability under the Non-Domestic Rating (Collection and Enforcement) (Local Lists) Regulations 1989, SI 1989/1058, reg 24.

14 Ie under regulations under the Local Government Finance Act 1988 s 55: see PARA 199.

15 Non-Domestic Rating (Collection and Enforcement) (Local Lists) Regulations 1989, SI 1989/1058, reg 24(8).

16 Ie an appeal made under regulations which have been made under the Local Government Finance Act 1988 s 55: see PARA 199. As to the alteration of lists see PARA 202 et seq. As to appeals in respect of the alteration to lists see PARA 242 et seq.

17 See the Non-Domestic Rating (Collection and Enforcement) (Local Lists) Regulations 1989, SI 1989/1058, reg 23(1), applied by reg 24(7). The proceedings referred to are proceedings under reg 24: see reg 24(7).

18 As to local non-domestic rating lists see PARA 191 et seq.

19 As to the meaning of 'billing authority' see PARA 53.

20 See the Non-Domestic Rating (Collection and Enforcement) (Local Lists) Regulations 1989, SI 1989/1058, reg 23(2) (amended by SI 1993/616), applied by the Non-Domestic Rating (Collection and Enforcement) (Local Lists) Regulations 1989, SI 1989/1058, reg 24(7).

(iii) Central Non-domestic Rating Lists

A. DEMAND

(A) Demand Notices

306. Demand notices and their service.

For each chargeable financial year[1], the appropriate national authority[2] must in accordance with the central non-domestic rating lists regulations[3] serve a notice in writing[4] (a 'demand notice')[5] on every person who is a ratepayer[6] in relation to the year[7]. Different demand notices must be served for different chargeable financial years[8].

Any notice which is required or authorised by the central non-domestic rating lists regulations[9] to be served on a person by the appropriate national authority may be served:

(1) in the case of a body corporate, by addressing the notice or information to the secretary of the body, and:
  (a) delivering it to him[10];
  (b) leaving it at or by sending it by post to him at the registered or principal office of the body[11]; or
  (c) sending it to him by electronic communication[12] to such address[13] as may be notified by him for that purpose[14]; and
(2) in any other case:
  (a) by delivering the notice or information to the person[15];
  (b) by leaving it at or sending it by post to him at his last place of abode or an address given by him at which service will be accepted[16]; or
  (c) by sending it to him by electronic communication to such an address as may be notified by him for that purpose[17].

For the purpose of any legal proceedings, a notice given by the means described in head (1)(c) or (2)(c) above must, unless the contrary is proved, be treated as served on the second business day after it was sent[18].

1 As to the meaning of 'chargeable financial year' see PARA 24 note 1.
2 Ie the Secretary of State or, in relation to Wales, the Welsh Ministers. The functions of the Secretary of State under the Non-Domestic Rating (Collection and Enforcement) (Central Lists) Regulations 1989, SI 1989/2260, so far as exercisable in relation to Wales, were transferred to the National Assembly for Wales (see the National Assembly for Wales (Transfer of Functions) Order 1999, SI 1999/672, arts 2, 3, Sch 1) and are now vested in the Welsh Ministers (see the Government of Wales Act 2006 s 162(1), Sch 11 para 30). As to the Secretary of State and the Welsh Ministers see PARA 4 note 18. As to the meaning of 'Wales' see PARA 2 note 16.
3 Ie in accordance with the Non-Domestic Rating (Collection and Enforcement) (Central Lists) Regulations 1989, SI 1989/2260, regs 5–7: see PARA 307 et seq. As to central non-domestic rating lists see PARA 196 et seq.
4 As to the meaning of 'writing' see PARA 21 note 3.
5 'Demand notice' means the notice required to be served by the Non-Domestic Rating (Collection and Enforcement) (Central Lists) Regulations 1989, SI 1989/2260, reg 4(1): reg 2(1).
6 'Ratepayer', in relation to a chargeable financial year, means a person liable to pay an amount under the Local Government Finance Act 1988 s 54 (see PARA 142) in respect of the year: Non-Domestic Rating (Collection and Enforcement) (Central Lists) Regulations 1989, SI 1989/2260, reg 2(1). As to the meaning of 'person' see PARA 11 note 13.
7 Non-Domestic Rating (Collection and Enforcement) (Central Lists) Regulations 1989, SI 1989/2260, reg 4(1). As to the time for service of demand notices see PARA 307.
8 Non-Domestic Rating (Collection and Enforcement) (Central Lists) Regulations 1989, SI 1989/2260, reg 4(2). As from 15 February 2012, in relation to England only, where, but for reg 4(3), notices would fall to be served in accordance with the Non-Domestic Rating (Collection and

Enforcement) (Central Lists) Regulations 1989, SI 1989/2260, on a ratepayer at the same time in relation to a financial year not then ended and any earlier financial year, nothing in reg 4(2) requires a billing authority to serve more than one notice: see reg 4(2), (3) (reg 4(2) amended, reg 4(3), (4) added, by SI 2012/24); Non-Domestic Rating (Collection and Enforcement) (Amendment) (England) Regulations 2012, SI 2012/24, reg 1. If a single demand notice relates to the amount payable with respect to more than one financial year, the amounts due under it and the times at which they fall due, must be determined as if separate notices were issued in respect of each financial year: Non-Domestic Rating (Collection and Enforcement) (Central Lists) Regulations 1989, SI 1989/2260, reg 4(4) (as so added). As to the meaning of 'England' see PARA 2 note 16.

9 Ie by the Non-Domestic Rating (Collection and Enforcement) (Central Lists) Regulations 1989, SI 1989/2260.

10 Non-Domestic Rating (Collection and Enforcement) (Central Lists) Regulations 1989, SI 1989/2260, reg 3(1)(a)(i) (reg 3 substituted, in relation to England, by SI 2006/237; and, in relation to Wales, by SI 2009/2706).

11 Non-Domestic Rating (Collection and Enforcement) (Central Lists) Regulations 1989, SI 1989/2260, reg 3(1)(a)(ii) (as substituted: see note 10). Where a company registered outside the United Kingdom has an office in the United Kingdom, that office is to be treated for the purpose of reg 3(1)(a)(ii) as its principal office; and where it has more than one office in the United Kingdom its principal office in the United Kingdom is to be treated as its principal office for that purpose: reg 3(5) (as so substituted). As to service by post generally see PARA 139 note 3. As to the registered office of a company see COMPANIES vol 14 (2016) PARA 124. As to the meaning of 'United Kingdom' see PARA 4 note 10.

12 'Electronic communication' means a communication transmitted (whether from one person to another, from one device to another or from a person to a device or vice versa) by means of an electronic communications network within the meaning of the Communications Act 2003 s 32(1) (see TELECOMMUNICATIONS vol 97 (2015) PARA 53), or by other means but while in electronic form: Non-Domestic Rating (Collection and Enforcement) (Central Lists) Regulations 1989, SI 1989/2260, reg 2(1) (definition added, in relation to England, by SI 2006/237; and, in relation to Wales, by SI 2009/2706).

13 'Address', in relation to electronic communications, includes any number or address used for the purposes of such communications: Non-Domestic Rating (Collection and Enforcement) (Central Lists) Regulations 1989, SI 1989/2260, reg 2(1) (definition added, in relation to England, by SI 2006/237; and, in relation to Wales, by SI 2009/2706).

14 Non-Domestic Rating (Collection and Enforcement) (Central Lists) Regulations 1989, SI 1989/2260, reg 3(1)(a)(iii) (as substituted: see note 10). A person who has notified an address for the purpose of reg 3(1)(a)(iii) or reg 3(1)(b)(iii) (see head (2)(c) in the text) must, by notice in writing to the appropriate national authority, advise the appropriate national authority of any change in that address; and the change takes effect on the third business day after the date on which the notice is received by the appropriate national authority: reg 3(3) (as so substituted). A person who has notified an address for the purpose of reg 3(1)(a)(iii) or reg 3(1)(b)(iii) may, by notice in writing to the appropriate national authority, withdraw that notification; and the withdrawal takes effect on the third business day after the date on which the notice is received by the appropriate national authority: reg 3(4) (as so substituted). 'Business day' means any day except a Saturday or Sunday, Christmas Day, Good Friday or a day which is a bank holiday under the Banking and Financial Dealings Act 1971 (see TIME vol 97 (2015) PARAS 313, 321) in England and Wales: Non-Domestic Rating (Collection and Enforcement) (Central Lists) Regulations 1989, SI 1989/2260, reg 2(1) (definition added, in relation to England, by SI 2006/237; and, in relation to Wales, by SI 2009/2706).

15 Non-Domestic Rating (Collection and Enforcement) (Central Lists) Regulations 1989, SI 1989/2260, reg 3(1)(b)(i) (as substituted: see note 10).

16 Non-Domestic Rating (Collection and Enforcement) (Central Lists) Regulations 1989, SI 1989/2260, reg 3(1)(b)(ii) (as substituted: see note 10).

17 Non-Domestic Rating (Collection and Enforcement) (Central Lists) Regulations 1989, SI 1989/2260, reg 3(1)(b)(iii) (as substituted: see note 10). See also note 14.

18 Non-Domestic Rating (Collection and Enforcement) (Central Lists) Regulations 1989, SI 1989/2260, reg 3(2) (as substituted: see note 10).

307. Time of service of demand notices.

A demand notice[1] must be served[2] on or as soon as practicable after:

(1) except in a case falling within head (2) below, 1 April in the relevant year[3]; or

(2) if the ratepayer's[4] name is not shown in a central list[5] for that day, the first day after that day for which it is so shown[6].

A demand notice may, if the non-domestic multiplier for the relevant year has been determined[7], be served before the beginning of the relevant year on a person[8] whose name, for the day on which it is issued[9], is shown[10] in a central list[11].

1 As to the meaning of 'demand notice' see PARA 306 note 5.
2 Ie subject to the Non-Domestic Rating (Collection and Enforcement) (Central Lists) Regulations 1989, SI 1989/2260, reg 5(2) (see the text to notes 7–11): see reg 5(1). As to the service of notices see PARA 306.
3 Non-Domestic Rating (Collection and Enforcement) (Central Lists) Regulations 1989, SI 1989/2260, reg 5(1)(a). 'Relevant year' in relation to a notice means the chargeable financial year to which the notice relates: reg 2(1). As to the meaning of 'chargeable financial year' see PARA 24 note 1.
4 As to the meaning of 'ratepayer' see PARA 306 note 6.
5 As to central non-domestic rating lists see PARA 196 et seq.
6 Non-Domestic Rating (Collection and Enforcement) (Central Lists) Regulations 1989, SI 1989/2260, reg 5(1)(b).
7 Ie under the Local Government Finance Act 1988 Sch 7: see PARA 156.
8 As to the meaning of 'person' see PARA 11 note 13.
9 Where references are made in the Non-Domestic Rating (Collection and Enforcement) (Central Lists) Regulations 1989, SI 1989/2260, to the day on which a notice is issued, they are to be taken to be references:
   (1) if the notice is served in the manner described in reg 3 (see PARA 306) by being left at, or sent by post to, a person's last-known place of abode or a body's registered or principal office (as the case may be), to the day on which it is so left or posted (reg 2(2)(a)); or
   (2) in any other case, to the day on which it is served (reg 2(2)(b)).
10 Ie or would be so shown if a list sent under the Local Government Finance Act 1988 s 52(5) were in force: see PARA 196.
11 Non-Domestic Rating (Collection and Enforcement) (Central Lists) Regulations 1989, SI 1989/2260, reg 5(2). If a demand notice is so served, references to a ratepayer are, in relation to that notice and so far as the context permits, to be construed as references to that person: reg 5(2).

308. Payments under demand notices.

If a demand notice[1] is issued before or during the relevant year[2] and the ratepayer's[3] name is shown in a central list[4] for the day on which it is issued[5], the notice must require payment of an amount equal to the estimate made by the appropriate national authority[6] of the amount payable[7] for the year, made as respects periods after the issue of the notice on the assumption that the ratepayer's name will be shown in a central list for every day in the relevant year after that day[8].

If a demand notice is issued after the end of the relevant year, it must require payment of the amount payable for the year[9].

1 As to the meaning of 'demand notice' see PARA 306 note 5.
2 As to the meaning of 'relevant year' see PARA 307 note 3. As to the time of service of demand notices see PARA 307.
3 As to the meaning of 'ratepayer' see PARA 306 note 6.
4 Ie or would be so shown if a list sent under the Local Government Finance Act 1988 s 52(5) were in force: see PARA 196. As to central non-domestic rating lists see PARA 196 et seq.
5 As to references to the day on which a notice is issued see PARA 307 note 9.
6 Ie the Secretary of State or, in relation to Wales, the Welsh Ministers. The functions of the Secretary of State under the Non-Domestic Rating (Collection and Enforcement) (Central Lists) Regulations 1989, SI 1989/2260, so far as exercisable in relation to Wales, were transferred to the National Assembly for Wales (see the National Assembly for Wales (Transfer of Functions) Order 1999, SI 1999/672, arts 2, 3, Sch 1) and are now vested in the Welsh Ministers (see the Government of Wales Act 2006 s 162(1), Sch 11 para 30). As to the Secretary of State and the

Welsh Ministers see PARA 4 note 18. As to the meaning of 'Wales' see PARA 2 note 16.

7 The 'amount payable' for a chargeable financial year (or part of a chargeable financial year) in relation to a ratepayer and a hereditament is defined by the Non-Domestic Rating (Collection and Enforcement) (Central Lists) Regulations 1989, SI 1989/2260, reg 2(1) (definition substituted by SI 1991/142) as:

(1) the amount the ratepayer is liable to pay to the appropriate national authority as regards the hereditament in respect of the year or part under the Local Government Finance Act 1988 s 54 (see PARA 142); or

(2) where an amount falls to be credited by the appropriate national authority against the ratepayer's liability in respect of the year (or part), the amount (if any) by which the amount referred to in head (1) exceeds the amount falling to be so credited.

As to the meaning of 'chargeable financial year' see PARA 24 note 1. As to the meaning of 'hereditament' see PARA 106.

8 Non-Domestic Rating (Collection and Enforcement) (Central Lists) Regulations 1989, SI 1989/2260, reg 6(1). If a demand notice is issued during the relevant year but reg 6(1) does not apply, the notice must require payment of an amount equal to the amount payable by the ratepayer for the period in the year to the day for which his name is last shown in a central list: reg 6(2). If, after a notice to which reg 6(2) applies is served, the ratepayer's name is shown again in a central list for a day in the relevant year, a further notice must be served on him requiring payments with respect to the amount payable for the period in the relevant year beginning with the day for which his name is so shown again in the list; and regs 5–8 (and, so far as applicable, the Sch 1 (see PARAS 307, 310–316)) are to apply to the further notice with respect to that period as if it were a demand notice and his name had not been shown in a central list for a day before that period begins: reg 6(3).

Special provision is made as to deferred payments under demand notices, in relation to England, relating to financial years beginning on 1 April 2009, 1 April 2010 and 1 April 2011 (see reg 7A, Sch 1A (both added by SI 2009/1597)); and financial years beginning on 1 April 2012, 1 April 2013 and 1 April 2014 (see the Non-Domestic Rating (Collection and Enforcement) (Central Lists) Regulations 1989, SI 1989/2260, reg 7C, Sch 1C (both added by SI 2012/994); and, in relation to Wales, relating to financial years beginning on 1 April 2008 and 1 April 2012 (see the Non-Domestic Rating (Collection and Enforcement) (Central Lists) Regulations 1989, SI 1989/2260, reg 7B, Sch 1B (both added by SI 2009/2154; substituted and amended respectively by SI 2012/466).

9 Non-Domestic Rating (Collection and Enforcement) (Central Lists) Regulations 1989, SI 1989/2260, reg 6(4).

309. Demand notices: final adjustment.

Where:

(1) a notice has been issued[1] by the appropriate national authority[2] requiring a payment or payments to be made by a ratepayer[3] in respect of the amount payable[4] for a chargeable financial year or part of a chargeable financial year[5];

(2) the payment or payments required to be paid are found to be in excess of or less than the amount payable for the year or the part[6]; and

(3) provision for adjusting the amounts required under the notice and (as appropriate) for the making of additional payments or the repaying or crediting of any amount overpaid is not made by any other provision[7],

the appropriate national authority must as soon as practicable after the expiry of the year or the part of a year serve a further notice[8] on the ratepayer stating the amount payable for the year or part and adjusting (by reference to that amount) the amounts required to be paid under the notice referred to in head (1) above[9].

1 Ie under the Non-Domestic Rating (Collection and Enforcement) (Central Lists) Regulations 1989, SI 1989/2260.

2 Ie the Secretary of State or, in relation to Wales, the Welsh Ministers. The functions of the Secretary of State under the Non-Domestic Rating (Collection and Enforcement) (Central Lists) Regulations 1989, SI 1989/2260, so far as exercisable in relation to Wales, were transferred to the

National Assembly for Wales (see the National Assembly for Wales (Transfer of Functions) Order 1999, SI 1999/672, arts 2, 3, Sch 1) and are now vested in the Welsh Ministers (see the Government of Wales Act 2006 s 162(1), Sch 11 para 30). As to the Secretary of State and the Welsh Ministers see PARA 4 note 18. As to the meaning of 'Wales' see PARA 2 note 16.

3 As to the meaning of 'ratepayer' see PARA 306 note 6.

4 As to the meaning of 'amount payable' see PARA 308 note 7.

5 Non-Domestic Rating (Collection and Enforcement) (Central Lists) Regulations 1989, SI 1989/2260, reg 9(1)(a). As to the meaning of 'chargeable financial year' see PARA 24 note 1.

6 Non-Domestic Rating (Collection and Enforcement) (Central Lists) Regulations 1989, SI 1989/2260, reg 9(1)(b).

7 Non-Domestic Rating (Collection and Enforcement) (Central Lists) Regulations 1989, SI 1989/2260, reg 9(1)(c). The provision referred to is any other provision of the Non-Domestic Rating (Collection and Enforcement) (Central Lists) Regulations 1989, SI 1989/2260, the Local Government Finance Act 1988, or any agreement entered into under the Non-Domestic Rating (Collection and Enforcement) (Central Lists) Regulations 1989, SI 1989/2260, reg 7(3) (see PARA 310): see reg 9(1)(c).

8 As to the service of notices see PARA 306.

9 Non-Domestic Rating (Collection and Enforcement) (Central Lists) Regulations 1989, SI 1989/2260, reg 9(2). If the amount stated in the further notice is greater than the amount required to be paid under the notice referred to in reg 9(1)(a) (see head (1) in the text), the amount of the difference for which such other provision as is mentioned in reg 9(1)(c) (see note 7) is not made is due from the ratepayer to the appropriate national authority on the expiry of such period (being not less than 14 days) after the day of issue of the notice as is specified in it: reg 9(3).

If there has been an overpayment in respect of any liability of the ratepayer under the Non-Domestic Rating (Collection and Enforcement) (Central Lists) Regulations 1989, SI 1989/2260, the amount overpaid for which such other provision as is mentioned in reg 9(1)(c) is not made:

(1) must be repaid if the ratepayer so requires (reg 9(4)(a)); or

(2) in any other case must (as the appropriate national authority determines) either be repaid or be credited against any subsequent liability of the ratepayer to pay anything to the appropriate national authority by way of non-domestic rate (reg 9(4)(b)).

(B) Payment by Instalments

(a) In General

310. Payment by instalments.

The appropriate national authority[1] and a ratepayer[2] may agree that the estimate of the amount payable[3] which is required to be paid[4] should be paid in such manner as is provided by the agreement, rather than in accordance with the non-domestic rate instalment scheme[5].

If such an agreement[6] in relation to the relevant year[7] has been reached between the appropriate national authority and the ratepayer before the demand notice is issued, a notice[8] must require the estimate of the amount payable to be paid in accordance with that agreement[9].

Unless such an agreement[10] in relation to the relevant year has been reached between the ratepayer and the appropriate national authority before the demand notice is issued, a notice[11] must require the estimate of the amount payable to be paid by instalments[12].

A notice with retrospective application[13] must require payment of the amount payable on the expiry of such period (being not less than 14 days) after the day of issue of the notice[14] as is specified in it[15].

No payment in respect of the amount payable by a ratepayer for any chargeable financial year[16] (whether interim, final or sole) need be made unless a notice duly served[17] requires it[18].

In relation to England, the following provisions apply where a ratepayer gives notice in writing to the Secretary of State that the ratepayer wishes to pay the estimate of the amount payable for each chargeable financial year by 12 monthly instalments until further notice[19]. An instalment notice[20] may be given either before or after a demand notice is issued and may specify that it is to take effect starting in relation to the relevant year or the year following the relevant year[21]. Where an instalment notice relates to the relevant year, a demand notice[22] must be issued as soon as reasonably practicable after the date on which the instalment notice is received by the Secretary of State and must require the estimate of the amount payable to be paid in instalments in accordance with the relevant provision[23].

Where an instalment notice relates to the year following the relevant year, as soon as reasonably practicable after the date on which the instalment notice is received by the Secretary of State, the Secretary of State must write to confirm that the estimate of the amount payable for that year is to be paid in instalments in accordance with the relevant statutory provision[24].

For each subsequent chargeable financial year for which the Secretary of State issues a demand notice to the ratepayer[25] after an instalment notice has been given, the demand notice must require payment of the estimate of the amount payable for the year in accordance with the relevant statutory provision[26].

A ratepayer may give notice in writing to the Secretary of State that the statutory provision as to payment by instalments[27] is no longer to apply[28]. A notice so given takes effect at the expiry of the chargeable financial year in which it was received[29].

1 Ie the Secretary of State or, in relation to Wales, the Welsh Ministers. The functions of the Secretary of State under the Non-Domestic Rating (Collection and Enforcement) (Central Lists) Regulations 1989, SI 1989/2260, so far as exercisable in relation to Wales, were transferred to the National Assembly for Wales (see the National Assembly for Wales (Transfer of Functions) Order 1999, SI 1999/672, arts 2, 3, Sch 1) and are now vested in the Welsh Ministers (see the Government of Wales Act 2006 s 162(1), Sch 11 para 30). As to the Secretary of State and the Welsh Ministers see PARA 4 note 18. As to the meaning of 'Wales' see PARA 2 note 16.

2 As to the meaning of 'ratepayer' see PARA 306 note 6.

3 As to the meaning of 'amount payable' see PARA 308 note 7.

4 Ie under a notice to which the Non-Domestic Rating (Collection and Enforcement) (Central Lists) Regulations 1989, SI 1989/2260, reg 6(1) applies: see PARA 308.

5 Non-Domestic Rating (Collection and Enforcement) (Central Lists) Regulations 1989, SI 1989/2260, reg 7(3). The non-domestic rate instalment scheme is that set out in Sch 1 (see PARAS 311–315): see reg 7(3).

Notwithstanding anything in reg 7(1), (2) (see the text to notes 6–12) or in reg 7(3), such an agreement may be entered into either before or after the demand notice concerned is issued, and may make provision for the cessation or adjustment of payments, and for the making of fresh estimates, in the event of the estimate mentioned in reg 6(1) (see PARA 308) turning out to be wrong; and if it is entered into after the demand notice has been issued, it may make provision dealing with the treatment for the purposes of the agreement of any sums paid in accordance with Sch 1 before it was entered into: reg 7(4). As to the meaning of 'demand notice' see PARA 306 note 5.

Special provision is made as to deferred payments under demand notices, in relation to England, relating to financial years beginning on 1 April 2009, 1 April 2010 and 1 April 2011 (see reg 7A, Sch 1A (both added by SI 2009/1597)); and financial years beginning on 1 April 2012, 1 April 2013 and 1 April 2014 (see the Non-Domestic Rating (Collection and Enforcement) (Central Lists) Regulations 1989, SI 1989/2260, reg 7C, Sch 1C (both added by SI 2012/994); and, in relation to Wales, relating to financial years beginning on 1 April 2008 and 1 April 2012 (see the Non-Domestic Rating (Collection and Enforcement) (Central Lists) Regulations 1989, SI 1989/2260, reg 7B, Sch 1B (both added by SI 2009/2154; substituted and amended respectively by SI 2012/466).

6 Ie under the Non-Domestic Rating (Collection and Enforcement) (Central Lists) Regulations 1989, SI 1989/2260, reg 7(3): see the text to notes 1–5.
7 As to the meaning of 'relevant year' see PARA 307 note 3.
8 Ie a notice to which the Non-Domestic Rating (Collection and Enforcement) (Central Lists) Regulations 1989, SI 1989/2260, reg 6(1) applies: see PARA 308.
9 Non-Domestic Rating (Collection and Enforcement) (Central Lists) Regulations 1989, SI 1989/2260, reg 7(2).
10 Ie under the Non-Domestic Rating (Collection and Enforcement) (Central Lists) Regulations 1989, SI 1989/2260, reg 7(3): see the text to notes 1–5.
11 Ie a notice to which the Non-Domestic Rating (Collection and Enforcement) (Central Lists) Regulations 1989, SI 1989/2260, reg 6(1) applies: see PARA 308.
12 Non-Domestic Rating (Collection and Enforcement) (Central Lists) Regulations 1989, SI 1989/2260, reg 7(1). The instalments must be paid in accordance with Sch 1 Pt I (paras 1–5) (see PARA 311); and where such instalments are required, Sch 1 Pt II (paras 6–8) (see PARAS 312–315) applies for their cessation or adjustment in the circumstances described in Sch 1 Pt II: see reg 7(1).
13 Ie a notice to which the Non-Domestic Rating (Collection and Enforcement) (Central Lists) Regulations 1989, SI 1989/2260, reg 6(2) or reg 6(4) applies: see PARA 308.
14 As to references to the day on which a notice is issued see PARA 307 note 9.
15 Non-Domestic Rating (Collection and Enforcement) (Central Lists) Regulations 1989, SI 1989/2260, reg 7(5).
16 As to the meaning of 'chargeable financial year' see PARA 24 note 1.
17 Ie under the Non-Domestic Rating (Collection and Enforcement) (Central Lists) Regulations 1989, SI 1989/2260. As to the service of notices see PARA 306.
18 Non-Domestic Rating (Collection and Enforcement) (Central Lists) Regulations 1989, SI 1989/2260, reg 7(6).
19 Non-Domestic Rating (Collection and Enforcement) (Central Lists) Regulations 1989, SI 1989/2260, reg 7(1B) (reg 7(1A)–(1H) added, in relation to England, by SI 2014/479).
20 In the Non-Domestic Rating (Collection and Enforcement) (Central Lists) Regulations 1989, SI 1989/2260, reg 7 and in Sch 1 para 1, 'instalment notice' means a notice given by a ratepayer to the Secretary of State under reg 7(1B): reg 7(1A) (as added: see note 19).
21 Non-Domestic Rating (Collection and Enforcement) (Central Lists) Regulations 1989, SI 1989/2260, reg 7(1C) (as added: see note 19).
22 Ie a notice to which the Non-Domestic Rating (Collection and Enforcement) (Central Lists) Regulations 1989, SI 1989/2260, reg 6(1) (see PARA 308) applies.
23 Non-Domestic Rating (Collection and Enforcement) (Central Lists) Regulations 1989, SI 1989/2260, reg 7(1D) (as added: see note 19). The relevant provision is Sch 1 para 1(2B): reg 7(1D) (as so added).
24 Non-Domestic Rating (Collection and Enforcement) (Central Lists) Regulations 1989, SI 1989/2260, reg 7(1E) (as added: see note 19). The relevant provision is Sch 1 para 1(2B): reg 7(1E) (as so added).
25 Ie in accordance with the Non-Domestic Rating (Collection and Enforcement) (Central Lists) Regulations 1989, SI 1989/2260, reg 6(1): see PARA 308.
26 Non-Domestic Rating (Collection and Enforcement) (Central Lists) Regulations 1989, SI 1989/2260, reg 7(1F) (as added: see note 19). The relevant provision is Sch 1 para 1(2B): reg 7(1F) (as so added).
27 Ie the Non-Domestic Rating (Collection and Enforcement) (Central Lists) Regulations 1989, SI 1989/2260, Sch 1 para 1(2B): see PARA 311 note 6.
28 Non-Domestic Rating (Collection and Enforcement) (Central Lists) Regulations 1989, SI 1989/2260, reg 7(1G) (as added: see note 19).
29 Non-Domestic Rating (Collection and Enforcement) (Central Lists) Regulations 1989, SI 1989/2260, reg 7(1H) (as added: see note 19). This is subject to reg 7(3) (see the text to notes 1–5): reg 7(1H) (as so added).

311. Payment of the aggregate amount under the non-domestic rate instalment scheme.

The following provisions apply where the demand notice[1] is issued on or before 31 December in the relevant year[2].

The aggregate amount[3] is payable in monthly instalments[4], the number of such instalments being ten or, if less, the number of whole months[5] remaining in the relevant year after the issue of the notice less one[6]. The months in which the instalments are payable must be uninterrupted but, subject to that[7], are to be such months in the relevant year as are specified in the notice; and the instalments are to be payable on such day in each month as is so specified[8].

If the aggregate amount divided by the number of instalments gives an amount which is a multiple of a pound, the instalments are to be of that amount[9]. However, if the aggregate amount so divided would not give such an amount, a statutory formula must be applied in respect of calculating the instalments due[10].

The demand notice must be issued at least 14 days before the day on which the first instalment is due under it[11].

1 As to the meaning of 'demand notice' see PARA 306 note 5.

2 Non-Domestic Rating (Collection and Enforcement) (Central Lists) Regulations 1989, SI 1989/2260, Sch 1 para 1(1) (Sch 1 numbered as such, in relation to England, by SI 2009/1597). As to the meaning of 'relevant year' see PARA 307 note 3. Schedule 1 para 1 has effect subject to Sch 1 para 3, which applies special provisions to cases where instalments payable in accordance with Sch para 1 would produce an amount for an instalment of less than £50: see Sch 1 paras 1, 3 (as so numbered).

3 For the purposes of the Non-Domestic Rating (Collection and Enforcement) (Central Lists) Regulations 1989, SI 1989/2260, Sch 1 Pt I (paras 1–5), the 'aggregate amount' means the amount of the estimate referred to in reg 6(1) (see PARA 308): Sch 1 para 5 (Sch 1 as so numbered: see note 2).

4 Ie except where the demand notice is issued between 1 January and 31 March in the relevant year, in which case the aggregate amount is payable in a single instalment on such day as is specified in the notice: see the Non-Domestic Rating (Collection and Enforcement) (Central Lists) Regulations 1989, SI 1989/2260, Sch 1 para 2 (Sch 1 as so numbered: see note 2).

5 As to the meaning of 'month' see PARA 11 note 1.

6 Non-Domestic Rating (Collection and Enforcement) (Central Lists) Regulations 1989, SI 1989/2260, Sch 1 para 1(2) (Sch 1 as so numbered: see note 2).

In relation to England, Sch 1 para 1(2) is subject to Sch 1 para 1(2A), (2B): Sch 1 para 1(2) (so numbered; amended by SI 2014/479). Schedule 1 para 1(2B) applies where a demand notice is issued to a ratepayer that has served an instalment notice on the Secretary of State: Sch 1 para 1(2A) (Sch 1 para 1(2A), (2B) added by SI 2014/479). The aggregate amount is to be payable in monthly instalments, the number of such instalments being:

(1) where the demand notice is issued on or before 15 April in the relevant year (including where it is issued before the beginning of the relevant year), 12 (Non-Domestic Rating (Collection and Enforcement) (Central Lists) Regulations 1989, SI 1989/2260, Sch 1 para 1(2B)(a) (as so added));

(2) where the demand notice is issued on or after 16 April in the relevant year, the number of whole months remaining in the relevant year after the issue of the demand notice (Sch 1 para 1(2B)(b) (as so added)).

7 Ie subject also to the Non-Domestic Rating (Collection and Enforcement) (Central Lists) Regulations 1989, SI 1989/2260, Sch 1 para 4: see the text to note 11.

8 Non-Domestic Rating (Collection and Enforcement) (Central Lists) Regulations 1989, SI 1989/2260, Sch 1 para 1(3) (Sch 1 as so numbered: see note 2).

9 Non-Domestic Rating (Collection and Enforcement) (Central Lists) Regulations 1989, SI 1989/2260, Sch 1 para 1(4) (Sch 1 as so numbered: see note 2).

10 See the Non-Domestic Rating (Collection and Enforcement) (Central Lists) Regulations 1989, SI 1989/2260, Sch 1 para 1(5) (Sch 1 as so numbered: see note 2).

11 Non-Domestic Rating (Collection and Enforcement) (Central Lists) Regulations 1989, SI 1989/2260, Sch 1 para 4 (Sch 1 as so numbered: see note 2).

(b) Cessation and Adjustment of Instalments

312. Ratepayer's name no longer shown in a central list.

Where the demand notice[1] has been served on a ratepayer[2] by the appropriate national authority[3], and for a day in the relevant year[4] after its issue (the 'relevant day') the ratepayer's name is no longer shown in a central list[5], no payments of instalments falling due after the relevant day are payable under the notice[6].

The appropriate national authority must, on the relevant day or as soon as practicable after that day, serve a notice[7] on the ratepayer stating the amount payable[8] for the period in the relevant year up to the relevant day[9].

If these provisions[10] apply in relation to a demand notice, and after the relevant day the ratepayer's name is shown again in a central list for a day in the relevant year, a further notice must be served on him requiring payments with respect to the amount payable for the period in the relevant year beginning with the day for which his name is so shown again in the list[11].

1 As to the meaning of 'demand notice' see PARA 306 note 5.

2 As to the meaning of 'ratepayer' see PARA 306 note 6.

3 Ie the Secretary of State or, in relation to Wales, the Welsh Ministers. The functions of the Secretary of State under the Non-Domestic Rating (Collection and Enforcement) (Central Lists) Regulations 1989, SI 1989/2260, so far as exercisable in relation to Wales, were transferred to the National Assembly for Wales (see the National Assembly for Wales (Transfer of Functions) Order 1999, SI 1999/672, arts 2, 3, Sch 1) and are now vested in the Welsh Ministers (see the Government of Wales Act 2006 s 162(1), Sch 11 para 30). As to the Secretary of State and the Welsh Ministers see PARA 4 note 18. As to the meaning of 'Wales' see PARA 2 note 16.

4 As to the meaning of 'relevant year' see PARA 307 note 3.

5 Non-Domestic Rating (Collection and Enforcement) (Central Lists) Regulations 1989, SI 1989/2260, Sch 1 para 6(1) (Sch 1 numbered as such, in relation to England, by SI 2009/1597). As to central non-domestic rating lists see PARA 196 et seq.

6 Non-Domestic Rating (Collection and Enforcement) (Central Lists) Regulations 1989, SI 1989/2260, Sch 1 para 6(2) (Sch 1 as so numbered: see note 5). This provision is subject to Sch 1 para 6(5) (see note 9) and Sch 1 para 6(6) (see notes 10–11): see Sch 1 para 6(2) (as so numbered).

7 As to the service of notices see PARA 306.

8 As to the meaning of 'amount payable' see PARA 308 note 7.

9 Non-Domestic Rating (Collection and Enforcement) (Central Lists) Regulations 1989, SI 1989/2260, Sch 1 para 6(3) (Sch 1 as so numbered: see note 5). If the amount stated in Sch 1 para 6(3) is less than the aggregate amount of any instalments which have fallen due on or before the relevant day, the difference is to go in the first instance to discharge any liability to pay the instalments (to the extent that they remain unpaid); and any residual overpayment in respect of any liability of the ratepayer under the Non-Domestic Rating (Collection and Enforcement) (Central Lists) Regulations 1989, SI 1989/2260:

(1) must be repaid if the ratepayer so requires (Sch 1 para 6(4)(a) (as so numbered)); or

(2) in any other case must (as the appropriate national authority determines) either be repaid or credited against any subsequent liability of the ratepayer to pay anything to the appropriate national authority by way of non-domestic rate (Sch 1 para 6(4)(b) (as so numbered)).

If the amount stated in Sch 1 para 6(3) is greater than the aggregate amount of any instalments which have fallen due on or before the relevant day, the difference between the two is due from the ratepayer to the appropriate national authority on the expiry of such period (being not less than 14 days) after the day of issue of the notice served under Sch 1 para 6(3) as is specified in it: Sch 1 para 6(5) (as so numbered).

10 Ie the Non-Domestic Rating (Collection and Enforcement) (Central Lists) Regulations 1989, SI 1989/2260, Sch 1 para 6.

11 Non-Domestic Rating (Collection and Enforcement) (Central Lists) Regulations 1989, SI 1989/2260, Sch 1 para 6(6) (Sch 1 as so numbered: see note 5). Regulations 5–8 (and, as far as applicable, Sch 1) (see PARAS 307–310, 313 et seq) apply to the further notice with respect to that period as if it were a demand notice and his name had not been shown in a central list for a day before that period begins: see Sch 1 para 6(6).

313. False factor or assumption made in relation to estimate.

Subject to transitional provisions[1], where the demand notice[2] has been served on a ratepayer[3] by the appropriate national authority[4], any factor or assumption by reference to which the estimate[5] was calculated is shown to be false in respect of a day (the 'relevant day'), and the required event[6] has not occurred as regards the ratepayer[7], the appropriate national authority must, on or as soon as practicable after the relevant day:

(1) adjust the instalments (if any) payable on or after the adjustment day[8] (the 'remaining instalments') so that they accord with the amounts prescribed[9]; and

(2) serve a notice[10] on the ratepayer stating the amount of the revised estimate[11], and the amount of any remaining instalment[12].

The amount of the revised estimate is the revised estimate of the appropriate national authority of the amount payable[13] for the relevant year[14].

The aggregate amount of the remaining instalments payable is equal to the amount by which the revised estimate exceeds the aggregate amount of the instalments payable under the demand notice before the adjustment day; and the amount of each remaining instalment (if there are more than one) is calculated[15] as if references to the aggregate amount and to instalments were references to the aggregate amount of the remaining instalments and to the remaining instalments respectively[16].

If the revised estimate exceeds the aggregate amount of the instalments payable under the demand notice before the adjustment day, but no instalments are payable under it on or after that day, the amount of the excess is due from the ratepayer to the appropriate national authority in a single instalment on the expiry of such period (being not less than 14 days) after the day of issue of the notice[17] as is specified in it; and if in any case the revised estimate is less than the aggregate amount of the instalments payable before the adjustment day, any overpayment in respect of any liability of the ratepayer[18]:

(a) must be repaid if the ratepayer so requires[19]; or

(b) in any other case, must (as the appropriate national authority determines) either be repaid or credited against any subsequent liability of the ratepayer to pay anything to the appropriate national authority by way of non-domestic rate[20].

1 Ie subject to the Non-Domestic Rating (Collection and Enforcement) (Central Lists) Regulations 1989, SI 1989/2260, Sch 1 para 7(1A): see Sch 1 para 7(1) (Sch 1 numbered as such, in relation to England, by SI 2009/1597; the Non-Domestic Rating (Collection and Enforcement) (Central Lists) Regulations 1989, Sch 1 para 7(1) amended, para 7(1A) added, by SI 1992/1513). Accordingly, the Non-Domestic Rating (Collection and Enforcement) (Central Lists) Regulations 1989, SI 1989/2260, Sch 1 para 7 does not apply in a case to which Sch 1 paras 7A, 7B (see PARA 314) apply, except as provided in Sch 1 para 8(2) (see PARA 315): see Sch 1 para 7(1A) (as so added and numbered).

2 As to the meaning of 'demand notice' see PARA 306 note 5.

3 As to the meaning of 'ratepayer' see PARA 306 note 6.

4 Ie the Secretary of State or, in relation to Wales, the Welsh Ministers. The functions of the Secretary of State under the Non-Domestic Rating (Collection and Enforcement) (Central Lists) Regulations 1989, SI 1989/2260, so far as exercisable in relation to Wales, were transferred to the National Assembly for Wales (see the National Assembly for Wales (Transfer of Functions) Order 1999, SI 1999/672, arts 2, 3, Sch 1) and are now vested in the Welsh Ministers (see the Government of Wales Act 2006 s 162(1), Sch 11 para 30). As to the Secretary of State and the Welsh Ministers see PARA 4 note 18. As to the meaning of 'Wales' see PARA 2 note 16.

5 Ie the estimate made under the Non-Domestic Rating (Collection and Enforcement) (Central Lists) Regulations 1989, SI 1989/2260, reg 6(1) for the purpose of the notice: see PARA 308.

6 Ie the event mentioned in the Non-Domestic Rating (Collection and Enforcement) (Central Lists) Regulations 1989, SI 1989/2260, Sch 1 para 6(1): see PARA 312.

7 Non-Domestic Rating (Collection and Enforcement) (Central Lists) Regulations 1989, SI 1989/2260, Sch 1 para 7(1) (as so numbered and amended: see note 1).

8 'Adjustment day' means the day 14 days after the day the notice served under the Non-Domestic Rating (Collection and Enforcement) (Central Lists) Regulations 1989, SI 1989/2260, Sch 1 para 7(2) (see head (2) in the text) is issued: Sch 1 para 7(7) (Sch 1 as so numbered: see note 1).

9 Non-Domestic Rating (Collection and Enforcement) (Central Lists) Regulations 1989, SI 1989/2260, Sch 1 para 7(2)(a) (Sch 1 as so numbered (see note 1); Sch 1 para 7(2) substituted by SI 1991/142). The amounts prescribed are those mentioned in the Non-Domestic Rating (Collection and Enforcement) (Central Lists) Regulations 1989, SI 1989/2260, Sch 1 para 7(4) (see the text to notes 15–16): see Sch 1 para 7(2)(a) (as so numbered and substituted).

10 As to the service of notices see PARA 306.

11 Non-Domestic Rating (Collection and Enforcement) (Central Lists) Regulations 1989, SI 1989/2260, Sch 1 para 7(2)(b)(i) (as substituted and so numbered: see notes 1, 9). The amount of the revised estimate is that mentioned in Sch 1 para 7(3) (see the text to notes 13–14): see Sch 1 para 7(2)(b)(i) (as so substituted and numbered).

12 Non-Domestic Rating (Collection and Enforcement) (Central Lists) Regulations 1989, SI 1989/2260, Sch 1 para 7(2)(b)(ii) (as substituted and so numbered: see notes 1, 9).

13 Ie amount payable for the relevant year made on the assumption mentioned in the Non-Domestic Rating (Collection and Enforcement) (Central Lists) Regulations 1989, SI 1989/2260, reg 6(1) (see PARA 308) and as if the notice mentioned in that provision were the notice referred to in Sch 1 para 7(2) (see head (2) in the text): see Sch 1 para 7(3) (Sch 1 as so numbered: see note 1). As to the meaning of 'amount payable' see PARA 308 note 7. As to the meaning of 'relevant year' see PARA 307 note 3.

14 Non-Domestic Rating (Collection and Enforcement) (Central Lists) Regulations 1989, SI 1989/2260, Sch 1 para 7(3) (Sch 1 as so numbered: see note 1).

15 Ie in accordance with the Non-Domestic Rating (Collection and Enforcement) (Central Lists) Regulations 1989, SI 1989/2260, Sch 1 para 1(4), (5): see PARA 311.

16 Non-Domestic Rating (Collection and Enforcement) (Central Lists) Regulations 1989, SI 1989/2260, Sch 1 para 7(4) (Sch 1 as so numbered: see note 1).

17 Ie the notice served under the Non-Domestic Rating (Collection and Enforcement) (Central Lists) Regulations 1989, SI 1989/2260, Sch 1 para 7(2): see head (2) in the text.

18 Ie under the Non-Domestic Rating (Collection and Enforcement) (Central Lists) Regulations 1989, SI 1989/2260.

19 Non-Domestic Rating (Collection and Enforcement) (Central Lists) Regulations 1989, SI 1989/2260, Sch 1 para 7(5)(a) (Sch 1 as so numbered: see note 1).

20 Non-Domestic Rating (Collection and Enforcement) (Central Lists) Regulations 1989, SI 1989/2260, Sch 1 para 7(5)(b) (Sch 1 as so numbered: see note 1). Where a notice has been given under Sch 1 para 7(2) (see head (2) in the text), as respects any further notice that may fall to be given under it, references in Sch 1 para 7 to the demand notice and to amounts in respect of instalments payable under it must be construed (so far as the context permits) as references to the demand notice and amounts in respect of instalments payable under the notice, as from time to time previously adjusted under Sch 1 para 7; and in calculating the aggregate amount of instalments payable under a demand notice before the adjustment day for the purposes of Sch 1 para 7(4) (see the text to notes 15–16) and Sch 1 para 7(5) in consequence of the calculation of the revised estimate mentioned in Sch 1 para 7(3) (see the text to notes 13–14), there is not to count as so payable any amount in respect of such instalments which has fallen to be repaid (or credited) under Sch 1 para 7(5) on the occasion of the giving of a previous notice under Sch 1 para 7(2), or has been paid (or credited) by way of interest under the Non-Domestic Rating (Payment of Interest) Regulations 1990, SI 1990/1904 (see PARA 199): Non-Domestic Rating (Collection and Enforcement) (Central Lists) Regulations 1989, SI 1989/2260, Sch 1 para 7(6) (as so numbered; amended by SI 1991/142).

314. Cessation and adjustment of instalments required by transitional provisions.

The central non-domestic rating lists regulations[1] contain special provision where the original estimate for the purposes of the demand notice[2] was shown to be false by reason of transitional charging provisions which were introduced subsequently in either the Non-Domestic Rating Act 1992[3] or the Non-Domestic Rating Act 1993[4].

1 Ie the Non-Domestic Rating (Collection and Enforcement) (Central Lists) Regulations 1989, SI 1989/2260.

2 Ie the original estimate which was made by the Secretary of State under the Non-Domestic Rating (Collection and Enforcement) (Central Lists) Regulations 1989, SI 1989/2260, reg 6(1) (see PARA 308) before the coming into force of the respective transitional provisions. As to the meaning of 'demand notice' see PARA 306 note 5.

3 Ie the Non-Domestic Rating Act 1992 ss 1–3.
4 See the Non-Domestic Rating (Collection and Enforcement) (Central Lists) Regulations 1989, SI 1989/2260, Sch 1 paras 7A, 7B, 7C (Sch 1 numbered as such, in relation to England, by SI 2009/1597; the Non-Domestic Rating (Collection and Enforcement) (Central Lists) Regulations 1989, SI 1989/2260, Sch 1 paras 7A, 7B added by SI 1992/1513; the Non-Domestic Rating (Collection and Enforcement) (Central Lists) Regulations 1989, SI 1989/2260, Sch 1 para 7C added by SI 1993/1494). The relevant provision of the Non-Domestic Rating Act 1993 was s 1: see the Non-Domestic Rating (Collection and Enforcement) (Central Lists) Regulations 1989, SI 1989/2260, Sch 1 para 7C (as so added and numbered).

315. Multiple adjustments.

More than one adjustment of amounts paid or payable[1] under a demand notice[2] may be made[3] as the circumstances require[4].

1 As to the meaning of 'amount payable' see PARA 308 note 7.
2 As to the meaning of 'demand notice' see PARA 306 note 5.
3 Ie under the Non-Domestic Rating (Collection and Enforcement) (Central Lists) Regulations 1989, SI 1989/2260, Sch 1 Pt II (paras 6–8) (see PARAS 312–314).
4 Non-Domestic Rating (Collection and Enforcement) (Central Lists) Regulations 1989, SI 1989/2260, Sch 1 para 8(1) (Sch 1 numbered as such, in relation to England, by SI 2009/1597; the Non-Domestic Rating (Collection and Enforcement) (Central Lists) Regulations 1989, SI 1989/2260, Sch 1 para 8 substituted by SI 1992/1513). Special provision was made where a further adjustment fell to be made under the Non-Domestic Rating (Collection and Enforcement) (Central Lists) Regulations 1989, SI 1989/2260, Sch 1 Pt II (paras 6–8) after the service of a transitional adjustment notice pursuant to Sch 1 paras 7A, 7B (see PARA 314): see Sch 1 para 8(2) (as so substituted and numbered).

(c) Failure to Pay Instalments

316. Failure to pay instalments.

Where:

(1) a demand notice[1] has been served by the appropriate national authority[2] on a ratepayer[3];
(2) instalments are payable under the notice[4] in accordance with the non-domestic rate instalment scheme[5]; and
(3) any such instalment is not paid in accordance with the scheme[6],

the appropriate national authority must (unless all the instalments have fallen due) serve a further notice[7] on the ratepayer stating the instalments required to be paid[8].

If, after the service of such a further notice, the ratepayer:

(a) fails to pay, before the expiry of the period of seven days beginning with the day of service of the further notice, any instalments which fall due before the expiry of that period under the demand notice concerned[9]; or
(b) fails to pay any instalment which falls due after the expiry of that period under the demand notice concerned on or before the day on which it falls due[10],

the unpaid balance of the estimated amount[11] becomes payable by him at the expiry of a further period of seven days beginning with the day of the failure[12].

If any factor or assumption by reference to which the estimated amount was calculated is shown to be false before the amount payable is capable of final determination[13], the appropriate national authority may, and if so required by the ratepayer must, make a calculation of the appropriate amount[14] with a view to adjusting the ratepayer's liability in respect of the estimated amount and (as appropriate) to:

(i) requiring an interim payment from the ratepayer if the appropriate amount is greater than the estimated amount[15]; or

(ii) making an interim repayment to the ratepayer if the appropriate amount is less than the amount of the estimated amount paid[16].

On calculating the appropriate amount, the appropriate national authority must notify the ratepayer in writing of it[17]; and a payment required from the ratepayer under head (i) above is due from the ratepayer to the appropriate national authority on the expiry of such period (being not less than 14 days) after the day of issue of the notice as is specified in it[18].

1 As to the meaning of 'demand notice' see PARA 306 note 5.

2 Ie the Secretary of State or, in relation to Wales, the Welsh Ministers. The functions of the Secretary of State under the Non-Domestic Rating (Collection and Enforcement) (Central Lists) Regulations 1989, SI 1989/2260, so far as exercisable in relation to Wales, were transferred to the National Assembly for Wales (see the National Assembly for Wales (Transfer of Functions) Order 1999, SI 1999/672, arts 2, 3, Sch 1) and are now vested in the Welsh Ministers (see the Government of Wales Act 2006 s 162(1), Sch 11 para 30). As to the Secretary of State and the Welsh Ministers see PARA 4 note 18. As to the meaning of 'Wales' see PARA 2 note 16.

3 Non-Domestic Rating (Collection and Enforcement) (Central Lists) Regulations 1989, SI 1989/2260, reg 8(1)(a). As to the meaning of 'ratepayer' see PARA 306 note 6.

4 Ie in accordance with the Non-Domestic Rating (Collection and Enforcement) (Central Lists) Regulations 1989, SI 1989/2260, Sch 1: see PARAS 311–315.

5 See the Non-Domestic Rating (Collection and Enforcement) (Central Lists) Regulations 1989, SI 1989/2260, reg 8(1)(b).

6 See the Non-Domestic Rating (Collection and Enforcement) (Central Lists) Regulations 1989, SI 1989/2260, reg 8(1)(c).

7 As to the service of notices see PARA 306.

8 Non-Domestic Rating (Collection and Enforcement) (Central Lists) Regulations 1989, SI 1989/2260, reg 8(1).

Special provision is made as to payments under demand notices, in relation to England, relating to financial years beginning on 1 April 2009, 1 April 2010 and 1 April 2011 (see reg 7A, Sch 1A (both added by SI 2009/1597)); and financial years beginning on 1 April 2012, 1 April 2013 and 1 April 2014 (see the Non-Domestic Rating (Collection and Enforcement) (Central Lists) Regulations 1989, SI 1989/2260, reg 7C, Sch 1C (both added by SI 2012/994); and, in relation to Wales, relating to financial years beginning on 1 April 2008 and 1 April 2012 (see the Non-Domestic Rating (Collection and Enforcement) (Central Lists) Regulations 1989, SI 1989/2260, reg 7B, Sch 1B (both added by SI 2009/2154; substituted and amended respectively by SI 2012/466).

9 Non-Domestic Rating (Collection and Enforcement) (Central Lists) Regulations 1989, SI 1989/2260, reg 8(2)(a).

10 Non-Domestic Rating (Collection and Enforcement) (Central Lists) Regulations 1989, SI 1989/2260, reg 8(2)(b).

11 'Estimated amount' means the amount last estimated under the Non-Domestic Rating (Collection and Enforcement) (Central Lists) Regulations 1989, SI 1989/2260, reg 6(1) (see PARA 308) for the purposes of the demand notice mentioned in reg 8(1)(a) (see head (1) in the text) or any subsequent notice given under Sch 1 para 7(2) (see PARA 313) or, as the case may be, Sch 1 paras 7A, 7B (see PARA 314) prior to the failure mentioned in reg 8(2), save that if in any case an interim adjustment has been required or made under reg 8(5) (see the text to notes 15–16), it means in relation to the next payment, repayment or interim adjustment in that case under reg 8, if any, the appropriate amount by reference to which the previous interim adjustment was so made: reg 8(8) (amended by SI 1992/1513).

12 Non-Domestic Rating (Collection and Enforcement) (Central Lists) Regulations 1989, SI 1989/2260, reg 8(2). If the amount payable for the relevant year proves to be greater than the estimated amount, an additional sum equal to the difference between the two is, on the service by the appropriate national authority on the ratepayer of a notice stating the amount payable, due from the person to the appropriate national authority on the expiry of such period (being not less than 14 days) after the day of issue of the notice as is specified in it: reg 8(3). As to the meaning of 'relevant year' see PARA 307 note 3.

If the amount payable for the relevant year proves to be less than the estimated amount, the appropriate national authority must notify the ratepayer in writing of the amount payable; and any overpayment in respect of any liability of the ratepayer under the Non-Domestic Rating (Collection and Enforcement) (Central Lists) Regulations 1989, SI 1989/2260:

(1) must be repaid if the ratepayer so requires (reg 8(4)(a)); or
(2) in any other case, must (as the appropriate national authority determines) either be repaid or be credited against any subsequent liability of the ratepayer to pay anything to the appropriate national authority by way of non-domestic rate (reg 8(4)(b)).

As to the meaning of 'amount payable' see PARA 308 note 7. As to the meaning of 'writing' see PARA 21 note 3.

13 Ie for the purposes of the Non-Domestic Rating (Collection and Enforcement) (Central Lists) Regulations 1989, SI 1989/2260, reg 8(3), (4): see note 12.
14 The 'appropriate amount' is the amount which would be required to be paid under a demand notice if such a notice were issued with respect to the relevant year and the ratepayer on the day that the notice under the Non-Domestic Rating (Collection and Enforcement) (Central Lists) Regulations 1989, SI 1989/2260, reg 8(7) (see the text to note 17) is issued; and more than one calculation of the appropriate amount and interim adjustment may be made under reg 8(5) according to the circumstances: reg 8(6), (8).
15 Non-Domestic Rating (Collection and Enforcement) (Central Lists) Regulations 1989, SI 1989/2260, reg 8(5)(a).
16 Non-Domestic Rating (Collection and Enforcement) (Central Lists) Regulations 1989, SI 1989/2260, reg 8(5)(b).
17 Non-Domestic Rating (Collection and Enforcement) (Central Lists) Regulations 1989, SI 1989/2260, reg 8(7).
18 Non-Domestic Rating (Collection and Enforcement) (Central Lists) Regulations 1989, SI 1989/2260, reg 8(7).

B. ENFORCEMENT

317. Recovery in a court of competent jurisdiction.

A sum which has become payable under the central non-domestic rating lists regulations[1], whether to the appropriate national authority[2] or by way of repayment, and which has not been paid, is recoverable in a court of competent jurisdiction[3]. However, any matter which could be the subject of an appeal as regards matters connected with the alteration of rating lists[4] may not be raised in such recovery proceedings[5].

The contents of a central non-domestic rating list[6] (or an extract from such a list) may be proved in such recovery proceedings by production of a copy of the list (or relevant part of the list) purporting to be credited by or on behalf of the appropriate national authority to be a true copy[7].

1 Ie under the Non-Domestic Rating (Collection and Enforcement) (Central Lists) Regulations 1989, SI 1989/2260.
2 Ie the Secretary of State or, in relation to Wales, the Welsh Ministers. The functions of the Secretary of State under the Non-Domestic Rating (Collection and Enforcement) (Central Lists) Regulations 1989, SI 1989/2260, so far as exercisable in relation to Wales, were transferred to the National Assembly for Wales (see the National Assembly for Wales (Transfer of Functions) Order 1999, SI 1999/672, arts 2, 3, Sch 1) and are now vested in the Welsh Ministers (see the Government of Wales Act 2006 s 162(1), Sch 11 para 30). As to the Secretary of State and the Welsh Ministers see PARA 4 note 18. As to the meaning of 'Wales' see PARA 2 note 16.
3 Non-Domestic Rating (Collection and Enforcement) (Central Lists) Regulations 1989, SI 1989/2260, reg 10(1).
4 Ie an appeal made under regulations which have been made under the Local Government Finance Act 1988 s 55: see PARA 199.
5 Non-Domestic Rating (Collection and Enforcement) (Central Lists) Regulations 1989, SI 1989/2260, reg 10(2).
6 As to central non-domestic rating lists see PARA 196 et seq.
7 Non-Domestic Rating (Collection and Enforcement) (Central Lists) Regulations 1989, SI 1989/2260, reg 10(3).

318. Outstanding liabilities on death.

Where a person dies and at any time before his death he was or is alleged to have been subject to a central non-domestic rate[1], and:

(1) before the deceased's death, a sum has become payable by him under the central non-domestic rating collection regulations[2] or by way of relevant costs[3] in respect of a central non-domestic rate but has not been paid[4]; or

(2) after the deceased's death, a sum would, but for his death (and whether or not on the service of a notice) become payable by him[5] in respect of a central non-domestic rate[6],

his executor or administrator is[7] liable to pay the sum and may deduct out of the assets and effects of the deceased any payments made (or to be made)[8].

Where, before the deceased's death, a sum in excess of his liability[9] (including relevant costs payable by him) in respect of a central non-domestic rate has been paid (whether the excess arises because of his death or otherwise) and has not been repaid or credited under the central non-domestic rating collection regulations[10], his executor or administrator is entitled to the sum[11].

In so far as is relevant to such liability[12] in the administration of the deceased's estate, the executor or administrator may institute, continue or withdraw proceedings[13].

1 See the Non-Domestic Rating (Collection and Enforcement) (Local Lists) Regulations 1989, SI 1989/1058, reg 24(1) (applied by the Non-Domestic Rating (Collection and Enforcement) (Central Lists) Regulations 1989, SI 1989/2260, reg 11). The Non-Domestic Rating (Collection and Enforcement) (Local Lists) Regulations 1989, SI 1989/1058, reg 24 has effect as if references to Pt II (regs 3–9) included a reference to the Non-Domestic Rating (Collection and Enforcement) (Central Lists) Regulations 1989, SI 1989/2260: reg 11(a).

2 Ie under the Non-Domestic Rating (Collection and Enforcement) (Central Lists) Regulations 1989, SI 1989/2260.

3 'Relevant costs' include costs in respect of which an order of a court has been made in proceedings under the Non-Domestic Rating (Collection and Enforcement) (Central Lists) Regulations 1989, SI 1989/2260, reg 10(1) (see PARA 317): reg 11(b). As to the meaning of 'relevant costs' see PARA 305 note 3.

4 See the Non-Domestic Rating (Collection and Enforcement) (Local Lists) Regulations 1989, SI 1989/1058, reg 24(2)(a) (amended by SI 1990/145) (as applied: see note 1).

5 Ie under the Non-Domestic Rating (Collection and Enforcement) (Central Lists) Regulations 1989, SI 1989/2260.

6 See the Non-Domestic Rating (Collection and Enforcement) (Local Lists) Regulations 1989, SI 1989/1058, reg 24(2)(b) (as applied: see note 1). Where head (2) in the text applies, the liability of the executor or administrator does not arise until the service on him of a notice requiring payment of the sum: reg 24(3) (as so applied). As to the service of notices see PARA 306.

7 Ie subject to the Non-Domestic Rating (Collection and Enforcement) (Local Lists) Regulations 1989, SI 1989/1058, reg 24(3) (see note 6) and to the extent that it is not in excess of the deceased's liability under the Local Government Finance Act 1988 or, in relation to England, the Business Rate Supplements Act 2009 (including relevant costs payable by him) in respect of the rate: see the Non-Domestic Rating (Collection and Enforcement) (Local Lists) Regulations 1989, SI 1989/1058, reg 24(2) (as applied (see note 1); amended, in relation to England, by SI 2010/187).

8 See the Non-Domestic Rating (Collection and Enforcement) (Local Lists) Regulations 1989, SI 1989/1058, reg 24(2) (as applied: see note 1). A sum payable under reg 24(2) is enforceable in the administration of the deceased's estate as a debt of the deceased: see reg 24(6) (as so applied). The Non-Domestic Rating (Collection and Enforcement) (Central Lists) Regulations 1989, SI 1989/2260, reg 10(2), (3) (see PARA 317) applies to enforce a liability arising under the Non-Domestic Rating (Collection and Enforcement) (Local Lists) Regulations 1989, SI 1989/1058, reg 24 (as so applied) as it applies to proceedings under the Non-Domestic Rating (Collection and Enforcement) (Central Lists) Regulations 1989, SI 1989/2260, reg 10(1): Non-Domestic Rating (Collection and Enforcement) (Local Lists) Regulations 1989, SI 1989/1058, reg 24(7) (as so applied; substituted for this purpose by SI 1989/2260). As to executors and administrators see WILLS AND INTESTACY vol 103 (2016) PARA 605 et seq.

9 Ie his liability under the Local Government Finance Act 1988 or, in relation to England, the Business Rate Supplements Act 2009.
10 Ie under the Non-Domestic Rating (Collection and Enforcement) (Central Lists) Regulations 1989, SI 1989/2260.
11 See the Non-Domestic Rating (Collection and Enforcement) (Local Lists) Regulations 1989, SI 1989/1058, reg 24(4) (as applied (see note 1); amended, in relation to England, by SI 2010/187). Interest is usually due on such payments: see the Non-Domestic Rating (Payment of Interest) Regulations 1990, SI 1990/1904; and PARA 199.
12 Ie his liability under the Non-Domestic Rating (Collection and Enforcement) (Local Lists) Regulations 1989, SI 1989/1058, reg 24 (as applied: see note 1).
13 See the Non-Domestic Rating (Collection and Enforcement) (Local Lists) Regulations 1989, SI 1989/1058, reg 24(8) (as applied: see note 1).

(11) Bid Levy on Non-domestic Ratepayers

(i) Arrangements for Business Improvement Districts

A. IN GENERAL

319. Arrangements with respect to business improvement districts.

A billing authority[1] may make arrangements[2] ('BID arrangements') with respect to an area (a 'business improvement district') comprising all or part of the area of the authority[3]. The purpose of BID arrangements is to enable:

(1) the projects specified in the arrangements to be carried out for the benefit of the business improvement district or those who live, work or carry on any activity in the district[4]; and
(2) those projects to be financed (in whole or in part) by a levy ('BID levy') imposed on the non-domestic ratepayers[5], or a class of such ratepayers, in the district[6].

The appropriate national authority[7] may by regulations[8] make provision for or in connection with enabling two or more billing authorities to make BID arrangements with respect to a business improvement district comprising all or part of the area of each of the authorities[9].

The following persons, namely:

(a) the billing authority which has made the arrangements[10];
(b) a county council or parish council in England, or a community council in Wales, any part of whose area falls within the business improvement district[11]; and
(c) any other person authorised or required to do so in accordance with the arrangements[12],

may make financial contributions or take action for the purpose of enabling the projects specified in BID arrangements to be carried out[13].

Where BID arrangements are in force, the billing authority which made the arrangements must comply with them[14].

The appropriate national authority may by regulations make further provision in respect of business improvement districts[15].

1 'Billing authority' means, in relation to England, a district council, a unitary county council, a London borough council, the Common Council of the City of London or the Council of the Isles of Scilly; and, in relation to Wales, a county council or county borough council: Local Government Act 2003 s 59(1). As to the meanings of 'England' and 'Wales' see PARA 2 note 16. As to local government areas and authorities in England and Wales see LOCAL GOVERNMENT vol 69 (2018) PARA 36 et seq.

2 Ie in accordance with the Local Government Act 2003 Pt 4 (ss 41–59).
3 Local Government Act 2003 s 41(1). The Local Government Act 2003 Pt 4 (ss 41–59) binds the Crown: s 57. The White Paper *Strong Local Leadership – Quality Public Services* (Cm 5237) (2001) stated that the starting point in establishing a business improvement district will be the identification of a gap or weakness in the services provided by local authorities, being a source of concern to local businesses (see para 7.19). The geographical boundaries of a BID area will be decided locally, as part of the BID proposal, and all ratepayers in that area will have a vote on the proposed BID (see para 7.20). As to the procedure for making and approving proposals for BID arrangements see PARA 320 et seq.
4 Local Government Act 2003 s 41(2)(a).
5 'Non-domestic ratepayer', in relation to any area, means a person subject to a non-domestic rate under the Local Government Finance Act 1988 s 43 (see PARAS 133, 143 et seq) or s 45 (see PARAS 135–136, 148) because he is the owner or occupier of a hereditament situated in that area: Local Government Act 2003 s 59(1). As to the meaning of 'person' see PARA 11 note 13. As to the meaning of 'hereditament' see PARA 106; and as to the meanings of 'owner' and 'occupier' see PARA 86 (definitions applied by s 59(2)).
6 Local Government Act 2003 s 41(2)(b). As to the BID levy see PARA 324 et seq.
7 Ie the Secretary of State or, in relation to Wales, the Welsh Ministers. In their application in relation to Wales, the Local Government Act 2003 ss 41–44 have effect as if for each reference in those provisions to the Secretary of State there were substituted a reference to the National Assembly for Wales: see s 58(2)(a). The functions of the National Assembly for Wales are now vested in the Welsh Ministers: see the Government of Wales Act 2006 s 162(1), Sch 11 para 30. As to the Secretary of State and the Welsh Ministers see PARA 4 note 18. As to the meaning of 'Wales' see PARA 2 note 16.
8 The provision which may be made by regulations under the Local Government Act 2003 s 42 includes provision which modifies any provision made by or under Pt 4 (ss 41–59) in its application to such arrangements: s 42(2). At the date at which this volume states the law, no such regulations had been made.
9 Local Government Act 2003 s 42(1).
10 Local Government Act 2003 s 43(2)(a).
11 Local Government Act 2003 ss 43(2)(b), 58(2)(b). As to parish councils in England see LOCAL GOVERNMENT vol 69 (2018) PARA 41 et seq. As to community councils in Wales see LOCAL GOVERNMENT vol 69 (2018) PARA 63 et seq.
12 Local Government Act 2003 s 43(2)(c).
13 Local Government Act 2003 s 43(1).
14 Local Government Act 2003 s 44.
15 The appropriate national authority may by regulations make such supplementary, incidental, consequential or transitional provision as it considers necessary or expedient for the purposes of, in consequence of, or for giving full effect to, any provision made by or under the Local Government Act 2003 Pt 4 (ss 41–59): s 56(1). The provision which may be made under s 56(1) includes provision amending any enactment (whenever passed or made): s 56(2). However, no regulations under s 56(1) which include provision amending an Act are to be made by the Secretary of State unless a draft of the statutory instrument containing the regulations (whether containing them alone or with other provisions) has been laid before, and approved by a resolution of, each House of Parliament: see ss 56(3), 58(1). 'Enactment' includes an enactment contained in a local or private Act or comprised in subordinate legislation within the meaning of the Interpretation Act 1978 (see PARA 111 note 1): Local Government Act 2003 s 59(1). As to the regulations made under s 56 see the Business Improvement Districts (England) Regulations 2004, SI 2004/2443 (amended by SI 2011/2085, SI 2013/2265, SI 2014/600 and SI 2014/3199); and the Business Improvement Districts (Wales) Regulations 2005, SI 2005/1312 (amended by SI 2011/2085, SI 2014/600 and SI 2017/327).

B. PROCEDURE FOR APPROVING PROPOSALS FOR BID ARRANGEMENTS

320. BID proposals.

BID arrangements[1] are not to come into force unless proposals for the arrangements ('BID proposals') are approved by a ballot of the non-domestic ratepayers[2] in the proposed business improvement district[3] who are to be liable for the proposed BID levy[4].

The appropriate national authority[5] may by regulations[6] make provision:

(1) as to the persons[7] who may draw up BID proposals[8];
(2) as to the procedures to be followed in connection with the drawing up of BID proposals[9];
(3) as to the matters to be included in BID proposals[10]; and (4) as to the date which may be provided under BID proposals for the coming into force of BID arrangements which give effect to the proposals[11].

1 As to the meaning of 'BID arrangements' see PARA 319.
2 As to the meaning of 'non-domestic ratepayer' see PARA 319 note 5. As to ballots to approve proposals for BID arrangements see PARAS 321–322.
3 As to the meaning of 'business improvement district' see PARA 319.
4 Local Government Act 2003 s 49(1). As to the meaning of 'BID levy' see PARA 319. As to liability for the BID levy see PARA 324.
5 Ie the Secretary of State or, in relation to Wales, the Welsh Ministers. In its application in relation to Wales, the Local Government Act 2003 s 49 has effect as if for each reference to the Secretary of State there were substituted a reference to the National Assembly for Wales: see s 58(2)(a). The functions of the National Assembly for Wales are now vested in the Welsh Ministers: see the Government of Wales Act 2006 s 162(1), Sch 11 para 30. As to the Secretary of State and the Welsh Ministers see PARA 4 note 18. As to the meaning of 'Wales' see PARA 2 note 16.
6 As to the regulations made see the Business Improvement Districts (England) Regulations 2004, SI 2004/2443 (amended by SI 2011/2085, SI 2013/2265, SI 2014/600 and SI 2014/3199); and the Business Improvement Districts (Wales) Regulations 2005, SI 2005/1312 (amended by SI 2011/2085, SI 2014/600 and SI 2017/327).
7 As to the meaning of 'person' see PARA 11 note 13.
8 Local Government Act 2003 s 49(2)(a).
9 Local Government Act 2003 s 49(2)(b).
10 Local Government Act 2003 s 49(2)(c).
11 Local Government Act 2003 s 49(2)(d).

321. Ballot to approve BID proposals.

BID proposals[1] are not to be regarded as approved by a ballot[2] unless the following two conditions are satisfied[3]:

(1) the first condition is that a majority of the persons voting in the ballot[4] have voted in favour of the BID proposals[5]; and
(2) the second condition is that the aggregate of the rateable values of each hereditament[6] in respect of which a person voting in the ballot has voted in favour of the BID proposals ('A')[7] exceeds the aggregate of the rateable values of each hereditament in respect of which a person voting in the ballot has voted against the BID proposals ('B')[8].

The appropriate national authority[9] may by regulations[10] make provision in relation to ballots[11]. The provision which may be made by such regulations includes provision[12]:

(a) as to the timing of ballots[13];
(b) as to the non-domestic ratepayers[14] entitled to vote in a ballot[15];
(c) as to the question to be asked in a ballot[16];
(d) as to the form that ballots may take[17];
(e) as to the persons who are to hold ballots[18];
(f) as to the conduct of ballots[19];
(g) conferring power on the appropriate national authority to declare ballots void in cases of material irregularity[20];
(h) for or in connection with enabling a billing authority[21] to recover the costs of a ballot from such persons and in such circumstances as may be prescribed[22].

1 As to BID proposals see PARA 320.
2 Ie a ballot held for the purposes of the Local Government Act 2003 s 49(1): see PARA 320.

3 Local Government Act 2003 s 50(1). These conditions apply also to a ballot held to renew BID arrangements: see PARA 323.
4 As to eligibility to vote in a ballot on BID proposals see PARA 320. As to the meaning of 'person' see PARA 11 note 13.
5 Local Government Act 2003 s 50(2).
6 For these purposes, the rateable value of a hereditament is that shown on the day of the ballot under the Local Government Finance Act 1988 s 42(4) (see PARA 194): Local Government Act 2003 s 50(6). As to the meaning of 'hereditament' see PARA 106 (definition applied by s 59(2)).
7 Local Government Act 2003 s 50(3), (4).
8 Local Government Act 2003 s 50(3), (5).
9 Ie the Secretary of State or, in relation to Wales, the Welsh Ministers. In its application in relation to Wales, the Local Government Act 2003 s 55 (except s 55(4): see note 15) has effect as if for each reference to the Secretary of State there were substituted a reference to the National Assembly for Wales: see s 58(2)(a). The functions of the National Assembly for Wales are now vested in the Welsh Ministers: see the Government of Wales Act 2006 s 162(1), Sch 11 para 30. As to the Secretary of State and the Welsh Ministers see PARA 4 note 18. As to the meaning of 'Wales' see PARA 2 note 16.
10 As to the regulations made see the Business Improvement Districts (England) Regulations 2004, SI 2004/2443 (amended by SI 2011/2085, SI 2013/2265, SI 2014/600 and SI 2014/3199); and the Business Improvement Districts (Wales) Regulations 2005, SI 2005/1312 (amended by SI 2011/2085, SI 2014/600 and SI 2017/327).
11 Local Government Act 2003 s 55(1). For these purposes, 'ballot' means a ballot held for the purposes of s 49(1) (BID proposals) (see PARA 320) or s 54(2) (renewal of BID arrangements) (see PARA 323): s 55(5).

As to provision that may be made specifically by or under Pt 4 (ss 41–59) see PARA 255 note 11.

12 Local Government Act 2003 s 55(2). Nothing in s 55(2) is to be taken as limiting the power conferred by s 55(1) (see the text to notes 9–11): s 55(3).
13 Local Government Act 2003 s 55(2)(a).
14 As to the meaning of 'non-domestic ratepayer' see PARA 319 note 5.
15 Local Government Act 2003 s 55(2)(b). No regulations under s 55(1) which include provision of the kind mentioned in s 55(2)(b) are to be made by the Secretary of State unless a draft of the statutory instrument containing the regulations (whether containing them alone or with other provisions) has been laid before, and approved by a resolution of, each House of Parliament: s 55(4).
16 Local Government Act 2003 s 55(2)(c).
17 Local Government Act 2003 s 55(2)(d).
18 Local Government Act 2003 s 55(2)(e).
19 Local Government Act 2003 s 55(2)(f).
20 Local Government Act 2003 s 55(2)(g).
21 As to the meaning of 'billing authority' see PARA 319 note 1.
22 Local Government Act 2003 s 55(2)(h). 'Prescribed' means prescribed by the regulations: see s 59(1).

322. Outcome of ballot.

Where BID proposals[1] are approved by a ballot[2], the billing authority[3] to which the proposals relate may, in prescribed[4] circumstances, veto the proposals within such period from the date of the ballot as may be prescribed[5]. In deciding whether to exercise the veto, a billing authority is to have regard to such matters as may be prescribed[6]. If a billing authority vetoes BID proposals, it must give notice of the exercise of the veto to the persons[7] entitled to vote in the ballot[8].

Where a billing authority vetoes BID proposals, any person who was entitled to vote in the ballot may appeal to the appropriate national authority[9]. The appropriate national authority may by regulations make provision in relation to such appeals[10], including provision:

(1) as to the time by which an appeal is to be made[11];
(2) as to the manner in which an appeal is to be made[12];
(3) as to the procedure to be followed in connection with an appeal[13]; and

(4) as to the matters to be taken into account in deciding whether to allow an appeal[14].

1 As to BID proposals see PARA 320.
2 Ie a ballot held for the purposes of the Local Government Act 2003 s 49(1) (see PARA 320): see s 51(1).
3 As to the meaning of 'billing authority' see PARA 319 note 1.
4 'Prescribed' means prescribed by regulations made by the appropriate national authority: see the Local Government Act 2003 s 59(1). 'Appropriate national authority' means the Secretary of State or, in relation to Wales, the Welsh Ministers. In their application in relation to Wales, ss 51, 52 (see the text to notes 9–14) have effect as if for each reference to the Secretary of State there were substituted a reference to the National Assembly for Wales: see s 58(2)(a). The functions of the National Assembly for Wales are now vested in the Welsh Ministers: see the Government of Wales Act 2006 s 162(1), Sch 11 para 30. As to the Secretary of State and the Welsh Ministers see PARA 4 note 18. As to the meaning of 'Wales' see PARA 2 note 16.
As to the regulations made under the Local Government Act 2003 ss 51, 52 see the Business Improvement Districts (England) Regulations 2004, SI 2004/2443 (amended by SI 2011/2085, SI 2013/2265, SI 2014/600 and SI 2014/3199); and the Business Improvement Districts (Wales) Regulations 2005, SI 2005/1312 (amended by SI 2011/2085, SI 2014/600 and SI 2017/327).
5 Local Government Act 2003 s 51(2).
6 Local Government Act 2003 s 51(3).
7 As to the meaning of 'person' see PARA 11 note 13.
8 Local Government Act 2003 s 51(4). The notice must set out the reasons for the exercise of the veto, and must give details of the right of appeal under s 52 (see the text to notes 9–14): s 51(5). A copy of the notice must be sent to the appropriate national authority: s 51(6). As to eligibility to vote in a ballot on BID proposals see PARA 320.
9 Local Government Act 2003 s 52(1).
10 As to the regulations made see note 4. As to the provisions that apply where an appeal against a veto of BID proposals is successful see PARA 323.
11 Local Government Act 2003 s 52(2)(a).
12 Local Government Act 2003 s 52(2)(b).
13 Local Government Act 2003 s 52(2)(c).
14 Local Government Act 2003 s 52(2)(d).

C. COMMENCEMENT AND DURATION OF BID ARRANGEMENTS

323. Commencement and duration of BID arrangements.

Where BID proposals[1] are approved by a ballot[2], the billing authority[3] concerned must ensure that BID arrangements[4] which give effect to the proposals are made by the time the arrangements are to come into force[5].

BID arrangements are to come into force on such day as may be provided under the BID proposals[6]. However, if the BID proposals are vetoed[7], BID arrangements which give effect to the proposals are not to come into force unless the appropriate national authority[8] allows an appeal[9] against the veto[10].

BID arrangements are to have effect for such period (not exceeding five years) as may be specified in the arrangements[11]. BID arrangements may be renewed for one or more periods (each of which must not exceed five years) but only if the renewal of the arrangements on that or each occasion is approved by a ballot of the non-domestic ratepayers in the business improvement district[12] who are liable for the BID levy[13].

The appropriate national authority may by regulations make provision[14] as to the alteration of BID arrangements[15], and as to the termination of BID arrangements[16].

1 As to BID proposals see PARA 320.
2 Ie a ballot held for the purposes of the Local Government Act 2003 s 49(1) (see PARA 320): s 53(1).
3 As to the meaning of 'billing authority' see PARA 319 note 1.
4 As to the meaning of 'BID arrangements' see PARA 319.

5 Local Government Act 2003 s 53(2).
6 Local Government Act 2003 s 53(3).
7 Ie under the Local Government Act 2003 s 51: see PARA 322.
8 Ie the Secretary of State or, in relation to Wales, the Welsh Ministers. In their application in relation to Wales, the Local Government Act 2003 ss 53, 54 (except s 54(7): see note 14) have effect as if for each reference to the Secretary of State there were substituted a reference to the National Assembly for Wales: see s 58(2)(a). The functions of the National Assembly for Wales are now vested in the Welsh Ministers: see the Government of Wales Act 2006 s 162(1), Sch 11 para 30. As to the Secretary of State and the Welsh Ministers see PARA 4 note 18. As to the meaning of 'Wales' see PARA 2 note 16.
9 Ie under the Local Government Act 2003 s 52: see PARA 322.
10 Local Government Act 2003 s 53(4). Where the appropriate national authority allows such an appeal, BID arrangements which give effect to the proposals are to come into force on such day as the appropriate national authority may determine: s 53(5). The day determined under s 53(5) must not be earlier than the day mentioned in s 53(3) (see the text to note 6): s 53(6). As to the meaning of 'person' see PARA 11 note 13. As to the meaning of 'non-domestic ratepayer' see PARA 319 note 5.
11 Local Government Act 2003 s 54(1).
12 As to the meaning of 'business improvement district' see PARA 319.
13 Local Government Act 2003 s 54(2). The renewal of BID arrangements is not to be regarded as approved by a ballot held for the purposes of s 54(2) unless the two conditions in s 50 (see PARA 321), which apply to the approval of BID proposals, are satisfied in relation to the renewal of the arrangements: s 54(3). As to the meaning of 'BID levy' see PARA 319. As to liability for the BID levy see PARA 324.
14 Local Government Act 2003 s 54(4). No such regulations are to be made by the Secretary of State unless a draft of the statutory instrument containing the regulations (whether containing them alone or with other provisions) has been laid before, and approved by a resolution of, each House of Parliament: s 54(7). The provision which may be made by virtue of s 54(4)(a), (b) (see the text and notes 15–16) includes provision preventing or restricting the alteration or early termination of BID arrangements: s 54(5). However, nothing in s 54(5) is to be taken as limiting the power conferred by s 54(4): s 54(6).

As to the regulations made under s 54 see the Business Improvement Districts (England) Regulations 2004, SI 2004/2443 (amended by SI 2011/2085, SI 2013/2265, SI 2014/600 and SI 2014/3199); and the Business Improvement Districts (Wales) Regulations 2005, SI 2005/1312 (amended by SI 2011/2085, SI 2014/600 and SI 2017/327).
15 Local Government Act 2003 s 54(4)(a). See also note 14.
16 Local Government Act 2003 s 54(4)(b). See also note 14.

(ii) Business Improvement District Levy

A. IN GENERAL

324. BID levy.

BID levy[1] is to be imposed in a business improvement district[2] only for periods ('chargeable periods') falling within the period in which BID arrangements[3] are in force in respect of the district[4]. The length of any chargeable period, and the day on which it begins, are to be such as may be specified in the BID arrangements[5]. The amount of BID levy for any chargeable period:

(1) is to be calculated in such manner as may be provided in the BID arrangements[6]; and
(2) may be different for different cases[7].

BID arrangements must specify the description of non-domestic ratepayers[8] in the business improvement district who are to be liable for BID levy for a chargeable period[9]. A person[10] is to be liable for BID levy for a chargeable period if he falls within that description at any time within the period[11]; and the amount of a person's liability for BID levy for any chargeable period is to be determined in accordance with the BID arrangements[12]. Any amount of BID levy for which a person is liable is to be paid to the billing authority which made the arrangements[13].

The appropriate national authority[14] may by regulations[15] make provision with respect to the imposition, administration, collection, recovery and application of BID levy[16].

1 As to the meaning of 'BID levy' see PARA 319.
2 As to the meaning of 'business improvement district' see PARA 319.
3 As to the meaning of 'BID arrangements' see PARA 319.
4 Local Government Act 2003 s 45(1).
5 Local Government Act 2003 s 45(2).
6 Local Government Act 2003 s 45(3)(a).
7 Local Government Act 2003 s 45(3)(b).
8 As to the meaning of 'non-domestic ratepayer' see PARA 319 note 5.
9 Local Government Act 2003 s 46(1).
10 As to the meaning of 'person' see PARA 11 note 13.
11 Local Government Act 2003 s 46(2).
12 Local Government Act 2003 s 46(3).
13 Local Government Act 2003 s 46(4). Amounts paid to the authority by way of BID levy must be credited to the BID Revenue Account: see PARA 325.
14 Ie the Secretary of State or, in relation to Wales, the Welsh Ministers. In its application in relation to Wales, the Local Government Act 2003 s 48 has effect as if for each reference to the Secretary of State there were substituted a reference to the National Assembly for Wales: see s 58(2)(a). The functions of the National Assembly for Wales are now vested in the Welsh Ministers: see the Government of Wales Act 2006 s 162(1), Sch 11 para 30. As to the Secretary of State and the Welsh Ministers see PARA 4 note 18. As to the meaning of 'Wales' see PARA 2 note 16.
15 As to the regulations made under the Local Government Act 2003 s 48 see the Business Improvement Districts (England) Regulations 2004, SI 2004/2443 (amended by SI 2011/2085, SI 2013/2265, SI 2014/600 and SI 2014/3199); and the Business Improvement Districts (Wales) Regulations 2005, SI 2005/1312 (amended by SI 2011/2085, SI 2014/600 and SI 2017/327).
16 Local Government Act 2003 s 48(1). The provision which may be made by regulations under s 48 includes provision:
  (1) corresponding to any provision which may be made by regulations under the Local Government Finance Act 1988 s 50 (joint owners or occupiers of hereditament: see PARA 86), s 63 (liability on death of ratepayer: see PARA 277) or Sch 9 (administration of non-domestic rating: see PARA 226 et seq) (Local Government Act 2003 s 48(2)(a));
  (2) modifying or applying with modifications any provision made by regulations under any of those provisions (s 48(2)(b)).

  However, nothing in s 48(2) is to be taken as limiting the power conferred by s 48(1): s 48(3).

B. ADMINISTRATION OF BID LEVY

325. BID revenue account.

A billing authority[1] which has made BID arrangements[2] must, in accordance with proper practices, keep an account, to be called the 'BID Revenue Account'[3]. Amounts paid to the authority by way of BID levy[4] must be credited to the BID Revenue Account[5]; and amounts are to be debited to the BID Revenue Account only in accordance with BID arrangements[6].

The appropriate national authority[7] may by regulations[8] make further provision in relation to the BID Revenue Account[9].

1 As to the meaning of 'billing authority' see PARA 319 note 1.
2 As to the meaning of 'BID arrangements' see PARA 319.
3 Local Government Act 2003 s 47(1).
4 As to the meaning of 'BID levy' see PARA 319. As to liability to BID levy see PARA 324.
5 Local Government Act 2003 s 47(2).
6 Local Government Act 2003 s 47(3).

7 Ie the Secretary of State or, in relation to Wales, the Welsh Ministers. In its application in relation to Wales, the Local Government Act 2003 s 47 has effect as if for each reference to the Secretary of State there were substituted a reference to the National Assembly for Wales: see s 58(2)(a). The functions of the National Assembly for Wales are now vested in the Welsh Ministers: see the Government of Wales Act 2006 s 162(1), Sch 11 para 30. As to the Secretary of State and the Welsh Ministers see PARA 4 note 18. As to the meaning of 'Wales' see PARA 2 note 16.

8 As to the regulations made under the Local Government Act 2003 s 47 see the Business Improvement Districts (England) Regulations 2004, SI 2004/2443 (amended by SI 2011/2085, SI 2013/2265, SI 2014/600 and SI 2014/3199); and the Business Improvement Districts (Wales) Regulations 2005, SI 2005/1312 (amended by SI 2011/2085, SI 2014/600 and SI 2017/327).

9 Local Government Act 2003 s 47(4).

(12) Business Rate Supplement Levy

(i) Power to Impose Business Rate Supplements

326. Power to impose a BRS.

A levying authority[1] has power to impose a levy, to be called a 'business rate supplement', on non-domestic ratepayers[2] in its area[3]. The purpose of imposing a business rate supplement is to raise money for expenditure on a project that the authority is satisfied will promote economic development in its area[4].

The Business Rate Supplements Act 2009 binds the Crown[5].

1 'Levying authority' means:

(1) the Greater London Authority (Business Rate Supplements Act 2009 s 2(1)(a));
(2) a county council in England (s 2(1)(b));
(3) a district council for an area in England for which there is no county council (s 2(1)(c));
(4) a county council or county borough council in Wales (s 2(1)(d)).

As to the Greater London Authority see LONDON GOVERNMENT vol 71 (2013) PARA 67 et seq. As to local government areas and authorities in England and Wales see LOCAL GOVERNMENT vol 69 (2018) PARA 36 et seq. As to the meanings of 'England' and 'Wales' see PARA 2 note 16.

At the date at which this volume states the law, the Business Rate Supplements Act 2009 is in force in relation to England only (see the Business Rate Supplements Act 2009 (Commencement No 1) (England) Order 2009, SI 2009/2202, art 2); and will be brought into force in relation to Wales on a day to be appointed under the Business Rate Supplements Act 2009 s 32(2). At the date at which this volume states the law no such day had been appointed.

2 A person is a 'non-domestic ratepayer' in the area of a levying authority if the person is, as regards a hereditament in the authority's area, subject to a non-domestic rate under the Local Government Finance Act 1988 s 43 (occupiers of properties: see PARAS 133, 143 et seq), or s 45 (owners of empty properties: see PARA 135): Business Rate Supplements Act 2009 s 1(3). As to the meaning of 'person' see PARA 11 note 13. As to the meaning of 'hereditament' see PARA 106 (definition applied by s 30(2)).

3 Business Rate Supplements Act 2009 s 1(1). The power conferred on a levying authority by s 1(1) may be exercised jointly with one or more other levying authorities: s 2(2). Where two or more levying authorities are so acting jointly, a reference to a levying authority is (except where there is contrary provision) to be read as a reference to those authorities acting jointly: s 2(3). In carrying out its functions a levying authority must have regard to guidance: see PARA 341.

4 Business Rate Supplements Act 2009 s 1(2).

5 Business Rate Supplements Act 2009 s 31. As to the Crown see CONSTITUTIONAL AND ADMINISTRATIVE LAW vol 20 (2014) PARA 150; CROWN AND CROWN PROCEEDINGS vol 29 (2014) PARA 1 et seq.

327. Use of money raised by a BRS.

A levying authority[1] must secure that the sums it receives in respect of a business rate supplement[2] are used only for expenditure:

(1) on the project to which the business rate supplement relates[3]; and

(2) that the authority would not have incurred had it not imposed the business rate supplement[4].

A levying authority may use sums it receives in respect of a business rate supplement to make payments in respect of money loaned for the purpose of providing funding for the project to which the business rate supplement relates[5].

A levying authority must not use sums it receives in respect of a business rate supplement to provide[6]:

(a) housing[7];
(b) social services[8];
(c) education services[9];
(d) services for children[10];
(e) health services[11];
(f) services that the authority provides in the discharge of functions imposed by or under the Planning Acts[12].

The Greater London Authority may make arrangements with a functional body[13] for some or all of the sums that the Authority receives in respect of a business rate supplement imposed by it to be used by the body for expenditure on the project to which the business rate supplement relates[14].

1 As to the meaning of 'levying authority' see PARA 326 note 1. In carrying out its functions a levying authority must have regard to guidance: see PARA 341.

2 As to business rate supplements see PARA 326. A reference to sums that a levying authority receives in respect of a business rate supplement includes a reference to financial contributions made to it for the purpose of enabling the project to which the business rate supplement relates to be carried out: Business Rate Supplements Act 2009 s 3(6). The reference in s 3(6) to financial contributions made to a levying authority includes, where the levying authority is not a billing authority, financial contributions:

(1) made for the purpose specified in s 3(6) to a billing authority which is a lower-tier authority in relation to the levying authority (s 3(7)(a)); and
(2) transferred to the levying authority (s 3(7)(b)).

A 'lower-tier authority' is:

(a) in relation to the Greater London Authority, a London borough council, or the Common Council of the City of London in its capacity as a local authority (s 3(8)(a));
(b) in relation to a county council in England, a district council whose area forms part of the county council's area (s 3(8)(b)).

As to the meaning of 'billing authority' see PARA 53 (definition applied by s 30(2)). As to the Greater London Authority see LONDON GOVERNMENT vol 71 (2013) PARA 67 et seq. As to the London boroughs and their councils see LONDON GOVERNMENT vol 71 (2013) PARAS 15, 20–22, 55 et seq. As to the Common Council of the City of London see LONDON GOVERNMENT vol 71 (2013) PARAS 34–38. As to local government areas and authorities in England see LOCAL GOVERNMENT vol 69 (2018) PARA 36 et seq.

At the date at which this volume states the law, the Business Rate Supplements Act 2009 is in force in relation to England only (see the Business Rate Supplements Act 2009 (Commencement No 1) (England) Order 2009, SI 2009/2202, art 2); and will be brought into force in relation to Wales on a day to be appointed under the Business Rate Supplements Act 2009 s 32(2). At the date at which this volume states the law no such day had been appointed. As to the meanings of 'England' and 'Wales' see PARA 2 note 16.

3 Business Rate Supplements Act 2009 s 3(1)(a).

4 Business Rate Supplements Act 2009 s 3(1)(b). As to the application of this provision in certain circumstances see PARA 328 note 7.

5 Business Rate Supplements Act 2009 s 3(2).

6 Business Rate Supplements Act 2009 s 3(3). Regulations may amend s 3(3) so as to add, vary or omit a reference to a matter: s 3(4). At the date at which this volume states the law, no such regulations had been made.

7 Business Rate Supplements Act 2009 s 3(3)(a). As to local authorities as local housing authorities see HOUSING vol 56 (2017) PARA 11.

8 Business Rate Supplements Act 2009 s 3(3)(b). As to the social services functions of local authorities see SOCIAL SERVICES vol 95 (2017) PARA 315.

9 Business Rate Supplements Act 2009 s 3(3)(c). As to the duties and functions of local authorities in relation to education see EDUCATION vol 35 (2015) PARA 25 et seq.

10 Business Rate Supplements Act 2009 s 3(3)(d). As to local authorities as children's services authorities see CHILDREN AND YOUNG PERSONS vol 9 (2017) PARA 212 et seq.

11 Business Rate Supplements Act 2009 s 3(3)(e).

12 Business Rate Supplements Act 2009 s 3(3)(f). 'The Planning Acts' means that expression as defined by the Town and Country Planning Act 1990 (see PLANNING vol 81 (2018) PARA 4): see the Business Rate Supplements Act 2009 s 3(3)(f).

13 'Functional body' has the meaning given in the Greater London Authority Act 1999 s 424 (see LONDON GOVERNMENT vol 71 (2013) PARA 148): see the Business Rate Supplements Act 2009 s 30(2).

14 Business Rate Supplements Act 2009 s 3(5). Where the Greater London Authority makes arrangements under s 3(5) with a functional body, s 3 applies to the body's use of sums that it receives in respect of the business rate supplement as it applies to the Authority's use of sums that the Authority receives in respect of the business rate supplement: s 3(9). A reference to sums that a functional body receives in respect of a business rate supplement is a reference to:

(1) sums that the Greater London Authority transfers to the body for the purposes of arrangements under s 3(5) that relate to the business rate supplement (s 3(10)(a)); and

(2) financial contributions made to the body for the purpose specified in s 3(6) (see note 2) (s 3(10)(b)).

In s 3(1)(b) (see head (2) in the text) as it is applied to a functional body by virtue of s 3(9), the reference to expenditure of the levying authority is to be read as a reference to expenditure of the functional body: s 3(11).

328. Special introductory provision.

The chargeable period[1] of a business rate supplement[2] must not begin before 1 April 2010[3].

A levying authority[4] may impose a business rate supplement for the purpose of raising money for expenditure on a project beginning before 19 August 2009[5] only if the levying authority's area is in England[6], and the chargeable period of the business rate supplement begins on or before 1 April 2012[7].

1 As to the meaning of 'chargeable period' see PARA 332 note 11.

2 As to business rate supplements see PARA 326.

3 See the Business Rate Supplements Act 2009 s 27(1). At the date at which this volume states the law, the Business Rate Supplements Act 2009 is in force in relation to England only (see the Business Rate Supplements Act 2009 (Commencement No 1) (England) Order 2009, SI 2009/2202, art 2); and will be brought into force in relation to Wales on a day to be appointed under the Business Rate Supplements Act 2009 s 32(2). At the date at which this volume states the law no such day had been appointed. As to the meanings of 'England' and 'Wales' see PARA 2 note 16.

4 As to the meaning of 'levying authority' see PARA 326 note 1. In carrying out its functions a levying authority must have regard to guidance: see PARA 341.

5 Ie the date of the commencement of the Business Rate Supplements Act 2009 s 1: see s 27(2); Business Rate Supplements Act 2009 (Commencement No 1) (England) Order 2009, SI 2009/2202, art 2.

6 Business Rate Supplements Act 2009 s 27(2)(a).

7 Business Rate Supplements Act 2009 s 27(2)(b). Any guidance given by the Secretary of State in anticipation of the passing of the Business Rate Supplements Act 2009 or the commencement of a provision of the Act ('pre-commencement guidance') may be relied on for the purpose of imposing a business rate supplement in reliance on s 27(2) (s 27(3)(a)) and in the case of a business rate supplement imposed in reliance on s 27(2) (s 27(3)(b)). Pre-commencement guidance is to be treated as given by the Secretary of State under s 26 (see PARA 341): s 27(4). Anything done in anticipation of the passing of the Business Rate Supplements Act 2009 or the commencement of a provision of the Act is, in so far as it is done in reliance on and in accordance with pre-commencement guidance, to be treated as done in accordance with the Act: s 27(5). The Business Rate Supplements Act 2009 was passed (ie received Royal Assent) on 2 July 2009. As to the Secretary of State see PARA 4 note 18.

Section 3(1)(b) (see PARA 327), s 7(1) (see PARA 330) and s 10(7) (see PARA 331) do not apply to a business rate supplement that the Greater London Authority proposes to impose, or imposes, in reliance on s 27(2) if the chargeable period of the business rate supplement begins on or before 1 April 2011: s 27(6). The Secretary of State may by regulations make other provision about:

(1) the exercise by the Greater London Authority of the power to impose a business rate supplement in reliance on s 27(2) (s 27(7)(a));

(2) the operation of the Act in relation to a business rate supplement imposed by the Authority in reliance on s 27(2) (s 27(7)(b)).

The regulations may, in particular:

(a) confer or impose a function (which may include the exercise of a discretion) on the Greater London Authority, a lower-tier authority in relation to it or a functional body (s 27(8)(a));

(b) disapply a provision of the Act (s 27(8)(b));

(c) apply a provision of the Act with modifications (s 27(8)(c)).

As to the meaning of 'lower-tier authority' see PARA 327 note 2. As to the meaning of 'functional body' see PARA 327 note 13. At the date at which this volume states the law, no such regulations had been made.

(ii) Involvement of Ratepayers, Etc

329. Conditions for imposing a BRS.

A levying authority[1] may not impose a business rate supplement[2] unless:

(1) it has published a document that sets out the proposal for the imposition of the business rate supplement (an 'initial prospectus')[3];

(2) it has consulted[4] the relevant persons on the proposal[5];

(3) a ballot has been held and the imposition of the BRS approved[6]; and

(4) it has published a document that sets out the arrangements for the imposition of the business rate supplement (a 'final prospectus')[7].

The levying authority must publish a revised version of an initial prospectus if, in the light of the consultation on the proposal in the prospectus, the authority thinks that it is necessary or appropriate to do so[8].

Any initial or final prospectus must include the prescribed information[9], and may include such other information as the levying authority thinks appropriate[10]. The function of the levying authority of approving a final prospectus before publication is a function that must be discharged only by the whole authority[11].

After publishing an initial or final prospectus, a levying authority[12] must place an electronic copy of the published prospectus on its website[13], and make copies of the published prospectus available for inspection at its principal office at all reasonable times of the day[14].

1 As to the meaning of 'levying authority' see PARA 326 note 1. In carrying out its functions a levying authority must have regard to guidance: see PARA 341.

2 As to business rate supplements see PARA 326.

3 Business Rate Supplements Act 2009 s 4(a). At the date at which this volume states the law, the Business Rate Supplements Act 2009 is in force in relation to England only (see the Business Rate Supplements Act 2009 (Commencement No 1) (England) Order 2009, SI 2009/2202, art 2); and will be brought into force in relation to Wales on a day to be appointed under the Business Rate Supplements Act 2009 s 32(2). At the date at which this volume states the law no such day had been appointed. As to the meanings of 'England' and 'Wales' see PARA 2 note 16.

4 As to the exercise of the duty to consult see JUDICIAL REVIEW vol 61 (2010) PARA 627.

5 Business Rate Supplements Act 2009 s 4(b). The 'relevant persons' for the purposes of consultation on the proposal in an initial prospectus are:

(1) each person who will be liable to pay the business rate supplement (s 6(1)(a));

(2) each lower-tier authority in relation to the levying authority (s 6(1)(b));

(3) such other persons as the levying authority thinks appropriate (s 6(1)(c)).

A person is to be regarded for the purposes of head (1) above as a person who will be liable to pay a business rate supplement if:

(a) the levying authority thinks that the person will be liable to pay a chargeable amount for the first day of the chargeable period of the business rate supplement (s 6(2));

(b) the levying authority thinks that the person would, but for s 13(7) or (8) (see PARA 332), be liable to pay a chargeable amount for the first day of the chargeable period of the business rate supplement (s 6(3));
(c) the levying authority thinks that the person would, but for s 15 (see PARA 333) or s 16 (see PARA 334), be liable to pay a chargeable amount for the first day of the chargeable period of the business rate supplement (s 6(4)(a)), and will be liable to pay a chargeable amount before the end of that period (s 6(4)(b)).

A reference in s 6(2), (3) or (4) to a chargeable amount does not include a reference to a chargeable amount of zero: s 6(8).

For the purposes of head (3) above, a levying authority must, in particular, think whether it would be appropriate to consult persons who the authority thinks might become liable to pay a chargeable amount before the end of the chargeable period of the business rate supplement: s 6(5). As to the meaning of 'person' see PARA 11 note 13. As to liability to pay business rate supplement see PARA 332. As to the meaning of 'lower-tier authority' see PARA 327 note 2. As to the meanings of 'chargeable amount' and 'chargeable period' see PARA 332 note 11.

6 Business Rate Supplements Act 2009 s 4(c) (amended, in relation to England only, by the Localism Act 2011 s 68(1), (2)); Localism Act 2011 (Commencement No 2 and Transitional and Saving Provision) Order 2012, SI 2012/57, art 3. The amendments made by the Localism Act 2011 s 68 do not apply in relation to a business rate supplement imposed before 15 January 2012 in relation to England (ie the date s 68 came into force) (whether or not the chargeable period of the business rate supplement has begun before that date): s 68(7). As to the meaning of 'chargeable period' see PARA 332 note 11 (definition applied by s 68(8)).

7 Business Rate Supplements Act 2009 s 4(d).

8 Business Rate Supplements Act 2009 s 6(6). A reference in s 5 (see the text to notes 9–14) to an initial prospectus includes a reference to an initial prospectus revised under s 6(6): s 6(7).

9 Ie the information specified in the Business Rate Supplements Act 2009 Sch 1: see s 5(1), Sch 1 (Sch 1 paras 19, 20 substituted by the Localism Act 2011 s 68(1), (6)). The information to be included in a prospectus is:

(1) information relating to the project (see the Business Rate Supplements Act 2009 Sch 1 paras 1–11);
(2) information as to the amount of the business rate supplement (see Sch 1 paras 12–13);
(3) information as to liability to the business rate supplement (see Sch 1 paras 14–18);
(4) information required in relation to a ballot on the imposition of the BRS (see Sch 1 paras 19–20 (as so substituted)); and
(5) information as to the authority's policy for variations and contingencies (see Sch 1 paras 21–23).

Regulations may amend Sch 1 so as to add, vary or omit a description of information: s 5(5). At the date at which this volume states the law, no such regulations had been made.

10 Business Rate Supplements Act 2009 s 5(1).

11 Business Rate Supplements Act 2009 s 5(2). However, this does not apply in the case of the Greater London Authority: see s 5(2). In a case where two or more levying authorities are acting jointly by virtue of s 2 (see PARA 326), each authority must separately discharge the function of approving a final prospectus before publication: s 5(4)(a). As to the Greater London Authority see LONDON GOVERNMENT vol 71 (2013) PARA 67 et seq.

12 In a case where two or more levying authorities are acting jointly by virtue of the Business Rate Supplements Act 2009 s 2 (see PARA 326), each authority must separately comply with the duty imposed by s 5(3): s 5(4)(b).

13 Business Rate Supplements Act 2009 s 5(3)(a).

14 Business Rate Supplements Act 2009 s 5(3)(b).

330. Ballots.

Regulations[1] may make provision in relation to the holding of a ballot on the imposition of a business rate supplement[2]. The provision which may be made includes, in particular, provision about:

(1) the timing of a ballot[3];
(2) the form that a ballot may take[4];
(3) who is to hold a ballot[5];
(4) the conduct of a ballot[6].

The regulations may, in particular:

(a) confer functions on a levying authority[7];
(b) enable a levying authority to appoint an officer of its to exercise on its behalf a function conferred by virtue of head (a) (a 'ballot function')[8];
(c) enable a levying authority to delegate to a lower-tier authority[9] in relation to it the exercise of a ballot function in the area of that lower-tier authority[10];
(d) enable a levying authority to delegate to a lower-tier authority in relation to it the exercise of a ballot function in the area of each other lower-tier authority in relation to the levying authority[11];
(e) enable a lower-tier authority to which the exercise of a ballot function is delegated by virtue of head (c) or (d) to appoint an officer of its to exercise the function on its behalf[12].

The regulations may also make provision as to who may cast a vote in a case where the person[13] eligible to vote is a body corporate, partnership or unincorporated association[14].

The proposition to be voted on in a ballot on the imposition of a business rate supplement is: 'The [insert name of levying authority] proposes to introduce a business rate supplement. The proposal is set out in [insert title of prospectus]. Should the proposed business rate supplement be introduced?'[15].

A person is eligible to vote in a ballot on the imposition of a business rate supplement if he is within the statutory criteria[16].

The imposition of a business rate supplement is approved if[17]:

(i) a majority of the persons voting in the ballot have voted in favour of the imposition of the business rate supplement[18]; and
(ii) the aggregate of the rateable values of each hereditament[19] in respect of which a person voting in the ballot has voted in favour of the imposition of the business rate supplement exceeds the aggregate of the rateable values of each hereditament in respect of which a person voting in the ballot has voted against the imposition of the business rate supplement[20].

1 At the date at which this volume states the law, no such regulations had been made.
2 Business Rate Supplements Act 2009 s 9(1). Nothing in s 9(2)–(4) (see the text to notes 3–14) is to be taken as limiting the power conferred by s 9(1): s 9(5). As to business rate supplements see PARA 326.
At the date at which this volume states the law, the Business Rate Supplements Act 2009 is in force in relation to England only (see the Business Rate Supplements Act 2009 (Commencement No 1) (England) Order 2009, SI 2009/2202, art 2); and will be brought into force in relation to Wales on a day to be appointed under the Business Rate Supplements Act 2009 s 32(2). At the date at which this volume states the law no such day had been appointed. As to the meanings of 'England' and 'Wales' see PARA 2 note 16.
3 Business Rate Supplements Act 2009 s 9(2)(a).
4 Business Rate Supplements Act 2009 s 9(2)(b).
5 Business Rate Supplements Act 2009 s 9(2)(c).
6 Business Rate Supplements Act 2009 s 9(2)(d).
7 Business Rate Supplements Act 2009 s 9(3)(a). As to the meaning of 'levying authority' see PARA 326 note 1.
8 Business Rate Supplements Act 2009 s 9(3)(b).
9 As to the meaning of 'lower-tier authority' see PARA 327 note 2.
10 Business Rate Supplements Act 2009 s 9(3)(c).
11 Business Rate Supplements Act 2009 s 9(3)(d).
12 Business Rate Supplements Act 2009 s 9(3)(e).
13 As to the meaning of 'person' see PARA 11 note 13.
14 Business Rate Supplements Act 2009 s 9(4).
15 Business Rate Supplements Act 2009 s 7(3).
16 See the Business Rate Supplements Act 2009 s 7(4). The statutory criteria are those of s 6(2), (3)

or (4) (see PARA 329): see s 7(4).

17 Business Rate Supplements Act 2009 s 8(1) (amended, in relation to England only, by the Localism Act 2011 s 68(1), (4)); Localism Act 2011 (Commencement No 2 and Transitional and Saving Provision) Order 2012, SI 2012/57, art 3. The amendments made by the Localism Act 2011 s 68 do not apply in relation to a business rate supplement imposed before 15 January 2012, in relation to England, (ie the date s 68 came into force) (whether or not the chargeable period of the business rate supplement has begun before that date): s 68(7). As to the meaning of 'chargeable period' see PARA 332 note 11 (definition applied by s 68(8)).

18 Business Rate Supplements Act 2009 s 8(1)(a).

19 As to the meaning of 'hereditament' see PARA 106 (definition applied by the Business Rate Supplements Act 2009 s 30(2)).

20 See the Business Rate Supplements Act 2009 s 8(1)(b), (2). For these purposes, the rateable value of a hereditament is its rateable value on the day of the ballot: s 8(3). As to the meaning of 'rateable value' see s 12(9); and PARA 332 note 13 (definition applied by s 30(2)).

331. Variations.

A levying authority[1] may vary a business rate supplement[2] in so far as the variation is of a kind that may be made in accordance with the final prospectus[3]; but a variation the purpose of which is to increase the number of persons liable to pay a chargeable amount[4] may not be made in reliance on this power[5].

Otherwise, a levying authority may vary a business rate supplement only if:

(1) it has published a document that sets out the proposal for the variation[6];
(2) it has consulted the relevant persons on the proposal[7];
(3) a ballot[8] on the proposal has been held and the variation approved[9]; and
(4) it has published a document that sets out the arrangements for making the variation[10].

The proposition to be voted on in a ballot on a proposal to vary a business rate supplement is: 'The [insert name of levying authority] proposes to vary the business rate supplement set out in [insert title of prospectus and title of any document setting out a variation to the business rate supplement]. The proposal is set out in [insert title of document setting out proposal]. Should the proposed variation be made?'[11].

A person is eligible to vote in a ballot on a proposal to vary a business rate supplement if he is within the statutory criteria[12].

1 As to the meaning of 'levying authority' see PARA 326 note 1. In carrying out its functions a levying authority must have regard to guidance: see PARA 341.

2 As to business rate supplements see PARA 326.

3 Business Rate Supplements Act 2009 s 10(1). As to the meaning of 'final prospectus' see PARA 329. At the date at which this volume states the law, the Business Rate Supplements Act 2009 is in force in relation to England only (see the Business Rate Supplements Act 2009 (Commencement No 1) (England) Order 2009, SI 2009/2202, art 2); and will be brought into force in relation to Wales on a day to be appointed under the Business Rate Supplements Act 2009 s 32(2). At the date at which this volume states the law no such day had been appointed. As to the meanings of 'England' and 'Wales' see PARA 2 note 16.

4 As to the meaning of 'person' see PARA 11 note 13. As to the meaning of 'chargeable amount' see PARA 332. As to liability to business rate supplement see PARA 332.

5 See the Business Rate Supplements Act 2009 s 10(12). Section 10(1) (see the text to notes 1–3) is to be read accordingly: see s 10(12).

6 Business Rate Supplements Act 2009 s 10(2)(a). A document published for the purposes of s 10(2)(a) or (d) (see head (4) in the text) must:

(1) specify the amount that the authority expects to raise from the imposition of the business rate supplement on the assumption that the variation is made (the specified amount to include the amount already raised from the imposition of the business rate supplement) (s 10(3)(a));
(2) specify the authority's estimate of the total cost of the project to which the business rate supplement relates (s 10(3)(b));
(3) specify the day on which the variation will, if made, take effect (s 10(3)(c)); and

(4) include, to the extent that the authority thinks appropriate, such other information as would be included in an initial or final prospectus if the proposal or arrangements were for the imposition of the business rate supplement as varied (s 10(3)(d)).

As to the meaning of 'initial prospectus' see PARA 329. Section 5 (see PARA 329) applies as follows in relation to the publication of a document for the purposes of s 10(2)(a) or (d):

(a) s 5(2) applies to the approval of a document before publication for the purposes of s 10(2)(d) as it applies to the approval of a final prospectus before publication (s 10(4)(a));

(b) s 5(3) applies to a document published for the purposes of s 10(2)(a) or (d) as it applies to a published initial or final prospectus (s 10(4)(b));

(c) s 5(4) applies so far as necessary for the purposes of the applications made by heads (a) and (b) (s 10(4)(c)).

Section 6(6) (see PARA 329) applies in relation to a document published for the purposes of s 10(2)(a) as it applies in relation to an initial prospectus: s 10(6).

7 Business Rate Supplements Act 2009 s 10(2)(b). The 'relevant persons' for the purposes of consultation on a proposal to vary a business rate supplement are those who would be the relevant persons if the proposal were for the imposition of the business rate supplement as varied; for that purpose, s 6 (see PARA 329) applies as if references to the first day of the chargeable period of the business rate supplement were references to the day specified for the purposes of s 10(3)(c) (see note 6): s 10(5). As to the exercise of the duty to consult see JUDICIAL REVIEW vol 61 (2010) PARA 627.

8 As to ballots see PARA 330.

9 Business Rate Supplements Act 2009 s 10(2)(c) (amended by the Localism Act 2011 ss 68(1), (5)(a), 237, Sch 25 Pt 9); Localism Act 2011 (Commencement No 2 and Transitional and Saving Provision) Order 2012, SI 2012/57, arts 3(a), (c), 4(1)(ee)(ii). The amendments made by the Localism Act 2011 s 68 do not apply in relation to a business rate supplement imposed in England before 15 January 2012 (ie the date s 68 came into force) (whether or not the chargeable period of the business rate supplement has begun before that date): s 68(7). As to the meaning of 'chargeable period' see PARA 332 note 11 (definition applied by s 68(8)).

10 Business Rate Supplements Act 2009 s 10(2)(d). See also note 6.

11 Business Rate Supplements Act 2009 s 10(10).

12 See the Business Rate Supplements Act 2009 s 10(11). The statutory criteria are those of s 6(2), (3) or (4) (see PARA 329) (as applied by s 10(5): see note 7); and ss 8 and 9 (see PARA 330) apply to a ballot on a proposal to vary a business rate supplement as they apply to a ballot on a proposal for the imposition of a business rate supplement: see s 10(11).

(iii) Liability to Business Rate Supplements

332. Liability of non-domestic ratepayers.

A person[1] who, as regards a hereditament[2], is subject to a non-domestic rate[3] in respect of a financial year[4] is, in relation to that hereditament and in respect of that year, subject to such business rate supplements as are imposed for that year[5] by the levying authority[6] in whose area the hereditament is situated[7].

A person who is subject to a business rate supplement in relation to a hereditament in respect of a financial year is liable to pay in respect of that year an amount calculated by finding the chargeable amount for each chargeable day[8], and totalling the amounts so found[9]. The 'chargeable amount' for a chargeable day in relation to a hereditament is calculated by using the appropriate statutory formula[10]. A 'chargeable day' is a day which falls within the financial year and the chargeable period[11] of the business rate supplement[12], and on which the rateable value condition is met in relation to the hereditament[13].

1 As to the meaning of 'person' see PARA 11 note 13.

2 As to the meaning of 'hereditament' see PARA 106 (definition applied by the Business Rate Supplements Act 2009 s 30(2)).

3 Ie under the Local Government Finance Act 1988 s 43 (see PARAS 133, 143 et seq) or s 45 (see PARA 135).

4 See the Business Rate Supplements Act 2009 s 11(1). As to the meaning of 'financial year' see PARA

24 note 1 (definition applied by s 30(2)). At the date at which this volume states the law, the Business Rate Supplements Act 2009 is in force in relation to England only (see the Business Rate Supplements Act 2009 (Commencement No 1) (England) Order 2009, SI 2009/2202, art 2); and will be brought into force in relation to Wales on a day to be appointed under the Business Rate Supplements Act 2009 s 32(2). At the date at which this volume states the law no such day had been appointed. As to the meanings of 'England' and 'Wales' see PARA 2 note 16.

5 A reference to a business rate supplement imposed for a financial year is to a business rate supplement the chargeable period of which is or includes the whole or part of the financial year in question: Business Rate Supplements Act 2009 s 11(8). As to business rate supplements see PARA 326.

6 As to the meaning of 'levying authority' see PARA 326 note 1.

7 Business Rate Supplements Act 2009 s 11(2). But a person subject to a non-domestic rate under the Local Government Finance Act 1988 s 45 (see PARA 135) (a 'section 45 ratepayer') is not subject to a business rate supplement if:
  (1) s 45A (empty properties: zero rating for charities and amateur sports clubs: see PARA 147) applies to the hereditament (Business Rate Supplements Act 2009 s 11(3)(a)); or
  (2) the final prospectus for the business rate supplement states that section 45 ratepayers are not to be subject to the business rate supplement (s 11(3)(b)).

Section 11(3)(b) does not apply if, by virtue of s 10 (see PARA 331), section 45 ratepayers become subject to the business rate supplement: s 11(9). As to the meaning of 'final prospectus' see PARA 329. As to business rate supplement relief see PARA 333.

8 Business Rate Supplements Act 2009 s 11(4)(a).

9 See the Business Rate Supplements Act 2009 s 11(4)(b).

10 See the Business Rate Supplements Act 2009 ss 13, 14 (both amended by the Telecommunications Infrastructure (Relief from Non-Domestic Rates) Act 2018 Schedule para 8).

11 The 'chargeable period' of a business rate supplement is the period for which the business rate supplement is imposed (Business Rate Supplements Act 2009 s 11(6)(a)), and must not begin before the day on which the business rate supplement is imposed (s 11(6)(b)). The length of the chargeable period of a business rate supplement must not exceed:
  (1) the length of the period specified as the chargeable period in the final prospectus (s 11(7)(a)); or
  (2) if the length of the chargeable period is varied in accordance with s 10 (see PARA 331), the length of the period as varied (s 11(7)(b)).

12 Business Rate Supplements Act 2009 s 11(5)(a).

13 Business Rate Supplements Act 2009 s 11(5)(b). The rateable value condition is met in relation to a hereditament:
  (1) unless s 12(2) applies, on any day on which the rateable value of the hereditament exceeds the amount prescribed by regulations (s 12(1));
  (2) if s 12(2) applies, on any day on which the rateable value of the occupied part exceeds the amount prescribed under s 12(1) (s 12(3)).

Section 12(2) applies if part only of a hereditament is occupied (s 12(2)(a)), and section 45 ratepayers are not subject to the business rate supplement (s 12(2)(b)). For the purposes of a case where s 12(2) applies, the levying authority may require the valuation officer for the authority (or, where it is not a billing authority, for the billing authority in whose area the hereditament is situated):
  (a) to apportion the rateable value of the hereditament between the occupied and unoccupied parts (s 12(4)(a)); and
  (b) to certify the apportionment to the levying authority (s 12(4)(b)).

The levying authority may, for those purposes, rely on an apportionment under the Local Government Finance Act 1988 s 44A (see PARA 134) if satisfied that the apportionment will be accurate for those purposes: Business Rate Supplements Act 2009 s 12(5). Regulations may make provision:
  (i) for the proposal of alterations to a certificate under s 12(4) (s 12(6)(a));
  (ii) for an appeal in relation to such a certificate to a valuation tribunal for the purposes of the Local Government Finance Act 1988 s 55 (see PARA 199) (Business Rate Supplements Act 2009 s 12(6)(b)).

Regulations under s 12(6):
  (A) may include such provision for the purposes of the Business Rate Supplements Act 2009 as may be included in regulations under the Local Government Finance Act 1988 s 55(3)–(7) for the purposes of that Act (Business Rate Supplements Act 2009 s 12(7)(a));

(B) may amend, or apply (with or without modifications), any provision of regulations made under any of those subsections (s 12(7)(b)).

Accordingly, provision by virtue of s 12(6) as to the period for which or day from which an alteration to a certificate is to have effect may have retrospective effect; and provision by virtue of that subsection may require the retrospective effect to be indicated on the certificate as altered: s 12(8). As to valuation officers see PARA 54. As to the meaning of 'billing authority' see PARA 53 (definition applied by s 30(2)). As to occupation see PARA 86.

The 'rateable value' of a hereditament on a day is the rateable value of that hereditament shown for that day in the local non-domestic rating list maintained for the billing authority in whose area the hereditament is situated: s 12(9). As to local non-domestic rating lists see PARA 191 et seq.

As to the regulations made under s 12 see the Business Rate Supplements (Rateable Value Condition) (England) Regulations 2009, SI 2009/2542, prescribing £50,000 as the amount.

333. BRS relief.

A levying authority[1] that imposes a business rate supplement[2] may apply such reliefs in relation to the business rate supplement as it thinks appropriate[3].

If a levying authority applies a relief in relation to a business rate supplement, the chargeable amount[4] for a chargeable day[5] in relation to a hereditament[6] is determined in accordance with the rules set by the authority for the application of the relief[7]. A levying authority may not apply a relief in relation to a business rate supplement unless the rules for the application of the relief[8]:

(1) are set out in the final prospectus[9] for the business rate supplement or have effect by virtue[10] of a variation[11];
(2) operate by reference to the rateable value[12] of a hereditament in respect of which the liability arises[13];
(3) apply consistently to hereditaments in the levying authority's area regardless of the purpose for which they may be used or the basis on which they are owned or occupied[14]; and
(4) apply uniformly throughout the levying authority's area[15].

1 As to the meaning of 'levying authority' see PARA 326 note 1. In carrying out its functions a levying authority must have regard to guidance: see PARA 341.
2 As to business rate supplements see PARA 326.
3 Business Rate Supplements Act 2009 s 15(1). As to liability to business rate supplement see PARA 332. At the date at which this volume states the law, the Business Rate Supplements Act 2009 is in force in relation to England only (see the Business Rate Supplements Act 2009 (Commencement No 1) (England) Order 2009, SI 2009/2202, art 2); and will be brought into force in relation to Wales on a day to be appointed under the Business Rate Supplements Act 2009 s 32(2). At the date at which this volume states the law no such day had been appointed. As to the meanings of 'England' and 'Wales' see PARA 2 note 16.
4 As to the meaning of 'chargeable amount' see PARA 332.
5 As to the meaning of 'chargeable day' see PARA 332.
6 As to the meaning of 'hereditament' see PARA 106 (definition applied by the Business Rate Supplements Act 2009 s 30(2)).
7 Business Rate Supplements Act 2009 s 15(2).
8 Business Rate Supplements Act 2009 s 15(3). Regulations may amend s 15(3) so as to add, vary or omit a condition to be met in relation to the rules for the application of a relief under s 15: s 15(4). At the date at which this volume states the law, no such regulations had been made.
9 As to the meaning of 'final prospectus' see PARA 329.
10 Ie by virtue of the Business Rate Supplements Act 2009 s 10: see PARA 331.
11 See the Business Rate Supplements Act 2009 s 15(3)(a). See also note 8.
12 As to the meaning of 'rateable value' see the Business Rate Supplements Act 2009 s 12(9); and PARA 332 note 13 (definition applied by s 30(2)).
13 Business Rate Supplements Act 2009 s 15(3)(b). See also note 8.
14 Business Rate Supplements Act 2009 s 15(3)(c). See also note 8. As to ownership and occupation see PARA 86.
15 Business Rate Supplements Act 2009 s 15(3)(d). See also note 8.

334. Interaction with BID levy.

A levying authority[1] must set rules[2] for the purposes of cases where a person[3] is, by reference to a hereditament[4], liable for BID levy[5] for the whole or part of a financial year[6] in respect of which the person is, in relation to that hereditament, subject to a business rate supplement imposed by the authority[7].

The chargeable amount[8] in relation to the hereditament for a chargeable day[9] for which the person is also liable for BID levy by reference to the hereditament is the amount found by offsetting the amount of the person's liability for BID levy for the day against the amount that the person would[10] be liable to pay in respect of the business rate supplement for that day, to the extent specified in the rules[11].

In specified circumstances a billing authority[12] may make arrangements ('BRS-BID arrangements') in respect of a business improvement district[13] in its area[14].

1 As to the meaning of 'levying authority' see PARA 326 note 1. In carrying out its functions a levying authority must have regard to guidance: see PARA 341.

2 Rules set for the purposes of cases within the Business Rate Supplements Act 2009 s 16(1) must:
   (1) accord with such rules as are set out for those purposes in the final prospectus for the business rate supplement or as have effect for those purposes by virtue of s 10 (see PARA 331) (s 16(4)(a));
   (2) apply consistently in relation to BID levies (s 16(4)(b)); and
   (3) apply uniformly throughout the levying authority's area (s 16(4)(c)).

As to the meaning of 'final prospectus' see PARA 329. As to business rate supplements see PARA 326. As to the meaning of 'BID levy' see PARA 319 (definition applied by s 30(2)).

At the date at which this volume states the law, the Business Rate Supplements Act 2009 is in force in relation to England only (see the Business Rate Supplements Act 2009 (Commencement No 1) (England) Order 2009, SI 2009/2202, art 2); and will be brought into force in relation to Wales on a day to be appointed under the Business Rate Supplements Act 2009 s 32(2). At the date at which this volume states the law no such day had been appointed. As to the meanings of 'England' and 'Wales' see PARA 2 note 16.

3 As to the meaning of 'person' see PARA 11 note 13.

4 As to the meaning of 'hereditament' see PARA 106 (definition applied by the Business Rate Supplements Act 2009 s 30(2)).

5 As to liability to BID levy see PARA 324.

6 As to the meaning of 'financial year' see PARA 24 note 1 (definition applied by the Business Rate Supplements Act 2009 s 30(2)).

7 Business Rate Supplements Act 2009 s 16(1). As to liability to business rate supplement see PARA 332.

8 As to the meaning of 'chargeable amount' see PARA 332.

9 As to the meaning of 'chargeable day' see PARA 332.

10 Ie apart from the Business Rate Supplements Act 2009 s 16.

11 See the Business Rate Supplements Act 2009 s 16(2), (3).

12 As to the meaning of 'billing authority' see PARA 53 (definition applied by the Business Rate Supplements Act 2009 s 30(2)).

13 As to the meaning of 'business improvement district' see PARA 319 (definition applied by the Business Rate Supplements Act 2009 Sch 2 para 11).

14 The Business Rate Supplements Act 2009 Sch 2 (BRS-BID arrangements) has effect; and s 16(1)–(4) (see the text to notes 1–11) applies in relation to BRS-BID levy (within the meaning given by Sch 2) as it applies in relation to BID levy, but the rules relating to BRS-BID levy need not be the same as the rules relating to BID levy: s 16(5). Schedule 2 applies in the following four cases:
   (1) the first case is where a levying authority whose area is in England imposes a business rate supplement, and at the time of the imposition, all or part of the authority's area is comprised in a business improvement district (Sch 2 para 1(1), (2));
   (2) the second case is where a levying authority whose area is in England may impose a business rate supplement (the conditions in s 4 having been satisfied), and all or part of the authority's area is comprised in a business improvement district (Sch 2 para 1(1), (3));
   (3) the third case is where a billing authority whose area is in England makes BID arrangements, and the business improvement district in respect of which the

arrangements are made comprises all or part of an area in which a business rate supplement has been imposed (and the imposition has not come to an end) (Sch 2 para 1(1), (4));

(4) the fourth case is where a billing authority whose area is in England makes BID arrangements, and the business improvement district in respect of which the arrangements are made comprises all or part of an area in which a business rate supplement may be imposed (the conditions in s 4 having been satisfied) (Sch 2 para 1(1), (5)).

Detailed provision as to the making of BRS-BRD arrangements is set out in Sch 2 paras 2–10. See also the Business Improvement Districts (Property Owners) (England) Regulations 2014, SI 2014/3204. As to BID arrangements see PARA 319.

335. Regulations to deal with joint ownership, joint occupation or death.

Regulations may make provision for cases where a hereditament[1] is owned or occupied[2] by more than one person[3] at a particular time[4].

Regulations may also make provision for cases where a person who has died was (or is alleged to have been) subject to a business rate supplement[5].

1 As to the meaning of 'hereditament' see PARA 106 (definition applied by the Business Rate Supplements Act 2009 s 30(2)).

2 As to ownership and occupation see PARA 86.

3 As to the meaning of 'person' see PARA 11 note 13.

4 Business Rate Supplements Act 2009 s 17(1). Such regulations:

(1) may include such provision for the purposes of the Business Rate Supplements Act 2009 as may be included in regulations under the Local Government Finance Act 1988 s 50 (cases of joint ownership or occupation: see PARA 86) for the purposes of that Act (Business Rate Supplements Act 2009 s 17(2)(a));

(2) may amend, or apply (with or without modifications), a provision of regulations made under the Local Government Finance Act 1988 s 50 (Business Rate Supplements Act 2009 s 17(2)(b)).

At the date at which this volume states the law, no regulations had been made under s 17(1), (2).

At the date at which this volume states the law, the Business Rate Supplements Act 2009 is in force in relation to England only (see the Business Rate Supplements Act 2009 (Commencement No 1) (England) Order 2009, SI 2009/2202, art 2); and will be brought into force in relation to Wales on a day to be appointed under the Business Rate Supplements Act 2009 s 32(2). At the date at which this volume states the law no such day had been appointed. As to the meanings of 'England' and 'Wales' see PARA 2 note 16.

5 Business Rate Supplements Act 2009 s 17(3). As to business rate supplements see PARA 326. Regulations under s 17(3):

(1) may include such provision for the purposes of the Business Rate Supplements Act 2009 as may be included in regulations under the Local Government Finance Act 1988 s 63 (cases of death: see PARA 277) for the purposes of that Act (Business Rate Supplements Act 2009 s 17(4)(a));

(2) may amend, or apply (with or without modifications), any provision of regulations made under the Local Government Finance Act 1988 s 63 (Business Rate Supplements Act 2009 s 17(4)(b)).

As to the regulations made under s 17(3), (4) see the Business Rate Supplements (Collection and Enforcement) (England) Regulations 2010, SI 2010/187, which make amendments to the Non-Domestic Rating (Collection and Enforcement) (Local Lists) Regulations 1989, SI 1989/1058, reg 24 (see PARA 305) and the Council Tax and Non-Domestic Rating (Demand Notices) (England) Regulations 2003, SI 2003/2613, reg 3, Sch 2 (see PARA 282) so as to apply those provisions to the Business Rate Supplements Act 2009.

(iv) Administration of Business Rate Supplements

336. Notices to billing authorities.

A levying authority[1] which is not a billing authority[2] must, for each financial year[3] for which it intends to impose a business rate supplement[4], give a written[5] notice relating to the business rate supplement to each billing authority which is a lower-tier authority[6] in relation to it[7]. The notice must:

(1) if the business rate supplement is to be imposed for part only of the year, specify the part of the year for which it is to be imposed[8];

(2) specify the multiplier for the business rate supplement for the year[9];

(3) state whether persons[10] who, as regards hereditaments[11] in the billing authority's area, are section 45 ratepayers[12] are to be subject to the business rate supplement[13];

(4) specify whether a relief[14] is to be applied in relation to the business rate supplement (and, if so, set out the rules for its application)[15]; and

(5) set out the rules for cases[16] in which there is also a liability to BID levy[17].

The notice must be given before 1 March in the financial year preceding that for which the levying authority intends to impose the business rate supplement[18]. Where more than one business rate supplement is to be imposed by the levying authority for the year, the notice may relate to some or all of the business rate supplements in question[19].

If:

(a) a levying authority which is not a billing authority intends to impose a business rate supplement for a financial year[20], but has not, for that year, given a notice[21] in relation to the business rate supplement[22]; or

(b) a levying authority varies[23] a business rate supplement[24], and thinks that, as a result of the variation, new calculations are required to find the chargeable amounts[25] that some or all of those subject to the business rate supplement are liable to pay[26],

the levying authority must give a written notice relating to the business rate supplement to each billing authority which is a lower-tier authority in relation to it[27].

1 As to the meaning of 'levying authority' see PARA 326 note 1. In carrying out its functions a levying authority must have regard to guidance: see PARA 341.

2 As to the meaning of 'billing authority' see PARA 53 (definition applied by the Business Rate Supplements Act 2009 s 30(2)).

3 As to the meaning of 'financial year' see PARA 24 note 1 (definition applied by the Business Rate Supplements Act 2009 s 30(2)).

4 As to business rate supplements see PARA 326. As to the meaning of 'impose a business rate supplement for a financial year' see PARA 332 note 5.

5 As to the meaning of 'written' see PARA 21 note 3.

6 As to the meaning of 'lower-tier authority' see PARA 327 note 2.

7 Business Rate Supplements Act 2009 s 18(1). At the date at which this volume states the law, the Business Rate Supplements Act 2009 is in force in relation to England only (see the Business Rate Supplements Act 2009 (Commencement No 1) (England) Order 2009, SI 2009/2202, art 2); and will be brought into force in relation to Wales on a day to be appointed under the Business Rate Supplements Act 2009 s 32(2). At the date at which this volume states the law no such day had been appointed. As to the meanings of 'England' and 'Wales' see PARA 2 note 16.

8 Business Rate Supplements Act 2009 s 18(2)(a).

9 Business Rate Supplements Act 2009 s 18(2)(b).

10 As to the meaning of 'person' see PARA 11 note 13.

11 As to the meaning of 'hereditament' see PARA 106 (definition applied by the Business Rate Supplements Act 2009 s 30(2)).

12 As to the meaning of 'section 45 ratepayers' see PARA 332 note 7.

13 Business Rate Supplements Act 2009 s 18(2)(c).

14 Ie under the Business Rate Supplements Act 2009 s 15: see PARA 333.

15 Business Rate Supplements Act 2009 s 18(2)(d).

16 Ie cases within the Business Rate Supplements Act 2009 s 16(1): see PARA 334.

17 Business Rate Supplements Act 2009 s 18(2)(e).

18 Business Rate Supplements Act 2009 s 18(3).

19 Business Rate Supplements Act 2009 s 18(4)(a). If the notice does so it must set out the information required under s 18(2) (see the text to heads (1)–(5) in the text) separately for each business rate supplement to which the notice relates: see s 18(4)(b).
20 Business Rate Supplements Act 2009 s 19(1)(a).
21 Ie under the Business Rate Supplements Act 2009 s 18: see the text to notes 1–19.
22 Business Rate Supplements Act 2009 s 19(1)(b).
23 Ie in accordance with the Business Rate Supplements Act 2009 s 10: see PARA 331.
24 Business Rate Supplements Act 2009 s 19(2)(a).
25 As to the meaning of 'chargeable amount' see PARA 332.
26 Business Rate Supplements Act 2009 s 19(2)(b).
27 Business Rate Supplements Act 2009 s 19(3). A notice given for the purposes of a case within s 19(1) (see head (a) in the text) must comply with s 18(2) (see heads (1)–(5) in the text): s 19(4). A notice given for the purposes of a case within s 19(2) (see head (b) in the text) must specify the variation (s 19(5)(a)), and the day specified for the purposes of s 10(3)(c) in the document published for the purposes of s 10(2)(d) (see PARA 331) (s 19(5)(b)).

337. Calculations for financial year.

A billing authority[1] which is a levying authority[2] must calculate the chargeable amount[3] which each person[4] who is to be subject to a business rate supplement[5] imposed by it for a financial year[6] is to be liable to pay in respect of that year[7].

If a billing authority which is a lower-tier authority[8] in relation to a levying authority receives a notice[9] from the levying authority[10], the billing authority must calculate the chargeable amount that each person who is to be subject to the business rate supplement to which the notice relates is to be liable to pay in respect of the financial year[11].

Any such calculation must be made in accordance with the appropriate statutory provision[12].

1 As to the meaning of 'billing authority' see PARA 53 (definition applied by the Business Rate Supplements Act 2009 s 30(2)).
2 As to the meaning of 'levying authority' see PARA 326 note 1. In carrying out its functions a levying authority must have regard to guidance: see PARA 341.
3 As to the meaning of 'chargeable amount' see PARA 332.
4 As to the meaning of 'person' see PARA 11 note 13.
5 As to business rate supplements see PARA 326.
6 As to the meaning of 'financial year' see PARA 24 note 1 (definition applied by the Business Rate Supplements Act 2009 s 30(2)). As to the meaning of 'impose a business rate supplement for a financial year' see PARA 332 note 5.
7 Business Rate Supplements Act 2009 s 20(1). As to liability to business rate supplement see PARA 332. At the date at which this volume states the law, the Business Rate Supplements Act 2009 is in force in relation to England only (see the Business Rate Supplements Act 2009 (Commencement No 1) (England) Order 2009, SI 2009/2202, art 2); and will be brought into force in relation to Wales on a day to be appointed under the Business Rate Supplements Act 2009 s 32(2). At the date at which this volume states the law no such day had been appointed. As to the meanings of 'England' and 'Wales' see PARA 2 note 16.
8 As to the meaning of 'lower-tier authority' see PARA 327 note 2.
9 Ie under the Business Rate Supplements Act 2009 s 18 or s 19: see PARA 336.
10 Business Rate Supplements Act 2009 s 20(2).
11 Business Rate Supplements Act 2009 s 20(3). If a billing authority receives a notice given for the purposes of a case within s 19(2) (see PARA 336), the duty imposed on the authority by s 20(3) applies only in so far as new calculations are required to be made as a result of the variation specified in the notice: s 20(4).
12 A calculation under the Business Rate Supplements Act 2009 s 20 must be made in accordance with s 11(4) (see PARA 332): s 20(5).

338. Collection and enforcement.

Regulations may make provision in relation to the collection and recovery of sums due under the Business Rate Supplements Act 2009[1].

After the imposition of a business rate supplement[2] has come to an end, a billing authority[3] may seek to collect or recover sums in respect of the business rate supplement in so far as the sums became payable to it before the imposition of the business rate supplement came to an end[4].

Regulations[5] may authorise a billing authority[6] to use a prescribed proportion of such sums as it collects or recovers in respect of a business rate supplement[7] to meet expenses it incurs in the collection or recovery ('administrative expenses')[8].

In so far as a billing authority which is not a levying authority incurs administrative expenses in response to a notice given by the levying authority[9], those expenses must be met by the levying authority[10]; but the levying authority may not meet those expenses by:

(1) using sums that it receives in respect of the business rate supplement[11]; or

(2) directing the billing authority to retain from sums it is required to transfer to the levying authority in respect of the business rate supplement a sum equivalent to the amount that the levying authority is required to pay[12].

1 Business Rate Supplements Act 2009 s 21(1). The regulations:

(1) may include such provision for the purposes of the Business Rate Supplements Act 2009 as may be included in regulations under the Local Government Finance Act 1988 Sch 9 paras 1–4A (collection and recovery of non-domestic-rates: see PARAS 272–276) for the purposes of that Act (Business Rate Supplements Act 2009 s 21(2)(a));

(2) may amend, or apply (with or without modifications), any provision of regulations made under any of the Local Government Finance Act 1988 Sch 9 paras 1–4A (Business Rate Supplements Act 2009 s 21(2)(b));

(3) may confer on a billing authority for the purposes of the Business Rate Supplements Act 2009 a power corresponding to that conferred on a billing authority by the Local Government Finance Act 1988 s 62A (taking control of goods: see PARA 295) for the purposes of that Act (Business Rate Supplements Act 2009 s 21(2)(c)).

As to the regulations made see the Business Rate Supplements (Administrative Expenses) (England) Regulations 2010, SI 2010/134; the Business Rate Supplements (Collection and Enforcement) (England) Regulations 2010, SI 2010/187; the Non-Domestic Rating and Business Rate Supplements (England) (Amendment) Regulations 2011, SI 2011/255; the Non-Domestic Rating and Business Rate Supplements (Deferred Payments) (England) Regulations 2012, SI 2012/994; and the Non-Domestic Rating (Demand Notices) (Amendment) (England) Regulations 2017, SI 2017/39.

At the date at which this volume states the law, the Business Rate Supplements Act 2009 is in force in relation to England only (see the Business Rate Supplements Act 2009 (Commencement No 1) (England) Order 2009, SI 2009/2202, art 2); and will be brought into force in relation to Wales on a day to be appointed under the Business Rate Supplements Act 2009 s 32(2). At the date at which this volume states the law no such day had been appointed. As to the meanings of 'England' and 'Wales' see PARA 2 note 16.

2 As to business rate supplements see PARA 326.

3 As to the meaning of 'billing authority' see PARA 53 (definition applied by the Business Rate Supplements Act 2009 s 30(2)).

4 Business Rate Supplements Act 2009 s 21(3). Regulations may provide that, if the project to which a business rate supplement relates is abandoned (or, where a business rate supplement relates to only certain aspects of a project, those aspects are abandoned), the imposition of the business rate supplement is to be treated for the purposes of s 21(3) as having come to an end at the time of the abandonment (s 21(4)(a)), or at such other time as may be prescribed (s 21(4)(b)). At the date at which this volume states the law, no regulations had been made for these purposes. Section 21(3) does not apply where the imposition of a business rate supplement comes to an end as a result of s 24: see s 24(7); and PARA 342.

5 Ie regulations under the Business Rate Supplements Act 2009 s 21: see the text to notes 1–4. As to the regulations made for these purposes see the Business Rate Supplements (Administrative Expenses) (England) Regulations 2010, SI 2010/134.

6 If the chargeable period of a business rate supplement begins, or a variation of a business rate supplement takes effect, later than the first day of a financial year, the levying authority may not, in respect of that financial year, act in reliance on provision made by virtue of the Business Rate Supplements Act 2009 s 22(1): s 22(3). As to the meaning of 'chargeable period' see PARA 332 note 11. As to variations see PARA 331. As to the meaning of 'financial year' see PARA 24 note 1 (definition applied by s 30(2)). As to the meaning of 'levying authority' see PARA 326 note 1.

7 A reference to sums that a billing authority collects in respect of a business rate supplement includes a reference to financial contributions made to it for the purpose of enabling the project to which the business rate supplement relates to be carried out: Business Rate Supplements Act 2009 s 22(7).

8 Business Rate Supplements Act 2009 s 22(1). Provision by virtue of s 22(1) may, in particular, amend the Local Government Finance Act 1988 s 90 (payments to and from collection funds: see PARA 581): Business Rate Supplements Act 2009 s 22(2).

9 Ie under the Business Rate Supplements Act 2009 s 19: see PARA 336.

10 Business Rate Supplements Act 2009 s 22(4). The amount that a levying authority is required to pay under s 22(4) must not exceed such amount as may be prescribed by regulations under s 21 (see the text to notes 1–4) (or as is to be determined in accordance with such formula as may be prescribed by regulations under that section): s 22(6). As to the regulations made see the Business Rate Supplements (Administrative Expenses) (England) Regulations 2010, SI 2010/134.

11 Business Rate Supplements Act 2009 s 22(5)(a).

12 Business Rate Supplements Act 2009 s 22(5)(b).

339. Accounting.

A levying authority[1] that imposes a business rate supplement[2] must, in accordance with proper practices, keep a revenue account that is solely for that business rate supplement[3], and must secure that such sums as the authority receives in respect of the business rate supplement[4] are credited to that account[5].

Regulations[6] may make provision:

(1) for sums collected in respect of a business rate supplement by a billing authority[7] which is a levying authority to be transferred from its collection fund to its revenue account for the business rate supplement[8];

(2) for sums collected in respect of a business rate supplement by a billing authority which is not a levying authority to be transferred from the billing authority's collection fund to the levying authority's revenue account for the business rate supplement[9].

Regulations[10] may provide for refunds or credits to be given in a case where the imposition of a business rate supplement has come to an end[11] and the levying authority's, or a functional body's, revenue account for the business rate supplement is in credit[12].

Regulations may make further provision in relation to revenue accounts for business rate supplements[13].

1 In a case where two or more levying authorities are acting jointly by virtue of the Business Rate Supplements Act 2009 s 2 (see PARA 326), each authority must comply separately with the duties imposed by Sch 3 para 1(1): s 23, Sch 3 para 1(3). As to the meaning of 'levying authority' see PARA 326 note 1. In carrying out its functions a levying authority must have regard to guidance: see PARA 341.

A functional body with which the Greater London Authority makes arrangements under s 3(5) (see PARA 327) must, in accordance with proper practices, keep a revenue account that is solely for the business rate supplement to which the arrangements relate (Sch 3 para 1(2)(a)), and must secure that such sums as the body receives in respect of the business rate supplement are credited to that account (Sch 3 para 1(2)(b)). As to the meaning of 'functional body' see PARA 327 note 13. As to the meaning of 'sums received by a functional body in respect of business rate supplement' see PARA 327 note 14.

At the date at which this volume states the law, the Business Rate Supplements Act 2009 is in force in relation to England only (see the Business Rate Supplements Act 2009 (Commencement No 1) (England) Order 2009, SI 2009/2202, art 2); and will be brought into force in relation to Wales on a day to be appointed under the Business Rate Supplements Act 2009 s 32(2). At the date at which this volume states the law no such day had been appointed. As to the meanings of 'England' and 'Wales' see PARA 2 note 16.

2 As to business rate supplements see PARA 326.

3 Business Rate Supplements Act 2009 Sch 3 para 1(1)(a).

4 As to the meaning of 'sums received by a levying authority in respect of a business rate supplement' see PARA 327 note 2.

5 Business Rate Supplements Act 2009 Sch 3 para 1(1)(b). As to collection of business rate supplement see PARA 338.

6 Regulations under the Business Rate Supplements Act 2009 Sch 3 para 2:

(1) may include such provision for the purposes of the Business Rate Supplements Act 2009 as may be included in regulations under the Local Government Finance Act 1988 s 89 (see PARA 581) or s 99 (see PARA 583) for the purposes of that Act (Business Rate Supplements Act 2009 Sch 3 para 2(2)(a));

(2) may amend, or apply (with or without modifications), any provision of regulations made under either of those sections (Sch 3 para 2(2)(b));

(3) are to have effect subject to such provision (if any) as is made by virtue of s 22(1) (see PARA 338) (Sch 3 para 2(2)(c)).

As to the regulations made under the Business Rate Supplements Act 2009 Sch 3 see the Business Rate Supplements (Transfers to Revenue Accounts) (England) Regulations 2009, SI 2009/2543 (amended by SI 2010/403 and SI 2011/255); the Business Rate Supplements (Accounting) (England) Regulations 2010, SI 2010/403; and the Non-Domestic Rating and Business Rate Supplements (England) (Amendment) Regulations 2011, SI 2011/255.

7 As to the meaning of 'sums collected by a billing authority in respect of a business rate supplement' see PARA 338 note 7. As to the meaning of 'billing authority' see PARA 53 (definition applied by the Business Rate Supplements Act 2009 s 30(2)).

8 Business Rate Supplements Act 2009 Sch 3 para 2(1)(a).

9 Business Rate Supplements Act 2009 Sch 3 para 2(1)(b).

10 The regulations may, in particular:

(1) if the levying authority is not a billing authority, require it to transfer the sum standing to the credit of its revenue account in equal proportions to each billing authority which is a lower-tier authority in relation to it (Business Rate Supplements Act 2009 Sch 3 para 3(2)(a));

(2) if the levying authority is a billing authority, authorise it to use a prescribed proportion of the sum standing to the credit of its revenue account to meet administrative expenses (Sch 3 para 3(2)(b));

(3) authorise a billing authority which is a lower-tier authority in relation to the levying authority to use a prescribed proportion of the sum it receives by virtue of head (1) above to meet administrative expenses (Sch 3 para 3(2)(c));

(4) require a functional body to transfer the sum standing to the credit of its revenue account to the levying authority's revenue account (Sch 3 para 3(2)(d)).

For these purposes, 'administrative expenses', in relation to an authority, are expenses it incurs in giving a credit or refund by virtue of Sch 3 para 3: Sch 3 para 3(3).

As to the meaning of 'lower-tier authority' see PARA 327 note 2. As to the regulations made see note 6.

11 Business Rate Supplements Act 2009 Sch 3 para 3(1)(a).

12 Business Rate Supplements Act 2009 Sch 3 para 3(1)(b).

13 Business Rate Supplements Act 2009 Sch 3 para 5. As to the regulations made see note 6.

340. Provision of information.

A levying authority[1] may require[2] a billing authority which is a lower-tier authority[3] in relation to it to provide it with:

(1) the address and rateable value[4] of each hereditament[5] shown in the local non-domestic rating list[6] maintained for the billing authority[7];

(2) the name and address of each person[8] who, as regards a hereditament shown in the list, is subject[9] to a non-domestic rate[10];

(3) such other information for the purposes of the Business Rate Supplements Act 2009 as the levying authority may specify[11].

A billing authority must comply with such a requirement[12].

A levying authority:

(a) may not use information provided to it[13] except in so far as is necessary for the purposes of the Business Rate Supplements Act 2009[14]; and

(b) may not disclose the information (except in accordance with an enactment, in pursuance of an order of a court or with the consent of any person to whom the information relates)[15].

1 As to the meaning of 'levying authority' see PARA 326 note 1. In carrying out its functions a levying authority must have regard to guidance: see PARA 341.

2 A requirement must be in writing (Business Rate Supplements Act 2009 s 25(3)(a)), and must be accompanied by such fee (if any) as the billing authority may charge for complying with the requirement (s 25(3)(b)). As to the meaning of 'writing' see PARA 21 note 3. As to the meaning of 'billing authority' see PARA 53 (definition applied by s 30(2)).

At the date at which this volume states the law, the Business Rate Supplements Act 2009 is in force in relation to England only (see the Business Rate Supplements Act 2009 (Commencement No 1) (England) Order 2009, SI 2009/2202, art 2); and will be brought into force in relation to Wales on a day to be appointed under the Business Rate Supplements Act 2009 s 32(2). At the date at which this volume states the law no such day had been appointed. As to the meanings of 'England' and 'Wales' see PARA 2 note 16.

3 As to the meaning of 'lower-tier authority' see PARA 327 note 2.

4 As to the meaning of 'rateable value' see the Business Rate Supplements Act 2009 s 12(9); and PARA 332 note 13 (definition applied by s 30(2)).

5 As to the meaning of 'hereditament' see PARA 106 (definition applied by the Business Rate Supplements Act 2009 s 30(2)).

6 As to local non-domestic rating lists see PARA 191 et seq.

7 Business Rate Supplements Act 2009 s 25(1)(a).

8 As to the meaning of 'person' see PARA 11 note 13.

9 Ie under the Local Government Finance Act 1988 s 43 (see PARAS 133, 143 et seq) or s 45 (see PARA 135).

10 Business Rate Supplements Act 2009 s 25(1)(b).

11 Business Rate Supplements Act 2009 s 25(1)(c).

12 See the Business Rate Supplements Act 2009 s 25(2).

13 Ie under the Business Rate Supplements Act 2009 s 25.

14 Business Rate Supplements Act 2009 s 25(4)(a).

15 Business Rate Supplements Act 2009 s 25(4)(b).

341. Guidance.

In carrying out functions imposed by or by virtue of the Business Rate Supplements Act 2009, a levying authority[1] must have regard to such guidance as the appropriate national authority[2] may give[3]. Guidance may, in particular, relate to:

(1) the kinds of projects which may, and may not, be regarded as appropriate ones in relation to which to impose business rate supplements[4];

(2) the carrying out by a levying authority of an assessment[5] of the likely impact of the imposition of the business rate supplement on businesses in the authority's area and the likely benefits of the related project for its area[6];

(3) the discharge of the duty imposed[7] in relation to the use of money raised by a business rate supplement[8];

(4) expenditure which may, and may not, be regarded as an appropriate use for money raised from the imposition of a business rate supplement[9];

(5) the contents of an initial or final prospectus[10] or a document required to be published for the purposes[11] of the variation of a business rate supplement (in particular, the level of detail to provide)[12];

(6) the holding of a ballot on the imposition of a business rate supplement or on a proposal to vary a business rate supplement[13].

1 As to the meaning of 'levying authority' see PARA 326 note 1.

2 'Appropriate national authority' means:

(1) in relation to a levying authority whose area is in England or in relation to hereditaments in England, the Secretary of State (Business Rate Supplements Act 2009 s 30(1)(a));

(2) in relation to a levying authority whose area is in Wales or in relation to hereditaments in Wales, the Welsh Ministers (s 30(1)(b)).

As to the meanings of 'England' and 'Wales' see PARA 2 note 16. As to the meaning of 'hereditament' see PARA 106 (definition applied by s 30(2)). As to the Secretary of State and the Welsh Ministers see PARA 4 note 18.

At the date at which this volume states the law, the Business Rate Supplements Act 2009 is in force in relation to England only (see the Business Rate Supplements Act 2009 (Commencement No 1) (England) Order 2009, SI 2009/2202, art 2); and will be brought into force in relation to Wales on a day to be appointed under the Business Rate Supplements Act 2009 s 32(2). At the date at which this volume states the law no such day had been appointed.

3 Business Rate Supplements Act 2009 s 26(1).

4 Business Rate Supplements Act 2009 s 26(2)(a). As to business rate supplements see PARA 326.

5 Ie for the purposes of the Business Rate Supplements Act 2009 Sch 1 para 5: see PARA 329.

6 Business Rate Supplements Act 2009 s 26(2)(b).

7 Ie by the Business Rate Supplements Act 2009 s 3(1) (see PARA 327) (in particular, its discharge in a case within s 27: see PARA 328).

8 See the Business Rate Supplements Act 2009 s 26(2)(c).

9 Business Rate Supplements Act 2009 s 26(2)(d).

10 As to the meanings of 'initial prospectus' and 'final prospectus' see PARA 329.

11 Ie for the purposes of the Business Rate Supplements Act 2009 s 10(2)(a) or (d): see PARA 331.

12 Business Rate Supplements Act 2009 s 26(2)(e).

13 Business Rate Supplements Act 2009 s 26(2)(f). As to ballots see PARA 330. As to variations see PARA 331.

(v) Powers of Appropriate National Authority

342. Power to cancel a business rate supplement.

If the appropriate national authority[1] thinks that a levying authority[2] has, in relation to a business rate supplement[3] imposed by it, acted in a way that is materially inconsistent with information provided by it[4], including information provided:

(1) in the final prospectus for the business rate supplement[5];

(2) in a document published[6] about a proposal to vary the business rate supplement[7];

(3) in the course of consultation on the proposal for the imposition of the business rate supplement or on a proposal to vary the business rate supplement[8];

(4) in connection with the holding of a ballot on the imposition of the business rate supplement or on a proposal to vary the BRS[9],

the appropriate national authority:

(a) may direct the levying authority to cancel the imposition of the business rate supplement[10];

(b) may direct the levying authority to refund the sums received by it in respect of the business rate supplement or, where the levying authority is not a billing authority[11], direct it to return to a billing authority that is a lower-tier authority[12] in relation to it sums transferred to it by the billing authority[13];

(c) may direct a billing authority that is a lower-tier authority in relation to the levying authority to refund the sums collected by it in respect of the business rate supplement but not transferred to the levying authority[14];

(d) may direct a functional body[15] to transfer to the Greater London Authority[16] sums received by the body in respect of the business rate supplement but not used by it[17]; and

(e) may take such other steps as the appropriate national authority thinks appropriate[18].

The appropriate national authority may, in connection with the exercise or proposed exercise of such power under these provisions, require the levying authority[19], a billing authority that is a lower-tier authority in relation to it[20], or a functional body[21], to provide such information relating to a business rate supplement as the appropriate national authority may specify[22].

A levying authority, a billing authority or a functional body must comply with any such direction given to it, or requirement imposed on it[23].

1 As to the meaning of 'appropriate national authority' see PARA 341 note 2.
2 As to the meaning of 'levying authority' see PARA 326 note 1.
3 As to business rate supplements see PARA 326.
4 Business Rate Supplements Act 2009 s 24(1). At the date at which this volume states the law, the Business Rate Supplements Act 2009 is in force in relation to England only (see the Business Rate Supplements Act 2009 (Commencement No 1) (England) Order 2009, SI 2009/2202, art 2); and will be brought into force in relation to Wales on a day to be appointed under the Business Rate Supplements Act 2009 s 32(2). At the date at which this volume states the law no such day had been appointed. As to the meanings of 'England' and 'Wales' see PARA 2 note 16.
5 Business Rate Supplements Act 2009 s 24(2)(a). As to the meaning of 'final prospectus' see PARA 329.
6 Ie for the purposes of the Business Rate Supplements Act 2009 s 10(2)(d): see PARA 331.
7 Business Rate Supplements Act 2009 s 24(2)(b).
8 Business Rate Supplements Act 2009 s 24(2)(c). As to consultation on the imposition of a business rate supplement see PARA 329. As to consultation on the variation of a business rate supplement see PARA 331.
9 Business Rate Supplements Act 2009 s 24(2)(d). As to ballots see PARA 330. As to variations see PARA 331.
10 Business Rate Supplements Act 2009 s 24(3)(a).
11 As to the meaning of 'billing authority' see PARA 53 (definition applied by the Business Rate Supplements Act 2009 s 30(2)).
12 As to the meaning of 'lower-tier authority' see PARA 327 note 2.
13 Business Rate Supplements Act 2009 s 24(3)(b).
14 Business Rate Supplements Act 2009 s 24(3)(c). Where the appropriate national authority gives a direction to a billing authority which is not a levying authority, the appropriate national authority may direct the levying authority to meet the expenses incurred by the billing authority in complying with the direction: s 24(4).
15 As to the meaning of 'functional body' see PARA 327 note 13.
16 As to the Greater London Authority see LONDON GOVERNMENT vol 71 (2013) PARA 67 et seq.
17 Business Rate Supplements Act 2009 s 24(3)(d).
18 Business Rate Supplements Act 2009 s 24(3)(e).
19 Business Rate Supplements Act 2009 s 24(5)(a).
20 Business Rate Supplements Act 2009 s 24(5)(b).
21 Business Rate Supplements Act 2009 s 24(5)(c).
22 Business Rate Supplements Act 2009 s 24(5).

23 Business Rate Supplements Act 2009 s 24(6). Section 21(3) (power of billing authority to seek to collect or recover sums in respect of the business rate supplement in so far as the sums became payable to it before the imposition of the business rate supplement came to an end: see PARA 338) does not apply where the imposition of a business rate supplement comes to an end as a result of s 24: s 24(7).

343. Power to make consequential provision.

The Secretary of State[1] or the Welsh Ministers[2] may by regulations[3] make supplementary, incidental or consequential provision:

(1) for the general purposes, or any particular purpose, of the Business Rate Supplements Act 2009[4]; or

(2) in consequence of, or for giving full effect to, a provision made by or under the Act[5].

The regulations may, in particular:

(a) amend or repeal, or apply with modifications, a provision of an Act (including the Business Rate Supplements Act 2009 and any Act passed before, or in the same session as, that Act)[6];

(b) amend or revoke, or apply with modifications, a provision of subordinate legislation[7] made before the passing of the Business Rate Supplements Act 2009[8].

1 As to the Secretary of State see PARA 4 note 18.

2 The power conferred by the Business Rate Supplements Act 2009 s 28 is also exercisable by the Welsh Ministers in so far as it is exercisable in relation to matters with respect to which functions are exercisable by the Welsh Ministers: s 28(3). As to functions exercisable by the Welsh Ministers see PARAS 341, 342. As to the Welsh Ministers see PARA 4 note 18.

At the date at which this volume states the law, the Business Rate Supplements Act 2009 is in force in relation to England only (see the Business Rate Supplements Act 2009 (Commencement No 1) (England) Order 2009, SI 2009/2202, art 2); and will be brought into force in relation to Wales on a day to be appointed under the Business Rate Supplements Act 2009 s 32(2). At the date at which this volume states the law no such day had been appointed. As to the meanings of 'England' and 'Wales' see PARA 2 note 16.

3 At the date at which this volume states the law, no such regulations had been made.

4 Business Rate Supplements Act 2009 s 28(1)(a).

5 Business Rate Supplements Act 2009 s 28(1)(b).

6 Business Rate Supplements Act 2009 s 28(2)(a). The amendments or modifications that may be made by virtue of s 28(2) are in addition to those made by or by virtue of any other provision of the Business Rate Supplements Act 2009: s 28(4). The Business Rate Supplements Act 2009 was passed, ie received Royal Assent, on 2 July 2009.

7 'Subordinate legislation' has the same meaning as in the Interpretation Act 1978 (see PARA 111 note 1): Business Rate Supplements Act 2009 s 28(5).

8 Business Rate Supplements Act 2009 s 28(2)(b). See also note 6.

5. COUNCIL TAX

(1) In General

344. Legislative developments leading to the council tax.

Until 1 April 1990, local authorities were authorised to raise money from the public by virtue of the general rate[1], whereby the occupier or owner of a hereditament was liable for a charge based upon the value of the hereditament[2].

With effect from 1 April 1990, rating was abolished in relation to domestic property, and a community charge was introduced which was based on the chargepayer rather than the value of the hereditament[3]. The new charge was payable by every person over 18 years of age except those expressly excluded[4].

With effect from 1 April 1993, the community charge was abolished[5] and replaced with the council tax[6]. The law governing council tax is derived from statute and delegated legislation, the principal Act governing the making and levying of council tax being the Local Government Finance Act 1992, which introduced a new system of taxation of residential and domestic hereditaments on the model of the non-domestic rating system[7]. The new system imposes liability for council tax[8], and also empowers local authorities to set and levy council tax[9].

1 See the General Rate Act 1967 (repealed with savings). As to the general historical background to the modern law of rating and council tax see PARA 50.

2 This system of rating survives but only in so far as it applies to non-domestic hereditaments: see the Local Government Finance Act 1988 Pt III (ss 41–67); and PARA 51 et seq.

3 See the Local Government Finance Act 1988 Pt I (ss 1–31), Pt II (ss 32–40) (all repealed). The capitation basis of this system of taxation gave rise to the community charge's soubriquet: 'poll tax'.

4 See the Local Government Finance Act 1988 s 2, Sch 1 (both repealed). Appeals in relation to the contents of the register were made to a valuation and community charge tribunal: see ss 23, 24 (both repealed).

5 See the Local Government Finance Act 1992 ss 100, 117, Sch 13, Sch 14; and as to saving provisions enabling the collection of outstanding amounts of community charge see s 118.

6 As to the council tax see PARA 345 et seq.

7 As to the citation, commencement and extent of the Local Government Finance Act 1992 see s 119. Nothing in any private or local Act (whenever passed) in any way affects the operation of the 1992 Act or of anything done under it: s 116(2).

8 See PARA 348 et seq.

9 See PARA 346.

345. The Secretary of State and the Welsh Ministers.

The council tax legislation confers the functions of central government in relation to the council tax system upon the 'Secretary of State' without reference to a particular department or ministry[1], but in practice the Secretary of State for Housing, Communities and Local Government has responsibility for council tax[2]. Many statutory functions vested in a Secretary of State or a Minister of the Crown are transferred so as to be exercisable in relation to Wales[3] by the Welsh Ministers[4].

Any power of the Secretary of State, the Minister for the Cabinet Office[5], the Treasury[6] or the Welsh Ministers[7] under the Local Government Finance Act 1992 to make orders or regulations[8] may be so exercised as to make different provision for different cases or descriptions of case, including different provision for different areas or for different authorities[9]. Any such power to make orders or regulations includes power to make incidental, consequential, transitional or supplementary provision[10]. Any power of the Secretary of State, the Minister for the Cabinet Office, the Treasury or the Welsh Ministers to make orders or regulations is exercisable by statutory instrument[11].

The Secretary of State or, as appropriate, the Welsh Ministers may designate or nominate an authority if the amount calculated by the authority as its annual budgetary requirement is excessive or represents an excessive increase over the preceding financial year[12].

The appropriate national authority[13] may at any time by order make such supplementary, incidental, consequential or transitional provision as appears to it to be necessary or expedient for the general purposes or any particular purposes of the Local Government Finance Act 1992 or in consequence of any of its provisions or for giving full effect to it[14]. Any such provision is in addition and without prejudice to any other provision of the Local Government Finance Act 1992[15]; and no other provision of the Act is to be construed as prejudicing the generality of these powers[16].

The Secretary of State and the Welsh Ministers may issue Practice Notes in relation to the council tax system[17].

In circumstances where:

(1) the appropriate national authority serves a notice on a relevant authority[18] or relevant officer[19] requiring it or him to supply to the appropriate national authority information[20] specified in the notice[21];

(2) the information is required by the appropriate national authority for the purpose of deciding whether to exercise its powers (and how to perform its functions) under the Local Government Finance Act 1992[22] or under the Greater London Authority Act 1999[23]; and

(3) the information is not personal information[24],

the authority or officer must supply the information required, and must do so in such form and manner and at such time as the appropriate national authority specifies in the notice[25]. If an authority or officer fails so to comply, the appropriate national authority may assume the information required to be such as it sees fit; and in such a case the appropriate national authority may decide in accordance with the assumption whether to exercise those powers (and how to perform those functions)[26]. In so deciding whether to exercise its powers (and how to perform its functions) the appropriate national authority may also take into account any other information available to it, whatever its source and whether or not obtained under a provision contained in or made under the Local Government Finance Act 1992[27] or any other enactment[28].

1 As to the Secretary of State see PARA 4 note 18.

2 As to the Secretary of State in relation to non-domestic rating see PARA 51.

3 As to the meaning of 'Wales' see PARA 2 note 16.

4 As to the Welsh Ministers and the general legislative competence of the Welsh Assembly see PARA 4 note 18. Where functions have been transferred this is referred to in the paragraphs concerned.

5 As to the Cabinet Office see CONSTITUTIONAL LAW vol 20 (2014) PARAS 234–236.

6 As to the meaning of 'the Treasury' see PARA 30 note 15.

7 The Local Government Finance Act 1992 s 113 refers to the National Assembly for Wales. The functions of the National Assembly for Wales are now vested in the Welsh Ministers: see the Government of Wales Act 2006 s 162(1), Sch 11 para 30.

8 Ie other than the power to make orders under the Local Government Finance Act 1992 s 52X(6): see PARA 21.

9 Local Government Finance Act 1992 s 113(1) (amended by the Local Government Act 1999 s 30, Sch 1 Pt II paras 2, 9(a); the Local Government Act 2003 s 127(1), Sch 7 paras 40, 52(1), (2); and the Localism Act 2011 s 80(1), (4); and by SI 2013/2597 and SI 2016/997).

10 See the Local Government Finance Act 1992 s 113(2) (amended by the Local Government Act 2003 Sch 7 paras 40, 52(1)–(3); and the Localism Act 2011 s 80(1), (4), (5); and by SI 2013/2597 and SI 2016/997).

11 See the Local Government Finance Act 1992 s 113(3), (4) (s 113(3) amended by SI 2013/2597 and SI 2016/997; the Local Government Finance Act 1992 s 113(4) added by the Local Government Act 2003 Sch 7 paras 40, 52(1), (5); and amended by the Localism Act 2011 s 80(1), (6)). Except in the case of regulations under the Local Government Finance Act 1992 s 14A, 14B, 14C or 52ZQ, or orders under s 5(4), 11(3), 22B(1A), 52F(4), 52H(2), 52Q(2), 52S(2), 52X(6), 74(3), 79(3) or 119(2) or Sch 12 para 1, such orders or regulations made by the Secretary of State, the Minister for the Cabinet Office, the Treasury are subject to annulment in pursuance of a resolution of either House of Parliament: s 113(3) (amended by the Local Government Act 1999 Sch 1, Pt II paras 2, 9(b); the Council Tax (New Valuation Lists for England) Act 2006 s 1(6); the Localism Act 2011 s 72(2), Sch 6 paras 1, 32; and the Local Government Finance Act 2012 s 14(1), (4)).

12 See the Local Government Finance Act 1992 Pt I Ch IVA (ss 52A–52Y); and PARAS 21–22.

13 Ie the Secretary of State or, in relation to Wales, the Welsh Ministers. The functions of the Secretary of State under the Local Government Finance Act 1992 s 68 (see the text to notes 17–27), s 114 so far as exercisable in relation to Wales, were transferred to the National Assembly for Wales (see the National Assembly for Wales (Transfer of Functions) Order 1999, SI 1999/672, art 2, Sch 1) and are now vested in the Welsh Ministers (see the Government of Wales Act 2006 s 162(1), Sch 11 para 30).

14 Local Government Finance Act 1992 s 114(1). An order under s 114 may in particular make provision for amending, repealing or revoking (with or without savings) any provision of an Act passed before or in the same session as the Local Government Finance Act 1992, or of an instrument made under an Act before the passing of the Local Government Finance Act 1992, and for making savings or additional savings from the effect of any amendment or repeal made by the Local Government Finance Act 1992: s 114(2). For these purposes, 'Act' includes a private or local Act: see s 114(5).

15 See the Local Government Finance Act 1992 s 114(3).

16 See the Local Government Finance Act 1992 s 114(4).

17 There is no express statutory authority for this practice.

18 'Relevant authority' means a billing authority or a precepting authority or a functional body within the meaning of the Greater London Authority Act 1999 (see LONDON GOVERNMENT vol 71 (2013) PARA 148): Local Government Finance Act 1992 s 68(5) (definition amended by the Greater London Authority Act 1999 s 109(3), (6)). As to the meaning of 'precepting authority' see PARA 23 note 1. As to the meaning of 'billing authority' see PARA 346.

19 'Relevant officer' means a proper officer within the meaning of the Local Government Act 1972 (see LOCAL GOVERNMENT vol 69 (2018) PARA 477) of a relevant authority: Local Government Finance Act 1992 s 68(5).

20 'Information' includes accounts, estimates and returns: Local Government Finance Act 1992 s 116(1).

21 Local Government Finance Act 1992 s 68(1)(a).

22 Ie under the Local Government Finance Act 1992 Pt I (ss 1–69).

23 Local Government Finance Act 1992 s 68(1)(b) (amended by the Greater London Authority Act 1999 s 109(3), (4)). The relevant provisions of the Greater London Authority Act 1999 for these purposes are those of Pt III (ss 81–140) (financial provisions: see LONDON GOVERNMENT vol 71 (2013) PARA 150 et seq): see the Local Government Finance Act 1992 s 68(1)(b) (as so amended). For provision as to council tax in Greater London generally see the Greater London Authority Act 1999 ss 81–99; and LONDON GOVERNMENT vol 71 (2013) PARA 150.

24 Local Government Finance Act 1992 s 68(1)(c). 'Personal information':

(1) is information which relates to an individual (living or dead) who can be identified from that information or from that and other information supplied to any person by the authority or officer concerned (s 68(6)(a)); and

(2) includes any expression of opinion about the individual and any indication of the intentions of any person in respect of the individual (s 68(6)(b)).

As to the meaning of 'person' see PARA 11 note 13.

25 Local Government Finance Act 1992 s 68(2).

26 Local Government Finance Act 1992 s 68(3) (amended by the Greater London Authority Act 1999 s 109(3), (5)).

27 Ie under the Local Government Finance Act 1992 Pt I (ss 1–69).

28 Local Government Finance Act 1992 s 68(4).

346. Billing authorities.

In relation to England[1], a district council[2] or London borough council[3], the Common Council of the City of London[4] or the Council of the Isles of Scilly[5] and, in relation to Wales[6], a county council or county borough council[7] is a 'billing authority'[8] charged with the levying and collection of the council tax[9] which is payable in respect of dwellings situated in its area[10].

Certain functions of an authority in relation to council tax must be discharged only by the authority[11]; but subject thereto, various functions of a billing authority in relation to the administration and enforcement of council tax may, to the prescribed extent, be exercised by, or by the employees of, such person[12] as may be authorised to exercise them by the authority whose functions they are[13].

Where an order making structural or boundary change in relation to local government in England[14] transfers the functions of district councils in relation to any area to a council for a county consisting of that area, the county council is, for any financial year[15] beginning at the same time as or after that transfer, a billing authority for the purposes of the Local Government Finance Act 1992[16] in relation to the area[17].

1 As to the meaning of 'England' see PARA 2 note 16.

2 As to local government areas and authorities in England see LOCAL GOVERNMENT vol 69 (2018) PARA 36 et seq.

3 As to the London boroughs and their councils see LONDON GOVERNMENT vol 71 (2013) PARAS 15, 20–22, 55 et seq.

4 For these purposes, the Inner Temple and the Middle Temple are to be taken to fall within the area of the Common Council of the City of London: see the Local Government Finance Act 1992 s 69(3). As to the Common Council of the City of London see LONDON GOVERNMENT vol 71 (2013) PARAS 34–38. As to the Temples see LONDON GOVERNMENT vol 71 (2013) PARA 17.

5 Local Government Finance Act 1992 s 1(2)(a) (s 1(2) substituted by the Local Government (Wales) Act 1994 s 35(5)). As to the Council of the Isles of Scilly see LOCAL GOVERNMENT vol 69 (2018) PARA 50.

6 As to the meaning of 'Wales' see PARA 2 note 16.

7 Local Government Finance Act 1992 s 1(2)(b) (as substituted: see note 5). As to local government areas and authorities in Wales see LOCAL GOVERNMENT vol 69 (2018) PARA 51 et seq.

8 Local Government Finance Act 1992 s 1(2) (as substituted: see note 5).

9 As to the administration of council tax see PARA 437 et seq.

10 See the Local Government Finance Act 1992 s 1(1); and PARA 348 et seq. As to billing authorities for the purposes of non-domestic rating see PARA 53.

11 See the Local Government Finance Act 1992 s 67(1); and PARA 11.

12 As to the meaning of 'person' see PARA 11 note 13.

13 See the Local Authorities (Contracting Out of Tax Billing, Collection and Enforcement Functions) Order 1996, SI 1996/1880, art 3 (amended, in relation to England, by SI 2013/502; and, in relation to Wales, by SI 2013/695).

14 Ie an order under the Local Government and Public Involvement in Health Act 2007 Pt 1 Ch 1 (ss 1–23): see LOCAL GOVERNMENT vol 69 (2018) PARA 95 et seq.

15 For these purposes, 'financial year' means 12 months beginning with 1 April: Local Government and Public Involvement in Health Act 2007 s 19(3). As to the meaning of 'month' see PARA 11 note 1.

16 Ie for the purposes of the Local Government Finance Act 1992 Pt I (ss 1–69).

17 See the Local Government and Public Involvement in Health Act 2007 s 19(1)(a); and the Local Government (Structural Changes) (Finance) Regulations 2008, SI 2008/3022, reg 7(1), (2)(a). The Local Government and Public Involvement in Health Act 2007 s 19 does not limit any power to make provision by order under Pt 1 Ch 1 (ss 1–23) or any power to make incidental, consequential, transitional or supplementary provision in connection with the provisions of any such order: s 19(2). As to further provision made in relation to billing authorities where such an order is made see the Local Government (Structural Changes) (Finance) Regulations 2008, SI 2008/3022, regs

8–11. As to the power to equalise the council tax payable in the areas subject to such an order see regs 12–22 (regs 12, 15, 16 amended, reg 15A added, by SI 2012/20; the Local Government (Structural Changes) (Finance) Regulations 2008, SI 2008/3022, reg 12 further amended by SI 2012/2914).

347. Listing officers.

The Commissioners for Her Majesty's Revenue and Customs[1] must appoint a listing officer for each billing authority[2].

The functions of the Commissioners in relation to council tax include the duty to value dwellings in England and Wales[3] and to furnish listing officers with certain information[4].

A listing officer or any other officer of the Commissioners appointed to carry out their functions may enter on, survey and value a hereditament[5]; and listing officers and the Commissioners each have the power to request certain information relating to property if they reasonably believe it will assist them in carrying out any of their functions[6].

A person may require a listing officer to provide access to such information as will enable him to establish what is the state of a list, or has been its state at any time since it came into force[7].

1 As to the Commissioners for Her Majesty's Revenue and Customs see INCOME TAXATION vol 58 (2014) PARAS 33–34.

2 Local Government Finance Act 1992 s 20(1) (amended by virtue of the Commissioners for Revenue and Customs Act 2005 s 50). As to the meaning of 'billing authority' see PARA 346. In the Local Government Finance Act 1992 Pt I (ss 1–69), 'listing officer' must be construed in accordance with s 20: s 69(1). Any reference in Pt I Ch II (ss 20–29) to a listing officer's or the Commissioners' functions is a reference to the functions imposed or conferred on him or them by or under that chapter: s 20(3).

The remuneration of, and any expenses incurred by, listing officers in carrying out their functions (including the remuneration and expenses of persons, whether or not in the service of the Crown, to assist them) must be paid out of money provided by Parliament: Local Government Finance Act 1992 s 20(2).

3 As to the meanings of 'England' and 'Wales' see PARA 2 note 16.

4 See the Local Government Finance Act 1992 s 21; and PARA 408.

5 See the Local Government Finance Act 1992 ss 25A, 26; and PARAS 413, 414.

6 See the Local Government Finance Act 1992 s 27; and PARA 415.

7 See the Local Government Finance Act 1992 s 28; and PARA 416.

(2) Liability to Council Tax

(i) In General

348. Council tax in respect of dwellings.

As regards the financial year[1], each billing authority[2] must, in accordance with the council tax provisions which have effect in relation to England and Wales[3], levy and collect a tax ('council tax'), which is payable in respect of dwellings[4] situated in its area[5].

Liability to pay council tax is determined on a daily basis[6]. For the purposes of determining for any day:

(1) whether any property is a chargeable dwelling[7];

(2) which valuation band[8] is shown in the billing authority's valuation list[9] as applicable to any chargeable dwelling[10];

(3) the person liable to pay council tax in respect of any such dwelling[11]; or

(4) whether any amount of council tax is subject to a discount and (if so) the amount of the discount[12],

it is to be assumed that any state of affairs subsisting at the end of the day had subsisted throughout the day[13].

1 Ie the financial year beginning in 1993 and subsequent financial years: see the Local Government Finance Act 1992 s 1(1). As to the meaning of 'financial year' see PARA 11 note 1.
2 As to the meaning of 'billing authority' see PARA 346.
3 Ie in accordance with the Local Government Finance Act 1992 Pt I (ss 1–69).
4 As to the meaning of 'dwelling' see PARA 349.
5 Local Government Finance Act 1992 s 1(1). For the purposes of Pt I (ss 1–69), the Secretary of State or, in relation to Wales, the Welsh Ministers may make regulations containing rules for treating a dwelling as situated in a billing authority's area if part only of the dwelling falls within the area: s 1(3). The power to make regulations under s 1(3), so far as exercisable in relation to Wales, was transferred to the National Assembly for Wales except as regards a dwelling part only of which falls within the area of a Welsh billing authority (see the National Assembly for Wales (Transfer of Functions) Order 1999, SI 1999/672, art 2, Sch 1) and is now vested in the Welsh Ministers (see the Government of Wales Act 2006 s 162(1), Sch 11 para 30). The function of the Secretary of State under the Local Government Finance Act 1992 s 1(3) is, as regards a dwelling part only of which falls within the area of a Welsh billing authority, exercisable only with the agreement of the Welsh Ministers: see the National Assembly for Wales (Transfer of Functions) Order 1999, SI 1999/672, art 5, Sch 2. As to the Secretary of State and the Welsh Ministers see PARA 4 note 18. As to the meaning of 'Wales' see PARA 2 note 16.
   As to the regulations made see the Council Tax (Situation and Valuation of Dwellings) Regulations 1992, SI 1992/550, Pt II (regs 2–5) (amended by SI 1994/1747).
6 Local Government Finance Act 1992 s 2(1).
7 Local Government Finance Act 1992 s 2(2)(a). As to the meaning of 'chargeable dwelling' see PARA 350.
8 As to valuation bands see PARA 361.
9 As to valuation lists see PARA 408 et seq.
10 Local Government Finance Act 1992 s 2(2)(b).
11 Local Government Finance Act 1992 s 2(2)(c). As to the persons liable see PARA 354 et seq.
12 Local Government Finance Act 1992 s 2(2)(d). As to discounts see PARA 362 et seq.
13 Local Government Finance Act 1992 s 2(2).

(ii) Chargeable Dwellings

349. Meaning of 'dwelling'.

For the purposes of the council tax provisions which have effect in relation to England and Wales[1], provision is made for determining what is a dwelling[2]. A 'dwelling' is any property which[3]:

(1) would have been a hereditament for the purposes of the General Rate Act 1967 (now repealed)[4] if that Act remained in force[5]; and
(2) is not for the time being shown or required to be shown in a local or a central non-domestic rating list in force at that time[6]; and
(3) is not for the time being exempt[7] from local non-domestic rating[8].

In applying heads (2) and (3), no account is to be taken of any rules as to Crown exemption[9].

A hereditament which:

(a) is a composite hereditament for the purposes of the Local Government Finance Act 1988[10]; and
(b) would still be such a hereditament if certain provisions relating to the definition of domestic property for those purposes[11] were omitted[12],

is also a dwelling for council tax purposes[13].

None of the following property, namely:

(i) a yard, garden, outhouse or other appurtenance belonging to or enjoyed with property used wholly for the purposes of living accommodation[14]; or
(ii) a private garage which either has a floor area of not more than 25 square metres or is used wholly or mainly for the accommodation of a private motor vehicle[15]; or
(iii) private storage premises used wholly or mainly for the storage of articles of domestic use[16],

is a dwelling except in so far as it forms part of a larger property which is itself a dwelling by virtue of heads (1) to (3) above[17].

The appropriate national authority[18] may by order provide that in such cases as may be prescribed by or determined under the order:

(A) anything which would (apart from the order) be one dwelling is to be treated as two or more dwellings[19]; and
(B) anything which would (apart from the order) be two or more dwellings is to be treated as one dwelling[20].

The appropriate national authority may by order amend any definition of 'dwelling' which is for the time being effective for council tax purposes[21].

1 Ie for the purposes of the Local Government Finance Act 1992 Pt I (ss 1–69).
2 See the Local Government Finance Act 1992 s 3(1).
3 Local Government Finance Act 1992 s 3(2). This provision is expressed to be subject to s 3(3)–(6) (see the text to notes 10–21): see s 3(2). There is no need to imply that s 3(2) only applies to houses as the provision provides a satisfactory and working definition of 'dwelling' without that implication being made: see *Lewis v Christchurch Borough Council* [1996] RA 229 (beach huts held to be dwellings under the Local Government Finance Act 1992 s 3(2)).
4 Ie by virtue of the definition of 'hereditament' in the General Rate Act 1967 s 115(1) (repealed): see the Local Government Finance Act 1992 s 3(2)(a). For the purposes of the General Rate Act 1967, 'hereditament' was defined as property which is or may become liable to a rate, being a unit of such property which is, or would fall to be, shown as a separate item in the valuation list: see s 115(1) (repealed). As to rateable hereditaments under the Local Government Finance Act 1988 (the Act which repealed and replaced the General Rate Act 1967 and uses the same definition of 'hereditament' for its own purposes) see PARA 80 et seq.
5 Local Government Finance Act 1992 s 3(2)(a). See *Wilson v Jo Coll (Listing Officer)* [2011] EWHC 2824 (Admin), [2012] PTSR 1313, [2011] All ER (D) 114 (Oct) (the tribunal had confused the issue of the valuation of the hereditament and the issue of whether a hereditament existed or not; the question whether a hereditament existed or not is a question of fact not law).
6 Local Government Finance Act 1992 s 3(2)(b). See *Stubbs v Hartnell (Listing Officer)* [1997] EWCA Civ 1817, [2002] RVR 90 (appellant's plot of land and mooring, together with his houseboat moored to it, was properly regarded as a hereditament for the purposes of the charge to council tax). As to local non-domestic rating lists see PARA 191 et seq; and as to central non-domestic rating lists see PARA 196 et seq.
7 Ie for the purposes of the Local Government Finance Act 1988 Pt III (ss 41–67). As to exemptions from non-domestic rating see PARA 110 et seq.
8 Local Government Finance Act 1992 s 3(2)(c).
9 Local Government Finance Act 1992 s 3(2). As to Crown exemption from non-domestic rating see PARA 111; and as to Crown exemption from council tax see PARA 359.
10 Ie for the purposes of the Local Government Finance Act 1988 Pt III (ss 41–67) (see PARA 106): see the Local Government Finance Act 1992 s 3(3)(a).
11 Ie the provisions contained in the Local Government Finance Act 1988 s 66(1)(b)–(d): see PARA 190.
12 Local Government Finance Act 1992 s 3(3)(b).
13 See the Local Government Finance Act 1992 s 3(3). This provision is expressed to be subject to s 3(6) (see the text to note 21): see s 3(3). A property is a composite hereditament for the purposes of council tax if at least one room is used exclusively for the purposes of a dwelling: see *Williams v Bristol District Valuation Officer* [1995] RA 189 (maisonette above a shop is a dwelling even if access is only through the shop). Similarly, a house may be a composite hereditament if one or more rooms are used mainly for the conduct of a business: see *Fotheringham v Wood (Valuation*

Officer) [1995] RA 315, Lands Tribunal (rates liability arose where one room used mainly for business, another partly so); cf *Tully v Jorgensen (Valuation Officer)* [2003] RA 233, Lands Tribunal (rates liability did not arise in this case where a room was used to carry out employment-related office work because the use remained for the purposes of ordinary domestic living accommodation); and see PARA 190 (definition of 'domestic property' for non-domestic rating purposes).

Where part of a property is wholly or mainly used in the course of business for short-stay accommodation, that part may fall to be rated as a non-domestic hereditament: see PARA 190. See also *Skott v Pepperell (Valuation Officer)* [1995] RA 243, Lands Tribunal.

14 Local Government Finance Act 1992 s 3(4)(a).

15 Local Government Finance Act 1992 s 3(4)(b).

16 Local Government Finance Act 1992 s 3(4)(c).

17 Local Government Finance Act 1992 s 3(4). This provision is expressed to be subject to s 3(6) (see the text to note 21): see s 3(4). Subject to s 3(6) (see the text to note 21), domestic property falling within the Local Government Finance Act 1988 s 66(1A) (see PARA 190) is not a dwelling except in so far as it forms part of a larger property which is itself a dwelling by virtue of the Local Government Finance Act 1992 s 3(2): s 3(4A) (added by SI 2013/468).

18 Ie the Secretary of State or, in relation to Wales, the Welsh Ministers. The functions of the Secretary of State under the Local Government Finance Act 1992 s 3, so far as exercisable in relation to Wales, were transferred to the National Assembly for Wales (see the National Assembly for Wales (Transfer of Functions) Order 1999, SI 1999/672, art 2, Sch 1) and are now vested in the Welsh Ministers (see the Government of Wales Act 2006 s 162(1), Sch 11 para 30). As to the Secretary of State and the Welsh Ministers see PARA 4 note 18. As to the meaning of 'Wales' see PARA 2 note 16.

19 Local Government Finance Act 1992 s 3(5)(a). Accordingly, where a single property contains more than one self-contained unit, for the purposes of the Local Government Finance Act 1992 Pt I (ss 1–69), the property is to be treated as comprising as many dwellings as there are such units included in it and each such unit is to be treated as a dwelling: Council Tax (Chargeable Dwellings) Order 1992, SI 1992/549, art 3 (amended in relation to England by SI 2003/3121; and in relation to Wales by SI 2004/2921 and SI 2014/2653).

A care home is to be treated as comprising the number of dwellings found by adding one to the number of self-contained units occupied by (or, if currently unoccupied, provided for the purpose of accommodating) the person registered in respect of it in accordance with the Care Standards Act 2000 Pt II (ss 11–42) (see HEALTH SERVICES vol 54A (2017) PARA 633 et seq) in relation to Wales or the Health and Social Care Act 2008 Pt 1 (ss 1–97), in relation to England, and each such unit is to be treated as a dwelling: Council Tax (Chargeable Dwellings) Order 1992, SI 1992/549, art 3A (added in relation to England by SI 2003/3121; and in relation to Wales by SI 2004/2921; and amended by SI 2012/1915). For these purposes, 'care home' means a care home within the meaning of the Care Standards Act 2000 (see HEALTH SERVICES vol 54 (2009) PARA 748 et seq), in respect of which a person is registered in accordance with Pt II in relation to Wales or the Health and Social Care Act 2008 Pt 1, in relation to England: Council Tax (Chargeable Dwellings) Order 1992, SI 1992/549, art 2 (definition added in relation to England by SI 2003/3121; and in relation to Wales by SI 2004/2921; and amended by SI 2012/1915). 'Self-contained unit' means a building or a part of a building which has been constructed or adapted for use as separate living accommodation: Council Tax (Chargeable Dwellings) Order 1992, SI 1992/549, art 2 (definition substituted by SI 1997/656). 'Single property' means property which would, apart from the Council Tax (Chargeable Dwellings) Order 1992, SI 1992/549, be one dwelling within the meaning of the Local Government Finance Act 1992 s 3: Council Tax (Chargeable Dwellings) Order 1992, SI 1992/549, art 2.

A flat and a house within a single property are treated as two self-contained units for the purposes of the Council Tax (Chargeable Dwellings) Order 1992, SI 1992/549, where both have the usual features of separate accommodation, such as bathing and cooking facilities, and are not affected by the fact that one is accessed through the other: *McColl v Sabacchi (Listing Officer)* [2001] EWHC Admin 712, [2001] RA 342, [2001] All ER (D) 04 (Sep). More generally, there have been various responses to the question of how to determine whether part of a building is a self-contained unit for the purposes of the Council Tax (Chargeable Dwellings) Order 1992, SI 1992/549, art 3. In *Williams (Listing Officer) v Royal National Institute for the Blind* [2003] EWHC 1308 (Admin), [2003] RA 158, [2003] All ER (D) 249 (May), it was held that the question as to whether a building or part of a building has been constructed or adapted for use as separate living accommodation, is to be answered in the light of all the objective circumstances, including the use for which the rest of the building had been built, and that case considered factors identified in previous judgments, including those factors which should not be taken into account at all, such as the use to which a part of a building is actually put (*Batty v Burfoot* [1995] RA 299, [1995] 2 EGLR 142; *Beaseley v National Council of the YMCA* [2000] RA 429) or the impracticability of the sale of part of a building (*Batty v Burfoot* above) or the subjective intention of the builder or developer (*Coleman (Listing Officer) v Rotzstein* [2003] EWHC 1057 (Admin), [2003] RA 152, [2003] All ER (D) 371 (Apr)) and those factors which should not be treated as of decisive effect, such as the terms of the grant of planning permission (*Batty v Burfoot* above) or the absence of a bath or shower within the unit (*Clement (Listing Officer) v Bryant* [2003] EWHC 422 (Admin), [2003] RA 133, [2003] All ER (D) 216 (Feb)). The case of *Jorgensen (Listing Officer) v Gomperts* [2006] EWHC 1885 (Admin), [2006] RA 300, [2006] All ER (D) 01 (Jul) found that, having regard to case law, the correct test to be applied was an objective 'bricks and mortar' test which looked at the reality of what had been constructed and/or how it had been adapted; the intention and use, whether actual or prospective, are irrelevant to the determination. See also *Daniels (Listing Officer) v Aristides* [2006] EWHC 3052 (Admin), [2006] RVR 379 (house and a studio in the garden of the house had to be listed separately for council tax purposes; intention of developer and actual use both irrelevant). The primacy of the 'bricks and mortar', or more accurately the 'physical characteristics of the building', test was emphasised again in *Coll (Listing Officer) v Mooney* [2016] EWHC 485 (Admin), [2016] RA 125, [2016] All ER (D) 57 (Apr), where a building originally designed as single dwelling which had been subdivided was reinstated to a single dwelling but the listing officer maintained two entries in the valuation list, classing the lower ground floor as a self-contained unit. The High Court upheld the successful appeal to the tribunal, noting the relevant physical characteristics of the building and the absence of a kitchen and cooking facilities on the lower ground floor, and it was further held that, although the manner in which the building was being used by particular occupiers was not the legislative test, evidence of actual use might properly be considered, so the tribunal could have regard to the evidence that the house was in use as a single household whose sole kitchen facilities were on the ground floor and sole laundry facilities on the lower ground floor.

Planning conditions restricting or regulating use of the property are not necessarily relevant to the issue of actual self-containment of units, nor is it relevant to assess the degree of communal living or the fact that a part of the dwelling might be sold as a separate unit: see *Rodd v Ritchings* [1995] RA 299, 159 LG Rev 829.

As to exceptions from the general rule that each unit is a separate dwelling see PARAS 351–352.

20 Local Government Finance Act 1992 s 3(5)(b). Accordingly, where a multiple property:

(1) consists of a single self-contained unit, or such a unit together with or containing premises constructed or adapted for non-domestic purposes (Council Tax (Chargeable Dwellings) Order 1992, SI 1992/549, art 4(1)(a)); and

(2) is occupied as more than one unit of separate living accommodation (art 4(1)(b)),

the listing officer may, if he thinks fit, treat the property as one dwelling (art 4(1)). In so exercising his discretion, the listing officer must have regard to all the circumstances of the case, including the extent, if any, to which the parts of the property separately occupied have been structurally altered: art 4(2). For these purposes, 'multiple property' means property which would, apart from the Council Tax (Chargeable Dwellings) Order 1992, SI 1992/549, be two or more dwellings within the meaning of the Local Government Finance Act 1992 s 3: Council Tax (Chargeable Dwellings) Order 1992, SI 1992/549, art 2. As to listing officers see PARA 347.

In Wales, a refuge must be treated as a single dwelling: art 3B (added, in relation to Wales, by SI 2014/2653). 'Refuge' means a building in Wales which is operated by a person otherwise than for profit and is used wholly or mainly for the temporary accommodation of persons who have been subject to any incident or pattern of incidents of:

(a) controlling, coercive or threatening behaviour;

(b) physical violence;

(c) abuse of any other description (whether physical or mental in nature); or

(d) threats of any such violence or abuse,

from persons to whom they are or were married, are or were in a civil partnership or with whom they are or were co-habiting: Council Tax (Chargeable Dwellings) Order 1992, SI 1992/549, art 2 (definition added, in relation to Wales, by SI 2014/2653).

Where a property consisting of two or more flats is converted into a single property, a new dwelling is created for council tax purposes: see *R v East Sussex Valuation Tribunal, ex p Silverstone* [1996] RVR 203n.

21 See the Local Government Finance Act 1992 s 3(6). At the date at which this volume states the law no such order had been made.

350. Dwellings chargeable to council tax.

Council tax[1] is payable in respect of any dwelling[2] which is not an exempt dwelling[3]. 'Chargeable dwelling' means[4] any dwelling in respect of which council tax is payable[5].

1 As to council tax see PARA 348.
2 As to the meaning of 'dwelling' see PARA 349.
3 Local Government Finance Act 1992 s 4(1). As to the meaning of 'exempt dwelling' see PARA 351.
4 Ie for the purposes of the Local Government Finance Act 1992 Pt I Ch I (ss 1–19).
5 Local Government Finance Act 1992 s 4(2). A floating home without means of propulsion, although not constituting real property, may be a chargeable dwelling for council tax purposes: see *Nicholls v Wimbledon Valuation Office Agency* [1995] RVR 171.

351. Power to exempt dwellings.

An 'exempt dwelling' is[1] any dwelling[2] of a class prescribed by an order made by the appropriate national authority[3]. For these purposes, a class of dwellings may be prescribed by reference to such factors as the appropriate national authority sees fit[4]. In particular, a class of dwellings may be prescribed by reference to one or more of the following factors[5], namely:

(1) the physical characteristics of dwellings[6];
(2) the fact that dwellings are unoccupied or are occupied for prescribed purposes or are occupied or owned by persons[7] of prescribed descriptions[8].

1 Ie for the purposes of the Local Government Finance Act 1992 Pt I Ch I (ss 1–19).
2 As to the meaning of 'dwelling' see PARA 349.
3 Local Government Finance Act 1992 s 4(2). As to the order made see the Council Tax (Exempt Dwellings) Order 1992, SI 1992/558; and PARA 352. The specification of a class of exempt dwelling in an order of the appropriate national authority under the Local Government Finance Act 1992 s 4(2) may not be questioned except by an application for judicial review: see s 66(1), (2)(a). If, on an application for judicial review, the court decides to grant relief in respect of any of the matter, it must quash the determination: s 66(3) (amended by the Local Government Finance Act 2012 s 10(2), (3)(b), Sch 4 paras 3, 5(1), (3)). As to judicial review see JUDICIAL REVIEW vol 61 (2010) PARA 601 et seq.

The appropriate national authority means the Secretary of State or, in relation to Wales, the Welsh Ministers. The functions of the Secretary of State under the Local Government Finance Act 1992 s 4, so far as exercisable in relation to Wales, were transferred to the National Assembly for Wales (see the National Assembly for Wales (Transfer of Functions) Order 1999, SI 1999/672, art 2, Sch 1) and are now vested in the Welsh Ministers (see the Government of Wales Act 2006 s 162(1), Sch 11 para 30). As to the Secretary of State and the Welsh Ministers see PARA 4 note 18. As to the meaning of 'Wales' see PARA 2 note 16.
4 Local Government Finance Act 1992 s 4(3).
5 See the Local Government Finance Act 1992 s 4(4).
6 Local Government Finance Act 1992 s 4(4)(a).
7 As to the meaning of 'person' see PARA 11 note 13.
8 Local Government Finance Act 1992 s 4(4)(b).

352. Prescribed classes of exempt dwellings.

For the purposes of determining whether or not council tax is payable[1], a dwelling[2] is an exempt dwelling[3] on a particular day if on that day it falls within one of the following classes[4], namely:

(1) Class A: in relation to Wales, a dwelling which is vacant[5] and:
 (a) requires or is undergoing major repair work[6] to render it habitable[7]; or
 (b) is undergoing structural alteration[8]; or

(c) has undergone major repair work to render it habitable (if less than six months have elapsed since the date on which the work was substantially completed and the dwelling has continuously remained vacant since that date)[9]; or

(d) has undergone structural alteration (if less than six months have elapsed since the date on which the alteration was substantially completed and the dwelling has continuously remained vacant since that date)[10],

but which has not been such a dwelling for a continuous period of 12 months or more ending immediately before the day in question[11];

(1) Class B: in relation to England or Wales, a dwelling owned by a body established for charitable purposes only, which is unoccupied[12] and has been so for a period of less than six months and was last occupied in furtherance of the objects of the charity[13];

(2) Class C: in relation to Wales, a vacant dwelling[14] which has been such for a continuous period of less than six months ending immediately before the day in question[15];

(3) Class D: in relation to England or Wales, an unoccupied dwelling[16] which either:

(a) would be the sole or main residence of a person who is an owner or tenant[17] of the dwelling and is detained elsewhere[18], but for his detention[19]; or

(b) was previously his sole or main residence, if he has been a relevant absentee[20] for the whole period since it last ceased to be such[21];

(4) Class E: in relation to England or Wales, an unoccupied dwelling which was previously the sole or main residence of a person who is an owner or tenant of the dwelling[22], and who:

(a) has his sole or main residence elsewhere[23]; and

(b) has been a relevant absentee[24] for the whole of the period since the dwelling last ceased to be his sole or main residence[25];

(5) Class F: in relation to England or Wales, an unoccupied[26] dwelling which has been unoccupied since the date of death of a person (the 'deceased')[27] and in relation to which one of the following conditions is satisfied[28], namely:

(a) the deceased had, at the date of his death, a freehold interest in the dwelling, or a leasehold interest in the dwelling which was granted for a term of six months or more[29], and:

(b) no person is a qualifying person[30] in respect of the dwelling[31]; or

(c) a person is a qualifying person in respect of the dwelling acting in his capacity as executor or administrator, and no person is a qualifying person in any other capacity[32]; or

(d) the deceased was a tenant of the dwelling at the date of his death, and an executor or administrator acting in his capacity as such is liable for rent (or, as the case may be, a licence fee) for the day[33];

(6) Class G: in relation to Wales, an unoccupied dwelling the occupation of which is prohibited by law, or which is kept unoccupied by reason of action taken under powers conferred by or under any Act of Parliament, with a view to prohibiting its occupation or to acquiring it[34]; or, in relation to England, an unoccupied dwelling:

(a) the occupation of which is restricted by a condition which prevents occupancy[35], and is imposed by any planning permission granted or deemed to be granted under the Town and Country Planning Act 1990[36]; or

(b) the occupation of which is otherwise prohibited by law[37]; or

(c) which is kept unoccupied by reason of other action taken under powers conferred by or under any Act of Parliament, with a view to prohibiting its occupation or to acquiring it[38];

(7) Class H: in relation to England or Wales, an unoccupied dwelling which is held for the purpose of being available for occupation by a minister of any religious denomination as a residence from which to perform the duties of his office[39];

(8) Class I: in relation to England or Wales, an unoccupied dwelling which was previously the sole or main residence of a person who is an owner or tenant of the dwelling[40], and who:

(a) for the purpose of receiving personal care required by that person by reason of old age, disablement, illness, past or present alcohol or drug dependence or past or present mental disorder has his sole or main residence in another place[41]; and

(b) has been a relevant absentee[42] for the whole of the period since the dwelling last ceased to be his residence[43];

(9) Class J: in relation to England or Wales, an unoccupied dwelling which was previously the sole or main residence of a person who is an owner or tenant of the dwelling[44], and who:

(a) has his sole or main residence in another place for the purpose of providing (or better providing) personal care for a person who requires such care by reason of old age, disablement, illness, past or present alcohol or drug dependence or past or present mental disorder[45]; and

(b) has been a relevant absentee[46] for the whole of the period since the dwelling last ceased to be his residence[47];

(10) Class K: in relation to England or Wales, an unoccupied dwelling:

(a) which was last occupied as the sole or main residence of a qualifying person (the 'last occupier')[48]; and

(b) in relation to which every qualifying person is a student[49], and either:

(c) has been a student throughout the period since the last occupier ceased to occupy the dwelling as his sole or main residence[50]; or

(d) has become a student within six weeks of the day mentioned in head (11)(b)(i) above[51];

(11) Class L: in relation to England or Wales, an unoccupied dwelling where a mortgagee is in possession under the mortgage[52];

(12) Class M: in relation to England or Wales, a dwelling comprising a hall of residence provided predominantly for the accommodation of students which is either:

(a) owned or managed by an institution[53] or by a body established for charitable purposes only[54]; or

(b) the subject of an agreement allowing such an institution to nominate the majority of the persons who are to occupy the accommodation so provided[55];

(13) Class N: in relation to England or Wales, a dwelling which is either:

(a) occupied by one or more residents all of whom are relevant persons[56];
(b) occupied only by one or more relevant persons as term time accommodation[57];

(14) Class O: in relation to England or Wales, a dwelling of which the Secretary of State for Defence[58] is the owner, held for the purposes of armed forces accommodation (other than accommodation for visiting forces)[59];

(15) Class P: in relation to England or Wales, a dwelling in respect of which at least one person (who would be liable to pay council tax but for this provision) satisfies the condition[60] that he has a relevant association[61] with a body, contingent or detachment of the forces of a country to which any provision in the Visiting Forces Act 1952 applies on that day[62];

(16) Class Q: in relation to England or Wales, an unoccupied dwelling in relation to which a person is a qualifying person in his capacity as a trustee in bankruptcy[63];

(17) Class R: in relation to England or Wales, a dwelling consisting of a pitch or a mooring which is not occupied by a caravan or, as the case may be, a boat[64];

(18) Class S: in relation to England or Wales, a dwelling occupied only by a person or persons aged under 18[65];

(19) Class T: in relation to England or Wales, an unoccupied dwelling which:
(a) forms part of a single property[66] which includes another dwelling[67]; and
(b) may not be let separately from that other dwelling without a breach of planning control[68];

(20) Class U: in relation to England or Wales, a dwelling occupied only:
(a) by one or more severely mentally impaired[69] persons, where (but for these provisions) either such a person, or a relevant person[70], would be liable to pay the council tax[71]; or
(b) by one or more severely mentally impaired persons, together with one or more relevant persons[72];

(21) Class V: in relation to England or Wales, a dwelling in respect of which at least one person (who would be liable to pay council tax but for this class) satisfies the following conditions[73], namely:
(a) that he has certain privileges and immunities conferred or that he qualifies otherwise for relief[74]; and
(b) that there is no other dwelling in the United Kingdom which is the main residence of that person, or is the main residence within the United Kingdom of that person[75];

(22) Class W: in relation to England or Wales, a dwelling which forms part of a single property including at least one other dwelling and which is the sole or main residence of a dependent relative[76] of a person who is resident in that other dwelling (or, as the case may be, one of those other dwellings)[77].

1 Ie for the purposes of the Local Government Finance Act 1992 s 4: see PARAS 350–351.
2 As to the meaning of 'dwelling' see PARA 349.
3 As to the meaning of 'exempt dwelling' see PARA 351.
4 Council Tax (Exempt Dwellings) Order 1992, SI 1992/558, art 3.

5 In relation to Wales, for the purposes of the Council Tax (Exempt Dwellings) Order 1992, SI 1992/558, art 3 Class A and Class C (see head (3) in the text), a dwelling is vacant on any day if on the day:
   (1) in the case of a dwelling consisting of a pitch occupied by a caravan or a mooring occupied by a boat, the caravan or boat is unoccupied (art 2(2)(a)(i) (art 2(2) substituted by SI 1994/539; revoked, in relation to England, by SI 2012/2965)); and
   (2) in any other case, the dwelling is unoccupied and substantially unfurnished (Council Tax (Exempt Dwellings) Order 1992, art 2(2)(a)(ii) (as so substituted)).

In considering whether a dwelling has been vacant for any period, any one period, not exceeding six weeks, during which it was not vacant is to be disregarded: art 2(2)(b) (as so substituted).

'Caravan' is to be construed in accordance with the Caravan Sites and Control of Development Act 1960 Pt I (ss 1–32) (see PLANNING vol 83 (2018) PARA 1137): Council Tax (Exempt Dwellings) Order 1992, SI 1992/558, art 2(1) (definition added by SI 1994/539). 'Unoccupied dwelling' means, subject to the Council Tax (Exempt Dwellings) Order 1992, SI 1992/558, art 2(3) (see note 12), a dwelling in which no one lives; and 'occupied' is to be construed accordingly: art 2(1) (definition amended by SI 1994/539).

6 For these purposes, 'major repair work' includes structural repair work: Council Tax (Exempt Dwellings) Order 1992, SI 1992/558, art 3 Class A para (3) (art 3 Class A substituted in relation to England by SI 2000/424; and in relation to Wales by SI 2000/1025; revoked, in relation to England, by SI 2012/2865).

7 Council Tax (Exempt Dwellings) Order 1992, SI 1992/558, art 3 Class A para (2)(a) (as substituted: see note 6).

8 Council Tax (Exempt Dwellings) Order 1992, SI 1992/558, art 3 Class A para (2)(b) (as substituted: see note 6).

9 Council Tax (Exempt Dwellings) Order 1992, SI 1992/558, art 3 Class A para (2)(c) (as substituted: see note 6). As to the meaning of 'month' see PARA 11 note 1.

10 Council Tax (Exempt Dwellings) Order 1992, SI 1992/558, art 3 Class A para (2)(d) (as substituted: see note 6).

11 Council Tax (Exempt Dwellings) Order 1992, SI 1992/558, art 3 Class A para (1) (as substituted: see note 6).

12 For the purposes of the Council Tax (Exempt Dwellings) Order 1992, SI 1992/558, art 3 Class B and Class F (see head (6) in the text), in considering whether a dwelling has been unoccupied for any period, any one period (not exceeding six weeks) during which it was occupied must be disregarded: art 2(3) (added by SI 1993/150; substituted by SI 1994/539). As to the meaning of 'unoccupied dwelling' generally see note 5.

13 Council Tax (Exempt Dwellings) Order 1992, SI 1992/558, art 3 Class B (amended by SI 1994/539). In *Ealing London Borough Council v Notting Hill Housing Trust* [2015] EWHC 161 (Admin), [2015] RA 233, [2015] All ER (D) 83 (Feb) the High Court overruled the president of the tribunal who, having noted the four elements to the exemption, found that the trust was entitled to an exemption in respect of void periods between lettings and that for charitable social housing providers there was a presumption that the second and fourth elements were satisfied with a consequential reversal of the normal burden of proof.

Nevertheless, the court recommended that the Secretary of State should consider promulgating a revision to the exemption relating to charitable purposes since, while it could see the need for the presumption referred to, that should be done by the relevant Secretary of State and approved by Parliament, not by an impermissible and artificial stretching of the plain words of the existing law by the tribunal.

As to charitable purposes see CHARITIES vol 8 (2015) PARA 2 et seq.

14 See note 5.

15 Council Tax (Exempt Dwellings) Order 1992, SI 1992/558, art 3 Class C (substituted by SI 1993/150; revoked, in relation to England, by SI 2012/2965).

16 As to the meaning of 'unoccupied dwelling' generally see note 5. For the purposes of the Council Tax (Exempt Dwellings) Order 1992, SI 1992/558, art 3 Class D para (1), a dwelling is to be regarded as unoccupied if its only occupant or occupants are persons detained elsewhere in the circumstances there mentioned: art 3 Class D para (2).

17 For these purposes, 'tenant' is defined by the Council Tax (Exempt Dwellings) Order 1992, SI 1992/558, art 2(1) (definition added by SI 1994/539; amended by SI 1997/74) as a person who:
   (1) has a leasehold interest in a dwelling which was granted for a term of less than six months;
   (2) is a secure, introductory or statutory tenant of a dwelling; or
   (3) has a contractual licence to occupy a dwelling.

'Introductory tenant' means a tenant within the meaning of the Housing Act 1996 Pt V Ch I (ss

124–143) (see LANDLORD AND TENANT vol 63 (2016) PARA 1103 et seq): Council Tax (Exempt Dwellings) Order 1992, SI 1992/558, art 2(1) (definition added by SI 1997/74). 'Secure tenant' means a tenant under a secure tenancy within the meaning of the Housing Act 1985 Pt IV (ss 79–117) (see LANDLORD AND TENANT vol 63 (2016) PARA 1037 et seq): Council Tax (Exempt Dwellings) Order 1992, SI 1992/558, art 2(1) (definition added by SI 1994/539). 'Statutory tenant' means a statutory tenant within the meaning of the Rent Act 1977 or the Rent (Agriculture) Act 1976 (see LANDLORD AND TENANT vol 63 (2013) PARA 653 et seq): Council Tax (Exempt Dwellings) Order 1992, SI 1992/558, art 2(1) (definition added by SI 1994/539).

18 Ie in the circumstances specified in the Local Government Finance Act 1992 Sch 1 para 1 (see PARA 368): see the Council Tax (Exempt Dwellings) Order 1992, SI 1992/558, art 3 Class D para (1)(a) (amended by SI 1994/539).

19 Council Tax (Exempt Dwellings) Order 1992, SI 1992/558, art 3 Class D para (1)(a) (as amended: see note 18).

20 For these purposes, 'relevant absentee', in relation to a dwelling, means a person who is detained elsewhere in the circumstances mentioned in the Council Tax (Exempt Dwellings) Order 1992, SI 1992/558, art 3 Class D para (1)(a) (see head (4)(a) in the text): art 2(1).

21 Council Tax (Exempt Dwellings) Order 1992, SI 1992/558, art 3 Class D para (1)(b) (substituted by SI 1993/150).

22 See the Council Tax (Exempt Dwellings) Order 1992, SI 1992/558, art 3 Class E (amended by SI 1994/539).

23 Ie, in relation to Wales, in the circumstances specified in the Local Government Finance Act 1992 Sch 1 para 6 (hospital patients: see PARA 372) or Sch 1 para 7 (patients in homes in England and Wales: see PARA 373) or Sch 1 para 8 (patients in homes in Scotland) (see the Council Tax (Exempt Dwellings) Order 1992, SI 1992/558, art 3 Class E para (a)) or, in relation to England, in the circumstances specified in the Local Government Finance Act 1992 Sch 1 para 6 or Sch 1 para 7 or in accommodation provided in Scotland by a care home service within the meaning of the Public Services Reform (Scotland) Act 2010 Sch 12 para 2 (see the Council Tax (Exempt Dwellings) Order 1992, SI 1992/558, art 3 Class E para (a) (substituted in relation to England by SI 2005/2865; and amended by SI 2011/2581)). As to the meanings of 'England' and 'Wales' see PARA 2 note 16.

24 For these purposes, 'relevant absentee', in relation to a dwelling, means a person who has his sole or main residence elsewhere in the circumstances mentioned in the Council Tax (Exempt Dwellings) Order 1992, SI 1992/558, art 3 Class E para (a) (see head (5)(a) in the text): art 2(1).

25 Council Tax (Exempt Dwellings) Order 1992, SI 1992/558, art 3 Class E para (b).

26 See note 12.

27 Council Tax (Exempt Dwellings) Order 1992, SI 1992/558, art 3 Class F para (1)(a) (art 3 Class F substituted by SI 1994/539).

28 Council Tax (Exempt Dwellings) Order 1992, SI 1992/558, art 3 Class F para (1)(b) (as substituted: see note 27).

29 Council Tax (Exempt Dwellings) Order 1992, SI 1992/558, art 3 Class F para (2)(a) (as substituted: see note 27).

30 For these purposes, 'qualifying person' means a person who would, but for the provisions of the Council Tax (Exempt Dwellings) Order 1992, SI 1992/558, be liable for the council tax in respect of a dwelling on a particular day as the owner, whether or not jointly with any other person: art 2(1).

31 Council Tax (Exempt Dwellings) Order 1992, SI 1992/558, art 3 Class F para (2)(a)(i) (as substituted: see note 27).

32 Council Tax (Exempt Dwellings) Order 1992, SI 1992/558, art 3 Class F para (2)(a)(ii) (as substituted: see note 27). Article 3 Class F para (2)(a)(ii) only applies, in a case where a grant of probate or letters of administration has been made, if less than six months have elapsed since the date of the grant: art 3 Class F para (3) (as so substituted). As to the grant of probate see WILLS AND INTESTACY vol 103 (2016) PARA 707 et seq. As to letters of administration see WILLS AND INTESTACY vol 103 (2016) PARA 754 et seq.

33 Council Tax (Exempt Dwellings) Order 1992, SI 1992/558, art 3 Class F para (2)(b) (as substituted: see note 27). Article 3 Class F para (2)(b) only applies, in a case where a grant of probate or letters of administration has been made, if less than six months have elapsed since the date of the grant: art 3 Class F para (3) (as so substituted).

34 Council Tax (Exempt Dwellings) Order 1992, SI 1992/558, art 3 Class G. See *Watson v Rhonnda Cynon Taff County Council* [2001] EWHC Admin 913, [2002] RVR 132 (notices to repair issued from local authority were not notices which constituted an action with a view to prohibiting occupation of the property in question).

35 Council Tax (Exempt Dwellings) Order 1992, SI 1992/558, art 3 Class G para (a)(i) (art 3 Class G substituted, in relation to billing authorities in England, by SI 2006/2318). As to the meaning of 'billing authority' see PARA 346.

36 Council Tax (Exempt Dwellings) Order 1992, SI 1992/558, art 3 Class G para (a)(ii) (as substituted: see note 35). The relevant provisions of the Town and Country Planning Act 1990 are those of Pt III (ss 55–106B) (see PLANNING vol 81 (2018) PARA 333 et seq): see the Council Tax (Exempt Dwellings) Order 1992, SI 1992/558, art 3 Class G para (a)(ii) (as so substituted).

37 Council Tax (Exempt Dwellings) Order 1992, SI 1992/558, art 3 Class G para (b) (as substituted: see note 35).

38 Council Tax (Exempt Dwellings) Order 1992, SI 1992/558, art 3 Class G para (c) (as substituted: see note 35).

39 Council Tax (Exempt Dwellings) Order 1992, SI 1992/558, art 3 Class H.

40 Council Tax (Exempt Dwellings) Order 1992, SI 1992/558, art 3 Class I (substituted in relation to England by SI 2003/3121; and in relation to Wales by SI 2004/2921).

41 Council Tax (Exempt Dwellings) Order 1992, SI 1992/558, art 3 Class I para (a) (as substituted: see note 40). Another place means another place not being a hospital, care home, independent hospital or hostel within the meaning of the Local Government Finance Act 1992 Sch 1 para 6 (hospital patients: see PARA 372) or Sch 1 para 7 (patients in homes in England and Wales: see PARA 373) or in accommodation provided in Scotland by a care home service within the meaning of the Public Services Reform (Scotland) Act 2010 Sch 12 para 2: see the Council Tax (Exempt Dwellings) Order 1992, SI 1992/558, art 3 Class I para (a) (as so substituted; amended by SI 2011/2581).

42 For these purposes, 'relevant absentee', in relation to a dwelling, means a person who has his sole or main residence elsewhere in the circumstances mentioned in the Council Tax (Exempt Dwellings) Order 1992, SI 1992/558, art 3 Class I para (a) (see head (9)(a) in the text): art 2(1).

43 Council Tax (Exempt Dwellings) Order 1992, SI 1992/558, art 3 Class I para (b) (as substituted: see note 40).

44 Council Tax (Exempt Dwellings) Order 1992, SI 1992/558, art 3 Class J (amended by SI 1994/539).

45 Council Tax (Exempt Dwellings) Order 1992, SI 1992/558, art 3 Class J para (a).

46 For these purposes, 'relevant absentee', in relation to a dwelling, means a person who has his sole or main residence elsewhere in the circumstances mentioned in the Council Tax (Exempt Dwellings) Order 1992, SI 1992/558, art 3 Class J para (a) (see head (10)(a) in the text): art 2(1).

47 Council Tax (Exempt Dwellings) Order 1992, SI 1992/558, art 3 Class J para (b).

48 Council Tax (Exempt Dwellings) Order 1992, SI 1992/558, art 3 Class K para (a) (art 3 Class K substituted by SI 1993/150).

49 Council Tax (Exempt Dwellings) Order 1992, SI 1992/558, art 3 Class K para (b) (as substituted: see note 48). As to the meaning of 'student' see PARA 371 note 2 (definition applied by art 2(1)).

50 Council Tax (Exempt Dwellings) Order 1992, SI 1992/558, art 3 Class K para (b)(i) (as substituted: see note 48).

51 Council Tax (Exempt Dwellings) Order 1992, SI 1992/558, art 3 Class K para (b)(ii) (as substituted: see note 48).

52 Council Tax (Exempt Dwellings) Order 1992, SI 1992/558, art 3 Class L.

53 As to the meaning of 'institution' see PARA 371 note 4 (definition applied by the Council Tax (Exempt Dwellings) Order 1992, SI 1992/558, art 3 Class M para (a) (amended by SI 1994/539)).

54 Council Tax (Exempt Dwellings) Order 1992, SI 1992/558, art 3 Class M para (a) (as amended: see note 53).

55 Council Tax (Exempt Dwellings) Order 1992, SI 1992/558, Class M para (b) (substituted by SI 1993/150).

56 Council Tax (Exempt Dwellings) Order 1992, SI 1992/558, art 3 Class N para (1)(a) (Class N substituted by SI 1993/150). For these purposes, 'relevant person' means:

(1) a student (Council Tax (Exempt Dwellings) Order 1992, SI 1992/558, art 3 Class N para (2)(a)(i) (art 3 Class N as so substituted; art 3 Class N para (2)(a) further substituted by SI 1995/619));

(2) a student's spouse, civil partner or dependant being in each case a person who is not a British citizen and who is prevented, by the terms of his leave to enter or remain in the United Kingdom, from taking paid employment or from claiming benefits (Council Tax (Exempt Dwellings) Order 1992, SI 1992/558, art 3 Class N para (2)(a)(ii) (art 3 Class N para (2)(a) as so substituted; art 3 Class N para (2)(a)(ii) amended in relation to England by SI 2005/2865; and in relation to Wales by SI 2005/3302)); or

(3) a person to whom the Council Tax (Additional Provision for Discount Disregards) Regulations 1992, SI 1992/552, reg 3(1) Class C (school and college leavers: see PARA

371) applies (Council Tax (Exempt Dwellings) Order 1992, SI 1992/558, art 3 Class N para (2)(a)(iii) (as so substituted)).

As to civil partnership see MATRIMONIAL AND CIVIL PARTNERSHIP LAW vol 72 (2015) PARA 3. As to the meaning of 'United Kingdom' see PARA 4 note 10. As to the meaning of 'British citizen' see BRITISH NATIONALITY vol 4 (2011) PARA 421 et seq.

A non-British spouse of a student who is prevented by the terms of her leave to enter from claiming benefits, but is not prevented from taking paid employment, is exempt from liability to pay council tax: *Harrow London Borough Council v Ayiku* [2012] EWHC 1200 (Admin), [2012] RA 270, [2012] All ER (D) 105 (May).

57 Council Tax (Exempt Dwellings) Order 1992, SI 1992/558, art 3 Class N para (1)(b) (as substituted: see note 56). A dwelling is to be regarded as occupied by a relevant person as term time accommodation during any vacation in which he:

(1) holds a freehold or leasehold interest in or licence to occupy the whole or any part of the dwelling (art 3 Class N para (2)(b)(i) (as so substituted)); and

(2) has previously used or intends to use the dwelling as term time accommodation (art 3 Class N para (2)(b)(ii) (as so substituted)).

58 As to the Secretary of State for Defence see CONSTITUTIONAL AND ADMINISTRATIVE LAW vol 20 (2014) PARA 266.

59 Council Tax (Exempt Dwellings) Order 1992, SI 1992/558, art 3 Class O (amended by SI 1992/2941). As to the meaning of 'visiting forces' see the Visiting Forces Act 1952 s 12(1) (see ARMED FORCES vol 3 (2011) PARA 410) (definition applied by the Council Tax (Exempt Dwellings) Order 1992, SI 1992/558, art 3 Class O (as so amended)).

60 Council Tax (Exempt Dwellings) Order 1992, SI 1992/558, art 3 Class P para (1) (art 3 Class P added by SI 1992/2941).

61 Ie within the meaning of the Visiting Forces Act 1952 Pt I (ss 1–12): see the Council Tax (Exempt Dwellings) Order 1992, SI 1992/558, art 3 Class P para (2) (as added: see note 60). References in the Visiting Forces Act 1952 Pt I to a person's having at any time a relevant association with a visiting force are references to his being at that time a person of one or other of the following descriptions, that is to say:

(1) a member of that visiting force or a member of a civilian component of that force (s 12(2)(a));

(2) a person, not being a citizen of the United Kingdom and Colonies or ordinarily resident in the United Kingdom, but being a dependant of a member of that visiting force or of a civilian component of that force (s 12(2)(b)).

For these purposes, the expression 'dependant', in relation to a person, means any of the following, that is to say:

(a) the wife or husband of that person (s 12(4)(a)); and

(b) any other person wholly or mainly maintained by him or in his custody, charge or care (s 12(4)(b)).

As to British nationality and citizenship see BRITISH NATIONALITY vol 4 (2011) PARAS 403, 421 et seq.

62 Council Tax (Exempt Dwellings) Order 1992, SI 1992/558, art 3 Class P para (2) (as added: see note 60). The relevant provisions of the Visiting Forces Act 1952 for these purposes are those of Pt I (ss 1–12) (see ARMED FORCES vol 3 (2011) PARA 322): see the Council Tax (Exempt Dwellings) Order 1992, SI 1992/558, art 3 Class P para (2) (as so added).

63 Council Tax (Exempt Dwellings) Order 1992, SI 1992/558, art 3 Class Q (added by SI 1993/150). For these purposes, a trustee in bankruptcy is one under the Bankruptcy Act 1914 (repealed with savings) or the Insolvency Act 1986 (see BANKRUPTCY AND INDIVIDUAL INSOLVENCY vol 5 (2013) PARA 314 et seq): see the Council Tax (Exempt Dwellings) Order 1992, SI 1992/558, art 3 Class Q (as so added).

64 Council Tax (Exempt Dwellings) Order 1992, SI 1992/558, art 3 Class R (added by SI 1994/539).

65 Council Tax (Exempt Dwellings) Order 1992, SI 1992/558, art 3 Class S (art 3 Classes S–U added by SI 1995/619).

66 For these purposes, 'single property' means property which would, apart from the Council Tax (Chargeable Dwellings) Order 1992, SI 1992/549, be one dwelling within the meaning of the Local Government Finance Act 1992 s 3 (see PARA 349): Council Tax (Exempt Dwellings) Order 1992, SI 1992/558, art 2(1) (definition added by SI 1997/656).

67 Council Tax (Exempt Dwellings) Order 1992, SI 1992/558, art 3 Class T para (a) (as added: see note 65).

68 Council Tax (Exempt Dwellings) Order 1992, SI 1992/558, art 3 Class T para (b) (as added: see note 65). As to the meaning of 'breach of planning control' for these purposes see the Town and

Country Planning Act 1990 s 171A (see PLANNING vol 82 (2018) PARA 854) (definition applied by the Council Tax (Exempt Dwellings) Order 1992, SI 1992/558, art 3 Class T para (b) (as so added)).

69 As to the meaning of 'severely mentally impaired' see PARA 369 note 2 (definition applied by the Council Tax (Exempt Dwellings) Order 1992, SI 1992/558, art 3 Class U para (2)(b) (art 3 Class U as added (see note 65); substituted by SI 1999/536)).

70 As to the meaning of 'relevant person' see note 56 (definition applied by the Council Tax (Exempt Dwellings) Order 1992, SI 1992/558, art 3 Class U para (2)(a) (as added and substituted: see note 69)).

71 Council Tax (Exempt Dwellings) Order 1992, SI 1992/558, art 3 Class U para (1)(a) (as added and substituted: see note 69).

72 Council Tax (Exempt Dwellings) Order 1992, SI 1992/558, art 3 Class U para (1)(b) (as added and substituted: see note 69).

73 Council Tax (Exempt Dwellings) Order 1992, SI 1992/558, art 3 Class V para (1) (art 3 Classes V, W added by SI 1997/656).

74 Council Tax (Exempt Dwellings) Order 1992, SI 1992/558, art 3 Class V para (2) (as added: see note 73). The privileges and immunities or other qualification referred to are that the person:

(1) is a person on whom privileges and immunities are conferred by the Diplomatic Privileges Act 1964 (see INTERNATIONAL RELATIONS LAW vol 61 (2010) PARA 263 et seq) (Council Tax (Exempt Dwellings) Order 1992, SI 1992/558, art 3 Class V para (2)(a) (as so added)); or

(2) is a person on whom privileges and immunities are conferred under the Commonwealth Secretariat Act 1966 s 1(2), Schedule Pt II para 5(1) (staff of the Secretariat: see COMMONWEALTH vol 13 (2017) PARA 623) (Council Tax (Exempt Dwellings) Order 1992, SI 1992/558, art 3 Class V para (2)(b) (as so added)); or

(3) is a person on whom privileges and immunities are conferred by the Consular Relations Act 1968 s 1 (see INTERNATIONAL RELATIONS LAW vol 61 (2010) PARA 290 et seq) (Council Tax (Exempt Dwellings) Order 1992, SI 1992/558, art 3 Class V para (2)(c) (as so added)); or

(4) is (in relation to any organisation specified in an Order in Council made under the International Organisations Act 1968 s 1(2)) within a class of persons mentioned in s 1(3) to which the relevant Order extended relief from rates as specified in Sch 1 Pt II para 9 (see INTERNATIONAL RELATIONS LAW vol 61 (2010) PARA 317) (Council Tax (Exempt Dwellings) Order 1992, SI 1992/558, art 3 Class V para (2)(d) (as so added)); or

(5) is a person on whom privileges and immunities are conferred by the Commonwealth Countries and Republic of Ireland (Immunities and Privileges) Order 1985, SI 1985/1983, arts 3–4 (see COMMONWEALTH vol 13 (2017) PARA 626) (Council Tax (Exempt Dwellings) Order 1992, SI 1992/558, art 3 Class V para (2)(e) (as so added)); or

(6) is the head of any office established as described in the Hong Kong Economic Trade Act 1996 s 1(1) (Council Tax (Exempt Dwellings) Order 1992, SI 1992/558, art 3 Class V para (2)(f) (as so added));

and is not:

(a) a British citizen, a British overseas territories citizen, a British national (overseas) or a British overseas citizen (art 3 Class V para (2)(i) (as so added; amended by virtue of the British Overseas Territories Act 2002 s 2(3))); or

(b) a person who under the British Nationality Act 1981 is a British subject (see BRITISH NATIONALITY vol 4 (2011) PARAS 407, 469–475) (Council Tax (Exempt Dwellings) Order 1992, SI 1992/558, art 3 Class V para (2)(ii) (as so added)); or

(c) a British protected person (within the meaning of the British Nationality Act 1981: see BRITISH NATIONALITY vol 4 (2011) PARAS 408, 476–481) (Council Tax (Exempt Dwellings) Order 1992, SI 1992/558, art 3 Class V para (2)(iii) (as so added)); or

(d) a permanent resident of the United Kingdom (art 3 Class V para (2)(iv) (as so added)).

As to the meaning of 'British citizen' see BRITISH NATIONALITY vol 4 (2011) PARAS 406, 421–444. As to the meaning of 'British overseas territories citizen' see BRITISH NATIONALITY vol 4 (2011) PARAS 406, 445–458. As to the meaning of 'British National (Overseas)' see BRITISH NATIONALITY vol 4 (2011) PARAS 406, 465–468. As to the meaning of 'British Overseas citizen' see BRITISH NATIONALITY vol 4 (2011) PARAS 406, 459–464.

75 Council Tax (Exempt Dwellings) Order 1992, SI 1992/558, art 3 Class V para (3) (as added: see note 73).

76 For these purposes, a person is to be regarded as the relative of another if (Council Tax (Exempt Dwellings) Order 1992, SI 1992/558, art 2(5) (added by SI 1997/656; substituted by SI 1998/291)):

(1) he is the spouse or civil partner of that person (Council Tax (Exempt Dwellings) Order 1992, SI 1992/558, art 2(5)(a) (art 2(5) as so added and substituted; art 2(5)(a) amended in relation to England by SI 2005/2865; and in relation to Wales by SI 2005/3302)); or

(2) he is that person's parent, child, grandparent, grandchild, brother, sister, uncle or aunt, nephew or niece, great-grandparent, great-grandchild, great-uncle, great-aunt, great-nephew or great-niece (Council Tax (Exempt Dwellings) Order 1992, SI 1992/558, art 2(5)(b) (as so added and substituted)); or

(3) he is that person's great-great-grandparent, great-great-grandchild, great-great-uncle, great-great-aunt, great-great-nephew or great-great-niece (art 2(5)(c) (as so added and substituted)).

For these purposes:

(a) a relationship by marriage or civil partnership is to be treated as a relationship by blood (art 2(5)(i) (art 2(5) as so added and substituted; art 2(5)(i) amended in relation to England by SI 2005/2865; and in relation to Wales by SI 2005/3302));

(b) a relationship between a man and a woman living together as husband and wife is to be treated as a relationship by marriage and a relationship between two persons of the same sex living together as if they were civil partners is to be treated as a relationship by civil partnership (Council Tax (Exempt Dwellings) Order 1992, SI 1992/558, art 2(5)(ii) (art 2(5) as so added and substituted; art 2(5)(ii) amended in relation to England by SI 2005/2865; and in relation to Wales by SI 2005/3302));

(c) the stepchild of a person is to be treated as his child (Council Tax (Exempt Dwellings) Order 1992, SI 1992/558, art 2(5)(iii) (as so added and substituted)); and

(d) the child of the civil partner of a person ('A') is to be treated as A's child (Council Tax (Exempt Dwellings) Order 1992, SI 1992/558, art 2(5)(iv) (art 2(5) as so added and substituted; art 2(5)(iv) added in relation to England by SI 2005/2865; and in relation to Wales by SI 2005/3302)).

A relative is to be regarded as dependent if he is:

(i) aged 65 years or more (Council Tax (Exempt Dwellings) Order 1992, SI 1992/558, art 2(4)(a) (art 2(4) added by SI 1997/656)); or

(ii) severely mentally impaired (Council Tax (Exempt Dwellings) Order 1992, SI 1992/558, art 2(4)(b) (as so added)); or

(iii) substantially and permanently disabled (whether by illness, injury, congenital deformity or otherwise) (art 2(4)(c) (as so added)).

As to the meaning of 'severely mentally impaired' see PARA 369 note 2 (definition applied by art 2(4)(b) (as so added)). As to the construction of references to any relationship between two persons see the Interpretation Act 1978 s 5, Sch 1; the Family Law Reform Act 1987 s 1; and CHILDREN AND YOUNG PERSONS vol 9 (2017) PARA 141; STATUTES AND LEGISLATIVE PROCESS vol 96 (2012) PARA 1214.

Marriage includes marriage of a same sex couple: see the Marriage (Same Sex Couples) Act 2013 Sch 3 para 1(1)(a), (2), (3); and MATRIMONIAL AND CIVIL PARTNERSHIP LAW vol 72 (2015) PARA 1 et seq.

77 Council Tax (Exempt Dwellings) Order 1992, SI 1992/558, art 3 Class W (as added: see note 73).

353. Completion of new dwellings.

Where:

(1) a completion notice is served[1]; and

(2) the building[2] to which the notice relates is not completed on or before the relevant day[3],

any dwelling[4] in which the building or any part of it will be comprised is deemed, for the purposes of the council tax provisions[5], to have come into existence on that day[6].

Where:

(a) a day is determined[7] as the completion day in relation to a new building[8]; and

(b) the building is one produced by the structural alteration of a building which is comprised in one or more existing dwellings[9], the existing dwelling or dwellings is or are deemed for the purposes of the council tax provisions[10] to have ceased to exist on that day[11].

1 Ie under the Local Government Finance Act 1988 Sch 4A (see PARA 138 et seq): see the Local Government Finance Act 1992 s 17(3)(a). Subject to the provisions of s 17, the Local Government Finance Act 1988 Sch 4A (which makes provision for the determination of a completion day in relation to a new building), with the exception of Sch 4A para 6 (see PARA 141), applies for the purposes of the Local Government Finance Act 1992 Pt I (ss 1–69) as it applies for the purposes of the Local Government Finance Act 1988 Pt III (ss 41–67): Local Government Finance Act 1992 s 17(1). Any reference in s 17 to the Local Government Finance Act 1988 Sch 4A is a reference to that Schedule as it applies for the purposes of the Local Government Finance Act 1992 Pt I: see s 17(2). Any reference in the Local Government Finance Act 1988 Sch 4A to the valuation officer is to be construed for these purposes as a reference to the listing officer: see the Local Government Finance Act 1992 s 17(7). As to listing officers see PARA 347.

2 Any reference in the Local Government Finance Act 1992 s 17 to a 'building' includes a reference to a part of a building: see s 17(7).

3 Local Government Finance Act 1992 s 17(3)(b). The 'relevant day' in relation to a completion notice is:
   (1) where no appeal against the notice is brought under the Local Government Finance Act 1988 Sch 4A para 4 (see PARA 141) (as it applies for these purposes: see note 1), the day stated in the notice (see the Local Government Finance Act 1992 s 17(2), (4)(a) (s 17(4)(a), (b) amended by the Local Government Act 2003 s 127(1), Sch 7 paras 40, 43(1))); and
   (2) where an appeal against the notice is brought under the Local Government Finance Act 1988 Sch 4A para 4, the day determined under Sch 4A (see PARA 141) (as it applies for these purposes: see note 1) as the completion day in relation to the building to which the notice relates (see the Local Government Finance Act 1992 s 17(2), (4)(b) (as so amended)).

4 As to the meaning of 'dwelling' see PARA 349.

5 Ie for the purposes of the Local Government Finance Act 1992 Pt I (ss 1–69).

6 Local Government Finance Act 1992 s 17(3).

7 Ie under the Local Government Finance Act 1988 Sch 4A (see PARA 138 et seq) (as it applies for these purposes: see note 1).

8 Local Government Finance Act 1992 s 17(5)(a). Any reference in s 17 or in the Local Government Finance Act 1988 Sch 4A (see PARA 138 et seq) (as it applies for these purposes: see note 1) to a 'new building' includes a reference to a building produced by the structural alteration of an existing building where:
   (1) the existing building or any part of it is comprised in a dwelling which, by virtue of the alteration, becomes or becomes part of a different dwelling or different dwellings (see the Local Government Finance Act 1992 s 17(2), (6)(a)); or
   (2) neither the existing dwelling nor any part of it is, except by virtue of the alteration, comprised in any dwelling (see s 17(2), (6)(b)).

9 Local Government Finance Act 1992 s 17(5)(b).

10 Ie for the purposes of the Local Government Finance Act 1992 Pt I (ss 1–69).

11 Local Government Finance Act 1992 s 17(5).

(iii) Persons Liable

354. Persons liable to pay council tax.

The person who is liable to pay council tax[1] in respect of any chargeable dwelling[2] and any day is the person who falls within the first of heads (1) to (7) below to apply, taking head (1) first, head (2) next, and so on[3]. Accordingly, a person is liable to pay council tax in relation to any chargeable dwelling and any day if, on that day:

(1) he is a resident[4] of the dwelling and has a freehold interest in the whole or any part of it[5]; or

(2) he is such a resident and has a leasehold interest in the whole or any part of the dwelling which is not inferior to another such interest held by another such resident[6]; or
(3) he is both such a resident and a statutory[7], secure[8] or introductory tenant[9] of the whole or any part of the dwelling[10]; or
(4) he is such a resident and has a contractual licence to occupy the whole or any part of the dwelling[11]; or
(5) he is such a resident[12]; or
(6) prospectively, in the case of a dwelling situated in the area of a billing authority[13] in England, the person is a mortgagee in possession of the owner's interest in the dwelling[14];
(7) he is the owner[15] of the dwelling[16].

Where, in relation to any chargeable dwelling and any day, two or more persons fall within the first of heads (1) to (7) above to apply, they are each jointly and severally liable to pay the council tax in respect of the dwelling and that day[17]. However, as respects any day on which one or more of the persons so mentioned fall to be disregarded for the purposes of discount, either on grounds of severe mental impairment[18] or owing to their status as a student, apprentice or trainee[19], and one or more of them do not, liability to pay the council tax in respect of the dwelling and that day must be determined as follows[20]:

(a) if only one of those persons does not fall to be so disregarded, he is solely liable[21];
(b) if two or more of those persons do not fall to be so disregarded, they are each jointly and severally liable[22].

In prescribed cases, these provisions relating to liability to pay council tax do not apply, and other provisions have effect in substitution, by virtue of which liability falls on the owner[23].

1 As to council tax see PARA 344 et seq.

2 As to the meaning of 'chargeable dwelling' see PARA 350.

3 Local Government Finance Act 1992 s 6(1). Thus liability falls first on the person who is resident in the dwelling and has the principal legal interest in it; but if there is no resident, the non-resident owner is liable (eg liability attaches to holiday homes and second homes, although there may be a discount).

4 Unless the context otherwise requires, 'resident', in relation to any dwelling, means an individual who has attained the age of 18 years and has his sole or main residence in the dwelling: Local Government Finance Act 1992 ss 6(5), 69(1). The time at which a person attains a particular age expressed in years is the commencement of the relevant anniversary of the date of his birth: see the Family Law Reform Act 1969 s 9; and CHILDREN AND YOUNG PERSONS vol 9 (2017) PARA 2.

Where a person owns more than one property, it is a question of fact and degree which of the properties is the sole or main residence: see *Frost (Inspector of Taxes) v Feltham* [1981] 1 WLR 452, [1981] STC 115. 'Mainly' may be defined as indicating that more than half of the total time is spent in a certain property: see *Fawcett Properties Ltd v Buckinghamshire County Council* [1961] AC 636 at 669, [1960] 3 All ER 503 at 512, HL, per Lord Morton. However, the individual circumstances of each case must be weighed: see *Ward v Kingston-upon-Hull City Council* [1993] RA 71 (house with security of tenure but occupied only for six to nine weeks a year held to be main residence despite remaining time spent in rented accommodation tied to employment abroad). In *Williams v Horsham District Council* [2004] EWCA Civ 39, [2004] 3 All ER 30, [2004] 1 WLR 1137, [2004] RA 49, it was held that, rather than attach too much weight to the issues of 'security of tenure' and the 'intention to return', a tribunal should view a person's main residence as being the dwelling that a reasonable onlooker, with knowledge of the material facts, would regard as that person's home at the material time, the words 'sole or main residence' in the Local Government Finance Act 1992 s 6(5) referring to premises in which a taxpayer actually resided but allowing for the fact that a person could reside in more than one place. See also *Parry v Derbyshire Dales District Council* [2006] EWHC 988 (Admin), [2006] RA 252, [2006] All ER (D) 70 (May) (the question of residence is one of fact, not simply one of law; while status for income tax purposes might not be determinative of his liability for council tax, it seemed anomalous that a person should be non-resident in the United Kingdom for income tax purposes, but mainly resident for the purpose of liability for council tax).

On the issue of residence see also *Doncaster Borough Council v Stark* [1998] RVR 80; *Bennett v Copeland Borough Council* [2004] EWCA Civ 672 at [33], [2004] RA 171 at [33] per Rix LJ (actual residence is critical to an understanding of the Local Government Finance Act 1992 s 6(2)). Also relevant are cases decided in relation to the community charge, where sole or main occupation was a determinative criterion: see *Bradford Metropolitan City Council v Anderton* [1991] RA 45, 89 LGR 681 (length of time spent at an address an obviously relevant factor); *Codner v Wiltshire Valuation and Community Charge Tribunal* [1994] RVR 169 (relevant to consider joint ownership of a family home and location of family although working week passed elsewhere). See also *Cox v London (South West) Valuation and Community Charge Tribunal and Poole Borough Council Community Charge Registration Office* [1994] RVR 171. Other relevant factors include the degree of permanence, including where the majority of a person's possessions are kept: *Frost (Inspector of Taxes) v Feltham* (above). Matters of lesser weight include the person's own view as to his main residence, and where a person sleeps: *Mullaney v Watford Borough Council and Hertfordshire Valuation Tribunal* [1997] RA 225.

Some of the cases cited in this paragraph were decided under earlier legislation, and they must therefore now be considered in relation to the provisions of the Local Government Finance Act 1992.

5 Local Government Finance Act 1992 s 6(2)(a).

6 Local Government Finance Act 1992 s 6(2)(b). See *Regentford Ltd v Shepway District Council* [2006] EWHC 3200 (Admin), [2006] RVR 377, [2006] All ER (D) 295 (Oct).

7 'Statutory tenant' means a statutory tenant within the meaning of the Rent Act 1977 or the Rent (Agriculture) Act 1976 (see LANDLORD AND TENANT vol 63 (2016) PARA 653 et seq): Local Government Finance Act 1992 s 6(6).

8 'Secure tenant' means a tenant under a secure tenancy within the meaning of the Housing Act 1985 Pt IV (ss 79–117) (see LANDLORD AND TENANT vol 63 (2016) PARA 1037 et seq): Local Government Finance Act 1992 s 6(6).

9 'Introductory tenant' means a tenant under an introductory tenancy within the meaning of the Housing Act 1996 Pt V Ch I (ss 124–143) (see LANDLORD AND TENANT vol 63 (2016) PARA 1103 et seq): Local Government Finance Act 1992 s 6(6) (definition added by SI 1997/74).

10 Local Government Finance Act 1992 s 6(2)(c) (amended by SI 1997/74). See *Regentford Ltd v Shepway District Council* [2006] EWHC 3200 (Admin), [2006] RVR 377, [2006] All ER (D) 295 (Oct).

11 Local Government Finance Act 1992 s 6(2)(d).

12 Local Government Finance Act 1992 s 6(2)(e).

13 As to the meaning of 'billing authority' see PARA 346.

14 Local Government Finance Act 1992 s 6(2)(ea) (added, as from a day to be appointed, by the Local Government Finance Act 2012 s 13(1)). At the date at which this volume states the law, no such day had been appointed.

15 Unless the context otherwise requires, 'owner', in relation to any dwelling, means the person as regards whom the following conditions are fulfilled (Local Government Finance Act 1992 ss 6(5), 69(1)), namely that:

(1) he has a material interest in the whole or any part of the dwelling; and

(2) at least part of the dwelling (or, as the case may be, at least part of the part of the dwelling concerned) is not subject to a material interest inferior to his interest.

'Material interest' means a freehold interest or a leasehold interest which was granted for a term of six months or more: s 6(6). See *Leeds City Council v Broadley* [2016] EWCA Civ 1213, [2016] All ER (D) 59 (Dec) (landlord was owner where tenancy was granted for fixed term and then continued from month to month, even where tenant no longer occupied). As to the meaning of 'month' see PARA 11 note 1.

16 Local Government Finance Act 1992 s 6(2)(f). As to the relationship between this head and head (1) in the text see *Parry v Derbyshire Dales District Council* [2006] EWHC 988 (Admin), [2006] RA 252, [2006] All ER (D) 70 (May) (the person who is the owner of a dwelling is not, without more, resident in it and there has to be a resident of a dwelling if it is to be a person's residence; the fact that a legal impediment to residence by the freehold owner is removed does not, of itself, result in his residing in the dwelling). As to the issue of residence see the cases cited in note 4.

17 Local Government Finance Act 1992 s 6(3). As to apportionment in the case of joint taxpayers see the Council Tax (Administration and Enforcement) Regulations 1992, SI 1992/613, reg 27; and PARA 452. As to the liability of spouses see PARA 357.

18 Ie by virtue of the Local Government Finance Act 1992 Sch 1 para 2: see PARA 369.
19 Ie by virtue of the Local Government Finance Act 1992 Sch 1 para 4: see PARA 371.
20 Local Government Finance Act 1992 s 6(4) (amended by the Local Government Act 2003 s 74(1)).
21 Local Government Finance Act 1992 s 6(4)(a).
22 Local Government Finance Act 1992 s 6(4)(b).
23 See PARAS 355–356.

355. Liability in respect of caravans and boats.

The following provisions have effect in substitution for the general provisions[1] relating to liability to pay council tax[2].

Where, in relation to any chargeable dwelling[3] which consists of a pitch occupied by a caravan[4], or a mooring occupied by a boat[5], on any day, the owner of the caravan or boat[6] is not, but some other person is, a resident[7] of the dwelling, that other person is liable to pay the council tax in respect of the dwelling and that day[8]. Where on any day this is not the case[9], the owner of the caravan or boat is liable to pay the council tax in respect of the dwelling and that day[10].

Where, on any day, two or more persons are liable to pay the council tax[11], they are each jointly and severally so liable in respect of the dwelling and that day[12].

1 Ie the Local Government Finance Act 1992 s 6: see PARA 354.
2 See the Local Government Finance Act 1992 s 7(1). As to council tax see PARA 344 et seq.
3 As to the meaning of 'chargeable dwelling' see PARA 350.
4 For these purposes, 'caravan' is to be construed in accordance with the Caravan Sites and Control of Development Act 1960 Pt I (ss 1–32) (see PLANNING vol 83 (2018) PARA 1137): Local Government Finance Act 1992 s 7(6).
5 See the Local Government Finance Act 1992 s 7(1).
6 Any reference in the Local Government Finance Act 1992 s 7 to the owner of a caravan or boat is to be construed:
    (1) in relation to a caravan or boat which is subject to an agreement for hire-purchase or conditional sale, as a reference to the person in possession under the agreement (s 7(7)(a));
    (2) in relation to a caravan or boat which is subject to a bill of sale or mortgage, as a reference to the person entitled to the property in it apart from the bill or mortgage (s 7(7)(b)).

  As to hire-purchase and conditional sale agreements see CONSUMER CREDIT vol 21 (2016) PARAS 38, 64. As to bills of sale see FINANCIAL INSTRUMENTS AND TRANSACTIONS vol 49 (2015) PARA 403 et seq. As to mortgages of personalty see MORTGAGE vol 77 (2016) PARA 205.
7 As to the meaning of 'resident' see PARA 354 note 4.
8 Local Government Finance Act 1992 s 7(2).
9 Ie where on any day the Local Government Finance Act 1992 s 7(2) (see the text to notes 3–8) does not apply: see s 7(3).
10 Local Government Finance Act 1992 s 7(3).
11 Ie where on any day two or more persons fall within the Local Government Finance Act 1992 s 7(2) or (3): see the text to notes 3–11.
12 See the Local Government Finance Act 1992 s 7(4). Section 6(4) applies for the purposes of s 7(4) as it applies for the purposes of s 6(3) (see PARA 354): s 7(5).

356. Liability in prescribed cases.

The following provisions[1] have effect in substitution for the general provisions relating to liability to pay council tax[2] and those[3] relating to liability in respect of caravans and boats[4].

In relation to any chargeable dwelling[5] that is of a class prescribed for the purpose[6], the owner[7] of the dwelling is liable to pay the council tax in respect of the dwelling and any day on which the provisions allowing for prescription have effect in relation to the dwelling[8]. Where, on any day, two or more persons are so liable, they are each jointly and severally liable to pay the council tax in respect of the dwelling and that day[9].

1 Ie the Local Government Finance Act 1992 s 8(3), (4): see the text to notes 5–9.
2 Ie the Local Government Finance Act 1992 s 6: see PARA 354. As to council tax see PARA 344 et seq.
3 Ie the Local Government Finance Act 1992 s 7: see PARA 355.
4 See the Local Government Finance Act 1992 s 8(1), (2).
5 As to the meaning of 'chargeable dwelling' see PARA 350.
6 Ie:
  (1) prescribed for the purposes of the Local Government Finance Act 1992 s 8(1) (see s 8(1)); or
  (2) prescribed for the purposes of s 8(2), if the billing authority so determines in relation to all dwellings of that class which are situated in its area (see s 8(2)).

A determination made under s 8(2) may not be questioned except by an application for judicial review: see s 66(1), (2)(b) (s 66(2)(b) amended by the Local Government Act 2003 s 127(1), Sch 7 paras 40, 49). If, on an application for judicial review, the court decides to grant relief in respect of any matter, it must quash the determination: see the Local Government Finance Act 1992 s 66(3) (amended by the Local Government Finance Act 2012 s 10(2), (3)(b), Sch 4 paras 3, 5(1), (3)). As to the meaning of 'billing authority' see PARA 346. As to judicial review see JUDICIAL REVIEW vol 61 (2010) PARA 601 et seq.

'Prescribed' means prescribed by regulations made by the Secretary of State or, in relation to Wales, by the Welsh Ministers: s 116(1). The functions of the Secretary of State under the Local Government Finance Act 1992 s 8, so far as exercisable in relation to Wales, were transferred to the National Assembly for Wales (see the National Assembly for Wales (Transfer of Functions) Order 1999, SI 1999/672, art 2, Sch 1) and are now vested in the Welsh Ministers (see the Government of Wales Act 2006 s 162(1), Sch 11 para 30). As to the Secretary of State and the Welsh Ministers see PARA 4 note 18. As to the meaning of 'Wales' see PARA 2 note 16.

A class of dwellings may be prescribed by reference to such factors as the Secretary of State or the Welsh Ministers sees fit: see the Local Government Finance Act 1992 s 4(3) (s 4(3), (4) applied by s 8(7)). Without prejudice to the generality of s 4(3), a class of dwellings may be prescribed by reference to one or more of the following factors:
  (a) the physical characteristics of dwellings (s 4(4)(a) (as so applied));
  (b) the fact that dwellings are unoccupied or are occupied for prescribed purposes or are occupied or owned by persons of prescribed descriptions (s 4(4)(b) (as so applied)).

The following classes of chargeable dwellings are prescribed for the purposes of s 8(1):
  (i) Class A: Residential care homes, etc (see the Council Tax (Liability for Owners) Regulations 1992, SI 1992/551, reg 2 Class A (substituted, in relation to England, by SI 2003/3125; and, in relation to Wales, by SI 2004/2920; amended by SI 2012/1915 and SI 2016/211));
  (ii) Class B: Dwellings inhabited by religious communities (see the Council Tax (Liability for Owners) Regulations 1992, SI 1992/551, reg 2 Class B);
  (iii) Class C: Houses in multiple occupation, etc (see reg 2 Class C (substituted by SI 1993/151; amended by SI 1995/620));
  (iv) Class D: Dwellings inhabited by resident staff (see the Council Tax (Liability for Owners) Regulations 1992, SI 1992/551, reg 2 Class D);
  (v) Class E: Dwellings inhabited by ministers of religion (see reg 2 Class E);
  (vi) Class F: Dwellings provided to asylum seekers (see reg 2 Class F (added, relation to England, by SI 2000/537; and, in relation to Wales, by SI 2000/1024)).

As to head (i), see *Henriques v Lambeth London Borough Council* [2007] EWHC 2974 (Admin), [2007] All ER (D) 295 (Nov) (evidence did not suggest that premises in which appellant had been residing was a residential care home and in any case was not a registered care home).

As to head (iii), see *Hayes v Humberside Valuation Tribunal and Kingston upon Hull City Council* [1997] RA 236; affd [1998] RA 37, CA (test required no more than a consideration of whether dwelling was suitable for occupation by persons who did not constitute a single household); *UHU Property Trust v Lincoln City Council* [2000] RA 419 (valuation tribunal must look at the realities of the arrangements, not just at the written tenancy agreement); *Hardy v Sefton Metropolitan Borough Council* [2006] EWHC 1928 (Admin), [2007] RA 140, [2006] All ER (D) 409 (Jul) (individuals, each having a tenancy agreement to occupy a named room within a certain rented property, did not constitute a single household; liability to council tax fell upon the owner);

R (on the application of Watts) v Preston City Council [2009] EWHC 2179 (Admin), [2009] RA 334, [2009] All ER (D) 264 (Oct); *R (on the application of Goremsandu) v Harrow London Borough Council* [2010] EWHC 1873 (Admin), [2010] All ER (D) 279 (Jul).

At the date at which this volume states the law, no regulations had been made under the Local Government Finance Act 1992 s 8(2).

7 As to the meaning of 'owner' see PARA 354 note 15. Regulations prescribing a class of chargeable dwellings for the purposes of the Local Government Finance Act 1992 s 8(1) or s 8(2) (see note 6) may provide that, in relation to any dwelling of that class, s 8(3) has effect as if for the reference to the owner of the dwelling there were substituted a reference to the person falling within such description as may be prescribed: s 8(6). Accordingly, in relation to a dwelling within the Council Tax (Liability for Owners) Regulations 1992, SI 1992/551, reg 2 Class C (see note 6 head (iii)), the Local Government Finance Act 1992 s 8(3) has effect as if, for the reference to the owner, there were substituted a reference to the person who has a relevant material interest which is not subject to a relevant material interest inferior to it, or, if there is no such person, the person who has a freehold interest in the whole or any part of the dwelling: Council Tax (Liability for Owners) Regulations 1992, SI 1992/551, reg 2A(1) (reg 2A added by SI 1993/151). For these purposes, 'relevant material interest' means a freehold or leasehold interest in the whole of the dwelling: Council Tax (Liability for Owners) Regulations 1992, SI 1992/551, reg 2A(2) (as so added).

In relation to a dwelling within reg 2 Class E (see note 6 head (v)) where a minister of the Church of England is the inhabitant and the owner of the dwelling and is in receipt of a stipend, the Local Government Finance Act 1992 s 8(3) has effect as if, for the reference to the owner, there were substituted a reference to the diocesan board of finance of the diocese in which the dwelling is situated: Council Tax (Liability for Owners) Regulations 1992, SI 1992/551, reg 3 (amended by SI 1995/620). As to the Church of England see ECCLESIASTICAL LAW vol 34 (2011) PARA 50 et seq; and as to diocesan boards of finance see ECCLESIASTICAL LAW vol 34 (2011) PARAS 241–242.

8 See the Local Government Finance Act 1992 s 8(3).

9 Local Government Finance Act 1992 s 8(4). Section 6(4) applies for the purposes of s 8(4) above as it applies for the purposes of s 6(3) (see PARA 354): s 8(5).

357. Liability of spouses and civil partners.

Where:

(1) a person who is liable to pay council tax[1] in respect of any chargeable dwelling[2] of which he is a resident[3] and any day is married to[4], or is the civil partner of[5], another person[6]; and

(2) that other person is also a resident of the dwelling on that day but would not, apart from this provision, be so liable[7],

those persons are each jointly and severally liable to pay the council tax in respect of the dwelling and that day[8]. However, this provision as to liability does not apply as respects any day on which the other person there mentioned falls to be disregarded for the purposes of discount, either on grounds of severe mental impairment[9] or owing[10] to their status as a student, apprentice or trainee[11].

1 As to council tax see PARA 344 et seq. As to persons liable to pay council tax see PARAS 354 et seq.

2 As to the meaning of 'chargeable dwelling' see PARA 350.

3 As to the meaning of 'resident' see PARA 354 note 4.

4 For these purposes, two persons are married to each other if they are a man and a woman:

(1) who are married to each other (Local Government Finance Act 1992 s 9(3)(a)); or

(2) who are not married to each other but are living together as husband and wife (s 9(3)(b)).

Marriage includes marriage of a same sex couple: see the Marriage (Same Sex Couples) Act 2013 Sch 3 para 1(1)(a), (2), (3); and MATRIMONIAL AND CIVIL PARTNERSHIP LAW vol 72 (2015) PARA 1 et seq.

5 For these purposes, two persons are civil partners of each other if they are of the same sex and either:

(1) they are civil partners of each other (Local Government Finance Act 1992 s 9(4)(a) (s 9(4) added by the Civil Partnership Act 2004 s 261(1), Sch 27 para 140(2))); or

(2) they are not civil partners of each other but are living together as if they were civil partners (Local Government Finance Act 1992 s 9(4)(b) (as so added)).

As to civil partnership see MATRIMONIAL AND CIVIL PARTNERSHIP LAW vol 72 (2015) PARA 3.

6 Local Government Finance Act 1992 s 9(1)(a) (amended by the Civil Partnership Act 2004 Sch 27 para 140(1)).

7 Local Government Finance Act 1992 s 9(1)(b).

8 Local Government Finance Act 1992 s 9(1). See *Gardiner v Swindon Borough Council* [2003] EWHC 515 (Admin), [2003] RVR 242, [2003] All ER (D) 355 (Feb).

9 Ie by virtue of the Local Government Finance Act 1992 Sch 1 para 2: see PARA 369.

10 Ie by virtue of the Local Government Finance Act 1992 Sch 1 para 4: see PARA 371.

11 See the Local Government Finance Act 1992 s 9(2) (amended by the Local Government Act 2003 s 74(2)).

358. Death of persons liable.

The appropriate national authority[1] may make such regulations[2] as it thinks fit to deal with any case where a person dies, and at any time before his death:

(1) he was (or is alleged to have been) liable to pay council tax[3] through his residence in or ownership of a chargeable dwelling[4];

(2) he was (or is alleged to have been) so liable[5] as spouse or civil partner[6]; or

(3) a penalty was imposed[7] on him[8].

The regulations may[9]:

(a) provide that where, before his death, a sum has become payable by the deceased but has not been paid, his executor or administrator is liable to pay the sum and may deduct out of the assets and effects of the deceased any payments made (or to be made)[10];

(b) provide that where, before his death, a sum in excess of his liability has been paid (whether the excess arises because of his death or otherwise) and has not been repaid or credited, his executor or administrator is entitled to the sum[11];

(c) provide for the recovery of any sum which is payable under the regulations and is not paid[12];

(d) provide that proceedings (whether by way of appeal or otherwise) may be instituted, continued or withdrawn by the deceased's executor or administrator[13].

1 Ie the Secretary of State or, in relation to Wales, the Welsh Ministers. The functions of the Secretary of State under the Local Government Finance Act 1992 s 18, so far as exercisable in relation to Wales, were transferred to the National Assembly for Wales (see the National Assembly for Wales (Transfer of Functions) Order 1999, SI 1999/672, art 2, Sch 1) and are now vested in the Welsh Ministers (see the Government of Wales Act 2006 s 162(1), Sch 11 para 30). As to the Secretary of State and the Welsh Ministers see PARA 4 note 18. As to the meaning of 'Wales' see PARA 2 note 16.

2 As to the regulations made see the Council Tax (Civil Partners) (England) Regulations 2005, SI 2005/2866, and the Council Tax (Administration and Enforcement) (Amendment) (England) Regulations 2013, SI 2013/590, which amend various other provisions.

3 Ie under the Local Government Finance Act 1992 s 6 (see PARA 354), s 7 (see PARA 355) or s 8 (see PARA 356). As to council tax see PARA 344 et seq.

4 See the Local Government Finance Act 1992 s 18(1)(a).

5 Ie under the Local Government Finance Act 1992 s 9: see PARA 357.

6 Local Government Finance Act 1992 s 18(1)(b) (amended by the Civil Partnership Act 2004 s 261(1), Sch 27 para 140(3)).

7 Ie under regulations under the Local Government Finance Act 1992 s 14C (see PARA 438) or under Sch 3 para 1 (see PARA 471).

8 Local Government Finance Act 1992 s 18(1)(c) (amended by the Local Government Finance Act 2012 s 14(1), (3)).

9 Nothing in the Local Government Finance Act 1992 s 18(3)–(6) prejudices the generality of s 18(1) (see the text to notes 1–8): s 18(2).
10 Local Government Finance Act 1992 s 18(3). As to executors and administrators see WILLS AND INTESTACY vol 103 (2016) PARA 605 et seq.
11 Local Government Finance Act 1992 s 18(4).
12 Local Government Finance Act 1992 s 18(5).
13 Local Government Finance Act 1992 s 18(6). As to appeals see PARA 513.

(iv) Exclusion of Crown Exemption

359. Exclusion of Crown exemption in certain cases.

In the case of a dwelling[1] provided and maintained by an authority mentioned in any of heads (1) to (7) below for purposes connected with the administration of justice, police purposes or other Crown purposes[2], any rules as to Crown exemption which would have applied apart from this provision do not prevent either the dwelling being a chargeable dwelling[3] or any person being liable to pay council tax[4] in respect of the dwelling[5]. The authorities that are so excluded from such exemption are:

(1) a billing authority[6] other than the Council of the Isles of Scilly[7];
(2) a county council[8];
(3) the Greater London Authority[9];
(4) any functional body within the meaning of the Greater London Authority Act 1999[10];
(5) a police and crime commissioner[11];
(6) the Receiver for the Metropolitan Police District[12];
(7) the Residuary Body for Wales ('Corff Gweddilliol Cymru')[13].

The appropriate national authority[14] may by order[15] provide that these provisions[16] are also to apply in relation to any dwelling of a class prescribed by the order[17].

1 As to the meaning of 'dwelling' see PARA 349.
2 See the Local Government Finance Act 1992 s 19(1).
3 Local Government Finance Act 1992 s 19(2)(a). As to the meaning of 'chargeable dwelling' see PARA 350.
4 As to council tax see PARA 344 et seq. As to persons liable to pay council tax see PARAS 354–357.
5 Local Government Finance Act 1992 s 19(2)(b).
6 As to the meaning of 'billing authority' see PARA 346.
7 Local Government Finance Act 1992 s 19(3)(a). As to the Council of the Isles of Scilly see LOCAL GOVERNMENT vol 69 (2018) PARA 50.
8 Local Government Finance Act 1992 s 19(3)(b). As to local government areas and authorities see LOCAL GOVERNMENT vol 69 (2018) PARA 36 et seq.
9 Local Government Finance Act 1992 s 19(3)(bb) (s 19(3)(bb), (bc) added by the Greater London Authority Act 1999 s 137). As to the Greater London Authority see LONDON GOVERNMENT vol 71 (2013) PARA 67 et seq.
10 Local Government Finance Act 1992 s 19(3)(bc) (as added: see note 9). As to what constitutes a functional body within the meaning of the Greater London Authority Act 1999 see LONDON GOVERNMENT vol 71 (2013) PARA 148.
11 Local Government Finance Act 1992 s 19(3)(c) (substituted by the Police Reform and Social Responsibility Act 2011 s 99 Sch 16 para 212). As to police and crime commissioners see POLICE AND INVESTIGATORY POWERS vol 84 (2013) PARA 56 et seq.
12 Local Government Finance Act 1992 s 19(3)(e) (amended by the Police and Magistrates' Courts Act 1994 s 93, Sch 9 Pt I). As from a day to be appointed under the Greater London Authority Act 1999 s 425(2), the Local Government Finance Act 1992 s 19(3)(e) is repealed by the Greater London Authority Act 1999 s 423, Sch 34 Pt I. At the date at which this volume states the law, no such day had been appointed.

13 Local Government Finance Act 1992 s 19(3)(g) (added by the Local Government (Wales) Act 1994 s 39(2), Sch 13 para 33). The Residuary Body for Wales has been wound up and abolished: see LOCAL GOVERNMENT vol 69 (2018) PARA 18.

14 Ie the Secretary of State or, in relation to Wales, the Welsh Ministers. The functions of the Secretary of State under the Local Government Finance Act 1992 s 19, so far as exercisable in relation to Wales, were transferred to the National Assembly for Wales (see the National Assembly for Wales (Transfer of Functions) Order 1999, SI 1999/672, art 2, Sch 1) and are now vested in the Welsh Ministers (see the Government of Wales Act 2006 s 162(1), Sch 11 para 30). As to the Secretary of State and the Welsh Ministers see PARA 4 note 18. As to the meaning of 'Wales' see PARA 2 note 16.

15 At the date at which this volume states the law no such order had been made.

16 Ie the Local Government Finance Act 1992 s 19(2): see the text to notes 1–5.

17 Local Government Finance Act 1992 s 19(4). For these purposes, a class of dwellings may be prescribed by reference to such factors as the appropriate national authority sees fit: s 4(3) (s 4(3), (4) applied by s 19(5)). In particular, a class of dwellings may be prescribed by reference to one or more of the following factors, namely:
   (1) the physical characteristics of dwellings (s 4(4)(a) (as so applied));
   (2) the fact that dwellings are unoccupied or are occupied for prescribed purposes or are occupied or owned by persons of prescribed descriptions (s 4(4)(b) (as so applied)).

(3) Amount of Council Tax

(i) Basic Amount

360. Basic amounts payable.

Subject to the provisions regarding discounts and reduced amounts[1], a person who is liable to pay council tax[2] in respect of any chargeable dwelling[3] and any day must, as respects the dwelling and the day, pay to the billing authority[4] for the area in which the dwelling is situated[5] an amount calculated in accordance with a specified formula[6].

1 Ie subject to the Local Government Finance Act 1992 ss 11–13A: see PARA 362 et seq.

2 As to persons liable to pay council tax see PARA 354 et seq. As to council tax see PARA 344 et seq.

3 As to the meaning of 'chargeable dwelling' see PARA 350.

4 As to the meaning of 'billing authority' see PARA 346.

5 For the purposes of the Local Government Finance Act 1992 Pt I (ss 1–69), the Secretary of State or, in relation to Wales, the Welsh Ministers may make regulations containing rules for ascertaining in what part of a billing authority's area a dwelling is situated (whether situated in the area in fact or by virtue of regulations made under s 1(3) (see PARA 348)): s 10(2). As to the regulations made see the Council Tax (Situation and Valuation of Dwellings) Regulations 1992, SI 1992/550, Pt II (regs 2–5) (reg 3 amended by SI 1994/1747).

The functions of the Secretary of State under the Local Government Finance Act 1992 s 10, so far as exercisable in relation to Wales, were transferred to the National Assembly for Wales (see the National Assembly for Wales (Transfer of Functions) Order 1999, SI 1999/672, art 2, Sch 1) and are now vested in the Welsh Ministers (see the Government of Wales Act 2006 s 162(1), Sch 11 para 30). As to the Secretary of State and the Welsh Ministers see PARA 4 note 18. As to the meaning of 'Wales' see PARA 2 note 16.

6 See the Local Government Finance Act 1992 s 10(1) (amended by the Local Government Finance Act 2012 s 10(2), (3)(b), Sch 4 paras 3, 4).

361. Different amounts for dwellings in different valuation bands.

For the purposes of calculating liability for council tax[1], dwellings[2] are categorised according to their value into different valuation bands. The amounts of council tax payable[3] in respect of dwellings situated in the same billing authority's[4] area (or the same part of such an area) and listed in different valuation bands[5] must be in the proportion specified[6].

The valuation bands for dwellings in England are[7]:

(1) valuation band A: values not exceeding £40,000[8];
(2) valuation band B: values exceeding £40,000 but not exceeding £52,000[9];
(3) valuation band C: values exceeding £52,000 but not exceeding £68,000[10];
(4) valuation band D: values exceeding £68,000 but not exceeding £88,000[11];
(5) valuation band E: values exceeding £88,000 but not exceeding £120,000[12];
(6) valuation band F: values exceeding £120,000 but not exceeding £160,000[13];
(7) valuation band G: values exceeding £160,000 but not exceeding £320,000[14];
(8) valuation band H: values exceeding £320,000[15].

The valuation bands for dwellings in Wales are[16]:

(a) valuation band A: values not exceeding £44,000[17];
(b) valuation band B: values exceeding £44,000 but not exceeding £65,000[18];
(c) valuation band C: values exceeding £65,000 but not exceeding £91,000[19];
(d) valuation band D: values exceeding £91,000 but not exceeding £123,000[20];
(e) valuation band E: values exceeding £123,000 but not exceeding £162,000[21];
(f) valuation band F: values exceeding £162,000 but not exceeding £223,000[22];
(g) valuation band G: values exceeding £223,000 but not exceeding £324,000[23];
(h) valuation band H: values exceeding £324,000 but not exceeding £424,000[24];
(i) valuation band I: values exceeding £424,000[25].

The appropriate national authority[26] may by order[27], as regards financial years beginning on or after such date as is specified in the order:

(i) substitute another proportion for that which is for the time being effective[28] for the above purposes[29]; or
(ii) substitute other valuation bands for those which are for the time being effective[30] for the above purposes[31].

The appropriate national authority[32] may by regulations make provision for the purpose of smoothing changes in council tax liability resulting from the coming into force in relation to a billing authority of such an order[33]. Such regulations may make different provision for different financial years[34]; and may, in particular:

(A) make provision about the circumstances in which changes are to be smoothed[35];
(B) make provision for changes to be smoothed over such one or more financial years as may be specified in the regulations[36];

(C) make provision for liability for any financial year to be determined in accordance with such rules as may be so specified, which may result in liability being the same as or different from what it would otherwise be[37].

1 As to council tax see PARA 344 et seq. As to persons liable to pay council tax see PARA 354 et seq.
2 As to the meaning of 'dwelling' see PARA 349.
3 Any reference in the Local Government Finance Act 1992 Pt I (ss 1–69) to an amount payable in respect of council tax for any financial year includes a reference to an amount payable in respect of council tax for any period falling within that year: s 69(2)(b). As to the meaning of 'financial year' see PARA 11 note 1.
4 As to the meaning of 'billing authority' see PARA 346.
5 Any reference in the Local Government Finance Act 1992 Pt I (ss 1–69) to dwellings listed in a particular valuation band is to be construed as a reference to dwellings to which that valuation band is shown as applicable in the billing authority's valuation list: ss 5(6), 69(2)(a). As to valuation lists see PARA 408 et seq.
6 See the Local Government Finance Act 1992 s 5(1). In relation to dwellings situated in England, the specified proportion is as follows: 6:7:8:9:11:13:15:18, where 6 is for dwellings listed in valuation band A (see head (1) in the text), 7 is for dwellings listed in valuation band B (see head (2) in the text), and so on: see s 5(1). For the purposes of the application of s 5(1) to dwellings situated in Wales, for the purposes of financial years beginning on or after 1 April 2005, for the proportion specified in s 5(1) there is substituted the following proportion: 6:7:8:9:11:13:15:18:21: s 5(1A) (added by SI 2003/3046). As to revaluation and the compilation of new lists see PARA 411 et seq. As to the meanings of 'England' and 'Wales' see PARA 2 note 16.
7 Local Government Finance Act 1992 s 5(2).
8 See the Local Government Finance Act 1992 s 5(2), Table.
9 See the Local Government Finance Act 1992 s 5(2), Table.
10 See the Local Government Finance Act 1992 s 5(2), Table.
11 See the Local Government Finance Act 1992 s 5(2), Table.
12 See the Local Government Finance Act 1992 s 5(2), Table.
13 See the Local Government Finance Act 1992 s 5(2), Table.
14 See the Local Government Finance Act 1992 s 5(2), Table.
15 See the Local Government Finance Act 1992 s 5(2), Table.
16 Local Government Finance Act 1992 s 5(3).
17 See the Local Government Finance Act 1992 s 5(3), Table (Table substituted by SI 2003/3046).
18 See the Local Government Finance Act 1992 s 5(3), Table (Table as substituted: see note 17).
19 See the Local Government Finance Act 1992 s 5(3), Table (Table as substituted: see note 17).
20 See the Local Government Finance Act 1992 s 5(3), Table (Table as substituted: see note 17).
21 See the Local Government Finance Act 1992 s 5(3), Table (Table as substituted: see note 17).
22 See the Local Government Finance Act 1992 s 5(3), Table (Table as substituted: see note 17).
23 See the Local Government Finance Act 1992 s 5(3), Table (Table as substituted: see note 17).
24 See the Local Government Finance Act 1992 s 5(3), Table (Table as substituted: see note 17).
25 See the Local Government Finance Act 1992 s 5(3), Table (Table as substituted: see note 17).
26 Ie the Secretary of State or, in relation to Wales, the Welsh Ministers. The functions of the Secretary of State under the Local Government Finance Act 1992 s 5 so far as exercisable in relation to Wales, were transferred to the National Assembly for Wales (see the National Assembly for Wales (Transfer of Functions) Order 1999, SI 1999/672, art 2, Sch 1) and are now vested in the Welsh Ministers (see the Government of Wales Act 2006 s 162(1), Sch 11 para 30). As to the Secretary of State and the Welsh Ministers see PARA 4 note 18.
27 No such order may be made by the Secretary of State unless a draft of the order has been laid before and approved by resolution of the House of Commons: see the Local Government Finance Act 1992 s 5(5). As to the equivalent procedure in relation to subordinate legislation made by the Welsh Ministers see the Government of Wales Act 2006 Sch 11 paras 33–35; and STATUTES AND LEGISLATIVE PROCESS vol 96 (2012) PARA 1035.
28 Ie effective for the purposes of the Local Government Finance Act 1992 s 5(1): see the text to notes 1–6.
29 Local Government Finance Act 1992 s 5(4)(a).
30 Ie effective for the purposes of the Local Government Finance Act 1992 s 5(2) (see the text to notes 7–15) or s 5(3) (see the text to notes 16–25), as the case may be: see s 5(4)(b).

31 Local Government Finance Act 1992 s 5(4)(b). The power under s 5(4)(b) includes power to make provision for a different number of valuation bands from those which are for the time being effective for the purposes of s 5(2) or 5(3): s 5(4A) (added by the Local Government Act 2003 s 78). The Council Tax (Valuation Bands) (Wales) Order 2003, SI 2003/3046 (an amending provision as to which see notes 6, 17), has been made.

32 The functions under the Local Government Finance Act 1992 s 13B(2) were formerly vested in the National Assembly for Wales and are now exercisable by the Welsh Ministers by virtue of the Government of Wales Act 2006 s 162(1), Sch 11 paras 30, 32.

33 See the Local Government Finance Act 1992 s 13B(1), (2) (s 13B added by the Local Government Act 2003 s 79). To the extent that he would not have power to do so apart from this provision, the Secretary of State may:

(1) include in regulations made by him under the Local Government Finance Act 1992 s 13B such amendments of any social security instrument as he thinks expedient in consequence of the regulations (s 13B(5)(a) (as so added));

(2) include in any social security instrument such provision as he thinks expedient in consequence of regulations under s 13B (s 13B(5)(b) (as so added)).

'Social security instrument' has the meaning given by s 13(10) (see PARA 377 note 27): s 13B(6) (as so added). The following regulations have been made in relation to Wales under s 13B(2): the Council Tax (Transitional Arrangements) (Wales) Regulations 2004, SI 2004/3142 (amended by SI 2005/702), which make transitional arrangements for the period from 1 April 2005 to 31 March 2008.

34 Local Government Finance Act 1992 s 13B(4) (as added: see note 33). This provision is expressed to be without prejudice to s 113(1) (see PARA 345): see s 13B(4) (as so added).

35 Local Government Finance Act 1992 s 13B(3)(a) (as added: see note 33).

36 Local Government Finance Act 1992 s 13B(3)(b) (as added: see note 33).

37 Local Government Finance Act 1992 s 13B(3)(c) (as added: see note 33).

(ii) Discounts and Premiums

A. IN GENERAL

362. Discounts.

The amount of council tax payable[1] in respect of any chargeable dwelling[2] and any day is subject to a discount equal to the appropriate percentage[3] of that amount if on that day[4]:

(1) there is only one resident[5] of the dwelling and he does not fall to be disregarded for the purposes of discount[6]; or

(2) there are two or more residents of the dwelling and each of them except one falls to be disregarded for those purposes[7].

Subject to the special provisions made in relation to England and Wales respectively[8], the amount of council tax payable in respect of any chargeable dwelling and any day is subject to a discount equal to twice the appropriate percentage of that amount if on that day[9]:

(a) there is no resident of the dwelling[10]; or

(b) there are one or more residents of the dwelling and each of them falls to be disregarded for the purposes of discount[11].

1 As to references to an amount payable in respect of council tax see PARA 361 note 3. As to council tax see PARA 344 et seq. As to persons liable to pay council tax see PARA 354 et seq.

2 As to the meaning of 'chargeable dwelling' see PARA 350.

3 'Appropriate percentage' means 25% or, if the Secretary of State or, in relation to Wales, the Welsh Ministers by order so provide in relation to the financial year in which the day falls, such other percentage as is specified in the order: see the Local Government Finance Act 1992 s 11(3) (amended by the Local Government Act 2003 s 127(2), Sch 8 Pt 1). As to the meaning of 'financial year' see PARA 11 note 1. No such order may be made by the Secretary of State unless a draft of the order has been laid before and approved by resolution of the House of Commons: see the Local Government Finance Act 1992 s 11(4). As to the equivalent procedure in relation to subordinate legislation made by the Welsh Ministers see the Government of Wales Act 2006 Sch 11 paras

33–35; and STATUTES AND LEGISLATIVE PROCESS vol 96 (2012) PARA 1035. At the date at which this volume states the law no such order had been made.

The functions of the Secretary of State under the Local Government Finance Act 1992 s 11, so far as exercisable in relation to Wales, were transferred to the National Assembly for Wales (see the National Assembly for Wales (Transfer of Functions) Order 1999, SI 1999/672, art 2, Sch 1) and are now vested in the Welsh Ministers (see the Government of Wales Act 2006 s 162(1), Sch 11 para 30). As to the Secretary of State and the Welsh Ministers see PARA 4 note 18. As to the meaning of 'Wales' see PARA 2 note 16.

4 Local Government Finance Act 1992 s 11(1). For the purposes of determining for any day whether any amount of council tax is subject to a discount and (if so) the amount of the discount, it must be assumed that any state of affairs subsisting at the end of the day had subsisted throughout the day: see s 2(2)(d); and PARA 348.

5 As to the meaning of 'resident' see PARA 354 note 4. See *Bennett v Copeland Borough Council* [2004] EWCA Civ 672 at [33], [2004] RA 171 at [33] per Rix LJ (actual residence is critical to an understanding of the Local Government Finance Act 1992 s 11).

6 Local Government Finance Act 1992 s 11(1)(a). As to the persons to be disregarded for the purposes of discount see Sch 1; and PARAS 368–376.

7 Local Government Finance Act 1992 s 11(1)(b).

8 Ie subject to the Local Government Finance Act 1992 ss 11A, 11B (England) (see PARAS 363—364) and ss 12, 12A, 12B (Wales) (see PARAS 365, 366, 367). As to the meaning of 'England' see PARA 2 note 16.

9 Local Government Finance Act 1992 s 11(2) (amended by the Local Government Act 2003 s 127(1), Sch 7 paras 40, 41; the Local Government Finance Act 2012 s 12(1), (3); and, in relation to Wales, the Housing (Wales) Act 2014 s 139(1), (3), Sch 3 para 29(1), (2)).

10 Local Government Finance Act 1992 s 11(2)(a).

11 Local Government Finance Act 1992 s 11(2)(b).

363. Special provision for discounts where dwellings in England have no resident.

The Secretary of State[1] may for any financial year[2] by regulations prescribe[3] one or more classes of dwelling[4] in England[5] for the purposes[6] of allowing a billing authority[7] in England by determination[8] to provide in relation to all dwellings of that class in its area[9] (or in such part of its area as it may specify in the determination) that the discount which applies to the amount payable in respect of council tax where there is no resident of the dwelling[10]:

(1) is to be such lesser percentage of at least ten as it may so specify[11]; or
(2) does not apply[12] or is to be such lesser percentage as it may so specify[13]; or
(3) does not apply or is to be such percentage (which may be 100) as it may so specify, in relation to all dwellings of that class in its area, or in relation to such description of dwellings of that class as it may specify in the determination[14].

A billing authority may make a determination varying or revoking any such determination for a financial year, but only before the beginning of the year[15]. A billing authority which makes a determination[16] must publish a notice of it in at least one newspaper circulating in its area and do so before the end of the period of 21 days beginning with the date of the determination[17]; but a failure to comply with this requirement does not affect the validity of a determination[18].

For each financial year beginning on or after 1 April 2013, the following classes are prescribed as classes of dwellings for the purposes of head (2) above[19]:

(a) Class A: comprising every chargeable dwelling[20] in England:
 (i) which is not the sole or main residence of an individual[21];
 (ii) which is furnished[22]; and

(iii) the occupation of which is restricted by a planning condition preventing occupancy for a continuous period of at least 28 days in the relevant year[23];

except that the class of dwellings so described is not to include any dwelling which is excluded from that class by virtue of head (A) or head (B) below[24];

(b) Class B: comprising every chargeable dwelling in England:

(i) which is not the sole or main residence of an individual[25];

(ii) which is furnished[26]; and

(iii) the occupation of which is not restricted by a planning condition preventing occupancy for a continuous period of at least 28 days in the relevant year[27];

except that the class of dwellings so described is not to include any dwelling which is excluded from that class by virtue of head (A) or head (B) below[28].

except that the class of dwellings so described is not to include any dwelling which is excluded from that class by virtue of head (A) or head (B) below[28].

Neither Class A nor Class B is to include:

(A) any dwelling which consists of a pitch occupied by a caravan[29], or a mooring occupied by a boat[30]; or

(B) any dwelling where a qualifying person[31] in relation to that dwelling is a qualifying person in relation to another dwelling in England, Wales[32] or Scotland which for him is job-related[33], or which for a qualifying person is job-related where that person is a qualifying person in relation to another dwelling in England, Wales or Scotland[34].

For each financial year beginning on or after 1 April 2013, the classes of dwellings prescribed for the purposes of head (3) above are:

(I) Class C[35] which comprises every chargeable dwelling in England which is unoccupied[36] and which is substantially unfurnished[37]; and

(II) Class D[38]: comprising every chargeable dwelling in England:

(AA) which satisfies the requirement set out in head (BB) unless it has been such a dwelling for a continuous period of 12 months or more ending immediately before the day in question[39];

(BB) the requirement referred to in head (AA) is that the dwelling is vacant[40] and requires or is undergoing major repair work[41] to render it habitable[42], or is undergoing structural alteration[43] or has undergone major repair work to render it habitable, if less than six months have elapsed since the date on which the alteration was substantially completed and the dwelling has continuously remained vacant since that date[44].

1 As to the Secretary of State see PARA 4 note 18.

2 As to the meaning of 'financial year' see PARA 11 note 1.

3 Ie for the purposes set out in the Local Government Finance Act 1992 s 11A(3) (see head (1) in the text), s 11A(4) (see head (2) in the text) or s 11A(4A) (see head (3) in the text). As to the regulations made see the text to notes 19–44.

4 As to the meaning of 'dwelling' see PARA 349. A class of dwellings may be prescribed under the Local Government Finance Act 1992 s 11A(1) by reference to such factors as the Secretary of State sees fit and may, in particular, be prescribed by reference to:

(1) the physical characteristics of dwellings (s 11A(2)(a) (s 11A added by the Local Government Act 2003 s 75(1))); or

(2) the fact that dwellings are unoccupied (Local Government Finance Act 1992 s 11A(2)(b) (as so added)).

5 As to the meaning of 'England' see PARA 2 note 16.

6 See the Local Government Finance Act 1992 s 11A(1) (as added (see note 4); amended by the Local Government Finance Act 2012 s 11(2)).
7 As to the meaning of 'billing authority' see PARA 346.
8 The making of a determination under the Local Government Finance Act 1992 s 11A may be discharged only by the billing authority: see s 67(1), (2)(a) (s 67(2)(a) amended by the Local Government Act 2003 s 127(1), Sch 7 paras 40, 50(a)). A determination made under the Local Government Finance Act 1992 s 11A may not be questioned except by an application for judicial review: see s 66(1), (2)(b) (s 66(2)(b) amended by the Local Government Act 2003 Sch 7 paras 40, 49(a)). If on an application for judicial review the court decides to grant relief, it must quash the determination: see the Local Government Finance Act 1992 s 66(3) (amended by the Local Government Finance Act 2012 s 10(2), (3)(b), Sch 4 paras 3, 5(1), (3)). As to judicial review see JUDICIAL REVIEW vol 61 (2010) PARA 601 et seq.
9 As to the power of the Secretary of State to make regulations containing rules for ascertaining in what part of a billing authority's area a dwelling is situated see the Local Government Finance Act 1992 s 10(2); and PARA 360; and as to the power to make regulations containing rules for treating a dwelling as situated in a billing authority's area if part only of the dwelling falls within the area see s 1(3); and PARA 348.
10 Ie the discount under the Local Government Finance Act 1992 s 11(2)(a): see PARA 362.
11 See the Local Government Finance Act 1992 s 11A(3) (as added: see note 4).
12 See the Local Government Finance Act 1992 s 11A(4)(a) (as added: see note 4).
13 See the Local Government Finance Act 1992 s 11A(4)(b) (as added: see note 4).
14 See the Local Government Finance Act 1992 s 11A(4A) (s 11A as added (see note 4); s 11A(4A), (4B) added by the Local Government Finance Act 2012 s 11(1)). Where a class of dwellings is prescribed for the purposes of the Local Government Finance Act 1992 s 11A(4A) by reference to the period of time for which a condition is met, a billing authority may not, under s 11A(4A)(b), specify a description of dwellings of that class by reference (wholly or partly) to a shorter such period: s 11A(4B) (as so added). Section 11A(3), (4), (4A) is are subject to s 11B(4) (see PARA 364): s 11A(4C) (added by the Local Government Finance Act 2012 s 12(1), (4)).
15 Local Government Finance Act 1992 s 11A(5) (as added (see note 4); amended by the Local Government Finance Act 2012 s 11(2)).
16 Ie a determination under the Local Government Finance Act 1992 s 11A.
17 Local Government Finance Act 1992 s 11A(6) (as added: see note 4).
18 Local Government Finance Act 1992 s 11A(7) (as added: see note 4).
19 See the Council Tax (Prescribed Classes of Dwellings) (England) Regulations 2003, SI 2003/3011, reg 3(1) (reg 3 substituted by SI 2012/2964).
20 As to the meaning of 'chargeable dwelling' see PARA 350.
21 Council Tax (Prescribed Classes of Dwellings) (England) Regulations 2003, SI 2003/3011, reg 4(a). As to the meaning of 'resident' and what constitutes a sole or main residence see PARA 354 note 4.
22 Council Tax (Prescribed Classes of Dwellings) (England) Regulations 2003, SI 2003/3011, reg 4(b).
23 Council Tax (Prescribed Classes of Dwellings) (England) Regulations 2003, SI 2003/3011, reg 4(c). For these purposes, 'relevant year' means the financial year for which a billing authority makes a determination under the Local Government Finance Act 1992 s 11A (see the text to notes 1–18): Council Tax (Prescribed Classes of Dwellings) (England) Regulations 2003, SI 2003/3011, reg 2(1) (reg 2 substituted by SI 2012/2964). As to the conditional grant of planning permission see PLANNING vol 82 (2018) PARA 466 et seq.
24 Council Tax (Prescribed Classes of Dwellings) (England) Regulations 2003, SI 2003/3011, reg 4.
25 Council Tax (Prescribed Classes of Dwellings) (England) Regulations 2003, SI 2003/3011, reg 5(a).
26 Council Tax (Prescribed Classes of Dwellings) (England) Regulations 2003, SI 2003/3011, reg 5(b).
27 Council Tax (Prescribed Classes of Dwellings) (England) Regulations 2003, SI 2003/3011, reg 5(c).
28 Council Tax (Prescribed Classes of Dwellings) (England) Regulations 2003, SI 2003/3011, reg 5.
28 Council Tax (Prescribed Classes of Dwellings) (England) Regulations 2003, SI 2003/3011, reg 5.
29 'Caravan' is to be construed in accordance with the Caravan Sites and Control of Development Act 1960 Pt I (ss 1–32) (see PLANNING vol 83 (2018) PARA 1137): Council Tax (Prescribed Classes of Dwellings) (England) Regulations 2003, SI 2003/3011, reg 2(1) (as substituted: see note 23).
30 Council Tax (Prescribed Classes of Dwellings) (England) Regulations 2003, SI 2003/3011, reg 6(1).

31 'Qualifying person' means a person who is liable for the council tax in respect of a dwelling on a particular day (whether or not jointly with any other person) or who would be liable for the council tax in respect of a dwelling on a particular day if that dwelling did not fall within the Council Tax (Exempt Dwellings) Order 1992, SI 1992/558, art 3 Class O (see PARA 352) or the Council Tax (Liability for Owners) Regulations 1992, SI 1992/551, reg 2 Class E (see PARA 356): see the Council Tax (Prescribed Classes of Dwellings) (England) Regulations 2003, SI 2003/3011, reg 2(1) (as substituted: see note 23). As to persons liable to pay council tax see PARA 354 et seq.

32 As to the meaning of 'Wales' see PARA 2 note 16.

33 Council Tax (Prescribed Classes of Dwellings) (England) Regulations 2003, SI 2003/3011, reg 6(2)(a) (amended by SI 2005/416). For these purposes, a dwelling is job-related if it falls within the description set out in the Council Tax (Prescribed Classes of Dwellings) (England) Regulations 2003, SI 2003/3011, Schedule para 1, 2 or 2A: see reg 6(3), Schedule (reg 6(3) substituted by SI 2004/926; the Council Tax (Prescribed Classes of Dwellings) (England) Regulations 2003, SI 2003/3011, Schedule amended by SI 2004/926 and SI 2005/2866).

34 Council Tax (Prescribed Classes of Dwellings) (England) Regulations 2003, SI 2003/3011, reg 6(2)(b) (amended by SI 2005/416). For these purposes, a dwelling is job-related if it falls within the description set out in the Council Tax (Prescribed Classes of Dwellings) (England) Regulations 2003, SI 2003/3011, Schedule para 1 or 2: see reg 6(3), Schedule (as substituted and amended: see note 32).

35 See the Council Tax (Prescribed Classes of Dwellings) (England) Regulations 2003, SI 2003/3011, reg 3(2) (as substituted: see note 19).

36 Council Tax (Prescribed Classes of Dwellings) (England) Regulations 2003, SI 2003/3011, reg 7(a). For these purposes, 'unoccupied dwelling' means a dwelling in which no-one lives: reg 2(1) (as substituted: see note 23).

37 Council Tax (Prescribed Classes of Dwellings) (England) Regulations 2003, SI 2003/3011, reg 7(b).

38 See the Council Tax (Prescribed Classes of Dwellings) (England) Regulations 2003, SI 2003/3011, reg 3(2) (as substituted: see note 19).

39 Council Tax (Prescribed Classes of Dwellings) (England) Regulations 2003, SI 2003/3011, reg 8(a) (reg 8 added by SI 2012/2964).

40 For the purposes of Class D:

(1) a dwelling is vacant on any day if on the day:

(a) in the case of a dwelling consisting of a pitch occupied by a caravan or a mooring occupied by a boat, the caravan or boat is unoccupied (Council Tax (Prescribed Classes of Dwellings) (England) Regulations 2003, SI 2003/3011, reg 2(2)(a)(i) (as substituted: see note 23)); and

(b) in any other case, the dwelling is unoccupied and substantially unfurnished (reg 2(2)(a)(ii) (as so substituted)); and

(2) in considering whether a dwelling has been vacant for any period, any one period, not exceeding six weeks, during which it was not vacant shall be disregarded (reg 2(2)(b) (as so substituted)).

41 For the purposes of the Council Tax (Prescribed Classes of Dwellings) (England) Regulations 2003, SI 2003/3011, reg 8, 'major repair work' includes structural repair work: reg 8(c) (as added: see note 39).

42 Council Tax (Prescribed Classes of Dwellings) (England) Regulations 2003, SI 2003/3011, reg 8(b)(i) (as added: see note 39).

43 Council Tax (Prescribed Classes of Dwellings) (England) Regulations 2003, SI 2003/3011, reg 8(b)(ii) (as added: see note 39).

44 Council Tax (Prescribed Classes of Dwellings) (England) Regulations 2003, SI 2003/3011, reg 8(b)(iiii) (as added: see note 39).

364. Higher amount of council tax for long-term empty dwellings: England.

For any financial year[1], a billing authority[2] in England[3] may by determination[4] provide in relation to its area, or such part of its area as it may specify in the determination[5], that if on any day a dwelling[6] is a long-term empty dwelling[7]:

(1) the discount which applies to the amount payable in respect of council tax where there is no resident of the dwelling[8] is not to apply[9]; and

(2) the amount of council tax payable in respect of that dwelling and that day is to be increased by such percentage of not more than 50 as it may so specify[10].

Where a determination under these provisions has effect in relation to a class of dwellings, the billing authority may not make a determination that the discount is to be a lesser percentage or is not to apply[11] in relation to that class, and any such determination that has been made ceases to have effect in relation to that class[12].

A billing authority may make a determination varying or revoking a determination in respect of a long term empty dwelling for a financial year, but only before the beginning of the year[13]. A billing authority which makes a determination must publish a notice of it in at least one newspaper circulating in its area and do so before the end of the period of 21 days beginning with the date of the determination[14]; but a failure to comply with this requirement does not affect the validity of a determination[15].

The Secretary of State may by regulations prescribe one or more classes of dwelling in relation to which a billing authority may not make such a determination[16]. For each financial year beginning on or after 1 April 2013, the following classes are prescribed as classes of dwellings for this purpose[17]:

(a) Class E: comprising every chargeable dwelling[18] in England which:
   (i) is the sole or main residence[19] of an individual where that individual is a qualifying person[20] in relation to another dwelling provided by the Secretary of State for Defence for the purposes of armed forces accommodation, and which for that individual is job-related[21]; or
   (ii) would be the sole or main residence of an individual if that individual were not a qualifying person in relation to another dwelling provided by the Secretary of State for Defence for the purposes of armed forces accommodation, and which for that individual is job-related[22].
(b) Class F: comprising every chargeable dwelling in England:
   (i) which forms part of a single property[23] which includes at least one other dwelling[24]; and
   (ii) which is being used by a resident of that other dwelling, or as the case may be, one of those other dwellings, as part of their sole or main residence[25].

1 As to the meaning of 'financial year' see PARA 11 note 1.
2 As to the meaning of 'billing authority' see PARA 346.
3 As to the meaning of 'England' see PARA 2 note 16.
4 The making of a determination under the Local Government Finance Act 1992 s 11B may be discharged only by the billing authority: see s 67(1), (2)(a) (s 67(2)(a) amended by the Local Government Act 2003 s 127(1), Sch 7 paras 40, 50(a); and the Local Government Finance Act 2012 s 12(1), (7)). A determination made under the Local Government Finance Act 1992 s 11B may not be questioned except by an application for judicial review: see s 66(1), (2)(b) (s 66(2)(b) amended by the Local Government Act 2003 s 127(1), Sch 7 paras 40, 49(a); and the Local Government Finance Act 2012 s 12(1), (6)). If on an application for judicial review the court decides to grant relief, it must quash the determination: see the Local Government Finance Act 1992 s 66(3) (amended by the Local Government Finance Act 2012 s 10(2), (3)(b), Sch 4 paras 3, 5(1), (3)). As to judicial review see JUDICIAL REVIEW vol 61 (2010) PARA 601 et seq.
5 As to the power of the Secretary of State to make regulations containing rules for ascertaining in what part of a billing authority's area a dwelling is situated see the Local Government Finance Act 1992 s 10(2); and PARA 360; and as to the power to make regulations containing rules for treating a dwelling as situated in a billing authority's area if part only of the dwelling falls within the area see s 1(3); and PARA 348. As to the Secretary of State see PARA 4 note 18.
6 As to the meaning of 'dwelling' see PARA 349.

7 Local Government Finance Act 1992 s 11B(1) (s 11B added by the Local Government Finance Act 2012 s 12(1), (2)). For the purposes of the Local Government Finance Act 1992 s 11B, a dwelling is a 'long-term empty dwelling' on any day if for a continuous period of at least two years ending with that day:
(1) it has been unoccupied (s 11B(8)(a) (as so added)); and
(2) it has been substantially unfurnished (s 11B(8)(b) (as so added)).
In determining whether a dwelling is a long-term empty dwelling, no account is to be taken of any one or more periods of not more than six weeks during which either of the conditions in s 11B(8)(a) and (b) is not met (or neither of them is met): s 11B(9) (as so added). The Secretary of State may by regulations substitute a different period, of not less than six weeks, for the period which is for the time being specified in s 11B(9): s 11B(10) (as so added).
8 Ie the discount under the Local Government Finance Act 1992 s 11(2)(a): see PARA 362.
9 Local Government Finance Act 1992 s 11B(1)(a) (as added: see note 7).
10 Local Government Finance Act 1992 s 11B(1)(b) (as added: see note 7).
11 Ie under the Local Government Finance Act 1992 s 11A(3), (4) or (4A): see PARA 363.
12 Local Government Finance Act 1992 s 11B(4) (as added: see note 7).
13 Local Government Finance Act 1992 s 11B(5) (as added: see note 7).
14 Local Government Finance Act 1992 s 11B(6) (as added: see note 7).
15 Local Government Finance Act 1992 s 11B(7) (as added: see note 7).
16 Local Government Finance Act 1992 s 11B(2) (as added: see note 7). A class of dwellings may be prescribed under s 11B(2) by reference to such factors as the Secretary of State thinks fit (s 11B(3) (as so added)) and may, in particular, be prescribed by reference to:
(1) the physical characteristics of, or other matters relating to, dwellings (s 11B(3)(a) (as so added));
(2) the circumstances of, or other matters relating to, any person who is liable to the amount of council tax concerned (s 11B(3)(b) (as so added)).
For regulations made under s 11B(2), (3) see the Council Tax (Prescribed Classes of Dwellings) (England) (Amendment) Regulations 2012, SI 2012/2964.
17 See the Council Tax (Prescribed Classes of Dwellings) (England) Regulations 2003, SI 2003/3011, reg 3(3) (reg 3 substituted by SI 2012/2964).
18 As to the meaning of 'chargeable dwelling' see PARA 350.
19 As to the meaning of 'resident' and what constitutes a sole or main residence see PARA 354 note 4.
20 As to the meaning of 'qualifying person' see PARA 363 note 31.
21 Council Tax (Prescribed Classes of Dwellings) (England) Regulations 2003, SI 2003/3011, reg 9(1)(a) (reg 9 added by SI 2012/2964). For the purposes of the Council Tax (Prescribed Classes of Dwellings) (England) Regulations 2003, SI 2003/3011, reg 9(1), a dwelling is job-related if it falls within the description set out in the Schedule para 1: see reg 9(2), Schedule para 1 (reg 9(2) as so added; Schedule para 1 amended by SI 2005/2866).
22 Council Tax (Prescribed Classes of Dwellings) (England) Regulations 2003, SI 2003/3011, reg 9(1)(b) (as added: see note 21).
23 For the purposes of the Council Tax (Prescribed Classes of Dwellings) (England) Regulations 2003, SI 2003/3011, 'single property' means property which would apart from the Council Tax (Chargeable Dwellings) Order 1992, SI 1992/549, be one dwelling within the meaning of the Local Government Finance Act 1992 s 3 (see PARA 349): Council Tax (Prescribed Classes of Dwellings) (England) Regulations 2003, SI 2003/3011, reg 10(2) (reg 10 added by SI 2012/2964).
24 Council Tax (Prescribed Classes of Dwellings) (England) Regulations 2003, SI 2003/3011, reg 10(1)(a) (as added: see note 23).
25 Council Tax (Prescribed Classes of Dwellings) (England) Regulations 2003, SI 2003/3011, reg 10(1)(b) (as added: see note 23).

365. Special provision for discounts where dwellings in Wales have no resident.

The Welsh Ministers[1] may for any financial year[2] by regulations prescribe[3] one or more classes of dwelling[4] in Wales[5] for the purposes[6] of allowing a billing authority[7] in Wales by determination[8] to provide in relation to all dwellings of that class in its area[9] (or in such part of its area as it may specify in the determination) that the discount which applies to the amount payable in respect of council tax where there is no resident of the dwelling[10], either:

(1) is to be such lesser percentage of at least ten as it may so specify[11]; or

(2) does not apply[12] or is to be such lesser percentage as it may so specify[13]. A billing authority may make a determination varying or revoking a determination under head (1) or (2) above for a financial year, but only before the beginning of the year[14]. A billing authority which makes a determination[15] must publish a notice of it in at least one newspaper circulating in its area and do so before the end of the period of 21 days beginning with the date of the determination[16]; but a failure to comply with this requirement does not affect the validity of a determination[17].

For each financial year beginning on or after 1 April 1998, the following classes are prescribed as classes of dwellings for the purposes of both heads (1) and (2) above[18]:

(a) Class A: comprising every dwelling in Wales:
  (i) of which there is no resident[19];
  (ii) which is substantially furnished[20]; and
  (iii) the occupation of which is prohibited by law for a continuous period of at least 28 days in the relevant year[21];

  except that the class of dwellings so described is not to include any dwelling which is excluded from that class by virtue of heads (A) to (C) below[22];

(b) Class B: comprising every dwelling in Wales:
  (i) of which there is no resident[23];
  (ii) which is substantially furnished[24]; and
  (iii) the occupation of which is not prohibited by law for a continuous period of at least 28 days in the relevant year[25];

  except that the class of dwellings so described is not to include any dwelling which is excluded from that class by virtue of heads (A) to (C) below[26].

Neither Class A nor Class B includes:

(A) any dwelling which consists of a pitch occupied by a caravan[27], or a mooring occupied by a boat[28]; or

(B) any unoccupied dwelling[29] in relation to which a person is a qualifying person[30] in his capacity as personal representative[31], if no person is a qualifying person in any other capacity[32], and either no grant of probate or of letters of administration has been made, or less than 12 months[33] have elapsed since the day on which such a grant was made[34];

(C) any dwelling where a qualifying person in relation to that dwelling is a qualifying person in relation to another dwelling which for him is job-related[35].

For each financial year beginning on or after 1 April 2004, there is also prescribed as a class of dwellings for the purposes of head (2) above, Class C[36] which comprises every chargeable dwelling[37] in Wales which is unoccupied[38], and which is substantially unfurnished[39].

1 The functions under the Local Government Finance Act 1992 s 12 were formerly vested in the National Assembly for Wales and are now exercisable by the Welsh Ministers by virtue of the Government of Wales Act 2006 s 162(1), Sch 11 paras 30, 32. As to the Welsh Ministers see PARA 4 note 18.

2 As to the meaning of 'financial year' see PARA 11 note 1.

3 Ie for the purposes set out in either the Local Government Finance Act 1992 s 12(3) (see head (1) in the text) or s 12(4) (see head (2) in the text). As to the regulations made see the text to notes 18–39.

4 A class of dwellings may be prescribed under the Local Government Finance Act 1992 s 12(1) by reference to such factors as the Welsh Ministers see fit and may, in particular, be prescribed by reference to:

(1) the physical characteristics of dwellings (s 12(2)(a) (s 12 substituted by the Local Government Act 2003 s 75(2))); or
(2) the fact that dwellings are unoccupied (Local Government Finance Act 1992 s 12(2)(b) (as so substituted)).

As to the meaning of 'dwelling' see PARA 349.

5 As to the meaning of 'Wales' see PARA 2 note 16.
6 See the Local Government Finance Act 1992 s 12(1) (as substituted: see note 4).
7 As to the meaning of 'billing authority' see PARA 346.
8 The making of a determination under the Local Government Finance Act 1992 s 12 may be discharged only by the billing authority: see s 67(1), (2)(a) (s 67(2)(a) amended by the Local Government Act 2003 s 127(1), Sch 7 paras 40, 50(b); and the Housing (Wales) Act 2014 s 139(1), (3), Sch 3 para 29(1), (6)). A determination made under the Local Government Finance Act 1992 s 12 may not be questioned except by an application for judicial review: see s 66(1), (2)(b) (s 66(2)(b) amended by the Local Government Act 2003 s 127(1), Sch 7 paras 40, 49(b); and the Housing (Wales) Act 2014 Sch 3 para 29(1), (5)). If on an application for judicial review the court decides to grant relief, it must quash the determination: see the Local Government Finance Act 1992 s 66(3) (amended by the Local Government Finance Act 2012 s 10(2), (3)(b), Sch 4 paras 3, 5(1), (3)). As to judicial review see JUDICIAL REVIEW vol 61 (2010) PARA 601 et seq.
9 As to the power of the Welsh Ministers to make regulations containing rules for ascertaining in what part of a billing authority's area a dwelling is situated see the Local Government Finance Act 1992 s 10(2); and PARA 360; and as to the power to make regulations containing rules for treating a dwelling as situated in a billing authority's area if part only of the dwelling falls within the area see s 1(3); and PARA 348.
10 Ie the discount under the Local Government Finance Act 1992 s 11(2)(a) (see PARA 362): see the Local Government Finance Act 1992 s 12(3), (4) (as substituted: see note 4).
11 See the Local Government Finance Act 1992 s 12(3) (as substituted: see note 4). Section 12(3) is subject to s 12A(6) and 12B(7) (see PARAS 366, 367): s 12(4A) (added by the Housing (Wales) Act 2014 Sch 3 para 29(1), (3)).
12 See the Local Government Finance Act 1992 s 12(4)(a) (as substituted: see note 4).
13 See the Local Government Finance Act 1992 s 12(4)(b) (as substituted: see note 4). Section 12(4) is subject to s 12A(6) and 12B(7) (see PARAS 366, 367): s 12(4A) (as added: see note 11).
14 Local Government Finance Act 1992 s 12(5) (as substituted: see note 4).
15 Ie under the Local Government Finance Act 1992 s 12: see the text to notes 1–14.
16 Local Government Finance Act 1992 s 12(6) (as substituted: see note 4).
17 Local Government Finance Act 1992 s 12(7) (as substituted: see note 4).
18 See the Council Tax (Prescribed Class of Dwellings) (Wales) Regulations 1998, SI 1998/105, reg 3(1) (renumbered by SI 2004/452).
19 Council Tax (Prescribed Class of Dwellings) (Wales) Regulations 1998, SI 1998/105, reg 4(a) (substituted by SI 2017/42). As to the meaning of 'resident' see PARA 354 note 4.
20 Council Tax (Prescribed Class of Dwellings) (Wales) Regulations 1998, SI 1998/105, reg 4(b) (amended by SI 2017/42).
21 Council Tax (Prescribed Class of Dwellings) (Wales) Regulations 1998, SI 1998/105, reg 4(c). For these purposes, 'relevant year' means the financial year for which a billing authority makes a determination under the Local Government Finance Act 1992 s 12 (see the text to notes 1–14): Council Tax (Prescribed Class of Dwellings) (Wales) Regulations 1998, SI 1998/105, reg 2.
22 Council Tax (Prescribed Class of Dwellings) (Wales) Regulations 1998, SI 1998/105, reg 4.
23 Council Tax (Prescribed Class of Dwellings) (Wales) Regulations 1998, SI 1998/105, reg 5(a) (substituted by SI 2017/42).
24 Council Tax (Prescribed Class of Dwellings) (Wales) Regulations 1998, SI 1998/105, reg 5(b) (amended by SI 2017/42).
25 Council Tax (Prescribed Class of Dwellings) (Wales) Regulations 1998, SI 1998/105, reg 5(c).
26 Council Tax (Prescribed Class of Dwellings) (Wales) Regulations 1998, SI 1998/105, reg 5.
27 'Caravan' is to be construed in accordance with the Caravan Sites and Control of Development Act 1960 Pt I (ss 1–32) (see PLANNING vol 83 (2018) PARA 1137): Council Tax (Prescribed Class of Dwellings) (Wales) Regulations 1998, SI 1998/105, reg 2.
28 Council Tax (Prescribed Class of Dwellings) (Wales) Regulations 1998, SI 1998/105, reg 6(1).
29 'Unoccupied dwelling' means a dwelling in which no-one lives: Council Tax (Prescribed Class of Dwellings) (Wales) Regulations 1998, SI 1998/105, reg 2.
30 'Qualifying person' means a person who is liable for the council tax in respect of a dwelling on a particular day, whether or not jointly with any other person, or who would be liable for the council tax in respect of a dwelling on a particular day if that dwelling did not fall within the Council Tax

(Exempt Dwellings) Order 1992, SI 1992/558, art 3 Class O (see PARA 352): Council Tax (Prescribed Class of Dwellings) (Wales) Regulations 1998, SI 1998/105, reg 2 (definition substituted by SI 2010/612). As to council tax see PARA 344 et seq. As to persons liable to pay council tax see PARA 354 et seq.

31 As to personal representatives see WILLS AND INTESTACY vol 103 (2016) PARA 608.

32 Council Tax (Prescribed Class of Dwellings) (Wales) Regulations 1998, SI 1998/105, reg 6(2)(a).

33 As to the meaning of 'month' see PARA 11 note 1.

34 Council Tax (Prescribed Class of Dwellings) (Wales) Regulations 1998, SI 1998/105, reg 6(2)(b).

35 Council Tax (Prescribed Class of Dwellings) (Wales) Regulations 1998, SI 1998/105, reg 6(3). A dwelling is job-related if it falls within the description set out in either Schedule para 1 or Schedule para 2: see the reg 6(4), Schedule (Schedule amended by SI 2004/452, SI 2005/3302 and SI 2014/107).

36 See the Council Tax (Prescribed Class of Dwellings) (Wales) Regulations 1998, SI 1998/105, reg 3(2) (added by SI 2004/452; amended by SI 2004/3094).

37 As to the meaning of 'chargeable dwelling' see PARA 350.

38 Council Tax (Prescribed Class of Dwellings) (Wales) Regulations 1998, SI 1998/105, reg 5A(a) (reg 5A added by SI 2004/452).

39 Council Tax (Prescribed Class of Dwellings) (Wales) Regulations 1998, SI 1998/105, reg 5A(b) (as added: see note 38).

366. Higher amount of council tax for long-term empty dwellings: Wales.

For any financial year[1], a billing authority[2] in Wales[3] may by determination[4] provide in relation to its area that if on any day a dwelling[5] is a long-term empty dwelling[6]:

(1) the discount which applies to the amount payable in respect of council tax where there is no resident of the dwelling[7] does not apply[8]; and

(2) the amount of council tax payable in respect of that dwelling and that day is increased by such percentage of not more than 100 as it may specify in the determination[9].

A billing authority may specify different percentages for different dwellings based on the length of time for which they have been long-term empty dwellings[10]. In exercising its functions under these provisions a billing authority must have regard to any guidance issued by the Welsh Ministers[11].

Where a determination has effect in relation to a class of dwellings, the billing authority may not make a determination that the discount is to be a lesser percentage or is not to apply[12] in relation to that class, and any such determination that has been made ceases to have effect in relation to that class[13].

A billing authority may make a determination varying or revoking a determination in respect of a long term empty dwelling for a financial year, but only before the beginning of the year[14]. Where a billing authority makes a determination it must publish a notice of it in at least one newspaper circulating in its area[15]. The notice must be published before the end of the period of 21 days beginning with the date of the determination[16]. However, the validity of a determination is not affected by a failure to comply with these requirements[17].

The Welsh Ministers may, by regulations, prescribe one or more classes of dwelling in relation to which a billing authority may not make a determination relating to long-term empty dwellings[18]. For each financial year beginning on or after 1 April 2016, the following classes are prescribed as classes of dwellings for this purpose[19]:

(a) Class 1: comprising every dwelling in Wales that falls within head (i) or (ii) below unless it has been such a dwelling for a period of one year or more[20]:

(i) a dwelling that is being marketed for sale[21] at a price that is reasonable for the sale of the dwelling[22];

(ii) a dwelling in relation to which an offer to purchase the dwelling has been accepted (whether or nor the acceptance is subject to contract) but the sale has not been completed[23].

After the end of an excepted period[24] a dwelling does not fall within Class 1 for a further period unless the dwelling has been the subject of a relevant transaction[25].

(b) Class 2: comprising every dwelling in Wales that falls within head (i) or (ii) below unless it has been such a dwelling for a period of one year or more[26]:

(i) a dwelling that is being marketed for let under a tenancy on terms and conditions, including the proposed rent, that are reasonable for letting the dwelling[27];

(ii) a dwelling in relation to which an offer to rent the dwelling has been accepted (whether or not the acceptance is subject to contract) but the tenancy has not started[28].

After the end of an excepted period[29] a dwelling does not fall within Class 2 for a further period unless it has been subject to a tenancy that was granted for a term of six months or more[30].

(c) Class 3: comprising every dwelling in Wales[31]:

(i) that forms part of a single property[32] that includes at least one other dwelling[33]; and

(ii) that is being used by a resident of that other dwelling, or as the case may be, those other dwellings, as part of their residence[34].

(d) Class 4: comprising every dwelling in Wales which would be the sole or main residence[35] of an individual if that individual were not residing in armed forces accommodation[36].

1 As to the meaning of 'financial year' see PARA 11 note 1.

2 As to the meaning of 'billing authority' see PARA 346.

3 As to the meaning of 'Wales' see PARA 2 note 16.

4 The making of a determination under the Local Government Finance Act 1992 s 12A may be discharged only by the billing authority: see s 67(1), (2)(a) (s 67(2)(a) amended by the Local Government Act 2003 s 127(1), Sch 7 paras 40, 50(a); and the Housing (Wales) Act 2014 s 139(1), (3), Sch 3 para 29(1), (6)). A determination made under the Local Government Finance Act 1992 s 12A may not be questioned except by an application for judicial review: see s 66(1), (2)(b) (s 66(2)(b) amended by the Local Government Act 2003 s 127(1), Sch 7 paras 40, 49(a); and the Housing (Wales) Act 2014 Sch 3 para 29(1), (5)). If on an application for judicial review the court decides to grant relief, it must quash the determination: see the Local Government Finance Act 1992 s 66(3) (amended by the Local Government Finance Act 2012 s 10(2), (3)(b), Sch 4 paras 3, 5(1), (3)). As to judicial review see JUDICIAL REVIEW vol 61 (2010) PARA 601 et seq.

5 As to the meaning of 'dwelling' see PARA 349.

6 Local Government Finance Act 1992 s 12A(1) (s 12A added by the Housing (Wales) Act 2014 s 139(1), (2)). For the purposes of the Local Government Finance Act 1992 s 12A a dwelling is a 'long-term empty dwelling' on any day if for a continuous period of at least one year ending with that day:

(1) it has been unoccupied (s 12A(11)(a) (as so added)); and

(2) it has been substantially unfurnished (s 12A(11)(b) (as so added)).

In determining whether a dwelling is a long-term empty dwelling, no account is to be taken of:

(a) any period which pre-dates the coming into force of s 12A, ie 1 April 2016 (s 12A(12)(a) (as so added));

(b) any one or more periods of not more than six weeks during which one or both of the conditions in s 12A(11) are not met (s 12A(12)(b) (as so added)).

As to the commencement of s 12A see the Housing (Wales) Act 2014 (Commencement No 5) Order 2015, SI 2015/2046, art 2(2).

The Welsh Ministers may by regulations:

(i) substitute a different percentage limit for the limit which is for the time being specified in the Local Government Finance Act 1992 s 12A(1)(b) (see head (2) in the text) (s 12A(13)(a) (as so added));

(ii) substitute a different period, of not less than one year, for the period which is for the time being specified in s 12A(11) (s 12A(13)(b) (as so added));

(iii) substitute a different period, of not less than six weeks, for the period which is for the time being specified in s 12A(12)(b) (s 12A(13)(c) (as so added)).

A statutory instrument containing regulations made under s 12A(13)(a) or (b) may not be made unless a draft of the instrument has been laid before, and approved by resolution of, the National Assembly for Wales: s 12A(14) (as so added). Any other statutory instrument containing regulations made under s 12A is subject to annulment in pursuance of a resolution of the National Assembly for Wales: s 12A(15) (as so added). As to the Welsh Ministers see PARA 4 note 18.

7 Ie the discount under the Local Government Finance Act 1992 s 11(2)(a): see PARA 362.

8 Local Government Finance Act 1992 s 12A(1)(a) (as added: see note 6).

9 Local Government Finance Act 1992 s 12A(1)(b) (as added: see note 6).

10 Local Government Finance Act 1992 s 12A(2) (as added: see note 6).

11 Local Government Finance Act 1992 s 12A(3) (as added: see note 6).

12 Ie under the Local Government Finance Act 1992 s 12(3) or (4): see PARA 365.

13 Local Government Finance Act 1992 s 12A(6) (as added: see note 6).

14 Local Government Finance Act 1992 s 12A(7) (as added: see note 6).

15 Local Government Finance Act 1992 s 12A(8) (as added: see note 6).

16 Local Government Finance Act 1992 s 12A(9) (as added: see note 6).

17 Local Government Finance Act 1992 s 12A(10) (as added: see note 6).

18 Local Government Finance Act 1992 s 12A(4) (as added: see note 6). A class of dwellings may be prescribed under s 12A(4) by reference to such factors as the Welsh Ministers think fit (s 12A(5) (as so added)) and may, amongst other factors, be prescribed by reference to:

(1) the physical characteristics of, or other matters relating to, dwellings (s 12A(5)(a) (as so added));

(2) the circumstances of, or other matters relating to, any person who is liable to the amount of council tax concerned (s 12A(5)(b) (as so added)).

For regulations made under s 12A(4), (5) see the Council Tax (Exceptions to Higher Amounts) (Wales) Regulations 2015, SI 2015/2068.

19 See the Council Tax (Exceptions to Higher Amounts) (Wales) Regulations 2015, SI 2015/2068, reg 3(1).

20 Council Tax (Exceptions to Higher Amounts) (Wales) Regulations 2015, SI 2015/2068, reg 4(1).

21 Marketing a dwelling for sale includes the marketing for sale of the freehold or of a leasehold for a term of seven years or more: Council Tax (Exceptions to Higher Amounts) (Wales) Regulations 2015, SI 2015/2068, reg 4(3)(a).

22 Council Tax (Exceptions to Higher Amounts) (Wales) Regulations 2015, SI 2015/2068, reg 4(1)(a).

23 Council Tax (Exceptions to Higher Amounts) (Wales) Regulations 2015, SI 2015/2068, reg 4(1)(b).

24 For this purpose, the 'excepted period' is the period during which a dwelling falls within Class 1: Council Tax (Exceptions to Higher Amounts) (Wales) Regulations 2015, SI 2015/2068, reg 4(3)(b).

25 Council Tax (Exceptions to Higher Amounts) (Wales) Regulations 2015, SI 2015/2068, reg 4(2). 'Relevant transaction' means a transfer on sale of the freehold or a transfer on sale of the leasehold for a term of seven years or more: reg 4(3)(c).

26 Council Tax (Exceptions to Higher Amounts) (Wales) Regulations 2015, SI 2015/2068, reg 5(1).

27 Council Tax (Exceptions to Higher Amounts) (Wales) Regulations 2015, SI 2015/2068, reg 5(1)(a).

28 Council Tax (Exceptions to Higher Amounts) (Wales) Regulations 2015, SI 2015/2068, reg 5(1)(b).

29 For this purpose, the 'excepted period' is the period during which a dwelling falls within Class 2: Council Tax (Exceptions to Higher Amounts) (Wales) Regulations 2015, SI 2015/2068, reg 5(3).

30 Council Tax (Exceptions to Higher Amounts) (Wales) Regulations 2015, SI 2015/2068, reg 5(2).

31 Council Tax (Exceptions to Higher Amounts) (Wales) Regulations 2015, SI 2015/2068, reg 6(1).

32 For this purpose, 'single property' means a property that would, apart from the Council Tax (Chargeable Dwellings) Order 1992, SI 1992/549, be one dwelling within the meaning of the Local Government Finance Act 1992 s 3 (see PARA 349): Council Tax (Exceptions to Higher Amounts) (Wales) Regulations 2015, SI 2015/2068, reg 6(2).

33 Council Tax (Exceptions to Higher Amounts) (Wales) Regulations 2015, SI 2015/2068, reg 6(1)(a).

34 Council Tax (Exceptions to Higher Amounts) (Wales) Regulations 2015, SI 2015/2068, reg 6(1)(b).

35 As to the meaning of 'resident' and what constitutes a sole or main residence see PARA 354 note 4.

36 Council Tax (Exceptions to Higher Amounts) (Wales) Regulations 2015, SI 2015/2068, reg 7(1). For this purpose, 'armed forces accommodation' is accommodation which is provided to:
(1) a member of any of Her Majesty's forces; or
(2) a member of the family of a member of any of Her Majesty's forces,
for the purposes of any of Her Majesty's forces: reg 7(2)(a). A person is a member of another's family if:
(a) he or she is the spouse or civil partner of that person (reg 7(2)(b)(i)); or
(b) he or she is that person's parent, grandparent, child, grandchild, brother, sister, uncle, aunt, nephew or niece (reg 7(2)(b)(ii)).
In the Council Tax (Exceptions to Higher Amounts) (Wales) Regulations 2015, SI 2015/2068, references to the spouse of a person include references to a person who is living with the other as if they were that person's spouse; and references to the civil partner of a person include references to a person of the same sex who is living with the other as if they were that person's civil partner: reg 2. Marriage includes marriage of a same sex couple: see the Marriage (Same Sex Couples) Act 2013 Sch 3 para 1(1)(a), (2), (3); and MATRIMONIAL AND CIVIL PARTNERSHIP LAW vol 72 (2015) PARA 1 et seq.

367. Higher amount of council tax for dwellings occupied periodically: Wales.

For any financial year[1], a billing authority[2] in Wales[3] may by determination[4] provide in relation to its area that if on any day conditions (a) and (b) below are satisfied in respect of a dwelling[5]:

(1) the discount which applies to the amount payable in respect of council tax where there is no resident of the dwelling[6] does not apply[7]; and
(2) the amount of council tax payable in respect of that dwelling and that day is increased by such percentage of not more than 100 as it may specify in the determination[8].

The conditions are:

(a) there is no resident of the dwelling[9]; and
(b) the dwelling is substantially furnished[10].

A billing authority's first determination must be made at least one year before the beginning of the financial year to which it relates[11]. In exercising its functions under these provisions a billing authority must have regard to any guidance issued by the Welsh Ministers[12].

Where a determination under these provisions has effect in relation to a class of dwellings, the billing authority may not make a determination that the discount is to be a lesser percentage or is not to apply[13] in relation to that class, and any such determination that has been made ceases to have effect in relation to that class[14].

A billing authority may make a determination varying or revoking a determination in respect of dwellings occupied periodically for a financial year, but only before the beginning of the year[15]. Where a billing authority makes such a determination it must publish a notice of the determination in at least one newspaper circulating in its area[16]. The notice must be published before the end of the period of 21 days beginning with the date of the determination[17]. However, the validity of a determination is not affected by a failure to comply with these requirements[18].

The Welsh Ministers may by regulations specify a different percentage limit for the limit which is for the time being specified in head (2)[19].

The Welsh Ministers may, by regulations, prescribe one or more classes of dwelling in relation to which a billing authority may not make a determination relating to dwellings occupied periodically[20]. For each financial year beginning on or after 1 April 2016, the following classes are prescribed as classes of dwellings for this purpose[21]:

(i) Classes 1, 2, 3 and 4[22] as prescribed in respect of long-term empty dwellings[23].

(ii) Class 5: comprising every dwelling in Wales which consists of a pitch occupied by a caravan[24] or a mooring occupied by a boat[25].

(iii) Class 6: comprising every dwelling in Wales the occupation of which is restricted by a planning condition[26] preventing occupancy for a continuous period of at least 28 days in any one year period[27].

(iv) Class 7: comprising every dwelling in Wales:

 (A) where a qualifying person[28] in relation to that dwelling is resident in another dwelling which, for that person, is job-related[29]; or

 (B) which, for a qualifying person, is job-related[30].

1 As to the meaning of 'financial year' see PARA 11 note 1.

2 As to the meaning of 'billing authority' see PARA 346.

3 As to the meaning of 'Wales' see PARA 2 note 16.

4 The making of a determination under the Local Government Finance Act 1992 s 12B may be discharged only by the billing authority: see s 67(1), (2)(a) (s 67(2)(a) amended by the Local Government Act 2003 s 127(1), Sch 7 paras 40, 50(a); and the Housing (Wales) Act 2014 s 139(1), (3), Sch 3 para 29(1), (6)). A determination made under the Local Government Finance Act 1992 s 12B may not be questioned except by an application for judicial review: see s 66(1), (2)(b) (s 66(2)(b) amended by the Local Government Act 2003 s 127(1), Sch 7 paras 40, 49(a); and the Housing (Wales) Act 2014 Sch 3 para 29(1), (5)). If on an application for judicial review the court decides to grant relief, it must quash the determination: see the Local Government Finance Act 1992 s 66(3) (amended by the Local Government Finance Act 2012 s 10(2), (3)(b), Sch 4 paras 3, 5(1), (3)). As to judicial review see JUDICIAL REVIEW vol 61 (2010) PARA 601 et seq.

5 Local Government Finance Act 1992 s 12B(1) (s 12B added by the Housing (Wales) Act 2014 s 139(1), (2)). As to the meaning of 'dwelling' see PARA 349.

6 Ie the discount under the Local Government Finance Act 1992 s 11(2)(a): see PARA 362.

7 Local Government Finance Act 1992 s 12B(1)(a) (as added: see note 5).

8 Local Government Finance Act 1992 s 12B(1)(b) (as added: see note 5).

9 Local Government Finance Act 1992 s 12B(2)(a) (as added: see note 5).

10 Local Government Finance Act 1992 s 12B(2)(b) (as added: see note 5).

11 Local Government Finance Act 1992 s 12B(3) (as added: see note 5).

12 Local Government Finance Act 1992 s 12B(4) (as added: see note 5).

13 Ie under the Local Government Finance Act 1992 s 12(3) or (4): see PARA 365.

14 Local Government Finance Act 1992 s 12B(7) (as added: see note 5).

15 Local Government Finance Act 1992 s 12B(8) (as added: see note 5).

16 Local Government Finance Act 1992 s 12B(9) (as added: see note 5).

17 Local Government Finance Act 1992 s 12B(10) (as added: see note 5).

18 Local Government Finance Act 1992 s 12B(11) (as added: see note 5).

19 Local Government Finance Act 1992 s 12B(12) (as added: see note 5). A statutory instrument containing regulations made under s 12B(12) may not be made unless a draft of the instrument has been laid before, and approved by resolution of, the National Assembly for Wales: s 12B(13) (as so added). Any other statutory instrument containing regulations made under s 12B is subject to annulment in pursuance of a resolution of the National Assembly for Wales: s 12B(14) (as so added).

20 Local Government Finance Act 1992 s 12B(5) (as added: see note 5). A class of dwellings may be prescribed under s 12B(5) by reference to such factors as the Welsh Ministers think fit and may, amongst other factors, be prescribed by reference to:

 (1) the physical characteristics of, or other matters relating to, dwellings (s 12B(6)(a) (as so added));

 (2) the circumstances of, or other matters relating to, any person who is liable to the amount of council tax concerned (s 12B(6)(b) (as so added)).

For regulations made under s 12B(5), (6) see the Council Tax (Exceptions to Higher Amounts) (Wales) Regulations 2015, SI 2015/2068.

21 See the Council Tax (Exceptions to Higher Amounts) (Wales) Regulations 2015, SI 2015/2068, reg 3.

22 See PARA 366.

23 Council Tax (Exceptions to Higher Amounts) (Wales) Regulations 2015, SI 2015/2068, reg 3(1).

24 As to the meaning of 'caravan' see PARA 355 note 4 (definition applied by the Council Tax (Exceptions to Higher Amounts) (Wales) Regulations 2015, SI 2015/2068, reg 8(2)).

25 Council Tax (Exceptions to Higher Amounts) (Wales) Regulations 2015, SI 2015/2068, reg 8(1).

26 For the purpose of the Council Tax (Exceptions to Higher Amounts) (Wales) Regulations 2015, SI 2015/2068, reg 9 'planning condition' means any condition imposed on planning permission granted or deemed to be granted under the Town and Country Planning Act 1990 Pt III (ss 55–106C) (see PLANNING vol 81 (2018) PARA 333 et seq).

27 Council Tax (Exceptions to Higher Amounts) (Wales) Regulations 2015, SI 2015/2068, reg 9(1).

28 For this purpose, 'qualifying person' means:

(1) a person who is liable for council tax in respect of a dwelling on a particular day, whether or not jointly with another person (Council Tax (Exceptions to Higher Amounts) (Wales) Regulations 2015, SI 2015/2068, reg 10(3)(a)); or

(2) a person who would be liable for the council tax in respect of a dwelling on a particular day, whether or not jointly with another person, if that dwelling did not fall within the Council Tax (Exempt Dwellings) Order 1992, SI 1992/558, art 3 Class O (see PARA 352) or the Council Tax (Liability for Owners) Regulations 1992, SI 1992/551, reg 2 Class E (see PARA 356) (Council Tax (Exceptions to Higher Amounts) (Wales) Regulations 2015, SI 2015/2068, reg 10(3)(b)).

29 Council Tax (Exceptions to Higher Amounts) (Wales) Regulations 2015, SI 2015/2068, reg 10(1)(a). For the purpose of reg 10 a dwelling is job-related for a person if it falls within one of the descriptions set out in the Schedule para 1, 2 or 3: reg 10(2), Schedule.

30 Council Tax (Exceptions to Higher Amounts) (Wales) Regulations 2015, SI 2015/2068, reg 10(1)(b).

B. PERSONS DISREGARDED FOR DISCOUNT

368. Persons in detention.

A person is to be disregarded for the purposes of discounts which may be applied to the amount payable in respect of council tax on a particular day[1] if, on the day[2]:

(1) he is detained[3] in a prison, a hospital or any other place by virtue of an order[4] of a court in the United Kingdom[5], or an order or award (whether or not of a court) made (anywhere) in proceedings in respect of a service offence within the meaning of the Armed Forces Act 2006[6];

(2) he is detained under the Immigration Act 1971 pending deportation[7]; or

(3) he is detained[8] under various powers under the Mental Health Act 1983[9].

The appropriate national authority[10] may by order[11] provide that a person is to be disregarded for the purposes of discount on a particular day if on the day he is in service custody[12] and such conditions as may be prescribed by the order are fulfilled[13].

1 As to discounts applicable to an amount payable in respect of council tax see PARAS 362–367.

2 See the Local Government Finance Act 1992 s 11(5), Sch 1 para 1(1).

3 If a person:

(1) is temporarily discharged under the Prison Act 1952 s 28 (power to discharge prisoners temporarily on account of ill health: see PRISONS AND PRISONERS vol 85 (2012) PARA 592) or temporarily released under rules under s 47(5) (power to release temporarily certain prisoners after conviction and sentencing: see PRISONS AND PRISONERS vol 85 (2012) PARA 404) (Local Government Finance Act 1992 Sch 1 para 1(3)(a));

(2) is temporarily released under rules under the Armed Forces Act 2006 s 300 (see ARMED FORCES vol 3 (2011) PARA 652) (Local Government Finance Act 1992 Sch 1 para 1(3)(aa) (added by the Armed Forces Act 2006 s 378(1), Sch 16 para 123(1), (2)(c))); or

(3) is temporarily discharged under the Prisons (Scotland) Act 1989 s 27, or temporarily released under rules under s 39(6) (Local Government Finance Act 1992 Sch 1 para 1(3)(b)),

he must be treated as detained for the purposes of Sch 1 para 1(1): Sch 1 para 1(3).

4 'Order' includes a sentence, direction, warrant or other means of giving effect to the decision of the court concerned: Local Government Finance Act 1992 Sch 1 para 1(5).

5 See the Local Government Finance Act 1992 Sch 1 para 1(1)(a), (2)(a) (Sch 1 para 1(1)(a) amended, Sch 1 para 1(2) substituted, by the Armed Forces Act 2006 Sch 16 para 123(1), (2)). As to the meaning of 'United Kingdom' see PARA 4 note 10.

6 See the Local Government Finance Act 1992 Sch 1 para 1(1)(a), (2)(b) (as amended and substituted: see note 5). As to the meaning of 'service offence' in the Armed Forces Act 2006 see ARMED FORCES vol 3 (2011) PARA 569. The Local Government Finance Act 1992 Sch 1 para 1(1) does not apply where the person:

(1) is detained under regulations made under Sch 4 para 8 (see PARA 498) (Sch 1 para 1(4)(a)); or

(2) is detained under the Magistrates' Courts Act 1980 s 76 (see MAGISTRATES vol 71 (2013) PARAS 627, 634, 678) or under the Powers of Criminal Courts (Sentencing) Act 2000 s 108 (see SENTENCING vol 92 (2015) PARA 551) for default in payment of a fine (Local Government Finance Act 1992 Sch 1 para 1(4)(b) (amended by the Powers of Criminal Courts (Sentencing) Act 2000 s 165(1), Sch 9 para 152)).

As from a day to be appointed the Local Government Finance Act 1992 Sch 1 para 1(4)(b) is amended by the omission of the reference to the Powers of Criminal Courts (Sentencing) Act 2000 s 108: see the Local Government Finance Act 1992 Sch 1 para 1(4)(b) (as so amended; prospectively further amended by the Criminal Justice and Court Services Act 2000 s 75, Sch 8; at the date at which this volume states the law, no such day had been appointed).

7 Ie he is detained under the Immigration Act 1971 Sch 3 para 2 (see IMMIGRATION AND ASYLUM vol 57 (2012) PARA 197): Local Government Finance Act 1992 Sch 1 para 1(1)(b).

8 Ie under the Mental Health Act 1983 Pt II (ss 2–34) (see MENTAL HEALTH AND CAPACITY vol 75 (2013) PARA 767 et seq) or s 46 (repealed), s 47 (removal to hospital of persons serving sentences of imprisonment: see MENTAL HEALTH AND CAPACITY vol 75 (2013) PARA 892), s 48 (removal to hospital of certain prisoners: see MENTAL HEALTH AND CAPACITY vol 75 (2013) PARA 893) or s 136 (mentally disordered persons found in public places: see MENTAL HEALTH AND CAPACITY vol 75 (2013) PARA 923).

9 See the Local Government Finance Act 1992 Sch 1 para 1(1)(c).

10 Ie the Secretary of State or, in relation to Wales, the Welsh Ministers. The functions of the Secretary of State under the Local Government Finance Act 1992 Sch 1, so far as exercisable in relation to Wales, were transferred to the National Assembly for Wales (see the National Assembly for Wales (Transfer of Functions) Order 1999, SI 1999/672, art 2, Sch 1) and are now vested in the Welsh Ministers (see the Government of Wales Act 2006 s 162(1), Sch 11 para 30). As to the Secretary of State and the Welsh Ministers see PARA 4 note 18. As to the meaning of 'Wales' see PARA 2 note 16.

11 As to the order made see note 13.

12 Local Government Finance Act 1992 Sch 1 para 1(6)(a) (amended by the Armed Forces Act 2006 Sch 16 para 123(1), (2)(d)).

13 Local Government Finance Act 1992 Sch 1 para 1(6)(b). Under Sch 1 para 1(6), a person is to be disregarded for the purposes of discount on a particular day if on the day he is imprisoned under, or in service custody for the purposes of, the Armed Forces Act 2006 and, where a person is in custody, the custody forms part of a continuous period exceeding 48 hours: Council Tax (Discount Disregards) Order 1992, SI 1992/548, art 2 (substituted by SI 2009/2054).

369. Severely mentally impaired persons.

A person is to be disregarded for the purposes of discounts which may be applied to the amount payable in respect of council tax on a particular day[1]:

(1) if, on the day, he is severely mentally impaired[2];

(2) if, as regards any period which includes the day, he is stated in a certificate of a registered medical practitioner[3] to have been or to be likely to be severely mentally impaired[4]; and

(3) if, as regards the day, he fulfils such conditions as may be prescribed by order made by the appropriate national authority[5].

1 As to discounts applicable to an amount payable in respect of council tax see PARAS 362–367.

2 Local Government Finance Act 1992 s 11(5), Sch 1 para 2(1)(a). For these purposes, a person is severely mentally impaired if he has a severe impairment of intelligence and social functioning (however caused) which appears to be permanent: Sch 1 para 2(2). The Secretary of State or, in relation to Wales, the Welsh Ministers (the 'appropriate national authority') may by order substitute another definition for the definition in Sch 1 para 2(2) as for the time being effective for the purposes of Sch 1 para 2: see Sch 1 para 2(3). At the date at which this volume states the law no such order had been made.

The functions of the Secretary of State under the Local Government Finance Act 1992 Sch 1, so far as exercisable in relation to Wales, were transferred to the National Assembly for Wales (see the National Assembly for Wales (Transfer of Functions) Order 1999, SI 1999/672, art 2, Sch 1) and are now vested in the Welsh Ministers (see the Government of Wales Act 2006 s 162(1), Sch 11 para 30). As to the Secretary of State and the Welsh Ministers see PARA 4 note 18. As to the meaning of 'Wales' see PARA 2 note 16.

3 As to the meaning of 'registered medical practitioner' see MEDICAL PROFESSIONS vol 74 (2011) PARA 176.

4 Local Government Finance Act 1992 Sch 1 para 2(1)(b).

5 See the Local Government Finance Act 1992 Sch 1 para 2(1)(c). The condition so prescribed is that the person in question is either entitled to one of the qualifying benefits, or meets other specified requirements: see the Council Tax (Discount Disregards) Order 1992, SI 1992/548, art 3 (amended by SI 1994/543, SI 1995/619, SI 1996/636, SI 1996/3143, SI 1997/656; in relation to England by SI 2013/388, SI 2013/591 and SI 2013/630; and in relation to Wales by SI 2013/638 and SI 2013/1048).

370. Persons in respect of whom child benefit is payable.

A person is to be disregarded for the purposes of discounts which may be applied to the amount payable in respect of council tax on a particular day[1] if, on the day, he:

(1) has attained the age of 18 years[2]; but

(2) is a person in respect of whom another person is (or would be[3]) entitled to child benefit[4].

1 As to discounts applicable to an amount payable in respect of council tax see PARAS 362–367.

2 Local Government Finance Act 1992 s 11(5), Sch 1 para 3(1)(a). As to the day on which a person attains a particular age see PARA 354 note 4.

3 Ie but for the Social Security Contributions and Benefits Act 1992 Sch 9 para 1(c); WELFARE BENEFITS AND STATE PENSIONS vol 104 (2014) PARA 165.

4 Local Government Finance Act 1992 Sch 1 para 3(1)(b). As to child benefit generally see WELFARE BENEFITS AND STATE PENSIONS vol 104 (2014) PARA 155 et seq. The Secretary of State or, in relation to Wales, the Welsh Ministers may by order substitute another provision for Sch 1 para 3(1)(b) as for the time being effective for the purposes of Sch 1 para 3: Sch 1 para 3(2). At the date at which this volume states the law no such order had been made.

The functions of the Secretary of State under the Local Government Finance Act 1992 Sch 1, so far as exercisable in relation to Wales, were transferred to the National Assembly for Wales (see the National Assembly for Wales (Transfer of Functions) Order 1999, SI 1999/672, art 2, Sch 1) and are now vested in the Welsh Ministers (see the Government of Wales Act 2006 s 162(1), Sch 11 para 30). As to the Secretary of State and the Welsh Ministers see PARA 4 note 18. As to the meaning of 'Wales' see PARA 2 note 16.

371. Students etc.

A person is to be disregarded for the purposes of discounts which may be applied to the amount payable in respect of council tax on a particular day[1]:

(1) if, on the day he is a student, student nurse, apprentice or youth training trainee[2]; and

(2) if such conditions as may be prescribed by order made by the appropriate national authority are fulfilled[3].

An institution[4] must, on request, supply a certificate to any person who is following or[5] has followed a course of education at that institution as a student or student nurse[6]. Such a certificate must contain such information[7] about the person to whom it refers as may be prescribed by order made by the appropriate national authority[8]. An institution may refuse to comply with a request made more than one year after the person making it has ceased to follow a course of education at that institution[9].

1 As to discounts applicable to an amount payable in respect of council tax see PARAS 362–367.

2 Local Government Finance Act 1992 s 11(5), Sch 1 para 4(1)(a). For these purposes, 'apprentice', 'student', 'student nurse' and 'youth training trainee' have the meanings for the time being assigned to them by order made by the Secretary of State or, in relation to Wales, the Welsh Ministers: see Sch 1 para 4(2). In this paragraph the Secretary of State and the Welsh Ministers are together referred to as the 'appropriate national authority'. The functions of the Secretary of State under the Local Government Finance Act 1992 Sch 1, so far as exercisable in relation to Wales, were transferred to the National Assembly for Wales (see the National Assembly for Wales (Transfer of Functions) Order 1999, SI 1999/672, art 2, Sch 1) and are now vested in the Welsh Ministers (see the Government of Wales Act 2006 s 162(1), Sch 11 para 30). As to the Secretary of State and the Welsh Ministers see PARA 4 note 18. As to the meaning of 'Wales' see PARA 2 note 16.

The terms 'apprentice', 'student', 'student nurse' and 'youth training trainee' are defined for the purposes of the Local Government Finance Act 1992 Sch 1 para 4 by the Council Tax (Discount Disregards) Order 1992, SI 1992/548, art 4, Sch 1 (art 4 amended by SI 1994/543 and, in relation to Wales, SI 2003/673; the Council Tax (Discount Disregards) Order 1992, SI 1992/548, Sch 1 amended by SI 1995/619, SI 1996/636, SI 2004/1771 and SI 2011/948; in relation to England by SI 2006/3396, SI 2010/677, SI 2010/1941, SI 2012/956 and SI 2015/971; and in relation to Wales by SI 2003/673, SI 2007/580, SI 2010/2448 and SI 2016/236).

See *Southwark London Borough Council v Mohammed* [2006] EWHC 305 (Ch), [2006] RVR 124, a case in which a bankrupt contended that no council tax was payable by him for the whole of the disputed period, based primarily on the contention that he was in full-time education throughout that time. See also *Wirral Borough Council v Farthing* [2008] EWHC 1919 (Ch), [2008] RA 303; *R (on the application of Fayad) v London South East Valuation Tribunal* [2008] EWHC 2531 (Admin), [2009] RA 157, [2008] All ER (D) 78 (Nov); *Feller v Cambridge City Council* [2011] EWHC 1252 (Admin),[2011] All ER (D) 349 (Mar) (in which consideration was given as to what constitutes a course of full-time education for the purposes of the definition of 'student'); and on that issue see also *R (on the application of Hakeem) v Enfield London Borough Council* [2013] EWHC 1026 (Admin), [2013] All ER (D) 177 (Jan); *R (on the application of Earl) v Winchester City Council* [2014] EWHC 195 (Admin), [2014] ELR 225, [2014] All ER (D) 55 (Feb); and *Jagoo v Bristol City Council* [2017] EWHC 926 (Admin), [2017] RA 159, [2017] All ER (D) 06 (May).

3 Local Government Finance Act 1992 Sch 1 para 4(1)(b). At the date at which this volume states the law no such order had been made for these purposes.

4 Ie any such educational establishment or other body as may be prescribed by order made by the appropriate national authority: see the Local Government Finance Act 1992 Sch 1 para 5(4). As to the prescribed establishments and bodies in the case of students see the Council Tax (Discount Disregards) Order 1992, SI 1992/548, art 5(2)(a), Sch 2 Pt I (paras 1–3) (art 5(2), Sch 2 paras 1, 2 substituted by SI 2011/948); and, in the case of student nurses see the Council Tax (Discount Disregards) Order 1992, SI 1992/548, art 5(2)(b), Sch 2 Pt II (para 4) (art 5(2) as so substituted).

5 Ie subject to the Local Government Finance Act 1992 Sch 1 para 5(3): see the text to note 9.

6 Local Government Finance Act 1992 Sch 1 para 5(1). 'Student' and 'student nurse' have the same meanings as in Sch 1 para 4 (see note 2): see Sch 1 para 5(4).

7 As to the meaning of 'information' see PARA 345 note 20.

8 Local Government Finance Act 1992 Sch 1 para 5(2). The information prescribed to be contained in a certificate is:

(1) the name and address of the prescribed educational establishment by whom the certificate is issued (Council Tax (Discount Disregards) Order 1992, SI 1992/548, art 5(1)(a));

(2) the full name of the person to whom it is issued (art 5(1)(b));
(3) his date of birth (where this is known to the establishment and where the person is to be regarded as a person undertaking a qualifying course of education by Sch 1 Pt II para 5 (see note 2)) (art 5(1)(c));
(4) a statement certifying that he is following or has followed a course of education as a student or, as the case may be, a student nurse (art 5(1)(d));
(5) the date when the person became a student or a student nurse at the establishment and the date when his course has come or is expected to come to an end (art 5(1)(e)).

9 Local Government Finance Act 1992 Sch 1 para 5(3).

372. Hospital patients.

A person is to be disregarded for the purposes of discounts which may be applied to the amount payable in respect of council tax on a particular day[1] if, on the day, he is a patient who has his sole or main residence in a hospital[2].

1 As to discounts applicable to an amount payable in respect of council tax see PARAS 362–367.

2 Local Government Finance Act 1992 s 11(5), Sch 1 para 6(1). For these purposes, 'hospital' means:
(1) a health service hospital within the meaning of the National Health Service Act 2006, the National Health Service (Wales) Act 2006 (see HEALTH SERVICES vol 54 (2017) PARA 26) or the National Health Service (Scotland) Act 1978 s 108(1) (interpretation) (Local Government Finance Act 1992 Sch 1 para 6(2)(a) (amended by the National Health Service (Consequential Provisions) Act 2006 s 2, Sch 1 paras 151, 152)); and
(2) a military, air-force or naval unit or establishment at or in which medical or surgical treatment is provided for persons subject to service law within the meaning of the Armed Forces Act 2006 (see ARMED FORCES) (Local Government Finance Act 1992 Sch 1 para 6(2)(b) (amended by the Armed Forces Act 2006 s 378(1), Sch 16 para 123(1), (3))).

The Secretary of State or, in relation to Wales, the Welsh Ministers may by order substitute another definition for the definition in the Local Government Finance Act 1992 Sch 1 para 6(2) as for the time being effective for the purposes of Sch 1 para 6: Sch 1 para 6(3). At the date at which this volume states the law, no such order had been made.

The functions of the Secretary of State under the Local Government Finance Act 1992 Sch 1, so far as exercisable in relation to Wales, were transferred to the National Assembly for Wales (see the National Assembly for Wales (Transfer of Functions) Order 1999, SI 1999/672, art 2, Sch 1) and are now vested in the Welsh Ministers (see the Government of Wales Act 2006 s 162(1), Sch 11 para 30). As to the Secretary of State and the Welsh Ministers see PARA 4 note 18. As to the meaning of 'Wales' see PARA 2 note 16.

373. Patients in care homes etc.

A person is to be disregarded for the purposes of discounts which may be applied to the amount payable in respect of council tax on a particular day[1] if, on the day:
(1) he has his sole or main residence[2] in a care home[3], independent hospital[4] or hostel[5] in England and Wales[6]; and
(2) he is receiving care or treatment (or both) in the home, hospital or hostel[7].

A person must also be disregarded for the purposes of discounts on a particular day if on the day:
(a) either he has as his sole or main residence a private hospital in Scotland, or a care home service provides, in Scotland, accommodation which is his sole or main residence; and
(b) he is receiving care or treatment (or both) in the hospital or in the accommodation so provided[8].

1 As to discounts applicable to an amount payable in respect of council tax see PARAS 362–367.

2 As to the meaning of 'resident' and what constitutes a sole or main residence see PARA 354 note 4.

3 For these purposes, 'care home' means:

(1) a care home within the meaning of the Care Standards Act 2000 (see CHILDREN AND YOUNG PERSONS vol 10 (2017) PARA 1017) (Local Government Finance Act 1992 s 11(5), Sch 1 para 7(2)(a) (Sch 1 para 7(2) substituted by the Care Standards Act 2000 s 116, Sch 4 para 20(c)));

(2) a building or part of a building in which accommodation is provided for an adult under the Social Services and Well-being (Wales) Act 2014 Pt 4 (ss 32–58) (see SOCIAL SERVICES vol 95 (2017) PARA 2 et seq) (Local Government Finance Act 1992 Sch 1 para 7(2)(b) (Sch 1 para 7(2) as so substituted; Sch 1 para 7(2)(b) substituted by SI 2016/413)); or

(3) a building or part of a building in which accommodation is provided under the Care Act 2014 Pt 1 (ss 1–80) (see SOCIAL SERVICES vol 95 (2017) PARA 1 et seq) (Local Government Finance Act 1992 Sch 1 para 7(2)(c) (Sch 1 para 7(2) as so substituted; Sch 1 para 7(2)(c) added by SI 2015/914)).

See *Bogdal v Kingston upon Hull City Council* [1998] RA 45 (whether unregistered home was fairly treated as a domestic home rather than a care home).

The Secretary of State or, in relation to Wales, the Welsh Ministers may by order substitute another definition for any definition of 'care home' for the time being effective for the purposes of Sch 1 para 7: see Sch 1 para 7(3) (amended by the Care Standards Act 2000 Sch 4 para 20(d)). At the date at which this volume states the law no such order had been made.

The functions of the Secretary of State under the Local Government Finance Act 1992 Sch 1, so far as exercisable in relation to Wales, were transferred to the National Assembly for Wales (see the National Assembly for Wales (Transfer of Functions) Order 1999, SI 1999/672, art 2, Sch 1) and are now vested in the Welsh Ministers (see the Government of Wales Act 2006 s 162(1), Sch 11 para 30). As to the Secretary of State and the Welsh Ministers see PARA 4 note 18. As to the meaning of 'Wales' see PARA 2 note 16.

4 For these purposes, 'independent hospital' means (see the Local Government Finance Act 1992 Sch 1 para 7(2) (as substituted (see note 3); definition further substituted by SI 2010/813):

(1) in relation to England, a hospital as defined by the National Health Service Act 2006 s 275 (see HEALTH SERVICES vol 54A (2017) PARA 633) that is not a health service hospital as defined by that section; and

(2) in relation to Wales, has the same meaning as in the Care Standards Act 2000 (see SOCIAL SERVICES vol 95 (2017) PARA 69).

As to the meaning of 'England' see PARA 2 note 16. The Secretary of State or, in relation to Wales, the Welsh Ministers may by order substitute another definition for any definition of 'independent hospital' for the time being effective for the purposes of Sch 1 para 7: see Sch 1 para 7(3) (as amended: see note 3). The Health and Social Care Act 2008 (Consequential Amendments No 2) Order 2010, SI 2010/813, has been made: see the definition above.

5 For these purposes, 'hostel' means anything which falls within any definition of hostel for the time being prescribed by order made by the Secretary of State or, in relation to Wales, the Welsh Ministers under the Local Government Finance Act 1992 Sch 1 para 7(2): see Sch 1 para 7(2) (as substituted: see note 3). Accordingly, 'hostel' means:

(1) premises approved under the Criminal Justice and Court Services Act 2000 s 9(1) (repealed) (Council Tax (Discount Disregards) Order 1992, SI 1992/548, art 6(a) (art 6 substituted in relation to England by SI 2003/3121; and in relation to Wales by SI 2004/2921)); or

(2) a building or part of a building:

(a) which is solely or mainly used for the provision of residential accommodation in other than separate and self-contained sets of premises, together with personal care, for persons who require such personal care by reason of old age, disablement, past or present alcohol or drug dependence or past or present mental disorder (Council Tax (Discount Disregards) Order 1992, SI 1992/548, art 6(b)(i) (as so substituted)); and

(b) which is not a care home or independent hospital for the purposes of the Local Government Finance Act 1992 Sch 1 para 7 (Council Tax (Discount Disregards) Order 1992, SI 1992/548, art 6(b)(ii) (as so substituted)).

6 Local Government Finance Act 1992 Sch 1 para 7(1)(a) (amended by the Care Standards Act 2000 Sch 4 para 20(a)).

7 Local Government Finance Act 1992 Sch 1 para 7(1)(b) (amended by the Care Standards Act 2000 Sch 4 para 20(b)).

8 See the Local Government Finance Act 1992 Sch 1 para 8 (amended by the Regulation of Care (Scotland) Act 2001 s 79, Sch 3 para 18; and by SSI 2005/465).

374. Care workers.

A person is to be disregarded for the purposes of discounts which may be applied to the amount payable in respect of council tax on a particular day[1]:

(1) if, on the day, he is engaged in providing care or support (or both) to another person or other persons[2]; and

(2) if such conditions as may be prescribed[3] are fulfilled[4].

Without prejudice to the generality of head (2) above, the conditions may:

(a) require the care or support (or both) to be provided on behalf of a charity or a person[5] fulfilling some other description[6];

(b) relate to the period for which the person is engaged in providing care or support (or both)[7];

(c) require his income for a prescribed period (which contains the day concerned) not to exceed a prescribed amount[8];

(d) require his capital not to exceed a prescribed amount[9];

(e) require him to be resident in prescribed premises[10];

(f) require him not to exceed a prescribed age[11];

(g) require the other person or persons to fulfil a prescribed description (whether relating to age, disablement or otherwise)[12].

1 As to discounts applicable to an amount payable in respect of council tax see PARAS 362–367.

2 Local Government Finance Act 1992 s 11(5), Sch 1 para 9(1)(a).

3 'Prescribed' means prescribed by regulations made by the Secretary of State or, in relation to Wales, the Welsh Ministers: see the Local Government Finance Act 1992 s 116(1). The functions of the Secretary of State under the Local Government Finance Act 1992 Sch 1, so far as exercisable in relation to Wales, were transferred to the National Assembly for Wales (see the National Assembly for Wales (Transfer of Functions) Order 1999, SI 1999/672, art 2, Sch 1) and are now vested in the Welsh Ministers (see the Government of Wales Act 2006 s 162(1), Sch 11 para 30). As to the Secretary of State and the Welsh Ministers see PARA 4 note 18. As to the meaning of 'Wales' see PARA 2 note 16.

4 Local Government Finance Act 1992 Sch 1 para 9(1)(b). The conditions prescribed for these purposes are that, on the day in question, the person fulfils either the requirements set out in the Council Tax (Additional Provisions for Discount Disregards) Regulations 1992, SI 1992/552, Schedule Pt I or those set out in Schedule Pt II: see reg 2, Schedule (Schedule amended by SI 1994/540 and SI 1996/637; in relation to England by SI 2005/2866, SI 2006/3395, SI 2013/388, SI 2013/591 and SI 2013/725; and in relation to Wales by SI 2005/3302, SI 2007/581, SI 2013/639 and SI 2013/1049).

5 As to the meaning of 'person' in this context see PARA 11 note 13.

6 Local Government Finance Act 1992 Sch 1 para 9(2)(a).

7 Local Government Finance Act 1992 Sch 1 para 9(2)(b).

8 Local Government Finance Act 1992 Sch 1 para 9(2)(c).

9 Local Government Finance Act 1992 Sch 1 para 9(2)(d).

10 Local Government Finance Act 1992 Sch 1 para 9(2)(e).

11 Local Government Finance Act 1992 Sch 1 para 9(2)(f).

12 Local Government Finance Act 1992 Sch 1 para 9(2)(g).

375. Residents of certain dwellings.

A person is to be disregarded for the purposes of discounts which may be applied to the amount payable in respect of council tax on a particular day[1] if, on the day, he has his sole or main residence in a dwelling[2]:

(1) which is for the time being providing residential accommodation, whether as a hostel or night shelter or otherwise[3]; and

(2) if the accommodation is predominantly provided:

  (a) otherwise than in separate and self-contained sets of premises[4];

  (b) for persons of no fixed abode and no settled way of life[5]; and

  (c) under licences to occupy which do not constitute tenancies[6].

1 As to discounts applicable to an amount payable in respect of council tax see PARAS 362–367.

2 See the Local Government Finance Act 1992 s 11(5), Sch 1 para 10(1). As to the meaning of 'dwelling' see PARA 349. As to the meaning of 'resident' and what constitutes a sole or main residence see PARA 354 note 4.
3 Local Government Finance Act 1992 Sch 1 para 10(2)(a).
4 Local Government Finance Act 1992 Sch 1 para 10(2)(b)(i).
5 Local Government Finance Act 1992 Sch 1 para 10(2)(b)(ii).
6 Local Government Finance Act 1992 Sch 1 para 10(2)(b)(iii).

376. Persons of other descriptions.

A person is to be disregarded for the purposes of discounts which may be applied to the amount payable in respect of council tax on a particular day[1]:

(1) if, on the day, he falls within such description as may be prescribed[2]; and
(2) such conditions as may be prescribed are fulfilled[3].

1 As to discounts applicable to an amount payable in respect of council tax see PARAS 362–367.
2 Local Government Finance Act 1992 s 11(5), Sch 1 para 11(a). 'Prescribed' means prescribed by regulations made by the Secretary of State or, in relation to Wales, the Welsh Ministers: see s 116(1). The functions of the Secretary of State under the Local Government Finance Act 1992 Sch 1, so far as exercisable in relation to Wales, were transferred to the National Assembly for Wales (see the National Assembly for Wales (Transfer of Functions) Order 1999, SI 1999/672, art 2, Sch 1) and are now vested in the Welsh Ministers (see the Government of Wales Act 2006 s 162(1), Sch 11 para 30). As to the Secretary of State and the Welsh Ministers see PARA 4 note 18. As to the meaning of 'Wales' see PARA 2 note 16.

The descriptions prescribed for the purposes of the Local Government Finance Act 1992 Sch 1 para 11, and the conditions to be fulfilled in respect of those descriptions on a particular day (see head (2) in the text), are that a person is within one of the following classes (Council Tax (Additional Provisions for Discount Disregards) Regulations 1992, SI 1992/552, reg 3(1)):

(1) Class A: a member or a dependant of a member (within the meanings given by the International Headquarters and Defences Organisations Act 1964 s 1(2), Schedule) of a headquarters or organisation which is on that day the subject of a designation by an Order in Council under s 1 (see ARMED FORCES vol 3 (2011) PARA 420) (see the Council Tax (Additional Provisions for Discount Disregards) Regulations 1992, SI 1992/552, reg 3(1) Class A);
(2) Class B: a person who is a member of a religious community, the principal occupation of which consists of prayer, contemplation, education, the relief of suffering (or any combination of these) and who has no income or capital of his own (disregarding any income by way of a pension in respect of former employment) and is dependent on the community to provide for his material needs (see reg 3(1) Class B);
(3) Class C: a person who is under the age of 20 and has within a relevant period ceased to undertake a qualifying course of education or a full-time course of education (see reg 3(1) Class C (substituted by SI 1993/149));
(4) Class D: a person who has a relevant association (within the meaning of the Visiting Forces Act 1952 Pt I (ss 1–12): see PARA 352 note 61) with a body, contingent or detachment of the forces of a country, to which any provision in Pt I applies on that day (see ARMED FORCES vol 3 (2011) PARA 407 et seq) (see the Council Tax (Additional Provisions for Discount Disregards) Regulations 1992, SI 1992/552, reg 3(1) Class D (added by SI 1992/2942));
(5) Class E: a person who is the spouse or civil partner or dependant of a student within the meaning of the Local Government Finance Act 1992 Sch 1 para 4 (see PARA 371), and is not a British citizen, and who is prevented (by the terms of his leave to enter or remain in the United Kingdom) from taking paid employment or from claiming benefits (see the Council Tax (Additional Provisions for Discount Disregards) Regulations 1992, SI 1992/552, reg 3(1) Class E (added by SI 1995/620; amended in relation to England by SI 2005/2866; and in relation to Wales by SI 2005/3302));
(6) Class F: a person who is:
    (a) a person on whom privileges and immunities are conferred by the Diplomatic Privileges Act 1964 (see INTERNATIONAL RELATIONS LAW vol 61 (2010) PARA 275) (Council Tax (Additional Provisions for Discount Disregards) Regulations 1992, SI 1992/552, reg 3(1) Class F para (a) (Class F added by SI 1997/657)); or

(b) a person on whom privileges and immunities are conferred under the Commonwealth Secretariat Act 1966 s 1(2), Schedule Pt II para 5(1) (staff of the Secretariat: see COMMONWEALTH vol 13 (2017) PARA 623) (Council Tax (Additional Provisions for Discount Disregards) Regulations 1992, SI 1992/552, reg 3(1) Class F para (b) (as so added));
(c) a person on whom privileges and immunities are conferred by the Consular Relations Act 1968 s 1 (see INTERNATIONAL RELATIONS LAW vol 61 (2010) PARA 290 et seq) (Council Tax (Additional Provisions for Discount Disregards) Regulations 1992, SI 1992/552, reg 3(1) Class F para (c) (as so added)); or
(d) in relation to any organisation specified in an Order in Council made under the International Organisations Act 1968 s 1(2), within a class of persons mentioned in s 1(3) to which the relevant Order extended relief from rates as specified in Sch 1 Pt II para 9 (see INTERNATIONAL RELATIONS LAW vol 61 (2010) PARA 317) (Council Tax (Additional Provisions for Discount Disregards) Regulations 1992, SI 1992/552, reg 3(1) Class F para (d) (as so added)); or
(e) a person on whom privileges and immunities are conferred by the Commonwealth Countries and Republic of Ireland (Immunities and Privileges) Order 1985, SI 1985/1983, arts 3–4 (see COMMONWEALTH vol 13 (2017) PARA 626) (Council Tax (Additional Provisions for Discount Disregards) Regulations 1992, SI 1992/552, reg 3(1) Class F para (e) (as so added)); or
(f) the head of any office established as described in the Hong Kong Economic Trade Act 1996 s 1(1) (Council Tax (Additional Provisions for Discount Disregards) Regulations 1992, SI 1992/552, reg 3(1) Class F para (f) (as so added));

and is not

(i) a British citizen, a British overseas territories citizen, a British national (overseas) or a British overseas citizen (reg 3(1) Class F para (i) (as so added; amended by virtue of the British Overseas Territories Act 2002 s 2(3))); or
(ii) a person who under the British Nationality Act 1981 is a British subject (BRITISH NATIONALITY vol 4 (2011) PARA 407, 469–475) (Council Tax (Additional Provisions for Discount Disregards) Regulations 1992, SI 1992/552, reg 3(1) Class F para (ii) (as so added)); or
(iii) a British protected person (within the meaning of the British Nationality Act 1981: see BRITISH NATIONALITY vol 4 (2011) PARA 408, 476–481) (Council Tax (Additional Provisions for Discount Disregards) Regulations 1992, SI 1992/552, reg 3(1) Class F para (iii) (as so added)); or
(iv) a permanent resident of the United Kingdom (reg 3(1) Class F para (iv) (as so added)).

For the purposes of head (3) above, 'relevant period' means the period after 30 April and before 1 November in any year; 'qualifying course of education' and 'full-time course of education' have the same meanings as in the Council Tax (Discount Disregards) Order 1992, SI 1992/548, Sch 1 Pt II (paras 2–6) (see PARA 371 note 2); and the day in question must be within the same relevant period as that in which the cessation takes place: see the Council Tax (Additional Provisions for Discount Disregards) Regulations 1992, SI 1992/552, reg 3(2) (substituted by SI 1993/149). As to the meaning of 'United Kingdom' see PARA 4 note 10. As to British citizens see BRITISH NATIONALITY vol 4 (2011) PARAS 406, 421–444. As to British overseas citizens see BRITISH NATIONALITY vol 4 (2011) PARAS 406, 459–464. As to British overseas territories citizens see BRITISH NATIONALITY vol 4 (2011) PARAS 406, 445–458.

3 Local Government Finance Act 1992 Sch 1 para 11(b). As to the conditions so prescribed see note 2.

(iii) Other Relief

377. Central government's power to reduce amounts of council tax payable.

The appropriate national authority[1] may make regulations[2] as regards any case where:

(1) a person is liable to pay an amount to a billing authority[3] in respect of council tax[4] for any financial year[5] which is prescribed[6]; and
(2) prescribed conditions are fulfilled[7],

which regulations may provide that the amount he is liable to pay is to be an amount which is less than the amount it would be apart from the regulations[8], and is determined in accordance with prescribed rules[9].

The conditions mentioned in head (2) above may be prescribed by reference to such factors as the appropriate national authority thinks fit[10]. In particular, such factors may include the making of an application by the person concerned, and all or any of the following factors[11], namely:

(a) community charges for a period before 1 April 1993[12];
(b) the circumstances of, or other matters relating to, the person concerned[13];
(c) an amount relating to the authority concerned and specified (or to be specified) for the purposes of the regulations in a report laid (or to be laid) before the House of Commons or the National Assembly for Wales, as the case may be[14];
(d) such other amounts as may be prescribed or arrived at in a prescribed manner[15];

or all or any of the following factors[16], namely:

(i) a disabled person having his sole or main residence in the dwelling concerned[17];
(ii) the circumstances of, or other matters relating to, that person[18];
(iii) the physical characteristics of, or other matters relating to, that dwelling[19].

The regulations may include[20]:

(A) provision requiring the appropriate national authority to specify in a report, for the purposes of the regulations, an amount in relation to each billing authority[21];
(B) provision requiring the Secretary of State to lay the report before the House of Commons or the Welsh Ministers to lay the report before the National Assembly for Wales, as the case may be[22];
(C) provision for the review of any prescribed decision of a billing authority relating to the application or operation of the regulations[23];
(D) provision that[24] no appeal may be made to a valuation tribunal in respect of such a decision[25].

To the extent that he would not have power to do so otherwise, the Secretary of State[26] may include in such regulations such amendments of any social security instrument[27] as he thinks expedient in consequence of such regulations[28]; and he may include in any social security instrument such provision as he thinks expedient in consequence of such regulations[29].

1 Ie the Secretary of State or, in relation to Wales, the Welsh Ministers. The functions of the Secretary of State under the Local Government Finance Act 1992 s 13 (except under s 13(9) (see the text to notes 26–29)), so far as exercisable in relation to Wales, were transferred to the National Assembly for Wales (see the National Assembly for Wales (Transfer of Functions) Order 1999, SI 1999/672, art 2, Sch 1) and are now vested in the Welsh Ministers (see the Government of Wales Act 2006 s 162(1), Sch 11 para 30). As to the Secretary of State and the Welsh Ministers see PARA 4 note 18. As to the meaning of 'Wales' see PARA 2 note 16.

2 As to the regulations made see note 6.

3 As to the meaning of 'billing authority' see PARA 346.

4 The Local Government Finance Act 1992 s 13 applies whether the amount mentioned in s 13(1) is determined under s 10 (basic amounts payable: see PARA 360) or under s 10 read with s 11 (discounts: see PARA 362), s 11A (special provision for discounts where dwellings in England have no resident: see PARA 363), s 11B (higher amount of council tax for long-term empty dwellings in England: see PARA 364), s 12 (special provision for discounts where dwellings in Wales have no resident: see PARA 365), s 12A (higher amount of council tax for long-term empty dwellings in

Wales: see PARA 366) or s 12B (higher amount of council tax for dwellings in Wales occupied periodically: see PARA 367): s 13(3) (amended by the Local Government Act 2003 s 127(1), Sch 7 paras 40, 42; the Local Government Finance Act 2012 s 12(1), (5); and the Housing (Wales) Act 2014 s 139(1), (3), Sch 3 para 29(1), (4)). As to the meaning of references to an amount payable in respect of council tax see PARA 361 note 3. As to council tax see PARA 344 et seq. As to a billing authority's power to reduce the amount of council tax payable see PARA 378.

5 As to the meaning of 'financial year' see PARA 11 note 1.

6 Local Government Finance Act 1992 s 13(1)(a). 'Prescribed' means prescribed by the regulations: see s 116(1). Regulations have made provision for reduced amounts to be payable where special facilities for disabled persons have placed a property in a higher valuation band: see the Council Tax (Reductions for Disabilities) Regulations 1992, SI 1992/554 (amended by SI 1993/195 and SI 1999/1004; and in relation to Wales by SI 2005/702; modified by SI 1995/3150 and SI 2004/3142). As to valuation bands see PARA 361.

There must be an appropriate causal link between the disability and the requirement for the use of the accommodation: see *Howell-Williams v Wirral Borough Council* (1981) 79 LGR 697, [1981] RA 189, CA; *Luton Borough Council v Ball* [2001] EWHC Admin 328, [2001] RVR 198, [2001] All ER (D) 323 (Mar) (the purpose of the statutory instrument was to relieve eligible persons from an increase in their council tax liability when they needed an extra room to meet their needs); *Sandwell Metropolitan Borough Council v Perks* [2003] EWHC 1749 (Admin), [2003] RVR 317, [2003] All ER (D) 118 (Jul); *South Gloucestershire Council v Titley* [2006] EWHC 3117 (Admin), [2007] RA 27, [2006] All ER (D) 89 (Dec) (no basis in the regulations for a requirement that without the room or extra feature the disabled person must find it physically impossible or extremely difficult to live in the dwelling, or that his health would suffer or the disability would be likely to become more severe); and see *Hanson v Middlesbrough Borough Council* [2006] EWHC 1700 (Admin), [2006] RA 320, [2006] All ER (D) 340 (Jun).

Regulations, now largely of historical interest, have also made provision for payment of reduced amounts under transitional arrangements: see the Council Tax (Transitional Reduction Scheme) (England) Regulations 1993, SI 1993/175 (amended by SI 1993/253 and SI 1993/401); the Council Tax (Transitional Reduction Scheme) (England) Regulations 1994, SI 1994/135; the Council Tax (Transitional Reduction Scheme) (England) Regulations 1995, SI 1995/209; the Local Government Reorganisation (Wales) (Council Tax Reduction Scheme) Regulations 1996, SI 1996/309; the Local Government Reorganisation (Wales) (Council Tax Reduction Scheme) Regulations 1997, SI 1997/261; the Council Tax Reduction Scheme (Wales) Regulations 1998, SI 1998/266; the Local Government Changes for England (Council Tax) (Transitional Reduction) Regulations 1999, SI 1999/259; the Council Tax Reduction Scheme (Wales) Regulations 1999, SI 1999/347; the Council Tax (Reduction Scheme) and (Demand Notices Transitional Provisions) (Wales) Regulations 2000, SI 2000/501; the Council Tax (Transitional Arrangements) (Wales) Regulations 2004, SI 2004/3142 (amended by SI 2005/702); and the Council Tax (Reductions for Annexes) (England) Regulations 2013, SI 2013/2977.

7 Local Government Finance Act 1992 s 13(1)(b). As to the regulations made see note 6.

8 Local Government Finance Act 1992 s 13(2)(a).

9 Local Government Finance Act 1992 s 13(2)(b). The regulations may be prescribed by reference to such factors as the appropriate national authority thinks fit; and in particular such factors may include all or any of the factors mentioned in s 13(5) (see heads (a)–(d) in the text) or s 13(6)(b) or (c) (see heads (ii), (iii) in the text): s 13(7). As to the regulations made see note 6.

10 Local Government Finance Act 1992 s 13(4).

11 Local Government Finance Act 1992 s 13(4)(a).

12 Local Government Finance Act 1992 s 13(5)(a). With effect from 1 April 1993, the community charge was abolished and replaced with the council tax: see PARA 344 et seq.

13 Local Government Finance Act 1992 s 13(5)(b).

14 See the Local Government Finance Act 1992 s 13(5)(c); and the Government of Wales Act 2006 Sch 11 para 36.

15 Local Government Finance Act 1992 s 13(5)(d).

16 Local Government Finance Act 1992 s 13(4)(b).

17 Local Government Finance Act 1992 s 13(6)(a). As to the meaning of 'dwelling' see PARA 349. As to the meaning of 'resident' and what constitutes a sole or main residence see PARA 354 note 4.

18 Local Government Finance Act 1992 s 13(6)(b).

19 Local Government Finance Act 1992 s 13(6)(c).

20 Local Government Finance Act 1992 s 13(8). This provision is expressed to be without prejudice to s 113(2) (see PARA 345): see s 13(8).

21 Local Government Finance Act 1992 s 13(8)(a).

22 See the Local Government Finance Act 1992 s 13(8)(b); and the Government of Wales Act 2006 Sch 11 para 36.
23 Local Government Finance Act 1992 s 13(8)(c).
24 Ie notwithstanding the provisions of the Local Government Finance Act 1992 s 16(1): see PARA 513.
25 Local Government Finance Act 1992 s 13(8)(d).
26 This function of the Secretary of State has not been transferred to the Welsh Ministers: see note 1.
27 'Social security instrument' means:
(1) an order or regulations made, or falling to be made, by the Secretary of State under the Social Security Acts, ie the Social Security Contributions and Benefits Act 1992 and the Social Security Administration Act 1992 (Local Government Finance Act 1992 s 13(10)(a) (designated as such by SI 2013/388)); or
(2) regulations made, or falling to be made, under the Welfare Reform Act 2012 Pt 4 (ss 77–95) (Local Government Finance Act 1992 s 13(10)(b) (added by SI 2013/388)).
28 Local Government Finance Act 1992 s 13(9)(a).
29 Local Government Finance Act 1992 s 13(9)(b).

378. Billing authority's power to reduce amounts of council tax payable.

The amount of council tax[1] which a person is liable to pay in respect of any chargeable dwelling[2] and any day[3]:

(1) in the case of a dwelling situated in the area of a billing authority[4] in England[5], is to be reduced to the extent, if any, required by the authority's council tax reduction scheme[6];
(2) in the case of a dwelling situated in the area of a billing authority in Wales[7], is to be reduced to the extent, if any, required by any council tax reduction scheme made under regulations made by the Welsh Ministers[8] that applies to that dwelling[9];
(3) in any case, may be reduced to such extent (or, if the amount has been reduced under head (1) or (2), such further extent) as the billing authority for the area in which the dwelling is situated thinks fit[10].

Each billing authority in England must make a scheme specifying the reductions which are to apply to amounts of council tax payable, in respect of dwellings situated in its area[11], by:

(a) persons whom the authority considers to be in financial need[12]; or
(b) persons in classes consisting of persons whom the authority considers to be, in general, in financial need[13].

The Welsh Ministers may by regulations[14]:

(i) require a person or body specified in the regulations to make a scheme specifying the reductions which are to apply to amounts of council tax payable, in respect of dwellings to which the scheme applies, by persons to whom the scheme applies[15];
(ii) impose requirements on that person or body regarding the matters which must be included in that scheme[16]; and
(iii) make other provision for and in connection with such schemes[17].

Each billing authority in England must make a council tax reduction scheme no later than 31 January 2013; and the first financial year to which that scheme relates must be the year beginning with 1 April 2013[18].

Where a billing authority in England or a specified authority[19] in Wales makes a council tax reduction scheme[20], or a billing authority exercises the power under head (3) above by determining a class of case in which liability is to be reduced[21], then:

(A) where the scheme or the determination provides for liability to be reduced to nil, any dwelling in relation to which the reduction applies is to be treated for the purposes of council tax administration[22] as an exempt dwelling[23];

(B) where the scheme or the determination provides for liability to be reduced otherwise than to nil, any amount in relation to which the reduction applies is to be treated for the purposes of council tax administration[24] as subject to a discount equal to the amount of the reduction[25].

The Secretary of State must make provision for an independent review of all council tax reduction schemes made under the provisions of the Local Government Finance Act 2012 to consider their effectiveness, efficiency, fairness and transparency and their impact on the localism agenda, and to make recommendations as to whether such schemes should be brought within universal credit[26]. Such a review must take place within three years after the Local Government Finance Act 2012 comes into effect (ie 31 October 2102)[27].

1 As to council tax see PARA 344 et seq. As to persons liable to pay council tax see PARA 354 et seq.
2 As to the meaning of 'dwelling' see PARA 349. As to the meaning of 'chargeable dwelling' see PARA 350.
3 Ie as determined in accordance with the Local Government Finance Act 1992 ss 10–13: see PARAS 360, 362 et seq.
4 As to the meaning of 'billing authority' see PARA 346. As to the power to make regulations containing rules for ascertaining in what part of a billing authority's area a dwelling is situated see the Local Government Finance Act 1992 s 10(2); and PARA 360; and as to the power to make regulations containing rules for treating a dwelling as situated in a billing authority's area if part only of the dwelling falls within the area see s 1(3); and PARA 348.
5 As to the meaning of 'England' see PARA 2 note 16.
6 Local Government Finance Act 1992 s 13A(1)(a) (s 13A added by the Local Government Act 2003 s 76; and substituted by the Local Government Finance Act 2012 s 10(1)).
7 As to the meaning of 'Wales' see PARA 2 note 16.
8 Ie regulations under the Local Government Finance Act 1992 s 13A(4): see the text and notes 14–17. As to the Welsh Ministers see PARA 4 note 18.
9 Local Government Finance Act 1992 s 13A(1)(b) (as added and substituted: see note 6).
10 Local Government Finance Act 1992 s 13A(1)(c) (as added and substituted: see note 6). The power under s 13A(1)(c) includes power to reduce an amount to nil: s 13A(6) (as so added). The power under s 13A(1)(c) may be exercised in relation to particular cases or by determining a class of case in which liability is to be reduced to an extent provided by the determination: s 13A(7) (as so added).
11 Local Government Finance Act 1992 s 13A(2) (as added and substituted: see note 6). Provision about schemes is made by Sch 1A (added by the Local Government Finance Act 2012 s 10(2), (3)(a), Sch 4 para 1; and amended by SI 2017/1305): Local Government Finance Act 1992 s 13A(3) (as added and substituted: see note 6).

It is the authority itself which must discharge the function of making or revising a council tax reduction scheme under s 13A(2): s 67(1), (2)(aa) (s 67(2)(aa) added by the Local Government Finance Act 2012 s 10(2), (3)(b), Sch 4 paras 3, 6).

In exercise of the powers conferred by the Local Government Finance Act 1992 Sch 1A (as so added), the following regulations have been made: the Council Tax Reduction Schemes (Prescribed Requirements) (England) Regulations 2012, SI 2012/2885 (amended by SI 2012/3085, SI 2013/3181, SI 2014/107, SI 2014/448, SI 2014/3255, SI 2014/3312, SI 2015/643, SI 2015/971, SI 2015/1985, SI 2015/2041, SI 2016/211, SI 2016/1262, SI 2017/204, SI 2017/422 and SI 2017/1305); the Council Tax Reduction Schemes (Default Scheme) (England) Regulations 2012, SI 2012/2886 (amended by SI 2012/3085, SI 2015/971, SI 2015/1985, SI 2016/211 and SI 2017/422); the Council Tax Reduction Schemes (Transitional Provision) (England) Regulations 2013, SI 2013/215; and the Jobseeker's Allowance (Schemes for Assisting Persons to Obtain Employment) Regulations 2013, SI 2013/276 (amended by SI 2013/2584, SI 2014/2103 and SI 2015/336).

See also *R (on the application of Moseley) v Haringey London Borough Council* [2014] UKSC 56, [2014] 1 WLR 3947, [2014] All ER (D) 332 (Oct) (failure to refer to alternatives invalidated public consultation) (as to this case see What Constitutes a Fair Public Consultation? Andrew Eaton: 165 NLJ 7636 (*Moseley* is the first case in which the United Kingdom's highest court has considered the law on the duty to consult)).

12 Local Government Finance Act 1992 s 13A(2)(a) (as added and substituted: see note 6).

13 Local Government Finance Act 1992 s 13A(2)(b) (as added and substituted: see note 6).

14 Local Government Finance Act 1992 s 13A(4) (as added and substituted: see note 6). No regulations under s 13A(4) are to be made unless a draft of the statutory instrument containing them has been laid before, and approved by a resolution of, the National Assembly for Wales: s 13A(8) (as so added and substituted). Further provision about regulations under s 13A(4) and about schemes under those regulations is made by Sch 1B: s 13A(5) (as so added and substituted).

In exercise of the powers conferred by Sch 1B (added by the Local Government Finance Act 2012 s 10(2), (3)(a), Sch 4 para 1), the following regulations have been made in relation to Wales: the Council Tax Reduction Schemes (Transitional Provisions) (Wales) Regulations 2013, SI 2013/111; the Council Tax Reduction Schemes and Prescribed Requirements (Wales) Regulations 2013, SI 2013/3029 (amended by SI 2014/66, SI 2014/825, SI 2014/852, SI 2015/44, SI 2015/971, SI 2016/50, SI 2017/46 and SI 2018/14); and the Council Tax Reduction Schemes (Default Scheme) (Wales) Regulations 2013, SI 2013/3035 (amended by SI 2014/66, SI 2014/825, SI 2014/852, SI 2015/44, SI 2015/971, SI 2016/50, SI 2017/46 and SI 2018/14).

15 Local Government Finance Act 1992 s 13A(4)(a) (as added and substituted: see note 6).

16 Local Government Finance Act 1992 s 13A(4)(b) (as added and substituted: see note 6).

17 Local Government Finance Act 1992 s 13A(4)(c) (as added and substituted: see note 6).

18 Local Government Finance Act 2012 s 10(4). The Secretary of State may by order made by statutory instrument amend s 10(4) by substituting a different date or a later financial year (or both): s 10(5). As to the Secretary of State see PARA 4 note 18.

A council tax reduction scheme, or any revision of such a scheme, may not be questioned except by an application for judicial review (see JUDICIAL REVIEW vol 61 (2010) PARA 601 et seq): see the Local Government Finance Act 1992 s 66(1), (2)(ba) (s 66(2)(ba) added by the Local Government Finance Act 2012 Sch 4 paras 3, 5(1), (2)). A scheme was quashed in *R (on the application of Winder) Sandwell Metropolitan Borough Council* [2014] EWHC 2617 (Admin), [2015] RVR 47 (no power to define a class for purposes of the Local Government Finance Act 1992 s 13A(2)(b) by reference to non-financial need criterion of length of residence), but a challenge on the basis of indirect discrimination failed in *R (on the application of Logan) v Havering London Borough* [2015] EWHC 3193 (Admin), [2015] All ER (D) 73 (Nov).

19 Ie within the meaning of the Local Government Finance Act 1992 Sch 1B.

20 For the purposes of the Local Government Finance Act 1992 Pt I (ss 1–69) 'council tax reduction scheme' means a scheme under s 13A(2) or regulations under s 13A(4): s 13A(9) (as added and substituted: see note 6).

21 See the Local Government Finance Act 1992 Sch 2 para 21(1) (Sch 2 para 21 added by the Local Government Act 2003 s 127(1), Sch 7 paras 40, 53(1), (3); the Local Government Finance Act 1992 Sch 2 para 21(1) substituted by the Local Government Finance Act 2012 Sch 4 paras 3, 7(1), (2)).

22 Ie for the purposes of the Local Government Finance Act 1992 Sch 2: see PARA 437.

23 Local Government Finance Act 1992 Sch 2 para 21(2) (as added (see note 21); amended by the Local Government Finance Act 2012 Sch 4 paras 3, 7(1), (3)).As to the meaning of 'exempt dwelling' see PARA 351.

24 Ie for the purposes of the Local Government Finance Act 1992 Sch 2: see PARA 437.

25 Local Government Finance Act 1992 Sch 2 para 21(3) (as added (see note 21); amended by the Local Government Finance Act 2012 Sch 4 paras 3, 7(1), (3)). As to discounts generally applicable to an amount payable in respect of council tax see PARA 362 et seq.

26 Local Government Finance Act 2012 s 9(1).

27 Local Government Finance Act 2012 s 9(2). The Act received the Royal Assent on 31 October 2012 and s 9 came into force on that day.

379. Central government's power to smooth changes in council tax liability.

The Secretary of State[1], in relation to a billing authority[2] in England[3], or the Welsh Ministers[4], in relation to a billing authority in Wales[5], may by regulations[6] make provision for the purpose of smoothing changes in council tax liability[7] resulting from the coming into force of:

(1) an order[8] varying the provisions by which dwellings in different valuation bands attract different amounts of council tax[9]; or

(2) a list made[10] pursuant to the provisions which govern the compilation and maintenance of new lists[11].

1 As to the Secretary of State see PARA 4 note 18.
2 As to the meaning of 'billing authority' see PARA 346.
3 As to the meaning of 'England' see PARA 2 note 16.
4 As to the Welsh Ministers see PARA 4 note 18.
5 As to the meaning of 'Wales' see PARA 2 note 16.
6 As to the regulations made see the Council Tax (Transitional Arrangements) (Wales) Regulations 2004, SI 2004/3142 (amended by SI 2005/702), which made transitional arrangements for the period from 1 April 2005 to 31 March 2008 in relation to Wales.
7 As to council tax see PARA 344 et seq. As to persons liable to pay council tax see PARA 354 et seq.
8 Ie an order under the Local Government Finance Act 1992 s 5: see PARA 361.
9 See the Local Government Finance Act 1992 s 13B(1)(a), (2)(a) (s 13B added by the Local Government Act 2003 s 79). See further PARA 361.
10 Ie under the Local Government Finance Act 1992 s 22B: see PARA 411.
11 See the Local Government Finance Act 1992 s 13B(1)(b), (2)(b) (as added: see note 9). See further PARA 411.

(iv) Calculation

380. Amounts for different categories of dwellings.

For each financial year[1] and each category of dwellings[2] in its area[3], a billing authority[4] must set an amount of council tax[5]. An amount so set is to be calculated by taking the aggregate of:

(1) the amount which, in relation to the year and the category of dwellings, has been calculated (or last calculated) by the authority in accordance with the requisite calculations[6]; and

(2) any amounts which, in relation to the year and the category of dwellings, have been calculated[7] and have been stated (or last stated) in accordance with the provisions with regard to the issue of precepts[8] in precepts issued to the authority by major precepting authorities[9].

Where the aggregate amount so given is a negative amount, the amount set must be nil[10].

A billing authority must assume for these purposes that each of the valuation bands is shown in its valuation list[11] as applicable to one or more dwellings situated in its area or (as the case may be) each part of its area as respects which different calculations have been so made[12].

Any amount must be set before 11 March in the financial year preceding that for which it is set, but is not invalid merely because it is set on or after that date[13]. No amount may be set:

(a) before the earlier of the following:
    (i) 1 March in the financial year preceding that for which the amount is set[14];
    (ii) the date of the issue to the authority of the last precept capable of being issued to it (otherwise than by way of substitute) by a major precepting authority for the financial year for which the amount is set[15];

(b) unless the authority has made in relation to the year the requisite calculations[16].

1 As to the meaning of 'financial year' see PARA 11 note 1.

2 As to the meaning of 'dwelling' see PARA 349. Dwellings fall within different categories for the purposes of the Local Government Finance Act 1992 s 30(1), (2) (see the text to notes 6–9) according as different calculations have been made in relation to them in accordance with (s 30(4)):
   (1) in the case of a billing authority in England, ss 31A, 31B (see PARAS 382–383) and ss 34–36 (see PARA 386), or ss 42A, 42B, 45–47 (see PARAS 12–13), or both (s 30(4)(a) (s 30(4)(a), (b) substituted by the Localism Act 2011 s 79, Sch 7 paras 7, 8(1), (3)); or
   (2) in the case of a billing authority in Wales, the Local Government Finance Act 1992 ss 32, 33 (see PARAS 384–385) and ss 34–36, or ss 43–47 (see PARA 14), or both (s 30(4)(b) (as so substituted)).

As to the meanings of 'England' and 'Wales' see PARA 2 note 16.

Where the major precepting authority in question is the Greater London Authority, the Local Government Finance Act 1992 s 30(2)(b) (see head (2) in the text) and s 30(4) have effect as if the references to ss 43–47 were references to the appropriate Greater London provisions: s 30(10) (s 30(10), (11) added by the Greater London Authority Act 1999 s 81). 'Appropriate Greater London provisions' means the Local Government Finance Act 1992 s 47 (see PARA 11) and the Greater London Authority Act 1999 ss 85–90 (see LONDON GOVERNMENT vol 71 (2013) PARA 150) or, in the case of calculations by way of substitute, ss 85, 86 (see LONDON GOVERNMENT vol 71 (2013) PARA 150) and ss 88–90, and Sch 7 (see LONDON GOVERNMENT vol 71 (2013) PARA 150) and the Local Government Finance Act 1992 s 47: s 30(11) (as so added).

3 As to the power to make regulations containing rules for ascertaining in what part of a billing authority's area a dwelling is situated see the Local Government Finance Act 1992 s 10(2); and PARA 360; and as to the power to make regulations containing rules for treating a dwelling as situated in a billing authority's area if part only of the dwelling falls within the area see s 1(3); and PARA 348.

4 As to the meaning of 'billing authority' see PARA 346.

5 Local Government Finance Act 1992 s 30(1). As to council tax see PARA 344 et seq. The setting of an amount of council tax for a financial year (whether originally or by way of substitute) must be discharged only by the authority: see s 67(1), (2)(c). As to substituted amounts see PARA 381. The setting of an amount of council tax for a financial year (whether originally or by way of substitute) may not be questioned except by an application for judicial review: see s 66(1), (2)(d). If on an application for judicial review the court decides to grant relief, it must quash the setting: see s 66(3) (amended by the Local Government Finance Act 2012 s 10(2), (3)(b), Sch 4 paras 3, 5(1), (3)). As to judicial review see JUDICIAL REVIEW vol 61 (2010) PARA 601 et seq. Sums received by a billing authority in respect of council tax set by it in accordance with s 30 must be paid into the authority's collection fund: see the Local Government Finance Act 1988 s 90(1); and PARA 581.

The Local Government Finance Act 1992 ss 30, 36 are modified where, following an order creating a single tier local authority area, an authority makes a determination with a view to equalising council tax payable in respect of dwellings situated in the predecessor areas of a reorganised area: see the Local Government (Structural Changes) (Finance) Regulations 2008, SI 2008/3022, reg 15(5), (6), Sch 2 paras 1, 4 (reg 15(6) amended and Sch 2 substituted by SI 2012/20). As to the transfer of functions in relation to council tax following local government re-organisation see PARA 346.

6 Local Government Finance Act 1992 s 30(2)(a). The requisite calculations are those made in accordance with:
   (1) in the case of a billing authority in England, ss 31A, 31B (see PARAS 382–383) and ss 34–36 (see PARA 386) (s 30(2)(a)(i) (s 30(2)(a)(i), (ii) substituted by the Localism Act 2011 Sch 7 paras 7, 8(1), (2)(a))); or
   (2) in the case of a billing authority in Wales, the Local Government Finance Act 1992 ss 32–36 (see PARAS 384–386) (s 30(2)(a)(ii) (as so substituted)).

Accordingly, the amount to be taken into account under s 30(2)(a) for any financial year in respect of a category of dwellings listed in a particular valuation band is to be calculated by applying a formula: see the Local Government Finance Act 1992 s 36(1).

Dwellings fall within different categories for the purposes of s 36 according as different calculations have been made in relation to them under s 34: s 36(2). As to the meaning of dwellings listed in a particular valuation band see PARA 361 note 5. As to valuation bands see PARA 361.

7 Ie, in the case of a billing authority in England, in accordance with the Local Government Finance Act 1992 ss 42A, 42B, 45–47 (see PARAS 12–13); or, in the case of a billing authority in Wales, in accordance with ss 43, 44 and ss 45–47 (see PARA 14).

8 Ie, in the case of a billing authority in England or Wales, in accordance with the Local Government

Finance Act 1992 s 40: see PARA 11.
9 Local Government Finance Act 1992 s 30(2)(b) (amended by the Localism Act 2011 Sch 7 paras 7, 8(1), (2)(b)). As to the meaning of 'major precepting authority' see PARA 11 note 2.
10 Local Government Finance Act 1992 s 30(3).
11 As to valuation lists see PARA 408 et seq.
12 Local Government Finance Act 1992 s 30(5).
13 Local Government Finance Act 1992 s 30(6).
14 Local Government Finance Act 1992 s 30(7)(a). A purported setting of an amount, if done in contravention of s 30(7) or s 30(8) (see the text to note 16), is to be treated as not having occurred: s 30(9).
15 Local Government Finance Act 1992 s 30(7)(b). See note 14.
16 Local Government Finance Act 1992 s 30(8). The calculations referred to are those required by Pt I Ch III (ss 30–38) (see note 6): see s 30(8). See also note 14.

381. Substituted amounts.

Where a billing authority[1] has set amounts for council tax for a financial year[2], and at any later time:

(1) it makes[3] substitute calculations[4]; or
(2) substitute calculations it has made[5] have effect[6]; or
(3) it is issued with a precept for the year (originally or by way of substitute) by a major precepting authority[7],

it must as soon as reasonably practicable after that time set amounts in substitution so as to give effect to those calculations or that precept[8].

Where a billing authority so sets any amount in substitution (a 'new amount'), anything paid to it by reference to the amount for which it is substituted (the 'old amount') is to be treated as paid by reference to the new amount[9]. If the old amount exceeds the new amount, the following applies as regards anything paid if it would not have been paid had the old amount been the same as the new amount:

(a) it must be repaid if the person by whom it was paid so requires[10];
(b) in any other case it must (as the billing authority determines) either be repaid or be credited against any subsequent liability of the person to pay in respect of any council tax set[11] by the authority[12].

Where an authority sets amounts in substitution under head (2) above, it may recover from the major precepting authority administrative expenses incurred by it in, or in consequence of, so doing[13].

1 As to the meaning of 'billing authority' see PARA 346.
2 Ie under the Local Government Finance Act 1992 s 30: see PARA 380. As to the meaning of 'financial year' see PARA 11 note 1. As to council tax see PARA 344 et seq.
3 Ie under the Local Government Finance Act 1992 s 36A (see PARA 387), s 37 (see PARA 388) or ss 52I, 52T (see PARA 22).
4 Local Government Finance Act 1992 s 31(1)(a) (amended by the Local Government Act 1999 s 30, Sch 1 Pt II paras 2, 3; and the Localism Act 2011 s 79, Sch 7 paras 7, 9).
5 Ie under the Local Government Finance Act 1992 s 52ZF: see PARA 394.
6 Ie by virtue of the Local Government Finance Act 1992 s 52ZH (see PARA 396) or s 52ZI (see PARA 397): s 31(1)(aa) (added by the Localism Act 2011 s 72(2), Sch 6 paras 1, 2(1), (2)).
7 Local Government Finance Act 1992 s 31(1)(b). As to the meaning of 'major precepting authority' see PARA 11 note 2. As to the issue of precepts by major precepting authorities see PARA 11 et seq.
8 Local Government Finance Act 1992 s 31(1). Any amount set in substitution under s 31(1) must be set in accordance with s 30 (see PARA 380), but s 30(6) (amount to be set before 11 March in the preceding financial year) is to be ignored for this purpose: s 31(2). The setting of an amount of council tax for a financial year (whether originally or by way of substitute) must be discharged only by the authority: see s 67(1), (2)(c). The setting of an amount of council tax for a financial year (whether originally or by way of substitute) may not be questioned except by an application for judicial review: see s 66(1), (2)(d). If on an application for judicial review the court decides to grant relief, it must quash the setting: see s 66(3) (amended by the Local Government Finance Act 2012

s 10(2), (3)(b), Sch 4 paras 3, 5(1), (3)). As to judicial review see JUDICIAL REVIEW vol 61 (2010) PARA 601 et seq.

9 Local Government Finance Act 1992 s 31(3).

10 Local Government Finance Act 1992 s 31(4)(a). As to persons liable to pay council tax see PARA 354 et seq.

11 Ie in accordance with the Local Government Finance Act 1992 s 30: see PARA 380.

12 Local Government Finance Act 1992 s 31(4)(b).

13 Local Government Finance Act 1992 s 31(5). This provision is expressed to be subject to any provision made by regulations under s 31(6): see s 31(5) (amended by the Localism Act 2011 Sch 6 paras 1, 2(1), (4)). Subject to any provision made by regulations under the Local Government Finance Act 1992 s 31(6), where an authority sets amounts in substitution under s 31(1)(a) (see head (1) in the text) in the circumstances described in s 52ZO(6) (see PARA 403) or s 52ZP(6) or (8) (see PARA 404), it may recover from the local precepting authority in question administrative expenses incurred by it in, or in consequence of, so doing: s 31(4A) (added by the Localism Act 2011 Sch 6 paras 1, 2(1), (3)). As to the meaning of 'local precepting authority' see PARA 18 note 2.

The Secretary of State may by regulations make provision for cases in which the Local Government Finance Act 1992 s 31(4A) or (5) does not apply, or that subsection applies with modifications: s 31(6) (added by the Localism Act 2011 Sch 6 paras 1, 2(1), (5)). As to the Secretary of State see PARA 4 note 18. The Local Authority (Referendums Relating to Council Tax Increases) Regulations 2012, SI 2012/460, have been made under the Local Government Finance Act 1992 s 31(6).

382. Calculation of council tax requirement by authorities in England.

In relation to each financial year[1] a billing authority[2] in England[3] must make the following calculations[4].

The authority must calculate the aggregate of[5]:

(1) the expenditure which the authority estimates it will incur in the year in performing its functions and will charge to a revenue account, other than a BID revenue account[6], for the year in accordance with proper practices[7];

(2) such allowance as the authority estimates will be appropriate for contingencies in relation to amounts to be charged or credited to a revenue account for the year in accordance with proper practices[8];

(3) the financial reserves which the authority estimates it will be appropriate to raise in the year for meeting its estimated future expenditure[9];

(4) such financial reserves as are sufficient to meet so much of the amount estimated by the authority to be a revenue account deficit for any earlier financial year as has not already been provided for[10];

(5) any amounts which it estimates will be transferred[11] in the year from its general fund to its collection fund[12];

(6) any amounts which it estimates will be transferred[13] in the year from its general fund to its collection fund[14]; and

(7) any amounts which it estimates will be transferred from its general fund to its collection fund[15] and charged to a revenue account for the year[16].

The authority must also calculate the aggregate of[17]:

(a) the income which it estimates will accrue to it in the year and which it will credit to a revenue account, other than a BID revenue account, for the year in accordance with proper practices[18];

(b) any amounts which it estimates will be transferred[19] in the year from its collection fund to its general fund[20];

(c) any amounts which it estimates will be transferred[21] in the year from its collection fund to its general fund[22];

(d) any amounts which it estimates will be transferred from its collection fund to its general fund[23] and will be credited to a revenue account for the year[24]; and

(e) the amount of the financial reserves which the authority estimates it will use in order to provide for the items mentioned in heads (1), (2), (6) and (7) above[25].

If the aggregate calculated under heads (1) to (7) above exceeds that calculated under heads (a) to (e) above, the authority must calculate the amount equal to the difference; and the amount so calculated is to be its council tax requirement for the year[26].

The Secretary of State may by regulations[27] do either or both of the following:

(i) alter the constituents of any calculation to be made under the above provisions (whether by adding, deleting or amending items)[28];

(ii) alter[29] the rules governing the making of any such calculation[30].

Calculations to be made in relation to a particular financial year must be made before 11 March in the preceding financial year, but they are not invalid merely because they are made on or after that date[31].

1 As to the meaning of 'financial year' see PARA 11 note 1.

2 As to the meaning of 'billing authority' see PARA 346.

3 As to the meaning of 'England' see PARA 2 note 16.

4 Local Government Finance Act 1992 s 31A(1) (s 31A added by the Localism Act 2011 s 74). The Local Government Finance Act 1992 s 31A is subject to s 52ZS (which requires a direction to a billing authority that the referendum provisions in Pt 1 Ch 4ZA (ss 52ZA–52ZY) are not to apply to the authority for a financial year to state the amount of the authority's council tax requirement for the year: see PARA 406): s 31A(12) (as so added).

Before a billing authority makes its calculations (otherwise than by way of substitute, as to which see PARA 387) in relation to the financial year under s 31A, it must consult persons or bodies appearing to it to be representative of persons subject to non-domestic rates under the Local Government Finance Act 1988 s 43 (see PARAS 82, 133, 143 et seq) and s 45 (see PARAS 135–136, 147–148) as regards hereditaments situated in the authority's area: see the Local Government Finance Act 1992 s 65(1), (3), (4)(a) (s 65(3) amended by the Greater London Authority Act 1999 s 423, Sch 34 Pt I; the Police Reform and Social Responsibility Act 2011 s 26(1), (3); and the Policing and Crime Act 2017 s 6, Sch 1 para 71(1), (3); the Local Government Finance Act 1992 s 65(4)(a) amended by the Localism Act 2011 s 79, Sch 7 paras 7, 28). As to the meaning of 'person' see PARA 11 note 13. As to non-domestic rating see PARA 52 et seq. Consultations must be made as to each financial year, and must be about the authority's proposals for expenditure (including capital expenditure) in that financial year; and the Secretary of State may by regulations prescribe matters which are to be treated as expenditure for this purpose: Local Government Finance Act 1992 s 65(2). At the date at which this volume states the law, no such regulations had been made.

In performing the duty to consult, an authority must have regard to any guidance issued by the Secretary of State concerning:

(1) persons or bodies to be regarded for these purposes as representative of persons subject to non-domestic rates as regards hereditaments situated in the authority's area (s 65(5)(a)); and

(2) the timing and manner of the consultations (s 65(5)(b)).

An authority must make available to persons or bodies it proposes to consult such information as may be prescribed and is in its possession or control; and it must do so in such form and manner, and at such time, as may be prescribed: s 65(6). As to the regulations made see the Non-Domestic Ratepayers (Consultation) Regulations 1992, SI 1992/3171.

The function of making a calculation under the Local Government Finance Act 1992 s 31A must be discharged only by the authority: see s 67(1), (2)(b) (s 67(2)(b) amended by the Localism Act 2011 Sch 7 paras 7, 30). Where an authority to which the Local Government Finance Act 1992 s 31A applies is making calculations in accordance with that section, the chief finance officer of the authority must report to it on matters such as the robustness of the estimates made for the purposes of the calculations, and the adequacy of the proposed financial reserves, and must review those calculations throughout the year: see the Local Government Act 2003 s 25; and PARA 16.

A calculation made in accordance with the Local Government Finance Act 1992 s 31A may not be questioned except by an application for judicial review: see s 66(1), (2)(c) (s 66(2)(c) amended by the Localism Act 2011 Sch 7 paras 7, 29). If, on an application for judicial review, the court decides to grant relief in respect of any matter, it must quash the calculation: see the Local Government Finance Act 1992 s 66(3) (amended by the Local Government Finance Act 2012 s 10(2), (3)(b), Sch 4 paras 3, 5(1), (3)). As to judicial review see JUDICIAL REVIEW vol 61 (2010) PARA 601 et seq.

5 In making the calculation under the Local Government Finance Act 1992 s 31A(2) the authority must ignore payments which must be met from its collection fund under the Local Government Finance Act 1988 s 90(2) (see PARA 581) or from a trust fund, and subject to the Local Government Finance Act 1992 s 31A(2)(da), (e) and (f) (see heads (5)–(7) in the text), sums which have been or are to be transferred from its general fund to its collection fund: Local Government Finance Act 1992 s 31A(5) (as added (see note 4); amended by SI 2014/389).

6 'BID revenue account' has the same meaning as in the Local Government Act 2003 Pt 4 (ss 41–59) (see PARA 325): Local Government Finance Act 1992 s 31A(13) (as added: see note 4). As to accounts generally see PARA 588 et seq.

7 Local Government Finance Act 1992 s 31A(2)(a) (as added: see note 4). As to the meaning of 'proper practices' see PARA 590 note 4. In estimating under s 31A(2)(a) the authority must take into account:

(1) the amount of any expenditure which it estimates it will incur in the year in making any repayments of grants or other sums paid to it by the Secretary of State (s 31A(6)(a) (as so added)); and

(2) the amount of any precept issued to it for the year by a local precepting authority and the amount of any levy or special levy issued to it for the year (s 31A(6)(b) (as so added)).

But (except as provided by regulations under s 41 (see PARA 18) or regulations under the Local Government Finance Act 1988 s 74 or s 75 (see PARA 24)) the authority must not anticipate a precept, levy or special levy not issued: Local Government Finance Act 1992 s 31A(7) (as so added). As to the Secretary of State see PARA 4 note 18. As to grants see PARA 29 et seq. As to the meaning of 'levy' see PARA 12 note 5. As to the meaning of 'special levy' see PARA 384 note 5. As to precepts see PARA 11 et seq. As to the meaning of 'local precepting authority' see PARA 18 note 2.

8 Local Government Finance Act 1992 s 31A(2)(b) (as added: see note 4).

9 Local Government Finance Act 1992 s 31A(2)(c) (as added: see note 4). For these purposes an authority's estimated future expenditure is:

(1) that which the authority estimates it will incur in the financial year following the year in question, will charge to a revenue account for the year in accordance with proper practices and will have to defray in the year before the following sums are sufficiently available (s 31A(8)(a) (as so added)):

  (a) sums which will be payable for the year into its general fund and in respect of which amounts will be credited to a revenue account for the year in accordance with proper practices (s 31A(8)(a)(i) (as so added)); and

  (b) sums which will be transferred as regards the year from its collection fund to its general fund (s 31A(8)(a)(ii) (as so added)); and

(2) that which the authority estimates it will incur in the financial year referred to in head (1) or any subsequent financial year in performing its functions and which will be charged to a revenue account for that or any other year in accordance with proper practices (s 31A(8)(b) (as so added)).

As to collection and general funds see PARA 579.

In relation to the estimation of financial reserves for the purpose of calculations in accordance with s 31A, in the case of a controlled reserve, it is not to be regarded as appropriate for the balance of the reserve at the end of the financial year under consideration to be less than the minimum amount determined in accordance with regulations made by the appropriate person: see the Local Government Act 2003 s 26(1)(a), (2), (3) (s 26(1) amended by the Localism Act 2011 Sch 7 paras 42, 44). As to the meanings of 'controlled reserve' and 'appropriate person' see PARA 16 note 8. At the date at which this volume states the law, no such regulations had been made. The provisions relating to the making of a report by the chief finance officer on the inadequacy of controlled reserves and budget monitoring also apply: see the Local Government Act 2003 ss 27, 28; and PARAS 16–17.

10 Local Government Finance Act 1992 s 31A(2)(d) (as added: see note 4). See also note 9.

11 Ie in accordance with regulations under the Local Government Finance Act 1988 s 97(2B): see PARA 582.

12 Local Government Finance Act 1992 s 31A(2)(da) (s 31A as added (see note 4); s 31A(2)(da) added by SI 2013/733).
13 Ie in accordance with the Local Government Finance Act 1988 s 97(4): see PARA 582.
14 Local Government Finance Act 1992 s 31A(2)(e) (as added: see note 4).
15 Ie pursuant to a direction under the Local Government Finance Act 1988 s 98(5): see PARA 582.
16 Local Government Finance Act 1992 s 31A(2)(f) (as added: see note 4).
17 In making the calculation under the Local Government Finance Act 1992 s 31A(3) the authority must ignore:
(1) payments which must be made into its collection fund under the Local Government Finance Act 1988 s 90(1) (see PARA 581) or to a trust fund (Local Government Finance Act 1992 s 31A(9)(a) (as added: see note 4)); and
(2) subject to s 31A(3)(aa), (b), (c) (see heads (b), (c), (d) in the text), sums which have been or are to be transferred from its collection fund to its general fund (s 31A(9)(b) (as so added; amended by SI 2013/733)).
18 Local Government Finance Act 1992 s 31A(3)(a) (as added: see note 4).
19 Ie in accordance with regulations under the Local Government Finance Act 1988 s 97(2A): see PARA 582.
20 Local Government Finance Act 1992 s 31A(3)(aa) (s 31A as added (see note 4); s 31A(3)(aa) added by SI 2013/733).
21 Ie in accordance with the Local Government Finance Act 1988 s 97(3): see PARA 582.
22 Local Government Finance Act 1992 s 31A(3)(b) (as added: see note 4).
23 Ie pursuant to a direction under the Local Government Finance Act 1988 s 98(4): see PARA 582.
24 Local Government Finance Act 1992 s 31A(3)(c) (as added: see note 4).
25 Local Government Finance Act 1992 s 31A(3)(d) (as added: see note 4).
26 Local Government Finance Act 1992 s 31A(4) (as added: see note 4).
27 At the date at which this volume states the law, no such regulations had been made.
28 Local Government Finance Act 1992 s 31A(10)(a) (as added: see note 4).
29 Ie whether by deleting or amending the Local Government Finance Act 1992 s 31A(5)–(9) (see notes 5, 7, 9, 15), or any of those provisions, or by adding other provisions, or by a combination of those methods.
30 Local Government Finance Act 1992 s 31A(10)(b) (as added: see note 4).
31 Local Government Finance Act 1992 s 31A(11) (as added: see note 4).

383. Calculation of basic amount of tax by authorities in England.

In relation to each financial year[1] a billing authority in England[2] must calculate the basic amount of its council tax[3] by applying a specified formula[4].

The Secretary of State[5] must make regulations[6] containing rules for making for any year certains calculations relating to the formula[7].

The Secretary of State may by regulations[8] do either or both of the following:

(1) alter the constituents of any calculation to be made under the above provisions (whether by adding, deleting or amending items[9];
(2) provide for rules[10] governing the making of any such calculation[11].

1 As to the meaning of 'financial year' see PARA 11 note 1.
2 As to the meaning of 'billing authority' see PARA 346. As to the meaning of 'England' see PARA 2 note 16.
3 The function of setting an amount of council tax for a financial year under the Local Government Finance Act 1992 Pt I Ch III (ss 30–38), whether originally or by way of substitute, must be discharged only by the authority (see s 67(1), (2)(c) (s 67(1) amended by the Local Government Act 2003 s 84(1), (2)) but this does not apply to the determination of an amount for item 'T' in the Local Government Finance Act 1992 s 31B(1) (see the text to notes 6–8) (s 67(2A)(za) (s 67(2A) added by the Local Government Act 2003 s 84(1), (3); the Local Government Finance Act 1992 s 67(2A)(za) added by the Localism Act 2011 s 79, Sch 7 paras 7, 30(1), (3))). However, that function may, if the authority so directs, be exercised by a committee of the authority appointed by it for that purpose; and as respects a committee so appointed the number of members and their term of office must be fixed by the authority, and each member must be a member of the authority: see the Local Government Finance Act 1992 s 67(3) (amended by the Localism Act 2011 Sch 7 paras 7, 30(1), (4)).

4 See the Local Government Finance Act 1992 s 31B. Regulations may be made in relation to the formula: see s 31B(4) (as so added). At the date at which this volume states the law, no such regulations had been made.
5 As to the Secretary of State see PARA 4 note 18.
6 See the Local Authorities (Calculation of Council Tax Base) (England) Regulations 2012, SI 2012/2914.
7 Local Government Finance Act 1992 s 31B(3) (as added: see note 5).
8 As to regulations made under the Local Government Finance Act 1992 s 31B(5) see the Local Authorities (Calculation of Council Tax Base) (England) Regulations 2012, SI 2012/2914.
9 Local Government Finance Act 1992 s 31B(5)(a) (as added: see note 5).
10 Ie whether by adding provisions to, or deleting or amending provisions of, the Local Government Finance Act 1992 s 31B, or by a combination of those methods.
11 Local Government Finance Act 1992 s 31B(5)(b) (as added: see note 5).

384. Calculation of budget requirement by authorities in Wales.

In relation to each financial year[1], a billing authority in Wales[2] must make the requisite calculations[3] by:

(1) calculating the aggregate of[4]:
  (a) the expenditure which the authority estimates it will incur in the year in performing its functions and will charge to a revenue account for the year[5];
  (b) the expenditure that the authority estimates it will incur in the year in making repayments of grant paid to it by the Secretary of State or the Welsh Ministers, or of amounts paid to it by the Welsh Ministers in respect of redistributed non-domestic rates[6];
  (c) such allowance as the authority estimates will be appropriate for contingencies in relation to expenditure to be charged to a revenue account for the year[7];
  (d) the financial reserves which the authority estimates it will be appropriate to raise in the year for meeting its estimated future expenditure[8]; and
  (e) such financial reserves as are sufficient to meet so much of the amount estimated by the authority to be a revenue account deficit for any earlier financial year as has not already been provided for[9]; and
(2) calculating the aggregate of[10]:
  (a) the sums which it estimates will be payable for the year into its council fund[11] and in respect of which amounts will be credited to a revenue account for the year, other than sums which it estimates will be so payable in respect of redistributed non-domestic rates[12], BID levy[13] or financial contribution towards enabling the projects specified in BID arrangements to be carried out[14], revenue support grant[15], its council tax reduction scheme[16] or additional grant[17];
  (b) the sums that it estimates will be payable to it for an earlier financial year in respect of redistributed non-domestic rates, revenue support grant or additional grant[18]; and
  (c) the amount of the financial reserves which the authority estimates that it will use in order to provide for the items mentioned in heads (1)(a) and (1)(c) above[19].

If the aggregate calculated under head (1) above exceeds that calculated under head (2) above, the authority must calculate the amount equal to the difference; and the amount so calculated is to be its budget requirement for the year[20].

Calculations to be made in relation to a particular financial year under these provisions must be made before 11 March in the preceding financial year, but they are not invalid merely because they are made on or after that date[21].

1 As to the meaning of 'financial year' see PARA 11 note 1.

2 As to the meaning of 'billing authority' see PARA 346. As to the meaning of 'Wales' see PARA 2 note 16.

3 See the Local Government Finance Act 1992 s 32(1) (amended by the Localism Act 2011 s 79, Sch 7 paras 7, 10(1), (3)). Before a billing authority makes its calculations (otherwise than by way of substitute, as to which see PARA 388) in relation to the financial year under the Local Government Finance Act 1992 s 32, it must consult persons or bodies appearing to it to be representative of persons subject to non-domestic rates under the Local Government Finance Act 1988 s 43 (see PARAS 82, 133, 143 et seq) and s 45 (see PARAS 135–136, 147–148) as regards hereditaments situated in the authority's area: see the Local Government Finance Act 1992 s 65(1), (3), (4)(a) (s 65(3) amended by the Greater London Authority Act 1999 s 423, Sch 34 Pt I; the Police Reform and Social Responsibility Act 2011 s 26(1), (3); and the Policing and Crime Act 2017 s 6, Sch 1 para 71(1), (3); the Local Government Finance Act 1992 s 65(4)(a) amended by the Localism Act 2011 s 79, Sch 7 paras 7, 28). As to the meaning of 'person' see PARA 11 note 13. As to non-domestic rating see PARA 52 et seq. Consultations must be made as to each financial year, and must be about the authority's proposals for expenditure (including capital expenditure) in that financial year; and the Welsh Ministers may by regulations prescribe matters which are to be treated as expenditure for this purpose: see the Local Government Finance Act 1992 s 65(2). At the date at which this volume states the law, no such regulations had been made.

In performing the duty to consult, an authority must have regard to any guidance issued by the Welsh Ministers concerning:

(1) persons or bodies to be regarded for these purposes as representative of persons subject to non-domestic rates under the Local Government Finance Act 1988 ss 43, 45 as regards hereditaments situated in the authority's area (see the Local Government Finance Act 1992 s 65(5)(a)); and

(2) the timing and manner of consultations under s 65 (s 65(5)(b)).

An authority must make available to persons or bodies it proposes to consult such information as may be prescribed and is in its possession or control, and it must do so in such form and manner and at such time as may be prescribed: see s 65(6). 'Prescribed' means prescribed by regulations: see s 116(1). As to the meaning of 'information' see PARA 345 note 20. As to the regulations made under s 65(6) see the Non-Domestic Ratepayers (Consultation) Regulations 1992, SI 1992/3171.

Where an authority to which the Local Government Finance Act 1992 s 32 applies is making calculations in accordance with that section, the chief finance officer of the authority must report to it on matters such as the robustness of the estimates made for the purposes of the calculations, and the adequacy of the proposed financial reserves, and must review those calculations throughout the year: see the Local Government Act 2003 s 25; and PARA 16.

4 Local Government Finance Act 1992 s 32(2). In making the calculation under s 32(2) the authority must ignore:

(1) payments which must be met from a trust fund (s 32(5)(a) (s 32(5) substituted by the Localism Act 2011 Sch 7 paras 7, 10(1), (7)));

(2) payments to be made to the Welsh Ministers under the Local Government Finance Act 1988 Sch 8 para 5 or regulations made under Sch 8 para 5(15) (see PARA 49) (Local Government Finance Act 1992 s 32(5)(b) (as so substituted; amended by SI 2012/521));

(3) payments to be made in respect of the amount of any precept issued by a major precepting authority under the Local Government Finance Act 1992 Pt I (ss 1–69) (but not payments to be so made in respect of interest on such an amount) (s 32(5)(c) (as so substituted)); and

(4) payments to be made to another person in repaying, under regulations under the Local Government Finance Act 1988 or the Local Government Finance Act 1992 Pt I, excess receipts by way of non-domestic rates or council tax (s 32(5)(d) (as so substituted)).

As to the meaning of 'major precepting authority' see PARA 11 note 2.

5 Local Government Finance Act 1992 s 32(2)(a) (substituted by SI 2013/216). The expenditure mentioned in the Local Government Finance Act 1992 s 32(2)(a) does not include expenditure which the authority estimates it will charge to a BID Revenue Account: s 32(2A) (added by SI 2013/216). 'BID revenue account' has the same meaning as in the Local Government Act 2003 Pt 4 (ss 41–59) (see PARA 325): Local Government Finance Act 1992 s 32(12A) (added by SI 2013/216). As to accounts generally see PARA 588 et seq.

In making its estimation under the Local Government Finance Act 1992 s 32(2)(a), the authority must take into account:

(1) the amount of any precept issued to it for the year by a local precepting authority (s 32(6)(a)); and

(2) the amount of any levy or special levy issued to it for the year (s 32(6)(b)),

but, except as provided by regulations under s 41 (see PARA 18) or regulations under the Local Government Finance Act 1988 s 74 (levies: see PARA 24) or s 75 (special levies: see PARA 24), must not anticipate a precept, levy or special levy not issued: Local Government Finance Act 1992 s 32(6). As to the meaning of 'levy' see PARA 12 note 5. 'Special levy' means a levy under regulations made under s 75: Local Government Finance Act 1992 s 69(1). As to the meaning of 'local precepting authority' see PARA 18 note 2.

6 Local Government Finance Act 1992 s 32(2)(aa) (added by SI 2013/216).

7 Local Government Finance Act 1992 s 32(2)(b).

8 Local Government Finance Act 1992 s 32(2)(c) (amended by the Localism Act 2011 Sch 7 paras 7, 10(1), (4)). For these purposes, an authority's estimated future expenditure is:

(1) that which the authority estimates it will incur in the financial year following the year in question, will charge to a revenue account for the year and will have to defray in the year before the following sums are sufficiently available, namely sums which will be payable for the year into its council fund and in respect of which amounts will be credited to a revenue account for the year (Local Government Finance Act 1992 s 32(7)(a)(i) (amended by the Local Government (Wales) Act 1994 Sch 12 para 4(4); and the Localism Act 2011 ss 79, 237, Sch 7 paras 7, 10(1), (8), Sch 25 Pt 13)); and

(2) that which the authority estimates it will incur in the financial year referred to in head (1) above or any subsequent financial year in performing its functions and which will be charged to a revenue account for that or any other year (Local Government Finance Act 1992 s 32(7)(b)).

In relation to the estimation of financial reserves for the purpose of calculations in accordance with s 32, in the case of a controlled reserve, it is not to be regarded as appropriate for the balance of the reserve at the end of the financial year under consideration to be less than the minimum amount determined in accordance with regulations made by the appropriate person: see the Local Government Act 2003 s 26(1)(a), (2), (3) (s 26(1) amended by the Localism Act 2011 Sch 7 paras 42, 44). As to the meanings of 'controlled reserve' and 'appropriate person' see PARA 16 note 8. At the date at which this volume states the law, no such regulations had been made. The provisions relating to the making of a report by the chief finance officer on the inadequacy of controlled reserves and budget monitoring also apply: see ss 27, 28; and PARAS 16–17.

9 Local Government Finance Act 1992 s 32(2)(d). See also note 8.

10 Local Government Finance Act 1992 s 32(3).

11 The Local Government Finance Act 1992 s 32(3)(a) does not require the estimation of sums payable into a billing authority's council fund in respect of council tax, non-domestic rates or the grant paid to it under the Local Government Finance Act 1988 s 88A (see PARA 38): Local Government Finance Act 1992 s 32(3A) (added by the Local Government (Wales) Act 1994 s 38(11), Sch 12 para 4; and amended by the Localism Act 2011 Sch 7 paras 7, 10(1), (6), Sch 25 Pt 13; and by SI 1995/56). As to council funds see PARA 585.

12 In the Local Government Finance Act 1992 ss 32, 33 (see PARA 385) references to sums payable for the financial year in respect of redistributed non-domestic rates are references to sums so payable in accordance with the local government finance report for the year under the Local Government Finance Act 1988 s 84G (see PARA 34) relating to the authority (including as amended by a report under Sch 8 para 13) (see PARA 49): Local Government Finance Act 1992 s 32(12)(a) (s 32(12) substituted by SI 2013/216). 'Redistributed non-domestic rates' means any sums payable by the Welsh Ministers under the Local Government Finance Act 1988 Sch 8 para 12 or 15 (see PARA 49): Local Government Finance Act 1992 s 69(1) (definition amended by SI 2013/733).

13 'BID levy' has the same meaning as in the Local Government Act 2003 Pt 4 (ss 41–59) (see PARA 319): Local Government Finance Act 1992 s 32(12A) (as added: see note 5).

14 Ie under the Local Government Act 2003 s 43: see PARA 319. As to the meaning of 'bid arrangements' see PARA 319.

15 References in the Local Government Finance Act 1992 ss 32, 33 (see PARAS 384–385) to sums payable for the financial year in respect of revenue support grant are references to sums so payable in accordance with the local government finance report for the year under the Local Government Finance Act 1988 s 84G (including as amended by a report under s 84L) (see PARA 34): Local Government Finance Act 1992 s 32(12)(b) (as substituted: see note 12).

16 As to the meaning of 'council tax reduction scheme' see PARA 378 note 20. In the Local Government Finance Act 1992 ss 32, 33 (see PARAS 384–385), references to sums payable for a financial year in respect of an authority's council tax reduction scheme are to sums payable by the Welsh Ministers under the Local Government Act 2003 s 31 in respect of a scheme which applies in accordance with regulations under s 13A or in default in accordance with regulations under s 13A and Sch 1B para 6: Local Government Finance Act 1992 s 32(12)(c) (as substituted: see note 12).

17 Local Government Finance Act 1992 s 32(3)(a) (amended by the Local Government (Wales) Act 1994 s 38(11), Sch 12 para 4(2); the Localism Act 2011 Sch 7 paras 7, 10(1), (5)(c), Sch 25 Pt 13; and by SI 1994/246, SI 1995/234, SI 2012/521 and SI 2013/216). 'Additional grant' has the meaning given by the Local Government Finance Act 1988 s 86A(2) (see PARA 36): Local Government Finance Act 1992 s 69(1) (definition amended by the Local Government Finance Act 2012 s 3(5), (8)). References in the Local Government Finance Act 1992 ss 32, 33 to sums payable for a financial year in respect of additional grant are to sums so payable in accordance with a report for the year under the Local Government Finance Act 1988 s 86A: Local Government Finance Act 1992 s 32(12)(d) (as substituted: see note 12).

18 Local Government Finance Act 1992 s 32(3)(aa) (added by SI 2013/216).

19 Local Government Finance Act 1992 s 32(3)(c) (amended by the Localism Act 2011 Sch 7 paras 7, 10(1), 5(c)).

20 Local Government Finance Act 1992 s 32(4). The Welsh Ministers may by regulations do one or both of the following (s 32(9) (amended by the Localism Act 2011 s 79, Sch 7, paras 10(1), (10)(a)):

(1) alter the constituents of any calculation to be made under the Local Government Finance Act 1992 s 32(2) (see head (1) in the text) or s 32(3) (see head (2) in the text), whether by adding, deleting or amending items (s 32(9)(a));

(2) alter the rules governing the making of any calculation under s 32(2) or s 32(3), whether by deleting or amending s 32(5)–(7), or any of them, or by adding other provisions, or by a combination of those methods (s 32(9)(b) (amended by the Localism Act 2011 Sch 7 paras 7, 10(1), (10)(b))).

The following regulations have been made under the Local Government Finance Act 1992 s 32(9): the Local Authorities (Alteration of Requisite Calculations) (Wales) Regulations 1999, SI 1999/296 (amended by the Localism Act 2011 Sch 25 Pt 13); the Local Authorities (Alteration of Requisite Calculations) (Wales) Regulations 2000, SI 2000/717 (amended by the Localism Act 2011 Sch 25 Pt 13); the Local Authorities (Alteration of Requisite Calculations) (Wales) Regulations 2006, SI 2006/344; the Local Authorities (Alteration of Requisite Calculations) (Wales) Regulations 2007, SI 2007/571; Local Authorities (Alteration of Requisite Calculations) (Wales) Regulations 2008, SI 2008/476; the Local Authorities (Alteration of Requisite Calculations) (Wales) Regulations 2009, SI 2009/267; the Local Authorities (Alteration of Requisite Calculations) (Wales) Regulations 2010, SI 2010/317; the Local Authorities (Alteration of Requisite Calculations) (Wales) Regulations 2011, SI 2011/446; the Local Authorities (Alteration of Requisite Calculations) (Wales) Regulations 2012, SI 2012/521; and the Local Authorities (Alteration of Requisite Calculations) (Wales) Regulations 2013, SI 2013/216.

21 Local Government Finance Act 1992 s 32(10).

385. Calculation of basic amount of tax by authorities in Wales.

In relation to each financial year[1], a billing authority in Wales[2] must calculate the basic amount of its council tax[3] by applying a formula[4]. Regulations may make provision for the calculation of such a formula[5].

1 As to the meaning of 'financial year' see PARA 11 note 1.

2 As to the meaning of 'billing authority' see PARA 346. As to the meaning of 'Wales' see PARA 2 note 16.

3 As to council tax see PARA 344 et seq.

4 See the Local Government Finance Act 1992 s 33(1) (amended by the Local Government (Wales) Act 1994 s 38(11), Sch 12 para 5; the Localism Act 2011 s 79, Sch 7 paras 7, 11(1), (3); and SI 1994/246, SI 2012/521 and SI 2013/216).

5 See the Local Government Finance Act 1992 s 33(4) (amended by Localism Act 2011 ss 79, 237, Sch 7 paras 7, 11(1), (6), Sch 25 Pt 13); National Assembly for Wales (Transfer of Functions) Order 1999, SI 1999/672, art 2, Sch 1; Government of Wales Act 2006 s 162(1), Sch 11 para 30. The following regulations have been made under the Local Government Finance Act 1992 s 33(4): the Local Authorities (Alteration of Requisite Calculations) (Wales) Regulations 2011, SI 2011/446; and the Local Authorities (Alteration of Requisite Calculations) (Wales) Regulations

2012, SI 2012/521; and the Local Authorities (Alteration of Requisite Calculations) (Wales) Regulations 2013, SI 2013/216. See also the Local Authorities (Calculation of Council Tax Base) (Wales) Regulations 1995, SI 1995/2561, reg 8 (amended by SI 2004/3094).

386. Additional calculations where special items relate to part only of area: England and Wales.

Where, for any financial year[1], an item (a 'special item')[2] relates to a part only of a billing authority's area[3], the authority must calculate the basic amount of its council tax[4] for dwellings in a part of its area[5] to which no special item relates by applying a specific formula[6].

The authority must calculate the basic amount of its council tax for dwellings in a part of its area to which one or more special items relate by adding to the amount given by the above formula the aggregate of the amounts which, in relation to each of those special items, are given by a specified calculation[7]. The appropriate national authority[8] must make regulations[9] containing rules relating to the calculations[10].

The special items referred to for these purposes are:

(1) any precept issued to or anticipated by the authority which is or is believed to be applicable to a part of its area and was taken into account by it in making the calculation (or last calculation)[11] in relation to the year[12]; and

(2) any expenses of the authority which are its special expenses and were taken into account by it in making that calculation[13].

For the purposes of heads (1) and (2) above:

(a) provided a resolution of a billing authority to the following effect is in force, the expenses of meeting a levy or special levy[14] issued to or anticipated by it are its special expenses or (if the resolution relates to some only of those expenses) those to which the resolution relates are its special expenses[15];

(b) any expenses which a billing authority believes will have to be met out of amounts transferred or to be transferred from its collection fund to its general fund[16], and which arise out of its possession of property held in trust for a part of its area, are its special expenses[17];

(c) any expenses which a billing authority believes will have to be met out of amounts transferred or to be transferred from its collection fund to its general fund, and which relate to a part of its area, are its special expenses provided that expenses of the same kind which relate to another part of its area are to be met out of property held in trust for that part[18];

(d) any expenses incurred by a billing authority in performing in a part of its area a function performed elsewhere in its area by the sub-treasurer of the Inner Temple, the under-treasurer of the Middle Temple[19], a parish or community council or the chairman of a parish meeting[20] are the authority's special expenses unless a resolution of the authority to the contrary effect is in force[21]; and

(e) provided a resolution of a billing authority to the following effect is in force, the expenses incurred by it in performing in a part of its area a function performed elsewhere in its area by a body with power to issue a levy or special levy to it are its special expenses or (if the resolution relates to some only of those expenses) those to which the resolution relates are its special expenses[22].

The following rules apply to the making of a resolution under head (e) above by a billing authority:

(i) no such resolution may be made unless the body mentioned in head (e) above is one in relation to which the billing authority has made under head (a) above a resolution which is in force[23];

(ii) the resolution under head (e) above may not be made so as to be in force at any time when that under head (a) above is not in force[24];

(iii) the fact that the resolution under head (a) above relates to all the expenses concerned does not mean that the resolution under head (e) above must relate to all the expenses concerned[25]; and

(iv) the fact that the resolution under head (a) above relates to part of the expenses concerned does not mean that the resolution under head (e) above must relate to part, or any particular part, of the expenses concerned[26].

1 As to the meaning of 'financial year' see PARA 11 note 1.

2 'Special item' means any item mentioned in the Local Government Finance Act 1992 s 35(1) (see heads (1) and (2) in the text) which relates to a part only of a billing authority's area: see s 34(1). As to the meaning of 'billing authority' see PARA 346.

3 See the Local Government Finance Act 1992 s 34(1). The Local Government Finance Act 1992 s 34 is modified where, following an order creating a single tier local authority area, an authority makes a determination with a view to equalising council tax payable in respect of dwellings situated in the predecessor areas of a reorganised area: see the Local Government (Structural Changes) (Finance) Regulations 2008, SI 2008/3022, reg 15(5), (6), Sch 2 para 3 (Sch 2 substituted by SI 2012/20). As to the transfer of functions in relation to council tax following local government reorganisation see PARA 346.

4 As to council tax see PARA 344 et seq.

5 As to the meaning of 'dwelling' see PARA 349. As to the power to make regulations containing rules for ascertaining in what part of a billing authority's area a dwelling is situated see the Local Government Finance Act 1992 s 10(2); and PARA 360; and as to the power to make regulations containing rules for treating a dwelling as situated in a billing authority's area if part only of the dwelling falls within the area see s 1(3); and PARA 348.

6 See the Local Government Finance Act 1992 s 34 (amended by the Localism Act 2011 s 97, Sch 7 paras 7, 12; and the Local Government Finance Act 2012 s 15(1)).

7 See the Local Government Finance Act 1992 s 34(3).

8 Ie the Secretary of State or, in relation to Wales, the Welsh Ministers. The functions of the Secretary of State under the Local Government Finance Act 1992 s 34, so far as exercisable in relation to Wales, were transferred to the National Assembly for Wales (see the National Assembly for Wales (Transfer of Functions) Order 1999, SI 1999/672, art 2, Sch 1) and are now vested in the Welsh Ministers (see the Government of Wales Act 2006 s 162(1), Sch 11 para 30). As to the Secretary of State and the Welsh Ministers see PARA 4 note 18. As to the meaning of 'Wales' see PARA 2 note 16.

9 As to the regulations made see: the Local Authorities (Calculation of Council Tax Base) (England) Regulations 2012, SI 2012/2914; and the Local Authorities (Calculation of Council Tax Base) (Wales) Regulations 1995, SI 1995/2561 (amended by SI 1999/2935, SI 2004/3094 and SI 2016/969).

10 Local Government Finance Act 1992 s 34(4). Regulations under s 34(4) that apply to billing authorities in England may contain different rules for the purposes of calculating item TP in relation to different kinds of special item: s 34(5) (added by the Local Government Finance Act 2012 s 15(1)).

11 Ie under the Local Government Finance Act 1992 s 31A(2) (see PARA 382) or s 32(2) (see PARA 384).

12 Local Government Finance Act 1992 s 35(1)(a) (amended by the Localism Act 2011 Sch 7 paras 7, 13). As to precepts see PARA 11 et seq.

13 Local Government Finance Act 1992 s 35(1)(b). Expenses of a billing authority are not to be treated as its special expenses for the purposes of s 35(1) if they are expenses of meeting a levy issued to it by, or anticipated by it from, a National Park authority in relation to a National Park in Wales: s 35(5) (added by the Local Government (Wales) Act 1994 s 38(11), Sch 12 para 6; amended by the Environment Act 1995 ss 78, 120(3), Sch 10 para 35, Sch 24). As to the meaning

of 'levy' see PARA 12 note 5. As to National Park authorities see OPEN SPACES AND COUNTRYSIDE vol 78 (2010) PARA 526.

14 As to the meaning of 'special levy' see PARA 384 note 5.

15 Local Government Finance Act 1992 s 35(2)(a).

16 Any reference to a billing authority's general fund is to be construed in relation to the Common Council of the City of London as a reference to the City fund: Local Government Finance Act 1992 s 69(2)(c). As to what constitutes the Common Council of the City of London for these purposes see PARA 346 note 4. As to the funds established for the purposes of local government finance see PARA 579 et seq.

17 Local Government Finance Act 1992 s 35(2)(b). In relation to a Welsh county council or county borough council s 35(2)(b) is substituted so as to read: 'any expenses incurred by a billing authority and arising in connection with property which it holds in trust for a part of its area are its special expenses': see s 35(4) (added by the Local Government (Wales) Act 1994 s 38(11), Sch 12 para 6).

18 Local Government Finance Act 1992 s 35(2)(c). In relation to a Welsh county council or county borough council s 35(2)(c) is substituted so as to read: 'any expenses incurred by a billing authority which relate to a part of its area and which are of the same kind as expenses which both relate to another part of its area and are to be met out of property held in trust for that part, are its special expenses': see s 35(4) (as added: see note 22).

19 As to the Inner and Middle Temples see LONDON GOVERNMENT vol 71 (2013) PARA 17. See also PARA 346 note 4.

20 As to parish councils see LOCAL GOVERNMENT vol 69 (2018) PARA 41 et seq. As to community councils see LOCAL GOVERNMENT vol 69 (2018) PARA 63 et seq. As to parish meetings see LOCAL GOVERNMENT vol 69 (2018) PARA 48.

21 Local Government Finance Act 1992 s 35(2)(d).

22 Local Government Finance Act 1992 s 35(2)(e).

23 Local Government Finance Act 1992 s 35(3)(a).

24 Local Government Finance Act 1992 s 35(3)(b).

25 Local Government Finance Act 1992 s 35(3)(c).

26 Local Government Finance Act 1992 s 35(3)(d).

387. Substitute calculations: England.

An authority in England[1] which has made the requisite calculations[2] in relation to a financial year[3] (originally or by way of substitute) may make calculations in substitution[4] in relation to the year[5].

1 As to the meaning of 'England' see PARA 2 note 16.

2 Ie in accordance with the Local Government Finance Act 1992 ss 31A, 31B (see PARAS 382–383) and ss 34–36 (see PARAS 380, 386).

3 As to the meaning of 'financial year' see PARA 11 note 1.

4 Ie in accordance with the Local Government Finance Act 1992 ss 31A, 31B (see PARAS 382– 383) and ss 34–36 (see PARAS 380, 386) but ignoring s 31A(11) for this purpose.

5 Local Government Finance Act 1992 s 36A(1) (s 36A added by the Localism Act 2011 s 79, Sch 7 paras 7, 15). None of the substitute calculations is to have any effect if:

(1) the amount calculated under the Local Government Finance Act 1992 s 31A(4) (see PARA 382), or any amount calculated under s 31B(1) (see PARA 383) or s 34(2) or (3) (see PARA 386) as the basic amount of council tax applicable to any dwelling, would exceed that so calculated in the previous calculations (s 36A(2)(a) (as so added)); or

(2) the billing authority fails to comply with s 36A(3) below in making the substitute calculations (s 36A(2)(b) (as so added)).

As to the meaning of 'dwelling' see PARA 349. For the purposes of head (1) above, one negative amount is to be taken to exceed another if it is closer to nil (so that minus £1 is to be taken to exceed minus £2): s 36A(4) (as so added).

In making substitute calculations under s 31B(1) or s 34(3), the billing authority must use any amount determined in the previous calculations for item 'T' in s 31B(1) or item 'TP' in s 34(3): s 36A(3) (as so added). The provisions of s 36A(2), (3) do not apply if the previous calculations have been quashed because of a failure to comply with ss 31A, 31B and ss 34–36 in making the calculations: s 36A(5) (as so added).

388. Substitute calculations: Wales.

A billing authority in Wales[1] which has made the requisite calculations[2] in relation to a financial year[3] (originally or by way of substitute) may make calculations in substitution in relation to the year[4].

1 As to the meaning of 'billing authority' see PARA 346. As to the meaning of 'Wales' see PARA 2 note 16.

2 Ie in accordance with the Local Government Finance Act 1992 ss 32–36: see PARAS 384–386.

3 As to the meaning of 'financial year' see PARA 11 note 1.

4 Local Government Finance Act 1992 s 37(1) (amended by the Localism Act 2011 s 79, Sch 7 paras 7, 16). Such calculations are to be made in accordance with the Local Government Finance Act 1992 ss 32–36 (see PARAS 384–386), ignoring s 32(10) (see PARA 384): see s 37(1).

None of the substitute calculations is to have any effect if:

(1) the amount calculated under s 32(4) (see PARA 384), or any amount calculated under s 33(1) (see PARA 385) or s 34(2) or s 34(3) (see PARA 386) as the basic amount of council tax applicable to any dwelling, would exceed that so calculated in the previous calculations (s 37(2)(a)); or

(2) the billing authority fails to comply with s 37(3) in making the substitute calculations (s 37(2)(b)).

As to the meaning of 'dwelling' see PARA 349. As to council tax see PARA 344 et seq. For the purposes of s 37(2)(a), one negative amount must be taken to exceed another if it is closer to nil (so that minus £1 must be taken to exceed minus £2): s 37(4). In making substitute calculations under s 33(1) or s 34(3), the billing authority must use any amount determined in the previous calculations for item 'P' or item 'T' in s 33(1) or item 'TP' in s 34(3): s 37(3). For the purposes of s 37(3), the billing authority may treat any amount determined in the previous calculations for item 'P' in s 33(1) as increased by the amount of any sum which:

(a) it estimates will be payable for the year into its general fund or (as the case may be) council fund in respect of additional grant (s 37(5)(a) (amended by the Local Government (Wales) Act 1994 s 38(11), Sch 12 para 7)); and

(b) was not taken into account by it in making those calculations (Local Government Finance Act 1992 s 37(5)(b)).

As to the meaning of 'additional grant' see PARA 384 note 17. As to the funds established for the purposes of local government finance generally see PARA 579 et seq. As to the meaning of references to a billing authority's general fund see PARA 386 note 16.

However, s 37(2), (3) does not apply if the previous calculations have been quashed because of a failure to comply with ss 32–36 in making the calculations: s 37(6).

389. Information for purposes of the setting of council tax: England and Wales.

If the appropriate national authority[1] so requires by regulations[2], a precepting authority[3] must supply prescribed information[4] within a prescribed period to any billing authority[5] to which it has power to issue a precept[6].

A billing authority which has set amounts for different categories of dwellings[7] (originally or by way of substitute) must, before the end of the period of 21 days beginning with the day of doing so, publish a notice of the amounts in at least one newspaper circulating in the authority's area[8]. However, failure to comply with this requirement does not make the setting of amounts invalid[9].

1 Ie the Secretary of State or, in relation to Wales, the Welsh Ministers. The functions of the Secretary of State under the Local Government Finance Act 1992 s 38, so far as exercisable in relation to Wales, were transferred to the National Assembly for Wales (see the National Assembly for Wales (Transfer of Functions) Order 1999, SI 1999/672, art 2, Sch 1) and are now vested in the Welsh Ministers (see the Government of Wales Act 2006 s 162(1), Sch 11 para 30). As to the Secretary of State and the Welsh Ministers see PARA 4 note 18. As to the meaning of 'Wales' see PARA 2 note 16.

2 As to the regulations made see the Local Authorities (Calculation of Council Tax Base) (Supply of Information) Regulations 1992, SI 1992/2904 (amended by SI 1995/3150 and, in relation to England, SI 2012/2914).

3 As to the meaning of 'precepting authority' see PARA 23 note 1.

4 'Prescribed' means prescribed by regulations made by the appropriate national authority: see the Local Government Finance Act 1992 s 116(1). As to the meaning of 'information' see PARA 345 note 20.
5 As to the meaning of 'billing authority' see PARA 346.
6 Local Government Finance Act 1992 s 38(1). As to precepts see PARA 11 et seq.
7 Ie in accordance with the Local Government Finance Act 1992 s 30: see PARA 380.
8 Local Government Finance Act 1992 s 38(2).
9 Local Government Finance Act 1992 s 38(3).

390. Limitation of council tax.

Provision is made as to limitation of council tax in relation to Wales[1].

1 See the Local Government Finance Act 1992 ss 52A–52N; and PARA 21.

(v) Referendums Relating to Council Tax Increases: England

A. DETERMINATION OF WHETHER INCREASE EXCESSIVE

391. Duty to determine whether council tax excessive.

A billing authority[1] in England[2] must determine whether its relevant basic amount of council tax for a financial year[3] is excessive[4]. Where the amount is excessive the statutory provisions[5] relating to the duty to hold a referendum in the case of an excessive council tax increase by a billing authority apply[6].

A major precepting authority[7] in England must determine whether its relevant basic amount of council tax[8] for a financial year is excessive[9]. Where the amount is excessive the statutory provisions[10] relating to the duty to hold a referendum in the case of an excessive council tax increase by a major precepting authority apply[11].

A local precepting authority in England must determine whether its relevant basic amount of council tax[12] for a financial year is excessive[13]. Where the amount is excessive the statutory provisions[14] relating to the duty to hold a referendum in the case of an excessive council tax increase by a local precepting authority apply[15].

A determination under the above provisions for a financial year must be made as soon as is reasonably practicable after the principles[16] for that year as to whether an authority's relevant basic amount of council tax is excessive are approved[17] by a resolution of the House of Commons[18].

1 As to the meaning of 'billing authority' see PARA 346.
2 As to the meaning of 'England' see PARA 2 note 16.
3 Any reference in the Local Government Finance Act 1992 Pt I Ch 4ZA (ss 52ZA–52ZY) to a billing authority's relevant basic amount of council tax for a financial year is a reference to the amount that would be calculated by it in relation to the year under s 31B(1) (see PARA 383) if s 31A (see PARA 382) did not require or permit it to take into account the amount of any precepts:
   (1) issued to it for the year by local precepting authorities (s 52ZX(1)(a) (ss 52ZA, 52ZB, 52ZX added by the Localism Act 2011 s 72(1), Sch 5; the Local Government Finance Act 1992 s 52ZX(1)(a), (b) substituted by the Local Audit and Accountability Act 2014 s 41(1), (10)); or
   (2) or anticipated by it in pursuance of regulations under the Local Government Finance Act 1992 s 41 (see PARA 191) (Local Government Finance Act 1992 s 52ZX(1)(b) (as so added and substituted)).

In the application of s 52ZX any calculation for which another has been substituted is to be disregarded: s 52ZX(9) (as so added). As to the meaning of 'financial year' see PARA 11 note 1. As to precepts see PARA 11 et seq. As to the meaning of 'local precepting authority' see PARA 18 note 2. As to the meaning of 'levy' see PARA 12 note 5. As to the meaning of 'special levy' see PARA 384 note 5.

4 Local Government Finance Act 1992 ss 52ZA(1)(a), 52ZB(1) (as added: see note 3).
5 Ie the Local Government Finance Act 1992 ss 52ZF–52ZI: see PARAS 394–397.
6 See the Local Government Finance Act 1992 s 52ZB(2) (as added: see note 3).
7 As to the meaning of 'major precepting authority' see PARA 11 note 2.
8 In the case of a major precepting authority other than the Greater London Authority, any reference in the Local Government Finance Act 1992 Pt I Ch 4ZA to the authority's relevant basic amount of council tax for a financial year is a reference to the amount calculated by it in relation to the year under s 42B(1) (see PARA 13): s 52ZX(2) (as added (see note 3); amended by the Local Audit and Accountability Act 2014 s 41(1), (11)). In the case of a major precepting authority that is the Greater London Authority, any such reference to the authority's relevant basic amount of council tax for a financial year is a reference to:
 (1) the amount (referred to in Pt 1 Ch 4ZA as the Greater London Authority's unadjusted relevant basic amount of council tax for the year) calculated by it in relation to the year under the Greater London Authority Act 1999 s 88(2) (see LONDON GOVERNMENT vol 71 (2013) PARA 150) (Local Government Finance Act 1992 s 52ZX(4)(a) (as so added; s 52ZX(4)(a), (b) substituted by the Local Audit and Accountability Act 2014 s 41(1), (13))); or
 (2) any amount (referred to in the Local Government Finance Act 1992 Pt I Ch 4ZA as the Greater London Authority's adjusted relevant basic amount of council tax for the year) calculated by it in relation to the year under the Greater London Authority Act 1999 s 89(3) (see LONDON GOVERNMENT vol 71 (2013) PARA 150) (Local Government Finance Act 1992 s 52ZX(4)(b) (as so added and substituted)).

 In the application of s 52ZX any calculation for which another has been substituted is to be disregarded: s 52ZX(9) (as so added).

 For provision permitting the Secretary of State to consider the impact of previous levy increases when setting referendum principles for the financial year beginning 1 April 2014 see the Local Audit and Accountability Act 2014 s 41(14)–(17).
9 Local Government Finance Act 1992 ss 52ZA(1)(b), 52ZB(3) (as added: see note 3).
10 Ie the Local Government Finance Act 1992 s 52ZJ, s 52ZK (see PARAS 398–399) and ss 52ZN–52ZP (see PARAS 402–404).
11 See the Local Government Finance Act 1992 s 52ZB(4) (as added: see note 3).
12 Any reference in the Local Government Finance Act 1992 Pt I Ch 4ZA to a local precepting authority's relevant basic amount of council tax for a financial year is a reference to the amount found by applying a specified formula: see s 52ZX(5), (6) (as added: see note 3).

 The Secretary of State must make regulations containing rules for making for any year the calculation required in s 52ZX(5) above; and the billing authority concerned must make the calculations for any year in accordance with the rules for the time being effective (as regards the year) under the regulations: s 52ZX(7) (as so added). Regulations prescribing a period for purposes relating to s 52ZX(5) may provide that, in any case where a billing authority fails to notify its calculation to the precepting authority concerned within that period, that item must be determined in the prescribed manner by such authority or authorities as may be prescribed: s 52ZX(8) (as so added). In the application of s 52ZX any calculation for which another has been substituted is to be disregarded: s 52ZX(9) (as so added). As to the Secretary of State see PARA 4 note 18. 'Prescribed' means prescribed by the regulations: see s 116(1). As to regulations made under s 52ZX(7), (8) see the Local Authority (Referendums Relating to Council Tax Increases) Regulations 2012, SI 2012/460; and the Local Authorities (Calculation of Council Tax Base) (England) Regulations 2012, SI 2012/2914.
13 Local Government Finance Act 1992 ss 52ZA(1)(c), 52ZB(5) (as added: see note 3).
14 Ie the Local Government Finance Act 1992 ss 52ZL–52ZP: see PARAS 400–404.
15 See the Local Government Finance Act 1992 s 52ZB(6) (as added: see note 3).
16 Ie the principles under the Local Government Finance Act 1992 s 52ZC: see PARA 392.
17 Ie under the Local Government Finance Act 1992 s 52ZD: see PARA 392.
18 Local Government Finance Act 1992 s 52ZB(7) (as added: see note 3).

392. Determination of whether increase is excessive.

The question whether an authority's[1] relevant basic amount of council tax[2] for a financial year[3] ('the year under consideration') is excessive must be decided in accordance with a set of principles determined by the Secretary of State[4] for the year[5].

A set of principles may contain one principle or two or more principles[6]; and must constitute or include a qualifying comparison[7]. A comparison is a qualifying comparison if it is between the authority's relevant basic amount of council tax for the year under consideration[8], and the authority's relevant basic amount of council tax for the financial year immediately preceding the year under consideration[9].

If for these purposes the Secretary of State determines categories of authority for the year under consideration any principles determined for the year must be such that the same set is determined for all authorities (if more than one) falling within the same category[10]; and, as regards an authority which does not fall within any of the categories, the authority's relevant basic amount of council tax for the year is not capable[11] of being excessive[12]. If the Secretary of State does not determine such categories, any principles determined for the year under consideration must be such that the same set is determined for all authorities[13]. In determining categories of authorities for the year under consideration the Secretary of State must take into account any information that he thinks is relevant[14].

The principles for a financial year must be set out in a report which must be laid before the House of Commons[15]. If a report for a financial year is not laid before the specified date[16] or, if so laid, is not approved by resolution of the House of Commons on or before the specified date, no principles have effect for that year[17] and, accordingly, no authority's relevant basic amount of council tax for the year is capable[18] of being excessive[19]. If the Secretary of State does not propose to determine a set of principles for a financial year, the Secretary of State must lay a report before the House of Commons before the specified date giving his reasons for not doing so[20].

1 In the Local Government Finance Act 1992 Pt I Ch 4ZA (ss 52ZA–52ZY) a reference to an 'authority' is to a billing authority in England, a major precepting authority in England and a local precepting authority in England: see s 52ZA(1), (2)(a) (ss 52ZA, 52ZC, 52ZD added by the Localism Act 2011 s 72(1), Sch 5). As to the meaning of 'billing authority' see PARA 346. As to the meaning of 'major precepting authority' see PARA 11 note 2. As to the meaning of 'local precepting authority' see PARA 18 note 2. As to the meaning of 'England' see PARA 2 note 16.

2 As to the meaning of 'relevant basic amount of council tax' see PARA 391 notes 3, 8, 12.

3 As to the meaning of 'financial year' see PARA 11 note 1.

4 As to the Secretary of State see PARA 4 note 18.

5 Local Government Finance Act 1992 s 52ZC(1) (as added: see note 1).

6 Local Government Finance Act 1992 s 52ZC(2)(a) (as added: see note 1).

7 See the Local Government Finance Act 1992 s 52ZC(2)(b) (as added: see note 1). A principle that applies to the Greater London Authority and that constitutes or includes a qualifying comparison may only provide for:

(1) a comparison between unadjusted relevant basic amounts of council tax (see s 52ZC(6)(a) (as so added));

(2) a comparison between adjusted relevant basic amounts of council tax (s 52ZC(6)(b) (as so added)); or

(3) a comparison within head (1) and a comparison within head (2) (s 52ZC(6)(c) (as so added)).

As to the meanings of 'unadjusted relevant basic amounts of council tax' and 'adjusted relevant basic amounts of council tax' see PARA 391 note 8.

8 Local Government Finance Act 1992 s 52ZC(3)(a) (as added: see note 1).

9 Local Government Finance Act 1992 s 52ZC(3)(b) (as added: see note 1).

10 Local Government Finance Act 1992 s 52ZC(4)(a) (as added: see note 1).

11 Ie for the purposes of the Local Government Finance Act 1992 Pt I Ch4ZA.

12 Local Government Finance Act 1992 s 52ZC(4)(b) (as added: see note 1).

13 Local Government Finance Act 1992 s 52ZC(5) (as added: see note 1).

14 Local Government Finance Act 1992 s 52ZC(6) (as added: see note 1).

15 Local Government Finance Act 1992 s 52ZD(1) (as added: see note 1). As to the laying of

documents before Parliament see STATUTES AND LEGISLATIVE PROCESS vol 96 (2013) PARA 1052.

16 'The specified date', in relation to a financial year, means the date on which the local government finance report for the year under the Local Government Finance Act 1988 Sch 7B para 5(1) (see PARA 59) is approved by resolution of the House of Commons: Local Government Finance Act 1992 s 52ZD(4) (as added (see note 1); amended by SI 2013/733).

17 Local Government Finance Act 1992 s 52ZD(2)(a) (as added: see note 1).

18 Ie for the purposes of the Local Government Finance Act 1992 Pt I Ch 4ZA.

19 Local Government Finance Act 1992 s 52ZD(2)(b) (as added: see note 1).

20 Local Government Finance Act 1992 s 52ZD(3) (as added: see note 1).

393. Alternative notional amounts.

The Secretary of State[1] may make a report specifying an alternative notional amount in relation to any year under consideration[2] and any authority[3]. An 'alternative notional amount' is an amount which the Secretary of State thinks should be used as the basis of any comparison in applying the set of principles[4] in place of the authority's relevant basic amount of council tax[5] for the preceding year[6].

A report:

(1) may relate to two or more authorities[7];

(2) may be amended by a subsequent such report[8];

(3) must contain such explanation as the Secretary of State thinks desirable of the need for the calculation of the alternative notional amount and the method for that calculation[9];

(4) must be laid before the House of Commons[10].

1 As to the Secretary of State see PARA 4 note 18.

2 'Year under consideration' has the same meaning as in the Local Government Finance Act 1992 s 52ZC (see PARA 392): s 52ZE(6) (s 52ZE added by the Localism Act 2011 s 72(1), Sch 5).

3 Local Government Finance Act 1992 s 52ZE(1) (as added: see note 2). As to the meaning of 'authority' see PARA 392 note 1.

4 Ie in applying the Local Government Finance Act 1992 s 52ZC: see PARA 392.

5 As to the meaning of 'relevant basic amount of council tax' see PARA 391 notes 3, 8, 12.

6 Local Government Finance Act 1992 s 52ZE(2) (as added: see note 2).

7 Local Government Finance Act 1992 s 52ZE(3)(a) (as added: see note 2).

8 Local Government Finance Act 1992 s 52ZE(3)(b) (as added: see note 2).

9 Local Government Finance Act 1992 s 52ZE(3)(c) (as added: see note 2).

10 Local Government Finance Act 1992 s 52ZE(3)(d) (as added: see note 2). If a report for a financial year is approved by resolution of the House of Commons on or before the date on which the report under s 52ZD (see PARA 392) for that year is approved by resolution of the House of Commons (s 52ZE(4) (as so added)), s 52ZC (see PARA 392) has effect, as regards the year under consideration and any authority to which the report relates, as if the reference in s 52ZC(3) to the authority's relevant basic amount of council tax for the financial year immediately preceding the year under consideration were a reference to the alternative notional amount for that year (s 52ZE(5) (as so added)). As to the meaning of 'financial year' see PARA 11 note 1. As to the laying of documents before Parliament see STATUTES AND LEGISLATIVE PROCESS vol 96 (2013) PARA 1052.

B. EXCESSIVE INCREASE IN COUNCIL TAX BY BILLING AUTHORITY

394. Billing authority's duty to make substitute calculations.

Where the relevant basic amount of council tax determined by a billing authority in England is excessive[1], the authority must make substitute calculations for the financial year[2] in compliance with these provisions[3]; but those calculations do not have effect for the purposes of setting the council tax[4] except in accordance with the statutory provisions[5] relating to referendums[6].

Substitute calculations for a financial year comply with these provisions if they are made in accordance with the appropriate statutory provisions[7], and the relevant basic amount of council tax produced[8] is not excessive by reference to the principles determined[9] by the Secretary of State[10] for the year[11].

1 See the Local Government Finance Act 1992 ss 52ZA(1)(a), 52ZB(1), (2); and PARA 391. As to the meaning of 'relevant basic amount of council tax' see PARA 391 note 3. As to the meaning of 'billing authority' see PARA 346. As to the meaning of 'England' see PARA 2 note 16.

2 As to the meaning of 'financial year' see PARA 11 note 1.

3 Ie in compliance with the Local Government Finance Act 1992 s 52ZF. The functions under s 52ZF must be discharged only by the authority: see s 67(1), (2)(b) (amended by the Localism Act 2011 s 72(2), Sch 6 paras 1, 30(a)). A calculation made in accordance with the Local Government Finance Act 1992 s 52ZF may not be questioned except by an application for judicial review: see s 66(1), (2)(c) (s 66(2)(c) amended by the Localism Act 2011 Sch 6 paras 1, 29(a)). If on an application for judicial review the court decides to grant relief, it must quash the calculation: see the Local Government Finance Act 1992 s 66(3) (amended by the Local Government Finance Act 2012 s 10(2), (3)(b), Sch 4 paras 3, 5(1), (3)). As to judicial review see JUDICIAL REVIEW vol 61 (2010) PARA 601 et seq.

4 Ie for the purposes of the Local Government Finance Act 1992 Pt I Ch III (ss 30–38): see PARA 380 et seq.

5 Ie the Local Government Finance Act 1992 ss 52ZH, 52ZI: see PARAS 396–397.

6 See the Local Government Finance Act 1992 s 52ZF(1) (s 52ZF added by the Localism Act 2011 s 72(1), Sch 5).

7 Ie they must be made in accordance with the Local Government Finance Act 1992 s 31A (see PARA 382), s 31B (see PARA 383) and ss 34–36 (see PARAS 380, 386), ignoring s 31A(11) for this purpose (see s 52ZF(2)(a) (as added: see note 6)), and in accordance with s 52ZF (see s 52ZF(2)(c) (as so added)).

In making the substitute calculations, the authority must:

(1) use the amount determined in the previous calculation for the year under s 31A(3) so far as relating to amounts which the authority estimates it will accrue in the year in respect of locally retained non-domestic rates, revenue support grant, special grant or (in the case of the Common Council of the City of London only) police grant (s 52ZF(3)(a) (as so added); amended by the Local Government Finance Act 2012 s 3(5), (6)(a); and SI 2013/733)); and

(2) use the amount determined in the previous calculation for the year for item 'T' in the Local Government Finance Act 1992 s 31B(1) and (where applicable) item 'TP' in s 34(3) (s 52ZF(3)(b) (as so added)).

In Pt 1 Ch 4ZA (ss 52ZA–52ZY), 'locally retained non-domestic rates', in relation to a billing authority or a major precepting authority, means amounts received by the authority under, or under regulations under, the Local Government Finance Act 1988 Sch 7B (see PARA 58 et seq), or under regulations under s 99(3) (see PARA 583) in connection with the operation of Sch 7B: Local Government Finance Act 1992 s 52ZF(3A) (added by SI 2013/733).

8 Ie by applying the Local Government Finance Act 1992 s 52ZX (see PARA 391 note 8) to the calculations.

9 Ie under the Local Government Finance Act 1992 s 52ZC: see PARA 392.

10 As to the Secretary of State see PARA 4 note 18.

11 See the Local Government Finance Act 1992 s 52ZF(2)(b) (as added: see note 6).

395. Arrangements for referendum.

Where the relevant basic amount of council tax determined by a billing authority in England is excessive[1], the authority must[2] make arrangements to hold a referendum in relation to the authority's relevant basic amount of council tax for the financial year[3].

Subject as follows, the referendum is to be held on a date decided by the billing authority[4]. That date must be not later than the first Thursday in May in the financial year[5] or such other date in that year as the Secretary of State[6] may specify by order[7].

The persons entitled to vote in the referendum are those who, on the day of the referendum would be entitled to vote as electors at an election for members for an electoral area[8] of the billing authority[9], and are registered in the register of local government electors[10] at an address within the billing authority's area[11].

As soon as is reasonably practicable after determining that it is required to hold a referendum in relation to its relevant basic amount of council tax for the financial year, the billing authority must notify that fact in writing to any body that has issued a levy or a special levy to it for the financial year[12].

1 See the Local Government Finance Act 1992 ss 52ZA(1)(a), 52ZB(1), (2); and PARA 391. As to the meaning of 'relevant basic amount of council tax' see PARA 391 note 3. As to the meaning of 'billing authority' see PARA 346. As to the meaning of 'England' see PARA 2 note 16.

2 Ie in accordance with the Local Government Finance Act 1992 s 52ZG.

3 Local Government Finance Act 1992 s 52ZG(1) (s 52ZG added by the Localism Act 2011 s 72(1), Sch 5). The Local Government Finance Act 1992 s 52ZG is subject to regulations under s 52ZQ (see PARA 405): s 52ZG(7) (as so added). As to the meaning of 'financial year' see PARA 11 note 1.

4 Local Government Finance Act 1992 s 52ZG(2) (as added: see note 3).

5 Local Government Finance Act 1992 s 52ZG(3)(a) (as added: see note 3).

6 As to the Secretary of State see PARA 4 note 18.

7 Local Government Finance Act 1992 s 52ZG(3)(b) (as added: see note 3). Such an order must be made not later than:

(1) 1 February in the financial year preceding the year mentioned in s 52ZG(3)(b) (s 52ZG(4)(a) (as so added)); or

(2) in the case of an order affecting more than one financial year, 1 February in the financial year preceding the first of those years (s 52ZG(4)(b) (as so added)).

The date specified for the purposes of s 52ZG(3)(b) is 22 May 2014: see the Local Authority (Referendums Relating to Council Tax Increases) (Date of Referendum) (England) Order 2013, SI 2013/2862, art 2.

8 'Electoral area' means:

(1) where the billing authority is a district council, a London borough council or the Common Council of the City of London, a ward (Local Government Finance Act 1992 s 52ZG(6)(a) (as added: see note 3));

(2) where the billing authority is a county council, an electoral division (s 52ZG(6)(b) (as so added));

(3) where the billing authority is the Council of the Isles of Scilly, a parish (s 52ZG(6)(c) (as so added)).

As to the establishment of electoral areas for the purpose of local government elections see ELECTIONS AND REFERENDUMS vol 37 (2013) PARA 74.

9 Local Government Finance Act 1992 s 52ZG(5)(a) (as added: see note 3).

10 'Register of local government electors' means the register of local government electors kept in accordance with the provisions of the Representation of the People Acts (see ELECTIONS AND REFERENDUMS vol 37 (2013) PARA 112): Local Government Finance Act 1992 s 52ZG(6) (as added: see note 3).

11 Local Government Finance Act 1992 s 52ZG(5)(b) (as added: see note 3).

12 Local Government Finance Act 1992 s 52ZG(5A) (s 52ZG as added (see note 3); s 52ZG(5A) added by the Local Audit and Accountability Act 2014 s 41(1), (2)). As to the meaning of 'levy' see PARA 12 note 5. As to the meaning of 'special levy' see PARA 384 note 5.

396. Effect of referendum.

The billing authority[1] must inform the Secretary of State[2], and any body the authority was required to notify about the holding of the referendum[3], of the result of the referendum[4].

If the result is that the billing authority's relevant basic amount of council tax[5] for the financial year[6] is approved by a majority of persons voting in the referendum[7], the authority's calculations from which that amount was derived continue to have effect[8] for that year[9]. If the result is that the billing authority's relevant basic amount of council tax for the financial year is not approved by a majority of persons voting in the referendum[10], the substitute calculations made[11] in relation to the year have effect in relation to the authority and the financial year[12].

1 Ie the billing authority in England: see the Local Government Finance Act 1992 s 52ZA(1)(a) (ss 52ZA, 52ZH added by the Localism Act 2011 s 72(1), Sch 5). As to the meaning of 'billing authority' see PARA 346. As to the meaning of 'England' see PARA 2 note 16.
2 As to the Secretary of State see PARA 4 note 18.
3 Ie under the Local Government Finance Act 1992 s 52ZG(5A): see PARA 395.
4 Local Government Finance Act 1992 s 52ZH(1) (as added (see note 1); amended by the Local Audit and Accountability Act 2014 s 41(1), (3)). As to arrangements for referendums see PARA 395.
5 As to the meaning of 'relevant basic amount of council tax' see PARA 391 note 3.
6 As to the meaning of 'financial year' see PARA 11 note 1.
7 Local Government Finance Act 1992 s 52ZH(2) (as added: see note 1). As to the persons entitled to vote in referendums see PARA 395.
8 Ie for the purposes of the Local Government Finance Act 1992.
9 Local Government Finance Act 1992 s 52ZH(3) (as added: see note 1).
10 Local Government Finance Act 1992 s 52ZH(4) (as added: see note 1).
11 Ie under the Local Government Finance Act 1992 s 52ZF: see PARA 394.
12 Local Government Finance Act 1992 s 52ZH(5) (as added: see note 1).

397. Failure to hold referendum.

If the billing authority[1] fails to hold a referendum[2], the substitute calculations made[3] in relation to the year have effect in relation to the authority and the financial year[4]. If the authority has not made those substitute calculations, during the period of restriction[5] the authority has no power to transfer any amount from its collection fund to its general fund[6].

1 Ie the billing authority in England: see the Local Government Finance Act 1992 s 52ZA(1)(a) (ss 52ZA, 52ZI added by the Localism Act 2011 s 72(1), Sch 5). As to the meaning of 'billing authority' see PARA 346. As to the meaning of 'England' see PARA 2 note 16.
2 Ie in accordance with the Local Government Finance Act 1992 Pt I Ch 4ZA. As to arrangements for referendums see PARA 395.
3 Ie under the Local Government Finance Act 1992 s 52ZF: see PARA 394.
4 Local Government Finance Act 1992 s 52ZI(1) (as added: see note 1). As to the meaning of 'financial year' see PARA 11 note 1.
5 'The period of restriction' means the period beginning with the latest date on which the referendum could have been held (Local Government Finance Act 1992 s 52ZI(3)(a) (as added: see note 1)), and ending with the date (if any) when the billing authority makes the substitute calculations (s 52ZI(3)(b) (as so added)).
6 Local Government Finance Act 1992 s 52ZI(2) (as added: see note 1). The Local Government Finance Act 1988 ss 97, 98 (see PARA 582) have effect accordingly: see the Local Government Finance Act 1992 s 52ZI(2) (as so added). In relation to the Common Council of the City of London the reference to a billing authority's general fund is a reference to the City fund: see s 69(2)(c). As to general funds and collection funds see PARA 579 et seq. As to the City Fund see PARA 586.

C. EXCESSIVE INCREASE IN COUNCIL TAX BY PRECEPTING AUTHORITY

398. Major precepting authority's duty to make substitute calculations.

Where the relevant basic amount of council tax determined by a major precepting authority in England is excessive[1], the authority must make substitute calculations for the financial year[2] in compliance with the following provisions[3].

Substitute calculations made for a financial year by a major precepting authority other than the Greater London Authority[4] comply with these provisions if they are made in accordance with the appropriate statutory provisions[5], and the relevant basic amount of council tax for the year produced by the calculations is not excessive by reference to the principles determined by the Secretary of State[6] for the year[7].

1 See the Local Government Finance Act 1992 ss 52ZA(1)(b), 52ZB(3), (4); and PARA 391. As to the meaning of 'relevant basic amount of council tax' see PARA 391 notes 8, 12. As to the meaning of 'major precepting authority' see PARA 11 note 2. As to the meaning of 'England' see PARA 2 note 16.

2 As to the meaning of 'financial year' see PARA 11 note 1.

3 See the Local Government Finance Act 1992 s 52ZJ(1) (s 52ZJ added by the Localism Act 2011 s 72(1), Sch 5). The functions under the Local Government Finance Act 1992 s 52ZJ must be discharged only by the authority: see s 67(1), (2)(b) (s 67(2)(b) amended by the Localism Act 2011 s 72(2), Sch 6 paras 1, 30(b)). A calculation made in accordance with the Local Government Finance Act 1992 s 52ZJ may not be questioned except by an application for judicial review: see s 66(1), (2)(c) (s 66(2)(c) amended by the Localism Act 2011 Sch 6 paras 1, 29(b)). If on an application for judicial review the court decides to grant relief, it must quash the calculation: see the Local Government Finance Act 1992 s 66(3) (amended by the Local Government Finance Act 2012 s 10(2), (3)(b), Sch 4 paras 3, 5(1), (3)). As to judicial review see JUDICIAL REVIEW vol 61 (2010) PARA 601 et seq.

4 Substitute calculations made for a financial year by the Greater London Authority comply with the Local Government Finance Act 1992 s 52ZJ if:

(1) they are made by applying the relevant London provisions and ss 47, 48 (see PARAS 149–150) to the Authority's substitute consolidated council tax requirement for the year (s 52ZJ(3)(a) (as added: see note 3)); and

(2) they are made in accordance with s 52ZJ (s 52ZJ(3)(b) (as so added)).

In making the substitute calculations, the Greater London Authority must use any amount determined in the previous calculations for item 'T' in the Greater London Authority Act 1999 s 88(2) (see LONDON GOVERNMENT vol 71 (2013) PARA 150) or for item 'TP2' in s 89(4) (see LONDON GOVERNMENT vol 71 (2013) PARA 150): Local Government Finance Act 1992 s 52ZJ(6) (as so added). In Pt 1 Ch 4ZA (ss 52ZA–52ZY), 'the relevant London provisions' means the Greater London Authority Act 1999 s 88 and (where applicable) s 89; and 'the Authority's substitute consolidated council tax requirement', in relation to a financial year, means the Authority's substitute consolidated council tax requirement agreed under the Greater London Authority Act 1999 Sch 6 (see LONDON GOVERNMENT vol 71 (2013) PARA 150), or set out in its substitute consolidated budget as agreed under that Schedule, as the case may be: Local Government Finance Act 1992 s 52ZJ(7) (as so added). As to the Greater London Authority see LONDON GOVERNMENT vol 71 (2013) PARA 67 et seq.

5 Ie in accordance with the Local Government Finance Act 1992 s 42A (see PARA 12), s 42B (see PARA 13) and ss 45–48 (see PARAS 12–13) (s 52ZJ(2)(a) (as added: see note 3)), and in accordance with s 52ZJ (s 52ZJ(2)(c) (as so added)).

In making the substitute calculations, a major precepting authority other than the Greater London Authority must:

(1) use the amount determined in the previous calculation under s 42A(3) so far as relating to amounts which the authority estimates it will accrue in the year in respect of locally retained non-domestic rates, revenue support grant, special grant or police grant (s 52ZJ(4)(a) (as so added; amended by the Local Government Finance Act 2012 s 3(5), (7)(a); and by SI 2013/733)); and

(2) use the amount determined in the previous calculation for item 'T' in the Local Government Finance Act 1992 s 42B(1) or (where applicable) item 'TP' in s 45(3) (s 52ZJ(4)(b) (as so added)).

6 Ie under the Local Government Finance Act 1992 s 52ZC: see PARA 392. As to the Secretary of State see PARA 4 note 18.

7 Local Government Finance Act 1992 s 52ZJ(2)(b) (as added: see note 3).

399. Major precepting authority's duty to notify appropriate billing authorities.

Where the relevant basic amount of council tax determined by a major precepting authority in England is excessive[1], the authority must notify each appropriate billing authority[2] that its relevant basic amount of council tax for a financial year[3] is excessive[4], and that the billing authority is required to hold[5] a referendum[6]. Such a notification must include a precept[7].

As soon as is reasonably practicable after determining that its relevant basic amount of council tax for the financial year is excessive, the major precepting authority must also notify the matters mentioned above[8] in writing to any body that has issued a levy[9] to it for the financial year or, in the case of the Greater London Authority, has issued a levy to any constituent body[10] for the financial year[11].

The Secretary of State[12] must by regulations prescribe a date by which a notification to appropriate billing authorities must be made[13].

1 See the Local Government Finance Act 1992 ss 52ZA(1)(b), 52ZB(3), (4); and PARA 391. As to the meaning of 'relevant basic amount of council tax' see PARA 391 note 8. As to the meaning of 'major precepting authority' see PARA 11 note 2. As to the meaning of 'England' see PARA 2 note 16.

2 As to the meaning of 'billing authority' see PARA 346.

3 As to the meaning of 'financial year' see PARA 11 note 1.

4 Local Government Finance Act 1992 s 52ZK(1)(a) (s 52ZK added by the Localism Act 2011 s 72(1), Sch 5). The Local Government Finance Act 1992 s 52ZK does not require the Greater London Authority to notify a billing authority to which this provision applies unless the Authority's unadjusted relevant basic amount of council tax for the year is excessive: s 52ZK(9) (as so added). Section 52ZK(9) applies to a billing authority if the special item within the meaning of the Greater London Authority Act 1999 s 89(2) (see LONDON GOVERNMENT vol 71 (2013) PARA 150) does not apply to any part of the authority's area: s 52ZK(10) (as so added). As to the meaning of 'the Authority's unadjusted relevant basic amount of council tax for the year' see PARA 391 note 8.

5 Ie in accordance with the Local Government Finance Act 1992 Pt I Ch 4ZA. As to arrangements for referendums see PARA 402.

6 Local Government Finance Act 1992 s 52ZK(1)(b) (as added: see note 4).

7 See the Local Government Finance Act 1992 s 52ZK(2) (as added (see note 4); amended by the Local Audit and Accountability Act 2014 s 41(1), (6)). The precept must be in accordance with the Local Government Finance Act 1992 s 52ZK(3)–(10) (see below and note 4); but that precept does not have effect for the purposes of Pt I Ch III (ss 30–38) and Ch IV (ss 39–52) except in accordance with s 52ZO (see PARA 403) and s 52ZP (see PARA 404): see s 52ZK(2) (as so added).

A precept issued to a billing authority under s 52ZK by a major precepting authority other than the Greater London Authority must state:

(1) the amount which, in relation to the year and each category of dwellings in the billing authority's area, has been calculated by the precepting authority in accordance with ss 42A, 42B and ss 45–47 as applied by s 52ZJ (see PARA 398) (s 52ZK(3)(a) (as so added)); and

(2) the amount which has been calculated by the precepting authority in accordance with s 48 as applied by s 52ZJ as the amount payable by the billing authority for the year (s 52ZK(3)(b) (as so added)).

Dwellings fall within different categories for the purposes of s 52ZK(3) according as different calculations have been made in relation to them as mentioned in s 52ZK(3)(a): s 52ZK(4) (as so added).

A precept issued to a billing authority under s 52ZK by the Greater London Authority must state:

(a) the amount which, in relation to the year and each category of dwellings in the billing authority's area, has been calculated by applying, in accordance with s 52ZJ, the relevant London provisions and s 47 (see PARAS 149–150) to the Authority's substitute consolidated council tax requirement (s 52ZK(5)(a) (as so added)); and

(b) the amount which has been calculated by the Authority in accordance with s 48 as applied by s 52ZJ as the amount payable by the billing authority for the year (s 52ZK(5)(b) (as so added)).

Dwellings fall within different categories for the purposes of s 52ZK(5) according as different calculations have been made in relation to them as mentioned in s 52ZK(5)(a): s 52ZK(6) (as so added). As to the meaning of 'dwelling' see PARA 349. As to the meanings of 'the relevant London provisions' and 'the Authority's substitute consolidated council tax requirement' see PARA 398 note 4.

A major precepting authority must assume for the purposes of s 52ZK(3), (5) that each of the valuation bands is shown in the billing authority's valuation list as applicable to one or more dwellings situated in its area or (as the case may be) each part of its area as respects which different calculations have been made: s 52ZK(7) (as so added). As to valuation bands see PARA 361. As to valuation lists see PARA 408 et seq.

8 Ie the matters mentioned in the Local Government Finance Act 1992 s 52ZK(1).

9 As to the meaning of 'levy' see PARA 12 note 5.

10 As to the meaning of 'constituent body' see PARA 406 note 9.

11 Local Government Finance Act 1992 s 52ZK(1A) (s 52ZK as added (see note 4); s 52ZK(1A) added by the Local Audit and Accountability Act 2014 s 41(1), (5)).

12 As to the Secretary of State see PARA 4 note 18.

13 Local Government Finance Act 1992 s 52ZK(8) (as added (see note 4); amended by the Local Audit and Accountability Act 2014 s 41(1), (7)). As to regulations made under the Local Government Finance Act 1992 s 52ZK(8) see the Local Authority (Referendums Relating to Council Tax Increases) Regulations 2012, SI 2012/460.

400. Local precepting authority's duty to make substitute calculations.

Where the relevant basic amount of council tax determined by a local precepting authority in England is excessive[1], the authority must make substitute calculations for the financial year[2] in compliance with these provisions[3].

Substitute calculations for a financial year comply with these provisions if:

(1) they are made in accordance with the appropriate statutory provisions[4]; and

(2) the relevant basic amount of council tax produced[5] is not excessive by reference to the principles determined by the Secretary of State[6] for the year[7].

1 See the Local Government Finance Act 1992 ss 52ZA(1)(c), 52ZB(5), (6); and PARA 391. As to the meaning of 'relevant basic amount of council tax' see PARA 391 note 12. As to the meaning of 'local precepting authority' see PARA 18 note 2. As to the meaning of 'England' see PARA 2 note 16.

2 As to the meaning of 'financial year' see PARA 11 note 1.

3 Local Government Finance Act 1992 s 52ZL(1) (s 52ZL added by the Localism Act 2011 s 72(1), Sch 5).

4 Ie they are made in accordance with the Local Government Finance Act 1992 s 49A (see PARA 19): s 52ZL(2)(a) (as added: see note 3).

5 Ie by applying the Local Government Finance Act 1992 s 52ZX to the calculations: see PARA 391 note 12.

6 Ie under the Local Government Finance Act 1992 s 52ZC: see PARA 392. As to the Secretary of State see PARA 4 note 18.

7 Local Government Finance Act 1992 s 52ZL(2)(b) (as added: see note 3).

401. Local precepting authority's duty to notify appropriate billing authority.

Where the relevant basic amount of council tax determined by a local precepting authority in England is excessive[1], the authority must notify its appropriate billing authority[2] that its relevant basic amount of council tax for a financial year[3] is excessive[4], and that the billing authority is required to hold[5] a referendum[6]. Such a notification must include a precept[7].

The Secretary of State[8] must by regulations[9] prescribe a date by which the notification must be made[10].

1 See the Local Government Finance Act 1992 ss 52ZA(1)(c), 52ZB(5), (6); and PARA 391. As to the meaning of 'relevant basic amount of council tax' see PARA 391 note 12. As to the meaning of 'local precepting authority' see PARA 18 note 2. As to the meaning of 'England' see PARA 2 note 16.

2 As to the meaning of 'billing authority' see PARA 346.

3 As to the meaning of 'financial year' see PARA 11 note 1.
4 Local Government Finance Act 1992 s 52ZM(1)(a) (s 52ZM added by the Localism Act 2011 s 72(1), Sch 5).
5 Ie in accordance with the Local Government Finance Act 1992 Pt I Ch 4ZA (ss 52ZA–52ZY).
6 Local Government Finance Act 1992 s 52ZM(1)(b) (as added: see note 4). As to arrangements for referendums see PARA 402.
7 See the Local Government Finance Act 1992 s 52ZM(2) (as added: see note 4). The precept must be in accordance with s 52ZM(3); but that precept does not have effect for the purposes of Pt I Ch III (ss 30–38) and Ch IV (ss 39–52) except in accordance with s 52ZO (see PARA 403) and s 52ZP (see PARA 404): s 52ZM(2) (as so added). The precept must state, as the amount payable by the billing authority for the year, the amount which has been calculated by the local precepting authority under s 49A as applied by s 52ZL (see PARA 400): s 52ZM(3) (as so added).
8 As to the Secretary of State see PARA 4 note 18.
9 See the Local Authority (Referendums Relating to Council Tax Increases) Regulations 2012, SI 2012/460.
10 Local Government Finance Act 1992 s 52ZM(4) (as added: see note 4).

402. Arrangements for referendum.

A billing authority in England[1] that is notified[2] by a precepting authority[3] that its relevant basic amount of council tax[4] for a financial year[5] is excessive, must make arrangements[6] to hold a referendum in relation to the precepting authority's relevant basic amount of council tax for the financial year[7].

Where the referendum is one of two or more referendums required to be held in respect of the same calculation, it is to be held on the first Thursday in May in the financial year[8], or such other date as the Secretary of State[9] may specify by order[10]. Otherwise the referendum is to be held on a date decided by the billing authority[11]; but that date must be not later than the first Thursday in May in the financial year[12], or such other date in that year as the Secretary of State may specify by order[13].

The persons entitled to vote in the referendum are those who, on the day of the referendum would be entitled to vote as electors at an election for members for an electoral area[14] of the billing authority that falls wholly or partly within the precepting authority's area[15], and are registered in the register of local government electors[16] at an address that is within both the precepting authority's area[17] and the billing authority's area[18].

Subject to regulations made by the Secretary of State[19], the billing authority may recover from the precepting authority the expenses that are incurred by the billing authority in connection with the referendum[20].

1 See the Local Government Finance Act 1992 s 52ZA(1)(a) (ss 52ZA, 52ZN added by the Localism Act 2011 s 72(1), Sch 5). As to the meaning of 'billing authority' see PARA 346. As to the meaning of 'England' see PARA 2 note 16.
2 Ie under the Local Government Finance Act 1992 s 52ZK (see PARA 399) or s 52ZM (see PARA 401).
3 Ie a major precepting authority in England or a local precepting authority in England: see the Local Government Finance Act 1992 s 52ZA(1)(b), (c), (2)(b) (as added: see note 1). As to the meaning of 'major precepting authority' see PARA 11 note 2. As to the meaning of 'local precepting authority' see PARA 18 note 2.
4 As to the meaning of 'relevant basic amount of council tax' see PARA 391 note 3.
5 As to the meaning of 'financial year' see PARA 11 note 1.
6 Ie in accordance with the Local Government Finance Act 1992 s 52ZN.
7 Local Government Finance Act 1992 s 52ZN(1) (as added: see note 1). Section 52ZN is subject to regulations under s 52ZQ (see PARA 405): s 52ZN(10) (as so added). As to the effect of a referendum see PARA 403. As to failure to hold a referendum see PARA 404.
8 Local Government Finance Act 1992 s 52ZN(2)(a) (as added: see note 1).
9 As to the Secretary of State see PARA 4 note 18.

10 Local Government Finance Act 1992 s 52ZN(2)(b) (as added: see note 1). Such an order must be made not later than:

(1) 1 February in the financial year preceding the year mentioned in s 52ZN(2)(b) (see s 52ZN(5)(a) (as so added)); or

(2) in the case of an order affecting more than one financial year, 1 February in the financial year preceding the first of those years (see s 52ZN(5)(b) (as so added)).

The date specified for the purposes of s 52ZN(2)(b) is 22 May 2014: Local Authority (Referendums Relating to Council Tax Increases) (Date of Referendum) (England) Order 2013, SI 2013/2862.

11 See the Local Government Finance Act 1992 s 52ZN(3) (as added: see note 1).

12 Local Government Finance Act 1992 s 52ZN(3), (4)(a) (as added: see note 1).

13 Local Government Finance Act 1992 s 52ZN(3), (4)(b) (as added: see note 1). Such an order must be made not later than:

(1) 1 February in the financial year preceding the year mentioned in s 52ZN(4)(b) (see s 52ZN(5)(a) (as so added)); or

(2) in the case of an order affecting more than one financial year, 1 February in the financial year preceding the first of those years (see s 52ZN(5)(b) (as so added)).

The date specified for the purposes of s 52ZN(4)(b) is 22 May 2014: Local Authority (Referendums Relating to Council Tax Increases) (Date of Referendum) (England) Order 2013, SI 2013/2862.

14 'Electoral area' means the following (Local Government Finance Act 1992 s 52ZN(9) (as added: see note 1)):

(1) in relation to a district council, a London borough council or the Common Council of the City of London, a ward;

(2) in relation to a county council, an electoral division;

(3) in relation to the Council of the Isles of Scilly, a parish.

As to the establishment of electoral areas for the purpose of local government elections see ELECTIONS AND REFERENDUMS vol 37 (2013) PARA 74.

15 Local Government Finance Act 1992 s 52ZN(6)(a) (as added: see note 1).

16 'Register of local government electors' means the register of local government electors kept in accordance with the provisions of the Representation of the People Acts (see ELECTIONS AND REFERENDUMS vol 37 (2013) PARA 112): Local Government Finance Act 1992 s 52ZN(9) (as added: see note 1).

17 Local Government Finance Act 1992 s 52ZN(6)(b)(i) (as added: see note 1).

18 Local Government Finance Act 1992 s 52ZN(6)(b)(ii) (as added: see note 1).

19 The Secretary of State may by regulations make provision for cases in which the Local Government Finance Act 1992 s 52ZN(7) does not apply (s 52ZN(8)(a) (as added: see note 1)), or in which s 52ZN(7) applies with modifications (s 52ZN(8)(b) (as so added)). See the Local Authority (Referendums Relating to Council Tax Increases) Regulations 2012, SI 2012/460.

20 Local Government Finance Act 1992 s 52ZN(7) (as added: see note 1).

403. Effect of referendum.

The precepting authority[1] must inform the Secretary of State[2] and any body the authority was required to notify about the holding of the referendum[3] of the result of the referendum or (as the case may be) each of them[4].

If:

(1) in a case where one referendum is held in respect of the precepting authority's relevant basic amount of council tax[5] for the financial year[6], that amount is approved by a majority of persons voting in the referendum[7]; or

(2) in a case where two or more referendums are held in respect of that amount, that amount is approved by a majority of persons voting in all of those referendums taken together[8],

the precepting authority's calculations that include that amount or (as the case may be) from which that amount was derived continue to have effect[9] for the year[10].

If:

(a) in a case where one referendum is held in respect of the precepting authority's relevant basic amount of council tax for a financial year, that amount is not approved by a majority of persons voting in the referendum[11]; or

(b) in a case where two or more referendums are held in respect of that amount, that amount is not approved by a majority of persons voting in all of those referendums taken together[12],

any precept issued to a billing authority[13] as part of a notification that triggered the referendum has effect[14] as a precept issued to that billing authority for the year[15].

1 Ie a major precepting authority in England or a local precepting authority in England: see the Local Government Finance Act 1992 s 52ZA(1)(b), (c), (2)(b) (ss 52ZA, 52ZO added by the Localism Act 2011 s 72(1), Sch 5). As to the meaning of 'major precepting authority' see PARA 11 note 2. As to the meaning of 'local precepting authority' see PARA 18 note 2. As to the meaning of 'England' see PARA 2 note 16.

2 As to the Secretary of State see PARA 4 note 18.

3 Ie under the Local Government Finance Act 1992 s 52ZK(1A): see PARA 399.

4 Local Government Finance Act 1992 s 52ZO(1) (as added (see note 1); amended by the Local Audit and Accountability Act 2014 s 41(1), (8)). As to arrangements for referendums see PARA 402.

5 As to the meaning of 'relevant basic amount of council tax' see PARA 391 notes 3, 8, 12.

6 As to the meaning of 'financial year' see PARA 11 note 1.

7 Local Government Finance Act 1992 s 52ZO(2)(a) (as added: see note 1). As to the persons entitled to vote in a referendum see PARA 402.

8 Local Government Finance Act 1992 s 52ZO(2)(b) (as added: see note 1).

9 Ie for the purposes of the Local Government Finance Act 1992.

10 Local Government Finance Act 1992 s 52ZO(3) (as added: see note 1).

11 Local Government Finance Act 1992 s 52ZO(4)(a) (as added: see note 1).

12 Local Government Finance Act 1992 s 52ZO(4)(b) (as added: see note 1).

13 Ie under the Local Government Finance Act 1992 s 52ZK (see PARA 399) or s 52ZM (see PARA 401). As to the meaning of 'billing authority' see PARA 346.

14 Ie for the purposes of the Local Government Finance Act 1992 Pt I Ch III (ss 30–38): see PARA 380 et seq.

15 Local Government Finance Act 1992 s 52ZO(5) (as added: see note 1). Where the precept was issued to a billing authority by a local precepting authority under s 52ZM (see PARA 401), s 36A (see PARA 387) has effect in relation to the billing authority as if it required the authority to make calculations in substitution on the basis of the precept (rather than permitting it to do so): s 52ZO(6) (as so added).

In the case of a major precepting authority other than the Greater London Authority, s 30 (see PARA 380) has effect by virtue of s 52ZO(5) in relation to that precept as if:

(1) references to amounts calculated under Pt I Ch IV (ss 39–52) were to amounts calculated as mentioned in s 52ZJ(2) (see PARA 398) (s 52ZO(7)(a) (as so added)); and

(2) the reference to the amount stated in accordance with s 40 (see PARA 11) were to the amount stated in accordance with s 52ZK(3)(b) (see PARA 399) (s 52ZO(7)(b) (as so added)).

In the case of the Greater London Authority, s 30 has effect by virtue of s 52ZO(5) in relation to that precept as if:

(a) references that are to be read as amounts calculated under the Greater London Authority Act 1999 Pt III Ch I (ss 81–99) (see LONDON GOVERNMENT vol 71 (2013) PARA 150) were to amounts calculated as mentioned in the Local Government Finance Act 1992 s 52ZJ(3) (see PARA 398) (s 52ZO(8)(a) (as so added)); and

(b) the reference to the amount stated in accordance with s 40 were to the amount stated in accordance with s 52ZK(5)(b) (see PARA 399) (s 52ZO(8)(b) (as so added)).

If the precepting authority has already issued a precept for the financial year (originally or by way of substitute) to the billing authority:

(i) s 42(3), (4) (see PARA 23) applies to the precept within s 52ZO(5) as it applies to a precept issued in substitution under that section (s 52ZO(9)(a) (as so added)); but

(ii) the references in those subsections to the amount of the new precept are to be read as references to the amount stated in the precept within s 52ZO(5) in accordance with s 52ZK(3)(b) or (5)(b) (s 52ZO(9)(b) (as so added)).

404. Failure to hold referendum.

If a billing authority in England[1] that is required to be notified[2] by a precepting authority[3] that its relevant basic amount of council tax[4] for a financial year[5] is excessive and that the billing authority is required to hold a referendum fails to hold[6] a referendum[7]:

(1) if the precepting authority has failed to so notify the billing authority[8], the precepting authority must issue a precept for the year[9] to the billing authority[10]; and during the period of restriction[11] no billing authority to which the precepting authority has power to issue a precept has power to pay anything in respect of a precept issued by the precepting authority for the year[12];

(2) if the precepting authority has so notified the billing authority, the precept issued to the billing authority[13] as part of the notification has effect[14] as a precept issued to that billing authority for the year[15].

1 See the Local Government Finance Act 1992 s 52ZA(1)(a) (ss 52ZA, 52ZP added by the Localism Act 2011 s 72(1), Sch 5). As to the meaning of 'billing authority' see PARA 346. As to the meaning of 'England' see PARA 2 note 16.

2 Ie under the Local Government Finance Act 1992 s 52ZK (see PARA 399) or s 52ZM (see PARA 401).

3 Ie a major precepting authority in England or a local precepting authority in England: see the Local Government Finance Act 1992 s 52ZA(1)(b), (c), (2)(b) (as added: see note 1). As to the meaning of 'major precepting authority' see PARA 11 note 2. As to the meaning of 'local precepting authority' see PARA 18 note 2.

4 As to the meaning of 'relevant basic amount of council tax' see PARA 391 notes 3, 8, 12.

5 As to the meaning of 'financial year' see PARA 11 note 1.

6 Ie in accordance with the Local Government Finance Act 1992 Pt I Ch 4ZA (ss 52ZA–52ZY). As to arrangements for referendums see PARA 402.

7 See the Local Government Finance Act 1992 s 52ZP(1) (as added: see note 1).

8 See the Local Government Finance Act 1992 s 52ZP(2) (as added: see note 1).

9 Ie in accordance with the Local Government Finance Act 1992 s 52ZK (see PARA 399) or s 52ZM (see PARA 401).

10 Local Government Finance Act 1992 s 52ZP(3) (as added: see note 1). Such a precept has effect for the purposes of Pt I Ch III (ss 30–38) (see PARA 380 et seq): see s 52ZP(3) (as so added). Where a precept under s 52ZP(3) is issued to a billing authority by a local precepting authority, s 36A (see PARA 387) has effect in relation to the billing authority as if it required the authority to make calculations in substitution on the basis of the precept (rather than permitting it to do so): s 52ZP(6) (as so added). Section 52ZO(7)–(9) (see PARA 403) applies to a precept within s 52ZP(3) as it applies to a precept within s 52ZO(5): see s 52ZP(9) (as so added).

11 'The period of restriction' means the period beginning with the date on which the referendum would have been required to be held or (as the case may be) the latest date on which it could have been held if the notification had been made (Local Government Finance Act 1992 s 52ZP(5)(a) (as added: see note 1)), and ending with the date (if any) when the precepting authority complies with s 52ZP(3) (see the text to notes 9–10) (s 52ZP(5)(b) (as so added)). As to the date for the holding of a referendum see PARA 402.

12 Local Government Finance Act 1992 s 52ZP(4) (as added: see note 1).

13 Ie under the Local Government Finance Act 1992 s 52ZK (see PARA 399) or s 52ZM (see PARA 401).

14 Ie for the purposes of the Local Government Finance Act 1992 Pt I Ch III (ss 30–38): see PARA 380 et seq.

15 Local Government Finance Act 1992 s 52ZP(7) (as added: see note 1). Section 52ZO(7)–(9) (see PARA 403) applies to a precept within s 52ZP(7) as it applies to a precept within s 52ZO(5): see s 52ZP(9) (as so added). Where the precept was issued to a billing authority by a local precepting

authority under s 52ZM (see PARA 401), s 36A (see PARA 387) has effect in relation to the billing authority as if it required the authority to make calculations in substitution on the basis of the precept (rather than permitting it to do so): s 52ZP(8) (as so added).

D. REGULATORY PROVISIONS

405. Regulations about referendums.

The Secretary of State or the Minister for the Cabinet Office[1] may by regulations[2] make provision:

(1) as to the conduct of referendums[3] relating to council tax increases[4];
(2) for the combination of polls at two or more such referendums[5];
(3) for the combination of polls at such referendums with polls at any elections or any referendums otherwise[6] held[7].

The provision which may be made includes, in particular, provision:

(a) as to the question to be asked in a referendum[8];
(b) as to the publicity to be given in connection with a referendum (including the publicity to be given with respect to the consequences of the referendum and its result)[9];
(c) about the limitation of expenditure in connection with a referendum[10];
(d) as to the conduct of the authority[11], members of the authority and officers of the authority in relation to a referendum[12];
(e) as to when, where and how voting in a referendum is to take place[13];
(f) as to how the votes cast in a referendum are to be counted[14];
(g) for disregarding alterations in a register of electors[15];
(h) for the questioning of the result of a referendum by a court or tribunal[16].

The regulations may apply or incorporate, with or without modifications or exceptions, any provision of any enactment[17] (whenever passed or made) relating to elections or referendums[18]; but where the regulations apply or incorporate (with or without modifications) any provision that creates an offence, the regulations may not impose a penalty greater than is provided for in respect of that offence[19].

Before making any such regulations, the Secretary of State or the Minister for the Cabinet Office must consult the Electoral Commission[20]; and no such regulations are to be made unless a draft of the regulations has been laid before and approved by resolution of each House of Parliament[21].

1 As to the Secretary of State see PARA 4 note 18. As to the Cabinet Office see CONSTITUTIONAL LAW vol 20 (2014) PARAS 234–236.

2 See the Local Authorities (Conduct of Referendums) (Council Tax Increases) (England) Regulations 2012, SI 2012/444 (amended by SI 2013/409, SI 2014/231, SI 2014/356 and SI 2017/67).

3 Ie referendums under the Local Government Finance Act 1992 Pt I Ch 4ZA (ss 52ZA–52ZY). As to referendums see PARAS 395, 402.

4 See the Local Government Finance Act 1992 s 52ZQ(1) (s 52ZQ added by the Localism Act 2011 s 72(1), Sch 5; the Local Government Finance Act 1992 s 52ZQ(1), (2), (6) amended by SI 2013/2597 and SI 2016/997).

5 See the Local Government Finance Act 1992 s 52ZQ(2)(a) (as added and amended: see note 4).

6 Ie otherwise than under the Local Government Finance Act 1992 Pt I Ch 4ZA (ss 52ZA–52ZY).

7 See the Local Government Finance Act 1992 s 52ZQ(2)(b) (as added and amended: see note 4).

8 Local Government Finance Act 1992 s 52ZQ(4)(a) (as added: see note 4).

9 Local Government Finance Act 1992 s 52ZQ(4)(b) (as added: see note 4).

10 Local Government Finance Act 1992 s 52ZQ(4)(c) (as added: see note 4).

11 As to the meaning of 'authority' see PARA 392 note 1.

12 Local Government Finance Act 1992 s 52ZQ(4)(d) (as added: see note 4). Such provision may include provision modifying the effect of the Local Government Act 1986 s 2 (prohibition of

political publicity: see LOCAL GOVERNMENT vol 69 (2018) PARA 607): see the Local Government Finance Act 1992 s 52ZQ(4)(d) (as so added).
13 Local Government Finance Act 1992 s 52ZQ(4)(e) (as added: see note 4).
14 Local Government Finance Act 1992 s 52ZQ(4)(f) (as added: see note 4).
15 Local Government Finance Act 1992 s 52ZQ(4)(g) (as added: see note 4).
16 Local Government Finance Act 1992 s 52ZQ(4)(h) (as added: see note 4).
17 'Enactment' includes an enactment contained in a local Act or comprised in subordinate legislation (within the meaning of the Interpretation Act 1978: see PARA 111 note 1): Local Government Finance Act 1992 s 52ZQ(8) (as added: see note 4). As to local Acts see STATUTES AND LEGISLATIVE PROCESS vol 96 (2012) PARA 626.
18 Local Government Finance Act 1992 s 52ZQ(3) (as added: see note 4).
19 Local Government Finance Act 1992 s 52ZQ(5) (as added: see note 4).
20 Local Government Finance Act 1992 s 52ZQ(6) (as added and amended: see note 4). As to the Electoral Commission see ELECTIONS AND REFERENDUMS vol 37 (2013) PARA 34.
21 Local Government Finance Act 1992 s 52ZQ(7) (as added: see note 4). As to the laying of documents before Parliament see STATUTES AND LEGISLATIVE PROCESS vol 96 (2013) PARA 1052.

406. Direction that referendum provisions are not to apply.

The Secretary of State[1] may give a direction to an authority[2] other than the Greater London Authority[3] if it appears to the Secretary of State that, unless the authority's council tax calculations[4] are such as to produce a relevant basic amount of council tax[5] that is excessive by reference to the principles determined by the Secretary of State for the year[6]:

(1) the authority will be unable to discharge its functions in an effective manner[7]; or

(2) the authority will be unable to meet its financial obligations[8].

The Secretary of State may give a direction to the Greater London Authority if it appears to the Secretary of State that, unless the Authority's council tax calculations are such as to produce a relevant basic amount of council tax that is excessive by reference to the principles determined by the Secretary of State for the year:

(a) one or more of the Authority's constituent bodies[9] will be unable to discharge its functions in an effective manner[10], or

(b) one or more of those bodies will be unable to meet its financial obligations[11].

The effect of a direction is that the referendum provisions[12] do not apply for the financial year[13] to, and no further step is to be taken for the financial year under the referendum provisions by, the authority to whom it is made[14] and, where that authority is a precepting authority[15], a billing authority as a result of any notification[16] by the precepting authority[17].

A direction may be given to an authority other than the Greater London Authority whether or not the authority has carried out its council tax calculations for the financial year[18], and, in the case of a billing authority, whether or not the authority has set[19] an amount of council tax for the financial year[20]. A direction may be given to the Greater London Authority only if it has carried out its council tax calculations for the financial year[21]. However, a direction may not be given to an authority if a referendum has been held relating to the authority's relevant basic amount of council tax for the financial year[22] and that amount has not been approved[23].

If the Secretary of State gives a direction to a billing authority the direction must state the amount that is to be the amount of the billing authority's council tax requirement for the financial year[24]. If the Secretary of State gives a direction to a major precepting authority other than the Greater London Authority the direction must state the amount that is to be the amount of the major precepting authority's council tax requirement for the financial year[25]. If the Secretary of State gives a direction to a local precepting authority the direction must state the amount that is to be the amount of the local precepting authority's council tax requirement for the financial year[26].

An authority that is required to make substitute calculations for a financial year[27] must make the calculations[28] and, in the case of a major precepting authority, must issue any precepts in substitution required[29] in consequence[30], before the end of the period of 21 days beginning with the day on which the authority receives the direction[31]. In the case of a billing authority, the authority has no power during the period of restriction[32] to transfer any amount from its collection fund to its general fund[33]. In the case of a precepting authority, no authority to which it has power to issue a precept has power during the period of restriction to pay anything in respect of a precept issued by the precepting authority for the financial year[34].

1 As to the Secretary of State see PARA 4 note 18.
2 As to the meaning of 'authority' see PARA 392 note 1.
3 As to the Greater London Authority see LONDON GOVERNMENT vol 71 (2013) PARA 67 et seq.
4 'Council tax calculations' means (Local Government Finance Act 1992 s 52ZR(8) (ss 52ZA, 52ZR–52ZW added by the Localism Act 2011 s 72(1), Sch 5)):
  (1) in relation to a billing authority, calculations under the Local Government Finance Act 1992 s 31A (see PARA 382), s 31B (see PARA 383) and ss 34–36 (see PARAS 380, 386);
  (2) in relation to a major precepting authority other than the Greater London Authority, calculations under s 42A (see PARA 12), s 42B (see PARA 13) and ss 45–48 (see PARAS 12–13);
  (3) in relation to the Greater London Authority, calculations under the Greater London Authority Act 1999 ss 85–90 (see LONDON GOVERNMENT vol 71 (2013) PARA 150) and the Local Government Finance Act 1992 ss 47–48 (see PARA 11); and
  (4) in the case of a local precepting authority, calculations under s 49A (see PARA 19).
5 As to the meaning of 'relevant basic amount of council tax' see PARA 391 notes 3, 8, 12.
6 As to such principles see PARA 392.
7 Local Government Finance Act 1992 s 52ZR(1)(a) (as added: see note 4).
8 Local Government Finance Act 1992 s 52ZR(1)(b) (as added: see note 4).
9 'Constituent body' means the Mayor of London, the London Assembly, or a functional body within the meaning of the Greater London Authority Act 1999 s 424 (see LONDON GOVERNMENT vol 71 (2013) PARA 148): Local Government Finance Act 1992 s 52ZR(8) (as added: see note 4). As to the Mayor of London see LONDON GOVERNMENT vol 71 (2013) PARA 69. As to the London Assembly see LONDON GOVERNMENT vol 71 (2013) PARA 70.
10 Local Government Finance Act 1992 s 52ZR(2)(a) (as added: see note 4).
11 Local Government Finance Act 1992 s 52ZR(2)(b) (as added: see note 4).
12 'The referendum provisions' means (Local Government Finance Act 1992 s 52ZR(8) (as added: see note 4):
  (1) where the direction is given to a billing authority, s 52ZB (see PARA 391) and ss 52ZF–52ZI (see PARAS 394–397);
  (2) where the direction is given to a major precepting authority, s 52ZB, s 52ZJ (see PARA 398), s 52ZK (see PARA 399) and ss 52ZN–52ZP (see PARAS 402–404); and
  (3) where the direction is given to a local precepting authority, s 52ZB, s 52ZL (see PARA 400), s 52ZM (see PARA 401) and ss 52ZN–52ZP.
13 As to the meaning of 'financial year' see PARA 11 note 1.
14 Local Government Finance Act 1992 s 52ZR(3)(a) (as added: see note 4).
15 Ie a major precepting authority in England or a local precepting authority in England: see the Local Government Finance Act 1992 s 52ZA(1)(b), (c), (2)(b) (as added: see note 4).
16 Ie under the Local Government Finance Act 1992 s 52ZK (see PARA 399) or s 52ZM (see PARA 401).
17 Local Government Finance Act 1992 s 52ZR(3)(b) (as added: see note 4).
18 Local Government Finance Act 1992 s 52ZR(4)(a) (as added: see note 4).

19 Ie under the Local Government Finance Act 1992 s 30: see PARA 380.
20 Local Government Finance Act 1992 s 52ZR(4)(b) (as added: see note 4).
21 Local Government Finance Act 1992 s 52ZR(5) (as added: see note 4).
22 Local Government Finance Act 1992 s 52ZR(6)(a) (as added: see note 4).
23 Ie that amount has not been approved as mentioned in the Local Government Finance Act 1992 s 52ZH (where the authority is a billing authority) (see PARA 396) or s 52ZO (where the authority is a precepting authority) (see PARA 403): s 52ZR(6)(b) (as added: see note 4).
24 Local Government Finance Act 1992 s 52ZS(1), (2) (as added: see note 4). If the direction is given before the billing authority has carried out its council tax calculations for the financial year, that amount is to be treated for all purposes as the amount calculated by the billing authority under s 31A (see PARA 382): s 52ZS(3) (as so added). If the direction is given after the billing authority has carried out its council tax calculations for the financial year (whether or not it has set an amount of council tax for the year) those calculations are of no effect (s 52ZS(4)(a) (as so added)), and the authority must make substitute calculations for the year in accordance with s 36A (see PARA 387) (s 52ZS(4)(b) (as so added)). For the purposes of those and any subsequent substitute calculations and the application of Pt I Ch III (ss 30–38) to them:
(1) the amount stated in the direction as the amount of the billing authority's council tax requirement for the financial year is to be treated as the amount calculated by the billing authority under s 31A (s 52ZS(5)(a) (as so added)); and
(2) s 36A(2)(a), (4) is to be ignored (s 52ZS(5)(b) (as so added)).
25 Local Government Finance Act 1992 s 52ZT(1), (2) (as added: see note 4). If the direction is given before the major precepting authority has carried out its council tax calculations for the financial year, that amount is to be treated for all purposes as the amount calculated by the major precepting authority under s 42A (see PARA 12): s 52ZT(3) (as so added). If the direction is given after the major precepting authority has carried out its council tax calculations for the financial year (whether or not it has issued a precept for the year) those calculations are of no effect (s 52ZT(4)(a) (as so added)), and the authority must make substitute calculations for the year in accordance with s 49 (see PARA 13) (s 52ZT(4)(b) (as so added)). For the purposes of those and any subsequent substitute calculations and the application of Pt I Ch III and Ch IV (ss 39–52) to them:
(1) the amount stated in the direction as the amount of the major precepting authority's council tax requirement for the financial year is to be treated as the amount calculated by the billing authority under s 42A (s 52ZT(5)(a) (as so added)); and
(2) s 49(2)(za) (see PARA 13) is to be ignored (s 52ZT(5)(b) (as so added)).
As to directions to the Greater London Authority see further ss 52ZU, 52ZW (both as so added).
26 Local Government Finance Act 1992 s 52ZV(1), (2) (as added: see note 4). That amount is to be treated for all purposes as the amount calculated by the local precepting authority under s 49A (see PARA 19): s 52ZV(3) (as so added). If the direction is given after the local precepting authority has issued a precept for the financial year, that amount is to be treated for all purposes as an amount calculated by the authority in substitution in relation to the year in accordance with that section (so that, in particular, s 42 (see PARA 23) applies accordingly): s 52ZV(4) (as so added).
27 Ie by virtue of any of the Local Government Finance Act 1992 ss 52ZS–52ZU: see the text to notes 23–26.
28 Local Government Finance Act 1992 s 52ZW(1)(a) (as added: see note 4).
29 Ie under the Local Government Finance Act 1992 s 42: see PARA 23.
30 Local Government Finance Act 1992 s 52ZW(1)(b) (as added: see note 4).
31 See the Local Government Finance Act 1992 s 52ZW(1), (3)(b) (as added: see note 4). A local precepting authority to which s 52ZV(4) applies (see note 26) must issue any precepts in substitution required in consequence under s 42 before the end of such period: see s 52ZW(2) (as so added).
32 'The period of restriction' is the period beginning at the end of the period mentioned in the Local Government Finance Act 1992 s 52ZW(3) (see the text to note 31) (s 52ZW(6)(a) (as added: see note 4)), and ending at the time (if any) when the authority complies with s 52ZW(1) or (2) (as the case may be) (see the text to notes 27–31) (s 52ZW(6)(b) (as so added)).
33 Local Government Finance Act 1992 s 52ZW(4) (as added: see note 4). The Local Government Finance Act 1988 ss 97, 98 (see PARA 582) have effect accordingly: see the Local Government Finance Act 1992 s 52ZW(4) (as so added). As to collection and general funds see PARA 579 et seq.
34 Local Government Finance Act 1992 s 52ZW(5) (as added: see note 4). As to precepts generally see PARA 11 et seq.

407. Information.

The Secretary of State[1] may serve on an authority[2] a notice requiring it to supply to him such information[3] as is specified in the notice and required for the purposes of the performance of his functions[4] in relation to council tax referendums[5].

The authority must supply the information required if it is in its possession or control, and must do so in such form and manner and at such time as the Secretary of State specifies in the notice[6]. If an authority fails to comply with this obligation, the Secretary of State may exercise his functions on the basis of such assumptions and estimates as he thinks fit[7]; and in exercising those functions, the Secretary of State may also take into account any other available information, whatever its source and whether or not obtained under a provision contained in or made under the Local Government Finance Act 1992 or any other Act[8].

1 As to the Secretary of State see PARA 4 note 18.
2 As to the meaning of 'authority' see PARA 392 note 1.
3 As to the meaning of 'information' see PARA 345 note 20.
4 Ie under the Local Government Finance Act 1992 Pt I Ch 4ZA (ss 52ZA–52ZY).
5 Local Government Finance Act 1992 s 52ZY(1) (s 52ZY added by the Localism Act 2011 s 72(1), Sch 5).
6 Local Government Finance Act 1992 s 52ZY(2) (as added: see note 5).
7 Local Government Finance Act 1992 s 52ZY(3) (as added: see note 5).
8 Local Government Finance Act 1992 s 52ZY(4) (as added: see note 5).

(4) Valuation Lists: England and Wales

(i) Compilation and Maintenance of Lists

408. Valuations for purposes of lists.

The Commissioners for Her Majesty's Revenue and Customs[1] must:

(1) carry out such valuations of dwellings[2] in England and Wales[3];
(2) furnish listing officers[4] with such information[5] obtained in carrying out the valuations or in the exercise of their powers[6] to obtain information about properties[7]; and
(3) disclose to such officers such contents of particulars delivered documents[8],

as they consider necessary or expedient for the purpose of facilitating the compilation and maintenance by those officers of valuation lists in accordance with the statutory provisions[9]. The valuations must be carried out by reference to the appropriate date[10] and on such assumptions and in accordance with such principles as may be prescribed[11].

Without prejudice to the generality of their powers, the Commissioners for Her Majesty's Revenue and Customs may appoint persons[12] who are not in the service of the Crown to assist them in carrying out the valuations[13]; and, for the purposes of the valuations, the Commissioners may disclose to a person so appointed:

(a) any survey report obtained for any purpose of rating, including non-domestic rating[14]; and
(b) any information obtained in the exercise of their powers[15] to obtain information about properties[16].

If any person to whom any report or information is so disclosed uses or discloses the report or information, in whole or in part, otherwise than for the purposes of the valuations, he commits an offence[17].

1 As to the Commissioners for Her Majesty's Revenue and Customs see INCOME TAXATION vol 58 (2014) PARAS 33–34.
2 As to the meaning of 'dwelling' see PARA 349.
3 Local Government Finance Act 1992 s 21(1)(a). As to the meanings of 'England' and 'Wales' see PARA 2 note 16. As to powers of entry for the purposes of valuation see PARA 413.
4 As to the meaning of 'listing officer' see PARA 347 note 2.
5 As to the meaning of 'information' see PARA 345 note 20.
6 Ie the powers conferred by the Local Government Finance Act 1992 s 27: see PARA 415.
7 Local Government Finance Act 1992 s 21(1)(b).
8 Local Government Finance Act 1992 s 21(1)(c). 'Particulars delivered document' means any document which, having been (whether before or after 6 March 1992):
   (1) produced to the Commissioners for Her Majesty's Revenue and Customs in pursuance of the Finance Act 1931 s 28; or
   (2) furnished to them in pursuance of Sch 2,

   is for the time being in their possession or under their control: Local Government Finance Act 1992 s 69(1) (definition amended by virtue of the Commissioners for Revenue and Customs Act 2005 s 50).
9 Local Government Finance Act 1992 s 21(1) (amended by virtue of the Commissioners for Revenue and Customs Act 2005 s 50). The statutory provisions referred to are those of the Local Government Finance Act 1992 Pt I Ch II (ss 20–29) (valuation lists) (see PARAS 347, 409 et seq): see s 21(1). As to the compilation and maintenance of new lists see PARA 411.
10 The 'appropriate date' is:
   (1) in relation to a list under the Local Government Finance Act 1992 s 22 (see PARA 409), 1 April 1991 (s 21(2A)(a) (s 21(2A), (2B) added by the Local Government Act 2003 s 127(1), Sch 7 paras 40, 44)); and
   (2) in relation to a list under the Local Government Finance Act 1992 s 22B (see PARA 411), the later of:
      (a) two years before the date on which the list falls to be compiled (s 21(2A)(b)(i) (as so added)); and
      (b) such date, if any, within that two year period as may be specified by regulations (s 21(2A)(b)(ii) (as so added)).

   The power to make regulations under head (2)(b) is exercisable:
   (i) in relation to a list to be compiled for a billing authority in England, by the Secretary of State (s 21(2B)(a) (as so added)); and
   (ii) in relation to a list to be compiled for a billing authority in Wales, by the Welsh Ministers (s 21(2B)(b) (as so added)).

   As to the meaning of 'billing authority' see PARA 346. As to the Secretary of State and the Welsh Ministers see PARA 4 note 18. At the date at which this volume states the law, no regulations had been made under s 21(2A), (2B).

   The functions under the Local Government Finance Act 1992 s 21(2B)(b) were formerly vested in the National Assembly for Wales and are now exercisable by the Welsh Ministers by virtue of the Government of Wales Act 2006 s 162(1), Sch 11 paras 30, 32.
11 Local Government Finance Act 1992 s 21(2) (amended by the Local Government Act 2003 Sch 7 paras 40, 44). 'Prescribed' means prescribed by regulations made by the Secretary of State or, in relation to Wales, the Welsh Ministers: see the Local Government Finance Act 1992 s 116(1). As to the regulations made under s 21(2) see the Council Tax (Situation and Valuation of Dwellings) Regulations 1992, SI 1992/550, Pt III (regs 6–7) (reg 6 amended by SI 1994/1747, SI 2005/701 and SI 2008/315). See *Call v Brannan; Call v Kozak* [2015] EWHC 920 (Admin), [2015] All ER (D) 44 (Apr) (pursuant to the Council Tax (Situation and Valuation of Dwellings) Regulations 1992, SI 1992/550 reg 6, flats were to be valued on the basis that they would be subject to conventional long leases at nominal rent, rather than subject to shared ownership leases). The method of valuation prescribed by reg 7 (valuation of dwelling which is, or is contained in, a composite hereditament) is discussed in *Atkinson v Cumbria Valuation Tribunal* (1997) 96 LGR 721, CA, sub nom *Atkinson v Lord (Listing Officer)* [1997] RA 413, CA.

The functions of the Secretary of State under the Local Government Finance Act 1992 s 21(2), so far as exercisable in relation to Wales, were transferred to the National Assembly for Wales (see the National Assembly for Wales (Transfer of Functions) Order 1999, SI 1999/672, art 2, Sch 1) and are now vested in the Welsh Ministers (see the Government of Wales Act 2006 s 162(1), Sch 11 para 30).

12 As to the meaning of 'person' see PARA 11 note 13.

13 Local Government Finance Act 1992 s 21(3).

14 Local Government Finance Act 1992 s 21(4)(a). As to non-domestic rating lists see PARA 188 et seq.

15 Ie the powers conferred by the Local Government Finance Act 1992 s 27: see PARA 415.

16 Local Government Finance Act 1992 s 21(4)(b). Except as provided by s 21(4), nothing in s 21 permits the disclosure to any person appointed under s 21(3) of information which is subject to the rules of confidentiality applicable to the Commissioners for Her Majesty's Revenue and Customs (see INCOME TAXATION vol 58 (2014) PARA 33): s 21(6).

17 See the Local Government Finance Act 1992 s 21(5). The penalty for such an offence is:

(1) on conviction on indictment, imprisonment for a term not exceeding two years or a fine or both (s 21(5)(a)); and

(2) on summary conviction, imprisonment for a term not exceeding six months or a fine not exceeding the statutory maximum or both (s 21(5)(b)).

As to the powers of magistrates' courts to issue fines on summary conviction see SENTENCING vol 92 (2015) PARA 176.

409. Compilation and maintenance of first valuation lists.

The listing officer[1] for a billing authority[2] had to compile a list for the authority (to be called its 'valuation list') in accordance with the statutory provisions[3]. The list was to be compiled on 1 April 1993 (and came into force on that day)[4]. As soon as reasonably practicable after compiling a list the listing officer had to send a copy of it to the authority[5]; and as soon as reasonably practicable after receiving the copy the authority had to deposit it at its principal office[6].

The list remains in force until a new list[7] for the authority is compiled[8]. The listing officer is under a duty to maintain the list[9]; and the list must be maintained for so long as was necessary for the purposes of the Local Government Finance Act 1992[10].

1 As to the meaning of 'listing officer' see PARA 347 note 2.

2 As to the meaning of 'billing authority' see PARA 346.

3 See the Local Government Finance Act 1992 s 22(1). The statutory provisions referred to are those of Pt I Ch II (ss 20–29): see s 22(1). Before the first list was compiled, the listing officer had to take such steps as were reasonably practicable in the time available to ensure that it was accurately compiled on 1 April 1993: see s 22(3). Any valuation of a dwelling carried out by the listing officer in pursuance of s 22(3) had to be carried out in accordance with s 21(2) (see PARA 408): see s 22(4). At the following times, namely:

(1) not later than 1 September 1992; and

(2) not earlier than 15 November 1992 and not later than 1 December 1992,

the listing officer had to send to the billing authority a copy of the list which he proposed (on the information then before him) to compile: see s 22(5). As soon as reasonably practicable after receiving the copy the authority had to deposit it at its principal office and take such steps as it thought most suitable for giving notice of it: see s 22(6). As to amalgamated valuation lists for Wales see PARA 410.

4 See the Local Government Finance Act 1992 s 22(2).

5 See the Local Government Finance Act 1992 s 22(7).

6 See the Local Government Finance Act 1992 s 22(8).

7 Ie compiled under the Local Government Finance Act 1992 s 22B: see PARA 411.

8 See the Local Government Finance Act 1992 s 22(2) (amended by the Local Government Act 2003 s 127(1), Sch 7 paras 40, 45).

9 See the Local Government Finance Act 1992 s 22(1).

10 See the Local Government Finance Act 1992 s 22(9).

410. Amalgamated valuation lists for Welsh billing authorities.

Following the reorganisation of local government in Wales under the Local Government (Wales) Act 1994[1], every new listing officer appointed for a new billing authority[2] had, on 1 April 1996, to compile a list (the 'amalgamated list') for that authority, based on the information provided for him[3]. A new listing officer's amalgamated list was to be treated, for the purposes of the Local Government Finance Act 1992, as the valuation list for his new billing authority and was deemed to have come into force on 1 April 1993[4].

1 As to local government areas and authorities in Wales see LOCAL GOVERNMENT vol 69 (2018) PARA 51 et seq.

2 'New billing authority' means an authority which is a new principal council within the meaning of the Local Government (Wales) Act 1994 (see LOCAL GOVERNMENT vol 69 (2018) PARA 51): Local Government Finance Act 1992 s 22A(11) (s 22A added by the Local Government (Wales) Act 1994 s 36).

3 See the Local Government Finance Act 1992 s 22A(1)–(3), (5)–(10) (as added: see note 2). As to the compilation and maintenance of new lists see PARA 411.

4 See the Local Government Finance Act 1992 s 22A(4) (as added: see note 2).

411. Compilation and maintenance of new lists: England and Wales.

The listing officer[1] for a billing authority[2] must compile, and then maintain, new lists for the authority in accordance with the statutory provisions[3] (each such list to be called its 'valuation list')[4].

A new list must be compiled:

(1) in relation to billing authorities in England[5], on 1 April in each year specified by order made by the Secretary of State[6]; and

(2) in relation to billing authorities in Wales[7], on 1 April 2005[8], and, after that, on 1 April in each year specified by order made by the Welsh Ministers[9].

A new list comes into force on the day on which it is compiled and remains in force until the next such list is compiled[10]. The duty to maintain a new list[11] continues for so long as is necessary for the purposes of the Local Government Finance Act 1992[12] and is not affected by the list ceasing to be in force[13].

Before a new list is compiled[14], the listing officer must take such steps as are reasonably practicable in the time available to ensure that it is accurately compiled on the date on which it is to be compiled[15].

Where a new list is to be compiled[16], the listing officer for a billing authority must send the authority a copy of the list he proposes to compile (on the information[17] then before him) not later than 1 September before the date on which it is to be compiled[18]. As soon as reasonably practicable after receiving such a copy list, a billing authority must deposit it at its principal office and take such steps as it thinks most suitable for giving notice of it[19].

As soon as reasonably practicable after the listing officer for a billing authority has compiled a new list[20], he must send a copy of it to the authority[21]. As soon as reasonably practicable after receiving such a copy list, a billing authority must deposit it at its principal office[22].

The appropriate national authority[23] may by regulations make provision for the purpose of smoothing changes in council tax liability[24] resulting from the coming into force[25] in relation to a billing authority of a new list[26]. Such regulations may, in particular:

(a) make provision about the circumstances in which changes are to be smoothed[27];

(b) make provision for changes to be smoothed over such one or more financial years[28] as may be specified in the regulations[29];

(c) make provision for liability for any financial year to be determined in accordance with such rules as may be so specified, which may result in liability being the same as or different from what it would otherwise be[30],

and may make different provision for different financial years[31].

1 As to the meaning of 'listing officer' see PARA 347 note 2.

2 As to the meaning of 'billing authority' see PARA 346.

3 Ie in accordance with the Local Government Finance Act 1992 Pt I Ch II (ss 20–29).

4 Local Government Finance Act 1992 s 22B(1) (s 22B added by the Local Government Act 2003 s 77).

5 As to the meaning of 'England' see PARA 2 note 16.

6 Local Government Finance Act 1992 s 22B(1A) (s 22B as added (see note 4); s 22B(1A) added by the Council Tax (New Valuation Lists for England) Act 2006 s 1(1), (2)). No such order may be made unless a draft of the order has been laid before, and approved by resolution of, the House of Commons: Local Government Finance Act 1992 s 22B(11) (as so added; amended by the Council Tax (New Valuation Lists for England) Act 2006 s 1(1), (5)). At the date at which this volume states the law, no such order had been made. As to the Secretary of State see PARA 4 note 18. As to the laying of documents before Parliament see STATUTES AND LEGISLATIVE PROCESS vol 96 (2013) PARA 1052. As to the compilation of first valuation lists see PARA 409.

7 As to the meaning of 'Wales' see PARA 2 note 16.

8 Local Government Finance Act 1992 s 22B(2) (as added (see note 4); amended by the Council Tax (New Valuation Lists for England) Act 2006 s 1(1), (3)). As to amalgamated valuation lists in Wales see PARA 410.

9 Local Government Finance Act 1992 s 22B(3) (as added (see note 4); amended by the Council Tax (New Valuation Lists for England) Act 2006 s 1(1), (4); and the Localism Act 2011 s 80(1), (2))). No such order may be made unless a draft of the statutory instrument containing it has been laid before, and approved by a resolution of, the National Assembly for Wales: Local Government Finance Act 1992 s 22B(12) (added by the Localism Act 2011 s 80(1), (3)). At the date at which this volume states the law, no such order had been made. As to the Welsh Ministers see PARA 4 note 18. As to the National Assembly for Wales see CONSTITUTIONAL AND ADMINISTRATIVE LAW vol 20 (2014) PARA 351 et seq.

10 Local Government Finance Act 1992 s 22B(4) (as added: see note 4).

11 Ie a list compiled under the Local Government Finance Act 1992 s 22B.

12 Ie the purposes of the Local Government Finance Act 1992 Pt I (ss 1–69).

13 Local Government Finance Act 1992 s 22B(5) (as added: see note 4).

14 Ie under the Local Government Finance Act 1992 s 22B.

15 Local Government Finance Act 1992 s 22B(6) (as added: see note 4).

16 Ie under the Local Government Finance Act 1992 s 22B.

17 As to the meaning of 'information' see PARA 345 note 20.

18 Local Government Finance Act 1992 s 22B(7) (as added: see note 4).

19 Local Government Finance Act 1992 s 22B(8) (as added: see note 4).

20 Ie under the Local Government Finance Act 1992 s 22B.

21 Local Government Finance Act 1992 s 22B(9) (as added: see note 4).

22 Local Government Finance Act 1992 s 22B(10) (as added: see note 4).

23 Ie the Secretary of State or, in relation to Wales, the Welsh Ministers. The functions of the Secretary of State under the Local Government Finance Act 1992 s 13B, so far as exercisable in relation to Wales, were transferred to the National Assembly for Wales (see the National Assembly for Wales (Transfer of Functions) Order 1999, SI 1999/672, art 2, Sch 1) and are now vested in the Welsh Ministers (see the Government of Wales Act 2006 s 162(1), Sch 11 para 30).

24 As to persons liable to pay council tax see PARA 354 et seq.

25 Ie under the Local Government Finance Act 1992 s 22B: see the text to notes 1–22.

26 See the Local Government Finance Act 1992 s 13B(1)(b), (2)(b) (s 13B added by the Local Government Act 2003 s 79). To the extent that he would not have power to do so apart from this provision, the Secretary of State may:

(1) include in regulations made by him under the Local Government Finance Act 1992 s 13B such amendments of any social security instrument as he thinks expedient in consequence of the regulations (s 13B(5)(a) (as so added));

(2) include in any social security instrument such provision as he thinks expedient in consequence of regulations under s 13B (s 13B(5)(b) (as so added)).

As to the meaning of 'social security instrument' see PARA 377 note 27 (definition applied by s 13B(6) (as so added)).

As to the regulations made under s 13B(2) see the Council Tax (Transitional Arrangements) (Wales) Regulations 2004, SI 2004/3142 (amended by SI 2005/702), which make transitional arrangements for the period from 1 April 2005 to 31 March 2008 in relation to Wales.

27 Local Government Finance Act 1992 s 13B(3)(a) (as added: see note 26).
28 As to the meaning of 'financial year' see PARA 11 note 1.
29 Local Government Finance Act 1992 s 13B(3)(b) (as added: see note 26).
30 Local Government Finance Act 1992 s 13B(3)(c) (as added: see note 26).
31 See the Local Government Finance Act 1992 s 13B(4) (as added: see note 26). This provision is expressed to be without prejudice to s 113(1) (see PARA 345): see s 13B(4) (as so added).

412. Contents of lists.

A valuation list[1] must show, for each day for which it is in force, each dwelling[2] which is situated in the billing authority's area[3]. For each day on which a dwelling is shown in a list, the list must also show which of the valuation bands[4] is applicable to the dwelling[5]; and must contain such information[6] about dwellings shown in it as may be prescribed[7].

For each day on which a dwelling is shown in a valuation list[8], the list must also contain[9]:

(1) the reference number ascribed to the dwelling by the listing officer[10];
(2) if it be the case, an indication that the dwelling is a composite hereditament[11];
(3) where the list is altered as regards the dwelling[12], an indication:
    (a) of the period for which (or, as the case may be, the day from which) the alteration has effect[13]; and
    (b) if it be the case, that the alteration was made pursuant to the order of a valuation tribunal or the High Court[14].

The omission from a list of any matter required to be included in it does not of itself render the list invalid[15]. Any rules as to Crown exemption which otherwise would have applied[16] do not prevent a list showing a dwelling, showing the valuation band applicable to a dwelling and containing any prescribed information about a dwelling[17].

1 As to valuation lists see PARAS 408–436.
2 As to the meaning of 'dwelling' see PARA 349.
3 Local Government Finance Act 1992 s 23(1). As to the meaning of 'billing authority' see PARA 346. As to the power to make regulations containing rules for ascertaining in what part of a billing authority's area a dwelling is situated see s 10(2); and PARA 360; and as to the power to make regulations containing rules for treating a dwelling as situated in a billing authority's area if part only of the dwelling falls within the area see s 1(3); and PARA 348.
4 As to valuation bands see PARA 361.
5 Local Government Finance Act 1992 s 23(2).
6 As to the meaning of 'information' see PARA 345 note 20.
7 Local Government Finance Act 1992 s 23(3). 'Prescribed' means prescribed by regulations made by the Secretary of State or, in relation to Wales, the Welsh Ministers: see s 116(1). As to the regulations made under s 23(3) see the text to notes 8–14.

The functions of the Secretary of State under the Local Government Finance Act 1992 s 23, so far as exercisable in relation to Wales, were transferred to the National Assembly for Wales (see the National Assembly for Wales (Transfer of Functions) Order 1999, SI 1999/672, art 2, Sch 1) and are now vested in the Welsh Ministers (see the Government of Wales Act 2006 s 162(1), Sch 11 para 30). As to the Secretary of State and the Welsh Ministers see PARA 4 note 18. As to the meaning of 'Wales' see PARA 2 note 16.

8 Ie a valuation list compiled under the Local Government Finance Act 1992 s 22 (see PARA 409)

or s 22A (see PARA 410): see the Council Tax (Contents of Valuation Lists) Regulations 1992, SI 1992/553, reg 1(2) (amended by SI 1996/619).

9 Council Tax (Contents of Valuation Lists) Regulations 1992, SI 1992/553, reg 2. The information specified in heads (1) to (3) in the text is in addition to the matters required to be shown by the Local Government Finance Act 1992 s 23(1), (2) (see the text to notes 1–5): see the Council Tax (Contents of Valuation Lists) Regulations 1992, SI 1992/553, reg 2.

10 Council Tax (Contents of Valuation Lists) Regulations 1992, SI 1992/553, reg 2(a). As to the meaning of 'listing officer' see PARA 347 note 2.

11 Council Tax (Contents of Valuation Lists) Regulations 1992, SI 1992/553, reg 2(b). A dwelling is a composite hereditament if it is one to which the Local Government Finance Act 1992 s 3(3) (see PARA 349) applies: see the Council Tax (Contents of Valuation Lists) Regulations 1992, SI 1992/553, reg 2(b).

12 As to alterations to valuation lists see PARA 417 et seq.

13 Council Tax (Contents of Valuation Lists) Regulations 1992, SI 1992/553, reg 2(c)(i).

14 Council Tax (Contents of Valuation Lists) Regulations 1992, SI 1992/553, reg 2(c)(ii). As to orders of a valuation tribunal see PARA 531. As to orders of the High Court see PARAS 560, 562.

15 Local Government Finance Act 1992 s 23(4).

16 Ie would have applied apart from the Local Government Finance Act 1992 s 23(5). As to Crown exemption from council tax see PARA 359.

17 Local Government Finance Act 1992 s 23(5).

413. Powers of entry: England.

If a valuation officer[1] needs to value a dwelling[2] in England[3] for the purpose of carrying out any of the officer's functions, the officer and any servant of the Crown authorised by the officer in writing[4] may enter on, survey and value the dwelling if the conditions in heads (1) and (2) and (where it applies) head (3) below[5] are fulfilled[6]:

(1) the valuation officer must obtain the approval of the tribunal[7] before the officer or a person authorised by the officer exercises the power of entry[8];

(2) after the tribunal has given its approval, at least three days' notice in writing must be given of the proposed exercise of the power[9];

(3) in a case where a person authorised by a valuation officer proposes to exercise the power, that person must if required produce the authorisation[10].

A person who intentionally delays or obstructs a person in the exercise of such power of entry commits an offence[11].

The tribunal may:

(a) determine any application brought under these provisions and any question arising from that application[12];

(b) specify the arrangements by which any entry approved by it must be conducted, including whether the entry may occur on more than one day[13].

1 In the Local Government Finance Act 1992 s 25A, 'valuation officer' means any listing officer and any other officer of Revenue and Customs who is for the time being appointed by the Commissioners of Her Majesty's Revenue and Customs to carry out any of their functions: s 25A(9) (s 25A added by SI 2015/982). As to the meaning of 'listing officer', and as to the meaning of references to the functions of listing officers and the Commissioners, see PARA 347 note 2. As to the Commissioners for Her Majesty's Revenue and Customs see INCOME TAXATION vol 58 (2014) PARAS 33–34.

2 As to the meaning of 'dwelling' see PARA 349. As to valuations see PARA 408.

3 As to the meaning of 'England' see PARA 2 note 16. As to powers of entry in relation to houses in Wales see PARA 414.

4 As to the meaning of 'writing' see PARA 21 note 3.

5 Ie the Local Government Finance Act 1992 s 25A(2), (4) and (where it applies) s 25A(5).

6 Local Government Finance Act 1992 s 25A(1) (as added: see note 1).

7 Ie the Upper Tribunal: Local Government Finance Act 1992 s 25A(9) (as added: see note 1). As to the Upper Tribunal see COURTS AND TRIBUNALS vol 24 (2010) PARA 874 et seq.
8 Local Government Finance Act 1992 s 25A(2) (as added: see note 1). The tribunal must not give its approval unless it is satisfied that the valuation officer needs to value the dwelling: s 25A(3) (as so added).
9 Local Government Finance Act 1992 s 25A(4) (as added: see note 1). For the purpose of the requirement under s 25A(4), the following days are to be disregarded (s 25A(7) (as so added)):
(1) a Saturday, a Sunday, Christmas Day or Good Friday (s 25A(7)(a) (as so added));
(2) a day which is a bank holiday (see TIME vol 97 (2015) PARA 321) under the Banking and Financial Dealings Act 1971 in England and Wales (Local Government Finance Act 1992 s 25A(7)(b) (as so added)).
10 Local Government Finance Act 1992 s 25A(5) (as added: see note 1).
11 Local Government Finance Act 1992 s 25A(6) (as added: see note 1). The penalty for such an offence is, on summary conviction, a fine not exceeding level 1 on the standard scale: see s 25A(6) (as so added). As to the powers of magistrates' courts to issue fines on summary conviction see SENTENCING vol 92 (2015) PARA 176.
12 Local Government Finance Act 1992 s 25A(8)(a) (as added: see note 1).
13 Local Government Finance Act 1992 s 25A(8)(b) (as added: see note 1).

414. Powers of entry: Wales.

If a valuation officer[1] needs to value a dwelling[2] in Wales[3] for the purpose of carrying out any of his functions, he and any servant of the Crown authorised by him in writing[4] may enter on, survey and value the dwelling, so long as the conditions in heads (1) and (2) below are fulfilled[5]:

(1) at least three clear days' notice in writing of the proposed exercise of the power is given[6]; and
(2) in a case where a person authorised by a valuation officer proposes to exercise the power, that person (if required) produces his authority[7].

If a person intentionally delays or obstructs a person in the exercise of such power of entry, he commits an offence[8].

1 In the Local Government Finance Act 1992 ss 26, 27 (see PARA 415), 'valuation officer' means any listing officer and any other officer of the Commissioners for Her Majesty's Revenue and Customs who is for the time being appointed by them to carry out any of their functions: Local Government Finance Act 1992 s 26(5) (amended by virtue of the Commissioners for Revenue and Customs Act 2005 s 50). As to the meaning of 'listing officer', and as to the meaning of references to the functions of listing officers and the Commissioners, see PARA 347 note 2. As to the Commissioners for Her Majesty's Revenue and Customs see INCOME TAXATION vol 58 (2014) PARAS 33–34.
2 As to the meaning of 'dwelling' see PARA 349. As to valuations see PARA 408.
3 As to the meaning of 'Wales' see PARA 2 note 16. As to powers of entry in relation to houses in England see PARA 403.
4 As to the meaning of 'writing' see PARA 21 note 3.
5 See the Local Government Finance Act 1992 s 26(1) (amended by SI 2015/982).
6 Local Government Finance Act 1992 s 26(2). There must be disregarded for this purpose:
(1) any day which is a Saturday, a Sunday, Christmas Day or Good Friday (s 26(2)(a)); or
(2) a day which is a bank holiday under the Banking and Financial Dealings Act 1971 (see TIME vol 97 (2015) PARA 321) in England and Wales (Local Government Finance Act 1992 s 26(2)(b)).
7 Local Government Finance Act 1992 s 26(3).
8 See the Local Government Finance Act 1992 s 26(4). The penalty for such an offence is, on summary conviction, a fine not exceeding level 2 on the standard scale: see s 26(4). As to the powers of magistrates' courts to issue fines on summary conviction see SENTENCING vol 92 (2015) PARA 176.

415. Information about properties: England and Wales.

In any case where:

(1) a notice is served by a listing officer[1] or the Commissioners for Her Majesty's Revenue and Customs[2] on a charging or billing authority[3], a community charges registration officer[4] or any other person prescribed for these purposes[5];

(2) the notice requests the supply of information[6] of a description specified in the notice[7]; and

(3) the information relates to property and is information which the listing officer or the Commissioners reasonably believe will assist him or them in carrying out any of his or their functions[8],

the authority, officer or other person must supply the information requested, and must do so in such form and manner and at such time as the listing officer or the Commissioners specify in the notice[9].

For the purpose of carrying out any of his functions, a valuation officer[10] may serve on a person who is or has been an owner[11] or occupier of any dwelling[12] a notice:

(a) requesting him to supply to the officer information which is of a description specified in the notice[13]; and

(b) stating that the officer believes the information requested will assist him in carrying out his functions[14].

A person on whom such a notice is served must supply the information requested if it is in his possession or control, and must do so in such form and manner as is specified in the notice and within the period of 21 days beginning with the day on which the notice is served[15]. If a person on whom such a notice has been served[16] fails without reasonable excuse to comply with this provision, he commits an offence[17]. If a person[18], in supplying information in purported compliance with a request for information from a valuation officer, either makes a statement which he knows to be false in a material particular[19] or recklessly makes a statement which is false in a material particular[20], he commits an offence[21].

If in the course of the exercise of its functions any information comes to the notice of a charging or billing authority which it considers would assist a listing officer in carrying out any of his functions, it is the authority's duty to inform the listing officer[22].

In carrying out any of his or their functions, a listing officer or the Commissioners for Her Majesty's Revenue and Customs may also take into account any other information available to him or them, whatever its source and whether or not obtained under a provision contained in or made under the Local Government Finance Act 1992 or any other Act[23].

1 As to the meaning of 'listing officer' see PARA 347 note 2.

2 As to the Commissioners for Her Majesty's Revenue and Customs see INCOME TAXATION vol 58 (2014) PARAS 33–34.

3 'Charging authority' is to be construed in accordance with the Local Government Finance Act 1988 s 144(1) (see PARA 24 note 2): Local Government Finance Act 1992 s 27(8). As to the meaning of 'billing authority' see PARA 346.

4 'Community charges registration officer' is to be construed in accordance with the Local Government Finance Act 1988 s 26 (repealed): Local Government Finance Act 1992 s 27(8). With effect from 1 April 1993, the community charge was abolished and replaced with the council tax: see PARA 344 et seq.

5 Local Government Finance Act 1992 s 27(1)(a). 'Prescribed' means prescribed by regulations made by the Secretary of State or, in relation to Wales, the Welsh Ministers: see s 116(1). As to the meaning of 'person' see PARA 11 note 13. At the date at which this volume states the law, no such regulations had been made.

The functions of the Secretary of State under the Local Government Finance Act 1992 s 27, so far as exercisable in relation to Wales, were transferred to the National Assembly for Wales (see the National Assembly for Wales (Transfer of Functions) Order 1999, SI 1999/672, art 2, Sch 1) and are now vested in the Welsh Ministers (see the Government of Wales Act 2006 s 162(1), Sch 11 para 30). As to the Secretary of State and the Welsh Ministers see PARA 4 note 18. As to the meaning of 'Wales' see PARA 2 note 16.

6 As to the meaning of 'information' see PARA 345 note 20.

7 Local Government Finance Act 1992 s 27(1)(b).

8 Local Government Finance Act 1992 s 27(1)(c). As to the meaning of references to the functions of listing officers and the Commissioners see PARA 347 note 2.

9 Local Government Finance Act 1992 s 27(1).

10 As to the meaning of 'valuation officer' see PARA 413 note 1.

11 As to the meaning of 'owner' see PARA 354 note 15.

12 As to the meaning of 'dwelling' see PARA 349.

13 Local Government Finance Act 1992 s 27(2)(a).

14 Local Government Finance Act 1992 s 27(2)(b).

15 Local Government Finance Act 1992 s 27(3).

16 Ie under the Local Government Finance Act 1992 s 27(2): see the text to notes 10–14.

17 See the Local Government Finance Act 1992 s 27(4). The penalty for such an offence is, on summary conviction, a fine not exceeding level 2 on the standard scale: s 27(4). As to the powers of magistrates' courts to issue fines on summary conviction see SENTENCING vol 92 (2015) PARA 176.

18 Ie a person on whom a notice has been served under the Local Government Finance Act 1992 s 27(2): see the text to notes 10–14.

19 Local Government Finance Act 1992 s 27(5)(a). As to knowledge in these circumstances see PARA 226 note 8.

20 Local Government Finance Act 1992 s 27(5)(b). As to recklessness in criminal law see CRIMINAL LAW vol 25 (2016) PARA 11.

21 See the Local Government Finance Act 1992 s 27(5). The penalty for such an offence is, on summary conviction, imprisonment for a term not exceeding three months or a fine not exceeding level 3 on the standard scale or both: s 27(5). As from a day to be appointed under the Criminal Justice Act 2003 s 336(3), the reference in the Local Government Finance Act 1992 s 27(5) to 'imprisonment for a term not exceeding three months' (and the corresponding reference to 'or both') is repealed: see s 27(5) (prospectively amended by the Criminal Justice Act 2003 s 332, Sch 37 Pt 9). At the date at which this volume states the law, no such day had been appointed.

22 Local Government Finance Act 1992 s 27(6).

23 Local Government Finance Act 1992 s 27(7).

416. Information about valuation lists.

A person[1] may require a listing officer[2] to give him access to such information[3] as will enable him to establish what is the state of a list[4] (or has been its state at any time since it came into force) if:

(1) the officer is maintaining the list[5]; and

(2) the list is in force or has been in force at any time in the preceding five years[6].

A person may require a billing authority[7] to give him access to such information as will enable him to establish what is the state of a copy of a list (or has been its state at any time since it was deposited)[8] if:

(a) the authority has deposited such a copy[9]; and

(b) the list is in force or has been in force at any time in the preceding five years[10].

A person may also require a billing authority to give him access to such information as will enable him to establish what is the state of a copy of a proposed list[11] if:

(i) the authority has deposited such a copy[12]; and

(ii) the list itself is not yet in force[13].

Any such requirement for access to information[14] must be complied with at a reasonable time and place and without payment being sought; but the information may be in documentary or other form, as the person or authority of whom the requirement is made thinks fit[15]. Where access is given to information in documentary form, the person to whom access is given may make copies of (or of extracts from) the document[16]; and may require a person having custody of the document to supply to him a photographic copy of (or of extracts from) the document[17]. Where access is given to information in a form which is not documentary, the person to whom access is given may make transcripts of (or of extracts from) the information[18]; and may require a person having control of access to the information to supply to him a copy in documentary form of (or of extracts from) the information[19]. If a reasonable charge is required for the copying or transcribing of (or extracting from) documents[20], the facility may not be made available to a person[21] unless the person seeking to avail himself of the facility pays the charge[22].

If without reasonable excuse a person having custody of a document containing (or having control of access to) information access to which is sought[23]:

(A) intentionally obstructs a person in exercising any right[24] of access to (or of copying, transcribing or extracting from) any such document[25]; or

(B) refuses to comply with a requirement[26] to supply a copy of the information (or of extracts from the information) in photographic or documentary form[27],

he commits an offence[28].

1 As to the meaning of 'person' see PARA 11 note 13.
2 As to the meaning of 'listing officer' see PARA 347 note 2.
3 As to the meaning of 'information' see PARA 345 note 20.
4 As to valuation lists see PARAS 409–411.
5 Local Government Finance Act 1992 s 28(1)(a). As to the duty of a listing officer to maintain a list PARAS 409–412.
6 Local Government Finance Act 1992 s 28(1)(b).
7 As to the meaning of 'billing authority' see PARA 346.
8 Local Government Finance Act 1992 s 28(2).
9 See the Local Government Finance Act 1992 s 28(2)(a) (amended by the Local Government (Wales) Act 1994 s 66(6), Sch 16 para 97; and the Local Government Act 2003 s 127(1), Sch 7 paras 40, 48). The deposit of a copy referred to is that under the Local Government Finance Act 1992 s 22(8) (see PARA 409), s 22A(10) (see PARA 410) or s 22B(10) (see PARA 411): see s 28(2)(a) (as so amended).
10 Local Government Finance Act 1992 s 28(2)(b).
11 Local Government Finance Act 1992 s 28(3).
12 Local Government Finance Act 1992 s 28(3)(a) (amended by the Local Government Act 2003 Sch 7 paras 40, 48). The deposit of a copy referred to is that under the Local Government Finance Act 1992 s 22(6) (see PARA 409) or s 22B(8) (see PARA 411): see s 28(3)(a) (as so amended).
13 Local Government Finance Act 1992 s 28(3)(b).
14 Ie a requirement under the Local Government Finance Act 1992 s 28(1), (2) or (3): see the text to notes 1–13.
15 Local Government Finance Act 1992 s 28(4).
16 Local Government Finance Act 1992 s 28(5)(a).
17 Local Government Finance Act 1992 s 28(5)(b).
18 Local Government Finance Act 1992 s 28(6)(a).
19 Local Government Finance Act 1992 s 28(6)(b).
20 Ie if a reasonable charge is required for a facility under the Local Government Finance Act 1992 s 28(5) (see the text to notes 16–17) or s 28(6) (see the text to notes 18–19).
21 Ie the Local Government Finance Act 1992 s 28(5) (see the text to notes 16–17) or s 28(6) (see the text to notes 18–19), as the case may be, does not apply.
22 Local Government Finance Act 1992 s 28(7).
23 Ie under the Local Government Finance Act 1992 s 28.

24 Ie a right under the Local Government Finance Act 1992 s 28(1), (2), (3) (see the text to notes 1–13), s 28(5)(a) (see the text to note 16) or s 28(6)(a) (see the text to note 18).
25 See the Local Government Finance Act 1992 s 28(8)(a).
26 Ie a requirement under the Local Government Finance Act 1992 s 28(5)(b) (see the text to note 17) or s 28(6)(b) (see the text to note 19).
27 See the Local Government Finance Act 1992 s 28(8)(b).
28 See the Local Government Finance Act 1992 s 28(8). The penalty for such an offence is, on summary conviction, a fine not exceeding level 2 on the standard scale: s 28(8). As to the powers of magistrates' courts to issue fines on summary conviction see SENTENCING vol 92 (2015) PARA 176.

(ii) Alteration of Lists

A. IN GENERAL

417. Power to make regulations about the alteration of lists.

The appropriate national authority[1] may make regulations[2] about the alteration by listing officers[3] of valuation lists which have been compiled under the statutory provisions[4].

The regulations may include provision:

(1) that where a listing officer intends to alter the list with a view to its being accurately maintained, he must not alter it unless prescribed[5] conditions (as to notice or otherwise) are fulfilled[6];
(2) that any valuation of a dwelling[7] carried out in connection with a proposal for the alteration of the list must be carried out in accordance with the relevant statutory provision[8];
(3) that no alteration may be made of a valuation band[9] shown in the list as applicable to any dwelling unless[10]:
   (a) since the valuation band was first shown in the list as applicable to the dwelling:
   (b) there has been a material increase[11] in the value of the dwelling and a relevant transaction[12] has been subsequently carried out in relation to the whole or any part of it[13];
   (c) there has been a material reduction[14] in the value of the dwelling[15];
   (d) the dwelling has become or ceased to be a composite hereditament for the purposes of the non-domestic rating provisions[16]; or
   (e) in the case of a dwelling which continues to be such a hereditament, there has been an increase or reduction in its domestic use[17], and (in any case) prescribed conditions are fulfilled[18];
   (f) the listing officer is satisfied that a different valuation band should have been determined by him as applicable to the dwelling[19] or the valuation band shown in the list is not that determined by him as so applicable[20]; or
   (g) an order of a valuation tribunal or of the High Court requires the alteration to be made[21];
(4) as to who (other than a listing officer) may make a proposal for the alteration of the list with a view to its being accurately maintained[22];
(5) as to the manner and circumstances in which a proposal may be made and the information to be included in a proposal[23];
(6) as to the period within which a proposal must be made[24];

(7) as to the procedure for and subsequent to the making of a proposal[25];

(8) as to the circumstances in which and the conditions upon which a proposal may be withdrawn[26];

(9) requiring the listing officer to inform other prescribed persons of the proposal in a prescribed manner[27];

(10) that, where there is a disagreement between the listing officer and another person making a proposal for the alteration of a list either about the validity of the proposal or about the accuracy of the list, an appeal may be made to a valuation tribunal[28];

(11) as to the period for which or day from which an alteration of a list is to have effect (including provision that it is to have retrospective effect)[29];

(12) requiring a list to be altered so as to indicate the effect (retrospective or otherwise) of the alteration[30];

(13) requiring the listing officer to inform prescribed persons of an alteration within a prescribed period[31];

(14) requiring the listing officer to keep for a prescribed period a record of the state of the list before the alteration was made[32];

(15) as to financial adjustments to be made as a result of alterations, including provision requiring payments or repayments to be made[33]; and provision as to the recovery (by deduction or otherwise) of sums due[34];

(16) that where the listing officer for a billing authority has informed the authority of an alteration of the list[35], and where a copy of the list has been deposited by the authority at its principal office[36], the authority must alter the copy accordingly[37].

1 Ie the Secretary of State or, in relation to Wales, the Welsh Ministers. The functions of the Secretary of State under the Local Government Finance Act 1992 s 24, so far as exercisable in relation to Wales, were transferred to the National Assembly for Wales (see the National Assembly for Wales (Transfer of Functions) Order 1999, SI 1999/672, art 2, Sch 1) and are now vested in the Welsh Ministers (see the Government of Wales Act 2006 s 162(1), Sch 11 para 30). As to the Secretary of State and the Welsh Ministers see PARA 4 note 18. As to the meaning of 'Wales' see PARA 2 note 16.

2 As to the regulations made see the Council Tax (Alteration of Lists and Appeals) Regulations 1993, SI 1993/290 (revoked, in relation to England, by SI 2009/2270; amended by SI 1994/1746, SI 1996/619, SI 2005/181, SI 2009/1307, SI 2010/613, SI 2010/77 and SI 2010/713); the Valuation Tribunal for England (Council Tax and Rating Appeals) (Procedure) Regulations 2009, SI 2009/2269 (amended by SI 2011/434, SI 2013/465 and SI 2017/156); the Council Tax (Alteration of Lists and Appeals) (England) Regulations 2009, SI 2009/2270 (amended by SI 2013/467); the Valuation Tribunal for Wales Regulations 2010, SI 2010/713 (amended by SI 2013/547, SI 2014/554, SI 2016/481 and SI 2017/941); and PARAS 419 et seq, 428 et seq, 514 et seq.

3 As to the meaning of 'listing officer' see PARA 347 note 2.

4 Local Government Finance Act 1992 s 24(1). The statutory provisions referred to are those of Pt I Ch II (ss 20–29): see s 24(1). The provisions of s 24(2)–(10) (see the text to notes 5–37) apply for the purposes of s 24(1): see s 24(1). As to valuation lists see PARAS 409–411.

5 'Prescribed' means prescribed by regulations made by the appropriate national authority: see the Local Government Finance Act 1992 s 116(1).

6 Local Government Finance Act 1992 s 24(2). As to the duty of a listing officer to maintain a valuation list see PARAS 409–412.

7 As to the meaning of 'dwelling' see PARA 349.

8 Local Government Finance Act 1992 s 24(3). The relevant statutory provision is s 21(2) (see PARA 408): see s 24(3).

9 As to valuation bands see PARA 361.

10 Local Government Finance Act 1992 s 24(4).

11 'Material increase', in relation to the value of a dwelling, means any increase which is caused (in whole or in part) by any building, engineering or other operation carried out in relation to the dwelling, whether or not constituting development for which planning permission is required: Local Government Finance Act 1992 s 24(10). As to the meaning of development in relation to planning permission see PLANNING vol 81 (2018) PARA 333.
12 'Relevant transaction' means a transfer on sale of the fee simple, a grant of a lease for a term of seven years or more or a transfer on sale of such a lease: Local Government Finance Act 1992 s 24(10).
13 Local Government Finance Act 1992 s 24(4)(a)(i).
14 'Material reduction', in relation to the value of a dwelling, means any reduction which is caused (in whole or in part) by the demolition of any part of the dwelling, any change in the physical state of the dwelling's locality or any adaptation of the dwelling to make it suitable for use by a physically disabled person: Local Government Finance Act 1992 s 24(10). For these purposes, it has been held that an increase in noise and fumes caused by an intensification in the use of a nearby road is not capable of being a 'change in the physical state of the dwelling's locality': see *Chilton-Merryweather v Hunt* [2008] EWCA Civ 1025, [2008] RA 357, [2008] All ER (D) 96 (Sep).
15 Local Government Finance Act 1992 s 24(4)(a)(ii).
16 Local Government Finance Act 1992 s 24(4)(a)(iii). The relevant provisions are those of the Local Government Finance Act 1988 Pt III (ss 41–67) (see PARA 80 et seq): see the Local Government Finance Act 1992 s 24(4)(a)(iii).
17 Local Government Finance Act 1992 s 24(4)(a)(iv). 'Domestic use', in relation to a dwelling, means use in such a manner as to constitute it domestic property for the purposes of the Local Government Finance Act 1988 Pt III (ss 41–67) (see PARA 190): Local Government Finance Act 1992 s 24(10).
18 Local Government Finance Act 1992 s 24(4)(a).
19 Local Government Finance Act 1992 s 24(4)(b)(i).
20 Local Government Finance Act 1992 s 24(4)(b)(ii).
21 Local Government Finance Act 1992 s 24(4)(c).
22 Local Government Finance Act 1992 s 24(5)(a).
23 Local Government Finance Act 1992 s 24(5)(b).
24 Local Government Finance Act 1992 s 24(5)(c).
25 Local Government Finance Act 1992 s 24(5)(d).
26 Local Government Finance Act 1992 s 24(5)(e).
27 Local Government Finance Act 1992 s 24(5)(f). As to the meaning of 'person' see PARA 11 note 13.
28 Local Government Finance Act 1992 s 24(6).
29 Local Government Finance Act 1992 s 24(7)(a).
30 Local Government Finance Act 1992 s 24(7)(b).
31 Local Government Finance Act 1992 s 24(7)(c).
32 Local Government Finance Act 1992 s 24(7)(d).
33 Local Government Finance Act 1992 s 24(8)(a).
34 Local Government Finance Act 1992 s 24(8)(b).
35 Local Government Finance Act 1992 s 24(9)(a).
36 Ie under the Local Government Finance Act 1992 s 22(8) (see PARA 409), s 22A(10) (see PARA 410) or s 22B(10) (see PARA 411): s 24(9)(b) (amended by the Local Government (Wales) Act 1994 s 66(6), Sch 16 para 96; and the Local Government Act 2003 s 127(1), Sch 7 paras 40, 46).
37 Local Government Finance Act 1992 s 24(9).

418. Information about proposals and appeals.

A person[1] may, at a reasonable time and without making payment, inspect any proposal made or notice of appeal given under regulations relating to the alteration of lists[2], if made or given as regards a list which is in force when inspection is sought (or which has been in force at any time in the preceding five years)[3].

A person may:

(1) make copies of (or of extracts from) such a document[4]; or
(2) require a person having custody of such a document to supply to him a photographic copy of (or of extracts from) the document[5].

If a reasonable charge is required for a facility under head (1) or head (2) above, the facility may not be made available unless the person seeking to avail himself of the facility pays the charge[6].

If without reasonable excuse a person having custody of a document[7]:

(a) intentionally obstructs a person in exercising either a right of inspection[8] or a right under head (1) above[9]; or

(b) refuses to supply a copy to a person entitled to it under head (2) above[10],

he commits an offence[11].

1 As to the meaning of 'person' see PARA 11 note 13.
2 Ie regulations made under the Local Government Finance Act 1992 s 24: see PARA 417.
3 Local Government Finance Act 1992 s 29(1). As to valuation lists see PARAS 409–411.
4 Local Government Finance Act 1992 s 29(2)(a).
5 Local Government Finance Act 1992 s 29(2)(b).
6 Local Government Finance Act 1992 s 29(3).
7 Ie a document mentioned in the Local Government Finance Act 1992 s 29(1): see the text to notes 1–3.
8 Ie a right under the Local Government Finance Act 1992 s 29(1): see the text to notes 1–3.
9 See the Local Government Finance Act 1992 s 29(4)(a).
10 Local Government Finance Act 1992 s 29(4)(b).
11 See the Local Government Finance Act 1992 s 29(4). The penalty for such an offence is, on summary conviction, a fine not exceeding level 2 on the standard scale: s 29(4). As to the powers of magistrates' courts to issue fines on summary conviction see SENTENCING vol 92 (2015) PARA 176.

B. ENGLAND

419. Restriction on alteration of valuation bands.

No alteration[1] may be made of a valuation band[2] shown in a list as applicable to any dwelling in England unless[3]:

(1) since the valuation band was first shown in the list as applicable to the dwelling:
  (a) there has been a material increase[4] in the value of the dwelling and a relevant transaction[5] has been subsequently carried out in relation to the whole or any part of it[6]; or
  (b) there has been a material reduction[7] in the value of the dwelling[8]; or
  (c) the dwelling has[9] become or ceased to be a composite hereditament[10]; or
  (d) in the case of a dwelling which continues to be a composite hereditament, there has been an increase or reduction in its domestic use[11]; or

(2) the listing officer[12] is satisfied that:
  (a) a different valuation band should have been determined by the listing officer as applicable to the dwelling[13]; or
  (b) the valuation band shown in the list is not that determined by the listing officer as so applicable[14]; or

(3) an order of the Valuation Tribunal for England[15], a valuation tribunal[16] or the High Court[17] requires the alteration to be made[18].

1 'Alteration' means alteration of a list in relation to a particular dwelling, and 'alter' must be construed accordingly: Council Tax (Alteration of Lists and Appeals) (England) Regulations 2009, SI 2009/2270, reg 2(1). 'List' means a valuation list compiled under the Local Government Finance Act 1992 s 22 (see PARA 409): Council Tax (Alteration of Lists and Appeals) (England) Regulations 2009, SI 2009/2270, reg 2(1). As to the meaning of 'dwelling' see PARA 349.
2 As to valuation bands see PARA 361.

3 Council Tax (Alteration of Lists and Appeals) (England) Regulations 2009, SI 2009/2270, reg 3(1). The Council Tax (Alteration of Lists and Appeals) (England) Regulations 2009, SI 2009/2270, apply in relation to England only: see reg 1(2). As to the equivalent regulations in relation to Wales see the Council Tax (Alteration of Lists and Appeals) Regulations 1993, SI 1993/290, Pt II (regs 3–15); and PARA 428 et seq. As to the meanings of 'England' and 'Wales' see PARA 2 note 16.

4 As to the meaning of 'material increase' see PARA 417 note 11.

5 As to the meaning of 'relevant transaction' see PARA 417 note 12. For the purposes of the Council Tax (Alteration of Lists and Appeals) (England) Regulations 2009, SI 2009/2270, reg 3(1)(a)(i), the relevant transaction must be one other than the grant of a lease described in reg 3(2B) or the transfer on sale of such a lease: reg 3(2A) (reg 3(2A), (2B) added by SI 2013/467). The lease referred to is a lease for the purposes of the installation of plant or equipment for the generation of electricity or the production of heat by a source of energy or a technology mentioned in the Climate Change and Sustainable Energy Act 2006 s 26(2) (see ENERGY AND CLIMATE CHANGE vol 42 (2011) PARA 114) (Council Tax (Alteration of Lists and Appeals) (England) Regulations 2009, SI 2009/2270, reg 3(2B) (as so added), where:
   (1) the majority of the electricity or heat is generated or produced for use by such persons as may be in the dwelling (reg 3(2B)(a) (as so added)); or
   (2) the plant or equipment used to generate the electricity or produce the heat has a capacity not exceeding 10 kilowatts or 45 kilowatts thermal, as the case may be (reg 3(2B)(b) (as so added)).

6 Council Tax (Alteration of Lists and Appeals) (England) Regulations 2009, SI 2009/2270, reg 3(1)(a)(i) (amended by SI 2013/467). In determining whether the valuation band shown in a list as applicable to any dwelling may be altered on the ground specified in the Council Tax (Alteration of Lists and Appeals) (England) Regulations 2009, SI 2009/2270, reg 3(1)(a)(i), where:
   (1) the circumstances which caused the increase referred to in that provision arose before an alteration made to correct an inaccuracy in the list had effect in relation to the dwelling in accordance with reg 11(6), (7) or (8) (see PARA 426) ('the previous alteration') (reg 3(2)(a)); and
   (2) the previous alteration has had effect before a relevant transaction has been carried out (reg 3(2)(b)),

   the previous alteration is deemed to have had effect before the circumstances which caused the material increase arose: reg 3(2).

7 As to the meaning of 'material reduction' see PARA 417 note 14.

8 Council Tax (Alteration of Lists and Appeals) (England) Regulations 2009, SI 2009/2270, reg 3(1)(a)(ii). This provision is expressed to be subject to reg 3(3): see reg 3(1)(a)(ii) (amended by SI 2013/467). Where a material reduction in the value of a dwelling is caused wholly by the demolition of any part of the dwelling, the valuation band must not be altered if the works of demolition are part of, or connected with, a building, engineering or other operation carried out, in progress or proposed to be carried out in relation to the dwelling: reg 3(3). The reference in reg 3(3) to an operation does not include the repair of any damage caused to the dwelling in the course of demolition: reg 3(4). As to building, engineering or other operations for the purposes of development in relation to planning permission see PLANNING vol 81 (2018) PARA 333.

9 Ie for the purposes of the Local Government Finance Act 1988 Pt III (ss 41–67): see PARA 106 note 6.

10 Council Tax (Alteration of Lists and Appeals) (England) Regulations 2009, SI 2009/2270, reg 3(1)(a)(iii).

11 Council Tax (Alteration of Lists and Appeals) (England) Regulations 2009, SI 2009/2270, reg 3(1)(a)(iv). As to the meaning of 'domestic use' see PARA 417 note 17.

12 'Listing officer', in relation to a list, means the officer charged with its maintenance under the Local Government Finance Act 1992 s 22 (see PARA 409): Council Tax (Alteration of Lists and Appeals) (England) Regulations 2009, SI 2009/2270, reg 2(1).

13 Council Tax (Alteration of Lists and Appeals) (England) Regulations 2009, SI 2009/2270, reg 3(1)(b)(i).

14 Council Tax (Alteration of Lists and Appeals) (England) Regulations 2009, SI 2009/2270, reg 3(1)(b)(ii).

15 As to appeals to the Valuation Tribunal for England see PARA 513 et seq. As to the Valuation Tribunal for England see PARA 232.

16 'Valuation tribunal' means a valuation tribunal established in England before 1 October 2009 under the Local Government Finance Act 1988 Sch 11 para 1 (repealed, as from that date, in relation to England): Council Tax (Alteration of Lists and Appeals) (England) Regulations 2009, SI 2009/2270, reg 2(1).

17 As to appeals to the High Court see PARA 560.
18 Council Tax (Alteration of Lists and Appeals) (England) Regulations 2009, SI 2009/2270, reg 3(1)(c).

420. Circumstances and periods in which proposals for alteration may be made.

Subject to the following provisions[1], where a billing authority[2] or an interested person[3] is of the opinion that a list[4] is inaccurate because:

(1) it shows as a dwelling property[5] which ought not to be shown[6]; or
(2) it fails to show a dwelling which ought to be shown[7]; or
(3) the listing officer has determined as applicable to the dwelling a valuation band[8] other than that which should have been determined as so applicable[9]; or
(4) since the valuation band was first shown in the list as applicable to the dwelling, one (or more) of the prescribed events[10] has occurred[11]; or
(5) in relation to a matter shown in it, account has not been taken (whether as regards a particular dwelling or a class of dwelling) of a relevant decision of the Valuation Tribunal for England[12], a valuation tribunal[13] or the High Court[14],

that authority or person may make a proposal for the alteration of the list[15].

No proposal in relation to the matter mentioned in head (5) above may be made after the expiry of the period of six months[16] beginning on the day on which the decision in question was made[17].

Where, in relation to a dwelling shown in a list on the day on which it is compiled, a billing authority or an interested person is of the opinion that the list is inaccurate because the listing officer has determined as applicable to the dwelling a valuation band other than that which should have been determined as so applicable, any proposal for the alteration of that list as regards that matter must be made not later than the end of the period of six months beginning on the day on which the list is compiled[18].

A person who on any day during the period in which a list is in force becomes the taxpayer in respect of a particular dwelling shown in the list may make a proposal for the alteration of the list in respect of that dwelling where:

(a) he has not during that period previously been the taxpayer in respect of that dwelling[19]; or
(b) the dwelling is first shown in the list after the day on which it was compiled[20].

However, no such proposal may be made[21] where:

(i) six months has expired since the day on which the person first became the taxpayer[22];
(ii) a proposal to alter the same list in relation to the same dwelling and arising from the same facts has been considered and determined by the Valuation Tribunal for England[23] or by the High Court[24];
(iii) the new taxpayer is a company which is a subsidiary of the immediately preceding taxpayer[25];
(iv) the immediately preceding taxpayer is a company which is a subsidiary of the new taxpayer[26];
(v) both the new and the immediately preceding taxpayers are companies which are subsidiaries of the same company[27]; or
(vi) the change of taxpayer has occurred solely by reason of the formation of a new partnership in relation to which any of the partners was a partner in the previous partnership[28].

Where the listing officer has altered the list in respect of a dwelling, a billing authority or an interested person may, within six months of the service of the notice of alteration[29], make a proposal for either or both of the following[30]:

(A) the restoration of the list to its state before the alteration was made[31];

(B) a further alteration of the list in respect of that dwelling[32].

1 Ie subject to the Council Tax (Alteration of Lists and Appeals) (England) Regulations 2009, SI 2009/2270, reg 4(2)–(7): see the text to notes 16–32.

The Council Tax (Alteration of Lists and Appeals) (England) Regulations 2009, SI 2009/2270, apply in relation to England only: see reg 1(2). As to the equivalent regulations in relation to Wales see the Council Tax (Alteration of Lists and Appeals) Regulations 1993, SI 1993/290, Pt II (regs 3–15); and PARA 428 et seq. As to the meanings of 'England' and 'Wales' see PARA 2 note 16.

2 'Billing authority', in relation to a dwelling, means the billing authority in whose area the dwelling is situated: Council Tax (Alteration of Lists and Appeals) (England) Regulations 2009, SI 2009/2270, reg 2(1). Any reference in the Council Tax (Alteration of Lists and Appeals) (England) Regulations 2009, SI 2009/2270, to a dwelling being situated in the area of a billing authority includes a reference to its being treated as so situated: reg 2(2)(b). As to the meaning of 'dwelling' see PARA 349. As to the meaning of 'billing authority' see PARA 346. As to the power to make regulations containing rules for ascertaining in what part of a billing authority's area a dwelling is situated see the Local Government Finance Act 1992 s 10(2); and PARA 360; and as to the power to make regulations containing rules for treating a dwelling as situated in a billing authority's area if part only of the dwelling falls within the area see s 1(3); and PARA 348.

3 'Interested person', in relation to a dwelling and a day, is defined by the Council Tax (Alteration of Lists and Appeals) (England) Regulations 2009, SI 2009/2270, reg 2(1), as:

(1) the owner;

(2) where the Local Government Finance Act 1992 s 8(3) (see PARA 356) has effect on the day, and regulations provide for that subsection to have effect as if, for the reference to the owner, there were substituted a reference to another person, that other person;

(3) in relation to an exempt dwelling or a dwelling in respect of which the amount set under s 30 (see PARA 380) for the financial year is nil, any person (other than the owner) who would be liable to pay council tax if the dwelling were not an exempt dwelling or, as the case may be, the amount so set were other than nil; and

(4) any other person who is a taxpayer in respect of the dwelling.

As to the meaning of 'owner' see PARA 354 note 15. As to the meaning of 'person' see PARA 11 note 13. As to the meaning of 'exempt dwelling' see PARA 351. As to persons liable to pay council tax see PARA 354 et seq. 'Taxpayer', in relation to a dwelling and a day, means the person who is liable (whether solely or jointly and severally) to pay council tax in respect of the dwelling and the day: reg 2(1).

4 As to the meaning of 'list' see PARA 419 note 1.

5 Ie including property shown as one dwelling which, by virtue of the Council Tax (Chargeable Dwellings) Order 1992, SI 1992/549, art 3 (see PARA 349) falls to be shown as a number of dwellings, but excluding property in respect of which a determination of the listing officer under art 4 of that Order (see PARA 349) is for the time being effective for the purposes of the Local Government Finance Act 1992 Pt I (ss 1–69): see the Council Tax (Alteration of Lists and Appeals) (England) Regulations 2009, SI 2009/2270, reg 4(1)(a). As to the meaning of 'listing officer' see PARA 419 note 12.

6 Council Tax (Alteration of Lists and Appeals) (England) Regulations 2009, SI 2009/2270, reg 4(1)(a).

7 Council Tax (Alteration of Lists and Appeals) (England) Regulations 2009, SI 2009/2270, reg 4(1)(b).

8 As to valuation bands see PARA 361.

9 Council Tax (Alteration of Lists and Appeals) (England) Regulations 2009, SI 2009/2270, reg 4(1)(c).

10 Ie the events mentioned in the Council Tax (Alteration of Lists and Appeals) (England) Regulations 2009, SI 2009/2270, reg 3(1)(a): see PARA 419.

11 Council Tax (Alteration of Lists and Appeals) (England) Regulations 2009, SI 2009/2270, reg 4(1)(d).

12 As to appeals to the Valuation Tribunal for England see PARA 515 et seq. As to the Valuation Tribunal for England see PARA 232.

13 As to the meaning of 'valuation tribunal' see PARA 419 note 16.

14 Council Tax (Alteration of Lists and Appeals) (England) Regulations 2009, SI 2009/2270, reg 4(1)(e). As to appeals to the High Court see PARA 560.
15 Council Tax (Alteration of Lists and Appeals) (England) Regulations 2009, SI 2009/2270, reg 4(1). As to the meaning of 'alteration' see PARA 419 note 1.
16 As to the meaning of 'month' see PARA 11 note 1.
17 Council Tax (Alteration of Lists and Appeals) (England) Regulations 2009, SI 2009/2270, reg 4(2).
18 Council Tax (Alteration of Lists and Appeals) (England) Regulations 2009, SI 2009/2270, reg 4(3). This provision is expressed to be subject to reg 4(4) (see the text to notes 19–20) and reg 7(3)(a) (see PARA 422): see reg 4(3).
19 Council Tax (Alteration of Lists and Appeals) (England) Regulations 2009, SI 2009/2270, reg 4(4)(a).
20 Council Tax (Alteration of Lists and Appeals) (England) Regulations 2009, SI 2009/2270, reg 4(4)(b).
21 Ie under the Council Tax (Alteration of Lists and Appeals) (England) Regulations 2009, SI 2009/2270, reg 4(4): see the text to notes 19–20.
22 Council Tax (Alteration of Lists and Appeals) (England) Regulations 2009, SI 2009/2270, reg 4(5)(a).
23 Ie otherwise than as mentioned in the Valuation Tribunal for England (Council Tax and Rating Appeals) (Procedure) Regulations 2009, SI 2009/2269, reg 32 (hearing in a party's absence): see PARA 528.
24 Council Tax (Alteration of Lists and Appeals) (England) Regulations 2009, SI 2009/2270, reg 4(5)(b).
25 Council Tax (Alteration of Lists and Appeals) (England) Regulations 2009, SI 2009/2270, reg 4(5)(c). 'Company' and 'subsidiary' have the same meanings as in the Companies Act 2006 (see COMPANIES vol 14 (2016) PARAS 1, 22): Council Tax (Alteration of Lists and Appeals) (England) Regulations 2009, SI 2009/2270, reg 2(1).
26 Council Tax (Alteration of Lists and Appeals) (England) Regulations 2009, SI 2009/2270, reg 4(5)(d).
27 Council Tax (Alteration of Lists and Appeals) (England) Regulations 2009, SI 2009/2270, reg 4(5)(e).
28 Council Tax (Alteration of Lists and Appeals) (England) Regulations 2009, SI 2009/2270, reg 4(5)(f).
29 Ie under the Council Tax (Alteration of Lists and Appeals) (England) Regulations 2009, SI 2009/2270, reg 12: see PARA 427.
30 Council Tax (Alteration of Lists and Appeals) (England) Regulations 2009, SI 2009/2270, reg 4(6). Regulation 4(6) does not apply to the extent that the alteration in question:
    (1) consists of:
        (a) the insertion or alteration of a reference number (reg 4(7)(a)(i));
        (b) the alteration of an address (reg 4(7)(a)(ii));
        (c) the correction of a clerical error (reg 4(7)(a)(iii)); or
        (d) the entry of the day from which an alteration has effect where the day is the completion day determined under the Local Government Finance Act 1988 Sch 4A as it applies for the purposes of the Local Government Finance Act 1992 Pt I (ss 1–69) (see s 17; and PARA 353) in relation to the dwelling concerned (Council Tax (Alteration of Lists and Appeals) (England) Regulations 2009, SI 2009/2270, reg 4(7)(a)(iv)); or
    (2) reflects a change in the area of the billing authority or a decision of the Valuation Tribunal for England or the High Court in relation to the dwelling concerned (reg 4(7)(b)).
31 Council Tax (Alteration of Lists and Appeals) (England) Regulations 2009, SI 2009/2270, reg 4(6)(a).
32 Council Tax (Alteration of Lists and Appeals) (England) Regulations 2009, SI 2009/2270, reg 4(6)(b).

421. Manner of making proposals and information to be included.

A proposal[1] must be made by notice in writing[2] served on the listing officer[3]; and the notice must[4]:

(1) state the name and address of the proposer[5], and the capacity in which the proposer makes the proposal[6];
(2) identify the dwelling[7] to which it relates[8];

(3) identify the respects in which it is proposed the list be altered[9]; and
(4) include:
  (a) a statement of the reasons for believing the list to be inaccurate[10];
  (b) if the proposal is made in relation to one or more of the prescribed events having taken place[11], a statement of the reasons for the belief that such an event has occurred and of the date on which the event occurred[12];
  (c) if the proposal is made in relation to the failure to take into account a prescribed decision[13], a statement identifying the property to which the decision in question relates and the date of that decision and (as the case may be) that the decision was a decision of the Valuation Tribunal for England or the High Court[14];
  (d) if the proposal is made in relation to an inaccuracy in a list in prescribed circumstances[15], a statement of the day on which the proposer became the taxpayer[16];
  (e) if the proposal disputes the accuracy of an alteration made by the listing officer, a statement of the day on which the listing officer served[17] the relevant notice[18];
  (f) if the proposal disputes the day from which an alteration should have effect, a statement of the day proposed in its place[19].

A proposal may deal with more than one dwelling:
(i) in the prescribed circumstances[20]; or
(ii) where the proposer makes the proposal in the same capacity as respects each dwelling, and each of the dwellings is within the same building as each other dwelling or, where any of them is not within a building, it is within the same curtilage as the other or others[21].

Unless he serves an invalidity notice[22], the listing officer must, within the period of 28 days beginning on the day on which he receives a proposal, by notice in writing served on the proposer acknowledge its receipt[23].

Within six weeks beginning on the day on which a proposal is served on him, the listing officer must serve a copy of the proposal on each of the following (not being the proposer):
(A) any person who then appears to him to be the taxpayer as regards any dwelling to which the proposal relates[24]; and
(B) the billing authority[25], where that authority has served notice on the listing officer that it wishes to receive a copy of a class or classes of proposal, and the proposal falls within any such class[26].

1 'Proposal' means a proposal for the alteration of a list: Council Tax (Alteration of Lists and Appeals) (England) Regulations 2009, SI 2009/2270, reg 2(1). As to the meaning of 'alteration' see PARA 419 note 1. As to the meaning of 'list' see PARA 419 note 1. As to the circumstances in which proposals may be made see PARA 420.
2 As to the meaning of 'writing' see PARA 21 note 3.
3 As to the meaning of 'listing officer' see PARA 419 note 12.
4 Council Tax (Alteration of Lists and Appeals) (England) Regulations 2009, SI 2009/2270, reg 5(1). The Council Tax (Alteration of Lists and Appeals) (England) Regulations 2009, SI 2009/2270, apply in relation to England only: see reg 1(2). As to the equivalent regulations in relation to Wales see the Council Tax (Alteration of Lists and Appeals) Regulations 1993, SI 1993/290, Pt II (regs 3–15); and PARA 428 et seq. As to the meanings of 'England' and 'Wales' see PARA 2 note 16.
5 'Proposer' means the person making a proposal: Council Tax (Alteration of Lists and Appeals) (England) Regulations 2009, SI 2009/2270, reg 2(1). As to the meaning of 'person' see PARA 11 note 13.
6 Council Tax (Alteration of Lists and Appeals) (England) Regulations 2009, SI 2009/2270, reg

5(1)(a). As to the persons by whom proposals may be made see PARA 420.
7 As to the meaning of 'dwelling' see PARA 349.
8 Council Tax (Alteration of Lists and Appeals) (England) Regulations 2009, SI 2009/2270, reg 5(1)(b).
9 Council Tax (Alteration of Lists and Appeals) (England) Regulations 2009, SI 2009/2270, reg 5(1)(c).
10 Council Tax (Alteration of Lists and Appeals) (England) Regulations 2009, SI 2009/2270, reg 5(1)(d)(i).
11 Ie in the circumstances mentioned in the Council Tax (Alteration of Lists and Appeals) (England) Regulations 2009, SI 2009/2270, reg 4(1)(d): see PARA 420.
12 See the Council Tax (Alteration of Lists and Appeals) (England) Regulations 2009, SI 2009/2270, reg 5(1)(d)(ii).
13 Ie in the circumstances mentioned in the Council Tax (Alteration of Lists and Appeals) (England) Regulations 2009, SI 2009/2270, reg 4(1)(e): see PARA 420.
14 See the Council Tax (Alteration of Lists and Appeals) (England) Regulations 2009, SI 2009/2270, reg 5(1)(d)(iii).
15 Ie in the circumstances mentioned in the Council Tax (Alteration of Lists and Appeals) (England) Regulations 2009, SI 2009/2270, reg 4(3): see PARA 420.
16 See the Council Tax (Alteration of Lists and Appeals) (England) Regulations 2009, SI 2009/2270, reg 5(1)(d)(iv). As to the meaning of 'taxpayer' see PARA 420 note 3.
17 Ie under the Council Tax (Alteration of Lists and Appeals) (England) Regulations 2009, SI 2009/2270, reg 12: see PARA 427.
18 Council Tax (Alteration of Lists and Appeals) (England) Regulations 2009, SI 2009/2270, reg 5(1)(d)(v).
19 Council Tax (Alteration of Lists and Appeals) (England) Regulations 2009, SI 2009/2270, reg 5(1)(d)(vi).
20 Ie in the circumstances mentioned in the Council Tax (Alteration of Lists and Appeals) (England) Regulations 2009, SI 2009/2270, reg 4(1)(a) (see PARA 420): reg 5(2)(a).
21 Council Tax (Alteration of Lists and Appeals) (England) Regulations 2009, SI 2009/2270, reg 5(2)(b).
22 The Council Tax (Alteration of Lists and Appeals) (England) Regulations 2009, SI 2009/2270, reg 6(1) does not apply where the listing officer serves a notice under reg 7 (see PARA 422) in respect of the proposal: reg 6(2).
23 Council Tax (Alteration of Lists and Appeals) (England) Regulations 2009, SI 2009/2270, reg 6(1). A notice must specify the date of receipt of the proposal; and must be accompanied by a statement of the effect of regs 8–12 (see the text to notes 24–26 and PARAS 423–424, 426–427): reg 6(3).
24 Council Tax (Alteration of Lists and Appeals) (England) Regulations 2009, SI 2009/2270, reg 8(1)(a). Each copy of a proposal served under reg 8(1)(a) must be accompanied by a statement of the effect of regs 9–12 (see PARAS 423–424, 426–427): reg 8(2).
25 As to the meaning of 'billing authority' see PARA 420 note 2.
26 Council Tax (Alteration of Lists and Appeals) (England) Regulations 2009, SI 2009/2270, reg 8(1)(b).

422. Proposals treated as invalid.

Where the listing officer[1] is of the opinion that a proposal[2] has not been validly made[3], he may, within four weeks of its service, serve notice (an 'invalidity notice') on the proposer[4] that he is of that opinion[5] and stating the reasons for that opinion[6]. The listing officer may at any time withdraw an invalidity notice by notice in writing[7] served on the proposer; and on such withdrawal any appeal against the invalidity notice must be treated as having been withdrawn[8].

Unless an invalidity notice has been so withdrawn, the person[9] on whom it is served may, within four weeks of its service:

(1) make a further proposal in relation to the same dwelling[10], notwithstanding the previous expiry of any period[11] for the making of proposals[12]; or
(2) appeal against the notice to the Valuation Tribunal for England[13].

An appeal against an invalidity notice must be made by the proposer serving on the Valuation Tribunal for England a copy of the invalidity notice together with a written statement of the following matters to the extent that they are not included in the invalidity notice:

(a) the address of the dwelling to which the proposal relates[14];
(b) the reasons for the appeal against the invalidity notice[15]; and
(c) the names and addresses of the proposer[16] and the listing officer[17].

Where the listing officer withdraws an invalidity notice after an appeal against it has been made, he must, as soon as reasonably practicable, inform the tribunal of the withdrawal[18].

Until it is finally decided[19] that the proposal to which an invalidity notice relates was validly made, the statutory provisions relating to the procedure subsequent to the making of proposals[20] do not apply in relation to the proposal; and where it is finally decided as so mentioned, those provisions have effect as if the proposal had been served on the listing officer on the date of that final decision[21].

Nothing done under the above provisions is to be construed as preventing any party to an appeal in respect of a disagreement as to a proposed alteration[22] from contending for the purposes of that appeal that the proposal to which the appeal relates was not validly made[23].

1 As to the meaning of 'listing officer' see PARA 419 note 12.
2 As to the meaning of 'proposal' see PARA 421 note 1.
3 As to the making of proposals see PARAS 420–421.
4 As to the meaning of 'proposer' see PARA 421 note 5.
5 Council Tax (Alteration of Lists and Appeals) (England) Regulations 2009, SI 2009/2270, reg 7(1). The Council Tax (Alteration of Lists and Appeals) (England) Regulations 2009, SI 2009/2270, apply in relation to England only: see reg 1(2). As to the equivalent regulations in relation to Wales see the Council Tax (Alteration of Lists and Appeals) Regulations 1993, SI 1993/290, Pt II (regs 3–15); and PARA 428 et seq. As to the meanings of 'England' and 'Wales' see PARA 2 note 16.
6 Council Tax (Alteration of Lists and Appeals) (England) Regulations 2009, SI 2009/2270, reg 7(1)(a). The notice must also state the effect of reg 7(3)–(6) (see the text to notes 9–17): reg 7(1)(b).
7 As to the meaning of 'writing' see PARA 21 note 3.
8 Council Tax (Alteration of Lists and Appeals) (England) Regulations 2009, SI 2009/2270, reg 7(2).
9 As to the meaning of 'person' see PARA 11 note 13.
10 As to the meaning of 'dwelling' see PARA 349.
11 Ie applicable under the Council Tax (Alteration of Lists and Appeals) (England) Regulations 2009, SI 2009/2270, reg 4: see PARA 420.
12 See the Council Tax (Alteration of Lists and Appeals) (England) Regulations 2009, SI 2009/2270, reg 7(3)(a). No proposal may be made under reg 7(3)(a) where the proposal to which the invalidity notice relates was made under reg 7(3)(a) or after the expiry of any period applicable under reg 4 (see PARA 420): reg 7(4). Where a proposal is made under reg 7(3)(a), the proposal in respect of which the invalidity notice was served must be treated as having been withdrawn: reg 7(5).
13 Council Tax (Alteration of Lists and Appeals) (England) Regulations 2009, SI 2009/2270, reg 7(3)(b). As to appeals to the tribunal see PARA 514 et seq. As to the Valuation Tribunal for England see PARA 232.
14 Council Tax (Alteration of Lists and Appeals) (England) Regulations 2009, SI 2009/2270, reg 7(6)(a).
15 Council Tax (Alteration of Lists and Appeals) (England) Regulations 2009, SI 2009/2270, reg 7(6)(b).
16 Council Tax (Alteration of Lists and Appeals) (England) Regulations 2009, SI 2009/2270, reg 7(6)(c)(i).
17 Council Tax (Alteration of Lists and Appeals) (England) Regulations 2009, SI 2009/2270, reg 7(6)(c)(ii).
18 Council Tax (Alteration of Lists and Appeals) (England) Regulations 2009, SI 2009/2270, reg 7(7).
19 For these purposes, a final decision is made:
    (1) where the invalidity notice is withdrawn, on the day of the withdrawal (Council Tax (Alteration of Lists and Appeals) (England) Regulations 2009, SI 2009/2270, reg 7(9)(a));

(2) in any other case, on the day on which:
   (a) the tribunal having determined the appeal, the period within which an appeal may be made to the High Court under the Valuation Tribunal for England (Council Tax and Rating Appeals) (Procedure) Regulations 2009, SI 2009/2269, reg 45 (notification of further proceedings) expires without such an appeal being made (Council Tax (Alteration of Lists and Appeals) (England) Regulations 2009, SI 2009/2270, reg 7(9)(b)(i)); or
   (b) the High Court determines the appeal (reg 7(9)(b)(ii)).

Note: there is no Valuation Tribunal for England (Council Tax and Rating Appeals) (Procedure) Regulations 2009, SI 2009/2269, reg 45 as referred to in head (2)(a) above; as to the relevant provision see reg 44; and PARA 560.

20 Ie the Council Tax (Alteration of Lists and Appeals) (England) Regulations 2009, SI 2009/2270, regs 8–12: see PARAS 421, 423–424, 426–427.

21 Council Tax (Alteration of Lists and Appeals) (England) Regulations 2009, SI 2009/2270, reg 7(8).

22 Ie an appeal under the Council Tax (Alteration of Lists and Appeals) (England) Regulations 2009, SI 2009/2270, reg 10: see PARA 424.

23 Council Tax (Alteration of Lists and Appeals) (England) Regulations 2009, SI 2009/2270, reg 7(10).

423. Listing officer's decision.

Within the period of four months[1] beginning on the date on which the proposer[2] served the proposal[3] on the listing officer[4]:

(1) the listing officer must decide whether:
   (a) the whole of the proposal is well-founded[5];
   (b) only part of the proposal is well-founded[6]; or
   (c) the whole of the proposal is not well-founded[7]; and
(2) in relation to any dwelling[8] to which the proposal relates:
   (a) where the decision is that referred to in head (1)(a) above, the listing officer must decide to alter[9] the list[10] accordingly[11];
   (b) where the decision is that referred to in head (1)(b) above, the listing officer may reach an agreement with the proposer on an alteration of the list[12] in terms which are partly different from those contained in the proposal but otherwise in accordance with the proposal[13];
   (c) where the decision is that referred to in head (1)(c) above the listing officer may reach an agreement with the proposer on an alteration of the list[14] in terms which are wholly different from those contained in the proposal[15];
   (d) where the decision is that referred to in head (1)(b) or (1)(c) above and the listing officer decides not to, or is unable to, reach an agreement with the proposer on an alteration of the list, the listing officer must decide whether or not to alter the list in relation to any dwelling to which the proposal relates[16].

As soon as reasonably practicable after making a decision or reaching an agreement, in accordance with any of heads (2)(a) to (d) above, the listing officer must serve a written[17] notice (a 'decision notice') on:

(i) the proposer[18];
(ii) any other person[19] who then appears to the listing officer to be the taxpayer[20] as regards any dwelling to which the proposal relates[21]; and
(iii) where the decision notice relates to a decision under head (2)(d) above, any other person who then appears to the listing officer to be a competent person[22] as regards any dwelling to which the proposal relates[23].

The notice must give particulars of the decision made or agreement reached[24].

Where the listing officer has made a decision in accordance with head (2)(a) or (d) above, he must, within the period of six weeks beginning on the date on which the decision notice was served on the proposer, alter the list in accordance with the decision[25]. Where the listing officer has reached an agreement in accordance with head (2)(b) or (c) above, he must, within the period of six weeks beginning on the date on which the agreement was reached, alter the list in accordance with the terms of the agreement[26].

1 As to the meaning of 'month' see PARA 11 note 1.
2 As to the meaning of 'proposer' see PARA 421 note 5.
3 As to the meaning of 'proposal' see PARA 421 note 1.
4 Council Tax (Alteration of Lists and Appeals) (England) Regulations 2009, SI 2009/2270, reg 9(1). As to the meaning of 'listing officer' see PARA 419 note 12. As to service of a proposal see PARA 421.

The Council Tax (Alteration of Lists and Appeals) (England) Regulations 2009, SI 2009/2270, apply in relation to England only: see reg 1(2). As to the equivalent regulations in relation to Wales see the Council Tax (Alteration of Lists and Appeals) Regulations 1993, SI 1993/290, Pt II (regs 3–15); and PARA 428 et seq. As to the meanings of 'England' and 'Wales' see PARA 2 note 16.

5 Council Tax (Alteration of Lists and Appeals) (England) Regulations 2009, SI 2009/2270, reg 9(1)(a)(i).
6 Council Tax (Alteration of Lists and Appeals) (England) Regulations 2009, SI 2009/2270, reg 9(1)(a)(ii).
7 Council Tax (Alteration of Lists and Appeals) (England) Regulations 2009, SI 2009/2270, reg 9(1)(a)(iii).
8 As to the meaning of 'dwelling' see PARA 349.
9 As to the meaning of 'alter' see PARA 419 note 1.
10 As to the meaning of 'list' see PARA 419 note 1.
11 Council Tax (Alteration of Lists and Appeals) (England) Regulations 2009, SI 2009/2270, reg 9(1)(b)(i).
12 Ie which is in accordance with the Council Tax (Alteration of Lists and Appeals) (England) Regulations 2009, SI 2009/2270, Pt 2 (regs 3–12): see PARA 419 et seq.
13 Council Tax (Alteration of Lists and Appeals) (England) Regulations 2009, SI 2009/2270, reg 9(1)(b)(ii).
14 Ie which is in accordance with the Council Tax (Alteration of Lists and Appeals) (England) Regulations 2009, SI 2009/2270, Pt 2 (regs 3–12): see PARA 419 et seq.
15 Council Tax (Alteration of Lists and Appeals) (England) Regulations 2009, SI 2009/2270, reg 9(1)(b)(iii).
16 Council Tax (Alteration of Lists and Appeals) (England) Regulations 2009, SI 2009/2270, reg 9(1)(b)(iv).
17 As to the meaning of 'written' see PARA 21 note 3.
18 Council Tax (Alteration of Lists and Appeals) (England) Regulations 2009, SI 2009/2270, reg 9(2)(a).
19 As to the meaning of 'person' see PARA 11 note 13.
20 As to the meaning of 'taxpayer' see PARA 420 note 3.
21 Council Tax (Alteration of Lists and Appeals) (England) Regulations 2009, SI 2009/2270, reg 9(2)(b).
22 'Competent person', in relation to a proposal and an appeal, means a person (other than the proposer) who, at the date on which the decision notice in respect of that proposal was served on the proposer, would have been competent to make the proposal: Council Tax (Alteration of Lists and Appeals) (England) Regulations 2009, SI 2009/2270, reg 2(1). As to the persons who may make a proposal see PARA 420.
23 Council Tax (Alteration of Lists and Appeals) (England) Regulations 2009, SI 2009/2270, reg 9(2)(c).
24 See the Council Tax (Alteration of Lists and Appeals) (England) Regulations 2009, SI 2009/2270, reg 9(2).
25 Council Tax (Alteration of Lists and Appeals) (England) Regulations 2009, SI 2009/2270, reg 9(3).
26 Council Tax (Alteration of Lists and Appeals) (England) Regulations 2009, SI 2009/2270, reg 9(4).

424. Disagreement as to proposed alteration.

Where the listing officer[1] has:

(1) after making a decision that only part of a proposal is well founded or that the whole of a proposal is not well founded, decided whether or not to alter the list in relation to any dwelling to which the proposal relates[2]; and

(2) served[3] a decision notice on the proposer[4],

the proposer or any competent person[5] may appeal to the Valuation Tribunal for England[6] against the listing officer's decision[7].

Such an appeal must be made within the period of three months[8] beginning on the date on which the decision notice was served on the proposer[9]. However, where an appeal is made after the end of that period[10], and the president of the tribunal[11] is satisfied that the failure to initiate the appeal within that period has arisen by reason of circumstances beyond the control of the proposer or a competent person (as the case may be)[12], the president may authorise the appeal and must notify the appellant as soon as reasonably practicable of the authorisation[13].

An appeal must be made by the appellant serving on the tribunal a copy of the decision notice together with a written[14] statement of the prescribed matters to the extent that they are not included in the decision notice[15].

An appeal made by a competent person may not proceed where the proposer appeals or where another competent person has already made an appeal in relation to the same decision notice[16].

1 As to the meaning of 'listing officer' see PARA 419 note 12.

2 Ie a decision under the Council Tax (Alteration of Lists and Appeals) (England) Regulations 2009, SI 2009/2270, reg 9(1)(b)(iv) (see PARA 423): see reg 10(1)(a).

The Council Tax (Alteration of Lists and Appeals) (England) Regulations 2009, SI 2009/2270, apply in relation to England only: see reg 1(2). As to the equivalent regulations in relation to Wales see the Council Tax (Alteration of Lists and Appeals) Regulations 1993, SI 1993/290, Pt II (regs 3–15); and PARA 428 et seq. As to the meanings of 'England' and 'Wales' see PARA 2 note 16.

3 Ie in accordance with the Council Tax (Alteration of Lists and Appeals) (England) Regulations 2009, SI 2009/2270, reg 9(2): see PARA 423.

4 Council Tax (Alteration of Lists and Appeals) (England) Regulations 2009, SI 2009/2270, reg 10(1)(b). As to the meaning of 'proposer' see PARA 421 note 5.

5 As to the meaning of 'competent person' see PARA 423 note 22.

6 As to the Valuation Tribunal for England see PARA 232.

7 Council Tax (Alteration of Lists and Appeals) (England) Regulations 2009, SI 2009/2270, reg 10(1). As to the conduct of appeals to the Valuation Tribunal for England see PARA 515 et seq.

8 As to the meaning of 'month' see PARA 11 note 1.

9 Council Tax (Alteration of Lists and Appeals) (England) Regulations 2009, SI 2009/2270, reg 10(2).

10 See the Council Tax (Alteration of Lists and Appeals) (England) Regulations 2009, SI 2009/2270, reg 10(3)(a).

11 As to the president of the Valuation Tribunal for England see PARA 233.

12 Council Tax (Alteration of Lists and Appeals) (England) Regulations 2009, SI 2009/2270, reg 10(3)(b).

13 Council Tax (Alteration of Lists and Appeals) (England) Regulations 2009, SI 2009/2270, reg 10(3).

14 As to the meaning of 'written' see PARA 21 note 3.

15 Council Tax (Alteration of Lists and Appeals) (England) Regulations 2009, SI 2009/2270, reg 10(5). The prescribed matters are:

(1) the address of any dwelling to which the decision notice relates (reg 10(5)(a));

(2) the reasons for the appeal (reg 10(5)(b)); and

(3) the names and addresses of:

(a) the appellant (reg 10(5)(c)(i));

(b) the proposer (where the proposer is not the appellant) (reg 10(5)(c)(ii));

(c) the listing officer (reg 10(5)(c)(iii));

(d) where the appellant knows the name and address of any person (who is neither the proposer nor the appellant) who appears to be a taxpayer as regards any dwelling to which the decision notice relates, that person (reg 10(5)(c)(iv)); and
(e) where the appellant knows the name and address of any other person who appears to be an interested person as regards any dwelling to which the decision notice relates, that person (reg 10(5)(c)(v)).

As to the meaning of 'dwelling' see PARA 349. As to the meaning of 'person' see PARA 11 note 13. As to the meaning of 'taxpayer' see PARA 420 note 3. As to the meaning of 'interested person' see PARA 420 note 3.

16 Council Tax (Alteration of Lists and Appeals) (England) Regulations 2009, SI 2009/2270, reg 10(4). This provision is expressed to be subject to Valuation Tribunal for England (Council Tax and Rating Appeals) (Procedure) Regulations 2009, SI 2009/2269, reg 19 (withdrawals and deemed withdrawals: see PARA 526): see the Council Tax (Alteration of Lists and Appeals) (England) Regulations 2009, SI 2009/2270, reg 10(4).

425. Post-appeal agreements.

After an appeal in respect of a disagreement as to a proposed alteration of a list[1] has been made, but before the commencement of a hearing or consideration of written representations[2], the listing officer[3] may reach an agreement on an alteration of the list in accordance with the following provisions[4].

Such an agreement must be reached with all the prescribed persons[5], and must provide for the alteration of the list to be of a prescribed description[6] and to have effect from the day[7] that is relevant to an alteration of the description concerned[8]. Where such an agreement is reached, the listing officer must:

(1) as soon as reasonably practicable serve a written[9] notice on the Valuation Tribunal for England[10] that an agreement has been reached[11];
(2) serve a copy of the notice on the other parties to the agreement[12]; and
(3) not later than six weeks after the date on which the agreement was reached, alter the list to give effect to the agreement[13].

An appeal in relation to which such a notice has been served must be treated as withdrawn on the date on which the notice is served on the Valuation Tribunal for England[14].

1 Ie an appeal under the Council Tax (Alteration of Lists and Appeals) (England) Regulations 2009, SI 2009/2270, reg 10: see PARA 424. As to the meanings of 'alteration' and 'list' see PARA 419 note 1.
2 As to the procedure for appeals see PARA 515 et seq.
3 As to the meaning of 'listing officer' see PARA 419 note 12.
4 Council Tax (Alteration of Lists and Appeals) (England) Regulations 2009, SI 2009/2270, reg 13(1). The Council Tax (Alteration of Lists and Appeals) (England) Regulations 2009, SI 2009/2270, apply in relation to England only: see reg 1(2). As to the equivalent regulations in relation to Wales see the Council Tax (Alteration of Lists and Appeals) Regulations 1993, SI 1993/290, Pt II (regs 3–15); and PARA 428 et seq. As to the meanings of 'England' and 'Wales' see PARA 2 note 16.
5 Council Tax (Alteration of Lists and Appeals) (England) Regulations 2009, SI 2009/2270, reg 13(2)(a). The prescribed persons are:
(1) the appellant (reg 13(4)(a));
(2) any other person who at the date of the agreement is a taxpayer as regards any dwelling to which the appeal relates and whose name and address the listing officer knows (reg 13(4)(b)); and
(3) any other person who at the date of the agreement is a party to the appeal and whose name and address the listing officer knows (reg 13(4)(c)).

As to the meaning of 'person' see PARA 11 note 13. As to the meaning of 'taxpayer' see PARA 420 note 3. As to the meaning of 'dwelling' see PARA 349. Any reference in the Council Tax (Alteration of Lists and Appeals) (England) Regulations 2009, SI 2009/2270, to a party to an appeal must be construed in accordance with the Valuation Tribunal for England (Council Tax and Rating Appeals) (Procedure) Regulations 2009, SI 2009/2269, reg 2(3)(a) (see PARA 515 note 4): Council Tax (Alteration of Lists and Appeals) (England) Regulations 2009, SI 2009/2270, reg 2(2)(a).

Subject to reg 13(6), where, at the date of the agreement, more than one person is a taxpayer as regards any dwelling to which the appeal relates, the requirement in reg 13(2)(a), in so far as it relates to the agreement of the taxpayer, must be treated as satisfied where one of the taxpayers as regards the dwelling is a party to the agreement: reg 13(5). This does not prevent the appellant, any other person who is a competent appellant or any competent party from being a party to the agreement: reg 13(6).

6 See the Council Tax (Alteration of Lists and Appeals) (England) Regulations 2009, SI 2009/2270, reg 13(2)(b)(i). The prescribed descriptions of alteration are those specified in any of reg 11(1)–(4) and (6)–(9) (see PARA 426): see reg 13(2)(b)(i).

7 Ie the day ascertained in accordance with the Council Tax (Alteration of Lists and Appeals) (England) Regulations 2009, SI 2009/2270, reg 11(1)–(4) or (6)–(9): see PARA 426.

8 See the Council Tax (Alteration of Lists and Appeals) (England) Regulations 2009, SI 2009/2270, reg 13(2)(b)(ii).

9 As to the meaning of 'written' see PARA 21 note 3.

10 As to the Valuation Tribunal for England see PARA 232.

11 Council Tax (Alteration of Lists and Appeals) (England) Regulations 2009, SI 2009/2270, reg 13(3)(a).

12 Council Tax (Alteration of Lists and Appeals) (England) Regulations 2009, SI 2009/2270, reg 13(3)(b).

13 Council Tax (Alteration of Lists and Appeals) (England) Regulations 2009, SI 2009/2270, reg 13(3)(c).

14 Council Tax (Alteration of Lists and Appeals) (England) Regulations 2009, SI 2009/2270, reg 13(7).

426. Day from which alteration has effect.

Subject to the following provisions[1], an alteration[2] made so as to show in or, as the case may be, to delete from a list[3] any dwelling[4] which, since the list was compiled:

(1) has come into existence or ceased to exist[5]; or

(2) has ceased to be situated, or has become situated, in the area of the billing authority[6] for whose area the list was compiled[7],

has effect from the day on which the circumstances giving rise to the alteration occurred[8].

An alteration reflecting a material increase[9] in the value of a dwelling has effect from the day on which the alteration is entered in the list[10].

An alteration reflecting a material reduction[11] in the value of a dwelling has effect from the day on which the circumstances which caused that reduction arose[12].

An alteration reflecting an increase or reduction in the domestic use[13] of a dwelling which is or becomes or ceases to be a composite hereditament[14] has effect from the day on which the circumstances which caused that increase or reduction arose[15].

Where an alteration is made to correct an inaccuracy in a list[16] and the inaccuracy was to show as one dwelling property which should have been treated[17] as two or more dwellings[18], the alteration has effect from the day on which the alteration is entered in the list[19].

An alteration made to correct an inaccuracy in a list on the day it was compiled has effect[20]:

(a) in a case where the inaccuracy was to show as applicable to a dwelling a valuation band[21] which is lower than the band which should have been determined or shown as applicable to it, from the day on which the alteration is entered in the list[22]; and

(b) in any other case, from the day on which the list was compiled[23].

Where an alteration is made to correct an inaccuracy in a list (other than an alteration which falls to have effect as provided in the foregoing provisions)[24], and the inaccuracy arose in the course of making a previous alteration and was to show as applicable to a dwelling a valuation band which is lower than the band which should have been determined or shown as applicable to it[25], the alteration has effect from the day on which the alteration is entered in the list[26].

An alteration made to correct an inaccuracy in a list (other than an alteration which falls to have effect as provided in the foregoing provisions)[27] has effect:

(i) in a case where the alteration is made to correct an inaccuracy in the list which arose in the course of making a previous alteration[28] and the previous alteration fell to have effect in accordance with the foregoing provisions[29], from the day on which the previous alteration had effect, or, but for the inaccuracy, would have had effect[30]; and

(ii) in any other case, from the day on which the list became inaccurate[31].

These provisions[32] do not apply, as regards the date from which an alteration is to have effect, where provision for that date is made under a consent order[33] or other order[34] made by the Valuation Tribunal for England[35].

1 Ie subject to the Council Tax (Alteration of Lists and Appeals) (England) Regulations 2009, SI 2009/2270, reg 11(2)–(12): see the text to notes 10–35.

The Council Tax (Alteration of Lists and Appeals) (England) Regulations 2009, SI 2009/2270, apply in relation to England only: see reg 1(2). As to the equivalent regulations in relation to Wales see the Council Tax (Alteration of Lists and Appeals) Regulations 1993, SI 1993/290, Pt II (regs 3–15); and PARA 428 et seq. As to the meanings of 'England' and 'Wales' see PARA 2 note 16.

2 As to the meaning of 'alteration' see PARA 419 note 1.

3 As to the meaning of 'list' see PARA 419 note 1.

4 As to the meaning of 'dwelling' see PARA 349.

5 Council Tax (Alteration of Lists and Appeals) (England) Regulations 2009, SI 2009/2270, reg 11(1)(a). Any reference in reg 11 to a dwelling ceasing to exist or coming into existence includes a reference to a dwelling:

(1) the day of whose coming into existence or ceasing to exist is provided for as mentioned in the Local Government Finance Act 1992 s 17(3) or (5) (completion of new dwellings: see PARA 353) (Council Tax (Alteration of Lists and Appeals) (England) Regulations 2009, SI 2009/2270, reg 11(10)(a)); or

(2) which ceases to exist or comes into existence:

(a) by virtue of property which was a dwelling:

(i)becoming liable (as such or together with other property) to non-domestic rating by reason of its consisting entirely of non-domestic property (reg 11(10)(b)(i)(aa)); or

(ii)ceasing (otherwise than as mentioned in head (i)) to satisfy the requirements of the Local Government Finance Act 1992 s 3 (see PARA 349) (see the Council Tax (Alteration of Lists and Appeals) (England) Regulations 2009, SI 2009/2270, reg 11(10)(b)(i)(bb));

(a) by virtue of a hereditament consisting entirely of property which is non-domestic becoming a composite hereditament which satisfies the requirements of the Local Government Finance Act 1992 s 3 (Council Tax (Alteration of Lists and Appeals) (England) Regulations 2009, SI 2009/2270, reg 11(10)(b)(ii));

(b) by virtue of property which was one dwelling for the purposes of the Local Government Finance Act 1992 Pt I (ss 1–69) being treated for those purposes as two or more dwellings (Council Tax (Alteration of Lists and Appeals) (England) Regulations 2009, SI 2009/2270, reg 11(10)(b)(iii)); or

(c) by virtue of property which was two or more dwellings for those purposes being treated for those purposes as one dwelling (reg 11(10)(b)(iv)).

As to the meaning of 'hereditament' see PARA 106 (definition applied by reg 11(11)).

6 As to the meaning of 'billing authority' and as to references to a dwelling being situated in a billing authority's area see PARA 420 note 2.

7 Council Tax (Alteration of Lists and Appeals) (England) Regulations 2009, SI 2009/2270, reg 11(1)(b).

8 Council Tax (Alteration of Lists and Appeals) (England) Regulations 2009, SI 2009/2270, reg 11(1).

9 As to the meaning of 'material increase' see PARA 417 note 11.

10 Council Tax (Alteration of Lists and Appeals) (England) Regulations 2009, SI 2009/2270, reg 11(2).

11 As to the meaning of 'material reduction' see PARA 417 note 14.
12 Council Tax (Alteration of Lists and Appeals) (England) Regulations 2009, SI 2009/2270, reg 11(3). Where for the purposes of reg 11(3) or (4) (see the text to notes 13–15) the day on which the relevant circumstances arose is not reasonably ascertainable:
    (1) where the alteration is made in pursuance of a proposal, the alteration has effect from the day on which the proposal was served on the listing officer (reg 11(5)(a));
    (2) in any other case, the alteration has effect from the day on which it is entered in the list (reg 11(5)(b)).

    As to the meaning of 'proposal' see PARA 421 note 1. As to the meaning of 'listing officer' see PARA 419 note 12.
13 As to the meaning of 'domestic use' see PARA 417 note 17.
14 Ie for the purposes of the Local Government Finance Act 1988 Pt III (ss 41–67) (non-domestic rating: see PARA 106 note 6) (otherwise than in the circumstances mentioned in the Council Tax (Alteration of Lists and Appeals) (England) Regulations 2009, SI 2009/2270, reg 11(10)(a)(ii)): see reg 11(4). Note: there is no reg 11(10)(a)(ii); see reg 11(10)(b)(i)(bb); and note 5 head (2)(a)(ii).
15 Council Tax (Alteration of Lists and Appeals) (England) Regulations 2009, SI 2009/2270, reg 11(4). See also reg 11(5); and note 12.
16 Council Tax (Alteration of Lists and Appeals) (England) Regulations 2009, SI 2009/2270, reg 11(6)(a).
17 Ie by virtue of the Council Tax (Chargeable Dwellings) Order 1992, SI 1992/549, art 3: see PARA 349.
18 Council Tax (Alteration of Lists and Appeals) (England) Regulations 2009, SI 2009/2270, reg 11(6)(b).
19 Council Tax (Alteration of Lists and Appeals) (England) Regulations 2009, SI 2009/2270, reg 11(6). This provision is expressed to be subject to reg 3(2) (see PARA 419): see reg 11(6).
20 Council Tax (Alteration of Lists and Appeals) (England) Regulations 2009, SI 2009/2270, reg 11(7). This provision is expressed to be subject to reg 3(2) (see PARA 419): see reg 11(7).
21 As to valuation bands see PARA 361.
22 Council Tax (Alteration of Lists and Appeals) (England) Regulations 2009, SI 2009/2270, reg 11(7)(a).
23 Council Tax (Alteration of Lists and Appeals) (England) Regulations 2009, SI 2009/2270, reg 11(7)(b).
24 Council Tax (Alteration of Lists and Appeals) (England) Regulations 2009, SI 2009/2270, reg 11(8)(a). The foregoing provisions are those of reg 11(1)–(7) (see the text to notes 1–23): see reg 11(8)(a).
25 Council Tax (Alteration of Lists and Appeals) (England) Regulations 2009, SI 2009/2270, reg 11(8)(b).
26 Council Tax (Alteration of Lists and Appeals) (England) Regulations 2009, SI 2009/2270, reg 11(8). This provision is expressed to be subject to reg 3(2) (see PARA 419): see reg 11(8).
27 The foregoing provisions are those of the Council Tax (Alteration of Lists and Appeals) (England) Regulations 2009, SI 2009/2270, reg 11(1)–(8) (see the text to notes 1–26): see reg 11(9).
28 Council Tax (Alteration of Lists and Appeals) (England) Regulations 2009, SI 2009/2270, reg 11(9)(a)(i).
29 Council Tax (Alteration of Lists and Appeals) (England) Regulations 2009, SI 2009/2270, reg 11(9)(a)(ii).
30 Council Tax (Alteration of Lists and Appeals) (England) Regulations 2009, SI 2009/2270, reg 11(9)(a).
31 Council Tax (Alteration of Lists and Appeals) (England) Regulations 2009, SI 2009/2270, reg 11(9)(b).
32 Ie the Council Tax (Alteration of Lists and Appeals) (England) Regulations 2009, SI 2009/2270, reg 11(1)–(9): see the text to notes 1–31.
33 Ie under the Valuation Tribunal for England (Council Tax and Rating Appeals) (Procedure) Regulations 2009, SI 2009/2269, reg 35: see PARA 531.
34 Ie under the Valuation Tribunal for England (Council Tax and Rating Appeals) (Procedure) Regulations 2009, SI 2009/2269, reg 38(3): see PARA 531.
35 See the Council Tax (Alteration of Lists and Appeals) (England) Regulations 2009, SI 2009/2270, reg 11(12).

427. Notification of alteration.

Within six weeks of altering[1] a list[2] the listing officer[3] must serve notice on the billing authority[4] stating the effect of the alteration[5]. The billing authority must as soon as is reasonably practicable alter the copy of the list deposited by it[6] at its principal office[7].

Within six weeks of making an alteration the listing officer must also serve notice[8] on the person[9] who then appears to him to be the taxpayer[10] as regards any dwelling[11] to which the alteration relates stating the effect of the alteration[12] and the application of the relevant statutory provisions in relation to the alteration[13]. However, this duty[14] does not apply in relation to alterations made solely for the purpose of correcting a clerical error, or for reflecting:

(1) a decision of the listing officer that the whole of a proposal[15] is well-founded[16];

(2) an agreement[17] between the listing officer and the proposer[18];

(3) a change in the address of the dwelling concerned[19];

(4) a change in the area of the billing authority[20]; or

(5) the decision of the Valuation Tribunal for England[21], the relevant valuation tribunal[22] or the High Court[23] in relation to the dwelling concerned[24].

1 As to the meaning of 'alter' see PARA 419 note 1.

2 As to the meaning of 'list' see PARA 419 note 1.

3 As to the meaning of 'listing officer' see PARA 419 note 12.

4 As to the meaning of 'billing authority' see PARA 420 note 2.

5 Council Tax (Alteration of Lists and Appeals) (England) Regulations 2009, SI 2009/2270, reg 12(1). The Council Tax (Alteration of Lists and Appeals) (England) Regulations 2009, SI 2009/2270, apply in relation to England only: see reg 1(2). As to the equivalent regulations in relation to Wales see the Council Tax (Alteration of Lists and Appeals) Regulations 1993, SI 1993/290, Pt II (regs 3–15); and PARA 428 et seq. As to the meanings of 'England' and 'Wales' see PARA 2 note 16.

6 Ie under the Local Government Finance Act 1992 s 22(8): see PARA 409.

7 Council Tax (Alteration of Lists and Appeals) (England) Regulations 2009, SI 2009/2270, reg 12(1).

8 The listing officer must take such steps as are reasonably practicable to secure that any notice under the Council Tax (Alteration of Lists and Appeals) (England) Regulations 2009, SI 2009/2270, reg 12(2) is served not later than the corresponding notice under reg 12(1) (see the text to notes 1–5): reg 12(4).

9 As to the meaning of 'person' see PARA 11 note 13.

10 As to the meaning of 'taxpayer' see PARA 420 note 3.

11 As to the meaning of 'dwelling' see PARA 349.

12 Council Tax (Alteration of Lists and Appeals) (England) Regulations 2009, SI 2009/2270, reg 12(2)(a).

13 See the Council Tax (Alteration of Lists and Appeals) (England) Regulations 2009, SI 2009/2270, reg 12(2)(b). The relevant statutory provisions are those of Pt 2 (regs 3–12) and Pt 3 (reg 13) (see PARA 419 et seq): see reg 12(2)(b).

14 Ie the Council Tax (Alteration of Lists and Appeals) (England) Regulations 2009, SI 2009/2270, reg 12(2): see the text to notes 8–13.

15 As to the meaning of 'proposal' see PARA 421 note 1.

16 Council Tax (Alteration of Lists and Appeals) (England) Regulations 2009, SI 2009/2270, reg 12(3)(a). As to decisions of the listing officer see PARA 423.

17 Ie under the Council Tax (Alteration of Lists and Appeals) (England) Regulations 2009, SI 2009/2270, reg 9: see PARA 423.

18 See the Council Tax (Alteration of Lists and Appeals) (England) Regulations 2009, SI 2009/2270, reg 12(3)(b). As to the meaning of 'proposer' see PARA 421 note 5.

19 Council Tax (Alteration of Lists and Appeals) (England) Regulations 2009, SI 2009/2270, reg 12(3)(c).

20 Council Tax (Alteration of Lists and Appeals) (England) Regulations 2009, SI 2009/2270, reg 12(3)(d). As to the power to make regulations containing rules for ascertaining in what part of a billing authority's area a dwelling is situated see the Local Government Finance Act 1992 s 10(2); and PARA 360; and as to the power to make regulations containing rules for treating a dwelling as situated in a billing authority's area if part only of the dwelling falls within the area see s 1(3);

and PARA 348.

21 As to appeals to the Valuation Tribunal for England see PARA 514 et seq.

22 'Relevant valuation tribunal' means the valuation tribunal for the area in which is situated the dwelling to which the alteration relates: Council Tax (Alteration of Lists and Appeals) (England) Regulations 2009, SI 2009/2270, reg 12(5). As to the meaning of 'valuation tribunal' see PARA 419 note 16.

23 As to appeals to the High Court see PARA 560.

24 Council Tax (Alteration of Lists and Appeals) (England) Regulations 2009, SI 2009/2270, reg 12(3)(e).

C. WALES

428. Restriction on alteration of valuation bands.

No alteration[1] may be made of a valuation band[2] shown in a list as applicable to any dwelling in Wales unless[3]:

(1) since the valuation band was first shown in the list as applicable to the dwelling:

(a) there has been a material increase[4] in the value of the dwelling and a relevant transaction[5] has been subsequently carried out in relation to the whole or any part of it[6]; or

(b) there has been a material reduction[7] in the value of the dwelling[8]; or

(c) the dwelling has[9] become or ceased to be a composite hereditament[10]; or

(d) in the case of a dwelling which continues to be a composite hereditament, there has been an increase or reduction in its domestic use[11]; or

(2) the listing officer[12] is satisfied that:

(a) a different valuation band should have been determined by the listing officer as applicable to the dwelling[13]; or

(b) the valuation band shown in the list is not that determined by the listing officer as so applicable[14]; or

(3) an order of a valuation tribunal[15] or of the High Court[16] requires the alteration to be made[17].

1 'Alteration' means alteration of a list in relation to a particular dwelling, and 'alter' must be construed accordingly: Council Tax (Alteration of Lists and Appeals) Regulations 1993, SI 1993/290, reg 3. 'List' means, other than in reg 5(1A), (3) and (3A) (see PARA 429), a valuation list compiled under the Local Government Finance Act 1992 s 22 (see PARA 409), s 22A (see PARA 410) or s 22B (see PARA 411): Council Tax (Alteration of Lists and Appeals) Regulations 1993, SI 1993/290, reg 2(1) (definition substituted by SI 2005/181). As to the meaning of 'dwelling' see PARA 349.

2 As to valuation bands see PARA 361.

3 Council Tax (Alteration of Lists and Appeals) Regulations 1993, SI 1993/290, reg 4(1). The Council Tax (Alteration of Lists and Appeals) Regulations 1993, SI 1993/290, apply in relation to Wales only: see PARA 417 note 2. As to the equivalent regulations in relation to England see the Council Tax (Alteration of Lists and Appeals) (England) Regulations 2009, SI 2009/2270; and PARA 419 et seq. As to the meanings of 'England' and 'Wales' see PARA 2 note 16.

4 As to the meaning of 'material increase' see PARA 417 note 11.

5 As to the meaning of 'relevant transaction' see PARA 417 note 12.

6 Council Tax (Alteration of Lists and Appeals) Regulations 1993, SI 1993/290, reg 4(1)(a)(i). In determining whether the valuation band shown in a list as applicable to any dwelling may be altered on the ground specified in reg 4(1)(a)(i), where:

(1) the circumstances which caused the increase referred to in that provision arose before an alteration made to correct an inaccuracy in the list had effect in relation to the dwelling in accordance with reg 14(6)(a), or (7) (see PARA 435) ('the previous alteration') (reg 4(1A)(a) (reg 4(1A) added by SI 1994/1746)); and

(2) the previous alteration has had effect before a relevant transaction has been carried out (Council Tax (Alteration of Lists and Appeals) Regulations 1993, SI 1993/290, reg 4(1A)(b) (as so added)),

the previous alteration is deemed to have had effect before the circumstances which caused the material increase arose: reg 4(1A) (as so added).

7 As to the meaning of 'material reduction' see PARA 417 note 14.

8 Council Tax (Alteration of Lists and Appeals) Regulations 1993, SI 1993/290, reg 4(1)(a)(ii). This provision is expressed to be subject to reg 4(2). Where a material reduction in the value of a dwelling is caused wholly by the demolition of any part of the dwelling, the valuation band must not be altered if the works of demolition are part of, or connected with, a building, engineering or other operation carried out, in progress or proposed to be carried out in relation to the dwelling: reg 4(2). The reference in reg 4(2) to an operation does not include the repair of any damage caused to the dwelling in the course of demolition: reg 4(3). As to building, engineering or other operations for the purposes of development in relation to planning permission see PLANNING vol 81 (2018) PARA 333.

9 Ie for the purposes of the Local Government Finance Act 1988 Pt III (ss 41–67): see PARA 106 note 6.

10 Council Tax (Alteration of Lists and Appeals) Regulations 1993, SI 1993/290, reg 4(1)(a)(iii).

11 Council Tax (Alteration of Lists and Appeals) Regulations 1993, SI 1993/290, reg 4(1)(a)(iv). As to the meaning of 'domestic use' see PARA 417 note 17.

12 'Listing officer', in relation to a list, means the officer charged with its maintenance under the Local Government Finance Act 1992 s 22 (see PARA 409): Council Tax (Alteration of Lists and Appeals) Regulations 1993, SI 1993/290, reg 2(1).

13 Council Tax (Alteration of Lists and Appeals) Regulations 1993, SI 1993/290, reg 4(1)(b)(i).

14 Council Tax (Alteration of Lists and Appeals) Regulations 1993, SI 1993/290, reg 4(1)(b)(ii).

15 Ie the Valuation Tribunal for Wales (see PARA 534 et seq): Council Tax (Alteration of Lists and Appeals) Regulations 1993, SI 1993/290, reg 3 (definition substituted by SI 2010/713). As to the Valuation Tribunal for Wales see PARA 236 et seq.

16 As to appeals to the High Court see PARA 562.

17 Council Tax (Alteration of Lists and Appeals) Regulations 1993, SI 1993/290, reg 4(1)(c).

429. Circumstances and periods in which proposals for alteration may be made.

Subject to the following provisions[1], where a billing authority[2] or an interested person[3] is of the opinion that a list[4] is inaccurate because:

(1) it shows as a dwelling property[5] which ought not to be shown[6]; or

(2) it fails to show a dwelling which ought to be shown[7]; or

(3) the listing officer has determined as applicable to the dwelling a valuation band[8] other than that which should have been determined as so applicable[9]; or

(4) since the valuation band was first shown in the list as applicable to the dwelling, one (or more) of the prescribed events[10] has occurred[11]; or

(5) in relation to a matter shown in it, account has not been taken (whether as regards a particular dwelling or a class of dwelling) of a relevant decision of a valuation tribunal[12] or of the High Court[13],

that authority or person may make a proposal for the alteration of the list[14].

No proposal in relation to the matter mentioned in head (5) above may be made after the expiry of the period of six months[15] beginning on the day on which the decision in question was made[16].

Where, in relation to a dwelling shown in a list[17] on the day on which it is compiled, a billing authority or an interested person is of the opinion that the list is inaccurate because the listing officer has determined as applicable to the dwelling a valuation band other than that which should have been determined as so applicable, any proposal for the alteration of that list as regards that matter must be made not later than 30 November 1993[18].

A person who on any day during the period in which a list is in force becomes the taxpayer in respect of a particular dwelling shown in the list may make a proposal for the alteration of the list in respect of that dwelling where:

(a) he has not during that period previously been the taxpayer in respect of that dwelling[19]; or

(b) the dwelling is first shown in the list after the day on which it was compiled[20].

However, no such proposal may be made[21] where:

(i) six months has expired since the day on which the person first became the taxpayer[22];

(ii) a proposal to alter the same list in relation to the same dwelling and arising from the same facts has been considered and determined by a valuation tribunal[23] or by the High Court[24];

(iii) the new taxpayer is a company which is a subsidiary of the immediately preceding taxpayer[25];

(iv) the immediately preceding taxpayer is a company which is a subsidiary of the new taxpayer[26];

(v) both the new and the immediately preceding taxpayers are companies which are subsidiaries of the same company[27]; or

(vi) the change of taxpayer has occurred solely by reason of the formation of a new partnership in relation to which any of the partners was a partner in the previous partnership[28].

Where the listing officer has altered the list in respect of a dwelling, a billing authority or an interested person may, within six months of the service of the notice of alteration[29], make a proposal for either or both of the following[30]:

(A) the restoration of the list to its state before the alteration was made[31];

(B) a further alteration of the list in respect of that dwelling[32].

1 Ie subject to the Council Tax (Alteration of Lists and Appeals) Regulations 1993, SI 1993/290, reg 5(1A)–(7): see the text to notes 14–32.

The Council Tax (Alteration of Lists and Appeals) Regulations 1993, SI 1993/290, apply in relation to Wales only: see PARA 417 note 2. As to the equivalent regulations in relation to England see the Council Tax (Alteration of Lists and Appeals) (England) Regulations 2009, SI 2009/2270; and PARA 419 et seq. As to the meanings of 'England' and 'Wales' see PARA 2 note 16.

2 'Billing authority', in relation to a dwelling, means the billing authority in whose area the dwelling is situated: Council Tax (Alteration of Lists and Appeals) Regulations 1993, SI 1993/290, reg 2(1). Any reference in the Council Tax (Alteration of Lists and Appeals) Regulations 1993, SI 1993/290, to a dwelling being situated in the area of a billing authority includes a reference to its being treated as so situated: reg 2(2)(b). As to the meaning of 'dwelling' see PARA 349. As to the meaning of 'billing authority' see PARA 346. As to the power to make regulations containing rules for ascertaining in what part of a billing authority's area a dwelling is situated see the Local Government Finance Act 1992 s 10(2); and PARA 360; and as to the power to make regulations containing rules for treating a dwelling as situated in a billing authority's area if part only of the dwelling falls within the area see s 1(3); and PARA 348.

3 'Interested person', in relation to a dwelling and a day, is defined by the Council Tax (Alteration of Lists and Appeals) Regulations 1993, SI 1993/290, reg 2(1), as:

(1) the owner;

(2) where the Local Government Finance Act 1992 s 8(3) (see PARA 356) has effect on the day, and regulations provide for that subsection to have effect as if, for the reference to the owner, there were substituted a reference to another person, that other person;

(3) in relation to an exempt dwelling or a dwelling in respect of which the amount set under s 30 (see PARA 380) for the financial year is nil, any person (other than the owner) who would be liable to pay council tax if the dwelling were not an exempt dwelling or, as the case may be, the amount so set were other than nil; and

(4) any other person who is a taxpayer in respect of the dwelling.

As to the meaning of 'owner' see PARA 354 note 15. As to the meaning of 'person' see PARA 11 note 13. As to the meaning of 'exempt dwelling' see PARA 351. As to persons liable to pay council tax see PARA 354 et seq. 'Taxpayer', in relation to a dwelling and a day, means the person who is liable (whether solely or jointly and severally) to pay council tax in respect of the dwelling and the day: reg 2(1).

4 As to the meaning of 'list' see PARA 428 note 1.

5 Ie including property shown as one dwelling which, by virtue of the Council Tax (Chargeable Dwellings) Order 1992, SI 1992/549, art 3 (see PARA 349) falls to be shown as a number of dwellings, but excluding property in respect of which a determination of the listing officer under art 4 of that Order (see PARA 349) is for the time being effective for the purposes of the Local Government Finance Act 1992 Pt I (ss 1–69): see the Council Tax (Alteration of Lists and Appeals) Regulations 1993, SI 1993/290, reg 5(1)(a). As to the meaning of 'listing officer' see PARA 428 note 12.

6 Council Tax (Alteration of Lists and Appeals) Regulations 1993, SI 1993/290, reg 5(1)(a).

7 Council Tax (Alteration of Lists and Appeals) Regulations 1993, SI 1993/290, reg 5(1)(b).

8 As to valuation bands see PARA 361.

9 Council Tax (Alteration of Lists and Appeals) Regulations 1993, SI 1993/290, reg 5(1)(c).

10 Ie the events mentioned in the Council Tax (Alteration of Lists and Appeals) Regulations 1993, SI 1993/290, reg 4(1)(a): see PARA 428.

11 Council Tax (Alteration of Lists and Appeals) Regulations 1993, SI 1993/290, reg 5(1)(d).

12 As to the meaning of 'valuation tribunal' see PARA 428 note 15. As to appeals to a valuation tribunal PARA 513 et seq.

13 Council Tax (Alteration of Lists and Appeals) Regulations 1993, SI 1993/290, reg 5(1)(e). As to appeals to the High Court see PARA 562.

14 Council Tax (Alteration of Lists and Appeals) Regulations 1993, SI 1993/290, reg 5(1). No proposal may be made later than 31 December 2005 in relation to a list compiled under the Local Government Finance Act 1992 s 22 (see PARA 409) or s 22A PARA 410) other than in respect of the Council Tax (Alteration of Lists and Appeals) Regulations 1993, SI 1993/290, reg 5(2), (6) and reg 8(3)(a), (9) (see PARA 431): reg 5(1A) (added by SI 2005/181). Any valuation of a dwelling carried out in connection with a proposal for the alteration of a list must be carried out in accordance with the Local Government Finance Act 1992 s 21(2) (see PARA 408): Council Tax (Alteration of Lists and Appeals) Regulations 1993, SI 1993/290, reg 36. As to the meaning of 'alteration' see PARA 428 note 1.

15 As to the meaning of 'month' see PARA 11 note 1.

16 Council Tax (Alteration of Lists and Appeals) Regulations 1993, SI 1993/290, reg 5(2).

17 Ie a list compiled under the Local Government Finance Act 1992 s 22 (see PARA 409) or s 22A (see PARA 410).

18 Council Tax (Alteration of Lists and Appeals) Regulations 1993, SI 1993/290, reg 5(3) (amended by SI 2005/181). This provision is expressed to be subject to the Council Tax (Alteration of Lists and Appeals) Regulations 1993, SI 1993/290, reg 5(4) (see the text to notes 19–20) and reg 8(3)(a) (see PARA 431): see reg 5(3). Subject to reg 5(4) and reg 8(3)(a), where, in relation to a dwelling shown in a list compiled under the Local Government Finance Act 1992 s 22B (see PARA 411) on the day on which it is compiled, a billing authority or an interested person is of the opinion that the list is inaccurate because the listing officer has determined as applicable to the dwelling a valuation band other than that which should have been determined as so applicable, any proposal for the alteration of that list as regards that matter must be made not later than 30 September 2006: Council Tax (Alteration of Lists and Appeals) Regulations 1993, SI 1993/290, reg 5(3A) (added by SI 2005/181).

19 Council Tax (Alteration of Lists and Appeals) Regulations 1993, SI 1993/290, reg 5(4)(a).

20 Council Tax (Alteration of Lists and Appeals) Regulations 1993, SI 1993/290, reg 5(4)(b).

21 Ie under the Council Tax (Alteration of Lists and Appeals) Regulations 1993, SI 1993/290, reg 5(4): see the text to notes 19–20.

22 Council Tax (Alteration of Lists and Appeals) Regulations 1993, SI 1993/290, reg 5(5)(a).

23 Ie otherwise than as mentioned in the Council Tax (Alteration of Lists and Appeals) Regulations 1993, SI 1993/290, reg 25(4) (dismissal on failure of parties to appear): see PARA 539.

24 Council Tax (Alteration of Lists and Appeals) Regulations 1993, SI 1993/290, reg 5(5)(b).

25 Council Tax (Alteration of Lists and Appeals) Regulations 1993, SI 1993/290, reg 5(5)(c). 'Company' and 'subsidiary' have the same meanings as (now) in the Companies Act 2006 (see COMPANIES vol 14 (2016) PARAS 1, 22): Council Tax (Alteration of Lists and Appeals) Regulations 1993, SI 1993/290, reg 3.

26 Council Tax (Alteration of Lists and Appeals) Regulations 1993, SI 1993/290, reg 5(5)(d).

27 Council Tax (Alteration of Lists and Appeals) Regulations 1993, SI 1993/290, reg 5(5)(e).
28 Council Tax (Alteration of Lists and Appeals) Regulations 1993, SI 1993/290, reg 5(5)(f).
29 Ie under the Council Tax (Alteration of Lists and Appeals) Regulations 1993, SI 1993/290, reg 15: see PARA 436. As to service of notices see PARA 535.
30 Council Tax (Alteration of Lists and Appeals) Regulations 1993, SI 1993/290, reg 5(6). Regulation 5(6) does not apply to the extent that the alteration in question:
 (1) consists of:
  (a) the insertion or alteration of a reference number (reg 5(7)(a)(i));
  (b) the alteration of an address (reg 5(7)(a)(ii));
  (c) the correction of a clerical error (reg 5(7)(a)(iii)); or
  (d) the entry of the day from which an alteration has effect where the day is the completion day determined under the Local Government Finance Act 1988 Sch 4A as it applies for the purposes of the Local Government Finance Act 1992 Pt I (ss 1–69) (see s 17; and PARA 353) in relation to the dwelling concerned (Council Tax (Alteration of Lists and Appeals) Regulations 1993, SI 1993/290, reg 5(7)(a)(iv)); or
 (2) reflects a change in the area of the billing authority or a decision of a valuation tribunal or the High Court in relation to the dwelling concerned (reg 5(7)(b)).
31 Council Tax (Alteration of Lists and Appeals) Regulations 1993, SI 1993/290, reg 5(6)(a).
32 Council Tax (Alteration of Lists and Appeals) Regulations 1993, SI 1993/290, reg 5(6)(b).

430. Manner of making proposals and information to be included.

A proposal[1] must be made by notice in writing[2] served on the listing officer[3]; and the notice must[4]:

(1) state the name and address of the proposer[5], and the capacity in which the proposer makes the proposal[6];
(2) identify the dwelling[7] to which it relates[8];
(3) identify the respects in which it is proposed the list be altered[9]; and
(4) include:
 (a) a statement of the reasons for believing the list to be inaccurate[10];
 (b) if the proposal is made in relation to one or more of the prescribed events having taken place[11], a statement of the reasons for the belief that such an event has occurred and of the date on which the event occurred[12];
 (c) if the proposal is made in relation to the failure to take into account a prescribed decision[13], a statement identifying the property to which the decision in question relates and the date of that decision and (as the case may be) that the decision was a decision of the valuation tribunal or the High Court[14];
 (d) if the proposal is made in relation to an inaccuracy in a list in prescribed circumstances[15], a statement of the day on which the proposer became the taxpayer[16];
 (e) if the proposal disputes the accuracy of an alteration made by the listing officer, a statement of the day on which the listing officer served[17] the relevant notice[18];
 (f) if the proposal disputes the day from which an alteration should have effect, a statement of the day proposed in its place[19].

A proposal may deal with more than one dwelling:

(i) in the prescribed circumstances[20]; or
(ii) where the proposer makes the proposal in the same capacity as respects each dwelling, and each of the dwellings is within the same building as each other dwelling or, where any of them is not within a building, it is within the same curtilage as the other or others[21].

Unless he serves an invalidity notice[22], the listing officer must, within the period of 28 days beginning on the day on which he receives a proposal, by notice in writing served on the proposer acknowledge its receipt[23].

Within six weeks beginning on the day on which a proposal is served on him, the listing officer must serve a copy of the proposal on each of the following (not being the proposer):

(A) any person who then appears to him to be the taxpayer as regards any dwelling to which the proposal relates[24]; and

(B) the billing authority[25], where that authority has served notice on the listing officer that it wishes to receive a copy of a class or classes of proposal, and the proposal falls within any such class[26].

1 'Proposal' means a proposal for the alteration of a list: Council Tax (Alteration of Lists and Appeals) Regulations 1993, SI 1993/290, reg 2(1). As to the meaning of 'alteration' see PARA 428 note 1. As to the meaning of 'list' see PARA 428 note 1. As to the circumstances in which proposals may be made see PARA 429.

2 In the Council Tax (Alteration of Lists and Appeals) Regulations 1993, SI 1993/290, any reference to a written notice includes a reference to a notice in electronic form: reg 35(8) (reg 35 substituted in relation to Wales by SI 2010/613). As to the meaning of 'writing' see PARA 21 note 3.

3 As to service of notices see PARA 535. As to the meaning of 'listing officer' see PARA 428 note 12.

4 Council Tax (Alteration of Lists and Appeals) Regulations 1993, SI 1993/290, reg 5(1). The Council Tax (Alteration of Lists and Appeals) Regulations 1993, SI 1993/290, apply in relation to Wales only: see PARA 417 note 2. As to the equivalent regulations in relation to England see the Council Tax (Alteration of Lists and Appeals) (England) Regulations 2009, SI 2009/2270; and PARA 419 et seq. As to the meanings of 'England' and 'Wales' see PARA 2 note 16.

5 'Proposer' means the person making a proposal: Council Tax (Alteration of Lists and Appeals) Regulations 1993, SI 1993/290, reg 2(1). As to the meaning of 'person' see PARA 11 note 13.

6 Council Tax (Alteration of Lists and Appeals) Regulations 1993, SI 1993/290, reg 6(1)(a). As to the persons by whom proposals may be made see PARA 429.

7 As to the meaning of 'dwelling' see PARA 349.

8 Council Tax (Alteration of Lists and Appeals) Regulations 1993, SI 1993/290, reg 6(1)(b).

9 Council Tax (Alteration of Lists and Appeals) Regulations 1993, SI 1993/290, reg 6(1)(c).

10 Council Tax (Alteration of Lists and Appeals) Regulations 1993, SI 1993/290, reg 6(1)(d)(i).

11 Ie in the circumstances mentioned in the Council Tax (Alteration of Lists and Appeals) Regulations 1993, SI 1993/290, reg 5(1)(d): see PARA 429.

12 See the Council Tax (Alteration of Lists and Appeals) Regulations 1993, SI 1993/290, reg 6(1)(d)(ii).

13 Ie in the circumstances mentioned in the Council Tax (Alteration of Lists and Appeals) Regulations 1993, SI 1993/290, reg 5(1)(e): see PARA 429.

14 See the Council Tax (Alteration of Lists and Appeals) Regulations 1993, SI 1993/290, reg 6(1)(d)(iii).

15 Ie in the circumstances mentioned in the Council Tax (Alteration of Lists and Appeals) Regulations 1993, SI 1993/290, reg 5(4): see PARA 429.

16 See the Council Tax (Alteration of Lists and Appeals) Regulations 1993, SI 1993/290, reg 6(1)(d)(iv). As to the meaning of 'taxpayer' see PARA 429 note 3.

17 Ie under the Council Tax (Alteration of Lists and Appeals) Regulations 1993, SI 1993/290, reg 15: see PARA 436.

18 Council Tax (Alteration of Lists and Appeals) Regulations 1993, SI 1993/290, reg 6(1)(d)(v).

19 Council Tax (Alteration of Lists and Appeals) Regulations 1993, SI 1993/290, reg 6(1)(d)(vi).

20 Ie in the circumstances mentioned in the Council Tax (Alteration of Lists and Appeals) Regulations 1993, SI 1993/290, reg 5(1)(a) (see PARA 429): reg 6(2)(a).

21 Council Tax (Alteration of Lists and Appeals) Regulations 1993, SI 1993/290, reg 6(2)(b).

22 The Council Tax (Alteration of Lists and Appeals) Regulations 1993, SI 1993/290, reg 7(1) does not apply where the listing officer serves a notice under reg 8 (see PARA 431) in respect of the proposal: reg 7(2).

23 Council Tax (Alteration of Lists and Appeals) Regulations 1993, SI 1993/290, reg 7(1). A notice must specify the date of receipt of the proposal; and must be accompanied by a statement of the effect of regs 8–12 (see the text to notes 24–26 and PARAS 432–434, 435–436): reg 7(3).

24 Council Tax (Alteration of Lists and Appeals) Regulations 1993, SI 1993/290, reg 9(1)(a). Each copy of a proposal served under reg 9(1)(a) must be accompanied by a statement of the effect of regs 10–13 (see PARAS 432–434, 435–436): reg 9(2).
25 As to the meaning of 'billing authority' see PARA 429 note 2.
26 Council Tax (Alteration of Lists and Appeals) Regulations 1993, SI 1993/290, reg 9(1)(b).

431. Proposals treated as invalid.

Where the listing officer[1] is of the opinion that a proposal[2] has not been validly made[3], he may, within four weeks of its service on him, serve notice (an 'invalidity notice') on the proposer[4] that he is of that opinion[5] and stating the reasons for that opinion[6]. The listing officer may at any time withdraw an invalidity notice by notice in writing[7] served on the proposer; and on such withdrawal any appeal against the invalidity notice must be treated as having been withdrawn[8].

Unless an invalidity notice has been so withdrawn, the person[9] on whom it is served may, within four weeks of its service on him:

(1) make a further proposal in relation to the same dwelling[10], notwithstanding the previous expiry of any period[11] for the making of proposals[12]; or
(2) appeal against the notice to the relevant valuation tribunal[13].

An appeal against an invalidity notice must be initiated by serving notice of disagreement on the listing officer[14]. Unless the listing officer withdraws the invalidity notice within four weeks of the service of the notice of disagreement, on the expiry of that period he must inform the clerk of the relevant valuation tribunal[15] of:

(a) the entry in the list (if any) which is proposed to be altered[16];
(b) the grounds on which the proposal was made[17]; and
(c) the reasons for his opinion that the proposal has not been validly made[18].

Where information relating to an invalidity notice has been supplied in accordance with heads (a) to (c) above and the notice is withdrawn, the listing officer must, as soon as practicable, inform the clerk of the relevant valuation tribunal of the withdrawal[19].

Until it is finally decided[20] that the proposal to which an invalidity notice relates was validly made, the statutory provisions relating to the procedure subsequent to the making of proposals[21] do not apply in relation to the proposal; and where it is finally decided as so mentioned, those provisions have effect as if the proposal had been served on the listing officer on the date of that final decision[22].

Nothing done under the above provisions is to be construed as preventing any party to an appeal in respect of a disagreement as to a proposed alteration[23] from contending for the purposes of that appeal that the proposal to which the appeal relates was not validly made[24].

1 As to the meaning of 'listing officer' see PARA 428 note 12.
2 As to the meaning of 'proposal' see PARA 430 note 1.
3 As to the making of proposals see PARAS 429–430.
4 As to the meaning of 'proposer' see PARA 430 note 5.
5 Council Tax (Alteration of Lists and Appeals) Regulations 1993, SI 1993/290, reg 8(1). The Council Tax (Alteration of Lists and Appeals) Regulations 1993, SI 1993/290, apply in relation to Wales only: see PARA 417 note 2. As to the equivalent regulations in relation to England see the Council Tax (Alteration of Lists and Appeals) (England) Regulations 2009, SI 2009/2270; and PARA 419 et seq. As to the meanings of 'England' and 'Wales' see PARA 2 note 16.
6 Council Tax (Alteration of Lists and Appeals) Regulations 1993, SI 1993/290, reg 8(1)(a). The notice must also state the effect of reg 8(3)–(6) (see the text to notes 9–14): reg 8(1)(b). As to service of notices see PARA 535.

7 As to the meaning of 'written notice' see PARA 430 note 2. As to the meaning of 'writing' see PARA 21 note 3.
8 Council Tax (Alteration of Lists and Appeals) Regulations 1993, SI 1993/290, reg 8(2).
9 As to the meaning of 'person' see PARA 11 note 13.
10 As to the meaning of 'dwelling' see PARA 349.
11 Ie applicable under the Council Tax (Alteration of Lists and Appeals) Regulations 1993, SI 1993/290, reg 5: see PARA 429.
12 See the Council Tax (Alteration of Lists and Appeals) Regulations 1993, SI 1993/290, reg 8(3)(a). No proposal may be made under reg 8(3)(a) where the proposal to which the invalidity notice relates was made under reg 8(3)(a) or after the expiry of any period applicable under reg 5 (see PARA 429): reg 8(4). Where a proposal is made under reg 8(3)(a), the proposal in respect of which the invalidity notice was served must be treated as having been withdrawn: reg 8(5).
13 Council Tax (Alteration of Lists and Appeals) Regulations 1993, SI 1993/290, reg 8(3)(b). 'The relevant valuation tribunal', means the Valuation Tribunal for Wales: reg 3 (definition substituted by SI 2010/713). As to appeals to the tribunal see PARA 513 et seq. As to the Valuation Tribunal for Wales see PARA 236 et seq.
14 Council Tax (Alteration of Lists and Appeals) Regulations 1993, SI 1993/290, reg 8(6).
15 Council Tax (Alteration of Lists and Appeals) Regulations 1993, SI 1993/290, reg 8(7).
16 Council Tax (Alteration of Lists and Appeals) Regulations 1993, SI 1993/290, reg 8(7)(a).
17 Council Tax (Alteration of Lists and Appeals) Regulations 1993, SI 1993/290, reg 8(7)(b).
18 Council Tax (Alteration of Lists and Appeals) Regulations 1993, SI 1993/290, reg 8(7)(c).
19 Council Tax (Alteration of Lists and Appeals) Regulations 1993, SI 1993/290, reg 8(8).
20 For these purposes, a final decision is made:
   (1) where the invalidity notice is withdrawn, on the day of the withdrawal (Council Tax (Alteration of Lists and Appeals) Regulations 1993, SI 1993/290, reg 8(10)(a));
   (2) in any other case, on the day on which:
      (a) the valuation tribunal having determined the appeal, the period within which an appeal may be made to the High Court under reg 32 (appeals: see PARA 562) expires without such an appeal being made (reg 8(10)(b)(i)); or
      (b) the High Court determines the appeal (reg 8(10)(b)(ii)).
21 Ie the Council Tax (Alteration of Lists and Appeals) Regulations 1993, SI 1993/290, regs 9–13: see PARAS 430, 432–434, 435–436.
22 Council Tax (Alteration of Lists and Appeals) Regulations 1993, SI 1993/290, reg 8(9).
23 Ie an appeal under the Council Tax (Alteration of Lists and Appeals) Regulations 1993, SI 1993/290, reg 13: see PARA 434.
24 Council Tax (Alteration of Lists and Appeals) Regulations 1993, SI 1993/290, reg 8(11).

432. Proposals agreed by listing officer.

Where the listing officer[1] is of the opinion that a proposal[2] is well-founded, he must:

(1) serve notice[3] on:
   (a) the proposer[4]; and
   (b) any person[5] (not being the proposer) who then appears to him to be the taxpayer[6] as regards any dwelling[7] to which the proposal relates,

   that he proposes to alter the list[8] accordingly[9]; and

(2) within six weeks of the date of the notice so alter the list[10].

1 As to the meaning of 'listing officer' see PARA 428 note 12.
2 As to the meaning of 'proposal' see PARA 430 note 1.
3 As to service of notices see PARA 535.
4 As to the meaning of 'proposer' see PARA 430 note 5.
5 As to the meaning of 'person' see PARA 11 note 13.
6 As to the meaning of 'taxpayer' see PARA 429 note 3.
7 As to the meaning of 'dwelling' see PARA 349.
8 As to the meanings of 'alter' and 'list' see PARA 428 note 1.
9 Council Tax (Alteration of Lists and Appeals) Regulations 1993, SI 1993/290, reg 10(a). The Council Tax (Alteration of Lists and Appeals) Regulations 1993, SI 1993/290, apply in relation to

Wales only: see PARA 417 note 2. As to the equivalent regulations in relation to England see the Council Tax (Alteration of Lists and Appeals) (England) Regulations 2009, SI 2009/2270; and PARA 419 et seq. As to the meanings of 'England' and 'Wales' see PARA 2 note 16.

10 Council Tax (Alteration of Lists and Appeals) Regulations 1993, SI 1993/290, reg 10(b).

433. Agreed alterations following proposals.

Where, following the making of a proposal[1], all the prescribed persons[2] agree on an alteration of the list[3] in accordance with the relevant statutory provisions[4] in terms other than those contained in the proposal, and that agreement is signified in writing[5]:

(1) the listing officer[6] must not later than the expiry of six weeks beginning on the day on which the agreement was made alter the list to give effect to the agreement[7]; and

(2) the proposal is to be treated as having been withdrawn[8].

1 As to the meaning of 'proposal' see PARA 430 note 1.

2 Ie all the persons mentioned in the Council Tax (Alteration of Lists and Appeals) Regulations 1993, SI 1993/290, reg 12(2). The prescribed persons are:

(1) the listing officer (reg 12(2)(a));

(2) the proposer (reg 12(2)(b));

(3) subject to reg 12(3), (4), the taxpayer, at the date of the proposal, in relation to the dwelling to which it relates (reg 12(2)(c));

(4) subject to reg 12(4), the taxpayer, at the date of the agreement, in relation to the dwelling to which it relates (reg 12(2)(d));

(5) subject to reg 12(3), any other person who:

(a) at the date of the proposal would have been competent to make the proposal (reg 12(2)(e)(i)); and

(b) has within three months beginning on the day on which the proposal was served on the listing officer served notice on him in writing to the effect that he wishes to be party to the proceedings in respect of the proposal (reg 12(2)(e)(ii)).

As to the meaning of 'person' see PARA 11 note 13. As to the meaning of 'proposer' see PARA 430 note 5. As to the meaning of 'taxpayer' see PARA 429 note 3. As to the meaning of 'dwelling' see PARA 349. As to the meaning of 'month' see PARA 11 note 1.

Where:

(i) a person who was at the date of the proposal the taxpayer in respect of the dwelling is, at the date on which all the other persons mentioned in heads (1)–(5) above have agreed on an alteration of the list as mentioned in reg 12(1), no longer the taxpayer in respect of the dwelling, and the listing officer has taken all reasonable steps to ascertain the whereabouts of that person, but they have not been ascertained (reg 12(3)(a)); or

(ii) a person who has given notice as mentioned in head (5) above cannot be contacted at the address supplied to the listing officer (whether in that notice or otherwise) (reg 12(3)(b)),

the agreement of that person under reg 12(1), (2) is not required: reg 12(3).

Where, at the date of the proposal or agreement, more than one person is a taxpayer in respect of dwelling concerned, such of the requirements of reg 12(1) as relate to the agreement of persons referred to in head (3) or, as the case may be, head (4) above are to be treated as satisfied where the agreement of one of the persons to whom the description in the relevant head applies has been signified: reg 12(4).

3 As to the meanings of 'alteration' and 'list' see PARA 428 note 1.

4 Ie in accordance with the Council Tax (Alteration of Lists and Appeals) Regulations 1993, SI 1993/290, Pt II (regs 3–15).

5 As to the meaning of 'in writing' see PARA 21 note 3.

6 As to the meaning of 'listing officer' see PARA 428 note 12.

7 Council Tax (Alteration of Lists and Appeals) Regulations 1993, SI 1993/290, reg 12(1)(a). This is subject to reg 12(5): see reg 12(1)(a). Where the period of six weeks mentioned in reg 12(1)(a) would expire before the period of three months mentioned in reg 12(2)(e) (see note 5), the alteration required by reg 12(1)(a) must, where no notice is served as mentioned in reg 12(2)(e), be made as soon as practicable after the expiry of that period of three months: reg 12(5).

8 Council Tax (Alteration of Lists and Appeals) Regulations 1993, SI 1993/290, reg 12(1)(b).

The Council Tax (Alteration of Lists and Appeals) Regulations 1993, SI 1993/290, apply in relation to Wales only: see PARA 417 note 2. As to the equivalent regulations in relation to England see the Council Tax (Alteration of Lists and Appeals) (England) Regulations 2009, SI 2009/2270; and PARA 419 et seq. As to the meanings of 'England' and 'Wales' see PARA 2 note 16.

434. Disagreement as to proposed alteration.

Where the listing officer[1] is of the opinion that a proposal[2] is not well-founded and:

(1) the proposal is not withdrawn[3]; and
(2) there is no agreement[4] as to alterations[5],

the disagreement must, no later than the expiry of the period of six months[6] beginning on the day on which the proposal was served[7] on him, be referred by the listing officer to the relevant valuation tribunal[8], as an appeal by the proposer[9] against the listing officer's refusal to alter the list[10].

A referral must take place by means of the transmission to the clerk of the tribunal of a statement of the following matters[11]:

(a) the entry in the list (if any) which is proposed to be altered[12];
(b) the date of service of the proposal[13];
(c) the names and addresses (where known to the listing officer) of all persons whose agreement to alter the list[14] is required[15]; and
(d) the grounds on which the proposal was made[16].

1 As to the meaning of 'listing officer' see PARA 428 note 12.
2 As to the meaning of 'proposal' see PARA 430 note 1.
3 Council Tax (Alteration of Lists and Appeals) Regulations 1993, SI 1993/290, reg 13(1)(a).
The Council Tax (Alteration of Lists and Appeals) Regulations 1993, SI 1993/290, apply in relation to Wales only: see PARA 417 note 2. As to the equivalent regulations in relation to England see the Council Tax (Alteration of Lists and Appeals) (England) Regulations 2009, SI 2009/2270; and PARA 419 et seq. As to the meanings of 'England' and 'Wales' see PARA 2 note 16.
4 Ie as provided in the Council Tax (Alteration of Lists and Appeals) Regulations 1993, SI 1993/290, reg 12: see PARA 433.
5 Council Tax (Alteration of Lists and Appeals) Regulations 1993, SI 1993/290, reg 13(1)(b).
6 As to the meaning of 'month' see PARA 11 note 1.
7 As to service of a proposal see PARA 430.
8 Ie the Valuation Tribunal for Wales: see PARA 431 note 13. As to appeals to the tribunal see PARA 513 et seq. As to the Valuation Tribunal for Wales see PARA 236 et seq.
9 As to the meaning of 'proposer' see PARA 430 note 5.
10 Council Tax (Alteration of Lists and Appeals) Regulations 1993, SI 1993/290, reg 13(1). As to the meanings of 'alteration' and 'list' see PARA 428 note 1.
11 Council Tax (Alteration of Lists and Appeals) Regulations 1993, SI 1993/290, reg 13(2).
12 Council Tax (Alteration of Lists and Appeals) Regulations 1993, SI 1993/290, reg 13(2)(a).
13 Council Tax (Alteration of Lists and Appeals) Regulations 1993, SI 1993/290, reg 13(2)(b).
14 Ie under the Council Tax (Alteration of Lists and Appeals) Regulations 1993, SI 1993/290, reg 12: see PARA 433.
15 Council Tax (Alteration of Lists and Appeals) Regulations 1993, SI 1993/290, reg 13(2)(c).
16 Council Tax (Alteration of Lists and Appeals) Regulations 1993, SI 1993/290, reg 13(2)(d).

435. Day from which alteration has effect.

Subject to the following provisions[1], an alteration[2] effected so as to show in or, as the case may be, to delete from a list[3] any dwelling[4] which, since the list was compiled:

(1) has come into existence or ceased to exist[5]; or
(2) has ceased to be situated, or has become situated, in the area of the billing authority[6] for whose area the list was compiled[7],

has effect from the day on which the circumstances giving rise to the alteration occurred[8].

An alteration reflecting a material increase[9] in the value of a dwelling has effect from the day on which the relevant transaction, as regards that dwelling (or part of it) and that increase, was completed[10].

An alteration reflecting a material reduction[11] in the value of a dwelling has effect from the day on which the circumstances which caused that reduction arose[12].

An alteration reflecting an increase or reduction in the domestic use[13] of a dwelling which is or becomes or ceases to be a composite hereditament[14] has effect from the day on which the circumstances which caused that increase or reduction arose[15].

An alteration made to correct an inaccuracy in a list on the day it was compiled has effect[16]:

(a) in any case where the inaccuracy was to show:
   (i) as applicable to a dwelling a valuation band[17] which is lower than the band which should have been determined or shown as applicable to it[18]; or
   (ii) as one dwelling property which should have been treated[19] as two or more dwellings[20],

   from the day on which the alteration is entered in the list[21];

(b) in a case where the inaccuracy was to show as applicable to a dwelling a valuation band which is higher than the band which should have been determined or shown as applicable to it, from the later of:
   (i) the day on which the list was compiled[22]; and
   (ii) the day six years before the day on which the alteration is entered in the list[23]; and

(c) in any other case, from the day on which the list was compiled[24].

Where an alteration is made to correct an inaccuracy in a list (other than an alteration which falls to have effect as provided in the foregoing provisions)[25], and the inaccuracy arose in the course of making a previous alteration and was to show:

(A) as applicable to a dwelling a valuation band which is lower than the band which should have been determined or shown as applicable to it[26]; or

(B) as one dwelling property which should have been treated[27] as two or more dwellings[28],

the alteration has effect from the day on which the alteration is entered in the list[29].

An alteration made to correct an inaccuracy in a list (other than an alteration which falls to have effect as provided in the foregoing provisions)[30] has effect:

(I) in a case where the alteration is made to correct an inaccuracy in the list which arose in the course of making a previous alteration[31] and the previous alteration fell to have effect in accordance with the foregoing provisions[32], from the day on which the previous alteration had effect, or, but for the inaccuracy, would have had effect[33]; and

(II) in any other case, from the day on which the list became inaccurate[34].

1 Ie subject to the Local Government Finance Act 1992 s 17(3), (5) (completion of new dwellings: see PARA 353), the Council Tax (Alteration of Lists and Appeals) Regulations 1993, SI 1993/290, reg 29 (see PARA 542) and reg 14(2)–(10) (see the text to notes 9–34).

The Council Tax (Alteration of Lists and Appeals) Regulations 1993, SI 1993/290, apply in relation to Wales only: see PARA 417 note 2. As to the equivalent regulations in relation to England see the Council Tax (Alteration of Lists and Appeals) (England) Regulations 2009, SI 2009/2270; and PARA 419 et seq. As to the meanings of 'England' and 'Wales' see PARA 2 note 16.

2 As to the meaning of 'alteration' see PARA 428 note 1.
3 As to the meaning of 'list' see PARA 428 note 1.
4 As to the meaning of 'dwelling' see PARA 349.
5 Council Tax (Alteration of Lists and Appeals) Regulations 1993, SI 1993/290, reg 14(1)(a) (reg 14 substituted by SI 2010/77). Any reference in the Council Tax (Alteration of Lists and Appeals) Regulations 1993, SI 1993/290, reg 14(1)–(8) to a dwelling ceasing to exist or coming into existence includes a reference to a dwelling which ceases to exist or comes into existence:
    (1) by virtue of property which was a dwelling:
        (a) becoming liable (as such or together with other property) to non-domestic rating by reason of its consisting entirely of non-domestic property (reg 14(9)(a)(i) (as so substituted)); or
        (b) ceasing (otherwise than as mentioned in head (a)) to satisfy the requirements of the Local Government Finance Act 1992 s 3 (see PARA 349) (Council Tax (Alteration of Lists and Appeals) Regulations 1993, SI 1993/290, reg 14(9)(a)(ii) (as so substituted));
    (2) by virtue of a hereditament consisting entirely of property which is non-domestic becoming a composite hereditament which satisfies the requirements of the Local Government Finance Act 1992 s 3 (Council Tax (Alteration of Lists and Appeals) Regulations 1993, SI 1993/290, reg 14(9)(b) (as so substituted));
    (3) by virtue of property which was one dwelling for the purposes of Part I of the Local Government Finance Act 1992 Pt I (ss 1–69) being treated for those purposes as two or more dwellings (Council Tax (Alteration of Lists and Appeals) Regulations 1993, SI 1993/290, reg 14(9)(c) (as so substituted)); or
    (4) by virtue of property which was two or more dwellings for those purposes being treated for those purposes as one dwelling (reg 14(9)(d) (as so substituted)).

  As to the meaning of 'hereditament' see PARA 106 (definition applied by reg 14(10)).
6 As to the meaning of 'billing authority' and as to references to a dwelling being situated in a billing authority's area see PARA 429 note 2.
7 Council Tax (Alteration of Lists and Appeals) Regulations 1993, SI 1993/290, reg 14(1)(b) (as substituted: see note 5).
8 Council Tax (Alteration of Lists and Appeals) Regulations 1993, SI 1993/290, reg 14(1) (as substituted: see note 5).
9 As to the meaning of 'material increase' see PARA 417 note 11.
10 Council Tax (Alteration of Lists and Appeals) Regulations 1993, SI 1993/290, reg 14(2) (as substituted: see note 5).
11 As to the meaning of 'material reduction' see PARA 417 note 14.
12 Council Tax (Alteration of Lists and Appeals) Regulations 1993, SI 1993/290, reg 14(3) (as substituted: see note 5). Where for the purposes of reg 14(3) or (4) (see the text to notes 13–15) the day on which the relevant circumstances arose is not reasonably ascertainable:
    (1) where the alteration is made in pursuance of a proposal, the alteration has effect from the day on which the proposal was served on the listing officer (reg 14(5)(a) (as so substituted));
    (2) in any other case, the alteration has effect from the day on which it is entered in the list (reg 14(5)(b) (as so substituted)).

  As to the meaning of 'proposal' see PARA 430 note 1. As to the meaning of 'listing officer' see PARA 428 note 12.
13 As to the meaning of 'domestic use' see PARA 417 note 17.
14 Ie for the purposes of the Local Government Finance Act 1988 Pt III (ss 41–67) (non-domestic rating: see PARA 106 note 6) (otherwise than in the circumstances mentioned in the Council Tax (Alteration of Lists and Appeals) Regulations 1993, SI 1993/290, reg 14(9)(a)(ii)): see reg 14(4); and note 5 head (1)(b).
15 Council Tax (Alteration of Lists and Appeals) Regulations 1993, SI 1993/290, reg 14(4) (as substituted: see note 5). See also reg 14(5); and note 12.
16 Council Tax (Alteration of Lists and Appeals) Regulations 1993, SI 1993/290, reg 14(6) (as substituted: see note 5). This provision is expressed to be subject to reg 4(1A) (see PARA 428): see reg 14(6) (as so substituted).
17 As to valuation bands see PARA 361.
18 Council Tax (Alteration of Lists and Appeals) Regulations 1993, SI 1993/290, reg 14(6)(a)(i) (as substituted: see note 5).
19 Ie by virtue of the Council Tax (Chargeable Dwellings) Order 1992, SI 1992/549, art 3: see PARA 349.

20 Council Tax (Alteration of Lists and Appeals) Regulations 1993, SI 1993/290, reg 14(6)(a)(ii) (as substituted: see note 5).
21 Council Tax (Alteration of Lists and Appeals) Regulations 1993, SI 1993/290, reg 14(6)(a) (as substituted: see note 5).
22 Council Tax (Alteration of Lists and Appeals) Regulations 1993, SI 1993/290, reg 14(6)(b)(i) (as substituted: see note 5).
23 Council Tax (Alteration of Lists and Appeals) Regulations 1993, SI 1993/290, reg 14(6)(b)(ii) (as substituted: see note 5).
24 Council Tax (Alteration of Lists and Appeals) Regulations 1993, SI 1993/290, reg 14(6)(c) (as substituted: see note 5).
25 Council Tax (Alteration of Lists and Appeals) Regulations 1993, SI 1993/290, reg 14(7) (as substituted: see note 5). This provision is expressed to be subject to reg 4(1A) (see PARA 428): see reg 14(7) (as so substituted).
26 Council Tax (Alteration of Lists and Appeals) Regulations 1993, SI 1993/290, reg 14(7)(a) (as substituted: see note 5).
27 Ie by virtue of the Council Tax (Chargeable Dwellings) Order 1992, SI 1992/549, art 3: see PARA 349.
28 Council Tax (Alteration of Lists and Appeals) Regulations 1993, SI 1993/290, reg 14(7)(b) (as substituted: see note 5).
29 Council Tax (Alteration of Lists and Appeals) Regulations 1993, SI 1993/290, reg 14(7) (as substituted: see note 5).
30 Council Tax (Alteration of Lists and Appeals) Regulations 1993, SI 1993/290, reg 14(8) (as substituted: see note 5). The foregoing provisions are those of reg 14(1)–(7) (see the text to notes 1–29): see reg 14(8) (as so added).
31 Council Tax (Alteration of Lists and Appeals) Regulations 1993, SI 1993/290, reg 14(8)(a)(i) (as substituted: see note 5).
32 Council Tax (Alteration of Lists and Appeals) Regulations 1993, SI 1993/290, reg 14(8)(a)(ii) (as substituted: see note 5).
33 Council Tax (Alteration of Lists and Appeals) Regulations 1993, SI 1993/290, reg 14(8)(a) (as substituted: see note 5).
34 Council Tax (Alteration of Lists and Appeals) Regulations 1993, SI 1993/290, reg 14(8)(b) (as substituted: see note 5).

436. Notification of alteration.

Within six weeks of altering[1] a list[2] the listing officer[3] must serve notice on the billing authority[4] stating the effect of the alteration[5]. The billing authority must as soon as is reasonably practicable alter the copy of the list deposited by it[6] at its principal office[7].

Within six weeks of effecting an alteration the listing officer must also serve notice[8] on the person[9] who then appears to him to be the taxpayer[10] as regards any dwelling[11] to which the alteration relates stating the effect of the alteration[12] and the application of the relevant statutory provisions in relation to the alteration[13]. However, this duty[14] does not apply in relation to alterations made solely for the purpose of correcting a clerical error[15], or for reflecting:

(1) a decision of the listing officer that a proposal[16] is well-founded[17];
(2) an agreement[18] between the listing officer and the proposer[19];
(3) a change in the address of the dwelling concerned[20];
(4) a change in the area of the billing authority[21]; or
(5) the decision of a valuation tribunal[22] or the High Court[23] in relation to the dwelling concerned[24].

1 As to the meaning of 'alter' see PARA 428 note 1.
2 As to the meaning of 'list' see PARA 428 note 1.
3 As to the meaning of 'listing officer' see PARA 428 note 12.
4 As to service of notices see PARA 535. As to the meaning of 'billing authority' see PARA 429 note 2.
5 Council Tax (Alteration of Lists and Appeals) Regulations 1993, SI 1993/290, reg 15(1). The Council Tax (Alteration of Lists and Appeals) Regulations 1993, SI 1993/290, apply in relation to

Wales only: see PARA 417 note 2. As to the equivalent regulations in relation to England see the Council Tax (Alteration of Lists and Appeals) (England) Regulations 2009, SI 2009/2270; and PARA 419 et seq. As to the meanings of 'England' and 'Wales' see PARA 2 note 16.

6 Ie under the Local Government Finance Act 1992 s 22(8) (see PARA 409), s 22A(10) (see PARA 410) or s 22B(10) (see PARA 411).

7 Council Tax (Alteration of Lists and Appeals) Regulations 1993, SI 1993/290, reg 15(1) (amended by SI 2005/181).

8 The listing officer must take such steps as are reasonably practicable to secure that any notice under the Council Tax (Alteration of Lists and Appeals) Regulations 1993, SI 1993/290, reg 15(2) is served not later than the corresponding notice under reg 15(1) (see the text to notes 1–5): reg 15(4).

9 As to the meaning of 'person' see PARA 11 note 13.

10 As to the meaning of 'taxpayer' see PARA 429 note 3.

11 As to the meaning of 'dwelling' see PARA 349.

12 Council Tax (Alteration of Lists and Appeals) Regulations 1993, SI 1993/290, reg 15(2)(a).

13 See the Council Tax (Alteration of Lists and Appeals) Regulations 1993, SI 1993/290, reg 15(2)(b). The relevant statutory provisions are those of Pt II (regs 3–15) (see PARA 428 et seq) and Pt III (regs 16–34) (appeals: see PARA 513 et seq): see reg 15(2)(b).

14 Ie the Council Tax (Alteration of Lists and Appeals) Regulations 1993, SI 1993/290, reg 15(2): see the text to notes 8–13.

15 Council Tax (Alteration of Lists and Appeals) Regulations 1993, SI 1993/290, reg 15(3).

16 As to the meaning of 'proposal' see PARA 430 note 1.

17 Council Tax (Alteration of Lists and Appeals) Regulations 1993, SI 1993/290, reg 15(3)(a). As to decisions of the listing officer see PARA 432.

18 Ie under the Council Tax (Alteration of Lists and Appeals) Regulations 1993, SI 1993/290, reg 10: see PARA 432.

19 See the Council Tax (Alteration of Lists and Appeals) Regulations 1993, SI 1993/290, reg 15(3)(b). As to the meaning of 'proposer' see PARA 430 note 5.

20 Council Tax (Alteration of Lists and Appeals) Regulations 1993, SI 1993/290, reg 15(3)(c).

21 Council Tax (Alteration of Lists and Appeals) Regulations 1993, SI 1993/290, reg 15(3)(d). As to the power to make regulations containing rules for ascertaining in what part of a billing authority's area a dwelling is situated see the Local Government Finance Act 1992 s 10(2); and PARA 360; and as to the power to make regulations containing rules for treating a dwelling as situated in a billing authority's area if part only of the dwelling falls within the area see s 1(3); and PARA 348.

22 Ie the Valuation Tribunal for Wales: see PARA 428 note 15. (see): As to the Valuation Tribunal for Wales see PARA 236 et seq. As to appeals to the tribunal see PARA 513 et seq.

23 As to appeals to the High Court see PARA 562.

24 Council Tax (Alteration of Lists and Appeals) Regulations 1993, SI 1993/290, reg 15(3)(e).

(5) Administration of Council Tax

(i) In General

437. Power to make regulations for administration of council tax.

The appropriate national authority[1] may make regulations[2] containing such provision as it thinks fit in relation to[3]:

(1) the collection of amounts persons are liable to pay in respect of council tax[4]; and

(2) other aspects of administration as regards council tax[5].

Regulations relating to the collection of council tax may include provision for making payments on account[6], for the supply of information to authorities[7] and for the service of notices[8]. Regulations may also include provision relating to payment by instalment[9], payment by persons who are jointly and severally liable[10], discounts and increases[11], reductions for lump sum payment[12], exempt dwellings[13], supply of information by other authorities and certain officers[14], and the use of information by authorities[15].

1 Ie the Secretary of State or, in relation to Wales, the Welsh Ministers. The functions of the Secretary of State under the Local Government Finance Act 1992 Sch 2, so far as exercisable in relation to Wales, were transferred to the National Assembly for Wales, with the functions under Sch 2 paras 14 and 15 (see the text to note 14) being exercisable by the Assembly concurrently with the Secretary of State: see the National Assembly for Wales (Transfer of Functions) Order 1999, SI 1999/672, art 2, Sch 1. These functions are now vested in the Welsh Ministers: see the Government of Wales Act 2006 s 162(1), Sch 11 para 30. As to the Secretary of State and the Welsh Ministers see PARA 4 note 18. As to the meaning of 'Wales' see PARA 2 note 16.

2 As to the regulations made see: the Council Tax (Administration and Enforcement) Regulations 1992, SI 1992/613 (amended by SI 1992/1741, SI 1992/3008, SI 1993/196, SI 1993/773, SI 1994/505, SI 1995/22, SI 1996/675, SI 1996/1880, SI 1996/2405, SI 1997/393, SI 1998/295, SI 1999/534, SI 2005/617, SI 2012/672 and SI 2014/600; in relation to England by SI 2000/2026, SI 2001/362, SI 2001/2237, SI 2003/768, SI 2003/2211, SI 2003/2604, SI 2004/927, SI 2005/2866, SI 2006/3395, SI 2007/501, SI 2010/752, SI 2012/3086, SI 2013/590, SI 2013/630 and SI 2013/2977; and in relation to Wales by SI 2001/1076, SI 2002/808, SI 2003/522, SI 2003/1715, SI 2004/785, SI 2005/3302, SI 2007/582, SI 2009/2706, SI 2011/528, SI 2013/62, SI 2013/570, SI 2014/129 and SI 2017/41); the Council Tax (Administration and Enforcement) (Attachment of Earnings Order) (Wales) Regulations 1992, SI 1992/1741; the Council Tax (Demand Notices) (Wales) Regulations 1993, SI 1993/255 (amended by SI 1995/160, SI 1996/310, SI 1996/1880, SI 2004/460, SI 2006/217, SI 2013/63, SI 2014/122 and SI 2017/40); the Council Tax and Non-Domestic Rating (Demand Notices) (England) Regulations 2003, SI 2003/2613 (amended by SI 2003/3081, SI 2004/3389, SI 2006/217, SI 2006/492, SI 2006/3395, SI 2007/501, SI 2008/387, SI 2008/3264, SI 2009/355, SI 2009/1597, SI 2010/140, SI 2010/187, SI 2012/538, SI 2012/2914, SI 2013/694, SI 2015/427, SI 2016/316 and SI 2017/39); the Council Tax (Demand Notices) (England) Regulations 2009, SI 2009/3193 (amended by SI 2012/2914 and SI 2017/863); the Council Tax (Demand Notices) (England) Regulations 2010, SI 2010/2990; and the Council Tax (Demand Notices) (England) Regulations 2011, SI 2011/3038 (amended by SI 2012/3087, SI 2013/2977, SI 2016/188 and SI 2017/13); and see PARA 439 et seq.

3 Local Government Finance Act 1992 ss 14(1), 97(3), Sch 2 para 1(1).

4 Local Government Finance Act 1992 Sch 2 para 1(1)(a). As to council tax see PARA 344 et seq. As to persons liable to pay council tax see PARA 354 et seq. See *R (on the application of Salmon) v Feltham Magistrates' Court* [2008] EWHC 3507 (Admin), [2009] RVR 160, [2008] All ER (D) 317 (Nov) (claim regulations ultra vires the Local Government Finance Act 1992 Sch 2 dismissed).

5 Local Government Finance Act 1992 Sch 2 para 1(1)(b).

6 See the Local Government Finance Act 1992 Sch 2 paras 2(1), (2), 20(a); and PARA 458.

7 See the Local Government Finance Act 1992 Sch 2 paras 2(3), 20(b); and PARA 440 et seq. Any reference in Sch 2 to an 'authority' is a reference to a billing authority: see Sch 2 para 1(2) (amended by the Local Government etc (Scotland) Act 1994 s 180(1), Sch 13 para 176(16)). As to the meaning of 'billing authority' see PARA 346.

8 See the Local Government Finance Act 1992 Sch 2 para 2(4); and PARAS 439, 452 et seq.

9 See the Local Government Finance Act 1992 Sch 2 para 2(5); and PARA 463 et seq.

10 See the Local Government Finance Act 1992 Sch 2 para 3; and PARA 460.

11 See the Local Government Finance Act 1992 Sch 2 paras 4, 5; and PARA 450 et seq.

12 See the Local Government Finance Act 1992 Sch 2 paras 6, 7; and PARA 468.

13 See the Local Government Finance Act 1992 Sch 2 paras 8, 9, 10, 21; and PARAS 378, 445 et seq.

14 See the Local Government Finance Act 1992 Sch 2 paras 11–17; and PARA 441.

15 See the Local Government Finance Act 1992 Sch 2 paras 18, 18A; and PARA 444.

438. Power to make regulations for specific purposes.

The appropriate national authority[1] may by regulations provide for the exercise, for prescribed council tax purposes[2], of:

(1) powers to require the provision of information[3];

(2) powers to require a person to enter into arrangements under which access is permitted to the person's electronic records[4].

The appropriate authority may by regulations make provision about arrangements for access to electronic records for prescribed council tax purposes where the arrangements are entered into otherwise than under a requirement of the kind mentioned in head (2)[5]. The appropriate authority may by regulations:

(a) make provision about the persons by whom powers conferred by regulations under these provisions may be exercised[6];

(b) make provision about the persons by whom arrangements under regulations under these provisions may be made[7];

(c) in particular, make provision for the authorisation by billing authorities[8] of persons to exercise those powers or make those arrangements[9].

The provision that may be made by regulations under these provisions includes, in particular, provision equivalent to:

(i) provision made by a relevant enactment[10]; or

(ii) provision that is capable of being made under a relevant enactment[11],

with such modifications as the appropriate authority thinks fit[12].

The appropriate authority may by regulations provide for the creation of offences that may be committed by a person in prescribed circumstances[13]:

(A) by intentionally delaying or obstructing a person in the exercise of a power conferred by regulations under heads (1) and (2) above[14] as to the provision of information[15];

(B) by refusing or failing to comply with any requirement under regulations under head (2) above[16] or with the requirements of any arrangements entered into in accordance with such regulations[17];

(C) by refusing or failing, when required to do so by or under the Local Government Finance Act 1992 or by or under regulations made under that Act, to provide any information or document in connection with a person's liability to pay council tax[18];

(D) by making a false statement or representation in connection with such liability[19];

(E) by providing, or causing or allowing to be provided, in connection with such liability, a document or information which is false[20];

(F) by failing to notify, or causing or allowing a person to fail to notify, a matter that is relevant to such liability (including in particular any matter that is required to be notified by or under the Local Government Finance Act 1992 or by or under regulations made under that Act)[21].

Regulations under head (A), (B) or (C) above must provide for an offence under the regulations to be triable only summarily[22]. Regulations under head (A), (B) or (C) may provide, in a case where a person is convicted of an offence under the regulations and the act or omission constituting the offence continues after the conviction, for the person to be guilty of a further offence and liable on summary conviction to a daily fine[23].

Regulations under head (D), (E) or (F) above that create an offence that may only be committed by a person acting dishonestly must provide for the offence to be triable summarily or on indictment[24]. Regulations under head (D), (E) or (F) that create an offence that may be committed by a person acting otherwise than dishonestly must provide for the offence to be triable only summarily[25].

The appropriate authority may by regulations make provision:

(I) about defences to an offence under regulations under heads (A) to (F) above[26];

(II) about the commission by a body corporate of such an offence[27];

(III) about the conduct of proceedings for such an offence[28];

(IV) about the time limits for bringing such proceedings[29];
(V) about the determination of issues arising in such proceedings[30];
(VI) about other matters of procedure and evidence in relation to such offences[31].

The appropriate authority may by regulations make provision for the imposition of a penalty by a billing authority on a person where in prescribed circumstances that person's act or omission results or could result in the amount of council tax that a person ('P') is liable to pay being reduced or subject to a discount, and P is not or will not be entitled to that reduction or discount[32].

The appropriate authority may by regulations make provision for the imposition of a penalty by a billing authority on a person where in prescribed circumstances that person's act or omission results or could result in a dwelling in respect of which a person ('P') would otherwise be liable to pay council tax being treated as an exempt dwelling for a period, and the dwelling is not or will not be an exempt dwelling for all or part of that period[33].

Regulations making provision for the imposition of a penalty must:

(AA) make provision with the effect that a penalty may only be imposed on a person where the person agrees to the imposition of the penalty as an alternative to criminal proceedings being taken against the person in respect of the act or omission to which the penalty relates[34];
(BB) make provision with the effect that a penalty may only be imposed on a person where the person has not been charged with an offence in respect of the act or omission to which the penalty relates[35]; or
(CC) make provision within heads (AA) and (BB)[36].

Where regulations specify a sum as a penalty (or a minimum or maximum penalty) and it appears to the Treasury that there has been a change in the value of money since those regulations were made or (as the case may be) the last occasion when an order under this provision was made, the Treasury may by order substitute for that sum such other sum as appears to it to be justified by the change[37].

1 Ie the Secretary of State in relation to England or, in relation to Wales, the Welsh Ministers: Local Government Finance Act 1992 s 14D(1) (ss 14A–14D added by the Local Government Finance Act 2012 s 14(1), (2)). As to the Secretary of State and the Welsh Ministers see PARA 4 note 18. As to the meaning of 'Wales' see PARA 2 note 16.

2 In the Local Government Finance Act 1992 s 14A, 'council tax purposes' means purposes relating to a person's liability to pay council tax: s 14A(7) (as added: see note 1). 'Prescribed' means prescribed by regulations made by the appropriate national authority: see the Local Government Finance Act 1992 s 116(1). 'Prescribed', in relation to regulations made by the Welsh Ministers, means prescribed by such regulations: s 14D(1) (as so added). As to council tax see PARA 344 et seq. As to persons liable to pay council tax see PARA 354 et seq.

3 Local Government Finance Act 1992 s 14A(1)(a) (as added: see note 1). Section 14A does not affect the operation of Sch 2 (administration of council tax: see PARA 437): s 14A(6) (as so added).

A statutory instrument containing regulations made by the Secretary of State under any of ss 14A–14C may not be made unless a draft of the instrument has been laid before and approved by a resolution of each House of Parliament: s 14D(2) (as so added). A statutory instrument containing regulations made by the Welsh Ministers under any of ss 14A–14C may not be made unless a draft of the instrument has been laid before and approved by a resolution of the National Assembly for Wales: s 14D(3) (as so added).

4 Local Government Finance Act 1992 s 14A(1)(b) (as added: see note 1). For regulations made under ss 14A–14C see the Council Tax Reduction Schemes (Detection of Fraud and Enforcement) (England) Regulations 2013, SI 2013/501; and the Council Tax Reduction Schemes (Detection of Fraud and Enforcement) (Wales) Regulations 2013, SI 2013/588 (amended by SI 2014/825). See also the Council Tax (Reductions for Annexes) (England) Regulations 2013, SI 2013/2977.

5 Local Government Finance Act 1992 s 14A(2) (as added: see note 1).

6 Local Government Finance Act 1992 s 14A(3)(a) (as added: see note 1).

7 Local Government Finance Act 1992 s 14A(3)(b) (as added: see note 1).
8 As to the meaning of 'billing authority' see PARA 346.
9 Local Government Finance Act 1992 s 14A(3)(c) (as added: see note 1).
10 Local Government Finance Act 1992 s 14A(4)(a) (as added: see note 1).
11 Local Government Finance Act 1992 s 14A(4)(b) (as added: see note 1). For the purposes of s 14A(4), each of the following enactments as it had effect on the day on which the Local Government Finance Act 2012 was passed (ie 31 October 2102) is a 'relevant enactment': the Social Security Administration Act 1992 s 109A(8) (application of s 109B to the Crown); s 109B (powers to require information); s 110A (authorisations by local authorities to exercise powers of investigation); s 110AA (power of local authority to require electronic access to information); s 121DA (interpretation of Pt VI); and s 191 (interpretation of that Act): Local Government Finance Act 1992 s 14A(5) (as so added). As to the enactments see WELFARE BENEFITS AND STATE PENSIONS vol 104 (2014) PARA 546 et seq.
12 Local Government Finance Act 1992 s 14A(4) (as added: see note 1).
13 Local Government Finance Act 1992 s 14B(1) (as added: see note 1).

The provision that may be made by regulations under s 14B includes, in particular, provision equivalent to:

(1) provision made by a relevant enactment; or
(2) provision that is capable of being made under a relevant enactment,

with such modifications as the appropriate authority thinks fit: s 14B(9) (as so added). For the purposes of s 14B(9), each of the following enactments as it had effect on the day on which the Local Government Finance Act 2012 was passed (ie 31 October 2012) is a 'relevant enactment': the Social Security Administration Act 1992 s 111 (offences relating to powers under that Act); s 111A (dishonest representations for obtaining benefit etc); s 112 (false representations for obtaining benefit etc); s 115 (offences by bodies corporate); s 116 (legal proceedings); s 121DA (interpretation of Pt VI); s 191 (interpretation of that Act): Local Government Finance Act 1992 s 14B(10) (as so added). As to the enactments see WELFARE BENEFITS AND STATE PENSIONS vol 104 (2014) PARA 580 et seq.
14 Ie under the Local Government Finance Act 1992 s 14A(1).
15 Local Government Finance Act 1992 s 14B(1)(a) (as added: see note 1).
16 Ie under the Local Government Finance Act 1992 s 14A(1)(b).
17 Local Government Finance Act 1992 s 14B(1)(b) (as added: see note 1).
18 Local Government Finance Act 1992 s 14B(1)(c) (as added: see note 1).
19 Local Government Finance Act 1992 s 14B(1)(d) (as added: see note 1).
20 Local Government Finance Act 1992 s 14B(1)(e) (as added: see note 1).
21 Local Government Finance Act 1992 s 14B(1)(f) (as added: see note 1).
22 Local Government Finance Act 1992 s 14B(2)(a) (as added: see note 1). Such regulations may not provide for such an offence to be punishable with a fine exceeding level 3 on the standard scale: s 14B(2)(a) (as so added). As to the powers of magistrates' courts to issue fines on summary conviction see SENTENCING vol 92 (2015) PARA 176.
23 Local Government Finance Act 1992 s 14B(3)(a) (as added: see note 1). Such regulations may not provide for the daily fine to exceed £40: s 14B(3)(b) (as so added).
24 Local Government Finance Act 1992 s 14B(4)(a) (as added: see note 1). Such regulations may not provide for the offence to be punishable on summary conviction with imprisonment for a term exceeding 12 months or with a fine exceeding the statutory maximum (s 14B(4)(b) (as so added)); and may not provide for the offence to be punishable on conviction on indictment with imprisonment for a term exceeding seven years (and may provide for the offence to be punishable on conviction on indictment with a fine) (s 14B(4)(c) (as so added)).

Regulations under s 14B that create an offence within s 14B(4) that may be committed before the date that the Criminal Justice Act 2003 s 154(1) comes into force may not provide for such an offence committed before that date to be punishable on summary conviction with imprisonment for a term exceeding six months: Local Government Finance Act 1992 s 14B(5) (as so added).
25 Local Government Finance Act 1992 s 14B(6)(a) (as added: see note 1). Such regulations may not provide for the offence to be punishable with imprisonment for a term exceeding 51 weeks or with a fine exceeding level 5 on the standard scale: s 14B(6)(b) (as so added). Regulations under s 14B that create an offence within s 14B(6) that may be committed before the date that the Criminal Justice Act 2003 s 281(5) comes into force may not provide for such an offence committed before that date to be punishable with imprisonment for a term exceeding three months: Local Government Finance Act 1992 s 14B(7) (as so added).
26 Local Government Finance Act 1992 s 14B(8)(a) (as added: see note 1).
27 Local Government Finance Act 1992 s 14B(8)(b) (as added: see note 1).
28 Local Government Finance Act 1992 s 14B(8)(c) (as added: see note 1).

29 Local Government Finance Act 1992 s 14B(8)(d) (as added: see note 1).
30 Local Government Finance Act 1992 s 14B(8)(e) (as added: see note 1).
31 Local Government Finance Act 1992 s 14B(8)(f) (as added: see note 1).
32 Local Government Finance Act 1992 s 14C(1) (as added: see note 1). Section 14C does not affect the operation of Sch 3 para 1 (penalties: see PARA 471): s 14C(6) (as so added).

The provision that may be made by regulations under s 14C includes, in particular, provision equivalent to:

(1) provision made by a relevant enactment; or
(2) provision that is capable of being made under a relevant enactment,

with such modifications as the appropriate authority thinks fit: s 14C(7) (as so added). For the purposes of s 14C(7), each of the following is a 'relevant enactment': the Social Security Administration Act 1992 s 115A (penalty as alternative to prosecution); s 115B (penalty as alternative to prosecution: colluding employers etc); s 115C (penalties in respect of incorrect statements etc); s 115D (penalties in respect of failures to disclose information); s 121DA (interpretation of Pt VI); and s 191 (interpretation of that Act): Local Government Finance Act 1992 s 14C(8) (as so added). The reference in s 14C(8):

(a) to the Social Security Administration Act 1992 s 115C or 115D is to that section without the repeals in it contained in the Welfare Reform Act 2012 Sch 14 Pt 1 (Local Government Finance Act 1992 s 14C(9)(a) (as so added));
(b) to any other provision of the Social Security Administration Act 1992 is to the provision as it had effect on the day on which the Local Government Finance Act 2012 was passed (ie 31 October 2012) (Local Government Finance Act 1992 s 14C(9)(b) (as so added)).

As to the enactments see WELFARE BENEFITS AND STATE PENSIONS vol 104 (2014) PARAS 548, 588, 592.

33 Local Government Finance Act 1992 s 14C(2) (as added: see note 1).
34 Local Government Finance Act 1992 s 14C(3)(a) (as added: see note 1).
35 Local Government Finance Act 1992 s 14C(3)(b) (as added: see note 1).
36 Local Government Finance Act 1992 s 14C(3)(c) (as added: see note 1).
37 Local Government Finance Act 1992 s 14C(4) (as added: see note 1). An order under s 14C(4) does not apply in relation to any act done or omission which began before the date on which the order comes into force: s 14C(5) (as so added). As to the meaning of 'the Treasury' see PARA 30 note 15.

439. Service of notices.

Where any notice which is required or authorised by the council tax administration and enforcement regulations[1] to be given to or served on any person[2] falls to be given or served by or on behalf of the Common Council of the City of London[3] it may be given or served in any manner in which it might be given or served under the Local Government Act 1972[4] if the Common Council were a local authority[5] for those purposes[6].

If the name of any person on whom a notice is to be served (either for the purposes of obtaining information from residents, owners or managing agents of a dwelling[7] or for the purposes of obtaining information from such persons relating to exempt dwellings[8]) cannot after reasonable inquiry be ascertained, the notice may be served by addressing it to 'The Resident'[9] or, as the case may be, 'The Owner'[10] or 'The Managing Agent'[11] of the dwelling concerned (naming the dwelling) without further name or description[12].

If the name of any person to whom a notice is to be given or on whom a notice is to be served in accordance with any of the billing provisions[13] cannot after reasonable inquiry be ascertained, the notice may be given or served by addressing it to 'The Council Tax Payer' of the dwelling concerned (naming the dwelling) without further name or description[14].

Any notice which is required or authorised[15] to be given to (or served by) a billing authority on any person in connection with obtaining information (including with regard to exempt dwellings) or for billing purposes[16]:

(1) may be so given, served or supplied by sending the notice or information to that person by electronic communication[17] to such address[18] as may be notified by that person for that purpose[19]; or

(2) is to be treated as given, served or supplied to that person where:
   (a) the billing authority and that person have agreed for that purpose that any documents containing the notice or information may be accessed by that person on a website[20];
   (b) the document is a document to which that agreement applies[21];
   (c) the billing authority has published the document on a website[22]; and
   (d) that person is notified, in a manner for the time being agreed for those purposes between him and the billing authority, of the publication of the document on a website[23], of the address of that website[24] and of the place on the website where the document may be accessed[25].

For the purpose of any legal proceedings, a notice given by a means described in heads (1) and (2) above must, unless the contrary is proved, be treated as served on the second business day after it was sent in accordance with head (1) above[26], or on the second business day after notification of its publication was given in accordance with head (2)(d) above[27].

Any information required by the demand notice regulations[28] to be supplied to any person when a demand notice[29] is served:

(i) may be so supplied by sending the information to that person by electronic communication to such address as may be notified by that person for that purpose[30]; or
(ii) is to be treated as supplied to that person where the billing authority has published the information on a website and that person is notified by way of the demand notice of:
   (A) the publication of the information on a website[31];
   (B) the address of that website[32]; and
   (C) the place on the website where the information may be accessed[33].

Head (ii) above does not apply where that person has requested a hard copy of the information[34]. Where a person requests a hard copy of the information in writing[35] either before or after the demand notice is issued the authority must supply it as soon as reasonably practicable following receipt of the request[36].

1 Ie the Council Tax (Administration and Enforcement) Regulations 1992, SI 1992/613.

2 As to the meaning of 'person' see PARA 11 note 13.

3 As to what constitutes the Common Council of the City of London for these purposes see PARA 346 note 4.

4 Ie under the Local Government Act 1972 s 233 (service of notices by local authorities): see LOCAL GOVERNMENT vol 69 (2018) PARA 648.

5 Ie within the meaning of the Local Government Act 1972 s 233: see LOCAL GOVERNMENT vol 69 (2018) PARA 648.

6 Council Tax (Administration and Enforcement) Regulations 1992, SI 1992/613, reg 2(1).

7 Ie in accordance with the Council Tax (Administration and Enforcement) Regulations 1992, SI 1992/613, reg 3 (information from residents etc): see PARA 440.

8 Ie in accordance with the Council Tax (Administration and Enforcement) Regulations 1992, SI 1992/613, reg 12 (information relating to exempt dwellings etc): see PARA 449. 'Exempt dwelling' means a dwelling which is exempt from council tax under the Council Tax (Exempt Dwellings) Order 1992, SI 1992/558 (see PARA 352) or a dwelling in relation to which no council tax is payable by virtue of a reduction under the Local Government Finance Act 1992 s 13A(1)(a) or 13A(1)(c) where a scheme under s 13A(2) provides, or the billing authority has determined under s 13A(7), that liability is to be reduced to nil (see PARA 378): see the Council Tax (Administration and Enforcement) Regulations 1992, SI 1992/613, reg 1(2) (definition added in relation to Wales by SI 2004/785; in relation to England by SI 2004/927; and substituted in relation to England by SI 2012/3086; and in relation to Wales by SI 2013/62). As to the meaning

of 'dwelling' see PARA 349. As to the meaning of 'billing authority' see PARA 346. As to council tax see PARA 344 et seq.

9 As to the meaning of 'resident' under the Local Government Finance Act 1992 see PARA 354 note 4.

10 As to the meaning of 'owner' under the Local Government Finance Act 1992 see PARA 354 note 15.

11 'Managing agent', in relation to a dwelling, means any person authorised to arrange lettings of the dwelling: Council Tax (Administration and Enforcement) Regulations 1992, SI 1992/613, reg 1(2) (definition added by SI 1992/3008; and amended in relation to England by SI 2013/630; and in relation to Wales by SI 2017/41).

12 Council Tax (Administration and Enforcement) Regulations 1992, SI 1992/613, reg 2(2) (amended by SI 1992/3008).

13 Ie in accordance with any provision of the Council Tax (Administration and Enforcement) Regulations 1992, SI 1992/613, Pt V (regs 17–31): see PARA 452 et seq.

14 Council Tax (Administration and Enforcement) Regulations 1992, SI 1992/613, reg 2(3).

15 Ie a notice required or authorised to be given by a provision of the Council Tax (Administration and Enforcement) Regulations 1992, SI 1992/613, Pt II (regs 3–6) (information: see PARA 440 et seq), Pt III (regs 7–12) (exempt dwellings: see PARA 445 et seq) or Pt V (billing: see PARA 452 et seq).

16 See the Council Tax (Administration and Enforcement) Regulations 1992, SI 1992/613, reg 2(4) (reg 2(4)–(8) added in relation to England by SI 2003/2604; and in relation to Wales by SI 2009/2706; the Council Tax (Administration and Enforcement) Regulations 1992, SI 1992/613, reg 2(4) amended in relation to England by SI 2012/3086; and in relation to Wales by SI 2013/62). The Council Tax (Administration and Enforcement) Regulations 1992, SI 1992/613, reg 2(4) is expressed to be without prejudice to the Local Government Act 1972 s 233 (service of notices by local authorities: see LOCAL GOVERNMENT vol 69 (2018) PARA 648) and the Council Tax (Administration and Enforcement) Regulations 1992, SI 1992/613, reg 2(1)–(3) (see the text to notes 1–14) and subject to reg 2(5)–(8) (see the text and notes 19, 26–27): see reg 2(4) (as so added).

17 'Electronic communication' means a communication transmitted (whether from one person to another, from one device to another or from a person to a device or vice versa) by means of an electronic communications network within the meaning of the Communications Act 2003 s 32(1) (see TELECOMMUNICATIONS vol 97 (2015) PARA 53), or by other means but while in electronic form: Council Tax (Administration and Enforcement) Regulations 1992, SI 1992/613, reg 1(2) (definition added in relation to England by SI 2003/2604, and substituted by SI 2006/237; definition added in relation to Wales by SI 2009/2706).

18 'Address', in relation to electronic communications, includes any number or address used for the purposes of such communications: Council Tax (Administration and Enforcement) Regulations 1992, SI 1992/613, reg 1(2) (definition added in relation to England by SI 2003/2604; and in relation to Wales by SI 2009/2706).

19 Council Tax (Administration and Enforcement) Regulations 1992, SI 1992/613, reg 2(4)(a) (as added: see note 16). A person who has notified an address for the purpose of reg 2(4)(a) or reg 2(4A)(a) (see head (i) in the text) must, by notice in writing to the billing authority, advise the billing authority of any change in that address; and the change takes effect on the third business day after the date on which the notice is received by the billing authority: reg 2(6) (as so added; amended in relation to England by SI 2012/3086; and in relation to Wales by SI 2013/62). A person who has notified an address for the purpose of the Council Tax (Administration and Enforcement) Regulations 1992, SI 1992/613, reg 2(4)(a) or reg 2(4A)(a) also may, by notice in writing to the billing authority, withdraw that notification; and the withdrawal takes effect on the third business day after the date on which the notice is received by the billing authority: reg 2(7) (as so added; amended in relation to England by SI 2012/3086; and in relation to Wales by SI 2013/62). As to the meaning of 'writing' see PARA 21 note 3. 'Business day' means any day except a Saturday or Sunday, Christmas Day, Good Friday or a day which is a bank holiday under the Banking and Financial Dealings Act 1971 (see TIME vol 97 (2015) PARAS 313, 321) in England and Wales: Council Tax (Administration and Enforcement) Regulations 1992, SI 1992/613, reg 1(2) (definition added in relation to England by SI 2003/2604; and in relation to Wales by SI 2009/2706).

20 Council Tax (Administration and Enforcement) Regulations 1992, SI 1992/613, reg 2(4)(b)(i) (as added: see note 16). A person who has entered into an agreement with the billing authority under reg 2(4)(b)(i) may, by notice in writing to the billing authority, inform the authority that he no

longer wishes to be a party to the agreement; and where such notice is given, the agreement is to be treated as revoked on the third business day after the date on which the notice is received by the billing authority: reg 2(8) (as so added).

21 Council Tax (Administration and Enforcement) Regulations 1992, SI 1992/613, reg 2(4)(b)(ii) (as added: see note 16).

22 Council Tax (Administration and Enforcement) Regulations 1992, SI 1992/613, reg 2(4)(b)(iii) (as added: see note 16).

23 Council Tax (Administration and Enforcement) Regulations 1992, SI 1992/613, reg 2(4)(b)(iv)(aa) (as added: see note 16).

24 Council Tax (Administration and Enforcement) Regulations 1992, SI 1992/613, reg 2(4)(b)(iv)(bb) (as added: see note 16).

25 Council Tax (Administration and Enforcement) Regulations 1992, SI 1992/613, reg 2(4)(b)(iv)(cc) (as added: see note 16).

26 Council Tax (Administration and Enforcement) Regulations 1992, SI 1992/613, reg 2(5)(a) (as added: see note 16).

27 Council Tax (Administration and Enforcement) Regulations 1992, SI 1992/613, reg 2(5)(b) (as added: see note 16).

28 'Demand notice regulations' means regulations under the Local Government Finance Act 1992 Sch 2 para 1 (see PARA 437) making provision either that a notice must contain prescribed matters (see Sch 2 para 2(4)(e)) or that the authority must supply prescribed information to the liable person when it serves a notice (see Sch 2 para 2(4)(j)): Council Tax (Administration and Enforcement) Regulations 1992, SI 1992/613, reg 1(2) (definition substituted by SI 1992/3008; amended in relation to England by SI 2003/2604; and in relation to Wales by SI 2009/2706).

As to the demand notice regulations so specified see the Council Tax (Demand Notices) (Wales) Regulations 1993, SI 1993/255; the Council Tax and Non-Domestic Rating (Demand Notices) (England) Regulations 2003, SI 2003/2613; the Council Tax (Demand Notices) (England) Regulations 2009, SI 2009/3193; the Council Tax (Demand Notices) (England) Regulations 2010, SI 2010/2990; the Council Tax (Demand Notices) (England) Regulations 2011, SI 2011/3038; and PARA 437 note 2.

29 Ie within the meaning of the Council Tax (Administration and Enforcement) Regulations 1992, SI 1992/613, Pt V: see PARA 452 note 5.

30 Council Tax (Administration and Enforcement) Regulations 1992, SI 1992/613, reg 2(4A)(a) (reg 2(4A)–(4C) added in relation to England by SI 2012/3086; and in relation to Wales by SI 2013/62). The Council Tax (Administration and Enforcement) Regulations 1992, SI 1992/613, reg 2(4A) is expressed to be without prejudice to the Local Government Act 1972 s 233 (see note 16) and subject to the Council Tax (Administration and Enforcement) Regulations 1992, SI 1992/613, reg 2(6), (7) (see note 19): see reg 2(4A) (as so added).

31 Council Tax (Administration and Enforcement) Regulations 1992, SI 1992/613, reg 2(4A)(b)(i) (as added: see note 30).

32 Council Tax (Administration and Enforcement) Regulations 1992, SI 1992/613, reg 2(4A)(b)(ii) (as added: see note 30).

33 Council Tax (Administration and Enforcement) Regulations 1992, SI 1992/613, reg 2(4A)(b)(iii) (as added: see note 30).

34 Council Tax (Administration and Enforcement) Regulations 1992, SI 1992/613, reg 2(4B) (as added: see note 30).

35 As to the meaning of 'writing' see PARA 21 note 3.

36 Council Tax (Administration and Enforcement) Regulations 1992, SI 1992/613, reg 2(4C) (as added: see note 30).

(ii) Information and Assumptions

440. Information from residents etc.

A person[1] who appears to a billing authority[2] to be a resident[3], owner[4] or managing agent[5] of a particular dwelling[6] must supply to the authority such information[7] as fulfils the following conditions, namely:

(1) it is in the possession or control of the person concerned[8];

(2) the authority requests (by notice given in writing)[9] the person concerned to supply it[10]; and

(3) it is requested by the authority for the purposes of identifying the person who, in respect of any period specified in the notice, is the liable person[11] in relation to the dwelling[12].

A person on whom such a notice is served must supply the information so requested within the period of 21 days beginning on the day on which the notice was served[13] and, if the authority so requires, in the form specified in the request[14].

1 As to the meaning of 'person' see PARA 11 note 13.
2 As to the meaning of 'billing authority' see PARA 346.
3 As to the meaning of 'resident' see PARA 354 note 4.
4 As to the meaning of 'owner' see PARA 354 note 15.
5 As to the meaning of 'managing agent' see PARA 439 note 11.
6 As to the meaning of 'dwelling' see PARA 349.
7 As to the meaning of 'information' see PARA 345 note 20.
8 Council Tax (Administration and Enforcement) Regulations 1992, SI 1992/613, reg 3(1)(a).
9 As to the service of notices see PARA 439. As to the meaning of 'writing' see PARA 21 note 3.
10 Council Tax (Administration and Enforcement) Regulations 1992, SI 1992/613, reg 3(1)(b).
11 The reference to the liable person is a reference to a person who is liable (whether solely or jointly and severally) to pay to a billing authority, in respect of a particular dwelling, an amount in respect of council tax; and includes a reference to a person who in the opinion of the authority will be so liable: Council Tax (Administration and Enforcement) Regulations 1992, SI 1992/613, reg 3(3) (substituted by SI 1992/3008). As to the meaning of references to an amount payable in respect of council tax see PARA 361 note 3. As to council tax see PARA 344 et seq. As to persons liable to pay council tax see PARA 354 et seq.
12 Council Tax (Administration and Enforcement) Regulations 1992, SI 1992/613, reg 3(1)(c).
13 Council Tax (Administration and Enforcement) Regulations 1992, SI 1992/613, reg 3(2)(a).
14 Council Tax (Administration and Enforcement) Regulations 1992, SI 1992/613, reg 3(2)(b). As to the power of a billing authority to impose a penalty in respect of a failure to provide information or the provision of inaccurate information see PARA 471.

441. Information from public bodies.

A billing authority[1] may, for the purpose of carrying out its functions under the Local Government Finance Act 1992[2], request (by notice given in writing)[3] any other billing authority[4], any precepting authority[5], any levying authority[6] and the electoral registration officer for any area in Great Britain[7] to supply to it such information[8] as is specified in the notice which does not fall within any of the following categories[9], namely that which is not:

(1) information obtained by the person[10] concerned or by a committee, any executive[11], a committee of any executive or a member of any executive, of such a person[12]:
   (a) in its capacity as police authority[13]; or
   (b) in its capacity as a constituent council of such an authority[14];
(2) information obtained by the person concerned in its capacity as an employer[15]; or
(3) information consisting of anything other than the name, address and any past or present place of residence of any person and the dates during which he is known or thought to have resided at that place[16].

A billing authority may also, for the purpose of carrying out those functions under the Local Government Finance Act 1992, request (by notice given in writing) community charges registration officers[17] to supply to it such information as is specified in the notice which does not consist of anything other than[18]:

(i) the name, address and any past or present place of residence of any person and the dates during which he is known or thought to have resided at that place[19];

(ii) information relevant to the status of any person as an exempt individual[20]; and

(iii) the days on which any person was an exempt individual[21].

Information so requested by a billing authority from any of the specified authorities[22] must be supplied by the person requested to supply it if it is in his possession or control, and it must be so supplied within 21 days of the day on which the request is made[23].

A billing authority may[24] supply relevant information[25] to another billing authority (or to a levying authority) even if it is not requested to supply the information[26].

1 As to the meaning of 'billing authority' see PARA 346.
2 Ie under the Local Government Finance Act 1992 Pt I (ss 1–69).
3 See the Council Tax (Administration and Enforcement) Regulations 1992, SI 1992/613, reg 4(1) (reg 4 substituted by SI 1992/3008). As to the service of notices see PARA 439. As to the meaning of 'writing' see PARA 21 note 3.
4 Council Tax (Administration and Enforcement) Regulations 1992, SI 1992/613, reg 4(2)(a) (as substituted: see note 3).
5 Council Tax (Administration and Enforcement) Regulations 1992, SI 1992/613, reg 4(2)(b) (as substituted: see note 3). As to the meaning of 'precepting authority' see PARA 23 note 1.
6 Council Tax (Administration and Enforcement) Regulations 1992, SI 1992/613, reg 4(2)(c) (as substituted: see note 3). The reference in the text to a levying authority applies to the administration of the council tax in Scotland, which may have an impact on the system in England, eg in relation to information confirming a person's sole or main residence (see PARA 354).
7 Council Tax (Administration and Enforcement) Regulations 1992, SI 1992/613, reg 4(2)(d) (as substituted: see note 3). As to the meaning of 'Great Britain' see PARA 4 note 10. As to electoral registration officers and their areas see ELECTIONS AND REFERENDUMS vol 37 (2013) PARA 139 et seq.
8 As to the meaning of 'information' see PARA 345 note 20.
9 Council Tax (Administration and Enforcement) Regulations 1992, SI 1992/613, reg 4(1)(a) (as substituted: see note 3).
10 As to the meaning of 'person' see PARA 11 note 13.
11 Ie within the meaning of the Local Government Act 2000 Pt II (ss 10–48): see LOCAL GOVERNMENT vol 69 (2018) PARA 335. Part II now applies in relation to Wales only; as to the equivalent provisions applicable in relation to England see Pt 1A (ss 9B–9R): see LOCAL GOVERNMENT vol 69 (2018) PARA 295 et seq.
12 See the Council Tax (Administration and Enforcement) Regulations 1992, SI 1992/613, reg 4(3)(a) (as substituted (see note 3); amended in relation to England by SI 2001/2237; and in relation to Wales by SI 2002/808).
13 Council Tax (Administration and Enforcement) Regulations 1992, SI 1992/613, reg 4(3)(a)(i) (as substituted: see note 3). As to police authorities see POLICE AND INVESTIGATORY POWERS vol 84 (2013) PARA 55 et seq.
14 Council Tax (Administration and Enforcement) Regulations 1992, SI 1992/613, reg 4(3)(a)(ii) (as substituted: see note 3).
15 See the Council Tax (Administration and Enforcement) Regulations 1992, SI 1992/613, reg 4(3)(b) (as substituted: see note 3).
16 See the Council Tax (Administration and Enforcement) Regulations 1992, SI 1992/613, reg 4(3)(c) (as substituted: see note 3).
17 Council Tax (Administration and Enforcement) Regulations 1992, SI 1992/613, reg 4(4) (as substituted: see note 3). References to community charges registration officers are to be construed, in relation to such officers in England or Wales, in accordance with the Local Government Finance Act 1988 s 26 (repealed): Council Tax (Administration and Enforcement) Regulations 1992, SI 1992/613, reg 4(9)(a) (as substituted: see note 3). As to the meanings of 'England' and 'Wales' see PARA 2 note 16. With effect from 1 April 1993, the community charge was abolished and replaced with the council tax: see PARA 344.
18 See the Council Tax (Administration and Enforcement) Regulations 1992, SI 1992/613, reg 4(1)(b) (as substituted: see note 3).

19 Council Tax (Administration and Enforcement) Regulations 1992, SI 1992/613, reg 4(5)(a) (as substituted: see note 3).

20 Council Tax (Administration and Enforcement) Regulations 1992, SI 1992/613, reg 4(5)(b) (as substituted: see note 3). References to an 'exempt individual' are to be construed, as regards any period during which the sole or main residence of the person concerned is or was in England or Wales, in accordance with the Local Government Finance Act 1988 s 2 and Sch 1 (repealed): see the Council Tax (Administration and Enforcement) Regulations 1992, SI 1992/613, reg 4(9)(b) (as so substituted).

21 Council Tax (Administration and Enforcement) Regulations 1992, SI 1992/613, reg 4(5)(c) (as substituted: see note 3).

22 Ie information requested under the Council Tax (Administration and Enforcement) Regulations 1992, SI 1992/613, reg 4(1): see the text to notes 1–21.

23 Council Tax (Administration and Enforcement) Regulations 1992, SI 1992/613, reg 4(6) (as substituted: see note 3).

24 Ie so far as it does not have the power to do so apart from under the Council Tax (Administration and Enforcement) Regulations 1992, SI 1992/613, Pt II (regs 3–6): see PARAS 440, 443–444.

25 Information is 'relevant information' for these purposes if:
(1) it was obtained by the billing authority in exercising its functions under the Local Government Finance Act 1992 Pt I (ss 1–69) (Council Tax (Administration and Enforcement) Regulations 1992, SI 1992/613, reg 4(8)(a) (as substituted (see note 3); amended in relation to England by SI 2012/3086; and in relation to Wales by SI 2013/62));
(2) it believes it would be useful to the other billing authority in exercising its functions under the Local Government Finance Act 1992 Pt I (or, in the case of a levying authority, its functions under Pt II (ss 70–99) (Scotland)) (Council Tax (Administration and Enforcement) Regulations 1992, SI 1992/613, reg 4(8)(b) (as so substituted)); and
(3) it was not supplied to the first-mentioned authority under the Local Government Finance Act 1992 Sch 2 para 15A (see PARAS 437, 442) or the Welfare Reform Act 2012 s 131 (see WELFARE BENEFITS AND STATE PENSIONS vol 104 (2014) PARA 555) (Council Tax (Administration and Enforcement) Regulations 1992, SI 1992/613, reg 4(8)(c) (added in relation to England by SI 2012/3086; and in relation to Wales by SI 2013/62)).

26 Council Tax (Administration and Enforcement) Regulations 1992, SI 1992/613, reg 4(7) (as substituted: see note 3).

442. Information from Revenue and Customs officials: England.

A Revenue and Customs official[1] may supply information[2] which is held by the Revenue and Customs[3] in connection with a function of the Revenue and Customs[4] to a qualifying person for prescribed[5] purposes relating to council tax[6].

The following are qualifying persons for this purpose[7]:
(1) a billing authority in England[8];
(2) a person authorised to exercise any function of such an authority relating to council tax[9];
(3) a person providing services to such an authority relating to council tax[10].

Information supplied under these provisions may be used for another prescribed purpose relating to council tax[11]. Information supplied under these provisions may be supplied to another qualifying person for a prescribed purpose relating to council tax (whether or not that is a purpose for which it was supplied)[12].

1 'Revenue and Customs official' has the same meaning as in the Commissioners for Revenue and Customs Act 2005 s 18 (see INCOME TAXATION vol 59 (2014) PARA 2325): Local Government Finance Act 1992 Sch 2 para 15A(5) (Sch 2 paras 15A–15D added by the Local Government Finance Act 2012 s 17(1), (2)).

2 As to the meaning of 'information' see PARA 345 note 20.

3 'The Revenue and Customs' has the same meaning as in the Commissioners for Revenue and Customs Act 2005 s 18 (see INCOME TAXATION vol 59 (2014) PARA 2325): Local Government Finance Act 1992 Sch 2 para 15A(5) (as added: see note 1).

4 'Function of the Revenue and Customs' has the same meaning as in the Commissioners for

Revenue and Customs Act 2005 s 18 (see INCOME TAXATION vol 59 (2014) PARA 2325): Local Government Finance Act 1992 Sch 2 para 15A(5) (as added: see note 1).

5 'Prescribed' means prescribed by regulations made by the appropriate national authority: see the Local Government Finance Act 1992 s 116(1).

6 Local Government Finance Act 1992 Sch 2 para 15A(1) (as added: see note 1). As to council tax see PARA 344 et seq. The purposes prescribed under Sch 2 para 15A(1) are:
   (1) making a council tax reduction scheme (Council Tax (Administration and Enforcement) Regulations 1992, SI 1992/613, reg 5A(a) (regs 5A–5C added in relation to England by SI 2013/590; and in relation to Wales by SI 2013/570));
   (2) determining a person's entitlement or continued entitlement to a reduction under a council tax reduction scheme (Council Tax (Administration and Enforcement) Regulations 1992, SI 1992/613, reg 5A(b) (as so added));
   (3) preventing, detecting, securing evidence of, or prosecuting the commission of, a council tax offence (reg 5A(c) (as so added)).

   As to the meaning of 'council tax reduction scheme' see PARA 378 note 20. 'Council tax offence' has the same meaning as in the Council Tax Reduction Schemes (Detection of Fraud and Enforcement) (England) Regulations 2013, SI 2013/501: Council Tax (Administration and Enforcement) Regulations 1992, SI 1992/613, reg 1(2) (definition added in relation to England by SI 2013/590; and in relation to Wales by SI 2013/570).

7 Local Government Finance Act 1992 Sch 2 para 15A(2) (as added: see note 1).

8 Local Government Finance Act 1992 Sch 2 para 15A(2)(a) (as added: see note 1). As to the meaning of 'billing authority' see PARA 346. As to the meaning of 'England' see PARA 2 note 16.

9 Local Government Finance Act 1992 Sch 2 para 15A(2)(b) (as added: see note 1).

10 Local Government Finance Act 1992 Sch 2 para 15A(2)(c) (as added: see note 1).

11 Local Government Finance Act 1992 Sch 2 para 15A(3) (as added: see note 1). The purposes prescribed under Sch 2 para 15A(3) are any purposes connected with:
   (1) making a council tax reduction scheme (Council Tax (Administration and Enforcement) Regulations 1992, SI 1992/613, reg 5B(a) (as added: see note 6));
   (2) determining a person's entitlement or continued entitlement to a reduction under a council tax reduction scheme (reg 5B(b) (as so added));
   (3) preventing, detecting, securing evidence of, or prosecuting the commission of, a council tax offence (reg 5B(c) (as so added));
   (4) any proceedings before the Valuation Tribunal for England in connection with a reduction under a council tax reduction scheme (reg 5B(d) (as so added)).

   As to proceedings before the Valuation Tribunal for England see PARA 513 et seq.

12 Local Government Finance Act 1992 Sch 2 para 15A(4) (as added: see note 1). The purposes prescribed under Sch 2 para 15A(4) are:
   (1) making a council tax reduction scheme (Council Tax (Administration and Enforcement) Regulations 1992, SI 1992/613, reg 5C(a) (as added: see note 6));
   (2) determining a person's entitlement or continued entitlement to a reduction under a council tax reduction scheme (reg 5C(b) (as so added));
   (3) preventing, detecting, securing evidence of, or prosecuting the commission of, a council tax offence (reg 5C(c) (as so added)).

443. Information as to deaths.

Within seven days of the registration of the death[1] of any person aged 18 or over[2], the registrar of births and deaths for the sub-district in which the death occurred[3] must supply to any billing authority[4] whose area includes all or part of, or falls within, that sub-district, the following particulars of the death:

(1) the name and surname of the deceased[5];
(2) the date of his death[6]; and
(3) his usual address[7].

The registrar must supply the particulars so specified either in writing[8] or in a form in which they can be processed by a computer[9].

1 As to the registration of deaths see REGISTRATION CONCERNING THE INDIVIDUAL vol 88 (2012) PARA 277 et seq.

2 As to the time at which a person attains a particular age see PARA 354 note 4.

3 As to registration officers see REGISTRATION CONCERNING THE INDIVIDUAL vol 88 (2012) PARA 337 et seq.

4 As to the meaning of 'billing authority' see PARA 346.
5 Council Tax (Administration and Enforcement) Regulations 1992, SI 1992/613, reg 5(1)(a).
6 Council Tax (Administration and Enforcement) Regulations 1992, SI 1992/613, reg 5(1)(b).
7 Council Tax (Administration and Enforcement) Regulations 1992, SI 1992/613, reg 5(1)(c).
8 As to the meaning of 'writing' see PARA 21 note 3.
9 Council Tax (Administration and Enforcement) Regulations 1992, SI 1992/613, reg 5(2).

444. Use of information by billing authority.

In carrying out its functions under the Local Government Finance Act 1992[1], a billing authority[2] may use information[3] obtained under any other enactment provided that it was not obtained by a committee of the authority in its capacity as a police authority[4].

A billing authority also may use information it has obtained for the purpose of carrying out those functions under Local Government Finance Act 1992:

(1) for the purpose of identifying vacant dwellings[5]; or
(2) for the purpose of taking steps to bring vacant dwellings back into use[6].

The power under head (1) or head (2) above, so far as relating to personal information[7], extends only to information which consists of an individual's name or an address or number for communicating with him[8].

1 Ie under the Local Government Finance Act 1992 Pt I (ss 1–69).
2 As to the meaning of 'billing authority' see PARA 346.
3 As to the meaning of 'information' see PARA 345 note 20.
4 Council Tax (Administration and Enforcement) Regulations 1992, SI 1992/613, reg 6(1)(a) (amended by SI 1995/22). As to police authorities see POLICE AND INVESTIGATORY POWERS vol 84 (2013) PARA 55 et seq.
5 Local Government Finance Act 1992 Sch 2 para 18A(1)(a) (Sch 2 para 18A added by the Local Government Act 2003 s 85). 'Vacant dwelling' means a dwelling in which no one lives and which is substantially unfurnished: Local Government Finance Act 1992 Sch 2 para 18A(3) (as so added). As to the meaning of 'dwelling' see PARA 349.
6 Local Government Finance Act 1992 Sch 2 para 18A(1)(b) (as added: see note 5).
7 'Personal information' means information which relates to an individual (living or dead) who can be identified, either from that information or from that information and other information of the authority, and includes any expression of opinion about the individual and any indication of the intentions of any person in respect of the individual: Local Government Finance Act 1992 Sch 2 para 18A(3) (as added: see note 5). As to the meaning of 'person' see PARA 11 note 13.
8 Local Government Finance Act 1992 Sch 2 para 18A(2) (as added: see note 5).

445. Information for owners of exempt dwellings etc.

A billing authority[1] which received a copy of a proposed first valuation list[2] had, as respects each dwelling[3] shown in the copy which in the opinion of the authority would be a relevant dwelling[4] on the day when the list came into force, to notify[5] the person concerned[6] of the valuation band[7] shown in the copy as applicable to the dwelling[8]. Where:

(1) a dwelling was not shown in the copy of such a proposed list but was shown in the copy of the list that was compiled and sent[9] to the authority[10]; and
(2) in the opinion of the authority the dwelling was a relevant dwelling on the day when the list came into force[11],

the authority had to notify the person concerned of the valuation band shown in the list as applicable to the dwelling[12].

1 As to the meaning of 'billing authority' see PARA 346.
2 Ie sent to it under the Local Government Finance Act 1992 s 22(5)(b): see PARA 409.
3 As to the meaning of 'dwelling' see PARA 349.
4 A dwelling was a 'relevant dwelling' on any day if:

(1) on the day the dwelling was an exempt dwelling (Council Tax (Administration and Enforcement) Regulations 1992, SI 1992/613, reg 7(6)(a)(i)); or
(2) in respect of the financial year in which the day falls and the dwelling, the amount set under the Local Government Finance Act 1992 s 30 (see PARA 380) was nil (Council Tax (Administration and Enforcement) Regulations 1992, SI 1992/613, reg 7(6)(a)(ii)).

As to the meaning of 'financial year' see PARA 11 note 1. As to the meaning of 'exempt dwelling' see PARA 439 note 8. As to dwellings that may be deemed to be exempt dwellings for the purposes of the Local Government Finance Act 1992 Sch 2 (regulations relating to the collection and administration of council tax) see PARA 378.

5 A notification required to be given by the Council Tax (Administration and Enforcement) Regulations 1992, SI 1992/613, reg 7(1) had to be given not later than 31 March 1993: see reg 7(4)(a) (substituted by SI 1992/3008). As to the service of notices see PARA 439.

6 For these purposes, any reference to the 'person concerned', in relation to a dwelling, is a reference to the person who would be liable (whether solely or jointly and severally) to pay to the authority an amount in respect of council tax for the particular day if the dwelling were not or had not been a relevant dwelling on that day: Council Tax (Administration and Enforcement) Regulations 1992, SI 1992/613, reg 7(6)(b). As to references to an amount payable in respect of council tax see PARA 361 note 3. As to persons liable to pay council tax see PARA 354 et seq. As to council tax see PARA 344 et seq.

7 As to valuation bands see PARA 361.

8 Council Tax (Administration and Enforcement) Regulations 1992, SI 1992/613, reg 7(1). This provision is expressed to be subject to reg 7(3A) and reg 7(5) (see note 12): see reg 7(1) (amended by SI 1992/3008). Accordingly, the Council Tax (Administration and Enforcement) Regulations 1992, SI 1992/613, reg 7(1)–(3) did not apply in the case of a relevant dwelling which was an exempt dwelling within the Council Tax (Exempt Dwellings) Order 1992, SI 1992/558, art 3 Class O (see PARA 352): see the Council Tax (Administration and Enforcement) Regulations 1992, SI 1992/613, regs 1(2), 7(3A) (definition in reg 1(2) substituted, reg 7(3A) added, by SI 1992/3008).

9 Ie under the Local Government Finance Act 1992 s 22(7): see PARA 409.

10 Council Tax (Administration and Enforcement) Regulations 1992, SI 1992/613, reg 7(2)(a).

11 Council Tax (Administration and Enforcement) Regulations 1992, SI 1992/613, reg 7(2)(b).

12 Council Tax (Administration and Enforcement) Regulations 1992, SI 1992/613, reg 7(2). This provision is expressed to be subject to the reg 7(3A) (see note 8): see reg 7(2) (amended by SI 1992/3008). Subject to the Council Tax (Administration and Enforcement) Regulations 1992, SI 1992/613, reg 7(3A), where:

(1) the valuation band shown as applicable to a dwelling in the copy of a proposed list sent to a billing authority under the Local Government Finance Act 1992 s 22(5)(b) (see PARA 409) was different from that shown as applicable to it in the copy of the list sent to the authority under s 22(7) (see PARA 409) (Council Tax (Administration and Enforcement) Regulations 1992, SI 1992/613, reg 7(3)(a)); and
(2) in the opinion of the authority, the dwelling was a relevant dwelling on the day when the list came into force (reg 7(3)(b)),

the authority had to notify the person concerned of the reason for the difference (reg 7(3) (amended by SI 1992/3008)).

A notification required to be given by the Council Tax (Administration and Enforcement) Regulations 1992, SI 1992/613, reg 7(2), (3) had to be given within the period of two months beginning on the day on which the authority received a copy of the list: reg 7(4)(b). If at the time when a person was notified as mentioned in reg 7(3) the authority had not yet given him a notification under reg 7(1) (see the text to notes 1–8), the authority was not required to give him such a notification: reg 7(5).

446. Inquiries and assumptions as to dwellings.

A billing authority[1] must, as regards each financial year[2] commencing with the financial year beginning on 1 April 1993, take reasonable steps to ascertain whether any dwellings[3] in its area[4] will be or were exempt dwellings[5] for any period during the year[6].

Where, having taken such steps:

(1) a billing authority has no reason to believe that a particular dwelling will be or was an exempt dwelling for any period during the year, it must assume, for billing purposes[7], that the dwelling will be or was a chargeable dwelling[8] for that period[9];

(2) a billing authority has reason to believe that a particular dwelling will be or was an exempt dwelling for a period during the year, it must, subject to head (3), assume, for billing purposes[10], that the dwelling will be or was an exempt dwelling for that period[11];

(3) a billing authority has reason to believe that a particular dwelling would be or would have been an exempt dwelling for a period during the year but for a determination made in relation to that dwelling in connection with a reduction scheme[12], it must assume, for billing purposes[13], that the dwelling will be or was a chargeable dwelling for that period[14].

1 As to the meaning of 'billing authority' see PARA 346.
2 As to the meaning of 'financial year' see PARA 11 note 1.
3 As to the meaning of 'dwelling' see PARA 349.
4 As to the power to make regulations containing rules for ascertaining in what part of a billing authority's area a dwelling is situated see the Local Government Finance Act 1992 s 10(2); and PARA 360; and as to the power to make regulations containing rules for treating a dwelling as situated in a billing authority's area if part only of the dwelling falls within the area see s 1(3); and PARA 348.
5 As to the meaning of 'exempt dwelling' see PARA 439 note 8.
6 Council Tax (Administration and Enforcement) Regulations 1992, SI 1992/613, reg 8.
7 Ie for the purposes of the Council Tax (Administration and Enforcement) Regulations 1992, SI 1992/613, Pt V (regs 17–31): see PARA 452 et seq.
8 As to the meaning of 'chargeable dwelling' see PARA 350.
9 Council Tax (Administration and Enforcement) Regulations 1992, SI 1992/613, reg 9(1).
10 Ie for the purposes of the Council Tax (Administration and Enforcement) Regulations 1992, SI 1992/613, Pt V: see PARA 452 et seq.
11 Council Tax (Administration and Enforcement) Regulations 1992, SI 1992/613, reg 9(2) (amended in relation to England by SI 2012/3086; and in relation to Wales by SI 2013/62). As to the notification of such assumptions see PARA 447. As to the correction of such assumptions see PARA 448.
12 Ie under para 118(1)(c) of the scheme prescribed in the Council Tax Reduction Schemes (Default Scheme) (England) Regulations 2012, SI 2012/2886, Schedule, or a provision contained in an authority's scheme under the Local Government Finance Act 1992 s 13A(2) by virtue of the Council Tax Reduction Schemes (Prescribed Requirements) (England) Regulations 2012, SI 2012/2885, Sch 8 para 14(1)(c). See PARA 378.
13 Ie for the purposes of the Council Tax (Administration and Enforcement) Regulations 1992, SI 1992/613, Pt V: see PARA 452 et seq.
14 Council Tax (Administration and Enforcement) Regulations 1992, SI 1992/613, reg 9(3) (added in relation to England by SI 2012/3086; and in relation to Wales by SI 2013/62; amended in relation to Wales by SI 2014/129).

447. Notification of assumption.

A billing authority[1] which has made an assumption[2] that a particular dwelling[3] will be or was an exempt dwelling[4] for a period during the financial year[5] must inform[6] the relevant person[7] of the assumption made in his case[8]. Such information must be given by notice in writing[9] and as soon as reasonably practicable after the assumption has been made[10].

Where the dwelling in respect of which the assumption is made is a dwelling in relation to which no council tax is payable by virtue of a reduction[11] where a scheme[12] provides that liability is to be reduced to nil, different notification requirements apply[13].

1 As to the meaning of 'billing authority' see PARA 346.

2 Ie under the Council Tax (Administration and Enforcement) Regulations 1992, SI 1992/613, reg 9(2): see PARA 446.
3 As to the meaning of 'dwelling' see PARA 349.
4 As to the meaning of 'exempt dwelling' see PARA 439 note 8.
5 As to the meaning of 'financial year' see PARA 11 note 1.
6 Ie in accordance with the Council Tax (Administration and Enforcement) Regulations 1992, SI 1992/613, reg 10(2): see the text to notes 9–10. Information need not be given under reg 10:
(1) where the dwelling in respect of which such an assumption is made is an exempt dwelling within the Council Tax (Exempt Dwellings) Order 1992, SI 1992/558, art 3 Class O (see PARA 352) (Council Tax (Administration and Enforcement) Regulations 1992, SI 1992/613, reg 10(6)(a) (reg 10(6) substituted by SI 1992/3008)); or
(2) in so far as it would be repetitive of information given to the person concerned in accordance with the Council Tax (Administration and Enforcement) Regulations 1992, SI 1992/613, reg 7 (see PARA 445) or any provision of demand notice regulations (reg 10(6)(b) (as so substituted)).

As to the meaning of 'demand notice regulations' see PARA 439 note 28.
7 For these purposes, references to the 'relevant person' are references to a person who, in respect of the particular dwelling, would be liable (whether solely or jointly and severally) to pay to the authority an amount in respect of council tax for the period to which the assumption relates if the dwelling were not or had not been an exempt dwelling for that period: Council Tax (Administration and Enforcement) Regulations 1992, SI 1992/613, reg 10(7). Where, as regards a particular dwelling and period, there is more than one relevant person, nothing in reg 10(1) requires information to be given, as regards that dwelling and period, to more than one of them: reg 10(5). As to references to an amount payable in respect of council tax see PARA 361 note 3. As to council tax see PARA 344 et seq. As to persons liable to pay council tax see PARA 354 et seq.
8 Council Tax (Administration and Enforcement) Regulations 1992, SI 1992/613, reg 10(1). This provision is expressed to be subject to reg 10(5) (see note 7) and reg 10(6) (see note 6): see reg 10(1).
9 As to the meaning of 'writing' see PARA 21 note 3. As to the service of notices see PARA 439.
10 Council Tax (Administration and Enforcement) Regulations 1992, SI 1992/613, reg 10(2). Subject to reg 10(6), (6A) (see notes 6, 13) (reg 10(3) (amended in relation to England by SI 2012/3086; and in relation to Wales by SI 2013/62)), a billing authority must supply with any notice given in accordance with the Council Tax (Administration and Enforcement) Regulations 1992, SI 1992/613, reg 10(2) a statement:
(1) specifying the valuation band shown in the authority's valuation list as applicable to the dwelling (reg 10(3)(a));
(2) summarising the effect of any regulations under the Local Government Finance Act 1992 s 24 (alteration of lists: see PARA 417) relevant to the making by a person (other than a billing authority) of a proposal for the alteration of that list (Council Tax (Administration and Enforcement) Regulations 1992, SI 1992/613, reg 10(3)(b));
(3) specifying:
(a) where the notice is given after the end of the financial year in which the period to which the assumption relates falls, the amount which, subject to reg 10(4), would have been payable in respect of council tax for that period if the dwelling had been a chargeable dwelling throughout that period (reg 10(3)(c)(i)); or
(b) in any other case, the authority's estimate of that amount (reg 10(3)(c)(ii));
(4) summarising the classes of dwelling which are for the time being exempt dwellings for the purposes of the Local Government Finance Act 1992 Pt I Ch I (ss 1–19) (see PARAS 351–352) (Council Tax (Administration and Enforcement) Regulations 1992, SI 1992/613, reg 10(3)(d)); and
(5) where the amount first set for the financial year in question under the Local Government Finance Act 1992 s 30 (see PARA 380) is nil, that, if the dwelling is or becomes a chargeable dwelling on any day of that year, no council tax is to be payable for that year in respect of the dwelling unless an amount is set in substitution for the nil amount (Council Tax (Administration and Enforcement) Regulations 1992, SI 1992/613, reg 10(3)(e)).

In determining an amount for the purpose of reg 10(3)(c) (see head (3) above), the authority must assume that, as regards each day of the period to which the assumption relates, the Local Government Finance Act 1992 s 11 (discounts: see PARA 362) and s 12 (special provision for discounts: see PARA 365), the Social Security Contributions and Benefits Act 1992 s 131 (council tax benefit: see WELFARE BENEFITS AND STATE PENSIONS vol 104 (2014) PARA 249) and regulations under the Local Government Finance Act 1992 s 13 (reduced amounts: see PARA 377) do not apply in the case of the person concerned: Council Tax (Administration and Enforcement) Regulations 1992, SI 1992/613, reg 10(4).

As to valuation bands see PARA 361. As to valuation lists see PARAS 409–411. As to the meaning of 'chargeable dwelling' see PARA 350.

11 Ie under the Local Government Finance Act 1992 s 13A(1)(a): see PARA 378.

12 Ie under the Local Government Finance Act 1992 s 13A(2): see PARA 378.

13 Council Tax (Administration and Enforcement) Regulations 1992, SI 1992/613, reg 10(6A) (added in relation to England by SI 2012/3086; and in relation to Wales by SI 2013/62; amended in relation to Wales by SI 2014/129). In such circumstances:

(1) the Council Tax (Administration and Enforcement) Regulations 1992, SI 1992/613, reg 10(3) (see note 10) does not apply (reg 10(6A)(a) (as so added and amended));

(2) the billing authority must supply with any notice given in accordance with reg 10(2) (see the text to notes 9–10) a statement:

(a) informing the person affected of the duty imposed by para 115(1) of the scheme prescribed by the Council Tax Reduction Schemes (Default Scheme) (England) Regulations 2012, SI 2012/2886, Schedule, or contained in the authority's scheme by virtue of the Council Tax Reduction Schemes (Prescribed Requirements) (England) Regulations 2012, SI 2012/2885, Sch 8 para 9(1), as the case may be (Council Tax (Administration and Enforcement) Regulations 1992, SI 1992/613, reg 10(6A)(b)(i) (as so added and amended));

(b) explaining the possible consequences (including prosecution) of failing to comply with that duty (reg 10(6A)(b)(ii) (as so added and amended)); and

(c) setting out the circumstances a change in which might affect entitlement to the reduction or its amount (reg 10(6A)(b)(iii) (as so added and amended)).

448. Correction of assumptions.

Where a person:

(1) has been informed[1] of an assumption[2] made in his case that a particular dwelling[3] will be or was an exempt dwelling[4] for a period during the financial year[5]; and

(2) at any time before the end of the financial year following the financial year in respect of which the assumption is made, he has reason to believe that the dwelling concerned[6] will not be or was not an exempt dwelling for the period concerned[7], or will be or was an exempt dwelling for a shorter period[8],

he must, within the period of 21 days beginning on the day on which he first has reason so to believe, notify the authority in writing[9] of his belief[10]. This does not apply, however, where a determination has been made in relation to that person under a council tax reduction scheme[11] which provides that liability is to be reduced to nil[12].

Where persons are jointly and severally liable to pay council tax[13] in respect of the dwelling and period concerned, the duty to supply information in this way is a duty of each of them, but is discharged if one of them supplies the information on behalf of both or all of them[14].

1 Ie in accordance with the Council Tax (Administration and Enforcement) Regulations 1992, SI 1992/613, reg 10(1) (see PARA 447) or as mentioned in reg 10(6) (see PARA 447).

2 Ie under the Council Tax (Administration and Enforcement) Regulations 1992, SI 1992/613, reg 9(2): see PARA 446.

3 As to the meaning of 'dwelling' see PARA 349.

4 As to the meaning of 'exempt dwelling' see PARA 439 note 8.

5 Council Tax (Administration and Enforcement) Regulations 1992, SI 1992/613, reg 11(1)(a). As to the meaning of 'financial year' see PARA 11 note 1.

6 References to the 'dwelling concerned' are to the dwelling to which the relevant assumption relates: Council Tax (Administration and Enforcement) Regulations 1992, SI 1992/613, reg 11(3).

7 References to the 'period concerned' are to the period to which the relevant assumption relates: Council Tax (Administration and Enforcement) Regulations 1992, SI 1992/613, reg 11(3).

8 Council Tax (Administration and Enforcement) Regulations 1992, SI 1992/613, reg 11(1)(b).
9 As to the meaning of 'writing' see PARA 21 note 3. As to the service of notices see PARA 439.
10 Council Tax (Administration and Enforcement) Regulations 1992, SI 1992/613, reg 11(1). This is subject to reg 11(1A), (2): see reg 11(1) (amended in relation to England by SI 2012/3086; and in relation to Wales by SI 2013/62). As to the power of a billing authority to impose a penalty in respect of a failure to give such notification see PARA 471.
11 Ie under the Local Government Finance Act 1992 s 13A(2): see PARA 378.
12 Council Tax (Administration and Enforcement) Regulations 1992, SI 1992/613, reg 11(1A) (added in relation to England by SI 2012/3086; and in relation to Wales by SI 2013/62; amended in relation to Wales by SI 2014/129).
13 As to persons liable to pay council tax see PARA 354 et seq. As to council tax see PARA 344 et seq.
14 Council Tax (Administration and Enforcement) Regulations 1992, SI 1992/613, reg 11(2).

449. Information relating to exempt dwellings etc.

A person who appears to a billing authority[1] to be a resident[2], owner[3] or managing agent[4] of a particular dwelling[5] in respect of which an assumption[6] has been made that the dwelling will be or was an exempt dwelling[7] for a period during the financial year, must supply to the authority such information as fulfils the following conditions[8], namely that:

(1) the information is in the possession or control of the person concerned[9];
(2) the authority requests (by notice in writing[10]) the person concerned to supply the information[11]; and
(3) the information is requested by the authority for the purposes of identifying the person who, in respect of any period specified in the notice, is or will be the relevant person[12] in relation to the dwelling[13].

A person on whom such a notice is served must supply the information so requested:

(a) within the period of 21 days beginning on the day on which the notice was served[14]; and
(b) if the authority so requires, in the form specified in the request[15].

1 As to the meaning of 'billing authority' see PARA 346.
2 As to the meaning of 'resident' see PARA 354 note 4.
3 As to the meaning of 'owner' see PARA 354 note 15.
4 As to the meaning of 'managing agent' see PARA 439 note 11.
5 As to the meaning of 'dwelling' see PARA 349.
6 Ie under the Council Tax (Administration and Enforcement) Regulations 1992, SI 1992/613, reg 9(2): see PARA 446.
7 As to the meaning of 'exempt dwelling' see PARA 439 note 8.
8 Council Tax (Administration and Enforcement) Regulations 1992, SI 1992/613, reg 12(1).
9 Council Tax (Administration and Enforcement) Regulations 1992, SI 1992/613, reg 12(1)(a).
10 As to the meaning of 'writing' see PARA 21 note 3. As to the service of notices see PARA 439.
11 Council Tax (Administration and Enforcement) Regulations 1992, SI 1992/613, reg 12(1)(b).
12 References to the 'relevant person' are references to a person who, in respect of the particular dwelling:

(1) is or will be liable (whether solely or jointly and severally) to pay to the authority an amount in respect of council tax for the period to which the assumption relates (Council Tax (Administration and Enforcement) Regulations 1992, SI 1992/613, reg 12(3)(a)); or
(2) would be so liable if the dwelling were not or had not been an exempt dwelling for that period (reg 12(3)(b)).

As to references to an amount payable in respect of council tax see PARA 361 note 3. As to council tax see PARA 344 et seq. As to persons liable to pay council tax see PARA 354 et seq.

13 Council Tax (Administration and Enforcement) Regulations 1992, SI 1992/613, reg 12(1)(c).
14 Council Tax (Administration and Enforcement) Regulations 1992, SI 1992/613, reg 12(2)(a).
15 Council Tax (Administration and Enforcement) Regulations 1992, SI 1992/613, reg 12(2)(b). As to the power of a billing authority to impose a penalty in respect of a failure to provide information or the provision of inaccurate information see PARA 471.

450. Ascertainment of entitlement to and assumptions as to discount or premium.

Before making any calculation of the chargeable amount[1] for the purposes of billing[2] in respect of any dwelling in its area[3], a billing authority must take reasonable steps to ascertain whether that amount is subject to any discount[4] or premium[5] and, if so, the amount of that discount or premium[6].

Where, having taken such steps, a billing authority has no reason to believe that the chargeable amount for the financial year concerned is subject to a discount or premium, it must assume, in making any calculation of the chargeable amount for the purposes of billing[7], that the chargeable amount is not subject to any discount or premium[8].

Where, having taken such steps, a billing authority has reason to believe that the chargeable amount for the financial year concerned is subject to a discount or premium of a particular amount, it must assume, in making any calculation of the chargeable amount for the purposes of billing that the chargeable amount is subject to a discount or premium of that amount[9].

Where, having taken such steps, a billing authority has reason to believe that the chargeable amount for the financial year concerned would be subject to a discount of a particular amount but for a determination made in relation to that discount[10] under a council tax reduction scheme, it must assume, in making any calculation of the chargeable amount for the purposes of billing, that the chargeable amount is not subject to a discount of that amount[11].

1 In the Council Tax (Administration and Enforcement) Regulations 1992, SI 1992/613, Pt IV (regs 13–16), any reference to the 'chargeable amount' is a reference to an amount which a person is liable to pay (whether solely or jointly and severally) in respect of a particular dwelling to a billing authority in respect of council tax for a financial year and includes, unless the context otherwise requires, an amount which in the opinion of the authority a person will be so liable to pay (reg 13(a)); and any reference to any calculation of the chargeable amount includes a reference to any estimate of the amount (reg 13(b)). As to the meaning of 'dwelling' see PARA 349. As to the meaning of 'financial year' see PARA 11 note 1. As to references to an amount payable in respect of council tax see PARA 361 note 3. As to council tax see PARA 344 et seq. As to persons liable to pay council tax see PARA 354 et seq. As to the meaning of 'billing authority' see PARA 346.

2 Ie for the purposes of the Council Tax (Administration and Enforcement) Regulations 1992, SI 1992/613, Pt V (regs 17–31): see PARA 452 et seq.

3 As to the power to make regulations containing rules for ascertaining in what part of a billing authority's area a dwelling is situated see the Local Government Finance Act 1992 s 10(2); and PARA 360; and as to the power to make regulations containing rules for treating a dwelling as situated in a billing authority's area if part only of the dwelling falls within the area see s 1(3); and PARA 348.

4 'Discount' means a discount under the Local Government Finance Act 1992 s 11 (discounts: see PARA 362) or s 11A (special provision for discounts where dwellings in England have no resident: see PARA 363) or a reduction in the amount of council tax payable for a dwelling under the Council Tax (Reductions for Annexes) (England) Regulations 2013, SI 2013/2977, or a reduction under the Local Government Finance Act 1992 s 13A(1)(a) or (c) (see PARA 378) where a scheme under s 13A(2) provides, or the billing authority has determined under s 13A(7), that liability is to be reduced otherwise than to nil: Council Tax (Administration and Enforcement) Regulations 1992, SI 1992/613, reg 1(2) (definition added in relation to Wales by SI 2004/785; and in relation to England by SI 2004/927; substituted relation to England by SI 2012/3086; and in relation to Wales by SI 2013/62; further substituted in relation to England by SI 2013/2977; and amended in relation to Wales by SI 2014/129).

5 'Premium' means an increase in the amount of council tax payable in respect of a dwelling under the Local Government Finance Act 1992 11B(1) (see PARA 364): Council Tax (Administration and Enforcement) Regulations 1992, SI 1992/613, reg 1(2) (definition added in relation to England by virtue of SI 2012/3086; and in relation to Wales by SI 2017/41).

6 Council Tax (Administration and Enforcement) Regulations 1992, SI 1992/613, reg 14 (substituted in relation to Wales by SI 2004/785; and in relation to England by SI 2004/927; amended in relation to England by SI 2012/3086; and in relation to Wales by SI 2017/41).

7 Ie for the purposes of the Council Tax (Administration and Enforcement) Regulations 1992, SI 1992/613, Pt V (regs 17–31): see PARA 452 et seq.

8 Council Tax (Administration and Enforcement) Regulations 1992, SI 1992/613, reg 15(1) (amended in relation to England by SI 2012/3086; and in relation to Wales by SI 2017/41).

9 Council Tax (Administration and Enforcement) Regulations 1992, SI 1992/613, reg 15(2) (amended in relation to England by SI 2012/3086; and in relation to Wales by SI 2017/41). This is subject to the Council Tax (Administration and Enforcement) Regulations 1992, SI 1992/613, reg 15(3): see reg 15(2) (amended in relation to England by SI 2012/3086; and in relation to Wales by SI 2013/62).

10 Ie under para 118(1)(c) of the scheme prescribed in the Council Tax Reduction Schemes (Default Scheme) (England) Regulations 2012, SI 2012/2886, Schedule, or a provision contained in an authority's scheme under the Local Government Finance Act 1992 s 13A(2) by virtue of the Council Tax Reduction Schemes (Prescribed Requirements) (England) Regulations 2012, SI 2012/2885, Sch 8 para 14(1)(c). See PARA 378.

11 Council Tax (Administration and Enforcement) Regulations 1992, SI 1992/613, reg 15(3) (added in relation to England by SI 2012/3086; and in relation to Wales by SI 2013/62; amended in relation to Wales by SI 2014/129).

451. Correction of discount or premium assumptions.

Where a person:

(1) has been informed in accordance with any provision of demand notice regulations[1] of an assumption as to discount[2] or premium[3] made in his case[4]; and

(2) at any time before the end of the financial year[5] following the financial year in respect of which the assumption is made, he has reason to believe that the chargeable amount[6] is not in fact subject to any discount or premium, or is subject to a discount or premium of a smaller or larger amount[7],

he must, within the period of 21 days beginning on the day on which he first has reason so to believe, notify the authority in writing[8] of his belief[9]. This does not apply, however, where a determination has been made in relation to that person under a council tax reduction scheme[10] which provides that liability is to be reduced otherwise than to nil[11].

Where persons are jointly and severally liable to pay council tax[12] in respect of the dwelling[13] and period concerned, the duty to supply information is a duty of each of them, but is discharged if one of them supplies the information on behalf of both or all of them[14].

For these purposes, the fact that any person concerned has wholly or partly discharged his liability to pay the amount must be ignored[15].

1 As to the meaning of 'demand notice regulations' see PARA 439 note 28.

2 As to the meaning of 'discount' for these purposes see PARA 450 note 4.

3 As to the meaning of 'premium' for these purposes see PARA 450 note 5.

4 Council Tax (Administration and Enforcement) Regulations 1992, SI 1992/613, reg 16(1)(a) (amended in relation to England by SI 2012/3086; and in relation to Wales by SI 2017/41).

5 As to the meaning of 'financial year' see PARA 11 note 1.

6 As to the meaning of references to the chargeable amount see PARA 450 note 1.

7 Council Tax (Administration and Enforcement) Regulations 1992, SI 1992/613, reg 16(1)(b) (amended in relation to England by SI 2012/3086; and in relation to Wales by SI 2013/62 and SI 2017/41).

8 As to the meaning of 'writing' see PARA 21 note 3. As to the service of notices see PARA 439.

9 Council Tax (Administration and Enforcement) Regulations 1992, SI 1992/613, reg 16(1). This is subject to reg 16(1A), (2): see reg 16(1) (amended in relation to England by SI 2012/3086; and in relation to Wales by SI 2013/62). As to the power of a billing authority to impose a penalty in respect of a failure to give such notification see PARA 471.

10 Ie under the Local Government Finance Act 1992 s 13A(2): see PARA 378.
11 Council Tax (Administration and Enforcement) Regulations 1992, SI 1992/613, reg 16(1A) (added in relation to England by SI 2012/3086; and in relation to Wales by SI 2013/62; amended in relation to Wales by SI 2014/129).
12 As to persons liable to pay council tax see PARA 354 et seq. As to council tax see PARA 344 et seq.
13 As to the meaning of 'dwelling' see PARA 349.
14 Council Tax (Administration and Enforcement) Regulations 1992, SI 1992/613, reg 16(2).
15 Council Tax (Administration and Enforcement) Regulations 1992, SI 1992/613, reg 16(3).

(iii) Demand Notices and Reminder Notices

452. The requirement for demand notices.

For each financial year[1], a billing authority[2] must serve[3] a notice in writing[4] (a 'demand notice'[5]) on every liable person[6]. However, where[7] notices would fall to be served in accordance with the billing provisions[8] at the same time[9] and in respect of the same dwelling[10], in relation to a financial year not then ended and any preceding financial year, a billing authority is not required thereby to serve more than one notice[11]. If a person is liable in any financial year to pay to the same billing authority different chargeable amounts in respect of different dwellings, a demand notice must be served in respect of each chargeable amount[12].

1 As to the meaning of 'financial year' see PARA 11 note 1.
2 As to the meaning of 'billing authority' see PARA 346.
3 Ie in accordance with the Council Tax (Administration and Enforcement) Regulations 1992, SI 1992/613, regs 19–21: see PARAS 457–458. As to the service of notices generally see PARA 439.
4 As to the meaning of 'writing' see PARA 21 note 3.
5 'Demand notice' means the notice required to be served under the Council Tax (Administration and Enforcement) Regulations 1992, SI 1992/613, reg 18(1): reg 17(1).
6 Council Tax (Administration and Enforcement) Regulations 1992, SI 1992/613, reg 18(1). Except where the context otherwise requires, and subject to reg 17(5), any reference in Pt V (regs 17–31) to the liable person (however expressed) is a reference:
    (1) to a person who is, or in the opinion of the billing authority will be, solely liable to pay to the authority, an amount in respect of council tax in respect of a particular dwelling and a day (reg 17(2)(a) (reg 17(2) substituted by SI 1992/3008)); or
    (2) where persons are joint taxpayers, to those persons (Council Tax (Administration and Enforcement) Regulations 1992, SI 1992/613, reg 17(2)(b) (as so substituted)).

'Joint taxpayers' means two or more persons who are (or in the opinion of the billing authority will be) jointly and severally liable to pay to the authority an amount in respect of council tax in respect of a particular dwelling and a day (whether such liability arises by virtue of the Local Government Finance Act 1992 s 6(3) or s 6(4)(b) (see PARA 354), s 7(4) or s 7(5) (see PARA 355), s 8(4) or s 8(5) (see PARA 356) or s 9(1) (see PARA 357)): Council Tax (Administration and Enforcement) Regulations 1992, SI 1992/613, reg 17(1) (definition added by SI 1992/3008).

The Council Tax (Administration and Enforcement) Regulations 1992, SI 1992/613, Pt V applies (amongst other matters) for the making of payments in relation to the chargeable amount for a financial year; but its application as regards persons who are joint taxpayers is subject to the provisions of regs 27, 28, 28A (see PARA 460): reg 17(5) (substituted by SI 1992/3008). Various provisions of the Council Tax (Administration and Enforcement) Regulations 1992, SI 1992/613, Pt V are modified by reg 27, which applies in the case of joint taxpayers, although its application to joint taxpayers on whom a joint taxpayers' notice (see PARA 460) is served is subject to reg 28A: see reg 27 (substituted by SI 1992/3008; and amended in relation to England by SI 2013/590; and in relation to Wales by SI 2013/570).

Any reference in the Council Tax (Administration and Enforcement) Regulations 1992, SI 1992/613, Pt V to the 'chargeable amount' is a reference to the amount the liable person is or will be liable to pay: Council Tax (Administration and Enforcement) Regulations 1992, SI 1992/613, reg 17(3). As to persons liable to pay council tax see PARA 354 et seq. As to council tax see PARA 344 et seq. As to the meaning of 'dwelling' see PARA 349. As to references to an amount payable in respect of council tax see PARA 361 note 3.

The liability to pay council tax requires a demand by the billing authority to transform it into a duty to pay: see *Regentford Ltd v Thanet District Council* [2004] EWHC 246 (Admin), [2004] RA 113, (2004) Times, 4 March (there is an analogy between liability for council tax and the liability in the ordinary sense of a guarantor who is at all times exposed to a potential duty to discharge the guaranteed obligation, but a duty that is triggered only when a demand is made of him).

7 Ie but for the Council Tax (Administration and Enforcement) Regulations 1992, SI 1992/613, reg 18.

8 Ie in accordance with the Council Tax (Administration and Enforcement) Regulations 1992, SI 1992/613, Pt V.

9 Council Tax (Administration and Enforcement) Regulations 1992, SI 1992/613, reg 18(2)(a). Any reference in Pt V to the day on or time at which a notice is issued, is a reference:
   (1) if the notice is served in the manner described in the Local Government Act 1972 s 233(2) (service of notices by local authorities: see LOCAL GOVERNMENT vol 69 (2018) PARA 648) by being left at, or sent by post to, a person's proper address, to the day on or time at which it is so left or posted (Council Tax (Administration and Enforcement) Regulations 1992, SI 1992/613, reg 17(4)(a)); or
   (2) in any other case, to the day on or time at which the notice is served (reg 17(4)(b)).

10 Council Tax (Administration and Enforcement) Regulations 1992, SI 1992/613, reg 18(2)(b).

11 Council Tax (Administration and Enforcement) Regulations 1992, SI 1992/613, reg 18(2) (amended by SI 1997/393).

12 Council Tax (Administration and Enforcement) Regulations 1992, SI 1992/613, reg 18(3).

453. Content of demand notices: England.

A demand notice[1] which relates to a year beginning on or after 1 April 2012[2] and is served by an English billing authority[3] or such an authority's authorised person[4], must contain the following matters[5]:

(1) the name (if any) of the person to whom the notice is issued[6];
(2) the date the notice is issued[7];
(3) the period to which the notice relates[8];
(4) the address of the dwelling[9];
(5) the applicable band[10];
(6) the amount of council tax set[11] by the billing authority[12];
(7) any precept issued[13] to the billing authority by a major precepting authority[14];
(8) the amount calculated[15] by the billing authority in relation to the tax for different valuation bands[16];
(9) where a local precepting authority has issued a precept to the billing authority[17] or the billing authority anticipates such a precept[18], the name of the local precepting authority and such amount of the precept or anticipated precept as is payable in respect of a dwelling in the applicable band and in the category of dwellings which includes the dwelling[19];
(10) if an authority's relevant basic amount of council tax is excessive[20], a footnote to the precept or amount mentioned in (as the case may be) head (7), (8) or (9) above stating that fact, that a referendum must be held, and that information regarding the referendum will be provided in due course[21];
(11) if it is the case, in relation to the year beginning in 2016 and to any subsequent year[22] a statement that the council tax attributable to the billing authority[23] or the major precepting authority[24] includes a precept to fund adult social care[25];
(12) the percentage change in each of the relevant amounts[26] from the preceding year[27] to the relevant year[28];
(13) certain information as to discounts, reductions and premiums applied[29];

(14) where an amount is being recovered under the notice in respect of a penalty[30] but the person on whom the notice is served has not previously been informed of the ground on which the penalty is imposed, a statement of that ground[31];

(15) any amount credited against the amount of council tax which would otherwise be payable[32];

(16) any penalty or overpayment of council tax benefit which is being recovered under the notice[33];

(17) where the notice requires the payment of an amount of council tax for any year before the relevant year and the person to whom the notice is issued has not previously been issued with a notice requiring the payment of that amount, a statement of the amount[34];

(18) the amount required to be paid under the notice, the instalments or other payments required to be paid and the manner in which those payments may be made[35];

(19) a statement of the address and telephone number to which any enquiries may be directed[36];

(20) explanatory notes, which must include the prescribed information[37].

When a billing authority serves a demand notice on a person it must also supply that person with the prescribed information[38].

1 As to the meaning of 'demand notice' see PARA 452 note 5 (definition applied by the Council Tax (Demand Notices) (England) Regulations 2011, SI 2011/3038, reg 2(1)).

2 See the Council Tax (Demand Notices) (England) Regulations 2011, SI 2011/3038, reg 1(2)(a). As to the appropriate regulations in relation to a demand notice relating to the year beginning on 1 April 2011 served by an English billing authority or such an authority's authorised person see the Council Tax (Demand Notices) (England) Regulations 2010, SI 2010/2990. As to the appropriate regulations in relation to a demand notice relating to the year beginning on 1 April 2010 served by an English billing authority or such an authority's authorised person see the Council Tax (Demand Notices) (England) Regulations 2009, SI 2009/3193 (amended by SI 2012/2914 and SI 2017/863). As to the appropriate regulations in relation to demand notices served by an English billing authority or an authorised person on behalf of such a billing authority in relation to financial years beginning on or after 1 April 2004 see the Council Tax and Non-Domestic Rating (Demand Notices) (England) Regulations 2003, SI 2003/2613 (as amended: see PARA 437 note 2).

The Council Tax (Demand Notices) (England) Regulations 2011, SI 2011/3038, apply in relation to England only; as to the equivalent regulations in relation to Wales see the Council Tax (Demand Notices) (Wales) Regulations 1993, SI 1993/255; and PARA 454. As to the meanings of 'England' and 'Wales' see PARA 2 note 16.

3 As to the meaning of 'billing authority' see PARA 346.

4 Council Tax (Demand Notices) (England) Regulations 2011, SI 2011/3038, reg 1(2)(b). 'Authorised person', in relation to a billing authority, means a person authorised in accordance with the Local Authorities (Contracting Out of Tax Billing, Collection and Enforcement Functions) Order 1996, SI 1996/1880 (see PARA 346) to exercise functions on the authority's behalf in relation to the administration of council tax: Council Tax (Demand Notices) (England) Regulations 2011, SI 2011/3038, reg 2(1). As to the meaning of 'person' see PARA 11 note 13.

5 See the Council Tax (Demand Notices) (England) Regulations 2011, SI 2011/3038, reg 5(1).

6 Council Tax (Demand Notices) (England) Regulations 2011, SI 2011/3038, Sch 1 para 2. Unless otherwise stated, a matter specified in Sch 1 is specified for the relevant year, and, where relevant to the matter, the applicable band and the category of dwellings which includes the dwelling: Sch 1 para 1(2). 'Relevant year', in relation to a notice, means the year to which the demand for payment made by the notice relates: reg 2(1). Any reference to a year is a reference to a financial year: reg 2(2)(c). As to the meaning of 'financial year' see PARA 11 note 1. 'Applicable band' means the relevant valuation band which applies to the dwelling for the relevant year; and 'relevant valuation band', in relation to a dwelling, means the valuation band shown as applicable to the dwelling in the billing authority's valuation list compiled under the Local Government Finance Act 1992 s 22 (compilation and maintenance of lists: see PARA 409) or s 22B (compilation and maintenance of new lists: see PARA 411): Council Tax (Demand Notices) (England) Regulations 2011, SI 2011/3038, Sch 1 para 1. 'Dwelling' means the dwelling to which the notice relates: Sch 1 para

1. As to the meaning of 'dwelling' generally see PARA 349.
7 Council Tax (Demand Notices) (England) Regulations 2011, SI 2011/3038, Sch 1 para 3.
8 Council Tax (Demand Notices) (England) Regulations 2011, SI 2011/3038, Sch 1 para 4.
9 Council Tax (Demand Notices) (England) Regulations 2011, SI 2011/3038, Sch 1 para 5.
10 Council Tax (Demand Notices) (England) Regulations 2011, SI 2011/3038, Sch 1 para 6.
11 Ie under the Local Government Finance Act 1992 s 30: see PARA 380.
12 See the Council Tax (Demand Notices) (England) Regulations 2011, SI 2011/3038, Sch 1 para 7. This is subject to Sch 1 para 7A: see Sch 1 para 7 (amended by SI 2016/188). The Council Tax (Demand Notices) (England) Regulations 2011, SI 2011/3038, Sch 1 para 7A applies instead of Sch 1 para 7:

(1) in relation to the year beginning in 2016 and to any subsequent year (Sch 1 para 7A(1)(a) (Sch 1 para 7A added by SI 2016/188; and amended by SI 2017/13));
(2) where the billing authority is an adult social care authority (Council Tax (Demand Notices) (England) Regulations 2011, SI 2011/3038, Sch 1 para 7A(1)(b) (as so added)); and
(3) where the amount set by the authority under the Local Government Finance Act 1992 s 30 includes an amount attributable to the adult social care precept in the relevant year or in any prior year (Sch 1 para 7A(1)(c) (as so added and amended)).

The notice must contain the matters specified in Sch 1 para 7A(3), (4): Sch 1 para 7A(2) (as so added; substituted by SI 2017/13). Those are:

(a) the amount set by the authority under the Local Government Finance Act 1992 s 30 less any amount which is attributable to the adult social care precept in the relevant year and in any prior year (Council Tax (Demand Notices) (England) Regulations 2011, SI 2011/3038, Sch 1 para 7A(3) (as so added and amended)); and
(b) the amount attributable to the adult social care precept (Sch 1 para 7A(4) (as so added)).

The amount referred to in Sch 1 para 7A(4) must represent the aggregate of:

(i) the amount attributable to the adult social care precept in the relevant year (Sch 1 para 7A(5)(a) (as so added; Sch 1 para 7A(5) substituted by SI 2017/13)); and
(ii) the amount attributable to the adult social care precept in any prior year (Council Tax (Demand Notices) (England) Regulations 2011, SI 2011/3038, Sch 1 para 7A(5)(b) (as so added and substituted)).

'Adult social care authority' means a local authority within the meaning of the Care Act 2014 s 1(4) (see SOCIAL SERVICES vol 95 (2017) PARA 1) and the Council of the Isles of Scilly: Council Tax (Demand Notices) (England) Regulations 2011, SI 2011/3038, reg 2(1) (definition added by SI 2016/188).

13 Ie under the Local Government Finance Act 1992 s 40(2)(a): see PARA 11. Any reference to a precept includes a reference to a substitute precept: Council Tax (Demand Notices) (England) Regulations 2011, SI 2011/3038, reg 2(2)(a).
14 Council Tax (Demand Notices) (England) Regulations 2011, SI 2011/3038, Sch 1 para 8. As to the meaning of 'major precepting authority' see PARA 11 note 2. This is subject to Sch 1 para 8A: see Sch 1 para 8 (amended by SI 2016/188). The Council Tax (Demand Notices) (England) Regulations 2011, SI 2011/3038, Sch 1 para 8A applies instead of Sch 1 para 8:

(1) in relation to the year beginning in 2016 and to any subsequent year (Sch 1 para 8A(1)(a) (Sch 1 para 8A added by SI 2016/188; and amended by SI 2017/13));
(2) where a major precepting authority which is an adult social care authority issues a precept to the billing authority under the Local Government Finance Act 1992s 40 (Council Tax (Demand Notices) (England) Regulations 2011, SI 2011/3038, Sch 1 para 8A(1)(b) (as so added)); and
(3) where an amount stated by the major precepting authority under the Local Government Finance Act 1992 s 40(2)(a) includes an amount attributable to the adult social care precept in the relevant year or in any prior year (Council Tax (Demand Notices) (England) Regulations 2011, SI 2011/3038, Sch 1 para 8A(1)(c) (as so added and amended)).

The notice must contain the matters specified in Sch 1 para 8(3), (4): Sch 1 para 8A(1)(c) (as so added; substituted by SI 2017/13). Those are:

(a) The amount of the precept issued by the major precepting authority under the Local Government Finance Act 1992 s 40(2)(a) less any amount which is attributable to the adult social care precept in the relevant year and in any prior year (Council Tax (Demand Notices) (England) Regulations 2011, SI 2011/3038, Sch 1 para 8A(3) (as so added and amended));
(b) the amount attributable to the adult social care precept (Sch 1 para 8A(4) (as so added)).
(c) The amount referred to in Sch 1 para 8A(4) must represent the aggregate of:

(d) the amount attributable to the adult social care precept in the relevant year (Sch 1 para 8A(5)(a) (as so added; Sch 1 para 8A(5) substituted by SI 2017/13)); and
(e) the amount attributable to the adult social care precept in any prior year (Council Tax (Demand Notices) (England) Regulations 2011, SI 2011/3038, Sch 1 para 8A(5)(b) (as so added and substituted)).

15 Ie under the Local Government Finance Act 1992 s 36 (see PARA 380) if s 31A (see PARA 382) did not require or permit the authority to take into account the amount of any precepts issued to it by local precepting authorities under s 41 (see PARA 18) or anticipated by it in pursuance of regulations under that section: see the Council Tax (Demand Notices) (England) Regulations 2011, SI 2011/3038, Sch 1 para 9. As to the meaning of 'local precepting authority' see PARA 18 note 2.
16 See the Council Tax (Demand Notices) (England) Regulations 2011, SI 2011/3038, Sch 1 para 9.
17 Ie under the Local Government Finance Act 1992 s 41: see PARA 18.
18 Ie in pursuance of regulations under the Local Government Finance Act 1992 s 41: see PARA 18.
19 See the Council Tax (Demand Notices) (England) Regulations 2011, SI 2011/3038, Sch 1 paras 10, 11.
20 As to excessive council tax see PARA 382 et seq.
21 See the Council Tax (Demand Notices) (England) Regulations 2011, SI 2011/3038, Sch 1 para 12.
22 Council Tax (Demand Notices) (England) Regulations 2011, SI 2011/3038, Sch 1 para 12A(1) (Sch 1 para 12A added by SI 2016/188; the Council Tax (Demand Notices) (England) Regulations 2011, SI 2011/3038, Sch 1 para 12A(1) amended by SI 2017/13).
23 Ie in a case to which the Council Tax (Demand Notices) (England) Regulations 2011, SI 2011/3038, Sch 1 para 7A applies (see note 12): Sch 1 para 12A(2) (as added: see note 22). The statement must read: 'The council tax attributable to [name of billing authority] includes a precept to fund adult social care' and must include, where indicated, the name of the billing authority serving the notice: see the Sch 1 para 12A(2) (as so added).
24 Ie in a case to which the Council Tax (Demand Notices) (England) Regulations 2011, SI 2011/3038, Sch 1 para 8A applies (see note 14): Sch 1 para 12A(3) (as added: see note 22). The statement must read: 'The council tax attributable to [name of major precepting authority] includes a precept to fund adult social care' and must include, where indicated, the name of the major precepting authority in question: Sch 1 para 12A(3) (as so added).
25 Council Tax (Demand Notices) (England) Regulations 2011, SI 2011/3038, Sch 1 para 12A (as added and amended: see note 22).
26 'Relevant amounts' means the amounts and precepts mentioned in the Council Tax (Demand Notices) (England) Regulations 2011, SI 2011/3038, Sch 1 paras 7–10 (see heads (6)–(9) in the text): Sch 1 para 1.
27 'Preceding year', in relation to a notice, means the year before the relevant year: Council Tax (Demand Notices) (England) Regulations 2011, SI 2011/3038, reg 2(1).
28 See the Council Tax (Demand Notices) (England) Regulations 2011, SI 2011/3038, Sch 1 paras 13–17 (Sch 1 para 13 amended by SI 2016/188) See also the Council Tax (Demand Notices) (England) Regulations 2011, SI 2011/3038, Sch 1 paras 17A, 17B (added by SI 2016/188; and amended by SI 2017/13).
29 See the Council Tax (Demand Notices) (England) Regulations 2011, SI 2011/3038, Sch 1 paras 18–20 (Sch 1 paras 18, 19 amended by SI 2012/3087 and SI 2013/2977). See also the Council Tax (Demand Notices) (England) Regulations 2011, SI 2011/3038, Sch 1 paras 18A, 19B (added by SI 2012/3087).
30 As to penalties see PARA 471 et seq.
31 Council Tax (Demand Notices) (England) Regulations 2011, SI 2011/3038, Sch 1 para 21.
32 Council Tax (Demand Notices) (England) Regulations 2011, SI 2011/3038, Sch 1 para 22.
33 Council Tax (Demand Notices) (England) Regulations 2011, SI 2011/3038, Sch 1 para 23. As to council tax benefit see WELFARE BENEFITS AND STATE PENSIONS vol 104 (2014) PARA 249.
34 Council Tax (Demand Notices) (England) Regulations 2011, SI 2011/3038, Sch 1 para 24.
35 Council Tax (Demand Notices) (England) Regulations 2011, SI 2011/3038, Sch 1 para 25.
36 Council Tax (Demand Notices) (England) Regulations 2011, SI 2011/3038, Sch 1 para 26.
37 See the Council Tax (Demand Notices) (England) Regulations 2011, SI 2011/3038, Sch 1 para 27 (amended by SI 2012/3087, SI 2013/2977 and SI 2017/13). A notice which is served on a person after the end of the relevant year and at the same time as a notice relating to another year not then ended is not required to contain such explanatory notes: see the Council Tax (Demand Notices) (England) Regulations 2011, SI 2011/3038, reg 5(2).

38 See the Council Tax (Demand Notices) (England) Regulations 2011, SI 2011/3038, reg 6(1), Sch 2 (Sch 2 amended by SI 2016/188 and SI 2017/13). The Council Tax (Demand Notices) (England) Regulations 2011, SI 2011/3038, reg 6(1) does not apply when a notice is served after the end of the relevant year: reg 6(2). Precepting authorities and levying bodies must supply a billing authority with certain information for these purposes: see regs 8, 9 (reg 8 amended by SI 2016/188 and SI 2017/13).

454. Content of demand notices: Wales.

A demand notice[1] issued by or on behalf of a Welsh billing authority must contain the following matters[2]:

(1) a statement of the name (if known) of the person on whom the notice is served[3];

(2) a statement of the day of issue of the notice[4];

(3) a statement of the period to which the notice relates[5];

(4) a statement of the address of the dwelling to which the notice relates ('the relevant dwelling')[6];

(5) a statement of the relevant valuation band[7] as regards the relevant dwelling[8];

(6) a statement as regards the relevant year, the category[9] of dwellings which includes the relevant dwelling, and the relevant valuation band[10] of the amount:

(a) set[11] by the billing authority[12];

(b) calculated[13] by the major precepting authority[14];

(c) referred to in head (a) above less the sum of the amounts referred to in heads (b) above and (d) below[15]; and

(d) calculated (if any)[16] in relation to the special item being the precept (whether issued or anticipated) of the relevant local precepting authority[17];

(7) a statement of the days (if any) as regards which it was assumed that the amount required to be paid under the notice falls to be calculated by reference to specified factors[18];

(8) where a statement falls to be given as mentioned in head (7) by reason of a specified[19] matter[20]:

(a) a statement of the basis on which the authority assumed that the chargeable amount for the relevant year was or should be subject to a discount of an amount equal to the appropriate percentage or (as the case may be[21]) twice the appropriate percentage[22];

(b) a statement that if at any time before the end of the financial year following the relevant year the person to whom the notice is issued has reason to believe that the chargeable amount for the relevant year is not in fact subject to any discount or is subject to a discount of a smaller amount, he is required, within the period of 21 days beginning on the day on which he first had that belief, to notify the authority of it[23]; and

(c) a statement that if the person fails without reasonable excuse to comply with a requirement contained in a statement pursuant to head (b) above, the authority may impose on him a penalty of £50[24].

(9) where a statement falls to be given as mentioned in head (7) by reason of a reduction[25] required by a council tax reduction scheme[26]:

(a) the reasons for the reduction and its amount[27];

(b) a statement:

(c) informing the person affected of the duty[28] to notify changes of circumstances[29];
(d) explaining the possible consequences (including prosecution) of failing to comply with that duty[30]; and
(e) setting out the circumstances a change in which might affect entitlement to the reduction or its amount[31];

(10) where a statement falls to be given as regards a matter referred to in head (7), a statement of the amount of the discount or reduction applicable to that matter[32];

(11) a statement of the days (if any) as regards which it was assumed that the amount required to be paid under the demand notice falls to be calculated by reference to a premium[33];

(12) where head (11) applies:
(a) the amount of the premium and the reasons for it[34];
(b) a statement that if at any time before the end of the following year the person to whom the notice is issued has reason to believe that the amount of council tax payable:
(i) is not subject to a premium; or
(ii) is subject to a premium of a smaller or larger amount;
the person must notify the billing authority of this belief within a period of 21 days beginning on the day on which the person first had that belief[35]; and
(c) a statement that if the person fails without reasonable excuse to comply head (b) above the authority may impose the specified[36] penalty[37];

(13) a statement of the amount (if any) falling to be credited against the amount of council tax which would otherwise be payable for the relevant year[38];

(14) a statement of the amount of any penalty or penalties, or any overpayment of council tax benefit, being recovered under the demand notice[39];

(15) Where:
(a) the demand notice requires the payment of an amount of council tax in respect of the relevant dwelling and a financial year preceding the relevant year; and
(b) there has not previously been served on the person to whom the notice is issued a demand notice requiring the payment of that amount,
a statement of that amount[40];

(16) a statement of the amount required to be paid under the notice, together with a statement of the instalments or other payments required to be paid and the manner in which those payments may be made[41];

(17) a statement of the address and telephone number to which enquiries may be directed as to any matter of which a statement is required to be given by any of heads (1) to (16) above[42].

When a billing authority serves a demand notice on a person it must also supply that person with the prescribed information[43].

1 'Demand notice' means a council tax demand notice within the meaning of the Council Tax (Administration and Enforcement) Regulations 1992, SI 1992/613, Pt V (regs 17–31) (see PARA 452 note 5) which is served by a billing authority or any person authorised by a billing authority to exercise any functions relating to the administration of the council tax: Council Tax (Demand Notices) (Wales) Regulations 1993, SI 1993/255, reg 2(1) (numbered as such by SI 2004/460;

definition amended by SI 1996/1880). 'Billing authority' means a Welsh billing authority: Council Tax (Demand Notices) (Wales) Regulations 1993, SI 1993/255, reg 2(1) (as so renumbered). As to the meaning of 'billing authority' see PARA 346.

The Council Tax (Demand Notices) (Wales) Regulations 1993, SI 1993/255, apply in relation to Wales only: see reg 1 (amended by SI 1996/1880). As to the equivalent regulations in relation to England see the Council Tax (Demand Notices) (England) Regulations 2011, SI 2011/3038; and PARA 453. As to the meanings of 'England' and 'Wales' see PARA 2 note 16.

2 Council Tax (Demand Notices) (Wales) Regulations 1993, SI 1993/255, reg 3(1). Nothing in reg 3 requires a notice to be given on a single sheet of paper, but if more than one sheet is used, the sheets must be issued together, whether or not attached, so as to comprise one notice: reg 3(2).

3 Council Tax (Demand Notices) (Wales) Regulations 1993, SI 1993/255, Sch 1 para 1.

4 Council Tax (Demand Notices) (Wales) Regulations 1993, SI 1993/255, Sch 1 para 2.

5 Council Tax (Demand Notices) (Wales) Regulations 1993, SI 1993/255, Sch 1 para 3.

6 Council Tax (Demand Notices) (Wales) Regulations 1993, SI 1993/255, Sch 1 para 4. As to the meaning of 'dwelling' generally see PARA 349.

7 Any reference in the Council Tax (Demand Notices) (Wales) Regulations 1993, SI 1993/255, to the relevant valuation band in relation to a dwelling is a reference to the valuation band shown as applicable to the dwelling:

(1) in the billing authority's valuation list (reg 2(2)(a) (reg 2(2), (3) added by SI 2004/460)); or

(2) if a new valuation list is due to come into force for the relevant year under the Local Government Finance Act 1992 s 22B(2)(b) or (3)(b), as the case may be (see PARA 411):

(a) except in a case to which the Council Tax (Demand Notices) (Wales) Regulations 1993, SI 1993/255, reg 2(3) applies, in the list proposed to be compiled as the new list, 'the proposed list', by the listing officer and sent to the billing authority under the Local Government Finance Act 1992 s 22B(7) (see PARA 411) (Council Tax (Demand Notices) (Wales) Regulations 1993, SI 1993/255, reg 2(2)(b)(i) (as so added)); or

(b) in a case to which reg 2(3) applies, in information which for the purposes of reg 2(2) is relevant information (reg 2(2)(b)(ii) (as so added)).

Regulation 2(3) applies where the listing officer supplies the authority with information relating to property shown in the proposed list (including information relating to the application to such property of the Council Tax (Chargeable Dwellings) Order 1992, SI 1992/549, art 3 or 4 (see PARA 349); and such information is relevant information for the purposes of the Council Tax (Demand Notices) (Wales) Regulations 1993, SI 1993/255, reg 2(2) to the extent that it differs from information contained in the proposed list: reg 2(3) (as so added). 'The relevant year', in relation to a demand notice, means the financial year to which the demand for payment made by the notice relates: reg 2(1) (as renumbered: see note 1). As to the meaning of 'listing officer' see PARA 347 note 2. As to the meaning of 'financial year' see PARA 11 note 1.

8 Council Tax (Demand Notices) (Wales) Regulations 1993, SI 1993/255, Sch 1 para 5.

9 For the purposes of the Council Tax (Demand Notices) (Wales) Regulations 1993, SI 1993/255, Sch 1 para 6(1), 'category' is to be construed in accordance with the Local Government Finance Act 1992 s 30(4) (see PARA 380 note 2); and where the demand notice is served before 1 April 1993, a dwelling must be treated as included in the category in which, in the opinion of the billing authority, it will be included on 1 April 1993: Council Tax (Demand Notices) (Wales) Regulations 1993, SI 1993/255, Sch 1 para 6(3).

10 Council Tax (Demand Notices) (Wales) Regulations 1993, SI 1993/255, Sch 1 para 6(1)(a)–(c).

11 Ie under the Local Government Finance Act 1992 s 30: see PARA 380.

12 Council Tax (Demand Notices) (Wales) Regulations 1993, SI 1993/255, Sch 1 para 6(1)(i).

13 Ie in accordance with the Local Government Finance Act 1992 s 47: see PARA 11.

14 Council Tax (Demand Notices) (Wales) Regulations 1993, SI 1993/255, Sch 1 para 6(1)(ii). 'The major precepting authority', in relation to a billing authority, means the new police authority which has power to issue a precept to the billing authority: reg 2(1) (as renumbered (see note 1); definition amended by SI 1995/160). 'New police authority' means a police authority established under the Police Act 1964 s 3 (now repealed): Council Tax (Demand Notices) (Wales) Regulations 1993, SI 1993/255, reg 2(1) (as so renumbered; definition added by SI 1995/160). As to police authorities see POLICE AND INVESTIGATORY POWERS vol 84 (2013) PARA 55 et seq.

15 Council Tax (Demand Notices) (Wales) Regulations 1993, SI 1993/255, Sch 1 para 6(1)(iii).

16 Ie in accordance with the Local Government Finance Act 1992 s 34(2): see PARA 386.

17 Council Tax (Demand Notices) (Wales) Regulations 1993, SI 1993/255, Sch 1 para 6(1)(iv), (2). 'Local precepting authority', in relation to a billing authority, means a community council which has power to issue a precept to the billing authority; and 'relevant local precepting authority', in relation to a demand notice and a dwelling, means the community council which has power to issue to the billing authority a precept which is applicable to the part of its area in which the dwelling is situated: reg 2(1) (as renumbered: see note 1). As to community councils see LOCAL GOVERNMENT vol 69 (2018) PARA 63 et seq.

18 Council Tax (Demand Notices) (Wales) Regulations 1993, SI 1993/255, Sch 1 para 7. The factors specified are:

(1) the Local Government Finance Act 1992 s 11 (discounts: see PARA 362) (Council Tax (Demand Notices) (Wales) Regulations 1993, SI 1993/255, Sch 1 para 7(a));

(2) a determination made under the Local Government Finance Act 1992 s 12 (discounts: special provision for Wales: see PARA 365) (Council Tax (Demand Notices) (Wales) Regulations 1993, SI 1993/255, Sch 1 para 7(b) (substituted by SI 2013/63));

(3) the Council Tax (Reductions for Disabilities) Regulations 1992, SI 1992/554 (see PARA 377) (Council Tax (Demand Notices) (Wales) Regulations 1993, SI 1993/255, Sch 1 para 7(c));

(4) the Council Tax Benefit Regulations 2006, SI 2006/215 (see WELFARE BENEFITS AND STATE PENSIONS vol 104 (2014) PARA 249) (Council Tax (Demand Notices) (Wales) Regulations 1993, SI 1993/255, Sch 1 para 7(d) (substituted by SI 2006/217));

(5) the Council Tax Benefit (Persons who have attained the qualifying age for state pension credit) Regulations 2006, SI 2006/126 (Council Tax (Demand Notices) (Wales) Regulations 1993, SI 1993/255, Sch 1 para 7(e) (added by SI 2006/217));

(6) a reduction made under the Local Government Finance Act 1992 s 13A(1)(b) (see PARA 378) (Council Tax (Demand Notices) (Wales) Regulations 1993, SI 1993/255, Sch 1 para 7(f) (added by SI 2013/63)); or

(7) a reduction made under the Local Government Finance Act 1992 s 13A(1)(c) (see PARA 378) (Council Tax (Demand Notices) (Wales) Regulations 1993, SI 1993/255, Sch 1 para 7(g) (added by SI 2013/63)).

19 Ie a matter referred to in the Council Tax (Demand Notices) (Wales) Regulations 1993, SI 1993/255, Sch 1 para 7(a), (b) or (g): see note 18 heads (1), (2), (7).

20 Council Tax (Demand Notices) (Wales) Regulations 1993, SI 1993/255, Sch 1 para 8 (amended by SI 2013/63).

21 Ie in relation to the Council Tax (Demand Notices) (Wales) Regulations 1993, SI 1993/255, Sch 1 para 7(a).

22 Council Tax (Demand Notices) (Wales) Regulations 1993, SI 1993/255, Sch 1 para 8(a).

23 Council Tax (Demand Notices) (Wales) Regulations 1993, SI 1993/255, Sch 1 para 8(b).

24 Council Tax (Demand Notices) (Wales) Regulations 1993, SI 1993/255, Sch 1 para 8(c).

25 Ie by reason of the matter referred to in the Council Tax (Demand Notices) (Wales) Regulations 1993, SI 1993/255, Sch 1 para 7(f): see note 18 head (6).

26 Council Tax (Demand Notices) (Wales) Regulations 1993, SI 1993/255, Sch 1 para 8A (Sch 1 para 8A added by SI 2013/63).

27 Council Tax (Demand Notices) (Wales) Regulations 1993, SI 1993/255, Sch 1 para 8A(a) (as added (see note 26); substituted by SI 2014/122).

28 Ie the duty imposed by para 113(1) of the scheme prescribed in the Council Tax Reduction Schemes (Default Scheme) (Wales) Regulations 2013, SI 2013/3035, Schedule or contained in the authority's scheme by virtue of the Council Tax Reduction Schemes and Prescribed Requirements (Wales) Regulations 2013, SI 2013/3029, Sch 13 para 7(1) as the case may be.

29 Council Tax (Demand Notices) (Wales) Regulations 1993, SI 1993/255, Sch 1 para 8A(b)(i) (as added (see note 26); substituted by SI 2014/122).

30 Council Tax (Demand Notices) (Wales) Regulations 1993, SI 1993/255, Sch 1 para 8A(b)(ii) (as added: see note 26).

31 Council Tax (Demand Notices) (Wales) Regulations 1993, SI 1993/255, Sch 1 para 8A(b)(iii) (as added: see note 26).

32 Council Tax (Demand Notices) (Wales) Regulations 1993, SI 1993/255, Sch 1 para 9.

33 Council Tax (Demand Notices) (Wales) Regulations 1993, SI 1993/255, Sch 1 para 9A (added by SI 2017/40). 'Premium' means a higher amount of council tax payable as a result of a determination made by a billing authority under the Local Government Finance Act 1992 s 12A(1) (higher amount for long-term empty dwellings: see PARA 366) or 12B(1) (higher amount for

dwellings occupied periodically: see PARA 367): Council Tax (Demand Notices) (Wales) Regulations 1993, SI 1993/255, reg 2(1) (as renumbered (see note 1); definition added by SI 2017/40).

34 Council Tax (Demand Notices) (Wales) Regulations 1993, SI 1993/255, Sch 1 para 9B(a) (Sch 1 para 9B added by SI 2017/40).

35 Council Tax (Demand Notices) (Wales) Regulations 1993, SI 1993/255, Sch 1 para 9B(b) (as added: see note 34).

36 Ie the penalty specified in the Local Government Finance Act 1992 Sch 3 para 1(2): see PARA 471.

37 Council Tax (Demand Notices) (Wales) Regulations 1993, SI 1993/255, Sch 1 para 9B(c) (as added: see note 34).

38 Council Tax (Demand Notices) (Wales) Regulations 1993, SI 1993/255, Sch 1 para 10.

39 Council Tax (Demand Notices) (Wales) Regulations 1993, SI 1993/255, Sch 1 para 11.

40 Council Tax (Demand Notices) (Wales) Regulations 1993, SI 1993/255, Sch 1 para 12.

41 Council Tax (Demand Notices) (Wales) Regulations 1993, SI 1993/255, Sch 1 para 13.

42 Council Tax (Demand Notices) (Wales) Regulations 1993, SI 1993/255, Sch 1 para 14.

43 See the Council Tax (Demand Notices) (Wales) Regulations 1993, SI 1993/255, reg 4(1), Sch 2 (Sch 2 amended by SI 1995/160, SI 1996/310, SI 2004/460 and SI 2017/40). The Council Tax (Demand Notices) (Wales) Regulations 1993, SI 1993/255, reg 4(1) does not apply when a demand notice is served after the end of the relevant year: reg 4(2). If it appears requisite to a billing authority when it serves a demand notice that the information mentioned in Sch 2 Pt I should be supplied in English and Welsh, instead of in English or in Welsh, it must be so supplied: reg 4(3). Major precepting authorities must supply a billing authority with certain information for these purposes: see regs 6, 7 (reg 6 amended by SI 1996/310).

455. Consequence of omissions: England.

In relation to a demand notice[1] which relates to a year beginning on or after 1 April 2012[2] and is served by an English billing authority[3] or such an authority's authorised person[4], if:

(1) as a consequence of a mistake a notice does not contain a specified matter[5] ('the relevant matter')[6]; but

(2) the amount required to be paid under the notice is demanded[7] in accordance with the appropriate statutory provisions[8],

the requirement to pay that amount is valid[9].

Where head (1) above applies, as soon as practicable after the mistake is discovered the billing authority must serve a statement of the relevant matter on the person[10] on whom the notice was served[11].

1 As to the meaning of 'demand notice' see PARA 452 note 5 (definition applied by the Council Tax (Demand Notices) (England) Regulations 2011, SI 2011/3038, reg 2(1)).

2 See the Council Tax (Demand Notices) (England) Regulations 2011, SI 2011/3038, reg 1(2)(a). As to the appropriate regulations in relation to a demand notice relating to the year beginning on 1 April 2011 served by an English billing authority or such an authority's authorised person see the Council Tax (Demand Notices) (England) Regulations 2010, SI 2010/2990. As to the appropriate regulations in relation to a demand notice relating to the year beginning on 1 April 2010 served by an English billing authority or such an authority's authorised person see the Council Tax (Demand Notices) (England) Regulations 2009, SI 2009/3193 (amended by SI 2012/2914 and SI 2017/863). As to the appropriate regulations in relation to demand notices served by an English billing authority or an authorised person on behalf of such a billing authority in relation to financial years beginning on or after 1 April 2004 see the Council Tax and Non-Domestic Rating (Demand Notices) (England) Regulations 2003, SI 2003/2613 (as amended: see PARA 437 note 2).

The Council Tax (Demand Notices) (England) Regulations 2011, SI 2011/3038, apply in relation to England only; as to the equivalent regulations in relation to Wales see the Council Tax (Demand Notices) (Wales) Regulations 1993, SI 1993/255; and PARA 456. As to the meanings of 'England' and 'Wales' see PARA 2 note 16.

3 As to the meaning of 'billing authority' see PARA 346.

4 Council Tax (Demand Notices) (England) Regulations 2011, SI 2011/3038, reg 1(2)(b). As to the meaning of 'authorised person' see PARA 453 note 4.

5 Ie a matter specified in the Council Tax (Demand Notices) (England) Regulations 2011, SI 2011/3038, Sch 1: see PARA 453.

6 Council Tax (Demand Notices) (England) Regulations 2011, SI 2011/3038, reg 7(1)(a).

7 Ie in accordance with the Council Tax (Administration and Enforcement) Regulations 1992, SI 1992/613, Pt V (regs 17–31): see PARA 452 et seq.
8 See the Council Tax (Demand Notices) (England) Regulations 2011, SI 2011/3038, reg 7(1)(b).
9 Council Tax (Demand Notices) (England) Regulations 2011, SI 2011/3038, reg 7(1).
10 As to the meaning of 'person' see PARA 11 note 13.
11 Council Tax (Demand Notices) (England) Regulations 2011, SI 2011/3038, reg 7(2).

456. Invalid demand notices: Wales.

Where:

(1) a demand notice[1] is invalid because it does not contain all the required matters[2];
(2) the failure so to comply was due to a mistake[3]; and
(3) the amounts required to be paid under the notice were demanded in accordance with the appropriate statutory provisions[4],

the requirement to pay those amounts will apply as if the notice were valid[5].

Where a requirement to pay an amount under an invalid notice subsists by virtue of heads (1) to (3) above, the billing authority[6] must as soon as practicable after the mistake is discovered issue to the liable person[7] concerned a statement of the matters which were not contained in the notice and which should have been so contained[8].

1 As to the meaning of 'demand notice' see PARA 454 note 1.
2 Ie it does not comply with the Council Tax (Demand Notices) (Wales) Regulations 1993, SI 1993/255, reg 3(1) (see PARA 454): reg 5(1)(a).
The Council Tax (Demand Notices) (Wales) Regulations 1993, SI 1993/255, apply in relation to Wales only: see reg 1 (amended by SI 1996/1880). As to the equivalent regulations in relation to England see the Council Tax (Demand Notices) (England) Regulations 2011, SI 2011/3038; and PARA 455. As to the meanings of 'England' and 'Wales' see PARA 2 note 16.
3 Council Tax (Demand Notices) (Wales) Regulations 1993, SI 1993/255, reg 5(1)(b).
4 Ie the Council Tax (Administration and Enforcement) Regulations 1992, SI 1992/613, Pt V (regs 17–31): see PARA 452 et seq: Council Tax (Demand Notices) (Wales) Regulations 1993, SI 1993/255, reg 5(1)(c).
5 Council Tax (Demand Notices) (Wales) Regulations 1993, SI 1993/255, reg 5(1).
6 As to the meaning of 'billing authority' see PARA 346.
7 As to the meaning of 'person' see PARA 11 note 13.
8 Council Tax (Demand Notices) (Wales) Regulations 1993, SI 1993/255, reg 5(2).

457. Service of demand notices: England and Wales.

The demand notice[1] is to be served[2] on or as soon as practicable after the day the billing authority[3] first sets an amount of council tax[4] for the relevant year[5] for the category[6] of dwellings which includes the chargeable dwelling[7] to which the notice relates[8].

1 As to the meaning of 'demand notice' see PARA 452 note 5. As to the requirement for demand notices see PARA 452.
2 As to the service of notices see PARA 439. The use of the words 'is to be' in the Council Tax (Administration and Enforcement) Regulations 1992, SI 1992/613, reg 19 admitted of the construction that a breach of that statutory duty by a billing authority did not operate in all cases as a windfall to the person liable, but precluded a claim to payment and a duty to pay only when the breach had occasioned some procedural or substantive prejudice: see *Regentford Ltd v Thanet District Council* [2004] EWHC 246 (Admin), [2004] RA 113, (2004) Times, 4 March.
3 As to the meaning of 'billing authority' see PARA 346.
4 As to the setting of council tax see PARA 380. As to council tax see PARA 344 et seq.
5 'Relevant year', in relation to a notice, means the financial year to which the notice relates: Council Tax (Administration and Enforcement) Regulations 1992, SI 1992/613, reg 17(1). As to the meaning of 'financial year' see PARA 11 note 1.
6 For these purposes, 'category' is to be construed in accordance with the Local Government Finance

Act 1992 s 30(4) (see PARA 380 note 2); and where a demand notice was served before 1 April 1993, a dwelling was to be treated as included in the category in which, in the opinion of the billing authority, it would be included on 1 April 1993: see the Council Tax (Administration and Enforcement) Regulations 1992, SI 1992/613, reg 19(2) (reg 19 substituted by SI 1992/3008). As to the meaning of 'dwelling' see PARA 349.

7 As to the meaning of 'chargeable dwelling' see PARA 350.

8 Council Tax (Administration and Enforcement) Regulations 1992, SI 1992/613, reg 19(1) (as substituted: see note 6).

458. Demand notices: payments required: England and Wales.

If the demand notice[1] is issued before or during the relevant year[2], the notice must require the making of payments on account of the following amount[3]:

(1) the billing authority's[4] estimate of the chargeable amount[5], made as respects the relevant year (or part, as the case may be) on the assumptions referred to in heads (a) to (h) below[6]; or

(2) where an amount falls to be credited[7] by the billing authority against the chargeable amount, the amount (if any) by which the amount estimated as mentioned in head (1) above exceeds the amount falling to be so credited[8].

The assumptions on which an estimate is to be made are:

(a) that the person will be liable to pay the council tax[9] to which the notice relates on every day after the issue of the notice[10];

(b) that, as regards the dwelling concerned, the relevant valuation band[11] on the day the notice is issued will remain the relevant valuation band for the dwelling as regards every day after the issue of the notice[12];

(c) if on the day the notice is issued the person satisfies conditions prescribed for the purposes of allowing reduced amounts to be paid[13] (and consequently the chargeable amount in his case is less than it would otherwise be), that he will continue to satisfy those conditions as regards every day after the issue of the notice[14];

(d) if[15] the dwelling to which the notice relates is assumed to be a chargeable dwelling[16] on the day the notice is issued, that it will continue to be a chargeable dwelling as regards every day after the issue of the notice[17];

(e) if[18] the chargeable amount is assumed not to be subject to a discount on the day the notice is issued, that it will not be subject to a discount as regards any day after the issue of the notice[19];

(f) if[20] the chargeable amount is assumed to be subject to a discount on the day the notice is issued, that it will continue to be subject to the same rate of discount as regards every day after the issue of the notice[21];

(g) if it is assumed[22] that the chargeable amount is not subject to a discount, that it will not be subject to a discount as regards any day after the issue of the notice[23]; and

(h) if on the day the notice is issued a determination as to council tax benefit to which the person is entitled is in effect, and by virtue of regulations which prescribe the nature of such benefits[24] the benefit allowed as regards that day takes the form of a reduction in the amount the person is liable to pay in respect of council tax for the relevant year, that as regards every day after that day he will be allowed the same reduction in that amount[25].

If the demand notice is issued during the relevant year and the liable person is not liable to pay an amount by way of council tax in respect of the day on which the notice is issued, the demand notice must require payment of[26]:

(i) the chargeable amount for the period in the year up to the last day in respect of which he was so liable[27]; or

(ii) where an amount falls to be credited by the billing authority against that chargeable amount, an amount equal to the amount (if any) by which that chargeable amount exceeds the amount falling to be so credited[28].

If the demand notice is issued after the end of the relevant year, it must require payment of[29]:

(A) the chargeable amount[30]; or

(B) where an amount falls to be credited by the billing authority against the chargeable amount, an amount equal to the amount (if any) by which the chargeable amount exceeds the amount falling to be so credited[31].

No payment on account of the chargeable amount (whether interim, final or sole) need be made unless a notice served under the billing provisions[32] requires it[33].

Unless:

(I) an agreement[34] in relation to the relevant year has been reached between the billing authority and the liable person before the demand notice is issued[35]; or

(II) the authority has resolved that a Part II scheme[36] is to have effect for the relevant year as regards dwellings[37] of a class which includes the dwelling in respect of which the chargeable amount falls to be paid[38],

a demand notice[39] must require the amount due[40] to be paid by instalments[41] in accordance with a council tax instalment scheme[42].

A billing authority and a liable person may agree that the amount[43] which is required to be paid under a demand notice must be paid in such manner as is provided by the agreement[44].

Where a liable person requests by notice in writing to the billing authority to pay the amount required to be paid by 12 monthly instalments, the following provisions apply[45]. Such a request may be made either before or after the demand notice is issued and may be made in relation to the relevant year or the year following the relevant year[46]. Where the request relates to the relevant year, a demand notice must be issued as soon as reasonably practicable after the date on which the notice to pay by 12 monthly instalments is received by the billing authority and must require the amount to be paid by instalments in accordance with the relevant provisions[47]. Where the request relates to the year following the relevant year, as soon as reasonably practicable after the date on which the notice is received by the billing authority, the billing authority must write to confirm that from such date as is requested in the notice the amount for that year is to be paid by instalments in accordance with the relevant provisions[48].

1 As to the meaning of 'demand notice' see PARA 452 note 5. As to the requirement for demand notices see PARA 452.

2 As to the meaning of 'relevant year' see PARA 457 note 5.

3 Council Tax (Administration and Enforcement) Regulations 1992, SI 1992/613, reg 20(1). The payments are generally to be paid by instalments: see the text to notes 34–48.

4 As to the meaning of 'billing authority' see PARA 346.

5 As to the meaning of 'chargeable amount' see PARA 452 note 6.

6 Council Tax (Administration and Enforcement) Regulations 1992, SI 1992/613, reg 20(2)(a).

7 The provisions of the Council Tax (Administration and Enforcement) Regulations 1992, SI 1992/613, Pt V (regs 17–31) which provide for the repayment or crediting of any amount or the adjustment of payments due under a notice have effect subject to the Local Government Finance Act 1992 s 31(4) (see PARA 381): Council Tax (Administration and Enforcement) Regulations 1992, SI 1992/613, reg 17(6).

8 Council Tax (Administration and Enforcement) Regulations 1992, SI 1992/613, reg 20(2)(b). This is subject to reg 20(2A): see reg 20(2)(b) (amended in relation to England by SI 2012/3086; and in relation to Wales by SI 2013/62). Where the billing authority has made a determination under:

(1) para 118(1)(c) of the scheme prescribed in the Council Tax Reduction Schemes (Default Scheme) (England) Regulations 2012, SI 2012/2886, Schedule; or

(2) a provision contained in an authority's scheme under the Local Government Finance Act 1992 s 13A(2) by virtue of the Council Tax Reduction Schemes (Prescribed Requirements) (England) Regulations 2012, SI 2012/2885, Sch 8 para 14(1)(c) (see PARA 378),

the Council Tax (Administration and Enforcement) Regulations 1992, SI 1992/613, reg 20 (2)(b) does not apply in relation to that amount: reg 20(2A) (added in relation to England by SI 2012/3086; and in relation to Wales by SI 2013/62).

9 As to liability to council tax generally see PARA 348 et seq.

10 Council Tax (Administration and Enforcement) Regulations 1992, SI 1992/613, reg 20(3)(a). As to the day on or time at which a notice is issued see PARA 452 note 9.

11 Any reference in the Council Tax (Administration and Enforcement) Regulations 1992, SI 1992/613, Pt V (regs 17–31) to the 'relevant valuation band' in relation to a dwelling is a reference to the valuation band shown as applicable to the dwelling in the billing authority's valuation list: reg 17(1A)(a) (reg 17(1A), (1B) added by SI 1993/196). If no such list is in force, the reference is to the valuation band shown as applicable to the dwelling:

(1) except in a case to which the Council Tax (Administration and Enforcement) Regulations 1992, SI 1992/613, reg 17(1B) applies, in the copy of the proposed list supplied to the authority between 15 November 1992 and 1 December 1992 (ie under the Local Government Finance Act 1992 s 22(5)(b): see PARA 409) (Council Tax (Administration and Enforcement) Regulations 1992, SI 1992/613, reg 17(1A)(b)(i) (as so added));

(2) in a case to which reg 17(1B) applies, in information which for the purposes of reg 17(1A) is relevant information (reg 17(1A)(b)(ii) (as so added)).

The provisions of reg 17(1B) apply where the listing officer supplies the authority with information relating to property shown in the proposed list (including information relating to the application to such property of the Council Tax (Chargeable Dwellings) Order 1992, SI 1992/549, art 3 or art 4 (see PARA 349)); and such information is relevant information for the purposes of the Council Tax (Administration and Enforcement) Regulations 1992, SI 1992/613, reg 17(1A)(b)(ii) to the extent that it differs from information contained in the proposed list: reg 17(1B) (as so added). As to valuation bands see PARA 361. As to valuation lists see PARAS 409–411. As to the meaning of 'listing officer' see PARA 347 note 2.

12 Council Tax (Administration and Enforcement) Regulations 1992, SI 1992/613, reg 20(3)(b).

13 Ie conditions prescribed for the purposes of regulations under the Local Government Finance Act 1992 s 13: see PARA 377.

14 Council Tax (Administration and Enforcement) Regulations 1992, SI 1992/613, reg 20(3)(c).

15 Ie by virtue of the Council Tax (Administration and Enforcement) Regulations 1992, SI 1992/613, reg 9(1): see PARA 446.

16 As to the meaning of 'chargeable dwelling' see PARA 350.

17 Council Tax (Administration and Enforcement) Regulations 1992, SI 1992/613, reg 20(3)(d).

18 Ie by virtue of the Council Tax (Administration and Enforcement) Regulations 1992, SI 1992/613, reg 15(1): see PARA 450.

19 Council Tax (Administration and Enforcement) Regulations 1992, SI 1992/613, reg 20(3)(e).

20 Ie by virtue of the Council Tax (Administration and Enforcement) Regulations 1992, SI 1992/613, reg 15(2): see PARA 450.

21 Council Tax (Administration and Enforcement) Regulations 1992, SI 1992/613, reg 20(3)(f) (amended in relation to England by SI 2012/3086; and in relation to Wales by SI 2013/62).

22 Ie by virtue of the Council Tax (Administration and Enforcement) Regulations 1992, SI 1992/613, reg 15(3): see PARA 450.

23 Council Tax (Administration and Enforcement) Regulations 1992, SI 1992/613, reg 20(3)(fa) (added in relation to England by SI 2012/3086; and in relation to Wales by SI 2013/62).

24 Ie regulations under the Social Security Administration Act 1992 s 138(1).

25 Council Tax (Administration and Enforcement) Regulations 1992, SI 1992/613, reg 20(3)(g).

26 Council Tax (Administration and Enforcement) Regulations 1992, SI 1992/613, reg 20(4). A notice to which reg 20(4) or reg 20(5) (see the text to notes 29–31) applies must (as the billing authority determines) require payment of the amount concerned:

(1) on the expiry of such period (being not less than 14 days) after the day of issue of the notice as is specified in it (reg 21(7)(a)); or
(2) by instalments of such amounts as are specified in the notice, payable at such intervals and on such day in each interval as is so specified (reg 21(7)(b)).

27 Council Tax (Administration and Enforcement) Regulations 1992, SI 1992/613, reg 20(4)(a).
28 Council Tax (Administration and Enforcement) Regulations 1992, SI 1992/613, reg 20(4)(b).
29 Council Tax (Administration and Enforcement) Regulations 1992, SI 1992/613, reg 20(5). See also note 26.
30 Council Tax (Administration and Enforcement) Regulations 1992, SI 1992/613, reg 20(5)(a).
31 Council Tax (Administration and Enforcement) Regulations 1992, SI 1992/613, reg 20(5)(b).
32 Ie the Council Tax (Administration and Enforcement) Regulations 1992, SI 1992/613, Pt V (regs 17–31).
33 Council Tax (Administration and Enforcement) Regulations 1992, SI 1992/613, reg 22.
34 Ie under the Council Tax (Administration and Enforcement) Regulations 1992, SI 1992/613, reg 21(5) (see the text to notes 43–44).
35 Council Tax (Administration and Enforcement) Regulations 1992, SI 1992/613, reg 21(1)(a). As to the meaning of references to the liable person see PARA 452 note 6.
36 'Part II scheme' means a scheme for the payment of the chargeable amount by instalments in accordance with a scheme complying with the requirements of the Council Tax (Administration and Enforcement) Regulations 1992, SI 1992/613, Sch 1 Pt II (see PARA 464): reg 17(1).
37 As to the meaning of 'dwelling' see PARA 349.
38 Council Tax (Administration and Enforcement) Regulations 1992, SI 1992/613, reg 21(1)(b).
39 Ie a notice to which the Council Tax (Administration and Enforcement) Regulations 1992, SI 1992/613, reg 20(1) applies (see the text to notes 1–3).
40 Ie the amount mentioned in the Council Tax (Administration and Enforcement) Regulations 1992, SI 1992/613, reg 20(2) (see heads (1), (2) in the text).
41 Ie in accordance with the Council Tax (Administration and Enforcement) Regulations 1992, SI 1992/613, Sch 1 Pt I (see PARA 463).
42 Council Tax (Administration and Enforcement) Regulations 1992, SI 1992/613, reg 21(1). Where a billing authority has resolved as mentioned in head (II) in the text, a notice to which reg 20(1) applies must require the amount mentioned in reg 21(2) to be paid by instalments in accordance with the provisions of the authority's Part II scheme: reg 21(2). Where instalments are required to be paid in accordance with a Part II scheme or under Sch 1 Pt I, Sch 1 Pt III (see PARAS 465–466) applies for their cessation or adjustment in the circumstances described in Sch 1 Pt III (subject, in the case of payments in accordance with a Part II scheme, to provision included in the scheme pursuant to Sch 1 Pt II para 8(6) (see PARA 464)): reg 21(3).
43 Ie the amount mentioned in the Council Tax (Administration and Enforcement) Regulations 1992, SI 1992/613, reg 20(2) (see heads (1), (2) in the text).
44 Council Tax (Administration and Enforcement) Regulations 1992, SI 1992/613, reg 21(5). If an agreement under reg 21(5) in relation to the relevant year has been reached between the billing authority and the liable person before the demand notice is issued, a notice to which reg 20(1) applies must require the amount mentioned in reg 20(2) to be paid in accordance with that agreement: reg 21(4). Notwithstanding the provisions of reg 21(1)–(5), such an agreement may be entered into either before or after the demand notice concerned is issued, and may make provision for the cessation or adjustment of payments, and for the making of fresh estimates, in the event of the estimate mentioned in reg 20(2) turning out to be wrong; and if it is entered into after the demand notice has been issued, it may make provision dealing with the treatment for the purposes of the agreement of any sums paid in accordance with Sch 1 Pt I or a Part II scheme before it was entered into: reg 21(6). See also note 7.
45 Council Tax (Administration and Enforcement) Regulations 1992, SI 1992/613, reg 21(1A) (reg 21(1A)–(1D) added in relation to England by SI 2012/3086; and in relation to Wales by SI 2013/62).
46 Council Tax (Administration and Enforcement) Regulations 1992, SI 1992/613, reg 21(1B) (as added: see note 45).
47 Council Tax (Administration and Enforcement) Regulations 1992, SI 1992/613, reg 21(1C) (as added: see note 45). The instalments must be paid in accordance with Sch 1 para 2(3A) (see PARA 463): reg 21(1C) (as so added).
48 Council Tax (Administration and Enforcement) Regulations 1992, SI 1992/613, reg 21(1D) (as added: see note 45). The instalments must be paid in accordance with Sch 1 para 2(3A) (see PARA 463): reg 21(1D) (as so added).

459. Procedure following referendum on excessive amount: England.

The following provisions apply where an increase of council tax of an excessive amount is not approved by a referendum[1], if:

(1) a billing authority[2] has served a demand notice[3] on a liable person[4] in respect of an amount set[5] for a financial year[6]; and

(2) as a consequence of a relevant event[7] the authority subsequently sets a different amount[8] in substitution for that amount[9].

The demand notice mentioned in head (1) will continue to have effect unless and until a notice as to the revised estimate of the amount payable is issued[10], but for the purposes of the enforcement provisions[11] the demand notice will have effect as if it did not include the additional amount[12] and accordingly no liability order may be issued and no enforcement action may be taken under those provisions in respect of that amount[13]. The billing authority may issue a notice as to the revised estimate[14] and must do so if the person mentioned in head (1) so requires[15].

The following provisions apply[16] where an increase of council tax of an excessive amount is approved by a referendum, if:

(a) a billing authority has served a demand notice on a liable person in respect of an amount set[17] for a financial year[18]; and

(b) as a consequence of a relevant event the authority subsequently sets a different amount[19] in substitution for that amount[20], and either:

 (i) the billing authority's relevant basic amount of council tax[21] for the financial year is subsequently given effect[22] for the purposes of the Local Government Finance Act 1992[23]; or

 (ii) a relevant precepting authority's[24] calculations from which its relevant basic amount of council tax was derived are subsequently given effect[25] for the financial year[26].

Where a notice of revised estimate has not been issued[27], the demand notice referred to in head (1) will continue to have effect[28]. Where a notice of revised estimate has been issued, the billing authority must issue a further notice[29] as to the revised estimate[30].

1 Ie the Council Tax (Administration and Enforcement) Regulations 1992, SI 1992/613, reg 21A: see reg 21A(1) (regs 21A, 21B added by SI 2012/672). As to council tax see PARA 344 et seq. As to referendums relating to council tax increases in England see PARA 391 et seq.

2 As to the meaning of 'billing authority' see PARA 346.

3 As to the meaning of 'demand notice' see PARA 452 note 5. As to the requirement for demand notices see PARA 452.

4 As to the meaning of references to the liable person see PARA 452 note 6.

5 Ie under the Local Government Finance Act 1992 s 30: see PARA 380.

6 Council Tax (Administration and Enforcement) Regulations 1992, SI 1992/613, reg 21A(1)(a) (as added: see note 1). As to the meaning of 'financial year' see PARA 11 note 1.

7 'Relevant event', in relation to a billing authority, means any of the following (Council Tax (Administration and Enforcement) Regulations 1992, SI 1992/613, reg 21A(5) (as added: see note 1)):

 (1) the authority's substitute calculations having effect in accordance with the Local Government Finance Act 1992 s 52ZH(5) (relevant basic amount of council tax not approved by majority in referendum: see PARA 396) or s 52ZI(1) (failure to hold referendum: see PARA 397) or the Local Authorities (Conduct of Referendums) (Council Tax Increases) (England) Regulations 2012, SI 2012/444, reg 22(5);

 (2) the making by the authority of substitute calculations mentioned in the Local Government Finance Act 1992 s 52ZI(3)(b) (see PARA 397);

 (3) substitute precepts issued to the authority having effect in accordance with s 52ZO(5) (relevant basic amount of council tax not approved by majority in referendum: see PARA

403) or s 52ZP(7) (failure to hold referendum: see PARA 404) or the Local Authorities (Conduct of Referendums) (Council Tax Increases) (England) Regulations 2012, SI 2012/444, reg 22(13);

(4) the issuing to the authority of a precept under the Local Government Finance Act 1992 s 52ZP(3) (see PARA 404).

8 Ie under the Local Government Finance Act 1992 s 31: see PARA 381.

9 Council Tax (Administration and Enforcement) Regulations 1992, SI 1992/613, reg 21A(1)(b) (as added: see note 1).

10 Ie under the Council Tax (Administration and Enforcement) Regulations 1992, SI 1992/613, reg 21A(3).

11 Ie the Council Tax (Administration and Enforcement) Regulations 1992, SI 1992/613, Pt VI (regs 32–57): see PARA 474 et seq.

12 'Additional amount' means the difference between the amount mentioned in the Council Tax (Administration and Enforcement) Regulations 1992, SI 1992/613, reg 21(1)(a) (see head (1) in the text) and the different amount mentioned in reg 21A(1)(b) (see head (2) in the text): reg 21A(5) (as added: see note 1).

13 Council Tax (Administration and Enforcement) Regulations 1992, SI 1992/613, reg 21A(2) (as added: see note 1).

14 Ie in accordance with the Council Tax (Administration and Enforcement) Regulations 1992, SI 1992/613, Sch 1 para 10 (see PARA 466) as modified by reg 21A(4).

15 Council Tax (Administration and Enforcement) Regulations 1992, SI 1992/613, reg 21A(3) (as added: see note 1). As to the modifications see reg 21A(4) (as so added).

16 Ie the Council Tax (Administration and Enforcement) Regulations 1992, SI 1992/613, reg 21B: see reg 21B(1) (as added: see note 1).

17 Ie under the Local Government Finance Act 1992 s 30: see PARA 380.

18 Council Tax (Administration and Enforcement) Regulations 1992, SI 1992/613, reg 21B(1)(a) (as added: see note 1).

19 Ie under the Local Government Finance Act 1992 s 31: see PARA 381.

20 Council Tax (Administration and Enforcement) Regulations 1992, SI 1992/613, reg 21B(1)(b) (as added: see note 1).

21 As to the meaning of 'relevant basic amount of council tax' see PARA 391 notes 3, 8, 12.

22 Ie by virtue of the Local Authorities (Conduct of Referendums) (Council Tax Increases) (England) Regulations 2012, SI 2012/444, reg 22(9) and the Local Government Finance Act 1992 s 52ZH(3): see PARA 403.

23 Council Tax (Administration and Enforcement) Regulations 1992, SI 1992/613, reg 21B(1)(b)(i) (as added: see note 1).

24 In the Council Tax (Administration and Enforcement) Regulations 1992, SI 1992/613, reg 21B, 'relevant precepting authority' means a precepting authority which issues a precept to the billing authority for the financial year concerned: reg 21B(5) (as added: see note 1). As to the meaning of 'precepting authority' see PARA 23 note 1.

25 Ie by virtue of the Local Authorities (Conduct of Referendums) (Council Tax Increases) (England) Regulations 2012, SI 2012/444, reg 22(17) and the Local Government Finance Act 1992 s 52ZO(3): see PARA 396.

26 Council Tax (Administration and Enforcement) Regulations 1992, SI 1992/613, reg 21B(1)(b)(ii) (as added: see note 1).

27 Ie in accordance with the Council Tax (Administration and Enforcement) Regulations 1992, SI 1992/613, reg 21A(3): see the text to notes 14–15.

28 Council Tax (Administration and Enforcement) Regulations 1992, SI 1992/613, reg 21B(2) (as added: see note 1). Regulation 21A(2) (see the text to notes 10–13) will no longer apply in relation to that notice: reg 21B(2) (as so added).

29 Ie in accordance with the Council Tax (Administration and Enforcement) Regulations 1992, SI 1992/613, Sch 1 para 10 (see PARA 466) as modified by reg 21B(4).

30 Council Tax (Administration and Enforcement) Regulations 1992, SI 1992/613, reg 21B(3) (as added: see note 1). As to the modifications see reg 21B(4) (as so added).

460. Joint taxpayers' notice: England and Wales.

An amount payable by way of council tax[1] is not payable by a person who is one of joint taxpayers[2] and on whom a demand notice[3] has not been served[4] unless a notice ('joint taxpayers' notice') is served on him in accordance with the following provisions[5]. A joint taxpayers' notice may not be served on a person after the expiry of the period of six years beginning with the first day of the financial year[6] to which the notice relates[7]. Where:

(1) a joint taxpayers' notice is served during the relevant year[8]; and

(2) the person on whom (as one of the joint taxpayers) a demand notice for that year was served (or, if more than one person was so served, each of them) is not on the day of issue of the notice[9] one of the joint taxpayers[10]; and

(3) the unpaid balance of the estimated amount has not[11] become due[12],

the notice must require the payment of the adjusted amount[13].

The amount required to be so paid is payable by instalments of such amounts, and at such intervals and on such days in each interval, as are specified in the notice; provided that the number of instalments is not less than the number of instalments payable under the agreement, the demand notice or any subsequent notice[14], as the case may be, as regards the period beginning on the day on which the joint taxpayers' notice is served and ending on the last day of the relevant year[15].

A joint taxpayers' notice which is issued after the end of the relevant year, or after the unpaid balance of the estimated amount has become due[16], must (as the billing authority determines) require payment of the amount concerned:

(a) on the expiry of such period (being not less than 14 days) after the issue of the notice as is specified in it[17]; or

(b) by instalments of such amounts as are specified in the notice, payable at such intervals and on such day in each interval as is so specified[18].

A billing authority and a person on whom a joint taxpayers' notice is served may agree that the amount required to be paid under the notice must be paid in such manner as is provided by the agreement[19].

If the amount required to be paid under a joint taxpayers' notice is shown to be incorrect, the billing authority must serve a further notice on every person on whom the joint taxpayers' notice was served stating the revised sum required to be paid[20]. If the amount stated in the further notice so served is greater than the amount required to be paid under the joint taxpayers' notice, the further notice must also state the revised amount of each remaining instalment or, as the case may be, the period (being not less than 14 days) after the issue of that further notice within which the further sum payable is required to be paid[21]. If the amount stated in the further notice so served is less than the amount required to be paid under the joint taxpayers' notice, any overpayment:

(i) must be repaid[22] if the person on whom the joint taxpayers' notice was served so requires[23]; or

(ii) in any other case must (as the billing authority determines) either be repaid or be credited against any subsequent liability of that person to make a payment in respect of council tax to the authority[24].

1 As to council tax see PARA 344 et seq.

2 As to the meaning of 'joint taxpayers' see PARA 452 note 6.

3 As to the meaning of 'demand notice' see PARA 452 note 5. As to the requirement for demand notices see PARA 452.

4 As to the service of demand notices see PARA 457. As to the service of notices generally see PARA 439.

5 Council Tax (Administration and Enforcement) Regulations 1992, SI 1992/613, reg 28(1) (reg 28 substituted, reg 28A added, by SI 1992/3008).

6 As to the meaning of 'financial year' see PARA 11 note 1.

7 Council Tax (Administration and Enforcement) Regulations 1992, SI 1992/613, reg 28(2) (as substituted: see note 5).

8 Council Tax (Administration and Enforcement) Regulations 1992, SI 1992/613, reg 28(3)(a) (as substituted: see note 5). As to the meaning of 'relevant year' see PARA 457 note 5.
9 As to the day on or time at which a notice is issued see PARA 452 note 9.
10 Council Tax (Administration and Enforcement) Regulations 1992, SI 1992/613, reg 28(3)(b) (as substituted: see note 5).
11 Ie as mentioned in the Council Tax (Administration and Enforcement) Regulations 1992, SI 1992/613, reg 23(3), (4): see PARA 461.
12 Council Tax (Administration and Enforcement) Regulations 1992, SI 1992/613, reg 28(3)(c) (as substituted: see note 5).
13 Council Tax (Administration and Enforcement) Regulations 1992, SI 1992/613, reg 28(3) (as substituted: see note 5). 'The adjusted amount' is defined by reg 28(4) (as so substituted; definition amended by SI 1994/505) as an amount equal to the lesser of:
(1) the billing authority's estimate of the chargeable amount made as respects the period to which the joint taxpayers' notice relates; and the Council Tax (Administration and Enforcement) Regulations 1992, SI 1992/613, reg 20(3) (see PARA 458) has effect for these purposes as it has effect in a case to which reg 27 (see PARA 452) applies and as if references in reg 27(2)(b) to the demand notice were references to the joint taxpayers' notice; and
(2) the relevant sum.
'The relevant sum' is defined by reg 28(4) (as so substituted) as an amount equal to the difference between:
(a) the amount estimated or last estimated as regards the dwelling concerned:
(i) for the purposes of an agreement under reg 21(5) (see PARA 458); or
(ii) under reg 20(2) (see PARA 458) for the purposes of the demand notice or any subsequent notice given under Sch 1 para 10 (see PARA 466); and
(b) the aggregate of the amounts paid to the authority under any such agreement or notice before the issue of the joint taxpayers' notice.
As to the meaning of 'billing authority' see PARA 346. As to the meaning of 'chargeable amount' see PARA 332. As to the meaning of 'dwelling' see PARA 349.
14 Ie given under the Council Tax (Administration and Enforcement) Regulations 1992, SI 1992/613, Sch 1 para 10: see PARA 466.
15 Council Tax (Administration and Enforcement) Regulations 1992, SI 1992/613, reg 28(5) (as substituted: see note 5). This provision is expressed to be subject to reg 28A(1) (see the text to note 19): see reg 28(5) (as so substituted).
16 Ie as mentioned in the Council Tax (Administration and Enforcement) Regulations 1992, SI 1992/613, reg 23(3), (4): see PARA 461.
17 Council Tax (Administration and Enforcement) Regulations 1992, SI 1992/613, reg 28(6)(a) (as substituted: see note 5).
18 Council Tax (Administration and Enforcement) Regulations 1992, SI 1992/613, reg 28(6)(b) (as substituted: see note 5).
19 Council Tax (Administration and Enforcement) Regulations 1992, SI 1992/613, reg 28A(1) (as added: see note 5). Regulation 21(6) applies with the necessary modifications in relation to an agreement under reg 28A(1) as it applies to an agreement under reg 21(5) (see PARA 458): see reg 28A(1) (as so added). Regulation 23 (failure to pay instalments: see PARA 461) applies with the necessary modifications in relation to instalments payable in accordance with a joint taxpayers' notice as it applies to instalments payable in accordance with Sch 1 Pt I or a Part II scheme: reg 28A(2) (as so added). As to the meaning of 'Part II scheme' see PARA 458 note 36.
20 Council Tax (Administration and Enforcement) Regulations 1992, SI 1992/613, reg 28A(3) (as added: see note 5).
21 Council Tax (Administration and Enforcement) Regulations 1992, SI 1992/613, reg 28A(4) (as added: see note 5).
22 As to the repayment or crediting of any amount or the adjustment of payments due under a notice see PARA 458 note 7.
23 Council Tax (Administration and Enforcement) Regulations 1992, SI 1992/613, reg 28A(5)(a) (as added: see note 5).
24 Council Tax (Administration and Enforcement) Regulations 1992, SI 1992/613, reg 28A(5)(b) (as added: see note 5).

461. Reminder notices: England and Wales.

In circumstances where:

(1) a demand notice[1] has been served by a billing authority[2] on a liable person[3];
(2) instalments in respect of the council tax to which the notice relates are[4] payable[5]; and
(3) any such instalment is not[6] so paid[7],

the billing authority must serve a notice ('reminder notice') on the liable person stating[8]:

(a) the amount which is the aggregate of the instalments which are due under the demand notice or any subsequent notice[9] and which are unpaid and the instalments that will become due within the period of seven days beginning with the day on which the reminder notice is issued[10];
(b) that the amount mentioned in head (a) above is required to be paid by him within the period there mentioned[11];
(c) the effect of the relevant statutory provisions relating to the liability that will be incurred by a failure to pay following the issue of a reminder notice[12] and the amount that will become payable by him in the circumstances mentioned in those provisions[13]; and
(d) where the notice is the second such notice as regards the relevant year[14], the effect of the relevant statutory provisions[15] relating to the liability that will be incurred by a failure to pay subsequent instalments[16].

If, within the period of seven days beginning with the day on which a reminder notice is issued, the liable person fails to pay any instalments which are or will become due before the expiry of that period, the unpaid balance of the estimated amount (or, as the case may be, the chargeable amount[17]) becomes payable by him at the expiry of a further period of seven days beginning with the day of the failure[18].

If, after making a payment in accordance with a reminder notice which is the second such notice as regards the relevant year, the liable person fails to pay any subsequent instalment as regards that year on or before the day on which it falls due, the unpaid balance of the estimated amount (or, as the case may be, the chargeable amount) becomes payable by him on the day following the day of the failure[19].

1 As to the meaning of 'demand notice' see PARA 452 note 5. As to the requirement for demand notices see PARA 452. As to the service of demand notices see PARA 457.
2 As to the meaning of 'billing authority' see PARA 346.
3 Council Tax (Administration and Enforcement) Regulations 1992, SI 1992/613, reg 23(1)(a). As to the meaning of references to the liable person see PARA 452 note 6.
4 Ie in accordance with the Council Tax (Administration and Enforcement) Regulations 1992, SI 1992/613 Sch 1 Pt I (see PARA 463) or, as the case may be, a Part II scheme or a determination under reg 21(7) (see PARA 458). As to the meaning of 'Part II scheme' see PARA 458 note 36.
5 Council Tax (Administration and Enforcement) Regulations 1992, SI 1992/613, reg 23(1)(b) (amended by SI 1997/393).
6 Ie in accordance with the Council Tax (Administration and Enforcement) Regulations 1992, SI 1992/613, Sch 1 (see PARA 463) or, as the case may be, the relevant Part II scheme or determination under reg 21(7) (see PARA 458).
7 Council Tax (Administration and Enforcement) Regulations 1992, SI 1992/613, reg 23(1)(c) (amended by SI 1997/393).
8 Council Tax (Administration and Enforcement) Regulations 1992, SI 1992/613, reg 23(1). Nothing in reg 23(1) requires the service of a reminder notice where all the instalments have fallen due (reg 23(2)(a)) or in the circumstances mentioned in reg 23(3), (4) (see the text to notes 17–19) (reg 23(2)(b)).
9 Ie given under the Council Tax (Administration and Enforcement) Regulations 1992, SI 1992/613, Sch 1 para 10: see PARA 466.

10 Council Tax (Administration and Enforcement) Regulations 1992, SI 1992/613, reg 23(1)(i) (reg 23(1)(i)–(iv) substituted by SI 1994/505). As to the day on or time at which a notice is issued see PARA 452 note 9.
11 Council Tax (Administration and Enforcement) Regulations 1992, SI 1992/613, reg 23(1)(ii) (as substituted: see note 10).
12 Ie the effect of the Council Tax (Administration and Enforcement) Regulations 1992, SI 1992/613, reg 23(3): see the text to notes 17–18.
13 Council Tax (Administration and Enforcement) Regulations 1992, SI 1992/613, reg 23(1)(iii) (as substituted: see note 10).
14 As to the meaning of 'relevant year' see PARA 457 note 5.
15 Ie the effect of the Council Tax (Administration and Enforcement) Regulations 1992, SI 1992/613, reg 23(4): see the text to note 19.
16 Council Tax (Administration and Enforcement) Regulations 1992, SI 1992/613, reg 23(1)(iv) (as substituted: see note 10).
17 As to the meaning of 'chargeable amount' see PARA 332.
18 Council Tax (Administration and Enforcement) Regulations 1992, SI 1992/613, reg 23(3) (amended by SI 1997/393).
19 Council Tax (Administration and Enforcement) Regulations 1992, SI 1992/613, reg 23(4) (amended by SI 1997/393).

462. Final adjustment: England and Wales.

In circumstances where:

(1) a notice has been issued by a billing authority[1] under the billing provisions[2] requiring a payment or payments to be made by a person in respect of his liability to pay council tax[3] for a financial year[4] or part of a financial year[5];

(2) the payment or payments required to be made are found to be in excess of or less than his liability for the year or the part[6]; and

(3) provision for adjusting the amounts required under the notice and (as appropriate) for the making of additional payments or the repaying or crediting of any amount[7] overpaid is not otherwise[8] made[9],

the billing authority must as soon as practicable after the expiry of the year or the part of a year serve[10] a further notice on the person stating the amount of his liability for the year or the part, and adjusting (by reference to that amount) the amounts required to be paid under the notice referred to in head (1) above[11].

If the amount stated in the further notice is greater than the amount required to be paid under the notice referred to in head (1) above, the amount of the difference for which such other provision as is mentioned in head (3) above is not made is due from the person to the billing authority on the expiry of such period (being not less than 14 days) after the day of issue of the notice[12] as is specified in it[13]. If there has been an overpayment, the amount overpaid for which such other provision as is mentioned in head (3) above is not made:

(a) must be repaid if the person so requires[14]; or

(b) in any other case, must (as the billing authority determines) either be repaid or be credited against any subsequent liability of the person to make a payment in respect of any council tax of the authority[15].

1 As to the meaning of 'billing authority' see PARA 346.
2 Ie under the Council Tax (Administration and Enforcement) Regulations 1992, SI 1992/613, Pt V (regs 17–31): see PARA 452 et seq.
3 As to the meaning of references to the liable person see PARA 452 note 6. As to council tax see PARA 344 et seq.
4 As to the meaning of 'financial year' see PARA 11 note 1.
5 Council Tax (Administration and Enforcement) Regulations 1992, SI 1992/613, reg 31(1)(a).
6 Council Tax (Administration and Enforcement) Regulations 1992, SI 1992/613, reg 31(1)(b).
7 As to the repayment or crediting of any amount or the adjustment of payments due under a notice

see PARA 458 note 7.

8 Ie is not made by any other provision of the Council Tax (Administration and Enforcement) Regulations 1992, SI 1992/613, Pt V (regs 17–31), of the Local Government Finance Act 1992 or of any agreement entered into under the Council Tax (Administration and Enforcement) Regulations 1992, SI 1992/613, reg 21(5) (see PARA 458).

9 Council Tax (Administration and Enforcement) Regulations 1992, SI 1992/613, reg 31(1)(c).

10 As to the service of notices see PARA 439.

11 Council Tax (Administration and Enforcement) Regulations 1992, SI 1992/613, reg 31(2).

12 As to the day on or time at which a notice is issued see PARA 452 note 9.

13 Council Tax (Administration and Enforcement) Regulations 1992, SI 1992/613, reg 31(3).

14 Council Tax (Administration and Enforcement) Regulations 1992, SI 1992/613, reg 31(4)(a).

15 Council Tax (Administration and Enforcement) Regulations 1992, SI 1992/613, reg 31(4)(b).

(iv) Payment

463. Payment of the aggregate amount: monthly instalments.

Where the demand notice[1] is issued on or before 31 December[2] in the relevant year[3], the aggregate amount[4] is payable in monthly instalments[5]. The number of such instalments[6]:

(1) where the notice is issued before the beginning of the relevant year or at any time in the period beginning on the first day of that year and ending on 30 April of that year, must be ten[7];

(2) where the notice is issued on or after 1 May in the relevant year, must be one less than the number of whole months[8] remaining in the relevant year after the issue of the notice[9].

The months in which the instalments are payable must be uninterrupted, but subject to that are to be such months in the relevant year as are specified in the notice; and the instalments are to be payable on such day in each month as is so specified[10].

If the aggregate amount divided by the number of instalments gives an amount which is a multiple of a pound, the instalments must be of that amount[11].

If the aggregate amount so divided would not give such an amount a specific calculation is applied[12]. If the calculation of instalments in accordance with this formula would produce an amount for an instalment of less than £5, the demand notice may require that the amount which[13] would be the second instalment must be added to the amount which[14] would be the first instalment, and the number of instalments must be reduced by one[15].

If amounts so calculated[16] would produce an amount for an instalment of less than £5[17], the demand notice may require the aggregate amount to be paid:

(a) where the aggregate amount is less than £10, in a single instalment payable on such day as is specified in the notice[18]; or

(b) where the aggregate amount is equal to or greater than £10, by a number of monthly instalments equal to the greatest whole number by which £5 can be multiplied to give a product which is less than or equal to the aggregate amount[19].

Where the demand notice is issued between 1 January and 31 March in the relevant year, the aggregate amount is to be payable in a single instalment on such day as is specified in the notice[20].

The demand notice must be issued at least 14 days before the day on which the first instalment is due under it[21].

The provisions above do not apply where, as regards the relevant year, instalments are payable in accordance with an authority's instalment scheme[22].

1 As to the meaning of 'demand notice' see PARA 452 note 5. As to the requirement for demand notices see PARA 452.
2 As to the day on or time at which a notice is issued see PARA 452 note 9.
3 See the Council Tax (Administration and Enforcement) Regulations 1992, SI 1992/613, Sch 1 para 2(1). As to the meaning of 'relevant year' see PARA 457 note 5. Schedule 1 para 2 has effect subject to Sch 1 para 3 (see the text to notes 18–21): see Sch 1 para 2(1).
4 For these purposes, 'aggregate amount' means the amount to in the Council Tax (Administration and Enforcement) Regulations 1992, SI 1992/613, reg 20(2) (see PARA 458): Sch 1 para 5.
5 Council Tax (Administration and Enforcement) Regulations 1992, SI 1992/613, Sch 1 para 2(2).
6 Council Tax (Administration and Enforcement) Regulations 1992, SI 1992/613, Sch 1 para 2(3). Schedule 1 para 2(3) is subject to Sch 1 para 2(3A), (7) (see note 9 and the text to notes 13–15): see Sch 1 para 2(3) (amended by SI 1995/22; and in relation to England by SI 2012/3086; and in relation to Wales by SI 2013/62).
7 Council Tax (Administration and Enforcement) Regulations 1992, SI 1992/613, Sch 1 para 2(3)(a) (Sch 1 para 2(3)(a), (b) amended by SI 1992/3008).
8 As to the meaning of 'month' see PARA 11 note 1.
9 Council Tax (Administration and Enforcement) Regulations 1992, SI 1992/613, Sch 1 para 2(3)(b) (as amended: see note 7).

The following provisions apply where a notice to which reg 20(1) applies has been issued in accordance with reg 21(1C) (see PARA 458): Sch 1 para 2(3A) (Sch 1 para 2(3A), (3B) added in relation to England by SI 2012/3086; and in relation to Wales by SI 2013/62; and amended by SI 2013/590). Subject to the Council Tax (Administration and Enforcement) Regulations 1992, SI 1992/613, Sch 1 para 2(7), the number of such instalments:

(1) where the notice is issued before the beginning of the relevant year or at any time in the period beginning on the first day of that year and ending on 15 April of that year, must be 12 (Sch 1 para 2(3A)(a)(i) (as so added));
(2) where the notice is issued on or after 16 April in the relevant year, must be the number of whole months remaining in the relevant year after the issue of the notice (Sch 1 para 2(3A)(a)(ii) (as so added)).

Where the aggregate amount was calculated by reference to a determination under the Local Government Finance Act 1992 s 11A(3), (4) or (4A) (discounts: special provision for England: see PARA 363) and the level of discount varies over the course of the relevant year, the monthly instalments do not need to be equal amounts but must be as specified in the notice: Council Tax (Administration and Enforcement) Regulations 1992, SI 1992/613, Sch 1 para 2(3B) (as so added)).

10 Council Tax (Administration and Enforcement) Regulations 1992, SI 1992/613, Sch 1 para 2(4).
11 Council Tax (Administration and Enforcement) Regulations 1992, SI 1992/613, Sch 1 para 2(5).
12 See the Council Tax (Administration and Enforcement) Regulations 1992, SI 1992/613, Sch 1 para 2(6).
13 Ie but for the Council Tax (Administration and Enforcement) Regulations 1992, SI 1992/613, Sch 1 para 2(7).
14 Ie but for the Council Tax (Administration and Enforcement) Regulations 1992, SI 1992/613, Sch 1 para 2(7).
15 Council Tax (Administration and Enforcement) Regulations 1992, SI 1992/613, Sch 1 para 2(7) (added by SI 1995/22).
16 Ie calculated in accordance with the Council Tax (Administration and Enforcement) Regulations 1992, SI 1992/613, Sch 1 para 2: see the text to notes 1–15.
17 Ie notwithstanding any adjustment of instalments made in accordance with the Council Tax (Administration and Enforcement) Regulations 1992, SI 1992/613, Sch 1 para 2(7): see the text to notes 13–15.
18 Council Tax (Administration and Enforcement) Regulations 1992, SI 1992/613, Sch 1 para 3(1)(a).
19 Council Tax (Administration and Enforcement) Regulations 1992, SI 1992/613, Sch 1 para 3(1)(b). The months in which the instalments under Sch 1 para 3(1)(b) are payable must be uninterrupted but subject to that are to be such of the months in which, but for Sch 1 para 3, the instalments would have been payable under Sch 1 para 2 (see the text to notes 1–15) as are specified in the demand notice; and the instalments are to be payable on such day in each month

as is so specified: Sch 1 para 3(2). Schedule 1 para 2(5)–(7) (see the text to notes 11–15) applies to instalments under Sch 1 para 3(1)(b) as it applies to instalments under Sch 1 para 2: Sch 1 para 3(3) (amended by SI 1995/22). See note 3.

20 Council Tax (Administration and Enforcement) Regulations 1992, SI 1992/613, Sch 1 para 4.

21 Council Tax (Administration and Enforcement) Regulations 1992, SI 1992/613, Sch 1 para 4A (added by SI 1992/3008).

22 The Council Tax (Administration and Enforcement) Regulations 1992, SI 1992/613, Sch 1 Pt I (paras 1–5) does not apply where, as regards the relevant year, instalments are payable in accordance with a Part II scheme: Sch 1 para 1. As to the meaning of 'Part II scheme' see PARA 458 note 36. As to payment under a Part II scheme see PARA 464.

464. Payment of the aggregate amount: authorities' instalment schemes.

Where the demand notice[1] is issued before or during the relevant year[2], then, except where, as regards the relevant year, instalments are payable under the provisions relating to payment by monthly instalments[3], a scheme made by a billing authority[4] for the payment by instalments of the aggregate amount[5] must comply with the following requirements[6].

The scheme must be expressed to have effect for all financial years[7] commencing with the financial year for which it first has effect unless varied or revoked[8]. The scheme must provide:

(1) that no variation may affect the operation of the scheme as regards a particular financial year unless the variation is made before the day on which the authority first sets an amount[9] for the year[10]; and

(2) that it may not be revoked later than 31 December immediately preceding the financial year from which it is desired that it should cease to have effect[11].

The scheme must provide for its application as regards chargeable dwellings[12] in the authority's area in respect of which the aggregate amount as regards the dwelling and the relevant year falls or, in the opinion of the authority, will fall to be paid by a person by whom an amount by way of rent for that dwelling for periods in that year is or, in the opinion of the authority, will be payable to the authority[13]. The scheme may provide for its continued application, as regards any period in the relevant year in respect of which rent is not so payable where such period follows a period in respect of which rent is so payable[14].

The scheme must provide:

(a) for the aggregate amount to be payable in instalments[15];

(b) subject to head (c) below, for the number of instalments to be not less than ten nor more than 52[16];

(c) for the first instalment to be required to be paid no earlier than 14 days after the day on which the demand notice was issued and for the last instalment to be required to be paid before the end of the relevant year but, subject to that, for instalments to be payable on such day in each interval as is specified in the scheme[17];

(d) for the determination of the amount of any instalment where the aggregate amount divided by the number of instalments does not give an amount which is a multiple of ten pence[18].

1 As to the meaning of 'demand notice' see PARA 452 note 5. As to the requirement for demand notices see PARA 452.

2 See the Council Tax (Administration and Enforcement) Regulations 1992, SI 1992/613, Sch 1 para 6(1). As to the meaning of 'relevant year' see PARA 457 note 5. As to the day on or time at which a notice is issued see PARA 452 note 9.

3 Ie the Council Tax (Administration and Enforcement) Regulations 1992, SI 1992/613, Sch 1 Pt II (paras 6–8) does not apply where, as regards the relevant year, instalments are payable under Sch 1 Pt I (paras 1–5) (see PARA 463): see Sch 1 para 6(1), (2).

4 As to the meaning of 'billing authority' see PARA 346.
5 For these purposes, 'aggregate amount' means the amount referred to in the Council Tax (Administration and Enforcement) Regulations 1992, SI 1992/613, reg 20(2) (see PARA 458): Sch 1 para 6(3).
6 See the Council Tax (Administration and Enforcement) Regulations 1992, SI 1992/613, Sch 1 para 7.
7 As to the meaning of 'financial year' see PARA 11 note 1.
8 Council Tax (Administration and Enforcement) Regulations 1992, SI 1992/613, Sch 1 para 8(1).
9 Ie under the Local Government Finance Act 1992 s 30: see PARA 380.
10 Council Tax (Administration and Enforcement) Regulations 1992, SI 1992/613, Sch 1 para 8(2)(a).
11 Council Tax (Administration and Enforcement) Regulations 1992, SI 1992/613, Sch 1 para 8(2)(b).
12 As to the meaning of 'chargeable dwelling' see PARA 350.
13 Council Tax (Administration and Enforcement) Regulations 1992, SI 1992/613, Sch 1 para 8(3).
14 Council Tax (Administration and Enforcement) Regulations 1992, SI 1992/613, Sch 1 para 8(4). This provision is expressed to be without prejudice to reg 21(5) (see PARA 458): see Sch 1 para 8(4).
15 Council Tax (Administration and Enforcement) Regulations 1992, SI 1992/613, Sch 1 para 8(5)(a).
16 Council Tax (Administration and Enforcement) Regulations 1992, SI 1992/613, Sch 1 para 8(5)(b).
17 Council Tax (Administration and Enforcement) Regulations 1992, SI 1992/613, Sch 1 para 8(5)(c) (amended by SI 1992/3008).
18 Council Tax (Administration and Enforcement) Regulations 1992, SI 1992/613, Sch 1 para 8(5)(d). The scheme must provide that where instalments fall to be adjusted in the circumstances mentioned in Sch 1 Pt III para 10 (see PARA 466), the remaining instalments mentioned in Sch 1 Pt III para 10(2) are to be calculated as if references in Sch 1 Pt II (paras 6–8) to the aggregate amount and to instalments were references to the aggregate amount of the remaining instalments and to the remaining instalments respectively: Sch 1 para 8(6). As to the repayment or crediting of any amount or the adjustment of payments due under a notice see PARA 458 note 7.

465. Cessation of instalments.

Where the demand notice[1] has been served on a liable person[2] by a billing authority[3] and after its issue[4] the person ceases to be the liable person in respect of the chargeable dwelling[5] and the period to which the notice relates[6], no payments of instalments falling due after the relevant day[7] are payable under the notice[8].

The billing authority must on the relevant day or as soon as practicable after that day serve a notice[9] on the liable person stating the amount of his liability in respect of the council tax to which the demand notice relates as it has effect for the period in the relevant year[10] up to the day on which he ceased to be so liable[11]. If the amount so stated is less than the aggregate amount of any instalments which have fallen due on or before the relevant day, the difference must go in the first instance to discharge any liability to pay the instalments (to the extent that they remain unpaid)[12]. Any residual overpayment must be repaid[13] if the liable person so requires[14]; or, in any other case, any residual overpayment must (as the billing authority determines) either be repaid or be credited against any subsequent liability of the person to make a payment in respect of any council tax of the authority[15]. However, if the amount so stated is greater than the aggregate amount of any instalments which have fallen due on or before the relevant day, the difference between the two is due from the liable person to the billing authority on the expiry of such period (being not less than 14 days) after the day of issue of the notice so served[16] as is specified in it[17].

If these provisions apply in relation to a demand notice[18], and after the person ceases to be liable to pay an amount in respect of council tax for the relevant year, he again becomes liable to make such a payment, a further notice must be served on the liable person requiring payments in respect of the council tax as it has effect for the period in the year after he becomes so liable[19].

1 As to the meaning of 'demand notice' see PARA 452 note 5. As to the requirement for demand notices see PARA 452.

2 As to the meaning of references to the liable person see PARA 452 note 6. As to the service of demand notices see PARA 457.

3 As to the meaning of 'billing authority' see PARA 346.

4 As to the day on or time at which a notice is issued see PARA 452 note 9.

5 As to the meaning of 'chargeable dwelling' see PARA 350.

6 See the Council Tax (Administration and Enforcement) Regulations 1992, SI 1992/613, reg 21, Sch 1 para 9(1).

7 For these purposes, 'relevant day' means the day on which the person ceases to be liable to make payments in respect of council tax: Council Tax (Administration and Enforcement) Regulations 1992, SI 1992/613, Sch 1 para 9(7).

8 Council Tax (Administration and Enforcement) Regulations 1992, SI 1992/613, Sch 1 para 9(2). This provision is expressed to be subject to Sch 1 para 9(5), (6) (see the text to notes 16–19): see Sch 1 para 9(2). As to payments of instalments see PARAS 463–464.

9 As to the service of notices see PARA 439.

10 As to the meaning of 'relevant year' see PARA 457 note 5.

11 Council Tax (Administration and Enforcement) Regulations 1992, SI 1992/613, Sch 1 para 9(3).

12 Council Tax (Administration and Enforcement) Regulations 1992, SI 1992/613, Sch 1 para 9(4).

13 As to the repayment or crediting of any amount or the adjustment of payments due under a notice see PARA 458 note 7.

14 Council Tax (Administration and Enforcement) Regulations 1992, SI 1992/613, Sch 1 para 9(4)(a).

15 Council Tax (Administration and Enforcement) Regulations 1992, SI 1992/613, Sch 1 para 9(4)(b). As to council tax see PARA 344 et seq.

16 Ie the notice served under the Council Tax (Administration and Enforcement) Regulations 1992, SI 1992/613, Sch 1 para 9(3): see the text to notes 9–11.

17 Council Tax (Administration and Enforcement) Regulations 1992, SI 1992/613, Sch 1 para 9(5).

18 Ie if the Council Tax (Administration and Enforcement) Regulations 1992, SI 1992/613, Sch 1 para 9 applies in relation to a demand notice: see Sch 1 para 9(6).

19 Council Tax (Administration and Enforcement) Regulations 1992, SI 1992/613, Sch 1 para 9(6). Regulations 19–23 (see PARAS 457–458, 461) (and, so far as applicable, Sch 1 (see PARAS 463–466)) apply to the further notice with respect to that period and the sums payable by the liable person with respect to that period, as if it were a different demand notice: see Sch 1 para 9(6).

466. Adjustment of instalments.

Where the demand notice[1] has been served on a liable person[2] by a billing authority[3], and after its issue the person continues to be the liable person in respect of the chargeable dwelling[4] and the period to which the notice relates[5], but it comes to the attention of the authority that one or more of the following events has occurred[6]:

(1) the notice was so served by reference to an amount set by the billing authority for the relevant year[7] and after the issue of the notice[8] the authority sets[9] a different amount in substitution for that amount[10];

(2) the notice was so served on the assumption that, as regards any day in the period to which the notice relates, the dwelling concerned would be or was a chargeable dwelling and the dwelling was not or has ceased to be a chargeable dwelling as regards any day in that period[11];

(3) the notice was so served on the assumption that, as regards any day in the period to which the notice relates, the dwelling concerned would be or was in a particular valuation band and the dwelling was not or has ceased to be in that band as regards any day in that period[12];

(4) the notice was so served on the assumption that, as regards any day in the period to which the notice relates, the person would be or was entitled to a discount and he was not or has ceased to be so entitled or was or is entitled to a discount of a smaller or larger amount than had been assumed[13];

(5) the notice was so served on the assumption that, as regards any day in the period to which the notice relates, the person was not or would not be entitled to a discount and he was or is so entitled[14];

(6) the notice was so served on the assumption that, as regards any day in the period to which the notice relates, the person would be or was liable to a premium and he was not or has ceased to be so liable or was or is liable to a premium of a smaller or larger amount than had been assumed[15];

(7) the notice was so served on the assumption that, as regards any day in the period to which the notice relates, the person was not or would not be liable to a premium and he was or is so liable[16];

(8) the notice was so served on the assumption that, as regards any day in the period to which the notice relates, the person was or would be liable to pay an amount in respect of council tax and, by virtue of regulations under the Local Government Finance Act 1992[17], he was or is liable to pay a greater or lesser amount than the amount stated in the notice[18];

(9) the notice was so served on the assumption that, as regards any day in the period to which the notice relates, the person was or would be entitled to a reduction in the amount he is liable to pay in respect of council tax under regulations made under the Social Security Administration Act 1992[19], and he was or is allowed a larger or smaller reduction than had been so assumed[20];

(10) the notice was so served on the assumption that, as regards any day in the period to which the notice relates, the person was not or would not be entitled to such a reduction as is mentioned in head (9) above, and he was or is so entitled[21],

the billing authority must on or as soon as practicable after the relevant day[22]:

(a) adjust the instalments (if any) payable on or after the adjustment day[23] (the 'remaining instalments') so that they accord with the appropriate amounts[24]; and

(b) serve a notice[25] on the liable person which is to state:

 (i) the amount of the revised estimate[26]; and

 (ii) the amount of any remaining instalments[27].

If the revised estimate referred to in head (b)(i) above exceeds the aggregate amount of the instalments payable under the demand notice before the adjustment day, but no instalments are payable under it on or after that day, the amount of the excess is due from the liable person to the billing authority in a single instalment on the expiry of such period (being not less than 14 days) after the day of issue of the notice so served as is specified in it[28]; and if in any case the revised estimate is less than the aggregate amount of the instalments payable before the adjustment day, any overpayment:

(A) must be repaid if the liable person so requires[29]; or

(B) in any other case, must (as the billing authority determines) either be repaid or be credited against any subsequent liability of the person to make a payment in respect of any council tax of the authority[30].

More than one adjustment of amounts paid or payable under a demand notice may be so made as the circumstances require[31].

1 As to the meaning of 'demand notice' see PARA 452 note 5. As to the requirement for demand notices see PARA 452.
2 As to the meaning of references to the liable person see PARA 452 note 6. As to the service of demand notices see PARA 457.
3 As to the meaning of 'billing authority' see PARA 346.
4 As to the meaning of 'chargeable dwelling' see PARA 350.
5 Ie where the event mentioned in the Council Tax (Administration and Enforcement) Regulations 1992, SI 1992/613, Sch 1 para 9(1) (see PARA 465) has not occurred in relation to the notice: see Sch 1 para 10(1).
6 Council Tax (Administration and Enforcement) Regulations 1992, SI 1992/613, Sch 1 para 10(1) (amended by SI 1992/3008).
7 As to the meaning of 'relevant year' see PARA 457 note 5.
8 As to the day on or time at which a notice is issued see PARA 452 note 9.
9 Ie under the Local Government Finance Act 1992 s 31: see PARA 381.
10 Council Tax (Administration and Enforcement) Regulations 1992, SI 1992/613, Sch 1 para 10(1)(a).
11 Council Tax (Administration and Enforcement) Regulations 1992, SI 1992/613, Sch 1 para 10(1)(b).
12 Council Tax (Administration and Enforcement) Regulations 1992, SI 1992/613, Sch 1 para 10(1)(c). As to valuation bands see PARA 361.
13 Council Tax (Administration and Enforcement) Regulations 1992, SI 1992/613, Sch 1 para 10(1)(d) (amended in relation to England by SI 2012/3086; and in relation to Wales by SI 2013/62). As to the meaning of 'discount' see PARA 450 note 4.
14 Council Tax (Administration and Enforcement) Regulations 1992, SI 1992/613, Sch 1 para 10(1)(e).
15 Council Tax (Administration and Enforcement) Regulations 1992, SI 1992/613, Sch 1 para 10(1)(ea) (added in relation to England by SI 2012/3086; and in relation to Wales by SI 2017/41). As to the meaning of 'premium' see PARA 450 note 5.
16 Council Tax (Administration and Enforcement) Regulations 1992, SI 1992/613, Sch 1 para 10(1)(eb) (added in relation to England by SI 2012/3086; and in relation to Wales by SI 2017/41).
17 Ie regulations under the Local Government Finance Act 1992 s 13: see PARA 377.
18 Council Tax (Administration and Enforcement) Regulations 1992, SI 1992/613, Sch 1 para 10(1)(f).
19 Ie under the Social Security Administration Act 1992 s 138(1).
20 Council Tax (Administration and Enforcement) Regulations 1992, SI 1992/613, Sch 1 para 10(1)(g).
21 Council Tax (Administration and Enforcement) Regulations 1992, SI 1992/613, Sch 1 para 10(1)(h) (added by SI 1992/3008).
22 Council Tax (Administration and Enforcement) Regulations 1992, SI 1992/613, Sch 1 para 10(2). 'Relevant day' means the day with respect to which the assumption mentioned in Sch 1 para 10(1) (see the text to notes 1–6) is wrong or the day the amount set in substitution mentioned in Sch 1 para 10(1)(a) (see head (1) in the text) is so set: Sch 1 para 10(8).
23 'Adjustment day' means the day 14 days after the day the notice served under the Council Tax (Administration and Enforcement) Regulations 1992, SI 1992/613, Sch 1 para 10(2) (see head (b) in the text) is issued: Sch 1 para 10(8).
24 See the Council Tax (Administration and Enforcement) Regulations 1992, SI 1992/613, Sch 1 para 10(2)(a). The appropriate amounts are those mentioned in Sch 1 para 10(4): see Sch 1 para 10(2)(a). As to the repayment or crediting of any amount or the adjustment of payments due under a notice see PARA 458 note 7.

Subject to Sch 1 para 10(6A), the aggregate amount of the remaining instalments payable must be equal to the amount by which the revised estimate mentioned in Sch 1 para 10(3) (see note 24) exceeds the aggregate amount of the instalments payable under the demand notice before the adjustment day; and, where instalments are payable in accordance with Sch 1 Pt I (paras 1–5) (see PARA 463), the amount of each remaining instalment (if there are more than one) must be calculated in accordance with Sch 1 Pt I, as if references in Sch 1 Pt I to the aggregate amount and to instalments were references to the aggregate amount of the remaining instalments and to the remaining instalments respectively: Sch 1 para 10(4) (amended by SI 1995/22). For the purposes of the Council Tax (Administration and Enforcement) Regulations 1992, SI 1992/613, Sch 1 para

10(4), the aggregate amount of the remaining instalments payable must be reduced by the amount of any payment to the authority on or after the relevant day and before the adjustment day with respect to an instalment, or part of an instalment, which is payable on or after the adjustment day: Sch 1 para 10(6A) (added by SI 1995/22).

In calculating the aggregate amount of instalments payable under a demand notice before the adjustment day for the purposes of the Council Tax (Administration and Enforcement) Regulations 1992, SI 1992/613, Sch 1 para 10(4), or for the purposes of Sch 1 para 10(5) in consequence of the making of a revised estimate under Sch 1 para 10(3) (see the text to notes 28–30):

(1) there must count as so payable any amount in respect of such instalments which has been treated as paid to the authority under the Local Government Finance Act 1992 s 31(3) or has been credited under s 31(4) (see PARA 381) or (on the occasion of the making of a previous revised estimate under the Council Tax (Administration and Enforcement) Regulations 1992, SI 1992/613, Sch 1 para 10(3)) under Sch 1 para 10(5) (Sch 1 para 10(6)(a));

(2) there must count as so payable any amount paid to the authority before the relevant day with respect to an instalment, or part of an instalment, which is payable on or after the adjustment day (Sch 1 para 10(6)(aa) (added by SI 1995/22)); and

(3) there must not count as so payable any amount in respect of such instalments which has been repaid under the Local Government Finance Act 1992 s 31 (see PARA 381) or under the Council Tax (Administration and Enforcement) Regulations 1992, SI 1992/613, Sch 1 para 10(5) (Sch 1 para 10(6)(b)).

Where a notice has been given under Sch 1 para 10(2), in the operation of Sch 1 para 10 as respects any further notice that may fall to be given under it, references in Sch 1 para 10 to the demand notice and to amounts in respect of instalments payable under it must be construed (so far as the context permits) as references to the demand notice, and amounts in respect of instalments payable under the notice, as from time to time previously adjusted under Sch 1 para 10: Sch 1 para 10(7).

25 As to the service of notices see PARA 439.

26 Council Tax (Administration and Enforcement) Regulations 1992, SI 1992/613, Sch 1 para 10(2)(b)(i). For these purposes, the revised estimate is the revised estimate of the billing authority of the amount that the person is liable to pay in respect of council tax for the relevant year made on the assumptions mentioned in reg 20(3) (see PARA 458) and as if the notice mentioned in reg 20(3) were the notice referred to in Sch 1 para 10(2): Sch 1 para 10(3).

27 Council Tax (Administration and Enforcement) Regulations 1992, SI 1992/613, Sch 1 para 10(2)(b)(ii).

28 Ie notice served under the Council Tax (Administration and Enforcement) Regulations 1992, SI 1992/613, Sch 1 para 10(2) (see head (b) in the text): see Sch 1 para 10(5).

29 Council Tax (Administration and Enforcement) Regulations 1992, SI 1992/613, Sch 1 para 10(5)(a).

30 Council Tax (Administration and Enforcement) Regulations 1992, SI 1992/613, Sch 1 para 10(5)(b).

31 See the Council Tax (Administration and Enforcement) Regulations 1992, SI 1992/613, Sch 1 para 11.

467. Payments: adjustments.

If the chargeable amount in respect of council tax[1] proves to be greater than the estimated amount[2], an additional sum equal to the difference between the two is, on the service by the billing authority[3] on the liable person[4] of a notice[5] stating the chargeable amount, due from him to the authority on the expiry of such period (being not less than 14 days) after the day of issue of the notice as is specified in it[6].

If the chargeable amount proves to be less than the estimated amount, the billing authority must notify the liable person in writing[7] of the chargeable amount; and any overpayment of the chargeable amount:

(1) must be repaid if the liable person so requires[8]; or

(2) in any other case, must (as the billing authority determines) either be repaid or be credited[9] against any subsequent liability of the liable person to make a payment in respect of any council tax of the authority[10].

If any assumption by reference to which the estimated amount was calculated is shown to be false before the chargeable amount is capable of final determination[11], the billing authority may, and if so required by the liable person must, make a calculation of the appropriate amount[12] with a view to adjusting the liable person's liability in respect of the estimated amount and (as appropriate) to:

(a) requiring an interim payment from the liable person if the appropriate amount is greater than the estimated amount[13]; or

(b) making an interim repayment to the liable person if the appropriate amount is less than the amount of the estimated amount paid[14].

On calculating the appropriate amount the billing authority must notify the liable person in writing of it; and a payment required under head (a) above is due from the liable person to the billing authority on the expiry of such period (being not less than 14 days) after the day of issue of the notice as is specified in it[15].

If the chargeable amount or the appropriate amount is less than the estimated amount in consequence of the liable person ceasing during the relevant year to be liable to make the payment to which the estimated amount relates, and he becomes liable, in respect of a different chargeable dwelling[16], to make a payment to the same billing authority by way of council tax in respect of the same day as that on which he so ceases, the billing authority may require that the amount of any overpayment[17] or any difference mentioned in head (b) above must, instead of being repaid, be credited against his liability in respect of the different dwelling[18].

1 As to the meaning of 'chargeable amount' see PARA 332.

2 'Estimated amount' means the amount last estimated under the Council Tax (Administration and Enforcement) Regulations 1992, SI 1992/613, reg 20(2) (see PARA 458) for the purposes of a demand notice or any subsequent notice given under Sch 1 para 10 (see PARA 466) prior to the failure mentioned in reg 23(3) (see PARA 461), save that if in any case an interim adjustment has been made under reg 24(3) (see the text to notes 11–14), it means in relation to the next payment, repayment or interim adjustment in that case under reg 24 (if any) the appropriate amount by reference to which the previous interim adjustment was so made: reg 24(7). As to the meaning of 'demand notice' see PARA 452 note 5. As to the requirement for demand notices see PARA 452.

See *R (on the Application of Daniels) v Barnet London Borough Council* [2007] EWHC 1885 (Admin), [2007] RVR 300, [2007] All ER (D) 236 (May) (billing authority has power to correct retrospectively the rate of discount allowed in any demand if information provided by the person liable to pay council tax was incorrect).

3 As to the meaning of 'billing authority' see PARA 346.

4 As to the meaning of references to the liable person see PARA 452 note 6.

5 As to the service of notices see PARA 439.

6 Council Tax (Administration and Enforcement) Regulations 1992, SI 1992/613, reg 24(1). As to the day on or time at which a notice is issued see PARA 452 note 9.

7 As to the meaning of 'writing' see PARA 21 note 3.

8 Council Tax (Administration and Enforcement) Regulations 1992, SI 1992/613, reg 24(2)(a). This provision is expressed to be subject to reg 24(6) (see the text to notes 16–18): see reg 24(2)(a).

9 As to the repayment or crediting of any amount or the adjustment of payments due under a notice see PARA 458 note 7.

10 Council Tax (Administration and Enforcement) Regulations 1992, SI 1992/613, reg 24(2)(b). As to council tax see PARA 344 et seq. As to liability to pay council tax generally see PARA 354 et seq.

11 Ie for the purposes of the Council Tax (Administration and Enforcement) Regulations 1992, SI 1992/613, reg 24(1), (2): see the text to notes 1–10.

12 For the purposes of the Council Tax (Administration and Enforcement) Regulations 1992, SI 1992/613, reg 24(3), the 'appropriate amount' is the amount which would be required to be paid under a demand notice if such a notice were issued with respect to the relevant year on the day that the notice under reg 24(5) (see the text to note 15) is issued; and more than one calculation of the appropriate amount and interim adjustment may be made under reg 24(3) according to the circumstances: see reg 24(4), (7). As to the meaning of 'relevant year' see PARA 457 note 5.

13 Council Tax (Administration and Enforcement) Regulations 1992, SI 1992/613, reg 24(3)(a).

14 Council Tax (Administration and Enforcement) Regulations 1992, SI 1992/613, reg 24(3)(b). This provision is expressed to be subject to reg 24(6) (see the text to notes 16–18): see reg 24(3)(b).
15 Council Tax (Administration and Enforcement) Regulations 1992, SI 1992/613, reg 24(5).
16 As to the meaning of 'chargeable dwelling' see PARA 350.
17 Ie mentioned in the Council Tax (Administration and Enforcement) Regulations 1992, SI 1992/613, reg 24(2): see the text to notes 7–10.
18 Council Tax (Administration and Enforcement) Regulations 1992, SI 1992/613, reg 24(6).

468. Lump sum payments.

A billing authority[1] may, subject to the conditions set out below, accept an amount payable in respect of council tax[2] in a single lump sum in such cases as it may determine and in satisfaction of any liability of a liable person[3] under a demand notice[4] to pay the estimated amount[5], being a lump sum which is of an amount determined by the authority and less than the estimated amount[6]. The conditions are that:

(1) such determinations as to the cases where a lump sum will be accepted and as to the amount of the sum in those cases must be made by the authority on or before the day on which it first sets[7] an amount for the relevant year[8];
(2) under those determinations persons liable to pay the same number of instalments in the relevant year must be treated alike, and so that in particular the proportion that the amount of the single lump sum to be accepted in relation to a person bears to the estimated amount payable by him must be the same as that applicable to all other persons liable to pay the same number of instalments in the relevant year[9]; and
(3) for a lump sum to be accepted under those determinations as they have effect in any case:
    (a) at least two instalments must fall to be paid[10] under the demand notice concerned[11]; and
    (b) the single lump sum payment must be made on or before the day on which the first instalment falls due under the notice[12].

Such a determination may be revoked at any time, and if revoked may (but only on or before the day mentioned in head (1) above) be replaced by a fresh determination[13].

If the chargeable amount[14] proves to be greater than the estimated amount, an additional sum equal to the difference between the two, proportionately reduced[15], is, on the service by the billing authority on the liable person of a notice[16] stating the chargeable amount, due from him to the authority on the expiry of such period (being not less than 14 days) after the day of issue of the notice as is specified in it[17]. If the chargeable amount proves to be less than the estimated amount, the billing authority must notify the liable person in writing[18] of the chargeable amount; and any overpayment of the chargeable amount, proportionately reduced[19], must be repaid if the liable person so requires[20] or, in any other case, must (as the billing authority determines) either be repaid or be credited[21] against any subsequent liability of the liable person to make a payment in respect of any council tax of the authority[22].

If any assumption by reference to which the estimated amount was calculated is shown to be false before the chargeable amount is capable of final determination[23], the billing authority may (and, if so required by the liable person, must) make a calculation of the appropriate amount[24] with a view to adjusting the liable person's liability in respect of the estimated amount and (as appropriate) to:

(i) requiring an interim payment from the liable person, proportionately reduced[25], if the appropriate amount is greater than the estimated amount[26]; or

(ii) making an interim repayment to the liable person, proportionately reduced[27], if the appropriate amount is less than the amount of the estimated amount paid[28].

On calculating the appropriate amount the billing authority must notify the liable person in writing of it; and a payment required under head (i) above is due from the liable person to the billing authority on the expiry of such period (being not less than 14 days) after the day of issue of the notice as is specified in it[29].

The proportion by reference to which a payment or repayment (or sum to be credited)[30] is to be reduced is to be the proportion determined under head (2) above in respect of the lump sum concerned in that case; but in determining whether there has been an overpayment of the chargeable amount or appropriate amount (and the amount of any sum to be repaid or credited before reduction) one payment of the lump sum must be treated as a payment of the estimated amount in full, and any other proportionately reduced payment or repayment already made must be treated as not having been so reduced[31].

1 As to the meaning of 'billing authority' see PARA 346.
2 As to council tax see PARA 344 et seq.
3 As to the meaning of references to the liable person see PARA 452 note 6.
4 Ie to which the Council Tax (Administration and Enforcement) Regulations 1992, SI 1992/613, reg 20(2) applies: see PARA 458. As to the meaning of 'demand notice' see PARA 452 note 5. As to the requirement for demand notices see PARA 452.
5 'Estimated amount' means the amount last estimated under the Council Tax (Administration and Enforcement) Regulations 1992, SI 1992/613, reg 20(2) (see PARA 458) for the purposes of a demand notice or any subsequent notice given under Sch 1 para 10 (see PARA 466) prior to the payment of the single lump sum mentioned in reg 25(1); save that if in any case an interim adjustment has been made under reg 25(6) (see the text to notes 23–28), in relation to the next payment, or interim adjustment in that case under reg 25 (if any), it means (except in reg 25(9): see the text to notes 30–31) the appropriate amount by reference to which the previous interim adjustment was so made: reg 25(10).
6 Council Tax (Administration and Enforcement) Regulations 1992, SI 1992/613, reg 25(1).
7 Ie under the Local Government Finance Act 1992 s 30: see PARA 380.
8 Council Tax (Administration and Enforcement) Regulations 1992, SI 1992/613, reg 25(2)(a). As to the meaning of 'relevant year' see PARA 457 note 5.
9 Council Tax (Administration and Enforcement) Regulations 1992, SI 1992/613, reg 25(2)(b).
10 Ie in accordance with the Council Tax (Administration and Enforcement) Regulations 1992, SI 1992/613, Sch 1 Pt I (see PARA 463), a Part II scheme or any agreement under reg 21(5) (see PARA 458): see reg 25(2)(c)(i). As to the meaning of 'Part II scheme' see PARA 458 note 36.
11 Council Tax (Administration and Enforcement) Regulations 1992, SI 1992/613, reg 25(2)(c)(i).
12 Council Tax (Administration and Enforcement) Regulations 1992, SI 1992/613, reg 25(2)(c)(ii).
13 Council Tax (Administration and Enforcement) Regulations 1992, SI 1992/613, reg 25(3).
14 As to the meaning of 'chargeable amount' see PARA 332.
15 Ie in accordance with the Council Tax (Administration and Enforcement) Regulations 1992, SI 1992/613, reg 25(9): see the text to notes 30–31.
16 As to the service of notices see PARA 439.
17 Council Tax (Administration and Enforcement) Regulations 1992, SI 1992/613, reg 25(4). As to the day on or time at which a notice is issued see PARA 452 note 9.
18 As to the meaning of 'writing' see PARA 21 note 3.
19 Ie in accordance with the Council Tax (Administration and Enforcement) Regulations 1992, SI 1992/613, reg 25(9): see the text to notes 30–31.
20 Council Tax (Administration and Enforcement) Regulations 1992, SI 1992/613, reg 25(5)(a).
21 As to the repayment or crediting of any amount or the adjustment of payments due under a notice see PARA 458 note 7.
22 Council Tax (Administration and Enforcement) Regulations 1992, SI 1992/613, reg 25(5)(b).

23 Ie for the purposes of the Council Tax (Administration and Enforcement) Regulations 1992, SI 1992/613, reg 25(4), (5): see the text to notes 14–22.
24 The 'appropriate amount' is the amount which would be required to be paid under a demand notice if such a notice were issued with respect to the relevant year on the day that the notice under the Council Tax (Administration and Enforcement) Regulations 1992, SI 1992/613, reg 25(8) (see the text to note 29) is issued; and more than one calculation of the appropriate amount and interim adjustment may be made under reg 25(6) according to the circumstances: see reg 25(7), (10).
25 Ie in accordance with the Council Tax (Administration and Enforcement) Regulations 1992, SI 1992/613, reg 25(9): see the text to notes 30–31.
26 Council Tax (Administration and Enforcement) Regulations 1992, SI 1992/613, reg 25(6)(a).
27 Ie in accordance with the Council Tax (Administration and Enforcement) Regulations 1992, SI 1992/613, reg 25(9): see the text to notes 30–31.
28 Council Tax (Administration and Enforcement) Regulations 1992, SI 1992/613, reg 25(6)(b).
29 Council Tax (Administration and Enforcement) Regulations 1992, SI 1992/613, reg 25(8).
30 Ie under the Council Tax (Administration and Enforcement) Regulations 1992, SI 1992/613, reg 25(4)–(6): see the text to notes 14–28.
31 Council Tax (Administration and Enforcement) Regulations 1992, SI 1992/613, reg 25(9).

469. Non-cash payments.

A billing authority[1] may, subject to the following conditions, accept an amount (the 'discounted amount') in such cases as it may determine and in satisfaction of any liability of a person[2] to pay to it any instalment or other payment due under a notice given under the billing provisions[3], being an amount determined by the authority and less than the amount of the instalment or other payment due[4]. The conditions are that:

(1) the discounted amount is paid to the authority otherwise than by either bank notes[5] or coin[6]; and

(2) the determinations as to the cases where a discounted amount will be accepted and as to the proportion that the amount is to bear to the amount of the instalment or other payment due in those cases must be made by the authority on or before the day on which it first sets an amount of council tax[7] for the relevant year[8].

Such a determination may be revoked at any time, and if revoked may (but only on or before the day mentioned in head (2) above) be replaced by a fresh determination[9].

For the purpose of determining whether an adjustment of any amount paid (whether by way of repayment[10], crediting or otherwise) falls to be made under the billing provisions[11] where a discounted amount has been accepted, the instalment or other payment by reference to which the discounted amount was accepted must be treated as having been paid in full; but any amount to be repaid or credited against any subsequent liability in any case must, in so far as it is attributable to such an instalment or other payment, be reduced in accordance with the proportion determined under head (2) above in respect of that case[12].

1 As to the meaning of 'billing authority' see PARA 346.
2 As to the meaning of references to the liable person see PARA 452 note 6.
3 Ie the Council Tax (Administration and Enforcement) Regulations 1992, SI 1992/613, Pt V (regs 17–31): see PARA 452 et seq.
4 Council Tax (Administration and Enforcement) Regulations 1992, SI 1992/613, reg 26(1).
5 Ie within the meaning of the Currency and Bank Notes Act 1954: see FINANCIAL INSTITUTIONS vol 48 (2015) PARAS 100–101.
6 Council Tax (Administration and Enforcement) Regulations 1992, SI 1992/613, reg 26(2)(a).
7 Ie under the Local Government Finance Act 1992 s 30: see PARA 380.
8 See the Council Tax (Administration and Enforcement) Regulations 1992, SI 1992/613, reg 26(2)(b). As to the meaning of 'relevant year' see PARA 457 note 5.

9 Council Tax (Administration and Enforcement) Regulations 1992, SI 1992/613, reg 26(3). The power to revoke under reg 26(3) has effect in any case subject to any agreement to the contrary between the billing authority and the person liable to pay the instalment or other payment concerned: see reg 26(5). As to agreements see PARA 458.

10 As to the repayment or crediting of any amount or the adjustment of payments due under a notice see PARA 458 note 7.

11 Ie under the Council Tax (Administration and Enforcement) Regulations 1992, SI 1992/613, Pt V (regs 17–31).

12 Council Tax (Administration and Enforcement) Regulations 1992, SI 1992/613, reg 26(4). Regulation 26(4) has effect in any case subject to any agreement to the contrary between the billing authority and the person liable to pay the instalment or other payment concerned: see reg 26(5).

470. Outstanding liabilities on death.

Where a person dies and at any time before his death:

(1) he was (or is alleged to have been) liable to pay council tax[1] under the Local Government Finance Act 1992[2]; or

(2) he was (or is alleged to have been) so liable[3], as spouse or civil partner[4]; or

(3) a penalty was imposed[5] on him[6];

and where:

(a) before the deceased's death a sum has become payable by him under the billing provisions[7] or by way of relevant costs[8] in respect of one of the matters mentioned in heads (1) to (3) above but has not been paid[9]; or

(b) after the deceased's death a sum would, but for his death (and whether or not on the service of a notice), become payable by him under the billing provisions[10] in respect of one of those matters[11],

his executor or administrator is, and to the extent that it is not in excess of the deceased's liability under the Local Government Finance Act 1992 (including relevant costs payable by him) in respect of the matter, liable to pay the sum and may deduct out of the assets and effects of the deceased any payments made (or to be made)[12].

Where before the deceased's death a sum in excess of his liability under the Local Government Finance Act 1992 (including relevant costs payable by him) in respect of one of the matters mentioned in heads (1) to (3) above has been paid (whether the excess arises because of his death or otherwise) and has not been repaid or credited under the billing provisions[13], his executor or administrator is entitled to the sum[14].

In so far as is relevant to his liability in the administration of the deceased's estate, the executor or administrator may institute, continue or withdraw proceedings (whether by way of appeal under the Local Government Finance Act 1992[15] or otherwise)[16].

1 Ie under the Local Government Finance Act 1992 s 6 (see PARA 354), s 7 (see PARA 355) or s 8 (see PARA 356). As to the meaning of references to the liable person see PARA 452 note 6. As to council tax see PARA 344 et seq.

2 See the Council Tax (Administration and Enforcement) Regulations 1992, SI 1992/613, reg 58(1)(a).

3 Ie under the Local Government Finance Act 1992 s 9: see PARA 357.

4 Council Tax (Administration and Enforcement) Regulations 1992, SI 1992/613, reg 58(1)(b) (amended in relation to England by SI 2005/2866; and in relation to Wales by SI 2005/3302). As to civil partnership see MATRIMONIAL AND CIVIL PARTNERSHIP LAW vol 72 (2015) PARA 3. Marriage includes marriage of a same sex couple: see the Marriage (Same Sex Couples) Act 2013 Sch 3 para 1(1)(a), (2), (3); and MATRIMONIAL AND CIVIL PARTNERSHIP LAW vol 72 (2015) PARA 1 et seq.

5 Ie under the Local Government Finance Act 1992 Sch 3 para 1(1)–(3) (see PARA 471) or under any of the Council Tax Reduction Schemes (Detection of Fraud and Enforcement) (England) Regulations 2013, SI 2013/501, regs 11–13.

6 Council Tax (Administration and Enforcement) Regulations 1992, SI 1992/613, reg 58(1)(c) (amended in relation to England by SI 2013/590; and in relation to Wales by SI 2013/570).

7 Ie under the Council Tax (Administration and Enforcement) Regulations 1992, SI 1992/613, Pt V (regs 17–31): see PARAS 452 et seq, 472.

8 Costs are 'relevant costs' if:

(1) an order or warrant (as the case may be) was made by the court in respect of them before the deceased's death under the Council Tax (Administration and Enforcement) Regulations 1992, SI 1992/613, reg 34(7)(b) or reg 34(8) (see PARA 478), reg 36A(5)(b) (see PARA 486), reg 47(4)(b) (see PARA 499) or reg 50(3)(c)(ii) (see PARA 484) (reg 58(5)(a) (amended in relation to England by SI 2005/2866)); or

(2) they are charges which may be recovered pursuant to the Taking Control of Goods (Fees) Regulations 2014, SI 2014/1 (see CIVIL PROCEDURE vol 12A (2015) PARA 1363 et seq) (Council Tax (Administration and Enforcement) Regulations 1992, SI 1992/613, reg 58(5)(b) (amended by SI 2014/600)).

9 Council Tax (Administration and Enforcement) Regulations 1992, SI 1992/613, reg 58(2)(a).

10 Ie under the Council Tax (Administration and Enforcement) Regulations 1992, SI 1992/613, Pt V (regs 17–31).

11 Council Tax (Administration and Enforcement) Regulations 1992, SI 1992/613, reg 58(2)(b).

12 Council Tax (Administration and Enforcement) Regulations 1992, SI 1992/613, reg 58(2). Where reg 58(2)(b) applies (see head (b) in the text), the liability of the executor or administrator does not arise until the service on him of a notice requiring payment of the sum: reg 58(3). As to the service of notices see PARA 439.

A sum payable under reg 58(2) is enforceable in the administration of the deceased's estate as a debt of the deceased and accordingly:

(1) no liability order need be applied for in respect of it after the deceased's death under reg 34 (see PARA 478) (reg 58(6)(a)); and

(2) the liability of the executor or administrator is a liability in his capacity as such (reg 58(6)(b)).

Regulation 57(1) (see PARA 506) applies to proceedings to enforce a liability arising under reg 58 as it applies to proceedings under Pt VI (regs 32–57): reg 58(7).

As to executors and administrators see WILLS AND INTESTACY vol 103 (2016) PARA 605 et seq.

13 Ie under the Council Tax (Administration and Enforcement) Regulations 1992, SI 1992/613, Pt V (regs 17–31). As to the repayment or crediting of any amount or the adjustment of payments due under a notice see PARA 458 note 7.

14 Council Tax (Administration and Enforcement) Regulations 1992, SI 1992/613, reg 58(4). See also reg 58(7); and note 12.

15 Ie under the Local Government Finance Act 1992 s 16: see PARA 513.

16 Council Tax (Administration and Enforcement) Regulations 1992, SI 1992/613, reg 58(8). See also reg 58(7); and note 12.

(6) Penalties

471. Imposition of penalties.

Where a person is requested by a billing authority[1] to supply information[2] under any provision included in regulations made for the purposes of administering the council tax[3], the authority may impose a penalty of £70 on him[4]:

(1) if he fails to supply the information in accordance with the provision[5]; or

(2) if, in purported compliance with the provision, he knowingly supplies information which is inaccurate in a material particular[6].

Where a penalty has been so imposed on a person and he is requested by the authority again to supply the same information under the same provision, the authority may impose a further penalty of £280 on him[7]:

(a) if he fails to supply the information in accordance with the provision[8]; or

(b) if, in purported compliance with the provision, he knowingly supplies information which is inaccurate in a material particular[9].

This power to impose further penalties applies each time the authority repeats a request[10].

In any case where a person is required by any provision included in regulations made for the purposes of administering the council tax[11] to notify a billing authority[12], and he fails without reasonable excuse to notify the authority in accordance with the provision[13], the authority may impose a penalty of £70 on him[14].

Any penalty imposed under these provisions[15] must be paid to the authority imposing it[16]. An authority may quash any penalty imposed by it[17].

A person may appeal to a valuation tribunal[18] if he is aggrieved by the imposition on him of such a penalty[19]. Where a penalty is imposed on a person, and he alleges that there is no power in the case concerned to impose a penalty of the amount imposed, he may appeal against the imposition[20].

A person ('P') may appeal to a valuation tribunal if aggrieved by the imposition on P of a penalty relating to an act or omission[21], unless P agreed to the imposition of the penalty as an alternative to criminal proceedings being taken against P in respect of the act or omission to which the penalty relates[22]. Where such a penalty is imposed on a person ('P'), and P alleges that there is no power in the case concerned to impose a penalty of the amount imposed, P may appeal to a valuation tribunal against the imposition[23].

Where a person is convicted of an offence, the conduct by reason of which he is convicted does not also allow a penalty in respect of failure to supply information or to notify a billing authority to be so imposed[24].

The appropriate national authority[25] may make regulations containing provision as to the collection of amounts payable as penalties[26]. The regulations may include:

(i) provision for the collection of such amounts (including provision about instalments and notices) which is equivalent to that made in other regulations[27] for the collection of amounts persons are liable to pay in respect of council tax subject to any modifications the appropriate national authority thinks fit[28];

(ii) provision that, where the imposition of a penalty is subject to an appeal[29], no amount is to be payable in respect of the penalty while the appeal is outstanding[30];

(iii) rules for ascertaining whether an imposition is subject to an appeal, and whether an appeal is outstanding; and the regulations may treat an appeal as outstanding unless it is finally disposed of or abandoned or fails for non-prosecution[31];

(iv) provisions dealing with any case where such a penalty is quashed or revoked, and may in particular provide for the repayment of an amount or the allowance of an amount by way of deduction against a sum due[32].

If it appears to the Treasury[33] that there has been a change in the value of money since the passing of the Local Government Finance Act 1992[34] or (as the case may be) the last occasion when the power to vary penalties[35] was exercised, it may by order substitute for any sum for the time being specified such other sum as appears to it to be justified by the change[36]. Such an order may not apply in relation to any failure which began or anything done before the date on which the order comes into force[37].

1 As to the meaning of 'billing authority' see PARA 346.
2 As to the meaning of 'information' see PARA 345 note 20.
3 Ie in regulations under the Local Government Finance Act 1992 Sch 2 para 2, 3, 9 or 10(2): see PARA 437.
4 See the Local Government Finance Act 1992 Sch 3 para 1(1) (amended, in relation to England, by SI 2008/981). In relation to Wales the penalty is £50: see the Local Government Finance Act 1992 Sch 3 para 1(1). As to the meanings of 'England' and 'Wales' see PARA 2 note 16.
5 Local Government Finance Act 1992 Sch 3 para 1(1)(a).
6 Local Government Finance Act 1992 Sch 3 para 1(1)(b).
7 See the Local Government Finance Act 1992 Sch 3 para 1(3) (amended, in relation to England, by SI 2008/981). In relation to Wales the penalty is £200: see the Local Government Finance Act 1992 Sch 3 para 1(3).
8 Local Government Finance Act 1992 Sch 3 para 1(3)(a).
9 Local Government Finance Act 1992 Sch 3 para 1(3)(b).
10 Local Government Finance Act 1992 Sch 3 para 1(4).
11 Ie in regulations under the Local Government Finance Act 1992 Sch 2 para 4, 5, 9 or 10(2): see PARA 437.
12 Local Government Finance Act 1992 Sch 3 para 1(2)(a).
13 Local Government Finance Act 1992 Sch 3 para 1(2)(b).
14 Local Government Finance Act 1992 Sch 3 para 1(2) (amended, in relation to England, by SI 2008/981). In relation to Wales the penalty is £50: see the Local Government Finance Act 1992 Sch 3 para 1(2).
15 Ie a penalty under the Local Government Finance Act 1992 Sch 3 para 1: see the text to notes 1–14.
16 Local Government Finance Act 1992 Sch 3 para 1(5).
17 Local Government Finance Act 1992 Sch 3 para 1(6).
18 As to the meaning of 'valuation tribunal' see PARA 512.
19 Local Government Finance Act 1992 Sch 3 para 3(1).
20 See the Local Government Finance Act 1992 Sch 3 para 3(3).
21 Ie under regulations under the Local Government Finance Act 1992 s 14C: see PARA 438.
22 Local Government Finance Act 1992 Sch 3 para 3(1A) (added by the Local Government Finance Act 2012 s 14(1), (5), (6)).
23 Local Government Finance Act 1992 Sch 3 para 3(4) (added by the Local Government Finance Act 2012 s 14(1), (5), (7)).
24 See the Local Government Finance Act 1992 Sch 3 para 4. Ie a penalty to be imposed under Sch 3 para 1.
25 Ie the Secretary of State or, in relation to Wales, the Welsh Ministers. The functions of the Secretary of State under the Local Government Finance Act 1992 Sch 3 para 6, so far as exercisable in relation to Wales, were transferred to the National Assembly for Wales (see the National Assembly for Wales (Transfer of Functions) Order 1999, SI 1999/672, art 2, Sch 1) and are now vested in the Welsh Ministers (see the Government of Wales Act 2006 s 162(1), Sch 11 para 30). As to the Secretary of State and the Welsh Ministers see PARA 4 note 18.
26 See the Local Government Finance Act 1992 Sch 3 para 6(1) (amended by the Local Government Finance Act 2012 s 14(1), (5), (8)). As to the regulations made see the Council Tax (Administration and Enforcement) Regulations 1992, SI 1992/613; and PARA 472.
27 Ie under the Local Government Finance Act 1992 Sch 2 paras 2, 3: see PARA 437.
28 See the Local Government Finance Act 1992 Sch 3 para 6(2).
29 In the application of the Local Government Finance Act 1992 Sch 3 para 6 to England and Wales, any reference to an appeal includes a reference to an arbitration in pursuance of regulations made under the Local Government Finance Act 1988 Sch 11 para 4 (see PARA 232): Local Government Finance Act 1992 Sch 3 para 6(6). As to arbitration see PARA 559.
30 Local Government Finance Act 1992 Sch 3 para 6(3).
31 Local Government Finance Act 1992 Sch 3 para 6(4).
32 Local Government Finance Act 1992 Sch 3 para 6(5) (amended by the Local Government Finance Act 2012 s 14(1), (5), (8)).

33 As to the meaning of 'the Treasury' see PARA 30 note 15. The power of the Treasury to vary penalties under the Local Government Finance Act 1992 Sch 3 para 5(1) in relation to Wales is not transferred to the Welsh Ministers: see the National Assembly for Wales (Transfer of Functions) Order 1999, SI 1999/672, art 2, Sch 1.
34 The Local Government Finance Act 1992 received the Royal Assent on 6 March 1992.
35 Ie the power conferred by the Local Government Finance Act 1992 Sch 3 para 5(1).
36 Local Government Finance Act 1992 Sch 3 para 5(1). As to the order made see the Local Government Finance (England) (Substitution of Penalties) Order 2008, SI 2008/981; and notes 4, 7, 14.
37 Local Government Finance Act 1992 Sch 3 para 5(2).

472. Collection of penalties.

Where a penalty is payable by a person to a billing authority[1] it may be collected, as the authority to which it is payable determines[2], either:

(1) by treating the penalty[3] as if it were part of the amount that the person is or will be liable to pay in respect of council tax[4] as regards any demand notice issued[5] after the penalty is imposed[6]; or
(2) by the service by the authority on the person of a notice[7] requiring payment of the penalty on the expiry of such period (being not less than 14 days) after the issue of the notice as is specified in it[8].

Where the imposition of a penalty is subject to an appeal or arbitration, no amount is payable in respect of the penalty while the appeal or arbitration is outstanding[9]. The imposition of a penalty is to be treated[10] as subject to an appeal or arbitration until such time as the matter is finally disposed of[11] or is abandoned or fails for non-prosecution; and the circumstances in which an appeal is to be treated as failing for non-prosecution include the expiry of any time prescribed[12] in consequence of which any such appeal would be required to be dismissed by a valuation tribunal[13]. A demand notice making provision for the recovery of a penalty which is subject to appeal or arbitration may not be issued under head (1) above during the period that the appeal or arbitration concerned is outstanding; and where a penalty becomes subject to appeal or arbitration after the issue of a demand notice which makes such provision, such proportion of the instalments due under it as are attributable to the penalty does not fall due until the appeal or arbitration is finally disposed of, abandoned or fails for non-prosecution[14].

Where an amount has been paid by a person in respect of a penalty which is quashed by the authority[15] or pursuant to the order of a valuation tribunal or the High Court[16], the billing authority which imposed the penalty may allow the amount to him by way of deduction against any other sum which has become due from him under the billing provisions[17] (whether in respect of another penalty or otherwise); and any balance must be repaid[18] to him[19].

1 Ie under the Local Government Finance Act 1992 Sch 3 para 1(1)–(3) (see PARA 471) or under any of the Council Tax Reduction Schemes (Detection of Fraud and Enforcement) (England) Regulations 2013, SI 2013/501, regs 11–13. As to the meaning of 'billing authority' see PARA 346.
2 Council Tax (Administration and Enforcement) Regulations 1992, SI 1992/613, reg 29(1) (amended in relation to England by SI 2013/590; and in relation to Wales by SI 2013/570). This provision is expressed to be subject to the Council Tax (Administration and Enforcement) Regulations 1992, SI 1992/613, reg 29(2)–(4) (see the text to notes 9–14): see reg 29(1).
3 Ie for the purposes of the Council Tax (Administration and Enforcement) Regulations 1992, SI 1992/613, regs 20, 21 (see PARA 458) and Sch 1 (see PARA 463 et seq).
4 As to the meaning of references to the liable person see PARA 452 note 6. As to council tax see PARA 344 et seq.
5 Ie issued pursuant to the Council Tax (Administration and Enforcement) Regulations 1992, SI 1992/613, reg 20(2): see PARA 458.
6 Council Tax (Administration and Enforcement) Regulations 1992, SI 1992/613, reg 29(1)(a).
7 As to the service of notices see PARA 439.

8 Council Tax (Administration and Enforcement) Regulations 1992, SI 1992/613, reg 29(1)(b). As to the day on or time at which a notice is issued see PARA 452 note 9.
9 Council Tax (Administration and Enforcement) Regulations 1992, SI 1992/613, reg 29(2).
10 Ie for the purposes of the Council Tax (Administration and Enforcement) Regulations 1992, SI 1992/613, reg 27 (see PARA 452) and reg 29.
11 Ie in accordance with regulations under the Local Government Finance Act 1988 Sch 11 para A3 in relation to England (see PARA 232) or Sch 11 para 4 in relation to Wales (see PARA 237).
12 Ie prescribed under the Local Government Finance Act 1988 Sch 11 para 8(2)(a): see PARA 240.
13 Council Tax (Administration and Enforcement) Regulations 1992, SI 1992/613, reg 29(3) (amended in relation to England by SI 2013/590). As to the meaning of 'valuation tribunal' see PARA 512.
14 Council Tax (Administration and Enforcement) Regulations 1992, SI 1992/613, reg 29(4).
15 Ie under the Local Government Finance Act 1992 Sch 3 para 1(6) (see PARA 471) or the Council Tax Reduction Schemes (Detection of Fraud and Enforcement) (England) Regulations 2013, SI 2013/501, reg 12(4) or reg 13(6).
16 As to such orders see PARA 472 et seq.
17 Ie under the Council Tax (Administration and Enforcement) Regulations 1992, SI 1992/613, Pt V (regs 17–31): see PARA 452 et seq.
18 As to the repayment or crediting of any amount or the adjustment of payments due under a notice see PARA 458 note 7.
19 Council Tax (Administration and Enforcement) Regulations 1992, SI 1992/613, reg 29(5) (amended in relation to England by SI 2013/590; and in relation to Wales by SI 2013/570).

(7) Recovery of Council Tax

(i) In General

473. Power to make regulations for recovery of sums payable.

The appropriate national authority[1] may make regulations[2]:

(1) in relation to the recovery[3] of any sum which has become payable to a billing authority[4] in relation to council tax[5] or penalties[6] and has not been paid[7];

(2) in relation to the recovery[8] of any sum in relation to council tax which has become payable (by way of repayment) to a person other than a billing authority[9] and has not been paid[10].

Regulations under head (1) above may apply any provision contained in or made under a relevant enactment[11], or may apply any such provision subject to prescribed[12] modifications, or may contain provision equivalent to any such provision (whether or not subject to prescribed modifications)[13].

1 Ie the Secretary of State or, in relation to Wales, the Welsh Ministers. The functions of the Secretary of State under the Local Government Finance Act 1992 Sch 4, so far as exercisable in relation to Wales, were transferred to the National Assembly for Wales (see the National Assembly for Wales (Transfer of Functions) Order 1999, SI 1999/672, art 2, Sch 1) and are now vested in the Welsh Ministers (see the Government of Wales Act 2006 s 162(1), Sch 11 para 30). As to the Secretary of State and the Welsh Ministers see PARA 4 note 18. As to the meaning of 'Wales' see PARA 2 note 16.
2 As to the regulations made under the Local Government Finance Act 1992 Sch 4 para 1, see the Council Tax (Administration and Enforcement) Regulations 1992, SI 1992/613; the Council Tax (Administration and Enforcement) (Attachment of Earnings Order) (Wales) Regulations 1992, SI 1992/1741 (amended by SI 1996/1880); the Council Tax (Deduction from Income Support) Regulations 1993, SI 1993/494 (amended by SI 1993/2113, SI 1996/2344, SI 1997/827, SI 1998/563, SI 1999/3178, SI 2002/1397, SI 2002/3019, SI 2008/1554 and SI 2013/612); and PARA 474 et seq.
3 Ie otherwise than under the Tribunals, Courts and Enforcement Act 2007 Sch 12 (taking control

of goods: see PARA 497): see the Local Government Finance Act 1992 Sch 4 para 1(1) (amended by the Tribunals, Courts and Enforcement Act 2007 s 62(3), Sch 13 paras 101, 107(1), (2)).

4 As to the meaning of 'billing authority' see PARA 346.

5 Ie under any provision included in regulations under the Local Government Finance Act 1992 Sch 2 paras 2, 3 or 6(2) or (3) (see PARA 437): see s 14(3), Sch 4 para 1(1)(a).

6 Ie under any provision included in regulations under the Local Government Finance Act 1992 Sch 3 para 6 (see PARA 471): see Sch 4 para 1(1)(b).

7 Local Government Finance Act 1992 Sch 4 para 1(1) (as amended: see note 3). References in Sch 4 para 1(1) and (2) (see head (2) in the text) to a sum which has become payable and has not been paid include references to a sum forming part of a larger sum which has become payable and the other part of which has been paid: Sch 4 para 1(3). Regulations under Sch 4 para 1(1) may make, in relation to the recovery of any sum falling within Sch 4 para 1(1) which a person is solely liable to pay, any such provision as is authorised by Sch 4 paras 3–20 (see PARA 476 et seq): Sch 4 para 2(1). Regulations under Sch 4 para 1(1) may make, in relation to any sum falling within Sch 4 para 1(1) which persons are jointly and severally liable to pay, provision equivalent to any so authorised subject to any modifications the appropriate national authority thinks fit: Sch 4 para 2(2).

No provision of Pt I (ss 1–69) (see PARA 345 et seq) which provides an express remedy is to prejudice any remedy available to a person (apart from that provision) in respect of a failure to observe a provision of Pt I; and references to Pt I include references to instruments made under it: see s 69(4). As to the meaning of 'person' see PARA 11 note 13.

8 Ie otherwise than under the Tribunals, Courts and Enforcement Act 2007 Sch 12 (taking control of goods: see PARA 497): see the Local Government Finance Act 1992 Sch 4 para 1(2) (amended by the Tribunals, Courts and Enforcement Act 2007 Sch 13 paras 101, 107(1), (2)).

9 Ie under any provision included in regulations under the Local Government Finance Act 1992 Sch 2 para 2, 3 or 6(2) or (3): see PARA 437.

10 Local Government Finance Act 1992 Sch 4 para 1(2) (as amended: see note 8). Regulations under Sch 4 para 1(2) may provide that any sum falling within Sch 4 para 1(2) is recoverable in a court of competent jurisdiction: Sch 4 para 2(3).

11 The relevant enactments are the Attachment of Earnings Act 1971 (see CIVIL PROCEDURE vol 12A (2015) PARA 1426 et seq), the Charging Orders Act 1979 (see CIVIL PROCEDURE vol 12A (2015) PARA 1462 et seq), the Social Security Administration Act 1992 Pt II (ss 17–70) (see WELFARE BENEFITS AND STATE PENSIONS vol 104 (2014) PARA 575) and any enactment applied by any of those enactments: Local Government Finance Act 1992 Sch 4 para 19(2).

12 'Prescribed' means prescribed by regulations made (in relation to England) by the Secretary of State and (in relation to Wales) by the Welsh Ministers: Local Government Finance Act 1992 Sch 4 para 20 (added by the Local Government Act 2003 s 127(1), Sch 7 paras 40, 54). As to the meaning of 'England' see PARA 2 note 16.

13 Local Government Finance Act 1992 Sch 4 para 19(1).

474. Repayments.

A sum which has become payable (by way of repayment) under the billing provisions[1] to a person other than a billing authority[2] but which has not been paid[3] is recoverable in a court of competent jurisdiction[4].

1 Ie under the Council Tax (Administration and Enforcement) Regulations 1992, SI 1992/613, Pt V (regs 17–31): see PARA 452 et seq.

2 As to the meaning of 'billing authority' see PARA 346.

3 References in the Council Tax (Administration and Enforcement) Regulations 1992, SI 1992/613, Pt VI (regs 32–57) to a sum which has become payable and which has not been paid include references to a sum forming part of a larger sum which has become payable and the other part of which has been paid: reg 32(4).

4 Council Tax (Administration and Enforcement) Regulations 1992, SI 1992/613, reg 55.

475. Joint and several liability.

The following provisions have effect with respect to the application of the enforcement provisions[1] to a sum for which persons are jointly and severally liable under the billing provisions[2].

A final notice served[3] on every person against whom the application for a liability order[4] is to be made may be addressed to two or more joint taxpayers[5] in joint names[6]. A liability order may be made against one or more joint taxpayers in respect of an amount for which they are jointly and severally liable[7]. Where a liability order has been made against two or more joint taxpayers[8]:

(1) an attachment of allowances order[9] or an attachment of earnings order[10] may be made against one of them, or different such orders may be made against more than one[11];

(2) the Schedule 12 procedure[12] may be used against one or more of them[13];

(3) a charging order[14] may be made against one of them, or against more than one jointly, or different such orders may be made against more than one of them (as the circumstances require)[15]; and

(4) deductions may be made under the Income Support Regulations[16] from any amount payable to one or more of them by way of income support or universal credit[17].

Where a liability order has been made against two or more joint taxpayers in respect of an amount, steps by way of any method specified in heads (1) to (4) above:

(a) may not be taken under it in respect of one of them while steps by way of that or another of those methods are being taken under it in respect of another of them[18]; and

(b) may be taken under it in respect of one of them notwithstanding that no steps by way of that or another of those methods have been taken under it in respect of another of them[19].

Where a liability order has been made against two or more joint taxpayers and an amount is payable to one of them by way of income support[20] or universal credit, and:

(i) deductions are being made under the Income Support Regulations from any such amount[21]; or

(ii) an application under the Income Support Regulations[22] has been made in respect of him to the appropriate national authority[23] and remains undetermined[24],

no steps, or no further steps, by way of attachment of allowances or earnings, the Schedule 12 procedure, commitment, bankruptcy or charging may be taken, under that or any other liability order, against him or any other of those joint taxpayers who is a member of his family[25].

Where the Schedule 12 procedure has been used against two or more joint taxpayers in respect of an amount, a warrant of commitment may[26] be applied for at any time against one of them or different warrants may be applied for against more than one of them; but no such application may be made in respect of any of them who has not attained the age of 18 years[27]. However, where a liability order has been made against two or more joint taxpayers in respect of an amount, a warrant of commitment may not be applied for unless:

(A) the Schedule 12 procedure has been used against all of them[28]; and

(B) the person using the Schedule 12 procedure reports to the authority that, in relation to each of them, he was unable (for whatever reason) to find any or sufficient goods[29].

Where a liability order has been made against two or more joint taxpayers in respect of an amount, and a warrant of commitment is issued against one of them or a term of imprisonment is fixed in the case of one of them[30], no steps, or no further steps, may be taken against any of them by way of attachment of allowances or earnings, the Schedule 12 procedure, bankruptcy or charging in relation to the relevant amount[31] in respect of which a warrant of commitment may be made[32].

Where a liability order has been made against persons who are joint taxpayers, and a warrant of commitment is issued against one of them or a term of imprisonment is fixed in the case of one of them[33], no steps, or further steps, may be taken under the Income Support Regulations in respect of any of them in relation to the relevant amount[34] in respect of which a warrant of commitment may be made[35].

Where a liability order has been made against two or more joint taxpayers in respect of an amount and in using the Schedule 12 procedure against one of them goods jointly owned by both or all of them are found, control may be taken of those goods with respect to that amount; but in any subsequent proceedings for commitment[36], charges arising[37] from the use of the Schedule 12 procedure must be treated as charges relating to the person against whose goods the Schedule 12 procedure was intended to be used when the joint goods were found, and not as charges relating to the other or others[38].

1 Ie the Council Tax (Administration and Enforcement) Regulations 1992, SI 1992/613, regs 33–53: see PARA 476 et seq.
2 See the Council Tax (Administration and Enforcement) Regulations 1992, SI 1992/613, reg 54(1). The billing provisions are those of Pt V (regs 17–31) (see PARA 452 et seq): see reg 54(1). As to the application of Pt V to joint taxpayers see PARA 452 note 6.
3 Ie in accordance with the Council Tax (Administration and Enforcement) Regulations 1992, SI 1992/613, reg 33: see PARA 477.
4 As to the meaning of 'liability order' see PARA 478 note 6.
5 'Joint taxpayers' means two or more individuals who are jointly and severally liable to pay an amount in respect of council tax: Council Tax (Administration and Enforcement) Regulations 1992, SI 1992/613, reg 54(2). As to council tax see PARA 344 et seq. As to persons liable to pay council tax see PARA 354 et seq.
6 Council Tax (Administration and Enforcement) Regulations 1992, SI 1992/613, reg 54(3). Likewise, a summons under reg 34(2) (application for liability order: see PARA 478) may be addressed to two or more joint taxpayers in joint names: see reg 54(3A) (added by SI 1992/3008).
7 Council Tax (Administration and Enforcement) Regulations 1992, SI 1992/613, reg 54(4).
8 Council Tax (Administration and Enforcement) Regulations 1992, SI 1992/613, reg 54(5) (amended by SI 1994/505). The Council Tax (Administration and Enforcement) Regulations 1992, SI 1992/613, reg 54(5) is subject to reg 54(6) (see the text to notes 17–18) and reg 54(6A) (see the text to notes 19–24): see reg 54(5) (as so amended).
9 As to the meaning of 'attachment of allowances order' see PARA 495.
10 As to the meaning of 'attachment of earnings order' see PARA 488.
11 Council Tax (Administration and Enforcement) Regulations 1992, SI 1992/613, reg 54(5)(a).
12 'The Schedule 12 procedure' means the procedure in the Tribunals, Courts and Enforcement Act 2007 Sch 12 (taking control of goods and selling them to recover a sum of money): Council Tax (Administration and Enforcement) Regulations 1992, SI 1992/613, reg 32(1) (definition added by SI 2014/600). As to the Schedule 12 procedure see PARA 497; and CIVIL PROCEDURE vol 12A (2015) PARA 1334 et seq.
13 Council Tax (Administration and Enforcement) Regulations 1992, SI 1992/613, reg 54(5)(b) (amended by SI 1994/505 and SI 2014/600).
14 As to the meaning of 'charging order' see PARA 484.
15 Council Tax (Administration and Enforcement) Regulations 1992, SI 1992/613, reg 54(5)(c) (amended by SI 1994/505).
16 The 'Income Support Regulations' means the Council Tax (Deduction from Income Support) Regulations 1993, SI 1993/494 (see PARAS 473, 501): Council Tax (Administration and Enforcement) Regulations 1992, SI 1992/613, reg 32(1) (definition added by SI 1993/773).
17 Council Tax (Administration and Enforcement) Regulations 1992, SI 1992/613, reg 54(5)(d) (added by SI 1994/505; amended in relation to England by SI 2013/630; and in relation to Wales by SI 2013/570). 'Universal credit' means universal credit under the Welfare Reform Act 2012 Pt 1 (ss 1–43): Council Tax (Administration and Enforcement) Regulations 1992, SI 1992/613, reg

1(2) (definition added in relation to England by SI 2013/630). As to universal credit see WELFARE BENEFITS AND STATE PENSIONS vol 104 (2014) PARA 1 et seq.

18 Council Tax (Administration and Enforcement) Regulations 1992, SI 1992/613, reg 54(6)(a) (amended by SI 1994/505).

19 Council Tax (Administration and Enforcement) Regulations 1992, SI 1992/613, reg 54(6)(b) (amended by SI 1994/505).

20 'Income support' means income support within the meaning of the Social Security Contributions and Benefits Act 1992 (see WELFARE BENEFITS AND STATE PENSIONS vol 104 (2014) PARA 292 et seq): Council Tax (Administration and Enforcement) Regulations 1992, SI 1992/613, reg 54(6B) (reg 54(6A), (6B) added by SI 1994/505).

21 Council Tax (Administration and Enforcement) Regulations 1992, SI 1992/613, reg 54(6A)(a) (as added: see note 20).

22 Ie under the Council Tax (Deductions from Income Support) Regulations 1993, SI 1993/494, reg 2: see PARA 473.

23 Ie the Secretary of State or, in relation to Wales, the Welsh Ministers. As to the Secretary of State and the Welsh Ministers see PARA 4 note 18. As to the meaning of 'Wales' see PARA 2 note 16.

24 Council Tax (Administration and Enforcement) Regulations 1992, SI 1992/613, reg 54(6A)(b) (as added: see note 20).

25 Council Tax (Administration and Enforcement) Regulations 1992, SI 1992/613, reg 54(6A) (as added (see note 20); amended by virtue of SI 2014/600; in relation to England by SI 2013/630; and in relation to Wales by SI 2013/570). 'Family' has the same meaning as in the Social Security Contributions and Benefits Act 1992 s 137(1) (see WELFARE BENEFITS AND STATE PENSIONS vol 104 (2014) PARA 250): Council Tax (Administration and Enforcement) Regulations 1992, SI 1992/613, reg 54(6B) (as so added).

26 Ie subject to the Council Tax (Administration and Enforcement) Regulations 1992, SI 1992/613, reg 54(8): see the text to notes 28–29.

27 Council Tax (Administration and Enforcement) Regulations 1992, SI 1992/613, reg 54(7) (amended by SI 2014/600). As to the time at which a person attains a particular age see PARA 354 note 4.

28 Council Tax (Administration and Enforcement) Regulations 1992, SI 1992/613, reg 54(8)(a) (amended by virtue of SI 2014/600).

29 Council Tax (Administration and Enforcement) Regulations 1992, SI 1992/613, reg 54(8)(b) (amended by virtue of SI 2014/600).

30 Ie under the Council Tax (Administration and Enforcement) Regulations 1992, SI 1992/613, reg 47(3): see PARA 499.

31 Ie the amount mentioned in the Council Tax (Administration and Enforcement) Regulations 1992, SI 1992/613, reg 47(4): see PARA 499.

32 See the Council Tax (Administration and Enforcement) Regulations 1992, SI 1992/613, reg 54(9) (amended by SI 2014/600).

33 Ie under the Council Tax (Administration and Enforcement) Regulations 1992, SI 1992/613, reg 47(3): see PARA 499.

34 Ie the amount mentioned in the Council Tax (Administration and Enforcement) Regulations 1992, SI 1992/613, reg 47(4): see PARA 499.

35 See the Council Tax (Administration and Enforcement) Regulations 1992, SI 1992/613, reg 54(9A) (added by SI 1993/773).

36 Ie under the Council Tax (Administration and Enforcement) Regulations 1992, SI 1992/613, reg 47: see PARA 499.

37 Ie under the Taking Control of Goods (Fees) Regulations 2014, SI 2014/1: see CIVIL PROCEDURE vol 12A (2015) PARA 1363 et seq.

38 Council Tax (Administration and Enforcement) Regulations 1992, SI 1992/613, reg 54(10) (amended by SI 2014/600). Where:

(1) a liability order has been made against more than one person in respect of an amount (Council Tax (Administration and Enforcement) Regulations 1992, SI 1992/613, reg 54(11)(a) (reg 54(11) substituted by SI 2014/600)); and

(2) a charge has arisen against one of them for the enforcement stage within the meaning of the Taking Control of Goods (Fees) Regulations 2014, SI 2014/1, reg 5 in respect of that amount (Council Tax (Administration and Enforcement) Regulations 1992, SI 1992/613, reg 54(11)(b) (as so substituted)),

no further charge for the enforcement stage or compliance stage (within the meaning of the Taking Control of Goods (Fees) Regulations 2014, SI 2014/1, reg 5) in consequence of any further use or attempted use of the Schedule 12 procedure in respect of that amount may be recovered from any of them; and a charge for the compliance stage must be treated for those purposes as a charge with respect to the others as well as that one (Council Tax (Administration and Enforcement) Regulations 1992, SI 1992/613, reg 54(11) (as so added).

(ii) Liability Orders

476. Provision for liability orders.

Regulations made under the provisions that govern the recovery of sums which have become payable to a billing authority[1] in respect of the council tax but have not been paid[2] may provide that:

(1) the authority concerned may apply to a magistrates' court for an order (a 'liability order') against the person by whom the sum is payable[3];

(2) the magistrates' court must make the order if it is satisfied that the sum has become payable by the person concerned and has not been paid[4].

The regulations may include provision:

(a) that the order must be made in respect of an amount equal to the aggregate of:
  (i) the sum payable[5]; and
  (ii) a sum (of a prescribed[6] amount or an amount determined in accordance with prescribed rules) in respect of the costs incurred in obtaining the order[7];

(b) that, where the sum payable is paid after the order has been applied for but before it is made, the magistrates' court must nonetheless make the order in respect of a sum (of a prescribed amount or an amount determined in accordance with prescribed rules) in respect of the costs incurred in applying for it[8];

(c) prescribing steps to be taken before an application may be made[9];

(d) that no application may be made after a prescribed period has expired[10];

(e) prescribing the procedure to be followed for the initiation of an application (which may include provision as to form)[11];

(f) prescribing the procedure to be followed in dealing with an application[12];

(g) prescribing the form and contents of an order[13].

Separate provision is made as to the circumstances in which, a liability order having been made, it may be quashed[14].

1 As to the meaning of 'billing authority' see PARA 346.

2 Ie regulations under the Local Government Finance Act 1992 Sch 4 para 1(1) (see PARA 473): see s 14(3), Sch 4 para 3(1). As to the regulations made see PARA 477 et seq. As to council tax see PARA 344 et seq.

3 Local Government Finance Act 1992 Sch 4 para 3(1)(a). Where a liability order has been made against a person under regulations made under the Local Government Finance Act 1992 Sch 4, the billing authority concerned may use the procedure in the Tribunals, Courts and Enforcement Act 2007 Sch 12 (taking control of goods: see CIVIL PROCEDURE vol 12A (2015) PARA 1334 et seq) to recover the amount in respect of which the order was made, to the extent that it remains unpaid: Local Government Finance Act 1992 s 14(4) (added by the Tribunals, Courts and Enforcement Act 2007 s 62(3), Sch 13 paras 105, 106).

4 Local Government Finance Act 1992 Sch 4 para 3(1)(b).

5 Local Government Finance Act 1992 Sch 4 para 3(2)(a).

6 'Prescribed' means prescribed by regulations made (in relation to England) by the Secretary of State and (in relation to Wales) by the Welsh Ministers: see the Local Government Finance Act 1992 Sch 4 para 20 (added by the Local Government Act 2003 s 127(1), Sch 7 paras 40, 54). As to the Secretary of State and the Welsh Ministers see PARA 4 note 18. As to the meanings of 'England'

and 'Wales' see PARA 2 note 16. The functions under the Local Government Finance Act 1992 Sch 4 were formerly vested in the National Assembly for Wales and are now exercisable by the Welsh Ministers by virtue of the Government of Wales Act 2006 s 162(1), Sch 11 paras 30, 32.
7 Local Government Finance Act 1992 Sch 4 para 3(2)(b).
8 Local Government Finance Act 1992 Sch 4 para 3(3).
9 Local Government Finance Act 1992 Sch 4 para 3(4)(a).
10 Local Government Finance Act 1992 Sch 4 para 3(4)(b).
11 Local Government Finance Act 1992 Sch 4 para 3(4)(c).
12 Local Government Finance Act 1992 Sch 4 para 3(4)(d).
13 Local Government Finance Act 1992 Sch 4 para 3(4)(e).
14 See the Local Government Finance Act 1992 Sch 4 para 12A; and PARA 485.

477. Preliminary steps in the application for a liability order.

Before a billing authority[1] applies for a liability order[2] it must serve on the person against whom the application is to be made a notice[3] (a 'final notice') which is to state every amount in respect of which the authority is to make the application[4]. A final notice may be served in respect of an amount at any time after it has become due[5].

1 As to the meaning of 'billing authority' see PARA 346.
2 As to the meaning of 'liability order' see PARA 478 note 6.
3 As to the service of notices see PARA 439.
4 Council Tax (Administration and Enforcement) Regulations 1992, SI 1992/613, reg 33(1) (amended by SI 1994/505). However, nothing in the Council Tax (Administration and Enforcement) Regulations 1992, SI 1992/613, reg 33(1) requires the service of a final notice in the circumstances mentioned in reg 23(3) (see PARA 461) (including reg 23(3) as applied as mentioned in reg 28A(2): see PARA 460): reg 33(3) (substituted by SI 1994/505).

The Council Tax (Administration and Enforcement) Regulations 1992, SI 1992/613, regs 33–53 apply for the recovery of a sum which has become payable to a billing authority under Pt V (regs 17–31) (see PARA 452 et seq) and which has not been paid; but their application in relation to a sum for which persons are jointly and severally liable under Pt V is subject to the provisions of reg 54 (see PARA 475): reg 32(3). As to the meaning of references to a sum which has become payable and which has not been paid see PARA 474 note 3.
5 Council Tax (Administration and Enforcement) Regulations 1992, SI 1992/613, reg 33(2). As to demands for payment of amounts due in respect of council tax see PARA 452 et seq.

478. Application for liability order.

If an amount in respect of council tax which has fallen due[1] is wholly or partly unpaid[2], or (in a case where a final notice is required[3]) the amount stated in the final notice is wholly or partly unpaid at the expiry of the period of seven days beginning with the day on which the notice was issued[4], the billing authority[5] may apply to a magistrates' court for an order (a 'liability order'[6]) against the person by whom it is payable[7]. The application is to be instituted by making complaint to a justice of the peace[8], and requesting the issue of a summons directed to that person to appear before the court to show why he has not paid the sum which is outstanding[9]. If, after a summons has been so issued but before the application is heard, there is paid or tendered to the authority an amount equal to the aggregate of:

(1) the sum specified in the summons as the sum outstanding or so much of it as remains outstanding (as the case may be)[10]; and
(2) a sum of an amount equal to the costs reasonably incurred by the authority in connection with the application up to the time of the payment or tender[11],

the authority must accept the amount and the application may not be proceeded with[12].

The court must make the order if it is satisfied that the sum has become payable by the defendant and has not been paid[13]. The order must be made in respect of an amount equal to the aggregate of[14]:

(a) the sum payable[15]; and

(b) a sum of an amount equal to the costs reasonably incurred by the applicant in obtaining the order[16].

Where the sum payable is paid after a liability order has been duly applied for[17] but before it is made, the court must nonetheless (if so requested by the billing authority) make the order in respect of a sum of an amount equal to the costs reasonably incurred by the authority in making the application[18].

The amount in respect of which a liability order is made is enforceable in accordance with the council tax enforcement provisions[19]; and accordingly, for the purposes of any of the provisions of the Magistrates' Courts Act 1980 relating to satisfaction and enforcement[20], it is not to be treated as a sum adjudged to be paid by order of the court[21].

1 Ie under the Council Tax (Administration and Enforcement) Regulations 1992, SI 1992/613, reg 23(3), (4) (see PARA 461) (including reg 23(3), (4) as applied as mentioned in reg 28A(2) (see PARA 460)): see reg 34(1) (amended by SI 1992/3008).

2 As to the meaning of references to a sum which has become payable and which has not been paid see PARA 474 note 3.

3 Ie under the Council Tax (Administration and Enforcement) Regulations 1992, SI 1992/613, reg 33: see PARA 477.

4 Any reference in the Council Tax (Administration and Enforcement) Regulations 1992, SI 1992/613, Pt VI (regs 32–57) to the day on or time at which a notice is issued, is a reference:

(1) if the notice is served in the manner described in the Local Government Act 1972 s 233(2) (see LOCAL GOVERNMENT vol 69 (2018) PARA 648) by being left at, or sent by post to, a person's proper address, to the day on or time at which it is so left or posted (Council Tax (Administration and Enforcement) Regulations 1992, SI 1992/613, reg 32(5)(a) (reg 32(5) added by SI 1992/3008)); or

(2) in any other case, to the day on or time at which the notice is served (Council Tax (Administration and Enforcement) Regulations 1992, SI 1992/613, reg 32(5)(b) (as so added)).

As to the service of notices see PARA 439.

5 As to the meaning of 'billing authority' see PARA 346.

6 'Liability order' means an order under the Council Tax (Administration and Enforcement) Regulations 1992, SI 1992/613, reg 34 or reg 36A(5) (see PARA 486): reg 32(1) (definition amended in relation to England by SI 2004/927; and in relation to Wales by SI 2004/785).

7 Council Tax (Administration and Enforcement) Regulations 1992, SI 1992/613, reg 34(1) (as amended: see note 1). As to the application of regs 33–53 see PARA 477 note 4. As to the magistrates' court, and as to the admissibility in proceedings under reg 34 of evidence derived from records compiled by the applicant authority (or by an authorised person) before such a court, see PARA 504.

A pending claim for council tax benefit (as to which see WELFARE BENEFITS AND STATE PENSIONS vol 104 (2014) PARA 249) is unlikely to give the taxpayer a defence to the billing authority's application for a liability order: see *R v Bristol City Magistrates' Court and Bristol City Council, ex p Willsman* [1991] RA 292, 156 LGR 442, CA; and see *R (on the application of Williams) v Pontefract Magistrates' Court* [2002] EWHC 1265 (Admin), [2002] RVR 259, [2002] All ER (D) 465 (May) (the issues for determination on an application for a liability order do not include a consideration of whether the defaulter should or should not have received council tax benefit).

As to the jurisdiction of a magistrates' court to set aside a liability order see *R (on the application of Newham London Borough Council) v Stratford Magistrates' Court* [2008] EWHC 125 (Admin), [2008] RA 108, [2008] All ER (D) 17 (Jan) (there are three criteria to be applied:

(1) a genuine and arguable dispute as to the liability to pay;

(2) the liability order had to have been made due to a substantive procedural defect, error or mishap; and

(3) the application to set aside had to have been made promptly after a defendant had had notice that a liability order had been made or might have been made).

Some of the cases cited in this paragraph were decided prior to the coming into force of the Local Government Finance Act 1992 but may continue to be of relevance: see PARA 50.

8 References to a justice of the peace in the Council Tax (Administration and Enforcement) Regulations 1992, SI 1992/613, reg 34(2) must be construed subject to the Justices' Clerks Rules 2005, SI 2005/545, r 3 (which authorises certain matters authorised to be done by a justice of the peace to be done by a justices' clerk: see MAGISTRATES vol 71 (2013) PARA 503): Council Tax (Administration and Enforcement) Regulations 1992, SI 1992/613, reg 53(3). As to justices of the peace see MAGISTRATES vol 71 (2013) PARA 401 et seq.

9 Council Tax (Administration and Enforcement) Regulations 1992, SI 1992/613, reg 34(2). As to the appropriate procedure where applications for liability orders are made as a result of incorrect service see *R (on the application of Tull) v Camberwell Green Magistrates' Court* [2004] EWHC 2780 (Admin), [2005] RA 31, [2004] All ER (D) 269 (Nov). See also *R (on the application of Clark-Darby) v Highbury Corner Magistrates' Court* [2001] EWHC Admin 959, [2002] RVR 35, [2001] All ER (D) 229 (Nov) (failure to give the taxpayer notice of hearing at which the billing authority obtained a liability order against her in respect of unpaid council tax amounted to a breach of natural justice for which judicial review was the appropriate remedy).

The Magistrates' Courts Act 1980 s 127(1) (limitation of time: see MAGISTRATES vol 71 (2013) PARA 526) does not apply to an application under the Council Tax (Administration and Enforcement) Regulations 1992, SI 1992/613, reg 34; but no application may be instituted in respect of a sum after the period of six years beginning with the day on which it became due under Pt V (regs 17–31): reg 34(3). Accordingly, the limitation period in reg 34(3) runs from the date of the demand under reg 18(1) (see PARA 452): see *Regentford Ltd v Thanet District Council* [2004] EWHC 246 (Admin), [2004] RA 113, (2004) Times, 4 March. However, the passage of more than six years after the making of the liability order does not prevent an authority from proceeding by way of a winding-up petition: see *Bolsover District Council v Ashfield Nominees Ltd* [2010] EWCA Civ 1129, [2010] RA 523, [2011] 2 BCLC 42.

A warrant must not be issued under the Magistrates' Courts Act 1980 s 55(2) (see MAGISTRATES vol 71 (2013) PARA 533) in any proceedings under the Council Tax (Administration and Enforcement) Regulations 1992, SI 1992/613, reg 34: reg 34(4). No liability order is to be made in pursuance of a summons issued under reg 34(2) unless 14 days have elapsed since the day on which the summons was served: reg 35(2A) (added by SI 1998/295). A summons issued under the Council Tax (Administration and Enforcement) Regulations 1992, SI 1992/613, reg 34(2) may be served on a person:

(1) by delivering it to him (reg 35(2)(a)); or
(2) by leaving it at his usual or last-known place of abode, or, in the case of a company, at its registered office (reg 35(2)(b)); or
(3) by sending it by post to him at his usual or last-known place of abode, or, in the case of a company, to its registered office (reg 35(2)(c)); or
(4) by leaving it at, or by sending it by post to him at, an address given by the person as an address at which service of the summons will be accepted (reg 35(2)(d)).

As to the registered office of a company see COMPANIES vol 14 (2016) PARA 124. As to service by post generally see PARA 139 note 3. A summons under reg 34(2) may be addressed to two or more joint taxpayers in joint names: see reg 54(3A); and PARA 475.

10 Council Tax (Administration and Enforcement) Regulations 1992, SI 1992/613, reg 34(5)(a). If a liability order has been made, and:

(1) by virtue of a notification which is given by the billing authority or an authorised person under reg 24(2) or (5) (see PARA 467), reg 25(5) or (8) (see PARA 468), reg 28(3) or (4) (see PARA 460) or reg 31(2) (see PARA 462), or Sch 1 Pt III para 9(3) (see PARA 465) or Sch 1 Pt III para 10(2)(a) (see PARA 466) (reg 57(2)(a) (amended by SI 1996/1880)); or
(2) by virtue of the Local Government Finance Act 1992 s 31(4) (see PARA 381) applying in any case (Council Tax (Administration and Enforcement) Regulations 1992, SI 1992/613, reg 57(2)(b)),

any part of the amount mentioned in reg 34(5)(a) in respect of which the order was made would (if paid) fall to be repaid or credited against any subsequent liability, that part is to be treated for the purposes of Pt VI (regs 32–57) as paid on the day the notification is given or the amount in substitution is set under the Local Government Finance Act 1992 s 31(2) (see PARA 381) and accordingly as no longer outstanding: Council Tax (Administration and Enforcement) Regulations 1992, SI 1992/613, reg 57(2) (amended by SI 1992/3008). 'Authorised person' means any person authorised by a billing authority to exercise any functions relating to the administration and enforcement of the council tax: Council Tax (Administration and Enforcement) Regulations 1992, SI 1992/613, reg 32(1) (definition added by SI 1996/1880). As to the meaning of 'person' see PARA

11 note 13. As to the power of billing authorities to authorise other persons to exercise certain of their functions relating to the administration and enforcement of the council tax see PARA 346.

11 Council Tax (Administration and Enforcement) Regulations 1992, SI 1992/613, reg 34(5)(b).

12 Council Tax (Administration and Enforcement) Regulations 1992, SI 1992/613, reg 34(5).

13 Council Tax (Administration and Enforcement) Regulations 1992, SI 1992/613, reg 34(6). Sums due following a liability order may be included in an administration order under the County Courts Act 1984 Pt VI (ss 112–117) (see BANKRUPTCY AND INDIVIDUAL INSOLVENCY vol 5 (2013) PARA 887 et seq) where the debtor is unable to pay the judgment sum immediately: see *Preston Borough Council v Riley* [1995] RA 227, (1995) Times, 19 April, CA.

14 A single liability order may deal with one person and one such amount (or aggregate amount) as is mentioned in the Council Tax (Administration and Enforcement) Regulations 1992, SI 1992/613, reg 34(7), (8) (see the text to notes 17–18), or, if the court thinks fit, may deal with more than one person and more than one such amount: reg 35(1) (amended in relation to England by SI 2003/2211; and in relation to Wales by SI 2003/1715).

15 Council Tax (Administration and Enforcement) Regulations 1992, SI 1992/613, reg 34(7)(a).

16 Council Tax (Administration and Enforcement) Regulations 1992, SI 1992/613, reg 34(7)(b). In relation to Wales, such costs, including those of instituting the application under reg 34(2) (see the text to notes 8–9), are not to exceed the prescribed amount of £70: see reg 34(7)(b) (amended, in relation to Wales, by SI 2011/528). As to the meaning of 'Wales' see PARA 2 note 16.

Before making an order, it is incumbent on justices to have sufficient information to be satisfied that costs were actually incurred and were reasonably incurred: *R (on the application of Reverend Nicolson) v Tottenham Magistrates* [2015] EWHC 1252 (Admin), [2015] All ER (D) 54 (May). For other challenges to the costs awarded, see *Ewing v Highbury Corner Magistrates' Court* [2015] EWHC 3788 (Admin), [2016] All ER (D) 26 (Jan); *Bexley London Borough Council v XXX* [2016] EWHC 711 (Admin), [2016] RA 251; *Williams v East Northamptonshire District Council* [2016] EWHC 470 (Admin), [2016] RA 191, [2016] All ER (D) 95 (Mar); and *Nicolson v Grant Thornton LLP* [2016] EWHC 710 (Admin), [2017] RVR 43.

17 Ie under the Council Tax (Administration and Enforcement) Regulations 1992, SI 1992/613, reg 34(2): see the text to notes 8–9.

18 Council Tax (Administration and Enforcement) Regulations 1992, SI 1992/613, reg 34(8). In relation to Wales, such costs, including those of instituting the application under reg 34(2) (see the text to notes 8–9), are not to exceed the prescribed amount of £70: see reg 34(8) (amended, in relation to Wales, by SI 2011/528). See also note 14.

19 Ie the Council Tax (Administration and Enforcement) Regulations 1992, SI 1992/613, Pt VI (regs 32–57): see PARAS 477, 480 et seq.

20 Ie the Magistrates' Courts Act 1980 Pt III (ss 75–96A): see MAGISTRATES vol 71 (2013) PARA 648 et seq.

21 Council Tax (Administration and Enforcement) Regulations 1992, SI 1992/613, reg 35(3).

479. Provision for information.

Regulations made under the provisions that govern the recovery of sums which have become payable in respect of the council tax but have not been paid[1] may provide that where a magistrates' court has made a liability order[2] against a person (the 'debtor') he is to be, during such time as the amount in respect of which the order was made remains wholly or partly unpaid, under a duty to supply relevant information[3] to the billing authority concerned[4]. The regulations may include provision that the information is to be supplied in a prescribed form and within a prescribed period of the request being made[5].

1 Ie regulations under the Local Government Finance Act 1992 Sch 4 para 1(1): see PARA 473. As to the regulations made see PARA 480. As to council tax see PARA 344 et seq.

2 As to the making of liability orders see PARA 478.

3 'Relevant information' is such information as fulfils the following conditions:

(1) it is in the debtor's possession or control (Local Government Finance Act 1992 s 14(3), Sch 4 para 4(2)(a));

(2) the authority requests him to supply it (Sch 4 para 4(2)(b)); and

(3) it falls within a prescribed description of information (Sch 4 para 4(2)(c)).

As to the meaning of 'information' see PARA 345 note 20. 'Prescribed' means prescribed by regulations made (in relation to England) by the Secretary of State and (in relation to Wales) by the Welsh Ministers: Sch 4 para 20 (added by the Local Government Act 2003 s 127(1), Sch 7 paras

40, 54). As to the Secretary of State and the Welsh Ministers see PARA 4 note 18. As to the meanings of 'England' and 'Wales' see PARA 2 note 16. The functions under the Local Government Finance Act 1992 Sch 4 were formerly vested in the National Assembly for Wales and are now exercisable by the Welsh Ministers by virtue of the Government of Wales Act 2006 s 162(1), Sch 11 paras 30, 32.

4 See the Local Government Finance Act 1992 Sch 4 para 4(1). As to the meaning of 'billing authority' see PARA 346.

5 Local Government Finance Act 1992 Sch 4 para 4(3).

480. Duties of debtors subject to liability order.

Where a liability order has been made[1], the debtor[2] against whom it was made is, during such time as the amount in respect of which the order was made remains wholly or partly unpaid[3], under a duty to supply relevant information[4] to the billing authority on whose application it was made[5]. Information is to be supplied within 14 days of the day on which the request is made[6].

1 As to the meaning of 'liability order' see PARA 478 note 6. As to the making of liability orders see PARA 478.

2 'Debtor' means a person against whom a liability order has been made: Council Tax (Administration and Enforcement) Regulations 1992, SI 1992/613, reg 32(1).

3 As to the meaning of references to a sum which has become payable and which has not been paid see PARA 474 note 3.

4 'Relevant information' is such information as fulfils the following conditions:

(1) it is in the debtor's possession or control (Council Tax (Administration and Enforcement) Regulations 1992, SI 1992/613, reg 36(2)(a));

(2) the billing authority requests him by notice given in writing to supply it (reg 36(2)(b)); and

(3) it falls within reg 36(3) (reg 36(2)(c)).

Information falls within reg 36(3) if it is specified in the notice mentioned in reg 36(2)(b) (see head (2) above) and it falls within one or more of the following descriptions:

(a) information as to the name and address of an employer of the debtor (reg 36(3)(a));

(b) information as to earnings or expected earnings of the debtor (reg 36(3)(b));

(c) information as to deductions and expected deductions from such earnings in respect of the matters referred to in heads (A)–(C) of the definition of 'net earnings' below or attachment of earnings orders (ie made under Pt VI (regs 32–57) (see PARA 487 et seq); the Community Charges (Administration and Enforcement) Regulations 1989, SI 1989/438, reg 32 (now lapsed); the Attachment of Earnings Act 1971 (see CIVIL PROCEDURE vol 12A (2015) PARA 1426 et seq); or the Child Support Act 1991 (see CHILDREN AND YOUNG PERSONS vol 9 (2017) PARA 642)) (Council Tax (Administration and Enforcement) Regulations 1992, SI 1992/613, reg 36(3)(c) (amended by SI 1993/773));

(d) information as to the debtor's work or identity number in an employment, or such other information as will enable an employer of the debtor to identify him (Council Tax (Administration and Enforcement) Regulations 1992, SI 1992/613, reg 36(3)(d));

(e) information as to sources of income of the debtor other than an employer of his (reg 36(3)(e));

(f) information as to whether another person is jointly and severally liable with the debtor for the whole or any part of the amount in respect of which the order was made (reg 36(3)(f)).

As to the meaning of 'information' see PARA 345 note 20. As to the meaning of 'billing authority' see PARA 346. As to the service of notices see PARA 439. As to the meaning of 'writing' see PARA 21 note 3.

'Earnings' means sums payable to a person by way of wages or salary (including any fees, bonus, commission, overtime pay or other emoluments payable in addition to wages or salary or payable under a contract of service) or by way of statutory sick pay: reg 32(1). However, in so far as the following would otherwise be treated as earnings, they must not be treated as such (reg 32(1) (definition amended by SI 1999/534; in relation to England by SI 2003/768 and SI 2013/630; and in relation to Wales by SI 2003/522 and SI 2013/570)):

(i) sums payable by any public department of the government of Northern Ireland or of a territory outside the United Kingdom;

(ii) pay or allowances payable to the debtor as a member of Her Majesty's forces other than pay or allowances payable by his employer to him as a special member of a reserve force (within the meaning of the Reserve Forces Act 1996: see ARMED FORCES vol 3 (2011) PARA 470 et seq);

(iii) allowances or benefit payable under the Social Security Contributions and Benefits Act 1992 and the Social Security Administration Act 1992 or universal credit;

(iv) a tax credit (within the meaning of the Tax Credits Act 2002: see WELFARE BENEFITS AND STATE PENSIONS vol 104 (2014) PARA 335 et seq);

(v) allowances payable in respect of disablement or disability (see WELFARE BENEFITS AND STATE PENSIONS vol 104 (2014) PARA 144 et seq); and

(vi) wages payable to a person as a seaman, other than wages payable to him as a seaman of a fishing boat.

For the purposes of head (vi), expressions used in the Merchant Shipping Act 1894 have the same meanings as in that Act: Council Tax (Administration and Enforcement) Regulations 1992, SI 1992/613, reg 32(2). As to the meaning of 'United Kingdom' see PARA 4 note 10. As to the meaning of 'universal credit' see PARA 475 note 17.

'Net earnings' in relation to an employment means (reg 32(1) (definition amended by SI 1993/773; in relation to England by SI 2005/2866; and in relation to Wales by SI 2005/3302)) the residue of earnings payable under the employment after deduction by the employer of:

(A) income tax;

(B) primary Class 1 contributions under the Social Security Contributions and Benefits Act 1992 Pt I (ss 1–19A) (see WELFARE BENEFITS AND STATE PENSIONS vol 104 (2014) PARA 380 et seq);

(C) amounts deductible under any enactment, or in pursuance of a request in writing by the debtor, for the purposes of a superannuation scheme, namely any enactment, rules, deed or other instrument providing for the payment of annuities or lump sum (either to the persons with respect to whom the instrument has effect on their retirement at a specified age or on becoming incapacitated at some earlier age or to the personal representatives or the widows, widowers, surviving civil partners, relatives or dependants of such persons on their death or otherwise) whether with or without any further or other benefits; and

(D) where an order under the Community Charges (Administration and Enforcement) Regulations 1989, SI 1989/438, reg 32 (now lapsed) made before the making of the attachment of earnings order concerned remains in force, any amount required to be deducted in accordance with that order.

As to the meaning of 'attachment of earnings order' see PARA 488.

5 Council Tax (Administration and Enforcement) Regulations 1992, SI 1992/613, reg 36(1). As to the application of regs 33–53 see PARA 477 note 4.

6 Council Tax (Administration and Enforcement) Regulations 1992, SI 1992/613, reg 36(4). It is an offence to fail to comply with a request to supply information or to supply information that is false: see reg 56; and PARA 510.

481. Provision for amount due under a liability order to be deemed a debt.

Regulations made under the provisions that govern the recovery of sums which have become payable in respect of the council tax but have not been paid[1] may provide that:

(1) where a magistrates' court has made a liability order[2] against a person (the 'debtor') and the debtor is an individual, the amount due[3] is deemed to be a debt for the purposes of the provisions of the Insolvency Act 1986[4] relating to the grounds for the issue of a creditor's petition[5];

(2) where a magistrates' court has made a liability order against a person (the 'debtor') and the debtor is a company, the amount due[6] is deemed to be a debt for the purposes of the provisions of the Insolvency Act 1986[7] relating to the winding up of companies[8].

1 Ie regulations under the Local Government Finance Act 1992 Sch 4 para 1(1): see PARA 473. As to the regulations made see PARA 482. As to council tax see PARA 344 et seq.

2 As to the making of liability orders see PARA 478.

3 The 'amount due' is an amount equal to any outstanding sum which is or forms part of the amount in respect of which the liability order was made: Local Government Finance Act 1992 s 14(3), Sch 4 para 9(2).

4 Ie the Insolvency Act 1986 s 267 (grounds of creditor's petition): see BANKRUPTCY AND INDIVIDUAL INSOLVENCY vol 5 (2013) PARA 132.

5 See the Local Government Finance Act 1992 Sch 4 para 9(1).

6 The 'amount due' is an amount equal to any outstanding sum which is or forms part of the amount in respect of which the liability order was made: Local Government Finance Act 1992 Sch 4 para 10(2).

7 Ie the Insolvency Act 1986 s 122(1)(f) (winding up of companies by the court: see COMPANY AND PARTNERSHIP INSOLVENCY vol 16 (2017) PARA 354) or, as the case may be, s 221(5)(b) (winding up of unregistered companies: see COMPANY AND PARTNERSHIP INSOLVENCY vol 17 (2017) PARA 1032).

8 See the Local Government Finance Act 1992 Sch 4 para 10(1).

482. Amount due under liability order deemed to be debt.

Where a liability order has been made[1] and the debtor[2] against whom it was made is an individual, the amount due[3] is deemed to be a debt for the purposes of the provisions of the Insolvency Act 1986[4] relating to the grounds for the issue of a creditor's petition[5].

Similarly, where a liability order has been made and the debtor against whom it was made is a company, the amount due is deemed to be a debt for the purposes of the provisions of the Insolvency Act 1986[6] relating to the winding up of companies[7].

1 As to the meaning of 'liability order' see PARA 478 note 6. As to the making of liability orders see PARA 478.

2 As to the meaning of 'debtor' see PARA 480 note 2.

3 For the purposes of the Council Tax (Administration and Enforcement) Regulations 1992, SI 1992/613, reg 49, the 'amount due' is an amount equal to any outstanding sum which is or forms part of the amount in respect of which the liability order was made: reg 49(3).

4 Ie the Insolvency Act 1986 s 267 (grounds of creditor's petition): see BANKRUPTCY AND INDIVIDUAL INSOLVENCY vol 5 (2013) PARA 132.

5 Council Tax (Administration and Enforcement) Regulations 1992, SI 1992/613, reg 49(1). As to the application of regs 33–53 see PARA 477 note 4. As to the relationship between remedies see reg 52; and PARA 501.

6 Ie the Insolvency Act 1986 s 122(1)(f) (winding up of companies by the court: see COMPANY AND PARTNERSHIP INSOLVENCY vol 16 (2017) PARA 354) or, as the case may be, s 221(5)(b) (winding up of unregistered companies: see COMPANY AND PARTNERSHIP INSOLVENCY vol 17 (2017) PARA 1032).

7 Council Tax (Administration and Enforcement) Regulations 1992, SI 1992/613, reg 49(2).

483. Provision for charging orders.

Regulations made under the provisions that govern the recovery of sums which have become payable in respect of the council tax but have not been paid[1] may provide that where a magistrates' court has made a liability order against a person[2] (the 'debtor') and prescribed[3] conditions are fulfilled:

(1) the billing authority[4] concerned may apply to a court for an order (a 'charging order') imposing, on any interest held by the debtor beneficially in the relevant dwelling[5], a charge for securing the due amount[6]; and

(2) a charge imposed by a charging order must have the like effect and must be enforceable in the same courts and in the same manner as an equitable charge created by the debtor by writing under his hand[7].

The regulations may include provision:

(a) as to the court to which an application may be made (which may be the High Court or the County Court)[8];
(b) as to the factors to be considered by the court in deciding whether to make a charging order[9];
(c) requiring an order to specify the dwelling and interest concerned, and such other matters as may be prescribed[10];
(d) requiring an order to be in a prescribed form[11];
(e) allowing an order to be made absolutely or subject to conditions[12];
(f) as to the discharge or variation of an order[13].

1 Ie regulations under the Local Government Finance Act 1992 Sch 4 para 1(1)(a) (see PARA 473): see s 14(3), Sch 4 para 11(1). This excludes regulations made under Sch 4 para 1(1)(b), ie those relating to the collection of amounts payable as penalties: see PARA 473. As to the regulations made see PARA 484. As to council tax see PARA 344 et seq.

2 Regulations under the Local Government Finance Act 1992 Sch 4 para 1(1)(a) (see PARA 473) may provide that two or more liability orders against the same person must be treated as a single liability order for the purposes of provision included by virtue of Sch 4 para 11 if an application under such provision could be made in respect of each of them in relation to the same dwelling: Sch 4 para 11A (added by the Local Government Act 2003 s 81). As to the meaning of 'dwelling' see PARA 349. As to the making of liability orders see PARA 478.

3 'Prescribed' means prescribed by regulations made (in relation to England) by the Secretary of State and (in relation to Wales) by the Welsh Ministers: see the Local Government Finance Act 1992 Sch 4 para 20 (added by the Local Government Act 2003 s 127(1), Sch 7 paras 40, 54). As to the Secretary of State and the Welsh Ministers see PARA 4 note 18. As to the meanings of 'England' and 'Wales' see PARA 2 note 16. The functions under the Local Government Finance Act 1992 Sch 4 were formerly vested in the National Assembly for Wales and are now exercisable by the Welsh Ministers by virtue of the Government of Wales Act 2006 s 162(1), Sch 11 paras 30, 32.

4 As to the meaning of 'billing authority' see PARA 346.

5 The 'relevant dwelling' is the dwelling in respect of which, at the time the application for the liability order was made, the debtor was liable to pay the sum falling within the Local Government Finance Act 1992 Sch 4 para 1(1)(a) (see PARA 473): Sch 4 para 11(2).

6 See the Local Government Finance Act 1992 Sch 4 para 11(1)(a). The 'due amount' is the aggregate of:
(1) an amount equal to any outstanding sum which is or forms part of the amount in respect of which the liability order was made (Sch 4 para 11(3)(a)); and
(2) a sum (of a prescribed amount or an amount determined in accordance with prescribed rules) in respect of costs connected with the charging order (Sch 4 para 11(3)(b)).

7 Local Government Finance Act 1992 Sch 4 para 11(1)(b). As to the meaning of 'writing' see PARA 21 note 3. As to equitable charges see MORTGAGE vol 77 (2016) PARA 221 et seq.

8 Local Government Finance Act 1992 Sch 4 para 11(4)(a) (amended by the Crime and Courts Act 2013 s 17(5), Sch 9 para 52(1)(b), (2)). As to the High Court of Justice in England and Wales see COURTS AND TRIBUNALS vol 24 (2010) PARA 695 et seq. As to County Court see COURTS AND TRIBUNALS vol 24 (2010) PARA 758 et seq.

9 Local Government Finance Act 1992 Sch 4 para 11(4)(b).

10 Local Government Finance Act 1992 Sch 4 para 11(4)(c).

11 Local Government Finance Act 1992 Sch 4 para 11(4)(d).

12 Local Government Finance Act 1992 Sch 4 para 11(4)(e).

13 Local Government Finance Act 1992 Sch 4 para 11(4)(f).

484. Charging orders.

Where:

(1) a magistrates' court has made[1] one or more liability orders[2];
(2) the amount[3] in respect of which the liability order was made, or, where more than one liability order was made, the aggregate of the amounts[4] in respect of which each such liability order was made, is an amount the debtor[5] is liable to pay under the billing provisions[6]; and

(3) at the time that the application is made at least £1,000 of the amount in respect of which the liability order was made, or, where more than one liability order was made, the aggregate of the amounts in respect of which those liability orders were made, remains outstanding[7],

an application to the appropriate court[8] may be made[9] by the authority concerned[10] for an order (a 'charging order')[11] imposing, on any interest held by the debtor beneficially in the relevant dwelling, a charge for securing the due amount[12]; and the court may make such an order on such an application[13].

In deciding whether to make a charging order, the court must consider all the circumstances of the case, and in particular any evidence before it as to:

(a) the personal circumstances of the debtor[14]; and
(b) whether any other person[15] would be likely to be unduly prejudiced by the making of the order[16].

A charging order must specify the dwelling concerned and the interest held by the debtor beneficially in it[17]; and may, as the court thinks fit, be made absolutely or subject to conditions as to the time when the charge is to become enforceable or as to other matters[18].

A charge imposed by a charging order has the like effect and is enforceable in the same courts and in the same manner as an equitable charge created by the debtor by writing under his hand[19]. The court by which a charging order was made may at any time, on the application of the debtor, the authority on whose application the order was made or any person interested in the dwelling, make an order discharging or varying the charging order[20].

1 Ie pursuant to the Council Tax (Administration and Enforcement) Regulations 1992, SI 1992/613, reg 34(6) (see PARA 478) or reg 36A(5) (see PARA 486).
2 Council Tax (Administration and Enforcement) Regulations 1992, SI 1992/613, reg 50(1)(a) (reg 50(1), (3) substituted in relation to England by SI 2004/927; and in relation to Wales by SI 2004/785). As to the application of the Council Tax (Administration and Enforcement) Regulations 1992, SI 1992/613, regs 33–53 see PARA 477 note 4.
3 Ie the amount mentioned in the Council Tax (Administration and Enforcement) Regulations 1992, SI 1992/613, reg 34(7)(a) (see PARA 478) or reg 36A(5)(a) (see PARA 486).
4 Ie the aggregate of the amounts mentioned in the Council Tax (Administration and Enforcement) Regulations 1992, SI 1992/613, reg 34(7)(a) (see PARA 478) or reg 36A(5)(a) (see PARA 486).
5 As to the meaning of 'debtor' see PARA 480 note 2.
6 Council Tax (Administration and Enforcement) Regulations 1992, SI 1992/613, reg 50(1)(b) (as substituted: see note 2). The billing provisions are those of Pt V (regs 17–31) (see PARA 452 et seq): see reg 50(1)(b) (as so substituted).
7 Council Tax (Administration and Enforcement) Regulations 1992, SI 1992/613, reg 50(1)(c) (as substituted: see note 2).
8 The 'appropriate court' is the County Court for the area in which the relevant dwelling is situated: Council Tax (Administration and Enforcement) Regulations 1992, SI 1992/613, reg 50(3)(d) (as substituted: see note 2). The 'relevant dwelling' is the dwelling in respect of which, at the time the application for the liability order was made, or, where more than one liability order was made, at the time the applications for the liability orders were made, the debtor was liable to pay council tax: reg 50(3)(b) (as so substituted). As to the meaning of 'dwelling' see PARA 349. As to persons liable to pay council tax see PARA 354 et seq. As to council tax see PARA 344 et seq. As to the County Court see COURTS AND TRIBUNALS vol 24 (2010) PARA 758 et seq.
9 See the Council Tax (Administration and Enforcement) Regulations 1992, SI 1992/613, reg 50(1), (2) (reg 50(1) as substituted: see note 2).
10 'The authority concerned' is the authority which applied for the one or more liability orders referred to in the Council Tax (Administration and Enforcement) Regulations 1992, SI 1992/613, reg 50(1)(a) (see head (1) in the text): reg 50(3)(a) (as substituted: see note 2).
11 'Charging order' means an order under the Council Tax (Administration and Enforcement) Regulations 1992, SI 1992/613, reg 50: reg 32(1).
12 The 'due amount' is the aggregate of:

(1) an amount equal to any outstanding sum which is or forms part of the amount in respect of which the one or more liability orders were made (Council Tax (Administration and Enforcement) Regulations 1992, SI 1992/613, reg 50(3)(c)(i) (as substituted: see note 2)); and

(2) a sum of an amount equal to the costs reasonably incurred by the applicant in obtaining the charging order (reg 50(3)(c)(ii) (as so substituted)).

13 Council Tax (Administration and Enforcement) Regulations 1992, SI 1992/613, reg 50(2). As to the relationship between remedies see reg 52; and PARA 501.

14 Council Tax (Administration and Enforcement) Regulations 1992, SI 1992/613, reg 51(1)(a).

15 As to the meaning of 'person' see PARA 11 note 13.

16 Council Tax (Administration and Enforcement) Regulations 1992, SI 1992/613, reg 51(1)(b).

17 Council Tax (Administration and Enforcement) Regulations 1992, SI 1992/613, reg 51(2)(a).

18 Council Tax (Administration and Enforcement) Regulations 1992, SI 1992/613, reg 51(2)(b).

19 Council Tax (Administration and Enforcement) Regulations 1992, SI 1992/613, reg 51(3). As to the meaning of 'writing' see PARA 21 note 3. As to equitable charges see MORTGAGE vol 77 (2016) PARA 221 et seq. The Land Charges Act 1972 (see REAL PROPERTY AND REGISTRATION vol 87 (2017) PARA 694 et seq) and the Land Registration Act 1925 (repealed) apply in relation to charging orders as they apply in relation to orders or writs issued or made for the purposes of enforcing judgments: Council Tax (Administration and Enforcement) Regulations 1992, SI 1992/613, reg 51(5).

20 Council Tax (Administration and Enforcement) Regulations 1992, SI 1992/613, reg 51(4). Where a charging order has been protected by an entry registered under the Land Charges Act 1972 (see REAL PROPERTY AND REGISTRATION vol 87 (2017) PARA 694 et seq) or the Land Registration Act 1925 (repealed), an order under the Council Tax (Administration and Enforcement) Regulations 1992, SI 1992/613, reg 51(4) discharging the charging order may direct that the entry be cancelled: reg 51(6).

485. Provision for quashing of liability orders on application.

Regulations made under the provisions that govern the recovery of sums which have become payable in respect of the council tax but have not been paid[1] may provide[2]:

(1) that, where on an application by the billing authority[3] concerned a magistrates' court is satisfied that a liability order should not have been made[4], it must quash the order[5];

(2) that, where on an application to a magistrates' court for the quashing of a liability order, the court is satisfied that, had the original application been for a liability order in respect of a lesser sum payable, such an order could properly have been made, it must substitute a liability order in respect of the aggregate of:

  (a) that lesser sum[6]; and

  (b) any sum included in the quashed order in respect of the costs incurred in obtaining it[7].

1 Ie regulations under the Local Government Finance Act 1992 Sch 4 para 1(1): see PARA 473. As to the regulations made see PARA 486. As to council tax see PARA 344 et seq.

2 Local Government Finance Act 1992 s 14(3), Sch 4 para 12A (Sch 4 para 12A added by the Local Government Act 2003 s 82).

3 As to the meaning of 'billing authority' see PARA 346.

4 As to the making of liability orders see PARA 478.

5 Local Government Finance Act 1992 Sch 4 para 12A(a) (as added: see note 2).

6 Local Government Finance Act 1992 Sch 4 para 12A(b)(i) (as added: see note 2).

7 Local Government Finance Act 1992 Sch 4 para 12A(b)(ii) (as added: see note 2).

486. Quashing and substitution of liability orders.

Where a magistrates' court has made[1] a liability order[2] and the authority on whose application the liability order was made considers that the order should not have been made[3], the authority may apply to a magistrates' court to have the liability order quashed[4]. Where, on such an application, the magistrates' court is satisfied that the liability order should not have been made, it must quash the order[5].

Where an authority makes such an application for a liability order (the 'original order') to be quashed, and a lesser amount than the amount for which the original order was made has fallen due[6] and is wholly or partly unpaid or, in a case where a final notice is required[7], the amount stated in the final notice is wholly or partly unpaid at the expiry of the period of seven days beginning with the day on which the notice was issued[8], the billing authority[9] may also apply to the magistrates' court for an order against the person by whom the lesser amount was payable[10].

Where, having quashed a liability order, the magistrates' court is satisfied that, had the original application for the liability order been for a liability order in respect of a lesser sum payable, such an order could properly have been made, it must make a liability order in respect of the aggregate of:

(1) the lesser sum payable[11]; and

(2) any sum included in the quashed order in respect of the costs reasonably incurred by the authority in obtaining the quashed order[12].

1 Ie pursuant to the Council Tax (Administration and Enforcement) Regulations 1992, SI 1992/613, reg 34(6): see PARA 478.

2 Council Tax (Administration and Enforcement) Regulations 1992, SI 1992/613, reg 36A(1)(a) (reg 36A added in relation to England by SI 2004/927; and in relation to Wales by SI 2004/785). As to the application of the Council Tax (Administration and Enforcement) Regulations 1992, SI 1992/613, regs 33–53 see PARA 477 note 4.

3 Council Tax (Administration and Enforcement) Regulations 1992, SI 1992/613, reg 36A(1)(b) (as added: see note 2).

4 Council Tax (Administration and Enforcement) Regulations 1992, SI 1992/613, reg 36A(1) (as added: see note 2). As to applications by a debtor for the setting aside of a liability order see the cases cited in PARA 478 notes 7, 9.

5 Council Tax (Administration and Enforcement) Regulations 1992, SI 1992/613, reg 36A(2) (as added: see note 2).

6 Ie under the Council Tax (Administration and Enforcement) Regulations 1992, SI 1992/613, reg 23(3), (4) (see PARA 461) (including reg 23(3), (4) as applied as mentioned in reg 28A(2) (see PARA 460)).

7 Ie under the Council Tax (Administration and Enforcement) Regulations 1992, SI 1992/613, reg 33: see PARA 477.

8 As to the day on or time at which a notice is issued see PARA 478 note 4.

9 As to the meaning of 'billing authority' see PARA 346.

10 Council Tax (Administration and Enforcement) Regulations 1992, SI 1992/613, reg 36A(3) (as added: see note 2). Regulation 34(2)–(5) (see PARA 478) applies to applications under reg 36A(3): reg 36A(4) (as so added).

11 Council Tax (Administration and Enforcement) Regulations 1992, SI 1992/613, reg 36A(5)(a) (as added: see note 2).

12 Council Tax (Administration and Enforcement) Regulations 1992, SI 1992/613, reg 36A(5)(b) (as added: see note 2).

(iii) Attachment of Earnings

487. Provision for attachment of earnings etc.

Regulations made under the provisions that govern the recovery of sums which have become payable in respect of the council tax but have not been paid[1] may provide that where a magistrates' court has made a liability order[2] against a person (the 'debtor') and the debtor is an individual:

(1) the billing authority[3] concerned may make an order (an 'attachment of earnings order') to secure the payment of the appropriate amount[4];

(2) such an order must be expressed to be directed to a person who has the debtor in his employment[5], and is to operate as an instruction to such a person to make deductions from the debtor's earnings[6] and to pay the amounts deducted to the authority[7];

(3) the authority may serve a copy of the order on a person who appears to the authority to have the debtor in his employment[8]; and

(4) a person who has the debtor in his employment must comply with the order if a copy of it is served on him[9].

The regulations may include:

(a) provision allowing an attachment of earnings order to be varied[10];

(b) provision requiring a person who has the debtor in his employment to comply with the order as varied if a copy of the order as varied is served on him[11];

(c) provision requiring an order to be in a prescribed form[12];

(d) provision requiring an order to specify the sum to which the order relates, the rate at which the debtor's earnings are to be applied to meet the sum, and such other particulars as may be prescribed[13];

(e) rules about the rate which may be so specified[14];

(f) provision allowing the person who deducts and pays amounts under the order to deduct from the debtor's earnings prescribed sums (or sums determined in accordance with prescribed rules) towards his administrative costs[15];

(g) provision requiring the person who deducts and pays amounts under the order to notify the debtor, in a prescribed manner and at any prescribed time, of the total amount of sums (including sums towards administrative costs) deducted up to the time of the notification or of the total amount of sums (including sums towards such costs) that will fall to be deducted after that time[16];

(h) provision requiring any person on whom a copy of the order is served to notify the authority in a prescribed manner and within a prescribed period if he does not have, or subsequently ceases to have, the debtor in his employment[17];

(i) provision that, where the whole amount to which the order relates has been paid, the authority must give notice of that fact to any person who appears to it to have the debtor in his employment and who has been served with a copy of the order[18];

(j) provision allowing or requiring an order to be discharged[19].

The regulations may include provision that while an attachment of earnings order is in force:

(i) the debtor must from time to time notify the authority concerned, in a prescribed manner and within a prescribed period, of each occasion when he leaves any employment or becomes employed or re-employed, and must include in such a notification a statement of his earnings and expected earnings from the employment concerned and of such other matters as may be prescribed[20];

(ii) any person who becomes the debtor's employer and knows that the order is in force and by what authority it was made must notify the authority concerned, in a prescribed manner and within a prescribed period, that he is the debtor's employer, and must include in such a notification a statement of the debtor's earnings and expected earnings from the employment concerned and of such other matters as may be prescribed[21].

The regulations may include provision with respect to the priority to be accorded as between:

(A) two or more orders made under the regulations[22]; and

(B) orders made under the regulations and orders made under the Attachment of Earnings Act 1971[23] or the Child Support Act 1991[24].

The regulations may include provision that a person may appeal to a magistrates' court if he is aggrieved by the making or the terms of an attachment of earnings order, or if there is a dispute whether payments constitute earnings or as to any other prescribed matter relating to the order[25]. The regulations may also include:

(I) provision prescribing the procedure to be followed for initiating an appeal[26];

(II) provision prescribing the procedure to be followed in dealing with an appeal[27];

(III) provision as to the powers of the court (which may include provision as to the quashing of an attachment of earnings order or the variation of the terms of such an order)[28].

1 Ie regulations under the Local Government Finance Act 1992 Sch 4 para 1(1): see PARA 473. As to the regulations made see PARA 488 et seq. As to council tax see PARA 344 et seq.

2 As to the making of liability orders see PARA 478.

3 As to the meaning of 'billing authority' see PARA 346.

4 Local Government Finance Act 1992 s 14(3), Sch 4 para 5(1)(a) (Sch 4 para 5(1)(a) amended by the Local Government Act 2003 s 80(1), (2)). The 'appropriate amount' is the aggregate of:

(1) any outstanding sum which is or forms part of the amount in respect of which the liability order was made (unless head (2) applies) (Local Government Finance Act 1992 Sch 4 para 5(1A)(a) (Sch 4 para 5(1A) added by the Local Government Act 2003 s 80(1), (3); and amended by the Tribunals, Courts and Enforcement Act 2007 s 62(3), Sch 13 paras 105, 107(1), (3)(a), (b))); and

(2) where a person authorised to act under the power conferred by the Local Government Finance Act 1992 s 14(4) (see PARA 476 note 3) has reported to the authority concerned that he was unable (for whatever reason) to find sufficient goods of the debtor to pay the amount outstanding (Sch 4 para 5(1A)(b) (as so added and amended)):

(a) the amount outstanding at the time when the attachment of earnings order is made (Sch 4 para 5(1A)(b)(i) (as so added and amended)); and

(b) if the authority has applied for the issue of a warrant committing the debtor to prison under provision included by virtue of Sch 4 para 8 (see PARA 498), a sum (of a prescribed amount or an amount determined in accordance with prescribed rules) in respect of the costs of the application (Sch 4 para 5(1A)(b)(ii) (as so added)).

As to the meaning of 'person' see PARA 11 note 13. For these purposes, 'amount outstanding' has the meaning given by the Tribunals, Courts and Enforcement Act 2007 Sch 12 para 50(3) (see CIVIL PROCEDURE vol 12A (2015) PARA 1356): Local Government Finance Act 1992 Sch 4 para 5(9) (added by the Tribunals, Courts and Enforcement Act 2007 Sch 13 paras 101, 107(1), (3)(c)).'Prescribed' means prescribed by regulations made (in relation to England) by the Secretary of State and (in relation to Wales) by the Welsh Ministers: see Sch 4 para 20 (added by the Local Government Act 2003 s 127(1), Sch 7 paras 40, 54). As to the Secretary of State and the Welsh Ministers see PARA 4 note 18. As to the meanings of 'England' and 'Wales' see PARA 2 note 16. The functions under the Local Government Finance Act 1992 Sch 4 were formerly vested in the National Assembly for Wales and are now exercisable by the Welsh Ministers by virtue of the Government of Wales Act 2006 s 162(1), Sch 11 paras 30, 32.

5 The provisions of the Local Government Finance Act 1992 Sch 4 para 5 (except Sch 4 para 5(3), (4)(b): see the text to notes 20–21, 23–24) apply to elected members of billing authorities or relevant precepting authorities as they apply to persons in employment; and for the purposes of the application of those provisions in relation to any such members any reference to a person having the debtor in his employment must be construed as a reference to such an authority having the

debtor as an elected member: Sch 4 para 5(7)(a). A 'relevant precepting authority' is a major precepting authority other than the Receiver for the Metropolitan Police District (Sch 4 para 5(8)(a)); and a person is an elected member of a relevant precepting authority other than a county council if he is appointed to the authority by a constituent council of which he is an elected member (Sch 4 para 5(8)(b)). As to the meaning of 'major precepting authority' see PARA 11 note 2. As from a day to be appointed, the words 'other than the Receiver for the Metropolitan Police District' in the Local Government Finance Act 1992 Sch 4 para 5(8)(a) are repealed by the Greater London Authority Act 1999 s 423, Sch 34 Pt I. At the date at which this volume states the law, no such day had been appointed.

6 The provisions of the Local Government Finance Act 1992 Sch 4 para 5 (except Sch 4 para 5(3), (4)(b): see the text to notes 20–21, 23–24) apply to elected members of billing authorities or relevant precepting authorities as they apply to persons in employment; and for the purposes of the application of those provisions in relation to any such members any reference to the debtor's earnings must be construed as a reference to allowances payable to the debtor by such an authority: Sch 4 para 5(7)(b).

7 Local Government Finance Act 1992 Sch 4 para 5(1)(b).

8 Local Government Finance Act 1992 Sch 4 para 5(1)(c).

9 Local Government Finance Act 1992 Sch 4 para 5(1)(d).

10 Local Government Finance Act 1992 Sch 4 para 5(2)(a).

11 Local Government Finance Act 1992 Sch 4 para 5(2)(b).

12 Local Government Finance Act 1992 Sch 4 para 5(2)(c).

13 Local Government Finance Act 1992 Sch 4 para 5(2)(d).

14 Local Government Finance Act 1992 Sch 4 para 5(2)(e).

15 Local Government Finance Act 1992 Sch 4 para 5(2)(f).

16 Local Government Finance Act 1992 Sch 4 para 5(2)(g).

17 Local Government Finance Act 1992 Sch 4 para 5(2)(h).

18 Local Government Finance Act 1992 Sch 4 para 5(2)(i).

19 Local Government Finance Act 1992 Sch 4 para 5(2)(j).

20 Local Government Finance Act 1992 Sch 4 para 5(3)(a).

21 Local Government Finance Act 1992 Sch 4 para 5(3)(b).

22 Local Government Finance Act 1992 Sch 4 para 5(4)(a).

23 See CIVIL PROCEDURE vol 12A (2015) PARA 1426 et seq.

24 Local Government Finance Act 1992 Sch 4 para 5(4)(b). As to the Child Support Act 1991 see CHILDREN AND YOUNG PERSONS vol 9 (2017) PARA 637 et seq.

25 Local Government Finance Act 1992 Sch 4 para 5(5).

26 Local Government Finance Act 1992 Sch 4 para 5(6)(a).

27 Local Government Finance Act 1992 Sch 4 para 5(6)(b).

28 Local Government Finance Act 1992 Sch 4 para 5(6)(c).

488. Making of attachment of earnings order.

Where a liability order[1] has been made and the debtor[2] against whom it was made is an individual, the billing authority[3] which applied for the order may[4] make an order (an 'attachment of earnings order')[5] to secure the payment of the appropriate amount[6]. However, an attachment of earnings order may not be made by an authority if the effect would be that the number of orders for the time being in force made by that authority in relation to the debtor in question exceeded two[7].

An attachment of earnings order remains in force until discharged[8] or until the whole amount to which it relates has been paid (whether by attachment of earnings or otherwise)[9].

The authority may serve[10] a copy of the order on a person[11] who appears to the authority to have the debtor in his employment; and a person on whom it is so served who has the debtor in his employment must comply with it[12]. If an authority so serves a copy of an attachment of earnings order, it must (unless it has previously done so) also serve a copy of the order on the debtor[13].

1 As to the meaning of 'liability order' see PARA 478 note 6.

2 As to the meaning of 'debtor' see PARA 480 note 2.

3 As to the meaning of 'billing authority' see PARA 346.

4 Ie subject to the Council Tax (Administration and Enforcement) Regulations 1992, SI 1992/613, reg 37(4): see the text to note 7.
5 'Attachment of earnings order' means an order under the Council Tax (Administration and Enforcement) Regulations 1992, SI 1992/613, reg 37: see reg 32(1).
6 See the Council Tax (Administration and Enforcement) Regulations 1992, SI 1992/613, reg 37(1) (amended by SI 1998/295; in relation to England by SI 2004/927; and in relation to Wales by SI 2004/785). An attachment of earnings order must be in the form specified in (and accordingly contain the matters specified in) the Council Tax (Administration and Enforcement) Regulations 1992, SI 1992/613, Sch 3: see reg 37(2)(a), Sch 3 (amended by SI 1992/1741, SI 1992/3008, SI 1993/773, SI 1999/534; in relation to England by SI 2007/501 and SI 2013/630; and in relation to Wales by SI 2013/570).

The 'appropriate amount' is the aggregate of any outstanding sum which is or forms part of the amount in respect of which the liability order was made: Council Tax (Administration and Enforcement) Regulations 1992, SI 1992/613, reg 37(1A) (added in relation to England by SI 2004/927; and in relation to Wales by SI 2004/785; amended by SI 2014/600).

As to the application of the Council Tax (Administration and Enforcement) Regulations 1992, SI 1992/613, regs 33–53 see PARA 477 note 4. As to the relationship between remedies see reg 52; and PARA 501.
7 See the Council Tax (Administration and Enforcement) Regulations 1992, SI 1992/613, reg 37(4) (added by SI 1998/295).
8 Ie under the Council Tax (Administration and Enforcement) Regulations 1992, SI 1992/613, reg 41(2): see PARA 492.
9 See the Council Tax (Administration and Enforcement) Regulations 1992, SI 1992/613, reg 37(2)(b).
10 As to the service of notices see PARA 439.
11 As to the meaning of 'person' see PARA 11 note 13.
12 Council Tax (Administration and Enforcement) Regulations 1992, SI 1992/613, reg 37(3). It is an offence to fail to comply with an order: see reg 56; and PARA 510. As to deductions under attachment of earnings orders see PARA 489. As to the obligations of employers in respect of such orders see further PARA 490.
13 Council Tax (Administration and Enforcement) Regulations 1992, SI 1992/613, reg 41(3).

489. Deductions under attachment of earnings order.

The sum to be deducted by an employer under an attachment of earnings order[1] on any pay-day is to be[2]:

(1) where the debtor's[3] earnings[4] from the employer are payable weekly, a sum equal to the appropriate percentage of the net earnings[5] otherwise payable on that pay-day[6];
(2) where his earnings from the employer are payable monthly, a sum equal to the appropriate percentage of the net earnings otherwise payable on that pay-day[7];
(3) where his earnings from the employer are payable at regular intervals of a whole number of weeks or months, the sum arrived at by:
    (a) calculating what would be his weekly or monthly net earnings by dividing the net earnings payable to him by the employer on the pay-day by that whole number (of weeks or months, as the case may be)[8];
    (b) ascertaining the specified percentage (or percentages)[9] within which the notional net earnings calculated under head (3)(a) above fall[10]; and
    (c) calculating the sum which equals the appropriate percentage (or percentages) of the notional net earnings for any of those weeks or months and multiplying that sum by the whole number of weeks or months, as appropriate[11].

Where a sum is to be deducted by an employer under an attachment of earnings order as set out above and the amount to be paid to the debtor on any pay-day includes an advance in respect of future pay, the sum to be deducted on that pay-day is the aggregate of the amount which would otherwise fall to be deducted[12], and:

(i) where the amount advanced would otherwise have been paid on a single pay-day, the sum which would have been deducted on that pay-day[13] if the amount advanced had been the amount of net earnings on that day[14]; or

(ii) where the amount advanced would otherwise have been paid on more than one pay-day, the sums which would have been deducted on each of the relevant pay-days[15] if an equal proportion of the amount advanced had been paid on each of those days[16] and if the net earnings of the debtor on each of those days had been an amount equal to that proportion[17].

Where the debtor's earnings from the employer are payable at regular intervals other than at the intervals mentioned above[18], the sum to be deducted on any pay-day is to be arrived at by[19]:

(A) calculating what would be his daily net earnings by dividing the net earnings payable to him by the employer on the pay-day by the number of days in the interval[20];

(B) ascertaining the specified percentage (or percentages)[21] within which the notional net earnings calculated under head (A) above fall[22]; and

(C) calculating the sum which equals the appropriate percentage (or percentages) of the notional daily net earnings and multiplying that sum by the number of days in the interval[23].

Where the debtor's earnings are payable at such intervals[24], and the amount to be paid to the debtor on any pay-day includes an amount advanced in respect of future pay, the amount of the debtor's notional net earnings under head (A) above must be calculated in accordance with a specific formula[25].

Where the debtor's earnings from the employer are payable at irregular intervals, the sums to be deducted on any pay-day are arrived at by[26]:

(I) calculating what would be his daily net earnings by dividing the net earnings payable to him by the employer on the pay-day by the number of days since earnings were last payable by the employer to him[27], or (if the earnings are the first earnings to be payable by the employer to him with respect to the employment in question) by the number of days since he began the employment[28];

(II) ascertaining the specified percentage (or percentages)[29] within which the notional net earnings calculated under head (aa) above fall[30]; and

(III) calculating the sum which equals the appropriate percentage (or percentages) of the daily net earnings and multiplying that sum by the same number as that of the divisor for the purposes of the calculation mentioned in head (aa) above[31].

Where on the same pay-day there are payable to the debtor by the employer both earnings payable at regular intervals and earnings payable at irregular intervals, for the purpose of arriving at the sum to be deducted on the pay-day under the above provisions[32] all the earnings must be aggregated and treated as earnings payable at the regular interval[33]. Where there are earnings payable to the debtor by the employer at regular intervals on one pay-day, and earnings are payable by the employer to him at irregular intervals on a different pay-day, the sum to be deducted on each of the pay-days on which the earnings which are payable at irregular intervals are so payable must be 20 per cent of the net earnings payable to him on the day[34].

1 As to attachment of earnings orders see PARA 488.
2 Council Tax (Administration and Enforcement) Regulations 1992, SI 1992/613, reg 38(1). As to the application of regs 33–53 see PARA 477 note 4.
3 As to the meaning of 'debtor' see PARA 480 note 2.
4 As to the meaning of 'earnings' see PARA 480 note 4.
5 As to the meaning of 'net earnings' see PARA 480 note 4. Where the Council Tax (Administration and Enforcement) Regulations 1992, SI 1992/613, reg 38(1) applies and the amount payable to the debtor on any pay-day is reduced by reason of an earlier advance of pay, the net earnings of the debtor on that day, for the purposes of reg 38(1), is the amount defined in reg 32(1) (see PARA 480 note 4) less the amount of the deduction: reg 38(3) (amended by SI 1995/22).
6 Council Tax (Administration and Enforcement) Regulations 1992, SI 1992/613, reg 38(1)(a) (amended by SI 1992/3008). For this purpose, the 'appropriate percentage' is the percentage (or percentages) specified in the Council Tax (Administration and Enforcement) Regulations 1992, SI 1992/613, Sch 4 Table A col 2 in relation to the band in Sch 4 Table A col 1 within which the net earnings fall: see reg 38(1)(a) (as so amended), Sch 4 (Sch 4 substituted by SI 1998/295; and amended in relation to England by SI 2006/3395 and SI 2007/501; and in relation to Wales by SI 2007/582).
7 Council Tax (Administration and Enforcement) Regulations 1992, SI 1992/613, reg 38(1)(b) (amended by SI 1992/3008). For this purpose, the 'appropriate percentage' is the percentage (or percentages) specified in the Council Tax (Administration and Enforcement) Regulations 1992, SI 1992/613, Sch 4 Table B col 2 in relation to the band in Sch 4 Table B col 1 within which the net earnings fall: see reg 38(1)(b) (as so amended), Sch 4 (as substituted and amended: see note 6).
8 Council Tax (Administration and Enforcement) Regulations 1992, SI 1992/613, reg 38(1)(c)(i).
9 Ie the percentage (or percentages) specified in the Council Tax (Administration and Enforcement) Regulations 1992, SI 1992/613, Sch 4 Table A col 2 opposite the band in Sch 4 Table A col 1 (see note 6) (if the whole number is of weeks) or the percentage (or percentages) specified in Sch 4 Table B col 2 opposite the band in Sch 4 Table B col 1 (see note 7) (if the whole number is of months): see reg 38(1)(c)(ii).
10 Council Tax (Administration and Enforcement) Regulations 1992, SI 1992/613, reg 38(1)(c)(ii).
11 Council Tax (Administration and Enforcement) Regulations 1992, SI 1992/613, reg 38(1)(c)(iii).
12 Ie which would otherwise fall to be deducted under the Council Tax (Administration and Enforcement) Regulations 1992, SI 1992/613, reg 38(1): see the text to notes 1–11.
13 Ie in accordance with the Council Tax (Administration and Enforcement) Regulations 1992, SI 1992/613, reg 38(1): see the text to notes 1–11.
14 Council Tax (Administration and Enforcement) Regulations 1992, SI 1992/613, reg 38(2)(a) (amended by SI 1992/3008).
15 Ie in accordance with the Council Tax (Administration and Enforcement) Regulations 1992, SI 1992/613, reg 38(1): see the text to notes 1–11.
16 Council Tax (Administration and Enforcement) Regulations 1992, SI 1992/613, reg 38(2)(b)(i) (amended by SI 1992/3008).
17 Council Tax (Administration and Enforcement) Regulations 1992, SI 1992/613, reg 38(2)(b)(ii).
18 Ie the intervals to which the Council Tax (Administration and Enforcement) Regulations 1992, SI 1992/613, reg 38(1) applies: see the text to notes 1–11.
19 Council Tax (Administration and Enforcement) Regulations 1992, SI 1992/613, reg 38(4). Regulation 38(3) (see note 5) applies in relation to reg 38(4) as it applies in relation to reg 38(1): reg 38(6).
20 Council Tax (Administration and Enforcement) Regulations 1992, SI 1992/613, reg 38(4)(a).
21 Ie the percentage (or percentages) specified in the Council Tax (Administration and Enforcement) Regulations 1992, SI 1992/613, Sch 4 Table C col 2 opposite the band in Sch 4 Table C col 1: see reg 38(4)(b), Sch 4 (as substituted and amended: see note 6).
22 Council Tax (Administration and Enforcement) Regulations 1992, SI 1992/613, reg 38(4)(b).
23 Council Tax (Administration and Enforcement) Regulations 1992, SI 1992/613, reg 38(4)(c).
24 Ie at the intervals mentioned in the Council Tax (Administration and Enforcement) Regulations 1992, SI 1992/613, reg 38(4): see the text to notes 18–23.
25 Council Tax (Administration and Enforcement) Regulations 1992, SI 1992/613, reg 38(5). See the Where earnings are payable to a debtor by the employer by two or more series of payments at regular intervals:
(1) if some or all of the intervals are of different lengths:

(a) for the purpose of arriving at the sum to be deducted, whichever of reg 38(1), (2), (3), (4), (5) and (6) (see also the text to notes 1–24) is appropriate applies to the series with the shortest interval (or, if there is more than one series with the shortest interval, such one of those series as the employer may choose) (reg 38(7)(a)(i)); and

(b) in relation to the earnings payable in every other series, the sum to be deducted is to be 20% of the net earnings or, where on any pay-day an amount advanced is also paid, 20% of the aggregate of the net earnings and the amount advanced (reg 38(7)(a)(ii));

(2) if all of the intervals are of the same length, whichever of reg 38(1), (2), (3), (4), (5) and (6) is appropriate applies to such series as the employer may choose and reg 38(7)(a)(ii) (see head (1)(b) above) applies to every other series (reg 38(7)(b)).

Regulation 38(3) (see note 5) applies in relation to reg 38(7)(a)(ii) as it applies in relation to reg 38(1): reg 38(7).

26 Council Tax (Administration and Enforcement) Regulations 1992, SI 1992/613, reg 38(8).
27 Council Tax (Administration and Enforcement) Regulations 1992, SI 1992/613, reg 38(8)(a)(i).
28 Council Tax (Administration and Enforcement) Regulations 1992, SI 1992/613, reg 38(8)(a)(ii).
29 Ie the percentage (or percentages) specified in the Council Tax (Administration and Enforcement) Regulations 1992, SI 1992/613, Sch 4 Table C col 2 opposite the band in Sch 4 Table C col 1: see reg 38(8)(b), Sch 4 (as substituted and amended: see note 6).
30 Council Tax (Administration and Enforcement) Regulations 1992, SI 1992/613, reg 38(8)(b).
31 Council Tax (Administration and Enforcement) Regulations 1992, SI 1992/613, reg 38(8)(c).
32 Ie under the Council Tax (Administration and Enforcement) Regulations 1992, SI 1992/613, reg 38(4)–(8): see the text to notes 18–31.
33 Council Tax (Administration and Enforcement) Regulations 1992, SI 1992/613, reg 38(9).
34 Council Tax (Administration and Enforcement) Regulations 1992, SI 1992/613, reg 38(10).

490. Ancillary powers and duties of employers and others served.

An employer who deducts and pays amounts under an attachment of earnings order[1] may, on each occasion that he makes such a deduction, also deduct from the debtor's[2] earnings[3] the sum of one pound towards his administrative costs[4].

An employer who deducts and pays amounts under an attachment of earnings order must notify the debtor in writing[5] of:

(1) the total amount of the sums (including such sums deducted towards administrative costs) deducted under the order up to the time of the notification[6]; or

(2) the total amount of the sums (including such sums deducted towards administrative costs) that will fall to be so deducted after that time[7].

Such a notification must be given at the time that the pay statement given by the employer to the debtor next after a deduction has been made is so given, or, if no such statements are usually issued by the employer, as soon as practicable after a deduction has been made[8].

A person[9] on whom a copy of an attachment of earnings order has been served must notify in writing the authority which made the order if he does not have the debtor against whom it was made in his employment or the debtor subsequently ceases to be in his employment[10]. Such a notification must be given within 14 days of the day on which the copy of the order was served on him or the debtor ceased to be in his employment (as the case may be)[11].

While an attachment of earnings order is in force, any person who becomes the debtor's employer and knows that the order is in force and by what authority it was made must notify that authority in writing that he is the debtor's employer[12]. Such a notification must be given within 14 days of the day on which the debtor became the person's employee or of the day on which the person first knows that the order is in force and the identity of the authority by which it was made, whichever is the later[13].

1 As to attachment of earnings orders see PARA 488. As to deductions made by an employer under

such orders see PARA 489.
2 As to the meaning of 'debtor' see PARA 480 note 2.
3 As to the meaning of 'earnings' see PARA 480 note 4.
4 Council Tax (Administration and Enforcement) Regulations 1992, SI 1992/613, reg 39(1). As to the application of regs 33–53 see PARA 477 note 4.
5 As to the meaning of 'writing' see PARA 21 note 3. As to the service of notices see PARA 439.
6 Council Tax (Administration and Enforcement) Regulations 1992, SI 1992/613, reg 39(2)(a).
7 Council Tax (Administration and Enforcement) Regulations 1992, SI 1992/613, reg 39(2)(b).
8 Council Tax (Administration and Enforcement) Regulations 1992, SI 1992/613, reg 39(3). It is an offence to fail to give such notification or to make a false statement in relation thereto: see reg 56(4); and PARA 510.
9 As to the meaning of 'person' see PARA 11 note 13.
10 Council Tax (Administration and Enforcement) Regulations 1992, SI 1992/613, reg 39(4). As to the service of attachment of earnings orders see PARA 488.
11 Council Tax (Administration and Enforcement) Regulations 1992, SI 1992/613, reg 39(5). It is an offence to fail to give such notification or to make a false statement in relation thereto: see reg 56(4); and PARA 510.
12 Council Tax (Administration and Enforcement) Regulations 1992, SI 1992/613, reg 39(6). As to the time for which an attachment of earnings order is in force see PARA 488.
13 Council Tax (Administration and Enforcement) Regulations 1992, SI 1992/613, reg 39(7). It is an offence to fail to give such notification or to make a false statement in relation thereto: see reg 56(4); and PARA 510.

491. Duties of debtor.

While an attachment of earnings order is in force[1], the debtor[2] in respect of whom the order has been made must notify in writing[3] the authority which made it of each occasion when he leaves an employment or becomes employed or re-employed, and (in a case where he becomes so employed or re-employed) must include in the notification a statement of:

(1) his earnings[4] and (so far as he is able) expected earnings from the employment concerned[5];
(2) the deductions and (so far as he is able) expected deductions from such earnings:
  (a) in respect of income tax[6];
  (b) in respect of primary Class 1 contributions under the Social Security Contributions and Benefits Act 1992[7];
  (c) for the purposes of a superannuation scheme[8];
(3) the name and address of the employer[9]; and
(4) his work or identity number in the employment (if any)[10].

Such notification must be given within 14 days of the day on which the debtor leaves or commences (or recommences) the employment (as the case may be), or (if later) the day on which he is informed by the authority that the order has been made[11].

1 As to attachment of earnings orders see PARA 488.
2 As to the meaning of 'debtor' see PARA 480 note 2.
3 As to the meaning of 'writing' see PARA 21 note 3.
4 As to the meaning of 'earnings' see PARA 480 note 4.
5 Council Tax (Administration and Enforcement) Regulations 1992, SI 1992/613, reg 40(1)(a). As to the application of regs 33–53 see PARA 477 note 4.
6 Council Tax (Administration and Enforcement) Regulations 1992, SI 1992/613, reg 40(1)(b)(i).
7 Ie primary Class 1 contributions under the Social Security Contributions and Benefits Act 1992 Pt I (ss 1–19A) (see WELFARE BENEFITS AND STATE PENSIONS vol 104 (2014) PARA 380 et seq): see the Council Tax (Administration and Enforcement) Regulations 1992, SI 1992/613, reg 40(1)(b)(ii).
8 See the Council Tax (Administration and Enforcement) Regulations 1992, SI 1992/613, reg 40(1)(b)(iii). For these purposes a superannuation scheme is such as is mentioned in the definition

of 'net earnings' in reg 32(1) (see PARA 480 note 4): see reg 40(1)(b)(iii).

9 Council Tax (Administration and Enforcement) Regulations 1992, SI 1992/613, reg 40(1)(c).

10 Council Tax (Administration and Enforcement) Regulations 1992, SI 1992/613, reg 40(1)(d).

11 Council Tax (Administration and Enforcement) Regulations 1992, SI 1992/613, reg 40(2). It is an offence to fail to give such notification or to make a false statement in relation thereto: see reg 56(4); and PARA 510.

492. Ancillary powers and duties of authority.

Where the whole amount to which an attachment of earnings order[1] relates has been paid (whether by attachment of earnings or otherwise), the authority by which it was made must give notice[2] of the fact to any person[3] who appears to it to have the debtor[4] in his employment and who has been served with a copy of the order[5].

The authority by which an attachment of earnings order was made may, on its own account or on the application of the debtor or an employer of the debtor, make an order discharging the attachment of earnings order; and if it does so it must give notice of that fact to any person who appears to it to have the debtor in his employment and who has been served with a copy of the order[6].

1 As to attachment of earnings orders see PARA 488.

2 As to the service of notices see PARA 439.

3 As to the meaning of 'person' see PARA 11 note 13.

4 As to the meaning of 'debtor' see PARA 480 note 2.

5 Council Tax (Administration and Enforcement) Regulations 1992, SI 1992/613, reg 41(1). As to the application of regs 33–53 see PARA 477 note 4. As to the service of attachment of earnings orders see PARA 488.

6 Council Tax (Administration and Enforcement) Regulations 1992, SI 1992/613, reg 41(2).

493. Priority as between orders.

Where an employer would otherwise[1] be obliged to make deductions on any pay-day under more than one attachment of earnings order[2], he must[3]:

(1) deal with the orders according to the respective dates on which they were made, disregarding any later order until an earlier one has been dealt with[4]; and

(2) deal with any later order as if the earnings[5] to which it relates were the residue of the debtor's[6] earnings after the making of any deduction to comply with any earlier order[7].

Where an employer would otherwise[8] be obliged to comply with one or more attachment of earnings orders and with one or more deduction orders[9], he must deal with the orders according to the respective dates on which they were made in like manner as under heads (1) and (2) above[10]. However, an employer must not deal with a deduction order made either wholly or in part in respect of the payment of a judgment debt[11] or payments under an administration order[12] until he has dealt with the attachment of earnings order or orders and any other deduction order[13].

1 Ie but for the Council Tax (Administration and Enforcement) Regulations 1992, SI 1992/613, reg 42(1): see the text to notes 1–7.

2 As to attachment of earnings orders see PARA 488. As to deductions made by an employer under such orders see PARA 489.

3 Council Tax (Administration and Enforcement) Regulations 1992, SI 1992/613, reg 42(1) (reg 42 substituted by SI 1992/3008; the Council Tax (Administration and Enforcement) Regulations 1992, SI 1992/613, reg 42(1) amended by SI 1999/534). As to the application of the Council Tax (Administration and Enforcement) Regulations 1992, SI 1992/613, regs 33–53 see PARA 477 note 4.

4 Council Tax (Administration and Enforcement) Regulations 1992, SI 1992/613, reg 42(1)(a) (as substituted: see note 3).
5 As to the meaning of 'earnings' see PARA 480 note 4.
6 As to the meaning of 'debtor' see PARA 480 note 2.
7 Council Tax (Administration and Enforcement) Regulations 1992, SI 1992/613, reg 42(1)(b) (as substituted: see note 3).
8 Ie but for the Council Tax (Administration and Enforcement) Regulations 1992, SI 1992/613, reg 42(2): see the text to notes 9–10.
9 'Deduction order' means an order under the Attachment of Earnings Act 1971 (see CIVIL PROCEDURE vol 12A (2015) PARA 1428 et seq) or the Child Support Act 1991 s 31(2) (see CHILDREN AND YOUNG PERSONS vol 9 (2017) PARA 642): Council Tax (Administration and Enforcement) Regulations 1992, SI 1992/613, reg 42(4) (as substituted: see note 3).
10 Council Tax (Administration and Enforcement) Regulations 1992, SI 1992/613, reg 42(2) (as substituted: see note 3).
11 As to judgment debts generally see CIVIL PROCEDURE vol 12A (2015) PARA 1307 et seq.
12 As to administration orders generally see BANKRUPTCY AND INDIVIDUAL INSOLVENCY vol 5 (2013) PARA 887 et seq.
13 Council Tax (Administration and Enforcement) Regulations 1992, SI 1992/613, reg 42(3) (as substituted: see note 3).

494. Persons employed under the Crown.

Where a debtor[1] is in the employment of the Crown and an attachment of earnings order[2] is made in respect of him, then for the purposes of the council tax enforcement provisions[3]:

(1) the chief officer for the time being of the department, office or other body in which the debtor is employed must be treated as having the debtor in his employment (any transfer of the debtor from one department, office or body to another being treated as a change of employment)[4]; and

(2) any earnings paid by the Crown or a Minister of the Crown[5], or out of the public revenue of the United Kingdom[6], must be treated as paid by that chief officer[7].

If any question arises as to what department, office or other body is concerned for these purposes, or as to who for these purposes is its chief officer, the question must be referred to and determined by the Minister for the Civil Service[8]. A document purporting to set out such a determination of the Minister and to be signed by an official of the office of that Minister is, in any proceedings arising in relation to an attachment of earnings order, admissible in evidence and is deemed to contain an accurate statement of such a determination unless the contrary is shown[9].

1 As to the meaning of 'debtor' see PARA 480 note 2.
2 The provisions of the Council Tax (Administration and Enforcement) Regulations 1992, SI 1992/613, Pt VI (regs 32–57) (see PARA 477 et seq) have effect in relation to attachment of earnings orders notwithstanding any enactment passed before 29 May 1970 and preventing or avoiding the attachment or diversion of sums due to a person in respect of services under the Crown, whether by way of remuneration, pension or otherwise: reg 43(4). As to attachment of earnings orders see PARA 488. As to the application of regs 33–53 generally see PARA 477 note 4.
3 Ie the Council Tax (Administration and Enforcement) Regulations 1992, SI 1992/613, Pt VI (regs 32–57): see PARA 477 et seq.
4 Council Tax (Administration and Enforcement) Regulations 1992, SI 1992/613, reg 43(1)(a).
5 As to Ministers of the Crown see CONSTITUTIONAL AND ADMINISTRATIVE LAW vol 20 (2014) PARA 151.
6 As to the meaning of 'United Kingdom' see PARA 4 note 10.
7 Council Tax (Administration and Enforcement) Regulations 1992, SI 1992/613, reg 43(1)(b).
8 Council Tax (Administration and Enforcement) Regulations 1992, SI 1992/613, reg 43(2). As to

the Minister for the Civil Service and CONSTITUTIONAL AND ADMINISTRATIVE LAW vol 20 (2014) PARA 234 et seq.

9 Council Tax (Administration and Enforcement) Regulations 1992, SI 1992/613, reg 43(3).

495. Attachment of allowances orders.

Where a liability order has been made[1] and the debtor[2] against whom it was made is an elected member of a relevant billing authority[3] or an elected member of a relevant precepting authority[4], the authority which applied for the order may make an order (an 'attachment of allowances order')[5] to secure the payment of any outstanding sum which is or forms part of the amount in respect of which the liability order was made[6]. Such an order must be expressed to be directed to the authority of whom the debtor is an elected member and operates as an instruction to the authority to make deductions from attachable allowances[7] payable to the debtor and to pay the sums so deducted to the authority by which the order was made[8]. The sum to be deducted by an authority under such an order on any day is a sum equal to 40 per cent of the aggregate of attachable allowances payable to the debtor on that day[9].

An attachment of allowances order remains in force until discharged or until the whole sum to which it relates has been paid (whether by attachment of allowances or otherwise)[10].

1 As to the meaning of 'liability order' see PARA 478 note 6. As to the making of liability orders see PARA 478.

2 As to the meaning of 'debtor' see PARA 480 note 2.

3 A 'relevant billing authority' is a billing authority other than the Common Council of the City of London: Council Tax (Administration and Enforcement) Regulations 1992, SI 1992/613, reg 44(2)(a). As to the meaning of 'billing authority' see PARA 346. As to what constitutes the Common Council of the City of London for these purposes see PARA 346 note 4.

4 A 'relevant precepting authority' is a major precepting authority other than the Receiver for the Metropolitan Police District: Council Tax (Administration and Enforcement) Regulations 1992, SI 1992/613, reg 44(2)(b). A person is an elected member of a relevant precepting authority other than a county council if he is appointed to the authority by a constituent council of which he is an elected member: reg 44(2)(c). As to the meaning of 'major precepting authority' see PARA 11 note 2.

5 'Attachment of allowances order' means an order under the Council Tax (Administration and Enforcement) Regulations 1992, SI 1992/613, reg 44: see reg 32(1).

6 See the Council Tax (Administration and Enforcement) Regulations 1992, SI 1992/613, reg 44(1), (3). As to the application of regs 33–53 see PARA 477 note 4. As to the relationship between remedies see reg 52; and PARA 501.

7 References to 'attachable allowances' are references to the allowances referred to in the Council Tax (Administration and Enforcement) Regulations 1992, SI 1992/613, reg 44(7)(b) (see head (2) below): see reg 44(2)(d). Regulation 37(3) (see PARA 488), reg 39(1)–(5) (see PARA 490) and reg 41(1), (2) (see PARA 492) apply to orders under reg 44 as they apply to attachment of earnings orders as if any reference in those provisions:

- (1) to an employer or a person having the debtor in his employment, were a reference to a relevant billing authority or a relevant precepting authority having the debtor as an elected member (reg 44(7)(a));
- (2) to the debtor's earnings, were a reference to allowances:
  - (a) payable to the debtor in accordance with a scheme under regulations under the Local Government and Housing Act 1989 s 18 (schemes for basic, attendance and special responsibility allowances for local authority members: see LOCAL GOVERNMENT vol 69 (2018) PARA 201) (Council Tax (Administration and Enforcement) Regulations 1992, SI 1992/613, reg 44(7)(b)(i)); or
  - (b) in the nature of an attendance allowance, payable to the debtor under the Local Government Act 1972 s 175 (allowances for attending conferences and meetings: see LOCAL GOVERNMENT vol 69 (2018) PARA 203) (Council Tax (Administration and Enforcement) Regulations 1992, SI 1992/613, reg 44(7)(b)(ii));

(3) to an attachment of earnings order (reg 44(7)(c)),
were a reference to an order under reg 44: reg 44(7). As to offences in relation to attachment of allowances orders see reg 56(2)–(4); and PARA 510.

8 Council Tax (Administration and Enforcement) Regulations 1992, SI 1992/613, reg 44(4).

9 Council Tax (Administration and Enforcement) Regulations 1992, SI 1992/613, reg 44(6).

10 Council Tax (Administration and Enforcement) Regulations 1992, SI 1992/613, reg 44(5).

496. Provision for deductions from income support.

Regulations made under the provisions that govern the recovery of sums which have become payable in respect of the council tax but have not been paid[1] may provide that where a magistrates' court has made a liability order[2] against a person (the 'debtor') and the debtor is entitled to universal credit, income support, a jobseeker's allowance, state pension credit or an employment and support allowance[3]:

(1) the billing authority[4] seeking to recover the sum may apply to the Secretary of State[5] asking him to deduct sums from any amounts payable to the debtor by way of that benefit, in order to secure the payment of any outstanding sum which is or forms part of the amount in respect of which the liability order was made[6]; and

(2) the Secretary of State may deduct such sums and pay them to the authority towards satisfaction of any such outstanding sum[7].

The regulations may include:

(a) provision allowing or requiring adjudication as regards an application, and provision as to appeals to appeal tribunals[8] and decisions[9];

(b) a scheme containing provision as to the circumstances and manner in which and times at which sums are to be deducted and paid, provision about the calculation of such sums (which may include provision to secure that amounts payable to the debtor by way of universal credit, income support, a jobseeker's allowance, state pension credit or an employment and support allowance do not fall below prescribed[10] figures), and provision as to the circumstances in which the Secretary of State is to cease making deductions[11];

(c) provision requiring the Secretary of State to notify the debtor, in a prescribed manner and at any prescribed time, of the total amount of sums deducted up to the time of the notification[12];

(d) provision that, where the whole amount to which the application relates has been paid, the authority must give notice of that fact to the Secretary of State[13].

1 Ie regulations under the Local Government Finance Act 1992 Sch 4 para 1(1): see PARA 473. As to the regulations made see the Council Tax (Deductions from Income Support) Regulations 1993, SI 1993/494 (amended by SI 1993/2113, SI 1996/2344, SI 1997/827, SI 1998/563, SI 1999/3178, SI 2002/1397, SI 2002/310, SI 2008/1554 and SI 2013/612). As to council tax see PARA 344 et seq.

2 As to liability orders see PARA 476 et seq.

3 Local Government Finance Act 1992 s 14(3), Sch 4 para 6(1) (Sch 4 para 6(1) amended by the Jobseekers Act 1995 s 41(4), (5), Sch 2 para 75(1), (2)(a), (2)(b), Sch 3; the State Pension Credit Act 2002 s 14, Sch 2 Pt 3 paras 32, 33(1), (2); the Welfare Reform Act 2007 s 28(1), Sch 3 para 11(1), (2)(a); and the Welfare Reform Act 2012 s 31, Sch 2 paras 32, 33(1), (2)(a)). As from a day to be appointed, the Local Government Finance Act 1992 Sch 4 para 6(1) is further amended by the repeal of the reference to 'income support': Sch 4 para 6(1) (as so amended; prospectively further amended by the Welfare Reform Act 2009 ss 9(3)(b), 58(1), Sch 7, Pt 1; and the Welfare Reform Act 2012 s 147, Sch 14 Pt 1). At the date at which this volume states the law no such day had been appointed.

As to income support see WELFARE BENEFITS AND STATE PENSIONS vol 104 (2014) PARA 292 et seq. As to jobseeker's allowance see WELFARE BENEFITS AND STATE PENSIONS vol 104 (2014) PARA 419 et seq.

4 As to the meaning of 'billing authority' see PARA 346.
5 As to the Secretary of State see PARA 4 note 18. The functions of the Secretary of State under the Local Government Finance Act 1992 Sch 4 para 6 in relation to Wales are not transferred to the Welsh Ministers: see the National Assembly for Wales (Transfer of Functions) Order 1999, SI 1999/672, art 2, Sch 1. As to the transfer of functions to the Welsh Ministers generally see PARA 345.
6 See the Local Government Finance Act 1992 Sch 4 para 6(1)(a) (amended by the Jobseekers Act 1995 Sch 2 para 75(1), (2)(c)).
7 Local Government Finance Act 1992 Sch 4 para 6(1)(b). As to the relationship between remedies see the Council Tax (Administration and Enforcement) Regulations 1992, SI 1992/613, reg 52; and PARA 501.
8 Ie constituted under the Social Security Act 1998 Pt I Ch I (ss 1–7): see WELFARE BENEFITS AND STATE PENSIONS vol 104 (2014) PARA 546 et seq.
9 Local Government Finance Act 1992 Sch 4 para 6(2)(a) (amended by the Social Security Act 1998 s 86(1), Sch 7 para 117). The decisions referred to are those under the Social Security Act 1998 s 9 or s 10 (see WELFARE BENEFITS AND STATE PENSIONS vol 104 (2014) PARA 558): see the Local Government Finance Act 1992 Sch 4 para 6(2)(a) (as so amended).
10 'Prescribed' means prescribed by regulations made by the Secretary of State: see the Local Government Finance Act 1992 s 116(1).
11 Local Government Finance Act 1992 Sch 4 para 6(2)(b) (amended by the Jobseekers Act 1995 Sch 2 para 75; the State Pension Credit Act 2002 Sch 2 Pt 3 paras 32, 33(1), (3); the Welfare Reform Act 2007 Sch 3 para 11(1), (2)(a); and the Welfare Reform Act 2012 Sch 14 Pt 1). As from a day to be appointed, the Local Government Finance Act 1992 Sch 4 para 6(2)(b) is further amended by the repeal of the reference to 'income support': Sch 4 para 6(2)(b) (as so amended; prospectively further amended by the Welfare Reform Act 2009 ss 9(3)(b), 58(1), Sch 7 Pt 1; and the Welfare Reform Act 2012 Sch 14 Pt 1). At the date at which this volume states the law no such day had been appointed.
12 Local Government Finance Act 1992 Sch 4 para 6(2)(c).
13 Local Government Finance Act 1992 Sch 4 para 6(2)(d).

(iv) Enforcement by Taking Control of Goods

497. Enforcement by taking control of goods.

Where a liability order[1] has been made, payment may be enforced by using the Schedule 12 procedure[2].

1 As liability orders see PARA 478 et seq.
2 Council Tax (Administration and Enforcement) Regulations 1992, SI 1992/613, reg 45 (substituted by SI 2014/600). See also the Local Government Finance Act 1992 s 14(4); and PARA 476 note 3. As to the meaning of 'Schedule 12 procedure' see PARA 475 note 12. As to the procedure for taking control of goods under the Tribunals, Courts and Enforcement Act 2007 Sch 12 see CIVIL PROCEDURE vol 12A (2015) PARA 1334 et seq.

(v) Commitment

498. Provision for commitment to prison.

Regulations made under the provisions that govern the recovery of sums which have become payable in respect of the council tax but have not been paid[1] may provide that:

(1) where the debtor[2] is an individual who has attained the age of 18 years[3], and there are insufficient goods to satisfy an amount due under a liability order in respect of which the procedure for enforcement by taking control of goods has been used[4], the authority may apply to a magistrates' court for the issue of a warrant committing the debtor to prison[5];

(2) on such application being made the court must (in the debtor's presence) inquire as to his means and inquire whether the failure to pay which has led to the application is due to his wilful refusal or culpable neglect[6];
(3) if (and only if) the court is of opinion that his failure is due to his wilful refusal or culpable neglect it may if it thinks fit issue a warrant of commitment against the debtor, or fix a term of imprisonment and postpone the issue of the warrant until such time and on such conditions (if any) as the court thinks just[7];
(4) the warrant must be made in respect of the relevant amount[8];
(5) the warrant must state that amount[9];
(6) the order in the warrant must be that the debtor be imprisoned for a time specified in the warrant (which must not exceed three months), unless the amount stated in the warrant is sooner paid[10];
(7) the period of imprisonment must be reduced by a prescribed amount in respect of part payment in prescribed circumstances[11];
(8) a warrant may be directed to the authority concerned and to such other persons (if any) as the court issuing it thinks fit[12];
(9) a warrant may be executed anywhere in England and Wales by any person to whom it is directed[13].

The regulations may include:
(a) provision that a single warrant must not be issued[14] against more than one person[15];
(b) provision as to the form of a warrant[16];
(c) provision allowing remission of payment where no warrant is issued or term of imprisonment fixed[17];
(d) provision allowing an application to be renewed where no warrant is issued or term of imprisonment fixed[18];
(e) provision that a statement in writing[19] to the effect that wages of any amount have been paid to the debtor during any period, purporting to be signed by or on behalf of his employer, is evidence of the facts there stated[20];
(f) provision that, for the purpose of enabling inquiry to be made as to the debtor's conduct and means, a justice of the peace may issue a summons to him to appear before a magistrates' court and (if he does not obey the summons) may issue a warrant for his arrest[21];
(g) provision that, for the purpose of enabling such inquiry, a justice of the peace may issue a warrant for the debtor's arrest without issuing a summons[22];
(h) provision as to the execution of a warrant for arrest (which may include provision allowing it to be executed anywhere in England and Wales)[23].

1 Ie regulations under the Local Government Finance Act 1992 Sch 4 para 1(1): see PARA 473. As to the regulations made see PARA 499. As to council tax see PARA 344 et seq.

2 As to the meaning of 'debtor' for these purposes see PARA 296 note 3.

3 As to the time at which a person attains a particular age see PARA 354 note 4.

4 Ie an amount under the Local Government Finance Act 1992 s 14(4): see PARA 476 note 3. The reference to insufficient goods to satisfy an amount under s 14(4) is a reference to circumstances where a person authorised to act under the power conferred by s 14(4) (power to use the procedure in Schedule 12 to the Tribunals, Courts and Enforcement Act 2007) has reported to the authority concerned that he was unable (for whatever reason) to find sufficient goods of the debtor to pay the amount outstanding: Local Government Finance Act 1992 s 14(3), Sch 4 para 8(1A) (Sch 4 para 8(1A) added by the Tribunals, Courts and Enforcement Act 2007 s 62(3), Sch 13 paras 105, 107(1), (5)(b)).

5 Local Government Finance Act 1992 Sch 4 para 8(1)(a) (amended by the Tribunals, Courts and Enforcement Act 2007 ss 62(3), 146, Sch 13 paras 101, 107(1), (5)(a), Sch 23 Pt 3).
6 Local Government Finance Act 1992 Sch 4 para 8(1)(b).
7 Local Government Finance Act 1992 Sch 4 para 8(1)(c).
8 Local Government Finance Act 1992 Sch 4 para 8(1)(d). The 'relevant amount' is the aggregate of:
(1) the amount outstanding at the time when the warrant of commitment is issued (Sch 4 para 8(2)(a) (substituted by the Tribunals, Courts and Enforcement Act 2007 Sch 13 paras 105, 107(1), (5)(c))); and
(2) a sum (of a prescribed amount or an amount determined in accordance with prescribed rules) in respect of the costs of commitment (Local Government Finance Act 1992 Sch 4 para 8(2)(b)).

For these purposes, 'amount outstanding' has the meaning given by the Tribunals, Courts and Enforcement Act 2007 Sch 12 para 50(3) (see CIVIL PROCEDURE vol 12A (2015) PARA 1356): Local Government Finance Act 1992 Sch 4 para 8(4) (added by the Tribunals, Courts and Enforcement Act 2007 Sch 13 paras 101, 107(1), (5)(d)).

'Prescribed' means prescribed by regulations made (in relation to England) by the Secretary of State and (in relation to Wales) by the Welsh Ministers: Local Government Finance Act 1992 Sch 4 para 20 (added by the Local Government Act 2003 s 127(1), Sch 7 paras 40, 54). As to the Secretary of State and the Welsh Ministers see PARA 4 note 18. As to the meanings of 'England' and 'Wales' see PARA 2 note 16. The functions under the Local Government Finance Act 1992 Sch 4 paras 8, 20 were formerly vested in the National Assembly for Wales and are now exercisable by the Welsh Ministers by virtue of the Government of Wales Act 2006 s 162(1), Sch 11 paras 30, 32.
9 Local Government Finance Act 1992 Sch 4 para 8(1)(e).
10 Local Government Finance Act 1992 Sch 4 para 8(1)(f). As to the meaning of 'month' see PARA 11 note 1.
11 Local Government Finance Act 1992 Sch 4 para 8(1)(g).
12 Local Government Finance Act 1992 Sch 4 para 8(1)(h).
13 Local Government Finance Act 1992 Sch 4 para 8(1)(i).
14 Ie under any provision included under the Local Government Finance Act 1992 Sch 4 para 8.
15 Local Government Finance Act 1992 Sch 4 para 8(3)(a).
16 Local Government Finance Act 1992 Sch 4 para 8(3)(b).
17 Local Government Finance Act 1992 Sch 4 para 8(3)(c).
18 Local Government Finance Act 1992 Sch 4 para 8(3)(d).
19 As to the meaning of 'writing' see PARA 21 note 3.
20 Local Government Finance Act 1992 Sch 4 para 8(3)(e).
21 Local Government Finance Act 1992 Sch 4 para 8(3)(f).
22 Local Government Finance Act 1992 Sch 4 para 8(3)(g).
23 Local Government Finance Act 1992 Sch 4 para 8(3)(h).

499. Commitment to prison.

Where:

(1) a billing authority[1] has sought[2] to enforce payment by use of the Schedule 12 procedure[3];
(2) the debtor[4] is an individual who has attained the age of 18 years[5]; and
(3) the enforcement agent[6] reports to the authority that he was unable (for whatever reason) to find any or sufficient goods of the debtor to enforce payment[7],

the authority may apply to a magistrates' court[8] for the issue of a warrant committing the debtor to prison[9].

On such application being made, the court must (in the debtor's presence) inquire as to his means and inquire whether the failure to pay which has led to the application is due to his wilful refusal or culpable neglect[10]. If (and only if) the court is of the opinion that his failure is due to his wilful refusal or culpable neglect it may if it thinks fit issue a warrant of commitment against the debtor[11], or fix a term of imprisonment and postpone the issue of the warrant until such time and on such conditions (if any) as the court thinks just[12].

The warrant must be made in respect of the relevant amount[13] and must state that relevant amount[14]. It may be directed to the authority making the application and to such other persons (if any) as the court issuing it thinks fit[15], and may be executed anywhere in England and Wales by any person to whom it is directed[16]. The order in the warrant must be that the debtor be imprisoned for a time specified in the warrant which must not exceed three months[17], unless the amount stated in the warrant is sooner paid[18]. A single warrant may not be issued against more than one person[19].

If:

(a) before a warrant has been issued, or a term of imprisonment fixed and the issue of a warrant postponed, the prescribed amount[20] is paid or tendered to the authority[21]; or

(b) after a term of imprisonment has been fixed and the issue of a warrant postponed, the amount (if any) the court has ordered the debtor to pay is paid or tendered to the authority[22]; or

(c) after a warrant has been issued, the amount stated in it is paid or tendered to the authority[23],

the authority must accept the amount concerned, no further steps may be taken as regards its recovery, and the debtor (if committed to prison) must be released[24].

Where an application for the issue of a warrant committing the debtor to prison has been made[25] and, after the making of the proper inquiries[26], no warrant is issued or term of imprisonment fixed, the court may remit all or part of the appropriate amount[27] with respect to which the application related[28]. Where such an application has been made but no warrant is issued or term of imprisonment fixed, the application may be renewed (except so far as regards any sum so remitted[29]) on the ground that the circumstances of the debtor have changed[30].

There is no express provision made in the regulations for a taxpayer to challenge an order for commitment to prison[31].

1 As to the meaning of 'billing authority' see PARA 346.

2 Ie under the Council Tax (Administration and Enforcement) Regulations 1992, SI 1992/613, reg 45: see PARA 497. As to the meaning of 'Schedule 12 procedure' see PARA 475 note 12.

3 See the Council Tax (Administration and Enforcement) Regulations 1992, SI 1992/613, reg 47(1) (amended by SI 2014/600). As to the application of the Council Tax (Administration and Enforcement) Regulations 1992, SI 1992/613, regs 33–53 see PARA 477 note 4.

4 As to the meaning of 'debtor' see PARA 480 note 2.

5 See the Council Tax (Administration and Enforcement) Regulations 1992, SI 1992/613, reg 47(1). As to the time at which a person attains a particular age see PARA 354 note 4.

6 As to the meaning of 'enforcement agent' see the Tribunals, Courts and Enforcement Act 2007 Sch 12 para 2; and CIVIL PROCEDURE vol 12A (2015) PARA 1334.

7 See the Council Tax (Administration and Enforcement) Regulations 1992, SI 1992/613, reg 47(1) (as amended: see note 3).

8 As to the magistrates' court, and as to the admissibility in proceedings under the Council Tax (Administration and Enforcement) Regulations 1992, SI 1992/613, reg 47 of evidence derived from records compiled by the applicant authority (or by an authorised person) before such a court, see PARA 504.

9 See the Council Tax (Administration and Enforcement) Regulations 1992, SI 1992/613, reg 47(1). Regulations 47 and 48 (see note 10 and the text to notes 19, 25–30) both have effect subject to the Criminal Justice Act 1982 Pt I (ss 1–11) (largely repealed) (treatment of young offenders) (see now the Powers of Criminal Courts (Sentencing) Act 2000; and see SENTENCING vol 92 (2015) PARA 551): Council Tax (Administration and Enforcement) Regulations 1992, SI 1992/613, reg 48(7).

The power of committal to prison for failure to pay local taxes or fines has been considered by the European Court of Human Rights in *Lloyd v United Kingdom* [2006] RA 329, ECtHR, and in *Beet v United Kingdom* [2006] RA 384, ECtHR. See also *Benham v United Kingdom* (1996) 22 EHRR 293, ECtHR; and *Perks v United Kingdom* (1999) 30 EHRR 33, ECtHR.

10 Council Tax (Administration and Enforcement) Regulations 1992, SI 1992/613, reg 47(2). See also note 9. A statement in writing to the effect that wages of any amount have been paid to the debtor during any period, purporting to be signed by or on behalf of his employer, is in any proceedings for committal evidence of the facts there stated: reg 48(4). As to the meaning of 'writing' see PARA 21 note 3.

For the purpose of enabling inquiry to be made as to the debtor's conduct and means, a justice of the peace may:

(1) issue a summons to him to appear before a magistrates' court and (if he does not obey the summons) issue a warrant for his arrest (reg 48(5)(a)); or

(2) issue a warrant for the debtor's arrest without issuing a summons (reg 48(5)(b)).

A warrant issued under head (1) or (2) above may be executed anywhere in England and Wales by any person to whom it is directed or by any constable acting within his police area; and the Magistrates' Courts Act 1980 s 125(3) (repealed) (execution of warrants) (see now s 125A; and MAGISTRATES vol 71 (2013) PARA 670) applies to such a warrant: Council Tax (Administration and Enforcement) Regulations 1992, SI 1992/613, reg 48(6). As to the meanings of 'England' and 'Wales' see PARA 2 note 16. As to the office of constable see POLICE AND INVESTIGATORY POWERS vol 84 (2013) PARA 1 et seq. 'Police area' has the meaning or effect described by the Police Act 1996 s 101(1) (see POLICE AND INVESTIGATORY POWERS vol 84 (2013) PARA 52): Interpretation Act 1978 s 5, Sch 1 (amended by the Police Act 1996 s 103, Sch 7 para 32).

11 Council Tax (Administration and Enforcement) Regulations 1992, SI 1992/613, reg 47(3)(a). See also note 9. See *R v Cannock Justices, ex p Swaffer* [1997] EWHC Admin 822, [2003] RVR 114 (imprisonment appeared to have been imposed out of pure retribution rather than for a proper purpose given the lack of evidence that there was likely to be means to pay). See also *R (on the application of Wandless) v Halifax Magistrates' Court* [2009] EWHC 1857 (Admin), [2010] RVR 6 (warrant quashed: failure by justices to make proper inquiries and to have in mind the purpose of a committal order as a method of last resort to extract payment and not to be used as a means of punishment); and *R (on the application of Woolcock) v Bridgend Magistrates' Court* [2017] EWHC 34 (Admin), [2017] All ER (D) 139 (Jan) (where no means inquiry was conducted). See also *R (on the application of Woolcock) v Bridgend Magistrates' Court* [2018] EWHC 17 (Admin), [2018] All ER (D) 120 (Jan) (no basis for a systemic challenge by way of judicial review to the system of council tax enforcement under the Council Tax (Administration and Enforcement) Regulations 1992, SI 1992/613 as the risk of unfairness arose in the ordinary course of individual decision-making, in that magistrates simply failed to comply with the scheme's requirements).

12 Council Tax (Administration and Enforcement) Regulations 1992, SI 1992/613, reg 47(3)(b). See also note 9. See *R v Newcastle Justices, ex p Ashley* [1993] RA 264 (community charge case, where the warrant was quashed because the magistrates failed to consider alternative ways of dealing with the debtor); *R v Highbury Corner Magistrates' Court, ex p Uchendu* [1994] RA 51, 158 LGR 481. See also non-domestic rating cases cited in PARA 296 which may be considered in this context.

As to the restriction on the taking of other steps under the enforcement provisions of the Council Tax (Administration and Enforcement) Regulations 1992, SI 1992/613, Pt VI (regs 32–57) where a warrant of commitment is issued against (or a term of imprisonment is fixed in the case of) a person, see reg 52(1); and PARA 501.

If, after a warrant is issued or term of imprisonment is fixed under reg 47(3), and before the term of imprisonment has begun or been fully served, a billing authority gives a notification under reg 24(2) or (5) (see PARA 467), reg 25(5) or (8) (see PARA 468), reg 28(3) or (4) (see PARA 460) or reg 31(2) (see PARA 462), or Sch 1 Pt III para 9(3) (see PARA 465) or Sch 1 Pt III para 10(2)(a) (see PARA 466) in the case in question, or sets an amount in substitution so that the Local Government Finance Act 1992 s 31(4) (see PARA 381) applies in the case in question, it must forthwith notify accordingly the designated officer for the court which issued the warrant and (if the debtor is detained) the governor or keeper of the prison or place where he is detained or such other person as has lawful custody of him: see the Council Tax (Administration and Enforcement) Regulations 1992, SI 1992/613, reg 57(3) (amended by SI 2005/617; in relation to England by SI 2001/362; and in relation to Wales by SI 2001/1076). If the debtor is treated as having paid an amount under the Council Tax (Administration and Enforcement) Regulations 1992, SI 1992/613, reg 57(2) (see PARA 478) on any day, and:

(1) that day falls after the completion of the service of a term of imprisonment imposed under reg 47 in respect of the amount he is treated as having paid (reg 57(4)(a)); or

(2) the debtor is serving a term of imprisonment imposed under reg 47 on that day and the amount he is treated as having paid exceeds the amount of any part payment which, if

made, would cause the expiry of the term of imprisonment pursuant to reg 47(7)(b) (see note 18) on that day (reg 57(4)(b)),

then the amount mentioned in head (1) above or the excess mentioned in head (2) above must be paid to the debtor or credited against any subsequent liability of his, as the debtor requires: reg 57(4).

13 Council Tax (Administration and Enforcement) Regulations 1992, SI 1992/613, reg 47(4). The relevant amount for this purpose is the aggregate of:

(1) an amount equal to the amount outstanding (within the meaning of the Tribunals, Courts and Enforcement Act 2007 Sch 12: see CIVIL PROCEDURE vol 12A (2015) PARA 1356) (Council Tax (Administration and Enforcement) Regulations 1992, SI 1992/613, reg 47(4)(a) (amended by SI 2014/600)); and

(2) a sum of an amount equal to the costs reasonably incurred by the applicant in respect of the application (Council Tax (Administration and Enforcement) Regulations 1992, SI 1992/613, reg 47(4)(b)).

14 See the Council Tax (Administration and Enforcement) Regulations 1992, SI 1992/613, reg 47(5)(a).

15 Council Tax (Administration and Enforcement) Regulations 1992, SI 1992/613, reg 47(5)(b).

16 Council Tax (Administration and Enforcement) Regulations 1992, SI 1992/613, reg 47(5)(c). See also note 9.

17 As to the meaning of 'month' see PARA 11 note 1.

18 Council Tax (Administration and Enforcement) Regulations 1992, SI 1992/613, reg 47(7). See also note 9. However, where a warrant is issued after a postponement under reg 47(3)(b) (see the text to note 12) and, since the term of imprisonment was fixed but before the issue of the warrant, the amount mentioned in reg 47(4)(a) (see note 13 head (1)) with respect to which the warrant would (but for the postponement) have been made has been reduced by a part payment, the period of imprisonment ordered under the warrant must be the term fixed under reg 47(3) (see the text to note 12) reduced by such number of days as bears to the total number of days in that term less one day the same proportion as the part paid bears to that amount: reg 47(7)(a). Where, after the issue of a warrant, a part payment of the amount stated in it is made, the period of imprisonment must be reduced by such number of days as bears to the total number of days in the term of imprisonment specified in the warrant less one day the same proportion as the part paid bears to the amount so stated: reg 47(7)(b). In calculating a reduction required under reg 47(7), any fraction of a day is to be left out of account; and the Magistrates' Courts Rules 1981, SI 1981/552, r 55(1)–(3) (payment after imprisonment imposed: see MAGISTRATES vol 71 (2013) PARA 648 et seq) applies (so far as is relevant) to a part payment as if the imprisonment concerned were imposed for want of sufficient goods being found under the Schedule 12 procedure to satisfy a sum adjudged to be paid by a magistrates' court: Council Tax (Administration and Enforcement) Regulations 1992, SI 1992/613, reg 47(8) (amended by virtue of SI 2014/600). As to the meaning of 'Schedule 12 procedure' see PARA 475 note 12.

19 Council Tax (Administration and Enforcement) Regulations 1992, SI 1992/613, reg 48(1) (amended in relation to England by SI 2003/2211; and in relation to Wales by SI 2003/1715). See also note 9.

20 The amount referred to is the aggregate of:

(1) the amount outstanding (within the meaning of the Tribunals, Courts and Enforcement Act 2007 Sch 12 (see note 13)) (Council Tax (Administration and Enforcement) Regulations 1992, SI 1992/613, reg 47(6A)(a) (reg 47(6A), (6B), Sch 6 added by SI 1994/505; the Council Tax (Administration and Enforcement) Regulations 1992, SI 1992/613, reg 47(6A)(a) amended by SI 2014/600)); and

(2) subject to the Council Tax (Administration and Enforcement) Regulations 1992, SI 1992/613, reg 47(6B), the authority's reasonable costs incurred up to the time of payment or tender in making one or more of the applications referred to in Sch 6 (see reg 47(6A)(b), Sch 6 (both as so added; Sch 6 substituted in relation to England by SI 2010/752; and in relation to Wales by SI 2011/528)).

For the purposes of the Council Tax (Administration and Enforcement) Regulations 1992, SI 1992/613, reg 47(6A)(b), the authority's reasonable costs in respect of any application must not exceed the amount specified for that application in Sch 6: reg 47(6B) (as so added).

21 See the Council Tax (Administration and Enforcement) Regulations 1992, SI 1992/613, reg 47(6)(a) (reg 47(6) substituted by SI 1994/505).

22 Council Tax (Administration and Enforcement) Regulations 1992, SI 1992/613, reg 47(6)(b) (as substituted: see note 21).

23 Council Tax (Administration and Enforcement) Regulations 1992, SI 1992/613, reg 47(6)(c) (as substituted: see note 21).

24 Council Tax (Administration and Enforcement) Regulations 1992, SI 1992/613, reg 47(6) (as substituted: see note 21).
25 Ie under the Council Tax (Administration and Enforcement) Regulations 1992, SI 1992/613, reg 47: see the text to notes 1–24.
26 Ie the inquiries mentioned in the Council Tax (Administration and Enforcement) Regulations 1992, SI 1992/613, reg 47(2): see the text to note 10.
27 Ie the appropriate amount mentioned in the Council Tax (Administration and Enforcement) Regulations 1992, SI 1992/613, reg 45(2): see PARA 497 note 2.
28 Council Tax (Administration and Enforcement) Regulations 1992, SI 1992/613, reg 48(2). See *R (on the application of Broadhurst) v Sheffield Justices* [2001] RVR 245 (the court should consider the question of remission of part or all of the sums due before it considers the question of imprisonment); and *Teignbridge District Council v Saunders* [2001] EWHC Admin 344, [2001] RVR 282, [2001] All ER (D) 94 (May) (justices had no discretion to rescind or cancel an order for imprisonment reasonably imposed at an earlier hearing and then to proceed to exercise their power of remission in the Council Tax (Administration and Enforcement) Regulations 1992, SI 1992/613, reg 48(2) which expressly applied only where no order for imprisonment had been made).
29 Ie under the Council Tax (Administration and Enforcement) Regulations 1992, SI 1992/613, reg 48(2): see the text to notes 25–28.
30 Council Tax (Administration and Enforcement) Regulations 1992, SI 1992/613, reg 48(3).
31 Accordingly, remedies must be sought by means outside the regulations: see eg *R (on the application of Nwankwo) v Hendon Magistrates' Court* [2003] EWHC 1659 (Admin), [2003] All ER (D) 27 (Jun) (on application for judicial review, the justices' decision to commit the taxpayer to prison was quashed on grounds that the hearing had been unfair and that the procedure set out under the Council Tax (Administration and Enforcement) Regulations 1992, SI 1992/613, governing the steps to be taken before committal is considered, had not been followed); and see *R v Newcastle upon Tyne Justices, ex p Devine* [1998] RA 97, 162 JP 602 (a community charge case). See also *R v Thanet District Council, ex p Haddow* [1992] RA 245 (a community charge case).

(vi) Procedural Matters

500. Provision for the relationship between remedies.

As regards a case where a magistrates' court has made a liability order[1], regulations made under the provisions that govern the recovery of sums which have become payable in respect of the council tax but have not been paid[2] may include provision that:

(1) attachment of earnings[3] may be resorted to more than once[4];
(2) deductions from universal credit may be resorted to more than once[5];
(3) deductions from income support[6], deductions from state pension credit[7] or deductions from an employment and support allowance[8] may be resorted to more than once[9];
(4) attachment of earnings, deductions from universal credit, deductions from income support[10], deductions from state pension credit, deductions from an employment and support allowance and the power of enforcement by taking possession of goods[11] (or any two of them) may be resorted to in any order or alternately (or both)[12];
(5) steps by way of attachment, deduction, exercise of the power of enforcement by taking possession of goods, commitment, bankruptcy, winding up or charging may not be taken while steps by way of another of those methods are being taken[13];

(6) where a warrant of commitment is issued against (or a term of imprisonment is fixed in the case of) the person concerned no steps, or no further steps, by way of attachment, deduction, exercise of the power of enforcement by taking possession of goods, bankruptcy or charging may be taken[14].

1 As to liability orders see PARA 478.

2 Ie regulations under the Local Government Finance Act 1992 Sch 4 para 1(1): see PARA 473. As to the regulations made see PARA 501. As to council tax see PARA 344 et seq.

3 Any reference to attachment of earnings includes a reference to attachment of allowances: Local Government Finance Act 1992 s 14(3), Sch 4 para 12(2). As to attachment of earnings and attachment of allowances see PARA 487 et seq.

4 Local Government Finance Act 1992 Sch 4 para 12(1)(a).

5 Local Government Finance Act 1992 Sch 4 para 12(1)(aa) (added by the Welfare Reform Act 2012 s 31, Sch 2 paras 32, 33(1), (3)(a)). As to universal credit see WELFARE BENEFITS AND STATE PENSIONS vol 104 (2014) PARA 1 et seq.

6 See the Local Government Finance Act 1992 Sch 4 para 12(1)(b) (repealed, as from a day to be appointed, by the Welfare Reform Act 2012 s 147, Sch 14 Pt 1; at the date at which this volume states the law, no such day had been appointed). As from a day to be appointed, the Local Government Finance Act 1992 Sch 4 para 12(1)(b) is amended so that for the reference to 'income support' there is substituted a reference to 'jobseeker's allowance payable to any person whose claim to the allowance is based on meeting the Jobseekers Act 1995 s 1A condition B': see the Local Government Finance Act 1992 Sch 4 para 12(1)(b) (prospectively amended by the Welfare Reform Act 2009 s 9(3)(a), Sch 2 para 4(a)). At the date at which this volume states the law no such day had been appointed. As to income support see WELFARE BENEFITS AND STATE PENSIONS vol 104 (2014) PARA 292 et seq. As to jobseekers allowance see WELFARE BENEFITS AND STATE PENSIONS vol 104 (2014) PARA 419 et seq.

7 See the Local Government Finance Act 1992 Sch 4 para 12(1)(bb) (added by the State Pension Credit Act 2002 s 14, Sch 2 Pt 3 paras 32, 34(a)).

8 See the Local Government Finance Act 1992 Sch 4 para 12(1)(bc) (added by the Welfare Reform Act 2007 s 28(1), Sch 3 para 11(1), (2)(b)).

9 See the Local Government Finance Act 1992 Sch 4 para 12(1)(b) (as prospectively amended and repealed: see note 6), Sch 4 para 12(1)(bb) (as added: see note 7), Sch 4 para 12(1)(bc) (as added: see note 8).

10 As from a day to be appointed, the Local Government Finance Act 1992 Sch 4 para 12(1)(d) is amended so that for the reference to 'income support' there is substituted a reference to 'jobseeker's allowance payable to any person whose claim to the allowance is based on meeting the Jobseekers Act 1995 s 1A condition B': see the Local Government Finance Act 1992 Sch 4 para 12(1)(d) (prospectively amended by the Welfare Reform Act 2009 Sch 2 para 4(b); and the Welfare Reform Act 2012 Sch 14 Pt 1). At the date at which this volume states the law no such day had been appointed.

11 Ie the power conferred by the Local Government Finance Act 1992 s 14(4): see PARAS 476 note 3, 497.

12 Local Government Finance Act 1992 Sch 4 para 12(1)(d) (amended by the State Pension Credit Act 2002 Sch 2 Pt 3 paras 32, 34(b); the Welfare Reform Act 2007 Sch 3 para 11(1), (2)(c); the Tribunals, Courts and Enforcement Act 2007 s 62(3), Sch 13 paras 105, 107(1), (6)(b); and the Welfare Reform Act 2012 Sch 2 paras 32, 33(1), (3)(b)).

13 Local Government Finance Act 1992 Sch 4 para 12(1)(e) (amended by the Tribunals, Courts and Enforcement Act 2007 Sch 13 paras 105, 107(1), (6)(c)).

14 Local Government Finance Act 1992 Sch 4 para 12(1)(f) (amended by the Tribunals, Courts and Enforcement Act 2007 Sch 13 paras 105, 107(1), (6)(d)).

501. Relationship between remedies.

Where a warrant of commitment is issued against (or a term of imprisonment is fixed in the case of) a person[1], no steps, or no further steps, may be taken under the council tax enforcement provisions[2], by way of attachment of allowances[3], attachment of earnings[4], the procedure for enforcement by taking control of goods[5], bankruptcy[6] or charging[7], or under the Income Support Regulations[8], in relation to the relevant amount[9].

Steps under the council tax enforcement provisions[10] by way of attachment of allowances, attachment of earnings, the Schedule 12 procedure, commitment, bankruptcy, winding up[11] or charging may not be taken in relation to a person against whom a liability order[12] has been made while[13]:

(1) steps by way of another of those methods are being taken against him under it[14]; or

(2) deductions are being made under the Income Support Regulations from any amount payable to him by way of income support, universal credit or jobseeker's allowance[15]; or

(3) an application under the Income Support Regulations[16] has been made in respect of him to the Secretary of State[17] and remains undetermined[18].

An application as mentioned in head (3) above[19] may not be made in respect of a person against whom a liability order has been made while steps under the council tax enforcement provisions[20] are being taken against him for the recovery of an amount equal to any outstanding sum which is or forms part of the amount in respect of which the liability order was made[21].

Attachment of allowances, attachment of earnings, deductions under the Income Support Regulations or the procedure for enforcement by taking control of goods may be resorted to more than once[22]; and attachment of allowances, attachment of earnings, deductions under the Income Support Regulations or the procedure for enforcement by taking control of goods may be resorted to in any order or alternately (or both)[23].

Where a step is taken for the recovery of an outstanding sum which is or forms part of an amount in respect of which a liability order has been made and under which additional costs or charges with respect to the step are also recoverable in accordance with the council tax enforcement provisions[24], any sum recovered thereby which is less than the aggregate of the amount outstanding and such additional costs and charges is to be treated as discharging first the costs and charges, the balance (if any) being applied towards the discharge of the outstanding sum[25].

1 Ie under the Council Tax (Administration and Enforcement) Regulations 1992, SI 1992/613, reg 47(3): see PARA 499.

2 Ie under the Council Tax (Administration and Enforcement) Regulations 1992, SI 1992/613, Pt VI (regs 32–57).

3 As to attachment of allowances orders see PARA 495.

4 As to attachment of earnings orders see PARA 488.

5 Ie 'the Schedule 12 procedure' (see PARA 475 note 12). See PARA 497.

6 As to bankruptcy see PARA 482.

7 As to charging orders see PARA 484.

8 As to the meaning of 'the Income Support Regulations' see PARA 475 note 16. As to deductions under those regulations see PARA 496.

9 Council Tax (Administration and Enforcement) Regulations 1992, SI 1992/613, reg 52(1) (amended by SI 1993/773 and SI 2014/600). The 'relevant amount' is that mentioned in the Council Tax (Administration and Enforcement) Regulations 1992, SI 1992/613, reg 47(4) (see PARA 499): see reg 52(1). As to the application of regs 33–53 see PARA 477 note 4.

10 Ie under the Council Tax (Administration and Enforcement) Regulations 1992, SI 1992/613, Pt VI.

11 As to winding up see PARA 482.

12 As to the meaning of 'liability order' see PARA 478 note 6. As to the making of liability orders see PARA 478.

13 Council Tax (Administration and Enforcement) Regulations 1992, SI 1992/613, reg 52(2) (amended by SI 1993/773 and SI 2014/600).

14 Council Tax (Administration and Enforcement) Regulations 1992, SI 1992/613, reg 52(2)(a) (reg 52(2)(a)–(c) added by SI 1993/773).

15 Council Tax (Administration and Enforcement) Regulations 1992, SI 1992/613, reg 52(2)(b) (as added (see note 14); amended by SI 1996/2405; in relation to England by SI 2013/630; and in relation to Wales by SI 2013/570).
16 Ie under the Council Tax (Deductions from Income Support) Regulations 1993, SI 1993/494, reg 2: see PARA 496.
17 As to the Secretary of State in this respect see PARA 496 note 5.
18 Council Tax (Administration and Enforcement) Regulations 1992, SI 1992/613, reg 52(2)(c) (as added: see note 14).
19 Ie an application under the Council Tax (Deductions from Income Support) Regulations 1993, SI 1993/494, reg 2: see PARA 496.
20 Ie under the Council Tax (Administration and Enforcement) Regulations 1992, SI 1992/613, Pt VI.
21 Council Tax (Administration and Enforcement) Regulations 1992, SI 1992/613, reg 52(2A) (added by SI 1993/773).
22 Council Tax (Administration and Enforcement) Regulations 1992, SI 1992/613, reg 52(3)(a) (reg 52(3)(a), (b) amended by SI 1994/505 and SI 2014/600). The Council Tax (Administration and Enforcement) Regulations 1992, SI 1992/613, reg 52(3)(a), (b) (see the text to note 23) are expressed to be subject to reg 52(1), (2) (see the text to notes 1–18): see reg 52(3).
23 Council Tax (Administration and Enforcement) Regulations 1992, SI 1992/613, reg 52(3)(b) (as amended: see note 22). See also note 22.
24 Ie under the Council Tax (Administration and Enforcement) Regulations 1992, SI 1992/613, Pt VI.
25 Council Tax (Administration and Enforcement) Regulations 1992, SI 1992/613, reg 52(4).

502. Provision for magistrates and justices.

Regulations made under the provisions that govern the recovery of sums which have become payable in respect of the council tax but have not been paid[1] may include:

(1) provision for determining what justices and magistrates' courts are to have jurisdiction in cases provided for by the regulations[2]; and

(2) provision as to the composition of magistrates' courts in cases provided for by the regulations[3].

1 Ie regulations under the Local Government Finance Act 1992 Sch 4 para 1(1): see PARA 473. As to the regulations made see PARA 504. As to council tax see PARA 344 et seq.
2 Local Government Finance Act 1992 s 14(3), Sch 4 para 13(a).
3 Local Government Finance Act 1992 Sch 4 para 13(b).

503. Provision for the admissibility of evidence in proceedings before a magistrates' court.

Regulations made under the provisions that govern the recovery of sums which have become payable in respect of the council tax but have not been paid[1] may include provision that, in any proceedings before a magistrates' court[2]:

(1) a statement[3] contained in a document of record[4] is admissible as evidence of any fact stated in it of which direct oral evidence would be admissible[5]; and

(2) a certificate which is made with respect to a document of record produced by a computer and purports to be signed by a responsible person[6] is admissible as evidence of anything which is stated in it to the best of his information and belief[7].

1 Ie regulations under the Local Government Finance Act 1992 Sch 4 para 1(1): see PARA 473. As to the regulations made see PARA 504. As to council tax see PARA 344 et seq.
2 Ie any proceedings before a magistrates' court under any provision included by virtue of the provisions of the Local Government Finance Act 1992 Sch 4 paras 1–13: see PARA 473 et seq.
3 'Statement' includes any representation of fact, whether made in words or otherwise: Local Government Finance Act 1992 s 14(3), Sch 4 para 14(2).
4 'Document of record' means a document constituting or forming part of a record compiled by the billing authority seeking to recover sums in respect of unpaid council tax: see the Local Government Finance Act 1992 Sch 4 para 14(2).

5 Local Government Finance Act 1992 Sch 4 para 14(1)(a).
6 'Responsible person' means a person occupying a responsible position in relation to the operation of the computer: Local Government Finance Act 1992 Sch 4 para 14(2).
7 Local Government Finance Act 1992 Sch 4 para 14(1)(b).

504. Magistrates' courts.

Subject to any other enactment authorising a District Judge (magistrates' courts) or other person to act by himself, a magistrates' court may not under the council tax enforcement provisions[1] hear a summons, entertain an application for a warrant or hold an inquiry as to means on such an application except when composed of at least two justices[2].

In any proceedings relating to:

(1) an application for a liability order[3]; or
(2) an application for the issue of a warrant committing a debtor to prison[4],

a statement[5] contained in a document constituting or forming part of a record compiled by the applicant authority or an authorised person[6] is admissible as evidence of any fact stated in it of which direct oral evidence would be admissible[7]. In proceedings where the applicant authority or an authorised person desires to give a statement in evidence in this way, and the document containing that statement is produced by a computer, a certificate:

(a) identifying the document containing the statement and the computer by which it was produced[8];
(b) containing a statement that at all material times the computer was operating properly, or if not, that any respect in which it was not operating properly or was out of operation was not such as to affect the production of the document or the accuracy of its contents[9];
(c) giving such explanation as may be appropriate of the content of the document[10]; and
(d) purporting to be signed by a person occupying a responsible position in relation to the operation of the computer[11],

is admissible as evidence of anything which is stated in it to the best of the signatory's information and belief[12].

1 Ie under the Council Tax (Administration and Enforcement) Regulations 1992, SI 1992/613, Pt VI (regs 32–57): see PARA 477 et seq.
2 Council Tax (Administration and Enforcement) Regulations 1992, SI 1992/613, reg 53(2) (amended in relation to England by SI 2000/2026; in relation to Wales by SI 2001/1076). As to the application of the Council Tax (Administration and Enforcement) Regulations 1992, SI 1992/613, regs 33–53 see PARA 477 note 4. As to District Judges (magistrates' courts) see MAGISTRATES vol 71 (2013) PARA 420 et seq. As to magistrates' courts see MAGISTRATES vol 71 (2013) PARA 470 et seq. See *R (on the application of Woolcock) v Secretary of State for Communities and Local Government* [2018] EWHC 17 (Admin), [2018] All ER (D) 120 (Jan).
3 Ie an application under the Council Tax (Administration and Enforcement) Regulations 1992, SI 1992/613, reg 34: see PARA 478.
4 Ie an application under the Council Tax (Administration and Enforcement) Regulations 1992, SI 1992/613, reg 47: see PARA 499. For these purposes, the reference to an application under reg 47 includes a reference to an application under reg 48(3) (see PARA 499): reg 53(6).
5 'Statement' includes any representation of fact, whether made in words or otherwise: see the Council Tax (Administration and Enforcement) Regulations 1992, SI 1992/613, reg 53(6).
6 As to the meaning of 'authorised person' see PARA 478 note 10.
7 Council Tax (Administration and Enforcement) Regulations 1992, SI 1992/613, reg 53(4) (amended by SI 1996/1880 and SI 2014/600).
8 Council Tax (Administration and Enforcement) Regulations 1992, SI 1992/613, reg 53(5)(a).
9 Council Tax (Administration and Enforcement) Regulations 1992, SI 1992/613, reg 53(5)(b).
10 Council Tax (Administration and Enforcement) Regulations 1992, SI 1992/613, reg 53(5)(c).
11 Council Tax (Administration and Enforcement) Regulations 1992, SI 1992/613, reg 53(5)(d).

12 Council Tax (Administration and Enforcement) Regulations 1992, SI 1992/613, reg 53(5) (amended by SI 1996/1880). As to the evidential effect of certificates admissible by statute see CIVIL PROCEDURE vol 12 (2015) PARA 955.

505. Provision for the exclusion of certain matters.

Regulations made under the provisions that govern the recovery of sums which have become payable in respect of the council tax but have not been paid[1] may provide that any matter which could be the subject of an appeal to a valuation tribunal[2], may not be raised in proceedings under the regulations[3].

1 Ie regulations under the Local Government Finance Act 1992 Sch 4 para 1(1): see PARA 473. As to the regulations made see PARA 506. As to council tax see PARA 344 et seq.

2 Ie an appeal under the Local Government Finance Act 1992 s 16 (see PARA 513), or regulations under s 24 (see PARA 417).

3 Local Government Finance Act 1992 s 14(3), Sch 4 para 15.

506. Exclusion of certain matters.

Any matter which could be the subject of an appeal to a valuation tribunal[1] may not be raised in proceedings[2] under the council tax enforcement provisions[3].

1 Ie an appeal under the Local Government Finance Act 1992 s 16 (see PARA 513), or regulations under s 24 (see PARA 417).

2 Ie proceedings under the Council Tax (Administration and Enforcement) Regulations 1992, SI 1992/613, Pt VI (regs 32–57): see PARA 477 et seq.

3 Council Tax (Administration and Enforcement) Regulations 1992, SI 1992/613, reg 57(1) (amended by SI 1992/3008). See also *Hardy v Sefton Metropolitan Borough Council* [2006] EWHC 1928 (Admin), [2007] RA 140, [2006] All ER (D) 409 (Jul) (assuming that a magistrates' court had jurisdiction to refuse to make a liability order where prejudice had been established, it did not follow that a tribunal had the same jurisdiction).

507. Provision as to costs.

Regulations made under the provisions that govern the recovery of sums which have become payable in respect of the council tax but have not been paid[1] may provide that where an authority has received in proceedings under the regulations an amount by way of costs it must pay a prescribed[2] amount, or an amount determined in accordance with prescribed rules, to a prescribed person[3] for the benefit of such court as is identified in accordance with prescribed rules[4].

1 Ie regulations under the Local Government Finance Act 1992 Sch 4 para 1(1): see PARA 473. At the date at which this volume states the law, no regulations had been made for the purposes referred to in this paragraph. As to council tax see PARA 344 et seq.

2 'Prescribed' means prescribed by regulations made (in relation to England) by the Secretary of State and (in relation to Wales) by the Welsh Ministers: Local Government Finance Act 1992 s 14(3), Sch 4 para 20 (Sch 4 para 20 added by the Local Government Act 2003 s 127(1), Sch 7 paras 40, 54). As to the Secretary of State and the Welsh Ministers see PARA 4 note 18. As to the meanings of 'England' and 'Wales' see PARA 2 note 16. The functions under the Local Government Finance Act 1992 Sch 4 paras 16, 20 were formerly vested in the National Assembly for Wales and are now exercisable by the Welsh Ministers by virtue of the Government of Wales Act 2006 s 162(1), Sch 11 paras 30, 32.

3 As to the meaning of 'person' see PARA 11 note 13.

4 Local Government Finance Act 1992 Sch 4 para 16.

508. Provision for the termination of proceedings.

Regulations made under the provisions that govern the recovery of sums which have become payable in respect of the council tax but have not been paid[1] may provide that in a case where:

(1) proceedings under the regulations have been taken as regards the recovery of any sum which has become payable in respect of the council tax but has not been paid[2]; and

(2) the outstanding amount[3] is paid or tendered to the billing authority to which it is payable[4],

the authority must accept the amount, no further steps must be taken as regards its recovery, and any person committed to prison in pursuance of the proceedings must be released[5].

In a case where costs and charges are relevant the outstanding amount is to be treated as augmented by a sum (of a prescribed[6] amount or an amount determined in accordance with prescribed rules) in respect of costs and charges incurred in the proceedings up to the time of payment or tender[7].

1 Ie regulations under the Local Government Finance Act 1992 Sch 4 para 1(1): see PARA 473. As to the regulations made see PARAS 478, 486, 497, 499. As to council tax see PARA 344 et seq.
2 Local Government Finance Act 1992 s 14(3), Sch 4 para 17(1)(a).
3 For these purposes, the outstanding amount is an amount equal to the sum concerned or to so much of it as remains outstanding (as the case may be): Local Government Finance Act 1992 Sch 4 para 17(2).
4 See the Local Government Finance Act 1992 Sch 4 para 17(1)(b). As to the meaning of 'billing authority' see PARA 346.
5 Local Government Finance Act 1992 Sch 4 para 17(1).
6 'Prescribed' means prescribed by regulations made (in relation to England) by the Secretary of State and (in relation to Wales) by the Welsh Ministers: Local Government Finance Act 1992 Sch 4 para 20 (added by the Local Government Act 2003 s 127(1), Sch 7 paras 40, 54). As to the Secretary of State and the Welsh Ministers see PARA 4 note 18. As to the meanings of 'England' and 'Wales' see PARA 2 note 16. The functions under the Local Government Finance Act 1992 Sch 4 paras 17, 20 were formerly vested in the National Assembly for Wales and are now exercisable by the Welsh Ministers by virtue of the Government of Wales Act 2006 s 162(1), Sch 11 paras 30, 32.
7 Local Government Finance Act 1992 Sch 4 para 17(3).

(vii) Offences

509. Provision for offences.

Regulations made under the provisions that govern the recovery of sums which have become payable in respect of the council tax but have not been paid[1] may provide that a person is guilty of an offence if he is required[2] to supply information[3], and:

(1) he fails without reasonable excuse to supply the information in accordance with the provision[4]; or

(2) in supplying information in purported compliance with the provision he makes a statement which he knows to be false in a material particular or recklessly makes a statement which is false in a material particular[5].

Such regulations may also provide that:

(a) a person is guilty of an offence if he is required[6] to comply with an attachment of earnings order and fails to do so[7];

(b) it is a defence for a person charged with such an offence to prove that he took all reasonable steps to comply with the order[8].

Such regulations may also provide that a person is guilty of an offence if he is required[9] to notify another person[10], and:

(i) he fails without reasonable excuse to notify the other person in accordance with the provision[11]; or

(ii) in notifying the other person in purported compliance with the provision he makes a statement which he knows to be false in a material particular or recklessly makes a statement which is false in a material particular[12].

Such regulations may provide that a person guilty of such an offence[13] is:

(A) (where the provision is included by virtue of head (1) or head (i) above) liable on summary conviction to a fine not exceeding level 2 on the standard scale[14]; or

(B) (where the provision is included by virtue of head (2) or head (a) or head (ii) above) liable on summary conviction to a fine not exceeding level 3 on the standard scale[15].

1 Ie regulations under the Local Government Finance Act 1992 Sch 4 para 1(1): see PARA 473. As to the regulations made see PARA 510. As to council tax see PARA 344 et seq.
2 Ie by any provision included by virtue of the Local Government Finance Act 1992 Sch 4 para 4: see PARA 479.
3 Local Government Finance Act 1992 s 14(3), Sch 4 para 18(1). As to the meaning of 'information' see PARA 345 note 20.
4 Local Government Finance Act 1992 Sch 4 para 18(1)(a).
5 Local Government Finance Act 1992 Sch 4 para 18(1)(b).
6 Ie by any provision included by virtue of the Local Government Finance Act 1992 Sch 4 para 5(1)(d) or Sch 4 para 5(2)(b): see PARA 487.
7 Local Government Finance Act 1992 Sch 4 para 18(2)(a).
8 Local Government Finance Act 1992 Sch 4 para 18(2)(b).
9 Ie by any provision included by virtue of the Local Government Finance Act 1992 Sch 4 para 5(2)(g), Sch 4 para 5(2)(h), Sch 4 para 5(3)(a) or Sch 4 para 5(3)(b): see PARA 487.
10 As to the meaning of 'person' see PARA 11 note 13.
11 Local Government Finance Act 1992 Sch 4 para 18(3)(a).
12 Local Government Finance Act 1992 Sch 4 para 18(3)(b).
13 Ie an offence under any provision included by virtue of the Local Government Finance Act 1992 Sch 4 para 18(1)–(3): see the text to notes 1–12.
14 See the Local Government Finance Act 1992 Sch 4 para 18(4)(a). As to the powers of magistrates' courts to issue fines on summary conviction see SENTENCING vol 92 (2015) PARA 176.
15 See the Local Government Finance Act 1992 Sch 4 para 18(4)(b).

510. Offences.

A person[1] is guilty of an offence if, following a request[2], he is under a duty to supply information[3], and:

(1) he fails without reasonable excuse to supply[4] the information[5]; or

(2) in supplying information in purported compliance with that request[6] he makes a statement which is false in a material particular or recklessly makes a statement which is false in a material particular[7].

A person is guilty of an offence if, following the service on him of a copy of an attachment of allowances order[8] or an attachment of earnings order[9], he is under a duty to comply with the order[10] and he fails to do so[11]. It is a defence for a person charged with such an offence to prove that he took all reasonable steps to comply with the order[12].

A person is guilty of an offence if he is under a duty to notify another person[13], and:

(a) he fails without reasonable excuse to notify the other person in accordance with the provision concerned[14]; or

(b) in notifying the other person in purported compliance with the provision concerned, he makes a statement which he knows to be false in a material particular or recklessly makes a statement which is false in a material particular[15].

1 As to the meaning of 'person' see PARA 11 note 13.
2 Ie under the Council Tax (Administration and Enforcement) Regulations 1992, SI 1992/613, reg 36(2)(b): see PARA 480.
3 As to the meaning of 'information' see PARA 345 note 20.
4 Ie in accordance with the Council Tax (Administration and Enforcement) Regulations 1992, SI 1992/613, reg 36: see PARA 480.
5 Council Tax (Administration and Enforcement) Regulations 1992, SI 1992/613, reg 56(1)(a). A person guilty of an offence under reg 56(1)(a) is liable on summary conviction to a fine not exceeding level 2 on the standard scale: see reg 56(5). As to the powers of magistrates' courts to issue fines on summary conviction see SENTENCING vol 92 (2015) PARA 176.
6 Ie in purported compliance with the Council Tax (Administration and Enforcement) Regulations 1992, SI 1992/613, reg 36: see PARA 480.
7 See the Council Tax (Administration and Enforcement) Regulations 1992, SI 1992/613, reg 56(1)(b). A person guilty of an offence under reg 56(1)(b) is liable on summary conviction to a fine not exceeding level 3 on the standard scale: see reg 56(6).
8 As to attachment of allowances orders see PARA 475.
9 As to attachment of earnings orders see PARA 488.
10 Ie by virtue of the Council Tax (Administration and Enforcement) Regulations 1992, SI 1992/613, reg 37(3) (see PARA 488), including reg 37(3) as applied for the purposes of attachment of allowances orders by reg 44(7) (see PARA 495): see reg 56(2).
11 Council Tax (Administration and Enforcement) Regulations 1992, SI 1992/613, reg 56(2). A person guilty of an offence under reg 56(2) is liable on summary conviction to a fine not exceeding level 3 on the standard scale: see reg 56(6).
12 Council Tax (Administration and Enforcement) Regulations 1992, SI 1992/613, reg 56(3).
13 Ie under the Council Tax (Administration and Enforcement) Regulations 1992, SI 1992/613, reg 39(2), (3) or under reg 39(4), (5) (see PARA 490) (including those provisions as applied for the purposes of attachment of allowances orders by reg 44(7) (see PARA 495)), reg 39(6), (7) (see PARA 490) or reg 40 (see PARA 491): see reg 56(4).
14 Council Tax (Administration and Enforcement) Regulations 1992, SI 1992/613, reg 56(4)(a). A person guilty of an offence under reg 56(4)(a) is liable on summary conviction to a fine not exceeding level 2 on the standard scale: see reg 56(5).
15 Council Tax (Administration and Enforcement) Regulations 1992, SI 1992/613, reg 56(4)(b). A person guilty of an offence under reg 56(4)(b) is liable on summary conviction to a fine not exceeding level 3 on the standard scale: see reg 56(6).

(viii) Restriction on Debtors Participating in Local Authority Proceedings

511. Council tax: restrictions on voting.

If, at any time, a sum[1] which has become payable by a specified member of a local authority[2] in respect of council tax has not been paid by him, and has remained unpaid for at least two months[3], and if such a member is present at a meeting of the authority or committee or, in the case of a local authority which is operating executive arrangements, the executive of that authority or any committee of that executive[4] at which any of the following matters is the subject of consideration, namely[5]:

(1) any calculation required by the provisions of the Local Government Finance Act 1992 which govern the setting of council tax[6] or precepts[7], or which govern the limitation of either council tax or precepts[8];

(2) any recommendation, resolution or other decision which might affect the making of any such calculation[9]; or

(3) the exercise of any functions[10] relating to the administration and enforcement of council tax[11],

he must at the meeting, and as soon as practicable after its commencement, disclose the fact that these conditions apply to him, and he must not vote on any question with respect to the matter[12].

If a person fails to comply with this requirement he commits an offence[13], unless he proves that he did not know either that these restrictions applied to him at the time of the meeting[14] or that the matter in question was the subject of consideration at the meeting[15]. A prosecution for such an offence may not be instituted except by or on behalf of the Director of Public Prosecutions[16].

1 Ie a sum falling within the Local Government Finance Act 1992 Sch 4 para 1(1)(a) (see PARA 473): see s 106(1)(a). Provision was also made in relation to a sum falling within the Local Government Finance Act 1988 Sch 4 para 1(1)(a), (b), (d) or (ee) (repealed with savings) (corresponding provisions with respect to community charges): see the Local Government Finance Act 1992 s 106(1)(b). With effect from 1 April 1993, the community charge was abolished and replaced with the council tax: see PARA 344. As to council tax see PARA 344 et seq.

2 Ie a member of a local authority, or a member of a committee of a local authority or a member of a joint committee of two or more local authorities (including in either case a sub-committee): see the Local Government Finance Act 1992 s 106(1) (amended, in relation to England, by SI 2001/2237; and, in relation to Wales, by the Local Government (Wales) Measure 2011 ss 34(9)(a), 176(2), Sch 4 Pt B; and SI 2002/808). 'Local authority' has the same meaning as in the Local Government Act 1972 ss 94, 97 (pecuniary interests: now repealed): Local Government Finance Act 1992 s 106(6). Section 106(1) is also expressed, in relation to England, to apply to a council manager within the meaning of the Local Government Act 2000 s 11(4)(b): see the Local Government Finance Act 1992 s 106(1) (as so amended). However, the Local Government Act 2000 Pt II (ss 10–48) now applies only in relation to Wales and the position of council manager no longer exists in either England or Wales: see the amendments to Pt II made by the Local Government and Public Involvement in Health Act 2007 Pt 3 (ss 62–74) and the Local Government (Wales) Measure 2011 Sch 4 Pt B; and LOCAL GOVERNMENT vol 69 (2018) PARAS 21, 335 et seq. As to the meanings of 'England' and 'Wales' see PARA 2 note 16.

3 See the Local Government Finance Act 1992 s 106(1) (as amended: see note 2). As to the meaning of 'month' see PARA 11 note 1.

4 'Executive' and 'executive arrangements' have the same meanings as in the Local Government Act 2000 Pt II (ss 10–48) (see LOCAL GOVERNMENT vol 69 (2018) PARA 335): Local Government Finance Act 1992 s 116(1) (definition added, in relation to England, by SI 2001/2237; and, relation to Wales, by SI 2002/808). The Local Government Act 2000 Pt II now applies in relation to Wales only; as to the equivalent provisions in England see Pt 1A (ss 9B–9R); and LOCAL GOVERNMENT vol 69 (2018) PARA 295 et seq.

5 See the Local Government Finance Act 1992 s 106(2) (amended, in relation to England, by SI 2001/2237; and in relation to Wales by the Local Government (Wales) Measure 2011 ss 34(9)(b), 176(2), Sch 4 Pt B; and SI 2002/808). In the case of an authority which is operating executive arrangements, if or to the extent that any matter listed in the Local Government Finance Act 1992 s 106(2)(a)–(c) (see heads (1)–(3) in the text) is the responsibility of the executive of that authority, no member of the executive to whom s 106 applies may take any action or discharge any function with respect to that matter: s 106(2A) (added in relation to England by SI 2001/2237; and, in relation to Wales, by SI 2002/808).

6 Ie the Local Government Finance Act 1992 Pt I Ch III (ss 30–38) (see PARA 380 et seq), and Pt I Ch 4ZA (ss 52ZA–52ZY) (see PARA 391 et seq).

7 Ie the Local Government Finance Act 1992 Pt I Ch IV (ss 39–52) (see PARA 11 et seq): see s 106(2)(a).

8 Ie the Local Government Finance Act 1992 Pt I Ch IVA (ss 52A–52Y) (see PARA 21 et seq): see s 106(2)(a) (amended by the Local Government Act 1999 s 30, Sch 1 Pt II paras 2, 8; and the Localism Act 2011 s 72(2), Sch 6 paras 1, 31).

9 Local Government Finance Act 1992 s 106(2)(b).

10 Ie any functions under the Local Government Finance Act 1992 Schs 2–4: see PARA 437 et seq.

11 Local Government Finance Act 1992 s 106(2)(c). Provision was also made in relation to functions under the Local Government Finance Act 1988 Schs 2–4 (repealed with savings) (corresponding provision with respect to community charges): see the Local Government Finance Act 1992 s 106(2)(c).

12 See the Local Government Finance Act 1992 s 106(2) (as amended: see note 6). The Local Government Act 1972 s 97(1)–(3) (removal or exclusion of liability etc: repealed) applies in relation to the Local Government Finance Act 1992 s 106 and any disability imposed by it as it applies in relation to the Local Government Act 1972 s 94 (repealed) and any disability imposed by it: Local Government Finance Act 1992 s 106(5).

13 The penalty for each such offence is, on summary conviction, a fine not exceeding level 3 on the standard scale: see the Local Government Finance Act 1992 s 106(3). As to the powers of magistrates' courts to issue fines on summary conviction see SENTENCING vol 92 (2015) PARA 176.

14 Local Government Finance Act 1992 s 106(3)(a).

15 Local Government Finance Act 1992 s 106(3)(b).

16 Local Government Finance Act 1992 s 106(4). As to the Director of Public Prosecutions see CRIMINAL PROCEDURE vol 27 (2015) PARA 25.

(8) Appeals Relating to Council Tax

(i) Valuation Tribunals

512. In general.

Valuation and community charge tribunals formerly established under the Local Government Finance Act 1988[1] are now known as valuation tribunals[2]; and 'valuation tribunal' means:

(1) in relation to England, the Valuation Tribunal for England[3]; and

(2) in relation to Wales, a valuation tribunal established under the Local Government Finance Act 1988[4].

In addition to the jurisdiction conferred on them by or under the Local Government Finance Act 1988[5], valuation tribunals exercise the jurisdiction conferred on them by or under the Local Government Finance Act 1992[6].

1 Ie under the Local Government Finance Act 1988 Sch 11 (as originally enacted).

2 See the Local Government Finance Act 1992 s 15(1).

3 See the Local Government Finance Act 1992 s 69(1) (definition substituted by the Local Government and Public Involvement in Health Act 2007 s 220(1), Sch 16 para 7). As to the Valuation Tribunal for England see PARA 232. As to the meaning of 'England' see PARA 2 note 16.

4 Ie under the Local Government Finance Act 1992 Sch 11 para 1 (see PARA 236): see s 69(1) (definition as substituted: see note 3). As to the meaning of 'Wales' see PARA 2 note 16.

5 As to the jurisdiction conferred on the Valuation Tribunal for England by the Local Government Finance Act 1988 see PARA 232; and as to the jurisdiction so conferred on valuation tribunals in Wales see PARA 237.

6 See the Local Government Finance Act 1992 s 15(2). The jurisdiction concerned is that conferred by:

(1) s 16 (see PARA 513) (s 15(2)(a));

(2) regulations made under s 24 (see PARA 417) (s 15(2)(b)); and

(3) Sch 3 para 3 (see PARA 471) (s 15(2)(c)).

(ii) Appeals to Valuation Tribunals

A. IN GENERAL

513. Appeals to valuation tribunals.

A person[1] may appeal to a valuation tribunal[2] if he is aggrieved by[3]:

(1) any decision of a billing authority[4] that a dwelling is a chargeable dwelling[5], or that he is liable to pay council tax[6] in respect of such a dwelling[7]; or

(2) any calculation made by such an authority of an amount[8] which he is liable to pay to the authority in respect of council tax[9].

No such appeal may be made unless the aggrieved person serves a written notice[10], and one of the following conditions is fulfilled[11], namely that:

(a) the aggrieved person is notified in writing, by the authority on which he served the notice, that the authority believes the grievance is not well founded, but the person is still aggrieved[12];

(b) the aggrieved person is notified in writing, by the authority on which he served the notice, that steps have been taken to deal with the grievance, but the person is still aggrieved[13];

(c) the period of two months[14], beginning with the date of service of the aggrieved person's notice, has ended without his being notified under head (a) or (b) above[15].

Where a written notice is served on an authority by an aggrieved person in this way[16], the authority must:

(i) consider the matter to which the notice relates[17];

(ii) include in any notification under head (a) above the reasons for the belief concerned[18];

(iii) include in any notification under head (b) above a statement of the steps taken[19].

1 As to the meaning of 'person' see PARA 11 note 13.

2 As to the meaning of 'valuation tribunal' see PARA 512.

3 Local Government Finance Act 1992 s 16(1). Section 16(1) does not apply where the grounds on which the person concerned is aggrieved fall within such category or categories as may be prescribed: s 16(3). 'Prescribed' means prescribed by regulations made by the Secretary of State or, in relation to Wales, the Welsh Ministers: see s 116(1). As to the Secretary of State and the Welsh Ministers see PARA 4 note 18. As to the meaning of 'Wales' see PARA 2 note 16. The functions of the Secretary of State under the Local Government Finance Act 1992 s 16, so far as exercisable in relation to Wales, were transferred to the National Assembly for Wales (see the National Assembly for Wales (Transfer of Functions) Order 1999, SI 1999/672, art 2, Sch 1) and are now vested in the Welsh Ministers (see the Government of Wales Act 2006 s 162(1), Sch 11 para 30).

The Local Government Finance Act 1992 s 16(1) does not apply where the ground on which the person concerned is aggrieved is that any assumption as to the future that is required by the Council Tax (Administration and Enforcement) Regulations 1992, SI 1992/613, Pt V (regs 17–31) (see PARA 452 et seq) to be made in the calculation of an amount may prove to be inaccurate: reg 30.

A valuation tribunal has no jurisdiction under the Local Government Finance Act 1992 s 16 to investigate the question whether the billing authority is in breach of its obligations in relation to demand notices under the Council Tax (Administration and Enforcement) Regulations 1992, SI 1992/613, reg 18 (see PARA 452) or reg 19 (see PARA 457): see *Hardy v Sefton Metropolitan Borough Council* [2006] EWHC 1928 (Admin), [2007] RA 140, [2006] All ER (D) 409 (Jul).

4 As to the meaning of 'billing authority' see PARA 346.

5 As to the meaning of 'dwelling' see PARA 349. As to the meaning of 'chargeable dwelling' see PARA 350.

6 As to persons liable to pay council tax see PARA 354 et seq. As to council tax see PARA 344 et seq.

7 Local Government Finance Act 1992 s 16(1)(a).

8 This reference to any calculation of an amount includes a reference to any estimate of the amount: see the Local Government Finance Act 1992 s 16(2).

9 Local Government Finance Act 1992 s 16(1)(b). As to the meaning of references to an amount payable in respect of council tax see PARA 361 note 3.

10 Local Government Finance Act 1992 s 16(4)(a). As to the meaning of 'written' see PARA 21 note 3. A notice under s 16(4) must be served on the billing authority concerned (s 16(5)); and must state the matter by which and the grounds on which the person is aggrieved (s 16(6)).

11 Local Government Finance Act 1992 s 16(4)(b).

12 Local Government Finance Act 1992 s 16(7)(a).

13 Local Government Finance Act 1992 s 16(7)(b).

14 As to the meaning of 'month' see PARA 11 note 1.

15 Local Government Finance Act 1992 s 16(7)(c).
16 Ie under the Local Government Finance Act 1992 s 16(4): see the text to notes 10–11.
17 Local Government Finance Act 1992 s 16(8)(a).
18 Local Government Finance Act 1992 s 16(8)(b).
19 Local Government Finance Act 1992 s 16(8)(c).

514. Jurisdiction.

Appeals to valuation tribunals[1] arise in relation to council tax where[2]:

(1) a person is aggrieved by any decision of a billing authority that a dwelling is a chargeable dwelling, or that he is liable to pay council tax in respect of such a dwelling[3]; or
(2) a person is aggrieved by any calculation made by a billing authority of an amount which he is liable to pay to the authority in respect of council tax[4];
(3) a person proposing an alteration to a valuation list objects to the proposal being treated as invalidly made[5];
(4) there is a disagreement as to a proposed alteration of a valuation list[6];
(5) a person objects to the service on him of a completion notice[7];
(6) a person is aggrieved by the imposition on him by a billing authority of a penalty[8].

1 As to the meaning of 'valuation tribunal' see PARA 512.
2 See the Valuation Tribunal for England (Council Tax and Rating Appeals) (Procedure) Regulations 2009, SI 2009/2269, reg 2(1); the Council Tax (Alteration of Lists and Appeals) Regulations 1993, SI 1993/290, reg 16; and the Valuation Tribunal for Wales Regulations 2010, SI 2010/713, reg 27(1).
3 Ie an appeal under the Local Government Finance Act 1992 s 16: see PARA 513.
4 Ie an appeal under the Local Government Finance Act 1992 s 16: see PARA 513.
5 Ie an appeal under the Council Tax (Alteration of Lists and Appeals) (England) Regulations 2009, SI 2009/2270, reg 7 (see PARA 422) or the Council Tax (Alteration of Lists and Appeals) Regulations 1993, SI 1993/290, reg 8 (see PARA 431).
6 Ie an appeal under the Council Tax (Alteration of Lists and Appeals) (England) Regulations 2009, SI 2009/2270, reg 10 (see PARA 424) or the Council Tax (Alteration of Lists and Appeals) Regulations 1993, SI 1993/290, reg 13 (see PARA 434).
7 Ie an appeal under the Local Government Finance Act 1988 Sch 4A para 4 as it applies for the purposes of the Local Government Finance Act 1992 Pt I (ss 1–69): see s 17; and PARA 353.
8 Ie an appeal under the Local Government Finance Act 1992 Sch 3 para 3: see PARA 471.

B. PROCEDURE: ENGLAND

515. Conduct of appeals.

In giving effect to the Valuation Tribunal for England (Council Tax and Rating Appeals) (Procedure) Regulations[1] and in exercising any of its functions under the regulations, the Valuation Tribunal for England[2] must have regard to:

(1) dealing with appeals[3] in ways which are proportionate to the importance of the appeal, the complexity of the issues, the anticipated costs and the resources of the parties[4];
(2) avoiding unnecessary formality and seeking flexibility in the proceedings[5];
(3) ensuring, so far as practicable, that the parties are able to participate fully in the proceedings[6];
(4) using any special expertise of the tribunal effectively[7]; and
(5) avoiding delay, so far as compatible with proper consideration of the issues[8].

The tribunal must acknowledge receipt of every notice of appeal within two weeks of its receipt and must send a copy of the notice of appeal and any accompanying documents to every party (other than the appellant) as soon as reasonably practicable after receiving the notice of appeal[9].

An irregularity resulting from failure to comply with any requirement in the regulations or a direction[10] does not of itself render void the proceedings or any step taken in the proceedings[11]. If a party has failed to comply with a requirement in the regulations or a direction, the tribunal may take such action as it considers just, which may include:

(a) waiving the requirement[12];
(b) requiring the failure to be remedied[13]; or
(c) exercising the power[14] to give a direction[15].

The tribunal may not make any order in respect of costs[16].

Provision is made as to the sending and delivery of documents[17]. An act required by the regulations or a direction to be done on or by a particular day must be done by 5 pm on that day[18].

1 Ie the Valuation Tribunal for England (Council Tax and Rating Appeals) (Procedure) Regulations 2009, SI 2009/2269. These regulations apply in England only: see reg 1. As to the equivalent regulations in relation to Wales see the Council Tax (Alteration of Lists and Appeals) Regulations 1993, SI 1993/290, Pt III (regs 16–34); and the Valuation Tribunal for Wales Regulations 2010, SI 2010/713, Pt 5 (regs 27–46); and see PARA 534 et seq. As to the meanings of 'England' and 'Wales' see PARA 2 note 16.

2 As to the Valuation Tribunal for England see PARA 232.

3 As to appeals in relation to council tax see PARA 514.

4 Valuation Tribunal for England (Council Tax and Rating Appeals) (Procedure) Regulations 2009, SI 2009/2269, reg 3(a). Any reference to a 'party':

(1) in relation to an appeal under the Local Government Finance Act 1992 s 16 (see PARA 513), means the appellant and the billing authority (Valuation Tribunal for England (Council Tax and Rating Appeals) (Procedure) Regulations 2009, SI 2009/2269, reg 2(3)(a));
(2) in relation to an appeal under the Council Tax (Alteration of Lists and Appeals) (England) Regulations 2009, SI 2009/2270, reg 7 or reg 10 (see PARAS 422, 424), includes the appellant and the listing officer and:
 (a) where the appeal is under reg 10, the taxpayer for the time being as regards any dwelling to which the decision notice relates, any competent appellant, and any competent party (Valuation Tribunal for England (Council Tax and Rating Appeals) (Procedure) Regulations 2009, SI 2009/2269, reg 2(3)(b)(i));
 (b) where the appeal is proceeding by virtue of reg 22 (new appellant's appeal: see PARA 527), includes the appellant and the listing officer, and:
  (i) any other person who, in response to the request in the tribunal's notice under reg 23(1) (other parties to new appeal: see PARA 526), has within the period specified in the notice served a notice informing the tribunal of that person's wish to be a party (reg 2(3)(b)(ii)(aa)); and
  (ii) any other person who becomes a competent party after the date on which the tribunal's notice was served under reg 23(1) (reg 2(3)(b)(ii)(bb));
(3) in relation to an appeal against imposition of a penalty, means the appellant and the authority which imposed the penalty (reg 2(3)(c));
(4) if the proceedings on an appeal have been concluded, means a person who was a party when the tribunal finally disposed of all issues in the proceedings (reg 2(3)(e)).

'Appellant', unless the context otherwise requires, means (reg 2(1)):

(A) a person who makes an appeal under the Local Government Finance Act 1992 s 16;
(B) a person who makes an appeal under the Council Tax (Alteration of Lists and Appeals) (England) Regulations 2009, SI 2009/2270, reg 7 or reg 10; or
(C) where a person has been substituted under the Valuation Tribunal for England (Council Tax and Rating Appeals) (Procedure) Regulations 2009, SI 2009/2269, reg 11(1) (see PARA 521), that person.

As to the meaning of 'billing authority' see PARA 346. 'Listing officer', in relation to a list, means the officer charged with its maintenance under the Local Government Finance Act 1992 s 22 (see

PARA 409); and 'list' means a valuation list compiled under s 22: Valuation Tribunal for England (Council Tax and Rating Appeals) (Procedure) Regulations 2009, SI 2009/2269, reg 2(1). 'Taxpayer', in relation to a dwelling and a day, means the person who is liable (whether solely or jointly and severally) to pay council tax in respect of the dwelling and the day: reg 2(1). As to the meaning of 'dwelling' see PARA 349. As to persons liable to pay council tax see PARA 354 et seq.

'Competent appellant', in relation to a proposal for the alteration of a list, an appeal under the Council Tax (Alteration of Lists and Appeals) (England) Regulations 2009, SI 2009/2270, reg 7 or 10 or the withdrawal of such an appeal, means a person who has appealed against the listing officer's decision in respect of the proposal or appeal (whether or not that person's appeal proceeds): Valuation Tribunal for England (Council Tax and Rating Appeals) (Procedure) Regulations 2009, SI 2009/2269, reg 2(1). As to the meaning of 'person' see PARA 11 note 13.

'Competent party', in relation to a proposal for the alteration of a list, an appeal under the Council Tax (Alteration of Lists and Appeals) (England) Regulations 2009, SI 2009/2270, regs 7 or 10 or the withdrawal of such an appeal, means an interested person who serves a notice on the listing officer and the tribunal in accordance with the Valuation Tribunal for England (Council Tax and Rating Appeals) (Procedure) Regulations 2009, SI 2009/2269, reg 27 (competent party to appeal: see PARA 520): reg 2(1). 'Interested person', in relation to a dwelling and a day, means (reg 2(1)):

(I) the owner;
(II) where the Local Government Finance Act 1992 s 8(3) (see PARA 356) has effect on the day, and regulations provide for that subsection to have effect as if, for the reference to the owner, there were substituted a reference to another person, that other person;
(III) in relation to an exempt dwelling or a dwelling in respect of which the amount set under s 30 (see PARA 380) for the financial year is nil, any person (other than the owner) who would be liable to pay council tax if the dwelling were not an exempt dwelling or, as the case may be, the amount so set were other than nil; and
(IV) any other person who is a taxpayer in respect of the dwelling.

As to the meaning of 'owner' see PARA 354 note 15. As to the meaning of 'exempt dwelling' see PARA 351.

5 Valuation Tribunal for England (Council Tax and Rating Appeals) (Procedure) Regulations 2009, SI 2009/2269, reg 3(b).
6 Valuation Tribunal for England (Council Tax and Rating Appeals) (Procedure) Regulations 2009, SI 2009/2269, reg 3(c).
7 Valuation Tribunal for England (Council Tax and Rating Appeals) (Procedure) Regulations 2009, SI 2009/2269, reg 3(d).
8 Valuation Tribunal for England (Council Tax and Rating Appeals) (Procedure) Regulations 2009, SI 2009/2269, reg 3(e).
9 Valuation Tribunal for England (Council Tax and Rating Appeals) (Procedure) Regulations 2009, SI 2009/2269, reg 28(2). If an appellant provides notice of appeal against the imposition of a penalty to the tribunal later than the time required by the Council Tax (Alteration of Lists and Appeals) (England) Regulations 2009, SI 2009/2270, or by an extension of time allowed under the Valuation Tribunal for England (Council Tax and Rating Appeals) (Procedure) Regulations 2009, SI 2009/2269, reg 6(3)(a) (appeal management powers: see PARA 516), the tribunal must not admit the notice of appeal unless the tribunal extends time for the notice of appeal under that provision: see reg 28(1). As to the power of the tribunal to correct errors in documents produced by it see PARA 521.
10 As to the power of the tribunal to give directions in relation to the conduct or disposal of proceedings see PARA 516. As to directions generally see PARA 521. As to directions relating to evidence and information see PARA 524.
11 Valuation Tribunal for England (Council Tax and Rating Appeals) (Procedure) Regulations 2009, SI 2009/2269, reg 9(1).
12 Valuation Tribunal for England (Council Tax and Rating Appeals) (Procedure) Regulations 2009, SI 2009/2269, reg 9(2)(a).
13 Valuation Tribunal for England (Council Tax and Rating Appeals) (Procedure) Regulations 2009, SI 2009/2269, reg 9(2)(b).
14 Ie under the Valuation Tribunal for England (Council Tax and Rating Appeals) (Procedure) Regulations 2009, SI 2009/2269, reg 8: see PARA 245.
15 Valuation Tribunal for England (Council Tax and Rating Appeals) (Procedure) Regulations 2009, SI 2009/2269, reg 9(2)(c).
16 Valuation Tribunal for England (Council Tax and Rating Appeals) (Procedure) Regulations 2009, SI 2009/2269, reg 12.

17 Any document to be provided to the tribunal under the regulations or a direction must be:
(1) sent by pre-paid post or delivered by hand to the address specified for the proceedings (Valuation Tribunal for England (Council Tax and Rating Appeals) (Procedure) Regulations 2009, SI 2009/2269, reg 15(1)(a));
(2) sent by fax to the number specified for the proceedings (reg 15(1)(b)); or
(3) sent or delivered by such other method and to such address as may be agreed by the tribunal and the person by whom the documents are to be sent or delivered (reg 15(1)(c)).

If a party provides a fax number, email address or other details for the electronic transmission of documents to it, that party must accept delivery of documents by that method: reg 15(2). However, if a party informs the tribunal and all other parties that a particular form of communication (other than pre-paid post or delivery by hand) should not be used to provide documents to that party, that form of communication must not be used: reg 15(3). If the tribunal or a party sends a document to a party or the tribunal by email or any other electronic means of communication, the recipient may request that the sender provide a hard copy of the document to the recipient (reg 15(4)); and such a request must be made as soon as reasonably practicable after the recipient receives the document electronically (reg 15(5)). The tribunal and each party may assume that the address provided by a party or its representative is and remains the address to which documents should be sent or delivered until receiving written notification to the contrary: reg 15(6). As to service by post generally see PARA 139 note 3.

18 Valuation Tribunal for England (Council Tax and Rating Appeals) (Procedure) Regulations 2009, SI 2009/2269, reg 14(1). If the time specified by the regulations or a direction for doing any act ends on a day other than a working day, the act is done in time if it is done on the next working day: reg 14(2). 'Working day' means any day except a Saturday or Sunday, Christmas Day, Good Friday or a bank holiday under the Bank and Financial Dealings Act 1971 s 1 (see TIME vol 97 (2015) PARA 321): Valuation Tribunal for England (Council Tax and Rating Appeals) (Procedure) Regulations 2009, SI 2009/2269, reg 14(3).

516. Appeal management.

It is the duty of the president of the Valuation Tribunal for England[1] to ensure that arrangements are made for the determination of appeals[2].

Subject as otherwise provided[3], the tribunal may regulate its own procedure[4]. The tribunal may give a direction in relation to the conduct or disposal of proceedings at any time, including a direction amending, suspending or setting aside an earlier direction[5]. In particular, and without restricting these general powers[6], the tribunal may:
(1) extend or shorten the time for complying with any regulation or direction[7];
(2) consolidate or hear together two or more sets of proceedings or parts of proceedings raising common issues, or treat[8] an appeal as a lead appeal[9];
(3) permit or require a party[10] to amend a document[11];
(4) permit or require a party or another person[12] to provide documents, evidence, information, or submissions to the tribunal or a party[13];
(5) deal with an issue in proceedings as a preliminary issue[14];
(6) hold a hearing to consider any matter, including a case management issue[15];
(7) decide the form of any hearing[16];
(8) adjourn or postpone a hearing[17];
(9) require a party to produce a bundle for a hearing[18];
(10) stay proceedings[19]; or
(11) suspend the effect of its own decision pending the determination by the Upper Tribunal[20] or a court of an application for permission to appeal against, and any appeal against or review of, that decision[21].

If two or more related appeals have been made[22] to the tribunal[23], and as regards each of the related appeals the tribunal has not made a decision disposing of the proceedings[24] and the related appeals give rise to common or related issues of fact or law[25], then the tribunal may give a direction specifying one or more of the related appeals as a lead appeal or lead appeals[26] and staying the other related appeals[27]. When the tribunal makes a decision in respect of the common or related issues, it must send a copy of that decision to each party in each of the related appeals[28]; and that decision is binding on each of those parties[29] unless, within one month[30] after the date on which the tribunal sends a copy of the decision to a party, that party applies in writing[31] for a direction that the decision does not apply to, and is not binding on the parties to, a particular related appeal[32].

If before the tribunal makes a decision in respect of the common or related issues the lead appeal is withdrawn[33] or, where there is more than one lead appeal, all of the lead appeals are withdrawn[34], the tribunal must give directions as to whether another appeal or other appeals are to be specified as a lead appeal or appeals[35].

1 As to the Valuation Tribunal for England see PARA 232. As to the president of the tribunal, and membership of the tribunal generally, see PARA 233. The Valuation Tribunal for England (Council Tax and Rating Appeals) (Procedure) Regulations 2009, SI 2009/2269, apply in relation to England only: see reg 1. As to the equivalent regulations in relation to Wales see the Council Tax (Alteration of Lists and Appeals) Regulations 1993, SI 1993/290, Pt III (regs 16–34); and the Valuation Tribunal for Wales Regulations 2010, SI 2010/713, Pt 5 (regs 27–46); and see PARA 534 et seq. As to the meanings of 'England' and 'Wales' see PARA 2 note 16.

2 See the Valuation Tribunal for England (Council Tax and Rating Appeals) (Procedure) Regulations 2009, SI 2009/2269, reg 5(1). As to appeals in relation to council tax see PARA 514. The arrangements must provide for appeals to be to be determined in accordance with the provisions of regs 6–44 (see the text to notes 3–35; and PARAS 515, 519 et seq); see reg 5(1). The tribunal must not deal with an appeal under the Council Tax (Alteration of Lists and Appeals) (England) Regulations 2009, SI 2009/2270, reg 10 (see PARA 424) until any appeal under reg 7 (see PARA 422) in respect of the same proposal has been decided: Valuation Tribunal for England (Council Tax and Rating Appeals) (Procedure) Regulations 2009, SI 2009/2269, reg 5(2). 'Proposal' means a proposal for the alteration of a list: reg 2(1). As to the meaning of 'list' see PARA 515 note 4. Where two or more appeals relating to the same dwelling or dwellings are referred under the Council Tax (Alteration of Lists and Appeals) (England) Regulations 2009, SI 2009/2270, reg 10, the order in which the appeals are dealt with must be the order in which the alterations in question would, but for the disagreements which occasion the appeals, have taken effect: see the Valuation Tribunal for England (Council Tax and Rating Appeals) (Procedure) Regulations 2009, SI 2009/2269, reg 5(3). As to the meaning of 'dwelling' see PARA 349. As to the alteration of lists see PARA 417 et seq.

3 Ie subject to the provisions of the Local Government Finance Act 1988 Sch 11 Pt I (see PARA 232) and the Valuation Tribunal for England (Council Tax and Rating Appeals) (Procedure) Regulations 2009, SI 2009/2269: see reg 6(1).

4 Valuation Tribunal for England (Council Tax and Rating Appeals) (Procedure) Regulations 2009, SI 2009/2269, reg 6(1).

5 Valuation Tribunal for England (Council Tax and Rating Appeals) (Procedure) Regulations 2009, SI 2009/2269, reg 6(2). As to directions see also PARAS 521, 524. As to the striking out of proceedings see PARA 521.

6 Ie the powers in the Valuation Tribunal for England (Council Tax and Rating Appeals) (Procedure) Regulations 2009, SI 2009/2269, reg 6(1), (2): see the text to notes 3–5.

7 Valuation Tribunal for England (Council Tax and Rating Appeals) (Procedure) Regulations 2009, SI 2009/2269, reg 6(3)(a). As to the calculation of time generally see reg 14; and PARA 515.

8 Ie whether in accordance with the Valuation Tribunal for England (Council Tax and Rating Appeals) (Procedure) Regulations 2009, SI 2009/2269, reg 7 (see the text to notes 22–35) or otherwise.

9 Valuation Tribunal for England (Council Tax and Rating Appeals) (Procedure) Regulations 2009, SI 2009/2269, reg 6(3)(b).

10 As to the meaning of 'party' see PARA 515 note 4.

11 Valuation Tribunal for England (Council Tax and Rating Appeals) (Procedure) Regulations 2009, SI 2009/2269, reg 6(3)(c) (amended by SI 2017/156).

12 As to the meaning of 'person' see PARA 11 note 13.

13 Valuation Tribunal for England (Council Tax and Rating Appeals) (Procedure) Regulations 2009, SI 2009/2269, reg 6(3)(d). This is subject to reg 17 (see PARA 524): reg 6(3)(d) (amended by SI 2017/156). As to the service and delivery of documents see the Valuation Tribunal for England (Council Tax and Rating Appeals) (Procedure) Regulations 2009, SI 2009/2269, reg 15; and PARA 515.
14 Valuation Tribunal for England (Council Tax and Rating Appeals) (Procedure) Regulations 2009, SI 2009/2269, reg 6(3)(e).
15 Valuation Tribunal for England (Council Tax and Rating Appeals) (Procedure) Regulations 2009, SI 2009/2269, reg 6(3)(f).
16 Valuation Tribunal for England (Council Tax and Rating Appeals) (Procedure) Regulations 2009, SI 2009/2269, reg 6(3)(g).
17 Valuation Tribunal for England (Council Tax and Rating Appeals) (Procedure) Regulations 2009, SI 2009/2269, reg 6(3)(h).
18 Valuation Tribunal for England (Council Tax and Rating Appeals) (Procedure) Regulations 2009, SI 2009/2269, reg 6(3)(i).
19 Valuation Tribunal for England (Council Tax and Rating Appeals) (Procedure) Regulations 2009, SI 2009/2269, reg 6(3)(j).
20 As to the Upper Tribunal see COURTS AND TRIBUNALS vol 24 (2010) PARA 874 et seq.
21 Valuation Tribunal for England (Council Tax and Rating Appeals) (Procedure) Regulations 2009, SI 2009/2269, reg 6(3)(k). As to appeals from decisions of the Valuation Tribunal for England see PARA 560.
22 Ie under the Council Tax (Alteration of Lists and Appeals) (England) Regulations 2009, SI 2009/2270, reg 10: see PARA 424.
23 See the Valuation Tribunal for England (Council Tax and Rating Appeals) (Procedure) Regulations 2009, SI 2009/2269, reg 7(1)(a)(i).
24 See the Valuation Tribunal for England (Council Tax and Rating Appeals) (Procedure) Regulations 2009, SI 2009/2269, reg 7(1)(b).
25 See the Valuation Tribunal for England (Council Tax and Rating Appeals) (Procedure) Regulations 2009, SI 2009/2269, reg 7(1)(c).
26 See the Valuation Tribunal for England (Council Tax and Rating Appeals) (Procedure) Regulations 2009, SI 2009/2269, reg 7(2)(a).
27 See the Valuation Tribunal for England (Council Tax and Rating Appeals) (Procedure) Regulations 2009, SI 2009/2269, reg 7(2)(b). The tribunal must give directions in respect of appeals which are so stayed, providing for the disposal of, or further directions in, those appeals: reg 7(5).
28 Valuation Tribunal for England (Council Tax and Rating Appeals) (Procedure) Regulations 2009, SI 2009/2269, reg 7(3)(a).
29 Valuation Tribunal for England (Council Tax and Rating Appeals) (Procedure) Regulations 2009, SI 2009/2269, reg 7(3)(b).
30 As to the meaning of 'month' see PARA 11 note 1.
31 As to the meaning of 'writing' see PARA 21 note 3.
32 See the Valuation Tribunal for England (Council Tax and Rating Appeals) (Procedure) Regulations 2009, SI 2009/2269, reg 7(4).
33 Valuation Tribunal for England (Council Tax and Rating Appeals) (Procedure) Regulations 2009, SI 2009/2269, reg 7(6)(a). As to the withdrawal of appeals see PARA 526.
34 Valuation Tribunal for England (Council Tax and Rating Appeals) (Procedure) Regulations 2009, SI 2009/2269, reg 7(6)(b).
35 Valuation Tribunal for England (Council Tax and Rating Appeals) (Procedure) Regulations 2009, SI 2009/2269, reg 7(6)(i). Any direction affecting the related appeals should be set aside or amended: reg 7(6)(ii).

517. Where notice of appeal is required.

An appeal against a decision of a billing authority that a dwelling is a chargeable dwelling, or that a person is liable to pay council tax in respect of such a dwelling, or against any calculation made by a billing authority of an amount which a person is liable to pay to the authority in respect of council tax[1], must be initiated by giving written[2] notice of appeal to the Valuation Tribunal for England[3].

A notice of appeal in such a case must include the following particulars[4]:

(1) the full name and address of the appellant[5];

(2) the address of the relevant chargeable dwelling[6], if different from the address referred to in head (1)[7];

(3) the date on which the written notice of the appellant's grievance[8] was served and the name of the authority on which it was served[9];

(4) the date, if applicable, on which the appellant was notified by the authority[10] that the authority believes the grievance is not well founded or that steps have been taken to deal with the grievance[11];

(5) the grounds on which the appellant is aggrieved[12];

(6) brief reasons why the appellant considers that the decision or calculation made by the authority was incorrect[13]; and

(7) where the appellant has also made an appeal to the First-tier Tribunal in connection with housing benefit[14] and the appeal raises common issues of fact with the appeal relating to council tax[15], a statement to that effect[16].

1 Ie an appeal under the Local Government Finance Act 1992 s 16: see PARA 513.
2 As to the meaning of 'written' see PARA 21 note 3.
3 Valuation Tribunal for England (Council Tax and Rating Appeals) (Procedure) Regulations 2009, SI 2009/2269, reg 20A(1) (reg 20A added by SI 2013/465). As to the Valuation Tribunal for England see PARA 232.

The Valuation Tribunal for England (Council Tax and Rating Appeals) (Procedure) Regulations 2009, SI 2009/2269, apply in relation to England only: see reg 1. As to the equivalent regulations in relation to Wales see the Council Tax (Alteration of Lists and Appeals) Regulations 1993, SI 1993/290, Pt III (regs 16–34); and the Valuation Tribunal for Wales Regulations 2010, SI 2010/713, Pt 5 (regs 27–46); and see PARA 534 et seq. As to the meanings of 'England' and 'Wales' see PARA 2 note 16.
4 Valuation Tribunal for England (Council Tax and Rating Appeals) (Procedure) Regulations 2009, SI 2009/2269, reg 20A(2) (as added: see note 3).
5 Valuation Tribunal for England (Council Tax and Rating Appeals) (Procedure) Regulations 2009, SI 2009/2269, reg 20A(2)(a) (as added: see note 3). As to the meaning of 'appellant' see PARA 515 note 4.
6 As to the meaning of 'dwelling' see PARA 349. As to the meaning of 'chargeable dwelling' see PARA 350.
7 Valuation Tribunal for England (Council Tax and Rating Appeals) (Procedure) Regulations 2009, SI 2009/2269, reg 20A(2)(b) (as added: see note 3).
8 Ie under the Local Government Finance Act 1992 s 16(4)(a):see PARA 513.
9 Valuation Tribunal for England (Council Tax and Rating Appeals) (Procedure) Regulations 2009, SI 2009/2269, reg 20A(2)(c) (as added: see note 3).
10 Ie in accordance with the Local Government Finance Act 1992 s 16(7)(a) or (b): see PARA 513.
11 Valuation Tribunal for England (Council Tax and Rating Appeals) (Procedure) Regulations 2009, SI 2009/2269, reg 20A(2)(d) (as added: see note 3).
12 Valuation Tribunal for England (Council Tax and Rating Appeals) (Procedure) Regulations 2009, SI 2009/2269, reg 20A(2)(e) (as added: see note 3).
13 Valuation Tribunal for England (Council Tax and Rating Appeals) (Procedure) Regulations 2009, SI 2009/2269, reg 20A(2)(f) (as added: see note 3).
14 Ie in accordance with the Housing Benefit and Council Tax Benefit (Decisions and Appeals) Regulations 2001, SI 2001/1002: see WELFARE BENEFITS AND STATE PENSIONS vol 104 (2014) PARA 329.
15 Ie the appeal made under the Local Government Finance Act 1992 s 16.
16 Valuation Tribunal for England (Council Tax and Rating Appeals) (Procedure) Regulations 2009, SI 2009/2269, reg 20A(2)(g) (as added: see note 3).

518. Time limits in relation to appeals.

If an appellant[1] provides notice of appeal[2] against a completion notice[3] or the imposition of a penalty to the Valuation Tribunal for England[4] later than the time required[5], the tribunal must not admit the notice of appeal unless the tribunal extends time[6] for the notice of appeal[7]. The tribunal must acknowledge receipt of every notice of appeal within two weeks of its receipt and must send[8] a copy of the notice of appeal and any accompanying documents to every party[9] (other than the appellant) as soon as reasonably practicable after receiving the notice of appeal[10].

The Valuation Tribunal for England must dismiss an appeal by a person[11] in relation to whom one or other of the qualifying conditions[12] is fulfilled unless the appeal is initiated within two months[13] of the date of service of the billing authority's notice[14]. Where the billing authority does not serve a notice[15] the tribunal must dismiss an appeal by an aggrieved person unless the appeal is initiated within four months of the date of service[16] of that person's notice[17].

The tribunal must dismiss an appeal against a penalty unless the appeal is initiated within two months of the date of service of written notice of the imposition of the penalty[18].

The tribunal must dismiss an appeal against a completion notice unless the appeal is initiated within 28 days of the date of service of the notice[19].

The president of the Valuation Tribunal for England[20] may authorise an appeal to be entertained where he is satisfied that the failure of the person aggrieved to initiate the appeal[21] has arisen by reason of circumstances beyond that person's control[22].

1 As to the meaning of 'appellant' see PARA 515 note 4.

2 As to appeals in relation to council tax see PARA 514.

3 'Completion notice' means a notice under the Local Government Finance Act 1988 Sch 4A para 1 (see PARA 138) as it applies for the purposes of the Local Government Finance Act 1992 Pt I (ss 1–69) (see s 17; and PARA 353): Valuation Tribunal for England (Council Tax and Rating Appeals) (Procedure) Regulations 2009, SI 2009/2269, reg 2(1).

4 As to the Valuation Tribunal for England see PARA 232. The Valuation Tribunal for England (Council Tax and Rating Appeals) (Procedure) Regulations 2009, SI 2009/2269, apply in relation to England only: see reg 1. As to the equivalent regulations in relation to Wales see the Council Tax (Alteration of Lists and Appeals) Regulations 1993, SI 1993/290, Pt III (regs 16–34); and the Valuation Tribunal for Wales Regulations 2010, SI 2010/713, Pt 5 (regs 27–46); and see PARA 534 et seq. As to the meanings of 'England' and 'Wales' see PARA 2 note 16.

5 Ie the time required by the Council Tax (Alteration of Lists and Appeals) (England) Regulations 2009, SI 2009/2270, or by an extension of time allowed under the Valuation Tribunal for England (Council Tax and Rating Appeals) (Procedure) Regulations 2009, SI 2009/2269, reg 6(3)(a) (appeal management powers: see PARA 516): see reg 28(1).

6 Ie under the Valuation Tribunal for England (Council Tax and Rating Appeals) (Procedure) Regulations 2009, SI 2009/2269, reg 6(3)(a): see PARA 516.

7 Valuation Tribunal for England (Council Tax and Rating Appeals) (Procedure) Regulations 2009, SI 2009/2269, reg 28(1).

8 As to the service and delivery of documents see PARA 515.

9 As to the meaning of 'party' see PARA 515 note 4.

10 Valuation Tribunal for England (Council Tax and Rating Appeals) (Procedure) Regulations 2009, SI 2009/2269, reg 28(2). Where a notice is received from a person who is an interested person for the purposes of reg 27(2) (see PARA 520), the tribunal must acknowledge receipt of the notice and send a copy of it to the listing officer concerned: reg 28(3). As to the meaning of 'interested person' see PARA 515 note 4. As to the meaning of 'listing officer' see PARA 515 note 4.

11 As to the meaning of 'person' see PARA 11 note 13.

12 Ie the condition mentioned in the Local Government Finance Act 1992 s 16(7)(a) or (b): see PARA 513.

13 As to the meaning of 'month' see PARA 11 note 1. As to the calculation of time see the Valuation Tribunal for England (Council Tax and Rating Appeals) (Procedure) Regulations 2009, SI 2009/2269, reg 14; and PARA 515.

14 Valuation Tribunal for England (Council Tax and Rating Appeals) (Procedure) Regulations 2009, SI 2009/2269, reg 21(2). The notice in question is that under the Local Government Finance Act 1992 s 16 (see PARA 513): see the Valuation Tribunal for England (Council Tax and Rating Appeals) (Procedure) Regulations 2009, SI 2009/2269, reg 21(2). Regulation 21(2) is subject to reg 21(6) (see the text to notes 20–22): see reg 21(1). As to the meaning of 'billing authority' see PARA 346.

15 Ie where the condition mentioned in the Local Government Finance Act 1992 s 16(7)(c) is fulfilled: see PARA 513.
16 Ie under the Local Government Finance Act 1992 s 16(4): see PARA 513.
17 See the Valuation Tribunal for England (Council Tax and Rating Appeals) (Procedure) Regulations 2009, SI 2009/2269, reg 21(3). Regulation 21(3) is subject to reg 21(6) (see the text to notes 20–22): see reg 21(1).
18 Valuation Tribunal for England (Council Tax and Rating Appeals) (Procedure) Regulations 2009, SI 2009/2269, reg 21(4). Regulation 21(4) is subject to reg 21(6) (see the text to notes 20–22): see reg 21(1).
19 Valuation Tribunal for England (Council Tax and Rating Appeals) (Procedure) Regulations 2009, SI 2009/2269, reg 21(5). Regulation 21(5) is subject to reg 21(6) (see the text to notes 20–22): see reg 21(1).
20 As to the president of the Valuation Tribunal for England see PARA 233.
21 Ie as provided by the Valuation Tribunal for England (Council Tax and Rating Appeals) (Procedure) Regulations 2009, SI 2009/2269, reg 21: see the text to notes 11–19.
22 Valuation Tribunal for England (Council Tax and Rating Appeals) (Procedure) Regulations 2009, SI 2009/2269, reg 21(6). As to appeals out of time see *Moghaddam v Hammersmith and Fulham London Borough Council* [2009] EWHC 1670 (Admin), [2009] RA 209, [2009] All ER (D) 144 (Jul) (decided under previous legislation).

519. Procedure subsequent to making of appeals concerning proposed alterations of valuation list.

Where the Valuation Tribunal for England[1] receives a copy of an invalidity notice[2] together with a written statement from the proposer[3], the tribunal must:

(1) within the period of two weeks beginning on the day on which those documents were received, serve on the proposer a written notice[4] acknowledging receipt of them and specifying the date of receipt[5]; and
(2) as soon as reasonably practicable serve a copy of the statement on the listing officer[6].

Where the Valuation Tribunal for England receives a copy of a decision notice in a case where there is disagreement as to a proposed alteration of a valuation list[7] together with an appeal statement[8] from an appellant[9], the tribunal must[10]:

(a) within the period of two weeks beginning on the day on which those documents were received, serve on the appellant a written notice acknowledging receipt of them and specifying the date of receipt[11];
(b) where the appellant is a competent appellant[12] and the proposer appeals in relation to the same decision notice[13], at the same time as serving the notice referred to in head (a) or as soon as reasonably practicable afterwards, serve on the appellant a written notice informing the appellant of the proposer's appeal[14]; and
(c) where the appellant is a competent appellant[15] and another competent appellant made an appeal in relation to the same decision notice before the appellant did so and that earlier appeal is proceeding[16], at the same time as serving the notice referred to in head (a) or as soon as reasonably practicable afterwards, serve on the appellant a written notice informing the appellant of the other competent appellant's earlier appeal[17].

Where the appeal is proceeding, the tribunal must, as soon as reasonably practicable:

(i) serve a copy of the appeal statement[18] on the listing officer[19]; and
(ii) serve a written notice[20] on any person who is a party[21] to the appeal or then appears to the tribunal to be an interested person[22] as regards any dwelling to which the decision notice relates (other than the appellant and the listing officer)[23], and whose name and address are included in the decision notice or the appeal statement or are otherwise known to the tribunal[24].

Where, in relation to an appeal, the listing officer receives a copy of an appeal statement[25] from the tribunal, he must serve on the tribunal a written notice of the name and address of any person who is a party to the appeal[26], or then appears to be an interested person as regards any dwelling to which the decision notice relates[27], whose name and address the listing officer knows but which were not included in the decision notice or the appeal statement[28]. Where the tribunal receives such a notice, as soon as reasonably practicable (where this has not already been done) the tribunal must serve a written notice on any person whose name and address the listing officer included in the notice[29].

1 As to the Valuation Tribunal for England see PARA 232. The Valuation Tribunal for England (Council Tax and Rating Appeals) (Procedure) Regulations 2009, SI 2009/2269, apply in relation to England only: see reg 1. As to the equivalent regulations in relation to Wales see the Council Tax (Alteration of Lists and Appeals) Regulations 1993, SI 1993/290, Pt III (regs 16–34); and the Valuation Tribunal for Wales Regulations 2010, SI 2010/713, Pt 5 (regs 27–46); and see PARA 534 et seq. As to the meanings of 'England' and 'Wales' see PARA 2 note 16.
2 As to invalidity notices see the Council Tax (Alteration of Lists and Appeals) (England) Regulations 2009, SI 2009/2270, reg 7(1); and PARA 422.
3 Ie under the Council Tax (Alteration of Lists and Appeals) (England) Regulations 2009, SI 2009/2270, reg 7(6): see PARA 422. 'Proposer' means the person making a proposal: Valuation Tribunal for England (Council Tax and Rating Appeals) (Procedure) Regulations 2009, SI 2009/2269, reg 2(1). As to the meaning of 'proposal' see PARA 516 note 2.
4 As to the meaning of 'written' see PARA 21 note 3. As to the service of notices by the tribunal see PARA 515. As to the calculation of time see PARA 515.
5 Valuation Tribunal for England (Council Tax and Rating Appeals) (Procedure) Regulations 2009, SI 2009/2269, reg 24(a).
6 Valuation Tribunal for England (Council Tax and Rating Appeals) (Procedure) Regulations 2009, SI 2009/2269, reg 24(b). As to the meaning of 'listing officer' see PARA 515 note 4.
7 As to decision notices see the Council Tax (Alteration of Lists and Appeals) (England) Regulations 2009, SI 2009/2270, reg 9(2); and PARA 423. As to the alteration of valuation lists see PARA 417 et seq.
8 Ie the written statement served by an appellant on the tribunal in accordance with the Council Tax (Alteration of Lists and Appeals) (England) Regulations 2009, SI 2009/2270, reg 10(5) (see PARA 424): see the Valuation Tribunal for England (Council Tax and Rating Appeals) (Procedure) Regulations 2009, SI 2009/2269, regs 20, 25(1).
9 As to the meaning of 'appellant' see PARA 515 note 4.
10 See the Valuation Tribunal for England (Council Tax and Rating Appeals) (Procedure) Regulations 2009, SI 2009/2269, reg 25(1).
11 Valuation Tribunal for England (Council Tax and Rating Appeals) (Procedure) Regulations 2009, SI 2009/2269, reg 25(1)(a).
12 Valuation Tribunal for England (Council Tax and Rating Appeals) (Procedure) Regulations 2009, SI 2009/2269, reg 25(1)(b)(i). As to the meaning of 'competent appellant' see PARA 515 note 4.
13 Valuation Tribunal for England (Council Tax and Rating Appeals) (Procedure) Regulations 2009, SI 2009/2269, reg 25(1)(b)(ii).
14 See the Valuation Tribunal for England (Council Tax and Rating Appeals) (Procedure) Regulations 2009, SI 2009/2269, reg 25(1)(b). The notice must also inform the appellant of the effect of the Council Tax (Alteration of Lists and Appeals) (England) Regulations 2009, SI 2009/2270, reg 10(4) (see PARA 424) and the Valuation Tribunal for England (Council Tax and Rating Appeals) (Procedure) Regulations 2009, SI 2009/2269, reg 22 (see PARA 527): reg 25(1)(b).
15 Valuation Tribunal for England (Council Tax and Rating Appeals) (Procedure) Regulations 2009, SI 2009/2269, reg 25(1)(c)(i).
16 Valuation Tribunal for England (Council Tax and Rating Appeals) (Procedure) Regulations 2009, SI 2009/2269, reg 25(1)(c)(ii).
17 See the Valuation Tribunal for England (Council Tax and Rating Appeals) (Procedure) Regulations 2009, SI 2009/2269, reg 25(1)(c). The notice must also inform the appellant of the effect of the Council Tax (Alteration of Lists and Appeals) (England) Regulations 2009, SI 2009/2270, reg 10(4) (see PARA 424) and the Valuation Tribunal for England (Council Tax and Rating Appeals) (Procedure) Regulations 2009, SI 2009/2269, reg 22 (see PARA 527): reg 25(1)(c).
18 See note 8.

19 Valuation Tribunal for England (Council Tax and Rating Appeals) (Procedure) Regulations 2009, SI 2009/2269, reg 25(2)(a).
20 See the Valuation Tribunal for England (Council Tax and Rating Appeals) (Procedure) Regulations 2009, SI 2009/2269, reg 25(2)(b). The notice must include the following matters (see reg 25(2)(b)):
(1) the address of any dwelling to which the appeal relates (reg 25(3)(a));
(2) the appellant's reasons for the appeal (reg 25(3)(b)); and
(3) the date on which the appeal was made (reg 25(3)(c)).
As to the meaning of 'dwelling' see PARA 349.
21 As to the meaning of 'party' see PARA 515 note 4.
22 As to the meaning of 'interested person' see PARA 515 note 4.
23 Valuation Tribunal for England (Council Tax and Rating Appeals) (Procedure) Regulations 2009, SI 2009/2269, reg 25(2)(b)(i).
24 Valuation Tribunal for England (Council Tax and Rating Appeals) (Procedure) Regulations 2009, SI 2009/2269, reg 25(2)(b)(ii).
25 See note 8.
26 Valuation Tribunal for England (Council Tax and Rating Appeals) (Procedure) Regulations 2009, SI 2009/2269, reg 26(1)(a)(i).
27 Valuation Tribunal for England (Council Tax and Rating Appeals) (Procedure) Regulations 2009, SI 2009/2269, reg 26(1)(a)(ii).
28 Valuation Tribunal for England (Council Tax and Rating Appeals) (Procedure) Regulations 2009, SI 2009/2269, reg 26(1)(a). The notice must be served as soon as reasonably practicable after the listing officer becomes aware of that information: see reg 26(1)(b).
29 See the Valuation Tribunal for England (Council Tax and Rating Appeals) (Procedure) Regulations 2009, SI 2009/2269, reg 26(2). The notice must include:
(1) the address of any dwelling to which the appeal relates (reg 26(2)(a));
(2) the appellant's reasons for the appeal (reg 26(2)(b)); and
(3) the date on which the appeal was made (reg 26(2)(c)).

520. Competent party to appeal.

Where an interested person[1], as regards any dwelling[2] to which the decision notice relating to a disagreement concerning a proposed alteration to a valuation list[3] relates, wishes to be a party[4] to any appeal[5], is not already a party to the appeal[6], is not the proposer[7], and would have been competent to make the proposal[8] in relation to which the appeal relates on the relevant date[9], he may, within the period of three months[10] beginning on the relevant date, serve a written[11] notice on the Valuation Tribunal for England[12] stating that he wishes to be a party to the appeal[13].

The tribunal must, within the period of two weeks beginning on the day on which it receives the interested person's notice, serve on him a written notice[14] acknowledging receipt of it and specifying the date of receipt[15]; and as soon as reasonably practicable serve a copy of the interested person's notice on the listing officer[16].

1 As to the meaning of 'interested person' see PARA 515 note 4.
2 As to the meaning of 'dwelling' see PARA 349.
3 As to decision notices see the Council Tax (Alteration of Lists and Appeals) (England) Regulations 2009, SI 2009/2270, reg 9(2); and PARA 423.
4 As to the meaning of 'party' see PARA 515 note 4.
5 Ie any appeal made under the Council Tax (Alteration of Lists and Appeals) (England) Regulations 2009, SI 2009/2270, reg 10 (see PARA 424) (including any appeal which is proceeding by virtue of the Valuation Tribunal for England (Council Tax and Rating Appeals) (Procedure) Regulations 2009, SI 2009/2269, reg 22: see PARA 527): see reg 27(1)(a).
6 Valuation Tribunal for England (Council Tax and Rating Appeals) (Procedure) Regulations 2009, SI 2009/2269, reg 27(1)(b).
7 Valuation Tribunal for England (Council Tax and Rating Appeals) (Procedure) Regulations 2009, SI 2009/2269, reg 27(1)(c). As to the meaning of 'proposer' see PARA 519 note 3.
8 As to the meaning of 'proposal' see PARA 516 note 2.

9 Valuation Tribunal for England (Council Tax and Rating Appeals) (Procedure) Regulations 2009, SI 2009/2269, reg 27(1)(d). The 'relevant date' is:
(1) the date on which the proposer appealed in accordance with the Council Tax (Alteration of Lists and Appeals) (England) Regulations 2009, SI 2009/2270, reg 10 (see PARA 424) (Valuation Tribunal for England (Council Tax and Rating Appeals) (Procedure) Regulations 2009, SI 2009/2269, reg 27(1)(d)(i)); or
(2) where the proposer has not appealed, the date on which a competent appellant appealed in accordance with that regulation or, if there is more than one competent appellant, the first date on which a competent appellant did so (reg 27(1)(d)(ii)).
As to the meaning of 'competent appellant' see PARA 515 note 4.
10 As to the meaning of 'month' see PARA 11 note 1. As to the calculation of time see the Valuation Tribunal for England (Council Tax and Rating Appeals) (Procedure) Regulations 2009, SI 2009/2269, reg 14; and PARA 515.
11 As to the meaning of 'written' see PARA 21 note 3.
12 As to the Valuation Tribunal for England see PARA 232. The Valuation Tribunal for England (Council Tax and Rating Appeals) (Procedure) Regulations 2009, SI 2009/2269, apply in relation to England only: see reg 1. As to the equivalent regulations in relation to Wales see the Council Tax (Alteration of Lists and Appeals) Regulations 1993, SI 1993/290, Pt III (regs 16–34); and the Valuation Tribunal for Wales Regulations 2010, SI 2010/713, Pt 5 (regs 27–46); and see PARA 534 et seq. As to the meanings of 'England' and 'Wales' see PARA 2 note 16.
13 Valuation Tribunal for England (Council Tax and Rating Appeals) (Procedure) Regulations 2009, SI 2009/2269, reg 27(2). The interested person must include in the notice:
(1) the address of the dwelling to which the decision notice relates (reg 27(3)(a)); and
(2) the names and addresses of the interested person, the proposer and the listing officer (reg 27(3)(b)).
As to the meaning of 'listing officer' see PARA 515 note 4.
14 As to the service of notices by the tribunal see PARA 515.
15 Valuation Tribunal for England (Council Tax and Rating Appeals) (Procedure) Regulations 2009, SI 2009/2269, reg 27(4)(a).
16 Valuation Tribunal for England (Council Tax and Rating Appeals) (Procedure) Regulations 2009, SI 2009/2269, reg 27(4)(b).

521. Directions.

The Valuation Tribunal for England[1] may give a direction on the application of one or more of the parties[2] or on its own initiative[3]. An application for a direction must state the reason for making that application[4], and may be made by sending or delivering a written[5] application to the tribunal[6] or orally during the course of a hearing[7]. Unless the tribunal considers that there is good reason not to do so, it must send written notice of any direction to every party and to any other person[8] affected by the direction[9]; and if a party or any other person sent such notice wishes to challenge the direction, he may do so by applying for another direction which amends, suspends or sets aside the first direction[10].

The tribunal may give a direction[11]:
(1) substituting a party if:
  (a) the wrong person has been named as a party[12]; or
  (b) the substitution has become necessary because of a change of circumstances since the start of proceedings[13];
(2) adding a person to the proceedings as a party[14].

The tribunal may at any time correct any clerical mistake or other accidental slip or omission in a direction or any document produced by it by sending notification of the amended direction, or a copy of the amended document, to all parties[15], and making any necessary amendment to any information published in relation to the direction or document[16].

1 As to the Valuation Tribunal for England see PARA 232. The Valuation Tribunal for England (Council Tax and Rating Appeals) (Procedure) Regulations 2009, SI 2009/2269, apply in relation

to England only: see reg 1. As to the equivalent regulations in relation to Wales see the Council Tax (Alteration of Lists and Appeals) Regulations 1993, SI 1993/290, Pt III (regs 16–34); and the Valuation Tribunal for Wales Regulations 2010, SI 2010/713, Pt 5 (regs 27–46); and see PARA 534 et seq. As to the meanings of 'England' and 'Wales' see PARA 2 note 16.
2 As to the meaning of 'party' see PARA 515 note 4.
3 Valuation Tribunal for England (Council Tax and Rating Appeals) (Procedure) Regulations 2009, SI 2009/2269, reg 8(1). As to the power of the tribunal to give directions in relation to the conduct or disposal of proceedings see PARA 516.
4 Valuation Tribunal for England (Council Tax and Rating Appeals) (Procedure) Regulations 2009, SI 2009/2269, reg 8(3).
5 As to the meaning of 'written' see PARA 21 note 3.
6 Valuation Tribunal for England (Council Tax and Rating Appeals) (Procedure) Regulations 2009, SI 2009/2269, reg 8(2)(a). As to the service of documents see PARA 515.
7 Valuation Tribunal for England (Council Tax and Rating Appeals) (Procedure) Regulations 2009, SI 2009/2269, reg 8(2)(b).
8 As to the meaning of 'person' see PARA 11 note 13.
9 Valuation Tribunal for England (Council Tax and Rating Appeals) (Procedure) Regulations 2009, SI 2009/2269, reg 8(4).
10 See the Valuation Tribunal for England (Council Tax and Rating Appeals) (Procedure) Regulations 2009, SI 2009/2269, reg 8(5).
11 If the tribunal gives a direction under the Valuation Tribunal for England (Council Tax and Rating Appeals) (Procedure) Regulations 2009, SI 2009/2269, reg 11(1) or (2), it may give such consequential directions as it considers appropriate: reg 11(3).
12 Valuation Tribunal for England (Council Tax and Rating Appeals) (Procedure) Regulations 2009, SI 2009/2269, reg 11(1)(a).
13 Valuation Tribunal for England (Council Tax and Rating Appeals) (Procedure) Regulations 2009, SI 2009/2269, reg 11(1)(b).
14 Valuation Tribunal for England (Council Tax and Rating Appeals) (Procedure) Regulations 2009, SI 2009/2269, reg 11(2).
15 Valuation Tribunal for England (Council Tax and Rating Appeals) (Procedure) Regulations 2009, SI 2009/2269, reg 39(a). The tribunal must make arrangements for the effect of each correction under reg 39 to be recorded: see reg 41; and PARA 533.
16 Valuation Tribunal for England (Council Tax and Rating Appeals) (Procedure) Regulations 2009, SI 2009/2269, reg 39(b).

522. Striking out proceedings.

The proceedings, or the appropriate part of them, will automatically be struck out if the appellant[1] has failed to comply with a direction[2] that stated that failure by a party[3] to comply with the direction would lead to the striking out of the proceedings or that part of them[4].

The Valuation Tribunal for England[5] must strike out the whole or part of the proceedings if it does not have jurisdiction in relation to the proceedings or that part of them[6]. The tribunal may strike out the whole or a part of the proceedings if:

(1) the appellant has failed to comply with a direction that stated that failure by the appellant to comply with the direction could lead to the striking out of the proceedings or that part of them[7];
(2) the appellant has failed to co-operate with the tribunal to such an extent that it cannot deal with the proceedings fairly and justly[8]; or
(3) the tribunal considers there is no reasonable prospect of the appellant's appeal, or part of it, succeeding[9].

However, the tribunal may not strike out the whole or part of the proceedings under the above powers[10] without first giving the appellant an opportunity to make representations in relation to the proposed striking out[11].

If the proceedings, or part of them, have been struck out in certain of the above circumstances[12], the appellant may apply for the proceedings, or part of them, to be reinstated[13].

The above provisions apply to a party to the proceedings other than the appellant as they apply to an appellant with certain exceptions[14].

Certain functions of the Valuation Tribunal for England[15], may be discharged on behalf of the Valuation Tribunal for England by the clerk of the Valuation Tribunal for England or by any other member of its staff[16].

1 As to the meaning of 'appellant' see PARA 515 note 4. As to appeals in relation to council tax see PARA 514.

2 As to the power of the tribunal to give directions in relation to the conduct or disposal of proceedings see PARA 516. As to directions generally see PARA 521. As to directions relating to evidence and information see PARA 524.

3 As to the meaning of 'party' see PARA 515 note 4.

4 Valuation Tribunal for England (Council Tax and Rating Appeals) (Procedure) Regulations 2009, SI 2009/2269, reg 10(1). The Valuation Tribunal for England (Council Tax and Rating Appeals) (Procedure) Regulations 2009, SI 2009/2269, apply in relation to England only: see reg 1. As to the equivalent regulations in relation to Wales see the Council Tax (Alteration of Lists and Appeals) Regulations 1993, SI 1993/290, Pt III (regs 16–34); and the Valuation Tribunal for Wales Regulations 2010, SI 2010/713, Pt 5 (regs 27–46); and see PARA 534 et seq. As to the meanings of 'England' and 'Wales' see PARA 2 note 16.

5 As to the Valuation Tribunal for England see PARA 232.

6 Valuation Tribunal for England (Council Tax and Rating Appeals) (Procedure) Regulations 2009, SI 2009/2269, reg 10(2). As to the jurisdiction of the tribunal see PARA 232.

7 Valuation Tribunal for England (Council Tax and Rating Appeals) (Procedure) Regulations 2009, SI 2009/2269, reg 10(3)(a).

8 Valuation Tribunal for England (Council Tax and Rating Appeals) (Procedure) Regulations 2009, SI 2009/2269, reg 10(3)(b). As to the general duty of the tribunal in relation to the conduct of appeals see PARA 515.

9 Valuation Tribunal for England (Council Tax and Rating Appeals) (Procedure) Regulations 2009, SI 2009/2269, reg 10(3)(c).

10 Ie under the Valuation Tribunal for England (Council Tax and Rating Appeals) (Procedure) Regulations 2009, SI 2009/2269, reg 10(2) or (3)(b) or (c): see the text to notes 5–6, 8–9.

11 Valuation Tribunal for England (Council Tax and Rating Appeals) (Procedure) Regulations 2009, SI 2009/2269, reg 10(4).

12 Ie under the Valuation Tribunal for England (Council Tax and Rating Appeals) (Procedure) Regulations 2009, SI 2009/2269, reg 10(1) or (3)(a): see the text to notes 1–4, 7.

13 Valuation Tribunal for England (Council Tax and Rating Appeals) (Procedure) Regulations 2009, SI 2009/2269, reg 10(5). An application must be made in writing and received by the tribunal within one month after the date on which it sent notification of the striking out to the appellant: reg 10(6). As to the meaning of 'month' see PARA 11 note 1. As to the meaning of 'writing' see PARA 21 note 3. As to the service and delivery of documents see reg 15; and PARA 515.

14 The Valuation Tribunal for England (Council Tax and Rating Appeals) (Procedure) Regulations 2009, SI 2009/2269, reg 10 applies to a party to the proceedings other than the appellant as it applies to an appellant except that:

(1) a reference to the striking out of the proceedings is to be read as a reference to the barring of that other party from taking further part in the proceedings (reg 10(7)(a)); and

(2) a reference to an application for the reinstatement of proceedings which have been struck out is to be read as a reference to an application for the lifting of the bar on that other party from taking further part in the proceedings (reg 10(7)(b)).

If a party other than the appellant has been barred from taking further part in the proceedings under reg 10 and that bar has not been lifted, the tribunal need not consider any response or other submission made by that party: reg 10(8).

15 Ie the functions of the tribunal under Valuation Tribunal for England (Council Tax and Rating Appeals) (Procedure) Regulations 2009, SI 2009/2269, regs 10(2), (3)(a), (4), 37 (see the text to notes 5–6, 7, 10–11; and PARA 530), so far as they relate to the striking out of proceedings in an appeal under the Local Government Finance Act 1992 s 16 (see PARA 513).

16 Valuation Tribunal for England (Council Tax and Rating Appeals) (Procedure) Regulations 2009, SI 2009/2269, reg 10(9) (reg 10(9), (10) added by SI 2013/465). 'Valuation Tribunal for England's staff' means the staff provided to the Valuation Tribunal for England by, or under arrangements made by, the Valuation Tribunal for England: Valuation Tribunal for England (Council Tax and Rating Appeals) (Procedure) Regulations 2009, SI 2009/2269, reg 10(10) (as so added).

523. Representatives.

A party[1] may appoint a representative (whether a legal representative or not) to represent that party in the proceedings[2], but the representative must not be a member of the Valuation Tribunal for England[3] or the Valuation Tribunal Service[4] or an employee of the Valuation Tribunal Service[5]. If a party appoints a representative, that party (or the representative if the representative is a legal representative) must send or deliver to the tribunal written notice[6] of the representative's name and address unless the representative's name and address have already been given to the listing officer[7]. If the tribunal receives such notice that a party has appointed a representative, it must send a copy of that notice to each other party[8]. A person[9] who receives due notice of the appointment of a representative must provide to the representative any document which is required to be provided to the represented party, and need not provide that document to the represented party[10]; and may assume that the representative is and remains authorised as such until he receives written notification that this is not so from the representative or the represented party[11].

Anything permitted or required to be done by a party[12] or a direction[13] may be done by the representative of that party, except signing a witness statement[14]. At a hearing a party may be accompanied by another person, other than a member of the tribunal or the Valuation Tribunal Service or an employee of that service, whose name and address has not been notified[15] to the tribunal; and that person may act as a representative or otherwise assist in presenting the party's case at the hearing[16].

1 As to the meaning of 'party' see PARA 515 note 4.
2 As to appeals in relation to council tax see PARA 514.
3 As to membership of the Valuation Tribunal for England see PARA 233. The Valuation Tribunal for England (Council Tax and Rating Appeals) (Procedure) Regulations 2009, SI 2009/2269, apply in relation to England only: see reg 1. As to the equivalent regulations in relation to Wales see the Council Tax (Alteration of Lists and Appeals) Regulations 1993, SI 1993/290, Pt III (regs 16–34); and the Valuation Tribunal for Wales Regulations 2010, SI 2010/713, Pt 5 (regs 27–46); and see PARA 534 et seq. As to the meanings of 'England' and 'Wales' see PARA 2 note 16.
4 As to the Valuation Tribunal Service see PARA 241.
5 Valuation Tribunal for England (Council Tax and Rating Appeals) (Procedure) Regulations 2009, SI 2009/2269, reg 13(1).
6 As to the meaning of 'written' see PARA 21 note 3. As to the service and delivery of documents see PARA 515.
7 See the Valuation Tribunal for England (Council Tax and Rating Appeals) (Procedure) Regulations 2009, SI 2009/2269, reg 13(2). As to the meaning of 'listing officer' see PARA 515 note 4.
8 Valuation Tribunal for England (Council Tax and Rating Appeals) (Procedure) Regulations 2009, SI 2009/2269, reg 13(3).
9 As to the meaning of 'person' see PARA 11 note 13.
10 Valuation Tribunal for England (Council Tax and Rating Appeals) (Procedure) Regulations 2009, SI 2009/2269, reg 13(5)(a).
11 Valuation Tribunal for England (Council Tax and Rating Appeals) (Procedure) Regulations 2009, SI 2009/2269, reg 13(5)(b).
12 Ie under the Valuation Tribunal for England (Council Tax and Rating Appeals) (Procedure) Regulations 2009, SI 2009/2269.
13 As to the power of the tribunal to give directions in relation to the conduct or disposal of proceedings see PARA 516. As to directions generally see PARA 521. As to directions relating to evidence and information see PARA 524.
14 Valuation Tribunal for England (Council Tax and Rating Appeals) (Procedure) Regulations 2009, SI 2009/2269, reg 13(4). As to witness statements see PARA 524.
15 Ie under the Valuation Tribunal for England (Council Tax and Rating Appeals) (Procedure) Regulations 2009, SI 2009/2269, reg 13(2): see the text to notes 6–7.

16 Valuation Tribunal for England (Council Tax and Rating Appeals) (Procedure) Regulations 2009, SI 2009/2269, reg 13(6). Regulation 13(2)–(5) (see the text to notes 6–14) does not apply in relation to a person who accompanies a party under reg 13(6): reg 13(7). As to hearings see PARA 528.

524. Evidence and submissions.

The Valuation Tribunal for England[1] may make an order[2] prohibiting the disclosure or publication of:

(1) specified documents or information relating to the proceedings[3]; or
(2) any matter likely to lead members of the public to identify any person[4] whom the tribunal considers should not be identified[5].

The tribunal may give a direction prohibiting the disclosure of information to a person if it is satisfied that such disclosure would be likely to cause that person or some other person serious harm[6], and it is satisfied, having regard to the interests of justice, that it is proportionate to give such a direction[7]. The tribunal must conduct proceedings as appropriate in order to give effect to such a direction[8].

The tribunal may give directions as to:

(a) issues on which it requires evidence or submissions[9];
(b) the nature of the evidence or submissions it requires[10];
(c) whether any parties are permitted or required to provide expert evidence[11];
(d) any limit on the number of witnesses whose evidence a party may put forward, whether in relation to a particular issue or generally[12];
(e) the manner in which any evidence or submissions are to be provided, which may include a direction for them to be given orally at a hearing[13] or by written[14] submissions or witness statement[15]; and
(f) the time at which any evidence or submissions are to be provided[16].

The tribunal may:

(i) admit evidence whether or not the evidence would be admissible in a civil trial in England[17]; or
(ii) exclude evidence that would otherwise be admissible where the evidence was not provided within the time allowed by a direction[18], or the evidence was otherwise provided in a manner that did not comply with a direction[19], or it would otherwise be unfair to admit the evidence[20].

Certain information[21] must not be used in any relevant proceedings[22] by a billing authority[23] or a listing officer[24] unless:

(A) not less than two weeks' notice[25], specifying in relation to any information to be so used the documents or other media in or on which that information is held and the dwelling[26] to which it relates, has previously been given to every other party to the proceedings[27];
(B) any person who has given not less than 24 hours' notice of his intention to do so has been permitted, at any reasonable time to inspect the documents or other media in or on which such information is held[28] and to make a copy (other than a photographic copy) of, or of any extract from, any document containing such information[29]; and
(C) for an appeal relating to the alteration of a valuation list[30], the information relates to a matter included in the notice of appeal or any document accompanying the notice of appeal, or in new or further evidence admitted[31].

The contents of a list may be proved by the production of a copy of it, or of the relevant part, purporting to be certified to be a true copy by the listing officer[32].

The contents of a completion notice[33] may be proved by the production of a copy of it purporting to be certified to be a true copy by the proper officer of the relevant authority[34].

1 As to the Valuation Tribunal for England see PARA 232. The Valuation Tribunal for England (Council Tax and Rating Appeals) (Procedure) Regulations 2009, SI 2009/2269, apply in relation to England only: see reg 1. As to the equivalent regulations in relation to Wales see the Council Tax (Alteration of Lists and Appeals) Regulations 1993, SI 1993/290, Pt III (regs 16–34); and the Valuation Tribunal for Wales Regulations 2010, SI 2010/713, Pt 5 (regs 27–46); and see PARA 534 et seq. As to the meanings of 'England' and 'Wales' see PARA 2 note 16.

2 As to the correction of errors in an order see PARA 531.

3 Valuation Tribunal for England (Council Tax and Rating Appeals) (Procedure) Regulations 2009, SI 2009/2269, reg 16(1)(a). As to appeals in relation to council tax see PARA 514.

4 As to the meaning of 'person' see PARA 11 note 13.

5 Valuation Tribunal for England (Council Tax and Rating Appeals) (Procedure) Regulations 2009, SI 2009/2269, reg 16(1)(b).

6 Valuation Tribunal for England (Council Tax and Rating Appeals) (Procedure) Regulations 2009, SI 2009/2269, reg 16(2)(a).

7 Valuation Tribunal for England (Council Tax and Rating Appeals) (Procedure) Regulations 2009, SI 2009/2269, reg 16(2)(b). If a party ('the first party') considers that the tribunal should give such a direction prohibiting the disclosure of information to another party ('the second party'), the first party must:

(1) exclude the relevant document or information from any documents that will be provided to the second party (reg 16(3)(a)); and

(2) provide to the tribunal the excluded document or information, and the reason for its exclusion, so that the tribunal may decide whether the document or information should be disclosed to the second party or should be the subject of a direction under reg 16(2) (reg 16(3)(b)).

As to the meaning of 'party' see PARA 515 note 4.

If the tribunal gives a direction under reg 16(2) which prevents disclosure to a party who has appointed a representative, the tribunal may give a direction that the documents or information be disclosed to that representative if it is satisfied that:

(a) disclosure to the representative would be in the interests of the party (reg 16(5)(a)); and

(b) the representative will act in accordance with reg 16(6) (reg 16(5)(b)).

Documents or information disclosed to a representative in accordance with a direction under reg 16(5) must not be disclosed either directly or indirectly to any other person without the tribunal's consent: reg 16(6). As to representatives see PARA 523. As to the correction of errors in directions see PARA 521.

8 Valuation Tribunal for England (Council Tax and Rating Appeals) (Procedure) Regulations 2009, SI 2009/2269, reg 16(4). As to the general duty of the tribunal in relation to the conduct of appeals see PARA 515.

9 Valuation Tribunal for England (Council Tax and Rating Appeals) (Procedure) Regulations 2009, SI 2009/2269, reg 17(1)(a). Regulation 17(1) is subject to reg 17(1A) (see reg 17(1) (amended by SI 2017/156)), but that applies only in relation to non-domestic rating appeals (see PARA 248).

10 Valuation Tribunal for England (Council Tax and Rating Appeals) (Procedure) Regulations 2009, SI 2009/2269, reg 17(1)(b).

11 Valuation Tribunal for England (Council Tax and Rating Appeals) (Procedure) Regulations 2009, SI 2009/2269, reg 17(1)(c).

12 Valuation Tribunal for England (Council Tax and Rating Appeals) (Procedure) Regulations 2009, SI 2009/2269, reg 17(1)(d).

13 Valuation Tribunal for England (Council Tax and Rating Appeals) (Procedure) Regulations 2009, SI 2009/2269, reg 17(1)(e)(i).

14 As to the meaning of 'written' see PARA 21 note 3.

15 Valuation Tribunal for England (Council Tax and Rating Appeals) (Procedure) Regulations 2009, SI 2009/2269, reg 17(1)(e)(ii).

16 Valuation Tribunal for England (Council Tax and Rating Appeals) (Procedure) Regulations 2009, SI 2009/2269, reg 17(1)(f). As to the calculation of time generally see reg 14; and PARA 515.

17 Valuation Tribunal for England (Council Tax and Rating Appeals) (Procedure) Regulations 2009, SI 2009/2269, reg 17(2)(a). As to the admissibility of evidence see *Moghaddam v Hammersmith and Fulham London Borough Council* [2009] EWHC 1670 (Admin), [2009] RA 209, [2009] All

ER (D) 144 (Jul) (decided under previous legislation). As to evidence in civil proceedings see CIVIL PROCEDURE vol 12 (2015) PARA 685 et seq.

18 Valuation Tribunal for England (Council Tax and Rating Appeals) (Procedure) Regulations 2009, SI 2009/2269, reg 17(2)(b)(i).

19 Valuation Tribunal for England (Council Tax and Rating Appeals) (Procedure) Regulations 2009, SI 2009/2269, reg 17(2)(b)(ii).

20 Valuation Tribunal for England (Council Tax and Rating Appeals) (Procedure) Regulations 2009, SI 2009/2269, reg 17(2)(b)(iii).

21 The Valuation Tribunal for England (Council Tax and Rating Appeals) (Procedure) Regulations 2009, SI 2009/2269, reg 17(4) applies to:

(1) information supplied in pursuance of the Local Government Finance Act 1992 s 27(1) or (3) (see PARA 415) or regulations made under s 13 (see PARA 377) or Sch 2 (see PARAS 437, 444), or supplied under Sch 2 para 15A (see 442) or the Welfare Reform Act 2012 s 131 for purposes relating to council tax (Valuation Tribunal for England (Council Tax and Rating Appeals) (Procedure) Regulations 2009, SI 2009/2269, reg 17(3)(a)(ii), (iii), (v), (vi) (reg 17(3)(a) substituted by SI 2011/434; and amended by SI 2013/465)); and

(2) information contained in:

(a) any document which, having been produced to the Commissioners for Her Majesty's Revenue and Customs in pursuance of the Finance Act 1931 s 28 or furnished to them in pursuance of Sch 2 to that Act, is for the time being in their possession or under their control (Valuation Tribunal for England (Council Tax and Rating Appeals) (Procedure) Regulations 2009, SI 2009/2269, reg 17(3)(b)(i)); or

(b) any land transaction return within the meaning of the Finance Act 2003 Pt 4 (ss 42–124) (stamp duty land tax) (Valuation Tribunal for England (Council Tax and Rating Appeals) (Procedure) Regulations 2009, SI 2009/2269, reg 17(3)(b)(ii)).

22 In the Valuation Tribunal for England (Council Tax and Rating Appeals) (Procedure) Regulations 2009, SI 2009/2269, reg 17(4) and (8) (see note 27), 'relevant proceedings' means any proceedings on or in consequence of an appeal under the Local Government Finance Act 1992 s 16 (see PARA 513) or the Council Tax (Alteration of Lists and Appeals) (England) Regulations 2009, SI 2009/2270 (see PARA 419 et seq) and any proceedings on or in consequence of a reference to arbitration under the Valuation Tribunal for England (Council Tax and Rating Appeals) (Procedure) Regulations 2009, SI 2009/2269, reg 4 (see PARA 559): see reg 17(11).

23 As to the meaning of 'billing authority' see PARA 346.

24 As to the meaning of 'listing officer' see PARA 515 note 4.

25 As to the service and delivery of documents see PARA 515.

26 As to the meaning of 'dwelling' see PARA 349.

27 See the Valuation Tribunal for England (Council Tax and Rating Appeals) (Procedure) Regulations 2009, SI 2009/2269, reg 17(4)(a). Subject to reg 17(7), any person to whom notice relating to any dwelling has been given under reg 17(4)(a) ('P') may before the hearing serve notice on the listing officer specifying other dwellings as being dwellings which are comparable in character or otherwise relevant to P's case (reg 17(5)), and requiring the listing officer:

(1) to permit P at any reasonable time specified in the notice to inspect and (if P so desires) to make a copy (other than a photographic copy) of, or of any extract from, any document containing information to which reg 17 applies which relates to those other dwellings and is in the possession of the listing officer (reg 17(5)(a)); and

(2) to produce at the hearing or to submit to the tribunal such documents as before the hearing P has informed the listing officer that P requires (reg 17(5)(b)).

The number of dwellings specified in a notice under reg 17(5) must not exceed four or, if greater, the number specified in the notice under reg 17(4)(a): see reg 17(7). Nothing in reg 17(5) is to be construed as requiring the making available for inspection or copying, or the production of, any document in so far as it contains information other than information which is reasonably required for the purposes of the relevant proceedings: see reg 17(8).

Where P has given notice to the listing officer under reg 17(5), and the listing officer refuses or fails to comply with the notice, P may apply to the tribunal or, as the case may be, the arbitrator appointed to determine the appeal; and the tribunal or the arbitrator may, if satisfied that it is reasonable to do so, direct the listing officer to comply with the notice as respects all the dwellings or such of them as the tribunal or the arbitrator may determine: see reg 17(9). If any document required to be made available for inspection in accordance with reg 17(5) is not maintained in documentary form, the duty to make it so available is satisfied if a print-out, photographic image or other reproduction of the document which has been obtained from the storage medium adopted in relation to the document is made available for inspection: see reg 17(10).

28 Valuation Tribunal for England (Council Tax and Rating Appeals) (Procedure) Regulations 2009, SI 2009/2269, reg 17(4)(b)(i).

29 Valuation Tribunal for England (Council Tax and Rating Appeals) (Procedure) Regulations 2009, SI 2009/2269, reg 17(4)(b)(ii).

30 As to the meaning of 'list' see PARA 515 note 4.

31 Valuation Tribunal for England (Council Tax and Rating Appeals) (Procedure) Regulations 2009, SI 2009/2269, reg 17(4)(c).

32 See the Valuation Tribunal for England (Council Tax and Rating Appeals) (Procedure) Regulations 2009, SI 2009/2269, reg 17(12).

33 As to the meaning of 'completion notice' see PARA 518 note 3.

34 Valuation Tribunal for England (Council Tax and Rating Appeals) (Procedure) Regulations 2009, SI 2009/2269, reg 17(13). 'Relevant authority', in relation to a dwelling, means the billing authority in whose area the dwelling is situated: reg 2(1).

525. Summoning of witnesses and orders to answer questions or produce documents.

On the application of a party[1] or on its own initiative, the Valuation Tribunal for England[2] may:

(1) by summons require any person[3] to attend as a witness at a hearing at the time and place specified in the summons[4];

(2) order any person to answer any questions or produce any documents in that person's possession or control which relate to any issue in the proceedings[5].

Any such summons or order must:

(a) state that the person on whom the requirement is imposed may apply to the tribunal to vary or set aside the summons or order if he has not had an opportunity to object to it[6]; and

(b) state the consequences of failure to comply with the summons or order[7].

A summons under head (1) above must give the person required to attend 14 days' notice of the hearing or such shorter period as the tribunal may direct[8], and, where the person is not a party, make provision for the person's necessary expenses of attendance to be paid, and state who is to pay them[9].

No person may be compelled to give any evidence or produce any document that the person could not be compelled to give or produce on a trial of an action in a court of law in England[10].

1 As to the meaning of 'party' see PARA 515 note 4.

2 As to the Valuation Tribunal for England see PARA 232. The Valuation Tribunal for England (Council Tax and Rating Appeals) (Procedure) Regulations 2009, SI 2009/2269, apply in relation to England only: see reg 1. As to the equivalent regulations in relation to Wales see the Council Tax (Alteration of Lists and Appeals) Regulations 1993, SI 1993/290, Pt III (regs 16–34); and the Valuation Tribunal for Wales Regulations 2010, SI 2010/713, Pt 5 (regs 27–46); and see PARA 534 et seq. As to the meanings of 'England' and 'Wales' see PARA 2 note 16.

3 As to the meaning of 'person' see PARA 11 note 13.

4 Valuation Tribunal for England (Council Tax and Rating Appeals) (Procedure) Regulations 2009, SI 2009/2269, reg 18(1)(a). As to the service and delivery of documents see PARA 515. As to appeals in relation to council tax see PARA 514. Regulation 18 is modified in relation to a non-domestic rating appeal: see regs 18(A1), 18A: and PARA 249.

5 Valuation Tribunal for England (Council Tax and Rating Appeals) (Procedure) Regulations 2009, SI 2009/2269, reg 18(1)(b).

6 Valuation Tribunal for England (Council Tax and Rating Appeals) (Procedure) Regulations 2009, SI 2009/2269, reg 18(4)(a).

7 Valuation Tribunal for England (Council Tax and Rating Appeals) (Procedure) Regulations 2009, SI 2009/2269, reg 18(4)(b).

8 Valuation Tribunal for England (Council Tax and Rating Appeals) (Procedure) Regulations 2009, SI 2009/2269, reg 18(2)(a). As to the calculation of time see reg 14; and PARA 515.
9 Valuation Tribunal for England (Council Tax and Rating Appeals) (Procedure) Regulations 2009, SI 2009/2269, reg 18(2)(b).
10 Valuation Tribunal for England (Council Tax and Rating Appeals) (Procedure) Regulations 2009, SI 2009/2269, reg 18(3). As to evidence in civil proceedings see CIVIL PROCEDURE vol 12 (2015) PARA 685 et seq. As to the production of documents in civil proceedings see CIVIL PROCEDURE vol 12 (2015) PARA 621 et seq.

526. Withdrawals and deemed withdrawals of appeals.

In respect of appeals relating to proposals for the alteration of a valuation list[1], a party[2] may give notice[3] of the withdrawal of its appeal, or any part of it:

(1) at any time before a hearing to consider the disposal of the proceedings (or, if the Valuation Tribunal for England[4] disposes of the proceedings without a hearing, before that disposal), by sending or delivering to the tribunal a written[5] notice of withdrawal[6]; or

(2) orally at a hearing[7].

A party which has withdrawn its appeal may apply to the tribunal for the appeal to be reinstated[8].

An appeal in relation to which a notice has been served on the tribunal[9] in relation to a post-appeal agreement must be treated as withdrawn on the date on which the notice is served on the tribunal[10].

Where, after an appeal has been made to the tribunal in respect of a disagreement as to a proposed alteration of a list[11], the listing officer[12] alters the list in accordance with the proposal to which the appeal relates, the listing officer must notify the tribunal of that fact; and the appeal must be treated as withdrawn on the date on which the notice is served on the tribunal[13].

Where, following the initiation of an appeal against imposition of a penalty[14] the billing authority[15] decides to remit the penalty, the billing authority must notify the tribunal of that fact; and the appeal must be treated as withdrawn on the date on which the notice is served on the tribunal[16].

The tribunal must notify each party in writing of a withdrawal under these provisions[17].

1 Ie appeals under the Council Tax (Alteration of Lists and Appeals) (England) Regulations 2009, SI 2009/2270, reg 7 or reg 10 (see PARA 424): see the Valuation Tribunal for England (Council Tax and Rating Appeals) (Procedure) Regulations 2009, SI 2009/2269, reg 19(1) (reg 19 substituted by SI 2011/434).

The Valuation Tribunal for England (Council Tax and Rating Appeals) (Procedure) Regulations 2009, SI 2009/2269, apply in relation to England only: see reg 1. As to the equivalent regulations in relation to Wales see the Council Tax (Alteration of Lists and Appeals) Regulations 1993, SI 1993/290, Pt III (regs 16–34); and the Valuation Tribunal for Wales Regulations 2010, SI 2010/713, Pt 5 (regs 27–46); and see PARA 534 et seq. As to the meanings of 'England' and 'Wales' see PARA 2 note 16.

2 As to the meaning of 'party' see PARA 515 note 4.
3 As to the service and delivery of documents see PARA 515.
4 As to the Valuation Tribunal for England see PARA 232.
5 As to the meaning of 'written' see PARA 21 note 3.
6 Valuation Tribunal for England (Council Tax and Rating Appeals) (Procedure) Regulations 2009, SI 2009/2269, reg 19(2)(a) (as substituted: see note 1). As to hearings see PARA 528.
7 Valuation Tribunal for England (Council Tax and Rating Appeals) (Procedure) Regulations 2009, SI 2009/2269, reg 19(2)(b) (as substituted: see note 1). Where a party gives notice of withdrawal at a hearing, the notice of withdrawal does not take effect unless the tribunal panel consents to the withdrawal: reg 19(3) (as so substituted). 'Tribunal panel', in relation to an appeal, means the members of the Valuation Tribunal for England selected to deal with the appeal in accordance with tribunal business arrangements: reg 2(1). As to tribunal business arrangements see PARA 234.

8 Valuation Tribunal for England (Council Tax and Rating Appeals) (Procedure) Regulations 2009, SI 2009/2269, reg 19(4) (as substituted: see note 1). An application under reg 19(4) must be made in writing and be received by the tribunal within one month after:
(1) the date on which the tribunal received the notice under reg 19(2)(a) (see head (1) in the text) (reg 19(5)(a) (as so substituted)); or
(2) the date of the hearing at which the appeal was withdrawn orally under reg 19(2)(b) (see head (2) in the text) (reg 19(5)(b) (as so substituted)).
As to the meaning of 'month' see PARA 11 note 1.
9 Ie under the Council Tax (Alteration of Lists and Appeals) (England) Regulations 2009, SI 2009/2270, reg 13(3)(a) (post-appeal agreements): see PARA 425.
10 Valuation Tribunal for England (Council Tax and Rating Appeals) (Procedure) Regulations 2009, SI 2009/2269, reg 19(6) (as substituted: see note 1).
11 Ie an appeal under the Council Tax (Alteration of Lists and Appeals) (England) Regulations 2009, SI 2009/2270, reg 10: see PARA 424. As to the meaning of 'list' see PARA 515 note 4.
12 As to the meaning of 'listing officer' see PARA 515 note 4.
13 Valuation Tribunal for England (Council Tax and Rating Appeals) (Procedure) Regulations 2009, SI 2009/2269, reg 19(7) (as substituted: see note 1).
14 Ie an appeal under the Local Government Finance Act 1992 Sch 3 para 3: see PARA 471.
15 As to the meaning of 'billing authority' see PARA 346.
16 Valuation Tribunal for England (Council Tax and Rating Appeals) (Procedure) Regulations 2009, SI 2009/2269, reg 19(8) (as substituted: see note 1).
17 Valuation Tribunal for England (Council Tax and Rating Appeals) (Procedure) Regulations 2009, SI 2009/2269, reg 19(9) (as substituted: see note 1). Where a withdrawal has effect by virtue of any of reg 19(6)–(8) (see the text to notes 9–16), the tribunal must serve on the appellant and on every other party to the appeal a written notice confirming that the appeal has been withdrawn and the date on which it is treated as withdrawn: see reg 19(9) (as so substituted).
Where the tribunal's notice under reg 19(9) relates to the withdrawal of an appeal under the Council Tax (Alteration of Lists and Appeals) (England) Regulations 2009, SI 2009/2270, reg 7 or reg 10 (see PARAS 422, 424), or any part of it, the notice must specify the date by which a party (other than the withdrawing party) may serve notice on the tribunal under the Valuation Tribunal for England (Council Tax and Rating Appeals) (Procedure) Regulations 2009, SI 2009/2269, reg 22(1): reg 19(10) (as so substituted). 'Withdrawing party' means a person who made an appeal under the Council Tax (Alteration of Lists and Appeals) (England) Regulations 2009, SI 2009/2270, reg 10 and serves a notice under the Valuation Tribunal for England (Council Tax and Rating Appeals) (Procedure) Regulations 2009, SI 2009/2269, reg 19(2) (see the text to notes 1–7): reg 19(11) (as so substituted). As to new appellant's appeals see PARA 527.

527. Alteration of lists: new appellant's appeal.

Before the date specified[1] in the Valuation Tribunal for England's[2] notice of withdrawal of an appeal[3], a competent appellant[4] or a competent party[5] ('the new appellant') may serve a written notice[6] on the tribunal stating[7]:

(1) that the new appellant wishes to proceed with an appeal in relation to the same decision notice[8]; and
(2) where the new appellant is not a competent appellant, the reasons for the new appeal[9].

Where the tribunal receives such a notice:

(a) within the period of two weeks beginning on the day on which the notice was received[10], the tribunal must serve on the new appellant a written notice stating the date of receipt of the new appellant's notice[11], and stating that the withdrawing party's[12] appeal is withdrawn[13]; and
(b) where the new appellant's notice was the first such notice received by the tribunal in relation to the withdrawal, the notice under head (a) must state that the new appellant's appeal is proceeding[14]; or in any other case, the notice under head (a) must state that the new appellant's appeal is not proceeding because an earlier new appeal is proceeding[15].

Where the new appellant[16] is a competent appellant, the appeal already made[17] proceeds as if any steps taken by the tribunal in relation to the withdrawing party's appeal[18] had been taken in relation to the new appeal[19]. Where the new appellant[20] is not a competent appellant the new appeal is deemed to have been made under the appropriate provisions[21], the reasons for the new appeal are those included in the notice served[22] on the tribunal[23], and the new appeal proceeds as if any steps taken by the tribunal in relation to the withdrawing party's appeal[24] had been taken in relation to the new appeal[25].

As soon as reasonably practicable after receiving a notice[26] the tribunal must serve on the withdrawing party and every party[27] to the withdrawing party's appeal (other than the new appellant[28]) a written notice ('the tribunal's notice'):

(i) specifying that the withdrawing party's appeal is withdrawn and that the new appellant's appeal is proceeding[29];
(ii) stating the new appellant's reasons for the appeal[30]; and
(iii) requesting the party (where the party is neither the listing officer[31] nor the withdrawing party) to inform the tribunal by written notice, within such period as is specified in the tribunal's notice, being not less than 21 days from the date on which that notice is served, whether the party wishes to be a party to the proceedings on the new appellant's appeal[32].

1 Ie in accordance with the Valuation Tribunal for England (Council Tax and Rating Appeals) (Procedure) Regulations 2009, SI 2009/2269, reg 19(10): see PARA 526.
2 As to the Valuation Tribunal for England see PARA 232. The Valuation Tribunal for England (Council Tax and Rating Appeals) (Procedure) Regulations 2009, SI 2009/2269, apply in relation to England only: see reg 1. As to the equivalent regulations in relation to Wales see the Council Tax (Alteration of Lists and Appeals) Regulations 1993, SI 1993/290, Pt III (regs 16–34); and the Valuation Tribunal for Wales Regulations 2010, SI 2010/713, Pt 5 (regs 27–46); and see PARA 534 et seq. As to the meanings of 'England' and 'Wales' see PARA 2 note 16.
3 Ie the notice under the Valuation Tribunal for England (Council Tax and Rating Appeals) (Procedure) Regulations 2009, SI 2009/2269, reg 19(9): see PARA 526.
4 As to the meaning of 'competent appellant' see PARA 515 note 4.
5 As to the meaning of 'competent party' see PARA 515 note 4.
6 As to the meaning of 'written' see PARA 21 note 3. As to the service and delivery of documents see PARA 515.
7 Valuation Tribunal for England (Council Tax and Rating Appeals) (Procedure) Regulations 2009, SI 2009/2269, reg 22(1) (amended by SI 2011/434).
8 Valuation Tribunal for England (Council Tax and Rating Appeals) (Procedure) Regulations 2009, SI 2009/2269, reg 22(1)(a).
9 Valuation Tribunal for England (Council Tax and Rating Appeals) (Procedure) Regulations 2009, SI 2009/2269, reg 22(1)(b).
10 As to the calculation of time see the Valuation Tribunal for England (Council Tax and Rating Appeals) (Procedure) Regulations 2009, SI 2009/2269, reg 14; and PARA 515.
11 Valuation Tribunal for England (Council Tax and Rating Appeals) (Procedure) Regulations 2009, SI 2009/2269, reg 22(2)(a)(i).
12 'Withdrawing party' means a person who made an appeal under the Council Tax (Alteration of Lists and Appeals) (England) Regulations 2009, SI 2009/2270, reg 10 (see PARA 424) and serves a notice under the Valuation Tribunal for England (Council Tax and Rating Appeals) (Procedure) Regulations 2009, SI 2009/2269, reg 19(2): reg 20 (definition amended by SI 2011/434). As to the meaning of 'person' see PARA 11 note 13.
13 Valuation Tribunal for England (Council Tax and Rating Appeals) (Procedure) Regulations 2009, SI 2009/2269, reg 22(2)(a)(ii).
14 Valuation Tribunal for England (Council Tax and Rating Appeals) (Procedure) Regulations 2009, SI 2009/2269, reg 22(2)(b)(i).
15 Valuation Tribunal for England (Council Tax and Rating Appeals) (Procedure) Regulations 2009, SI 2009/2269, reg 22(2)(b)(ii).
16 Where the tribunal receives a notice under the Valuation Tribunal for England (Council Tax and Rating Appeals) (Procedure) Regulations 2009, SI 2009/2269, reg 22(1) (see the text to notes 1–9) from more than one person in relation to the same withdrawal, reg 22(4) and reg 23 (see the text to notes 26–32) apply as if references to the new appellant are references to the person whose notice the tribunal receives first: reg 22(3).

17 Ie under the Council Tax (Alteration of Lists and Appeals) (England) Regulations 2009, SI 2009/2270, reg 10: see PARA 424.
18 Ie other than steps under the Valuation Tribunal for England (Council Tax and Rating Appeals) (Procedure) Regulations 2009, SI 2009/2269, reg 19: see PARA 526.
19 Valuation Tribunal for England (Council Tax and Rating Appeals) (Procedure) Regulations 2009, SI 2009/2269, reg 22(4)(a).
20 See note 16.
21 Ie under the Council Tax (Alteration of Lists and Appeals) (England) Regulations 2009, SI 2009/2270, reg 10 (see PARA 424): see the Valuation Tribunal for England (Council Tax and Rating Appeals) (Procedure) Regulations 2009, SI 2009/2269, reg 22(4)(b)(i).
22 Ie under the Valuation Tribunal for England (Council Tax and Rating Appeals) (Procedure) Regulations 2009, SI 2009/2269, reg 22(1): see the text to notes 1–9.
23 See the Valuation Tribunal for England (Council Tax and Rating Appeals) (Procedure) Regulations 2009, SI 2009/2269, reg 22(4)(b)(ii).
24 Ie other than steps under the Valuation Tribunal for England (Council Tax and Rating Appeals) (Procedure) Regulations 2009, SI 2009/2269, reg 19: see PARA 526.
25 Valuation Tribunal for England (Council Tax and Rating Appeals) (Procedure) Regulations 2009, SI 2009/2269, reg 22(4)(b)(iii).
26 Ie under the Valuation Tribunal for England (Council Tax and Rating Appeals) (Procedure) Regulations 2009, SI 2009/2269, reg 22(1): see the text to notes 1–9.
27 As to the meaning of 'party' see PARA 515 note 4.
28 See note 16.
29 Valuation Tribunal for England (Council Tax and Rating Appeals) (Procedure) Regulations 2009, SI 2009/2269, reg 23(1)(a).
30 Valuation Tribunal for England (Council Tax and Rating Appeals) (Procedure) Regulations 2009, SI 2009/2269, reg 23(1)(b).
31 As to the meaning of 'listing officer' see PARA 515 note 4.
32 Valuation Tribunal for England (Council Tax and Rating Appeals) (Procedure) Regulations 2009, SI 2009/2269, reg 23(1)(c). Where the tribunal receives a notice from a party under reg 23(1)(c), the tribunal must:
    (1) within the period of two weeks beginning on the day on which the tribunal received it, serve on the party a written notice acknowledging receipt of it and specifying the date of receipt (reg 23(2)(a)); and
    (2) as soon as reasonably practicable serve a copy of the party's notice on the listing officer (reg 23(2)(b)).

528. Hearings.

The Valuation Tribunal for England[1] must hold a hearing before making a decision which disposes of proceedings[2] unless each party[3] has consented to, or has not objected to, the matter being decided without a hearing[4], and the tribunal considers that it is able to decide the matter without a hearing[5]. However, the tribunal may, in any event, dispose of proceedings without a hearing under the provisions[6] relating to the striking out of proceedings[7].

The tribunal must give each party entitled to attend a hearing reasonable notice[8] of the time and place of the hearing (including any adjourned or postponed hearing) and any changes to the time and place of the hearing[9].

All hearings must be held in public[10]; but the tribunal or the tribunal panel[11] may give a direction that a hearing, or part of it, is to be held in private[12]. Where a hearing, or part of it, is to be held in private, the tribunal or the tribunal panel may determine who is permitted to attend the hearing or part of it[13].

Where the tribunal or the tribunal panel considers:

(1) that the conduct of any person is likely to disrupt the hearing[14];
(2) that the presence of any person is likely to prevent another person from giving evidence or making submissions freely[15]; or
(3) that the presence of any person is likely to defeat the purpose of the hearing[16],

the tribunal or the tribunal panel (as the case may be) may give a direction excluding the person from any hearing, or part of it[17]. The tribunal panel may give a direction excluding from any hearing, or part of it any person whose conduct the panel considers is disrupting the hearing[18]. The tribunal or the tribunal panel may give a direction excluding a witness from a hearing until that witness gives evidence[19].

If a party fails to attend a hearing the tribunal panel may proceed with the hearing if it is satisfied that the party has been notified of the hearing or that reasonable steps have been taken to notify the party of the hearing[20], and it considers that it is in the interests of justice to proceed with the hearing[21].

Where at the hearing of an appeal relating to a disagreement as to a proposed alteration of a valuation list[22] the listing officer[23] contends that the proposal was not validly made[24] and the tribunal panel does not uphold the contention[25], the panel must not immediately proceed to deal with the appeal unless every party present or represented at the hearing so agrees[26].

1 As to the Valuation Tribunal for England see PARA 232. The Valuation Tribunal for England (Council Tax and Rating Appeals) (Procedure) Regulations 2009, SI 2009/2269, apply in relation to England only: see reg 1. As to the equivalent regulations in relation to Wales see the Council Tax (Alteration of Lists and Appeals) Regulations 1993, SI 1993/290, Pt III (regs 16–34); and the Valuation Tribunal for Wales Regulations 2010, SI 2010/713, Pt 5 (regs 27–46); and see PARA 534 et seq. As to the meanings of 'England' and 'Wales' see PARA 2 note 16.

2 As to appeals in relation to council tax see PARA 514.

3 As to the meaning of 'party' see PARA 515 note 4.

4 Valuation Tribunal for England (Council Tax and Rating Appeals) (Procedure) Regulations 2009, SI 2009/2269, reg 29(1)(a).

5 Valuation Tribunal for England (Council Tax and Rating Appeals) (Procedure) Regulations 2009, SI 2009/2269, reg 29(1)(b).

6 Ie the Valuation Tribunal for England (Council Tax and Rating Appeals) (Procedure) Regulations 2009, SI 2009/2269, reg 10: see PARA 522.

7 Valuation Tribunal for England (Council Tax and Rating Appeals) (Procedure) Regulations 2009, SI 2009/2269, reg 29(2).

8 As to the service and delivery of documents see PARA 515.

9 Valuation Tribunal for England (Council Tax and Rating Appeals) (Procedure) Regulations 2009, SI 2009/2269, reg 30(1). The period of notice under reg 30(1) must be at least 14 days except that the tribunal may give shorter notice:
(1) with the parties' consent (reg 30(2)(a)); or
(2) in urgent or exceptional circumstances (reg 30(2)(b)).

10 Valuation Tribunal for England (Council Tax and Rating Appeals) (Procedure) Regulations 2009, SI 2009/2269, reg 31(1). This provision is expressed to be subject to reg 31(2)–(6) (see the text to notes 11–19): see reg 31(1).

11 As to the meaning of 'tribunal panel' see PARA 526 note 7.

12 Valuation Tribunal for England (Council Tax and Rating Appeals) (Procedure) Regulations 2009, SI 2009/2269, reg 31(2). As to the power of the tribunal to correct errors in a direction see PARA 521.

13 Valuation Tribunal for England (Council Tax and Rating Appeals) (Procedure) Regulations 2009, SI 2009/2269, reg 31(3).

14 Valuation Tribunal for England (Council Tax and Rating Appeals) (Procedure) Regulations 2009, SI 2009/2269, reg 31(4)(a).

15 Valuation Tribunal for England (Council Tax and Rating Appeals) (Procedure) Regulations 2009, SI 2009/2269, reg 31(4)(b).

16 Valuation Tribunal for England (Council Tax and Rating Appeals) (Procedure) Regulations 2009, SI 2009/2269, reg 31(4)(c).

17 Valuation Tribunal for England (Council Tax and Rating Appeals) (Procedure) Regulations 2009, SI 2009/2269, reg 31(4).

18 Valuation Tribunal for England (Council Tax and Rating Appeals) (Procedure) Regulations 2009, SI 2009/2269, reg 31(5).

19 Valuation Tribunal for England (Council Tax and Rating Appeals) (Procedure) Regulations 2009, SI 2009/2269, reg 31(6). As to witnesses see PARA 524.

20 Valuation Tribunal for England (Council Tax and Rating Appeals) (Procedure) Regulations 2009, SI 2009/2269, reg 32(a).
21 Valuation Tribunal for England (Council Tax and Rating Appeals) (Procedure) Regulations 2009, SI 2009/2269, reg 32(b). As to appeal management generally see PARA 516. As to the general duty of the tribunal in relation to appeals see PARA 515.
22 Ie an appeal under the Council Tax (Alteration of Lists and Appeals) (England) Regulations 2009, SI 2009/2270, reg 10: see PARA 424.
23 As to the meaning of 'listing officer' see PARA 515 note 4.
24 Valuation Tribunal for England (Council Tax and Rating Appeals) (Procedure) Regulations 2009, SI 2009/2269, reg 33(a).
25 Valuation Tribunal for England (Council Tax and Rating Appeals) (Procedure) Regulations 2009, SI 2009/2269, reg 33(b).
26 Valuation Tribunal for England (Council Tax and Rating Appeals) (Procedure) Regulations 2009, SI 2009/2269, reg 33.

529. Entry and inspection of premises.

The tribunal panel[1] may enter and inspect[2]:

(1) the dwelling[3] which is the subject of the appeal[4]; and
(2) so as far as is practicable, any comparable land or property to which the attention of the tribunal panel is drawn[5].

When the tribunal panel intends to enter any premises in accordance with this power it must give notice[6] to the parties[7], who are entitled to be represented at the inspection[8]. Where the tribunal panel considers it appropriate, representation at an inspection may be limited to one person to represent those parties having the same interest in the appeal[9].

1 As to the meaning of 'tribunal panel' see PARA 526 note 7.
2 Valuation Tribunal for England (Council Tax and Rating Appeals) (Procedure) Regulations 2009, SI 2009/2269, reg 34(1). Regulation 34(1) is expressed to be subject to reg 34(2) (see the text to notes 6–8): see reg 34(1).
The Valuation Tribunal for England (Council Tax and Rating Appeals) (Procedure) Regulations 2009, SI 2009/2269, apply in relation to England only: see reg 1. As to the equivalent regulations in relation to Wales see the Council Tax (Alteration of Lists and Appeals) Regulations 1993, SI 1993/290, Pt III (regs 16–34); and the Valuation Tribunal for Wales Regulations 2010, SI 2010/713, Pt 5 (regs 27–46); and see PARA 534 et seq. As to the meanings of 'England' and 'Wales' see PARA 2 note 16.
3 As to the meaning of 'dwelling' see PARA 349.
4 Valuation Tribunal for England (Council Tax and Rating Appeals) (Procedure) Regulations 2009, SI 2009/2269, reg 34(1)(a). As to appeals in relation to council tax see PARA 514.
5 Valuation Tribunal for England (Council Tax and Rating Appeals) (Procedure) Regulations 2009, SI 2009/2269, reg 34(1)(b).
6 As to the service and delivery of documents see PARA 515.
7 As to the meaning of 'party' see PARA 515 note 4.
8 Valuation Tribunal for England (Council Tax and Rating Appeals) (Procedure) Regulations 2009, SI 2009/2269, reg 34(2).
9 Valuation Tribunal for England (Council Tax and Rating Appeals) (Procedure) Regulations 2009, SI 2009/2269, reg 34(3).

530. Decisions.

The tribunal panel[1] may give a decision orally at a hearing[2]. As soon as reasonably practicable after the tribunal panel makes a decision which finally disposes of all issues in the proceedings, the Valuation Tribunal for England[3] must provide to each party[4]:

(1) a decision notice stating the tribunal panel's decision[5];
(2) in the case of an appeal relating to liability to council tax[6], notification of the right to request a written statement of reasons, where those written reasons have not already been provided[7];

(3) notification of any right of appeal against the decision and of any right to make an application for the review of the decision[8]; and
(4) notification of the time within which, and the manner in which, any right referred to in head (2) or (3) may be exercised[9].

As soon as reasonably practicable after the tribunal panel makes a decision which finally disposes of all issues in the proceedings on an appeal, the Valuation Tribunal for England must send to each party a written[10] statement of the tribunal panel's reasons for the decision[11].

The Valuation Tribunal for England may at any time correct any clerical mistake or other accidental slip or omission in a decision by sending notification of the amended decision to all parties[12] and making any necessary amendment to any information published in relation to the decision[13].

1 As to the meaning of 'tribunal panel' see PARA 526 note 7.

2 Valuation Tribunal for England (Council Tax and Rating Appeals) (Procedure) Regulations 2009, SI 2009/2269, reg 36(1). As to hearings see PARA 528. As to appeals in relation to council tax see PARA 514. As to records of decisions see PARA 533.

The Valuation Tribunal for England (Council Tax and Rating Appeals) (Procedure) Regulations 2009, SI 2009/2269, apply in relation to England only: see reg 1. As to the equivalent regulations in relation to Wales see the Council Tax (Alteration of Lists and Appeals) Regulations 1993, SI 1993/290, Pt III (regs 16–34); and the Valuation Tribunal for Wales Regulations 2010, SI 2010/713, Pt 5 (regs 27–46); and see PARA 534 et seq. As to the meanings of 'England' and 'Wales' see PARA 2 note 16.

3 As to the Valuation Tribunal for England see PARA 232.

4 As to the meaning of 'party' see PARA 515 note 4.

5 Valuation Tribunal for England (Council Tax and Rating Appeals) (Procedure) Regulations 2009, SI 2009/2269, reg 36(2)(a). As to the service and delivery of documents see PARA 515.

6 Ie an appeal under the Local Government Finance Act 1992 s 16: see PARA 513.

7 Valuation Tribunal for England (Council Tax and Rating Appeals) (Procedure) Regulations 2009, SI 2009/2269, reg 36(2)(aa) (added by SI 2013/465).

In the case of an appeal under the Local Government Finance Act 1992 s 16 the tribunal panel may give reasons for a decision which disposes of proceedings:

(1) orally at a hearing (Valuation Tribunal for England (Council Tax and Rating Appeals) (Procedure) Regulations 2009, SI 2009/2269, reg 37(3)(a) (reg 37(3)–(7) added by SI 2013/465)); or
(2) in a written statement of reasons to each party (Valuation Tribunal for England (Council Tax and Rating Appeals) (Procedure) Regulations 2009, SI 2009/2269, reg 37(3)(b) (as so added)).

Unless the tribunal panel has already provided a written statement of reasons under head (2), a party may request the tribunal panel to provide such written statement following a decision which finally disposes of all issues in the proceedings: reg 37(4) (as so added). Such a request must be made within two weeks beginning with the date on which the panel sent or otherwise provided to the party a decision notice relating to the decision which finally disposes of all issues in the proceedings: reg 37(5) (as so added). If a party makes such a request, the tribunal panel must send a written statement of reasons to each party within two weeks beginning with the date on which the request was made or as soon as reasonably practicable after the end of that period: reg 37(6) (as so added). Where a request under reg 37(4) is made in writing, it must be treated, for the purposes of reg 37(5), (6), as having been made on the date it is received by the tribunal: reg 37(7) (as so added).

8 Valuation Tribunal for England (Council Tax and Rating Appeals) (Procedure) Regulations 2009, SI 2009/2269, reg 36(2)(b). As to reviews of decisions see PARA 532. As to appeals see PARA 560.

9 Valuation Tribunal for England (Council Tax and Rating Appeals) (Procedure) Regulations 2009, SI 2009/2269, reg 36(2)(c) (amended by SI 2013/465).

10 As to the meaning of 'written' see PARA 21 note 3.

11 Valuation Tribunal for England (Council Tax and Rating Appeals) (Procedure) Regulations 2009, SI 2009/2269, reg 37(1). This is subject to reg 37(3) (see note 7): reg 37(1) (amended by SI 2013/465). In the case of an appeal against a completion notice, the tribunal must send notice of the decision to the listing officer for the relevant authority: see the Valuation Tribunal for England (Council Tax and Rating Appeals) (Procedure) Regulations 2009, SI 2009/2269, reg

37(2)(a). As to the meaning of 'completion notice' see PARA 518 note 3. As to the meaning of 'listing officer' see PARA 515 note 4. As to the meaning of 'relevant authority' see PARA 524 note 33. As to reasons for decisions see *Moghaddam v Hammersmith and Fulham London Borough Council* [2009] EWHC 1670 (Admin), [2009] RA 209, [2009] All ER (D) 144 (Jul) (decided under previous legislation).

12 See the Valuation Tribunal for England (Council Tax and Rating Appeals) (Procedure) Regulations 2009, SI 2009/2269, reg 39(a).

13 See the Valuation Tribunal for England (Council Tax and Rating Appeals) (Procedure) Regulations 2009, SI 2009/2269, reg 39(b).

531. Orders.

The Valuation Tribunal for England[1] may, at the request of the parties[2] but only if the tribunal considers it appropriate, make a consent order disposing of the proceedings[3] and making such other appropriate provision as the parties have agreed[4]. A consent order may provide for the alteration of a list[5] and, where it does, must specify the day from which the alteration is to have effect[6].

After dealing with an appeal relating to liability to council tax[7] the tribunal may by order require:

(1) an estimate to be quashed or altered[8];
(2) a penalty to be quashed[9];
(3) the decision of a billing authority to be reversed[10]; or
(4) a calculation (other than an estimate) of an amount to be quashed and the amount to be re-calculated[11].

After dealing with an appeal relating to a disagreement as to a proposed alteration of a list[12] the tribunal may by order require a listing officer[13] to alter a list in accordance with any provision made by or under the Local Government Finance Act 1992[14].

After dealing with an appeal against the imposition of a penalty, the tribunal may by order require a penalty to be quashed[15]. After dealing with an appeal against the imposition of a penalty, the tribunal may order the listing officer whose notice is the subject of the appeal to reduce or remit the penalty[16].

An order[17] may require any matter ancillary to its subject matter to be attended to[18].

The billing authority or the listing officer (as the case may be) must comply with an order[19] within two weeks of the day of its making[20].

The tribunal may at any time correct any clerical mistake or other accidental slip or omission in an order by sending notification[21] of the amended order to all parties[22], and making any necessary amendment to any information published in relation to the order[23].

1 As to the Valuation Tribunal for England see PARA 232. The Valuation Tribunal for England (Council Tax and Rating Appeals) (Procedure) Regulations 2009, SI 2009/2269, apply in relation to England only: see reg 1. As to the equivalent regulations in relation to Wales see the Council Tax (Alteration of Lists and Appeals) Regulations 1993, SI 1993/290, Pt III (regs 16–34); and the Valuation Tribunal for Wales Regulations 2010, SI 2010/713, Pt 5 (regs 27–46); and see PARA 534 et seq. As to the meanings of 'England' and 'Wales' see PARA 2 note 16.

2 As to the meaning of 'party' see PARA 515 note 4.

3 As to appeals in relation to council tax see PARA 514.

4 Valuation Tribunal for England (Council Tax and Rating Appeals) (Procedure) Regulations 2009, SI 2009/2269, reg 35(1). Notwithstanding any other provision of the Valuation Tribunal for England (Council Tax and Rating Appeals) (Procedure) Regulations 2009, SI 2009/2269, the tribunal need not hold a hearing before making an order under reg 35(1), or provide reasons for the order: reg 35(3). As to hearings see PARA 528. As to records of orders see PARA 533.

5 As to the meaning of 'list' see PARA 515 note 4.

6 Valuation Tribunal for England (Council Tax and Rating Appeals) (Procedure) Regulations 2009, SI 2009/2269, reg 35(2).

7 Ie an appeal under the Local Government Finance Act 1992 s 16: see PARA 513.
8 Valuation Tribunal for England (Council Tax and Rating Appeals) (Procedure) Regulations 2009, SI 2009/2269, reg 38(1)(a).
9 Valuation Tribunal for England (Council Tax and Rating Appeals) (Procedure) Regulations 2009, SI 2009/2269, reg 38(1)(b).
10 Valuation Tribunal for England (Council Tax and Rating Appeals) (Procedure) Regulations 2009, SI 2009/2269, reg 38(1)(c). As to the meaning of 'billing authority' see PARA 346.
11 Valuation Tribunal for England (Council Tax and Rating Appeals) (Procedure) Regulations 2009, SI 2009/2269, reg 38(1)(d).
12 Ie an appeal under the Council Tax (Alteration of Lists and Appeals) (England) Regulations 2009, SI 2009/2270, reg 10: see PARA 424.
13 As to the meaning of 'listing officer' see PARA 515 note 4.
14 Valuation Tribunal for England (Council Tax and Rating Appeals) (Procedure) Regulations 2009, SI 2009/2269, reg 38(2). Where it is decided that the valuation band applicable to the dwelling should be higher than:
(1) the valuation band shown in the list at the date of the proposal (reg 38(3)(a)); and
(2) the valuation band contended for in the proposal (reg 38(3)(b)),
the tribunal must order the listing officer to alter the list with effect from the day on which the tribunal panel made the decision; and the listing officer must so alter the list, notwithstanding any provision to the contrary in the Council Tax (Alteration of Lists and Appeals) (England) Regulations 2009, SI 2009/2270, reg 11 (day from which alteration has effect: see PARA 426): Valuation Tribunal for England (Council Tax and Rating Appeals) (Procedure) Regulations 2009, SI 2009/2269, reg 38(3). As to valuation bands see PARA 361. As to the meaning of 'dwelling' see PARA 349. As to the meaning of 'tribunal panel' see PARA 526 note 7.
15 See the Valuation Tribunal for England (Council Tax and Rating Appeals) (Procedure) Regulations 2009, SI 2009/2269, reg 38(7A) (added by SI 2013/465).
16 See the Valuation Tribunal for England (Council Tax and Rating Appeals) (Procedure) Regulations 2009, SI 2009/2269, reg 38(8).
17 Ie an order under the Valuation Tribunal for England (Council Tax and Rating Appeals) (Procedure) Regulations 2009, SI 2009/2269, reg 38: see the text to notes 7–16.
18 Valuation Tribunal for England (Council Tax and Rating Appeals) (Procedure) Regulations 2009, SI 2009/2269, reg 38(10).
19 Ie an order under the Valuation Tribunal for England (Council Tax and Rating Appeals) (Procedure) Regulations 2009, SI 2009/2269, reg 38: see the text to notes 7–16.
20 Valuation Tribunal for England (Council Tax and Rating Appeals) (Procedure) Regulations 2009, SI 2009/2269, reg 38(9). As to the calculation of time generally see reg 14; and PARA 515.
21 As to the service and delivery of documents see PARA 515.
22 See the Valuation Tribunal for England (Council Tax and Rating Appeals) (Procedure) Regulations 2009, SI 2009/2269, reg 39(a).
23 See the Valuation Tribunal for England (Council Tax and Rating Appeals) (Procedure) Regulations 2009, SI 2009/2269, reg 39(b).

532. Review of decisions.

A party[1] may apply to the Valuation Tribunal for England[2] in writing[3] for the review of the whole or part of a decision which disposes of proceedings on an appeal[4]. An application must be made within 28 days of the date on which notice of the decision was sent[5], and must be considered by the president of the tribunal[6]. The president of the tribunal must not grant an application unless at least one of the following conditions is satisfied[7]. The conditions are:

(1) a document relating to the proceedings was not sent to, or was not received at an appropriate time by, a party or a party's representative[8];
(2) a document relating to the proceedings was not sent to the tribunal at an appropriate time[9];
(3) a party or its representative was not present at a hearing relating to the proceedings and the party shows reasonable cause for its or its representative's absence[10];
(4) there has been some other procedural irregularity in the proceedings[11];

(5) the decision is affected by a decision of, or on appeal from, the Upper Tribunal or the High Court[12];

(6) where the decision relates to an appeal against a completion notice[13], new evidence, whose existence could not have been discovered by reasonable inquiry or could not have been foreseen, has become available since the conclusion of the proceedings[14].

The president of the tribunal also has power to direct that a review be undertaken of the whole or part of a decision which disposes of proceedings on an appeal[15].

Where an application[16] is granted or a direction is given[17], the tribunal must review the decision or part that is the subject of the review[18]; and if it considers that any of the conditions specified in heads (1) to (6) above is satisfied[19] and that it is in the interests of justice to do so[20], the tribunal must set aside the decision or part[21]. If the tribunal sets aside a decision it must revoke any order made in consequence of the decision[22] and notify the parties in writing of the revocation[23]. The tribunal must notify the parties in writing of the result of an application[24], of the result of a review[25] and if[26] it revokes an order[27].

1 As to the meaning of 'party' see PARA 515 note 4.

2 As to the Valuation Tribunal for England see PARA 232. The Valuation Tribunal for England (Council Tax and Rating Appeals) (Procedure) Regulations 2009, SI 2009/2269, apply in relation to England only: see reg 1. As to the equivalent regulations in relation to Wales see the Council Tax (Alteration of Lists and Appeals) Regulations 1993, SI 1993/290, Pt III (regs 16–34); and the Valuation Tribunal for Wales Regulations 2010, SI 2010/713, Pt 5 (regs 27–46); and see PARA 534 et seq. As to the meanings of 'England' and 'Wales' see PARA 2 note 16.

3 As to the meaning of 'writing' see PARA 21 note 3.

4 Valuation Tribunal for England (Council Tax and Rating Appeals) (Procedure) Regulations 2009, SI 2009/2269, reg 40(1). As to decisions see PARA 530. As to appeals in relation to council tax see PARA 514.

Where, on the day on which an application is made, an appeal to the Upper Tribunal or the High Court in relation to the same issue as is the subject of the application remains undetermined, the tribunal must notify the Upper Tribunal or the High Court as soon as reasonably practicable:

(1) after the application is made (reg 40(10)(a)); and

(2) after notice is given under any of reg 40(9)(a)–(c) (see the text to notes 24–27) (reg 40(10)(b)).

As to appeals from the tribunal see PARA 560.

Where a listing officer applies to the tribunal under reg 40 for the review of a decision in consequence of which an order requiring the alteration of a list was made the listing officer must, at the same time or as soon as reasonably practicable afterwards, notify the authority concerned of the application or appeal: see reg 44(1)(a). For these purposes, 'the authority concerned', in relation to an appeal under the Local Government Finance Act 1992 s 16 (see PARA 513), is the billing authority concerned: Valuation Tribunal for England (Council Tax and Rating Appeals) (Procedure) Regulations 2009, SI 2009/2269, reg 44(2)(a). As to the meaning of 'listing officer' see PARA 515 note 4. As to the meaning of 'list' see PARA 515 note 4. As to the service and delivery of documents see PARA 515. As to the meaning of 'billing authority' see PARA 346.

5 Valuation Tribunal for England (Council Tax and Rating Appeals) (Procedure) Regulations 2009, SI 2009/2269, reg 40(3)(a). As to the calculation of time see reg 14; and PARA 515.

6 Valuation Tribunal for England (Council Tax and Rating Appeals) (Procedure) Regulations 2009, SI 2009/2269, reg 40(3)(b). As to the president of the Valuation Tribunal for England see PARA 233.

7 Valuation Tribunal for England (Council Tax and Rating Appeals) (Procedure) Regulations 2009, SI 2009/2269, reg 40(4).

8 Valuation Tribunal for England (Council Tax and Rating Appeals) (Procedure) Regulations 2009, SI 2009/2269, reg 40(5)(a). As to representatives see PARA 523.

9 Valuation Tribunal for England (Council Tax and Rating Appeals) (Procedure) Regulations 2009, SI 2009/2269, reg 40(5)(b).

10 Valuation Tribunal for England (Council Tax and Rating Appeals) (Procedure) Regulations 2009, SI 2009/2269, reg 40(5)(c). As to hearings see PARA 528.

11 Valuation Tribunal for England (Council Tax and Rating Appeals) (Procedure) Regulations 2009, SI 2009/2269, reg 40(5)(d).
12 Valuation Tribunal for England (Council Tax and Rating Appeals) (Procedure) Regulations 2009, SI 2009/2269, reg 40(5)(e).
13 As to the meaning of 'completion notice' see PARA 518 note 3.
14 Valuation Tribunal for England (Council Tax and Rating Appeals) (Procedure) Regulations 2009, SI 2009/2269, reg 40(5)(f).
15 See the Valuation Tribunal for England (Council Tax and Rating Appeals) (Procedure) Regulations 2009, SI 2009/2269, reg 40(2).
16 Ie under the Valuation Tribunal for England (Council Tax and Rating Appeals) (Procedure) Regulations 2009, SI 2009/2269, reg 40(1): see the text to notes 1–14.
17 Ie under the Valuation Tribunal for England (Council Tax and Rating Appeals) (Procedure) Regulations 2009, SI 2009/2269, reg 40(2): see the text to note 15.
18 Valuation Tribunal for England (Council Tax and Rating Appeals) (Procedure) Regulations 2009, SI 2009/2269, reg 40(6). Tribunal business arrangements apply in relation to the selection of members of the tribunal to review a decision or part of a decision as if the review were an appeal: reg 40(7). As to tribunal business arrangements see PARA 234.
19 Valuation Tribunal for England (Council Tax and Rating Appeals) (Procedure) Regulations 2009, SI 2009/2269, reg 40(6)(a).
20 Valuation Tribunal for England (Council Tax and Rating Appeals) (Procedure) Regulations 2009, SI 2009/2269, reg 40(6)(b).
21 Valuation Tribunal for England (Council Tax and Rating Appeals) (Procedure) Regulations 2009, SI 2009/2269, reg 40(6).
22 As to orders see PARA 531.
23 Valuation Tribunal for England (Council Tax and Rating Appeals) (Procedure) Regulations 2009, SI 2009/2269, reg 40(8).
24 Valuation Tribunal for England (Council Tax and Rating Appeals) (Procedure) Regulations 2009, SI 2009/2269, reg 40(9)(a). See also note 4.
25 Ie a review under the Valuation Tribunal for England (Council Tax and Rating Appeals) (Procedure) Regulations 2009, SI 2009/2269, reg 40(6) (see the text to notes 16–21): see reg 40(9)(b). See also note 4.
26 Ie under the Valuation Tribunal for England (Council Tax and Rating Appeals) (Procedure) Regulations 2009, SI 2009/2269, reg 40(8): see the text to notes 22–23.
27 Valuation Tribunal for England (Council Tax and Rating Appeals) (Procedure) Regulations 2009, SI 2009/2269, reg 40(9)(c). See also note 4.

533. Records of decisions and orders.

The Valuation Tribunal for England[1] must make arrangements for each decision[2], each order[3], the effect of each correction of a decision, order, direction or other document[4], and each revocation of an order[5] to be recorded[6]. Each record must be retained for the period of six years beginning on the day on which an entry was last made in it[7].

Any person[8] may, at a reasonable time stated by or on behalf of the tribunal and without making payment, inspect such records[9]. A person having custody of such records commits an offence if, without reasonable excuse, he intentionally obstructs a person in exercising this right of inspection[10].

The production in any proceedings in any court of law of a document purporting to be certified by the president of the tribunal[11] or the clerk of the tribunal to be a true copy of a record of the tribunal is, unless the contrary is proved, sufficient evidence of the document and of the facts it records[12].

1 As to the Valuation Tribunal for England see PARA 232. The Valuation Tribunal for England (Council Tax and Rating Appeals) (Procedure) Regulations 2009, SI 2009/2269, apply in relation to England only: see reg 1. As to the equivalent regulations in relation to Wales see the Council Tax (Alteration of Lists and Appeals) Regulations 1993, SI 1993/290, Pt III (regs 16–34); and the Valuation Tribunal for Wales Regulations 2010, SI 2010/713, Pt 5 (regs 27–46); and see PARA 534 et seq. As to the meanings of 'England' and 'Wales' see PARA 2 note 16.
2 As to decisions see PARA 530.
3 Ie under the Valuation Tribunal for England (Council Tax and Rating Appeals) (Procedure)

Regulations 2009, SI 2009/2269, reg 35 or reg 38: see PARA 531.

4 Ie each correction under the Valuation Tribunal for England (Council Tax and Rating Appeals) (Procedure) Regulations 2009, SI 2009/2269, reg 39: see PARAS 521, 530–531.

5 Ie under the Valuation Tribunal for England (Council Tax and Rating Appeals) (Procedure) Regulations 2009, SI 2009/2269, reg 40(8): see PARA 532.

6 Valuation Tribunal for England (Council Tax and Rating Appeals) (Procedure) Regulations 2009, SI 2009/2269, reg 41(1). Records may be kept in any form, whether documentary or otherwise: reg 41(2) (amended by SI 2011/434).

Where a tribunal orders the listing officer for a billing authority to alter the authority's valuation list (Local Government Finance Act 1988 Sch 11 para 9(1)(d) (added by the Local Government Finance Act 1992 s 117(1), Sch 13 para 88(8))), if the order is recorded in accordance with any provision included in regulations under the Local Government Finance Act 1988 Sch 11 para A19 or Sch 11 para 1 (as to such regulations see PARA 235), the officer or authority ordered must:

(1) alter the register or list concerned accordingly (Sch 11 para 9(2)(a) (Sch 11 para 9(2) amended by the Local Government and Public Involvement in Health Act 2007 s 219(1), Sch 15 paras 1, 12)); and

(2) attend to any ancillary matter provided for in the order (such as the repayment of an amount, or the allowance of an amount by way of deduction against a sum due) (Local Government Finance Act 1988 Sch 11 para 9(2)(b) (as so amended)).

As to listing officers see PARA 347. As to billing authorities see PARA 346. As to valuation lists see PARA 408.

Where a tribunal orders a billing authority:

(a) to reverse a decision that a particular dwelling is a chargeable dwelling for the purposes of the Local Government Finance Act 1992 Pt I Ch I (ss 1–19) (see PARA 350), or that a particular person is liable to pay council tax in respect of such a dwelling (Local Government Finance Act 1988 Sch 11 para 10A(1)(a) (Sch 11 para 10A added by the Local Government Finance Act 1992 Sch 13 para 88(9)));

(b) to quash or alter an estimate of an amount which a person is liable to pay to the authority in respect of council tax (Local Government Finance Act 1988 Sch 11 para 10A(1)(b) (as so added));

(c) to quash a calculation (other than an estimate) of such an amount, or to recalculate the amount (Sch 11 para 10A(1)(c) (as so added)); or

(d) to quash a penalty imposed by the authority under regulations under the Local Government Finance Act 1992 s 14C (see PARA 438) or Sch 3 (see PARA 471) (Local Government Finance Act 1988 Sch 11 para 10A(1)(d) (as so added; amended by the Local Government Finance Act 2012 s 14(9))),

then, if the order is recorded in accordance with any provision included in regulations under Sch 11 para A19 or para 1 (see PARA 235), the authority ordered must (Sch 11 para 10A(2) (as so added; amended by the Local Government and Public Involvement in Health Act 2007 Sch 15 paras 1, 14)):

(i) reverse the decision, quash or alter the estimate, quash the calculation, recalculate the amount or quash the penalty accordingly (Local Government Finance Act 1988 Sch 11 para 10A(2)(a) (as so added)); and

(ii) attend to any ancillary matter provided for in the order (such as the repayment of an amount, or the allowance of an amount by way of deduction against a sum due) (Sch 11 para 10A(2)(b) (as so added)).

As to persons liable to pay council tax see PARA 354 et seq.

7 Valuation Tribunal for England (Council Tax and Rating Appeals) (Procedure) Regulations 2009, SI 2009/2269, reg 41(3).

8 As to the meaning of 'person' see PARA 11 note 13.

9 Valuation Tribunal for England (Council Tax and Rating Appeals) (Procedure) Regulations 2009, SI 2009/2269, reg 41(4).

10 See the Valuation Tribunal for England (Council Tax and Rating Appeals) (Procedure) Regulations 2009, SI 2009/2269, reg 41(5). The penalty for such an offence is, on summary conviction, a fine not exceeding level 1 on the standard scale: reg 41(5). As to the powers of magistrates' courts to issue fines on summary conviction see SENTENCING vol 92 (2015) PARA 176.

11 As to the president of the Valuation Tribunal for England see PARA 233.

12 Valuation Tribunal for England (Council Tax and Rating Appeals) (Procedure) Regulations 2009, SI 2009/2269, reg 41(6).

C. PROCEDURE: WALES

(A) Alteration of Lists

534. Arrangements for appeals.

It is the duty of the President of the Valuation Tribunal for Wales[1] to secure that arrangements are made for appeals[2] relating to the alteration of valuation lists to be determined in accordance with the relevant provisions[3]. A tribunal[4] must not hear an appeal relating to a disagreement as to a proposal for the alteration of a valuation list[5] until any appeal about the validity of a proposal[6] in respect of the same proposal has been determined[7]. Where two or more appeals for alteration of the valuation list relating to the same dwelling are referred, the order in which the appeals are dealt with is to be the order in which the alterations in question would, but for the disagreements which occasion the appeals, have taken effect[8].

1 As to the Valuation Tribunal for Wales see PARA 237. As to the president see PARA 238.

2 In the Council Tax (Alteration of Lists and Appeals) Regulations 1993, SI 1993/290, Pt III (regs 16–34) 'appeal', unless the context otherwise requires, means an appeal under reg 8 (see PARA 431) or reg 13 (see PARA 434): reg 16(1).

3 Council Tax (Alteration of Lists and Appeals) Regulations 1993, SI 1993/290, reg 18(1) (amended by SI 2010/713). The relevant provisions are the Council Tax (Alteration of Lists and Appeals) Regulations 1993, SI 1993/290, regs 18(2)–38.

The Council Tax (Alteration of Lists and Appeals) Regulations 1993, SI 1993/290, apply in relation to Wales only: see PARA 417 note 2. The procedure on other appeals relating to council tax in Wales is governed by the Valuation Tribunal for Wales Regulations 2010, SI 2010/713, Pt 5 (regs 27–46): see PARA 546 et seq. As to the equivalent regulations in relation to England see the Valuation Tribunal for England (Council Tax and Rating Appeals) (Procedure) Regulations 2009, SI 2009/2269; and see PARA 515 et seq. As to the meanings of 'England' and 'Wales' see PARA 2 note 16.

4 'Tribunal' means the members of the Valuation Tribunal for Wales convened in accordance with the Council Tax (Alteration of Lists and Appeals) Regulations 1993, SI 1993/290, Pt III for the purpose of disposing of an appeal: reg 16(1) (definition substituted by SI 2010/713). As to the Valuation Tribunal for Wales see PARA 237.

5 Ie an appeal under the Council Tax (Alteration of Lists and Appeals) Regulations 1993, SI 1993/290, reg 13: see PARA 434.

6 Ie an appeal under the Council Tax (Alteration of Lists and Appeals) Regulations 1993, SI 1993/290, reg 8: see PARA 431.

7 Council Tax (Alteration of Lists and Appeals) Regulations 1993, SI 1993/290, reg 18(2).

8 Council Tax (Alteration of Lists and Appeals) Regulations 1993, SI 1993/290, reg 18(3).

535. Service of notices.

Any notice[1] required or authorised to be served under the regulations relating to the alteration of lists and appeals[2] may be served either[3]:

(1) by delivering it[4]:
   (a) to the person[5] on whom it is to be served[6]; or
   (b) to any other person authorised by him to act as his agent for the purpose[7];
(2) by leaving it at or forwarding it by sending it by first class or second class post[8] to:
   (a) the usual or last-known address of that person[9]; or
   (b) in the case of a company, its registered office[10]; or
   (c) the usual or last-known address, place of business or registered office of any other person authorised as mentioned in head (1)(b)[11];

(3) by delivering it to some person in the dwelling[12] to which it relates or, if there is no person to whom it can so be delivered, then by fixing it to some conspicuous part of the dwelling[13]; or

(4) by sending it by electronic communication[14] to a relevant electronic address[15].

If the name of any taxpayer on whom a notice is required or authorised to be served cannot after reasonable inquiry be ascertained, the notice may be served by addressing it to 'The Council Tax Payer' of the dwelling concerned (naming the dwelling), without further name or description[16].

Any notice required or authorised to be served on a listing officer[17] may be served by addressing the notice to the listing officer for the area in question, without further description[18]; and

(i) delivering it, or sending it by first class or second class post, to his office[19];

(ii) delivering it, or sending it by first class or second class post, to the listing officer's office[20]; or

(iii) sending it by electronic communication to a relevant electronic address[21].

A person who has notified a relevant electronic address for the purpose of head (4) or (iii) above:

(A) must notify any change of that address[22]; and

(B) may withdraw the notification of that address[23],

by serving a written notice[24] on the relevant sender; and the change of address or the withdrawal, as the case may be, will take effect on the third business day after the day on which the notice is received by the relevant sender[25].

For the purposes of the regulations relating to the alteration of lists and appeals:

(I) a notice served by:

(AA) delivering it to a person after 5 pm on a business day or at any time on a day which is not a business day[26];

(BB) delivering it to, or leaving it at, the usual or last known address, place of business or office of a person[27]; or

(CC) fixing it to some part of the dwelling to which it relates[28],

is to be treated as served on the next business day after it was so delivered, left or fixed[29];

(II) a notice served by sending it by first class post is to be treated as served on the second business day after it was posted[30]; and

(III) a notice served by sending it by second class post is to be treated as served on the fourth business day after it was posted[31]; and

(IV) a notice served by the means described in head (4) or (iii) above is:

(AA) if sent by facsimile transmission on a business day before 4 pm, to be treated as served on that day[32];

(BB) if sent by facsimile transmission in any other case, to be treated as served on the next business day after the day on which it was sent[33]; and

(CC) in any other case, to be treated as served on the second business day after the day on which it was sent[34].

1 In the Council Tax (Alteration of Lists and Appeals) Regulations 1993, SI 1993/290, reg 35, any reference to a notice includes a reference to a proposal and any other document required or authorised to be served; and any reference to such requirement or authorisation is to a requirement or authorisation under those Regulations: reg 35(5)(a), (b) (reg 35 substituted in relation to Wales by SI 2010/613). As to the meaning of 'proposal' see PARA 430 note 1.

2 Ie the Council Tax (Alteration of Lists and Appeals) Regulations 1993, SI 1993/290. See PARAS 428 et seq, 534 et seq.

The Council Tax (Alteration of Lists and Appeals) Regulations 1993, SI 1993/290, apply in relation to Wales only: see PARA 417 note 2. The procedure on other appeals relating to council tax in Wales is governed by the Valuation Tribunal for Wales Regulations 2010, SI 2010/713, Pt 5 (regs 27–46): see PARA 546 et seq. As to the equivalent regulations in relation to England see the Valuation Tribunal for England (Council Tax and Rating Appeals) (Procedure) Regulations 2009, SI 2009/2269; and see PARA 515 et seq. As to the meanings of 'England' and 'Wales' see PARA 2 note 16.

3 Council Tax (Alteration of Lists and Appeals) Regulations 1993, SI 1993/290, reg 35(1) (as substituted: see note 1). This is without prejudice to the Local Government Act 1972 s 233 (service of notice by local authorities: LOCAL GOVERNMENT vol 69 (2018) PARA 648): Council Tax (Alteration of Lists and Appeals) Regulations 1993, SI 1993/290, reg 35(1) (as so substituted).

4 Council Tax (Alteration of Lists and Appeals) Regulations 1993, SI 1993/290, reg 35(1)(a) (as substituted: see note 1).

5 As to the meaning of 'person' see PARA 11 note 13.

6 Council Tax (Alteration of Lists and Appeals) Regulations 1993, SI 1993/290, reg 35(1)(a)(i) (as substituted: see note 1).

7 Council Tax (Alteration of Lists and Appeals) Regulations 1993, SI 1993/290, reg 35(1)(a)(ii) (as substituted: see note 1).

8 Council Tax (Alteration of Lists and Appeals) Regulations 1993, SI 1993/290, reg 35(1)(b) (as substituted: see note 1). In reg 35, any reference to first class post includes a reference to an alternative service which provides for delivery on the next business day: reg 35(5)(c) (as so substituted). 'Business day' means any day other than a Saturday, a Sunday, Christmas Day, Good Friday or a bank holiday in England and Wales; and 'bank holiday' means a day which is a bank holiday under the Banking and Financial Dealings Act 1971 (see TIME vol 97 (2015) PARAS 313, 321): Council Tax (Alteration of Lists and Appeals) Regulations 1993, SI 1993/290, reg 35(6) (as so substituted).

9 Council Tax (Alteration of Lists and Appeals) Regulations 1993, SI 1993/290, reg 35(1)(b)(i) (as substituted: see note 1).

10 Council Tax (Alteration of Lists and Appeals) Regulations 1993, SI 1993/290, reg 35(1)(b)(ii) (as substituted: see note 1). As to the registered office of a company see COMPANIES vol 14 (2016) PARA 124.

11 Council Tax (Alteration of Lists and Appeals) Regulations 1993, SI 1993/290, reg 35(1)(b)(iii) (as substituted: see note 1).

12 As to the meaning of 'dwelling' see PARA 349.

13 Council Tax (Alteration of Lists and Appeals) Regulations 1993, SI 1993/290, reg 35(1)(c) (as substituted: see note 1).

14 'Electronic communication' means a communication transmitted (whether from one person to another, from one device to another or from a person to a device or vice versa), either by means of an electronic communications network within the meaning of the Communications Act 2003 s 32(1) (see TELECOMMUNICATIONS vol 97 (2015) PARA 53) or by other means but while in an electronic form: Council Tax (Alteration of Lists and Appeals) Regulations 1993, SI 1993/290, reg 35(6) (as substituted: see note 1).

15 Council Tax (Alteration of Lists and Appeals) Regulations 1993, SI 1993/290, reg 35(1)(d) (as substituted: see note 1). 'Relevant electronic address' is defined by reg 35(6) (as so substituted) as an address which is notified:

(1) to the person serving a notice ('the relevant sender');
(2) by:
  (a) the person on whom the notice is to be served ('the recipient'); or
  (b) any other person authorised by the recipient to notify the relevant sender of the address; and
(3) for the purpose of enabling the notice to be sent by electronic communication.

'Address' in relation to an electronic communication includes any number or address used for the purposes of such communication: reg 35(6) (as so substituted).

16 Council Tax (Alteration of Lists and Appeals) Regulations 1993, SI 1993/290, reg 35(2) (as substituted: see note 1). As to the meaning of 'taxpayer' see PARA 429 note 3.

17 As to the meaning of 'listing officer' see PARA 428 note 12.

18 Council Tax (Alteration of Lists and Appeals) Regulations 1993, SI 1993/290, reg 35(3)(a) (as substituted: see note 1).

19 Council Tax (Alteration of Lists and Appeals) Regulations 1993, SI 1993/290, reg 35(3)(a)(i) (as substituted: see note 1).
20 Council Tax (Alteration of Lists and Appeals) Regulations 1993, SI 1993/290, reg 35(3)(a)(ii) (as substituted: see note 1).
21 Council Tax (Alteration of Lists and Appeals) Regulations 1993, SI 1993/290, reg 35(3)(a)(iii) (as substituted: see note 1).
22 Council Tax (Alteration of Lists and Appeals) Regulations 1993, SI 1993/290, reg 35(4)(a) (as substituted: see note 1).
23 Council Tax (Alteration of Lists and Appeals) Regulations 1993, SI 1993/290, reg 35(4)(b) (as substituted: see note 1).
24 In the Council Tax (Alteration of Lists and Appeals) Regulations 1993, SI 1993/290, any reference to a written notice includes a reference to a notice in electronic form: reg 35(8) (as substituted: see note 1).
25 Council Tax (Alteration of Lists and Appeals) Regulations 1993, SI 1993/290, reg 35(4) (as substituted: see note 1).
26 Council Tax (Alteration of Lists and Appeals) Regulations 1993, SI 1993/290, reg 35(7)(a)(i) (as substituted: see note 1).
27 Council Tax (Alteration of Lists and Appeals) Regulations 1993, SI 1993/290, reg 35(7)(a)(ii) (as substituted: see note 1).
28 Council Tax (Alteration of Lists and Appeals) Regulations 1993, SI 1993/290, reg 35(7)(a)(iii) (as substituted: see note 1).
29 Council Tax (Alteration of Lists and Appeals) Regulations 1993, SI 1993/290, reg 35(7)(a) (as substituted: see note 1).
30 Council Tax (Alteration of Lists and Appeals) Regulations 1993, SI 1993/290, reg 35(7)(b) (as substituted: see note 1).
31 Council Tax (Alteration of Lists and Appeals) Regulations 1993, SI 1993/290, reg 35(7)(c) (as substituted: see note 1).
32 Council Tax (Alteration of Lists and Appeals) Regulations 1993, SI 1993/290, reg 35(7)(d)(i) (as substituted: see note 1).
33 Council Tax (Alteration of Lists and Appeals) Regulations 1993, SI 1993/290, reg 35(7)(d)(ii) (as substituted: see note 1).
34 Council Tax (Alteration of Lists and Appeals) Regulations 1993, SI 1993/290, reg 35(7)(d)(iii) (as substituted: see note 1).

536. Withdrawal of appeals.

An appeal[1] may be withdrawn by notice in writing[2] given to the clerk[3] by the listing officer[4] before the commencement of a hearing[5] or of consideration of written representations[6]. Notice may not be given unless every other party to the appeal[7] has, by notice in writing[8] given to the listing officer, consented to the withdrawal[9]. This does not apply, however, where the withdrawal is attributable to:

(1) an agreement[10] as to alterations[11]; or
(2) in the case of an appeal as to the validity of a proposed alteration[12], an alteration of the list in accordance with the proposal[13].

1 As to the meaning of 'appeal' see PARA 534 note 2.
2 As to the meaning of 'writing' see PARA 21 note 3.
3 'Clerk', in relation to an appeal, means the clerk of the Valuation Tribunal for Wales: Council Tax (Alteration of Lists and Appeals) Regulations 1993, SI 1993/290, reg 16(1) (definition substituted by SI 2010/713).
4 As to the meaning of 'listing officer' see PARA 428 note 12.
5 As to hearings see PARA 539.
6 Council Tax (Alteration of Lists and Appeals) Regulations 1993, SI 1993/290, reg 19(1). This is without prejudice to reg 8(2) (see PARA 431), and subject to reg 19(2): reg 19(1). As to written representations see PARA 537.

The Council Tax (Alteration of Lists and Appeals) Regulations 1993, SI 1993/290, apply in relation to Wales only: see PARA 417 note 2. The procedure on other appeals relating to council tax in Wales is governed by the Valuation Tribunal for Wales Regulations 2010, SI 2010/713, Pt 5 (regs 27–46): see PARA 546 et seq. As to the equivalent regulations in relation to England see the Valuation Tribunal for England (Council Tax and Rating Appeals) (Procedure) Regulations 2009,

SI 2009/2269; and see PARA 515 et seq. As to the meanings of 'England' and 'Wales' see PARA 2 note 16.

7 Any reference in the Council Tax (Alteration of Lists and Appeals) Regulations 1993, SI 1993/290, Pt III (regs 16–34) to a party to an appeal includes the person making the appeal (reg 16(2)) and:
  (1) in relation to an appeal under reg 8, the listing officer (reg 16(2)(a));
  (2) in relation to an appeal under reg 13, every person whose agreement is required for the purposes of reg 12 (reg 16(2)(b)).

8 As to the meaning of 'writing' see PARA 21 note 3.

9 Council Tax (Alteration of Lists and Appeals) Regulations 1993, SI 1993/290, reg 19(2).

10 Ie under the Council Tax (Alteration of Lists and Appeals) Regulations 1993, SI 1993/290, reg 12: see PARA 433.

11 Council Tax (Alteration of Lists and Appeals) Regulations 1993, SI 1993/290, reg 19(3)(a).

12 Ie under the Council Tax (Alteration of Lists and Appeals) Regulations 1993, SI 1993/290, reg 13: see PARA 434.

13 Council Tax (Alteration of Lists and Appeals) Regulations 1993, SI 1993/290, reg 19(3)(b).

537. Disposal of appeal by written representations.

An appeal[1] may be disposed of on the basis of written[2] representations if all the parties have given their agreement in writing[3]. Where all the parties have given their agreement, the clerk[4] must serve notice on the parties accordingly[5]; and, within four weeks of service of such a notice on a party, each party may serve on the clerk a notice stating:

(1) the reasons or further reasons for the disagreement giving rise to the appeal[6]; or
(2) that party does not intend to make further representations[7].

A copy of any notice so served must be served by the clerk on the other party or parties to the appeal, and must be accompanied by a statement of the effect of the provisions[8] as to service of further notice[9]. Any party on whom such a notice is served may, within four weeks of that service, serve on the clerk a further notice stating that party's reply to the other party's statement, or that that party does not intend to make further representations, as the case may be; and the clerk must serve a copy of any such further notice on the other party or parties[10].

After the expiry of four weeks beginning with the expiry of the period of four weeks mentioned above the clerk must submit to a tribunal[11] copies of:

(a) any information transmitted to the clerk in connection with the appeal[12]; and
(b) any notice under the provisions above[13].

The tribunal to which an appeal is so referred may if it thinks fit:

(i) require any party to furnish in writing further particulars of the grounds relied on and of any relevant facts or contentions[14]; or
(ii) order that the appeal be disposed of on the basis of a hearing[15].

Where a tribunal requires any party to furnish any particulars under head (i), the clerk must serve a copy of such particulars on every other party, and each such party may within four weeks of such service serve on the clerk any further statement he wishes to make in response[16].

1 As to the meaning of 'appeal' see PARA 534 note 2.

2 As to the meaning of 'written' see PARA 21 note 3.

3 Council Tax (Alteration of Lists and Appeals) Regulations 1993, SI 1993/290, reg 20(1). As to references to a party to an appeal see PARA 536 note 7.

The Council Tax (Alteration of Lists and Appeals) Regulations 1993, SI 1993/290, apply in relation to Wales only: see PARA 417 note 2. The procedure on other appeals relating to council tax in Wales is governed by the Valuation Tribunal for Wales Regulations 2010, SI 2010/713, Pt 5 (regs 27–46): see PARA 546 et seq. As to the equivalent regulations in relation to England see the Valuation Tribunal for England (Council Tax and Rating Appeals) (Procedure) Regulations 2009,

SI 2009/2269; and see PARA 515 et seq. As to the meanings of 'England' and 'Wales' see PARA 2 note 16.

4 As to the meaning of 'clerk' see PARA 546 note 12.
5 Council Tax (Alteration of Lists and Appeals) Regulations 1993, SI 1993/290, reg 20(2). As to service of notices see PARA 535.
6 Council Tax (Alteration of Lists and Appeals) Regulations 1993, SI 1993/290, reg 20(2)(a).
7 Council Tax (Alteration of Lists and Appeals) Regulations 1993, SI 1993/290, reg 20(2)(b).
8 Ie the effect of the Council Tax (Alteration of Lists and Appeals) Regulations 1993, SI 1993/290, reg 20(4), (5): see the text to notes 10–13.
9 Council Tax (Alteration of Lists and Appeals) Regulations 1993, SI 1993/290, reg 20(3).
10 Council Tax (Alteration of Lists and Appeals) Regulations 1993, SI 1993/290, reg 20(4).
11 Ie a tribunal constituted as in the Council Tax (Alteration of Lists and Appeals) Regulations 1993, SI 1993/290, reg 25: see PARA 539.
12 Council Tax (Alteration of Lists and Appeals) Regulations 1993, SI 1993/290, reg 20(5)(a).
13 Council Tax (Alteration of Lists and Appeals) Regulations 1993, SI 1993/290, reg 20(5)(b).
14 Council Tax (Alteration of Lists and Appeals) Regulations 1993, SI 1993/290, reg 20(6)(a).
15 Council Tax (Alteration of Lists and Appeals) Regulations 1993, SI 1993/290, reg 20(6)(b). As to hearings see PARA 539.
16 Council Tax (Alteration of Lists and Appeals) Regulations 1993, SI 1993/290, reg 20(7).

538. Representation at hearing.

Any party to an appeal[1] which is to be decided at a hearing[2] may appear in person (with assistance from any person if he wishes), by counsel or solicitor, or any other representative (other than a person who is an employee or member of the Valuation Tribunal for Wales)[3].

1 As to the meaning of 'appeal' see PARA 534 note 2. As to references to a party to an appeal see PARA 536 note 7.
2 As to hearings see PARA 539.
3 Council Tax (Alteration of Lists and Appeals) Regulations 1993, SI 1993/290, reg 24 (amended by SI 2010/713). As to employees of the tribunal see PARA 238.

The Council Tax (Alteration of Lists and Appeals) Regulations 1993, SI 1993/290, apply in relation to Wales only: see PARA 417 note 2. The procedure on other appeals relating to council tax in Wales is governed by the Valuation Tribunal for Wales Regulations 2010, SI 2010/713, Pt 5 (regs 27–46): see PARA 546 et seq. As to the equivalent regulations in relation to England see the Valuation Tribunal for England (Council Tax and Rating Appeals) (Procedure) Regulations 2009, SI 2009/2269; and see PARA 515 et seq. As to the Valuation Tribunal for Wales see PARA 237.As to the meanings of 'England' and 'Wales' see PARA 2 note 16.

539. Hearings.

Where the appeal[1] is to be disposed of on the basis of a hearing, the clerk[2] must, not less than four weeks before the date in question, serve[3] on the parties notice of the date, time and place appointed for the hearing[4].

The clerk must advertise the date, time and place appointed for any hearing by causing a notice giving such information to be conspicuously displayed[5]:

(1) at the valuation tribunal's office[6];
(2) outside an office of the billing authority[7] appointed by the authority for that purpose[8]; or
(3) in another place within that authority's area[9].

The notice required to be advertised must name a place where a list of the appeals to be heard may be inspected[10].

Where the hearing of an appeal has been postponed, the clerk must take such steps as are reasonably practicable in the time available[11]:

(a) to notify the parties of the postponement[12]; and
(b) to advertise the postponement[13].

The Valuation Tribunal for Wales's functions of hearing or determining an appeal will be discharged by three members of the tribunal, who must include at least one chairman; and a chairman will preside[14]. However, where all parties to an appeal[15] who appear so agree, the appeal may be decided by two members of an appeal panel, and notwithstanding the absence of a chairman[16].

The hearing must take place in public unless the tribunal otherwise orders on the application of a party, and on being satisfied that the interests of that party would be prejudicially affected[17].

If at the hearing of an appeal every party other than the listing officer fails to appear, the tribunal may dismiss the appeal[18]. If at the hearing of an appeal any party does not appear, the tribunal may hear and determine the appeal in his absence[19].

The tribunal may require any witness to give evidence under oath or affirmation, and has power for that purpose to administer an oath or affirmation in due form[20]. Unless the tribunal determines otherwise, on the hearing of an appeal about the validity of a proposal[21], or arising from an alteration of a list by the listing officer, the listing officer must begin the hearing; and in any other case parties at the hearing may be heard in such order as the tribunal may determine[22]. Parties at the hearing may examine any witness before the tribunal and call witnesses[23].

A hearing may be adjourned for such time, to such place and on such terms (if any) as the tribunal thinks fit; and reasonable notice of the time and place to which the hearing has been adjourned must be given to every party[24].

If it thinks fit an appeal panel may, after notice to the parties inviting them to be present, inspect any dwelling which is the subject of an appeal[25].

Where on the hearing of an appeal as to a proposed alteration[26]:

(i) the listing officer contends that the proposal was not validly made[27]; and
(ii) the tribunal does not uphold his contention[28],

the tribunal must not immediately proceed to determine the appeal unless every party so agrees[29].

Subject to any specific provisions[30], the tribunal:

(A) must conduct the hearing in such manner as it considers most suitable to the clarification of the issues before it and generally to the just handling of the proceedings[31];
(B) must, so far as appears to it appropriate, seek to avoid formality in its proceedings[32]; and
(C) will not be bound by any enactment or rule of law relating to the admissibility of evidence before courts of law[33].

1 As to the meaning of 'appeal' see PARA 534 note 2.
2 As to the meaning of 'clerk' see PARA 546 note 12.
3 As to service of notices see PARA 535.
4 Council Tax (Alteration of Lists and Appeals) Regulations 1993, SI 1993/290, reg 22(1).
The Council Tax (Alteration of Lists and Appeals) Regulations 1993, SI 1993/290, apply in relation to Wales only: see PARA 417 note 2. The procedure on other appeals relating to council tax in Wales is governed by the Valuation Tribunal for Wales Regulations 2010, SI 2010/713, Pt 5 (regs 27–46): see PARA 546 et seq. As to the equivalent regulations in relation to England see the Valuation Tribunal for England (Council Tax and Rating Appeals) (Procedure) Regulations 2009, SI 2009/2269; and see PARA 515 et seq. As to the meanings of 'England' and 'Wales' see PARA 2 note 16.
5 Council Tax (Alteration of Lists and Appeals) Regulations 1993, SI 1993/290, reg 22(2).
6 Council Tax (Alteration of Lists and Appeals) Regulations 1993, SI 1993/290, reg 22(2)(a).
7 As to the meaning of 'billing authority' see PARA 346.
8 Council Tax (Alteration of Lists and Appeals) Regulations 1993, SI 1993/290, reg 22(2)(b).
9 Council Tax (Alteration of Lists and Appeals) Regulations 1993, SI 1993/290, reg 22(2)(c).
10 Council Tax (Alteration of Lists and Appeals) Regulations 1993, SI 1993/290, reg 22(3).

11 Council Tax (Alteration of Lists and Appeals) Regulations 1993, SI 1993/290, reg 22(4).
12 Council Tax (Alteration of Lists and Appeals) Regulations 1993, SI 1993/290, reg 22(4)(a).
13 Council Tax (Alteration of Lists and Appeals) Regulations 1993, SI 1993/290, reg 22(4)(b).
14 Council Tax (Alteration of Lists and Appeals) Regulations 1993, SI 1993/290, reg 25(1) (amended by SI 2010/713). As to members of the tribunal see PARA 238. A member of a relevant billing authority is disqualified from participating as a member in the hearing or determination of, or acting as clerk or officer of a tribunal in relation to, an appeal: reg 23(1). For this purpose, 'relevant billing authority' means the billing authority in whose area is situated the dwelling which is the subject of the appeal: reg 23(2).

A person shall be disqualified from participating as a member in the hearing or determination of, or acting as clerk or officer of a tribunal in relation to, an appeal if the appellant is his spouse or civil partner or he supports the appellant financially or is liable to do so: reg 23(3). A person is not otherwise disqualified from acting in any capacity in relation to an appeal by reason only of the fact that he is a member of an authority which derives revenue directly or indirectly from payments in respect of council tax which may be affected by the exercise of his functions: reg 23(4).

Marriage includes marriage of a same sex couple: see the Marriage (Same Sex Couples) Act 2013 Sch 3 para 1(1)(a), (2), (3); and MATRIMONIAL AND CIVIL PARTNERSHIP LAW vol 72 (2015) PARA 1 et seq. As to civil partnership see MATRIMONIAL AND CIVIL PARTNERSHIP LAW vol 72 (2015) PARA 3. As to the meaning of 'dwelling' see PARA 349. As to council tax see PARA 344 et seq.
15 As to references to a party to an appeal see PARA 536 note 7.
16 Council Tax (Alteration of Lists and Appeals) Regulations 1993, SI 1993/290, reg 25(2).
17 Council Tax (Alteration of Lists and Appeals) Regulations 1993, SI 1993/290, reg 25(3).
18 Council Tax (Alteration of Lists and Appeals) Regulations 1993, SI 1993/290, reg 25(4). As to the meaning of 'listing officer' see PARA 428 note 12.
19 Council Tax (Alteration of Lists and Appeals) Regulations 1993, SI 1993/290, reg 25(5).
20 Council Tax (Alteration of Lists and Appeals) Regulations 1993, SI 1993/290, reg 25(6). As to oaths and affirmations see CIVIL PROCEDURE vol 12 (2015) PARA 824 et seq.
21 Ie under the Council Tax (Alteration of Lists and Appeals) Regulations 1993, SI 1993/290, reg 8: see PARA 431.
22 Council Tax (Alteration of Lists and Appeals) Regulations 1993, SI 1993/290, reg 25(7).
23 Council Tax (Alteration of Lists and Appeals) Regulations 1993, SI 1993/290, reg 25(8).
24 Council Tax (Alteration of Lists and Appeals) Regulations 1993, SI 1993/290, reg 25(9).
25 Council Tax (Alteration of Lists and Appeals) Regulations 1993, SI 1993/290, reg 25(10).
26 Ie under the Council Tax (Alteration of Lists and Appeals) Regulations 1993, SI 1993/290, reg 13: see PARA 434.
27 Council Tax (Alteration of Lists and Appeals) Regulations 1993, SI 1993/290, reg 25(11)(a).
28 Council Tax (Alteration of Lists and Appeals) Regulations 1993, SI 1993/290, reg 25(11)(b).
29 Council Tax (Alteration of Lists and Appeals) Regulations 1993, SI 1993/290, reg 25(11).
30 Ie of the Council Tax (Alteration of Lists and Appeals) Regulations 1993, SI 1993/290, Pt III (regs 16–34).
31 Council Tax (Alteration of Lists and Appeals) Regulations 1993, SI 1993/290, reg 25(12)(a).
32 Council Tax (Alteration of Lists and Appeals) Regulations 1993, SI 1993/290, reg 25(12)(b).
33 Council Tax (Alteration of Lists and Appeals) Regulations 1993, SI 1993/290, reg 25(12)(c). As to evidence see PARA 540.

540. Evidence.

The following provisions apply to:

(1) information supplied[1] for purposes relating to non-domestic rating or council tax[2]; and

(2) information contained in any particulars delivered document[3].

Subject to what follows, information to which these provisions apply will in any relevant proceedings[4] be admissible as evidence of any fact stated in it[5]; and any document purporting to contain such information will, unless the contrary is shown, be presumed:

(a) to have been supplied by the person by whom it purports to have been supplied[6]; and

(b) to have been supplied by that person in any capacity in which it purports to have been supplied[7].

Information to which these provisions apply must not be used in any relevant proceedings by a listing officer[8] unless:

(i) not less than two weeks' notice, specifying in relation to any information to be so used the documents or other media in or on which that information is held and the dwelling[9] or dwellings to which it relates, has previously been given to every other party to the proceedings[10]; and

(ii) any person who has given not less than 24 hours' notice of his intention to do so has been permitted, at any reasonable time:

(A) to inspect the documents or other media in or on which such information is held[11]; and

(B) to make a copy (other than a photographic copy) of, or of any extract from, any document containing such information[12].

Nothing in the foregoing provisions[13] is to be construed as requiring the making available for inspection or copying, or the production of, any document in so far as it contains information other than information which is reasonably required for the purposes of the relevant proceedings[14].

If any document required to be made available for inspection in accordance with these provisions is not maintained in documentary form, the duty to make it so available is satisfied if a print-out, photographic image or other reproduction of the document which has been obtained from the storage medium adopted in relation to that information is made available for inspection[15].

The contents of a list[16] may be proved by the production of a copy of the list, or of the relevant part, purporting to be certified to be a true copy by the listing officer[17].

1 Ie in pursuance of the Local Government Finance Act 1988 Sch 9 (see PARA 226 et seq, PARAS 272–276) or the Local Government Finance Act 1992 s 27(1) or (3) (see PARA 415).

2 Council Tax (Alteration of Lists and Appeals) Regulations 1993, SI 1993/290, reg 26(1)(a).

The Council Tax (Alteration of Lists and Appeals) Regulations 1993, SI 1993/290, apply in relation to Wales only: see PARA 417 note 2. The procedure on other appeals relating to council tax in Wales is governed by the Valuation Tribunal for Wales Regulations 2010, SI 2010/713, Pt 5 (regs 27–46): see PARA 546 et seq. As to the equivalent regulations in relation to England see the Valuation Tribunal for England (Council Tax and Rating Appeals) (Procedure) Regulations 2009, SI 2009/2269; and see PARA 515 et seq. As to the meanings of 'England' and 'Wales' see PARA 2 note 16.

3 Council Tax (Alteration of Lists and Appeals) Regulations 1993, SI 1993/290, reg 26(1)(b). 'Particulars delivered document' has the same meaning as in the Local Government Finance Act 1992 Pt I (ss 1–69) (see PARA 408 note 8): Council Tax (Alteration of Lists and Appeals) Regulations 1993, SI 1993/290, reg 16(1). No rule of confidentiality applicable to the Commissioners of Revenue and Customs prevents the disclosure for the purposes of an appeal under the Council Tax (Alteration of Lists and Appeals) Regulations 1993, SI 1993/290, of particulars delivered documents: reg 37 (amended by virtue of the Commissioners for Revenue and Customs Act 2005 s 50).

4 In the Council Tax (Alteration of Lists and Appeals) Regulations 1993, SI 1993/290, reg 26 'relevant proceedings' means any proceedings on or in consequence of an appeal, and any proceedings on or in consequence of a reference to arbitration under reg 33 (see PARA 559): reg 26(8).

5 Council Tax (Alteration of Lists and Appeals) Regulations 1993, SI 1993/290, reg 26(2).

6 Council Tax (Alteration of Lists and Appeals) Regulations 1993, SI 1993/290, reg 26(2)(a). As to the meaning of 'person' see PARA 11 note 13.

7 Council Tax (Alteration of Lists and Appeals) Regulations 1993, SI 1993/290, reg 26(2)(b).

8 As to the meaning of 'listing officer' see PARA 428 note 12.

9 As to the meaning of 'dwelling' see PARA 349.

10 Council Tax (Alteration of Lists and Appeals) Regulations 1993, SI 1993/290, reg 26(3)(a). As to references to a party to an appeal see PARA 536 note 7.

Subject to reg 26(5), any person to whom notice relating to any dwelling has been given under reg 26(3)(a) may before the hearing serve notice on the listing officer specifying other dwellings as being dwellings which are comparable in character or otherwise relevant to that person's case, and requiring the listing officer:

(1) to permit him at any reasonable time specified in the notice to inspect and (if he so desires) to make a copy (other than a photographic copy) of, or of any extract from, any document containing information to which this regulation applies which relates to those other dwellings and is in the possession of the listing officer (reg 26(4)(a)); and

(2) to produce at the hearing or to submit to the tribunal such documents as before the hearing he has informed the listing officer that he requires (reg 26(4)(b)).

The number of dwellings specified in a notice under reg 26(4) must not exceed four or, if greater, the number specified in the notice under reg 26(3)(a) (see head (i) in the text): reg 26(5). Where a notice has been given to the listing officer under reg 26(4), and the listing officer refuses or fails to comply with the notice, the person who gave the notice may apply to the tribunal or, as the case may be, the arbitrator appointed to determine the appeal; and that tribunal or arbitrator may, if satisfied that it is reasonable to do so, direct the listing officer to comply with the notice as respects all the dwellings or such of them as the tribunal or arbitrator may determine: reg 26(7).

11 Council Tax (Alteration of Lists and Appeals) Regulations 1993, SI 1993/290, reg 26(3)(b)(i).

12 Council Tax (Alteration of Lists and Appeals) Regulations 1993, SI 1993/290, reg 26(3)(b)(ii).

13 Ie in the Council Tax (Alteration of Lists and Appeals) Regulations 1993, SI 1993/290, reg 26(1)–(5).

14 Council Tax (Alteration of Lists and Appeals) Regulations 1993, SI 1993/290, reg 26(6).

15 Council Tax (Alteration of Lists and Appeals) Regulations 1993, SI 1993/290, reg 26(8).

16 As to the meaning of 'list' see PARA 428 note 1.

17 Council Tax (Alteration of Lists and Appeals) Regulations 1993, SI 1993/290, reg 27.

541. Decisions on appeals.

An appeal[1] may be decided by a majority of the members participating; and where[2] it falls to be disposed of by two members and they are unable to agree, it must be remitted by the clerk[3] to be decided by a tribunal consisting of three different members[4].

Where an appeal is disposed of on the basis of a hearing, the decision may be reserved or given orally at the end of the hearing[5]. As soon as is reasonably practicable after a decision has been made, it must:

(1) in the case of a decision given orally, be confirmed[6];

(2) in any other case, be communicated[7],

by notice in writing[8] to the parties; and the notice must be accompanied by a statement of the reasons for the decision[9]. However, nothing in this provision will require notice to be given to a party[10] if it would be repetitive of any document supplied under the provision as to records[11] to that person[12].

1 As to the meaning of 'appeal' see PARA 534 note 2.

2 Ie pursuant to the Council Tax (Alteration of Lists and Appeals) Regulations 1993, SI 1993/290, reg 25(2): see PARA 539.

3 As to the meaning of 'clerk' see PARA 546 note 12.

4 Council Tax (Alteration of Lists and Appeals) Regulations 1993, SI 1993/290, reg 28(1). As to orders which can be made on an appeal see PARA 542.

The Council Tax (Alteration of Lists and Appeals) Regulations 1993, SI 1993/290, apply in relation to Wales only: see PARA 417 note 2. The procedure on other appeals relating to council tax in Wales is governed by the Valuation Tribunal for Wales Regulations 2010, SI 2010/713, Pt 5 (regs 27–46): see PARA 546 et seq. As to the equivalent regulations in relation to England see the Valuation Tribunal for England (Council Tax and Rating Appeals) (Procedure) Regulations 2009, SI 2009/2269; and see PARA 515 et seq. As to the meanings of 'England' and 'Wales' see PARA 2 note 16.

5 Council Tax (Alteration of Lists and Appeals) Regulations 1993, SI 1993/290, reg 28(2).

6 Council Tax (Alteration of Lists and Appeals) Regulations 1993, SI 1993/290, reg 28(3)(a).

7 Council Tax (Alteration of Lists and Appeals) Regulations 1993, SI 1993/290, reg 28(3)(b).

8 As to the meaning of 'writing' see PARA 21 note 3.

9 Council Tax (Alteration of Lists and Appeals) Regulations 1993, SI 1993/290, reg 28(3).

10 As to references to a party to an appeal see PARA 536 note 7.
11 Ie the Council Tax (Alteration of Lists and Appeals) Regulations 1993, SI 1993/290, reg 31: see PARA 545.
12 Council Tax (Alteration of Lists and Appeals) Regulations 1993, SI 1993/290, reg 28(4). As to the meaning of 'person' see PARA 11 note 13.

542. Orders.

On or after deciding an appeal[1] the tribunal[2] may, in consequence of the decision, by order require a listing officer[3] to alter a list[4], in accordance with any provision made by or under the Local Government Finance Act 1992[5]. The listing officer must comply with an order to alter a list within six weeks beginning on the day of its making[6].

Where the decision is that the valuation band[7] applicable to the dwelling[8] should be higher than:

(1) the valuation band shown in the list at the date of the proposal[9]; and
(2) the valuation band contended for in the proposal[10],

the order must require the list to be altered with effect from the day on which the decision is given[11]. This does not apply, however, where the alteration relates to any dwelling which has come into existence or ceased to exist[12].

An order under these provisions may require any matter ancillary to its subject matter to be attended to[13].

1 As to the meaning of 'appeal' see PARA 534 note 2. As to deciding an appeal see PARA 541.
2 As to the meaning of 'tribunal' see PARA 534 note 4.
3 As to the meaning of 'listing officer' see PARA 428 note 12.
4 As to the meaning of 'list' see PARA 428 note 1.
5 Council Tax (Alteration of Lists and Appeals) Regulations 1993, SI 1993/290, reg 29(1).
The Council Tax (Alteration of Lists and Appeals) Regulations 1993, SI 1993/290, apply in relation to Wales only: see PARA 417 note 2. The procedure on other appeals relating to council tax in Wales is governed by the Valuation Tribunal for Wales Regulations 2010, SI 2010/713, Pt 5 (regs 27–46): see PARA 546 et seq. As to the equivalent regulations in relation to England see the Valuation Tribunal for England (Council Tax and Rating Appeals) (Procedure) Regulations 2009, SI 2009/2269; and see PARA 515 et seq. As to the meanings of 'England' and 'Wales' see PARA 2 note 16.
6 Council Tax (Alteration of Lists and Appeals) Regulations 1993, SI 1993/290, reg 29(2). Before altering an entry in a list, the listing officer must ensure that a record (which need not be in documentary form) is made of the entry: reg 38(1). A record made under reg 38(1) must be retained until the expiry of six years beginning on the day on which it was made: reg 38(2).
7 As to valuation bands see PARA 361.
8 As to the meaning of 'dwelling' see PARA 349.
9 Council Tax (Alteration of Lists and Appeals) Regulations 1993, SI 1993/290, reg 29(3)(a).
10 Council Tax (Alteration of Lists and Appeals) Regulations 1993, SI 1993/290, reg 29(3)(b).
11 Council Tax (Alteration of Lists and Appeals) Regulations 1993, SI 1993/290, reg 29(3).
12 Council Tax (Alteration of Lists and Appeals) Regulations 1993, SI 1993/290, reg 29(4). Regulation 14(9) applies for the purposes of reg 29(4) as it applies for the purposes of reg 14 (see PARA 435 note 5): reg 29(4) (amended by SI 2010/77).
13 Council Tax (Alteration of Lists and Appeals) Regulations 1993, SI 1993/290, reg 29(5).

543. Review of decisions.

A tribunal[1] constituted as provided below[2] has power on the written[3] application of a party[4] to review or set aside by certificate under the hand of the presiding member any decision on the grounds that[5]:

(1) the decision was wrongly made as a result of clerical error[6];
(2) a party did not appear and can show reasonable cause why he did not do so[7];

(3) the decision is affected by a decision of, or a decision on appeal from, the High Court or the Upper Tribunal in relation to an appeal in respect of the dwelling which, or, as the case may be, the person who, was the subject of the tribunal's decision[8].

This does not apply where an appeal against the decision in question has been determined by the High Court[9]. An application may be dismissed if it is not made within the period of four weeks beginning on the day on which notice is given[10] of the decision in question[11].

So far as is reasonably practicable, the tribunal appointed to review a decision must consist of the same members as constituted the tribunal which took the decision[12].

If a tribunal sets aside a decision in pursuance of these provisions, it must revoke any order made in consequence of that decision and must order a re-hearing or redetermination before either the same or a different tribunal[13].

As soon as reasonably practicable after:

(a) a determination that the tribunal will not undertake a review[14];
(b) the determination of the tribunal not to set aside the decision in question[15];
(c) the issue of any certificate[16] by the tribunal[17]; and
(d) the revocation of any order[18],

the clerk must give written notice to the applicant and to every other party to the appeal of the occurrence of the relevant event[19].

Where, in relation to a decision in respect of which an application to review or set aside a decision is made, an appeal to the High Court remains undetermined on the relevant day[20], the clerk must notify the High Court as soon as reasonably practicable after the occurrence of the relevant event[21].

1 As to the meaning of 'tribunal' see PARA 534 note 4.
2 Ie under the Council Tax (Alteration of Lists and Appeals) Regulations 1993, SI 1993/290, reg 42(4): see the text to note 12.
3 As to the meaning of 'written' see PARA 21 note 3.
4 As to references to a party to an appeal see PARA 536 note 7.
5 Council Tax (Alteration of Lists and Appeals) Regulations 1993, SI 1993/290, reg 30(1). Regulation 30(1) is subject to reg 30(2), (3): see reg 30(1).
The Council Tax (Alteration of Lists and Appeals) Regulations 1993, SI 1993/290, apply in relation to Wales only: see PARA 417 note 2. The procedure on other appeals relating to council tax in Wales is governed by the Valuation Tribunal for Wales Regulations 2010, SI 2010/713, Pt 5 (regs 27–46): see PARA 546 et seq. As to the equivalent regulations in relation to England see the Valuation Tribunal for England (Council Tax and Rating Appeals) (Procedure) Regulations 2009, SI 2009/2269; and see PARA 515 et seq. As to the meanings of 'England' and 'Wales' see PARA 2 note 16.
6 Council Tax (Alteration of Lists and Appeals) Regulations 1993, SI 1993/290, reg 30(1)(a).
7 Council Tax (Alteration of Lists and Appeals) Regulations 1993, SI 1993/290, reg 30(1)(b).
8 Council Tax (Alteration of Lists and Appeals) Regulations 1993, SI 1993/290, reg 30(1)(c).
9 Council Tax (Alteration of Lists and Appeals) Regulations 1993, SI 1993/290, reg 30(3). As to determination by the High Court see PARA 561.
10 Ie whether in accordance with the Council Tax (Alteration of Lists and Appeals) Regulations 1993, SI 1993/290, reg 28(3) (see PARA 541) or reg 31(3) (see PARA 545).
11 Council Tax (Alteration of Lists and Appeals) Regulations 1993, SI 1993/290, reg 30(2).
12 Council Tax (Alteration of Lists and Appeals) Regulations 1993, SI 1993/290, reg 30(4).
13 Council Tax (Alteration of Lists and Appeals) Regulations 1993, SI 1993/290, reg 30(5).
14 Council Tax (Alteration of Lists and Appeals) Regulations 1993, SI 1993/290, reg 30(6)(a).
15 Council Tax (Alteration of Lists and Appeals) Regulations 1993, SI 1993/290, reg 30(6)(b).
16 Ie under the Council Tax (Alteration of Lists and Appeals) Regulations 1993, SI 1993/290, reg 30(1): see the text to motes 1–8.
17 Council Tax (Alteration of Lists and Appeals) Regulations 1993, SI 1993/290, reg 30(6)(c).
18 Council Tax (Alteration of Lists and Appeals) Regulations 1993, SI 1993/290, reg 30(6)(d). As to

orders see PARA 556.

19 Council Tax (Alteration of Lists and Appeals) Regulations 1993, SI 1993/290, reg 30(6). As to the meaning of 'clerk' see PARA 546 note 12.

20 'The relevant day' means the day on which, as the case may be, the application under the Council Tax (Alteration of Lists and Appeals) Regulations 1993, SI 1993/290, reg 30(1) is made or an event referred to in any of reg 30(6)(a)–(d) (see heads (a)–(d) in the text) occurs: reg 30(8).

21 Council Tax (Alteration of Lists and Appeals) Regulations 1993, SI 1993/290, reg 30(7). The relevant event', in relation to a relevant day, means the event occurring on that day: reg 30(8).

544. Notifications by listing officer.

Where a listing officer[1]:

(1) applies to a tribunal[2] for the review of a decision in consequence of which an order requiring the alteration of a list[3] was made[4]; or

(2) appeals to the High Court[5] against a decision in consequence of which such an order was made, or against such an order[6],

he must, at the same time or as soon as reasonably practicable thereafter, notify the billing authority[7] of the application or appeal[8].

1 As to the meaning of 'listing officer' see PARA 428 note 12.

2 Ie under the Council Tax (Alteration of Lists and Appeals) Regulations 1993, SI 1993/290, reg 30: see PARA 543. As to the meaning of 'tribunal' see PARA 534 note 4.

3 As to the meaning of 'list' see PARA 428 note 1.

4 Council Tax (Alteration of Lists and Appeals) Regulations 1993, SI 1993/290, reg 34(1)(a).

5 Ie under the Council Tax (Alteration of Lists and Appeals) Regulations 1993, SI 1993/290, reg 32: see PARA 561.

6 Council Tax (Alteration of Lists and Appeals) Regulations 1993, SI 1993/290, reg 34(1)(b).

7 As to the meaning of 'billing authority' see PARA 346.

8 Council Tax (Alteration of Lists and Appeals) Regulations 1993, SI 1993/290, reg 34(1).

The Council Tax (Alteration of Lists and Appeals) Regulations 1993, SI 1993/290, apply in relation to Wales only: see PARA 417 note 2. The procedure on other appeals relating to council tax in Wales is governed by the Valuation Tribunal for Wales Regulations 2010, SI 2010/713, Pt 5 (regs 27–46): see PARA 546 et seq. As to the equivalent regulations in relation to England see the Valuation Tribunal for England (Council Tax and Rating Appeals) (Procedure) Regulations 2009, SI 2009/2269; and see PARA 515 et seq. As to the meanings of 'England' and 'Wales' see PARA 2 note 16.

545. Records of decisions and orders.

It is the duty of the clerk[1] to make arrangements for each decision[2], each order[3] and the effect of each certificate and revocation[4] to be recorded[5]. Records may be kept in any form, whether documentary or otherwise, and must contain the specified[6] particulars[7].

A copy, in documentary form, of the relevant entry in the record must, as soon as reasonably practicable after the entry has been made, be sent to each party to the appeal to which the entry relates[8]. Each record must be retained for the period of six years beginning on the day on which an entry was last made in it[9].

Any person[10] may, at a reasonable time stated by or on behalf of the tribunal concerned[11] and without making payment, inspect the records which are required to be made[12]. If, without reasonable excuse, a person having custody of records intentionally obstructs a person in exercising this right, that person will be liable on summary conviction to a fine[13].

The member who presided at the hearing or determination of an appeal may authorise the correction of any clerical error in the record, and a copy of the corrected entry must be sent to the persons to whom a copy of the original entry was sent[14].

The production in any proceedings in any court of law of a document purporting to be certified by the clerk to be a true copy of a record of that tribunal will, unless the contrary is proved, be sufficient evidence of the document and of the facts it records[15].

1 As to the meaning of 'clerk' see PARA 546 note 12.
2 As to decisions see PARA 541.
3 Ie made under the Council Tax (Alteration of Lists and Appeals) Regulations 1993, SI 1993/290, reg 29: see PARA 542.
4 Ie made under the Council Tax (Alteration of Lists and Appeals) Regulations 1993, SI 1993/290, reg 30: see PARA 543.
5 Council Tax (Alteration of Lists and Appeals) Regulations 1993, SI 1993/290, reg 31(1).
The Council Tax (Alteration of Lists and Appeals) Regulations 1993, SI 1993/290, apply in relation to Wales only: see PARA 417 note 2. The procedure on other appeals relating to council tax in Wales is governed by the Valuation Tribunal for Wales Regulations 2010, SI 2010/713, Pt 5 (regs 27–46): see PARA 546 et seq. As to the equivalent regulations in relation to England see the Valuation Tribunal for England (Council Tax and Rating Appeals) (Procedure) Regulations 2009, SI 2009/2269; and see PARA 515 et seq. As to the meanings of 'England' and 'Wales' see PARA 2 note 16.
6 Ie specified in the Council Tax (Alteration of Lists and Appeals) Regulations 1993, SI 1993/290, Schedule. Those particulars are:
(1) the appellant's name and address;
(2) the matter appealed against;
(3) the date of the hearing or determination;
(4) the names of the parties who appeared, if any;
(5) the decision of the tribunal and its date;
(6) the reasons for the decision;
(7) any order made in consequence of the decision;
(8) the date of any such order;
(9) any certificate setting aside the decision;
(10) any revocation under reg 30(5).
7 Council Tax (Alteration of Lists and Appeals) Regulations 1993, SI 1993/290, reg 31(2).
8 Council Tax (Alteration of Lists and Appeals) Regulations 1993, SI 1993/290, reg 31(3). As to references to a party to an appeal see PARA 536 note 7.
9 Council Tax (Alteration of Lists and Appeals) Regulations 1993, SI 1993/290, reg 31(4).
10 As to the meaning of 'person' see PARA 11 note 13.
11 As to the meaning of 'tribunal' see PARA 534 note 4.
12 Council Tax (Alteration of Lists and Appeals) Regulations 1993, SI 1993/290, reg 31(5).
13 Council Tax (Alteration of Lists and Appeals) Regulations 1993, SI 1993/290, reg 31(6). The fine will not exceed level 1 on the standard scale: reg 31(6). As to the powers of magistrates' courts to issue fines on summary conviction see SENTENCING vol 92 (2015) PARA 176.
14 Council Tax (Alteration of Lists and Appeals) Regulations 1993, SI 1993/290, reg 31(7).
15 Council Tax (Alteration of Lists and Appeals) Regulations 1993, SI 1993/290, reg 31(8).

(B) Council Tax Appeals

546. Arrangements for appeals.

The president of the Valuation Tribunal for Wales[1] must secure that arrangements are made for appeals[2] to be determined in accordance with the relevant provisions[3]. Where a council tax appeal[4] and an appeal relating to the alteration of non-domestic rating or valuation lists[5] relate to the same property[6], the president will secure that the appeals are dealt with in such order as appears to the president best designed to secure the interests of justice[7]; and the valuation officer[8] or the listing officer[9] (as the case may be) and the billing authority[10] must be joined as a party to a council tax appeal[11]. The clerk[12] must as soon as is reasonably practicable serve a copy of the notice of appeal[13] on a person[14] who has been made a party in accordance with this provision[15].

1 As to the Valuation Tribunal for Wales see PARA 237. 'President' means the President of the Valuation Tribunal appointed under the Valuation Tribunal for Wales Regulations 2010, SI 2010/713, reg 11: reg 2(1). As to the president see PARA 238.

2 In the Valuation Tribunal for Wales Regulations 2010, SI 2010/713, Pt 5 (regs 27–46) 'appeal', unless the context otherwise requires, means an appeal under the Local Government Finance Act 1992 s 16 (appeals—general: see PARA 513), Sch 3 para 3(1) (penalties: see PARA 471) or under the Local Government Finance Act 1988 Sch 4A para 4 as it applies for the purposes of the Local Government Finance Act 1992 Pt I (ss 1–69) (see PARA 353) (in the Valuation Tribunal for Wales Regulations 2010, SI 2010/713, Pt 5 called an 'appeal against a completion notice'): reg 27(1).

The procedure for appeals under the Council Tax (Alteration of Lists and Appeals) Regulations 1993, SI 1993/290, reg 8 (see PARA 431) or reg 13 (see PARA 434) is governed by the Council Tax (Alteration of Lists and Appeals) Regulations 1993, SI 1993/290, Pt III (regs 16–34): see PARA 534 et seq.

The Valuation Tribunal for Wales Regulations 2010, SI 2010/713, apply in relation to Wales only: see reg 2. The Council Tax (Alteration of Lists and Appeals) Regulations 1993, SI 1993/290, also apply in relation to Wales only: see PARA 417 note 2. As to the equivalent regulations in relation to England see the Valuation Tribunal for England (Council Tax and Rating Appeals) (Procedure) Regulations 2009, SI 2009/2269; and see PARA 515 et seq. As to the meanings of 'England' and 'Wales' see PARA 2 note 16.

3 Valuation Tribunal for Wales Regulations 2010, SI 2010/713, reg 31(1). The relevant provisions are regs 31(2)–46.

4 Ie an appeal under the Valuation Tribunal for Wales Regulations 2010, SI 2010/713, Pt 5. As to council tax see PARA 344 et seq.

5 Ie an appeal under one or more of the following (Valuation Tribunal for Wales Regulations 2010, SI 2010/713, reg 31(2)):

(1) regulations made under the Local Government Finance Act 1988 s 55 (see PARA 199) (Valuation Tribunal for Wales Regulations 2010, SI 2010/713, reg 31(2)(a));

(2) regulations made under the Local Government Finance Act 1992 s 24 (see PARA 417) (Valuation Tribunal for Wales Regulations 2010, SI 2010/713, reg 31(2)(b)).

6 Valuation Tribunal for Wales Regulations 2010, SI 2010/713, reg 31(2).

7 Valuation Tribunal for Wales Regulations 2010, SI 2010/713, reg 31(3)(a).

8 'Valuation officer' means the officer appointed under the Local Government Finance Act 1988 s 61(1)(a) (see PARA 54): Valuation Tribunal for Wales Regulations 2010, SI 2010/713, reg 31(4).

9 'Listing officer' in relation to an appeal, means the officer appointed under the Local Government Finance Act 1992 s 20 for the authority in whose area the dwelling to which the appeal relates is situated: Valuation Tribunal for Wales Regulations 2010, SI 2010/713, reg 27(1). As to the meaning of 'dwelling' see PARA 349.

10 As to the meaning of 'billing authority' see PARA 346.

11 Valuation Tribunal for Wales Regulations 2010, SI 2010/713, reg 31(3).

12 'Clerk' means the chief executive and any other employee of the valuation tribunal appointed under the Valuation Tribunal for Wales Regulations 2010, SI 2010/713, reg 15(6) to whom some or all of the functions of the clerk in Pt 5 have been delegated: reg 27(1). See PARA 238.

13 'Notice of appeal' means a notice under the Valuation Tribunal for Wales Regulations 2010, SI 2010/713, reg 30(1) (see PARA 547): Valuation Tribunal for Wales Regulations 2010, SI 2010/713, reg 27(1).

14 As to the meaning of 'person' see PARA 11 note 13.

15 Valuation Tribunal for Wales Regulations 2010, SI 2010/713, reg 31(5).

547. Initiating appeal.

An appeal[1] to a valuation tribunal[2] must be initiated by serving on the clerk[3] a notice in writing[4]. Where the appeal relates to liability for council tax[5], the notice of appeal must contain the following information[6]:

(1) the grounds on which the appeal is made[7];

(2) the date on which the notice of the appellant's grievance[8] was served on the billing authority[9];

(3) the date, if any, on which the appellant was notified by the authority[10] that the authority believes the grievance is not well founded or that steps have been taken to deal with the grievance[11]; and

(4) where the appellant has also made an appeal to the First-tier Tribunal in connection with housing benefit[12] and the appeal raises common issues of fact with the appeal relating to council tax[13], a copy of the notice provided[14] and any other information required to be provided[15] in connection with the housing benefit appeal[16].

A notice of appeal given under heads (1) to (4) above must be accompanied by a copy of any written notification provided[17] by the billing authority[18].

Where the appeal is an appeal against a completion notice[19], the notice of appeal must be accompanied by:

(a) a copy of the completion notice[20]; and

(b) a statement of the grounds on which the appeal is made[21].

Where the appeal is against the imposition of a penalty[22], the notice of appeal must contain the following information[23]:

(i) the grounds on which the appeal is made[24]; and

(ii) the date of service of written notice of the imposition of a penalty[25].

The clerk must, within two weeks of service of the notice of appeal, notify the appellant that the clerk has received the notice, and must serve a copy of it on the billing authority whose decision, action or notice is the subject of the appeal, and any other billing authority appearing to the clerk to be concerned with the matter[26].

1 As to the meaning of 'appeal' see PARA 546 note 2.

2 As to the Valuation Tribunal for Wales see PARA 237. Where the appellant is:

(1) a former member of an old tribunal;

(2) a former employee of an old tribunal, of the old service or of the valuation tribunal; or

(3) an employee or member of the valuation tribunal,

the appeal must be dealt with by such members of the valuation tribunal as may be appointed for that purpose by the president: Valuation Tribunal for Wales Regulations 2010, SI 2010/713, reg 28(1). Where it appears to the president that by reason of a conflict of interests, or the appearance of such a conflict, it would be inappropriate for an appeal to be dealt with by particular members of the valuation tribunal, the president must appoint other members to deal with that appeal: reg 28(2). 'Old tribunal' means a valuation tribunal in Wales which existed immediately before 1 July 2010; and 'old service' means the Valuation Tribunal Service for Wales established by the Valuation Tribunals (Wales) Regulations 2005, SI 2005/3364 (revoked): Valuation Tribunal for Wales Regulations 2010, SI 2010/713, reg 2(1). As to the meaning of 'president' see PARA 546 note 1. As to the president, members and staff of the tribunal see PARA 238.

The Valuation Tribunal for Wales Regulations 2010, SI 2010/713, apply in relation to Wales only: see reg 2. As to the equivalent regulations in relation to England see the Valuation Tribunal for England (Council Tax and Rating Appeals) (Procedure) Regulations 2009, SI 2009/2269; and see PARA 515 et seq. As to the meanings of 'England' and 'Wales' see PARA 2 note 16.

The procedure for appeals under the Council Tax (Alteration of Lists and Appeals) Regulations 1993, SI 1993/290, reg 8 (see PARA 431) or reg 13 (see PARA 434) is governed by the Council Tax (Alteration of Lists and Appeals) Regulations 1993, SI 1993/290, Pt III (regs 16–34): see PARA 534 et seq.

3 As to the meaning of 'clerk' see PARA 546 note 12.

4 Valuation Tribunal for Wales Regulations 2010, SI 2010/713, reg 30(1).

5 Ie is made under the Local Government Finance Act 1992 s 16: see PARA 513. As to council tax see PARA 344 et seq.

6 Valuation Tribunal for Wales Regulations 2010, SI 2010/713, reg 30(2).

7 Valuation Tribunal for Wales Regulations 2010, SI 2010/713, reg 30(2)(a).

8 Ie under the Local Government Finance Act 1992 s 16(4):see PARA 513.

9 Valuation Tribunal for Wales Regulations 2010, SI 2010/713, reg 30(2)(b) (amended by SI 2013/547). As to the meaning of 'billing authority' see PARA 346.

10 Ie in accordance with the Local Government Finance Act 1992 s 16(7)(a) or (b): see PARA 513.

11 Valuation Tribunal for Wales Regulations 2010, SI 2010/713, reg 30(2)(c).
12 Ie in accordance with the Housing Benefit and Council Tax Benefit (Decisions and Appeals) Regulations 2001, SI 2001/1002: see WELFARE BENEFITS AND STATE PENSIONS vol 104 (2014) PARA 329.
13 Ie the appeal made under the Local Government Finance Act 1992 s 16.
14 Ie in accordance with the Housing Benefit and Council Tax Benefit (Decisions and Appeals) Regulations 2001, SI 2001/1002, reg 20(1).
15 Ie in accordance with the Housing Benefit and Council Tax Benefit (Decisions and Appeals) Regulations 2001, SI 2001/1002, reg 20.
16 Valuation Tribunal for Wales Regulations 2010, SI 2010/713, reg 30(2)(d) (added by SI 2013/547).
17 Ie in accordance with the Local Government Finance Act 1992 s 16(7)(a) or (b): see PARA 513.
18 Valuation Tribunal for Wales Regulations 2010, SI 2010/713, reg 30(2A) (added by SI 2013/547).
19 Ie under the Local Government Finance Act 1988 Sch 4A para 4 as it applies for the purposes of the Local Government Finance Act 1992 Pt I: see PARA 353.
20 Valuation Tribunal for Wales Regulations 2010, SI 2010/713, reg 30(3)(a).
21 Valuation Tribunal for Wales Regulations 2010, SI 2010/713, reg 30(3)(b).
22 Ie under the Local Government Finance Act 1992 Sch 3 para 3(1): see PARA 471.
23 Valuation Tribunal for Wales Regulations 2010, SI 2010/713, reg 30(4).
24 Valuation Tribunal for Wales Regulations 2010, SI 2010/713, reg 30(4)(a).
25 Valuation Tribunal for Wales Regulations 2010, SI 2010/713, reg 30(4)(b).
26 Valuation Tribunal for Wales Regulations 2010, SI 2010/713, reg 30(5).

548. Service of notices.

Any notice[1] to be served by the clerk[2] or listing officer[3] under the regulations relating to council tax appeals[4] may be served as follows[5]:

(1) by delivering it[6]:
  (a) to the person[7] on whom it is to be served[8]; or
  (b) to any other person authorised by them to act as their agent for the purpose[9];
(2) by leaving it at or forwarding it by post[10] to:
  (a) the usual or last-known place of business of that person[11]; or
  (b) in the case of a company, its registered office[12]; or
  (c) the usual or last-known place of business or registered office of any other person authorised as mentioned in head (1)(b)[13];
(3) by delivering it to some person on the premises to which it relates or, if there is no person on the premises to whom it can so be delivered, by fixing it to some conspicuous part of the premises[14];
(4) without prejudice to the foregoing provisions of this regulation, where premises to which the notice relates are a place of business of the person on whom it is to be served, by leaving it at, or forwarding it by post addressed to that person at, that place of business[15]; or
(5) by electronic communication[16].

Any notice to be served on the Valuation Tribunal for Wales[17], the clerk, the valuation officer[18] or the listing officer[19] in connection with a council tax appeal must be:

(i) sent by pre-paid post or delivered by hand to the address specified for the proceedings[20];
(ii) sent by fax to the number specified for the proceedings[21]; or
(iii) sent or delivered by such other method and to such address as may be agreed by the clerk, the valuation officer or the listing officer (as the case may be) and the person by whom the notice is to be served[22].

If a party provides a fax number, email address or other details for the electronic transmission of documents to them, that party must accept service of notices and delivery of documents by that method[23]. If a party informs the clerk and all other parties that a particular form of communication (other than post or delivery) should not be used to serve notice on, or provide documents to, that party, that form of communication must not be used[24].

If the clerk or a party sends a notice to a party or the clerk by email or any other electronic means of communication, the recipient may request that the sender provide a hard copy of the notice to the recipient[25]. Such a request must be made as soon as reasonably practicable after the recipient receives the notice or document electronically[26].

If the name of any taxpayer on whom a notice is required or authorised to be served cannot after reasonable inquiry be ascertained, the notice may be served by addressing it to 'The Council Tax Payer' of the dwelling concerned (naming the dwelling), without further name or description[27].

For the purpose of any legal proceedings, a notice given by electronic communication, is, unless the contrary is proved, to be treated as served on the second business day after it was sent[28].

A person who has notified an address for the purpose of electronic communication must, by notice in writing to the clerk and the other parties, advise the clerk and the other parties of any change in that address; and the change will take effect on the third business day after the date on which the notice is received by the clerk and the other parties, as the case may be[29].

The clerk and each party may assume that the address provided by a party or its representative is and remains the address to which documents should be sent or delivered until receiving written notification to the contrary[30].

1 In the Valuation Tribunal for Wales Regulations 2010, SI 2010/713, reg 46, any reference to a notice includes a reference to any other document required or authorised to be served (reg 46(11)(b)); and any reference to such requirement or authorisation is to a requirement or authorisation under those Regulations (reg 46(11)(c)).

The Valuation Tribunal for Wales Regulations 2010, SI 2010/713, apply in relation to Wales only: see reg 2. As to the equivalent regulations in relation to England see the Valuation Tribunal for England (Council Tax and Rating Appeals) (Procedure) Regulations 2009, SI 2009/2269; and see PARA 515 et seq. As to the meanings of 'England' and 'Wales' see PARA 2 note 16.

The procedure for appeals under the Council Tax (Alteration of Lists and Appeals) Regulations 1993, SI 1993/290, reg 8 (see PARA 431) or reg 13 (see PARA 434) is governed by the Council Tax (Alteration of Lists and Appeals) Regulations 1993, SI 1993/290, Pt III (regs 16–34): see PARA 534 et seq.

2 As to the meaning of 'clerk' see PARA 546 note 12.

3 As to the meaning of 'listing officer' see PARA 546 note 9.

4 Ie the Valuation Tribunal for Wales Regulations 2010, SI 2010/713, Pt 5 (regs 27–46). As to council tax see PARA 344 et seq.

5 Valuation Tribunal for Wales Regulations 2010, SI 2010/713, reg 46(1). This is without prejudice to the Local Government Act 1972 s 233 (service of notice by local authorities: LOCAL GOVERNMENT vol 69 (2018) PARA 648): Valuation Tribunal for Wales Regulations 2010, SI 2010/713, reg 46(1).

6 Valuation Tribunal for Wales Regulations 2010, SI 2010/713, reg 46(1)(a).

7 As to the meaning of 'person' see PARA 11 note 13.

8 Valuation Tribunal for Wales Regulations 2010, SI 2010/713, reg 46(1)(a)(i).

9 Valuation Tribunal for Wales Regulations 2010, SI 2010/713, reg 46(1)(a)(ii).

10 Valuation Tribunal for Wales Regulations 2010, SI 2010/713, reg 46(1)(b).

11 Valuation Tribunal for Wales Regulations 2010, SI 2010/713, reg 46(1)(b)(i).

12 Valuation Tribunal for Wales Regulations 2010, SI 2010/713, reg 46(1)(b)(ii). As to the registered office of a company see COMPANIES vol 14 (2016) PARA 124.

13 Valuation Tribunal for Wales Regulations 2010, SI 2010/713, reg 46(1)(b)(iii).

14 Valuation Tribunal for Wales Regulations 2010, SI 2010/713, reg 46(1)(c).

15 Valuation Tribunal for Wales Regulations 2010, SI 2010/713, reg 46(1)(d).

16 Valuation Tribunal for Wales Regulations 2010, SI 2010/713, reg 46(1)(e). Ie in accordance with reg 46(3) (see the text to note 23) but subject as mentioned in that paragraph: reg 46(1)(e). 'Electronic communication' has the meaning given in the Electronic Communications Act 2000 s 15(1) (see CIVIL PROCEDURE vol 11 (2015) PARA 61): Valuation Tribunal for Wales Regulations 2010, SI 2010/713, reg 46(11)(a).
17 As to the Valuation Tribunal for Wales see PARA 237.
18 As to valuation officers see PARA 54.
19 Ie under the Valuation Tribunal for Wales Regulations 2010, SI 2010/713.
20 Valuation Tribunal for Wales Regulations 2010, SI 2010/713, reg 46(2)(a).
21 Valuation Tribunal for Wales Regulations 2010, SI 2010/713, reg 46(2)(b).
22 Valuation Tribunal for Wales Regulations 2010, SI 2010/713, reg 46(2)(c).
23 Valuation Tribunal for Wales Regulations 2010, SI 2010/713, reg 46(3). As to references to a party to an appeal see PARA 551 note 3.
24 Valuation Tribunal for Wales Regulations 2010, SI 2010/713, reg 46(4).
25 Valuation Tribunal for Wales Regulations 2010, SI 2010/713, reg 46(5).
26 Valuation Tribunal for Wales Regulations 2010, SI 2010/713, reg 46(6).
27 Valuation Tribunal for Wales Regulations 2010, SI 2010/713, reg 46(7).
28 Valuation Tribunal for Wales Regulations 2010, SI 2010/713, reg 46(8).
29 Valuation Tribunal for Wales Regulations 2010, SI 2010/713, reg 46(9).
30 Valuation Tribunal for Wales Regulations 2010, SI 2010/713, reg 46(10).

549. Time limits in relation to appeals.

An appeal[1] by a person who has received notice from a billing authority[2] in relation to a grievance that the authority believes the grievance is not well founded, or that steps have been taken to deal with the grievance, but who is still aggrieved[3] will be dismissed unless it is initiated[4] not later than the expiry of two months[5] beginning with the date of service of the billing authority's notice[6].

When the period of two months, beginning with the date of service of the aggrieved person's notice, has ended without his being notified by the billing authority as above[7], an appeal by the aggrieved person will be dismissed unless it is initiated within four months of the date of service[8] of that person's notice of grievance[9].

An appeal against a penalty[10] will be dismissed unless it is initiated not later than the expiry of two months beginning with the date of service of written notice of the imposition of the penalty[11].

An appeal against a completion notice[12] will be dismissed unless it is initiated not later than the expiry of four weeks beginning with the date of service of the notice[13].

Notwithstanding the provisions above, the president of the Valuation Tribunal for Wales[14] may authorise an appeal to be entertained where the president is satisfied that the failure of the person aggrieved to initiate the appeal as so provided has arisen by reason of circumstances beyond that person's control[15].

1 As to the meaning of 'appeal' see PARA 546 note 2.
2 As to the meaning of 'person' see PARA 11 note 13. As to the meaning of 'billing authority' see PARA 346.
3 Ie a person in relation to whom the condition mentioned in the Local Government Finance Act 1992 16(7)(a) or (b) is fulfilled (see PARA 513): see the Valuation Tribunal for Wales Regulations 2010, SI 2010/713, reg 29(1).
4 Ie in accordance with the Valuation Tribunal for Wales Regulations 2010, SI 2010/713, Pt 5 (regs 27–46).
5 As to the meaning of 'month' see PARA 11 note 1.
6 Valuation Tribunal for Wales Regulations 2010, SI 2010/713, reg 29(1). As to the service of notices see PARA 548.

The Valuation Tribunal for Wales Regulations 2010, SI 2010/713, apply in relation to Wales only: see reg 2. As to the equivalent regulations in relation to England see the Valuation Tribunal for England (Council Tax and Rating Appeals) (Procedure) Regulations 2009, SI 2009/2269; and see PARA 515 et seq. As to the meanings of 'England' and 'Wales' see PARA 2 note 16.

The procedure for appeals under the Council Tax (Alteration of Lists and Appeals) Regulations 1993, SI 1993/290, reg 8 (see PARA 431) or reg 13 (see PARA 434) is governed by the Council Tax (Alteration of Lists and Appeals) Regulations 1993, SI 1993/290, Pt III (regs 16–34): see PARA 534 et seq.

7 Ie where the condition mentioned in the Local Government Finance Act 1992 16(7)(c) is fulfilled (see PARA 513): see the Valuation Tribunal for Wales Regulations 2010, SI 2010/713, reg 29(2).

8 Ie under the Local Government Finance Act 1992 16(4): see PARA 513.

9 Valuation Tribunal for Wales Regulations 2010, SI 2010/713, reg 29(2). This is subject to reg 29(2A): see reg 29(2) (amended by SI 2014/554). When the condition mentioned in the Local Government Finance Act 1992 s 16(7)(c) is fulfilled and the appeal by the aggrieved person relates to a billing authority's decision to award a reduction under its council tax reduction scheme, the appeal will be dismissed unless the notice required by s 16(4) was served on the billing authority in accordance with the Council Tax Reduction Schemes and Prescribed Requirements (Wales) Regulations 2013, SI 2013/3029, Sch 12 para 8(2) or Sch 1 para 8(2) of the scheme prescribed in the Council Tax Reduction Schemes (Default Scheme) (Wales) Regulations 2013, SI 2013/3035, as the case may be: Valuation Tribunal for Wales Regulations 2010, SI 2010/713, reg 29(2A) (added by SI 2014/554). 'Council tax reduction scheme' means a scheme made by a billing authority in accordance with the Council Tax Reduction Schemes and Prescribed Requirements (Wales) Regulations 2013, SI 2013/3029, or the scheme that applies in default by virtue of the Local Government Finance Act 1992 Sch 1B para 6(1)(e): Valuation Tribunal for Wales Regulations 2010, SI 2010/713, reg 27(1) (definition added by SI 2013/547; and amended by SI 2014/554). As to council tax reduction schemes see PARA 378.

10 Ie under the Local Government Finance Act 1992 Sch 3 para 3(1): see PARA 471.

11 Valuation Tribunal for Wales Regulations 2010, SI 2010/713, reg 29(3).

12 Ie under the Local Government Finance Act 1988 Sch 4A para 4 as it applies for the purposes of the Local Government Finance Act 1992 Pt I: see PARA 353.

13 Valuation Tribunal for Wales Regulations 2010, SI 2010/713, reg 29(4).

14 As to the meaning of 'president' see PARA 546 note 1. As to the president of the tribunal see PARA 238.

15 Valuation Tribunal for Wales Regulations 2010, SI 2010/713, reg 29(5). As to appeals out of time see *Moghaddam v Hammersmith and Fulham London Borough Council* [2009] EWHC 1670 (Admin), [2009] RA 209, [2009] All ER (D) 144 (Jul) (decided under previous legislation).

550. Withdrawal and striking out of appeals.

An appeal[1] may be withdrawn by notice in writing[2] given to the clerk[3] before the commencement of a hearing[4] or of consideration of written representations[5] by an appeal panel[6]. The clerk must notify the appellant when the notice of withdrawal has been received, and must serve a copy of the notice on all the other parties to the appeal[7].

The Valuation Tribunal for Wales may strike out an appeal or part of an appeal[8] where:

(1) the appeal, or part of the appeal, relates to a billing authority's decision to award a reduction under its council tax reduction scheme[9]; and

(2) the reduction awarded is the maximum reduction that the billing authority may have awarded under its scheme[10].

Where only part of an appeal falls within head (1), the valuation tribunal may only strike out that part of the appeal[11].

The valuation tribunal may not strike out an appeal, or part of an appeal, without first giving the appellant an opportunity to make representations in relation to the proposed striking out[12].

1 As to the meaning of 'appeal' see PARA 546 note 2.

2 As to the meaning of 'writing' see PARA 21 note 3.

3 As to the meaning of 'clerk' see PARA 546 note 12.

4 As to hearings see PARA 553.

5 As to written representations see PARA 551.

6 Valuation Tribunal for Wales Regulations 2010, SI 2010/713, reg 32(1). 'Appeal panel' means the members of the Valuation Tribunal for Wales convened in accordance with Pt 5 (regs 27–46) for the purpose of disposing of an appeal: regs 2(1), 27(1).

The Valuation Tribunal for Wales Regulations 2010, SI 2010/713, apply in relation to Wales only: see reg 2. As to the equivalent regulations in relation to England see the Valuation Tribunal for England (Council Tax and Rating Appeals) (Procedure) Regulations 2009, SI 2009/2269; and see PARA 515 et seq. As to the meanings of 'England' and 'Wales' see PARA 2 note 16.

The procedure for appeals under the Council Tax (Alteration of Lists and Appeals) Regulations 1993, SI 1993/290, reg 8 (see PARA 431) or reg 13 (see PARA 434) is governed by the Council Tax (Alteration of Lists and Appeals) Regulations 1993, SI 1993/290, Pt III (regs 16–34): see PARA 534 et seq.

7 Valuation Tribunal for Wales Regulations 2010, SI 2010/713, reg 32(2).

8 Valuation Tribunal for Wales Regulations 2010, SI 2010/713, reg 32A(1) (reg 32A added by SI 2013/547).

9 Valuation Tribunal for Wales Regulations 2010, SI 2010/713, reg 32A(1)(a) (as added: see note 8). As to the meaning of 'billing authority' see PARA 346. As to the meaning of 'council tax reduction scheme' see PARA 549 note 9; and as to such schemes see PARA 378. As to council tax see PARA 344 et seq.

10 Valuation Tribunal for Wales Regulations 2010, SI 2010/713, reg 32A(1)(b) (as added: see note 8).

11 Valuation Tribunal for Wales Regulations 2010, SI 2010/713, reg 32A(2) (as added: see note 8).

12 Valuation Tribunal for Wales Regulations 2010, SI 2010/713, reg 32A(3) (as added: see note 8).

551. Disposal of appeal by written representations.

An appeal[1] may be disposed of on the basis of written[2] representations if all the parties have given their agreement in writing[3]. Where all the parties have given their agreement, the clerk[4] must serve notice on the parties accordingly[5]; and, within four weeks of service of such a notice on a party, each party may serve on the clerk a notice stating:

(1) the reasons or further reasons for the disagreement giving rise to the appeal[6]; or

(2) that party does not intend to make further representations[7].

A copy of any notice so served must be served by the clerk on the other party or parties to the appeal, and must be accompanied by a statement of the effect of the provisions[8] as to service of further notice and notifying an appeal panel[9]. Any party on whom such a notice is served may, within four weeks of that service, serve on the clerk a further notice stating that party's reply to the other party's statement, or that that party does not intend to make further representations, as the case may be; and the clerk must serve a copy of any such further notice on the other party or parties[10].

After the expiry of four weeks beginning with the expiry of the period of four weeks mentioned above the clerk must submit to an appeal panel copies of:

(a) any information transmitted to the clerk in connection with the appeal[11]; and

(b) any notice under the provisions above[12].

The appeal panel to which an appeal is so referred may if it thinks fit:

(i) require any party to furnish in writing further particulars of the grounds relied on and of any relevant facts or contentions[13]; or

(ii) order that the appeal be disposed of on the basis of a hearing[14].

Where an appeal panel requires any party to furnish any particulars under head (i), the clerk must serve a copy of such particulars on every other party, and each such party may within four weeks of such service serve on the clerk any further statement they wish to make in response[15].

1 As to the meaning of 'appeal' see PARA 546 note 2.

2 As to the meaning of 'written' see PARA 21 note 3.

3 Valuation Tribunal for Wales Regulations 2010, SI 2010/713, reg 33(1). Any reference in Pt 5 (regs 27–46) to a party to an appeal, includes the appellant and any person entitled in pursuance of Pt 5 to be served with a copy of the appellant's notice of appeal: reg 27(2)(a).

The Valuation Tribunal for Wales Regulations 2010, SI 2010/713, apply in relation to Wales only: see reg 2. As to the equivalent regulations in relation to England see the Valuation Tribunal for England (Council Tax and Rating Appeals) (Procedure) Regulations 2009, SI 2009/2269; and see PARA 515 et seq. As to the meanings of 'England' and 'Wales' see PARA 2 note 16.

The procedure for appeals under the Council Tax (Alteration of Lists and Appeals) Regulations 1993, SI 1993/290, reg 8 (see PARA 431) or reg 13 (see PARA 434) is governed by the Council Tax (Alteration of Lists and Appeals) Regulations 1993, SI 1993/290, Pt III (regs 16–34): see PARA 534 et seq.

4 As to the meaning of 'clerk' see PARA 546 note 12.

5 Valuation Tribunal for Wales Regulations 2010, SI 2010/713, reg 33(2). As to service of notices see PARA 548.

6 Valuation Tribunal for Wales Regulations 2010, SI 2010/713, reg 33(2)(a).

7 Valuation Tribunal for Wales Regulations 2010, SI 2010/713, reg 33(2)(b).

8 Ie the effect of the Valuation Tribunal for Wales Regulations 2010, SI 2010/713, reg 33(4), (5): see the text to notes 10–13.

9 Valuation Tribunal for Wales Regulations 2010, SI 2010/713, reg 33(3). As to the meaning of 'appeal panel' see PARA 550 note 6.

10 Valuation Tribunal for Wales Regulations 2010, SI 2010/713, reg 33(4).

11 Valuation Tribunal for Wales Regulations 2010, SI 2010/713, reg 33(5)(a).

12 Valuation Tribunal for Wales Regulations 2010, SI 2010/713, reg 33(5)(b).

13 Valuation Tribunal for Wales Regulations 2010, SI 2010/713, reg 33(6)(a).

14 Valuation Tribunal for Wales Regulations 2010, SI 2010/713, reg 33(6)(b). As to hearings see PARA 553.

15 Valuation Tribunal for Wales Regulations 2010, SI 2010/713, reg 33(7).

552. Representation at hearing.

Any party to an appeal[1] which is to be decided at a hearing[2] may appear in person (with assistance, if wished, from any person), or be represented by counsel or solicitor, or any other representative (other than a person who is a member of the Valuation Tribunal for Wales[3] or the Governing Council[4] or an employee of the valuation tribunal)[5].

1 As to the meaning of 'appeal' see PARA 546 note 2. As to references to a party to an appeal see PARA 551 note 3.

2 As to hearings see PARA 553.

3 As to the Valuation Tribunal for Wales see PARA 237.

4 'Governing Council' means the Governing Council of the Valuation Tribunal for Wales established under the Valuation Tribunal for Wales Regulations 2010, SI 2010/713, reg 5 (see PARA 237): reg 2(1).

5 Valuation Tribunal for Wales Regulations 2010, SI 2010/713, reg 36. As to employees of the tribunal see PARA 238.

The Valuation Tribunal for Wales Regulations 2010, SI 2010/713, apply in relation to Wales only: see reg 2. As to the equivalent regulations in relation to England see the Valuation Tribunal for England (Council Tax and Rating Appeals) (Procedure) Regulations 2009, SI 2009/2269; and see PARA 515 et seq. As to the meanings of 'England' and 'Wales' see PARA 2 note 16.

The procedure for appeals under the Council Tax (Alteration of Lists and Appeals) Regulations 1993, SI 1993/290, reg 8 (see PARA 431) or reg 13 (see PARA 434) is governed by the Council Tax (Alteration of Lists and Appeals) Regulations 1993, SI 1993/290, Pt III (regs 16–34): see PARA 534 et seq.

553. Hearings.

Where the appeal[1] is to be disposed of on the basis of a hearing, the clerk[2] must, not less than four weeks before the date in question, serve[3] on the parties notice of the date, time and place appointed for the hearing[4].

The clerk will advertise the date, time and place appointed for any hearing by causing a notice giving such information to be conspicuously displayed:

(1) outside an office of the billing authority[5] appointed by the authority for that purpose[6]; or
(2) in another place within that authority's area[7].

The notice required to be advertised must name a place where a list of the appeals to be heard may be inspected[8].

Where the hearing of an appeal has been postponed, the clerk must take such steps as are reasonably practicable in the time available:

(a) to notify the parties of the postponement[9]; and
(b) to advertise the postponement[10].

The valuation tribunal's function of hearing or determining an appeal will be discharged by a panel of three members of the valuation tribunal ('an appeal panel') which must include at least one chairperson; and a chairperson will preside[11]. However, where all parties to an appeal who appear so agree, the appeal may be decided by two members of an appeal panel, and notwithstanding the absence of a chairperson[12].

The hearing must take place in public unless the appeal panel otherwise orders on being satisfied that it is in the interests of justice to hold a hearing, or part of a hearing, in private[13]. Where the hearing is to be held in private, the appeal panel may determine who is permitted to attend the hearing or part of the hearing[14].

If the appellant fails to appear at the hearing, the appeal panel may dismiss the appeal, and if any other party does not appear the appeal panel may hear and determine the appeal in that party's absence[15].

The appeal panel may require any witness to give evidence under oath or affirmation, and will have power for that purpose to administer an oath or affirmation in due form[16]. Parties at the hearing may be heard in such order as the appeal panel may determine, and may examine any witness before the appeal panel and call witnesses[17].

A hearing may be adjourned for such time, to such place and on such terms (if any) as the appeal panel thinks fit; and reasonable notice of the time and place to which the hearing has been adjourned must be given to every party[18].

If it thinks fit an appeal panel may, after notice to the parties inviting them to be present, inspect any dwelling which is the subject of an appeal[19].

Subject to any specific provisions[20], the appeal panel:

(i) must conduct the hearing in such manner as it considers most suitable to the clarification of the issues before it and generally to the just handling of the proceedings[21];
(ii) must, so far as appears to it appropriate, seek to avoid formality in its proceedings[22]; and
(iii) will not be bound by any enactment or rule of law relating to the admissibility of evidence before courts of law[23].

1 As to the meaning of 'appeal' see PARA 546 note 2.
2 As to the meaning of 'clerk' see PARA 546 note 12.
3 As to service of notices see PARA 548.
4 Valuation Tribunal for Wales Regulations 2010, SI 2010/713, reg 34(1).

The Valuation Tribunal for Wales Regulations 2010, SI 2010/713, apply in relation to Wales only: see reg 2. As to the equivalent regulations in relation to England see the Valuation Tribunal for England (Council Tax and Rating Appeals) (Procedure) Regulations 2009, SI 2009/2269; and see PARA 515 et seq. As to the meanings of 'England' and 'Wales' see PARA 2 note 16.

The procedure for appeals under the Council Tax (Alteration of Lists and Appeals) Regulations 1993, SI 1993/290, reg 8 (see PARA 431) or reg 13 (see PARA 434) is governed by the Council Tax (Alteration of Lists and Appeals) Regulations 1993, SI 1993/290, Pt III (regs 16–34): see PARA 534 et seq.
5 As to the meaning of 'billing authority' see PARA 346.

6 Valuation Tribunal for Wales Regulations 2010, SI 2010/713, reg 34(2)(a).
7 Valuation Tribunal for Wales Regulations 2010, SI 2010/713, reg 34(2)(b).
8 Valuation Tribunal for Wales Regulations 2010, SI 2010/713, reg 34(3).
9 Valuation Tribunal for Wales Regulations 2010, SI 2010/713, reg 34(4)(a).
10 Valuation Tribunal for Wales Regulations 2010, SI 2010/713, reg 34(4)(b).
11 Valuation Tribunal for Wales Regulations 2010, SI 2010/713, reg 37(1). As to members of the tribunal see PARA 238. A person will be disqualified from participating as a member in the hearing or determination of, or acting as clerk or officer of the valuation tribunal in relation to, an appeal if that person is a member of the relevant billing authority: reg 35(1). For this purpose, 'relevant billing authority' means:
(1) in the case of an appeal against a completion notice (see PARA 546 note 2), the billing authority in whose area is situated the dwelling which is the subject matter of the appeal (reg 35(2)(a)); and
(2) in any other case, the billing authority whose decision is being appealed against (reg 35(2)(b)).

A person will be disqualified from participating as a member in the hearing or determination of, or acting as clerk or officer of the valuation tribunal in relation to, an appeal if the appellant is that person's spouse, civil partner or that person supports the appellant financially or is liable to do so: reg 35(3). A person will not otherwise be disqualified from acting in any capacity in relation to an appeal by reason only of the fact that that person is a member of an authority which derives revenue directly or indirectly from payments in respect of council tax which may be affected by the exercise of that person's functions: reg 35(4).

Marriage includes marriage of a same sex couple: see the Marriage (Same Sex Couples) Act 2013 Sch 3 para 1(1)(a), (2), (3); and MATRIMONIAL AND CIVIL PARTNERSHIP LAW vol 72 (2015) PARA 1 et seq. As to civil partnership see MATRIMONIAL AND CIVIL PARTNERSHIP LAW vol 72 (2015) PARA 3. As to council tax see PARA 344 et seq.
12 Valuation Tribunal for Wales Regulations 2010, SI 2010/713, reg 37(2).
13 Valuation Tribunal for Wales Regulations 2010, SI 2010/713, reg 37(3) (substituted by SI 2013/547).
14 Valuation Tribunal for Wales Regulations 2010, SI 2010/713, reg 37(3A) (added by SI 2013/547). As to references to a party to an appeal see PARA 551 note 3.
15 Valuation Tribunal for Wales Regulations 2010, SI 2010/713, reg 37(4).
16 Valuation Tribunal for Wales Regulations 2010, SI 2010/713, reg 37(5). As to oaths and affirmations see CIVIL PROCEDURE vol 12 (2015) PARA 824 et seq.
17 Valuation Tribunal for Wales Regulations 2010, SI 2010/713, reg 37(6).
18 Valuation Tribunal for Wales Regulations 2010, SI 2010/713, reg 37(7).
19 Valuation Tribunal for Wales Regulations 2010, SI 2010/713, reg 37(8).
20 Ie of the Valuation Tribunal for Wales Regulations 2010, SI 2010/713, Pt 5 (regs 27–46).
21 Valuation Tribunal for Wales Regulations 2010, SI 2010/713, reg 37(9)(a).
22 Valuation Tribunal for Wales Regulations 2010, SI 2010/713, reg 37(9)(b).
23 Valuation Tribunal for Wales Regulations 2010, SI 2010/713, reg 37(9)(c). As to evidence see PARA 554.

554. Evidence.

The following provisions apply to information supplied[1] for purposes relating to council tax[2]. Subject to what follows, information to which these provisions apply will in any relevant proceedings[3] be admissible as evidence of any fact stated in it[4]; and any document purporting to contain such information will, unless the contrary is shown, be presumed:

(1) to have been supplied by the person by whom it purports to have been supplied[5]; and
(2) to have been supplied by that person in any capacity in which it purports to have been supplied[6].

Information to which these provisions apply must not be used in any relevant proceedings by a billing authority[7] unless:

(a) not less than two weeks' notice, specifying the information to be so used and the dwelling[8] or person to which or to whom it relates, has previously been given to every other party to the proceedings[9]; and

(b) any person who has given not less than 24 hours' notice of that person's intention to do so has been permitted by that authority at any reasonable time:
   (i) to inspect the documents and other media in or on which such information is held[10]; and
   (ii) to make a copy of, or of any extract from, any document containing such information[11].

If any information required to be made available for inspection in accordance with these provisions is not maintained in documentary form, the duty to make it so available is satisfied if a print-out, photographic image or other reproduction of the information, which has been obtained from the storage medium adopted in relation to that information, is made available for inspection[12].

The contents of a list[13] may be proved by the production of a copy of the list, or of the relevant part, purporting to be certified to be a true copy by the listing officer[14]. The contents of a completion notice may be proved by the production of a copy of it purporting to be certified to be a true copy by the proper officer of the billing authority[15].

1 Ie under regulations made under the Local Government Finance Act 1992 s 13 (see PARA 377) or Sch 2 (see PARAS 437, 444), or the Welfare Reform Act 2012 s 131. As to council tax see PARA 344 et seq.

2 Valuation Tribunal for Wales Regulations 2010, SI 2010/713, reg 38(1) (amended by SI 2013/547).

The Valuation Tribunal for Wales Regulations 2010, SI 2010/713, apply in relation to Wales only: see reg 2. As to the equivalent regulations in relation to England see the Valuation Tribunal for England (Council Tax and Rating Appeals) (Procedure) Regulations 2009, SI 2009/2269; and see PARA 515 et seq. As to the meanings of 'England' and 'Wales' see PARA 2 note 16.

The procedure for appeals under the Council Tax (Alteration of Lists and Appeals) Regulations 1993, SI 1993/290, reg 8 (see PARA 431) or reg 13 (see PARA 434) is governed by the Council Tax (Alteration of Lists and Appeals) Regulations 1993, SI 1993/290, Pt III (regs 16–34): see PARA 534 et seq.

3 In the Valuation Tribunal for Wales Regulations 2010, SI 2010/713, reg 38 'relevant proceedings' means any proceedings on or in consequence of an appeal, and any proceedings on or in consequence of a reference to arbitration under reg 45 (see PARA 559): reg 38(5).

4 Valuation Tribunal for Wales Regulations 2010, SI 2010/713, reg 38(2).

5 Valuation Tribunal for Wales Regulations 2010, SI 2010/713, reg 38(2)(a). As to the meaning of 'person' see PARA 11 note 13.

6 Valuation Tribunal for Wales Regulations 2010, SI 2010/713, reg 38(2)(b).

7 As to the meaning of 'billing authority' see PARA 346.

8 As to the meaning of 'dwelling' see PARA 349.

9 Valuation Tribunal for Wales Regulations 2010, SI 2010/713, reg 38(3)(a). As to references to a party to an appeal see PARA 551 note 3.

10 Valuation Tribunal for Wales Regulations 2010, SI 2010/713, reg 38(3)(b)(i).

11 Valuation Tribunal for Wales Regulations 2010, SI 2010/713, reg 38(3)(b)(ii).

12 Valuation Tribunal for Wales Regulations 2010, SI 2010/713, reg 38(4).

13 'List' means a valuation list compiled under the Local Government Finance Act 1992 Pt I Ch II (ss 20–29) (see PARA 408 et seq): Valuation Tribunal for Wales Regulations 2010, SI 2010/713, reg 27(1).

14 Valuation Tribunal for Wales Regulations 2010, SI 2010/713, reg 39(1). As to the meaning of 'listing officer' see PARA 546 note 9.

15 Valuation Tribunal for Wales Regulations 2010, SI 2010/713, reg 39(2). 'Proper officer' has the same meaning as in the Local Government Act 1972 (see LOCAL GOVERNMENT vol 69 (2018) PARA 477): Valuation Tribunal for Wales Regulations 2010, SI 2010/713, reg 39(3).

555. Decisions on appeals.

An appeal[1] may be decided by a majority of the members[2] participating; and where[3] it falls to be disposed of by two members and they are unable to agree, it must be remitted by the clerk[4] to be decided by an appeal panel consisting of three different members[5].

Where an appeal is disposed of on the basis of a hearing, the decision of the appeal panel may be reserved or given orally at the end of the hearing[6]. As soon as is reasonably practicable after a decision has been made, it must:

(1) in the case of a decision given orally, be confirmed[7];

(2) in any other case, be communicated[8],

by notice in writing[9] to the parties; and the notice must be accompanied by a statement of the reasons for the decision[10]. However, nothing in this provision will require notice to be given to a party[11] if it would be repetitive of any document supplied under the provision as to records[12] to that person[13].

In the case of an appeal against a completion notice[14], the clerk must send notice of the decision to the listing officer[15] appointed for the billing authority[16] which is a party to the appeal[17].

1 As to the meaning of 'appeal' see PARA 546 note 2.

2 In the Valuation Tribunal for Wales Regulations 2010, SI 2010/713, reg 40, 'member' means a member of an appeal panel: reg 40(6). As to the meaning of 'appeal panel' see PARA 550 note 6.

3 Ie pursuant to the Valuation Tribunal for Wales Regulations 2010, SI 2010/713, reg 37(2): see PARA 553.

4 As to the meaning of 'clerk' see PARA 546 note 12.

5 Valuation Tribunal for Wales Regulations 2010, SI 2010/713, reg 40(1). As to orders which can be made on an appeal see PARA 556.

The Valuation Tribunal for Wales Regulations 2010, SI 2010/713, apply in relation to Wales only: see reg 2. As to the equivalent regulations in relation to England see the Valuation Tribunal for England (Council Tax and Rating Appeals) (Procedure) Regulations 2009, SI 2009/2269; and see PARA 515 et seq. As to the meanings of 'England' and 'Wales' see PARA 2 note 16.

The procedure for appeals under the Council Tax (Alteration of Lists and Appeals) Regulations 1993, SI 1993/290, reg 8 (see PARA 431) or reg 13 (see PARA 434) is governed by the Council Tax (Alteration of Lists and Appeals) Regulations 1993, SI 1993/290, Pt III (regs 16–34): see PARA 534 et seq.

6 Valuation Tribunal for Wales Regulations 2010, SI 2010/713, reg 40(2).

7 Valuation Tribunal for Wales Regulations 2010, SI 2010/713, reg 40(3)(a).

8 Valuation Tribunal for Wales Regulations 2010, SI 2010/713, reg 40(3)(b).

9 As to the meaning of 'writing' see PARA 21 note 3.

10 Valuation Tribunal for Wales Regulations 2010, SI 2010/713, reg 40(3).

11 As to references to a party to an appeal see PARA 551 note 3.

12 Ie the Valuation Tribunal for Wales Regulations 2010, SI 2010/713, reg 43: see PARA 558.

13 Valuation Tribunal for Wales Regulations 2010, SI 2010/713, reg 40(4). As to the meaning of 'person' see PARA 11 note 13.

14 As to the meaning of 'appeal against a completion notice' see PARA 546 note 2.

15 As to the meaning of 'listing officer' see PARA 546 note 9.

16 As to the meaning of 'billing authority' see PARA 346.

17 Valuation Tribunal for Wales Regulations 2010, SI 2010/713, reg 40(5).

556. Orders.

On or after deciding an appeal[1] the appeal panel[2] may, in consequence of the decision, by order require[3]:

(1) an estimate to be quashed or altered[4];

(2) a penalty[5] to be quashed[6];

(3) the decision of a billing authority[7] to be reversed[8];

(4) a calculation (other than an estimate) of an amount to be quashed and the amount to be recalculated[9].

An order may require any matter ancillary to its subject matter to be attended to[10].

1 As to the meaning of 'appeal' see PARA 546 note 2. As to deciding an appeal see PARA 555.

2 As to the meaning of 'appeal panel' see PARA 550 note 6.

3 Valuation Tribunal for Wales Regulations 2010, SI 2010/713, reg 41(1).
The Valuation Tribunal for Wales Regulations 2010, SI 2010/713, apply in relation to Wales only: see reg 2. As to the equivalent regulations in relation to England see the Valuation Tribunal for England (Council Tax and Rating Appeals) (Procedure) Regulations 2009, SI 2009/2269; and see PARA 515 et seq. As to the meanings of 'England' and 'Wales' see PARA 2 note 16.
The procedure for appeals under the Council Tax (Alteration of Lists and Appeals) Regulations 1993, SI 1993/290, reg 8 (see PARA 431) or reg 13 (see PARA 434) is governed by the Council Tax (Alteration of Lists and Appeals) Regulations 1993, SI 1993/290, Pt III (regs 16–34): see PARA 534 et seq.
4 Valuation Tribunal for Wales Regulations 2010, SI 2010/713, reg 41(1)(a).
5 'Penalty' means a penalty imposed under the Local Government Finance Act 1992 Sch 3 para 1 (see PARA 471): Valuation Tribunal for Wales Regulations 2010, SI 2010/713, reg 27(1).
6 Valuation Tribunal for Wales Regulations 2010, SI 2010/713, reg 41(1)(b).
7 As to the meaning of 'billing authority' see PARA 346.
8 Valuation Tribunal for Wales Regulations 2010, SI 2010/713, reg 41(1)(c).
9 Valuation Tribunal for Wales Regulations 2010, SI 2010/713, reg 41(1)(d).
10 Valuation Tribunal for Wales Regulations 2010, SI 2010/713, reg 41(2).

557. Review of decisions.

An appeal panel[1] constituted as provided below[2] will have power on written[3] application by a party[4] to review or set aside by certificate under the hand of the presiding member[5]:

(1) any decision on any of the grounds mentioned in heads (a) to (d) below[6]; and
(2) a decision on an appeal against a completion notice[7], on the additional ground mentioned in head (e) below[8].

This does not apply where an appeal against the decision in question has been determined by the High Court[9]. An application may be dismissed if it is not made within the period of four weeks beginning on the day on which notice is given[10] of the decision in question[11].

So far as is reasonably practicable, the appeal panel appointed to review a decision will consist of the same members as constituted the appeal panel which took the decision[12].

The grounds referred to in head (1) above are[13]:

(a) that the decision was wrongly made as a result of clerical error[14];
(b) that a party did not appear and can show reasonable cause why that party did not do so[15];
(c) that the decision is affected by a decision of, or a decision on appeal from, the High Court or the Upper Tribunal in relation to an appeal in respect of the dwelling which, or, as the case may be, the person who, was the subject of the appeal panel's decision[16]; and
(d) the interests of justice otherwise require such a review[17].

The additional ground referred to in head (2) above is that new evidence, the existence of which could not have been ascertained by reasonably diligent inquiry or could not have been foreseen, has become available since the conclusion of the proceedings to which the decision relates[18].

If an appeal panel sets aside a decision in pursuance of these provisions, it must revoke any order made in consequence of that decision[19] and must order a re-hearing or redetermination before either the same or a different appeal panel[20].

The clerk must as soon as reasonably practicable notify the parties to the appeal in writing[21] of:

(i) a determination that the appeal panel will not undertake a review[22];
(ii) the determination of the appeal panel, having undertaken a review, that it will not set aside the decision concerned[23];

(iii) the issue of any certificate by the appeal panel[24]; and
(iv) the revocation of any order[25].

Where in relation to a decision in respect of which an application to review or set aside a decision is made, an appeal to the High Court remains undetermined on the relevant day[26], the clerk must notify the High Court as soon as reasonably practicable after the occurrence of the relevant event[27].

1 As to the meaning of 'appeal panel' see PARA 550 note 6.
2 Ie under the Valuation Tribunal for Wales Regulations 2010, SI 2010/713, reg 42(4): see the text to note 12.
3 As to the meaning of 'written' see PARA 21 note 3.
4 As to references to a party to an appeal see PARA 551 note 3.
5 Valuation Tribunal for Wales Regulations 2010, SI 2010/713, reg 42(1). Regulation 42(1) is subject to reg 42(2), (3): see reg 42(1). In reg 42, 'member' means a member of an appeal panel: reg 42(11).

The Valuation Tribunal for Wales Regulations 2010, SI 2010/713, apply in relation to Wales only: see reg 2. As to the equivalent regulations in relation to England see the Valuation Tribunal for England (Council Tax and Rating Appeals) (Procedure) Regulations 2009, SI 2009/2269; and see PARA 515 et seq. As to the meanings of 'England' and 'Wales' see PARA 2 note 16.

The procedure for appeals under the Council Tax (Alteration of Lists and Appeals) Regulations 1993, SI 1993/290, reg 8 (see PARA 431) or reg 13 (see PARA 434) is governed by the Council Tax (Alteration of Lists and Appeals) Regulations 1993, SI 1993/290, Pt III (regs 16–34): see PARA 534 et seq.

6 Valuation Tribunal for Wales Regulations 2010, SI 2010/713, reg 42(1)(a).
7 As to the meaning of 'appeal against a completion notice' see PARA 546 note 2.
8 Valuation Tribunal for Wales Regulations 2010, SI 2010/713, reg 42(1)(b).
9 Valuation Tribunal for Wales Regulations 2010, SI 2010/713, reg 42(2). As to determination by the High Court see PARA 562.
10 Ie whether in accordance with the Valuation Tribunal for Wales Regulations 2010, SI 2010/713, reg 40(3) (see PARA 555) or reg 43(3) (see PARA 558).
11 Valuation Tribunal for Wales Regulations 2010, SI 2010/713, reg 42(3).
12 Valuation Tribunal for Wales Regulations 2010, SI 2010/713, reg 42(4).
13 Valuation Tribunal for Wales Regulations 2010, SI 2010/713, reg 42(5).
14 Valuation Tribunal for Wales Regulations 2010, SI 2010/713, reg 42(5)(a).
15 Valuation Tribunal for Wales Regulations 2010, SI 2010/713, reg 42(5)(b).
16 Valuation Tribunal for Wales Regulations 2010, SI 2010/713, reg 42(5)(c).
17 Valuation Tribunal for Wales Regulations 2010, SI 2010/713, reg 42(5)(d).
18 Valuation Tribunal for Wales Regulations 2010, SI 2010/713, reg 42(6).
19 As to orders see PARA 556.
20 Valuation Tribunal for Wales Regulations 2010, SI 2010/713, reg 42(7).
21 Valuation Tribunal for Wales Regulations 2010, SI 2010/713, reg 42(8).
22 Valuation Tribunal for Wales Regulations 2010, SI 2010/713, reg 42(8)(a).
23 Valuation Tribunal for Wales Regulations 2010, SI 2010/713, reg 42(8)(b).
24 Valuation Tribunal for Wales Regulations 2010, SI 2010/713, reg 42(8)(c).
25 Valuation Tribunal for Wales Regulations 2010, SI 2010/713, reg 42(8)(d).
26 'The relevant day' means the day on which, as the case may be, the application under the Valuation Tribunal for Wales Regulations 2010, SI 2010/713, reg 42(1) is made or the event referred to in any of reg 42(8)(a)–(d) (see heads (i)–(iv) in the text) occurs: reg 42(10).
27 Valuation Tribunal for Wales Regulations 2010, SI 2010/713, reg 42(9). The relevant event', in relation to a relevant day, means the event occurring on that day: reg 42(10).

558. Records of decisions and orders.

It will be the duty of the clerk[1] to make arrangements for each decision[2], each order[3] and the effect of each certificate and revocation[4] to be recorded[5]. Records may be kept in any form, whether documentary or otherwise, and must contain the specified[6] particulars[7].

A copy, in documentary form, of the relevant entry in the record must, as soon as reasonably practicable after the entry has been made, be sent to each party to the appeal to which the entry relates[8]. Each record must be retained for the period of six years beginning on the day on which an entry was last made in it[9].

Any person[10] may, at a reasonable time stated by or on behalf of the Valuation Tribunal for Wales and without making payment, inspect the records which are required to be made[11]. If, without reasonable excuse, a person having custody of the record intentionally obstructs a person in exercising this right, that person will be liable on summary conviction to a fine[12].

The member who presided at the hearing or determination of an appeal may authorise the correction of any clerical error in the record, and a copy of the corrected entry must be sent to the persons to whom a copy of the original entry was sent[13].

The production in any proceedings in any court of law of a document purporting to be certified by the chief executive[14] or clerk of an appeal panel to be a true copy of a record or decision of that panel will, unless the contrary is proved, be sufficient evidence of the document and of the facts it records[15].

1 As to the meaning of 'clerk' see PARA 546 note 12.

2 As to decisions see PARA 555.

3 Ie made under the Valuation Tribunal for Wales Regulations 2010, SI 2010/713, reg 41: see PARA 556.

4 Ie made under the Valuation Tribunal for Wales Regulations 2010, SI 2010/713, reg 42: see PARA 557.

5 Valuation Tribunal for Wales Regulations 2010, SI 2010/713, reg 43(1).

The Valuation Tribunal for Wales Regulations 2010, SI 2010/713, apply in relation to Wales only: see reg 2. As to the equivalent regulations in relation to England see the Valuation Tribunal for England (Council Tax and Rating Appeals) (Procedure) Regulations 2009, SI 2009/2269; and see PARA 515 et seq. As to the meanings of 'England' and 'Wales' see PARA 2 note 16.

The procedure for appeals under the Council Tax (Alteration of Lists and Appeals) Regulations 1993, SI 1993/290, reg 8 (see PARA 431) or reg 13 (see PARA 434) is governed by the Council Tax (Alteration of Lists and Appeals) Regulations 1993, SI 1993/290, Pt III (regs 16–34): see PARA 534 et seq.

6 Ie specified in the Valuation Tribunal for Wales Regulations 2010, SI 2010/713, Sch 3. Those particulars are (Sch 3):

(1) the appellant's name and address;
(2) the date of the appeal;
(3) the matter appealed against;
(4) the name of the billing authority whose decision was appealed against;
(5) the date of the hearing or determination;
(6) the names of the parties who appeared, if any;
(7) the decision of the appeal panel and its date;
(8) the reasons for the decision;
(9) any order made in consequence of the decision;
(10) the date of any such order;
(11) any certificate setting aside the decision;
(12) any revocation under reg 42(7).

7 Valuation Tribunal for Wales Regulations 2010, SI 2010/713, reg 43(2).

8 Valuation Tribunal for Wales Regulations 2010, SI 2010/713, reg 43(3). As to references to a party to an appeal see PARA 551 note 3.

9 Valuation Tribunal for Wales Regulations 2010, SI 2010/713, reg 43(4).

10 As to the meaning of 'person' see PARA 11 note 13.

11 Valuation Tribunal for Wales Regulations 2010, SI 2010/713, reg 43(5).

12 Valuation Tribunal for Wales Regulations 2010, SI 2010/713, reg 43(6). The fine will not exceed level 1 on the standard scale: reg 43(6). As to the powers of magistrates' courts to issue fines on summary conviction see SENTENCING vol 92 (2015) PARA 176.

13 Valuation Tribunal for Wales Regulations 2010, SI 2010/713, reg 43(7).

14 As to the chief executive see PARA 238.

15 Valuation Tribunal for Wales Regulations 2010, SI 2010/713, reg 43(8).

(iii) Arbitration

559. Reference to arbitration.

In relation to England, where the persons[1] who, if a matter falling within the Valuation Tribunal for England's[2] jurisdiction were to be the subject of an appeal to the tribunal[3], would be the parties[4] to the appeal agree in writing[5] that the matter is to be referred to arbitration, the matter must be so referred[6].

Unless the tribunal considers that there is good reason not to do so, where at any time before the determination of an appeal by the tribunal, the parties to the proceedings on an appeal agree in writing that any matter arising in the proceedings is to be referred to arbitration, the matter must be so referred[7].

In any arbitration under these provisions the award may include any order[8] which could have been made by the tribunal in relation to the matter[9].

In relation to Wales, where at any time before the beginning of a hearing[10] or the consideration by an appeal panel[11] of written representations[12] it is so agreed in writing between the persons who, if a dispute were to be the subject of an appeal to the Valuation Tribunal for Wales[13], would be the parties to the appeal, the question will be referred to arbitration[14].

In any arbitration in pursuance of this provision, the award may include any order which could have been made by an appeal panel in relation to the question[15].

1 As to the meaning of 'person' see PARA 11 note 13.

2 As to the Valuation Tribunal for England see PARA 232. The Valuation Tribunal for England (Council Tax and Rating Appeals) (Procedure) Regulations 2009, SI 2009/2269, apply in relation to England only: see reg 1. As to the meanings of 'England' and 'Wales' see PARA 2 note 16.

3 As to appeals in relation to council tax see PARA 514.

4 As to the meaning of 'party' see PARA 515 note 4.

5 As to the meaning of 'writing' see PARA 21 note 3.

6 See the Valuation Tribunal for England (Council Tax and Rating Appeals) (Procedure) Regulations 2009, SI 2009/2269, reg 4(1), (2). The provisions of the Arbitration Act 1996 Pt I (ss 1–84) apply to any arbitration under the Valuation Tribunal for England (Council Tax and Rating Appeals) (Procedure) Regulations 2009, SI 2009/2269, reg 4: see the Arbitration Act 1996 s 94; and ARBITRATION vol 2 (2017) PARA 509.

7 Valuation Tribunal for England (Council Tax and Rating Appeals) (Procedure) Regulations 2009, SI 2009/2269, reg 4(3).

8 As to orders see PARA 531.

9 Valuation Tribunal for England (Council Tax and Rating Appeals) (Procedure) Regulations 2009, SI 2009/2269, reg 4(4). The Local Government Finance Act 1988 Sch 11 para 9 (see PARA 533) applies to such an order as it applies to an order recorded under the Valuation Tribunal for England (Council Tax and Rating Appeals) (Procedure) Regulations 2009, SI 2009/2269: see reg 4(4).

10 As to hearings see PARA 553.

11 As to the meaning of 'appeal panel' see PARA 550 note 6.

12 As to written representations see PARA 551.

13 As to the Valuation Tribunal for Wales see PARA 237.

14 Valuation Tribunal for Wales Regulations 2010, SI 2010/713, reg 45(1). See also the Council Tax (Alteration of Lists and Appeals) Regulations 1993, SI 1993/290, reg 33(1), (2). The Valuation Tribunal for Wales Regulations 2010, SI 2010/713, apply in relation to Wales only: see reg 2.

15 Valuation Tribunal for Wales Regulations 2010, SI 2010/713, reg 45(2). The Local Government Finance Act 1988 Sch 11 para 10A (see PARA 533 note 6) will apply to such an order as it applies to orders recorded in pursuance of the Valuation Tribunal for Wales Regulations 2010, SI 2010/713, Pt 5 (regs 27–46): reg 45(2). See also the Council Tax (Alteration of Lists and Appeals) Regulations 1993, SI 1993/290, reg 33(3). The Local Government Finance Act 1988 Sch 11 para 9 (see PARA 533) will apply to such and order as it applies to an order recorded in pursuance of the Council Tax (Alteration of Lists and Appeals) Regulations 1993, SI 1993/290: reg 33(3).

(iv) Appeal to the High Court

560. Appeals to the High Court: England.

An appeal lies to the High Court[1] on a question of law arising out of a decision or order[2] which is given or made by the Valuation Tribunal for England[3] on an appeal[4] in relation to council tax[5]. Such an appeal to the High Court may be dismissed if it is not made within four weeks[6] of the date on which notice is given of the decision or order that is the subject of the appeal or, in the case of an appeal as to council tax liability[7], within two weeks of the date on which written reasons for the decision are given[8], if later[9].

The High Court may confirm, vary, set aside, revoke or remit the decision or order, and may make any order the tribunal could have made[10]. Billing authorities and listing officers must act in accordance with any order made by the High Court[11].

1 As to the High Court of Justice in England and Wales see COURTS AND TRIBUNALS vol 24 (2010) PARA 695 et seq.

2 As to decisions see PARA 530. As to orders see PARA 531.

3 As to the Valuation Tribunal for England see PARA 232. The Valuation Tribunal for England (Council Tax and Rating Appeals) (Procedure) Regulations 2009, SI 2009/2269, apply in relation to England only: see reg 1. As to the equivalent provision in relation to Wales see the Council Tax (Alteration of Lists and Appeals) Regulations 1993, SI 1993/290, reg 32; the Valuation Tribunal for Wales Regulations 2010, SI 2010/713, reg 44; and PARAS 561, 562. As to the meanings of 'England' and 'Wales' see PARA 2 note 16.

4 Ie an appeal under the Local Government Finance Act 1992 s 16 or the Council Tax (Alteration of Lists and Appeals) (England) Regulations 2009, SI 2009/2270, or an appeal against a completion notice under the Local Government Finance Act 1988 Sch 4A para 1 as it applies for the purposes of the Local Government Finance Act 1992 Pt I (ss 1–69): see the Valuation Tribunal for England (Council Tax and Rating Appeals) (Procedure) Regulations 2009, SI 2009/2269, reg 43(1). As to appeals in relation to council tax see PARA 514.

5 Valuation Tribunal for England (Council Tax and Rating Appeals) (Procedure) Regulations 2009, SI 2009/2269, reg 43(1). See eg *Cselko v Listing Officer for Camden* [2001] RVR 280 (tribunal might have reached a different conclusion because its valuation of a number of flats together failed to have regard to the special circumstances relating to one of them).

Where a listing officer appeals to the High Court under reg 43 against a decision in consequence of which an order requiring the alteration of a list was made, or against such an order, the listing officer must, at the same time or as soon as reasonably practicable afterwards, notify the authority concerned of the application or appeal: see reg 44(1)(b). As to the meaning of 'listing officer' see PARA 515 note 4. As to the meaning of 'list' see PARA 515 note 4. As to the service and delivery of documents see PARA 515. As to the meaning of 'the authority concerned' see PARA 532 note 4.

Where, in relation to a decision or order made on an appeal under the Local Government Finance Act 1992 s 16 (see PARA 513), a billing authority appeals to the High Court under the Valuation Tribunal for England (Council Tax and Rating Appeals) (Procedure) Regulations 2009, SI 2009/2269, reg 43, or receives notice of such an appeal instituted by another party, it must, as soon as reasonably practicable afterwards, notify the tribunal of the appeal: reg 44(5). As to the meaning of 'billing authority' see PARA 346. As to the meaning of 'party' see PARA 515 note 4.

6 As to the calculation of time see PARA 515.

7 Ie an appeal under the Local Government Finance Act 1992 s 16: see PARA 513.

8 Ie in accordance with the Valuation Tribunal for England (Council Tax and Rating Appeals) (Procedure) Regulations 2009, SI 2009/2269, reg 37(6): see PARA 530 note 7.

9 Valuation Tribunal for England (Council Tax and Rating Appeals) (Procedure) Regulations 2009, SI 2009/2269, reg 43(2) (amended by SI 2013/465). However, where the appeal is made by a person whose application under the Valuation Tribunal for England (Council Tax and Rating Appeals) (Procedure) Regulations 2009, SI 2009/2269, reg 40(1) for the review of the decision relied (whether in whole or part) on satisfaction of the condition mentioned in reg 40(5)(c) (see PARA 532) (reg 43(3)(a)), and the tribunal gave notice that it would not undertake a review (reg 43(3)(b)(i)) or, having reviewed the decision or part, that it would not set aside the decision or part (reg 43(3)(b)(ii)), the appeal may be dismissed if it is not made within four weeks of the date of the

tribunal's notice (reg 43(3)). As to the meaning of 'person' see PARA 11 note 13.

Turner v South Cambridgeshire District Council [2016] EWHC 1017 (Admin), [2016] RVR 355, in rejecting a challenge as being made out of time without good reason, emphasised both that weight must be attached to timetabling rules for appeals brought as of right, and also that such challenges must not simply be an attempt to secure a review of the merits.

10 Valuation Tribunal for England (Council Tax and Rating Appeals) (Procedure) Regulations 2009, SI 2009/2269, reg 43(4).

11 Valuation Tribunal for England (Council Tax and Rating Appeals) (Procedure) Regulations 2009, SI 2009/2269, reg 43(5). For these purposes, the Local Government Finance Act 1988 Sch 11 para 10A (see PARA 533 note 6) has effect as if the reference to a tribunal included a reference to the High Court: see the Valuation Tribunal for England (Council Tax and Rating Appeals) (Procedure) Regulations 2009, SI 2009/2269, reg 43(5).

561. Appeals to the High Court: alteration of lists in Wales.

An appeal will lie to the High Court on a question of law arising out of a decision or order which is given or made by a tribunal[1] on an appeal[2]. Such an appeal may be dismissed if it is not made within four weeks of the date on which notice is given of the decision or order that is the subject of the appeal[3]. Further, where in relation to an application for review of a decision[4] made within four weeks of the date on which notice was given of the decision which is the subject matter of the appeal:

(1) notice is given[5] that the tribunal will not undertake a review[6]; or

(2) notice is given[7] of the determination of the tribunal not to set aside the decision in question[8],

the appeal may be dismissed if it is not made within four weeks of the service of that notice[9].

The High Court may confirm, vary, set aside, revoke or remit the decision or order of the tribunal, and may make any order which the tribunal could have made[10]. A listing officer[11] must act in accordance with any order made by the High Court[12].

1 As to the meaning of 'tribunal' see PARA 534 note 4.

2 Council Tax (Alteration of Lists and Appeals) Regulations 1993, SI 1993/290, reg 32(1). As to the meaning of 'appeal' see PARA 534 note 2.

The Council Tax (Alteration of Lists and Appeals) Regulations 1993, SI 1993/290, apply in relation to Wales only: see PARA 417 note 2. As to the procedure on other appeals relating to council tax in Wales see the Valuation Tribunal for Wales Regulations 2010, SI 2010/713, reg 44; and PARA 562. As to the equivalent provision in relation to England see the Valuation Tribunal for England (Council Tax and Rating Appeals) (Procedure) Regulations 2009, SI 2009/2269, reg 43; and PARA 560. As to the meanings of 'England' and 'Wales' see PARA 2 note 16.

3 Council Tax (Alteration of Lists and Appeals) Regulations 1993, SI 1993/290, reg 32(2).

4 Ie under the Council Tax (Alteration of Lists and Appeals) Regulations 1993, SI 1993/290, reg 30(1): see PARA 543.

5 Ie as mentioned in the Council Tax (Alteration of Lists and Appeals) Regulations 1993, SI 1993/290, reg 30(6)(a): see PARA 543 head (a).

6 Council Tax (Alteration of Lists and Appeals) Regulations 1993, SI 1993/290, reg 32(3)(a).

7 Ie as mentioned in the Council Tax (Alteration of Lists and Appeals) Regulations 1993, SI 1993/290, reg 30(6)(b): see PARA 543 head (b).

8 Council Tax (Alteration of Lists and Appeals) Regulations 1993, SI 1993/290, reg 32(3)(b).

9 Council Tax (Alteration of Lists and Appeals) Regulations 1993, SI 1993/290, reg 32(3). *Turner v South Cambridgeshire District Council* [2016] EWHC 1017 (Admin), [2016] RVR 355, in rejecting a challenge as being made out of time without good reason, emphasised both that weight must be attached to timetabling rules for appeals brought as of right, and also that such challenges must not simply be an attempt to secure a review of the merits.

10 Council Tax (Alteration of Lists and Appeals) Regulations 1993, SI 1993/290, reg 32(4).

11 As to the meaning of 'listing officer' see PARA 428 note 12.

12 Council Tax (Alteration of Lists and Appeals) Regulations 1993, SI 1993/290, reg 32(5). The

Local Government Finance Act 1988 Sch 11 para 9 (see PARA 533) will have effect subject to this requirement: Council Tax (Alteration of Lists and Appeals) Regulations 1993, SI 1993/290, reg 32(5).

562. Appeals to the High Court: council tax appeals in Wales.

An appeal will lie to the High Court on a question of law arising out of a decision or order which is given or made by an appeal panel[1] on an appeal[2] and may be made by any party to the appeal[3]. Such an appeal may be dismissed if it is not made within four weeks of the date on which notice is given of the decision or order that is the subject matter of the appeal[4]. Further, where in relation to an application for review of a decision[5] made within four weeks of the date on which notice was given of the decision which is the subject matter of the appeal:

(1) notice is given[6] that the appeal panel will not undertake a review[7]; or
(2) notice is given[8] that the appeal panel, having undertaken a review, will not set aside the decision concerned[9],

the appeal may be dismissed if it is not made within four weeks of the service of that notice[10].

The High Court may confirm, vary, set aside, revoke or remit the decision or order of an appeal panel, and may make any order which the appeal panel could have made[11]. Billing authorities[12] must act in accordance with any order made by the High Court[13].

1 As to the meaning of 'appeal panel' see PARA 550 note 6.
2 As to the meaning of 'appeal' see PARA 546 note 2.
3 Valuation Tribunal for Wales Regulations 2010, SI 2010/713, reg 44(1). As to references to a party to an appeal see PARA 551 note 3.
The Valuation Tribunal for Wales Regulations 2010, SI 2010/713, apply in relation to Wales only: see reg 2. As to the equivalent provision in relation to England see the Valuation Tribunal for England (Council Tax and Rating Appeals) (Procedure) Regulations 2009, SI 2009/2269, reg 43; and PARA 560. As to the equivalent provision in relation to appeals under the Council Tax (Alteration of Lists and Appeals) Regulations 1993, SI 1993/290, reg 8 (see PARA 431) or reg 13 (see PARA 434) see the Council Tax (Alteration of Lists and Appeals) Regulations 1993, SI 1993/290, reg 32; and PARA 561. As to the meanings of 'England' and 'Wales' see PARA 2 note 16.
4 Valuation Tribunal for Wales Regulations 2010, SI 2010/713, reg 44(2).
5 Ie under the Valuation Tribunal for Wales Regulations 2010, SI 2010/713, reg 42(1): see PARA 557 heads (1), (2).
6 Ie as mentioned in the Valuation Tribunal for Wales Regulations 2010, SI 2010/713, reg 42(8)(a): see PARA 557 head (i).
7 Valuation Tribunal for Wales Regulations 2010, SI 2010/713, reg 44(3)(a).
8 Ie as mentioned in the Valuation Tribunal for Wales Regulations 2010, SI 2010/713, reg 42(8)(b): see PARA 557 head (ii).
9 Valuation Tribunal for Wales Regulations 2010, SI 2010/713, reg 44(3)(b).
10 Valuation Tribunal for Wales Regulations 2010, SI 2010/713, reg 44(3). *Turner v South Cambridgeshire District Council* [2016] EWHC 1017 (Admin), [2016] RVR 355, in rejecting a challenge as being made out of time without good reason, emphasised both that weight must be attached to timetabling rules for appeals brought as of right, and also that such challenges must not simply be an attempt to secure a review of the merits.
11 Valuation Tribunal for Wales Regulations 2010, SI 2010/713, reg 44(4).
12 As to the meaning of 'billing authority' see PARA 346.
13 Valuation Tribunal for Wales Regulations 2010, SI 2010/713, reg 44(5). The Local Government Finance Act 1988 Sch 11 para 10A (see PARA 533 note 6) will have effect subject to this requirement: Valuation Tribunal for Wales Regulations 2010, SI 2010/713, reg 44(5).

6. OTHER SOURCES OF FINANCE

(1) Capital Finance

(i) In General

563. Information and guidance.

A local authority[1] must supply the appropriate national authority[2] with such information relating to capital finance[3], and at such time, as the appropriate national authority may request[4].

In carrying out its functions in relation to capital finance[5], a local authority[6] must have regard to such guidance as the appropriate national authority may issue[7] and to such other guidance as the appropriate national authority may by regulations specify for these purposes[8].

1 The following are local authorities for the purposes of the Local Government Act 2003 Pt 1 (ss 1–24):

(1) a county council (s 23(1)(a));
(2) a county borough council (s 23(1)(b));
(3) a district council (s 23(1)(c));
(4) the Greater London Authority (s 23(1)(d));
(5) a functional body, within the meaning of the Greater London Authority Act 1999 (see LONDON GOVERNMENT vol 71 (2013) PARA 148) (Local Government Act 2003 s 23(1)(e));
(6) a London borough council (s 23(1)(f));
(7) the Common Council of the City of London, in its capacity as a local authority, police authority or port health authority (s 23(1)(g));
(8) the Council of the Isles of Scilly (s 23(1)(h));
(9) an authority established under the Local Government Act 1985 s 10 (waste disposal authorities: see LOCAL GOVERNMENT vol 69 (2018) PARA 17) (Local Government Act 2003 s 23(1)(j));
(10) a joint authority established by the Local Government Act 1985 Pt IV (ss 23–42) (fire and rescue services and transport: LOCAL GOVERNMENT vol 69 (2018) PARAS 71, 72) (Local Government Act 2003 s 23(1)(k) (amended by the Civil Contingencies Act 2004 s 32(1), Sch 2 para 10(3)(e)));
(11) a joint planning board constituted for an area in Wales outside a National Park by an order under the Town and Country Planning Act 1990 s 2(1B) (see PLANNING vol 81 (2018) PARA 188) (Local Government Act 2003 s 23(1)(l));
(12) a fire and rescue authority constituted by a scheme under the Fire and Rescue Services Act 2004 s 2 or a scheme to which s 4 of that Act applies (see FIRE AND RESCUE SERVICES vol 51 (2013) PARAS 18–20) (Local Government Act 2003 s 23(1)(m) (substituted by the Fire and Rescue Services Act 2004 s 53(1), Sch 1 paras 99, 100));
(13) a fire and rescue authority created by an order under the Fire and Rescue Services Act 2004 s 4A (see FIRE AND RESCUE SERVICES) (Local Government Act 2003 s 23(1)(ma) (added by the Policing and Crime Act 2017 s 6 Sch 1 para 83(1), (2)));
(14) a police and crime commissioner (see POLICE AND INVESTIGATORY POWERS vol 84 (2013) PARA 56 et seq) (Local Government Act 2003 s 23(1)(n) (substituted by the Police Reform and Social Responsibility Act 2011 s 99, Sch 16 paras 316, 317));
(15) any other body specified for these purposes by regulations under the Local Government Act 2003 s 23(2) (s 23(1)(o)).

As to local government areas and authorities in England and Wales see LOCAL GOVERNMENT vol 69 (2018) PARA 36 et seq. As to the Greater London Authority see LONDON GOVERNMENT vol 71 (2013) PARA 67 et seq. As to the London boroughs and their councils see LONDON GOVERNMENT vol 71 (2013) PARAS 15, 20–22, 55 et seq. As to the Common Council of the City of London see LONDON GOVERNMENT vol 71 (2013) PARAS 34–38. As to the Council of the Isles of Scilly see LOCAL GOVERNMENT vol 69 (2018) PARA 50. As to the meanings of 'England' and 'Wales' see PARA 2 note 16.

The Secretary of State or, in relation to Wales, the Welsh Ministers may by regulations specify for the purposes of the Local Government Act 2003 s 23(1) any body which is (or any class of bodies each of which is):

(a) a levying body, within the meaning of the Local Government Finance Act 1988 s 74 (see PARA 24) (Local Government Act 2003 s 23(2)(a));

(b) a body to which the Local Government Finance Act 1988 s 75 applies (bodies with power to issue special levies: see PARA 24) (Local Government Act 2003 s 23(2)(b));

(c) a body to which the Local Government Finance Act 1988 s 118 applies (other bodies with levying powers: see PARA 24) (Local Government Act 2003 s 23(2)(c));

(d) a local precepting authority as defined in the Local Government Finance Act 1992 s 69 (see PARA 18 note 2) (Local Government Act 2003 s 23(2)(d)).

Such regulations may provide for Pt 1 to have effect, in relation to a body specified under s 23(2), subject to exceptions or modifications: s 23(3). In its application to Wales, Pt 1, except s 19 and Sch 1 (application to parish and community councils: see below), has effect as if for any reference to the Secretary of State there were substituted a reference to the Welsh Ministers: s 24(1) (numbered as such and amended by the Local Government and Public Involvement in Health Act 2007 ss 216(2), 238(3), Sch 14 para 5(1), (3)). The Local Government Act 2003 s 24(1) does not apply to s 21 to the extent that it confers functions on the Secretary of State in relation to a person or body that is a relevant authority for the purposes of the Local Audit and Accountability Act 2014 (see PARA 588 note 3), and exercises functions in relation to an area that is partly in England and partly in Wales: s 24(1A) (added by the Local Audit and Accountability Act 2014 s 45, Sch 12 paras 49, 52). As to the Secretary of State and the Welsh Ministers see PARA 4 note 18.

The following bodies are specified for the purposes of head (15) above:

(i) in relation to England: the Broads Authority; the Lee Valley Regional Park Authority; a National Park authority; the London Pensions Fund Authority; and the South Yorkshire Pensions Authority (see the Local Authorities (Capital Finance and Accounting) (England) Regulations 2003, SI 2003/3146, reg 32);

(ii) in relation to Wales, National Park authorities (see the Local Authorities (Capital Finance and Accounting) (Wales) Regulations 2003, SI 2003/3239, reg 26).

As to the Broads Authority see WATER AND WATERWAYS vol 101 (2009) PARA 734. As to National Park authorities see OPEN SPACES AND COUNTRYSIDE vol 78 (2010) PARA 526.

The Local Government Act 2003 Pt 1, other than ss 1–8 (see PARAS 567–568, 570), s 13 (see PARA 569) and s 17 (see PARA 566), applies in relation to an economic prosperity board established under the Local Democracy, Economic Development and Construction Act 2009 s 88 as it applies in relation to a local authority: Local Government Act 2003 s 23(4) (s 23(4), (5) added by the Local Democracy, Economic Development and Construction Act 2009 s 119, Sch 6 para 117(1), (2)). The Local Government Act 2003 Pt 1 applies in relation to a combined authority established under the Local Democracy, Economic Development and Construction Act 2009 s 103 as it applies in relation to a local authority, except that s 1 (see PARA 567) confers power on such a combined authority to borrow money for a purpose relevant to its transport functions only or in relation to any other functions of the authority that are specified for the purposes of this subsection in regulations made by the Secretary of State: Local Government Act 2003 s 23(5) (as so added; amended by the Cities and Local Government Devolution Act 2016 s 9(3)).

A function of a combined authority may be specified in regulations under the Local Government Act 2003 s 23(5) only with the consent of:

(A) each county council the whole or any part of whose area is within the area of the authority (s 23(6)(a) (s 23(6)–(10) added by the Cities and Local Government Devolution Act 2016 s 9(4));

(B) each district council whose area is within the area of the authority (Local Government Act 2003 s 23(6)(b) (as so added)); and

(C) in the case of regulations in relation to an existing combined authority, the combined authority (s 23(6)(c) (as so added)).

Section 23(6) is subject to the Local Democracy, Economic Development and Construction Act 2009 s 106A (which enables regulations to be made without the consent of every authority within heads (A) and (B) above in certain circumstances: see TRADE AND INDUSTRY vol 97 (2015) PARA 1094): Local Government Act 2003 s 23(7) (as so added).

The reference in s 23(5) to functions of the authority includes, in the case of a mayoral combined authority, mayoral functions: s 23(8) (as so added). In s 23(8), 'mayoral combined authority' has the meaning given by the Local Democracy, Economic Development and Construction Act 2009 s 107A(8); and 'mayoral functions' has the meaning given by s 107G(7) (see TRADE AND INDUSTRY): Local Government Act 2003 s 23(9) (as so added).

No regulations under s 23(5) may be made unless a draft of the statutory instrument containing the regulations (whether containing them alone or with other provisions) has been laid before, and approved by a resolution of, each House of Parliament: s 23(10) (as so added).

In s 2(3), (4) (see PARA 567), s 6 (see PARA 570), ss 9–13 (see PARAS 569, 572–574), s 15 (see PARA 563), s 16 (see PARA 572), s 17(1)(a), (b), (d)–(f), (2) (see PARA 566) and s 18 (see PARA 564), references to a local authority include a parish council, a community council and charter trustees: s 19(1). The Secretary of State or, in relation to Wales, the Welsh Ministers may by regulations:

(I) apply any of the other provisions of Pt 1 Ch 1 (ss 1–20) to parish or community councils or charter trustees, or parish or community councils or charter trustees of any description, with or without modifications (s 19(3)(a)); and

(II) make any corresponding disapplication of any of the provisions of Sch 1 (see PARA 567) (s 19(3)(b)).

As to the regulations made see the Local Authorities (Capital Finance and Accounting) (Wales) (Amendment) Regulations 2004, SI 2004/1010. As to parish councils see LOCAL GOVERNMENT vol 69 (2018) PARA 41 et seq. As to community councils see LOCAL GOVERNMENT vol 69 (2018) PARA 63 et seq. As to charter trustees see LOCAL GOVERNMENT vol 69 (2018) PARA 144.

2 Ie the Secretary of State or, in relation to Wales, the Welsh Ministers.

3 Ie relating to any of the matters dealt with in the Local Government Act 2003 Pt 1 Ch 1 (ss 1–20).

4 Local Government Act 2003 s 14.

5 Ie its functions under the Local Government Act 2003 Pt 1 Ch 1 (ss 1–20).

6 In the Local Government Act 2003 s 15, references to a local authority include a parish council, a community council and charter trustees: see s 19(1).

7 See the Local Government Act 2003 ss 15(1)(a), 24 (s 24 as amended: see note 1).

8 See the Local Government Act 2003 ss 15(1)(b), 24 (s 24 as amended: see note 1). The power under s 15(1)(b) is not to be read as limited to the specification of existing guidance: s 15(2). As to the regulations made see the Local Authorities (Capital Finance and Accounting) (England) Regulations 2003, SI 2003/3146 (amended by SI 2004/534, SI 2004/3055, SI 2006/521, SI 2007/573, SI 2008/414, SI 2009/321, SI 2010/454, SI 2012/711, SI 2012/265, SI 2012/1324, SI 2012/2269, SI 2013/472, SI 2013/476, SI 2013/1751, SI 2014/1375, SI 2015/341 and SI 2017/536); and the Local Authorities (Capital Finance and Accounting) (Wales) Regulations 2003, SI 2003/3239 (amended by SI 2004/1010, SI 2006/944, SI 2007/1051, SI 2008/588, SI 2009/560, SI 2010/685, SI 2014/481; SI 2016/102 and SI 2018/325).

564. Local authority companies.

The appropriate national authority[1] may[2] by regulations[3] make provision for things done by or to a specified body[4] to be treated, in such cases and to such extent as the regulations may provide, as done by or to a local authority specified in, or determined in accordance with, the regulations[5].

The regulations may include:

(1) provision for the application of any of the statutory provisions relating to capital finance[6] to members of a local authority group[7] subject to such modifications as the regulations may specify[8];

(2) provision as to the way in which:

 (a) dealings between members of a local authority group[9], or

 (b) changes in the capitalisation or capital structure of a company in a local authority group[10], are[11] to be brought into account[12].

1 Ie the Secretary of State or, in relation to Wales, the Welsh Ministers: see the Local Government Act 2003 s 24; and PARA 563 note 1. As to the Secretary of State and the Welsh Ministers see PARA 4 note 18. As to the meaning of 'Wales' see PARA 2 note 16.

2 Ie for the purposes of the Local Government Act 2003 Pt 1 Ch 1 (ss 1–20).

3 At the date at which this volume states the law, no such regulations had been made.

4 Ie a body mentioned in the Local Government Act 2003 s 18(2): see s 18(1). Those bodies are:

(1) a Passenger Transport Executive (s 18(2)(a)); and, until a day to be appointed:

(2) a company which, in accordance with the Local Government and Housing Act 1989 Pt V (ss 67–73) (companies in which local authorities have interests: see LOCAL GOVERNMENT vol 69 (2018) PARA 447 et seq), is under the control, or for the time being subject to the influence, of a local authority or a Passenger Transport Executive

(Local Government Act 2003 s 18(2)(b) (s 18(2)(b) prospectively substituted, s 18(2)(c) prospectively repealed, by the Local Government and Public Involvement in Health Act 2007 s 216(2), Sch 14 para 5(1), (2)(a))); and

(3) a trust to which the provisions of the Local Government and Housing Act 1989 s 69 (companies subject to local authority influence) are applicable because of an order under s 72 (trusts influenced by local authorities) (see LOCAL GOVERNMENT vol 69 (2018) PARA 448) (Local Government Act 2003 s 18(2)(c) (as so prospectively repealed)).

As to Passenger Transport Executives see ROAD TRAFFIC vol 89 (2011) PARA 47. As to the meaning of 'local authority' see PARA 563 note 1. In s 18, references to a local authority include a parish council, a community council and charter trustees: see s 19(1); and PARA 563 note 1.

As from a day to be appointed, heads (2) and (3) above are replaced by the following '(2) an entity which is, or the trustees of a trust which is under the control of a local authority or Passenger Transport Executive, subject to the influence of such an authority or Executive or jointly controlled by bodies that include such an authority or Executive' (s 18(2)(b) (prospectively substituted by the Local Government and Public Involvement in Health Act 2007 s 216(2), Sch 14 para 5(1), (2)(a))):

The references to:

(a) 'an entity under the control of' and 'a trust under the control of' a local authority or Passenger Transport Executive;

(b) 'an entity subject to the influence of' and 'a trust subject to the influence of' such an authority or Executive; and

(c) 'an entity jointly controlled by bodies that include' and 'a trust jointly controlled by bodies that include' such an authority or Executive,

have the meanings given by order under the Local Government and Public Involvement in Health Act 2007 s 217: Local Government Act 2003 s 18(2A) (added, as from a day to be appointed, by the Local Government and Public Involvement in Health Act 2007 Sch 14 para 5(1), (2)(b)). At the date at which this volume states the law no such day had been appointed. At the date at which this volume states the law no order had been made under the Local Government and Public Involvement in Health Act 2007 s 217.

As from a day to be appointed, in its application to Wales, the Local Government Act 2003 s 18 has effect as if any reference to a Passenger Transport Executive were omitted, and for the reference in s 18(2A) to the Local Government and Public Involvement in Health Act 2007 s 217 there were substituted a reference to s 218 of that Act: Local Government Act 2003 s 24(2) (added, as from a day to be appointed, by the Local Government and Public Involvement in Health Act 2007 s 216(2), Sch 14 para 5(1), (3); at the date at which this volume states the law, no such day had been appointed).

5 Local Government Act 2003 s 18(1).

6 Ie any of the provisions of the Local Government Act 2003 Pt 1 Ch 1 (ss 1–20).

7 A local authority to which the regulations and any body or bodies falling within the Local Government Act 2003 s 18(2)(a) or (b) (see note 4) with which the regulations link the authority are referred to as the members of a local authority group: s 18(3).

8 Local Government Act 2003 s 18(4)(a).

9 Local Government Act 2003 s 18(4)(b)(i).

10 Local Government Act 2003 s 18(4)(b)(ii).

11 Ie for the purposes of the Local Government Act 2003 Pt 1 Ch 1 (ss 1–20).

12 Local Government Act 2003 s 18(4)(b).

565. Private Finance Initiative.

The Private Finance Initiative (PFI) allows a local authority to purchase from the private sector, within the framework of a single contract, both services and any asset required for the provision of the service, spread over the period of the contract[1], commonly 25 to 30 years[2].

Central Government funding in the form of PFI credits is available towards the capital costs of projects[3]. While PFI projects are not now specifically provided for in the capital finance regime[4], those entered into before 1 April 2004 are required to continue to comply with the regime then in force[5].

Private Finance 2 (PF2) is a new approach to public private partnerships, following the reform of PFI. PF2 reaffirms the government's commitment to private sector involvement in infrastructure and services, while recognising recent changes to the economic context[6].

1 See the Local Government PFI Project Support Guide (20098–10), p 1, Communities and Local Government. PFI grant is paid under the Local Government Act 2003 s 31 (see PARA 41).
2 See eg the Private Finance Initiative: A Guide for Fire and Rescue Authorities, Introduction, Communities and Local Government, 2009.
3 See the Local Government PFI Project Support Guide (2008–10), p 1, Communities and Local Government; Project Review Group (PRG) — Process and Code of Practice, para 2.1, HM Treasury, 2009, version 3.
4 Ie under the Local Authorities (Capital Finance and Accounting) (England) Regulations 2003, SI 2003/3146, and the Local Authorities (Capital Finance and Accounting) (Wales) Regulations 2003, SI 2003/3229: see PARA 563.
5 Ie under the Local Authorities (Capital Finance) Regulations 1997, SI 1997/319 (lapsed).
6 See A new approach to public private partnerships, HM Treasury, December 2012.

566. External funds.

For the purposes of the statutory provisions relating to capital finance[1]:

(1) borrowing of money by a local authority[2] for the purposes of an external fund[3] must be treated as not being borrowing by the authority[4];
(2) the temporary use by a local authority of money forming part of an external fund, if not for a purpose of the fund, must be treated as borrowing by the authority[5];
(3) entry into a credit arrangement[6] by a local authority for the purposes of an external fund must be treated as not being entry into a credit arrangement by the authority[7];
(4) a disposal by a local authority of:
    (a) an interest in an asset which, at the time of the disposal, is an asset of an external fund[8]; or
    (b) an investment held for the purposes of such a fund[9], must be treated as not being a disposal by the authority[10];
(5) the making of an investment by a local authority for the purposes of an external fund must be treated as not being the making of an investment by the authority[11];
(6) expenditure incurred by a local authority in respect of payments out of an external fund must be treated as not being expenditure of the authority[12].

1 Ie for the purposes of the Local Government Act 2003 Pt 1 Ch 1 (ss 1–20).
2 As to the meaning of 'local authority' see PARA 563 note 1. In the Local Government Act 2003 s 17(1)(a), (b), (d)–(f), (2) (see heads (1), (2), (4)–(6) in the text and note 3) references to a local authority include a parish council, a community council and charter trustees: see s 19(1); and PARA 563 note 1.
3 References in the Local Government Act 2003 s 17 to an 'external fund', in relation to a local authority, are to:
    (1) a superannuation fund which the authority is required to keep by virtue of the Superannuation Act 1972 (see LOCAL GOVERNMENT vol 69 (2018) PARA 493) (Local Government Act 2003 s 17(2)(a)); or
    (2) a trust fund of which the authority is a trustee (s 17(2)(b)).
4 Local Government Act 2003 s 17(1)(a). As to borrowing see PARA 567 et seq.
5 Local Government Act 2003 s 17(1)(b).
6 As to the meaning of 'credit arrangement' see PARA 571 note 2.
7 Local Government Act 2003 s 17(1)(c).
8 Local Government Act 2003 s 17(1)(d)(i).
9 Local Government Act 2003 s 17(1)(d)(ii).
10 Local Government Act 2003 s 17(1)(d). As to the disposal of capital assets see PARA 572.
11 Local Government Act 2003 s 17(1)(e). As to the power of investment see PARA 574.
12 Local Government Act 2003 s 17(1)(f). As to local government expenditure see PARA 3 et seq.

(ii) Borrowing

567. Local authority power to borrow.

A local authority[1] may borrow money:

(1) for any purpose relevant to its functions under any enactment[2]; or

(2) for the purposes of the prudent management of its financial affairs[3].

A local authority may not borrow[4] money if doing so would result in a breach of:

(a) the borrowing limit for the time being determined[5] by or for it[6]; or

(b) any borrowing limit for the time being applicable[7] to it[8].

A local authority may not, without the consent of the Treasury[9], borrow otherwise than in sterling[10].

1 As to the meaning of 'local authority' see PARA 563 note 1. Specific provision is made about borrowing, and the making of loans, by parish and community councils and charter trustees: see Sch 1. As to parish councils see LOCAL GOVERNMENT vol 69 (2018) PARA 41 et seq. As to community councils see LOCAL GOVERNMENT vol 69 (2018) PARA 63 et seq. As to charter trustees see LOCAL GOVERNMENT vol 69 (2018) PARA 144.

2 Local Government Act 2003 s 1(a).

3 Local Government Act 2003 s 1(b). As to local government expenditure generally see PARA 3 et seq. The borrowing of money by a local authority for the purposes of an external fund is treated as not being borrowing by the authority; however, the temporary use by a local authority of money forming part of an external fund, if not for a purpose of the fund, is treated as borrowing by the authority: see s 17; and PARA 566.

4 The Local Government Act 2003 s 2 applies to borrowing under any power for the time being available to a local authority under any enactment, whenever passed: s 2(4). In s 2(3) (see the text to notes 9–10) and s 2(4), references to a local authority include a parish council, a community council and charter trustees: see s 19(1); and PARA 563 note 1.

5 Ie under the Local Government Act 2003 s 3: see PARA 568.

6 See the Local Government Act 2003 s 2(1)(a).

7 Ie under the Local Government Act 2003 s 4: see PARA 568.

8 See the Local Government Act 2003 s 2(1)(b). The Secretary of State or, in relation to Wales, the Welsh Ministers may, in relation to specific borrowing by a particular local authority, by direction disapply s 2(1)(b), so far as relating to any limit for the time being applicable under s 4(1) (see PARA 568): ss 2(2), 24(1) (s 24(1) numbered as such and amended by the Local Government and Public Involvement in Health Act 2007 ss 216(2), 238(3), Sch 14 para 5(1), (3)). Directions must be in writing (see the Local Government Act 2003 s 20(1)) and may be expressed to have effect in specified circumstances or subject to specified conditions (see s 20(2)). Any power to give a direction includes power to give a direction varying or revoking a previous direction given in exercise of the power: see s 20(3). As to the Secretary of State and the Welsh Ministers see PARA 4 note 18. As to the meaning of 'Wales' see PARA 2 note 16. As to the meaning of 'writing' see PARA 21 note 3.

9 As to the meaning of 'the Treasury' see PARA 30 note 15.

10 Local Government Act 2003 s 2(3). See also note 4.

568. Borrowing limits.

A local authority[1] must determine and keep under review how much money it can afford to borrow[2]. A local authority's function in relation to this duty must be discharged only by the authority[3].

The appropriate national authority[4] may by regulations make provision about the performance of this duty[5]. The regulations may, in particular:

(1) make provision about when a determination[6] is to be made[7], how such a determination is to be made[8], and the period for which such a determination is to be made[9];

(2) make provision about the monitoring of an amount determined[10];

(3) make provision about factors to which regard may be had in making a determination or in monitoring an amount determined under that determination[11].

The regulations may also include provision requiring a person[12] making a determination to have regard to one or more specified codes of practice, whether issued by the appropriate national authority or another[13].

The appropriate national authority may for national economic reasons by regulations[14] set limits in relation to the borrowing of money by local authorities[15]. The appropriate national authority may by direction[16] set limits in relation to the borrowing of money by a particular local authority for the purpose of ensuring that the authority does not borrow more than it can afford[17].

Any limit for the time being determined by or for a local authority[18], or applicable to it[19], must be treated[20] as increased by the amount of any payment which is due to the authority in the period to which the limit relates[21] but has not yet been received by it[22].

1 In the Local Government Act 2003 s 3, 'local authority' does not include the Greater London Authority or a functional body: s 3(11). As to the meaning of 'local authority' generally see PARA 563 note 1.

In the case of the Greater London Authority and a functional body, the Mayor of London must determine and keep under review how much money the authority can afford to borrow: s 3(2), (11). Before making any such determination the Mayor must consult the London Assembly (s 3(3)) and, in the case of a determination for a functional body, the Mayor must also consult that body (see s 3(4)). The Greater London Authority Act 1999 s 38(1) (delegation by Mayor: see LONDON GOVERNMENT vol 71 (2013) PARA 128) does not apply in relation to functions under the Local Government Act 2003 s 3(2): s 3(9). 'Functional body' has the same meaning as in the Greater London Authority Act 1999 (see LONDON GOVERNMENT vol 71 (2013) PARA 148): Local Government Act 2003 s 3(11). As to the Greater London Authority see LONDON GOVERNMENT vol 71 (2013) PARA 67 et seq. As to the Mayor of London see LONDON GOVERNMENT vol 71 (2013) PARA 69. As to the London Assembly see LONDON GOVERNMENT vol 71 (2013) PARA 70. As to the exercise of the duty to consult see JUDICIAL REVIEW vol 61 (2010) PARA 627.

2 Local Government Act 2003 s 3(1). As to the power to borrow see PARA 567.

3 See the Local Government Act 2003 s 3(8).

4 Ie the Secretary of State or, in relation to Wales, the Welsh Ministers: see the Local Government Act 2003 s 24; and PARA 563 note 1.

5 Local Government Act 2003 s 3(5). The duty referred to is that under s 3(1) or (2) (see the text to notes 1–2): see s 3(5). As to the regulations made see the Local Authorities (Capital Finance and Accounting) (England) Regulations 2003, SI 2003/3146; the Local Authorities (Capital Finance and Accounting) (Wales) Regulations 2003, SI 2003/3239; and PARA 563 note 8.

6 Ie under the Local Government Act 2003 s 3(1) or (2): see the text to notes 1–2.

7 Local Government Act 2003 s 3(6)(a)(i).

8 Local Government Act 2003 s 3(6)(a)(ii).

9 Local Government Act 2003 s 3(6)(a)(iii).

10 See the Local Government Act 2003 s 3(6)(b).

11 See the Local Government Act 2003 s 3(6)(c).

12 As to the meaning of 'person' see PARA 11 note 13.

13 See the Local Government Act 2003 s 3(7). The power under s 3(7) is not to be read as limited to the specification of an existing document: s 3(10).

14 At the date at which this volume states the law, no such regulations had been made.

15 Local Government Act 2003 s 4(1). Different limits may be set under s 4(1) in relation to different kinds of borrowing: see s 4(3).

A local authority subject to a limit set under s 4(1) may transfer any headroom it has in relation to the limit to another local authority subject to a corresponding limit: s 4(4). The appropriate national authority may by regulations make provision about the exercise of the right under s 4(4) ((s 4(5)) and may, in particular, make provision about:

(1) the circumstances in which a local authority is to be regarded as having headroom for those purposes (s 4(5)(a)); and

(2) the amount of headroom which it has for those purposes (s 4(5)(b)).

At the date at which this volume states the law, no such regulations had been made. Where an amount is transferred under s 4(4), Pt 1 Ch 1 (ss 1–20) has effect:
(a) in relation to the transferor, as if the limit in relation to which the headroom exists were reduced by that amount (s 4(6)(a)); and
(b) in relation to the transferee, as if the corresponding limit to which it is subject were increased by that amount (s 4(6)(b)).

16 Directions must be in writing (see the Local Government Act 2003 s 20(1)) and may be expressed to have effect in specified circumstances or subject to specified conditions (see s 20(2)). Any power to give a direction includes power to give a direction varying or revoking a previous direction given in exercise of the power: see s 20(3). As to the meaning of 'writing' see PARA 21 note 3.
17 Local Government Act 2003 s 4(2). Different limits may be set under s 4(2) in relation to different kinds of borrowing: see s 4(3).
18 Ie under the Local Government Act 2003 s 3: see the text to notes 1–13.
19 Ie under the Local Government Act 2003 s 4: see the text to notes 14–17.
20 Ie for the purposes of the Local Government Act 2003 Pt 1 Ch 1 (ss 1–20).
21 Local Government Act 2003 s 5(1)(a).
22 Local Government Act 2003 s 5(1)(b). In the case of a limit determined under s 3 (see the text to notes 1–13), or set under s 4(2) (see the text to notes 16–17), s 5(1) does not apply to any payment whose delayed receipt was taken into account in arriving at the limit: s 5(2).

569. Security for money borrowed.

Except as otherwise provided[1], a local authority[2] may not mortgage or charge any of its property as security for money which it has borrowed or which it otherwise owes[3]. Security given in breach of prohibition is unenforceable[4].

All money borrowed by a local authority[5], together with any interest on the money borrowed, must be charged indifferently on all the revenues of the authority[6]. All securities created by a local authority rank equally without any priority[7].

The High Court[8] may appoint a receiver on application by a person[9] entitled to principal or interest due in respect of any borrowing by a local authority if the amount due remains unpaid for a period of two months[10] after demand in writing[11]. However, no such application may be made unless the sum due in respect of the borrowing concerned amounts to not less than £10,000[12].

The High Court may appoint the receiver on such terms, and confer on him such powers, as it thinks fit[13]; and may confer on him any powers which the local authority has in relation to:

(1) collecting, receiving or recovering the revenues of the local authority[14];
(2) issuing levies or precepts[15]; or
(3) setting, collecting or recovering council tax[16].

1 Ie except as provided by the Local Government Act 2003 s 13(3): see the text to notes 5–6.
2 As to the meaning of 'local authority' see PARA 563 note 1. In the Local Government Act 2003 s 13, references to a local authority include a parish council, a community council and charter trustees: see s 19(1); and PARA 563 note 1.
3 Local Government Act 2003 s 13(1). As to the power to borrow see PARA 567.
4 See the Local Government Act 2003 s 13(2).
5 Ie whether before or after, in relation to Wales, 27 November 2003 or, in relation to England, 1 April 2004 (the dates of the coming into force of the Local Government Act 2003 s 13). As to the meanings of 'England' and 'Wales' see PARA 2 note 16.
6 Local Government Act 2003 s 13(3).
7 Local Government Act 2003 s 13(4).
8 As to the High Court of Justice in England and Wales see COURTS AND TRIBUNALS vol 24 (2010) PARA 695 et seq.
9 As to the meaning of 'person' see PARA 11 note 13.
10 As to the meaning of 'month' see PARA 11 note 1.
11 Local Government Act 2003 s 13(5). As to the meaning of 'writing' see PARA 21 note 3.

12 Local Government Act 2003 s 13(8). The Secretary of State or, in relation to Wales, the Welsh Ministers may by order substitute a different sum for the one for the time being specified in s 13(8): s 13(9). At the date at which this volume states the law no such order had been made. As to the Secretary of State and the Welsh Ministers see the Local Government Act 2003 s 24; and PARA 563 note 1.
13 See the Local Government Act 2003 s 13(6).
14 Local Government Act 2003 s 13(7)(a).
15 Local Government Act 2003 s 13(7)(b). As to precepts see PARA 11 et seq. As to levies see PARA 24.
16 Local Government Act 2003 s 13(7)(c). As to council tax see PARA 344 et seq.

570. Protection of lenders.

A person[1] lending money to a local authority[2] is not bound to enquire whether the authority has power to borrow[3] the money and is not prejudiced by the absence of any such power[4].

1 As to the meaning of 'person' see PARA 11 note 13.
2 As to the meaning of 'local authority' see PARA 563 note 1. In the Local Government Act 2003 s 6, references to a local authority include a parish council, a community council and charter trustees: see s 19(1); and PARA 563 note 1.
3 As to the power to borrow see PARA 567.
4 Local Government Act 2003 s 6. As to the doctrine of ultra vires in relation to the exercise of local authority functions see LOCAL GOVERNMENT vol 69 (2018) PARA 505. See also LOCAL GOVERNMENT vol 69 (2018) PARA 506 for the general subsidiary powers of local authorities and the cases cited there as to limitations on statutory powers.

571. Control of credit arrangements.

A local authority[1] may not enter into, or vary, a credit arrangement[2] if doing so would result in a breach of:

(1) the borrowing limit for the time being determined[3] by or for it[4]; or
(2) any borrowing limit for the time being applicable[5] to it[6]. In applying those limits for these purposes:
    (a) entry into a credit arrangement must be treated as the borrowing of an amount of money equal to the cost of the arrangement[7]; and
    (b) variation of a credit arrangement must be treated as the borrowing of an amount of money equal to the cost of the variation[8].

Public-private partnerships involve the public and private sectors working together to improve services[9], and the private finance initiative aims to provide value for money and to allocate risk between the public and private sectors[10]. Private finance transactions are a form of credit arrangement, under which a private sector contractor provides capital assets and certain services.

1 As to the meaning of 'local authority' see PARA 563 note 1.
2 A local authority is taken to have entered into a 'credit arrangement' where it enters into a transaction which gives rise to a liability on its part (Local Government Act 2003 s 7(1)(a)), and the liability is a qualifying liability (s 7(1)(b)). A transaction entered into by a local authority is to be taken for these purposes as giving rise to a liability on the part of the authority if:
    (1) it falls in accordance with proper practices to be treated for the purposes of the authority's accounts as giving rise to such a liability (s 7(2)(a)); or
    (2) it falls in accordance with regulations made by the Secretary of State or, in relation to Wales, the Welsh Ministers to be treated as falling within head (1) (s 7(2)(b)).

The reference in s 7(1)(b) to a 'qualifying liability' is to any liability other than:
    (a) a liability to repay money (s 7(3)(a));
    (b) a liability in respect of which the date for performance is less than 12 months after the date on which the transaction giving rise to the liability is entered into (s 7(3)(b)); and

(c) a liability of a description specified for the purposes of this provision by regulations made by the Secretary of State or, in relation to Wales, the Welsh Ministers (s 7(3)(c)).

As to financial administration and accounts see PARA 665 et seq. As to the Secretary of State and the Welsh Ministers see s 24; and PARA 563 note 1. As to the meaning of 'month' see PARA 11 note 1.

As to the regulations made under ss 7, 8(3) (see note 7) see the Local Authorities (Capital Finance and Accounting) (England) Regulations 2003, SI 2003/3146; and the Local Authorities (Capital Finance and Accounting) (Wales) Regulations 2003, SI 2003/3239; and PARA 563 note 8.

The entry into a credit arrangement by a local authority for the purposes of an external fund is treated as not being entry into a credit arrangement by the authority: see s 17; and PARA 566.

3 Ie under the Local Government Act 2003 s 3: see PARA 568.

4 Local Government Act 2003 s 8(1)(a).

5 Ie under the Local Government Act 2003 s 4: see PARA 568.

6 Local Government Act 2003 s 8(1)(b).

7 Local Government Act 2003 s 8(2)(a). The Secretary of State or, in relation to Wales, the Welsh Ministers may by regulations make provision about the calculation for the purposes of s 8(2) of the cost of a credit arrangement or a variation and may, in particular, make provision about the treatment of options: s 8(3). As to the regulations made see note 2.

8 Local Government Act 2003 s 8(2)(b). See also note 7.

9 As to public-private partnership agreements see the Greater London Authority Act 1999 s 210 et seq; and LONDON GOVERNMENT vol 71 (2013) PARA 167.

10 As to the private finance initiative see PARA 565.

(iii) Disposal of Capital Assets

572. Meaning of 'capital receipt'.

A 'capital receipt', in relation to a local authority[1], is a sum received by the authority in respect of the disposal by it of an interest in a capital asset[2]. An asset is a 'capital asset' for these purposes if, at the time of the disposal, expenditure on the acquisition of the asset would be capital expenditure[3]. 'Capital expenditure', in relation to a local authority, is expenditure of the authority which falls to be capitalised in accordance with proper practices[4].

The appropriate national authority[5] may by regulations[6] apply the above provisions[7] to cases where:

(1) a local authority makes a disposal of an interest in a capital asset[8] and the consideration for the disposal does not consist wholly of money payable to the authority[9]; or

(2) a local authority receives otherwise than in the form of money anything which, if received in that form, would[10] be a capital receipt[11].

The regulations may, in particular:

(a) make provision for a local authority to be treated as receiving a sum of such an amount as may be determined under the regulations[12];

(b) make provision about when the deemed receipt is to be treated as taking place[13].

1 As to the meaning of 'local authority' see PARA 563 note 1. In the Local Government Act 2003 ss 9, 10, 16, references to a local authority include a parish council, a community council and charter trustees: see s 19(1); and PARA 563 note 1.

2 See the Local Government Act 2003 s 9(1). This provision is expressed to be subject to s 9(3): see s 9(1). The Secretary of State or, in relation to Wales, the Welsh Ministers may by regulations:

(1) make provision for the whole of a sum received by a local authority in respect of the disposal by it of an interest in a capital asset, or such part of such a sum as may be determined under the regulations, to be treated as not being a capital receipt for the purposes of Pt 1 Ch 1 (ss 1–20) (s 9(3)(a));

(2) make provision for the whole of a sum received by a local authority otherwise than in respect of the disposal by it of an interest in a capital asset, or such part of such a sum as may be determined under the regulations, to be treated as being a capital receipt for those purposes (s 9(3)(b)).

As to the Secretary of State and the Welsh Ministers see s 24; and PARA 563 note 1.

Where a sum becomes payable to a local authority before it is actually received by the authority, it must be treated for the purposes of s 9 as received by the authority when it becomes payable to it: s 9(4). A disposal by a local authority of an interest in an asset which, at the time of the disposal, is an asset of an external fund, or an investment held for the purposes of such a fund, is treated as not being a disposal by the authority: see s 17; and PARA 566.

As to the regulations made under ss 9, 10, 16 (see the text to notes 4–13) see the Local Authorities (Capital Finance and Accounting) (England) Regulations 2003, SI 2003/3146; and the Local Authorities (Capital Finance and Accounting) (Wales) Regulations 2003, SI 2003/3239; and PARA 563 note 8.

3 Local Government Act 2003 s 9(2).

4 Local Government Act 2003 s 16(1). This provision is expressed to be subject to s 16(2): see s 16(1). The Secretary of State or, in relation to Wales, the Welsh Ministers may:

(1) by regulations provide that expenditure of local authorities must be treated for the purposes of Pt 1 Ch 1 (ss 1–20) as being, or as not being, capital expenditure (s 16(2)(a));

(2) by direction provide that expenditure of a particular local authority must be treated for those purposes as being, or as not being, capital expenditure (s 16(2)(b)).

As to the regulations made see note 2. Directions must be in writing (see s 20(1)) and may be expressed to have effect in specified circumstances or subject to specified conditions (see s 20(2)). Any power to give a direction includes power to give a direction varying or revoking a previous direction given in exercise of the power: see s 20(3). As to the meaning of 'writing' see PARA 21 note 3.

Expenditure incurred by a local authority in respect of payments out of an external fund is treated as not being expenditure of the authority: see s 17; and PARA 566.

5 Ie the Secretary of State or, in relation to Wales, the Welsh Ministers.

6 As to the regulations made see note 2.

7 Ie the Local Government Act 2003 s 9: see the text to notes 1–3.

8 Ie a disposal of the kind mentioned in the Local Government Act 2003 s 9(1): see the text to notes 1–2.

9 Local Government Act 2003 s 10(1)(a).

10 Ie under the Local Government Act 2003 s 9: see the text to notes 1–3.

11 Local Government Act 2003 s 10(1)(b).

12 Local Government Act 2003 s 10(2)(a).

13 Local Government Act 2003 s 10(2)(b).

573. Use of capital receipts.

The appropriate national authority[1] may by regulations[2] make provision about the use of capital receipts[3] by a local authority[4]. The regulations may, in particular:

(1) make provision requiring an amount equal to the whole or any part of a capital receipt to be used only to meet capital expenditure[5], or debts or other liabilities[6];

(2) make provision requiring an amount equal to the whole or any part of a capital receipt to be paid to the appropriate national authority[7].

The regulations may also include provision authorising the appropriate national authority to set off any amount which an authority in Wales is liable to pay to the appropriate national authority[8] against any amount which the appropriate national authority is liable to pay to the authority[9].

Where the Secretary of State is liable to repay an amount that has been overpaid by a local housing authority in England, the Secretary of State may set off against the amount of the repayment any amount that the authority is liable to pay the Secretary of State under specified[10] provisions[11].

1 Ie the Secretary of State or, in relation to Wales, the Welsh Ministers: see the Local Government Act 2003 s 24; and PARA 563 note 1.

2 As to the regulations made see the Local Authorities (Capital Finance and Accounting) (England) Regulations 2003, SI 2003/3146; and the Local Authorities (Capital Finance and Accounting) (Wales) Regulations 2003, SI 2003/3239; and PARA 563 note 8.

3 As to the meaning of 'capital receipt' see PARA 572.

4 Local Government Act 2003 s 11(1). As to the meaning of 'local authority' see PARA 563 note 1. In s 11, references to a local authority include a parish council, a community council and charter trustees: see s 19(1); and PARA 563 note 1.

5 Local Government Act 2003 s 11(2)(a)(i). As to the meaning of 'capital expenditure' see PARA 572.

6 Local Government Act 2003 s 11(2)(a)(ii).

7 Local Government Act 2003 s 11(2)(b). The power under s 11(1) (see the text to notes 1–4), so far as relating to provision of the kind mentioned in s 11(2)(b), only applies to receipts which a local authority derives from the disposal of an interest in housing land: s 11(3). The reference in s 11(3) to 'housing land' is to any land, house or other building in relation to which the local authority is, or has been, subject to the duty under the Local Government and Housing Act 1989 s 74 (duty to keep Housing Revenue Account: see HOUSING vol 56 (2017) PARA 356): Local Government Act 2003 s 11(4).

The Secretary of State and a local authority in England may enter into an agreement with the effect that a requirement imposed under s 11(2)(b) does not apply to, or is modified in its application to, capital receipts of the authority that are specified or described in the agreement: s 11(6) (added by the Localism Act 2011 s 174).

8 Ie under the Local Government Act 2003 s 11.

9 Local Government Act 2003 s 11(5) (amended by the Housing and Planning Act 2016 s 78(1), (2)).

10 Ie the Local Government Act 2003 s 11 or the Housing and Planning Act 2016 s 69 (payments in respect of vacant higher value housing: see HOUSING vol 56 (2017) PARA 363).

11 Local Government Act 2003 s 11(5A) (added by the Housing and Planning Act 2016 s 78(1), (3)).

(iv) Investment

574. Local authority power of investment.

A local authority[1] may invest[2]:

(1) for any purpose relevant to its functions under any enactment[3]; or

(2) for the purposes of the prudent management of its financial affairs[4].

1 As to the meaning of 'local authority' see PARA 563 note 1. In the Local Government Act 2003 s 12, references to a local authority include a parish council, a community council and charter trustees: see s 19(1); and PARA 563 note 1.

2 The making of an investment by a local authority for the purposes of an external fund is treated as not being the making of an investment by the authority: see the Local Government Act 2003 s 17; and PARA 566.

3 Local Government Act 2003 s 12(a).

4 Local Government Act 2003 s 12(b). As to the power to borrow see PARA 567.

(v) Local Government Reorganisation

575. Control of disposals, contracts and reserves: England.

In relation to a local authority in England[1] which is to be dissolved by virtue of an order implementing proposals for a single tier of local government for an area[2] or an order following a recommendation by the Boundary Committee for England as to a change of local government area boundaries[3], the Secretary of State[4] may direct that the authority may not without the written consent of a specified person or persons[5]:

(1) dispose of any land if the consideration for the disposal exceeds £100,000[6];

(2) enter into any capital contract which meets certain prescribed conditions[7];

(3) enter into any non-capital contract which meets certain prescribed conditions[8]; or

(4) include an amount of financial reserves in relation to prescribed calculations[9].

A disposal made in contravention of such a direction is void[10]; and a contract entered into by an authority in contravention of such a direction is not enforceable against a successor authority[11]. If an authority includes an amount in financial reserves in contravention of such a direction the authority is to be treated as not having made the appropriate statutory calculations[12].

1 'Local authority' means a county council or a district council in England or a London borough council: see the Local Government and Public Involvement in Health Act 2007 s 30(1). As to the meaning of 'England' see PARA 2 note 16. As to local government areas and authorities in England see LOCAL GOVERNMENT vol 69 (2018) PARA 36 et seq. As to the London boroughs and their councils see LONDON GOVERNMENT vol 71 (2013) PARAS 15, 20–22, 55 et seq.

2 Ie an order under the Local Government and Public Involvement in Health Act 2007 s 7: see LOCAL GOVERNMENT vol 69 (2018) PARA 98.

3 Ie an order under the Local Government and Public Involvement in Health Act 2007 s 10: see LOCAL GOVERNMENT vol 69 (2018) PARA 101.

4 As to the Secretary of State see PARA 4 note 18.

5 See the Local Government and Public Involvement in Health Act 2007 s 24(1). As to directions see further ss 25–27.

6 Local Government and Public Involvement in Health Act 2007 s 24(1)(a).

7 See the Local Government and Public Involvement in Health Act 2007 s 24(1)(b). 'Capital contract' means a contract as regards which the consideration payable by the relevant authority would be capital expenditure for the purposes of the Local Government Act 2003 Pt 1 Ch 1 (ss 1–20) (see PARA 572): Local Government and Public Involvement in Health Act 2007 s 24(3).

8 See the Local Government and Public Involvement in Health Act 2007 s 24(1)(c). 'Non-capital contract' means a contract which is not a capital contract: s 24(3).

9 See the Local Government and Public Involvement in Health Act 2007 s 24(1)(d). The prescribed calculations are those under the Local Government Finance Act 1992 s 31A(3) (see PARA 382) or s 42A(3) (see PARA 12): see the Local Government and Public Involvement in Health Act 2007 s 24(1)(d) (amended by the Localism Act 2011 s 79, Sch 7 paras 48, 49).

10 Local Government and Public Involvement in Health Act 2007 s 28(1).

11 See the Local Government and Public Involvement in Health Act 2007 s 28(2), (3). A contract which would be a certified contract for the purposes of the Local Government (Contracts) Act 1997 (see LOCAL GOVERNMENT vol 69 (2018) PARA 453) is not a certified contract for those purposes if it is entered into in contravention of a direction: see s 28(4).

12 See the Local Government and Public Involvement in Health Act 2007 s 28(5), (6) (amended by the Localism Act 2011 Sch 7 paras 48, 51).

576. Transfer of financial reserves.

On the reorganisation date[1] the financial reserves[2] vest in the successor council nominated by the Secretary of State[3] for these purposes (the 'nominated council') on trust for itself and the other successor councils concerned[4].

Within three months[5] of the reorganisation date, or such longer period as may be agreed between the successor councils concerned before the end of that three-month period, the nominated council must divide the financial reserves between itself and the other successor councils concerned in such proportion as may be agreed by all the successor councils concerned or, failing such agreement, as is determined by such person[6] as the Secretary of State appoints[7]. The nominated council must, as soon as practicable after the other successor councils' shares have been agreed or determined, transfer the shares so agreed or determined; and the trust so created ceases as soon as the transfer has been completed[8].

1 'Reorganisation date', in relation to a predecessor council and an order under the Local

Government and Public Involvement in Health Act 2007 s 7 (see LOCAL GOVERNMENT vol 69 (2018) PARA 98), means the date specified in the order as that on which the council is to be wound up and dissolved: Local Government (Structural Changes) (Transfer of Functions, Property, Rights and Liabilities) Regulations 2008, SI 2008/2176, reg 2(1). 'Predecessor council', in relation to an order under the Local Government and Public Involvement in Health Act 2007 s 7, means a county or district council for whose winding up and dissolution the order provides: Local Government (Structural Changes) (Transfer of Functions, Property, Rights and Liabilities) Regulations 2008, SI 2008/2176, reg 2(1).

2 'Financial reserves', in relation to a predecessor council and any successor council, means (Local Government (Structural Changes) (Transfer of Functions, Property, Rights and Liabilities) Regulations 2008, SI 2008/2176, reg 6(1) (definition substituted by SI 2009/5)):

(1) the total of such amounts (other than an amount which does not form part of the authority's capital receipts for the purposes of the Local Government Act 2003 Pt 1 Ch 1 (ss 1–20) (see PARA 572) and which is set aside for the year as provision to meet credit liabilities) which are set aside for the year as reasonably necessary for the purpose of providing for any liability or loss which is likely or certain to be incurred but is uncertain as to the amount or the date on which it will arise (or both) (ie such amounts of a description contained in the Local Government Finance Act 1992 s 69(2A)(b) (repealed)); and

(2) the total of the amount of the predecessor council's capital receipts, as defined for the purposes of the Local Government Act 2003 Pt 1 Ch 1.

'Successor council':

(a) in relation to a predecessor council whose entire area becomes part of the area of a sole single tier council on the reorganisation date, means that council;

(b) in relation to a predecessor council whose area becomes the area of more than one single tier council on the reorganisation date, means those councils,

but this is subject to the Local Government (Structural Changes) (Transfer of Functions, Property, Rights and Liabilities) Regulations 2008, SI 2008/2176, reg 2(2): reg 2(1).

Regulation 2(2) provides that, as regards any period:

(i) which, for the purposes of the order under the Local Government and Public Involvement in Health Act 2007 s 7 relevant to a predecessor council, is a shadow period or part of a transitional period before the reorganisation date; and

(ii) during which a provision of the Local Government (Structural Changes) (Transfer of Functions, Property, Rights and Liabilities) Regulations 2008, SI 2008/2176, requires or authorises steps to be taken by a successor council,

the definition of 'successor council' has effect as if, for 'that council' and 'those councils', there were substituted:

(A) as regards a shadow period, 'the shadow authority';

(B) as regards part of a transitional period before the reorganisation date, 'the preparing council'.

3 As to the Secretary of State see PARA 4 note 18.

4 Local Government (Structural Changes) (Transfer of Functions, Property, Rights and Liabilities) Regulations 2008, SI 2008/2176, reg 10(1). 'The successor councils concerned' means those councils that are the successor councils to the predecessor council to which the financial reserves relate: reg 10(4).

5 As to the meaning of 'month' see PARA 11 note 1.

6 As to the meaning of 'person' see PARA 11 note 13.

7 Local Government (Structural Changes) (Transfer of Functions, Property, Rights and Liabilities) Regulations 2008, SI 2008/2176, reg 10(2).

8 Local Government (Structural Changes) (Transfer of Functions, Property, Rights and Liabilities) Regulations 2008, SI 2008/2176, reg 10(3).

(2) Rents, Charges and Fees

577. Rents, charges and fees.

Among the sources of finance available to a local authority are receipts in the form of rents[1], charges and fees[2], which now form a significant proportion of local authority income.

1 The largest element of these receipts represents housing rents; as to the provision and management

of housing by local authorities see HOUSING vol 56 (2017) PARA 401 et seq.

2 As to the power of local authorities to charge for the provision of services see LOCAL GOVERNMENT vol 69 (2018) PARA 563 et seq.

(3) Profits from Undertakings

578. Profits from undertakings.

Local authorities may derive income from various undertakings which they have statutory powers to conduct such as transport undertakings[1], markets[2] and harbours[3]. However, local authorities must apply or dispose of the surplus revenue arising from any undertaking carried on by them in accordance with any enactment or instrument applicable to the undertaking[4].

1 As to transport undertakings see ROAD TRAFFIC vol 89 (2011) PARA 47 et seq.

2 See MARKETS vol 71 (2013) PARA 801 et seq.

3 See PORTS AND HARBOURS vol 85 (2012) PARA 4 et seq.

4 See the Local Government Act 1972 s 152.

7. FINANCIAL ADMINISTRATION AND ACCOUNTS

(1) Establishment and Maintenance of Funds

(i) General Funds and Collection Funds: England

579. Establishment and maintenance of general funds.

Every relevant authority in England[1] must establish, and then maintain, a fund (called the 'general fund') in accordance with the Local Government Finance Act 1988[2].

Subject to the following exceptions[3], the general fund had to be established on 1 April 1990[4]. However:

(1) in the case of a district council subsequently established for an area by an order[5], the general fund must be established on the date on which by virtue of the order the structural or boundary change[6] affecting the area comes into force[7];

(2) in the case of:
   (a) a county council which is established by such an order and to which are transferred by or in consequence of the order the functions of district councils in relation to the county council's area[8]; or
   (b) an existing county council to which are transferred by or in consequence of such an order the functions of district councils in relation to the county council's area[9], the general fund must be established on the date on which by virtue of the order the structural change comes into force[10];

(3) in the case of the Greater London Authority, the general fund must be established on a date specified in regulations[11];

(4) in the case of a district council or London borough council established by an order[12] relating to local government reorganisation[13], or a county council to which the functions of district councils in relation to the county council's area are transferred by or in consequence of such an order[14], the general fund must be established on a date specified in the order or in regulations[15].

The Secretary of State[16] may make regulations[17]:

(i) about the relationship of a relevant authority's general fund to its other funds[18];

(ii) providing for assets falling within a relevant authority's general fund to be held in separate funds within the general fund[19].

The regulations may provide that:

(A) any fund established by a relevant authority on or after 1 April 1990, other than its collection fund[20] or a trust fund, is to be maintained as a separate fund falling within its general fund[21];

(B) such assets as are transferred to a relevant authority's general fund[22] and fall within a prescribed[23] description must be held in separate funds falling within the general fund (the number and composition of the separate funds being such as are prescribed)[24].

1 The Local Government Finance Act 1988 Pt VI (ss 89–99) does not apply to a Welsh county council or county borough council (for whom provision as to the establishment of a council fund

is made by the Local Government (Wales) Act 1994 s 38: see PARA 585): Local Government Finance Act 1988 s 89A (added by the Local Government (Wales) Act 1994 s 38(11), Sch 12 para 2). As to the meanings of 'England' and 'Wales' see PARA 2 note 16.

Each of the following is a 'relevant authority':

(1) a district council (Local Government Finance Act 1988 ss 91(1)(a), 92(1));

(2) a county council to which have been transferred, by or in consequence of an order under the Local Government Finance Act 1992 s 17 (repealed) or the Local Government and Public Involvement in Health Act 2007 Pt 1 (ss 1–30) (see LOCAL GOVERNMENT vol 69 (2018) PARA 95 et seq), the functions of district councils in relation to the county council's area (Local Government Finance Act 1988 ss 91(1)(aa), 92(1) (s 91(1)(aa) added by SI 1994/2825; and amended by the Local Government and Public Involvement in Health Act 2007 s 22, Sch 1 Pt 2 para 16(1), (4)(a); and the Local Democracy, Economic Development and Construction Act 2009 s 146(1), Sch 7 Pt 4));

(3) the Greater London Authority (Local Government Finance Act 1988 ss 91(1)(ab), 92(1) (s 91(1)(ab) added by the Greater London Authority Act 1999 s 106(1), (2)));

(4) a London borough council (Local Government Finance Act 1988 ss 91(1)(b), 92(1)); and

(5) the Council of the Isles of Scilly (ss 91(1)(c), 92(1)).

As to local government areas and authorities see LOCAL GOVERNMENT vol 69 (2018) PARA 36 et seq. As to the Greater London Authority see LONDON GOVERNMENT vol 71 (2013) PARA 67 et seq. As to the London boroughs and their councils see LONDON GOVERNMENT vol 71 (2013) PARAS 15, 20–22, 55 et seq. As to the Council of the Isles of Scilly see LOCAL GOVERNMENT vol 69 (2018) PARA 50.

Each authority established under the Local Government Act 1985 Pt IV (ss 23–42) (see LOCAL GOVERNMENT vol 69 (2018) PARA 71), the London Fire and Emergency Planning Authority (see FIRE AND RESCUE SERVICES vol 51 (2013) PARA 17), a sub-national transport body established under the Local Transport Act 2008 s 102E (see ROAD TRAFFIC) and a combined authority established under the Local Democracy, Economic Development and Construction Act 2009 s 103 must also keep a general fund, as must waste regulation and disposal authorities (see ENVIRONMENTAL QUALITY AND PUBLIC HEALTH vol 46 (2010) PARA 620): see the Local Government Act 1985 s 72(1), (5) (s 72(5) added by the Greater London Authority Act 1999 s 328, Sch 29 Pt I para 40; and substituted by the Cities and Local Government Devolution Act 2016 s 23(1), Sch 5 paras 6, 7); and the Waste Regulation and Disposal (Authorities) Order 1985, SI 1985/1884, art 9(1). As from a day to be appointed, the reference to the London Fire and Emergency Planning Authority is replaced by a reference to the London Fire Commissioner: see the Local Government Act 1985 s 72(5) (amended, as from a day to be appointed, by the Policing and Crime Act 2017 s 9(3), Sch 2 paras 70, 71).

2 Local Government Finance Act 1988 s 91(2). The relevant provisions of the Local Government Finance Act 1988 for these purposes are those of Pt VI (ss 89–99): see s 91(2).

3 Ie subject to the Local Government Finance Act 1988 s 91(3A)–(3D): see the text to notes 5–15.

4 See the Local Government Finance Act 1988 s 91(3) (amended by the Greater London Authority Act 1999 s 106(1), (3); the Local Government and Public Involvement in Health Act 2007 s 22, Sch 1 Pt 2 para 16(1), (4)(b); and SI 1994/2825).

After 31 March 1990 no district council or London borough council was required to keep a general rate fund; and the assets held in the general rate fund of such an authority immediately before 1 April 1990 (other than assets forming part of a trust fund) had to be transferred to its general fund on that date: see the Local Government Finance Act 1988 s 91(6). After 31 March 1990 the Council of the Isles of Scilly was not required to keep any fund known as its general fund and required (apart from this provision) to be kept under any order made under the Local Government Act 1972 s 265 (see LOCAL GOVERNMENT vol 69 (2018) PARA 50); and the assets held in that fund immediately before 1 April 1990 (other than assets forming part of a trust fund) had to be transferred on that date to the council's general fund established under the Local Government Finance Act 1988 s 91: see s 91(7).

5 Ie in the case of a district council which is established for an area by an order under the Local Government Act 1992 s 17 (repealed) or the Regional Assemblies (Preparations) Act 2003 s 17 (repealed).

6 'Structural change' and 'boundary change' must be construed in accordance with the Local Government Act 1992 s 14 (repealed): see the Local Government Finance Act 1988 s 89(6) (added by SI 1994/2825).

7 Local Government Finance Act 1988 s 91(3A) (added by SI 1994/2825; and amended by the Regional Assemblies (Preparations) Act 2003 s 17(6), Schedule para 3(1), (4)(b)).

8 Local Government Finance Act 1988 s 91(3B)(a) (s 91(3B) added by SI 1994/2825).

9 Local Government Finance Act 1988 s 91(3B)(b) (as added: see note 8).

10 Local Government Finance Act 1988 s 91(3B) (as added (see note 8); amended by the Local Government and Public Involvement in Health Act 2007 ss 22, 241, Sch 1 Pt 2 para 16(1), (4)(c), Sch 18 Pt 1).

11 Local Government Finance Act 1988 s 91(3C) (added by the Greater London Authority Act 1999 s 106(1), (4)). At the date at which this volume states the law no such regulations had been made.

12 Ie an order under the under the Local Government and Public Involvement in Health Act 2007 Pt 1 (ss 1–30): see LOCAL GOVERNMENT vol 69 (2018) PARA 95 et seq.

13 See the Local Government Finance Act 1988 s 91(3D)(a) (s 91(3D) added by the Local Government and Public Involvement in Health Act 2007 s 22, Sch 1 Pt 2 para 16(1), (4)(d)).

14 Local Government Finance Act 1988 s 91(3D)(b) (as added: see note 13).

15 Local Government Finance Act 1988 s 91(3D) (as added: see note 13). The regulations concerned are any made under the Local Government and Public Involvement in Health Act 2007 s 14 (see LOCAL GOVERNMENT vol 69 (2018) PARA 102): see the Local Government Finance Act 1988 s 91(3D) (as so added). 1 April 2009 is the date specified for the purposes of s 91(3D) as regards a single tier council that is related to a predecessor council which is a shadow council, or a preparing council which is a county council: Local Government (Structural Changes) (Further Financial Provisions and Amendment) Regulations 2009, SI 2009/5, reg 4. As to the meanings of 'single tier council', 'predecessor council', 'shadow council' and 'preparing council', and as to when a single tier council is related to a predecessor council, see PARA 581 note 14.

The assets held in the county fund of a relevant county council immediately before the reorganisation date (other than assets forming part of a trust fund) must be transferred on that date to its general fund established under the Local Government Finance Act 1988 s 91: s 91(8) (added by SI 1994/2825; and amended by the Local Government and Public Involvement in Health Act 2007 Sch 1 Pt 2 para 16(1), (4)(e)). 'Relevant county council' means (Local Government Finance Act 1988 s 91(9) (added by the Local Government and Public Involvement in Health Act 2007 Sch 1 Pt 2 para 16(1), (4)(f))):

(1) a county council such as is referred to in the Local Government Finance Act 1988 s 91(3B)(b) (see the text to note 10); or

(2) an existing county council to which the functions of district councils in relation to the county council's area are transferred by or in consequence of an order under the Local Government and Public Involvement in Health Act 2007 Pt 1 (ss 1–30).

'The reorganisation date' means the date on which the council is required by the Local Government Finance Act 1988 s 91 to establish its general fund: s 91(9) (as so added).

16 As to the Secretary of State see PARA 4 note 18.

17 At the date at which this volume states the law, no such regulations had been made.

18 Local Government Finance Act 1988 s 92(2)(a). As to other funds see PARA 581 et seq.

19 Local Government Finance Act 1988 s 92(2)(b).

20 As to collection funds see PARA 581.

21 Local Government Finance Act 1988 s 92(3).

22 Ie under the Local Government Finance Act 1988 s 91(6) or (7) (see note 4) or s 91(8) (see note 15).

23 'Prescribed' means prescribed by the regulations: see the Local Government Finance Act 1988 s 146(6), (7).

24 Local Government Finance Act 1988 s 92(4) (amended by SI 1994/2825).

580. Receipts and payments into general funds.

Any sum received by a relevant authority[1] on or after the date on which it is required[2] to establish its general fund[3] must be paid into that fund; but this does not apply to a sum which is to be paid into its collection fund[4] or a trust fund[5]. Any payment to be made by a relevant authority on or after the date on which it is required to establish its general fund must be met from that fund; but this does not apply to a payment which is to be met from its collection fund or a trust fund[6].

Authorities established under the Local Government Act 1985[7] must carry all receipts into their general fund and pay all liabilities falling to be discharged by the authority out of that fund[8].

1 As to the meaning of 'relevant authority' see PARA 579 note 1.

2 Ie by the Local Government Finance Act 1988 s 91: see PARA 579.

3 As to general funds see PARA 579.

4 As to collection funds see PARA 581.
5 Local Government Finance Act 1988 s 91(4) (amended by SI 1994/2825). Local authorities stand in a fiduciary position in respect of those who contribute to the funds of such authorities: *Bromley London Borough Council v Greater London Council* [1983] 1 AC 768, [1982] 1 All ER 129, HL.
6 Local Government Finance Act 1988 s 91(5) (amended by SI 1994/2825).
7 Ie under the Local Government Act 1985 Pt IV (ss 23–42) (see LOCAL GOVERNMENT vol 69 (2018) PARA 71), and including also the London Fire and Emergency Planning Authority (see FIRE AND RESCUE SERVICES vol 51 (2013) PARA 17), a combined authority established under the Local Democracy, Economic Development and Construction Act 2009 s 103 and a waste regulation and disposal authority (see ENVIRONMENTAL QUALITY AND PUBLIC HEALTH vol 46 (2010) PARA 620): see the Local Government Act 1985 s 72(1), (5) (s 72(5) added by the Greater London Authority Act 1999 s 328, Sch 29 Pt I para 40; and substituted by the Cities and Local Government Devolution Act 2016 s 23(1), Sch 5 paras 6, 7); and the Waste Regulation and Disposal (Authorities) Order 1985, SI 1985/1884, art 9(1). As from a day to be appointed, the reference to the London Fire and Emergency Planning Authority is replaced by a reference to the London Fire Commissioner: see the Local Government Act 1985 s 72(5) (amended, as from a day to be appointed, by the Policing and Crime Act 2017 s 9(3), Sch 2 paras 70, 71). As to the requirement for such authorities to keep a general fund see PARA 579.
8 See the Local Government Act 1985 s 72(1). Nothing in s 72(1) is to be construed as requiring or authorising an authority to apply or dispose of the surplus revenue arising from any undertaking carried on by it otherwise than in accordance with any enactment or instrument applicable to the undertaking: s 72(4).

581. Establishment and maintenance of collection funds.

Every billing authority in England[1] is required to establish, and then maintain, a fund (called the 'collection fund') in accordance with the Local Government Finance Act 1988[2]. Subject to the following exceptions[3], the collection fund had to be established on 1 April 1990[4]. However:

(1) in the case of a district council subsequently established for an area by an order[5], the collection fund must be established on the date on which by virtue of the order the structural or boundary change[6] affecting the area comes into force[7];
(2) in the case of:
    (a) a county council which is established by such an order, to which the functions of district councils in relation to the county council's area are transferred by or in consequence of the order[8]; or
    (b) an existing county council, to which the functions of district councils in relation to the county council's area are transferred by or in consequence of such an order[9],

    the collection fund must be established on the date on which by virtue of the order the structural change concerned comes into force[10];
(3) in the case of a district council or London borough council established by an order[11] relating to local government reorganisation[12], or a county council to which the functions of district councils in relation to the county council's area are transferred by or in consequence of such an order[13], the collection fund must be established on a date specified in the order or in regulations[14].

Any sum paid into an authority's collection fund must be used in the making of payments which are to be met from that fund or of transfers which are to be made from it[15]. If not immediately required for the purpose of making those payments or transfers, the sum must be held, invested or otherwise used in such manner as may be prescribed by regulations made by the Secretary of State[16].

The following must be paid into the collection fund of a billing authority[17]:

(i) sums received by the authority in respect of council tax set by it[18] (but not sums received by way of penalty)[19];
(ii) sums received[20] by the authority from any major precepting authority or the Secretary of State[21];
(iii) sums received by the authority in respect of any non-domestic rate[22];
(iv) sums received by the authority in respect of any business rate supplement[23];
(v) sums received by the authority under certain statutory provisions[24] relating to the local retention of non-domestic rates that are of a kind specified by the Secretary of State as falling to be paid into a billing authority's collection fund[25];
(vi) sums received by the authority under provision made by regulations[26] relating to the local retention of non-domestic rates[27]; and
(vii) any other sums which the Secretary of State specifies[28] are to be paid into a billing authority's collection fund[29].

The following payments must be met from the collection fund of a billing authority[30]:

(A) payments to be made by the authority in respect of the amount of any precept issued by a major precepting authority[31] (but not payments to be so made in respect of interest on such an amount)[32];
(B) payments to be made[33] by the authority to any major precepting authority or the Secretary of State[34];
(C) payments to be made by the authority to a levying authority in accordance with provision made by or under the Business Rate Supplements Act 2009[35];
(D) payments to be made by the authority to the Secretary of State under certain statutory provisions[36] relating to the local retention of non-domestic rates[37];
(E) payments to be made by the authority under certain provisions[38] relating to the local retention of non-domestic rates[39];
(F) payments to be made by the authority to another person[40] in repaying[41] excess receipts by way of non-domestic rates or of council tax[42]; and
(G) any other payments which are to be made by the authority to another person and which the Secretary of State specifies are to be met from a billing authority's collection fund[43].

1 As to the meaning of 'billing authority' see PARA 346 (definition applied by the Local Government Finance Act 1988 s 144(2) (substituted by the Local Government Finance Act 1992 s 117(1), Sch 13 para 81(1); and amended by the Local Government Finance Act 2012 s 5(1), (2)(b), Sch 3 paras 23, 29)). The Local Government Finance Act 1988 Pt VI (ss 89–99) does not apply to a Welsh county council or county borough council (for whom provision as to the establishment of a council fund is made by the Local Government (Wales) Act 1994 s 38: see PARA 585): Local Government Finance Act 1988 s 89A (added by the Local Government (Wales) Act 1994 s 38(11), Sch 12 para 2). As to the meanings of 'England' and 'Wales' see PARA 2 note 16.

2 Local Government Finance Act 1988 s 89(1) (amended by the Local Government Finance Act 1992 s 104, Sch 10 para 19). The relevant provisions of the Local Government Finance Act 1988 for these purposes are those of Pt VI (ss 89–99): see s 89(1). The Local Government Act 1972 s 101(1)(b) (delegation: see LOCAL GOVERNMENT vol 69 (2018) PARA 399) does not apply as regards the functions of an authority in relation to its collection fund: Local Government Finance Act 1988 s 89(3).

3 Ie subject to the Local Government Finance Act 1988 s 89(2A)–(2C): see the text to notes 5–14.

4 Local Government Finance Act 1988 s 89(2) (amended by the Local Government and Public Involvement in Health Act 2007 s 22, Sch 1 Pt 2 para 16(1), (3)(a); and SI 1994/2825).

5 Ie under the Local Government Act 1992 s 17 (repealed).

6 As to the meanings of 'structural change' and 'boundary change' see PARA 579 note 6.

7 Local Government Finance Act 1988 s 89(2A) (added by SI 1994/2825; and amended by the Regional Assemblies (Preparations) Act 2003 s 17(6), Schedule paras 3(1), (3); and the Local Democracy, Economic Development and Construction Act 2009 s 146(1), Sch 7 Pt 4).
8 Local Government Finance Act 1988 s 89(2B)(a) (s 89(2B) added by SI 1994/2825).
9 Local Government Finance Act 1988 s 89(2B)(b) (as added: see note 8).
10 Local Government Finance Act 1988 s 89(2B) (as added: see note 8).
11 Ie under the Local Government and Public Involvement in Health Act 2007 Pt 1 (ss 1–30): see LOCAL GOVERNMENT vol 69 (2018) PARA 95 et seq.
12 Local Government Finance Act 1988 s 89(2C)(a) (s 89(2C) added by the Local Government and Public Involvement in Health Act 2007 Sch 1 Pt 2 para 16(1), (3)(b)).
13 Local Government Finance Act 1988 s 89(2C)(b) (as added: see note 12).
14 Local Government Finance Act 1988 s 89(2C) (as added: see note 12). The regulations concerned are any made under the Local Government and Public Involvement in Health Act 2007 s 14 (see LOCAL GOVERNMENT vol 69 (2018) PARA 102): see the Local Government Finance Act 1988 s 89(2C) (as so added).

As regards a single tier council that is related to a predecessor council which is a shadow council, or a preparing council which is a county council, the date specified for these purposes is the date that falls one day after the date on which the predecessor council makes its calculation under the Local Government Finance Act 1992 s 32 (calculation of budget requirement: see PARA 384) for the financial year beginning on the reorganisation date: Local Government (Structural Changes) (Further Financial Provisions and Amendment) Regulations 2009, SI 2009/5, reg 3. The Local Authorities (Funds) (England) Regulations 1992, SI 1992/2428 (see note 16) have effect with modifications: see the Local Government (Structural Changes) (Further Financial Provisions and Amendment) Regulations 2009, SI 2009/5, reg 5, Schedule. 'Single tier council' means a local authority which on and after the reorganisation date is the sole principal authority for an area; and 'predecessor council' means a local authority which, by or in consequence of an order under the Local Government and Public Involvement in Health Act 2007 s 7 (a 'section 7 order'), ceases to exist on the reorganisation date: Local Government (Structural Changes) (Further Financial Provisions and Amendment) Regulations 2009, SI 2009/5, reg 2(1).

A single tier council is related to a predecessor council if on the reorganisation date the area of the single tier council includes that of the predecessor council; and, where on the reorganisation date the area of a predecessor council comprises the areas of two or more single tier councils taken together, both or all of those single tier councils are related to the predecessor council: reg 2(2). 'Reorganisation date', in relation to a single tier council, means the date specified in the section 7 order as that on which a structural change comes into effect: reg 2(1). 'Shadow council' means an authority (not being a local authority) which, in accordance with a s 7 order, becomes a single tier council on the reorganisation date; and 'preparing council' means a local authority which, in accordance with a section 7 order, becomes a single tier council on the reorganisation date: reg 2(1). 'Local authority' means a county council in England, a district council in England or a London borough council: Local Government and Public Involvement in Health Act 2007 s 23(1). As to local government areas and authorities in England see LOCAL GOVERNMENT vol 69 (2018) PARA 36 et seq. As to the London boroughs and their councils see LONDON GOVERNMENT vol 71 (2013) PARAS 15, 20–22, 55 et seq.

15 Local Government Finance Act 1988 s 89(4) (amended by the Local Government and Housing Act 1989 s 139, Sch 5 para 62).
16 Local Government Finance Act 1988 s 89(5) (amended by the Local Government and Housing Act 1989 Sch 5 para 79(3)). For additional provisions which may be included in such regulations see the Local Government Finance Act 1988 s 98(3); and PARA 582. As to the regulations made see the Local Authorities (Funds) (England) Regulations 1992, SI 1992/2428 (amended by SI 1994/246, SI 1995/2910, SI 1999/3459, SI 2001/3649, SI 2009/5, SI 2009/2543 and SI 2013/2974). As to the Secretary of State see PARA 4 note 18.
17 Local Government Finance Act 1988 s 90(1) (s 90 substituted by the Local Government Finance Act 1992 Sch 10 para 20).
18 Ie the council tax set by it in accordance with the Local Government Finance Act 1992 s 30: see PARA 380.
19 Local Government Finance Act 1988 s 90(1)(a) (as substituted: see note 17). As to penalties in respect of council tax see PARA 471 et seq.
20 Ie under regulations made under the Local Government Finance Act 1988 s 99(3): see PARA 583.
21 Local Government Finance Act 1988 s 90(1)(b) (as substituted (see note 17); amended by the Local Government Finance Act 2012 s 5(1), (2)(b), Sch 3 paras 23, 24(1), (2)). As to the meaning of

'major precepting authority' see PARA 11 note 2 (definition applied by the Local Government Finance Act 1988 s 144(2) (as substituted and amended: see note 1)).

22 See the Local Government Finance Act 1988 s 90(1)(c) (as substituted: see note 17). As to non-domestic rating see PARA 49 et seq.

23 Local Government Finance Act 1988 s 90(1)(ca) (s 90 as substituted (see note 17); s 90(1)(ca), (1A) added by the Business Rate Supplements Act 2009 Sch 3 para 4(1), (2)). The reference in the Local Government Finance Act 1988 s 90(1)(ca) to sums received by a billing authority in respect of business rate supplements:

(1) includes a reference to financial contributions made to it for the purpose of enabling the project to which a business rate supplement relates to be carried out (s 90(1A)(a) (as so substituted and added)); but

(2) does not include a reference to sums returned or transferred to it by virtue of the Business Rate Supplements Act 2009 s 24(3)(b) or Sch 3 para 3(2)(a) (see PARA 339) (Local Government Finance Act 1988 s 90(1A)(b) (as so substituted and added)).

As to business rate supplements generally see PARA 326 et seq.

24 Ie the Local Government Finance Act 1988 Sch 7B para 14(2) (payments by Secretary of State following local government finance report: see PARA 62), Sch 7B para 14(9) or (10) (payments by Secretary of State following revised calculation: see PARA 62) or Sch 7B para 17(7) or (8) (payments by Secretary of State following amending report: see PARA 63): see the Local Government Finance Act 1988 s 90(1)(d)(i)–(iii) (s 90(1)(d) as substituted (see note 17); further substituted by the Local Government Finance Act 2012 s 5(1), (2)(b), Sch 3 paras 23, 24(1), (3)).

25 Local Government Finance Act 1988 s 90(1)(d) (as substituted: see notes 17, 24).

26 See the Local Government Finance Act 1988 s 90(1)(da)(i)–(vi) (s 90(1)(da) added by the Local Government Finance Act 2012 Sch 3 paras 23, 24(1), (3)). Ie provision made by regulations:

(1) under the Local Government Finance Act 1988 Sch 7B para 7 (regulations about administration of payments in respect of the central share: see PARA 60);

(2) under provision made by regulations under Sch 7B para 10 (administration of payments by billing authorities to major precepting authorities: see PARA 61) by virtue of Sch 7B para 10(2)(e) or (f) (reconciliation payments);

(3) under provision made by regulations under Sch 7B para 11 (regulations about payments by billing authorities to major precepting authorities out of deductions from the central share: see PARA 61);

(4) under provision made by regulations under Sch 7B para 33 (transitional protection payments: see PARA 68);

(5) under provision made by regulations under Sch 7B para 39 or 40 (designation of areas or classes of hereditament: see PARA 71) by virtue of Sch 7B para 41 (payments by billing authorities to relevant authorities: see PARA 72); or

(6) under provision made by regulations under Sch 7B para 42 (payments by Secretary of State following estimates of amounts relating to designated areas or classes: see PARA 72).

27 Local Government Finance Act 1988 s 90(1)(da) (as added: see note 26).

28 The power to specify under the Local Government Finance Act 1988 s 90:

(1) includes power to revoke or amend a specification made under the power (s 90(3)(a) (as substituted: see note 17)); and

(2) may be exercised differently in relation to different authorities (s 90(3)(b) (as so substituted)).

29 Local Government Finance Act 1988 s 90(1)(e) (as substituted: see note 17).

30 Local Government Finance Act 1988 s 90(2) (as substituted: see note 17).

31 Ie under the Local Government Finance Act 1992 Pt I (ss 1–69). As to precepts see PARA 11 et seq.

32 Local Government Finance Act 1988 s 90(2)(a) (as substituted: see note 17).

33 Ie under regulations made under the Local Government Finance Act 1988 s 99(3): see PARA 583.

34 Local Government Finance Act 1988 s 90(2)(b) (as substituted (see note 17); amended by the Local Government Finance Act 2012 Sch 3 paras 23, 24(1), (4)).

35 Local Government Finance Act 1988 s 90(2)(ba) (s 90 as substituted (see note 17); s 90(2)(ba) added by the Business Rate Supplements Act 2009 Sch 3 para 4(1)(c), (2)). As to levying authorities see PARA 326.

36 Ie the Local Government Finance Act 1988 Sch 7B para 14(1) (payments to Secretary of State following local government finance report: see PARA 62), Sch 7B para 14(9) or (10) (payments to Secretary of State following revised calculation: see PARA 62) or Sch 7B para 17(4) or (5)

(payments to Secretary of State following amending report: see PARA 63): see the Local Government Finance Act 1988 s 90(2)(c)(i)–(iii) (s 90(2)(c) as substituted (see note 17); further substituted by the Local Government Finance Act 2012 Sch 3 paras 23, 24(1), (5)).

37 Local Government Finance Act 1988 s 90(2)(c) (as substituted (see notes 17, 36).

38 See the Local Government Finance Act 1988 s 90(2)(ca)(i)–(vii) (s 90(2)(ca) added by the Local Government Finance Act 2012 Sch 3 paras 23, 24(1), (5)). Ie provision made:

(1) under the Local Government Finance Act 1988 Sch 7B para 6 or under provision made by regulations under Sch 7B para 7 (payments in respect of the central share: see PARA 60);

(2) under provision made by regulations under Sch 7B para 9 (payments by billing authorities to major precepting authorities: see PARA 61);

(3) under provision made by regulations under Sch 7B para 10 (administration of payments by billing authorities to major precepting authorities: see PARA 61) by virtue of Sch 7B para 10(2)(e) or (f) (reconciliation payments);

(4) under provision made by regulations under Sch 7B para 11 (regulations about payments by billing authorities to major precepting authorities out of deductions from the central share: see PARA 61);

(5) under provision made by regulations under Sch 7B para 33 (transitional protection payments: see PARA 68);

(6) under provision made by regulations under Sch 7B para 39 or 40 (designation of areas or classes of hereditament: see PARA 71) by virtue of Sch 7B para 41 (payments by billing authorities to relevant authorities: see PARA 72); or

(7) under provision made by regulations under Sch 7B para 42 (payments to Secretary of State following estimates of amounts relating to designated areas or classes: see PARA 72).

39 Local Government Finance Act 1988 s 90(2)(ca) (as added: see note 38).

40 As to the meaning of 'person' see PARA 11 note 13.

41 Ie under regulations under the Local Government Finance Act 1988 or the Local Government Finance Act 1992 Pt I (ss 1–69).

42 Local Government Finance Act 1988 s 90(2)(d) (as substituted: see note 17).

43 Local Government Finance Act 1988 s 90(2)(e) (as substituted: see note 17). See also note 24.

582. Transfers between general funds and collection funds.

A billing authority in England[1] which has made council tax calculations[2] (originally or by way of substitute) must transfer from its collection fund[3] to its general fund[4] an amount which must be calculated by applying a specified statutory formula[5]. However, where the amount so given is a negative amount, the authority must transfer the equivalent positive amount from its general fund to its collection fund[6].

The Secretary of State[7] may by regulations make provision requiring a billing authority to transfer from its collection fund to its general fund such amounts as may be specified in or determined in accordance with the regulations by reference to sums received by the authority in respect of non-domestic rates under the Local Government Finance Act 1988[8], and sums received by the authority in respect of local retention of non-domestic rates[9] and required[10] to be paid into its collection fund[11]. The Secretary of State may by regulations make provision requiring a billing authority to transfer from its general fund to its collection fund such amounts as may be specified in or determined in accordance with the regulations by reference to sums received by the authority in respect of non-domestic rates under the Local Government Finance Act 1988[12].

Where in accordance with regulations[13] a billing authority has estimated that there is a surplus in its collection fund for the preceding year, it must transfer from its collection fund to its general fund an amount equal to so much of the surplus as, in accordance with the regulations, the authority calculates to be its share[14]. Where in accordance with regulations[15] a billing authority has estimated that there is a deficit in its collection fund for the preceding year, it must transfer from its general fund to its collection fund an amount equal to so much of the deficit as, in accordance with the regulations, the authority calculates must be borne by it[16].

Regulations[17] may include provision that:

(1) any sum to which they relate must be transferred from an authority's collection fund to its general fund[18];

(2) the sum so transferred must be held, invested or otherwise used in such manner as may be prescribed[19];

(3) a sum equal to the sum transferred must be transferred to the authority's collection fund from its general fund[20].

In relation to each financial year[21] beginning in or after 1993 a billing authority must, in accordance with its schedule of instalments[22]:

(a) pay to its relevant precepting authorities[23] from its collection fund or its general fund (as the case may be)[24];

(b) transfer from its collection fund to its general fund[25]; and

(c) transfer from its general fund to its collection fund[26], such amounts, if any, as will discharge its liabilities[27] for that year[28].

Where a substitute precept or calculation[29] has been issued or made in relation to a financial year and that substitute precept or calculation has been issued or made on or after the day of the final instalment to be paid or transferred in accordance with the schedule of instalments in that year, any amounts to be paid or transferred by a billing authority in respect of its liabilities for that year which remain to be discharged immediately after the substitute precept or calculation is issued or made must be paid or transferred as soon as reasonably practicable after the issue of that precept or making of that calculation[30].

In relation to each financial year beginning in or after 1993 a billing authority must transfer from its general fund to its collection fund such amounts as will discharge its liability to transfer anything from its general fund[31] at such times and in such instalments as it determines, provided it discharges any such liability within the financial year to which it relates[32]. Where a billing authority makes a substitute calculation after the end of the financial year to which it relates and becomes liable to transfer an amount[33], any amounts to be transferred by that authority in respect of its liabilities which remain to be discharged immediately after the substitute calculation is made must be transferred as soon as reasonably practicable after the making of that calculation[34].

In relation to each financial year beginning in or after 1994 a billing authority must[35] discharge its liability to pay anything from its collection fund to a relevant major precepting authority in respect of so much of any surplus in that fund as that billing authority calculates[36] to be that major precepting authority's share as regards that year[37]. Any amount so calculated as regards the financial year in question must be paid by a billing authority to a relevant major precepting authority in no more than ten equal instalments during that financial year, provided that the first and final instalments are paid in that year no later than 31 May and 31 March respectively, and there are an equal number of days[38] between each instalment[39].

Any amount paid or transferred by a billing authority in respect of a liability for a financial year[40] must be treated as discharging that liability to the extent of the payment or transfer[41].

If the Secretary of State directs it to do so, a billing authority must transfer from its collection fund to its general fund such an amount as is specified in, or calculated in a manner specified in, the direction; and the transfer must be made at such time as is specified in the direction[42]. If the Secretary of State directs it do so, a billing authority must transfer to its collection fund from its general fund such an amount as is specified in, or calculated in a manner specified in, the direction; and the transfer must be made at such time as is specified in the direction[43]. Different directions may be given[44] to different authorities[45].

1 As to the meaning of 'billing authority' see PARA 346 (definition applied by the Local Government Finance Act 1988 s 144(2) (substituted by the Local Government Finance Act 1992 s 117(1), Sch 13 para 81(1); and amended by the Local Government Finance Act 2012 s 5(1), (2)(b), Sch 3 paras 23, 29)). The Local Government Finance Act 1988 Pt VI (ss 89–99) does not apply to a Welsh county council or county borough council (for whom provision as to the establishment of a council fund is made by the Local Government (Wales) Act 1994 s 38: see PARA 585): Local Government Finance Act 1988 s 89A (added by the Local Government (Wales) Act 1994 s 38(11), Sch 12 para 2). As to the meanings of 'England' and 'Wales' see PARA 2 note 16.

2 Ie calculations in accordance with the Local Government Finance Act 1992 ss 31A, 31B (see PARAS 382–383) and ss 34–36: see PARAS 380, 386.

3 As to collection funds see PARA 581.

4 As to general funds see PARA 579. For the purposes of the Local Government Finance Act 1988 ss 97, 98, 99 (see PARA 583), any reference to a billing authority's general fund must be construed in relation to the Common Council of the City of London as a reference to the City fund: s 97(5) (s 97 substituted by the Local Government Finance Act 1992 s 104, Sch 10 para 22). As to the City fund see PARA 586. As to the Common Council of the City of London see LONDON GOVERNMENT vol 71 (2013) PARAS 34–38.

5 See the Local Government Finance Act 1988 s 97(1) (as substituted (see note 4); amended by the Localism Act 2011 s 79, Sch 7 paras 1, 4). As to the formula see the Local Government Finance Act 1988 s 97(1) (as so substituted and amended).

6 Local Government Finance Act 1988 s 97(2) (as substituted: see note 4).

7 As to the Secretary of State see PARA 4 note 18.

8 As to non-domestic rating see PARA 49 et seq.

9 Ie under or by virtue of the Local Government Finance Act 1988 Sch 7B: see PARA 58 et seq.

10 Ie by virtue of provision made by or under the Local Government Finance Act 1988 s 90(1)(d) or (da): see PARA 581.

11 Local Government Finance Act 1988 s 97(2A) (s 97(2A), (2B) added by the Local Government Finance Act 2012 s 5(1), (2)(b), Sch 3 paras 23, 25(1), (2)).

12 Local Government Finance Act 1988 s 97(2B) (as added: see note 11).

13 Ie regulations under the Local Government Finance Act 1988 s 99(3): see PARA 583.

14 Local Government Finance Act 1988 s 97(3) (as substituted: see note 4).

15 Ie regulations under the Local Government Finance Act 1988 s 99(3): see PARA 583.

16 Local Government Finance Act 1988 s 97(4) (as substituted: see note 4).

17 Ie regulations under the Local Government Finance Act 1988 s 89(5): see PARA 581.

18 Local Government Finance Act 1988 s 98(3)(a) (amended by the Local Government Finance Act 1992 ss 104, 117(2), Sch 10 para 23(1), Sch 14).

19 Local Government Finance Act 1988 s 98(3)(b).

20 Local Government Finance Act 1988 s 98(3)(c) (amended by the Local Government Finance Act 1992 Sch 10 para 23(1), Sch 14).

21 As to the meaning of 'financial year' see PARA 24 note 1.

22 Any reference in the Local Authorities (Funds) (England) Regulations 1992, SI 1992/2428, reg 3 to an authority's schedule of instalments is a reference to the schedule of instalments determined by the authority in accordance with reg 4, or where the authority has amended its schedule in accordance with reg 6, to its schedule of instalments as it currently has effect: reg 3(11). 'Schedule of instalments' means a schedule determined by a billing authority, in accordance with regs 4 and 6, with respect to the times for and the number and amounts of payments or transfers from its collection fund or its general fund in respect of its liabilities: reg 2(1).

23 'Relevant precepting authority' in relation to a billing authority means each relevant major precepting authority and each relevant local precepting authority: Local Authorities (Funds) (England) Regulations 1992, SI 1992/2428, reg 2(1). 'Relevant major precepting authority' in relation to a billing authority means any major precepting authority having power to issue a precept to that billing authority but the Greater London Authority is, and the Secretary of State is not, a relevant major precepting authority for the purposes of regs 3(6), (7), (8) (see the text to notes 35–39) in respect of the period beginning on 12 January 2000 and ending with 2 July 2000, notwithstanding the transitional adaptation of the Local Government Finance Act 1992 s 39(1):

see the Local Authorities (Funds) (England) Regulations 1992, SI 1992/2428, reg 2(1) (definition amended by SI 1999/3459). 'Relevant local precepting authority' in relation to a billing authority means any local precepting authority having power to issue a precept to that billing authority: Local Authorities (Funds) (England) Regulations 1992, SI 1992/2428, reg 2(1). As to the meaning of 'major precepting authority' see PARA 11 note 2; and as to the meaning of 'local precepting authority' see PARA 18 note 2 (definitions applied by the Local Government Finance Act 1988 s 144(2) (substituted by the Local Government Finance Act 1992 s 117(1), Sch 13 para 81(1); and amended by the Local Government Finance Act 2012 s 5(1), (2)(b), Sch 3 paras 23, 29)). As to the Greater London Authority see LONDON GOVERNMENT vol 71 (2013) PARA 67 et seq.

24 Local Authorities (Funds) (England) Regulations 1992, SI 1992/2428, reg 3(1)(a).

25 Local Authorities (Funds) (England) Regulations 1992, SI 1992/2428, reg 3(1)(b).

26 Local Authorities (Funds) (England) Regulations 1992, SI 1992/2428, reg 3(1)(c).

27 Any reference in the Local Authorities (Funds) (England) Regulations 1992, SI 1992/2428 (however framed) to 'liabilities' in relation to a billing authority is a reference to the liability of a billing authority to:

(1) pay anything from its collection fund in respect of any precept issued by a relevant major precepting authority under the Local Government Finance Act 1992 Pt I (ss 1–69), after taking into account any amount credited by that major precepting authority under s 42(4) (see PARA 23) (Local Authorities (Funds) (England) Regulations 1992, SI 1992/2428, reg 2(2)(a));

(2) pay anything from its collection fund in respect of so much of any surplus in that fund as, in accordance with reg 11 (apportionment of and liability for surpluses and deficits), that billing authority calculates to be a relevant major precepting authority's share (reg 2(2)(b));

(3) pay anything from its general fund in respect of any precept issued by a relevant local precepting authority under the Local Government Finance Act 1992 Pt I, after taking into account any amount credited by that local precepting authority under s 42(4) (see PARA 23) (Local Authorities (Funds) (England) Regulations 1992, SI 1992/2428, reg 2(2)(c));

(4) transfer anything from its collection fund or its general fund under the Local Government Finance Act 1988 s 97(1) or (2) (see the text to notes 1–6) (as the case may be) (Local Authorities (Funds) (England) Regulations 1992, SI 1992/2428, reg 2(2)(d));

(5) transfer anything from its collection fund or its general fund under the Local Government Finance Act 1988 s 97(3) or (4) (see the text to notes 7–10) (as the case may be) in respect of so much of any surplus or deficit in its collection fund as, in accordance with the Local Authorities (Funds) (England) Regulations 1992, SI 1992/2428, reg 11, that billing authority calculates to be its share or calculates must be borne by it (reg 2(2)(e)); and

(6) pay anything from its collection fund in respect of a variation to any payment or instalment of a payment relating to a precept agreed between that billing authority and a major precepting authority under the Local Government Finance Act 1992 Sch 1A para 6(3)(b) (council tax reduction schemes: arrangements to deal with shortfall in council tax receipts) in the circumstances described in the Local Authorities (Funds) (England) Regulations 1992, SI 1992/2428, reg 10A or Sch 2 para 6(4A) (Local Authorities (Funds) (England) Regulations 1992, SI 1992/2428, reg 2(2)(f) (added by SI 2013/2974)).

As to precepts generally see PARA 11 et seq.

28 Local Authorities (Funds) (England) Regulations 1992, SI 1992/2428, reg 3(1). The requirement in reg 3(1) to make payments or transfers in accordance with a schedule of instalments does not apply where any of the provisions in reg 3(3)–(8) (see the text to notes 29–39) apply: reg 3(2).

29 Any reference to the making of a substitute calculation is a reference to the making of a substitute calculation by a billing authority in accordance with the Local Government Finance Act 1992 s 32(4) (see PARA 384): Local Authorities (Funds) (England) Regulations 1992, SI 1992/2428, reg 2(3).

30 Local Authorities (Funds) (England) Regulations 1992, SI 1992/2428, reg 3(3).

31 Ie under the Local Government Finance Act 1988 s 97(2): see the text to note 6.

32 Local Authorities (Funds) (England) Regulations 1992, SI 1992/2428, reg 3(4).

33 Ie under the Local Government Finance Act 1988 s 97(2): see the text to note 6.

34 Local Authorities (Funds) (England) Regulations 1992, SI 1992/2428, reg 3(5).

35 Ie in accordance with the Local Authorities (Funds) (England) Regulations 1992, SI 1992/2428, reg 3(7), (8): see the text to notes 38–39.

36 Ie in accordance with the Local Authorities (Funds) (England) Regulations 1992, SI 1992/2428, reg 11 (apportionment of and liability for surpluses and deficits).
37 Local Authorities (Funds) (England) Regulations 1992, SI 1992/2428, reg 3(6).
38 For the purposes of the computation of days under the Local Authorities (Funds) (England) Regulations 1992, SI 1992/2428, reg 3(7) a day which is a Saturday, Sunday or bank holiday must be excluded: see reg 3(8).
39 Local Authorities (Funds) (England) Regulations 1992, SI 1992/2428, reg 3(7) (amended by SI 1999/3459). Any amount so calculated by an authority (ie in accordance with the Local Authorities (Funds) (England) Regulations 1992, SI 1992/2428, Sch 2 para 6(5), (6), (7)) must be paid by a billing authority to the Greater London Authority in no more than eight instalments during the financial year beginning on 1 April 2000, provided that the first and final instalments are paid in that year no later than 6 July and 31 March respectively, and there are an equal number of days between each instalment: reg 3(7A) (added by SI 1999/3459). For the purposes of the computation of days under the Local Authorities (Funds) (England) Regulations 1992, SI 1992/2428, reg 3(7A) a day which is a Saturday, Sunday or bank holiday must be excluded: see reg 3(8) (amended by SI 1999/3459).
40 Ie whether or not paid or transferred in accordance with a schedule of instalments or in accordance with any of the provisions in the Local Authorities (Funds) (England) Regulations 1992, SI 1992/2428, reg 3(3)–(8) (see the text to notes 29–39).
41 Local Authorities (Funds) (England) Regulations 1992, SI 1992/2428, reg 3(9). For the purposes of reg 3(9), any amount paid or transferred which was treated in accordance with that provision as discharging a billing authority's liability, but which was subsequently repaid or credited by the relevant precepting authority concerned under the Local Government Finance Act 1992 s 42(2) (see PARA 23), or transferred under the Local Authorities (Funds) (England) Regulations 1992, SI 1992/2428, reg 9, must, to the extent of the amount repaid or credited or transferred under reg 9, cease to be treated as discharging that liability: reg 3(10).
42 Local Government Finance Act 1988 s 98(4) (amended by the Local Government Finance Act 1992 Sch 10 para 23, Sch 14).
43 Local Government Finance Act 1988 s 98(5) (amended by the Local Government Finance Act 1992 Sch 10 para 23, Sch 14).
44 Ie under the Local Government Finance Act 1988 s 98(4), (5): see the text to notes 42–42.
45 Local Government Finance Act 1988 s 98(6) (amended by the Local Government Finance Act 1992 Sch 10 para 23, Sch 14).

583. Power to make regulations in relation to funds.

The Secretary of State[1] may make regulations[2] about the discharge of the following liabilities of a billing authority in England[3]:

(1) the liability to pay anything from its collection fund[4] or its general fund[5] in respect of any precept issued[6] by a major or local precepting authority[7];
(2) the liability to transfer anything[8] from its collection fund[9]; and
(3) the liability to transfer anything[10] from its general fund[11].

The regulations may include provision:

(a) that anything falling to be paid or transferred must be paid or transferred within a prescribed period[12];
(b) that anything falling to be paid or transferred must be paid or transferred in instalments of such amounts, and at such times, as are determined by the billing authority in accordance with prescribed rules[13];
(c) that the billing authority must inform any precepting authorities when instalments will be paid and how they are to be calculated[14];
(d) that if an instalment is not paid to a precepting authority in accordance with the regulations, it is to be entitled to interest on the amount of the instalment[15];
(e) as to the circumstances in which the billing authority is to be treated as having discharged the liabilities mentioned in heads (1) to (3) above[16];

(f) as to the recovery (by deduction or otherwise) of any excess amount paid by the billing authority to any precepting authority in purported discharge of the liability mentioned in head (1) above[17]; and

(g) as to the transfer back of any excess amount transferred by the billing authority in purported discharge of the liability mentioned in head (2) or head (3) above[18].

The Secretary of State may by regulations make provision as regards any financial year[19]:

(i) that a billing authority must estimate at a prescribed time in the preceding financial year and in accordance with prescribed rules whether there is a deficit or surplus in its collection fund for that year and, if so, the amount of the deficit or surplus[20];

(ii) that any surplus or deficit so estimated must in the financial year concerned be shared among, or be borne between, the billing authority and one or more relevant authorities[21] in accordance with prescribed rules[22];

(iii) that the billing authority must within a prescribed period inform prescribed relevant authorities of the effects of any estimates and rules mentioned in heads (i) and (ii) above[23];

(iv) as to the manner in which any payments which fall to be made by a billing authority or a relevant authority by virtue of any provision included in regulations under head (i) or head (ii) above must be made[24];

(v) as to the period within which, or time or times at which, any such payments or instalments of such payments must be made[25]; and

(vi) as to the recovery (by deduction or otherwise) of any excess amount paid by a relevant authority or a billing authority in purported discharge of any liability arising by virtue of any provision included in regulations under head (i) or head (ii) above[26].

Regulations under heads (i) to (vi) above may make separate provision in relation to council tax and non-domestic rates[27], with the effect that:

(A) more than one estimate is to be made by a billing authority of whether there is a deficit or surplus in its collection fund for a financial year and, if so, of the amount of the deficit or surplus[28];

(B) each estimate takes into account different amounts to be paid into or met from that fund[29]; and

(C) each estimate has different consequences as to the payments to be made, or other functions to be exercised, by the billing authority, major precepting authorities or the Secretary of State[30].

The Secretary of State may make regulations requiring transfers between funds, or adjustments or assumptions, to be made to take account of any substitute calculation[31] of budget requirement[32].

The Secretary of State may make regulations providing that sums standing to the credit of a billing authority's collection fund at any time in a financial year must not exceed a total to be calculated in such manner as may be prescribed[33].

1 As to the Secretary of State see PARA 4 note 18.

2 As to the regulations made under the Local Government Finance Act 1988 s 99 see the Local Authorities (Funds) (England) Regulations 1992, SI 1992/2428 (amended by SI 1994/246, SI 1995/2910, SI 1999/3459, SI 2001/3649, SI 2009/5, SI 2009/2543 and SI 2013/2974); and the Local Authorities (Alteration of Requisite Calculations and Funds) Regulations 1994, SI 1994/246.

3 As to the meaning of 'billing authority' see PARA 346 (definition applied by the Local Government Finance Act 1988 s 144(2) (substituted by the Local Government Finance Act 1992 s 117(1),

Sch 13 para 81(1); and amended by the Local Government Finance Act 2012 s 5(1), (2)(b), Sch 3 paras 23, 29)). The Local Government Finance Act 1988 Pt VI (ss 89–99) does not apply to a Welsh county council or county borough council (for whom provision as to the establishment of a council fund is made by the Local Government (Wales) Act 1994 s 38: see PARA 585): Local Government Finance Act 1988 s 89A (added by the Local Government (Wales) Act 1994 s 38(11), Sch 12 para 2). As to the meanings of 'England' and 'Wales' see PARA 2 note 16.

4 As to collection funds see PARA 581.

5 As to general funds see PARA 579.

6 Ie under the Local Government Finance Act 1992 Pt I (ss 1–69): see PARA 11 et seq.

7 Local Government Finance Act 1988 s 99(1)(a) (s 99 substituted by the Local Government Finance Act 1992 s 104, Sch 10 para 24). As to the meaning of 'major precepting authority' see PARA 11 note 2; and as to the meaning of 'local precepting authority' see PARA 18 note 2 (definitions applied by the Local Government Finance Act 1988 s 144(2) (substituted by the Local Government Finance Act 1992 s 117(1), Sch 13 para 81(1); and amended by the Local Government Finance Act 2012 s 5(1), (2)(b), Sch 3 paras 23, 29)).

8 Ie under the Local Government Finance Act 1988 s 97(1), (3) or (4A) or regulations under s 97(2A): see PARA 582.

9 Local Government Finance Act 1988 s 99(1)(b) (as substituted (see note 7); amended by the Local Government Finance Act 2012 s 5(1), (2)(b), Sch 3 paras 23, 26(1), (2)).

10 Ie under the Local Government Finance Act 1988 s 97(2) or (4) or regulations under s 97(2B): see PARA 582.

11 Local Government Finance Act 1988 s 99(1)(c) (as substituted (see note 7); amended by the Local Government Finance Act 2012 Sch 3 paras 23, 26(1), (3)).

12 Local Government Finance Act 1988 s 99(2)(a) (as substituted: see note 7). 'Prescribed' means prescribed by the regulations: see s 146(6), (7).

13 Local Government Finance Act 1988 s 99(2)(b) (as substituted: see note 7).

14 Local Government Finance Act 1988 s 99(2)(c) (as substituted: see note 7).

15 Local Government Finance Act 1988 s 99(2)(d) (as substituted: see note 7).

16 Local Government Finance Act 1988 s 99(2)(e) (as substituted: see note 7).

17 Local Government Finance Act 1988 s 99(2)(f) (as substituted: see note 7).

18 Local Government Finance Act 1988 s 99(2)(g) (as substituted: see note 7).

19 As to the meaning of 'financial year' see PARA 24 note 1. As to the regulations made see note 2.

20 Local Government Finance Act 1988 s 99(3)(a) (as substituted: see note 7).

21 In the Local Government Finance Act 1988 s 99(3) 'relevant authority' means a major precepting authority or the Secretary of State: s 99(3C) (added by the Local Government Finance Act 2012 Sch 3 paras 23, 26(1), (6)).

22 Local Government Finance Act 1988 s 99(3)(b)(i) (as substituted (see note 7); amended by the Local Government Finance Act 2012 Sch 3 paras 23, 26(1), (4)(a)). In the case of the financial year beginning in 1993, the regulations may make provision that any surplus or deficit so estimated must belong solely to, or be borne solely by, the billing authority: see the Local Government Finance Act 1988 s 99(3)(b)(ii) (as so substituted).

23 Local Government Finance Act 1988 s 99(3)(c) (as substituted (see note 7); amended by the Local Government Finance Act 2012 Sch 3 paras 23, 26(1), (4)(b)).

24 Local Government Finance Act 1988 s 99(3)(d) (as substituted (see note 7); amended by the Local Government Finance Act 2012 Sch 3 paras 23, 26(1), (4)(c)).

25 Local Government Finance Act 1988 s 99(3)(e) (as substituted: see note 7).

26 Local Government Finance Act 1988 s 99(3)(f) (as substituted (see note 7); amended by the Local Government Finance Act 2012 Sch 3 paras 23, 26(1), (4)(c)).

27 Local Government Finance Act 1988 s 99(3D) (added by the Local Government Finance Act 2012 Sch 3 paras 23, 26(1), (6)).

28 Local Government Finance Act 1988 s 99(3D)(a) (as added: see note 27).

29 Local Government Finance Act 1988 s 99(3D)(b) (as added: see note 27).

30 Local Government Finance Act 1988 s 99(3D)(c) (as added: see note 27).

31 Ie under the Local Government Finance Act 1992 s 31A(4): see PARA 382.

32 See the Local Government Finance Act 1988 s 99(4) (as substituted (see note 7); amended by the Localism Act 2011 s 79, Sch 7 paras 1, 5). As to the regulations made see note 2.

33 Local Government Finance Act 1988 s 99(5) (as substituted: see note 7). Regulations under s 99(5) in their application to a particular financial year (including regulations amending others) are not effective unless they come into force before 1 January in the preceding financial year; but this does not affect regulations which merely revoke others: s 99(6) (as so substituted). As to the regulations made see note 2.

(ii) County Funds

584. County funds.

The council of each county in England[1] must keep a fund known as the 'county fund'[2]. All receipts of a county council must be carried to the county fund, and all liabilities falling to be discharged by that council must be discharged out of that fund[3].

Accounts must be kept of receipts carried to, and payments made out of the county fund[4]. Any account kept in respect of general expenses only of a principal area[5] must be called the 'general account' of that area and any account kept in respect of any class of special expenses only of any such area must be called a 'special account' of that area[6].

The assets held in the county fund of a relevant county council immediately before the date on which the council is required to establish its general fund (other than assets forming part of a trust fund) must be transferred on that date to its general fund[7].

1 The Local Government Act 1972 s 148 does not apply in relation to a Welsh county council or county borough council: Local Government Act 1972 s 148(6) (added by the Local Government (Wales) Act 1994 s 38(11), Sch 12 para 1). As to the provision made in relation to such councils for the establishment of a council fund see the Local Government (Wales) Act 1994 s 38; and PARA 585. As to the meanings of 'England' and 'Wales' see PARA 2 note 16. As to local government areas and authorities in England and Wales see LOCAL GOVERNMENT vol 69 (2018) PARA 36 et seq.

2 Local Government Act 1972 s 148(2) (amended by the Local Government Act 1985 s 102, Sch 17). This provision does not apply to the council for a county for any financial year for which that council is, by virtue of the Local Government Act 1992 s 18(1) (repealed), a billing authority for that year for the purposes of the Local Government Finance Act 1992 Pt I (ss 1–69) (see PARA 346): Local Government Act 1972 s 148(5A) (added by SI 1994/2825). 'Financial year' means the period of 12 months ending with 31 March in any year: Local Government Act 1972 s 270(1). As to the meaning of 'month' see PARA 11 note 1.

3 Local Government Act 1972 s 148(4) (substituted by SI 1991/1730). This provision does not apply to the council for a county for any financial year for which that council is, by virtue of the Local Government Act 1992 s 18(1) (repealed), a billing authority for that year for the purposes of Pt I (ss 1–69): Local Government Act 1972 s 148(5A) (as added: see note 2).

4 Local Government Act 1972 s 148(5)(a) (substituted by SI 1991/1730). Accounts must also be kept of receipts carried to, and payments made out of the collection fund and the general fund established under the Local Government Finance Act 1988 s 89 (see PARA 581) and s 91 (see PARA 579), in the case of a district or London borough: Local Government Act 1972 s 148(5)(b) (substituted by SI 1991/1730).

5 'Principal area' means a non-metropolitan county, a district or a London borough: see the Local Government Act 1972 s 270(1) (definition amended by the Local Government Act 1985 s 102, Sch 16 para 8).

6 Local Government Act 1972 s 148(5). For any financial year for which the council for a county is, by virtue of the Local Government Act 1992 s 18(1) (repealed), a billing authority for that year for the purposes of the Local Government Finance Act 1992 Pt I (ss 1–69), the Local Government Act 1972 s 148(5)(b) and not s 148(5)(a) (see the text to note 4) will apply in the case of the county: s 148(5B) (added by SI 1994/2825).

7 See the Local Government Finance Act 1988 s 91(8); and PARA 579.

(iii) Funds of Principal Councils in Wales

585. Funds of principal councils in Wales.

Each principal council[1] must establish, and then maintain, a fund to be known as its 'council fund'[2]. Any sums received by a principal council must be paid into its council fund[3], and all payments by a principal council must be made out of its council fund[4]. However, these provisions do not apply in relation to any sums to be paid into, or payments to be made out of, a trust fund[5].

Each principal council must keep accounts of sums paid into, and of payments made out of, its council fund[6]. Any account kept only in respect of the general expenses of a principal council is to be known as its 'general account' and any account kept only in respect of any class of its special expenses must be known as a 'special account'[7].

The Welsh Ministers[8] may make regulations[9]:

(1) requiring assets of a prescribed[10] description which fall within a council fund to be held in a separate fund within the council fund[11];

(2) requiring any fund (other than a trust fund) of a prescribed description which is established by a principal council to be maintained as a separate fund within its council fund[12].

The Welsh Ministers may by regulations:

(a) make provision with respect to the liability of principal councils to make payments from their council funds in respect of precepts issued[13] by precepting authorities[14];

(b) make provision for the sharing among a principal council and major precepting authorities[15], in accordance with rules specified in the regulations, of an amount equal to all or part of any deduction that[16] falls to be made in calculating the council's non-domestic rating contribution for a financial year[17].

Regulations under head (a) or (b) above may, in particular, include provision[18]:

(i) that anything falling to be paid must be paid within a prescribed period[19] and in instalments of such amounts, and at such times, as are determined by the billing authority[20] in accordance with prescribed rules[21];

(ii) that the billing authority must inform any precepting authorities when instalments will be paid and how they are to be calculated[22];

(iii) that if an instalment is not paid to a precepting authority in accordance with the regulations, it is to be entitled to interest on the amount of the instalment[23];

(iv) as to the circumstances in which the billing authority is to be treated as having discharged the liability mentioned in head (a) above or any liability arising under head (b) above[24];

(v) as to the recovery (by deduction or otherwise) of any excess amount paid by the billing authority to any precepting authority in purported discharge of the liability mentioned in head (a) above or any liability arising under head (b) above[25].

In relation to each financial year beginning in or after 1996 a billing authority must in accordance with its schedule of instalments[26] pay to its relevant precepting authorities[27] such amounts, if any, as will discharge its liabilities[28] for that financial year[29]. The requirement to make payments in accordance with a schedule of instalments does not apply where a substitute precept has been issued in relation to a financial year and that substitute precept has been issued on or after the day of the final instalment to be paid in accordance with the schedule of instalments for that financial year[30]. In such a case, any amounts to be paid by a billing authority in respect of its liability for that financial year which remain to be discharged immediately after the substitute precept is issued must be paid as soon as is reasonably practicable after the issue of that precept[31].

1 'Principal council' means a council elected for a county or county borough in Wales: see the Local Government Act 1972 s 270(1) (definition amended by the Local Government (Wales) Act 1994 s 1(8)) (definition applied by the Local Government (Wales) Act 1994 s 64(3)). As to the meaning of 'Wales' see PARA 2 note 16. As to local government areas and authorities in Wales see LOCAL GOVERNMENT vol 69 (2018) PARA 51 et seq.

2 See the Local Government (Wales) Act 1994 s 38(1). The Local Government Act 1972 s 101(1)(b) (delegation: see LOCAL GOVERNMENT vol 69 (2018) PARA 399) does not apply as regards the functions of a principal council in relation to its council fund: see the Local Government (Wales) Act 1994 s 38(5).

3 See the Local Government (Wales) Act 1994 s 38(2).

4 See the Local Government (Wales) Act 1994 s 38(3).

5 Local Government (Wales) Act 1994 s 38(4).

6 See the Local Government (Wales) Act 1994 s 38(6).

7 See the Local Government (Wales) Act 1994 s 38(7).

8 The functions of the Secretary of State under the Local Government (Wales) Act 1994 s 38, so far as exercisable in relation to Wales, were transferred to the National Assembly for Wales (see the National Assembly for Wales (Transfer of Functions) Order 1999, SI 1999/672, art 2, Sch 1) and are now vested in the Welsh Ministers (see the Government of Wales Act 2006 s 162(1), Sch 11 para 30). As to the Secretary of State and the Welsh Ministers see PARA 4 note 18.

9 At the date at which this volume states the law, no such regulations had been made.

10 'Prescribed' means prescribed by the regulations: see the Local Government (Wales) Act 1994 s 64(1).

11 Local Government (Wales) Act 1994 s 38(8)(a).

12 See the Local Government (Wales) Act 1994 s 38(8)(b).

13 Ie under the Local Government Finance Act 1992 Pt I Ch IV (ss 39–52): see PARA 11 et seq.

14 See the Local Government (Wales) Act 1994 s 38(9). As to the regulations made see the Local Authorities (Precepts) (Wales) Regulations 1995, SI 1995/2562: see the text to notes 27–31. As to precepts and precepting authorities see PARA 11 et seq.

15 As to the meaning of 'major precepting authority' see PARA 11 note 2 (definition applied by the Local Government (Wales) Act 1994 s 38(12) (added by the Local Government Act 2003 s 70(9))).

16 Ie in accordance with provision under the Local Government Finance Act 1988 Sch 8 para 4(4A) (local retention of rates): see PARA 75.

17 See the Local Government (Wales) Act 1994 s 38(9A) (added by the Local Government Act 2003 s 70(7)). 'Financial year' means the period of 12 months beginning with 1 April: Local Government (Wales) Act 1994 s 64(1). The functions under s 38(9A) were formerly vested in the National Assembly for Wales and are now exercisable by the Welsh Ministers by virtue of the Government of Wales Act 2006 s 162(1), Sch 11 paras 30, 32.

18 Local Government (Wales) Act 1994 s 38(10) (amended by the Local Government Act 2003 s 70(8)(a)).

19 Local Government (Wales) Act 1994 s 38(10)(a)(i).

20 As to billing authorities see PARA 346.

21 Local Government (Wales) Act 1994 s 38(10)(a)(ii).

22 Local Government (Wales) Act 1994 s 38(10)(b).

23 Local Government (Wales) Act 1994 s 38(10)(c).

24 Local Government (Wales) Act 1994 s 38(10)(d) (amended by the Local Government Act 2003 s 70(8)(b)).

25 Local Government (Wales) Act 1994 s 38(10)(e) (amended by the Local Government Act 2003 s 70(8)(b)).

26 'Schedule of instalments' is defined in the Local Authorities (Precepts) (Wales) Regulations 1995, SI 1995/2562, reg 2(1) as:

(1) a schedule determined, or to be determined, by a billing authority in accordance with the reg 4 and, where it applies, reg 6, with respect to the times for and the number and amounts of payments from its council fund in respect of its liabilities; and

(2) in relation to a financial year for which such a schedule has been so determined, means the schedule which currently has effect for that financial year.

As to the determination of schedules of instalments see reg 4, Schedule. As to the amendment of schedules of instalments see reg 6. As to information on schedules of instalments see reg 5.

27 'Relevant precepting authority', in relation to a billing authority, means the relevant major precepting authority and each relevant local precepting authority: Local Authorities (Precepts) (Wales) Regulations 1995, SI 1995/2562, reg 2(1). 'Relevant major precepting authority', in relation to a billing authority, means the police authority established under the Police Act 1964 s 3 (now repealed), having power to issue a precept to that billing authority: Local Authorities (Precepts) (Wales) Regulations 1995, SI 1995/2562, reg 2(1). 'Relevant local precepting authority', in relation to a billing authority, means any community council having power to issue a precept to that billing authority: reg 2(1). As to police authorities see POLICE AND INVESTIGATORY POWERS vol 84 (2013) PARA 55 et seq. As to community councils see LOCAL GOVERNMENT vol 69 (2018) PARA 63 et seq.

28 Any reference in the Local Authorities (Precepts) (Wales) Regulations 1995, SI 1995/2562 (however framed), to liability in relation to a billing authority is a reference to the liability of a billing authority to pay anything from its council fund in respect of any precept issued by a relevant precepting authority under the Local Government Finance Act 1992 Pt I Ch IV (ss 39–52) (see PARA 11 et seq), after taking into account any amount credited against that liability by that relevant precepting authority under s 42(4) (see PARA 23): Local Authorities (Precepts) (Wales) Regulations 1995, SI 1995/2562, reg 2(2).

29 Local Authorities (Precepts) (Wales) Regulations 1995, SI 1995/2562, reg 3(1). As to interest on instalments see regs 7, 8 (reg 8 amended by SI 2001/3649).

30 See the Local Authorities (Precepts) (Wales) Regulations 1995, SI 1995/2562, reg 3(2), (3).

31 Local Authorities (Precepts) (Wales) Regulations 1995, SI 1995/2562, reg 3(3). Any amount paid by a billing authority in respect of a liability for a financial year, whether or not paid in accordance with a schedule of instalments or in accordance with the provisions in reg 3(3), must be treated as discharging that liability to the extent of the payment: reg 3(4). For the purposes of reg 3(4), any amount paid which was treated as discharging a billing authority's liability, but was subsequently repaid or credited by the relevant precepting authority concerned under the Local Government Finance Act 1992 s 42(4) (see PARA 23), must, to the extent of the amount repaid or credited, cease to be treated as discharging that liability: Local Authorities (Precepts) (Wales) Regulations 1995, SI 1995/2562, reg 3(5).

(iv) The City Fund

586. The City fund.

The Common Council of the City of London[1] must establish, and then maintain, a fund (called 'the City fund')[2]. The City fund had to be established on 1 April 1990[3]. Any sum received by the Common Council of the City of London after 31 March 1990 must be paid into the City fund if it is not a sum which is to be paid into its collection fund[4] or a trust fund and:

(1) it is received in respect of the general rate, the poor rate or the St Botolph tithe rate[5]; or

(2) it would have fallen to be credited in aid of any of those rates had the Local Government Finance Act 1988 not been passed[6].

Any payment to be made by the Common Council of the City of London after 31 March 1990 must be met from the City fund if it is not a payment which is to be met from its collection fund or a trust fund and if, had the Local Government Finance Act 1988 not been passed, it would have fallen to be met out of:

(a) the general rate, the poor rate or the St Botolph tithe rate[7]; or

(b) sums which, had the Local Government Finance Act 1988 not been passed, would have fallen to be credited in aid of any of those rates[8].

No sum may be paid into, and no payment may be met from, the City fund except in accordance with these provisions[9].

The assets of the Common Council of the City of London subsisting immediately before 1 April 1990 had to be transferred to the City fund on that date if they were assets subsisting in respect of the general rate, the poor rate or the St Botolph tithe rate[10], or representing sums credited in aid of any of those rates[11].

The Secretary of State[12] may make regulations[13]:

(i) about the relationship of the City fund to other funds of the Common Council of the City of London[14];

(ii) providing for assets falling within the City fund to be held in separate funds within the City fund[15];

(iii) prohibiting the Common Council of the City of London from establishing funds[16].

The regulations may provide that:

(A) any fund established by the Common Council of the City of London on or after 1 April 1990, and falling within a prescribed[17] description, is to be maintained as a separate fund falling within the City fund[18];

(B) such assets as are transferred to the City fund[19] and fall within a prescribed description must be held in separate funds falling within the City fund; and the number and composition of the separate funds must be such as are prescribed[20];

(C) the Common Council of the City of London is not to establish or maintain on or after 1 April 1990 a fund into which both the following must or may be paid, namely, sums which must be paid into the City fund[21], and other sums[22];

(D) the Common Council of the City of London may not establish or maintain on or after 1 April 1990 a fund from which both the following must or may be met, namely, payments which must be met from the City fund[23], and other payments[24].

1 For these purposes the Inner Temple and the Middle Temple must be taken to fall within the area of the Common Council of the City of London: see the Local Government Finance Act 1988 s 146(5), (7). As to the Common Council of the City of London see LONDON GOVERNMENT vol 71 (2013) PARAS 34–38. As to the Inner and Middle Temples see LONDON GOVERNMENT vol 71 (2013) PARA 17.

2 See the Local Government Finance Act 1988 s 93(1).

3 Local Government Finance Act 1988 s 93(2).

4 As to collection funds see PARA 581.

5 Local Government Finance Act 1988 s 93(3)(a).

6 Local Government Finance Act 1988 s 93(3)(b).

7 Local Government Finance Act 1988 s 93(4)(a).

8 Local Government Finance Act 1988 s 93(4)(b).

9 Local Government Finance Act 1988 s 93(5). The provisions referred to are s 93(3), (4) (see the text to notes 4–8): see s 93(5).

10 Local Government Finance Act 1988 s 93(6)(a).

11 Local Government Finance Act 1988 s 93(6)(b).

12 As to the Secretary of State see PARA 4 note 18.

13 At the date at which this volume states the law, no such regulations had been made.

14 Local Government Finance Act 1988 s 94(1)(a).

15 Local Government Finance Act 1988 s 94(1)(b).

16 Local Government Finance Act 1988 s 94(1)(c).

17 'Prescribed' means prescribed by the regulations: see the Local Government Finance Act 1988 s 146(6), (7).

18 Local Government Finance Act 1988 s 94(2).

19 Ie under the Local Government Finance Act 1988 s 93(6): see the text to notes 10–11.

20 Local Government Finance Act 1988 s 94(3).

21 Ie under the Local Government Finance Act 1988 s 93(3): see the text to notes 4–6.

22 Local Government Finance Act 1988 s 94(4).

23 Ie under the Local Government Finance Act 1988 s 93(4): see the text to notes 7–8.

24 Local Government Finance Act 1988 s 94(5).

(v) Police Funds

587. Police funds.

Each elected local policing body must keep a fund to be known as the police fund[1]. All of an elected local policing body's receipts must be paid into the relevant police fund[2]; and all of an elected local policing body's expenditure must be paid out of the relevant police fund[3]. An elected local policing body must keep accounts of payments made into or out of the relevant police fund[4].

1 See the Police Reform and Social Responsibility Act 2011 s 21(1); and POLICE AND INVESTIGATORY POWERS vol 84 (2013) PARA 103.
2 See the Police Reform and Social Responsibility Act 2011 s 21(2); and POLICE AND INVESTIGATORY POWERS vol 84 (2013) PARA 103.
3 See the Police Reform and Social Responsibility Act 2011 s 21(3); and POLICE AND INVESTIGATORY POWERS vol 84 (2013) PARA 103.
4 See the Police Reform and Social Responsibility Act 2011 s 21(4); and POLICE AND INVESTIGATORY POWERS vol 84 (2013) PARA 103.

(2) Accounts and Audit

(i) In Relation to England

A. IN GENERAL

588. General requirements for accounts and audit.

The Local Audit and Accountability Act 2014 abolished the Audit Commission for Local Authorities and the National Health Service in England and the existing audit regime under the Audit Commission Act 1998[1]. The Local Audit and Accountability Act 2014 makes, inter alia, provision about the accounts of local and certain other public authorities and the auditing of those accounts[2]. Under the new regime, a relevant authority[3], other than a health service body[4], must keep adequate accounting records[5], and must prepare a statement of accounts[6] in respect of each financial year[7].

The accounts of a relevant authority for a financial year must be audited in accordance with the Local Audit and Accountability Act 2014 and provision made under it, and by an auditor (a 'local auditor') appointed in accordance with the Local Audit and Accountability Act 2014 or provision made under it[8].

1 See the Local Audit and Accountability Act 2014 s 1, Sch 1.
2 See PARAS 589, 592 et seq, 590 et seq. The Local Audit and Accountability Act 2014 does not apply to the accounts of a local government body in Wales. As to accounts and auditing in relation to Wales see PARA 615 et seq. As to the meaning of 'Wales' see PARA 2 note 16.
3 'Relevant authority' means a person or body listed in the Local Audit and Accountability Act 2014 Sch 2: s 2(1). Those persons or bodies are the following:
   (1) a county council in England (Sch 2 para 1);
   (2) a district council (Sch 2 para 2);
   (3) a London borough council (Sch 2 para 3);
   (4) a parish council (Sch 2 para 4);
   (5) a joint authority established under the Local Government Act 1985 Pt IV (ss 23–42) (see LOCAL GOVERNMENT vol 69 (2018) PARAS 71, 72) (Local Audit and Accountability Act 2014 Sch 2 para 5);
   (6) a Passenger Transport Executive (Sch 2 para 6);
   (7) the Greater London Authority (Sch 2 para 7);
   (8) a functional body (Sch 2 para 8);

(9) the London Pensions Fund Authority (Sch 2 para 9);
(10) the London Waste and Recycling Board (Sch 2 para 10);
(11) the Common Council of the City of London (Sch 2 para 11);
(12) a parish meeting (Sch 2 para 12);
(13) the Council of the Isles of Scilly (Sch 2 para 13);
(14) charter trustees (Sch 2 para 14);
(15) port health authority for a port health district that is wholly in England (Sch 2 para 15);
(16) the Broads Authority (Sch 2 para 16);
(17) a National Park authority for a National Park in England (Sch 2 para 17);
(18) a conservation board established by order of the Secretary of State under the Countryside and Rights of Way Act 2000 s 86 (see OPEN SPACES AND COUNTRYSIDE vol 78 (2010) PARA 660 (Local Audit and Accountability Act 2014 Sch 2 para 18);
(19) a police and crime commissioner for a police area in England (Sch 2 para 19);
(20) a chief constable for an area in England (Sch 2 para 20);
(21) the Commissioner of Police of the Metropolis (Sch 2 para 21);
(22) a fire and rescue authority in England constituted by a scheme under the Fire and Rescue Services Act 2004 s 2 or a scheme to which s 4 of that Act applies (see FIRE AND RESCUE SERVICES vol 51 (2013) PARAS 18–20) (Local Audit and Accountability Act 2014 Sch 2 para 22);
(23) a fire and rescue authority created by an order under the Fire and Rescue Services Act 2004 s 4A (Local Audit and Accountability Act 2014 Sch 2 para 22A (added by the Policing and Crime Act 2017 s 6, Sch 1 para 97(1), (2)));
(24) a clinical commissioning group (Local Audit and Accountability Act 2014 Sch 2 para 23);
(25) special trustees for a hospital (Sch 2 para 24 (repealed, as from a day to be appointed, by the NHS (Charitable Trusts Etc) Act 2016 s 1(9), Sch 1 paras 17, 18(i); at the date at which this volume states the law, no such day had been appointed));
(26) an internal drainage board for an internal drainage district that is wholly in England (Local Audit and Accountability Act 2014 Sch 2 para 26);
(27) an economic prosperity board established under the Local Democracy, Economic Development and Construction Act 2009 s 88 (see TRADE AND INDUSTRY vol 97 (2015) PARA 1086) (Local Audit and Accountability Act 2014 Sch 2 para 27);
(28) a combined authority (Sch 2 para 28);
(29) a sub-national transport body (Sch 2 para 28A (added by the Cities and Local Government Devolution Act 2016 s 23(1), Sch 5 para 37(1), (4));
(30) any person or body exercising functions in relation to an area wholly in England or partly in England and partly in Wales (Local Audit and Accountability Act 2014 Sch 2 para 29):
    (a) which was originally subject to audit provisions contained in an enactment passed before the Audit Commission Act 1998 (Local Audit and Accountability Act 2014 Sch 2 para 29(a)); and
    (b) to which the audit provisions of that Act applied by virtue of Sch 4 para 4(1) or 7 immediately before the repeal of s 2(1) by the Local Audit and Accountability Act 2014 (Sch 2 para 29(b)).

Note: The Local Audit and Accountability Act 2014 applies to the Common Council only to the extent that it exercises functions in relation to the collection fund of the Common Council, the City Fund or a pension fund maintained and administered by the Common Council under regulations under the Public Service Pensions Act 2013 s 1: Local Audit and Accountability Act 2014 Sch 2 item 11 note. The Local Audit and Accountability Act 2014 applies to special trustees for a hospital only if the trust of which they are trustees is not a charitable trust: Sch 2 item 24 note (added by SI 2015/975).

'Functional body' means a functional body within the meaning of the Greater London Authority Act 1999 s 424(1) (see LONDON GOVERNMENT vol 71 (2013) PARA 148): Local Audit and Accountability Act 2014 s 44(1). 'Parish meeting' means a parish meeting of a parish which does not have a separate parish council: s 44(1). 'Charter trustees' means charter trustees constituted under the Local Government Act 1972 s 246, by the Charter Trustees Regulations 1996, SI 1996/263, or under the Local Government and Public Involvement in Health Act 2007 Pt 1 (ss 1–30) (see LOCAL GOVERNMENT vol 69 (2018) PARA 144): Local Audit and Accountability Act 2014 s 44(1). 'Chief constable' means a chief constable for a police force for a police area; and 'police area' means a police area listed in the Police Act 1996 Sch 1 (police areas outside London) (see POLICE AND INVESTIGATORY POWERS vol 84 (2013) PARA 52 et seq): Local Audit and Accountability Act 2014 s 44(1). 'Area', in relation to a chief constable, means the police area of the chief constable's police force; and in relation to a clinical commissioning group, means the area specified in the group's constitution (see the National Health Service Act 2006 Sch 1A): Local Audit and Accountability Act 2014 s 44(1). 'Combined authority' means a combined authority established under the Local Democracy, Economic Development and Construction Act 2009 s 103 (see TRADE AND INDUSTRY vol 97 (2015) PARA 1092): Local Audit and Accountability Act 2014 s 44(1).

As to local government areas and authorities in England see LOCAL GOVERNMENT vol 69 (2018) PARA 36 et seq. As to the meaning of 'England' see PARA 2 note 16. As to the Greater London Authority see LONDON GOVERNMENT vol 71 (2013) PARA 67 et seq. As to Passenger Transport Executives see ROAD TRAFFIC vol 89 (2011) PARA 47. As to the Broads Authority see WATER AND WATERWAYS vol 101 (2009) PARA 734. As to the Common Council of the City of London see LONDON GOVERNMENT vol 71 (2013) PARAS 34–38. As to police and crime commissioners see POLICE AND INVESTIGATORY POWERS vol 84 (2013) PARA 56 et seq. As to clinical commissioning groups see HEALTH SERVICES vol 54 (2017) PARA 35 As to special trustees see HEALTH SERVICES vol 54 (2017) PARA 89 As to internal drainage boards see WATER AND WATERWAYS vol 101 (2009) PARA 569 et seq. As to collection funds see PARA 581. As to the City fund see PARA 586.

The application of the Local Audit and Accountability Act 2014 to a relevant authority is subject to any note forming part of the entry for that authority in Sch 2: s 2(2). The Secretary of State may by regulations amend Sch 2 by adding, modifying or removing an entry relating to a relevant authority: s 2(3). Regulations under s 2(3) may add an entry relating to a person or body to Sch 2 only if that person or body exercises functions of a public nature in relation to an area which is either wholly in England or partly in England and partly in Wales: s 2(4). The Secretary of State may by regulations or order make provision about the application of the Local Audit and Accountability Act 2014 or provision made under it to a person or body that comes to fall within Sch 2 (whether or not as a result of regulations under s 2(3)): s 2(5). The power in s 2(5) includes power:

(i) to amend the Local Audit and Accountability Act 2014 or provision made under it in its application to that person or body (s 2(6)(a)); or
(ii) to make provision for the Act or provision made under it to apply to that person or body with modifications (s 2(6)(b)).

A statutory instrument containing regulations under s 2(3) and regulations or an order under s 2(5) (whether alone or with other provision) may not be made unless a draft of the instrument has been laid before and approved by a resolution of each House of Parliament: s 43(3), (4)(a), (b). If a draft of a statutory instrument containing regulations or an order under s 2 would, apart from this provision, be treated for the purposes of the standing orders of either House of Parliament as a hybrid instrument (see STATUTES AND LEGISLATIVE PROCESS vol 96 (2012) PARA 1057), it is to proceed in that House as if it were not such an instrument: s 43(7). As to the Secretary of State see PARA 4 note 18.

4 'Health service body' means (Local Audit and Accountability Act 2014 ss 3(9), 44(1)):
(1) a clinical commissioning group (Local Audit and Accountability Act 2014 s 3(9)(a));
(2) special trustees appointed as mentioned in the National Health Service Act 2006 s 212(1) (special trustees for a university hospital or teaching hospital) for a hospital in England (referred to in the Local Audit and Accountability Act 2014 as 'special trustees for a hospital') (s 3(9)(b); repealed, as from a day to be appointed, by the NHS (Charitable Trusts Etc) Act 2016 s 1(9), Sch 1 paras 17, 18(a); at the date at which this volume states the law, no such day had been appointed).

See HEALTH SERVICES vol 54 (2017) PARA 35, 89.

5 Local Audit and Accountability Act 2014 s 3(1). 'Adequate accounting records' means records that are sufficient:
(1) to show and explain the relevant authority's transactions (Local Audit and Accountability Act 2014 s 3(2)(a));
(2) to disclose at any time, with reasonable accuracy, the financial position of the authority at that time (s 3(2)(b)); and
(3) to enable the authority to ensure that any statements of accounts required to be prepared by the authority comply with the requirements imposed by or under the Local Audit and Accountability Act 2014 (s 3(2)(c)).

6 In the Local Audit and Accountability Act 2014, references to accounts are to be construed in accordance with the following provisions: ss 4(2), 44(1). In relation to a relevant authority which is not a health service body, 'accounts' means:
(1) the authority's accounting records (s 4(3)(a)); and

(2) the authority's statement of accounts (s 4(3)(b)).

In relation to a clinical commissioning group, 'accounts' means:

(a) the annual accounts of the group prepared under the National Health Service Act 2006 Sch 1A para 17(2) (accounts and audit of clinical commissioning groups) (Local Audit and Accountability Act 2014 s 4(4)(a));

(b) any accounts of the group prepared under the National Health Service Act 2006 Sch 1A para 17(3) in respect of which a direction has been given under Sch 1A para 17(5) (see HEALTH SERVICES vol 54 (2017) PARA 162) (Local Audit and Accountability Act 2014 s 4(4)(b)).

In relation to special trustees for a hospital, 'accounts' means the annual accounts of the trustees prepared under the National Health Service Act 2006 Sch 15 para 3: Local Audit and Accountability Act 2014 s 4(5) (repealed, as from a day to be appointed, by the NHS (Charitable Trusts Etc) Act 2016 s 1(9), Sch 1 paras 17, 18(b); at the date at which this volume states the law, no such day had been appointed).

7 Local Audit and Accountability Act 2014 s 3(3). 'Financial year' means a period of 12 months ending with 31 March: s 3(4). The Secretary of State may by regulations:

(1) make provision for the financial year of a relevant authority, other than a health service body, for the purposes of the Local Audit and Accountability Act 2014 to be such period as is specified in the regulations (s 3(5)(a));

(2) make provision for any requirement in s 3 not to apply, or to apply with modifications, in relation to the relevant authorities, other than health service bodies, specified or described in the regulations (s 3(5)(b)).

Regulations under s 3(5)(a) may:

(a) amend the Local Audit and Accountability Act 2014 or provision made under it in its application to a relevant authority to which the regulations apply (s 3(6)(a)); or

(b) provide for that Act or provision made under it to apply in relation to such a relevant authority with modifications (s 3(6)(b)).

Regulations under s 3(5)(a) may make provision in relation to:

(i) all relevant authorities (other than health service bodies) (s 3(7)(a));

(ii) the relevant authorities specified or described in the regulations (s 3(7)(b)).

Section 32 enables the Secretary of State by regulations to make further provision about accounting records and statements of accounts: s 3(8); see PARA 605.

8 Local Audit and Accountability Act 2014 s 4(1).

589. Modification of audits of accounts of smaller authorities.

The Secretary of State[1] may by regulations provide for the audit of the accounts[2] of smaller authorities[3]. Such regulations may, in particular, provide for any provision of or made under the Local Audit and Accountability Act 2014 not to apply, or to apply with modifications, in relation to smaller authorities[4].

Regulations under these provisions may, in particular:

(1) provide for the appointment, by a person specified by the Secretary of State, of a local auditor in relation to the audit of the accounts of a smaller authority[5];

(2) make provision about the persons that may be specified by the Secretary of State[6];

(3) make provision about the procedure for specifying a person and for a person's specification to come to an end in specified circumstances[7];

(4) make provision about the consequences of a person's specification coming to an end, including for the exercise of functions by the Secretary of State and the transfer of the person's rights and liabilities arising by virtue of the regulations to the Secretary of State or another specified person[8];

(5) confer functions on a specified person[9], including in relation to:

   (a) the appointment of local auditors under the regulations[10];

   (b) the activities of such auditors[11]; and

   (c) the resignation or removal from office of such auditors[12];

(6) require a specified person to consult such persons as are specified in the regulations before exercising specified functions[13];

(7) make provision for the appointment of a local auditor in relation to the accounts of a smaller authority to which arrangements within head (1) apply where the specified person does not make an appointment under the regulations (and in particular for such an appointment to be made by the authority or the Secretary of State)[14].

Regulations may, in particular:

(i) make provision about the smaller authorities to which arrangements within head (1) above apply, including provision for them to apply to an authority that has opted into them or has not opted out of them[15];

(ii) make provision about the procedures to be followed in relation to opting into or out of those arrangements[16];

(iii) impose duties on smaller authorities to which those arrangements apply[17], including duties as to:

(A) the payment of fees to a specified person[18]; and

(B) the provision of information to a specified person[19];

(iv) make provision for the making of payments, in specified circumstances and by the smaller authorities to which those arrangements apply, to a fund of a specified kind for the purposes of meeting local auditors' costs of a specified kind[20].

Regulations may, in particular:

(I) make provision about the eligibility of a person to be appointed as a local auditor of the accounts of a smaller authority[21];

(II) make provision about the functions of a local auditor in relation to the accounts of a smaller authority[22];

(III) provide that, in specified circumstances, the accounts of a smaller authority of a specified description are to be exempt from specified audit requirements[23];

(IV) make provision for an exemption under head (III) not to apply or to cease to apply to an authority in specified circumstances[24].

1 As to the Secretary of State see PARA 4 note 18. The Local Audit and Accountability Act 2014 s 32 does not apply to the accounts of a local government body in Wales. As to accounts and audit regulations in relation to Wales see PARA 653. As to the meaning of 'Wales' see PARA 2 note 16.

2 As to the meaning of 'accounts' see PARA 588 note 6.

3 Local Audit and Accountability Act 2014 s 5(1). A relevant authority is a 'smaller authority' for a financial year if:

(1) where that year is the year in which the authority was established, the qualifying condition is met for that year (s 6(1)(a));

(2) where that year is the year following that in which the authority was established, the qualifying condition is met for that year or the previous year (s 6(1)(b)); and

(3) where that year is the second or any subsequent year following that in which the authority was established, the qualifying condition is met for that year or either of the two previous years (s 6(1)(c)).

The qualifying condition is met for a relevant authority and a financial year if the higher of the authority's gross income for the year and its gross expenditure for the year does not exceed £6·5 million: s 6(2). For the purpose of determining, at a time when a relevant authority's gross income or expenditure for a financial year cannot be accurately determined, whether s 6(2) applies or will apply to the authority, that provision is to be read as referring to the authority's estimated gross income or expenditure (as the case may be): s 6(3). The Secretary of State may by regulations make provision about the application of the Local Audit and Accountability Act 2014 (including in its application by virtue of s 5) or any provision made under it in a case where:

(a) an authority is treated as a smaller authority for a financial year (s 6(4)(a)); and

(b) the authority was not in fact a smaller authority for that year (s 6(4)(b)).

The Secretary of State may by regulations amend s 6: s 6(5).

As to the meaning of 'relevant authority' see PARA 588 note 3. As to the meaning of 'financial year' see PARA 588 note 7. As to regulations made under s 5 see the Local Audit (Smaller Authorities) Regulations 2015, SI 2015/184.

4 Local Audit and Accountability Act 2014 s 5(2). Section 5(2) applies to a provision of or made under the Local Audit and Accountability Act 2014 even if it makes specific provision about a smaller authority to which the regulations apply: s 5(3).
5 Local Audit and Accountability Act 2014 s 5(4)(a).
6 Local Audit and Accountability Act 2014 s 5(4)(b).
7 Local Audit and Accountability Act 2014 s 5(4)(c). In s 5 'specified' (except in the expressions 'person specified by the Secretary of State' and 'specified person') means specified in regulations under s 5(1): s 5(9).
8 Local Audit and Accountability Act 2014 s 5(4)(d).
9 Local Audit and Accountability Act 2014 s 5(4).
10 Local Audit and Accountability Act 2014 s 5(4)(e)(i).
11 Local Audit and Accountability Act 2014 s 5(4)(e)(ii).
12 Local Audit and Accountability Act 2014 s 5(4)(e)(iii).
13 Local Audit and Accountability Act 2014 s 5(4)(f).
14 Local Audit and Accountability Act 2014 s 5(4)(g).
15 Local Audit and Accountability Act 2014 s 5(5)(a).
16 Local Audit and Accountability Act 2014 s 5(5)(b).
17 Local Audit and Accountability Act 2014 s 5(5)(c).
18 Local Audit and Accountability Act 2014 s 5(5)(c)(i). Provision made by regulations under s 5(1) by virtue of s 5(5)(c)(i) may, in particular:
  (1) provide for fees to be paid in accordance with a scale or scales of fees determined by a specified person (s 5(6)(a)); and
  (2) provide for the payment in specified circumstances of a larger or smaller fee than is set out in the appropriate scale (s 5(6)(b)).
19 Local Audit and Accountability Act 2014 s 5(5)(c)(ii).
20 Local Audit and Accountability Act 2014 s 5(5)(d).
21 Local Audit and Accountability Act 2014 s 5(7)(a).
22 Local Audit and Accountability Act 2014 s 5(7)(b).
23 Local Audit and Accountability Act 2014 s 5(8)(a).
24 Local Audit and Accountability Act 2014 s 5(8)(b).

590. Accounting practices.

The appropriate national authority[1] may by regulations[2] make provision about the accounting practices to be followed by a local authority[3], in particular with respect to the charging of expenditure to a revenue account[4].

The appropriate national authority may issue guidance about the accounting practices to be followed by a local authority, in particular with respect to the charging of expenditure to a revenue account[5]. A local authority must have regard to any such guidance issued to it[6].

1 Ie the Secretary of State or, in relation to Wales, the Welsh Ministers. In its application to Wales, the Local Government Act 2003 ss 21, 22 have effect as if for any reference to the Secretary of State there were substituted a reference to the Welsh Ministers: see s 24(1) (numbered as such and amended by the Local Government and Public Involvement in Health Act 2007 s 238(3)). The Local Government Act 2003 s 24(1) does not apply to s 21 to the extent that it confers functions on the Secretary of State in relation to a person or body that is a relevant authority for the purposes of the Local Audit and Accountability Act 2014 (see PARA 588 note 3), and exercises functions in relation to an area that is partly in England and partly in Wales: s 24(1A) (added by the Local Audit and Accountability Act 2014 s 45, Sch 12 paras 49, 52).

As to the Secretary of State and the Welsh Ministers see PARA 4 note 18. As to the meaning of 'Wales' see PARA 2 note 16.

2 As to the regulations made see the Local Authorities (Capital Finance and Accounting) (England) Regulations 2003, SI 2003/3146 (amended by SI 2004/534, SI 2004/3055, SI 2006/521, SI 2007/573, SI 2008/414, SI 2009/321, SI 2010/454, SI 2012/711, SI 2012/265, SI 2012/1324, SI 2012/2269, SI 2013/472, SI 2013/476, SI 2013/1751, SI 2014/1375, SI 2015/341 and SI 2017/536); and the Local Authorities (Capital Finance and Accounting) (Wales) Regulations 2003, SI 2003/3239 (amended by SI 2004/1010, SI 2006/944, SI 2007/1051, SI 2008/588, SI 2009/560, SI 2010/685, SI 2014/481; SI 2016/102; and SI 2018/325).

3 In the Local Government Act 2003 ss 21, 22, 'local authority' includes the following (ss 21(6), 22(3) (substituted by the Local Audit and Accountability Act 2014 s 45, Sch 12 paras 49, 50(1), (3), 51)):

(1) a parish council (Local Government Act 2003 ss 21(6)(a), 22(3)(a) (as so substituted));
(2) a parish meeting of a parish which does not have a separate parish council (ss 21(6)(b), 22(3)(b) (as so substituted));
(3) a community council (ss 21(6)(c), 22(3)(c) (as so substituted));
(4) a Passenger Transport Executive (ss 21(6)(d), 22(3)(d) (as so substituted));
(5) the London Waste and Recycling Board (ss 21(6)(e), 22(3)(e) (as so substituted));
(6) charter trustees (within the meaning of the Local Audit and Accountability Act 2014: see PARA 588 note 3) (Local Government Act 2003 ss 21(6)(f), 22(3)(f) (as so substituted));
(7) a port health authority for a port health district that is wholly in England (ss 21(6)(g), 22(3)(g) (as so substituted));
(8) a conservation board established by order of the Secretary of State under the Countryside and Rights of Way Act 2000 s 86 (see OPEN SPACES AND COUNTRYSIDE vol 78 (2010) PARA 660) (Local Government Act 2003 ss 21(6)(h), 22(3)(h) (as so substituted));
(9) a chief constable for a police force for a police area in England (ss 21(6)(i), 22(3)(i) (as so substituted));
(10) the Commissioner of Police of the Metropolis (ss 21(6)(j), 22(3)(j) (as so substituted));
(11) an internal drainage board for an internal drainage district (ss 21(6)(k), 22(3)(k) (as so substituted)):
    (a) wholly in England (ss 21(6)(k)(i), 22(3)(k)(i) (as so substituted)); or
    (b) partly in England and partly in Wales (ss 21(6)(k)(ii), 22(3)(k)(ii) (as so substituted)); and
(12) any other person or body which for the time being is a relevant authority for the purposes of the Local Audit and Accountability Act 2014 (see PARA 588 note 3) (Local Government Act 2003 ss 21(6)(l), 22(3)(l) (as so substituted)) and:
    (a) is not listed in heads (1)–(11) above or the Local Government Act 2003 s 23(1) (see PARA 563 note 1) (ss 21(6)(l)(i), 22(3)(l)(i) (as so substituted));
    (b) is not a health service body (within the meaning of the Local Audit and Accountability Act 2014: see PARA 588 note 4) (Local Government Act 2003 ss 21(6)(l)(ii), 22(3)(l)(ii) (as so substituted));
    (c) is not specified in regulations under the Local Government Act 2003 s 23(2) (ss 21(6)(l)(iii), 22(3)(l)(iii) (as so substituted)); and
    (d) does not fall within a class of bodies so specified (ss 21(6)(l)(iv), 22(3)(l)(iv) (as so substituted)).

As to the meaning of 'local authority' generally see PARA 563 note 1. As to parish councils see LOCAL GOVERNMENT vol 69 (2018) PARA 41 et seq. As to community councils see LOCAL GOVERNMENT vol 69 (2018) PARA 63 et seq. As to Passenger Transport Executives see ROAD TRAFFIC vol 89 (2011) PARA 47. As to port health authorities see ENVIRONMENTAL QUALITY AND PUBLIC HEALTH vol 45 (2010) PARA 102. As to police and crime commissioners see POLICE AND INVESTIGATORY POWERS vol 84 (2013) PARA 56 et seq. As to internal drainage boards see WATER AND WATERWAYS vol 101 (2009) PARA 569 et seq.

4 Local Government Act 2003 s 21(1). References to a 'revenue account', in relation to a local authority, are to one of the following accounts for a financial year of the authority:

(1) a revenue account which the authority is required to keep by virtue of any enactment (s 22(1)(a));
(2) a revenue account which the authority is required to keep in order to comply with proper practices (s 22(1)(b));
(3) any other revenue account which the authority decides to keep in accordance with proper practices (s 22(1)(c)).

As to the meaning of 'financial year' see PARA 16 note 9.

Section 22 has effect for the purposes of:

(a) the Local Government and Housing Act 1989 (Local Government Act 2003 s 22(2)(a));
(b) any enactment passed after or in the same session as that Act (Local Government Act 2003 s 22(2)(b)); and
(c) any earlier enactment amended by that Act or an enactment falling within head (b) (Local Government Act 2003 s 22(2)(c)).

In any enactment contained in the Local Government Act 2003, any Act passed after or in the same session as that Act, the Local Government and Housing Act 1989, the Local Government Finance Act 1992, the Greater London Authority Act 1999, and subordinate legislation (within the meaning of the Interpretation Act 1978: see PARA 111 note 1) whenever made (see the Local Government Act 2003 s 21(2), (4) (amended by the Localism Act 2011 s 73; and the Local Audit and Accountability Act 2014 s 45, Sch 12 paras 49, 50(1), (2))), reference to 'proper practices', in relation to accounts of a local authority, is to those accounting practices:

(i) which the authority is required to follow by virtue of any enactment (Local Government Act 2003 s 21(2)(a)); or
(ii) which are contained in a code of practice or other document which is identified for the purposes of this provision by regulations made by the appropriate national authority (s 21(2)(b)).

In the event of conflict between practices falling within head (i) above and practices falling within head (ii) above, only those falling within head (i) are to be regarded as proper practices: s 21(3). The power under head (ii) is not to be read as limited to the identification of an existing document: s 21(5).

5 Local Government Act 2003 s 21(1A) (s 21(1A), (1B) added by the Local Government and Public Involvement in Health Act 2007 s 238(2)).
6 Local Government Act 2003 s 21(1B) (as added: see note 5).

B. LOCAL AUDITORS AND AUDITOR PANELS

591. Appointment of local auditor.

A relevant authority[1] must ensure that it has appointed a local auditor or local auditors to audit its accounts[2] for a financial year[3] not later than 31 December in the preceding financial year[4]. A relevant authority may appoint a local auditor to audit its accounts for more than one financial year[5]; and in such a case:

(1) the requirement to ensure that it has appointed a local auditor does not apply in relation to the second or any subsequent year for which the appointment is made[6]; but
(2) the authority must make a further appointment of a local auditor at least once every five years[7].

Two or more local auditors may be appointed to audit the accounts of a relevant authority[8], and those auditors may be appointed:

(a) to act jointly in relation to some or all parts of the accounts[9];
(b) to act separately in relation to different parts of the accounts[10];
(c) to carry out different functions in relation to the audit[11].

If, as a result of an appointment under head (b) or (c), a function under the Local Audit and Accountability Act 2014 may be exercised by two or more local auditors:

(i) it may be exercised by both or all of them acting jointly or by such one or more of them as they may determine[12]; and
(ii) references (however expressed) to the local auditor by whom the function is or has been exercised are to the auditors by whom it is or has been exercised[13].

A relevant authority must consult and take into account the advice of its auditor panel on the selection and appointment of a local auditor and, within the period of 28 days beginning with the day on which the appointment is made, must publish a notice about the appointment[14]. The relevant authority must, within the period of 28 days beginning with the day on which the appointment is made, publish a notice[15] that:

(A) states that it has made the appointment[16];
(B) identifies the local auditor that has been appointed[17];
(C) specifies the period for which the local auditor has been appointed[18];

(D) sets out the advice, or a summary of the advice, of its auditor panel about the selection and appointment of a local auditor[19]; and

(E) if it has not followed that advice, sets out the reasons why it has not done so[20].

The notice must be published, if the relevant authority has a website, on its website[21]; otherwise, in accordance with the following provisions[22]. A relevant authority publishes a notice as required if it does not have a website:

(I) in the case of a relevant authority other than a health service body[23], if it publishes the notice in such manner as it thinks is likely to bring the notice to the attention of persons who live in its area[24];

(II) in the case of a clinical commissioning group, if it publishes the notice in such manner as it thinks is likely to bring the notice to the attention of persons who live in the area of the group and persons who do not live in the area of the group but for whom the group is responsible[25];

(III) in the case of special trustees for a hospital, they publish the notice in such manner as they think is likely to bring the notice to the attention of persons to whom services are provided at that hospital[26].

The relevant authority must exclude from the notice information whose disclosure would prejudice commercial confidentiality, unless there is an overriding public interest in favour of its disclosure[27].

If a relevant authority, other than a clinical commissioning group, fails to appoint a local auditor[28], the authority must immediately inform the Secretary of State[29], who may direct the authority to appoint a specified auditor or may appoint a local auditor on behalf of the authority[30]. The Secretary of State must:

(AA) inform the relevant authority of the intention to give a direction or appoint a local auditor not less than 28 days before the direction is given or the appointment made[31]; and

(BB) consider any representations made by the relevant authority regarding the proposed direction or appointment[32].

However, the Secretary of State may give a direction or make an appointment without having complied with heads (AA) and (BB) if the Secretary of State thinks it is likely that a local auditor would have to exercise a function under the Local Audit and Accountability Act 2014 in relation to a relevant authority within the period of 60 days beginning with the day on which the direction is given or the appointment is made[33].

When a clinical commissioning group fails to appoint an auditor a similar procedure applies, but with the involvement of the National Health Service Commissioning Board[34].

The Secretary of State may by regulations make provision for the appointment, by a person specified by the Secretary of State, of a local auditor to audit the accounts of a relevant authority[35].

1 As to the meaning of 'relevant authority' see PARA 588 note 3.

2 As to the meaning of 'accounts' see PARA 588 note 6.

3 As to the meaning of 'financial year' see PARA 588 note 7.

4 Local Audit and Accountability Act 2014 s 7(1). Schedule 3 makes further provision in relation to specific types of relevant authorities and empowers the Secretary of State to make provision about the appointment of a local auditor to audit the accounts of a specified relevant authority or relevant authority of a specified description. Section 7 is subject to Sch 3 and provision made under it: s 7(8). As to the Secretary of State see PARA 4 note 18.

A local auditor appointed under s 7:

(1) must be eligible for appointment as a local auditor (see Pt 4 (s 18), Sch 5; and PARA 595) (s 7(5)(a)); and

(2) must not be prohibited from acting as a local auditor of the accounts of the relevant authority by virtue of the Companies Act 2006 s 1214 (independence requirement) as it has effect by virtue of the Local Audit and Accountability Act 2014 Sch 5 (s 7(5)(b)).

The Local Audit and Accountability Act 2014 does not apply to the accounts of a local government body in Wales. As to accounts and audit regulations in relation to Wales see PARA 653. As to the meaning of 'Wales' see PARA 2 note 16.

5 Local Audit and Accountability Act 2014 s 7(2).
6 Local Audit and Accountability Act 2014 s 7(2)(a).
7 Local Audit and Accountability Act 2014 s 7(2)(b). This does not prevent the relevant authority from re-appointing a local auditor: s 7(3). The Secretary of State may by regulations amend s 7(2)(b) so as to alter the period for the time being specified in it: s 7(4).
8 Local Audit and Accountability Act 2014 s 7(6).
9 Local Audit and Accountability Act 2014 s 7(6)(a).
10 Local Audit and Accountability Act 2014 s 7(6)(b).
11 Local Audit and Accountability Act 2014 s 7(6)(c).
12 Local Audit and Accountability Act 2014 s 7(7)(a).
13 Local Audit and Accountability Act 2014 s 7(7)(b).
14 Local Audit and Accountability Act 2014 s 8(1). As to auditor panels see PARA 592. Section 8 is subject to Sch 3 (further provision about appointment of local auditors) and provision made under it: s 8(6).
15 Local Audit and Accountability Act 2014 s 8(2).
16 Local Audit and Accountability Act 2014 s 8(2)(a).
17 Local Audit and Accountability Act 2014 s 8(2)(b).
18 Local Audit and Accountability Act 2014 s 8(2)(c).
19 Local Audit and Accountability Act 2014 s 8(2)(d).
20 Local Audit and Accountability Act 2014 s 8(2)(e).
21 Local Audit and Accountability Act 2014 s 8(3)(a).
22 Local Audit and Accountability Act 2014 s 8(3)(b).
23 As to the meaning of 'health service body' see PARA 588 note 4.
24 Local Audit and Accountability Act 2014 s 8(4)(a).
25 Local Audit and Accountability Act 2014 s 8(4)(b).
26 Local Audit and Accountability Act 2014 s 8(4)(c) (repealed, as from a day to be appointed, by the NHS (Charitable Trusts Etc) Act 2016 s 1(9), Sch 1 paras 17, 18(c); at the date at which this volume states the law, no such day had been appointed). As to special trustees see HEALTH SERVICES vol 54 (2017) PARA 89
27 Local Audit and Accountability Act 2014 s 8(5).
28 Ie in accordance with the Local Audit and Accountability Act 2014 Pt 3 (ss 7–17).
29 Local Audit and Accountability Act 2014 s 12(1). As to clinical commissioning groups see HEALTH SERVICES vol 54 (2017) PARA 35.
30 See the Local Audit and Accountability Act 2014 s 12(2). An appointment under s 12(2)(b) by the Secretary of State takes effect as if it had been made by the relevant authority and on such terms as the Secretary of State may direct: s 12(3).
31 Local Audit and Accountability Act 2014 s 12(4)(a).
32 Local Audit and Accountability Act 2014 s 12(4)(b).
33 Local Audit and Accountability Act 2014 s 12(5).
34 See the Local Audit and Accountability Act 2014 s 13. As to the National Health Service Commissioning Board see HEALTH SERVICES vol 54 (2017) PARA 32
35 See the Local Audit and Accountability Act 2014 s 17(1). Such regulations may, in particular:
   (1) make provision about the persons that may be specified as an appointing person (s 17(2)(a));
   (2) make provision about the procedure for specifying a person and for an appointing person's specification to come to an end in prescribed circumstances (s 17(2)(b));
   (3) make provision about the consequences of an appointing person's specification coming to an end, including:
      (a) for the exercise of functions by the Secretary of State (s 17(2)(c)(i)); and
      (b) for the transfer of the person's rights and liabilities arising by virtue of the regulations to the Secretary of State or another appointing person (s 17(2)(c)(ii));
   (4) confer functions on an appointing person, including in relation to:
      (a) the appointment of local auditors under the regulations (s 17(2)(d)(i));
      (b) the activities of such auditors (s 17(2)(d)(ii)); and
      (c) the resignation or removal from office of such auditors (s 17(2)(d)(iii));

(5) require an appointing person to consult prescribed persons before exercising prescribed functions (s 17(2)(e)).

In s 17, 'prescribed' means prescribed by regulations under s 17(1): s 17(10).

Regulations under s 17(1) may, in particular:

(i) make provision about the relevant authorities to which the arrangements under the regulations apply, including provision for them to apply to an authority that has opted into them or has not opted out of them (s 17(3)(a));

(ii) make provision about the procedures to be followed in relation to opting into or out of those arrangements (s 17(3)(b));

(iii) impose duties on relevant authorities to which those arrangements apply, including duties as to:

(A) the payment of fees to the appointing person in respect of an audit carried out by a local auditor appointed by that person (s 17(3)(c)(i)); and

(B) the provision of information to the appointing person (s 17(3)(c)(ii)).

Provision made by regulations under s 17(1) by virtue of s 17(3)(c)(i) may, in particular:

(I) provide for fees to be paid in accordance with a scale or scales of fees specified by the appointing person (s 17(4)(a)); and

(II) provide for the payment in prescribed circumstances of a larger or smaller fee than is specified by the appropriate scale (s 17(4)(b)).

Regulations under s 17(1) may, in particular, make provision about the functions of a local auditor appointed by an appointing person: s 17(5). Such regulations may, in particular, make provision for the appointment of a local auditor of the accounts of a relevant authority to which arrangements made by the regulations apply where the appointing person does not make an appointment under the regulations: s 17(6). Provision made by regulations under s 17(1) by virtue of s 17(6) may, in particular, provide for the appointment to be made by the authority or the Secretary of State: s 17(7).

Regulations under s 17(1) may, in particular provide for any provision of, or made under, Pt 3 not to apply, or to apply with modifications, in relation to a relevant authority to which regulations under s 17(1) apply; or for any other provision of, or made under, the Local Audit and Accountability Act 2014 not to apply, or to apply with modifications, in consequence of provision made by regulations under s 17(1): s 17(8). Section 17(8) applies to a provision of or made under the Local Audit and Accountability Act 2014 even if it makes specific provision about a relevant authority to which the regulations apply: s 17(9).

For regulations made under s 17(1) see the Local Audit (Appointing Person) Regulations 2015, SI 2015/192.

592. Auditor panels.

Each relevant authority[1], other than a chief constable and the Commissioner of Police of the Metropolis, must have an auditor panel to exercise the functions conferred on auditor panels by or under the Local Audit and Accountability Act 2014[2]. Provision is made for, among other options, the appointment of an auditor panel of a relevant authority for making a determination that a committee of a relevant authority is to be a relevant authority's auditor panel[3]; for the constitution and proceedings of auditor panels, and the terms of office of members[4]; the application of local authority enactments to auditor panels[5]; the status and expenses of auditor panels[6]; and in relation to connected entities[7].

A relevant authority's auditor panel must advise the authority on:

(1) the maintenance of an independent relationship with the local auditor appointed to audit its accounts[8];

(2) the selection and appointment of a local auditor to audit its accounts[9];

(3) any proposal by the authority to enter into a liability limitation agreement[10],

and a relevant authority must publish advice from its auditor panel[11].

The Secretary of State[12] may by regulations:

(a) provide more details about an auditor panel's functions under any of the provisions above[13];

(b) confer or impose other functions on a relevant authority's auditor panel in relation to the audit of the authority's accounts[14];

(c) enable a relevant authority to confer or impose other functions on its auditor panel in relation to the audit of its accounts[15].

An auditor panel must have regard to any guidance issued by the Secretary of State in exercising, or deciding whether to exercise, its functions[16]; and a relevant authority must have regard to any guidance issued by the Secretary of State in exercising, or deciding whether to exercise, its functions in relation to its auditor panel[17].

A relevant authority other than a health service body must, if asked to do so by its auditor panel, supply to the panel any documents or information held by the authority and required by the panel for the exercise of its functions[18]. A relevant authority's auditor panel, other than the auditor panel of a health service body, may require a member or officer of the authority to come to a meeting of the panel to answer its questions[19]. Such a person must comply with a requirement imposed by an auditor panel[20]. This does not require the person to answer any questions which the person would be entitled to refuse to answer in or for the purposes of proceedings in a court in England and Wales[21].

1 As to the meaning of 'relevant authority' see PARA 588 note 3.

2 Local Audit and Accountability Act 2014 s 9(1), (2). Schedule 4 makes further provision about auditor panels: s 9(3).

The Local Audit and Accountability Act 2014 does not apply to the accounts of a local government body in Wales. As to accounts and audit regulations in relation to Wales see PARA 653. As to the meaning of 'Wales' see PARA 2 note 16.

3 See the Local Audit and Accountability Act 2014 Sch 4 para 1.

4 See the Local Audit and Accountability Act 2014 Sch 4 paras 2–4 (Sch 4 para 2 amended by SI 2014/2845); the Local Audit (Auditor Panel) Regulations 2014, SI 2014/3224, regs 2–6; and the Local Audit (Health Service Bodies Auditor Panel and Independence) Regulations 2015, SI 2015/18, regs 2, 3, 5–10).

5 See the Local Audit and Accountability Act 2014 Sch 4 para 5; and the Local Audit (Auditor Panel) Regulations 2014, SI 2014/3224, regs 8–10.

6 See the Local Audit and Accountability Act 2014 Sch 4 paras 6, 7.

7 See the Local Audit and Accountability Act 2014 Sch 4 para 8 (amended by SI 2014/2845).

8 Local Audit and Accountability Act 2014 s 10(1). Advice under s 10(1) to a police and crime commissioner for an area must include advice on the maintenance of an independent relationship between the local auditor and the chief constable for the area: s 10(2). Advice under s 10(1) to the Mayor's Office for Policing and Crime must include advice on the maintenance of an independent relationship between the local auditor and the Commissioner of Police of the Metropolis: s 10(3). Advice under s 10(1) must be given if the relevant authority asks for it, and at other times, if the auditor panel thinks it is appropriate to do so: s 10(5). As to the meaning of 'accounts' see PARA 588 note 6. As to police and crime commissioners see POLICE AND INVESTIGATORY POWERS vol 84 (2013) PARA 56 et seq. As to the Mayor's Office for Policing and Crime see POLICE AND INVESTIGATORY POWERS vol 84 (2013) PARA 78 et seq.

9 Local Audit and Accountability Act 2014 s 10(4). Advice under s 10(4) must be given if the relevant authority asks for it, and at other times, if the auditor panel thinks it is appropriate to do so: s 10(5).

10 Local Audit and Accountability Act 2014 s 10(6). Advice under s 10(6) must be given if the authority asks for it: s 10(7). As to liability limitation agreements see s 14; and PARA 593.

11 Local Audit and Accountability Act 2014 s 10(9). Publication of advice must be in accordance with s 10(10): s 10(9). A relevant authority publishes advice in accordance with s 10(10) if:

(1) in the case of a relevant authority other than a health service body, it publishes the advice in such manner as it thinks is likely to bring the advice to the attention of persons who live in its area (s 10(10)(a));

(2) in the case of a clinical commissioning group, it publishes the advice in such manner as it thinks is likely to bring the advice to the attention of:

(a) persons who live in the area of the group (s 10(10)(b)(i)); and

(b) persons who do not live in the area of the group but for whom the group is responsible (s 10(10)(b)(ii));

(3) in the case of special trustees for a hospital, they publish the advice in such manner as they think is likely to bring the advice to the attention of persons to whom services are

provided at that hospital (s 10(10)(c) (repealed, as from a day to be appointed, by the NHS (Charitable Trusts Etc) Act 2016 s 1(9), Sch 1 paras 17, 18(d); at the date at which this volume states the law, no such day had been appointed).

As to the meaning of 'health service body' see PARA 588 note 4. As to clinical commissioning groups see HEALTH SERVICES vol 54 (2017) PARA 35 As to special trustees see HEALTH SERVICES vol 54 (2017) PARA 89

The relevant authority must exclude from advice published under the Local Audit and Accountability Act 2014 s 10(10) information whose disclosure would prejudice commercial confidentiality, unless there is an overriding public interest in favour of its disclosure: s 10(11).

12 As to the Secretary of State see PARA 4 note 18.
13 Local Audit and Accountability Act 2014 s 10(8)(a).
14 Local Audit and Accountability Act 2014 s 10(8)(b).
15 Local Audit and Accountability Act 2014 s 10(8)(c). See the Local Audit (Auditor Panel) Regulations 2014, SI 2014/3224, reg 7; and the Local Audit (Health Service Bodies Auditor Panel and Independence) Regulations 2015, SI 2015/18, reg 4.
16 Local Audit and Accountability Act 2014 s 10(12).
17 Local Audit and Accountability Act 2014 s 10(13).
18 Local Audit and Accountability Act 2014 s 11(1). The auditor panel of a police and crime commissioner for an area may also exercise the functions in s 11(1), (2) in relation to the chief constable for the area: s 11(6). The auditor panel of the Mayor's Office for Policing and Crime may also exercise the functions in s 11(1), (2) in relation to the Commissioner of Police of the Metropolis: s 11(7).
19 Local Audit and Accountability Act 2014 s 11(2). In the application of s 11(2) to a corporation sole, the reference to a member is a reference to a holder of that office: s 11(3). The auditor panel of a parish meeting may only exercise the function in s 11(2) in relation to the chairman of the parish meeting or the proper officer of the district council within whose area the parish lies: s 11(8). As to the meaning of 'parish meeting' see PARA 588 note 3. As to corporations sole see CORPORATIONS vol 24 (2010) PARA 314 et seq.
20 Local Audit and Accountability Act 2014 s 11(4).
21 Local Audit and Accountability Act 2014 s 11(5).

593. Local auditor liability limitation agreements.

A 'liability limitation agreement' is an agreement that purports to limit the amount of a liability owed to a relevant authority[1] by its local auditor[2] in respect of any negligence, default, breach of duty or breach of trust occurring in the course of the audit of accounts[3], of which the auditor may be guilty in relation to the authority[4]. A liability limitation agreement must comply with regulations made by the Secretary of State[5].

Such regulations may, in particular:

(1) make provision about the duration of a liability limitation agreement[6];
(2) make provision as to the amount to which a local auditor's liability may be limited by a liability limitation agreement (which may be an amount that is specified in, determined under or described in general terms in the regulations)[7].

Such regulations may:

(a) require a liability limitation agreement to contain provisions, or provisions of a description, specified in the regulations[8];
(b) prohibit a liability limitation agreement from containing provisions, or provisions of a description, specified in the regulations[9].

Regulations may provide:

(i) that a liability limitation agreement that does not comply with the regulations is void[10];
(ii) that a liability limitation agreement is effective only to the extent that it complies with the regulations[11];

(iii) that, in the circumstances specified in the regulations, a provision of a liability limitation agreement that does not comply with the regulations is to have effect as if it complied with the regulations[12].

The Secretary of State may by regulations make provision requiring a relevant authority that has entered into a liability limitation agreement to disclose such information about the agreement as may be specified in the regulations in such manner as may be so specified[13].

A liability limitation agreement must not contain provisions which make the duration of the agreement longer than the financial year[14] or years in relation to which the appointment of the local auditor applies, and a local auditor's liability may be limited by a liability limitation agreement to such amount as is fair and reasonable in all the circumstances of the case[15].

Before entering into a liability limitation agreement, a relevant authority other than a chief constable or the Commissioner of Police of the Metropolis must consult and take into account the advice of its auditor panel[16]. If a relevant authority is a local authority operating executive arrangements[17], the function of deciding whether to enter into a liability limitation agreement is not the responsibility of an executive of the authority under those arrangements[18]. If a relevant authority is a local authority[19], the power to arrange for the discharge of its functions by a committee, a sub-committee, an officer of the authority or any other local authority[20] does not apply to the authority's function of deciding whether to enter into a liability limitation agreement[21].

A decision to enter into a liability limitation agreement between a local auditor and the Greater London Authority must be taken by the Mayor of London and the London Assembly acting jointly on behalf of the Authority[22].

A decision to enter into a liability limitation agreement between a local auditor and a parish meeting[23] must be taken by the parish meeting itself (and not by its chairman on behalf of the parish meeting)[24].

1 As to the meaning of 'relevant authority' see PARA 588 note 3.
2 As to the appointment of local auditors see PARA 591.
3 As to the meaning of 'accounts' see PARA 588 note 6.
4 Local Audit and Accountability Act 2014 s 14(1).
5 Local Audit and Accountability Act 2014 s 14(2). A liability limitation agreement that complies with such regulations is not subject to the Unfair Contract Terms Act 1977 s 2(2) or s 3(2)(a) (see CONTRACT vol 22 (2012) PARAS 410, 411): Local Audit and Accountability Act 2014 s 14(7). As to the Secretary of State see PARA 4 note 18.
6 Local Audit and Accountability Act 2014 s 14(3)(a).
7 Local Audit and Accountability Act 2014 s 14(3)(b).
8 Local Audit and Accountability Act 2014 s 14(4)(a).
9 Local Audit and Accountability Act 2014 s 14(4)(b).
10 Local Audit and Accountability Act 2014 s 14(5)(a).
11 Local Audit and Accountability Act 2014 s 14(5)(b).
12 Local Audit and Accountability Act 2014 s 14(5)(c).
13 Local Audit and Accountability Act 2014 s 14(6).
14 As to the meaning of 'financial year' see PARA 588 note 7.
15 See the Local Audit (Liability Limitation Agreements) Regulations 2014, SI 2014/1628.
16 Local Audit and Accountability Act 2014 s 15(1). Before entering into a liability limitation agreement, a chief constable for an area must consult and take into account the advice of the auditor panel of the police and crime commissioner for the area: s 15(2). Before entering into a liability limitation agreement, the Commissioner of Police of the Metropolis must consult and take into account the advice of the auditor panel of the Mayor's Office for Policing and Crime: s 15(3). As to the Mayor's Office for Policing and Crime see POLICE AND INVESTIGATORY POWERS vol 84 (2013) PARA 78 et seq.
17 'Executive' and 'executive arrangements' have the same meaning as in the Local Government Act

2000 Pt 1A (ss 9B–99R): Local Audit and Accountability Act 2014 s 44(1). See LOCAL GOVERNMENT vol 69 (2018) PARA 295 et seq.
18 Local Audit and Accountability Act 2014 s 15(4).
19 Ie within the meaning of the Local Government Act 1972 s 101 (arrangements for discharge of functions).
20 Ie the Local Government Act 1972 s 101: see LOCAL GOVERNMENT vol 69 (2018) PARA 399.
21 Local Audit and Accountability Act 2014 s 15(5).
22 Local Audit and Accountability Act 2014 s 15(6). As to the Greater London Authority see LONDON GOVERNMENT vol 71 (2013) PARA 67 et seq. As to the Mayor of London see LONDON GOVERNMENT vol 71 (2013) PARA 69. As to the London Assembly see LONDON GOVERNMENT vol 71 (2013) PARA 70.
23 As to the meaning of 'parish meeting' see PARA 588 note 3.
24 Local Audit and Accountability Act 2014 s 15(7).

594. Resignation and renewal of local auditor.

The Secretary of State[1] may by regulations make provision about the resignation of a local auditor[2] of the accounts[3] of a relevant authority[4] from that office[5], and about the removal of a local auditor before the expiry of the term of that office[6].

Regulations about the resignation of a local auditor may, in particular, make provision about:

(1) the steps that must be taken by a person who is a local auditor to resign from that office[7];
(2) the time at which the resignation takes effect[8];
(3) the steps that must be taken in connection with the resignation by the relevant authority[9];
(4) the role of the authority's auditor panel or of a recognised supervisory body in connection with the resignation[10];
(5) the steps that must be taken by the relevant authority after the resignation[11].

Regulations about the removal of a local auditor may, in particular, make provision about:

(a) the steps that must be taken to remove a local auditor from that office[12];
(b) the person or persons by whom those steps must be taken and the way in which they must be taken[13];
(c) the steps that may be taken by the local auditor in connection with the local auditor's removal from that office[14];
(d) the role of the relevant authority's auditor panel[15] or of a recognised supervisory body[16] in connection with the removal of the local auditor from that office[17];
(e) the steps that must be taken by the relevant authority after the removal of the local auditor from that office[18].

Regulations under these provisions may, in particular:

(i) make provision for the Secretary of State to appoint, or direct the relevant authority to appoint, a replacement local auditor[19];
(ii) make provision that permits or requires, or enables the Secretary of State to permit or require, that appointment to have effect for a limited period or limited purposes only[20].

Regulations that confer functions on a recognised supervisory body may make provision about the supply to the body by a relevant authority of documents or information relating to the resignation or removal of a local auditor[21].

A local auditor resigning from that office must give notice of resignation in writing to the relevant authority accompanied by a statement in writing of the reasons for the local auditor ceasing to hold office and any matters connected with the local auditor ceasing to hold office that the local auditor considers need to be brought to the attention of the relevant authority or the relevant authority's auditor panel[22]. Where a local auditor resigns from office the relevant authority's auditor panel must, within three months of the date on which the resignation takes effect, investigate and report on the circumstances connected with the local auditor ceasing to hold office[23].

A relevant authority may remove its local auditor from that office before the expiry of the term of that office[24]. A relevant authority must notify certain bodies that the local auditor has ceased to hold office, and must appoint a new local auditor within three months[25].

1 As to the Secretary of State see PARA 4 note 18.
2 As to the appointment of local auditors see PARA 591.
3 As to the meaning of 'accounts' see PARA 588 note 6.
4 As to the meaning of 'relevant authority' see PARA 588 note 3.
5 Local Audit and Accountability Act 2014 s 16(1)(a).
6 Local Audit and Accountability Act 2014 s 16(1)(b).
7 Local Audit and Accountability Act 2014 s 16(2)(a).
8 Local Audit and Accountability Act 2014 s 16(2)(b).
9 Local Audit and Accountability Act 2014 s 16(2)(c).
10 Local Audit and Accountability Act 2014 s 16(2)(d).
11 Local Audit and Accountability Act 2014 s 16(2)(e).
12 Local Audit and Accountability Act 2014 s 16(3)(a).
13 Local Audit and Accountability Act 2014 s 16(3)(b). Regulations under s 16(1)(b) which make provision about the matter in s 16(3)(b) may provide, in relation to a local auditor of the accounts of a health service body, that some or all of the steps may be taken by the Secretary of State: s 16(4). As to the meaning of 'health service body' see PARA 588 note 4.
14 Local Audit and Accountability Act 2014 s 16(3)(c).
15 As to auditor panels see PARA 592.
16 'Recognised supervisory body' is to be construed in accordance with the Companies Act 2006 s 1217(4) and Sch 10 as they have effect by virtue of the Local Audit and Accountability Act 2014 Sch 5: s 44(1). See COMPANIES vol 15 (2016) PARA 1092 et seq.
17 Local Audit and Accountability Act 2014 s 16(3)(d).
18 Local Audit and Accountability Act 2014 s 16(3)(e).
19 Local Audit and Accountability Act 2014 s 16(5)(a). Regulations under s 16(1) which make provision as mentioned in s 16(5)(a) may apply s 12(3), (4) or (5) (see PARA 591) with modifications to a direction given or appointment made by the Secretary of State under such regulations: s 16(6).
20 Local Audit and Accountability Act 2014 s 16(5)(b).
21 Local Audit and Accountability Act 2014 s 16(7).
22 Local Audit (Auditor Resignation and Removal) Regulations 2014, SI 2014/1710, reg 3.
23 Local Audit (Auditor Resignation and Removal) Regulations 2014, SI 2014/1710, reg 4.
24 Local Audit (Auditor Resignation and Removal) Regulations 2014, SI 2014/1710, regs 5–7.
25 Local Audit (Auditor Resignation and Removal) Regulations 2014, SI 2014/1710, regs 8, 9. As to the application of the Local Audit (Auditor Resignation and Removal) Regulations 2014, SI 2014/1710, to a chief constable for an area in England and the Commissioner of Police of the Metropolis, see reg 2.

595. Eligibility and regulation of local auditors.

The provisions of the Companies Act 2006 relating to statutory auditors[1] apply, with modifications[2], in relation to the eligibility and regulation of local auditors[3].

1 Ie the Companies Act 2006 Pt 42 (ss 1209–1264), Sch 10: see COMPANIES vol 15 (2016) PARA 1092 et seq.

2 Ie the general modifications in the Local Audit and Accountability Act 2014 Sch 5 para 2 and the specific modifications in Sch 5 paras 1(2), (3), 3–29: s 18(1), Sch 5 para 1(1)(a), (b). The Secretary of State may by regulations amend Sch 5 if the Secretary of State considers it is appropriate to do so as a result of amendments made to the Companies Act 2006 Pt 42: Local Audit and Accountability Act 2014 s 18(2).

3 Local Audit and Accountability Act 2014 Sch 5 para 1(1). As to the modifications see Sch 5 paras 1(2), (3), 2–29 (Sch 5 para 1(3) substituted by SI 2016/649). See also the Local Audit (Professional Qualifications and Major Local Audit) Regulations 2014, SI 2014/1627.

C. CONDUCT OF LOCAL AUDIT

596. Codes of audit practice and guidance.

The Comptroller and Auditor General[1] must prepare one or more codes of audit practice prescribing the way in which local auditors are to carry out their functions under the Local Audit and Accountability Act 2014[2]. Different codes may be prepared for different relevant authorities[3] (but the Comptroller and Auditor General must ensure that each kind of relevant authority is covered by a code)[4]. A code may contain different provision for different relevant authorities[5]. A code must embody what the Comptroller and Auditor General considers to be the best professional practice with respect to the standards, procedures and techniques to be adopted by local auditors[6].

Before preparing a code, the Comptroller and Auditor General must consult[7]:

(1) such associations or representatives of relevant authorities as the Comptroller and Auditor General thinks appropriate[8];
(2) the recognised supervisory bodies[9];
(3) the persons appearing on the register of auditors kept under regulations[10] under the Companies Act 2006[11];
(4) the Secretary of State[12];
(5) the Treasury[13];
(6) each body to whom the Secretary of State has delegated[14] functions[15]; and
(7) such other bodies or persons as the Comptroller and Auditor General thinks appropriate[16].

After preparing a code of audit practice, the Comptroller and Auditor General must publish it in draft and send it to a Minister of the Crown, who must lay it before Parliament[17]. If, within the 40-day period[18], either House of Parliament resolves not to approve the code, it must not be published by the Comptroller and Auditor General and the Comptroller and Auditor General must prepare another code[19]. If no such resolution is made within that period, the Comptroller and Auditor General must publish the code[20]. These requirements do not apply to a code of audit practice prepared to replace an existing code of audit practice[21].

The Comptroller and Auditor General must keep each code of audit practice under review[22]. The Comptroller and Auditor General may prepare alterations to a code of audit practice[23]. The duty to consult[24] applies to alterations to a code as it applies to a code[25]. After preparing alterations to a code, the Comptroller and Auditor General must publish the code as altered in draft and send the code as altered to a Minister of the Crown, who must lay it before Parliament[26]. If, within the 40-day period, either House of Parliament resolves not to approve the code as altered, it must not be published by the Comptroller and Auditor General[27]. If no such resolution is made within that period, the Comptroller and Auditor General must publish the code as altered[28]. A code published as altered in draft or approved must show the alterations that are proposed to be made to it or (as the case may be) have been made to it in such manner as the Comptroller and Auditor General thinks appropriate[29].

The Comptroller and Auditor General may prepare a code of audit practice to replace a published[30] code[31]. The Comptroller and Auditor General must:

(a) use reasonable endeavours to ensure that a code is published[32] to replace a previous code[33] published ('the original code') before the end of five years beginning with the date on which the original code was published[34]; or

(b) if it does not prove possible to comply with head (a), ensure that a code of the kind referred to there is published[35] as soon as is reasonably practicable after the end of the period referred to there[36].

Heads (a) and (b) apply regardless of whether the original code has been published with alterations[37] in the meantime[38]. A replacement code prepared to comply with heads (a) and (b) need not make different provision from that made by the original code[39].

After preparing a replacement code, the Comptroller and Auditor General must publish it in draft and send it to a Minister of the Crown, who must lay it before Parliament[40]. If, within the 40-day period, either House of Parliament resolves not to approve the replacement code:

(i) the code must not be published by the Comptroller and Auditor General[41]; and

(ii) if the period of five years beginning with the date on which the original code was published has expired, the Comptroller and Auditor General must prepare another replacement code[42].

If no such resolution is made within that period, the Comptroller and Auditor General must publish the replacement code[43].

A code of audit practice may be published in such manner as the Comptroller and Auditor General thinks fit[44]. A code comes into force on the day on which it is published[45] unless it specifies a different commencement date[46]. Alterations to a code come into force on the day on which the code as altered is published[47] unless it specifies a different commencement date for those alterations[48]. A code may specify different commencement dates for different purposes and may include transitional provisions and savings[49]. A code may, in particular, provide that all or part of an existing code of audit practice has effect until all or part of the new code comes into force[50].

A relevant authority must provide the Comptroller and Auditor General with the information that the Comptroller and Auditor General reasonably requires for the purposes of these provisions[51].

The Comptroller and Auditor General may issue guidance as to the exercise by local auditors of their functions under the Local Audit and Accountability Act 2014[52]. Such guidance may, in particular, explain or supplement the provisions of a code of practice[53].

1 As to the Comptroller and Auditor General see CONSTITUTIONAL AND ADMINISTRATIVE LAW vol 20 (2014) PARA 494 et seq.

2 Local Audit and Accountability Act 2014 s 19, Sch 6 para 1(1). As to local auditors see PARA 591 et seq. Until replaced by a provision of a code of audit practice under Sch 6, a provision of a code of audit practice under the Audit Commission Act 1998 s 4 (repealed) continues in force: Local Audit and Accountability Act 2014 Sch 6 para 8(1). A provision of a code under the Audit Commission Act 1998 s 4 is to be read subject to the modifications necessary for it to have effect in relation to the functions of a local auditor under the Local Audit and Accountability Act 2014: Sch 6 para 8(2). A code under the Audit Commission Act 1998 s 4:

(1) is not to be treated as a code of audit practice for the purposes of the Local Audit and Accountability Act 2014 Sch 6 (other than Sch 6 para 8) (Sch 6 para 8(3)(a)); but
(2) is otherwise to be treated as a code of audit practice for the purposes of that Act (Sch 6 para 8(3)(b)).

As to the application of Sch 6 to auditors of NHS foundation trusts see Sch 6 para 10.

3 As to the meaning of 'relevant authority' see PARA 588 note 3.
4 Local Audit and Accountability Act 2014 Sch 6 para 1(2).
5 Local Audit and Accountability Act 2014 Sch 6 para 1(3).
6 Local Audit and Accountability Act 2014 Sch 6 para 1(4).
7 Local Audit and Accountability Act 2014 Sch 6 para 1(5).
8 Local Audit and Accountability Act 2014 Sch 6 para 1(5)(a).
9 Local Audit and Accountability Act 2014 Sch 6 para 1(5)(b). As to the meaning of 'recognised supervisory body' see PARA 594 note 16.
10 Ie under regulations under the Companies Act 2006 s 1239 as it has effect by virtue of the Local Audit and Accountability Act 2014 Sch 5 (see PARA 595).
11 Local Audit and Accountability Act 2014 Sch 6 para 1(5)(c).
12 Local Audit and Accountability Act 2014 Sch 6 para 1(5)(d). As to the Secretary of State see PARA 4 note 18.
13 Local Audit and Accountability Act 2014 Sch 6 para 1(5)(e). As to the Treasury see CONSTITUTIONAL AND ADMINISTRATIVE LAW vol 20 (2014) PARA 262 et seq.
14 Ie under the Companies Act 2006 s 1252 as it has effect by virtue of the Local Audit and Accountability Act 2014 Sch 5.
15 Local Audit and Accountability Act 2014 Sch 6 para 1(5)(f).
16 Local Audit and Accountability Act 2014 Sch 6 para 1(5)(g).
17 Local Audit and Accountability Act 2014 Sch 6 para 2(1).
18 In the Local Audit and Accountability Act 2014 Sch 6 'the 40-day period', in relation to a code laid before Parliament, means the period of 40 days beginning with:
(1) the day on which the code is laid (Sch 6 para 11(1)(a)); or
(2) if it is not laid before each House of Parliament on the same day, the later of the two days on which it is laid (Sch 6 para 11(1)(b)).

In calculating that period, no account is to be taken of any period during which Parliament is dissolved or prorogued or during which both Houses are adjourned for more than four days: Sch 6 para 11(2).

19 Local Audit and Accountability Act 2014 Sch 6 para 2(2).
20 Local Audit and Accountability Act 2014 Sch 6 para 2(3).
21 Local Audit and Accountability Act 2014 Sch 6 para 2(4). See, however, Sch 6 para 5; and the text to notes 31–43.
22 Local Audit and Accountability Act 2014 Sch 6 para 3.
23 Local Audit and Accountability Act 2014 Sch 6 para 4(1).
24 Ie the Local Audit and Accountability Act 2014 Sch 6 para 1(5): see heads (1)–(7) in the text.
25 Local Audit and Accountability Act 2014 Sch 6 para 4(2).
26 Local Audit and Accountability Act 2014 Sch 6 para 4(3).
27 Local Audit and Accountability Act 2014 Sch 6 para 4(4).
28 Local Audit and Accountability Act 2014 Sch 6 para 4(5).
29 Local Audit and Accountability Act 2014 Sch 6 para 4(6).
30 Ie under the Local Audit and Accountability Act 2014 Sch 6 para 2(3) or 5(7).
31 Local Audit and Accountability Act 2014 Sch 6 para 5(1).
32 Ie under the Local Audit and Accountability Act 2014 Sch 6 para 5(7).
33 Ie a code published under the Local Audit and Accountability Act 2014 Sch 6 para 2(3) or 5(7).
34 Local Audit and Accountability Act 2014 Sch 6 para 5(2)(a).
35 Ie under the Local Audit and Accountability Act 2014 Sch 6 para 5(7).
36 Local Audit and Accountability Act 2014 Sch 6 para 5(2)(b).
37 Ie under the Local Audit and Accountability Act 2014 Sch 6 para 4: see the text to notes 3–29.
38 Local Audit and Accountability Act 2014 Sch 6 para 5(3).
39 Local Audit and Accountability Act 2014 Sch 6 para 5(4).
40 Local Audit and Accountability Act 2014 Sch 6 para 5(5).
41 Local Audit and Accountability Act 2014 Sch 6 para 5(6)(a).
42 Local Audit and Accountability Act 2014 Sch 6 para 5(6)(b).
43 Local Audit and Accountability Act 2014 Sch 6 para 5(7).
44 Local Audit and Accountability Act 2014 Sch 6 para 6(1).
45 Ie under the Local Audit and Accountability Act 2014 Sch 6 para 2(3) or 5(7).
46 Local Audit and Accountability Act 2014 Sch 6 para 6(2).

47 Ie under the Local Audit and Accountability Act 2014 Sch 6 para 4(5).
48 Local Audit and Accountability Act 2014 Sch 6 para 6(3).
49 Local Audit and Accountability Act 2014 Sch 6 para 6(4).
50 Local Audit and Accountability Act 2014 Sch 6 para 6(5).
51 Local Audit and Accountability Act 2014 Sch 6 para 7.
52 Local Audit and Accountability Act 2014 Sch 6 para 9(1).
53 Local Audit and Accountability Act 2014 Sch 6 para 9(2).

597. Powers and duties of local auditors.

In auditing the accounts[1] of a relevant authority[2] other than a health service body[3], a local auditor[4] must, by examination of the accounts and otherwise, be satisfied[5]:

(1) that the accounts comply with the requirements of the enactments that apply to them[6];
(2) that proper practices have been observed in the preparation of the statement of accounts, and that the statement presents a true and fair view[7]; and
(3) that the authority has made proper arrangements for securing economy, efficiency and effectiveness in its use of resources[8].

On completion of the audit, the local auditor must enter on the statement of accounts a certificate that the auditor has completed the audit in accordance with the Local Audit and Accountability Act 2014 and the auditor's opinion on the statement[9]. A local auditor may enter an opinion on the statement of accounts on that statement before the audit is completed if[10]:

(a) the audit has not been completed because an objection has been made[11] and that objection has not been disposed of[12]; and
(b) the auditor thinks that, if the objection were resolved in the objector's favour, this would not affect the accuracy of the statement of accounts[13].

A local auditor must, in carrying out the auditor's functions in relation to the accounts of a relevant authority, comply with the code of audit practice applicable to the authority that is for the time being in force[14]. A local auditor must, in carrying out functions under the Local Audit and Accountability Act 2014, have regard to guidance issued[15] by the Comptroller and Auditor General[16].

A local auditor has a right of access at all reasonable times to every document (an 'audit document') that:

(i) relates to a relevant authority or an entity connected with a relevant authority[17]; and
(ii) the auditor thinks is necessary for the purposes of the auditor's functions under the Local Audit and Accountability Act 2014[18].

This includes power to inspect, copy or take away an audit document[19].

A local auditor may:

(A) require a person holding or accountable for, or who has at any time held or been accountable for, an audit document to provide such information or explanation as the auditor thinks is necessary for the purposes of the Local Audit and Accountability Act 2014[20]; and
(B) if the auditor thinks it necessary, require the person to meet the auditor to give the information or explanation or (if the person holds or is accountable for the document) to produce the document[21].

Where an audit document is in an electronic form, the power to require a person to produce the document includes power to require it to be produced in a form in which it is legible and can be taken away[22]. For the purpose of inspecting an audit document which is in an electronic form, a local auditor:

(I) may have access to, and inspect and check the operation of, any computer and associated apparatus or material which the auditor thinks is or has been used in connection with the document[23]; and

(II) may require a specified person[24] to give the auditor the reasonable assistance that the auditor needs for that purpose[25].

A local auditor may require any specified person[26] to provide such information or explanation as the auditor thinks is necessary for the purposes of the Local Audit and Accountability Act 2014[27] and, if the auditor thinks it necessary, require the person to meet the auditor to give the information or explanation[28]. A local auditor of the accounts of a parish meeting[29] may only exercise this function, so far as it applies to a person who is or was a member or officer of a relevant authority, in relation to a person who is or was the chairman of the parish meeting or the proper officer of the district council within whose area the parish lies[30].

A relevant authority or an entity connected with a relevant authority[31] must provide a local auditor with the facilities and information that the auditor reasonably requires for the purposes of the auditor's functions under the Local Audit and Accountability Act 2014[32].

A statement made by a person in response to a requirement under these provisions may not be used in evidence against that person in criminal proceedings other than proceedings for an offence relating to disclosure of information[33].

Nothing in these provisions compels a person to disclose information in respect of which a claim to legal professional privilege could be maintained in legal proceedings[34].

A person is guilty of an offence if, without reasonable excuse, the person:

(AA) obstructs the exercise of any power conferred by the provisions above[35]; or

(BB) fails to comply with any requirement of a local auditor under the provisions above[36].

The reasonable expenses[37] incurred by a local auditor in connection with proceedings for an offence alleged to have been committed by a specified person[38] in relation to the audit of the accounts of a relevant authority are recoverable from that authority so far as they are not recovered from any other source[39].

Until a day to be appointed[40], a local auditor may refer to the Secretary of State any matter arising from an audit under the Local Audit and Accountability Act 2014 if it appears that the matter may be relevant for the purposes of any of the functions of the Secretary of State relating to social security[41].

1 As to the meaning of 'accounts' see PARA 588 note 6.

2 As to the meaning of 'relevant authority' see PARA 588 note 3.

3 As to the meaning of 'health service body' see PARA 588 note 4. As to the requirements of a local auditor in auditing the accounts of a health service body, see Local Audit and Accountability Act 2014 s 21; and HEALTH SERVICES vol 54A (2017) PARA 550.

4 As to local auditors see PARA 591 et seq.

5 Local Audit and Accountability Act 2014 s 20(1).

6 Local Audit and Accountability Act 2014 s 20(1)(a).

7 Local Audit and Accountability Act 2014 s 20(1)(b).

8 Local Audit and Accountability Act 2014 s 20(1)(c). As to the duties of a local auditor see eg *Porter v Magill* [2001] UKHL 67, [2002] 1 All ER 465; and *Asher v Secretary of State for the Environment* [1974] Ch 208, [1974] 2 All ER 156, CA. As to the liability of a local auditor to an authority see *West Wiltshire District Council v Garland* [1993] Ch 409, [1993] 4 All ER 246.

9 Local Audit and Accountability Act 2014 s 20(2). If, for any part of the period for which a relevant authority is required to prepare a statement of accounts, the authority is required to maintain a pension fund under regulations under the Public Service Pensions Act 2013 s 1 as they relate to

local government workers (within the meaning of that Act), the authority's local auditor must give a separate opinion on the part of the statement that relates to the accounts of that pension fund: Local Audit and Accountability Act 2014 s 20(3).

10 Local Audit and Accountability Act 2014 s 20(4).

11 Ie under the Local Audit and Accountability Act 2014 s 27: see PARA 600.

12 Local Audit and Accountability Act 2014 s 20(4)(a).

13 Local Audit and Accountability Act 2014 s 20(4)(b).

14 Local Audit and Accountability Act 2014 s 20(5). As to codes of practice see PARA 596.

15 Ie under the Local Audit and Accountability Act 2014 Sch 6 para 9: see PARA 596.

16 Local Audit and Accountability Act 2014 s 20(6).

17 Local Audit and Accountability Act 2014 s 22(1)(a).

18 Local Audit and Accountability Act 2014 s 22(1)(b).

19 Local Audit and Accountability Act 2014 s 22(2).

20 Local Audit and Accountability Act 2014 s 22(3)(a).

21 Local Audit and Accountability Act 2014 s 22(3)(b).

22 Local Audit and Accountability Act 2014 s 22(4).

23 Local Audit and Accountability Act 2014 s 22(5)(a).

24 Ie a person within the Local Audit and Accountability Act 2014 s 22(6). A person is within s 22(6) who:

(1) is the person by whom or on whose behalf the computer is or has been used (s 22(6)(a)); or

(2) is a person in charge of, or otherwise involved in operating, the computer, apparatus or material (s 22(6)(b)).

25 Local Audit and Accountability Act 2014 s 22(5)(b).

26 Ie a person to whom the Local Audit and Accountability Act 2014 s 22(7) applies. Section 22(7) applies to:

(1) a member or officer of a relevant authority (s 22(8)(a));

(2) where a relevant authority is a corporation sole, the holder of that office (s 22(8)(b));

(3) a person elected or appointed:

  (a) as an entity connected with a relevant authority (s 22(8)(c)(i));

  (b) to such an entity (s 22(8)(c)(ii)); or

  (c) to an office of such an entity (s 22(8)(c)(iii));

(4) an employee of such an entity (s 22(8)(d));

(5) an auditor of the accounts of such an entity (s 22(8)(e)); or

(6) a person who fell within any of heads (1)–(5) at a time to which the information or explanation required by the local auditor relates (s 22(8)(f)).

As to corporations sole see CORPORATIONS vol 24 (2010) PARA 314 et seq.

27 Local Audit and Accountability Act 2014 s 22(7)(a).

28 Local Audit and Accountability Act 2014 s 22(7)(b).

29 As to the meaning of 'parish meeting' see PARA 588 note 3.

30 Local Audit and Accountability Act 2014 s 22(9).

31 References in the Local Audit and Accountability Act 2014 to an entity connected with a relevant authority or to a connected entity are to be construed in accordance with Sch 4 para 8: s 44(4). For the purposes of the Local Audit and Accountability Act 2014, an entity ('E') is connected with a relevant authority at any time if E is an entity other than the relevant authority and the relevant authority considers that, in accordance with proper practices in force at that time:

(1) the financial transactions, reserves, assets and liabilities of E are to be consolidated into the relevant authority's statement of accounts for the financial year in which that time falls (Sch 4 para 8(1)(a) (Sch 4 para 8 amended by SI 2014/2845));

(2) the relevant authority's share of the financial transactions, reserves, assets and liabilities of E is to be consolidated into the relevant authority's statement of accounts for that financial year (Local Audit and Accountability Act 2014 Sch 4 para 8(1)(b)); or

(3) the relevant authority's share of the net assets or net liabilities of E, and of the profit or loss of E, are to be brought into the relevant authority's statement of accounts for that financial year (Sch 4 para 8(1)(c)).

In Sch 4 para 8(1) 'entity' means any entity, whether or not a legal person: Sch 4 para 8(2). The Secretary of State may by regulations amend Sch 4 para 8(1) or (2): Sch 4 para 8(3). In Sch 4 para 8(1) as it applies in relation to a health service body, the reference to the relevant authority's statement of accounts is to be read as a reference to the body's accounts: Sch 4 para 8(4). As to the Secretary of State see PARA 4 note 18.

32 Local Audit and Accountability Act 2014 s 22(10).

33 Local Audit and Accountability Act 2014 s 22(11).

34 Local Audit and Accountability Act 2014 s 22(12).
35 Local Audit and Accountability Act 2014 s 23(1)(a).
36 Local Audit and Accountability Act 2014 s 23(1)(b). A person guilty of an offence under s 23(1) is liable on summary conviction to a fine not exceeding level 3 on the standard scale, and to an additional fine of not more than £20 for each day on which the offence continues after conviction for that offence: s 23(2). As to the powers of magistrates' courts to issue fines on summary conviction see SENTENCING vol 92 (2015) PARA 176.
37 'Expenses', in relation to anything done by a local auditor, means the expenses incurred by the auditor in doing that thing, including the auditor's costs of doing it; and 'costs', in relation to anything done by a local auditor, means the costs of the auditor's time to do that thing, whether or not the auditor charges on the basis of the time taken to do it: Local Audit and Accountability Act 2014 s 44(1).
38 Ie a person within the Local Audit and Accountability Act 2014 s 23(4). The persons within s 23(4) are:
(1) a member or officer of the relevant authority (s 23(4)(a));
(2) a person elected or appointed:
(a) as an entity connected with the relevant authority (s 23(4)(b)(i));
(b) to such an entity (s 23(4)(b)(ii)); or
(c) to an office of such an entity (s 23(4)(b)(iii)); and
(3) an employee of such an entity (s 23(4)(c)).
In s 23(4)(a) the reference to a member of the relevant authority, in relation to a corporation sole, is to the holder of that office: s 23(6).
39 Local Audit and Accountability Act 2014 s 23(3). Section 23(3) does not apply in relation to a parish meeting unless the offence is alleged to have been committed by the chairman of the parish meeting or the proper officer of the district council within whose area the parish lies: s 23(5).
40 Ie until the coming into force of the repeal of the Social Security Administration Act 1992 s 139D by the Welfare Reform Act 2012: Local Audit and Accountability Act 2014 s 37(3).
41 See the Local Audit and Accountability Act 2014 s 37(1). Modification is made by s 37(2) to the Social Security Administration Act 1992 s 139D(1).

598. Reports and recommendations.

The Local Audit and Accountability Act 2014[1] sets out detailed requirements for local auditors[2] to consider making public interest reports[3] and written recommendations[4], and for the procedures to be adopted following their issue[5]. These include provision about the supply of public interest reports[6], publicity for public interest reports[7], consideration of a report or recommendation[8], a bar on the delegation of functions relating to meetings[9], publicity for meetings[10], access to meetings and documents[11] and publicity for decisions[12].

1 See the Local Audit and Accountability Act 2014 s 24, Sch 7.
2 As to local auditors see PARA 591 et seq.
3 See the Local Audit and Accountability Act 2014 Sch 7 para 1.
4 See the Local Audit and Accountability Act 2014 Sch 7 para 2.
5 See the Local Audit and Accountability Act 2014 Sch 7 paras 3–10.
6 See the Local Audit and Accountability Act 2014 Sch 7 para 3.
7 See the Local Audit and Accountability Act 2014 Sch 7 para 4 (Sch 7 para 4(8)(c) repealed, as from a day to be appointed, by the NHS (Charitable Trusts Etc) Act 2016 s 1(9), Sch 1 paras 17, 18(j); at the date at which this volume states the law, no such day had been appointed).
8 See the Local Audit and Accountability Act 2014 Sch 7 paras 5, 6 (Sch 7 para 5(7) amended by the Policing and Crime Act 2017 s 6, Sch 1 para 97(1), (3); and, as from a day to be appointed, by the Policing and Crime Act 2017 s 9(3)(c), Sch 2 para 122(1), (3); at the date at which this volume states the law, no such day had been appointed). See also the Public Interest Reports and Recommendations (Modification of Consideration Procedure) Regulations 2014, SI 2014/1629.
9 See the Local Audit and Accountability Act 2014 Sch 7 para 7.
10 See the Local Audit and Accountability Act 2014 Sch 7 para 8.
11 See the Local Audit and Accountability Act 2014 Sch 7 para 9.
12 See the Local Audit and Accountability Act 2014 Sch 7 para 10.

599. Public inspection of accounts and documents.

Relevant authorities[1], other than health service bodies[2], must enable local government electors[3] to inspect and make copies of[4]:

(1) the statement of accounts prepared by the authority[5];
(2) the local auditor's certificate that the audit of the authority's accounts including that statement has been completed[6];
(3) the local auditor's opinion on the statement of accounts[7];
(4) any public interest report relating to the authority or an entity connected with it[8]; and
(5) any recommendation relating to the authority or an entity connected with it[9].

A relevant authority other than a health service body must ensure that a local government elector for its area may have copies of any document within heads (1) to (5) above supplied to the elector at the elector's request on payment of a reasonable sum for each copy[10]. The relevant authority must ensure that a local government elector may inspect a document within heads (1) to (5) above at all reasonable times and without payment[11].

These provisions apply in relation to a document only if the relevant authority has prepared the document or it has been made available to the authority[12].

At each audit of accounts under the Local Audit and Accountability Act 2014, other than an audit of accounts of a health service body, any persons interested or any journalist[13] may[14]:

(a) inspect the accounting records for the financial year to which the audit relates and all books, deeds, contracts, bills, vouchers, receipts and other documents relating to those records[15]; and
(b) make copies of all or any part of those records or documents[16].

At the request of a local government elector for any area to which the accounts relate, the local auditor must give the elector, or any representative of the elector, an opportunity to question the auditor about the accounting records[17]. These provisions do not entitle a person:

(i) to inspect or copy any part of any record or document containing information which is protected on the grounds of commercial confidentiality[18]; or
(ii) to require any such information to be disclosed in answer to any question[19];
(iii) to inspect or copy any part of any record or document containing personal information[20]; or
(iv) to require any personal information to be disclosed in answer to any question[21].

1 As to the meaning of 'relevant authority' see PARA 588 note 3.

2 As to the meaning of 'health service body' see PARA 588 note 4.

3 A reference in the Local Audit and Accountability Act 2014 to a local government elector for any area:

(1) in relation to a Passenger Transport Executive, is a reference to a local government elector for the area of the Integrated Transport Authority or combined authority for the area for which the Executive is established (s 44(6)(a));
(2) in relation to the Broads Authority, is a reference to a local government elector for the area of any participating authority (as defined by the Norfolk and Suffolk Broads Act 1988 s 25) (Local Audit and Accountability Act 2014 s 44(6)(b));
(3) in relation to a National Park authority which is the local planning authority for a National Park, is a reference to a local government elector for any area the whole or any part of which is comprised in that Park (s 44(6)(c)).

As to Passenger Transport Executives see ROAD TRAFFIC vol 89 (2011) PARA 47. As to the Broads Authority see WATER AND WATERWAYS vol 101 (2009) PARA 734. As to National Park authorities see OPEN SPACES AND COUNTRYSIDE vol 78 (2010) PARA 526.

4 Local Audit and Accountability Act 2014 s 25(1). References s 25 to copies of a document include a reference to copies of any part of it.

5 Local Audit and Accountability Act 2014 s 25(1)(a). As to the statement of accounts see PARA 588.
6 Local Audit and Accountability Act 2014 s 25(1)(b). As to the local auditor's certificate see PARA 597.
7 Local Audit and Accountability Act 2014 s 25(1)(c). As to the local auditor's opinion see PARA 597.
8 Local Audit and Accountability Act 2014 s 25(1)(d). As to public interest reports see PARA 598.
9 Local Audit and Accountability Act 2014 s 25(1)(d). As to recommendations see PARA 598. As to the meaning of 'connected with' see PARA 597 note 31.
10 Local Audit and Accountability Act 2014 s 25(2).
11 Local Audit and Accountability Act 2014 s 25(3).
12 Local Audit and Accountability Act 2014 s 25(4).
13 In the Local Audit and Accountability Act 2014 s 26(1) 'journalist' means any person who produces for publication journalistic material (whether paid to do so or otherwise): s 26(1A) (added by the Local Audit (Public Access to Documents) Act 2017 s 26(1), (3)). As to the meaning of 'any persons interested', and the use to which information obtained may be put, see *R (on the application of HTV) v Bristol City Council* [2004] EWHC 1219 (Admin), [2004] 1 WLR 2717; and *R (on the application of Veolia ES Nottinghamshire Ltd) v Nottinghamshire County Council* [2010] EWCA Civ 1214, [2011] LGR 95.
14 Local Audit and Accountability Act 2014 s 26(1) (amended by Local Audit (Public Access to Documents) Act 2017 s 1(1), (2)).
15 Local Audit and Accountability Act 2014 s 26(1)(a).
16 Local Audit and Accountability Act 2014 s 26(1)(b).
17 Local Audit and Accountability Act 2014 s 26(2). The local auditor's reasonable costs of complying with s 26(2) are recoverable from the relevant authority to which the accounts relate: s 26(3). As to the meaning of 'costs' see PARA 597 note 37.
18 Local Audit and Accountability Act 2014 s 26(4)(a). Information is protected on the grounds of commercial confidentiality if:
   (1) its disclosure would prejudice commercial confidentiality (s 26(5)(a)); and
   (2) there is no overriding public interest in favour of its disclosure (s 26(5)(b)).
19 Local Audit and Accountability Act 2014 s 26(4)(b).
20 Local Audit and Accountability Act 2014 s 26(6)(a). Information is personal information if it identifies a particular individual or enables a particular individual to be identified (but see s 26(8)): s 26(7). Information is not personal information merely because it relates to a business carried on by an individual as a sole trader: s 26(8). Information is personal information if it is information about an officer of the relevant authority which relates specifically to a particular individual and is available to the authority because:
   (1) the individual holds or has held an office or employment with that authority (s 26(9)(a)); or
   (2) payments or other benefits in respect of an office or employment under any other person are or have been made or provided to that individual by that authority (s 26(9)(b)).
   For the purposes of s 26(9):
   (a) 'the relevant authority' means the relevant authority whose accounts are being audited (s 26(10)(a)); and
   (b) payments made or benefits provided to an individual in respect of an office or employment include any payment made or benefit provided in respect of the individual ceasing to hold the office or employment (s 26(10)(b)).
21 Local Audit and Accountability Act 2014 s 26(6)(b).

600. Public objections to matters in audit.

The following provisions apply if, at an audit of accounts[1] under the Local Audit and Accountability Act 2014 other than an audit of accounts of a health service body[2], a local government elector[3] for an area to which the accounts relate makes an objection to the local auditor which meets the requirements below[4] and which:

(1) concerns a matter in respect of which the auditor could make a public interest report[5]; or
(2) concerns a matter in respect of which the auditor could apply[6] for a declaration[7].

The requirements are that:

(a) the objection is made in writing[8]; and
(b) a copy of the objection is sent to the relevant authority[9] whose accounts are being audited[10].

The local auditor must decide whether to consider the objection and, if the auditor does so, whether to take action within head (1) or (2) above in response[11]. The local auditor may decide not to consider the objection if, in particular, the auditor thinks that:

(i) the objection is frivolous or vexatious[12];
(ii) the cost of the auditor considering the objection would be disproportionate to the sums to which the objection relates[13]; or
(iii) the objection repeats an objection already considered[14] by a local auditor of the authority's accounts or by an auditor appointed under the Audit Commission Act 1998[15] in relation to those accounts[16].

If the local auditor decides not to take action within head (1) or (2) above, the auditor may recommend that the relevant authority should instead take action in response to the objection[17].

The local auditor's reasonable costs[18] of exercising functions under these provisions are recoverable from the relevant authority[19].

Information obtained in the exercise of functions under the Local Audit and Accountability Act 2014 which relates to a particular body or person and which is not available to the public may not be disclosed, except with the consent of the body or person to whom the information relates, for the purposes of any functions of a person under or by virtue of the Local Audit and Accountability Act 2014, or for other specified purposes[20].

1 As to the meaning of 'accounts' see PARA 588 note 6.
2 As to the meaning of 'health service body' see PARA 588 note 4. As to audits see PARA 597 et seq.
3 As to the meaning of 'local government elector' see PARA 599 note 3.
4 Ie the requirements of the Local Audit and Accountability Act 2014 s 27(2): s 27(1).
5 Local Audit and Accountability Act 2014 s 27(1)(a). As to public interest reports see PARA 598.
6 Ie under the Local Audit and Accountability Act 2014 s 28: see PARA 601.
7 Local Audit and Accountability Act 2014 s 27(1)(b).
8 Local Audit and Accountability Act 2014 s 27(2)(a).
9 As to the meaning of 'relevant authority' see PARA 588 note 3.
10 Local Audit and Accountability Act 2014 s 27(2)(b).
11 Local Audit and Accountability Act 2014 s 27(3).
12 Local Audit and Accountability Act 2014 s 27(4)(a).
13 Local Audit and Accountability Act 2014 s 27(4)(b). Section 27(4)(b) does not entitle the local auditor to refuse to consider an objection which the auditor thinks might disclose serious concerns about how the relevant authority is managed or led: s 27(5).
14 Ie under the Local Audit and Accountability Act 2014 s 27.
15 Ie under the Audit Commission Act 1998 s 16 (repealed).
16 Local Audit and Accountability Act 2014 s 27(4)(c).
17 Local Audit and Accountability Act 2014 s 27(6).
18 As to the meaning of 'costs' see PARA 597 note 37.
19 Local Audit and Accountability Act 2014 s 27(7).
20 See the Local Audit and Accountability Act 2014 s 36, Sch 11 paras 1–4. Disclosure in breach of Sch 11 is an offence: see Sch 11 para 5.

601. Declaration that item of account is unlawful.

If a local auditor[1] carrying out an audit of accounts[2] under the Local Audit and Accountability Act 2014, other than an audit of accounts of a health service body[3], thinks that an item of account[4] is contrary to law, the auditor may apply to the court for a declaration to that effect[5].

On such an application, the court:

(1) may make or refuse to make the declaration[6]; and

(2) if it makes the declaration, may also order rectification of the statement of accounts or accounting records[7].

A person who has objected concerning a matter in respect of which the auditor could apply for a declaration[8] and who is aggrieved by a decision of the local auditor not to consider the objection or not to apply for a declaration[9] may:

(a) within the period of six weeks beginning with the day after that on which the person is notified of the decision, require the auditor to provide written reasons for the decision[10]; and

(b) within the period of 21 days beginning with the day after that on which the person receives those written reasons, appeal against the decision to the court[11].

On an appeal, the court has the same powers in relation to the item of account to which the objection relates as it would have on an application by the local auditor for the declaration[12]. On an application or appeal under these provisions, the court may make an order for the payment by the relevant authority to which the application or appeal relates of expenses[13] incurred in connection with it by the local auditor or the person by whom the appeal is brought[14].

If a local auditor of the accounts of a relevant authority incurs costs[15] in determining whether to make an application for a declaration in relation to the authority, but the application is not in fact made[16], the local auditor may recover the reasonable costs so incurred from the relevant authority[17].

1 As to local auditors see PARA 591 et seq.
2 As to the meaning of 'accounts' see PARA 588 note 6.
3 As to the meaning of 'health service body' see PARA 588 note 4.
4 In the Local Audit and Accountability Act 2014, 'item of account', in relation to a relevant authority, means an item in the authority's accounting records or statement of accounts: s 28(9). As to the meaning of 'relevant authority' see PARA 588 note 3.
5 Local Audit and Accountability Act 2014 s 28(1). The High Court and the County Court have jurisdiction for the purposes of s 28: s 28(8). As to meaning of 'contrary to law' see *Roberts v Hopwood* [1925] AC 578, HL; *Pickwell v Camden London Borough Council* [1983] QB 962, [1983] 1 All ER 602; and *Allsop v North Tyneside Metropolitan Borough Council* (1992) 90 LGR 462, [1992] ICR 639, CA.
6 Local Audit and Accountability Act 2014 s 28(2)(a).
7 Local Audit and Accountability Act 2014 s 28(2)(b).
8 Ie under the Local Audit and Accountability Act 2014 s 27(1)(b): see PARA 600.
9 Local Audit and Accountability Act 2014 s 28(3).
10 Local Audit and Accountability Act 2014 s 28(3)(a).
11 Local Audit and Accountability Act 2014 s 28(3)(b).
12 Local Audit and Accountability Act 2014 s 28(4). For decisions expressing the view that the court should be slow to interfere with the discretion of the expert auditor see *R (on the application of Moss) v KPMG LLP* [2010] EWHC 2923 (Admin); and *Nicolson v Grant Thornton UK LLP* [2016] EWHC 710 (Admin), [2017] RVR 43.
13 As to the meaning of 'expenses' see PARA 597 note 37.
14 Local Audit and Accountability Act 2014 s 28(5).
15 As to the meaning of 'costs' see PARA 597 note 37.
16 Local Audit and Accountability Act 2014 s 28(6).
17 Local Audit and Accountability Act 2014 s 28(7).

D. PREVENTION OF UNLAWFUL EXPENDITURE

602. Power of local auditor to issue advisory notice.

A local auditor[1] of the accounts[2] of a relevant authority[3], other than a health service body[4], may issue an advisory notice[5] if the auditor thinks that the authority or an officer of the authority:

(1) is about to make or has made a decision which involves or would involve the authority incurring unlawful expenditure[6];
(2) is about to take or has begun to take a course of action which, if followed to its conclusion, would be unlawful and likely to cause a loss or deficiency[7]; or
(3) is about to enter an item of account, the entry of which is unlawful[8].

For the purposes of the statutory provisions relating to advisory notices[9] the actions of the following are to be treated as actions of the relevant authority itself[10]:

(a) a committee or sub-committee of the authority[11];
(b) any other person (other than an officer) authorised to act on behalf of the authority[12].

A copy of an advisory notice:

(i) in the case of a notice addressed to a relevant authority, must be served on the relevant authority[13];
(ii) in the case of a notice addressed to an officer, must be served on the relevant authority concerned[14] and the officer[15]; and
(iii) may be served on any other person the local auditor thinks appropriate[16].

If the relevant authority referred to in head (i) or (ii) is a connected entity[17], a copy of the notice must also be served on its related authority or authorities[18].

The local auditor must serve a statement of the auditor's reasons for the belief referred to in heads (1) to (3) above[19]:

(A) on the relevant authority concerned[20];
(B) on any officer on whom a copy of the notice was served under head (ii) above[21]; and
(C) if a copy of the notice was served on a related authority or authorities[22], on that authority or those authorities[23].

The statement must be served before the end of the period of seven days beginning with the day on which a copy of the notice was served on the person to whom it is addressed[24].

An advisory notice may at any time be withdrawn by the local auditor of the accounts of the relevant authority to which, or to an officer of which, the notice was addressed[25]. The local auditor must give notice in writing of the withdrawal to any person on whom a copy of the advisory notice was served[26].

While an advisory notice has effect, it is not lawful for the relevant authority concerned or any officer of that authority[27]:

(I) if the notice relates to a decision, to make or implement the decision[28];
(II) if the notice relates to a course of action, to take or continue to take the course of action[29]; or
(III) if the notice relates to an item of account, to enter the item of account[30].

This does not apply if:

(AA) the relevant authority has considered, in the light of the advisory notice and the statement of the auditor's reasons[31], the consequences of doing the thing mentioned in heads (I) to (III) which is relevant[32];
(BB) the relevant authority or officer has given the authority's local auditor and (where applicable) its related authority or each of its related authorities the period of notice in writing required[33] by the advisory notice[34]; and
(CC) that period has expired[35].

An advisory notice takes effect on the day on which a copy of the notice is served on the person to whom it is addressed, and ceases to have effect either, if a statement of reasons is not served in accordance with the statutory provision[36], at the end of the period specified[37] for service of the statement of reasons[38], or when it is withdrawn[39].

A local auditor may recover from a relevant authority the reasonable costs[40] of determining whether to issue an advisory notice to that authority or an officer of that authority[41], and the reasonable costs of issuing an advisory notice to that authority or an officer of that authority[42].

1 As to local auditors see PARA 591 et seq.

2 As to the meaning of 'accounts' see PARA 588 note 6.

3 As to the meaning of 'relevant authority' see PARA 588 note 3.

4 As to the meaning of 'health service body' see PARA 588 note 4. As to the powers of a local auditor of the accounts of a health service body see the Local Audit and Accountability Act 2014 s 30; and HEALTH SERVICES vol 54A (2017) PARA 550.

5 Local Audit and Accountability Act 2014 s 29, Sch 8 para 1(1). An advisory notice is a notice which:
(1) is addressed to the authority or officer concerned (Sch 8 para 1(2)(a));
(2) specifies the paragraph of Sch 8 para 1(1) (see heads (1)–(3) in the text) which is relevant and the decision, course of action or item of account to which the notice relates (Sch 8 para 1(2)(b));
(3) specifies that the notice will take effect on the day on which a copy of the notice is served on the person to whom it is addressed (Sch 8 para 1(2)(c)); and
(4) requires the authority or officer to give the authority's local auditor at least the specified number of days' notice in writing of the intention of the authority or officer to:
(a) make or implement the decision (Sch 8 para 1(2)(d)(i));
(b) take or continue to take the course of action (Sch 8 para 1(2)(d)(ii)); or
(c) enter the item of account (Sch 8 para 1(2)(d)(iii)),
(as the case may be) (Sch 8 para 1(2)(d)).
In Sch 8 para 1(2)(d) 'the specified number' means the number of days specified in the notice, which may not be more than 21: Sch 8 para 1(3).
See also PARA 603 as to the power of a local auditor to apply for judicial review.

6 Local Audit and Accountability Act 2014 Sch 8 para 1(1)(a).

7 Local Audit and Accountability Act 2014 Sch 8 para 1(1)(b).

8 Local Audit and Accountability Act 2014 Sch 8 para 1(1)(c).

9 Ie the Local Audit and Accountability Act 2014 Sch 8.

10 Local Audit and Accountability Act 2014 Sch 8 para 1(4).

11 Local Audit and Accountability Act 2014 Sch 8 para 1(4)(a).

12 Local Audit and Accountability Act 2014 Sch 8 para 1(4)(b).

13 Local Audit and Accountability Act 2014 Sch 8 para 2(1)(a). Schedule 8 para 4(2) applies if:
(1) before an advisory notice is served, a relevant authority enters into a contract to dispose of or acquire an interest in land (Sch 8 para 4(1)(a)); and
(2) before the disposal or acquisition is completed, an advisory notice takes effect as a result of which it is unlawful for the authority to complete the disposal or acquisition (Sch 8 para 4(1)(b)).
The existence of the advisory notice does not affect any remedy in damages which may be available to any person by reason of the relevant authority's failure to complete the contract: Sch 8 para 4(2). No action lies against a local auditor in respect of loss or damage alleged to have been caused by reason of the issue of an advisory notice which was issued in good faith: Sch 8 para 4(3).

14 In the Local Audit and Accountability Act 2014 Sch 8, 'the relevant authority concerned', in relation to an advisory notice, means the relevant authority to which, or to any officer of which, the notice is addressed: Sch 8 para 2(8).

15 Local Audit and Accountability Act 2014 Sch 8 para 2(1)(b). Where Sch 8 para 2 requires a document to be served on an officer of a relevant authority, it must be served by addressing it to the officer and delivering it to the officer or leaving it at, or sending it by post to, the office where the officer is employed: Sch 8 para 2(5).

16 Local Audit and Accountability Act 2014 Sch 8 para 2(1)(c). As to the meaning of 'person' see PARA 11 note 13.

17 As to the meaning of 'connected entity' see PARA 597 note 31.

18 Local Audit and Accountability Act 2014 Sch 8 para 2(2).
19 Local Audit and Accountability Act 2014 Sch 8 para 2(3).
20 Local Audit and Accountability Act 2014 Sch 8 para 2(3)(a).
21 Local Audit and Accountability Act 2014 Sch 8 para 2(3)(b).
22 Ie under the Local Audit and Accountability Act 2014 Sch 8 para 2(2): see the text to notes 17–18.
23 Local Audit and Accountability Act 2014 Sch 8 para 2(3)(c).
24 Local Audit and Accountability Act 2014 Sch 8 para 2(4).
25 Local Audit and Accountability Act 2014 Sch 8 para 2(6).
26 Local Audit and Accountability Act 2014 Sch 8 para 2(7).
27 Local Audit and Accountability Act 2014 Sch 8 para 3(1).
28 Local Audit and Accountability Act 2014 Sch 8 para 3(1)(a).
29 Local Audit and Accountability Act 2014 Sch 8 para 3(1)(b).
30 Local Audit and Accountability Act 2014 Sch 8 para 3(1)(c).
31 Ie the statement under the Local Audit and Accountability Act 2014 Sch 8 para 2(3): see the text to notes 19–23.
32 Local Audit and Accountability Act 2014 Sch 8 para 3(2)(a). The condition in Sch 8 para 3(2)(a) is met in relation to a parish meeting only if the matters referred to in that paragraph are considered by the parish meeting itself (and not by its chairman on behalf of the parish meeting): Sch 8 para 3(3). As to the meaning of 'parish meeting' see PARA 588 note 3.
33 Ie under the Local Audit and Accountability Act 2014 Sch 8 para 1(2)(d): see note 5 head (4).
34 Local Audit and Accountability Act 2014 Sch 8 para 3(2)(b).
35 Local Audit and Accountability Act 2014 Sch 8 para 3(2)(c).
36 Ie the Local Audit and Accountability Act 2014 Sch 8 para 2(3): see the text to notes 19–23.
37 Ie in the Local Audit and Accountability Act 2014 Sch 8 para 2(4): see the text to note 24.
38 Local Audit and Accountability Act 2014 Sch 8 para 3(4)(a).
39 Local Audit and Accountability Act 2014 Sch 8 para 3(4)(b).
40 As to the meaning of 'costs' see PARA 597 note 37.
41 Local Audit and Accountability Act 2014 Sch 8 para 3(5)(a). This applies regardless of whether the notice is in fact issued: Sch 8 para 3(6).
42 Local Audit and Accountability Act 2014 Sch 8 para 3(5)(b).

603. Power of local auditor to apply for judicial review.

A local auditor[1] appointed to audit the accounts[2] of a relevant authority[3] other than a health service body[4] may make an application for judicial review of a decision of that authority, or of a failure by that authority to act, which it is reasonable to believe would have an effect on the accounts of that body[5]. This does not affect the statutory requirement[6] to obtain the leave of the High Court to make the application[7]. The existence of the powers conferred on a local auditor under the Local Audit and Accountability Act 2014 is not a ground for refusing an application for judicial review (or an application for leave to make the application)[8].

On an application for judicial review made as mentioned above, the court may make such order as it thinks fit for the payment by the relevant authority of expenses[9] incurred by the local auditor in connection with the application[10].

If a local auditor of the accounts of a relevant authority incurs costs[11] in determining whether to make an application for judicial review in relation to the authority, but the application is not in fact made[12], the local auditor may recover the reasonable costs so incurred from the relevant authority[13].

1 As to local auditors see PARA 591 et seq.
2 As to the meaning of 'accounts' see PARA 588 note 6.
3 As to the meaning of 'relevant authority' see PARA 588 note 3.
4 As to the meaning of 'health service body' see PARA 588 note 4. As to the powers of a local auditor of the accounts of a health service body see the Local Audit and Accountability Act 2014 s 30; and HEALTH SERVICES vol 54A (2017) PARA 550.
5 Local Audit and Accountability Act 2014 s 31(1). As to judicial review see JUDICIAL REVIEW vol 61 (2010) PARA 601 et seq. See also PARA 602 as to the power of a local auditor to issue an advisory notice.

6 Ie in the Senior Courts Act 1981 s 31(3): see JUDICIAL REVIEW vol 61 (2010) PARA 660.
7 Local Audit and Accountability Act 2014 s 31(2).
8 Local Audit and Accountability Act 2014 s 31(3).
9 As to the meaning of 'expenses' see PARA 597 note 37.
10 Local Audit and Accountability Act 2014 s 31(4).
11 As to the meaning of 'costs' see PARA 597 note 37.
12 Local Audit and Accountability Act 2014 s 31(5).
13 Local Audit and Accountability Act 2014 s 31(6).

604. Data matching to assist in prevention and detection of fraud.

The Secretary of State or the Minister for the Cabinet Office ('the relevant minister')[1] may conduct data matching exercises or arrange for them to be conducted on the relevant minister's behalf, exercisable for the purpose of assisting in the prevention and detection of fraud[2]. A data matching exercise is an exercise involving the comparison of sets of data to determine how far they match (including the identification of any patterns and trends)[3].

A data matching exercise may not be used to identify patterns and trends in an individual's characteristics or behaviour which suggest nothing more than the individual's potential to commit fraud in the future[4].

The relevant minister must prepare, and keep under review, a code of practice with respect to data matching exercises, and regard must be had to the code in conducting and participating in any such exercise[5].

A relevant minister may require a person specified below to provide the minister or a person acting on the minister's behalf with such data (and in such form) as the minister or that person may reasonably require for the purpose of conducting data matching exercises[6]. Those persons are[7]:

(1) a relevant authority[8];
(2) a best value authority[9] which is not a relevant authority[10]; and
(3) an NHS foundation trust[11].

If a relevant minister thinks it appropriate to conduct a data matching exercise using data held by or on behalf of a body or person in England, the data may be disclosed to the minister or a person acting on the minister's behalf[12]. Certain data is excluded from disclosure[13]. A disclosure under this provision does not breach any obligation of confidence owed by a person making the disclosure[14], or any other restriction on the disclosure of information (however imposed)[15]. These provisions do not limit the circumstances in which data may be disclosed apart from them[16]. Data matching exercises may include data provided by a body or person outside England[17].

Provision is made as to the disclosure of the results of data matching exercises[18], publication of reports of data matching exercises[19] and fees which may be prescribed in connection with data matching exercises[20].

The relevant minister may amend the statutory provisions relating to data matching[21].

1 Local Audit and Accountability Act 2014 s 33, Sch 9 para 1(2). As to the Secretary of State see PARA 4 note 18. As to the Cabinet Office see CONSTITUTIONAL AND ADMINISTRATIVE LAW vol 20 (2014) PARAS 234–236.
2 Local Audit and Accountability Act 2014 Sch 9 para 1(1), (4).
3 Local Audit and Accountability Act 2014 Sch 9 para 1(3). In Sch 9, any reference to a data matching exercise is to an exercise conducted or arranged to be conducted under Sch 9 para 1: Sch 9 para 1(6).
4 Local Audit and Accountability Act 2014 Sch 9 para 1(5).
5 Local Audit and Accountability Act 2014 Sch 9 para 7(1), (2). Before preparing or altering the code, the relevant minister must consult:
(1) the persons within Sch 9 para 2(2) (see heads (1)–(3) in the text) (Sch 9 para 7(3)(a));

(2) such representatives of persons within Sch 9 para 2(2) as the minister thinks appropriate (Sch 9 para 7(3)(b));
(3) the Information Commissioner (Sch 9 para 7(3)(c)); and
(4) such other bodies or persons as the minister thinks appropriate (Sch 9 para 7(3)(d)).
The relevant minister must:
(a) lay a copy of the code, and of any alterations made to it, before Parliament (Sch 9 para 7(4)(a)); and
(b) from time to time publish the code as for the time being in force (Sch 9 para 7(4)(b)).
As to the Information Commissioner see CONFIDENCE AND INFORMATIONAL PRIVACY vol 19 (2011) PARA 109.

6 Local Audit and Accountability Act 2014 Sch 9 para 2(1).
7 Local Audit and Accountability Act 2014 Sch 9 para 2(2).
8 Local Audit and Accountability Act 2014 Sch 9 para 2(2)(a). As to the meaning of 'relevant authority' see PARA 588 note 3.
9 'Best value authority' has the meaning given by the Local Government Act 1999 s 1 (see LOCAL GOVERNMENT vol 69 (2018) PARA 779): Local Audit and Accountability Act 2014 Sch 9 para 2(3).
10 Local Audit and Accountability Act 2014 Sch 9 para 2(2)(b).
11 Local Audit and Accountability Act 2014 Sch 9 para 2(2)(c). As to NHS foundation trusts see HEALTH SERVICES vol 54 (2017) PARA 244 et seq.
12 Local Audit and Accountability Act 2014 Sch 9 para 3(1). This applies to the disclosure of data by a relevant authority, a best value authority or an NHS foundation trust otherwise than in response to a requirement under Sch 9 para 2 as it applies to other disclosures of data: Sch 9 para 3(2).
13 The Local Audit and Accountability Act 2014 Sch 9 para 3(1) does not authorise:
(1) a disclosure which contravenes the Data Protection Act 1998 (Local Audit and Accountability Act 2014 Sch 9 para 3(3)(a)); or
(2) a disclosure prohibited by (until a day to be appointed) the Regulation of Investigatory Powers Act 2000 Pt 1 or (as from a day to be appointed) any of the Investigatory Powers Act 2016 Pts 1–7 or Pt 9 Ch 1 (Local Audit and Accountability Act 2014 Sch 9 para 3(3)(b) (amended, as from a day to be appointed, by the Investigatory Powers Act 2016 s 271(1), Sch 10 para 31; at the date at which this volume states the law, no such day had been appointed).

Data may not be disclosed under the Local Audit and Accountability Act 2014 Sch 9 para 3(1) if the data comprise or include patient data: Sch 9 para 3(4). 'Patient data' means data relating to an individual which are held for medical purposes (within the meaning of the National Health Service Act 2006 s 251) and from which the individual can be identified: Local Audit and Accountability Act 2014 Sch 9 para 3(5).

14 Local Audit and Accountability Act 2014 Sch 9 para 3(6)(a).
15 Local Audit and Accountability Act 2014 Sch 9 para 3(6)(b).
16 Local Audit and Accountability Act 2014 Sch 9 para 3(7).
17 Local Audit and Accountability Act 2014 Sch 9 para 3(8). As to the meaning of 'England' see PARA 2 note 16.
18 See the Local Audit and Accountability Act 2014 Sch 9 para 4.
19 See the Local Audit and Accountability Act 2014 Sch 9 para 5.
20 See the Local Audit and Accountability Act 2014 Sch 9 para 6.
21 See the Local Audit and Accountability Act 2014 Sch 9 para 8.

E. ACCOUNTS AND AUDIT REGULATIONS

605. Power to make accounts and audit regulations.

The Secretary of State[1] may by regulations[2] applying to relevant authorities[3] other than health service bodies[4] make provision about[5]:

(1) the form and contents of accounting records[6];
(2) the form, contents, preparation and approval of statements of accounts[7];
(3) the preservation of accounting records or statements of accounts[8];
(4) the publication of accounting records, statements of accounts or other information[9];

(5) the exercise of any rights of objection or inspection[10] and the steps to be taken by any authority to enable those rights to be exercised[11];
(6) the financial management of relevant authorities[12];
(7) the maintenance by relevant authorities of systems of internal control (including arrangements for the management of risk)[13].

Before making any such regulations, the Secretary of State must consult[14]:

(a) the Comptroller and Auditor General[15];
(b) such representatives of relevant authorities as the Secretary of State thinks appropriate[16]; and
(c) the recognised supervisory bodies[17].

1 As to the Secretary of State see PARA 4 note 18. The Local Audit and Accountability Act 2014 s 32 does not apply to the accounts of a local government body in Wales. As to accounts and audit regulations in relation to Wales see PARA 653. As to the meaning of 'Wales' see PARA 2 note 16.
2 Any power of the Secretary of State to make regulations or an order under the Local Audit and Accountability Act 2014 is exercisable by statutory instrument: s 43(1). Any power of the Secretary of State to make regulations or an order under that Act includes:
 (1) power to make different provision for different cases or classes of case, including different provision for different authorities (s 43(2)(a));
 (2) power to make incidental, supplementary, consequential, transitional or transitory provision or savings (s 43(2)(b)).
 A statutory instrument containing regulations under s 32 is subject to annulment in pursuance of a resolution of either House of Parliament: s 43(5). As to the regulations made see the Accounts and Audit Regulations 2015, SI 2015/234; and PARA 606 et seq.
3 As to the meaning of 'relevant authority' see PARA 588 note 3. As to the power to modify the audit of accounts of smaller authorities see PARA 589.
4 As to the meaning of 'health service body' see PARA 588 note 4.
5 Local Audit and Accountability Act 2014 s 32(1).
6 Local Audit and Accountability Act 2014 s 32(1)(a).
7 Local Audit and Accountability Act 2014 s 32(1)(b). Regulations under s 32(1)(b) may, in particular, make provision about any information to be provided by way of notes to the accounts: s 32(2). As to the meaning of 'accounts' see PARA 588 note 6.
8 Local Audit and Accountability Act 2014 s 32(1)(c).
9 Local Audit and Accountability Act 2014 s 32(1)(d).
10 Ie conferred by the Local Audit and Accountability Act 2014 s 25, 26 or 27: see PARAS 599—600.
11 Local Audit and Accountability Act 2014 s 32(1)(e).
12 Local Audit and Accountability Act 2014 s 32(1)(f).
13 Local Audit and Accountability Act 2014 s 32(1)(g).
14 Local Audit and Accountability Act 2014 s 32(3).
15 Local Audit and Accountability Act 2014 s 32(3)(a). As to the Comptroller and Auditor General see CONSTITUTIONAL AND ADMINISTRATIVE LAW vol 20 (2014) PARA 494 et seq.
16 Local Audit and Accountability Act 2014 s 32(3)(b).
17 Local Audit and Accountability Act 2014 s 32(3)(c).

606. Responsibility for internal control and financial management.

A relevant authority[1] must ensure that it has a sound system of internal control[2] which:

(1) facilitates the effective exercise of its functions and the achievement of its aims and objectives[3];
(2) ensures that the financial and operational management of the authority is effective[4]; and
(3) includes effective arrangements for the management of risk[5].

A relevant authority must, each financial year:

(a) conduct a review of the effectiveness of the required system of internal control[6]; and
(b) prepare an annual governance statement[7].

If the relevant authority is a category 1 authority[8], following the review, it must:

(i) consider the findings of the review required by head (1), by a committee or by members of the authority meeting as a whole[9]; and

(ii) approve the annual governance statement prepared in accordance with head (b) by resolution of a committee or of members of the authority meeting as a whole[10].

If the relevant authority is a category 2 authority[11], following the review it must:

(A) consider the findings of the review by members of the authority meeting as a whole[12]; and

(B) approve the annual governance statement prepared in accordance with head (b) above by resolution of members of the authority meeting as a whole[13].

1 The Accounts and Audit Regulations 2015, SI 2015/234, apply to relevant authorities other than health service bodies: reg 1(3). As to the meaning of 'relevant authority' see PARA 588 note 3. As to the meaning of 'health service body' see PARA 588 note 4.

The Accounts and Audit Regulations 2015, SI 2015/234, being made under the Local Audit and Accountability Act 2014 ss 32, 43(2), 46, apply in relation to England only: see PARA 605. As to the equivalent regulations in relation to Wales see the Accounts and Audit (Wales) Regulations 2014, SI 2014/3362; and PARA 654 et seq. As to the meanings of 'England' and 'Wales' see PARA 2 note 16.

2 Accounts and Audit Regulations 2015, SI 2015/234, reg 3.

3 Accounts and Audit Regulations 2015, SI 2015/234, reg 3(a).

4 Accounts and Audit Regulations 2015, SI 2015/234, reg 3(b).

5 Accounts and Audit Regulations 2015, SI 2015/234, reg 3(c).

6 Accounts and Audit Regulations 2015, SI 2015/234, reg 6(1)(a).

7 Accounts and Audit Regulations 2015, SI 2015/234, reg 6(1)(b). The annual governance statement, referred to in reg 6(1)(b) must be:

(1) approved in advance of the relevant authority approving the statement of accounts in accordance with reg 9(2)(b) or 12(2)(b) (as the case may be) (see PARA 611) (reg 6(4)(a)); and

(2) prepared in accordance with proper practices in relation to accounts (reg 6(4)(b)).

As to the meaning of 'proper practices' see PARA 590 note 4.

8 'Category 1 authority' means a relevant authority that either is not a smaller authority; or is a smaller authority that has chosen to prepare its accounts for the purpose of a full audit in accordance with the Local Audit (Smaller Authorities) Regulations 2015, SI 2015/184, reg 8: Accounts and Audit Regulations 2015, SI 2015/234, reg 2(1). 'Smaller authority' is defined in the Local Audit and Accountability Act 2014 s 6 (see PARA 589 note 3); the qualifying condition to be met for a relevant authority and a financial year is that the higher of the authority's gross income for the year and its gross expenditure for the year does not exceed £6.5 million: see s 6(2). In the Local Audit (Smaller Authorities) Regulations 2015, SI 2015/184, 'smaller authority' does not include a health service body, the Mayor's Office for Policing and Crime, a police and crime commissioner for a police area in England, a chief constable for an area in England, the Commissioner of Police of the Metropolis or the Common Council of the City of London: reg 2.

9 Accounts and Audit Regulations 2015, SI 2015/234, reg 6(2)(a). Where a relevant authority is a corporation sole, references to 'members of the authority meeting as a whole' are to a holder of that office of corporation sole: reg 2(3). As to corporations sole see CORPORATIONS vol 24 (2010) PARA 314 et seq.

10 Accounts and Audit Regulations 2015, SI 2015/234, reg 6(2)(b).

11 'Category 2 authority' means a smaller authority which is not a category 1 authority: Accounts and Audit Regulations 2015, SI 2015/234, reg 2(1).

12 Accounts and Audit Regulations 2015, SI 2015/234, reg 6(3)(a).

13 Accounts and Audit Regulations 2015, SI 2015/234, reg 6(3)(b).

607. Accounting records, control systems and internal audit.

Subject as provided[1], and, in so far as they are not in conflict with those provisions, to any instructions given by a relevant authority[2] to its responsible financial officer[3], that officer must determine on behalf of the authority[4]:

(1) the form of its accounting records and supporting records[5]; and;

(2) its financial control systems[6].

The responsible financial officer for a relevant authority must ensure on behalf of that authority that the financial control systems determined by that officer in accordance with head (2) are observed and that the accounting records of the authority are kept up to date[7]. The accounting records must, in particular, contain[8]:

(a) entries from day to day of all sums of money received and expended by the authority and the matters to which its income and expenditure or receipts and payments relate[9]; and

(b) a record of the assets and liabilities of the authority[10].

The financial control systems determined in accordance with head (2) must include[11]:

(i) measures:

(A) to ensure that the financial transactions of the authority are recorded as soon as, and as accurately as, reasonably practicable[12];

(B) to enable the prevention and the detection of inaccuracies and fraud, and the reconstitution of any lost records[13]; and

(C) to ensure that risk is appropriately managed[14];

(ii) identification of the duties of officers dealing with financial transactions and division of responsibilities of those officers[15].

A relevant authority must undertake an effective internal audit to evaluate the effectiveness of its risk management, control and governance processes, taking into account public sector internal auditing standards or guidance[16]. Any officer or member of a relevant authority must, if required to do so for the purposes of the internal audit:

(I) make available such documents and records[17]; and

(II) supply such information and explanations[18],

as are considered necessary by those conducting the internal audit[19].

1 Ie subject to the Accounts and Audit Regulations 2015, SI 2015/234, reg 4(3), (4): see the text to notes 8–15.

2 As to the meaning of 'relevant authority' see PARA 588 note 3; and see PARA 606 note 1.

3 Any reference in the Accounts and Audit Regulations 2015, SI 2015/234, to the 'responsible financial officer' means:

(1) the person who, by virtue of:

(a) the Local Government Act 1972 s 151 (financial administration: see PARA 665);

(b) the Norfolk and Suffolk Broads Act 1988 s 17(1) (accounts) (see WATER AND WATERWAYS vol 101 (2009) PARA 735);

(c) the Local Government Finance Act 1988 s 112(1) (financial administration as to certain authorities: see PARA 665);

(d) the Local Government and Housing Act 1989 s 6(1) (officer responsible for financial administration of certain authorities: see PARA 665);

(e) the Environment Act 1995 Sch 7 para 13(6) (National Park Authorities: see OPEN SPACES AND COUNTRYSIDE vol 78 (2010) PARA 644);

(f) the Greater London Authority Act 1999 s 127(2): see LONDON GOVERNMENT vol 71 (2013) PARA 154;

(g) the Police Reform and Social Responsibility Act 2011 Sch 1 para 6(1)(b) (police and crime commissioners);

(h) the Police Reform and Social Responsibility Act 2011 Sch 2 para 4(1) (chief constables);

(i) the Police Reform and Social Responsibility Act 2011 Sch 4 para 1(1) (Commissioner of Police of the Metropolis), as the case may be, is responsible for the administration of the financial affairs of a relevant authority or, if no person is so responsible, the person who is responsible for keeping the accounts of such an authority (Accounts and Audit Regulations 2015, SI 2015/234, reg 2(2)(a)); or

(2) if the person referred to in head (1) ('P') is unable to act owing to absence or illness, such member of P's staff as is nominated by P for the purposes of the Local Government Finance Act 1988 s 114 (functions of responsible officer as regards reports: see PARA 667) or where that section does not apply to the relevant authority, such member of staff as is nominated by P for the purposes of the Accounts and Audit Regulations 2015, SI 2015/234 (reg 2(2)(b)).

4 Accounts and Audit Regulations 2015, SI 2015/234, reg 4(1).

The Accounts and Audit Regulations 2015, SI 2015/234, being made under the Local Audit and Accountability Act 2014 ss 32, 43(2), 46, apply in relation to England only: see PARA 605. As to the equivalent regulations in relation to Wales see the Accounts and Audit (Wales) Regulations 2014, SI 2014/3362; and PARA 654 et seq. As to the meanings of 'England' and 'Wales' see PARA 2 note 16.

5 Accounts and Audit Regulations 2015, SI 2015/234, reg 4(1)(a).

6 Accounts and Audit Regulations 2015, SI 2015/234, reg 4(1)(b).

7 Accounts and Audit Regulations 2015, SI 2015/234, reg 4(2). As to statements of accounts and other accounting statements see PARAS 608–609.

8 Accounts and Audit Regulations 2015, SI 2015/234, reg 4(3).

9 Accounts and Audit Regulations 2015, SI 2015/234, reg 4(3)(a).

10 Accounts and Audit Regulations 2015, SI 2015/234, reg 4(3)(b).

11 Accounts and Audit Regulations 2015, SI 2015/234, reg 4(4).

12 Accounts and Audit Regulations 2015, SI 2015/234, reg 4(4)(a)(i).

13 Accounts and Audit Regulations 2015, SI 2015/234, reg 4(4)(a)(ii).

14 Accounts and Audit Regulations 2015, SI 2015/234, reg 4(4)(a)(iii).

15 Accounts and Audit Regulations 2015, SI 2015/234, reg 4(4)(b).

16 Accounts and Audit Regulations 2015, SI 2015/234, reg 5(1).

17 Accounts and Audit Regulations 2015, SI 2015/234, reg 5(2)(a). In reg 5, 'documents and records' includes information recorded in an electronic form: reg 5(3).

18 Accounts and Audit Regulations 2015, SI 2015/234, reg 5(2)(b).

19 Accounts and Audit Regulations 2015, SI 2015/234, reg 5(2).

608. Statement of accounts: category 1 authority.

A statement of accounts prepared[1] by a category 1 authority[2] must be prepared in accordance with the relevant regulations[3] and proper practices[4] in relation to accounts[5]. The statement must include a note:

(1) except in relation to persons to whom head (2) below applies[6], of the number of employees[7] or senior police officers[8] in the year to which the accounts relate whose remuneration fell in each bracket of a scale in multiples of £5,000 starting with £50,000[9];

(2) of the remuneration, set out according to the specified categories[10], and the relevant body's contribution to the person's pension[11], by the relevant body during the relevant year of senior employees[12] or relevant police officers in respect of their employment by the relevant body or in their capacity as a police officer, whether on a permanent or temporary basis, to be listed individually in relation to such persons who must nevertheless be identified by way of job title only (except for persons whose salary is £150,000 or more per year, who must also be identified by name)[13];

(3) demonstrating whether the dedicated schools grant[14] has been deployed in accordance with the appropriate regulations[15].

In the case of a local authority which is required[16] to keep a housing revenue account, the statement of accounts must include also an account in respect of a reserve for major repairs to property of the authority (to be called a major repairs reserve)[17].

A category 1 authority must prepare a narrative statement in respect of each financial year[18]. A narrative statement so prepared must include comment by the authority on its financial performance and economy, efficiency and effectiveness in its use of resources over the financial year[19].

Provision is also made as to the preparation of accounts by a joint board, a combined authority or a National Park authority to which the regulations[20] apply[21].

1 Ie in accordance with the Local Audit and Accountability Act 2014 s 3(3). A relevant authority, other than a health service body, must prepare a statement of accounts in respect of each financial year: s 3(3). In the Local Audit and Accountability Act 2014 'financial year' means a period of 12 months ending with 31 March: s 3(4). As to the meaning of 'relevant authority' see PARA 588 note 3; and as to the meaning of 'health service body' see PARA 588 note 4.

2 As to the meaning of 'category 1 authority' see PARA 606 note 8.

3 Ie the Accounts and Audit Regulations 2015, SI 2015/234.

4 As to the meaning of 'proper practices' see PARA 590 note 4.

5 Accounts and Audit Regulations 2015, SI 2015/234, reg 7(1). The statement referred to in reg 7(1) must include such of the following accounting statements as are relevant to that authority's functions (reg 7(2)):
(1) housing revenue account (reg 7(2)(a));
(2) collection fund (reg 7(2)(b));
(3) firefighters' pension fund (reg 7(2)(c));
(4) any other statements relating to each and every other fund in relation to which the authority is required by any statutory provision to keep a separate account (reg 7(2)(d)).
As to collection funds and other funds see PARA 579 et seq. As to the signing, approval and publication of statements of accounts see PARA 611.

The Accounts and Audit Regulations 2015, SI 2015/234, being made under the Local Audit and Accountability Act 2014 ss 32, 43(2), 46, apply in relation to England only: see PARA 605. As to the equivalent regulations in relation to Wales see the Accounts and Audit (Wales) Regulations 2014, SI 2014/3362; and PARA 654 et seq. As to the meanings of 'England' and 'Wales' see PARA 2 note 16.

6 Accounts and Audit Regulations 2015, SI 2015/234, Sch 1 para 1(2).

7 'Employee' includes a member of the relevant authority, and a holder of an office under the relevant authority, but does not include a person who is an elected councillor, and 'employment' is to be construed accordingly: Accounts and Audit Regulations 2015, SI 2015/234, Sch 1 para 3.

8 'Senior police officer' means a member of a police force holding a rank above that of superintendent: Accounts and Audit Regulations 2015, SI 2015/234, Sch 1 para 3. As to ranks in a police force see POLICE AND INVESTIGATORY POWERS vol 84 (2013) PARA 163. 'Police force' has the meaning or effect described by the Police Act 1996 s 101(1) (see POLICE AND INVESTIGATORY POWERS vol 84 (2013) PARA 2): Interpretation Act 1978 s 5, Sch 1.

9 Accounts and Audit Regulations 2015, SI 2015/234, reg 7(3), Sch 1 para 1(1). 'Remuneration' means all amounts paid to or receivable by a person, and includes sums due by way of expenses allowance (so far as those sums are chargeable to United Kingdom income tax), and the estimated money value of any other benefits received by an employee otherwise than in cash: Sch 1 para 3.

10 The categories are:
(1) the total amount of salary, fees or allowances paid to or receivable by the person in the current and previous financial year (Accounts and Audit Regulations 2015, SI 2015/234, Sch 1 para 2(2)(a));
(2) the total amount of bonuses so paid or receivable in the current and previous financial year (Sch 1 para 2(2)(b));
(3) the total amount of sums paid by way of expenses allowance that are chargeable to United Kingdom income tax, and were paid to or receivable by the person (Sch 1 para 2(2)(c));
(4) the total amount of any compensation for loss of employment paid to or receivable by the person, and any other payments made to or receivable by the person in connection with the termination of their employment by the relevant authority, or, in the case of a relevant police officer, the total amount of any payment made to a relevant police officer who ceases to hold office before the end of a fixed term appointment (Sch 1 para 2(2)(d));

(5) the total estimated value of any benefits received by the person otherwise than in cash that do not fall within head (1)–(4) above, are emoluments of the person, and are received by the person in respect of their employment by the relevant authority or in their capacity as a police officer (Sch 1 para 2(2)(e)); and

(6) in relation to relevant police officers, any payments, whether made under the Police Regulations 2003, SI 2003/527, or otherwise, which do not fall within heads (1)–(5) above (Accounts and Audit Regulations 2015, SI 2015/234, Sch 1 para 2(2)(f)).

'Relevant police officer' is defined by Sch 1 para 3 as:

(a) in relation to a police force maintained under the Police Act 1996 s 2 (maintenance of police forces: see POLICE AND INVESTIGATORY POWERS vol 84 (2013) PARA 52), the chief constable;

(b) in relation to the metropolitan police force, the Commissioner of Police of the Metropolis;

(c) in relation to the City of London police force, the Commissioner of Police for the City of London; and

(d) any other senior police officer whose salary is £150,000 or more per year.

As to chief officers of police see POLICE AND INVESTIGATORY POWERS vol 84 (2013) PARA 112 et seq.

11 'Contribution to the person's pension' means an amount to be calculated as follows (Accounts and Audit Regulations 2015, SI 2015/234, Sch 1 para 3):

(1) in relation to contributions to the local government pension scheme established under the Public Service Pensions Act 2013 s 1 (see PERSONAL AND OCCUPATIONAL PENSIONS vol 80 (2013) PARA 320), the sum of:

(a) the primary rate of the employer's contribution specified in the rates and adjustment certificate prepared under the Local Government Pension Scheme Regulations 2013, SI 2013/2356, reg 62 (actuarial valuations of pension funds: see LOCAL GOVERNMENT vol 69 (2018) PARA 493) being the amount appropriate for that authority calculated in accordance with the certificate and reg 67(4) (employer's contributions: see LOCAL GOVERNMENT vol 69 (2018) PARA 493), multiplied by the person's pensionable pay; and

(b) if applicable, any additional contribution under reg 16 or 68(3) (see LOCAL GOVERNMENT vol 69 (2018) PARA 493);

(2) in relation to contributions to the firefighters' pension scheme established under the Fire Services Acts 1947 and 1959, the percentage of the aggregate of the pensionable pay calculated for the purposes of the Firemen's Pension Scheme Order 1992, SI 1992/129, Sch 2 para G2(3), (4) (see FIRE AND RESCUE SERVICES vol 51 (2013) PARA 49) multiplied by the person's pensionable pay;

(3) in relation to contributions to the firefighters' pension scheme established under the Fire and Rescue Services Act 2004, the percentage of the aggregate of the pensionable pay calculated for the purposes of the Firefighters' Pension Scheme (England) Order 2006, SI 2006/3432, Sch 1 Pt 13 Rule 2 paras (2) and (3) (see FIRE AND RESCUE SERVICES vol 51 (2013) PARA 48) multiplied by the person's pensionable pay;

(4) in relation to contributions to the firefighters' pension scheme established under the Firefighters' Pension Scheme (England) Regulations 2014, SI 2014/2848, the employer contribution rate on the member's pensionable earnings determined in accordance with reg 117, multiplied by the person's pensionable pay; or

(5) in relation to contributions to police pension schemes established under the Police Pensions Regulations 1987, SI 1987/257, or the Police Pensions Regulations 2006, SI 2006/3415 (see POLICE AND INVESTIGATORY POWERS vol 84 (2013) PARA 197 et seq) the percentage of pensionable pay specified in the Police Pension Fund Regulations 2007, SI 2007/1932, reg 5(1) (police authority contributions) multiplied by the person's pensionable pay.

12 'Senior employee' means an employee whose salary is £150,000 or more per year, or an employee whose salary is £50,000 or more per year (to be calculated pro rata for an employee employed for fewer than the usual full-time hours for the relevant authority concerned) who falls within at least one of the following categories (Accounts and Audit Regulations 2015, SI 2015/234, Sch 1 para 3):

(1) a person employed by a relevant authority to which the Local Government and Housing Act 1989 s 2 (politically restricted posts: see LOCAL GOVERNMENT vol 69 (2018) PARA 161) applies who has been designated as head of paid service under s 4(1)(a) (see

LOCAL GOVERNMENT vol 69 (2018) PARA 470), is a statutory chief officer within the meaning of s 2(6), or is a non-statutory chief officer within the meaning of s 2(7);
(2) a person who is the head of staff for any relevant authority to which s 4 does not apply; or
(3) a person who has responsibility for the management of the relevant authority to the extent that the person has power to direct or control the major activities of the authority (in particular activities involving the expenditure of money), whether solely or collectively with other persons.

13 Accounts and Audit Regulations 2015, SI 2015/234, reg 7(3), Sch 1 para 2(1).
14 Ie made under the Education Act 2002 s 14 (power of Secretary of State to give financial assistance for purposes related to education or children etc): see EDUCATION vol 35 (2015) PARA 78.
15 See the Accounts and Audit Regulations 2015, SI 2015/234, reg 7(4). The appropriate regulations are any made under School Standards and Framework Act 1998 s 45A (determination of specified budgets of local authority: see EDUCATION vol 35 (2015) PARA 315), s 45AA (power to require local authorities to make initial determination of schools budget: see EDUCATION vol 35 (2015) PARA 317), s 47 (determination of schools' budget share: see EDUCATION vol 35 (2015) PARA 316), s 48(1), (2) (local authorities' financial schemes: see EDUCATION vol 35 (2015) PARA 321), s 138(7) (orders and regulations), and Sch 14 para 1(7)(b) (see EDUCATION vol 35 (2015) PARA 322): see the Accounts and Audit Regulations 2015, SI 2015/234, reg 7(4)(a)–(f).
16 Ie by Local Government and Housing Act 1989 s 74: see HOUSING vol 56 (2017) PARA 356.
17 See the Accounts and Audit Regulations 2015, SI 2015/234, reg 7(5).
18 Accounts and Audit Regulations 2015, SI 2015/234, reg 8(1) (amended by SI 2018/91). The statement must be prepared in accordance with reg 8(2) (see the text to note 21): reg 8(1).
19 Accounts and Audit Regulations 2015, SI 2015/234, reg 8(2).
20 Ie the Accounts and Audit Regulations 2015, SI 2015/234.
21 See the Accounts and Audit Regulations 2015, SI 2015/234, reg 19. As to combined authorities see TRADE AND INDUSTRY vol 97 (2015) PARA 1092 et seq. As to National Park authorities see OPEN SPACES AND COUNTRYSIDE vol 78 (2010) PARA 644.

609. Statement of accounts: category 2 authority.

A category 2 authority[1] must ensure that required[2] the statement of accounts is prepared in accordance with the relevant regulations[3]. A statement of accounts so prepared by a category 2 authority must take the form of:

(1) an income and expenditure account[4]; and
(2) a statement of balances[5],

prepared in accordance with, and in the form specified in any annual return required by, proper practices[6] in relation to accounts[7].

However, where in relation to a category 2 authority and a financial year[8], the gross income or expenditure (whichever is the higher) was not more than £200,000 for that financial year or for either of the two immediately preceding financial years, the statement of accounts may, instead of complying with the above requirements, take the form of a record of receipts and payments of the authority in relation to that financial year[9]. Such a record must be prepared in accordance with, and in the form specified in any annual return required by, proper practices in relation to accounts[10].

1 As to the meaning of 'category 2 authority' see PARA 606 note 11.
2 Ie required by the Local Audit and Accountability Act 2014 s 3(3): see PARA 608 note 1.
3 Accounts and Audit Regulations 2015, SI 2015/234, reg 11(1). The Accounts and Audit Regulations 2015, SI 2015/234, being made under the Local Audit and Accountability Act 2014 ss 32, 43(2), 46, apply in relation to England only: see PARA 605. As to the equivalent regulations in relation to Wales see the Accounts and Audit (Wales) Regulations 2014, SI 2014/3362; and PARA 654 et seq. As to the meanings of 'England' and 'Wales' see PARA 2 note 16.
4 Accounts and Audit Regulations 2015, SI 2015/234, reg 11(2)(a).
5 Accounts and Audit Regulations 2015, SI 2015/234, reg 11(2)(b).
6 As to the meaning of 'proper practices' see PARA 590 note 4.
7 Accounts and Audit Regulations 2015, SI 2015/234, reg 11(2). As to the signing, approval and publication of accounting statements see PARAS 611–612.

8 As to the meaning of 'financial year' see PARA 608 note 1.
9 Accounts and Audit Regulations 2015, SI 2015/234, reg 11(3).
10 Accounts and Audit Regulations 2015, SI 2015/234, reg 11(4).

610. Greater London Authority.

The summary statement of accounts which the Greater London Authority ('the Authority') is required to prepare[1] must be prepared in accordance with proper practices[2] in relation to accounts and must include[3]:

(1) a summary of the income and expenditure of the Authority[4];
(2) a summary of the income and expenditure of each of the functional bodies[5] and the London Pensions Fund Authority[6];
(3) a summary of the capital expenditure of the Authority[7];
(4) a summary of the capital expenditure of each of the functional bodies and the London Pensions Fund Authority[8].

1 Ie under the Greater London Authority Act 1999 s 134 (summary statement of accounts of Authority and other bodies): see LONDON GOVERNMENT vol 71 (2013) PARA 153.
2 As to the meaning of 'proper practices' see PARA 590 note 4.
3 Accounts and Audit Regulations 2015, SI 2015/234, reg 18.
4 Accounts and Audit Regulations 2015, SI 2015/234, reg 18(a).
5 As to functional bodies see LONDON GOVERNMENT vol 71 (2013) PARA 148.
6 Accounts and Audit Regulations 2015, SI 2015/234, reg 18(b).
7 Accounts and Audit Regulations 2015, SI 2015/234, reg 18(c).
8 Accounts and Audit Regulations 2015, SI 2015/234, reg 18(d).

611. Signing and approval of statements of accounts and accounting statements.

The responsible financial officer[1] for a category 1 authority[2] must, on behalf of that authority, in the following order[3]:

(1) sign and date the statement of accounts[4], and confirm that they are satisfied that it presents a true and fair view of the financial position of the authority at the end of the financial year[5] to which it relates[6] and that authority's income and expenditure for that financial year[7];
(2) commence the period for the exercise of public rights[8]; and
(3) notify the local auditor of the date on which that period was so commenced[9].

A category 1 authority must, following the conclusion of the period for the exercise of public rights[10], in the following order[11]:

(a) consider, either by way of a committee or by the members meeting as a whole, the statement of accounts[12];
(b) approve the statement of accounts by a resolution of that committee or meeting[13];
(c) ensure that the statement of accounts is signed and dated by the person presiding at the committee or meeting at which that approval is given[14].

The responsible financial officer for a category 1 authority must re-confirm on behalf of that authority that they are satisfied that the statement of accounts presents a true and fair view of:

(i) the financial position of the authority at the end of the financial year to which it relates[15]; and
(ii) that authority's income and expenditure for that financial year[16],

before that authority approves it[17].

The responsible financial officer for a category 2 authority[18] must, on behalf of that authority[19]:

(A) in a case where the authority has prepared a record of receipts and payments[20], sign and date that record, and confirm that they are satisfied that it properly presents that authority's receipts and payments for the financial year to which the record relates[21]; or

(B) in any other case, sign and date the income and expenditure account and statement of balances, and confirm that they are satisfied that they present fairly the financial position of the authority at the end of the financial year to which they relate[22] and that authority's income and expenditure for that financial year[23].

When the responsible financial officer has complied with heads (A) and (B), a category 2 authority must, in the following order[24]:

(I) consider the statement of accounts by the members meeting as a whole[25];

(II) approve the statement of accounts by resolution[26]; and

(III) ensure the statement of accounts is signed and dated by the person presiding at the meeting at which that approval is given[27].

The responsible financial officer for a category 2 authority must, as soon as reasonably practicable after the date on which the authority complies with head (III), on behalf of that authority[28]:

(AA) commence the period for the exercise of public rights[29]; and

(BB) notify the local auditor[30] of the date on which that period was so commenced[31].

1 As to the meaning of 'responsible financial officer' see PARA 607 note 3.
2 As to the meaning of 'category 1 authority' see PARA 606 note 8.
3 Accounts and Audit Regulations 2015, SI 2015/234, reg 9(1). The Accounts and Audit Regulations 2015, SI 2015/234, being made under the Local Audit and Accountability Act 2014 ss 32, 43(2), 46, apply in relation to England only: see PARA 605. As to the equivalent regulations in relation to Wales see the Accounts and Audit (Wales) Regulations 2014, SI 2014/3362; and PARA 654 et seq. As to the meanings of 'England' and 'Wales' see PARA 2 note 16.
4 As to the statement of accounts see PARA 608.
5 As to the meaning of 'financial year' see PARA 608 note 1.
6 Accounts and Audit Regulations 2015, SI 2015/234, reg 9(1)(a)(i).
7 Accounts and Audit Regulations 2015, SI 2015/234, reg 9(1)(a)(ii).
8 Accounts and Audit Regulations 2015, SI 2015/234, reg 9(1)(b). The exercise of public rights is in accordance with regs 14, 15: see PARA 613. 'Period for the exercise of public rights' means the period of time referred to in reg 14 within which the rights of objection, inspection and questioning of the local auditor conferred by the Local Audit and Accountability Act 2014 ss 26, 27 may be exercised: Accounts and Audit Regulations 2015, SI 2015/234, reg 2(1).
9 Accounts and Audit Regulations 2015, SI 2015/234, reg 9(1)(c).
10 Ie in the Accounts and Audit Regulations 2015, SI 2015/234, reg 14.
11 Accounts and Audit Regulations 2015, SI 2015/234, reg 9(2).
12 Accounts and Audit Regulations 2015, SI 2015/234, reg 9(2)(a). As to references to the members meeting as a whole see PARA 606 note 9.
13 Accounts and Audit Regulations 2015, SI 2015/234, reg 9(2)(b).
14 Accounts and Audit Regulations 2015, SI 2015/234, reg 9(2)(c).
15 Accounts and Audit Regulations 2015, SI 2015/234, reg 9(3)(a).
16 Accounts and Audit Regulations 2015, SI 2015/234, reg 9(3)(b).
17 Accounts and Audit Regulations 2015, SI 2015/234, reg 9(3).
18 As to the meaning of 'category 2 authority' see PARA 606 note 11.
19 Accounts and Audit Regulations 2015, SI 2015/234, reg 12(1).
20 See PARA 609.
21 Accounts and Audit Regulations 2015, SI 2015/234, reg 12(1)(a).
22 Accounts and Audit Regulations 2015, SI 2015/234, reg 12(1)(b)(i).
23 Accounts and Audit Regulations 2015, SI 2015/234, reg 12(1)(b)(ii).
24 Accounts and Audit Regulations 2015, SI 2015/234, reg 12(2).
25 Accounts and Audit Regulations 2015, SI 2015/234, reg 12(2)(a).

26 Accounts and Audit Regulations 2015, SI 2015/234, reg 12(2)(b).
27 Accounts and Audit Regulations 2015, SI 2015/234, reg 12(2)(c).
28 Accounts and Audit Regulations 2015, SI 2015/234, reg 12(3).
29 Accounts and Audit Regulations 2015, SI 2015/234, reg 12(3)(a).
30 The references to a 'local auditor' in the Accounts and Audit Regulations 2015, SI 2015/234, reg 12(3)(b) must, where such a reference concerns a category 2 authority with exempt status, which is also an opted in authority within the meaning of the Local Audit (Smaller Authorities) Regulations 2015, SI 2015/184, be construed as a reference to the specified person under reg 3 of those Regulations: Accounts and Audit Regulations 2015, SI 2015/234, reg 2(4). 'Category 2 authority with exempt status' means a category 2 authority that has certified itself as exempt under the Local Audit (Smaller Authorities) Regulations 2015, SI 2015/184, reg 9(1): Accounts and Audit Regulations 2015, SI 2015/234, reg 2(1).
31 Accounts and Audit Regulations 2015, SI 2015/234, reg 12(3)(b).

612. Publication of statements of accounts and accounting statements.

A category 1 authority[1] must, after approving the statement of accounts[2] but not later than 31 July of the financial year[3] immediately following the end of the financial year to which the statement relates, publish (which must include publication on the authority's website)[4]:

(1) the statement of accounts together with any certificate or opinion, entered[5] by the local auditor[6];
(2) the approved[7] annual governance statement[8]; and
(3) the narrative statement prepared[9] for the financial year[10].

Where an audit of accounts has not been concluded before the date specified above, an authority must:

(a) publish (which must include publication on the authority's website) as soon as reasonably practicable on or after that date a notice stating that it has not been able to publish the statement of accounts and its reasons for this[11]; and
(b) comply with the requirement to publish as if for 'but not later than 31 July of the financial year immediately following the end of the financial year to which the statement relates' there were substituted 'as soon as reasonably practicable after the receipt of any report from the auditor which contains the auditor's final findings from the audit which is issued before the conclusion of the audit'[12].

Where documents are published[13] an authority must:

(i) keep copies of those documents for purchase by any person on payment of a reasonable sum[14]; and
(ii) ensure that those documents remain available for public access for a period of not less than five years beginning with the date on which those documents were first published in accordance with the provisions above[15].

A category 2 authority[16] must, after the conclusion of the period for the exercise of public rights[17] but not later than 30 September of the financial year immediately following the end of the financial year to which the statement relates, publish (which must include publication on that authority's website)[18]:

(A) the statement of accounts together with any certificate or opinion entered[19] by the local auditor[20]; and
(B) the approved[21] annual governance statement[22].

Where documents are published under these provisions, the authority must:

(I) keep copies of those documents for purchase by any person on payment of a reasonable sum[23]; and

(II) ensure that those documents remain available for public access for a period of not less than five years beginning with the date on which those documents were first published in accordance with the provisions above[24].

The above provisions[25] do not apply to a category 2 authority with exempt status[26]. A category 2 authority with exempt status must:

(AA) keep copies of its statement of accounts for purchase by any person on payment of a reasonable sum[27]; and

(BB) after the conclusion of the period for the exercise of public rights[28] in regulation 14, ensure that the statement of accounts that was published on the authority's website[29] remains available for public access for a period of not less than five years beginning with the date of such publication[30].

In the case of a category 2 authority which is a parish meeting, and where the authority has displayed its statement of accounts in a conspicuous place[31], head (BB) does not apply[32].

1 As to the meaning of 'category 1 authority' see PARA 606 note 8.
2 Ie in accordance with the Accounts and Audit Regulations 2015, SI 2015/234, reg 9(2): see PARA 611.
3 As to the meaning of 'financial year' see PARA 608 note 1.
4 Accounts and Audit Regulations 2015, SI 2015/234, reg 10(1). The Accounts and Audit Regulations 2015, SI 2015/234, being made under the Local Audit and Accountability Act 2014 ss 32, 43(2), 46, apply in relation to England only: see PARA 605. As to the equivalent regulations in relation to Wales see the Accounts and Audit (Wales) Regulations 2014, SI 2014/3362; and PARA 654 et seq. As to the meanings of 'England' and 'Wales' see PARA 2 note 16.
5 Ie in accordance with the Local Audit and Accountability Act 2014 s 20(2).
6 Accounts and Audit Regulations 2015, SI 2015/234, reg 10(1)(a).
7 Ie approved in accordance with the Accounts and Audit Regulations 2015, SI 2015/234, reg 6(2): see PARA 606.
8 Accounts and Audit Regulations 2015, SI 2015/234, reg 10(1)(b).
9 Ie in accordance with the Accounts and Audit Regulations 2015, SI 2015/234, reg 8: see PARA 608.
10 Accounts and Audit Regulations 2015, SI 2015/234, reg 10(1)(c).
11 Accounts and Audit Regulations 2015, SI 2015/234, reg 10(2)(a).
12 Accounts and Audit Regulations 2015, SI 2015/234, reg 10(2)(b).
13 Ie under the Accounts and Audit Regulations 2015, SI 2015/234, reg 10(1).
14 Accounts and Audit Regulations 2015, SI 2015/234, reg 10(3)(a).
15 Accounts and Audit Regulations 2015, SI 2015/234, reg 10(3)(b).
16 As to the meaning of 'category 2 authority' see PARA 606 note 11.
17 As to the meaning of 'period for the exercise of public rights' see PARA 611 note 8.
18 Accounts and Audit Regulations 2015, SI 2015/234, reg 13(1). Any reference in the Accounts and Audit Regulations 2015, SI 2015/234, to publication on an authority's website must be construed as:
   (1) in the case of a category 2 authority without its own website, a reference to publication on any website, provided that information so published is accessible by any member of the public without registration or payment (reg 2(5)(a));
   (2) in the case of a category 2 authority which is a parish meeting, a reference to:
      (a) publication on a website of the type specified in head (1) (reg 2(5)(b)(i)); or
      (b) displaying the information in question in a conspicuous place in the area of the authority for at least 14 days (reg 2(5)(b)(ii)).
19 Ie in accordance with the Local Audit and Accountability Act 2014 s 20(2).
20 Accounts and Audit Regulations 2015, SI 2015/234, reg 13(1)(a).
21 Ie in accordance with the Accounts and Audit Regulations 2015, SI 2015/234, reg 6(3): see PARA 606.
22 Accounts and Audit Regulations 2015, SI 2015/234, reg 13(1)(b).
23 Accounts and Audit Regulations 2015, SI 2015/234, reg 13(2)(a).
24 Accounts and Audit Regulations 2015, SI 2015/234, reg 13(2)(b).
25 Ie the Accounts and Audit Regulations 2015, SI 2015/234, reg 13(1), (2).
26 Accounts and Audit Regulations 2015, SI 2015/234, reg 13(3). As to the meaning of 'category 2

authority with exempt status' see PARA 611 note 30.
27 Accounts and Audit Regulations 2015, SI 2015/234, reg 13(4)(a).
28 Ie under the Accounts and Audit Regulations 2015, SI 2015/234, reg 14.
29 Ie in accordance with the Accounts and Audit Regulations 2015, SI 2015/234, reg 15(2): see PARA 613.
30 Accounts and Audit Regulations 2015, SI 2015/234, reg 13(4)(b).
31 Ie in accordance with the Accounts and Audit Regulations 2015, SI 2015/234, reg 2(5)(b)(ii): see note 18.
32 Accounts and Audit Regulations 2015, SI 2015/234, reg 13(5).

613. Inspection and notice procedure.

Any rights of objection, inspection and questioning of the local auditor[1] may only be exercised within a single period of 30 working days[2]. This period starts with the day on which the period for the exercise of public rights is treated[3] as having been commenced[4]. During the period for the exercise of public rights a relevant authority[5] must make the specified documents[6] available for inspection on reasonable notice at all reasonable times[7].

The responsible financial officer[8] for a relevant authority must, on behalf of the authority, ensure that commencement of the period for the exercise of public rights[9], takes place on such a day that ensures that the period referred to above includes[10]:

(1) the first ten working days of June of the financial year[11] immediately following the end of the financial year to which the statement relates, where that authority is a category 1 authority[12]; or
(2) the first 10 working days of July of the financial year immediately following the end of the financial year to which the statement relates, where that authority is a category 2 authority[13].

The responsible financial officer for a relevant authority must, on behalf of that authority, publish (which must include publication on the authority's website)[14]:

(a) the statement of accounts[15], accompanied by:
  (i) a declaration, signed by that officer to the effect that[16]:
  (ii) the status of the statement of accounts is unaudited and that the statement of accounts as published may be subject to change[17]; or
  (iii) in the case of a category 2 authority with exempt status[18], the statement of accounts will not be audited on account of that authority's self-certified status as exempt, unless either a request for an opportunity to question the auditor about the authority's accounting records[19] or an objection[20], results in the involvement of the local auditor; and that in either of those circumstances the audit will be limited[21];
  (iv) the annual governance statement[22], whether or not that statement has been approved[23] as required[24]; and
  (v) where the authority in question is a category 1 authority, the narrative statement prepared[25] by the authority[26];
(b) a statement that sets out[27]:
  (i) the period for the exercise of public rights[28];
  (ii) details of the manner in which notice should be given of an intention to inspect the accounting records and other documents[29];
  (iii) the name and address of the local auditor[30];
  (iv) the statutory provisions as to inspection of documents and the right to make objections at audit[31], as they have effect in relation to the authority in question[32]; and

(v) in the case of a category 2 authority with exempt status, the statutory provisions as to inspection of documents etc[33] as they have effect in relation to the authority in question[34].

The period for the exercise of public rights is treated as being commenced on the day following the day on which all of the obligations specified in heads (a) and (b) above have been fulfilled, in so far as they are applicable to the authority in question[35].

1 Ie conferred by the Local Audit and Accountability Act 2014 ss 26, 27.

2 Accounts and Audit Regulations 2015, SI 2015/234, reg 14(1). 'Working day' means any day other than a Saturday, a Sunday, Christmas Day, Good Friday or a day which is a bank holiday in England under the Banking and Financial Dealings Act 1971 (see TIME vol 97 (2015) PARA 321): Accounts and Audit Regulations 2015, SI 2015/234, reg 2(1).

The Accounts and Audit Regulations 2015, SI 2015/234, being made under the Local Audit and Accountability Act 2014 ss 32, 43(2), 46, apply in relation to England only: see PARA 605. As to the equivalent regulations in relation to Wales see the Accounts and Audit (Wales) Regulations 2014, SI 2014/3362; and PARA 654 et seq. As to the meanings of 'England' and 'Wales' see PARA 2 note 16.

3 Ie in accordance with the Accounts and Audit Regulations 2015, SI 2015/234, reg 15(3): see the text to note 35.

4 Accounts and Audit Regulations 2015, SI 2015/234, reg 14(2).

5 As to the meaning of 'relevant authority' see PARA 588 note 3.

6 Ie the documents referred to in the Local Audit and Accountability Act 2014 s 26(1).

7 Accounts and Audit Regulations 2015, SI 2015/234, reg 14(3).

8 As to the meaning of 'responsible financial officer' see PARA 607 note 3.

9 Ie under the Accounts and Audit Regulations 2015, SI 2015/234, reg 9(1)(b) or 12(3)(a) (as the case may be): see PARA 611. As to the meaning of 'period for the exercise of public rights' see PARA 611 note 8.

10 Accounts and Audit Regulations 2015, SI 2015/234, reg 15(1).

11 As to the meaning of 'financial year' see PARA 608 note 1.

12 Accounts and Audit Regulations 2015, SI 2015/234, reg 15(1)(a). As to the meaning of 'category 1 authority' see PARA 606 note 8.

13 Accounts and Audit Regulations 2015, SI 2015/234, reg 15(1)(b). As to the meaning of 'category 2 authority' see PARA 606 note 11.

14 Accounts and Audit Regulations 2015, SI 2015/234, reg 15(2). As to references to publication on an authority's website see PARA 612 note 18.

15 Accounts and Audit Regulations 2015, SI 2015/234, reg 15(2)(a). In reg 15, 'statement of accounts' means:

(1) in relation to a category 1 authority, a statement of accounts that has been signed, dated and confirmed in accordance with reg 9(1)(a) (see PARA 611) (reg 15(4)(a));

(2) in relation to a category 2 authority, a statement of accounts that has been considered, approved, signed and dated in accordance with the procedure set out in reg 12(2) (see PARA 611) (reg 15(4)(b));

but has not yet had entered on it a certificate in accordance with the Local Audit and Accountability Act 2014 s 20(2)(a) that the auditor has completed the audit in accordance with the Act: Accounts and Audit Regulations 2015, SI 2015/234, reg 15(4).

16 Accounts and Audit Regulations 2015, SI 2015/234, reg 15(2)(a)(i).

17 Accounts and Audit Regulations 2015, SI 2015/234, reg 15(2)(a)(i)(aa).

18 As to the meaning of 'category 2 authority with exempt status' see PARA 611 note 30.

19 Ie under the Local Audit and Accountability Act 2014 s 26(2).

20 Ie under the Local Audit and Accountability Act 2014 s 27(1). Any written notice of objection given under s 27 must state (Accounts and Audit Regulations 2015, SI 2015/234, reg 17):

(1) the facts on which the local government elector relies (reg 17(a));

(2) the grounds on which the objection is being made (reg 17(b)); and

(3) so far as is possible, particulars of:

(a) any item of account which is alleged to be contrary to law (reg 17(c)(i)); and

(b) any matter in respect of which it is proposed that the auditor could make a public interest report under the Local Audit and Accountability Act 2014 s 24, and Sch 7 para 1 (Accounts and Audit Regulations 2015, SI 2015/234, reg 17(c)(ii)).

21 Accounts and Audit Regulations 2015, SI 2015/234, reg 15(2)(a)(i)(bb). The audit will be limited to that required by the Local Audit and Accountability Act 2014 s 20 as modified by the Local Audit (Smaller Authorities) Regulations 2015, SI 2015/184: see the Accounts and Audit Regulations 2015, SI 2015/234, reg 15(2)(a)(i)(bb).
22 Ie the statement prepared in accordance with the Accounts and Audit Regulations 2015, SI 2015/234, reg 6(1)(b): see PARA 606.
23 Ie in accordance with the Accounts and Audit Regulations 2015, SI 2015/234, reg 6(2)(b) or (3)(b) as the case may be): see PARA 606.
24 Accounts and Audit Regulations 2015, SI 2015/234, reg 15(2)(a)(ii).
25 Ie prepared in accordance with the Accounts and Audit Regulations 2015, SI 2015/234, reg 8: see PARA 608.
26 Accounts and Audit Regulations 2015, SI 2015/234, reg 15(2)(a)(iii).
27 Accounts and Audit Regulations 2015, SI 2015/234, reg 15(2)(b).
28 Accounts and Audit Regulations 2015, SI 2015/234, reg 15(2)(b)(i).
29 Accounts and Audit Regulations 2015, SI 2015/234, reg 15(2)(b)(ii).
30 Accounts and Audit Regulations 2015, SI 2015/234, reg 15(2)(b)(iiii).
31 Ie the provisions contained in the Local Audit and Accountability Act 2014 s 26 (inspection of documents etc) and s 27 (right to make objections at audit).
32 Accounts and Audit Regulations 2015, SI 2015/234, reg 15(2)(b)(iv).
33 Ie the provisions contained in the Local Audit and Accountability Act 2014 s 25.
34 Accounts and Audit Regulations 2015, SI 2015/234, reg 15(2)(b)(v).
35 Accounts and Audit Regulations 2015, SI 2015/234, reg 15(3).

614. Steps following conclusion of audit.

As soon as reasonably practicable after conclusion of an audit, a relevant authority[1] must publish (which must include publication on the authority's website)[2] a statement of the following matters[3]. Those matters are[4]:

(1) a statement:
  (a) that the audit has been concluded and that the statement of accounts has been published[5]; and
  (b) of the rights of inspection conferred[6] on local government electors[7];
(2) the address at which, and the hours during which, those rights may be exercised[8].

These provisions do not apply to a category 2 authority with exempt status[9].

Where, following completion of an audit, a relevant authority receives any audit letter[10] from the local auditor, the members of the relevant authority, or, in the case of a category 1 authority[11], a committee of that authority, must meet to consider that letter as soon as reasonably practicable[12]. Following consideration of the letter authority must:

(i) publish (which must include publication on the authority's website) the audit letter received from the local auditor[13]; and
(ii) make copies available for purchase by any person on payment of such sum as the relevant authority may reasonably require[14].

1 As to the meaning of 'relevant authority' see PARA 588 note 3.
2 As to references to publication on an authority's website see PARA 612 note 18.
3 Accounts and Audit Regulations 2015, SI 2015/234, reg 16(1).

The Accounts and Audit Regulations 2015, SI 2015/234, being made under the Local Audit and Accountability Act 2014 ss 32, 43(2), 46, apply in relation to England only: see PARA 605. As to the equivalent regulations in relation to Wales see the Accounts and Audit (Wales) Regulations 2014, SI 2014/3362; and PARA 654 et seq. As to the meanings of 'England' and 'Wales' see PARA 2 note 16.
4 Accounts and Audit Regulations 2015, SI 2015/234, reg 16(2).
5 Accounts and Audit Regulations 2015, SI 2015/234, reg 16(2)(a)(i).
6 Ie under the Local Audit and Accountability Act 2014 s 25. As to inspection see PARA 613.
7 Accounts and Audit Regulations 2015, SI 2015/234, reg 16(2)(a)(ii).
8 Accounts and Audit Regulations 2015, SI 2015/234, reg 16(2)(b).

9 Accounts and Audit Regulations 2015, SI 2015/234, reg 16(3). As to the meaning of 'category 2 authority with exempt status' see PARA 611 note 30.
10 'Audit letter' means the annual audit letter to the relevant authority by the local auditor sent pursuant to the Code of Audit Practice published by the National Audit Office, 157-197 Buckingham Palace Road, Victoria, London SW1W 9SP and dated January 2015. Reference number: 10495-001: Accounts and Audit Regulations 2015, SI 2015/234, reg 2(1).
11 As to the meaning of 'category 1 authority' see PARA 606 note 8.
12 Accounts and Audit Regulations 2015, SI 2015/234, reg 20(1).
13 Accounts and Audit Regulations 2015, SI 2015/234, reg 20(2)(a).
14 Accounts and Audit Regulations 2015, SI 2015/234, reg 20(1)(b).

(ii) In Relation to Wales

A. IN GENERAL

615. The Auditor General for Wales.

The Government of Wales Act 2006 established the office of Auditor General for Wales ('Archwilydd Cyffredinol Cymru')[1]. The office of Auditor General for Wales (the 'Auditor General') is continued under the Public Audit (Wales) Act 2013[2]. The Auditor General is appointed by Her Majesty on the nomination of the National Assembly for Wales[3] and holds office for up to eight years[4]. The person may not be appointed again[5]. A person cannot be appointed as Auditor General, and a person ceases to be Auditor General, if the person is disqualified on any of certain specified grounds[6].

The Auditor General is to be the chief executive (but not an employee) the Wales Audit Office[7], and is to be the accounting officer for the Wales Audit Office[8].

1 See the Government of Wales Act 2006 s 145(1) (repealed). For provision about the Auditor General for Wales or Archwilydd Cyffredinol Cymru (referred to in the Government of Wales Act 2006 as 'the Auditor General') see Sch 8 and the Public Audit (Wales) Act 2013: Government of Wales Act 2006 s 145(2) (amended by the Public Audit (Wales) Act 2013 s 34, Sch 4 paras 70, 77(1), (3)). The Welsh Ministers must co-operate with the Auditor General where it seems to them appropriate to do so for the efficient and effective discharge of their functions in relation to Welsh NHS bodies: Government of Wales Act 2006 s 145(3). As to the meaning of 'Welsh NHS bodies' see PARA 616 note 2; definition applied by s 145(4). As to the Welsh Ministers see PARA 4 note 18. As to the Auditor General for Wales see further CONSTITUTIONAL AND ADMINISTRATIVE LAW vol 20 (2014) PARA 400 et seq.
2 Public Audit (Wales) Act 2013 s 2(1).
3 Public Audit (Wales) Act 2013 s 2(2). No nomination is to be made until the National Assembly for Wales is satisfied that reasonable consultation has been undertaken with such bodies as appear to the Assembly to represent the interests of local government bodies in Wales: s 2(3). For these purposes, 'local government body' has the meaning given in the Public Audit (Wales) Act 2004 s 12 (see PARA 618): Public Audit (Wales) Act 2013 s 32. The validity of any act or omission of a person appointed as Auditor General is not affected by any defect in the person's nomination or appointment: s 2(6). As to the National Assembly for Wales see CONSTITUTIONAL AND ADMINISTRATIVE LAW vol 20 (2014) PARA 351 et seq.

The office holder is a corporation sole: s 6(1). The Auditor General is not to be regarded as holding office under Her Majesty or as exercising any functions on behalf of the Crown: s 6(2). However, the Auditor General is to be taken to be a Crown servant for the purposes of the Official Secrets Act 1989: Public Audit (Wales) Act 2013 s 6(3). As to the Official Secrets Act 1989 see CRIMINAL LAW vol 26 (2016) PARA 503 et seq.

Provision is made as to the employment of a former Auditor General: see the Public Audit (Wales) Act 2013 s 5.

Before a person is appointed as Auditor General, remuneration arrangements are to be made in respect of that person by the National Assembly: s 7(1). Before those arrangements can be made, the First Minister must be consulted: s 7(2). The remuneration arrangements:

(1) may make provision for a salary, allowances, gratuities, arrangements for a pension and other benefits (s 7(3)(a)); and
(2) may include a formula or other mechanism for adjusting one or more of those elements from time to time (s 7(2)(b)).

But no element is to be performance-based: s 7(4).

The National Assembly Commission must make payments to the Minister for the Civil Service, at such times as the Minister may determine, of such amounts as may be so determined, in respect of:

(a) the provision of pensions, allowances, gratuities or other benefits by virtue of the Superannuation Act 1972 s 1 to or in respect of any person who holds or has ceased to hold office as Auditor General (Public Audit (Wales) Act 2013 s 7(5)(a)); and
(b) the expenses incurred in administering those pensions, allowances, gratuities or other benefits (s 7(5)(b)).

Amounts payable by virtue of s 7 are to be charged on, and paid out of, the Welsh Consolidated Fund: s 7(6). As to the Welsh Consolidated Fund see CONSTITUTIONAL AND ADMINISTRATIVE LAW vol 20 (2014) PARA 392 et seq.

4 Public Audit (Wales) Act 2013 s 2(4). A person appointed as Auditor General holds office until the end of the period for which the person was appointed (subject to s 3(2), (3): s 3(1). Her Majesty may relieve a person from office as Auditor General before the end of the period for which the person was appointed:

(1) at the person's request (s 3(2)(a)); or
(2) on Her Majesty being satisfied that the person is incapable for medical reasons of performing the duties of the office and of requesting to be relieved of it (s 3(2)(b)).

Her Majesty may remove a person from office as Auditor General before the end of the period for which the person was appointed on the making of a recommendation, on the ground of the person's misbehaviour, that Her Majesty should do so: s 3(3). A recommendation for the removal of a person from office as Auditor General may not be made unless:

(a) the National Assembly has resolved that the recommendation should be made (s 3(4)(a)); and
(b) the resolution of the Assembly is passed on a vote in which the number of Assembly members voting in favour is not less than two-thirds of the total number of Assembly seats (s 3(4)(b)).

5 Public Audit (Wales) Act 2013 s 2(5).
6 See the Public Audit (Wales) Act 2013 s 4; and CONSTITUTIONAL AND ADMINISTRATIVE LAW vol 20 (2014) PARA 400.
7 See the Public Audit (Wales) Act 2013 s 16(1). See also s 4(3)(f). As to the Wales Audit Office see CONSTITUTIONAL AND ADMINISTRATIVE LAW vol 20 (2014) PARAS 403–405
8 See the Public Audit (Wales) Act 2013 Sch 1 para 33(1).

616. Welsh NHS bodies.

The accounts prepared[1] by a Welsh NHS body[2] must be submitted by that body to the Auditor General for Wales[3] who must examine and certify them, and, no later than four months after the accounts are submitted to him, lay before the National Assembly for Wales[4] a copy of them as certified by him together with his report on them[5]. Where an officer of a Welsh NHS body receives money or other property on behalf of that body, or for which he ought to account to that body the officer must keep accounts, which must be audited by the Auditor General for Wales[6].

The Care Quality Commission has a duty to provide the Auditor General for Wales with relevant information[7].

1 Ie under the National Health Service (Wales) Act 2006 Sch 9 para 3(1): see HEALTH SERVICES vol 54A (2017) PARA 549.
2 As to the meaning of 'Welsh NHS body' see the Public Audit (Wales) Act 2004 s 60 (amended by the National Health Service (Consequential Provisions) Act 2006 s 2, Sch 1 paras 260, 261).
3 As to the Auditor General for Wales see PARA 615; and CONSTITUTIONAL AND ADMINISTRATIVE LAW vol 20 (2014) PARA 400 et seq.
4 As to the National Assembly for Wales see CONSTITUTIONAL AND ADMINISTRATIVE LAW vol 20 (2014) PARA 351 et seq.

5 See the Public Audit (Wales) Act 2004 s 61 (amended by the National Health Service (Consequential Provisions) Act 2006 s 2, Sch 1 para 62; the Health Act 2006 s 80(1), Sch 8 para 62; and the Public Audit (Wales) Act 2013 s 34, Sch 4 paras 20, 60). As to the Auditor General for Wales's duty to co-operate with the Welsh Ministers and the Care Quality Commission see the Public Audit (Wales) Act 2004 s 62 (amended by the Health and Social Care Act 2008 s 95, Sch 5 para 76; the Public Audit (Wales) Act 2013 Sch 4 paras 20, 61; and the Local Audit and Accountability Act 2014 s 45, Sch 12 paras 59, 62).

6 See the Public Audit (Wales) Act 2004 s 63.

7 See the Public Audit (Wales) Act 2004 s 64 (amended by the Health and Social Care Act 2008 s 95, Sch 5 para 77).

617. Assistance by Auditor General for Wales to inspectorates.

The Auditor General for Wales[1] may provide assistance[2] to:

(1) Her Majesty's Chief Inspector of Prisons[3];

(2) Her Majesty's Inspectors of Constabulary[4];

(3) Her Majesty's Chief Inspector of the Crown Prosecution Service[5]; and

(4) Her Majesty's Inspectorate of Probation for England and Wales[6],

in the discharge of any of their functions[7]. Any sums charged in relation to assistance provided under this provision may not exceed the full cost of providing that assistance[8].

1 As to the Auditor General for Wales see PARA 615; and CONSTITUTIONAL AND ADMINISTRATIVE LAW vol 20 (2014) PARA 400 et seq.

2 For these purposes assistance may be provided on such terms, including terms as to payment, as the Wales Audit Office and the body or person in question may agree, but any terms as to payment agreed by the Wales Audit Office must be made in accordance with a scheme for charging fees prepared under the Public Audit (Wales) Act 2013 s 24: Public Audit (Wales) Act 2004 s 67A(2) (s 67A added by the Police and Justice Act 2006 s 52, Sch 14 para 60; the Public Audit (Wales) Act 2004 s 67A(2) amended by the Public Audit (Wales) Act 2013 s 34, Sch 4 paras 20, 69(1)–(3)). As to the Wales Audit Office see CONSTITUTIONAL AND ADMINISTRATIVE LAW vol 20 (2014) PARAS 403–405

3 Public Audit (Wales) Act 2004 s 67A(1)(a) (as added: see note 2). As to Her Majesty's Chief Inspector of Prisons see PRISONS AND PRISONERS vol 85 (2012) PARA 409.

4 Public Audit (Wales) Act 2004 s 67A(1)(b) (as added: see note 2). As to Her Majesty's Inspectors of Constabulary see POLICE AND INVESTIGATORY POWERS vol 84 (2013) PARA 152.

5 Public Audit (Wales) Act 2004 s 67A(1)(c) (as added: see note 2). As to Her Majesty's Chief Inspector of the Crown Prosecution Service see CRIMINAL PROCEDURE vol 27 (2015) PARA 26.

6 Public Audit (Wales) Act 2004 s 67A(1)(d) (as added (see note 2); amended by SI 2008/612). As to Her Majesty's Inspectorate of Probation for England and Wales see SENTENCING vol 92 (2015) PARA 682.

7 Public Audit (Wales) Act 2004 s 67A(1) (as added (see note 2); amended by SI 2012/2401).

8 Public Audit (Wales) Act 2004 s 67A(3) (added by the Public Audit (Wales) Act 2013 Sch 4 paras 20, 69(1), (4)).

B. ACCOUNTS AND AUDIT OF PUBLIC BODIES

(A) Audit of Accounts

618. Audit of accounts.

For the purposes of the Public Audit (Wales) Act 2004[1], 'local government body in Wales' means any of the following[2]:

(1) a local authority in Wales[3];

(2) a committee of a local authority in Wales (including a joint committee of two or more local authorities in Wales)[4];

(3) a port health authority for a port health district wholly in Wales[5];

(4) a national park authority for a national park in Wales[6];

(5) a conservation board established by order of the Welsh Ministers[7];

(6) a police and crime commissioner for a police area in Wales[8];

(7) a chief constable of a police force maintained for a police area in Wales[9];
(8) a fire and rescue authority in Wales[10];
(9) an internal drainage board for an internal drainage district wholly in Wales[11];
(10) a local probation board for an area in Wales[12];
(11) A Welsh probation trust[13].

A local government body in Wales must make up its accounts each year to 31 March or such other date as the Welsh Ministers may generally or in any special case direct[14], and must ensure that its accounts are appropriately audited[15]. The Auditor General for Wales must audit the accounts of local government bodies in Wales[16].

1 Ie the Public Audit (Wales) Act 2004 Pt 2 (ss 12–59).
2 Public Audit (Wales) Act 2004 s 12(1). The Welsh Ministers may by order amend s 12(1) by adding a public body whose functions relate exclusively to Wales or an area of Wales, by omitting a body, or by altering the description of a body: s 12(2). For these purposes 'public body' means a body which exercises functions of a public nature, or is entirely or substantially funded from public money: s 12(3). 'Body' includes office: s 71. As to the Welsh Ministers see PARA 4 note 18.
3 Public Audit (Wales) Act 2004 s 12(1)(a). 'Local authority in Wales' means a county council, county borough council or community council in Wales: Public Audit (Wales) Act 2004 s 59(5). As to areas and authorities in Wales see LOCAL GOVERNMENT vol 69 (2018) PARA 51 et seq.
4 Public Audit (Wales) Act 2004 s 12(1)(b). As to committees and joint committees see LOCAL GOVERNMENT vol 69 (2018) PARA 400 et seq.
5 Public Audit (Wales) Act 2004 s 12(1)(c). As to port health authorities see ENVIRONMENTAL QUALITY AND PUBLIC HEALTH vol 45 (2010) PARA 102 et seq.
6 Public Audit (Wales) Act 2004 s 12(1)(d). As to national park authorities see OPEN SPACES AND COUNTRYSIDE vol 78 (2010) PARA 526 et seq.
7 Public Audit (Wales) Act 2004 s 12(1)(e). A conservation board is established by order under the Countryside and Rights of Way Act 2000 s 86: see OPEN SPACES AND COUNTRYSIDE vol 78 (2010) PARA 660.
8 Public Audit (Wales) Act 2004 s 12(1)(f) (amended by the Police Reform and Social Responsibility Act 2011 s 99, Sch 16 paras 336, 337(a). As to police and crime commissioners see POLICE AND INVESTIGATORY POWERS vol 84 (2013) PARA 56 et seq.
9 Public Audit (Wales) Act 2004 s 12(1)(fa) (added by the Police Reform and Social Responsibility Act 2011 Sch 16 paras 336, 337(b)). The text refers to a police force maintained under the Police Act 1996 s 2 (see POLICE AND INVESTIGATORY POWERS vol 84 (2013) PARA 52).
10 Public Audit (Wales) Act 2004 s 12(1)(g). A fire and rescue authority is constituted by a scheme under the Fire and Rescue Services Act 2004 s 2, or a scheme to which s 4 applies: see FIRE AND RESCUE SERVICES vol 51 (2013) PARAS 18–20.
11 Public Audit (Wales) Act 2004 s 12(1)(h). As to internal drainage boards see WATER AND WATERWAYS vol 101 (2009) PARA 569 et seq.
12 Public Audit (Wales) Act 2004 s 12(1)(i). A local probation board is established under the Criminal Justice and Court Services Act 2000 s 4: see SENTENCING vol 92 (2015) PARA 666 et seq.
13 Public Audit (Wales) Act 2004 s 12(1)(j) (added by the Offender Management Act 2007 s 5(6), Sch 1 para 13(5)(a)). A Welsh probation trust is defined in the Offender Management Act 2007 Sch 1 para 13(6).
14 Public Audit (Wales) Act 2004 s 13(1)(a) (s 13 substituted by the Public Audit (Wales) Act 2013 s 11(1)).
15 Public Audit (Wales) Act 2004 s 13(1)(b) (as substituted: see note 15). As to the Auditor General for Wales see PARA 615; and CONSTITUTIONAL AND ADMINISTRATIVE LAW vol 20 (2014) PARA 400 et seq. The text refers to accounts audited in accordance with the Public Audit (Wales) Act 2004 Pt 1 Ch 1 (ss 12–40).
16 Public Audit (Wales) Act 2004 s 13(2) (as substituted: see note 15).

619. General duties on audit of accounts.

In relation to the audit of the accounts of a local government body in Wales[1], the Auditor General for Wales[2] must, by examination of the accounts and otherwise, satisfy himself[3]:

(1) that the accounts are prepared in accordance with regulations under the Public Audit (Wales) Act 2004[4];

(2) that they comply with the requirements of all other statutory provisions applicable to the accounts[5];

(3) that proper practices have been observed in the compilation of the accounts[6];

(4) that the body has made proper arrangements for securing economy, efficiency and effectiveness in its use of resources[7];

(5) that the body, if required to publish information as to standards of performance[8], has made such arrangements for collecting and recording the information and for publishing it as are required for the performance of its duties[9].

1 Ie the audit of accounts under the Public Audit (Wales) Act 2004 Pt 2 Ch 1 (ss 12–40). As to the meaning of 'local government body in Wales' see PARA 618.

2 As to the Auditor General for Wales see PARA 615; and CONSTITUTIONAL AND ADMINISTRATIVE LAW vol 20 (2014) PARA 400 et seq.

3 See the Public Audit (Wales) Act 2004 s 17(1), (2) (s 17(2) amended by the Public Audit (Wales) Act 2013 s 34, Sch 4 paras 20, 23(1), (2)). As to the duties of an auditor see eg *Porter v Magill* [2001] UKHL 67, [2002] 1 All ER 465; and *Asher v Secretary of State for the Environment* [1974] Ch 208, [1974] 2 All ER 156, CA.

4 Public Audit (Wales) Act 2004 s 17(2)(a). The regulations referred to in the text are those made under the Public Audit (Wales) Act 2004 s 39: see PARA 653 et seq.

5 Public Audit (Wales) Act 2004 s 17(2)(b).

6 Public Audit (Wales) Act 2004 s 17(2)(c).

7 Public Audit (Wales) Act 2004 s 17(2)(d).

8 Ie in pursuance of a direction under the Public Audit (Wales) Act 2004 s 47: see PARA 644.

9 Public Audit (Wales) Act 2004 s 17(2)(e). The duties referred to are those under s 47: see PARA 644.

620. Fees in respect of functions exercised by Auditor General for Wales.

The Wales Audit Office[1] must, in accordance with a scheme for charging fees prepared by it[2] charge a fee in respect of functions exercised by the Auditor General for Wales[3] in auditing the accounts of local government bodies in Wales[4], and in undertaking studies[5] at the request of a local government body[6].

The Wales Audit Office must prescribe a scale or scales of fees payable for one or more financial years[7] in respect of the audit of accounts of local government bodies in Wales under the Public Audit (Wales) Act 2004[8]. Before prescribing any such scale of fees the Wales Audit Office must consult[9]:

(1) any associations of local government bodies in Wales which appear to the Wales Audit Office to be concerned[10]; and

(2) such other persons as the Wales Audit Office thinks fit[11].

A local government body in Wales must pay to the Wales Audit Office the fee payable in respect of the audit in accordance with the appropriate scale[12]. However, if it appears to the Wales Audit Office that the work involved in a particular audit differed substantially from that envisaged by the appropriate scale, the Wales Audit Office may charge a fee which differs from that referred to above[13]. A fee payable under these provisions may not exceed the full cost of exercising the function to which it relates[14].

1 As to the Wales Audit Office see CONSTITUTIONAL AND ADMINISTRATIVE LAW vol 20 (2014) PARAS 403–405

2 Ie under the Public Audit (Wales) Act 2013 s 24: CONSTITUTIONAL AND ADMINISTRATIVE LAW vol 20 (2014) para 405.

3 As to the Auditor General for Wales see para 615; and CONSTITUTIONAL AND ADMINISTRATIVE LAW vol 20 (2014) para 400 et seq.

4 Ie under the Public Audit (Wales) Act 2004 Pt 2 Ch 1 (ss 12–40): see para 619 et seq. As to the meaning of 'local government body in Wales' see para 618.
5 Ie under the Public Audit (Wales) Act 2004 s 44: see para 639.
6 Public Audit (Wales) Act 2004 s 20(A1) (added by the Public Audit (Wales) Act 2013 s 34, Sch 4 paras 20, 25(1), (2)).
7 'Financial year' means the 12 months ending with 31 March: Public Audit (Wales) Act 2004 s 71.
8 Public Audit (Wales) Act 2004 s 20(1) (amended by the Public Audit (Wales) Act 2013 Sch 4 paras 20, 25(1), (4)).
9 Public Audit (Wales) Act 2004 s 20(2) (amended by the Public Audit (Wales) Act 2013 Sch 4 paras 20, 25(1), (5)(a)).
10 Public Audit (Wales) Act 2004 s 20(2)(a) (amended by the Public Audit (Wales) Act 2013 Sch 4 paras 20, 25(1), (5)(b)).
11 Public Audit (Wales) Act 2004 s 20(2)(b) (substituted by the Public Audit (Wales) Act 2013 Sch 4 paras 20, 25(1), (5)(c)).
12 Public Audit (Wales) Act 2004 s 20(4) (amended by the Public Audit (Wales) Act 2013 Sch 4 paras 20, 25(1), (7)).
13 Public Audit (Wales) Act 2004 s 20(5) (amended by the Public Audit (Wales) Act 2013 Sch 4 paras 20, 25(1), (8)).
14 Public Audit (Wales) Act 2004 s 20(5A) (added by the Public Audit (Wales) Act 2013 Sch 4 paras 20, 25(1), (9)).

(B) Audit Reports and Recommendations

621. Auditor General's reports and recommendations.

In auditing accounts of a local government body in Wales[1] under the Public Audit (Wales) Act 2004[2], the Auditor General for Wales[3] must consider whether, in the public interest, he should make a report on any matter which comes to his notice in the course of the audit, in order for it to be considered by the body, or brought to the attention of the public[4]. If the Auditor General for Wales considers that, in the public interest, he should make such a report, he must consider whether the public interest requires the matter to be made the subject of an immediate report[5] and, if he decides it does, he must make the report immediately[6]. If the auditor considers that the public interest does not require the matter to be made the subject of an immediate report, he must make the report at the conclusion of the audit[7].

1 As to the meaning of 'local government body in Wales' see PARA 618.
2 Ie under the Public Audit (Wales) Act 2004 Pt 2 Ch 1 (ss 12–40): see PARA 619 et seq.
3 As to the Auditor General for Wales see PARA 615; and CONSTITUTIONAL AND ADMINISTRATIVE LAW vol 20 (2014) PARA 400 et seq.
4 Public Audit (Wales) Act 2004 s 22(1) (amended by the Public Audit (Wales) Act 2013 s 34, Sch 4 paras 20, 27(1), (2)).
5 Public Audit (Wales) Act 2004 s 22(2) (amended by the Public Audit (Wales) Act 2013 Sch 4 paras 20, 27(1), (2)).
6 See the Public Audit (Wales) Act 2004 s 22(3) (amended by the Public Audit (Wales) Act 2013 Sch 4 paras 20, 27(1), (2)). In a case within the Public Audit (Wales) Act 2004 s 22(3) the Auditor General for Wales must send the report to the body immediately after making it: s 22(5) (amended by the Public Audit (Wales) Act 2013 Sch 4 paras 20, 27(1)–(4)). As to additional publicity for immediate reports see PARA 622.
7 Public Audit (Wales) Act 2004 s 22(4) (amended by the Public Audit (Wales) Act 2013 Sch 4 paras 20, 27(1), (2)). In a case within the Public Audit (Wales) Act 2004 s 22(4), the Auditor General for Wales must send the report to the body before the end of the period of 14 days starting with the day on which he concludes the audit: s 22(6) (amended by the Public Audit (Wales) Act 2013 Sch 4 paras 20, 27(1)–(4)). As to additional publicity for non-immediate reports see PARA 623.

622. Additional publicity for immediate reports.

Where the Auditor General for Wales[1] has sent an immediate report[2] to a local government body in Wales[3], from the time when the report is received by the body any member of the public may[4]:

(1) inspect the report at all reasonable times without payment[5];
(2) make a copy of the report or any part of it at all reasonable times without payment[6];
(3) require the body to supply him on payment of a reasonable sum with a copy of the report or any part of it[7].

On receiving the report[8] a body must immediately ensure that a notice is published in one or more newspapers circulating in the area of the body, and supply a copy of the report to every member of the body[9]. The notice must identify the subject matter of the report, and state that any member of the public may inspect the report and make a copy of it or any part of it between such times and at such place or places as are specified in the notice[10].

The auditor who has made the report may notify any person that he has made the report, and supply a copy of the report or of any part of it to any person[11].

A person who has custody of an immediate report commits an offence if[12]:
(a) he obstructs a person in the exercise of a right conferred by head (1) or (2) above[13]; or
(b) he refuses to comply with a requirement under head (3) above[14].

1 As to the Auditor General for Wales see PARA 615; and CONSTITUTIONAL AND ADMINISTRATIVE LAW vol 20 (2014) PARA 400 et seq.
2 Ie a report made under the Public Audit (Wales) Act 2004 s 22(3), and sent under s 22(5): see PARA 621.
3 As to the meaning of 'local government body in Wales' see PARA 618.
4 See the Public Audit (Wales) Act 2004 s 27(1), (2) (s 27(1) amended by the Public Audit (Wales) Act 2013 s 34, Sch 4 paras 20, 32(1), (2)).
5 Public Audit (Wales) Act 2004 s 27(2)(a).
6 Public Audit (Wales) Act 2004 s 27(2)(b).
7 Public Audit (Wales) Act 2004 s 27(2)(c).
8 Ie the report sent to the body under the Public Audit (Wales) Act 2004 s 22(5): see PARA 621.
9 Public Audit (Wales) Act 2004 s 27(3). A body which fails to comply with a requirement of s 27(3) is guilty of an offence and is liable on summary conviction to a fine not exceeding level 3 on the standard scale: see s 27(8), (9). As to the powers of magistrates' courts to issue fines on summary conviction see SENTENCING vol 92 (2015) PARA 176.
10 Public Audit (Wales) Act 2004 s 27(4).
11 Public Audit (Wales) Act 2004 s 27(5) (amended by the Public Audit (Wales) Act 2013 Sch 4 paras 20, 32(1), (3)).
12 Public Audit (Wales) Act 2004 s 27(6). Such a person is liable on summary conviction to a fine not exceeding level 3 on the standard scale: s 27(7).
13 Public Audit (Wales) Act 2004 s 27(6)(a).
14 Public Audit (Wales) Act 2004 s 27(6)(b).

623. Additional publicity for non-immediate reports.

Where the Auditor General for Wales[1] has sent a non-immediate report[2] to a local government body in Wales[3], the Auditor General for Wales may[4]:
(1) notify any person that he has made the report[5];
(2) publish the report[6];
(3) supply a copy of the report or any part of it to any person[7].

From the time when the report is sent to the body:
(a) the Auditor General for Wales must ensure that any member of the public may:
  (i) inspect the report at all reasonable times without payment;
  (ii) make a copy of the report or any part of it at all reasonable times without payment[8];

(b) any member of the public may require the Auditor General for Wales to supply him on payment of a reasonable sum with a copy of the report or any part of it[9].

1 As to the Auditor General for Wales see PARA 615; and CONSTITUTIONAL AND ADMINISTRATIVE LAW vol 20 (2014) PARA 400 et seq.
2 Ie a report made under the Public Audit (Wales) Act 2004 s 22(4), and sent under s 22(6): see PARA 621.
3 As to the meaning of 'local government body in Wales' see PARA 618.
4 Public Audit (Wales) Act 2004 s 28(1), (2) (amended by the Public Audit (Wales) Act 2013 s 34, Sch 4 paras 20, 33(1), (2)).
5 Public Audit (Wales) Act 2004 s 28(2)(a).
6 Public Audit (Wales) Act 2004 s 28(2)(b).
7 Public Audit (Wales) Act 2004 s 28(2)(c).
8 Public Audit (Wales) Act 2004 s 28(3)(a) (amended by the Public Audit (Wales) Act 2013 Sch 4 paras 20, 33(1), (2)).
9 Public Audit (Wales) Act 2004 s 28(3)(b) (amended by the Public Audit (Wales) Act 2013 Sch 4 paras 20, 33(1), (2)).

624. General report.

When the Auditor General for Wales[1] has concluded his audit of a body's accounts[2], if a statement of accounts is required to be prepared by regulations[3], the Auditor General for Wales must enter on the statement (or, where no such statement is required to be prepared, on the accounts) a certificate that he has completed the audit in accordance with the Public Audit (Wales) Act 2004, and his opinion on the statement (or, as the case may be, on the accounts)[4]. However, if the Auditor General for Wales makes a report[5] at the conclusion of the audit, he may include the certificate and opinion referred to above in the report instead of making an entry on the statement or accounts[6].

1 As to the Auditor General for Wales see PARA 615; and CONSTITUTIONAL AND ADMINISTRATIVE LAW vol 20 (2014) PARA 400 et seq.
2 See the Public Audit (Wales) Act 2004 s 23(1) (amended by the Public Audit (Wales) Act 2013 s 34, Sch 4 paras 20, 28). The conclusion of an audit referred to in the text is under the Public Audit (Wales) Act 2004 Pt 2 Ch 1 (ss 12–40): see PARA 619 et seq.
3 Ie under the Public Audit (Wales) Act 2004 s 39: see PARA 653 et seq.
4 See the Public Audit (Wales) Act 2004 s 23(2), (3).
5 Ie under the Public Audit (Wales) Act 2004 s 22: see PARA 621.
6 Public Audit (Wales) Act 2004 s 23(4).

625. Consideration of reports in public interest.

If the Auditor General for Wales[1] makes a public interest report[2] on a matter which comes to his notice in the course of the audit, the body, if it is a port authority[3], conservation board[4], internal drainage board[5], local probation board[6] or a probation trust, must take the report into consideration as soon as practicable after receiving it[7].

In any other case where a body is required to take a report into consideration, or where the auditor sends to the body a written recommendation, and states in the document containing the recommendation that in his opinion the recommendation should be considered[8], the body must consider the report or recommendation at a meeting held by it before the end of the period of one month starting with the day on which the auditor sends the report or recommendation to it[9]. At the meeting the body must decide:

(1) if a report is considered at the meeting, whether the report requires it to take any action[10];

(2) if a recommendation is considered at the meeting, whether the recommendation is to be accepted[11]; and

(3) what action, if any, to take in response to the report or recommendation[12].

1 As to the Auditor General for Wales see PARA 615; and CONSTITUTIONAL AND ADMINISTRATIVE LAW vol 20 (2014) PARA 400 et seq.

2 Ie a report under the Public Audit (Wales) Act 2004 s 22: see PARA 621.

3 As to port health authorities see ENVIRONMENTAL QUALITY AND PUBLIC HEALTH vol 45 (2010) PARA 102 et seq.

4 As to conservation boards see OPEN SPACES AND COUNTRYSIDE vol 78 (2010) PARA 660.

5 As to internal drainage boards see WATER AND WATERWAYS vol 101 (2009) PARA 569 et seq.

6 As to local probation boards see SENTENCING vol 92 (2015) PARA 666 et seq.

7 See the Public Audit (Wales) Act 2004 s 24(1), (2)(a), (3) (s 24(1) amended by the Public Audit (Wales) Act 2013 s 34, Sch 4 paras 20, 29; the Public Audit (Wales) Act 2004 s 24(3) amended by the Offender Management Act 2007 s 5(6), Sch 1 para 13(5)(b)). The agenda supplied to members of the body for the meeting of the body at which the report is to be considered must be accompanied by the report: Public Audit (Wales) Act 2004 s 24(4). The following powers do not include power to exclude the report (s 24(6)):

(1) the power under the Public Bodies (Admission to Meetings) Act 1960 s 1(4)(b) (see LOCAL GOVERNMENT vol 69 (2018) PARA 733) to exclude items from the matter supplied under that provision (supply of agenda etc to newspapers) (Public Audit (Wales) Act 2004 s 24(5)(a));

(2) the power under the Local Government Act 1972 s 100B(2) to exclude documents from the documents open to inspection under s 100B(1), or exclude items from the matter supplied under s 100B(7) (see LOCAL GOVERNMENT vol 69 (2018) PARA 739) (public access to agenda and reports before meetings and supply of agenda etc to newspapers) (Public Audit (Wales) Act 2004 s 24(5)(b)).

The Local Government Act 1972 Pt VA (ss 100A–100K) (see LOCAL GOVERNMENT vol 69 (2018) PARA 737 et seq) has effect in relation to the report as if s 100C(1)(d) (public access to copies of reports for six years after meeting) were not limited to so much of the report as relates to an item during which the meeting was open to the public: Public Audit (Wales) Act 2004 s 24(7). Nothing in s 27 (see PARA 622) affects the operation of s 24(4)–(7): s 27(10).

8 See the Public Audit (Wales) Act 2004 ss 24(2)(b), 25(1), (2) (s 25(2) amended by the Public Audit (Wales) Act 2013 Sch 4 paras 20, 30(1), (2)).

9 See the Public Audit (Wales) Act 2004 s 25(4) (amended by the Public Audit (Wales) Act 2013 Sch 4 paras 20, 30(1), (3)). The Auditor General for Wales may extend the period of one month mentioned in the Public Audit (Wales) Act 2004 s 25(4) in relation to a report or recommendation if he is satisfied that it is reasonable to allow the body more time to comply with its duties under s 25(4), (5) in relation to the report or recommendation: s 25(6) (amended by the Public Audit (Wales) Act 2013 Sch 4 paras 20, 30(1), (4)). A period may be extended under the Public Audit (Wales) Act 2004 s 25(6) more than once: s 25(7).

10 Public Audit (Wales) Act 2004 s 25(5)(a).

11 Public Audit (Wales) Act 2004 s 25(5)(b).

12 Public Audit (Wales) Act 2004 s 25(5)(c). Nothing in the Local Government Act 1972 s 101 (delegation of functions) applies to a duty imposed on a body by the Public Audit (Wales) Act 2004 s 25: s 25(8). Section 25 does not affect any duties (so far as they relate to the subject matter of a report or recommendation) imposed by or under the Public Audit (Wales) Act 2004; the Local Government Finance Act 1988 ss 114–116 (reports by chief finance officers); the Local Government and Housing Act 1989 s 5 (functions of monitoring officers); or any other enactment: Public Audit (Wales) Act 2004 s 25(9).

626. Publicity for meetings.

If a body is required[1] to hold a meeting for consideration of the Auditor General for Wales's[2] report or recommendation, the meeting may be held on a particular day only if, at least seven clear days before that day, a notice[3] has been published in a newspaper circulating in the area of the body[4]. The notice must:

(1) state the time and place of the meeting[5];

(2) indicate that the meeting is to be held to consider the Auditor General for Wales's report or recommendation, as the case may be[6]; and
(3) describe the subject matter of the report or recommendation[7].

As soon as practicable after the meeting the body must:
(a) ensure that the Auditor General for Wales is notified of the decisions made by the body[8];
(b) obtain the approval of the Auditor General for Wales to a written summary of those decisions (the 'approved summary')[9]; and
(c) ensure that a notice containing the approved summary is published in one or more newspapers circulating in the area of the body[10].

1 Ie by virtue of the Public Audit (Wales) Act 2004 s 25(4): see PARA 625.
2 As to the Auditor General for Wales see PARA 615; and CONSTITUTIONAL AND ADMINISTRATIVE LAW vol 20 (2014) PARA 400 et seq.
3 Ie a notice complying with the Public Audit (Wales) Act 2004 s 26(3): see the text to note 5–7.
4 See the Public Audit (Wales) Act 2004 s 26(1), (2).
5 Public Audit (Wales) Act 2004 s 26(3)(a).
6 Public Audit (Wales) Act 2004 s 26(3)(b) (amended by virtue of the Public Audit (Wales) Act 2013 s 34, Sch 4 paras 20, 31).
7 Public Audit (Wales) Act 2004 s 26(3)(c).
8 Public Audit (Wales) Act 2004 s 26(4)(a) (amended by the Public Audit (Wales) Act 2013 Sch 4 paras 20, 31). The decisions referred to in the text are those made under the Public Audit (Wales) Act 2004 s 25(5): see PARA 625.
9 Public Audit (Wales) Act 2004 s 26(4)(b) (amended by the Public Audit (Wales) Act 2013 Sch 4 paras 20, 31).
10 Public Audit (Wales) Act 2004 s 26(4)(c). The approved summary need not summarise any decision made at the meeting while the public were excluded:
(1) under the Local Government Act 1972 s 100A(2) (see LOCAL GOVERNMENT vol 69 (2018) PARA 737) (confidential information) (Public Audit (Wales) Act 2004 s 26(5)(a));
(2) in pursuance of a resolution under s 100A(4) (see LOCAL GOVERNMENT vol 69 (2018) PARA 737) (exempt information) (Public Audit (Wales) Act 2004 s 26(5)(b));
(3) in pursuance of a resolution under the Public Bodies (Admission to Meetings) Act 1960 s 1(2) (protection of public interest) (Public Audit (Wales) Act 2004 s 26(5)(c)).

But if the Local Government Act 1972 ss 100C, 100D (see LOCAL GOVERNMENT vol 69 (2018) PARAS 740, 741) (availability for inspection after meeting of minutes, background papers and other documents) apply in relation to the meeting, the approved summary must indicate the documents in relation to the meeting which are open for inspection under those provisions: Public Audit (Wales) Act 2004 s 26(6). Section 26 does not affect any provisions made in relation to meetings of a body by s 24(4)–(7) (see PARA 625) or by or under the Local Government Act 1972; the Public Bodies (Admission to Meetings) Act 1960; or any other enactment: Public Audit (Wales) Act 2004 s 26(7).

(C) *Public Inspection and Objections*

627. Public inspections and objections.

A local government elector[1] for the area of a local government body in Wales[2] may:
(1) at all reasonable times and without payment inspect and make a copy[3] of any statement of accounts prepared by the body pursuant to regulations under the Public Audit (Wales) Act 2004[4];
(2) at all reasonable times and without payment inspect and make a copy of any report, other than an immediate report[5], made to the body[6] by the Auditor General for Wales[7];
(3) require a copy of a statement or report falling within head (1) or (2) to be delivered to him on payment of a reasonable sum for each copy[8].

A person who has custody of a document falling within head (1) or (2) commits an offence if he obstructs a person in the exercise of a right under these provisions to inspect or make a copy of the document, or if he refuses to supply a copy of the document to a person entitled to the copy under head (3)[9].

1 'Local government elector' means a person registered as a local government elector in the register of electors in accordance with the provisions of the Representation of the People Acts (see ELECTIONS AND REFERENDUMS vol 37 (2013) PARA 3): Public Audit (Wales) Act 2004 s 59(6). A reference to a local government elector for an area, in relation to a national park authority which is the local planning authority for a national park, is to a local government elector for any area the whole or part of which is comprised in the park: s 59(7). As to national park authorities see OPEN SPACES AND COUNTRYSIDE vol 78 (2010) PARA 526 et seq.
2 As to the meaning of 'local government body in Wales' see PARA 618.
3 For these purposes references to a copy of a document include a copy of any part of it: Public Audit (Wales) Act 2004 s 29(4).
4 Public Audit (Wales) Act 2004 s 29(1)(a). The regulations referred to in the text are those made under the Public Audit (Wales) Act 2004 s 39: see PARA 653 et seq.
5 Ie a report under the Public Audit (Wales) Act 2004 s 22(3) (see PARA 621).
6 As to the meaning of 'body' see PARA 618 note 2.
7 Public Audit (Wales) Act 2004 s 29(1)(b) (amended by the Public Audit (Wales) Act 2013 s 34, Sch 4 paras 20, 34(1), (2)).
8 Public Audit (Wales) Act 2004 s 29(1)(c).
9 Public Audit (Wales) Act 2004 s 29(2). A person guilty of an offence under s 29(2) is liable on summary conviction to a fine not exceeding level 3 on the standard scale: s 29(3). As to the powers of magistrates' courts to issue fines on summary conviction see SENTENCING vol 92 (2015) PARA 176.

628. Inspection of documents and questions at audit.

At an audit of accounts under the Public Audit (Wales) Act 2004[1] an interested person may inspect the accounts to be audited and all books, deeds, contracts, bills, vouchers and receipts relating to them, and may make a copy of all or any part of the accounts and of any of the other above documents[2]. At the request of a local government elector[3] for any area to which accounts to be audited relate, the Auditor General of Wales[4] must give the elector, or any representative of his, an opportunity to question the Auditor General about the accounts[5]. Nothing in the above provisions entitles a person to inspect any accounts or other document relating to a body[6] to the extent that the accounts contain, or the document contains, personal information[7], or to require any personal information to be disclosed by the Auditor General for Wales in answer to any question[8].

1 Ie under the Public Audit (Wales) Act 2004 Pt 2 Ch 1 (ss 12–40): see PARA 619 et seq.
2 Public Audit (Wales) Act 2004 s 30(1).
3 As to the meaning of 'local government elector' see PARA 627 note 1.
4 As to the Auditor General for Wales see PARA 615; and CONSTITUTIONAL AND ADMINISTRATIVE LAW vol 20 (2014) PARA 400 et seq.
5 Public Audit (Wales) Act 2004 s 30(2) (amended by the Public Audit (Wales) Act 2013 s 34, Sch 4 paras 20, 35(1), (2)).
6 As to the meaning of 'body' see PARA 618 note 2.
7 Public Audit (Wales) Act 2004 s 30(3)(a). For the purposes of the Public Audit (Wales) Act 2004 s 30(3) 'personal information' means information relating to an individual which is available to the body for reasons connected with either of the following (s 30(4)):
   (1) the fact that the individual holds or has held an office or employment under the body (s 30(4)(a)); or
   (2) the fact that payments or other benefits are or have been made or provided to the individual by the body in respect of an office or employment under another person (s 30(4)(b)).

   For the purposes of s 30(4) payments made or benefits provided to an individual in respect of an office or employment include any payment made or benefit provided to an individual in respect of his ceasing to hold the office or employment: s 30(5).
8 Public Audit (Wales) Act 2004 s 30(3)(b) (amended by the Public Audit (Wales) Act 2013 Sch 4 paras 20, 35(1), (2)). See also note 7.

629. Right to make objections at audit.

At an audit of accounts under the Public Audit (Wales) Act 2004[1] a local government elector[2] for the area to which the accounts relate, or any representative of his, may make objections before the Auditor General for Wales[3]. A local government elector proposing to make such an objection must give written notice to the Auditor General for Wales of the proposed objection and the grounds on which it is to be made, and, at the same time, send a copy of the notice to the body whose accounts are being audited[4].

1 Ie under the Public Audit (Wales) Act 2004 Pt 2 Ch 1 (ss 12–40): see PARA 619 et seq.

2 As to the meaning of 'local government elector' see PARA 627 note 1.

3 Public Audit (Wales) Act 2004 s 31(1) (s 31 amended by the Public Audit (Wales) Act 2013 s 34, Sch 4 paras 20, 36). Objections may be made as to:
   (1) any matter in respect of which the auditor has a power to apply for a declaration under the Public Audit (Wales) Act 2004 s 32 (see PARA 630) (s 31(1)(a) (as so amended)); or
   (2) any other matter in respect of which the auditor has the power to make a report under s 22 (see PARA 621) (s 31(1)(b) (as so amended)).

   As to the Auditor General for Wales see PARA 615; and CONSTITUTIONAL AND ADMINISTRATIVE LAW vol 20 (2014) PARA 400 et seq.

4 Public Audit (Wales) Act 2004 s 31(2) (as amended: see note 3)

(D) Unlawful Items of Account and Expenditure

630. Unlawful items of account and expenditure.

Where it appears to the Auditor General for Wales[1] in carrying out an audit under the Public Audit (Wales) Act 2004[2] that an item of account is contrary to law, he may apply to the court[3] for a declaration that the item is contrary to law[4]. On such an application the court may make or refuse to make the declaration applied for[5]. If it makes the declaration applied for it may also order rectification of the accounts[6].

If the Auditor General for Wales decides not to make an application for a declaration under these provisions in relation to an item of account, he must notify a person who has made an objection[7] in relation to the item of account of his decision[8]. A person so notified of the Auditor General for Wales's decision may require the Auditor General for Wales to state in writing the reasons for his decision before the end of the permitted period[9]. A person who receives reasons for the Auditor General for Wales's decision may appeal to the court against the decision before the end of the permitted period[10].

On such an appeal the court has the same powers in relation to the item of account as it would have if the Auditor General for Wales had applied to the court for a declaration[11] in relation to the item of account[12].

On an application or appeal under these provisions relating to the accounts of a body[13], the court may make such order as it thinks fit for the payment by the body of expenses incurred in connection with the application or appeal by the Auditor General for Wales or the person by whom the appeal is brought[14].

1 As to the Auditor General for Wales see PARA 615; and CONSTITUTIONAL AND ADMINISTRATIVE LAW vol 20 (2014) PARA 400 et seq.

2 Ie under the Public Audit (Wales) Act 2004 Pt 2 Ch 1 (ss 12–40): see PARA 619 et seq.

3 The High Court and the County Court have jurisdiction for the purposes of the Public Audit (Wales) Act 2004 s 32: s 32(10) (amended by the Crime and Courts Act 2013 s 17(5), Sch 9 para 124).

4 Public Audit (Wales) Act 2004 s 32(1) (amended by the Public Audit (Wales) Act 2013 s 34, Sch 4 paras 20, 37(1), (2)). As to meaning of 'contrary to law' see *Roberts v Hopwood* [1925] AC 578, HL; *Pickwell v Camden London Borough Council* [1983] QB 962, [1983] 1 All ER 602; and *Allsop v North Tyneside Metropolitan Borough Council* (1992) 90 LGR 462, [1992] ICR 639, CA.
5 Public Audit (Wales) Act 2004 s 32(2).
6 Public Audit (Wales) Act 2004 s 32(3).
7 Ie under the Public Audit (Wales) Act 2004 s 31(1)(a): see PARA 629.
8 Public Audit (Wales) Act 2004 s 32(4) (amended by the Public Audit (Wales) Act 2013 Sch 4 paras 20, 37(1), (3)). The Public Audit (Wales) Act 2004 s 32(4) does not apply if the person who has made the objection has failed to comply with s 31(2) (see PARA 629): s 32(5).
9 Public Audit (Wales) Act 2004 s 32(6) (amended by the Public Audit (Wales) Act 2013 Sch 4 paras 20, 37(1), (4)). The permitted period for these purposes is 14 days starting with the day on which the person is notified of the Auditor General for Wales's decision: Public Audit (Wales) Act 2004 s 32(6) (as so amended).
10 Public Audit (Wales) Act 2004 s 32(7) (amended by virtue of the Public Audit (Wales) Act 2013 Sch 4 paras 20, 37(1), (4)). The permitted period for these purposes is 28 days starting with the day on which the person receives the reasons: Public Audit (Wales) Act 2004 s 32(7).
11 Ie under the Public Audit (Wales) Act 2004 s 32(1): see the text and notes 1–4.
12 Public Audit (Wales) Act 2004 s 32(8) (amended by the Public Audit (Wales) Act 2013 Sch 4 paras 20, 37(1), (4)). For decisions expressing the view that the court should be slow to interfere with the discretion of the expert auditor see *R (on the application of Moss) v KPMG LLP* [2010] EWHC 2923 (Admin); and *Nicolson v Grant Thornton UK LLP* [2016] EWHC 710 (Admin), [2017] RVR 43.
13 As to the meaning of 'body' see PARA 618 note 2.
14 Public Audit (Wales) Act 2004 s 32(9) (amended by the Public Audit (Wales) Act 2013 Sch 4 paras 20, 37(1), (4)).

631. Advisory notices.

The Auditor General for Wales[1] may issue a notice under this provision (an 'advisory notice'[2]) if he has reason to believe that one or more of the following requirements[3] is met in respect of a local government body in Wales[4]:

(1) the body or an officer of the body is about to make or has made a decision which involves or would involve the body incurring expenditure which is unlawful[5];
(2) the body or an officer of the body is about to take or has begun to take a course of action which, if pursued to its conclusion, would be unlawful and likely to cause a loss or deficiency[6];
(3) the body or an officer of the body is about to enter an item of account, the entry of which is unlawful[7].

A copy of an advisory notice:

(a) must be served on the body to which, or to an officer of which, it is addressed[8];
(b) if the notice is addressed to an officer, must be served on him[9];
(c) may be served on any other person considered appropriate by the Auditor General for Wales[10].

An advisory notice may at any time be withdrawn by the Auditor General for Wales[11]. The Auditor General for Wales must give notice in writing of the withdrawal to any body or person on whom a copy of the advisory notice was served[12].

1 As to the Auditor General for Wales see PARA 615; and CONSTITUTIONAL AND ADMINISTRATIVE LAW vol 20 (2014) PARA 400 et seq.
2 An advisory notice is a notice which meets the following requirements (Public Audit (Wales) Act 2004 s 33(4)):
 (1) it is addressed to the body or officer (s 33(4)(a));
 (2) it specifies which of the requirements specified in s 33(2) is met and the decision, course of action or item of account to which the notice relates (s 33(4)(b));

(3) it specifies that the notice will take effect on the day a copy of it is served on the person to whom it is addressed (s 33(4)(c));

(4) it requires the body or officer to give the Auditor General for Wales not less than the specified period of notice in writing of the intention of the body or officer to:

(a) make or implement the decision to which the notice relates (s 33(4)(d)(i));

(b) take or continue to take the course of action to which the notice relates (s 33(4)(d)(ii)); or

(c) enter the item of account to which the notice relates (s 33(4)(d)(iii)).

For the purposes of head (4) the specified period of notice is the period (not exceeding 21 days) specified in the advisory notice: s 33(5). As to the meaning of 'body' see PARA 618 note 2.

3 Ie the requirements specified in the Public Audit (Wales) Act 2004 s 33(2).

4 See the Public Audit (Wales) Act 2004 s 33(1) (amended by the Public Audit (Wales) Act 2013 s 34, Sch 4 paras 20, 38(1), (2)). For the purposes of the Public Audit (Wales) Act 2004 s 33 the actions of any body or officer mentioned in s 33(2) (see notes 5–7) are to be treated as the actions of:

(1) a committee or sub-committee of the body (s 33(3)(a));

(2) a person (other than an officer of the body) authorised to act on behalf of the body (s 33(3)(b)).

As to the meaning of 'local government body in Wales' see PARA 618.

5 Public Audit (Wales) Act 2004 s 33(2)(a).

6 Public Audit (Wales) Act 2004 s 33(2)(b).

7 Public Audit (Wales) Act 2004 s 33(2)(c).

8 Public Audit (Wales) Act 2004 s 33(6)(a).

9 Public Audit (Wales) Act 2004 s 33(6)(b). A document to be served on an officer of a body under s 33 must be served on him by addressing it to him (s 33(9)) and:

(1) delivering it to him at an office of the body at which he is employed (s 33(9)(a));

(2) leaving it at such an office(s 33(9)(b)); or

(3) sending it by post to such an office (s 33(9)(c)).

10 Public Audit (Wales) Act 2004 s 33(6)(c) (amended by the Public Audit (Wales) Act 2013 Sch 4 paras 20, 38(1), (4)). The Auditor General for Wales must, before the end of the required period, serve a statement of his reasons for the belief referred to in the Public Audit (Wales) Act 2004 s 33(1) (see the text and notes 1–4) on the body, and, if the advisory notice is addressed to an officer of the body, the officer: s 33(7) (amended by the Public Audit (Wales) Act 2013 Sch 4 paras 20, 38(1), (5)). The required period for the purposes of the Public Audit (Wales) Act 2004 s 33(7) is seven days starting on the day on which a copy of the advisory notice was served on the person to whom it is addressed: s 33(8).

11 Public Audit (Wales) Act 2004 s 33(10) (amended by the Public Audit (Wales) Act 2013 Sch 4 paras 20, 38(1), (6)).

12 Public Audit (Wales) Act 2004 s 33(11) (amended by the Public Audit (Wales) Act 2013 Sch 4 paras 20, 38(1), (7)).

632. Effect of an advisory notice.

While an advisory notice[1] has effect, it is not lawful for the body concerned[2] or an officer of the body[3]:

(1) if the advisory notice relates to a decision, to make or implement the decision[4];

(2) if the advisory notice relates to a course of action, to take or continue to take the course of action[5];

(3) if the advisory notice relates to an item of account, to enter the item of account[6],

unless and until the following conditions are met:

(a) that the body has considered, in the light of the advisory notice and the statement of reasons for belief[7], the consequences of doing the thing mentioned in whichever of heads (1) to (3) above is applicable[8];

(b) that the body or officer has given the Auditor General for Wales[9] the period of notice in writing required by the advisory notice[10];

(c) that that period has expired[11].

An advisory notice takes effect on the day on which a copy of the notice is served on the person to whom it is addressed[12]. It ceases to have effect:

(i) if a statement of reasons is not served[13], at the end of the specified period[14];

(ii) in any other case, when it is withdrawn[15].

The Wales Audit Office may recover from the body concerned any expenses reasonably incurred by the Auditor General for Wales in or in connection with the issue of an advisory notice[16].

Where, before an advisory notice is served, a body enters into a contract to dispose of or acquire an interest in land, and before the disposal or acquisition is completed, an advisory notice takes effect as a result of which it is unlawful for the body to complete the disposal or acquisition, the existence of the advisory notice does not prejudice any remedy in damages which may be available to any person as a result of the body's failure to complete the contract[17].

No action lies against the Auditor General for Wales in respect of loss or damage alleged to have been caused as a result of the issue of an advisory notice which was issued in good faith[18].

1 As to the meaning of 'advisory notice' see PARA 631 note 2.
2 In the Public Audit (Wales) Act 2004 s 34 the 'body concerned', in relation to an advisory notice, means the body to which, or to an officer of which, the notice is addressed: s 34(9). For the purposes of s 34 the actions of any body or officer are to be treated as the actions of:
   (1) a committee or sub-committee of the body (s 33(3)(a));
   (2) a person (other than an officer of the body) authorised to act on behalf of the body (s 33(3)(b)).
3 See the Public Audit (Wales) Act 2004 s 34(1).
4 Public Audit (Wales) Act 2004 s 34(2).
5 Public Audit (Wales) Act 2004 s 34(3).
6 Public Audit (Wales) Act 2004 s 34(4).
7 Ie under the Public Audit (Wales) Act 2004 s 33(7): see PARA 631.
8 Public Audit (Wales) Act 2004 s 34(5)(a).
9 As to the Auditor General for Wales see PARA 615; and CONSTITUTIONAL AND ADMINISTRATIVE LAW vol 20 (2014) PARA 400 et seq.
10 Public Audit (Wales) Act 2004 s 34(5)(b) (amended by the Public Audit (Wales) Act 2013 s 34, Sch 4 paras 20, 39(1), (2)). The advisory notice referred to in the text is required under the Public Audit (Wales) Act 2004 s 33(4)(d): see PARA 631 note 2.
11 Public Audit (Wales) Act 2004 s 34(5)(c).
12 Public Audit (Wales) Act 2004 s 34(6).
13 Ie in accordance with the Public Audit (Wales) Act 2004 s 33(7): see PARA 631.
14 Ie the period specified in the Public Audit (Wales) Act 2004 s 33(8): see PARA 631.
15 Public Audit (Wales) Act 2004 s 34(7). The reference in the text to withdrawal is a reference to withdrawal under s 33(10): see PARA 631.
16 Public Audit (Wales) Act 2004 s 34(8) (amended by the Public Audit (Wales) Act 2013 Sch 4 paras 20, 39(1), (3)).
17 Public Audit (Wales) Act 2004 s 35(1), (2).
18 Public Audit (Wales) Act 2004 s 35(3) (amended by the Public Audit (Wales) Act 2013 Sch 4 paras 20, 40).

633. Power to make a claim for judicial review.

The Auditor General for Wales[1] may make a claim for judicial review with respect to a decision of a local government body in Wales[2] or a failure of the body to act, if it is reasonable to believe that the decision or failure to act would have an effect on the body's accounts[3]. The existence of the powers conferred on the Auditor General for Wales under the Public Audit (Wales) Act 2004[4] is not a ground for refusing such a claim, or for refusing an application for permission to make such a claim[5]. On a claim by the Auditor General for Wales for judicial review with respect to a decision of a body or a failure of a body to act, the court may make any order it thinks fit for the payment by the body of expenses incurred by the Auditor General for Wales or the Wales Audit Office in connection with the claim[6].

1 As to the Auditor General for Wales see PARA 615; and CONSTITUTIONAL AND ADMINISTRATIVE LAW vol 20 (2014) PARA 400 et seq.
2 As to the meaning of 'local government body in Wales' see PARA 618.
3 Public Audit (Wales) Act 2004 s 36(1) (amended by the Public Audit (Wales) Act 2013 s 34, Sch 4 paras 20, 41(1), (2)). The Public Audit (Wales) Act 2004 s 36(1) is subject to the Senior Courts Act 1981 s 31(3) (no claim for judicial review without permission of court) (see JUDICIAL REVIEW vol 61 (2010) PARA 656): Public Audit (Wales) Act 2004 s 36(2) (amended by virtue of the Constitutional Reform Act 2005 s 59(5), Sch 11 para 1(2)).
4 Ie under the Public Audit (Wales) Act 2004 Pt 2 (ss 12–60).
5 Public Audit (Wales) Act 2004 s 36(3) (amended by the Public Audit (Wales) Act 2013 Sch 4 paras 20, 41(1), (3)).
6 Public Audit (Wales) Act 2004 s 36(4) (amended by the Public Audit (Wales) Act 2013 Sch 4 paras 20, 41(1), (4)).

(E) Miscellaneous

634. Extraordinary audit.

The Auditor General for Wales[1] may hold an extraordinary audit[2] of the accounts of a local government body in Wales[3] if either of the following conditions[4] is met[5]:

(1) if it appears to the Auditor General for Wales to be desirable to hold an extraordinary audit of the body's accounts[6]; or

(2) if an application for an extraordinary audit of the body's accounts is made by a local government elector[7] for the area of the body[8].

The Welsh Ministers[9] may require the Auditor General for Wales to hold an extraordinary audit of the accounts of a local government body in Wales if it appears to the Welsh Ministers to be desirable in the public interest for an extraordinary audit of the body's accounts to be held[10].

An extraordinary audit of a body's accounts may be held only if three clear days' notice in writing of the audit is given to the body[11].

The expenditure incurred in holding an extraordinary audit of a body's accounts must be met in the first instance by the Auditor General for Wales[12]. The Wales Audit Office may recover all or part of the expenditure from the body[13].

1 As to the Auditor General for Wales see PARA 615; and CONSTITUTIONAL AND ADMINISTRATIVE LAW vol 20 (2014) PARA 400 et seq.
2 The following provisions apply to an extraordinary audit under the Public Audit (Wales) Act 2004 s 37 as they apply to an ordinary audit: ss 17–19 (see PARAS 619, 620), ss 22–28 (see PARA 621–626), ss 31, 32 (see PARAS 629, 630): s 37(5) (amended by the Public Audit (Wales) Act 2013 s 34, Sch 4 paras 20, 42(1), (5)).

Where, under the Public Audit (Wales) Act 2004 s 37, the Auditor General for Wales holds an extraordinary audit of accounts of a relevant body, the body must display a notice on its website and in at least one conspicuous place in the area of the body, concerning the right of any local government elector for the area to which the accounts relate to make objections to any of those accounts: Accounts and Audit (Wales) Regulations 2014, SI 2014/3362, reg 28(1) (substituted by SI 2018/91). Where the auditor referred to in the Accounts and Audit (Wales) Regulations 2014, SI 2014/3362, reg 28(1) is the Auditor General for Wales, the reference to the Auditor General directing an auditor to hold an extraordinary audit is to be read as the Auditor General for Wales holding an extraordinary audit: reg 28(2).
3 As to the meaning of 'local government body in Wales' see PARA 618. As to the meaning of 'body' see PARA 618 note 2.
4 Ie the conditions in the Public Audit (Wales) Act 2004 s 37(2) or (3): see the text to notes 6–8.
5 Public Audit (Wales) Act 2004 s 37(1) (amended by the Public Audit (Wales) Act 2013 Sch 4 paras 20, 42(1), (3)).

6 Public Audit (Wales) Act 2004 s 37(2).
7 As to the meaning of 'local government elector' see PARA 627 note 1.
8 Public Audit (Wales) Act 2004 s 37(3).
9 As to the Welsh Ministers see PARA 4 note 18.
10 Public Audit (Wales) Act 2004 s 37(4) (amended by the Public Audit (Wales) Act 2013 Sch 4 paras 20, 42(1), (2), (4)).
11 Public Audit (Wales) Act 2004 s 37(6).
12 Public Audit (Wales) Act 2004 s 37(7).
13 Public Audit (Wales) Act 2004 s 37(8) (amended by the Public Audit (Wales) Act 2013 Sch 4 paras 20, 42(1), (6)).

635. Audit of accounts of officers.

If an officer of a local government body in Wales[1] receives money or other property on behalf of the body[2], or for which he ought to account to the body[3], the Auditor General for Wales[4] must audit the officer's accounts[5].

1 As to the meaning of 'local government body in Wales' see PARA 618. As to officers see PARA 425 et seq.
2 Public Audit (Wales) Act 2004 s 38(1)(a).
3 Public Audit (Wales) Act 2004 s 38(1)(b).
4 As to the Auditor General for Wales see PARA 615; and CONSTITUTIONAL AND ADMINISTRATIVE LAW vol 20 (2014) PARA 400 et seq.
5 Public Audit (Wales) Act 2004 s 38(1), (2) (s 38(2) amended by the Public Audit (Wales) Act 2013 s 34, Sch 4 paras 20, 43). The following provisions of the Public Audit (Wales) Act 2004apply with the necessary modifications to the accounts and audit: s 13(1) (see PARA 618), ss 17–24 (see PARA 619 et seq), ss 27–32 (see PARAS 622–623, 627–630), s 37 (see PARA 634), and s 39 (see PARA 653 et seq): s 38(3).

636. Documents relating to police and crime commissioners or chief constables.

If the Auditor General for Wales[1] makes a public interest report[2] and the report relates to a police and crime commissioner for, or the chief constable of a police force[3] for, a police area in Wales[4], he must send a copy of the report to the Secretary of State and the Welsh Ministers[5].

If the Auditor General for Wales has sent a document, or a copy of a document, relating to one or more police and crime commissioners for police areas in Wales to a police and crime commissioner for a police area in Wales, he may send a copy of the document to the Secretary of State and the Welsh Ministers[6].

If the Auditor General for Wales has sent a document (or a copy of a document) relating to one or more chief constables of police forces for a police area in Wales, the Auditor General may send a copy of the document to the Secretary of State and the Welsh Ministers[7].

1 As to the Auditor General for Wales see PARA 615; and CONSTITUTIONAL AND ADMINISTRATIVE LAW vol 20 (2014) PARA 400 et seq.
2 Ie a report under the Public Audit (Wales) Act 2004 s 22(5), (6): see PARA 621.
3 As to police and crime commissioners see POLICE AND INVESTIGATORY POWERS vol 84 (2013) PARA 56 et seq.
4 Ie a police force maintained under the Police Act 1996 s 2: see POLICE AND INVESTIGATORY POWERS vol 84 (2013) PARA 52.
5 Public Audit (Wales) Act 2004 s 40(1) (amended by the Police Reform and Social Responsibility Act 2011 s 99, Sch 16 paras 336, 338(1), (3); and the Public Audit (Wales) Act 2013 s 34, Sch 4 paras 20, 45(1)–(3)). As to the Secretary of State and the Welsh Ministers see PARA 4 note 18.
6 Public Audit (Wales) Act 2004 s 40(2) (amended by the Police Reform and Social Responsibility Act 2011 Sch 16 paras 336, 338(1), (4); and the Public Audit (Wales) Act 2013 Sch 4 paras 20, 45(1), (3)).
7 Public Audit (Wales) Act 2004 s 40(3) (added by the Police Reform and Social Responsibility Act 2011 Sch 16 paras 336, 338(1), (5)).

C. STUDIES, PERFORMANCE STANDARDS AND OTHER FUNCTIONS

(A) Studies and Related Functions

637. Studies for improving economy, efficiency and effectiveness in the provision of services.

The Auditor General for Wales[1] must for each financial year[2] undertake studies designed to enable him to make recommendations[3]:

(1) for improving economy, efficiency and effectiveness in the discharge of the functions of local government bodies in Wales[4] that are Welsh improvement authorities[5];

(2) for improving economy, efficiency and effectiveness in the provision of services provided by other local government bodies in Wales[6];

(3) for improving the financial or other management of local government bodies in Wales[7].

The studies which the Auditor General for Wales is required to undertake include, in particular[8]:

(a) studies designed to enable the Auditor General for Wales to determine what directions he should give for requiring relevant bodies to publish specified information[9];

(b) studies of information published in pursuance of such directions[10] which are designed to enable the Auditor General for Wales to determine, in relation to each financial year, what comparative information to publish himself about the standards of performance achieved by bodies which are relevant bodies for these purposes[11].

The Auditor General for Wales may undertake other studies relating to the provision of services by local government bodies in Wales[12].

Where the Auditor General for Wales undertakes a study under these provisions, he must publish or otherwise make available the results of the study, and any recommendations made by him[13].

Before undertaking a study under these provisions, other than a study of a kind mentioned in head (a) or (b) above, the Auditor General for Wales must consult[14]:

(i) any associations of local government bodies in Wales which appear to him to be concerned[15]; and

(ii) any associations of employees which appear to him to be appropriate[16].

The Auditor General for Wales may undertake studies designed to enable him to make recommendations for improving economy, efficiency and effectiveness in the discharge of the functions of any relevant body[17] or bodies[18]. The Auditor General may also undertake or promote other studies relating to the provision of services by any relevant body or bodies[19]. However, these provisions[20] do not entitle the Auditor General to question the merits of the policy objectives of any relevant body[21]. In determining how to exercise these functions[22], the Auditor General must take into account the views of the audit committee as to the studies which he should undertake or promote[23].

1 As to the Auditor General for Wales see PARA 615; and CONSTITUTIONAL AND ADMINISTRATIVE LAW vol 20 (2014) PARA 400 et seq.

The Auditor General for Wales and the Welsh Ministers must co-operate with each other with respect to the exercise of their respective functions under s 41 and under the Health and Social Care (Community Health and Standards) Act 2003 ss 94, 95 (see SOCIAL SERVICES vol 95 (2017) PARA 339) (reviews, investigations and studies): Public Audit (Wales) Act 2004 s 41(6) (amended by the Public Audit (Wales) Act 2013 s 34, Sch 4 paras 20, 46(1), (4)). Prospectively, for the reference to the Health and Social Care (Community Health and Standards) Act 2003 ss 94, 95 there is substituted a reference to the Social Services and Well-being (Wales) Act 2014 ss 149A,

149B (reviews of studies and research and other reviews relating to local authority social services functions carried out by the Welsh Ministers): see the Public Audit (Wales) Act 2004 s 41(6) (amended, as from a day to be appointed, by the Regulation and Inspection of Social Care (Wales) Act 2016 s 185, Sch 3 paras 21, 22; at the date at which this volume states the law, no such day had been appointed). As to the Welsh Ministers see PARA 4 note 18.

Prospectively, in respect of the discharge of social services functions by local authorities in Wales, the Auditor General and the Social Care Wales must co-operate with each other with respect to the exercise of their respective functions under the Public Audit (Wales) Act 2004 s 41 and the Regulation and Inspection of Social Care (Wales) Act 2016 s 70 (studies by SCW as to economy etc): Public Audit (Wales) Act 2004 s 41(7), (8) (s 41(7)–(9) added, as from a day to be appointed, by the Regulation and Inspection of Social Care (Wales) Act 2016 Sch 3 paras 47, 48; at the date at which this volume states the law, no such day had been appointed). For these purposes, 'social services functions' has the same meaning as in the Social Services and Well-being (Wales) Act 2014: Public Audit (Wales) Act 2004 s 41(9) (as so added).

2 As to the meaning of 'financial year' see PARA 620 note 7.

3 Public Audit (Wales) Act 2004 s 41(1) (amended by the Public Audit (Wales) Act 2013 Sch 4 paras 20, 46(1), (2)).

4 As to the meaning of 'local government body in Wales' see PARA 618.

5 Public Audit (Wales) Act 2004 s 41(1)(a) (amended by the Local Government and Public Involvement in Health Act 2007 s 144(2), Sch 8, para 27(1), (2); the Local Government (Wales) Measure 2009 s 51(1), Sch 1 paras 34, 35; and the Public Audit (Wales) Act 2013 Sch 4 paras 20, 46(1), (3)). The text refers to a Welsh improvement authority for the purposes of the Local Government (Wales) Measure 2009 Pt 1 (ss 1–47) (see LOCAL GOVERNMENT vol 69 (2018) PARA 789 et seq).

6 Public Audit (Wales) Act 2004 s 41(1)(b).

7 Public Audit (Wales) Act 2004 s 41(1)(c).

8 Public Audit (Wales) Act 2004 s 41(2) (amended by the Public Audit (Wales) Act 2013 Sch 4 paras 20, 46(1), (2)).

9 Public Audit (Wales) Act 2004 s 41(2)(a). The directions referred to in the text are those given under the Public Audit (Wales) Act 2004 s 47 (publication of information as to standards of performance): see PARA 644.

10 Ie under the Public Audit (Wales) Act 2004 s 47: see PARA 644.

11 Public Audit (Wales) Act 2004 s 41(2)(b).

12 Public Audit (Wales) Act 2004 s 41(3) (amended by the Public Audit (Wales) Act 2013 Sch 4 paras 20, 46(1), (2)).

13 Public Audit (Wales) Act 2004 s 41(4) (amended by the Public Audit (Wales) Act 2013 Sch 4 paras 20, 46(1), (2)).

14 Public Audit (Wales) Act 2004 s 41(5) (amended by the Public Audit (Wales) Act 2013 Sch 4 paras 20, 46(1), (2)).

15 Public Audit (Wales) Act 2004 s 41(5)(a).

16 Public Audit (Wales) Act 2004 s 41(1)(b).

17 For these purposes each of the following is a 'relevant body':

(1) a person who prepares accounts or statements of accounts falling to be examined by the Auditor General for Wales in accordance with any provision made by or under the Government of Wales Act 1998 or any other Act (s 145A(5)(a) (as added (see note 18); substituted by the Government of Wales Act 2006 s 160(1), Sch 10 paras 41, 47));

(2) any other person (other than a local government body in Wales) in relation to whom, by virtue of provision made by or under this or any other Act, the Auditor General for Wales carries out examinations or studies relating to the economy, efficiency and effectiveness with which that person has used his resources in discharging his functions (Government of Wales Act 1998 s 145A(5)(b) (as so added));

(3) a person (other than a registered social landlord in Wales) in respect of whom the Auditor General for Wales has functions by virtue of provision made under s 146A (see CONSTITUTIONAL AND ADMINISTRATIVE LAW vol 20 (2014) PARA 402) (s 145A(5)(c) (as so added)).

For these purposes 'local government body in Wales' has the meaning given in the Public Audit (Wales) Act 2004 s 12(1) (see PARA 618); and 'registered social landlord in Wales' has the meaning given in the Government of Wales Act 1998 s 146A(2) (see CONSTITUTIONAL AND ADMINISTRATIVE LAW vol 20 (2014) PARA 402): s 145A(7) (as so added).

18 Government of Wales Act 1998 s 145A(1) (s 145A added by the Public Audit (Wales) Act 2004 s 3).

19 Government of Wales Act 1998 s 145A(2) (as added: see note 18).
20 Ie the provisions of the Government of Wales Act 1998 s 145A(1), (2): see the text and notes 17–19).
21 Government of Wales Act 1998 s 145A(3) (as added: see note 18).
22 Ie his functions under the Government of Wales Act 1998 s 145A.
23 Government of Wales Act 1998 s 145A(4) (as added: see note 18). Where the Auditor General for Wales undertakes or promotes a study under s 145A he may arrange for a report containing:
(1) the results of the study; and
(2) his recommendations (if any),
to be laid before the National Assembly for Wales: s 145A(6) (as so added).

638. Studies on impact of statutory provisions.

The Auditor General for Wales[1] must undertake studies designed to enable him to prepare reports as to the impact of[2]:

(1) the operation of any statutory provisions[3]; or
(2) any relevant directions or guidance given by the Welsh Ministers (whether or not under a statutory provision)[4],

on economy, efficiency and effectiveness in the discharge of the functions of local government bodies in Wales[5]. The Auditor General for Wales must from time to time lay before the National Assembly for Wales a report of any matters which, in his opinion, arise out of studies under this provision, and ought to be drawn to the attention of the Assembly[6].

Before undertaking any such study, the Auditor General for Wales must consult any associations of local government bodies in Wales which appear to him to be concerned, and any associations of employees which appear to him to be appropriate[7].

1 As to the Auditor General for Wales see PARA 615; and CONSTITUTIONAL AND ADMINISTRATIVE LAW vol 20 (2014) PARA 400 et seq. The Auditor General for Wales and the Welsh Ministers must co-operate with each other with respect to the exercise of their respective functions under the Health and Social Care (Community Health and Standards) Act 2003 s 95(2) (see SOCIAL SERVICES vol 95 (2017) PARA 339) (studies by Welsh Ministers on impact of statutory provisions): Public Audit (Wales) Act 2004 s 42(4) (amended by the Public Audit (Wales) Act 2013 s 34, Sch 4 paras 20, 47(1), (5)). Prospectively, for the reference to the Health and Social Care (Community Health and Standards) Act 2003 s 95(2) there is substituted a reference to the Social Services and Well-being (Wales) Act 2014 ss 149A, 149B (reviews of studies and research and other reviews relating to local authority social services functions carried out by the Welsh Ministers): see the Public Audit (Wales) Act 2004 s 42(4) (amended, as from a day to be appointed, by the Regulation and Inspection of Social Care (Wales) Act 2016 s 185, Sch 3 paras 21, 23; at the date at which this volume states the law, no such day had been appointed). As to the Welsh Ministers see PARA 4 note 18.
2 Public Audit (Wales) Act 2004 s 42(1) (amended by the Public Audit (Wales) Act 2013 Sch 4 paras 20, 47(1), (2)(a)).
3 Public Audit (Wales) Act 2004 s 42(1)(a).
4 Public Audit (Wales) Act 2004 s 42(1)(b) (amended by the Public Audit (Wales) Act 2013 Sch 4 paras 20, 47(1), (2)(b)).
5 Public Audit (Wales) Act 2004 s 42(1). As to the meaning of 'local government body in Wales' see PARA 618.
6 Public Audit (Wales) Act 2004 s 42(2) (amended by the Public Audit (Wales) Act 2013 Sch 4 paras 20, 47(1), (3)). As to the National Assembly for Wales see CONSTITUTIONAL AND ADMINISTRATIVE LAW vol 20 (2014) PARA 351 et seq.
7 Public Audit (Wales) Act 2004 s 42(3) (amended by the Public Audit (Wales) Act 2013 Sch 4 paras 20, 47(1), (4)).

639. Studies at request of local government bodies in Wales.

The Auditor General for Wales[1] may, at the request of a local government body in Wales[2], undertake studies designed to enable him to make recommendations for improving economy, efficiency and effectiveness in the discharge of the functions of the body[3].

Before making the request the body must consult any associations of employees which appear to it to be appropriate[4].

1 As to the Auditor General for Wales see PARA 615; and CONSTITUTIONAL AND ADMINISTRATIVE LAW vol 20 (2014) PARA 400 et seq.
2 As to the meaning of 'local government body in Wales' see PARA 618.
3 Public Audit (Wales) Act 2004 s 44(1) (amended by the Public Audit (Wales) Act 2013 s 34, Sch 4 paras 20, 48).
4 Public Audit (Wales) Act 2004 s 44(2).

640. Benefit administration studies for Secretary of State.

The Auditor General for Wales[1] may, at the request of the Secretary of State[2], conduct, or assist the Secretary of State in conducting, benefit administration studies[3]. Benefit administration studies are studies designed to enable recommendations to be made for improving economy, efficiency, and effectiveness and quality of performance in the discharge by one or more local authorities in Wales[4] of functions relating to the administration of housing benefit or council tax benefit (or both)[5].

Any information obtained in the course of a benefit administration study may be disclosed by the Auditor General for Wales to the Secretary of State for the purposes of any functions of the Secretary of State which are connected with housing benefit or council tax benefit[6].

The Auditor General for Wales must send to the Secretary of State a copy of a report of a benefit administration study carried out by the Auditor General for Wales[7], and the Secretary of State or the Auditor General for Wales may send a copy of the report to any local authority to which the study relates[8]. The Secretary of State may publish a report of a benefit administration study in conjunction with the Auditor General for Wales[9].

The Auditor General for Wales may conduct, or assist the Secretary of State in conducting, a benefit administration study only if the Secretary of State has made arrangements for the payment to the Wales Audit Office[10] of a fee in respect of the study[11].

1 As to the Auditor General for Wales see PARA 615; and CONSTITUTIONAL AND ADMINISTRATIVE LAW vol 20 (2014) PARA 400 et seq.
2 As to the Secretary of State see PARA 4 note 18.
3 Public Audit (Wales) Act 2004 s 45(1).
4 As to the meaning of 'local authority in Wales' see PARA 618 note 3.
5 Public Audit (Wales) Act 2004 s 45(2). As to housing benefit see WELFARE BENEFITS AND STATE PENSIONS vol 104 (2014) PARA 318 et seq. As to council tax benefit see WELFARE BENEFITS AND STATE PENSIONS vol 104 (2014) PARA 249.
6 Public Audit (Wales) Act 2004 s 45(3)
7 Public Audit (Wales) Act 2004 s 45(4).
8 Public Audit (Wales) Act 2004 s 45(5).
9 Public Audit (Wales) Act 2004 s 45(6).
10 As to the Wales Audit Office see CONSTITUTIONAL AND ADMINISTRATIVE LAW vol 20 (2014) PARAS 403–405
11 Public Audit (Wales) Act 2004 s 45(7) (amended by the Public Audit (Wales) Act 2013 s 34, Sch 4 paras 20, 49(1), (2)). The amount of the fee must be a reasonable amount agreed between the Secretary of State and the Wales Audit Office (but may not exceed the full cost incurred by the Auditor General for Wales in conducting, or assisting the Secretary of State to conduct, the study): Public Audit (Wales) Act 2004 s 45(8) (amended by the Public Audit (Wales) Act 2013 Sch 4 paras 20, 49(1), (3)). A fee payable under the Public Audit (Wales) Act 2004 s 45 must be charged in accordance with a scheme for charging fees prepared under the Public Audit (Wales) Act 2013 s

24 (see CONSTITUTIONAL AND ADMINISTRATIVE LAW vol 20 (2014) PARA 405): Public Audit (Wales) Act 2004 s 45(9) (added by the Public Audit (Wales) Act 2013 Sch 4 paras 20, 49(1), (4)).

641. Social security references and reports to Secretary of State.

The Auditor General for Wales[1] may refer to the Secretary of State[2] any matter arising from an audit or study under the Public Audit (Wales) Act 2004[3], if it appears that the matter may be relevant for the purposes of any of the functions of the Secretary of State relating to social security[4]. The Auditor General for Wales may send to the Secretary of State a copy of any public interest report made by him[5], and which contains observations on the administration by a local authority in Wales[6] of housing benefit or council tax benefit[7].

1 As to the Auditor General for Wales see PARA 615; and CONSTITUTIONAL AND ADMINISTRATIVE LAW vol 20 (2014) PARA 400 et seq.
2 As to the Secretary of State see PARA 4 note 18.
3 Ie under the Public Audit (Wales) Act 2004 Pt 2 (ss 12–59).
4 See the Public Audit (Wales) Act 2004 s 51(1). See generally WELFARE BENEFITS AND STATE PENSIONS vol 104 (2014) PARA 550.
5 Ie under the Public Audit (Wales) Act 2004 s 22: see PARA 621.
6 As to the meaning of 'local authority in Wales' see PARA 618 note 3.
7 Public Audit (Wales) Act 2004 s 51(3) (amended by the Public Audit (Wales) Act 2013 s 34, Sch 4 paras 20, 52(1), (3)). As to housing benefit see WELFARE BENEFITS AND STATE PENSIONS vol 104 (2014) PARA 318 et seq. As to council tax benefit see WELFARE BENEFITS AND STATE PENSIONS vol 104 (2014) PARA 249.

642. Studies at request of educational bodies.

The Auditor General for Wales[1] may undertake studies designed to enable him to make recommendations for improving economy, efficiency and effectiveness in the discharge of the functions of the following educational bodies[2]:

(1) the governing body of an institution in Wales within the higher education sector if requested to do so by the governing body or the Higher Education Funding Council for Wales[3];

(2) the governing body of an institution in Wales receiving financial support from the Higher Education Funding Council for Wales[4] if requested to do so by the governing body or the Higher Education Funding Council for Wales[5];

(3) the governing body of an institution in Wales within the further education sector if requested to do so by the governing body or the National Assembly for Wales[6].

The Auditor General for Wales may also, on request, give appropriate advice to certain educational bodies in Wales[7].

1 As to the Auditor General for Wales see PARA 615; and CONSTITUTIONAL AND ADMINISTRATIVE LAW vol 20 (2014) PARA 400 et seq.
2 See the Government of Wales Act 1998 s 145B(1) (s 145B added by the Public Audit (Wales) Act 2004 s 4). The Government of Wales Act 1998 s 145B(1) does not entitle the Auditor General for Wales to question the merits of the policy objectives of a body: s 145B(2) (as so added; amended by the Education Act 2011 s 16(1), Sch 5 para 15(1), (4)). Where the Auditor General for Wales undertakes such a study he may, with the consent of the body that requested the study, arrange for a report containing the results of the study, and his recommendations (if any), to be laid before the National Assembly for Wales: Government of Wales Act 1998 s 145B(3) (as so added; amended by the Education Act 2005 s 98, Sch 14 para 21(1), (5); and the Education Act 2011 Sch 5 para 15(1), (5)).
3 Government of Wales Act 1998 s 145B(1), Table (as added: see note 2). As to the Higher Education Funding Council for Wales see EDUCATION vol 35 (2015) PARA 691 et seq.
4 Ie under the Education Act 2005 s 86: see EDUCATION vol 36 (2015) PARA 1062.

5 Government of Wales Act 1998 s 145B(1), Table (as added (see note 2); amended by the Education Act 2005 Sch 14 para 21(1), (2)).

6 Government of Wales Act 1998 s 145B(1), Table (as added (see note 2); amended by SI 2005/3238).

7 See the Government of Wales Act 1998 s 145B(4)–(7) (as added (see note 2); s 145B(5) substituted by SI 2014/77).

643. Studies relating to registered social landlords.

The Welsh Ministers[1] and the Auditor General for Wales[2] may agree on one or more programmes of studies designed to enable the Auditor General for Wales to make recommendations for improving economy, efficiency and effectiveness in the discharge of the functions of registered social landlords[3]. If a programme is agreed, the Auditor General for Wales must ensure that studies giving effect to the programme are undertaken by him[4]. It must be a term of every such programme that the Welsh Ministers pay to the Wales Audit Office[5] a sum in respect of the costs incurred (which may not exceed the full cost incurred in undertaking the programme), in accordance with a scheme[6] for charging fees[7].

This power does not entitle the Auditor General for Wales to question the merits of the policy objectives of a registered social landlord[8].

A person commits an offence if without reasonable excuse he fails to comply with a requirement to give assistance, information or explanation to the Auditor General for Wales[9] in relation to such a study[10].

The Auditor General for Wales may disclose to the Welsh Ministers information obtained by him or a person acting on his behalf in the course of a study under these provisions[11].

The Auditor General for Wales may also, if he thinks it appropriate to do so, provide advice or assistance to a registered social landlord for the purpose of the exercise by the registered social landlord of its functions[12].

1 As to the Welsh Ministers see PARA 4 note 18.

2 As to the Auditor General for Wales see PARA 615; and CONSTITUTIONAL AND ADMINISTRATIVE LAW vol 20 (2014) PARA 400 et seq.

3 Government of Wales Act 1998 s 145C(1) (s 145C added by the Public Audit (Wales) Act 2004 s 5; the Government of Wales Act 1998 s 145C(1) amended by the Government of Wales Act 2006 s 160(1), Sch 10 paras 41, 48(1), (2); and by SI 2010/866). 'Registered social landlord' means a body which is registered as a social landlord under the Housing Act 1996 Pt I Ch I (ss 1–7) (see HOUSING vol 56 (2017) PARA 167 et seq): Government of Wales Act 1998 s 145C(9) (as so added; substituted by SI 2010/866).

4 Government of Wales Act 1998 s 145C(2) (as added (see note 3); amended by the Public Audit (Wales) Act 2013 s 34, Sch 4 paras 5, 6(1), (2)). Where a study is undertaken under the Government of Wales Act 1998 s 145C by the Auditor General for Wales or on his behalf, he may arrange for a report containing the results of the study, and his recommendations (if any), to be laid before the National Assembly for Wales: s 145C(5). In s 145C, a reference to a person acting on behalf of the Auditor General for Wales is a reference to a person acting on the Auditor's behalf by virtue of a delegation made under the Public Audit (Wales) Act 2013 s 18 (see CONSTITUTIONAL AND ADMINISTRATIVE LAW vol 20 (2014) PARA 402): Government of Wales Act 1998 s 145C(10) (added by the Public Audit (Wales) Act 2013 s 34, Sch 4 paras 5, 6(1), (4)).

5 As to the Wales Audit Office see CONSTITUTIONAL AND ADMINISTRATIVE LAW vol 20 (2014) PARAS 403–405

6 Ie a scheme prepared under the Public Audit (Wales) Act 2013 s 24: see CONSTITUTIONAL AND ADMINISTRATIVE LAW vol 20 (2014) PARA 405.

7 Government of Wales Act 1998 s 145C(3) (as added (see note 3); amended by the Government of Wales Act 2006 Sch 10 paras 41, 48(1), (3); and the Public Audit (Wales) Act 2013 Sch 4 paras 5, 6(1), (3)).

8 Government of Wales Act 1998 s 145C(4) (as added (see note 3); amended by SI 2010/866).

9 Ie the requirement imposed under the Government of Wales Act 2006 Sch 8 para 17(3)(a), (b): see CONSTITUTIONAL AND ADMINISTRATIVE LAW vol 20 (2014) PARA 402.

10 Government of Wales Act 1998 s 145C(6) (as added (see note 3); amended by the Government of Wales Act 2006 Sch 10 paras 41, 48(1), (4)). A person guilty of an offence under the Government of Wales Act 1998 s 145C(6) is liable on summary conviction to a fine not exceeding level 3 on the standard scale: s 145C(7) (as added: see note 3). As to the powers of magistrates' courts to issue fines on summary conviction see SENTENCING vol 92 (2015) PARA 176.

11 Government of Wales Act 1998 s 145C(8) (as added (see note 3); amended by the Government of Wales Act 2006 Sch 10 paras 41, 48(1), (5)).

12 Government of Wales Act 1998 s 145D(1) (s 145D added by the Local Government and Public Involvement in Health Act 2007 s 166; the Government of Wales Act 1998 s 145D(1) amended by SI 2010/866). See further s 145D(2)–(4) (as so added; amended by the Public Audit (Wales) Act 2013 Sch 4 paras 5, 7).

(B) Performance Standards

644. Publication of information as to standards of performance.

The Auditor General for Wales[1] must give any directions[2] which he thinks fit for requiring relevant bodies[3] to publish information[4] relating to their activities in a financial year[5] which will, in the opinion of the Auditor General for Wales, facilitate the making of appropriate comparisons[6]:

(1) between the standards of performance achieved by different relevant bodies in the financial year[7]; or

(2) between the standards of performance achieved by relevant bodies in different financial years[8].

The comparisons are to be made by reference to the criteria of cost, economy, efficiency and effectiveness[9].

If a relevant body is required by a direction under this provision to publish information in relation to a financial year, it must[10]:

(a) make arrangements for collecting and recording the information which secure that the information is available for publication and, so far as practicable, that everything published in pursuance of the direction is accurate and complete[11];

(b) publish the information in accordance with the direction and in a permitted method[12] before the end of the period of nine months starting immediately after the end of the financial year[13]; and

(c) keep a document containing any information published in pursuance of the direction available for inspection by local government electors[14] for its area[15].

1 As to the Auditor General for Wales see PARA 615; and CONSTITUTIONAL AND ADMINISTRATIVE LAW vol 20 (2014) PARA 400 et seq.

2 See further PARA 645.

3 Each of these local government bodies in Wales is a relevant body for the purposes of the Public Audit (Wales) Act 2004 ss 47–49:

(1) a local authority in Wales (s 46(1)(a));

(2) a committee of a local authority in Wales (including a joint committee of two or more local authorities in Wales) (s 46(1)(b));

(3) a national park authority for a national park in Wales (s 46(1)(c));

(4) a police and crime commissioner for a police area in Wales (s 46(1)(d) (amended by the Police Reform and Social Responsibility Act 2011 s 99, Sch 16 paras 336, 339));

(5) a fire and rescue authority in Wales constituted by a scheme under the Fire and Rescue Services Act 2004 s 2 or a scheme to which s 4 of that Act applies (see FIRE AND RESCUE SERVICES vol 51 (2013) PARAS 18–20) (Public Audit (Wales) Act 2004 s 46(1)(e)).

As to the meaning of 'local government body in Wales' see PARA 618. As to the meaning of 'local authority in Wales' see PARA 618 note 3, but note that for the purposes of s 46 'local authority in Wales' does not include a community council: see s 46(3). The Welsh Ministers may by order provide for ss 47–49 to have effect as if any other local government body in Wales were a relevant body for the purposes of those sections: s 46(2) (amended by the Public Audit (Wales) Act 2013 s 34, Sch 4 paras 20, 50). At the date at which this volume states the law no such orders had been made under the Public Audit (Wales) Act 2004 s 46. As to the Welsh Ministers see PARA 4 note 18.

As to national park authorities see OPEN SPACES AND COUNTRYSIDE vol 78 (2010) PARA 526 et seq. As to police and crime commissioners see POLICE AND INVESTIGATORY POWERS vol 84 (2013) PARA 56 et seq.

4 See the Public Audit (Wales) Act 2004 s 47(1).
5 As to the meaning of 'financial year' see PARA 620 note 7.
6 Public Audit (Wales) Act 2004 s 47(2).
7 Public Audit (Wales) Act 2004 s 47(2)(a).
8 Public Audit (Wales) Act 2004 s 47(2)(b).
9 Public Audit (Wales) Act 2004 s 47(3).
10 Public Audit (Wales) Act 2004 s 47(4).
11 Public Audit (Wales) Act 2004 s 47(4)(a).
12 Ie permitted by the Public Audit (Wales) Act 2004 s 48. The permitted methods of publication referred to in s 47(4)(b) are the following: s 48(1). The relevant body may publish the information in a newspaper which is printed for sale, and circulating in its area: s 48(2). If the relevant body ensures that the distribution condition is met with respect to the information, it may publish the information in a newspaper or periodical publication which is produced and distributed by another person, other than a local authority company (ie a company under the control of a local authority), and is free of charge to the recipient: s 48(3), (5). A relevant body ensures that the distribution condition is met with respect to information if:

(1) in any case, the body takes all reasonable steps to secure that a copy of a publication containing the information is distributed to each dwelling house in its area (s 48(4)(a)); and

(2) in a case where the body considers that the information is of concern to persons carrying on business in its area, the body takes such steps as it considers reasonable and practicable to secure that a copy of a publication containing the information is also distributed to business premises in its area (s 48(4)(b)).

The Local Government and Housing Act 1989 s 68(1) (see PARA 607) (company under control of local authority) has effect for the purposes of the Public Audit (Wales) Act 2004 s 48(5) as it has effect for the purposes of the Local Government and Housing Act 1989 Pt V (ss 67–73): Public Audit (Wales) Act 2004 s 48(6). The Welsh Ministers may by order define 'an entity under the control of a local authority' for the purposes of s 48(3): Local Government and Public Involvement in Health Act 2007 s 218(1)(e). At the date at which this volume states the law no such order had been made.

As from a day to be appointed the Public Audit (Wales) Act 2004 s 48 is amended by the Local Government and Public Involvement in Health Act 2007 s 216(2), Sch 14 para 6(1), (2) to replace the reference in the Public Audit (Wales) Act 2004 s 48(3) to a local authority company with a reference to an entity under the control of a local authority, to repeal s 48(5), (6) and to make provision with regard to entities under the control of a local authority in the new s 48(5)–(9). At the date at which this volume states the law no such day had been appointed.

13 Public Audit (Wales) Act 2004 s 47(4)(b). The Welsh Ministers may by order vary this period: s 47(5) (amended by the Public Audit (Wales) Act 2013 Sch 4 paras 20, 51). The period specified in an order under the Public Audit (Wales) Act 2004 s 47(5) must not be longer than nine months starting immediately after the end of the financial year in question: s 47(6). At the date at which this volume states the law no such orders had been made under s 47.
14 As to the meaning of 'local government elector' see PARA 627 note 1.
15 Public Audit (Wales) Act 2004 s 47(4)(c). A local government elector for the area of a relevant body may at all reasonable times and without payment, inspect and make copies of the whole or any part of a document kept available for inspection by the body under s 47(4)(c), and may require copies of the whole or part of any such document to be delivered to him on payment of a reasonable sum for each copy: s 47(7). A person who has custody of a document kept available for inspection under s 47(4)(c) commits an offence if he obstructs a person in the exercise of his rights in this regard, or he refuses to comply with a requirement to provide a copy of the document: s 47(8). A person guilty of such an offence is liable on summary conviction to a fine not exceeding level 3 on the standard scale: s 47(9). As to the powers of magistrates' courts to issue fines on summary conviction see SENTENCING vol 92 (2015) PARA 176.

645. Directions requiring publication of information about standards of performance.

A direction given by the Auditor General for Wales[1] requiring the publication of information must[2]:

(1) identify the financial year[3] or years in relation to which the information is to be published[4];

(2) specify or describe the activities to which the information is to relate[5]; and

(3) make provision as to the matters to be contained in the information and as to the form in which it is to be published[6].

A direction may be given so as to apply either to all relevant bodies[7] or to all relevant bodies of a description specified in the direction, and may be varied or revoked by a subsequent direction[8].

Before giving a direction which imposes a new requirement on a relevant body as to the publication of any information[9], the Auditor General for Wales must consult any associations of relevant bodies he thinks fit, and any other persons he thinks fit[10]. A direction imposing a new requirement on a relevant body as to the publication of any information must not be given later than the 31 December in the financial year which precedes the relevant financial year[11].

If the Auditor General for Wales gives a direction[12], he must:

(a) publish the direction in the manner he considers appropriate for bringing it to the attention of members of the public[13]; and

(b) send a copy of the direction to every relevant body on which duties are imposed by virtue of the direction[14].

1 Ie under the Public Audit (Wales) Act 2004 s 47: see PARA 644. As to the Auditor General for Wales see PARA 615; and CONSTITUTIONAL AND ADMINISTRATIVE LAW vol 20 (2014) PARA 400 et seq.
2 Public Audit (Wales) Act 2004 s 49(1).
3 As to the meaning of 'financial year' see PARA 620 note 7.
4 Public Audit (Wales) Act 2004 s 49(1)(a).
5 Public Audit (Wales) Act 2004 s 49(1)(b).
6 Public Audit (Wales) Act 2004 s 49(1)(c).
7 As to the meaning of 'relevant body' see PARA 644 note 3.
8 Public Audit (Wales) Act 2004 s 49(2).
9 References in the Public Audit (Wales) Act 2004 s 49 to the imposition of a new requirement on a relevant body as to the publication of information are to:
   (1) the imposition of a requirement by the first direction under s 47 (see PARA 644) to apply to the body (s 49(7)(a));
   (2) any subsequent extension of or addition to:
      (a) the matters to be contained in the information which the body is required to publish in relation to a financial year in pursuance of directions under s 47 (s 49(7)(b)(i)); or
      (b) the activities to which any such information is to relate (s 49(7)(b)(ii)).
10 Public Audit (Wales) Act 2004 s 49(3).
11 Public Audit (Wales) Act 2004 s 49(4). The relevant financial year is the financial year in relation to which the information is to be published: s 49(5).
12 Ie under the Public Audit (Wales) Act 2004 s 47: see PARA 644.
13 Public Audit (Wales) Act 2004 s 49(6)(a).
14 Public Audit (Wales) Act 2004 s 49(6)(b).

(C) Data Matching

646. Power to conduct data matching exercises.

The Auditor General for Wales[1] may conduct data matching exercises[2], exercisable for the purpose of assisting in the prevention and detection of fraud in or with respect to Wales[3]. That assistance may, but need not, form part of an audit[4].

A data matching exercise may not be used to identify patterns and trends in an individual's characteristics or behaviour which suggest nothing more than his potential to commit fraud in the future[5].

The Auditor General for Wales must prepare, and keep under review, a code of practice with respect to data matching exercises[6], and regard must be had to the code in conducting and participating in any such exercise[7].

He must lay a copy of the code, and of any alterations made to the code, before the National Assembly for Wales[8], and from time to time publish the code as for the time being in force[9].

1 As to the Auditor General for Wales see PARA 615; and CONSTITUTIONAL AND ADMINISTRATIVE LAW vol 20 (2014) PARA 400 et seq.

2 Public Audit (Wales) Act 2004 s 64A(1) (ss 64A, 64G, 64H added by the Serious Crime Act 2007 s 73, Sch 7 para 4; the Public Audit (Wales) Act 2004 s 64A(1) amended by the Public Audit (Wales) Act 2013 s 34, Sch 4 paras 20, 62). A data matching exercise is an exercise involving the comparison of sets of data to determine how far they match (including the identification of any patterns and trends): Public Audit (Wales) Act 2004 s 64A(2) (as so added). In the Public Audit (Wales) Act 2004 ss 64B–64H, reference to a data matching exercise is to an exercise conducted or arranged to be conducted under s 64A: s 64A(6) (as so added).

3 Public Audit (Wales) Act 2004 s 64A(3) (as added: see note 2).

The Secretary of State may by order amend the Public Audit (Wales) Act 2004 Pt 3A (ss 64A–64H) to add any of the following purposes to the purposes for which data matching exercises may be conducted, or to modify the application of those provisions in relation to a purpose so added: Public Audit (Wales) Act 2004 s 64H(1) (as so added). The purposes which may be added are:

(1) to assist in the prevention and detection of crime (other than fraud) in or with respect Wales (s 64H(2)(a) (as so added));

(2) to assist in the apprehension and prosecution of offenders in or with respect to Wales (s 64H(2)(b) (as so added));

(3) to assist in the recovery of debt owing to Welsh public bodies (s 64H(2)(c) (as so added)).

Before making such an order the Secretary of State must consult the Auditor General for Wales: s 64H(4) (as so added). An order under s 64H is to be made by statutory instrument and may include such incidental, consequential, supplemental or transitional provision as the Secretary of State thinks fit: s 64H(5) (as so added). No order under s 64H may be made unless a draft of the statutory instrument has been laid before, and approved by a resolution of, each House of Parliament: s 64H(6) (as so added). 'Welsh public body' means a public body (see PARA 618 note 2) whose functions relate exclusively to Wales or to an area of Wales: s 64H(7) (as so added). At the date at which this volume states the law no such orders had been made under s 64H. As to the Secretary of State see PARA 4 note 18.

4 Public Audit (Wales) Act 2004 s 64A(4) (as added: see note 2).

5 Public Audit (Wales) Act 2004 s 64A(5) (as added: see note 2).

6 Public Audit (Wales) Act 2004 s 64G(1) (as added: see note 2). Before preparing or altering the code, the Auditor General for Wales must consult the bodies mentioned in the Public Audit (Wales) Act 2004 s 64B(2) (see PARA 647), the Information Commissioner and such other bodies or persons as the Auditor General for Wales thinks fit: s 64G(3) (as so added). As to the Information Commissioner see CONFIDENCE AND INFORMATIONAL PRIVACY vol 19 (2011) PARA 109 et seq.

7 Public Audit (Wales) Act 2004 s 64G(2) (as added: see note 2).

8 Public Audit (Wales) Act 2004 s 64G(4)(a) (as added (see note 2); amended by the Public Audit (Wales) Act 2013 Sch 4 paras 20, 68).

9 Public Audit (Wales) Act 2004 s 64G(4)(b) (as added: see note 2).

647. Provision of data and fees.

The Auditor General for Wales[1] may require any local government body in Wales[2], any Welsh NHS body[3], and any officer or member of such a body, to provide him or a person acting on his behalf[4] with such data (and in such form) as he or that person may reasonably require for the purpose of conducting data matching exercises[5]. A person who without reasonable excuse fails to comply with such a requirement[6] is guilty of an offence and liable on summary conviction to a fine[7].

If the Auditor General for Wales thinks it appropriate to conduct a data matching exercise using data held by or on behalf of a body or person not subject to this requirement[8], the data may be disclosed to him or a person acting on his behalf[9]. Such a disclosure does not breach any obligation of confidence owed by a person making the disclosure, or any other restriction on the disclosure of information (however imposed)[10].

Data matching exercises may include data provided by a body or person outside England and Wales[11].

The Wales Audit Office may, in accordance with a scheme for charging fees[12] charge a fee in respect of a data matching exercise undertaken by the Auditor General for Wales[13]. The Wales Audit Office must prescribe a scale or scales of fees in respect of data matching exercises[14]. A body required[15] to provide data for a data matching exercise must pay to the Wales Audit Office the fee applicable to that exercise in accordance with the appropriate scale[16]. However, if it appears to the Wales Audit Office that the work involved in the exercise was substantially more or less than that envisaged by the appropriate scale, it may charge the body a fee which is larger or smaller than the fee generally applicable[17].

In addition to this power, the Wales Audit Office may charge a fee to any other body or person providing data for or receiving the results of a data matching exercise, such fee to be payable in accordance with terms agreed between the Wales Audit Office and that body or person[18].

If the Welsh Ministers[19] consider it necessary or desirable to do so, they may by regulations prescribe a scale or scales of fees to have effect, for such period as is specified in the regulations, in place of any scale or scales of fees prescribed by the Welsh Audit Office and, if they do so, references in these provisions to the appropriate scale are to be read as respects that period as references to the appropriate scale prescribed by the Welsh Ministers[20].

1 As to the Auditor General for Wales see PARA 615; and CONSTITUTIONAL AND ADMINISTRATIVE LAW vol 20 (2014) PARA 400 et seq.

2 As to the meaning of 'local government body in Wales' see PARA 618.

3 As to the meaning of 'Welsh NHS body' see PARA 616 note 2.

4 Ie by virtue of a delegation made under the Public Audit (Wales) Act 2013 s 18: see CONSTITUTIONAL AND ADMINISTRATIVE LAW vol 20 (2014) PARA 402.

5 See the Public Audit (Wales) Act 2004 s 64B(1), (2) (ss 64B, 64C, 64F, 64H added by the Serious Crime Act 2007 s 73, Sch 7 para 4; the Public Audit (Wales) Act 2004 s 64B(1) amended by the Public Audit (Wales) Act 2013 s 34, Sch 4 paras 20, 63(1), (2)). As to data matching exercises see PARA 646 note 2.

The Secretary of State may by order amend the Public Audit (Wales) Act 2004 Pt 3A (ss 64A–64H) (see PARA 646 et seq):

(1) to add a Welsh public body to the list of bodies in s 64B(2) (s 64H(3)(a) (as so added));
(2) to modify the application of Pt 3A in relation to a body so added (s 64H(3)(b) (as so added));
(3) to remove a body from that list (s 64H(3)(c) (as so added)).

Before making such an order the Secretary of State must consult the Auditor General for Wales: s 64H(4) (as so added). An order under s 64H is to be made by statutory instrument and may include such incidental, consequential, supplemental or transitional provision as the Secretary of State thinks fit: s 64H(5) (as so added). No order under s 64H may be made unless a draft of the statutory instrument has been laid before, and approved by a resolution of, each House of Parliament: s 64H(6) (as so added). As to the meaning of 'Welsh public body' see PARA 646 note 3. At the date at which this volume states the law no such orders had been made under s 64H. As to the Secretary of State see PARA 4 note 18.

6 Ie under the Public Audit (Wales) Act 2004 s 64B(1)(b): see the text to notes 1–5.

7 See the Public Audit (Wales) Act 2004 s 64B(3) (as added: see note 5). A person is liable on summary conviction to a fine not exceeding level 3 on the standard scale, and to an additional fine not exceeding £20 for each day on which the offence continues after conviction for that offence: s 64B(3)(a), (b) (as so added). If an officer or member of a body is convicted of an offence under s 64B(3), any expenses incurred by the Auditor General or by the Wales Audit Office in connection with proceedings for the offence, so far as not recovered from any other source, are recoverable from that body by the Wales Audit Office: s 64B(4) (as so added; amended by the Public Audit (Wales) Act 2013 Sch 4 paras 20, 63(1), (3)). As to the Wales Audit Office see CONSTITUTIONAL AND ADMINISTRATIVE LAW vol 20 (2014) PARAS 403–405 As to the powers of magistrates' courts to issue fines on summary conviction see SENTENCING vol 92 (2015) PARA 176.

8 Ie not subject to the Public Audit (Wales) Act 2004 s 64B: see the text and notes 1–7.

9 Public Audit (Wales) Act 2004 s 64C(1) (as added (see note 5); amended by the Public Audit (Wales) Act 2013 Sch 4 paras 20, 64). The text refers to a person acting by virtue of a delegation made under the Public Audit (Wales) Act 2013 s 18.

10 Public Audit (Wales) Act 2004 s 64C(2) (as added: see note 5). However, nothing in s 64C authorises a disclosure which contravenes the Data Protection Act 1998 (see CONFIDENCE AND INFORMATIONAL PRIVACY), or is prohibited by the Regulation of Investigatory Powers Act 2000 Pt I (ss 1–25) (see POLICE AND INVESTIGATORY POWERS vol 84A (2013) PARA 655 et seq): Public Audit (Wales) Act 2004 s 64C(3) (as so added). Prospectively, for the reference to the Regulation of Investigatory Powers Act 2000 Pt I there is substituted a reference to the Investigatory Powers Act 2016 Pts 1–7 (ss 1–226), Pt 9 Ch 1 (ss 248–259): see the Public Audit (Wales) Act 2004 s 64C(3) (as so added; amended, as from a day to be appointed, by the Investigatory Powers Act 2016 s 271(1), Sch 10 para 16; at the date at which this volume states the law, no such day had been appointed).

Nor may data be so disclosed if the data comprise or include patient data: Public Audit (Wales) Act 2004 s 64C(4) (as so added). 'Patient data' means data relating to an individual which are held for medical purposes (within the meaning of the National Health Service Act 2006 s 251 (see HEALTH SERVICES vol 54 (2017) PARA 78)) and from which the individual can be identified: Public Audit (Wales) Act 2004 s 64C(5) (as so added). Section 64C does not limit the circumstances in which data may be disclosed apart from this section: s 64C(6) (as so added).

11 Public Audit (Wales) Act 2004 s 64C(7) (as added: see note 5).

12 Ie a scheme prepared under the Public Audit (Wales) Act 2013 s 24: see CONSTITUTIONAL AND ADMINISTRATIVE LAW vol 20 (2014) PARA 405.

13 Public Audit (Wales) Act 2004 s 64F(A1) (s 64F as added (see note 5); s 64F(A1) added by the Public Audit (Wales) Act 2013 Sch 4 paras 20, 67(1), (2)). A fee charged under the Public Audit (Wales) Act 2004 s 64F may not exceed the full cost of exercising the function to which it relates: s 64F(10) (s 64F as so added; s 64F(10) added by the Public Audit (Wales) Act 2013 Sch 4 paras 20, 67(1), (7)).

14 Public Audit (Wales) Act 2004 s 64F(1) (as added (see note 5); amended by the Public Audit (Wales) Act 2013 Sch 4 paras 20, 67(1), (3)).

15 Ie required under the Public Audit (Wales) Act 2004 s 64B(1): see the text and notes 1–5.

16 Public Audit (Wales) Act 2004 s 64F(2) (as added (see note 5); amended by the Public Audit (Wales) Act 2013 Sch 4 paras 20, 67(1), (4)). Before prescribing a scale of fees under the Public Audit (Wales) Act 2004 s 64F, the Wales Audit Office must consult the bodies mentioned in s 64B(2) (see the text and notes 1–5) and such other bodies or persons as the Wales Audit Office thinks fit: s 64F(4) (as so added; amended by the Public Audit (Wales) Act 2013 Sch 4 paras 20, 67(1), (5)).

17 Public Audit (Wales) Act 2004 s 64F(3) (as added (see note 5); amended by the Public Audit (Wales) Act 2013 Sch 4 paras 20, 67(1), (5)).

18 Public Audit (Wales) Act 2004 s 64F(8) (as added (see note 5); amended by the Public Audit (Wales) Act 2013 Sch 4 paras 20, 67(1), (5)). Any terms as to payment agreed by the Wales Audit Office under the Public Audit (Wales) Act 2004 s 64F(8) must be in accordance with a scheme for charging fees prepared under the Public Audit (Wales) Act 2013 s 24: Public Audit (Wales) Act 2004 s 64F(9) (s 64F as so added; s 64F(9) added by the Public Audit (Wales) Act 2013 Sch 4 paras 20, 67(1), (7)).

19 As to the Welsh Ministers see PARA 4 note 18.

20 Public Audit (Wales) Act 2004 s 64F(5) (as added (see note 5); amended by the Public Audit (Wales) Act 2013 Sch 4 paras 20, 67(1), (5)). Before making any regulations under the Public Audit (Wales) Act 2004 s 64F(5), the Welsh Ministers must consult the Wales Audit Office and such other bodies or persons as they think fit: s 64F(6) (as so added; amended by the Public Audit

(Wales) Act 2013 Sch 4 paras 20, 67(1), (3)). The power under the Public Audit (Wales) Act 2004 s 64F(5) is exercisable by statutory instrument subject to annulment in pursuance of a resolution of the National Assembly for Wales: s 64F(7) (as so added; amended by the Public Audit (Wales) Act 2013 Sch 4 paras 20, 67(1), (6)).

648. Disclosure of results and publication.

Information relating to a particular body or person obtained by or on behalf of the Auditor General for Wales[1] for the purpose of conducting a data matching exercise[2], or the results of any such exercise, may be disclosed by or on behalf of the Auditor General for Wales if the disclosure is[3]:

(1) for or in connection with a purpose for which the data matching exercise is conducted[4];

(2) to a relevant body or person[5] (or a related party[6]) for or in connection with a function of that body or person corresponding or similar to the functions of the Auditor General for Wales with regard to audits and accounts of public bodies[7], or the functions of the Auditor General for Wales in relation to Welsh NHS bodies[8] or data matching[9]; or

(3) in pursuance of a duty imposed by or under a statutory provision[10].

Information so disclosed[11] may not be further disclosed except[12]:

(a) for or in connection with the purpose for which it was disclosed under head (1) or the function for which it was disclosed under head (2)[13];

(b) for the investigation or prosecution of an offence[14]; or

(c) in pursuance of a duty imposed by or under a statutory provision[15].

Except as authorised above[16], a person who discloses relevant information is guilty of an offence and liable on conviction to imprisonment, a fine or both[17].

Nothing in the above provisions prevents the Auditor General for Wales from publishing a report on a data matching exercise (including on the results of the exercise)[18]. However, the report may not include information relating to a particular body or person if[19]:

(i) the body or person is the subject of any data included in the data matching exercise[20];

(ii) the body or person can be identified from the information[21]; and

(iii) the information is not otherwise in the public domain[22].

A report so published may be published in such manner as the Auditor General for Wales considers appropriate for bringing it to the attention of those members of the public who may be interested[23].

Provision with regard to publication[24] does not affect any powers of the Auditor General for Wales where the data matching exercise in question forms part of an audit[25].

1 As to the Auditor General for Wales see PARA 615; and CONSTITUTIONAL AND ADMINISTRATIVE LAW vol 20 (2014) PARA 400 et seq.

2 As to data matching exercises see PARA 646 note 2.

3 Public Audit (Wales) Act 2004 s 64D(1), (2) (ss 64D, 64E added by the Serious Crime Act 2007 s 73, Sch 7 para 4). The Public Audit (Wales) Act 2004 s 54 (see PARA 616) does not apply to information to which s 64D applies: s 64D(9) (as so added).

4 Public Audit (Wales) Act 2004 s 64D(2)(a) (as added: see note 3). If the data used for a data matching exercise include patient data s 64D(2)(a) applies only so far as the purpose for which the disclosure is made relates to a relevant NHS body: s 64D(5)(a). As to the meaning of 'patient data' see PARA 647 note 10; definition applied by the Public Audit (Wales) Act 2004 s 64D(6)(a) (as so added). 'Relevant NHS body' means:

(1) a Welsh NHS body (see PARA 616 note 2) (s 64D(6)(b)(i) (as so added));

(2) a body mentioned in the Local Audit and Accountability Act 2014 Sch 9 para 4(12)(a), (b) or (c) ('relevant NHS body') (Public Audit (Wales) Act 2004 s 64D(6)(b)(ii) (as so added; substituted by the Local Audit and Accountability Act 2014 s 45, Sch 12 paras 59, 63(1), (6));
(3) an NHS body as defined in the Community Care and Health (Scotland) Act 2002 s 22(1) (Public Audit (Wales) Act 2004 s 64D(6)(b)(iii) (as so added));
(4) a health and social care body mentioned in the Health and Social Care (Reform) Act (Northern Ireland) 2009 s 1(5)(a)–(e) (Public Audit (Wales) Act 2004 s 64D(6)(b)(iv) (as so added; substituted by the Public Audit (Wales) Act 2013 s 34, Sch 4 paras 20, 65(1), (3))).

5 The bodies or persons are (Public Audit (Wales) Act 2004 s 64D(3) (as so added; amended by the Local Audit and Accountability Act 2014 Sch 12 paras 59, 63(1), (3))):
(1) the Secretary of State (Public Audit (Wales) Act 2004 s 64D(3)(a) (as so added; substituted by the Local Audit and Accountability Act 2014 Sch 12 paras 59, 63(1), (4)));
(2) the Minister for the Cabinet Office (Public Audit (Wales) Act 2004 s 64D(3)(aa) (added by the Local Audit and Accountability Act 2014 Sch 12 paras 59, 63(1), (4)));
(3) a local auditor within the meaning of the Local Audit and Accountability Act 2014 (Public Audit (Wales) Act 2004 s 64D(3)(ab) (added by the Local Audit and Accountability Act 2014 Sch 12 paras 59, 63(1), (4)));
(4) the Auditor General for Scotland (Public Audit (Wales) Act 2004 s 64D(3)(b) (as so added));
(5) the Accounts Commission for Scotland (s 64D(3)(c) (as so added));
(6) Audit Scotland (s 64D(3)(d) (as so added));
(7) the Comptroller and Auditor General for Northern Ireland (s 64D(3)(e) (as so added)); and
(8) a person designated as a local government auditor under the Local Government (Northern Ireland) Order 2005, SI 2005/1968, art 4 (Public Audit (Wales) Act 2004 s 64D(3)(f) (as so added)).

6 'Related party', in relation to a body or person mentioned in the Public Audit (Wales) Act 2004 s 64D(3), means (s 64D(4) (as added (see note 3); amended by the Local Audit and Accountability Act 2014 Sch 12 paras 59, 63(1), (5))):
(1) a body or person acting on its behalf (Public Audit (Wales) Act 2004 s 64D(4)(a) (as so added));
(2) a body whose accounts are required to be audited by it or by a person appointed by it (s 64D(4)(b) (as so added));
(3) a person appointed by it to audit those accounts (s 64D(4)(c) (as so added)).

7 Ie under the Public Audit (Wales) Act 2004 Pt 2 Ch 1 (ss 12–40): see PARA 619 et seq.

8 Ie under the Public Audit (Wales) Act 2004 Pt 3 (ss 60–64): see PARA 616.

9 Public Audit (Wales) Act 2004 s 64D(2)(b) (as added (see note 3); amended by the Public Audit (Wales) Act 2013 Sch 4 paras 20, 65(1), (2); and the Local Audit and Accountability Act 2014 Sch 12 paras 59, 63(1), (2)). The functions of the Auditor General for Wales referred to in the text are those under the Public Audit (Wales) Act 2004 Pt 3A (ss 64A–64G): see PARA 646 et seq.

If the data used for a data matching exercise include patient data s 64D(2)(b) applies only so far as the function for or in connection with which the disclosure is made relates to such a body: s 64D(5)(a) (as so added). As to the meaning of 'patient data' see PARA 647 note 10; definition applied by the Public Audit (Wales) Act 2004 s 64D(6)(a) (as so added).

10 Public Audit (Wales) Act 2004 s 64D(2)(c) (as added: see note 3). 'Statutory provision' means a provision contained in or having effect under an enactment: s 59(8); definition applied by s 64D(10) (as so added).

11 Ie disclosed under the Public Audit (Wales) Act 2004 s 64D(2): see the text and notes 1–10.

12 Public Audit (Wales) Act 2004 s 64D(7) (as added: see note 3).

13 Public Audit (Wales) Act 2004 s 64D(7)(a) (as added: see note 3).

14 Public Audit (Wales) Act 2004 s 64D(7)(b) (as added: see note 3). Section 64D(7)(b) applies in so far as the disclosure does not fall within s 64D(7)(a).

15 Public Audit (Wales) Act 2004 s 64D(7)(c) (as added: see note 3).

16 Ie under the Public Audit (Wales) Act 2004 s 64D(2), (7): see the text and notes 1–15.

17 Public Audit (Wales) Act 2004 s 64D(8) (as added: see note 3). A person guilty of such an offence is liable on conviction on indictment, to imprisonment for a term not exceeding two years, to a fine or to both (s 64D(8)(a) (as so added)), or on summary conviction, to imprisonment for a term not exceeding 12 months, to a fine not exceeding the statutory maximum or to both (s 64D(8)(b) (as so added)). As to the powers of magistrates' courts to issue fines on summary conviction see

SENTENCING vol 92 (2015) PARA 176.
18 Public Audit (Wales) Act 2004 s 64E(1) (as added: see note 3).
19 Public Audit (Wales) Act 2004 s 64E(2) (as added: see note 3).
20 Public Audit (Wales) Act 2004 s 64E(2)(a) (as added: see note 3).
21 Public Audit (Wales) Act 2004 s 64E(2)(b) (as added: see note 3).
22 Public Audit (Wales) Act 2004 s 64E(2)(c) (as added: see note 3).
23 Public Audit (Wales) Act 2004 s 64E(3) (as added: see note 3).
24 Ie under the Public Audit (Wales) Act 2004 s 64E.
25 Public Audit (Wales) Act 2004 s 64E(4) (as added (see note 3); amended by the Public Audit (Wales) Act 2013 Sch 4 paras 20, 66). The audit referred to in the text is an audit performed under the Public Audit (Wales) Act 2004 Pt 2 (ss 12–59), or Pt 3 (ss 60–64): see PARA 615; and CONSTITUTIONAL AND ADMINISTRATIVE LAW vol 20 (2014) PARA 400 et seq et seq.

D. PROVISION AND PUBLICATION OF INFORMATION

649. Rights of access to documents and information.

The Auditor General for Wales[1] has a right of access at all reasonable times to every document relating to a local government body in Wales[2] which appears to him necessary for the purposes of his functions under the Public Audit (Wales) Act 2004[3]. The documents relating to a body to which this right applies may include in particular[4]:

(1) a document which is held or controlled by a person who has received financial assistance from the body by means of a grant, loan or guarantee or as a result of the taking of an interest in any property or body corporate[5];

(2) a document which is held or controlled by a person who has supplied goods or services to the body in pursuance of a contract to which the body was party or who has supplied goods or services in pursuance of a relevant sub-contract[6];

(3) a document of a description specified in an order made by the Welsh Ministers[7].

The Auditor General for Wales may require a person who he thinks has certain information[8] to give him any assistance, information and explanation which the Auditor General for Wales thinks necessary for the purposes of his functions under the Public Audit (Wales) Act 2004[9], and to attend before him in person to give the assistance, information or explanation, or to produce any document which is held or controlled by the person and to which the right of access applies[10]. A person commits an offence if without reasonable excuse he fails to comply with these requirements[11].

Every local government body in Wales must provide the Auditor General for Wales with every facility and all information which he may reasonably need for the purposes of his functions[12].

1 As to the Auditor General for Wales see PARA 615; and CONSTITUTIONAL AND ADMINISTRATIVE LAW vol 20 (2014) PARA 400 et seq.
2 As to the meaning of 'local government body in Wales' see PARA 618.
3 Public Audit (Wales) Act 2004 s 52(1). The functions referred to in the text are those under Pt 2 (ss 12–59).
4 Public Audit (Wales) Act 2004 s 52(2).
5 Public Audit (Wales) Act 2004 s 52(2)(a).
6 Public Audit (Wales) Act 2004 s 52(2)(b). For the purposes of s 52(2)(b) a contract is a relevant sub-contract if its performance fulfils, or contributes to the fulfilment of, an obligation to supply goods or services to the body in another contract: Public Audit (Wales) Act 2004 s 52(3).
7 Public Audit (Wales) Act 2004 s 52(2)(c) (amended by the Public Audit (Wales) Act 2013 s 34, Sch 4 paras 20, 53(1), (2)). Before making an order under the Public Audit (Wales) Act 2004 s 52(2)(c) the Welsh Ministers must consult the Auditor General for Wales, and any associations of

local authorities in Wales which appear to them to be concerned: s 52(8) (amended by the Public Audit (Wales) Act 2013 Sch 4 paras 20, 53(1), (4)). A statutory instrument containing an order under the Public Audit (Wales) Act 2004 s 52(2)(c) is (unless a draft of the order has been laid before, and approved by a resolution of the National Assembly for Wales) subject to annulment in pursuance of a resolution of the Assembly: s 52(9) (added by the Public Audit (Wales) Act 2013 Sch 4 paras 20, 53(1), (5)). At the date at which this volume states the law no such orders had been made under the Public Audit (Wales) Act 2004 s 52. As to the meaning of 'local authority in Wales' see PARA 618 note 3. As to the Welsh Ministers see PARA 4 note 18.

8 Ie information which relates to:
(1) a local government body in Wales (Public Audit (Wales) Act 2004 s 52(5)(a));
(2) a document to which the right conferred by s 52(1) (see the text and notes 1–3) applies (s 52(5)(b));
(3) a person who holds or controls such a document (s 52(5)(c)).

9 Public Audit (Wales) Act 2004 s 52(4)(a). The function referred to in the text are those under Pt 2 (ss 12–59).

10 Public Audit (Wales) Act 2004 s 52(4)(b).

11 See the Public Audit (Wales) Act 2004 s 53(1). A person guilty of such an offence is liable on summary conviction to a fine not exceeding level 3 on the standard scale, and to an additional fine not exceeding £20 for each day on which the offence continues after he has been convicted of it: s 53(2). If a person is convicted of an offence under s 53(1), and expenses are incurred by the Auditor General for Wales or the Wales Audit Office in connection with proceedings for the offence, the expenses may be recovered by the Wales Audit Office from the convicted person or an appropriate person, to the extent that they are not recovered from any other source: s 53(3), (4) (amended by the Public Audit (Wales) Act 2013 s 34, Sch 4 paras 20, 54). An appropriate person is a person who controlled the document referred to in the Public Audit (Wales) Act 2004 s 52(5) at the time the requirement was imposed: s 53(5).)). As to the Wales Audit Office see CONSTITUTIONAL AND ADMINISTRATIVE LAW vol 20 (2014) PARAS 403–405 As to the powers of magistrates' courts to issue fines on summary conviction see SENTENCING vol 92 (2015) PARA 176.

12 Public Audit (Wales) Act 2004 s 52(7). The functions referred to in the text are those under Pt 2 (ss 12–59).

650. Restriction on disclosure of information.

No information relating to a particular body or other person obtained by the Auditor General for Wales[1] or by a person acting on behalf of the Auditor General for Wales[2], pursuant to a statutory provision relating to the accounts and audits of local government bodies in Wales[3] or in the course of an audit, study, assessment or inspection under such a provision, or in the course of a study relating to registered social landlords[4] may be disclosed except[5]:

(1) with the consent of the body or person to whom the information relates[6];
(2) for the purposes of any functions of the Auditor General for Wales under the statutory provisions as to the accounts and audits of local government bodies in Wales[7];
(3) for the purposes of the functions of the Secretary of State[8] relating to social security[9];
(4) for the purposes of the functions of the Public Services Ombudsman for Wales with regard to the conduct of local government members and employees[10];
(5) for the purposes of any functions of the Welsh Ministers which are connected with the discharge of social services functions[11] by local authorities in Wales[12];
(6) for the purposes of any criminal investigation which is being or may be carried out, whether in the United Kingdom or elsewhere[13];
(7) for the purposes of any criminal proceedings which have been or may be initiated, whether in the United Kingdom or elsewhere[14];

(8) for the purposes of the initiation or bringing to an end of any such investigation or proceedings[15];

(9) for the purpose of facilitating a determination of whether any such investigation or proceedings should be initiated or brought to an end[16].

A person who is, or acts on behalf of a person who is, a public authority for the purposes of the Freedom of Information Act 2000[17], may disclose such information under certain circumstances[18].

A person commits an offence if he discloses information in contravention of these provisions[19].

1 As to the Auditor General for Wales see PARA 615; and CONSTITUTIONAL AND ADMINISTRATIVE LAW vol 20 (2014) PARA 400 et seq.

2 Ie by virtue of a delegation made under the Public Audit (Wales) Act 2013 s 18: see CONSTITUTIONAL AND ADMINISTRATIVE LAW vol 20 (2014) PARA 402.

3 Ie the Public Audit (Wales) Act 2004 Pt 2 (ss 12–59) (see PARA 618 et seq) or the Local Government (Wales) Measure 2009 Pt 1 (ss 1–47) (see LOCAL GOVERNMENT vol 69 (2018) PARA 789 et seq).

4 Ie a study under the Government of Wales Act 1998 s 145C: see PARA 643.

5 See the Public Audit (Wales) Act 2004 s 54(1), (2) (s 54(1) amended by the Local Government (Wales) Measure 2009 s 51(1), Sch 1 paras 34, 36(a), (b); and the Public Audit (Wales) Act 2013 s 34, Sch 4 paras 20, 55(1)–(3)).

6 Public Audit (Wales) Act 2004 s 54(2)(a).

7 Public Audit (Wales) Act 2004 s 54(2)(b) (amended by the Local Government (Wales) Measure 2009 Sch 1 paras 34, 36(c); and the Public Audit (Wales) Act 2013 Sch 4 paras 20, 55(1), (4)(a)). The text refers to functions under the Public Audit (Wales) Act 2004 Pt 2 or the Local Government (Wales) Measure 2009 Pt 1.

8 As to the Secretary of State see PARA 4 note 18.

9 Public Audit (Wales) Act 2004 s 54(2)(c). As to functions of the Secretary of State relating to social security see WELFARE BENEFITS AND STATE PENSIONS vol 104 (2014) PARA 527 et seq.

10 Public Audit (Wales) Act 2004 s 54(2)(d) (amended by the Public Services Ombudsman (Wales) Act 2005 s 39(1), Sch 6 para 77). The functions with regard to conduct referred to in the text are those under the Local Government Act 2000 Pt III (ss 49–83): see LOCAL GOVERNMENT vol 69 (2018) PARA 264 et seq.

11 For these purposes 'social services functions' has the same meaning as in the Social Services and Well-being (Wales) Act 2014 s 143 (see SOCIAL SERVICES vol 95 (2017) PARA 373): Public Audit (Wales) Act 2004 s 54(5) (amended by SI 2016/413). As to the Welsh Ministers see PARA 4 note 18.

12 Public Audit (Wales) Act 2004 s 54(2)(e) (amended by the Public Audit (Wales) Act 2013 Sch 4 paras 20, 55(1), (4)(b)). As to the meaning of 'local authority in Wales' see PARA 618 note 3.

13 Public Audit (Wales) Act 2004 s 54(2)(g). See generally CRIMINAL LAW.

14 Public Audit (Wales) Act 2004 s 54(2)(h). See generally CRIMINAL LAW.

15 Public Audit (Wales) Act 2004 s 54(2)(i). See generally CRIMINAL LAW.

16 Public Audit (Wales) Act 2004 s 54(2)(j). See generally CRIMINAL LAW.

17 See CONSTITUTIONAL AND ADMINISTRATIVE LAW vol 20 (2014) PARA 425.

18 See the Public Audit (Wales) Act 2004 s 54(2ZA) (s 54(2ZA)–(2ZD) added by the Local Government and Public Involvement in Health Act 2007 s 167(1), (2)). A person referred to in the text may also disclose such information:

(1) in accordance with the Government of Wales Act 1998 s 145C(5) or (8) (see PARA 643) (Public Audit (Wales) Act 2004 s 54(2ZA)(a) (as so added)); or

(2) in any other circumstances, except where the disclosure would, or would be likely to, prejudice the effective performance of a function imposed or conferred on the person by or under an enactment (s 54(2ZA)(b) (as so added)).

A person who does not fall within s 54(2ZA) may also disclose such information in accordance with consent given by the Auditor General for Wales: s 54(2ZC) (as so added; amended by the Public Audit (Wales) Act 2013 Sch 4 paras 20, 55(1), (6)). Consent for the purposes of the Public Audit (Wales) Act 2004 s 54(2ZC) must be obtained in accordance with the following provisions: ss 54(2ZD), 54ZA(1) (s 54ZA added by the Local Government and Public Involvement in Health Act 2007 s 167(1), (6)). A person requesting consent (the 'applicant') must make a request for consent which:

(a) is in writing (s 54ZA(2)(a) (as so added));
(b) states the name of the applicant and an address for correspondence (s 54ZA(2)(b) (as so added));
(c) describes the information in relation to which consent is requested (s 54ZA(2)(c) (as so added)); and
(d) identifies the person to whom the information will be disclosed (s 54ZA(2)(d) (as so added)).

Consent must be given except where the disclosure would, or would be likely to, prejudice the effective performance of a function imposed or conferred on the Auditor General for Wales by or under an enactment: s 54ZA(3) (as so added; amended by the Public Audit (Wales) Act 2013 Sch 4 paras 20, 56(1), (2)). Consent may be given or refused orally or in writing; but where it is given or refused orally the consent or refusal must be confirmed in writing: Public Audit (Wales) Act 2004 s 54ZA(4) (as so added). A refusal (or, where the refusal is oral, the confirmation of the refusal) must contain the reasons for the refusal: s 54ZA(5) (as so added). The Auditor General for Wales must give or refuse consent not later than the twentieth working day following the day on which the request is received: s 54ZA(6) (as so added; amended by the Public Audit (Wales) Act 2013 Sch 4 paras 20, 56(1), (3)). 'Working day' means any day other than a Saturday, a Sunday, Christmas Day, Good Friday or a day which is a bank holiday under the Banking and Financial Dealings Act 1971 in any part of the United Kingdom: Public Audit (Wales) Act 2004 s 54ZA(7) (as so added). As to the meaning of 'United Kingdom' see PARA 4 note 10.

19 Public Audit (Wales) Act 2004 s 54(3) (amended by the Local Government and Public Involvement in Health Act 2007 s 167(1), (4)). A person guilty of an offence under the Public Audit (Wales) Act 2004 s 54(3) is liable on summary conviction to a fine not exceeding the statutory maximum: Public Audit (Wales) Act 2004 s 54(4) (amended by the Local Government and Public Involvement in Health Act 2007 ss 167(1), (5), 241, Sch 18 Pt 13). As to the powers of magistrates' courts to issue fines on summary conviction see SENTENCING vol 92 (2015) PARA 176.

651. Supply of benefit information to Auditor General for Wales.

The Secretary of State[1] may supply to the Auditor General for Wales[2] any information held by him which relates to housing benefit or council tax benefit[3], and appears to the Secretary of State to be relevant to the exercise of any function of the Auditor General for Wales[4].

1 As to the Secretary of State see PARA 4 note 18.

2 As to the Auditor General for Wales see PARA 615; and CONSTITUTIONAL AND ADMINISTRATIVE LAW vol 20 (2014) PARA 400 et seq.

3 As to housing benefit see WELFARE BENEFITS AND STATE PENSIONS vol 104 (2014) PARA 318 et seq. As to council tax benefit see WELFARE BENEFITS AND STATE PENSIONS vol 104 (2014) PARA 249.

4 Public Audit (Wales) Act 2004 s 55. As to the functions of the Auditor General for Wales see CONSTITUTIONAL AND ADMINISTRATIVE LAW vol 20 (2014) PARA 402.

652. Publication of information by Auditor General for Wales.

The Auditor General for Wales[1] may publish information with respect to any of these:

(1) the making[2] of a public interest report[3];
(2) the subject matter of a public interest report[4];
(3) the decision made and other action taken by a body in response to the receipt of a public interest report or to anything in such a report[5];
(4) a contravention by a body of regulations made under the Public Audit (Wales) Act 2004[6];
(5) a contravention by a body of an obligation imposed on it[7].

The information that may be published under head (1), (2) or (3) above does not include information excluded[8] from an approved summary[9].

The Auditor General for Wales must inform a body before publishing the information relating to it[10]. Information must be published in any manner which the Auditor General for Wales considers appropriate for bringing the information to the attention of members of the public who may be interested in it[11].

1 As to the Auditor General for Wales see PARA 615; and CONSTITUTIONAL AND ADMINISTRATIVE LAW vol 20 (2014) PARA 400 et seq.
2 A public interest report is a report under the Public Audit (Wales) Act 2004 s 22: see PARA 621.
3 Public Audit (Wales) Act 2004 s 56(1)(a) (amended by the Public Audit (Wales) Act 2013 s 34, Sch 4 paras 20, 57).
4 Public Audit (Wales) Act 2004 s 56(1)(b).
5 Public Audit (Wales) Act 2004 s 56(1)(c).
6 Public Audit (Wales) Act 2004 s 56(1)(d). The regulations referred to in the text are those made under the Public Audit (Wales) Act 2004 s 39: see PARA 653 et seq.
7 Public Audit (Wales) Act 2004 s 56(1)(e). The reference to an obligation imposed on a body is to an obligation imposed under s 47(4): see PARA 644.
8 Ie under the Public Audit (Wales) Act 2004 s 26(5): see PARA 626.
9 Public Audit (Wales) Act 2004 s 56(2). The reference to an approved summary is to a summary published under s 26(4)(c): see PARA 626.
10 Public Audit (Wales) Act 2004 s 56(3).
11 Public Audit (Wales) Act 2004 s 56(4).

E. ACCOUNTS AND AUDIT REGULATIONS

653. Accounts and audit regulations: Wales.

The Welsh Ministers[1] may by regulations[2] applying to local government bodies in Wales[3] make provision with respect to[4]:

(1) the keeping of accounts[5];
(2) the form, preparation and certification of accounts and of statements of accounts[6];
(3) the deposit of the accounts of a body at the offices of the body or at another place[7];
(4) the publication of information relating to accounts and the publication of statements of accounts[8];
(5) the exercise of any rights of objection or inspection[9] and the steps to be taken by a body for informing local government electors[10] for the area of the body of those rights[11].

Before making any such regulations the Welsh Ministers must consult[12]:

(a) the Auditor General for Wales[13];
(b) any associations of local authorities in Wales which appear to them to be concerned[14]; and
(c) any bodies of accountants which appear to them to be appropriate[15].

A person commits an offence if[16]:

(i) without reasonable excuse he contravenes a provision of regulations under these provisions[17]; and
(ii) the regulations declare that contravention of the provision is an offence[18].

If a person is convicted of committing such an offence in relation to a body, and expenses are incurred by the Auditor General for Wales or the Wales Audit Office in connection with proceedings for the offence, the expenses may be recovered by the Wales Audit Office from the convicted person or the body, to the extent that they are not recovered from any other source[19].

1 As to the Welsh Ministers see PARA 4 note 18. As to the meaning of 'Wales' see PARA 2 note 16.
2 As to the regulations made see the Accounts and Audit (Wales) Regulations 2014, SI 2014/3362; and PARA 606 et seq. See also the Local Government (Wales) Measure 2009 s 15; and LOCAL GOVERNMENT vol 69 (2018) PARA 796.
3 As to the meaning of 'local government body in Wales' see PARA 618.

4 Public Audit (Wales) Act 2004 s 39(1).
5 Public Audit (Wales) Act 2004 s 39(1)(a).
6 Public Audit (Wales) Act 2004 s 39(1)(b).
7 Public Audit (Wales) Act 2004 s 39(1)(c).
8 Public Audit (Wales) Act 2004 s 39(1)(d).
9 Ie under the Public Audit (Wales) Act 2004 s 29, 30 or 31.
10 As to the meaning of 'local government elector' see PARA 627 note 1.
11 Public Audit (Wales) Act 2004 s 39(1)(e).
12 Public Audit (Wales) Act 2004 s 39(2).
13 Public Audit (Wales) Act 2004 s 39(2)(a). As to the Auditor General for Wales see PARA 615; and CONSTITUTIONAL AND ADMINISTRATIVE LAW vol 20 (2014) PARA 400 et seq.
14 Public Audit (Wales) Act 2004 s 39(2)(b).
15 Public Audit (Wales) Act 2004 s 39(2)(c).
16 Public Audit (Wales) Act 2004 s 39(3). A person guilty of an offence under s 39(3) is liable on summary conviction to a fine not exceeding level 3 on the standard scale: s 39(4). As to the powers of magistrates' courts to issue fines on summary conviction see SENTENCING vol 92 (2015) PARA 176.
17 Public Audit (Wales) Act 2004 s 39(3)(a).
18 Public Audit (Wales) Act 2004 s 39(3)(b).
19 Public Audit (Wales) Act 2004 s 39(5), (6) (amended by the Public Audit (Wales) Act 2013 s 34, Sch 4 paras 20, 44(1), (4), (5)). As to the Wales Audit Office see CONSTITUTIONAL AND ADMINISTRATIVE LAW vol 20 (2014) PARA 403.

654. Responsibility for internal control and financial management: Wales.

The relevant authority[1] must ensure that there is a sound system of internal control which facilitates the effective exercise of that body's functions and which includes:

(1) arrangements for the management of risk[2]; and
(2) adequate and effective financial management[3].

The relevant body must conduct a review at least once in a year[4] of the effectiveness of its system of internal control[5]. The findings of the review must be considered:

(a) in the case of a larger relevant body, by the members of the body meeting as a whole or by a committee[6]; and
(b) in the case of a smaller relevant body, by the members of the body meeting as a whole[7].

Following the review, the body or committee must approve a statement on internal control prepared in accordance with proper practices[8]. The relevant body must ensure that the statement accompanies:

(i) any statement of accounts which it is obliged[9] to prepare[10]; or
(ii) any accounting statement which it is obliged[11] to prepare[12].

1 'Relevant body' means (as appropriate) a larger relevant body or a smaller relevant body: Accounts and Audit (Wales) Regulations 2014, SI 2014/3362, reg 2(1). 'Larger relevant body' means a county or county borough council, a fire and rescue authority, a National Park authority, a police and crime commissioner, a chief constable, or a body which is listed in the definition of 'smaller relevant body' in reg 2 but which does not meet the qualifying condition: reg 2(1). 'Smaller relevant body means a body which is a community council, a committee of a county or county borough council (including a joint committee), a port health authority, an internal drainage board or a conservation board, and being-either an established body, which meets the qualifying condition for the year concerned or for either of the two preceding years, or a newly established body, which meets the qualifying condition for its first or second year: reg 2(1). The 'qualifying condition' means that the relevant body's gross income or gross expenditure (whichever is higher) is not more than £2,500,000: reg 2(1).

'Fire and rescue authority' means an authority constituted by a scheme under the Fire and Rescue Services Act 2004 s 2 or a scheme to which s 4 of that Act applies (see FIRE AND RESCUE SERVICES vol 51 (2013) PARAS 18–20): Accounts and Audit (Wales) Regulations 2014, SI 2014/3362, reg 2(1). 'Joint committee' means a joint committee of two or more local authorities: reg 2(1). 'Port health authority' means a port health authority for a port health district wholly in Wales; and 'internal drainage board' means an internal drainage board for an internal drainage district wholly in Wales: reg 2(1). 'Conservation board' means a board established by order of the Welsh Ministers under the Countryside and Rights of Way Act 2000 s 86 (see OPEN SPACES AND COUNTRYSIDE vol 78 (2010) PARA 660): Accounts and Audit (Wales) Regulations 2014, SI 2014/3362, reg 2(1).

As to local government areas and authorities in Wales see LOCAL GOVERNMENT vol 69 (2018) PARA 51 et seq. As to National Park authorities see OPEN SPACES AND COUNTRYSIDE vol 78 (2010) PARA 526. As to police and crime commissioners see POLICE AND INVESTIGATORY POWERS vol 84 (2013) PARA 56 et seq. As to internal drainage boards see WATER AND WATERWAYS vol 101 (2009) PARA 569 et seq. As to port health authorities see ENVIRONMENTAL QUALITY AND PUBLIC HEALTH vol 45 (2010) PARA 102.

The Accounts and Audit (Wales) Regulations 2014, SI 2014/3362, apply only in relation to Wales: reg 1(2). As to the equivalent regulations in relation to England see the Accounts and Audit Regulations 2015, SI 2015/234; and PARA 606 et seq. As to the meanings of 'England' and 'Wales' see PARA 2 note 16.

2 Accounts and Audit (Wales) Regulations 2014, SI 2014/3362, reg 5(1)(a).
3 Accounts and Audit (Wales) Regulations 2014, SI 2014/3362, reg 5(1)(b).
4 'Year' means the 12 months ending with 31 March: Accounts and Audit (Wales) Regulations 2014, SI 2014/3362, reg 2(1).
5 Accounts and Audit (Wales) Regulations 2014, SI 2014/3362, reg 5(2).
6 Accounts and Audit (Wales) Regulations 2014, SI 2014/3362, reg 5(3)(a).
7 Accounts and Audit (Wales) Regulations 2014, SI 2014/3362, reg 5(3)(b).
8 Accounts and Audit (Wales) Regulations 2014, SI 2014/3362, reg 5(4). As to the meaning of 'proper practices' see PARA 590 note 4. See also PARA 654 note 8. For the purposes of the Local government Act 2003 s 21(2) (accounting practices: see PARA 590 note 4):
   (1) in relation to internal drainage boards, the accounting practices contained in the 'Governance and Accountability in Internal Drainage Boards in England: A Practitioners Guide 2006' (as revised in November 2007 and issued jointly by the Association of Drainage Authorities and the Department for Environment, Food and Rural Affairs) are proper practices (Accounts and Audit (Wales) Regulations 2014, SI 2014/3362, reg 4(a)); and
   (2) in relation to port health authorities which are not county councils or county borough councils, the accounting practices contained in the 'Governance and accountability for Local Councils in Wales: A Practitioners' Guide 2011 (Wales)' as may be amended or reissued from time to time (whether under the same title or not) issued jointly by One Voice Wales and the Society for Local Council Clerks are proper practices (Accounts and Audit (Wales) Regulations 2014, SI 2014/3362, reg 4(b)).
9 Ie in accordance with the Accounts and Audit (Wales) Regulations 2014, SI 2014/3362, reg 8: see PARA 656.
10 Accounts and Audit (Wales) Regulations 2014, SI 2014/3362, reg 5(5)(a).
11 Ie in accordance with the Accounts and Audit (Wales) Regulations 2014, SI 2014/3362, reg 14: see PARA 657.
12 Accounts and Audit (Wales) Regulations 2014, SI 2014/3362, reg 5(5)(b).

655. Accounting records, control systems and internal audit.

The responsible financial officer[1] of a relevant body[2] must determine on behalf of the body, after consideration, when relevant, of proper practices[3], its:

(1) accounting records, including the form of accounts and supporting accounting records[4]; and
(2) accounting control systems[5],

and that officer must ensure that the accounting control systems determined by that officer are observed and that the accounting records of the body are kept up to date and maintained in accordance with the requirements of any enactment and proper practices[6].

The accounting records determined in accordance with head (1) must:

(a) be sufficient to show and explain a relevant body's transactions and to enable the responsible financial officer to ensure that any statement of accounts or accounting statement which is prepared under the accounts and audit regulations[7] complies with those regulations[8]; and

(b) contain:

(i) entries from day to day of all sums of money received and expended by the body and the matters to which the income and expenditure or receipts and payments accounts relate[9];

(ii) a record of the assets and liabilities of the body[10]; and

(iii) a record of income and expenditure of the body in relation to claims made, or to be made, by it for contribution, grant or subsidy from the Welsh Ministers, any Minister of the Crown or a body to whom the Welsh Ministers or such a Minister may pay sums of money[11].

The accounting control systems determined in accordance with head (2) must include:

(A) measures to ensure that the financial transactions of the body are recorded as soon as reasonably practicable and as accurately as reasonably possible, measures to enable the prevention and detection of inaccuracies and fraud, and the ability to reconstitute any lost records[12];

(B) identification of the duties of officers dealing with financial transactions and division of responsibilities of those officers in relation to significant transactions[13];

(C) procedures to ensure that uncollectable amounts, including bad debts, are not written off except with the approval of the responsible financial officer, or such member of that person's staff as is nominated for this purpose, and that the approval is shown in the accounting records[14]; and

(D) measures to ensure that risk is appropriately managed[15].

A relevant body must maintain an adequate and effective system of internal audit of its accounting records and of its system of internal control[16]. Any officer or member of that body must, if the body requires:

(I) make available such documents of the body which relate to its accounting and other records as appear to that body to be necessary for the purpose of the audit[17]; and

(II) supply the body with such information and explanation as that body considers necessary for that purpose[18].

A larger relevant body[19] must, at least once in each year, conduct a review of the effectiveness of its internal audit[20]. The findings of the review must be considered, as part of the consideration of the system of internal control[21] by the members of the body meeting as a whole or by a committee[22].

1 Any reference in the Accounts and Audit (Wales) Regulations 2014, SI 2014/3362, to the 'responsible financial officer' means:

(1) the person who is responsible for the administration of the financial affairs of a relevant body by virtue of:

(a) the Local Government Act 1972 s 151 (financial administration: see PARA 665);

(b) the Local Government Finance Act 1988 s 112(1) (financial administration as to certain authorities: see PARA 665);

(c) the Environment Act 1995 Sch 7 para 13(6) (National Park Authorities: see OPEN SPACES AND COUNTRYSIDE vol 78 (2010) PARA 644),

or, if no person is so responsible, the person who is responsible for keeping the accounts of such a body (Accounts and Audit (Wales) Regulations 2014, SI 2014/3362, reg 2(2)(a)); or

(2) if the person referred to in head (1) is unable to act owing to absence or illness:

(a) such member of that person's staff as is nominated by that person for the purposes of the Local Government Finance Act 1988 s 114 (functions of responsible officer as regards reports: see PARA 667) (Accounts and Audit (Wales) Regulations 2014, SI 2014/3362, reg 2(2)(b)(i)); or

(b) if no nomination is made under the Local Government Finance Act 1988 s 114, such member of staff nominated by the person referred to in head (1) for the purposes of the Accounts and Audit (Wales) Regulations 2014, SI 2014/3362 (reg 2(2)(b)(ii)).

2 As to the meaning of 'relevant body' see PARA 654 note 1.

3 As to the meaning of 'proper practices' see PARA 590 note 4. See also PARA 654 note 8.

4 Accounts and Audit (Wales) Regulations 2014, SI 2014/3362, reg 6(1)(a).

5 Accounts and Audit (Wales) Regulations 2014, SI 2014/3362, reg 6(1)(b).

6 Accounts and Audit (Wales) Regulations 2014, SI 2014/3362, reg 6(1).

The Accounts and Audit (Wales) Regulations 2014, SI 2014/3362, apply only in relation to Wales: reg 1(2). As to the equivalent regulations in relation to England see the Accounts and Audit Regulations 2015, SI 2015/234; and PARA 606 et seq. As to the meanings of 'England' and 'Wales' see PARA 2 note 16.

7 Ie the Accounts and Audit (Wales) Regulations 2014, SI 2014/3362.

8 Accounts and Audit (Wales) Regulations 2014, SI 2014/3362, reg 6(2)(a).

9 Accounts and Audit (Wales) Regulations 2014, SI 2014/3362, reg 6(2)(b)(i).

10 Accounts and Audit (Wales) Regulations 2014, SI 2014/3362, reg 6(2)(b)(ii).

11 Accounts and Audit (Wales) Regulations 2014, SI 2014/3362, reg 6(2)(b)(iii).

12 Accounts and Audit (Wales) Regulations 2014, SI 2014/3362, reg 6(3)(a).

13 Accounts and Audit (Wales) Regulations 2014, SI 2014/3362, reg 6(3)(b).

14 Accounts and Audit (Wales) Regulations 2014, SI 2014/3362, reg 6(3)(c).

15 Accounts and Audit (Wales) Regulations 2014, SI 2014/3362, reg 6(3)(d).

16 Accounts and Audit (Wales) Regulations 2014, SI 2014/3362, reg 7(1).

17 Accounts and Audit (Wales) Regulations 2014, SI 2014/3362, reg 7(2)(a). In reg 5, 'documents and records' includes information recorded in an electronic form: reg 5(3).

18 Accounts and Audit (Wales) Regulations 2014, SI 2014/3362, reg 7(2)(b).

19 As to the meaning of 'larger relevant body' see PARA 654 note 1.

20 Accounts and Audit (Wales) Regulations 2014, SI 2014/3362, reg 7(3).

21 Ie the system of internal control referred to in the Accounts and Audit (Wales) Regulations 2014, SI 2014/3362, reg 5(3): see PARA 654.

22 Accounts and Audit (Wales) Regulations 2014, SI 2014/3362, reg 7(4).

656. Statement of accounts: larger relevant body.

A larger relevant body[1] must prepare for each year[2] a statement of accounts in accordance with the accounts and audit regulations[3] and proper practices[4] and the statement must include such of the following accounting statements as are relevant to the functions of the body[5]:

(1) housing revenue account[6];

(2) firefighters' pension fund[7];

(3) any other statements relating to each and every other fund in relation to which the body is required by any statutory provision to keep a separate account[8].

The statement of accounts must be accompanied by the notes referred to below[9].

The first note is a note of the relevant body's remuneration ratio information[10] (but this requirement does not apply to a relevant body which is a joint committee)[11].

The second note is a note of (except in relation to persons to whom the third note[12] applies) the number of employees[13] or police officers in the year to which the accounts relate whose remuneration fell in each bracket of a scale in multiples of £5,000 starting with £60,000[14].

The third note is a note of the remuneration (set out according to the specified categories[15]) and the contribution to the person's pension[16] by the relevant body of:

(a) senior employees[17]; or
(b) relevant police officers[18],

in respect of their employment by the relevant body or in their capacity as a police officer, whether on a permanent or temporary basis[19]. The remuneration and the pension contribution must be noted in respect of both the year to which the accounts relate and the previous year[20].

1 As to the meaning of 'larger relevant body' see PARA 654 note 1.
2 As to the meaning of 'year' see PARA 654 note 4.
3 Ie the Accounts and Audit (Wales) Regulations 2014, SI 2014/3362.
4 As to the meaning of 'proper practices' see PARA 590 note 4. See also PARA 654 note 8.
5 Accounts and Audit (Wales) Regulations 2014, SI 2014/3362, reg 8(1).
The Accounts and Audit (Wales) Regulations 2014, SI 2014/3362, apply only in relation to Wales: reg 1(2). As to the equivalent regulations in relation to England see the Accounts and Audit Regulations 2015, SI 2015/234; and PARA 606 et seq. As to the meanings of 'England' and 'Wales' see PARA 2 note 16.
6 Accounts and Audit (Wales) Regulations 2014, SI 2014/3362, reg 8(1)(a). Where a county council or a county borough council is required by the Local Government and Housing Act 1989 s 74 to maintain a Housing Revenue Account (see HOUSING vol 56 (2017) PARA 356), the statement of accounts required by the Accounts and Audit (Wales) Regulations 2014, SI 2014/3362, reg 8(1) must include a note prepared in accordance with proper practices in relation to any Major Repairs Allowance grant paid to the county council or county borough council under the Local Government Act 2003 s 31 (see PARA 41) detailing income and expenditure and any balance on any account used to record the grant: Accounts and Audit (Wales) Regulations 2014, SI 2014/3362, reg 8(2).
7 Accounts and Audit (Wales) Regulations 2014, SI 2014/3362, reg 8(1)(b).
8 Except accounts for pension funds administered in accordance with the Local Government Pension Scheme Regulations 2013, SI 2013/2356: Accounts and Audit (Wales) Regulations 2014, SI 2014/3362, reg 8(1)(c) (amended by SI 2018/91).
9 Accounts and Audit (Wales) Regulations 2014, SI 2014/3362, reg 9(1).
10 'Relevant body's remuneration ratio information' means (Accounts and Audit (Wales) Regulations 2014, SI 2014/3362, reg 9(8)):
(1) the remuneration of the body's chief executive during the year to which the accounts relate;
(2) the median remuneration of all the body's employees during the year to which the accounts relate; and
(3) the ratio of the amount in head (1) to the amount in head (2).
'Remuneration' means all amounts paid to or receivable by a person, and includes sums due by way of expenses allowance (so far as those sums are chargeable to United Kingdom income tax), and the estimated money value of any other benefits received by an employee otherwise than in cash: reg 9(8).
'Chief executive' means (reg 9(8)):
(a) in the case of a relevant body which is a county council or county borough council, fire and rescue authority or National Park authority, the head of the body's paid service designated under the Local Government and Housing Act 1989 s 4(1);
(b) in the case of a relevant body which is a chief constable, the chief constable;
(c) in the case of a relevant body which is a police and crime commissioner, the chief executive appointed by the commissioner under the Police Reform and Social Responsibility Act 2011 Sch 1;
(d) in the case of any other relevant body, the highest ranking employee.
As to local government areas and authorities in Wales see LOCAL GOVERNMENT vol 69 (2018) PARA 51 et seq. As to the meanings of 'fire and rescue authority' and National Park authority see PARA 654 note 1. As to police and crime commissioners see POLICE AND INVESTIGATORY POWERS vol 84 (2013) PARA 56 et seq.
11 Accounts and Audit (Wales) Regulations 2014, SI 2014/3362, reg 9(2). As to the meaning of 'joint committee' see PARA 654 note 1.
12 Ie the Accounts and Audit (Wales) Regulations 2014, SI 2014/3362, reg 9(4).

13 'Employee' includes a member of the relevant body and a holder of an office under the relevant body, but does not include a person who is an elected councillor, and 'employment' is to be construed accordingly: Accounts and Audit (Wales) Regulations 2014, SI 2014/3362, reg 9(8).

14 Accounts and Audit (Wales) Regulations 2014, SI 2014/3362, reg 9(3).

15 Ie the categories specified in the Accounts and Audit (Wales) Regulations 2014, SI 2014/3362, reg 9(7). Those categories are:

(1) the total amount of salary, fees or allowances paid to or receivable by the person (reg 9(7)(a));

(2) the total amount of bonuses paid to or receivable by the person (reg 9(7)(b));

(3) the total amount of sums paid by way of expenses allowance that are chargeable to United Kingdom income tax, and were paid to or receivable by the person (reg 9(7)(c));

(4) the total amount of any compensation for loss of employment paid to or receivable by the person, and any other payments made to or receivable by the person in connection with the termination of their employment by the relevant body, or, in the case of a relevant police officer, the total amount of any payment made to a relevant police officer who ceases to hold office before the end of a fixed term appointment (reg 9(7)(d));

(5) the total estimated value of any benefits received by the person otherwise than in cash which do not fall within heads (1)–(4) above, which are emoluments of the person, and which are received by the person in respect of their employment by the relevant body or in their capacity as a police officer (reg 9(7)(e)); and

(6) in relation to relevant police officers, any payments, whether made under the Police Regulations 2003, SI 2003/527, or otherwise, which do not fall within heads (1) to (5) above (reg 9(7)(f)).

16 'Contribution to the person's pension' means an amount to be calculated as follows (Accounts and Audit (Wales) Regulations 2014, SI 2014/3362, reg 9(8)):

(1) in relation to contributions to the relevant pension scheme established under the Superannuation Act 1972 s 7, the common rate of employer's contribution specified in a rates and adjustments certificate prepared under the Local Government Pension Scheme Regulations 2013, SI 2013/2356, reg 62 (actuarial valuations of pension funds: see LOCAL GOVERNMENT vol 69 (2018) PARA 493), being the amount appropriate for that body calculated in accordance with the certificate and reg 67 (employer's contributions) of those Regulations, multiplied by the person's pensionable pay;

(2) in relation to contributions to the firefighters' pension scheme established under the Fire Services Acts 1947 and 1959, the percentage of the aggregate of the pensionable pay calculated for the purposes of the Firemen's Pension Scheme Order 1992, SI 1992/129, Sch 2 para G2(3), (4) (see FIRE AND RESCUE SERVICES vol 51 (2013) PARA 49), multiplied by the person's pensionable pay;

(3) in relation to contributions to the firefighters' pension scheme established under the Fire and Rescue Services Act 2004, the percentage of the aggregate of the pensionable pay calculated for the purposes of the Firefighters' Pension Scheme (Wales) Order 2007, SI 2007/1073, Sch 1 Pt 13 rule 2(2), (3) multiplied by the person's pensionable pay;

(4) in relation to contributions to police pension schemes established under the Police Pensions Regulations 1987, SI 1987/257, or the Police Pensions Regulations 2006, SI 2006/3415 (see POLICE AND INVESTIGATORY POWERS vol 84 (2013) PARA 197 et seq), the percentage of pensionable pay specified in the Police Pension Fund Regulations 2007, SI 2007/1932, reg 5(1), multiplied by the person's pensionable pay.

17 Accounts and Audit (Wales) Regulations 2014, SI 2014/3362, reg 9(4)(i). 'Senior employee' means an employee whose salary is £150,000 or more per year, or an employee whose salary is £60,000 or more per year who falls within at least one of the following categories (reg 9(8)):

(1) a person employed by a relevant body to which the Local Government and Housing Act 1989 s 2 (politically restricted posts: see LOCAL GOVERNMENT vol 69 (2018) PARA 161) applies who:

(a) has been designated as head of paid service under s 4(1) (see LOCAL GOVERNMENT vol 69 (2018) PARA 470);

(b) is a statutory chief officer within the meaning of s 2(6); or

(c) is a non-statutory chief officer within the meaning of s 2(7);

(2) the person who is the head of staff for any relevant body to which s 4 does not apply; or

(3) a person who has responsibility for the management of the relevant body to the extent that the person has power to direct or control the major activities of the body (in particular activities involving the expenditure of money), whether solely or collectively with other persons.

The sums of £60,000 and £150,000 in reg 9 are to be reduced pro rata for an employee or officer who is employed or engaged on a temporary or part-time basis: reg 9(9).

18 Accounts and Audit (Wales) Regulations 2014, SI 2014/3362, reg 9(4)(ii). 'Relevant police officer' is defined by reg 9(8) as:

(1) in relation to a police force maintained under the Police Act 1996 s 2 (maintenance of police forces: see POLICE AND INVESTIGATORY POWERS vol 84 (2013) PARA 52), the chief constable;

(2) any other senior police officer whose salary is £150,000 (see note 17) or more per year.

'Senior police officer' means a member of a police force holding a rank above that of superintendent: reg 9(8). As to chief officers of police see POLICE AND INVESTIGATORY POWERS vol 84 (2013) PARA 112 et seq.

19 Accounts and Audit (Wales) Regulations 2014, SI 2014/3362, reg 9(4). The persons whose remuneration is to be noted under reg 9(4) must be listed individually and identified by way of job title only, except that those persons whose salary is £150,000 or more per year must also be identified by name: reg 9(5).

20 Accounts and Audit (Wales) Regulations 2014, SI 2014/3362, reg 9(6).

657. Accounting statement: smaller relevant body.

A smaller relevant body[1] must prepare for each year[2] accounting statements in accordance with the accounts and audit regulations[3] and proper practices[4].

1 As to the meaning of 'smaller relevant body' see PARA 654 note 1.

2 As to the meaning of 'year' see PARA 654 note 4.

3 Ie the Accounts and Audit (Wales) Regulations 2014, SI 2014/3362.

4 Accounts and Audit (Wales) Regulations 2014, SI 2014/3362, reg 14. As to the meaning of 'proper practices' see PARA 590 note 4. See also PARA 654 note 8.

The Accounts and Audit (Wales) Regulations 2014, SI 2014/3362, apply only in relation to Wales: reg 1(2). As to the equivalent regulations in relation to England see the Accounts and Audit Regulations 2015, SI 2015/234; and PARA 606 et seq. As to the meanings of 'England' and 'Wales' see PARA 2 note 16.

658. Signing and approval of statements of accounts and accounting statements.

The responsible financial officer[1] of a larger relevant body[2] must, no later than 31 May immediately following the end of a year[3], sign and date the statement of accounts[4], and certify that it presents a true and fair view of the financial position of the body at the end of the year to which it relates and of that body's income and expenditure for that year[5].

A larger relevant body must, no later than 31 July in the year immediately following the end of the year to which the statement relates[6]:

(1) consider either by way of a committee or by the members meeting as a whole the statement of accounts[7];

(2) following that consideration, approve the statement of accounts by a resolution of that committee or meeting[8];

(3) following approval, ensure that the statement of accounts is signed and dated by the person presiding at the committee or meeting at which that approval was given[9]; and

(4) publish (which must include publication on the body's website) the statement of accounts together with any certificate, opinion or report issued, given or made by the auditor[10] before the date of publication, or, if the publication takes place prior to the conclusion of the audit and no such opinion has been given, together with a declaration and explanation of the fact that at the date of publication the auditor has given no opinion[11].

The responsible financial officer must re-certify the presentation of the statement of accounts before the relevant body approves it[12]. If the responsible financial officer does not comply with the duty to sign and certify the accounts, the larger relevant body must:

(a) publish immediately a statement setting out the reasons for the officer's non-compliance[13]; and

(b) agree to a course of action to ensure compliance as soon as possible[14].

If the accounts were approved by the relevant body before the conclusion of an audit of those accounts, the accounts must be approved as soon as reasonably practicable after the receipt of any report from the auditor which contains the auditor's final findings from the audit and which is issued before the conclusion of the audit[15]. This approval is in addition to approval under heads (1) to (5) above[16].

Where any material amendment is made to the accounts, the responsible financial officer must report such amendment to the larger relevant body or the committee of that body immediately before the body or committee is to approve[17] the accounts[18].

A larger relevant body must keep copies of the documents mentioned in head (4) above for purchase by any person on payment of a reasonable sum[19].

Before the approval referred to in heads (i) to (iii) below is given, the responsible financial officer of a relevant body must:

(i) in a case where the body has prepared a statement of accounts, sign and date the statement of accounts, and certify that it presents a true and fair view of the financial position of the body at the end of the year to which it relates and of that body's income and expenditure for that year[20];

(ii) in a case where the body has prepared a record of receipts and payments, sign and date that record, and certify that it properly presents that body's receipts and payments for the year to which the record relates[21]; or

(iii) in any other case, sign and date the income and expenditure account and statement of balances, and certify that they present fairly the financial position of the body at the end of the year to which they relate and that body's income and expenditure for that year[22].

A smaller relevant body[23] must, no later than 30 June immediately following the end of a year:

(A) consider the accounting statements by the members meeting as a whole[24];

(B) following that consideration, approve the accounting statements for submission to the auditor by a resolution of the body[25]; and

(C) following approval, ensure that the accounting statements are signed and dated by the person presiding at the meeting at which that approval was given[26].

If the responsible financial officer does not comply with heads (a) to (c) above, the smaller relevant body must publish immediately a statement setting out the reasons for the officer's non-compliance and agree to a course of action to ensure compliance as soon as possible[27].

Where a smaller relevant body decides to amend its accounting statements following the receipt of a report from the auditor which contains the auditor's final findings and which is issued before the conclusion of the audit, the body must ensure that the amended accounting statements are signed and dated by the person presiding at the meeting at which the amendment was approved[28].

A smaller relevant body must, no later than 30 September in the year immediately following the end of the year to which the statement relates, either:

(I) publish the accounting statements by means other than solely by reference in the minutes of meetings[29], together with:

(AA) any certificate, opinion, or report issued, given or made[30] by the auditor[31]; or

(BB) if the publication takes place prior to the conclusion of the audit and no such opinion has been given, together with a declaration and explanation of the fact that at the date of publication the auditor has given no opinion[32]; or

(II) display a notice containing the documents mentioned in head (A) in at least one conspicuous place in the area of the body for a period of at least 14 days[33].

A smaller relevant body must keep copies of the documents mentioned in head (A) above for purchase by any person on payment of a reasonable sum[34].

1 As to the meaning of 'responsible financial officer' see PARA 655 note 1.
2 As to the meaning of 'larger relevant body' see PARA 654 note 1.
3 As to the meaning of 'year' see PARA 654 note 4.
4 As to the statement of accounts see PARA 656.
5 Accounts and Audit (Wales) Regulations 2014, SI 2014/3362, reg 10(1) (amended by SI 2018/91).
The Accounts and Audit (Wales) Regulations 2014, SI 2014/3362, apply only in relation to Wales: reg 1(2). As to the equivalent regulations in relation to England see the Accounts and Audit Regulations 2015, SI 2015/234; and PARA 606 et seq. As to the meanings of 'England' and 'Wales' see PARA 2 note 16. For modifications for the year ending on 31 March 2018 see reg 10A and for modifications for county and country borough councils for years ending 31 March 2019 and 31 March 2020 see reg 10B (regs 10A, 10B both added by SI 2018/91).
6 Accounts and Audit (Wales) Regulations 2014, SI 2014/3362, reg 10(2) (amended by SI 2018/91).
7 Accounts and Audit (Wales) Regulations 2014, SI 2014/3362, reg 10(2)(a).
8 Accounts and Audit (Wales) Regulations 2014, SI 2014/3362, reg 10(2)(b).
9 Accounts and Audit (Wales) Regulations 2014, SI 2014/3362, reg 10(2)(c).
10 Ie under the Public Audit (Wales) Act 2004 ss 23(2) (general report) and 33 (advisory notices): see PARAS 624, 631. 'Auditor' means a person whose appointment continues to have effect by virtue of the Public Audit (Wales) Act 2013 Sch 3 para 2(2) or, otherwise, the Auditor General for Wales: Accounts and Audit (Wales) Regulations 2014, SI 2014/3362, reg 2(1).
11 Accounts and Audit (Wales) Regulations 2014, SI 2014/3362, reg 10(2)(d).
12 Accounts and Audit (Wales) Regulations 2014, SI 2014/3362, reg 10(3).
13 Accounts and Audit (Wales) Regulations 2014, SI 2014/3362, reg 10(4)(a).
14 Accounts and Audit (Wales) Regulations 2014, SI 2014/3362, reg 10(4)(b).
15 Accounts and Audit (Wales) Regulations 2014, SI 2014/3362, reg 10(5).
16 Accounts and Audit (Wales) Regulations 2014, SI 2014/3362, reg 10(6).
17 Ie pursuant to the Accounts and Audit (Wales) Regulations 2014, SI 2014/3362, reg 10(2) or (5).
18 Accounts and Audit (Wales) Regulations 2014, SI 2014/3362, reg 10(7).
19 Accounts and Audit (Wales) Regulations 2014, SI 2014/3362, reg 10(8).
20 Accounts and Audit (Wales) Regulations 2014, SI 2014/3362, reg 15(1)(a). For modifications for committees of country or country borough councils see reg 15A (added by SI 2018/91).
21 Accounts and Audit (Wales) Regulations 2014, SI 2014/3362, reg 15(1)(b).
22 Accounts and Audit (Wales) Regulations 2014, SI 2014/3362, reg 15(1)(c).
23 As to the meaning of 'larger relevant body' see PARA 654 note 1.
24 Accounts and Audit (Wales) Regulations 2014, SI 2014/3362, reg 15(2)(a).
25 Accounts and Audit (Wales) Regulations 2014, SI 2014/3362, reg 15(2)(b).
26 Accounts and Audit (Wales) Regulations 2014, SI 2014/3362, reg 15(2)(c).
27 Accounts and Audit (Wales) Regulations 2014, SI 2014/3362, reg 15(3).
28 Accounts and Audit (Wales) Regulations 2014, SI 2014/3362, reg 15(4).
29 Accounts and Audit (Wales) Regulations 2014, SI 2014/3362, reg 15(5)(a).
30 Ie under the Public Audit (Wales) Act 2004 ss 23(2) and 33.
31 Accounts and Audit (Wales) Regulations 2014, SI 2014/3362, reg 15(5)(a)(i).
32 Accounts and Audit (Wales) Regulations 2014, SI 2014/3362, reg 15(5)(a)(ii).

33 Accounts and Audit (Wales) Regulations 2014, SI 2014/3362, reg 15(5)(b) (amended by SI 2018/91).
34 Accounts and Audit (Wales) Regulations 2014, SI 2014/3362, reg 15(6).

659. Public inspection of accounts.

The auditor[1] must, for the purpose of the exercise of rights of public inspection and objection[2], appoint a date on or after which those rights may be exercised, and must notify that date to the relevant body[3] concerned[4].

A relevant body so notified must make the accounts and other documents[5] available in accordance with the procedure specified for larger relevant bodies[6], or for smaller relevant bodies[7], as appropriate[8].

The procedure for public inspection of accounts for a larger relevant body, referred to above, is that it must make the documents referred to available for public inspection for 20 working days[9] before the date appointed[10] by the auditor[11].

The procedure for public inspection of accounts for a smaller relevant body, referred to above, is that the body must make the documents mentioned available for public inspection on reasonable notice, during a period of 20 working days before the date appointed[12] by the auditor[13].

A relevant body must give notice of public rights in accordance with the procedure specified for larger relevant bodies[14], or for smaller relevant bodies[15].

The procedure for a larger relevant body to give notice of public rights, referred to above, is that, not later than 14 days before the commencement of the period during which the accounts and other documents are made available[16], the body must display on its website and in at least one conspicuous place in its area a notice containing the specified[17] matters[18]. A larger relevant body must, on giving notice of public rights, notify the auditor immediately in writing that a notice has been given[19].

The procedure for a smaller relevant body to give notice of public rights, referred to above, is that it must display, in at least one conspicuous place in the area of the body for a period of at least 14 days immediately prior to the period during which the accounts and other documents are made available[20], a notice containing the specified[21] matters[22].

A smaller relevant body must on displaying a notice of public rights notify the auditor immediately in writing that a notice has been displayed[23].

1 As to the meaning of 'auditor' see PARA 658 note 10.
2 Ie under the Public Audit (Wales) Act 2004 ss 30(2) (inspection of documents and questions at audit) and 31(1) (right to make objections at audit): see PARAS 628, 629.
3 As to the meaning of 'relevant body' see PARA 654 note 1.
4 Accounts and Audit (Wales) Regulations 2014, SI 2014/3362, reg 21.
The Accounts and Audit (Wales) Regulations 2014, SI 2014/3362, apply only in relation to Wales: reg 1(2). As to the equivalent regulations in relation to England see the Accounts and Audit Regulations 2015, SI 2015/234; and PARA 606 et seq. As to the meanings of 'England' and 'Wales' see PARA 2 note 16.
5 Ie the documents mentioned in the Public Audit (Wales) Act 2004 s 30 (inspection of documents and questions at audit): see PARA 628.
6 Ie in the Accounts and Audit (Wales) Regulations 2014, SI 2014/3362, reg 11. As to the meaning of 'larger relevant body' see PARA 654 note 1.
7 Ie in the Accounts and Audit (Wales) Regulations 2014, SI 2014/3362, reg 16. As to the meaning of 'smaller relevant body' see PARA 654 note 1.
8 Accounts and Audit (Wales) Regulations 2014, SI 2014/3362, reg 22.
9 'Working day' means any day other than a Saturday, a Sunday, Christmas Day, Good Friday or any other day which is a bank holiday in Wales under the Banking and Financial Dealings Act

1971 (see TIME vol 97 (2015) PARA 321): Accounts and Audit (Wales) Regulations 2014, SI 2014/3362, reg 2(1).

10 Ie under the Accounts and Audit (Wales) Regulations 2014, SI 2014/3362, reg 21.

11 Accounts and Audit (Wales) Regulations 2014, SI 2014/3362, reg 11.

12 Ie under the Accounts and Audit (Wales) Regulations 2014, SI 2014/3362, reg 21.

13 Accounts and Audit (Wales) Regulations 2014, SI 2014/3362, reg 16.

14 Ie in the Accounts and Audit (Wales) Regulations 2014, SI 2014/3362, reg 12.

15 Accounts and Audit (Wales) Regulations 2014, SI 2014/3362, reg 24. The procedure for smaller relevant bodies is specified in reg 17.

16 Ie in pursuance of the Accounts and Audit (Wales) Regulations 2014, SI 2014/3362, reg 11.

17 Ie the matters set out in the Accounts and Audit (Wales) Regulations 2014, SI 2014/3362, reg 12(2). Those matters are:

(1) the period during which the accounts and other documents referred to in reg 12(1) will be available for inspection in accordance with reg 11 (reg 12(2)(a));
(2) the place at which, and the hours during which, they will be so available (reg 12(2)(b));
(3) the name and address of the auditor (reg 12(2)(c));
(4) the rights contained in the Public Audit (Wales) Act 2004 s 30 (inspection of documents and questions at audit) and s 31 (right to make objections at audit) (Accounts and Audit (Wales) Regulations 2014, SI 2014/3362, reg 12(2)(d)); and
(5) the date appointed under reg 21 for the exercise of rights of electors (reg 12(2)(e)).

18 Accounts and Audit (Wales) Regulations 2014, SI 2014/3362, reg 12(1) (amended by SI 2018/91).

19 Accounts and Audit (Wales) Regulations 2014, SI 2014/3362, reg 12(3).

20 Ie under the Accounts and Audit (Wales) Regulations 2014, SI 2014/3362, reg 16.

21 Ie the matters set out in the Accounts and Audit (Wales) Regulations 2014, SI 2014/3362, reg 17(2). Those matters are:

(1) the period during which the accounts and other documents referred to in reg 17(1) will be available for inspection in accordance with reg 16 (reg 17(2)(a));
(2) details of the manner in which notice should be given of an intention to inspect the accounts and other documents (reg 17(2)(b));
(3) the name and address of the auditor (reg 17(2)(c));
(4) the provisions contained in the Public Audit (Wales) Act 2004 s 30 (inspection of documents and questions at audit) and s 31 (right to make objections at audit) (Accounts and Audit (Wales) Regulations 2014, SI 2014/3362, reg 17(2)(d)); and
(5) the date appointed under reg 21 for the exercise of rights of electors (reg 17(2)(e)).

22 Accounts and Audit (Wales) Regulations 2014, SI 2014/3362, reg 17(1) (amended by SI 2018/91).

23 Accounts and Audit (Wales) Regulations 2014, SI 2014/3362, reg 17(3).

660. Steps following conclusion of audit.

As soon as reasonably possible after conclusion of an audit, a larger relevant body[1] must display on its website and in at least one conspicuous place in its area a notice stating that the audit has been concluded and that the statement of accounts[2] is available for inspection by local government electors[3] and including:

(1) a statement of the rights conferred[4] on local government electors[5];
(2) the address at which and the hours during which those rights may be exercised[6]; and
(3) details of where the last approved statement of accounts and auditor's reports can be found on the body's website[7].

As soon as reasonably possible after conclusion of an audit, a smaller relevant body must display a notice in at least one conspicuous place in the area of the body for a period of at least 14 days stating that the audit has been completed and that the last approved relevant accounting statements[8] and auditor's report are available for inspection by local government electors on reasonable notice[9] and including:

(a) a statement of the rights conferred[10] on local government electors[11];
(b) details of the manner in which notice should be given of an intention to exercise the right of inspection[12]; and

(c) if the body has a website, details of where the last approved statement of accounts and auditor's report can be found on that website[13].

1 As to the meaning of 'larger relevant body' see PARA 654 note 1.
2 As to the statement of accounts see PARA 656.
3 Accounts and Audit (Wales) Regulations 2014, SI 2014/3362, reg 13 (amended by SI 2018/91).
The Accounts and Audit (Wales) Regulations 2014, SI 2014/3362, apply only in relation to Wales: reg 1(2). As to the equivalent regulations in relation to England see the Accounts and Audit Regulations 2015, SI 2015/234; and PARA 606 et seq. As to the meanings of 'England' and 'Wales' see PARA 2 note 16.
4 Ie by the Public Audit (Wales) Act 2004 s 29 (inspection of statements of accounts and Auditor General for Wales' reports): see PARA 627.
5 Accounts and Audit (Wales) Regulations 2014, SI 2014/3362, reg 13(a).
6 Accounts and Audit (Wales) Regulations 2014, SI 2014/3362, reg 13(b).
7 Accounts and Audit (Wales) Regulations 2014, SI 2014/3362, reg 13(c).
8 Ie the relevant accounting statements required by the Accounts and Audit (Wales) Regulations 2014, SI 2014/3362: see PARA 657.
9 Accounts and Audit (Wales) Regulations 2014, SI 2014/3362, reg 18 (amended by SI 2018/91).
10 Ie by the Public Audit (Wales) Act 2004 s 29 (inspection of statements of accounts and Auditor General for Wales' reports): see PARA 627.
11 Accounts and Audit (Wales) Regulations 2014, SI 2014/3362, reg 18(a).
12 Accounts and Audit (Wales) Regulations 2014, SI 2014/3362, reg 18(b).
13 Accounts and Audit (Wales) Regulations 2014, SI 2014/3362, reg 18(c).

(iii) Other Provisions

661. Accounts of best value authorities.

Regulations made under the Local Government Act 1999 may make provision about the keeping of accounts by best value authorities[1].

1 See the Local Government Act 1999 s 23; and LOCAL GOVERNMENT vol 69 (2018) PARA 783.

662. Local financial returns.

Every local authority[1] and the chairman of the parish meeting[2] of every parish not having a separate parish council must make a return to the appropriate national authority[3] for each year ending on 31 March, or such other day as the appropriate national authority may direct, of its income and expenditure[4] and, in the case of any billing authority, of the amount payable to the authority by way of council tax[5] and non-domestic rates[6] and of the amount paid to any other authority in pursuance of a precept or levy[7].

The returns must be in such form, must contain such particulars, must be submitted to the appropriate national authority by such date in each year and must be certified in such manner as the appropriate national authority may direct[8]. The Secretary of State must make an annual summary of the returns and information he receives under these provisions and lay the summary before both Houses of Parliament[9].

1 For these purposes, 'local authority' means:
(1) a billing authority (see PARA 53) or a precepting authority (see PARA 23 note 1) as defined in the Local Government Finance Act 1992 s 69 (Local Government Act 1972 s 168(5)(a) (s 168(5) substituted by SI 1990/776; the Local Government Act 1972 s 168(5)(a) further substituted by the Local Government Finance Act 1992 s 117(1), Sch 13 para 34(2)));
(2) a fire and rescue authority in Wales constituted by a scheme under the Fire and Rescue Services Act 2004 s 2 or a scheme to which s 4 of that Act applies (see FIRE AND RESCUE SERVICES vol 51 (2013) PARAS 18–20) (Local Government Act 1972 s 168(5)(aa) (s 168(5) as so substituted; s 168(5)(aa) added by the Local Government

Finance Act 1992 Sch 13 para 34(2); and further substituted by the Fire and Rescue Services Act 2004 s 53(1), Sch 1 paras 38, 41(1), (2)));

(3) a levying body within the meaning of the Local Government Finance Act 1988 s 74 (see PARA 24) (Local Government Act 1972 s 168(5)(b) (s 168(5) as so substituted; s 168(5)(b) amended by the Greater London Authority Act 1999 ss 109(1), 423, Sch 34 Pt I; and the Fire and Rescue Services Act 2004 s 53(1), Sch 1 paras 38, 41(1), (3)));

(4) a body as regards which the Local Government Finance Act 1988 s 75 applies (see PARA 24) (Local Government Act 1972 s 168(5)(c) (s 168(5) as so substituted)); and

(5) a functional body within the meaning of the Greater London Authority Act 1999 (see LONDON GOVERNMENT vol 71 (2013) PARA 148) (Local Government Act 1972 s 168(5)(d) (s 168(5) as so substituted; s 168(5)(d) added by the Greater London Authority Act 1999 Sch 34 Pt I)).

2 As to parish meetings see LOCAL GOVERNMENT vol 69 (2018) PARA 48.

3 Ie the Secretary of State or, in relation to Wales, the Welsh Ministers. The functions of the Secretary of State under the Local Government Act 1972 s 168, so far as exercisable in relation to Wales, were transferred to the National Assembly for Wales (see the National Assembly for Wales (Transfer of Functions) Order 1999, SI 1999/672, art 2, Sch 1) and are now vested in the Welsh Ministers (see the Government of Wales Act 2006 s 162(1), Sch 11 para 30). As to the Secretary of State and the Welsh Ministers see PARA 4 note 18. As to the meaning of 'Wales' see PARA 2 note 16.

4 See the Local Government Act 1972 s 168(1)(a). In the case of the chairman of a parish meeting this is a return of the income and expenditure of the parish meeting: s 168(1)(a).

5 As to council tax see PARA 344 et seq.

6 As to non-domestic rating see PARA 49 et seq.

7 Local Government Act 1972 s 168(1)(b) (substituted by SI 1990/776; and amended by the Local Government Finance Act 1992 Sch 13 para 34(1)). As to precepts see PARA 11 et seq. As to levies see PARA 24.

8 Local Government Act 1972 s 168(2). Such a direction may impose different requirements in relation to returns of different classes: see s 168(2). If it appears to the appropriate national authority that sufficient information about any of the matters mentioned in s 168(1) (see the text to notes 1–7) has been supplied to it by a local authority, or by or on behalf of a parish meeting, under any other enactment, the appropriate national authority may exempt the local authority or chairman of the meeting from all or any of the requirements of s 168 so far as they relate to that matter: see s 168(3).

9 Local Government Act 1972 s 168(4). The summary must cover any information supplied to the Secretary of State under any other enactment in consequence of which he has granted an exemption under s 168(3) (see note 8): see s 168(4). As to the laying of documents before Parliament see STATUTES AND LEGISLATIVE PROCESS vol 96 (2012) PARA 1052. As to the laying of reports or statements by the Welsh Ministers before the National Assembly for Wales see the Government of Wales Act 2006 s 86; and CONSTITUTIONAL AND ADMINISTRATIVE LAW vol 20 (2014) PARA 384.

663. Generally accepted accounting practice: power to amend enactments.

The appropriate person[1] may by order[2] amend or repeal an enactment[3] relating to a local authority[4] if he considers it appropriate to do so in the light of generally accepted accounting practice as it applies to local government[5]. It does not matter for these purposes whether the enactment itself relates to the accounts of a local authority[6].

1 Ie, in relation to England, the Secretary of State; and, in relation to Wales, the Welsh Ministers: Local Government Act 2003 s 124. As to the Secretary of State and the Welsh Ministers see PARA 4 note 18. As to the meanings of 'England' and 'Wales' see PARA 2 note 16. The functions under the Local Government Act 2003 ss 117, 124 were formerly vested in the National Assembly for Wales and are now exercisable by the Welsh Ministers by virtue of the Government of Wales Act 2006 s 162(1), Sch 11 paras 30, 32.

2 No such order may be made by the Secretary of State unless a draft of the statutory instrument containing the order has been laid before, and approved by a resolution of, each House of Parliament: Local Government Act 2003 s 117(3). As to the equivalent procedure in relation to subordinate legislation made by the Welsh Ministers see the Government of Wales Act 2006 Sch 11 paras 33–35; and STATUTES AND LEGISLATIVE PROCESS vol 96 (2012) PARA 1035.

At the date at which this volume states the law no order had been made under the Local Government Act 2003 s 117(1).

3 'Enactment' includes an enactment contained in the Local Government Act 2003 or any Act passed after that Act: s 117(4). The Local Government Act 2003 was passed, ie received Royal Assent, on 18 September 2003.

4 'Local authority' means a body which is a local authority for the purposes of the Local Government Act 2003 Pt 1 (ss 1–24) (see PARA 563 note 1), or a parish council, a community council or charter trustees: s 117(4). As to parish councils see LOCAL GOVERNMENT vol 69 (2018) PARA 41 et seq. As to community councils see LOCAL GOVERNMENT vol 69 (2018) PARA 63 et seq. As to charter trustees see LOCAL GOVERNMENT vol 69 (2018) PARA 144.

5 Local Government Act 2003 s 117(1).

6 Local Government Act 2003 s 117(2).

(3) Officers and Reports

664. Financial assistance conditional on provision of information.

If in any financial year[1] a local authority[2] provides financial assistance[3] to a voluntary organisation[4] or to a specified body or fund[5], and the total amount[6] provided to that organisation, body or fund in that year exceeds the relevant minimum[7], then, as a condition of the assistance, the authority must require the organisation, body or fund, within the period of 12 months[8] beginning on the date when the assistance is provided[9], to furnish to the authority a statement in writing[10] of the use to which that amount has been put[11].

It is a sufficient compliance with a requirement imposed by the above provisions that there is furnished to the local authority concerned an annual report or accounts which contain the information required to be in the statement[12]. A statement (or any reports or accounts) provided to the local authority in pursuance of such a requirement must be deposited with the proper officer of the authority[13].

1 As to the meaning of 'financial year' see PARA 584 note 2.

2 In the Local Government Act 1972 s 137A, 'local authority' includes the Common Council of the City of London: see the Local Government Act 1972 ss 137A(6), 270(1) (s 137A added by the Local Government and Housing Act 1989 s 37). As to the meaning of 'local authority' see PARA 9 note 1. As to the Common Council of the City of London see LONDON GOVERNMENT vol 71 (2013) PARAS 34–38.

3 'Financial assistance' means assistance by way of grant or loan or by entering into a guarantee to secure any money borrowed: Local Government Act 1972 s 137A(2) (as added: see note 2).

4 Ie as defined in the Local Government Act 1972 s 137(2D) (see PARA 4 note 6): s 137A(1)(a) (as added: see note 2).

5 Ie specified in the Local Government Act 1972 s 137(3) (see PARA 4): see s 137A(1)(b) (as added: see note 2).

6 In relation to any financial assistance, any reference to the amount of the assistance is a reference to the amount of money granted or lent by the local authority or borrowed in reliance on the local authority's guarantee: Local Government Act 1972 s 137A(2)(a) (as added: see note 2).

7 The relevant minimum is £2,000 or such higher sum as the Secretary of State or, in relation to Wales, the Welsh Ministers may by order specify: see s 137A(3) (as added: see note 2). For the purposes of s 137A(1) the sum of £5,000 is specified as the relevant minimum for financial assistance provided by a local authority in Wales: Local Authorities (Discretionary Expenditure Limits) (Wales) Order 2000, SI 2000/990, art 2(2). At the date at which this volume states the law no such order had been made in relation to England.

The functions of the Secretary of State under the Local Government Act 1972 s 137A, so far as exercisable in relation to Wales, were transferred to the National Assembly for Wales (see the National Assembly for Wales (Transfer of Functions) Order 1999, SI 1999/672, art 2, Sch 1) and are now vested in the Welsh Ministers (see the Government of Wales Act 2006 s 162(1), Sch 11 para 30). As to the Secretary of State and the Welsh Ministers see PARA 4 note 18. As to the meaning of 'Wales' see PARA 2 note 16.

8 As to the meaning of 'month' see PARA 11 note 1.
9 In relation to any financial assistance, any reference to the date when the assistance is provided is a reference to the date on which the grant or loan is made or, as the case may be, on which the guarantee is entered into: Local Government Act 1972 s 137A(2)(b) (as added: see note 2).
10 As to the meaning of 'writing' see PARA 21 note 3.
11 Local Government Act 1972 s 137A(1) (as added: see note 2).
12 Local Government Act 1972 s 137A(4) (as added: see note 2).
13 Local Government Act 1972 s 137A(5) (as added: see note 2). The 'proper officer' is an officer appointed by a local authority for that purpose: see s 270(3), (4)(c). As to the proper officer generally see LOCAL GOVERNMENT vol 69 (2018) PARA 477.

665. Responsible officer.

Every local authority[1] must make arrangements for the proper administration of its financial affairs and must secure that one of its officers has responsibility for the administration of those affairs[2]. This is without prejudice to the general power of a local authority to do anything which is calculated to facilitate or is conducive or incidental to the discharge of any of its functions[3].

Similarly, any combined fire and rescue authority[4], any economic prosperity board[5], and authorities established under the Local Government Act 1985[6] must make arrangements for the proper administration of their financial affairs and must secure that one of their officers has responsibility for the administration of those affairs[7].

The Common Council of the City of London must make arrangements for the proper administration of such of its financial affairs as relate to it in its capacity as a local authority, police authority or port health authority[8], and secure that one of its officers has responsibility for the administration of those affairs[9].

While the responsible officer is a delegate of the local authority, the authority and its members retain responsibility for the proper administration of the finances of the authority[10]. Unless statutorily prevented from doing so, the responsible officer may delegate his duties[11] to other officers of the local authority[12].

1 As to the meaning of 'local authority' see PARA 664 note 2.
2 Local Government Act 1972 s 151. As to the qualifications required by such an officer see PARA 666. As to the duties of such an officer see PARAS 667, 669. As to responsibility for internal control and financial management see PARA 606.
3 Ie without prejudice to the Local Government Act 1972 s 111 (see LOCAL GOVERNMENT vol 69 (2018) PARA 506): see s 151.
4 Local Government Finance Act 1988 s 112(2)(b) (amended by the Fire and Rescue Services Act 2004 s 53(1), Sch 1 para 68(1), (3)). As to combined fire and rescue authorities see FIRE AND RESCUE SERVICES vol 51 (2013) PARA 17.
5 Ie an economic prosperity board established under the Local Democracy, Economic Development and Construction Act 2009 s 88 (see TRADE AND INDUSTRY vol 97 (2015) PARA 1086 et seq): see the Local Government Finance Act 1988 s 112(2)(c) (added by the Local Democracy, Economic Development and Construction Act 2009 s 119, Sch 6 paras 74, 78).
6 Ie any authority established by the Local Government Act 1985 Pt III (ss 18–22) (repealed) or Pt IV (ss 23–42) (see LOCAL GOVERNMENT vol 69 (2018) PARA 71) and including a sub-national transport body established under the Local Transport Act 2008 s 102E (see ROAD TRAFFIC) and a combined authority established under the Local Democracy, Economic Development and Construction Act 2009 s 103 (see TRADE AND INDUSTRY vol 97 (2015) PARA 1092 et seq): see the Local Government Act 1985 ss 73(2), 105(1) (s 73(2) added by the Local Democracy, Economic Development and Construction Act 2009 Sch 6 paras 59, 61(1), (3); and amended by the Cities and Local Government Devolution Act 2016 s 23(1), Sch 5 paras 6, 8).
7 See the Local Government Finance Act 1988 s 112(1); and the Local Government Act 1985 s 73(1) (numbered as such by the Local Democracy, Economic Development and Construction Act 2009 Sch 6 paras 59, 61(1), (2)). As to the qualifications required by such an officer see PARA 666. As

to the duties of such an officer see PARAS 667, 669. It is not necessary that the officer is an employee of the authority: *Pinfold North Ltd v Humberside Fire Authority* [2010] EWHC 2944 (QB), [2011] ICR 760, [2010] LGR 995 (combined fire and rescue service).

8 Local Government and Housing Act 1989 s 6(1)(a). As to the Common Council of the City of London see LONDON GOVERNMENT vol 71 (2013) PARAS 34–38.

9 Local Government and Housing Act 1989 s 6(1)(b). As to the qualifications required by such an officer see PARA 666.

10 *Lloyd v McMahon* [1987] AC 625, [1987] 1 All ER 1118, HL; *Provident Mutual Life Assurance Association v Derby City Council* [1981] 1 WLR 173, 79 LGR 297, HL.

11 Ie other than the reporting duty under the Local Government Finance Act 1988 s 114: see PARA 667. Note that this case was decided before the duty under s 114A (see PARA 669) was introduced.

12 *Provident Mutual Life Assurance Association v Derby City Council* [1981] 1 WLR 173, 79 LGR 297, HL.

666. Qualifications and appointment of responsible officer.

The person having responsibility[1] for the administration of the financial affairs of a relevant authority[2] must fulfil certain requirements[3]. That person (the 'responsible officer')[4] holds a politically restricted post for the purposes of the provisions of the Local Government and Housing Act 1989[5], and is therefore disqualified from becoming or remaining a member of a local authority[6]. The appointment of the responsible officer must be made on merit[7].

Where the relevant authority[8] proposes to appoint a chief officer[9], and it is not proposed that the appointment be made exclusively from among its existing officers, the authority must draw up a statement specifying the duties of the officer concerned and any qualifications or qualities to be sought in the person to be appointed[10], make arrangements for the to be advertised in such a way as is likely to bring it to the attention of persons who are qualified to apply for it[11] and make arrangements for a copy of the statement mentioned above to be sent to any person on request[12].

1 Ie under the Local Government Act 1972 s 151, the Local Government Act 1985 s 73 or the Local Government Finance Act 1988 s 112 (see PARA 665), or the Greater London Authority Act 1999 s 127 (see LONDON GOVERNMENT vol 71 (2013) PARA 154).

2 For the purposes of the Local Government Finance Act 1988 Pt VIII (ss 111–116), each of the following is a 'relevant authority':

(1) a county council (s 111(2)(a));

(2) a county borough council (s 111(2)(aa) (added by the Local Government (Wales) Act 1994 s 38(11), Sch 2));

(3) a district council (Local Government Finance Act 1988 s 111(2)(b));

(4) the Greater London Authority (s 111(2)(bb) (added by the Greater London Authority Act 1999 s 128(1), (2)));

(5) a functional body, within the meaning of the Greater London Authority Act 1999 (see LONDON GOVERNMENT vol 71 (2013) PARA 148) (Local Government Finance Act 1988 s 111(2)(bc) (added by the Greater London Authority Act 1999 s 128(1), (2)));

(6) the London Pensions Fund Authority (Local Government Finance Act 1988 s 111(2)(bd) (added by the Greater London Authority Act 1999 s 128(1), (2)));

(7) a London borough council (Local Government Finance Act 1988 s 111(2)(c));

(8) a police and crime commissioner (see POLICE AND INVESTIGATORY POWERS vol 84 (2013) PARA 56 et seq) (Local Government Finance Act 1988 s 111(2)(e) (substituted by the Police Reform and Social Responsibility Act 2011 s 99, Sch 16 paras 180, 186(a)));

(9) a chief officer of police (which, for this purpose, means a chief constable of a police force maintained under the Police Act 1996 s 2 (see POLICE AND INVESTIGATORY POWERS vol 84 (2013) PARA 52) or the Commissioner of Police of the Metropolis) (Local Government Finance Act 1988 s 111(2)(ea) (added by the Police Reform and Social Responsibility Act 2011 Sch 16 paras 180, 186(a)));

(10) a metropolitan county fire and rescue authority (Local Government Finance Act 1988 s 111(2)(g) (amended by the Civil Contingencies Act 2004 s 32(1), Sch 2 Pt 1 para 10(1), (2)));

(11) an integrated transport authority for an integrated transport area in England (Local Government Finance Act 1988 s 111(2)(i) (substituted by the Local Transport Act 2008 s 77(5), Sch 4 Pt 4 para 56(1), (3)));

(12) an economic prosperity board established under the Local Democracy, Economic Development and Construction Act 2009 s 88 (see TRADE AND INDUSTRY vol 97 (2015) PARA 1086 et seq) (Local Government Finance Act 1988 s 111(2)(ia) (s 111(2)(ia), (ib) added by the Local Democracy, Economic Development and Construction Act 2009 s 119, Sch 6 paras 74, 77));

(13) a combined authority established under the Local Democracy, Economic Development and Construction Act 2009 s 103 (see TRADE AND INDUSTRY vol 97 (2015) PARA 1092 et seq) (Local Government Finance Act 1988 s 111(2)(ib) (as so added));

(14) a waste disposal authority (s 111(2)(j));

(15) the Council of the Isles of Scilly (s 111(2)(k)); and

(16) a combined fire and rescue authority (s 111(2)(m) (amended by the Fire and Rescue Services Act 2004 s 53(1), Sch 1 para 68(1), (3))).

As to local government areas and authorities in England and Wales see LOCAL GOVERNMENT vol 69 (2018) PARA 36 et seq. As to the Greater London Authority see LONDON GOVERNMENT vol 71 (2013) PARA 67 et seq. As to the London boroughs and their councils see LONDON GOVERNMENT vol 71 (2013) PARAS 15, 20–22, 55 et seq. As to metropolitan county fire and rescue authorities see FIRE AND RESCUE SERVICES vol 51 (2013) PARA 17. As to integrated transport authorities see LOCAL GOVERNMENT vol 69 (2018) PARA 73. As to waste disposal authorities see LOCAL GOVERNMENT vol 69 (2018) PARA 17. As to combined fire and rescue authorities see LOCAL GOVERNMENT vol 69 (2018) PARA 72.

3 See the Local Government Finance Act 1988 s 113(1) (amended by the Greater London Authority Act 1999 s 129). In general, he must be a member of a specified body but, if he had responsibility for the administration of the financial affairs of an authority immediately before a certain date, this may be a sufficient qualification: see the Local Government Finance Act 1988 s 113(1), (2) (s 113(1) as so amended); the Local Government and Housing Act 1989 s 6(3), (6); and the Common Council and New Successor Bodies (Chief Finance Officer) Regulations 1991, SI 1991/445. The bodies specified are: the Institute of Chartered Accountants in England and Wales; the Institute of Chartered Accountants of Scotland; the Chartered Association of Certified Accountants; the Chartered Institute of Public Finance and Accountancy; the Institute of Chartered Accountants in Ireland; the Chartered Institute of Management Accountants; and any other body of accountants established in the United Kingdom and for the time being approved by the Secretary of State or, in relation to Wales, the Welsh Ministers for these purposes: see the Local Government Finance Act 1988 s 113(3); the Local Government and Housing Act 1989 s 6(5). As to the meaning of 'United Kingdom' see PARA 4 note 10.

The functions of the Secretary of State under the Local Government Finance Act 1988 s 113 and the Local Government and Housing Act 1989 s 6, so far as exercisable in relation to Wales, were transferred to the National Assembly for Wales (see the National Assembly for Wales (Transfer of Functions) Order 1999, SI 1999/672, art 2, Sch 1) and are now vested in the Welsh Ministers (see the Government of Wales Act 2006 s 162(1), Sch 11 para 30). As to the Secretary of State and the Welsh Ministers see PARA 4 note 18. As to the meaning of 'Wales' see PARA 2 note 16.

Similar provision is made in relation to the officer appointed by the Common Council of the City of London under the Local Government and Housing Act 1989 s 6 (see PARA 665) to have responsibility for the administration of such of its financial affairs as relate to it in its capacity as a local authority, police authority or port health authority: see s 6(3), (5).

4 Ie including the officer appointed by the Common Council of the City of London under the Local Government and Housing Act 1989 s 6: see PARA 665.

5 See the Local Government and Housing Act 1989 s 2(1)(b), (6)(d); and LOCAL GOVERNMENT vol 69 (2018) PARA 161. The relevant provisions of the Local Government and Housing Act 1989 are those of Pt I (ss 1–21): see s 2(1).

6 See the Local Government and Housing Act 1989 s 1(1); and LOCAL GOVERNMENT vol 69 (2018) PARA 160.

7 See the Local Government and Housing Act 1989 s 7; and LOCAL GOVERNMENT vol 69 (2018) PARA 466.

8 'Relevant authority' means a county or district council, the council of a London borough, the Common Council of the City of London and the Council of the Isles of Scilly in its capacity as a local authority, police authority or port health authority: Local Authorities (Standing Orders)

Regulations 1993, SI 1993/202, reg 1(2). The Local Authorities (Standing Orders) Regulations 1993 apply in relation to England and a National Park Authority in Wales only, having been revoked in relation to Wales for all other purposes: see the Local Authorities (Standing Orders) (Wales) Regulations 2006, SI 2006/1275, reg 10. As to the equivalent provision in relation to other authorities in Wales see the Local Authorities (Standing Orders) (Wales) Regulations 2006, SI 2006/1275. As to the standing orders of authorities in England operating executive arrangements or alternative arrangements under the Local Government Act 2000 Pt 1A (ss 9B–9R) (see LOCAL GOVERNMENT vol 69 (2018) PARA 295 et seq) see the Local Authorities (Standing Orders) (England) Regulations 2001, SI 2001/3384; and LOCAL GOVERNMENT vol 69 (2018) PARA 697.

9 'Chief officer', in relation to a relevant authority, includes the responsible officer: see the Local Authorities (Standing Orders) Regulations 1993, SI 1993/202, reg 1(2).

10 Local Authorities (Standing Orders) Regulations 1993, SI 1993/202, reg 2, Sch 1 Pt I standing order 1(a).

11 Local Authorities (Standing Orders) Regulations 1993, SI 1993/202, Sch 1 Pt I standing order 1(b). Where a post has been advertised as provided in standing order 1(b), the authority must interview all qualified applicants for the post or select a short list of such qualified applicants and interview those included on the short list: Sch 1 Pt I standing order 2(1). Where no qualified person has applied, the authority must make further arrangements for advertisement in accordance with Sch 1 Pt I standing order 1(b): Sch 1 Pt I standing order 2(2).

12 Local Authorities (Standing Orders) Regulations 1993, SI 1993/202, Sch 1 Pt I standing order 1(c).

667. Reports of responsible officer.

The person having responsibility[1] for the administration of the financial affairs of a relevant authority[2] (the 'chief finance officer') has the following duties, without prejudice to any other functions[3].

Except where a relevant authority is operating executive arrangements[4], the chief finance officer of a relevant authority must make a report if it appears to him that the authority, a committee[5] of the authority, a person holding any office or employment under the authority, a member of the relevant police force[6], or a joint committee[7] on which the authority is represented[8]:

(1) has made or is about to make a decision which involves or would involve the authority incurring expenditure which is unlawful[9];

(2) has taken or is about to take a course of action which, if pursued to its conclusion, would be unlawful and likely to cause a loss or deficiency on the part of the authority[10]; or

(3) is about to enter an item of account the entry of which is unlawful[11].

It is the duty of the chief finance officer of a relevant authority (except where the relevant authority is a chief officer of police), in preparing such a report, to consult so far as practicable with the person who is for the time being designated as the head of the authority's paid service[12] and with the person who is for the time being responsible for performing the duties of the authority's monitoring officer[13].

The chief finance officer of a relevant authority must also make a report if it appears to him that the expenditure of the authority incurred (including expenditure it proposes to incur) in a financial year[14] is likely to exceed the resources (including sums borrowed) available to it to meet that expenditure[15].

Where a chief finance officer of a relevant authority has made a report under the above provisions he must send a copy of it to:

(a) the person who at the time the report is made has the duty to audit the authority's accounts[16];

(b) in the case of:

 (i) a police and crime commissioner, the commissioner and each member of the police and crime panel for the commissioner's police area[17];

(ii) the Mayor's Office for Policing and Crime, that Office and each member of the police and crime panel of the London Assembly[18];

(iii) a chief officer of police, the chief officer and the elected local policing body[19]; and

(iv) any other relevant authority, each person who is at that time a member of the authority[20]; and

(c) in a case where the relevant authority has a mayor and council manager executive, the person who at the time the report is made is the council manager of that authority[21].

The duties of a chief finance officer of a relevant authority to make a report[22] must be performed by him personally[23]. However, if the chief finance officer is unable to act owing to absence or illness the duties must be performed:

(A) by such member of his staff as is a member of one or more of the specified professional bodies[24] and is for the time being nominated by the chief finance officer for the purpose[25]; or

(B) if no member of his staff is a member of one or more of those bodies, by such member of his staff as is for the time being nominated by the chief finance officer for the purpose[26].

A relevant authority must provide its chief finance officer with such staff, accommodation and other resources as are in his opinion sufficient to allow his duties to be performed[27].

Similar provisions apply to the chief finance officer of the Common Council of the City of London[28].

1 Ie under the Local Government Act 1972 s 151, the Local Government Act 1985 s 73 or the Local Government Finance Act 1988 s 112 (see PARA 665), the Greater London Authority Act 1999 s 127 (see LONDON GOVERNMENT vol 71 (2013) PARA 154) or the Police Reform and Social Responsibility Act 2011 Sch 1, 2 or 4 (see POLICE AND INVESTIGATORY POWERS vol 84 (2013) PARA 56 et seq, 112 et seq, 117 et seq).

2 As to the meaning of 'relevant authority' see PARA 666 note 2.

3 See the Local Government Finance Act 1988 s 114(1) (amended by the Greater London Authority Act 1999 s 130(1), (2); and the Police Reform and Social Responsibility Act 2011 s 99, Sch 16 paras 180, 188(1), (2)).

4 Where a relevant authority is operating executive arrangements, the chief finance officer of the relevant authority must not make a report under the Local Government Finance Act 1988 s 114(2) in respect of any action referred to in s 114(2)(a), (b) or (c) (see heads (1)–(3) in the text) unless it is action taken otherwise than by or on behalf of the relevant authority's executive: s 114(2A) (added, in relation to England, by SI 2001/2237; and, in relation to Wales, by SI 2002/808). 'Executive' and 'executive arrangements' have the same meaning as in the Local Government Act 2000 Pt II (ss 10–48) (see LOCAL GOVERNMENT vol 69 (2018) PARA 336): Local Government Finance Act 1988 s 111(3A) (added, in relation to England, by SI 2001/2237; and, in relation to Wales, by SI 2002/808). As to reports of the responsible officer where authorities are operating executive arrangements see PARA 669. The Local Government Act 2000 Pt II now applies in relation to Wales only; as to the equivalent provisions in England see Pt 1A (ss 9B–9R); and LOCAL GOVERNMENT vol 69 (2018) PARA 295 et seq.

5 References to a committee (joint or otherwise) include references to a sub-committee: Local Government Finance Act 1988 s 114(8)(b). As to the power of a local authority to appoint committees and sub-committees see LOCAL GOVERNMENT vol 69 (2018) PARA 400.

6 'Relevant police force', in relation to the chief finance officer of a relevant authority, means:

(1) in the case where the relevant authority is a chief officer of police, the police force of which that person is chief officer (Local Government Finance Act 1988 s 114(8A)(a) (s 114(8A) added by the Police Reform and Social Responsibility Act 2011 Sch 16 paras 180, 188(1), (6)));

(2) in any other case, the police force maintained by the relevant authority (Local Government Finance Act 1988 s 114(8A)(b) (as so added)).

'Police force' has the meaning or effect described by the Police Act 1996 s 101(1) (see POLICE AND INVESTIGATORY POWERS vol 84 (2013) PARA 2): Interpretation Act 1978 s 5, Sch 1.

7 References to a joint committee are to a committee on which two or more relevant authorities are represented: Local Government Finance Act 1988 s 114(8)(a). See also note 5. As to joint committees see LOCAL GOVERNMENT vol 69 (2018) PARA 410.
8 Local Government Finance Act 1988 s 114(2) (amended by the Police and Magistrates' Courts Act 1994 s 43, Sch 4 Pt I para 34; the Police Reform and Social Responsibility Act 2011 Sch 16 paras 180, 188(1), (3); and SI 2001/2237 and SI 2002/808).
9 Local Government Finance Act 1988 s 114(2)(a).
10 Local Government Finance Act 1988 s 114(2)(b).
11 Local Government Finance Act 1988 s 114(2)(c).
12 Ie under the Local Government and Housing Act 1989 s 4 (see LOCAL GOVERNMENT vol 69 (2018) PARA 470): see the Local Government Finance Act 1988 s 114(3A)(a) (s 114(3A) added by the Local Government and Housing Act 1989 s 139, Sch 5 para 66; and amended by the Police Reform and Social Responsibility Act 2011 Sch 16 paras 180, 188(1), (4)). Specific provision is made as to the application of the Local Government Finance Act 1988 s 114(3A) in relation to Transport for London: see s 114(3C), (3D) (s 114(3B)–(3D) added by the Greater London Authority Act 1999, s 130(1), (3); the Local Government Finance Act 1988 s 114(3B) repealed by the Localism Act 2011 s 237, Sch 25 Pt 32). As to Transport for London see LONDON GOVERNMENT vol 71 (2013) PARA 163 et seq.
13 Ie under the Local Government and Housing Act 1989 s 5 (see LOCAL GOVERNMENT vol 69 (2018) PARA 472): see the Local Government Finance Act 1988 s 114(3A)(b) (as added: see note 12).
14 As to the meaning of 'financial year' see PARA 24 note 1.
15 Local Government Finance Act 1988 s 114(3). As to the expenditure of local authorities generally see PARA 2.
16 Local Government Finance Act 1988 s 114(4)(a). As to the audit of accounts see PARA 588 et seq.
17 Local Government Finance Act 1988 s 114(4)(b)(i) (s 114(4)(b) substituted by the Police Reform and Social Responsibility Act 2011 Sch 16 paras 180, 188(1), (5)). As to police and crime commissioners see POLICE AND INVESTIGATORY POWERS vol 84 (2013) PARA 56 et seq.
18 Local Government Finance Act 1988 s 114(4)(b)(ii) (as substituted: see note 17). As to the Mayor's Office for Policing and Crime see POLICE AND INVESTIGATORY POWERS vol 84 (2013) PARA 78 et seq.
19 Local Government Finance Act 1988 s 114(4)(b)(iii) (as substituted: see note 17).
20 Local Government Finance Act 1988 s 114(4)(b)(iv) (as substituted: see note 17). As to the application of the duty under s 114(4)(b) where the relevant authority is the Greater London Authority or a functional body within the meaning of the Greater London Authority Act 1999, see the Local Government Finance Act 1988 s 114(4A) (added by the Greater London Authority Act 1999 s 130(1), (4)). As to the duties of the relevant authority where copies of a report have been sent under the Local Government Finance Act 1988 s 114(4) see PARA 668.
21 Local Government Finance Act 1988 s 114(4)(c) (added, in relation to England, by SI 2001/2237; and, in relation to Wales, by SI 2002/808). 'Council manager' and 'mayor and council manager executive' have the same meaning as in the Local Government Act 2000 Pt II (ss 10–48) (see LOCAL GOVERNMENT vol 69 (2018) PARA 336): Local Government Finance Act 1988 s 111(3A) (as added: see note 4). The Local Government Act 2000 Pt II now applies in relation to Wales only; as to the equivalent provisions in England see Pt 1A (ss 9B–9R); and LOCAL GOVERNMENT vol 69 (2018) PARA 295 et seq. The position of council manager no longer exists in either England or Wales: see LOCAL GOVERNMENT vol 69 (2018) PARAS 21, 335 et seq.
22 Ie the duties under the Local Government Finance Act 1988 s 114(2), (3): see the text to notes 4–11, 14–15.
23 Local Government Finance Act 1988 s 114(5).
24 Ie the bodies mentioned in the Local Government Finance Act 1988 s 113(3): see PARA 666.
25 Local Government Finance Act 1988 s 114(6)(a).
26 Local Government Finance Act 1988 s 114(6)(b).
27 Local Government Finance Act 1988 s 114(7).
28 See the Common Council and New Successor Bodies (Chief Finance Officer) Regulations 1991, SI 1991/445, which make provision equivalent to the Local Government Finance Act 1988 ss 114–116 and apply to the Common Council of the City of London in its capacity as a local authority, police authority or port health authority: see the Common Council and New Successor Bodies (Chief Finance Officer) Regulations 1991, SI 1991/445, reg 3. As to the Common Council of the City of London see LONDON GOVERNMENT vol 71 (2013) PARAS 34–38.

668. Authorities' duties once report is made.

Where copies of a report by the chief finance officer have been sent[1], the relevant authority[2] other than an elected local policing body or a chief officer of police must consider the report at a meeting where it must decide whether it agrees or disagrees with the views contained in the report and what action (if any) it proposes to take in consequence of it[3]. The meeting must be held not later than the end of the period of 21 days beginning with the day on which copies of the report are sent[4].

In the case of a report made by the chief finance officer of an elected local policing body, that body must consider the report and decide whether the body agrees or disagrees with the views contained in the report and what action (if any) the body proposes to take in consequence of it[5]. In the case of a report made by the chief finance officer of a chief officer of police, the chief officer of police must consider the report and decide whether the chief officer of police agrees or disagrees with the views contained in the report and what action (if any) the chief officer of police proposes to take in consequence of it[6]. The consideration and decision-making must be concluded not later than the end of the period of 21 days beginning with the day on which copies of the report are sent[7].

As soon as practicable after the elected local policing body, or the chief officer of police, has concluded the consideration of the chief finance officer's report, that body or chief officer must prepare a report[8] which specifies:

(1) what action (if any) that body or chief officer has taken in response to the report[9];

(2) what action (if any) that body or chief officer proposes to take in response to the report[10]; and

(3) the reasons for taking the action specified in the report or, as the case may be, for taking no action[11].

As soon as practicable after the elected local policing body has prepared a report, the elected local policing body must arrange for a copy of the report to be sent to:

(a) the chief finance officer[12];

(b) the person who at the time the report is made has the duty to audit the elected local policing body's accounts[13]; and

(c) each member of the police and crime panel for the police area for which the elected local policing body is established[14].

As soon as practicable after the chief officer of police has prepared a report, the chief officer of police must arrange for a copy of the report to be sent to:

(i) the chief finance officer[15];

(ii) the person who at the time the report is made has the duty to audit the chief officer's accounts[16]; and

(iii) the elected local policing body which maintains the police force in which the chief officer serves[17].

If the report sent was made concerning unlawful expenditure or conduct[18], then, during the prohibition period[19], the course of conduct which led to the report being made must not be pursued[20]. If the report was made concerning expenditure exceeding resources[21], then, during the prohibition period, the authority may not enter into any new agreement which may involve the incurring of expenditure (at any time) by the authority unless the chief finance officer of the authority authorises it to do so[22].

Where it is proposed to hold a meeting under these provisions[23], the authority's proper officer[24] must as soon as is reasonably practicable notify its auditor of the date, time and place of the proposed meeting[25]. As soon as is reasonably practicable after such a meeting is held, the authority's proper officer must notify its auditor of any decision made at the meeting[26]. In the case of an elected local policing body, the chief finance officer of that body must notify the body's auditor of any decisions taken by the body in accordance with the provisions above[27]. In the case of a chief officer of police, the chief officer of police's chief finance officer must notify that chief officer of police's auditor of any decisions taken by the chief officer of police in accordance with the provisions above[28].

Similar provisions apply to the Common Council of the City of London[29].

1 Ie where copies of a report under the Local Government Finance Act 1988 s 114 have been sent under s 114(4) (see PARA 667): see s 115(1).

2 As to the meaning of 'relevant authority' see PARA 666 note 2.

3 Local Government Finance Act 1988 s 115(2) (amended by the Police Reform and Social Responsibility Act 2011 s 99, Sch 16 paras 180, 189(1), (3)). The Local Government Act 1972 s 101 (delegation: see LOCAL GOVERNMENT vol 69 (2018) PARA 399) does not apply to the duty under the Local Government Finance Act 1988 s 115(2) where the authority is one to which that section would apply apart from s 115(4): s 115(4).

Where the report under s 114 is a report by the chief finance officer of the Greater London Authority, s 115A has effect in place of s 115(2), (3): s 115(1A) (ss 115(1A), (9A), (13)–(14), 115A added, s 115(10), (11) amended, by the Greater London Authority Act 1999 s 131). See ss 115(1A), (9A)–(11), (13)–(14), 115A (as so added and amended). As to the application of the Local Government Finance Act 1988 s 115 to Transport for London see s 115(4A) (added by the Greater London Authority Act 1999, s 131(1), (4); and amended by the Localism Act 2011 ss 195(2), 237, Sch 20 para 2, Sch 25 Pt 32). As to the Greater London Authority see LONDON GOVERNMENT vol 71 (2013) PARA 67 et seq. As to Transport for London see LONDON GOVERNMENT vol 71 (2013) PARA 163 et seq.

4 Local Government Finance Act 1988 s 115(3).

5 Local Government Finance Act 1988 s 115(1B) (s 115(1B)–(1G) added by the Police Reform and Social Responsibility Act 2011 s 99, Sch 16 paras 180, 189(1), (2)). 'Chief finance officer' has the same meaning as in the Local Government Finance Act 1988 s 114 (see PARA 667): s 115(14) (as added (see note 3); definition added by the Local Government Act 2003 s 30(3)).

6 Local Government Finance Act 1988 s 115(1C) (as added: see note 5).

7 Local Government Finance Act 1988 s 115(1D) (as added: see note 5).

8 Local Government Finance Act 1988 s 115(1E) (as added: see note 5).

9 Local Government Finance Act 1988 s 115(1E)(a) (as added: see note 5).

10 Local Government Finance Act 1988 s 115(1E)(b) (as added: see note 5).

11 Local Government Finance Act 1988 s 115(1E)(c) (as added: see note 5).

12 Local Government Finance Act 1988 s 115(1F)(a) (as added: see note 5).

13 Local Government Finance Act 1988 s 115(1F)(b) (as added: see note 5).

14 Local Government Finance Act 1988 s 115(1F)(c) (as added: see note 5).

15 Local Government Finance Act 1988 s 115(1G)(a) (as added: see note 5).

16 Local Government Finance Act 1988 s 115(1G)(b) (as added: see note 5).

17 Local Government Finance Act 1988 s 115(1G)(c) (as added: see note 5).

18 Ie if the report was made under the Local Government Finance Act 1988 s 114(2): see PARA 667.

19 'The prohibition period' means the period:

(1) beginning with the day on which copies of the report are sent (Local Government Finance Act 1988 s 115(9)(a)); and

(2) ending with the first business day to fall after the day (if any) on which the authority's consideration of the report under s 115(1B), (1C) or (2) (see the text to notes 3–6) is concluded (s 115(9)(b) (amended by the Police Reform and Social Responsibility Act 2011 Sch 16 paras 180, 189(1), (4)).

If the Local Government Finance Act 1988 s 115(1B), (1C) or (3) is not complied with, it is immaterial for the purposes of s 115(9)(b) (head (2) above): s 115(10) (amended by virtue of the Police Reform and Social Responsibility Act 2011 Sch 16 paras 180, 189(1), (5)). 'Business day' means any day other than a Saturday, a Sunday, Christmas Day, Good Friday or a day which is a bank holiday in England and Wales: Local Government Finance Act 1988 s 115(12). As to bank holidays see TIME vol 97 (2015) PARAS 313, 321.

20 Local Government Finance Act 1988 s 115(5). If s 115(5) is not complied with, and the authority makes any payment in the prohibition period as a result of the course of conduct being pursued, it must be taken not to have had power to make the payment (notwithstanding any obligation to make it under contract or otherwise): s 115(7).
21 Ie if the report was made under the Local Government Finance Act 1988 s 114(3): see PARA 667.
22 Local Government Finance Act 1988 s 115(6) (amended by the Local Government Act 2003 s 30(1)). The chief finance officer may only give authority for the purposes of the Local Government Finance Act 1988 s 115(6) if he considers that the agreement concerned is likely to:
(1) prevent the situation that led him to make the report from getting worse (s 115(6A)(a) (s 115(6A), (6B) added by the Local Government Act 2003 s 30(2)));
(2) improve the situation (Local Government Finance Act 1988 s 115(6A)(b) (as so added)); or
(3) prevent the situation from recurring (s 115(6A)(c) (as so added)).
Authority for the purposes of s 115(6) must:
(a) be in writing (s 115(6B)(a) (as so added));
(b) identify the ground on which it is given (s 115(6B)(b) (as so added)); and
(c) explain the chief finance officer's reasons for thinking that the ground applies (s 115(6B)(c) (as so added)).
As to the meaning of 'writing' see PARA 21 note 3.
If the Local Government Finance Act 1988 s 115(6) is not complied with, the authority must be taken not to have had power to enter into the agreement (notwithstanding any option to do so under contract or otherwise): s 115(8).
23 Ie under the Local Government Finance Act 1988 s 115: see the text to notes 1–22.
24 For the purposes of the Local Government Finance Act 1988 s 116:
(1) an authority's proper officer is the person to whom the authority has for the time being assigned responsibility to notify its auditor under s 116 (s 116(3)); and
(2) an authority's auditor is the person who for the time being has the duty to audit its accounts (s 116(4)).
As to the audit of accounts see PARA 588 et seq.
25 Local Government Finance Act 1988 s 116(1).
26 Local Government Finance Act 1988 s 116(2).
27 Local Government Finance Act 1988 s 116(2B) (s 116(2B), (2C) added by the Police Reform and Social Responsibility Act 2011 Sch 16 paras 180, 190(1), (3)).
28 Local Government Finance Act 1988 s 116(2C) (as added: see note 27).
29 See the Common Council and New Successor Bodies (Chief Finance Officer) Regulations 1991, SI 1991/445, which make provision equivalent to the Local Government Finance Act 1988 ss 114–116 and apply to the Common Council of the City of London in its capacity as a local authority, police authority or port health authority: see the Common Council and New Successor Bodies (Chief Finance Officer) Regulations 1991, SI 1991/445, reg 3. As to the Common Council of the City of London see LONDON GOVERNMENT vol 71 (2013) PARAS 34–38.

669. Reports of responsible officer: authorities operating executive arrangements.

The person having responsibility[1] for the administration of the financial affairs of a relevant authority[2] which is operating executive arrangements[3] (the 'chief finance officer') has the following duties, without prejudice to any other functions[4].

The chief finance officer must make a report to the executive[5] of the authority if it appears to him that, in the course of the discharge of functions of the authority, the executive or a person on behalf of the executive[6]:

(1) has made or is about to make a decision which involves or would involve the authority incurring expenditure which is unlawful[7];
(2) has taken or is about to take a course of action which, if pursued to its conclusion, would be unlawful and likely to cause a loss or deficiency on the part of the authority[8]; or
(3) is about to enter an item of account the entry of which is unlawful[9].

It is the duty of the chief finance officer, in preparing such a report, to consult so far as practicable with the person who is for the time being designated[10] as the head of the authority's paid service[11] and with the person who is for the time being responsible[12] for performing the duties of the authority's monitoring officer[13].

Where a chief finance officer has made such a report he must send a copy of it to:

(a) the person who at the time the report is made has the duty to audit the authority's accounts[14];

(b) each person who at that time is a member of the authority[15]; and

(c) where the authority has a mayor and council manager executive, the person who at that time is the council manager[16].

A relevant authority must provide its chief finance officer with such staff, accommodation and other resources as are in his opinion sufficient to allow these duties to be performed[17].

1 Ie under the Local Government Act 1972 s 151: see PARA 665.
2 As to the meaning of 'relevant authority' see PARA 666 note 2.
3 As to the meaning of 'executive arrangements' see PARA 667 note 4.
4 See the Local Government Finance Act 1988 s 114A(1) (s 114A added, in relation to England, by SI 2001/2237; and (subject to minor variation) in relation to Wales by SI 2002/808).
5 As to the meaning of 'executive' see PARA 667 note 4.
6 Local Government Finance Act 1988 s 114A(2) (as added: see note 4). The provisions of s 114(5), (6) (see PARA 667) apply in relation to duties under s 114A(2), (3) (see the text to notes 10–13) as they apply in relation to duties under s 114(2), (3): s 114A(5) (as so added).
7 Local Government Finance Act 1988 s 114A(2)(a) (as added: see note 4).
8 Local Government Finance Act 1988 s 114A(2)(b) (as added: see note 4).
9 Local Government Finance Act 1988 s 114A(2)(c) (as added: see note 4).
10 Ie under the Local Government and Housing Act 1989 s 4: see LOCAL GOVERNMENT vol 69 (2018) PARA 470.
11 Local Government Finance Act 1988 s 114A(3)(a) (as added: see note 4). See also note 6.
12 Ie under the Local Government and Housing Act 1989 s 5: see LOCAL GOVERNMENT vol 69 (2018) PARA 472.
13 Local Government Finance Act 1988 s 114A(3)(b) (as added: see note 4). See also note 6.
14 Local Government Finance Act 1988 s 114A(4)(a) (as added: see note 4). As to the audit of accounts see PARA 588 et seq.
15 Local Government Finance Act 1988 s 114A(4)(b) (as added: see note 4).
16 Local Government Finance Act 1988 s 114A(4)(c) (as added: see note 4). As to the meanings of 'mayor and council manager executive' and 'council manger' see PARA 667 note 21.
17 Local Government Finance Act 1988 s 114A(6) (as added: see note 4).

670. Authorities' duties: authorities operating executive arrangements.

Where copies of a report have been sent[1], the executive[2] of the relevant authority[3] must consider the report at a meeting where it must decide whether it agrees or disagrees with the views contained in the report and what action (if any) it proposes to take in consequence of it[4]. The meeting must be held not later than the end of the period of 21 days beginning with the day on which copies of the report are sent[5].

During the prohibition period[6] the course of conduct which led to the report being made must not be pursued[7].

As soon as practicable after the executive has concluded its consideration of the chief finance officer's report, the executive must prepare a report which specifies:

(1) what action (if any) the executive has taken in response to the chief finance officer's report[8];

(2) what action (if any) the executive proposes to take in response to the chief finance officer's report and when the executive proposes to take that action[9]; and

(3) the reasons for taking the action specified in the executive's report or, as the case may be, for taking no action[10].

As soon as practicable after the executive has prepared such a report, it must arrange for a copy of it to be sent to the person who at the time the report is made has the duty to audit the authority's accounts[11], each person who at that time is a member of the authority[12], and the chief finance officer[13].

1 Ie where copies of a report under the Local Government Finance Act 1988 s 114A have been sent under s 114A(4) (see PARA 669): see s 115B(1) (s 115B added, in relation to England, by SI 2001/2237; and (subject to minor variation) in relation to Wales by SI 2002/808).

2 As to the meaning of 'executive' see PARA 667 note 4.

3 As to the meaning of 'relevant authority' see PARA 666 note 2.

4 See the Local Government Finance Act 1988 s 115B(2) (as added: see note 1). Where it is proposed to hold a meeting under s 115B:

(1) where the authority has a mayor and cabinet executive, the elected mayor (s 116(1A)(a) (s 116(1A), (2A) added, in relation to England, by SI 2001/2237; and, in relation to Wales, by SI 2002/808));

(2) where the authority has a leader and cabinet executive, the executive leader (Local Government Finance Act 1988 s 116(1A)(b) (as so added)); or

(3) where the authority has a mayor and council manager executive, the council manager (s 116(1A)(c) (as so added)),

must as soon as is reasonably practicable notify, or instruct the authority's proper officer to notify, the authority's auditor of the date, time and place of the proposed meeting: s 116(1A) (as so added). As soon as is reasonably practicable after a meeting is held:

(a) where the authority has a mayor and cabinet executive, the elected mayor (s 116(2A)(a) (as so added));

(b) where the authority has a leader and cabinet executive, the executive leader (s 116(2A)(b) (as so added)); or

(c) where the authority has a mayor and council manager executive, the council manager (s 116(2A)(c) (as so added)),

must notify, or instruct the authority's proper officer to notify, the authority's auditor of any decision made at the meeting: s 116(2A) (as so added). As to the meanings of 'mayor and council manager executive' and 'council manger' see PARA 667 note 21. 'Elected mayor', 'executive leader' and 'mayor and cabinet executive' have the same meanings as in the Local Government Act 2000 Pt II (ss 10–48) (see LOCAL GOVERNMENT vol 69 (2018) PARA 336): Local Government Finance Act 1988 s 111(3A) (added, in relation to England, by SI 2001/2237; and, in relation to Wales, by SI 2002/808). 'Leader and cabinet executive' means, in relation to England, a leader and cabinet executive (England), and, in relation to Wales, a leader and cabinet executive (Wales); and for this purpose 'leader and cabinet executive (England)' and 'leader and cabinet executive (Wales)' have the same meanings as in the Local Government Act 2000 Pt II (see LOCAL GOVERNMENT vol 69 (2018) PARA 336): Local Government Finance Act 1988 s 111(3B) (added by the Local Government and Public Involvement in Health Act 2007 s 74(1), Sch 3 paras 20, 21(1), (3)). The Local Government Act 2000 Pt II now applies in relation to Wales only; as to the equivalent provisions in England see Pt 1A (ss 9B–9R); and LOCAL GOVERNMENT vol 69 (2018) PARA 295 et seq. As to the meanings of 'proper officer' and 'auditor' see PARA 668 note 24.

5 Local Government Finance Act 1988 s 115B(3) (as added: see note 1).

6 'The prohibition period' means the period:

(1) beginning with the day on which copies of the chief finance officer's report are sent (Local Government Finance Act 1988 s 115B(8)(b)(i) (as added: see note 1)); and

(2) ending with the first business day to fall after the day (if any) on which the executive's consideration of the report under s 115B(2) (see the text to notes 2–4) is concluded (s 115B(8)(b)(ii) (as so added)).

If s 115B(3) is not complied with, it is immaterial for the purposes of head (2) above: s 115B(9) (as so added). The nature of the decisions made at the meeting is immaterial for the purposes of head (2) above: s 115B(10) (as so added). 'Chief finance officer' has the same meaning as in s 114A (see PARA 669): s 115B(8)(a) (as so added). 'Business day' means any day other than a Saturday, a Sunday, Christmas Day, Good Friday or a day which is a bank holiday in England: s 115B(11) (as so added). As to bank holidays see TIME vol 97 (2015) PARA 321.

7 Local Government Finance Act 1988 s 115B(4) (as added: see note 1). If s 115B(4) is not complied with, and the executive makes any payment in the prohibition period as a result of the course of conduct being pursued, the executive must be taken not to have had power to make the payment (notwithstanding any obligation to make it under contract or otherwise): s 115B(5) (as so added).
8 Local Government Finance Act 1988 s 115B(6)(a) (as added: see note 1).
9 Local Government Finance Act 1988 s 115B(6)(b) (as added: see note 1).
10 Local Government Finance Act 1988 s 115B(6)(c) (as added: see note 1).
11 Local Government Finance Act 1988 s 115B(7)(a) (as added: see note 1). As to the audit of accounts see PARA 588 et seq.
12 Local Government Finance Act 1988 s 115B(7)(b) (as added: see note 1).
13 Local Government Finance Act 1988 s 115B(7)(c) (as added: see note 1).

INDEX

Local Government Finance